A Guide to Federal Terms and Acronyms

Second Edition

Edited by
Don Philpott

Lanham • Boulder • New York • London

Published by Bernan Press
An imprint of The Rowman & Littlefield Publishing Group, Inc.
4501 Forbes Boulevard, Suite 200, Lanham, Maryland 20706
www.rowman.com
800-865-3457; info@bernan.com

Unit A, Whitacre Mews, 26-34 Stannary Street, London SE11 4AB

Copyright © 2018 by Bernan Press

All rights reserved. No part of this book may be reproduced in any form or by any electronic or mechanical means, including information storage and retrieval systems, without written permission from the publisher, except by a reviewer who may quote passages in a review. Bernan Press does not claim copyright in U.S. government information.

The reader should not rely on this publication to address specific questions that apply to a particular set of facts. The author and the publisher make no representation or warranty, express or implied, as to the completeness, correctness, or utility of the information in this publication. In addition, the author and the publisher assume no liability of any kind whatsoever resulting from the use of or reliance upon the contents of this book.

British Library Cataloguing in Publication Information Available

Library of Congress Cataloging-in-Publication Data Available

ISBN 9781598889291 (cloth : alk. paper)
ISBN 9781598889307 (electronic)

∞™ The paper used in this publication meets the minimum requirements of American National Standard for Information Sciences—Permanence of Paper for Printed Library Materials, ANSI/NISO Z39.48-1992.

Printed in the United States of America

Contents

Preface	v
Acquisitions	1
Administration on Intellectual and Developmental Disabilities	79
AIDS and HIV-Related Terms	83
Alzheimer's-Dementia	125
Alcohol, Tobacco and Firearms	129
Agriculture	139
Building Protection and Real Estate	157
Census	173
Chemical, Biological and Radiological	187
Children	191
Child Support Enforcement, Office of	201
Central Intelligence Agency	213
Coast Guard	217
Congress	241
Contracts and Contracting	251
Defense	257
Disaster and Emergency Management	345
Drugs	421
Education	437
Energy	443
Environmental Health	567
Environmental Protection	573
Equal Opportunities	659
Family Violence	663
Federal Aviation Administration	671
Federal Budget	681
Federal Highway Administration	715
Food Safety	741

Health and Human Services	761
Health—Long-Term Care	797
Health—Medicare	801
Homeland Security	807
Housing and Urban Development	815
Information Technology	831
Immigration and Naturalization	837
Internal Revenue Service	849
Justice	855
Justice—U.S. Courts	867
Labor—Employment Benefits	877
Labor Statistics	891
Small Business Administration	905
Transportation	909
Veterans Affairs	915
Water Quality	923

Preface

Trying to navigate through bureaucratic red tape can be a nightmare. You not only have to know the right procedures and protocols to follow but also often need to understand a completely different language.

If you have ever had to attend a meeting with federal government officials, you will know how difficult it can be most of the time to follow the conversation. Officials tend to talk their own department jargon, using abbreviations and acronyms on the assumption that everyone present knows what they mean.

After you have been to a few meetings, you begin to get the hang of it and even start using department-speak yourself. The problem, however, arises again when you start talking to another department.

Federal departments' documents are littered with acronyms, abbreviations and terms that mean little or nothing to the outsider. For instance, in government contracting the COTR reports to the CO about compliance with FAR, GPRA, SARA and FASA. Confused? Have you any idea was MIL-STD-129P is all about? (It is the standard for military shipping label requirements.)

A Guide to Federal Terms and Acronyms is a desktop reference that provides lists of terms, acronyms and abbreviations and hundreds of thousands of definitions arranged by subject matter. It is not a comprehensive list of all federal department glossaries because that would require several volumes. One Department of Agriculture glossary on agricultural chemical terms alone runs to more than a million words.

This revised, expanded and updated desktop reference does, however, include the most commonly used terms, acronyms and abbreviations and will, hopefully, be an invaluable reference to anyone who does business with the government—or simply wants to translate a jargon-rich government document. This new edition contains comprehensive new sections on AIDS, the federal budget, long-term health care, Alzheimer's and dementia, and the U.S. legal system.

The glossary consists of a series of lists of definitions, acronyms and abbreviations sorted alphabetically by subject matter. Where necessary, these lists have been further subdivided into more specific subjects to assist the reader in searches. For instance, the section on Disaster and Emergency Management is subdivided into sections on Disaster Housing, FEMA, Flooding and so on.

As mentioned above, this glossary does not claim to be a complete reference of all terms used by federal departments, but if you think there are omissions that should have been included, we would welcome your comments.

Acquisitions

GLOSSARY OF ACQUISITION TERMS

8(a) Section 8(a) of the Small Business Act. (FAR 19.800(a))

8(a) Contract A contract with the Small Business Administration under a program established by Section 8(a) of the Small Business Act. Under that program, the Small Business Administration is authorized to enter into all types of contracts with other agencies and let subcontracts for performing those contracts to firms eligible for program participation. (FAR 19.800(a))

8(a) Contractor A Small Business Administration subcontractor under an 8(a) contract. (FAR 19.800(a))

Acceptance Also referred to as acceptance of offer. In contract law, the act accepting an offer (e.g., awarding a contract based on an offer under a request for proposals). Also referred to as acceptance of work. The act of an authorized representative of the Government by which the Government, for itself or as agent of another, assumes ownership of existing identified supplies tendered or approves specific services rendered as partial or complete performance of the contract. (FAR 46.101)

Acceptance of Offer See acceptance.

Acceptance of Work See acceptance.

Acceptance Period The number of calendar days available to the Government for awarding a contract from the date specified in the solicitation for receipt of offers. (FAR 52.214-16)

Acceptance The process followed by Government personnel during acceptance of a supply or Procedures service.

Acceptance Time A definite period of time that one party to a negotiation has to accept an offer by another party. Instead of forcing a quick decision, this tactic can be used to deliberately give the other negotiator more time to grasp a solution or ideas.

Accessory Item An item that facilitates or enhances the operation of plant equipment but which is not essential for its operation. (FAR 45.501)

Accrual of a Claim Also referred to as claim accrual. Occurs on the date when all events, which fix the alleged liability of either the Government or the contractor and permit assertion of the claim, were known or should have been known. For liability to be fixed, some injury must have occurred. However, monetary damages need not have been incurred. (FAR 33.201)

Accrued Benefit Cost Method An actuarial cost method under which units of benefit (e.g., a pension benefit) are assigned to each cost accounting period and are valued as they accrue (i.e., based on the services performed by each employee in the period involved). The measure of normal cost under this method for each cost accounting period is the present value of the units of benefit deemed to be credited to employees for service in that period. The measure of the actuarial liability at a plan's inception date is the present value of the units of benefit credited to employees for service prior to that date. (FAR 31.001)

Accumulating Costs Collecting cost data in an organized manner, such as through a system of accounts. (FAR 31.001)

Acquisition The acquiring by contract with appropriated funds of supplies or services (including construction) by and for the use of the Federal Government through purchase or lease, whether the supplies or services are already in existence or must be created, developed, demonstrated, and evaluated. Acquisition begins at the point when agency needs are established and includes the description of requirements to satisfy agency needs, solicitation and selection of sources, award of contracts, contract financing, contract performance, contract administration, and those technical and management functions directly related to the process of fulfilling agency needs by contract. (FAR 2.101)

Acquisition Plan A document used to facilitate acquisition planning. It must address all the technical, business, management, and other considerations that will control the acquisition. It must identify those milestones at which decisions should be made. Specific content will vary, depending on the nature, circumstances, and stage of the acquisition. Plans for service contracts must describe the strategies for implementing performance-based contracting methods or provide rationale for not using such methods. (FAR 7.105)

Acquisition Planning The process by which the efforts of all personnel responsible for an acquisition are coordinated and integrated through a comprehensive plan for fulfilling the agency need in a timely manner and at a reasonable cost. It includes developing the overall strategy for managing the acquisition. (FAR 7.101)

Acquisition Savings In value engineering, savings resulting from the application of a value engineering change proposal (VECP) to contracts awarded by the same contracting office or its successor for essentially the same unit. They include: Instant contract savings; Concurrent contract savings; and Future contract savings. (FAR 48.001)

Acquisition Streamlining Any effort that results in more efficient and effective use of resources to design and develop or produce quality systems. This includes ensuring that only necessary and cost-effective requirements are included, at the most appropriate time in the acquisition cycle, in solicitations and resulting contracts for the design, development, and production of new systems, or for modifications to existing systems that involve redesign of systems or subsystems. (FAR 7.101)

Acquisition Team All participants in Government acquisition including not only representatives of the technical, supply, and procurement communities but also the customers they serve, and the contractors who provide the products and services. (FAR 1.102(c))

Actual Cash Value The cost of replacing damaged property with other property of like kind and quality in the physical condition of the property immediately before the damage. (FAR 31.001)

Actual Costs Amounts determined on the basis of costs incurred, as distinguished from forecasted costs. Actual costs include standard costs properly adjusted for applicable variances. (FAR 31.001)

Actuarial Valuation The determination, as of a specified date, of the normal cost, actuarial liability, value of the assets of a pension fund, and other relevant values for the pension plan. (FAR 31.001)

Adequate Evidence Information sufficient to support the reasonable belief that a particular act or omission has occurred. (FAR 9.403)

Adequate Price Competition Adequate price competition exists when two or more responsible offerors, competing independently, submit priced offers that satisfy the Government's expressed requirement and: a. Award will be made to the offeror whose proposal represents the best value where price is a substantial factor in source selection; and b. There is no finding that the price of the otherwise successful offeror is unreasonable. Any finding that the price is unreasonable must be supported by a statement of the facts and approved at a level above the Contracting Officer. (FAR 15.403-1(c)(i))

Administrative Change A unilateral contract modification, in writing, that does not affect the substantive rights of the parties (e.g., a change in the paying office or the appropriation data). (FAR 43.101)

Administrative Contracting Officer (ACO) A Contracting Officer who is administering contracts. (FAR 2.101)

Administrator, Wage and Hour Division The Administrator of the Wage and Hour Division, Employment Standards Administration, U.S. Department of Labor, or an authorized representative. (FAR 22.001)

Advance Agreement An agreement on the treatment of special or unusual costs, before those costs are incurred. The purpose of the agreement is to avoid possible subsequent disallowance or dispute based on unreasonableness, unallocability, or unallowability under specific cost principles. (FAR 31.109(a))

Advance Notice A notice of projected Government construction requirements distributed to reach as many prospective offerors as practicable. (FAR 36.211)

Advance Notification Under cost-reimbursement contracts, even if the contractor has an approved purchasing system and consent to subcontract is not required, the contractor is required by statute to notify the agency before the award of: a. Any cost-plus-fixed-fee subcontract; or b. Any fixed-price subcontract that exceeds limits identified in the FAR. (FAR 44.201-2)

Advance Payment Bond A bond that secures fulfillment of the contractor's obligations under an advance payment provision. (FAR 28.001)

Advance Payments Advances of money by the Government to a prime contractor before, in anticipation of, and for the purpose of complete performance under one or more contracts. They are expected to be liquidated from payments due to the contractor incident to performance of the contracts. Since they are not measured by performance, they differ from partial, progress, or other payments based on the performance or partial performance of a contract. Advance payments may be made to prime contractors for the purpose of making advances to subcontractors. (FAR 32.102(a))

Advance Payments for Non-Commercial Contract Items A payment made before any performance of work under a non-commercial-item. Generally, the least preferred method of contract financing. (FAR 32.402)

Advertisement Any single message prepared for placement in communication media, regardless of the number of placements. (FAR 5.501)

Advertising The use of media to promote the sale of products or services and accomplish other activities identified in the FAR, regardless of the medium employed, when the advertiser has control over the form and content of what will appear, the media in which it will appear, and when it will appear. Advertising media include but are not limited to conventions, exhibits, free goods, samples, magazines, newspapers, trade papers, direct mail, dealer cards, window displays, outdoor advertising, radio, and television. (FAR 31.205-1(b))

Advertising Material Material designed to acquaint the Government with a prospective contractor's present products, services, or potential capabilities, or designed to stimulate the Government's interest in buying such products or services. (FAR 15.601)

Advisory and Assistance Services Means:
a. Services provided under contract by nongovernmental sources to: (1) Support or improve: organizational policy development; decision-making; management and administration; program and/or project management and administration; or R&D activities. (2) Furnish professional advice or assistance rendered to improve the effectiveness of Federal management processes or procedures (including those of an engineering and technical nature).
b. In rendering the foregoing services, outputs may take the form of information, advice, opinions, alternatives, analyses, evaluations, recommendations, training, and the day-to-day aid of support personnel needed for the successful performance of ongoing Federal operations. All advisory and assistance services are classified in one of the following definitional subdivisions:
  (1) Management and professional support services;
  (2) Studies, analyses and evaluations; or
  (3) Engineering and technical services. (FAR 37.201)

Affiliates 1. Associated business concerns or individuals if, directly or indirectly:
a. Either one controls or can control the other; or b. A third party controls or can control both. (FAR 2.101) 2. Business concerns, organizations, or individuals are affiliates of each other if, directly or indirectly: a. Either one controls or has the power to control the other, or b. A third party controls or has the power to control both. Indicia of control include, but are not limited to, interlocking management or ownership, identity of interests among family members, shared facilities and equipment, common use of employees, or a business entity organized following the debarment, suspension, or proposed debarment of a contractor which has the same or similar management, ownership, or principal employees as the contractor that was debarred, suspended, or proposed for debarment. (FAR 9.403); 3. Business concerns are affiliates of each other if, directly or indirectly, either one controls or has the power to control the other, or another concern controls or has the power to control both. In determining whether affiliation exists, consider all appropriate factors including common ownership, common management, and contractual relationships; provided, that restraints imposed by a franchise agreement are not considered in determining whether the franchiser controls or has the power to control the franchisee, if the franchisee has the right to profit from its effort, commensurate with ownership, and bears the risk of loss or failure.

Any business entity may be found to be an affiliate, whether or not it is organized for profit or located inside the United States. (FAR 19.101)

Affirmative Action Program A contractor's program that complies with Department of Labor regulations to ensure equal opportunity in employment to minorities and women. (FAR 22.801)

After-Imposed Federal Tax 1. Any new or increased Federal excise tax or duty, or tax that was exempted or excluded on the contract date but whose exemption was later revoked or reduced during the contract period, on the transactions or property covered by a contract that the Contractor is required to pay or bear as the result of legislative, judicial, or administrative action taking effect after the contract date. It does not include Social Security tax or other employment taxes. (FAR 52.229-3(a)). 2. Any new or increased Federal excise tax or duty, or tax that was exempted or excluded on the contract date but whose exemption was later revoked or reduced during the contract period, on the transactions or property covered by a contract that the Contractor is required to pay or bear as the result of legislative, judicial, or administrative action taking effect after the contract date. It does not include Social Security tax or other employment taxes. (FAR 52.229-4(a)) .

After-Relieved Federal Tax Any amount of Federal excise tax or duty, except Social Security or other employment taxes, that would otherwise have been payable on the transactions or property covered by a contract, but which the Contractor is not required to pay or bear, or for which the Contractor obtains a refund or drawback, as the result of legislative, judicial, or administrative action taking effect after the contract date. (FAR 52.229-3(a))

Any amount of Federal excise tax or duty, except Social Security or other employment taxes, that would otherwise have been payable on the transactions or property covered by a contract, but which the Contractor is not required to pay or bear, or for which the Contractor obtains a refund or drawback, as the result of legislative, judicial, or administrative action taking effect after the contract date. (FAR 52.229-4(a))

Agency 1. In contract law, a legal relationship in which a agent acts under the direction of a principal for the principal's benefit. 2. Any executive department, military department or defense agency, or other agency or independent establishment of the executive branch. (FAR 9.403). 3. Any executive department, military department, Government corporation, Government controlled corporation, or other establishment in the executive branch of the Government (including the Executive Office of the President), or any independent regulatory agency. (FAR 24.101). 4. See executive agency.

Agency Ethics Official The designated agency ethics official and any other designated person, including: a. Deputy ethics officials, to whom authority has been delegated by the designated agency ethics official; and b. Alternate designated agency ethics. (FAR 3.104-3)

Agency Head See head of the agency. (FAR 2.101)

Agency Labor Advisor An individual responsible for advising contracting agency officials on Federal contract labor matters. (FAR 22.1001)

Agency Procurement Protest See agency protest.

Agency Protest Also referred to as agency procurement protest. A protest made to the agency responsible for the procurement. (FAR 33.103)

Agency Screening The procedure for screening certain types of property only within the contracting agency. The screening period begins on the date the plant clearance officer receives acceptable inventory schedules and ends 30 days later. (FAR 45.608-3)

Agency-Peculiar Property Government-owned personal property that is peculiar to the mission of one agency (e.g., military or space property). It excludes Government material, special test equipment, special tooling, and facilities. (FAR 45.301)

Agent A person who acts under the direction of a principal for the principal's benefit in a legal relationship known as agency.

Aggregate Price Index Number A quantity that measures relative price changes for a group of related products over time.

Air Act The Clean Air Act. (FAR 52.223-2(a))

Air Freight Forwarder An indirect air carrier that is responsible for the transportation of property from the point of receipt to the point of destination, and utilizes for the whole or any part of such transportation the services of a direct air carrier or its agent, or of another air freight forwarder. (FAR 47.401)

All Applicable Federal, State, and Local Taxes and Duties All taxes and duties, in effect on the contract date, that the taxing authority is imposing and collecting on the transactions or property covered by the contract. (FAR 52.229-3(a))

All Applicable Taxes and Duties All taxes and duties, in effect on the contract date, that the taxing authority is imposing and collecting on the transactions or property covered by the contract, pursuant to written ruling or regulation in effect on the contract date. (FAR 52.229-6(b))

All Employment Openings All positions except executive and top management, those positions that will be filled from within the contractor's organization, and positions lasting 3 days or less. This term includes full-time employment, temporary employment of more than 3 days' duration, and part-time employment. (FAR 52.222-35(a))

Allocability A cost is allocable if it is assignable or chargeable to one or more cost objectives on the basis of relative benefits received or other equitable relationship. (FAR 31.201-4)

Allocate To assign an item of cost, or a group of items of cost, to one or more cost objectives. This term includes both direct assignment of cost and the reassignment of a share from an indirect cost pool. (FAR 31.001)

Allocation An action taken by a central nonprofit agency to designate the participating nonprofit agencies that will furnish definite quantities of supplies or perform specific services upon receipt of orders from ordering offices. (FAR 8.701)

Allowable Cost A cost that meets the tests of: a. Reasonableness; b. Allocability to the contract; c. Accounting in accordance with standards promulgated by the Cost Accounting Standards Board, if applicable; otherwise, generally accepted accounting principles and practices appropriate to the particular circumstances; d. The terms of the contract; and e. Any limitations set forth in the FAR cost principles. (FAR 31.201-2(a))

Alternate A substantive variation of a basic provision or clause prescribed for use in a defined circumstance. It: a. Adds wording to; b. Deletes wording from; or c. Substitutes specified wording for a portion of the basic provision or clause. (FAR 52.101)

Alternate Liquidation Rate See liquidation rate—alternate method.

Alternative Dispute Resolution (ADR) Any procedure or combination of procedures voluntarily used to resolve issues in controversy without the need to resort to litigation. These procedures may include, but are not limited to, assisted settlement negotiations, conciliation, facilitation, mediation, fact-finding, mini-trials, and arbitration. (FAR 33.201)

Alternative Positions By offering two or more alternative positions at the same time, a negotiator can indicate a willingness to accept more than one way of settling a particular issue or group of issues.

Amendment A change in a solicitation prior to contract award. (FAR 14.208 and FAR 15.206)

Analysis of Variance The terms used to analyze variation/variance in the regression model. These terms are (ANOVA) commonly summarized in a format known as an ANOVA table.

Annual Bid Bond A bond that secures all bids (on other than construction contracts) requiring bonds submitted during a specific Government fiscal year. (FAR 28.001)

Annual Performance Bond A single bond furnished by a bidder, in lieu of separate bonds. It is furnished by a contractor, in lieu of separate performance bonds, to secure fulfillment of the contractor's obligations under contracts (other than construction contracts) requiring bonds entered into during a specific Government fiscal year. (FAR 28.001)

Annual Receipts A measure of the revenue received by a business concern each year.

a. For a concern that has been in business for three or more complete fiscal years, the annual average gross revenue of the concern taken for the last 3 fiscal years. Details for revenue calculation are presented in the FAR. b. For a concern that has been in business for less than 3 complete fiscal years, the total receipts for the period it has been in business, divided by the number of weeks including fractions of a week that it has been in business, and multiplied by 52. Details for revenue calculation are presented in the FAR. (FAR 19.101)

Anti-Deficiency Act Requires that no officer or employee of the Government may create or authorize an obligation in excess of the funds available or in advance of appropriations unless otherwise authorized by law. (FAR 32.702)

Apparent Withdrawal A negotiator using this tactic gives the impression that his/her organization is withdrawing from the negotiation when that is not the actual intent. Instead, there is a plan to resume negotiations at some later time.

Applied Research 1. An effort which: a. Normally follows basic research, but may not be severable from the related basic research; b. Attempts to determine and exploit the potential of scientific discoveries or improvements in technology, materials, processes, methods, devices, or techniques; and c. Attempts to advance the state of the art. Applied research does not include efforts whose principal aim is design, development, or test of specific items or services to be considered for sale. (FAR 31.205-18(a))

2. An effort that: a. Normally follows basic research, but may not be severable from the related basic research; b. Attempts to determine and exploit the potential of scientific discoveries or improvements in technology, materials, processes, methods, devices, or techniques; and c. Attempts to advance the state of the art. When being used by contractors in cost principle applications, this term does not include efforts whose principal aim is the design, development, or testing of specific items or services to be considered for sale; these efforts are within the definition of development. (FAR 35.001)

Appointment Letter Document used by the contacting officer to assign contractual responsibility to another Government official. The letter or memorandum specifies the official's authority and is signed by the Contracting Officer.

Apprentice A person: a. Employed and individually registered in a bona fide apprenticeship program registered with the U.S. Department of Labor, Employment and Training Administration, Bureau of Apprenticeship and Training, or with a State Apprenticeship Agency recognized by the Bureau, or b. In the first 90 days of probationary employment as an apprentice in such an apprenticeship program, who is not individually registered in the program, but who has been certified by the Bureau of Apprenticeship and Training or a State Apprenticeship Agency (where appropriate) to be eligible for probationary employment as an apprentice. (FAR 22.401)

Appropriate Office of the State Employment Service System The local office of the Federal-State national system of public employment offices with assigned responsibility to serve the area where an employment opening is to be filled, including the District of Columbia, Guam, the Commonwealth of Puerto Rico, and the Virgin Islands. (FAR 52.222-35(a))

Approved Purchasing System A contractor's purchasing system that has been reviewed and approved in accordance with FAR requirements. (FAR 44.101)

Arbitrary Deadline Every contract negotiation has real deadlines (e.g., funding availability or required delivery) that might be used to put pressure on one party or the other. However, an arbitrary deadline is a point in time set by one of the parties to the negotiation simply to put pressure on another party.

Architect-Engineer Evaluation Board A panel composed of members who, collectively, have experience in architecture, engineering, construction, and Government and related acquisition matters. Members shall be appointed from among highly qualified professional employees of the agency or other agencies, and if authorized by agency procedures, private practitioners of architecture, engineering, or related professions. One Government member of each board shall be designated as the chairperson. Under the general direction of the head of the contracting activity, an evaluation board must perform the following functions: a. Review the current data files on eligible firms and responses to a public notice concerning the particular project; b. Evaluate the firms in accordance with the selection criteria; c. Hold discussions with at least three of the most highly qualified firms regarding concepts and the relative utility of alternative methods of furnishing the required services; and d. Prepare a selection report for the agency head or other designated selection Evaluation Board authority recommending, in order of preference, at least three firms that are considered to be the most highly qualified to perform the required services. The report must include a description of the discussions and evaluation conducted by the board to allow the selection authority to review the considerations upon which the recommendations are based. (FAR 36.602-2(a) and 36.602-3)

Architect-Engineer Selection Authority The person who makes the final selection decision. That person may be the agency head or a designated selection authority. (FAR 36.602-4)

Architect-Engineer Services a. Professional services of an architectural or engineering nature, as defined by State law, if applicable, which are required to be performed or approved by a person licensed, registered, or certified to provide such services; b. Professional services of an architectural or engineering nature performed by contract that are associated with research, planning, development, design, construction, alteration, or repair of real property; and c. Such other professional services of an architectural or engineering nature, or incidental services, which members of the architectural and engineering professions (and individuals in their employ) may logically or justifiably perform, including studies, investigations, surveying and mapping, tests, evaluations, consultations, comprehensive planning, program management, conceptual designs, plans and specifications, value engineering, construction phase services, soils engineering, drawing reviews, preparation of operating and maintenance manuals, and other related services. (FAR 36.102)

Areawide Contract A contract entered into between the General Services Administration and a utility service supplier to cover utility service needs of Federal agencies within the franchise territory of the supplier. Each areawide contract includes an authorization form for requesting service, connection, disconnection, or change in service. (FAR 41.101)

As-Built Drawings See record drawings. (FAR 36.102)

Asphalt A solid or semi-solid cementitious material that: a. Gradually liquefies when heated, b. Has bitumens as its predominating constituents, and c. Is obtained in refining crude oil. (FAR 25.108(d)(2)(ii)(A))

Assignment of Claims The transfer or making over by the contractor to a bank, trust company, or other financing institution, as security for a loan to the contractor, of its right to be paid by the Government for contract performance. (FAR 32.801)

Assignment of Contract Administration Also referred to as delegation of contract administration. As provided in agency procedures, Contracting Officers may delegate contract administration or specialized support services, either through interagency agreements or by direct request to the cognizant Contract Administration Office listed in the Federal Directory of Contract Administration Services Components. (FAR 42.202(a))

Assignment of Contract Audit Services As provided in agency procedures or interagency agreements, Contracting Officers may request audit services directly from the responsible audit agency cited in the Directory of Federal Contract Audit Offices. a. The audit request should include a suspense date and should identify any information needed by the Contracting Officer. b. The responsible audit agency may decline requests for services on a case-by-case basis, if resources of the audit agency are inadequate to accomplish the tasks. Declinations shall be in writing. (FAR 42.102)

Attorney-in-Fact An agent, independent agent, underwriter, or any other company or individual holding a power of attorney granted by a surety. See also power of attorney. (FAR 28.001)

Audit 1. A review of an offeror's or contractor's books and financial records to evaluate reporting accuracy, financial risk, or cost reasonableness and report to the Contracting Officer or another Government official. 2. A document prepared by an auditor submitting information and advice to the requesting activity related to the auditor's: a. Analysis of the contractor's financial and accounting records or other related data as to the acceptability of the contractor's incurred and estimated costs; b. Review of the financial and accounting aspects of the contractor's cost control systems; and c. Other analysis or review that required access to the contractor's financial and accounting records supporting proposed and incurred costs. (FAR 42.101(a))

Auditor 1. A person with general access to an offeror's or contractor's books and financial records to perform an audit. (FAR 15.404-2(c)(3)) 2. A person responsible for: a. Submitting information and advice to the requesting activity, based on the auditor's analysis of the contractor's financial and accounting records or other related data as to the acceptability of the contractor's incurred and estimated costs; b. Reviewing the financial and accounting aspects of the contractor's cost control systems; and c. Performing other analyses and reviews that require access to the contractor's financial and accounting records supporting proposed and incurred costs. (FAR 42.101(a))

Authorization Also referred to as authorization form. The document executed by the ordering agency and the utility supplier to order service under an area-wide contract. (FAR 41.101)

Authorization Form See authorization.

Authorized Individual A person who has been granted authority, in accordance with agency procedures, to acquire supplies and services in accordance with FAR Part 13. (FAR 13.001)

Auxiliary Item An item without which the basic unit of plant equipment cannot operate. (FAR 45.501)

Average The arithmetic mean—the measure of central tendency most commonly used in contract pricing.

Bad Debts Actual or estimated losses arising from uncollectible accounts receivable due from customers and other claims, and any directly associated costs (e.g., collection costs and legal costs). (FAR 31.205-3)

Bargaining Persuasion, alteration of assumptions and positions, give-and-take, that may apply to price, schedule, technical requirements, type of contract, or other terms of a proposed contract. (FAR 15.306(d))

Bargaining Power The power of each party in the bargaining process is relative. It comes in many forms and is never totally one-sided, because both parties have bargaining strengths and weaknesses. It must be perceived by at least one party to have an effect on negotiations. In fact, the power does not have to be real as long it is perceived.

Based on Adequate Price Competition A price is based on adequate price competition if: a. There is adequate price competition to satisfy the Government's expressed requirement; b. There was a reasonable expectation, based on market research or other assessment, that two or more responsible offerors, competing independently, would submit priced offers in response to the solicitation's expressed requirement, even though only one offer is received from a responsible offeror and if: (1) Based on the offer received, the Contracting Officer can reasonably conclude that the offer was submitted with the expectation of competition, e.g., circumstances indicate that: a. The offeror believed that at least one other offeror was capable of submitting a meaningful offer; and b. The offeror had no reason to believe that other potential offerors did not intend to submit an offer; and (2) The determination that the proposed price is based on adequate price competition, is reasonable, and is approved at a level above the Contracting Officer; or c. Price analysis clearly demonstrates that the proposed price is reasonable in comparison with current or recent prices for the same or similar items, adjusted to reflect changes in market conditions, economic conditions, quantities, or terms and conditions under contracts that resulted from adequate price competition. (FAR 15.403-1)

Based on Prices Set by Law or Regulation A price is based on prices set by law or regulation if the price is set by pronouncements in the form of periodic rulings, reviews, or similar actions of a governmental body, or embodied in the law. (FAR 15.403-1)

Basic Agreement A basic agreement is not a contract. It is a written instrument of understanding, negotiated between an agency or contracting activity and a contractor, that: a. Contains contract clauses applying to future contracts between the parties during its term; and b. Contemplates separate future contracts that will incorporate by reference or attachment the required and applicable clauses agreed upon in the basic agreement. (FAR 16.702(a))

Basic Ordering A basic ordering agreement is not a contract. It is a written instrument of Agreement understanding, negotiated between an agency, contracting activity, or contracting office and a contractor that contains: a. Terms and clauses applying to future contracts (orders) between the parties during its term; b. A description, as specific as practicable, of supplies or services to be provided; and c. Methods for pricing, issuing, and delivering future orders under the basic ordering agreement. (FAR 16.703(a))

Basic Research 1. Research directed toward the increase of knowledge in science. The primary aim of basic research is a fuller knowledge or understanding of the subject under study, rather than any practical application thereof. (FAR 31.205-18(a)) 2. Research directed toward increasing knowledge in science. The primary aim of basic research is a fuller knowledge or understanding of the subject under study, rather than any practical application of that knowledge. (FAR 35.001)

Benefit-Cost Analysis See cost-benefit analysis.

Best Alternative to Negotiated Agreement (BATNA) An analysis of negotiator alternatives if negotiations fail. It provides a measure of relative bargaining power and the long-term effect of negotiations. For example, sometimes accepting an unreasonable negotiation result may be better than the available alternatives (e.g., a contractor may accept an unreasonably low price in an effort to limit future competition).

Best Practices Techniques that agencies may use to help detect problems in the acquisition, management, and administration of service contracts. Best practices are practical techniques gained from experience that agencies may use to improve the procurement process. (FAR 37.501)

Best Value The expected outcome of an acquisition that, in the Government's estimation, provides the greatest overall benefit in response to the requirement. (FAR 2.101)

Bid Also referred to as sealed bid. An offer in response to an invitation for bids. (FAR 2.101)

Bid and Proposal (B&P) Costs Costs incurred in preparing, submitting, and supporting bids and proposals (whether or not solicited) on potential Government or non-Government contracts. The term does not include the costs of effort sponsored by a grant or cooperative agreement, or required in the performance of a contract. (FAR 31.205-18(a))

Bid Guarantee A form of security assuring that the bidder not: a. Not withdraw a bid within the period specified for acceptance; and b. Execute a written contract and furnish required bonds, including any necessary coinsurance or reinsurance agreements, within the time specified in the bid, unless a longer time allowed, after receipt of the specified forms. (FAR 28.001)

Bid Opening For unclassified bids, the bid opening officer (or delegated assistant) must decide when the time set for opening bids in the solicitation has arrived and inform those present of that decision. The bid opening officer (or delegated assistant) must: a. Personally and publicly open all bids received before that time. b. If practical, read the bids aloud to the persons present. c. Have the bids recorded. The original of each bid must be carefully safeguarded, particularly until the abstract of bids has been made and its accuracy verified. d. Permit the examination of bids by interested persons if it does not interfere unduly with the conduct of Government business. (FAR 14.402-1)

Bid Protest See protest.

Bid Sample 1. A sample to be furnished by a bidder to show the characteristics of the product offered in a bid. (FAR 14.202-4). 2. Item sample submissions required of bidders to show those characteristics of the offered products that cannot adequately be described by specifications or purchase descriptions (e.g., balance, facility of use, or pattern). (FAR 52.214-20(a))

Bidder Any person who has submitted a bid in response to an invitation for bids.

Bilateral Modification A contract modification that is signed by the contractor and the Contracting Officer. Bilateral modifications are used to: a. Make negotiated equitable adjustments resulting from the issuance of a change order; b. Definitize letter contracts; and c. Reflect other agreements of the parties modifying the terms of contracts. (FAR 43.103(a))

Billing Rate An indirect cost rate: a. Established temporarily for interim reimbursement of incurred indirect costs; and b. Adjusted as necessary pending establishment of final indirect cost rates. (FAR 42.701)

Blanket Purchase Agreement (BPA) A simplified method of filling anticipated repetitive needs for supplies or services by establishing charge accounts with qualified sources of supply. (FAR 13.303-1(a))

Blanketing A negotiation approach designed to get all the issues on the table at the beginning of the negotiation. Negotiators using the blanketing tactic open the negotiation by outlining all their demands at once.

Bogey A bogey is standard of performance set up as a mark to be attained. A negotiator using the bogey tactic blames the negotiation position on a standard set by a third party or a situation beyond the negotiator's control (e.g., management policy). Any reason might be used as long as it is beyond the negotiator's control.

Bona Fide 1. Genuine. 2. Made honestly and in good faith.

Bona Fide Agency An established commercial or selling agency, maintained by a contractor for the purpose of securing business, that neither exerts nor proposes to exert improper influence to solicit or obtain Government contracts nor holds itself out as being able to obtain any Government contract or contracts through improper influence. (FAR 3.401)

Bona Fide Employee A person, employed by a contractor and subject to the contractor's supervision and control as to time, place, and manner of performance, who neither exerts nor proposes to exert improper influence to solicit or obtain Government contracts nor holds out as being able to obtain any Government contract or contracts through improper influence. (FAR 3.401)

Bond A written instrument executed by a bidder or contractor (the principal), and a second party (the surety or sureties), to assure fulfillment of the principal's obligations to a third party (the obligee or Government), identified in the bond. If the principal's obligations are not met, the bond assures payment, to the extent stipulated, of any loss sustained by the obligee. (FAR 28.001)

Bonding Costs Costs arise when the Government or the contract requires assurance against financial loss to itself or others by reason of the act or default of the contractor.

Bonuses and Incentive Compensation Incentive compensation for management employees, cash bonuses, suggestion awards, safety awards, and incentive compensation based on production, cost reduction, or efficient performance. (FAR 31.205-6(f)(1))

Borrower A contractor, subcontractor (at any tier), or other supplier who receives a guaranteed loan. (FAR 32.301)

Both-Win Outcome See win/win outcome.

Bracketing A bracket is a group or class of issues or solutions that are linked together. Negotiators can use this technique to identify issues that are critical to a mutually satisfactory result.

Brainstorming A technique to develop alternative solutions through an unrestrained exchange of ideas. Negotiators using this tactic think out loud and openly discuss many alternative solutions or ways to resolve issues. No value judgment is placed on any idea during the brainstorming session. Ideas are simply recorded for later evaluation and possible use.

Break Even A situation that exists when cost and revenue (e.g., contract price) are equal. Profit is zero.

Broad Agency Announcement A general announcement of an agency's research interest including criteria for selecting proposals and soliciting the participation of all offerors capable of satisfying the Government's needs. (FAR 35.001)

Building Construction activity as distinguished from manufacturing, furnishing of materials, or servicing and maintenance work. The term includes, without limitation, buildings, structures, and improvements of all types, such as bridges, dams, plants, highways, parkways, streets, subways, tunnels, sewers, mains, power lines, pumping stations, heavy generators, railways, airports, terminals, docks, piers, wharves, ways, lighthouses, buoys, jetties, breakwaters, levees, canals, dredging, shoring, rehabilitation and reactivation of plants, scaffolding, drilling, blasting, excavating, clearing, and landscaping. The manufacture or furnishing of materials, articles, supplies, or equipment (whether or not a Federal or state agency acquires title to such materials, articles, supplies, or equipment during the course of the manufacture or furnishing, or owns the materials from which they are manufactured or furnished) is not building within the meaning of this definition unless conducted in connection with and at the site of such building as is described in the foregoing sentence, or under the United States Housing Act of 1937 and the Housing Act of 1949 in the construction or development of the project. (FAR 22.401)

Building Construction The construction of sheltered enclosures with walk-in access, for housing persons, machinery, equipment, or supplies. It typically includes all construction of such structures, installation of utilities and equipment (both above and below grade level), as well as incidental grading, utilities and paving, unless there is an established area practice to the contrary. (FAR 22.404-2(c)(1))

Building Service Contract A contract for recurring services related to the maintenance of a public building. Recurring services are services that are required to be performed regularly or periodically throughout the course of a contract, and throughout the course of the succeeding or follow-on contract(s), at one or more of the same public buildings.

a. Building service include, but are not limited to, contracts for the recurring provision of custodial or janitorial services; window washing; laundry; food services; guard or other protective services; landscaping and grounds keeping services; and inspection, maintenance, and repair of fixed equipment such as elevators, air conditioning, and heating systems. b. Building service contracts do not include:

(1) Contracts that provide maintenance services only on a non-recurring or irregular basis (e.g., a contract to provide servicing of fixed equipment once a year, or to mulch a garden on a one-time or annual basis, is a non-recurring maintenance contract); (2) Contracts for day-care services in a Federal office building; or (3) Concessions for sales of goods or services other than food services or laundry services. (FAR 22.1202)

Burden See indirect cost.

Burden Rate See indirect cost rate.

Bureau Helium Distributor A private helium distributor which has established and maintains eligibility to distribute helium purchased from the Bureau of Land Management. (FAR 8.501)

Bureau of Land Management Department of the Interior, Bureau of Land Management. (FAR 8.501)

Business Unit Any segment of an organization, or an entire business organization which is not divided into segments. (FAR 31.001)

Buy Item An item or work effort to be produced or performed by a subcontractor. (FAR 15.407-2(b))

Buying-In Submitting an offer below anticipated costs, expecting to: a. Increase the contract amount after award (e.g., through unnecessary or excessively priced change orders); or b. Receive follow-on contracts at artificially high prices to recover losses incurred on the buy-in contract. (FAR 3.501-1)

C. & f. Destination Free of expense to the Government delivered on board the ocean vessel to the specified point of destination, with the cost of transportation paid by the Contractor. (FAR 52.247-41(a))

C.i.f. Destination Free of expense to the Government delivered on board the ocean vessel to the specified point of destination, with the cost of transportation and marine insurance paid by the Contractor. (FAR 52.247-42(a))

Canadian End Product An article that: a. Is wholly the growth, product, or manufacture of Canada; or b. In the case of an article which consists in whole or in part of materials from another country or instrumentality, has been substantially transformed in Canada into a new and different article of commerce with a name, character, or use distinct from that of the article or articles from which it was transformed. The term refers to a product offered for purchase under a supply contract, but for purposes of calculating the value of the end product includes services (except transportation services) incidental to its supply; provided, that the value of those incidental services does not exceed that of the product itself. (FAR 25.401)

Cancellation The cancellation (within a contractually specified time) of the total requirements of all remaining program years of a multi-year contract. Cancellation results when the Contracting Officer a. Notifies the cancellation contractor of nonavailability of funds for contract performance for any subsequent program year; or b. Fails to notify the contractor that funds are available for performance of the succeeding program year requirement. (FAR 17.103)

Cancellation Ceiling The maximum cancellation charge that the contractor can receive in the event of multi-year contract. (FAR 17.103)

Cancellation Charge The amount of unrecovered costs which would have been recouped through amortization over the full term of a multi-year contract, including the term canceled. (FAR 17.103)

Capital Asset Tangible property, including durable goods, equipment, buildings, installations, and land. (OMB Circular A-94, App A)

Capital Property Contractor's plant, equipment, and other facilities subject to depreciation. (FAR 31.205-11(c))

Carrier A common carrier or a contract carrier. (FAR 47.001)

CAS-Covered Contract Any negotiated contract or subcontract in which a CAS clause is required to be included. (FAR 9903.301(a))

Central Nonprofit Agency The nonprofit agency designated to represent a specific group under the Javits-Wagner-O'Day Act. National Industries for the Blind (NIB) has been designated to represent people who are blind. NISH has been designated to represent participating nonprofit agencies serving people with severe disabilities other than blindness. (FAR 8.701)

Certificate of Competency (COC) A document issued by the Small Business Administration stating that the holder is responsible (with respect to all elements of responsibility, including, but not limited to, capability, competency, capacity, credit, integrity, perseverance, tenacity, and limitations on subcontracting) for the purpose of receiving and performing a specific Government contract. (FAR 19.601(a))

Certificate of Conformance A certificate signed by a contractor representative that the supplies or services required by the contract have been furnished in accordance with all applicable contract requirements. The certificate further states that the supplies or services are of the quality specified and conform in all respects with the contract requirements, including specifications, drawings, preservation, packaging, packing, marking requirements, and physical item identification (part number), and are in the quantity shown on this or on the attached acceptance document. (FAR 46.315 and 52.246-15)

Certificate of Current Cost or Pricing Data A certificate in a FAR-prescribed format that cost or pricing data submitted, either actually or by specific identification in writing, are accurate, complete, and current as of the date that negotiations were concluded and price agreement reached or (if applicable) an earlier date agreed upon between the parties that is as close as practicable to the date of agreement on price. (FAR 15.406-2(a))

Certificate of Indirect Costs A certificate that the contractor's final indirect cost rate proposal does not include any costs which are expressly unallowable under applicable cost principles of the FAR or its supplements. The certificate is required as part of any final indirect rate proposal and a proposal must not be accepted and no agreement made to establish final indirect cost rates unless the costs have been certified by the contractor. However, the agency head, or designee, can waive the certification requirement under certain circumstances. (FAR 42.703-2 and 52.242-4)

Certified Invoice An invoice certified for payment under the terms of the contract in lieu of a separate receiving report. It must contain the information described in paragraphs required for a receiving report. (FAR 32.905(f)(7))

Change Order A written order, signed by the Contracting Officer, directing the contractor to make a change that the Changes clause authorizes the Contracting Officer to order without the contractor's consent. (FAR 43.101)

Change-of-Name Agreement A legal instrument executed by the contractor and the Government that recognizes the legal change of name of the contractor without disturbing the original contractual rights and obligations of the parties. (FAR 42.1201)

Civil Aircraft and Related Articles Includes: a. All aircraft other than aircraft to be purchased for use by the Department of Defense or the U.S. Coast Guard; b. The engines (and parts and components for incorporation into the engines) of these aircraft; c. Any other parts, components, and subassemblies for incorporation into the aircraft; and d. Any ground flight simulators, and parts and components of these simulators, for use with respect to the aircraft, whether to be used as original or replacement equipment in the manufacture, repair, maintenance, rebuilding, modification, or conversion of the aircraft, and without regard to whether the aircraft or articles receive duty-free treatment under the Trade Agreements Act of 1979. (FAR 25.101)

Civil Judgment A judgment or finding of a civil offense by any court of competent jurisdiction. (FAR 9.403)

Claim A written demand or written assertion by one of the contracting parties seeking, as a matter of right, the payment of money in a sum certain, the adjustment or interpretation of contract terms, or other relief arising under or relating to the contract. A claim arising under a contract, unlike a claim relating to that contract, is a claim that can be resolved under a contract clause that provides for the relief sought by the claimant. However, a written demand or written assertion by the contractor seeking the payment of money exceeding $100,000 is not a claim under the Contract Disputes Act of 1978 until certified as required by the Act and the FAR. A voucher, invoice, or other routine request for payment that is not in dispute when submitted is not a claim. The submission may be converted to a claim, by written notice to the Contracting Officer, if it is disputed either as to liability or amount or is not acted upon in a reasonable time. (FAR 33.201)

Claim Accrual See accrual of a claim.

Clarifications Limited exchanges, between the Government and offerors, that may occur after receipt of proposals when award without discussions is contemplated. (FAR 15.306(a))

Class Determinations and Findings A determination and findings that provides authority for a class of contracting actions. A class may consist of contracting actions for the same or related supplies or services or other contracting actions that require essentially identical justification. The findings must fully support the proposed action either for the class as a whole or for each action. The class determination and finding must be for a specified period, with the expiration date stated in the document. (FAR 1.703)

Class Deviations A FAR deviation that affects more than one contracting action. (FAR 1.404)

Classified Acquisition An acquisition that consists of one or more contracts in which offerors would be required to have access to classified information (confidential, secret, or top secret) to properly submit an offer or quotation, to understand the performance requirements of a classified contract under the acquisition, or to perform the contract. (FAR 4.401)

Classified Bid Any bid that contains classified information (confidential, secret, or top secret).

Classified Contract Any contract that requires, or will require, access to classified information (confidential, secret, or top secret) by the contractor or its employees in the performance of the contract. A contract may be a classified contract even though the contract document is not classified. (FAR 4.401)

Classified Information Any information or material, regardless of its physical form or characteristics, that is owned by, produced by or for, or under the control of the United States Government, and determined pursuant to Executive Order 12356, April 2, 1982 or prior orders to require protection against unauthorized disclosure, and is so designated. (FAR 4.401)

Clause See contract clause.

Code of Ethical Conduct A code set forth in E.O. 11222, which reads "Where Government is based on consent of the governed, every citizen is entitled to have complete confidence in the integrity of his Government. Each individual officer, employee, or advisor of Government must help to earn and must honor that trust by his own integrity and conduct in all official actions." (Executive Order 11222)

Coefficient of Determination A measure of the strength of the association between the independent and dependent variables. Coefficient values can range from zero and one. A value of zero indicates that there is no relationship between the independent and dependent variables. A value of one indicates that there is a perfect relationship. The closer the coefficient is to one, the better the regression line fits the data set. For example, a coefficient value of .90 indicates that 90 percent of the variation in the dependent variable has been explained by its relationship with the independent variable.

Coefficient of Variation A measure of relative dispersion between two samples when sample means are not equal.

Cognizant Administrative Contracting Officer (ACO) The Administrative Contracting Officer responsible for a particular contract or group of contracts at business unit.

Cognizant Audit Office The office responsible for performing audits at a particular business unit.

Cognizant Auditor The auditor responsible for performing audits of a particular contract or group of contracts at a business unit.

Cognizant Federal Agency The Federal agency that, on behalf of all Federal agencies, is responsible for establishing final indirect cost rates and forward pricing rates, if applicable, and administering cost accounting standards for all contracts in a business unit. (FAR 42.001)

Collateral Costs In value engineering, agency costs of operation, maintenance, logistic support, or Government-furnished property. (FAR 48.001)

Collateral Savings In value engineering, those measurable net reductions resulting from a value engineering change proposal in the agency's overall projected collateral costs, exclusive of acquisition savings, whether or not the acquisition cost changes. (FAR 48.001)

Commerce Business Daily (CBD) The public notification media by which U.S. Government agencies identify proposed contract actions and contract awards. It is published in five or six daily editions weekly, as necessary. (FAR 5.101)

Commercial Advance Payment A payment made before any performance of work under a commercial-item contract. The aggregate of these payments must not exceed 15 percent of the contract price. These payments are contract financing payments for prompt payment purposes (i.e., not subject to the interest penalty provisions of the Prompt Payment Act). These payments are not subject to the requirements that apply to advance payments for noncommercial items. (FAR 32.202-2)

Commercial Carrier   See carrier.

Commercial Component   Any component that is a commercial item. (FAR 2.101)

Commercial Interim Payment   Any payment that is not a commercial advance payment or a delivery payment. These payments are contract financing payments for prompt payment purposes (i.e., not subject to the interest penalty provisions of the Prompt Payment Act). A commercial interim payment is given to the contractor after some work has been done, whereas a commercial advance payment is given to the contractor when no work has been done. (FAR 32.202-2)

Commercial Item   Includes: a. Any item, other than real property, that is of a type customarily used for nongovernmental purposes and that: (1) Has been sold, leased, or licensed to the general public; or, (2) Has been offered for sale, lease, or license to the general public; b. Any item that evolved from an item described in Paragraph 1 of this definition through advances in technology or performance and that is not yet available in the commercial marketplace, but will be available in the commercial marketplace in time to satisfy the delivery requirements under a Government solicitation; c. Any item that would satisfy a criterion expressed in Paragraphs 1 or 2 of this definition, but for:
(1) Modifications of a type customarily available in the commercial marketplace; or (2) Minor modifications of a type not customarily available in the commercial marketplace made to meet Federal Government requirements. Minor modifications means modifications that do not significantly alter the nongovernmental function or essential physical characteristics of an item or component, or change the purpose of a process. Factors to be considered in determining whether a modification is minor include the value and size of the modification and the comparative value and size of the final product. Dollar values and percentages may be used as guideposts, but are not conclusive evidence that a modification is minor; d. Any combination of items meeting the requirements of Paragraphs a, b, c, or e of this definition that are of a type customarily combined and sold in combination to the general public; e. Installation services, maintenance services, repair services, training services, and other services if such services are procured for support of an item referred to in Paragraphs a, b, c, or d of this definition, and if the source of such services (1) Offers such services to the general public and the Federal Government contemporaneously and under similar terms and conditions; and (2) Offers to use the same work force for providing the Federal Government with such services as the source uses for providing such services to the general public; f. Services of a type offered and sold competitively in substantial quantities in the commercial marketplace based on established catalog or market prices for specific tasks performed under standard commercial terms and conditions. This does not include services that are sold based on hourly rates without an established catalog or market price for a specific service performed; g. Any item, combination of items, or service referred to in Paragraphs a through f, notwithstanding the fact that the item, combination of items, or service is transferred between or among separate divisions, subsidiaries, or affiliates of a contractor; or h. A nondevelopmental item, if the procuring agency determines the item was developed exclusively at private expense and sold in substantial quantities, on a competitive basis, to multiple State and local governments. (FAR 2.101)

Commercial Item Offer   An offer of a commercial item that the vendor wishes to see introduced in the Government's supply system as an alternate or a replacement for an existing supply item. This term does not include innovative or unique configurations or uses of commercial items that are being offered for further development and that may be submitted as an unsolicited proposal. (FAR 15.601)

Commercial Plan   A subcontracting plan (including goals) that covers the offeror's fiscal year and that applies to the entire production of commercial items sold by either the entire company or a portion thereof (e.g., division, plant, or product line). (FAR 19.701)

Committee   The Committee for Purchase from People Who Are Blind or Severely Disabled. (FAR 8.701)

Common Carrier   1. A person holding itself out to the general public to provide transportation for compensation. (FAR 47.001) 2. A person holding itself out to the general public to provide telecommunications services for compensation.

Common Item   Material that is common to the applicable Government contract and the contractor's other work. (FAR 45.601)

Common Parent   1. Corporate entity that owns or controls an affiliated group of corporations that files its Federal income tax returns on a consolidated basis, and of which the offeror is a member. (FAR 4.901) 2. Corporate entity that owns or controls an affiliated group of corporations that files its Federal income tax returns on a consolidated basis, and of which the offeror is a member. (FAR 52.204-3(a))

Communications   Exchanges, between the Government and offerors, after receipt of proposals, leading to establishment of the competitive range. (FAR 15.306(b))

Company All divisions, subsidiaries, and affiliates of the contractor under common control. (FAR 31.205-18(a))

Compensated Personal Absence Any absence from work for reasons such as illness, vacation, holidays, jury duty, military training, or personal activities for which an employer pays compensation directly to an employee in accordance with a plan or custom of the employer. (FAR 31.001)

Compensation Wages, salaries, honoraria, commissions, professional fees, and any other form of compensation, provided directly or indirectly for services rendered. Compensation is indirectly provided if it is paid to an entity other than the individual, specifically in exchange for services provided by the individual. (FAR 3.104-3)

Compensation for Personal Services All remuneration paid currently or accrued, in whatever form and whether paid immediately or deferred, for services rendered by employees to the contractor during the period of contract performance (except as otherwise provided for in the FAR). It includes, but is not limited to, salaries; wages; directors' and executive committee members' fees; bonuses (including stock bonuses); incentive awards; employee stock options, and stock appreciation rights; employee stock ownership plans; employee insurance; fringe benefits; contributions to pension, other postretirement benefits, annuity, and employee incentive compensation plans; and allowances for off-site pay, incentive pay, location allowances, hardship pay, severance pay, and cost of living differential. (FAR 31.205-6(a))

Competitive Range Based on the ratings of each proposal against all evaluation criteria, all of the most highly rated proposals, unless the range is further reduced for purposes of efficiency. (FAR 15.306(c))

Completion Form A form of cost-plus-fixed-fee contract that describes the scope of work by stating a definite goal or target and specifying an end product. It normally requires the contractor to complete and deliver the specified end product (e.g., a final report of research accomplishing the goal or target) within the estimated cost, if possible, as a condition for payment of the entire fixed fee. However, in the event the work cannot be completed within the estimated cost, the Government may require more effort without increase in fee, provided the Government increases the estimated cost. (FAR 16.306(d)(1))

Compliance Compliance with: a. Clean air or water standards; or b. A schedule or plan ordered or approved by a court of competent jurisdiction, the EPA, or an air or water pollution control agency under the requirements of the Air Act or Water Act and related regulations. (FAR 52.223-2(a))

Component Any item supplied to the Federal Government as part of an end item or of another component. (FAR 2.101)

Components 1. Those articles, materials, and supplies incorporated directly into the end products. (FAR 25.101). 2. Those articles, materials, and supplies incorporated directly into construction materials. (FAR 25.201). 3. Those articles, materials, and supplies incorporated directly into the end products. (FAR 25.225-9(a))

Computer Software Concern Computer programs, computer data bases, and documentation thereof. (FAR 27.401). Any business entity organized for profit (even if its ownership is in the hands of a nonprofit entity) with a place of business located in the United States and which makes a significant contribution to the U.S. economy through payment of taxes and/or use of American products, material and/or labor, etc. It includes but is not limited to an individual, partnership, corporation, joint venture, association, or cooperative. (FAR 19.001)

Concurrent Contract Savings In value engineering, net reductions in the prices of other contracts that are definitized and ongoing at the time the value engineering change proposal is accepted. (FAR 48.001)

Confidence Interval A probability statement about an interval which is likely to contain the true population mean.

Confidence Level A measure of the confidence that a particular interval includes the population mean.

Connection Charge All nonrecurring costs, whether refundable or nonrefundable, to be paid by the Government to the utility supplier for the required connecting facilities, which are installed, owned, operated, and maintained by the utility supplier. (FAR 41.101)

Conscious Nonverbal Messages Senders are aware that they are sending a nonverbal message and the general meaning of that message. Receivers of conscious nonverbal communication are aware that they received the message and the meaning intended by the sender. For example, the individuals extending a hug know that they are embracing someone and that action is normally perceived as indicating affection. The receiver of a hug generally realizes that the message is a sign of friendship.

Consent of Surety An acknowledgment by a surety that its bond given in connection with a contract continues to apply to the contract as modified. (FAR 28.001)

Consent to Subcontract 1. The Contracting Officer's written consent for the prime contractor to enter into a particular subcontract. (FAR 44.101) 2. The requirement for the Contracting Officer responsible for contract administration to consent to identified subcontract actions: a. If the contractor has an approved purchasing system, consent is required for subcontracts specifically identified by the Contracting Officer in the subcontracts clause of the contract. b. If the contractor does not have an approved purchasing system, consent to the subcontract is required for cost-reimbursement, time-and-materials, labor-hour, or letter contracts, and also for many unpriced actions (including unpriced modifications and unpriced delivery orders) under fixed-price contracts that exceed the simplified acquisition threshold. (FAR 44.201-1)

Consideration In contract law, something of value. It may be money, an act, or a promise. It is one of the key elements required to have a binding contract.

Constant Dollar Values Economic units measured in terms of constant purchasing power. Constant dollar values are not affected by general price inflation. (OMB Circular A-94, App A)

Construction 1. Construction, alteration, or repair of any public building or public work in the United States. (FAR 25.201) 2. Construction, alteration, or repair (including dredging, excavating, and painting) of buildings, structures, or other real property. For purposes of this definition, the terms buildings, structures, or other real property include but are not limited to improvements of all types, such as bridges, dams, plants, highways, parkways, streets, subways, tunnels, sewers, mains, power lines, cemeteries, pumping stations, railways, airport facilities, terminals, docks, piers, wharves, ways, lighthouses, buoys, jetties, breakwaters, levees, canals, and channels. Construction does not include the manufacture, production, furnishing, construction, alteration, repair, processing, or assembling of vessels, aircraft, or other kinds of personal property. (FAR 36.102)

Construction Equipment Equipment (including marine equipment) in sound workable condition, either owned or controlled by the contractor or the subcontractor at any tier, or obtained from a commercial rental source, and furnished for use under Government contracts. (FAR 31.105(d)(2))

Construction Material An article, material, or supply brought to the construction site for incorporation into the building or work. Construction material also includes an item brought to the site pre-assembled from articles, materials, and supplies. However, emergency life safety systems, such as emergency lighting, fire alarm, and audio evacuation systems, which are discrete systems incorporated into a public building or work and which are produced as a complete system, shall be evaluated as a single and distinct construction material regardless of when or how the individual parts or components of such systems are delivered to the construction site. (FAR 25.201)

Construction Work The construction, rehabilitation, alteration, conversion, extension, demolition, or repair of buildings, highways, or other changes or improvements to real property, including facilities providing utility services. The term also includes the supervision, inspection, and other on-site functions incidental to the actual construction. (FAR 22.801)

Construction Alteration, or Repair All types of work done on a particular building or work at the site thereof, including without limitation, altering, remodeling, installation (if appropriate) on the site of the work of items fabricated off-site, painting and decorating, the transporting of materials and supplies to or from the building or work by the employees of the construction contractor or construction subcontractor, and the manufacturing or furnishing of materials, articles, supplies, or equipment on the site of the building or work by persons employed by the contractor or subcontractor. (FAR 22.401)

Constructive Change A Government action or inaction that constitutes an unauthorized modification of contract requirements. The Contracting Officer may be required to follow agency ratification procedures, prior to considering formalization of the modification.

Consumer Price Index (CPI) Published monthly by the U.S. Department of Labor, Bureau of Labor Statistics (BLS), measures changes in consumer prices for a fixed mix of goods selected from the following categories: food; clothing; shelter and fuels; transportation; and medical services.

Consumer Product Any article (other than an automobile) that: a. Consumes energy; and b. Is distributed in commerce for personal use or consumption by individuals. (FAR 23.202)

Continental United States (CONUS) The 48 contiguous states and the District of Columbia. (FAR 47.001)

Contingency A possible future event or condition arising from presently known or unknown causes, the outcome of which is indeterminable at the present time. (FAR 31.205-7(a))

Contingent Fee Any commission, percentage, brokerage, or other fee that is contingent upon the success that a person or concern has in securing a Government contract. (FAR 3.401)

Continued Portion of the Contract The portion of a partially terminated contract that the contractor must continue to perform. (FAR 49.001)

Contract A mutually binding legal relationship obligating the seller to furnish the supplies or services (including construction) and the buyer to pay for them. It includes all types of commitments that obligate the Government to an expenditure of appropriated funds and that, except as otherwise authorized, are in writing. In addition to bilateral instruments, contracts include (but are not limited to) awards and notices of awards; job orders or task letters issued under basic ordering agreements; letter contracts; orders, such as purchase orders, under which the contract becomes effective by written acceptance or performance; and bilateral contract modifications. Contracts do not include grants and cooperative agreements. (FAR 2.101)

Contract Action An action resulting in a contract, including contract modifications for additional supplies or services, but not including contract modifications that are within the scope and under the terms of the contract, such as contract modifications issued pursuant to the Changes clause, or funding and other administrative changes. (FAR 32.001)

Contract Adjustment Boards An agency head may establish a contract adjustment board with authority to approve, authorize, and direct appropriate extraordinary contractual actions and to make all appropriate determinations and findings. The decisions of the board shall not be subject to appeal; however, the board may reconsider and modify, correct, or reverse its previous decisions. The board must determine its own procedures and have authority to take all action necessary or appropriate to conduct its functions. (FAR 50.202)

Contract Administration File File which contains the document supporting all actions reflecting the basis for and the performance of contract administration responsibilities. Included are the copy of the contract and all modifications, together with official record copies of supporting documents executed by the Contract Administration Office. (FAR 4.802)

Contract Administration Office An office that performs: a. Assigned postaward functions related to the administration of contracts; and b. Assigned preaward functions. (FAR 2.101)

Contract Administration Plan The Contracting Officer's scheme for performing the functions required for contract administration.

Contract Carrier 1. A person providing transportation for compensation under continuing agreements with one person or a limited number of persons. (FAR 47.001)

2. A person providing telecommunications services for compensation under continuing agreements with one person or a limited number of persons.

Contract Clause A term or condition used in contracts or in both solicitations and contracts, and applying after contract award or both before and after award. (FAR 52.101)

Contract Closeout Action taken in accordance with the FAR and agency procedures to close the contract and dispose of the contract file after receipt of evidence of physical contract completion. (FAR 4.804-5 and 4.805)

Contract Date 1. The date set for bid opening or, if this is a negotiated contract or a modification, the effective date of a contract or modification.

(FAR 52.229-3(a)) 2. The effective date of a contract and, for any modification to a contract, the effective date of a modification. (FAR 52.229-4(a))

Contract Disputes Act of 1978 Establishes procedures and requirements for asserting and resolving claims subject to the Act. In addition, the Act provides for: a. The payment of interest on contractor claims; b. Certification of contractor claims; and c. A civil penalty for contractor claims that are fraudulent or based on a misrepresentation of fact. (FAR 33.202)

Contract Elements To be legally enforceable, a contract must include the following: an offer, an acceptance, consideration, execution by competent parties, legality of purpose, and clear terms and conditions.

Contract Financing Payment A Government disbursement of monies to a contractor under a contract clause or other authorization prior to acceptance of supplies or services by the Government. Contract financing payments include advance payments, progress payments based on cost, progress payments based on a percentage or stage of completion (other than those made under fixed-price construction or architect-engineer contracts), and interim payments on cost-type contracts. Contract financing payments do not include invoice payments or payments for partial deliveries. (FAR 32.902)

Contract Modification Also referred to as a modification. Any written change in the terms of a contract. (FAR 43.101)

Contract Price 1. The award price of a contract or, for requirements contracts, the price payable for the estimated quantity; or for indefinite-delivery type contracts, the price payable for the specified minimum quantity. (FAR 52.228-15(a)) 2. The total amount of a contract for the term of the contract (excluding options, if any) or, for requirements contracts, the price payable for the estimated quantity; or for indefinite-delivery type contracts, the price payable for the specified minimum quantity. (FAR 52.228-16(a))

Contract Quality Requirements The technical requirements in the contract relating to the quality of the product or service and those contract clauses prescribing inspection, and other quality controls incumbent on the contractor, to assure that the product or service conforms to the contractual requirements. (FAR 46.101)

Contract Type Also referred to as type of contract. Categories of contracts that are differentiated according to: a. The degree and timing of the responsibility assumed by the contractor for the costs of performance; and b. The amount and nature of the profit incentive offered to the contractor for achieving or exceeding specified standards or goals. (FAR 16.101(a))

Contract Work Hours and Safety Standards Act Requires that certain contracts contain a clause specifying that no laborer or mechanic doing any part of the work contemplated by the contract shall be required or permitted to work more than 40 hours in any workweek unless paid for all additional hours at not less than 1 1/2 times the basic rate of pay. (FAR 22.403-3)

Contracting Purchasing, renting, leasing, or otherwise obtaining supplies or services from nonfederal sources. Contracting includes description (but not determination) of supplies and services required, selection and solicitation of sources, preparation and award of contracts, and all phases of contract administration. It does not include making grants or cooperative agreements. (FAR 2.101)

Contracting Action An action resulting in a contract, including contract modifications for additional supplies or services, but not including contract modifications that are within the scope and under the terms of the contract, such as contract modifications issued pursuant to the contract Changes clause, or funding and other administrative changes. (FAR 5.001)

Contracting Activity An element of an agency designated by the agency head and delegated broad authority regarding acquisition functions. (FAR 2.101)

Contracting Agency Any department, agency, establishment, or instrumentality in the Executive Branch of the Government, including any wholly owned Government corporation that enters into contracts. (FAR 22.801)

Contracting Office 1. An office that awards or executes a contract for supplies or services and performs postaward functions not assigned to a contract administration office. (FAR 2.101) 2. Any contracting office that the acquisition is transferred to, such as another branch of the agency or another agency's office that is performing a joint acquisition action. (FAR 48.001)

Contracting Officer 1. A person with the authority to enter into, administer, and/or terminate contracts (CO) and make related determinations and findings. The term includes certain authorized representatives of the Contracting Officer acting within the limits of their authority as delegated by the Contracting Officer. A single Contracting Officer may be responsible for duties in any or all of these areas. FAR reference to the Administrative or Termination Contracting Officer does not: a. Require that a duty be performed at a particular office or activity; or b. Restrict in any way a Contracting Officer in the performance of any duty properly assigned. (FAR 2.101) 2. Does not include any representative of the Contracting Officer. (FAR 52.243-7(a))

Contracting Officer Representative (COR) Also referred to as Contracting Officer Technical Representative. A person designated by the Contracting Officer to assist in the technical monitoring or administration of a contract. Procedures vary from agency to agency, but generally a COR must be designated in writing with a copy furnished to the contractor and the contract administration office. The designation does not include any authority to make any commitments or changes that affect price, quality, quantity, delivery, or other terms and conditions of the contract.

Contracting Officer Technical Representative (COTR) See Contracting Officer Representative.

Contractor 1. Any individual or other legal entity that: a. Directly or indirectly (e.g., through an affiliate) submits offers for or is awarded, or reasonably may be expected to submit offers for or be awarded, a Government contract, including a contract for carriage under Government or commercial bills of lading, or a subcontract under a Government contract; or b. Conducts business, or reasonably may be expected to conduct business, with the Government as an agent or representative of another contractor. (FAR 9.403) 2. Includes the terms "prime contractor" and "subcontractor." (FAR 22.801) 3. Includes a subcontractor at any tier whose subcontract is subject to the provisions of the Services Contract Act. (FAR 22.1001) 4. For subcontracting requirements, the total contractor organization or a separate entity of it, such as an affiliate, division, or plant, that performs its own purchasing. (FAR 44.101)

Contractor-Acquired Property Property acquired or otherwise provided by the contractor for performing a contract and to which the Government has title. (FAR 45.101)

Contractor Acquisition Team Contractor members of the Acquisition Team.

Contractor Bid Information See contractor proposal information.

Contractor's Development and Implementation Costs In value engineering, those costs the contractor incurs on a value engineering change proposal specifically in developing, testing, preparing, and submitting the value engineering change proposal (VECP), as well as those costs the contractor incurs to make the contractual changes required by Government acceptance of a VECP. (FAR 48.001)

Contractor's Managerial Personnel Also referred to as contractor's principal officials, the Contractor's directors, officers, and any of the contractor's managers, superintendents, or equivalent representatives who have supervision or direction of: a. All or substantially all of the contractor's business; b. All or substantially all of the contractor's operation at any one plant or separate location at which the contract is being performed; or c. A separate and complete major industrial operation connected with performing a contract. (FAR 52.245-2(g)(1) Alternate)

Contractor's Plant The term includes contractor facilities and contractor-operated Government facilities. (FAR 45.601)

Contractor's Principal Officials See contractor's managerial personnel.

Contractor Inventory Any property: a. Acquired by and in the possession of a contractor or subcontractor under a contract for which title is vested in the Government and which exceeds the amounts needed to complete full performance under the entire contract; b. That the Government is obligated or has the option to take over under any type of contract as a result either of any changes in the specifications or plans thereunder or of the termination of the contract (or subcontract thereunder), before completion of the work, for the convenience or at the option of the Government; and c. Furnished by the Government that exceeds the amounts needed to complete full performance under the entire contract. (FAR 45.601)

Contractor Proposal Information Any of the following information submitted to a Federal agency as part of or in connection with a bid or proposal to enter into a Federal agency procurement contract, if that information has not been previously made available to the public or disclosed publicly: a. Cost or pricing data; b. Indirect costs and direct labor rates; c. Proprietary information about manufacturing processes, operations, or techniques marked by the contractor in accordance with applicable law or regulation; d. Information marked by the contractor as "contractor bid or proposal information" in accordance with applicable law or regulation; or e. Information marked by the contractor with the restrictions prescribed in FAR 52.215-1(e). (FAR 3.104-3)

Contractor Purchasing System Review (CPSR) The complete evaluation of a contractor's purchasing of material and services, subcontracting, and subcontract management from development of the requirement through completion of subcontract performance. The review provides the Administrative Contracting Officer a basis for granting, withholding, or withdrawing approval of the contractor's purchasing system. (FAR 44.101 and 44.301)

Contractor Team Arrangement An arrangement in which: a. Two or more companies form a partnership or joint venture to act as a potential prime contractor; or b. A potential prime contractor agrees with one or more other companies to have them act as its subcontractors under a specified Government contract or acquisition program. (FAR 9.601)

Contracts with Commercial Organizations All contracts and contract modifications for supplies, services, or experimental, developmental, or research work negotiated with organizations other than educational institutions, construction and architect-engineer contracts, State and local governments, and nonprofit organizations on the basis of cost.

Contribution A concept, suggestion, or idea presented to the Government for its use with no indication that the source intends to devote any further effort to it on the Government's behalf. (FAR 15.601)

Contribution Income The difference between revenue and variable cost required to provide a supply or service.

Controlled Materials The various shapes and forms of steel, copper, aluminum, and nickel alloys specified in Schedule II, and defined in Schedule III, of the DPAS. (FAR 11.601)

Conviction 1. A judgment or conviction of a criminal offense by any court of competent jurisdiction, whether entered upon a verdict or a plea, and includes a conviction entered upon a plea of nolo contendere. (FAR 9.403) 2. A finding of guilt (including a plea of nolo contendere) or imposition of sentence, or both, by any judicial body charged with the responsibility to determine violations of the Federal or State criminal drug statutes. (FAR 23.503)

Copeland (Anti-Kickback) Act Makes it unlawful to induce, by force, intimidation, threat of procuring dismissal from employment, or otherwise, any person employed in the construction or repair of public buildings or public works, financed in whole or in part by the United States, to give up any part of the compensation to which that person is entitled under a contract of employment. The Act also requires each contractor and subcontractor to furnish weekly a statement of compliance with respect to the wages paid each employee during the preceding week. Contracts subject to the Act must contain a clause requiring contractors and subcontractors to comply with the regulations issued by the Secretary of Labor under the Act. (FAR 22.403-2)

COR Workplan Plan of action for the Contracting Officer Representative (COR).

Corporate Administrative Contracting Officer (CACO) Contractors with more than one operational location (e.g., division, plant, or subsidiary) often have corporate-wide policies, procedures, and activities requiring Government review and approval and affecting the work of more than one Administrative Contracting Officer. In these circumstances, effective and consistent contract administration may require the assignment of a corporate Administrative Contracting Officer to deal with corporate management and to perform selected contract administration functions on a corporate-wide basis. (FAR 42.601)

Corporate Surety A corporation licensed under various insurance laws and, under its charter, has legal power to act as surety for others. (FAR 28.001)

Correction The elimination of a defect. (FAR 46.701)

Cost Accounting Practice Any disclosed or established accounting method or technique which is used for allocation of cost to cost objectives, assignment of cost to cost accounting periods, or measurement of cost. (FAR 9903.302-1)

Cost Accounting Standards (CAS) Accounting requirements designed to achieve uniformity and consistency in the cost accounting practices governing measurement, assignment, and allocation of costs to contracts with the United States Government. (FAR 9901.302)

Cost Accounting Standards Board (CASB) A 5-member board that has the exclusive authority to make, promulgate, amend, and rescind cost accounting standards and regulations, including interpretations thereof, designed to achieve uniformity and consistency in the cost accounting practices governing measurement, assignment, and allocation of costs to contracts with the United States Government. (FAR 9901.302 and 9901.304)

Cost Analysis The review and evaluation of the separate cost elements and profit in an offeror's or contractor's proposal (including cost or pricing data or information other than cost or pricing data), and the application of judgment to determine how well the proposed costs represent what the cost of the contract should be, assuming reasonable economy and efficiency. (FAR 15.404-1(c)(1))

Cost Contract A cost-reimbursement contract in which the contractor receives no fee. May be appropriate for research and development work, particularly with nonprofit educational institutions or other nonprofit organizations, and for facilities contracts. (FAR 16.302)

Cost Estimating Relationship A technique used to estimate a particular cost or price by using an established relationship with an independent variable.

Cost Input The cost, except general and administrative (G&A) expenses, which for contract; costing purposes is allocable to the production of goods and services during a cost accounting period. (FAR 31.001)

Cost Objective A function, organizational subdivision, contract, or other work unit for which cost data are desired and for which provision is made to accumulate and measure the cost of processes, products, jobs, capitalized projects, etc. (FAR 31.001)

Cost of Capital Committed to Facilities An imputed cost determined by applying a cost of money rate to facilities capital. (FAR 31.001)

Cost or Price Negotiation Objectives Goals for contract action cost or price. Without an overall price objective, negotiations will often flounder and result in settlements that can be neither explained nor defended.

Cost or Pricing Data All facts that, as of the date of price agreement or, if applicable, an earlier date agreed upon between the parties that is as close as practicable to the date of agreement on price, prudent buyers and sellers would reasonably expect to affect price negotiations significantly. Cost or pricing data are data requiring certification. Cost or pricing data are factual, not judgmental; and are verifiable. While they do not indicate the accuracy of the prospective contractor's judgment about estimated future costs or projections, they do include the data forming the basis for that judgment. Cost or pricing data are more than historical accounting data; they are all the facts that can be reasonably expected to contribute to the soundness of estimates of future costs and to the validity of determinations of costs already incurred. They also include such factors as: vendor quotations; nonrecurring costs; information on changes in production methods and in production or purchasing volume; data supporting projections of business prospects and objectives and related operations costs; unit-cost trends such as those associated with labor efficiency; make-or-buy decisions; estimated resources to attain business goals; and information on management decisions that could have a significant bearing on costs. (FAR 15.401)

Cost or Pricing Data Index An offeror listing of all cost or pricing data and information accompanying or identified in a proposal. It includes any supplemental additions and/or revisions, up to the date of agreement on price, or an earlier date agreed upon by the parties. (FAR Table 15-2)

Cost or Pricing Data Submission The requirement for submission of cost or pricing data is met when all accurate cost or pricing data reasonably available to the offeror have been submitted, either actually or by specific identification, to the Contracting Officer or an authorized representative. The requirement for submission of cost or pricing data continues up to the time of agreement on price, or an earlier date agreed upon between the parties if applicable. (FAR Table 15-2)

Cost or Pricing Data Threshold The threshold for obtaining cost or pricing data. Currently $500,000 for new contracts. The threshold for each existing contract is specified in the contract. (FAR 15.403-4(a)(1))

Cost Principles for Commercial Contracts Principles for determining the allowable costs of contracts and subcontracts with commercial contractors presented in FAR 31.2. (FAR 31.2)

Cost Principles for Nonprofit Organizations Principles for determining the costs applicable to work performed by nonprofit organizations under contracts (also grants and other agreements) with the Government presented in Office of Management and Budget Circular A-122, Cost Principles for Nonprofit Organizations. (FAR 31.702)

Cost Principles for State and Local Governments Principles for determining the allowable costs of contracts and subcontracts with State, local, and

Federally recognized Indian tribal governments presented in Office of Governments Management and Budget Circular A-87, Cost Principles for State and Local (FAR 31.602)

Cost Realism The costs in an offeror's proposal are realistic for the work to be performed; reflect a clear understanding of the requirements; and are consistent with the various elements of the offeror's technical proposal. (FAR 15.401)

Cost Realism Analysis The process of independently reviewing and evaluating specific elements of each offeror's proposed cost estimate to determine whether the estimated proposed cost elements are realistic for the work to be performed; reflect a clear understanding of the requirements; and are consistent with the unique methods of performance and materials described in the offeror's technical proposal. (FAR 15.404-1(d)(1))

Cost Sharing An explicit arrangement under which the contractor bears some of the burden of reasonable, allocable, and allowable contract cost. (FAR 35.001)

Cost-Benefit Analysis Also referred to as benefit-cost analysis. A systematic quantitative method of assessing the desirability of Government projects or policies when it is important to take a long view of future effects and a broad view of possible side-effects. (OMB Circular A-94, App A)

Cost-Effectiveness A systematic quantitative method for comparing the costs of alternative means of achieving the same stream of benefits or a given objective. (OMB Circular A-94, App A)

Cost-Plus-Award-Fee Contract A cost-reimbursement contract that provides for a fee consisting of a. A base amount fixed at inception of the contract; and b. An award amount that the contractor may earn in whole or in part during performance and that is sufficient to provide motivation for excellence in such areas as quality, timeliness, technical ingenuity, and cost-effective management. The amount of the award fee to be paid is determined by the Government's judgmental evaluation of the contractor's performance in terms of the criteria stated in the contract. This determination is made unilaterally by the Government and is not subject to the Disputes clause. (FAR 16.405-2(a))

Cost-Plus-Fixed-Fee Contract A cost-reimbursement contract that provides for payment to the contractor of a negotiated fee that is fixed at the inception of the contract. The fixed fee does not vary with actual cost, but may be adjusted as a result of changes in the work to be performed under the contract. This contract type permits contracting for efforts that might otherwise present too great a risk to contractors, but it provides the contractor only a minimum incentive to control costs. (FAR 16.306(a))

Cost-Plus-Incentive-Fee Contract A cost-reimbursement contract that provides for the initially negotiated fee to be adjusted later by a formula based on the relationship of total allowable costs to total target costs. This contract type specifies a target cost, a target fee, minimum and maximum fees, and a fee adjustment formula. After contract performance, the fee payable to the contractor is determined in accordance with the formula. The formula provides, within limits, for increases in fee above target fee when total allowable costs are less than target costs, and decreases in fee below target fee when total allowable costs exceed target costs. This increase or decrease is intended to provide an incentive for the contractor to manage the contract effectively. When total allowable cost is greater than or less than the range of costs within which the fee-adjustment formula operates, the contractor is paid total allowable costs, plus the minimum or maximum fee. (FAR 16.405-1(a))

Cost-Reimbursement Contract A contract that provides for payment of allowable incurred costs, to the extent prescribed in the contract. These contracts establish an estimate of total cost for the purpose of obligating funds and establishing a ceiling that the contractor may not exceed (except at its own risk) without the approval of the Contracting Officer. (FAR 16.301-1)

Cost-Sharing Contract A cost-reimbursement contract in which the contractor receives no fee and is reimbursed only for an agreed-upon portion of its allowable costs. May be used when the contractor agrees to absorb a portion of the costs, in the expectation of substantial compensating benefits. (FAR 16.303)

Cost-Volume-Profit Analysis An examination of the relationship between revenue, fixed cost, variable cost, and profit.

Cost-Volume-Profit Equation An used in cost-volume-profit analysis. In the equation, revenue is equal to fixed cost plus variable cost plus profit.

Costs 1. Allowable costs in accordance with Part 31 of the Federal Acquisition Regulation (FAR) in effect on the date of a contract. (FAR 52.216-5(b)). 2. Include, but are not limited to, administrative and clerical expenses; the costs of legal services, whether performed by in-house or private counsel; the costs of the services of accountants, consultants, or others retained by the contractor to assist it; costs of employees, officers, and directors; and any similar costs incurred before, during, and after commencement of a judicial or administrative proceeding which bears a direct relationship to the proceeding. (FAR 31.205-47)

Costs of Idle Facilities or Idle Capacity Costs such as maintenance, repair, housing, rent, and other costs related to idle facilities (e.g., property taxes, insurance, and depreciation). (FAR 31.205-17(a))

Cosurety One of two or more sureties jointly liable for the penal sum of a bond. A limit of liability for each surety may be stated. (FAR 28.001)

Counterfeit Competition Negotiators using counterfeit competition openly and blatantly praise the benefits of false alternative choices which are supposedly at least as attractive as successfully completing the current negotiation. Presumably, the alternative would become increasingly attractive if the negotiator was forced to make further concessions during negotiations.

Country Concerned Any country, other than the United States, its possessions, and Puerto Rico, in which expenditures under a contract are made. (FAR 52.229-6(b))

Covered Area The geographical area described in a solicitation for a contract. (FAR 52.222-27(a))

Covered Federal Action Any of the following Federal actions are covered by the Limitation on Payments to Influence Certain Federal Transactions Clause:
a. The awarding of any Federal contract;
b. The making of any Federal grant;
c. The making of any Federal loan;
d. The entering into of any cooperative agreement; or
e. The extension, continuation, renewal, amendment, or modification of any Federal contract, grant, loan, or cooperative agreement. (FAR 52.203-12(a))

Covered Personnel In service contracting:
a. An officer or an individual who is appointed in the civil service by one of the following acting in an official capacity:
  1. The President;
  2. A Member of Congress;
  3. A member of the uniformed services;
  4. An individual who is an employee under 5 U.S.C. 2105;
  5. The head of a Government-controlled corporation; or
  6. An adjutant general appointed by the Secretary concerned.
b. A member of the Armed Services of the United States.
c. A person assigned to a Federal agency who has been transferred to another position in the competitive service in another agency. (FAR 37.201)

Covered Product A consumer product of one of the following types:
a. Central air conditioners.
b. Clothes dryers.
c. Clothes washers.
d. Dishwashers.
e. Freezers.
f. Furnaces.
g. Home heating equipment, not including furnaces.
h. Humidifiers and dehumidifiers.
i. Kitchen ranges and ovens.
j. Refrigerators and refrigerator-freezers.
k. Room air conditioners.
l. Television sets.
m. Water heaters.
n. Any other type of product that the Secretary of Energy classifies as a covered product. (FAR 23.202)

Criminal Drug Statute 1. A Federal or non-Federal criminal statute involving the manufacture, distribution, dispensing, possession, or use of any controlled substance. (FAR 23.503). 2. A Federal or non-Federal criminal statute involving the manufacture, distribution, dispensing, possession, or use of any controlled substance. (FAR 52.223-6(a))

Critical Nonconformance A nonconformance that is likely to result in hazardous or unsafe conditions for individuals using, maintaining, or depending upon the supplies or services; or is likely to prevent performance of a vital agency mission. (FAR 46.101)

Criticality Designator A code (A, B, or C) assigned by the contacting officer to identify the relative importance of the contract to Government operation and need for close production surveillance. (FAR 42.1105)

Crude Oil Crude petroleum, as it is produced at the wellhead, and liquids (under atmospheric conditions) that have been recovered from mixtures of hydrocarbons that existed in a vaporous phase in a reservoir and that are not natural gas products. (FAR 25.108(d)(2)(i))

Crunch This tactic is designed to take another bite at the other party's position no matter how reasonable it is. The user of this tactic is never satisfied and responds in words such as "You have to do better than that," or "That is not good enough."

Cumulative Average Improvement Curve An improvement curve model based on the assumption that as the total volume of units produced doubles the average cost per unit decreases by some constant percentage.

Custodial Records Written memoranda of any kind, such as requisitions, issue hand receipts, tool checks, and stock record books, used to control items issued from tool cribs, tool rooms, and stockrooms. (FAR 45.501)

Customary Contract Financing That financing deemed by an agency to be available for routine use by Contracting Officers. Most customary contract financing arrangements should be usable by Contracting Officers without specific reviews or approvals by higher management. The following contract financing arrangements are customary contract financing when

provided in accordance with the FAR and agency regulations:
  a. Financing of shipbuilding, or ship conversion, alteration, or repair, when agency regulations provide for progress payments based on a percentage or stage of completion;
  b. Financing of construction or architect-engineer services;
  c. Financing of contracts for supplies or services awarded under the sealed bid method of procurement or under the competitive negotiation method of procurement through progress payments based on costs;
  d. Financing of contracts for supplies or services awarded under a sole-source acquisition through either progress payments based on costs or performance-based payments. Performance-based payments are the preferred method when the Contracting Officer finds them practical, and the contractor agrees to their use;
  e. Financing of contracts for supplies or services through advance payments;
  f. Financing of contracts for supplies or services through guaranteed loans; or
  g. Financing of contracts for supplies or services through any appropriate combination of advance payments, guaranteed loans, and either performance-based payments or progress payments but not both. (FAR 32.001 and FAR 32.113)

Customary Progress Payment Rate The rate(s) identified in the FAR as customary for progress payments. Normally, there are different rates for contracts with small business and other concerns. The Department of Defense may establish other customary rates for foreign military sales and for flexible progress payments.

Customary Progress Payments Progress payments based on cost made using the customary progress payment rate, the cost base, and frequency of payment established in the Progress Payments clause, and either the ordinary liquidation method or the alternate method. (FAR 32.501)

Customs Territory of The United States The States, the District of Columbia, and Puerto Rico. (FAR 25.601)

Data Recorded information, regardless of form or the media on which it may be recorded. The term includes technical data and computer software. The term does not include information incidental to contract administration, such as financial, administrative, cost or pricing or management information. (FAR 27.401)

Davis-Bacon Act Provides that contracts in excess of $2,000 to which the United States or the District of Columbia is a party for construction, alteration, or repair (including painting and decorating) of public buildings or public works within the United States, must contain a clause that no laborer or mechanic employed directly upon the site of the work must less than the prevailing wage rates as determined by the Secretary of Labor. (FAR 22.403-1)

Day 1. Unless otherwise specified, a calendar day. (FAR 2.101). 2. In the computation of any time period: a. The day of the act, event, or default from which the designated period of time begins to run is not included; and b. The last day after the act, event, or default is included unless: (1) The last day is a Saturday, Sunday, or Federal holiday; or (2) In the case of a filing of a paper at any appropriate administrative forum, the last day is a day on which weather or other conditions cause the closing of the forum for all or part of the day, in which event the next day on which the appropriate administrative forum is open is included. (3) In the case of the 5-day period after a debriefing date and the 10-day period after contract award for filing a protest resulting in a suspension, Saturdays, Sundays, and legal holidays must be counted. (FAR 33.101)

Deadlock See lose/lose outcomes.

Debarment Action taken by a debarring official to exclude a contractor from Government contracting and Government-approved subcontracting for a reasonable, specified period. (FAR 9.403).

Debarred Excluded from Government contracting and Government-approved subcontracting for a reasonable, specified period. (FAR 9.403)

Debarring Official An agency head or a designee authorized by the agency head to impose debarment. (FAR 9.403)

Decoy A person or thing that lures someone into danger. In negotiations, the danger is an unsatisfactory outcome. The lure is a position or issue that appears important to the negotiator using the tactic, but in reality is not. The issue or position can be completely fabricated or one whose importance is simply blown way out of proportion.

Decrement Factor 1. A percentage used to indicate the relative difference between a proposed price and a recommended should-pay price. 2. A percentage by which a subcontract reduces its subcontract price, if, for example, the prime contractor purchases more than a specified amount of supplies.

Defect Any condition or characteristic in any supplies or services furnished by the Contractor under the contract that is not in compliance with the requirements of the contract. (FAR 52.246-19(a))

Defective Certification With respect to a claim, a certificate which alters or otherwise deviates from the language in the FAR or which is not executed by a person duly authorized to bind the contractor with respect to the claim. Failure to certify must not be deemed to be a defective certification. (FAR 33.201)

Defective Cost or Pricing Data Cost or pricing data found after contract award to be inaccurate, incomplete, or noncurrent as of the date of final agreement on price or an earlier date agreed upon by the parties given on the contractor's or subcontractor's Certificate of Current Cost or Pricing Data. (FAR 15.407-1(b)(1))

Defense Contract Audit Agency (DCAA) For contractors other than educational institutions and nonprofit organizations, the Defense Contract Audit Agency (DCAA) is normally the agency responsible for performing Government contract audits. (FAR 42.101(b))

Defense Contract Management Command (DCMC) An element of the Defense Logistics Agency that performs a wide variety of contract administration and support services for the Department of Defense and other agencies. (FAR 42.201(b))

Defense Priorities and Allocation System (DPAS) A Department of Commerce system controlling the use of critical material and facilities. Goals are to: a. Assure the timely availability of industrial resources to meet current defense requirements; and b. Provide a framework for rapid industrial expansion in case of a national emergency. (FAR 11.600)

Defense Production Act of 1950 Under Title I of the Defense Production Act of 1950, as amended, the President is authorized: a. To require that contracts in support of the national defense be accepted and performed on a preferential or priority basis over all other contracts, and b. To allocate materials and facilities in such a manner as to promote the national defense. (FAR 11.602(a))

Defense Production Pool A pool formed to obtain and perform defense production contracts. (FAR 9.701)

Defense Research and Development A pool formed to obtain and perform defense research and development contracts. (FAR 9.701)

Deferred Compensation An award made by an employer to compensate an employee in a future cost accounting period or periods for services rendered in one or more cost accounting periods before the date of the receipt of compensation by the employee. This definition must not include the amount of yearend accruals for salaries, wages, or bonuses that are to be paid within a reasonable period of time after the end of a cost accounting period. (FAR 31.001)

Deficiency A material failure of a proposal to meet a Government requirement or a combination of significant weaknesses in a proposal that increases the risk of unsuccessful contract performance to an unacceptable level. (FAR 15.301)

Defined-Benefit Pension Plan A pension plan in which the benefits to be paid, or the basis for determining such benefits, are established in advance and the contributions are intended to provide the stated benefits. (FAR 31.001)

Defined-Contribution Pension Plan A pension plan in which the contributions to be made are established in advance and the benefits are determined thereby. (FAR 31.001)

Definite-Quantity Contract An indefinite-delivery contract that provides for delivery of a definite quantity of specific supplies or services for a fixed period, with deliveries or performance to be scheduled at designated locations upon order. (FAR 16.502)

Deflation Decreases in the price for identical or similar items that results in a decrease in purchasing power.

Delegate Agency An agency of the U.S. Government authorized by delegation from Department of Commerce to place priority ratings on contracts that support authorized programs. Schedule I of the DPAS lists the Delegate Agencies. (FAR 11.601)

Delegated Agency An agency that has received a written delegation of authority from GSA to contract for utility services for periods not exceeding ten years. (FAR 41.101)

Delegation of Contract Administration See assignment of contract administration.

Delivery Order An order for supplies placed against an established contract or with Government sources. (FAR 2.101)

Delivery Order Contract A contract for supplies that does not procure or specify a firm quantity of supplies (other than a minimum or maximum quantity) and that provides for the issuance of orders for the delivery of supplies during the period of the contract. (FAR 16.501-1)

Delivery Payment A payment for accepted supplies or services, including payments for accepted partial deliveries. Commercial financing payments are liquidated by deduction from these payments. Delivery payments are invoice payments for prompt payment purposes. (FAR 32.202-2)

Demand for Payment See demand for payment of contract debt.

Demand for Payment of Contract Debt Also referred to as demand for payment or demand letter. A demand for a refund due the Government. It must include the following:

  a. A description of the debt, including the debt amount.
  b. Notification that any amounts not paid within 30 days from the date of the demand will bear interest from the date of the demand, or from any earlier date specified in the contract, and that the interest rate must be the rate established by the Secretary of the Treasury, for the period affected, under Public Law 92-41. In case of a debt arising

from a price reduction for defective pricing, or as specifically set forth in a Cost Accounting Standards (CAS) clause in the contract, that interest will run from the date of overpayment by the Government until repayment by the contractor at the underpayment rate established by the Secretary of the Treasury, for the periods affected.

c. A notification that the contractor may submit a proposal for deferment of collection if immediate payment is not practicable or if the amount is disputed.

d. Identification of the responsible official designated for determining the amount of the debt and for its collection. (FAR 32.610(b))

Demand Letter See demand for payment of contract debt.

Depreciation A charge to current operations which distributes the cost of a tangible capital asset, less estimated residual value, over the estimated useful life of the asset in a systematic and logical manner. It does not involve a process of valuation. Useful life refers to the prospective period of economic usefulness in a particular contractor's operations as distinguished from physical life; it is evidenced by the actual or estimated retirement and replacement practice of the contractor. (FAR 31.205-11(a))

Descriptive Literature 1. Information, such as cuts, illustrations, drawings, and brochures, which shows the characteristics or construction of a product or explains its operation. It is furnished by bidders as a part of their bids to describe the products offered. The term includes only information required to determine acceptability of the product. It excludes other information such as that furnished in connection with the qualifications of a bidder or for use in operating or maintaining equipment. (FAR 14.202-5). 2. Information (e.g., cuts, illustrations, drawings, and brochures) that is submitted as part of a bid. Descriptive literature is required to establish, for the purpose of evaluation and award, details of the product offered that are specified elsewhere in the solicitation and pertain to significant elements such as (1) design; (2) materials; (3) components; (4) performance characteristics; and (5) methods of manufacture, assembly, construction, or operation. The term includes only information required to determine the technical acceptability of the offered product. It does not include other information such as that used in determining the responsibility of a prospective Contractor or for operating or maintaining equipment. (FAR 52.214-21(a))

Descriptive Statistics A large variety of methods for summarizing or describing a set of numbers. These methods may involve computational or graphical analysis.

Design In construction, defining the construction requirement (including the functional relationships and technical systems to be used, such as architectural, environmental, structural, electrical, mechanical, and fire protection), producing the technical specifications and drawings, and preparing the construction cost estimate. (FAR 36.102)

Design-Bid-Build The traditional delivery method where design and construction are sequential and contracted for separately with two contracts and two contractors. (FAR 36.102)

Design-Build Combining design and construction in a single contract with one contractor. (FAR 36.102)

Design-to-Cost A concept that establishes cost elements as management goals to achieve the best balance between life-cycle cost, acceptable performance, and schedule. Under this concept, cost is a design constraint during the design and development phases and a management discipline throughout the acquisition and operation of the system or equipment. (FAR 7.101)

Designated Agency Any department or agency of the executive branch of the United States Government. (FAR 32.801)

Designated Billing Office The office or person (Governmental or nongovernmental) designated in the contract where the contractor first submits invoices and contract financing requests. This might be the Government disbursing office, contract administration office, office accepting the supplies delivered or services performed by the contractor, contract audit office, or a nongovernmental agent. In some cases, different offices might be designated to receive invoices and contract financing requests. (FAR 32.902)

Designated Country A country or instrumentality designated under the Trade Agreements Act of 1979 and identified in the FAR. (FAR 25.401)

Designated Country Construction Material Construction material that: a. Is wholly the growth, product, or manufacture of a designated country; or b. In the case of a construction material which consists in whole or in part of materials from another country or instrumentality, has been substantially transformed in a designated country into a new and different construction material distinct from the materials from which it was transformed. (FAR 25.401)

Designated Country End Product 1. An article that: a. Is wholly the growth, product, or manufacture of the designated country, or b. In the case of an article which consists in whole or in part of materials from another country or instrumentality, has been substantially transformed into a new and different article of commerce with a name, character, or use distinct from that of the article or articles from which it was so transformed. The term refers to a product offered for purchase under a supply contract, but for purposes of calculating the value of the end product includes services (except transportation services) incidental to its supply; provided, that the value of incidental services does not exceed that of the product itself. (FAR 25.401)

2. An article that: a. Is wholly the growth, product, or manufacture of the designated country, or b. In the case of an article which consists in whole or in part of materials from another country or instrumentality, has been substantially transformed into a different article of commerce with a name, character, or use distinct from that of the article or articles from which it was so transformed. The term refers to a product offered for purchase under a supply contract, but for purposes of calculating the value of the end product includes services (except transportation services) incidental to its supply, provided that the value of incidental services does not exceed that of the product itself. (FAR 52.225-9(a))

Designated Payment The place designated in the contract to make invoice payments or contract financing Office payments. Normally, this will be the Government disbursing office. (FAR 32.902)

Detailed Requirement Contract requirement stated in detail (e.g., detailed product design requirements).

Determination and Findings A special form of written approval by an authorized official that is required by statute or regulation as a prerequisite to taking certain contracting actions. The determination is a conclusion or decision supported by the findings. The findings are statements of fact or rationale essential to support the determination and must cover each requirement of the statute or regulation. (FAR 1.701)

Development 1. The systematic use, under whatever name, of scientific and technical knowledge in the design, development, test, or evaluation of a potential new product or service (or of an improvement in an existing product or service) for the purpose of meeting specific performance requirements or objectives.
  a. Development includes the functions of design engineering, prototyping, and engineering testing.
  b. Development excludes:
     (1) Subcontracted technical effort which is for the sole purpose of developing an additional source for an existing product; or
     (2) Development effort for manufacturing or production materials, systems, processes, methods, equipment, tools, and techniques not intended for sale. (FAR 31.205-18(a))

2. The systematic use of scientific and technical knowledge in the design, development, testing, or evaluation of a potential new product or service (or of an improvement in an existing product or service) to meet specific performance requirements or objectives. It includes the functions of design engineering, prototyping, and engineering testing; it excludes subcontracted technical effort that is for the sole purpose of developing an additional source for an existing product. (FAR 35.001)

Deviation Also referred to as a FAR deviation. Any one or combination of the following:
  a. The issuance or use of a policy, procedure, solicitation provision, contract clause, method, or practice of conducting acquisition actions of any kind at any stage of the acquisition process that is inconsistent with the FAR.
  b. The omission of any solicitation provision or contract clause when its prescription requires its use.
  c. The use of any solicitation provision or contract clause with modified or alternate language that is not authorized by the FAR.
  d. The use of a solicitation provision or contract clause prescribed by the FAR on a "substantially as follows" or "substantially the same as" basis if such use is inconsistent with the intent, principle, or substance of the prescription or related coverage on the subject matter in the FAR.
  e. The authorization of lesser or greater limitations on the use of any solicitation provision, contract clause, policy, or procedure prescribed by the FAR.
  f. The issuance of policies or procedures that govern the contracting process or otherwise control contracting relationships that are not incorporated into agency acquisition regulations. (FAR 1.401)

Direct Cost Any cost that can be identified specifically with a particular final cost objective.
  a. Costs identified specifically with the contract are direct costs of the contract and to be charged directly to the contract.
  b. No final cost objective must have allocated to it as a direct cost any cost, if other costs incurred for the same purpose in like circumstances have been included in any indirect cost pool to be allocated to that or any other final cost objective.
  c. All costs specifically identified with other final cost objectives of the contractor are direct costs of those cost objectives and are not to be charged to the contract directly or indirectly.
  d. For reasons of practicality, any direct cost of minor dollar amount may be treated as an indirect cost if the accounting treatment:
     (1) Is consistently applied to all final cost objectives; and
     (2) Produces substantially the same results as treating the cost as a direct cost. (FAR 31.202)

Directly Associated Cost Any cost which is generated solely as a result of the incurrence of another cost, and which would not have been incurred had the other cost not been incurred. (FAR 31.001)

Directly Engaged 1. Includes all direct-cost employees and any other contract employee who has other than a minimal impact or involvement in contract performance. (FAR 23.503). 2. Includes all direct-cost employees and any other Contractor employee who has other than a minimal impact or involvement in contract performance. (FAR 52.223-6(a))

Director 1. The Director, Office of Federal Contract Compliance Programs (OFCCP), United States Department of Labor. (FAR 22.801) 2. Director, Office of Federal Contract Compliance Programs (OFCCP), United States Department of Labor, or any person to whom the Director delegates authority. (FAR 52.222-27(a))

Directory of Federal Contract Audit Offices
A publication maintained and distributed by the Defense Contract Audit Agency that identifies cognizant audit offices and the contractors over which they have cognizance. (FAR 42.103(a))

Disclosure Statement A written description of a contractor's cost accounting practices and procedures. Submission of a new or revised Disclosure Statement is not required for any non-CAS-covered contract or from any small business concern. (FAR 9903.202-1(a))

Discount Factor The factor that translates expected benefits or costs in any given future year into where it is the interest present value terms. The discount factor is equal to 1/(1 + i)rate and t is the number of years from the date of initiation for the program or policy until the given future year. (OMB Circular A-94, App A)

Discount for Prompt Payment An invoice payment reduction voluntarily offered by the contractor, in conjunction with the Discounts for Prompt Payment clause if payment is made by the Government prior to the due date. The due date is calculated from the date of the contractor's invoice. If the contractor has not placed a date on the invoice, the due date is calculated from the date the designated billing office receives a proper invoice, provided the agency annotates such invoice with the date of receipt at the time of receipt. When the discount date falls on a Saturday, Sunday, or legal holiday when Federal Government offices are closed and Government business is not expected to be conducted, payment may be made on the following business day and a discount may be taken. (FAR 32.902)

Discount Rate The interest rate used in calculating the present value of expected yearly benefits and costs. (OMB Circular A-94, App A)

Discrepancies Incident All deficiencies incident to shipment of Government property to or from a contractor's to Shipment facility whereby differences exist between the property purported to have been and property actually received. Such deficiencies include loss, damage, destruction, improper status and condition coding, errors in identity or classification, and improper consignment. (FAR 45.501)

Discussions Negotiations that occur after establishment of the competitive range that may, at the Contracting Officer's discretion, result in the offeror being allowed to revise its proposal. (FAR 15-306(d) and 52.215-1(a))

Dismissal Wages See severance pay.

Display Room A location maintained by an organization, without charge to the public, to display requirements for the benefit of prospective offerors, subcontractors, and material suppliers. (FAR 36.211)

DO Rating A priority rating under DPAS. All DO-rated orders have equal priority with each other and take preference over unrated orders. (FAR 11.603(a))

Domestic and Foreign Differential Pay
For personal services performed in a foreign country, compensation may also include a differential that may properly consider all expenses associated with foreign employment such as housing, cost of living adjustments, transportation, bonuses, additional Federal, State, local or foreign income taxes resulting from foreign assignment, and other related expenses. (FAR 31.205-6(e)(1))

Domestic Construction Material a. An unmanufactured construction material mined or produced in the United States, or b. A construction material manufactured in the United States, if the cost of its components mined, produced, or manufactured in the United States exceeds 50 percent of the cost of all its components. (In determining whether a construction material is domestic, only consider the construction material and its components.) The cost of each component includes transportation costs to the place of incorporation into the construction material and any applicable duty (whether or not a duty-free entry certificate is issued). Components of foreign origin of the same class or kind which the head of the contracting activity or designee determines are not mined, produced, or manufactured in the United States in sufficient and reasonably available commercial quantities of a satisfactory quality are treated as domestic. (FAR 25.201)

Domestic End Product a. An unmanufactured end product mined or produced in the United States, or b. An end product manufactured in the United States, if the cost of its components mined, produced, or manufactured in the United States exceeds 50 percent of the cost of all its components. (In determining if an end product is domestic, only consider the end product and its components.) The cost of each component includes transportation costs to the place of incorporation into the end product and any applicable duty (whether or not a duty-free entry certificate is issued). Components of foreign origin of the same class or kind that are not mined, produced, or manufactured in the United States in sufficient and reasonably available commercial quantities of a satisfactory quality or which the agency head determines that domestic preference would be inconsistent with the public interest are treated as domestic. Scrap generated, collected, and prepared for processing in the United States is considered domestic. (FAR 25.101) A component shall also be considered to have been mined, produced, or manufactured in the United States (regardless of its source in fact) if the end product in which it is incorporated is manufactured in the United States and the component is of a class or kind:

(1) Determined by the Government to be not mined, produced, or manufactured in the United States in sufficient and reasonably available commercial quantities of a satisfactory quality, or

(2) To which the agency head concerned has determined that it would be inconsistent with the public interest to apply the restrictions of the Buy American Act. (FAR 52.225-9(a))

Domestic Offer An offered price for a domestic end product, including transportation to destination. (FAR 25.101)

Domestic Services Services performed in the United States. If services provided under a single contract are performed both inside and outside the United States, they must be considered domestic if 25 percent or less of their total cost is attributable to services (including incidental supplies used in connection with these services) performed outside the United States. (FAR 25.301)

Donation Screening Screening by the General Services Administration for possible donation. (FAR 45.608-2)

Double Moving Average Data collected over two or more time periods (normally at least three) are summed and divided by the number of time periods. A second moving average is then calculated using the averages from your first moving average as observations. These two moving averages are then used to forecast for future time periods. Forecasts assume that there is a trend in the data.

Draft Request for Proposals (RFP) A tentative solicitation submitted to prospective offerors for review and comment. (FAR 15.201(c))

Drug-Free Workplace The site(s) for the performance of work done by the contractor in connection with a specific contract at which employees of the contractor are prohibited from engaging in the unlawful manufacture, distribution, dispensing, possession, or use of a controlled substance. (FAR 23.503)

Dry Bulk Carrier A vessel used primarily for the carriage of shipload lots of homogeneous unmarked nonliquid cargoes such as grain, coal, cement, and lumber. (FAR 47.501)

Dry Cargo Liner A vessel used for the carriage of heterogeneous marked cargoes in parcel lots. However, any cargo may be carried in these vessels, including part cargoes of dry bulk items or, when carried in deep tanks, bulk liquids such as petroleum and vegetable oils. (FAR 47.501)

Due Date The date on which payment should be made. (FAR 32.902)

DX Rating A priority rating under DPAS. All DX-rated orders have equal priority with each other and take preference over DO-rated orders and unrated orders. This rating is used for special defense programs designated by the President to be of the highest national priority. (FAR 11.603(a))

Economic Planning Costs Costs of generalized long-range management planning that is concerned with the future overall development of the contractor's business and that may take into account the eventual possibility of economic dislocations or fundamental alterations in those markets in which the contractor currently does business. They do not include organization or reorganization costs. (FAR 31.205-12(a))

Economic Purchase Quantity A supply acquisition quantity that produces economic benefit to the Government. Evaluation should consider the costs related to purchasing and holding the supply item. (FAR 7.203 and 52.207-4)

Educational Institution Public or nonprofit institution of higher education, e.g., an accredited college or university, as defined in Section 1201(a) of the Higher Education Act of 1965. (FAR 9903.201-2(c)(2))

Effective Competition A market condition which exists when two or more contractors, acting independently, actively contend for the Government's business in a manner which ensures that the Government will be offered the lowest cost or price alternative or best technical design meeting its minimum needs. (FAR 34.001)

Effective Date 1. For a solicitation amendment, change order, or administrative change, the effective date must be the issue date of the amendment, change order, or administrative change. 2. For a supplemental agreement, the effective date must be the date agreed upon by the contracting parties. 3. For a modification issued as a confirming notice of termination for the convenience of the Government, the effective date of the confirming notice must be the same as the effective date of the initial notice. 4. For a modification converting a termination for default to a termination for the convenience of the Government, the effective date must be the same as the effective date of the termination for default. 5. For a modification confirming the Termination Contracting Officer's previous letter determination of the amount due in settlement of a contract termination for convenience, the effective date must be the same as the effective date of the previous letter determination. (FAR 43.101)

Effective Date of Termination The date on which the notice of termination requires the contractor to stop performance under the contract. If the termination notice is received by the contractor subsequent to the date fixed for termination, then the effective date of termination means the date the notice is received. (FAR 49.001)

Efficiency Factor A measure of overall performance used in a work measurement system. It is calculated by dividing the standard time to perform the work by the actual time.

Electronic Bid A bid submitted using electronic commerce. (FAR 14.202-8)

Electronic Commerce (EC) A paperless process including electronic mail, electronic bulletin boards, electronic funds transfer, electronic data interchange, and similar techniques for accomplishing business transactions. The use of terms commonly associated with paper transactions (e.g., copy, document, page, printed, sealed envelope, and stamped) must not be interpreted to restrict the use of electronic commerce. Contracting Officers may supplement electronic transactions by using other media to meet the requirement of any contract action governed by FAR (e.g., transmission of a hard copy of drawings). (FAR 4.502(a))

Electronic Data Interchange (EDI) A technique for electronically transferring and storing formatted information between computers utilizing established and published formats and codes, as authorized by the applicable Federal Information Processing Standards. (FAR 4.501)

Electronic Funds System. A transfer payment transaction instruction given to the Federal Reserve. (FAR Transfer (EFT) 32.902)

Eligible Product 1. A designated, North American Free Trade Agreement (NAFTA), or Caribbean Basin country end product. (FAR 25.401). 2. A designated, North American Free Trade Agreement (NAFTA), or Caribbean Basin country end product. (FAR 52.225-9(a))

Emerging Small Business Concern A small business concern whose size is no greater than 50 percent of the numerical size standard applicable to the standard industrial classification code assigned to a contracting opportunity. (FAR 19.1002)

Employee An employee of a contractor directly engaged in the performance of work under a Government contract. (FAR 23.503)

Employee of an Agency Includes the following individuals who are employed by an agency:
   a. An individual who is appointed to a position in the Government, including a position under a temporary appointment;
   b. A member of the uniformed services;
   c. A special Government employee; and
   d. An individual who is a member of a Federal advisory committee. (FAR 3.801)

Employer's Identification Number The Federal Social Security number used on the employer's quarterly Federal tax return, U.S. Treasury Department Form 941. (FAR 52.222-27(a))

Employment Cost Index (ECI) Published monthly by the U.S. Department of Labor, Bureau of Labor Statistics (BLS), measures changes in labor costs.

End Product Those articles, materials, and supplies to be acquired for public use under the contract. (FAR 25.101)

End Products Those articles, materials, and supplies to be acquired under the contract for public use. (FAR 52.225-9(a))

Energy Efficiency Standard A performance standard that: a. Prescribes a minimum level of energy efficiency for a covered product; and b. Includes any other requirements that the Secretary of Energy may prescribe. (FAR 23.202)

Energy Use and Efficiency Label A label provided by a manufacturer of a covered product. (FAR 23.202)

Engineering and Technical Services Contract services used to support the program office during the acquisition cycle by providing such services as systems engineering and technical direction to ensure the effective operation and maintenance of a weapon system or major system or to provide direct support of a weapon system that is essential to research, development, production, operation or maintenance of the system. (FAR37.201)

Entertainment Costs Costs of amusement, diversions, social activities, and any directly associated costs such as tickets to shows or sports events, meals, lodging, rentals, transportation, and gratuities. (FAR 31.205-14)

Entity of the Government See Government.

Environmentally Preferable Products or services that have a lesser negative effect on human health or the environment when compared with competing products or services that serve the same purpose. This comparison should use principles recommended in guidance issued by the Environmental Protection Agency and may consider raw materials acquisition, production, manufacturing, packaging, distribution, reuse, operation, maintenance, or disposal of the product or service. (FAR 23.703)

EPA-Designated Item An item:
a. That is or can be made with recovered material;
b. That is listed by EPA in a procurement guideline; and
c. For which EPA has provided purchasing recommendations in a related Recovered Materials Advisory Notice (RMAN). (FAR 23.402)

Estimating Costs The process of forecasting a future result in terms of cost, based upon information available at the time. (FAR 31.001)

Estimating Equation A quantitative relationship use to estimate cost or price. The relationship may be linear or nonlinear and may include one or more independent variables.

Estimating Factor A multiple used to estimate cost or price based on a linear relationship with a product characteristic or an element of cost.

Estimating System The contractor's policies, procedures, and practices for generating cost estimates and other data included in proposals submitted to customers in the expectation of receiving contract awards. Components include the contractor's:
a. Organizational structure;
b. Established lines of authority, duties, and responsibilities;
c. Internal controls and managerial reviews;
d. Flow of work, coordination, and communications; and
e. Estimating methods, techniques, accumulation of historical costs, and other analyses used to generate cost estimates. (DFARS 252.215-7002)

Ex Dock, Pier, or Warehouse Importation Free of expense to the Government delivered on the designated dock or pier or in the warehouse at the specified port of importation. (FAR 52.247-40(a))

Excepted Tax Social Security or other employment taxes, net income and franchise taxes, excess profits taxes, capital stock taxes, transportation taxes, unemployment compensation taxes, and property taxes. It does not include gross income taxes levied on or measured by sales or receipts from sales, property taxes assessed on completed supplies covered by a contract, or any tax assessed on the Contractor's possession of, interest in, or use of property, title to which is in the Government. (FAR 52.229-4(a))

Exception When related to Government forms, means an approved departure from the established design, content, printing specifications, or conditions for use of any standard form. (FAR 53.001)

Excess Personal Property Any personal property under the control of a Federal agency that the agency head or a designee determines is not required for its needs and for the discharge of its responsibilities. (FAR 8.101)

Execution The final consummation of a contract action including all formalities (e.g., signature and any necessary approvals) needed to complete the action. (FAR 4.1)

Executive Agency Also referred to as an agency. An executive department, a military department, or any independent establishment within the meaning of 5 U.S.C. 101, 102, and 104(1), respectively, and any wholly owned Government corporation within the meaning of 31 U.S.C. 9101. (FAR 2.101)

Executive Agreement A government-to-government agreement, including agreements with international organizations, to which the United States is a party. (FAR 1.405(a))

Express Warranty Warranty terms defined in the contract. For commercial contracts, a express warranty must be included in the contract by addendum. (FAR 12.404(b))

Expressly Unallowable Cost A particular item or type of cost which, under the express provisions of an applicable law, regulation, or contract, is specifically named and stated to be unallowable. (FAR 31.001)

Extraordinary Contractual Action P.L. 93-155, as amended, and Executive Order 10789, dated November 14, 1958, as amended empower the President to authorize agencies exercising functions in connection with the national defense to enter into, amend, and modify contracts, without regard to other provisions of law related to making, performing, amending, or modifying contracts, whenever the President considers that such action would facilitate the national defense. (FAR 50.101)

F.a.s. Vessel, Port of Shipment Free of expense to the Government delivered alongside the ocean vessel and within reach of its loading tackle at the specified port of shipment. (FAR 52.247-36(a))

F.o.b. Designated Air Carrier's Terminal Point of Exportation Free of expense to the Government loaded aboard the aircraft, or delivered to the, custody of the air carrier (if only the air carrier performs the loading), at the air carrier's terminal specified in the contract. (FAR 52.247-43(a))

F.o.b. Designated Air Carrier's Terminal Point of Importation Free of expense to the Government delivered to the air carrier's terminal at the point of importation specified in the contract. (FAR 52.247-44(z))

F.o.b. Destination Free on board at destination (i.e., the seller or consignor delivers the goods on seller's or consignor's conveyance at destination). Unless the contract provides otherwise, cost of shipping and risk of loss are borne by the seller or consignor. (FAR 47.001)

F.o.b. Destination Within Consignee's Premises Free of expense to the Government delivered and laid down within the doors of the consignee's premises, including delivery to specific rooms within a building if so specified. (FAR 52.247-35(a))

F.o.b. Inland Carrier Point of Exportation Free of expense to the Government, on board the conveyance of the inland carrier, delivered to the specified point of exportation. (FAR 52.247-38(a))

F.o.b. Inland Point, Country of Importation Free of expense to the Government, on board the indicated type of conveyance of the carrier, delivered to the specified inland point where the consignee's facility is located. (FAR 247-39(a))

F.o.b. Origin Free on board at origin (i.e., the seller or consignor places the goods on the conveyance by which they are to be transported). Unless the contract provides otherwise, cost of shipping and risk of loss are borne by the buyer or consignee. (FAR 47.001)

F.o.b. Origin, Contractor's Facility Free of expense to the Government delivered on board the indicated type of conveyance of the carrier (or of the Government, if specified) at the designated facility, on the named street or highway, in the city, county, and State from which the shipment will be made. (FAR 52.247-30(a))

F.o.b. Origin, Freight Allowed Means: a. Free of expense to the Government delivered: (1) On board the indicated type of conveyance of the carrier (or of the Government, if specified) at a designated point in the city, county, and State from which the shipments will be made and from which line-haul transportation service (as distinguished from switching, local drayage, or other terminal service) will begin; (2) To, and placed on, the carrier's wharf (at shipside within reach of the ship's loading tackle when the shipping point is within a port area having water transportation service) or the carrier's freight station; (3) To a U.S. Postal Service facility; or (4) If stated in the solicitation, to any Government-designated point located within the same city or commercial zone as the f.o.b. origin point specified in the contract (commercial zones are prescribed by the Interstate Commerce Commission at 49 CFR 1048); and b. An allowance for freight, based on applicable published tariff rates (or Government rate tenders) between the points specified in the contract, is deducted from the contract price. (FAR 52.247-31(a))

F.o.b. Origin, Freight Prepaid Means: a. Free of expense to the Government delivered: (1) On board the indicated type of conveyance of the carrier (or of the Government, if specified) at a designated point in the city, county, and State from which the shipments will be made and from which line-haul transportation service (as distinguished from switching, local drayage, or other terminal service) will begin; (2) To, and placed on, the carrier's wharf (at shipside, within reach of the ship's loading tackle, when the shipping point is within a port area having water transportation service) or the carrier's freight station; (3) To a U.S. Postal Service facility; or (4) If stated in the solicitation, to any Government-designated point located within the same city or commercial zone as the f.o.b. origin point specified in the contract (commercial zones are prescribed by the Interstate Commerce Commission at 49 CFR 1048); and b. The cost of transportation, ultimately the Government's obligation, is prepaid by the contractor to the point specified in the contract. (FAR 52.247-32(a))

F.o.b. Origin, with Differentials Means: a. Free of expense to the Government delivered: (1) On board the indicated type of conveyance of the carrier (or of the Government, if specified) at a designated point in the city, county, and State from which the shipments will be made and from which line-haul transportation service (as distinguished from switching, local drayage, or other terminal service) will begin; (2) To, and placed on, the carrier's wharf (at shipside, within reach of the ship's loading tackle, when the shipping point is within a port area having water transportation service) or the carrier's freight station; (3) To a U.S. Postal Service facility; or (4)If stated in the solicitation, to any Government-designated point located within the same city or commercial zone as the f.o.b. origin point specified in the contract (commercial zones are prescribed by the Interstate Commerce Commission at 49 CFR 1048); and b. Differentials for mode of transportation, type of vehicle, or place of delivery as indicated in Contractor's offer may be added to the contract price. (FAR 52.247-33(a))

F.o.b. Vessel, Port of Shipment Free of expense to the Government loaded, stowed, and trimmed on board the ocean vessel at the specified port of shipment. (FAR 52.247-37(a))

Facilities 1. Plant or any portion thereof (including land integral to the operation), equipment, individually or collectively, or any other tangible capital asset, wherever located, and whether owned or leased by the contractor. (FAR 31.205-17(a)) 2. Property used for production, maintenance, research, development, or testing. It includes plant equipment and real property. It does not include material, special test equipment, special tooling, or agency-peculiar property. (FAR 45.301) 3. All property provided under a facilities contract. (FAR 52.245-7(a))

Facilities Capital The net book value of tangible capital assets and of those intangible capital assets that are subject to amortization. (FAR 31.001)

Facilities Capital Cost of Money (FCCOM) An imputed cost determined by applying a cost-of-money rate to facilities capital employed in contract performance. A cost-of-money rate determined by the Treasury Secretary is uniformly imputed to all contractors. Capital employed is determined without regard to whether its source is equity or borrowed capital. The resulting cost of money is not a form of interest on borrowings. (FAR 31.205-10(a)(1)(i))

Facilities Contract A contract under which Government facilities are provided to a contractor or subcontractor by the Government for use in connection with performing one or more related contracts for supplies or services. It is used occasionally to provide special tooling or special test equipment. Facilities contracts may take any of the following forms: a. A facilities acquisition contract providing for the acquisition, construction, and installation of facilities. b. A facilities use contract providing for the use, maintenance, accountability, and disposition of facilities. c. A consolidated facilities contract, which is a combination of a facilities acquisition and a facilities use contract. (FAR 45.301)

Facility Any building, plant, installation, structure, mine, vessel or other floating craft, location, or site of operations, owned, leased, or supervised by a Contractor or subcontractor, used in the performance of a contract or subcontract. When a location or site of operations includes more than one building, plant, installation, or structure, the entire location or site must be deemed a facility except when the Administrator, or a designee, of the Environmental Protection Agency determines that independent facilities are collocated in one geographical area. (FAR 52.223-2(a))

Facsimile 1. Electronic equipment that communicates and reproduces both printed and handwritten material. 2. If used in conjunction with a reference to a document (e.g., facsimile bid, the terms refers to a document) that has been transmitted to and received by the Government via facsimile. (FAR 2.101)

Facsimile Bid A bid, modification of a bid, or withdrawal of a bid that is transmitted to and received by the Government via electronic equipment that communicates and reproduces both printed and handwritten material. (FAR 52.214-31(a))

Facsimile Proposal A proposal, revision or modification of a proposal, or withdrawal of a proposal that is transmitted to and received by the Government via facsimile machine. (FAR 52.215-5(a))

Fact-Finding An exchange with an offeror or contractor to obtain a clear understanding of all the contractor's proposal, Government requirements, and any alternatives proposed by the contractor. (FAR 15.406-1)

Fair Market Price A price based on reasonable costs under normal competitive conditions and not on lowest possible cost. (FAR 19.001)

Fait Accompli A fait accompli is an accomplished fact. A negotiator using this tactic hopes that the other party will accept a position because related actions have already been completed.

FAR Deviation See deviation.

Fax A facsimile document.

Federal Acquisition Computer Network Architecture (FACNET) A Government-wide system that provides universal user access, employs nationally and internationally recognized data formats, and allows the electronic data interchange of acquisition information between the private sector and the Federal Government. FACNET qualifies as the single, Government-wide point of entry pending designation by the Administrator of the Office of Federal Procurement Policy (OFPP). (FAR 2.101)

Federal Agency Any executive agency or any independent establishment in the legislative or judicial branch of the Government (except the Senate, the House of Representatives, the Architect of the Capitol, and any activities under the Architect's direction). (FAR 2.101)

Federal Directory of Contract Administration Services Components The Defense Contract Management Command (DCMC) maintains and distributes the Federal Directory of Contract Administration Services Components. The directory lists the names and telephone numbers of those DCMC and other agency offices that offer contract administration services within designated geographic areas and at specified contractor plants. (FAR 42.203)

Federal Excise Tax A tax levied on the sale or use of particular supplies or services by the Federal Government. (FAR 29.201(a))

Federal Power and Water Marketing Agency A Government entity that produces, manages, transports, controls, and sells electrical and water supply service to customers. (FAR 41.101)

Federal Prison Industries, Inc. (FPI) Also referred to as UNICOR. A self-supporting, wholly owned Government corporation of the District of Columbia. It provides training and employment of prisoners confined in Federal penal and correctional institutions through he sale of its supplies and services to Government agencies. (FAR 8.601)

Federal Reserve Board The Board of Governors of the Federal Reserve System. (FAR 32.301)

Federal Supply Schedule (FSS) Publications issued by the GSA schedule contracting office containing the information for placing delivery or task orders under indefinite delivery contracts (including requirements contracts) established with commercial firms to obtain commonly used commercial supplies and services associated with volume buying. Ordering offices issue delivery or task orders directly to the schedule contractors. (FAR 8.401)

Federal Supply Schedule Program A program to provide Federal agencies with a simplified process for acquiring commonly used supplies and services in varying quantities at lower prices while obtaining discounts associated with volume buying. Indefinite delivery contracts (including requirements contracts) are awarded, using competitive procedures, to commercial firms to provide supplies and services at stated prices for given periods of time, for delivery within the 48 continuous states, Washington, DC, and possibly Alaska, Hawaii, and overseas deliveries. (FAR 38.101)

Federal Travel Regulations (FTR) Regulations, prescribed by the General Services Administration, for travel in the conterminous 48 United States. (FAR 31.20546(a)(2)(i))

Federally Funded Research and Development Center An activity that is sponsored under a broad charter by a Government agency (or agencies) for the purpose of performing, analyzing, integrating, supporting, and/or managing basic or applied research and/or development, and which receive 70 percent (FFRDC) or more of its financial support from the Government; a long-term relationship is contemplated; most or all of the facilities are owned or funded by the Government; and the FFRDC has access to Government and supplier data, employees, and facilities beyond that which is common in a normal contractual relationship. The National Science Foundation maintains the master list of FFRDCs. (FAR 35.001)

Feinting The use of a pretense or action designed to mislead. In negotiations, this tactic normally involves the use of true but misleading statement or behavior. It gives the other negotiator a false impression or deceives the negotiator into believing something that is not true.

FEMA-Authorized Program A program approved by the Federal Emergency Management Agency (FEMA) for priorities and allocations support under the Defense Production Act of 1950,amended, to promote the national defense. Schedule I of the DPAS lists currently authorized programs. (FAR 11.601)

Field Pricing Assistance Generally, technical, audit, and special reports associated with cost elements of a proposal, including subcontracts. It may also include information related to offeror: pricing practices and history; or business, technical, production, or other capabilities. (FAR 15.404-2(a)(2))

Filed The complete receipt of any document by an agency before its close of business. Documents received after close of business are considered filed as of the next day. Unless otherwise stated, the agency close of business is presumed to be 4:30 p.m., local time. (FAR 33.101)

Final Conviction A conviction, whether entered on a verdict or plea, including a plea of nolo contendere, for which a sentence has been imposed. (FAR 3.702)

Final Cost Objective A cost objective that has allocated to it both direct and indirect costs and, in the contractor's accumulation system, is one of the final accumulation points. (FAR 31.001)

Final Indirect Cost Rate The indirect cost rate established and agreed upon by the Government and the contractor and not subject to change. It is usually established after the close of the contractor's fiscal year (unless the parties decide upon a different period) to which it applies. In the case of cost-reimbursement research and development contracts with educational institutions, it may be predetermined; that is, established for a future period on the basis of cost experience with similar contracts, together with supporting data. (FAR 42.701)

Finished Products Any one or more of several petroleum oils identified in the FAR, or a mixture or combination of those oils, to be used without further processing except blending by mechanical means. (FAR 25.108(d)(2)(ii))

Firm Any individual, partnership, corporation, association, or other legal entity permitted by law to practice the professions of architecture or engineering. (FAR 36.102)

Firm Fixed-Price Contract A contract that provides for a price that is not subject to any adjustment on the basis of the contractor's cost experience in performing the contract. (FAR 16.202-1)

Firm Fixed-Price, Level-of-Effort Term Contract Also referred to as fixed-price-level-of-effort contract. A contract that requires: a. The contractor to provide a specified level of effort, over a stated period of time, on work that can be stated only in general terms; and b. The Government to pay the contractor a fixed dollar amount. (FAR 16.207-1)

First-In-First-Out For inventory accounting purposes, the first unit into the inventory is assumed to be the first unit to be drawn out. The inventory value assigned to any unit drawn out is the value of the first unit recorded as still being in inventory. It does not matter which unit is physically drawn out of inventory.

First-Tier Subcontractor A subcontractor holding a subcontract with a prime contractor. (FAR 22.801)

Fiscal Year The accounting period for which annual financial statements are regularly prepared, generally a period of 12 months, 52 weeks, or 53 weeks. (FAR 31.001)

Fixed Cost Costs that remain constant as production volume varies in the relevant range of production. Fixed cost per unit decreases as total fixed cost is spread over an increasing number of units.

Fixed-Ceiling-Price Contract with Retroactive Price Redetermination A contract that provides for: a. A fixed ceiling price; and b. Retroactive price redetermination within the ceiling after completion of the contract. (FAR 16.206-1)

Fixed-Price Award- Fee Contract See fixed-price contract with award fee.

Fixed-Price Contract A contract that provides for a firm price or, in appropriate cases, an adjustable price. Fixed-price contracts providing for an adjustable price may include a ceiling price, a target price, or both. Unless otherwise specified in the contract, the ceiling price or target price is subject to adjustment only by operation of contract clauses providing for an equitable adjustment or other revision of the contract price under stated circumstances. (FAR 16.201)

Fixed-Price Contract with Award Fee Also referred to as fixed-price award-fee contract. A contract that provides for: a. A fixed price (including normal profit) for the contract effort. This price will be paid for satisfactory contract performance. b. An award fee that will be paid (if earned) will be paid in addition to that fixed price; and c. Periodic evaluation of the contractor's performance against an award-fee plan to determine the amount of fee (if any) due the contractor. (FAR 16.404(a))

Fixed-Price Contract with Economic Price Adjustment A contract that provides for upward and downward revision of the stated contract price upon the occurrence of specified contingencies. Economic price adjustments may be based on: a. Established prices; b. Actual costs of labor or material; or c. Cost indexes of labor or material. (FAR 16.203-1)

Fixed-Price Contract with Prospective Price Redetermination A contract that provides for: a. A firm fixed price for an initial period of contract deliveries or performance and b. Prospective redetermination, at a stated time or times during performance, of the price for subsequent periods of performance. (FAR 16.205-1)

Fixed-Price Incentive (Firm Target) Contract Also referred to as fixed-price incentive firm contract. A contract that specifies a target cost, a target profit, a price ceiling (but not a profit ceiling or floor), and a profit adjustment formula. These elements are all negotiated at the outset. The price ceiling is the maximum that may be paid to the contractor, except for any adjustment under other contract clauses. When the contractor completes performance, the parties negotiate the final cost, and the final price is established by applying the formula. When the final cost is less than the target cost, application of the formula results in a final profit greater than the target profit; conversely, when final cost is more than target cost, application of the formula results in a final profit less than the target profit, or even a net loss. If the final negotiated cost exceeds the price ceiling, the contractor absorbs the difference as a loss. (FAR 16.403 1(a))

Fixed-Price Incentive (Successive Targets) Contract A contract that: a. Specifies the following elements, all of which are negotiated at the outset: (1) An initial target cost. (2) An initial target profit. (3) An initial profit adjustment formula to be used for establishing the firm target profit, including a ceiling and floor for the firm target profit. (This formula normally provides for a lesser degree of contractor cost responsibility than would a formula for establishing final profit and price.) (4) The production point at which the firm target cost and firm target profit will be negotiated (usually before delivery or shop completion of the first item). (5) A ceiling price that is the maximum that may be paid to the contractor, except for any adjustment under other contract clauses providing for equitable adjustment or other revision of the contract price under stated circumstances. b. When the production point specified in the contract is reached, the parties negotiate the firm target cost, giving consideration to cost experience under the contract and other pertinent factors. The firm target profit is established by the formula. At this point, the parties have two alternatives, as follows: (1) They may negotiate a firm fixed-price, using the firm target cost plus the firm target profit as a guide. (2) If negotiation of a firm fixed-price is inappropriate, they may negotiate a formula for establishing the final price using the firm target cost and firm target profit. The final cost is then negotiated at completion, and the final profit is established by formula, as under the fixed-price incentive (firm target) contract. (FAR 16.403-2(a))

Fixed-Price Incentive A fixed-price contract that provides for adjusting profit and establishing the final contract price by application of a formula based on the relationship of total final negotiated cost to total target cost. The final price is subject to a price ceiling, negotiated at the outset. The two forms of fixed-price incentive contracts are firm target and successive targets. (FAR 16.403(a))

Fixed-Price Incentive Firm Contract See fixed-price incentive (firm target) contract.

Fixed-Price-Level-of-Effort Contract See firm fixed-price, level-of-effort term contract.

Flexible Progress Payments A method of making progress payments used by the Department of Defense for certain negotiated contracts performed in the United States. It tailors the progress payment rate to more closely match the contractor's cash needs for financing contract performance. (DFARS 232.502-71)

Follower Company A company designated under a leader company contract to receive assistance and know-how from a developer or sole producer of a product or system, so they it can become a source of supply for that product or system. (FAR 17.401)

Forbearance The act of refraining or abstaining from action. In negotiation it allows both parties to agree to disagree and move on to the next issue without making a commitment one way or another.

Foreign Construction Material A construction material other than a domestic construction material. (FAR 25.201)

Foreign Contractor A contractor or subcontractor organized or existing under the laws of a country other than the United States, its territories, or possessions. (FAR 25.901)

Foreign End Product 1. An end product other than a domestic end product. (FAR 25.101) 2. An end product other than a domestic end product. (FAR 52.225-9(a))

Foreign Military Sale (FMS) Department of Defense acquisition on behalf of a foreign government or international organization under Section 22 of the Arms Export Control Act. Acquisitions for FMS are conducted under the same acquisition and contract management procedures as other defense contracts. (DFARS 225.7300(a) and 225.7301(b))

Foreign Offer An offered price for a foreign end product, including transportation to destination and duty (whether or not a duty-free entry certificate is issued). (FAR 25.101)

Foreign Services Services other than domestic services. (FAR 25.301)

Foreign-Flag Vessel Any vessel of foreign registry including vessels owned by U.S. citizens but registered in a nation other than the United States. (FAR 47.501)

Form, Fit, and Function Data Data relating to items, components, processes that are sufficient to enable physical and functional interchangeability, as well as data identifying source, size, configuration, mating and attachment characteristics, functional characteristics, and performance requirements; except that for computer software it means data identifying source, functional characteristics, and performance requirements, but specifically excludes the source code, algorithm, process, formulae, and flow charts of the software. (FAR 27.401)

Forward Pricing Rate Agreement (FPRA) A written agreement negotiated between a contractor and the Government to make certain rates available during a specified period for use in pricing contracts or modifications. Such rates represent reasonable projections of specific costs that are not easily estimated for, identified with, or generated by a specific contract, contract end item, or task. These projections may include rates for such things as labor, indirect costs, material obsolescence and usage, spare parts provisioning, and material handling. (FAR 15.401)

Forward Pricing Rate Recommendation A rate set unilaterally by the Administrative Contracting Officer for use by the Government in negotiations or other contract actions when forward pricing rate agreement negotiations have not been completed or when the contractor will not agree to a forward pricing rate agreement. (FAR 15.401)

Franchise Territory A geographical area that a utility supplier has a right to serve based upon a franchise, a certificate of public convenience and necessity, or other legal means. (FAR 41.101)

Fraud Acts: a. Of fraud or corruption or attempts to defraud the Government or to corrupt its agents; b. Which constitute a cause for debarment or suspension; and c. Which violate the False Claims Act or the Anti-Kickback Act. (FAR 31.205-47)

Free on Board (f.o.b.) A term is used in conjunction with a physical point to determine: a. The responsibility and basis for payment of freight charges; and b. Unless otherwise agreed, the point at which title for goods passes to the buyer or consignee. (FAR 47.001)

Freedom of Information Act (FOIA) Specifies, among other things, how agencies must make their records available upon public request, imposes strict time standards for agency responses, and exempts certain records from public disclosure. (FAR 24.203(a))

Freight Supplies, goods, and transportable property. (FAR 47.001)

Fringe Benefits Allowances and services provided by the contractor to its employees as compensation in addition to regular wages and salaries. Fringe benefits include, but are not limited to, the cost of vacations, sick leave, holidays, military leave, employee insurance, and supplemental unemployment benefit plans. (FAR 31.205-6(m)(1))

Fuel Oil A liquid or liquefiable petroleum product burned for lighting or for the generation of heat or power and derived directly or indirectly from crude oil, such as kerosene, range oil, distillate fuel oils, gas oil, diesel fuel, topped crude oil, or residues. (FAR 25.108(d)(2)(ii)(B))

Full and Open Competition All responsible sources are permitted to compete for a contract action. (FAR 6.003)

Full Coverage Requires that the business unit comply with all cost accounting standards (CAS) that are in effect on the date of the contract award and with any CAS that become applicable because of later award of a CAS-covered contract. (FAR 9903.201-2(a))

Full Production A contract for full production of a successfully tested major system. (FAR 34.005-6)

Functional Requirement Contract requirement stated in terms of the objectives that must be achieved under the contract. Each offeror is permitted to define how those objectives will be achieved in its contract proposal.

Funded Pension Cost The portion of pension costs for a current or prior cost accounting period that has been paid to a funding agency. (FAR 31.001)

Funny Money Many issues in Government contract negotiations relate to percentages, factors, or other estimating relationships. Bargaining on these relationships is essential to reaching a mutually satisfactory result. However, these relationships can become funny money if a negotiator uses them to distract another party from considering their effect on the total contract.

Future Contract Savings In value engineering, savings which are the product of the future value engineering unit cost reduction multiplied by the number of future contract units scheduled for delivery during the sharing period. If the instant contract is a multi-year contract, future contract savings include savings on quantities funded after value engineering change proposal acceptance. (FAR 48.001)

Future Unit Cost Reduction In value engineering, the instant unit cost reduction adjusted as the Contracting Officer considers necessary for projected learning or changes in quantity during the sharing period. It is calculated at the time the value engineering change proposal is accepted and applies either: a. Throughout the sharing period, unless the Contracting Officer decides that recalculation is necessary because conditions are significantly different from those previously anticipated, or b. To the calculation of a lump-sum payment, which cannot later be revised. (FAR 48.001)

Gasoline A refined petroleum distillate that, by its composition, is suitable for use as a carburant in internal combustion engines. (FAR 25.108(d)(2)(ii)(C))

Gateway Airport The airport from which the traveler last embarks en route to the United States or abroad which the traveler first debarks incident to travel from the United States. (FAR 47.401)

Gateway Airport in the United States The last U.S. airport from which the traveler's flight departs or the first U.S. airport at which the traveler's flight arrives. (FAR 47.401)

General Accounting Office (GAO) Protest A procurement protest made to the General Accounting Office. (FAR 33.104)

General and Administrative (G&A) Expense Any management, financial, and other expense which is incurred by or allocated to a business unit and which is for the general management and administration of the business unit as a whole. G&A expense does not include those management expenses whose beneficial or causal relationship to cost objectives can be more directly measured by a base other than a cost input base representing the total activity of a business unit during a cost accounting period. (FAR 31.001)

General and Administrative (G&A) Expense Rate The indirect cost rate used by a concern to recover G&A Expense.

General Freight Supplies, goods, and transportable property not encompassed in the definitions of household goods or office furniture. (FAR 47.201)

General Wage Determination Contains prevailing wage rates for the types of construction designated in the determination, and is used in contracts performed within a specified geographical area. General wage determinations contain no expiration date and remain valid until modified, superseded, or canceled by a notice in the Federal Register by the Department of Labor. Once incorporated in a contract, a general wage determination normally remains effective for the life of the contract. (FAR 22.404-1(a))

Good Guy/Bad Guy This negotiation tactic involves role playing by members of the negotiating team. One member plays an easy-going good guy role while another team member plays the hard-core or difficult bad guy. The bad guy's position may even involve a serious personal threat.

Goodwill An unidentifiable intangible asset, that originates under the purchase method of accounting for a business combination when the price paid by the acquiring company exceeds the sum of the identifiable individual assets acquired less liabilities assumed, based upon their fair values. Goodwill may arise from the acquisition of a company as a whole or a portion thereof. (FAR 31.205-49)

Government Also referred to as entity of the Government. Any entity of the legislative or judicial branch, any executive agency, military department, Government corporation, or independent establishment, the U.S. Postal Service, or any nonappropriated-fund instrumentality of the Armed Forces. (FAR 8.701)

Government Acquisition Team Government members of the Acquisition Team including representatives of the technical, supply, procurement, and the customers they serve.

Government Contract Any agreement or modification thereof between a Government contracting agency and any person for the furnishing of supplies or services, or for the use of real or personal property including lease arrangements. The term does not include: a. Agreements in which the parties stand in the relationship of employer and employee, and b. Contracts for the sale of real and personal property by the Government. (FAR 22.801)

Government Contract Quality Assurance The various functions, including inspection, performed by the Government to determine whether a contractor has fulfilled the contract obligations pertaining to quality and quantity. (FAR 46.101)

Government Costs In value engineering, those agency costs that result directly from developing and implementing the value engineering change proposal (VECP), such as any net increases in the cost of testing, operations, maintenance, and logistics support. The term does not include the normal administrative costs of processing the VECP or any increase in instant contract cost or price resulting from negative instant contract savings. (FAR 48.001)

Government Delay of Work Delays and interruptions in the contract work caused by the acts, or failures to act, of the Contracting Officer. The Federal Government Delay of Work clause provides for the administrative settlement of contractor claims that arise from any delay caused by the Government. (FAR 42.1304(a))

Government Financing Payments made to a contractor before supplies have been delivered or services rendered, including: a. Advance payments; b. Progress payments based on cost; c. Loan guarantees; d. Partial payments; e. Progress payments based on a percentage or stage of completion; or f. Performance-based payments. (FAR 32.102)

Government Printing Printing, binding, and blankbook work for the use of an executive department, independent agency, or establishment of the Government. (FAR 8.801)

Government Production and Research Property Government-owned facilities, Government-owned special test equipment, and special tooling to which the Government has title or the right to acquire title. (FAR 45.301)

Government Property All property owned by or leased to the Government or acquired by the Government under the terms of the contract. It includes both Government-furnished property and contractor-acquired property. (FAR 45.101)

Government Vessel A vessel owned by the U.S. Government and operated directly by the Government or for the Government by an agent or contractor, including a privately owned U.S.-flag vessel under bareboat charter to the Government. (FAR 47.501)

Government-Furnished Material Government property that may be incorporated into or attached to a deliverable end item or that may be consumed or expended in performing a contract. Property includes assemblies, components, parts, raw and processed materials, and small tools and supplies. (FAR 45.101 and 45.301)

Government- Furnished Property Property in the possession of, or directly acquired by, the Government and subsequently made available to the contractor. (FAR 45.101)

Governmentwide Commercial Purchase Card A purchase card, similar in nature to a commercial credit card, issued to authorized agency personnel to use to acquire and to pay for supplies and services. (FAR 13.001)

Governmentwide Point of Entry See single, Government wide point of entry.

GSA Advantage An on-line shopping service that enables ordering offices to search product information, review delivery options, place orders directly with contractors (or ask GSA to place orders on the agency's behalf), and pay contractors for orders using the Government wide commercial purchase card. The service can be accessed through the GSA Federal Supply Service Home Page (http:www.fss.gsa.gov). (FAR 8.402(c))

Guaranteed Loan Also referred to as a V loan. A loan, revolving credit fund, or other financial arrangement made pursuant to Regulation V of the Federal Reserve Board, under which the guaranteeing agency is obligated, on demand of the lender, to purchase a stated percentage of the loan and to share any losses in the amount of the guaranteed percentage. (FAR 32.301)

Guaranteeing Agency Any agency that the President has authorized to guarantee loans, through Federal Reserve Banks, for expediting national defense production. (FAR 32.301)

Hazardous Material Includes any material defined as hazardous under the latest version of Federal Standard No. 313 (including revisions adopted during the term of the contract). (FAR 52.223-3(a))

Head of the Agency Also referred to as Agency Head. The Secretary, Attorney General, Administrator, Governor, Chairperson, or other chief official of an executive agency, unless otherwise indicated, including any deputy or assistant chief official of an executive agency; and the term authorized representative means any person, persons, or board (other than the Contracting Officer) authorized to act for the head of the agency or Secretary. (FAR 2.101)

Head of the Contracting Activity The official who has overall responsibility for managing the contracting activity. (FAR 2.101)

Heavy Construction Those projects that are not properly classified as either building, residential, or highway, and is of a catch-all nature. Such heavy projects may sometimes be distinguished on the basis of their individual characteristics, and separate schedules issued (e.g., dredging, water and sewer line, dams, flood control, etc.). (FAR 22.404-2(c)(4))

Helium Requirement Forecast An estimate by the contractor or subcontractor of the amount of helium required for performance of the contract or subcontract. (FAR 8.501)

High-Value Item A contract end item that: a. Has a high unit cost (normally exceeding $100,000 per unit), such as an aircraft, an aircraft engine, a communication system, a computer system, a missile, or a ship, and b. Is designated by the Contracting Officer as a high-value item. (FAR 46.802)

Higher-Tier Subcontractor A subcontractor with at least one subcontract.

Highway Construction The construction, alteration, or repair of roads, streets, highways, runways, taxiways, alleys, parking areas, and other similar projects that are not incidental to building, residential, or heavy construction. (FAR 22.404-2(c)(3))

Hire See leasing.

Historically Black College or University An institution determined by the Secretary of Education to meet the requirements for such designation. For DoD, NASA, and the Coast Guard, the term also includes any nonprofit research institution that was an integral part of such a college or university before November 14, 1986. (FAR 26.301)

Home Office An office responsible for directing or managing two or more, but not necessarily all, segments of an organization. It typically establishes policy for, and provides guidance to, the segments in their operations. It usually performs management, supervisory, or administrative functions, and may also perform service functions in support of the operations of the various segments. An organization which has intermediate levels, such as groups, may have several home offices which report to a common home office. An intermediate organization may be both a segment and a home office. (FAR 31.001)

Household Goods Personal property that belongs to a person and that person's immediate family and includes, but is not limited to household furnishings, equipment and appliances, furniture, clothing, books, and similar property. (FAR 47.201)

Identical Bids Bids for the same line item that are determined to be identical as to unit price or total line item amount, with or without the application of evaluation factors (e.g., transportation cost). (FAR 3.302)

Idle Capacity The unused capacity of partially used facilities. a. It is the difference between that which a facility could achieve under 100 percent operating time on a one-shift basis, less operating interruptions resulting from time lost for repairs, setups, unsatisfactory materials, and other normal delays, and the extent to which the facility was actually used to meet demands during the accounting period. b. A multiple-shift basis may be used in the calculation instead of a one-shift basis if it can be shown that this amount of usage could normally be expected for the type of facility involved. (FAR 31.205-17(a))

Idle Facilities Completely unused facilities that are excess to the contractor's current needs. (FAR 31.205-17(a))

Immediate-Gain Actuarial Cost Method Any of the several actuarial cost methods under which actuarial gains and losses are included as part of the unfunded actuarial liability of the pension plan, rather than as part of the normal cost of the plan. (FAR 31.001)

Implied Warranty of Merchantability The implication by sale of the item that it is reasonably fit for the ordinary purposes for which items are used. Items must be of at least average, fair, or medium-grade quality and must be comparable in quality to those that will pass without objection in the trade or market for items of the same description. (FAR 12.404(a))

Imprest Fund A cash fund of a fixed amount established by an advance of funds, without charge to an appropriation, from an agency finance or disbursing officer to a duly appointed cashier, for disbursement as needed from time to time in making payment in cash for relatively small amounts. (FAR 13.001)

Improper Influence Any influence that induces or tends to induce a Government employee or officer to give consideration or to act regarding a Government contract on any basis other than the merits of the matter. (FAR 3.401)

Improvement Curve An estimating technique based on the concept that the resources (labor and/or material) required to produce each additional unit of a product decline as the total number of units produced over the item's entire production history increases. The concept further holds that decline in unit cost can be predicted mathematically.

In Writing Also referred to as written. Any worded or numbered expression which can be read, reproduced, and later communicated, and includes electronically transmitted and stored information. (FAR 2.101)

Incumbent Contractor Current contractor on an ongoing contractual requirement program.

Indefinite-Delivery Contract A contract that may be used to acquire supplies and/or services when the exact times and/or exact quantities of future deliveries are not known at the time of contract award. There are three types: definite quantity; requirements; and indefinite quantity. (FAR 16.501-2(a))

Indefinite-Quantity Contract An indefinite-delivery contract that provides for an indefinite quantity, within stated limits (minimum and maximum), of supplies or services to be furnished during a fixed period, with deliveries or performance to be scheduled by placing orders with the contractor. (FAR 16.504(a))

Independent Research and Development (IR&D) Cost The cost of effort which is neither sponsored by a grant, nor required in performing a contract, and which falls within any of the following four areas: a. Basic research; b. Applied research; c. Development; and d. Systems and other concept formulation studies. (FAR 31.001 and 31.205-18(a))

Indian Any person who is a member of any Indian tribe, band, group, pueblo, or community which is recognized by the Federal Government as eligible for services from the Bureau of Indian Affairs (BIA) and any Native as defined in the Alaska Native Claims Settlement Act. (FAR 26.101)

Indian Organization The governing body of any Indian tribe or entity established or recognized by the governing body of an Indian tribe. (FAR 26.101)

Indian Tribe Any Indian tribe, band, pueblo, or community, including native villages and native groups (including corporations organized by Kenai, Juneau, Sitka, and Kodiak) as defined in the Alaska Native Claims Settlement Act, which is recognized by the Federal Government as eligible for services from Bureau of Indian Affairs (BIA). (FAR 26.101)

Indian-Owned Economic Enterprise Any Indian-owned (as determined by the Secretary of the Interior) commercial, industrial, or business activity established or organized for the purpose of profit, provided that Indian ownership must constitute not less than 51 percent of the enterprise. (FAR 26.101)

Indictment Indictment for a criminal offense. An information or other filing by competent authority charging a criminal offense must be given the same effect as an indictment. (FAR 9.403)

Indirect Cost Also referred to as burden. Any cost not directly identified with a single, final cost objective, but identified with two or more final cost objectives or an intermediate cost objective. An indirect cost must not be allocated to a final cost objective if other costs incurred for the same purpose in like circumstances have been included as a direct cost of that or any other final cost objective. a. Indirect costs are accumulated by logical cost groupings with due consideration of the reasons for incurring such costs. Each grouping should be determined so as to permit distribution of the grouping on the basis of the benefits accruing to the several cost objectives. Commonly, manufacturing overhead, selling expenses, and general and administrative (G&A) expenses are separately grouped. Similarly, the particular case may require subdivision of these groupings, e.g., building occupancy costs might be separable from those of personnel administration within the manufacturing overhead group. b. A distribution base common to all cost objectives is used to allocate the grouping to those objectives. The base should be selected so as to permit allocation of the grouping on the basis of the benefits accruing to the several cost objectives. When substantially the same results can be achieved through less precise methods, the number and composition of cost groupings should be governed by practical considerations and should not unduly complicate the allocation. (FAR 31.203)

Indirect Cost Allocation Base The base used to calculate indirect cost rates. It should be selected so as to permit allocation indirect costs on the basis of the benefits accruing to the several cost objectives. (FAR 31.203(b))

Indirect Cost Pools Groupings of incurred costs identified with two or more cost objectives but not identified specifically with any final cost objective. (FAR 31.001)

Indirect Cost Rate Also referred to as a burden rate. The percentage or dollar factor that expresses the ratio of indirect expense incurred in a given period to direct labor cost, manufacturing cost, or another appropriate base for the same period. (FAR 42.701)

Indirect Cost Rate Certification Certain contracts require certification of the indirect cost rates proposed for final payment purposes. If a contractor includes unallowable costs in a final indirect cost settlement proposal, a penalty may be assessed. (FAR 31.110(a))

Individual 1. An offeror/contractor that has no more than one employee including the offeror/contractor. (FAR 23.503) 2. A citizen of the United States or an alien lawfully admitted for permanent residence. (FAR 24.101) 3. An offeror/contractor that has no more than one employee including the offeror/contractor. (FAR 52.223-6(a))

Individual Contract Plan A subcontracting plan that covers the entire contract period (including option periods), applies to a specific contract, and has goals that are based on the offeror's planned subcontracting in support of the specific contract, except that indirect costs incurred for common or joint purposes may be allocated on a prorated basis to the contract. (FAR 19.701)

Individual Deviation A FAR deviation that affects only one contracting action. (FAR 1.403)

Individual Item Record A separate card, form, document, or specific line(s) of computer data used to account for one item of property. (FAR 45.501)

Individual Surety One person, as distinguished from a business entity, who is liable for the entire penal amount of a bond. (FAR 28.001)

Inductive Statistics See inferential statistics.

Industry All concerns primarily engaged in similar lines of activity, as listed and described in the Standard Industrial Classification (SIC) Manual. (FAR 19.001)

Ineligible Excluded from Government contracting (and subcontracting, if appropriate) pursuant to statutory, Executive order, or regulatory authority other than the FAR and its implementing and supplementing regulations (e.g., pursuant to the Davis-Bacon Act and its related statutes and implementing regulations, the Service Contract Act, the Equal Employment Opportunity Acts and Executive orders, the Walsh-Healey Public Contracts Act, the Buy American Act, or the Environmental Protection Acts and Executive orders). (FAR 9.403)

Inferential Statistics Also referred to as inductive statistics. Methods of using a sample data taken from a statistical population to make actual decisions, predictions, and generalizations related to a problem of interest.

Inflation The proportionate rate of change in the general price level, as opposed to the proportionate increase in a specific price. Inflation is usually measured by a broad-based price index, such as the implicit deflator for the Consumer Price Index. (OMB Circular A-94, App A)

Influencing or Attempting to Influence Making, with the intent to influence, any communication to or appearance before an officer or employee of any agency, a Member of Congress, an officer or employee of Congress, or an employee of a Member of Congress in connection with any covered Federal action. (FAR 52.203-12(a))

Information Other Than Cost or Pricing Data Any type of information that is not required to be certified and is necessary to determine price reasonableness or cost realism. For example, such information may include pricing, sales, or cost information, and includes cost or pricing data for which certification is determined inapplicable after submission. (FAR 15.401)

Information Technology Any equipment, or interconnected system(s) or subsystem(s) of equipment, that is used in the automatic acquisition, storage, manipulation, management, movement, control, display, switching, interchange, transmission, or reception of data or information by the agency. a. For purposes of this definition, equipment is used by an agency if the equipment is used by the agency directly or is used by a contractor under a contract with the agency which: (1) Requires the use of such equipment; or (2) requires the use, to a significant extent, of such equipment in the performance of a service or the furnishing of a product. b. The term information technology includes computers, ancillary equipment, software, firmware and similar procedures, services (including support services), and related resources. c. The term information technology does not include: (1) Any equipment that is acquired by a contractor incidental to a contract; or (2) Any equipment that contains imbedded information technology that is used as an integral part of the product, but the principal function of which is not the acquisition, storage, manipulation, management, movement, control, display, switching, interchange, transmission, or reception of data or information. For example, heating, ventilation, and air conditioning equipment such as thermostats or temperature control devices, and medical equipment where information technology is integral to its operation, are not information technology. (FAR 2.101)

Inherently Governmental Function A function that is so intimately related to the public interest as to mandate performance by the Government. Such functions include activities that require either the exercise of discretion in applying Government authority (i.e., the act of governing) or the making of value judgments related to Government monetary transactions and entitlements. (FAR 7.501)

Inspection Examining and testing supplies or services (including, when appropriate, raw materials, components, and intermediate assemblies) to determine whether they conform to contract requirements. (FAR 46.101)

Inspector General An Inspector General appointed under the Inspector General Act of 1978, as amended. In the Department of Defense that is the DOD Inspector General. In the case of an executive agency that does not have an Inspector General, the duties must be performed by an official designated by the head of the executive agency. (FAR 3.901)

Installment Payment Financing Payment by the Government to a contractor of a fixed number of equal interim financing payments prior to delivery and acceptance of a contract item. (FAR 32.206(g))

Instant Contract In value engineering, the contract under which the value engineering change proposal (VECP) is submitted. It does not include increases in quantities after acceptance of the VECP that are due to contract modifications, exercise of options, or additional orders. If the contract is a multiyear contract, the term does not include quantities funded after VECP acceptance. In a fixed-price contract with prospective price redetermination, the term refers to the period for which firm prices have been established. (FAR 48.001)

Instant Contract Savings In value engineering, the net cost reductions on the contract under which the value engineering change proposal (VECP) is submitted and accepted, and which are equal to the instant unit cost reduction multiplied by the number of instant contract units affected by the VECP, less the contractor's allowable development and Implementation costs. (FAR 48.001)

Instant Unit Cost Reduction In value engineering, the amount of the decrease in unit cost of performance (without deducting any contractor's development or implementation costs) resulting from using the value engineering change proposal (VECP) on the instant contract. In service contracts, the instant unit cost reduction is normally equal to the number of hours per line-item task saved by using the VECP on the instant contract, multiplied by the appropriate contract labor rate. (FAR 48.001)

Instrumentality Does not include an agency or division of the government of a country, but may be construed to include arrangements such as the European Union. (FAR 25.101)

Insurance A contract which provides that for a stipulated consideration, one party undertakes to indemnify another against loss, damage, or liability arising from an unknown or contingent event. (FAR 28.001)

Insurance Administration Expenses The contractor's costs of administering an insurance program (e.g., the costs of operating an insurance or risk-management department, processing claims, actuarial fees, and service fees paid to insurance companies, trustees, or technical consultants). (FAR 31.001)

Intangible Capital Asset An asset that has no physical substance, has more than minimal value, and is expected to be held by an enterprise for continued use or possession beyond the current accounting period for the benefits it yields. (FAR 31.001)

Interagency Acquisition A procedure by which an agency needing supplies or services (the requesting agency) obtains them from another agency (the servicing agency). (FAR 17.501)

Interdivisional Transfers See interorganizational transfers.

Interested Party 1. A prime contractor or an actual or prospective offeror whose direct economic interest would be affected by the award of a subcontract or by the failure to award a subcontract. (FAR 26.101) 2. For the purpose of filing a protest, an actual or prospective offeror whose direct economic interest would be affected by the award of a contract or by the failure to award a contract. (FAR 33.101)

International Air Transportation Transportation by air between a place in the United States and a place outside the United States or between two places both of which are outside the United States. (FAR 47.401)

Interorganizational Transfers Also referred to as interdivisional transfers. Materials, supplies, or services that are sold or transferred between any divisions, subdivisions, subsidiaries, or affiliates of the contractor under a common control. (FAR 31.205-26(e))

Intervention Action by GSA or a delegated agency to formally participate in a utility regulatory proceeding on behalf of all Federal executive agencies. (FAR 41.101)

Invention Any invention or discovery that is or may be patentable or otherwise protectable under the U.S. Code or any novel variety of plant that is or may be protectable under the Plant Variety Protection Act. (FAR 27.301)

Inventory Basis Generally, the preferred basis for settlement proposals under fixed-price contracts terminated for convenience. (FAR 49.206-2(a))

Invitation for Bids (IFB) A solicitation for offers under sealed bidding.

Invoice A contractor's bill or written request for payment under the contract for supplies delivered or services performed. (FAR 32.902)

Invoice Payment A Government disbursement of monies to a contractor under a contract or other authorization for supplies or services accepted by the Government. This includes payments for partial deliveries that have been accepted by the Government and final cost or fee payments where amounts owed have been settled between the Government and the contractor. Invoice payments also include all payments made under the Payments Under Fixed-Price Construction Contracts clause or the Payments Under Fixed-Price Architect-Engineer Contracts clause. Invoice payments do not include contract financing payments. (FAR 32.902)

Irrevocable Letter of Credit (ILC) 1. A written commitment by a Federally insured financial institution to pay all or part of a stated amount of money until the expiration date of the letter, upon presentation by the Government (the beneficiary) of a written demand therefore. Neither the financial institution nor the offeror/contractor can revoke or condition the letter of credit. (FAR 28.001) 2. A written commitment by a Federally insured financial institution to pay all or part of a stated amount of money, until the expiration date of the letter, upon presentation by the Government (the beneficiary) of a written demand therefore. Neither the financial institution nor the offeror/contractor can revoke or condition the letter of credit. (FAR 52.228-14(a))

Issue in Controversy A material disagreement between the Government and the contractor which: a. May result in a claim; or b. Is all or part of an existing claim. (FAR 33.201)

Item of Supply Any individual part, component, subassembly, assembly, or subsystem integral to a major system, and other property which may be replaced during the service life of the system. The term includes spare parts and replenishment parts, but does not include packaging or labeling associated with shipment or identification of an item. (FAR 34.101)

Javits-Wagner-O'Day (JWOD) Requires the Government to purchase supplies or services on the Procurement List, at prices established by the Committee, from JWOD participating nonprofit agencies if Act they are available within the period required. When identical supplies or services are on the Procurement List and the Schedule of Products issued by Federal Prison Industries, Inc., ordering offices shall purchase supplies and services in the priority presented in the FAR. (FAR 8.704)

Jet Fuel A refined petroleum distillate used to fuel jet propulsion engines. (FAR 25.108(d)(2)(ii)(D))

Job A homogeneous cluster of work tasks, the completion of which serves an enduring purpose for the organization. Taken as a whole, the collection of tasks, duties, and responsibilities constitutes the assignment for one or more individuals whose work is of the same nature and is performed at the same skill/

responsibility level—as opposed to a position, which is a collection of tasks assigned to a specific individual. Within a job, there may be pay categories which are dependent on the degree of supervision required by the employee while performing assigned tasks which are performed by all persons with the same job. (FAR 31.001)

Job Class of Employees Employees performing in positions within the same job. (FAR 31.001)

Joint Settlement Joint negotiation of two or more termination settlement proposals from the same contractor under different contracts. (FAR 49.109-6(a))

Joint Travel Regulation (JTR) Regulations prescribed by the Department of Defense, for travel in Alaska, Hawaii, The Commonwealth of Puerto Rico, and territories and possessions of the United States. (FAR 31.205-46(a)(2)(ii))

Kickback 1. Any money, fee, commission, credit, gift, gratuity, thing of value, or compensation of any kind which is provided, directly or indirectly, to any prime contractor, prime contractor employee, subcontractor, or subcontractor employee for the purpose of improperly obtaining or rewarding favorable treatment in connection with a prime contract or in connection with a subcontract relating to a prime contract. (FAR 3.502-1) 2. Any money, fee, commission, credit, gift, gratuity, thing of value, or compensation of any kind which is provided, directly or indirectly, to any prime contractor, prime contractor employee, subcontractor, or subcontractor employee for the purpose of improperly obtaining or rewarding favorable treatment in connection with a prime contract or in connection with a subcontract relating to a prime contract. (FAR 52.3203-7(a))

Labor Cost at Standard A preestablished measure of the labor element of cost, computed by multiplying labor-rate standard by a labor-time standard. (FAR 31.001)

Labor Market A place where individuals exchange their labor for compensation. Labor markets are identified and defined by a combination of the following factors: a. Geography; b. Education and/or technical background required; c. Experience required by the job; d. Licensing or certification requirements; e. Occupational membership; and f. Industry. (FAR 31.001)

Labor Relations Costs Costs incurred in maintaining satisfactory relations between the contractor and its employees, including costs of shop stewards, labor management committees, employee publications, and other related activities. (FAR 31.205-21)

Labor Standard See labor-time standard.

Labor Surplus Area A geographical area identified by the Department of Labor as an area of concentrated unemployment or underemployment or an area of labor surplus. (FAR 19.001)

Labor Surplus Area Concern A concern that together with its first-tier subcontractors will perform substantially in labor surplus areas. Performance is substantially in labor surplus areas if the costs incurred under the contract on account of manufacturing, production, or performance of appropriate services in labor surplus areas exceed 50 percent of the contract price. (FAR 19.001)

Labor-Hour Contract A variation of the time-and-materials contract, differing only in that materials are not supplied by the contractor. (FAR 16.602)

Labor-Rate Standard A preestablished measure, expressed in monetary terms, of the price of labor. (FAR 31.001)

Labor-Time Standard Also referred to as labor standard. A preestablished measure, expressed in temporal terms, of the quantity of labor. (FAR 31.001)

Laborers or Mechanics The term: a. Includes: (1) Those workers, utilized by a contractor or subcontractor at any tier, whose duties are manual or physical in nature (including those workers who use tools or who are performing the work of a trade), as distinguished from mental or managerial. (2) Apprentices, trainees, helpers, and, in the case of contracts subject to the Contract Work Hours and Safety Standards Act, watchmen and guards. (FAR 22.401) (3) Working foremen who devote more than 20 percent of their time during a workweek performing duties of a laborer or mechanic, and who do not meet the required criteria, for the time so spent; and (4) Every person performing the duties of a laborer or mechanic, regardless of any contractual relationship alleged to exist between the contractor and those individuals. b. Does not include: (1) Workers whose duties are primarily executive, supervisory (except working foremen as provided above), administrative, or clerical, rather than manual; or (2) Persons employed in a bona fide executive, administrative, or professional capacity. (FAR 22.401)

Last-In-First-Out For inventory accounting purposes, the last unit into the inventory is assumed to be the first unit to be drawn out. The inventory value assigned to any unit drawn out is the value of the last unit recorded as still being in inventory. It does not matter which unit is physically drawn out of inventory.

Late Bid A bid received in the office designated in the invitation for bids after the exact time set for opening. (FAR 14.304-1)

Latent Defect A defect which exists at the time of acceptance but cannot be discovered by a reasonable inspection. (FAR 46.101)

Leader Company A developer or sole producer of a product or system designated under a leader company contract to furnish assistance and know-how to one or more designated follower companies, so they can become a source of supply. (FAR 17.401)

Leader Company Contract A developer or sole producer of a product or system is designated under this acquisition technique to be the leader company, and to furnish assistance and know-how under an approved contract to one or more designated follower companies, so they can become a source of supply. The objectives of this technique are one or more of the following: a. Reduce delivery time. b. Achieve geographic dispersion of suppliers. c. Maximize the use of scarce tooling or special equipment. d. Achieve economies in production. e. Ensure uniformity and reliability in equipment, compatibility or standardization of components, and interchangeability of parts. f. Eliminate problems in the use of proprietary data that cannot be resolved by more satisfactory solutions. g. Facilitate the transition from development to production and to subsequent competitive acquisition of end items or major components. (FAR 17.401)

Leasing Also referred to as rent or hire. Acquisition from private or commercial sources other than by purchase. (FAR 8.1101)

Legal Proceedings Any civil judicial proceeding to which the Government is a party or any criminal proceeding. The term includes appeals from such proceedings. (FAR 9.403)

Legitimacy The state or condition of complying with established rules and standards. Negotiators often rely on commonly accepted standards (e.g., past practice, official policy, or written documents) to support a negotiation position. Win/lose negotiators might use questionable or nonexistent standards to support their negotiation position.

Letter Contract A written preliminary contractual instrument that authorizes the contractor to begin immediately manufacturing supplies or performing services. (FAR 16.603-1)

Life-Cycle Cost 1. The total cost to the Government of acquiring, operating, supporting, and (if applicable) disposing of the items being acquired. (FAR 7.101) 2. The sum of all costs over the useful life of a building, system or product. It includes the cost of design, construction, acquisition, operation, maintenance, and salvage (resale) value, if any. (FAR 52.248-2(b)) 3. The overall estimated cost for a particular program alternative over the time period corresponding to the life of the program, including direct and indirect initial costs plus any periodic or continuing costs of operation and maintenance. (OMB Circular A-94, App A)

Limitation of Cost A limitation on the funds available under a cost-reimbursement contract. The parties estimate that the contract cost will not exceed the limitation of cost. The contractor agrees to use its best efforts to perform the work specified in the contract and all obligations under the contract within the estimated cost, which, if the contract is a cost-sharing contract, includes both the Government's and contractor's share of cost. (FAR 52.232-20)

Limitation of Funds A limit on the funds currently available under a cost-reimbursement contract when the available funding is less than the estimated amount of the contract. The parties contemplate that the Government will allot additional funds incrementally to the contract up to the full estimated cost to the Government specified in the Schedule, exclusive of any fee. The contractor agrees to perform, or have performed, work on the contract up to the point at which the total amount paid and payable by the Government under the contract approximates but does not exceed the total amount actually allotted by the Government to the contract. (FAR 52.232-22)

Limited Authority When large organizations are involved, most negotiators have limited authority. For example, Government negotiator authority is limited by the funds available and any required management approvals. However, negotiators using this tactic claim they have very little or no authority to negotiate a key issue or issues. Win/lose negotiators use limited authority to identify your negotiation limits without making any commitment or divulging any information themselves.

Limited Rights The rights of the Government in limited rights data, as set forth in Limited Rights Notice if included in a Data Rights clause of the contract. (FAR 27.401)

Limited Rights Data 1. Data, other than computer software, that embody trade secrets or are commercial or financial and confidential or privileged, to the extent that such data pertain to items, components, or processes developed at private expense, including minor modifications thereof. (FAR 27.401) 2. (Agencies may adopt the following alternate definition) Data developed at private expense that embody trade secrets or are commercial or financial and confidential or privileged. (FAR 27.401)

Limited Screening Screening by General Services Administration (GSA) of items (except special tooling) that are scrap or salvage or that otherwise have a limited potential for use and not ordinarily subject to standard or agency screening. The plant clearance officer must include listings of such property in a special file, which must be made available to GSA. (FAR 45.608-4)

Line Item 1. An item of supply or service that must be separately priced in a quote, offer, or contract. (FAR 3.302) 2. A single line entry on a reporting form that indicates a quantity of property having the same description and condition code from any one contract at any one reporting location. (FAR 45.601)

Liquefied Gases Hydrocarbon gases recovered from natural gas or produced from petroleum refining and kept under pressure to maintain a liquid state at ambient temperatures. (FAR 25.108(d)(2)(ii)(E))

Liquidated Damages A stipulation in a contract on monetary amount that must be paid by the contractor if the contractor fails to deliver supplies or perform services as specified in the contract or any modification. Payments are in lieu of actual damages related to the failure. The rate (e.g., dollars per day of delay) is fixed in the contract and must be reasonable considering probable actual damages related to any failure in contract performance. (FAR 11.502(b) and 52.211-11(a))

Liquidation Rate Progress payments are recouped by the Government through the deduction of liquidations from payments that would otherwise be due to the contractor for completed contract items. To determine the amount of the liquidation, a liquidation rate is applied to the contract price of contract items delivered and accepted. (FAR 32.503-8)

Liquidation Rate—Alternate Method Also referred to as alternate liquidation rate. The ordinary progress payment liquidation rate must apply throughout the period of contract performance unless the Contracting Officer adjusts the liquidation rate under the alternate method. The objective of the alternate liquidation rate method is to permit the contractor to retain the earned profit element of the contract prices for completed items in the liquidation process. The Contracting Officer may reduce the liquidation rate if: a. The contractor requests a reduction in the rate; b. The rate has not been reduced in the preceding 12 months; c. The contract delivery schedule extends at least 18 months from the contract award date; d. Data on actual costs are available (1) For the products delivered, or (2) If no deliveries have been made, for a performance period of at least 12 months; e. The reduced liquidation rate would result in the Government recouping under each invoice the full extent of the progress payments applicable to the costs allocable to that invoice; f. The contractor would not be paid for more than the costs of items delivered and accepted (less allocable progress payments) and the earned profit on those items; g. The unliquidated progress payments would not exceed the limit prescribed in the Progress Payments clause; h. The parties agree on an appropriate rate; and i. The contractor agrees to certify annually, or more often if requested by the Contracting Officer, that the alternate rate continues to meet FAR requirements. The certificate must be accompanied by adequate supporting information. (FAR 32.503-9)

Liquidation Rate—Ordinary Method Also referred to as ordinary liquidation rate. The ordinary method is to liquidate progress payments using a liquidation rate that is the same as the progress payment rate. (FAR 32.503-8)

List of Parties Excluded from Federal Procurement and Nonprocurement Programs A list compiled, maintained and distributed by the General Services Administration (GSA) containing the names and other information about parties: a. Debarred, suspended, or voluntarily excluded under the Nonprocurement Common Rule or the FAR; b. Proposed for debarment under the FAR; and c. Determined to be ineligible. (FAR 9.403)

Loan Guarantees Guarantees made by Federal Reserve banks, on behalf of designated guaranteeing agencies, to enable contractors to obtain financing from private sources under contracts for the acquisition of supplies or services for the national defense. (FAR 32.102(c))

Local Government Unit of government in a State and, if chartered, established, or otherwise recognized by a State for the performance of a governmental duty, including a local public authority, a special district, an intrastate district, a council of governments, a sponsor group representative organization, and any other instrumentality of a local government. (FAR 3.801)

Local Taxes 1. See state and local taxes. 2. Includes taxes imposed by a possession of the United States or by Puerto Rico. (FAR 52.229-5)

Lose/Lose Outcome Also referred to as a deadlock. Occurs when final agreement cannot be obtained. As a result both parties involved lose.

Loss A situation that exists when cost is greater than revenue (e.g., contract price). Profit is negative.

Loss Contract A contract under which the sum of the total costs incurred plus the estimated costs to complete the performance are likely to exceed the contract price. (FAR 32.503-6(g)(1))

Loss Ratio Factor A factor computed by the Contracting Officer and used adjust future progress payments to exclude the element of loss under a loss contract. It is computed as follows: a. Revise the current contract price used in progress payment computations (the current ceiling price under fixed-price incentive contracts) to include any pending change orders and unpriced orders to the extent funds for the orders have been obligated. b. Divide the revised contract price by the sum of the total costs incurred to date plus the estimated additional costs of completing the contract performance. (FAR 32.503-6(g)(1))

Lower-Tier Subcontractor A concern participating in a contract action as a subcontractor to a higher-tier subcontractor.

Lubricating Oil A refined petroleum distillate or specially treated petroleum residue used to lessen friction between surfaces. (FAR 25.108(d)(2)(ii)(F))

Made The conception or first actual reduction to practice of an invention. (FAR 27.301)

Maintain Maintain, collect, use, or disseminate. (FAR 24.101)

Maintenance and Repair Costs Costs necessary for the upkeep of property (including Government property, unless otherwise provided for) that neither add to the permanent value of the property nor appreciably prolong its intended life, but keep it in an efficient operating condition. (FAR 31.205-24(a))

Major Helium Requirement A helium requirement during a calendar month of 5,000 or more standard cubic feet (measured at 14.7 pounds per square inch absolute pressure and 70 degrees Fahrenheit temperature), including liquid helium gaseous equivalent. In any month in which the major requirement threshold is met, all helium purchased during that month is considered part of the major helium requirement. (FAR 8.501)

Major Nonconformance A nonconformance, other than critical, that is likely to result in failure of the supplies or services, or to materially reduce the usability of the supplies or services for their intended purpose. (FAR 46.101)

Major System That combination of elements that will function together to produce the capabilities required to fulfill a mission need. The elements may include hardware, equipment, software, or any combination thereof, but exclude construction or other improvements to real property. A system must be considered a major system if: a. The Department of Defense is responsible for the system and the total expenditures for research, development, test, and evaluation for the system are estimated to be more than $115 million (based on fiscal year 1990 constant dollars) or the eventual total expenditure for the acquisition exceeds $540 million (based on fiscal year 1990 constant dollars); b. A civilian agency is responsible for the system and total expenditures for the system are estimated to exceed $750,000 (based on fiscal year 1980 constant dollars) or the dollar threshold for a major system established by the agency pursuant to Office of Management and Budget Circular A-109, Major System Acquisitions, whichever is greater; or c. The system is designated a major system by the head of the agency responsible for the system. (FAR 2.101)

Make Item An item or work effort to be produced or performed by the prime contractor or its affiliates, subsidiaries, or divisions. (FAR 15.407-2(b))

Make-or-Buy Program That part of a contractor's written plan for a contract identifying those major items to be produced or work efforts to be performed in the prime contractor's facilities and those to be subcontracted. (FAR 15.407-2(b))

Management and Operating Contract An agreement under which the Government contracts for the operation, maintenance, or support, on its behalf, of a Government-owned or -controlled research, development, special production, or testing establishment wholly or principally devoted to one or more major programs of the contracting Federal agency. (FAR 17.601)

Management and Professional Support Services Contract services that provide assistance, advice or training for the efficient and effective management and operation of organizations, activities (including management and support services for R&D activities), or systems. These services are normally closely related to the basic responsibilities and mission of the agency originating the requirement for the acquisition of services by contract. Included are efforts that support or contribute to improved organization of program management, logistics management, project monitoring and reporting, data collection, budgeting, accounting, performance auditing, and administrative/technical support for conferences and training programs. (FAR 37.201)

Mandatory Federal Supply Schedule A Federal Supply Schedule that identifies an agency as a required user. For that agency the schedule as a mandatory source of supply. (FAR 8.404(c))

Manufacture To manufacture, produce, assemble, or import. (FAR 23.202)

Manufacturer Any business that, or person who, manufactures a consumer product. (FAR 23.202)

Manufacturers' Excise Tax An excise tax imposed on certain motor-vehicle articles, tires and inner tubes, gasoline, lubricating oils, coal, fishing equipment, firearms, shells, and cartridges sold by manufacturers, producers, or importers. (FAR 29.201(a))

Market Research Collecting and analyzing information about capabilities within the market to satisfy agency needs. (FAR 2.101)

Marketing Consultant Any independent contractor who furnishes advice, information, direction, or assistance to an offeror or any other contractor in support of the preparation or submission of an offer for a Government contract by that offeror. An independent contractor is not a marketing consultant when rendering: a. Services excluded in FAR Subpart 37.2; b. Routine engineering and technical services (e.g., installation, operation, or maintenance of systems, equipment, software, components, or facilities); c. Routine legal, actuarial, auditing, and accounting services; and d. Training services. (FAR 9.501)

Master Plan A subcontracting plan that contains all the required elements of an individual contract plan, except goals, and may be incorporated into individual contract plans, provided the master plan has been approved. (FAR 19.701)

Master Solicitation A document containing special clauses and provisions that have been identified as essential for the acquisition of a specific type of supply or service that is acquired repetitively. (FAR 14.203-3)

Material Property that may be incorporated into or attached to a deliverable end item or that may be consumed or expended in performing a contract. It includes assemblies, components, parts, raw and processed materials, and small tools and supplies that may be consumed in normal use in performing a contract. (FAR 45.301)

Material Cost at Standard A preestablished measure of the material elements of cost, computed by multiplying material-price standard by material-quantity standard. (FAR 31.001)

Material Costs The costs of such items as raw materials, parts, sub-assemblies, components, and manufacturing supplies, whether purchased or manufactured by the contractor, and may include such collateral items as inbound transportation and intransit insurance. In computing material costs, consider reasonable overruns, spoilage, or defective work (unless otherwise provided in the contract). (FAR 31.205-26(a))

Material-Price Standard A pre-established measure, expressed in monetary terms, of the price of material. (FAR 31.001)

Material-Quantity Standard A pre-established measure, expressed in physical terms, of the quantity of material. (FAR 31.001)

Materials 1. Building materials, supplies, fixtures, and equipment that become a part of or are annexed to any building or structure erected, altered, or repaired under a contract. (FAR 52.229-2(a)) 2.Includes data when the contract does not include the Warranty of Data clause. (FAR 52.246-6(a))

May Denotes the permissive. However, the words "no person may . . ." mean that no person is required, authorized, or permitted to do the act described. (FAR 2.101)

Mean The arithmetic mean (or simply the mean or average) is the measure of central tendency most commonly used in contract pricing. To calculate the mean, sum all observations in a data set and divide by the total number of observations involved.

Mean Absolute Deviation (MAD) The average absolute difference between observed values in a data set and the arithmetic mean (average) for those values.

Measure of Central Tendency The central value (e.g., mean, mode, or median) around which data observations (e.g., historical prices) tend to cluster. It is the central value of the distribution.

Measure of Dispersion An indication of how closely values in a data set are clustered around the mean.

Median The middle value of a data set when the observations are arrayed from the lowest to the highest (or from the highest to the lowest). If the data set contains an even number of observations, the median is the arithmetic mean of the two middle observations. It is often used to measure central tendency when a few observations might pull the measure from the center of the remaining data.

Mexican End Product An article that: a. Is wholly the growth, product, or manufacture of Mexico; or b. In the case of an article which consists in whole or in part of materials from another country or instrumentality, has been substantially transformed in Mexico into a new and different article of commerce with a name, character, or use distinct from that of the article or articles from which it was transformed. The term refers to a product offered for purchase under a supply contract, but for purposes of calculating the value of the end product includes services (except transportation services) incidental to its supply; provided, that the value of those incidental services does not exceed that of the product itself. (FAR 25.401)

Micro-Purchase An acquisition of supplies or services (except construction), the aggregate amount of which does not exceed $2,500, except that in the case of construction, the limit is $2,000. (FAR 2.101)

Micro-Purchase Threshold $2,500. (FAR 2.101)

Minor Nonconformance A nonconformance that is not likely to materially reduce the usability of the supplies or services for their intended purpose, or is a departure from established standards having little bearing on the effective use or operation of the supplies or services. (FAR 46.101)

Minority The following: a. American Indian or Alaskan Native (all persons having origins in any of the original peoples of North America and maintaining identifiable tribal affiliations through membership and participation or community identification). b. Asian and Pacific Islander (all persons having origins in any of the original peoples of the Far East, Southeast Asia, the Indian Subcontinent, or the Pacific Islands); c. Black (all persons having origins in any of the black African racial groups not of Hispanic origin); and d. Hispanic (all persons of Mexican, Puerto Rican, Cuban, Central or South American, or other Spanish culture or origin, regardless of race). (FAR 52.222-27(a))

Minority Institution An institution of higher education meeting the requirements of the Higher Education Act of 1965 which includes a Hispanic-serving institution of higher education. (FAR 26.301)

Misrepresentation of Fact A false statement of substantive fact, or any conduct which leads to the belief of a substantive fact material to proper understanding of the matter in hand, made with intent to deceive or mislead. (FAR 33.201)

Mode The observed value that occurs most often in the data set (i.e., the value with the highest frequency). It is often used to estimate which specific value is most likely to occur in the future. However, a data set may have more than one mode.

Modification 1. A minor change in the details of a provision or clause that is specifically authorized by the FAR and does not alter the substance of the provision or clause. (FAR 52.101) 2. See contract modification.

Modified Coverage Requires that the contractor comply with Cost Accounting Standards: 401, Consistency in Estimating, Accumulating, and Reporting Costs; 402, Consistency in Allocating Costs Incurred for the Same Purpose; 405, Accounting for Unallowable Costs, and 406, Cost Accounting Standard-Cost Accounting Period. (FAR 9903.201-2(b))

Modular Contracting Use of one or more contracts to acquire information technology systems in successive, interoperable increments. (FAR 39.002)

Monitoring Methods Techniques and procedures used by the Contracting Officer or a representative of the Contracting Officer to observe and document contractor performance.

Motor Vehicle An item of equipment, mounted on wheels and designed for highway and/or land use, that: a. Derives power from a self-contained power unit; or b. Is designed to be towed by and used in conjunction with self-propelled equipment. (FAR 8.1101)

Moving Average Cost An inventory costing method under which an average unit cost is computed after each acquisition by adding the cost of the newly acquired units to the cost of the units of inventory on hand and dividing this figure by the new total number of units. (FAR 31.001)

Multi-Year Contract A contract for the purchase of supplies or services for more than one, but not more than five, program years. A multi-year contract may provide that performance under the contract during the second and subsequent years of the contract is contingent upon the appropriation of funds, and (if it does so provide) may provide for a cancellation payment to be made to the contractor if appropriations are not made. The key distinguishing difference between multi-year contracts and multiple year contracts is that multi-year contracts, buy more than one year's requirement (of a product or service) without establishing and having to exercise an option for each program year after the first. (FAR 17.103)

Multiple Service Locations The various locations or delivery points in the utility supplier's service area to which it provides service under a single contract. (FAR 41.101)

Multiple-Year Contracts Contracts having a term of more than 1 year regardless of fiscal year funding. The term includes multi-year contracts. (FAR 22.1001)

NAFTA Country See North American Free Trade Agreement Country.

NAFTA Country Construction Material A construction material that: a. Is wholly the growth, product, or manufacture of a NAFTA country; or b. In the case of a construction material which consists in whole or in part of materials from another country or instrumentality, has been substantially transformed in a NAFTA country into a new and different construction material distinct from the materials from which it was transformed. (FAR 25.401)

NAFTA Country End Product 1. A Canadian end product or a Mexican end product. (FAR 25.401) 2. An article that: a. Is wholly the growth, product, or manufacture of a NAFTA country, or b. In the case of an article which consists in whole or in part of materials from another country or instrumentality, has been substantially transformed in a NAFTA country into a new and different article of commerce with a name, character, or use distinct from that of the article or articles from which it was transformed. The term refers to a product offered for purchase under a supply contract, but for purposes of calculating the value of the end product includes services (except transportation services) incidental to its supply; provided, that the value of those incidental services does not exceed that of the product itself. (FAR 52.225-9(a))

Naphtha A refined petroleum distillate falling within a distillation range overlapping the higher gasoline and the lower kerosenes. (FAR 25.108(d)(2)(ii)(G))

National Defense Any activity related to programs for military or atomic energy production or construction, military assistance to any foreign nation, stockpiling, or space. (FAR 2.101)

National Industries for the Blind (NIB) Nonprofit agency designated to represent people who are blind in Government contracting under the Javits-Wagner-O'Day Act. (FAR 8.701)

National Security System Any telecommunications or information system operated by the United States Government, the function, operation, or use of which: a. Involves intelligence activities; b. Involves cryptologic activities related to national security; c. Involves command and control of military forces; d. Involves equipment that is an integral part of a weapon or weapons system; or e. Is critical to the direct fulfillment of military or intelligence missions. This does not include a system that is to be used for routine administrative and business applications, such as payroll, finance, logistics, and personnel management applications. (FAR 39.002)

Natural Gas Products Liquids (under atmospheric conditions), including natural gasoline, that: a. Are recovered by a process of absorption, adsorption, compression, refrigeration, cycling, or a combination of these processes, from mixtures of hydrocarbons that existed in a vaporous phase in a reservoir, and b. When recovered and without processing in a refinery fuel oil, gasoline, jet fuel, or naphtha. (FAR 25.108(d)(2)(ii)(H))

Negative Instant Contract Savings In value engineering, the increase in the instant contract cost or price when the acceptance of a value engineering change proposal results in an excess of the contractor's allowable development and implementation costs over the product of the instant unit cost reduction multiplied by the number of instant contract units affected. (FAR 48.001)

Negotiation Outcome In general, there are three possible outcomes to every negotiation. These outcomes are known as "win/win," "win/lose," and "lose/lose." Any negotiation can conceivably result in any of these outcomes, but different negotiation styles can make one or the another more likely.

Negotiation Plan Contents may vary based on agency and contracting activity requirements, but the plan should include information such as the following: a. Background (e.g., contract, contractor, and negotiation situation); b. Major and minor negotiation issues and objectives (both price and non-price); c. Negotiation priorities and positions on key issues (including minimum, objective, and maximum positions on price); and d. Negotiation approach.

Negotiations Exchanges, in either a competitive or sole source environment, between the Government and offerors, that are undertaken with the intent of allowing the offeror to revise its proposal. (FAR 15.306(d))

Net Acquisition Savings In value engineering, total acquisition savings, including instant, concurrent, and future contract savings, less Government costs. (FAR 48.001)

Net Present Value The difference between the discounted present value of benefits and the discounted present value of costs. (OMB Circular A-94, App A)

Neutral Person An impartial third party, who serves as a mediator, fact finder, or arbitrator, or otherwise functions to assist the parties to resolve the issues in controversy. A neutral person may be a permanent or temporary officer or employee of the Federal Government or any other individual who is acceptable to the parties. A neutral person must have no official, financial, or personal conflict of interest with respect to the issues in controversy, unless such interest is fully disclosed in writing to all parties and all parties agree that the neutral person may serve. (FAR 33.201)

New Composed of previously unused components, whether manufactured from virgin material, recovered material in the form of raw material, or materials and by-products generated from, and reused within, an original manufacturing process; provided that the supplies meet contract requirements, including but not limited to, performance, reliability, and life expectancy. (FAR 52.211-5(a))

NISH Nonprofit agency designated to represent participating nonprofit agencies serving people with severe disabilities other than blindness in Government contracting under the Javits-Wagner-O'Day Act. (FAR 8.701)

No-Cost Settlement A termination settlement at no cost to the Government or the contractor. (FAR 49.109-4)

No-Setoff Commitment A contractual undertaking pledging that, to the extent permitted by the Assignment of Claims Act, payments by the designated agency to the assignee under an assignment of claims will not be reduced to liquidate the indebtedness of the contractor to the Government. (FAR 32.801)

Nominal Interest Rate An interest rate that is not adjusted to remove the effects of actual or expected inflation. Market interest rates are generally nominal interest rates. (OMB Circular A-94, App A)

Nominal Values Economic units measured in terms of purchasing power of the date in question. A nominal value reflects the effects of general price inflation. (OMB Circular A-94, App A)

Nonconforming Services Services that do not conform in all respects to contract requirements. (FAR 46.407(a))

Nonconforming Supplies Supplies that do not conform in all respects to contract requirements. (FAR 46.407(a))

Nondevelopmental Item Means: a. Any previously developed item of supply used exclusively for Governmental purposes by a Federal agency, a State or local government, or a foreign government with which the United States has a mutual defense cooperation agreement; b. Any item described in Paragraph a of this definition that requires only minor modification or modifications of a type customarily available in the commercial marketplace in order to meet the requirements of the procuring department or agency; or c. Any item of supply being produced that does not meet the requirements of Paragraph a or b solely because the item is not yet in use. (FAR 2.101)

Nonmanufacturer Rule A contractor under a small business set-aside or 8(a) contract must be a small business under the applicable size standard and must provide either its own product or that of another domestic small business manufacturing or processing concern. (FAR 19.001)

Nonpersonal Services Contract A contract under which the personnel rendering the services are not subject, either by the contract's terms or by the manner of its administration, to the supervision and control usually prevailing in relationships between the Government and its employees. (FAR 37.101)

Nonprocurement Common Rule The procedures used by Federal Executive Agencies to suspend, debar, or exclude individuals or entities from participation in nonprocurement transactions under Executive Order 12549. Examples of nonprocurement transactions are grants, cooperative agreements, scholarships, fellowships, contracts of assistance, loans, loan guarantees, subsidies, insurance, payments for specified use, and donation agreements. (FAR 9.403)

Nonprofit Agency Serving People Who Are Blind A qualified nonprofit agency employing people who are blind approved by the Committee to furnish a commodity or a service to the Government under the Javits-Wagner-O'Day Act. (FAR 8.701)

Nonprofit Agency Serving People with Other Severe Disabilities A qualified nonprofit agency employing people who have severe disabilities other than blindness approved by the Committee to furnish a commodity or a service to the Government under the Javits-Wagner-O'Day Act. (FAR 8.701)

Nonprofit Organization 1. A university or other institution of higher education or an organization granted nonprofit status under the Internal Revenue Code of 1954 and exempt from taxation under the Internal Revenue Code, or any nonprofit scientific or educational organization qualified under a State nonprofit organization statute. (FAR 27.301) 2. Any corporation, foundation, trust, or institution operated for scientific, educational, or medical purposes, not organized for profit, and no part of the net earnings of which inures to the benefit of any private shareholder or individual. (FAR 45.301)

Nonrecurring Costs Those costs which are generally incurred on a one-time basis and include such costs as plant or equipment relocation, plant rearrangement, special tooling, special test equipment, preproduction engineering, initial spoilage and rework, and specialized work force training. (FAR 17.103)

Nonsegregated Facilities Facilities that are not segregated. See segregated facilities.

Nonseverable Property that cannot be removed after erection or installation without substantial loss of value or damage to the property or to the premises where installed. (FAR 45.301)

Nonsponsor Any other organization, in or outside of the Federal Government, which funds specific work to be performed by the Federally Funded Research and Development Center and is not a party to the sponsoring agreement. (FAR 35.017)

Nonverbal Communication Verbal exchanges account for only a fraction of the messages people send and receive. Research has shown that between 70 and 90 percent of the entire communication spectrum is nonverbal, including: a. Body language; b. Physical environment; and c. Personal attributes such as: (1) Physical appearance; (2) Vocal cues; and (3) Touch.

Normal Cost The annual cost attributable, under the actuarial cost method in use, to years subsequent to a particular valuation date. (FAR 31.001)

Normal Distribution See normal probability distribution.

Normal Probability Distribution Also referred to as a Normal Distribution. The continuous distribution most commonly used in statistics to make inferences about a population from sample data.

Normal Workweek A workweek of 40 hours. Outside the United States, its possessions, and Puerto Rico, a workweek longer than 40 hours must be considered normal if: a. The workweek does not exceed the norm for the area, as determined by local custom, tradition, or law; and b. The hours worked in excess of 40 in the workweek are not compensated at a premium rate of pay. (22.103-1)

North American Free Trade Agreement (NAFTA) Country Canada or Mexico. (FAR 25.401)

Notice Standard Form (SF) 98, Notice of Intention to Make a Service Contract and Response to Notice, and SF 98a, Attachment A. (FAR 22.1001)

Notice of Award In construction, a notice to the contractor of contract award that includes: a. Identification of the invitation for bids; b. Identification of the contractor's bid; c. The award price; d. Advice to the contractor that any required payment and performance bonds must be promptly executed and returned to the Contracting Officer; e. The date of commencement of work, or advise that a notice to proceed will be issued. (FAR 36.213-4)

Notice of Termination A written notice to the contractor that the contract is being terminated for convenience or default. (FAR 49.102(a))

Novation Agreement A legal instrument: a. Executed by the: (1) Contractor (transferor), (2) Successor in interest (transferee), and (3) Government; b. By which, among other things, the transferor guarantees performance of the contract, the transferee assumes all obligations under the contract, and the Government recognizes the transfer of the contract and related assets. (FAR 42.1201)

Number of Employees A measure of the average employment of a business concern and means its average employment, including the employees of its domestic and foreign affiliates, based on the number of persons employed on a full-time, part-time, temporary, or other basis during each of the pay periods of the preceding 12 months. a. If a business has not been in existence for 12 months, it is the average employment of such concern and its affiliates during the period that such concern has been in existence based on the number of persons employed during each of the pay periods of the period that such concern has been in business. b. If a business has acquired an affiliate during the applicable 12-month period, include the affiliate's number of employees during the entire period, rather than only its employees during the period in which it has been an affiliate. c. Do not include the employees of a former affiliate, even if such concern had been an affiliate during a portion of the applicable 12-month period. (FAR 19.101)

Off-the-Shelf Item An item produced and placed in stock by a contractor, or stocked by a distributor, before receiving orders or contracts for its sale. The item may be commercial or produced to military or Federal specifications or description. (FAR 46.101)

Offer A response to a solicitation that, if accepted, would bind the offeror to perform the resultant contract. A response to an invitation for bids or a request for proposals is an offer. A response to a request for quotations is a quote not an offer. (FAR 2.101)

Offeror Any person who has submitted an offer.

Office Furniture Furniture, equipment, fixtures, records, and other equipment and materials used in Government offices, hospitals, and similar establishments. (FAR 47.201)

Office of Federal Procurement Policy Act Established the requirements for the Federal Acquisition Regulation system. (FAR 1.103)

Officer of an Agency See employee of an agency.

Operation of a System of Records 1. Performance of any of the activities associated with maintaining the system of records, including the collection, use, and dissemination of records. (FAR 24.101) 2. Performance of any of the activities associated with maintaining the system of records, including the collection, use, and dissemination of records.

Option A unilateral right in a contract by which, for a specified time, the Government may elect to purchase additional supplies or services called for by the contract, or may elect to extend the term of the contract. (FAR 17.201)

Optional Use Federal Supply Schedule When an agency is not identified as a mandatory schedule user, schedule use is optional. Orders should be placed with the schedule contractor that provides the best value. (FAR 8.404(b))

Ordering Office 1. Any activity in an entity of the Government that places orders for the purchase of supplies or services under the Javits-Wagner-O'Day Act Program. (FAR 8.701) 2. Any Government activity issuing a purchase order for supplies or services. 3. Any Government activity issuing a delivery order or task order under an indefinite delivery contract.

Ordinary Liquidation Rate See liquidation rate—ordinary method.

Organization Costs Except as provided in Paragraph b below, the term includes: a. Expenditures in connection with: (1) Planning or executing the organization or reorganization of the corporate structure of a business, including mergers and acquisitions; (2) Resisting or planning to resist the reorganization of the corporate structure of a business or a change in the controlling interest in the ownership of a business; and (3) Raising capital (net worth plus long-term liabilities). b. The cost of activities primarily intended to provide compensation are considered compensation for personal services, not organizational costs. (FAR 31.205-27)

Organizational Conflict of Interest Because of other activities or relationships with other persons, a person is unable or potentially unable to render impartial assistance or advice to the Government, the person's objectivity in performing the contract work is or might be otherwise impaired, or a person has an unfair competitive advantage. (FAR 9.501)

Original Complement of Low Cost Equipment A group of items acquired for the initial outfitting of a tangible capital asset or an operational unit, or a new addition to either. The items in the group individually cost less than the minimum amount established by the contractor for capitalization for the classes of assets acquired but in the aggregate they represent a material investment. The group, as a complement, is expected to be held for continued service beyond the current period. Initial outfitting of the unit is completed when the unit is ready and available for normal operations. (FAR 31.001)

Other Work Any current or scheduled work of the contractor, whether Government or commercial, other than work related to the terminated contract. (FAR 49.001)

Overhead 1. Indirect costs other than those related to general and administrative expense and selling expenses. (FAR 31.203(b)) 2. A general term often used to identify any indirect cost.

Overhead Rate The indirect cost rate used by a concern to recover overhead.

Overhead Should-Cost Review Should-cost review to evaluate indirect costs, such as fringe benefits, shipping and receiving, facilities and equipment, depreciation, plant maintenance and security, taxes, and general and administrative activities. It is normally used to evaluate and negotiate a forward pricing rate agreement with the contractor. When an overhead should-cost review is conducted, a separate audit report is required. (FAR 15.407-4(c)(1))

Overprinting Standard and optional forms used in Government contracting may be overprinted with names, addresses, and other uniform entries that are consistent with the purpose of the form and that do not alter the form in any way. Exception approval for overprinting is not needed. (FAR 53.104)

Overriding Negotiation Themes Government negotiators should always keep in mind the following basic attitudes when negotiating Government contracts: a. Think win/win; b. Sell your position; c. Win results not arguments; d. Everything is negotiable; and e. Make it happen.

Overtime Time worked by a contractor's employee in excess of the employee's normal workweek. (FAR 22.103-1)

Overtime Premium The difference between the contractor's regular rate of pay to an employee for the shift involved and the higher rate paid for overtime. It does not include shift premium. (FAR 22.103-1)

Ozone-Depleting Substance Any substance designated as: a. Class I by the Environmental Protection Agency, including but not limited to chlorofluorocarbons, halons, carbon tetrachloride, and methyl chloroform; or b. Class II by the Environmental Protection Agency, including but not limited to hydrochlorofluorocarbons. (FAR 23.802)

Paramount Lien If the security for Government financing is in the form of a lien, such lien is paramount to all other liens and is effective immediately upon the first payment, without filing, notice, or other action by the United States. a. The contract must specify what the lien is upon (e.g., the work in process, the contractor's plant, or the contractor's inventory). The contract must also give the Government a right to verify the existence and value of the assets. b. Provision of Government financing must be conditioned upon a contractor certification that the assets subject to the lien are free from any prior encumbrances. Prior liens may result from such things as capital equipment loans, installment purchases, working capital loans, various lines of credit, and revolving credit arrangements. (FAR 32.202-4(b))

Partial Payments Payments for accepted supplies and services that are only a part of the contract requirements are authorized under law. Office of Management and Budget Circular A-125, Prompt Payment, requires agencies to pay for partial delivery of supplies or partial performance of services unless specifically prohibited by the contract. Although partial payments generally are treated as a method of payment and not as a method of contract financing, using partial payments can assist contractors to participate in Government contracts without, or with minimal, contract financing. (FAR 32.102(d))

Partial Set-Aside for Small Business Also referred to as a partial small business set-aside. A portion of an acquisition restricted for participation by small business concerns. (FAR 19.502-3(a))

Partial Small Business Set-Aside See partial set-aside for small business.

Partial Termination The termination of a part, but not all, of the work that has not been completed and accepted under a contract. (FAR 49.001)

Past Performance File Location for maintaining contractor performance evaluations. Location can be a separate file or database, but must be readily accessed by contracting office personnel. Interim evaluations should be retained for the duration of the contract and included with the final evaluation in the file. The evaluations must not be retained to provide source selection information for longer than three years after completion of contract performance. (FAR 42.1503)

Past Performance Information Relevant information, for future source selection purposes, regarding a contractor's actions under previously awarded contracts. It includes, for example, the contractor's record of conforming to contract requirements and to standards of good workmanship; the contractor's record of forecasting and controlling costs; the contractor's adherence to contract schedules, including the administrative aspects of performance; the contractor's history of reasonable and cooperative behavior and commitment to customer satisfaction; and generally, the contractor's business-like concern for the interest of the customer. (FAR 42.1501)

Patent Defect Any defect which exists at the time of acceptance and is not a latent defect. (FAR 46.101)

Patent Infringement Bond A bond that secures fulfillment of the contractor's obligations under a patent provision. (FAR 28.001)

Pay-as-You-Go Cost Method A method of recognizing pension cost only when benefits are paid to retired employees or their beneficiaries. (FAR 31.001)

Payment Payment is an essential contract element consideration. It satisfies the Government's obligation to compensate the contractor according to the terms of the contract.

Payment Bond A bond that assures payments as required by law to all persons supplying labor or material in the prosecution of the work provided for in the contract. (FAR 28.001)

Payment Date The date on which a check for payment is dated or, for an electronic funds transfer the specified payment date. (FAR 32.902)

Penal Amount See penal sum. Also referred to as penal amount. The amount of money specified in a bond (or a Penal Sum percentage of the bid price in a bid bond) as the maximum payment for which the surety is obligated or the amount of security required to be pledged to the Government in lieu of a corporate or individual surety for the bond. (FAR 28.001)

Pension Plan A deferred compensation plan established and maintained by one or more employers to provide systematically for the payment of benefits to plan participants after their retirements; provided, that the benefits are paid for life or are payable for life at the option of the employees. Additional benefits such as permanent and total disability and death payments, and survivorship payments to beneficiaries of deceased employees may be an integral part of a pension plan. (FAR 31.001)

Pension Plan Participant Any employee or former employee of an employer or any member or former member of an employee organization, who is or may become eligible to receive a benefit from a pension plan which covers employees of such employer or members of such organization who have satisfied the plan's participation requirements, or whose beneficiaries are receiving or may be means eligible to receive any such benefit. A participant whose employment status with the employer has not been terminated is an active participant of the employer's pension plan. (FAR 31.001)

Performance Bond A bond that secures performance and fulfillment of the contractor's obligations under the contract. (FAR 28.001(f))

Performance Requirement Contract requirement stated in terms of performance required under the contract.

Performance-Based Contracting Also referred to as performance-based service contracting. Structuring all aspects of an acquisition around the purpose of the work to be performed as opposed to either the manner by which the work is to be performed or broad and imprecise statements of work. (FAR 37.101)

Performance-Based Contracts A service contract that: a. Describes requirements in terms of results required rather than the methods of performance of the work; b. Uses measurable performance standards (i.e., terms of quality, timeliness, quantity, etc.) and quality assurance surveillance plans; c. Specifies procedures for reductions of fee or for reductions to the price of a fixed-price contract when services are not performed or do not meet contract requirements; and d. Includes performance incentives where appropriate. (FAR 37.601)

Performance-Based Payments Contract financing payments made on the basis of a. Performance measured by objective, quantifiable methods; b. Accomplishment of defined events; or c. Other quantifiable measures of results. (FAR 32.102(f))

Performance-Based Service Contracting See performance-based contracting.

Person 1. A corporation, partnership, business association of any kind, trust, joint-stock company, or individual. (FAR 3.502-1) 2. A corporation, partnership, business association of any kind, trust, joint-stock company, or individual. (FAR 52.203-7(a)) 3. An individual, corporation, company, association, authority, firm, partnership, society, State, and local government, regardless of whether such entity is operated for profit or not for profit. This term excludes an Indian tribe, tribal organization, or any other Indian organization with respect to expenditures specifically permitted by other Federal law. (FAR 3.801)

Personal, Fatigue, and Delay (PF&D) Allowance A combination of allowances used in labor-time standard development to consider worker personal needs, fatigue, and unavoidable delays associated with the work.

Personal Property Property of any kind or interest in it except real property, records of the Federal Government, and naval vessels of the following categories: battleships, cruisers, aircraft carriers, destroyers, and submarines. (FAR 45.601)

Personal Services Contract A contract that, by its express terms or as administered, makes the contractor personnel appear, in effect, to be Government employees (see 37.104). (FAR 37.101)

Planner The designated person or office responsible for developing and maintaining a written plan, or for the planning function in those acquisitions not requiring a written plan. (FAR 7.101)

Plans and Drawings Specifications Plans and drawings specifications, and other data for and preliminary to the construction. (FAR 36.102)

Plant Clearance All actions relating to the screening, redistribution, and disposal of contractor inventory from a contractor's plant or work site. The term "contractor's plant" includes a contractor operated Government facility. (FAR 45.601)

Plant Clearance Officer An authorized representative of the Contracting Officer assigned responsibility for plant clearance. (FAR 45.601)

Plant Clearance Period The period beginning on the effective date of contract completion or termination and ending 90 days (or such longer period as may be agreed to) after receipt by the Contracting Officer of acceptable inventory schedules for each property classification. The final phase of the plant clearance period means that period after receipt of acceptable inventory schedules. (FAR 45.601)

Plant Equipment Personal property of a capital nature (including equipment, machine tools, test equipment, furniture, vehicles, and accessory and auxiliary items) for use in manufacturing supplies, in performing services, or for any administrative or general plant purpose. It does not include special tooling or special test equipment. (FAR 45.101)

Plant Protection Costs Costs of items such as: a. Wages, uniforms, and equipment of personnel engaged in plant protection; b. Depreciation on plant protection capital assets; and c. Necessary expenses to comply with military requirements. (FAR 31.205-29)

Plant Reconversion Costs Costs incurred in restoring or rehabilitating the contractor's facilities to approximately the same condition existing immediately before the start of the Government contract, fair wear and tear excepted. (FAR 31.205-31)

Pollution Prevention Any practice that: a. Reduces the amount of any hazardous substance, pollutant, or contaminant entering any waste stream or otherwise released into the environment (including fugitive emissions) prior to recycling, treatment, or disposal, and reduces the hazards to public health and the environment associated with the release of such substances, pollutants, and contaminants; or b. Reduces or eliminates the creation of pollutants through increased efficiency in the use of raw materials, energy, water, or other resources. (FAR 23.703)

Pool 1. A group of concerns that have: a. Associated together in order to obtain and perform, jointly or in conjunction with each other, defense production or research and development contracts; b. Entered into an agreement governing their organization, relationship, and procedures; and c. Obtained approval of the agreement by either: (1) The Small Business Administration under Section 9 or 11 of the Small Business Act; or (2) A designated official under Part V of Executive Order 10480, August 14, 1953 and Section 708 of the Defense Production Act of 1950. (FAR 9.701) 2. See also indirect cost pool.

Population 1.The set of all possible observations of a phenomenon under analysis. 2. A group of individual persons, objects, or item from which samples are taken for statistical analysis.

Positions That Will Be Filled from Within Employment openings for which no consideration will be given to persons outside the Contractor's organization (including any affiliates, subsidiaries, and parent companies) the Contractor's and includes any openings that the Contractor proposes to fill from regularly Organization established recall lists. (FAR 52.222-35(a))

Possessions The Virgin Islands, Johnston Island, American Samoa, Guam, Wake Island, Midway Island, and the Guano Islands, but does not include Puerto Rico, leased bases, or trust territories. (FAR 2.101)

Postaward Conference A meeting between Government and contractor representatives after award of a contract and prior to commencement of work to discuss significant elements of administering the contract including any unusual or significant contract requirements (e.g., labor clause requirements). (FAR 42.503-1)

Postaward Conference Report Prepared and signed by the Conference Chairperson appointed by the Contracting Officer, the report must cover all items discussed, including areas requiring resolution, controversial matters, the names of the participants assigned responsibility for further actions, and the due dates for the actions. (FAR 42.503-3)

Postaward Letter A letter or other written form of postaward orientation. It should identify the Government representative responsible for administering the contract and cite any unusual or significant contract requirements. (FAR 42.504)

Postaward Orientation A postaward conference, letter, or other form of written communication to aid both Government and contractor personnel to achieve a clear and mutual understanding of all contract requirements, and identify and resolve potential problems. (FAR 42.500 and 42.501(a))

Postconsumer Material A material or finished product that has served its intended use and has been diverted or recovered from waste destined for disposal, having completed its useful life as a consumer item. Postconsumer material is a part of the broader category of recovered material. (FAR 23.402)

Postmark A printed, stamped, or otherwise placed impression (exclusive of a postage meter machine impression) that is readily identifiable without further action as having been supplied and affixed by employees of the U.S. or Canadian Postal Service on the date of mailing. (FAR 52.215-1(c)(3)(iii))

Power of Attorney The authority given one person or corporation to act for and obligate another, as specified in the instrument creating the power; in corporate suretyship, an instrument under seal which appoints an attorney-in-fact to act in behalf of a surety company in signing bonds. See also attorney-in-fact. (FAR 28.001)

Practical Application To manufacture, in the case of a composition or product; to practice, in the case of a process or method; or to operate, in the case of a machine or system; and, in each case, under such conditions as to establish that the invention is being utilized and that its benefits are, to the extent permitted by law or Government regulations, available to the public on reasonable terms. (FAR 27.301)

Preaward Survey An evaluation by a surveying activity of a prospective contractor's capability to perform a proposed contract. (FAR 9.101)

Prebid Conference A meeting used, generally in complex acquisitions, as a means of briefing prospective bidders and explaining complicated specifications and requirements to them as early as possible after the invitation for bids (IFB) has been issued and before the bids are opened. It must never be used as a substitute for amending a defective or ambiguous invitation for bids. (FAR 14.207)

Precious Metals Uncommon and highly valuable metals characterized by their superior resistance to corrosion and oxidation. Included are silver, gold, and the platinum group metals—platinum, palladium, iridium, osmium, rhodium, and ruthenium. (FAR 45.601)

Preconstruction Conference An orientation meeting between representatives of the Government and a successful construction contract offeror prior to the start of construction at the work site (FAR 36.212)

Preconstruction Letter An orientation letter or other written communication from the Contracting Officer to a successful construction contract offeror prior to the start of construction at the worksite. (FAR 36.212)

Preconstruction Orientation A conference or letter to inform the successful construction contract offeror of significant matters of interest related to the contract, including: a. Statutory matters such as labor standards and subcontracting plan requirements; and b. Other matters of significant interest, including who has authority to decide matters such as contractual, administrative (e.g., security, safety, and fire and environmental protection), and construction responsibilities. (FAR 36.212(a))

Precontract Costs Costs incurred before the effective date of the contract directly pursuant to the negotiation and in anticipation of the contract award when such incurrence is necessary to comply with the proposed contract delivery schedule. (FAR 31.205-32)

Prediction Interval A range of values which you are confident contains the true value of the cost or price which you are trying to predict using a regression equation. For example, a prediction interval could permit you to state that you are 90 percent confident that the range includes the true value of the dependent variable.

Preliminary Meeting A meeting to prepare Government representatives for a postaward conference. Purposes include: Establishing an understanding of conference roles and responsibilities; developing a conference agenda; forming a unified Government team; and identifying any unusual or significant contract requirements. (FAR 42.503-1(a)(5))

Prenegotiation Objectives The Government's initial negotiation position. (FAR 15.406-1(a)). Objectives for a negotiation that are established prior to initiating negotiations.

Preponderance of the Evidence Proof by information that, compared with that opposing it, leads to the conclusion that the fact at issue is more probably true than not. (FAR 9.403)

Present Value The relative worth of a benefit received or cost expended at a specified time in the future when the applicable discount rate is considered.

Presolicitation Conference A meeting held prior to issuing the solicitation to involve potential offerors in the acquisition process. (FAR 10.002(b)(2)(viii))

Presolicitation Notice 1. A notice sent to concerns on the solicitation mailing list, in lieu of initially forwarding complete bid sets. Use is at the discretion of the Contracting Officer, but is particularly suitable when invitations for bids and solicitation mailing lists are lengthy. It must: a. Specify the final date for receipt of requests for a complete bid set, b. Briefly describe the requirement and furnish other essential information to enable concerns to determine whether they have an interest in the invitation, and c. Notify concerns that, if no bid is to be submitted, they should advise the issuing office in writing if future invitations are desired for the type of supplies or services involved. Drawings, plans, and specifications normally will not be furnished with the presolicitation notice. The return date of the notice must be sufficiently in advance of the mailing date of the invitation for bids to permit an accurate estimate of the number of bid sets required. Bid sets must be sent to concerns that request them in response to the notice. (FAR 14.205-4(c)) 2. A notice sent to prospective bidders about a construction requirement sufficiently in advance of the invitation for bids to stimulate the interest of the greatest number of prospective bidders. Such notices must: a. Describe the proposed work in sufficient detail to disclose the nature and volume of work (in terms of physical characteristics and estimated price range); b. State the location of the work; c. Include tentative dates for issuing invitations, opening bids, and completing contract performance; d. State where plans will be available for inspection without charge; e. Specify a date by which requests for the invitation for bids should be submitted; f. Notify recipients that if they do not submit a bid they should advise the issuing office as to whether they want to receive future presolicitation notices; g. State whether award is restricted to small businesses; h. Specify any amount to be charged for solicitation documents; and i. Be publicized in the Commerce Business Daily. (FAR 36.213-2)

Price 1. Cost plus any fee or profit applicable to the contract type. (FAR 15.401) 2. The amount paid for a supply or service.

Price Analysis The process of examining and evaluating a proposed price without evaluating its separate cost elements and proposed profit. (FAR 15.404-1(b)(1))

Price Based on Adequate Price A price is based on adequate price competition if: a. Two or more responsible offerors, competing independently, submit priced offers competition that satisfy the Government's expressed requirement and if: (1) Award will be made to the offeror whose proposal represents the best value where price is a substantial factor in source selection; and (2)There is no finding that the price of the otherwise successful offeror is unreasonable. Any finding that the price is unreasonable must be supported by a statement of the facts and approved at a level above the Contracting Officer; b. There was a reasonable expectation, based on market research or other assessment, that two or more responsible offerors, competing independently, would submit priced offers in response to the solicitation's expressed requirement, even though only one offer is received from a responsible offeror and if: (1) Based on the offer received, the Contracting Officer can reasonably conclude that the offer was submitted with the expectation of competition, e.g., circumstances indicate that: (A) The offeror believed that at least one other offeror was capable of submitting a meaningful offer; and (B) The offeror had no reason to believe that other potential offerors did not intend to submit an offer; and (2) The determination that the proposed price is based on adequate price competition, is reasonable, and is approved at a level above the Contracting Officer; or c. Price analysis clearly demonstrates that the proposed price is reasonable in comparison with current or recent prices for the same or similar items, adjusted to reflect changes in market conditions, economic conditions, quantities, or terms and conditions under contracts that resulted from adequate price competition. (FAR 15.403-1(c)(i))

Price Evaluation A price adjustment factor set by the Department of Commerce that is used in the Adjustment for Small evaluation of offerors submitted by a small disadvantaged business concerns in Disadvantaged competitive acquisitions that exceed the simplified acquisition threshold, unless the Business Concerns acquisition is set-aside for small business concerns or awarded under the 8(a) program. (FAR 19.1101 and 19.1102)

Price Index Number A quantity that measures relative price changes from one time period to another.

Price Set by Law or Regulation A price set by a pronouncements in the form of a periodic ruling, review, or similar action of a Governmental body, or embodied in the law. (FAR 15.403-1(c)(3)(i)(2))

Price-Related Factors Elements that can be quantified and used with price to determine the most advantageous bid for the Government. They include: a. Foreseeable costs or delays to the Government resulting from such factors as differences in inspection, locations of supplies, and transportation; b. Changes made, or requested by the bidder, in any of the provisions of the invitation for bids, if the change does not constitute a ground for bid rejection; c. Advantages or disadvantages to the Government that might result from making more than one award; d. Federal, state, and local taxes; and e. Origin of supplies, and, if foreign, the application of the Buy American Act or any other prohibition on foreign purchases. (FAR 14.201-8)

Pricing The process of establishing a reasonable amount or amounts to be paid for supplies or services. (FAR 31.001)

Primary Sponsor The lead agency responsible for managing, administering, or monitoring overall use of the Federally Funded Research and Development Center under a multiple sponsorship agreement. (FAR 35.017)

Prime Contract 1. A contract or contractual action entered into by the United States for the purpose of obtaining supplies, materials, equipment, or services of any kind. (FAR 3.502-1). 2. A contract or contractual action entered into by the United States for the purpose of obtaining supplies, materials, equipment, or services of any kind. (FAR 52.203-7(a))

Prime Contractor 1. A person who has entered into a prime contract with the United States. (FAR 3.502-1). 2. Any person who holds, or has held, a Government contract subject to E.O. 11246. (FAR 22.801). 3. A person who has entered into a prime contract with the United States. (FAR 52.203-7(a))

Prime Contractor Employee 1. Any officer, partner, employee, or agent of a prime contractor. (FAR 3.502-1). 2. Any officer, partner, employee, or agent of a prime contractor. (FAR 52.203-7(a))

Privately Owned U.S.- Flag Commercial Vessel A vessel: a. Registered and operated under the laws of the United States; b. Used in commercial trade of the United States; c. Owned and operated by U.S. citizens, including a vessel under voyage or time charter to the Government; and d. A Government-owned vessel under bareboat charter to, and operated by, U.S. citizens. (FAR 47.501)

Procurement All stages involved in the process of acquiring supplies or services, beginning with the determination of a need for supplies of services and ending with contract completion or closeout.

Procurement Executive See senior procurement executive.

Procurement List A list of supplies (including military resale commodities) and services that the Committee has determined are suitable for purchase by the Government under the Javits-Wagner-O'Day Act. (FAR 8.701)

Procuring Activity 1. A component of an executive agency having a significant acquisition function and designated as such by the head of the agency. Unless agency regulations specify otherwise, the term is synonymous with the term "contracting activity." (FAR 6.003) 2. A component of an executive agency having a significant acquisition function and designated as such by the head of the agency. Unless agency regulations specify otherwise, the term procuring activity is synonymous with "contracting activity." (FAR 9.201)

Procuring Contracting Officer (PCO) A Contracting Officer who enters into contracts on behalf of the Government. May assign postaward administration functions to an Administrative Contracting Officer or termination functions to a Termination Contracting Officer.

Producer Price Index (PPI) Published monthly by the U.S. Department of Labor, Bureau of Labor Statistics (BLS) measures price changes at the producer/wholesale level for 15 major commodity groups.

Production Surveillance A function of contract administration used to determine contractor progress and to identify any factors that may delay performance. It involves Government review and analysis of: a. Contractor performance plans, schedules, controls, and industrial processes; and b. The contractor's actual performance under them. (FAR 42.1101)

Professional and Consultant Services Services rendered by persons who are members of a particular profession or possess a special skill and who are not officers or employees of the contractor. Examples include those services acquired by contractors or subcontractors in order to enhance their legal, economic, financial, or technical positions. Professional and consultant services are generally acquired to obtain information, advice, opinions, alternatives, conclusions, recommendations, training, or direct assistance, such as studies, analyses, evaluations, liaison with Government officials, or other forms of representation. (FAR 31.205-33)

Professional Employee The term embraces members of those professions having a recognized status based upon acquiring professional knowledge through prolonged study. Examples of these professions include accountancy, actuarial computation, architecture, dentistry, engineering, law, medicine, nursing, pharmacy, the sciences (e.g., biology, chemistry, and physics, and teaching). To be a professional employee, a person must not only be a professional but must be involved essentially in discharging professional duties. (FAR 22.1102)

Profit 1. The difference between total cost and revenue. 2. The amount realized by a contractor after the cost of performance (both direct and indirect) are deducted from the amount to be paid under the terms of the contract.

Profit Center The smallest organizationally independent segment of a company charged by management with profit and loss responsibilities. (FAR 31.001)

Program Manager The person responsible for program plans, funding, schedules, and timely completion within cost limitations. Planning responsibilities include developing acquisition strategies and promoting full and open competition.

Program Should-Cost Review Should-cost review conducted to evaluate significant elements of direct costs, such as material and labor, and associated indirect costs, usually associated with the production of major systems. When a program should-cost review is conducted relative to a contractor's proposal, a separate audit report on the proposal is required. (FAR 15.407-4(b)(1))

Progress Payments Based on a Percentage Completion May be used as a payment method under agency procedures. Agency procedures must ensure that payments are commensurate with work accomplished, which meets the Stage of quality standards established under the contract. These payments may not exceed 80 percent of the eligible costs of work accomplished on undefinitized contract actions. (FAR 32.102(e))

Progress Payments Based on Costs Payments for contractor progress under a fixed-price contract. Payments are based on a percentage (e.g., 80 percent) of the costs incurred by the contractor in performing the contract considering limits related to the fixed-price. This form of contract financing does not include: a. Payments based on the percentage or stage of completion accomplished; b. Payments for partial deliveries accepted by the Government; c. Partial payments for a contract termination proposal; or d. Performance-based payments. (FAR 32.102(b) and FAR 32.501)

Project Inspector See Quality Assurance Inspector.

Project Wage Determination Issued at the specific request of a contracting agency. It is used only when no general wage determination applies, and is effective for 180 calendar days from the date of the determination. However, if a determination expires before contract award, it may be possible to obtain an extension to the 180-day life of the determination. Once incorporated in a contract, a project wage determination normally remains effective for the life of the contract. (FAR 22.404-1(b))

Projected Average Loss The estimated long-term average loss per period for periods of comparable exposure to risk of loss. (FAR 31.001)

Projected Benefit Cost Method Any of the several actuarial cost methods which distribute the estimated total cost of all the employees' prospective benefits over a period of years, usually their working careers. (FAR 31.001)

Prompt Payment The Government has strict policies on making invoice payments to contractors. Most payments are due the 30th day after the designated billing office has received a proper invoice from the contractor or the 30th day after Government acceptance of supplies delivered or services performed by the contract, whichever is later. Agencies must pay an interest penalty, without request from the contractor, for late invoice payments or improperly taken discounts. (FAR 32.903 and 32.905)

Prompt Payment Discount See discount for prompt payment.

Proper Invoice A bill or written request for payment which meets the minimum standards specified in the applicable prompt payment and other terms and conditions contained in the contract for invoice submission. (FAR 32.902)

Property 1. All property, both real and personal. It includes facilities, material, special tooling, special test equipment, and agency-peculiar property. (FAR 45.101) 2. All of the below-described items acquired or produced by a contractor that are or should be allocable or properly chargeable to a contract under sound and generally accepted accounting principles and practices. a. Parts, materials, inventories, and work in process; b. Special tooling and special test equipment to which the Government is to acquire title under any other clause of a contract; c. Nondurable (i.e., noncapital) tools, jigs, dies, fixtures, molds, patterns, taps, gauges, test equipment, and other similar manufacturing aids, title to which would not be obtained as special tooling; and d. Drawings and technical data, to the extent the Contractor or subcontractors are required to deliver them to the Government by other clauses of a contract. (FAR 52.232-16(d)(2)) 3. As used in payment clauses, includes all of the below-described items acquired or produced by a contractor that are or should be allocable or properly chargeable to a contract under sound and generally accepted accounting principles and practices. a. Parts, materials, inventories, and work in process; b. Special tooling and special test equipment to which the Government is to acquire title under any other clause of a contract; c. Nondurable (i.e., noncapital) tools, jigs, dies, fixtures, molds, patterns, taps, gauges, test equipment, and other similar manufacturing aids, title to which would not be obtained as special tooling; and d. Drawings and technical data, to the extent the Contractor or subcontractors are required to deliver them to the Government by other clauses of a contract. (FAR 52.232-32(f)(2))

Property Administrator An authorized representative of Contracting Officer assigned to administer the contract requirements and obligations relating to Government property. (FAR 45.501)

Proposal 1. An offer in response to a request for proposals. (FAR 2.101) 2. Any offer or other submission used as a basis for pricing a contract, contract modification, or termination settlement or for securing payments thereunder. (FAR 31.001) 3. Means: a. A final indirect cost rate proposal submitted by the Contractor after the expiration of its fiscal year which: (1) Relates to any payment made on the basis of billing rates; or (2) Will be used in negotiating the final contract price; or b. The final statement of costs incurred and estimated to be incurred under the Incentive Price Revision clause, which is used to establish the final contract price. (FAR 52.242-3(a))

Proposal Modification 1. A change made to a proposal before the solicitation closing date and time, or made in response to an amendment, or made to correct a mistake at any time before award. (FAR 15.001) 2. A change made to a proposal before the solicitation's closing date and time, or made in response to an amendment, or made to correct a mistake at any time before award. (FAR 52.215-1(a))

Proposal Revision 1. A change to a proposal made after the solicitation closing date, at the request of or as allowed by a Contracting Officer, as the result of negotiations. (FAR 15.001) 2. A change to a proposal made after the solicitation closing date, at the request of or as allowed by a Contracting Officer as the result of negotiations. (FAR 52.215-1(a))

Protest Also referred to as a bid protest or protest against award. A written objection by an interested party to any of the following: a. A solicitation or other request by an agency for offers for a contract for the procurement of property or services; b. The cancellation of the solicitation or other request; c. An award or proposed award of the contract; or d. A termination or cancellation of an award of the contract, if the written objection contains an allegation that the termination or cancellation is based in whole or in part on improprieties concerning the award of the contract. (FAR 33.101)

Protest After Award A protest filed before contract award.

Protest Against Award See protest.

Protest Before Award A protest filed before contract award.

Provision See solicitation provision.

Public Body Any State, Territory, or possession of the United States, any political subdivision thereof, the District of Columbia, the Commonwealth of Puerto Rico, any agency or instrumentality of any of the foregoing, any Indian tribe, or any agency of the Federal Government. (FAR 45.601)

Public Building 1. Also referred to as a public work. A building, the construction, prosecution, completion, or repair of which, is carried on directly by authority of, or with funds of, a Federal agency to serve the interest of the general public regardless of whether title thereof is in a Federal agency. (FAR 22.401) 2. Any building owned by the United States that is generally suitable for office or storage space or both for the use of one or more Federal agencies or mixed ownership corporations, its grounds, approaches, and appurtenances. a. Public buildings do not include any building on the public domain. b. Buildings on the following are not public buildings: (1) Properties of the United

States in foreign countries; (2) Native American and Native Eskimo properties held in trust by the United States; (3)Lands used in connection with Federal programs for agricultural, recreational, and conservation purposes, including research in connection therewith; (4) Lands used in connection with river, harbor, flood control, reclamation, or power projects; or for chemical manufacturing or development projects; or for nuclear production, research, or development projects; (5) Land used in connection with housing and residential projects; (6) Properties of the United States Postal Service; (7) Military installations (including any fort, camp, post, naval training station, airfield, proving ground, military supply depot, military school, or any similar facility of the Department of Defense, but not including the Pentagon); (8) Installations of the National Aeronautics and Space Administration, except regular office buildings; and (9) Department of Veterans Affairs installations used for hospital or domiciliary purposes. c. Buildings leased to the Government are not public buildings unless the building is leased pursuant to a lease-purchase contract. (FAR 22.1202)

Public Relations All functions and activities dedicated to: a. Maintaining, protecting, and enhancing the image of a concern or its products; or b. Maintaining or promoting reciprocal understanding and favorable relations with the public at large, or any segment of the public. The term "public relations" includes activities associated with areas such as advertising, customer relations, etc. (FAR 31.205-1(a))

Public Relations and Advertising Costs Include the costs of media time and space, purchased services performed by outside organizations, as well as the applicable portion of salaries, travel, and fringe benefits of employees engaged in public relations and advertising activities. (FAR 31.205-1(c))

Public Work See public building.

Public-Work Contract Any contract for a fixed improvement or for any other project, fixed or not, for the public use of the United States or its allies, involving construction, alteration, removal, or repair, including projects or operations under service contracts and projects in connection with the national defense or with war activities, dredging, harbor improvements, dams, roadways, and housing, as well as preparatory and ancillary work in connection therewith at the site or on the project. (FAR 28.305(a))

Publication Means: a. The placement of an advertisement in a newspaper, magazine, trade or professional journal, or any other printed medium; or b. The broadcasting of an advertisement over radio or television. (FAR 5.501)

Purchase Order An offer by the Government to buy supplies or services, including construction and research and development, upon specified terms and conditions, using simplified acquisition procedures. (FAR 13.001)

Qualification Requirement A Government requirement for testing or other quality assurance demonstration that must be completed before award of a contract. (FAR 9.201) A Government requirement for testing or other quality assurance demonstration that must be completed before award. (FAR 52.209-1(a))

Qualified Bidders List (QBL) A list of bidders who have had their products examined and tested and who have satisfied all applicable qualification requirements for that product or have otherwise satisfied all applicable qualification requirements. (FAR 9.201)

Qualified Manufacturers List (QML) A list of manufacturers who have had their products examined and tested and who have satisfied all applicable qualification requirements for that product. (FAR 9.201)

Qualified Products List (QPL) A list of products which have been examined, tested, and have satisfied all applicable qualification requirements. (FAR 9.201)

Quality Assurance Representative See Quality Assurance Inspector.

Quality Assurance Inspector Also referred to as a Quality Assurance Representative or Project Specialist. An authorized representative of Contracting Officer responsible for inspecting and accepting or recommending rejection of supplies or services. In executing that responsibility, they must determine whether the contractor has satisfied its contract obligations pertaining to item quality and quantity.

Quantity Price Discount Voluntarily price reduction offered by a firm to customers acquiring quantities of a product. Unit prices normally decline as volume increases, primarily because fixed costs are being divided by an increasing number of units.

Questioning The use of questions to probe the position of the other party.

Quick-Closeout Procedure A procedure used for contract closeout in advance of the determination of final indirect cost rates. Contracting officers must use the procedure if: a. The contract is physically complete; b. The amount of unsettled indirect cost to be allocated to the contract is relatively insignificant as defined in the FAR; and c. Agreement can be reached on a reasonable estimate of dollars allocable to the contract. (FAR 42.708(a))

Quick-Closeout Rates Indirect cost rates used in contract closeout using the quick-closeout procedure. (FAR 42.708(a))

Quotation See quote.

Quote Also referred to as a quotation. 1. A statement of current prices. 2. Response to a request for quotations. A quote is not considered an offer that could bind the quoter to a contract if accepted. (FAR 2.101)

Quoter Any person who has submitted a quote.

Range The difference between the highest and lowest observed values in a data set.

Rated Order A prime contract for any product, service, or material (including controlled materials) placed by a Delegate Agency under the provisions of the DPAS in support of an authorized program and which require preferential treatment, and includes subcontracts and purchase orders resulting under such contracts. (FAR 11.601)

Rates May include rate schedules, riders, rules, terms and conditions of service, and other tariff and service charges, e.g., facilities use charges. (FAR 41.101)

Ratification The act of approving an unauthorized commitment by an official who has the authority to do so. (FAR 1.602-3(a))

Real Dollar Values See constant dollar values. (OMB Circular A-94, App A)

Real Interest Rate An interest rate that has been adjusted to remove the effect of expected or actual inflation. Real interest rates can be approximated by subtracting the expected or actual inflation rate from a nominal interest rate. (OMB Circular A-94, App A)

Real Property Land and rights in land, ground improvements, utility distribution systems, and buildings and other structures. It does not include foundations and other work necessary for installing special tooling, special test equipment, or plant equipment. (FAR 45.101)

Realization Factor A measure of overall performance used in a work measurement system. It is calculated by dividing the actual time to perform the work by the standard time.

Reasonable Compensation With respect to a regularly employed officer or employee of any person, compensation that is consistent with the normal compensation for such officer or employee for work that is not furnished to, not funded by, or not furnished in cooperation with the Federal Government. (FAR 52.203-12(a))

Reasonable Payment 1. A payment in an amount that is consistent with the amount normally paid for such services in the private sector. (FAR 3.801) 2. A payment in an amount that is consistent with the amount normally paid for such services in the private sector. (FAR 52.203-12(a))

Reasonableness A cost is reasonable if, in its nature and amount, it does not exceed that which would be incurred by a prudent person in the conduct of competitive business. (FAR 31.201-3(a))

Receiving Report Written evidence which indicates Government acceptance of supplies delivered or services performed by the contractor. It must, as a minimum, include the following: a. Contract number or other authorization for supplies delivered or services performed; b. Description of supplies delivered or services performed; c. Quantities of supplies received and accepted or services performed, if applicable; d. Date supplies delivered or services performed; e. Date supplies or services were accepted by the designated Government official (or progress payment request was approved if being made under the Payments Under Fixed-Price Construction Contracts clause or the Payments Under Fixed-Price Architect-Engineer Contracts clause); f. Signature, or when permitted by agency regulations, electronic equivalent, printed name, title, mailing address, and telephone number of the designated Government official responsible for acceptance or approval functions; and g. If the contract provides for the use of Government certified invoices in lieu of a separate receiving report, the Government certified invoice also must contain this information. (FAR 32.902 and 32.905(f))

Recipient Includes the contractor and all subcontractors. This term excludes Indian tribes, tribal organizations, or any other Indian organization with respect to expenditures specifically permitted by other Federal law.

Reconditioned 1. Restored to the original normal operating condition by readjustments and material replacement. (FAR 11.001) 2. Restored to the original normal operating condition by readjustments and material replacement. (FAR 52.211-5(a))

Record 1. Item, collection, or grouping of information about an individual that is maintained by an agency, including, but not limited to, education, financial transactions, medical history, and criminal or employment history, and that contains the individual's name, or the identifying number, symbol, or other identifying particular assigned to the individual, such as a fingerprint or voiceprint or a photograph. (FAR 24.101) 2. Item, collection, or grouping of information about an individual that is maintained by an agency, including, but not limited to, education, financial transactions, medical history, and criminal or employment history, and that contains the individual's name, or the identifying number, symbol, or other identifying particular assigned to the individual, such as a fingerprint or voiceprint or a photograph. (FAR 52.224-2(c)(3))

Record Drawings Drawings submitted by a contractor or subcontractor at any tier to show the construction of a particular structure or work as actually completed under the contract. (FAR 36.102)

Records Includes books, documents, accounting procedures and practices, and other data, regardless of type and regardless of whether such items are in written form, in the form of computer data, or in any other form. (FAR 52.214-26(a))

Recoupment The recovery by the Government of Government-funded nonrecurring costs from contractors that sell, lease, or license the resulting products or technology to buyers other than the Federal Government. (FAR 35.001)

Recovered Material 1. Waste materials and by-products which have been recovered or diverted from solid waste including postconsumer material, but such term does not include those materials and by-products generated from, and commonly reused within, an original manufacturing process. (FAR 23.402) 2. Waste materials and by-products which have been recovered or diverted from solid waste including postconsumer material, but such term does not include those materials and by-products generated from, and commonly reused within, an original manufacturing process. (FAR 52.211-5(a))

Recruiting and Training Agency Any person who refers workers to any contractor or subcontractor or provides or supervises apprenticeship or training for employment by any contractor or subcontractor. (FAR 22.801)

Recurring Costs Costs that vary with the quantity being produced, such as labor and materials. (FAR 17.103)

Recycling The series of activities, including collection, separation, and processing, by which products or other materials are recovered from the solid waste stream for use in the form of raw materials in the manufacture of products other than fuel for producing heat or power by combustion. (FAR 23.703)

Regression Analysis A quantitative technique used to establish a line-of-best-fit through a set of data to establish a relationship between one or more independent variable and a dependent variable. That line is then used with a projected value of the independent variable(s) to estimate a value for the dependent variable.

Regularly Employed 1. With respect to an officer or employee of a person requesting or receiving a Federal contract, an officer or employee who is employed by such person for at least 130 working days within 1 year immediately preceding the date of the submission that initiates agency consideration of such person for receipt of such contract. An officer or employee who is employed by such person for less than 130 working days within 1 year immediately preceding the date of the submission that initiates agency consideration of such person must be considered to be regularly employed as soon as he or she is employed by such person for 130 working days. (FAR 3.801) 2. With respect to an officer or employee of a person requesting or receiving a Federal contract, an officer or employee who is employed by such person for at least 130 working days within 1 year immediately preceding the date of the submission that initiates agency consideration of such person for receipt of such contract. An officer or employee who is employed by such person for less than 130 working days within 1 year immediately preceding the date of the submission that initiates agency consideration of such person must be considered to be regularly employed as soon as he or she is employed by such person for 130 working days. (FAR 52.203-12(a))

Reinsurance A transaction which provides that a surety, for a consideration, agrees to indemnify another surety against loss which the latter may sustain under a bond which it has issued. (FAR 28.001)

Related Contract A Government contract or subcontract for supplies or services under which the use of the facilities is or may be authorized. (FAR 52.245-7(a))

Relocation Costs Costs incident to the permanent change of duty assignment (for an indefinite period or for a stated period, but in either event for not less than 12 months) of an existing employee or upon recruitment of a new employee. (FAR 31.205-35)

Remanufactured 1. Factory rebuilt to original specifications. (FAR 11.001) 2. Factory rebuilt to original specifications. (FAR 52.211-5(a))

Remedy Coordination Official The person or entity in the agency who coordinates within that agency the administration of criminal, civil, administrative, and contractual remedies resulting from investigations of fraud or corruption related to procurement activities. (FAR 32.006-2)

Rent See leasing.

Reportable Property Contractor inventory that must be reported for screening before disposition as surplus. (FAR 45.601)

Reporting Activity The Government activity that initiates the Report of Excess Personal Property (or when acceptable to GSA, by data processing output). (FAR 45.601)

Request for Information (RFI) A document used to obtain price, delivery, other market information, or capabilities for planning purposes when the Government does not presently intend to issue a solicitation. (FAR 15.202(e))

Request for Proposals (RFP) A solicitation for offers under negotiation procedures.

Request for Quotations (RFQ) A solicitation for quotes. Commonly used under simplified acquisition procedures.

Requirements Contract An indefinite-delivery contract that provides for filling all actual purchase requirements of designated Government activities for supplies or services during a specified contract period, with deliveries or performance to be scheduled by placing orders with the contractor. (FAR 16.503(a))

Residential Construction   The construction, alteration, or repair of single-family houses or apartment buildings of no more than four (4) stories in height, and typically includes incidental items such as site work, parking areas, utilities, streets and sidewalks, unless there is an established area practice to the contrary. (FAR 22.404-2(c)(2))

Residual Fuel Oil   A topped crude oil or viscous residuum that, as obtained in refining or after blending with other fuel oil, meets or is the equivalent of Military Specification Mil-F-859 for Navy Special Fuel Oil and any more viscous fuel oil, such as No. 5 or Bunker C. (FAR 25.108(d)(2)(ii)(I))

Residual Value   The proceeds, less removal and disposal costs, if any, realized upon disposition of a tangible capital asset. It usually is measured by the net proceeds from the sale or other disposition of the asset, or its fair value if the asset is traded in on another asset. The estimated residual value is a current forecast of the residual value. (FAR 31.001)

Responsible Audit Agency   The agency that is responsible for performing all required contract audit services at a business unit. (FAR 42.001)

Responsible Official   The Contracting Officer or other official designated under agency procedures to administer the collection of contract debts and applicable interest. (FAR 32.601)

Responsible Prospective Contractor   A contractor that: a. Has adequate financial resources to perform the contract, or the ability to obtain them; b. Is able to comply with the required or proposed delivery or performance schedule, taking into consideration all existing commercial and governmental business commitments; c. Has a satisfactory performance record; d. Has a satisfactory record of integrity and business ethics; e. Has the necessary organization, experience, accounting and operational controls, and technical skills, or the ability to obtain them; f. Has the necessary production, construction, and technical equipment and facilities, or the ability to obtain them; and g. Is otherwise qualified and eligible to receive an award under applicable laws and regulations. (FAR 9.101 and 9.104)

Restricted Computer   1. Computer software developed at private expense and that is a trade secret; is Software commercial or financial and confidential or privileged; or is published copyrighted computer software; including minor modifications of such computer software. (FAR 27.401) 2. Computer software developed at private expense and that is a trade secret; is commercial or financial and is confidential or privileged; or is published copyrighted computer software, including minor modifications of such computer software. (FAR 52.227-14(a))

Restricted Rights   1.The rights of the Government in restricted computer software as set forth in a Restricted Rights Notice, if included in a data rights clause of the contract, or as otherwise may be included or incorporated in the contract. (FAR 27.401) 2. The rights of the Government in restricted computer software, as set forth in a Restricted Rights Notice or as otherwise may be provided in a collateral agreement incorporated in and made part of a contract, including minor modifications of such computer software. (FAR 52.227-14(a))

Retainage   A percentage of a progress payment withheld based on unsatisfactory contract progress under a construction contract. The percentage withheld must not exceed 10 percent of the approved estimated amount of progress under the terms of the contract and may be adjusted as the contract approaches completion to recognize better than expected performance, the ability to rely on alternative safeguards, and other factors. Upon contract completion of all contract requirements, retained amounts must be paid promptly. (FAR 32.103)

Royalties   Any costs or charges in the nature of royalties, license fees, patent or license amortization costs, or the like, for the use of or for rights in patents and patent applications in connection with performing a contract or any subcontract. (FAR 52.227-9(b))

Rule of Thumb   In cost estimating, a relationship commonly used to estimate product cost or price.

Salami   The negotiator using this tactic makes one demand at a time rather than requesting everything all at once.

Salvage   Property that, because of its worn, damaged, deteriorated, or incomplete condition or specialized nature, has no reasonable prospect of sale or use as serviceable property without major repairs, but has some value in excess of its scrap value. (FAR 45.501)

Sample   A subset of the population of interest that is selected in order to make some inference about the whole population.

Sanctioned EU End Product   An article that: a. Is wholly the growth product or manufacture of a sanctioned member state of the EU; or b. In the case of an article which consists in whole or in part of materials from another country or instrumentality, has been substantially transformed into a new and different article of commerce with a name, character, or use distinct from that from which it was so transformed in a sanctioned member state of the EU. The term refers to a product offered for purchase under a supply contract, but for purposes of calculating the value of the end product includes services (except transportation services) incidental to its supply; provided, that the value of these incidental services does not exceed that of the product itself. (FAR 25.1001)

Sanctioned EU Services Services to be performed in a sanctioned member state of the EU when the contract is awarded by a contracting activity located in the United States or its territories. (FAR 25.1001)

Sanctioned European Union (EU) Construction Construction to be performed in a sanctioned member state of the EU and the contract is awarded by a contracting activity located in the United States or its territories. (FAR 25.1001)

Sanctioned Member State of the EU Austria, Belgium, Denmark, Finland, France, Ireland, Italy, Luxembourg, the Netherlands, Sweden, and the United Kingdom. (FAR 25.1001)

Scrap Screening Personal property that has no value except for its basic material content. (FAR 45.501) Serviceable or usable property included in the contractor's inventory schedules that is not purchased or retained by the prime contractor or subcontractor or returned to suppliers must be screened for use by Government agencies before disposition by donation or sale. Agencies must assure the widespread dissemination of information concerning the availability of contractor inventory. (FAR 45.608-1)

Screening Completion Date The date on which all screening is to be completed. It includes screening within the Government and the donation screening period. (FAR 45.601)

Sealed Bid See bid.

Sealed Bidding A method of contracting that employs competitive bids, public bid opening, and awards. Award is made to that responsible bidder whose bid, conforming to the invitation for bids, will be most advantageous to the Government consider only price and price-related factors included in the invitation. (FAR 14.101)

Secondary Delegation of Contract A contract administration office (CAO) that has been delegated administration of a contract or a contracting office retaining contract administration may request Administration supporting contract administration from the CAO cognizant of the contractor location where performance of specific contract administration functions is required. (FAR 42.202(e))

Segment 1. One of two or more divisions, product departments, plants, or other subdivisions of an organization reporting directly to a home office, usually identified with responsibility for profit and/or producing a product or service. The term includes Government-owned contractor-operated (GOCO) facilities, and joint ventures and subsidiaries (domestic and foreign) in which the organization has a majority ownership. The term also includes those joint ventures and subsidiaries (domestic and foreign) in which the organization has less than a majority of ownership, but over which it exercises control. (FAR 31.001)

2. One of two or more divisions, campus locations, or other subdivisions of an educational institution that operate as independent organizational entities under the auspices of the parent educational institution and report directly to an intermediary group office or the governing central system office of the parent educational institution. Two schools of instruction operating under one division, campus location or other subdivision would not be separate segments unless they follow different cost accounting practices, for example, the School of Engineering should not be a treated as a separate segment from the School of Humanities if they both are part of the same division's cost accounting system and are subject to the same cost accounting practices. The term includes Government-owned contractor-operated (GOCO) facilities, Federally Funded Research and Developments Centers (FFRDCs), and joint ventures and subsidiaries (domestic and foreign) in which the institution has a majority ownership. The term also includes those joint ventures and subsidiaries (domestic and foreign) in which the institution has less than a majority of ownership, but over which it exercises control. (FAR 9903.201-2(c)(2))

Segregated Facilities Any waiting rooms, work areas, rest rooms and wash rooms, restaurants and other eating areas, time clocks, locker rooms and other storage or dressing areas, parking lots, drinking fountains, recreation or entertainment areas, transportation, and housing facilities provided for employees, that are segregated by explicit directive or are in fact segregated on the basis of race, color, religion, or national origin because of habit, local custom, or otherwise. (FAR 52.222-21(a))

Self-Insurance The assumption or retention of the risk of loss by the contractor, whether voluntarily or involuntarily. Self-insurance includes the deductible portion of purchased insurance. (FAR 31.001)

Self-Insurance Charge A cost which represents the projected average loss under a self-insurance plan. (FAR 31.001)

Selling Expense Indirect costs related to selling the product(s) produced by the firm. (FAR 31.203(b))

Semivariable Cost Costs that include both fixed and variable cost elements. Costs may increase in steps or increase relatively smoothly from a fixed base.

Senior Procurement Executive Also referred to as procurement executive. The appointed individual responsible for management direction of the acquisition system of the executive agency, including implementation of the unique acquisition policies, regulations, and standards of the executive agency. (FAR 2.101)

Sensitive Property Government property for which the theft, loss, or misplacement could be potentially dangerous to the public health or safety, or which must be subject to exceptional physical security, protection, control, maintenance or accountability, including but not limited to hazardous property, precious metals, arms, ammunition, and explosives and classified property.

Separate Contract A utility services contract (other than a GSA areawide contract, an authorization under an areawide contract, or an interagency agreement), to cover the acquisition of utility services. (FAR 41.101)

Service Contract 1. Any Government contract, the principal purpose of which is to furnish services in the United States through the use of service employees, except as exempted under Section 7 of the Service Contract Act, or any subcontract at any tier thereunder. (FAR 22.1001) 2. A contract that directly engages the time and effort of a contractor whose primary purpose is to perform an identifiable task rather than to furnish an end item of supply. A service contract may be either a nonpersonal or personal contract. It can also cover services performed by either professional or nonprofessional personnel whether on an individual or organizational basis. Some of the areas in which service contracts are found include the following: a. Maintenance, overhaul, repair, servicing, rehabilitation, salvage, modernization, or modification of supplies, systems, or equipment; b. Routine recurring maintenance of real property; c. Housekeeping and base services; d. Advisory and assistance services; e. Operation of Government-owned equipment facilities, and systems; f. Communications services; g. Architect-Engineering; h. Transportation and related services; and i. Research and development. (FAR 37.101)

Service Contract Act The Service Contract Act of 1965, as amended. It requires that service contracts over $2,500 contain mandatory provisions regarding minimum wages and fringe benefits, safe and sanitary working conditions, notification to employees of the minimum allowable compensation, and equivalent Federal employee classifications and wage rates. (FAR 22.1001 and 22.1002-1)

Service Employee Any person engaged in the performance of a service contract other than any person employed in a bona fide executive, administrative, or professional capacity. The term includes all such persons regardless of any contractual relationship that may be alleged to exist between a contractor or subcontractor and such persons. (FAR 22.1001 and 22.1202)

Service Life The period of usefulness of a tangible capital asset (or group of assets) to its current owner. The period may be expressed in units of time or output. The estimated service life of a tangible capital asset (or group of assets) is a current forecast of its service life and is the period over which depreciation cost is to be assigned. (FAR 31.001)

Serviceable Property Also referred to as usable property. Property that has a reasonable prospect of use or sale either in its existing form or after minor repairs or alterations. (FAR 45.601)

Services 1. (For the New Mexico Gross Receipts and Compensating Tax) All activities engaged in for other persons for a consideration, which activities involve predominately the performance of a service as distinguished from selling or leasing property. Services include: a. Activities performed by a person for its members or shareholders. In determining what is a service, the intended use, principal objective or ultimate objective of the contracting parties must not be controlling. b. Construction activities and all tangible personal property that will become an ingredient or component part of a construction project. Such tangible personal property retains its character as tangible personal property until it is installed as an ingredient or component part of a construction project in New Mexico. However, sales of tangible personal property that will become an ingredient or component part of a construction project to persons engaged in the construction business are sales of tangible personal property. (FAR 29.401-6) 2. Includes services performed, workmanship, and material furnished or utilized in the performance of services. (FAR 52.246-4(a))

Set-Aside for Small Business The reserving of an acquisition exclusively for participation by small business concerns. A set-aside may be open to all small businesses. A set-aside of a single acquisition or a class of acquisitions may be total or partial. (FAR 19.501(a))

Setoff A reduction in contract payment to liquidate the indebtedness of the contractor to the Government. (FAR 32.611)

Settlement Agreement A written agreement in the form of an amendment to a contract settling all or a severable portion of a settlement proposal. (FAR 49.001)

Settlement by Determination If the contractor and TCO cannot agree on a termination settlement, or if a settlement proposal is not submitted within the period required by the termination clause, the TCO must issue a determination of the amount due consistent with the termination clause, including any cost principles incorporated by reference. (FAR 49.109-7)

Settlement Negotiation Memorandum A memorandum prepared by the Termination Contracting Officer at the conclusion of negotiations the principal elements of the settlement for inclusion in the termination case file and for use by reviewing authorities. (FAR 49.110(a))

Settlement Proposal A proposal for effecting settlement of a contract terminated in whole or in part, submitted by a contractor or subcontractor in the form, and supported by the data, required by this part.

A settlement proposal is included within the generic meaning of the word "claim" under false claims acts. (FAR 49.001)

Severance Pay Also referred to as dismissal wages. A payment in addition to regular salaries and wages by contractors to workers whose employment is being involuntarily terminated. (FAR 31.205-6(g)(1))

Shall The imperative. (FAR 2.101)

Sharing Base In value engineering, the number of affected end items on contracts of the contracting office accepting the value engineering change proposal. (FAR 48.001)

Sharing Period In value engineering, the period beginning with acceptance of the first unit incorporating the value engineering change proposal (VECP) and ending at the later of: a. 3 years after the first unit affected by the VECP is accepted or, b. The last scheduled delivery date of an item affected by the VECP under the instant contract delivery schedule in effect at the time the VECP is accepted. (FAR 48.001)

Shift Premium The difference between the contractor's regular rate of pay to an employee and the higher rate paid for extra-pay-shift work. (FAR 22.103-1)

Shipment Freight transported or to be transported. (FAR 47.001)

Shop Drawings Drawings submitted by the construction contractor or a subcontractor at any tier or required under a construction contract, showing in detail: a. The proposed fabrication and assembly of structural elements; b. The installation (i.e., form, fit, and attachment details) of materials or equipment; or c. Both. (FAR 36.102)

Should-Cost Review A specialized form of cost analysis. A should-cost review differs from traditional evaluation methods because it do not assume that a contractor's historical costs reflect efficient and economical operation. Instead, the review evaluates the economy and efficiency of the contractor's existing work force, methods, materials, facilities, operating systems, and management. The review is accomplished by a multi-functional team of Government contracting, contract administration, pricing, audit, and engineering representatives. The objective is to promote both short and long-range improvements in the contractor's economy and efficiency in order to reduce the cost of performance of Government contracts. In addition, by providing rationale for any recommendations and quantifying their impact on cost, the Government will be better able to develop realistic objectives for negotiation. (FAR 15.407-4(a))

Should-Pay Estimate See should-pay price.

Should-Pay Price Also referred to as should-pay estimate. An estimate of the price that you should pay for a supply or service based on available information.

Signature or Signed The discrete, verifiable symbol of an individual which, when affixed to a writing with the knowledge and consent of the individual, indicates a present intention to authenticate the writing. This includes electronic symbols. (FAR 2.101)

Significant Revision A revision that alters the substantive meaning of any coverage in the FAR system having a significant cost or administrative impact on contractors or offerors, or significant effect beyond the internal operating procedures of the issuing agency. It does not include editorial, stylistic, or other revisions that have no impact on the basic meaning of the coverage being revised. (FAR 1.501-1)

Significant Weakness A proposal flaw that appreciably increases the risk of unsuccessful contract performance. (FAR 15.301)

Silence The absence of mention in negotiations. In other words, a negotiator using this tactic does not say anything about a negotiation point. The primary hope is that the issue will not come up. If the issue does come up, the negotiator remains silent or avoids it by talking about something else. This tactic is generally used when negotiators do not want to disclose weaknesses in their position.

Simple Price Index Number A quantity that measures relative price changes for a single item over time.

Simplified Acquisition Procedures The methods prescribed in FAR Part 13 for making purchases of supplies or services. (FAR 2.101)

Simplified Acquisition Threshold $100,000, except that in the case of any contract to be awarded and performed, or purchase to be made, outside the United States in support of a contingency operation or a humanitarian or peacekeeping operation, the term means $200,000. (FAR 2.101)

Simplified Contract Format For firm-fixed-price or fixed-price with economic price adjustment acquisitions of noncommercial supplies and services, the Contracting Officer may use the simplified contract format in lieu of the uniform contract format. The Contracting Officer has flexibility in preparation and organization of the simplified contract format. However, the following format should be used to the maximum practical extent: a. Solicitation/contract form; b. Contract schedule; c. Clauses; d. List of documents and attachments (if necessary); and e. Representations and instructions.

Single Moving Average Data collected over two or more time periods (normally at least three) are summed and divided by the number of time periods. That average then becomes a forecast for future time periods. Forecasts assume that there is no trend in the data.

Single, Governmentwide Point of Entry (Also referred to as Governmentwide point of entry) One point of entry to be designated by the Administrator of the Office of Federal Procurement Policy that will allow the private sector to electronically access procurement opportunities Governmentwide. (FAR 4.501)

Single-Movement Contracts Contracts awarded for unique transportation services that are not otherwise available under carrier tariffs or covered by Department of Defense or General Services Administration contracts (e.g., special requirements at origin and/or destination). (FAR 47.204)

Site Inspection and Examination of Data Also referred to as a site visit. An opportunity arranged by the Contracting Officer for prospective offerors to inspect the work site and to examine data available to the Government which may provide information concerning the performance of the work, such as boring samples, original boring logs, and records and plans of previous construction. The data should be assembled in one place and made available for examination. The solicitation should notify offerors of the time and place for the site inspection and data examination. If it is not feasible for offerors to inspect the site or examine the data on their own, the solicitation should also designate an individual who will show the site or data to the offerors. (FAR 36.210)

Site of Construction The general physical location of any building, highway, or other change or improvement to real property that is undergoing construction, rehabilitation, alteration, conversion, extension, demolition, or repair; and any temporary location or facility at which a contractor, subcontractor, or other participating party meets a demand or performs a function relating to a Government contract or subcontract. (FAR 22.801)

Site of the Work In construction: a. The term is limited to the physical place or places where the construction called for in the contract will remain when work on it is completed, and nearby property (as described in Paragraph b of this definition) used by the contractor or subcontractor during construction that, because of proximity, can reasonably be included in the site. b. Except as provided in Paragraph c of this definition, fabrication plants, mobile factories, batch plants, borrow pits, job headquarters, tool yards, etc., are parts of the "site of the work," provided they are dedicated exclusively, or nearly so, to performance of the contract or project, and are so located in proximity to the actual construction location that it would be reasonable to include them. c. The term does not include permanent home offices, branch plant establishments, fabrication plants, or tool yards of a contractor or subcontractor whose locations and continuance in operation are determined wholly without regard to a particular Federal contract or project. In addition, fabrication plants, batch plants, borrow pits, job headquarters, yards, etc., of a commercial supplier or material man which are established by a supplier of materials for the project before opening of bids and not on the project site, are not included in the term. Such permanent, previously established facilities are not a part of the "site of the work," even if the operations for a period of time may be dedicated exclusively, or nearly so, to the performance of a contract. (FAR 22.401)

Site Visit 1. Offerors or quoters are urged and expected to inspect the site where services are to be performed and to satisfy themselves regarding all general and local conditions that may affect the cost of contract performance, to the extent that the information is reasonably obtainable. (FAR 52.237-1(a)) 2. See site inspection and examination of data.

Size Standard A maximum level of average employment or annual revenue at which a firm can qualify as a small business.

Small Business Concern A concern, including its affiliates, that is independently owned and operated, not dominant in the field of operation in which it is bidding on Government contracts, and qualified as a small business under the appropriate criteria and size standards presented in the FAR. (FAR 19.001)

Small Business Concern Owned and Controlled by Women See woman-owned small business concern.

Small Business Firm A small business concern as defined under law and implementing regulations of the Administrator of the Small Business Administration. (FAR 27.301)

Small Business Innovation Research (SBIR) Rights The rights in SBIR data set forth in the SBIR Rights Notice. (FAR 52.227-20)

Small Business (SBIR) Innovation Research Act Requires agencies with a budget for extramural research and development of more than $10 million to spend 1.25 percent of their budget with small businesses in SBIR contracts.

Small Business Innovation Research(SBIR) Contracts Contracts issued in two phases under the provisions of the SBIR Act. Phase I provides $50,000 to demonstrate the feasibility of the proposed innovation. Phase II provides for development of the proposed innovation.

Small Business Innovation Research(SBIR) Data Data first produced by a Contractor that is a small business firm in performance of a small business innovation research contract which are not generally known, and which data without obligation as to its confidentiality have not been made available to others by the Contractor or are not already available to the Government. (FAR 52.227-20)

Small Business Set-Aside See set-aside for small business.

Small Business Subcontractor Any concern that: a. In connection with subcontracts of $10,000 or less has a number of employees, including its affiliates, that does not exceed 500 persons; and b. In connection with subcontracts exceeding $10,000, has a number of employees or average annual receipts, including its affiliates, that does not exceed the size standard set forth in the FAR for the product or service it is providing on the subcontract. (FAR 19.701)

Small Disadvantaged Business Concern Means: a. For subcontractors, a small business concern that is at least 51 percent unconditionally owned by one or more individuals who are both socially and economically disadvantaged, or a publicly owned business that has at least 51 percent of its stock unconditionally owned by one or more socially and economically disadvantaged individuals and that has its management and daily business controlled by one or more such individuals. This term also means a small business concern that is at least 51 percent unconditionally owned by an economically disadvantaged Indian tribe or Native Hawaiian Organization, or a publicly owned business that has at least 51 percent of its stock unconditionally owned by one of these entities, that has its management and daily business controlled by members of an economically disadvantaged Indian tribe or Native Hawaiian Organization, and that meets the requirements of 13 CFR 124. b. For prime contractors, generally an offeror that represents, as part of its offer, that it is a small business under the size standard applicable to the acquisition; and either: (1) It has received certification from the Small Business Administration as a small disadvantaged business concern consistent with 13 CFR 124, Subpart B, and (i) No material change in disadvantaged ownership and control has occurred since its certification; (ii) Where the concern is owned by one or more disadvantaged individuals, the net work of each individual upon whom the certification is based does not exceed $750,000 after taking into account the applicable exclusions set forth at 13 CFR 124.104(c)(2); and (iii) It is listed, on the date of its representation, on the register of small disadvantaged business concerns maintained by the Small Business Administration; or (2)It has submitted a completed application to the Small Business Administration or a Private Certifier to be certified as a small disadvantaged business concern in accordance with 13 CFR 124, Subpart B, and a decision on that application is pending, and that no material change in disadvantaged ownership and control has occurred since its application was submitted. In this case a contractor must receive certification as an SDB by the SBA prior to contract award. (FAR 19.001)

Sole Source Acquisition A contract for the purchase of supplies or services that is entered into or proposed to be entered into by an agency after soliciting and negotiating with only one source. (FAR 6.003)

Solicitation 1.A document sent to prospective contractors by a Government agency requesting submission of an offer, quote, or information. 2.The process of issuing a document requesting submission of an offer, quote, or information and obtaining responses.

Solicitation Provision Also referred to as a provision. A term or condition used only in solicitations and applying only before contract award. (FAR 52.101)

Source Selection The process of identifying which offeror(s) will receive a contract in a competitive negotiated acquisition. (FAR 15.300)

Source Selection Authority (SSA) The person responsible for making the source selection decision. While the SSA may use reports and analyses prepared by others, the source selection decision must represent the SSA's independent judgment. (FAR 15.308)

Source Selection Decision The decision on which offeror(s) will receive a contract in a competitive negotiated acquisition.

Source Selection Evaluation Board Any board, team, council, or other group that evaluates bids or proposals. (FAR 3.104-3)

Source Selection Information Any of the following information which is prepared for use by a Federal agency for the purpose of evaluating a bid or proposal to enter into a Federal agency procurement contract, if that information has not been previously made available to the public or disclosed publicly: a. Bid prices submitted in response to a Federal agency invitation for bids, or lists of those bid prices before bid opening. b. Proposed costs or prices submitted in response to a Federal agency solicitation, or lists of those proposed costs or prices. c. Source selection plans. d. Technical evaluation plans. e. Technical evaluations of proposals. f. Cost or price evaluations of proposals. g. Competitive range determinations that identify proposals that have a reasonable chance of being selected for award of a contract. h. Rankings of bids, proposals, or competitors. i. Reports and evaluations of source selection panels, boards, or advisory councils. j. Other information marked as source selection information based on a case-by-case determination by the head of the agency or designee, or the Contracting Officer, that its disclosure would jeopardize the integrity or successful completion of the Federal agency procurement to which the information relates. (FAR 3.104-3)

Source Selection Plan A plan established prior to solicitation release to guide the source selection process. The format of the plan will depend on agency and contracting activity policies. However, it should include or provide for the following: a. Basis for the best value decision; b. Source selection organization; c. Proposal evaluation criteria; and d. Evaluation procedures.

Spearman's Rank Correlation Comparison of a calculated coefficient with a table value tests the existence of a trend in a data set. Commonly used to test for a trend in time-series data to support a coefficient decision on what estimating technique to use in developing a forecast.

Special Competency A special or unique capability, including qualitative aspects, developed incidental to the primary functions of the Federally Funded Research and Development Center to meet some special need. (FAR 35.017)

Special Fuels Excise Tax An excise tax imposed at the retail level on diesel fuel and special motor fuels. (FAR 29.201(a))

Special Items Screening Special screening procedures established for the following types of property: a. Special test equipment with standard components; b. Special test equipment without standard components; c. Printing equipment; and d. Nuclear materials. (FAR 45.608-5)

Special Test Equipment Either single or multipurpose integrated test units engineered, designed, fabricated, or modified to accomplish special purpose testing in performing a contract. It consists of items or assemblies of equipment including standard or general purpose items or components that are interconnected and interdependent so as to become a new functional entity for special testing purposes. It does not include material, special tooling, facilities (except foundations and similar improvements necessary for installing special test equipment), and plant equipment items used for general plant testing purposes. (FAR 45.101)

Special Tooling Jigs, dies, fixtures, molds, patterns, taps, gauges, other equipment and manufacturing aids, all components of these items, and replacement of these items, which are of such a specialized nature that without substantial modification or alteration their use is limited to the development or production of particular supplies or parts thereof or to the performance of particular services. It does not include material, special test equipment, facilities (except foundations and similar improvements necessary for installing special tooling), general or special machine tools, or similar capital items. (FAR 45.101)

Specifically Authorized Representative (SAR) A person designated in writing by the Contracting Officer as a representative to communicate with the contractor interpreting requirements of a negotiated research and development or supply contract for the acquisition of a major weapon system or principal subsystem. (FAR 52.243-7(a))

Specification A document intended primarily for use in acquisition that clearly describes the essential technical requirements for items, materials, or services, including the criteria for determining that requirements have been met.

Specified Payment Date The date which the Government has placed in the electronic funds transfer payment transaction instruction given to the Federal Reserve System as the date on which the funds are to be transferred to the contractor's account by the financial agent. If no date has been specified in the instruction, the specified payment date is 3 business days after the payment office releases the EFT payment transaction instruction. (FAR 32.902)

Sponsor The executive agency which manages, administers, monitors, funds, and is responsible for the overall use of a Federally Funded Research and Development Center. Multiple agency sponsorship is possible as long as one agency agrees to act as the primary sponsor. In the event of multiple sponsors, the term "sponsor" refers to the primary sponsor. (FAR 35.017)

Spread-Gain Actuarial Cost Method Any of the several projected benefit actuarial cost methods under which actuarial gains and losses are included as part of the current and future normal costs of the pension plan. (FAR 31.001)

Standard Cost Any cost computed with the use of preestablished measures. (FAR 31.001)

Standard Deviation In statistical analysis, the square root of the variance. It is one of the two most popular measures of dispersion. The other is the variance.

Standard Error of the Estimate (SEE) A measure of the accuracy of the regression equation. It indicates the variability of the observed points around the points predicted by the regression line. Given a value for the independent variable and the SEE, you should be able to establish a probability statement that a stated range includes the true value of the dependent variable.

Standard Error of the Mean The standard error of the mean is equal to the population standard deviation divided by the square root of sample size when the population is normally distributed. When population standard deviation is known, use the sample standard deviation to estimate the population standard deviation.

Standard Industrial Classification (SIC) A code published by the Government in the Standard Industrial Classification Manual. These codes classify and define activities by industry categories and is the source used by the Small Business Administration as a guide in defining industries for small business size standards. (FAR 19.102(g))

Standard Screening Screening of serviceable property with a line item value of $1,000 or more ($500 for furniture) that does not meet the criteria for another screening category. (FAR 45.608-2)

Standard Time A measure of the time it should take a qualified worker to perform a particular task.

State 1. A State of the United States, the District of Columbia, the Commonwealth of Puerto Rico, a territory or possession of the United States, an agency or instrumentality of a State, and multi-State, regional, or interstate entity having governmental duties and powers. (FAR 3.801) 2. A State of the United States, the District of Columbia, the Commonwealth of Puerto Rico, a territory or possession of the United States, an agency or instrumentality of a State, and multi-State, regional, or interstate entity having governmental duties and powers. (FAR 52.203-12(a))

State and Local Taxes Taxes levied by the States, the District of Columbia, Puerto Rico, possessions of the United States, or their political subdivisions. (FAR 29.301)

Statement of Work Also referred to as a work statement. A document that defines service contract requirements in clear, concise language identifying specific work to be accomplished. It must be individually tailored to consider the period of performance, deliverable items, if any, and the desired degree of performance. In the case of task order contracts, the statement of work for the basic contract need only define the scope of the overall contract. Individual task orders must define specific task requirements. (FAR 37.602-1)

Statistic A numerical characteristic of a sample.

Statistical Analysis An examination of available data using statistics.

Statistics A science which involves collecting, organizing, summarizing, analyzing, and interpreting data in order to facilitate the decision-making process. These data can be facts, measurements, or observations.

Stock Record A perpetual inventory record which shows by nomenclature the quantities of each item received and issued and the balance on hand. (FAR 45.501)

Stop-Work Order Under a negotiated fixed-price supply, cost-reimbursement supply, research and development, or service contract, a contract clause permits the Contracting Officer to order the contractor to stop work, if a work stoppage is required for reasons such as advancement in the state-of-the-art, production or engineering breakthroughs, or realignment of programs. Generally, a stop-work order will be issued only if it is advisable to suspend work pending a decision by the Government and a supplemental agreement providing for the suspension is not feasible. Issuance of a stop-work order must be approved at a level higher than the Contracting Officer. (FAR 42.1303)

Stratified Sampling A method of drawing a sample from a population that allows the analyst to concentrate on the items meriting 100 percent analysis while using random sampling procedures to identify any general pattern of other items in the population.

Studies, Analyses and Evaluation Services Contract services that provide organized, analytical assessments/evaluations in support of policy development, decision-making, management, or administration. Included are studies in support of R&D activities. Also included are acquisitions of models, methodologies, and related software supporting studies, analyses or evaluations. (FAR 37.201)

Subcontract 1. A contract or contractual action entered into by a prime contractor or subcontractor for the purpose of obtaining supplies, materials, equipment, or services of any kind under a prime contract. (FAR 3.502-1) 2. A transfer of commercial items between divisions, subsidiaries, or affiliates of a contractor or subcontractor. (FAR 12.001) 3. Includes a transfer of commercial items between divisions, subsidiaries, or affiliates of a contractor or a subcontractor. (FAR 15.401) 4. Any agreement (other than one involving an employer-employee relationship) entered into by a Government prime contractor or subcontractor calling for supplies and/or services required for performance of the contract, contract modification, or subcontract. (FAR 19.701) 5. Any agreement or arrangement between a contractor and any person (in which the parties do not stand in the relationship of an employer and an employee) --a. For the furnishing of supplies or services or for use of real or personal property, including lease arrangements that, in whole or in part, is necessary to the performance of any one or more Government contracts, or b. Under which any portion of the contractor's obligation under any one or more Government contracts is performed, undertaken, or assumed. (FAR 22.801) 6. Any contract entered into by a subcontractor to furnish supplies or services for performance of a prime contract or a subcontract. It includes but is not limited to purchase orders, and changes and modifications to purchase orders. (FAR 44.101) 7. A contract or contractual action entered into by a prime Contractor or subcontractor for the purpose of obtaining supplies, materials, equipment, or services of any kind under a prime contract. (FAR 52.203-7(a))

Subcontractor 1. Any person, other than the prime contractor, who offers to furnish or furnishes any supplies, materials, equipment, or services of any kind under a prime contract or a subcontract entered into in connection with such prime contract. The term includes any person who offers to furnish or furnishes general supplies to the prime contractor or a higher tier subcontractor. (FAR 3.502-1) 2. Any person who holds, or has held, a subcontract subject to E.O. 11246. (FAR 22.801) 3. Any supplier, distributor, vendor, or firm that furnishes supplies or services to or for a prime contractor or another subcontractor. (FAR 44.101) 4. Any person, other than the prime contractor, who offers to furnish or furnishes any supplies, materials, equipment, or services of any kind under a prime contract or a subcontract entered into in connection with such prime contract. The term includes any person who offers to furnish or furnishes general supplies to the prime contractor or a higher-tier subcontractor. (FAR 52.203-7(a))

Subcontractor Employee Any officer, partner, employee, or agent of a subcontractor. (FAR 52.203-7(a))

Subject Invention Any invention of the contractor conceived or first actually reduced to practice in the performance of work under a Government contract; provided, that in the case of a variety of plant, the date of determination defined in the Plant Variety Protection Act must also occur during the period of contract performance. (FAR 27.301)

Subject Matter Expert An individual possessing the prerequisite knowledge skills and abilities demonstrating competence in a field of endeavor.

Subliminal Nonverbal Messages Messages are communicated to the subconscious mind of the receiver. Receivers of subliminal messages are not consciously aware of the message. For example, police and military uniforms subliminally communicate the authority of those wearing them.

Subordination Agreement An agreement whereby a contractor's creditor subordinates its security interest in contractor-held property to the security interest held by the Government. In other words, the creditor agrees to relinquish its claim to any property properly claimed by the Government under the agreement.

Substantial Evidence Information sufficient to support the reasonable belief that a particular act or omission has occurred. (FAR 32.006-2)

Substantially as Follows Also referred to as substantially the same as. That authorization is granted to prepare and utilize a variation of that provision or clause to accommodate requirements that are peculiar to an individual acquisition; provided, that the variation includes the salient features of the FAR provision or clause, and is not inconsistent with the intent, principle, and substance of the FAR provision or clause or related coverage of the subject matter. (FAR 52.101)

Substantially the Same as See substantially as follows.

Substantive Performance Performance that deviates only in minor respects from contract requirements.

Summary Record A separate card, form, document or specific line(s) of computer data used to account for multiple quantities of a line item of special tooling, special test equipment, or plant equipment costing less than $5,000 per unit. (FAR 45.501)

Sunk Cost A cost incurred in the past that will not be affected by any present or future decision. Sunk costs should be ignored in determining whether a new investment is worthwhile. (OMB Circular A-94, App A)

Supplemental Agreement A contract modification that is accomplished by the mutual action of the parties. (FAR 43.101)

Supplies 1. All property except land or interest in land. It includes (but is not limited to) public works, buildings, and facilities; ships, floating equipment, and vessels of every character, type, and description, together with parts and accessories; aircraft and aircraft parts, accessories, and equipment; machine tools; and the alteration or installation of any of the foregoing. (FAR 2.101) 2. Includes but is not limited to raw materials, components, intermediate assemblies, end products, and lots of supplies. (FAR 52.246-2(a)) 3. Includes but is not limited to raw materials, components, intermediate assemblies, end products, lots of supplies, and, when the contract does not include the Warranty of Data clause, data. (FAR 52.246-3(a)) 4. The end item furnished by the Contractor and related services required under the contract. The word does not include data. (FAR 52.246-17(a)) 5. The end items furnished by the Contractor and related services required under a contract. The word does not include data. (FAR 52.246-18(a)) 6. The end items furnished by the Contractor and related services required under a contract. Except when a contract includes the clause entitled Warranty of Data, supplies also means data. (FAR 52.246-19(a))

Surety An individual or corporation legally liable for the debt, default, or failure of a principal to satisfy a contractual obligation. (FAR 28.001)

Surplus Property Contractor inventory not required by any Federal agency. (FAR 45.601)

Surplus Release Date (SRD) The date on which screening of personal property for Federal use is completed and the property is not needed for any Federal use. On that date, property becomes surplus and is eligible for donation. (FAR 45.601)

Surprise Negotiators may introduce a behavior, issue, or goal at an unexpected point in the proceedings. The negotiator plans an apparently spontaneous event (e.g., an emotional outburst) to surprise or shock the other negotiator. In general, the surprise tactic is used to disrupt negotiations and move the other negotiator away from the negotiation plan.

Surveying Activity The cognizant contract administration office or, if there is no such office, another organization designated by the agency to conduct preaward surveys. (FAR 9.101)

Suspended A contractor temporarily disqualified from Government contracting and Government-approved subcontracting. (FAR 9.403)

Suspending Official An agency head or a designee authorized by the agency head to impose suspension. (FAR 9.403)

Suspension Action taken by a suspending official to disqualify a contractor temporarily from Government contracting and Government-approved subcontracting; a contractor so disqualified is suspended. (FAR 9.403)

Suspension of Work Under construction or architect-engineer contracts, a contract clause permits the Contracting Officer to order the contractor to suspend work for a reasonable period of time. If the suspension is unreasonable, the contractor may submit a written claim for increases in the cost of performance, excluding profit. (FAR 42.1302)

Synopsis 1. A notice of a proposed contract action exceeding $25,000 furnished by an agency for publication in the Commerce Business Daily as required by the Small Business Act (15 U.S.C. 637(e)) and the Office of Federal Procurement Policy Act (41 U.S.C. 416). (FAR 5.201) 2. A notice furnished by an agency for publication in the Commerce Business Daily of a contract action exceeding $25,000 (the dollar threshold is not a prohibition against publicizing an award of a smaller amount when publicizing would be advantageous to industry or to the Government) that is: a. Subject to the Trade Agreements Act; or b. Likely to result in the award of any subcontracts. (FAR 5.301)

System of Records on Individuals 1. A group of any records under the control of any agency from which information is retrieved by the name of the individual or by some identifying number, symbol, or other identifying particular assigned to the individual. (FAR 24.101) 2. A group of any records under the control of any agency from which information is retrieved by the name of the individual or by some identifying number, symbol, or other identifying particular assigned to the individual. (FAR 52.224-2(c)(3))

Systems and Other Concept Formulation Studies Analyses and study efforts either related to specific independent research and development efforts or directed toward identifying desirable new systems, equipment or components, or modifications and improvements to existing systems, equipment, or components. (FAR 31.205-18(a))

t Distribution A distribution commonly used in statistics to make inferences about a population from sample data. As the sample size increases, the shape of the t distribution approaches the shape of the normal probability distribution.

T-test for the Significance Comparison of a calculated T value with a table value tests the significance of a regression equation. It permits analysts to identify situations where, because of sampling error, a regression relationship may have a rather high coefficient of determination when there is no real relationship between the independent and dependent variables (i.e., there is no statistical significance).

Take It or Leave It A negotiator using this tactic presents two alternatives, take the current offer as proposed or give up any chance of reaching an agreement. A negotiator using this tactic might use words such as "My best offer is on the table, and I have no room to compromise further."

Tangible Capital Asset An asset that has physical substance, more than minimal value, and is expected to be held by an enterprise for continued use or possession beyond the current accounting period for the services it yields. (FAR 31.001)

Tanker A vessel used primarily for the carriage of bulk liquid cargoes such as liquid petroleum products, vegetable oils, and molasses. (FAR 47.501)

Target Cost The estimated cost of a contract as initially negotiated, adjusted for any change in contract requirements. (FAR 52.216-10(b)(1))

Target Fee The fee initially negotiated on the assumption that a contract would be performed for a cost equal to the estimated cost initially negotiated, adjusted for any change in contract requirements. (FAR 52.216-10(b)(2))

Task Order An order for services placed against an established contract or with Government sources. (FAR 2.101)

Task Order Contract A contract for services that does not procure or specify a firm quantity of services (other than a minimum or maximum quantity) and that provides for the issuance of orders for the performance of tasks during the period of the contract. (FAR 16.501-1)

Tax Includes fees and charges for doing business that are levied by the government of the country concerned or by its political subdivisions. (FAR 52.229-6(b))

Taxpayer Identification Number (TIN) 1. The number required by the IRS to be used by the offeror in reporting income tax and other returns. (FAR 4.901) 2. The number required by the IRS to be used by the offeror in reporting income tax and other returns. (FAR 52.204-3(a))

Technical Analysis Review by personnel having specialized knowledge, skills, experience, or capability in engineering, science, or management of the proposed types and quantities of materials, labor, processes, special tooling, facilities, the reasonableness of scrap and spoilage, and other factors set forth in the proposal(s) in order to determine the need for and reasonableness of the proposed resources, assuming reasonable economy and efficiency. (FAR 15.404-1(e)(1))

Technical Data 1. Data other than computer software, which are of a scientific or technical nature.

(FAR 27.401) 2. Data (other than computer software) which are of a scientific or technical nature. (FAR 52.227-14(a))

Technical Direction An interpretation of Statement of Work requirements provided by a representative of the Contracting Officer. Representatives of the Contracting Officer have no authority to alter Statement of Work. The Statement of Work can only be altered through use of a contract modification signed by the Contracting Officer.

Technical Negotiation Objectives Goals based on Government's requirements and its evaluation of the contractor's technical proposal based on those requirements. Generally, they should center on whether the contractor can effectively and efficiently meet Government requirements.

Telecommunications Carrier A person engaged in providing telecommunications services.

Telegraphic Bid A bid submitted by telegraph or mailgram. (FAR 14.202-2)

Term Form A form of cost-plus-fixed-fee contract that describes the scope of work in general terms and obligates the contractor to devote a specified level of effort for a stated time period. If contract performance is considered satisfactory by the Government, the fixed-fee is payable at the expiration of the agreed-upon period, upon contractor statement that the level-of-effort specified in the contract has been expended in performing the contract work. Renewal for further periods of performance is a new acquisition that involves new cost and fee arrangements. (FAR 16.306(d)(2))

Terminated Portion of the Contract The portion of a terminated contract that relates to work or end items not completed and accepted before the effective date of termination that the contractor is not to continue to perform. For construction contracts that have been completely terminated for convenience, it means the entire contract, notwithstanding the completion of, and payment for, individual items of work before termination. (FAR 49.001)

Termination Case File A separate case file for each termination established by the Termination Contracting Officer responsible for negotiating the final settlement. This file will include memoranda and records of all actions relative to the settlement. (FAR 49.105-3)

Termination Contracting Officer (TCO) 1. A Contracting Officer who is settling terminated contracts. (FAR 2.101) 2. A Contracting Officer who is settling terminated contracts. (FAR 49.001)

Termination Costs The incurrence of costs or the special treatment of costs that would not have arisen had the contract not been terminated. (FAR 31.205-42)

Termination for Convenience 1. The Contracting Officer may terminate performance of work under the contract in whole or, from time to time, in part if the Contracting Officer determines that a termination is in the Government's interest. (FAR 52.249-2(a)) 2. The procedure which may apply to any Government contract, including multi-year contracts. As contrasted with cancellation, termination can be effected at any time during the life of the contract (cancellation is effected between fiscal years) and can be for the total quantity or a partial quantity (whereas cancellation must be for all subsequent fiscal years' quantities). (FAR 17.103)

Termination for Default The exercise of the Government's contractual right to completely or partially terminate a contract because of the contractor's actual or anticipated failure to perform its contractual obligations. (FAR 49.401)

Termination Gain or Loss An actuarial gain or loss resulting from the difference between the assumed and actual rates at which pension plan participants separate from employment for reasons other than retirement, disability, or death. (FAR 31.001)

Termination Inventory Any property purchased, supplied, manufactured, furnished, or otherwise acquired for the performance of a contract subsequently terminated and properly allocable to the terminated portion of the contract. It includes Government-furnished property. It does not include any facilities, material, special test equipment, or special tooling that are subject to a separate contract or to a special contract requirement governing their use or disposition. (FAR 45.601)

Termination Liability A contingent Government obligation to pay a utility supplier the unamortized portion of a connection charge and any other applicable nonrefundable service charge as defined in the contract in the event the Government terminates the contract before the cost of connection facilities has been recovered by the utility supplier. (FAR 41.101)

Testing That element of inspection that determines the properties or elements, including functional operation of supplies or their components, by the application of established scientific principles and procedures. (FAR 46.101)

Third-Party Draft An agency bank draft, similar to a check, that is used to acquire and to pay for supplies and services. (FAR 13.001)

Time Calculated using calendar days, unless otherwise specified, and will include Saturdays, Sundays, and legal holidays. However, if the last day falls on a Saturday, Sunday, or legal holiday, then the period includes the next working day. (FAR 52.215-1(a))

Time-and-Materials Contract A contract that provides for acquiring supplies or services on the basis of: a. Direct labor hours at specified fixed hourly rates that include wages, overhead, general and administrative expenses, and profit; and b. Materials at cost, including, if appropriate, material handling costs as part of material costs. (FAR 16.601(a))

Time-Series Analysis Identification of a trend related to time and using the trend to forecast future costs or events.

Title III Industrial Resource Materials, services, processes, or manufacturing equipment (including the processes, technologies, and ancillary services for the use of such equipment) established or maintained under the authority of Title III, Defense Production Act. (FAR 52.234-1(a))

Title III Project Contractor A contractor that has received assistance for the development or manufacture of an industrial resource under the Defense Production Act. (FAR 52.234-1(a))

Total Contract Cost The sum of direct and indirect costs allocable to a contract, incurred or to be incurred, less any allocable credits, plus any allocable cost of money. (FAR 31.201-1(a))

Total Cost Basis When use of the inventory basis is not practicable or will unduly delay settlement, the total-cost basis may be used to settle a fixed-price contract termination for convenience if approved in advance by the Termination Contracting Officer. (FAR 49.206-2(b))

Total Set-Aside for Small Business Also referred to as a total small business set-aside. An individual acquisition or class of acquisitions restricted for participation by small business concerns. (FAR 19.502-2)

Total Small Business Set-Aside See total set-aside for small business.

Toxic Chemicals Reportable chemicals currently listed and added pursuant to Emergency Planning and Community Right-to-Know Act (EPCRA), except for those chemicals deleted by the Environmental Protection Agency using the statutory criteria of EPCRA. (FAR 23.904)

Tradeoff Process In a negotiated acquisition, a procedure that permits consideration of tradeoffs among cost or price and non-cost factors and allows the Government to accept other than the lowest priced proposal. The perceived benefits of the higher priced proposal must merit the additional cost and the rationale must for tradeoffs must be documented in the contract file. (FAR 15.101-1(c))

Trainee A person registered and receiving on-the-job training in a construction occupation under a program which has been approved in advance by the U.S. Department of Labor, Employment and Training Administration, as meeting its standards for on-the-job training programs and which has been so certified by that Administration. (FAR 22.401)

Transportation Costs Include freight, express, cartage, and postage charges relating to goods purchased, in process, or delivered. (FAR 31.205-45)

Transportation Term Contracts Indefinite delivery requirements contracts for transportation or for transportation-related services. They are particularly useful for local drayage and office relocations within a metropolitan area. (FAR 47.203(a))

Travel Costs Costs for transportation, lodging, meals, and incidental expenses. (FAR 31.205-46(a))

Trial Balloon A tentative plan offered to test the reaction of a particular audience.

Two-Phase Design- Build Selection Procedures A selection method in which a limited number of offerors (normally five or fewer) is selected during Phase One to submit detailed proposals for Phase Two. (FAR 36.102)

Two-Step Sealed Bidding A combination of competitive procedures designed to obtain the benefits of sealed bidding when adequate specifications are not available. a. Step 1 consists of the request for, submission, evaluation, and (if necessary) discussion of a technical proposal. No pricing is involved. b. Step 2, involves the submission of sealed priced bids by those who have submitted acceptable technical proposals in Step 1. (FAR 14.501)

Type of Contract See contract type.

U.S.-Flag Air Carrier An air carrier holding a certificate under section 401 of the Federal Aviation Act of 1958 (49 U.S.C. 1371). (FAR 47.401)

U.S.-Flag Vessel Either a Government vessel or a privately owned U.S.-flag commercial vessel. (FAR 47.501)

Unallowable Cost Any cost which, under the provisions of any pertinent law, regulation, or contract, cannot be included in prices, cost-reimbursements, or settlements under a Government contract to which it is allocable. (FAR 31.001)

Unauthorized Commitment An agreement that is not binding solely because the Government representative who made it lacked the authority to enter into that agreement on behalf of the Government. (FAR 1.602-3(a))

Unbalanced Pricing Despite an acceptable total evaluated price, the price of one or more contract line items is significantly over or understated as indicated by the application of cost or price analysis techniques. (FAR 15.404-1(g)(1))

Unclassified Bid Any bid that does not contain classified information (confidential, secret, or top secret).

Uncompensated Overtime The hours worked without additional compensation in excess of an average of 40 hours per week by direct charge employees who are exempt from the Fair Labor Standards Act.

Compensated personal absences such as holidays, vacations, and sick leave must be included in the normal work week for purposes of computing uncompensated overtime hours. (FAR 52.237-10(a))

Uncompensated Overtime Rate The rate that results from multiplying the hourly rate for a 40-hour work week by 40, and then dividing by the proposed hours per week. For example, 45 hours proposed on a 40-hour work week basis at $20 per hour would be converted to an uncompensated overtime rate of $17.78 per hour (($20.00 x 40) ÷ 45 = $17.78). (FAR 52.237-10(a))

Undermining The negotiator using this tactic attempts to put the other party on the defensive using threats, insults, or ultimatums. Although this tactic often backfires because most people resent verbal attacks, it can sometimes be effective when used against an easily intimidated negotiator.

Unfair Trade Practices The commission of any of the following acts by a contractor: a. A violation of Section 337 of the Tariff Act of 1930 as determined by the International Trade Commission. b. A violation, as determined by the Secretary of Commerce, of any agreement of the group known as the "Coordination Committee" for purposes of the Export Administration Act of 1979, or any similar bilateral or multilateral export control agreement. c. A knowingly false statement regarding a material element of a certification concerning the foreign content of an item of supply, as determined by the Secretary of the Department or the head of the agency to which such certificate was furnished. (FAR 9.403)

Unfinished Oils One or more of several petroleum oils identified in the FAR, or a mixture or combination of those oils, that are to be further processed other than by blending by mechanical means. (FAR 25.108(d)(2)(iii))

Unfunded Pension A defined benefit pension plan for which no funding agency is established for the Plan accumulation of contributions. (FAR 31.001)

UNICOR See Federal Prison Industries, Inc.

Uniform Contract Format (UCF) The solicitation and contract format commonly used for most noncommercial supplies and services. The format is divided in parts and sections:

Part I—The Schedule:
    A Solicitation/contract form;
    B Supplies or services and prices;
    C Description/specifications;
    D Packaging and marking;
    E Inspection and acceptance;
    F Deliveries or performance;
    G Contract administration data; and
    H Special contract requirements.

Part II—Contract Clauses:
    I Contract clauses.

Part III—List of Documents, Exhibits, and Other Attachments:
    J List of documents, exhibits, and other attachments.

Part IV—Representations and Instructions:
    K Representations, certifications, and other statements of bidders;
    L Instructions, conditions, and notices to bidders; and
    M Evaluation factors for award. (FAR 15.204-1(a), FAR Table 15-1)

Unilateral Modification A contract modification that is signed only by the Contracting Officer. Unilateral modifications are used, for example, to a. Make administrative changes; b. Issue change orders; c. Make changes authorized by clauses other than a changes clause (e.g., Property clause, Options clause, Suspension of Work clause, etc.); and d. Issue termination notices. (FAR 43.103(b))

Unique and Innovative Concept When used relative to an unsolicited research proposal, it means that in the opinion and to the knowledge of the Government evaluator, the meritorious proposal is the product of original thinking submitted in confidence by one source; contains new, novel, or changed concepts, approaches, or methods; was not submitted previously by another; and is not otherwise available within the Federal Government. In this context, does not mean that the source has the sole capability of performing the research. (FAR 6.003)

Unit In value engineering, the item or task to which the Contracting Officer and the contractor agree the value engineering change proposal applies. (FAR 48.001)

Unit Credit Cost Method See accrued benefit cost method.

Unit Improvement Curve An improvement curve model based on the assumption that as the total volume of units produced doubles the cost per unit decreases by some constant percentage.

United States 1. The 50 States and the District of Columbia. (FAR 2.101) 2. The States, the District of Columbia, the Virgin Islands, the Commonwealth of Puerto Rico, and the possessions of the United States. (FAR 22.801) 3. Includes any State of the United States, the District of Columbia, Puerto Rico, the Virgin Islands, Outer Continental Shelf Lands as defined in the Outer Continental Shelf Lands, American Samoa, Guam, Northern Mariana Islands, Wake Island, and Johnston Island but does not include any other territory under U.S. jurisdiction or any U.S. base or possession within a foreign country. (FAR 22.1001) 4.

Includes the States, the District of Columbia, the Virgin Islands, the Commonwealth of Puerto Rico, and Guam. (FAR 22.1308(a)(1)(i)) 5. For the Buy American Act, the United States, its possessions, Puerto Rico, and any other place subject to its jurisdiction, but does not include leased bases or trust territories. (FAR 25.101) 6. The 50 States, the District of Columbia, the Commonwealth of Puerto Rico, and possessions of the United States. (FAR 47.401) 7. The United States, its territories and possessions, the Commonwealth of Puerto Rico, the U.S. Trust Territory of the Pacific Islands, and the District of Columbia. (FAR 52.219-23(a)) 8. The 50 States, the District of Columbia, the Commonwealth of Puerto Rico, and possessions of the United States. (FAR 52.247-63(a))

Unlimited Rights 1. The rights of the Government to use, disclose, reproduce, prepare derivative works, distribute copies to the public, and perform publicly and display publicly, in any manner and for any purpose, and to have or permit others to do so. (FAR 27.401) 2. The right of the Government to use, disclose, reproduce, prepare derivative works, distribute copies to the public, and perform publicly and display publicly, in any manner and for any purpose, and to have or permit others to do so. (FAR 52.227-14(a))

Unsettled Contract Change Any contract change or contract term for which a definitive modification is required but has not been executed. (FAR 49.001)

Unsolicited Proposal A written proposal for a new or innovative idea that is submitted to an agency on the initiative of the offeror for the purpose of obtaining a contract with the Government, and that is not in response to a request for proposals, Broad Agency Announcement, Small Business Innovation Research topic, Small Business Technology Transfer Research topic, Program Research and Development Announcement, or any other Government-initiated solicitation or program. (FAR 15.601)

Unusual Contract Financing Any financing not deemed customary contract financing by the agency. Unusual contract financing is financing that is legal and proper under applicable laws, but that the agency has not authorized Contracting Officers to use without specific reviews or approvals by higher management. (FAR 32.001)

Unusual Progress Payments Any progress payments based on cost that do not meet the limits set forth for customary progress payments. Use must be approved by the head of the contracting activity. (FAR 32.501)

Usable Property See serviceable property.

Utility Distribution System Includes distribution and transmission lines, substations, or installed equipment forming an integral part of the system by which gas, water, steam, electricity, sewerage, or other utility services are transmitted between the outside building or structure in which the services are used and the point of origin, disposal, or connection with some other system. It does not include communication services. (FAR 45.501)

Utility Service A service such as furnishing electricity, natural or manufactured gas, water, sewerage, thermal energy, chilled water, steam, hot water, or high temperature hot water. (FAR 41.101)

V Loan See guaranteed loan.

Value Engineering 1. An analysis of the functions of a program, project, system, product, item of equipment, building, facility, service, or supply of an executive agency, performed by qualified agency or contractor personnel, directed at improving performance, reliability, quality, safety, and life-cycle costs. (FAR 48.001). An organized effort to analyze the functions of systems, equipment, facilities, services, and supplies for the purpose of achieving the essential functions at the lowest life cycle cost consistent with required performance, reliability, quality, and safety. (FAR 52.248-2(b))

Value Engineering Change Proposal (VECP) A proposal that: a. Requires a change to the instant contract to implement; and b. Results in reducing the overall projected cost to the agency without impairing essential functions or characteristics; provided, that it does not involve a change: (1) In deliverable end item quantities only; (2) In research and development (R&D) items or R&D test quantities that are due solely to results of previous testing under the instant contract; or (3) To the contract type only. (FAR 48.001)

Value Engineering Proposal 1. In connection with an A-E contract, a change proposal developed by employees of the Federal Government or contractor value engineering personnel under contract to an agency to provide value engineering services for the contract or program. (FAR 48.001) 2. In connection with an A-E contract, a change proposal developed by employees of the Federal Government or contractor value engineering personnel under contract to an agency to provide value engineering services for the contract or program. (FAR 52.248-2(b))

Variable Cost In cost-volume-profit analysis, costs of each unit that remain constant no matter how many units are made in the relevant range of production. Total variable cost increases as the total number of units produced increases.

Variance 1. The difference between a preestablished measure and an actual measure. (FAR 31.001) 2. In statistical analysis, the variance of a sample is the average of the squared deviations between each observation and the mean. It is one of the two most popular measures of dispersion. The other is the standard deviation.

Veteran of the Vietnam Era A person who: a. Served on active duty for a period of more than 180 days, any part of which occurred between August 5, 1964, and May 7, 1975, and was discharged or released therefrom with other than a dishonorable discharge; or b. Was discharged or released from active duty for a service-connected disability if any part of such active duty was performed between August 5, 1964, and May 7, 1975. (FAR 52.222-35(a))

Virgin Material 1. Previously unused raw material, including previously unused copper, aluminum, lead, zinc, iron, other metal or metal ore, or any undeveloped resource that is, or with new technology will become, a source of raw materials. (FAR 11.001) 2. Previously unused raw material, including previously unused copper, aluminum, lead, zinc, iron, other metal or metal ore, or any undeveloped resource that is, or with new technology will become, a source of raw materials. (FAR 52.211-5(a))

Vocal Cues Nonverbal messages communicated by the sound of the human voice, can provide valuable information.

Vocational Training Preparing and maintaining a noncollege level program of instruction, including but not limited to on-the-job, classroom, and apprenticeship training, designed to increase the vocational effectiveness of employees. (FAR 31.205-44)

Wage and Hour Division The unit in the Employment Standards Administration of the Department of Labor to which is assigned functions of the Secretary of Labor under the Service Contract Act. (FAR 22.1001)

Wage Determination A determination of minimum wages or fringe benefits made under the Service Contract Act applicable to the employment in a given locality of one or more classes of service employees. (FAR 22.1001)

Wages The basic hourly rate of pay; any contribution irrevocably made by a contractor or subcontractor to a trustee or to a third person pursuant to a bona fide fringe benefit fund, plan, or program; and the rate of costs to the contractor or subcontractor which may be reasonably anticipated in providing bona fide fringe benefits to laborers and mechanics pursuant to an enforceable commitment to carry out a financially responsible plan or program, which was communicated in writing to the laborers and mechanics affected. The fringe benefits enumerated in the Davis-Bacon Act include medical or hospital care, pensions on retirement or death, compensation for injuries or illness resulting from occupational activity, or insurance to provide any of the foregoing; unemployment benefits; life insurance, disability insurance, sickness insurance, or accident insurance; vacation or holiday pay; defraying costs of apprenticeship or other similar programs; or other bona fide fringe benefits. Fringe benefits do not include benefits required by other Federal, state, or local law. (FAR 22.401)

Walsh-Healey Act See Walsh-Healey Public Contracts Act.

Walsh-Healey Public Contracts Act Also referred to as the Walsh-Healey Public Contracts Act. Requires that (unless exempted), all contracts subject to the Act and entered into by any executive department, independent establishment, or other agency or instrumentality of the United States, or by the District of Columbia, or by any corporation (all the stock of which is beneficially owned by the United States) for the manufacture or furnishing of materials, supplies, articles, and equipment (referred to in this subpart as supplies) in any amount exceeding $10,000, must include or incorporate by reference the stipulations required by the Act pertaining to such matters as minimum wages, maximum hours, child labor, convict labor, and safe and sanitary working conditions. (FAR 22.602)

Warranty A promise or affirmation given by a contractor to the Government regarding the nature, usefulness, or condition of the supplies or performance of services furnished under the contract. (FAR 46.701)

Warranty Costs Costs arising from fulfillment of any contractual obligation of a contractor to correct defects in the products, replace defective parts, or make refunds in the case of inadequate performance. (FAR 31.205-39)

Waste Prevention Any change in the design, manufacturing, purchase, or use of materials or products (including packaging) to reduce their amount or toxicity before they become municipal solid waste. Waste prevention also refers to the reuse of products or materials. (FAR 23.703)

Waste Reduction Preventing or decreasing the amount of waste being generated through waste prevention, recycling, or purchasing recycled and environmentally preferable products. (FAR 23.703)

Water Act Clean Water Act. (FAR 52.223-2(a))

Weakness A proposal flaw that increases the risk of unsuccessful contract performance. A significant weakness in the proposal is a flaw that appreciably increases the risk of unsuccessful contract performance. (FAR 15.301)

Weighted Average Cost An inventory costing method under which an average unit cost is computed periodically by dividing the sum of the cost of beginning inventory plus the cost of acquisitions by the total number of units included in these two categories. (FAR 31.001)

Wet Noodle A wet noodle is slick and difficult to pin down. The same can be said of negotiators using the wet noodle tactic. They are difficult to pin down on any issue because they give qualified or noncommittal responses. Users of this tactic avoid making firm commitments or concessions whenever possible.

Win/Lose Negotiation Style Negotiation based on power and using that power to force one negotiator's will on the other. That power could be real or only perceived by the other negotiator.

Win/Lose Outcome Occurs when one party involved in a negotiation is perceived as having done significantly better at the expense of the other. This type of negotiation tends to be highly competitive, with a large degree of mistrust on both sides.

Win/Win Negotiation Style Negotiation based on the merits of the situation to obtain a satisfactory result.

Win/Win Outcome Also referred to as a both-win outcome. Occurs when both sides achieve long-term satisfaction with negotiation results. Negotiations emphasize developing a mutually beneficial agreement. For example, awarding a contract at a fair and reasonable price is in the best interest of both the contractor and the Government.

Women-Owned Business Concern A concern which is at least 51 percent owned by one or more women; or in the case of any publicly owned business, at least 51 percent of the stock of which is owned by one or more women; and whose management and daily business operations are controlled by one or more women. (FAR 52.204-5(b))

Women-Owned Small Business Concern A small business concern: a. Which is at least 51 percent owned by one or more women; or, in the case of any publicly owned business, at least 51 percent of the stock of which is owned by one or more women; and b. Whose management and daily business operations are controlled by one or more women. (FAR 19.001)

Work 1. See building for definition related to construction. 2. Includes data when the contract does not include the Warranty of Data clause. (FAR 52.246-8(a)) 3. Includes, but is not limited to, materials, workmanship, and manufacture and fabrication of components. (FAR 52.246-12(a))

Work Hours and Safety Standards Act Requires that certain contracts contain a clause specifying that no laborer or mechanic doing any part of the work contemplated by the contract shall be required or permitted to work more than 40 hours in any workweek unless paid for all such overtime hours at not less than 1 1/2 times the basic rate of pay. (FAR 22.301)

Work Measurement The use of labor-time standards to measure and control the time required to perform a particular task or group of tasks.

Work Measurement System A management system designed to analyze the touch labor content of an operation, establish labor-time standards for that operation, measure and analyze variances from those standards, and continuously improve both the operation and the labor standards used in that operation.

Work Measurement System Plan A program for implementing, operating, and maintaining work measurement of operation activities.

Work Statement See statement of work.

Work-in-Process Material that has been released to manufacturing, engineering, design or other services under the contract and includes undelivered manufactured parts, assemblies, and products, either complete or incomplete. (FAR 45.501)

Written See in writing.

Year 2000 Compliant Information technology that accurately processes date/time data (including, but not limited to, calculating, comparing, and sequencing) from, into, and between the twentieth and twenty-first centuries, and the years 1999 and 2000 and leap year calculations, to the extent that other information technology, used in combination with the information technology being acquired, properly exchanges date/time data with it. (FAR 39.002)

ADMINISTRATION FOR NATIVE AMERICANS

Abbreviations and Acronyms

ACF	Administration for Children and Families
ANA	The Administration for Native Americans
CFDA	Catalog of Federal Domestic Assistance
CFR	Code of Federal Regulations
COB	Carry Over Budget
DoP	ANA Division of Policy
DPEP	ANA Division of Program Evaluation and Planning
DPM	Division of Payment Management
DPO	ANA Division of Program Operations
DUNS	Data Universal Numbering System
FOA	Funding Opportunity Announcement
GPS	Grants Policy Statement
HHS	Department of Health and Human Services
NAPA	Native American Programs Act of 1974, as amended
NCC	Non-Competing Continuation
NCE	No Cost Extension
NFS	Non-Federal Share
NGA	Notice of Grant Award
NOA	Notice of Award Letter
OER	Objective Evaluation Report
OGM	ACF Office of Grants Management
OMB	Office of Management and Budget
OPR	Objective Progress Report
OWP	Objective Work Plan

PIP Project Improvement Plan
SEDS Social and Economic Development Strategies
SF Standard Form
T/TA Training and Technical Assistance

GLOSSARY OF TERMS

Amendments (Formerly called Grant Actions) Non-routine grant actions that require special approval and do not automatically occur for every grant, such as:
- Budget Modification
- Change in Key Personnel
- Carry-Over Budget
- Supplemental Award

Change in Objective Work Plan or Impact Indicators, No Cost Extensions (NCE), Supplements, and Non-Competing Continuations (NCC) are not initiated under "Manage Amendments." You must contact your program specialist to initiate NCEs and Supplements. Continuing grantees are informed by ANA when the NCC applications are posted on GrantSolutions.

Authorized Official (AO) (Also referred to as the Authorized Certifying Official on ANA's Objective Progress Report from or Authorized Representative on the SF-424 form.) The individual named by the recipient organization who is authorized to act for the recipient, and to assume the obligations imposed by the Federal laws, regulations, requirements, and conditions that apply to grant applications or awards. The AO is able to upload amendments into GrantSolutions.

Authorized Organizational Representative The individual, named by the applicant/recipient organization, who is authorized to act for the applicant/recipient and to assume the obligations imposed by the federal laws, regulations, requirements and conditions that apply to grant applications or awards.

Budget Narrative A description of how the categorical costs are derived, which includes the necessity, reasonableness, and allocation of the proposed costs. The Budget Narrative should include all individual line items found in the line item budget. The Budget Narrative should be separate from the line item budget, and should be separated by year.

Budget Period The interval of time (usually 12 months) into which a project period is divided for budgetary and funding purposes. The Budget Period also is the "period of funding availability," as specified in 45 CFR Part 74 and Part 92.

Carryover of Budget (COB) Unobligated balance of funds at the end of a budget period which is carried forward into the next budget period to complete activities that were not completed in the budget period to which funds were originally awarded.

Construction Construction of a new building, including the installation of fixed equipment, but excluding the purchase of land and ancillary improvements, for example, parking lots or roads.

Contingency Plan A set of specific actions to reduce anticipated negative impacts on a project in the event challenges arise.

Core Administration Salaries and other expenses for those functions that support the applicant's organization as a whole or for purposes unrelated to the actual management or implementation of the ANA-funded project.

Direct Costs Costs that can be specifically identified with a particular project or activity.

Equipment An article of nonexpendable, tangible personal property, having a useful life of more than one year and an acquisition cost that equals or exceeds the lesser of: (a) the capitalization level established by the organization for the financial statement purposes, or (b) $5,000.

Federal Share Financial assistance provided by ANA in the amount of 80 percent of the approved costs of the project.

Governing Body A body (1) consisting of duly elected or designated representatives, (2) appointed by duly elected official, or (3) selected in accordance with traditional tribal means. The Governing Body must have authority to enter into contracts, agreements, and grants on behalf of the organization or individuals who elected, designated, appointed, or selected them.

Impact Indicators Measurement descriptions used to verify the impact of the project or the achievement of the project goal. Impact Indicators must be quantifiable and documented, and include target numbers and tracking systems. As of FY 2008, ANA requires three Impact Indicators per project. Impact indicators are separate from the results and benefits section of the Objective Work Plan.

Indirect Cost Rate A mechanism for determining what proportions of indirect costs each program/project should bear. An Indirect Cost Rate represents the ratio between the total indirect costs and benefiting direct costs, after excluding and/or reclassifying unallowable costs, and extraordinary or distorting expenditures. The Indirect Cost Rate is negotiated between the organization and the cognizant Federal agency. Indirect costs cannot be charged to the project without an Indirect Cost Rate agreement from the cognizant Federal agency.

Indirect Costs Costs incurred for common or joint objectives, which therefore cannot be identified readily and specifically with a particular sponsored project, program, or activity but are nevertheless necessary to the operations of the organization. For example, the costs of operating and maintaining facilities, depreciation, or administrative salaries. Indirect Costs are shared costs between projects, and they are distributed by an Indirect Cost Rate, which is identified by the Indirect Cost Rate agreement between the cognizant Federal agency and the organization or tribe. Indirect Costs are restricted funds that cannot be spent on direct costs. All Indirect Costs must be negotiated with ANA.

In-Kind Contribution The value of goods and services that benefit a Federally-assisted project, and are provided without charge to a recipient (or subrecipient or contractor under a grant).

Language Nest (As defined by P.L. 109-394) A site-based educational program that: provides native language instruction and child care through the use of a Native American language for at least 10 children under the age of 7, for an average of at least 500 hours per year per student; provides classes in a Native American language for parents (or legal guardians) of students enrolled in a Native American Language Nest (including Native American language-speaking parents); and ensures that a Native American language is the dominant medium of instruction in the Native American Language Nest.

Language Restoration Program An educational program that: operates at least one Native American language program for the community in which it serves; provides training programs for teachers of Native American languages; develops instructional materials for the programs; works towards a goal of increasing language proficiency and fluency in at least one Native American language; and provides instruction in at least one Native American language.

Language Survival School A site-based educational program for school-aged students that: provides an average of at least 500 hours of native language instruction through the use of 1 or more Native American language, for at least 15 students for whom a Native American Language Survival School is their principal place of instruction; develops instructional courses and materials for learning Native American languages and for instruction through the use of Native American languages; provides for teacher training; works toward a goal of all students achieving fluency in a Native American language and academic proficiency in mathematics, reading (or language arts), and science; and is located in areas that have high numbers or percentages of Native American students.

Letter of Commitment A letter documenting the commitment to provide cash or in-kind contributions to meet the match requirement. The Letter of Commitment may be from the applicant or a third-party. The letter of commitment must state the dollar amount (if applicable), the length of time the commitment will be honored, and the conditions under which the organization will support the ANA project. If a dollar amount is included, the amount must be based on market and historical rates charged and paid. The in-kind contributions to be committed may be human, natural, physical, or financial, and may include other Federal and non-Federal resources.

Leveraged Resource Any resource, other than the Federal share and non-Federal contribution, expressed as a dollar figure, acquired or utilized during the project period that supports the project. Leveraged Resources may include natural, financial, personnel, and physical resources provided to assist in the successful completion of the project.

Line Item Budget A budget that lists the individual costs of all budgeted items, such as personnel participating in the project, fringe benefits, travel, equipment, and supplies. A Line Item Budget should always be separate from the budget narrative and identify each budget period separately.

Non-Federal Share (NFS) The total dollar value of all non-ANA funded project costs. These include in-kind and cash contributions given to the project, but do not include other Federal funds unless those Federal funds have been identified by the NAPA legislation, specifically under section 803C(e)(1)(B)(ii), as being available for use as non-Federal funds. An applicant/grantee is required to provide at least 20 percent NFS match of the approved ANA-funded project costs.

Notice of Grant Award (NGA) (Formerly called Financial Assistance Award, or FAA.) Notifies the applicant or grantee that an application for funding, increase in budget, or amendment has been approved. Please keep in mind that Section 16 (Approved Budget) will now show the total amount of Federal and Non-Federal Share together for each budget category. Section 17 (Award Computation) will still show the total amount of Federal and Non-Federal Share, as well as the respective percentages of the total budget.

Objective A statement of the specific outcomes or results to be achieved within the project period, which directly contribute to the achievement of the project goals and support the community's long-range goals.

Objective Work Plan (OWP) The plan for achieving the project objectives and producing the results and benefits expected for each objective. The OWP is a blueprint for the project and includes the project goal, objectives, and activities.

Partnership A collaborative effort between two or more parties that supports the development and implementation of the project.

Principal Investigator/Program Director (PI/PD) The individual the grantee designates as the contact person on the SF-424 form. The PI/PD is the person whom the ANA Program Specialist will contact if they have any questions or concerns regarding the grant. The PI/PD is able to upload amendments into GrantSolutions.

Problem Statement A clear and concise description of the condition or issues that will be addressed by the project.

Project Goal The purpose or specific result expected from the project and achieved through the project objectives and activities.

Project Period The total time for which Federal support has been programmatically approved, as shown in the Notice of Grant Award (NGA). It is important to note that the Project Period shown in the NGA does not constitute a commitment by the Federal government to fund the entire period.

Real Property Land, including land improvements, structures, and appurtenances thereto, excluding movable machinery and equipment.

Renovation or Alteration Work that changes the interior arrangements or other physical characteristics of an existing facility or installed equipment so that it can be more effectively used for its current designated purpose, or adapted to an alternative use to meet a programmatic requirement. A minor Renovation or Alteration is distinguished from construction and major renovations, and must not exceed the lesser of $150,000 or 25 percent of total direct costs approved for the entire project period; it must be essential for the project.

Self-Sufficiency The ability to generate resources to meet a community's needs in a sustainable manner. A community's progress toward Self-Sufficiency is based on its efforts to plan, organize, and direct resources in a comprehensive manner that is consistent with its established long-range goals. For a community to self-sufficient, it must have local access to, control of, and coordination of services and programs that safeguard the health, well-being, and culture of the people that reside and work in the community.

Sustainable Project An ongoing program or service that can be maintained without additional ANA funds.

Administration on Intellectual and Developmental Disabilities

American Indian Consortium Any confederation of 2 or more recognized American Indian tribes, created through the official action of each participating tribe, that has a combined total resident population of 150,000 enrolled tribal members and a contiguous territory of Indian lands in 2 or more States.

Areas of emphasis The areas related to quality assurance activities, education activities and early intervention activities, child care-related activities, health-related activities, employment-related activities, housing-related activities, transportation-related activities, recreation-related activities, and other services available or offered to individuals in a community, including formal and informal community supports, that affect their quality of life.

Assistive technology device Any item, piece of equipment, or product system, whether acquired commercially, modified or customized, that is used to increase, maintain, or improve functional capabilities of individuals with developmental disabilities.

Assistive technology service Any service that directly assists an individual with a developmental disability in the selection, acquisition, or use of an assistive technology device. Such term includes conducting an evaluation of the needs of an individual with a developmental disability, including a functional evaluation of the individual in the individual's customary environment; purchasing, leasing, or otherwise providing for the acquisition of an assistive technology device by an individual with a developmental disability; selecting, designing, fitting, customizing, adapting, applying, maintaining, repairing or replacing an assistive technology device; coordinating and using another therapy, intervention, or service with an assistive technology device, such as a therapy, intervention, or service associated with an education or rehabilitation plan or program; providing training or technical assistance for an individual with a developmental disability, or, where appropriate, a family member, guardian, advocate, or authorized representative of an individual with a developmental disability; and providing training or technical assistance for professionals (including individuals providing education and rehabilitation services), employers, or other individuals who provide services to, employ, or are otherwise substantially involved in the major life functions of, an individual with developmental disabilities.

Center A University Center for Excellence in Developmental Disabilities Education, Research, and Service established under subtitle D.

Child care–related activities. The term means advocacy, capacity building, and systemic change activities that result in families of children with developmental disabilities having access to and use of child care services, including before-school, after-school, and out-of-school services, in their communities.

Culturally competent Used with respect to services, supports, or other assistance, means services, supports, or other assistance that is conducted or provided in a manner that is responsive to the beliefs, interpersonal styles, attitudes, language, and behaviors of individuals who are receiving the services, supports, or other assistance, and in a manner that has the greatest likelihood of ensuring their maximum participation in the program involved.

Developmental disability A severe, chronic disability of an individual that is attributable to a mental or physical impairment or combination of mental and physical impairments; is manifested before the individual attains age 22; is likely to continue indefinitely; results in substantial functional limitations in 3 or more of the following areas of major life activity: Self-care, Receptive and expressive language, Learning, Mobility, Self-direction. Capacity for independent living, Economic self-sufficiency; and reflects the individual's need for a combination and sequence of special, interdisciplinary, or generic services, individualized supports, or other forms of assistance that are of lifelong or extended duration and are individually planned and coordinated.

Early intervention activities The term means advocacy, capacity building, and systemic change activities provided to individuals described in paragraph (8)(B) and their families to enhance the development of the individuals to maximize their potential; and the capacity of families to meet the special needs of the individuals.

Education activities This means advocacy, capacity building, and systemic change activities that result in individuals with developmental disabilities being able to access appropriate supports and modifications when necessary, to maximize their educational potential, to benefit from lifelong educational activities, and to be integrated and included in all facets of student life.

Employment-related activities Advocacy, capacity building, and systemic change activities that result in individuals with developmental disabilities acquiring, retaining, or advancing in paid employment, including supported employment or self-employment, in integrated settings in a community.

Family support services
- ***In general***, services, supports, and other assistance provided to families with members who have developmental disabilities that are designed to strengthen the family's role as primary caregiver; prevent inappropriate out-of-the-home placement of the members and maintain family unity; and reunite families with members who have been placed out of the home whenever possible.
- ***Specific services*** include respite care, provision of rehabilitation technology and assistive technology, personal assistance services, parent training and counseling, support for families headed by aging caregivers, vehicular and home modifications, and assistance with extraordinary expenses, associated with the needs of individuals with developmental disabilities.

Health-related activities Advocacy, capacity building, and systemic change activities that result in individuals with developmental disabilities having access to and use of coordinated health, dental, mental health, and other human and social services, including prevention activities, in their communities.

Housing-related activities Advocacy, capacity-building, and systemic change activities that result in individuals with developmental disabilities having access to and use of housing and housing supports and services in their communities, including assistance related to renting, owning, or modifying an apartment or home.

Inclusion Used with respect to individuals with developmental disabilities and means the acceptance and encouragement of the presence and participation of individuals with developmental disabilities, by individuals without disabilities, in social, educational, work, and community activities, that enables individuals with developmental disabilities to have friendships and relationships with individuals and families of their own choice; live in homes close to community resources, with regular contact with individuals without disabilities in their communities; enjoy full access to and active participation in the same community activities and types of employment as individuals without disabilities; and take full advantage of their integration into the same community resources as individuals without disabilities, living, learning, working, and enjoying life in regular contact with individuals without disabilities.

Individualized supports Means supports that enable an individual with a developmental disability to exercise self-determination, be independent, be productive, and be integrated and included in all facets of community life; are designed to enable such individual to control such individual's environment, permitting the most independent life possible; prevent placement into a more restrictive living arrangement than is necessary; and enable such individual to live, learn, work, and enjoy life in the community; and include early intervention services; respite care; personal assistance services; family support services; supported employment services; support services for families headed by aging caregivers of individuals with developmental disabilities; and provision of rehabilitation technology and assistive technology, and assistive technology services.

Infants and young children An individual from birth to age 9, inclusive, who has a substantial developmental delay or specific congenital or acquired condition, may be considered to have a developmental disability without meeting 3 or more of the criteria described in clauses (i) through (v) of subparagraph (A) if the individual, without services and supports, has a high probability of meeting those criteria later in life.

Integration When used with respect to individuals with developmental disabilities, means exercising the equal right of individuals with developmental disabilities to access and use the same community resources as are used by and available to other individuals.

Not-for-profit When used with respect to an agency, institution, or organization, means an agency, institution, or organization that is owned or operated by 1 or more corporations or associations, no part of the net earnings of which inures, or may lawfully inure, to the benefit of any private shareholder or individual.

Personal assistance services A range of services, provided by 1 or more individuals, designed to assist an individual with a disability to perform daily activities, including activities on or off a job that such individual would typically perform if such individual did not have a disability. Such services shall be designed to increase such individual's control in life and ability to perform everyday activities, including activities on or off a job.

Prevention activities Activities that address the causes of developmental disabilities and the exacerbation of functional limitation, such as activities that eliminate or reduce the factors that cause or pre-dispose individuals to developmental disabilities or that increase the prevalence of developmental disabilities; increase the early identification of problems to eliminate circumstances that create or increase functional limitations; and mitigate against the effects of developmental disabilities throughout the lifespan of an individual.

Productivity Engagement in income-producing work that is measured by increased income, improved employment status, or job advancement; or engagement in work that contributes to a household or community.

Protection and advocacy system A protection and advocacy system established in accordance with section 143.

Quality assurance activities Advocacy, capacity building, and systemic change activities that result in improved consumer and family-centered quality assurance and that result in systems of quality assurance and consumer protection that include monitoring of services, supports, and assistance provided to an individual with developmental disabilities that ensures that the individual will not experience abuse, neglect, sexual or financial exploitation, or violation of legal or human rights; and will not be subject to the inappropriate use of restraints or seclusion; include training in leadership, self-advocacy, and self-determination for individuals with developmental disabilities, their families, and their guardians to ensure that those individuals will not experience abuse, neglect, sexual or financial exploitation, or violation of legal or human rights; and will not be subject to the inappropriate use of restraints or seclusion; or include activities related to interagency coordination and systems integration that result in improved and enhanced services, supports, and other assistance that contribute to and protect the self-determination, independence, productivity, and integration and inclusion in all facets of community life, of individuals with developmental disabilities.

Recreation- related activities Advocacy, capacity building, and systemic change activities that result in individuals with developmental disabilities having access to and use of recreational, leisure, and social activities, in their communities.

Rehabilitation technology The systematic application of technologies, engineering methodologies, or scientific principles to meet the needs of, and address the barriers confronted by, individuals with developmental disabilities in areas that include education, rehabilitation, employment, transportation, independent living, and recreation. Such term includes rehabilitation engineering, and the provision of assistive technology devices and assistive technology services.

Secretary The Secretary of Health and Human Services.

Self-determination activities Activities that result in individuals with developmental disabilities, with appropriate assistance, having the ability and opportunity to communicate and make personal decisions; the ability and opportunity to communicate choices and exercise control over the type and intensity of services, supports, and other assistance the individuals receive; the authority to control resources to obtain needed services, supports, and other assistance; opportunities to participate in, and contribute to, their communities; and support, including financial support, to advocate for themselves and others, to develop leadership skills, through training in self-advocacy, to participate in coalitions, to educate policymakers, and to play a role in the development of public policies that affect individuals with developmental disabilities.

State Except as otherwise provided, includes, in addition to each of the several States of the United States, the District of Columbia, the Commonwealth of Puerto Rico, the United States Virgin Islands, Guam, American Samoa, and the Commonwealth of the Northern Mariana Islands.

State Council on Developmental Disabilities A Council established under section 125.

Supported employment services Services that enable individuals with developmental disabilities to perform competitive work in integrated work settings, in the case of individuals with developmental disabilities for whom competitive employment has not traditionally occurred; or for whom competitive employment has been interrupted or intermittent as a result of significant disabilities; and who, because of the nature and severity of their disabilities, need intensive supported employment services or extended services in order to perform such work.

Transportation-related activities Advocacy, capacity building, and systemic change activities that result in individuals with developmental disabilities having access to and use of transportation.

Unserved and underserved Includes populations such as individuals from racial and ethnic minority backgrounds, disadvantaged individuals, individuals with limited English proficiency, individuals from underserved geographic areas (rural or urban), and specific groups of individuals within the population of individuals with developmental disabilities, including individuals who require assistive technology in order to participate in and contribute to community life.

AIDS and HIV-Related Terms

ABC Abacavir, a medication used to prevent and treat HIV/AIDS

Abruptio Placentae Premature separation of the placenta from the site of implantation on the uterus before delivery of the fetus.

Absolute Contraindication When a particular treatment or procedure should not be used under any circumstance because of the severe and potentially life-threatening risks involved.

Abstinence A popular HIV/AIDS prevention message (also Be Faithful, Use Condoms)

Accidental Inoculation An occupational exposure to HIV that occurs during the performance of job duties (by a nurse or doctor, for example). Includes a needlestick or cut with a sharp object, contact of mucous membranes (mouth, eyes), or contact of skin (especially when the exposed skin is chapped, abraded, or afflicted with dermatitis—skin rash or sores—or the contact is prolonged or involving an extensive area) with blood, tissues, or other body fluids (stool, urine, vaginal secretions, saliva, mucous) to which universal precautions apply.

Acanthosis Nigricans A skin disorder characterized by velvety, light brown-to-black markings that develop mainly in the folds of the body, such as in the armpits, groin, and creases of the neck. Acanthosis nigricans can be an inherited condition or can occur as the result of an endocrine disorder, cancer, or use of certain medications.

ACP AIDS Control Program

Acquired Immunity Immunity that develops during a person's lifetime. There are two types of acquired immunity: active immunity and passive immunity.

Acquired Immunodeficiency Syndrome (AIDS) The most severe manifestation of infection with the Human Immunodeficiency Virus (HIV). The Centers for Disease Control and Prevention (CDC), the World Health Organization, and many national governments list numerous opportunistic infections and cancers that, in the presence of HIV infection, result in an AIDS diagnosis. AIDS is also defined on the basis of the degree of immunodeficiency in an HIV-infected individual. AIDS can also affect the central nervous system and can result in neurological problems, infections, or cancers.

Acquired Resistance When a drug-resistant strain of HIV emerges while a person is on antiretroviral therapy (ART) for the treatment of HIV infection.

Active Immunity Protection from a disease as a result of previous exposure to the disease-causing infectious agent or part of the infectious agent (antigen). The protection can be a result of having had the disease or having received a vaccine to prevent getting the disease.

Active Tuberculosis Active disease caused by Mycobacterium tuberculosis, as evidenced by a confirmatory culture, or, in the absence of culture, suggestive clinical symptoms, including productive cough lasting >3 weeks, chest pain, hemoptysis, fever, night sweats, weight loss, and easy fatigability. Active TB is a communicable disease that is treatable, curable, and preventable. Persons with active TB disease should be under the care of a health care provider. Active TB disease may indicate immune deficiency. For HIV-infected persons, active TB disease is considered an opportunistic infection and a qualifying condition for AIDS.

Acute HIV Infection The period following infection when there is rapid production of virus. An estimated 80 to 90% of individuals with primary HIV infection develop an acute syndrome (disorder) characterized by flulike symptoms of fever, fatigue, swollen lymph nodes, sore throat, headache, aching muscles, and sometimes skin rash. Following infection, the immune system produces antibody and a cellular response to the virus (seroconversion) and a broad HIV-1 specific immune response occurs, usually within an average of 3 weeks after HIV infection. High levels of virus (HIV RNA) can be found in the blood at this time.

Acute Infection and Early Diseases Research Program (AIEDRP) A federally funded research program that studies how HIV infects humans and how the disease progresses to AIDS.

Acute Inflammatory Demyelinating Polyneuropathy Guillain-Barré syndrome

Acute Retroviral Syndrome Flu-like symptoms of acute HIV Infection that may appear approximately 1 to 4 weeks after infection. Symptoms such as fever, headache, fatigue, and swollen lymph nodes can last from 1 to 4 weeks, and then subside. During the acute stage of HIV infection, many, but not all, people will have symptoms of acute retroviral syndrome.

Adenopathy Any disease involving or causing enlargement of lymph nodes.

Adenovirus A group of viruses that use DNA as their genetic material and commonly cause respiratory and eye infections. People with weakened immune systems, including people with HIV, have a greater risk for serious complications from an adenovirus infection than people with healthy immune systems.

Adherence Taking medications (or other treatment) exactly as instructed by a health care provider. The benefits of strict adherence to an HIV regimen include sustained viral suppression, reduced risk of drug resistance, improved overall health and quality of life, and decreased risk of HIV transmission.

Adjuvant An ingredient added to a prescription or solution that increases or modifies the action of the principal ingredient. May be used in treatment of HIV or for HIV vaccines.

Adverse Drug Reaction (ADR) Any unintended, undesirable response to a drug taken at a normal dose for normal use. Adverse drug reactions (ADRs) are classified by onset, severity, and type.

Adverse Event (AE) Any undesirable experience associated with the use of a drug or other medical product.

Aerosolized A form of giving a drug in which a drug, such as pentamidine, is turned into a fine spray or mist by a nebulizer and inhaled.

Agammaglobulinemia A nearly total absence of antibodies (immunoglobulins) resulting in the loss of ability to produce immune antibodies.

Agency for Healthcare Research and Quality (AHRQ) A federally funded agency that produces evidence to make health care safer, higher quality, more accessible, equitable, and affordable and that works with partners to ensure that the evidence is understood and used.

Agranulocytopenia See Granulocytopenia.

AIDS See Acquired Immunodeficiency Syndrome (AIDS).

AIDS Case Definition Diagnostic criteria for AIDS established by the Centers for Disease Control and Prevention (CDC). To be diagnosed with AIDS, a person with HIV must have an AIDS-defining condition or have a CD4 count less than 200 cells/mm3 (regardless of whether the person has an AIDS-defining condition).

AIDS Clinical Trials Group (ACTG) Formerly called Adult AIDS Clinical Trials Group (AACTG). Federally funded program that supports the largest network of HIV/AIDS researchers and clinical trial units in the world. AIDS Clinical Trials Group (ACTG) develops and conducts research related to HIV infection and its complications.

AIDS Dementia Complex (ADC) (HIV-Associated Dementia, or HAD) A degenerative (destructive) neurological condition attributed to HIV infection, characterized by a group of clinical presentations including loss of coordination, mood swings, loss of inhibitions, and widespread inability to think. It is the most common central nervous system complication of HIV infection.

AIDS Drug Assistance Programs (ADAPs) Federally funded programs that provide medications and other HIV-related services to low-income, uninsured, and underinsured people with HIV/AIDS. Services of AIDS Drug Assistance Programs (ADAPs) are available in all 50 states and U.S. territories.

AIDS Education and Training Centers (AETCs) Regional centers that conduct education and training programs for health care providers who treat people living with HIV/AIDS. Training is targeted to providers who serve minority populations, the homeless, rural communities, prisoners, community and migrant health centers, and Ryan White HIV/AIDS Program-funded sites. AIDS Education and Training Centers (AETCs) serve all 50 states and many U.S. territories.

AIDS Encephalopathy See AIDS Dementia Complex.

AIDS-Related Cancers Several cancers are more common or more aggressive in persons living with HIV. These malignancies include certain types of immune system cancers known as lymphomas, Kaposi sarcoma, and anogenital cancers that primarily affect the anus and the cervix.

AIDS-Related Complex (ARC) (Early symptomatic HIV infection) A group of common complications found in early stages of HIV infection. They include progressive generalized lymphadenopathy (PGL), recurrent fever, unexplained weight loss, swollen lymph nodes, diarrhea, herpes, hairy leukoplakia, fungus infection of the mouth and throat, and the presence of HIV antibodies. Also includes symptoms that appear to be related to infection by HIV such as an unexplained, chronic deficiency of white blood cells (leukopenia) or a poorly functioning lymphatic system with swelling of the lymph nodes (lymphadenopathy) lasting for >3 months without the opportunistic infections required for a diagnosis of AIDS. See AIDS Wasting Syndrome.

AIDS Service Organization (ASO) A nongovernmental organization that provides services related to the prevention and treatment of HIV/AIDS.

AIDS Wasting Syndrome An AIDS-defining condition that includes at least 10% weight loss in the presence of diarrhea, chronic weakness, and documented fever for at least 30 days that is not the result of another infection or disease. In developing countries, it is often called "slim disease."

AIDSinfo The federal website offering HIV/AIDS medical practice guidelines and information on

HIV-related clinical trials and drugs for health care providers, researchers, people affected by HIV/AIDS, and the general public. Information is also available by phone, e-mail, and postal mail.

Alanine Aminotransferase (ALT) A liver enzyme that plays a role in protein metabolism. Abnormally high blood levels of ALT are a sign of liver inflammation or damage from infection or drugs. A normal level is below approximately 50 IU/L.

Alanine Transaminase See Alanine Aminotransferase.

Albumin A protein made by the liver and found in high concentrations in blood. This protein may be measured as part of a liver function test.

Albuminuria Proteinuria.

Alkaline Phosphatase (ALP) An enzyme normally present in certain cells within the liver, bone, kidney, intestine, and placenta. When the cells are destroyed in those tissues, more of the enzyme leaks into the blood, and levels rise in proportion to the severity of the condition. Measurement of this enzyme is used as an indication of the health of the liver.

Alopecia Loss of hair that frequently occurs in patients undergoing treatment for cancer or suffering from other diseases, such as AIDS, where cell-killing, or cytotoxic, drugs are used.

Alpha Interferon (Interferon Alpha, IFN) A protein produced by the immune system in response to infection that assists in controlling virus infection.

Alternate Test Site A site that provides only HIV services. Sometimes referred to as an anonymous test site.

Alternative Medicine A broad category of treatment systems (e.g., chiropractic, herbal medicine, acupuncture, homeopathy, naturopathy, and spiritual devotions) or culturally based healing traditions such as Chinese, Ayurvedic, and Christian Science. Alternative medicines share the common characteristic of nonacceptance by the biomedical (i.e., mainstream Western) establishment. Alternative medicine is also referred to as "complementary medicine." The designation "alternative medicine" is not equivalent to holistic medicine, a narrower term.

Amebiasis An inflammation of the intestines caused by infection with *Entamoeba histolytica* (a type of ameba) and characterized by frequent, loose stools flecked with blood and mucus.

American Trypanosomiasis Chagas disease.

Amino Acids The chemical building blocks of proteins.

Anal Intercourse/ Anal Sex A type of sexual intercourse in which a man inserts his penis in his partner's anus. Anal sex can be insertive or receptive.

Anaphylactic Shock A life-threatening allergic reaction characterized by a swelling of body tissues (including the throat) and a sudden decrease in blood pressure. Symptoms include difficulty breathing, violent coughing, and tightness of the chest.

ANC Antenatal clinic.

Anemia A blood disorder caused by reduced number or function of red blood cells, Symptoms may include shortness of breath, fatigue, and rapid heartbeat, HIV-associated causes of anemia include progression of HIV disease, opportunistic infections, and certain antiretroviral (ARV) drugs.

Anergy The loss or weakening of the body's immunity to an irritating agent, or antigen. Patients may be so immunodeficient that they are unable to produce a reaction to an infectious agent. For example, such patients will usually not test positive for tuberculosis (TB) on a tuberculin skin test (or Mantoux test).

Anogenital Related to the anal (rectum) and/or genital (sexual) area of the body.

Anonymous Without an ability to identify a person. In anonymous testing, patient-identifying information is not linked to testing information, including the request for tests or test results.

Anorexia The lack or loss of appetite that leads to significant decline in weight.

Antenatal Occurring before birth.

Antenatal The period between conception and birth. Same as prenatal.

Antepartum The time period before childbirth; antepartum refers to the mother.

Antibiotic A natural or manufactured substance that prevents the growth of bacteria or fungi. Some antibiotics are used to treat infectious diseases.

Antibody Substances in the blood or other body fluids that destroy bacteria, viruses, or other harmful agents (antigens). They are members of a class of proteins known as immunoglobulins, which are produced by special white blood cells called B-lymphocytes.

Antibody-Dependent Cell-Mediated Cytotoxicity (ADCC) An immune response in which antibodies bind to target cells, identifying them for attack by the immune system.

Antibody Differentiation Test A type of antibody test that can distinguish HIV-1 antibodies from HIV-2 antibodies. When an initial HIV antibody test result is positive, an antibody differentiation test is done to determine whether a person is infected with HIV-1 or HIV-2, The test is done using a sample of blood.

Antibody-Mediated Immunity Also called humoral immunity. Immunity that results from the activity of antibodies in blood and lymphoid tissue.

Anticoagulant A drug used to prevent the blood from clotting.

Antifungal A substance that kills or slows the growth of a fungus.

Antigen A substance that, when introduced into the body, stimulates production of an antibody.

Antigen/Antibody Combination Test A type of HIV test that can detect HIV-1 and HIV-2 antibodies and HIV-1 p24 antigen (a protein that forms the HIV core). Antigen/antibody combination tests can detect HIV earlier than tests that only detect HIV antibodies. The test is done using a sample of blood.

Antigen-Antibody Complex Immune complex.

Antigen-Presenting Cell (APC) A type of immune cell that enables a T lymphocyte (T cell) to recognize an antigen and mount an immune response against the antigen. Antigen-presenting cells (APCs) include macrophages, dendritic cells, and B lymphocytes (B cells).

Antineoplastic A substance that prevents the development or growth of cancer cells.

Antiprotozoal A substance that kills or inhibits the growth of single-celled microorganisms called protozoa, such as *Pneumocystis jiroveci*.

Antiretroviral A substance that kills or suppresses a retrovirus, such as HIV.

Antiretroviral Drugs Substances used to kill or stop the multiplication of retroviruses such as HIV.

Antiretroviral Pregnancy Registry A project established to monitor prenatal exposures to antiretroviral (ARV) drugs and to detect any potential increase in the risk of related birth defects. Pregnant women exposed to ARV drugs voluntarily enroll in the Registry through their health care providers. Information provided to the Registry includes no identifying patient information.

Antiretroviral Therapy (ART) The daily use of a combination of HIV medicines (called an HIV regimen) to treat HIV infection. A person's initial HIV regimen generally includes three antiretroviral (ARV) drugs from at least two different HIV drug classes.

Antiretroviral Toxic Neuropathy Nerve damage that is due to antiretroviral (ARV) drugs.

Antisense Antiviral A drug made of short segments of DNA or RNA that can bind to and alter or suppress the function of viral DNA or RNA. Antisense antivirals prevent viruses from replicating.

Antiviral A substance or process that destroys a virus or suppresses its replication (i.e., reproduction).

Aphthous Ulcer A painful mouth or throat sore of unknown cause. Aphthous ulcers are common in persons living with HIV.

Apoptosis The deliberate, programmed death of a cell. Apoptosis is a normal biological process that helps the body stay healthy by eliminating old or damaged cells. One of the ways that HIV infection gradually destroys the immune system is by causing apoptosis of CD4 T lymphocytes (CD4 cells).

Approved Drug A drug approved by the Food and Drug Administration (FDA) for sale in the United States. The extensive FDA drug approval process includes many steps, including preclinical laboratory and animal studies, safety and efficacy clinical trials in humans, filing of a New Drug Application by the drug manufacturer, FDA review of the application, and FDA approval or rejection of the application.

APV Amprenavir.

ARC See AIDS-Related Complex (ARC).

Area Under the Curve (AUC) A measure of how much drug reaches a person's bloodstream in a given period of time after a dose is given. The information is useful for determining dosing and for identifying potential drug interactions.

Arm A group or subgroup of participants in a clinical trial that receives specific interventions, or no intervention, according to the study protocol.

Arrhythmia Any irregularity in rhythm or rate of the heartbeat.

ART Antiretroviral therapy.

Arthralgia A pain in a joint.

ARV See Antiretroviral.

Aspartate Aminotransferase (AST) An enzyme found especially in heart, muscle, and liver cells. Aspartate aminotransferase may be measured as part of a liver function test.

Aspergillosis A fungal infection—resulting from the fungus Aspergillus—of the lungs that can spread through the blood to other organs. Symptoms include fever, chills, difficulty in breathing, and coughing up blood.

Assay A qualitative or quantitative analysis of a substance; a test.

Assembly The sixth of seven steps in the HIV life cycle. During assembly, new HIV RNA and HIV proteins made by the host CD4 cell move to the surface of the cell and assemble into immature (noninfectious) HIV.

Asthenia Weakness; lack or loss of energy or strength.

Asymptomatic Without symptoms or not sick. Usually used in HIV/AIDS literature to describe a person who has a positive reaction to one of several tests for HIV antibodies but who shows no clinical symptoms of the disease and who is not sick. Even though a person is asymptomatic, he or she may still infect another person with HIV.

Asymptomatic HIV Infection Chronic HIV infection.

Ataxia Impaired coordination of voluntary muscle movements. Ataxia may be an adverse effect of drugs used to treat either HIV or opportunistic infections or may be caused by neurological conditions associated with HIV.

Atherosclerosis The gradual build-up of plaque inside of artery walls. (Plaque is made up of fat, cholesterol, calcium, and other substances found in blood.) Over time, the plaque hardens and narrows the arteries, decreasing the flow of oxygen-rich blood to organs and other parts of the body.

Attachment Binding.

Attenuated Weakened or decreased. For example, an attenuated virus can no longer produce disease but might be used to produce a vaccine.

Autoimmune Disorder A condition that occurs when the immune system mistakenly attacks and destroys healthy body tissue. Autoimmune disorders may be caused by drugs used to treat opportunistic infections.

Avascular Necrosis (AVN) Death of bone tissue (osteonecrosis) due to a lack of blood supply. Avascular necrosis (AVN) most commonly affects the hip. Symptoms include pain in the affected area of the body, limited range of motion, joint stiffness, muscle spasms, and limping. AVN is associated with several medical conditions, including cancer and HIV infection.

AZT See Zidovudine.

B Lymphocytes (B Cells) One of the two major classes of lymphocytes (white blood cells); they are involved in the production of antibodies.

Backbone The two nucleoside reverse transcriptase inhibitors (NRTIs) upon which an initial HIV regimen is built. To complete the HIV regimen, the two NRTIs are combined with a third antiretroviral HIV drug from either the non-nucleoside reverse transcriptase inhibitor (NNRTI), protease inhibitor (PI), or integrase strand transfer inhibitor (INSTI) drug class.

Bactericide A drug used to kill bacteria.

Bacteriostat A drug used to prevent the growth of bacteria. Bacteriostats do not kill bacteria.

Bacteriostatic Capable of slowing the growth of bacteria.

Bartonellosis A group of infections caused by the bacteria Examples of the various infections include cat scratch disease, trench fever, bacillary angiomatosis (BA), and bacillary peliosis hepatis. BA and bacillary peliosis hepatis occur only in people with weakened immune systems, such as people with HIV.

Bacterium A single-celled microorganism. Bacteria occur naturally almost everywhere on earth, including in humans, Some bacteria can cause disease in humans, People with weakened immune systems, including people with HIV, are at a higher risk for bacterial infections than people with healthy immune systems.

Bactrim Brand name of trimethoprim/sulphamethoxazole. See Trimethoprim/Sulphamethoxazole; Cotrimoxazole.

Baseline An initial measurement used as the basis for future comparison. For people infected with HIV, baseline testing includes CD4 count, viral load (HIV RNA), and resistance testing. Baseline test results are used to guide HIV treatment choices and monitor effectiveness of antiretroviral therapy (ART).

Basophil A type of white blood cell that helps the body fight infection by triggering an inflammatory response to an antigen.

B-Cell Lymphoma A type of lymphoma (cancer of the lymphatic system) that starts in the lymphocyte (B cells). People with weakened immune systems, including people with HIV, are at a higher risk for B-cell lymphomas than people with healthy immune systems. In people infected with HIV, certain B-cell lymphomas are considered AIDS-defining conditions.

BCG Bacille of Calmette and Guerin—a TB vaccine.

bDNA Test See Branched DNA Assay.

Best Practice See Standard of Care.

BID Twice each day.

Bilirubin A yellow pigment occurring in liver bile, blood, and urine. Its measurement can be used as an indication of the health of the liver. Bilirubin is the product of the breakdown of red blood cells. An elevated level of bilirubin in blood is an indication of liver disease or drug-induced liver impairment.

Binding The first of seven steps in the HIV life cycle. When HIV attacks a CD4 cell, the virus binds (attaches itself) to molecules on the surface of the CD4 cell: first a CD4 receptor and then either a CCR5 or CXCR4 coreceptor.

Bioavailability A measure of the rate and extent to which a drug is absorbed and becomes available at the site of drug action in the body.

Biopsy Surgical removal of a piece of tissue from a person for microscopic examination to make a diagnosis (e.g., to determine whether abnormal cells such as cancer cells are present).

Bisexual Having sexual relations with both females and males.

BIW Twice each week.

Black Box Warning See Boxed Warning.

Blinded Study A clinical research study in which participants are unaware as to whether they are receiving the experimental drug. See Double-Blind Study.

Blip A temporary, detectable increase in the amount of HIV in the blood (viral load) that occurs after antiretroviral therapy (ART) has effectively suppressed the virus to an undetectable level. Isolated blips are not considered a sign of virologic failure.

Blood-Brain Barrier A semi-permeable layer of tightly joined cells that separate the brain from circulating blood. The blood-brain barrier prevents potentially dangerous substances in the blood, such as disease-causing organisms or chemical compounds, from entering the brain tissue. Certain antiretroviral

(ARV) drugs can cross the blood-brain barrier and may help stop or slow HIV damage to the brain.

Blood Thinner Anticoagulant.

BMI Body mass index (kilogram/meter^2).

BMS See Breast Milk Substitute.

Body Fluids Any fluid in the human body, such as blood, urine, saliva (spit), sputum, tears, semen, mother's milk, or vaginal secretions. Only blood, semen, mother's milk, and vaginal secretions have been linked directly to the transmission of HIV.

Body Habitus Changes Noticeable physical changes in body shape or appearance. In people with HIV, these changes may be due to HIV infection, opportunistic infections, or antiretroviral (ARV) drugs.

Body Surface Area (BSA) A measure of the overall surface of a person calculated from height and weight. Body surface area is expressed in meters squared (m^2).

Bone Density Test Dual energy x-ray absorptiometry.

Bone Marrow The soft, sponge-like tissue in the center of bones. There are two types of bone marrow: yellow (made up of mostly fat cells) and red (the source of red blood cells, platelets, and most white blood cells).

Bone Marrow Suppression Myelosuppression.

Booster A second or later dose of a vaccine given to increase the immune response to the original dose.

Boosting Using an antiretroviral (ARV) drug (or other drug) to increase the *R* effectiveness of another ARV drug. For example, drugs in the protease *S* inhibitor ARV drug class (called PIs) are often boosted with the ARV drug ritonavir. Ritonavir interferes with the breakdown of the PI, which allows the PI to remain in the body longer at a higher concentration.

Boxed Warning The strongest form of warning required by the Food and Drug Administration (FDA) for prescription drug labeling. A boxed warning alerts health care providers and consumers to increased risk of serious adverse reactions associated with use of a drug or to restrictions on use of a drug. The boxed warning is presented in a box surrounded by a black border and is placed on the drug label and any package inserts or promotional materials intended for the prescriber or patient.

Brain Attack Stroke.

Branched DNA Assay (bDNA test) A test developed by Bayer for measuring the amount of HIV (as well as other viruses) in blood plasma. Test results are calibrated in numbers of virus particle equivalents per milliliter of plasma.

Breakthrough Infection An infection caused by the infectious agent the substance is designed to protect against. As it pertains to a vaccine trial, the infection may be caused by exposure to the infectious agent, such as HIV, before the vaccine has taken effect, before all doses of the vaccine have been given, or because the vaccine is not effective.

Breast Abscess This is a collection of pus in part of the breast. It results in painful swelling of the breast and usually requires a surgical incision for drainage.

Breast-Feeding Feeding a child breast milk (direct from the breast or expressed). Breast-feeding practices may be further described according to timing and frequency. See Exclusive Breast-Feeding.

Breast Milk Substitute Any food being marketed or otherwise presented as partial or total replacement for breast milk, whether or not suitable for that purpose. A breast milk substitute can be commercial infant formula or home-modified animal milk.

Bronchopneumonia Pneumonia.

Bronchoscopy Examination of the bronchial (lung) passages through the tube of an endoscope (usually a curved flexible tube containing fibers that carry light down the tube and project an enlarged image up the tube to the viewer) that is inserted into the upper lungs.

Bronchospasm Sudden, involuntary contraction of the muscles of the bronchii (airways in the lungs).

Budding The final step of seven steps in the HIV life cycle. During budding, immature (noninfectious) HIV pushes itself out of the host CD4 cell. (Noninfectious HIV can't infect another CD4 cell.) Once outside the CD4 cell, the new HIV releases protease, an HIV enzyme. Protease acts to break up the long protein chains that form the noninfectious virus. The smaller HIV proteins combine to form mature, infectious HIV.

Buffalo Hump Dorsocervical fat pad.

Burkitt Lymphoma A fast-growing type of B-cell non-Hodgkin's lymphoma (cancer of the lymphatic system). In people with HIV, Burkitt lymphoma is considered an AIDS-defining cancer.

C/S See Cesarean Section.

Cachexia General ill health and malnutrition, marked by weakness and emaciation, usually associated with serious disease. See AIDS Wasting Syndrome.

Campylobacteriosis An enteric (intestinal) infection. Symptoms of campylobacteriosis, if any, include diarrhea (often bloody), abdominal cramping and pain, nausea and vomiting, fever, and fatigue. Some people with campylobacteriosis may develop Guillain-Barré syndrome. Certain bacterial enteric infections, including campylobacteriosis, occur at a much higher rate in people with HIV than in the general population.

Candida Yeastlike fungi commonly found in the normal flora of the mouth, skin, intestinal tract, and vagina, which can become infectious in individuals with an abnormal immune system. See Candidiasis; Fungus; Thrush.

Candidiasis An infection with a yeastlike fungus of the Candida family, generally Candida albicans. Candidiasis of the esophagus, trachea, bronchi, or lungs is an indicator disease for AIDS. Oral or recurrent vaginal candida infection is an early sign of immune system abnormalities. See Opportunistic Infection; Thrush; Vaginal Candidiasis.

Capsid The bullet-shaped center of HIV. The HIV capsid contains the genetic information (two single strands of RNA) and three enzymes needed for HIV to replicate.

Carcinogen Any cancer-producing substance.

Cardiomyopathy Disease of the heart muscle. Cardiomyopathy weakens the heart muscle, making it hard for the heart to pump blood to the rest of the body. HIV infection or use of some antiretroviral (ARV) drugs may cause cardiomyopathy.

Cardiovascular Relating to or involving the heart and blood vessels. Use of some antiretroviral (ARV) drugs may increase the risk of cardiovascular disease.

Casual Contact Can be defined as normal day-to-day contact among people at home, school, work, or in the community. A contagious infectious agent (e.g., chicken pox, flu) can be transmitted by casual contact.

CBC See Complete Blood Count (CBC).

CCR5 A protein on the surface of certain immune system cells, including CD4 T lymphocytes (CD4 cells). CCR5 can act as a coreceptor (a second receptor binding site) for HIV when the virus enters a host cell.

CCR5 Antagonist Antiretroviral (ARV) HIV drug class. CCR5 antagonists block the CCR5 coreceptor on the surface of certain immune cells, such as CD4 T lymphocytes (CD4 cells). This prevents HIV from entering the cell.

CCR5 Inhibitor CCR5 Receptor Blocker.

CD4 (T4) or CD4+ Cells A type of lymphocyte involved in protecting against viral, fungal, and protozoal infections. They are also known as T helper cells. They are HIV's preferred targets for infection. Destruction of CD4+ lymphocytes is the major cause of the immunodeficiency observed in AIDS, and decreasing CD4+ lymphocyte levels appear to be the best indicator for developing opportunistic infections.

CD4 Count A test that measures the number of CD4 lymphocytes in the blood, thus reflecting the state of the immune system. A normal count in a healthy adult is 600-1,200 cells/µL. When the CD4 count of an adult falls below 200 cells/µL, there is a high risk of opportunistic infection.

CD4 Percentage Percentage of white blood cells that are CD4 T lymphocytes (CD4 cells). In certain cases, such as during acute HIV infection or HIV infection in children younger than 5 years of age, CD4 percentage is used rather than CD4 count to assess HIV progression or response to antiretroviral therapy (ART).

CD4 Receptor One of the protein structures on the surface of a human cell that allows HIV to attach, enter, and thus infect the cell. Present on CD4 cells (helper T lymphocytes) among others.

CD4 T Lymphocyte A type of lymphocyte. CD4 T lymphocytes (CD4 cells) help coordinate the immune response by stimulating other immune cells, such as macrophages, B lymphocytes (B cells), and CD8 T lymphocytes (CD8 cells), to fight infection. HIV weakens the Immune system by destroying CD4 cells.

CD8 (T8) Cells White blood cells (lymphocytes) with the CD8 protein on their surface. These white blood cells kill some cancer cells and cells infected by bacteria and viruses. Also called cytotoxic T cells, T8 cells, cytotoxic T lymphocytes.

CDC See Centers for Disease Control and Prevention (CDC).

Cell-Mediated Immunity (CMI) Part of the immune system that deals with viruses and other infectious agents as well as cancer cells.

Cellular Immunity See Cell-Mediated Immunity (CMI).

Centers for Disease Control and Prevention (CDC) The U.S. Department of Health and Human Services agency with the mission to promote health and quality of life by preventing and controlling disease, injury, and disability.

Centers for Medicare and Medicaid Services (CMS) A federal agency that administers the Medicare program and monitors the Medicaid programs offered by each state, including the Children's Health Insurance Program.

Central Nervous System (CNS) The central nervous system is composed of the brain, spinal cord, and meanings (protective membranes surrounding them). The central nervous system is often affected in advanced AIDS, causing dementia. See AIDS Dementia Complex (ADC).

Central Nervous System (CNS) Damage Blood monocytes and macrophages that are infected by HIV appear to be relatively resistant to killing. However, these cells travel throughout the body and carry HIV to various organs, especially the lungs and the brain. Persons living with HIV often experience abnormalities in the central nervous system such as dementia (deterioration in intellectual function and emotional disturbances). Investigators have hypothesized that an accumulation of HIV in brain and nerve cells or the inappropriate release of chemical or toxic byproducts of infected cells that reach the central nervous system may be to blame for the neurological manifestations of HIV disease.

Cerebrospinal Fluid (CSF) Fluid that bathes the brain and the spinal cord.

Cervical Cancer A cancer of the uterine cervix. See Cervical Dysplasia; Cervix; Pap Smear.

Cervical Dysplasia Abnormality in the size, shape, and organization of adult cells of the cervix. It is often found before cancer cells appear. A precursor lesion for cervical cancer. Studies indicate an increase of cervical dysplasia among women living with HIV.

Cervical Intraepithelial Neoplasia (CIN) An abnormality of the epithelium (lining) of the cervix, often precancerous. Considerable evidence implicates a virus called human papilloma virus (HPV) in the development of CIN.

Cervix The lower part of the uterus that extends into the lower vagina and contains a narrow canal connecting the upper and lower parts of a woman's reproductive tract.

Cesarean Section A delivery procedure for the baby that involves making a cut through the abdominal wall to remove the baby from the uterus.

Chagas Disease A disease caused by a parasite (a type of protozoa). Chagas disease is most commonly transmitted when people come into contact with the feces of an infected bug, a blood-sucking insect that feeds on humans and animals. In the earliest stage of infection, Chagas disease usually has few signs or symptoms. However, if untreated, the disease becomes a lifelong infection. In people with HIV, reactivation of chronic Chagas disease infection can cause inflammation of the brain and meninges (meningoencephalitis).

Chancroid A highly contagious sexually transmitted disease caused by the *Haemophilus ducreyi* bacterium with symptoms appearing 3 to 5 days after exposure.

Chemokine Receptor An alternate receptor used by HIV to infect cells.

Chemokines Chemokines are messenger molecules secreted by CD8 cells whose major function is to attract immune cells to sites of infection. Several chemokines—called RANTES, MIP-1A, and MIP-1B—interfere with HIV multiplication by occupying these receptors.

Chemoprevention Use of specific drugs, vitamins, or other substances to reverse, suppress, or prevent a disease.

Chemoprophylaxis Chemotherapy. Use of chemical-based agents, such as drugs, to treat or control a disease. Similar to HIV infection, chemotherapy may result in immunosuppression.

Chemotherapy In general, it is the use of medicines to treat any disease. It is more commonly used to describe medicines to treat cancer.

Child-Turcotte-Pugh Classification System A classification system used to measure liver function, especially in people with chronic liver disease. The system may be used to assess liver function in people who have HIV/hepatitis C virus (HCV) coinfection.

Chlamydia A sexually transmitted disease (STD) caused by *Chlamydia trachomatis* that infects the genital tract. The infection is frequently asymptomatic (i.e., shows no symptoms), but if left untreated, it can cause sterility in women.

Cholangiopathy Bile duct disease. (Bile ducts are tubes that carry bile from the gallbladder to the small intestine, where the bile is used to digest fats.) Cholangiopathy may occur as a complication of AIDS or may be caused by certain opportunistic infections.

Cholesterol A waxy, fat-like substance that is made by the liver or absorbed from animal food sources such as eggs, meat, and dairy products. The body uses cholesterol to insulate nerves, make cell tissues, and produce certain hormones. Excess cholesterol, however, can clog the arteries and lead to heart disease. Some antiretroviral (ARV) drugs may cause high cholesterol levels.

Chorioamnionitis An infection of the placental tissues and amniotic fluid occurring during pregnancy. Can cause blood infection in the mother and may lead to premature birth and serious infection in the newborn baby.

Chromosome A thread-like structure found within a cell. Chromosomes, which are made of DNA coiled around proteins, carry all of the genetic information essential to the life of the cell.

Chronic HIV Infection The stage of HIV infection between acute HIV infection and the onset of AIDS. During chronic HIV infection, HIV levels gradually increase and the number of CD4 cells decrease. Declining CD4 cell levels indicate increasing damage to the immune system. Antiretroviral therapy (ART) can prevent HIV from destroying the immune system and advancing to AIDS.

Chronic Inflammatory Demyelinating Polyneuropathy (CIDP) A rare neurological disorder in which the immune system mistakenly attacks part of the peripheral nervous system. Chronic inflammatory demyelinating polyneuropathy (CIDP) primarily destroys the myelin that covers the peripheral nerves, causing the nerve signals to slow down. This damage can gradually weaken the legs and, to a lesser extent, the arms. CIDP has been associated with HIV infection.

Circumoral Pertaining to the area of the face around the mouth.

Clade Also called a subtype. A clade is a group of related HIV viruses classified according to their degree of virus similarity. There are currently three groups of HIV-1 M, N, and O. Isolate M (major strains) consists of at least 10 clades, A through J. Group O (outer strains) may consist of a similar number of clades.

Class-Sparing Regimen An antiretroviral (ARV) drug regimen that purposefully excludes all ARV drugs from a specific drug class. Class-sparing regimens are used to save specific ARV drugs for future use in case a regimen needs to be changed because of toxicity or drug resistance. A class-sparing regimen may also be used to avoid adverse effects associated with a specific drug class.

Clastogenic Causing breaks in chromosomes, which results in sections of a chromosome being deleted or rearranged. Before being approved, drugs—including antiretroviral (ARV) drugs—are tested to assess their potential for clastogenic effects.

Clinical Pertaining to observations, tests, or treatment of patients.

Clinical Alert An early notice of urgent findings from federally funded clinical trials. Clinical alerts are disseminated in a variety of ways, including online, to advise health care professionals and others of research findings that could affect patient care.

Clinical Endpoint In a clinical trial, an outcome or event used to objectively measure the effect of a drug or other intervention being studied. Common endpoints include severe toxicity, disease progression, and death.

Clinical Failure A type of HIV treatment failure. The occurrence or recurrence of an HIV-related complication (excluding IRIS) after more than 3 months of antiretroviral therapy (ART) is considered clinical failure.

Clinical Latency The period of time a virus or bacteria or other organism is living or developing in the body without causing symptoms. The period of time in which a person with HIV infection does not exhibit any evidence of disease or sickness.

Clinical Progression Advance of disease that can be measured by observable and diagnosable signs or symptoms. For example, HIV progression can be measured by change in CD4 count.

Clinical Trial A scientifically designed study of the effects of a drug, vaccine, biologic, or behavior in humans. The goal is to define the safety, the benefit, and side effects of the drug. Most countries require strict testing of all new drugs and vaccines prior to their approval for use.

Cmax A pharmacokinetic measure used to determine drug dosing. Cmax is the highest concentration of a drug in the blood, cerebrospinal fluid, or target organ after a dose is given.

Cmin A pharmacokinetic measure used to determine drug dosing. Cmin is the lowest concentration of a drug in the blood, cerebrospinal fluid, or target organ after a dose is given.

CMV Retinitis See Cytomegalovirus (CMV) Retinitis.

CNS See Central Nervous System (CNS).

Coagulopathy A disease or condition that affects the blood's ability to coagulate (clot) normally.

Coccidioidomycosis An infectious fungal disease caused by the breathing in of *Coccidioides immitis*, which are carried on windblown dust particles.

Cognitive Impairment Loss of the ability to process, learn, and remember information.

Cohort A group of individuals with some characteristics in common.

Coinfection When a person has two or more infections at the same time, For example, a person infected with HIV may be coinfected with hepatitis C (HCV) or tuberculosis (TB) or both.

Colitis Inflammation of the colon, the lower part of the intestine.

Colostrum The first thick yellow milk secreted by a woman beginning lactation. Colostrum contains high levels of proteins and antibodies.

Combination Therapy Two or more drugs or treatments used together to obtain the best results against HIV infection and/or AIDS. Combination drug therapy (treatment) has proven more effective than monotherapy (single-drug therapy) in controlling the growth of the virus. An example of combination therapy would be the use of two drugs such as zidovudine and lamivudine together.

Combination Treatment See Combination Therapy.

Combined Antiretroviral Therapy Antiretroviral Therapy.

Comfort Care Palliative Care.

Commercial Sex Worker (CSW) A woman or man who offers sexual intercourse for a fee. The terms prostitute or prostitution are used more frequently outside the AIDS area.

Communicable Disease An infectious disease that is contagious and that can be transmitted from one source to another by infectious bacteria or viral organisms.

Community Planning Community planning groups are responsible for developing HIV prevention, treatment, and care plans that are used in their communities. The goal of HIV community planning is to improve the effectiveness of HIV programs and to be certain that the needs of the community are being met.

Community-Based Organization (CBO) A service organization that provides social, support, education, and care services at the local level.

Community Programs for Clinical Research on AIDS (CPCRA) A federally sponsored program that conducts HIV-related clinical research through a national network of community-based research units. A primary objective of Community Programs for Clinical Research on AIDS (CPCRA) is to involve community-based primary care providers and their patients in HIV/AIDS research.

Comorbid Condition When a person has two or more diseases or conditions at the same time. For example, a person with high blood pressure may also have heart disease.

Compassionate Use Complementary and Alternative Medicine (CAM) Health care practices and products that are not considered part of conventional (Western) medicine. Complementary medicine refers to use of nonstandard treatments together with conventional treatments. Alternative medicine refers to use of nonstandard treatments in place of conventional treatments. Examples of complementary and alternative medicine (CAM) include use of herbal medicines, acupuncture, and massage therapy.

Complementary and Alternative Therapy Broad range of healing approaches and treatments that Western (conventional) medicine does not commonly use to improve health conditions. Examples include acupuncture, herbs, etc. See Alternative Medicine.

Complementary Feeding Any food, whether manufactured or locally prepared, suitable as a complement to breast milk or to infant formula, when either become insufficient to satisfy the nutritional requirements of the infant. Such food is commonly called "weaning food" or "breast milk supplement."

Complete Blood Count (CBC) A frequently ordered blood test that provides the white count, red blood cell count, hematocrit, and hemoglobulin in a microliter of whole blood. The CBC is used to assess overall health and to diagnose and guide treatment of numerous diseases.

Comprehensive Metabolic Panel (CMP) A blood test that measures several parameters, including blood sugar (glucose), proteins, electrolytes (such as sodium and potassium), waste products (such as blood urea nitrogen [BUN] and creatinine), and enzymes. The comprehensive metabolic panel is used to assess overall health and to diagnose and guide treatment of numerous diseases.

Computed Tomography Scan See C-T Scan (Computed Tomography Scan).

Concomitant Drugs Drugs that are taken together. Certain concomitant medications may have adverse interactions.

Concordant Couple A couple in which both partners are infected with the same sexually transmitted infection (STI), for example, HIV.

Condyloma A wartlike skin growth usually on the external genitalia or perianal area.

Condyloma Acuminatum A wart in the genital and perianal area. Although the lesions are usually few in number, they may aggregate to form large cauliflower-like masses. Caused by the human papilloma virus (HPV), it is infectious and capable of being transmitted from one part of the body to another. Also called genital warts, venereal warts, or verruca acuminata.

Confidential HIV Test Performing an HIV test and being certain that the result remains confidential. See Confidentiality.

Confidentiality Relating to a piece of information about a person that should not be given to another person without that person's permission. An example would be the result, whether positive or negative, of an HIV test.

Confirmatory Test Because the diagnosis of HIV infection is so important, a second test, to show that the first test was correct, is recommended. A confirmatory test for an ELISA test is usually the Western blot. A confirmatory test could also be another HIV test such as a rapid test or a DNA or RNA PCR test.

Confirmed Positive For HIV, a blood sample that is positive on an initial ELISA test, repeatedly positive on a second ELISA run on the same specimen, or confirmed positive on Western blot or other supplemental test indicates that the client is infected.

Contagious Any infectious disease capable of being transmitted by direct or indirect contact from one person to another.

Contagious Disease A very communicable disease that can spread rapidly from person to person through direct contact (touching an infected person), indirect contact (touching a contaminated object), or droplet contact (inhaling droplets made when an infected person coughs, sneezes, or talks).

Contraindication Any condition that renders a particular line of treatment improper or undesirable. Some drugs may be contraindicated when given together (e.g., zidovudine and lamivudine).

Control Arm In a clinical trial, the group of participants that is not given the experimental intervention being studied. The control arm can receive an intervention that is considered effective (the standard), a placebo, or no intervention. Outcomes in the control arm are compared with those in the experimental arm to determine any differences, for example, in safety and effectiveness.

Controlled Clinical Trials Performing a study in humans in which a control is used. A control is a standard against which study observations may be evaluated. For example, in clinical trials, one group of patients is given an experimental drug, while another group (i.e., the control group) is given either the normal treatment for the disease or a placebo.

Cord Traction A maneuver in which the umbilical cord is pulled gently with one hand while the other hand pushes the uterus up from the pubis. This is done to prevent uterine inversion.

Coreceptor A protein on the surface of a cell that serves as a second binding site for a virus or other molecule. In order to enter a host cell, HIV must bind to two sites on the cell: the primary CD4 receptor and either the CCR5 or CXCR4 coreceptor.

Cotrimoxazole Also known as trimethoprim/sulphamethoxazole, Bactrim, or Septra. A combination antibiotic drug effective at preventing and treating *Pneumocystis jiroveci* pneumonia (PCP); also serves as a prophylaxis against toxoplasmosis. The drug is also active against certain bacterial infections. See Trimethoprim/Sulphamethoxazole.

Counseling Confidential dialogue between individuals and their health care providers. The term can refer to discussions between health care workers and clients/patients specific to HIV testing to help clients examine their risk of acquiring or transmitting HIV infection.

Creatinine A protein found in muscles and blood, and excreted by the kidneys in the urine. The level of creatinine in the blood or urine provides a measure of kidney function.

Cross-Resistance The process in which an infectious agent that acquires resistance to one drug through direct exposure also turns out to have resistance to one or more other drugs to which it has not been exposed.

Cross Sensitivity A sensitivity reaction to a drug that predisposes a person to react similarly to a different, but related, drug, For example, a person who has an allergic reaction to penicillin may also have an allergic reaction to amoxicillin, a related antibiotic.

Cryotherapy A minimally invasive treatment in which liquid nitrogen or argon gas is used to freeze and destroy tissue. Cryotherapy is used to remove warts and precancerous skin lesions.

Crypto Cryptosporidiosis.

Cryptococcal Meningitis A life-threatening infection of the membranes surrounding the brain and the spinal cord caused by the fungus Cryptococcus neoformans. Symptoms include headache, dizziness, stiff neck, and, if untreated, coma and death. See Cryptococcus Neoformans.

Cryptococcosis An infectious disease due to the fungus Cryptococcus neoformans, which is acquired via the respiratory tract. It can spread from the lungs to the central nervous system (especially the membranes surrounding the brain), the skin, the skeletal system, and the urinary tract. It is considered an AIDS-defining opportunistic infection in persons infected with HIV. See Cryptococcal Meningitis.

Cryptococcus Neoformans A fungus found in soil contaminated by bird droppings. Most people have been exposed to this organism, which does not usually cause disease in healthy people. In persons with AIDS, this organism can cause illness and death.

Cryptosporidiosis A diarrheal disease caused by the protozoa *Cryptosporidium* that grows in the intestines. Symptoms include abdominal cramps and severe chronic diarrhea. It is considered an AIDS-defining opportunistic infection in persons with HIV infection as immunological deterioration progresses.

Cryptosporidium The protozoan (parasite *Cryptosporidium parvum*), which causes cryptosporidiosis. The parasite is found in the intestines of animals and may be transmitted to humans by direct contact with an infected animal, by eating contaminated food, or by drinking contaminated water. The parasite grows in the intestines and in people with HIV disease causes cryptosporidiosis. See Cryptosporidiosis.

Crystalluria Crystals in the urine. (Crystals are tiny stones composed of chemicals such as calcium.) Use of antiretroviral (ARV) drugs may cause crystalluria.

CSF See Cerebrospinal Fluid (CSF).

C-T Scan (Computed Tomography Scan) An x-ray in which a three-dimensional image of a body structure is constructed by computer from a series of images. See Magnetic Resonance Imaging (MRI).

CTL See Cytotoxic T Lymphocyte (CTL).

CTX See Cotrimoxazole.

Cutaneous Of, pertaining to, or affecting the skin.

CXCR4 A protein on the surface of certain immune system cells, including CD4 T lymphocytes (CD4 cells). CXCR4 can act as a coreceptor (a second receptor binding site) for HIV when the virus enters a host cell.

CYP3A4 An enzyme that plays a key role in the metabolism of approximately half the drugs in use today. CYP3A4 is a member of the cytochrome P450 family of enzymes.

Cystoisosporiasis An intestinal infection caused by the protozoan parasite (formerly called Isosporiasis) that can be spread by ingesting food or water contaminated with the parasite. Symptoms of Isosporiasis include watery diarrhea, abdominal pain, anorexia, and low-grade fever. In people with HIV, chronic Isosporiasis (lasting over 1 month) is an AIDS-defining condition.

Cytochrome P450 (CYP450) A group of enzymes involved in the breakdown of drugs in the liver. Many drugs can inhibit or enhance the activity of these enzymes, causing drug levels in the blood to increase or decrease. Cytochrome P450 (CYP450) enzymes metabolize all protease inhibitors (Pis) and nonnucleoside reverse transcriptase inhibitors (NNRTIs) and can cause drug interactions that may result in adverse effects.

Cytokine A family of proteins produced by cells, especially by immune cells. Cytokines act as chemical messengers between cells to regulate immune responses.

Cytomegalovirus (CMV) A common herpes virus that is a common cause of opportunistic diseases in persons with AIDS and other persons with immune suppression. CMV has infected most adults; however the virus does not cause disease in healthy people. Because the virus remains in the body for life, it can cause disease if the immune system becomes severely damaged by drugs. While CMV can infect most organs of the body, persons with AIDS are most susceptible to CMV retinitis (disease of the eye) and colitis (disease of the colon). See Cytomegalovirus (CMV) Retinitis.

Cytomegalovirus (CMV) Retinitis An eye disease caused by the CMV virus, common among persons who are living with HIV. Without treatment, persons with CMV retinitis can lose their vision. CMV infection can affect both eyes and is the most common cause of blindness among persons with AIDS.

Cytopenia Deficiency in the cellular elements of the blood.

Cytotoxic An agent or process that is toxic or destructive to cells.

Cytotoxic T Lymphocyte (CTL) A lymphocyte (white blood cell) that is able to kill foreign cells marked for destruction by the cellular immune system. CTLs can destroy cancer cells and cells infected with viruses, fungi, or certain bacteria. CTLs are also known as killer T cells; they carry the CD8 marker.

D4T Stavudine, an antiretroviral drug belonging to the reverse transcriptase class that inhibits HIV growth.

Data and Safety Monitoring Board (DSMB) A committee of clinical research experts, such as physicians and statisticians, and patient advocates who monitor the progress of a clinical trial and review safety and effectiveness data while the trial is ongoing. This committee is independent of the people, organizations, and institutions conducting the clinical trial. Data and safety monitoring boards can recommend that a trial be stopped early because of concerns about participant safety or because the main research question has been answered.

DDC Zalcitabine, a reverse transcriptase inhibitor.

DDI Didanosine stavudine, an antiretroviral drug belonging to the reverse transcriptase class that inhibits HIV growth.

Dementia Chronic impairment of thinking (i.e., loss of mental capacity) that affects a person's ability to function in a social or occupational setting. See AIDS Dementia Complex (ADC).

Demyelination Destruction, removal, or loss of the myelin sheath of a nerve or nerves.

Dendritic Cells Immune system cells that may initiate HIV infection by carrying the virus from the site of the infection to the lymph nodes, where other cells, such as CD4 T-cells, become infected. Dendritic cells circulate through the body and bind to infectious agents in tissues, such as the skin and membranes lining the intestinal tract, lungs, and reproductive tract. Once in contact with CD4 T-cells they initiate an immune response to the virus.

Dendritic Cell Vaccine An experimental vaccine that uses dendritic cells to boost the immune system. Dendritic cell vaccines are currently being studied as a possible way to treat people with HIV.

Deoxyribonucleic Acid (DNA) The twisted double-stranded molecular chain found in genes within the nucleus of each cell. DNA carries the genetic information that enables cells to reproduce and transmit hereditary characteristics.

Department of Health and Human Services (HHS) The primary federal agency for protecting the health of all Americans and providing essential human services. The Department of Health and Human Services (HHS) works closely with state and local governments, and many HHS-funded services are provided at the local level by state or county agencies, or through private sector grantees. The agency's 11 operating divisions, including the Centers for Disease Control and Prevention (CDC), the Food and Drug Administration (FDA), and the National Institutes of Health (NIH), collectively administer more than 300 HHS programs.

Depression A mood disorder characterized by sadness, inactivity, and inability to take pleasure or interest in usual activities. The changes in mood can interfere with daily life and normal functioning. Use of some antiretroviral (ARV) drugs may cause depression.

Desensitization Gradually increasing the dose of a medicine in order to overcome severe reactions.

Diabetes Mellitus (DM) A disorder of carbohydrate (sugar) metabolism characterized by elevated blood glucose (blood sugar) levels and glucose in the urine resulting from inadequate production or use of insulin (e.g., hyperglycemia).

Diagnosis The decision that a patient has a specific disease or infection, usually accomplished by evaluating clinical symptoms and laboratory tests.

Diarrhea Uncontrolled, loose, and frequent bowel movements caused by diet, infection, medication, and irritation or inflammation of the intestine. Severe or prolonged diarrhea can lead to weight loss and malnutrition. The excessive loss of fluid that may occur with AIDS-related diarrhea can be life threatening. There are many possible causes of diarrhea in persons who have AIDS. The most common infectious organisms causing AIDS-related diarrhea include Cytomegalovirus (CMV), the parasites *Cryptosporidium*, *Microsporidia*, and *Giardia lamblia*, and the bacteria *Mycobacterium* *avium* and *Mycobacterium intracellulare*. Other bacteria and parasites that cause diarrheal symptoms in otherwise healthy people may cause more severe, prolonged, or recurrent diarrhea in persons with HIV or AIDS.

Diplopia Double vision.

Directly Observed Therapy (DOT) A method of drug administration in which a health care professional watches as a person takes each dose of a medication. Directly observed therapy (DOT) is used to ensure the person receives and takes all medications as prescribed and to monitor response to treatment. DOT is widely used to manage tuberculosis (TB) disease. In HIV treatment, DOT is sometimes called directly administered antiretroviral therapy (DAART).

Discordant Couple A couple in which one partner is infected with a sexually transmitted infection (STI), for example HIV, and the other partner is **not** infected with the same STI.

Disseminated Spread of a disease throughout the body.

Distal Sensory Polyneuropathy (DSP) A type of peripheral neuropathy seen in people infected with HIV. Symptoms of distal sensory polyneuropathy (DSP) include tingling, numbness, or burning pain that normally begins in the legs and feet and may spread to the hands. There are two types of DSP: HIV-DSP, which is due to HIV infection itself, and antiretroviral (ARV)-DSP, which is caused by certain ARV drugs.

Division of Acquired Immunodeficiency Syndrome (DAIDS) A division of the National Institute of Allergy and Infectious Diseases (NIAID) that develops and supports global research to prevent and treat HIV/AIDS, its related coinfections, and co-morbidities.

DLV Delavirdine, a drug in the non-nucleoside reverse transcriptase inhibitor class.

D-M/Tropic Virus HIV that includes a combination of CCR5-tropic virus and CXCR4-tropic virus (mixed-tropic virus) and/or virus that uses either the CCR5 or the CXCR4 coreceptor (dual-tropic virus).

DNA See Deoxyribonucleic Acid (DNA).

Dormant Inactive infection that is still present in the body.

Dorsocervical Fat Pad An accumulation of fat on the back of the neck between the shoulders. A dorsocervical fat pad may be due to use of some antiretroviral (ARV) drugs.

DOT (S) Directly observed therapy (short course). Treatment that is given under the observation of a health care worker.

Double-Blind Study A clinical trial design in which neither the patient nor the study staff know which patients are receiving the experimental drug and which are receiving a placebo (or another therapy).

Drug Antagonism An interaction between two or more drugs that have opposite effects on the body. Drug antagonism may block or reduce the effectiveness of one or more of the drugs.

Drug Class A group of drugs that share common properties, including a similar mechanism of action, chemical structure, or approved use. Antiretroviral (ARV) HIV drugs are classified into six drug classes based on how each drug interferes with the HIV life cycle. These six classes include the nucleoside reverse transcriptase inhibitors (NRTIs), non-nucleoside reverse transcriptase inhibitors (NNRTIs), protease inhibitors (Pis), fusion and entry inhibitors, pharmacokinetic enhancers, and integrase strand transfer inhibitors (INSTIs).

Drug Concentration The amount of a drug in a given volume of blood plasma, measured as the number of micrograms per milliliter.

Drug-Food Interaction A change in a drug's effect on the body when the drug is taken together with certain foods (or beverages). Not all drugs are affected by food, and some drugs are affected by only certain foods. A drug-food interaction can delay, decrease, or enhance absorption of a drug. This can decrease or increase the action of the drug or cause adverse effects.

Drug Interaction A reaction between two (or more) drugs or between a drug and a food or supplement. An existing medical condition can also cause a drug interaction. A drug interaction can decrease or increase the action of the drug(s) or cause adverse effects.

Drug Resistance The ability of some disease-causing infectious agents, such as bacteria and viruses, to adapt themselves, grow, and multiply even in the presence of drugs that usually kill them. See Cross-Resistance.

Drug-Susceptible When a strain of HIV is sensitive to one or more antiretroviral (ARV) drugs, Antiretroviral therapy (ART) will likely be effective against a drug-susceptible strain of HIV.

Drug Synergism An interaction between two or more drugs that causes the total effect of the drugs to be greater than the sum of the individual effects of each drug. A synergistic effect can be beneficial or harmful.

Dual Energy X-Ray Absorptiometry (DXA) A test that uses low-dose x-rays to measure bone mineral density, including calcium content, in a section of bone. Dual energy x-ray absorptiometry (DXA) scans are used to detect osteoporosis and predict the risk of bone fracture.

Dual/Mixed Tropic Virus HIV that includes a combination of CCR5-tropic virus and CXCR4-tropic virus (mixed-tropic virus) and/or virus that uses either the CCR5 or the CXCR4 coreceptor (dual-tropic virus). To enter a host CD4 cell, HIV must first attach to a CD4 receptor, then attach to either a CCR5 or CXCR4 coreceptor, and finally fuse its membrane with the CD4 cell membrane.

Dyslipidemia Abnormal levels of lipids (fats), including cholesterol and triglycerides, in the blood. Dyslipidemia can refer to either decreased or elevated levels of lipids. Dyslipidemia may be an adverse effect of some antiretroviral (ARV) drugs.

Dysplasia Any abnormal development of tissues or organs.

Dyspnea Difficult or labored breathing.

EBM Expressed breast milk.

Ecchymosis A blue or purplish bruise that results from bleeding under the skin.

EDD Expected date of delivery.

Edema Abnormal swelling caused by excess accumulation of fluid in tissues or body cavities.

Efficacy The maximum ability of a drug or treatment to produce a result regardless of the drug dose.

EFV Efavirenz.

EFZ Efavirenz.

EGPAF Elizabeth Glaser Pediatric AIDS Foundation.

EIA Enzyme-linked immunosorbent assay.

Eligibility Criteria Factors used to determine whether a person is eligible (inclusion criteria) or not eligible (exclusion criteria) to participate in a clinical trial, Eligibility criteria may include disease type and stage, other medical conditions, previous treatment history, age, and gender.

ELISA (Enzyme-linked immunosorbent assay) A type of enzyme immunoassay to determine the presence of antibodies to HIV in the blood or oral fluids. Repeatedly (i.e., two or more) reactive ELISA test results should be confirmed with a second test such as the Western blot test, a rapid HIV test, or a DNA or RNA PCR. Availability of the confirmatory test often determines which one is performed.

Elite Controllers A very small subset of people infected with HIV who are able to maintain suppressed viral loads for years without antiretroviral therapy (ART). However, because HIV continues to replicate even in elite controllers, ART is recommended for those rare controllers who have declining CD4 counts or who develop HIV-related complications.

Encephalitis A brain inflammation of viral or other infectious disease origin. Symptoms include headaches, neck pain, fever, nausea, vomiting, and nervous system problems. Several types of opportunistic infections can cause encephalitis.

Encephalopathy Any degenerative disease of the brain.

Endemic Pertaining to diseases associated with particular locations or population groups.

Endogenous Relating to or produced by the body.

Endoscopy Viewing the inside of a body cavity (e.g., colon or throat) with an endoscope, a device using flexible fiber optics.

Endotoxin A toxin present inside a bacterial cell.

Endpoint A category of data used to compare the outcome of a clinical trial. Common endpoints are severe toxicity, disease progression, or death.

End-Stage Disease Final period or phase in the course of a disease leading to a person's death.

Enfuvirtide (T-20) A fusion inhibitor drug that inhibits HIV by interfering with the binding of the virus to CD4 cell receptors.

Engorgement/Engorged Breasts Breasts that are overly full, partly with milk and partly with increased tissue fluid and blood. As a result, milk flow is inhibited. Engorged breasts are often painful, shiny, and diffusely red. Nipples may be stretched tight and flat. The condition may be accompanied by fever lasting 24 hours or less.

Enteric Pertaining to the intestines.

Enteric-Coated (EC) When a tablet or capsule is coated with a substance that prevents the medication from being released until it reaches the small intestine, where it can then be absorbed.

Enteritis Inflammation of the intestine.

Entry Inhibitors Compounds designed to prevent the interactions between the HIV virus and the cell surface. These compounds can block or prevent HIV binding to human cell surface receptors.

Enzyme A molecule, usually a protein, that catalyzes (increases the rate of) chemical reactions in the body, enzymes are essential to all body functions. HIV requires specific enzymes, such as reverse transcriptase or integrase, to replicate.

Eosinophil A type of white blood cell, called granulocyte, that can digest infectious agents.

Eosinophilia The formation and accumulation of an abnormally large number of eosinophils in the blood. Eosinophils are a type of white blood cell that helps to destroy infectious agents. Increased numbers are seen in allergy and parasitic infection.

Epidemic A disease that spreads rapidly through a part of the human population—such as everyone in a given geographic area, a military base, school, or village—or everyone of a certain age or sex, such as the children or women of a region. Epidemic diseases can be spread from person to person or from a contaminated source such as food or water.

Epidemiologic Surveillance The ongoing organizing and collection, analysis, and interpretation of facts about a disease or health condition.

Epidemiology The branch of medical science that deals with the study and distribution and control of a disease in a population.

Episiotomy A surgical incision into the perineum and vagina at the time of delivery to prevent traumatic tearing during delivery.

Epithelium The covering of the internal and external organs of the body. Also the lining of blood vessels, body cavities, glands, and organs.

Epstein-Barr Virus (EBV) A herpes like virus that causes one of the two kinds of mononucleosis (the other is caused by CMV). It infects the nose and throat and is contagious. It has been associated with Burkitt lymphoma and hairy leukoplakia.

Eradication The total elimination of a pathogen, such as a bacterium, from the body. Eradication can also refer to the complete elimination of a disease from the world, such as the global eradication of smallpox.

Erythema Redness or inflammation of the skin or mucous membranes.

Erythema Multiforme A type of hypersensitivity reaction (rash) that occurs in response to drugs, infections, or illness. The exact cause is unknown. A severe form of this condition is called Stevens-Johnson syndrome.

Erythrocyte Sedimentation Rate (ESR) A test that measures the rate at which red blood cells settle through a column of liquid. This test is used to detect and monitor inflammation in the body.

Erythrocytes Red blood cells whose major function is to carry oxygen to cells.

ESR See Erythrocyte Sedimentation Rate (ESR).

Etiology The study or theory of the factors that cause disease.

Evaluation The study of a patient to determine the cause and effect of an illness, the study of a set of facts to determine what the facts mean, or the study of a program to determine its effectiveness.

Exclusion/Inclusion Criteria The medical determining of whether a patient may or may not be allowed to participate in a clinical trial. For example, some trials may not include persons with chronic liver disease, or may exclude persons with certain drug allergies.

Exclusive Breast-Feeding Feeding an infant only breast milk from his/her mother or a wet nurse, or expressed breast milk and no other liquids or solids with the exception of drops or syrups consisting of vitamins, mineral supplements, or medicines.

Exogenous Developed or originating outside the body.

Exotoxin A toxic substance made by bacteria released outside the bacterial cell that causes illness in a patient.

Expanded Access Legal use of an investigational drug outside of a clinical trial to treat a person who has a serious or immediately life-threatening disease and who has no approved treatment options. The Food and Drug Administration (FDA) regulates expanded access to investigational drugs on a case-by-case basis for an individual patient or groups of patients who do not meet criteria to participate in a clinical trial. Drug companies must have permission from the FDA to make an investigational drug available for expanded access.

Experimental Drug A drug that is not approved or licensed for use in humans.

Extensively Drug Resistant Tuberculosis (XDR-TB) A relatively rare type of multiple-drug-resistant tuberculosis (MDR-TB). Extensively drug-resistant tuberculosis (XDR-TB) occurs when a strain becomes resistant to drugs used to treat TB, including the two most effective first-line antibiotics (isoniazid and rifampin) and most of the second-line drugs. XDR-TB progresses more rapidly and is more severe in people coinfected with HIV than in people infected with XDR-TB alone.

Failure to Thrive (FTT) Weight loss or gradual but steady deterioration in weight gain as compared with the expected growth, as indicated in a child's growth chart.

False Negative A test result that is not correct. This may be a result of performing the test incorrectly or using a test that is not accurate. A false negative test in HIV would be a test that is negative in a person who is actually infected.

False Positive A test result that is not correct. This may be a result of performing the test incorrectly or using a test that is not accurate. A false positive test in HIV would be a test that is positive in a person who is not infected. For this reason, a second confirmatory test is recommended when a person tests HIV positive.

Fanconi Syndrome A hereditary or acquired kidney disorder that impairs the reabsorption of electrolytes, glucose, amino acids, and other nutrients into the bloodstream when blood passes through the kidneys. Acquired Fanconi syndrome may be caused by use of certain antiretroviral (ARV) drugs.

Fat Redistribution Also called body fat redistribution syndrome (BFR). Changes in body fat distribution, sometimes referred to as "lipodystrophy syndrome" or "fat redistribution syndrome," have been observed in patients taking protease inhibitors. Changes may include abdominal fat accumulation ("protease paunch"), fat accumulation over the back of the neck ("buffalo hump"), wasting of legs and arms with prominence of the veins, facial thinning, and breast enlargement.

FHI Family Health International.

First-Line Therapy A treatment that is accepted as best for the initial treatment of a condition or disease. The recommended first-line HIV treatment regimens include antiretroviral (ARV) drugs that are safe, effective, and convenient for most people with HIV who have never taken ARVs before.

Fixed-Dose Combination of one or more drugs contained in a single dosage form, such as a capsule or tablet. An example of a fixed-dose combination HIV drug is Atripla (a combination of efavirenz, emtricitabine, and tenofovir). By reducing the number of pills a person must take each day, fixed-dose combination drugs can help improve adherence to an HIV treatment regimen.

Food and Drug Administration (FDA) The U.S. Department of Health and Human Services agency responsible for ensuring the safety and effectiveness of all drugs, biologics, vaccines, and medical devices, including those used in the diagnosis, treatment, and prevention of HIV infection, AIDS, and AIDS-related opportunistic infections.

FP Family planning.

Fungus One of a group of primitive, nonvascular organisms including mushrooms, yeasts, rusts, and molds.

Fusion The second of seven steps in the HIV life cycle. After HIV attaches itself to a host CD4 cell, the HIV viral envelope fuses with the CD4 cell membrane. Fusion allows HIV to enter the CD4 cell. Once inside the CD4 cell, the virus releases HIV RNA and HIV enzymes, such as reverse transcriptase and integrase.

Fusion Inhibitor A class of antiretroviral agents that binds to the envelope protein and blocks the structural changes necessary for the virus to fuse with the host CD4 cell. A recently approved drug in this class is enfuvirtide (T-20).

Gamma Interferon A T-cell-derived stimulating substance that suppresses virus reproduction, stimulates other T cells, and activates macrophage cells.

Gamma Globulin One of the proteins in blood serum that contains antibodies obtained from pooled human plasma. See Globulins; Immunoglobulin G (IgG).

Gamma-Glutamyl Transpeptidase (GGT) An enzyme found in many organs in the body, including the liver. Gamma-glutamyl transpeptidase may be measured as part of a liver function test.

Gastrointestinal (GI) Relating to the stomach and intestines.

Gay Having sexual relations with an individual of the same sex. Usually refers to male-male relations. The term lesbian is most often used for female-female sexual relationships.

Gene The basic physical unit of inheritance. A gene is a short segment of DNA (or in the case of some viruses, RNA) that contains instructions for making proteins.

Gene Therapy Manipulating genes to treat or prevent disease. Gene therapy techniques being researched include replacing a defective gene with a healthy copy of the gene, repairing an abnormal gene, inactivating an improperly functioning gene, and introducing a new disease-fighting gene.

Generic Drug A drug that has the same active ingredients, dosage, formulation, safety, strength, route of administration, quality, effectiveness, and intended use as a brand-name drug. For example, ibuprofen is a generic drug that has several manufacturers and brand names, including Advil and Motrin. Generic drugs are usually less expensive than brand-name drugs.

Genetic Engineering Using biotechnological techniques to modify an organism by changing its genetic material (DNA or RNA). For example, bacteria can be genetically engineered to produce insulin, which can then be used to treat diabetes.

Genital Ulcer Disease Ulcerative lesions on the genitals usually caused by a sexually transmitted disease such as herpes, syphilis, or chancroid. The presence of genital ulcers may increase the risk of transmitting HIV.

Genital Warts See Condyloma.

Genitals The area of the sexual organs. In the male, the penis and scrotum. In the female, the vulva and vagina.

Genitourinary Tract The organs concerned with the production and excretion of urine and those concerned with reproduction. Also called genitourinary system, urogenital system, or urogenital tract.

Genome The complete genetic material of an organism, including all of its genes. The genome is contained in a set of chromosomes in humans, a single chromosome in bacteria, and a DNA or RNA molecule in viruses, The HIV genome consists of an RNA molecule and includes nine genes.

Genotype The genetic makeup of an individual organism such as HIV. In reference to HIV, genotypic resistance testing determines whether the HIV genetic structure contains certain mutations that make it resistant to a drug. Contrast with Phenotype.

Genotypic Antiretroviral Resistance Test (GART) A type of resistance test that detects drug-resistant mutations in HIV genes, Resistance testing is used to guide selection of an HIV regimen when initiating or changing antiretroviral therapy (ART).

Gestation Pregnancy.

Giardiasis A common protozoal infection of the small intestine, spread via contaminated food and water and direct person-to-person contact.

Globulins Simple proteins found in the blood serum containing various substances that function in the immune system function. See Immunoglobulin (Ig).

Gonorrhea An infection caused by Neisseria gonorrhoeae. Although gonorrhea is considered primarily a sexually transmitted disease, it can also be transmitted to newborns during the birth process.

gp120 A glycoprotein on the HIV envelope. gp120 binds to a CD4 receptor on a host cell, such as a CD4 T lymphocyte (CD4 cell). This starts the process by which HIV fuses its viral membrane with the host cell membrane and enters the host cell.

Granulocyte A type of white blood cell filled with granules of compounds that digest infectious agents. Granulocytes are part of the innate immune system and have broad-based activity.

Granulocyte Colony-Stimulating Factor (G-CSF) A substance (cytokine) that stimulates the growth of granulocytes, a type of white blood cell. G-CSF improves the neutropenia that is a side effect of certain drugs and infections.

Granulocyte Macrophage Colony-Stimulating Factor (GM-CSF) A substance secreted by cells (cytokine) that stimulates the growth of granulocytes and macrophages. Like the granulocyte colony-stimulating factor (G-CSF), it improves neutropenia.

Granulocytopenia A lack or low level of granulocytes in the blood. Often used interchangeably with neutropenia.

Guillain-Barré Syndrome (GBS) A rare acute neurological disorder in which the immune system mistakenly attacks part of the peripheral nervous system. Guillain-Barré syndrome (GBS) primarily destroys the myelin that covers the peripheral nerves, causing the nerve signals to slow down. This damage can result in weakness and sometimes paralysis of the legs, arms, face, and breathing muscles. GBS is often preceded by a bacterial or viral infection and can occur early in the course of HIV infection.

Gynecomastia Development of larger-than-normal breasts in males. Gynecomastia is due to excess growth of breast tissue, not fat tissue. Gynecomastia is sometimes caused by natural hormonal changes, but it can also be due to use of certain medications, including antiretroviral (ARV) drugs.

HAART See Highly Active Antiretroviral Therapy (HAART).

Hairy Leukoplakia See Oral Hairy Leukoplakia (OHL).

Half-Life The time it takes a drug to lose half its original concentration or activity after being introduced into the body. Drug half-life is considered when determining drug dosing.

Harm Reduction A prevention activity that aims to provide services to HIV-infected persons and their sex and needle-sharing partners so they can reduce their risk for infection or, if already infected, prevent transmission of HIV to others. It also seeks to help partners gain earlier access to individualized counseling, HIV testing, medical evaluation, treatment, and other prevention and support services.

HCW Healthcare worker.

Health Resources and Services Administration (HRSA) The primary federal agency for improving access to health care services for people who are uninsured, isolated, or medically vulnerable. Through its HIV/AIDS bureau, the Health Resources and Services Administration (HRSA) administers the Ryan White HIV/AIDS Program, the largest federal program focused exclusively on HIV/AIDS care.

HELLP Syndrome A rare but life-threatening complication of pregnancy that is characterized by **H**emolysis (breakdown of red blood cells), **E**levated **L**iver enzyme levels, and a **L**ow **P**latelet count. HELLP develops late in pregnancy, or sometimes after birth.

Helper T Cells Lymphocytes bearing the CD4 marker that are responsible for many immune system functions, including turning antibody production on and off.

Helper/Suppressor Ratio (of T Cells) T cells are lymphocytes (white blood cells) that are formed in the thymus and are part of the immune system. They have been found to be abnormal in persons with AIDS. The normal ratio of helper T cells (also known as CD4+ T cells) to suppressor T cells (also known as CD8+ T cells) is approximately 2 to 1. This ratio becomes inverted in persons with AIDS but also may be abnormal for other temporary reasons.

Hematocrit A laboratory measurement that determines the percentage of packed red blood cells in a given volume of blood. In women red blood cells are normally 37 to 47 percent of their blood, and in men red blood cells are normally 40 to 54 percent of their blood.

Hematotoxic Poisonous to the blood or bone marrow.

Hematuria Blood in the urine.

Hemoglobin (HGB) The red, iron-based pigment in red blood cells that enables them to transport oxygen; normal hemoglobin values are 14-18 g/dL in men and 12-16 g/dL in women. Normal values in resource-poor countries may be lower.

Hemolysis The rupture of red blood cells.

Hepatic Pertaining to the liver.

Hepatitis An inflammation of the liver. May be caused by bacterial or viral infection, parasitic infestation, alcohol, drugs, toxins, or transfusion of incompatible blood. Although many cases of hepatitis are not a serious threat to health, the disease can become chronic and can sometimes lead to liver failure and death. There are four major types of viral hepatitis: A, B, C, and D.

Hepatitis A Caused by infection with the hepatitis A virus, which is spread by fecal-oral contact.

Hepatitis B Caused by infection with the hepatitis B virus (HBV), which is most commonly passed on to a partner during sexual intercourse, especially during anal sex, as well as through sharing of drug needles.

Hepatitis C Approximately 40% of patients infected with HIV are also infected with the hepatitis C virus (HCV), mainly because both viruses share the same routes of transmission. HCV is one of most important causes of chronic liver disease in the United States. Clinical studies have demonstrated that HIV infection causes a more rapid progression of chronic hepatitis C to liver failure in HIV-infected persons.

Hepatomegaly   Enlargement of the liver.

Hepatosplenomegaly   Abnormal enlargement of both the liver and the spleen.

Hepatotoxicity   Liver damage due to toxic effects of poisons or drugs. Early damage is usually detected by measuring liver enzymes.

Herpes Simplex Virus 1 (HSV-1)   A virus that causes cold sores or fever blisters on the mouth or around the eyes, and can be transmitted to the genital region. Stress, trauma, other infections, or suppression of the immune system can reactivate the latent virus.

Herpes Simplex Virus 2 (HSV-2)   A virus causing painful sores of the anus or genitals that may lie dormant in nerve tissue. It can be reactivated to produce symptoms. HSV-2 may be transmitted to a newborn during birth from an infected mother, causing retardation and/or other serious complications. HSV-2 is a precursor of cervical cancer.

Herpes Varicella Zoster Virus (VZV)   The varicella virus causes chicken pox in children and may reappear in adults as herpes zoster. Also called shingles, herpes zoster consists of very painful blisters on the skin that follow nerve pathways.

Herpes Viruses   A group of viruses that includes herpes simplex type 1 (HSV-1), herpes simplex type 2 (HSV-2), Cytomegalovirus (CMV), Epstein-Barr virus (EBV), varicella zoster virus (VZV), human herpes virus type 6 (HHV-6), and HHV-8, a herpes virus associated with Kaposi sarcoma. See entries under names of some of the individual viruses.

Herpes Zoster   A painful infection with the varicella virus that normally causes chicken pox. The virus may be dormant for many years in the cells of the nervous system. When reactivated it appears on the skin in various locations as painful sores. Also called shingles.

Highly Active Antiretroviral Therapy (HAART)   The name given to treatment regimens recommended by HIV experts to aggressively decrease viral multiplication and progress of HIV disease. The usual HAART treatment combines three or more different drugs, such as two nucleoside reverse transcriptase inhibitors (NRTIs) and a protease inhibitor, two NRTIs and a non-nucleoside reverse transcriptase inhibitor (NNRTI), or other combinations. These treatment regimens have been shown to reduce the amount of virus so that it becomes undetectable in a patient's blood.

High-Risk Behavior   A reported sexual, injection drug use, or other non-work-related HIV exposure that might put a patient at high risk for acquiring HIV infection.

Histoplasmosis   A fungal infection, commonly of the lungs, caused by the fungus *Histoplasma capsulatum*. This fungus is commonly found in bird and bat droppings. It is spread by breathing in the spores of the fungus. Persons with severely damaged immune systems, such as those with AIDS, are susceptible to a very serious disease known as progressive disseminated histoplasmosis.

HIV   Human Immunodeficiency Virus. See Human Immunodeficiency Virus Type 1 (HIV-1); Human Immunodeficiency Virus Type 2 (HIV-2).

HIV Prevention Counseling   Provision of information on how HIV is transmitted, how an individual becomes infected, and how to prevent infection. Encompasses all modes of transmission including sexual (homosexual and bisexual), intravenous drug use, mother-to-child transmission, breast-feeding, accidental exposure from an infected patient, and HIV-infected blood transfusion.

HIV Set Point   The point where the level of virus stabilizes and remains at a particular level in each individual after the period of primary infection.

HIV Viral Load   See Viral Load Test.

HIV-1   See Human Immunodeficiency Virus Type 1 (HIV-1).

HIV-2   See Human Immunodeficiency Virus Type 2 (HIV-2).

HIV-Associated Dementia   See AIDS Dementia Complex (ADC).

HIV-Exposed Infant   An infant born to a mother infected with HIV and exposed to HIV during pregnancy, childbirth, or breast-feeding.

Hodgkin's Disease   A progressive cancer of the lymphatic system. Symptoms include lymphadenopathy, wasting, weakness, fever, itching, night sweats, and anemia. Treatment includes radiation and chemotherapy.

Home Sample Collection Test   A test kit that a consumer purchases and uses to collect blood (or other bodily fluid) to send away for testing.

Homosexual   Pertaining to sexual activity with a person of the same sex.

Hormone   An active chemical substance formed in one part of the body and carried in the blood to other parts of the body where it stimulates or suppresses cell and tissue activity.

Host Factors   The body's mechanisms for containing HIV, including immune system cells.

HPV   See Human Papilloma Virus (HPV).

HTLV-1; HTLV-2   HTLV-I and HTLV-II, like all retroviruses, are single-stranded RNA that divide through DNA made possible by the presence of a enzyme, reverse transcriptase, which converts a single-stranded viral RNA into a double-stranded DNA. HTLV-I attacks T lymphocytes; it appears to be the causative agent of certain T-cell leukemias, T-cell lymphomas, and HTLV-I-associated neurologic disease.

Human Herpesvirus 6 (HHV-6) Infection An infection caused by human herpesvirus 6 (HHV-6). HHV-6 is primarily transmitted through saliva and usually causes disease only in children or people with weakened immune systems. HHV-6 can cause neurological diseases, such as encephalitis and febrile seizures. HHV-6 can also cause fever and rash (roseola), which mostly affects children between 6 months and 2 years old.

Human Herpesvirus 7 (HHV-7) A type of herpesvirus found in saliva of people infected with human herpesvirus 7 (HHV-7). HHV-7 has not been definitively documented to cause a specific disease.

Human Herpesvirus 8 Sarcoma-associated herpesvirus.

Human Immunodeficiency Virus Type 1 (HIV-1) The retrovirus isolated and recognized as the etiologic (i.e., causing or contributing to the cause of a disease) agent of AIDS. HIV-1 is classified as a lentivirus in a subgroup of retroviruses. Also, the genetic material of a retrovirus such as HIV is the RNA itself. HIV inserts its own RNA into the host cell's DNA, preventing the host cell from carrying out its natural functions and turning it into an HIV factory. See Lentivirus; Retrovirus.

Human Immunodeficiency Virus Type 2 (HIV-2) A virus closely related to HIV-1 that has also been found to cause AIDS. It was first isolated in West Africa. Although HIV-1 and HIV-2 are similar in how they are transmitted and result in similar opportunistic infections, they have differed in their geographic patterns of infection. HIV-1 remains the most common cause of AIDS and represents the major type distributed worldwide.

Human Papilloma Virus (HPV) HPV is transmitted through sexual contact and is the virus that causes genital warts and plays a causative role in cervical dysplasia and cervical cancer.

Humoral Immunity The branch of the immune system that relies primarily on antibodies. See Cell-Mediated Immunity (CMI).

Hypercholesterolemia Abnormally high levels of cholesterol in the bloodstream. High cholesterol levels contribute to heart disease.

Hypergammaglobulinemia Abnormally high levels of immunoglobulins in the blood. Common in persons with HIV.

Hyperglycemia An abnormally high concentration of glucose (sugar) in the circulating blood, seen especially in patients with diabetes mellitus. Hyperglycemia, new onset diabetes mellitus, diabetic ketoacidosis, and worsening of existing diabetes mellitus in patients receiving protease inhibitors have been reported.

Hyperlipidemia An increase in the blood levels of triglycerides and cholesterol (fats) that can lead to heart disease and inflammation of the pancreas. As related to HIV, hyperlipidemia is a side effect of HAART. (All protease inhibitors have been shown to cause hyperlipidemia in clinical studies.)

Hyperplasia Abnormal increase in the parts of tissue or cells.

Hypersensitivity An exaggerated Immune response to a specific antigen or drug. Hypersensitivity reactions, including allergic reactions, can be life-threatening. Use of some antiretroviral (ARV) drugs may cause a hypersensitivity reaction.

Hypertriglyceridemia Elevated levels of triglycerides (fatty acid compounds) in the bloodstream. High levels contribute to heart disease.

Hypogammaglobulinemia Abnormally low levels of immunoglobulins. See Antibody.

Hypothesis An assumption as a basis for reasoning or argument, or as a guide to experimental investigation.

Hypoxia Reduction of oxygen supply to tissues.

Idiopathic Without a known cause.

Idiopathic Thrombocytopenia Low level of platelets without a cause.

IDU Intravenous (injection) drug user.

IDV Indinavir.

Immune Deficiency A breakdown or inability of certain parts of the immune system to function, thus making a person susceptible to certain diseases that they would not ordinarily develop.

Immune Reconstitution Inflammatory Syndrome (IRIS) In HIV infection, an exaggerated inflammatory reaction to a disease-causing microorganism that sometimes occurs when the immune system begins to recover following treatment with antiretroviral (ARV) drugs, Immune reconstitution inflammatory syndrome (IRIS) occurs in two forms: "unmasking" IRIS refers to the flare-up of an underlying, previously undiagnosed infection soon after antiretroviral therapy (ART) is started; "paradoxical" IRIS refers to the worsening of a previously treated infection after ART is started, IRIS can be mild or life-threatening.

Immune Response The activity of the immune system against foreign substances.

Immune System The body's complicated natural defense against disruption caused by invading foreign agents (e.g., bacteria, viruses). Acquired, or learned, immune response arises when specialized cells (dendritic cells and macrophages) process pieces of infectious agents. The ultimate result is the creation of antibody-producing B cells and cytotoxic T lymphocytes.

Immune Thrombocytopenic Purpura (ITP) Also called idiopathic immune thrombocytopenic purpura. A condition in which the body produces antibodies against the platelets in the blood, which are cells responsible for blood clotting. ITP is very common in persons infected with HIV.

Immunity A natural or acquired resistance to a specific disease. Immunity may be partial or complete, long lasting or temporary.

Immunization Protection against an infectious disease by vaccination, usually with a weakened (attenuated) or killed form of the disease-causing microorganism. While people are usually immunized against an infectious disease by getting vaccinated, having a disease such as measles, mumps, or rubella one time usually prevents or "immunizes" a person from getting this disease again.

Immunocompetent Capable of developing an immune response; possessing a normal immune system.

Immunocompromised Refers to an immune system in which the ability to resist or fight off infections and tumors is subnormal.

Immunodeficiency Breakdown of the immune system in which certain parts of the immune system no longer function. This condition makes a person more susceptible to certain diseases.

Immunogen (Antigen) A substance capable of provoking an immune response.

Immunogenicity The ability of an antigen or vaccine to stimulate an immune response.

Immunoglobulin (Ig) Also called immune serum globulin. A class of proteins also known as antibodies made by the B cells of the immune system in response to a specific antigen. There are five classes of immunoglobulins.

Immunoglobulin A (IgA) A class of antibodies that is secreted into bodily fluids such as saliva. IgA protects the body's mucosal surfaces from infections.

Immunoglobulin D (IgD) A class of antibodies that is present in low concentration in serum.

Immunoglobulin E (IgE) A class of antibodies involved in antiparasite immunity and in allergies.

Immunoglobulin G (IgG) The dominant class of antibodies and the one that provides long-term protection against infection. In pregnancy, IgG crosses the placenta to the fetus and protects it against infection. Also called gammaglobulin.

Immunoglobulin M (IgM) A class of antibodies that is made by the body as the initial response to an infection or immunization. If IgM is made in response to an immunization, a booster shot will result in a "switch" from IgM to mostly immunoglobulin G.

Immunomodulator Any substance that influences the immune system.

Immunostimulant Any agent or substance that triggers or enhances the body's defense; also called immunopotentiator.

Immunosuppression A state of the body in which the immune system is damaged and does not perform its normal functions. Immunosuppression may be induced by drugs (e.g., in chemotherapy) or result from certain disease processes, such as HIV infection.

Immunotherapy Treatment aimed at restoring an impaired immune system.

Immunotoxin A plant or animal toxin (i.e., poison) that is attached to an antibody and used to destroy a specific target cell.

In Utero Before birth; literally, in the uterus.

In Vitro An artificial environment created outside a living organism (e.g., a test tube or culture plate) used in experimental research to study a disease or process.

In Vivo ("In life") Within living organisms. (Often refers to animal or human studies.)

Incidence The number of new cases (e.g., of a disease) occurring in a given population over a certain period of time. Also called seroincidence.

Inclusion/Exclusion Criteria The medical or social standards determining whether a person may or may not be allowed to enter a clinical trial. For example, some trials may not allow persons with chronic liver disease or with certain drug allergies; others may exclude men or women, or include only persons with a lowered T-cell count.

Incubation Period The time interval between the initial infection with an infectious agent (e.g., HIV) and the appearance of the first symptom or sign of disease.

Indeterminate Test Result A laboratory test result that does not give a clear answer. Either additional laboratory studies should be performed or the test should be repeated.

Infection The state or condition in which the body (or part of the body) is invaded by an infectious agent (e.g., a bacterium, fungus, or virus), which multiplies and produces an injurious effect (active infection). As related to HIV, infection typically begins when HIV encounters a CD4+ cell.

Infectious An infection capable of being transmitted by direct or intimate contact (e.g., sex).

Informed Consent A process during which the patient learns the key facts about HIV testing—including what will occur during HIV testing and counseling and the purpose and benefits of HIV testing—before deciding whether to allow testing to proceed.

Infusion The process of administering fluid, other than blood, to an individual by slowly injecting a solution of the compound into a vein. Infusions are often used when the drug is too toxic or the volume is too large to be given by quick injection.

INH See Isoniazid (INH).

Injection Drug Use A method of illicit drug use. The drugs are injected directly into the body—into a vein, into a muscle, or under the skin—with a needle and syringe. Blood-borne viruses, including HIV and hepatitis, can be transmitted via shared needles or other drug injection equipment.

Injection Site Reaction An adverse reaction, such as rash or redness, at the site of an injection.

Innate Immunity Immunity that a person is born with. Innate immunity includes certain physical barriers, such as skin and mucous membranes, and fast-acting immune cells, such as natural killer cells.

Inoculation The introduction of a substance (inoculum; e.g., a vaccine, serum, or virus) into the body to produce or to increase immunity to the disease or condition associated with the substance. See Vaccine.

Institutional Review Board (IRB) A committee of physicians, statisticians, researchers, community advocates, and others that ensures that a clinical trial is ethical and that the rights of study participants are protected.

Insulin Resistance A condition in which the body is unable to respond to and use the insulin it produces. As a result, the pancreas secretes more insulin into the bloodstream in an effort to reduce blood glucose levels.

Integrase A little-understood enzyme that plays a vital role in the HIV infection process. Integrase inserts HIV's genes into a cell's normal DNA.

Integrase Inhibitors A class of experimental anti-HIV drugs that prevents the HIV integrase enzyme from inserting viral DNA into a host cell's normal DNA.

Intent to Treat Analysis of clinical trial results that includes all data from patients in the groups to which they were randomized (i.e., assigned through random distribution) even if they never received the treatment.

Interaction See Drug-Drug Interaction.

Interferon One of a number of antiviral proteins that control the immune response. Interferon (IFN) alpha is secreted by a virally infected cell and strengthens the defenses of nearby uninfected cells. A manufactured version of IFN alpha (trade names Roferon, Intron A) is an FDA-approved treatment for Kaposi sarcoma, hepatitis B, and hepatitis C. Interferon gamma is synthesized by immune system cells (natural killer cells and CD4 cells). It activates macrophages and helps promote cellular immunity.

Interleukins Substances (cytokines) that are released from immune and other cells. There are many types referred to as Interleukin (IL) 1, 2, 3, 4, 5, etc.

International Maternal Pediatric Adolescent AIDS Clinical Trials (IMPAACT) Group A global collaboration of institutions, investigators, and other partners that conduct clinical trials on interventions to treat and prevent HIV infection and its consequences in infants, children, adolescents, and pregnant/postpartum women.

International Network for Strategic Initiatives in Global HIV Trials (INSIGHT) A clinical trials network that conducts studies worldwide in order to define optimal strategies for the management of HIV and other infectious diseases.

Interstitial Relating to or situated in the small, narrow spaces between tissues or parts of an organ.

Intervention An action or strategy to change a particular problem or outcome or accomplish a specific result (e.g., use of ART to prevent HIV disease progression).

Intramuscular (IM) Injected directly into a muscle.

Intrapartum Time during labor and delivery.

Intravenous (IV) Of or pertaining to the inside of a vein, as of a thrombus. An injection made directly into a vein.

Intravenous Immunoglobulin (IVIG) A sterile solution of concentrated antibodies extracted from healthy people. IVIG is used to prevent bacterial infections in persons with low or abnormal antibody production. IVIG is injected into a vein.

Invasive Pertaining to an infection or disease that spreads to surrounding tissues or to other parts of the body. Invasive can also refer to a medical procedure that involves entering a part of the body, such as through an incision.

Investigational Drug A drug that is approved by the Food and Drug Administration (FDA) for testing in humans for a specified condition but not approved for commercial marketing and sale.

Investigational New Drug (IND) Application A drug sponsor's request to the Food and Drug Administration (FDA) for approval to test an investigational drug in humans (Phase 1-4 clinical trials). FDA review of an investigational new drug (IND) application ensures that the drug is safe for testing in humans and that testing will not put study participants at unreasonable risk.

IRB See Institutional Review Board (IRB).

Isolate An individual part of an organism (such as a spore or a bacteria or virus) that has been separated (as from diseased tissue, contaminated water, or the air) from the whole.

Isoniazid (INH) An orally administered drug used to eliminate tuberculosis infection in people without active disease. INH is also administered in combination with other drugs to treat active tuberculosis

ITP See Immune Thrombocytopenic Purpura (ITP).

IVIG See Intravenous Immunoglobulin (IVIG).

Jaundice Yellow pigmentation of the skin, mucous membranes, whites of the eyes, and body fluids caused by elevated blood levels of bilirubin. The condition is associated with either liver or gallbladder disease or excessive destruction of red blood cells.

JC Virus See Progressive Multifocal Leukoencephalopathy (PML); Papilloma.

Kaposi Sarcoma (KS) An AIDS-defining illness consisting of individual cancerous sores caused by an overgrowth of blood vessels. KS typically appears as pink or purple painless spots or nodules on the surface of the skin or mouth. KS also can occur internally, especially in the intestines, lymph nodes, and lungs, and in this case is life threatening. A species of herpes virus—also referred to as Kaposi sarcoma herpes virus (KSHV) or HHV-8—similar to the Epstein-Barr virus is the probable cause.

Karnofsky Score A score from 0 to 100 assigned by a physician based on observations of a patient's ability to perform common tasks. Thus, 100 signifies normal physical abilities with no evidence of disease. Decreasing numbers indicate a reduced ability to perform activities of daily living.

Ketoacidosis Increased acid in the bloodstream accompanied by the accumulation of ketone bodies. Ketones are a byproduct of fat metabolism. When glucose levels are inadequate, the liver converts fatty acids to ketones, which are used as fuel by the muscles.

Killer T Cells Because viruses lurk inside host (e.g., human) cells where antibodies cannot reach them, the only way they can be eliminated is by killing the infected host cell. To do this, the immune system uses a kind of white blood cell, called killer T cells. Also known as cytotoxic T cells (or cytotoxic T lymphocytes). See Natural Killer (NK) Cells; T Cells.

KSHV Kaposi sarcoma herpes virus. See Kaposi Sarcoma (KS).

Lactic Acidosis A buildup of lactic acid in the blood, accompanied by low blood pH. This is a potentially fatal condition characterized by nausea, abdominal pain, fatigue, muscle weakness, and shortness of breath. Also referred to as lactic acidemia.

Lactoferrin Iron-binding protein of very high affinity found in milk, tears, mucus, bile, and some white blood cells. Lactoferrin has antibiotic, antioxidant, antifungal, and antiviral properties.

Lamivudine (3TC) Nucleoside analogue with anti-HIV and anti-hepatitis B activity.

Latency The period when an infecting organism is in the body but is not producing any clinically noticeable ill effects or symptoms. In HIV disease, clinical latency is an asymptomatic period in the early years of HIV infection. The period of latency is characterized by near-normal CD4+ T-cell counts. Recent research indicates that HIV remains quite active in the lymph nodes during this period.

Latent See Latency.

Latent HIV Reservoir Resting CD4 cells (or other cells) that are infected with HIV but not actively producing HIV. Latent HIV reservoirs are established during the earliest stage of HIV infection. Although antiretroviral therapy (ART) can reduce the level of HIV in the blood to an undetectable level, latent reservoirs of HIV continue to survive. When a latently infected cell is reactivated, the cell begins to produce HIV again. For this reason, ART cannot cure HIV infection.

Lentivirus "Slow" virus characterized by a long time between infection and the onset of symptoms. HIV is a lentivirus, as is the simian immunodeficiency virus (SIV) that infects nonhuman primates.

Lesion A general term to describe an area of altered tissue (e.g., the infected patch or sore in a skin disease).

Leukocytes Any of the various white blood cells that together make up the immune system. Neutrophils, lymphocytes, and monocytes are all leukocytes.

Leukocytosis An abnormally high number of leukocytes in the blood. This condition can occur during many types of infection and inflammation.

Leukopenia A decrease in the number of white blood cells. The threshold value for leukopenia is usually taken as <5,000 white blood cells per cubic millimeter of blood.

Leukoplakia See Oral Hairy Leukoplakia (OHL).

LFT See Liver Function Test (LFT).

LGBTQ Acronym for lesbian, gay, bisexual, transgender, and questioning.

Linear Gingival Erythema A condition in which the edge of the gums near the teeth become red and inflamed. Linear gingival erythema is common with HIV infection.

LIP See Lymphoid Interstitial Pneumonitis (LIP).

Lipid Any of a group of fats and fatlike compounds, including sterols, fatty acids, and many other substances.

Lipoatrophy Loss of fat from specific areas of the body, especially from the face, arms, legs, and buttocks, Use of some antiretroviral (ARV) drugs may cause lipoatrophy.

Lipodystrophy A disturbance in the way the body produces, uses, and distributes fat. Lipodystrophy is also referred to as buffalo hump, protease paunch, or Crixivan potbelly. In HIV disease, lipodystrophy has come to refer to a group of symptoms that seem to be related to the use of protease inhibitor and NRTI drugs.

Lipohypertrophy Abnormal accumulation of fat, particularly within the abdominal cavity, the upper back (buffalo hump), and subcutaneous tissue (peripheral lipomatosis), Use of some antiretroviral (ARV) drugs may cause lipohypertrophy,

Lipoma Benign (not cancerous) lumps of fat that develop under the skin. Lipomas can develop as a result of lipodystrophy, which may be caused by certain antiretroviral (ARV) drugs.

Listeriosis Infection with one of the Listeria bacteria, which are capable of causing miscarriage, stillbirth, and premature birth.

Live Attenuated A disease-causing virus or bacterium that is weakened in a laboratory so it cannot cause disease (or only mild disease). Live attenuated viruses are often used as vaccines because, although weakened, they can stimulate a strong immune response. However, because of remote possibility that a live attenuated virus could cause disease, people infected with HIV should not receive most live attenuated vaccines.

Live Vector Vaccine As pertaining to HIV, a vaccine that uses an attenuated (i.e., weakened) virus or bacterium to carry pieces of HIV into the body to directly stimulate a cell-mediated immune response.

Liver Function Test (LFT) A test that measures the blood serum level of any of several enzymes (e.g., SGOT and SGPT) produced by the liver. An elevated liver function test is a sign of possible liver damage.

Lochia Vaginal discharge of blood, mucus, and tissue that takes place during the first week or two after childbirth.

Log10 A mathematical term used to describe changes in viral load (HIV RNA). For example, if the viral load is 20,000 copies/mL, then a 1-log increase equals a 10-fold (10 times) increase, or 200,000 copies/mL. A 2-log increase equals a 100-fold increase, or 2,000,000 copies/mL.

Long-Term Nonprogressors Individuals who have been living with HIV for at least 7 to 12 years (different authors use different time spans) and have stable CD4+ T-cell counts of 600 or more cells per cubic millimeter of blood, no HIV-related diseases, and no previous antiretroviral therapy. Data suggest that this phenomenon is associated with the maintenance of the integrity of the lymphoid tissues and with less virus trapping in the lymph nodes than is seen in other individuals living with HIV.

Lumbar Lower back region.

Lumbar Puncture A procedure in which cerebrospinal fluid from the subarachnoid space in the lumbar region is removed for examination. Also known as spinal tap.

Lymph A transparent, slightly yellow fluid that carries lymphocytes. Lymph is derived from tissue fluids collected from all parts of the body and is returned to the blood via lymphatic vessels.

Lymph Nodes Small, bean-sized organs of the immune system, distributed widely throughout the body. Lymph fluid is filtered through the lymph nodes in which all types of lymphocytes take up temporary residence. Lymph nodes contain T cells, B cells, as well as other cells of the immune system.

Lymphadenopathy Swollen or enlarged lymph nodes.

Lymphadenopathy Syndrome (LAS) Swollen, firm, and possibly tender lymph nodes. The cause may range from an infection such as HIV, the flu, or mononucleosis to lymphoma (cancer of the lymph nodes).

Lymphocyte A white blood cell. Present in the blood, lymph, and lymphoid tissue. See B Lymphocytes (B Cells); T Cells.

Lymphogranuloma Venereum (LGV) A chronic infection of the lymphatic system caused by three strains of the bacterium. Lymphogranuloma venereum (LGV) is a sexually transmitted infection. Symptoms include genital or rectal ulcers. LGV may increase the risk for sexual transmission of HIV.

Lymphoid Interstitial Pneumonitis (LIP) A type of pneumonia that affects 35 to 40% of children with AIDS, and which causes hardening of the lung membranes involved in absorbing oxygen. LIP is an AIDS-defining illness in children. The cause of LIP is not clear. There is no established treatment for LIP, but the use of corticosteroids for progressive LIP has been advocated.

Lymphoid Organs Include tonsils, adenoids, lymph nodes, spleen, thymus, and other tissues. These organs act as the body's filtering system, trapping any invading foreign particles (e.g., bacteria and viruses) and presenting them to squadrons of immune cells that congregate there.

Lymphoid Tissue See Lymphoid Organs.

Lymphokines Chemical products of the lymphatic cells that stimulate the production of disease-fighting agents and the activities of other cells of the immune system. Among the lymphokines are the interferons and interleukins.

Lymphoma Cancer of the lymphoid tissues. Lymphomas are often described as being large-cell or small-cell types, cleaved or noncleaved, or diffuse or nodular. The different types often have different prognoses (i.e., prospect of survival or recovery). Lymphomas can also be referred to by the organs where they are active, such as CNS lymphomas, which are in the central nervous system, and GI lymphomas, which are in the gastrointestinal tract. The types of lymphomas most commonly associated with HIV infection are called non-Hodgkin's lymphomas or B-cell lymphomas. In these types of cancers, certain cells of the lymphatic system grow abnormally. They divide rapidly, growing into tumors.

Lymphopenia A relative or absolute reduction in the number of lymphocytes in the circulating blood.

Lymphoproliferative Response A specific immune response that results in a rapid T-cell replication.

Lysis Rupture and destruction of a cell.

MAC See Mycobacterium Avium Complex (MAC).

Macrophage A large immune cell that destroys invading infectious agents. Macrophages can hide large quantities of HIV without being killed, acting as reservoirs of the virus.

Macrophage-Tropic Virus HIV strains that infect macrophages. They readily fuse with cells that have both CD4 and CCR5 molecules on their surfaces, whereas the same viral isolates fail to fuse with cells expressing only CD4. These isolates are the main ones found in patients during the symptom-free stage of HIV disease.

Magnetic Resonance Imaging (MRI) A noninvasive, non-x-ray diagnostic technique that provides computer-generated images of the body's internal tissues and organs.

MAI See Mycobacterium Avium Complex (MAC).

Maintenance Therapy Also referred to as secondary prophylaxis. A therapy that prevents reoccurrence of an infection that has been brought under control.

Malabsorption Syndrome Decreased intestinal absorption of foods and nutrients resulting in loss of appetite, muscle pain, and weight loss. See AIDS Wasting Syndrome.

Malaise A generalized, nonspecific feeling of discomfort or tiredness.

Malaria An infectious disease characterized by cycles of chills, fever, and sweating, caused by a parasite transmitted by a host mosquito.

Malignant Refers to cells or tumors growing in an uncontrolled fashion. Such growths may spread to and disrupt nearby normal tissue, or reach distant sites via the bloodstream. By definition, cancers are always malignant, and the term "malignancy" implies cancer. See Metastasis.

Mast Cell A granulocyte found in tissue. The contents of the mast cells, along with those of basophils, are responsible for the symptoms of allergy.

Mastitis An inflammation of the breast. It is a condition that commonly results from inadequate or poor drainage of milk from the breast. Mastitis can be infective or noninfective in origin. Noninfective mastitis, which is most common, is usually the result of a blocked milk duct, which causes inflammation of the breast tissue. Mastitis frequently affects only one breast (whereas engorgement often occurs bilaterally) and is characterized by hard swelling, severe pain, fever (24 hours or longer), and localized redness around the affected area. Other causes include infrequent feeds or ineffective suckling; breast trauma and tissue damage; and pressure on the breasts from clothes, fingers, or other sources that inhibit milk flow and cause milk stasis leading to breast tissue inflammation. Infective mastitis is the result of bacterial infection. Poor breast attachment causing nipple fissures is a common pathway to infectious mastitis.

MCH Maternal Child Health.

Meconium The first stools of the newborn. Typically thick, viscous, sticky, and dark green; usually sterile and odorless.

Medication Event Monitoring System (MEMS) A device used to monitor medication adherence. A medication event monitoring system (MEMS) monitor consists of a conventional medicine container fitted with a special closure that records the time and date each time the container is opened and closed.

Medline A federal database that contains references and summaries for biomedical and life science publications from around the world. Most of the publications are scholarly journals. Medline is a service of the U.S. National Library of Medicine.

Memory T Cells A subset of T lymphocytes that have been exposed to specific antigens and can then proliferate (i.e., reproduce) on subsequent immune system encounters with the same antigen.

Meninges Membranes surrounding the brain or spinal cord. Part of the so-called blood-brain barrier. See Meningitis.

Meningitis An inflammation of the meninges (membranes surrounding the brain or spinal cord), which may be caused by a bacterium, fungus, or virus. See Central Nervous System (CNS); Cryptococcal Meningitis.

Metaanalysis A quantitative method of combining the results of independent studies (usually drawn from the published literature) and synthesizing summaries and conclusions.

Metabolic Syndrome A combination of risk factors that increase the risk for heart disease, diabetes, and stroke. To be diagnosed with metabolic syndrome, a person must have at least three of the following metabolic risk factors: high blood pressure, abdominal obesity, high triglyceride levels, low levels of high-density lipoprotein (HDL) cholesterol, or high fasting blood sugar levels. Use of some antiretroviral (ARV) drugs may cause or worsen risk factors associated with metabolic syndrome.

Metabolism The chemical changes in living cells by which energy is provided for vital processes and activities and new material is assimilated.

Metastasis The spread of a disease (e.g., cancer) from an original site to other sites in the body.

Microbes Microscopic living organisms, including bacteria, protozoa, viruses, and fungi.

Microbicide An agent (e.g., a chemical or antibiotic) that destroys microbes. Research is being carried out to evaluate the use of rectal and vaginal microbicides to inhibit the transmission of sexually transmitted diseases, including HIV.

Microbicide Trials Network (MTN) A federally funded clinical trials network. Many Microbicide Trials Network (MTN) trials focus on evaluating microbicides and other promising HIV prevention approaches.

Micronutrients Vitamins or minerals that are necessary to maintain health and that the body must obtain from outside sources.

Microsporidiosis An intestinal infection that causes diarrhea and wasting in persons with HIV. It results from two species of microsporidia, a protozoal parasite. In HIV infection, it generally occurs when CD4+ T-cell counts fall below 100. See AIDS Wasting Syndrome; Pathogen; Protozoa.

Mitochondria A rod-shaped or oval portion on the inside of a cell that produces most of the cell's energy.

Mitochondrial Toxicity Also referred to as mitochondrial dysfunction. A possible side effect of certain anti-HIV drugs, primarily NRTIs, that results in mitochondrial damage. This damage can cause symptoms in the heart, nerves, muscles, pancreas, kidney, and liver, and it can also cause changes in lab tests. Some of the common conditions related to mitochondrial toxicity are muscle and nerve disease and inflammation of the pancreas.

Mixed-Tropic HIV HIV that includes both CCR5-tropic and CXCR4-tropic virus.

Modified Directly Observed Therapy (m-DOT) A variation of directly observed therapy (DOT). Modified-DOT (m-DOT) is when a health care professional watches a person take some, but not all, medication doses.

Molluscum Contagiosum A disease of the skin and mucous membranes caused by a poxvirus (molluscum contagiosum virus, MCV) infection. It is characterized by pearly white or flesh-colored papules (bumps) on the face, neck, and genital region. In persons living with HIV, molluscum contagiosum is often a progressive disease, resistant to treatment. When CD4+ cell counts fall below 200, the lesions tend to proliferate and spread.

Monocyte A large white blood cell that ingests infectious agents or other cells and foreign particles. When a monocyte enters tissues, it develops into a macrophage.

Monoinfection When a person has only one infection.

Mononeuropathy Neuropathy that damages only one nerve, resulting in symptoms that are linked specifically to the affected nerve.

Monotherapy Use of a single drug or therapy to treat a disease or condition.

Monovalent Vaccine A vaccine that is specific for only one antigen.

Morbidity The condition of being diseased or sick; also the incidence of disease or rate of sickness.

MRI See Magnetic Resonance Imaging (MRI).

MSM Men who have sex with men; a term created to include those who do not identify as gay or bisexual.

MSMW Acronym for men who have sex with men and women.

MTCT Mother-to-child transmission (of HIV).

Mucocutaneous Anything that concerns or pertains to mucous membranes and the skin (e.g., mouth, eyes, vagina, lips, or anal area).

Mucosa See Mucous Membrane.

Mucosal Immunity Resistance to infection across the mucous membranes. Dependent on immune cells and antibodies present in the lining of the urogenital tract, gastrointestinal tract, and other parts of the body exposed to the outside world.

Mucous Membrane Moist layer of tissue lining the digestive, respiratory, urinary, and reproductive tracts—all the body cavities with openings to the outside world except the ears.

Multicenter AIDS Cohort Study (MACS) Started in 1984, the study involves collection of biological specimens and medical and behavioral data on MSM (men who have sex with men) in order to study the natural and treated history of HIV, The Multicenter AIDS Cohort Study (MACS) has significantly contributed to the understanding of HIV, AIDS, and the effects of antiretroviral therapy (ART).

Multiple Drug-Resistant Tuberculosis (MDR-TB) A strain of TB that does not respond to two or more standard anti-TB drugs. MDR-TB usually occurs when treatment is interrupted, thus allowing organisms in which mutations for drug resistance have occurred to proliferate. See Tuberculosis (TB).

Mutation In biology, a sudden change in a gene or unit of hereditary material that results in a new inheritable characteristic. As related to HIV: During the course of HIV disease, mutated HIV strains may emerge in an infected individual. These mutated strains may differ widely in their ability to infect and kill different cell types, as well as in their rate of replication. Of course, HIV does not mutate into another type of virus.

Myalgia Diffuse muscle pain or tenderness, usually accompanied by malaise (vague feeling of discomfort or weakness).

Mycobacterium Any bacterium of the genus Mycobacterium or a closely related genus.

Mycobacterium Avium Complex (MAC) A common opportunistic infection caused by two very similar mycobacterial organisms, *Mycobacterium avium* and *Mycobacterium intracellulare* (MAI), found in soil and dust particles. A bacterial infection that can be localized (limited to a specific organ or area of the body) or disseminated throughout the body. It is a life-threatening disease, although new treatments offer promise for both prevention and treatment. MAC disease is extremely rare in persons who are not infected with HIV. It generally occurs when the CD4+ T-cell count falls below 50.

Mycobacterium Avium-Intracellulare (MAI) Infection An infection caused by two closely related and hard-to-distinguish bacteria. These two bacteria can be found in drinking water, dirt, and household dust. Most people are not affected by the bacteria, but for people with severely weakened immune systems, the bacteria can cause infection.

Mycosis Any disease caused by a fungus.

Myelin A substance that sheathes nerve cells, acting as an electric insulator that facilitates the conduction of nerve impulses.

Myelopathy Any disease of the spinal cord.

Myelosuppression Suppression of bone marrow activity, causing decreased production of red blood cells (anemia), white blood cells (leukopenia), or platelets (thrombocytopenia). Myelosuppression is a side effect of some drugs, such as AZT.

Myelotoxic Destructive to bone marrow.

Myocardial Refers to the heart's muscle mass.

Myopathy Progressive muscle weakness. Myopathy may arise as a toxic reaction to AZT or as a consequence of the HIV infection itself.

Nadir The lowest level to which viral load falls after starting antiretroviral treatment. Studies have shown that the nadir of the viral load is the best predictor of long-term viral suppression.

National Cancer Institute (NCI) The lead federal agency responsible for cancer-related research and training. The National Cancer Institute (NCI) is also responsible for disseminating cancer-related information and evaluating the incorporation of state-of-the-art cancer treatments into clinical practice. Programs at NCI focus on the cause, diagnosis, prevention, and treatment of cancer; rehabilitation from cancer; and continuing care of people with cancer and their families.

National Center for Complementary and Integrative Health (NCCIH) The primary federal agency for scientific research on the diverse medical and health care systems, practices, and products that are not generally considered part of conventional (Western) medicine.

National Institute of Allergy and Infectious Diseases (NIAID) A federal agency that supports basic and applied research to prevent, diagnose, and treat infectious and immune-mediated illnesses, including HIV/AIDS and other sexually transmitted infections. The Institute also supports medical research studies on tuberculosis (TB), malaria, autoimmune disorders, asthma, allergies, and illnesses from potential bioterrorism agents.

National Institutes of Health (NIH) In the United States, a multi-institute agency of the U.S. Department of Health and Human Services. NIH is the federal focal point for health research. It conducts research in its own laboratories and supports research in universities, medical schools, hospitals, and research institutions throughout the United States and abroad. Internet address: http://www.nih.gov/

National Library of Medicine (NLM) A federal institute that serves as the world's largest medical library and is the creator of PubMed, MEDLINE, and MedlinePlus. The National Library of Medicine (NLM) collects materials in all areas of biomedicine and health care. NLM makes its resources available around the world, primarily through its electronic information services.

Natural History Study Study of the natural development of something (such as an organism or a disease) over a period of time.

Natural Killer (NK) Cells A type of lymphocyte.

Nebulized See Aerosolized.

Nemaline Rod Myopathy (NM) A rare neuromuscular disorder characterized by the presence of rodlike structures (nemaline bodies) in the muscle fibers and by muscle weakness. Muscle weakness can occur throughout the body, but is typically most severe in the neck, face, and limbs. Nemaline rod myopathy (NM) in its most severe form can be life-threatening. NM can occur as a complication of HIVinfection.

Neonatal Concerning the first 6 weeks of life after birth.

Neoplasm An abnormal and uncontrolled growth of tissue; a tumor.

Nephritis Inflammation of the kidney.

Nephrolithiasis Calculi (stones) in the kidney. Use of some antiretroviral (ARV) drugs may cause nephrolithiasis.

Nephrotoxic Poisonous to the kidneys.

Neuralgia A sharp, shooting pain along a nerve pathway.

NeuroAIDS A group of neurological disorders caused primarily by HIV damage to the central and peripheral nervous systems. Examples of neuroAIDS disorders include myelopathy, sensory neuropathy, and AIDS dementia.

Neurological Related to the brain, spinal cord, or nerves.

Neurological Complications of AIDS See Central Nervous System (CNS) Damage.

Neuropathy The name given to a group of disorders involving nerves. Symptoms range from a tingling sensation or numbness in the toes and fingers to paralysis. It is estimated that 35% of persons with HIV disease have some form of neuropathy. See Peripheral Neuropathy.

Neutralization The process by which an antibody binds to specific antigens, thereby "neutralizing" the microorganism.

Neutralizing Antibody An antibody that keeps a virus from infecting a cell, usually by blocking receptors on the cell or the virus.

Neutropenia An abnormal decrease in the number of neutrophils (the most common type of white blood cell) in the blood. The decrease may be relative or absolute. Neutropenia may also be associated with HIV infection or may be drug induced.

Neutrophil A type of white blood cell (leukocyte) that engulfs and kills foreign microorganisms such as bacteria.

Nevirapine (NVP) A non-nucleoside reverse transcriptase inhibitor (NNRTI), FDA approved for treatment of HIV-infected adults in combination with nucleoside analogues. The drug is effective in preventing HIV transmission from mothers to infants and is widely used in developing countries because of ease of use and low cost; Viramune (trade name). See Viramune.

New Drug Application (NDA) A drug sponsor's request to the Food and Drug Administration (FDA) for approval to sell and market a new drug in the United States. A new drug application (NDA) includes enough information for the FDA to determine whether the new drug is safe and effective; whether the drug's benefits outweigh its risks; whether the proposed drug label (package insert) is appropriate; and whether the drug manufacturing standards are adequate. Information included in a NDA is based on laboratory and animal preclinical studies and testing in humans (Phase 1-4 clinical trials).

NFV Nelfinavir.

NGO Nongovernmental organization.

Night Sweats Extreme sweating during sleep. Although they can occur with other conditions, night sweats are also a symptom of HIV disease.

NIH See National Institutes of Health (NIH).

NK Cells See Natural Killer (NK) Cells.

NNRT See Non-Nucleoside Reverse Transcriptase Inhibitors (NNRTI).

NNRTI-Sparing Regimen Combination antiretroviral therapy (ART) that does not include antiretroviral (ARV) drugs from the non-nucleoside reverse transcriptase inhibitor (NNRTI) drug class. Excluding NNRTIs from an HIV treatment regimen saves drugs in the NNRTI class for future use.

Non-A, Non-B Hepatitis Non-A, non-B hepatitis, caused by the hepatitis C virus, which appears to be spread through sexual contact as well as through sharing of drug needles. (Another type of non-A, non-B hepatitis is caused by the hepatitis E virus, principally spread through contaminated water.)

Non-Hodgkin's Lymphoma (NHL) A lymphoma made up of B cells and characterized by nodular or diffuse tumors that may appear in the stomach, liver, brain, and bone marrow of persons with HIV. After Kaposi sarcoma, NHL is the most common opportunistic cancer in persons with AIDS.

Non-Inferiority Trial A clinical trial designed to show that a new drug (or other intervention) is at least as effective as the drug to which it is compared.

Non-Nucleoside Reverse Transcriptase Inhibitors (NNRTI) A group of structurally different compounds that bind to the catalytic site of HIV-1's reverse transcriptase. They are quite specific; unlike the nucleoside reverse transcriptase inhibitors, the NNRTIs have no activity against HIV-2. Included in this class of drugs are nevirapine, delavirdine, efavirenz, and tenofovir.

Non-Occupational Post-Exposure Prophylaxis (nPEP) Short-term treatment started as soon as possible after high-risk non-occupational exposure to an infectious agent, such as HIV, hepatitis B virus (HBV), or hepatitis C virus (HCV). Non-occupational exposure refers to exposure to an infectious agent that occurs outside of one's work, for example during sex or when needle sharing to inject street drugs, The purpose of non-occupational post-exposure prophylaxis (nPEP) is to reduce the risk of infection.

Non-Steroidal Anti-Inflammatory Drug (NSAID) A classification of drugs called nonsteroidal anti-inflammatory drugs. NSAIDs reduce inflammation and are used to treat arthritis and mild-to-moderate pain.

NRTI See Nucleoside Reverse Transcriptase Inhibitor (NRTI).

Nucleic Acid Amplification Testing See Nucleic Acid Test.

Nucleic Acid Test A technology that allows detection of very small amounts of genetic material (DNA or RNA) in blood, plasma, and tissue. A nucleic acid test can detect any number of viruses in blood or blood products, thereby better assuring the safety of the blood supply.

Nucleoside A building block of nucleic acids, DNA, or RNA, the genetic material found in living organisms. Nucleosides are nucleotides without the phosphate groups.

Nucleoside Analogue An artificial copy of a nucleoside. When incorporated into the DNA or RNA of a virus during viral growth, the nucleoside analogue acts to prevent production of new virus.

Nucleoside Reverse Transcriptase Inhibitor (NRTI) A nucleoside analogue antiretroviral drug whose chemical structure constitutes a modified version of a natural nucleoside. These compounds suppress replication of retroviruses by interfering with the reverse transcriptase enzyme. The nucleoside analogues cause premature termination of the proviral (viral precursor) DNA chain.

Nucleotide Nucleotides are the building blocks of nucleic acids, DNA, and RNA. Nucleotides are composed of phosphate groups, a five-sided sugar molecule (ribose sugars in RNA, deoxyribose sugars in DNA), and nitrogen-containing bases.

Nucleotide Analogues Nucleotide analogues are drugs that are structurally related to nucleotides; they are chemically altered to inhibit production or activity of disease-causing proteins.

Nucleus The central controlling body within a living cell, usually a spherical unit enclosed in a membrane and containing genetic codes for maintaining the life systems of the organism and for issuing commands for growth and reproduction.

NVP Nevirapine (generic name); Viramune (trade name). See Viramune.

Observational Trial A type of clinical trial. In observational trials, researchers do not assign participants to a treatment or other intervention. Instead, the researchers observe participants or measure certain outcomes to determine health outcomes.

Occupational Exposure Contact with a potentially harmful physical, chemical, or biological agent as a result of one's work. For example, a health care professional may be exposed to HIV or another infectious agent through a needlestick injury.

Occupational HIV Exposure Exposure to HIV as a result of work (job). Exposure may include accidental exposure to HIV-infected blood following a needlestick injury or cut from a surgical instrument.

Occupational Post-Exposure Prophylaxis (oPEP) Short-term treatment started as soon as possible after high-risk occupational exposure to an infectious agent, such as HIV, hepatitis B virus (HBV), or hepatitis C virus (HCV). The purpose of occupational postexposure prophylaxis (oPEP) is to reduce the risk of infection. An example of a high-risk occupational exposure is exposure to an infectious agent as the result of a needlestick injury.

Office of AIDS Research (OAR) The office of the National Institutes of Health (NIH) that coordinates the scientific, budgetary, legislative, and policy elements of the NIH AIDS research program.

Office of Minority Health (OMH) A federal office whose primary responsibility is to improve the health of racial and ethnic minority populations, including African Americans, Hispanic Americans, American Indians, Alaskan Natives, and Pacific Islanders. The Office of Minority Health (OMH) develops or advances policies, programs, and practices that address health, social, economic, environmental, and other factors that impact the health of minority populations, including those specifically affected by HIV/AIDS.

Off-Label Use The legal, prescribed use of a drug In a manner different from that described on the Food and Drug Administration (FDA)-approved drug label. Off-label use can include using a drug for a different disease or medical condition or giving a drug at a different dose or via a different route of administration than approved by FDA.

OI See Opportunistic Infection.

Oncology The branch of medicine that studies cancers or other tumors.

Open-Label Trial A type of clinical trial. In open-label trials, both the researchers and participants know which drug (or other intervention) is being given to participants.

Opportunistic Infection An illness caused by various organisms, some of which usually do not cause disease in persons with normal immune systems. Persons living with advanced HIV infection suffer opportunistic infections of the lungs, brain, eyes, and other organs. Opportunistic infections common in persons diagnosed with AIDS include *Pneumocystis jiroveci* pneumonia; Kaposi sarcoma; cryptosporidiosis; histoplasmosis; other parasitic, viral, and fungal infections; and some types of cancer.

Optimized Background Therapy (OBT) When a new drug is added to a failing HIV regimen, the other drugs in the regimen (the "background therapy") may also be changed. Any changes are made on the basis of a person's resistance test results and treatment history. Optimized background therapy gives a new HIV regimen (or an experimental HIV drug being studied in a clinical trial) the best chance of succeeding.

Opt In In HIV testing, a procedure whereby an individual is counseled about HIV and is given the option of accepting or rejecting an HIV test. They "opt in" when they agree to have the tested done.

Opt Out In HIV testing, a procedure whereby an individual is counseled about HIV and is only given the option of refusing an HIV test. If they refuse the test they have "opted out" of HIV testing. Studies have shown that more individuals agree to HIV testing when an opt out approach is used.

OPV Oral polio vaccine.

Oral Fluid Test A test using oral mucosal fluid. To differentiate this fluid from saliva, an absorbent material is left in the mouth for several minutes. In an HIV-infected person, oral mucosal fluid is likely to contain HIV antibodies.

Oral Hairy Leukoplakia (OHL) A whitish lesion that appears on the side of the tongue and inside the cheeks. The lesion appears raised, with a ribbed or hairy surface. OHL occurs mainly in persons with declining immunity and may be caused by Epstein-Barr virus infection. OHL was not observed before the HIV epidemic.

Oral Sex A type of sexual intercourse in which the partner's genitals are stimulated by mouth and tongue.

Oropharyngeal Relating to the division of the pharynx between the soft palate and the epiglottis. The pharynx is a tube that connects the mouth and nasal passages with the esophagus, the connection to the stomach. The epiglottis is a thin, valvelike structure that covers the glottis, the opening of the upper part of the larynx (the part of the throat containing the vocal cords), during swallowing.

Oropharynx The area beginning at the lips and extending to the back of the mouth.

Osteopenia Lower-than-normal bone mass and bone mineral density. Osteopenia often precedes more severe bone loss (osteoporosis). Osteopenia frequently develops in people taking antiretroviral (ARV) drugs; however, the association between ARV drugs and osteopenia is unclear.

Osteoporosis Progressive loss of bone mass and bone mineral density, resulting in an increased risk of fractures. Osteoporosis frequently develops in people taking antiretroviral (ARV) drugs; however, the association between ARV drugs and osteoporosis is unclear.

Otitis Inflammation of the ear, which may be marked by pain, fever, abnormalities of hearing, hearing loss, tinnitus, and vertigo.

Otitis Media Infection and inflammation of the middle ear space and eardrum.

OVC Orphans and vulnerable children.

Oxytocin A peptide hormone from the hypothalamus that induces smooth muscle contraction in the uterus and mammary glands.

P24 A bullet-shaped part of a protein that surrounds the viral RNA within the envelope of HIV. The p24 antigen test looks for the presence of this protein in a patient's blood. A positive result for the p24 antigen suggests active HIV multiplication.

Package Insert A document, approved by the FDA and furnished by the manufacturer of a drug (inserted into the package), for use when dispensing the drug. The document indicates approved uses, contraindications, and potential side effects.

Palliative A treatment that provides symptomatic relief but not a cure.

Palliative Care Palliative care is an approach to life-threatening chronic illnesses, especially at the end of life. Palliative care combines active and compassionate therapies to comfort and support patients who are living with life-ending illnesses and their families. Palliative care strives to meet physical needs through relieving pain and maintaining quality of life while emphasizing the patient's and family's rights to participate in informed discussions and to make choices. This patient- and family-centered approach uses the skills of interdisciplinary team members to provide a comprehensive continuum of care, including spiritual and emotional needs.

Pancreas A gland situated near the stomach that secretes a digestive fluid into the intestine through one or more ducts and also secretes the hormone insulin.

Pancreatitis Inflammation of the pancreas that can produce severe pain and debilitating illness. Its onset can be predicted by rises in blood levels of the pancreatic enzyme amylase.

Pancytopenia Deficiency of all cell elements of the blood.

Pandemic A disease prevalent throughout an entire country or continent, or the whole world. See Epidemic.

Pap Smear A method for the early detection of cancer and other abnormalities of the female genital tract, especially of the cervix.

Papilloma A benign tumor (as a wart, condyloma, or polyp) resulting from an overgrowth of epithelial tissue. An epithelial tumor caused by a virus. See Condyloma; Epithelium; JC Virus.

Parasite A plant or animal that lives and feeds on or within another living organism (host), causing some degree of harm to the host organism.

Parenteral A route other than in or through the digestive system. For example, parenteral can pertain to blood being drawn from a vein in the arm or introduced into that vein via a transfusion (intravenous), or to injection of medications or vaccines through the skin (subcutaneous) or into muscle (intramuscular).

Paresthesia Abnormal sensations such as burning, tingling, or a "pins-and-needles" feeling. Paresthesia may constitute the first group of symptoms of nerve involvement in HIV infection.

Parotid Of, pertaining to, or in the region of the parotid gland, which is one of the salivary glands situated just in front of or below the ear. It is the largest of the salivary glands in man, and its duct opens into the interior of the mouth opposite the second molar of the upper jaw.

Parotitis Inflammation of the parotid gland, which is located at the angle of the jaw. Mumps is the most frequent cause of parotid swelling. Parotid swelling associated with HIV infection is seen in patients with lymphadenopathy syndrome.

Partogram A series of charted measurements used to assess the progress of labor. Partograms usually record information on fetal heart rate, cervical dilatation, fetal head descent, uterine contractions, amniotic fluid, maternal urine, drugs given (including ARV prophylaxis), maternal blood pressure, pulse, and temperature. In HIV-infected women, the number of vaginal examinations may also be charted. Also known as a partograph.

Passive Antibody Transfer The transfer of antibodies from another person or from an animal, either naturally—as from mother to fetus or to the newborn via breast milk—or by intentional inoculation as in gammaglobulin treatment.

Passive Immunity Immunity that does not come form immunization. It comes from another individual and is given to a patient in the form of antibodies such gammaglobulin.

Passive Immunotherapy Process in which individuals with advanced disease (who have low levels of HIV antibody production) are infused with plasma rich in HIV antibodies or an immunoglobulin concentrate (HIVIG) from such plasma. The plasma is obtained from asymptomatic HIV-positive individuals with high levels of HIV antibodies.

Pathogen Any disease-producing microorganism or material.

Pathogenesis The origin and development of a disease.

PCP See Pneumocystis Jiroveci Pneumonia (PCP).

PCR See Polymerase Chain Reaction (PCR).

Pediatric AIDS Clinical Trials Group (PACTG) A large clinical trials network that evaluates treatments for HIV-infected children and adolescents and that develops new therapeutic approaches for preventing mother-to-child transmission of HIV. Originally an independent network, Pediatric AIDS Clinical Trials Group (PACTG) investigators are now merged with the International Maternal Pediatric Adolescent AIDS Clinical Trials (IMPAACT) Group.

Pediatric AIDS Clinical Trials Group 076 (PACTG 076) A federally funded study that determined that the risk of mother-to-child transmission (MTCT) of HIV could be reduced by nearly 70% if the antiretroviral (ARV) drug zidovudine was given to a woman during pregnancy and labor and delivery and to the newborn. The Pediatric AIDS Clinical Trials Group 076 (PACTG 076) study contributed greatly to preventing MTCT of HIV.

Pelvic Inflammatory Disease (PID) Gynecological condition caused by an infection (usually sexually transmitted) that spreads from the vagina to the upper parts of a woman's reproductive tract in the pelvic cavity. PID takes different courses in different women, but can cause abscesses and constant pain almost anywhere in the genital tract. If left untreated, it can cause infertility or more frequent periods.

Penicillium Marneffei Infection A fungus disease which is endemic in Southeast Asia (especially Northern Thailand). Symptoms include fever, anemia, weight loss, and skin lesions. Infection occurs mostly in people with weakened immune systems, such as people with HIV. Without timely antifungal treatment, the disease can be fatal.

PEP See Postexposure Prophylaxis (PEP).

Peptides Amino acids that are chemically linked to one another. Proteins are made of peptides.

Perianal Around the anus.

Perinatal Pertaining to or occurring in the period shortly before and after birth, variously defined as beginning with completion of the 20th to 28th week of gestation and ending 7 to 28 days after birth.

Perinatal Transmission Transmission of a pathogen, such as HIV, from mother to baby before, during, or after the birth process.

Peripartum See Perinatal.

Peripheral Blood Mononuclear Cell (PBMC) A type of white blood cell that contains one nucleus, such as a lymphocyte or macrophage.

Peripheral Nervous System (PNS) The part of the nervous system that is made up of the nerves outside of the brain and spinal cord, The peripheral nervous system (PNS) transmits information from the brain and spinal cord to the rest of the body; it also transmits sensory information back to the brain and spinal cord, HIV infection or use of certain antiretroviral (ARV) drugs can cause damage to the PNS.

Peripheral Neuritis Inflammation of far portion of the nerves or the nerve endings, usually associated with pain, muscle wasting, and loss of reflexes.

Peripheral Neuropathy Condition characterized by sensory loss, pain, muscle weakness, and wasting of muscle in the hands or legs and feet. It may start with burning or tingling sensations or numbness in the toes and fingers. In severe cases, paralysis may result. Peripheral neuropathy may arise from an HIV-related condition or be the side effect of certain drugs, some of the nucleoside analogues in particular.

Peritonitis Inflammation of the peritoneum (the lining of the abdominal cavity).

Persistent Generalized Lymphadenopathy (PGL) Chronic, diffuse, noncancerous lymph node enlargement. Typically it has been found in persons with persistent bacterial, viral, or fungal infections. PGL in HIV infection is a condition in which lymph nodes are chronically swollen in at least two areas of the body for 3 months or more with no obvious cause other than the HIV infection.

PGL See Persistent Generalized Lymphadenopathy (PGL).

Phagocyte A cell that is able to ingest and destroy foreign matter, including bacteria.

Phagocytosis The process of ingesting and destroying a virus or other foreign matter by phagocytes. See Macrophage; Monocyte.

Pharmacokinetic Enhancers (CYP3A Inhibitors) A drug class. A pharmacokinetic enhancer is used to boost the effectiveness of another drug. When the two drugs are given together, the pharmacokinetic enhancer Interferes with the breakdown of the other drug, which allows the drug to remain in the body longer at a higher concentration. Pharmacokinetic enhancers are included in some HIV treatment regimens.

Pharmacokinetics The processes (in a living organism) of absorption, distribution, metabolism, and excretion of a drug or vaccine.

Pharmacology The study of drugs. Pharmacology includes the study of a drug's composition, pharmacokinetics, therapeutic use, and toxicity.

Phenotype The genetic makeup of an organism such as HIV as it interacts with the environment. In the case of HIV, the virus may interact with cells and drugs. Phenotypic resistance testing determines whether an organism is susceptible to a specific drug in a test tube. Contrast with genotype.

Phase 1 Trial The first step in testing an experimental drug (or other treatment) in humans. Phase 1 trials evaluate the drug's safety and toxicity at different dose levels and determine drug pharmacokinetics. Because little is known about the possible risks and benefits of the drug being tested, Phase 1 trials usually include only a small number of participants (approximately 20 to 100). Testing of other biomedical interventions, such as diagnostic tests or medical devices, also begins with Phase 1 trials.

Phase 2 Trial The second step in testing an experimental drug (or other treatment) in humans. Typically, Phase 2 trials are done only if Phase 1 trials have shown that the drug is safe, but sometimes Phase 1 and Phase 2 trials are combined. Phase 2 trials are designed to evaluate the drug's effectiveness in people with the disease or condition being studied and to determine the common short-term adverse effects and risks associated with the drug. Phase 2 trials involve more participants (often several hundred) and typically last longer than Phase 1 trials.

Phase 3 Trial The third step in testing an experimental drug (or other treatment) in humans. Phase 3 trials are conducted to confirm and expand on safety and effectiveness results from Phase 1 and 2 trials, to compare the drug to standard therapies for the disease or condition being studied, and to evaluate the overall risks and benefits of the drug. This trial phase recruits a large group of people with the disease or condition, usually ranging from 1,000 to 3,000 participants. The Food and Drug Administration (FDA) reviews results from Phase 3 trials when considering a drug for approval.

Phase 4 Trial Preclinical Testing in humans that occurs after a drug (or other treatment) has already been approved by the Food and Drug Administration (FDA) and is being marketed for sale. Phase 4 trials are conducted to determine long-term safety and effectiveness and to identify adverse effects that may not have been apparent in prior trials. Thousands of participants are usually recruited to volunteer for this phase of clinical testing.

Phenotypic Assay A type of resistance test that measures the extent to which a person's strain of HIV will multiply in different concentrations of antiretroviral (ARV) drugs. Resistance testing is used to guide selection of an HIV regimen when initiating or changing antiretroviral therapy (ART).

Photosensitivity Abnormal sensitivity to light. Symptoms may include reddening and blistering of the skin. Use of some antiretroviral (ARV) drugs may cause photosensitivity reactions.

PI See Protease Inhibitors.

Pill Burden The number of tablets, capsules, or other dosage forms that a person takes on a regular basis. A high pill burden can make it difficult to adhere to an HIV treatment regimen.

Pi-Sparing Regimen Combination antiretroviral therapy (ART) that does not include antiretroviral (ARV) drugs from the protease inhibitor (PI) drug class. Excluding PIs from an HIV treatment regimen saves drugs in the PI class for future use.

Placebo A substance that has no activity, often used in a clinical study so that participants do no know if they are receiving the active (study drug) or the inactive placebo. This approach assists in performing clinical studies and determining whether a drug is active against a disease.

Placebo-Controlled Study A method of investigation of drugs in which 1an inactive substance (placebo) is given to one group of patients, while the drug being tested is given to another group. The results obtained in the two groups are then compared to see if the investigational treatment is more effective in treating the condition.

Placebo Effect A physical or emotional change, occurring after a substance is taken or administered, that is not the result of any special property of the substance. The change may be beneficial, reflecting the expectations of the patient and, often, the expectations of the person giving the substance.

Placenta Previa Positioning of the placenta over the opening to the birth canal so that separation usually precedes the infant's birth. This is an important cause of painless third-trimester bleeding.

Placental Barrier A temporary organ separating the mother and fetus. The placenta transfers oxygen and nutrients from the mother to the fetus and permits the release of carbon dioxide and waste products from the fetus through the mother.

Plasma The liquid part of the blood and lymph that contains nutrients, electrolytes (dissolved salts), gases, albumin, clotting factors, wastes, and hormones.

Platelets Active agents of inflammation that are released when damage occurs to a blood vessel. The platelets stick to the blood vessel walls, forming clots to prevent the loss of blood. Some persons living with HIV develop thrombocytopenia, a condition characterized by a platelet count of <100,000 platelets per cubic millimeter of blood.

PLHA People living with HIV/AIDS.

PLWHA People living with HIV/AIDS.

PML See Progressive Multifocal Leukoencephalopathy (PML).

PMTCT Prevention of mother-to-child transmission (of HIV).

Pneumocystis Jiroveci Pneumonia (PCP) An infection of the lungs caused by *Pneumocystis jiroveci*, which is thought to be a protozoan but may be more closely related to a fungus. *P. carinii* grows rapidly in the lungs of persons with AIDS and is a frequent AIDS-related cause of death. *P. carinii* infection sometimes may occur elsewhere in the body (skin, eye, spleen, liver, or heart).

Polymerase Chain Reaction (PCR) A laboratory process that selects a DNA segment from a mixture of DNA chains and rapidly multiplies it to create a large sample of a piece of DNA. It is a sensitive laboratory technique that can detect and measure HIV in a person's blood or lymph nodes (also called RT-PCR). It is also a means of measuring the amount of virus in the blood (viral load).

Polyneuritis Inflammation of many nerves at once.

Polyneuropathy Damage or degeneration of several nerves.

Polyvalent Vaccine A vaccine that is active against multiple viral strains.

Positive Test Any result that indicates that a person has a disease or infection. For HIV, a positive test indicates that the person has been infected with HIV.

Postexposure Prophylaxis (PEP) As it relates to HIV disease, a potentially preventative treatment using antiretroviral drugs to treat individuals within 72 hours of a high-risk exposure (e.g., needlestick injury, unprotected sex, needle sharing) to prevent HIV infection.

Postnatal Occurring after birth, especially during the period immediately after birth.

Postpartum See Postnatal.

PPD Test See Purified Protein Derivative (PPD).

Preconception Counseling Recommended for all women of childbearing age as a component of their primary medical care. The purpose of preconception care is to identify risk factors for adverse maternal or fetal outcome, provide education and counseling targeted to the patient's individual needs, and treat or stabilize medical conditions prior to conception in order to optimize maternal and fetal outcomes.

Pre-Exposure Prophylaxis (PrEP) An HIV prevention method for people who are HIV negative and at high risk of HIV infection. Pre-exposure prophylaxis (PrEP) involves taking a specific combination of HIV medicines daily. PrEP is even more effective when it is combined with condoms and other prevention tools.

Prenatal The period preceding birth, during which the fetus develops in the uterus.

Prepartum See Prenatal.

President's Emergency Plan for AIDS Relief (PEPFAR) The U.S. government global initiative to combat the HIV/AIDS epidemic. The President's Emergency Plan for AIDS Relief (PEPFAR) works with governmental and non-governmental partners worldwide to support integrated HIV prevention, treatment, and care programs. PEPFAR places emphasis on improving health outcomes, increasing program sustainability and integration, and strengthening health systems.

Presumptive Based on a reasonable assumption. In non-breastfed infants born to HIV-infected mothers, presumptive exclusion of HIV infection is based on two or more negative HIV tests, one at age 14 days or older and the other at age 1 month or older. Additional testing is necessary to definitively exclude HIV infection.

Prevalence A measure of the proportion of people in a population affected with a particular disease at a given time.

Preventive HIV Vaccine A vaccine to prevent HIV infection in people who do not have HIV. To date, no preventive HIV vaccine exists, but research is underway.

Primary HIV Infection See Acute HIV Infection.

Primary Immune Complex Reaction A type of hypersensitivity reaction that results from interactions between a drug and the immune system. During a primary immune complex reaction, antigens and antibodies clump together to form immune complexes. These immune complexes then damage body tissue. This rare but serious drug reaction can occur with use of certain antiretroviral (ARV) drugs.

Primary Isolate HIV taken from an infected individual (as opposed to being grown in laboratory cultures).

Primary Prevention Drugs or other forms of treatment used to prevent the development of a disease in a person who is at risk for but with no prior history of the disease. For example, primary prophylaxis is used to prevent people with advanced HIV infection from developing opportunistic infections, such as toxoplasmosis.

Probability The chance, or likelihood, that a certain event will occur.

Proctitis Inflammation of the rectum.

Prodrome A symptom that indicates the onset of a disease.

Products of Conception Tissues resulting from a pregnancy, such as the placenta.

Progressive Multifocal Leukoencephalopathy (PML) A rapidly debilitating opportunistic infection caused by the JC virus that infects brain tissue and causes damage to the brain and the spinal cord. Symptoms vary from patient to patient but include loss of muscle control, paralysis, blindness, problems with speech, and an altered mental state. PML can lead to coma and death.

Prophylactic Drug A drug that helps to prevent a disease or initial infection. See Prophylaxis.

Prophylaxis Treatment to prevent the onset of a particular disease (primary prophylaxis), or the recurrence of symptoms in an existing infection that has been brought under control (secondary prophylaxis, maintenance therapy).

Protease An enzyme that breaks down proteins into their component peptides. HIV's protease enzyme breaks apart long strands of viral protein into the separate proteins making up the viral core. The enzyme acts as new virus particles are budding off a cell membrane. Protease is the first HIV protein whose three-dimensional structure has been characterized. See Proteins.

Protease Inhibitors Antiviral drugs that act by inhibiting the virus' protease enzyme, thereby preventing viral replication. Specifically, these drugs block the protease enzyme from breaking apart long strands of viral proteins to make the smaller, active HIV proteins that comprise the virion. If the larger HIV proteins are not broken apart, they cannot assemble themselves into new functional HIV particles. HIV protease inhibitors include indinavir, ritonavir, saquinavir, nelfinavir, amprenavir, atazanavir, and fosamprenavir.

Protease-Sparing Regimen An antiretroviral drug regimen that does not include a protease inhibitor.

Proteins Highly complex organic compounds found naturally in all living cells. Proteins are a source of heat and energy to the body. They are essential for growth, the building of new tissue, and the repair of injured tissue.

Proteinuria Excess protein in the urine. Proteinuria is a sign of chronic kidney disease, which can result from diabetes, high blood pressure, and diseases that cause inflammation in the kidneys. Proteinuria can also occur if antiretroviral (ARV) drugs damage the kidneys.

Protocol The detailed plan for conducting clinical studies. It states the trial's rationale, purpose, drug or vaccine dosages, length of study, routes of administration, who may participate (Inclusion/Exclusion Criteria), and other aspects of trial design. See Inclusion/Exclusion Criteria.

Protozoa Large group of one-celled (unicellular) animals, including amoebas. Some protozoa cause parasitic diseases in persons with AIDS, notably toxoplasmosis and cryptosporidiosis. See Pneumocystis Jiroveci Pneumonia (PCP).

Provirus An inactive viral form that has been integrated into the genes of a host cell. For example, when HIV enters a host CD4 cell, HIV RNA is first changed to HIV DNA (provirus). The HIV provirus then gets inserted into the DNA of the CD4 cell. When the CD4 cell replicates, the HIV provirus is passed from one cell generation to the next, ensuring ongoing replication of HIV.

Pruritis Itching.

PubMed A service of the U.S. National Library of Medicine that provides free access to an extensive database of citations and abstracts for biomedical literature, life science journals, and online books. Citations may include links to full-text content and to related resources.

Pulmonary Pertaining to the lungs.

Purified Protein Derivative (PPD) Material used in the tuberculin skin test (TST); the most common test for exposure to Mycobacterium tuberculosis, the bacterium that causes tuberculosis (TB). PPD is sometimes used synonymously with TST. In the PPD test, a small amount of protein from TB is injected under the skin. If patients have been previously infected, they will mount a delayed-type hypersensitivity reaction, characterized by a hard red bump called an induration.

Purpura (ITP) See Immune Thrombocytopenic Purpura (ITP).

PWA Person with AIDS. Also known as PLWA, person living with AIDS.

QD Once each day.

QID Four times each day.

Quality Assurance An examination that reviews a study, manufacture of a drug or other process in order to certify that correct methods were followed.

Qualitative Transcription-Mediated Amplification Assay A type of viral load test. Viral load tests are used to diagnose acute HIV infection, guide treatment choices, and monitor response to antiretroviral therapy (ART).

Quantitative Branched DNA Assay (bDNA) A type of viral load test. Viral load tests are used to diagnose acute HIV infection, guide treatment choices, and monitor response to antiretroviral therapy (ART).

Quasispecies A group of viruses found in the same host. The viruses in the group develop similar genetic mutations over time. During HIV infection, HIV can mutate into multiple quasispecies, which may reduce the immune system's ability to control HIV infection. Antiretroviral therapy (ART) started in the early stages of HIV infection can control HIV replication and development of quasispecies.

R5-Tropic Virus A strain of HIV that enters and infects a host CD4 cell by attaching to the CCR5 coreceptor on the CD4 cell. To enter a CD4 cell, HIV must first attach to a CD4 receptor, then attach to either the CCR5 or CXCR4 coreceptor, and finally fuse its membrane with the CD4 cell membrane. HIV is usually R5-tropic (uses CCR5) during the early stages of infection, but the virus may later switch to using either only CXCR4 (X4-tropic) or both CCR5 and CXCR4 (dual-tropic). Antiretroviral (ARV) drugs in the CCR5 inhibitor drug class block HIV from attaching to the CCR5 coreceptor, preventing HIV entry into the CD4 cell.

Radiology The science of diagnosis and treatment of disease using radioactive substances, including x-rays, radioactive isotopes, ionizing radiation, and C-T scans.

Randomized Trial A study in which participants are randomly (i.e., by chance) assigned to one of two or more treatment arms or regimens of a clinical study. Occasionally, placebos are utilized.

Rapid HIV Test A screening test for detecting antibody to HIV that produces very quick results, usually in 5 to 30 minutes. For diagnosis of HIV infection, a positive rapid test is confirmed with a second rapid test made by a different manufacturer.

Reagent A substance used in a chemical reaction to detect, analyze, or produce another substance.

Rebound An increase in viral load following a previous decrease due to anti-HIV therapy.

Receptor A molecule on the surface of a cell that serves as a recognition or binding site for antigens, antibodies, or other cellular or immunological components.

Rechallenge Restarting a drug that was stopped because it was considered the likely cause of an adverse effect. When the drug is restarted, the person is closely monitored for any signs of the adverse effect.

Recombinant DNA produced in a laboratory by joining segments of DNA from different sources. Recombinant can also describe proteins, cells, or organisms made by genetic engineering.

Red Blood Cell Blood cells that carry oxygen to all parts of the body. Red blood cells have a high concentration of hemoglobin, a protein that binds to oxygen from the lungs and that gives blood its red color.

Referral A suggestion that a patient see another individual (usually a specialist) for another opinion.

Refractory Referring to a disease that does not readily respond to treatment.

Regimen Simplification Making changes to an HIV treatment regimen to make medication adherence easier. Simplifying an HIV regimen can include reducing the number of antiretroviral (ARV) drugs in the regimen or changing to a combination ARV drug that provides a one-pill, once-daily complete regimen. Other changes can include switching to ARV drugs that cause fewer adverse effects or to ARV drugs that can be taken without food. Benefits of regimen simplification include long-term medication adherence, reduced risk of treatment failure, and improved quality of life.

Regulatory T Lymphocyte A type of lymphocyte. Regulatory T lymphocytes (regulatory T cells) prevent the immune system from becoming over-active during an immune response and from attacking normal cells.

Reinfection/Superinfection The infection of an already HIV-infected person with another strain of HIV. The superinfection can be with a more aggressive strain of HIV.

Relapse The recurrence of a disease after a period of remission or apparent recovery.

Relative Contraindication When a particular treatment or procedure should be used with caution. The risk of using the treatment or procedure is acceptable because the benefits outweigh the risks.

Remission The lessening in the severity of symptoms or duration of an outbreak of a disease.

Renal Pertaining to the kidneys.

Replacement Feeding The process of feeding a child who is not receiving any breast milk with a diet that provides all the nutrients the child needs. During the first 6 months this should be with a suitable breast-milk substitute—commercial formula, or home-prepared formula with micronutrient supplements. After 6 months it preferably should be with a suitable breast-milk substitute and complementary foods made from appropriately prepared and nutrient-enriched family foods, given three times a day. If suitable breast-milk substitutes are not available, appropriately prepared family foods should be further enriched and given five times a day.

Replication The process of duplicating or reproducing.

Rescue Therapy See Salvage Therapy.

Resistance Reduction in a microorganism's sensitivity to a particular drug. Resistance is thought to result usually from a genetic mutation. In HIV, such mutations can change the structure of viral enzymes and proteins so that an antiviral drug can no longer bind with them as well as it used to.

Resistance Testing The evaluation of bacteria or viruses such as HIV to determine whether they are resistant to the effects of drugs used for treatment. Resistance testing is an important tool to determine whether a patient with HIV infection is getting sicker because ARV drugs are no longer working.

Retina Light-sensitive tissue at the back of the eye that transmits visual impulses to the brain via the optic nerve. See Retinitis.

Retinal Detachment Condition in which a portion of the retina becomes separated from the inner wall of the eye. In AIDS patients, it can result from retinal disease such as Cytomegalovirus (CMV) retinitis.

Retinitis Inflammation of the retina, linked in AIDS to Cytomegalovirus (CMV) infection. Untreated, it can lead to blindness.

Retrospective Study A type of medical research study. Retrospective studies look back in time to compare a group of people with a particular disease or condition to a group of people who do not have the disease or condition. Researchers study the medical and lifestyle histories of the people in each group to learn what factors may be associated with the disease or condition.

Retrovirus A type of virus that, when not infecting a cell, stores its genetic information on a single-stranded RNA molecule instead of the more usual double-stranded DNA. HIV is an example of a retrovirus.

Reverse Transcriptase (RT) An enzyme capable of copying RNA into DNA during the HIV multiplication cycle. Several anti-HIV drugs—such as AZT, ddI, and ddC—are chemicals that act against the reverse transcriptase enzyme.

Reverse Transcriptase Inhibitors (RTI) A series of nucleoside analogues that inhibit the reverse transcriptase of HIV. Included in this category are the drugs zidovudine, lamivudine, abacavir, didanosine, stavudine, zalcitabine, and emtricitabine.

Reverse Transcriptase Polymerase Chain Reaction (RT-PCR) An FDA-approved test to measure viral load. The test is also known as PCR (polymerase chain reaction). See Polymerase Chain Reaction (PCR).

Reverse Transcription The third of seven steps in the HIV life cycle. Once inside a CD4 cell, HIV releases and uses reverse transcriptase (an HIV enzyme) to convert its genetic material—HIV RNA—into HIV DNA. The conversion of HIV RNA to HIV DNA allows HIV to enter the CD4 cell nucleus and combine with the cell's genetic material.

Rhinitis Inflammation of the mucous membrane of the nose.

Ribonucleic Acid (RNA) A nucleic acid, found mostly in the cytoplasm of cells (rather than in the nucleus) that is important in the synthesis of proteins.

Risk Assessment Risk assessment is a fundamental part of an HIV prevention counseling session in which the individual is encouraged to identify, acknowledge, and discuss in detail his or her personal risk for acquiring or transmitting HIV.

RNA See Ribonucleic Acid (RNA).

RTI See Reverse Transcriptase Inhibitors (RTI).

RT-PCR See Reverse Transcriptase Polymerase Chain Reaction (RT-PCR).

RTV Ritonavir.

Rupture of Membranes Also known as water breaking. A term used to define the rupture of the amniotic sac, releasing the amniotic fluid and heralding the onset of labor.

Ryan White HIV/AIDS Program The largest federally funded program providing HIV-related services to low-income, uninsured, and underinsured people with HIV/AIDS. The program's services are available in all 50 states and U.S. territories.

Salmonella A family of gram-negative bacteria, found in undercooked poultry or eggs, that are a common cause of food poisoning, and that can cause serious disseminated disease in HIV-infected persons.

Salmonella Septicemia A life-threatening infection that has spread to the bloodstream. Septicemia can be caused by any of the bacteria, which are found in contaminated food and water. The infection is systemic and affects virtually every organ system. The most common symptom is a fever that comes and goes. In people with HIV, recurrent septicemia is an AIDS-defining condition.

Salvage Therapy Also referred to as rescue therapy. A treatment effort for people whose antiretroviral regimens have failed at least two times and who have had extensive prior exposure to antiretroviral agents.

Sarcoma A malignant (cancerous) tumor of the skin and soft tissue.

Seborrheic Dermatitis A chronic inflammatory disease of the skin of unknown cause or origin, characterized by moderate redness; dry, moist, or greasy scaling; and yellow crusted patches on various areas, including the mid-parts of the face, ears, above the orbit of the eye, umbilicus (the navel), genitalia, and especially the scalp.

Secondary Prophylaxis See Maintenance Therapy.

Secondary Transmission The transfer (spread) of HIV that mainly occurs during sex or needle sharing as the result of contact with the semen, vaginal fluid, or blood of an HIV-infected partner. (HIV transmission from mother to child during pregnancy, labor and delivery, or breastfeeding is called vertical transmission.)

Self-Administered Therapy (SAT) A method of drug administration in which a person takes medication without being observed by a health care professional.

Semen A thick, whitish fluid that is discharged from the male penis during ejaculation. Semen contains sperms and various secretions. HIV can be transmitted through the semen of a man with HIV.

Semen-Derived Enhancer of Virus Infection (SEVI) Protein fibers found in semen that can trap HIV and help HIV attach to cells. Semen-derived enhancer of virus infection (SEVI) increases the risk of sexual transmission of HIV.

Sensitivity (of a Test) The sensitivity of a test is the probability of it giving a positive result if infection is truly present. As the sensitivity of the test increases the proportion of false negatives decreases.

Sepsis The presence of harmful microorganisms or associated toxins in the blood.

Septra Trade name of trimethoprim/sulphamethoxazole. See Trimethoprim/sulphamethoxazole.

Seroconversion The development of antibodies to a particular bacteria, virus, or vaccine. When people develop antibodies to HIV, they seroconvert from antibody-negative to antibody-positive. It may take from as little as 1 week to several months or more after infection with HIV for antibodies to the virus to develop. After antibodies to HIV appear in the blood, a person should test positive on antibody tests. See Incubation Period; Window Period.

Seroincidence The rate of new infections within a specific target population in a time period.

Serologic Test Any number of tests that are performed on the clear fluid portion of blood. Often refers to a test that determines the presence of antibodies to antigens such as viruses.

Seroprevalence As related to HIV infection, the proportion of persons who have serologic (i.e., pertaining to serum) evidence of HIV infection at any given time.

Serostatus Results of a blood test for specific antibodies.

Serum The clear, thin, and sticky fluid portion of the blood that remains after coagulation (clotting). Serum contains no blood cells, platelets, or fibrinogen.

Set Point The measurable holding point or balance between the virus and the body's immune system reported as the viral load measurement. The viral set point is established within a few weeks to a few months after infection and is thought to remain steady for an indefinite period of time. Set points are thought to determine how long it will take for disease progression to occur.

Sexually Transmitted Disease (STD) Also called venereal disease (VD) (an older public health term) or sexually transmitted infection (STI). STDs are infections spread by the transfer of organisms from person to person during sexual contact. In addition to the "traditional" STDs (syphilis and gonorrhea), the spectrum of STDs now includes HIV infection, which causes AIDS; Chlamydia trachomatis infections; human papilloma virus (HPV) infection; genital herpes; chancroid; genital mycoplasmas; hepatitis B; trichomoniasis; enteric infections; and ectoparasitic diseases (i.e., diseases caused by organisms that live on the outside the host's body). The complexity and scope of STDs have increased dramatically since the 1980s; more than 20 microorganisms and syndromes are now recognized as belonging in this category.

SGOT (Serum glutamic oxaloacetic transaminase) Also known as AST (aspartate aminotransaminase), a liver enzyme that plays a role in protein metabolism. Elevated serum levels of SGOT are a sign of liver damage from disease or drugs.

SGPT (Serum glutamic pyruvate transaminase) Also known as ALT (alanine aminotransaminase), a liver enzyme that plays a role in protein metabolism similar to that of SGOT. Elevated serum levels of SGPT are a sign of liver damage from disease or drugs.

Shigellosis An enteric (intestinal) bacterial infection which is typically transmitted through contact with contaminated human feces. Symptoms usually include watery or bloody diarrhea, abdominal pain, nausea, and fever. Certain bacterial enteric infections, including shigellosis, occur at a much higher rate in people with HIV than in people with healthy immune systems.

Shingles See Herpes Zoster.

SHIV (Simian Human Immunodeficiency Virus) A genetically engineered virus having an HIV envelope and an SIV core.

Side Effects The actions or effects of a drug (or vaccine) other than those desired. The term usually refers to undesired or negative effects, such as headache, skin irritation, or liver damage. Experimental drugs must be evaluated for both immediate and long-term side effects.

Simian Immunodeficiency Virus (SIV) An HIV-like virus that infects monkeys, chimpanzees, and other nonhuman primates.

Single-Blind Study A type of clinical trial in which either the investigators or the participants are unaware of the treatment (or other intervention) that the participants are receiving.

Sinusitis Inflammation of the nasal cavity and sinuses.

SIV See Simian Immunodeficiency Virus (SIV).

Specificity (of a Test) The specificity of a test is the probability of the test providing a negative result if the disease is truly absent. As the specificity of a test increases, the proportion of false positives decreases.

Sperm Washing A laboratory procedure used to separate semen (the fluid part of ejaculate) from sperm. Sperm washing can be considered as a reproductive option for an HIV discordant couple in which the man is the HIV-Infected partner. Because the seminal fluid contains the highest concentration of HIV, the "washed" sperm contains little if any HIV. However, because sperm washing has not been proven completely effective, couples using the procedure should be counseled regarding the potential risks for transmission of HIV.

Spermicide A topical preparation or substance used during sexual intercourse to kill sperm. Although spermicides may prevent pregnancy, they do not protect against HIV infection or other sexually transmitted infections. Irritation of the vagina and rectum that sometimes occurs with use of spermicides may increase the risk of sexual transmission of HIV.

Spinal Tap See Lumbar Puncture.

Spleen Large lymphatic organ in the upper left of the abdominal cavity with several functions, including trapping of foreign matter in the blood, destruction of degraded red blood cells and foreign matter by macrophages, formation of new lymphocytes and antibody production, and storage of excess red blood cells.

Splenomegaly An enlarged spleen.

Sputum Mucus and other matter that is brought up from the lungs by coughing.

Sputum Analysis Method of detecting certain infections (especially tuberculosis) by culturing of sputum—the mucus matter that collects in the respiratory and upper digestive passages and is expelled by coughing.

SQV Saquinavir.

SSA Sub-Saharan Africa.

Standards of Care Treatment regimen or medical management based on state-of-the-art patient care.

Staphylococcus Type of bacteria that may cause various types of infection.

STD/STI See Sexually Transmitted Disease (STD).

Stem Cells Cells from which all blood cells derive. Bone marrow is rich in stem cells.

Stevens-Johnson Syndrome A severe and sometimes fatal form of erythema multiforme that is characterized by severe skin manifestations; conjunctivitis (eye inflammation), which often results in blindness; Vincent's angina (trench mouth); and ulceration of the genitals and anus.

Stomatitis Any of numerous inflammatory diseases of the mouth (e.g., canker sores, thrush, fever blisters) having various causes, such as mechanical trauma, irritants, allergy, vitamin deficiency, or infection.

Strain Subgroup of a species. For HIV, different types of HIV such as HIV-1, HIV-2, clade A, clade B, etc.

Streptococcus Pneumonia Infection Bacterial infection which is spread through contact with respiratory droplets from a person who is infected with or carrying the bacteria. The bacteria are a major cause of common illnesses, such as inflammation of the sinuses (sinusitis), but can also result in life-threatening infections, including meningitis and pneumonia. People with weakened immune systems, including people with HIV, are at higher risk for bacterial pneumonia, including infection, than people with healthy immune systems.

Stroke An interruption of blood flow to the brain, caused by a broken or blocked blood vessel. A stroke results in sudden loss of brain function, such as loss of consciousness, paralysis, or changes in speech. Stroke is a medical emergency and can be life-threatening.

Structured Treatment Interruption (STI) A planned break from treatment, during which a person stops taking medications. Structured treatment interruptions (STIs) may be used to reduce toxic effects of medications, to enhance a medication's effectiveness when restarted, or as a step towards stopping treatment all together. Structured interruption of HIV treatment is not recommended outside of controlled clinical trials.

Study Endpoint A primary or secondary outcome used to judge the effectiveness of a treatment.

Subclinical Infection An infection, or phase of infection, without readily apparent symptoms or signs of disease.

Subcutaneous (SQ) Beneath the skin or introduced beneath the skin (e.g., subcutaneous injections).

Subcutaneous Adipose Tissue (SAT) Fat tissue located right under the skin. HIV-associated lipodystrophy can include changes in subcutaneous adipose tissue (SAT) and may be related to use of certain antiretroviral (ARV) drugs.

Suboptimal Immunologic Response After antiretroviral therapy (ART) is initiated, the failure to achieve and maintain adequate CD4 counts despite viral suppression.

Subunit HIV Vaccine A vaccine that is based on only part of the HIV molecule.

Substance Abuse and Mental Health Services Administration (SAMHSA) The lead federal agency for reducing the impact of substance abuse and mental illness in the United States. The Substance Abuse and Mental Health Services Administration (SAMHSA) provides grant funding to address issues of HIV, AIDS, and viral hepatitis.

Subtype A subgroup of genetically related HIV-1 viruses. HIV-1 can be classified into four groups: M Group, N Group, 0 Group, and P Group. Viruses within each group can then be further classified by subtype. For example, the HIV-1 M group includes at least nine subtypes: A1, A2, B, C, D, FI, F2, G, H, J, and K.

Sulfa Drug A sulfonamide drug used to treat bacterial infections. These drugs inhibit the action of p-aminobenzoic acid, a substance bacteria need in order to reproduce.

Sulfonamides Synthetic derivatives of p-aminobenzene sulfonamide. See Sulfa Drug.

Superinfection When a person who is already infected with HIV becomes infected with a second, different strain of HIV. Superinfection may cause HIV to advance more rapidly. Superinfection can also complicate treatment if the newly acquired strain of HIV is resistant to antiretroviral (ARV) drugs in the person's current HIV treatment regimen.

Superiority Trial A clinical trial designed to show that a new drug (or other intervention) is more effective than the drug to which it is compared.

Suppressor T Cells (T8, CD8) Subset of T cells that halts antibody production and other immune responses.

Surrogate Endpoint Substitute measure for a clinical endpoint. Because it can be difficult to measure clinical endpoints in studies running for several years, researchers often use surrogate endpoints as substitute measures for clinical endpoints. For example, in HIV-related clinical trials, rising CD4 count is used as a surrogate endpoint for progression of HIV infection.

Surrogate Markers Variables (measures) that are followed in clinical trials when the variable of interest cannot be conveniently observed in a direct manner. Two commonly used surrogate markers in HIV studies are CD4+ T-cell counts and quantitative plasma HIV RNA (viral load).

Surveillance See Epidemiologic Surveillance.

Susceptible Vulnerable or predisposed to a disease or infection.

Sustained Virologic Response The continuous, long-term suppression of a person's viral load (HIV RNA)—generally to undetectable levels—as the result of treatment with antiretroviral (ARV) drugs.

Symptoms Any perceptible, subjective change in the body or its functions that indicates disease or phases of disease, as reported by the patient.

Syncytium A large cell-like structure that forms when many cells fuse together. Syncytia can form during viral infection. In some people with HIV, syncytia formation has been linked to more rapid progression of HIV infection.

Syndrome A group of symptoms as reported by the patient and signs as detected in an examination that together are characteristic of a specific condition.

Synergism, Synergistic An interaction between two or more treatments (e.g., drugs) that produces or enhances an effect that is greater than the sum of the effects produced by the individual treatments.

Syphilis A primarily sexually transmitted disease resulting from infection with the spirochete (a bacterium) Treponema pallidum. Syphilis can also be acquired in the uterus during pregnancy.

Systemic Concerning or affecting the body as a whole. A systemic therapy is one that the entire body is exposed to, rather than just the target tissues affected by a disease.

3TC Lamivudine.

T Cells (T lymphocytes) T cells are white blood cells derived from the thymus gland that participate in a variety of cell-mediated immune reactions. Three fundamentally different types of T cells are recognized helper, killer, and suppressor. They are essential for a normal functioning immune system.

T Lymphocytes See T Cells.

T Suppressor Cells T lymphocytes responsible for turning off the immune response after an infection is cleared. They are a subset of the CD8+ lymphocytes.

T4 Cell (Also called T-helper cell.) Antibody-triggered immune cells that seek and attack invading microorganisms. Macrophages summon T4 cells to the infection site. There, the T4 cell reproduces and secretes potent chemicals that stimulate B cells to produce antibodies, signal natural killer or cytotoxic (cell-killing) T cells, and summon other macrophages to the infection site. In healthy immune systems, T4 cells are twice as common as T8 cells.

Tachycardia Abnormal rapid heartbeat. In adults, a rate over 100 beats per minute is usually considered tachycardia. Tachycardia can occur as part of lactic acidosis, which may be caused by advanced HIV infection or some antiretroviral (ARV) drugs.

Tachypnea Abnormal increased rate of breathing. Tachypnea can occur as part of lactic acidosis, which may be caused by advanced HIV infection or antiretroviral (ARV) drugs.

Tanner Staging A scale used to classify the onset and progression of puberty in children and adolescents. The scale describes five stages of physical development on the basis of sex characteristics, such as pubic hair growth, development of genitalia in boys, and development of breasts in girls. Because children mature at different rates, health care providers use Tanner staging (in addition to age) to determine appropriate dosing of drugs to treat HIV infection and opportunistic infections.

TB, TBC   See Tuberculosis (TB).

T-Cell Exhaustion   The gradual decrease in T-cell function that can occur with chronic infections and cancers. T-cell exhaustion weakens the immune system making it difficult for the body to fight off infections or kill cancer-causing cells.

TDF   Tenofovir disoproxil fumarate.

Teratogenicity   The production of physical defects in offspring in utero (i.e., causing birth defects). Teratogenicity is a potential side effect of some drugs, such as thalidomide.

Tetanus   An acute, often fatal infectious disease caused by the bacterium *Clostridium tetani*. The agent usually enters the body through contaminated puncture wounds (e.g., those caused by metal nails, wood splinters, or insect bites), although other portals of entry include burns, surgical wounds, the umbilical stump of neonates, and the postpartum uterus. The disease can be prevented by immunizing with tetanus toxoid.

Therapeutic Drug Monitoring (TDM)   Measuring the concentration of a drug in the blood at scheduled intervals. Therapeutic drug monitoring (TDM) is used to determine the dose at which a drug will be most safe and effective. Although TDM is not generally recommended for routine use in HIV treatment, it may be considered in some situations.

Therapeutic HIV Vaccine   Also called treatment vaccine. A vaccine designed to boost the immune response to HIV infection. A therapeutic vaccine is different from a preventive vaccine, which is designed to prevent an infection or disease from becoming established in a person.

Therapeutic Index (TI)   A ratio that compares the blood concentration at which a drug becomes toxic and the concentration at which the drug is effective. The larger the therapeutic index (TI), the safer the drug is. If the TI is small (the difference between the two concentrations is very small), the drug must be dosed carefully and the person receiving the drug should be monitored closely for any signs of drug toxicity.

Therapy   Any form of treatment. Drugs, radiation, and psychiatric counseling are forms of therapy.

Thrombocytopenia   A decreased number of blood platelets (cells important for blood clotting). See Platelets; Immune Thrombocytopenic Purpura (ITP).

Thrush   Sore patches in the mouth caused by the fungus *Candida albicans*. Thrush is one of the most frequent early symptoms or signs of an immune disorder. The fungus commonly lives in the mouth, but only causes problems when the body's resistance is reduced either by antibiotics that have reduced the number of competitive organisms in the mouth or by an immune deficiency such as HIV disease. See Candidiasis.

Thymus   A mass of glandular tissue (lymphoid organ) found in the upper chest under the breastbone in humans. The thymus is essential to the development of the body's system of immunity beginning in fetal life (i.e., before birth). The thymus processes white blood cells (lymphocytes), which kill foreign cells and stimulate other immune cells to produce antibodies.

TID   Three times each day.

Tissue   A collection of similar cells acting together to perform a particular function. There are four basic tissues in the body: epithelial, connective, muscle, and nerve.

Titer (Titre)   A laboratory measurement of the amount—or concentration—of a given compound in solution.

TIW   Three times each week.

TMP/SMZ   Trimethoprim/sulfamethoxazole (generic name); Cotrimoxazole, Bactrim, Septra (trade names).

Tolerance   The ability to tolerate a drug when given as prescribed, in other words, tolerance means benefiting from the drug without having any adverse effects that would make it impossible to continue taking the drug.

Topical   Pertaining to a drug or treatment applied to the outer surface of the body, such as the skin or mucous membranes.

TOT   Training of trainers.

Total Lymphocyte Count   A count of the number of lymphocytes (white blood cells) in the blood.

Toxic Epidermal Necrolysis (TEN)   A severe form of Stevens-Johnson syndrome involving at least 30% of the total body skin area.

Toxicity   The extent, quality, or degree of being poisonous or harmful to the body.

Toxoplasmic Encephalitis   See Toxoplasmosis.

Toxoplasmosis (toxo)   An opportunistic infection caused by the protozoan parasite Toxoplasma gondii, which is found in undercooked meat and cat feces. A common manifestation is toxoplasmic encephalitis, characterized by brain swelling, confusion, lethargy, and possible coma.

Transaminase   A liver enzyme. A laboratory test that measures transaminase levels is used to assess the functioning of the liver.

Transfusion   The process of transfusing fluid (such as blood) into a vein.

Transmission   In the context of HIV disease, HIV is spread most commonly by sexual contact with an infected partner. The virus can enter the body through the mucosal lining of the vagina, vulva, penis, rectum, or, rarely, the mouth during sex. The likelihood of transmission is increased by factors that may damage these linings, especially other sexually transmitted diseases that cause ulcers or inflammation. HIV also is spread through contact with infected blood, most often by the sharing of drug needles or syringes contaminated with minute quantities of blood containing the virus. Children can contract HIV from their infected mothers either during pregnancy or birth, or postnatally through breast-feeding. In developed countries, HIV is now rarely transmitted by transfusion of blood or blood products because of screening measures.

Transmitted Resistance When a person becomes infected with a strain of HIV that is already resistant to certain antiretroviral (ARV) drugs.

Transplacental Across or through the placenta. Usually refers to the exchange of nutrients, waste products, and other materials (e.g., drugs) between the developing fetus and the mother. Also refers to transmission of virus such as HIV across the placenta to the infant.

Treatment Failure Inability of a medical therapy to achieve the desired results.

Treatment Regimen A structured treatment plan designed to improve and maintain health. Recommended regimens for the initial treatment of HIV include a combination of three or more antiretroviral (ARV) drugs from at least two different HIV drug classes.

Triglyceride A compound made up of a fatty acid (such as oleic, palmitic, or stearic acid) and glycerol. Triglycerides make up most animal and vegetable fats and are the basic water-insoluble substances (lipids) that appear in the blood where they circulate.

Trimethoprim/Sulphamethoxazole (Cotrimoxazole, Bactrim) A combination antibiotic drug effective at preventing and treating *Pneumocystis jiroveci* pneumonia (PCP); also serves as a prophylaxis against toxoplasmosis.

Triple-Class Experienced When an HIV-infected person has received antiretroviral (ARV) drugs from three drug classes.

True Negative A negative test result that correctly indicates that the condition being tested for is not present. For example, a true negative HIV test correctly indicates that a person is not infected with HIV.

True Positive A positive test result that correctly indicates that the condition being tested for is present. For example, a true positive HIV test correctly indicates that a person is infected with HIV.

Tuberculin Skin Test (TST) A purified protein derivative (PPD) of the tubercle bacilli, called tuberculin, is introduced into the skin by scratch, puncture, or intradermal injection. If a raised, red, or hard zone forms around the test site, the person is said to be sensitive to tuberculin, and the test is read as positive.

Tuberculosis (TB) Infection with the bacteria Mycobacterium tuberculosis, as evidenced by a positive tuberculin skin test (TST) that screens for infection with this organism. Sometimes, TST is called a purified protein derivative (PPD) or Mantoux test. A positive skin test might or might not indicate active TB disease. Thus, any person with a positive TST should be screened for active TB and, once active TB is excluded, evaluated for treatment to prevent the development of TB disease. TB infection alone is not considered an opportunistic infection indicating possible immune deficiency.

UNAIDS Joint United Nations Program on AIDS.

Undetectable Viral Load When the amount of HIV in the blood is too low to be detected with a viral load (HIV RNA) test. Antiretroviral (ARV) drugs may reduce a person's viral load to an undetectable level; however, that does not mean the person is cured. Some HIV, in the form of latent HIV reservoirs, remain inside cells and in body tissues.

Universal Precautions A simple set of effective practices designed to protect health workers and patients from infection with a range of pathogens, including blood-borne viruses. These practices are used when caring for all patients regardless of diagnosis.

Uptake Usually, the numbers of individuals who agree to a procedure such as the number of pregnant women who agree to take an HIV test or agree to participate in prenatal care.

Urolithiasis Calculi (stones) in the urinary tract. Use of some antiretroviral (ARV) drugs may cause urolithiasis.

Urticaria Raised, swollen, itchy areas on the skin or mucous membranes, usually caused by an allergic reaction to a drug or food.

Vaccination Inoculation of a substance (i.e., vaccine) into the body for the purpose of producing active immunity against a disease. Initially associated with smallpox vaccination but now often used interchangeably with immunization. See Vaccine.

Vaccine A substance that contains antigenic components from an infectious microorganism. By stimulating an immune response—but not the disease—it protects against subsequent infection by that organism. There can be preventive vaccines (e.g., measles or mumps) as well as therapeutic (treatment) vaccines. See Therapeutic HIV Vaccine; Antigen.

Vaccinia The pox-type virus used in the vaccine that eradicated smallpox. Researchers are studying the possibility of using a modified, milder version of the vaccinia virus to develop a vaccine against HIV infection.

Vacuolar Myelopathy A neurological disorder associated with advanced HIV infection. Vacuolar myelopathy causes the protective myelin sheath to pull away from nerve cells of the spinal cord, forming small holes (vacuoles) in nerve fibers. Symptoms of vacuolar myelopathy include weak and stiff legs and unsteadiness when walking.

Vaginal Candidiasis Infection of the vagina caused by the yeastlike fungus Candida (especially *Candida albicans*). Symptoms include, pain, itching, redness, and white patches in the vaginal wall. It can occur in all women, but it is especially common in women with HIV infection. The usual treatment is a cream applied locally to the vagina. Women with HIV infection may experience frequent reoccurrence of symptoms and may require systemic medications in order to treat these symptoms successfully. See Candidiasis.

Vaginal Intercourse A type of sexual intercourse in which the man's penis enters the woman's vagina.

Vaginal Sex Vaginal intercourse.

Valley Fever See Coccidioidomycosis.

Varicella Zoster Virus (VZV) A virus in the herpes family that causes chicken pox during childhood and may reactivate later in life to cause shingles in immunosuppressed individuals.

VCT Voluntary counseling and testing.

VDRL (Venereal diseases research laboratory) A test for syphilis.

Vector In genetically engineered vaccines, a vector is a bacterium or virus that transports antigen-coding genes into the body to provoke an immune response. (The vector itself does not provoke an immune response or cause disease.) A vector may also refer to an organism, especially an insect, that transmits disease-causing agents.

Venipuncture The puncture of a vein (usually in the arm) with a hollow-bore needle for the purpose of obtaining a blood specimen.

Vertical Transmission Transmission of a pathogen such as HIV from mother to fetus or baby during pregnancy or birth. See Perinatal Transmission.

Viral Burden/Viral Load The amount of HIV in the circulating blood. Monitoring a person's viral burden is important because of the apparent correlation between the amount of virus in the blood and the severity of the disease. Sicker patients generally have more virus than those with less advanced disease. A sensitive, rapid test—called the viral load assay for HIV-1 infection—can be used to monitor the HIV viral burden. This procedure may help clinicians decide when to give anti-HIV therapy or to switch drugs. It may also help investigators determine more quickly whether experimental HIV therapies are effective. See Viral Load Test; Polymerase Chain Reaction (PCR); Branched DNA Assay.

Viral Culture A laboratory method for growing viruses.

Viral Evolution The change in the genetic makeup of a virus population as the viruses mutate and multiply over time. HIV evolves rapidly because of its high mutation and replication rates. Antiretroviral therapy (ART) and the body's immune response can also influence HIV evolution.

Viral Latency When a virus is present in the body but exists in a resting (latent) state without producing more virus. A latent viral infection usually does not cause any noticeable symptoms and can last a long period of time before becoming active and causing symptoms. HIV is capable of viral latency, as seen in the reservoirs of latent HIV-infected cells that persist in a person's body despite antiretroviral therapy (ART).

Viral Load Test In relation to HIV, a test that measures the quantity of HIV RNA in the blood. Results are expressed as the number of copies per milliliter of blood plasma. Research indicates that viral load is a better predictor of the risk of HIV disease progression than the CD4 count. The lower the viral load, the longer the time to AIDS diagnosis and the longer the survival time. Viral load testing for HIV infection is being used to determine when to initiate and/or change therapy. See Viral Burden/Viral Load.

Viral Rebound When a person on antiretroviral therapy (ART) has persistent, detectable levels of HIV in the blood after a period of undetectable levels. Causes of viral rebound can include drug resistance or poor adherence to an HIV treatment regimen.

Viral Tropism When HIV selectively attaches to a particular coreceptor on the surface of a host CD4 cell. HIV can attach to either the CCR5 coreceptor (R5-tropic) or the CXCR4 coreceptor (X4-tropic) or both (dual-tropic).

Viramune See Nevirapine (NVP).

Viremia The presence of virus in the bloodstream. See Sepsis.

Viricide Any agent that destroys or inactivates a virus.

Virion A virus particle existing freely outside a host cell. A mature virus.

Virologic Failure A type of HIV treatment failure. Virologic failure occurs when antiretroviral therapy (ART) fails to suppress and sustain a person's viral load to less than 200 copies/mL. Factors that can contribute to virologic failure include drug resistance, drug toxicity, and poor treatment adherence.

Virologic Suppression Suppression of viral replication (e.g., HIV) by antiviral therapy.

Virology The study of viruses and viral disease.

Virus Organism composed mainly of nucleic acid within a protein coat. When viruses enter a living plant, animal, or bacterial cell, they make use of the host cell's chemical energy, protein, and nucleic acid-synthesizing ability to multiply. Some viruses do not kill cells but transform them into a cancerous state. Some cause illness and then seem to disappear, while remaining dormant and later causing another, sometimes much more severe, form of disease. In humans, viruses cause measles, mumps, yellow fever, poliomyelitis, influenza, and the common cold, among others. Some viral infections can be treated with drugs.

Visceral Involving the major organs inside the body.

Visceral Adipose Tissue (VAT) Fat tissue located deep in the abdomen and around internal organs, Use of certain antiretroviral (ARV) drugs can cause excessive accumulation of visceral adipose tissue (VAT), which increases the risk of heart attack, stroke, and diabetes.

VL See Viral Burden/Viral Load.

Voluntary HIV Testing An individual is usually counseled regarding HIV prevention and how HIV infection occurs. Participants have the opportunity to accept or refuse HIV testing.

VTC Voluntary testing and counseling.

VTR Vertical transmission rate.

Wasting Syndrome An involuntary loss of more than 10% of body weight (especially muscle mass), plus at least 30 days of either diarrhea or weakness and fever. HIV-associated wasting syndrome is an AIDS-defining condition. See AIDS Wasting Syndrome.

Western Blot A laboratory test for specific antibodies to confirm repeatedly positive results on the HIV ELISA or EIA tests. In the United States, Western blot is the validation test used most often for confirmation of these other tests. In developing countries, a rapid HIV test is utilized most commonly. A positive rapid HIV test should be confirmed by a second rapid HIV test made by a different manufacturer.

White Blood Cells See Leukocytes.

Wild-Type Virus The original type of HIV, unchanged by having developed any resistance to antiretroviral drugs. Also, the most common type of a virus in the host population before genetic manipulation or mutation; virus that is isolated from a host as opposed to one that is grown in a laboratory culture. See Primary Isolate.

Window Period Time from infection with HIV until antibodies are detected.

Women's Interagency HIV Study (WIHS) Started in 1993, the Women's Interagency HIV Study (WIHS) is an ongoing federally funded study on women who have HIV or who are at risk for HIV. Analysis of biological specimens and medical and behavioral data collected on WIHS participants has contributed to the understanding of HIV, AIDS, and the effects of antiretroviral therapy (ART) in women.

X4 Virus A strain of HIV that enters and infects a host CD4 cell by attaching to the CXCR4 coreceptor on the CD4 cell. To enter a CD4 cell, HIV must first attach to a CD4 receptor, then attach to either the CCR5 or CXCR4 coreceptor, and finally fuse its membrane with the CD4 cell membrane. HIV is usually R5-tropic (uses CCR5) during the early stages of infection, but the virus may later switch to using either only CXCR4 (X4-tropic) or both CCR5 and CXCR4 (dual-tropic).

Yeast Infection See Candidiasis.

ZDV Zidovudine

Zidovudine (ZDV; AZT; Retrovir (trade name)) A nucleoside analogue for treatment of HIV infection and also approved for preventing maternal-fetal HIV transmission.

Alzheimer's-Dementia

Accredited facility An accredited facility is a nursing home, assisted living center or hospital that meets very high standards of care. These standards are set by organizations such as The Joint Commission (JTO). To stay accredited, a facility must be inspected every 18 months to three years.

Activities of daily living (ADLs) Activities of daily living (ADLs) include eating, bathing, grooming, dressing and going to the toilet. People with dementia may need aid to perform these tasks. Questions about ADLs help decide what type of care a person needs.

Activity director An activity director plans group singing, art projects and other activities. Such activities help residents of a long-term care facility stay active, alert and sociable.

Acute care (hospital care) Acute care is a medical setting such as a hospital, intensive care unit or emergency department.

Administrator An administrator runs a care facility, such as a nursing home.

Adult day centers Adult day centers offer people with Alzheimer's and other dementias the opportunity to be social and to participate in activities in a safe environment.

Advance directive An advance directive is a legal document. It tells what kind of medical treatment a person would like when he or she cannot communicate wishes.

Allowable cost Allowable cost is the highest fee the state will pay for people on Medicaid. Other insurance plans may also set allowable costs for the services they cover.

Alzheimer's disease Alzheimer's is a type of dementia that causes problems with memory, thinking and behavior. Symptoms usually develop slowly and get worse over time, becoming severe enough to interfere with daily tasks.

Assessment An assessment of mental status is a test of a person's ability to think, feel and react to others. A doctor usually performs a mental status assessment.

Assistive device An assistive device is an aid, such as eyeglasses, a cane, a wheelchair or a hearing aid.

Assisted living Assisted living is a residential care facility that generally provides 24-hour staff, recreational activities, meals, housekeeping, laundry and transportation. Definitions of assisted living and the specific regulations differ from state to state. Residents may choose which services they receive from the residence such as house cleaning, help with grooming or medication reminders.

Attorney (elder law) An elder law attorney handles general estate planning issues and counsels clients about planning for the future with alternative decision-making documents. The attorney can also assist the client in planning for possible long-term care needs, including nursing home care. Not all attorneys specialize in elder law. Your local bar association or the National Academy of Elder Law Attorneys and your local chapter can refer you to elder law attorneys in your area.

Audiologist An audiologist deals with ear problems, including hearing loss, tinnitus (ringing in the ears or "head noise") and lack of balance. Audiologists provide hearing aids and other listening devices.

Bed-bound or bed-fast A person who is bed-bound cannot walk or get out of bed without help from another person or a mechanical lift.

Behaviors Alzheimer's disease and related dementias can cause a person to act in different and unpredictable ways. Some individuals with Alzheimer's exhibit behaviors such as agitation, repetition, hallucinations and suspicion.

Caregiver Anyone who provides care to a person with Alzheimer's disease or dementia. Caregivers can be family members or friends, or paid professional caregivers. Caregivers may provide full- or part-time help to the person with Alzheimer's.

Case management Case management describes the care and services planned by health care workers.

Catheter A catheter is a bendable plastic tube that goes into the bladder to help a person urinate.

Certified nursing assistant (CNA); also certified nurse's aide A certified nursing assistant helps feed and care for disabled adults. To learn these skills, CNAs attend at least 75 hours of classes. A CNA works under a nurse's supervision and must keep taking classes to stay certified.

Chaplain A chaplain offers spiritual counseling to people in nursing homes and hospitals.

Charge nurse A charge nurse supervises the staff and residents of a floor or unit of a nursing home. The charge nurse's shift usually lasts eight hours. On each shift, day or night, a charge nurse should be available.

Clinical trials Clinical trials are research studies conducted in people to determine whether treatments are safe and effective. Clinical trials are the best way for researchers to find new ways to detect, slow, treat and hopefully someday prevent Alzheimer's disease.

Contractures Contractures—shortenings of the tendons and muscles—can make the knees, arms, hands or feet curl up. Physical therapy can sometimes prevent or treat this condition. But contractures following a stroke or dementia may be permanent.

Custodial care Custodial care helps a person accomplish the activities of daily living (ADLs). Custodial care can also include preparing special diets and giving medications.

Daily plan A daily plan provides structure for the person with Alzheimer's or dementia. A plan should include activities that provide the person meaning and enjoyment.

Decubitus ulcers (pressure ulcers, pressure sores or bedsores) Decubitus ulcers are skin sores caused by constant pressure.

Deficiencies Deficiencies are problems an inspector notes while visiting a nursing home or other facility. The facility must correct any deficiencies. Otherwise, it may be fined and dropped from Medicare or Medicaid participation.

Dementia Dementia is not a specific disease. It's an overall term that describes a wide range of symptoms associated with a decline in memory or other thinking skills severe enough to reduce a person's ability to perform everyday activities. Alzheimer's disease is the most common type of dementia.

Dentist A staff or contract dentist cares for the teeth and gums of a facility's residents. Medicare does not cover dental services, but Medicaid covers some dental expenses. Regular dental care is a key to staying healthy.

Dietician A dietician makes sure that a facility's residents eat a healthy, nutritious diet.

Director of nursing services (DON) The Director of Nursing oversees all nursing activities. These include scheduling and making sure staff members get continuing education. The DON is a registered nurse who has graduated from an accredited school of nursing.

Discharge Discharge is the release of an individual from a hospital or other facility such as a nursing home. The attending doctor must give an order for the discharge.

Do Not Resuscitate (DNR) order A DNR order, signed by a doctor based on a patient's wishes, instructs medical personnel to not perform life-saving CPR or other procedures to restart the heart or breathing once they have ceased. Once signed, the DNR directive must be placed in the patient's chart. (see Advance directive).

Elder law attorney An elder law attorney handles general estate planning issues and counsels clients about planning for the future with alternative decision-making documents. The attorney can also assist the client in planning for possible long-term care needs, including nursing home care. Not all attorneys specialize in elder law. Your local bar association or the National Academy of Elder Law Attorneys and your local chapter can refer you to elder law attorneys in your area.

Family/designated representative or other caregiver "Family members" can include people who are important to the resident, whether or not they are related.

Feeding tube A feeding tube is a plastic or rubber tube to give food and water to someone who cannot eat or drink. A feeding tube can be put in through the nose (nasogastric) or the stomach wall (PEG tube).

Financial Planner A financial planner can help the client make decisions that make the most of financial resources while at the same time help negotiate the financial barriers that inevitably arise in every stage of life.

Functional impairment Functional impairment means being unable to dress, use the toilet, eat, bathe or walk without help.

Geriatric care manager A geriatric care manager will help create a plan of care that meets the needs of the older adult and will explain what resources and options are available.

Geriatric psychiatrist A geriatric psychiatrist is trained to diagnose and treat mental disorders in older adults. These disorders include dementia, depression, anxiety and late-life schizophrenia.

Geri chair A geri chair is a high-backed cushioned recliner with a leg and foot rest. The staff can push it on wheels, but the resident cannot move it. A geri chair is a restraint, so it can be used only on a physician's order.

Guardian/conservator A court-appointed guardian or conservator manages a resident's money and makes health care and living decisions. Becoming a guardian or conservator requires a court order.

Home health aides Individuals who provide non-medical health care to people at home. Training or certification requirements vary from state-to-state, but typical services include assistance with activities of daily living, managing medications and some household tasks.

Hospice A program that offers support for dying persons to live as fully and comfortably as they can.

In-home care These care services involve professionals coming to the home to help the caregiver and the person with dementia. Services vary in type and can include companion services, personal care services and homemaker services.

Instrumental activities of daily living (IADLs) Instrumental activities of daily living (IADLs) are important daily living activities, such as cooking, shopping and managing finances.

The Joint Commission The Joint Commission (JT), formerly the Joint Commission on Accreditation of Healthcare Organizations (JCAHO). JT is an independent, not-for-profit organization that accredits and certifies health care organizations and programs in the United States. (see Accredited facility).

Long-distance caregiving Family members or friends who live in another city, state or country, and who are responsible for caring for a person with Alzheimer's disease or dementia.

Long-term care facility A long-term care facility is a nursing home or assisted living center designed for disabled adults.

Medicaid Medicaid is a government health program for low-income people.

Medicaid-certified A Medicaid-certified facility can offer services to people who are on Medicaid.

Medical director The medical director is a doctor who oversees medical care in a facility, such as a nursing home. The medical director may be the attending doctor for some residents and may offer emergency medical care for other residents.

Medicare Medicare is a government health insurance program for people aged 65 and older and for disabled people.

Medicare-certified A Medicare-certified facility can offer services to people who are on Medicare.

Mini-Mental State Examination (MMSE) The Mini-Mental State Examination (MMSE) is a short test to measure a person's basic skills. These skills include short-term memory, long-term memory, writing and speaking.

Minimum Data Set (MDS) The Minimum Data Set (MDS) summarizes information on the abilities of people who live in long-term care facilities. To keep their Medicare and Medicaid certification, long-term care facilities must submit their MDS data regularly.

Nurse A nurse who works in a nursing home takes care of residents and oversees certified nurses' aides (CNAs) and custodial caregivers. A registered nurse (RN) is a graduate trained nurse who has been licensed by a state authority after passing qualifying examinations for registration. A licensed practical nurse (LPN) is a person who has undergone training and obtained a state license to provide routine care for the sick. Some states use the term licensed vocational nurse or LVN.

Nurse practitioners (NPs) and physician assistants (PAs) Nurse practitioners (NPs) and physician assistants (PAs) are specially trained and may help oversee residents' care. In many states, doctor-supervised NPs and PAs write orders for treatment and medication.

Occupational therapist (OT) An occupational therapist helps residents change their activities or environment so they can eat, dress and bathe. An OT may also help with other tasks, such as cooking, taking medication or driving. And OTs may guide family members and caregivers.

Ombudsman An ombudsman in a long-term care facility helps residents and their families keep their rights and resolve complaints.

Owner/operator The owner is the individual, agency or company that owns the facility. The owner may hire an operator to direct the facility.

Palliative care Palliative care includes medical or surgical methods to ease the pain of a serious or incurable illness.

Personal care People with Alzheimer's disease or dementia may need help with personal care activities, including grooming, bathing and dressing.

Personal health record A personal health record (PHR) is a regularly updated collection of important health information. If you have dementia or are caring for someone with dementia, a PHR will help you work with your care team.

Pharmacist A pharmacist offers information about prescriptions, reviews patients' drugs, teaches caregivers and gives out medications.

Physical therapist A physical therapist treats physical disabilities and works with residents to improve general fitness. A physical therapist may also teach a resident how to use a walker, artificial limb or wheelchair.

Physician A physician, or doctor, helps develop a medical care plan for each resident of a long-term care facility. Physicians make medical decisions, such as what medications residents take. They visit nursing home residents. They may also meet with a resident's family to discuss medical conditions or treatments.

Power of attorney A power of attorney is a legal form that names someone to act as your substitute.

Psychologist A psychologist detects and treats emotional problems. Personality and intelligence testing can help a psychologist diagnose these problems. Treatments include individual, family, and group therapy sessions. Psychologists in long-term care facilities also teach staff members how to interact with residents.

Quality indicators Quality indicators describe the care in a long-term facility. For example, one quality indicator is the percent of residents whose need for help with daily activities has increased. The government's Nursing Home Compare website uses quality indicators to score every nursing home in the United States.

Recreational therapist   A recreational therapist helps residents enjoy activities. For example, the recreational therapist might offer special tools, such as large-print song sheets, to encourage participation.

Resident   A resident is someone who lives in a long-term care facility, such as a nursing home.

Respite care   Respite care provides temporary relief from caregiving tasks. Such care could include in-home assistance, a short nursing home stay or adult day care.

Social worker   A social worker offers residents and their families therapy, support services and planning for discharge. Social workers may also teach and counsel staff members.

Speech-language pathologist   A speech-language pathologist tests, diagnoses and treats people with speech and swallowing problems.

Staff-resident ratio   The staff-resident ratio compares the number of staff members to the number of residents they care for.

Stages   A framework for the progression of Alzheimer's disease.

Support groups   A group of Alzheimer's caregivers who connect to share experiences, provide support and give advice. Support groups can meet face-to-face with a support group leader or meet online.

Survey   The state health department takes an unannounced survey of each nursing home about once a year. This survey helps make sure a facility is giving good care. A nursing home must participate to keep its license. Each facility has to post its latest survey results. These required surveys differ from the surveys of The Joint Commission (JT) that a nursing home may request (see Accredited facility).

Wandering   Anyone who has memory problems and is able to walk is at risk for wandering. A person with Alzheimer's or dementia may not remember his or her name or address, and can become disoriented and lost, even in familiar places.

Younger-onset   Younger-onset (also known as early-onset) Alzheimer's affects people younger than age 65. Many people with early-onset are in their 40s and 50s. They have families, careers or are even caregivers themselves when Alzheimer's disease strikes.

Alcohol, Tobacco and Firearms

Abatement Relief from a liability that has been assessed.

Added brandy Brandy or wine spirits for use in fortification of wine as permitted by internal revenue law.

Adjacent Adjoining.

Age Distilled Spirits: The period during which, after distillation and before bottling, distilled spirits have been stored in oak containers. "Age" for bourbon whisky, rye whisky, wheat whisky, malt whisky, or rye malt whisky, and straight whiskies other than straight corn whisky, means the period the whisky has been stored in charred new oak containers.

Agricultural wine Wine made from suitable agricultural products other than the juice of grapes, berries, or other fruits.

Alcohol for fuel 1. Fuel alcohol. 2. Distilled spirits that have been rendered unfit for beverage use at an alcohol fuel plant.

Alcoholic beverage This includes any beverage in liquid form which contains not less than one-half of one percent (0.5%) alcohol by volume and is intended for human consumption.

Alcoholic flavoring materials Distilled Spirits: Any nonbeverage product on which drawback has been or will be claimed under 26 U.S.C. 5131-5134 or flavors imported free of tax which are unfit for beverage purposes. The term includes eligible flavors but does not include flavorings or flavoring extracts manufactured on the bonded premises of a distilled spirits plant (DSP) as an intermediate product.

Alternation of premises Multiple operations alternating the equipment and premises operated by the same person (i.e., Bonded Wine Premises/DSP/Brewery/Taxpaid Wine Bottling House).

Alternation of proprietors Multiple persons alternating the use of/sharing bonded premises and equipment.

Amelioration The addition to juice or natural wine before, during, or after fermentation of either water or pure dry sugar, or a combination of water and sugar, to adjust the acid level.

"Appropriate TTB officer" An officer or employee of the Alcohol and Tobacco Tax and Trade Bureau (TTB) authorized to perform any functions relating to the administration or enforcement of parts by TTB Orders, Delegation of the Administrator's Authorities in Title 27 of the Code of Federal Regulations (CFR).

Articles A product, containing denatured spirits, which was manufactured under 27 CFR part 20 or part 19.

Artificially Carbonated Wine Effervescent wine artificially charged with carbon dioxide and containing more than 0.392 grams of carbon dioxide per 100 milliliters.

Assessment An action that establishes a tax liability.

Balling The percent by weight of dissolved solids at 60°F present in wort and beer, usually determined by a balling saccharometer.

Banking day Any day during which a bank is open to the public for carrying on substantially all of its banking functions.

Barrel 1. For Beer only: When used as a unit of measure, the quantity equal to 31 U.S. gallons. 2. When used as a container, a consumer package or keg containing a quantity of beer listed in Sec. 25.156, or other size authorized by the appropriate TTB officer.

Basic permit A document issued under the Federal Alcohol Administration Act authorizing a person to engage in activities at a particular location.

Beer Beer, ale, porter, stout, and other similar fermented beverages (including saké and similar products) of any name or description containing one-half of one percent (0.5%) or more of alcohol by volume, brewed or produced from malt, wholly or in part, or from any substitute for malt.

Blend For Wine: the mixing together of wines of two or more tax classes.

Blended whisky Blended whisky is a mixture which contains straight whisky or a blend of straight whiskies at not less than 20 percent on a proof gallon basis, excluding alcohol derived from added harmless coloring, flavoring or blending materials, and, separately, or in combination, whisky or neutral spirits.

Blended wine 1. In bond: wines of different tax classes mixed together; a reportable activity on the operational report. 2. Taxpaid: wines of the same tax class, but different national origins, mixed together as specified in 27 CFR 24.296.

Bond An insurance agreement pledging surety for financial loss.

Bonded premises An area or dwelling confined to the stipulations of the bond. 1. For Wine: Premises established under the provisions of 27 CFR Part 24 on which operations in untaxpaid wine are authorized to be conducted. 2. For Distilled Spirits: The premises of a distilled spirits plant, or part thereof, as described in the application for registration, on which distilled spirits operations defined in 26 U.S.C. 5002 are authorized to be conducted. 3. For Beer: The premises of a brewery as described in the Brewer's Notice on which operations defined in 26 U.S.C. 5411 are authorized to be conducted

Bonded wine cellar (BWC) Premises established under the provisions of Part 24, other than for the production of wine.

Bonded wine premises Premises established under the provisions of Part 24 on which untaxpaid wine operations are authorized to be conducted.

Bonded winery (BW) Premises established under the provisions of 27 CFR 24.107 on which wine production operations are conducted and other authorized operations may be conducted.

Bottle 1. For Wine: A container four liters or less in capacity, regardless of the material from which it is made, used to store wine or to remove wine from the wine premises. 2. For Distilled Spirits: Any container, irrespective of the material from which it is made, used for the sale of distilled spirits at retail. 3. For Beer: A bottle, can, or similar container.

Bottler 1. For Wine: A proprietor of wine premises, established under the provisions of part 24, who fills wine into a container of 4 liters or less. 2. For Distilled Spirits: A proprietor of a distilled spirits plant qualified under Part 19 as a processor who bottles distilled spirits. 3. For Beer: Any person who places malt beverages in containers of a capacity of one gallon or less.

Brand label 1. For Wine: The label carrying, in the usual distinctive design, the brand name of the wine. 2. For Distilled Spirits: The principal display panel that is most likely to be displayed, presented, shown, or examined under normal and customary conditions of display for retail sale, and any other label appearing on the same side of the bottle as the principal display panel. The principal display panel appearing on a cylindrical surface is that 40 percent of the circumference which is most likely to be displayed, presented, shown, or examined under normal and customary conditions of display for retail sale. 3. For Beer: The label carrying, in the usual distinctive design, the brand name of the malt beverage.

Brandy An alcoholic distillate from the fermented juice, mash, or wine of fruit, or from their residue, produced at less than 190% proof in such manner that the distillate possesses the taste, aroma, and characteristics generally attributed to the product. It is bottled at not less than 80% proof.

Brewer Any person who brews beer (except a person who produces only beer exempt from tax under 26 U.S.C. 5053(e)) and any person who produces beer for sale.

Brewery The land and buildings described in the Brewer's Notice, Form 5130.10, where beer is to be produced and packaged.

Brix The quantity of dissolved solids is expressed as grams of sucrose in 100 grams of solution at 60F (20C) (percent by weight of sugar). The measurement is expressed in degrees.

Brix adjustment See Chaptalization.

Bulk Quantities over: 1. 60 liters (Wine) 2. One standard gallon (Distilled Spirits) 3. 31 gallons (Beer)

Business day (breweries) The 24-hour cycle of operations in effect at the brewery and described on the Brewer's Notice, Form 5130.10.

Business day (wineries and distilleries) Any day, other than Saturday, Sunday, or a legal holiday. (The term "legal holiday" includes all holidays in the District of Columbia and statewide holidays in a particular State in which a claim, report, or return, as the case may be, is required to be filed, or the act is required to be performed.)

BW See Bonded Winery.

BWC See Bonded Wine Cellar.

Calendar quarter A three-month period during the year as follows: January 1 through March 31; April 1 through June 30; July 1 through September 30; and October 1 through December 31.

Carbonated When used with wine, artificially carbonated wine.

Carrier Any person, company, corporation, or organization, including a proprietor, owner, consignor, consignee, or bailee, who transports distilled spirits, denatured spirits, or wine in any manner for himself or for others.

Case For Wine: Two or more bottles, or one or more containers larger than four liters, enclosed in a box or fastened together by some other method.

CBW See Customs Bonded Warehouse.

CDA Completely denatured alcohol.

Cereal beverage A beverage, produced either wholly or in part from malt (or a substitute for malt), and either fermented or unfermented, which contains, when ready for consumption, less than one-half of one percent (0.5%) of alcohol by volume.

CFR Code of Federal Regulations.

Champagne Semi-generic term for a type of sparkling wine.

Chaptalization (Brix Adjustment) The addition of sugar or concentrated juice of the same kind of fruit to juice before or during fermentation of wine, to develop alcohol by fermentation.

Chewing tobacco Any leaf tobacco that is not intended to be smoked.

Cigar Any roll of tobacco wrapped in leaf tobacco or in any substance containing tobacco (other than any roll of tobacco which is a cigarette within the meaning of paragraph (2) of the definition for cigarette). See below.

Cigarette (1) Any roll of tobacco wrapped in paper or in any substance not containing tobacco, and (2) Any roll of tobacco wrapped in any substance containing tobacco which, because of its appearance, the type of tobacco used in the filler, or its packaging and labeling, is likely to be offered to, or purchased by, consumers as a cigarette described in paragraph (1) of this definition.

Cigarette paper Paper, or any other material except tobacco, prepared for use as a cigarette wrapper.

Cigarette tube Cigarette paper made into a hollow cylinder for use in making cigarettes.

COLA TTB Form 5100.31, Application for and Certification/Exemption of Label/Bottle Approval.

Collateral bond Cash or securities (Treasury note or Treasury bond) pledged to TTB to cover the tax liability on products in bond.

Concentrate 1. For Beer: Concentrate produced from beer by the removal of water under the provisions of subpart R of part 25. The processes of concentration of beer and reconstitution of beer are considered authorized processes in the production of beer. 2. For Wine: Volatile fruit-flavor concentrate: Any volatile fruit-flavor concentrate (essence) produced by any process which includes evaporations from any fruit mash or juice.

Consent of surety A document that extends the terms of a bond.

Consignee The consignee is the receiver when a manufacturer sends a quantity of goods from one site to the other.

Consignor The consignor is the sender when a quantity of goods is sent from one site to the other.

Container 1. For Wine: Any bottle, barrel, cask, or other closed receptacle, regardless of the size or of the material from which it is made, for the sale of wine at retail. 2. For Distilled Spirits: A receptacle, vessel, or form of bottle, can, package, tank, or pipeline (where specifically included) used or capable of being used to contain, store, transfer, convey, remove, or withdraw spirits and denatured spirits.

Contiguous Touching, near, or bordering.

Conveyance A method of transportation; a vehicle.

Cooperage Barrels.

Cordials, liqueurs Products obtained by mixing or redistilling distilled spirits with, or over, fruits, flowers, plants, or their pure juices, or other natural flavoring materials, or with extracts derived from infusions, percolation, or maceration of such materials, and containing sugar, dextrose, or levulose, or a combination thereof, in an amount not less than two and one-half percent (2.5%) by weight of the finished product.

Cover over Monies collected on rum imports that are returned to the treasuries of Puerto Rico or the Virgin Islands.

Curtailment of premises Realignment of the boundaries of the bonded premises, to place some of the property off bond.

Customs officer Any officer of the U.S. Customs and Border Protection Service or any commissioned, warrant, or petty officer of the Coast Guard, or any agent or other person authorized by law or designated by the Secretary of the Treasury to perform any duties of an officer of the Customs Service.

Customs bonded warehouse (CBW) A warehouse established under the provisions of U.S. Customs and Border Protection Service regulations.

Decolorizing material An agent (substance) that removes color.

Degrees Brix See Brix.

Denaturant Any material authorized under 27 CFR part 21 for addition to spirits in the production of denatured spirits.

Denaturation To add a substance or materials to an alcoholic liquid to make it unfit for beverage use.

Determine To establish enough information about taxable products at the time of removal to calculate the tax, specifically the quantity (gallons, barrels, proof gallons, pounds, or number) and kind (e.g., wine, beer, spirits, cigarettes, snuff, paper, or tubes).

For Tobacco: Where the tax rate depends on additional information (such as number of cigarette papers to a set before January 1, 2000, or sale price of large cigars), that information must also be established as part of tax determination.

Distilled spirits operations Any authorized distilling, warehousing, or processing operations conducted on the bonded premises of a plant qualified under 27 CFR part 19.

Distilled spirits plant (DSP) An establishment qualified under part 19 of 27 CFR for producing, warehousing, or processing of distilled spirits (including denatured spirits), or manufacturing of articles. An establishment qualified under part 19 for distilling, warehousing, processing or any combination of these.

Distilling material Any fermented or other alcoholic substance capable of, or intended for use in, the original distillation or other original processing of spirits.

Drawback A return or rebate, in whole or in part, of excise taxes previously paid. A drawback is granted when the claimant has complied with certain statutory requirements. For TTB purposes, drawback is not a "refund."

DSP See Distilled Spirits Plant.

Dump The practice of bringing spirits, wine, or flavorings into a bonded wine premises or distilled spirits plant and depositing to bulk.

Ebuilliometer An instrument used to measure the percentage of alcohol in wine.

Effective Tax Rate The net tax rate after reduction for any credit allowable under 26 U.S.C. 5010 for wine and flavor content at which the tax imposed on distilled spirits by 26 U.S.C. 5001 or 7652 is paid or determined.

Effervescent Wine containing more than 0.392 grams of carbon dioxide per 100 ml.

EFT See Electronic Funds Transfer.

Electronic Funds Transfer (EFT) Any transfer of funds effected by a proprietor's financial institution, either directly or through a correspondent banking relationship, via the Federal Reserve Communications System (FRCS) or Fedwire, to the Treasury Account at the Federal Reserve Bank.

Eligible flavor A flavor which: (1) Is of a type that is eligible for drawback of tax under 26 U.S.C. 5134, (2) Was not manufactured on the premises of a distilled spirits plant, and (3) Was not subjected to distillation on distilled spirits plant premises such that the flavor does not remain in the finished product.

Eligible wine Wine on which tax would be imposed by paragraph (1), (2), or (3) of 26 U.S.C. 5041(b) but for its removal to distilled spirits plant premises and which has not been subject to distillation at a distilled spirits plant after receipt in bond.

Engaged in the business Conducting operations authorized by TTB.

Entry for deposit The practice of recording spirits as they come off the still for entry into the storage or processing account.

Export warehouse For Tobacco: A bonded internal revenue warehouse for the storage of tobacco products and cigarette papers and tubes, upon which the internal revenue tax has not been paid for subsequent shipment to a foreign country, Puerto Rico, the Virgin Islands, or a possession of the United States, or for consumption beyond the jurisdiction of the internal revenue laws of the United States.

Extension of premises Realignment of the bonded premises, to place more of the property on bond.

Factory The premises of a manufacturer of tobacco products as described in his permit issued under 26 U.S.C. chapter 52, or the premises of a manufacturer of cigarette papers and tubes on which such business is conducted.

Fermenting material For Distilled Spirits: Any material which is to be subjected to a process of fermentation to produce distilling material. For Wine: materials which are in the process of being fermented.

Firearms Any portable weapons, such as rifles, carbines, machine guns, shotguns, or fowling pieces, from which a shot, bullet, or other projectile may be discharged by an explosive.

Fiscal year The period which begins October 1 and ends on the following September 30.

Flavor Substance added to impart or help impart a taste or aroma in food. 21 CFR 170.3 (o)(12)

Flavoring agent See Flavor.

Flavoring adjuvant See Flavor.

Foreign-trade zone (FTZ) A foreign-trade zone established and operated in accordance with the Act of June 18, 1934, as amended.

Foreign wine Wine produced outside the United States.

Formula wine Special natural wine, agricultural wine, and other than standard wine (except for distilling material and vinegar stock) produced on bonded wine premises under an approved formula.

Fruit flavor concentrate Concentrated material used for making juices.

Fruit wine Wine made from the juice of sound, ripe fruit (other than grapes). Fruit wine also includes wine made from berries or wine made from a combination of grapes and other fruit (including berries).

Fuel alcohol See Alcohol for Fuel.

Gallon—wine gallon A United States gallon of liquid measure equivalent to the volume of 231 cubic inches at 60°F.

Gauge The determination of the proof and quantity of spirits.

General Use Formulas Standardized formulas given in the regulations for the production of specific articles.

Generic For Wine: Name of a type of wine that originated in a particular place, but is no longer associated with that place of origin, e.g., Vermouth.

Gin A product obtained by original distillation from mash or by the redistillation of distilled spirits or by mixing neutral spirits with, or over, juniper berries and other aromatics, or with, or over, extracts from infusions, percolations, or maceration of materials. It is bottled at not less than 80% proof.

GRAS An acronym for "generally recognized as safe." The term means that the treating material has a U.S. Food and Drug Administration (FDA) listing in 21 CFR part 182 or part 184, or is considered to be generally recognized as safe by the FDA.

Hard cider Still wine derived primarily from apples or apple concentrate and water (apple juice, or the equivalent amount of concentrate reconstituted to the original brix of the juice prior to concentration, must represent more than 50 percent of the volume of the finished product) containing no other fruit product nor any artificial product which imparts a fruit flavor other than apple; containing at least one-half of one percent (0.5%) and less than seven percent alcohol by volume; having the taste, aroma, and characteristics generally attributed to hard cider; and sold or offered for sale as hard cider.

High-proof concentrate For Wine: A volatile fruit-flavor concentrate (essence) that has an alcohol content of more than 24 percent by volume and is unfit for beverage use (nonpotable) because of its natural constituents, i.e., without the addition of other substances.

Importer 1. Any person who imports distilled spirits, wines, or beer into the United States. 2. Any person who brings a taxable article into the United States from a source outside the United States, or who withdraws such an article from a Customs bonded warehouse for sale or use in the United States. 3. Tobacco: Any person in the United States to whom non-taxpaid tobacco products or cigarette papers or tubes manufactured in a foreign country, Puerto Rico, the Virgin Islands, or a possession of the United States are shipped or consigned; any person who removes cigars for sale or consumption in the United States from a Customs bonded manufacturing warehouse; and any person who smuggles or otherwise unlawfully brings tobacco products or cigarette papers or tubes into the United States.

In bond 1. For Wine: When used with respect to wine or spirits, "in bond" refers to wine or spirits possessed under bond to secure the payment of the taxes imposed by 26 U.S.C. Chapter 51, and on which such taxes have not been determined. The term includes any wine or spirits on the bonded wine premises or a distilled spirits plant, or in transit between bonded premises (including in the case of wine, bonded wine premises). Additionally, the term refers to wine withdrawn without payment of tax under 26 U.S.C. 5362 and to spirits withdrawn without payment of tax under 26 U.S.C. 5214 (a)(5) or (a)(13) with respect to which relief from liability has not yet occurred. 2. For Distilled Spirits: When used with respect to spirits, denatured spirits, articles, or wine refers to spirits, denatured spirits, articles, or wine possessed under bond to secure the payment of the taxes imposed by 26 U.S.C. Chapter 51, and on which such taxes have not been determined. The term includes such spirits, denatured spirits, articles, or wine on the bonded premises of a distilled spirits plant, such spirits, denatured spirits, or wines in transit between bonded premises (including, in the case of wine, bonded wine cellar premises). Additionally, the term refers to spirits in transit from Customs custody to bonded premises, and spirits withdrawn without payment of tax under 26 U.S.C. 5214, and with respect to which relief from liability has not occurred under the provisions of 26 U.S.C. 5005(e)(2). 3. For Tobacco: The status of tobacco products and cigarette papers and tubes, which come within the coverage of a bond securing the payment of internal revenue taxes imposed by 26 U.S.C. 5701 or 7652, and in respect to which such taxes have not been determined as provided by regulations in this chapter, including (a) such articles in a factory, (b) such articles removed, transferred, or released, pursuant to 26 U.S.C. 5704, and with respect to which relief from the tax liability has not occurred, and (c) such articles on which the tax has been determined, or with respect to which relief from the tax liability has occurred, which have been returned to the coverage of a bond.

Industrial use (for non-beverage purposes) 1. As applied to wines, shall have the meaning ascribed in 27 CFR 1.61: for use in vinegar, for experimental or research use by a university, for use of the Government, or which has been rendered unfit for beverage use. 2. As applied to spirits, shall have the meaning ascribed in 27 CFR 1.60: For use of the Government, for non-beverage purposes, or if denatured.

Intermediate product For distilled spirits: Any product manufactured pursuant to an approved formula under 27 CFR part 5, not intended for sale as such but for use in the manufacture of a distilled spirits product.

I.R.C. The Internal Revenue Code of 1954, as amended.

Jeopardy to the revenue Any possible circumstances where tax collection may suffer.

Kind 1. As applied to wines, kind shall mean the classes and types of wines as prescribed in 27 CFR part 4. 2. As applied to spirits, except as provided in Sec. 19.597, kind shall mean class and type as prescribed in 27 CFR part 5.

Knockdown condition For firearms: A taxable article that is unassembled but complete as to all component parts.

Large cigarettes Cigarettes weighing more than three pounds per thousand.

Large cigars Cigars weighing more than three pounds per thousand.

Liable for tax Obligated to pay a tax.

Liquor Distilled spirits.

Liquor bottle A bottle made of glass or earthenware, or of other suitable material approved by the Food and Drug Administration, which has been designed or is intended for use as a container for distilled spirits for sale for beverage purposes and which has been determined by the appropriate TTB officer to protect the revenue adequately.

Liqueurs See Cordials.

Litre (liter) 1. Wine: (a) A metric unit of capacity equal to 1,000 cubic centimeters and equivalent to 33.814 U.S. fluid ounces. For purposes of 27 CFR part 4, a liter is subdivided into 1,000 milliliters (ml). (b) For purposes of regulation, one liter of wine is defined as that quantity (mass) of wine occupying a one-liter volume at 20° C (68°F). 2. Distilled Spirits: A metric unit of capacity equal to 1,000 cubic centimeters of distilled spirits at 15.56 C (60°F.), and equivalent to 33.814 U.S. fluid ounces. A liter is subdivided into 1,000 milliliters. Milliliter or milliliters may be abbreviated as "ml."

Losses Known quantities of a commodity lost due to breakage, casualty, or other unusual cause.

Lot Wine of the same type. When used with reference to a "lot of wine bottled," lot means the same type of wine bottled or packed on the same date into containers.

Malt beverage A beverage made by the alcoholic fermentation of an infusion or decoction, or combination of both, in potable brewing water, of malted barley with hops, or their parts, or their products, and with or without other malted cereals, and with or without the addition of unmalted or prepared cereals, other carbohydrates or products prepared from these, and with or without the addition of carbon dioxide, and with or without other wholesome products suitable for human food consumption. Standards applying to the use of processing methods and flavors in malt beverage production appear in Sec. 7.11.

Manufacturer of cigarette papers and tubes Any person who manufactures cigarette paper, or makes up cigarette paper into tubes, except for his own personal use or consumption.

Manufacturer of tobacco products Any person who manufactures cigars, cigarettes, smokeless tobacco, pipe tobacco, or roll-your-own tobacco but does not include: (1) A person who produces tobacco products solely for that person's own consumption or use; or (2) A proprietor of a Customs bonded manufacturing warehouse with respect to the operation of such warehouse.

Marks For Wine: The required markings on each container larger than four liters or each case used to remove wine for consumption or sale as specified in 27 CFR 24.259. Distilled Spirits: The required markings on cases, drums, or barrels as specified in 27 CFR part 19. Beer: The requirements for beer marks are specified in 27 CFR part 25 subpart J. Tobacco: Every package of tobacco products, packaged in a domestic factory will, before removal subject to tax, have adequately imprinted on it, or on a label securely affixed to it, a mark as specified in 27 CFR 40.212.

Mash, wort, wash Any fermented material capable of, or intended for, use as a distilling material.

Mingling Mixing or consolidating.

Must For Wine: Unfermented juice or any mixture of juice, pulp, skins, and seeds prepared from grapes or other fruit (including berries).

Nano brewery: A very small brewery operation.

Natural wine The product of the juice or must of sound, ripe grapes or other sound, ripe fruit, made with such cellar treatment as may be authorized under 26 U.S.C. 5382.

Neutral spirits Distilled spirits produced from any material at or above 190% proof. If they are bottled, they are bottled at not less than 80% proof.

Nonbeverage alcohol Alcohol that is unfit for use for beverage purposes.

Nonbeverage wine Wine, or wine products made from wine, rendered unfit for beverage use in accordance with 27 CFR 24.215.

Non-contiguous Not adjacent or touching.

Non-generic Name of a type of wine that originated in a particular place and is still exclusively associated with that place (e.g., Bordeaux).

Nonindustrial use As applied to spirits, shall have the meaning ascribed in 27 CFR Part 1.60.

Notice 1. Reports of changes to the premises or permits of industry members filed by the industry member. 2. A brewer's qualification document. 3. A step in collecting taxes.

Obscuration The difference between true proof and apparent proof due to dissolved solids in the spirits. These are solid materials in spirits that prevent obtaining the true proof.

Operating permit For Distilled Spirits: The document issued pursuant to 26 U.S.C. 5171(d), authorizing the person named in the document to engage in the business or operation described in the document.

Other than standard wine Wines products that are classified in 27 CFR Part 24 Subpart J as not standard wine, including nonbeverage wine products, heavy bodied blending wine, vinegar stock and artificially flavored wine. A formula is required for the production of Other than Standard Wine.

Packages 1. A cask or barrel or similar wooden container, or a drum or similar metal container that contains alcohol. 2. For Tobacco: The immediate container in which tobacco products or cigarette papers or tubes are put up in by the manufacturer and offered for sale or delivery to the consumer.

Packer 1. For Wine: Any person who places wine in containers in excess of four liters. 2. For Beer: Any person who places malt beverages in containers of a capacity in excess of one gallon.

Penal sum The dollar amount of a bond.

Percent or percentage of alcohol content TTB measures alcohol content in percent by volume.

Permanent discontinuance The closing of the permission to operate a business regulated by TTB.

Permittee For Wine and Distilled Spirits: A person holding a basic permit under the Federal Alcohol Administration Act.

Pipe tobacco Any tobacco which, because of its appearance, type, packaging, or labeling, is suitable for use and likely to be offered to, or purchased by, consumers as tobacco to be smoked in a pipe.

Pistols Small projectile firearms which have a short one-hand stock or butt at an angle to the line of bore and a short barrel or barrels, and which are designed, made, and intended to be aimed and fired from one hand. The term does not include gadget devices, guns altered or converted to resemble pistols, or small portable guns erroneously referred to as pistols.

P. R. Puerto Rico.

Prepayment The excise tax payment made on or before the date products are removed from bond.

Processing The manufacturing, mixing, bottling, or denaturing of spirits or the manufacturing of distilled spirits articles.

Processor Except as otherwise provided under 26 U.S.C. 5002(a)(6), any person qualified under this part who manufactures, mixes, bottles, or otherwise processes distilled spirits or denatured spirits, or manufactures any article.

Produced at For distilled spirits: As used in 27 CFR 5.22 and 5.52 in conjunction with specific degrees of proof to describe the standards of identity, this term means the composite proof of the spirits after completion of distillation and before reduction in proof.

Proof The ethyl alcohol content of a liquid at 60°F, stated as twice the percent of ethyl alcohol by volume.

Proof gallon A gallon of liquid at 60°F, which contains 50 percent by volume of ethyl alcohol having a specific gravity of 0.7939 at 60°F, referred to water at 60°F, as unity, or the alcoholic equivalent.

Proprietary solvents Solvents that are manufactured with specially denatured alcohol under the proprietary solvent general-use formula in 27 CFR part 20.

Proprietor The person qualified under the regulations to operate regulated premises.

For wine: The person qualified under 27 CFR Part 24 to operate a wine premises, and includes the term "winemaker" when the context so requires.

Pure condensed must The dehydrated juice or must of sound, ripe grapes, or other fruit or agricultural products, concentrated to not more than 80 percent (balling), the composition thereof remaining unaltered except for removal of water.

Pursuant to the application In response to, in accordance with, or after the application.

Racking 1. For Wine: Pumping wine off the lees, or settlings. 2. For Beer: The filling of kegs or barrels.

Reconditioning 1. For Distilled Spirits: The dumping of distilled spirits products in bond after their bottling or packaging, for purposes other than destruction, denaturation, redistillation, or rebottling. The term may include the filtration, clarification, stabilization, or reformulation of a product. 2. For Wine: The conduct of operations, after original bottling or packing, to restore wine to a merchantable condition. The term includes relabeling or recasing operations.

Reconsignment Changing the destination (or recipient) of a shipment that is already in progress.

Recover To salvage alcohol after initial use.

Recovered article An article containing specially denatured spirits salvaged without all of its original ingredients, or an article containing completely denatured alcohol salvaged without all of the denaturants for completely denatured alcohol, under 27 CFR part 20.

Redenaturation To denature spirits again, by adding a substance or materials to an alcoholic liquid to make it unfit for beverage use.

Redistillation To distill spirits again after the initial distillation.

Relanded Any product that has been labeled or shipped for exportation and returned to the United States.

Remission A decision which indicates that a particular tax is not owed.

Removal—Alcohol Withdrawal of alcoholic beverages from a regulated plant. Removals are further categorized as Taxable Removals or Non-Taxable Removals.

Removal—Beer (a) The sale and transfer of possession of beer for consumption at the brewery, or (b) any removal of beer from the brewery.

Removal—Tobacco The removal of tobacco products or cigarette papers or tubes from the factory or release from Customs custody, including the smuggling of other unlawful importation of such articles into the United States.

Restored pure condensed must Pure condensed must to which has been added an amount of water not exceeding the amount removed in the dehydration process.

Restoration To return alcohol to its original state.

Return period Specified time period for determining taxes due. The amount of time for which a tax return must be filed.

Revolvers Small projectile firearms of the pistol type, having a breech-loading chambered cylinder so arranged that the cocking of the hammer or movement of the trigger rotates it and brings the next cartridge in line with the barrel for firing.

Roll-your-own tobacco Any tobacco which, because of its appearance, type, packaging, or labeling, is suitable for use and likely to be offered to, or purchased by, consumers as tobacco for making cigarettes.

Rum An alcoholic distillate from the fermented juice of sugar cane, sugar cane syrup, sugar cane molasses, or other sugar cane byproducts, produced at less than 190% proof in such manner that the distillate possesses the taste, aroma, and characteristics generally attributed to rum, and bottled at not less than 80% proof; and also includes mixtures solely of such distillates.

Sale price The price for which large cigars are sold by the manufacturer, determined in accordance with 27 CFR 40.22 and used for computation of the tax.

SDA Specially denatured alcohol.

Season The period from January 1 through June 30, is the spring season. The period from July 1 through December 31, is the fall season.

Secretary The Secretary of the Treasury or his or her delegate.

Segregation of operations Separating operations to comply with regulations.

Sets Any collection, grouping, or packaging of cigarette papers made up by any person for delivery to the consumer as a unit.

Shells and cartridges Includes any article consisting of a projectile, explosive, and container that is designed, assembled, and ready for use without further manufacture in firearms, pistols, or revolvers. A person who reloads used shell or cartridge casings is a manufacturer of shells or cartridges within the meaning of section 4181 if such reloaded shells or cartridges are sold by the reloader.

Shortage An unaccounted for discrepancy (missing quantity) of beer disclosed by physical inventory.

Small cigarettes Cigarettes weighing not more than three pounds per thousand.

Small cigars Cigars weighing not more than three pounds per thousand.

Small domestic producers wine credit Tax reduction available to small wineries if they meet certain criteria.

Smokeless tobacco Tobacco products that are not intended to be smoked such as snuff and chewing tobacco.

Snuff Any finely cut, ground, or powdered tobacco that is not intended to be smoked.

Sparkling wine An effervescent wine containing more than 0.392 gram of carbon dioxide per 100 milliliters of wine resulting solely from the secondary fermentation of the wine within a closed container.

Special Industrial Solvents Finished articles made in accordance with 27 CFR 20.112.

Special natural wine Natural wine with added natural flavors. A formula is required for the production of special natural wines.

Specially denatured Spirits that are denatured under the specially denatured alcohol formulas prescribed in 27 CFR part 21.

Specifically sweetened natural wine Natural wine with extra sugar, concentrate, or juice added.

Spirits or distilled spirits That substance known as ethyl alcohol, ethanol, or spirits of wine in any form (including all dilutions or mixtures thereof, from whatever source or by whatever process produced), but not denatured spirits unless specifically stated. The term does not include mixtures of distilled spirits and wine, bottled at 48 percent proof or less, if the mixture contains more than 50 percent wine on a proof gallon basis.

Spirits residues Residues, containing distilled spirits, of a manufacturing process related to the production of an article under 27 CFR part 20.

Standard wine Natural, special natural, specially sweetened natural, and agricultural wines under the provisions of 27 CFR Part 24.

Standards of fill Authorized sizes of containers of alcohol.

Stick An individual cigarette.

Still Any apparatus capable of being used for separating alcoholic or spirituous vapors, or spirituous solutions, or spirits, from spirituous solutions or mixtures, but shall not include stills used for laboratory purposes or stills used for distilling water or other nonalcoholic materials where the cubic distilling capacity is one gallon or less.

Still wine Wine containing not more than 0.392 gram of carbon dioxide per 100 milliliters.

Sugar Pure dry sugar, liquid sugar, and invert sugar syrup: 1. Pure dry sugar: Refined sugar 95 percent or more by weight dry, having a dextrose equivalent of not less than 95 percent on a dry basis, and produced from cane, beets, or fruit, or from grain or other sources of starch. 2. Liquid sugar: A substantially colorless refined sugar and water solution containing not less than the equivalent of 60 percent pure dry sugar by weight (60 degrees Brix). 3. Invert sugar syrup: A substantially colorless solution of invert sugar which has been prepared by recognized methods of inversion from pure dry sugar and contains not less than 60 percent sugar by weight (60 degrees Brix).

Surety bond An agreement with a federally approved insurance company covering the tax liability on products in bond.

Tax deferral Delay of excise tax payment until the due date of the tax return.

Tax determination The point at which a proprietor establishes the amount of tax due.

Tax-determined spirits When used with respect to the tax on any distilled spirits to be withdrawn from bond on determination of tax, shall mean that the taxable quantity of spirits has been established.

Tax-exempt cider Cider produced in accordance with 27 CFR 24.76.

Tax gallon A gallon of liquid at 60°F which contains 50 percent by volume of ethyl alcohol having a specific gravity of 0.7939 at 60°F referred to water at 60°F, as unity, or the alcoholic equivalent of it.

Tax year For Special Occupational Tax purposes: The period from July 1 of one calendar year through June 30 of the following year.

Taxpaid spirits When used with respect to distilled spirits, this term means that all applicable taxes imposed by law in respect to such spirits have been determined or paid as provided by law.

Taxpaid wine Wine on which the tax, imposed by law, has been determined regardless of whether the tax has been paid or whether the payment has been deferred.

Taxpaid wine bottling house Premises established under the provisions of 27 CFR part 24, primarily for bottling or packing taxpaid wine.

Taxpaid wine premises Premises established under the provision of 27 CFR part 24 on which taxpaid wine operations (other than bottling) are authorized.

Tequila An alcoholic distillate from a fermented mash derived from the Agave Tequilana Weber distilled in a manner so that the distillate has the taste, aroma, and characteristics attributed to Tequila. It is bottled at not less than 80% proof and it includes mixtures only of such distillates. This is a distinctive product of Mexico, manufactured in Mexico in compliance with the laws of Mexico regulating the manufacture of Tequila for consumption in that country.

Tobacco products Cigarettes, cigars, smokeless tobacco, pipe tobacco, and roll-your-own tobacco.

Total solids The degrees Brix of unfermented juice or dealcoholized wine.

TPWBH See Taxpaid Wine Bottling House.

Transfer in bond The removal of spirits, denatured spirits, and wines from one bonded premises to another bonded premises.

Transferee in bond Receiver of alcohol shipped from one bonded premises to another. When one proprietor sends a shipment of untaxpaid product to another, the recipient (the transferee) assumes the tax liability under his/her bond.

TTB Alcohol and Tobacco Tax and Trade Bureau.

Unconcentrated Natural form of juice or other material.

Unfinished spirits Spirits in the production system prior to production gauge.

Unmerchantable Wine which has been taxpaid, removed from bonded wine premises, and subsequently returned to a bonded wine premises under the provisions of 27 CFR 24.295 for the purpose of reconditioning, reformulation, or destruction.

Untaxpaid Articles on which taxes have not been paid.

Variance An alternate method or procedure approved by TTB.

V. I. Virgin Islands.

Vinegar A wine or wine product not for beverage use produced in accordance with the provisions of this part and having not less than 4.0 grams (4%) of volatile acidity (calculated as acetic acid and exclusive of sulfur dioxide) per 100 milliliters of wine.

Viticultural Area Any region where grapes are grown. An "American Viticultural Area" is a specific grape growing area defined in 27 CFR Part 9.

Vodka Neutral spirits so distilled, or so treated after distillation with charcoal or other materials, as to be without distinctive character, aroma, taste, or color.

Waiver Relief from a liability that has not been assessed.

Warehouseman A proprietor of a distilled spirits plant qualified under 27 CFR part 19 to store bulk distilled spirits.

Warning or warning letter A formal reprimand by TTB for regulatory violations.

Wine 1. For purposes of taxation, registry, bonding and reports:

When used without qualification, the term includes every class and type of product, produced on a bonded wine premises, from grapes, other fruit (including berries), or other suitable agricultural products. It contains not more than 24 percent of alcohol by volume. The term includes all imitation, other than standard, or artificial wine and compounds sold as wine. A wine product containing less than one-half of one percent alcohol by volume (0.5%) is not taxable as wine when removed from the bonded wine premises. See 27 CFR 24.10. 2. For purposes of labeling, advertising, basic permits, trade practices: (a) Wine as defined in section 610 and section 617 of the Revenue Act of 1918 (26 U.S.C. 3036, 3044, 3045) and (b) other alcoholic beverages not so defined, but made in the manner of wine, including sparkling and carbonated wine, wine made from condensed grape must, wine made from other agricultural products than the juice of sound, ripe grapes, imitation wine, compounds sold as wine, vermouth, cider, perry, and sake; in each instance only if containing not less than 7 percent, and not more than 24 percent of alcohol by volume, and if for nonindustrial use. See 27 CFR 4.10.

Wine gallon Standard gallon of liquid.

Wine products not for beverage use Products made from wine that are not taxed because they are not suitable for beverage use (e.g., sauces, jellies, salted cooking wines, and wine vinegar).

Wine spirits Brandy or wine spirits authorized under 26 U.S.C. 5373 for use in wine production.

Withdraw without payment of tax Removing alcohol from the bonded premises without payment of tax on those items.

Withdraw of spirits Removing spirits from distilled spirits bonded premises as specified in 27 CFR Part 19.

Wort The product of brewing before fermentation which results in beer.

Zone operator The person to which the privilege of establishing, operating, and maintaining a foreign-trade zone has been granted by the Foreign-Trade Zones Board created by the Act of June 18, 1934, as amended.

Agriculture

FARM AND COMMODITY POLICY GLOSSARY

0,50/85-92 provisions Refers to the so-called 50/85 and 50/92 provisions for rice and cotton and the 0/85 and 0/92 provisions for wheat and feed grains that were in effect in various forms from 1986 through 1995. Under these provisions, farmers could idle all or part of their permitted acreage, putting the idled land in a conserving use, and still receive deficiency payments for part of the acreage. A minimum planting requirement of 50 percent of maximum payment acreage was required in order to receive these payments in the case of rice and cotton.

1614 data Data which tracks the benefits provided, directly or indirectly, to individuals and entities under titles I and II and the amendments made by those titles. 1614 refers to the section in the 2002 Farm Act that required USDA to track benefits.

1862 colleges/universities The original land grant colleges and universities established by the Land Grant College Act of 1862 (see Land-Grant Institutions).

1890s colleges/universities These institutions resulted from provisions of the second Morrill Act, which prohibited racial discrimination in Land-Grant Colleges and Universities. States had the option of creating separate institutions to serve African-American students. The Southern States elected to have separate educational institutions, sometimes referred to as "historically black colleges and universities." While not a land-grant college, Tuskegee University traditionally has been associated with the African-American land-grant institutions. It was granted 25,000 acres of land by the U.S. Congress in 1899 and has espoused the land-grant philosophy throughout its history.

1938 Farm Act See Agricultural Adjustment Act (AAA) of 1938.

1949 Farm Act See Agricultural Act of 1949.

1985 Farm Act See Food Security Act of 1985.

1990 Farm Act See Food, Agriculture, Conservation and Trade Act of 1990.

1994 Institutions Land-Grant Institutions that traditionally served Native Americans. The Equity in Educational Land-Grant Status Act of 1994 conferred land-grant status for 29 tribal colleges that address agriculture and mechanical arts.

1996 Farm Act See Federal Agriculture Improvement and Reform Act of 1996.

2002 Farm Act See Farm Security and Rural Investment Act of 2002.

ACRE actual farm revenue The actual commodity farm yield X the ACRE national average market price.

ACRE actual State revenue The ACRE actual State yield X the ACRE national average market price.

ACRE actual State yield The crop year commodity production (quantity) produced in the State per planted acre.

ACRE benchmark farm revenue The 5-year Olympic average farm crop yields X [ACRE program guarantee price – crop insurance premiums per acre]

ACRE benchmark State yield The 5-year Olympic average commodity yield per planted acre in the State.

ACRE farm-specific productivity ratio A ratio of the 5-year Olympic average farm crop yield divided by the ACRE benchmark State yield.

ACRE national average market price The greater of (A) the national average commodity market price received by producers during the 12-month marketing year; or (B) the reduced marketing assistance commodity loan rate.

ACRE program guarantee The optional ACRE program guarantee of 90% of the [5-year ACRE benchmark State yield X 2-year ACRE program guarantee price] for the crop year and respective commodity.

ACRE program guarantee price The commodity-specific 2-year national average market price received by producers.

Acreage reduction program (ARP) An annual land retirement system for wheat, feed grains, cotton, or rice in which farmers participating in Federal commodity programs idled a crop-specific, nationally set portion of their crop acreage base in order to be eligible for benefits such as Commodity Credit Corporation (CCC) crop loans and deficiency payments. No deficiency payments were made on the idled ARP land. The 1996 and 2002 Farm Acts did not reauthorize ARPs.

Additional or buy-up coverage Any coverage level greater than catastrophic coverage.

Additional peanuts See peanuts, additional.

Adjusted gross revenue (AGR) A plan of insurance that bases coverage on adjusted gross revenue calculated from Schedule F income tax data.

Adjusted world price, cotton (AWP) As part of the upland cotton marketing assistance loan program, USDA calculates and publishes a loan repayment rate, on a weekly basis, known as the adjusted world price. The AWP is the prevailing world price for upland cotton, adjusted to account for U.S. quality and location. Producers who have taken out USDA marketing assistance loans may choose to repay them at either the lesser of the established commodity loan rate for upland cotton, plus interest, or the announced AWP for that week. The AWP for cotton also was used for determining Step 2 cotton program payments prior to suspension of Step 2 in 2006.

Adjusted world price, rice (AWP) As part of the rice marketing assistance loan program, USDA calculates and publishes a loan repayment rate, the world price for each class of milled rice (long grain, medium grain, and short grain) based on the prevailing world market price for each of the classes, modified to reflect U.S. quality and the U.S. cost of exporting milled rice. USDA sets this prevailing market price after reviewing milled rice prices in major world markets, and taking into account the effects of supply-demand changes, government-assisted sales, and other relevant price indicators. The steps for calculating and announcing the world prices are prescribed in more detail in Federal regulations.

Aggregate measurement of support (AMS) See aggregate measurement of support in ERS WTO Briefing Room Glossary.

Agreement on Agriculture See Agreement on Agriculture in ERS WTO Briefing Room Glossary.

Agricultural Act of 1949 P.L. 89-439 (October 31, 1949), along with the Agricultural Adjustment Act of 1938, makes up the major part of permanent law that mandates commodity price and farm income support. The original 1949 Act designated mandatory support for basic commodities and the following nonbasic commodities: wool and mohair, tung nuts, honey, Irish potatoes (excluded in the Agricultural Act of 1954), as well as milk, butterfat, and their products. Provisions of this law are generally superseded by more current legislation. If the current legislation expires and new legislation is not enacted, the law reverts back to the permanent provisions of the 1938 and 1949 Acts, unless Congress enacts an extension of current legislation.

Agricultural Adjustment Act (AAA) of 1938 P.L. 75-430 (February 16, 1938) was enacted to replace farm subsidy policies found unworkable in the AAA legislation of 1933. The 1938 Act was the first to make price support mandatory for corn, cotton, and wheat to help maintain a sufficient supply in low production periods, along with marketing quotas to keep supply in line with market demand. It established permissive supports for butter, dates, figs, hops, turpentine, rosin, pecans, prunes, raisins, barley, rye, grain sorghum, wool, winter cover-crop seeds, mohair, peanuts, and tobacco for the 1938-40 period. Title V of the Act established the Federal Crop Insurance Corporation. The 1938 Act is considered part of permanent legislation for commodity programs and farm income support (along with the Commodity Credit Corporation Charter Act and the Agricultural Act of 1949). Provisions of the law are generally superseded by more current legislation.

Agricultural and food science Congress defines "agricultural and food science" as basic, applied, and developmental research, extension, and teaching activities in food and fiber, agricultural, renewable natural resources, forestry, and physical and social sciences.

Agricultural Management Assistance (AMA) program Established under the Agricultural Risk Protection Act of 2000 and amended under the 2002 Farm Act, the Agricultural Management Assistance program provides financial assistance for conserving practices under 3- to 10-year contracts. The program focuses on producers in 15 States where participation in the Federal Crop Insurance Program has historically been low. The 2008 Farm Act added Hawaii to the list of designated states.

Agricultural Market Transition Act (AMTA) Title I of the 1996 Act allowed farmers who participated in the wheat, feed grain, cotton, and rice programs in any one of the previous 5 years to enter into 7-year production flexibility contracts for 1996-2002 and receive payments based on the enrolled acreage. Total production flexibility contract payment levels for each fiscal year were fixed. The AMTA allowed farmers to plant 100 percent of their total contract acreage to any crop, except for limitations on fruits and vegetables, and receive a full payment. Land had to be maintained in agricultural uses, including idling or conserving uses. Unlimited haying and grazing were allowed, as was the planting and harvesting of alfalfa and other forage corps—with no reduction in payments. Production flexibility contract payments, also referred to as AMTA payments, were replaced with direct payments in the 2002 Farm Act and the payment rates were fixed.

Agricultural Risk Protection Act of 2000 (ARPA) Federal crop insurance legislation amended to strengthen the safety net for agricultural producers. Included a provision recognizing organic farming as a "good farming practices" that would be covered by Federal crop insurance.

Agricultural use Refers to cropland planted to an agricultural crop, used for haying or grazing, idled for weather-related reasons or natural disasters, or diverted from crop production to an approved cultural practice that prevents erosion or other degradation.

Amber box policies See amber box policies in ERS WTO Briefing Room Glossary.

Appropriations An appropriations act of Congress permits USDA or other federal agencies to incur financial obligations to be drawn from the Federal Treasury. Appropriations do not represent cash actually set aside in the Treasury for the purposes specified in the appropriations act; they represent limitations of amounts that agencies may obligate for the purposes and during the time periods specified in the appropriations act. Appropriations may be annual (one year in duration), multiple-year (a definite period in excess of one fiscal year), or no-year (available indefinitely). Appropriations are definite (for a specific amount of money) or indefinite (for an unspecified amount of money), and either current (for the immediate fiscal year in question) or permanent (always available).

Area plan of insurance Crop yield or revenue insurance coverage based on county-level yield or revenue.

Authorization Legislation that establishes or continues the legal operation of a Federal program or agency, either indefinitely or for a specific period of time, or that sanctions a particular type of expenditure. An authorization normally is a prerequisite for an appropriation or other kind of budget authority. An authorization also may limit the amount of budget authority to be provided or may authorize the appropriation of "such sums as may be necessary."

Average crop revenue election (ACRE) An optional revenue-based program provision introduced in the 2008 farm legislation that replaces counter-cyclical payments for those producers who elect to participate in ACRE. Once producers elect to participate, participation continues until 2012. Producers continue to receive reduced direct payments and are eligible for reduced loan deficiency payments.

Base acreage (or crop acreage base) A farm's crop-specific acreage of wheat, feed grains, upland cotton, rice, oilseeds, pulse crops, or peanuts eligible to participate in commodity programs. Base acreage includes land that would have been eligible to receive production flexibility contract payments in 2002 and acreage (specified in legislation) planted to other covered commodities (oilseed and peanut producers). Base acreage refers to cropland on a farm, not to specific parcels of land. For a description of rules for determining base see Crop Acreage Bases and Program Payment Yields, 1981 Through 2002 Farm Acts.

Beginning farmer or rancher These are farmers and ranchers (or all members of the entity) who (a) have not operated a farm or ranch for more than 10 consecutive years, and (b) will materially or substantially participate in the operation of the farm or ranch.

Beginning farmer or rancher loans To qualify as a beginning farmer or rancher under USDA's Farm Service Agency guidelines, the loan applicant must be an individual or entity who (1) has not operated a farm or ranch for more than 10 years; (2) meets the loan eligibility requirements of the program to which he/she is applying; and (3) substantially participates in the operation. For farm ownership (FO) loan purposes, applicant cannot own a farm greater than 30 percent of the average size farm in the county. For direct FO loans, applicant must have participated in business operation of a farm for at least 3 years. If the applicant is an entity, all members must be related by blood or marriage, and all stockholders in a corporation must be eligible beginning farmers.

Beneficial interest When a producer controls the commodity and retains the ability to make all decisions affecting the commodity, including movement, sale and the request for and repayment of a loan or LDP.

Bill Emerson Humanitarian Trust See Emerson Humanitarian Trust.

Broadband A descriptive term for communication technologies that can provide consumers integrated access to voice, high-speed data service, video-demand services, and interactive delivery services.

Capacity and infrastructure programs Programs that improve overall effectiveness and ability. Some important Capacity and Infrastructure Programs include Hatch funds for State Agricultural Experiment Stations, McIntire-Stennis funds for forestry research, and Smith-Lever funds for cooperative extension.

Capped entitlement Under an entitlement program, eligible individuals must be allowed to participate, regardless of the cost. Agricultural examples include loan deficiency payments and marketing loan gains. Capped entitlements are entitlement programs with spending ceilings ("capped spending"). However, because they are still entitlements, and anyone who is eligible can participate, stringent eligibility requirements are used to limit participation to the number of individuals or farms for which funds are available. For example, the Conservation Security Program is open to all farms that are located in a watershed there the program is offered in a given year and meet all other eligibility criteria. Once available funds are expended, however, enrollment is suspended.

Catastrophic coverage (CAT) Minimum coverage level available under the Federal crop insurance program. CAT coverage is 50 percent of expected yield, indemnified at 55 percent of the price election.

Commodity certificates (Certs) Commodity certificates, issued by the Commodity Credit

Corporation (CCC), can be purchased at the posted county price for wheat, feed grains, and oilseeds or at the effective adjusted world price for rice or upland cotton. The certificates are available for producers to use immediately in acquiring crop collateral they pledged to the CCC for a commodity loan. When the posted county price or effective adjusted world price is below the loan rate, producers who are facing payment limits can benefit from the lower loan repayment rates. The use of commodity certificates to repay loans ends after the 2009 crop year. Certificates were also used during the mid-1980s in lieu of cash to compensate program beneficiaries and to reduce the large, costly, and price-depressing commodity surpluses held by the CCC.

Commodity Credit Corporation (CCC) A federally owned and operated corporation within the USDA created to stabilize and support agricultural prices and farm income by making loans and payments to producers, purchasing commodities, and engaging in various other operations. The CCC handles all money transactions for agricultural price and income support and related programs.

Commodity Exchange Act The Commodity Exchange Act, 7 USC 1, et seq., provides for the Federal regulation of commodity futures and options trading. See Commodity Futures Modernization Act.

Commodity Futures Modernization Act The Commodity Futures Modernization Act of 2000 (CFMA), Pub. L. No. 106-554, 114 Stat. 2763, reauthorized the Commodity Futures Trading Commission for 5 years and overhauled the Commodity Exchange Act to create a flexible structure for the regulation of futures and options trading. Significantly, the CFMA codified an agreement between the CFTC and the Securities and Exchange Commission to repeal the 18-year-old ban on the trading of single stock futures.

Commodity Futures Trading Commission The Federal regulatory agency established by the Commodity Futures Trading Act of 1974 to administer the Commodity Exchange Act.

Commodity loan rate The price per unit (pound, bushel, bale, or hundredweight) at which the Commodity Credit Corporation provides commodity-secured loans to farmers for a specified period of time.

Commodity Supplemental Food Program Program providing food to supplement the diets of low-income pregnant and breastfeeding women, other new mothers up to 1 year postpartum, infants, children up to age 6, and the elderly. Predecessor to the WIC Program. Funded under the authority of the Agriculture and Consumer Protection Act of 1973.

Community Food Projects Competitive Grant Program Established in 1996 to encourage development of community food projects that help promote the self-sufficiency of low-income communities. Grants provided to support projects that seek to increase food security in communities by establishing linkages among local groups to develop and support the local food system.

Competitive grants Funds that are allocated by panels of relevant professional peers after consideration of research proposals submitted to the review panel.

Congressional Hunger Fellows An anti-hunger leadership program of the Congressional Hunger Center. Initially funded with a challenge grant from VISTA and through private donations. In 1999, Congress provided supporting funds through USDA to establish the Mickey Leland International and Bill Emerson National Hunger Fellowships.

Conservation activities Conservation systems, practices, or management measures designed to address a resource concern. Structural, vegetative, and land management measures (including agricultural drainage management systems), and planning needed to address a resource concern are included.

Conservation Compliance Requires producers who cropped highly erodible land (HEL) before December 23, 1985 to implement a soil conservation plan or risk losing their Federal farm program benefits, including most commodity, conservation, and disaster payments. Conservation compliance requirements are similar to those of the Sodbuster requirements, (compliance on newly planted land) but tend to be less stringent.

Conservation measurement tool Procedure to estimate the level of environmental gain achieved by a producer in implementing conservation activities, including indices or other measures developed by the Secretary.

Conservation of Private Grazing Land Initiative The 1996 Farm Act authorized a coordinated technical, educational, and related assistance program for owners and managers of private grazing lands, including rangeland, pasture land, grazed forest land, and hay land. The purpose of the program is to promote improved management of grazing land resources for enhanced economic uses and environmental services.

Conservation plan A combination of land uses and farming practices to protect and improve soil productivity and water quality and prevent deterioration of natural resources on all or part of a farm. Conservation plans must be both technically and economically feasible.

Conservation practice Any technique or measure used to protect or improve natural resources and environmental quality, for which standards and specifications for installation, operation, or maintenance have been developed. Practices approved by the Natural

Resources Conservation Service are compiled at each conservation district in its field office technical guide.

Conservation Reserve Enhancement Program (CREP) Initiated following the 1996 Farm Act, CREP is a State-Federal conservation partnership program targeted to address specific State and nationally significant water quality, soil erosion, and wildlife habitat issues related to agriculture. The program offers additional financial incentives beyond the Conservation Reserve Program to encourage farmers and ranchers to enroll in 10-15 year contracts to retire land from production. CREP is funded through the Commodity Credit Corporation.

Conservation Reserve Program (CRP) Established in 1985 and administered by USDA's Farm Service Agency, CRP is the latest version of long-term land retirement programs used in the 1930s and 1960s. CRP provides farm owners or operators with an annual per-acre rental payment and half the cost of establishing a permanent land cover, in exchange for retiring environmentally sensitive cropland from production for 10-15 years. In 1996, Congress limited enrollment to 36.4 million acres at any time. The 2002 Farm Act increased the enrollment limit to 39.2 million acres. Beginning in 2010, the 2008 Farm Act will limit enrollment to 32 million acres. Producers can offer land for competitive bidding based on an Environmental Benefits Index during periodic signups or automatically enroll more limited acreages in such practices as riparian buffers, field windbreaks, and grass strips on a continuous basis. CRP is funded through the Commodity Credit Corporation.

Conservation Reserve Program (CRP) Continuous Sign-up Initiated following the 1996 Farm Act, continuous sign-up allows enrollment of land in riparian buffers, filter strips, grass waterways, and other high priority practices at any time and without competition. Eligible land is automatically accepted into the program. Continuous sign-up acreage is under the overall CRP acreage cap.

Conservation Security Program (CSP) Established in the 2002 Farm Act, CSP provides payments to producers for maintaining or adopting structural and/or land management practices that address a wide range of local and/or national resource concerns. As with the Environmental Quality Incentives Program, a wide range of practices can be subsidized. But CSP will focus on land-based practices and specifically excludes livestock waste handling facilities. Producers can participate at one of three tiers; higher tiers require greater conservation effort and offer higher payments. Participants must use the lowest cost practices that meet conservation standards. After September 30, 2008, new enrollment will be prohibited, but existing contracts will continue until they expire. CSP is replaced by a new, but similar program, The Conservation Stewardship Program.

Conservation Stewardship Program (CSP) Established in the 2008 Farm Act, CSP provides payments to producers for adopting or maintaining wide range of conservation management and land-based structural practices that address 1 or more resources of concern, such as soil, water, and wildlife habitat.

Conservation Technical Assistance (CTA) Since 1936, CTA, administered by USDA's Natural Resources Conservation Service (NRCS) and local conservation districts, has provided technical assistance to farmers for planning and implementing conservation practices.

Conserving use acreage Farmland diverted from crop production to an approved cultural practice that prevents erosion or other degradation. Though crops are not produced, conserving use is considered an agricultural use of the land.

Considered planted Acreage idled for weather-related reasons or natural disasters, acreage devoted to conservation purposes or planted to certain other allowed commodities, and acreage USDA determined as necessary to include for fair and equitable treatment. A provision of the Agricultural Act of 1949 used to implement the base acreage and yield system for 1991-95 crops and used to determine acreage planted within the 2008 ACRE program.

Contract acreage Land voluntarily enrolled in a production flexibility contract (PFC) under the 1996 Farm Act. Land was eligible for the PFC enrollment the landowner had at least one crop acreage base for a contract crop that would have been in effect for 1996 under previous farm law. A farmer could voluntarily choose to reduce contract acreage in subsequent years. Base acreage under previous farm law could, upon leaving the Conservation Reserve Program, be entered into a PFC. Otherwise, the maximum amount of contract acreage was established during the one-time signup for the PFC in 1996. Landowners could convert contract acreage to base acreage under the 2002 Farm Act.

Contract crops The term that referred to crops eligible for production flexibility contract payments under Title I of the 1996 Act: wheat, corn, sorghum, barley, oats, rice, and upland cotton.

Cost-sharing Payments to producers to cover a specified portion of the cost of installing, implementing, or maintaining a conservation (structural or land management) practice.

Counter-cyclical payments Counter-cyclical payments are available to producers with historic program payment acres and yields of wheat, corn, barley, grain sorghum, oats, upland cotton, long-grain and medium-grain rice, soybeans, other oilseeds, peanuts, and pulse crops (dry peas, lentils, small and large chickpeas). Payments are made whenever the current effective commodity price is less than the target price. The effective price is calculated by adding: 1) the national average farm price for the marketing year, or the commodity national loan rate, whichever is higher, and 2) the direct payment rate for the commodity.

Covered commodity (aka program commodity) Commodities for which Federal support programs are available to producers, including wheat, corn, barley, grain sorghum, oats, upland cotton, medium and long grain rice, oilseeds, and pulse crops (small and large chickpeas, dry beans and lentils). Programs for peanuts are separate in the 2002 and 2008 Farm Acts but are similar to those for covered commodities.

Crop insurance Insurance that protects farmers from crop losses due to natural hazards. A subsidized multiperil Federal insurance program, administered by the USDA's Risk Management Agency, is available to most farmers. Federal crop insurance is sold and serviced through private insurance companies. The Federal Government subsidizes a portion of the premium, as well as some administrative and operating expenses of the private companies. The Federal Crop Insurance Corporation reinsures the companies by absorbing the losses of the program when indemnities exceed total premiums. Various types of yield and revenue insurance products are available for major crops. Hail and fire insurance are offered through private companies without Federal subsidy.

Cropland Land used primarily for production of row crops, close-growing crops, and fruit and nut crops. It includes cultivated and noncultivated acreage, but not land enrolled in the Conservation Reserve Program. For details on land use of U.S. non-Federal lands, see USDA National Resources Conservation Services' National Resources Inventory.

Crop year (marketing year) The 12-month period starting with the month when the harvest of a specific crop typically begins. The 2008 wheat crop year, for example, is June 1, 2008, through May 30, 2009. The amount harvested during this time is then considered the "2008 crop."

Dairy Export Incentive Program A program that offers subsidies to exporters of U.S. dairy products based on the volume of exports. The intent is to make U.S. products more competitive in world markets, thereby increasing U.S. exports. The Commodity Credit Corporation receives export-price bids from exporters and makes the payments either in cash or through certificates redeemable for commodities. The program was originally authorized by the 1985 Farm Act, and reauthorized by subsequent Acts.

Decoupled payments See decoupled payments in ERS WTO Briefing Room Glossary.

Deficiency payments Direct government payments made prior to 1996 to farmers who participated in an annual commodity program for wheat, feed grains, rice, or cotton. The crop-specific payment rate for a particular crop year was based on the difference between an established target price and the higher of the commodity loan rate or the national average market price for the commodity during a specified time period. Deficiency payments are not the same as loan deficiency payments.

De minimis rule See de minimis rule in ERS WTO Briefing Room Glossary.

Department of Defense Fresh Fruit and Vegetable Program USDA, in collaboration with the Department of Defense, procures fresh fruits and vegetables from the Defense Supply Center Philadelphia (DSCP) for use in USDA school meals programs. DSCP operates a nationwide system to purchase and distribute a wide variety of high-quality fresh produce to military installations, Federal prisons, and veterans' hospitals. States and/or schools place orders directly with DSCP's field offices for a variety of available, U.S.-grown fresh products.

Direct loan "Direct" farm loans are made by USDA's Farm Service Agency (FSA) to family-size farmers and ranchers who cannot obtain commercial credit from conventional lenders. The FSA also services these loans and provides supervision and credit counseling so borrowers have a better chance for success. Farm Ownership (FO), Operating (OL), Emergency, and Youth loans are the main types of loans available under the Direct farm loan programs. Direct loan funds are also set aside each year for loans to minority applicants and beginning farmers. Direct loan applications are made at the local FSA office.

Direct payments Fixed payments for eligible historic production of wheat, corn, barley, grain sorghum, oats, upland cotton, long- and medium-grain rice, soybeans, other oilseeds, and peanuts. Producers enroll annually in the program to receive payments based on payment rates specified in the Farm Act and their historic program payment acres and yields.

Direct-to-Consumers Marketing Program Program administered by USDA's Agricultural Marketing Service to improve direct market access for operators of small and medium-size farms, enabling them to compete outside the supermarket system and other large wholesale market channels. Program includes farmers' markets, farm stands, roadside stands, community-supported agriculture, pick-your-own farms, Internet marketing, and niche markets.

Disaster payments Payments made to producers through existing or special legislation due to crop and livestock losses because of natural disasters such as floods, drought, hail, excessive moisture, or related conditions.

Diversion payment See paid land diversion.

Earmarks Congressional designations of funding for specific projects. When using this practice,

Congress, in report language or law, directs that appropriated funds go to a specific performer or designates awards for certain types of performers or geographic locations.

Easement Voluntary sale or donation of specific use rights to land. Examples of rights that could be sold include the rights to use land for cropping purposes (in Wetlands Reserve Program and Grassland Reserve Program) or the rights to develop land for urban uses (Farmland Preservation Program). Landowners who sell or donate an easement retain all other ownership rights to the land, including the right to sell the land. Future owners of land subject to an easement are legally required to abide by easement terms. Easements are perpetual or are long-term, 25 years or more.

Ecosystem service Those components of nature that are directly valued by people, or combined with other factors to produce valued goods and services.

Electronic Benefit Transfer (EBT) Debit card technology used for issuing food stamp benefits.

Emergency farm loan The USDA's Farm Service Agency (FSA) provides emergency loans to help farmers and ranchers recover from production and physical losses due to drought, flooding, other natural disasters, or quarantine. The farmers or ranchers must own or operate land in a county declared a disaster area by the President or designated by the Secretary of Agriculture as a disaster or quarantine area. The FSA administrator may authorize emergency loan assistance for physical losses only. The farmer or rancher must have suffered at least a 30-percent loss in crop production or a physical loss to livestock, livestock products, real estate, or chattel property.

Emerson Humanitarian Trust A special wheat, corn, grain sorghum, and rice reserve to be used for humanitarian food aid purposes. The Trust was formerly the Food Security Commodity Reserve and the Food Security Wheat Reserve. Created by the Agriculture Act of 1980 (P.L. 96-494), the reserve is generally used to provide famine and other emergency relief when commodities are not available under P.L. 480 (Food for Peace Program). The 1996 Farm Act expanded the reserve to include corn, grain sorghum, and rice in addition to wheat, and made other administrative changes. Commodity Credit Corporation also is authorized to hold money as well as commodities in the reserve.

Environmental Benefits Index The Environmental Benefits Index (EBI) is used to rank contract proposals for acceptance in the Conservation Reserve Program general sign-up. Environmental scores are based on potential to create wildlife habitat, reduce soil erosion, improve water quality, improve air quality, or sequester carbon. Contract cost is also an important factor.

Environmental Quality Incentives Program (EQIP) EQIP was established by the 1996 Farm Act to consolidate and better target the functions of the Agricultural Conservation Program, Water Quality Incentives Program, Great Plains Conservation Program, and Colorado River Basin Salinity Program. The objective of EQIP is to encourage farmers and ranchers to adopt practices that reduce environmental and resource problems through 1- to 10-year contracts. The program provides education and technical assistance, as well as financial assistance through cost-share payments for structural and vegetative practices and incentive payments for management practices. EQIP is run by the Natural Resources Conservation Service and is funded through Commodity Credit Corporation.

Erodibility Index (EI) A measure of the potential for soil productivity to be damaged by soil erosion. The higher the index, the higher the likelihood of soil damage in the absence of soil conservation measures. EI scores above 8 are equated to highly erodible land.

Exempt commercial market An electronic trading facility that trades exempt commodities on a principal-to-principal basis solely between persons that are eligible commercial entities.

Export Enhancement Program (EEP) Program started in May 1985 under the Commodity Credit Corporation Charter Act to help U.S. exporters meet competitors' prices in subsidized markets. Under the EEP, exporters received subsidies based on the volume of exports to specifically targeted countries. The program was reauthorized by the 1985 Farm Act and subsequent farm acts, until it was repealed by the 2008 Farm Bill.

Farm Credit System (FCS) A network of cooperatively owned lending institutions and related service organizations serving all 50 States and the Commonwealth of Puerto Rico. The FCS specializes in providing farm real estate and rural homeowner loans, operating credit, and related services to farmers, ranchers, and producers or harvesters of aquatic products.

Farm Credit System Insurance Corporation (FCSIC) An entity of the Farm Credit System (FCS), established by law in 1987, to insure the timely repayment of principal and interest on FCS debt securities.

Farm ownership loan (FO) Farm Ownership (FO) loans may be made by the Farm Service Agency (FSA) to purchase farmland, construct or repair buildings and other fixtures, develop farmland to promote soil and water conservation, or to refinance debt. FO loans are made under both guaranteed and direct loan programs, and are made to producers unable to obtain credit from conventional lenders.

Farm Security and Rural Investment Act of 2002 (2002 Farm Act) (P.L. 107-171) The omnibus food and agriculture legislation (2002 Farm Act) that provided a framework for the Secretary of Agriculture to administer various agricultural and food programs from 2002 to 2007. The legislation was signed into law on May 13, 2002. This farm act replaced production flexibility contract payments of the 1996 Farm Act with direct payments, and introduced counter-cyclical payments and the Conservation Security Program. The 2002 Act was the first farm act to include a separate energy title.

Farmed wetland Farmed wetlands are wetlands that have been partially drained or are naturally dry enough to allow crop production in some years but otherwise meet the soil, hydrological, and vegetative criteria defining a wetland.

Farmland Protection Program (FPP) Established in the 1996 Farm Act, FPP provides funding to State, local, and tribal entities and nongovernmental organizations with existing farmland protection programs to purchase conservation easements or other interests in land that limit nonagricultural uses of the land. The Natural Resources Conservation Service purchases conservation easements by partnering with eligible entities that have pending offers for the acquisition of conservation easements.

Farmers' Markets Promotion Program See Direct-to-Consumers Marketing Program.

Federal Agriculture Improvement and Reform Act of 1996 (1996 Farm Act) (P.L. 104-127) The omnibus food and agriculture legislation (Farm Act) signed into law on April 4, 1996, provided a 7-year framework (1996-2002) for the Secretary of Agriculture to administer various agricultural and food programs. The 1996 Act redesigned income support and supply management programs for producers of wheat, corn, grain sorghum, barley, oats, rice, and upland cotton. Production flexibility contract payments were made available under Title I of the 1996 Act (see Agricultural Market Transition Act). The legislation also suspended acreage reduction programs, revised and consolidated Federal milk marketing orders. Made program changes for sugar and peanuts, and consolidated and extended environmental programs.

Federal Agricultural Mortgage Corporation An organization more commonly referred to as Farmer Mac, which is a secondary (resale) market for agricultural mortgages. Farmer Mac was authorized by the Agricultural Credit Act of 1987

Federal Crop Insurance Act Legislation that provides a framework for the operation of the Federal crop insurance program. Enacted in 1938, with major amendments in 1980, 1994, and 2000. The 2000 amendment is referred to as the Agricultural Risk Protection Act of 2000.

Federal Crop Insurance Corporation (FCIC) Federally owned and operated corporation within USDA that promotes the economic stability of agriculture through a sound system of crop insurance and provides the means for the research and experience necessary to devise and establish such insurance.

Federal Crop Insurance Program See crop insurance.

Federal milk marketing orders Regulations issued by the Secretary of Agriculture specifying minimum prices that regulated handlers must pay for milk and other conditions under which milk can be bought and sold within a specified area. The orders establish minimum class prices according to the products for which milk is used that are then "blended" as a weighted average. The 1996 Farm Act required consolidation of the Federal milk marketing orders into 10-14 regional orders, down from 33. In 2008, there are 10 Federal milk marketing orders.

Flex acreage See normal flex acreage and optional flex acreage.

Food, Agriculture, Conservation and Trade Act of 1990 (1990 Farm Act) (P.L. 101-624) Omnibus food and agriculture legislation (Farm Act) signed into law on November 28, 1990, provided a 5-year framework (1991-95) for the Secretary of Agriculture to administer various agricultural and food programs. Commodity programs were continued, with modifications, such as creation of optional flex acreage, making the programs more market oriented.

Food Distribution Program on Indian Reservations (FDPIR) Program created in 1977 as an alternative to the FSP because many Native Americans live in remote areas where food costs are high and access to food stamp offices and grocery stores is limited. FDPIR provides monthly food packages to low-income individuals and families living on reservations, and to American Indian households living in approved areas near reservations and in approved service areas in Oklahoma. In fiscal year 2003, 5 States and 98 tribal authorities administered the program on 243 reservations.

Food Security Act of 1985 (1985 Farm Act) (P.L. 99-198) Omnibus food and agriculture legislation (Farm Act) signed into law on December 23, 1985, provided a 5-year framework (1986-90) for the Secretary of Agriculture to administer various agricultural and food programs. The law provided for lower price and income supports and a dairy herd buy-out program, and established marketing loans, loan deficiency payments, and the Conservation Reserve Program.

Food Security Commodity Reserve See the Bill Emerson Humanitarian Trust.

Food Stamp Employment and Training (FSE&T) See the Supplemental Nutrition Assistance Program Employment and Training.

Food Stamp Nutrition Education (FSNE) Program See Supplemental Nutrition Assistance Program Nutrition Education (SNAP-Ed).

Food Stamp Program (FSP) See Supplemental Nutrition Assistance Program (SNAP).

Forex Over-the-counter market for foreign exchange transactions. Also called the foreign exchange market.

Formula funds The amount of funds provided for agricultural research and extension to land-grant institutions (1862, 1890, and 1994 institutions), schools of forestry, and schools of veterinary medicine through several formula program authorities. The funds to each institution are determined by formula, often statutorily defined, that may include variables such as the rural population or farm population. Local or regional university leaders decide which specific projects will be supported by an institution's formula fund allotment. These decisions are informed, in part, by stakeholders who both conduct and use agricultural research and extension.

Fruit and vegetable planting restrictions Planting for harvest of fruits, vegetables (other than lentils, mung beans, and dry peas), and wild rice is prohibited on base acres of commodity program participants, except in certain situations specified in farm legislation (e.g., if the farm has a history of planting a specific crop in these categories). These restrictions were initiated in 1990 and extended in the 1996, 2002, and 2008 Farm Acts.

FSP administration FSP benefits are Federally funded, but the program is administered jointly with State and local welfare agencies. Interactions with clients are handled by State and local agencies that determine eligibility and calculate and issue benefits. USDA, FNS authorizes and monitors retail stores that redeem food stamp benefits. Federal and State authorities cooperate in developing and implementing nutrition education and outreach plans and in administering a nationwide quality control system that monitors accuracy of benefit determination.

FSP benefit formula An individual household's food stamp allotment equal to the maximum benefit for that household's size, less 30 percent of the household's net income. Households with no countable income receive the maximum allotment. Allotment levels are higher for Alaska, Hawaii, Guam, and the Virgin Islands, reflecting higher food prices in those areas.

FSP countable resources Assets applied to the resource limit, including cash on hand, checking and savings accounts, saving certificates, stocks and bonds, individual retirement accounts (IRAs), and Keogh plans, as well as some less liquid assets, such as vehicles and property not producing income. Not included are residential equity, business assets, personal property, lump-sum earned income tax credit payments and other nonrecurring payments, burial plots, the cash value of life insurance policies, and pension plans (other than Keogh plans and IRAs).

FSP dependent care deduction Deduction for dependent care that was needed to allow work, training, or education activities. Capped at $200 per month per child 2 and under and $175 for others.

FSP maximum benefit The maximum monthly benefit depends on the number of people in the household and the cost of the Thrifty Food Plan (which is annually indexed for inflation.) For FY 2008 the maximum benefit is $162 for a 1 person household; $298 for 2; $426 for 3; $542 for 4; $643 for 5; $772 for 6; $853 for 7, $975 for 8, and $122 for each additional person. Maximum benefits are higher for Alaska, Hawaii, Guam, and the Virgin Islands, reflecting higher food prices in those areas.

FSP minimum benefit Minimum benefit ($10) for eligible households with 1 or 2 members.

Fundamental or basic research Research conducted primarily to increase scientific understanding, not necessarily for direct application or new commercial products or processes. Also known as "basic research."

General Agreement on Tariffs and Trade (GATT) See General Agreement on Tariffs and Trade (GATT) in ERS WTO Briefing Room Glossary.

Grassland Reserve Program (GRP) Program established in the 2002 Farm Act to assist owners, through long-term contracts or easements, in restoring grassland and conserving virgin grassland. Restored, improved, or natural grassland, rangeland, and pasture, including prairie, can be enrolled. Eligible grassland can be enrolled under long term contracts or easements. The program is administered jointly by the Natural Resources Conservation Service, Farm Service Agency, and Forest Service.

Green box policies See green box policies in ERS WTO Briefing Room Glossary.

Guaranteed loan Farm Service Agency (FSA) guarantees loans lenders (e.g., banks, Farm Credit System institutions, credit unions) up to 95 percent of any loss of principal and interest on a loan. The guarantee permits lenders to extend agricultural credit to farmers who do not meet the lenders' normal underwriting criteria. FSA guaranteed loans are made for both farm ownership (FO) and operating (OL) purposes. FSA can guarantee OL or FO loans up to $949,000 (amount adjusted annually based on inflation).

High-tier tariff rate See over-quota tariff in ERS WTO Briefing Room Glossary.

Highly erodible land (HEL) Soils with an erodibility index (EI) equal to or greater than eight are defined as HEL. An EI of eight indicates that without any cover or conservation practices, the soil will erode at a rate eight times the soil tolerance level. Fields containing at least one-third or 50 acres (whichever is less) of HEL are designated as highly erodible for the purpose of Highly-Erodible Land Conservation Provisions.

Highly erodible land conservation Includes conservation compliance and sodbuster provisions.

Homestead property A family's principle property composed of a house and a lot, which can be filed as a homestead by State law. The homestead status protects USDA farm loan borrowers who lack the financial means to make timely payments, is ineligible for a restructured loan, and is unable to buy out the loan at the net recovery value of the collateral property by allowing them to instead convey the property to USDA in lieu of loan payments.

Horticulture crops See specialty crops.

Incentive payments Payments to producers in an amount or at a rate necessary to encourage producers to adopt one or more land management practices.

Indirect costs Portion of a grant that its recipient can use to cover general, administrative, and other costs not specifically related to the purposes of the grant.

Indirect (grant) costs The portion of a grant that covers general operating expenses and administrative activities not directly related to activities sponsored by the grant.

Initiative for Future Agriculture and Food Systems (IFAFS) Authorized in the Agricultural Research, Extension and Education Reform Act of 1998. Implements research, extension, and education grants to address critical emerging agricultural issues related to 1) future food production, 2) environmental quality and natural resource management, or 3) farm income; and activities authorized by the Alternative Agricultural Research and Commercialization Act of 1990.

In-quota tariff See in-quota tariff in ERS WTO Briefing Room Glossary.

Insular Areas of the United States The Commonwealth of Puerto Rico, the U.S. Virgin Islands, Guam, American Samoa, the Commonwealth of the Northern Mariana Islands, the Federated States of Micronesia, the Republic of the Marshall Islands, and the Republic of Palau.

Jones Act Cargo preference legislation that requires shipping of most government cargo, including foreign food aid, on U.S.-built, owned, crewed, and operated vessels.

Land-Grant Institutions A land-grant college or university is an institution designated by its State legislature or Congress to receive benefits of the Morrill Acts of 1862 and 1890. A principal mission of these institutions, set forth in the first Morrill Act (Land-Grant Act), was to teach agriculture and the mechanical arts. This law gave each State a grant of Federal land to be sold to provide an endowment for at least one land-grant institution. Additional colleges and universities have been established with land-grant status and certain existing institutions have received land-grant status (see 1890s colleges/universities and 1994 institutions).

Land management practice See management practice.

Limited-resource farmer or rancher Farmers and ranchers with (a) direct or indirect gross farm sales of $116,800 or less (adjusted for inflation starting in 2005) in each of the previous 2 years and (b) total household income at or below the national poverty level for a family of 4 OR less than 50 percent of county median household income in each of the previous 2 years.

Loan commodity Wheat, corn, grain sorghum, barley, oats, upland cotton, extra long staple cotton, long-grain rice, medium-grain rice, soybeans, other oilseeds, graded wool, nongraded wool, mohair, honey, dry peas, lentils, small chickpeas, and large chickpeas.

Loan deficiency payments A provision initiated in the Food Security Act of 1985 that gives the Secretary of Agriculture discretion to provide direct payments for loan commodities to producers who agree not to obtain a commodity loan on their production for a particular crop year. Loan deficiency payments (LDP) continue to be available for all loan commodities except extra-long staple cotton. LDPs are also available for unshorn pelts or hay and silage derived from a loan commodity. The LDP provision is applicable only if a marketing loan repayment provision has been implemented (i.e., if the market price of a commodity is below the commodity loan rate). The intent of the LDP provision (as well as the marketing loan repayment provision) is to minimize accumulation and storage of stocks by the government and allow U.S. commodities to be marketed freely and competitively. The LDP payment amount is determined by multiplying the local marketing loan repayment rate by the amount of the commodity eligible for a loan. Loan deficiency payments are not the same as deficiency payments.

Loan rate See commodity loan rate.

Loan repayment rate See marketing loan repayment rate.

Make allowance (or milk manufacturing marketing adjustment) Used by USDA in its calculation of Commodity Credit Corporation purchase prices for butter, nonfat dry milk, and cheese. It is intended to reflect manufacturing cost for the products purchased. This margin is administratively set so that manufacturers who receive the purchase price for their outputs should be able to pay dairy farmers the equivalent of the support price. The USDA make allowance is not a guaranteed margin to manufacturers.

Management practices Changes in the management of agricultural production in the context of environmental programs, e.g., nutrient or manure management, integrated pest management, irrigation management, tillage or residue management, and grazing management.

Market Access Program (MAP) Formerly the Market Promotion Program, designed to encourage development, maintenance, and expansion of commercial commodity exports to specific export markets. Participating organizations include nonprofit trade associations, State and regional trade groups, and private companies. Activities financed include consumer promotions, market research, technical assistance, and trade servicing.

Market loss assistance payments Direct payments to producers to partially offset financial losses due to severe weather and other natural disasters or stressful economic conditions, such as low commodity prices or pest and animal disease outbreaks.

Marketing allotments When in effect, these provide each processor or producer of a specified commodity a specific limit on sales for the year, above which penalties would apply. Sugar allotments, for example, were authorized during 1991-95, suspended by the 1996 Farm Act, and reauthorized under the 2002 and 2008 Farm Acts.

Marketing assessments A fee paid by producers, processors, or handlers to help cover costs of commodity programs.

Marketing loan gain The difference between the announced commodity loan rate and the marketing loan repayment rate. This represents a program benefit to producers and is aimed at reducing government costs of stock accumulation.

Marketing loan program Provisions that allow producers to repay nonrecourse commodity loans at less than the announced loan rate whenever the world price or loan repayment rate for the commodity is less than the loan rate. Marketing loan provisions are aimed at reducing government costs of stock accumulation. Marketing loan provisions were originally mandated only for rice and upland cotton. Marketing loan provisions are implemented for feed grains, wheat, rice, upland cotton, all oilseeds, peanuts, small and large chickpeas, lentils, dry beans, wool, mohair, and honey.

Marketing loan repayment rate Rate at which farmers are allowed to repay their loans when market prices are below the commodity loan rate. This lower repayment rate is based on the local, posted county prices (PCPs) for wheat, feed grains, or oilseeds; on the adjusted world price for rice or upland cotton; and on the national posted price for peanuts. Any accrued interest on the loan is waived.

Marketing orders Federal marketing orders authorize agricultural producers in a designated region to take various actions to promote orderly marketing, such as influencing supply and quality and pooling funds for promotion and research. Marketing orders are initiated by the industry, but must be approved by the Secretary of Agriculture and by a vote among affected producers. Once approved, a marketing order is mandatory for all producers in the marketing order area. There are marketing orders for a number of fruits, nuts, and vegetables, and for milk. (See also Federal milk marketing orders.)

Marketing year See crop year.

Market News A program administered by USDA's Agricultural Marketing Service to provide current, unbiased price and sales data to assist in the orderly marketing and distribution of farm commodities. Reports include prices, volume, quality, condition, and other market data on agricultural commodities in specific markets and marketing areas, domestically and in international markets.

Matching funds Funds that a grant recipient must provide personally or from another source as a condition for receiving grant funds.

Milk marketing orders See Federal milk marketing orders.

Minor oilseeds See other oilseeds.

National Organic Program USDA organic regulatory program for organic agriculture established under the Organic Foods Production Act of 1990.

National posted price Weekly price announced by the CCC for peanuts used to determine the loan repayment rate.

National Research Initiatives for Food, Agriculture and Environment of 1990 The 1990 Farm Act extended the role of competitive grants within USDA by formalizing the competitive process via the National Research Initiatives for Food, Agriculture and Environment.

National School Lunch Program Federally assisted meal program operating in public and nonprofit private schools and residential child care institutions. Established under the National School Lunch Act in 1946. It provides nutritionally balanced, low-cost lunches that are free to children in households with incomes at or below 130 percent of poverty and reduced price for those in households with incomes between 130 and 185 percent of poverty.

NIFA National Institute for Food and Agriculture.

No net cost A requirement that a price support program be operated at no cost to the Federal Government. The No-Net-Cost Act of 1982 required participants in the 1982 and subsequent tobacco programs to pay an assessment to cover potential losses in operating the tobacco price support program. A no-net-cost provision for sugar was initiated under the Food Security Act of 1985, suspended under the 1996 Farm Act, and reimplemented under the 2002 Farm Act and is continued in the 2008 Farm Act.

Noninsured Crop Disaster Assistance Program (NAP) Program that provides coverage similar to CAT insurance to producers of noninsurable crops. Administered by USDA's Farm Service Agency.

Nonrecourse loan program Program providing commodity-secured loan funds to producers for a specified period of time (typically 9 months), after which producers may either repay the loan and accrued interest or transfer ownership of the commodity amount pledged as collateral to the Commodity Credit Corporation (CCC) as full settlement of the loan, without penalty. These loans, also referred to as "commodity loans," are available on a crop year basis for wheat, feed grains, cotton, peanuts, rice, oilseeds, pulse crops, wool, mohair and honey. Sugar processors are also eligible for nonrecourse loans. Participants in commodity loan programs receive loan funds based on the commodity-specific, per-unit loan rate specified in legislation. The loans are called nonrecourse because, at the producer's option, the CCC has no recourse but to accept the commodity as full settlement of the loan. Under the Marketing Loan Program, producers of eligible commodities may repay the loan at the world price (rice and upland cotton), posted county price (wheat, feed grains, and oilseeds) or national posted price (peanuts) when these prices are below the year's set commodity loan rate, thus providing a disincentive to crop forfeiture. Some commodity loans are recourse loans, meaning producers must pay back the loans in cash.

Nontariff barriers (NTB) See nontariff barriers in ERS WTO Briefing Room Glossary.

Normal flex acreage A term given to the 15 percent of a farmer's acreage base that was not eligible for deficiency payments during 1991-95 but could receive nonrecourse loans and marketing loans for the commodity produced. Producers were allowed to plant any crop on this normal flex acreage, except fruits, vegetables, and some other prohibited crops, without a reduction in their crop acreage base.

NRI The National Research Initiatives for Food, Agriculture, and Environment of 1990.

Oilseeds Soybeans, sunflower seed, canola, rapeseed, safflower, mustard seed, and flaxseed.

Olympic average An average during a 5-year period, dropping the highest and lowest values.

The Omnibus Budget Reconciliation Act of 1990 (P.L. 101-508) A law covering a range of government budget issues that amended the 1990 Farm Act to address budgetary concerns for 1991-95. It mandated a reduction in payment acreage equal to 15 percent of base acreage and established assessments for certain crop loans and incentive payments.

Operating loan (OL) Farm Service Agency (FSA) operating loans (OL) may be used to purchase livestock, farm equipment, feed, seed, fuel, farm chemicals, insurance, and other operating expenses. Operating loans can also be used to pay for minor improvements to buildings, costs associated with land and water development, family living expenses, and to refinance debts under certain conditions. Operating loans are made under both direct and guaranteed programs, to producers who cannot obtain funding from conventional lenders.

Optional flex acreage Under the planting flexibility provision of the 1990 Farm Act, producers of specific crops could choose to plant up to 25 percent of their base acreage for a specific crop to other CCC-specified crops (except fruits and vegetables) without a reduction in their base acreage. Optional flex acreage is a term given to the 10 percent of a farmer's acreage base in 1991-95 beyond the 15-percent normal flex acreage that farmers could choose to plant to crops other than the base program crop. Optional flex acreage was eligible for deficiency payments when planted to the original program crop. However, no deficiency payments would be received on optional flex acreage if planted to another crop. The optional flex acreage planting provision was eliminated in the 1996 Farm Act.

Organic certification Agricultural products grown and processed according to USDA's national organic standards and certified by a USDA-accredited State or private certification organization. Certifying agents review applications from farmers and processors for certification eligibility and qualified inspectors conduct annual onsite inspections of organic operations. Certifying agents determine whether operators are in compliance with organic production standards.

Organic production Production system managed in accordance with the Organic Foods Production Act of 1990 and subsequent Federal regulations. Organic production systems respond to site-specific conditions by integrating cultural, biological, and mechanical practices that foster cycling of resources, promote ecological balance, and conserve biodiversity.

Other oilseeds Term referring to oilseed crops other than soybeans: sunflower seed, canola, rapeseed, safflower, mustard seed, flaxseed, crambe, and sesame seed. Also referred to as minor oilseeds. Additional oilseeds may be designated by the Secretary.

Over-quota tariff See over-quota tariff in ERS WTO Briefing Room Glossary.

Over-the-counter (OTC) Trading of commodities, contracts, or other instruments not listed on any exchange. OTC transactions can occur electronically or over the telephone. Also referred to as Off-Exchange.

Paid land diversion Programs that offered payments to producers to reduce planted acreage of program crops, if the Secretary determined that crop-specific planted acreage should be reduced more than under the acreage reduction program. Farmers were given a specific payment per acre idled in a given year that exceeded acreage reduction program requirements.

Parity-based support prices Commodity-specific support prices (such as loan rates or commodity program purchase prices) whose level in a given year is mandated to be calculated in a way that will maintain the commodity's purchasing power at the level of the 1910-14 base period. Under "permanent legislation" (whose provisions would automatically apply in the absence of current farm acts), the prices of some commodities would be supported at 50-90 percent of parity through direct government purchases or nonrecourse loans.

Payment acres Equal to 85 percent of the base acres for calculating direct and counter-cyclical payments. The 2008 Farm Act set payment acres at 83.3 percent of base acres for crop years 2009-11.

Payment limitation The maximum annual amount of commodity program benefits a person can receive by law. The total amount of payments must be attributed (linked) to a person, by taking into account direct and indirect ownership interests of the person in a legal entity, such as limited partnerships, corporations, associations, trusts, and estates, that are actively engaged in farming. Payment limits are set at $40,000 per person per crop year for direct payments and $65,000 for counter-cyclical payments. The 2008 Farm Act eliminated payment limits for marketing loan benefits. For producers who elect the Average Crop Revenue Election (ACRE) program the limit on direct payments is reduced by 20 percent. The limit on ACRE payments is $65,000 plus the 20 percent reduction in direct payments. The 2008 Farm Act established separate limits on the farm and nonfarm components of adjusted gross income based on the type of payment. These new limits include two applicable to nonfarm income and one applicable to farm income.

Payment yield (also called program yield) Farm's yield of record (per acre) for a specific commodity, determined by a procedure outlined in farm legislation and used in calculating direct payments and counter-cyclical payments.

Peanut poundage quota The maximum quantity of peanuts eligible for the higher of two price support loan rates under the peanut program ended by the 2002 Farm Act. The 1977 Farm Act initiated the two-tier price support program for peanuts. Each producer received a share of a national poundage quota. Producers could market more than their quota, but only the quota amount was eligible for domestic edible use. Over-quota marketings or "additional peanuts" could be sold only for export or processing (crush). Quota peanuts were eligible for a higher commodity loan rate than additionals. The 1996 Farm Act permitted the sale, lease, and transfer of a quota across county lines within a State up to specified amounts of quota annually.

Peanuts, additional Under the peanut program prior to 2002, these were peanuts sold from a farm in any marketing year in excess of the farm's peanut poundage quota. The higher of two price-support loan rate levels applied only to the quantity of peanuts within the annually determined poundage quota. "Additional peanuts" were eligible only for the lower price-support loan rate, the level of which was determined by the Secretary of Agriculture, taking into consideration the demand for peanut oil and meal, expected prices of other vegetable oils and protein meals, and the demand for peanuts in foreign markets.

Permanent legislation Legislation on which the major farm programs are based and that would be in effect in the absence of or expiration of a current farm act. Farm acts are essentially temporary amendments to permanent legislation that includes provisions of the Agricultural Adjustment Act of 1938, the Commodity Credit Corporation Charter Act of 1948, and the Agricultural Act of 1949. Generally, each new farm act suspends the permanent legislation for a specified period.

Personal Responsibility and Work Opportunity Reconciliation Act of 1996 Legislation enacted in 1996 that reformed the Nation's public assistance programs, replacing the cash welfare entitlement under the AFDC program with State-designed temporary assistance programs (TANF) that encouraged parents to work.

Planted yield Crop year commodity production (quantity) per planted acre.

Posted county price (PCP) Calculated for wheat, feed grains, and oilseeds for each county by USDA's Farm Service Agency, the PCP reflects price changes in major terminal grain markets (of which there are 18 in the United States) corrected for the cost of transporting grain from county to terminal. Under the marketing loan repayment provisions and loan deficiency payment provisions of the commodity programs, PCP is used as the loan repayment rate, allowing wheat, feed grain, and oilseed producers to repay commodity loans at less than the original loan rate.

Precision agriculture An integrated information and production-based farming system designed to increase long-term, site-specific, and whole-farm production efficiencies, productivity, and profitability while minimizing unintended impacts on wildlife and the environment.

Prevented planting acreage Land on which a farmer intended to plant a program crop or insurable crop but was unable to do so because of drought, flood, or other natural disaster or condition. Used in the calculation of disaster payments and crop insurance indemnity payments.

Price election Crop price at which indemnities are paid. When enrolling in crop insurance, producers choose a percentage of the price election at which to insure.

Price support loans See nonrecourse loan program.

Producer An owner, operator, landlord, tenant, or sharecropper who shares in the risk of producing a crop and is entitled to share in the crop available for marketing from the farm, or would have shared had the crop been produced.

Production flexibility contract (AMTA) payments Payments during 1996-2002 to farmers who enrolled "contract acreage," under Title I, Subtitle B of the 1996 Farm Act in a one-time sign-up in 1996. The annual total amount, specified in legislation, was allocated to specific crops (wheat, rice, feed grains, and upland cotton) based on percentage allocation factors established in the 1996 Act. Each participating producer of a contract crop received payments determined by multiplying their production flexibility contract payment quantity by the national average production flexibility contract payment rate (see below). Farmers could plant 100 percent of their total contract acreage to any crop, except for limitations on fruits and vegetables, Production Flexibility contract payments were replaced with direct payments under the 2002 Farm Act.

Production flexibility contract payment quantity The quantity of a farm's production eligible for production flexibility contract payments under the 1996 Farm Act. Payment quantity was calculated as the farm's payment yield (per acre) multiplied by 85 percent of the farm's contract acreage.

Production flexibility contract payment rate The amount paid to farmers per unit of participating production under the 1996 Farm Act. A farm's contract acreage and farm program payment yield was established in 1996 during the one-time sign-up period. The national average per-unit payment rate for each crop was calculated annually based on the total amount to be paid out for the crop (largely predetermined by the 1996 Act), divided by the total contract payment quantity of the commodity for the fiscal year.

Program crops Crops for which Federal support programs are available to producers, including wheat, corn, barley, grain sorghum, oats, extra long staple and upland cotton, rice, oilseeds, peanuts, and sugar.

Program yield See payment yield.

Public Law 480 (P.L. 480) Common name for the Agricultural Trade Development and Assistance Act of 1954, which seeks to expand foreign markets for U.S. agricultural products, combat hunger, and encourage economic progress in developing countries. Title I of P.L. 480, also called the Food for Peace Program, makes U.S. agricultural commodities available through long-term dollar credit sales at low interest rates for up to 30 years. Government donations for humanitarian food needs are provided under Title II. Title III authorizes government-to-government "food for development" grants, with donated commodities sold in the developing countries and the revenue used for economic development programs.

Pulse crops Term used in North American agriculture that commonly refers to dry (mature) peas, lentils and small and large chickpeas (garbanzo beans) used as food or feed crops (with "food" referring to human use and "feed" to animal use).

Recourse loan program A provision allowing farmers or processors participating in Government commodity programs to pledge a quantity of a commodity as collateral and obtain a loan from the Commodity Credit Corporation (CCC), which the borrower must repay with interest within a specified period. This provision is unlike nonrecourse loans, which allow producers to settle their loans by delivering the collateral to the CCC.

REEO Research Extension and Education Office.

Regional Equity Provision enacted in the 2002 Farm Act that requires that each State be allocated an amount of conservation funding through specific conservation programs, that collectively exceeds a predetermined minimum amount. The programs that are subject to this provision include the Environmental Quality Incentives Program, the Farmland Protection Program, the Wildlife Habitat Incentives Program and the Grassland Reserve Program.

Reinsurance year Year used to administer risk sharing and other terms of the Standard Reinsurance Agreement. The reinsurance year is from July 1 to June 30; the number of the year is the year containing June. For example, reinsurance year 2012 is July 1, 2011–June 30, 2012.

Revenue insurance An insurance policy offered to farmers that pays indemnities based on revenue shortfalls. These programs are subsidized and reinsured by USDA's Risk Management Agency.

RFP Request for proposals to provide specific government-commissioned work.

Risk Management Agency (RMA) USDA agency that administers programs of the Federal Crop Insurance Corporation.

SAES State Agricultural Experiment Stations.

Safety net A policy that ensures a minimum income, consumption, or wage level for everyone in a society or subgroup. It may also provide persons (including businesses) with protection against risks, such as lost income, limited access to credit, or devastation from natural disasters.

School Breakfast Program Provides nutritional meals to students at participating schools (and to children in a few residential child care institutions). Certified low-income students receive free or reduced-price breakfasts.

Section 32 Section 32 of Agricultural Adjustment Act Amendment of 1935 was enacted to widen market outlets for surplus agricultural commodities as one means of strengthening farm prices. Section 32 programs are financed by a permanent appropriation equal to 30 percent of the import duties collected on all items entering the United States under the customs laws, plus any unused balances up to $300 million. Most funds are annually transferred by appropriators to pay for child nutrition programs.

Section 416 Section 416 of the Agricultural Act of 1949 provides for the disposition of agricultural commodities held by the Commodity Credit Corporation to prevent waste. Disposal is usually carried out by donation of commodities to charitable groups and foreign governments.

Senior Farmers' Market Nutrition Program Program providing low-income seniors with coupons that can be exchanged for eligible foods at farmers' markets, roadside stands, and community-supported agriculture programs through grants awarded to States, U.S. territories, and federally recognized Indian tribal organizations. Participants receive nutrition education and a Federal food benefit of $20-$50 per year.

Simplified reporting A State food stamp option that allows States to minimize the information that food stamp recipients must provide to the food stamp office during the food stamp certification period. Households report only those changes in circumstances that result in income exceeding the food stamp eligibility limit of 130 percent of the Federal poverty level. At 6 months, a State must recertify the household or, if it uses a 12-month certification period, require the household to submit a semiannual report that will be used to update its eligibility and benefit level.

Smith-Lever 3(b) and 3(c) extension funds Federal funds for USDA cooperative extension activities.

Smith-Lever 3(d) special emphasis extension funds Smith-Lever 3(d) funds provide support to State and territory programs in Integrated Pest Management (IPM); Sustainable Agriculture Research and Education Farm Safety funds, which support health and safety efforts in the agricultural sector; and National Children, Youth, and Families at Risk, Federally Recognized Tribes Extension Program and Expanded Food and Nutrition Education Program, which support the nutritional education needs of the underserved, targeting citizens with limited incomes.

Socially-disadvantaged farmer or rancher (SDA) A farmer or rancher who is a member of a group whose members have been subjected to racial or ethnic (and in some cases gender) prejudice because of his or her identity as a member of the group. The definition of SDA farmers varies by Title.

Sodbuster Requires producers who began cropping highly erodible land (HEL) after December 23, 1985 to implement a soil conservation plan or risk losing their Federal farm program benefits, including most commodity, conservation, and disaster payments. Sodbuster requirements are similar to those of conservation compliance, but tend to be less stringent.

Special grants The Special Research Grants Act of 1965 created a mechanism outside the competitive grants process for the distribution of funds to State Agricultural Experiment Stations, public institutions, and individuals to study specific problems of concern to USDA, as defined by Congress. (See also definition for earmarks.)

Specialty crops Fruits, vegetables, tree nuts, dried fruits, nursery crops, and floriculture. Also referred to as horticulture crops.

Standard Reinsurance Agreement A cooperative financial assistance agreement between Federal Crop Insurance Corporation and approved insurance providers to deliver eligible crop insurance contracts.

State Agricultural Experiment Stations (SAES) SAES work with land-grant universities to carry out a joint research-teaching-extension mission. The Hatch Act of 1887 offered States the option of establishing stations to perform science-based research and acquire and disseminate information of use to the agricultural sector. Each State (as well as some territories) now has an SAES, and some States have additional substations. The experiment stations cooperate closely with USDA.

Step 2 payments for upland cotton Issued to exporters and domestic mill users of U.S. upland cotton on a weekly basis subject to price conditions in the United States and Northern Europe. Payments were made in cash or certificates to domestic users on documented raw cotton consumption, and to exporters on documented export shipments. Program terminated on August 1, 2006.

Stewardship threshold The level of natural resource conservation and environmental management required, as determined by the Secretary using conservation measurement tools, to improve and conserve the quality and condition of a resource.

Structural practice A practice that involves a constructed facility, land shaping, or permanent vegetative cover designed to preserve soil; reduce runoff of nutrient, sediment, and pesticides; enhance wildlife habitat; or other purposes. Examples include animal waste-management facilities, terraces, grassed waterways, contour grass strips, filter strips, tailwater pits, permanent wildlife habitats, and constructed wetlands.

Supplemental Agricultural Disaster Assistance Disaster assistance payments provided to producers of eligible commodities (crops, farm-raised fish, honey, and livestock) in counties declared by the Secretary to be "disaster counties."

Supplemental Nutrition Assistance Program (SNAP) New name for the former Food Stamp Program (FSP). SNAP provides monthly benefits to eligible low-income households and is designed to alleviate hunger and malnutrition by enabling participants to obtain a more nutritious diet. Benefits can be used to purchase food at authorized food stores. The 2008 Farm Act changed the name of the Food Stamp Program to the Supplemental Nutrition Assistance Program (SNAP), effective on October 1, 2008.

Supplemental Nutrition Assistance Program Employment and Training (SNAP E&T) Program requirement that certain members of participating households must register for work, accept suitable job offers, and fulfill work or training requirements (such as looking or training for a job) established by State welfare agencies. The Food Security Act of 1985 required all States to implement a Food Stamp Employment Training (FSE&T) Program to improve work opportunities for program participants. Funds for E&T were made available to States by Federal grants, with additional funding available on a 50 percent matching basis. Legislation in 1997 and 1998 targeted E&T funding to nonworking adults without dependents.

Supplemental Nutrition Assistance Program Nutrition Education (SNAP-Ed) A component of SNAP supporting nutrition education activities. SNAP-Ed focuses on improving the likelihood that SNAP participants and other low-income Americans will make healthy food choices within a limited budget and choose active lifestyles consistent with the Dietary Guidelines for Americans and MyPyramid food guidance system. State agencies have the option of participating in SNAP-Ed if they are willing to match Federal funding. USDA's Food and Nutrition Service approves State plans on an annual basis and then reimburses States for 50 percent of allowable expenditures.

Supplemental Revenue Assistance Payments Payments made to eligible producers on farms in disaster counties that incurred crop production or crop quality losses or both during the crop year.

Swampbuster Wetland conservation provision first established farm legislation in 1985. Producers who drain a wetland to make it ready for crop production can lose Federal farm program benefits, including most commodity, conservation, and disaster payments. Natural Resources Conservation Service certifies technical compliance, and USDA's Farm Services Agency administers changes in farm program benefits.

Target price Unit price level (e.g., for bushel, pound, or ton) established in the 2002 Farm Act used for calculating counter-cyclical payments for covered (program) commodities. Prior to 1996, target prices were used to calculate deficiency payments.

Tariff See tariff in ERS WTO Briefing Room Glossary.

Tariff-rate quota (TRQ) See tariff-rate quota (TRQ) in ERS WTO Briefing Room Glossary.

Temporary Assistance for Needy Families (TANF) A Federal-State, block-grant program that replaced AFDC program in 1996. TANF provides cash benefits to low-income families with children. Under TANF, States have flexibility to determine eligibility requirements and benefit levels, but benefits are subject to a 5-year Federal time limit and work requirements.

The Emergency Food Assistance Program (TEFAP) Provides commodities for distribution through the private emergency food system. Provides mandatory multiyear funding and commodity donations from excess CCC inventories of foodstuffs for food distribution by emergency feeding organizations serving the needy and homeless. TEFAP buys and donates commodities and provides grants for State and local costs of transporting, storing, and distributing them to emergency feeding organizations, soup kitchens, and food banks serving low-income persons.

Three-entity rule Limits the number of farms from which a person can receive program payments. Under the rule, an individual can receive a full payment directly and up to a half payment from two additional entities.

Thrifty Food Plan One of 4 USDA-designed food plans specifying foods and amounts of foods to provide adequate nutrition. Used as the basis for designing Food Stamp Program (FSP) benefits, it is the lowest cost food plan that can be priced monthly using the price data collected for the consumer price index. The monthly cost of the TFP used for the FSP represents a national average of prices (4-person household consisting of an adult couple and 2 school-age children) adjusted for other household sizes through the use of a formula reflecting economies of scale. For food stamp purposes, the TFP as priced each June sets maximum benefit levels for the fiscal year beginning the following October.

Transitional benefits Up to 5 months of transitional food stamp benefits provided by States to families that leave welfare without requiring the family to reapply or submit any additional paperwork or other information.

During the transitional period, the household's benefit level is frozen at the amount it received prior to its TANF case closure, adjusted for the loss of TANF income.

Uruguay Round (UR) See Uruguay Round (UR) in ERS WTO Briefing Room Glossary.

Wetlands Conservation See swampbuster.

Wetlands Reserve Program (WRP) Established in 1985 Farm Act and administered by the Natural Resources Conservation Service in consultation with USDA's Farm Service Agency and other Federal agencies. WRP is funded through Commodity Credit Corporation and has an acreage enrollment cap. All landowners who choose to participate in WRP must implement an approved wetlands restoration and protection plan. They may sell a permanent or 30-year conservation easement to USDA and receive payments, or enter into a 10-year cost-share restoration agreement to restore and protect wetlands. The landowner voluntarily limits future use of the land yet retains private ownership.

Wildlife Habitat Incentives Program (WHIP) The 1996 Farm Act created WHIP to provide cost-sharing and technical assistance to landowners for developing habitat for upland wildlife, wetland wildlife, threatened and endangered species, fish, and other types of wildlife. Participating landowners, with the assistance of the Natural Resources Conservation Service district office, develop plans for wildlife habitat restoration and development. Standard contracts are generally 5-10 years in length. Cost-share payments may be used to establish and maintain practices. Cooperating State wildlife agencies and nonprofit or private organizations may provide additional expertise and funding. WHIP funds are distributed to States based on State, regional, and national priorities, which may involve wildlife habitat areas, targeted species and their habitats, or specific practices.

World price (cotton) See adjusted world price, cotton.

World price (rice) See adjusted world price, rice.

World Trade Organization (WTO) An international organization established by the Uruguay Round trade agreement to replace the institution created by the General Agreement on Tariffs and Trade, known as the GATT. The Uruguay Round trade agreement modified the code and the framework and established the WTO on January 1, 1995. The WTO provides a code of conduct for international commerce and a framework for periodic multilateral negotiations on trade liberalization and expansion.

Youth loan The Farm Service Agency (FSA) makes loans to individual rural youths to establish and operate income-producing projects of modest size in connection with their participation in 4-H clubs, Future Farmers of America, and similar organizations. Each project must be part of an organized and supervised program of work. The project must be planned and operated with the help of the organization adviser, produce sufficient income to repay the loan, and provide the youth with practical business and educational experience. The project adviser must recommend the project and the loan, and agree to provide adequate supervision. The applicant cannot be less than 10 years or more than 20 years old and must live in a town of less than 10,000 people. The maximum amount for FSA youth loans is $5,000.

SOILS

Acre A unit of measurement of land. It is equal to the area of land inside a square that is about 209 feet on each side (43,560 square feet).

Bacteria Microscopic organisms that live on water and on land. They help break down organic materials into simpler nutrients in a process called decay. Bacteria release nutrients to the soil.

Bedrock A more or less solid layer of rock found on the surface of the land or below the soil.

Complex, Soil A map unit of two or more kinds of soil in such an intricate pattern or so small in area that it is not practical to map them separately at the selected scale of mapping. The pattern and proportion of the soils are somewhat similar in all areas.

Contour Stripcropping Growing crops in strips that follow the contour. Strip of grass or close-growing crops are alternated with strip of clean-tilled crops or summer fallow.

Drainage Class Refers to the frequency and duration of periods of saturation or partial saturation during soil formation, as opposed to altered drainage, which is commonly the result of artificial drainage or irrigation but may be caused by the sudden deepening of channels or the blocking of drainage outlets.

Eluviation The movement of material in true solution of colloidal suspension from one place to another within the soil. Soil horizons that have lost material through eluviation are eluvial; those that have received material are illuvial.

Evaporation Changing a liquid to a gas; for example, when water turns into steam or water vapor.

Fungi (plural of fungus) A group of non-green plants, such as molds, and mushrooms, that live on dead or dying organic matter. Fungi release nutrients to the soil.

Humus Highly decomposed plant and animal residue that is a part of soil.

Hydrologic Cycle The cycle of water movement from the atmosphere to the earth and back again through these steps; evaporation, transpiration, condensation, precipitation, percolation, runoff and storage.

Illuviation The movement of soil material from one horizon to another in the soil profile. Generally, material is removed from an upper horizon and deposited in a lower horizon.

Leaching The removal of soluble minerals from soil by the downward movement of water.

Mineral A naturally occurring inorganic substance with definite chemical and physical properties and a definite crystal structure.

Mottling, Soil Irregular spots of different colors that vary in number and size. Mottling generally indicates poor aeration and impeded drainage.

Munsell Notation A designation of color by degrees of three simple variables—hue, value, and chroma. For example, a notation of 10YR 6/4 is a color with hue of 10YR, value of 6, and chroma of 4.

Nematodes Microscopic, elongated worms that live on other organisms in the soil.

Nutrient A substance that supplies nourishment for an organism to live. It can be food or chemical depending upon the organism.

Nutrient Exchange The process by which plant roots exchange an acid for nutrients from the soil.

Organic Matter Plant and animal material in various stages of decomposition that may be part of the soil.

Parent Material The earthy materials—both mineral and organic—from which soil is formed.

Percolation The downward movement of water in soil.

Permeability The quality of soil that allows air or water to move through it.

pH Value A numerical designation of acidity and alkalinity in soil. (See Reaction, soil)

Pore Spaces The area of the soil through which water and air move. The space between soil particles.

Precipitation Rain, snow, and other forms of water that fall to earth.

Reaction, Soil A measure of acidity or alkalinity of a soil. expressed in pH -values. A soil that tests to pH 7.0 is described as precisely neutral in reaction because it is neither acid or alkaline.

Regolith The unconsolidated mantle of weathered rock and soil material on the earth's surface; the loose earth material above the solid rock.

Rock Fragments Rock or mineral fragments having a diameter of 2 millimeters or more; for example, pebbles, cobbles, stones, and boulders.

Root Zone The part of the soil that can be penetrated by plant roots.

Runoff Water that flows off land into streams and other waterways.

Sand As a soil separate, individual rock or mineral fragments from 0.05 millimeter to 2.0 millimeters in diameter. Most sand grains consist of quartz. As a soil textural class, a soil that is 85% or more sand and not more than 10% clay.

Silt As a soil separate, individual mineral particles that range in diameter from the upper limit of clay (0.002 mm) to the lower limit of very fine sand (0.05 mm). As soil textural class, soil that is 80% or more silt and less than 12% clay.

Soil A naturally occurring mixture of minerals, organic matter, water and air which has definite structure and composition and forms on the surface of the land.

Soil Color The color of a sample of soil

Soil Horizon A layer of soil that is nearly parallel to the land surface and is different from layers above and below.

Soil Mineral That portion of the soil that is inorganic and neither air nor water.

Soil Survey The identification, classification, mapping interpretation and explanation of the soil.

Soil Texture The relative amounts of sand, sift, and clay in a given soil sample.

Subsoil Technically, the B horizon; roughly, the part of the solum below plow depth.

Substratum The part of the soil below the solum.

Subsurface Layer Any surface soil horizon (A, E, AB, or EB) below the surface layer.

Surface Layer The soil ordinarily moved in tillage, or it equivalent in uncultivated soil, ranging in depth from about 4 to 10 inches (10 to 25 centimeters). Frequently designated as the plow layer, or the Ap horizon.

Top soil The upper part of the soil, which is the most favorable material for plant growth. It is ordinarily rich in organic matter and is used to topdress road banks, lawns, and land affected by mining.

Zone of Accumulation The layer in a soil into which soluble compounds are moved and deposited by water.

Zone of Decomposition Surface layers in a soil in which organic matter decays.

Zone of Leaching The layers in a soil from which soluble nutrients are removed by water.

Building Protection and Real Estate

11-B A congressionally required study in which GSA reports to Congress regarding the housing needs of a specific locality. This study may or may not recommend a new project. If it does, then the need for the project must be justified through a study such as a Local Portfolio Plan or a Prospectus Development Study.

Access control Any combination of barriers, gates, electronic security equipment, and/or guards that can deny entry to unauthorized personnel or vehicles.

Access control point (ACP) A station at an entrance to a building or a portion of a building where identification is checked and people and hand-carried items are searched.

Access control system (ACS) Also referred to as an Electronic Entry Control Systems; an electronic system that controls entry and egress from a building or area.

Access control system elements Detection measures used to control vehicle or personnel entry into a protected area. Access Control System elements include locks, Electronic Entry Control Systems, and guards.

Access controls Procedures and controls that limit or detect access to minimum essential infrastructure resource elements (e.g., people, technology, applications, data, and/or facilities), thereby protecting these resources against loss of integrity, confidentiality, accountability, and/or availability.

Access group A software configuration of an Access Control System that groups together access points or authorized users for easier arrangement and maintenance of the system.

Access road Any roadway such as a maintenance, delivery, service, emergency, or other special limited use road that is necessary for the operation of a building or structure.

Accountability The explicit assignment of responsibilities for oversight of areas of control to executives, managers, staff, owners, providers, and users of minimum essential infrastructure resource elements.

Acoustic eavesdropping The use of listening devices to monitor voice communications or other audibly transmitted information with the objective to compromise information.

Active vehicle barrier An impediment placed at an access control point that may be manually or automatically deployed in response to detection of a threat.

Aerosol Fine liquid or solid particles suspended in a gas (e.g., fog or smoke).

Aggressor Any person seeking to compromise a function or structure.

Airborne contamination Chemical or biological agents introduced into and fouling the source of supply of breathing or conditioning air.

Airlock A building entry configuration with which airflow from the outside can be prevented from entering a toxic-free area. An airlock uses two doors, only one of which can be opened at a time, and a blower system to maintain positive air pressures and purge contaminated air from the airlock before the second door is opened.

Alarm assessment Verification and evaluation of an alarm alert through the use of closed circuit television or human observation. Systems used for alarm assessment are designed to respond rapidly, automatically, and predictably to the receipt of alarms at the security center.

Alarm printers Alarm printers provide a hard-copy of all alarm events and system activity, as well as limited backup in case the visual display fails.

Alarm priority A hierarchy of alarms by order of importance. This is often used in larger systems to give priority to alarms with greater importance.

Allowance document Transfers the appropriated funds to the Region.

Annunciation A visual, audible, or other indication by a security system of a condition.

Antiterrorism (AT) Defensive measures used to reduce the vulnerability of individuals, forces, and property to terrorist acts.

Architect/Engineer (A/E) The architecture/engineering firm selected to perform the design of a project.

Area Commander A military commander with authority in a specific geographical area or military installation.

Area lighting Lighting that illuminates a large exterior area.

Areas of potential compromise Categories where losses can occur that will impact either a department's or an agency's minimum essential infrastructure and its ability to conduct core functions and activities.

Assessment The evaluation and interpretation of measurements and other information to provide a basis for decision-making.

Assessment system elements Detection measures used to assist guards in visual verification of Intrusion Detection System Alarms and Access Control System functions and to assist in visual detection by guards. Assessment System elements include closed circuit television and protective lighting.

Asset A resource of value requiring protection. An asset can be tangible (e.g., people, buildings, facilities, equipment, activities, operations, and information) or intangible (e.g., processes or a company's information and reputation).

Asset Business Plan (ABP) A document that provides all information, strategy, and long-term plans necessary to manage the business of operating and optimizing an asset. The GSA Asset Business Plan is a Web-based asset management tool that provides building history and projections for many areas, including space and income, that are used to develop long-range strategies for the asset, reinvestment plans, and capital investment priorities.

Asset protection Security program designed to protect personnel, facilities, and equipment, in all locations and situations, accomplished through planned and integrated application of combating terrorism, physical security, operations security, and personal protective services, and supported by intelligence, counterintelligence, and other security programs.

Asset value The degree of debilitating impact that would be caused by the incapacity or destruction of an asset.

Attack A hostile action resulting in the destruction, injury, or death to the civilian population, or damage or destruction to public and private property.

Audible alarm device An alarm device that produces an audible announcement (e.g., bell, horn, siren, etc.) of an alarm condition.

Balanced magnetic switch A door position switch utilizing a reed switch held in a balanced or center position by interacting magnetic fields when not in alarm condition.

Ballistics attack An attack in which small arms (e.g., pistols, submachine guns, shotguns, and rifles) are fired from a distance and rely on the flight of the projectile to damage the target.

Barbed tape or concertina A coiled tape or coil of wires with wire barbs or blades deployed as an obstacle to human trespass or entry into an area.

Barbed wire A double strand of wire with four-point barbs equally spaced along the wire deployed as an obstacle to human trespass or entry into an area.

Barcode A black bar printed on white paper or tape that can be easily read with an optical scanner.

Basis of Design (BOD) The documentation by the design team of the primary thought processes and assumptions behind design decisions that are made to meet the Owner's Project Requirements. The BOD describes the assumptions used for sizing and selection of systems (i.e., codes, standards, operating conditions, design conditions, weather data, interior environmental criteria, other pertinent design assumptions, etc.).

Biological agents Living organisms or the materials derived from them that cause disease in or harm to humans, animals, or plants or cause deterioration of material. Biological agents may be used as liquid droplets, aerosols, or dry powders.

Biometric reader A device that gathers and analyzes biometric features.

Biometrics The use of physical characteristics of the human body as a unique identification method.

Blast curtains Heavy curtains made of blast-resistant materials that could protect the occupants of a room from flying debris.

Blast-resistant glazing Window opening glazing that is resistant to blast effects because of the interrelated function of the frame and glazing material properties frequently dependent upon tempered glass, polycarbonate, or laminated glazing.

Blast vulnerability envelope The geographical area in which an explosive device will cause damage to assets.

Bollard A vehicle barrier consisting of a cylinder, usually made of steel and sometimes filled with concrete, placed on end in the ground and spaced about 3 feet apart to prevent vehicles from passing, but allowing entrance of pedestrians and bicycles.

Boundary penetration sensor An interior intrusion detection sensor that detects attempts by individuals to penetrate or enter a building.

Building Evaluation Report (BER) The Building Condition Assessment is done through a BER that documents the condition and deficiencies of a building. GSA will identify the BER work (called work items) that is to be addressed by the Prospectus Development Study (PDS). However, a PDS also must recognize other impacted work that may not be fully described in the BER work items or the Feasibility Study.

Building hardening Enhanced construction that reduces vulnerability to external blast and ballistic attacks.

Building Owners and Managers Association (BOMA) Provides information to and a network forum for industry professionals.

Building separation The distance between closest points on the exterior walls of adjacent buildings or structures.

Business Continuity Program (BCP) An ongoing process supported by senior management and funded to ensure that the necessary steps are taken to identify the impact of potential losses, maintain viable recovery strategies and recovery plans, and ensure continuity services through personnel training, plan testing, and maintenance.

Cable barrier Cable or wire rope anchored to and suspended off the ground or attached to chain-link fence to act as a barrier to moving vehicles.

Capacitance sensor A device that detects an intruder approaching or touching a metal object by sensing a change in capacitance between the object and the ground.

Card reader A device that gathers or reads information when a card is presented as an identification method.

Categorial Exclusion (CATEX) Under the National Environmental Policy Act, a CATEX is an action that normally does not require the preparation of an Environmental Assessment or an Environmental Impact Statement.

CCTV pan-tilt-zoom camera (PTZ) A CCTV camera that can move side to side, up and down, and zoom in or out.

CCTV pan-tilt-zoom control The method of controlling the PTZ functions of a camera.

CCTV pan-tilt-zoom controller The operator interface for performing PTZ control.

CCTV switcher A piece of equipment capable of presenting multiple video images to various monitors, recorders, etc.

Chemical agent A chemical substance that is intended to kill, seriously injure, or incapacitate people through physiological effects. Generally separated by severity of effect (e.g., lethal, blister, and incapacitating).

Chimney effect Air movement in a building between floors caused by differential air temperature (differences in density), between the air inside and outside the building. It occurs in vertical shafts, such as elevators, stairwells, and conduit/wiring/piping chases. Hotter air inside the building will rise and be replaced by infiltration with colder outside air through the lower portions of the building. Conversely, reversing the temperature will reverse the flow (down the chimney). Also known as stack effect.

Clear zone An area that is clear of visual obstructions and landscape materials that could conceal a threat or perpetrator.

Closed-circuit television (CCTV) An electronic system of cameras, control equipment, recorders, and related apparatus used for surveillance or alarm assessment.

Collateral damage Injury or damage to assets that are not the primary target of an attack.

Combating terrorism The full range of federal programs and activities applied against terrorism, domestically and abroad, regardless of the source or motive.

Commissioning (Cx) The National Conference on Building Commissioning has established an official definition of 'Total Building Commissioning' as follows: "Systematic process of assuring by verification and documentation, from the design stage to a minimum of one year after construction, that all facility systems perform interactively in accordance with the design documentation and intent, and in accordance with the owner's operational needs, including preparation of operation personnel"

Commissioning Agent (CxA) The qualified person, company or agency that plans, coordinates and oversees the entire commissioning process.

Commissioning plan The document prepared for each project that describes all aspects of the commissioning process including schedules, responsibilities, documentation requirements and communication structures.

Commissioning record The complete set of commissioning documentation for the project which is turned over to GSA at the end of the construction phase.

Communications Plan Identifies spokespersons for GSA, the customer agency, and stakeholders; schedules key communications to be disseminated in conjunction with project milestones; identifies potential issues; and includes strategies for responding to those issues.

Community A political entity that has the authority to adopt and enforce laws and ordinances for the area under its jurisdiction. In most cases, the community is an incorporated town, city, township, village, or unincorporated area of a county; however, each state defines its own political subdivisions and forms of government.

Components and cladding Elements of the building envelope that do not qualify as part of the main wind-force resisting system.

Computer-aided design (CAD) All new construction and major renovations entail drawings created in a standard GSA format, with the help of computer-based programs such as CAD.

Confidentiality The protection of sensitive information against unauthorized disclosure and sensitive facilities from physical, technical, or electronic penetration or exploitation.

Consequence management Measures to protect public health and safety, restore essential government services, and provide emergency relief to governments, businesses, and individuals affected by the consequences of terrorism. State and local governments exercise the primary authority to respond to the consequences of terrorism.

Construction checklist A checklist to ensure that the specified equipment has been provided, is properly installed, and initially started and checked out adequately in preparation for full operation and functional testing.

Contamination The undesirable deposition of a chemical, biological, or radiological material on the surface of structures, areas, objects, or people.

Continuity of services and operations Controls to ensure that, when unexpected events occur, departmental/agency minimum essential infrastructure services and operations, including computer operations, continue without interruption or are promptly resumed, and that critical and sensitive data are protected through adequate contingency and business recovery plans and exercises.

Control center A centrally located room or facility staffed by personnel charged with the oversight of specific situations and/or equipment.

Controlled area An area into which access is controlled or limited. It is that portion of a restricted area usually near or surrounding a limited or exclusion area. Correlates with exclusion zone.

Controlled lighting Illumination of specific areas or sections.

Controlled perimeter A physical boundary at which vehicle and personnel access is controlled at the perimeter of a site. Access control at a controlled perimeter should demonstrate the capability to search individuals and vehicles.

Conventional construction Building construction that is not specifically designed to resist weapons, explosives, or chemical, biological, and radiological effects. Conventional construction is designed only to resist common loadings and environmental effects such as wind, seismic, and snow loads.

Coordinate To advance systematically an exchange of information among principals who have or may have a need to know certain information in order to carry out their roles in a response.

Cost benchmark The cost model, based on real, similar facilities, used to evaluate project costs for a similar type of building.

Customer Billing Record (CBR) The mechanism that GSA uses to establish rent billing and is created through an Occupancy Agreement.

Counterintelligence Information gathered and activities conducted to protect against: espionage, other intelligence activities, sabotage, or assassinations conducted for or on behalf of foreign powers, organizations, or persons; or international terrorist activities, excluding personnel, physical, document, and communications security programs.

Counterterrorism (CT) Offensive measures taken to prevent, deter, and respond to terrorism.

Covert entry Attempts to enter a facility by using false credentials or stealth.

Crash bar A mechanical egress device located on the interior side of a door that unlocks the door when pressure is applied in the direction of egress.

Crime Prevention Through Environmental Design (CPTED) A crime prevention strategy based on evidence that the design and form of the built environment can influence human behavior. CPTED usually involves the use of three principles: natural surveillance (by placing physical features, activities, and people to maximize visibility); natural access control (through the judicial placement of entrances, exits, fencing, landscaping, and lighting); and territorial reinforcement (using buildings, fences, pavement, signs, and landscaping to express ownership).

Crisis management (CM) The measures taken to identify, acquire, and plan the use of resources needed to anticipate, prevent, and/or resolve a threat or act of terrorism.

Critical assets Those assets essential to the minimum operations of the organization, and to ensure the health and safety of the general public.

Critical infrastructure Primary infrastructure systems (e.g., utilities, telecommunications, transportation, etc.) whose incapacity would have a debilitating impact on the organization's ability to function.

Damage assessment The process used to appraise or determine the number of injuries and deaths, damage to public and private property, and the status of key facilities and services (e.g., hospitals and other health care facilities, fire and police stations, communications networks, water and sanitation systems, utilities, and transportation networks) resulting from a manmade or natural disaster.

Data-gathering panel A local processing unit that retrieves, processes, stores, and/or acts on information in the field.

Data transmission equipment A path for transmitting data between two or more components (e.g., a sensor and alarm reporting system, a card reader and controller, a CCTV camera and monitor, or a transmitter and receiver).

Decontamination The reduction or removal of a chemical, biological, or radiological material from the surface of a structure, area, object, or person.

Defense layer Building design or exterior perimeter barriers intended to delay attempted forced entry.

Defensive measures Protective measures that delay or prevent attack on an asset or that shield the asset from weapons, explosives, and CBR effects. Defensive measures include site work and building design.

Delay rating A measure of the effectiveness of penetration protection of a defense layer.

Design Basis Threat (DBT) The threat (e.g., tactics and associated weapons, tools, or explosives) against which assets within a building must be protected and upon which the security engineering design of the building is based.

Design constraint Anything that restricts the design options for a protective system or that creates additional problems for which the design must compensate.

Design excellence For projects that require significant architectural and engineering treatment, programming direction must reflect GSA's commitment to design excellence. General design principles and philosophies are presented in the architecture and interior design chapter of the *Facilities Standards for the Public Buildings Handbook*.

Design opportunity Anything that enhances protection, reduces requirements for protective measures, or solves a design problem.

Design team A group of individuals from various engineering and architectural disciplines responsible for the protective system design.

Detection layer A ring of intrusion detection sensors located on or adjacent to a defensive layer or between two defensive layers.

Detection measures Protective measures that detect intruders, weapons, or explosives; assist in assessing the validity of detection; control access to protected areas; and communicate the appropriate information to the response force. Detection measures include detection systems, assessment systems, and access control system elements.

Detection system elements Detection measures that detect the presence of intruders, weapons, or explosives. Detection system elements include Intrusion Detection systems, weapons and explosives detectors, and guards.

Disaster An occurrence of a natural catastrophe, technological accident, or human-caused event that has resulted in severe property damage, deaths, and/or multiple injuries.

Disaster Field Office (DFO) The office established in or near the designated area of a presidentially declared major disaster to support federal and state response and recovery operations.

Disaster Recovery Center (DRC) Places established in the area of a presidentially declared major disaster, as soon as practicable, to provide victims the opportunity to apply in person for assistance and/or obtain information relating to that assistance.

Domestic terrorism The unlawful use, or threatened use, of force or violence by a group or individual based and operating entirely within the United States or Puerto Rico without foreign direction committed against persons or property to intimidate or coerce a government, the civilian population, or any segment thereof in furtherance of political or social objectives.

Door position switch A switch that changes state based on whether or not a door is closed. Typically, a switch mounted in a frame that is actuated by a magnet in a door.

Door strike, electronic An electromechanical lock that releases a door plunger to unlock the door. Typically, an electronic door strike is mounted in place of or near a normal door strike plate.

Dose rate (radiation) A general term indicating the quantity (total or accumulated) of ionizing radiation or energy absorbed by a person or animal, per unit of time.

Dosimeter An instrument for measuring and registering total accumulated exposure to ionizing radiation.

Dual technology sensor A sensor that combines two different technologies in one unit.

Due diligence A term that describes the responsibilities of a landowner, such as GSA, to conduct an appropriate inquiry prior to the purchase or development of a parcel of commercial real estate and ensure that all "recognized conditions" have been identified.

Duress alarm devices Also known as panic buttons, these devices are designated specifically to initiate a panic alarm.

Effective stand-off distance A stand-off distance at which the required level of protection can be shown to be achieved through analysis or can be achieved through building hardening or other mitigating construction or retrofit.

Electromagnetic pulse (EMP) A sharp pulse of energy radiated instantaneously by a nuclear detonation that may affect or damage electronic components and equipment. EMP can also be generated in lesser intensity by non-nuclear means in specific frequency ranges to perform the same disruptive function.

Electronic emanations Electromagnetic emissions from computers, communications, electronics, wiring, and related equipment.

Electronic-emanations eavesdropping Use of electronic-emanation surveillance equipment from outside a facility or its restricted area to monitor electronic emanations from computers, communications, and related equipment.

Electronic entry control systems (EECS) Electronic devices that automatically verify authorization for a person to enter or exit a controlled area.

Electronic security system (ESS) An integrated system that encompasses interior and exterior sensors, closed circuit television systems for assessment of alarm conditions, electronic entry control systems, data transmission media, and alarm reporting systems for monitoring, control, and display of various alarm and system information.

Emergency Any natural or human-caused situation that results in or may result in substantial injury or harm to the population or substantial damage to or loss of property.

Emergency Alert System (EAS) A communications system of broadcast stations and interconnecting facilities authorized by the Federal Communications Commission (FCC). The system provides the president and other national, state, and local officials the means to broadcast emergency information to the public before, during, and after disasters.

Emergency environmental health services Services required to correct or improve damaging environmental health effects on humans, including inspection for food contamination, inspection for water contamination, and vector control; providing for sewage and solid waste inspection and disposal; cleanup and disposal of hazardous materials; and sanitation inspection for emergency shelter facilities.

Emergency medical services (EMS) Services including personnel, facilities, and equipment required to ensure proper medical care for the sick and injured from the time of injury to the time of final disposition, including medical disposition within a hospital, temporary medical facility, or special care facility; release from the site; or declared dead. Further, emergency medical services specifically include those services immediately required to ensure proper medical care and specialized treatment for patients in a hospital and coordination of related hospital services.

Emergency mortuary services Services required to assure adequate death investigation, identification, and disposition of bodies; removal, temporary storage, and transportation of bodies to temporary morgue facilities; notification of next of kin; and coordination of mortuary services and burial of unclaimed bodies.

Emergency Operations Center (EOC) The protected site from which state and local civil government officials coordinate, monitor, and direct emergency response activities during an emergency.

Emergency operations plan (EOP) A document that describes how people and property will be protected in disaster and disaster threat situations; details who is responsible for carrying out specific actions; identifies the personnel, equipment, facilities, supplies, and other resources available for use in the disaster; and outlines how all actions will be coordinated.

Emergency Planning Zones (EPZ) Areas around a facility for which planning is needed to ensure prompt and effective actions are taken to protect the health and safety of the public if an accident or disaster occurs. In the Radiological Emergency Preparedness Program, the two EPZs are: **Plume Exposure Pathway** (10-mile EPZ). A circular geographic zone (with a 10-mile radius centered at the nuclear power plant) for which plans are developed to protect the public against exposure to radiation emanating from a radioactive plume caused as a result of an accident at the nuclear power plant. **Ingestion Pathway** (50-mile EPZ). A circular geographic zone (with a 50-mile radius centered at the nuclear power plant) for which plans are developed to protect the public from the ingestion of water or food contaminated as a result of a nuclear power plant accident. In the Chemical Stockpile Emergency Preparedness Program (CSEPP), the EPZ is divided into three concentric circular zones: **Immediate Response Zone** (IRZ). A circular zone ranging from 10 to 15 kilometers (6 to 9 miles) from the potential chemical event source, depending on the stockpile location on-post. Emergency response plans developed for the IRZ must provide for the most rapid and effective protective actions possible, because the IRZ will have the highest concentration of agent and the least amount of warning time. **Protective Action Zone** (PAZ). An area that extends beyond the IRZ to approximately 16 to 50 kilometers (10 to 30 miles) from the stockpile location. The PAZ is that area where public protective actions may still be necessary in case of an accidental release of chemical agent, but where the available warning and response time is such that most people could evacuate. However, other responses (e.g., sheltering) may be appropriate for institutions and special populations that could not evacuate within the available time. **Precautionary Zone** (PZ). The outermost portion of the EPZ for CSEPP, extending from the PAZ outer boundary to a distance where the risk of adverse impacts to humans is negligible. Because of the increased warning and response time available for implementation of response actions in the PZ, detailed local emergency planning is not required, although consequence management planning may be appropriate.

Emergency public information (EPI) Information that is disseminated primarily in anticipation of an emergency or at the actual time of an emergency and, in addition to providing information frequently directs actions, instructs, and transmits direct orders.

Emergency response team (ERT) An interagency team, consisting of the lead representative from each federal department or agency assigned primary responsibility for an ESF and key members of the FCO's staff, formed to assist the FCO in carrying out his/her coordination responsibilities.

Emergency Response Team Advance Element (ERT-A) For federal disaster response and recovery activities under the Stafford Act, the portion of the ERT that is first deployed to the field to respond to a disaster incident. The ERT-A is the nucleus of the full ERT.

Emergency Response Team National (ERT-N) An ERT that has been established and rostered for deployment to catastrophic disasters where the resources of the FEMA Region have been, or are expected to be, overwhelmed. Three ERT-Ns have been established.

Emergency Support Function (ESF) In the Federal Response Plan (FRP), a functional area of response activity established to facilitate the delivery of federal assistance required during the immediate response phase of a disaster to save lives, protect property and public health, and to maintain public safety. ESFs represent those types of federal assistance that the state will most likely need because of the impact of a catastrophic or significant disaster on its own resources and response capabilities, or because of the specialized or unique nature of the assistance required. ESF missions are designed to supplement state and local response efforts.

Emergency Support Team (EST) An interagency group operating from FEMA Headquarters. The EST oversees the national-level response support effort under the FRP and coordinates activities with the ESF primary and support agencies in supporting federal requirements in the field.

Entity-wide security Planning and management that provides a framework and continuing cycle of activity for managing risk, developing security policies, assigning responsibilities, and monitoring the adequacy of the entity's physical and cyber security controls.

Entry control point A continuously or intermittently manned station at which entry to sensitive or restricted areas is controlled.

Entry control stations Entry control stations should be provided at main perimeter entrances where security personnel are present. Entry control stations should be located as close as practical to the perimeter entrance to permit personnel inside the station to maintain constant surveillance over the entrance and its approaches.

Environmental Assessment (EA) A concise public document that is prepared pursuant to the National Environmental Policy Act (NEPA) to determine whether a federal action would significantly affect the environment and thus require preparation of a more detailed Environmental Impact Statement (EIS). It also
- Briefly provides sufficient evidence and analysis for determining whether to prepare an EIS or a Finding of No Significant Impact (FONSI);
- Aids in an agency's compliance with the NEPA when no EIS is necessary, which leads to a FONSI; and
- Facilitates preparation of an EIS when one is necessary.

Environmental Impact Statement (EIS) The National Environmental Policy Act requires that federal agencies prepare an EIS for major projects or legislative proposals that significantly affect the environment. It is a decision-making tool that describes the positive and negative effects of the undertaking and lists alternative actions. An EIS is a detailed study that leads to a Record of Decision. It records decisions made and mitigation measures that relate to the environmental impacts of a project.

Environmental Site Assessment (ESA) A study of a property's past use, the environmental conditions at the site and adjoining sites, and the likely presence of hazardous substances. An ESA can contribute to the "innocent landowner" defense under the Comprehensive Environmental Response, Compensation, and Liability Act (CERCLA).

Equipment closet A room where field control equipment such as data gathering panels and power supplies are typically located.

Evacuation Organized, phased, and supervised dispersal of people from dangerous or potentially dangerous areas.

Evacuation, mandatory or directed This is a warning to persons within the designated area that an imminent threat to life and property exists and individuals MUST evacuate in accordance with the instructions of local officials.

Evacuation, spontaneous Residents or citizens in the threatened areas observe an emergency event or receive unofficial word of an actual or perceived threat and, without receiving instructions to do so, elect to evacuate the area. Their movement, means, and direction of travel are unorganized and unsupervised.

Evacuation, voluntary This is a warning to persons within a designated area that a threat to life and property exists or is likely to exist in the immediate future. Individuals issued this type of warning or order are NOT required to evacuate; however, it would be to their advantage to do so.

Evacuees All persons removed or moving from areas threatened or struck by a disaster.

Exclusion area A restricted area containing a security interest. Uncontrolled movement permits direct access to the item. See controlled area and limited area.

Exclusion zone An area around an asset that has controlled entry with highly restrictive access. See controlled area.

Explosives disposal container A small container into which small quantities of explosives may be placed to contain their blast pressures and fragments if the explosive detonates.

Facial recognition A biometric technology that is based on features of the human face.

Facilities Standards for the Public Buildings Service The *P-100* is the primary GSA design criteria/standards document and is typically referenced for compliance in architecture/engineering firm contracts.

Feasibility study GSA uses this study to evaluate Prospectus-level proposed projects to ensure that they meet tenant agency space needs and government-owned facility requirements. This study also determines the preferred alternative and basis for preparing a Prospectus Development Study, which will meet the housing needs of the customer agency.

Federal Coordinating Officer (FCO) The person appointed by the FEMA Director to coordinate federal assistance in a Presidentially declared emergency or major disaster.

Federal On-scene Commander The FBI official designated upon JOC activation to ensure appropriate coordination of the overall United States government response with federal, state, and local authorities, until such time as the Attorney General transfers the LFA role to FEMA.

Federal Response Plan (FRP) The FRP establishes a process and structure for the systematic, coordinated, and effective delivery of federal assistance to address the consequences of any major disaster or emergency.

Fence protection An intrusion detection technology that detects a person crossing a fence by various methods such as climbing, crawling, cutting, etc.

Fence sensor An exterior intrusion detection sensor that detects aggressors as they attempt to climb over, cut through, or otherwise disturb a fence.

Fiber optics A method of data transfer by passing bursts of light through a strand of glass or clear plastic.

Field Assessment Team (FAsT) A small team of pre-identified technical experts that conduct an assessment of response needs (not a PDA) immediately following a disaster.

Field of view The visible area in a video picture.

First responder Local police, fire, and emergency medical personnel who first arrive on the scene of an incident and take action to save lives, protect property, and meet basic human needs.

Flash flood Follows a situation in which rainfall is so intense and severe and runoff so rapid that it precludes recording and relating it to stream stages and other information in time to forecast a flood condition.

Flood A general and temporary condition of partial or complete inundation of normally dry land areas from overflow of inland or tidal waters, unusual or rapid accumulation or runoff of surface waters, or mudslides/mudflows caused by accumulation of water.

Forced entry Entry to a denied area achieved through force to create an opening in fence, walls, doors, etc., or to overpower guards.

Fragment retention film (FRF) A thin, optically clear film applied to glass to minimize the spread of glass fragments when the glass is shattered.

Frame rate In digital video, a measurement of the rate of change in a series of pictures, often measured in frames per second (fps).

Frangible construction Building components that are designed to fail to vent blast pressures from an enclosure in a controlled manner and direction.

Functional tests Tests that evaluate the dynamic function and operation of equipment and systems using direct observation or other monitoring methods. Functional testing is the assessment of the system's (rather than just component's) ability to perform within the parameters set up within the Owner's Project Requirements and Basis of Design. Functional tests are performed after construction checklists are complete.

Funding appropriation Funding set aside by Congress for a project or a particular use.

Funding authorization Funding approved by Congress for a project or a particular use. (Funds must be authorized and appropriated before becoming available for a project.)

General Construction Cost Review Guide (GCCRG) The Public Buildings Service *General Construction Cost Review Guide*, which is generally published yearly, provides costs to construct space by space type, escalation and location factors by localities, and a system for developing cost benchmarks.

Glare security lighting Illumination projected from a secure perimeter into the surrounding area, making it possible to see potential intruders at a considerable distance while making it difficult to observe activities within the secure perimeter.

Glass-break detector An intrusion detection sensor that is designed to detect breaking glass either through vibration or acoustics.

Glazing A material installed in a sash, ventilator, or panes (e.g., glass, plastic, etc., including material such as thin granite installed in a curtain wall).

Governor's Authorized Representative (GAR) The person empowered by the governor to execute, on behalf of the State, all necessary documents for disaster assistance.

Grid wire sensor An intrusion detection sensor that uses a grid of wires to cover a wall or fence. An alarm is sounded if the wires are cut.

Hand geometry A biometric technology that is based on characteristics of the human hand.

Hazard A source of potential danger or adverse condition.

Hazard mitigation Any action taken to reduce or eliminate the long-term risk to human life and property from hazards. The term is sometimes used in a stricter sense to mean cost-effective measures to reduce the potential for damage to a facility or facilities from a disaster event.

Hazardous material (HazMat) Any substance or material that, when involved in an accident and released in sufficient quantities, poses a risk to people's health, safety, and/or property. These substances and materials include explosives, radioactive materials, flammable liquids or solids, combustible liquids or solids, poisons, oxidizers, toxins, and corrosive materials.

High-hazard areas Geographic locations that, for planning purposes, have been determined through historical experience and vulnerability analysis to be likely to experience the effects of a specific hazard (e.g., hurricane, earthquake, hazardous materials accident, etc.), resulting in vast property damage and loss of life.

High-risk target Any material resource or facility that, because of mission sensitivity, ease of access, isolation, and symbolic value, may be an especially attractive or accessible terrorist target.

Human-caused hazard Human-caused hazards are technological hazards and terrorism. They are distinct from natural hazards primarily in that they originate from human activity. Within the military services, the term threat is typically used for human-caused hazard. See definitions of technological hazards and terrorism for further information.

Hurricane A tropical cyclone, formed in the atmosphere over warm ocean areas, in which wind speeds reach 74 miles per hour or more and blow in a large spiral around a relatively calm center or "eye." Circulation is counter-clockwise in the Northern Hemisphere and clockwise in the Southern Hemisphere.

Impact analysis A management level analysis that identifies the impacts of losing the

entity's resources. The analysis measures the effect of resource loss and escalating losses over time in order to provide the entity with reliable data upon which to base decisions on hazard mitigation and continuity planning.

Incident command system (ICS) A standardized organizational structure used to command, control, and coordinate the use of resources and personnel that have responded to the scene of an emergency. The concepts and principles for ICS include common terminology, modular organization, integrated communication, unified command structure, consolidated action plan, manageable span of control, designated incident facilities, and comprehensive resource management.

Indoor environmental quality (IEQ) The artificial environment that exists in a building that includes the factors of thermal comfort, illumination, noise, ventilation and level of indoor air pollutants.

Input document An input document is a supporting document, study, or report used to complete the feasibility study.

Insider compromise A person authorized access to a facility (an insider) compromises assets by taking advantage of that accessibility.

Intercom door/gate station Part of an intercom system where communication is typically initiated, usually located at a door or gate.

Intercom master station Part of an intercom system that monitors one or more intercom door/gate stations; typically, where initial communication is received.

Intercom switcher Part of an intercom system that controls the flow of communications between various stations.

Intercom system An electronic system that allows simplex, half-duplex, or full-duplex audio communications.

International terrorism Violent acts or acts dangerous to human life that are a violation of the criminal laws of the United States or any state, or that would be a criminal violation if committed within the jurisdiction of the United States or any state. These acts appear to be intended to intimidate or coerce a civilian population, influence the policy of a government by intimidation or coercion, or affect the conduct of a government by assassination or kidnapping. International terrorist acts occur outside the United States, or transcend national boundaries in terms of the means by which they are accomplished, the persons they appear intended to coerce or intimidate, or the locale in which their perpetrators operate or seek asylum.

Intrusion detection sensor A device that initiates alarm signals by sensing the stimulus, change, or condition for which it was designed.

Intrusion detection system (IDS) The combination of components, including sensors, control units, transmission lines, and monitor units, integrated to operate in a specified manner.

Isolated fenced perimeters Fenced perimeters with 100 feet or more of space outside the fence that is clear of obstruction, making approach obvious.

Issues log A formal and ongoing record of problems or concerns, as well as associated priorities, implications and resolutions.

Jersey barrier A protective concrete barrier initially and still used as a highway divider that now also functions as an expedient method for traffic speed control at entrance gates and to keep vehicles away from buildings.

Joint Information Center (JIC) A central point of contact for all news media near the scene of a large-scale disaster. News media representatives are kept informed of activities and events by Public Information Officers who represent all participating federal, state, and local agencies that are collocated at the JIC.

Joint Information System (JIS) Under the FRP, connection of public affairs personnel, decision-makers, and news centers by electronic mail, fax, and telephone when a single federal-state-local JIC is not a viable option.

Joint Interagency Intelligence Support Element (JIISE) An interagency intelligence component designed to fuse intelligence information from the various agencies participating in a response to a WMD threat or incident within an FBI JOC. The JIISE is an expanded version of the investigative/intelligence component that is part of the standardized FBI command post structure. The JIISE manages five functions, including security, collections management, current intelligence, exploitation, and dissemination.

Joint Operations Center (JOC) Established by the LFA under the operational control of the federal OSC, as the focal point for management and direction of on-site activities, coordination/establishment of state requirements/priorities, and coordination of the overall federal response.

Jurisdiction Typically counties and cities within a state, but states may elect to define differently in order to facilitate their assessment process.

Laminated glass A flat lite of uniform thickness consisting of two monolithic glass plies bonded together with an interlayer material as defined in Specification C1172.

Many different interlayer materials are used in laminated glass.

Landscaping The use of plantings (shrubs and trees), with or without landforms and/or large boulders, to act as a perimeter barrier against defined threats.

Laser card A card technology that uses a laser reflected off of a card for uniquely identifying the card.

Layers of protection A traditional approach in security engineering using concentric circles extending out from an area to be protected as demarcation points for different security strategies.

Lead Agency The federal department or agency assigned lead responsibility under U.S. law to manage and coordinate the federal response in a specific functional area.

Lead Federal Agency (LFA) The agency designated by the President to lead and coordinate the overall federal response is referred to as the LFA and is determined by the type of emergency. In general, an LFA establishes operational structures and procedures to assemble and work with agencies providing direct support to the LFA in order to provide an initial assessment of the situation, develop an action plan, monitor and update operational priorities, and ensure each agency exercises its concurrent and distinct authorities under U.S. law and supports the LFA in carrying out the President's relevant policy. Specific responsibilities of an LFA vary, according to the agency's unique statutory authorities.

Leadership in Energy and Environmental Design (LEED) GSA has adopted the LEED rating system of the U.S. Green Building Council as a measure for sustainable design. The *P-100* and the Capital Investment and Leasing Program (CILP) require that all new and fully renovated building projects meet criteria for basic LEED Certification (higher levels of achievement are Silver, Gold, and Platinum). As of fiscal year 2003, all new and fully renovated buildings must meet a Silver LEED rating.

Lease Construction Lease construction is new construction of a facility for government use in response to GSA's formal solicitation for offers. The construction may be on either a preselected site assigned by GSA to the successful offeror or the offeror's site.

Level of protection (LOP) The degree to which an asset is protected against injury or damage from an attack.

Liaison An agency official sent to another agency to facilitate interagency communications and coordination.

Limited area A restricted area within close proximity of a security interest. Uncontrolled movement may permit access to the item. Escorts and other internal restrictions may prevent access to the item. See controlled area and exclusion area.

Line of sight (LOS) Direct observation between two points with the naked eye or hand-held optics.

Line-of-sight sensor A pair of devices used as an intrusion detection sensor that monitor any movement through the field between the sensors.

Line supervision A data integrity strategy that monitors the communications link for connectivity and tampering. In intrusion detection system sensors, line supervision is often referred to as two-state, three-state, or four-state in respect to the number of conditions monitored. The frequency of sampling the link also plays a big part in the supervision of the line.

Local government Any county, city, village, town, district, or political subdivision of any state, and Indian tribe or authorized tribal organization, or Alaska Native village or organization, including any rural community or unincorporated town or village or any other public entity.

Local portfolio plan (LPP) The LPP is a document that provides the method for managing local portfolios and client needs within a specific locality.

The LPP provides the basis for market considerations; long-term tenant needs; existing leased and owned facilities; and community considerations to make decisions related to markets, tenant housing, and hold/divest decision-making.

Long List A long list is a list of all prospective sites considered in the site selection process.

Magnetic lock An electromagnetic lock that unlocks a door when power is removed.

Magnetic stripe A card technology that uses a magnetic stripe on the card to encode data used for unique identification of the card.

Mail-bomb delivery Bombs or incendiary devices delivered to the target in letters or packages.

Man-trap An access control strategy that uses a pair of interlocking doors to prevent tailgating. Only one door can be unlocked at a time.

Mass care The actions that are taken to protect evacuees and other disaster victims from the effects of the disaster. Activities include providing temporary shelter, food, medical care, clothing, and other essential life support needs to those people who have been displaced from their homes because of a disaster or threatened disaster.

Mass notification Capability to provide real-time information to all building occupants or personnel in the immediate vicinity of a building during emergency situations.

Microwave motion sensor An intrusion detection sensor that uses microwave energy to sense movement within the sensor's field of view. These sensors work similar to radar by using the Doppler effect to measure a shift in frequency.

Military installations Army, Navy, Air Force, and Marine Corps bases, posts, stations, and annexes (both contractor and government operated), hospitals, terminals, and other special mission facilities, as well as those used primarily for military purposes.

Minimum essential infrastructure resource elements The broad categories of resources, all or portions of which constitute the minimal essential infrastructure necessary for a department, agency, or organization to conduct its core mission(s).

Minimum measures Protective measures that can be applied to all buildings regardless of the identified threat. These measures offer defense or detection opportunities for minimal cost, facilitate future upgrades, and may deter acts of aggression.

Mitigation Those actions taken to reduce the exposure to and impact of an attack or disaster.

Motion detector An intrusion detection sensor that changes state based on movement in the sensor' field of view.

Moving vehicle bomb An explosive-laden car or truck driven into or near a building and detonated.

Mutual Aid Agreement A pre-arranged agreement developed between two or more entities to render assistance to the parties of the agreement.

Natural hazard Naturally occurring events such as floods, earthquakes, tornadoes, tsunami, coastal storms, landslides, and wildfires that strike populated areas. A natural event is a hazard when it has the potential to harm people or property (FEMA 386-2, Understanding Your Risks). The risks of natural hazards may be increased or decreased as a result of human activity; however, they are not inherently human-induced.

Natural protective barriers Natural protective barriers are mountains and deserts, cliffs and ditches, water obstacles, or other terrain features that are difficult to traverse.

Non-exclusive zone An area around an asset that has controlled entry, but shared or less restrictive access than an exclusive zone.

Non-persistent agent An agent that, upon release, loses its ability to cause casualties after 10 to 15 minutes. It has a high evaporation rate, is lighter than air, and will disperse rapidly. It is considered to be a short-term hazard; however, in small, unventilated areas, the agent will be more persistent.

Notice of Intent (NOI) Describes the proposed action, possible alternatives, and the proposed NEPA scoping process. It states the name and address of a person within GSA who can answer questions about the proposed action and EIS.

Nuclear, biological, or chemical weapons Also called weapons of mass destruction (WMD). Weapons that are characterized by their capability to produce mass casualties.

Nuclear detonation An explosion resulting from fission and/or fusion reactions in nuclear material, such as that from a nuclear weapon.

Occupancy agreement (OA) Similar to a lease between GSA and each tenant agency in a building that establishes the rent and space assignment for each agency.

On-scene coordinator (OSC) The federal official pre-designated by the EPA and U.S. Coast Guard to coordinate and direct response and removals under the National Oil and Hazardous Substances Pollution Contingency Plan.

Open systems architecture A term borrowed from the IT industry to claim that systems are capable of interfacing with other systems from any vendor, which also uses open system architecture. The opposite would be a proprietary system.

Operator interface The part of a security management system that provides that user interface to humans.

Organizational areas of control Controls consist of the policies, procedures, practices, and organization structures designed to provide reasonable assurance that business objectives will be achieved and that undesired events will be prevented or detected and corrected.

Owner's project requirements The documentation that provides the owner's vision for the planned facility, functional performance requirements and expectations for how it will be used and operated. It also provides benchmarks and criteria for performance.

Passive infrared motion sensor A device that detects a change in the thermal energy pattern caused by a moving intruder and initiates an alarm when the change in energy satisfies the detector' alarm-criteria.

Passive vehicle barrier A vehicle barrier that is permanently deployed and does not require esponse to be effective.

Patch panel A concentrated termination point that separates backbone cabling from devices cabling for easy maintenance and troubleshooting.

Perimeter barrier A fence, wall, vehicle barrier, landform, or line of vegetation applied along an exterior perimeter used to obscure vision, hinder personnel access, or hinder or prevent vehicle access.

Persistent agent An agent that, upon release, retains its casualty-producing effects for an extended period of time, usually anywhere from 30 minutes to several days. A persistent agent usually has a low evaporation rate and its vapor is heavier than air; therefore, its vapor cloud tends to hug the ground. It is considered to be a long-term hazard. Although inhalation hazards are still a concern, extreme caution should be taken to avoid skin contact as well.

Physical security The part of security concerned with measures/concepts designed to safeguard personnel; to prevent unauthorized access to equipment, installations, materiel, and documents; and to safeguard them against espionage, sabotage, damage, and theft.

Planter barrier A passive vehicle barrier, usually constructed of concrete and filled with dirt (and flowers for aesthetics). Planters, along with bollards, are the usual street furniture used to keep vehicles away from existing buildings. Overall size and the depth of installation below grade determine the vehicle stopping capability of the individual planter.

Plume Airborne material spreading from a particular source; the dispersal of particles, gases, vapors, and aerosols into the atmosphere.

Polycarbonate glazing A plastic glazing material with enhanced resistance to ballistics or blast effects.

Predetonation screen A fence that causes an anti-tank round to detonate or prevents it from arming before it reaches its target.

Preliminary Damage Assessment (PDA) A mechanism used to determine the impact and magnitude of damage and the resulting unmet needs of individuals, businesses, the public sector, and the community as a whole. Information collected is used by the state as a basis for the governor's request for a presidential declaration, and by FEMA to document the recommendation made to the president in response to the governor's request. PDAs are made by at least one state and one federal representative. A local government representative familiar with the extent and location of damage in the community often participates; other state and federal agencies and voluntary relief organizations also may be asked to participate, as needed.

Preparedness Establishing the plans, training, exercises, and resources necessary to enhance mitigation of and achieve readiness for response to, and recovery from all hazards, disasters, and emergencies, including WMD incidents.

Pressure mat A mat that generates an alarm when pressure is applied to any part of the mat's surface, such as when someone steps on the mat. Pressure mats can be used to detect an intruder approaching a protected object, or they can be placed by doors and windows to detect entry.

Primary asset An asset that is the ultimate target for compromise by an aggressor. Primary gathering building. Inhabited buildings routinely occupied by 50 or more personnel. This designation applies to the entire portion of a building that meets the population density requirements for an inhabited building.

Probability of detection (POD) A measure of an intrusion detection sensor's performance in detecting an intruder within its detection zone.

Probability of intercept The probability that an act of aggression will be detected and that a response force will intercept the aggressor before the asset can be compromised.

Pro forma Analyzes the predicted return on investment and income potential of the project.

Program of Requirements (POR) Defines the scope of the project and the tenant improvements or reimbursables associated with a project.

Progressive collapse A chain reaction failure of building members to an extent disproportionate to the original localized damage. Such damage may result in upper floors of a building collapsing onto lower floors.

Project Development Rating Index (PDRI) The GSA project team performs a project evaluation, utilizing the Construction Industry Institute's PDRI process, prior to submitting the Feasibility Study or Prospectus Development Study for funding a capital project. This process determines the Project Team's effectiveness in preparing a quality submission and assures minimization of risks and mitigation of potential negative issues. This self-evaluation aids in determining areas of project development that may need additional work or study prior to the project's submission for funding.

Project Management Plan (PMP) This is defined on the GSA/PBS website. For Project Management Plan requirements, visit their website.

Prospectus A formal document sent to the Office of Management and Budget and Congress to receive funding authorization. It includes project scope information, budget, and schedule, plus a housing plan. This, if approved, results in authorization letters from both the House and Senate that approve the project, whereas an appropriations bill actually funds the project.

Protective barriers Define the physical limits of a site, activity, or area by restricting,

channeling, or impeding access and forming a continuous obstacle around the object.

Protective measures Elements of a protective system that protect an asset against a threat. Protective measures are divided into defensive and detection measures.

Protective system An integration of all of the protective measures required to protect an asset against the range of threats applicable to the asset.

Proximity sensor An intrusion detection sensor that changes state based on the close distance or contact of a human to the sensor. These sensors often measure the change in capacitance as a human body enters the measured field.

Public Buildings Service (PBS) The General Services Administration's Public Buildings Service organization manages, owns, and constructs space for housing federal agencies.

Public information officer (PIO) A federal, state, or local government official responsible for preparing and coordinating the dissemination of emergency public information.

Radiation High-energy particles or gamma rays that are emitted by an atom as the substance undergoes radioactive decay. Particles can be either charged alpha or beta particles or neutral neutron or gamma rays.

Radiation sickness The symptoms characterizing the sickness known as radiation injury, resulting from excessive exposure of the whole body to ionizing radiation.

Radiological monitoring The process of locating and measuring radiation by means of survey instruments that can detect and measure (as exposure rates) ionizing radiation.

Recommissioning The process of commissioning a facility beyond project development and warranty phases. The purpose of recommissioning is to assure the facility performs as expected over its useful life.

Recovery The long-term activities beyond the initial crisis period and emergency response phase of disaster operations that focus on returning all systems in the community to a normal status or to reconstitute these systems to a new condition that is less vulnerable.

Regional Operations Center (ROC) The temporary operations facility for the coordination of federal response and recovery activities located at the FEMA Regional Office (or Federal Regional Center) and led by the FEMA Regional Director or Deputy Director until the DFO becomes operational. After the ERT-A is deployed, the ROC performs a support role for federal staff at the disaster scene.

Report printers A separate, dedicated printer attached to the Electronic Security Systems used for generating reports utilizing information stored by the central computer.

Request-to-exit device Passive infrared motion sensors or push buttons that are used to signal an electronic entry control system that egress is imminent or to unlock a door.

Resolution The level to which video details can be determined in a CCTV scene is referred to as resolving ability or resolution.

Resource management Those actions taken by a government to identify sources and obtain resources needed to support disaster response activities; coordinate the supply, allocation, distribution, and delivery of resources so that they arrive where and when most needed; and maintain accountability for the resources used.

Response Executing the plan and resources identified to perform those duties and services to preserve and protect life and property as well as provide services to the surviving population.

Response force The people who respond to an act of aggression. Depending on the nature of the threat, the response force could consist of guards, special reaction teams, military or civilian police, an explosives ordnance disposal team, or a fire department.

Response time The length of time from the instant an attack is detected to the instant a security force arrives on site.

Restricted area Any area with access controls that is subject to these special restrictions or controls for security reasons. See controlled area, limited area, exclusion area, and exclusion zone.

Retinal pattern A biometric technology that is based on features of the human eye.

RF data transmission A communications link using radio frequency to send or receive data.

Risk The potential for loss of, or damage to, an asset. It is measured based upon the value of the asset in relation to the threats and vulnerabilities associated with it.

Rotating drum or rotating plate vehicle barrier An active vehicle barrier used at vehicle entrances to controlled areas based on a drum or plate rotating into the path of the vehicle when signaled.

Routinely occupied For the purposes of these standards, an established or predictable pattern of activity within a building that terrorists could recognize and exploit.

RS-232 data IEEE Recommended Standard 232; a point-to-point serial data protocol with a maximum effective distance of 50 feet.

RS-422 data IEEE Recommended Standard 422; a point-to-point serial data protocol with a maximum effective distance of 4,000 feet.

RS-485 data IEEE Recommended Standard 485; a multi-drop serial data protocol with a maximum effective distance of 4,000 feet.

Sacrificial roof or wall Roofs or walls that can be lost in a blast without damage to the primary asset.

Safe haven Secure areas within the interior of the facility. A safe haven should be designed such that it requires more time to penetrate by aggressors than it takes for the response force to reach the protected area to rescue the occupants. It may be a haven from a physical attack or air-isolated haven from CBR contamination.

Scramble keypad A keypad that uses keys on which the numbers change pattern with each use to enhance security by preventing eavesdropping observation of the entered numbers.

Secondary asset An asset that supports a primary asset and whose compromise would indirectly affect the operation of the primary asset.

Secondary hazard A threat whose potential would be realized as the result of a triggering event that of itself would constitute an emergency (e.g., dam failure might be a secondary hazard associated with earthquakes).

Secure/access mode The state of an area monitored by an intrusion detection system in regards to how alarm conditions are reported.

Security analysis The method of studying the nature of and the relationship between assets, threats, and vulnerabilities.

Security console Specialized furniture, racking, and related apparatus used to house the security equipment required in a control center.

Security engineering The process of identifying practical, risk managed short- and long-term solutions to reduce and/or mitigate dynamic manmade hazards by integrating multiple factors, including construction, equipment, manpower, and procedures.

Security engineering design process The process through which assets requiring protection are identified, the threat to and vulnerability of those assets is determined, and a protective system is designed to protect the assets.

Security management system database In a security management system, a database that is transferred to various nodes or panels throughout the system for faster data processing and protection against communications link downtime.

Security management system distributed processing In a security management system, a method of data processing at various nodes or panels throughout the system for faster data processing and protection against communications links downtime.

Segregation of duties Policies, procedures, and an organizational structure established so that one individual cannot control key aspects of physical and/or computer-related operations and thereby conduct unauthorized actions or gain unauthorized access to minimum essential infrastructure resource elements.

Semi-isolated fenced perimeters Fence lines where approach areas are clear of obstruction for 60 to 100 feet outside of the fence and where the general public or other personnel seldom have reason to be in the area.

Senior FEMA Official (SFO) The official appointed by the Director of FEMA, or his representative, that is responsible for deploying to the JOC to serve as the senior interagency consequence management representative on the Command Group, and to manage and coordinate activities taken by the Consequence Management Group.

Serial interface An integration strategy for data transfer where components are connected in series.

Shielded wire Wire with a conductive wrap used to mitigate electromagnetic emanations.

Short list The sites on the short list are the best candidates from the long list and are further evaluated to develop a recommendation for site acquisition. The short list typically includes three sites.

Site Directive (also referred to as Limited Site Directive) The Office of the Chief Architect issues the Site Directive either after the President's proposed Budget (which includes the Site Design and Prospectus) is submitted to Congress or after Congress approves and the President signs the Budget. With receipt of the Site Directive, Regions are authorized to begin formal site selection actions (and acquisition and professional services procurement actions) up to the point of award. The award is contingent upon project authorization and funding appropriation by Congress.

Situational crime prevention A crime prevention strategy based on reducing the opportunities for crime by increasing the effort required to commit a crime, increasing the risks associated with committing the crime, and reducing the target appeal or vulnerability (whether property or person). This opportunity reduction is achieved by management and use policies such as procedures and training, as well as physical approaches such as alteration of the built environment.

Smart card A newer card technology that allows data to be written, stored, and read on a card typically used for identification and/or access.

Software level integration An integration strategy that uses software to interface systems. An example of this would be digital video displayed in the same computer application window and linked to events of a security management system.

Specific threat Known or postulated aggressor activity focused on targeting a particular asset.

Stand-off distance A distance maintained between a building or portion thereof and the potential location for an explosive detonation or other threat.

Stand-off weapons Weapons such as anti-tank weapons and mortars that are launched from a distance at a target.

State Coordinating Officer (SCO) The person appointed by the Governor to coordinate state, commonwealth, or territorial response and recovery activities with FRP-related activities of the Federal Government, in cooperation with the FCO.

State Liaison A FEMA official assigned to a particular state, who handles initial coordination with the state in the early stages of an emergency.

Stationary vehicle bomb An explosive-laden car or truck stopped or parked near a building.

Storm surge A dome of sea water created by the strong winds and low barometric pressure in a hurricane that causes severe coastal flooding as the hurricane strikes land.

Strain sensitive cable Strain sensitive cables are transducers that are uniformly sensitive along their entire length and generate an analog voltage when subjected to mechanical distortions or stress resulting from fence motion. They are typically attached to a chain-link fence about halfway between the bottom and top of the fence fabric with plastic ties.

Structural protective barriers Manmade devices (e.g., fences, walls, floors, roofs, grills, bars, roadblocks, signs, or other construction) used to restrict, channel, or impede access.

Superstructure The supporting elements of a building above the foundation.

Supplies-bomb delivery Bombs or incendiary devices concealed and delivered to supply or material handling points such as loading docks.

System events Events that occur normally in the operation of a security management system. Examples include access control operations and changes of state in intrusion detection sensors.

System software Controls that limit and monitor access to the powerful programs and sensitive files that control the computer hardware and secure applications supported by the system.

System for Tracking and Administering Real Property (STAR) GSA's building inventory database for space management, leases, and rent billing.

Tactics The specific methods of achieving the aggressor's goals to injure personnel, destroy assets, or steal materiel or information.

Tamper switch Intrusion detection sensor that monitors an equipment enclosure for breach.

Tangle-foot wire Barbed wire or tape suspended on short metal or wooden pickets outside a perimeter fence to create an obstacle to approach.

Taut wire sensor An intrusion detection sensor utilizing a column of uniformly spaced horizontal wires, securely anchored at each end and stretched taut. Each wire is attached to a sensor to indicate movement of the wire.

Technical assistance The provisioning of direct assistance to states and local jurisdictions to improve capabilities for program development, planning, and operational performances related to responses to WMD terrorist incidents.

Technological hazards Incidents that can arise from human activities such as manufacture, transportation, storage, and use of hazardous materials. For the sake of simplicity, it is assumed that technological emergencies are accidental and that their consequences are unintended.

TEMPEST An unclassified short name referring to investigations and studies of compromising emanations. It is sometimes used synonymously for the term "compromising emanations" (e.g., TEMPEST tests, TEMPEST inspections).

Terrorism The unlawful use of force and violence against persons or property to intimidate or coerce a government, the civilian population, or any segment thereof, in furtherance of political or social objectives.

Thermally tempered glass (TTG) Glass that is heat-treated to have a higher tensile strength and resistance to blast pressures, although with a greater susceptibility to airborne debris.

Threat Any indication, circumstance, or event with the potential to cause loss of, or damage to an asset.

Threat analysis A continual process of compiling and examining all available information concerning potential threats and human-caused hazards. A common method to evaluate terrorist groups is to review the factors of existence, capability, intentions, history, and targeting.

Time/date stamp Data inserted into a CCTV video signal with the time and date of the video as it was created.

TNT equivalent weight The weight of TNT (trinitrotoluene) that has an equivalent energetic output to that of a different weight of another explosive compound.

Tornado A local atmospheric storm, generally of short duration, formed by winds rotating at very high speeds, usually in a counter-clockwise direction. The vortex, up to several hundred yards wide, is visible to the observer as a whirlpool-like column of winds rotating about a hollow cavity or funnel. Winds may reach 300 miles per hour or higher.

Toxic-free area An area within a facility in which the air supply is free of toxic chemical or biological agents.

Toxicity A measure of the harmful effects produced by a given amount of a toxin on a living organism.

Transaction Screen The Transaction Screen (see ASTM E 1528-93, Environmental Site Assessments) is an inquiry process designed to meet CERCLA's "innocent landowner" defense, but does not require the judgment of an environmental professional. It includes a questionnaire with guidelines for interviewing owners and occupants of a property, observing site conditions, and conducting limited research. Based on the results, the user can determine whether additional information is required, proceed to a Phase I ESA, or research other areas of concern. The same type of process can be applied to other lines of inquiry.

Triple-standard concertina (TSC) wire This type of fence uses three rolls of stacked concertina. One roll will be stacked on top of two other rolls that run parallel to each other while resting on the ground, forming a pyramid.

Tsunami Sea waves produced by an undersea earthquake. Such sea waves can reach a height of 80 feet and can devastate coastal cities and low-lying coastal areas.

Twisted pair wire Wire that uses pairs of wires twisted together to mitigate electromagnetic interference.

Two-person rule A security strategy that requires two people to be present in or gain access to a secured area to prevent unobserved access by any individual.

Unobstructed space Space around an inhabited building without obstruction large enough to conceal explosive devices 150 mm (6 inches) or greater in height.

Unshielded wire Wire that does not have a conductive wrap.

Vault A reinforced room for securing items.

Vertical rod Typical door hardware often used with a crash bar to lock a door by inserting rods vertically from the door into the doorframe.

Vibration sensor An intrusion detection sensor that changes state when vibration is present.

Video intercom system. An intercom system that also incorporates a small CCTV system for verification.

Video motion detection. Motion-detection technology that looks for changes in the pixels of a video image.

Video multiplexer A device used to connect multiple video signals to a single location for viewing and/or recording.

Visual displays A display or monitor used to inform the operator visually of the status of the electronic security system.

Visual surveillance The aggressor uses ocular and photographic devices (such as binoculars and cameras with telephoto lenses) to monitor facility or installation operations or to see assets.

Voice recognition A biometric technology that is based on nuances of the human voice. Volumetric motion sensor. An interior intrusion detection sensor that is designed to sense aggressor motion within a protected space.

Vulnerability Any weakness that can be exploited by an aggressor or, in a nonterrorist threat environment, make an asset susceptible to hazard damage.

Warning The alerting of emergency response personnel and the public to the threat of extraordinary danger and the related effects that specific hazards may cause.

Watch Indication in a defined area that conditions are favorable for the specified type of severe weather (e.g., flash flood watch, severe thunderstorm watch, tornado watch, tropical storm watch).

Waterborne contamination Chemical, biological, or radiological agent introduced into and fouling a water supply.

Weapons-grade material Nuclear material considered most suitable for a nuclear weapon. It usually connotes uranium enriched to above 90 percent uranium-235 or plutonium with greater than about 90 percent plutonium-239.

Weapons of mass destruction (WMD) Any device, material, or substance used in a manner, in a quantity or type, or under circumstances showing an intent to cause death or serious injury to persons, or significant damage to property. An explosive, incendiary, or poison gas, bomb, grenade, rocket having a propellant charge of more than 4 ounces, or a missile having an explosive incendiary charge of more than 0.25 ounce, or mine or device similar to the above; poison gas; weapon involving a disease organism; or weapon that is designed to release radiation or radioactivity at a level dangerous to human life.

Weigand protocol A security industry standard data protocol for card readers.

Work plan A key tool that the team can use to manage the site selection process. The work plan includes information relating to a project's staff, schedule, scope, budget, approvals, controls, and communications

Zoom The ability of a CCTV camera to close and focus or open and widen the field of view.

Census

Accuracy of survey results refers to how closely the results from a sample can reproduce the results that would be obtained from a complete count (i.e., census) conducted using the same techniques at the same time. The difference between a sample result and the result from a complete census taken under the same conditions and at the same time is an indication of the precision of the sample result.

Administrative records and *administrative record data* refer to micro data records contained in files collected and maintained by administrative or program agencies and commercial entities. Government and commercial entities maintain these files for the purpose of administering programs and providing services. Administrative records (e.g., Title 26 data) are distinct from systems of information collected exclusively for statistical purposes, such as data from censuses and surveys that are collected under the authority of Titles 13 or 15 of the United States Code (U.S.C.). For the most part, the Census Bureau draws upon administrative records developed by federal agencies. To a lesser degree, it may use information from state, local, and tribal governments, as well as commercial entities. To obtain these data, the Census Bureau must adhere to a number of regulatory requirements.

The *Administrative Records Tracking System (ARTS)* is an electronic database on the Census Bureau's Intranet. It tracks Census Bureau administrative records agreements, agreement commitments, administrative data projects, and relevant external contacts.

Administratively restricted information (as defined in Data Stewardship Policy DS007, *Information Security Management Program*) consists of agency documentation that is not intended as a public information product and other pre-release or embargoed public information. Examples of administratively restricted information include:

- "For Official Use Only" (FOUO) information: Internal Census Bureau documentation consisting of program or operational materials (e.g., contracting, financial, budget, security, legal, policy documents) determined by management to be either protected under the Freedom of Information Act and/or of a nature that release could negatively impact the mission of the Census Bureau.
- Embargoed data or reports that have not been released, but meet Disclosure Review Board requirements for public release.
- Proprietary contractor information, such as its cost proposal and labor rates.
- All information not otherwise protected by statutory authority, but that is subject to access and/or use restrictions, as provided in a valid Agreement with the government agency or other entity supplying the information.
- All personally identifiable information (PII) not protected by an existing legal authority.
- All business identifiable information (BII) not protected by an existing legal authority.

Allocation involves using statistical procedures, such as within-household or nearest neighbor matrices populated by donors, to impute for missing values.

American National Standards Institute codes (ANSI codes) are a standardized set of numeric or alphabetic codes issued by the American National Standards Institute (ANSI) to ensure uniform identification of geographic entities through all federal government agencies.

The *autocorrelation function* of a random process describes the correlation between the processes at different points in time.

Automated record linkage is the pairing of data, primarily via computer software.

An *autoregressive integrated moving average (ARIMA)* model is a generalization of an autoregressive moving average or (ARMA) model for nonstationary time series. A nonstationary time series is a time series not in equilibrium about a constant mean level. In a nonstationary time series, the mean or variance of the series may not be the same at all time periods. The model is generally referred to as an ARIMA(p,d,q) model where p, d, and q are integers greater than or equal to zero and refer to the order of the autoregressive, integrated (differencing), and moving average parts of the model, respectively.

An *autoregressive moving average (ARMA)* model is a stationary model of time series data where the current data point and current stochastic error are each modeled as finite linear regressions of previous data points or stochastic errors, respectively. The regression for the data points is referred to as an autoregression. The regression for the stochastic errors is referred to as a moving average. Symbolically, the model is denoted as an ARMA (p,q) model where p and q are integers greater than or equal to zero and refer to the order of the autoregressive and moving average parts of the model, respectively. A stationary time series is a time series in equilibrium about a constant mean level. These models are fitted to time series data either to better understand the data or to predict future points in the series.

Behavior coding of respondent/interviewer interactions involves systematic coding of the interaction between interviewers and respondents from live or taped field or telephone interviews to collect quantitative information. When used for questionnaire assessment, the behaviors that are coded focus on behaviors indicative of a problem with the question, the response categories, or the respondent's ability to form an adequate response.

Bias is the difference between the expected value of an estimator and the actual population value.

Blocking is grouping the records of a set into mutually exclusive, exhaustive pieces by using a set of fields (e.g., state, last name, first initial). Usually used in the context of record linkage.

Bonferroni correction is a method used to address the problem of multiple comparisons. It is based on the idea that if an experimenter is testing n dependent or independent hypotheses on a set of data, then one way of maintaining the family-wise error rate is to test each individual hypothesis at a statistical significance level of 1/n times what it would be if only one hypothesis were tested.

Bottom-coding is a disclosure limitation technique that involves limiting the minimum value of a variable allowed on the file to prevent disclosure of individuals or other units with extreme values in a distribution.

A *bridge study* continues an existing methodology concurrent with a new methodology for the purpose of examining the relationship between the new and old estimates.

Business identifiable information is information defined in the Freedom of Information Act (FOIA) as trade secrets or commercial or financial information, that is obtained from a person representing a business entity, and which is privileged and confidential (e.g., Title 13) and exempt from automatic release under FOIA. Also included is commercial or other information that, although it may not be exempt from release under the FOIA, is exempt from disclosure by law (e.g., Title 13). Also see **Personally identifiable information**.

The *calibration* approach to estimation for finite populations consists of: (a) a computation of weights that incorporate specified auxiliary information and are restrained by calibration equation(s); (b) the use of these weights to compute linearly weighted estimates of totals and other finite population parameters: weight times variable value, summed over a set of observed units; (c) an objective to obtain nearly design unbiased estimates as long as nonresponse and other nonsampling errors are absent.

Cell suppression is a disclosure limitation technique where sensitive cells are generally deleted from a table and flags are inserted to indicate this condition.

A *census* is a data collection that seeks to obtain data directly from all eligible units in the entire target population. It can be considered a sample with a 100 percent sampling rate. The Economic Census may use administrative records data rather than interviews for some units.

Census Bureau publications are information products that are backed and released by the Census Bureau to the public. "Backed and released by the Census Bureau" means that the Census Bureau's senior management officials (at least through the Associate Director responsible for the product) have reviewed and approved the product and the Census Bureau affirms its content. Because publications do not contain personal views, these information products do not include a disclaimer.

Clerical record linkage is record matching that is primarily performed manually.

A *cluster* is a set of units grouped together on the basis of some well-defined criteria. For example, the cluster may be an existing grouping of the population such as a city block, a hospital, or a household; or may be conceptual such as the area covered by a grid imposed on a map.

Coding is the process of categorizing response data using alphanumeric values so that the responses can be more easily analyzed.

Coefficient of variation (CV) is a measure of dispersion calculated by dividing the standard deviation of an estimate by its mean. It is also referred to as the relative standard error.

Cognitive interviews are used as a pretesting technique consisting of one-on-one interviews using a draft questionnaire to find out directly from respondents about their problems with the questionnaire In a typical cognitive interview, respondents report aloud everything they are thinking as they attempt to answer a survey question.

Computer-assisted personal interviewing (CAPI) is an interviewing technique similar to computer-assisted telephone interviewing, except that the interview takes place in person instead of over the telephone. The interviewer sits in front of a computer terminal and enters the answers into the computer.

Computer-assisted telephone interviewing (CATI) is an interviewing technique, conducted using a telephone, in which the interviewer follows a script provided by a software application. The software is able to customize the flow of the questionnaire based on the answers provided, as well as information already known about the participant.

A *confidence interval* is a range of values determined in the process of estimating a population parameter. The likelihood that the true value of the parameter falls in that range is chosen in advance and determines the length of the interval. That likelihood is called the confidence level. Confidence intervals are displayed as (lower bound, upper bound) or as *estimate ± MOE, where MOE = z-value * standard error of the associated estimate (when the confidence level = 90%, the z-value = 1.645).*

Confidentiality involves the protection of personally identifiable information and business identifiable information from unauthorized release.

Controlled rounding is a form of random rounding, but it is constrained to have the sum of the published entries in each row and column equal the appropriate published marginal totals.

Controlled tabular adjustment is a perturbative method for statistical disclosure limitation in tabular data. This method perturbs sensitive cell values until they are considered safe and then rebalances the non-sensitive cell values to restore additivity.

A **convenience sample** is a nonprobability sample, from which inferences cannot be made. Convenience sampling involves selecting the sample from the part of the population that is convenient to reach. Convenience sampling is not allowed for Census Bureau information products.

Covariance is a characteristic that indicates the strength of relationship between two variables. It is the expected value of the product of the deviations of two random variables, x and y, from their respective means.

Coverage refers to the extent to which elements of the target population are listed on the sampling frame. **Overcoverage** refers to the extent that elements in the population are on the frame more than once and **undercoverage** refers to the extent that elements in the population are missing from the frame.

Coverage error which includes both undercoverage and overcoverage, is the error in an estimate that results from (1) failure to include all units belonging to the target population or failure to include specified units in the conduct of the survey (undercoverage), and (2) inclusion of some units erroneously either because of a defective frame or because of inclusion of unspecified units or inclusion of specified units more than once in the actual survey (overcoverage).

A *coverage ratio* is the ratio of the population estimate of an area or group to the independent estimate for that area or group. The coverage ratio is sometimes referred to as a coverage rate and may be presented as percentage.

Cross-sectional studies (also known as cross-sectional analysis) form a class of research methods that involve observation of some subset of a population of items all at the same time. The fundamental difference between cross-sectional and longitudinal studies is that cross-sectional studies take place at a single point in time and that a longitudinal study involves a series of measurements taken on the same units over a period of time. See **Longitudinal survey**.

Cross-validation is the statistical practice of partitioning a sample of data into subsets such that the analysis is initially performed on a single subset, while the other subset(s) are retained for subsequent use in confirming and validating the initial analysis.

Custom tabulations are tables prepared by the Census Bureau at the request of a data user or program sponsor. This terminology does not apply to tables produced by Census Bureau software (e.g., FERRET or American Fact Finder).

A *cut-off sample* is a nonprobability sample that consists of the units in the population that have the largest values of a key variable (frequently the variable of interest from a previous time period). For example, a 90 percent cut-off sample consists of the largest units accounting for at least 90 percent of the population total of the key variable. Sample selection is usually done by sorting the population in decreasing order by size, and including units in the sample until the percent coverage exceeds the established cut-off.

Data capture is the conversion of information provided by a respondent into electronic format suitable for use by subsequent processes.

Data collection involves activities and processes that obtain data about the elements of a population, either directly by contacting respondents to provide the data or indirectly by using administrative records or other data sources. Respondents may be individuals or organizations.

Data collection instrument refers to the device used to collect data, such as a paper questionnaire or computer assisted interviewing system.

A *data program* is a program that generates information products, often on a regular schedule. These programs include efforts such as the censuses and surveys that collect data from respondents. Data programs also include operations that generate information products from administrative records and operations that combine data from multiple sources, such as various surveys, censuses, and administrative records. Specific examples of multiple source data programs include the Small Area Income and Poverty Estimates (SAIPE) program, the Population Division's "Estimates and Projections" program, the National Longitudinal Mortality Study, and the Annual Survey of Manufactures (ASM). One-time surveys also are considered data programs.

Data-use agreements for administrative records are signed documents between the Census Bureau and other agencies to acquire restricted state or federal data or data from vendors. These are often called Memoranda of Understanding (MOU).

Derived statistics are calculated from other statistical measures. For example, population figures are statistical measures, but population-per-square-mile is a derived quantity.

The *design effect* is the ratio of the variance of a statistic, obtained from taking the complex sample design into account, to the variance of the statistic from a simple random sample with the same number of cases. Design effects differ for different subgroups and different statistics; no single design effect is universally applicable to any given survey or analysis.

A *direct comparison* is a statement that explicitly points out a difference between estimates.

Direct estimates are estimates of the true values of the target populations, based on the sample design and resulting survey data collected on the variable of interest, only from the time period of interest and only from sample units in the domain of interest. Direct estimates may be adjusted using explicit or implicit models (e.g., ratio adjustment, hot or cold deck imputation, and non-response adjustment) to correct for nonresponse and coverage errors.

Disclosure is the release of personally identifiable information or business identifiable information outside the Census Bureau.

Dissemination means Census Bureau-initiated or sponsored distribution of information to the public (e.g., publishing information products on the Census Bureau Internet Web site). Dissemination does not include distribution limited to government employees or agency contractors or grantees; intra-agency or inter-agency use or sharing of government information; and response to requests for agency records under the Freedom on Information Act, the Privacy Act, or other similar law. This definition also does not include distribution limited to correspondence with individuals or persons, press releases, archival records, public filings, subpoenas, or adjudicative processes.

A *dress rehearsal* is a complete test of the data collection components on a small sample under conditions that mirror the full-implementation. See **Field test**.

Editing is the process of identifying and examining missing, invalid, and inconsistent entries and changing these entries according to predetermined rules, other data sources, and recontacts with respondents with the intent to produce more accurate, cohesive, and comprehensive data. Some of the editing checks involve logical relationships that follow directly from the concepts and definitions. Others are more empirical in nature or are obtained through the application of statistical tests or procedures.

Equivalent quality data is data obtained from another source than the respondent, which have quality equivalent to data reported by the respondent. Equivalent quality data have three possible sources: 1) data directly substituted from another census or survey (for the same reporting unit, question wording, and time period); 2) data from administrative records; or 3) data obtained from some other equivalent source that has been validated by a study approved by the program manager in collaboration with the appropriate Research and Methodology area (e.g., company annual reports, Securities and Exchange Commission (SEC) filings, and trade association statistics).

An *estimate* is a numerical quantity for some characteristic or attribute calculated from sample data as an approximation of the true value of the characteristic in the entire population. An estimate can also be developed from models or algorithms that combine data from various sources, including administrative records.

Estimation is the process of using data from a survey or other sources to provide a value for an unknown population parameter (such as a mean, proportion, correlation, or effect size), or to provide a range of values in the form of a confidence interval.

Exploratory studies (also called **Feasibility studies**) are common methods for specifying and evaluating survey content relative to concepts. In economic surveys, these studies often take the form of company or site visits.

External users See **Users**.

Fax imaging is properly called Paperless Fax Imaging Retrieval System (PFIRS). This collection method mails or faxes a paper instrument to respondents. The respondents fax it back to the Census Bureau, where it is automatically turned into an image file.

Feasibility studies (also called **Exploratory studies**) are common methods for specifying and evaluating survey content relative to concepts. In economic surveys, these studies often take the form of company or site visits.

Field follow-up is a data collection procedure involving personal visits by enumerators to housing units to perform the operations such as, resolving inconsistent and/or missing data items on returned questionnaires, conducting a vacant/delete check, obtaining information for blank or missing questionnaires, and visiting housing units for which no questionnaire was checked in.

A *field test* is a test of some of the procedures on a small scale that mirrors the planned full-scale implementation. See **Dress rehearsal**.

A *focus group* is a pretesting technique whereby respondents are interviewed in a group setting to guide the design of a questionnaire based on the respondent's reaction to the subject matter and the issues raised during the discussion.

A *frame* consists of one or more lists of the units comprising the universe from which respondents can be selected (e.g., Census Bureau employee telephone directory). The frame may include elements not in the universe (e.g., retired employees). It may also miss elements that are in the universe (e.g., new employees).

The *frame population* is the set of elements that can be enumerated prior to the selection of a sample.

Geocoding is the conversion of spatial information into computer-readable form. As such, geocoding, both the process and the concepts involved, determines the type, scale, accuracy, and precision of digital maps.

A *geographic entity* is a spatial unit of any type, legal or statistical, such as a state, county, place, county subdivision, census tract, or census block.

A *geographic entity code (geocode)* is a code used to identify a specific geographic entity. For example, the geocodes needed to identify a census block for Census 2000 data are the state code, county code, census tract number, and block number. Every geographic entity recognized by the Census Bureau is assigned one or more geographic codes. "To geocode" means to assign an address, living quarters, establishment, etc., to one or more geographic codes that identify the geographic entity or entities in which it is located.

A *generalized variance function* is a mathematical model that describes the relationship between a statistic (such as a population total) and its corresponding variance. Generalized variance function models are used to approximate standard errors of a wide variety of characteristics of the target population.

Goodness-of-fit means how well a statistical model fits a set of observations. Measures of goodness of fit typically summarize the discrepancy between observed values and the values expected under a model. Such measures can be used in statistical hypothesis testing (e.g., to test for normality of residuals, to test whether two samples are drawn from identical distributions, or to test whether outcome frequencies follow a specified distribution).

A *graphical user interface (GUI)* emphasizes the use of pictures for output and a pointing device such as a mouse for input and control whereas a command line interface requires the user to type textual commands and input at a keyboard and produces a single stream of text as output.

Random variables are **heteroscedastic** if they have different variances. The complementary concept is called homoscedasticity.

Random variables are **homoscedastic** if they have the same variance. This is also known as homogeneity of variance. The complement is called heteroscedasticity.

A *housing unit* is a house, an apartment, a mobile home or trailer, a group of rooms or a single room occupied as separate living quarters or, if vacant, intended for occupancy as separate living quarters. The Census Bureau's estimates program prepares estimates of housing units for places, counties, states, and the nation.

Hypothesis testing draws a conclusion about the tenability of a stated value for a parameter. For example, sample data may be used to test whether an estimated value of a parameter (such as the difference between two population means) is sufficiently different from zero that the null hypothesis, designated H0 (no difference in the population means), can be rejected in favor of the alternative hypothesis, H1 (a difference between the two population means).

An *implied comparison* between two (or more) estimates is one that readers might infer, either because of proximity of the two estimates in the text of the report or because the discussion presents the estimates in a manner that makes it likely readers will compare them. For an implied comparison to exist between two estimates:

- The estimates must be for similar subgroups that it makes sense to compare (e.g., two age subgroups, two race subgroups).
- The estimates must be of the same type (e.g., percentages, rates, levels).
- The subgroups must differ by only one characteristic (e.g., teenage males versus teenage females; adult males versus adult females; teenage males versus adult males). If they differ by more than one characteristic an implied comparison does not exist (e.g., teenage males versus adult females).
- The estimates appear close enough to each other in the report that the reader would make a connection between them. Two estimates in the same paragraph that satisfy the first three criteria will always constitute an implied comparison. However, if the two estimates were in different sections of a report they would not constitute an implied comparison.

Estimates presented in tables do not constitute implied comparisons. However, if a table displays the difference between two estimates, it is a direct comparison.

Imputation is a procedure for entering a value for a specific data item where the response is missing or unusable.

Information products may be in print or electronic format and include news releases; Census Bureau publications; working papers (including technical papers or reports); professional papers (including journal articles, book chapters, conference papers, poster sessions, and written discussant comments); abstracts; research reports used to guide decisions about Census Bureau programs; presentations at public events (e.g., seminars or conferences); handouts for presentations; tabulations and custom tabulations; public-use data files; statistical graphs, figures, and maps; and the documentation disseminated with these information products.

Information quality is an encompassing term comprising utility, objectivity, and integrity.

Integration testing is the phase of software testing in which individual software modules are combined and tested as a group. The purpose of integration testing is to verify functional, performance and reliability requirements placed on major design items. Integration testing can expose problems with the interfaces among program components before trouble occurs in real-world program execution.

Integrity refers to the security of information—protection of the information from unauthorized access or revision, to ensure that the information is not compromised through corruption or falsification.

Internal users See **Users**.

Interviewer debriefing has traditionally been the primary method used to evaluate field or pilot tests of interviewer-administered surveys. Interviewer debriefing consists of group discussions or structured questionnaires with the interviewers who conducted the test to obtain their views of questionnaire problems.

An **item allocation rate** is the proportion of the estimated (weighted) total (T) of item t that was imputed using statistical procedures, such as within-household or nearest neighbor matrices populated by donors, for that item.

Item nonresponse occurs when a respondent provides some, but not all, of the requested information, or if the reported information is not useable.

Joint partners refers to projects where both the Census Bureau and another agency are collecting the data together, but for their own use. It is a collaborative effort to reduce overall costs to the government and increase efficiency.

Key from image (KFI) is an operation in which keyers enter questionnaire responses by referring to a scanned image of a questionnaire for which entries could not be recognized by optical character or optical mark recognition with sufficient confidence.

Key from paper (KFP) is an operation in which keyers enter information directly from a hard-copy questionnaire that could not be read by optical character or optical mark recognition with sufficient confidence.

Key variables are main classification variables (e.g., geography, demographic attributes, economic attributes, industry etc.) of units to be studied.

Latent class analysis is a method for estimating one or more components of the mean squared error or an estimator.

Linear regression is a method that models a parametric relationship between a dependent variable Y, explanatory variables X and a random term ε. This method is called "linear" because the relation of the response (the dependent variable Y) to the independent variables is assumed to be a linear function of the parameters.

Linking See **Record linkage**.

Load testing is the process of putting demand on a system or device and measuring its response. Load testing generally refers to the practice of modeling the expected usage of a software program by simulating multiple users accessing the program concurrently.

Logistic regression is a model used for prediction of the probability of occurrence of an event.

A *longitudinal survey* is a correlational research study that involves repeated observations of the same items over long periods of time, often many decades.

Longitudinal studies are often used in psychology to study developmental trends across the life span. The reason for this is that unlike cross-sectional studies, longitudinal studies track the same unit of observation, and therefore the differences observed in those people are less likely to be the result of cultural differences across generations.

Mail-out/mail-back is a method of data collection in which the U.S. Postal Service delivers addressed questionnaires to housing units. Residents are asked to complete and mail the questionnaires to a specified data capture center.

The *margin of error (MOE)* is a measure of the precision of an estimate at a given level of confidence (e.g., 90%). The larger the margin of error, the less confidence one should have that the reported results are close to the "true" figures; that is, the figures for the whole population.

Master Address File (MAF)/Topologically Integrated Geographic Encoding and Referencing (TIGER) is a topologically integrated geographic database in which the topological structures define the location, connection, and relative relationship of streets, rivers, railroads, and other features to each other, and to the numerous geographic entities for which the Census Bureau tabulates data for its censuses and sample surveys.

Matching See **Record linkage**.

Measurement error is the difference between the true value of the measurement and the value obtained during the measurement process.

Metadata are data about data. Metadata are used to facilitate the understanding, use and management of data. An item of metadata may describe an individual datum or content item, or a collection of data including multiple content items.

Methodological expert reviews are independent evaluations of an information product conducted by one or more technical experts. These experts may be within the Census Bureau or outside the Census Bureau, such as advisory committees. See also **Peer reviews**.

A *microdata* file includes the detailed information about people or establishments. Microdata come from interviews and administrative records.

A *model* is a formal (e.g., mathematical) description of a natural system. The formal system is governed by rules of inference; the natural system consists of some collection of observable and latent variables. It is presumed that the rules of inference governing the formal system mimic in some important respect the causal relations that govern the natural system (e.g., the formal laws of arithmetic apply to counting persons).

Model validation involves testing a model's predictive capabilities by comparing the model results to "known" sources of empirical data.

Monte Carlo simulation is a technique that converts uncertainties in input variables of a model into probability distributions. By combining the distributions and randomly selecting values from them, it recalculates the simulated model many times and brings out the probability of the output.

Multicollinearity is a statistical term for the existence of a high degree of linear correlation amongst two or more explanatory variables in a multiple regression model. In the presence of multicollinearity, it is difficult to assess the effect of the independent variables on the dependent variable.

In *multistage sampling*, a sample of clusters is selected and then a subsample of units is selected within each sample cluster. If the subsample of units is the last stage of sample selection, it is called a two-stage design. If the subsample is also a cluster from which units are again selected, it is called a three-stage design, etc.

Multivariate analysis is a generic term for many methods of analysis that are used to investigate relationships among two or more variables.

Noise infusion is a method of disclosure avoidance in which values for each establishment are perturbed prior to table creation by applying a random noise multiplier to the magnitude data (e.g., characteristics such as first-quarter payroll, annual payroll, and number of employees) for each company.

Nonresponse means the failure to obtain information from a sample unit for any reason (e.g., no one home or refusal). There are two types of nonresponse (see **Unit nonresponse** and **Item nonresponse**).

Nonresponse bias is the deviation of the expected value of an estimate from the population parameter due to differences between respondents and nonrespondents. The impact of nonresponse on a given estimate is affected by both the degree of nonresponse and the degree that the respondents' reported values differ from what the nonrespondents would have reported.

Nonresponse error is the overall error observed in estimates caused by differences between respondents and nonrespondents. It consists of a variance component and nonresponse bias.

Nonresponse follow-up is an operation whose objective is to obtain completed questionnaires from housing units for which the Census Bureau did not have a completed questionnaire in mail areas (mailout/mailback, update/leave, and urban update/leave).

Nonresponse subsampling is a method for reducing nonresponse bias in which new attempts are made to obtain responses from a subsample of sampling units that did not provide responses to the first attempt.

Nonsampling errors are survey errors caused by factors other than sampling (e.g., nonsampling errors include errors in coverage, response errors, nonresponse errors, faulty questionnaires, interviewer recording errors, and processing errors).

The *North American Industry Classification System (NAICS)* is the standard used by Federal statistical agencies in classifying business establishments for the purpose of collecting, analyzing, and publishing statistical data related to the U.S. business economy. Canada, Mexico, and the U.S. jointly developed the NAICS to provide new comparability in statistics about business activity across North America. NAICS coding has replaced the U.S. Standard Industrial Classification (SIC) system (for more information, see www.census.gov/epcd/www/naics.html).

Objectivity focuses on whether information is accurate, reliable, and unbiased, and is presented in an accurate, clear, complete, and unbiased manner.

Optical character recognition (OCR) is a technology that uses an optical scanner and computer software to "read" human handwriting and convert it into electronic form.

Optical mark recognition (OMR) is a technology that uses an optical scanner and computer software to recognize the presence of marks in predesignated areas and assign a value to the mark depending on its specific location and intensity on a page.

Outliers in a set of data are values that are so far removed from other values in the distribution that their presence cannot be attributed to the random combination of chance causes.

The *p-value* is the probability that the observed value of the test statistic or a value that is more extreme in the direction of the alternative hypothesis, calculated when H0 is true, is obtained.

Parameters are unknown, quantitative measures (e.g., total revenue, mean revenue, total yield or number of unemployed people) for the entire population or for specified domains that are of interest. A parameter is a constant in the equation of a curve that can be varied to yield a family of similar curves or a quantity (such as the mean, regression coefficient, or variance) that characterizes a statistical population and that can be estimated by calculations from sample data.

Participation means that the employee takes an active role in the event.

A *peer review* is an independent evaluation of an information product conducted by one or more technical experts.

Personally identifiable information refers to any information about an individual maintained by the Census Bureau which can be used to distinguish or trace an individual's identity, such as their name, Social Security number, date and place of birth, biometric records, etc., including any other personal information which is linked or linkable to an individual. Also see **Business identifiable information**.

Census Bureau information products must not contain *policy views.* The Census Bureau's status as a statistical agency requires us to absolutely refrain from taking partisan political positions. Furthermore, there is an important distinction between producing data and using that data to advocate for program and policy changes. The Census Bureau's duty is to produce high quality, relevant data that the nation's policy makers can use to formulate public policy and programs. The Census Bureau should not, however, insert itself into a debate about the program or policy implications of the statistics it produces. We produce poverty statistics; we do not advocate for programs to alleviate poverty.

Population estimates (post-censal or intercensal estimates) are prepared for demographic groups and geographic areas. These estimates usually are developed from separate measures of the components of population change (births, deaths, domestic net migration, and net international migration) in each year but may be supplemented with other methodologies in the absence of current measures of components.

Post-stratification is applied to survey data by stratifying sample units after data collection using information collected in the survey and auxiliary information to adjust weights to population control totals or for nonresponse adjustment.

Precision of survey results refers to how closely the results from a sample can be obtained across repeated samples conducted using the same techniques from the same population at the same time. A precise estimate is stable over replications.

Pretesting is a broad term that incorporates many different techniques for identifying problems for both respondents and interviewers with regard to question content, order/context effects, skip instructions, and formatting.

Primary sampling units (PSU) are clusters of reporting units selected in the first stage of a multistage sample.

Probabilistic methods for survey sampling are any of a variety of methods for sampling that give a known, non-zero probability of selection to each member of the frame. The advantage of probabilistic sampling methods is that sampling error can be calculated without reference to a model assumption. Such methods include random sampling, systematic sampling, and stratified sampling.

The *probability of selection* is the probability that a population (frame) unit will be drawn in a sample. In a simple random selection, this probability is the number of elements drawn in the sample divided by the number of elements on the sampling frame.

Probability sampling is an approach to sample selection that satisfies certain conditions:

(1) We can define the set of samples that are possible to obtain with the sampling procedure.
(2) A known probability of selection is associated with each possible sample.
(3) The procedure gives every element in the population a nonzero probability of selection.
(4) We select one sample by a random mechanism under which each possible sample receives exactly its probability of selection.

A *project* is a temporary endeavor undertaken to create a unique product, service, or result.

A *projection* is an estimate of a future value of a characteristic based on trends.

Protected information (as defined in Data Stewardship Policy DS007, *Information Security Management Program*) includes information about individuals, businesses, and sensitive statistical methods that are protected by law or regulation. The Census Bureau classifies the following as protected information:

- Individual census or survey responses.
- Microdata or paradata, containing original census or survey respondent data and/or administrative records data that do not meet the disclosure avoidance requirements.
- Address lists and frames, including the Master Address File (MAF).
- Pre-release Principal Economic Indicators and Demographic Time-Sensitive Data.
- Aggregate statistical information produced for internal use or research that do not meet the Disclosure Review Board disclosure avoidance requirements, or that have not been reviewed and approved for release.
- Internal use methodological documentation in support of statistical products such as the primary selection algorithm, swapping rates, or Disclosure Review Board checklists.
- All personally identifiable information (PII) protected by an existing legal authority (such as Title 13, Title 15, Title 5, and Title 26).
- All business identifiable information (BII) protected by an existing legal authority.

A *public event* means that the event is open to the general public, including events that require a registration fee.

A *qualified user* is a user with the experience and technical skills to meaningfully understand and analyze the data and results. For example, a qualified user of direct estimates produced from samples understands sampling, estimation, variance estimation, and hypothesis testing.

A *quantity response rate* is the proportion of the estimated (weighted) total (T) of data item t reported by tabulation units in the sample (expressed as a percentage). [Note: Because the value of economic data items can be negative (e.g., income), the absolute value must be used in the numerators and denominators in all calculations.]

A *questionnaire* is a set of questions designed to collect information from a respondent. A questionnaire may be interviewer-administered or respondent-completed, using paper-and-pencil methods for data collection or computer-assisted modes of completion.

Raking is a method of adjusting sample estimates to known marginal totals from an independent source. For a two-dimensional case, the procedure uses the sample weights to proportionally adjust the weights so that the sample estimates agree with one set of marginal totals. Next, these adjusted weights are proportionally adjusted so that the sample estimates agree with the second set of marginal totals. This two-step adjustment process is repeated enough times until the sample estimates converge simultaneously to both sets of marginal totals.

In *random rounding*, cell values are rounded, but instead of using standard rounding conventions a random decision is made as to whether they will be rounded up or down.

Ratio estimation is a method of estimating from sample data. In ratio estimation, an auxiliary variate xi, correlated with yi is obtained for each unit in the sample. The population total X of the xi must be known. The goal is to obtain increased precision by taking advantage of the correlation between yi and xi.

Readily accessible means that users can access the documentation when they need it, not that it is only available on request.

Recoding is a disclosure limitation technique that involves collapsing/regrouping detail categories of a variable so that the resulting categories are safe.

Record linkage is the process of linking or matching two or more records that are determined to refer to the same person or establishment.

Regression is a statistical method which tries to predict the value of a characteristic by studying its relationship with one or more other characteristics.

A *regression model* is a statistical model used to depict the relationship of a dependent variable to one or more independent variables.

Reimbursable projects are those for which the Census Bureau receives payment (in part or in total) from a customer for products or services rendered.

Reinterview is repeated measurement of the same unit intended to estimate measurement error (response error reinterview) or designed to detect and deter falsification (quality control reinterview).

A *release phase* refers to the point in the statistical process where you release the data. It may be to the public, the sponsor, or any other user for whom the data was created.

Releases of information products are the delivery or the dissemination of information products to government agencies, organizations, sponsors, or individuals outside the Census Bureau, including releases to the public.

Replication methods are variance estimation methods that take repeated subsamples, or replicates, from the data, re-compute the weighted estimate for each replicate, and then compute the variance based on the deviations of these replicate estimates from the full-sample estimate. The subsamples are generated to properly reflect the variability due to the sample design.

Reproducibility means that the information is capable of being substantially reproduced, subject to an acceptable degree of imprecision. For information judged to have more (less) important impacts, the degree of imprecision that is tolerated is reduced (increased). If the Census Bureau applies the reproducibility test to specific types of original or supporting data, the associated guidelines shall provide relevant definitions of reproducibility (e.g., standards for replication of laboratory data). With respect to analytic results, "capable of being substantially reproduced" means that independent analysis of the original or supporting data using identical methods would generate similar analytic results, subject to an acceptable degree of imprecision or error.

A *residual* is the observed value minus the predicted value.

Respondent burden is the estimated total time and financial resources expended by the respondent to generate, maintain, retain, and provide census or survey information.

Respondent debriefing is a pretesting technique that involves using a structured questionnaire following data collection to elicit information about respondents' interpretations of survey questions.

A **response analysis survey** is a technique for evaluating questionnaires from the perspective of the respondent. It is typically a respondent debriefing conducted after a respondent has completed the main survey.

Response error is the difference between the true answer to a question and the respondent's answer. It may be caused by the respondent, the interviewer, the questionnaire, the survey procedure or the interaction between the respondent and the interviewer.

A *response rate* measures the proportion of the selected sample that is represented by the responding units.

Revisions history is a stability diagnostic to compare regARIMA modeling and seasonal adjustment results over lengthening time spans. History analysis begins with a shortened series. Series values are added, one at a time, and the regARIMA model and seasonal adjustment are reestimated. Comparing different sets of adjustment options for the same series may indicate that one set of options is more stable. Among adjustment options whose other diagnostics indicate acceptable quality, options that result in fewer large revisions, that is, fewer large changes as data are added, usually are preferred.

The *sample design* describes the target population, frame, sample size, and the sample selection methods.

The *sample size* is the number of population units or elements selected for the sample, determined in relation to the required precision and available budget for observing the selected units.

A *sample survey* is a data collection that obtains data from a sample of the population.

The *sampled population* is the collection of all possible observation units (objects on which measurements are taken) that might have been chosen in the sample. For example, in a presidential poll taken to determine who people will vote for, the target population might be all persons who are registered to vote. The sampled population might be all registered voters who can be reached by telephone.

Sampling is the process of selecting a segment of a population to observe and facilitate the estimation and analysis of something of interest about the population. The set of sampling units selected is referred to as the sample. If all the units are selected, the sample is referred to as a census.

Sampling error is the uncertainty associated with an estimate that is based on data gathered from a sample of the population rather than the full population.

A *sampling frame* is any list or device that, for purposes of sampling, de-limits, identifies, and allows access to the sampling units, which contain elements of the frame population. The frame may be a listing of persons, housing units, businesses, records, land segments, etc. One sampling frame or a combination of frames may be used to cover the entire frame population.

Sampling units are the basic components of a sampling frame. The sampling unit may contain, for example, defined areas, houses, people, or businesses.

Sampling weight is a weight assigned to a given sampling unit that equals the inverse of the unit's probability of being included in the sample and is determined by the sample design. This weight may include a factor due to subsampling.

Sanitized data, used for testing, may be totally fictitious or based on real data that have been altered to eliminate the ability to identify the information of any entity represented by the data.

Scheffé's method is a method for adjusting significance levels in a linear regression analysis to account for multiple comparisons. It is particularly useful in analysis of variance, and in constructing simultaneous confidence bands for regressions involving basis functions. Scheffé's method is a single-step multiple comparison procedure which applies to the set of estimates of all possible contrasts among the factor level means, not just the pairwise differences considered by the Tukey method.

A *scoring weight* is the amount of value assigned when a pair of records agree or disagree on the same matching variable. Each matching variable is assigned two scoring weights—a positive weight for agreement and a negative weight for disagreement. After comparing all matching variables on a matching variable by matching variable basis, the resulting set of assigned weights are added to get a total score for the total record. Pairs of records with scores above a predetermined cut-off are classified as a match; pairs of records with scores below a second predetermined cut-off are classified as a non-match.

Seasonal adjustment is a statistical technique that consists of estimating seasonal factors and applying them to a time series to remove the seasonal variations in the estimates.

Sensitivity analysis is designed to determine how the variation in the output of a model (numerical or otherwise) can be apportioned, qualitatively or quantitatively, to changes in input parameter values and assumptions. This type of analysis is useful in ascertaining the capability of a given model, as well its robustness and reliability.

Sequential sampling is a sampling method in which samples are taken one at a time or in successive predetermined groups, until the cumulative result of their measurements (as assessed against predetermined limits) permits a decision to accept or reject the population or to continue sampling. The number of observations required is not determined in advance, but the decision to terminate the operation depends, at each stage, on the results of the previous observations. The plan may have a practical, automatic termination after a certain number of units have been examined.

Significance level refers to the probability of rejecting a true null hypothesis.

Simple random sampling (SRS) is a basic probability selection scheme that uses equal probability sampling with no strata.

A *skip pattern* in a data collection instrument is the process of skipping over non-applicable questions depending upon the answer to a prior question.

Sliding spans diagnostics are seasonal adjustment stability diagnostics for detecting adjustments that are too unstable. X-12-ARIMA creates up to four overlapping subspans of the time series, seasonally adjusts each span, then compares the adjustments of months (quarters with quarterly data) common to two or more spans. Months are flagged whose adjustments differ by more than a certain cutoff. (The default cut-off is 3% for most comparisons.) If too many months are flagged, the seasonal adjustment is rejected for being too unstable. The series should not be adjusted unless other software options are found that lead to an adjustment with an acceptable number of flagged months. Sliding spans diagnostics can include comparisons of seasonally adjusted values, seasonal factors, trading day factors, month-to-month changes and year-to-year changes. (Year-to-year change results are not used to accept or reject an adjustment.)

Small area estimation is a statistical technique involving the estimation of parameters for small sub-populations where a sample has insufficient or no sample for the sub-populations to be able to make accurate estimates for them. The term "small area" may refer strictly to a small geographical area such as a county, but may also refer to a "small domain," i.e., a particular demographic within an area. Small area estimation methods use models and additional data sources (such as census data) that exist for these small areas in order to improve estimates for them.

Special sworn status (SSS) is conferred upon individuals for whom the Census Bureau approves access to confidential Census Bureau data in furtherance of a Title 13 purpose. SSS individuals are subject to same legal penalties for violation of confidentiality as employees.

Spectral graphs are diagnostic graphs that indicate the presence of seasonal or trading day effects. Visually significant peaks at the marked seasonal and/or trading day frequencies usually indicate the presence of these effects, in some cases as residual effects after an adjustment that is not fully successful for the span of data from which the spectrum is calculated. Spectral graphs are available for the prior-adjusted series (or original series if specified), regARIMA model residuals, seasonally adjusted series, and modified irregular.

Split panel tests refer to controlled experimental testing of questionnaire variants or data collection modes to determine which one is "better" or to measure differences between them.

Stakeholders include Congress, federal agencies, sponsors, state and local government officials, advisory committees, trade associations, or organizations that fund data programs, use the data, or are affected by the results of the data programs.

The *standard deviation* is the square root of the variance and measures the spread or dispersion around the mean of a data set.

The *standard error* is a measure of the variability of an estimate due to sampling.

The *Standard Occupational Classification System (SOC)* is used to classify workers into occupational categories for the purpose of collecting, calculating, or disseminating data (for more information, see www.bls.gov/soc/).

Statistical attribute matching consists of comparing two records, determining if they refer to "similar" entities (but not necessarily the same entity), and augmenting data from one record to the other.

Statistical inference is inference about a population from a random or representative sample drawn from it. It includes point estimation, interval estimation, and statistical significance testing.

A *statistical model* consists of a series of assumptions about a data generating process that explicitly involve probability distributions and functions on those distributions, in order to construct an estimate or a projection of one or more phenomena.

Statistical purposes refer to the description, estimation, or analysis of the characteristics of groups without identifying the individuals or organizations that compose such groups.

Statistical significance is attained when a statistical procedure applied to a set of observations yields a *p*-value that exceeds the level of probability at which it is agreed that the null hypothesis will be rejected.

Strata are created by partitioning the frame and are generally defined to include relatively homogeneous units within strata.

Stratification involves dividing the sampling frames into subsets (called strata) prior to the selection of a sample for statistical efficiency, for production of estimates by stratum, or for operational convenience. Stratification is done such that each stratum contains units that are relatively homogeneous with respect to variables that are believed to be highly correlated with the information requested in the survey.

Stratified sampling is a sampling procedure in which the population is divided into homogeneous subgroups or strata and the selection of samples is done independently in each stratum.

Sufficient data is determined for a survey by whether the respondent completes enough items for the case to be considered a completed response.

Supplemental reinterview allows the regional offices to select any field representative (FR) with an original interview assignment for reinterview. All assigned cases that are not selected for reinterview are available as inactive supplemental reinterview cases. The regional office may place a field representative in supplemental reinterview for various reasons: the FR was not selected for reinterview; the FR was hired during the assignment period; or the regional office needs to reinterview additional cases to investigate the FR for suspected falsification.

Swapping is a disclosure limitation technique that involves selecting a sample of records, finding a match in the database on a set of predetermined variables, and swapping all other variables.

Synthetic data are microdata records created to improve data utility while preventing disclosure of confidential respondent information. Synthetic data is created by statistically modeling original data and then using those models to generate new data values that reproduce the original data's statistical properties. Users are unable to identify the information of the entities that provided the original data.

Systematic sampling is a method of sample selection in which the sampling frame is listed in some order and every kth element is selected for the sample, beginning from a random start between 1 and k.

A *systems test* is used to test the data collection instrument along with the data management systems.

The *target population* is the complete collection of observations under study. For example, in a presidential poll taken to determine who people will vote for, the target population might be all persons who are registered to vote. The sampled population might be all registered voters who can be reached by telephone.

A *Taylor series* is a representation of a function as an infinite sum of polynomial terms calculated from the values of its derivatives at a single point.

The *Taylor series method for variance estimation* is used to estimate variances for non-linear estimators such as ratio estimators. If the sample size is large enough so that estimator can be closely approximated by the first order (linear) terms in the Taylor series, then the variances can be approximated by using variance methods appropriate for linear statistics.

Testing is a process used to ensure that methods, systems or other components function as intended.

A *time series* is a sequence of data values obtained over a period of time, usually at uniform intervals.

Timeliness of information reflects the length of time between the information's availability and the event or phenomenon it describes.

Top-coding is a disclosure limitation technique that involves limiting the maximum value of a variable allowed on the file to prevent disclosure of individuals or other units with extreme values in a distribution.

Topologically Integrated Geographic Encoding and Referencing (TIGER) See definition for Master Address File (MAF)/Topologically Integrated Geographic Encoding and Referencing (TIGER).

A *total quantity response rate* is the proportion of the estimated (weighted) total (T) of data item t reported by tabulation units in the sample or from sources determined to be equivalent-quality-to-reported data (expressed as a percentage).

Touch-tone data entry (TDE) is a data collection method that uses an electronic instrument to collect and capture data by telephone.

Transparency refers to providing documentation about the assumptions, methods, and limitations of an information product to allow qualified third parties to reproduce the information, unless prevented by confidentiality or other legal constraints.

Truth decks are used to test imputation methods by comparing the imputed values to the original values for the items flagged as missing. The truth deck originates as a file of true responses. Certain responses are then blanked in a manner that reflects the probable nonresponse in the sample. The truth deck is then run through the imputation process in order to evaluate the accuracy of the imputed values.

Tukey's method is a single-step multiple comparison procedure and statistical test generally used in conjunction with an ANOVA to find which means are significantly different from one another. Named after John Tukey, it compares all possible pairs of means, and is based on a studentized range distribution q (this distribution is similar to the distribution of t from the t-test).

Unduplication involves the process of deleting units that are erroneously in the frame more than once to correct for overcoverage.

Unit nonresponse occurs when a sampled unit fails to respond or a sampled unit response does not meet a minimum threshold and is classified as not having responded at all.

Usability testing in surveys is the process whereby a group of representative users are asked to interact and perform tasks with survey materials (e.g., computer-assisted forms) to determine if the intended users can carry out planned tasks efficiently, effectively, and satisfactorily.

A ***user interface*** is the aspects of a computer system or program that can be seen (or heard or otherwise perceived) by the human user, and the commands and mechanisms the user uses to control its operation and input data.

Users are organizations, agencies, the public, or any others expected to use the information products. Census Bureau employees, contractors, and other Special Sworn Status individuals affiliated with the Census Bureau are **internal users**. Users outside of the Census Bureau, including Congress, federal agencies, sponsors, other Special Sworn Status individuals, and the public, are **external users**.

Utility refers to the usefulness of the information for its intended users.

Variance is a measurement of the error associated with nonobservation, that is, the error that occurs because all members of the frame population are not measured. The measurement is the average of the squared differences between data points and the mean.

Version Control is the establishment and maintenance of baselines and the identification of changes to baselines that make it possible to return to the previous baseline. A baseline, in the context of documentation, is a document that has been formally reviewed and agreed on.

Weights are values associated with each sample unit that are intended to account for probabilities of selection for each unit and other errors such as nonresponse and frame undercoverage so that estimates using the weights represent the entire population. A weight can be viewed as an estimate of the number of units in the population that the sampled unit represents.

Working papers are information products that are prepared by Census Bureau employees (or contractors), but the Census Bureau does not necessarily affirm their content. They include technical papers or reports, division reports, research reports, and similar documents that discuss analyses of subject matter topics or methodological, statistical, technical or operational issues. The Census Bureau releases working papers to the public, generally on the Census Bureau's Web site. Working papers must include a disclaimer, unless the Associate Director responsible for the program determines that a disclaimer is not appropriate.

Chemical, Biological and Radiological

CHEMICAL TERMS

Acetylcholinesterase An enzyme that hydrolyzes the neurotransmitter acetylcholine. The action of this enzyme is inhibited by nerve agents.

Aerosol Fine liquid or solid particles suspended in a gas (e.g., fog or smoke).

Atropine A compound used as an antidote for nerve agents.

Casualty (toxic) agents Produce incapacitation, serious injury, or death, and can be used to incapacitate or kill victims. They are the blister, blood, choking, and nerve agents.

- *Blister agents* Substances that cause blistering of the skin. Exposure is through liquid or vapor contact with any exposed tissue (eyes, skin, lungs). Examples are distilled mustard (HD), nitrogen mustard (HN), lewisite (L), mustard/lewisite (HL), and phenodichloroarsine (PD).
- *Blood agents* Substances that injure a person by interfering with cell respiration (the exchange of oxygen and carbon dioxide between blood and tissues). Examples are arsine (SA), cyanogens chloride (CK), hydrogen chloride (HCl), and hydrogen cyanide (AC).
- *Choking/lung/pulmonary agents* Substances that cause physical injury to the lungs. Exposure is through inhalation. In extreme cases, membranes swell and lungs become filled with liquid. Death results from lack of oxygen; hence, the victim is "choked." Examples are chlorine (CL), diphosgene (DP), cyanide (KCN), nitrogen oxide (NO), perfluororisobutylene (PHIB), phosgene (CG), red phosphorous (RP), sulfur trioxide-chlorosulfonic acid (FS), Teflon and PHIB, titanium tetrachloride (FM), and zinc oxide (HC).
- *Nerve agents* Substances that interfere with the central nervous system. Exposure is primarily through contact with the liquid (skin and eyes) and secondarily through inhalation of the vapor. Three distinct symptoms associated with nerve agents are pin-point pupils, an extreme headache, and severe tightness in the chest. See also G-series and V-series nerve agents.

Chemical agents Substances that are intended for use in military operations to kill, seriously injure, or incapacitate people through its physiological effects. Excluded from consideration are riot control agents, and smoke and flame materials. The agent may appear as a vapor, aerosol, or liquid; it can be either a casualty/toxic agent or an incapacitating agent.

Cutaneous Pertaining to the skin.

Decontamination The process of making any person, object, or area safe by absorbing, destroying, neutralizing, making harmless, or removing the hazardous material.

G-series nerve agents Chemical agents of moderate to high toxicity developed in the 1930s. Examples are tabun (GA), sarin (GB), soman (GD), phosphonofluoridic acid, ethyl-, 1-methylethyl ester (GE), and cyclohexyl sarin (GF).

Incapacitating agents Produce temporary physiological and/or mental effects via action on the central nervous system. Effects may persist for hours or days, but victims usually do not require medical treatment; however, such treatment speeds recovery.

- *Vomiting agents* Produce nausea and vomiting effects; can also cause coughing, sneezing, pain in the nose and throat, nasal discharge, and tears. Examples are adamsite (DM), diphenylchloroarsine (DA), and diphenylcyanoarsine (DC).
- *Tear (riot control) agents* Produce irritating or disabling effects that rapidly disappear within minutes after exposure ceases. Examples are bromobenzylcyanide (CA), chloroacetophenone (CN or commercially known as Mace), chloropicrin (PS), CNB (CN in benzene and carbon tetrachloride), CNC (CN in chloroform), CNS (CN and chloropicrin in chloroform, CR (dibenz-(b,f)-1,4-oxazepine, a tear gas), CS (tear gas), and Capsaicin (pepper spray).
- *Central nervous system depressants* Compounds that have the predominant effect of depressing or blocking the activity of the central nervous system. The primary mental effects include the disruption of the ability to think, sedation, and lack of motivation.

- **Central nervous system stimulants** Compounds that have the predominant effect of flooding the brain with too much information. The primary mental effect is loss of concentration, causing indecisiveness and the inability to act in a sustained, purposeful manner. Examples of the depressants and stimulants include agent 15 (suspected Iraqi BZ), BZ (3-quinulidinyle benzilate), cannibiods, fentanyls, LSD (lysergic acid diethylamide), and phenothiazines.

Industrial agents Chemicals developed or manufactured for use in industrial operations or research by industry, government, or academia. These chemicals are not primarily manufactured for the specific purpose of producing human casualties or rendering equipment, facilities, or areas dangerous for use by man. Hydrogen cyanide, cyanogen chloride, phosgene, chloropicrin, and many herbicides and pesticides are industrial chemicals that also can be chemical agents.

Liquid agents Chemical agents that appear to be an oily film or droplets. The color ranges from clear to brownish amber.

Nonpersistent agents Agents that, upon release, lose the ability to cause casualties after 10 to 15 minutes. They have a high evaporation rate and are lighter than air and will disperse rapidly. They are considered to be short-term hazards; however, in small unventilated areas, these agents will be more persistent.

Organophosphorous compound A compound containing the elements phosphorus and carbon, whose physiological effects include inhibition of acetylcholinesterase. Many pesticides (malathione and parathion) and virtually all nerve agents are organophosphorous compounds.

Percutaneous agents Agents that are able to be absorbed by the body through the skin.

Persistent agents Agents that, upon release, retain their casualty-producing effects for an extended period of time, usually anywhere from 30 minutes to several days. A persistent agent usually has a low evaporation rate and its vapor is heavier than air. Therefore, its vapor cloud tends to hug the ground. They are considered to be long-term hazards. Although inhalation hazards are still a concern, extreme caution should be taken to avoid skin contact as well.

Protection Any means by which an individual protects his or her body. Measures include masks, self-contained breathing apparatuses, clothing, structures such as buildings, and vehicles.

V-series nerve agents Chemical agents of moderate to high toxicity developed in the 1950s. They are generally persistent. Examples are VE (phosphonothioic acid, ethyl-, S-(diethylamino)ethyl] O-ethylester), VG (phosphorothioic acid, S-[2-(diethylamino)ethyl] O, O-diethyl ester), VM (phosphonothioic acid, methyl-, S-[2-(diethylamino) ethyl] O-ethyl ester), VS (phosphonothioic acid, ethyl, S-[2-bis(1-methylethyl)amino] ethyl O-ethyl ester), and VX (phosphonothioic acid, methyl-, S-[2-[bis(1-methylethyl)amino]ethyl] O-ethyl ester).

Vapor agents A gaseous form of a chemical agent. If heavier than air, the cloud will be close to the ground. If lighter than air, the cloud will rise and disperse more quickly.

Volatility A measure of how readily a substance will vaporize.

BIOLOGICAL TERMS

Aerosol Fine liquid or solid particles suspended in a gas (e.g., fog or smoke).

Antibiotic A substance that inhibits the growth of or kills microorganisms.

Antisera The liquid part of blood containing antibodies that react against disease-causing agents such as those used in biological warfare.

Bacteria Single-celled organisms that multiply by cell division and that can cause disease in humans, plants, or animals.

Biochemicals The chemicals that make up or are produced by living things.

Biological warfare The intentional use of biological agents as weapons to kill or injure humans, animals, or plants, or to damage equipment.

Biological warfare agents Living organisms or the materials derived from them that cause disease in or harm to humans, animals, or plants, or cause deterioration of material. Biological agents may be used as liquid droplets, aerosols, or dry powders.

Bioregulators Biochemicals that regulate bodily functions. Bioregulators that are produced by the body are termed "endogenous." Some of these same bioregulators can be chemically synthesized.

Causative agents The organism or toxin that is responsible for causing a specific disease or harmful effect.

Contagious Capable of being transmitted from one person to another.

Culture A population of microorganisms grown in a medium.

Decontamination The process of making people, objects, or areas safe by absorbing, destroying, neutralizing, making harmless, or removing the hazardous material.

Fungi Any of a group of plants mainly characterized by the absence of chlorophyll, the green-colored compound found in other plants. Fungi range from microscopic single-celled plants (such as molds and mildews) to large plants (such as mushrooms).

Host An animal or plant that harbors or nourishes another organism.

Incapacitating agents Agents that produce physical or psychological effects, or both, that may persist for hours or days after exposure, rendering victims incapable of performing normal physical and mental tasks.

Infectious agents Biological agents capable of causing disease in a susceptible host.

Infectivity (1) The ability of an organism to spread. (2) The number of organisms required to cause an infection to secondary hosts. (3) The capability of an organism to spread out from the site of infection and cause disease in the host organism. Infectivity also can be viewed as the number of organisms required to cause an infection.

Line-source delivery system A delivery system in which the biological agent is dispersed from a moving ground or air vehicle in a line perpendicular to the direction of the prevailing wind. (See also "point-source delivery system.")

Microorganism Any organism, such as bacteria, viruses, and some fungi, that can be seen only with a microscope.

Mycotoxin A toxin produced by fungi.

Nebulizer A device for producing a fine spray or aerosol.

Organism Any individual living thing, whether animal or plant.

Parasite Any organism that lives in or on another organism without providing benefit in return.

Pathogen Any organism (usually living), such as bacteria, fungi, and viruses, capable of producing serious disease or death.

Pathogenic agents Biological agents capable of causing serious disease.

Point-source delivery system A delivery system in which the biological agent is dispersed from a stationary position. This delivery method results in coverage over a smaller area than with the line-source system. See also line-source delivery system.

Route of exposure (entry) The path by which a person comes into contact with an agent or organism (e.g., through breathing, digestion, or skin contact).

Single-cell protein Protein-rich material obtained from cultured algae, fungi, protein, and bacteria, and often used as food or animal feed.

Spore A reproductive form some microorganisms can take to become resistant to environmental conditions, such as extreme heat or cold, while in a "resting stage."

Toxicity A measure of the harmful effect produced by a given amount of a toxin on a living organism. The relative toxicity of an agent can be expressed in milligrams of toxin needed per kilogram of body weight to kill experimental animals.

Toxins Poisonous substances produced by living organisms.

Vaccine A preparation of killed or weakened microorganism products used to artificially induce immunity against a disease.

Vector An agent, such as an insect or rat, capable of transferring a pathogen from one organism to another.

Venom A poison produced in the glands of some animals (e.g., snakes, scorpions, or bees).

Virus An infectious microorganism that exists as a particle rather than as a complete cell. Particle sizes range from 20 to 400 nanometers (one-billionth of a meter). Viruses are not capable of reproducing outside of a host cell.

RADIOLOGICAL TERMS

Acute radiation syndrome Consists of three levels of effects: hernatopoletic (blood cells, most sensitive); gastrointestinal (GI cells, very sensitive); and central nervous system (brain/muscle cells, insensitive). The initial signs and symptoms are nausea, vomiting, fatigue, and loss of appetite. Below about 200 rems, these symptoms may be the only indication of radiation exposure.

Alpha particles Alpha particles have a very short range in air and a very low ability to penetrate other materials, but also have a strong ability to ionize materials. Alpha particles are unable to penetrate even the thin layer of dead cells of human skin and consequently are not an external radiation hazard. Alpha-emitting nuclides inside the body as a result of inhalation or ingestion are a considerable internal radiation hazard.

Beta particles High-energy electrons emitted from the nucleus of an atom during radioactive decay. They normally can be stopped by the skin or a very thin sheet of metal.

Cesium-137 (Cs-137) A strong gamma ray source and can contaminate property, entailing extensive cleanup. It is commonly used in industrial measurement gauges and for irradiation of material. Its half-life is 30.2 years.

Cobalt-60 (Co-60) A strong gamma ray source, and is extensively used as a radiotherapeutic for treating cancer, food and material irradiation, gamma radiography, and industrial measurement gauges. Its half-life is 5.27 years.

Curie (Ci) A unit of radioactive decay rate defined as 3.7×10^{10} disintegrations per second.

Decay The process by which an unstable element is changed to another isotope or another element by the spontaneous emission of radiation from its nucleus. This process can be measured by using radiation detectors such as Geiger counters.

Decontamination The process of making people, objects, or areas safe by absorbing, destroying, neutralizing, making harmless, or removing the hazardous material.

Dose A general term for the amount of radiation absorbed over a period of time.

Dosimeter A portable instrument for measuring and registering the total accumulated dose to ionizing radiation.

Gamma ray A high-energy photon emitted from the nucleus of atoms; similar to an x-ray. It can penetrate deeply into body tissue and many materials. Cobalt-60 and Cesium-137 are both strong gamma-emitters. Shielding against gamma radiation requires thick layers of dense materials, such as lead. Gamma rays are potentially lethal to humans.

Half-life The amount of time needed for half of the atoms of a radioactive material to decay.

Highly enriched uranium (HEU) Uranium that is enriched to above 20 percent.Uranium-235 (U-235). Weapons-grade HEU is enriched to above 90 percent in U-235.

Ionize To split off one or more electrons from an atom, thus leaving it with a positive electric charge. The electrons usually attach to one of the atoms or molecules, giving them a negative charge.

Iridium-192 A gamma ray emitting radioisotope used for gamma radiography. Its half-life is 73.83 days.

Isotope A specific element always has the same number of protons in the nucleus. That same element may, however, appear in forms that have different numbers of neutrons in the nucleus. These different forms are referred to as "isotopes" of the element; for example, deuterium (2H) and tritium (3H) are isotopes of ordinary hydrogen (H).

Lethal dose (50/30) The dose of radiation expected to cause death within 30 days to 50 percent of those exposed without medical treatment. The generally accepted range is from 400-500 rem received over a short period of time.

Nuclear reactor A device in which a controlled, self-sustaining nuclear chain reaction can be maintained with the use of cooling to remove generated heat.

Plutonium-239 (Pu-239) A metallic element used for nuclear weapons. Its half-life is 24,110 years.

Rad A unit of absorbed dose of radiation defined as deposition of 100 ergs of energy per gram of tissue. A rad amounts to approximately one ionization per cubic micron.

Radiation High energy alpha or beta particles or gamma rays that are emitted by an atom as the substance undergoes radioactive decay.

Radiation sickness Symptoms resulting from excessive exposure to radiation of the body.

Radioactive waste Disposable, radioactive materials resulting from nuclear operations. Wastes are generally classified into two categories, high-level and low-level.

Radiological Dispersal Device (RDD) A device (weapon or equipment), other than a nuclear explosive device, designed to disseminate radioactive material in order to cause destruction, damage, or injury by means of the radiation produced by the decay of such material.

Radioluminescence The luminescence produced by particles emitted during radioactive decay.

Roentgen Equivalent Man (REM or rem) A unit of absorbed dose that takes into account the relative effectiveness of radiation that harms human health.

Shielding Materials (lead, concrete, etc.) used to block or attenuate radiation for protection of equipment, materials, or people.

Special Nuclear Material (SNM) Plutonium and uranium enriched in the isotopes Uranium-233 or Uranium-235.

Uranium 235 (U-235) Naturally occurring U-235 is found at 0.72 percent enrichment. U-235 is used as a reactor fuel or for weapons; however, weapons typically use U-235 enriched to 90 percent. Its half-life is 7.04×10^8 years.

X-ray An invisible, highly penetrating electromagnetic radiation of much shorter wavelength (higher frequency) than visible light. Very similar to gamma rays.

Children

CHILD ABUSE AND NEGLECT

Adoption services Services or activities provided to assist in bringing about the adoption of a child.

Adoptive parent A person with the legal relation of parent to a child not related by birth, with the same mutual rights and obligations that exist between children and their birth parents.

Age Age calculated in years at the time of the report of abuse or neglect, or as of December 31 of the reporting year.

Alcohol abuse Compulsive use of alcohol that is not of a temporary nature. Applies to infants addicted at birth, or who are victims of Fetal Alcohol Syndrome, or who may suffer other disabilities due to the use of alcohol during pregnancy.

Alleged perpetrator report source An individual who reports an alleged incident of child abuse or neglect in which he/she caused or knowingly allowed the maltreatment of a child.

Alleged victim Child about whom a report regarding maltreatment has been made to a CPS agency.

Alleged victim report source A child who alleges to have been a victim of child maltreatment and who makes a report of the allegation.

American Indian/Alaskan Native A person having racial origins in any of the original peoples of North and South America (including Central America), and who maintains tribal or community affiliation.

Anonymous or unknown report source An individual who reports a suspected incident of child maltreatment without identifying himself or herself; or the type of reporter is unknown.

Asian A person having racial origins in any of the original peoples of the Far East, Southeast Asia, or the Indian sub-continent, including, for example, Cambodia, China, Guam, India, Japan, Korea, Malaysia, Pakistan, the Philippine Islands, Thailand, and Vietnam.

Assessment A process by which the CPS agency determines whether the child and/or other persons involved in the report of alleged maltreatment is in need of services.

Behavior problem Behavior of the child in the school and/or community that adversely affects socialization, learning, growth, and moral development. May include adjudicated or non-adjudicated behavior problems. Includes running away from home or a placement.

Biological parent The birth mother or father of the child rather than the adoptive or foster parent or the stepparent.

Black/African-American A person whose ancestry is any of the black racial groups of Africa.

Caretaker A person responsible for the care and supervision of the child who was reported.

Case management services Activities for the arrangement, coordination, and monitoring of services to meet the needs of children and their families.

Child A person less than 18 years of age or considered to be a minor under State law.

Child date of birth The month, day and year of the child's birth. If the child is abandoned or the date of birth is otherwise unknown, approximate date of birth.

Child day care provider A person with a temporary caretaker responsibility for the child who is not related to the child, such as a day care center staff member, a family day care provider, or a baby-sitter. Does not include persons with legal custody or guardianship of the child.

Child ID A unique identification assigned to each child. This identification is not the State child identification but is an encrypted identification assigned by the State for the purposes of the NCANDS data collection.

Child victim A child for whom an incident of abuse or neglect has been substantiated or indicated by an investigation or assessment. A State may include some children with other dispositions as victims.

Children/families in need of services Disposition by a child welfare agency after an assessment; children or families with this assessment are generally not considered to be victims of maltreatment.

Closed without a finding Disposition that does not conclude with a specific finding because the investigation could not be completed for such reasons as the family moved out of the jurisdiction; the family could not be located; or necessary diagnostic or other reports were not received within required time limits.

Counseling services Beneficial activities that apply the therapeutic processes to personal, family, situational or occupational problems in order to bring about a positive resolution of the problem or improved individual or family functioning or circumstances.

Court action Legal action initiated by a representative of the CPS agency on behalf of the child. This includes, for instance, authorization to place the child, filing for temporary custody, dependency, or termination of parental rights. It does not include criminal proceedings against a perpetrator.

Court-appointed representative A person required to be appointed by the court to represent a child in a neglect or abuse proceeding. May be an attorney or a court-appointed special advocate (or both) and is often referred to as a guardian ad litem. Makes recommendations to the court concerning the best interests of the child.

County of report The geopolitical substate jurisdiction from which the report of child maltreatment originated. The unique identification number assigned to the county under the Federal Information Processing Standards (FIPS) guidelines is preferred.

County of residence The geopolitical substate jurisdiction in which the child subject of a report was residing at the time of the report. The unique identification number assigned to the county under the Federal Information Processing Standards (FIPS) guidelines is preferred.

Day care services Beneficial activities provided to a child or children in a setting that meets applicable standards of State and local law, in a center or in a home, for a portion of a 24-hour day.

Domestic violence Incidents of inter-spousal physical or emotional abuse perpetrated by one of the spouses or parent figures upon the other spouse or parent figure in the child victim's home environment.

Drug abuse Compulsive use of drugs that is not of a temporary nature. Applies to infants addicted at birth.

Education and training services Beneficial activities provided to improve knowledge or daily living skills and to enhance cultural opportunities.

Education personnel An employee of a public or private educational institution or program; includes teachers, teacher assistants, administrators and others directly associated with the delivery of educational services.

Emotionally disturbed A condition, which must be clinically diagnosed, exhibiting one or more of the following characteristics over a long period of time and to a marked degree an inability to build or maintain satisfactory interpersonal relationships; inappropriate types of behavior or feelings under normal circumstances; a general pervasive mood of unhappiness or depression; or a tendency to develop physical symptoms or fears associated with personal problems. Includes persons who are schizophrenic or autistic.

Employment services Beneficial activities provided to assist individuals in securing employment or acquiring learning skills that promote opportunities for employment.

Family A group of two or more persons related by birth, marriage, adoption, or emotional ties.

Family planning services Educational, comprehensive medical or social activities which enable individuals, including minors, to determine freely the number and spacing of their children and to select the means by which this may be achieved.

Family preservation services Activities designed to protect children from harm and to assist families at risk or in crisis, including services to prevent placement, to support the reunification of children with their families, or to support the continued placement of children in adoptive homes or other permanent living arrangements.

Family support services Community-based preventative activities designed to alleviate stress and promote parental competencies and behaviors that will increase the ability of families to successfully nurture their children, enable families to use other resources and opportunities available in the community, and create supportive networks to enhance child-rearing abilities of parents.

Financial problem A risk factor related to the family's inability to provide sufficient financial resources to meet minimum needs.

Foster care Twenty-four-hour substitute care for children placed away from their parents or guardians and for whom the State agency has placement and care responsibility. This includes, but is not limited to, family foster homes, foster homes of relatives, group homes, emergency shelters, residential facilities, child care institutions, and pre-adoptive homes regardless of whether the facility is licensed and whether payments are made by the State or local agency for the care of the child, or whether there is Federal matching of any payments made.

Foster care services Beneficial activities associated with 24-hour substitute care for children placed away from their parents or guardians and for whom the State agency has placement and care responsibility.

Foster parent Individual licensed to provide a home for orphaned, abused, neglected, delinquent or disabled children, usually with the approval of the government or a social service agency. May be a relative or a non-relative.

Friend A non-relative acquainted with the child, the parent, or caretaker including landlords, clergy, or youth group workers (e.g., Scouts, Little League coaches), etc.

Health-related and home health services Activities provided to attain and maintain a favorable condition of health.

Hispanic or Latino A Mexican, Puerto Rican, Cuban, Central or South American person, or person of other Spanish cultural origin, regardless of race. Whether a person is Hispanic is determined by how others define him or by how he defines himself.

Home-based services In-home activities provided to individuals or families to assist with household or personal care and improve or maintain adequate family well-being. Includes homemaker, chore, home maintenance, and household management services.

Housing services Beneficial activities designed to assist individuals or families in locating, obtaining or retaining suitable housing.

Inadequate housing A risk factor related to substandard, overcrowded, or unsafe housing conditions, including homelessness.

Independent and transitional living services Beneficial activities designed to help older youth in foster care or homeless youth make the transition to independent living.

Indicated or reason to suspect An investigation disposition that concludes that maltreatment cannot be substantiated under State law or policy, but there is reason to suspect that the child may have been maltreated or was at risk of maltreatment. This is applicable only to States that distinguish between substantiated and indicated dispositions.

Information and referral services Resources or activities designed to provide facts about services made available by public and private providers, after a brief assessment of client needs (but not a diagnosis and evaluation) to facilitate appropriate referral to these community resources.

Initial investigation Face-to-face contact with the alleged victim, when this is appropriate, or contact with another person who can provide information essential to the disposition of the investigation or assessment.

Intentionally false Unsubstantiated investigation disposition about which it has been concluded that the person reporting the alleged incident of maltreatment knew that the allegation was false.

Investigation The gathering and assessment of objective information to determine if a child has been or is at risk of being maltreated. Generally includes face-to-face contact with the victim and results in a disposition as to whether the alleged report is substantiated or not.

Investigation disposition A determination made by a social service agency that evidence is or is not sufficient under State law to conclude that maltreatment occurred.

Juvenile court petition A legal document filed with the court of original jurisdiction overseeing matters affecting children requesting that the court take action regarding the child's status as a result of an investigation; usually a petition requesting the child be declared a dependent or delinquent child, or that the child be placed in an out-of-home setting.

Learning disability A disorder in basic psychological processes involved in understanding or using language, spoken or written, that may manifest itself in an imperfect ability to listen, think, speak, read, write, spell or use mathematical calculations. The term includes conditions such as perceptual disability, brain injury, minimal brain dysfunction, dyslexia, and developmental aphasia.

Legal, law enforcement, or criminal justice personnel A person employed by a local, State, tribal, or Federal justice agency including law enforcement, courts, district attorney's office, probation or other community corrections agency, and correctional facilities.

Legal services Beneficial activities provided by a lawyer, or other person(s) under the supervision of a lawyer, to assist individuals in seeking or obtaining legal help in civil matters such as housing, divorce, child support, guardianship, paternity and legal separation.

Living arrangement The environment, e.g., family or foster care, in which a child was residing at the time of a report.

Maltreatment An act or failure to act by a parent, caretaker, or other person as defined under State law which results in physical abuse, neglect, medical neglect, sexual abuse, emotional abuse, or an act or failure to act which presents an imminent risk of serious harm to a child.

Maltreatment death Death of a child as a result of abuse or neglect, because either (a) an injury resulting from the abuse or neglect was the cause of death; or (b) abuse and/or neglect were contributing factors to the cause of death.

Maltreatment disposition level The disposition of an alleged maltreatment. The disposition level may be substantiated, indicated (reason to suspect), unsubstantiated, closed (no finding), other, or unknown.

Maltreatment type A particular form of child maltreatment determined by investigation to be substantiated or indicated under State law. Types include physical abuse, neglect or deprivation of necessities, sexual abuse, psychological or emotional maltreatment, and other forms included in State law.

Medical neglect A type of maltreatment caused by failure by the caretaker to provide for the appropriate health care of the child although financially able to do so, or offered financial or other means to do so.

Medical personnel A person employed by a medical facility or practice, including physicians, physician assistants, nurses, emergency medical technicians, dentists, dental assistants and technicians, chiropractors and coroners.

Mental health personnel A person employed by a mental health facility or practice, including psychologists, psychiatrists, therapists, etc.

Mental health services Beneficial activities which aim to overcome issues involving emotional disturbance or maladaptive behavior adversely affecting socialization, learning, or development. Usually provided by public or private mental health agencies and includes both residential and non-residential activities.

Mental retardation Significantly subaverage general cognitive and motor functioning existing concurrently with deficits in adaptive behavior that adversely affect socialization and learning; must be clinically diagnosed.

Military family member A person who is the legal dependent of an individual on active duty in the Armed Services of the United States.

Military member A person on active duty in the Armed Services of the United States, including Army, Navy, Air Force, or Marine Corps; excludes Inactive Reserve, National Guard, and retired.

Native Hawaiian or other Pacific Islander A person having racial origins in any of the original peoples of Hawaii, Guam, Samoa, or other Pacific Islands.

Neglect or deprivation of necessities A type of maltreatment that refers to the failure by the caretaker to provide needed, age-appropriate care although financially able to do so, or offered financial or other means to do so.

Neighbor A person living in close geographical proximity to the child or family.

Non-caretaker A person who is not responsible for the care and supervision of the child, including school personnel, friends, neighbors, etc.

Not substantiated Investigation disposition that determines that there is not sufficient evidence under State law or policy to conclude that the child has been maltreated or is at risk of being maltreated.

Notifications Mandated or courtesy contacting of other agencies with overlapping or potentially overlapping jurisdiction concerning a report of child maltreatment.

Other The State coding for this field is something other than the codes in the NCANDS record layout.

Out-of-court contact Contact, which is not part of the actual judicial hearing, between the court-appointed representative and the child victim. Such contacts enable the court-appointed representative to obtain a first-hand understanding of the situation and needs of the child victim, and to make recommendations to the court concerning the best interests of the child.

Parent The birth mother/father, adoptive mother/father, or stepmother/father of the child.

Perpetrator The person who has been determined to have caused or knowingly allowed the maltreatment of the child.

Perpetrator age at report Age of an individual determined to have caused or knowingly allowed the maltreatment of a child. Age is calculated in years at the time of the report of child maltreatment.

Perpetrator ID A unique identification assigned to each perpetrator. This identification is not the actual State perpetrator identification but is an encrypted identification assigned by the State for purposes of the NCANDS data collection.

Perpetrator maltreatment Type of substantiated maltreatment a specific perpetrator was involved in the on the record for a specific child.

Perpetrator prior abuser Perpetrator with previous substantiated or indicated incidents of child maltreatment.

Perpetrator relationship Primary role of the perpetrator with a child victim of maltreatment.

Petition date The month, day, and year that a juvenile court petition was filed.

Physical abuse Type of maltreatment that refers to physical acts that caused or could have caused physical injury to the child.

Physically disabled Having a physical condition that adversely affects the day-to-day motor functioning, such as cerebral palsy, spina bifida, multiple sclerosis, orthopedic impairments, and other physical disabilities.

Post-investigation services Beneficial activities provided or arranged by the child protective services agency, social services agency, and/or the child welfare agency for the child/family as a result of needs discovered during the course of the investigation. Include such services as Family Preservation, Family Support, and foster care provided as a result of the report of alleged child maltreatment, or offered prior to the report and continued after the disposition of the investigation. Post-investigation services are delivered within the first 90 days after the disposition of the report.

Pregnancy and parenting services for young parents Beneficial activities for married or unmarried adolescent parents and their families to assist them in coping with social, emotional, and economic problems related to pregnancy and to plan for the future.

Preventive services Beneficial activities aimed at preventing child abuse and neglect. Such activities may be directed at specific populations identified as being at increased risk of becoming abusive and may be designed to increase the strength and stability of families, to increase parents' confidence and competence in their parenting abilities, and to afford children a stable and supportive environment. They include child abuse and neglect preventive services provided through Federal funds such as the Child Abuse and Neglect State Grant, the Community-Based Family Resource and Support Grant, the Promoting Safe and Stable Families Program (title IV-B, subpart 2), Maternal and Child Health Block Grant, Social Services Block Grant (Title XX), and State and local funds. Such activities do not include public awareness campaigns.

Prior victim A child victim with previous substantiated or indicated incidents of maltreatment.

Psychological or emotional maltreatment Type of maltreatment that refers to acts or omissions, other than physical abuse or sexual abuse, that caused, or could have caused, conduct, cognitive, affective, or other mental disorders. Includes emotional neglect, psychological abuse, mental injury, etc. Frequently occurs as verbal abuse or excessive demands on a child's performance and may cause the child to have a negative self-image and disturbed behavior.

Public assistance Any one or combination of the following welfare or social services programs: AFDC, General Assistance, Medicaid, SSI, Food Stamps, etc.

Race The primary taxonomic category of which the individual identifies himself or herself as a member, or of which the parent identifies the child as a member.

Receipt of report The log-in of a call to the agency from a reporter alleging child maltreatment.

Removal date The month, day, and year that the child was removed from the care and supervision of his parents or parental substitutes, during or as a result of an investigation by the child protective services or social services agency. If a child has been removed more than once, the removal date is the first removal in concert with the investigation.

Removed from the home The removal of the child from his/her normal place of residence to a substitute care setting by a CPS or social services agency.

Report Notification to the CPS agency of suspected child maltreatment; can include one or more children.

Report date The month, day, and year that the responsible agency was notified of the suspected child maltreatment.

Report disposition The conclusion reached by the responsible agency regarding the report of maltreatment pertaining to the child.

Report disposition date The month, day, and year that a decision was made by the child protective services agency or court regarding the disposition of a report or investigation of alleged child maltreatment.

Report ID A unique identification assigned to each report of child maltreatment. This identification is not the actual State report identification but is an encrypted identification assigned by the State for the purposes of the NCANDS data collection.

Report source The category or role of the person who makes a report of alleged maltreatment.

Reporting period The 12-month period for which data are submitted to the NCANDS; generally refers to the calendar year.

Residential facility staff An employee of a public or private group residential facility, including emergency shelters, group homes, and institutions.

Respite care services Beneficial activities involving temporary care of the child(ren) to provide relief to the caretaker. May involve care of the children outside of the caretaker's own home for a brief period of time, such as overnight or for a weekend. Not considered by the State to be foster care or other placement.

Response time with respect to the initial investigation The time from the log-in of a call to the agency from a reporter alleging child maltreatment to the face-to-face contact with the alleged victim, where this is appropriate, or to contact with another person who can provide information.

Response time with respect to the provision of services The time from the log-in of a call to the agency from a reporter alleging child maltreatment to the opening of a case for ongoing services.

Service date Date of the report disposition or a date decided by the State to be more appropriate. The service date for cases for which services were continued (or changed) as a result of the investigation disposition is the date of the most recent case opening prior to the receipt of the report.

Services Noninvestigative public or private beneficial activities provided or continued as a result of an investigation or assessment. In general, such activities occur within 90 days of the report.

Sex The gender of a person at the time of the report.

Sexual abuse A type of maltreatment that refers to the involvement of the child in sexual activity to provide sexual gratification or financial benefit to the perpetrator, including contacts for sexual purposes, molestation, statutory rape, prostitution, pornography, exposure, incest, or other sexually exploitative activities.

Social services personnel An employee of a public or private social services or social welfare agency, or other social worker or counselor who provides similar services.

Source of report Person who makes a report to the CPS agency alleging child maltreatment.

Special services-disabled Beneficial activities for persons with developmental or physical disabilities, or visual or auditory impairments, to maximize their potential, help alleviate the effects of physical, mental or emotional disabilities, and enable them to live in the least restrictive environment possible.

Special services-juvenile delinquent Beneficial activities for youth (and their families) who are, or who may become, involved with the juvenile justice system.

State/territory The U.S. Postal Service two-character abbreviation used to indicate the State/Territory.

Stepparent The husband or wife, by a subsequent marriage, of the child victim's mother or father.

Substance abuse services Beneficial activities designed to deter, reduce, or eliminate substance abuse or chemical dependency.

Substantiated A type of investigation disposition that concludes that the allegation of maltreatment or risk of maltreatment was supported or founded by State law or State policy. This is the highest level of finding by a State agency.

Substitute care provider A person providing out-of-home care to children, such as a foster parent or residential facility staff.

Transportation services Beneficial provision of or arrangement for travel, including travel costs of individuals, in order to access social services, or obtain medical care or employment.

Unknown The State collects data for this field, but the data for this particular report (or child) were not captured or are missing.

Visually or hearing impaired A clinically diagnosed handicapping condition related to a visual impairment or permanent or fluctuating hearing or speech impairment that may significantly affect functioning or development.

White A person of European, North African, or Middle Eastern origin.

CHILD SUPPORT

Administration for Children and Families. U.S. Department of Health and Human Services.

absent parent See noncustodial parent.

accrual The sum of child support payments that are due or overdue.

adjudication The entry of a judgment, decree, or order by a judge or other decision-maker such as a master, referee, or hearing officer based on the evidence submitted by the parties.

administrative process A statutory system granting authority to an executive agency (instead of courts or judges) to determine child support legal obligations, including paternity establishment, order establishment, enforcement, and modifications.

AFDC The nation's welfare program was replaced under the Personal Responsibility and Work Opportunity Reconciliation Act of 1996 (PRWORA) by the Temporary Assistance for Needy Families (TANF) block grant program.

affidavit A written statement signed under oath or by affirmation, which is usually notarized.

Aid to Families with Dependent Children Title IV-A of the Social Security Act. Cash and/or medical support paid from government funds to a parent or other approved guardian on behalf of children who do not have the financial support of one of their parents due to death, disability, or absence from the home.

alleged father A person who has been named as the father of a child born out of wedlock, but who has not been legally determined to be the father; also referred to as putative father.

arrearage The total unpaid child support obligation for past periods owed by a parent who is obligated to pay.

assessment Putting the child support case together to determine what child support services are appropriate. The first step in the child support enforcement process.

assignment of support rights As a condition of eligibility for public assistance (TANF), the custodial parent must agree to turn over to the State any right to child support, including arrearages, paid by the obligated parent in exchange for receipt of cash assistance or other benefits. The State may keep support paid, up to the amount of the support order or the amount of the assistance payment, whichever is less, for the period the child receives TANF to offset the cost of the assistance.

burden of proof The duty of a party to produce the greater weight of evidence on a point at issue.

case A collection of people associated with a particular support order, court hearing, and/or request for IV-D services. A case typically includes a custodial parent, a dependent or dependents, and a noncustodial parent and/or putative father. In addition to names and identifying information about its members, a case includes information such as wage data, court order details, and payment history.

case ID Unique ID number assigned to a case.

CCEJ See Court of Continuing Exclusive Jurisdiction.

central registry A centralized unit maintained by every jurisdiction responsible for receiving, distributing, and responding to inquiries on all incoming IV-D cases.

child support Financial resources contributed by noncustodial parents to provide the necessities of living (food, shelter, clothing, medical support) to their children.

Child Support Enforcement Amendments (1984) Required equal services for AFDC and non-AFDC families, mandatory practices, Federal incentives, and improved interstate enforcement.

Child Support Recovery Act (1992) Made it a Federal crime to fail to pay past-due child support obligation for a child living in another State.

Cost of Living Adjustment (COLA) Modification of the amount of a support obligation, based on the economy's increasing or decreasing cost of the necessities of life, such as food, shelter, and clothing.

complainant Person who seeks to initiate court proceedings against another person. In a civil case, the complainant is the plaintiff; in a criminal case, the complainant is the State.

complaint A formal written document filed in court whereby the person initiating the action provides the names the parties involved, the allegations, and the request for relief sought; the initial pleading, sometimes called the petition.

consent agreement A voluntary written admission of paternity or responsibility for support.

cooperation As a condition of TANF eligibility, the recipient is required to cooperate with the child support agency in identifying and locating the noncustodial parent, establishing paternity, and/or obtaining child support payments.

cooperative agreement An agreement between the child support agencies and local jurisdictions for the provision of certain child support enforcement services. This type of agreement sets out the responsibilities of the State agency and the local agencies under the contractual relationship.

Court of Continuing Exclusive Jurisdiction Defined in UIFSA policy, states that there is to be one and only one court which maintains exclusive jurisdiction over a case. CCEJ helps avoid the problem of support orders from multiple States that occurred before the passage of UIFSA. The CCEJ is the only court that can make decisions on a current support order and continues to have jurisdiction until another court takes it away.

court order A legally binding edict from a court of law by a magistrate, judge, or properly empowered administrative officer. A court order related to child support dictates issues such as how often, how much, or what kind of support a noncustodial parent (NCP) is to pay; how long he/she is to pay it; and whether an employer must withhold support from an NCP's wages.

CP See below.

custodial parent Parent who has primary care of the child(ren), which may include having legal custody of the child.

Custody Legal custody is a legally binding determination which establishes with whom a child should live. **Physical custody** is a physical possession of a child, regardless of the legal custody status. **Joint custody** occurs when two persons share legal and/or physical custody of the child. **Split custody** occurs when children from the same parents are in the legal, sole custody of different parents.

customer The people assisted in obtaining child support. The primary customers of child support enforcement agencies are the children in need of support. The secondary customers are the parents of these children.

default The failure of a defendant to file an answer or response or appear in a civil case within the required time frame after having been properly served with a summons and complaint.

default judgment A decision made by the court or administrative authority when the defendant fails to respond or appear.

defendant A person against whom a civil or criminal proceeding is begun

dependent child Any person who has not reached the age of emancipation or been legally declared emancipated.

disbursement The paying out of collected child support funds.

distribution The rules covering the priority order for allocating child support collections. Welfare reform legislation changes distribution priorities to provide that families leaving welfare receive priority in payment of arrears.

disposition The court's decision of what should be done about a dispute that has been brought to its attention (e.g., the disposition of the court action may be that child support is ordered).

due process The conduct of legal proceedings according to those rules and principles which have been established in our system of law for the enforcement and protection of private rights. It is a safeguard against unreasonable, arbitrary, and capricious decisions.

enforcement A means for obtaining payment of a child or medical support obligation. Enforcement methods include income withholding, State and Federal income tax refunds offset, and liens against real and personal property.

establishment of paternity See paternity establishment.

Family Support Act (1988) Increased emphasis on enforcement remedies and simplified procedures for establishing paternity. Required States to automate procedures.

federal financial participation Federal reimbursement to the State for a percentage of their administrative costs associated with child support enforcement.

Federal Income Tax Offset Program A program under the Federal Office of Child Support Enforcement which makes available to State child support enforcement agencies a means for securing the income tax refund of parents who have been certified as owing at least a specified minimum amount of child support. State IV-D agencies also operate State income tax refund offset programs.

Federal Parent Locator Service A computerized national location network operated by the Federal Office of Child Support Enforcement to help the States locate parents in order to obtain child support payments. FPLS obtains address and employer information from Federal agencies and the National Directory of New Hires.

FFP See federal financial participation.

foster care A situation in which a child is raised in household by someone other than his or her own parents.

FPLS Federal Parent Locator Service.

full faith and credit A doctrine under which a State must honor an order or judgment entered in another State.

garnishment A legal proceeding whereby a person's property, money, or credit, in the possession of or under the control of a third party person (garnishee) is withheld from the defendant and applied to the payment of the defendant's debt to the plaintiff.

genetic testing Scientific analysis of inherited factors (usually by blood or tissue test) of mother, child, and alleged father which can help prove or disprove that the man is the biological father of the child.

good cause A legal reason for which a TANF recipient is excused from cooperating with the child support enforcement process. Includes cases involving rape, incest, and potential for harm to the custodial parent or child from the noncustodial parent.

guidelines A standard method for calculating child support obligations based on the income of the parent(s) and other factors as determined by State law. The Family Support Act of 1988 requires States to use guidelines as the rebuttably correct amount of support for each family.

initiating jurisdiction In interstate cases, the State/county/court which sends a request for action to another jurisdiction. In review and adjustment cases, the State in which one of the parties requests the review.

income tax refund offset See Federal Income Tax Offset Program.

intake See assessment.

interstate Cases in which the dependent child and noncustodial parent live in different States, or where two or more States are involved in some case activity, such as enforcement.

IV-D agency A single and separate organizational unit in a State that has the responsibility for administering the State Plan for child support under Title IV-D of the Social Security Act.

judgment The official decision or finding of a judge or administrative agency hearing officer upon the respective rights and claims of the parties to an action; also known as a decree or order and may include the "findings of fact and conclusions of law."

judicial process The use of courts or tribunals in determining child support legal obligations, including paternity establishment, order establishment, enforcement, and modification of orders.

jurisdiction The legal authority which a court or administrative agency has over particular persons or property and over certain types of cases. The jurisdiction may be limited to the court's county, circuit, district, or State.

legal custody See custody.

legal father A man who is recognized by law as the male parent of another person.

lien An encumbrance on any real or personal property. Real estate liens (mortgages) are usually filed where the property exists. Personal property liens are either filed Statewide or in the county where the owner resides.

locate Finding or attempting to find a noncustodial or absent parent. Key data such as Social Security number, date of birth, residential address, and employer are collected in an attempt to locate the individual.

long arm statute A law which permits one State to claim jurisdiction over nonresident parties. There must be some meaningful connection between the person and the State in which the jurisdiction is exercised in order for it to be constitutional to reach beyond the court's normal jurisdictional border.

medical support Legal provision for payment of medical and dental bills or premiums which can be linked to a parent's access to medical insurance.

National Directory of New Hires Under PRWORA, all States are mandated to establish New Hire Reporting programs as a tool for locating child support obligors. All employers are required to report certain information about newly hired employees to the State Directory of New Hires. The State Directory must perform database matching against lists of non-paying parents.

NCP See noncustodial parent.

NDNH See National Directory of New Hires.

new hires See National Directory of New Hires.

non-AFDC An individual who does not receive public assistance benefits but who receives child support services from the IV-D agency.

noncustodial parent A legal/natural parent who resides outside the home and does not have primary custody of a dependent. Also known as an absent parent.

obligation The amount of money to be paid as support by the noncustodial parent on an ongoing basis and the manner by which it is to be paid.

obligee The person, jurisdiction, or political subdivision to whom a duty of support is owed. Also referred to as the custodial parent when money is owed to the parent who resides with the child.

obligor The person owing the duty of support. Also referred to as the noncustodial parent.

OBRA See Omnibus Budget Reconciliation Act.

OCSE See below.

Office of Child Support Enforcement The Federal agency within the Administration for Children and Families in the Department of Health and Human Services that is responsible for the administration of the child support program. OCSE's mission is to assure that assistance in obtaining support (both financial and medical) is available to children through locating parents, establishing paternity and support obligations, and enforcing those obligations.

offset See Federal Income Tax Offset Program.

Omnibus Budget Reconciliation Act Simplified paternity establishment process and established medical support provisions for all children.

order A directive of a court or administrative authority.

pass-through The amount of child support money that is determined by the State in TANF cases to be passed through to the custodial parent.

paternity establishment The process of determining fatherhood by court order, administrative order, acknowledgment, or other method provided for under State law.

partners The people and organizations who help operate the child support program. The Child Support Enforcement program is a partnership which includes the Office of Child Support Enforcement (OCSE), including ACF Regional Offices, Federal, State, and local child support enforcement agencies, and Courts, law enforcement agencies, tribunals and other entities operating under cooperative agreements with child support enforcement agencies.

payee The person who, or entity that, receives money from a person paying child support. Used interchangeably with recipient or custodial parent in TANF cases.

Personal Responsibility and Work Opportunity Reconciliation Act (1996) Legislation which overhauled the nation's welfare system requiring work in exchange for time-limited assistance. The law contains strong work requirements, a performance bonus to reward States for moving welfare recipients into jobs, comprehensive child support enforcement, and supports for families moving from welfare to work including increased funding for child care and guaranteed medical coverage. Tough child support measures under welfare reform include a national new hire reporting system; streamlined paternity establishment; uniform interstate child support laws; computerized Statewide collections, and tough new penalties.

physical custody See custody.

plaintiff A person who brings an action; the party who complains or sues in a civil case.

pleadings Statements or allegations, presented in logical and legal form, which constitute a plaintiff's cause of action or defendant's grounds of defense.

proceeding The conduct of business before a judge or hearing officer.

private case A support case in which there is no IV-A or IV-D involvement.

PRWORA Personal Responsibility and Work Opportunity Reconciliation Act.

public assistance Monies provided from the Federal or State Government to families in need of and eligible for support.

putative father See alleged father.

quasi-judicial process A framework or procedure under the auspices of a State's judicial branch in which court officers other than judges process, establish, enforce, and modify support orders, usually subject to judicial review. The court officer may be a magistrate, a clerk, a master or court examiner. He or she may or may not have to be an attorney, depending on the State's laws.

reciprocity Generally, a relationship between States or countries whereby favors (recognition) or privileges granted by one are returned by the other.

region Breakdown of the United States and its U.S. Possessions into 10 Federal regions for the administration of child support enforcement.

responding jurisdiction The State/county/court which has or will have jurisdiction over a noncustodial parent under a URESA or UIFSA order in response to a request from an initiating State. In review and adjustment, the responding State is the State that is requested by the initiating State to do a review of the existing support order to determine if modification is warranted.

review and adjustment The review of child support orders for modification in accordance with the applicable child support guidelines. The Personal Responsibility and Work Opportunity Reconciliation Act of 1996 specified three methods for making adjustments to child support orders: Apply State guidelines to adjust the order; Apply a cost-of-living adjustment to the order (may be contested); Use automated methods to identify orders eligible for review, conduct the review, and apply the appropriate adjustment (may be contested).

service of process The delivery of a writ or summons to the party to whom it is directed for the purpose of obtaining jurisdiction over that party.

Social Services Amendments (1975) Comprehensive Child Support Legislation which enacted Title IV-D of the Social Security Act. Officially established the Federal Office of Child Support Enforcement (OCSE).

split custody See custody.

SPLS See State Parent Locator Service.

spousal support Court ordered support of an ex-spouse. Also referred to as maintenance or alimony.

State Parent Locator Service A unit within the IV-D program mandated to perform activities relating to the location of noncustodial parents. The SPLS is operated by the State Child Support Enforcement Agencies to locate noncustodial parents to establish paternity and to establish and enforce child support obligations.

Stakeholders Those individuals or organizations who have a legitimate interest in how our customers are served. Stakeholders include national or community-based organizations that serve the interests of our customers or partners; Congress and State legislators; Federal, State, and local governments such as welfare, foster care, and Medicaid agencies; hospitals, birthing centers, and other places where paternity can be acknowledged; employers, taxpayers; the general public.

State Plan Formalized plan developed by each State in conjunction with the Office of Child Support Enforcement. The State Plan includes procedures for implementing State policy and the allocation of necessary resources.

support order A legally binding edict from a court of law that dictates conditions of support that a noncustodial parent must pay. It can include how much is paid, how long it is paid, and whether an employer must withhold support from the noncustodial parent's wages. The order can be for child, medical, and/or spousal support.

TANF See below.

Temporary Assistance for Needy Families Time limited assistance payments to lower income families. The program provides parents with job preparation, work and support services to help them become self-sufficient.Replaced Aid to Families with Dependent Children (AFDC).

third-party liability A public assistance recipient may have medical insurance in addition to the medical coverage provided by TANF or medical support. The insurance provider is billed by Third Party Liability for medical expenses incurred by the recipient. The State pays the difference between the amount of the medical bill and the amount the insurance company has paid.

Title IV-A Part A of Title IV of the Social Security Act contains provisions for the Temporary Assistance for Needy Families Program (TANF) which replaced the AFDC Program.

Title IV-D Part D of Title IV of the Social Security Act mandates and contains the statutory provisions for the child support enforcement program.

Title IV-E Part E of Title IV of the Social Security Act Contains provisions for the AFDC-Foster Care Program.

Title XIX Title XIX of the Social Security Act mandates Medicaid coverage by the States for AFDC recipients, and certain other means-tested categories of persons.

TPL See third-party liability.

tribunal An official entity which establishes, enforces, and modifies support orders. Includes courts, as well as administrative agencies.

UIFSA See below.

Uniform Interstate Family Support Act Supercedes URESA. A 1992 law developed for States to replace URESA as the new interstate statute to govern the establishment, enforcement, and modification of child support orders and the establishment of paternity in cases where the noncustodial parent lives in a different State than his/her child(ren). PRWORA required all states and jurisdictions to adopt the revised version of UIFSA into their State law no later than January 1, 1998.

Uniform Reciprocal Enforcement of Support Act A model law established in 1950 that provided a mechanism for establishing, enforcing, and modifying support obligations in interstate cases.URESA was replaced by the Uniform Interstate Family Support Act (UIFSA), required in all states by January 1, 1998.

URESA See above.

voluntary acknowledgment of paternity An acknowledgement by a man, or both parents, that the man is the father of a child, usually provided in writing on an affidavit or form.

wage withholding A procedure by which automatic deductions are made from wages or income to pay a debt such as child support. The Family Support Act of 1988 required immediate wage withholding for all support, current, and past due.

welfare reform See Personal Responsibility and Work Opportunity Reconciliation Act.

Child Support Enforcement, Office of

ACRONYMS

ACF Administration for Children and Families
AFDC Aid to Families with Dependent Children
AT Action Transmittal
CCPA Consumer Credit Protection Act
CEJ Continuing Exclusive Jurisdiction
CHIP Children's Health Insurance Program
CP Custodial Party
CSE Child Support Enforcement
CSENet Child Support Enforcement Network
DCL Dear Colleague Letter
DNA Deoxyribonucleic Acid
DOB Date of Birth
DOD Department of Defense
EDI Electronic Data Interchange
EFT Electronic Funds Transfer
E-IWO Electronic Income Withholding Order
EVS Enumeration and Verification System
FCR Federal Case Registry of Child Support Orders
FEIN Federal Employer Identification Number
FFCCSOA Full Faith and Credit for Child Support Orders Act
FFP Federal Financial Participation
FIDM Financial Institution Data Match
FMS Financial Management Service
FOP Federal Offset Program
FPLS Federal Parent Locator Service FRC Foreign Reciprocating Country
FSA Family Support Act
FVI Family Violence Indicator
GSA Government Services Administration
HHS United States Department of Health and Human Services
ICR Interstate Case Reconciliation
IM Information Memorandum
IRG Intergovernmental Referral Guide
IRS Internal Revenue Service
IV-A Title IV-A of the Social Security Act
IV-D Title IV-D of the Social Security Act
IV-E Title IV-E of the Social Security Act
IWO Income Withholding Order
MAO Medical Assistance Only
MSFI Multistate Financial Institution

MSFIDM Multistate Financial Institution Data Match
MSO Monthly Support Obligation
NACHA National Automated Clearing House Association
NCP Noncustodial Parent
NDNH National Directory of New Hires
NH New Hire
NMSN National Medical Support Notice
NPRC National Personnel Records Center
NPRM Notice of Proposed Rule Making
OCSE Federal Office of Child Support Enforcement
OPM Office of Personnel Management
PF Putative Father
PIQ Policy Interpretation Question
PRWORA Personal Responsibility and Work Opportunity Reconciliation Act of 1996
QW Quarterly Wage
RURESA Enforcement of Support Act
SCR State Case Registry of Child Support Orders
SDNH State Directory of New Hires
SDU State Disbursement Unit
SESA State Employment Security Agency, now called "State Workforce Agency"
SPLS State Parent Locator Service
SSA Social Security Administration
SSN Social Security Number
SVES State Verification Enumeration Service
SWA State Workforce Agency
TANF Temporary Assistance for Needy Families
TCSE Tribal Child Support Enforcement
UDC Undistributed Collections
UI Unemployment Insurance
UIFSA Uniform Interstate Family Support Act
UPA Uniform Parentage Act
URA Unreimbursed Public Assistance
URESA Uniform Reciprocal Enforcement of Support Act

Adjudication The entry of a judgment, decree, or order by a judge or other decision-maker such as a master, referee, or hearing officer, based on the evidence submitted by the parties.

Administration for Children and Families (ACF) The agency that houses the Office of Child Support Enforcement (OCSE) within the Department of Health and Human Services (HHS).

Administrative Offset The process of withholding all or part of an administrative (non-tax related) payment that is paid by the federal government to a person or entity that owes an outstanding delinquent non-tax debt to the government, and then applying the funds to reduce or satisfy the debt. Administrative Procedure A method by which support orders are made and enforced by an executive agency rather than by courts and judges.

Affidavit A written statement, usually notarized, that is signed under oath or by affirmation.

Agent of the Child A person, usually a parent, who has the legal authority to act on behalf of a minor.

Aid to Families with Dependent Children (AFDC) Former entitlement program that made public assistance payments on behalf of children who did not have the financial support of one of their parents by reason of death, disability, or continued absence from the home; known in many states as AFDC (Aid to Families with Dependent Children). Replaced with Temporary Aid for Needy Families (TANF) under the Personal Responsibility and Work Opportunity Reconciliation Act (PRWORA). (See also Personal Responsibility and Work Opportunity Reconciliation Act)

Alleged Father A man named as the father of a child born of unmarried parents who has not been legally determined to be the father. The alleged father is also referred to as the putative father.

Allowable Disposable Income This is the maximum amount available for child support withholding, calculated by applying a state's limitations or the Consumer Credit Protection Act (CCPA) limits to the noncustodial parent's disposable income. (See also disposable income)

Arrearage Past due, unpaid child support owed by the noncustodial parent. If the parent has arrearages, he or she is said to be "in arrears."

Assignment of Support Rights The legal procedure by which a person receiving public assistance agrees to turn over to the state or tribe any right to child support, including arrearages, paid by the noncustodial parent in exchange for receipt of a cash assistance grant and other benefits. States and tribes can then use a portion of said child support to defray or recoup the public assistance expenditure.

Biological Father The man who provided the paternal genes of a child. The biological father is sometimes referred to as the natural father.

Burden of Proof The duty of a party to produce the greater weight of evidence on a point at issue.

Case A legal action. Also the group of people associated with a particular child support order, court hearing or request for child support services. This typically includes a custodial party (CP), dependent(s), and a noncustodial parent (NCP) or putative father (PF). In addition to names and identifying information about its members, every child support case has a unique case identification number and includes information such as CP and NCP wage data, court order details, and NCP payment history. (See also Child Support; IV-D Case; IV-A Case; IV-E Case)

Central Registry A centralized unit maintained by a state child support agency that is responsible for receiving, distributing, and responding to inquiries on interstate child support cases. Tribal programs currently do not have a centralized unit.

Child Support Financial support paid by parents to help support a child or children of whom they do not have custody. Child support can be entered into voluntarily or ordered by a court or a properly empowered administrative agency, depending on state or tribal laws. Child support can involve different types of cases:

- ***IV-A Case*** A case in which a state provides public assistance under the state's IV-A program, which is funded under Title IV-A of the Social Security Act where the child(ren) have been determined to be eligible for Temporary Assistance for Needy Families (TANF). The children's support rights have been assigned to the state or tribe, and a referral to the child support agency has been made.
- ***IV-D Case*** A case in which a state provides child support services as directed by the state or tribal child support program that is authorized by Title IV-D of the Social Security Act. A IV-D case is comprised of: a dependent child or children; a custodial party who may be a parent, caretaker relative or other custodian, including an entity such as a foster care agency; and a noncustodial parent or parents, a mother, a father, or a putative father whose paternity has not been legally established.
- ***IV-E Case (Foster Care and Adoption Assistance)*** A case in which a state currently provides benefits or services for foster care maintenance to children entitled to foster care maintenance under the state's IV-E Program authorized under Title IV-E of the Social Security Act. These cases are also eligible for IV-D services.
- ***Non-IV-D Case*** A case where the order is entered into privately and the CSE agency is not providing locate, enforcement, or collection services; often entered into during divorce proceedings. Non-IV-D cases are for payment processing only.

- *Current Assistance IV-D (Child Support) Case* A case where the children are: (1) recipients of Temporary Assistance for Needy Families (TANF) under Title IV-A of the Social Security Act or (2) entitled to Foster Care maintenance payments under Title IV-E of the Social Security Act. In addition, the children's support rights have been assigned by a caretaker relative to a state or tribe, and a referral to the state or tribal child support agency has been made. Also a TANF IV-D Case or Foster Care IV-D Case.
- *Never Assistance IV-D Case* A case where the children are receiving services under the Title IV-D program, but are not currently determined to be eligible for and have not previously received assistance under Titles IV-A or IV-E of the Social Security Act. A child support case is set up when a person requests a child support office to help them get child support money. The case file will have important papers such as birth certificates, court orders, information on the absent parent, etc. A never assistance case includes cases where the family is receiving child support services as a result of a written application for IV-D services, including cases where the children are receiving state (not Title IV-E) foster care services, or a case in which they are Medicaid recipients not receiving additional assistance. Tribal and international cases are considered never assistance cases if the case status is unknown.
- *Former Assistance IV-D Case* A case where the children formerly received Title IV-A (AFDC or TANF) or Title IV-E foster care services.

Child Support Enforcement Agency The agency that exists in every state or tribe to locate noncustodial parents or putative fathers; establish, enforce, and modify child support orders; and collect and distribute child support money. The agency is operated by state, tribal or local government according to the Child Support Enforcement program guidelines as set forth in Title IV-D of the Social Security Act. Also known as a "IV-D Agency."

Child Support Enforcement Program The federal/state/local partnership established under Title IV-D of the Social Security Act to locate parents, establish paternity and child support orders, and collect on those orders.

Child Support Order The document that sets: (1) an amount of money that is to be provided by a parent for the support of the parent's child(ren) and/or (2) the responsibility to provide health insurance or medical support for the child(ren). This amount or responsibility must be established by court order or administrative process, voluntary agreement (in states or tribes where such agreements are filed in the court or agency of the administrative process as an order and are legally enforceable) or other legal process. It may include a judgment for child support arrears.

Child Support Pass-Through Provision by which states can disburse part of a child support payment collected on behalf of a public assistance recipient instead of keeping the funds to reimburse the state and disregard the payment in determining eligibility for assistance. Tribal programs also have a choice in adopting pass-through. Also known as child support "disregard." (See also Public Assistance)

Complaint The formal written document filed in a court which sets forth the names of the parties, the allegations, and the request for relief sought. Sometimes called the initial pleading or petition.

Consent Agreement Voluntary written admission of paternity or responsibility for child support.

Consumer Credit Protection Act (CCPA) Federal law that limits the amount that may be withheld from earnings to satisfy child support obligations and other garnishments. State or tribal law may further limit the amount that can be withheld from a person's paycheck.

Continuing Exclusive Jurisdiction (CEJ) The authority that only one tribunal has to modify an order for support.

Controlling Order The one order that must be used by all states and tribes for enforcement and modification actions going forward. In cases involving multiple orders issued prior to the enactment of UIFSA, UIFSA provides rules for determining the controlling order, the one order to be prospectively enforced. UIFSA does not apply to tribes.

Cost of Living Adjustment (COLA) Modification of the amount of a support obligation based on the economy's increasing or decreasing cost of the necessities of life, such as food, shelter, and clothing.

Criminal Non-Support Criminal charges that can be brought when a noncustodial parent willfully fails to pay child support. There are criminal offenses for failure to support at both the state and federal levels. Federal actions require some interstate activity.
- *Child Support Recovery Act (CSRA) (1992)* This Act makes it a federal crime to willfully fail to pay a past-due child support obligation for a child living in another state. The past-due obligation must be either greater than $5,000 or must have remained unpaid for more than one year.
- *Deadbeat Parents Punishment Act of 1998 (DPPA)* A federal law that imposes criminal penalties on parents who repeatedly fail to support children living in another state or who flee across state lines to avoid supporting them; the Deadbeat Parents Punishment Act established felony violations for the willful failure to pay legal child support obligations in interstate cases.

Custodial Parent / Custodial Party (CP) The person who has primary care, custody, and control of the child. Can also be custodial party—a relative or other person with legal custody of the child.

Custody Order Legally binding determination that establishes with whom a child shall live. The meaning of different types of custody terms (e.g., joint custody, shared custody, split custody) varies from state to state and tribe to tribe.

Debt Check A program developed by the Treasury Department's Financial Management Service that allows agencies and outside lenders to determine whether applicants for federal loans, loan insurance or loan guarantees owe delinquent child support or non-tax debt to the federal government. Federal agencies are required to deny loans, loan insurance, or loan guarantees to individuals who owe delinquent child support if those debts have been referred to the Treasury Offset Program (TOP) for administrative offset.

Default The failure of a defendant to file an answer or appear in a civil case within the prescribed time after having been properly served with a summons and complaint. The tribunal hearing the case can enter an order based on information presented without any challenge if the responding party does not answer the claim or appear in court as requested. This is called a default order.

Default Judgment Decision made by the tribunal when the defendant fails to respond.

Defendant The person against whom a civil or criminal proceeding is begun.

Dependent A person who is under the care of a parent, relative or other caretaker and cannot live on his/her own. Most children who are eligible to receive child support must be dependents. The child ceases to be a dependent when he or she reaches the "age of emancipation," as determined by state or tribal law, but may remain eligible for child support for a period after he or she is emancipated or reaches the "age of majority" depending on the state's or tribe's provisions.

Disbursement The process of money being sent out to the custodial parent once child support has been received; the paying out of collected child support funds.

Disestablishment Procedure by which a tribunal can nullify an order or a determination of paternity generally.

Disposable Income The portion of an employee's earnings that remains after deductions required by law (taxes, Social Security, FICA) and that is used to determine the amount of an employee's pay subject to a garnishment, attachment, or child support withholding order. Also, the money due an employee after taxes and other required deductions. (See also Garnishment)

Distribution The allocation of child support collected to the various types of debt (e.g., monthly support obligations, arrears, ordered arrears) within a child support case as specified in 45 CFR 302.51 (45 CFR 309.115 for procedures governing tribal child support programs); the process of how the total child support payment amount is divided between all those owed under the support orders, including reimbursement for public assistance.

DNA Testing The analysis of human cells to facilitate the establishment of paternity.

Due Process The principle of fairness in legal proceedings so that a person has a right to know what action is being taken and has an opportunity to be heard.

Electronic Disbursement Process by which a child support payment is electronically transmitted to an account. The most common forms of electronic disbursement are direct deposit to a bank or other financial institution or through an electronic payment card (stored value card). The process when child support payment or any other payments are sent to banks accounts by computer systems.

Electronic Funds Transfer (EFT) Process by which money is transmitted electronically from one bank account to another.

Enforcement The application of remedies to obtain payment of a child or medical support obligation contained in a child or spousal support order. Examples of remedies include garnishment of wages, seizure of assets, liens placed on assets, revocation of licenses (e.g., drivers, business, medical), denial of U.S. passports, contempt of court proceedings, etc. The processes that can be used to collect payments from the noncustodial parent or to require compliance with some other provision of the order.

Emancipation A child ceases to be a dependent upon reaching the "age of majority" as determined by state or tribal law; however, depending on the state's provisions, may remain eligible for child support for a period after emancipation. The age a person is no longer considered a minor (child) under government laws. This law is different from state to state and tribe to tribe.

Establishment The process of determining legal paternity and/or obtaining a court or administrative order to put a child support obligation in place.

Family Violence Indicator (FVI) A designation that resides in the Federal Case Registry placed on a participant in a case or order by a state or tribe that indicates the participant is at risk of child abuse or domestic violence. Used to prevent disclosure of the location of a party or a child believed by the state or tribe to be at risk of family violence.

Federal Case Registry (FCR) A national database of information on individuals in all IV-D cases and all non-IV-D orders entered or modified on or after October 1, 1998. The FCR receives this case information on a daily basis from the State Case Registry located in every state, and proactively matches it with previous submissions to the FCR and with employment information contained in the National Directory of New Hires (NDNH). Any successful matches are returned to the appropriate state(s) for processing. The FCR and the NDNH are both part of the Federal Parent Locator Service maintained by OCSE.

Federal Financial Participation (FFP) The portion of a state's child support expenditures that are paid by a federal government match. Most child support costs are matched two to one. In other words, the federal share of most child support costs is 66 percent.

Federal Offset Program (FOP) The program that provides several enforcement tools to collect past-due child support from noncustodial parents, including federal income tax refund and administrative offset, Passport Denial Program, MSFIDM and Debt Check.

Federal Parent Locator Service (FPLS) A computerized, national location network operated by OCSE. The FPLS obtains address, employer information, and data on child support cases in every state, and then compares the data and returns matches to the appropriate states. This helps state and local child support agencies locate noncustodial parents and putative fathers for the purposes of establishing custody and visitation rights, establishing and enforcing child support obligations, investigating parental kidnapping, and processing adoption or foster care cases. The expanded FPLS includes the Federal Case Registry (FCR) and the National Directory of New Hires (NDNH).

Federal Tax Refund Offset Program The process that collects past-due child support amounts from noncustodial parents through interception of their federal income tax refunds.

Financial Institution Data Match (FIDM) A process whereby information on accounts held by banks, savings and loan companies, brokerage houses, and other financial institutions is matched against child support obligors who owe past-due support (arrearages).

Financial Management Service (FMS) Acting as the U.S. government's money manager, FMS provides centralized payment, collection, and reporting services, and using a centralized process, collects delinquent debts (e.g., federal student, mortgage, or small business loans; federal salary or benefit overpayments; fines or penalties assessed by federal agencies) owed to the U.S. government, as well as income tax debts owed to states and past-due child support payments owed to custodial parents.

Finding A formal determination by a court or administrative process that has legal standing.

Foreign Reciprocating Country A foreign country with which the United States has signed a bilateral agreement ensuring reciprocity in child support enforcement.

Foster Care A federal/state/tribal program that provides financial support to people, families or institutions that are raising children that are not their own. (See also IV-E Case)

Full Faith and Credit Doctrine under which a state or tribe must honor an order or judgment entered in another state or tribe and enforce it as if it were an order within its own territory, but may not modify the order unless properly petitioned to do so. This principle was specifically applied to child support orders in federal law that took effect in 1994, under the Full Faith and Credit for Child Support Orders Act (FFCCSOA). FFCCSOA requires states and federally funded tribal child support agencies to enforce child support orders made by other states or tribes if: the issuing state or tribe's tribunal had subject-matter jurisdiction to hear and resolve the matter and enter an order; the issuing state or tribe's tribunal had personal jurisdiction over the parties; and the parties were given reasonable notice and the opportunity to be heard. FFCCSOA also sets limits on state and tribal authority to modify another state or tribe's child support orders in instances when the state or tribe seeking to modify the order has jurisdiction to do so and the tribunal that originally issued the order no longer has continuing exclusive jurisdiction over the order either because the child and the parties to the case are no longer residents of the issuing state, or the parties to the case have filed written consent to transfer continuing exclusive jurisdiction to the tribunal seeking to make the modification.

Garnishment A legal proceeding under which part of a person's wages or assets are withheld for payment of a debt. This term is usually used to specify that an income or wage withholding is involuntary. (See also Income Withholding; Wage Withholding; Direct Income Withholding; Immediate Wage Withholding)

Genetic Testing Analysis of inherited factors to determine legal fatherhood or paternity. (See also Legal Father; Paternity; Putative Fathers; DNA Testing)

Good Cause A legal reason for which a Temporary Assistance for Needy Families (TANF) recipient is excused from cooperating with the child support enforcement process, such as past physical harm by the child's noncustodial parent. It also includes situations where rape or incest resulted in the conception of the child and situations where the mother is considering placing the child for adoption. (See also Temporary Assistance for Needy Families; IV-A Case)

Guidelines—Child Support A standard method for setting child support obligations, using a mathematical formula and based on the income of one or both parent(s) and other factors determined by state or tribal law. The Family Support Act of 1988 requires states to use guidelines to determine the amount of support for each family, unless they are rebutted by a written finding that applying the guidelines would be inappropriate to the case. (See also Income; Disposable Income; Imputed Income) IV-D (Four-D) Refers to Part D of title IV of the Social Security Act. Title IV-D established the child support program.

Imputed Income Income that may be attributed to an individual who refuses to obtain employment, chooses not to work for personal reasons, or chooses to earn less than is typical for someone with the individual's training, education and skill. An individual cannot be forced to work, but the court or decision-maker can attribute certain income levels to a person based on the person's education or training, skill, and work history. Some states consider assets, for example, if the obligor is self-employed or owns real estate. This also may be the amount of income the court or administrator determines that an obligor is capable of earning if he or she does not appear at a hearing after proper service. Some will also attribute income to a custodial parent who chooses to remain unemployed. (See also Disposable Income; Guidelines)

In-Kind Support Non-cash support payments, for example, food or clothing, provided to a custodial parent or child in lieu of cash support payments. Income For child support purposes, any periodic form of payment to an individual, regardless of source, including wages, salaries, commissions, bonuses, worker's compensation, disability, pension, or retirement program payments and interest; remuneration for work performed or any payment made in lieu of remuneration for worked performed, such as Social Security benefits or retirement pay.

Income Withholding An order that requires an employer to withhold support from a noncustodial parent's wages and transfer that withholding to the appropriate agency (the Centralized Collection Unit, the State Disbursement Unit or tribal child support agency). Sometimes referred to as a wage withholding or garnishment.

- *Direct Income Withholding* A procedure, whereby an income withholding order from one state can be sent directly to the noncustodial parent's employer in another state, without the need to use the child support agency or court system in the noncustodial parent's state.
- *Immediate Wage Withholding* An automatic deduction from income that starts as soon as the order for support is established and an income withholding order/notice is received and implemented by the noncustodial parent's employer.

Indian Tribe Any Indian or Alaskan Native tribe, band, nation, pueblo, village, or community the Secretary of the Interior acknowledges as an Indian tribe and includes in the list of federally recognized Indian tribal governments.

Initiating Jurisdiction The state, tribal or county court, or administrative agency that sends a request for action to another court or agency that can exercise legal authority against a party to an action. In cases where a state is trying to establish an initial child support order on behalf of a resident custodial parent and does not have Long-Arm Jurisdiction (cannot legally claim personal jurisdiction over a person who is not a resident), it must file a Two-State Action under the Uniform Interstate Family Support Act (UIFSA) guidelines. (Tribes are not subject to UIFSA.) (See also Long Arm Jurisdiction; Two-State Action; Uniform Interstate Family Support Act)

Intercept A method of securing child support by taking a portion of non-wage payments made to a noncustodial parent. Non-wage payments subject to interception include federal tax refunds, state tax refunds, unemployment benefits, and disability benefits. (See also Federal Tax Refund Offset Program)

Intergovernmental Reference Guide (IRG) An online compilation of state, tribal, and international child support agencies' contact and policy information.

Intergovernmental Case A case in which the dependent child and noncustodial parent live in different states, tribes, territories or countries, or where two or more agencies or tribunals are involved in some case activity, such as enforcement. (Also called Interstate or Interjurisdictional Case.)

International IV-D Case A case under the state's child support program received from or referred to a foreign country that has entered into an agreement with the United States under section 459A of the Social Security Act (a Foreign Reciprocating Country or FRC) or a foreign country with which the state has entered a reciprocal agreement. International cases also include child support cases in which there is an application for services from an individual who resides in a foreign country.

Interstate An action that takes place involving two or more states, typically where the order for support is in one state and one of the parties resides elsewhere. Can also be between two tribes or a state and a tribe; also called interjurisdictional or intergovernmental.

Interstate Case Reconciliation An OCSE program that matches cases that two states may have in common, identifies missing or incorrect data, and provides corrected data back to the states. The data include case ID, case status, and participant information.

Interstate Central Registry The unit in each state child support agency that is responsible for receiving, distributing and responding to inquiries on all incoming interstate cases.

Interstate IV-D Case A child support case in which the noncustodial parent lives or works in a different state from the custodial parent and child. Unless otherwise specified, the term applies both to one state and two state interstate cases.

Judgment The official decision or finding of a judge or administrative agency hearing officer upon the respective rights and claims of the parties to an action; also known as a decree or order. It may include the "findings of fact and conclusions of law."

Judicial Process The use of tribunals in determining child support legal obligations, including paternity establishment, order establishment, enforcement, and modifications of orders.

Jurisdiction The legal authority that a court or administrative agency has over particular persons and over certain types of cases, usually in a defined geographical area. Also, a term used to signify a geographic location such as a state or tribe with a tribunal that exercises such authority. (See also Initiating Jurisdiction; Long Arm Jurisdiction; Two-State Action)

Legal Father A man who is recognized by law as the male parent of a child. (See also Putative Father; Paternity; Genetic Testing, DNA Testing)

Levy The seizure and possible subsequent sale of assets, including personal property, to satisfy a child support debt.

Lien A claim upon property to prevent sale or transfer of that property until a debt is satisfied.

Litigation An action in which a controversy is brought before the court.

Locate Process by which a party or putative father is found for the purpose of establishing paternity, establishing and/or enforcing a child support obligation, establishing custody and visitation rights, processing adoption or foster care cases, and investigating parental kidnapping.

Locate Information Data used to locate putative fathers, noncustodial parents or custodial parents. May include their Social Security number, date of birth, residential address, and employer.

Long-Arm Jurisdiction Legal provision that permits one state or tribe to claim personal jurisdiction over someone who lives in another state or tribe. There must be some meaningful connection between the person and the state, tribe or district that is asserting jurisdiction in order for a court or agency to reach beyond its normal jurisdictional border. Also called Extended Personal Jurisdiction. (See also Initiating Jurisdiction; Two-State Action; Uniform Interstate Family Support Act)

Long Arm Statute A law that permits one state to claim personal jurisdiction over someone who lives in another state.

Medical Assistance Only (MAO) Form of public assistance administered by a state's IV-A program that provides benefits to recipients only in the form of medical, rather than financial, assistance.

Medical Coverage Medical coverage is any health coverage provided for a child or children, including: (1) private health insurance, (2) publicly-funded health coverage, (3) cash medical support, or (4) payment of medical bills (including dental or eye care). Medical coverage may be provided by the custodial parent, noncustodial parent or other person, such as a stepparent. (See also Medical Support)

Medical Support Medical coverage provided for a child or children pursuant to an order. This includes: (1) private health insurance, (2) publicly-funded health coverage if a parent is ordered by a court or administrative process to provide cash medical support payments to help pay the cost of Medicaid or Children's Health Insurance Program (CHIP), (3) cash medical support, including payment of health insurance premiums, and (4) payment of medical bills (including dental or eye care). Indian Health Service and Tricare are acceptable forms of medical support. Medical support may be provided by the custodial parent, noncustodial parent or another person, such as a stepparent. (See also Medical Coverage; National Medical Support Notice (NMSN))

Motion An application to the court requesting an order or ruling in favor of the party that is filing the motion. Motions are generally made in reference to a pending action and may address a matter in the court's discretion or concern a point of law.

Monthly Support Obligation (MSO) The amount of money a noncustodial parent or party is required to pay each month for child and/or spousal support.

Multistate Employer An employer that conducts business in two or more states. As with single-state employers, multistate employers are required by law to report all new hires to the State Directory of New Hires (SDNH) operated by their state government. However, unlike single-state employers, a multistate employer may report all of their new hires to the SDNH of only one state in which they do business rather than to each of them.

Multistate Financial Institution (MSFI) A financial institution that conducts business in two or more states.

Multistate Financial Institution Data Match (MSFIDM) Process by which delinquent child support obligors are matched with accounts held in financial institutions doing business in more than one state.

National Automated Clearing House Association (NACHA) The association that establishes the standards, rules, and procedures that enable financial institutions to exchange payments on a national basis.

The Electronic Funds Transfer and the child support Electronic Data Interchange formats are established by NACHA. NACHA also establishes rules and procedures that govern use of the stored value cards.

National Directory of New Hires (NDNH) A national database containing new hire and quarterly wage data from every State Directory of New Hires and federal agency, and Unemployment Insurance data from State Workforce Agencies. OCSE maintains the NDNH as part of the expanded Federal Parent Locator Service. (Tribes can choose to obtain access to the NDNH by agreements with a state.) (See also New Hire Data; Quarterly Wage Date; Unemployment Insurance Claim Data)

National Medical Support Notice (NMSN) The standard form sent to an employer from the state child support agency ordering the employer and its health care plan administrator to enroll a noncustodial parent's child in health care coverage when coverage is available through the employer and required as part of a child support order. When properly completed, the NMSN constitutes a Qualified Medical Child Support Order, a document necessary for health care plans to enroll dependents who are not residing with the covered parent. The NMSN is designed to simplify the work of employers and plan administrators by providing a uniform document to request health care coverage.

New Hire Reporting Program under which employers submit data on a new employee within 20 days of hire to the State Directory of New Hires in the state where they do business. Minimum data required includes the employee's name, address, and Social Security number, and the employer's name, address, and Federal Employer Identification Number. Some states request additional data. A multistate employer has the option of reporting all new hires to a single state in which they do business. The data is then submitted to the National Directory of New Hires (NDNH) and compared against child support order information contained in the Federal Case Registry for possible enforcement of child support obligations by wage garnishment. New hire data may also be used at the state level by other agencies to detect fraud; for example, to find new hires that have been receiving unemployment insurance or other public benefits for which they may no longer be eligible. Federal agencies report new hire data directly to the NDNH. (Tribal programs can have access to NDNH data by agreement with a state.) (See also State Directory of New Hires; National Directory of New Hires)

Noncustodial Parent (NCP) The parent who does not have primary care, custody, or control of the child, and who may have an obligation to pay child support. Also referred to as the obligor. (See also Custodial Party; Obligor)

Non-IV-D Order A child support order handled by a private attorney or parties representing themselves as opposed to an order where the action was brought by the state or local child support (IV-D) agency. A nonIV-D order is one where the state: 1) Is not currently providing services under the state's Title IV-A, Title IV-D, Title IV-E, or Title XIX programs. 2) Has no current application or applicable fee for services paid by either parent.

Nondisclosure Finding A finding that the health, safety, or liberty of a party or child would be unreasonably put at risk by the disclosure of identifying information. Interstate petitions must include certain identifying information regarding the parties and child(ren) unless a tribunal makes a nondisclosure finding by ordering that the address or identifying information not be disclosed. In such cases, the finding would be identified by a Family Violence Indicator (FVI). The procedures for obtaining a nondisclosure finding vary from state to state. Obligation The amount of money to be paid as support by a parent or spouse in the form of financial support for the child support, medical support, or spousal support.

Obligee The person, state or tribal agency, or other entity to which child support is owed (also referred to as a custodial party when the money is owed to the person with primary custody of the child).

Obligor The person obligated to pay child support (also referred to as a noncustodial parent or NCP).

Office of Child Support Enforcement (OCSE) The federal agency responsible for the administration of the Child Support Enforcement program. Created by Title IV-D of the Social Security Act in 1975, OCSE is responsible for developing child support policy; oversight, evaluation, and audits of state and tribal child support programs; and providing technical assistance and training to those programs. OCSE operates the Federal Parent Locator Service, which includes the National Directory of New Hires and the Federal Case Registry. OCSE is part of the Administration for Children and Families (ACF) within the Department of Health and Human Services (HHS). The following documents provide guidance, information, and direction to state and tribal child support programs:

- ***Action Transmittal (AT)*** Document sent out by the federal Office of Child Support Enforcement, which instructs state or federally funded tribal child support programs on the actions they must take to comply with new and amended federal laws. Has basis in federal law and regulation.
- ***Dear Colleague Letter (DCL)*** Letter sent out to those in the child support community, and interested partners, that conveys information on child support enforcement program activities.

- *Information Memorandum (IM)* Document that provides state and tribal child support enforcement agencies with information on program practices that can be useful to program improvement.
- *Policy Interpretation Question (PIQ)* An official reply from the federal Office of Child Support Enforcement to an inquiry submitted by a state or tribal child support agency concerning application of policy. Although questions often arise from a specific practice or situation, the responses are official statements of OCSE policy on the issue. The federal government, through the child support program, shares the cost of the state program with Federal Financial Participation (FFP).

Offset The process of reducing funds paid by the federal government to an obligor and applying the funds toward the balance of the delinquent debt. Also the amount of money that is intercepted from an obligor's state or federal income tax refund or from an administrative payment, such as federal retirement benefits, in order to satisfy a child support debt.

Order A legally binding decision that sets forth the responsibilities of the parties to an action. It can include a determination of parentage and a support obligation, and set forth other rights of the parties. It can be issued by a judge, master or other administrative entity authorized to enter orders. It can also be a consent agreement between the parties that has been ratified by an appropriate official. Order/Notice to Withhold Child Support The form to be used by all states that standardizes the information used to request income withholding for child support by an employer from a noncustodial parent's earnings. (See also Direct Income Withholding; Income Withholding; Garnishment)

Parentage The legal mother-child relationship and father-child relationship as determined by the state.

Passport Denial Program Program created by the Personal Responsibility and Work Opportunity Reconciliation Act (PRWORA) of 1996 that is operated under the auspices of the Federal Offset Program (FOP). Under the Passport Denial Program, cases in which an obligor owes child support arrearages that are greater than the federally mandated threshold and are submitted to the FOP are forwarded to the U.S. Department of State, which flags the obligor's name and refuses to issue a passport in the event he or she applies for one. After the obligor makes arrangements to satisfy the arrears, states can notify OCSE to request the State Department remove him/her from the program. This program is automatic, meaning that any obligor who is eligible will be submitted to the State Department unless the state submitting the case for tax refund offset specifically excludes him/her from the Passport Denial Program. (Tribes can choose to have access based on an agreement with the state.) (See also Federal Offset Program)

Paternity The legal establishment of fatherhood for a child, either by court determination, administrative process, tribal custom or voluntary acknowledgment. A paternity acknowledgment involves the legal establishment of fatherhood for a child through a voluntary acknowledgment signed by both parents as part of an in-hospital or other acknowledgement service.

Payee Person or organization in whose name child support money is paid.

Payor Person who makes a payment, usually a noncustodial parent or someone acting on their behalf.

Personal Responsibility and Work Opportunity Reconciliation Act of 1996 (PRWORA) Legislation that provides a number of requirements for employers, public licensing agencies, financial institutions, as well as state, tribal and federal child support agencies to assist in locating noncustodial parents and establishing, enforcing, and collecting child support. This legislation created the New Hire Reporting program and the State and Federal Case Registries. Otherwise known as Welfare Reform. (See also Aid to Families with Dependent Children)

Petitioner The person, state or tribal agency initiating a petition or motion.

Plaintiff A person who brings an action; the party who complains or sues in a civil case.

Pleadings Statements or allegations, presented in logical and legal form, which constitute a plaintiff's cause of action or a defendant's grounds of defense.

Presumption of Paternity A rule of law that permits a court to assume a man is the father of a child if certain facts exist. This rule may be rebutted by presenting factual information that shows the man could not be the father.

Private Case Known as a non-IV-D case, it is a support case where the custodial party to whom child support is owed is not receiving IV-A benefits or IV-D services.

Proactive Matching Process in which child support case data newly submitted to the Federal Case Registry is automatically compared with previous submissions, as well as with the employment data in the National Directory of New Hires. The resulting locate information is then returned to the appropriate State(s) for processing.

Probability of Paternity The probability that the alleged father is the biological father of the child as indicated by genetic test results.

Proceeding The conduct of business before a judge or administrative hearing officer.

Pro se When a party represents himself in a legal matter, rather than being represented by a lawyer.

PRWORA (Personal Responsibility and Work Opportunity Reconciliation Act) Legislation passed in 1996, also known as Welfare Reform. Public Assistance Money granted from the state, tribal, or federal programs to a person or family for living expenses. Eligibility is based on need and varies between programs. Applicants for certain types of public assistance (for example, Temporary Assistance for Needy Families or TANF) are automatically referred to their state or tribal child support agency, which will identify and locate the noncustodial parent, establish paternity where appropriate, and obtain child support payments. This allows the state or tribe to recoup or defray some of its public assistance expenditures with funds from the noncustodial parent and may enable the custodial party to become self-sufficient.

Putative Father (PF) The person alleged to be the father of the child but who has not yet been medically or legally declared to be the legal father. (See also Legal Father; Paternity; Genetic Testing)

Qualified Medical Child Support Order (QMCSO) An order, decree, or judgment, including approval of a settlement agreement, issued by a court or administrative agency of competent jurisdiction that provides for medical support for a child of a participant under a group health plan. A QMCSO must contain specific information to meet the requirements of the Employee Retirement Income Security Act (ERISA), which allows a plan administrator to enroll a child in the parent's health plan. A properly completed National Medical Support Notice (NMSN) is a QMSCO.

Quarterly Wage (QW) Data Data on all employees that must be submitted by employers on a quarterly basis to the State Workforce Agency in the state in which they operate. The data is then submitted to the National Directory of New Hires (NDNH). Minimum information must include the employee's name, address, Social Security number, wage amount, and the reporting period, and the employer's name, address, and Federal Employer Identification Number (FEIN). The data are then compared against child support order information contained in the Federal Case Registry (FCR) for possible enforcement of child support obligations by wage garnishment. Federal agencies report the data directly to the NDNH. (See also National Directory of New Hires)

Quasi-Judicial A framework or procedure under the auspices of a state's judicial branch or tribal court in which court officers other than judges process, establish, enforce and modify support orders, usually subject to judicial review. The court officer may be a magistrate, a clerk, master, or court examiner. He or she may or may not have to be an attorney, depending on the state or tribal law.

Reciprocity The process by which one jurisdiction grants certain privileges to another jurisdiction on the condition that it receives the same privileges.

Recognized Order The controlling order as identified by applying the rules of the Full Faith and Credit for Child Supports Orders Act (FFCCSOA) used for enforcement from the present time forward. (See also Full Faith and Credit)

Referral Request sent to a child support agency from another jurisdiction or a non-IV-D agent or agency asking that a child support case be established.

Registration The formal filing process by which an order of one jurisdiction is recognized in another jurisdiction. After registration, an action can be taken in a tribunal of the responding jurisdiction as if the order was issued in that jurisdiction. An order may be registered for enforcement, modification or both.

Respondent The party answering a petition or motion.

Responding Jurisdiction The court or administrative agency with authority over a noncustodial parent or child support order on which an initiating jurisdiction has requested action.

Review and Adjustment Periodic process in which current information is obtained from both parties in a child support case and evaluated to decide if a support order needs to be adjusted.

Service of Process The actual delivery of legal paperwork that requires a person to respond or appear to that person or his/her agent.

Service by Publication Service of process accomplished by publishing a notice in a newspaper or by posting it on a bulletin board of a courthouse or other public facility, after a court determines that other means of service are impractical or have been unsuccessful. This method of service is not available in every jurisdiction.

Show Cause An order directing a person to appear and bring forth any evidence as to why the remedies requested should not be granted. A show cause order is usually based on a motion and affidavit asking for relief.

Spousal Support Court-ordered support of a spouse or ex-spouse; also referred to as maintenance or alimony.

State Case Registry (SCR) A database maintained by each state that contains information on individuals in child support cases. Information submitted to the SCR is transmitted to the Federal Case Registry (FCR), where it is compared to cases submitted to the FCR by other states, as well as to employment data in the National Directory of New Hires (NDNH). Matches found are returned to the appropriate states for processing. (See also Federal Case Registry; IV-D Case; Non-IV-D Order)

State Directory of New Hires (SDNH) A database maintained by each state that contains information about individuals submitted by their employer within 20 days of hire. The data are transmitted to the NDNH, where they are compared to the employment data from other states as well as child support data in the Federal Case Registry. Matches found are returned to the appropriate states for processing. (See also National Directory of New Hires; New Hire Reporting Program)

State Disbursement Unit (SDU) The single site in most states where all child support payments are sent for processing. (See also Centralized Collection Unit)

State Parent Locator Service (SPLS) A service provided by the state child support agencies to locate parents in order to establish and enforce child support obligations, visitation, and custody orders or to establish paternity. This information is accessible to tribes through agreement made with a state.

State/Tribal IV-D Case A case under the state's child support program received from, or sent to, a tribal child support program for case processing.

State Workforce Agencies (SWA) Agencies in each state that process unemployment insurance claims and maintain databases of employment information and quarterly wage data submitted by employers. Formerly called State Employment Security Agencies (SESAs).

Statute of Limitations The cutoff point on the length of time a person has to take a legal action.

Stay An order by a court that suspends all or some of the proceedings in a case.

Stored Value Card A form of electronic disbursement in which the child support payment is electronically transmitted to the custodial party via a debit card. Also referred to as Electronic Payment Card.

Subpoena A process issued by a court compelling a witness to appear at a judicial proceeding. Sometimes the process will also direct the witness to bring documentary evidence to the court.

Summons A notice to a defendant that an action against him or her has been commenced in the court and that a judgment will be issued against him or her if the complaint is not answered within a certain time.

Temporary Assistance for Needy Families (TANF) Time-limited public assistance payments made to poor families, based on Title IV-A of the Social Security Act. TANF replaced Aid to Families with Dependent Children when the Personal Responsibility and Work Opportunity Reconciliation Act (PRWORA) was signed into law in 1996. The program provides parents with job preparation, work, and support services to help them become self-sufficient. Applicants for TANF benefits are automatically referred to their state or tribal child support agency in order to establish paternity and child support for their children from the noncustodial parent. This allows the state or tribe to recoup or defray some of its public assistance expenditures with funds from the noncustodial parent. (See also Personal Responsibility and Work Opportunity Reconciliation Act; Good Cause)

Third-Party Liability The responsibility that an entity, other than the parties to an action (CP and NCP, usually the parents), has to the state provider of health care coverage for reimbursement.

Tribal IV-A Program A TANF program administered by a federally recognized Indian tribe or tribal organization (Tribal TANF). Tribal IV-D Program A child support program administered by a federally recognized Indian tribe or tribal organization and funded under title IV-D of the Social Security Act.

Tribal Organizations Organizations run by Native American tribes. Tribe Any Indian or Alaskan Native tribe, band, nation, pueblo, village, or community the Secretary of the Interior acknowledges to exist as an Indian tribe and includes in the list of federally recognized Indian tribal governments. (See also Indian Tribe)

Tribunal The court, administrative agency, or quasi-judicial agency authorized to establish or modify support orders or to determine parentage.

Two-State Action Action a state must file under the Uniform Interstate Family Support Act (UIFSA) when it does not have Long Arm Jurisdiction (that is, it cannot legally claim personal jurisdiction over a noncustodial parent who lives in another state). This usually occurs in cases where a state is trying to establish paternity or an initial child support order on behalf of a custodial party. (See also Initiating Jurisdiction; Uniform Interstate Family Support Act)

Unclaimed Funds Support payment that cannot be disbursed because the identity of the payor or the case information is unknown, or the address of the payee is unknown.

Undistributed Collections (UDC) Child support payments that have been collected by child support agencies but have not yet been sent to custodial parents or other government agencies or returned to noncustodial parents.

Uniform Interstate Family Support Act (UIFSA) Law enacted by all states that provides mechanisms for establishing and enforcing child support obligations in interstate cases (when a noncustodial parent lives in a different state from the child and the custodial party). Among the law's provisions is ability of state child support agencies to send withholding orders to employers across state lines. (UIFSA does not apply to tribes.) (See also Continuing Exclusive Jurisdiction; Two-State Action; Long Arm Jurisdiction: Direct Income Withholding)

Unreimbursed Public Assistance (UPA) The cumulative amount of assistance money paid to the family for all months, which has not been repaid by assigned child support payments collected.

Visitation The right of a noncustodial parent to visit or spend time with his or her children.

Voluntary Acknowledgment of Paternity An acknowledgment by a man, or both parents, that the man is the father of a child, usually provided in writing on an affidavit or form.

Wage Assignment A voluntary agreement by an employee to transfer (or assign) portions of future wage payments to pay certain debts, such as child support.

Wage Attachment An involuntary transfer of a portion of an employee's wage payment to satisfy a debt. In some states this term is used interchangeably with Wage or Income Withholding; in other states there are distinctions between an attachment and withholding. The most common terms used are Wage or Income Withholding. (See also Wage Withholding; Income Withholding)

Wage Withholding A procedure by which scheduled deductions are automatically made from wages or income to pay an obligation, such as child support. The provision dictates that an employer must withhold support from a noncustodial parent's wages and transfer that withholding to the appropriate agency (the Centralized Collection Unit or State Disbursement Unit). Also known as income withholding. (See also Income Withholding; Direct Income Withholding; Garnishment)

Central Intelligence Agency

ACIC	Army Counter Intelligence Center.
ACIS	Arms Control Intelligence Staff.
ADCI/C	Assistant Director of Central Intelligence for Collection.
ADCI/A&P	Assistant Director of Central Intelligence for Analysis and Production.
AD/NE	Assistant Director for National Estimates.
AEC	Atomic Energy Commission.
AFOSI	Air Force Office of Special Investigations.
ATAC	Anti-Terrorism Alert, Center, Under NCIS.
ATC	Applied Technology Center.
ATO	Advanced Technology Office.
BMEWS	Ballistic Missile Early Warning System.
BNE	Board of National Estimates.
BW	Biological Weapons.
CBJB	Congressional Budget Justification Book.
CBW	Chemical and Biological Warfare.
C3I	Command, Control, Communications and Intelligence.
CCP	Consolidated Cryptologic Program.
CI	Counterintelligence.
CIG	Central Intelligence Group, precursor of CIA.
CINC	Commander in Chief.
CINCLANT	Commander in Chief, Atlantic Fleet.
CI&SCM	Counterintelligence and Security Countermeasures.
CIA	Central Intelligence Agency.
CIAP	Central Intelligence Agency Program.
CIARDS	Central Intelligence Agency Retirement and Disability System.
CIS	Commonwealth of Independent States.
CISO	Counterintelligence Support Officer at Unified Commands.
CITAC	Computer Investigations and Infrastructure Threat Assessment Center.
CLANSIG	Clandestine Signals Intelligence.
CMA	Community Management Account.
CMO	Central MASINT Organization.
CMS	Community Management Staff.
CNC	Crime and Narcotics Center.
COE	Common Operating Environment.
COMINT	Communications Intelligence. Technical and operational intelligence information derived from the intercept of foreign communications; it does not include the monitoring of foreign public media or the intercept of communications obtained during the course of counterintelligence investigations within the United States.
CONUS	Continental United States.
COSPO	Community Open Source Program Office.
COVCOM	Covert Communications.
CPCC	Community Personnel Coordinating Committee.
CTBT	Comprehensive Test Ban Treaty.
CT	Counterterrorism.
CTC	Counterterrorism Center.
CW	Chemical Weapons.
CWC	Chemical Weapons Convention.
DAO	Defense Attaché Office.
DCI	Director of Central Intelligence.
DCID	Director of Central Intelligence Directive.
DCIIS	Defense Counterintelligence Integrated Information System.
DDCI	Deputy Director of Central Intelligence.
DDCI/CM	Deputy Director of Central Intelligence for Community Management.
DDI	Deputy Director for Intelligence.
DDO	Deputy Director for Operations.
DDP	Deputy Director for Plans.
DDS	Defense Dissemination System.
DEPSECDEF	Deputy Secretary of Defense.
DHS	Defense HUMINT Service.
DIA	Defense Intelligence Agency.
DIAC	Defense Intelligence Analysis Center.
D/NFAC	Director, National Foreign Assessment Center.
DNI	Director of Naval Intelligence.
DO	Directorate of Operations.
DOD	Department of Defense.
DOD/FCIP	Department of Defense Foreign Counterintelligence Program.
DOE	Department of Energy.

DP	Directorate of Plans (from 1973, the Directorate of Operations).
DSS	Defense Security Service.
EDRB	Expanded Defense Resources Board.
EIC	Economic Intelligence Committee.
ELINT	Electronic Intelligence. Technical and operational intelligence information derived from foreign non-communications electromagnetic radiation emanating from other than atomic detonation or radioactive sources.
ETF	Environmental Task Force.
EXDIR/ICA	Executive Director/Intelligence Community Affairs.
FBI	Federal Bureau of Investigation.
FBI/FCI	Federal Bureau of Investigation Foreign Counterintelligence Program.
FBI/SCM	Federal Bureau of Investigation Security Countermeasures Program.
FBIS	Foreign Broadcast Information Service.
FCI	Foreign Counterintelligence.
FIA	Future Imagery Architecture.
FISA	Foreign Intelligence Surveillance Act.
FIS	Foreign Intelligence Service.
FISINT	Foreign Instrumentation Signals Intelligence. A category of intelligence derived from telemetry, beacons, and other related electromagnetic signals.
FLC	Foreign Language Committee.
FOIA	Freedom of Information Act.
FSU	Former Soviet Union.
FYDP	Future Years Defense Program. Previously called the Five-Year Defense Program, the current name was adopted to avoid changing the acronym but still reflect the fact that the two-year defense budgeting cycle requires a six-year planning budget to be developed every other year.
GATT	General Agreement on Tariffs and Trade.
GDIP	General Defense Intelligence Program.
GMAIC	Guided Missile and Astronautics Intelligence Committee.
GMIC	Guided Missile Intelligence Committee.
GSM	Global System for Mobile Communications.
HF	High Frequency. The portion of the electromagnetic spectrum associated with many radio signals of intelligence interest.
HOCNET	HUMINT Operational Communications Network.
HUMINT	Human Source Intelligence. A category of intelligence information derived from human sources.
IAB	Intelligence Advisory Board.
IAC	Intelligence Advisory Committee.
IC	Intelligence Community.
ICBM	Inter-Continental Ballistic Missile.
IC CIO	Intelligence Community Chief Information Officer.
IG	Inspector General.
IO	Information Operations.
IMINT	Imagery Intelligence and Geospatial Information.
INR	Department of State Bureau of Intelligence and Research.
IPRG	Intelligence Program Review Group.
IW	Information Warfare.
JAEIC	Joint Atomic Energy Intelligence Committee.
JCS	Joint Chiefs of Staff.
JIC	Joint Intelligence Center.
JIS	Joint Intelligence Staff.
JIVA	Joint Intelligence Virtual Architecture.
JMIP	Joint Military Intelligence Program. Interservice military intelligence programs in the Department of Defense. Part of the Tactical Intelligence and Related Activities (TIARA) program in the past, but presented as a separate program in FY 1996.
JTF	Joint Task Force.
JWICS	Joint Worldwide Intelligence Communications System maintained by the Department of Defense.
MAAG	Military Assistance and Advisory Group.
MAG	Military Assistance Group.
MASINT	Measurement and Signature Intelligence. Intelligence derived from the measurement and signature analysis of radar, laser, infrared, and other emanations.
MBB	Mission Based Budgeting.
NACIC	National Counterintelligence Center.
NAFTA	North American Free Trade Agreement.
NAIC	National Air Intelligence Center.
NBC	Nuclear, Biological, Chemical weapons.
NCIOB	National Counterintelligence Operations Board.
NCIPB	National Counterintelligence Policy Board.
NCIS	Naval Criminal Investigative Service.
NDIC	National Drug Intelligence Center.
NFAC	National Foreign Assessment Center.
NFIB	National Foreign Intelligence Board.
NFIP	National Foreign Intelligence Program.
NIA	National Intelligence Authority.
NIC	National Intelligence Council.
NICB	National Intelligence Collection Board.
NIE	National Intelligence Estimate.

NIMA	National Imagery and Mapping Agency.	*PNIO*	Priority National Intelligence Objective.
NIMAP	National Imagery and Mapping Agency Program.	*R&A*	Research and Analysis Branch of the Office of Strategic Services.
NIPB	National Intelligence Producers Board.	*R&D*	Research and Development.
NIS	National Intelligence Survey [a reference document, largely geographical in nature, prepared on a country-by-country basis]	*Reports Officer*	An intelligence officer responsible for the immediate evaluation of intelligence data collected in the field.
		SAFE	Support to the Analysts' File Environment.
NIST	National Intelligence Support Team.	*SE*	Special Estimate.
NPC	Nonproliferation Center.	*SEC*	Scientific Estimates Committee.
NRO	National Reconnaissance Office.	*SIC*	Scientific Intelligence Committee, successor to SEC.
NRP	National Reconnaissance Program.	*SIE*	Special Intelligence Estimate.
NSA	National Security Agency.	*SIGINT*	Signals intelligence. Intelligence information derived from all communications intelligence, electronics intelligence, and foreign instrumentation signals intelligence, however transmitted or collected.
NSA/CSS	National Security Agency/Central Security Service.		
NSCID	National Security Council Intelligence Directive.		
OCI	Office of Current Intelligence.		
OER	Office of Economic Reports.	*SLBM*	Submarine Launched Ballistic Missile.
OMB	Office of Management and Budget.		
ONE	Office of National Estimates.	*SNIE*	Special National Intelligence Estimate.
ONI	Office of Naval Intelligence.		
O/O	Office of Operations.	*SSO*	Special Security Office/Officer.
OPM	Office of Personnel Management.	*TECH ELINT*	Technical Electronic Intelligence.
ORD	Office of Research and Development.	*TIARA*	Tactical Intelligence and Related Activities. The military service intelligence programs separate from the NFIP and (starting in FY 1996) from the JMIP.
ORE	Office of Reports and Estimates.		
ORR	Office of Research and Reports.		
OSD	Office of the Secretary of Defense.		
OSI	Office of Scientific Intelligence.		
OSIS	Open-Source Information System.	*TR*	Terms of Reference.
OSR	Office of Strategic Research.	*UCA*	Unified Cryptologic Architecture.
OSS	Office of Strategic Services.	*USACOM*	US Atlantic Command.
PA&EO	Program Assessment and Evaluation Office, Community Management Staff.	*USCENTCOM*	US Central Command.
		USCIB	United States Communications Intelligence Board.
PDD	Presidential Decision Directive.	*USCS*	US Cryptologic System.
PFIAB	President's Foreign Intelligence Advisory Board.	*USEUCOM*	US European Command.
		USIB	United States Intelligence Board.

Coast Guard

Ability The quality of being able to do something, especially the physical, mental, financial, or legal power to accomplish something. A natural or acquired skill or talent. State or quality of being able (capability, flexibility, availability, etc.)

Accession Means of increasing or adding to the workforce. Examples include: enlisted recruiting, officer commissions, Chief Warrant Officer Appointments, civilian hiring, recall of retired or reserve personnel.

Accession Training Minimum essential training designed to provide basic skills required for service-entry or job-entry level performance. Includes Recruit, Class "A" Schools, OCS, Academy, CWO Indoctrination, Direct Commission, Basic Flight, CSPI, PPEP, NAPS.

Accomplishment A tangible achievement. An accomplishment may be a degree, license, certification, language proficiency, test score, honor, award or membership of an individual. Accomplishments have specified achievement dates and may have defined durations or expiration dates.

Accrual Process Date Used on the Vacation Request (leave) page. Date vacation entitlement (leave balance) was credited.

Active Duty Full-time duty in an active military service of the United States. It includes duty on the active list, full-time training duty, annual training duty, and attendance while in the active military service, at a school designated as a service school by law or by the Secretary of the military department concerned. (10 U.S.C. 101)

Active Duty for Special Work (ADSW-AC) ADSW-AC is Active Duty for Special Work performed by a reservist in support of the Active Component (formerly called TEMAC). Long-term ADSW-AC is duty performed consecutively in excess of 139 days. Short-term ADSW-AC is duty performed consecutively for 139 days or less. Reserve personnel on ADSW-AC do not fill an active duty PAL billet.

Active Duty for Special Work (ADSW-RC) ADSW-RC is Active Duty for Special Work performed by a reservist in support of the Reserve Component (formerly called SADT). Long-term ADSW-RC is duty performed consecutively in excess of 139 days. Short-term ADSW-RC is duty performed consecutively for 139 days or less. Reserve personnel on ADSW-RC do not fill an active duty PAL billet.

Active Duty for Training (ADT) A tour of active duty for training members of the Reserve component to provide trained units and qualified persons to fill needs of the Armed Forces during war or national emergency and such other times as national security requires. It includes annual training, special tours of ADT, school tours, and the initial duty of training performed by non-prior service enlistees.

Active Duty Other Than Training (ADOT) A tour of Active Duty that is used for support of Coast Guard missions. ADOT includes Active duty for Special Work (ADSW), Emergency Voluntary Active Duty, and Involuntary Active Duty.

Active Duty Promotion List (ADPL) A list of Coast Guard Officers on active duty in the rank of CWO2 and above who are not Reserve Program Administrators, Permanent Commissioned Teaching Staff, or Retired Officers recalled to Active Duty. The ADPL is used principally to determine precedence for promotion and is displayed in the Register of Officers.

Activity Guide The Activity Guide simplifies navigation by grouping separate tasks into one area.

Advanced Education Formal training or education which provides officer and enlisted personnel with the skills and knowledge required to become subject matter experts in various occupational specialties. Includes all Duty-under-Instruction, including post-graduate; ACET; Physician Assistant; Senior Service Schools.

AFC-01 Military pay, compensation, subsistence rations and entitlements for active duty, cadets, and reserve members undergoing Initial Active Duty Training (IADT).

AFC-08 Compensation, entitlements, and relocation costs for civilian employees.

AFC-20 Permanent Change of Station (PCS), travel and transportation expenses incident to PCS orders for military and dependents. Civilian relocation costs are funded from the AFC-08 account.

AFC-30 General operating and unit-level maintenance expenses.

AFC-30 "T" These are AFC-56 which has been converted to AFC-30 to facilitate further transfer to the field and headquarters units.

AFC-56 Formal training performed as TAD for civilian and military personnel, including Reserve members in the RK, RP and RY programs, and Auxiliarists.

AFC-57 General expenses to support health care of military members and their dependents.

AFC-90 Reserve expenses including repayments to other Coast Guard appropriations.

Agility Organizational ability to adjust and/or respond to new or changing conditions or requirements.

Airport Terminal The Airport Terminal provides commands with the ability to view pending arrivals and departures of personnel and to view member job related information. PCS orders will appear on the Airport Terminal until the PMIS transactions for the transfer have processed through the system.

Allotment Fund Control (AFC) AFC codes represent a breakdown of Operating Expenses (OE), Reserve Training (RT) and administrative operating targets (AOT) for specified purposes.

Annual Count of Officers 14 USC 42 requires the Secretary of Transportation to conduct a count of all officers on the ADPL at least once each year (usually in late May). The number of reimbursable officers (serving in joint commands) is subtracted from the total, and the remainder determines the maximum number of LCDR-RADM officers allowed on the ADPL.

Annual Training (ADT-AT) The specified period of active duty (normally 12 days) required annually of all members of the Selected Reserve. It may be performed in increments of one or more days depending upon mission requirements and budget constraints. The training must be related to the reservist's rate, RPAL billet requirement, or unit mission.

Applicant Someone who applies for a job.

Application Portal A Web site that helps you navigate to other web-based applications and content. This is usually your entry point when you launch your browser. You may customize it to include PeopleSoft application links, external links, and intranet links.

Appropriation An annual authorization by an Act of Congress to incur obligations for specified purposes and to make payments out of the Treasury. Appropriations are subdivided into budget activities, subheads, programs, projects, etc.

Assigned Billets/Positions Specific billets/positions at units or locations, listed by rating and paygrade (enlisted), specialty and paygrade (officer), or grade and series (civilian). These are approved and controlled by G-CCS, and are included on the Personnel Allowance List (PAL). Military personnel fill billets. Civilian personnel fill positions. In the Direct Access data structure all billets and positions are now referred to as positions.

Attendance The status of an employee's training or training request (e.g., completed, incomplete, course wait, or session wait).

Attrition All personnel losses from the Coast Guard, including resignation, death, administrative discipline, retirement, etc. May also be used to express losses from specific training courses or other programs.

Authorized Grade Distribution The total number of commissioned officers on the ADPL authorized to hold (by promotion) each grade as determined by the annual count of officers in accordance with 14 USC 42.

Authorized Strength The maximum number of personnel on active duty at the end of the fiscal year, as set by Congress in the current Coast Guard Authorization Act. The authorized strength of the Selected Reserve is set in the current National Defense Authorization Act.

Bargaining Unit Employee An employee included in an appropriate bargaining unit for which a labor organization has been granted exclusive recognition.

Billet/Position A billet is the authorization for a full time military position. It represents the duties, skills, responsibilities, pay grade and command relationships assigned to the military member. The parallel civilian term was position, but in the Direct Access data structure all billets and positions are now referred to as positions.

Breadcrumbs A small horizontal menu of links that is always present across the top of your page. The links show what pages, components, or menu navigation links you used to get to the current page.

Bundle A function used to group selected information and email it in one single email.

Business Process Re-engineering Changing practices, policies, and/or programs to improve overall performance. Based on an assessment of why the practice, policy and/or program exists, what it is intended to achieve, and what alternative methods could be used to better achieve the same objective.

Business Strategy The long-term goals and directions of an organization.

C4IT Electronics & IT Support Center.

Career Development Any activity or intervention that increase or changes an individual's knowledge, ability, or level of competency in areas that are designed to have direct linkage to a person's FUTURE job performance or career potential.

Causal Loop Generic: A description of the relationships among entities, quantities, properties, actions, whether constant or variable, such that the influence of one on another or others can be understood. Special use: a description of a circle of causality in which every element is both a cause and an effect, characterized by feedback, delays, and capable of generating behavior as a function of its structure. Usually used to describe a system, its components, its structure, and its predictable behavior.

CGHRMS Coast Guard Human Resources Management System.

Change Notice The electronic notification to G-CPA that the PAL should be changed based on delegated reprogramming authority as described in chapter 1 of this Personal Resources Reprogramming Manual.

CHRTT Civilian Human Resources Transformation Team.

CIAO Commandant's Intent Action Order.

Civilian Staffing Requirements (CSR) The CSR is a projection of the near-term civilian staffing needs of the Coast Guard. The CSR uses known budgetary changes and known reprogramming to predict the size and composition of the workforce. The CSR is then used in workforce planning.

Classification The process of determining the proper title, series, and grade level of a position, based on an in depth review of the duties and responsibilities, conducted through a Command's servicing Command Staff Advisor (CSA). A Position Description (PD) is tentatively classified when the process of determining the proper title, series, and grade level of a position has been completed with the exception of the PD cover sheet being certified and signed by the Classification Specialist.

Closed Rating This term is used in the CFTRR process to refer to a rating having more personnel in its enlisted peer group than ideal peer group. To be categorized as closed, the number of personnel in the rating must be greater than or equal to the number of authorized billets based on projected end-of-fiscal year personnel levels.

Collateral Duty Duty assigned to an individual by the commanding officer which is in addition to the individuals primary duty. These duties are normally performed at the individual's permanent duty station.

College Student Pre-Commissioning Initiative (CSPI) Formerly known as Minority Officer Recruiting Program (MORE). Offered at Historically Black Colleges and Universities (HBCU), Hispanic Association of Colleges and Universities (HACU) and other institutions approved by CGRC. Applicants are selected from sophomore and junior year civilian and Coast Guard reservists attending designated institutions that offer an accredited 4-year bachelor degree program. CSPI is a fully funded scholarship program which may pay up to two academic years of college tuition, books, and essential supplies for full-time students. While enrolled in school the CSPI candidate is enlisted in the regular Coast Guard, as an E-3, with a four-year active duty obligation.

Command Staff Advisor (CSA)/Human Resource Specialist Provide front line civilian personnel advisory services to management and employees. They are located in Washington, DC, Baltimore, MD, Norfolk, VA, Elizabeth City, NC, Boston, MA, USCG Academy, Miami, FL, New Orleans, LA, Alameda, CA, Seattle, WA, Kodiak, AK, and Honolulu, HI.

Command User A permission list/user role, which allows unit administrators access to the Airport Terminal, Unit Roster, Unit Personnel Allowance List (PAL), review and approved orders, reserve drills, career intentions worksheets and Employee Review (enlisted evaluations).

Competencies Competencies is a PeopleSoft term used to describe a person's skills, training, achievements and awards. In the Coast Guard, we use the Competencies module to record the following information about our personnel: Competencies (formerly known as Qualification Codes) Education and Degree Information Languages Honors and Awards Test Results from Armed Services Vocational Aptitude Battery (ASVAB) tests and retests. School completions, including Class "A" and "C" schools that are entered through the Training Administration System (TAS). Licenses & Certifications Memberships

Competency A skill, ability, behavior (other), or knowledge directly related to an employee's current position. Replaced Qual Code or Experience Indicator.

Competency Dictionary The definitive list of all competencies available for use. Includes the Competency Code, Title, Description, Eligibility, Sponsor, Special Status.

Competency Model Set of job competencies that together make up a profile for success for a particular job.

Competency Type Broad grouping of competencies establishing the functional area of a competency; Cutter Ops, Aviation, Communications. Competency Types can usually be directly related to Job Codes and/or Positions.

Component A group of related pages that pertain to a specific task. You access components from the menu. Components contain folder tabs with each tab containing a related page.

Contingency Personnel Requirements List (CPRL) The consolidated listing of forces (as contained in Contingency Plans) required by Operational Commanders and Headquarters to conduct contingency operations in time of war or national emergencies. The skills, rates, and ratings needed for CPRL-driven Reserve force requirements are reflected in the Reserve billets contained on the PAL as prioritized during the Reserve Workforce Structure Board process.

Contract Manpower Equivalent (CME) The number of man-years required if in-house employees perform contract workload at the same level of performance required in the contract's Performance Work Statement (PWS).

Controlled Enlisted Paygrades The grades E-8 and E-9 are controlled grades per 10 USC 517. This cap is set as a percentage of the active duty enlisted workforce at 1% for E-9 and 2.5% for E-8.

Controlled Officer Paygrades The number of officers on the ADPL serving in paygrades O4-O8 is limited to certain percentages prescribed by 14 USC 42. The exact number is determined at the beginning of the promotion year through the annual count process and maintained through promotion to vacancy. O9 and O10 are controlled by 14 USC by position not number.

Core Values The personal attributes expected of each member of Team Coast Guard.

Cost Benefit Analysis Compares what efforts will cost to expected in order to determine which is greater.

Course Session The instance of a course at a facility on a date. Each session has a sequence number. Replaced Scheduled Course Convene

Critical Skills Retention Bonus (CSRB) A retention bonus paid to active duty officers and enlisted who are qualified in a designated critical skill. By accepting the CSRB, the member agrees to an additional obligated service of not less than one year. A critical skill is a military skill designated as critical by the Secretary of Homeland Security.

CRRT CIAO Reorganization Review Team.

Culture A complex of typical behavior or standardized social characteristics peculiar to a specific group, occupation, or profession.

Culture Shifts Managing readiness requires more than an information system, it requires a fundamental shift in our attitude and behavior. The paradigms of our past will hinder our future success.

Customer Anyone internal or external to the service for whom the organization provides goods or services.

Dashboard Collection of measurement indicators.

DCMS Deputy Commandant for Mission Support.

DCO Deputy Commandant for Operations.

Deciding Official Term used in civilian employee relations. Management or supervisory official in the line of authority over the grievant has the responsibility to decide informal and formal grievances. Grievance-deciding officials must be at a higher administrative level than the official who initiated the subject action. At the informal step, an employee presents a grievance involving performance ratings to the approving official for reconsideration. The employee then presents the formal grievance, to the next level supervisor in the chain of command.

Department A unit or subordinate element of a unit. Used in place of the terms Unit or subunit.

Department ID/DeptID A number used to identify a department. Replaced ATU/OPFAC.

Department Type Refers to Unit Type (e.g., MSO, Air Station, etc.).

Dependent/Beneficiary List of Employee's Dependents.

Dependent Life Servicemember's Group Life Insurance for Dependents.

Direct Commission Officer (DCO) Category of accession programs. Provides officers with specialized skill sets to fill junior officer billets. Examples include Direct Commission lawyers, aviators, and Kings Point graduates.

Downgrade To lower the paygrade to a PAL position.

DSF Deployable Special Forces.

e-Interview Process used to endorse the e-Resume.

e-Resume The e-Resume, Job Basket and e-Interview functions are new terms used to describe the functionality that replaced the Electronic Assignment Data Card (e-ADC), Shopping List and the e-ADC endorsement process. The applications are accessed via the Coast Guard intranet (CGWEB), and consist of multiple web pages, which users complete, or review.

Education Instruction which provides the learner with knowledge and skills desired or required for future application in the accomplishment of general tasks or combinations of tasks, usually related to a particular discipline

Effectiveness The level of success in achieving established objectives or meeting established standards. A ratio of accomplishment to objective.

Efficiency A measure of how well resources are being utilized; the absence of waste in a process.

Employee Class/Empl Class Indicates the employee's affiliation with the Coast Guard. Replaced Member Type codes.

Employee ID/Emplid A system-generated unique identifier for an employee (7-digit number). The Emplid replaces the Social Security number as the primary method of accessing member records. This ID is not Privacy Act or FOIA sensitive.

Employee Review An employee performance evaluation. Replaces Enlisted Performance Evaluation Review (EPER) or Officer Evaluation Report (OER)

Employee Scope Policies and procedures extend to resent non-bargaining unit employees except for probationary, intermittent, and temporary employees not entitled to grievance rights.

Employee Status/Empl Status Indicates the employee's status in relation to the empl class (i.e., Regular(class), Active(status)). Replaces Member Type Three, Duty Dtatus Code.

End Strength The number of officer and enlisted requirements that can be authorized (funded) based on approved budgets.

Enlisted Force An ideal proportion of billets for each rate as a percentage of the total enlisted structure E-4 through E-9. The ideal enlisted force structure is based on Time In Grade goals which are common to the whole enlisted workforce; realistic attrition rates for each rating/paygrade; and statutory limits on the total number of E-9s (1%) and E-8s (2.5%) authorized as a percentage of the overall enlisted workforce.

Enlisted Selective Early Retirement Board (ESERB) Form of compensation in which a control board selects senior retirement eligible enlisted personnel for early mandatory retirement ensuring best qualified individuals are retained. This method gives responsibility to a select group to make an informed decision on the promotion ability of senior enlisted personnel based on their performance.

External Applicant A person who is not employed by the company and applies for a position.

Facility The location at which the session is conducted—typically a CG Training Center or DOD site.

Fact Finder Term used in civilian employee relations. An individual the formal grievance-deciding official appoints to investigate an issue(s) raised in a grievance. The fact finder must be a person uninvolved in the subject issue and who holds a position equal to any official who recommended, advised, decided or otherwise is or was involved in the contended matter. The fact finder may be an employee within the Coast Guard command or of another Coast Guard command, or any other person competent to carry out the fact-finding investigation.

Feedback The amount of clear information received regarding how well or how poorly one's job has been performed.

Fiscal Year (FY) The twelve-month period beginning 1 October and ending 30 September, which serves as the basis for the Federal Budget Cycle.

Folder tabs Folder tabs correspond to panel group items. Multiple panels are grouped into a panel group in PeopleSoft applications to organize information that cannot effectively fit onto one panel.

Force An aggregation of military personnel, weapon systems, and necessary support or combination of such elements.

Force/Rating Managers Force managers are experts assigned to an Assistant Commandant who advise on rating specific or specialty issues and changes.

Force Structure The proportion of billets in each paygrade to the total for a specific force.

Full-Time Equivalent (FTE) The equivalent of 2,080 work hours, which is the standard work year. The term FTE is sometimes used interchangeably with the term man-years.

Full-Time Permanent Positions (FTP) Positions that are authorized without a time limit and which provide for a regular 40 hour workweek. Although typically used to describe civilian positions, the term FTP can also be used to describe billets or positions in the Coast Guard budget.

Function The aggregation of occupationally related tasks within a mission.

General Detail A necessary part of the military workforce that accounts for personnel who are not filling an assigned unit billet. The purpose of the General Detail is to account for accession and some follow on training of the military workforce, and for extended period of absence due to disciplinary, medical, or transient reasons. In other words, the General Detail is the overhead required to ensure that all assigned billets can be filled all the time with no lapse. The General Detail is composed of the Support Allowance and the Training Allowance.

Geocentric Staffing An international staffing method that ignores nationality in favor of ability and seeks the best people for key jobs.

Grade A step or degree in a graduated scale of military rank or civilian grade that has been established by law or regulation.

Grid A method of presenting data in rows and columns. This is similar to a spreadsheet.

Grievance An employee's or group of employees' written request for personal relief in a matter of concern or dissatisfaction about their employment subject to the commanding officers' for MWR and CGES managers' control.

GUI Stands for Graphical User Interface. A computer display that takes advantage of graphics capabilities in order to make a program easier to use. Well-designed graphical user interfaces can free the user from learning complex command languages.

Guiding Principles Overarching values that govern the conduct of Coast Guard business.

GWIS Global Workforce Information Solution. Provides capability to view personnel data for members under your area of responsibility. Provides the conduit for review of data and an awareness of the quality level.

Hearing Examiner The formal grievance-deciding official authorizes to conduct a hearing on an issue(s) raised in a grievance. The hearing examiner mush have been trained to conduct hearings, is uninvolved in the contended matter, and occupies a position equal to an official who recommended, advised, decide, or otherwise was involved in the contended matter.

High-level key The field in a row of data in a PeopleSoft database that uniquely identifies that row from the other rows in the database.

High Year Tenure (HYT) Prescribes professional growth points (PGP) that must be achieved if an individual is to remain on active duty. These PGPs indicate the pay grade a member must reach within a certain time. See PERSMAN Chapter 12.G.

Hire Hiring someone into the company is the process of making an applicant an employee. The hire process includes gathering personal information, recording payroll data, assigning benefit programs, etc.

HR Generalist Administers or coordinate programs that span several HR functions.

HR Planning A process that forecasts personnel needs for an organization and develops programs and activities to meet those needs.

HR Specialist Has expertise in a discrete HR functional area.

HR&A Human Resources and Admin.

HSWL Health, Safety, and Work-Life.

Human Capital Consists of combined knowledge, skills, and experience of a company's employees.

Human Resource Management (HRM) Is the function that assists organizations in achieving goals by obtaining and maintaining effective employees.

Incumbent The person currently holding a specific position.

Indicator A gauge on the dashboard. Can be a weighted index of measures.

Individual Development Any activity or intervention that increases or changes an individual's knowledge, ability, or level of competency.

Internal Applicant A person who is already employed by the company and applies for a different position within the company.

Job Basket The Job Basket serves as a holding area to store your job selections for inclusion on your e-Resume. The Job Basket is accessible from the View Job Postings page. Jobs stay in your job basket until you remove them

Job Competencies Basic characteristics that can link individuals or teams to enhanced performance; critical success factors needed to perform a given role in an organization. To help understand the scope of this notion, most research and most competency models suggest that there are up to about 20 competencies involved in any single job.

Job Family A named grouping of jobcodes. BM, HS, and TC are examples of Job Families (Ratings).

Job Requisition A request to have a vacant position filled by an applicant. When an employee leaves a job or a new job is created, a job requisition containing relevant job information is created.

Jobcode A numeric code that represents an enlisted person's pay grade or an officer's rank (Rate, Grade, or Rank).

Lagging Indicator Measure of performance that has already occurred. Examples include the number of deaths in recreational boating last year, number of lives saved, number of gallons spilled and number of pounds of drugs seized.

Language Proficiency Description of a member's ability to speak, read, or write in a foreign language. See the user aid for full description of the codes used and their meaning. Replaced Language code.

LCs Logistics Centers.

Leading Indicators Measures that can be assessed to predict future performance. For example, the trend in percentages of new boaters taking boating safety courses.

Loss Rate The rate at which members leave any specified workforce or other identified entity. It includes both attrition and transition to other workforces or components. For example, losses from Enlisted to Officer programs; transitions from Active Duty to the Reserve and visa versa. Loss rate is calculated by dividing all losses during a year by the strength of the specified workforce at the beginning of the year.

LTPIO Logistics Transformation Program Integration Office.

Maintain Gross A special tax withholding status utilized by members who desire not to have federal tax withheld from their pay. Note: If indicated, wages will continue to be reported to the IRS. Additionally, status must be renewed annually by 1 February.

Man-Hour A unit measuring work. It is equivalent to one person working at a normal pace for 30 minutes, or similar combination of people working at a normal pace for a period of time equal to 60 minutes.

Man-Hour Availability Factor (MAF) The average number of man-hours per month an assigned individual is available to perform primary duties. Required man-hours are divided by MAF times the overload factor to determine the manpower requirement.

Management Study An analysis of an organization's products and services, customers, suppliers, processes, metrics and resources for the purpose of developing the most efficient organization (MEO). The MEO is the in-house organizational and product/service task structure which best meets the requirements of the a performance work statement (PWS) while using minimal amount of resources.

Manning The specific inventory of personnel at an activity in terms of numbers, grades, and occupational groups.

Manpower Determinant A means of quantifying manpower requirements. Determinants may cover a wide variety of methodologies including but not limited to manpower standards, models, and guides.

Manpower Management The methodical process of determining validating, and using manpower requirements as a basis for budget decisions, determining manpower authorization priorities based on available funding and personnel inventory; and the ability to link all these factors together.

Manpower Requirement The expression of skilled labor needed to accomplish a job, workload, mission or program. There are two types of manpower requirements: funded and unfunded. Funded manpower requirements are those that have been validated and allocated and are reflected in the most recent Military Staffing Requirement. Unfunded requirements are validated manpower needs but deferred because of budgetary constraints.

Manpower Standard A quantitative expression representing manpower requirements in response to varying levels of workload. A standard also includes a description of the workload, associated conditions on which the standard is built, a grade and skill level table, approved variances, and a product/service task analysis summary.

Menus A three-column navigation list that contains menu headings and links you can click to move between the pages of your system.

Metrics Individual data points.

Military Essential Positions that directly contribute to prosecution of war (combat support), exercise Uniform Code of Military Justice authority, are required by law, military due to customs or traditions, are needed for overseas rotations, or require a skill not available in the civilian workforces. Other workloads are not military essential and should be performed and should be performed by in-service civilians or contract services.

Military Skill Skill associated with a military that is not considered to be part of a person's occupational specialty.

Military Staffing Requirements (MSR) The MSR is a projection of the near-term staffing needs of the Coast Guard. The MSR uses known budgetary changes and known reprogramming to predict the size and composition of the workforce. The MSR/CSR is then used in workforce planning of accessions, training, and promotion.

Minimal Crewing The overriding goal of minimal crewing is to determine the smallest quantity of people required to operate and maintain a platform without due regard for total system support, lifetime sustainability, and total ownership cost implications. This results in an imbalance between the shipboard personnel requirement and the enabling personnel support elements such as training, assignments, billet backfill supply/demand, skill/experience supply/demand, quality of service, etc. The upshot is that a quest for lowest life-cycle cost for a platform by minimizing the size of its crew likely results in greater total ownership costs, risk, and adverse impacts with respect to the full range of human resources considerations.

Mission The task, together with the purpose, that clearly states and indicates the action to be taken and reason therefore. A duty assigned to an individual or unit.

Mission Demand/Resource Capability Gap The delta between the required ability to respond and accomplish specific or multiple mission areas identified by a threat assessment and the reality of utilizing resources that are not necessarily designed or best suited for that specific mission area.

Mission Requirements A statement of manpower needed to accomplish a job, workload, mission, or program. There are two types of manpower requirements: funded and unfunded. Funded manpower requirements are those that have been validated and allocated. Unfunded requirements are validated manpower needs which are deferred because of budgetary constraints.

Monthly Summary of Military Billets (MSMB) Report which provides the monthly distribution of military billets by pay grade on the Personnel Allowance List (PAL). These billets are identified as assigned, other allowances, training, and support allowance billets.

MSLT Mission Support Leadership Team.

MSPAIT Mission Support Planning and Integration Team.

Multi-part key The combination of fields in a row of data in a PeopleSoft database that uniquely identifies that row from the other rows in the database.

National ID Social Security number (SSN). A sequence of numbers which identifies one specific individual.

Naval Academy Preparatory School (NAPS) School designed to provide qualified enlisted personnel with the educational skills required to compete effectively for appointments to the Coast Guard Academy. NAPS is specifically aimed at personnel who may have been educationally or culturally deprived, but who have demonstrated that they possess the potential to become a Coast Guard officer.

Navigation Header The header area in PeopleSoft Internet Architecture that remains static as you navigate through your pages. The navigation header contains links back to your homepage and a Signoff button. If you are running the portal, the navigation header also has a Categories, Favorites, and Search feature.

Needs Analysis Process by which an organization's human resource development needs are identified and articulated in order to help the organization accomplish its objectives; also called assessment or needs assessment.

Needs Assessment Process by which an organization's human resource development needs are identified and articulated in order to help the organization accomplish its objectives; also called assessment or needs analysis.

NEPA National Environmental Policy Act.

Nonemployee, Applicant A person who will attend Coast Guard sponsored training or is in the process of becoming a Coast Guard employee. An applicant will have an employee ID that begins with an "A."

NVQ Unit National Vocational Code. NVQs are qualifications for work and show you can actually do a job, and not simply that you know how to do it in theory.

Officer Corps Consist of commissioned officers between the paygrades of O-1 (ensign) and O-10 (admiral). Includes officers serving on regular active duty, reserve officers serving on extended active duty (EAD) contracts, retired officers in recall status (on "retired recall"), members of the Permanent Commissioned Teaching Staff (for the CG Academy), and reserve officers serving on active duty as Reserve Program Administrators (RPA). While chaplains and uniformed members of the Public Health service do wear the Coast Guard uniform, they are not considered part of the Officer Corp. Federal Law limits the overall size of the officer corps to 6,200 officers. In addition to limiting the overall size of the officer corps, Federal law limits the number of officers serving in paygrades O-4 (lieutenant commander) and above. Currently, the number of flag officers (O-7 & O-8) cannot exceed 0.75% of the active duty officer corps. Likewise, captains (O-6) are limited to 6%, commanders (O-5) are limited to 12%, and lieutenant commanders (O-4) are limited to 18% of the active duty officer corps.

Officer Specialty Managers The officer specialty manager performs a similar function to the Enlisted Rating/Force Manager. Specialty Managers are not listed in any formal Coast Guard publication, but are typically assigned as a collateral duty on the staff of a given Headquarters Program Manager. The concept of officer specialty management has taken shape for the officer corps to deal with specific officer specialty accession, training, and assignment needs.

Open Rate List (ORL) A list of rates (rating/paygrade) into which recruiters may recruit prior CG and/or DOD personnel. These ratings may have temporary shortages and/or require special skills that are currently not available in the CG.

Operating Facilities of the Coast Guard (OPFAC) An OPFAC is a Coast Guard unit or facility, including assigned boats and aircraft. The listing of all OPFACs in the Coast Guard is found at the G-CPA Intranet site. By definition, an OPFAC is a manned facility, thus having personnel resources allocated to accomplishing the assigned missions. This intranet OPFAC listing outlines the command relationships for every unit and sub-unit in the Coast Guard. OPFACs have unique identification numbers that are integrated in the assignment, pay, and logistics systems of the Coast Guard. The PAL on G-CPA's Intranet site has been modified so that Direct Access "Department IDs" can be cross-referenced with OPFAC numbers.

Operating Facility Change Orders (OFCO) An OFCO is a change to an OPFAC. An OFCO is required under many circumstances, including commissioning, decommissioning, relocating, or renaming a unit. OFCOs must always address personnel resource changes, and thus are a primary input to the Personnel Resource Management System. Operating Facility Change Order Procedures, COMDTINST M5440.3 (series) details the OFCO process.

Operator ID/OprID The code an employee uses to access CGHRMS. This can be the same as your employee ID or your name or a combination of the two.

Optimal Crewing First and foremost, optimal crewing is not minimum crewing! Rather, it is an analytically determined crew size consistent with risk, affordability, human performance capability, and human workload. The largest single component of life cycle cost for a naval ship is manpower, including recruiting, training, assigning, and supporting Sailors for operations, maintenance and support. The primary benefits of optimal crewing are improved total system performance and a significant reduction in ownership costs. Other benefits include an increased emphasis on supporting human performance, productivity, safety, and quality of life, resulting in enhanced crew satisfaction and greater acceptance of technology initiatives. There are several critical factors required to achieve optimal crewing. Acquisition and design processes for ship systems must foster a design approach that encompasses human roles and requirements while reducing workload allocated to the human. Additionally, current policies for personnel and training and supporting infrastructure and the means to support a new and potentially different crew composition in a competitive personnel resource market environment, must be reviewed. Finally, the laws, regulations, doctrine, and cultural drivers for all of these policies must be addressed. An optimal crewing strategy begins with an assumed manning level of zero (0). Human involvement must be justified through a top down functional and task analysis. Human involvement requirements must be defined by a human-centered systems engineering process, called human systems integration (HSI). HSI brings to systems design a concern for the human as a part of the total system. It is an application of total systems engineering with emphasis on the roles, responsibilities, and requirements for the human. The process, tools and data required to integrate human performance into a system are also part of HSI, as are the traditional human factors engineering areas, such as manpower, personnel, training, safety, and life support. Through HSI, mission function and task allocation can be analytically applied to hardware, software, or people in terms of life cycle cost and performance tradeoffs.

Organization Analysis A method for evaluating organizational structure. It examines the structure's effectiveness and efficiency in supporting the organization's mission and it includes development of a suitable organization.

Organization Reengineering Study A holistic analysis of an organization's mission and structure, products and services, customers, suppliers, tasks, metrics, resources and operating environment for the purpose of developing the most efficient and effective delivery of the products and services needed to meet mission requirements.

Organizational Culture Is the shared attitudes and perceptions in an organization.

Output The amount of something produced by a system or process during a given span of time.

Page The individual display and data-entry screens for each part of your PeopleSoft application. Pages appear in the browser window. In PeopleSoft 7.5, this was called a panel.

Parameter A characteristic or property of a population.

Pareto Chart Shows how several items contribute to a total effect.

Performance The ability to generate the highest level of results at the least cost.

Performance Cycle View the chart at: http://mycg.uscg.mil/uscg_docs/portal/MyCG/Editorial/20031009/Performance.cycle.graph.pdf

Performance Standards The expectations of management translated into behaviors and results that employees can deliver.

Permission Lists The permission lists are the objects that control what a user can and can't access in the system. In most cases, users have a collection of permission lists. A collection of permission lists is a Role. See Role User.

PERSCEN Personnel Service Center (not the old PSC Topka, which is now PPC, Pay and Personnel Center).

Personal Development Areas that are for purely personal benefit without direct linkage to a person's job performance or career potential (e.g., estate planning, managing credit, marriage workshop, lawn repair). Any activity or intervention that increases or changes an individual's knowledge, ability, or level of competency in areas that are for purely personal benefit without direct linkage to a person's job performance or career potential (e.g., estate planning, managing credit, marriage workshop, lawn mower repair).

Personal Relief A specific remedy directly benefiting the grievant(s); it may not include a request for disciplinary or other action affecting another employee or individual.

Personnel Allowance Amendment (PAA) A document (CGHQ-9750A) used to modify any attributes of military billets or civilian positions on the Personnel Allowance List (PAL).

Personnel Allowance List (PAL) The PAL is a database listing of authorized full-time permanent civilian positions, selected reserve military billets and active duty military billets (including General Detail) that includes relevant information related to that billet (OPFAC; position number; OBC; appropriation, program, and sponsor codes; source; special training and qualification requirements; OPM series classification codes). PAL is the personnel resource allocation tool for the Coast Guard.

Personnel Assigned A tabulation of all officer and enlisted personnel charged to an activity.

Personnel Inventory Number of personnel available by occupational classification, paygrade and distribution category.

Position Billet (military) and position (civilian).

Position Description (PD) A position description is a written record of duties, responsibilities and supervision received for each civilian position. A PD is tentatively classified when the process of determining the proper title, series, and grade level of a position has been completed with the exception of the PD cover sheet being certified and signed by the Classification Specialist.

Position Number Identifies a position. Replaced Billet Control Number (BCN).

Position Number (PN) Numbering systems used in Direct Access to identify billets and positions on the PAL. The PAL on G-CPA's Intranet site has been modified so that Direct Access Position Numbers can be cross-referenced with POSITION NUMBERs/POSITION NUMBERs.

Precommissioning Program for Enlisted Personnel (PPEP) Enables selected enlisted personnel with associate degrees to attend college full-time for up to two years with a goal of qualifying to attend OCS. The program serves as an upward mobility mechanism for qualified enlisted members to become commissioned officers.

Preparedness A process intended to ensure that response plans, capability, and the organization are ready for prompt and effective reaction to incidents, with the goal of minimizing impacts.

Prevention The procedures undertaken by the public and private sector to minimize either the likelihood of occurrence of certain acts or events or the consequences of their occurrence.

Professional Development Any activity or intervention that increase or changes an individual's knowledge, ability, or level of competency in areas that are designed to have direct linkage to a person's CURRENT job performance.

Proficiency Level Proficiency levels relate to the POSITION, not the PERSON in the position. These levels describe the level of proficiency required of a competency that is needed in order to accomplish the duties and tasks of a position.

Program Manager An individual who has the responsibility of advocating for, setting performance standards for, and monitoring the successful use of resources engaged in pursuing the goals of a program.

Programming The process of transplanting planned force requirements into time-phased manpower.

Projected Workload An amount of work proposed or anticipated in the future to meet the requirement of a program/function.

PSD Personnel Support Division.

Quality Control Those actions taken by the performing organization to control the production of goods or services so that they will meet the requirements of the performance work statement.

Readiness Management Period (RMP, formerly known as "Appropriate Duty") A special period of Inactive Duty Training (IDT) for reservists (differing from single and multiple drills), under orders of three to eight hours duration, normally performed on one calendar day. However, one period may be performed incrementally within one calendar week. One RMP is equivalent to a single IDT drill for pay and point purposes.

Recruitment Bonus A one-time payment, up to 25% base pay, to fill a newly appointed civilian position from outside the Federal Government, when in absence of such a bonus, difficulty would be encountered in filling the position.

Reduction-In-Force (RIF) An involuntary separation of civilian employees involving layoffs, furloughs for more than 30 days or involuntary retirement (demotion without separation could be considered a RIF). Under the RIF system, employees compete for retention in their jobs based on the following retention factors (specified by law): (1) Type of appointment (tenure) (2) Veterans preference (3) Total length of civilian and creditable military service (4) Performance ratings.

Reengineering A holistic, methodical approach to reviewing the products and services of an enterprise, the associated processes and tasks, and the resources to accomplish them so as to construct an organization that matches people and available resources to products/services and track in the best, most efficient way to meet customer requirement.

Reimbursable Agreement Numbers Reimbursement is an amount collected and credited to an appropriation for items and services furnished, usually on an occasional basis. An interagency agreement provides budget authority to the performing agency in addition to that provided by its own appropriation. In simple terms, this means that the Coast Guard's budget authority is increased to cover the obligations incurred by these additional services. The Coast Guard uses reimbursable agreements to provide services to other agencies. For example, Coast Guard reservists may be ordered to duty to support the Federal Emergency Management Agency (FEMA) for hurricane, oil or hazardous chemical responses. Another example would be Coast Guard support to the Selective Service System (SSS).

Relocation Bonus A one-time payment to a civilian employee of up to 25% of basic pay, to entice a current high quality Federal employee to accept a position in a different commuting area.

Reprogramming The act of reallocating financial or personnel resources from one use to another, which produces no net change to the overall Coast Guard appropriation on number of billets/positions. For example, the reprogramming of funds from AFC-01 to AFC-08 is neutral to the overall Operating Expenses appropriation. Similarly, moving a YN2 billet from one unit to another is neutral. While most reprogrammings are not simple, they all result in no net change to Coast Guard appropriations

Reserve Personnel Allowance List (RPAL) A listing of Coast Guard billet requirements for selected reservists based on contingency needs, augmentation, and training opportunities. SELRES member accessions, assignments, and advancements are based upon RPAL, which includes a POSITION NUMBER, a rating and grade, and any required qualification code for each billet. The Reserve Personnel Allowance List (RPAL) is integrated with the Personnel Allowance List (PAL).

Reserve Program Administrator An officer of the Coast Guard Reserve assigned on extended active duty for the purpose of performing duty in connection with organizing, administering, recruiting, instructing, and training the Reserve component of the Coast Guard (see 10 U.S.C. 10211).

Retention Generally, a measure of the voluntary component of turnover: those who, having a choice to leave, choose to stay. This may be a measure ("retention is increasing") or an action to influence the decision ("our retention programs include bonuses and . . ."). Specific to the military, the number of people who, after the end of their service obligation, remain in the service.

Retention Allowance Is an ongoing payment, up to 25% of basic pay to retain a current federal employee in his or her present position. These allowances are intended to be used in unusual cases.

Risk Analysis A technique for assessing the risk associated with reducing or eliminating functions/sub-functions. This is accomplished by assigning a priority code to all functions/subfunctions. Impact statements for lowest priority work are developed for use by management in deciding whether to eliminate or reduce low priority tasking.

Role User Role users are the User Profiles or users that have membership to a particular role. Users inherit most of their permissions from the role(s) assigned to the User Profile.

Run Control A run control is a database record that provides values for these settings. Instead of entering the same values each time you run a report, you create (and save) a run control with those settings. The next time you run the report, you select the run control, and the system fills in the settings.

Run Control IDs Each run control you create receives a unique run control ID. When you select a report from a menu, a search dialog box appears, asking for a run control ID. If you're in Add mode, enter a new ID for the run control you're about to define. If you're in Update/Display mode, enter an existing run control ID or press Enter and select from the list of available run control IDs.

Same Day Transfer A term used on orders directing a change of station where both stations are located within the same corporate limits and, therefore, do not require traveling.

Scrollbar Scrollbars are provided when grids contain more information than what will fit on the screen. Click the scrollbar arrows to view hidden rows and columns.

SCs Support Centers.

Selected Reserve (SELRES) That portion of the Ready Reserve consisting of units and, as designated by the Secretary concerned, of individual reservists with the highest priority for mobilization who participate in inactive duty training periods and annual training in a pay status. Also includes persons performing initial active duty for training.

Selective Early Retirement Board (SERB) A workforce management tool designed to force military members to retire earlier than prescribed by other mandatory retirement laws. Currently used as a continuation board for CWO4s.

Selective Reenlistment Bonus (SRB) This bonus is a cash payment which the Coast Guard uses as an incentive to retain members in specialties experiencing personnel shortages. (A reenlistment bonus that is used as an incentive to encourage the retention of individuals in designated critical ratings.)

Service Contract A contract which delivers a task or service rather than furnishing an end item of supply.

SFLC Surface Forces Logistics Center.

Shared Vision A unified set of objectives held by everyone in the entire organization to focus on completing priorities.

Signal Number Each officer on the ADPL and IDPL is assigned a signal number annually. This number designates their seniority in relation to other active duty officers at the beginning of the calendar year.

SILC Shore Infrastructure Logistics Center.

Skills Inventories Data files containing information on knowledge, skills, abilities, and experience of current employees.

Source Indicates whether a position is active duty, reserve, or civilian.

Special Salary Rate Pay rates which are set higher than the minimum for all civilian employees in a particular occupation and location where there is significant recruitment and retention problems. Coast Guard requests must be submitted through DOT and OPM before special rates can be established.

Specialty Training Training needed by an individual to function in a specific assigned billet. Specialty training is typically received between the notification for PCS orders and the reporting date at the new unit. Mandatory ("pipeline") training must be received prior to reporting. Suggested training is desirable before reporting. Includes "C" Schools greater than 20 weeks in duration; all mandatory pre-arrival ("pipeline") training and Aviation Student Engineering.

Staffing Standards A Staffing Standard defines the quantitative and qualitative manpower required to accomplish identified workloads for a class of units, unit or activities. A staffing standard identifies the skill levels, series, rating and paygrades needed to perform Coast Guard work activity. Staffing standards, determined by studies, are contained in the Staffing Standards Manual, COMDTINST M5312.11 (series).

Standard Personnel Costs (SPC) Standard Personnel Costs provide estimates of the total costs associated with the employment of a civilian or military member for an entire year. It is broken down by paygrade and includes all pay and allowances as well as travel expenses. For military members, the costs associated with retirement are not included as because this is a separate mandatory appropriation. These costs should be used when preparing budget documents for the relevant budget year and for other internal purposes such as Resource Proposals, Planning Proposals, etc. SPCs are maintained by the Director of Finance & Procurement.

Standards An exact value, a physical entity, or an abstract concept established and defined by authority, custom, or common consent to serve as a reference, model, or rule in measuring quantities or qualities, establishing practices or procedures, or evaluating results ..a fixed quantity or quality.

Standby Reserve A category of the Reserve composed of members other than the Ready Reserve and Retired Reserve, who are liable for active duty in time of war or national emergency declared by Congress, or when otherwise authorized by law. No member of the Standby Reserve may be involuntarily ordered to active duty until it has been determined that there are not enough of the required types of units of personnel in the Ready Reserve who are readily available. (10 U.S.C. 373, 10 U.S.C. 674).

Strategic Objectives Goals and or vision formulated and approved at the highest level of the organization. Strategic objectives encompass operational and tactical objectives.

STT Strategic Transformation & Alignment Team.

Sub-Department Division or branch within a unit.

Succession Planning The process of identifying long-range needs and cultivating a supply of talent to meet those needs.

Superior Qualifications Appointment Setting pay for a newly appointed civilian employee, higher than the minimum rate of his/her grade due to 1) the superior qualifications of the employee or the employee meets a special need of the agency; and 2) the individual's existing pay.

Support Allowance The Support Allowance is the part of the General Detail which accounts for work-years of personnel who are not assigned to a Coast Guard unit, but who are not available to fill assigned billets or Training Allowance Billets. This part of the General Detail accounts for the work-years of labor consumed while hospitalized, in correctional custody, assigned to a unit in excess of its authorization, or in transit (change of station) between one unit and the next.

System As any element, platform, unit (or collection of units) that work together to execute CG missions. The Coast Guard is a system of systems.

TAS The Training Administration System. This application is used by training schedulers at Training Quota Management Center and Coast Guard Personnel Command, to maintain course sessions, enroll students, complete course sessions, create Travel Order Numbers, and start the orders issuing process. Schedulers can verify member level enrollment data, view course sessions that are currently set up, enter unit funded training for a member, and enroll/wait list members for Class "A" or "C" schools. Training Centers access the application to complete courses sessions.

Task A subdivision of work within a particular category.

TEMAC See Active Duty for Special Work (ADSW).

Temporary Early Retirement Authority (TERA) (Also referred to as the 15 year retirement). A drawdown tool that permits early retirement for selected military members with more than 15 years, but less than 20 years of military service.

TONO An acronym for travel order number.

Training Instruction which provides the learner with knowledge and skills required for immediate application in the accomplishment of a specific task or combinations of tasks.

Training Allowance The training allowance is part of the General Detail that accounts for total work-years of personnel undergoing training and education.

Training Allowance Billet (TAB) A billet or position specifically linked to a training program. In most cases, TAB is really an accounting notion, representing the accumulation of training into one work year of consumed labor. For example, CG Recruit Training is approximately 2months (1/6 of a year) in duration. If the CG anticipates sending 3600 recruits through Boot Camp this fiscal year, the TAB requirement for that training would be 3600 X 1/6 or 600 TABs. In other cases such as Post Graduate Training or Flight Training, members receive PCS orders to a TAB position that is located at the training site.

Training Program The set of courses for a position. Commonly referred to as "Pipeline Training." Replaced T Billet.

Training Requirements The documented (in policy, guidance, or doctrine) skills, knowledge and expertise usually obtained through some level of school house or classroom indoctrination.

Travel & Transportation Expenses Agencies may pay the travel and transportation expenses of a newly hired Federal employee going to the first post of duty.

Unit Roster The Unit Roster, accessed via the Airport Terminal, provides a listing of all personnel and positions at a department.

URL Abbreviation for Uniform Resource Locator, which is the global address of documents and other resources on the World Wide Web.

User ID See Operator ID.

Variance A condition that adds to or subtracts from the core workload or impacts the way the work is performed, the grade of a position, or the resource used to fill the position. Variances result from environmental, mission, or technological differences and can be negative, positive, or neutral.

Voluntary Early Out Authority (VERA) Subject to Office of Personnel Management (OPM) and Departmental criteria Coast Guard may officer civilian employees eligible for early retirement.

Voluntary Early Release A downsizing tool which waives obligated military service requirements (i.e. enlistment, academy commitment). There are no monetary separation incentives offered with this type of program. It should not be confused with DOD's voluntary incentive programs (VSI and SSB), which offer a monetary incentive to service members who separate.

Voluntary Separation Incentive (VSI) and Special Separation Benefit (SSB) Voluntary downsizing tools usually designated as "buyouts." The programs are open to selected military members with more than six years, but less than twenty years of service. Both of these programs were established solely to assist with the drawdown. They are not envisioned to become management tools nor are they expected to be authorized after the drawdown is completed.

Voluntary Separation Incentive Pay (VSIP) VSIP, also known as "buyouts," is used to encourage civilian employees to retire early. Buyouts are payments of a cash incentive to encourage federal employees to leave the federal service by resigning, by taking early retirement, if qualified, or simply by retiring. (Buyouts help lessen the need for mandatory RIFs in order to meet downsizing goals.)

Work Area The physical location in which work is accomplished.

Work Distribution Analysis A technique to improve production that helps find out what work is being done, how much time is spent on it, and who is doing it.

Work Measurement A technique employed independently or in conjunction with cost accounting for the collection of data on work-hours and production by work units, so that the relationship between work performed and work-hours expended can be calculated and used as the basis for manpower planning, scheduling, production, budget justification, performance evolution, and cost control.

Work Sampling A work measurement technique which is based on the laws of probability and which consists of taking observations at random intervals. Inferences are drawn, from the proportion of observations in each category concerning the work area under study.

Work Unit The basic identification of work accomplished or services performed. Work units should be easy to identify, convenient for obtaining productive count, and usable for scheduling, planning, and costing.

Workforce Management The execution of plans and actions associated with recruiting, training, assigning and promoting individuals to the right jobs at the right time.

Workforce Management Tools Used for shaping and/or down-sizing the workforce.

Workforce Optimization The multi-disciplinary practice of allocating human resources to meet mission performance objectives as efficiently as possible. Optimization involves analysis and selection/assignment of one, or a mix of, active duty, reserve, civilian, or auxiliary forces. Contracting for specific tasks also may be considered. Solutions to performance discrepancies that involve training may be considered as a way to change existing skills.

Workforce Planning The process which forecasts long and short term human resource needs; coordinates those needs (demand) with the availability of human resources (supply) to provide the best force mix and structure to support Coast Guard missions.

Worklist A list of items that requires your attention.

Workload An expression of the amount of work, identified by the number of work units or volume of a workload factor, that a work center has on hand at any given time or is responsible for performing during a specified period of time.

Workload Indicator A broad index used to measure work and establish a relationship between workload and manpower requirements.

COAST GUARD TELECOMMUNICATIONS ACRONYMS

A/D   Analog to Digital
A/K   Matrix Audio and keyline switching matrix device.
AAC   Authorization & Access Control
AAL ATM   Adaptation Layer—a protocol that adapts xfer characteristics of the ATM "layer" to the needs of higher-layer protocols or network services.
AAL Type 1   A protocol designed to meet the needs of CDR network services. Uses 1 octet per cell payload to support unstructured circuit transport (UCT).

AAL Type 3/4   Protocol defined to support the needs of SMDS connectionless service. Uses combo of 4 octets per cell payload and 8 octets per frame to provide its functions.
ABS   Automatic Broadcast Scheduler
AC&I   Acquisition, Construction & Improvement
ACC   Access Control Center (w/Blacker) Access Line Portion of a leased line that permanently connects the user w/serving central office (CO).
ACCUNET   AT&T data-oriented digital service
ACI   Adjacent Channel Interference
ACK   Control code for a positive ACKnowledgment of rcvd transmission
ACS   Alternate Control Station
ACTS   Advance Communications Technology Satellite
ADP   Automated Data Processing
ADPCM   Adaptive Differential Pulse Code Modulation
AFSAT   Air Force Satellite System
AGC   Automatic Gain Control
AGT   AUTODIN Gateway Terminal—A comms-computer system that interfaces the MDT with an ASC. (Also see Gateguard.)
AJ   Anti-Jam
ALE   Automatic Link Establishment
AM   Amplitude Modulation
AMME   Army Automated Multi-media Message Exchange
AMPE   Automated Message Processing Equipment
ANDVT   Advanced Narrowband Digital Voice Terminal (KYV-5)
ANSI   American National Standards Institute
Application Layer   The 7th and topmost layer of the "OSI Stack" that interfaces to the network user.
APR   Agency Procurement Request.
Architecture   A framework that describes how the components of a system fit together.
ARPA   Advanced Research Projects Agency
ARQ   Automatic Repeat ReQuest—method of automatic error correction used for handshake of SITOR terminals in point to point communications to ensure accurate communications.
ASC   Automatic Switching Center (i.e., AUTODIN ASC)
ASCII   American National Standard Code for Information Interchange
ASDS   ACCUNET Spectrum of Digital Services, a fractional T1 service tariffed by AT&T
ASIC   Application Specific Integrated Circuit
ASK   Amplitude Shift Keying—Asynchronous data transmission that isn't related to specific freq or timing. Start/Stop transmission—bytes encapsulated w/start-stop bits
AT&T   American Telephone & Telegraph
ATM   Asynchronous Transfer Mode—a form of packet switching; a subset of cell relay that uses 53 byte cells as the basic transport unit. A high-speed transmission technology—cell switching and multiplexing technology. Key concept is that all information is carried in short, fixed-length blocks called "cells."
AUTODIN   AUTOmatic Digital Information Network, DOD secure record message system for teletype data
AUTOVON   Automatic Voice Network
AWACS   Airborne Early Warning & Control System
B8ZS   Bipolar 8-Zero Substitution
B-ISDN   Broadband Integrated Services Digital Data Network
Backbone   A network designed to interconnect lower speed channels
BACS   Bay Area Communications System—A microwave system extending from Monterey to Humbolt Bay controlled by D11 and maintained by SUPRTCEN Alameda providing telephone and data services.
Bandwidth   The range of frequencies a device can handle. For a digital circuit it is the "bit speed" (BPS) governing the rate at which individual bits are carried.
BCST   Broadcast—transmitting to all users at once.
BER   Bit Error Rate
BFES   Blacker Front Ends (on Milnet)
BFSK   Binary Frequency Shift Keying
BICI   Broadband Inter-Carrier Interface (lets ATM services of public carriers interrelate)
BLACKER   NSA Cryptographic device (X.25)
BLOS   Beyond Line of Sight
BPS   Bits Per Second—measure of speed at which information is transferred.
BPSK   Binary Phase Shift Keying
BPV   Bipolar Violation
Bridge   An internetworking device that connects LANS together at the Media Access Control (MAC) or LINK layer of the OSI model (bottom two layers). They are typically cheaper and easier to install and manage than routers. Transparent bridges look at every packet on one network and forward those packets destined for another network through

	the appropriate port. Source-routing bridges use special info embedded inside the packet by the orig device to forward the frame toward the packets destination.
Broadband	Supporting a wide range of frequencies
Bus	A LAN topology where all interconnected computers are aware of all transmissions, but each computer receives only those transmissions addressed to it.
C2	Command & Control
C3(I)	Command, Control, Communications (& Intelligence)
C4(I)	Command, Control, Computers, Communications & Intelligence
C&A	Certification & Accreditation
CAMS	Communications Area Master Station.
CAMSLANT	Communications Area Master Station AtLANTic, operational control of COMMSTAs in their Area. Chesapeake, VA
CAMSPAC	Communications Area Master Station PACific, operational control of COMMSTAs in their Area. Point Reyes, CA
CAP	Component Approval Process (DMS)
CARRIER	Public/Common provider of communications facility
CASREP	Casualty Report: sent to operational commander on equipment/system casualty. NWP10 provides requirements for message and format.
CASCOR	Casualty Corrected: Report sent to operational commander on equipment/system casualty correction. NWP10 provides requirements for message and format.
CBR	Constant Bit Rate
CCITT	Consultative Committee; International Telegraph and Telephone
CCC	Clear Channel Capacity—ability use use the entire 64Kbs channel without the 8Kb overhead (resulting effective data rate at 56Kbs)
CCS	Communications Control System, an automated COMMSTA equipment control system.
CDAN	Component Deployment Approval Notice
CDM	Code Division Multiplexing
CDMA	Code Division Multiple Access
Cell	A fixed-length unit of data
Cellular	A radio comms technology where coverage areas are defined by "cells" and low-power frequencies are used.
CGDN	Coast Guard Data Network, a CG wide data network on SPRINTNET for EMAIL, data and message transfer. Was called HDN or X.25. Channel Logical or physical connection between two end points Channel Groups Multiple NxDSO's circuit switching an "open pipe" technique that establishes a temporary dedicated connection between two points.
CISS	Center for Information Systems Security
Clear Channel	Ability to use all 64 KBps of a DS0 for capability user data
Cloud	A homogenous data network. The "public network" (you don't know where it goes, as long as it comes out the other end).
CMS	Communications Security Material System: accountability system for cryptographic materials
CMW	Compartmented Mode Workstation
CO	Telephone company Central Office
COAX	Coaxial cable
COMDAC	Electronic sensor, weapons and display system used on 270 foot WMEC
COMPUSEC	Computer Security
COMSAT	Communications Satellite
COMSEC	Communications Security
COMMSTA	COMmunication STAtion
CONOPS	CONcept of OPerationS
CONUS	Continental United States
COTS	Commercial Off-the-Shelf
CP	Crypto-Peripheral (see WSP)
CPE	Customer Premise Equipment
CRC	Cyclic Redundancy Code
CRL	Certificate Revocation List (related to DMS)
Crossbanding	Translating a signals frequency from one major band to another (i.e., EHF to UHF)
CRTT	CAMSPAC keyed, Secure Pacific Radio Teletype broadcast. CAMSPAC simultaneously keys transmitters in Honolulu and Kodiak, AK.
CRYPTO	A device to encrypt or decrypt voice or data transmissions.
CSMA	Carrier-Sense Multiple Access with Collision Detection
CSU	Channel Service Unit: equipment that terminates the long-distance circuit in the customer's location. Often paired with a digital service unit (DSU).
CUDIXS	Common User Digital Information Exchange System
CW	Continuous Wave Morse Code transmission.
CWO	Communications Watch Officer.
D4	T1 framing technique dividing T1 into 24 channels, a D4 frame being 192 x 8000 / 24 = 64 Kbps or a DS0

D/A	Digital to Analog	DII	Defense Information Infrastructure
DAA	Designated Approving Authority	DISA	Defense Information Systems Agency
DACS	Digital Access and Cross-Connect System	DISN	Defense Information System Network (replacement for DDN) provides global multi-media connectivity
DAMA	Demand Assigned Multiplex Access—Multiplexing system for Satellite Communications to operate several different types of information over one Satellite channel.		
		Distributed Backbone Topology	A network configuration where local sites connect to other sites through intermediate, higher capacity sites.
Datagram	A finite length packet with sufficient information to be routed from source to destination independently of previous transmissions	DITSO	Defense Information Technology Services Organization
		DMS	Defense Messaging System—Replacement for AUTODIN—Secure, multilevel (U-TS/SCI) desktop to desktop message system.
dB	Decibel		
dBM	Decibels referred to 1 Milliwatt of Power		
DBMS	DataBase Management System		
DBOF	Defense Budget Operating Fund	DOD	Department of Defense
DBPSK	Differential Binary Phase Shift Keying	DONCAF	Department of the Navy Central Adjudication Facility, Washington Navy Yard for background investigation adjudications and security clearances
dBW	Decibel referenced to 1 watt		
DCA	Defense Communications Agency		
DCS	Defense Communications System		
DDN	Defense Data Network—X.25 common user packet switched communications network	DPA	Departmental Procurement Approval (by DOT for big $$$)
		DPCM	Differential Pulse Code Modulation
DDP	Distributed Data Processing	DPSK	Differential Phase Shift Keying
DDS	Dataphone Digital Service—a carrier offering that uses 2.4-56 Kbs	DS0	Digital Signal, Level 0 (64 Kbps)
		DS1	Digital Signal, Level 1 (1.544 Mbps)
DEC	Digital Electronics Corporation, computer manufacturer.	DS3	Digital Signal, Level 3 (44.736 Mbps)
		DSA	Directory System Agent
Dedicated	A private, leased or owned, communications path. Lines between specific sites.	DSCS	Defense Satellite Communications System
		DSI	Digital Speech Interpolation
Demod	Demodulator: A device to convert received teletype audio tones to teletype data.	DSN	Defense Switching Network, DOD telephone system for voice and low speed data.
Demux	Demultiplex		
DES	Commercial Digital Encryption Standard, encryption method used for voice or data for UNCLASSIFIED sensitive information. NOT AUTHORIZED for classified information.	DSNET1	Defense Secure Network 1—Secret Segment of DDN
		DSNET2	Defense Secure Network 2—Top Secret segment of DDN
		DSNET3	Defense Secure Network 3—SCI segment of DDN
DDN	Defense Digital Network for high speed DOD data systems.		
		DSS	Digital Signature Standard (an NIST standard) (DMS)
DDS	Digital Data Service		
DGG	Defense Global Grid	DSU	Digital Service Unit: a synchronous serial data interface that buffers and controls the flow of data between a network portal, such as a bridge or router, and the channel service unit (CSU).
Dialup	A communications path through a telephone line using tones to establish the connection		
		DTS	Diplomatic Telecommunications Service
		DUA	Directory User Agent (DMS)
		EAM	Emergency Action Message (e.g. USAF Global EAM) Earth Station A place where satellite signals are received and processed

Digital Data Three types:

1. Circuit Switched: similar to std phone line, dial up-xfer data-hang up.
2. Leased Lines: permanent circuit connections that are always available without any required setup time.
3. Packet Switched:
    (a) X.25: "low speed"/low volume w/lots of error checking
    (b) Frame Relay: "stripped down" version of X.25, w/higher speed, less error checking

EBLOS	Extended Beyond Line of Sight
EC	Earth Coverage
ECAC	Electromagnetic Compatibility Analysis Center, Annapolis, MD

ECCM	Electronic Counter-Countermeasures	FLEETSATCOM	Navy Satellite Communications System
EDI	Electronic Data Interchange	Flow Control	Ability of network node to manage different data rates by means of buffering schemes or by reducing the data flow from a sending station
EECEN	USCG Electronics Engineering Center, Wildwood, NJ		
EEPROM	Electronically Erasable Programmable Read-Only Memory		
EGP	Exterior Gateway Protocol	FOC	Full Operational Capability
EHF	Extremely High Frequency (>30 GHz)	FOW	Forward Orderwire
EILSP	Electronics Integrated Logistics Support Plan	Fractional T1 NxDS0	Portion of T1 bandwidth
EIP	Embedded INFOSEC Product	Frame Relay	A high speed data "packet" transfer scheme; an upgrade of X.25 packet switching
EIRP	Effective Isotropic Radiated Power		
EKMS	Electronic Key Management System (EKMC Finksburg, MD)	FREQ HOP	Randomize transmission frequencies to provide AJ and LPI.
ELF	Extremely Low Frequency (0-3 KHz) Submarine traffic	FRTT	COMMSTA Boston keyed, Secure Atlantic Radio Teletype broadcast.
ELF	Encrypted Link Filter (Direct interface for e-mail and modem service for SDN)	FSB	DOD/USN Fleet Satellite Broadcast (UHF)
ELINT	Electronic Intelligence e-mail Electronic Mail	FSK	Frequency Shift Keying, a method of data transmission by shifting a center frequency to higher a lower frequencies creating marks and spaces.
EMI	Electromagnetic Interference		
EMP	Electromagnetic Pulse		
ENCODE	Add check bits to data stream to allow for error correction at receiver.	FT1	Fractional T1, individual 64Kb channels of the 1.54Mb T1
ENCRYPT	Scramble data to provide Communications Security	FTAM	File Transfer, Access & Management
		FTP	File Transfer Protocol
EOM	End of Message	FTS2000	GSA contract with AT&T to provide telephone and telephone networks for non-DOD government agencies.
ERP	Effective Radiated Power		
ERPAL	Electronics Repair Parts Allowance List		
ES	End System	FY	Fiscal Year
ESF	Extended Superframe Format—T1 line framing technique using 24 D4 frames per ESF frame to provide "robust" line diagnostics, monitoring and control	G	Billion
		GAIN	Concentration of signal in preferred direction.
		GATEGUARD	
		GATEWAY	A device that interconnects dissimilar LAN's that employ different high-level protocols
ETHERNET	A local area newtwork (fiber, twisted pair or coax) used to connect computing devices Facility Communications link or circuit		
		GBA	Gimballed Antenna
		GCCS	Global Command & Control System
FAX	Facsimile	GDA	Gimballed Dish Antenna
FCC	Federal Communications Commission	GEOS	Geostationary Satellite. A satellite in a synchronous orbit above the equator.
FDDI	Fiber Distributed Data Interface—a fiber optic local area network (LAN) connecting computing devices	GHz	Gigahertz—billions of cycles per second
		Global Dial Tone	A concept of universal, everywhere, anytime simple to use communications.
FDDI-II	a variation of FDDI that supports isochronous traffic	GLORI	Global Radio Interface
FDM	Frequency Division Multiplexing	GOSIP	Government Open Systems Interconnection Protocol. Defines a common set of data communication protocols that enable systems developed by different vendors to interoperate and users of different applications on those systems to exchange information.
FDMA	Frequency Division Multiple Access		
FEC	Forward Error Correction, used for the broadcast mode of SITOR.		
Fiber	Fiber Optic Cable		
FIPS	Federal Information Processing Standard		

GOTS	Government Off the Shelf
GMCC	Gateway Monitoring & Control Center
GMDSS	Global Maritime Distress and Safety System.
GPS	Global Positioning System
Groom	Efficient allocation/assignment of DS0's on T1
HDN	Hybrid Data Network. (now CGDN)
HDN	Heterogeneous Data Networks—Networks with dissimilar data formats.
HDR	High Data Rate (Tx rate greater than 1.544 Mbps)
HEMP	High Altitude Electro-magnetic Pulse
HF	High Frequency (3-30 MHz or 3000-30000 KHz)
HFCW	High Frequency Morse CW (3-30 MHz).
HFDL	High Frequency Data Link; (Low volume) Mode for packet HF transmission used by WPB, WLB, WAGB, and LORAN Stations for communications.
HFRWI	High Frequency Radio Wireline Interface, Secure phone patch from desktop STU-III to ship via HF or Satellite (Navy)
HHR	High Hop Rate
HI-CAP	Telephone Company reference to a T-1 digital circuit.
HOBA	HOrizonal Broadband Antenna
HPA	High Power Amp
HPBW	Half Power Beam Width
HPCC	High Performance Computing & Communications
Hz	Hertz (aka: cycles per second)
I&A	Identification & Authentication
I&T	Integration & Test
I/O	Input/Output
IADS	International ACCUNET Digital Service
IBR	Intermediate Bit Rate (see IDR)
IC	Integrated Circuit
ICA	Integrated Communications Architecture
ICD	International Code Designator
IDR	Intermediate Data Rate (64, 128, 255, 384, 512, 768 KBps)
IDSCP	Initial Defense Satellite Communications Program
IEEE	Institute for Electrical & Electronic Engineers; has letter designators to define certain frequency bands for convenience; they are:

    Desig Frequency Range
    "A" 160-186 MHz
    "G" 186-225 MHz
    "P" 225-390 MHz
    "L" 390-1550 MHz
    "S" 1550-4200 MHz
    "C" 4200-7000 MHz
    "X" 7000-11000 MHz
    "K" 11000-33000 MHz
    "Q" 33000-46000 MHz
    "V" 46000-56000 MHz

IETF	Internet Engineering Task Force
IF	Intermediate Frequency
IFL	Inter-facility Link
IGRP	Internet Gateway Routing Protocol
IHFDL	Integrated High Frequency Data Link, used when the HFDL terminal is communicating between ship and Group Office via the SDN without CAMS/COMMSTA intervention.
ILSP	Integrated Logistics Support Plan
IMO	International Maritime Organization
INE	In-line Network Encryptors
INMARSAT	International Mobile satellite Organization; was International MARitime SATellite Organization, international company headquartered in London providing analog and digital satellite communications at a tariffed rate. COMSAT Inc. is the United States representative for this monopoly.
Intelligent Gateway	A process that uses external variables to dynamically select communications paths. Translates data formats between heterogeneous sub networks.
INTERNET	A network that interconnects two or more other networks
Interoperable	Ability to communicate between processes.
IOC	Initial Operational Capability
IOC	Inter-Office Channel
IP	Internet Protocol
IPR	In Process Review
IS	Information System
ISDN	Integrated Services Digital Network—CCITT defined high speed digital network
ISSA	Inter-Service Support Agreement
ITDS	Information Transfer Distribution System, used to transfer messages from SSAMPS throughout the Coast Guard via CGDN. (Formerly called MTDS.)
ITSDN	Integrated Tactical Secure Data Network
IXC	Inter-Exchange Carrier
Isochronous	Equally timed; timing info is transmitted on the channel along with date—sending asynchronous data by synchronous means sending asynch characters between each pair of start and stop bits.
JRSC	Jam Resistant Secure Communications
K	Thousand

KBPS	KiloBits Per Second (BPS x 1000)	*LOS*	Line of Sight
KDC	Key Distribution Center (Finksburg, MD operated by NSA)	*LPC*	Linear Predictive Coding
		LPI	Low Probability of Intercept
KEA	Key Encryption Algorithm	*LSO*	Local Servicing Office
Keyer	A device to convert teletype data to a 2000Hz audio tone with a shift of either +/-85 or +/- 425Hz for transmission.	*LUF*	Lowest usable frequency
		LUT	Local Users Terminal
		M	Million
		MAISRC	Major Acquisition System Review Council
KG-84C	CRYPTO box for decrypting and encrypting secure point to point RATT circuits over HF. (GPEE)	*MAP*	Manual Assist Position, a PC used to access the Thrane & Thrane SITOR equipment for message processing.
KG-84A	CRYPTO box for decrypting and encrypting secure point to point data over landline. (GPEE)		
		MBA	Multi-Beam Antenna
		MBPS	MegaBits Per Second (BPS x 1,000,000)
KHz	Kilohertz (cycles per second x 1000)	*MBS*	Multi-year Budget Strategy
KRL	Key Revocation List (related to DMS)	*MCM*	Multi-Chip Module
kW	Kilo Watt (Watt x 1000)	*MCW*	Modulated Continuous Wave.
KWT-46	CRYPTO box for encrypting or decrypting secure RATT broadcasts. (Vallor system)	*MDR*	Medium Data Rate (Tx rate 4800-1.544 Mbps)
KY-75	Old generation (PARKHILL) of Secure Voice CRYPTO being replaced by	*MDT*	Message Distribution Terminal, a Zenith PC used for office automation. Coast Guard uses it on the AUTODIN/NAV-COMPARS circuits for connectivity to DOD message system.
KYV-5	New Secure Voice (ANDVT) CRYPTO that replaces KY-75 (PARKHILL).		
L-band	Frequency band from 390 MHz-1550 MHz		
LA	Local Authority		
LAN	Local Area Network: Any data network that spans a local or limited geographic area. (i.e., office, building, campus environ) ownership by user organization	*MEGACOM*	AT&T MEGACOM 800 Service for large WATS customers
		MEK	Message Encryption Key
		MF	Medium Frequency (300-3000 KHz)
LATA	Local Access and Transport Area—local TELCO serving area	*MFCW*	Medium Frequency Morse CW (400-512 KHz)
		MFSK	Multiple Frequency Shift Keying
LATENCY	The time it takes for data to transit from source to destination	*MHz*	MegaHertz (millions of cycles per second)
		MIL-COM	Commercial contractor that does the majority of installation work for NAVELEX both ship and shore.
LAW	Local Authority Workstation—network security mgmt services (i.e., programming "TESSERA" cards, loading keymat, & user authentication certificates).		
		MILNET	Military Network—unclassified segment of DDN
LCCE	Life Cycle Cost Estimates	*MILSATCOM*	Military Satellite Communications—A DOD UHF military satellite system for transmission of voice, data and imagery.
LDMX	Navy Local Digital Message Exchange		
LDR	Low Data Rate (Tx rate 75-2400 bps)		
LEASAT	Leased Satellite	*MILSTAR*	MILitary STrategic And Relay (Satellite)
LEC	Local Exchange Carrier	*MIMIC*	Microwave/Millimeter Wave Monolithic Integrated Circuit
LEIS	Law Enforcement Information System		
LEOS	Low Earth Orbiting Satellite	*MISSI*	(NSA's) Multilevel Information Systems Security Initiative—MISSI products provide: writer-to-reader info security services including data integrity, access control, authentication, non-repudiation and confidentiality. Support for e-mail, file transfer, remote login, database mgmt. Compatibility w/commercial computing & networking technology. Protection against unauthorized disclosure or modification of information while allowing integration of systems w/different sensitivity levels.
LF	Low Frequency (30-300 KHz)		
LHR	Low Hop Rate		
Link 11	A datalink system to exchange tactical data less than 5 seconds old between ships using HF radio.		
Link 16	A SHF Satellite system used between battle group commands for real time tactical data. Distributed to battle group by Link 11		
LL	Local Loop		
LMD	Local Management Device		
LNA	Low Noise Amplifier		
LO	Local Oscillator		
LOC	Limited Operational Capability		

MLA	Mail List Agent (in DMS)—e-mail "exploder" for e-mail sent to a distribution list.
MLS	Multi-Level Security
MMDF-II	Multichannel Memorandum Distribution Facility
MMS	Multi-level Mail Server
MNS	Mission Needs Statement
MODEM	Modulator-Demodulator combination
MOSAIC	Message Security Protocol, NSA owned/produced government furnished software provided to vendors for "multi-level secure architecture," public/private data encryption key. A "workstation product" using NSA "Type II" algorithm, provides security services for sensitive but unclassified (SBU) electronic mail.
MROC	Multi-command Required Operational Capability
MSK	Minimal Shift Keying
MSP	Message Security Protocol (w/DMS)
MTA	Message Transfer Agent (DMS)
MTBF	Mean Time Between Failures
MTDS	Message Transfer Distribution System (now called ITDS)
MTTR	Mean Time to Repair
Multimedia	The ability to process audio, video, text, graphics and fax.
Multiple	A local device that allows one audio source input to generate outputs to multiple transmitters.
MUX	Multiplex(er)
NAVCAMS	US Naval Communications Area Master Station
NAVCOMPARS	NAVy COMmunications Processing And Routing System used for sending secure message to AUTODIN from ship, stations or mobile units.
NAVTEX	NAVigational TEXt, an international broadcast on 518 KHz that provides the mariner a printed copy of up to 26 different types of information.
NB	Narrowband
NBAM	Narrowband Amplitude Modulation
NBFM	Narrowband Frequency Modulation
NCA	National Command Authority
NCCS	Network Communications & Control Station
NCTS	Naval Computer & Telecommunications Station
NEACP	National Emergency Airborne Command Post
NEC	Numeric Electromagnetics Code
NES	Network Encryption System (NOT NINTENDO Entertainment System)
NESP	Navy EHF Satellite Program
Network	The pieces & parts of a communications system that connect computing devices.
Network Management	The process of managing the devices and software within a network. This may include phone lines, fiber optic cables, radios, satellite services, repeaters, bridges, routers, gateways, etc.
NIC	Network Information Center (Internet)
N-ISDN	Narrow-band Integrated Services Digital Network
NIST	National Institute of Science & Technology (old National Bureau of Standards)
NLSP	Network Level Security Protocol
NMA	Communications Station Miami, FL Radio call sign.
NMC	CAMSPAC San Francisco, CA Radio call sign.
NMCC	National Military Command Center
NMCS	National Military Command System
NMF	Communications Station Boston, MA Radio call sign.
NMG	Communications Station New Orleans, LA Radio call sign.
NMN	CAMSLANT Portsmouth, VA Radio call sign.
NMO	Communications Station Honolulu, HI Radio call sign.
NNI	Network to Network Interface
NOAA	National Oceanographic and Atmospheric Administration
NODE	termination point for two or more communication links
NOJ	Communications Station Kodiak, AK Radio call sign.
NPR	Noise-Power Ratio
NRV	Communications Station Guam Radio call sign.
NWS	National Weather Service
OC-3	155 MBs optical "pipe"
OC-12	622 MBs optical "pipe" (ie: SONET)
OE	Operating Expenses
OG-30	Operating Guide 30—Operating & Maintenance Funds
OG-42	Operating Guide 42—Repair & Replacement Funds
ON	Organizational Notary
OPCEN	Operations Center
Optical Fiber	Any filament or fiber made of dielectric materials and consisting of a core (to carry laser generated light signals) and a surrounding cladding that reflects the signal back into the core. May be glass or plastic.
ORBCON	A low earth orbiting satellite communications service provider.

ORD	Operational Requirements Document	PRF	Pulse Repetition Frequency
OSC	USCG Operations Systems Center, Martinsburg, WV	PRT	Packet Radio Terminal
OSI	Open Systems Interconnection enables multivendor systems to intercommunicate—protocol suite—X.400 message transfer agent (MTA), X.500 directory system agent (DSA)	Producer Push	A concept where data is sent from producers to users. As opposed to User Pull, where data is retrieved by a user as required.
		Protocol	The rules and conventions between communicating processes.
OSI	Stack Open Systems Interconnection—An international set of standard protocols between end systems. The stack consists of seven layers:	PSK	Phase Shift Keying
		PSN	Public Switched Network.
		PSTN	Public Switched Telephone Network.
(7) Application		Public Network	See "Cloud"
(6) Presentation		PVC	Permanent Virtual Connection
(5) Session		"Q" Signals	Operating signals used on both commercial and military circuits. From International Telecommunications Union Radio Regulations.
(4) Transport			
(3) Network			
(2) Datalink			
(1) Physical		QRY	A CW "Q" signal meaning: Your number is.
P/P	An abbreviation for either patch panel or Phone Patch.	QUALCOM	A geosynchronous satellite communications service provider.
PABX	Private Automatic Branch EXchange for local telephone service.	QUERY	A request for data from a remote data base.
Packet	A unit of data, consisting of binary digits including data and call-control signals, that is switched and transmitted as a composite whole.	R&D	Research & Development
		RAM	Random Access Memory
		RATT	Radio Teletype
		RCCOW	Return Control Channel Orderwire
Packet Switching	A data-transmission technique whereby physical resources on a path are switched on a per-packet basis, using control information in the header of each packet; it can operate in either connection-oriented or connectionless mode.	RCP	Resource Change Proposal
		RCS	Receiver Control System
		RD	Routing Domain
		RF	Radio Frequency
		RFL	A manufacturer of FSK and VFCT type terminal modems for multiplexing.
		RISC	Reduced Instruction Set Computer rlogin Remote Log-In
PBS	Private Branch Exchange. A small or local phone switching service.	RLPA	Rotatable Log Periodic Antenna
PCM	Pulse Code Modulation	ROBUST	The ability to operate, or degrade gracefully, under adverse or damaged conditions.
PCMCIA	Personal Computer Memory Card International Association		
		ROM	Read Only Memory
PCMT	Personal Computer Message Terminal	Router	A process that connects homogeneous networks. A device used to connect the wires from one or more networks together. Routers examine the network address of each packet. Those packets that contain a network address different from the originating PC's address are forwarded onto an adjoining network. Routers also have network-management and filtering capabilities, and many newer routers incorporate bridging capabilities as well. More expensive and harder to install than a bridge.
PDU	Protocol Data Unit		
Pipe	A communications path.		
PLA	Plain Language Address		
PM	Phase Modulation		
PMO	Program Management Office		
PMSP	Pre-Message Security Protocol (w/ DMS)—provides encryption, integrity and non-repudiation for Unclassified-Sensitive E-mail		
POC	Proof of Concept		
POM	Program Objective Memorandum		
POP	Point of Presence		
POTS	Plain Old Telephone Service.	ROW	Return Orderwire
PP	Project Plan	RRPSH	Root Registry Public Signature key
PPBES	Planning, Programming, Budgeting, Evaluation System	RX	Receiver
		S/a	Service/agency

S-band	Frequency band from 1550 MHz-5200 MHz	SHF	Super High Frequency (3-30 GHz or 3000-30000 MHz)
S/N	Signal to Noise Ratio	SINA	Static Integrated Network Access
SACS	STU-III Secure Access Control System. The newest generation of secure telephone for landline use with voice or data and is automatic answering.	SITOR	SImplex Teletype Over Radio, a narrow band direct printing teletype using ARQ protocol for error free data communications from ship to ship or ship to shore. Coast Guard sends SITOR navigational warnings broadcasts using the FEC mode.
SAFENET	Survivable, Adaptable, Fiberoptic, Embedded network. A Navy standard fiberoptic LAN.		
SAG	Secure Air to Ground, normally voice over specific HF Radio frequencies using PARKHILL or ANDVT.	SMDS	Switched Multi-megabit Data Service
		SMEF	System Management Engineering Facility
SAMPS	Semi-Automated Message Processing System	SMG	SNS Mail Guard—used to control traffic between networks (i.e., between a Secret high and a SBU network to allow exchange of SBU information) (see SNS)
SARSAT	Search And Rescue SATelite		
SATCOM	Satellite Communication	SMTP	Simple Mail Transfer Protocol
Satellite	Frequency Bands (fixed)	SNS	Secure Network Server—goes beyond SMG functionality—SNS will have MOSAIC and CP capability allowing confidentiality for classified data to the WSP workstation level.
SBU	Sensitive But Unclassified		
SCCN	Secure Command & Control Network		
SCF	Satellite Control Facility		
SCI(F)	Sensitive Compartmented Information (Facility)		
		SOM	Start of Message
SCN	System Control Network, an unclassified voice circuit over HF Radio for Coast Guard and Commercial vessel.	SONET	Synchronous Optical Network
		SOP	Standard Operating Procedure
		SOVT	System Operation Verification Test
SCPC	Single Channel Per Carrier	SOW	Statement of Work
SCT	Single Channel Transponder	SP3	Security Protocol 3 (Network Layer)
SDH	(CCITT) Synchronous Digital Hierarchy (aka: SONET) Worldwide digital hierarchy for broadband transmission systems. 155 Mbps network to network transport interface standard.	SP4	Security Protocol 4 (Transport Layer)
		SPWG	Security Policy Working Group
		SRD	Site Routing Domain. A "local" physical area over which routing occurs. (i.e. base, CGC, etc.)
SDLS	Satellite Data Link System	SS	Spread Spectrum
SDM	Subrate Data Multiplexing	SSA	Solid State Amplifier
SDMA	Space Division Multiple Access	SSAMPS	"Super" SAMPS: An automatic message processing system.
SDN	Secure Data Network, a SACS STU-III and SWS based system for secure message transmission.		
		SSIX	Submarine Satellite Information Exchange System
SDN	Softward Defined Network	SSMA	Spread Spectrum Multiple Access
SDNS	Secure Data Network System (w/DMS) DOD/DON Secure network that provides user to user security through Message Security Protocol (MSP) and Pre-Message	SSR-1	Receive Only terminal for Fleet Broadcast
		STU-III	Secure Telephone Unit (3rd Generation) The newest generation of secure telephone for landline. (Replaced the KY-71 STU-II)
Security Protocol (PMSP)	Message encryption from workstation to workstation		
		SVC	Secure Voice Conferencing
		SVN	Secure Voice Network, for ship to ship or ship to shore communications over HF Radio using ANDVT.
SDS	Satellite Data System		
SERVER	A process that answers a query.	SWS	Standard Work Station
SGLS	Space (Satellite) to Ground Link System	T1	Digital multiplexed carrier system provided by long distance carriers for voice or data transmission that will handle up
SH	System High		
SHA	Signature Hash Algorithm		

	to 24-64Kb voice channels or 1.544 Mbps of unchannelized data.
T3	AT&T standard for dialed-up or leased line circuits. Digital multiplexed carrier system that will handle up to 28 T-1's, 45 Mbps (44.736Mbps) of data.
TAC	Terminal Access Controller or Tactical Application Computer
TACSAT	Tactical Satellite
TAIS	Target Architecture & Implementation Strategy
TBD	"T" Budget Database
TCC	Telecommunications Center or Transportable Communications Center
TCF	Technical Control Facility
TDM	Time Division Multiplexing (fixed bandwidth)
TDMA	Time Division Multiple Access
Technology Insertion	The process of upgrading or adding new technology in a piecemeal manner.
TEMP	Test and Evaluation Master Plan
Terrestrial WAN	A land-based data network that covers a large geographic area.
TH	Time Hopping
Thrane	The manufacturer of the SITOR modem used by the Thrane Coast Guard CAMS/COMMSTAs. Sometimes called TRONTRON's.
TISCOM	USCG Telecommunications & Information Systems Command, Alexandria, VA
TOPOLOGY	A geometric or physical configuration of a communications network.
TR	Trouble Report
TRANSEC	Transmission Security
TRD	Transit Routing Domain: A facility that connects site routing domains through other transit routing domains.
TREE	Transient Radiation Effects on Electronics
Trunk	Facility between customer premise and LEC CO, and between carrier CO's.
TS	Top Secret
TTNR	Test Tone to Noise Ratio
TTY	Teletype
TX	Transmitter
Type I	Crypto item that secures classified or unclassified sensitive data
Type II	Crypto item that protects sensitive but unclassified info only
Type 2	A standard PCMCIA interface
U	Unclassified
UA	User Agent (DMS)
UCT	Unstructured Circuit Transport—transfer of bits at a constant rate between two points
UET	Unattended Earth Terminal
UHF	Ultra-High Frequency (300-3000 MHZ)
UMS	Universal Modem System
UNI	User to Network Interface
UPS	Uninterruptable Power Supply
User Pull	A concept where data is retrieved by a user. (Opposite of Producer Push.)
VAN	Value Added Network—A packetl-switched network that offers high reliability and such services as protocol conversion and data buffering.
VFCT	Voice-Frequency Carrier Telegraph, a composite tone pack of up to 16 different data signals in a 3000Hz voice channel.
VGPL	Voice Grade Private Line (analog)
VHF	Very-High Frequency (30-300 MHZ)
VHSIC	Very High Speed Integrated Circuit
Video Conferencing	Using high-speed data communications to establish two-way television.
VLF	Very Low Frequency
VLSI	Very Large Scale Integration
VOBRA	VOice BRoadcast Automation
VSAT	Very Small Aperture Terminal
W	Watt
WAIS	Wide Area Information Server
WAN	Wide Area Network
WATS	Wide Area Telephone Service
WB	Wide Band
WBAM	Wide Band Amplitude Modulation
WBFM	Wide Band Frequency Modulation
WBS	Work Breakdown Structure
WESTAR	Western Union Satellite
WHCA	White House Communications Agency
WORM	Write Once, Read Many
WS	Workstation
WSA	Workstation Security Applique (aka: Applique)—converts COTS workstations into "trusted" devices. Consists of a "WSP" and Security Monitor software.
WSP	Workstation Security Package (similar to MOSAIC but uses NSA "Type I" crypto algorithm) provides security services for classified information. Uses a PCMCIA card called "CP" (see CP).
WWABNCP	World Wide AirBorne Command Post
WWMCCS	World Wide Military Command & Control System
X-band Frequency	Band from 5200 MHz to 10,900 MHz

X.25	A CCITT standard—A data packet format used to pass relatively low speed data through communications networks. Error checking/ARQ is performed at each node in the network.	*X.500*	CCITT/ISO Directory Service Standard
		"Z"	Signals Operating signals on Military communications circuits.
		ZNI1	A Secure TTY position.
		ZNI2	A unclas TTY position.
X.121	CCITT terminal addressing scheme	*ZYB*	An administrative message. The ZYB is put after the date time group.
X.400	CCITT/ISO Message Handling System (MHS) standard		

Congress

Accompanying papers Petitions, affidavits, letters, and other papers that support or oppose claims for damages, pensions, or other forms of relief for which a private bill has been introduced, or papers relating to public bills. Accompanying papers appeared as a separate House series from the 39th through the 57th Congress (1865-1903). Before 1865 these records were filed with **committee papers**. The series known as "papers accompanying specific bills and resolutions" begins in the 58th Congress (1903-5) and includes published and unpublished records relating to specific bills and resolutions.

Adjournment sine die Adjournment without definitely fixing a day for reconvening; literally "adjournment without a day." Usually used to denote the final adjournment of a session of Congress.

Administrative records See **Housekeeping records**. Act (1) As used by Congress, a bill that has been passed by one House and engrossed. (2) As commonly used, a bill that has been passed by both Houses of Congress, enrolled, and either signed by the President or passed over his veto. See also **Bill**, **Private law**, **Public law** and **Veto**.

Amendment (1) A change made in proposed legislation after it has been formally introduced. An amendment may be proposed by the committee to which the bill was referred, or it may be proposed by a Member from the floor of either House when it is brought up for consideration. All amendments must be agreed to by a majority of the Members voting in the House where the amendment is proposed. (2) A change in the Constitution. Such an amendment is usually proposed in the form of a **joint resolution** of Congress, which may originate in either House. If passed, it does not go to the President for his approval but is submitted directly to the States for ratification.

Architect of the Capitol The official who acts as the agent of Congress and is responsible for the maintenance of the Capitol and its grounds, House and Senate office buildings, Capitol Power Plant, Senate garage, R. A. Taft Memorial, buildings and grounds of the Supreme Court and Library of Congress, and operation of the Botanic Gardens and the Senate and House restaurants. The architect is responsible for the acquisition of property and the planning and construction of congressional buildings. He or she assists in deciding which works of art, historical objects, and exhibits are to be accepted for display in the Capitol and the House and Senate office buildings. The flag office that flies American flags over the Capitol is under the Architect's direction.

Archives (1) The noncurrent records of an organization preserved because of their enduring value; also referred to, in this sense, as archival materials or holdings. See also **Permanent records**. (2) The agency responsible for preserving this material. (3) The building where such materials are located.

Arrangement (1) The order in which documents are filed. (2) A logical plan for organizing records, such as chronologically, numerically, or alphabetically by name or subject. (3) The process of packing, labeling, and shelving of records and manuscripts intended to achieve physical or administrative control and basic identification of the holdings. The term *unarranged* refers to materials that have no apparent systematic order applied to them.

Bill A written presentation to a legislative body proposing certain legislation for enactment into law. Bills may originate in either House, except as noted below, and must be passed by both Houses and approved by the President before they become law or, if disapproved by the President, must be passed over his veto by a two-thirds vote of each House. If a bill is passed within the 10-day period preceding the adjournment of Congress, the President may withhold approval and the bill will die (pocket veto). Bills for raising revenue, according to the Constitution, must originate in the House of Representatives, and bills for appropriating money customarily originate in the House. A bill is referred to in the following manner: H.R. 120, 70th Cong. 1st session.

- *Original bill* A bill in the form in which it was introduced, handwritten or typewritten or a printed copy of a like bill that had been introduced in an earlier Congress. A bill, after introduction, is assigned a number and is printed.
- *Bill file* A type of case file containing materials relating to a particular bill. It may include some or all of the following: copies of bills, reports, committee prints, and printed hearings

and transcripts of executive session hearings. Before the establishment of a systematic collection of bill files in 1903, material on certain bills and resolutions for the 39th through 57th Congresses is found in the **accompanying papers** series. Another and equivalent term is "papers accompanying specific bills and resolutions." See also **case file**.

- *Reported copy of a bill* The copy of a bill that has been discharged by a committee for consideration on the floor of the House. Such a bill is usually placed on one of the House calendars but may be brought up for immediate consideration without being placed on a calendar.
- *Engrossed bill* The final printed copy of a bill as it passed the House of origin and is sent to the other House for further action, or having passed the other House also, is sent back to the House of origin for enrollment. The engrossed copy of a bill that has passed both Houses together with its engrossed amendments is the official working copy from which an enrolled bill is prepared.
- *Enrolled bill* The final copy of an engrossed bill that has passed both Houses, embodying all amendments. Such a bill is printed on paper (formerly copied by a clerk in a fair, round hand on parchment) and is signed first by the Speaker of the House and second by the President of the Senate. On the back is an attestation by the Clerk of the House or the Secretary of the Senate, as the case may be, indicating the House of origin. The enrolled bill is presented to the President for his approval or disapproval. Some enrolled bills that were vetoed are among the records of the House of Representatives or Senate. Approved bills are in the General Records of the U.S. Government in the National Archives, those approved before May 24, 1950, having been received from the Secretary of State. Those after that date were received from the Office of the Federal Register. See also **Veto**.

Calendar A record of the order in which bills are to be taken up for consideration.

- *Committee calendar* A chronological listing that is used by a committee to record bills and resolutions referred to the committee and to indicate the status of matters the committee is considering. Committees sometimes include additional information in their published calendar. See also **docket**.
- *Consent calendar* A calendar that is used by Members to speed consideration of measures that are considered non-controversial. Bills are called up for consideration regularly twice a month.
- *Discharge calendar* The calendar to which motions to discharge are referred when the discharge motion has the required 218 Members' signatures. A motion to discharge a committee is an action to relieve a committee from jurisdiction over a measure before it. This is attempted more often in the House than in the Senate, and is rarely successful. Any Member may file a discharge motion 30 days after a bill is referred to committee. Such a motion requires 218 signatures in the House and is delayed seven days after the signatures have been obtained. On the second and fourth Mondays of each month a signing Member may be recognized to move that the committee be discharged. This seldom-used calendar forces debate on discharge motions on the House floor because a bill or resolution has been bottled up in committee for more than 30 days, and a majority of the House wants to consider that measure. See also **Quorum**.
- *House Calendar* A calendar or scheduling for action by the House on which are placed all public bills or joint resolutions not raising revenue or directly or indirectly appropriating money or property.
- *Private Calendar* A calendar of the Committee of the Whole House on which all bills or joint resolutions of a private character are placed. See also Private law.
- *Union Calendar* A calendar of the Committee of the Whole House on the State of the Union, on which are placed revenue bills, general appropriation bills, and bills of a public character directly or indirectly appropriating money or property.

Case file A file unit containing material relating to a specific transaction, event, person, project, or subject. A legislative case file (also known as a **bill file**) may cover one or many subjects that relate to a particular piece of legislation. A project case file may also cover many subjects pertaining to one main activity. The contents of investigative case files vary greatly depending on the practice of individual committees. See also **Program records**.

Chronological file See **Reading file**.

Clerk of the House The chief administrative officer of the House. The Clerk acts as presiding officer pending the election of the Speaker; makes up the roll of House Members from certificates of election; makes up and publishes a list of reports that are, by law, to be submitted to Congress; prepares and prints the *Journal*; certifies the passage of bills and resolutions; attests and seals warrants and subpoenas; keeps contingent and stationery accounts; acts as custodian of property; pays the salaries of all House personnel except those of Members and Delegates; is custodian of all noncurrent records; and supervises the House Library. See also *Delegate*.

Committee A body of Members, usually limited in number, appointed under House rules or by resolution, to consider some matter of business (e.g., investigations or legislation) and to report thereon to the House for further action. Only a full committee can report legislation for action by the House or Senate.

- *Committee of the Whole House* A committee that is formed by the House resolving itself into a committee. The Committee of the Whole House can act with a quorum of only 100 Members instead of the 218 required for action by the House itself. It does not originate resolutions or bills but receives those devised by standing or select committees and referred to it. Any legislation favorably acted on by the Committee of the Whole House must be reported to the House for further action. Such measures, however, must first have passed through the regular legislative or appropriation committees and be placed on the appropriate **calendar**. When the Committee of the Whole House reports, the House usually acts at once on the report without referring the matter again to select or other committees.
- *Conference committee* A committee appointed by the Speaker and the President of the Senate to resolve disagreements on a bill passed in different versions in each House. It is composed usually of the ranking Members of the committees of each House that originally considered the legislation.
- *Select or special committee* A committee appointed to perform a special function that is beyond the authority or capacity of a standing committee. A select committee is usually created by a simple resolution, which outlines its duties and powers, and its Members are appointed under the rules of their respective Houses. A select committee expires on completion of its assigned duties. Most special committees are investigative in nature rather than legislative.
- *Joint committee* A committee consisting of Members of both Houses and having jurisdiction over matters of joint interest. Most joint committees are standing committees, but special joint committees are created at times.
- *Standing committee* A committee permanently authorized by House and Senate rules. The **Legislative Reorganization Act of 1946** greatly reduced the number of committees. The powers and duties of each committee are set forth in the rules of the House and Senate, and the membership is elected on motion or resolution from the floor at the beginning of each Congress.
- *Subcommittee* A subdivision of a standing committee that considers specified matters and reports back to the full committee.

Committee hearings See **Hearings**.

Committee jurisdiction Subjects each committee is expected to cover as specified in rules published in House and Senate manuals. Jurisdictions can never be drawn to cover all contingencies and intercommittee cooperation is essential.

Committee meeting minutes See **Minute book**.

Committee papers A series of documents created or received by a committee in the course of considering proposed legislation or in conducting investigations that may assist in formulating legislation. The series may consist of correspondence, hearings, reports, minutes of meetings, dockets, calendars, and miscellaneous work papers. The content of this series varies considerably through time. Papers that relate to private bills and some papers that relate to public bills were filed as accompanying papers from the 39th Congress through the 57th Congress.

Committee print A general term used for a variety of publications issued by congressional committees on subjects related to their legislative or research activities. These publications are generally viewed as internal background information publications, and some are not announced for public distribution. Committee prints are of two kinds: (1) reports related to legislative activities such as investigative and oversight hearings, and (2) reports of results of research activities. Some committees have their own research staffs; others use outside consultants, and most use the staff of the Congressional Research Service of the Library of Congress to produce situation studies, statistical or historical information reports, or legislative analyses.

Concurrent resolution See *Resolution*.

Conference A meeting of representatives of the two Houses for the purpose of reaching agreement on conflicting versions of a bill or joint resolution or parts thereof passed in each House in order to have an agreed-upon version to send to the President. The conference version of the bill approved by a majority of the members appointed by each chamber to this ad hoc committee must be passed by both Houses before being sent to the President. See Committee, thereunder **Conference committee**; see also **Report**, thereunder **Conference report**.

Congress (1) The national legislature as a whole, including both the House and the Senate. (2) The united body of senators and representatives for any term of two years for which the whole body is chosen. A Congress lasts for a period of two years and usually has two sessions, but it may consist of three or more sessions. Before the adoption of the 20th amendment to the Constitution in 1933, a session of Congress began on the first Monday in December of each year, each odd-numbered year marking the beginning of a new Congress. Now a regular session of Congress begins on January 3 of each year and a new Congress begins January 3 of every odd-numbered year.

Congressional Record The daily, printed account of the proceedings in both the House and Senate Chambers, recording floor debates, statements, and floor actions. Highlights of legislative and committee action are embodied in a "Daily Digest" section of the **Record**, and Members are entitled to have their extraneous remarks printed in an appendix known as "Extension of Remarks." Members may edit and revise remarks made on the floor during debate, and quotations from debate reported by the press are not always found in the **Record**. The **Congressional Record** is printed for the convenience of the Members. The only official record kept of the proceedings of the Senate or House is the **Journal** of each body.

Congressional Serial Set A special edition of publications of the U.S. House and Senate and such other publications as Congress orders to be printed in it, also known as the Congressional Edition, the Congressional Set, and the United States Serial Set. The reports and documents of the House or Senate that comprise the set are assigned numbers within each Congress and category. The volumes of the set are numbered serially beginning in 1817 and continuing in an unbroken sequence to the present. The Serial Set is available at designated **depository libraries** throughout the United States. Each publication is entered and identified in the **Monthly Catalog**. Since 1969, items in the *Congressional Serial Set* are cited in the following manner: H. Doc. 91-1, etc. See also **Document** and **Report**.

Contingent fund A sum appropriated for lawful but miscellaneous expenses of each House. The Clerk of the House maintains that body's account which includes purchase of stationery, newspapers, and other incidental expenses.

Delegate A nonvoting representative of one of the territories or of a district organized by law who receives the compensation, allowances, and benefits of a Member of the House and is entitled to the privileges and immunities of Members. Delegates have a right to vote in committee and otherwise participate in House floor activities. The citizens of Puerto Rico are represented by a Resident Commissioner who has the same rights as a Delegate. At the organization of the House during the opening of the first session, Delegates and the Resident Commissioner are sworn but the Clerk of the House does not put them on the roll for voting.

Depository libraries Selected libraries that participate in the congressionally established Depository Library Program. The program's plan makes available Government publications to each State's citizens. The object is to make selected Government publications widely available for the free use of the general public. The number of libraries located in each State corresponds to the number of congressional districts. Regional depository libraries (two per state) permanently keep depository material received from the Superintendent of Public Documents.

Discharge a committee See **Calendar**, thereunder **Discharge calendar**.

Docket A book in which all matters referred to a committee for its consideration are registered numerically, together with the actions taken on them. See also **Calendar**, thereunder **Committee calendar**.

Document (1) A physical entity of any substance on which is recorded all or part of a work or multiple works. Documents include books and booklike materials, printed sheets, graphics, manuscripts, audiorecordings, videorecordings, motion pictures, and machine-readable data files. (2) A general term used to designate official materials issued in the name of the House. (3) Beginning with the 15th Congress, the copy of material that was printed by order of the House or Senate. Printed documents from the 30th through the 53d Congress were identified as either miscellaneous or executive documents, which see below. This distinction has disappeared and House documents are referred to in the following manner: H. Doc. 25, 54th Cong., 1st sess.

- *Executive document* A document that originated with an agency in the executive branch of the Government and was printed by order of the House or Senate. House executive documents were numbered in each Congress and were designated in the following manner: H. Ex. Doc. 49, 30th Cong., 1st sess. In 1895 the series was consolidated with the Miscellaneous Document series, and the resulting series became known as House Documents.
- *Miscellaneous documents* Petitions, memorials, communications from non-governmental sources, special reports, reports from independent agencies, and other miscellaneous items that were ordered printed by the House. These were numbered in each Congress in the following manner: H. Misc. Doc. 23, 53d Cong., 1st sess. In 1895 this series was consolidated with the Executive Document series, and the resulting series became known simply as House Documents.
- See also **Executive communications** and **Presidential messages**.

Electoral college See **Electors**.

Electoral vote (1) The vote cast by an elector for the President of the United States. (2) The aggregation of the votes of all electors in a Presidential election.

Electors Those chosen by vote of the people to the electoral college, the function of which is to elect the President of the United States. Each state has as many electors as it has Members of the House of Representatives plus its two Members of the Senate.

Endorsement The writing on the outside or cover of a bill, report, petition or memorial, or other document, giving a brief description of the document, by whom submitted or presented, date of referral, and either the name of the committee to which it was referred or other disposition that might have been made.

Executive communications Texts of various communications to the Congress which are recorded as House **Documents**. They include **Presidential messages** proposing new legislation for consideration by the Congress or vetoing legislation passed by the Congress. Also included for a signed bill is the statement by the President that describes the benefits to be derived from the new law and acknowledges the legislators and other interested parties who were closely associated with promoting the legislation. In addition, annual and special reports to Congress from various executive agencies are published as House and, occasionally, Senate Documents. Often these agency reports are transmitted by Presidential message. However, they may come directly from the reporting agency.

Executive department One of the major functional subdivisions of the executive branch of the Government, the head of which is a member of the President's Cabinet. See also **Independent agency**.

Executive document See **Document**.

Executive hearing See **Hearings**.

Federal Register (1) The daily publication, *Federal Register*. (2) The office in the National Archives and Records Administration that compiles and publishes the daily *Federal Register* of rules, regulations, and notices from government agencies; the *Code of Federal Regulations*; the *United States Government Manual*; *Compilation of Presidential Documents*; *Public Papers of the Presidents*; *United States Statutes at Large*; and **slip laws**.

Filibuster A time-delaying tactic associated with the Senate and used by a minority in an effort to prevent a vote on a bill or amendment that probably would pass if voted on directly. The most common method is to take advantage of the Senate's rules permitting unlimited debate, but other forms of parliamentary maneuvering may be used. The stricter rules used by the House make filibusters more difficult, but delaying tactics are employed occasionally through various procedural devices allowed by House rules.

Finding aids The descriptive matter, published and unpublished, created by an originating office, an archival agency, or a manuscript repository, to establish physical or administrative and intellectual control over records and other holdings.

Fiscal year The 12-month period used in accounting for the receipt and expenditure of funds from the U.S. Treasury. The Government operated on a calendar fiscal year basis from 1789 through 1842. A separate report was issued for the first six months of 1843. Thereafter, the fiscal year was defined as July 1 to the following June 30 for the years from 1843 through 1975. The 1976 fiscal year began July 1, 1975, but did not end until September 30, 1976. The 1977 fiscal year and all succeeding fiscal years began on October 1 and continued through the following September 30.

Government Printing Office The agency in the legislative branch that prints and binds, either in-house or on a commercial contract, all congressional publications as well as publications of departments and agencies of the Federal Government. Responsibilities include furnishing inks, paper, and printing supplies to governmental agencies on request; distributing and selling Government publications; cataloging and maintaining a library collection of its publications; and operating an exchange account for publications allotted to Members. See also *Congressional Record*, *Monthly Catalog*, *United States Code*, and *Congressional Serial Set*.

Hearing (1) A meeting of a House committee at which interested parties give testimony during the consideration of proposed legislation or during an investigation. (2) The recorded testimony presented at such a hearing. At hearings on legislation, witnesses usually include experts in the matter under consideration, governmental officials, and representatives of persons affected by the bill or bills under study. Hearings related to special investigations bring forth a variety of witnesses. Committees sometimes use their subpoena power to summon reluctant witnesses.

- *Executive hearing* (1) Closed hearings that bar the public and the press. (2) Recorded testimony presented at such a hearing and rarely printed. If not a separate series, the recorded testimony is typically found among **committee papers**.
- *Public hearing* (1) A hearing that is open to the public and press. (2) The recorded testimony presented at such a hearing usually printed and distributed by the committee conducting the hearing.

House document See **Document**.

Housekeeping records Records of a committee or an officer of Congress that relate to the administrative budget of Congress, including accounting, personnel, supply, and similar administrative or facilitative operations normally common to most organizations, as distinguished from program or substantive records that relate to the organization's primary functions. See **Program records**.

Impeachment The bringing of charges against an official of the Government that question his or her right or qualifications to hold office. Maladministration or misconduct while in office is usually the basis of the charges. Impeachment charges are made by the House of Representatives. The trial of an impeached officer is conducted before the Senate. The Chief Justice of the United States presides when the President of the United States is being tried.

Independent agency An agency of the executive branch of the government that operates independently of any **executive department**. The head of an independent agency is not a member of the President's Cabinet.

Intrinsic value In manuscript appraisal, the worth, in monetary terms, of a document, dependent upon some unique factor, such as its age, the circumstances regarding its creation, a signature, or an attached seal. In archival terms, it is those permanently valuable records that have qualities and characteristics that make the records in their original form the only archivally acceptable form for preservation.

Inventory (1) A basic archival **finding aid** usually describing the records of a Federal agency or part of an agency. It generally includes a brief history of the organization and functions of the agency whose records are being described; a description of each record series (giving as a minimum such data as title, dates, quantity, and arrangement, and sometimes relationships to other series and description of significant subject content); and, if appropriate, appendices that provide such supplementary information as a filing scheme, a glossary of abbreviations and special terms, lists of folder headings on special subjects, or indexes. (2) In records management, a survey of records prior to development of records disposition schedules.

Investigative case files See **Case files**.

Joint resolution: See **Resolution**.

Journal The official record (required by the Constitution in Article 1, section 5) of the proceedings on the floor of the House, which is read each day and approved. The *Journal* records the actions taken, but, unlike the **Congressional Record**, it does not include the substantially verbatim report of speeches, debates, etc. The *Journal* is printed, but the manuscript may be available in two forms, rough and finished. The rough journal consists of the first draft of the proceedings that is drafted from **minute books**. The finished journal is generally prepared from the rough journal after it has been revised and corrected. The finished journal is used as copy for the printer. The manuscript journal, after being edited and proofread by the Public Printer, is bound and returned to the Clerk of the House.

Jurisdiction The sphere or limits of authority of a House standing committee. A House rule defines each committee's jurisdiction. The Speaker must refer public bills and Members' private bills to the appropriate committee, but the House itself may refer a bill to any committee without regard to jurisdiction. A committee may not report a bill if the subject matter has not been referred to the committee by the House establishing jurisdiction by precedent. See also **Committee** and **Refer**.

Law See **Private law** and **Public law**.

Lay on the table See **Table**.

Legislative case file See **Case file**.

Legislative Reorganization Act of 1946 An act (60 Stat. 812), under which the 44 House committees of the 79th Congress were consolidated into 19, effective January 2, 1947. The jurisdiction of each new committee was specified, and committees were required to exercise continuous oversight over the agencies under their jurisdiction. All official committee records were to be kept separate from the congressional office records of the Member serving as chairman.

Legislative Reorganization Act of 1970 The act (84 Stat. 1140) that removed much of the secrecy surrounding Members' actions and positions on issues and legislation. All roll-call votes taken in committees were required to be made public. House Members' positions on floor amendments were individually recorded and printed in the **Congressional Record**.

Majority Leader The officer who is elected by his party colleagues as the majority party's legislative strategist and second ranking leader after the Speaker.

Majority Whip In effect, the assistant majority leader, in either House. His job is to help marshal majority forces in support of party strategy and legislation.

Manual The official handbook in each House prescribing in detail its organization, procedures, and operations. (See Chapter 1, para. 1.90.)

Memorial See **Petition**.

Minority Leader Floor leader for the minority party in each Chamber.

Minority Whip The assistant leader for the minority party.

Minute book (1) A record of the proceedings of either House that contains a brief outline of proceedings as they occur. The minute book is used to prepare the *Journal*. (2) A committee record in the form of notes or brief summary of the committee's proceedings.

Miscellaneous document See **Document**.

Monthly Catalog The **Monthly Catalog of United States Government Publications** which is issued by the Superintendent of Documents, U.S. **Government Printing Office**. Subjects are derived from Library of Congress subject headings. The catalog consists of an entry for each new publication and seven indexes-author, title, subject, series/report number, contract number, stock number, and title keyword. The catalog was first issued in 1895.

Motion   A proposal made to a deliberative body for its approval or disapproval. A motion may be made orally. However, in the House, the Speaker may require a motion to be put in writing. The precedence of motions, and whether they are debatable, is set forth in the House and Senate manuals.

Motion to discharge   See **Committee**.

Nonrecord   Material not usually included within the definition of records, such as unofficial copies of documents kept only for convenience or reference, stocks of publications and processed documents, and library or museum material intended solely for reference or exhibition.

Office of record   An office designated as the official custodian of records for specified programs, activities, or transactions of the House or Senate. For example, the House Administration Committee maintains permanent records of the hiring of consultants by committees and the Senate Disbursing Office keeps official Senate personnel records.

Order   A direction to carry out an action that has already been agreed to by the House. Orders can be addressed to committees, or individual Members, or officials of the House. When the House commands, it is by an "order," but fact, principles, and the Members' own opinions and purposes are expressed in the form of **resolutions**.

Overriding of a Veto   Enacting a bill without the President's signature after the President has disapproved it and returned it to Congress with his objections. To override a veto the Constitution (Article 1, section 7) requires a two-thirds majority recorded vote in each chamber. The question put to each House is: "Shall the bill pass, the objections of the President to the contrary notwithstanding?" See also Veto. **Papers** (1) A natural accumulation of personal and family materials, as distinct from **records**. (2) A general term used to designate more than one type of manuscript material. See also **Personal papers** (of a **Member**).

Parliamentarian   The officer who is responsible for advising presiding officers and Members on parliamentary procedures; for preparing and maintaining compilations of the precedents of the House; and for referral of bills, resolutions, and other communications to the appropriate committees at the direction of the Speaker.

Permanent records   Records of an office or committee of the legislative branch appraised by the National Archives as having enduring value because they document the organization and functions of the committee or office that created or received them and/or because they contain significant information on persons, things, problems, and conditions with which the committee or office dealt.

Personal papers   (of a **Member**): An accumulation of private documents of an individual, belonging to him or her and subject to his or her disposition.

Petition   A type of document, similar to a **memorial**, submitted to the Congress asking that some action be taken by the Government or taking a positive stand on an issue. Generally speaking, in the late 18th and 19th centuries a petition, unlike a **memorial**, included a prayer (e.g., petition of John Smith praying that his claim be granted). **Memorials** also express opposition to ("remonstrate against") some pending action. In modern usage, there is no apparent difference between a **memorial** and a petition, and petition has become the commonly accepted generic term. A similar document transmitted to Congress by a legislative body such as a State legislature takes the form of a **resolution** and is sometimes termed a memorial. See also **Refer**.

Petition book   A register in which the receipt of petitions and subsequent actions on them are recorded. It is kept in the office of the Clerk of the House. See also **Refer**.

Pocket veto   See **Veto**.

Precedent   A preceding instance or case that serves as an example for subsequent cases. The Speaker gives precedent its proper influence and is directed to prepare an updated compilation of House precedents every two years. Several publications of compiled precedents prepared by the House **Parliamentarian** have been issued and are known variously by the compiler's name, Hinds, Cannon, and Deschler. (See Chapter 1, para 1.91). Compiled while Thomas Jefferson was Vice President, *Jefferson's Manual* is published with each revised edition of Rules of the House.

Preliminary inventory: See **Inventory**.

Preservation (archival)   (1) Adequate protection, care, and maintenance of archives and manuscripts. (2) Specific measures, individual and collective, undertaken for the repair, maintenance, restoration, or protection of documents. (3) A basic responsibility of an archival repository.

Presidential messages   Communications to Congress delivered by the President in person or in writing as provided for under the Constitution (Article 2, section 3). Those in writing are usually communicated on the same day to both Houses. Only messages of great importance are delivered in person. See **Executive communications**.

Private law   An act granting a pension, authorizing payment of a claim, or affording another form of relief to a private individual or legal entity. See **Calendar**, thereunder **Private calendar**.

Program records Records created or received and maintained by a committee in the conduct of the substantive functions (legislative and oversight) for which it is responsible. A program correspondence file may include correspondence on a number of subjects, as distinguished from a **case file** that contains correspondence about specific legislation or a specific investigation.

Public hearings See **Hearings**.

Public law A act that is of universal application, that is clothed with any public interest, or that applies to a class of persons as opposed to a private law that applies only to a specified individual or legal entity.

Quorum The number of Members whose presence is necessary for the transaction of business. In the Senate and House, it is a majority of the membership. When there are no vacancies, this is 51 in the Senate and 218 in the House. A quorum is 100 in the **Committee of the Whole House**. If a point of order is made that a quorum is not present, the only business that is in order is a motion to adjourn or a motion to direct the Sergeant at Arms to request the attendance of absentees. See also **Calendar**, thereunder **Discharge calendar**.

Reading file A folder containing copies of documents, frequently letters sent, arranged in chronological order, sometimes known as a chronological or "chron" file or a day file. A reading file may be circulated to other persons for reference; chronological files are usually retained by the author for his or her reference.

Record group In Federal archives, a body of organizationally related records established on the basis of provenance with particular regard for the administrative history, the complexity, and the volume of the records and archives of the institution or organization involved. See also **Series**.

Record series See **Series**.

Records In Federal archives, all books, papers, maps, photographs, motion pictures, sound or video recordings, machine-readable materials, or other documentary materials, regardless of physical form or characteristics, made or received by agencies of the U.S. Government under Federal law or in connection with the transaction of public business and preserved or deemed appropriate for preservation by that agency or its legitimate successor as evidence of the organization, functions, policies, decisions, procedures, operations, or other activities of the Government or because of the informational value of the data in them.

Refer To assign a bill, communication, or other document to a committee for its consideration. The House or Senate *Journal* indicates the committee to which any bill or document was referred. The Speaker or presiding officer of the Senate may refer measures to several committees because of the jurisdictional complexities of modern legislation. There are three types of multiple referral: joint referral of a bill concurrently to two or more committees; sequential referral of a bill successively to one committee, then a second, and so on; and split referral of various parts of a bill to different committees for consideration.

Register A list of events, letters sent and received, actions taken, etc., usually in simple sequence, as by date or number, and often serving as a finding aid to the records, such as a register of letters sent or a register of visitors.

Report (1) To bring back to the House or Senate, with recommendations, a bill or other matter that was referred to a committee or that originated in the committee. (2) A document presenting a committee's findings, or the findings of a conference committee or an executive agency that is required by law to submit them. Beginning with the 16th Congress (1819-21), committee reports were printed in a separate series. They are usually numbered and indicate the bills or other matters to which they refer; they are identified in the following manner: H. Rept. 240, 70th Cong., 2d sess. Reports from executive agencies or other sources frequently are printed as House Documents. See also **Document**.

- *Committee report* A document explaining a committee's position on legislation when a bill is discharged from a committee. When expressed, minority views will also be included in such a report.

- *Conference committee report* A two-part presentation that includes: (1) a bill, called the conference version, which has been approved by a majority of the managers appointed by each chamber to an ad hoc committee, the **conference committee**, and which reconciles the differences in form and provisions of bills passed on the same subject by the two Houses. The conference version of the bill sent to both Chambers for approval contains the language agreed to and recommended by the managers. Approval of the conference version will ensure passage of legislation in identical language by both Chambers as required to complete legislative action on a bill; and (2) a descriptive statement of the provisions of the conference version. A conference committee report is numbered and designated in the same way as a regular committee report. See **Committee**, thereunder **Conference committee**.

Resolution A formal expression of position by one or both Houses not having the force of law, a means of providing procedural arrangements between the two Houses, or, if a joint resolution, an enactment

having the authority of legislation. There are three types of resolutions:
- *Simple resolution* A measure that deals with matters entirely within the prerogatives of one House or the other. It does not contain legislation and does not require concurrence of the other House or Presidential approval. Its authority extends only to the House in which it originates. It is designated H. Res. if it originates in the House of Representatives and S. Res. if it originates in the Senate. Such a resolution is used to amend the rules or procedures of one chamber; to express the will or sentiments of the House originating it; to create select or special committees; to authorize the printing of special reports or additional copies of reports or hearings; to give advice on foreign policy or other executive business; to authorize funds to conduct investigations, either select or special, or to fund an investigative subcommittee; and to request information from administrative agencies.
- *Concurrent resolution* A measure that is used as a vehicle for expressing the sense of Congress on various foreign policy and domestic issues. It is similar to a simple resolution except that it indicates joint action and requires the concurrence of both Houses. It contains no legislation and its authority does not extend beyond Congress. Also, it is used, for example, to set the time for an **adjournment sine die**, to correct enrolled bills, to express the will of Congress, and to create special joint committees. It does not require Presidential approval. Concurrent resolutions are usually printed and are assigned numbers by the House of origin. They are referred to in the following manner: H. Con. Res. 25, 70th Cong., 1st session.
- *Joint resolution* (1) A form of proposed legislation similar to a bill, which in former usage served a limited purpose or was temporary in its effect. In present usage, however, a joint resolution is almost identical to a bill. A joint resolution (except a joint resolution proposing an amendment to the Constitution) requires the signature of the President or passage over his veto before it becomes law. It is designated in the following manner: H.J. Res. 25, 70th Cong., 1st sess. There may also be original joint resolutions; reported, calendar, and desk copies of joint resolutions; engrossed joint resolutions, and enrolled joint resolutions. (2) The approved measure which is treated as an act and which, since 1941, has been numbered in the same series as acts that originated as bills. Joint resolutions are generally used in dealing with limited matters, such as a single appropriation for a special purpose.

Roll call (1) The calling of the roll for the purpose of determining the presence of a quorum or for recording the yeas and nays on a specific measure. (2) The record of roll calls taken. Records of roll calls are numbered in sequence and are retained in the files. See also **Yeas and nays**.

Rough Pertaining to a first draft from which a finished or "smooth" copy is transcribed or printed, as in the rough journal.

Rule (1) A standing order governing the conduct of House or Senate business. The permanent rules of either Chamber deal with duties of officers, the order of business, admission to the floor, parliamentary procedures on handling amendments and voting, jurisdictions of committees, and other procedures. (2) In the House, a resolution reported by the Rules Committee to govern the handling of a particular bill on the floor. The committee may report a "rule," also called a "special order," in the form of a simple resolution. If the resolution is adopted by the House, the temporary rule becomes as valid as any standing rule and lapses only after action has been completed on the measure to which it pertains. A rule may set the time limit on general debate. It also may waive points of order against provisions, such as non-germane language of the bill in question or against certain amendments intended to be proposed to the bill from the floor. A rule may even forbid all amendments or all amendments except those proposed by the legislative committee that handled the bill. In this instance, the rule is known as a "closed" or "gag" rule as opposed to an "open" rule, which puts no limitation on floor amendments, thus leaving the bill completely open to alteration by the adoption of germane amendments.

Secret journal A journal of proceedings that were ordered to be kept secret.

Sergeant at Arms A House officer whose duties include enforcing attendance at sessions of the House; enforcing House Rules and maintaining decorum; keeping the Mace, the symbol of legislative power and authority; operating the House bank for Members; maintaining a check cashing facility for House employees; providing for the security of the building, visitors, and all foreign delegations visiting the House; and serving on a rotational basis as chairman of the Capitol Police Board and Capitol Guide Board.

Series In archives, file units or documents arranged in accordance with a filing system or maintained as a unit because they relate to a particular subject or function, result from the same activity, or have a particular form.

Session A meeting of the Congress that continues from day to day until **adjournment sine die**. Two or more sessions may occur within the 2-year period covered by a Congress.

Slip law The first official publication of a bill that has been enacted and signed into law. Each is published separately in unbound single-sheet or pamphlet form.

Speaker The permanent presiding officer of the House, selected by the caucus of the majority party and formally elected by the whole House. The Speaker can vote on all matters, but normally does not do so except in case of a tie vote.

Speaker pro tempore Member appointed by the Speaker to perform the duties of the chair in the Speaker's absence. Such appointments do not extend beyond three legislative days. In case of illness, the Speaker may, with the approval of the House, appoint a Speaker pro tempore for a period of 10 days. Under certain circumstances, the House may elect a Speaker pro tempore for the period of the Speaker's absence.

Special committee A select committee. See **Committee**, thereunder **Select committee**.

Special session A session of Congress held after it has adjourned sine die, completing its regular session. Special sessions are convened by the President of the United States under his constitutional powers.

Statute A law enacted by a legislative body. The laws enacted by Congress are published in a series of volumes entitled *Statutes at Large*.

Statutes at Large A chronological arrangement of the laws enacted in each session of Congress. Though indexed, the laws are not arranged by subject, nor is there an indication of how they affect previously enacted laws. See also **United States Code**.

Table To dispose of a matter finally and adversely without debate. A motion to "lay on the table" is not debatable in either House. In the Senate different language is sometimes used, and a motion may be worded to let a bill "lie on the table," perhaps for subsequent "picking up." This motion is more flexible, merely keeping the bill pending for later action, if desired. Tabling motions on amendments are effective debate-ending devices in the Senate.

Transcription A copy or verbatim written record of a committee hearing.

United States Code An official Government publication that consolidates and codifies the general and permanent laws of the United States arranged by subject under 50 titles, the first six dealing with general or political subjects, and the other 44 alphabetically arranged from "agriculture" to "war and national defense." The code is revised every 6 years, and a supplement is published after each session of Congress by the Office of the Law Revision Counsel of the House of Representatives. This office is conducting a project to codify all laws of the United States and eventually at the project's completion it will be unnecessary for researchers to refer to **Statutes at Large** for any current law text.

United States Serial Set See **Congressional Serial Set**.

Veto (1) Presidential disapproval of a bill by returning it without signing it within 10 days (Sunday excepted) after it is presented to the President. Such a bill is usually accompanied by a veto message stating the President's reasons for disapproval. It is returned to the House of origin and becomes a question of high privilege in the relative priority of motions and actions to be made in the chamber. (2) Presidential disapproval of a bill by failing to sign it (pocket veto) less than 10 days before the adjournment of Congress. Joint resolutions may be vetoed in the same ways. See **Bill**.

Yeas and nays The record of the vote on a matter by the Members of the House. See also **Roll call**.

Contracts and Contracting

CONTRACTING

Acceptance The act of an authorized representative of the Government by which the Government, for itself or as agent of another, assumes ownership of existing identified supplies or approves specific services rendered as partial or complete performance of a contract.

Acquisition The acquiring by contract with appropriated funds of supplies or services (including construction) by and for the use of the Federal Government through purchase, lease, or barter, whether the supplies or services are already in existence or must be created, developed, demonstrated, and evaluated.

Administrative Contracting Officer (ACO) A Government contracting officer, often at a location other than the one that made the contract, who handles the business administration of the contract.

Allocation Funds made available for departmental subdivisions from the department allocation: a control point.

Allotment Authorization by an agency head to an agency subdivision to incur obligations within a specified amount.

Alternative Dispute Resolution (ADR) Any procedure or combination of procedures voluntarily used to resolve issues in controversy without the need to resort to litigation. ADR procedures may include assisted settlement negotiations, conciliation, facilitation, mediation and fact-finding, mini-trials, and arbitration.

Apportionment Statutory authorization to spend from VA for specified purposes.

Best and Final Offer (BAFO) An advanced step in the Source Selection process which permits an offeror to submit revised technical and cost proposals, after clarification and discussion of the offeror's original proposal(s).

Best Practices are defined as techniques that agencies may use to help detect and avoid problems in the acquisition, management, and administration of contracts. Best practices are practical techniques gained from practical experience that may be used to improve the procurement process.

Bid A prospective contractor's (bidder's) reply to a sealed bid solicitation document (IFB). Needs only Government acceptance to constitute a binding contract. Sealed Bid as identified under Title VII—Competition in Contract Act of 1984.

Bidders Conference In sealed bid acquisitions, a meeting of prospective bidders arranged by the Contracting Officer during the solicitation period to help solicited firms fully understand the Government's requirement and to give them an opportunity to ask questions.

Bidders List (Solicitation Mailing List) List of sources maintained by the procuring office from which bids (sealed bidding) or proposals or quotations may be solicited.

Bilateral Modification Contract modifications accomplished by mutual action of the involved parties. Bilateral modifications are used to make negotiated equitable adjustments resulting from change orders and to reflect other agreements of the parties modifying the terms of contracts.

Blanket Purchase Agreement (BPA) A negotiated agreement between a contractor and the Government under which individual "calls" may be placed for a specified period of time and within a stipulated amount.

Breach of Contract A breach occurs when the Government or the contractor fails to fulfill the terms and conditions of the contract and there is no relief available under the terms of the contract or the contractor has committed fraud or a gross mistake amounting to fraud.

Budget The Federal administrative package presented to Congress each year by the President as the nation's basic financial planning document.

Change Order Unilateral direction to a contractor to modify a contractual requirement within the scope of the contract, pursuant to the Changes clause contained in the contract

Claim A written demand by one of the contracting parties seeking payment of money for a certain amount, adjustment or interpretation of contract terms, or other relief arising under or relating to the contract. A claim can be "under a contract," meaning that it is directly connected to that contract, or "relating to a contract," meaning that it is indirectly associated with that contract.

Closeout Administrative closeout of a contract after receiving evidence of its physical completion. When completed, the closeout procedures ensure that all administrative tasks were accomplished.

Commerce Business Daily (CBD) Publication synopsizing proposed Government acquisitions, sales, and contract awards. Also publishes information on subcontracting opportunities and advance notices of acquisitions.

Commitment A firm administrative reservation of funds authorizing subsidiary activities to start action leading to an acquisition obligation.

Competitive Proposal Technical and Cost Proposals for negotiated acquisitions as cited in Title VII—Competition in Contracting Act of 1984.

Competitive Range In competitive negotiations, the group of firms, which have the potential to receive the contract award(s).

Comptroller General Head of the General Accounting Office appointed by the President (and confirmed by the Senate) for a 15-year term.

Constructive Change A constructive change occurs when the Contracting Officer, or a duly authorized representative, changes the contract without following the required legal procedures to formally modify a contract. A constructive change can result from either a specific action or a failure to act.

Contracts All types of agreements and orders for obtaining supplies or services. Includes awards and notices of award; contracts of a fixed-price, cost, cost-plus-a-fee, or the issuance of job orders, task orders or task letters; letter contracts, purchase orders and supplemental agreements, to name a few.

Contract Financing Payment A disbursement of monies to a contractor under a contract clause or other authorization prior to acceptance of supplies or services by the Government. Contract financing payments include advance payments; delivery payments; partial payments; progress payments based on percentage or stage of completion; payments under fixed-price construction contracts; payments under fixed-price Architect-Engineer contracts; and interim payments on cost-type contracts. Contract financing payments do not include invoice payments or payments for partial deliveries. No interest penalty is paid to the contractor as a result of delayed contract financing payments.

Contract Modification Describes any written change in the terms of the contract.

Contract Type A reference to the pricing terms of the agreement between a buyer and a seller; may refer to the special nature of other important terms in the agreement.

Contracting (Sometimes referred to as procurement) Purchasing, renting, leasing or otherwise obtaining supplies or services. Includes description (but not determination) of supplies and services required, solicitation of sources, preparation and award of contracts, and all phases of contract administration.

Cost Overrun The amount by which a contractor exceeds (i) the estimated cost and/or (ii) the final limitation of his contract.

Cost Reimbursement Contracts In general, a category of contracts whose use is based on payment by the Government to a contractor of allowable costs as prescribed by the contract. Normally, only "best efforts" of the contractor are involved. Includes (i) cost, (ii) cost sharing, (iii) cost-plus-fixed-fee, (iv) cost-plus incentive-fee and (v) cost-plus-award fee contracts.

Data All recorded information to be delivered under a contract. Technical data excludes management and financial data.

Delay Failure to perform the service or provide the product during the performance or delivery period established in the contract. Delays can be either excusable or non-excusable.

Determination & Findings (D&F) Written justification by a Contracting Officer for such things as: (i) entering into contracts by negotiation, (ii) making advance payments in negotiated acquisitions, (iii) determining the type of contract to use.

Economic Price Adjustment Provision Contractual provision for resetting the contract price when a contingency, such as a change in cost of labor or materials occurs: commonly used in gasoline or heating oil contracts.

Excusable Delays Excusable delays are beyond the control and without the fault or negligence of a contractor or its subcontractors at any tier. A delay is excusable when the contractor can prove the following: Excusable delays may also be caused by Government performance. When Government actions cause the contractor to stop performing, the contractor may be excused from complying with the schedule.

Federal Acquisition Regulation (FAR) The primary regulation for use by all Federal Executive agencies in the acquisition of supplies and services with appropriated funds.

Fee An amount, in addition to allowable costs, paid to contractors having CPFF, CPAF, or CPIF contracts. In CPFF contracts, the fee is fixed a percentage (stated in dollar amount) of the initially estimated cost of the acquisition.

Fixed-Price Contracts In general, a category of contracts whose use is based on the establishment of a firm price to complete the required work. Includes

(i) firm fixed price, (ii) fixed price with escalation, (iii) fixed price redeterminable, and (iv) fixed price with incentive provisions contracts

Government Property Refers to all property owned by, leased to, or otherwise acquired by the Government under the terms of the contract.

Indefinite Delivery/Indefinite Quantity Used when the precise quantity of items or specific time of delivery desired is not known. Usually will specify a maximum and/or minimum quantity. Such acquisition is effected via (i) a definite quantity contract, (ii) a requirement contract, or (iii) an indefinite quantity contract. May be established through either sealed bid or negotiated procedures.

Inspection The act of examining and testing supplies or services (including, when appropriate, raw materials, components, and intermediate assemblies) to determine whether they conform to contract requirements.

Invitation for Bid (IFB) A solicitation document used in sealed bidding acquisitions.

Joint Consolidated List for Debarred, Ineligible, and Suspended Contractors A list of contractors who, for various reasons, are partially or wholly prevented from award of Government contracts.

Letter Contract An interim type of contractual agreement, sometimes called a "Letter of Intent," authorizing the commencement of manufacturing of supplies or performance of services. Used in negotiated acquisitions only when a definitized fixed-price or cost-reimbursement contract cannot be written until a later date.

Material Anything incorporated into, or consumed in, the manufacture of an end item. Includes raw and processed material, parts, components, assemblies and usable tools.

Modifications Any formal revision of the terms of a contract, either within or outside the scope of the agreement. Includes Change Orders.

Negotiation The method of acquisition used when one or more of the basic conditions incident to sealed bidding is absent and/or when there is justification under one or more of the 7 exceptions provided by the Competition in Contracting Act of 1984.

Negotiation Authority Authority to negotiate a contract under one of the 7 statutory exceptions granted by Congress, rather than the sealed bid method of acquisition.

Nonconformance Occurs when the contractor presents a deliverable to the Government that does not conform to contract requirements. A nonconformance is evaluated to determine if it is a major (substantive) discrepancy or a minor one. Minor nonconformities may be accepted as is when the savings realized by the contractor does not exceed the cost to the Government for processing a formal modification.

Non-Excusable Delays When a contractor cannot justify a delay as being beyond their control. Contractors are responsible for meeting contract delivery or performance schedule requirements and for all costs incurred in making up for the "lost time" associated with other than an excusable delay.

Obligation A monetary liability of the Government limited in amount of the legal liability of the Government at the time of recording. Must be supported by documentary evidence of the transaction involved.

Offer/Proposal/Quotation A prospective contractor's response to the solicitation form (RFP/RFQ) used for a negotiated acquisition.

Office of Management & Budget Basic financial control agency in the executive branch. Reports directly to the President.

Office of Small and Disadvantaged Business Utilization (OSDBU) VA's program office with responsibility for advocating small business concerns. Serves as liaison office with SBA on certificates of competency

Option A contractual clause permitting an increase in the quantity of supplies beyond that originally stipulated or an extension in the time for which services on a time basis may be required.

Partial Payment A method of payment based on acceptance of a particular part of contract performance.

Past-Performance Information Relevant information for future source-selection decisions regarding contractor actions under previously awarded contracts.

Performance-Based Payments Contract financing payments that are not payment for accepted items and are not subject to the interest penalty provisions of prompt payment. These payments are fully recoverable in the same manner as progress payments, in the event the contractor defaults.

Performance Monitoring Activities that a Contracting Officer and other Government personnel use to ensure supplies and/or services acquired under contracts conform to prescribed quality, quantity, and other requirements. Monitoring activities include, but are not limited to, inspection and acceptance, as well as quality assurance techniques.

Post-Award Orientation A planned, structured discussion between Government and contractor that focuses on understanding the technical aspects of the contract, identifying and resolving oversights, preventing problems, averting misunderstandings, deciding how to solve problems that may occur later, and reaching agreement on common issues.

Pre-Award Phase That period of time that covers actions taken once the requirement has been identified and before the procurement is awarded to a contractor(s). The pre-award phase includes the pre-solicitation phase.

Pre-Award Survey Study of a prospective contractor's financial, organizational and operational capability, and managerial status, made prior to contract award, to determine his responsibility and eligibility for Government acquisition.

Pre-Solicitation Conference A meeting held with potential contractors prior to a formal Conference solicitation to discuss technical and other problems connected with a proposed acquisition. The conference is also used to elicit the interest of prospective contractors in pursuing the task.

Price and Fee Ceiling Price The negotiated monetary limit—in a fixed-price-type contract—to the amount that the Government is obligated to pay. Costs incurred beyond this point must be absorbed by the contractor.

Progress Payments Payments made to the prime contractor during the life of a fixed-price-type contract on the basis of percentage of the total incurred cost or total direct labor and material cost. Very common in construction contracts.

Progressing The monitoring of contract performance by personnel of the Government agency or of the prime contractor.

Prompt Payment When the Government pays the contractor prior to the invoice payment date. The prompt payment discount is an invoice payment reduction voluntarily offered to the Government by the contractor for prompt payment and is made before the due date stated on the invoice.

Property Personal property, and includes materials, special tooling, special test equipment, and agency-particular property.

Property Administrator An authorized representative of the Contracting Officer assigned to administer contract requirements and obligations relating to Government property.

Property Control System A contractor's method to establish to record, identify, and mark Government property used while working under a Government contract.

Protest A formal action by an interested party, which challenges VA's ability to progress with a solicitation or contract performance until the challenger's issues are resolved.

Purchase Order (PO) A contractual acquisition document used primarily to purchase supplies and non-personal services when the aggregate amount involved in any one transaction is relatively small (i.e., not exceeding $25,000).

Purchase Request (PR) Document that describes the required supplies or services so that an acquisition can be initiated. Some activities actually refer to the document by this title; others use different titles, such as Purchase Directive, etc. Requests must be placed on forms established by VA Acquisition Regulation.

Qualified Products List (QPL) A list of products that are pre-tested in advance of actual acquisition to determine which suppliers can comply properly with specification requirements.

Quality Assurance The function, including inspections, performed by the Government to determine whether a contractor has fulfilled contract obligations pertaining to quality and quantity.

Request for Proposal (RFP) A formal solicitation form. Acceptance by VA is legally binding upon the offeror.

Request for Quotation (RFQ) An informal solicitation form, commonly used in small purchase procedures. Acceptance is not legally binding upon the offeror.

Request for Technical Proposal (RTP) Solicitation document used in Step One of Two-Step Sealed Bidding. Normally in letter form, it asks only for technical information. Price and cost breakdowns are solicited only during Step Two.

Requiring Activity Any activity originating a request for supplies or services.

Sealed Bid See Bid.

Small Business Administration (SBA) A Federal agency created to foster and protect the interests of small business concerns.

Solicitation-Award Phase The solicitation-award phase is that period of time covering actions taken once the Contracting Officer has issued a solicitation and before award is made.

Statement of Work Although varying widely in precise definition, the term generally covers that portion of a contract that describes the actual work to be done by means of specifications or other minimum requirements, quantities, performance dates, and a statement of requisite quality.

Stop Work Order A written or oral order to stop work under a contract. If an oral stop work order is given to the contractor, it is only binding when confirmed in writing by the Contracting Officer and signed by the contractor.

Subcontract A contract between a buyer (usually the prime contractor) and a seller in which a significant part of the supplies or services being obtained is for eventual use in a Government contract. The term frequently implies a substantial dollar value and/or non-standard specifications.

Supplemental Agreement Bilateral written amendment to a contract by which the Government and the contractor settle price and/or performance adjustments to the basic contract.

Technical Analysis An analysis prepared by the COTR focusing on the technical aspects of a contractor's response to a Government request. The technical analysis is used by the Contracting Officer for making decisions to change the contract.

Technical Evaluation Analysis of activities and functions that cause costs or other changes to occur within a contract. The analysis is a means for determining the impact of any delivery delays on the requirement, value of proposed consideration other than price or acceptability of a value, acceptability of a value-engineering proposal, or acceptability of substitute material. The technical evaluation indicates if the Government will be harmed and include documentation supporting any modification request.

Termination The canceling of all or part of a prime contract or a subcontract prior to its completion through performance. May be for the convenience of the Government, or default of the contractor due to non-performance.

Termination for Convenience Termination for convenience occurs when the Government requires the contractor to discontinue performance because completion of the work is no longer in the Government's best interest. The Government has the right to terminate without cause and limit contractor recovery to costs incurred, profit on work done, and cost of preparing a termination settlement proposal. Recovery of anticipated profit is precluded. Termination for convenience should be considered when the requirement is no longer needed, the quantity needed has been reduced, or when there has been a radical change in the requirement beyond the contractor's expertise.

Termination for Default (or Cause) Termination for default (or cause) occurs when the contractor fails to perform in accordance with the contract. The Government will terminate a contract either for default or cause, when it is determined that to do so would be in its best interest. The word "cause" relates to a termination action and is normally used in the commercial marketplace. The word "default" is traditionally used in Government contracting. A contract is terminated for default (or cause) when there is no other alternative for obtaining performance, given contractor problems and deficiencies, and the Government has a sustainable case for default.

Time and Materials/Labor Hour Contract Negotiated contracts based on specified fixed hourly rates to complete a given task. Used only in situations where it is not possible at the outset to estimate the extent or duration of the work involved or to anticipate cost with any substantial accuracy. Least desirable contract type for the Government.

Unilateral Modification Unilateral modifications are changes to a contract signed only by the Government Contracting Officer. This type of modification is used to make administrative changes that are minor in nature and do not materially affect contract performance, issue change orders that are authorized by the Changes clause, make changes authorized by other contract clauses, such as stop-work, termination, or option clauses, or exercise of an option.

Unsolicited Proposal Innovative ideas, either written or oral, made to the Government by organizations or individuals acting in their own behalf. Such proposals have no relation to a particular solicitation used by the Government as a basis for acquisition.

Value Engineering An incentive plan used to encourage cost reduction and cost avoidance by providing contractors with profit incentives for developing changes that will reduce overall cost while maintaining accomplishment of the required function of the item or service being acquired.

CONTRACTING

AA Alternative Analysis.
ATO Authority to Operate.
Board Procedures Provides the IRB charter that includes its roles and responsibilities.
CA Certification and Accreditation.
CC Clinger-Cohen Act of 1996 (Clinger-Cohen).
CFO Chief Financial Officer.
COs Contracting Officers.
Cost-Benefit Analysis Provides guidance on completing a cost-benefit analysis (CBA).
CPIC Capital Planning and Investment Control (CPIC) process.
CPIC Process Checklist Provides a checklist of the process steps investments must complete for each CPIC phase.
CSO Chief Security Officer.
CY Current Year.
Cyber Security Infrastructure Guide Provides guidance concerning cyber security information to support the investment.
DME Development, Modernization, or Enhancements.
DOD Department of Defense.
EA Enterprise Architecture.
Earned Value Management Provides guidance on conducting earned value analysis.
E-Government Provides guidance on E-Government information to support the investment.
Enterprise Architecture Provides guidance on matters related to the Agency enterprise architecture.

ERC   Executive Review Committee.
ESPC   Energy Savings Performance Contract.
EVM   Earned Value Management.
FASA   Federal Acquisition Streamlining Act of 1994.
FCIO   Federal Chief Information Officer.
FEAF   Federal Enterprise Architecture Framework.
FISMA   Federal Information Security Management Act (FISMA).
GAO   Government Accountability Office.
GPEA   The Government Paperwork Elimination Act of 1998.
IEAC   Independent Estimate at Completion.
IGCE   Independent Government Cost Estimates.
IPT   Integrated Project / Program Teams.
IRB   Investment Review Board.
ISSO   Information Systems Security Officer.
IT   Information Technology.
LCC   Life-Cycle Cost.
MAC   Multi-Agency Collaboration.
Mission Needs Statement   Provides a template for evaluating the mission need(s) for a new Major IT/Non-IT Assets investments.
OBPA   Office of Budget and Program Analysis.
OCIO   Office of the Chief Information Officer.
OM   Operational System.
OMB   Office of Management and Budget.
OMB Requirements   Provides a summary of the data required for OMB using WorkLenz.
Operational Analysis Review   Provides a form to use that defines the basic elements needed for an operational analysis review.
Performance Measurement   Provides guidance on developing performance measures for Major IT/Non-IT Assets investments.
PIA   Privacy Impact Assessment.
PIO   Performance Improvement Officer.
PIR   Post Implementation Review (Provides guidance on conducting a post-implementation review).
PM   Project Manager.
PRA   Paperwork Reduction Act of 1995.
Project Management   Provides guidance on managing Major IT/Non-IT Assets investments.
Quarterly/Milestone Control and Evaluate Review Checklist   Lists the critical areas the Control and Evaluate review team discusses during each quarterly/milestone review.
Risk Assessment   Provides guidance on conducting a risk assessment for Major IT/Non-IT Assets capital planning.
ROI   Return on Investment.
SDLC   System Development Life Cycle.
SORN   Systems of Records Notice.
Telecommunications Reference Manual   Provides guidance on telecommunications information to support the investment.
TOC   Total Ownership Cost estimates.

Defense

AA&E	arms, ammunition, and explosives	*CD-ROM*	compact-disk, read-only memory
ABCS	Army Battle Command System	*cdr*	commander
AC	alternating current	*CG*	command guidance
admin	administration	*chap*	chapter
ADP	automated data processing	*CIA*	Central Intelligence Agency
AF	Air Force	*CID*	Criminal Investigation Division
AFB	Air Force base	*CINC*	commander in chief
AFM	Air Force manual	*CISO*	counterintelligence support officer
AFMAN	Air Force manual	*CMU*	concrete-masonry unit
AFOSI	Air Force Office of Special Investigations	*CONEX*	container express
		CONPLAN	contingency plan
AFR	Air Force regulation	*CONUS*	continental United States
AIQC	Antiterrorism Instructor Qualification Course	*CP*	command post
		CPWG	crime-prevention working group
AIS	automated information system	*CQ*	charge of quarters
AL	Alabama	*CRIMP*	Crime Reduction Involving Many People
AM	amplitude-modulated	*CTA*	common table of allowance
AMC	Army Materiel Command	*DA*	Department of the Army
AMS	Army management structure	*DARE*	Drug Abuse Resistance and Education
AO	area of operations	*DC*	direct current
AP	armor piercing	*DC*	District of Columbia
Apr	April	*Dec*	December
AR	Army regulation	*DIA*	Defense Intelligence Agency
AR-PERSCOM	Army Reserve Personnel Command	*DOD*	Department of Defense
ASP	ammunition supply point	*DOE*	Department of Energy
AT	antitank	*DOJ*	Department of Justice
AT/FP	antiterrorism/force protection	*DOS*	Department of State
attn	attention	*DOT*	Department of Transportation
Aug	August	*DS*	direct support
AWG	American wire gauge	*DTM*	data-transmission media
bldg	building	*DTOC*	division tactical operations center
BMS	balanced magnetic switch	*EDM*	emergency-destruct measures
BTO	barbed-tape obstacle	*EECS*	electronic entry-control system
BUPERS	Bureau of Naval Personnel	*EOD*	explosive-ordnance disposal
C2	command and control	*EOR*	element of resource
C3	command, control, and communications	*EPW*	enemy prisoner of war
		equip	equipment
cav	cavalry	*ESS*	electronic security system
CB	citizen's band	*FAA*	Federal Aviation Administration
CCB	Community Counterterrorism Board	*FBI*	Federal Bureau of Investigation
		FCC	Federal Communications Commission
CCIR	commander's critical information requirements	*Feb*	February
		FIS	foreign-intelligence services
CCTV	closed-circuit television	*FM*	field manual

FM	frequency-modulated
ft	foot, feet
FY	fiscal year
G2	Assistant Chief of Staff, G2 (Intelligence)
GHz	gigahertz
GTA	graphic training aid
HN	host nation
HQ	headquarters
HUD	Housing and Urban Development Administration
HUMINT	human intelligence
Hz	hertz
IAW	in accordance with
ICP	initial control point
ID	identification
IDS	intrusion-detection system
IED	improvised explosive device
IG	inspector general
IID	improvised incendiary device
in	inch(es)
INSCOM	US Army Intelligence and Security Command
INTAC	Individual Terrorism Awareness Course
IPB	intelligence preparation of the battlefield
IR	infrared
ISS	information systems security
J2	Intelligence Directorate (Joint Command)
Jan	January
JS	Joint Service
JSAT	Joint Security Assistance Training
JSCP	Joint Strategic Capabilities Plan
JSIIDS	Joint-Service Interior Intrusion-Detection System
Jul	July
Jun	June
K	one thousand
kHz	kilohertz
LED	light-emitting diode
liq	liquid
LOS	line of sight
LOTS	logistics over the shore
LP	listening post
LRA	local reproduction authorized
MACOM	major Army command
maint	maintenance
Mar	March
MCO	Marine Corps order
MDEP	management decision package
MDMP	military decision-making process
METT-TC	mission, enemy, terrain, troops, time available, and civilian considerations
MEVA	mission-essential or vulnerable area
MI	military intelligence
MILCON	military construction
MILPO	military personnel office
MILVAN	military van
min	minimum
mm	millimeter(s)
MO	modus operandi
MOU	memorandum of understanding
MP	military police
MPACS	Military Police Automated Control System
MPMIS	Military Police Management Information System
MPR	military-police report
MS-DOS	Microsoft®-disk operating system
MWD	military working dog
N/A	not applicable
naut	nautical
NAVATAC	Navy Antiterrorism Analysis Center
NBC	nuclear, biological, and chemical
NCIC	National Crime Information Center
NCO	noncommissioned officer
NISCOM	Naval Investigative Service Command
No.	number
Nov	November
NSA	National Security Agency
NTAV	nontactical armored vehicle
NVD	night-vision device
O	official
OASD	Office of the Assistant Secretary of Defense
OCOKA	observation and fields of fire, cover and concealment, obstacles, key terrain, and avenues of approach
OCONUS	outside the continental United States
Oct	October
OMA	operations and maintenance, Army
OPA	operations and procurement, Army
OPLAN	operation plan
OPORD	operations order
OPSEC	operations security
Pam	pamphlet
PAO	public affairs office(r)
PD	probability of detection
PERSCOM	Personnel Command
PHOTINT	photographic intelligence
PI	police intelligence
PIR	passive infrared
PM	provost marshal
PMO	provost marshal office
POL	petroleum, oil, and lubricants
POM	Program Objective Memorandum
POV	privately owned vehicle
PS	physical security
PSD	protective security detail
PSI	physical-security inspector

PTO	Parent-Teacher Organization
PX	post exchange
R&D	research and development
RD&E	research, development, and engineering
ref	reference(s)
RF	radio frequency
RII	relevant information and intelligence
ROI	report of investigation
RORO	roll on/roll off
RPG	rocket-propelled grenade
/s/	signed
S2	Intelligence Officer (US Army)
SAW	squad automatic weapon
SDNCO	staff duty noncommissioned officer
SDO	staff duty officer
Sep	September
SIGINT	signal intelligence
SJA	staff judge advocate
SO/LIC	Special Operations/Low-Intensity Conflict
SOFA	status of forces agreement
SOP	standing operating procedure
St.	Saint
STANO	surveillance, target acquisition, and night observation
stat	statute
STC	sound-transmission coefficient
STD	standard
STU	secure telephone unit
TAACOM	Theater Army Area Command
TB	technical bulletin
TDY	temporary duty
TECOM	US Army Test and Evaluation Command
TEMPEST	Terminal Electromagnetic-Pulse Emanation Standard
THREATCON	threat conditions
TM	technical manual
TMDE	test, measurement, and diagnostic equipment
TNT	trinitrotoluene
TRADOC	US Army Training and Doctrine Command
TSC	triple-standard concertina
UCMJ	Uniform Code of Military Justice
UFR	unfinanced requirement
US	United States
USACE	US Army Corps of Engineers
USACIDC	US Army Criminal Investigation Command
USAMPS	US Army Military Police School
USCG	US Coast Guard
VA	vulnerability assessment
VIP	very important person
vol	volume

ABBREVIATIONS AND ACRONYMS

A	analog
A&P	administrative and personnel; analysis and production
A2C2	Army airspace command and control
A-3	Operations Directorate (COMAFFOR)
A-4	Air Force logistics directorate
A-5	Plans Directorate (COMAFFOR)
AA	assessment agent; avenue of approach
AAA	antiaircraft artillery; arrival and assembly area; assign alternate area
AAAS	amphibious aviation assault ship
AABB	American Association of Blood Banks
AABWS	amphibious assault bulk water system
AAC	activity address code
AACG	arrival airfield control group
AADC	area air defense commander
AADP	area air defense plan
AA&E	arms, ammunition, and explosives
AAEC	aeromedical evacuation control team
AAFES	Army and Air Force Exchange Service
AAFIF	automated air facility information file
AAFS	amphibious assault fuel system
AAFSF	amphibious assault fuel supply facility
AAGS	Army air-ground system
AAI	air-to-air interface
AAM	air-to-air missile
AAMDC	US Army Air and Missile Defense Command
AAOE	arrival and assembly operations element
AAOG	arrival and assembly operations group
AAP	Allied administrative publication; assign alternate parent
AAR	after action report; after action review
AAST	aeromedical evacuation administrative support team
AAT	automatic analog test; aviation advisory team
AATCC	amphibious air traffic control center
AAU	analog applique unit
AAV	amphibious assault vehicle
AAW	antiair warfare
AB	airbase
ABCA	American, British, Canadian, Australian Armies Program
ABCS	Army Battle Command System
ABD	airbase defense
ABFC	advanced base functional component
ABFDS	aerial bulk fuel delivery system
ABFS	amphibious bulk fuel system
ABGD	air base ground defense
ABL	airborne laser

ABLTS	amphibious bulk liquid transfer system	ACOC	area communications operations center
ABM	antiballistic missile	ACOCC	air combat operations command center
ABN	airborne	ACOS	assistant chief of staff
ABNCP	Airborne Command Post	ACP	access control point; air commander's pointer; airspace control plan; Allied Communications Publication; assign common pool
ABO	air base operability; blood typing system		
ABP	air battle plan		
A/C	aircraft		
AC	Active Component; aircraft commander; alternating current	ACR	armored cavalry regiment (Army); assign channel reassignment
AC2	airspace command and control	ACS	agile combat support; air-capable ship; airspace control system; auxiliary crane ship
AC-130	Hercules		
ACA	airlift clearance authority; airspace control authority; airspace coordination area		
		ACSA	acquisition and cross-servicing agreement; Allied Communications Security Agency
ACAA	automatic chemical agent alarm		
ACAPS	area communications electronics capabilities		
		AC/S, C4I	Assistant Chief of Staff, Command, Control, Communications, Computers, and Intelligence (USMC)
ACAT	aeromedical evacuation command augmentation team		
		ACT	activity; advance civilian team; Allied Command Transformation
ACB	amphibious construction battalion		
ACC	Air Combat Command; air component commander; area coordination center; Army Contracting Command	ACU	assault craft unit
		ACV	aircraft cockpit video; armored combat vehicle
ACCE	air component coordination element		
ACCON	acoustic condition	ACW	advanced conventional weapons
ACCS	air command and control system	A/D	analog-to-digital
ACCSA	Allied Communications and Computer Security Agency	AD	active duty; advanced deployability; air defense; automatic distribution; priority add-on
ACDO	assistant command duty officer		
ACE	airborne command element (USAF); air combat element (NATO); Allied Command Europe; aviation combat element; aviation combat element Marine air-ground task force (MAGTF)	ADA	aerial damage assessment; air defense artillery
		A/DACG	arrival/departure airfield control group
		ADAFCO	air defense artillery fire control officer
		ADAL	authorized dental allowance list
		ADAM	air defense airspace management
ACEOI	automated communications-electronics operating instructions	ADAM/BAE	air defense airspace management/ brigade aviation element
ACF	air contingency force	ADAMS	Allied Deployment and Movement System
ACI	assign call inhibit		
ACIC	Army Counterintelligence Center	ADANS	Air Mobility Command Deployment Analysis System
ACINT	acoustic intelligence		
ACK	acknowledgement	ADC	air defense commander; area damage control
ACL	access control list; allowable cabin load		
ACLANT	Allied Command Atlantic	ADCAP	advanced capability
ACLP	affiliated contingency load planning	A/DCG	arrival/departure control group
ACM	advanced conventional munitions; advanced cruise missile; air combat maneuver; air contingency Marine air-ground task force (MAGTF); airspace coordinating measure	ADCI/MS	Associate Director of Central Intelligence for Military Support
		ADCON	administrative control
		ADD	assign on-line diagnostic
		ADDO	Assistant Deputy Director for Operations
ACMREQ	airspace control means request; airspace coordination measures request	ADDO(MS)	Assistant Deputy Director for Operations/ Military Support
ACN	assign commercial network		
ACO	administrative contracting officer; airspace control order	ADE	assign digit editing
		ADF	automatic direction finding
ACOA	adaptive course of action client	ADIZ	air defense identification zone

ADKC/RCU	Automatic Key Distribution Center/Rekeying Control Unit
ADL	advanced distributed learning; armistice demarcation line; assign XX (SL) routing
ADMIN	administration
ADN	Allied Command Europe desired ground zero number
ADNET	anti-drug network
ADOC	air defense operations center
ADP	air defense plan; automated data processing
ADPE	automated data processing equipment
ADPS	automatic data processing system
ADR	accident data recorder; aircraft damage repair; armament delivery recording
ADRA	Adventist Development and Relief Agency
ADS	air defense section; air defense sector; amphibian discharge site
ADSIA	Allied Data Systems Interoperability Agency
ADSW	active duty for special work
ADT	active duty for training; assign digital transmission group; automatic digital tester
ADUSD(TP)	Assistant Deputy Under Secretary of Defense, Transportation Policy
ADVON	advanced echelon
ADW	air defense warnings
ADWC	air defense warning condition
ADZ	amphibious defense zone
A/E	ammunition/explosives
AE	aeromedical evacuation; assault echelon; attenuation equalizer
AEC	aeromedical evacuation crew
AECA	Arms Export Control Act
AECC	aeromedical evacuation coordination center
AECM	aeromedical evacuation crew member
AECS	aeromedical evacuation command squadron
AECT	aeromedical evacuation control team
AEF	air and space expeditionary force
AEG	air expeditionary group
AELT	aeromedical evacuation liaison team
AEOS	aeromedical evacuation operations squadron
AEOT	aeromedical evacuation operations team
AEPS	aircrew escape propulsion system
AEPST	aeromedical evacuation plans and strategy team
AES	aeromedical evacuation squadron; aeromedical evacuation system
AESC	aeromedical evacuation support cell
AET	airport emergency team
AETC	Air Education and Training Command
AETF	air and space expeditionary task force
A/ETF	automated/electronic target folder
AEU	assign essential user bypass
AEW	air and space expeditionary wing; airborne early warning
AEW&C	airborne early warning and control
AF	amphibious force
AFAARS	Air Force After Action Reporting System
AFARN	Air Force air request net
AFATDS	Advanced Field Artillery Tactical Data System
AFB	Air Force base
AFC	area frequency coordinator; automatic frequency control
AFCA	Air Force Communications Agency
AFCAP	Air Force contract augmentation program; Armed Forces contract augmentation program
AFCB	Armed Forces Chaplains Board
AFCC	Air Force Component Commander
AFCCC	Air Force Combat Climatology Center
AFCEE	Air Force Center for Environmental Excellence
AFCENT	Allied Forces Central Europe (NATO)
AFCERT	Air Force computer emergency response team
AFCESA	Air Force Civil Engineering Support Agency
AFCS	automatic flight control system
AFD	assign fixed directory
AFDC	Air Force Doctrine Center
AFDD	Air Force doctrine document
AFDIGS	Air Force digital graphics system
AFDIL	Armed Forces DNA Identification Laboratory
AFDIS	Air Force Weather Agency Dial In Subsystem
AF/DP	Deputy Chief of Staff for Personnel, United States Air Force
AFE	Armed Forces Entertainment
AFEES	Armed Forces Examining and Entrance Station
AFFIS	Air Facilities File Information System
AFFMA	Air Force Frequency Management Agency
AFFOR	Air Force forces
AFH	Air Force handbook
AFI	Air Force instruction
AFID	anti-fratricide identification device
AF/IL	Deputy Chief of Staff for Installations and Logistics, USAF
AFIP	Armed Forces Institute of Pathology
AFIS	American Forces Information Service

AFIRB	Armed Forces Identification Review Board	AFSOD	Air Force special operations detachment
AFIWC	Air Force Information Warfare Center	AFSOE	Air Force special operations element
AFJI	Air Force joint instruction	AFSOF	Air Force special operations forces
AFJMAN	Air Force Joint Manual	AFSOUTH	Allied Forces, South (NATO)
AFLC	Air Force Logistics Command	AFSPACE	United States Space Command Air Force
AFLE	Air Force liaison element	AFSPC	Air Force Space Command
AFLNO	Air Force liaison officer	AFSPOC	Air Force Space Operations Center
AFMAN	Air Force manual	AFTAC	Air Force Technical Applications Center
AFMC	Air Force Materiel Command	AFTH	Air Force Theater Hospital
AFMD	Air Force Mission Directive	AFTN	Aeronautical Fixed Telecommunications Network
AFME	Armed Forces Medical Examiner	AFTO	Air Force technical order
AFMES	Armed Forces Medical Examiner System	AFTRANS	Air Force Transportation Component
AFMIC	Armed Forces Medical Intelligence Center	AFTTP	Air Force tactics, techniques, and procedures; Air Force technical training publication
AFMLO	Air Force Medical Logistics Office	AFTTP(I)	Air Force tactics, techniques, and procedures (instruction)
AFMS	Air Force Medical Service	AFW	Air Force Weather
AFNORTH	Air Force North; Allied Forces Northern Europe (NATO)	AFWA	Air Force Weather Agency
AFNORTHWEST	Allied Forces North West Europe (NATO)	AFWCF	Air Force working capital fund
		AFWIN	Air Force Weather Information Network
AFNSEP	Air Force National Security and Emergency Preparedness Agency	AF/XO	Deputy Chief of Staff for Plans and Operations, United States Air Force
AFOE	assault follow-on echelon	AF/XOI	Air Force Director of Intelligence, Surveillance, and Reconnaissance
AFOSI	Air Force Office of Special Investigations	AF/XOO	Director of Operations, United States Air Force
AFPAM	Air Force pamphlet	A/G	air to ground
AFPC	Air Force Personnel Center	AG	adjutant general (Army)
AFPD	Air Force policy directive	AGARD	Advisory Group for Aerospace Research and Development
AFPEO	Armed Forces Professional Entertainment Overseas	AGCCS	Army Global Command and Control System
AFR	Air Force Reserve; assign frequency for network reporting	AGE	aerospace ground equipment
AFRC	Air Force Reserve Command; Armed Forces Recreation Center	AGI	advanced geospatial intelligence
		AGIL	airborne general illumination lightself
AFRCC	Air Force rescue coordination center	AGL	above ground level
AFRL	Air Force Research Laboratory	AGM-28A	Hound Dog
AFRRI	Armed Forces Radiobiology Research Institute	AGM-65	Maverick
		AGM-69	short range attack missile
AFRTS	Armed Forces Radio and Television Service	AGR	Active Guard and Reserve
AFS	aeronautical fixed service	AGS	aviation ground support
AFSATCOM	Air Force satellite communications (system)	AHA	alert holding area
		AHD	antihandling device
AFSB	Army field support brigade	AI	airborne interceptor; air interdiction; area of interest
AFSC	Armed Forces Staff College; United States Air Force specialty code	AIA	Air Intelligence Agency
AFSCN	Air Force Satellite Control Network	AIASA	annual integrated assessment for security assistance
AFSOB	Air Force special operations base		
AFSOC	Air Force Special Operations Command; Air Force special operations component	AIC	air intercept controller; assign individual compressed dial; Atlantic Intelligence Command
AFSOCC	Air Force special operations control center	AICF/USA	Action Internationale Contre La Faim (International Action Against Hunger)

AIDS	acquired immune deficiency syndrome	ALCC	airlift control center
AIF	automated installation intelligence file	ALCE	airlift control element
		ALCF	airlift control flight
		ALCG	analog line conditioning group
AIFA	AAFES Imprest Fund Activity	ALCM	air launched cruise missile
AIG	addressee indicator group	ALCOM	United States Alaskan Command
AIIRS	automated intelligence information reporting system	ALCON	all concerned
		ALCS	airlift control squadron
AIK	assistance in kind	ALCT	airlift control team
AIM	Airman's Information Manual	ALD	airborne laser designator; available-to-load date
AIM-7	Sparrow		
AIM-9	Sidewinder	ALE	airlift liaison element
AIM-54A	Phoenix	ALERFA	alert phase (ICAO)
AIMD	aircraft intermediate maintenance department	ALERT	attack and launch early reporting to theater
AIQC	antiterrorism instructor qualification course	ALERTORD	alert order
		ALLOREQ	air allocation request; allocation request
AIRBAT	Airborne Intelligence, Surveillance, and Reconnaissance Requirements-Based Allocation Tool	ALLTV	all light level television
		ALMSNSCD	airlift mission schedule
		ALN	ammunition lot number
		ALNOT	alert notice; search and rescue alert notice
AIRCENT	Allied Air Forces Central Europe (NATO)		
		ALO	air liaison officer
AIRES	advanced imagery requirements exploitation system	ALOC	air line of communications
		ALORD	alert launch order
AIREVACCONFIRM	air evacuation confirmation	ALP	Allied Logistic Publication
AIREVACREQ	air evacuation request	ALSA	Air Land Sea Application (Center)
AIREVACRESP	air evacuation response	ALSS	advanced logistic support site
AIRNORTHWEST	Allied Air Forces North West Europe (NATO)	ALT	acquisition, logistics, and technology
		ALTD	airborne laser target designator
AIRREQRECON	air request reconnaissance	ALTRV	altitude reservation
AIRSOUTH	Allied Air Forces Southern Europe (NATO)	ALTTSC	alternate Tomahawk strike coordinator
		A/M	approach and moor
AIRSUPREQ	air support request	AM	amplitude modulation
AIS	automated information system	AMAL	authorized medical allowance list
AIT	aeromedical isolation team; automated identification technology	AMB	air mobility branch; ambassador
		AMBUS	ambulance bus
		AMC	airborne mission coordinator; Air Mobility Command; Army Materiel Command: midpoint compromise search area
AIU	Automatic Digital Network Interface Unit		
AJ	anti-jam		
AJBPO	area joint blood program office	AMCC	allied movement coordination center; alternate military command center
AJCC	alternate joint communications center		
		AMCIT	American citizen
AJ/CM	anti-jam control modem	AMCM	airborne mine countermeasures
AJF	allied joint force	AMCT	air mobility control team
AJFP	adaptive joint force packaging	AMD	air and missile defense; air mobility division
AJMRO	area joint medical regulating office		
		AME	antenna mounted electronics
AJNPE	airborne joint nuclear planning element	AMEDD	Army Medical Department
		AMEDDCS	U.S. Army Medical Department Center and School
AJP	Allied joint publication		
AK	commercial cargo ship	AMedP	Allied Medical Publication
AKNLDG	acknowledge message	AMEMB	American Embassy
ALARA	as low as reasonably achievable	AMF(L)	ACE Mobile Force (Land) (NATO)

AMH	automated message handler	AOA	amphibious objective area
AMIO	alien migrant interdiction operations	AOB	advanced operations base; aviation operations branch
AMLO	air mobility liaison officer		
AMMO	ammunition	AOC	air and space operations center (USAF); air operations center; Army operations center
AMOC	Air Marine Operations Center		
AMOCC	air mobility operations control center		
AMOG	air mobility operations group	AOCC	air operations control center
AMOPES	Army Mobilization and Operations Planning and Execution System	AOC-E	Aviation Operations Center-East (USCS)
AMOPS	Army mobilization and operations planning system; Army mobilization operations system	AOCU	analog orderwire control unit
		AOC-W	Aviation Operations Center-West (USCS)
AMOS	air mobility operations squadron	AOD	air operations directive; on-line diagnostic
AMOSS	Air and Marine Operations Surveillance System		
		AOF	azimuth of fire
AMOW	air mobility operations wing	AOI	area of interest
AMP	amplifier; analysis of mobility platform	AOL	area of limitation
AMPE	automated message processing exchange	AOP	air operations plan; area of probability
		AOR	area of responsibility
AMPN	amplification	AOS	area of separation
AMP-PAT	analysis of mobility platform suite of port analysis tools	AOSS	aviation ordnance safety supervisor
		AOTR	Aviation Operational Threat Response
AMPSSO	Automated Message Processing System Security Office (or Officer)	AP	allied publication; antipersonnel; average power
AMRAAM	advanced medium-range air-to-air missile		
		APA	Army pre-positioned afloat
AMS	aerial measuring system; air mobility squadron; Army management structure; Asset Management System	APAN	Asia-Pacific Area Network
		APC	aerial port commander; armored personnel carrier; assign preprogrammed conference list
AMSS	air mobility support squadron		
AMT	aerial mail terminal		
AMVER	automated mutual-assistance vessel rescue system	APCC	alternate processing and correlation center
		APES	Automated Patient Evacuation System
AMW	air mobility wing; amphibious warfare	APF	afloat pre-positioning force
AN	alphanumeric; analog nonsecure	APG	aimpoint graphic
ANCA	Allied Naval Communications Agency	APHIS	Animal and Plant Health Inspection Service
ANDVT	advanced narrowband digital voice terminal		
		APIC	allied press information center
ANG	Air National Guard	APL	antipersonnel land
ANGLICO	air-naval gunfire liaison company	APO	afloat pre-positioning operations; Air Force post office; Army post office
ANGUS	Air National Guard of the United States		
A/NM	administrative/network management	APOD	aerial port of debarkation
ANMCC	Alternate National Military Command Center	APOE	aerial port of embarkation
		APORT	aerial port
ANN	assign NNX routing	APORTSREP	air operations bases report
ANR	Alaskan North American Aerospace Defense Command Region	APP	allied procedural publication
		APPS	analytical photogrammetric positioning system
ANSI	American National Standards Institute		
ANX	assign NNXX routing	APR	assign primary zone routing
ANY	assign NYX routing	APS	aerial port squadron; afloat pre-positioning ship; Army pre-positioned stocks
ANZUS	Australia-New Zealand-United States Treaty		
AO	action officer; administration officer; air officer; area of operations; aviation ordnance person	APS-3	afloat pre-positioning stocks
		APU	auxiliary power unit
		AR	air refueling; Army regulation; Army reserve
AO&M	administration, operation, and maintenance		

ARB	alternate recovery base; assign receive bypass lists
ARBS	angle rate bombing system
ARC	air Reserve Components; American Red Cross
ARCENT	United States Army Central Command
ARCP	air refueling control point
ARCT	air refueling control team; air refueling control time
ARDF	automatic radio direction finding
AREC	air resource element coordinator
ARFOR	Army forces
ARG	amphibious ready group
ARGO	automatic ranging grid overlay
ARINC	Aeronautical Radio Incorporated
ARIP	air refueling initiation point
ARL-M	airborne reconnaissance low-multi-function
ARM	antiradiation missile
ARNG	Army National Guard
ARNGUS	Army National Guard of the United States
ARNORTH	US Army North
ARP	air refueling point
ARPERCEN	United States Army Reserve Personnel Center
ARQ	automatic request-repeat
ARRC	Allied Command Europe Rapid Reaction Corps (NATO)
ARRDATE	arrival date
ARS	acute radiation syndrome; air rescue service
ARSOA	Army special operations aviation
ARSOC	Army special operations component
ARSOF	Army special operations forces
ARSOTF	Army special operations task force
ARSPACE	Army Space Command
ARSPOC	Army space operations center
ARSST	Army space support team
ART	air reserve technician
ARTCC	air route traffic control center
ARTS III	Automated Radar Tracking System
ARTYMET	artillery meteorological
AS	analog secure; aviation ship
A/S	anti-spoofing
ASA	automatic spectrum analyzer
ASA(ALT)	Assistant Secretary of the Army for Acquisition, Logistics, and Technology
ASAP	as soon as possible
ASARS	Advanced Synthetic Aperture Radar System
ASAS	All Source Analysis System
ASAT	antisatellite weapon
ASB	naval advanced support base
ASBP	Armed Services Blood Program
ASBPO	Armed Services Blood Program Office
ASC	acting service chief; Aeronautical Systems Center; Air Systems Command; Army Sustainment Command; assign switch classmark; Automatic Digital Network switching center
ASCC	Air Standardization Coordinating Committee; Army Service component command; Army Service component commander
ASCIET	all Services combat identification evaluation team
ASCII	American Standard Code for Information Interchange
ASCOPE	areas, structures, capabilities, organizations, people, and events
ASCS	air support control section; air support coordination section
ASD	Assistant Secretary of Defense
ASD(A&L)	Assistant Secretary of Defense (Acquisition and Logistics)
ASD(C)	Assistant Secretary of Defense (Comptroller)
ASD(C3I)	Assistant Secretary of Defense (Command, Control, Communications, and Intelligence)
ASD(FM&P)	Assistant Secretary of Defense (Force Management and Personnel)
ASD(FMP)	Assistant Secretary of Defense (Force Management Policy)
ASD(HA)	Assistant Secretary of Defense (Health Affairs)
ASD(HD)	Assistant Secretary of Defense (Homeland Defense)
ASD(HD&ASA)	Assistant Secretary of Defense (Homeland Defense and Americas' Security Affairs)
ASDI	analog simple data interface
ASDIA	All-Source Document Index
ASD(ISA)	Assistant Secretary of Defense (International Security Affairs)
ASD(ISP)	Assistant Secretary of Defense (International Security Policy)
ASD(LA)	Assistant Secretary of Defense (Legislative Affairs)
ASD(NII)	Assistant Secretary of Defense (Networks and Information Integration)
ASD(P&L)	Assistant Secretary of Defense (Production and Logistics)
ASD(PA)	Assistant Secretary of Defense (Public Affairs)
ASD(PA&E)	Assistant Secretary of Defense (Program Analysis and Evaluation)

ASD(RA)	Assistant Secretary of Defense (Reserve Affairs)	ASWC	antisubmarine warfare commander
ASD(RSA)	Assistant Secretary of Defense (Regional Security Affairs)	AT	annual training; antitank; antiterrorism
		At	total attainable search area
ASD(S&R)	Assistant Secretary of Defense (Strategy and Requirements)	ATA	Airlift Tanker Association; airport traffic area
ASD(SO/LIC)	Assistant Secretary of Defense (Special Operations and Low-Intensity Conflict)	ATAC	antiterrorism alert center (Navy)
		ATACC	advanced tactical air command center
		ATACMS	Army Tactical Missile System
		ATACO	air tactical actions control officer
ASD(SO/LIC&IC)	Assistant Secretary of Defense for Special Operations and Low-Intensity Conflict and Interdependent Capabilities	ATACS	Army Tactical Communications System
		ATAF	Allied Tactical Air Force (NATO)
		ATBM	antitactical ballistic missile
		ATC	Air Threat Conference; air traffic control; air transportable clinic (USAF)
ASE	aircraft survivability equipment; automated stabilization equipment	ATCA	Allied Tactical Communications Agency
		ATCAA	air traffic control assigned airspace
ASF	aeromedical staging facility	ATCALS	air traffic control and landing system
ASG	area support group	ATCC	air traffic control center; Antiterrorism Coordinating Committee
ASH	Assistant Administrator for Security and Hazardous Materials		
		ATCC-SSG	Antiterrorism Coordinating Committee-Senior Steering Group
ASI	assign and display switch initialization		
		ATCRBS	Air Traffic Control Radar Beacon System
ASIC	Air and Space Interoperability Council	ATCS	air traffic control section
		ATDL1	Army tactical data link 1
ASIF	Airlift Support Industrial Fund	ATDLS	Advanced Tactical Data Link System
ASL	allowable supply list; archipelagic sea lane; assign switch locator (SL) routing; authorized stockage list (Army)	ATDM	adaptive time division multiplexer
		ATDS	airborne tactical data system
		ATEP	Antiterrorism Enterprise Portal
ASM	air-to-surface missile; armored scout mission; automated scheduling message	ATF	Advanced Targeting FLIR; amphibious task force; Bureau of Alcohol, Tobacco and Firearms (TREAS)
ASMD	antiship missile defense	AT/FP	antiterrorism/force protection
ASN(RD&A)	Assistant Secretary of the Navy for Research, Development and Acquisition	ATG	amphibious task group; assign trunk group cluster
		ATGM	antitank guided missile; antitank guided munition
ASO	advanced special operations; air support operations		
		ATH	air transportable hospital; assign thresholds
ASOC	air support operations center		
ASOFDTG	as of date/time group	ATHS	Airborne Target Handover System
ASP	ammunition supply point	ATM	advanced trauma management; air target material; assign traffic metering
ASPA	American Service-Members' Protection Act		
		ATMCT	air terminal movement control team
ASPP	acquisition systems protection program	ATMP	Air Target Materials Program
		ATN	assign thresholds
ASPPO	Armed Service Production Planning Office	ATO	air tasking order; antiterrorism officer
		ATOC	air tactical operations center; air terminal operations center
ASR	air support request; available supply rate		
		ATP	advance targeting pod; allied tactical publication
ASSETREP	transportation assets report		
AST	assign secondary traffic channels	ATR	attrition reserve
ASTS	aeromedical staging squadron	ATS	air traffic service; assign terminal service
ASW	antisubmarine warfare; average surface wind	ATSD(AE)	Assistant to the Secretary of Defense (Atomic Energy)
ASWBPL	Armed Services Whole Blood Processing Laboratories	ATSD(IO)	Assistant to the Secretary of Defense (Intelligence Oversight)

ATSD(NCB)	Assistant to the Secretary of Defense for Nuclear and Chemical and Biological Defense Programs
ATT	assign terminal type
ATTP	Army tactics, techniques, and procedures
ATTU	air transportable treatment unit
ATWG	antiterrorism working group
AUEL	automated unit equipment list
AUF	airborne use of force
AUG	application user group
AUIC	active duty unit identification code
AUTODIN	Automatic Digital Network
AUX	auxiliary
AV	air vehicle; asset visibility
AV-8	Harrier
AVCAL	aviation consolidated allowance list
AVDTG	analog via digital trunk group
AVGAS	aviation gasoline
AVIM	aviation intermediate maintenance
AVL	assign variable location
AVOU	analog voice orderwire unit
AVOW	analog voice orderwire
AVS	asset visibility system; audiovisual squadron
AVUM	aviation unit maintenance
AV/VI	audiovisual/visual information
AW	acoustic warfare; air warfare
AWACS	Airborne Warning and Control System
AWC	air warfare commander
AWCAP	airborne weapons corrective action program
AWCCM	acoustic warfare counter-countermeasures
AWCM	acoustic warfare countermeasures
AWDS	automated weather distribution system
AWN	Automated Weather Network
AWOL	absent without leave
AWS	Air Weather Service
AWSE	armament weapons support equipment
AWSIM	air warfare simulation model
AWSR	Air Weather Service regulation
AXP	ambulance exchange point
AXX	assign XXX routing
AZR	assign zone restriction lists
B	cross-over barrier pattern
B-52	Stratofortress
B&A	boat and aircraft
BAE	brigade aviation element
BAF	backup alert force
BAG	baggage
BAH	basic allowance for housing
BAI	backup aircraft inventory; battlefield air interdiction
BALO	battalion air liaison officer
BAS	basic allowance for subsistence; battalion aid station
BATF	Bureau of Alcohol, Tobacco, and Firearms
B/B	baseband
BB	breakbulk
BBL	barrel (42 US gallons)
BC	bottom current
BCA	border crossing authority
BCAT	beddown capability assessment tool
BCD	battlefield coordination detachment
BCI	bit count integrity
BCL	battlefield coordination line
BCN	beacon
BCOC	base cluster operations center
BCR	baseline change request
BCT	brigade combat team
BCTP	battle command training program
BCU	beach clearance unit
BDA	battle damage assessment
BDAREP	battle damage assessment report
BDC	blood donor center
BDE	brigade
BDL	beach discharge lighter
BDOC	base defense operations center
BDR	battle damage repair
BDRP	Biological Defense Research Program
BE	basic encyclopedia
BEAR	base expeditionary airfield resources
BEE	bioenvironmental engineering officer
BEN	base encyclopedia number
BE number	basic encyclopedia number
BER	bit error ratio
BES	budget estimate submission
BFT	blue force tracking
BfV	*Bundesamt für Verfassungsschutz* (federal office for defending the Constitution)
BGC	boat group commander
BHR	Bureau of Humanitarian Response
BI	battlefield injury; battle injury
BIA	behavioral influences analysis; Bureau of Indian Affairs
BIAS	Battlefield Illumination Assistance System
BIDDS	Base Information Digital Distribution System
BIDE	basic identity data element
BIFC	Boise Interagency Fire Center
BIH	International Time Bureau (Bureau International d'l'Heure)
BII	base information infrastructure
BINM	Bureau of International Narcotics Matters
BIO	biological; Bureau of International Organizations
BIS	Bureau of Industry and Security
BISS	base installation security system

BIT	built-in test	BPWRS	bulk petroleum war reserve stocks
BITE	built-in test equipment	BR	budget review
BIU	beach interface unit	BRAC	base realignment and closure
BKA	*Bundeskriminalamt* (federal criminal office)	BRACE	Base Resource and Capability Estimator
BL	biocontainment level	BRC	base recovery course
BLCP	beach lighterage control point	BS	battle staff; broadcast source
BLDREP	blood report	BSA	beach support area; brigade support area
BLDSHIPREP	blood shipment report		
BLM	Bureau of Land Management	BSB	brigade support battalion
BLOS	beyond line of sight	BSC	black station clock
BLS	beach landing site	BSC ro	black station clock receive out
BLT	battalion landing team	BSCT	behavioral science consultation team
BM	ballistic missile; battle management; beachmaster	BSD	blood supply detachment
		BSI	base support installation
BMC4I	Battle Management Command, Control, Communications, Computers, and Intelligence	BSP	base support plan
		BSSG	brigade service support group
		BSU	blood supply unit
BMCT	begin morning civil twilight	BT	bathythermograph
BMD	ballistic missile defense	BTB	believed-to-be
BMDO	Ballistic Missile Defense Organization	BTC	blood transshipment center
		BTG	basic target graphic
BMET	biomedical equipment technician	BTOC	battalion tactical operations center
BMEWS	ballistic missile early warning system	BTS	Border and Transportation Security (DHS)
BMNT	begin morning nautical twilight		
BMU	beachmaster unit	BTU	beach termination unit
BN	battalion	BULK	bulk cargo
BND	*Bundesnachrichtendienst* (federal intelligence service)	BUMEDINST	Bureau of Medicine and Surgery instruction
BOA	basic ordering agreement	BVR	beyond visual range
BOC	base operations center; bomb on coordinate	BW	bandwidth; biological warfare; biological weapon
BOCCA	Bureau of Coordination of Civil Aircraft (NATO)	BWC	Biological Weapons Convention
		BZ	buffer zone
BOG	beach operations group	C	Celsius; centigrade; clock; compromise band; coverage factor; creeping line pattern
BOH	bottom of hill		
BORFIC	Border Patrol Field Intelligence Center		
BOS	base operating support; battlefield operating system	C&A	certification and accreditation
		C&E	communications and electronics
BOSG	base operations support group	C&LAT	cargo and loading analysis table
BOSS	base operating support service	C2	command and control
BOT	bomb on target	C2-attack	an offensive form of command and control warfare
BP	battle position; block parity		
BPA	blanket purchase agreement	C2E	command and control element
BPD	blood products depot	C2IP	Command and Control Initiatives Program
BPG	beach party group		
BPI	bits per inch	C2IPS	Command and Control Information Processing System
BPO	blood program office		
BPPBS	bi-annual planning, programming, and budget system	C2P	command and control protection
		C2-protect	a defensive form of command and control warfare
bps	bits per second		
BPSK	biphase shift keying	C2S	command and control support
BPT	beach party team	C-2X	coalition Intelligence Directorate counterintelligence and human intelligence staff element
BPWRR	bulk petroleum war reserve requirement		

C3	command, control, and communications
C3AG	Command, Control, and Communications Advisory Group
C3CM	command, control, and communications countermeasures
C3I	command, control, communications, and intelligence
C3IC	coalition coordination, communications, and integration center
C3SMP	Command, Control, and Communications Systems Master Plan
C4CM	command, control, communications, and computer countermeasures
C4I	command, control, communications, computers, and intelligence
C4IFTW	command, control, communications, computers, and intelligence for the Warrior
C4ISR	command, control, communications, computers, intelligence, surveillance, and reconnaissance
C4S	command, control, communications, and computer systems
C4 systems	command, control, communications, and computer systems
C-5	Galaxy
C-17	Globemaster III
C-21	Learjet
C-27	Spartan
C-130	Hercules
C-141	Starlifter
CA	chaplain assistant; civil administration; civil affairs; combat assessment
C/A	course acquisition
CAA	civil air augmentation; combat aviation advisors; command arrangement agreement
CAAF	contractors authorized to accompany the force
CAB	combat aviation brigade
CAC	common access card; current actions center
CACOM	Civil Affairs command
CACTIS	community automated intelligence system
CAD	Canadian Air Division; cartridge actuated device; collective address designator
CADRS	concern and deficiency reporting system
CADS	containerized ammunition distribution system
CAE	command assessment element
CAF	Canadian Air Force; combat air forces; commander, airborne/air assault force
CAFMS	computer-assisted force management system
CAG	carrier air group; civil affairs group; collective address group
CAGO	contractor acquired government owned
CAIMS	conventional ammunition integrated management system
CAINS	carrier aircraft inertial navigation system
CAISE	civil authority information support element
CAL	caliber; critical asset list
CALA	Community Airborne Library Architecture
CALCM	conventional air-launched cruise missile
CALICS	communication, authentication, location, intentions, condition, and situation
CALMS	computer-aided load manifesting system
CAM	chemical agent monitor; crisis action module
CAMPS	Consolidated Air Mobility Planning System
CAMT	countering air and missile threats
CANA	convulsant antidote for nerve agent
CANADA COM	Canada Command
CANR	Canadian North American Aerospace Defense Command Region
CANUS	Canada-United States
CAO	chief administrative officer; civil affairs operations; counterair operation
CAOC	combat air operations center; combined air operations center
CAO SOP	standing operating procedures for coordination of atomic operations
CAP	Civil Air Patrol; civil augmentation program; combat air patrol; configuration and alarm panel; Consolidated Appeals Process (UN); crisis action planning
CAPT	civil affairs planning team
CAR	Chief of the Army Reserve
CARDA	continental United States airborne reconnaissance for damage assessment; continental United States area reconnaissance for damage assessment
CARE	Cooperative for Assistance and Relief Everywhere (CAREUSA)
CARIBROC	Caribbean Regional Operations Center
CARP	computed air release point; contingency alternate route plan

CARS	combat arms regimental system	CbT-RIF	Combating Terrorism Readiness Initiatives Fund
CARVER	criticality, accessibility, recuperability, vulnerability, effect, and recognizability	CBTZ	combat zone
		CBU	cluster bomb unit; conference bridge unit; construction battalion unit
CAS	casualty; civil aviation security; close air support	CBW	chemical and biological warfare
CASEVAC	casualty evacuation	C/C	cabin cruiser; cast off and clear
CASF	contingency aeromedical staging facility	CC	command center; component command (NATO); critical capability
CASP	computer-aided search planning	CC&D	camouflage, concealment, and deception
CASPER	contact area summary position report	CCA	carrier-controlled approach; central contracting authority; circuit card assembly; container control activity; contamination control area; contingency capabilities assessment; contract construction agent (DOD)
CASREP	casualty report		
CASREQ	close air support request		
CAT	category; crisis action team		
CATCC	carrier air traffic control center		
CATF	commander, amphibious task force		
CAU	crypto ancillary unit; cryptographic auxiliary unit	CCAP	combatant command AFRTS planner
		CCAS	contingency contract administration services
CAVU	ceiling and visibility unlimited		
CAW	carrier air wing	CCAS-C	contingency contract administration services commander
CAW/ESS	crisis action weather and environmental support system		
		CCATT	critical care air transport team
CAX	computer-assisted exercise	CCB	Community Counterterrorism Board; Configuration Control Board
C-B	chemical-biological		
CB	chemical-biological; construction battalion (SEABEES)	CCC	coalition coordination cell; coalition coordination center; crisis coordination center; critical control circuit; crosscultural communications course
CBBLS	hundreds of barrels		
CBD	chemical, biological defense		
CBFS	cesium beam frequency standard	CCD	camouflage, concealment, and deception
CBIRF	chemical-biological incident response force	CCDR	combatant commander
		CCE	container control element; continuing criminal enterprise
CBLTU	common battery line terminal unit		
CBMR	capabilities-based munitions requirements	CCEB	Combined Communications-Electronics Board
CBMU	construction battalion maintenance unit	CCF	collection coordination facility
		CCG	crisis coordination group
CBP	capabilities-based planning; Customs and Border Protection	CCGD	commander, Coast Guard district
		CCIB	command center integration branch
CBPO	Consolidated Base Personnel Office	CCIF	Combatant Commander Initiative Fund
CBPS	chemical biological protective shelter	CCIP	continuously computed impact point
CBR	chemical, biological, and radiological	CCIR	commander's critical information requirement; International Radio Consultative Committee
CBRN	Caribbean Basin Radar Network; chemical, biological, radiological, and nuclear		
		CCIS	common channel interswitch signaling
CBRNE	chemical, biological, radiological, nuclear, and high-yield explosives	CCITT	International Telegraph and Telephone Consultative Committee
CBRN hazard	chemical, biological, radiological, and nuclear hazard	CCIU	CEF control interface unit
		CCJTF	commander, combined joint task force
CBRN passive defense	chemical, biological, radiological, and nuclear passive defense	CCL	communications/computer link
		CCLI	computer control list item
CBRT	chemical-biological response team	CCO	central control officer; combat cargo officer; command and control office; complex contingency operation; contingency contracting officer
CBS	common battery signaling		
CBT	common battery terminal		
CbT	combating terrorism	CCOI	critical contact of interest

CCP	casualty collection point; consolidated cryptologic program; consolidation and containerization point
CCPDS	command center processing and display system
CCR	closed circuit refueling
CCRD	combatant commander's required delivery date
C-CS	communication and computer systems
CCS	central control ship; container control site
CCSA	containership cargo stowage adapter
CCSD	command communications service designator; control communications service designator
CCT	collaborative contingency targeting; combat control team
CCTI	Chairman of the Joint Chiefs of Staff commended training issue
CCTV	closed circuit television
CCW	1980 United Nations Convention on Conventional Weapons; continuous carrier wave
CD	channel designator; compact disc; counterdrug; customer direct
C-day	unnamed day on which a deployment operation begins
CDC	Centers for Disease Control and Prevention
CDE	collateral damage estimation
CDERA	Caribbean Disaster Emergency Response Agency
CDF	combined distribution frame
CDI	cargo disposition instructions; conditioned diphase
C di	conditioned diphase
CDHAM	Center for Disaster and Humanitarian Assistance Medicine
CDIP	combined defense improvement project
CDIPO	counterdrug intelligence preparation for operations
CDLMS	common data link management system
CDM	cable driver modem
CDMGB	cable driver modem group buffer
CDN	compressed dial number
CDO	command duty officer; commander, detainee operations
CDOC	counterdrug operations center
CDOPS	counterdrug operations
CDP	commander's dissemination policy; landing craft air cushion departure point
CDR	commander; continuous data recording
CDRAFSOF	commander, Air Force special operations forces
CDRARNORTH	Commander, US Army North
CDRCFCOM	Commander, Combined Forces Command
CDRESC	commander, electronic security command
CDREUDAC	Commander, European Command Defense Analysis Center (ELINT) or European Data Analysis Center
CDRFORSCOM	Commander, Forces Command
CDRG	catastrophic disaster response group (FEMA)
CDRJSOTF	commander, joint special operations task force
CDRL	contract data requirements list
CDRMTMC	Commander, Military Traffic Management Command
CDRNORAD	Commander, North American Aerospace Defense Command
CD-ROM	compact disc read-only memory
CDRTSOC	commander, theater special operations command
CDRUNC	Commander, United Nations Command
CDRUSAINSCOM	Commander, United States Army Intelligence and Security Command
CDRUSCENTCOM	Commander, United States Central Command
CDRUSELEMNORAD	Commander, United States Element, North American Aerospace Defense Command
CDRUSEUCOM	Commander, United States European Command
CDRUSJFCOM	Commander, United States Joint Forces Command
CDRUSNAVEUR	Commander, United States Naval Forces, Europe
CDRUSNORTHCOM	Commander, United States Northern Command
CDRUSPACOM	Commander, United States Pacific Command
CDRUSSOCOM	Commander, United States Special Operations Command
CDRUSSOUTHCOM	Commander, United States Southern Command
CDRUSSTRATCOM	Commander, United States Strategic Command
CDRUSTRANSCOM	Commander, United States Transportation Command

CDS	Chief of Defence Staff (Canada); container delivery system
CDSSC	continuity of operations plan designated successor service chief
CDU	counterdrug update
C-E	communications-electronics
CE	casualty estimation; circular error; command element (MAGTF); communications-electronics; core element; counterespionage
CEA	captured enemy ammunition
CEB	combat engineer battalion
CEC	civil engineer corps
CECOM	communications-electronics command
CEDI	commercial electronic data interface
CEDREP	communications-electronics deployment report
CEE	captured enemy equipment
CEF	civil engineering file; common equipment facility
CEG	common equipment group
CEI	critical employment indicator
CEM	combined effects munition
CEMC	communications-electronics management center
CENTRIXS	Combined Enterprise Regional Information Exchange System
CEOI	communications-electronics operating instructions
CEP	cable entrance panel; circular error probable
CEPOD	communications-electronics post-deployment report
CERF	Central Emergency Revolving Fund (UN)
CERFP	CBRNE enhanced response force package
CERP	Commanders' Emergency Response Program
CERT	computer emergency response team
CERTSUB	certain submarine
CES	coast earth station
CESE	civil engineering support equipment; communications equipment support element
CESG	communications equipment support group
CESO	civil engineer support office
CESPG	civil engineering support plan group; civil engineering support planning generator
CEXC	combined explosives exploitation cell
CEW	Civilian Expeditionary Workforce
CF	Canadian forces; carrier furnished; causeway ferry; conventional forces; drift error confidence factor
CFA	Committee on Food Aid Policies and Programmes (UN)
CFACC	combined force air component commander
CFB	Canadian forces base
CFC	Combined Forces Command, Korea
CF-COP	counterfire common operational picture
CFL	Contingency Planning Facilities List; coordinated fire line
CFM	cubic feet per minute
CFO	chief financial officer
CFR	Code of Federal Regulations
CFS	CI force protection source
CFSO	counterintelligence force protection source operations
CFST	coalition forces support team
CG	Chairman's guidance; Coast Guard; commanding general; Comptroller General
CGAS	Coast Guard Air Station
CGAUX	Coast Guard Auxiliary
CGC	Coast Guard Cutter
CGCAP	Coast Guard capabilities plan
CGDEFOR	Coast Guard defense force
CGFMFLANT	Commanding General, Fleet Marine Forces, Atlantic
CGFMFPAC	Commanding General, Fleet Marine Forces, Pacific
CGIS	US Coast Guard Investigative Service
CGLSMP	Coast Guard logistic support and mobilization plan
CGRS	common geographic reference system
CGS	common ground station; continental United States ground station
CGUSAREUR	Commanding General, United States Army, Europe
CH	channel; contingency hospital
CH-53	Sea Stallion
CHAMPUS	Civilian Health and Medical Program for the Uniformed Services
CHARC	counterintelligence and human intelligence analysis and requirements cell
CHB	cargo handling battalion
CHCS	composite health care system
CHCSS	Chief, Central Security Service
CHE	cargo-handling equipment; container-handling equipment
CHET	customs high endurance tracker
CHOP	change of operational control
CHPPM	US Army Center for Health Promotion and Preventive Medicine
CHRIS	chemical hazard response information system

CHSTR	characteristics of transportation resources
CHSTREP	characteristics of transportation resources report
CI	civilian internee; counterintelligence
CIA	Central Intelligence Agency
CIAP	Central Intelligence Agency program; central intelligence architecture plan; command, control, communications, computers, intelligence surveillance, reconnaissance (C4ISR) integrated architecture program; command intelligence architecture plan; command intelligence architecture program
CIAS	counterintelligence analysis section
CIAT	counterintelligence analytic team
CIB	combined information bureau; controlled image base
CIC	combat information center; combat intelligence center (Marine Corps); combined intelligence center; communications interface controller; content indicator code; counterintelligence center
CICA	counterintelligence coordination authority
CICAD	Inter-American Drug Abuse Control Commission
CID	combat identification; combat intelligence division; criminal investigation division
CIDB	common intelligence database
CIDC	Criminal Investigation Division Command
CIE	collaborative information environment
CIEG/CIEL	common information exchange glossary and language
CIFA	counterintelligence field activity
CIG	communications interface group
CIHO	counterintelligence/human intelligence officer
CIIR	counterintelligence information report
CI/KR	critical infrastructure/key resources
CIL	command information library; critical item list
CILO	counterintelligence liaison officer
CIM	civil information management; compartmented information management
CIMIC	civil-military cooperation
CIN	cargo increment number
CIO	chief information officer; command intelligence officer
CIOTA	counterintelligence operational tasking authority
CIP	communications interface processor; critical infrastructure protection
CIPSU	communications interface processor pseudo line
CIR	continuing intelligence requirement
CIRM	International Radio-Medical Center
CIRV	common interswitch rekeying variable
CIRVIS	communications instructions for reporting vital intelligence sightings
CIS	common item support; Commonwealth of Independent States; communications interface shelter
CISD	critical incident stress debriefing
CISO	counterintelligence staff office; counterintelligence support officer
CITP	counter-IED targeting program
CIV	civilian
CIVPOL	civilian police
CIWG	communications interoperability working group
CJ-4	combined-joint logistics officer
CJATF	commander, joint amphibious task force
CJB	Congressional Justification Book
CJCS	Chairman of the Joint Chiefs of Staff
CJCSAN	Chairman of the Joint Chiefs of Staff Alerting Network
CJCSI	Chairman of the Joint Chiefs of Staff instruction
CJCSM	Chairman of the Joint Chiefs of Staff manual
CJDA	critical joint duty assignment
CJMAB	Central Joint Mortuary Affairs Board
CJMAO	Central Joint Mortuary Affairs Office; Chief, joint mortuary affairs office
CJPOTF	combined joint psychological operations task force
CJSOTF	combined joint special operations task force
CJTF	combined joint task force (NATO); commander, joint task force
CJTF-CS	Commander, Joint Task Force—Civil Support
CJTF-NCR	Commander, Joint Task Force—National Capital Region
C-JWICS	Containerized Joint Worldwide Intelligence Communications System
CKT	circuit
CL	class
CLA	landing craft air cushion launch area
CLB	combat logistics battalion
CLD	compact laser designator
CLEA	civilian law enforcement agency
C-level	category level
CLF	cantilever lifting frame; combat logistics force; commander, landing force
CLG	combat logistics group
CLGP	cannon-launched guided projectile
CLIPS	communications link interface planning system

CLPSB	combatant commander logistic procurement support board	CMX	crisis management exercise
CLPT	contingency load planning team	CN	counternarcotic
CLR	combat logistics regiment	CNA	computer network attack
CLS	contracted logistic support	CNAC	Customs National Aviation Center (USCS)
CLSS	combat logistic support squadron	C-NAF	component numbered air force
CLT	civil liaison team; combat lasing team	CNASP	chairman's net assessment for strategic planning
CLZ	craft landing zone; cushion landing zone; landing craft air cushion landing zone	CNC	Crime and Narcotics Center
CM	Chairman's memorandum; collection manager; configuration management; consequence management; control modem; countermine	CNCE	communications nodal control element
		CND	computer network defense; counternarcotics division
		CNE	computer network exploitation; Counter Narcotics Enforcement
C_m	mean coverage factor	CNGB	Chief, National Guard Bureau
cm	centimeter	CNM	classified notice to mariners
CMA	collection management authority	CNO	Chief of Naval Operations; computer network operations
CMAA	Cooperative Military Airlift Agreement		
CMAH	commander of a combatant command's Mobile Alternate Headquarters	CNOG	Chairman, Nuclear Operations Group
		CNRF	Commander, Naval Reserve Forces
CMAT	consequence management advisory team	CNSG	Commander, Naval Security Group
CMC	Commandant of the Marine Corps; crew management cell	CNTY	country
		CNWDI	critical nuclear weapons design information
C_{mc}	midpoint compromise coverage factor		
CMCB	civil-military coordination board	CO	commanding officer
CMCC	combined movement coordination center	COA	course of action
CMD	command; cruise missile defense	COAA	course-of-action analysis
CMHT	consequence management home team	COAMPS	Coupled Ocean Atmosphere Mesoscale Prediction System
CMMA	collection management mission application	COB	collocated operating base; contingency operating base
CMO	Central Measurement and Signature Intelligence (MASINT) Organization; chief medical officer; chief military observer; civil-military operations; collection management office(r); configuration management office	COBOL	common business-oriented language
		COC	combat operations center
		CoC	Code of Conduct
		COCOM	combatant command (command authority)
		COD	carrier onboard delivery; combat operations division
CMOC	Cheyenne Mountain Operations Center; civil-military operations center	COE	Army Corps of Engineers; common operating environment; concept of employment
CMOS	cargo movement operations system; complementary metal-oxide semiconductor		
		COEDMHA	Center for Excellence in Disaster Management and Humanitarian Assistance
CMP	communications message processor; contractor management plan		
CMPF	commander, maritime pre-positioned force	COF	conduct of fire
		COFC	container on flatcar
CMPT	consequence management planning team	COG	center of gravity; continuity of government
CM R&A	consequence management response and assessment		
		COGARD	Coast Guard
CMRT	consequence management response team	COI	community of interest; contact of interest
CMS	cockpit management system; command management system; community management staff; community security materiel system; contingency mutual support; crisis management system	COIN	counterinsurgency
		COLDS	cargo offload and discharge system
		COLISEUM	community on-line intelligence system for end-users and managers
CMST	consequence management support team	COLPRO	collective protection
CMTS	comments		
CMTU	cartridge magnetic tape unit		
CMV	commercial motor vehicle		

COLT	combat observation and lasing team
COM	chief of mission; collection operations management; command; commander
COMACC	Commander, Air Combat Command
COMAFFOR	commander, Air Force forces
COMAFSOC	Commander, Air Force Special Operations Command
COMAJF	commander, allied joint force
COMALF	commander airlift forces
COMALOC	commercial air line of communications
COMARFOR	commander, Army forces
COMCAM	combat camera
COMCARGRU	commander, carrier group
COMCRUDESGRU	commander, cruiser destroyer group
COMDCAEUR	Commander, Defense Communications Agency Europe
COMDESRON	commander destroyer squadron
COMDT COGARD	Commandant, United States Coast Guard
COMDTINST	Commandant, United States Coast Guard instruction
COMICEDEFOR	Commander, United States Forces, Iceland
COMIDEASTFOR	Commander, Middle East Forces
COMINEWARCOM	Commander, Mine Warfare Command
COMINT	communications intelligence
COMJCSE	Commander, Joint Communications Support Element
COMJIC	Commander, Joint Intelligence Center
COMJSOTF	commander, joint special operations task force
COMLANDFOR	commander, land forces
COMLANTAREACOGARD	Commander, Coast Guard Atlantic Area
COMLOGGRU	combat logistics group
COMM	communications
COMMARFOR	commander, Marine Corps forces
COMMARFORNORTH	Commander, Marine Corps Forces North
COMMDZ	Commander, Maritime Defense Zone
COMMZ	communications zone
COMNAV	Committee for European Airspace Coordination Working Group on Communications and Navigation Aids
COMNAVAIRLANT	Commander, Naval Air Force, Atlantic
COMNAVAIRPAC	Commander, Naval Air Force, Pacific
COMNAVAIRSYSCOM	Commander, Naval Air Systems Command
COMNAVCOMTELCOM	Commander, Naval Computer and Telecommunications Command
COMNAVFOR	commander, Navy forces
COMNAVMETOCCOM	Commander, Naval Meteorology and Oceanography Command
COMNAVSEASYSCOM	Commander, Naval Sea Systems Command
COMNAVSECGRP	Commander, United States Navy Security Group
COMNAVSURFLANT	Commander, Naval Surface Force, Atlantic
COMNAVSURFPAC	Commander, Naval Surface Force, Pacific
COMP	component
COMPACAF	Commander, Pacific Air Forces
COMPACAREACOGARD	Commander, Coast Guard Pacific Area
COMPACFLT	Commander, Pacific Fleet
COMPASS	common operational modeling, planning, and simulation strategy; Computerized Movement Planning and Status System
COMPES	contingency operations mobility planning and execution system
COMPLAN	communications plan
COMPUSEC	computer security
COMSAT	communications satellite
COMSC	Commander, Military Sealift Command
COMSCINST	Commander, Military Sealift Command instruction
COMSEC	communications security
COMSOC	Commander, Special Operations Command
COMSOCCENT	Commander, Special Operations Command,

	United States Central Command	CONCAP	construction capabilities contract (Navy); Construction Capabilities Contract Process; construction capabilities contract program
COMSOCEUR	Commander, Special Operations Command, United States European Command		
		CONEX	container express
		CONEXPLAN	contingency and exercise plan
COMSOCPAC	Commander Special Operations Command, United States Pacific Command	CONOPS	concept of operations
		CONPLAN	concept plan; operation plan in concept format
COMSOCSOUTH	Commander Special Operations Command, United States Southern Command	CONR	continental United States North American Aerospace Defense Command Region
		CONUS	continental United States
COMSOF	commander, special operations forces	CONUSA	Continental United States Army
		COOP	continuity of operations
COMSTAT	communications status	COP	common operational picture
COMSUBLANT	Commander Submarine Force, United States Atlantic Fleet	COP-CSE	common operational picture-combat support enabled
		COPG	chairman, operations planners group
COMSUBPAC	Commander Submarine Force, United States Pacific Fleet	COPPERHEAD	name for cannon-launched guided projectile
COMSUPNAVFOR	commander, supporting naval forces	COPS	communications operational planning system
COMTAC	tactical communications	COR	contracting officer representative
COMUSAFE	Commander, United States Air Force in Europe	CORE	contingency response program
		COS	chief of staff; chief of station; critical occupational specialty
COMUSARCENT	Commander, United States Army Forces, Central Command	COSCOM	corps support command
		COSMIC	North Atlantic Treaty Organization (NATO) security category
COMUSCENTAF	Commander, United States Air Force, Central Command	COSPAS	*cosmicheskaya sistyema poiska avariynch sudov*—space system for search of distressed vessels (Russian satellite system)
COMUSFLTFORCOM	Commander, United States Fleet Forces Command		
COMUSFORAZ	Commander, United States Forces, Azores	COSR	combat and operational stress reactions
COMUSJ	Commander, United States Forces, Japan	COT	commanding officer of troops; crisis operations team
COMUSK	Commander, United States Forces, Korea	COTHEN	Customs Over-the Horizon Enforcement Network
COMUSLANTFLT	Commander, US Atlantic Fleet	COTP	captain of the port
		COTS	cargo offload and transfer system; commercial off-the-shelf; container offloading and transfer system
COMUSMARCENT	Commander, United States Marine Forces, Central Command		
		COU	cable orderwire unit
COMUSNAVCENT	Commander, United States Navy, Central Command	counter C3	counter command, control, and communications
		COVCOM	covert communications
COMUSPACFLT	Commander, US Pacific Fleet	CP	check point; collection point; command post; contact point; control point; counterproliferation
COMUSSOCJFCOM	Commander Special Operations Command, United States Joint Forces Command		
		CP&I	coastal patrol and interdiction
		CPA	Chairman's program assessment; closest point of approach

CPD	combat plans division
CPE	customer premise equipment
CPFL	contingency planning facilities list
CPG	central processor group; Commander, Amphibious Group; Contingency Planning Guidance
CPI	crash position indicator
CPIC	coalition press information center
CPM	civilian personnel manual
CPO	chief petty officer; complete provisions only
CPR	cardiopulmonary resuscitation; Chairman's program recommendation
CPRC	coalition personnel recovery center
CPS	characters per second; collective protective shelter
CPT	common procedural terminology
CPU	central processing unit
CPX	command post exercise
CR	critical requirement
CRA	command relationships agreement; continuing resolution authority; coordinating review authority
CRAF	Civil Reserve Air Fleet
CRAM	control random access memory
CRB	configuration review board
CRC	circuit routing chart; civil response corps; control and reporting center; CONUS replacement center; COOP response cell; cyclic redundancy rate
CRD	capstone requirements document; chemical reconnaissance detachment; combatant commander's required date
CRE	contingency response element; control reporting element
CREST	casualty and resource estimation support tool
CRF	channel reassignment function
CRG	contingency response group
CRI	collective routing indicator
CRIF	cargo routing information file
CRITIC	critical information; critical intelligence communication; critical message (intelligence)
CRITICOMM	critical intelligence communications system
CRM	collection requirements management; comment resolution matrix; crew resource management
CrM	crisis management
CRO	combat rescue officer
CROP	common relevant operational picture
CRP	control and reporting post
CRRC	combat rubber raiding craft
CRS	Catholic Relief Services; Chairman's readiness system; coastal radio station; community relations service; container recovery system; Coordinator for Reconstruction and Stabilization
CRT	cathode ray tube; contingency response team
CRTS	casualty receiving and treatment ship
CR-UAV	close-range unmanned aerial vehicle
CRW	contingency response wing
CRYPTO	cryptographic
CS	call sign; Chaplain Service (Air Force); circuit switch; civil support; coastal station; combat service; combat support; content staging; controlled space; creeping line singleunit; critical source
CSA	Chief of Staff, United States Army; combat support agency; container stuffing activity
CSAAS	combat support agency assessment system
CSADR	combat support agency director's report
CSAF	Chief of Staff, United States Air Force
CSAM	computer security for acquisition managers
CSAR	combat search and rescue
CSAR3	combat support agency responsiveness and readiness report
CSARTE	combat search and rescue task element
CSARTF	combat search and rescue task force
CSB	contracting support brigade
CSB (ME)	combat support brigade (maneuver enhancement)
CSC	combat support center; community support center; convoy support center; creeping line single-unit coordinated; International Convention for Safe Containers
CSCC	coastal sea control commander
CSE	client server environment; combat support enhanced; combat support equipment; contingency support element
CSEL	circuit switch select line; combat survivor evader locator; command senior enlisted leader
CSEP	Chairman of the Joint Chiefs of Staff–sponsored exercise program
CSG	carrier strike group; Chairman's Staff Group; coordinating subgroup; cryptologic services group; Cryptologic Support Group
CSGN	coordinating subgroup for narcotics
CSH	combat support hospital
CSI	critical sustainability item
CSIF	communications service industrial fund

CSIP	contract support integration plan	CTRIF	Combating Terrorism Readiness Initiative Fund
CSIPG	circuit switch interface planning guide	CTS	commodity tracking system
CSL	combat stores list; cooperative security location	CTSS	central targeting support staff
CSNP	causeway section, nonpowered	CTU	commander, task unit
CSNP(BE)	causeway section, nonpowered (beach end)	CU	cubic capacity; common unit
CSNP(I)	causeway section, nonpowered (intermediate)	CUL	common-user logistics
		CULT	common-user land transportation
CSNP(SE)	causeway section, nonpowered (sea end)	CV	aircraft carrier; carrier; critical vulnerability; curriculum vitae
CSO	Center for Special Operations (USSOCOM); communications support organization	CVAMP	Core Vulnerability Assessment Management Program
CSOA	combined special operations area	CVN	aircraft carrier, nuclear
CSOB	command systems operations branch	CVR	cockpit voice recorder
CSOD	command systems operation division	CVS	commercial vendor services
CSP	call service position; career sea pay; causeway section, powered; commence search point; contracting support plan; crisis staffing procedures (JCS); cryptologic support package	CVSD	continuous variable slope delta
		CVT	criticality-vulnerability-threat
		CVW	carrier air wing; cryptovariable weekly (GPS)
		CVWC	carrier strike group air wing commander
CSPAR	combatant commander's preparedness assessment report	CW	carrier wave; chemical warfare; continuous wave
CSR	central source registry; combatant commander's summary report; commander's summary report; controlled supply rate	CWC	Chemical Weapons Convention; composite warfare commander
		CWDE	chemical warfare defense equipment
		CWMD	combating weapons of mass destruction
CSRF	common source route file		
CSS	central security service; combat service support; communications subsystem; coordinator surface search	CWO	communications watch officer
		CWP	causeway pier
		CWPD	Conventional War Plans Division, Joint Staff (J-7)
CSSA	combat service support area		
CSSB	combat sustainment support battalion	CWR	calm water ramp
CSSC	coded switch set controller	CWT	combat weather team; customer wait time
CSSE	combat service support element (MAGTF)		
CSST	combat service support team	CY	calendar year
CSSU	combat service support unit	D	total drift, data
CST	contingency support team; customer service team	d	surface drift
		D&D	denial and deception
CSW	compartment stowage worksheet; coordinate seeking weapons	D&F	determinations and findings
		D&M	detection and monitoring
CT	control telemetry; counterterrorism; country team	D&R	debrief and reintegrate
		D3A	decide, detect, deliver, and assess
CTA	common table of allowance	D/A	digital-to-analog
CTAF	counterterrorism analytical framework	DA	data adapter aerospace drift; data administrator; Department of the Army; Development Assistance; direct action; Directorate for Administration (DIA); double agent
CTAPS	contingency Theater Air Control System automated planning system		
CTC	cargo transfer company (USA); counterterrorist center		
CTF	combined task force	Da	aerospace drift
CTG	commander, task group	DA&M	Director of Administration and Management
CTID	communications transmission identifier		
CTL	candidate target list	DAA	designated approving authority; display alternate area routing lists
CTM	core target material		
CTOC	corps tactical operations center		
CTP	common tactical picture	DAADC(AMD)	deputy area air defense commander for air and missile defense
CTR	cooperative threat reduction		

DAAS	defense automatic addressing system
DAASO	defense automatic addressing system office
DAB	Defense Acquisition Board
DAC	Defense Intelligence Agency (DIA) counterintelligence and security activity; Department of Army civilians
DACB	data adapter control block
DACG	departure airfield control group
DACM	data adapter control mode
DADCAP	dawn and dusk combat air patrol
DAF	Department of the Air Force
DAFL	directive authority for logistics
DAICC	domestic air interdiction coordinator center
DAL	defended asset list
DALIS	Disaster Assistance Logistics Information System
DALS	downed aviator locator system
DAMA	demand assigned multiple access
DAMES	defense automatic addressing system (DAAS) automated message exchange system
DAN	Diver's Alert Network
DAO	defense attaché office; defense attaché officer; department/agency/organization
DAP	designated acquisition program
DAR	Defense Acquisition Regulation; distortion adaptive receiver
DARO	Defense Airborne Reconnaissance Office
DARPA	Defense Advanced Research Projects Agency
DART	disaster assistance response team; downed aircraft recovery team; dynamic analysis and replanning tool
DAS	deep air support (USMC); defense attaché system; direct access subscriber; direct air support
DAS3	decentralized automated service support system
DASA	Department of the Army (DA) staff agencies
DASC	direct air support center
DASC(A)	direct air support center (airborne)
DASD	Deputy Assistant Secretary of Defense
DASD-CN	Deputy Assistant Secretary of Defense for Counternarcotics
DASD(H&RA)	Deputy Assistant Secretary of Defense (Humanitarian & Refugee Affairs)
DASD(I)	Deputy Assistant Secretary of Defense (Intelligence)
DASD(PK/HA)	Deputy Assistant Secretary of Defense (Peacekeeping and Humanitarian Affairs)
DASD(S&IO)	Deputy Assistant Secretary of Defense (Security and Information Operations)
DASSS	decentralized automated service support system
DAT	deployment action team
DATT	defense attaché
DATU	data adapter termination unit
dB	decibel
DBA	database administrator
DBDB	digital bathymetric database
DBG	database generation
DBI	defense budget issue
DBMS	database management system; Defense-Business Management System
DBSS	Defense Blood Standard System
DBT	design basis threat
D/C	downconverter
DC	Deputies Committee; direct current; dislocated civilian
DCA	Defense Communications Agency; Defense Cooperation Agreements; defensive counterair; dual-capable aircraft
DCAA	Defense Contract Audit Agency
DCAM	Defense Medical Logistics Standard Support (DMLSS) customer assistance module
DCAPES	Deliberate and Crisis Action Planning and Execution Segments
DCC	damage control center; deployment control center
DCCC	defense collection coordination center
DCCEP	developing country combined exercise program
DCD	data collection device
DCE	defense coordinating element
D-cell	deployment cell
DCGS	distributed common ground/surface system
DCHA	Bureau for Democracy, Conflict, and Humanitarian Assistance
DCI	defense critical infrastructure; Director of Central Intelligence; dual channel interchange
D/CI&SP	Director, Counterintelligence and Security Programs
DCID	Director of Central Intelligence directive
DCIIS	Defense Counterintelligence Information System

DCIO	defense criminal investigative organization	*DDI*	Deputy Director of Intelligence (CIA)
DCIP	Defense Critical Infrastructure Program	*DDL*	digital data link
		DDM	digital data modem
DCIS	Defense Criminal Investigative Services	*DDMA*	Defense Distribution Mapping Activity
DCJTF	deputy commander, joint task force	*DDMS*	Deputy Director for Military Support
DCM	data channel multiplexer; deputy chief of mission	*DDO*	Deputy Director of Operations (CIA)
		DDOC	Deployment and Distribution Operations Center (USTRANSCOM)
DCMA	Defense Contract Management Agency	*DDP*	detailed deployment plan
DCMC	Office of Deputy Chairman, Military Committee	*DDR*	disarmament, demobilization, and reintegration
DCMO	deputy chief military observer	*DDR&E*	director of defense research and engineering
DCNO	Deputy Chief of Naval Operations	*DDRRR*	disarmament, demobilization, repatriation, reintegration, and resettlement
DCO	defense connect online; defense coordinating officer (DOD); dial central office	*DDS*	defense dissemination system; Deployable Disbursing System; dry deck shelter
DCP	Defense Continuity Program; detainee collection point	*DDSM*	Defense Distinguished Service Medal
DCPA	Defense Civil Preparedness Agency	*DDS&T*	Deputy Director for Science & Technology (CIA)
DCPG	digital clock pulse generator		
DCR	DOTMLPF change recommendation	*DDWSO*	Deputy Director for Wargaming, Simulation, and Operations
DCS	Defense Communications System; Defense Courier Service; deputy chief of staff; digital computer system	*DE*	damage expectancy; delay equalizer; directed energy
DCSCU	dual capability servo control unit	*De*	total drift error
DC/S for RA	Deputy Chief of Staff for Reserve Affairs	*de*	individual drift error
		DEA	Drug Enforcement Administration
DCSINT	Deputy Chief of Staff for Intelligence	*dea*	aerospace drift error
DCSLOG	Deputy Chief of Staff for Logistics, US Army	*DEACN*	Drug Enforcement Administration Communications Network
DCSOPS	Deputy Chief of Staff for Operations and Plans, United States Army	*DEAR*	disease and environmental alert report
		DEARAS	Department of Defense (DOD) Emergency Authorities Retrieval and Analysis System
DCSPER	Deputy Chief of Staff for Personnel, United States Army		
DCST	Defense Logistics Agency (DLA) contingency support team	*DeCA*	Defense Commissary Agency
		DECL	declassify
DCTS	Defense Collaboration Tool Suite	*DEFCON*	defense readiness condition
DD	Department of Defense (form); destroyer (Navy ship)	*DEFSMAC*	Defense Special Missile and Aerospace Center
DDA	Deputy Director for Administration (CIA); designated development activity	*DEL*	deployable equipment list
		DEMARC	demarcation
		de max	maximum drift error
D-day	unnamed day on which operations commence or are scheduled to commence	*DEMIL*	demilitarization
		de min	minimum drift error
		de minimax	minimax drift error
DDC	data distribution center; defense distribution center	*DeMS*	deployment management system
		DEMUX	demultiplex
DDCI	Deputy Director of Central Intelligence (CIA)	*DEP*	Delayed Entry Program; deployed
		DEP&S	Drug Enforcement Plans and Support
DDCI/CM	Deputy Director of Central Intelligence for Community Management	*DEPCJTF*	deputy commander, joint task force
		DEPID	deployment indicator code
DDED	defense distribution expeditionary depot	*DEPMEDS*	deployable medical systems
		DepOpsDeps	Service deputy operations deputies
DDG	guided missile destroyer	*DEPORD*	deployment order

DESC	Defense Energy Support Center
DESCOM	Depot System Command (Army)
DESIGAREA	designated area message
DEST	destination; domestic emergency support team
DET	detachment; detainee
DETRESFA	distress phase (ICAO)
DEW	directed-energy warfare
DF	direction finding; dispersion factor; disposition form
DFARS	Department of Defense Federal Acquisition Regulation Supplement
DFAS	Defense Finance and Accounting Service
DFAS-DE	Defense Finance and Accounting Service-Denver
DFC	deputy force commander; detention facility commander
DFE	Defense Joint Intelligence Operations Center forward element; division force equivalent
DFM	deterrent force module
DFO	disaster field office (FEMA)
DFR	Defense Fuel Region
DFR/E	Defense Fuel Region, Europe
DFRIF	Defense Freight Railway Interchange Fleet
DFR/ME	Defense Fuel Region, Middle East
DFSC	Defense Fuel Supply Center
DFSP	Defense Fuel Support Point
DFT	deployment for training
DG	defense guidance
DGIAP	Defense General Intelligence and Applications Program
DGM	digital group multiplex
DGZ	desired ground zero
DH	death due to hostilities; Directorate for Human Intelligence (DIA)
DHA	detainee holding area
DHB	Defense Health Board
DHE	Department of Defense (DOD) human intelligence (HUMINT) element
DHHS	Department of Health and Human Services
DHM	Department of Defense human intelligence manager
DHMO	Department of Defense human intelligence management office
DHS	Defense Human Intelligence (HUMINT) Service; Department of Homeland Security; Director of Health Services
DI	Defense Intelligence Agency (DIA) Directorate for Analysis DIA Directorate for Intelligence Production; discrete identifier; dynamic interface
DIA	Defense Intelligence Agency
DIAC	Defense Intelligence Analysis Center
DIA/DHX	Defense Intelligence Agency, Directorate of Human Intelligence, Office of Document and Media Operations
DIAM	Defense Intelligence Agency manual; Defense Intelligence Agency memorandum
DIAP	Defense Intelligence Analysis Program; Drug Interdiction Assistance Program
DIAR	Defense Intelligence Agency (DIA) regulation
DIB	defense industrial base
DIBITS	digital in-band interswitch trunk signaling
DIBRS	defense incident-based reporting system
DIBTS	digital in-band trunk signaling
DICO	Data Information Coordination Office
DIDHS	Deployable Intelligence Data Handling System
DIDO	designated intelligence disclosure official
DIDS	Defense Intelligence Dissemination System
DIEB	Defense Intelligence Executive Board
DIEPS	Digital Imagery Exploitation Production System
DIG	digital
DIGO	Defence Imagery and Geospatial Organisation
DII	defense information infrastructure
DII-COE	defense information infrastructure-common operating environment
DIILS	Defense Institute of International Legal Studies
DIJE	Defense Intelligence Joint Environment
DILPA	diphase loop modem-A
DIMA	drilling individual mobilization augmentee
DIN	defense intelligence notice
DINET	Defense Industrial Net
DINFOS	Defense Information School
DIOC	drug interdiction operations center
DIOCC	Defense Intelligence Operations Coordination Center
DIPC	defense industrial plant equipment center
DIPFAC	diplomatic facility
DIPGM	diphase supergroup modem

DIRINT	Director of Intelligence (USMC)	DLQ	deck landing qualification
DIRJIATF	director, joint inter-agency task force	DLR	depot-level repairable
		DLSA	Defense Legal Services Agency
DIRLAUTH	direct liaison authorized	DLSS	Defense Logistics Standard Systems
DIRM	Directorate for Information and Resource Management	DLTM	digital line termination module
		DLTU	digital line termination unit
DIRMOBFOR	director of mobility forces	DM	detection and monitoring
DIRNSA	Director, National Security Agency	dmax	maximum drift distance
DIRSPACEFOR	director of space forces (USAF)	DMB	datum marker buoy
DIS	daily intelligence summary; defense information system; Defense Investigative Service; distributed interactive simulation	DMC	data mode control
		DMD	digital message device
		DMDC	defense management data center; defense manpower data center
DISA	Defense Information Systems Agency	DME	distance measuring equipment
		DMHS	Defense Message Handling System
DISA-LO	Defense Information Systems Agency—liaison officer	DMI	director military intelligence
		DMIGS	Domestic Mobile Integrated Geospatial-Intelligence System
DISANMOC	Defense Information Systems Agency Network Management and Operations Center	dmin	minimum drift distance
		DML	data manipulation language
DisasterAWARE	Disaster All-Hazard Warnings, Analysis, and Risk Evaluation System	DMLSS	Defense Medical Logistics Standard Support
		DMO	directory maintenance official
DISCOM	division support command (Army)	DMOS	duty military occupational specialty
DISGM	diphase supergroup	DMPI	designated mean point of impact; desired mean point of impact
DISN	Defense Information Systems Network		
		DMRD	defense management resource decision
DISN-E	Defense Information Systems Network—Europe		
		DMRIS	defense medical regulating information system
DISO	defense intelligence support office		
DISP	drug investigation support program (FAA)	DMS	defense message system; defense meteorological system; director of military support
DISUM	daily intelligence summary		
DITDS	defense information threat data system; defense intelligence threat data system	DMSB	Defense Medical Standardization Board
		DMSM	Defense Meritorious Service Medal
DITSUM	defense intelligence terrorist summary	DMSO	Defense Modeling and Simulation Office; director of major staff office; Division Medical Supply Office
DJIOC	Defense Joint Intelligence Operations Center		
		DMSP	Defense Meteorological Satellite Program
DJS	Director, Joint Staff		
DJSM	Director, Joint Staff memorandum	DMSSC	defense medical systems support center
DJTFAC	deployable joint task force augmentation cell		
		DMT	disaster management team (UN)
DJTFS	deputy joint task force surgeon	DMU	disk memory unit
DLA	Defense Logistics Agency	DMZ	demilitarized zone
DLAM	Defense Logistics Agency manual	DN	digital nonsecure
DLAR	Defense Logistics Agency regulation	DNA	Defense Nuclear Agency; deoxyribonucleic acid
DLEA	drug law enforcement agency	DNAT	defense nuclear advisory team
DLED	dedicated loop encryption device	DNBI	disease and nonbattle injury
DLIS	Defense Logistics Information Service	DNBI casualty	disease and nonbattle injury casualty
		DNC	digital nautical chart
DLP	data link processor	DND	Department of National Defence
DLPMA	diphase loop modem A	DNDO	Domestic Nuclear Detection Office

DNGA	Director of National Geospatial-Intelligence Agency
DNI	Director of National Intelligence; Director of Naval Intelligence
DNIF	duty not involving flying
DNMSP	driftnet monitoring support program
DNSO	Defense Network Systems Organization
DNVT	digital nonsecure voice terminal
DNY	display area code (NYX) routing
DOA	dead on arrival; director of administration
DOB	date of birth; dispersal operating base
DOC	Department of Commerce; designed operational capability
DOCC	deep operations coordination cell
DOCDIV	documents division
DOCEX	document exploitation
DOCNET	Doctrine Networked Education and Training
DOD	Department of Defense
DODAAC	Department of Defense activity address code
DODAAD	Department of Defense Activity Address Directory
DODAC DOD	ammunition code
DODD	Department of Defense directive
DODDS	Department of Defense Dependent Schools
DODEX	Department of Defense intelligence system information system extension
DODFMR	Department of Defense Financial Management Regulation
DODI	Department of Defense instruction
DODIC	Department of Defense identification code
DODID	Department of Defense Intelligence Digest
DODIIS	Department of Defense Intelligence Information System
DODIPC	Department of Defense intelligence production community
DODIPP	Department of Defense Intelligence Production Program
DOD-JIC	Department of Defense Joint Intelligence Center
DODM	data orderwire diphase modem
DOE	Department of Energy
DOF	degree of freedom
DOI	Defense Special Security Communications System (DSSCS) Operating Instructions; Department of Interior
DOJ	Department of Justice
DOL	Department of Labor
DOM	day of month
DOMS	director of military support
DON	Department of the Navy
DOPMA	Defense Officer Personnel Management Act
DOR	date of rank
DOS	date of separation; days of supply; denial of service; Department of State; disk operating system
DOT	Department of Transportation
DOTEO	Department of Transportation emergency organization
DOTMLPF	doctrine, organization, training, materiel, leadership and education, personnel, and facilities
DOW	data orderwire; died of wounds
DOX-T	direct operational exchange-tactical
DOY	day of year
DP	Air Force component plans officer (staff); decisive point; Directorate for Policy Support (DIA); displaced person
dp	parachute drift
DPA	Defense Production Act
DPAP	Defense Procurement and Acquisition Policy
DPAS	Defense Priorities and Allocation System
DPC	deception planning cell; Defense Planning Committee (NATO)
DPEC	displaced person exploitation cell
DPG	Defense Planning Guidance
DPI	desired point of impact
dpi	dots per inch
DPICM	dual purpose improved conventional munitions
DPKO	Department of Peacekeeping Operations
DPLSM	dipulse group modem
DPM	dissemination program manager
DPMO	Defense Prisoner of War/Missing Personnel Office
DPO	distribution process owner
DPP	data patch panel; distributed production program
DPPDB	digital point positioning database
DPQ	defense planning questionnaire (NATO)
DPR	display non-nodal routing
DPRB	Defense Planning and Resources Board
DPRE	displaced persons, refugees, and evacuees
DPS	data processing system
DPSC	Defense Personnel Support Center
DPSK	differential phase shift keying
DR	dead reckoning; digital receiver; disaster relief
DRB	Defense Resources Board
DRe	dead reckoning error

DRMD	deployments requirements manning document
DRMO	Defense Reutilization and Marketing Office
DRMS	Defense Reutilization and Marketing Service; distance root-mean-square
DRN	Disaster Response Network
DRO	departmental requirements office
DRRS	Defense Readiness Reporting System
DRS	detainee reporting system
DRSN	Defense Red Switched Network
DRT	dead reckoning tracer
DRTC	designated reporting technical control
DS	Directorate for Information Systems and Services (DIA); direct support; doctrine sponsor
DSA	defense special assessment (DIA); defensive sea area
DSAA	Defense Security Assistance Agency
DSAR	Defense Supply Agency regulation
DSB	digital in-band trunk signaling (DIBTS) signaling buffer
DSC	defensive space control; digital selective calling
DSCA	Defense Security Cooperation Agency; defense support of civil authorities
DSCP	Defense Supply Center Philadelphia
DSCR	Defense Supply Center Richmond
DSCS	Defense Satellite Communications System
DSCSOC	Defense Satellite Communications System operations center
DSDI	digital simple data interface
DSG	digital signal generator
DSI	defense simulation internet
DSL	display switch locator (SL) routing
DSMAC	digital scene-matching area correlation
DSN	Defense Switched Network
DSNET	Defense Secure Network
DSNET-2	Defense Secure Network-2
DSO	defensive systems officer
DSOE	deployment schedule of events
DSP	Defense Satellite Program; Defense Support Program
DSPD	defense support to public diplomacy
DSPL	display system programming language
DSPS	Director, Security Plans and Service
DSR	defense source registry
DSS	Defense Security Service; Distribution Standard System
DSS/ALOC	direct support system/air line of communications
DSSCS	Defense Special Security Communications System
DSSM	Defense Superior Service Medal
DSSO	data system support organization; defense sensitive support office; defense systems support organization
DSSR	Department of State Standardized Regulation
DST	Defense Logistics Agency (DLA) support team; deployment support team
DSTP	Director of Strategic Target Planning
DSTR	destroy
DSTS-G	DISN Satellite Transmission Services—Global
DSVL	doppler sonar velocity log
DSVT	digital subscriber voice terminal
DT	Directorate for MASINT and Technical Collection (DIA)
DTA	Defense Threat Assessment; dynamic threat assessment
DTAM	defense terrorism awareness message
DTCI	Defense Transportation Coordination Initiative
DTD	detailed troop decontamination
DTE	data terminal equipment; developmental test and evaluation
DTED	digital terrain elevation data
DTG	date-time group; digital trunk group (digital transmission group)
DTIP	Disruptive Technology Innovations Partnership (DIA)
DTL	designator target line
DTMF	dual tone multi-frequency
DTMR	defense traffic management regulation
DTO	division transportation office; drug trafficking organization
DTOC	division tactical operations center
DTR	defense transportation regulation
DTRA	Defense Threat Reduction Agency
DTRACS	Defense Transportation Reporting and Control System
DTRATCA	Defense Threat Reduction and Treaty Compliance Agency
DTS	Defense Transportation System; Defense Travel System; diplomatic telecommunications service
DTTS	Defense Transportation Tracking System
DU	depleted uranium
DUSD(CI&S)	Deputy Under Secretary of Defense for Counterintelligence and Security
DUSDL	Deputy Under Secretary of Defense for Logistics
DUSD(L&MR)	Deputy Under Secretary of Defense for Logistics and Materiel Readiness
DUSDP	Deputy Under Secretary of Defense for Policy

DUSTWUN	duty status-whereabouts unknown
DV	distinguished visitor
DVA	Department of Veterans Affairs
DVD	digital video device; digital video disc
DVITS	Digital Video Imagery Transmission System
DVOW	digital voice orderwire
DVT	deployment visualization tool
DWAS	Defense Working Capital Accounting System
DWMCF	double-wide modular causeway ferry
DWRIA	died of wounds received in action
DWT	deadweight tonnage
DWTS	Digital Wideband Transmission System
DX	Directorate for External Relations (DIA)
DZ	drop zone
DZC	drop zone controller
DZCO	drop zone control officer
DZSO	drop zone safety officer
DZST	drop zone support team
DZSTL	drop zone support team leader
E	total probable error
E&DCP	evaluation and data collection plan
E&E	emergency and extraordinary expense authority; evasion and escape
E&EE	emergency and extraordinary expense
E&I	engineering and installation
E&M	ear and mouth; special signaling leads
E1	Echelon 1
E2	Echelon 2
E3	Echelon 3; electromagnetic environmental effects
E4	Echelon 4
E5	Echelon 5
E-8C	joint surveillance, target attack radar system (JSTARS) aircraft
EA	electronic attack; emergency action; evaluation agent; executive agent; executive assistant
ea	each
EAC	echelons above corps (Army); emergency action; emergency action committee
EACS	expeditionary aeromedical evacuation crew member support
EACT	expeditionary aeromedical evacuation coordination team
EAD	earliest arrival date; echelons above division (Army); extended active duty
EADRU	Euro-Atlantic disaster response unit
EADS	Eastern Air Defense Sector
EAES	expeditionary aeromedical evacuation squadron
EAF	expeditionary aerospace forces
EAI	executive agent instruction
EALT	earliest anticipated launch time
EAM	emergency action message
EAP	emergency action plan; emergency action procedures
EAPC	Euro-Atlantic Partnership Council
EAP-CJCS	emergency action procedures of the Chairman of the Joint Chiefs of Staff
EARLY	evasion and recovery supplemental data report
E-ARTS	en route automated radar tracking system
EASF	expeditionary aeromedical staging facility
EAST	expeditionary aeromedical evacuation staging team
EASTPAC	eastern Pacific Ocean
EBCDIC	extended binary coded decimal interchange code
EBS	environmental baseline survey
EC	electronic combat; enemy combatant; error control; European Community
ECAC	Electromagnetic Compatibility Analysis Center
ECB	echelons corps and below (Army)
ECC	engineer coordination cell; evacuation control center
ECHA	Executive Committee for Humanitarian Affairs
ECHO	European Community Humanitarian Aid Department
ECM	electronic countermeasures
ECN	electronic change notice; Minimum Essential Emergency Communications Network
ECO	electronic combat officer
ECOSOC	Economic and Social Council (UN)
ECP	emergency command precedence; engineering change proposal; entry control point
ECS	expeditionary combat support
ECU	environmental control unit
ED	envelope delay; evaluation directive
EDA	Excess Defense Articles
EDC	estimated date of completion
EDD	earliest delivery date
EDI	electronic data interchange
EDSS	equipment deployment and storage system
EE	emergency establishment
EEA	environmental executive agent
EEBD	emergency escape breathing device
EECT	end evening civil twilight
EED	electro-explosive device; emergency-essential designation
EEDAC	emergency essential Department of the Army civilian
EEE	emergency and extraordinary expense

EEFI	essential elements of friendly information	EM	electromagnetic; executive manager
EEI	essential element of information	EMAC	emergency management assistance compact
EELV	evolved expendable launch vehicle	E-mail	electronic mail
		EMALL	electronic mall
EEO	equal employment opportunity	EMC	electromagnetic compatibility
EEPROM	electronic erasable programmable read-only memory	EMCON	emission control
		EMCON orders	emission control orders
EER	enlisted employee review; extended echo ranging	EMD	effective miss distance
		EME	electromagnetic environment
EEZ	exclusive economic zone	EMEDS	Expeditionary Medical Support
EFA	engineering field activity	EMF	expeditionary medical facility
EFAC	emergency family assistance center	EMI	electromagnetic interface; electromagnetic interference
EFD	engineering field division	EMIO	expanded maritime interception operations
EFST	essential fire support task		
EFT	electronic funds transfer	EMP	electromagnetic pulse
EFTO	encrypt for transmission only	EMR hazards	electromagnetic radiation hazards
EGM	Earth Gravity Model	EMS	electromagnetic spectrum; emergency medical services
EGS	Earth ground station		
EH	explosive hazard	EMSEC	emanations security
EHCC	explosive hazards coordination cell	EMT	emergency medical technician; emergency medical treatment
EHF	extremely high frequency	EMTF	expeditionary mobility task force
EHO	environmental health officer	EMV	electromagnetic vulnerability
EHRA	environmental health risk assessment	ENCOM	engineer command (Army)
		ENDEX	exercise termination
EHSA	environmental health site assessment	ENL	enlisted
		ENSCE	enemy situation correlation element
EHT	explosive hazard team	ENWGS	Enhanced Naval Warfare Gaming System
EI	environmental information; exercise item		
		EO	electro-optical; end office; equal opportunity; executive order; eyes only
EIA	Electronic Industries Association		
EID	electrically initiated device		
EIS	Environmental Impact Statement	EOB	electronic order of battle; enemy order of battle
ELBA	emergency locator beacon		
ELCAS	elevated causeway system	EOC	early operational capability; emergency operating center; emergency operations center
ELCAS(M)	elevated causeway system (modular)		
ELCAS(NL)	elevated causeway system (Navy lighterage)	EOD	explosive ordnance disposal
		EOI	electro-optic(al) imagery
ELD	emitter locating data	EO-IR	electro-optical-infrared
ELECTRO-OPTINT	electro-optical intelligence	EO-IR CM	electro-optical-infrared countermeasure
ELINT	electronic intelligence		
ELIST	enhanced logistics intratheater support tool	EOL	end of link
		EOM	end of message
ELOS	extended line of sight	EOP	emergency operating procedures
ELPP	equal level patch panel	E-O TDA	electro-optical tactical decision aid
ELR	extra-long-range aircraft	EOW	engineering orderwire
ELSEC	electronics security	EP	electronic protection; emergency preparedness; emergency procedures; execution planning
ELT	emergency locator transmitter		
ELV	expendable launch vehicle		
ELVA	emergency low visibility approach	EPA	Environmental Protection Agency; evasion plan of action

EPBX	electronic private branch exchange
EPC	Emergency Procurement Committee
EPF	enhanced palletized load system (PLS) flatrack
EPH	emergency planning handbook
EPIC	El Paso Intelligence Center
EPIRB	emergency position-indicating radio beacon
EPLO	emergency preparedness liaison officer
EPROM	erasable programmable read-only memory
EPW	enemy prisoner of war
EPW/CI	enemy prisoner of war/civilian internee
ERC	exercise related construction
ERDC	Engineer Research and Development Center
ERGM	extended range guided munitions
ERO	engine running on or offload
ERRO	Emergency Response and Recovery Office
ERSD	estimated return to service date
ERT	emergency response team (FEMA); engineer reconnaissance team
ERT-A	emergency response team—advance element
ERU	emergency response unit
ES	electronic warfare support
ESB	engineer support battalion
ESC	Electronics Systems Center; expeditionary sustainment command
ESF	Economic Support Fund; emergency support function
ESG	executive steering group; expeditionary strike group
ESGN	electrically suspended gyro navigation
ESI	extremely sensitive information
ESK	electronic staff weather officer kit
ESM	expeditionary site mapping
ESO	embarkation staff officer; environmental science officer
ESOC	Emergency Supply Operations Center
ESORTS	Enhanced Status of Resources and Training System
ESP	engineer support plan
ESR	external supported recovery
EST	embarked security team; emergency service team; emergency support team (FEMA); en route support team
ETA	estimated time of arrival
ETAC	emergency tactical air control; enlisted terminal attack controller
ETD	estimated time of departure
ETF	electronic target folder
ETI	estimated time of intercept
ETIC	estimated time for completion; estimated time in commission
ETM	electronic transmission
ETPL	endorsed TEMPEST products list
ETR	export traffic release
ETS	European telephone system
ETSS	extended training service specialist
ETX	end of text
EU	European Union
E-UAV	endurance unmanned aerial vehicle
EUB	essential user bypass
EURV	essential user rekeying variable
EUSA	Eighth US Army
EUSC	effective United States control/controlled
EUSCS	effective United States-controlled ships
EVC	evasion chart
EVE	equal value exchange
EW	early warning; electronic warfare
EWC	electronic warfare coordinator
EWCC	electronic warfare coordination cell
EWCS	electronic warfare control ship
EW/GCI	early warning/ground-controlled intercept
EWIR	electronic warfare integrated reprogramming
EWO	electronic warfare officer
EXCIMS	Executive Council for Modeling and Simulations
ExCom	executive committee
EXDIR	Executive Director (CIA)
EXDIR/ICA	Executive Director for Intelligence Community Affairs (USG)
EXECSEC	executive secretary
EXER	exercise
EXORD	execute order
EXPLAN	exercise plan
EZ	exchange zone
EZCO	extraction zone control officer
EZM	engagement zone manager
F	Fahrenheit; flare patterns; flash
F2T2EA	find, fix, track, target, engage, and assess
F&ES	fire and emergency services
FA	feasibility assessment; field artillery
FAA	Federal Aviation Administration; Foreign Assistance Act
FAAR	facilitated after-action review
FAC	forward air controller
FAC(A)	forward air controller (airborne)
FACE	forward aviation combat engineering
FACSFAC	fleet area control and surveillance facility
FACT	field advance civilian team; field assessment and coordination team
FAD	feasible arrival date

F/AD	force/activity designator	*FDSSS*	flight deck status and signaling system
FAE	fuel air explosive	*FDT*	forward distribution team
FALD	Field Administration and Logistics Division	*FDUL*	fixed directory unit list
		FDX	full duplex
FALOP	Forward Area Limited Observing Program	*FE*	facilities engineering
FAM	functional area manager	*FEA*	front-end analysis
FAMP	forward area minefield planning	*FEBA*	forward edge of the battle area
FAO	Food and Agriculture Organization (UN); foreign area officer	*FEC*	forward error correction
		FECC	fires and effects coordination cell
FAPES	Force Augmentation Planning and Execution System	*FED-STD*	federal standard
		FEK	frequency exchange keying
FAR	Federal Acquisition Regulation; Federal Aviation Regulation	*FEMA*	Federal Emergency Management Agency
		FEP	fleet satellite (FLTSAT) extremely high frequency (EHF) package
FARC	Revolutionary Armed Forces of Colombia		
FARP	forward arming and refueling point	*FEPP*	federal excess personal property; foreign excess personal property
FAS	Foreign Agricultural Service (USDA); frequency assignment subcommittee; fueling at sea; functional account symbol	*FEST*	foreign emergency support team; forward engineer support team
		FET	facility engineer team
FASCAM	family of scatterable mines	*FEU*	forty-foot equivalent unit
FAST	field assessment surveillance team; fleet antiterrorism security team	*FEZ*	fighter engagement zone
		FF	navy fast frigate
FAX	facsimile	*Ff*	fatigue correction factor
FB	forward boundary	*FFA*	free-fire area
FBI	Federal Bureau of Investigation	*FFC*	force fires coordinator
FBIS	Foreign Broadcast Information Service	*FFCC*	flight ferry control center; force fires coordination center
FBO	faith-based organization		
FC	field circular; final coordination; fires cell (Army); floating causeway; floating craft; force commander	*FFD*	foundation feature data
		FFE	field force engineering; fire for effect; flame field expedients
FCA	Foreign Claims Act; functional configuration audit	*FFG*	guided missile frigate
		FFH	fast frequency hopping
FCC	Federal Communications Commission; Federal coordinating center; functional combatant commander	*FFH-net*	fast-frequency-hopping net
		FFHT-net	fast-frequency-hopping training net
		FFIR	friendly force information requirement
FCE	forward command element	*FFP*	Food for Peace; fresh frozen plasma
FCG	foreign clearance guide	*FFTU*	forward freight terminal unit
FCM	foreign consequence management	*FG*	fighter group
FCO	federal coordinating officer	*FGMDSS*	Future Global Maritime Distress and Safety System
FCP	fire control party		
FCT	firepower control team	*FGS*	final governing standard
FD	from temporary duty	*FH*	fleet hospital
FDA	Food and Drug Administration	*FHA*	Bureau for Food and Humanitarian Assistance; Federal Highway Administration; foreign humanitarian assistance
FDBM	functional database manager		
FDC	fire direction center		
FDESC	force description	*FHC*	family help center
FDL	fast deployment logistics	*F-hour*	effective time of announcement by the Secretary of Defense to the Military Departments of a decision to mobilize Reserve units
FDLP	flight deck landing practice		
FDM	frequency division multiplexing		
FDO	fire direction officer; flexible deterrent option; flight deck officer; foreign disclosure officer		
		FHP	force health protection
FDR/FA	flight data recorder/fault analyzer	*FHWA*	Federal Highway Administration
FDS	fault detection system	*FI*	foreign intelligence
FDSL	fixed directory subscriber list	*FIA*	functional interoperability architecture
FDSS	fault detection subsystem	*FIC*	force indicator code

FID	foreign internal defense	FMA-net	frequency management A-net
FIDAF	foreign internal defense augmentation force	FMAS	foreign media analysis subsystem
		FMAT	financial management augmentation team
FIE	fly-in echelon		
FIFO	first-in-first-out	FMC	force movement characteristics; full mission-capable
FinCEN	Financial Crimes Enforcement Network		
		FMCH	fleet multichannel
FIR	first-impressions report; flight information region	FMCR	Fleet Marine Corps Reserve
		FMCSA	Federal Motor Carrier Safety Administration
FIRCAP	foreign intelligence requirements capabilities and priorities		
		FMI	field manual-interim
		FMF	Fleet Marine Force
1st IOC	1st Information Operations Command (Land)	FMFP	foreign military financing program
		FMID	force module identifier
FIS	flight information service; Foreign Intelligence Service	FMO	frequency management office; functional manager office
FISC	fleet and industrial supply center	FMP	force module package; foreign materiel program
FISINT	foreign instrumentation signals intelligence	FMS	force module subsystem; foreign military sales
FISS	foreign intelligence and security services	FMSC	frequency management sub-committee
		FMT-net	frequency management training net
FIST	fire support team; fleet imagery support terminal; fleet intelligence support team	FMV	full motion video
		FN	foreign nation
		FNMOC	Fleet Numerical Meteorology and Oceanography Center
FIWC	fleet information warfare center		
		FNMOD	Fleet Numerical Meteorological and Oceanographic Detachment
FIXe	navigational fix error		
FLAR	forward-looking airborne radar	FNOC	Fleet Numerical Oceanographic Command
FLENUMMETOCCEN	Fleet Numerical Meteorology and Oceanography Center	FNS	foreign nation support
		FO	fiber optic; flash override; forward observer
FLENUMMETOCDET	Fleet Numerical Meteorological and Oceanographic Detachment		
		FOB	forward operating base; forward operations base
FLETC	Federal Law Enforcement Training Center	FOC	full operational capability; future operations cell
FLIP	flight information publication; flight instruction procedures	FOD	field operations division; foreign object damage
FLIR	forward-looking infrared	FOFW	fiber optic field wire
FLITE	federal legal information through electronics	FOG	Field Operations Guide for Disaster Assessment and Response
FLO/FLO	float-on/float-off	FOI	fault detection isolation
FLOLS	fresnel lens optical landing system	FOIA	Freedom of Information Act
		FOIU	fiber optic interface unit
FLOT	forward line of own troops	FOL	fiber optic link; forward operating location
FLP	force level planning		
FLS	forward logistic site	FON	freedom of navigation (operations)
FLSG	force logistic support group	FOO	field ordering officer
FLTSAT	fleet satellite	FORSCOM	United States Army Forces Command
FLTSATCOM	fleet satellite communications	FORSTAT	force status and identity report
FM	field manual (Army); financial management; flare multiunit; force module; frequency modulation; functional manager	FOS	forward operating site; full operational status
		FOT	follow-on operational test
		FOUO	for official use only

FOV	field of view	FSR	field service representative
FP	firing point; force protection; frequency panel	FSS	fast sealift ship; fire support station; flight service station
FPA	foreign policy advisor	FSSG	force service support group (USMC)
FPC	final planning conference; future plans cell	FSST	forward space support to theater
		FST	fleet surgical team
FPCON	force protection condition	FSU	former Soviet Union; forward support unit
FPD	force protection detachment; foreign post differential		
		FSW	feet of seawater
FPF	final protective fire	ft	feet; foot
FPM	Federal personnel manual	ft3	cubic feet
FPO	fleet post office	FTC	Federal Trade Commission
FPOC	focal point operations center	FTCA	Foreign Tort Claims Act
FPS	force protection source	FTP	file transfer protocol
FPTAS	flight path threat analysis simulation	FTRG	fleet tactical readiness group
FPTS	forward propagation by tropospheric scatter	FTS	Federal Telecommunications System; Federal telephone service; file transfer service
FPWG	force protection working group		
FR	final report; frequency response	FTU	field training unit; freight terminal unit
FRA	Federal Railroad Administration (DOT)	FTX	field training exercise
FRAG	fragmentation code	FUAC	functional area code
FRAGORD	fragmentary order	FUNCPLAN	functional plan
FRC	federal resource coordinator; forward resuscitative care	F/V	fishing vessel
		Fv	aircraft speed correction factor
FRD	formerly restricted data	FVT	Force Validation Tool
FREQ	frequency	FW	fighter wing; fixed-wing; weather correction factor
FRERP	Federal Radiological Emergency Response Plan		
		FWD	forward
FRF	fragment retention film	FWDA	friendly weapon danger area
FRMAC	Federal Radiological Monitoring and Assessment Center (DOE)	FWF	former warring factions
		FY	fiscal year
FRN	force requirement number	FYDP	Future Years Defense Program
FROG	free rocket over ground	G-1	Army or Marine Corps component manpower or personnel staff officer (Army division or higher staff, Marine Corps brigade or higher staff)
FRP	Federal response plan (USG)		
FRRS	frequency resource record system		
FS	fighter squadron; file separator; file server; flare single-unit	G-2	Army or Marine Corps component intelligence staff officer (Army division or higher staff, Marine Corps brigade or higher staff)
fs	search radius safety factor		
FSA	fire support area		
FSB	fire support base; forward staging base; forward support base; forward support battalion	G-3	Army or Marine Corps component operations staff officer (Army division or higher staff, Marine Corps brigade or higher staff)
FSC	fire support cell; fire support coordinator (USMC)		
FSCC	fire support coordination center	G-4	Army or Marine Corps component logistics staff officer (Army division or higher staff, Marine Corps brigade or higher staff); Assistant Chief of Staff for Logistics
FSCL	fire support coordination line		
FSCM	fire support coordination measure		
FSCOORD	fire support coordinator (Army)		
FSE	fire support element		
FSEM	fire support execution matrix	G-6	Army or Marine Corps component command, control, communications, and computer systems staff officer; assistant chief of staff for communications
FSF	foreign security forces		
FSK	frequency shift key		
FSN	foreign service national		
FSO	fire support officer; flight safety officer; foreign service officer	G-7	information operations staff officer (ARFOR)

G/A	ground to air
GA	Tabun, a nerve agent
GAA	general agency agreement; geospatial intelligence assessment activity
GAFS	General Accounting and Finance System
GAMSS	Global Air Mobility Support System
GAO	General Accounting Office; Government Accountability Office
GAR	gateway access request
GARS	Global Area Reference System
GAT	governmental assistance team
GATB	guidance, apportionment, and targeting board
GATES	Global Air Transportation Execution System
GB	group buffer; Sarin, a nerve agent
GBL	government bill of lading
GBR	ground-based radar
GBS	Global Broadcast Service; Global Broadcast System
GBU	guided bomb unit
GC	general counsel; Geneva Convention; Geneva Convention Relative to the Protection of Civilian Persons in Time of War
GC3A	global command, control, and communications assessment
GC4A	global command, control, communications, and computer assessment
GCA	ground controlled approach
GCC	geographic combatant commander; global contingency construction
GCCC	Global Contingency Construction Contract
GCCS	Global Command and Control System
GCCS-A	Global Command and Control System-Army
GCCS-I3	Global Command and Control System Integrated Imagery and Intelligence
GCCS-J	Global Command and Control System-Joint
GCCS-M	Global Command and Control System-Maritime
GCE	ground combat element (MAGTF)
GCI	ground control intercept
GCM	global container manager
GCP	geospatial-intelligence contingency package; ground commander's pointer
GCRI	general collective routing indicator (RI)
GCS	ground control station
GCSC	Global Contingency Service Contract
GCSS-J	Global Combat Support System—Joint
GCTN	global combating terrorism network
GD	Soman, a nerve agent
GDF	gridded data field; Guidance for Development of the Force
GDIP	General Defense Intelligence Program
GDIPP	General Defense Intelligence Proposed Program
GDP	General Defense Plan (SACEUR): gross domestic product
GDSS	Global Decision Support System
GE	general engineering
GEF	Guidance for Employment of the Force
GEM	Global Information Grid (GIG) Enterprise Management
GENADMIN	general admin (message)
GENSER	general service (message)
GENTEXT	general text
GEO	geosynchronous Earth orbit
GEOCODE	geographic code
GEOFILE	geolocation code file; standard specified geographic location file
GEOINT	geospatial intelligence
GEOLOC	geographic location; geographic location code
GEOREF	geographic reference; world geographic reference system
GF	a nerve agent
GFE	government-furnished equipment
GFI	government-furnished information
GFM	Global Force Management; global freight management; government-furnished material
GFMB	Global Force Management Board
GFMIG	Global Force Management Implementation Guidance
GFMPL	Graphics Fleet Mission Program Library
GFOAR	global family of operation plans assessment report
GFU	group framing unit
GHz	gigahertz
GI	geomatics and imagery
GI&S	geospatial information and services
GIAC	graphic input aggregate control
GIC	(*gabarit international de chargement*) international loading gauge
GIE	global information environment
GIG	Global Information Grid
GII	global information infrastructure
GIP	gridded installation photograph
GIS	geographic information system; geospatial information systems
GL	government leased
GLCM	ground launched cruise missile
GLINT	gated laser intensifier
GLO	ground liaison officer
GLTD	ground laser target designator
GM	group modem
GMD	global missile defense; ground-based midcourse defense; group mux and/or demux

GMDSS	Global Maritime Distress and Safety System
GMF	ground mobile force
GMFP	global military force policy
GMI	general military intelligence
GMR	graduated mobilization response; ground mobile radar
GMRS	global mobility readiness squadron
GMS	global mobility squadron
GMTI	ground moving target indicator
GNC	Global Network Operations Center
GND	Global Information Grid (GIG) Network Defense
GO	government owned
GOCO	government-owned, contractor-operated
GOES	geostationary operational environmental satellite
GOGO	government-owned, government-operated
GOS	grade of service
GOSG	general officer steering group
GOTS	government off-the-shelf
GP	general purpose; group
GPC	government purchase card
GPD	gallons per day
GPE	geospatial intelligence preparation of the environment
GPEE	general purpose encryption equipment
GPL	Geospatial Product Library
GPM	gallons per minute; global pallet manager
GPMDM	group modem
GPMRC	Global Patient Movement Requirements Center
GPS	Global Positioning System
GPW	Geneva Convention Relative to the Treatment of Prisoners of War
GQ	general quarters
GR	graduated response
GRASP	general retrieval and sort processor
GRCA	ground reference coverage area
GRG	gridded reference graphic
GRL	global reach laydown
GRREG	graves registration
GS	general service; general support; ground speed; group separator
GSA	General Services Administration; general support artillery
GSE	ground support equipment
GSI	glide slope indicator
GSM	ground station module
GSO	general services officer
GSORTS	Global Status of Resources and Training System
GS-R	general support-reinforcing
GSR	general support-reinforcing; ground surveillance radar
GSSA	general supply support area
gt	gross ton
GTAS	ground-to-air signals
GTL	gun-target line
GTM	global transportation management
GTN	Global Transportation Network
GUARD	US National Guard and Air Guard
GUARDS	General Unified Ammunition Reporting Data System
G/VLLD	ground/vehicle laser locator designator
GW	guerrilla warfare
GWC	global weather central
GWEN	Ground Wave Emergency Network
GWOT	global war on terrorism
GWS	Geneva Convention for the Amelioration of the Condition of the Wounded and Sick in Armed Forces in the Field
GWS Sea	Geneva Convention for the Amelioration of the Condition of the Wounded, Sick, and Shipwrecked Members of the Armed Forces at Sea
H&I	harassing and interdicting
H&S	headquarters and service
HA	holding area; humanitarian assistance
HAARS	high-altitude airdrop resupply system
HAB	high altitude burst
HAC	helicopter aircraft commander
HACC	humanitarian assistance coordination center
HAHO	high-altitude high-opening parachute technique
HALO	high-altitude low-opening parachute technique
HAP	humanitarian assistance program
HAP-EP	humanitarian assistance program-excess property
HARM	high-speed antiradiation missile
HARP	high altitude release point
HAST	humanitarian assistance survey team
HATR	hazardous air traffic report
HAZ	hazardous cargo
HAZMAT	hazardous materials
HB	heavy boat
HBCT	heavy brigade combat team
HCA	head of contracting activity; humanitarian and civic assistance
HCAS	hostile casualty
HCL	hydrochloride
HCO	helicopter control officer
HCP	hardcopy printer
HCS	helicopter combat support (Navy); helicopter coordination section
HCT	human intelligence (HUMINT) collection team
HD	a mustard agent; harmonic distortion; homeland defense
HDC	harbor defense commander; helicopter direction center

HDCU	harbor defense command unit
HDO	humanitarian demining operations
HDPLX	half duplex
HDR	humanitarian daily ration
HDTC	Humanitarian Demining Training Center
HE	heavy equipment; high explosive
HEAT	helicopter external air transport; high explosive antitank
HEC	helicopter element coordinator
HEFOE	hydraulic electrical fuel oxygen engine
HEI	high explosives incendiary
HEL-H	heavy helicopter
HEL-L	light helicopter
HEL-M	medium helicopter
HELO	helicopter
HEMP	high-altitude electromagnetic pulse
HEMTT	heavy expanded mobile tactical truck
HEO	highly elliptical orbit
HEPA	high efficiency particulate air
HERF	hazards of electromagnetic radiation to fuels
HERO	electromagnetic radiation hazards; hazards of electromagnetic radiation to ordnance
HERP	hazards of electromagnetic radiation to personnel
HET	heavy equipment transporter; human intelligence (HUMINT) exploitation team
HEWSweb	Humanitarian Early Warning Service
HF	high frequency
HFDF	high frequency direction-finding
HFRB	high frequency regional broadcast
HH	homing pattern
HHC	headquarters and headquarters company
HHD	headquarters and headquarters detachment
H-hour	seaborne assault landing hour; specific time an operation or exercise begins
HHQ	higher headquarters
HHS	Department of Health and Human Services
HIC	humanitarian information center
HICAP	high-capacity firefighting foam station
HIDACZ	high-density airspace control zone
HIDTA	high-intensity drug trafficking area
HIFR	helicopter in-flight refueling
HIMAD	high to medium altitude air defense
HIMARS	High Mobility Artillery Rocket System
HIMEZ	high-altitude missile engagement zone
HIRSS	hover infrared suppressor subsystem
HIRTA	high intensity radio transmission area
HIU	humanitarian information unit
HIV	human immuno-deficiency virus
HJ	crypto key change
HLPS	heavy-lift pre-position ship
HLZ	helicopter landing zone
HM	hazardous material
HMA	humanitarian mine action
HMH	Marine heavy helicopter squadron
HMIRS	Hazardous Material Information Resource System
HMIS	Hazardous Material Information System
HMLA	Marine light/attack helicopter squadron
HMM	Marine medium helicopter squadron
HMMWV	high mobility multipurpose wheeled vehicle
HMOD	harbormaster operations detachment
HMW	health, morale, and welfare
HN	host nation
HNS	host-nation support
HNSA	host-nation support agreement
HNSCC	host-nation support coordination cell
HOB	height of burst
HOC	human intelligence operations cell; humanitarian operations center
HOCC	humanitarian operations coordination center
HOD	head of delegation
HOGE	hover out of ground effect
HOIS	hostile intelligence service
HOM	head of mission
HOSTAC	helicopter operations from ships other than aircraft carriers (USN publication)
HPA	high power amplifier
HPMSK	high priority mission support kit
HPT	high-payoff target
HPTL	high-payoff target list
HQ	HAVE QUICK; headquarters
HQCOMDT	headquarters commandant
HQDA	Headquarters, Department of the Army
HQFM-net	HAVE QUICK frequency modulation net
HQFMT-net	HAVE QUICK frequency modulation training net
HQMC	Headquarters, Marine Corps
HR	helicopter request; hostage rescue
HRB	high-risk billet
HRC	high-risk-of-capture
HRJTF	humanitarian relief joint task force
HRO	humanitarian relief organizations
HRP	high-risk personnel; human remains pouch
HRS	horizon reference system
HRT	hostage rescue team
HS	helicopter antisubmarine (Navy); homeland security; homing single-unit
HSAC	Homeland Security Advisory Council
HSAS	Homeland Security Advisory System
HSB	high speed boat
HSC	helicopter sea combat (Navy); Homeland Security Council

HSCDM	high speed cable driver modem
HSC/PC	Homeland Security Council Principals Committee
HSC/PCC	Homeland Security Council Policy Coordination Committee
HSD	human intelligence support detachment
HSE	headquarters support element; human intelligence support element (DIA)
HSEP	hospital surgical expansion package (USAF)
HSI	hyperspectral imagery
HSLS	health service logistic support
HSM	humanitarian service medal
HSPD	homeland security Presidential directive
HSPR	high speed pulse restorer
HSS	health service support
HSSDB	high speed serial data buffer
HST	helicopter support team
HT	hatch team
HTERRCAS	hostile terrorist casualty
HTG	hard target graphic
HTH	high test hypochlorite
HU	hospital unit
HUD	head-up display
HUMINT	human intelligence; human resources intelligence
HUMRO	humanitarian relief operation
HUMRO OCP	humanitarian relief operation operational capability package
HUS	hardened unique storage
HVA	high value asset
HVAA	high value airborne asset
HVAC	heating, ventilation, and air conditioning
HVI	high-value individual
HVT	high-value target
HW	hazardous waste
HWM	high water mark
HYE	high-yield explosives
Hz	hertz
I	immediate; individual
I&A	Office of Intelligence and Analysis
I&W	indications and warning
IA	implementing arrangement; individual augmentee; information assurance; initial assessment
IAC	Interagency Advisory Council
IACG	interagency coordination group
IADB	Inter-American Defense Board
IADS	integrated air defense system
IAEA	International Atomic Energy Agency (UN)
IAF	initial approach fix
IAIP	Information Analysis and Infrastructure Protection
IAM	inertially aided munition
IAMSAR	International Aeronautical and Maritime Search and Rescue manual
IAP	international airport
IAR	interoperability assessment report
IASC	Interagency Standing Committee (UN); interim acting service chief
IATA	International Air Transport Association
IATACS	Improved Army Tactical Communications System
IATO	interim authority to operate
IAVM	information assurance vulnerability management
IAW	in accordance with
I/B	inboard
IBB	International Broadcasting Bureau
IBCT	infantry brigade combat team
IBES	intelligence budget estimate submission
IBM	International Business Machines
IBS	Integrated Booking System; integrated broadcast service; Integrated Broadcast System
IBU	inshore boat unit
IC	incident commander; intelligence community; intercept
IC3	integrated command, control, and communications
ICAD	individual concern and deficiency
ICAF	Interagency Conflict Assessment Framework
ICAO	International Civil Aviation Organization
ICBM	intercontinental ballistic missile
ICC	information coordination center; Intelligence Coordination Center; International Criminal Court; Interstate Commerce Commission
ICD	international classifications of diseases; International Cooperation and Development Program (USDA)
ICDC	Intelligence Community Deputies Committee
ICDS	improved container delivery system
ICE	Immigration and Customs Enforcement
ICEDEFOR	Iceland Defense Forces
IC/EXCOM	Intelligence Community Executive Committee
ICF	intelligence contingency funds
ICG	interagency core group
ICIS	integrated consumable item support
ICITAP	International Crime Investigative Training Assistance Program (DOJ)
ICM	image city map; improved conventional munitions; integrated collection management

ICN	idle channel noise; interface control net
ICNIA	integrated communications, navigation, and identification avionics
ICOD	intelligence cutoff data
ICODES	integrated computerized deployment system
ICON	imagery communications and operations node; intermediate coordination node
ICP	incident command post; intertheater communications security (COMSEC) package; interface change proposal; inventory control point
ICPC	Intelligence Community Principals Committee
ICR	Intelligence Collection Requirements
ICRC	International Committee of the Red Cross
ICRI	interswitch collective routing indicator
ICS	incident command system; internal communications system; inter-Service chaplain support
ICSF	integrated command communications system framework
ICSAR	interagency committee on search and rescue
ICU	intensive care unit; interface control unit
ICVA	International Council of Voluntary Agencies
ICW	in coordination with
ID	identification; identifier; initiating directive
IDAD	internal defense and development
IDB	integrated database
IDCA	International Development Cooperation Agency
IDDF	intermediate data distribution facility
IDEAS	Intelligence Data Elements Authorized Standards
IDEX	imagery data exploitation system
IDF	intermediate distribution frame
IDHS	intelligence data handling system
ID/IQ	indefinite delivery/indefinite quantity
IDM	improved data modem; information dissemination management
IDNDR	International Decade for Natural Disaster Reduction (UN)
IDO	installation deployment officer
IDP	imagery derived product; imminent danger pay; internally displaced person
IDRA	infectious disease risk assessment
IDS	individual deployment site; integrated deployment system; interface design standards; intrusion detection system
IDSS	interoperability decision support system
IDT	inactive duty training
IDZ	inner defense zone
IEB	intelligence exploitation base
IED	improvised explosive device
IEDD	improvised explosive device defeat
IEEE	Institute of Electrical and Electronics Engineers
IEL	illustrative evaluation scenario
IEMATS	improved emergency message automatic transmission system
IER	information exchange requirement
IES	imagery exploitation system
IESS	imagery exploitation support system
IEW	intelligence and electronic warfare
IF	intermediate frequency
IFC	intelligence fusion center
IFCS	improved fire control system
IFF	identification, friend or foe
IFFN	identification, friend, foe, or neutral
IFF/SIF	identification, friend or foe/selective identification feature
IFP	integrated force package
IFR	instrument flight rules
IFRC	International Federation of Red Cross and Red Crescent Societies
IFSAR	interferometric synthetic aperture radar
IG	inspector general
IGE	independent government estimate
IGL	intelligence gain/loss
IGO	intergovernmental organization
IGSM	interim ground station module (JSTARS)
IHADSS	integrated helmet and display sight system (Army)
IHC	International Humanitarian Community
IHO	industrial hygiene officer
IHS	international health specialist
IIB	interagency information bureau
IICL	Institute of International Container Lessors
IIM	intelligence information management
IIP	Bureau of International Information Programs (DOS); interagency implementation plan; international information program; interoperability improvement program
IIR	imagery interpretation report; imaging infrared; intelligence information report
IJC3S	initial joint command, control, and communications system; Integrated Joint Command, Control, and Communications System
IL	intermediate location
ILO	International Labor Organization (UN)
ILOC	integrated line of communications
ILS	integrated logistic support
IM	information management
IMA	individual mobilization augmentee
IMAAC	Interagency Modeling and Atmospheric Assessment Center
IMC	instrument meteorological conditions; International Medical Corps
IMDC	isolated, missing, detained, or captured
IMDG	international maritime dangerous goods (UN)
IMET	international military education and training
IMETS	Integrated Meteorological System

IMF	International Monetary Fund (UN)	*INSCOM*	United States Army Intelligence and Security Command
IMI	international military information		
IMINT	imagery intelligence	*INTAC*	individual terrorism awareness course
IMIT	international military information team		
		INTACS	integrated tactical communications system
IMLTU	intermatrix line termination unit		
IMM	integrated materiel management	*INTELSAT*	International Telecommunications Satellite Organization
IMMDELREQ	immediate delivery required		
IMO	information management officer; International Maritime Organization	*INTELSITSUM*	intelligence situation summary
		InterAction	American Council for Voluntary International Action
IMOSAR	International Maritime Organization (IMO) search and rescue manual		
		INTERCO	International Code of signals
IMOSS	interim mobile oceanographic support system	*INTERPOL*	International Criminal Police Organization
IMP	implementation; information management plan; inventory management plan	*INTERPOL-USNCB*	International Criminal Police Organization, United States National Central Bureau (DOJ)
IMPT	incident management planning team	*INTREP*	intelligence report
IMRL	individual material requirements list	*INTSUM*	intelligence summary
IMS	information management system; Interagency Management System; international military staff; international military standardization	*INU*	inertial navigation unit; integration unit
		INV	invalid
		INVOL	involuntary
IMSU	installation medical support unit	*I/O*	input/output
IMU	inertial measuring unit; intermatrix unit	*IO*	information objectives; information operations; intelligence oversight
IN	Air Force component intelligence officer (staff); impulse noise; instructor	*IOC*	Industrial Operations Command; initial operational capability; intelligence operations center; investigations operations center
INCERFA	uncertainty phase (ICAO)		
INCNR	increment number		
INCSEA	incidents at sea		
INDRAC	Interagency Combating Weapons of Mass Destruction Database of Responsibilities, Authorities, and Capabilities	*IOI*	injured other than hostilities or illness
		IOM	installation, operation, and maintenance; International Organization for Migration
INF	infantry		
INFLTREP	inflight report		
INFOCON	information operations condition	*IOP*	interface operating procedure
INFOSEC	information security	*IOSS*	Interagency Operations Security (OPSEC) Support Staff
ING	Inactive National Guard		
INID	intercept network in dialing	*IOT*	information operations team
INJILL	injured or ill	*IOU*	input/output unit
INL	Bureau for International Narcotics and Law Enforcement Affairs (USG)	*IOWG*	information operations working group
INM	international narcotics matters	*IP*	initial point; initial position; instructor pilot; internet protocol
INMARSAT	international maritime satellite		
INR	Bureau of Intelligence and Research, Department of State		
		IPA	intelligence production agency
INREQ	information request	*IPB*	intelligence preparation of the battlespace
INRP	Initial National Response Plan		
INS	Immigration and Naturalization Service; inertial navigation system; insert code	*IPBD*	intelligence program budget decision
		IPC	initial planning conference; integration planning cell; interagency planning cell
INSARAG	International Search and Rescue Advisory Group		

IPDM	intelligence program decision memorandum	*IRT*	Initial Response Team
IPDP	inland petroleum distribution plan	*IS*	information superiority; information system; interswitch
IPDS	imagery processing and dissemination system; inland petroleum distribution system (Army)	*ISA*	international standardization agreement; inter-Service agreement
		ISAF	International Security Assistance Force
IPE	individual protective equipment; industrial plant equipment	*ISB*	intermediate staging base
		ISDB	integrated satellite communications (SATCOM) database
IPG	isolated personnel guidance		
IPI	indigenous populations and institutions	*ISE*	intelligence support element
IPIR	initial photo interpretation report	*ISG*	information synchronization group
IPL	imagery product library; integrated priority list	*ISMCS*	international station meteorological climatic summary
IPO	International Program Office	*ISMMP*	integrated continental United States (CONUS) medical mobilization plan
IPOE	intelligence preparation of the operational environment	*ISN*	Bureau of International Security and Nonproliferation; internment serial number
IPOM	intelligence program objective memorandum		
		ISO	International Organization for Standardization; isolation
IPP	impact point prediction; industrial preparedness program	*ISOO*	Information Security Oversight Office
IPR	in-progress review; intelligence production requirement	*ISOPAK*	International Organization for Standardization package
IPRG	intelligence program review group	*ISOPREP*	isolated personnel report
IPS	illustrative planning scenario; Interim Polar System; interoperability planning system	*ISP*	internet service provider
		ISR	intelligence, surveillance, and reconnaissance
IPSG	intelligence program support group	*ISRD*	intelligence, surveillance, and reconnaissance division
IPSP	intelligence priorities for strategic planning		
		ISS	in-system select
IPT	integrated planning team; integrated process team; Integrated Product Team	*ISSA*	inter-Service support agreement
		ISSG	Intelligence Senior Steering Group
I/R	internment/resettlement	*ISSM*	information system security manager
IR	incident report; information rate; information requirement; infrared; intelligence requirement	*ISSO*	information systems security organization
		IST	integrated system test; interswitch trunk
		ISU	internal airlift or helicopter slingable container unit
IRA	Provisional Irish Republican Army		
IRAC	interdepartment radio advisory committee	*IT*	information technology
I/R BN	internment/resettlement battalion	*ITA*	international telegraphic alphabet
IRC	International Red Cross; International Rescue Committee; internet relay chat	*ITAC*	intelligence and threat analysis center (Army)
IRCCM	infrared counter countermeasures	*ITALD*	improved tactical air-launched decoy
IRCM	infrared countermeasures	*ITAR*	international traffic in arms regulation (coassembly)
IRDS	infrared detection set		
IRF	Immediate Reaction Forces (NATO); incident response force	*ITF*	intelligence task force (DIA)
		ITG	infrared target graphic
IRINT	infrared intelligence	*ITL*	intelligence task list
IRISA	Intelligence Report Index Summary File	*ITO*	installation transportation officer
IRO	international relief organization	*ITRO*	inter-Service training organization
IR pointer	infrared pointer	*ITU*	International Telecommunications Union
IRR	Individual Ready Reserve; integrated readiness report	*ITV*	in-transit visibility
		ITW/AA	integrated tactical warning and attack assessment
IRS	Internal Revenue Service		
IRST	infrared search and track	*IUWG*	inshore undersea warfare group
IRSTS	infrared search and track sensor; Infrared Search and Track System	*IV*	intravenous
		IVR	initial voice report

IVSN	Initial Voice Switched Network
IW	irregular warfare
IWC	information operations warfare commander
IW-D	defensive information warfare
IWG	intelligence working group; interagency working group
IWSC	Information Warfare Support Center
IWW	inland waterway
IWWS	inland waterway system
J-1	manpower and personnel directorate of a joint staff; manpower and personnel staff section
J-2	intelligence directorate of a joint staff; intelligence staff section
J-2A	deputy directorate for administration of a joint staff
J2-CI	Joint Counterintelligence Office
J-2J	deputy directorate for support of a joint staff
J-2M	deputy directorate for crisis management of a joint staff
J-2O	deputy directorate for crisis operations of a joint staff
J-2P	deputy directorate for assessment, doctrine, requirements, and capabilities of a joint staff
J-2T	Deputy Directorate for Targeting, Joint Staff Intelligence Directorate
J-2T-1	joint staff target operations division
J-2T-2	Target Plans Division
J-2X	joint force counterintelligence and human intelligence staff element
J-3	operations directorate of a joint staff; operations staff section
J-4	logistics directorate of a joint staff; logistics staff section
J-5	plans directorate of a joint staff; plans staff section
J-6	communications system directorate of a joint staff; command, control, communications, and computer systems staff section
J-7	engineering staff section; Joint Staff Operational Plans and Joint Force Development Directorate; operational plans and interoperability directorate of a joint staff
J-7/JED	exercises and training directorate of a joint staff
J-8	Director for Force Structure, Resource, and Assessment, Joint Staff; force structure, resource, and assessment directorate of a joint staff
J-9	civil-military operations staff section
JA	judge advocate
J-A	judge advocate directorate of a joint staff
JAAR	joint after-action report
JAARS	Joint After-Action Reporting System
JAAT	joint air attack team
JA/ATT	joint airborne and air transportability training
JAC	joint analysis center
JACC	joint airspace control center
JACCC	joint airlift coordination and control cell
JACC/CP	joint airborne communications center/command post
JACCE	joint air component coordination element
JACS	joint automated communication-electronics operating instructions system
JADO	joint air defense operations
JADOCS	Joint Automated Deep Operations Coordination System
JAFWIN	JWICS Air Force weather information network
JAG	Judge Advocate General
JAGMAN	Manual of the Judge Advocate General (US Navy)
JAI	joint administrative instruction; joint airdrop inspection
JAIC	joint air intelligence center
JAIEG	joint atomic information exchange group
JAMPS	Joint Interoperability of Tactical Command and Control Systems (JINTACCS) automated message preparation system
JANAP	Joint Army, Navy, Air Force publication
JAO	joint air operations
JAOC	joint air operations center
JAOP	joint air operations plan
JAPO	joint area petroleum office
JAR	joint activity report
JARB	joint acquisition review board
JARCC	joint air reconnaissance control center
JARN	joint air request net
JARS	joint automated readiness system
JASC	joint action steering committee
JASSM	Joint Air-to-Surface Standoff Missile
JAT	joint acceptance test
JATACS	joint advanced tactical cryptological support
JAT Guide	Joint Antiterrorism Program Manager's Guide
JAWS	Joint Munitions Effectiveness Manual (JMEM)/air-to-surface weaponeering system
JBP	Joint Blood Program
JBPO	joint blood program office
JC2WC	joint command and control warfare center
JCA	jamming control authority; Joint Capability Area
JCASREP	joint casualty report
JCAT	joint crisis action team
JCC	joint command center; joint contracting center; joint course catalog
JCCB	Joint Configuration Control Board

JCCC	joint combat camera center	JDEC	joint document exploitation center
JCCP	joint casualty collection point	JDEIS	Joint Doctrine, Education, and Training Electronic Information System
JCE	Joint Intelligence Virtual Architecture (JIVA) Collaborative Environment	JDIG	Joint Drug Intelligence Group
JCEOI	joint communications-electronics operating instructions	JDISS	joint deployable intelligence support system
JCET	joint combined exchange training; joint combined exercise for training	JDN	joint data network
		JDNO	joint data network operations officer
JCEWR	joint coordination of electronic warfare reprogramming	JDOG	joint detention operations group
		JDOMS	Joint Director of Military Support
JCEWS	joint force commander's electronic warfare staff	JDPC	Joint Doctrine Planning Conference
		JDPO	joint deployment process owner
JCGRO	joint central graves registration office	JDSS	Joint Decision Support System
JCIDO	Joint Combat Identification Office	JDSSC	Joint Data Systems Support Center
JCIOC	joint counterintelligence operations center	JDTC	Joint Deployment Training Center
JCISA	Joint Command Information Systems Activity	JE	joint experimentation
		JEAP	Joint Electronic Intelligence (ELINT) Analysis Program
JCISB	Joint Counterintelligence Support Branch	JECE	Joint Elimination Coordination Element
JCLL	joint center for lessons learned		
JCMA	joint communications security monitor activity	JECG	joint exercise control group
		JECPO	Joint Electronic Commerce Program Office
JCMB	Joint Collection Management Board		
JCMC	joint crisis management capability	JEDD	Joint Education and Doctrine Division
JCMEB	joint civil-military engineering board	JEEP	joint emergency evacuation plan
JCMEC	joint captured materiel exploitation center	JEL	Joint Electronic Library
JCMO	joint communications security management office	JEM	joint exercise manual
		JEMB	joint environmental management board
JCMOTF	joint civil-military operations task force		
JCMPO	Joint Cruise Missile Project Office	JEMP	joint exercise management package
JCMT	joint collection management tools	JEPES	joint engineer planning and execution system
JCN	joint communications network		
JCS	Joint Chiefs of Staff	JET	Joint Operation Planning and Execution System (JOPES) editing tool
JCSAN	Joint Chiefs of Staff Alerting Network		
JCSAR	joint combat search and rescue	JEWC	Joint Electronic Warfare Center
JCSB	joint contracting support board	JEZ	joint engagement zone
JCSC	joint communications satellite center	JFA	joint field activity
JCSE	joint communications support element	JFACC	joint force air component commander
JCSM	Joint Chiefs of Staff memorandum	JFAST	Joint Flow and Analysis System for Transportation
JCSP	joint contracting support plan		
JCSS	joint communications support squadron	JFC	joint force commander
JCTN	joint composite track network	JFCC	joint functional component command
JDA	joint duty assignment	JFCC-IMD	Joint Functional Component Command for Integrated Missile Defense
JDAAP	Joint Doctrine Awareness Action Plan		
JDAL	Joint Duty Assignment List		
JDAM	Joint Direct Attack Munition	JFCC-ISR	Joint Functional Component Command for Intelligence, Surveillance, and Reconnaissance
JDAMIS	Joint Duty Assignment Management Information System		
		JFCC NW	Joint Functional Component Command for Network Warfare
JDC	joint deployment community; Joint Doctrine Center		
		JFCC SPACE	Joint Functional Component Command for Space
JDD	joint doctrine distribution		
JDDC	joint doctrine development community	JFCH	joint force chaplain
JDDE	Joint Deployment and Distribution Enterprise	JFE	joint fires element
		JFHQ	joint force headquarters
JDDOC	joint deployment and distribution operations center		

JFHQ-NCR	Joint Force Headquarters—National Capital Region
JFHQ-State	Joint Force Headquarters—State
JFIIT	Joint Fires Integration and Interoperability Team
JFIP	Japanese facilities improvement project
JFLCC	joint force land component commander
JFMC	joint fleet mail center
JFMCC	joint force maritime component commander
JFMO	Joint Frequency Management Office
JFO	joint field office; joint fires observer
JFP	joint force package (packaging)
JFRB	Joint Foreign Release Board
JFRG	joint force requirements generator
JFRG II	joint force requirements generator II
JFS	joint force surgeon
JFSOC	joint force special operations component
JFSOCC	joint force special operations component commander
JFTR	joint Federal travel regulations
JFUB	joint facilities utilization board
JHMCS	joint helmet-mounted cueing system
JI	joint inspection
JIACG	joint interagency coordination group
JIADS	joint integrated air defense system
JIATF	joint interagency task force
JIATF-E	joint interagency task force—East
JIATF-S	joint interagency task force—South
JIATF-W	joint interagency task force—West
JIB	joint information bureau
JIC	joint information center
JICC	joint information coordination center; joint interface control cell
JICO	joint interface control officer
JICPAC	Joint Intelligence Center, Pacific
JICTRANS	Joint Intelligence Center for Transportation
JIDC	joint intelligence and debriefing center; joint interrogation and debriefing center
JIEO	joint interoperability engineering organization
JIEP	joint intelligence estimate for planning
JIES	joint interoperability evaluation system
JIG	joint interrogation group
JILE	joint intelligence liaison element
JIMB	joint information management board
JIMP	joint implementation master plan
JIMPP	joint industrial mobilization planning process
JIMS	joint information management system
JINTACCS	Joint Interoperability of Tactical Command and Control Systems
JIO	joint interrogation operations
JIOC	joint information operations center; joint intelligence operations center
JIOCPAC	Joint Intelligence Operations Center, Pacific
JIOC-SOUTH	Joint Intelligence Operations Center, South
JIOC TRANS	Joint Intelligence Operations Center—Transportation
JIOP	joint interface operational procedures
JIOP-MTF	joint interface operating procedures-message text formats
JIOWC	Joint Information Operations Warfare Command
JIPC	joint imagery production complex
JIPCL	joint integrated prioritized collection list
JIPOE	joint intelligence preparation of the operational environment
JIPTL	joint integrated prioritized target list
JIS	joint information system
JISE	joint intelligence support element
JITC	joint interoperability test command
JITF-CT	Joint Intelligence Task Force for Combating Terrorism
JIVA	Joint Intelligence Virtual Architecture
JKDDC	Joint Knowledge Development and Distribution Capability
JLCC	joint lighterage control center; joint logistics coordination center
JLE	joint logistics environment
JLLP	Joint Lessons Learned Program
JLNCHREP	joint launch report
JLOC	joint logistics operations center
JLOTS	joint logistics over-the-shore
JLRC	joint logistics readiness center
JLSB	joint line of communications security board
JLSE	joint legal support element
JM&S	joint modeling and simulation
JMAARS	joint model after-action review system
JMAG	Joint METOC Advisory Group
JMAO	joint mortuary affairs office; joint mortuary affairs officer
JMAR	joint medical asset repository
JMAS	joint manpower automation system
JMAT	joint medical analysis tool; joint mobility assistance team
JMB	joint meteorology and oceanography board
JMC	joint military command; joint movement center
JMCC	joint meteorological and oceanographic coordination cell
JMCG	joint movement control group

JMCIS	joint maritime command information system
JMCO	joint meteorological and oceanographic coordination organization
JMCOMS	joint maritime communications system
JMD	joint manning document
JMeDSAF	joint medical semi-automated forces
JMEM	Joint Munitions Effectiveness Manual
JMET	joint mission-essential task
JMETL	joint mission-essential task list
JMIC	Joint Military Intelligence College; joint modular intermodal container
JMICS	Joint Worldwide Intelligence Communications System (JWICS) mobile integrated communications system
JMIE	joint maritime information element
JMIP	joint military intelligence program
JMISC	Joint Military Information Support Command
JMITC	Joint Military Intelligence Training Center
JMLO	joint medical logistics officer
JMMC	Joint Material Management Center
JMMT	joint military mail terminal
JMNA	joint military net assessment
JMO	joint maritime operations; joint meteorological and oceanographic officer
JMO(AIR)	joint maritime operations (air)
JMOC	joint medical operations center
JMP	joint manpower program
JMPA	joint military postal activity; joint military satellite communications (MILSATCOM) panel administrator
JMRC	joint mobile relay center
JMRO	Joint Medical Regulating Office
JMRR	Joint Monthly Readiness Review
JMSEP	joint modeling and simulation executive panel
JMSWG	Joint Multi-Tactical Digital Information Link (Multi-TADIL) Standards Working Group
JMT	joint military training
JMTCA	joint munitions transportation coordinating activity
JMTCSS	Joint Maritime Tactical Communications Switching System
JMUA	Joint Meritorious Unit Award
JMV	joint METOC viewer
JMWG	joint medical working group
JNACC	joint nuclear accident coordinating center
JNCC	joint network operations control center
JNOCC	Joint Operation Planning and Execution System (JOPES) Network Operation Control Center
JNPE	joint nuclear planning element
JOA	joint operations area
JOAF	joint operations area forecast
JOC	joint operations center; joint oversight committee
JOCC	joint operations command center
JOERAD	joint spectrum center ordnance E3 risk assessment database
JOG	joint operations graphic
JOGS	joint operation graphics system
JOPES	Joint Operation Planning and Execution System
JOPESIR	Joint Operation Planning and Execution System Incident Reporting System
JOPESREP	Joint Operation Planning and Execution System Reporting System
JOPP	joint operation planning process
JOPPA	joint operation planning process for air
JOR	joint operational requirement
JORD	joint operational requirements document
JOSG	joint operational steering group
JOT&E	joint operational test and evaluation
JOTS	Joint Operational Tactical System
JP	joint publication
JPAC	joint planning augmentation cell; Joint POW/MIA Accounting Command
JPADS	joint precision airdrop system
JPAG	Joint Planning Advisory Group
JPASE	Joint Public Affairs Support Element
JPATS	joint primary aircraft training system
JPAV	joint personnel asset visibility
JPC	joint planning cell; joint postal cell
JPD	joint planning document
JPEC	joint planning and execution community
JPERSTAT	joint personnel status and casualty report
JPG	joint planning group
JPME	joint professional military education
JPMRC	joint patient movement requirements center
JPMT	joint patient movement team
JPN	joint planning network
JPO	joint petroleum office; Joint Program Office
JPOC	joint planning orientation course
JPOI	joint program of instruction
JPOM	joint preparation and onward movement
JPO-STC	Joint Program Office for Special Technology Countermeasures
JPOTF	joint psychological operations task force
JPOTG	joint psychological operations task group
JPRA	Joint Personnel Recovery Agency
JPRC	joint personnel recovery center
JPRSP	joint personnel recovery support product
JPS	joint processing system

JPTTA	joint personnel training and tracking activity	JSO	joint security operations; joint specialty officer or joint specialist
JQR	joint qualification requirements	JSOA	joint special operations area
JQRR	joint quarterly readiness review	JSOAC	joint special operations air component; joint special operations aviation component
JRADS	Joint Resource Assessment Data System		
JRB	Joint Requirements Oversight Council (JROC) Review Board	JSOACC	joint special operations air component commander
JRC	joint reception center; joint reconnaissance center	JSOC	joint special operations command
		JSOFI	Joint Special Operations Forces Institute
JRCC	joint reception coordination center	JSOTF	joint special operations task force
JRERP	Joint Radiological Emergency Response Plan	JSOU	Joint Special Operations University
JRFL	joint restricted frequency list	JSOW	joint stand-off weapon
JRG	joint review group	JSPA	joint satellite communications (SATCOM) panel administrator
JRIC	joint reserve intelligence center		
JRMB	Joint Requirements and Management Board	JSPD	joint strategic planning document
JROC	Joint Requirements Oversight Council	JSPDSA	joint strategic planning document supporting analyses
JRS	joint reporting structure		
JRSC	jam-resistant secure communications; joint rescue sub-center	JSPOC	Joint Space Operations Center
		JSPS	Joint Strategic Planning System
JRSOI	joint reception, staging, onward movement, and integration	JSR	joint strategy review
		JSRC	joint subregional command (NATO)
JRTC	joint readiness training center	JSS	joint surveillance system
JRX	joint readiness exercise	JSSA	joint Services survival, evasion, resistance, and escape (SERE) agency
JS	the Joint Staff		
JSA	joint security area	JSSIS	joint staff support information system
JSAC	joint strike analysis cell; joint strike analysis center	JSST	joint space support team
		JSTAR	joint system threat assessment report
JSAM	joint security assistance memorandum; Joint Service Achievement Medal; joint standoff surface attack missile	JSTARS	Joint Surveillance Target Attack Radar System
		JSTE	joint system training exercise
JSAN	Joint Staff automation for the nineties	JSTO	joint space tasking order
JSAP	Joint Staff action package	JT&E	joint test and evaluation
JSAS	joint strike analysis system	JTA	joint technical architecture
JSC	joint security coordinator; Joint Spectrum Center	JTAC	joint technical augmentation cell; joint terminal attack controller; Joint Terrorism Analysis Center
JSCAT	joint staff crisis action team		
JSCC	joint security coordination center; joint Services coordination committee	JTACE	joint technical advisory chemical, biological, radiological, and nuclear element
JSCM	joint Service commendation medal	JTADS	Joint Tactical Air Defense System (Army); Joint Tactical Display System
JSCP	Joint Strategic Capabilities Plan		
JSDS	Joint Staff doctrine sponsor	JTAGS	joint tactical ground station (Army); joint tactical ground station (Army and Navy); joint tactical ground system
J-SEAD	joint suppression of enemy air defenses		
JSEC	joint strategic exploitation center		
JSHO	joint shipboard helicopter operations	JTAO	joint tactical air operations
JSIDS	joint Services imagery digitizing system	JTAR	joint tactical air strike request
JSIR	joint spectrum interference resolution	JTASC	joint training analysis and simulation center
JSISC	Joint Staff Information Service Center	JTASG	Joint Targeting Automation Steering Group
JSIT	Joint Operation Planning and Execution System (JOPES) information trace	JTAV	joint total asset visibility
		JTAV-IT	joint total asset visibility-in theater
JSIVA	Joint Staff Integrated Vulnerability Assessment	JTB	Joint Transportation Board
		JTC	joint technical committee; Joint Training Confederation
JSM	Joint Staff Manual		
JSME	joint spectrum management element		
JSMS	joint spectrum management system	JTCB	joint targeting coordination board

JTCC	joint transportation coordination cell; joint transportation corporate information management center	JUIC	joint unit identification code
		JULL	Joint Universal Lessons Learned (report)
		JULLS	Joint Universal Lessons Learned System
JTCG/ME	Joint Technical Coordinating Group for Munitions Effectiveness	JUO	joint urban operation
		JUSMAG	Joint United States Military Advisory Group
JTD	joint table of distribution; joint theater distribution		
		JUWTF	joint unconventional warfare task force
JTDC	joint track data coordinator	JV	Joint Vision
JTF	joint task force	JV 2020	Joint Vision 2020
JTF-6	joint task force-6	JVB	Joint Visitors Bureau
JTF-AK	Joint Task Force—Alaska	JVIDS	Joint Visual Integrated Display System
JTF-B	joint task force-Bravo	JVSEAS	Joint Virtual Security Environment Assessment System
JTFCEM	joint task force contingency engineering management		
		JWAC	Joint Warfare Analysis Center
JTF-CM	joint task force—consequence management	JWARS	Joint Warfare Analysis and Requirements System
JTF-CS	Joint Task Force-Civil Support	JWC	Joint Warfare Center
JTF-E	joint task force—elimination	JWCA	joint warfighting capabilities assessment
JTF-GNO	Joint Task Force-Global Network Operations	JWFC	Joint Warfighting Center
		JWG	joint working group
JTF-GTMO	Joint Task Force-Guantanamo	JWICS	Joint Worldwide Intelligence Communications System
JTF-HD	Joint Task Force-Homeland Defense		
JTF HQ	joint task force headquarters	JWID	joint warrior interoperability demonstration
JTF-MAO	joint task force—mortuary affairs office		
JTF-N	Joint Task Force-North	k	thousand
JTFP	Joint Tactical Fusion Program	Ka	Kurtz-above band
JTF-PO	joint task force-port opening	KAL	key assets list
JTFS	joint task force surgeon	KAPP	Key Assets Protection Program
JTF-State	Joint Task Force-State	kb	kilobit
JTIC	joint transportation intelligence center	kbps	kilobits per second
JTIDS	Joint Tactical Information Distribution System	KC-135	Stratotanker
		KDE	key doctrine element
JTL	joint target list	KEK	key encryption key
JTLM	Joint Theater Logistics Management	KG	key generator
JTLS	joint theater-level simulation	kg	kilogram
JTM	joint training manual	kHz	kilohertz
JTMD	joint table of mobilization and distribution; Joint Terminology Master Database	KIA	killed in action
		K-Kill	catastrophic kill
		km	kilometer
JTMP	joint training master plan	KMC	knowledge management center
JTMS	joint theater movement staff; joint training master schedule	KNP	Korean National Police
		KP	key pulse
JTP	joint test publication; joint training plan	kph	kilometers per hour
JTR	joint travel regulations	KPP	key performance parameter
JTRB	joint telecommunication resources board	KQ ID	tactical location identifier
JTS	Joint Targeting School	kt	kiloton(s); knot (nautical miles per hour)
JTSG	joint targeting steering group	Ku	Kurtz-under band
JTSSCCB	Joint Tactical Switched Systems Configuration Control Board	kVA	kilo Volt-Amps
		KVG	key variable generator
JTSST	joint training system support team	kW	kilowatt
JTT	joint targeting toolbox; joint training team	KWOC	keyword-out-of-context
JTTF	joint terrorism task force	L	length
JUH-MTF	Joint User Handbook-Message Text Formats	l	search subarea length

LA	lead agent; legal adviser; line amplifier; loop key generator (LKG) adapter
LAADS	low altitude air defense system
LAAM	light anti-aircraft missile
LABS	laser airborne bathymetry system
LACH	lightweight amphibious container handler
LACV	lighter, air cushioned vehicle
LAD	latest arrival date
LAMPS	Light Airborne Multipurpose System (helicopter)
LAN	local area network
LANDCENT	Allied Land Forces Central Europe (NATO)
LANDSAT	land satellite
LANDSOUTH	Allied Land Forces Southern Europe (NATO)
LANTIRN	low-altitude navigation and targeting infrared for night
LAO	limited attack option
LARC	lighter, amphibious resupply, cargo
LARC-V	lighter, amphibious resupply, cargo, 5 ton
LARS	lightweight airborne recovery system
LASH	lighter aboard ship
LASINT	laser intelligence
LAT	latitude
LAV	light armored vehicle
lb	pound
LBR	Laser Beam Rider
LC	lake current; legal counsel
LCAC	landing craft, air cushion
LCAP	low combat air patrol
LCB	line of constant bearing
LCC	amphibious command ship; land component commander; launch control center; lighterage control center; link communications circuit; logistics component command
LCCS	landing craft control ship
LCE	logistics capability estimator; logistics combat element (MAGTF); logistics combat element (Marine)
LCES	line conditioning equipment scanner
LCM	landing craft, mechanized; letter-class mail; life-cycle management
LCMC	life cycle management command
LCO	landing craft air cushion control officer; lighterage control officer
LCP	lighterage control point
LCPL	landing craft personnel (large)
LCS	landing craft air cushion control ship
LCSR	life cycle systems readiness
LCU	landing craft, utility; launch correlation unit
LCVP	landing craft, vehicle, personnel
LD	line of departure
LDA	limited depository account
LDF	lightweight digital facsimile
LDI	line driver interface
LDO	laser designator operator
LDR	leader; low data rate
LE	law enforcement; low-order explosives
LEA	law enforcement agency
LEAP	Light ExoAtmospheric Projectile
LEASAT	leased satellite
LEAU	Law Enforcement Assistance Unit (FAA)
LECIC	Law Enforcement and Counterintelligence Center (DOD)
LED	law enforcement desk; light emitting diode
LEDET	law enforcement detachment
LEGAT	legal attaché
LEO	law enforcement operations; low Earth orbit
LEP	laser eye protection; linear error probable
LERSM	lower echelon reporting and surveillance module
LERTCON	alert condition
LES	law enforcement sensitive; leave and earnings statement; Lincoln Laboratories Experimental Satellite
LESO	Law Enforcement Support Office
LET	light equipment transport
LF	landing force; low frequency
LFA	lead federal agency
LFORM	landing force operational reserve material
LFSP	landing force support party
LfV	Landesamt für Verfassungsschutz (regional authority for constitutional protection)
LG	deputy chief of staff for logistics
LGB	laser-guided bomb
LGM	laser-guided missile; loop group multiplexer
LGM-30	Minuteman
LGW	laser-guided weapon
LHA	amphibious assault ship (general purpose)
LHD	amphibious assault ship (multipurpose)
L-hour	specific hour on C-day at which a deployment operation commences or is to commence
LHT	line-haul tractor
LIDAR	light detection and ranging
LIF	light interference filter
LIMDIS	limited distribution
LIMFAC	limiting factor
LIPS	Logistics Information Processing System
LIS	logistics information system
LIWA	land information warfare activity
LKG	loop key generator
LKP	last known position

LL	lessons learned	LO/RO	lift-on/roll-off
LLLGB	low-level laser-guided bomb	LOROP	long range oblique photography
LLLTV	low-light level television	LOS	line of sight
LLSO	low-level source operation	LOTS	logistics over-the-shore
LLTR	low-level transit route	LOX	liquid oxygen
LM	loop modem	LP	listening post
LMARS	Logistics Metrics Analysis Reporting System	LPD	amphibious transport dock; low probability of detection
LMAV	laser MAVERICK	LPH	amphibious assault ship, landing platform helicopter
LMF	language media format		
LMSR	large, medium speed roll-on/roll-off	LPI	low probability of intercept
LN	lead nation	LPSB	logistics procurement support board
LNA	low voice amplifier	LPU	line printer unit
LNO	liaison officer	LPV	laser-protective visor
LO	low observable	LRC	logistics readiness center
LOA	Lead Operational Authority; letter of assist; letter of authorization; letter of offer and acceptance; lodgment operational area; logistics over-the-shore (LOTS) operation area	LRD	laser range finder-detector
		LRF	laser range finder
		LRF/D	laser range finder/detector
		LRG	long-range aircraft
		LRM	low rate multiplexer
LOAC	law of armed conflict	LRP	load and roll pallet
LOAL	lock-on after launch	LRRP	long range reconnaissance patrol
LOBL	lock-on before launch	LRS	launch and recovery site
LOC	line of communications; logistics operations center	LRST	long-range surveillance team
		LRSU	long-range surveillance unit
LOC ACC	location accuracy	LSA	logistic support analysis; logistics supportability analysis
LOCAP	low combat air patrol		
LOCE	Linked Operational Intelligence Centers Europe; Linked Operations-Intelligence Centers Europe	LSB	landing support battalion; lower sideband
		LSCDM	low speed cable driver modem
		LSD	dock landing ship; least significant digit
LOD	line of departure	LSE	landing signalman enlisted; logistic support element
LOE	letter of evaluation		
LOG	logistics	LSO	landing safety officer; landing signals officer
LOGAIR	logistics aircraft	LSPR	low speed pulse restorer
LOGAIS	logistics automated information system	LSS	laser spot search; local sensor subsystem
LOGCAP	logistics civil augmentation program	LST	landing ship, tank; laser spot tracker; tank landing ship
LOGCAT	logistics capability assessment tool		
LOGDET	logistics detail		
LOGEX	logistics exercise	LSU	logistics civil augmentation program support unit
LOGFAC	Logistics Feasibility Assessment Capability		
		LSV	logistics support vessel
LOGFOR	logistics force packaging system	LT	large tug; local terminal; long ton
LOGMARS	logistics applications of automated marking and reading symbols	L/T	long ton
		LTD	laser target designator
		LTD/R	laser target designator/ranger
LOGMOD	logistics module	LTF	logistics task force
LOGPLAN	logistics planning system	LTG	local timing generator
LOGSAFE	logistic sustainment analysis and feasibility estimator	LTL	laser-to-target line
		LTON	long ton
LOI	letter of instruction; loss of input	LTS	low-altitude navigation and targeting infrared for night (LANTIRN) targeting system
LO/LO	lift-on/lift-off		
LOMEZ	low-altitude missile engagement zone	LTT	loss to theater
LONG	longitude	LTU	line termination unit
LOO	line of operations	LUT	local user terminal
LOP	line of position	LVS	Logistics Vehicle System (USMC)
LORAN	long-range aid to navigation	LW	leeway

LWR	Lutheran World Relief	MARDIV	Marine division
LZ	landing zone	MARFOR	Marine Corps forces
LZCO	landing zone control officer	MARFOREUR	Marine Corps Forces, Europe
M&S	modeling and simulation	MARFORLANT	Marine Corps Forces, Atlantic
M88A1	recovery vehicle	MARFORNORTH	Marine Corps Forces, North
MA	master; medical attendant; mortuary affairs	MARFORPAC	Marine Corps Forces, Pacific
		MARFORSOUTH	Marine Corps Forces, South
mA	milliampere(s)	MARFORSTRAT	United States Marine Corps Forces, United States Strategic Command
MAAG	military assistance advisory group		
MAAP	master air attack plan	MARINCEN	Maritime Intelligence Center
MAC	Mortuary Affairs Center	MARLE	Marine liaison element
MACA	military assistance to civil authorities	MARLO	Marine liaison officer
		MAROP	marine operators
MACB	multinational acquisition and contracting board	MARPOL	International Convention for the Prevention of Pollution from Ships
MACCS	Marine air command and control system		
		MARS	Military Auxiliary Radio System
MACDIS	military assistance for civil disturbances	MARSA	military assumes responsibility for separation of aircraft
MACG	Marine air control group	MARSOC	Marine Corps special operations command
MACOM	major command (Army)		
MACP	mortuary affairs collection point	MARSOF	Marine Corps special operations forces
MACSAT	multiple access commercial satellite		
		MART	mobile Automatic Digital Network (AUTODIN) remote terminal
MAD	*Militärischer Abschirmdienst* (military protection service); military air distress		
		MASCAL	mass casualty
MADCP	mortuary affairs decontamination collection point	MASF	mobile aeromedical staging facility
		MASH	mobile Army surgical hospital
MAEB	mean area of effectiveness for blast	MASINT	measurement and signature intelligence
MAEF	mean area of effectiveness for fragments		
		MASLO	measurement and signature intelligence (MASINT) liaison officer
MAF	mobility air forces		
MAFC	Marine air-ground task force (MAGTF) all-source fusion center		
		MAST	military assistance to safety and traffic; mobile ashore support terminal
MAG	Marine aircraft group		
MAGTF	Marine air-ground task force		
MAGTF ACE	Marine air-ground task force aviation combat element	MAT	medical analysis tool
		MATCALS	Marine air traffic control and landing system
MAJCOM	major command (USAF)		
MANFOR	manpower force packaging system	MATCS	Marine air traffic control squadron
		M/ATMP	Missiles/Air Target Materials Program
MANPADS	man-portable air defense system		
MANPER	manpower and personnel module	MAW	Marine aircraft wing
MAOC-N	Maritime Analysis and Operations Center-Narcotics	MAX	maximum
		MAXORD	maximum ordinate
MAP	Military Assistance Program; missed approach point; missed approach procedure	MB	medium boat; megabyte
		MBA	main battle area
		MBBLs	thousands of barrels
MAR	METOC assistance request	MBCDM	medical biological chemical defense materiel
MARAD	Maritime Administration		
MARCORMATCOM	Marine Corps Materiel Command		
		MBI	major budget issue
MARCORSYSCOM	Marine Corps Systems Command	Mbps	megabytes per second
		Mbs	megabits per second

MC	Military Committee (NATO); military community; mission-capable
MC-130	Combat Talon (I and II)
MCA	mail control activity; maximum calling area; military civic action; mission concept approval; movement control agency
MCAG	maritime civil affairs group
MCAP	maximum calling area precedence
MCAS	Marine Corps air station
MCAT	maritime civil affairs team
MCB	movement control battalion
MCBAT	medical chemical biological advisory team
MCC	Marine component commander; maritime component commander; master control center; military cooperation committee; military coordinating committee; mission control center; mobility control center; movement control center
MCCC	mobile consolidated command center
MCCDC	Marine Corps Combat Development Command
MCCISWG	military command, control, and information systems working group
MCD	medical crew director
MCDA	military and civil defense assets (UN)
MCDP	Marine Corps doctrine publication
MCDS	modular cargo delivery system
MCEB	Military Communications-Electronics Board
MCEWG	Military Communications-Electronics Working Group
MC/FI	mass casualty/fatality incident
MCIA	Marine Corps Intelligence Activity
MCIO	military criminal investigative organization
MCIOC	Marine Corps Information Operations Center
MCIP	Marine Corps information publication; military command inspection program
MCJSB	Military Committee Joint Standardization Board
MCM	Manual for Courts-Martial; military classification manual; mine countermeasures
MCMC	mine countermeasures commander
MCMG	Military Committee Meteorological Group (NATO)
MCMO	medical civil-military operations
MCMOPS	mine countermeasures operations
M/CM/S	mobility, countermobility, and/or survivability
MCMREP	mine countermeasure report
MCO	Mapping Customer Operations; Marine Corps order
MCOO	modified combined obstacle overlay
MCRP	Marine Corps reference publication
MCS	maneuver control system; Military Capabilities Study; mine countermeasures ship; modular causeway system
MCSF	mobile cryptologic support facility
MCSFB	Marine Corps security force battalion
MCT	movement control team
MCTC	Midwest Counterdrug Training Center
MCTFT	Multijurisdictional Counterdrug Task Force Training
MCU	maintenance communications unit
MCW	modulated carrier wave
MCWP	Marine Corps warfighting publication
MCX	Marine Corps Exchange
MDA	Magen David Adom (Israeli equivalent of the Red Cross); maritime domain awareness
M-DARC	military direct access radar channel
M-day	mobilization day; unnamed day on which mobilization of forces begins
MDCI	multidiscipline counterintelligence
MDDOC	Marine air-ground task force (MAGTF) deployment and distribution operations center
MDF	Main Defense Forces (NATO); main distribution frame
MDITDS	migration defense intelligence threat data system; Modernized Defense Intelligence Threat Data System
MDMA	methylenedioxymethamphetamine
MDR	medium data rate
MDRO	mission disaster response officer
MDS	Message Dissemination Subsystem; mission design series
MDSS II	Marine air-ground task force (MAGTF) Deployment Support System II
MDSU	mobile diving and salvage unit
MDW	Military District of Washington
MDZ	maritime defense zone
MEA	munitions effect assessment; munitions effectiveness assessment
MEB	Marine expeditionary brigade
MEBU	mission essential backup
MEC	medium endurance cutter
ME/C	medical examiner and/or coroner
MED	manipulative electronic deception
MEDAL	Mine Warfare Environmental Decision Aids Library
MEDCAP	medical civic action program
MEDCC	medical coordination cell
MEDCOM	medical command; US Army Medical Command
MEDEVAC	medical evacuation
MEDINT	medical intelligence

MEDLOG	medical logistics (USAF AIS)
MEDLOGCO	medical logistics company
MEDLOG JR	medical logistics, junior (USAF)
MEDMOB	Medical Mobilization Planning and Execution System
MEDNEO	medical noncombatant evacuation operation
MEDREG	medical regulating
MEDREGREP	medical regulating report
MEDRETE	medical readiness training exercise
MEDS	meteorological data system
MEDSOM	medical supply, optical, and maintenance unit
MEDSTAT	medical status
MEF	Marine expeditionary force
MEFPAKA	manpower and equipment force packaging
MEL	maintenance expenditure limit; minimum equipment list
MEO	medium Earth orbit; military equal opportunity
MEP	mobile electric power
MEPCOM	military entrance processing command
MEPES	Medical Planning and Execution System
MEPRS	Military Entrance Processing and Reporting System
MERCO	merchant ship reporting and control
MERSHIPS	merchant ships
MES	medical equipment set
MESAR	minimum-essential security assistance requirements
MESF	maritime expeditionary security force
MET	medium equipment transporter; mobile environmental team
METAR	meteorological airfield report; meteorological aviation report
METARS	routine aviation weather report (roughly translated from French; international standard code format for hourly surface weather observations)
METCON	control of meteorological information (roughly translated from French); meteorological control (Navy)
METL	mission-essential task list
METMF	meteorological mobile facility
METMR(R)	meteorological mobile facility (replacement)
METOC	meteorological and oceanographic
METSAT	meteorological satellite
METT-T	mission, enemy, terrain and weather, troops and support available—time available
METT-TC	mission, enemy, terrain and weather, troops and support available-time available and civil considerations (Army)
MEU	Marine expeditionary unit
MEU(SOC)	Marine expeditionary unit (special operations capable)
MEVA	mission essential vulnerable area
MEWSG	Multi-Service Electronic Warfare Support Group (NATO)
MEZ	missile engagement zone
MF	medium frequency; mobile facility; multi-frequency
MFC	multinational force commander
MFDS	Modular Fuel Delivery System
MFE	manpower force element
MFFIMS	mass fatality field information management system
MFO	multinational force and observers
MFP	major force program
MFPC	maritime future plans center
MFPF	minefield planning folder
MFS	multifunction switch
MGB	medium girder bridge
MGM	master group multiplexer
MGRS	military grid reference system
MGS	mobile ground system
MGT	management
MGW	maximum gross weight
MHC	management headquarters ceiling
MHE	materials handling equipment
MHU	modular heat unit
MHW	mean high water
MHz	megahertz
MI	military intelligence; movement instructions
MIA	missing in action
MIAC	maritime intelligence and analysis center
MIB	Military Intelligence Board
MIC	Multinational Interoperability Council
MICAP	mission capable/mission capability
MICON	mission concept
MICRO-MICS	micro-medical inventory control system
MICRO-SNAP	micro-shipboard non-tactical automated data processing system
MIDAS	model for intertheater deployment by air and sea
MIDB	modernized integrated database; modernized intelligence database
MIDDS-T	Meteorological and Oceanographic (METOC) Integrated Data Display System-Tactical
MIF	maritime interception force

MIJI	meaconing, interference, jamming, and intrusion	*MLEA*	Maritime Law Enforcement Academy
MILALOC	military air line of communications	*MLG*	Marine logistics group
MILCON	military construction	*MLI*	munitions list item
MILDEC	military deception	*MLMC*	medical logistics management center
MILDEP	Military Department	*MLO*	military liaison office
MILGP	military group (assigned to American Embassy in host nation)	*MLP*	message load plan
		MLPP	multilevel precedence and preemption
MILOB	military observer	*MLPS*	Medical Logistics Proponent Subcommittee
MILOC	military oceanography group (NATO)		
MILPERS	military personnel	*MLRS*	Multiple Launch Rocket System
MILSATCOM	military satellite communications	*MLS*	microwave landing system; multilevel security
MILSPEC	military specification		
MILSTAMP	military standard transportation and movement procedures	*MLSA*	mutual logistics support agreement
		MLW	mean low water
MILSTAR	military strategic and tactical relay system	*MMA*	military mission area
		MMAC	military mine action center
MIL-STD	military standard	*MMC*	materiel management center
MILSTRAP	military standard transaction reporting and accounting procedure	*MMG*	DOD Master Mobilization Guide
		MMI	man/machine interface
MILSTRIP	military standard requisitioning and issue procedure	*MMLS*	mobile microwave landing system
		MMS	mast-mounted sight
MILTECH	military technician	*MMT*	military mail terminal
MILU	multinational integrated logistic support unit	*MNCC*	multinational coordination center
		MNF	multinational force
MILVAN	military van (container)	*MNFACC*	multinational force air component commander
MIM	maintenance instruction manual		
MIMP	Mobilization Information Management Plan	*MNFC*	multinational force commander
		MNFLCC	multinational force land component commander
MINEOPS	joint minelaying operations		
MIO	maritime interception operations	*MNFMCC*	multinational force maritime component commander
MIO-9	information operations threat analysis division (DIA)		
		MNFSOCC	multinational force special operations component commander
MIP	Military Intelligence Program		
MIPE	mobile intelligence processing element	*MNJLC*	multinational joint logistics component
MIPOE	medical intelligence preparation of the operational environment	*MNL*	multinational logistics
		MNLC	multinational logistic center
MIPR	military interdepartmental purchase request	*MNP*	master navigation plan
		MNS	mine neutralization system (USN); mission needs statement
MIS	maritime intelligence summary		
MISCAP	mission capability	*MNTF*	multinational task force
MISREP	mission report	*MO*	medical officer; month
MISS	missing	*MOA*	memorandum of agreement; military operating area
MIST	military information support team		
MITASK	mission tasking	*MOADS*	maneuver-oriented ammunition distribution system
MITO	minimum interval takeoff		
MITT	mobile integrated tactical terminal	*MOB*	main operating base; main operations base; mobilization
MIUW	mobile inshore undersea warfare		
MIUWU	mobile inshore undersea warfare unit	*MOBCON*	mobilization control
MIW	mine warfare	*MOBREP*	military manpower mobilization and accession status report; mobilization report
MJCS	Joint Chiefs of Staff memorandum		
MJLC	multinational joint logistic center	*MOC*	maritime operations center; media operations center
M-Kill	mobility kill		
MLA	mission load allowance	*MOCC*	measurement and signature intelligence (MASINT) operations coordination center; mobile operations control center
MLAYREP	mine laying report		
MLE	maritime law enforcement		

MOD	Minister (Ministry) of Defense
MODEM	modulator/demodulator
MODLOC	miscellaneous operational details, local operations
MOD T-AGOS	modified tactical auxiliary general ocean surveillance
MOE	measure of effectiveness
MOG	maximum (aircraft) on ground; movement on ground (aircraft); multinational observer group
MOGAS	motor gasoline
MOLE	multichannel operational line evaluator
MOMAT	mobility matting
MOMSS	mode and message selection system
MOP	measure of performance; memorandum of policy
MOPP	mission-oriented protective posture
MOR	memorandum of record
MOS	military occupational specialty
MOSC	meteorological and oceanographic operations support community
MOTR	maritime operational threat response
MOU	memorandum of understanding
MOUT	military operations in urban terrain; military operations on urbanized terrain
MOVREP	movement report
MOW	maintenance orderwire
MP	military police (Army and Marine); multinational publication
MPA	maritime patrol aircraft; mission and payload assessment; mission planning agent
MPAT	military patient administration team; Multinational Planning Augmentation Team
MPC	mid-planning conference; military personnel center
MPE/S	maritime pre-positioning equipment and supplies
MPF	maritime pre-positioning force
MPG	maritime planning group; mensurated point graphic
mph	miles per hour
MPLAN	Marine Corps Mobilization Management Plan
MPM	medical planning module
MPNTP	Master Positioning Navigation and Timing Plan
MPO	military post office
MPP	maritime procedural publication
MPR	maritime patrol and reconnaissance
MPRS	multi-point refueling system
MPS	maritime pre-positioning ship; message processor shelter; Military Postal Service
MPSA	Military Postal Service Agency
MPSRON	maritime pre-positioning ships squadron
MR	milliradian; mobile reserve
MRAALS	Marine remote area approach and landing system
MRAT	medical radiobiology advisory team
MRCI	maximum rescue coverage intercept
MRE	meal, ready to eat
MRG	movement requirements generator
MRI	magnetic resonance imaging
MRMC	US Army Medical Research and Materiel Command
MRO	mass rescue operation; materiel release order; medical regulating office; medical regulating officer
MROC	multicommand required operational capability
MRR	minimum-risk route
MRRR	mobility requirement resource roster
MRS	measurement and signature intelligence (MASINT) requirements system; meteorological radar subsystem; movement report system
MRSA	Materiel Readiness Support Agency
MRT	maintenance recovery team
MRU	mountain rescue unit
MS	message switch
ms	millisecond
MSC	major subordinate command; maritime support center; Military Sealift Command; military staff committee; mission support confirmation
MSCA	military support to civil authorities; military support to civilian authorities
MSCD	military support to civil defense
MSCLEA	military support to civilian law enforcement agencies
MSCO	Military Sealift Command Office
MSD	marginal support date; mobile security division
MS-DOS	Microsoft disk operating system
MSDS	mission specific data set
MSE	mission support element; mobile subscriber equipment;
MSECR	HIS 6000 security module
MSEL	master scenario events list
MSF	*Medicins Sans Frontieres* ("Doctors Without Borders"); mission support force; mobile security force; multiplex signal format
MSG	Marine Security Guard; message

MSGID	message identification	*MTL*	mission tasking letter
MSHARPP	mission, symbolism, history, accessibility, recognizability, population, and proximity	*MTMS*	maritime tactical message system
		MTN	multi-tactical data link network
		MTO	message to observer; mission type order
MSI	modified surface index; multispectral imagery	*MTOE*	modified table of organization and equipment
MSIC	Missile and Space Intelligence Center	*MTON*	measurement ton
MSIS	Marine safety information system	*MTP*	maritime task plan; mission tasking packet
MSK	mission support kit		
MSL	master station log	*MTS*	Movement Tracking System
MSNAP	merchant ship naval augmentation program	*MTS/SOF-IRIS*	multifunction system
		MTT	magnetic tape transport; mobile training team
MSO	map support office; marine safety office(r); maritime security operations; military satellite communications (MILSATCOM) systems organization; military source operation; military strategic objective; military support operations; mobilization staff officer	*MTTP*	multi-Service tactics, techniques, and procedures
		MTW	major theater war
		MTX	message text format
		MU	marry up
		MUL	master urgency list (DOD)
MSOC	Marine special operations company	*MULE*	modular universal laser equipment
MSP	mission support plan; mobile sensor platform	*MUREP*	munitions report
		MUSARC	major United States Army reserve commands
MSPES	mobilization stationing, planning, and execution system	*MUSE*	mobile utilities support equipment
MSPS	mobilization stationing and planning system	*MUST*	medical unit, self-contained, transportable
MSR	main supply route; maritime support request; mission support request	*MUX*	multiplex
		MV	merchant vessel; motor vessel
MSRON	maritime expeditionary security squadron	*mV*	millivolt
MSRR	modeling and simulation resource repository	*MWBP*	missile warning bypass
		MWC	Missile Warning Center (NORAD)
MSRV	message switch rekeying variable	*MWD*	military working dog
MSS	medical surveillance system; meteorological satellite subsystem	*MWDT*	military working dog team
		MWF	medical working file
MSSG	Marine expeditionary unit (MEU) service support group	*MWG*	mobilization working group
		MWOD	multiple word-of-day
MST	Marine expeditionary force (MEF) weather support team; meteorological and oceanographic support team; mission support team	*MWR*	missile warning receiver; morale, welfare, and recreation
		MWSG	Marine wing support group
		MWSS	Marine wing support squadron
M/T	measurement ton	*N*	number of required track spacings; number of search and rescue units (SRUs)
MT	measurement ton; military technician; ministry team		
MTA	military training agreement	*N-1*	Navy component manpower or personnel staff officer
MTAC	Multiple Threat Alert Center		
MTBF	mean time between failures	*N-2*	Director of Naval Intelligence; Navy component intelligence staff officer
MT Bn	motor transport battalion		
MTCR	missile technology control regime	*N-3*	Navy component operations staff officer
MT/D	measurement tons per day		
MTF	medical treatment facility; message text format	*N-4*	Navy component logistics staff officer
		N-5	Navy component plans staff officer
MTG	master timing generator	*N-6*	Navy component communications staff officer
MTI	moving target indicator		
MTIC	Military Targeting Intelligence Committee		

NA	nation assistance
NAAG	North Atlantic Treaty Organization (NATO) Army Armaments Group
NAC	North American Aerospace Defense Command (NORAD) Air Center; North Atlantic Council (NATO)
NACE	National Military Command System (NMCS) Automated Control Executive
NACISA	North Atlantic Treaty Organization (NATO) Communications and Information Systems Agency
NACISC	North Atlantic Treaty Organization (NATO) Communications and Information Systems Committee
NACSEM	National Communications Security/Emanations Security (COMSEC/EMSEC) Information Memorandum
NACSI	national communications security (COMSEC) instruction
NACSIM	national communications security (COMSEC) information memorandum
NADEFCOL	North Atlantic Treaty Organization (NATO) Defense College
NADEP	naval aircraft depot
NAE	Navy acquisition executive
NAEC-ENG	Naval Air Engineering Center—Engineering
NAF	naval air facility; nonappropriated funds; numbered air force
NAFAG	North Atlantic Treaty Organization (NATO) Air Force Armaments Group
NAI	named area of interest
NAIC	National Air Intelligence Center
NAK	negative acknowledgement
NALC	Navy ammunition logistics code
NALE	naval and amphibious liaison element
NALSS	naval advanced logistic support site
NAMP	North Atlantic Treaty Organization (NATO) Annual Manpower Plan
NAMS	National Air Mobility System
NAMTO	Navy material transportation office
NAOC	national airborne operations center (E-4B aircraft)
NAPCAP	North Atlantic Treaty Organization (NATO) Allied Pre-Committed Civil Aircraft Program
NAPMA	North Atlantic Treaty Organization (NATO) Airborne Early Warning and Control Program Management Agency
NAPMIS	Navy Preventive Medicine Information System
NAR	nonconventional assisted recovery; notice of ammunition reclassification
NARAC	national atmospheric release advisory capability
NARC	non-automatic relay center
NAS	naval air station
NASA	National Aeronautics and Space Administration
NASAR	National Association for Search and Rescue
NAS computer	national airspace system computer
NASIC	National Air and Space Intelligence Center
NAT	nonair-transportable (cargo)
NATO	North Atlantic Treaty Organization
NATOPS	Naval Air Training and Operating Procedures Standardization
NAU	Narcotics Assistance Unit
NAVAID	navigation aid
NAVAIDS	navigational aids
NAVAIR	naval air; Naval Air Systems Command
NAVAIRSYSCOM	Naval Air Systems Command (Also called NAVAIR)
NAVATAC	Navy Antiterrorism Analysis Center; Navy Antiterrorist Alert Center
NAVCHAPDET	naval cargo handling and port group detachment
NAVCHAPGRU	Navy cargo handling and port group
NAVCOMSTA	naval communications station
NAVELSG	Navy Expeditionary Logistic Support Group
NAVEODTECHDIV	Naval Explosives Ordnance Disposal Technology Division
NAVEURMETOCCEN	Naval Europe Meteorology and Oceanography Center
NAVFAC	Naval Facilities Engineering Command
NAVFACENGCOM	Naval Facilities Engineering Command
NAVFAC-X	Naval Facilities Engineering Command-expeditionary
NAVFAX	Navy facsimile
NAVFOR	Navy forces
NAVICECEN	Naval Ice Center
NAVLANTMETOCCEN	Naval Atlantic Meteorology and Oceanography Center
NAVMAG	naval magazine
NAVMED	Navy Medical; Navy medicine
NAVMEDCOMINST	Navy medical command instruction
NAVMEDLOGCOM	Navy Medical Logistical Command
NAVMEDP	Navy medical pamphlet

NAVMETOCCOM	Naval Meteorology and Oceanography Command
NAVMTO	naval military transportation office; Navy Material Transportation Office
NAVOCEANO	Naval Oceanographic Office
NAVORD	naval ordnance
NAVORDSTA	naval ordnance station
NAVPACMETOCCEN	Naval Pacific Meteorology and Oceanography Center
NAVSAFECEN	naval safety center
NAVSAT	navigation satellite
NAVSEA	Naval Sea Systems Command
NAVSEAINST	Naval Sea Systems Command instruction
NAVSEALOGCEN	naval sea logistics center
NAVSEASYSCOM	Naval Sea Systems Command
NAVSO	United States Navy Forces, Southern Command
NAVSOC	Naval Satellite Operations Center; naval special operations command; naval special operations component; naval special warfare special operations component; Navy special operations component
NAVSOF	naval special operations forces; Navy special operations forces
NAVSPACECOM	Naval Space Command
NAVSPECWARCOM	Naval Special Warfare Command
NAVSPOC	Naval Space Operations Center
NAVSUP	naval supply; Naval Supply Systems Command
NAVSUPINST	Navy Support Instruction
NAVSUPSYSCOM	Naval Supply Systems Command
NAVWAR	navigation warfare
NAWCAD	Naval Air Warfare Center, Aircraft Division
NB	narrowband
NBC	nuclear, biological, and chemical
NBCCS	nuclear, biological, and chemical (NBC) contamination survivability
NBDP	narrow band direct printing
NBG	naval beach group
NBI	nonbattle injury
NBS	National Bureau of Standards
NBST	narrowband secure terminal
NBVC	Naval Base Ventura County
NC3A	nuclear command, control, and communications (C3) assessment
NCAA	North Atlantic Treaty Organization (NATO) Civil Airlift Agency
NCAGS	naval cooperation and guidance for shipping
NCAPS	naval coordination and protection of shipping
NCB	national central bureau; naval construction brigade
NCC	National Coordinating Center; naval component commander; Navy component command; Navy component commander; network control center; North American Aerospace Defense Command (NORAD) Command Center
NCCS	Nuclear Command and Control System
NCD	net control device
NCDC	National Climatic Data Center
NCESGR	National Committee of Employer Support for the Guard and Reserve
NCF	naval construction force
NCFSU	naval construction force support unit
NCHB	Navy cargo handling battalion
NCHF	Navy cargo handling force
NCIC	National Crime Information Center
NCI&KA	national critical infrastructure and key assets
NCIS	Naval Criminal Investigative Service
NCISRA	Naval Criminal Investigative Service resident agent
NCISRO	Naval Criminal Investigative Service regional office
NCISRU	Naval Criminal Investigative Service resident unit
NCIX	National Counterintelligence Executive
NCMP	Navy Capabilities and Mobilization Plan
NCO	noncombat operations; noncommissioned officer
NCOB	National Counterintelligence Operations Board
NCOIC	noncommissioned officer in charge
NCOS	naval control of shipping
NCP	National Oil and Hazardous Substances Pollution Contingency Plan
NCR	National Capital Region (US); national cryptologic representative; National Security Agency/Central Security Service representative; naval construction regiment
NCRCC	National Capital Region Coordination Center
NCRCG	National Cyber Response Coordination Group
NCRDEF	national cryptologic representative defense

NCR-IADS	National Capital Region—Integrated Air Defense System
NCS	National Clandestine Service; National Communications System; naval control of shipping; net control station
NCSC	National Computer Security Center
NCSE	national intelligence support team (NIST) communications support element
NCT	network control terminal
NCTAMS	naval computer and telecommunications area master station
NCTC	National Counterterrorism Center; North East Counterdrug Training Center
NCTS	naval computer and telecommunications station
NCWS	naval coastal warfare squadron
NDA	national defense area
NDAA	National Defense Authorization Act
NDAF	Navy, Defense Logistics Agency, Air Force
N-day	day an active duty unit is notified for deployment or redeployment
NDB	nondirectional beacon
NDCS	national drug control strategy
NDDOC	US Northern Command Deployment and Distribution Operations Center
NDHQ	National Defence Headquarters, Canada
NDIC	National Drug Intelligence Center
NDL	national desired ground zero list
NDMC	North Atlantic Treaty Organization (NATO) Defense Manpower Committee
NDMS	National Disaster Medical System
NDOC	National Defense Operations Center
NDP	national disclosure policy
NDPB	National Drug Policy Board
NDPC	National Disclosure Policy Committee
NDRC	national detainee reporting center
NDRF	National Defense Reserve Fleet
NDS	national defense strategy
NDSF	National Defense Sealift Fund
NDU	National Defense University
NEA	Northeast Asia
NEAT	naval embarked advisory team
NECC	Navy Expeditionary Combat Command
NEMT	National Emergency Management Team
NEO	noncombatant evacuation operation
NEOCC	noncombatant evacuation operation coordination center
NEPA	National Environmental Policy Act
NEREP	Nuclear Execution and Reporting Plan
NES	National Exploitation System
NESDIS	National Environmental Satellite, Data and Information Service (DOC)
NEST	nuclear emergency support team
NETOPS	network operations
NETS	Nationwide Emergency Telecommunications System
NETT	new equipment training team
NETWARCOM	Naval Network Warfare Command
NEW	naval expeditionary warfare; net explosive weight
NEWAC	North Atlantic Treaty Organization (NATO) Electronic Warfare Advisory Committee
NEWCS	NATO electronic warfare core staff
NEXCOM	Navy Exchange Command
NFA	no-fire area
NFD	nodal fault diagnostics
NFELC	Naval Facilities Expeditionary Logistics Center
NFESC	Naval Facilities Engineering Service Center
NFI	national foreign intelligence
NFIB	National Foreign Intelligence Board
NFIP	National Flood Insurance Program (FEMA); National Foreign Intelligence Program
NFLIR	navigation forward-looking infrared
NFLS	naval forward logistic site
NFN	national file number
NFO	naval flight officer
NG	National Guard
NGA	National Geospatial-Intelligence Agency
NGB	National Guard Bureau
NGB-OC	National Guard Bureau—Office of the Chaplain
NGF	naval gun fire
NGFS	naval gunfire support
NGIC	National Ground Intelligence Center
NGLO	naval gunfire liaison officer
NGO	nongovernmental organization
NGP	National Geospatial-Intelligence Agency Program
NGRF	National Guard reaction force
NHCS	nonhostile casualty
NI	national identification (number); noted item
NIBRS	National Incident-Based Reporting System
NIC	National Intelligence Council; naval intelligence center
NICCP	National Interdiction Command and Control Plan
NICI	National Interagency Counternarcotics Institute
NID	naval intelligence database

NIDMS	National Military Command System (NMCS) Information for Decision Makers System	NMET	naval mobile environmental team
NIDS	National Military Command Center (NMCC) information display system	NMFS	National Marine Fisheries Services
		NMIC	National Maritime Intelligence Center
NIE	national intelligence estimate	NMIST	National Military Intelligence Support Team (DIA)
NIEX	no-notice interoperability exercise	NMOC	network management operations center
NIEXPG	No-Notice Interoperability Exercise Planning Group	NMOSW	Naval METOC Operational Support Web
NIFC	national interagency fire center		
NII	national information infrastructure	NMP	national media pool
NIIB	National Geospatial Intelligence Agency imagery intelligence brief	NMPS	Navy mobilization processing site
		NMR	news media representative
NIL	National Information Library	NMRC	Naval Medical Research Center
NIMCAMP	National Information Management and Communications Master Plan	NMS	National Military Strategy
		NMSA	North Atlantic Treaty Organization (NATO) Mutual Support Act
NIMS	National Incident Management System		
NIOC	Navy Information Operations Command	NMS-CO	National Military Strategy for Cyberspace Operations
NIP	National Intelligence Program		
NIPRNET	Non-Secure Internet Protocol Router Network	NMS-CWMD	National Military Strategy to Combat Weapons of Mass Destruction
NIPS	Naval Intelligence Processing System	NMSP-WOT	National Military Strategic Plan for the War on Terrorism
NIRT	Nuclear Incident Response Team		
NISH	noncombatant evacuation operation (NEO) intelligence support handbook	NNAG	North Atlantic Treaty Organization (NATO) Naval Armaments Group
NISP	national intelligence support plan; Nuclear Weapons Intelligence Support Plan	NNSA	National Nuclear Security Administration
NIST	National Institute of Standards and Technology; national intelligence support team	NOAA	National Oceanic and Atmospheric Administration
		NOACT	Navy overseas air cargo terminal
NITES	Navy Integrated Tactical Environmental System	NOC	National Operations Center; network operations center
NITF	national imagery transmission format	NOCONTRACT	not releasable to contractors or consultants
NIU	North Atlantic Treaty Organization (NATO) interface unit	NODDS	Naval Oceanographic Data Distribution System
NIWA	naval information warfare activity		
NL	Navy lighterage	NOE	nap-of-the-earth
NLO	naval liaison officer	NOEA	nuclear operations emergency action
.NL.	not less than		
NLT	not later than	NOFORN	not releasable to foreign nationals
NLW	nonlethal weapon	NOG	Nuclear Operations Group
NM	network management	NOGAPS	Navy Operational Global Atmospheric Prediction System
nm	nautical mile		
NMAWC	Naval Mine and Anti-Submarine Warfare Command	NOHD	nominal ocular hazard distance
		NOIC	Naval Operational Intelligence Center
NMB	North Atlantic Treaty Organization (NATO) military body		
		NOK	next of kin
NMCB	naval mobile construction battalion	NOLSC	Naval Operational Logistics Support Center
NMCC	National Military Command Center		
NMCM	not mission capable, maintenance	NOMS	Nuclear Operations Monitoring System
NMCS	National Military Command System; not mission capable, supply		
		NOP	nuclear operations
NMD	national missile defense	NOPLAN	no operation plan available or prepared
NMEC	National Media Exploitation Center		

NORAD	North American Aerospace Defense Command
NORM	normal; not operationally ready, maintenance
NORS	not operationally ready, supply
NOSC	network operations and security center
NOSSA	Navy Ordnance Safety and Security Activity
NOTAM	notice to airmen
NOTMAR	notice to mariners
NP	nonproliferation
NPC	Nonproliferation Center
NPES	Nuclear Planning and Execution System
NPG	nonunit personnel generator
NPOESS	National Polar-orbiting Operational Environmental Satellite System
NPS	National Park Service; nonprior service; Nuclear Planning System
NPT	national pipe thread; Treaty on the Non-proliferation of Nuclear Weapons
NPWIC	National Prisoner of War Information Center
NQ	nonquota
NR	North Atlantic Treaty Organization (NATO) restricted; number
NRC	National Response Center; non-unit-related cargo
NRCC	national response coordination center
NRCHB	Naval Reserve cargo handling battalion
NRCHF	Naval Reserve cargo handling force
NRCHTB	Naval Reserve cargo handling training battalion
NRF	National Response Framework
NRFI	not ready for issue
NRG	notional requirements generator
NRL	nuclear weapons (NUWEP) reconnaissance list
NRO	National Reconnaissance Office
NROC	Northern Regional Operations Center (CARIBROC-CBRN)
NRP	National Response Plan; non-unit-related personnel
NRPC	Naval Reserve Personnel Center
NRT	near real time
NRTD	near-real-time dissemination
NRZ	non-return-to-zero
NS	nuclear survivability
NSA	national security act; National Security Agency; national security area; national shipping authority; North Atlantic Treaty Organization (NATO) Standardization Agency
NSA/CSS	National Security Agency/Central Security Service
NSAWC	Naval Strike and Air Warfare Center
NSC	National Security Council
NSC/DC	Deputies Committee of the National Security Council
NSCID	National Security Council intelligence directive
NSC/IWG	National Security Council/Interagency Working Group
NSC/PC	National Security Council/Principals Committee
NSC/PCC	National Security Council Policy Coordinating Committee
NSCS	National Security Council System
NSCTI	Naval Special Clearance Team One
NS-CWMD	National Strategy to Combat Weapons of Mass Destruction
NSD	National Security Directive; National Security Division (FBI)
NSDA	non-self-deployment aircraft
NSDD	national security decision directive
NSDM	national security decision memorandum
NSDS-E	Navy Satellite Display System-Enhanced
NSE	national support element; Navy support element
NSEP	national security emergency preparedness
NSF	National Science Foundation
NSFS	naval surface fire support
NSG	National System for Geospatial Intelligence; north-seeking gyro
NSGI	National System for Geospatial Intelligence
NSHS	National Strategy for Homeland Security
NSI	not seriously injured
NSL	no-strike list
NSM	national search and rescue (SAR) manual
NSMS	National Strategy for Maritime Security
NSN	national stock number
NSNF	nonstrategic nuclear forces
NSO	non-Single Integrated Operational Plan (SIOP) option
NSOC	National Security Operations Center; National Signals Intelligence (SIGINT) Operations Center; Navy Satellite Operations Center
NSOOC	North Atlantic Treaty Organization (NATO) Staff Officer Orientation Course
NSP	national search and rescue plan
N-Sp/CC	North American Aerospace Defense Command (NORAD)-US Space Command/Command Center
NSPD	national security Presidential directive
NSRL	national signals intelligence (SIGINT) requirements list
NSS	National Search and Rescue Supplement; National Security Strategy; national security system; non-self-sustaining
NSSA	National Security Space Architect

NSSE	national special security event	NUCINT	nuclear intelligence
NSST	naval space support team	NUDET	nuclear detonation
NST	National Geospatial-Intelligence Agency support team	NUDETS	nuclear detonation detection and reporting system
NSTAC	National Security Telecommunications Advisory Committee	NUFEA	Navy-unique fleet essential aircraft
		NUP	non-unit-related personnel
NSTISSC	National Security Telecommunications and Information Systems Security Committee	NURC	non-unit-related cargo
		NURP	non-unit-related personnel
		NUWEP	policy guidance for the employment of nuclear weapons
NSTL	national strategic targets list		
NSTS	National Secure Telephone System	NVD	night vision device
NSW	naval special warfare	NVDT	National Geospatial-Intelligence Agency voluntary deployment team
NSWCDD	Naval Surface Warfare Center Dahlgren Division		
		NVG	night vision goggle(s)
NSWCOM	Naval Special Warfare Command	NVS	night vision system
NSWG	naval special warfare group	NW	network warfare; not waiverable
NSWTE	naval special warfare task element	NWARS	National Wargaming System
NSWTF	naval special warfare task force	NWB	normal wideband
NSWTG	naval special warfare task group	NWBLTU	normal wideband line termination unit
NSWTU	naval special warfare task unit	NWDC	Navy Warfare Development Command
NSWU	naval special warfare unit	NWFP	Northwest Frontier Province (Pakistan)
NT	nodal terminal	NWP	Navy warfare publication; numerical weather prediction
NTACS	Navy tactical air control system		
NTAP	National Track Analysis Program	NWREP	nuclear weapons report
NTB	national target base	NWS	National Weather Service
NTBC	National Military Joint Intelligence Center Targeting and Battle Damage Assessment Cell	NWT	normal wideband terminal
		1MC	general announcing system
		1NCD	1st Naval Construction Division
NTC	National Training Center	O	contour pattern
NTCS-A	Navy Tactical Command System Afloat	O&I	operations and intelligence
NTDS	naval tactical data system	O&M	operation and maintenance
NTF	nuclear task force	OA	objective area; operating assembly; operational area; Operations Aerology shipboard METOC division
N-TFS	New Tactical Forecast System		
NTIC	Navy Tactical Intelligence Center		
NTISS	National Telecommunications and Information Security System	OADR	originating agency's determination required
NTISSI	National Telecommunications and Information Security System (NTISS) Instruction	OAE	operational area evaluation
		OAF	Operation ALLIED FORCE
		OAFME	Office of the Armed Forces Medical Examiner
NTISSP	National Telecommunications and Information Security System (NTISS) Policy		
		OAG	operations advisory group
NTM	national or multinational technical means of verification; notice to mariners	OAI	oceanographic area of interest
		OAJCG	Operation Alliance joint control group
		OAP	offset aimpoint
NTMPDE	National Telecommunications Master Plan for Drug Enforcement	OAR	Chairman of the Joint Chiefs of Staff operation plans assessment report
NTMS	national telecommunications management structure	OAS	offensive air support; Organization of American States
NTPS	near-term pre-positioned ships		
NTRP	Navy tactical reference publication	OASD	Office of the Assistant Secretary of Defense
NTS	night targeting system; noncombatant evacuation operation tracking system		
		OASD(PA)	Office of the Assistant Secretary of Defense (Public Affairs)
NTSB	National Transportation Safety Board		
NTSS	National Time-Sensitive System	OASD(RA)	Office of the Assistant Secretary of Defense (Reserve Affairs)
NTTP	Navy tactics, techniques, and procedures		
NTU	new threat upgrade	OAU	Organization of African Unity
NUC	non-unit-related cargo; nuclear	O/B	outboard

OB	operating base; order of battle
OBA	oxygen breathing apparatus
OBFS	offshore bulk fuel system
OBST	obstacle
OBSTINTEL	obstacle intelligence
OC	oleoresin capsicum ; operations center
OCA	offensive counterair; operational control authority
OCC	Operations Computer Center (USCG)
OCCA	Ocean Cargo Clearance Authority
OCD	orderwire clock distributor
OCDEFT	organized crime drug enforcement task force
OCE	officer conducting the exercise
OCEANCON	control of oceanographic information
OCHA	Office for the Coordination of Humanitarian Affairs
OCJCS	Office of the Chairman of the Joint Chiefs of Staff
OCJCS-PA	Office of the Chairman of the Joint Chiefs of Staff–Public Affairs
OCMI	officer in charge, Marine inspection
OCO	offload control officer
OCONUS	outside the continental United States
OCOP	outline contingency operation plan
OCP	operational configuration processing
OCR	Office of Collateral Responsibility
OCU	orderwire control unit (Types I, II, and III)
OCU-1	orderwire control unit-1
OD	operational detachment; other detainee
ODA	operational detachment-Alpha
ODATE	organization date
O-Day	off-load day
ODB	operational detachment-Bravo
ODC	Office of Defense Cooperation
ODCSLOG	Office of the Deputy Chief of Staff for Logistics (Army)
ODCSOPS	Office of the Deputy Chief of Staff for Operations and Plans (Army)
ODCSPER	Office of the Deputy Chief of Staff for Personnel (Army)
ODIN	Operational Digital Network
ODJS	Office of the Director, Joint Staff
ODR	Office of Defense representative
ODZ	outer defense zone
OEBGD	Overseas Environmental Baseline Guidance Document
OE	operational environment
OEF	Operation ENDURING FREEDOM
OEG	operational experts group; operational exposure guide; operations security (OPSEC) executive group
OEH	occupational and environmental health
OEM	original equipment manufacturer
OER	officer evaluation report; operational electronic intelligence (ELINT) requirements
OES	office of emergency services
OET	Office of Emergency Transportation (DOT)
OF	officer (NATO)
OFAC	Office of Foreign Assets Control
OFCO	offensive counterintelligence operation
OFDA	Office of US Foreign Disaster Assistance
OFHIS	operational fleet hospital information system
OFOESA	Office of Field Operational and External Support Activities
OGA	other government agency
OGS	overseas ground station
OH	overhead
OHDACA	Overseas Humanitarian, Disaster, and Civic Aid
OHDM	Office of Humanitarian Assistance, Disaster Relief, and Mine Action
OI	Office of Intelligence (USCS); operating instruction
OI&A	Office of Intelligence and Analysis (DHS)
OIC	officer in charge
OICC	officer in charge of construction; operational intelligence coordination center
OID	operation order (OPORD) identification
OIF	Operation IRAQI FREEDOM
OIR	operational intelligence requirements; other intelligence requirements
OJT	on-the-job training
OL	operating location
OLD	on-line tests and diagnostics
OLS	operational linescan system; optical landing system
OM	contour multiunit
OMA	Office of Military Affairs (CIA)
OMB	Office of Management and Budget; operations management branch
OMC	Office of Military Cooperation; optical memory card
OMF	officer master file
OMS	Office of Mission Support
OMT	operations management team; orthogonal mode transducer
OMT/OMTP	operational maintenance test(ing)/test plan
ONDCP	Office of National Drug Control Policy
ONE	Operation NOBLE EAGLE
ONI	Office of Naval Intelligence
OOB	order of battle
OOD	officer of the deck

OODA	observe, orient, decide, act
OOS	out of service
OP	observation post; operational publication (USN); ordnance publication
OPARS	Optimum Path Aircraft Routing System
OPBAT	Operation Bahamas, Turks, and Caicos
OPCEN	operations center (USCG)
OPCOM	operational command (NATO)
OPCON	operational control
OPDEC	operational deception
OPDS	offshore petroleum discharge system
OPE	operational preparation of the environment
OPELINT	operational electronic intelligence
OPFOR	opposing force; opposition force
OPG	operations planning group
OPGEN	operation general matter
OPLAN	operation plan
OPLAW	operational law
OPM	Office of Personnel Management; operations per minute
OPMG	Office of the Provost Marshal General
OPNAVINST	Chief of Naval Operations instruction
OPORD	operation order
OPP	off-load preparation party; orderwire patch panel
OPR	office of primary responsibility
OPREP	operational report
OPROJ	operational project
OPS	operational project stock; operations; operations center
OPSCOM	Operations Committee
OPSDEPS	Service Operations Deputies
OPSEC	operations security
OPSTK	operational stock
OPSUM	operation summary
OPT	operational planning team
OPTAR	operating target
OPTASK	operation task
OPTASKLINK	operations task link
OPTEMPO	operating tempo
OPTINT	optical intelligence
OPZONE	operation zone
OR	operational readiness; other rank(s) (NATO)
ORBAT	order of battle
ORCON	originator controlled
ORD	Operational Requirements Document
ORDREF	order reference
ORDTYP	order type
ORG	origin (GEOLOC)
ORIG	origin
ORM	operational risk management
ORP	ocean reception point
ORS	operationally responsive space
OS	operating system
OSA	operational support airlift
OSAT	out-of-service analog test
OSC	offensive space control; on-scene commander; on-site commander; operational support command; operations support center
OSCE	Organization for Security and Cooperation in Europe
OSD	Office of the Secretary of Defense
OSE	on scene endurance; operations support element
OSEI	operational significant event imagery
OSG	operational support group
OSI	open system interconnection; operational subsystem interface
OSIA	on-site inspection activity
OSINT	open-source intelligence
OSIS	open-source information system
OSO	operational support office
OSOCC	on-site operations coordination center
OSP	operations support package
OSPG	overseas security policy group
OSRI	originating station routing indicator
OSV	ocean station vessel
OT	operational test
OT&E	operational test and evaluation
OTC	officer in tactical command; over the counter
OTG	operational target graphic
OTH	other; over the horizon
OTH-B	over-the-horizon backscatter (radar)
OTHT	over-the-horizon targeting
OTI	Office of Transition Initiatives
OTS	Officer Training School; one-time source
OUB	offshore petroleum discharge system (OPDS) utility boat
OUSD	Office of the Under Secretary of Defense
OUSD(AT&L)	Office of the Under Secretary of Defense (Acquisition, Technology, and Logistics)
OUSD(C)	Office of the Under Secretary of Defense (Comptroller)
OUSD(P)	Office of the Under Secretary of Defense (Policy)
OUT	outsize cargo
OVE	on-vehicle equipment
OVER	oversize cargo
OVM	Operation Vigilant Mariner
OW	orderwire

OWS	operational weather squadron	PC-LITE	processor, laptop imagery transmission equipment
P	parallel pattern; priority; publication	PCM	pulse code modulation
PA	parent relay; physician assistant; primary agency; probability of arrival; public affairs	PCO	primary control officer; procuring contracting officer
PAA	position area of artillery; primary aircraft authorization	PCRTS	primary casualty receiving and treatment ship
PABX	private automatic branch exchange (telephone)	PCS	permanent change of station; personal communications system; primary control ship; processing subsystem; processor controlled strapping
PACAF	Pacific Air Forces		
PAD	patient administration director; positional adjustment; precision aircraft direction	PCT	personnel control team
		PCTC	pure car and truck carrier
PADD	person authorized to direct disposition of human remains	PCZ	physical control zone
		PD	position description; Presidential directive; priority designator; probability of damage; probability of detection; procedures description; program definition; program directive; program director; public diplomacy
PADRU	Pan American Disaster Response Unit		
PADS	position azimuth determining system		
PAG	public affairs guidance		
PAI	primary aircraft inventory		
PAL	permissive action link; personnel allowance list; program assembler language		
		Pd	drift compensated parallelogram pattern
PALS	precision approach landing system		
PAM	preventive and aerospace medicine; pulse amplitude modulation	PDA	preliminary damage assessment
		PDAI	primary development/test aircraft inventory
PaM	passage material		
PANS	procedures for air navigation services	PDC	Pacific Disaster Center
PAO	public affairs office; public affairs officer	PDD	Presidential decision directive
PAR	performance assessment report; population at risk; precision approach radar	PDDA	power driven decontamination apparatus
		PDDG	program directive development group
PARC	principal assistant for contracting		
PARKHILL	high frequency cryptological device	PDG	positional data graphic
PARPRO	peacetime application of reconnaissance programs	PDM	program decision memorandum
		PDOP	position dilution of precision
PAS	personnel accounting symbol	PDS	position determining system; primary distribution site; protected distribution system
PAT	public affairs team		
PAV	policy assessment visit		
PAWS	phased array warning system		
PAX	passengers; public affairs plans	PDSC	public diplomacy and strategic communication
PB	particle beam; patrol boat; peace building; President's budget		
		PDU	psychological operations distribution unit
PB4T	planning board for training		
PBA	performance-based agreement; production base analysis	PDUSD(P&R)	Principal Deputy Under Secretary of Defense (Personnel & Readiness)
PBCR	portable bar code recorder	PE	peace enforcement; peacetime establishment; personal effects; program element
PBD	program budget decision		
PC	patrol craft; personal computer; pilot in command; preliminary coordination; Principals Committee		
		PEAD	Presidential emergency action document
Pc	cumulative probability of detection	PEAS	psychological operations (PSYOP) effects analysis subsystem
P,C,&H	packing, crating, and handling		
PCA	Posse Comitatus Act	PEC	program element code
PCC	policy coordination committee; primary control center	PECK	patient evacuation contingency kit
		PECP	precision engagement collaboration process
PCF	personnel control facility		
PCL	positive control launch		

PED	processing, exploitation, dissemination
PEDB	planning and execution database
PEGEO	personnel geographic location
PEI	principal end item
PEM	program element monitor
PEO	peace enforcement operations; program executive officer
PEP	personnel exchange program
PER	personnel
PERE	person eligible to receive effects
PERID	period
PERMREP	permanent representative (NATO)
PERSCO	personnel support for contingency operations
PERSCOM	personnel command (Army)
PERSINS	personnel information system
PES	preparedness evaluation system
PFA	primary federal agency
PFD	personal flotation device
PFDB	planning factors database
PFIAB	President's Foreign Intelligence Advisory Board
PFID	positive friendly identification
PFO	principal federal official
PFP	Partnership for Peace (NATO)
PGI	procedures, guidance, and information
PGM	precision-guided munition
pH	potential of hydrogen
PHEO	public health emergency officer
PHIBCB	amphibious construction battalion
PHIBGRU	amphibious group
PHIBOP	amphibious operation
PHIBRON	amphibious squadron
PHO	posthostilities operations
PHS	Public Health Service
PI	point of impact; probability of incapacitation; procedural item; purposeful interference
PIC	parent indicator code; payment in cash; person identification code; pilot in command; press information center (NATO)
PID	plan identification number
PIDD	planned inactivation or discontinued date
PIF	problem identification flag
PII	pre-incident indicators
PIM	pretrained individual manpower
PIN	personnel increment number
PINS	precise integrated navigation system
PIO	press information officer; public information officer
PIPS	plans integration partitioning system
PIR	priority intelligence requirement
PIRAZ	positive identification and radar advisory zone
PIREP	pilot report
PIRT	Purposeful Interference Response Team
PIW	person in water
PJ	pararescue jumper
PK	peacekeeping; probability of kill
PKG-POL	packaged petroleum, oils, and lubricants
PKI	public key infrastructure
PKO	peacekeeping operations
PKP	purple k powder
PL	phase line; public law
PLA	plain language address
PLAD	plain language address directory
PLANORD	planning order
PLAT	pilot's landing aid television
PLB	personal locator beacon
PLC	power line conditioner
PLGR	precise lightweight global positioning system (GPS) receiver
PLL	phase locked loop
PLL/ASL	prescribed load list/authorized stock level
PLRS	position location reporting system
PLS	palletized load system; personal locator system; personnel locator system; pillars of logistic support; precision location system
PLT	platoon; program library tape
PM	Bureau of Political-Military Affairs (DOS); parallel track multiunit; passage material; patient movement; peacemaking; political-military affairs; preventive medicine; program management; program manager; provost marshal
PMA	political/military assessment
PMAA	Production Management Alternative Architecture
PMAI	primary mission aircraft inventory
P/M/C	passengers/mail/cargo
PMC	parallel multiunit circle
PMCF	post maintenance check flight
PMCT	port movement control team
PMD	program management directive
PME	professional military education
PMEL	precision measurement equipment laboratory
PMESII	political, military, economic, social, information, and infrastructure
PMGM	program manager's guidance memorandum
PMI	patient movement item
PMIS	psychological operations (PSYOP) management information subsystem
PMN	parallel track multiunit non-return
PMO	production management office(r); program management office

PMOS	primary military occupational specialty	POV	privately owned vehicle
PMR	parallel track multiunit return; patient movement request; patient movement requirement	POW	prisoner of war
		P/P	patch panel
		p-p	peak-to-peak
PMRC	patient movement requirements center	PPA	personnel information system (PERSINS) personnel activity
PMS	portable meteorological subsystem	PPAG	proposed public affairs guidance
PN	partner nation; pseudonoise	PPBE	Planning, Programming, Budgeting, and Execution
PNID	precedence network in dialing		
PNT	positioning, navigation, and timing	PPD	program planning document
PNVS	pilot night vision system	PPDB	point positioning database
P/O	part of	PPE	personal protective equipment
PO	peace operations; petty officer	PPF	personnel processing file
POA	plan of action	Pplan	programming plan
POADS	psychological operations automated data system	PPLI	precise participant location and identification
POAI	primary other aircraft inventory	ppm	parts per million
POAS	psychological operations automated system	PPP	power projection platform; primary patch panel; priority placement program
POAT	psychological operations assessment team		
		PPR	prior permission required
POB	persons on board; psychological operations battalion	PPS	precise positioning service
		PPTO	petroleum pipeline and terminal operating
POC	point of contact		
POCD	port operations cargo detachment	PR	personnel recovery; Phoenix Raven; primary zone; production requirement; program review
POD	plan of the day; port of debarkation; probability of detection		
POE	port of embarkation; port of entry	PRA	patient reception area; primary review authority
POES	polar operational environment satellite		
POF	priority of fires	PRANG	Puerto Rican Air National Guard
POG	port operations group; psychological operations group	PRBS	pseudorandom binary sequence
		PRC	populace and resources control; Presidential Reserve Call-up
POI	program of instruction		
POL	petroleum, oils, and lubricants	PRCC	personnel recovery coordination cell
POLAD	policy advisor; political advisor	PRD	personnel readiness division; Presidential review directive
POLCAP	bulk petroleum capabilities report		
POLMIL	political-military	PRDO	personnel recovery duty officer
POM	program objective memorandum	PRECOM	preliminary communications search
POMCUS	pre-positioning of materiel configured to unit sets	PREMOB	pre-mobilization
		PREPO	pre-positioned force, equipment, or supplies; prepositioning
POMSO	Plans, Operations, and Military Support Office(r) (NG)		
		PREREP	pre-arrival report
POP	performance oriented packaging	PRF	personnel resources file; pulse repetition frequency
POPS	port operational performance simulator		
POR	proposed operational requirement	PRG	program review group
PORTS	portable remote telecommunications system	PRI	movement priority for forces having the same latest arrival date (LAD); priority; progressive routing indicator
PORTSIM	port simulation model		
POS	peacetime operating stocks; Point of Sale; probability of success		
		PRIFLY	primary flight control
POSF	port of support file	Prime BEEF	Prime Base Engineer Emergency Force
POSSUB	possible submarine	PRISM	Planning Tool for Resource, Integration, Synchronization, and Management
POSTMOB	post mobilization		
POTF	psychological operations task force	PRM	Bureau of Population, Refugees, and Migration (DOS); Presidential review memorandum
POTG	psychological operations task group		
POTUS	President of the United States		

PRMFL	perm file
PRMS	personnel recovery mission software
PRN	pseudorandom noise
PRO	personnel recovery officer
PROBSUB	probable submarine
PROC	processor; Puerto Rican Operations Center
PROFIS	professional officer filler information system
PROM	programmable read-only memory
PROPIN	caution—proprietary information involved
PROVORG	providing organization
proword	procedure word
PRP	personnel reliability program
PRRIS	Puerto Rican radar integration system
PRSL	primary zone/switch location
PRT	pararescue team; patient reception team; provincial reconstruction team
PRTF	personnel recovery task force
PRU	pararescue unit; primary reporting unit
PS	parallel track single-unit; processing subsystem
PSA	port support activity
PSB	poststrike base
PSC	port security company; principal subordinate command
PSD	planning systems division
PSE	peculiar support equipment; psychological operations support element
PS/HD	port security/harbor defense
PSHDGRU	port security and harbor defense group
PSI	personnel security investigation; Proliferation Security Initiative
psi	pounds per square inch
PSK	phase shift keying
PSL	parallel track single-unit long-range aid to navigation (LORAN)
PSMS	Personnel Status Monitoring System
PSN	packet switching node; public switch network
PSO	peace support operations (NATO); post security officer
PSP	perforated steel planking; portable sensor platform; power support platform
PSPS	psychological operations (PSYOP) studies program subsystem
PSS	parallel single-unit spiral; personnel services support
P-STATIC	precipitation static
PSTN	public switched telephone network
PSU	port security unit
PSV	pseudosynthetic video
PSYOP	psychological operations
PTA	position, time, altitude
PTAI	primary training aircraft inventory
PTC	peace through confrontation; primary traffic channel
PTDO	prepare to deploy order
PTT	postal telephone and telegraph; public telephone and telegraph; push-to-talk
PTTI	precise time and time interval
pub	publication
PUK	packup kit
PUL	parent unit level
PV	prime vendor
PVNTMED	preventive medicine
PVT	positioning, velocity, and timing
PW	prisoner of war
pW	picowatt
PWB	printed wiring board (assembly)
PWD	programmed warhead detonation
PWF	personnel working file
PWIS	Prisoner of War Information System
PWR	pre-positioned wartime reserves
PWRMR	pre-positioned war materiel requirement
PWRMS	pre-positioned war reserve materiel stock
PWRR	petroleum war reserve requirements
PWRS	petroleum war reserve stocks; pre-positioned war reserve stock
PWS	performance work statement
PZ	pickup zone
QA	quality assurance
QAM	quadrature amplitude modulation
QAT	quality assurance team
QC	quality control
QD	quality distance
QDR	quality deficiency report
QEEM	quick erect expandable mast
QHDA	qualified hazardous duty area
QM	quartermaster
QPSK	quadrature phase shift keying
QRA	quick reaction antenna
QRCT	quick reaction communications terminal
QRE	quick reaction element
QRF	quick response force
QRG	quick response graphic
QRP	quick response posture
QRS	quick reaction strike
QRSA	quick reaction satellite antenna
QRT	quick reaction team
QS	quality surveillance
Q-ship	decoy ship
QSR	quality surveillance representative
QSTAG	quadripartite standardization agreement
QTY	quantity
QUADCON	quadruple container
R	routine; search radius

R&D	research and development
R&R	rest and recuperation
R&S	reconnaissance and surveillance
R2P2	rapid response planning process
RA	response action; risk analysis; risk assessment
RAA	redeployment assembly area
RABFAC	radar beacon forward air controller
RAC	responsible analytic center
RAC-OT	readiness assessment system—output tool
RAD	routine aerial distribution
RADAY	radio day
RADBN	radio battalion
RADC	regional air defense commander
RADCON	radiological control team
RADF	radarfind
RADHAZ	electromagnetic radiation hazards
RADINT	radar intelligence
RADS	rapid area distribution support (USAF)
RAE	right of assistance entry
RAF	Royal Air Force (UK)
R-AFF	regimental affiliation
RAM	raised angle marker; random access memory; random antiterrorism measure
RAMCC	regional air movement coordination center
RAOB	rawindsonde observation
RAOC	rear area operations center; regional air operations center
RAP	Radiological Assistance Program (DOE); rear area protection; Remedial Action Projects Program (JCS)
RAS	recovery activation signal; refueling at sea
RAS-OT	readiness assessment system—output tool
RAST	recovery assistance, securing, and traversing systems
RASU	random access storage unit
RATT	radio teletype
RB	radar beacon; short-range coastal or river boat
RBC	red blood cell
RBE	remain-behind equipment
RBECS	Revised Battlefield Electronic Communications, Electronics, Intelligence, and Operations (CEIO) System
RBI	RED/BLACK isolator
RB std	rubidium standard
RC	receive clock; regional coordinator; Reserve Component; river current
RCA	residual capabilities assessment; riot control agent
RCAT	regional counterdrug analysis team
RCC	regional contracting center; relocation coordination center
RCCPDS	Reserve Component common personnel data system
RCEM	regional contingency engineering management
RCHB	reserve cargo handling battalion
RCIED	radio-controlled improvised explosive device
RCM	Rules for Courts-Martial
RCMP	Royal Canadian Mounted Police
RC NORTH	Regional Command North (NATO)
RCO	regional contracting office
RCP	resynchronization control panel
RCS	radar cross section
RC SOUTH	Regional Command South (NATO)
RCSP	remote call service position
RCT	regimental combat team; rescue coordination team (Navy)
RCTA	Regional Counterdrug Training Academy
RCU	rate changes unit; remote control unit
RCVR	receiver
RD	receive data; ringdown
RDA	research, development, and acquisition
R-day	redeployment day
RDCFP	Regional Defense Counterterrorism Fellowship Program
RDD	radiological dispersal device; required delivery date
RDECOM	US Army Research, Development, and Engineering Command
RDF	radio direction finder; rapid deployment force
RDO	request for deployment order
RDT&E	research, development, test and evaluation
REACT	rapid execution and combat targeting
REAC/TS	radiation emergency assistance center/training site (DOE)
READY	resource augmentation duty program
RECA	Residual Capability Assessment
RECAS	residual capability assessment system
RECAT	residual capability assessment team
RECCE	reconnaissance
RECCEXREP	reconnaissance exploitation report
RECMOB	reconstitution-mobilization
RECON	reconnaissance
RED	radiological exposure device
RED HORSE	Rapid Engineers Deployable Heavy Operations Repair Squadron, Engineers
REF	reference(s)
REGT	regiment
REL	relative
RELCAN	releasable to Canada
REMT	regional emergency management team
REMUS	remote environmental monitoring unit system

REPOL	bulk petroleum contingency report; petroleum damage and deficiency report; reporting emergency petroleum, oils, and lubricants
REPSHIP	report of shipment
REPUNIT	reporting unit
REQCONF	request confirmation
REQSTATASK	air mission request status tasking
RES	radiation exposure status
RESA	research, evaluation, and system analysis
RESCAP	rescue combat air patrol
RESCORT	rescue escort
RESPROD	responsible production
RET	retired
RF	radio frequency; reserve force; response force
RFA	radio frequency authorization; request for assistance; restrictive fire area
RFC	request for capabilities; response force commander
RF CM	radio frequency countermeasures
RFD	revision first draft
RF/EMPINT	radio frequency/electromagnetic pulse intelligence
RFF	request for feedback; request for forces
RFI	radio frequency interference; ready for issue; request for information
RFID	radio frequency identification
RFL	restrictive fire line
RFP	request for proposal
RFS	request for service
RFW	request for waiver
RG	reconstitution group
RGR	Rangers
RGS	remote geospatial intelligence services
RH	reentry home
Rh	Rhesus factor
RHIB	rigid hull inflatable boat
RI	radiation intensity; Refugees International; routing indicator
RIB	rubberized inflatable boat
RIC	routing indicator code
RICO	regional interface control officer
RIG	recognition identification group
RIK	replacement in kind
RIMS	registrant information management system
RIP	register of intelligence publications
RIS	reconnaissance information system
RISOP	red integrated strategic offensive plan
RISTA	reconnaissance, intelligence, surveillance, and target acquisition
RIT	remote imagery transceiver
RIVRON	riverine squadron
RJTD	reconstitution joint table of distribution
RLD	ready-to-load date
RLE	rail liaison element
RLG	regional liaison group; ring laser gyro
RLGM	remote loop group multiplexer
RLGM/CD	remote loop group multiplexer/cable driver
RLP	remote line printer
RM	recovery mechanism; resource management; risk management
RMC	remote multiplexer combiner; rescue mission commander; Resource Management Committee (CSIF); returned to military control
RMKS	remarks
RMO	regional Marine officer
RMP	religious ministry professional
RMS	requirements management system; root-mean-square
RMU	receiver matrix unit
RNAV	area navigation
RNP	remote network processor
R/O	receive only
Ro	search radius rounded to next highest whole number
ROA	restricted operations area
ROC	regional operations center; rehearsal of concept; required operational capability
ROCU	remote orderwire control unit
ROE	rules of engagement
ROEX	rules of engagement exercise
ROG	railhead operations group
ROICC	resident officer in charge of construction
ROK	Republic of Korea
ROM	read-only memory; restriction of movement; rough order of magnitude
RON	remain overnight
RO/RO	roll-on/roll-off
ROS	reduced operating status
ROTC	Reserve Officer Training Corps
ROTHR	relocatable over-the-horizon backscatter radar (USN)
ROWPU	reverse osmosis water purification unit
ROZ	restricted operations zone
RP	reconstitution priority; release point (road); religious program specialist; retained personnel
RPG	rocket propelled grenade
RPM	revolutions per minute
RPO	rendezvous and proximity operations
RPPO	Requirements, Plans, and Policy Office

RPT	report	RTCH	rough terrain container handler
RPTOR	reporting organization	RTD	returned to duty
RPV	remotely piloted vehicle	RTF	regional task force; return to force
RQMT	requirement	RTFL	rough terrain forklift
RQT	rapid query tool	RTG	radar target graphic
RR	reattack recommendation	RTL	restricted target list
RRC	regional reporting center	RTLP	receiver test level point
RRCC	regional response coordination center	RTM	real-time mode
RRDF	roll-on/roll-off (RO/RO) discharge facility	RTOC	rear tactical operations center
RRF	rapid reaction force; rapid response force; Ready Reserve Fleet; Ready Reserve Force	RTS	remote transfer switch
		RTTY	radio teletype
RRPP	rapid response planning process	RU	release unit; rescue unit
RS	rate synthesizer; religious support; requirement submission	RUF	rules for the use of force
		RUIC	Reserve unit identification number
RSA	retrograde storage area	RUSCOM	rapid ultrahigh frequency (UHF) satellite communications
RSC	red station clock; regional service center; rescue sub-center	RV	long-range seagoing rescue vessel; reentry vehicle; rekeying variable; rendezvous
RSD	reporting of supply discrepancy		
RSE	retrograde support element		
RSG	reference signal generator	RVR	runway visibility recorder
RSI	rationalization, standardization, and interoperability	RVT	remote video terminal
		RW	rotary-wing
RSL	received signal level	RWCM	regional wartime construction manager
RSN	role specialist nation	RWR	radar warning receiver
RSO	regional security officer	RWS	rawinsonde subsystem
RSOC	regional signals intelligence (SIGINT) operations center	RX	receive; receiver
		RZ	recovery zone; return-to-zero
RSOI	reception, staging, onward movement, and integration	618th TACC	618th Tanker Airlift Control Center
		S&F	store-and-forward
RSP	recognized surface picture; Red Switch Project (DOD); religious support plan; religious support policy	S&M	scheduling and movement
		S&R	search and recovery
		S&T	science and technology; scientific and technical
RSPA	Research and Special Programs Administration		
		S&TI	scientific and technical intelligence
RSS	radio subsystem; remote sensors subsystem; root-sum-squared	S-2	battalion or brigade intelligence staff officer (Army; Marine Corps battalion or regiment)
RSSC	regional satellite communications (SATCOM) support center; regional satellite support cell; regional signals intelligence (SIGINT) support center (NSA); regional space support center		
		S-3	battalion or brigade operations staff officer (Army; Marine Corps battalion or regiment)
		S-4	battalion or brigade logistics staff officer (Army; Marine Corps battalion or regiment)
RSSC-LO	regional space support center liaison officer		
		SA	security assistance; selective availability (GPS); senior adviser; situational awareness; staging area; stand-alone switch
RST	religious support team		
RSTA	reconnaissance, surveillance, and target acquisition		
		SAA	senior airfield authority
RSTV	real-time synthetic video	SAAFR	standard use Army aircraft flight route
RSU	rapid support unit; rear support unit; remote switching unit	SAAM	special assignment airlift mission
		SAB	scientific advisory board (USAF)
R/T	receiver/transmitter	SABER	situational awareness beacon with reply
RT	recovery team; remote terminal; rough terrain		
		SAC	special actions cell; special agent in charge; supporting arms coordinator
RTA	residual threat assessment		
RTB	return to base		
RTCC	rough terrain container crane	SACC	supporting arms coordination center

SACEUR	Supreme Allied Commander, Europe (NATO)
SACLANT	Supreme Allied Command, Atlantic
SACS	secure telephone unit (STU) access control system
SACT	Supreme Allied Commander Transformation
SADC	sector air defense commander
SADL	situation awareness data link
SAF	Secretary of the Air Force
SAFE	secure analyst file environment; selected area for evasion
SAFE-CP	selected area for evasion-contact point
SAFER	evasion and recovery selected area for evasion (SAFE) area activation request
SAFWIN	secure Air Force weather information network
SAG	surface action group
SAI	sea-to-air interface; single agency item
SAL	small arms locker
SAL-GP	semiactive laser-guided projectile (USN)
SALM	single-anchor leg mooring
SALT	supporting arms liaison team
SALTS	streamlined automated logistics transfer system; streamlined automated logistics transmission system
SALUTE	size, activity, location, unit, time, and equipment
SAM	space available mail; special airlift mission; surface-to-air missile
SAMM	security assistance management manual
SAMS	School of Advanced Military Studies
SAO	security assistance office/officer; security assistance organization; selected attack option
SAOC	sector air operations center
SAP	special access program
SAPI	special access program for intelligence
SAPO	subarea petroleum office
SAPR	sexual assault prevention and response
SAR	satellite access request; search and rescue; special access requirement; suspicious activity report; synthetic aperture radar
SARC	sexual assault response coordinator; surveillance and reconnaissance center
SARDOT	search and rescue point
SARIR	search and rescue incident report
SARMIS	search and rescue management information system
SARNEG	search and rescue numerical encryption group
SARREQ	search and rescue request
SARSAT	search and rescue satellite-aided tracking
SARSIT	search and rescue situation summary report
SARTEL	search and rescue (SAR) telephone (private hotline)
SARTF	search and rescue task force
SAS	sealed authenticator system; special ammunition storage
SASP	special ammunition supply point
SASS	supporting arms special staff
SASSY	supported activities supply systems
SAT	satellite; security alert team
SATCOM	satellite communications
SAW	surface acoustic wave
SB	standby base
SBCT	Stryker brigade combat team
SBIRS	space-based infrared system
SBL	space-based laser
SBPO	Service blood program officer
SBR	special boat squadron
SBRPT	subordinate reporting organization
SBS	senior battle staff; support battle staff
SBSS	science-based stockpile stewardship
SBT	special boat team
SBSO	sustainment brigade special operations
SBU	special boat unit
SC	sea current; search and rescue coordinator; station clock; strategic communication
SCA	space coordinating authority; support to civil administration
SCAR	strike coordination and reconnaissance
SCAS	stability control augment system
SCATANA	security control of air traffic and navigation aids
SC ATLANTIC	Strategic Command, Atlantic (NATO)
SCATMINE	scatterable mine
SCATMINEWARN	scatterable minefield warning
SCC	security classification code; shipping coordination center; Standards Coordinating Committee
SCC-WMD	United States Strategic Command Center for Combating Weapons of Mass Destruction
SCDL	surveillance control data link
SCE	Service cryptologic element
SC EUROPE	Strategic Command, Europe (NATO)
SCF(UK)	Save the Children Fund (United Kingdom)

SCF(US)	Save the Children Federation (United States)
SCG	Security Cooperation Guidance; switching controller group
SCI	sensitive compartmented information
SCIF	sensitive compartmented information facility
SCL	standard conventional load
SCM	security countermeasure; Service container manager
SCMP	strategic command, control, and communications (C3) master plan
SCNE	self-contained navigation equipment
SCO	secondary control officer; senior contracting official; state coordinating officer
SCOC	systems control and operations concept
SCONUM	ship control number
SCP	secure conferencing project; security cooperation plan; system change proposal
SCPT	strategic connectivity performance test
SCRB	software configuration review board
SCT	shipping coordination team; single channel transponder
SCTIS	single channel transponder injection system
SCTS	single channel transponder system
SCT-UR	single channel transponder ultrahigh frequency (UHF) receiver
SCUD	surface-to-surface missile system
SD	strategy division
SDA	Seventh-Day Adventist (ADRA)
S-day	day the President authorizes selective reserve call-up
SDB	Satellite Communications Database
SDDC	Surface Deployment and Distribution Command
SDDCTEA	Surface Deployment and Distribution Command Transportation Engineering Agency
SDF	self defense force
SDIO	Strategic Defense Initiative Organization
SDLS	satellite data link standards
SDMX	space division matrix
SDN	system development notification
SDNRIU	secure digital net radio interface unit
SDO	senior defense official; ship's debarkation officer
SDP	strategic distribution platform
SDR	system design review
SDSG	space division switching group
SDSM	space division switching matrix
SDV	sea-air-land team (SEAL) delivery vehicle; submerged delivery vehicle
SE	spherical error
SEA	Southeast Asia
SEABEE	Navy construction engineer; sea barge
SEAD	suppression of enemy air defenses
SEAL	sea-air-land team
SEC	submarine element coordinator
SECAF	Secretary of the Air Force
SECARMY	Secretary of the Army
SecDef	Secretary of Defense
SECDHS	Secretary of the Department of Homeland Security
SECHS	Secretary of Homeland Security
SECNAV	Secretary of the Navy
SECNAVINST	Secretary of the Navy instruction
SECOMP	secure en route communications package
SECORD	secure cord switchboard
SECRA	secondary radar data only
SECSTATE	Secretary of State
SECTRANS	Secretary of Transportation
SED	signals external data
SEDAS	spurious emission detection acquisition system
SEF	sealift enhancement feature
SEHS	special events for homeland security
SEI	specific emitter identification
SEL	senior enlisted leader
SEL REL	selective release
SELRES	Selected Reserve
SEMA	special electronic mission aircraft
SEMS	standard embarkation management system
SEO/SEP	special enforcement operation/special enforcement program
SEP	signal entrance panel; spherical error probable
SEPLO	state emergency preparedness liaison officer
SERE	survival, evasion, resistance, and escape
SERER	survival, evasion, resistance, escape, recovery
SES	senior executive service
SETA	system engineering and technical assistance
SEW	shared early warning
S/EWCC	signals intelligence/electronic warfare coordination center
SEWG	Special Events Working Group
S/EWOC	signals intelligence/electronic warfare operations center
SEWS	satellite early warning system
SF	security force; security forces (Air Force or Navy); single frequency; special forces; standard form
SFA	security force assistance

SFAF	standard frequency action format
SFCP	shore fire control party
SFG	security forces group; special forces group
SFI	spectral composition
SFLEO	senior federal law enforcement official
SFMS	special forces medical sergeant
SFOB	special forces operations base
SFOD-A/B/C	special forces operational detachment-A/B/C
SFOR	Stabilization Force
SFS	security forces squadron
SG	strike group; supergroup; Surgeon General
SGEMP	system-generated electromagnetic pulse
SGSA	squadron group systems advisor
SHAPE	Supreme Headquarters Allied Powers, Europe
SHD	special handling designator
SHF	super-high frequency
SHORAD	short-range air defense
SHORADEZ	short-range air defense engagement zone
SI	special intelligence; United States Strategic Command strategic instruction
SIA	station of initial assignment
SIAGL	survey instrument azimuth gyroscope lightweight
SIC	subject identification code
SICO	sector interface control officer
SICR	specific intelligence collection requirement
SID	secondary imagery dissemination; standard instrument departure
SIDAC	single integrated damage analysis capability
SIDL	standard intelligence documents list
SIDO	senior intelligence duty officer
SIDS	secondary imagery dissemination system
SIF	selective identification feature; strategic internment facility
SIG	signal
SIGINT	signals intelligence
SIGSEC	signal security
SII	seriously ill or injured; statement of intelligence interest
SIM	system impact message
SIMLM	single integrated medical logistics management; single integrated medical logistics manager
SINCGARS	single-channel ground and airborne radio system
SINS	ship's inertial navigation system
SIO	senior intelligence officer; special information operations
SIOP	Single Integrated Operational Plan
SIOP-ESI	Single Integrated Operational Plan-Extremely Sensitive Information
SIPRNET	SECRET Internet Protocol Router Network
SIR	serious incident report; specific information requirement
SIRADS	stored imagery repository and dissemination system
SIRMO	senior information resources management official
SIS	special information systems
SITLM	single integrated theater logistic manager
SITREP	situation report
SIV	special interest vessel
SJA	staff judge advocate
SJFHQ	standing joint force headquarters
SJFHQ(CE)	standing joint force headquarters (core element)
SJFHQ-N	Standing Joint Force Headquarters—North
SJS	Secretary, Joint Staff
SKE	station-keeping equipment
SL	sea level; switch locator
SLA	service level agreement
SLAM	stand-off land attack missile
SLAR	side-looking airborne radar
SLBM	submarine-launched ballistic missile
SLC	satellite laser communications; single line concept
SLCM	sea-launched cruise missile
SLCP	ship lighterage control point; ship's loading characteristics pamphlet
SLD	system link designator
SLEP	service life extension program
SLGR	small, lightweight ground receiver (GPS)
SLIT	serial-lot item tracking
SLO	space liaison officer
SLOC	sea line of communications
SLP	seaward launch point
SLWT	side loadable warping tug
SM	Secretary, Joint Staff, memorandum; Service manager; staff memorandum; system manager
SMART	special medical augmentation response team
SMART-AIT	special medical augmentation response—aeromedical isolation team
SMC	midpoint compromise track spacing; search and rescue mission coordinator; system master catalog

SMCA	single manager for conventional ammunition	*SOCA*	special operations communications assembly
SMCC	strategic mobile command center	*SOCC*	Sector Operations Control Center (NORAD)
SMCM	surface mine countermeasures		
SMCOO	spectrum management concept of operations	*SOCCE*	special operations command and control element
SMCR	Selected Marine Corps Reserve	*SOCCENT*	Special Operations Component, United States Central Command
SMD	strategic missile defense		
SMDC	Space & Missile Defense Command (Army)	*SOCCET*	special operations critical care evacuation team
SMDC/ARSTRAT	United States Army Space and Missile Defense Command/United States Army Forces Strategic Command	*SOCCT*	special operations combat control team
		SOCEUR	Special Operations Component, United States European Command
		SOCEX	special operations capable exercise
SME	subject matter expert	*SOCJFCOM*	Special Operations Command, Joint Forces Command
SMEB	significant military exercise brief		
SMEO	small end office	*SOCOORD*	special operations coordination element
SMFT	semi-trailer mounted fabric tank		
SMI	security management infrastructure	*SOCP*	special operations communication package
SMIO	search and rescue (SAR) mission information officer	*SOCPAC*	Special Operations Component, United States Pacific Command
SMO	senior meteorological and oceanographic officer; strategic mobility office(r); support to military operations	*SOCRATES*	Special Operations Command, Research, Analysis, and Threat Evaluation System
		SOCSOUTH	Special Operations Component, United States Southern Command
SMP	sub-motor pool		
SMPT	School of Military Packaging Technology	*SOD*	special operations division; strategy and options decision (Planning, Programming, and Budgeting System)
SMRI	service message routing indicator		
SMS	single mobility system	*SODARS*	special operations debrief and retrieval system
SMTP	simple message transfer protocol		
SMU	special mission unit; supported activities supply system (SASSY) management unit	*SOE*	special operations executive
		SOF	special operations forces; supervisor of flying
S/N	signal to noise	*SOFA*	status-of-forces agreement
SN	serial number	*SOFAR*	sound fixing and ranging
SNCO	staff noncommissioned officer	*SOFLAM*	special operations laser marker
SNF	strategic nuclear forces	*SOFME*	special operations forces medical element
SNIE	special national intelligence estimates		
		SOFSA	special operations forces support activity
SNLC	Senior North Atlantic Treaty Organization (NATO) Logisticians Conference	*SOG*	special operations group
		SOI	signal of interest; signal operating instructions; space object identification
SNM	system notification message		
SNOI	signal not of interest	*SOIC*	senior officer of the Intelligence Community
SO	safety observer; special operations		
SOA	separate operating agency; special operations aviation; speed of advance; status of action; sustained operations ashore	*SOLAS*	safety of life at sea
		SOLE	special operations liaison element
		SOLIS	signals intelligence (SIGINT) On-line Information System
SOAF	status of action file	*SOLL*	special operations low-level
SOAGS	special operations air-ground system	*SOM*	satellite communications operational manager; start of message; system operational manager
SOC	security operations center; special operations commander		
		SOMA	status of mission agreement

SOMARDS	Standard Operation and Maintenance Army Research and Development System
SOMARDS NT	Standard Operation and Maintenance Army Research and Development System Non-Technical
SOMPF	special operations mission planning folder
SONMET	special operations naval mobile environment team
SoO	ship of opportunity
SOOP	Center for Operations, Plans, and Policy
SOP	standard operating procedure; standing operating procedure
SO-peculiar	special operations-peculiar
SOR	statement of requirement
SORTIEALOT	sortie allotment message
SORTS	Status of Resources and Training System
SOS	special operations squadron
SOSB	special operations support battalion
SOSC	special opertions support command (theater army)
SOSCOM	special operations support command
SOSE	special operations staff element
SOSG	station operations support group
SOSR	suppress, obscure, secure, and reduce
SOTA	signals intelligence (SIGINT) operational tasking authority
SOTAC	special operations terminal attack controller
SOTF	special operations task force
SOTSE	special operations theater support element
SOUTHAF	Southern Command Air Forces
SOUTHROC	Southern Region Operational Center (USSOUTHCOM)
SOW	special operations wing; standoff weapon; statement of work
SOWT	special operations weather team
SOWT/TE	special operations weather team/tactical element
SP	security police
SPA	special psychological operations (PSYOP) assessment; submarine patrol area
SPACEAF	Space Air Forces
SPACECON	control of space information
SPCC	ships parts control center (USN)
SPEAR	strike protection evaluation and antiair research
SPEC	specified
SPECAT	special category
SPECWAR	special warfare
SPG	Strategic Planning Guidance
SPI	special investigative (USAF)
SPINS	special instructions
SPINTCOMM	special intelligence communications handling system
SPIREP	spot intelligence report
SPLX	simplex
SPM	single point mooring; single port manager
SPMAGTF	special purpose Marine air-ground task force
SPO	system program office
SPOC	search and rescue (SAR) points of contact; space command operations center
SPOD	seaport of debarkation
SPOE	seaport of embarkation
SPOTREP	spot report
SPP	Security and Prosperity Partnership of North America; shared production program; state partnership program
SPR	software problem report
SPRINT	special psychiatric rapid intervention team
SPS	special psychological operations (PSYOP) study; standard positioning service
SPSC	system planning and system control
SPTCONF	support confirmation
SPTD CMD	supported command
SPTG CMD	supporting command
SPTREQ	support request
sqft	square feet
SR	special reconnaissance
SRA	specialized-repair activity
SRAM	short-range air-to-surface attack missile; system replacement and modernization
SRB	software release bulletin; system review board (JOPES)
SRC	security risk category; service reception center; Single Integrated Operational Plan (SIOP) response cell; standard requirements code; survival recovery center
SRCC	service reserve coordination center
SRF	secure Reserve force
SRG	Seabee readiness group; short-range aircraft
SRI	surveillance, reconnaissance, and intelligence (Marine Corps)
SRIG	surveillance, reconnaissance, and intelligence group (USMC)
SROC	Senior Readiness Oversight Council; Southern Region Operational Center, United States Southern Command

SROE	standing rules of engagement	SSS	Selective Service System; shelter subsystem
SRP	Sealift Readiness Program; sealift reserve program; seaward recovery point; Single Integrated Operational Plan (SIOP) reconnaissance plan	SSSC	surface, subsurface search surveillance coordination
		SST	special support team (National Security Agency)
SRP/PDS	stabilization reference package/position determining system	SSTR	stability, security, transition, and reconstruction
SRR	search and rescue region	ST	short ton; small tug; special tactics; strike team
SRS	search and rescue sector		
SRSG	special representative of the Secretary-General	S/T	short ton
SRT	scheduled return time; special reaction team; standard remote terminal; strategic relocatable target	ST&E	security test and evaluation
		STA	system tape A
		STAB	space tactical awareness brief
		STA clk	station clock
SRTD	signals research and target development	STAMMIS	standard Army multi-command management information system
S/RTF	search and recovery task force		
SRU	search and rescue unit	STAMP	standard air munitions package (USAF)
SR-UAV	short-range unmanned aerial vehicle		
SRUF	standing rules for the use of force	STANAG	standardization agreement (NATO)
SRWBR	short range wide band radio		
S/S	steamship	STANAVFORLANT	Standing Naval Forces, Atlantic (NATO)
SS	submarine		
SSA	software support activity; space situational awareness; special support activity (NSA); strapdown sensor assembly; supply support activity; supply support area	STAR	scheduled theater airlift route; sensitive target approval and review; standard attribute reference; standard terminal arrival route; surface-to-air recovery; system threat assessment report
SSB	single side band; support services branch; surveillance support branch		
SSBN	fleet ballistic missile submarine		
SSB-SC	single sideband-suppressed carrier	STARC	state area coordinators
SSC	small scale contingency; surveillance support center	STARS	Standard Accounting and Reporting System
SSCO	shipper's service control office	START	Strategic Arms Reduction Treaty
SSCRA	Soldiers and Sailors Civil Relief Act		
SSD	strategic studies detachment	STARTEX	start of exercise
SSE	satellite communications (SATCOM) systems expert; sensitive site exploitation; space support element	STB	super tropical bleach
		STC	secondary traffic channel
		STD	sexually transmitted disease
SSF	software support facility	STDM	synchronous time division multiplexer
SSI	standing signal instruction		
SSM	surface-to-surface missile	STE	secure telephone equipment
SSMI	special sensor microwave imager	STEL STU III	Standford telecommunications (secure telephone)
SSMS	single shelter message switch		
SSN	attack submarine, nuclear; Social Security number; space surveillance network	STEP	software test and evaluation program; standardized tactical entry point; standard tool for employment planning
SS (number)	sea state (number)		
SSO	special security office(r); spot security office	STG	seasonal target graphic
		STICS	scalable transportable intelligence communications system
SSP	signals intelligence (SIGINT) support plan		
		STO	special technical operations
SSPM	single service postal manager	STOC	special technical operations coordinator
SSPO	strategic systems program office		
SSR	security sector reform		

STOD	special technical operations division
STOL	short takeoff and landing
STOMPS	stand-alone tactical operational message processing system
STON	short ton
STOVL	short takeoff and vertical landing aircraft
STP	security technical procedure
STR	strength
STRAPP	standard tanks, racks and pylons packages (USAF)
STRATOPS	strategic operations division
STREAM	standard tensioned replenishment alongside method
STS	special tactics squadron
STT	small tactical terminal; special tactics team
STU	secure telephone unit
STU-III	secure telephone unit III
STW	strike warfare
STWC	strike warfare commander
STX	start of text
SU	search unit
SUBJ	subject
sub-JIB	subordinate-joint information bureau
SUBOPAUTH	submarine operating authority
sub-PIC	subordinate-press information center
SUBROC	submarine rocket
SUC	surf current
SUIC	service unit identification code
SUMMITS	scenario unrestricted mobility model of intratheater simulation
SUPE	supervisory commands program
SUPPO	supply officer
SURG	surgeon
SUROBS	surf observation
SURPIC	surface picture
SUST BDE	sustainment brigade
SUW	surface warfare
SUWC	surface warfare commander
S/V	sailboat
SVC	Service
SVIP	secure voice improvement program
SVLTU	service line termination unit
SVR	surface vessel radar
SVS	secure voice system
Sw	switch
SWA	Southwest Asia
SWAT	special weapons and tactics
SWBD	switchboard
SWC	strike warfare commander; swell/wave current
SWI	special weather intelligence
SWO	staff weather officer
SWORD	submarine warfare operations research division
SWPC	Space Weather Prediction Center
SWSOCC	Southwest Sector Operation Control Center North American Aerospace Defense Command (NORAD)
SWXS	Space Weather Squadron
SYDP	six-year defense plan
SYG	Secretary General (UN)
SYNC	synchronization
SYS	system
SYSCOM	systems command
SYSCON	systems control
SZ	surf zone
2-D	two-dimensional
2E	Role 2 enhanced
2LM	Role 2 light maneuver
3-D	three-dimensional
T	search time available; short ton; trackline pattern
T&DE	test and diagnostic equipment
T&E	test and evaluation
T2	technology transfer
TA	target acquisition; target audience; technical arrangement; theater Army; threat assessment
TAA	tactical assembly area; target audience analysis
TAACOM	theater Army area command
TAADS	The Army Authorization Document System
TAAMDCOORD	theater Army air and missile defense coordinator
TAB	tactical air base
TAC	tactical advanced computer; terminal access controller; terminal attack control; terminal attack controller
TAC(A)	tactical air coordinator (airborne)
TACAIR	tactical air
TACAMO	take charge and move out (E-6A/B aircraft)
TACAN	tactical air navigation
TACC	tactical air command center (Marine Corps); tactical air control center (Navy)
TAC-D	tactical deception
TACDAR	tactical detection and reporting
TACINTEL	tactical intelligence
TACLAN	tactical local area network
TACLOG	tactical-logistical
TACM	tactical air command manual
TACO	theater allied contracting office

TACON	tactical control	TAMCA	theater Army movement control agency
TACOPDAT	tactical operational data	TAMCO	theater Army movement control center
TA/CP	technology assessment/control plan	TAMD	theater air and missile defense
TACP	tactical air control party	TAMMC	theater army material management command
TACRON	tactical air control squadron	TAMMIS	theater Army medical management information system
T-ACS	auxiliary crane ship		
TACS	tactical air control system; theater air control system	TAMS	transportation analysis, modeling, and simulation
TACSAT	tactical satellite	tanalt	tangent altitude
TACSIM	tactical simulation	TAO	tactical action officer
TACSTANS	tactical standards	TAOC	tactical air operations center (USMC)
TACT	tactical aviation control team	TAP	troopship
TACTRAGRULANT	Tactical Training Group, Atlantic	TAR	tactical air request; Training and Administration of the Reserve
TAD	tactical air direction; temporary additional duty (non-unit-related personnel); theater air defense; time available for delivery	TARBS	transportable amplitude modulation and frequency modulation radio broadcast system
		TARBUL	target bulletin
TADC	tactical air direction center	TARE	tactical record evaluation
TADCS	tactical airborne digital camera system	TAREX	target exploitation; target plans and operations
TADIL	tactical digital information link	TARS	tethered aerostat radar system
TADL	tactical digital information link	TARWI	target weather and intelligence
TADS	Tactical Air Defense System; target acquisition system and designation sight	TAS	tactical atmospheric summary; true air speed
		T-ASA	Television Audio Support Agency
TAES	theater aeromedical evacuation system	TASCID	tactical Automatic Digital Network (AUTODIN) satellite compensation interface device
TAF	tactical air force		
TAFDS	tactical airfield fuel dispensing system	TASCO	tactical automatic switch control officer
		TASIP	tailored analytic intelligence support to individual electronic warfare and command and control warfare projects
TAFIM	technical architecture framework for information management		
		TASKORD	tasking order
TAFS	tactical aerodrome forecasts	TASMO	tactical air support for maritime operations
TAFT	technical assistance field team		
TAG	technical assessment group; the adjutant general; Tomahawk land-attack missile aimpoint graphic	TASOSC	theater Army special operations support command
		TASS	tactical automated security system; tactical automated switch system
T-AGOS	tactical auxiliary general ocean surveillance	TASWC	theater antisubmarine warfare commander
TAGS	theater air-ground system	TAT	tactical analysis team; technical assistance team
T-AH	hospital ship		
TAI	target area of interest; total active inventory	TATC	tactical air traffic control
		T-AVB	aviation logistics support ship
TAIS	transportation automated information systems	TAW	tactical airlift wing
		TBD	to be determined
TAK	cargo ship	TBM	tactical ballistic missile; theater ballistic missile
T-AKR	fast logistics ship		
TALD	tactical air-launched decoy	TBMCS	theater battle management core system
TALON	Threat and Local Observation Notice	TBMD	theater ballistic missile defense
		TBP	to be published

TBSL	to be supplied later	TDF	tactical digital facsimile
TBTC	transportable blood transshipment center	TDIC	time division interface controller
		TDIG	time division interface group
TC	tidal current; transmit clock and/or telemetry combiner; training circular; Transportation Corps (Army)	TDIM	time division interface module
		TDL	tactical data link
		TDM	time division multiplexed
TCA	terminal control area; time of closest approach; traditional combatant commander activity	TDMA	time division multiple access
		TDMC	theater distribution management cell
		TDMF	time division matrix function
TC-ACCIS	Transportation Coordinator's Automated Command and Control Information System	TDMM	time division memory module
		TDMX	time division matrix
		TDN	target development nomination
TC-AIMS	Transportation Coordinator's Automated Information for Movement System	TDP	theater distribution plan
		TDR	transportation discrepancy report
		TDRC	theater detainee reporting center
TC-AIMS II	Transportation Coordinator's Automated Information for Movement System II	TDSG	time division switching group
		TDSGM	time division switching group modified
TCAM	theater Army medical management information system (TAMMIS) customer assistance module	TDT	theater display terminal
		TDY	temporary duty
		TE	transaction editor
TCC	transmission control code; transportation component command	TEA	Transportation Engineering Agency
		tech	technical
TCCF	tactical communications control facility	TECHCON	technical control
		TECHDOC	technical documentation
TCEM	theater contingency engineering management	TECHELINT	technical electronic intelligence
		TECHEVAL	technical evaluation
TCF	tactical combat force; technical control facility	TECHINT	technical intelligence
		TECHOPDAT	technical operational data
TCM	theater construction manager; theater container manager	TECS II	Treasury Enforcement Communications System
TCMD	transportation control and movement document	TED	trunk encryption device
		TEK	TeleEngineering Kit
TCN	third country national; transportation control number	TEL	transporter-erector-launcher (missile platform)
TCP	theater campaign plan	TELEX	teletype
TCS	theater communications system	TELINT	telemetry intelligence
TCSEC	trusted computer system evaluation criteria	TELNET	telecommunication network
		TEMPER	tent extendible modular personnel
TCSP	theater consolidation and shipping point	TENCAP	tactical exploitation of national capabilities program
TD	temporary duty; theater distribution; tie down; timing distributor; total drift; transmit data	TEOB	tactical electronic order of battle
		TEP	test and evaluation plan; theater engagement plan
TDA	Table of Distribution and Allowance	TERCOM	terrain contour matching
TDAD	Table of Distribution and Allowance (TDA) designation	TERF	terrain flight
		TERPES	tactical electronic reconnaissance processing and evaluation system
T-day	effective day coincident with Presidential declaration of a National Emergency and authorization of partial mobilization	TERPROM	terrain profile matching
		TERS	tactical event reporting system
		TES	theater event system
TDBM	technical database management	TESS	Tactical Environmental Support System
TDBSS	Theater Defense Blood Standard System		
TDD	target desired ground zero (DGZ) designator; time-definite delivery	TET	targeting effects team

TEU	technical escort unit; twenty-foot equivalent unit	*TISG*	technical interoperability standards group
TEWLS	Theater Enterprise Wide Logistics System	*TISS*	thermal imaging sensor system
		TJAG	the judge advocate general
TF	task force	*T-JMC*	theater-joint movement center
TFA	toxic free area	*T-JTB*	theater-joint transportation board
TFADS	Table Formatted Aeronautic Data Set	*TJTN*	theater joint tactical network
TFCICA	task force counterintelligence coordinating authority	*TL*	team leader
		TLAM	Tomahawk land attack missile
TFE	tactical field exchange; transportation feasibility estimator	*TLAMM*	theater lead agent for medical materiel
		TLAM/N	Tomahawk land attack missile/nuclear
TFLIR	targeting forward-looking infrared	*TLC*	traffic load control
TFMS-M	Transportation Financial Management System-Military	*TLCF*	teleconference
		TLE	target location error
TFR	temporary flight restriction	*TLM*	topographic line map
TFS	tactical fighter squadron; Tactical Forecast System	*TLP*	transmission level point
		TLR	trailer
TG	task group	*TLX*	teletype
TGC	trunk group cluster	*TM*	tactical missile; target materials; team member; technical manual; theater missile; TROPO modem
TGEN	table generate		
TGM	trunk group multiplexer		
TGMOW	transmission group module and/or orderwire	*TMAO*	theater mortuary affairs officer
		TMD	tactical munitions dispenser; theater missile defense
TGO	terminal guidance operations		
TGT	target	*TMEP*	theater mortuary evacuation point
TGTINFOREP	target information report	*TMG*	timing
TGU	trunk compatibility unit	*TMIP*	theater medical information program
TI	threat identification; training instructor	*TMIS*	theater medical information system
TIAP	theater intelligence architecture program	*TML*	terminal
		TMLMC	theater medical logistic management center
TIARA	tactical intelligence and related activities		
		TMMMC	theater medical materiel management center
TIB	toxic industrial biological		
TIBS	tactical information broadcast service	*TMN*	trackline multiunit non-return
TIC	target information center; toxic industrial chemical	*TMO*	traffic management office; transportation management office
TIDP	technical interface design plan	*TMP*	target materials program; telecommunications management program; theater manpower forces
TIDS	tactical imagery dissemination system		
TIF	theater internment facility		
TIFF	tagged image file format	*TMR*	trackline multiunit return
TII	total inactive inventory	*T/M/S*	type, model, and/or series (also as TMS)
TIM	theater information management; toxic industrial material	*TNAPS*	tactical network analysis and planning system
TIO	target intelligence officer	*TNAPS+*	tactical network analysis and planning system plus
TIP	target intelligence package; trafficking in persons		
		TNC	theater network operations (NETOPS) center
TIPG	telephone interface planning guide		
TIPI	tactical information processing interpretation	*TNCC*	theater network operations (NETOPS) control center
TIPS	tactical optical surveillance system (TOSS) imagery processing system	*TNCO*	transnational criminal organization
		T-net	training net
TIR	toxic industrial radiological	*TNF*	theater nuclear force
TIROS	television infrared observation satellite	*TNL*	target nomination list
		T/O	table of organization
TIS	technical interface specification; thermal imaging system	*TO*	technical order; theater of operations

TO&E	table of organization and equipment
TOA	table of allowance
TOAI	total overall aircraft inventory
TOC	tactical operations center; tanker airlift control center (TALCE) operations center
TOCU	tropospheric scatter (TROPO) orderwire control unit
TOD	tactical ocean data; time of day
TOE	table of organization and equipment
TOF	time of flight
TOFC	trailer on flatcar
TOH	top of hill
TOI	track of interest
TOPINT	technical operational intelligence
TOR	term of reference; time of receipt
TOS	time on station
TOSS	tactical optical surveillance system
TOT	time on target
TOW	tube launched, optically tracked, wire guided
TP	technical publication; transportation priority; turn point
TPB	tactical psychological operations battalion
TPC	tactical pilotage chart
TPC/PC	tactical pilotage chart and/or pilotage chart
TPED	tasking, processing, exploitation, and dissemination
TPERS	type personnel element
TPFDD	time-phased force and deployment data
TPFDL	time-phased force and deployment list
TPL	technical publications list; telephone private line
TPME	task, purpose, method, and effects
TPMRC	theater patient movement requirements center
TPO	task performance observation
TPRC	theater planning response cell
TPT	tactical petroleum terminal
TPTRL	time-phased transportation requirements list
TPU	tank pump unit
TQ	tactical questioning
TRA	technical review authority
TRAC2ES	transportation command regulating and command and control evacuation system
TRACON	terminal radar approach control facility
TRADOC	United States Army Training and Doctrine Command
TRAM	target recognition attack multisensor
TRANSEC	transmission security
TRAP	tactical recovery of aircraft and personnel (Marine Corps); tactical related applications; tanks, racks, adapters, and pylons; terrorism research and analysis program
TRC	tactical radio communication; threat reduction cooperation; transmission release code
TRCC	tactical record communications center
TRE	tactical receive equipment
TREAS	Department of the Treasury
TREE	transient radiation effects on electronics
TRIADS	Tri-Wall Aerial Distribution System
TRICON	triple container
TRI-TAC	Tri-Service Tactical Communications Program
TRK	truck; trunk
TRNG	training
TRO	training and readiness oversight
TROPO	troposphere; tropospheric scatter
TRP	target reference point
TRS	tactical reconnaissance squadron
TS	terminal service; top secret
TSA	target system analysis; theater storage area; Transportation Security Administration; travel security advisory
TSB	technical support branch; trunk signaling buffer
TSBn	transportation support battalion (USMC)
TSC	theater security cooperation; theater support command; theater sustainment command
TSCIF	tactical sensitive compartmented information facility
TSCM	technical surveillance countermeasures
TSCO	target selection confusion of the operator; top secret control officer
TSCP	theater security cooperation plan
TSCR	time sensitive collection requirement
TSE	tactical support element
TSEC	transmission security
TSG	targeting support group; test signal generator
TSGCE	tri-Service group on communications and electronics
TSGCEE	tri-Service group on communications and electronic equipment (NATO)
TSM	trunk signaling message
TSN	trackline single-unit non-return; track supervision net
TSO	technical standard order; telecommunications service order
TSOC	theater special operations command
TSP	telecommunications service priority
TSR	telecommunications service request; theater source registry; theater support representative; trackline single-unit return

TSS	tactical shelter system; target sensing system; timesharing system; time signal set; traffic service station	UAS	unmanned aircraft system
		UAV	unmanned aerial vehicle
		U/C	unit cost; upconverter
TSSP	tactical satellite signal processor	UCFF	Unit Type Code Consumption Factors File
TSSR	tropospheric scatter (TROPO)-satellite support radio	UCMJ	Uniform Code of Military Justice
TST	tactical support team; theater support team; time-sensitive target	UCP	Unified Command Plan
		UCT	underwater construction team
TSWA	temporary secure working area	UDAC	unauthorized disclosure analysis center
TT	terminal transfer	UDC	unit descriptor code
TT&C	telemetry, tracking, and commanding	UDESC	unit description
TTB	transportation terminal battalion	UDL	unit designation list
TTD	tactical terrain data; technical task directive	UDP	unit deployment program
		UDT	underwater demolition team
TTFACOR	targets, threats, friendlies, artillery, clearance, ordnance, restrictions	UE	unit equipment
		UFC	Unified Facilities Criteria
TTG	thermally tempered glass	UFO	ultrahigh frequency follow-on
TTL	transistor-transistor logic	UFR	unfunded requirement
TTM	threat training manual; training target material	UGA	ungoverned area
		UGIRH	Urban Generic Information Requirements Handbook
TTP	tactics, techniques, and procedures; trailer transfer point	UGM-84A	Harpoon
		UGM-96A	Trident I
TTR	tactical training range	UHF	ultrahigh frequency
TTT	time to target	UHV	Upper Huallaga Valley
TTU	transportation terminal unit	UIC	unit identification code
TTY	teletype	UICIO	unit identification code information officer
TUBA	transition unit box assembly		
TUCHA	type unit characteristics file	UIRV	unique interswitch rekeying variable
TUCHAREP	type unit characteristics report	UIS	unit identification system
TUDET	type unit equipment detail file	UJTL	Universal Joint Task List
TV	television	UK	United Kingdom
TVA	Tennessee Valley Authority	UK(I)	United Kingdom and Ireland
TW/AA	tactical warning and attack assessment	ULC	unit level code
TWC	Office for Counterterrorism Analysis (DIA); total water current	ULF	ultra low frequency
		ULLS	unit level logistics system
TWCF	Transportation Working Capital Fund	ULN	unit line number
TWCM	theater wartime construction manager	UMCC	unit movement control center
TWD	transnational warfare counterdrug analysis	UMCM	underwater mine countermeasures
		UMD	unit manning document; unit movement data
TWDS	tactical water distribution system		
TWI	Office for Information Warfare Support (DIA)	UMIB	urgent marine information broadcast
		UMMIPS	uniform material movement and issue priority system
TWPL	teletypewriter private line		
TWX	teletypewriter exchange	UMO	unit movement officer
TX	transmitter; transmit	UMPR	unit manpower personnel record
TYCOM	type commander	UMT	unit ministry team
U	wind speed	UN	United Nations
UA	unmanned aircraft	UNAMIR	United Nations Assistance Mission in Rwanda
UAOBS	upper air observation		
UAR	unconventional assisted recovery	UNC	United Nations Command
UARCC	unconventional assisted recovery coordination cell	UNCLOS	United Nations Convention on the Law of the Sea
UARM	unconventional assisted recovery mechanism	UNCTAD	United Nations Conference on Trade and Development
UART	unconventional assisted recovery team		

UND	urgency of need designator
UNDAC	United Nations disaster assessment and coordination
UNDHA	United Nations Department of Humanitarian Affairs
UN-DMT	United Nations disaster management team
UNDP	United Nations development programme
UNDPKO	United Nations Department for Peacekeeping Operations
UNEF	United Nations emergency force
UNEP	United Nations environment program
UNESCO	United Nations Educational, Scientific, and Cultural Organization
UNHCHR	United Nations High Commissioner for Human Rights
UNHCR	United Nations Office of the High Commissioner for Refugees
UNICEF	United Nations Children's Fund
UNIFIL	United Nations Interim Force in Lebanon
UNIL	unclassified national information library
UNITAF	unified task force
UNITAR	United Nations Institute for Training and Research
UNITREP	unit status and identity report
UNJLC	United Nations Joint Logistic Centre
UNLOC	United Nations logistic course
UNMIH	United Nations Mission in Haiti
UNMILPOC	United Nations military police course
UNMOC	United Nations military observers course
UNMOVCC	United Nations movement control course
UNO	unit number
UNOCHA	United Nations Office for the Coordination of Humanitarian Affairs
UNODC	United Nations Office on Drugs and Crime
UNODIR	unless otherwise directed
UNOSOM	United Nations Operations in Somalia
UNPA	United Nations Participation Act
UNPROFOR	United Nations protection force
UNREP	underway replenishment
UNREP CONSOL	underway replenishment consolidation
UNRWA	United Nations Relief and Works Agency for Palestine Refugees in the Near East
UNSC	United Nations Security Council
UNSCR	United Nations Security Council resolution
UNSG	United Nations Secretary-General
UNSOC	United Nations staff officers course
UNTAC	United Nations Transition Authority in Cambodia
UNTSO	United Nations Truce and Supervision Organization
UNV	United Nations volunteer
UOF	use of force
UP&TT	unit personnel and tonnage table
UPU	Universal Postal Union
URDB	user requirements database
USA	United States Army
USAB	United States Army barracks
USACCSA	United States Army Command and Control Support Agency
USACE	United States Army Corps of Engineers
USACFSC	United States Army Community and Family Support Center
USACHPPM	US Army Center for Health Promotion and Preventive Medicine
USACIDC	United States Army Criminal Investigation Command
USAF	United States Air Force
USAFE	United States Air Forces in Europe
USAFEP	United States Air Force, Europe pamphlet
USAFLANT	United States Air Force, Atlantic Command
USAFR	United States Air Force Reserve
USAFRICOM	United States Africa Command
USAFSOC	United States Air Force, Special Operations Command
USAFSOF	United States Air Force, Special Operations Forces
USAFSOS	USAF Special Operations School
USAID	United States Agency for International Development
USAITAC	United States Army Intelligence Threat Analysis Center
USAJFKSWC	United States Army John F. Kennedy Special Warfare Center
USAMC	United States Army Materiel Command
USAMMA	United States Army Medical Materiel Agency
USAMPS	United States Army Military Police School
USAMRICD	US Army Medical Research Institute for Chemical Defense
USAMRIID	US Army Medical Research Institute of Infectious Diseases

USAMRMC	US Army Medical Research and Materiel Command
USANCA	United States Army Nuclear and Combating Weapons of Mass Destruction Agency
USAO	United States Attorney Office
USAR	United States Army Reserve
USARCENT	United States Army, Central Command
USAREUR	United States Army, European Command
USARIEM	United States Army Research Institute of Environmental Medicine
USARJ	United States Army, Japan
USARNORTH	US Army Forces North
USARPAC	United States Army, Pacific Command
USARSO	United States Army, Southern Command
USASOC	United States Army Special Operations Command
USB	upper side band
USBP	United States Border Patrol
USC	United States Code; universal service contract
USCENTAF	United States Central Command Air Forces
USCENTCOM	United States Central Command
USCG	United States Coast Guard
USCGR	United States Coast Guard Reserve
USCIS	US Citizenship and Immigration Services
USCS	United States Cryptologic System; United States Customs Service
USDA	United States Department of Agriculture
USD(A&T)	Under Secretary of Defense for Acquisition and Technology
USDAO	United States defense attaché office
USD(AT&L)	Under Secretary of Defense for Acquisition, Technology, and Logistics
USD(C)	Under Secretary of Defense (Comptroller)
USDELMC	United States Delegation to the NATO Military Committee
USD(I)	Under Secretary of Defense for Intelligence
USD(P)	Under Secretary of Defense for Policy
USD(P&R)	Under Secretary of Defense for Personnel and Readiness
USDR	United States defense representative
USD(R&E)	Under Secretary of Defense for Research and Engineering
USELEMCMOC	United States Element Cheyenne Mountain Operations Center
USELEMNORAD	United States Element, North American Aerospace Defense Command
USERID	user identification
USERRA	Uniformed Services Employment and Reemployment Rights Act
USEUCOM	United States European Command
USFJ	United States Forces, Japan
USFK	United States Forces, Korea
USFORAZORES	United States Forces, Azores
USFS	United States Forest Service
USFWS	United States Fish and Wildlife Service
USG	United States Government
USGS	United States Geological Survey
USIA	United States Information Agency
USIC	United States interdiction coordinator
USIS	United States Information Service
USJFCOM	United States Joint Forces Command
USLANTFLT	United States Atlantic Fleet
USLO	United States liaison officer
USMARFORCENT	United States Marine Component, Central Command
USMARFORLANT	United States Marine Component, Atlantic Command
USMARFORPAC	United States Marine Component, Pacific Command
USMARFORSOUTH	United States Marine Component, Southern Command
USMC	United States Marine Corps
USMCEB	United States Military Communications-Electronics Board
USMCR	United States Marine Corps Reserve
USMER	United States merchant ship vessel locator reporting system
USMILGP	United States military group
USMILREP	United States military representative
USMOG-W	United States Military Observer Group—Washington
USMS	United States Marshals Service
USMTF	United States message text format

USMTM	United States military training mission	UW	unconventional warfare
USN	United States Navy	UWOA	unconventional warfare operating area
USNAVCENT	United States Naval Forces, Central Command	UXO	unexploded explosive ordnance; unexploded ordnance
USNAVEUR	United States Naval Forces, Europe	V	search and rescue unit ground speed; sector pattern; volt
USNAVSO	US Naval Forces Southern Command	v	velocity of target drift
USNCB	United States National Central Bureau (INTERPOL)	VA	Veterans Administration; victim advocate; vulnerability assessment
USNMR	United States National Military representative	V&A	valuation and availability
USNMTG	United States North Atlantic Treaty Organization (NATO) Military Terminology Group	VAAP	vulnerability assessment and assistance program
		VAC	volts, alternating current
USNO	United States Naval Observatory	VARVAL	vessel arrival data, list of vessels available to marine safety offices and captains of the port
USNORTHCOM	United States Northern Command		
USNR	United States Navy Reserve	VAT B	(weather) visibility (in miles), amount (of clouds, in eighths), (height of cloud) top (in thousands of feet), (height of cloud) base (in thousands of feet)
USNS	United States Naval Ship		
USPACAF	United States Air Forces, Pacific Command		
USPACFLT	United States Pacific Fleet		
USPACOM	United States Pacific Command	VBIED	vehicle-borne improvised explosive device
USPFO(P&C)	United States Property and Fiscal Office (Purchasing and Contracting)	VBS	visit, board, search
		VBSS	visit, board, search, and seizure
		VCC	voice communications circuit
		VCG	virtual coordination group
USPHS	United States Public Health Service	VCJCS	Vice Chairman of the Joint Chiefs of Staff
USPS	United States Postal Service	VCNOG	Vice Chairman, Nuclear Operations Group
USREPMC	United States representative to the military committee (NATO)		
		VCO	voltage controlled oscillator
USSOCOM	United States Special Operations Command	VCOPG	Vice Chairman, Operations Planners Group
		VCR	violent crime report
USSOUTHAF	United States Air Force, Southern Command	VCXO	voltage controlled crystal oscillator; voltage controlled oscillator
USSOUTHCOM	United States Southern Command	VDC	volts, direct current
USSS	United States Secret Service (TREAS); United States Signals Intelligence (SIGINT) System	VDJS	Vice Director, Joint Staff
		VDL	video downlink
		VDR	voice digitization rate
USSTRATCOM	United States Strategic Command	VDS	video subsystem
USTRANSCOM	United States Transportation Command	VDSD	visual distress signaling device
		VDU	visual display unit
USUN	United States Mission to the United Nations	VDUC	visual display unit controller
		VE	vertical error
USW	undersea warfare	VEE	Venezuelan equine encephalitis
USW/USWC	undersea warfare and/or undersea warfare commander	VEH	vehicle; vehicular cargo
		VEO	violent extremist organization
USYG	Under Secretary General	VERTREP	vertical replenishment
UT1	unit trainer; Universal Time	VF	voice frequency
UTC	Coordinated Universal Time; unit type code	VFR	visual flight rules
		VFS	validating flight surgeon
UTM	universal transverse mercator	VFTG	voice frequency telegraph
UTO	unit table of organization	VHF	very high frequency
UTR	underwater tracking range	VI	visual information
UUV	unmanned underwater vehicle	VICE	advice
UVEPROM	ultraviolet erasable programmable read-only memory	VID	visual identification information display
		VIDOC	visual information documentation

VINSON	encrypted ultrahigh frequency communications system
VIP	very important person; visual information processor
VIRS	verbally initiated release system
VIS	visual imaging system
VISA	Voluntary Intermodal Sealift Agreement
VISOBS	visual observer
VIXS	video information exchange system
VLA	vertical line array; visual landing aid
VLF	very low frequency
VLR	very-long-range aircraft
VLZ	vertical landing zone
VMap	vector map
VMAQ	Marine tactical electronic warfare squadron
VMC	visual meteorological conditions
VMF	variable message format
VMGR	Marine aerial refueler and transport squadron
VMI	vendor managed inventory
VNTK	target vulnerability indicator designating degree of hardness; susceptibility of blast; and K-factor
VO	validation office
VOCODER	voice encoder
VOCU	voice orderwire control unit
VOD	vertical onboard delivery
VOL	volunteer
vol	volume
VOLS	vertical optical landing system
VOR	very high frequency omnidirectional range station
VORTAC	very high frequency omnidirectional range station and/or tactical air navigation
VOX	voice actuation (keying)
VP	video processor
VPB	version planning board
VPD	version planning document
VPV	virtual prime vendor
VS	sector single-unit
VS&PT	vehicle summary and priority table
VSAT	very small aperture terminal
VSG	virtual support group
VSII	very seriously ill or injured
VSP	voice selection panel
VSR	sector single-unit radar
V/STOL	vertical and/or short takeoff and landing aircraft
VSW	very shallow water
VTA	voluntary tanker agreement
VTC	video teleconferencing
VTOL	vertical takeoff and landing
VTOL-UAV	vertical takeoff and landing unmanned aerial vehicle
VTS	vessel traffic service
VTT	video teletraining
VU	volume unit
VV&A	verification, validation, and accreditation
VV&C	verification, validation, and certification
VX	nerve agent (O-Ethyl S-Diisopropylaminomethyl Methylphosphonothiolate)
W	sweep width
w	search subarea width
WAAR	Wartime Aircraft Activity Report
WACBE	World Area Code Basic Encyclopedia
WADS	Western Air Defense Sector
WAGB	icebreaker (USCG)
WAI	weather area of interest
WAN	wide-area network
WARM	wartime reserve mode
WARMAPS	wartime manpower planning system
WARNORD	warning order
WARP	web-based access and retrieval portal
WAS	wide area surveillance
WASP	war air service program
WATCHCON	watch condition
WB	wideband
WBGTI	wet bulb globe temperature index
WC	wind current
WCA	water clearance authority
WCCS	Wing Command and Control System
WCDO	War Consumables Distribution Objective
WCO	World Customs Organization
WCS	weapons control status
W-day	declared by the President, W-day is associated with an adversary decision to prepare for war
WDT	warning and display terminal
WEAX	weather facsimile
WES	weapon engagement status
WETM	weather team
WEU	Western European Union
WEZ	weapon engagement zone
WFE	warfighting environment
WFP	World Food Programme (UN)
WG	working group
WGS	Wideband Global Satellite Communications (SATCOM); World Geodetic System
WGS-84	World Geodetic System 1984
WH	wounded due to hostilities
WHEC	high-endurance cutter (USCG)

WHNRS	wartime host-nation religious support
WHNS	wartime host-nation support
WHNSIMS	Wartime Host Nation Support Information Management System
WHO	World Health Organization (UN)
WIA	wounded in action
WISDIM	Warfighting and Intelligence Systems Dictionary for Information Management
WISP	Wartime Information Security Program
WIT	weapons intelligence team
WLG	Washington Liaison Group
WMD	weapons of mass destruction
WMD CM	weapons of mass destruction consequence management
WMD-CST	weapons of mass destruction-civil support team
WMEC	Coast Guard medium-endurance cutter
WMO	World Meteorological Organization
WMP	Air Force War and Mobilization Plan; War and Mobilization Plan
WOC	wing operations center (USAF)
WOD	wind-over deck; word-of-day
WORM	write once read many
WOT	war on terrorism
WP	white phosphorous; Working Party (NATO)
WPA	water jet propulsion assembly
WPAL	wartime personnel allowance list
WPARR	War Plans Additive Requirements Roster
WPB	Coast Guard patrol boat
WPC	Washington Planning Center
WPM	words per minute
WPN	weapon
WPR	War Powers Resolution
WPS	Worldwide Port System
WR	war reserve; weapon radius
WRA	Office of Weapons Removal and Abatement (DOS)
WRAIR	Walter Reed Army Institute of Research
WRC	World Radiocommunication Conference
WRL	weapons release line
WRM	war reserve materiel
WRMS	war reserve materiel stock
WRR	weapons response range (as well as wpns release rg)
WRS	war reserve stock
WRSA	war reserve stocks for allies
WRSK	war readiness spares kit; war reserve spares kit
WSE	weapon support equipment
WSES	surface effect ship (USCG)
WSESRB	Weapon System Explosive Safety Review Board
WSM	waterspace management
WSR	weapon system reliability
WT	gross weight; warping tug; weight
WTCA	water terminal clearance authority
WTCT	weapons of mass destruction technical collection team
WTLO	water terminal logistic office
W_u	uncorrected sweep width
WVRD	World Vision Relief and Development, Inc.
WWABNCP	worldwide airborne command post
WWII	World War II
WWSVCS	Worldwide Secure Voice Conferencing System
WWX	worldwide express
WX	weather
X	initial position error
XCVR	transceiver
XMPP	presence protocol
XO	executive officer
XSB	barrier single unit
Y	search and rescue unit (SRU) error
YR	year
Z	zulu
z	effort
ZF	zone of fire
Z_t	total available effort
ZULU	time zone indicator for Universal Time

Disaster and Emergency Management

CONTRACTS

Antitrust Laws The term "antitrust laws" has the meaning given to such term in subsection (a) of the first section of the Clayton Act [15 U.S.C. 12-27], except that such term includes section 5 of the Federal Trade Commission Act [15 U.S.C. 45-58] to the extent that such section 5 applies to unfair methods of competition.

Civilian Needs Any domestic economic activity supporting the United States population except:
i. Military production and construction, military assistance to foreign nations, stockpiling, outer space, and directly related activities; and
ii. Energy production and construction, distribution and use, and directly related activities.

Civil Transportation Movement of persons and property by all modes of transportation in interstate, intrastate, or foreign commerce within the United States, its territories and possessions, and the District of Columbia, and without limitation, related public storage and warehousing, ports, services, equipment and facilities, such as transportation carrier shop and repair facilities. However, "civil transportation" shall not include transportation owned or controlled by the Department of Defense, use of petroleum and gas pipelines, and coal slurry pipelines used only to supply energy production facilities directly. As applied herein, "civil transportation" shall include direction, control, and coordination of civil transportation capacity regardless of ownership.

Contractor Many prime contractor, subcontractor, or supplier in the supply chain supporting a rated order.

Critical Component The term "critical component" includes such components, subsystems, systems, and related special tooling and test equipment essential to the production, repair, maintenance, or operation of weapon systems or other items of equipment identified by the President as being essential to the execution of the national security strategy of the United States. Components identified as critical by a National Security Assessment conducted pursuant to section 113(i) of title 10, United States Code, or by a Presidential determination as a result of a petition filed under section 232 of the Trade Expansion Act of 1962 [19 U.S.C. App. § 1862] shall be designated as critical components for purposes of this Act [50 U.S.C. App. § 2061-2171], unless the President determines that the designation is unwarranted.

Critical Industry for National Security The term "critical industry for national security" means any industry (or industry sector) identified pursuant to section 2503(6) of title 10, United States Code, and such other industries or industry sectors as may be designated by the President as essential to provide industrial resources required for the execution of the national security strategy of the United States.

Critical Infrastructure Any systems and assets, whether physical or cyber-based, so vital to the United States that the degradation or destruction of such systems and assets would have a debilitating impact on national security, including, but not limited to, national economic security and national public health or safety.

Critical Technology The term "critical technology" includes any designated by the President to be essential to the national defense.

Critical Technology Item Materials directly employing, derived from, or utilizing a critical technology.

Defense Contractor Any person who enters into a contract with the United States
i. to furnish materials, industrial resources, or a critical technology for the national defense; or
ii. to perform services for the national defense.

Domestic Defense Industrial Base Domestic sources which are providing, or which would be reasonably expected to provide, materials or services to meet national defense requirements during peacetime, graduated mobilization, national emergency, or war.

Domestic Source A business concern
i. that performs in the United States or Canada substantially all of the research and development, engineering, manufacturing, and production activities required of such business concern under a contract with the United States relating

to a critical component or a critical technology item; and

ii. that procures from business concerns described in subparagraph (A) substantially all of any components and assemblies required under a contract with the United States relating to a critical component or critical technology item.

DHS-Approved Program A program involving civilian needs determined, in accordance with subsection 202(c) of E.O. 12919, to be necessary or appropriate to promote the national defense.

DPAS Officer A FEMA employee, who has completed required training in DPAS policy and procedures and has been appointed to address DPAS issues. The functions of a DPAS Officer may be performed as collateral duties.

Emergency Preparedness All those activities and measures designed or undertaken to prepare for or minimize the effects of a hazard upon the civilian population, to deal with the immediate emergency conditions which would be created by the hazard, and to effectuate emergency repairs to, or the emergency restoration of, vital utilities and facilities destroyed or damaged by the hazard. Such term includes the following:

i. Measures to be undertaken in preparation for anticipated hazards (including the establishment of appropriate organizations, operational plans, and supporting agreements, the recruitment and training of personnel, the conduct of research, the procurement and stockpiling of necessary materials and supplies, the provision of suitable warning systems, the construction or preparation of shelters, shelter areas, and control centers, and, when appropriate, the non-military evacuation of civil population).

ii. Measures to be undertaken during a hazard (including the enforcement of passive defense regulations prescribed by duly established military or civil authorities, the evacuation of personnel to shelter areas, the control of traffic and panic, and the control and use of lighting and civil communications).

iii. Measures to be undertaken following a hazard (including activities for fire fighting, rescue, emergency medical, health and sanitation services, monitoring for specific dangers of special weapons, unexploded bomb reconnaissance, essential debris clearance, emergency welfare measures, and immediately essential emergency repair or restoration of damaged vital facilities).

Energy All forms of energy including petroleum, gas (both natural and manufactured), electricity, solid fuels (including all forms of coal, coke, coal chemicals, coal liquification [liquefaction], and coal gasification), and atomic energy, and the production, conservation, use, control, and distribution (including pipelines) of all of these forms of energy.

Facilities All types of buildings, structures, or other improvements to real property (but excluding farms, churches or other places of worship, and private dwelling houses), and services relating to the use of any such building, structure, or other improvement.

Farm Equipment Equipment, machinery, and repair parts manufactured for use on farms in connection with the production or preparation for market use of food resources.

Fertilizer Any product or combination of products that contain one or more of the elements—nitrogen, phosphorus, and potassium—for use as a plant nutrient.

Food Resource Facilities Plants, machinery, vehicles (including on-farm), and other facilities required for the production, processing, distribution, and storage (including cold storage) of food resources, livestock and poultry feed and seed, and for the domestic distribution of farm equipment and fertilizer (excluding transportation thereof).

Food Resources All commodities and products, simple, mixed, or compound, or complements to such commodities or products, that are capable of being ingested by either human beings or animals, irrespective of other uses to which such commodities or products may be put, at all stages of processing from the raw commodity to the products thereof in vendible form for human or animal consumption. "Food resources" also means all starched, sugars, vegetable and animal or marine facts and oils, cotton, tobacco, wool mohair, hemp, flax fiber, and naval stores, but does not mean any such material after it loses its identity as an agricultural commodity or agricultural product.

Foreign Source A business entity other than a "domestic source."

Functions Powers, duties, authority, responsibilities, and discretion.

Hazard An emergency or disaster resulting from a natural disaster or an accidental or man-caused event.

Health Resources Materials, facilities, health supplies, and equipment including pharmaceutical, blood collecting and dispensing supplies, biological, surgical textiles, and emergency surgical instruments and supplies) required to prevent the impairment of, improve, or restore the physical and mental health conditions of the population.

Homeland Security Includes efforts —
a. to prevent terrorist attacks within the United States;

b. to reduce the vulnerability of the United States to terrorism; to minimize damage from a terrorist attack in the United States; and
c. to recover from a terrorist attack in the United States.

Industrial Resources All materials (including construction materials), services, and facilities, except the following: (1) food resources, food resource facilities, and the domestic distribution of farm equipment and commercial fertilizer; (2) all forms of energy; (3) health resources; (4) all forms of civil transportation; and (5) water resources.

Materials (1) Any raw materials (including minerals, metals, and advanced processed materials), commodities, articles, components (including critical components), products, and items of supply; and (2) any technical information or services ancillary to the use of any such materials, commodities, articles, components, products, or items.

Metals and Minerals All raw materials of mineral origin (excluding energy) including their refining, smelting, or processing, but excluding their fabrication.

National Defense Programs for military and energy production or construction, military or critical infrastructure assistance to any foreign nation, homeland security, stockpiling, space, and any directly related activity. Such term includes emergency preparedness activities conducted pursuant to title VI of The Robert T. Stafford Disaster Relief and Emergency Assistance Act [42 U.S.C. Â§ 5195 et seq.] and critical infrastructure protection and restoration.

Natural Disaster Any hurricane, tornado, storm, flood, high water, wind-driven water, tidal wave, tsunami, earthquake, volcanic eruption, landslide, mudslide, snowstorm, drought, fire, or other catastrophe in any part of the United States which causes, or which may cause, substantial damage or injury to civilian property or persons.

Person An individual, corporation, partnership, association, or any other organized group of persons, or legal successor or representative thereof, or any State or local government or agency thereof.

Plan of Action The term "plan of action" means any of 1 or more documented methods adopted by participants in an existing voluntary agreement to implement that agreement.

Program Official A FEMA employee who is authorized to direct placement of contracts and orders in support of FEMA programs.

Rated Order A contract or order containing a priority rating, in accordance with the DPAS.

Services Any effort that is needed for or incidental to
a. the development, production, processing, distribution, delivery, or use of an industrial resource or a critical technology item;
b. the construction of facilities;
c. the movement of individuals and property by all modes of civil transportation; or
d. other national defense programs and activities.

Title VI of the Stafford Act The purpose of this title is to provide a system of emergency preparedness for the protection of life and property in the United States from hazards and to vest responsibility for emergency preparedness jointly in the Federal Government and the States and their political subdivisions. This title states that the Federal Government shall provide necessary direction, coordination, and guidance, and shall provide necessary assistance, as authorized in this title so that a comprehensive emergency preparedness system exists for all hazards.

Voluntary Agreement An association entered into freely by two or more representatives of industry, business, financing, agriculture, labor, or other private interests to engage in specified activities in support of the national defense that could constitute violations of antitrust laws under normal circumstances. Participants in a voluntary agreement are granted relief from antitrust laws under the provisions of DPA Section 708.

Water Resources All usable water, from all sources, within the jurisdiction of the United States, which can be managed, controlled, and allocated to meet emergency requirements.

DISASTER AND EMERGENCY MANAGEMENT

Advanced Life Support (ALS) Ambulance An ambulance service capable of delivering advanced skills performed by Emergency Medical Services (EMS) practitioners (e.g., intravenous [IV] fluids and drug administration).

Air Ambulance A rotary-wing aircraft configured, staffed, and equipped to respond, care for, and transport patients. A rotary-wing aircraft must be approved/licensed by a State to do so.

Air Conditioner/Heater A specialized climate-controlled piece of equipment used to support cooling and/or heating requirements within enclosed structures. Requires mobilization to the desired site, along with set-up requirements, such as power hookup and duct installation. Amps can range from 24 to 260 or more. Equipment used to accommodate schools and malls to small office and tent settings.

Air Search and Rescue Team Team provides search and rescue emergency airlift and other special services at the request of, and to support, State and county agency needs.

Air Search Team (Fixed-Wing) Team provides airborne search, emergency airlift, airborne communications, and other special services. Varying levels of specialized management support and command and control capabilities are included in team structures.

Air Tanker (Fixed-Wing Firefighting Aircraft Tanker) Any fixed-wing aircraft certified by the Federal Aviation Administration (FAA) as being capable of transport and delivery of fire retardant solutions.

Airborne Communications Relay Team (Fixed-Wing), Civil Air Patrol (CAP) CAP Airborne Communications Relay Team provides airborne communications relay using fixed-wing platforms to support Federal, State, and local agency needs. Relays are primarily conducted through aircrews, but can also be accomplished through electronic repeaters carried aboard Civil Air Patrol (CAP) aircrafts. Varying levels of specialized management support and command and control capabilities are included in team structures.

Airborne Reconnaissance (Fixed-Wing) An airborne reconnaissance fixed-wing observation aircraft is capable of flying back video or still imagery from an incident/disaster scene.

Airborne Transport (Fixed-Wing) Team, Civil Air Patrol (CAP) A CAP Airborne Transport (Fixed-Wing) Team provides limited airborne transportation and emergency airlift to support Federal, State, and local agency needs using light fixed-wing platforms owned by the Civil Air Patrol (CAP). Varying levels of specialized management support and command and control capabilities are included in team structures.

Aircraft Rescue Firefighting (ARFF) A motor-driven vehicle, designed and constructed for the purpose of aircraft rescue and fighting fires and capable of delivering Class B Foam, providing a specified level of pumping, water, hose, and rescue capacity and personnel.

All-Terrain Cranes A self-propelled, all-terrain, hydraulic crane capable of traveling over primary, secondary, and off-road surfaces at the tactical support level.

Technical characteristics include diesel engine, power shift transmission, three-mode steering, and independently controlled hydraulic outriggers telescoping boom. Comes in various lifting capabilities and is used for construction, maintenance, bridging, and resupply activities. Mobilization of larger all-terrain cranes requires tractor-trailer support for booms and jibs along with additional escort services.

Alpine Search and Rescue Team (Snow and Ice Rescue) Team conducts search and rescue operations for individuals in a highaltitude alpine environment.

Ambulance Strike Team An Ambulance Strike Team is a group of five ambulances of the same type with common communications and a leader. It provides an operational grouping of ambulances complete with supervisory elements for organization command and control. The strike teams may be all ALS or all BLS.

Ambulance Task Force An Ambulance Task Force is a group of any combination of ambulances, within span of control, with common communications and a leader.

Animal Health Incident Management Team Team provides overall management of animal-related volunteers and donations.

Animal Health Technician Technician performs variety of animal health care duties to assist veterinarians in settings such as veterinarians' clinics, zoos, research laboratories, kennels, and commercial facilities. Prepares treatment room for examination of animals and holds or restrains animals during examination, treatment, or inoculation.

Animal Rescue Team A team proficient in animal handling and capture and management (minimum teams of two). Environments include water (swift water and flood), wildfire, and hazardous materials (HazMat) conditions. Operations include communications and/or evacuations to effect animal rescue.

Animal Sheltering Team A team proficient in animal handling, animal care, and animal shelter management and manages the setup, management, and staffing of temporary animal shelters.

Animal Treatment Team – Small A self-equipped team proficient in the medical treatment of companion animals affected by disasters.

Area Command Team, Firefighting An Area Command Team is an interagency organization under the auspices of NWCG (1) oversee the management of multiple incidents that are each being handled by an incident management team (IMT) organization; or (2) to oversee the management of a very large incident that has multiple IMTs assigned to it. Area Command has the responsibility to set overall strategy and priorities, allocate critical resources based on priorities, ensure incidents are properly managed, and that objectives are met and strategies followed.

Backhoe Loader (Wheel Loader; Backhoe) This is dual-purpose equipment used for loading materials and excavating. Components are located at each end of the equipment. The loading attachments are usually to the front end and the excavating attachment is to the rear. Equipment is available with all-wheel or two-wheel drive. Various sizes are available. Mobilization can be self-propelled and/or on a flat bed trailer. Refer to definitions of wheel loaders (medium to small) and hydraulic excavators for a sampling of capabilities.

Basic Life Support (BLS) Ambulance An ambulance service capable of delivering basic emergency interventions performed by Emergency Medical Services (EMS) practitioners trained and credentialed to do so (e.g., splinting, bandaging, oxygen administration).

Biological Agent Living organisms or the materials derived from them (such as bacteria, viruses, fungi, and toxins) that cause disease in or harm to humans, animals, or plants, or cause deterioration of material.

Boat, Fire A vessel or watercraft designed and constructed for the purpose of fighting fires providing specified level of pumping capacity. The boat is designed with the ability to carry firefighting foam and personnel for the extinguishments of fires in the marine environment.

Bomb Squad/Explosives Teams A public safety agency specializing in the investigation and disarming of suspected explosive devices.

Bomb Suits Suits made of Kevlar® (inner material) and Nomex 3 (outer material to protect from fire).

Breathing Apparatus Support (SCBA Support; Breathing Air, Firefighting) A mobile unit designed and constructed for the purpose of providing specified level of breathing air support capacity and personnel capable of refilling self-contained breathing apparatus (SCBA) at remote incident locations (Compressor Systems or Cascade).

Brush Patrol Unit, Firefighting (Brush Patrol) Any light, mobile vehicular unit with limited pumping and water capacity for off-road operations.

Canine Recovery Team (Cadaver Dog Team; K-9 Recovery Team) Team provides highly trained air scent recovery dog teams for search and recovery operations for deceased victims.

Canine Search Team (Search Dog Team; Dog Rescue Team; K-9 Rescue Team) Team provides highly trained search dog teams for search and rescue operations for living and deceased victims in a variety of environments. Teams can be broken into three capabilities: air scent (primary), tracking/trailing, and disaster dogs.

Cave Search and Rescue Team (Technical Rescue Team) Team performs search and rescue services to locate and remove injured, lost, or deceases individuals from caves and caverns. Team members work in totally dark environments that may include vertical drops, narrow or small spaces, boulder fields and scree slopes, cold, and water hazards.

Chemical/Biological (C/B) Protective Ensemble A compliant vapor-protective ensemble that is also certified as being compliant with the additional requirements for protection against C/B warfare agents such as vapors, gases, liquids, and particulate. (National Fire Protection Association [NFPA] Standard # 1991)

Chemical Warfare Agent A chemical substance (such as a nerve agent, blister agent, blood agent, choking agent, or irritating agent) used to kill, seriously injure, or incapacitate people through its physiological effects.

Chillers and Air Handlers A portable system that produces cold water through a series of components. When equipped with an air handler, cold air is generated and distributed. Requires mobilization to the desired site along with setup requirements, such as power hookup, water connections, and duct installation.

Collapse Search and Rescue Team (Technical Rescue Team) Team responds to locate, rescue, and recover individuals trapped in a fallen structure or buried in structural collapse.

Communications Support Team, Civil Air Patrol (CAP) A CAP Communications Support Team establishes and maintains CAP communications infrastructure in support of Federal, State, and local agencies.

Confined Space Search and Rescue Team (Mine Search and Rescue) Team provides search and rescue services to individuals in an enclosed area with limited entry or egress, which has a configuration not designed for human occupancy, such that an entrant could become trapped or asphyxiated. An Occupational Safety and Health Administration (OSHA) permit is required for confined space operations.

Crawler Cranes Crawler cranes have a steel undercarriage. Usually used for long-term applications where significant weights and reaches are a factor. Stabilization is accomplished through precise boom and counterweight configuration. Best used on level working areas. Several mobilization units will be required to transport boom units and counterweights. Set-up time can be accomplished with relative ease and speed once all components are available for assembly.

Crew Transport Any vehicle capable of transporting a specified number of crew personnel in a specified manner.

Critical Care Transport (CCT) An ambulance transport of a patient from a scene or a clinical setting whose condition warrants care commensurate with the scope of practice of a physician or registered nurse (e.g., capable of providing advanced hemodynamic support and monitoring, use of ventilators, infusion pumps, advanced skills, therapies, and techniques).

Critical Incident Stress Management Team (CISMT) A Critical Incident Stress Management Team is responsible for the prevention and mitigation of disabling stress among emergency responders in accordance with the standards of the International Critical Incident Stress Foundation (ICISF). Team composition, management, membership and governance vary, but can include psychologists, psychiatrists, social workers, and licensed professional counselors.

Debris Management Monitoring Team Team manages oversight of the removal, collection, and disposal of debris following a disaster, to mitigate against any potential threat to the health, safety, and welfare of the impacted citizens, and expedite recovery efforts in the impacted area, and address any threat of significant damage to improved public or private property. To act as the representing agent for the owner/agency hiring for this service providing overall coordination with all levels of government and other Emergency Support Functions (ESFs).

Provides daily reports as required. Required liability coverage for all aspects of operations and financial capabilities to manage progressive monitoring processes.

Debris Management Site Reduction Team A debris management site reduction team is designed to reduce debris from affected areas, and aims at limiting the modification of the site to the extent practicable to minimize site closure and restoration activities and cost. Teams must have knowledge and expertise to perform varying debris reduction separation techniques, including at minimum four categories: woody vegetative debris, construction or building rubble, hazardous materials [HazMat], and recyclable materials (e.g., aluminum, cast iron, steel, or household white goods or appliances). These methods of debris reduction separation could include grinding or mulching, air curtain incineration or ash, compaction, recycling, or other specialized separation techniques. Teams should have appropriate education and training in managing inspection stations located at such debris reduction sites, recycling locations, or temporary debris staging reduction sites. The management of said inspection stations shall at all times comply with OSHA, ADA, and other regulatory requirements. Routine maintenance of temporary debris staging reduction sites will be undertaken regularly to ensure no additional environmental impacts and that regulatory requirements are met. Upon completion of debris removal, teams shall provide a timely closeout of the debris reduction site by testing soil and water samples to compare with pre-use baselines, remove all unnecessary debris and equipment from the site, conduct environmental audits, and develop a restoration plan for the site. For quality assurance, teams shall provide debris monitors to observe and provide guidance to workers, whether government or contractual, that may assist in the process. All debris collected, separated, and analyzed by such debris reduction site management teams shall be done so in accordance with Federal, State, territorial, Tribal, or local laws, standards, and regulations.

Debris Management Team Team facilitates and coordinates the removal, collection, and disposal of debris following a disaster, to mitigate against any potential threat to the health, safety, and welfare of the impacted citizens, and expedite recovery efforts in the impacted area, and address any threat of significant damage to improved public or private property. Team mobilization will vary depending on the team selection, need, and or emergency. Debris removal process will vary depending on the team selection and need.

Decontamination The physical or chemical process of reducing and preventing the spread of contaminants from persons and equipment used at a hazardous materials (HazMat) incident. (National Fire Protection Association [NFPA] Standard # 472)

Deployable Portable Morgue Unit (DPMU) Mobile equipment and operations facility, fully equipped to support DMORT functions. Add-on to DMORT when no local morgue facilities are available. Supports either standard DMORT or DMORT-WMD.

Deployment Departure of team or personnel from home unit or base.

Desert Search and Rescue Team (Wilderness Rescue Team) Conducts search and rescue missions, evidence searches, and responds to other disaster or emergency situations in a desert environment.

Disaster Assessment Team Governed by type and magnitude of the disaster, the structure of the team consists of people most knowledgeable about the collection or material inventory of the disaster site, and assessing the magnitude and extent of impact on both the population and infrastructure of society. Trained specifically for disaster assessment techniques, team members are multidisciplinary and can include health personnel, engineering specialists, logisticians, environmental experts, and communications specialists. Responsibilities include recording observations and decisions made by the team, photographing and recording disaster site damage, and investigating where damage exists. Teams also analyze the significance of affected infrastructures, estimate the extent of damages, and establish initial priorities for recovery. Disaster assessment teams can perform an initial assessment that comprises situational and needs assessments in the early, critical stages of a disaster to determine the type of relief needed for an emergency response, or they may carry out a much more expedited process termed a rapid assessment.

Disaster Medical Assistance Team (DMAT) – Basic, National Disaster Medical System (NDMS) A DMAT is a volunteer group of medical and nonmedical individuals, usually from the same State or region of a State, which has formed a response team under the guidance of the NDMS (or under similar State or local auspices). Usually includes a mix of physicians, nurses, nurse practitioners, physician's assistants, pharmacists, emergency medical technicians, other allied health professionals, and support staff. Standard DMAT has 35 deployable personnel.

Disaster Medical Assistance Team (DMAT) – Burn Specialty, National Disaster Medical System (NDMS) A Burn Specialty DMAT is a volunteer group of medical and non-medical individuals, usually from the same State or region of a State, that has formed a response team under the guidance of the NDMS (or State or local auspices), and whose personnel have specific training/skills in the acute management of burn trauma patients. Members of the burn team are especially trained surgeons, nurses, and support personnel that include physical and occupational therapists, social workers, child life specialists, psychologists, nutrition and pharmacy consultants, respiratory therapists, chaplains, and volunteers. Team composition is usually determined ad hoc, based on the mission at hand.

Disaster Medical Assistance Team (DMAT) – Crush Injury Specialty, National Disaster Medical System (NDMS) A Crush Injury Specialty DMAT is a volunteer group of medical and nonmedical individuals, usually from the same State or region of a State, that has formed a response team under the guidance of the NDMS (or State or local auspices), and whose personnel have specific training/skills in the management of crush injury patients. Crush teams deal with crush and penetrating injuries. Usually includes a mix of physicians, nurses, nurse practitioners, physician's assistants, pharmacists, emergency medical technicians, other allied health professionals, and support staff. Team composition is usually determined ad hoc, based on the mission at hand.

Disaster Medical Assistance Team (DMAT) – Mental Health Specialty, National Disaster Medical System (NDMS) A Mental Health Specialty DMAT is a volunteer group of medical and nonmedical individuals, usually from the same State or region of a State, that has formed a response team under the guidance of the NDMS (or State or local auspices), and whose personnel have specific training/skills in the management of psychiatric patients. A multidisciplinary staff of specially trained and licensed mental health professionals provides emergency mental health assessment and crisis intervention services. Usually includes a mix of physicians, nurses, nurse practitioners, physician's assistants, pharmacists, emergency medical technicians, other allied health professionals, and support staff. Team composition is usually determined ad hoc, based on the mission at hand.

Disaster Medical Assistance Team (DMAT) – Pediatric Specialty, National Disaster Medical System (NDMS) A Pediatric Specialty DMAT is a volunteer group of medical and nonmedical individuals, usually from the same State or region of a State, that has formed a response team under the guidance of the NDMS (or State or local auspices), and whose personnel have specific training/skills in the management of pediatric patients. Usually includes a mix of physicians, nurses, nurse practitioners, physician's assistants, pharmacists, emergency medical technicians, other allied health professionals, and support staff. Team composition is usually determined ad hoc, based on the mission at hand.

Disaster Mortuary Operational Response Team (DMORT), National Disaster Medical System (NDMS) A DMORT is a volunteer group of medical and forensic personnel, usually from the same geographic region, that has formed a response team under the guidance of the NDMS (or State or local auspices), and whose personnel have specific training/ skills in victim identification, mortuary services, and forensic pathology and anthropology methods. Usually includes a mix of medical examiners, coroners, pathologists, forensic anthropologists, medical records technicians, fingerprint technicians, forensic odontologists, dental assistants, radiologists, funeral directors, mental health professionals, and support personnel. DMORTs are missiontailored on an ad-hoc basis, and usually deploy only with personnel and equipment specifically required for current mission.

Disaster Mortuary Operational Response Team (DMORT) – Weapons of Mass Destruction (WMD), National Disaster Medical System (NDMS) Same as DMORT except adds additional capability to deal with deceased persons residually contaminated by chemical, biological, or radiological agents.

Disaster Recovery Team A Disaster Recovery team is governed by type and magnitude of the disaster, the structure of the team consists of people most knowledgeable about the collection or material inventory of the disaster site, as they direct their efforts to recovery of both the population and infrastructure of society.

Responsibilities include separating collections and other materials to be salvaged, moving material to be recovered from affected areas to work or other storage locations for drying materials, and packing materials that will require shipment to another facility. Other responsibilities include maintaining records and photographs of the recovery effort, and establishing inventories and data collection of items as they are sent out of the building/affected location to off-site storage or other facilities. The Disaster Recovery Team may also label items that have lost inventory numbers, label or re-label boxes with locator information, and label boxes for shipment.

Donations Coordinator The Donations Coordinator is a subsection of a Donations Management Team and has working knowledge of the Individual Assistance and Public Assistance functions under FEMA/State agreement. A Donations Coordinator also has working knowledge of establishing long-term recovery committees on local levels following events. A Donations Coordinator possesses an operational knowledge of all aspects of donations coordination, including management of solicited and unsolicited funds, goods and services from concerned citizens and private organizations following a catastrophic disaster situation.

Donations Management Team A donations management team consists of one or two persons trained and experienced in all aspects of donations management. The team will be deployed to a disaster-affected jurisdiction after impact to assist in the organization and operations of State or local donations management in support of the affected jurisdiction.

Dozer (Bulldozer; Track Dozer) A dozer is specialized equipment used for leveling dirt, debris, and other materials. Equipment is usually associated with large mass movement of various materials. Often used for reducing or increasing grade elevations for roads, airports, and land clearing operations. It is also capable of ripping and moving of ledge rock and other rock materials through the use of a special attachment. Also used for cross-country lying of communication infrastructure through special attachments.

Dump Trailer Truck with a trailer attachment that has a dump body permanently attached. Dump body capacities will usually range from 20 yards to 50 yards. The equipment requires a level surface for dumping. The requirements from hauling over the road necessitate the equipment to be licensed by appropriate local jurisdictions. This equipment must meet specific standards for safety for hauling over the road whereby operators are usually required to have a commercial driver's license. This equipment is capable of transporting various aggregates along with construction and demolition debris. Typically used for long hauls.

Dump Truck, Off Road Truck with a dump body permanently attached. Equipment is usually used in an off-road situation. Equipment is usually all wheel drive with large mass capacities. It can maneuver in steep, semi-wet conditions and various weather elements. The equipment requires a semi-level surface for dumping. Often used for large mass projects where earth materials are moved within the project area. Often used in airport/road construction and open pit mining.

Dump Truck, On Road Truck with a dump body permanently attached. Dump body capacities will usually range from 3 yards to 20 yards. This equipment is capable of transporting various aggregates along with construction and demolition debris.

Electrical Power Restoration Team The electrical power restoration team is dependent upon event or disaster size and will be supported by various personal expertise. The teams are usually activated through power company mutual aid agreements. The assignment of personnel and equipment will be dependent upon availability of the releasing mutual aid partner, and will have an agreed timeframe for the release of these said resources. The restoration team coordinates and supports resources of energy producers to quickly restore electrical power to afflicted areas. The host recipients will provide or assist with accommodations for the duration of the team stay. Teams should possess the experience and financial capabilities to support equipment, personnel, and to maintain operations for an indefinite period of time.

EMAC Advanced Team (EMAC A-Team) The EMAC Advance Team is a team (typically comprised of 2 staff) of EMAC trained and experienced personnel designated to deploy to a State to facilitate interState mutual aid assistance under the Emergency Management Assistance Compact (EMAC). The mission of the EMAC Advance Team is to implement EMAC on behalf of the requesting State by coordinating and facilitating the provision of assistance from other member States in accordance with procedures set forth in the EMAC Standard Operating Procedures.

Emergency Medical Task Force An Emergency Medical Task Force is any combination (within span of control) of resources (Ambulances, Rescues, Engines, Squads, etc) assembled for a medical mission, with common communications, and a leader (supervisor). Self-sufficient for 12 hour operational periods, although it may be deployed longer, depending on need.

Emergency Medical Technician (EMT) A practitioner credentialed by a State to function as an EMT by a State Emergency Medical Services (EMS) system.

Emergency Operations Center (EOC) Management Support Team Team provides support to an Incident Commander (IC). An IC is an optional member of the team, because it is assumed that an Incident Command/lead has already been established under which these support functions will operate. Typically comprised of an information officer, liaison officer, safety officer, logistics officer, and administrative aide.

Emergency Response Team – Advance Element (ERT-A) The portion of the ERT-A first deployed to the field, usually the State Emergency Operations Center (EOC), and the disaster site to join State emergency management personnel to coordinate Federal assistance, determine the extent and focus of initial disaster response activities, and identify a suitable DFO site.

Emergency Response Team – National (ERTN) Team provides coordination for Federal response and recovery activities within a State. Once the ERT-N is operational at the Disaster Field Office (DFO), it assumes responsibility from the Regional Operations Center (ROC) staff for management of the Federal response and recovery operation. Major organizational elements of the ERT-N include operations, logistics, information and planning, and administration sections. These four sections coordinate at the staff level and provide mutual support to accomplish priority missions. This coordination includes interaction, consultation, planning, information sharing, operational decision-making, and commitment of resources.

EMS Strike Team A team comprised of five resources or less of the same type with a supervisor and common communications capability. Whether it is five resources or less, a specific number must be identified for the team. For instance, a basic life support (BLS) strike team would be five BLS units and a supervisor or, for example, an advanced life support (ALS) strike team would be comprised of five ALS units and a supervisor.

EMS Task Force A team comprised of five resources or less of the same type with a supervisor and common communications capability. Whether it is five resources or less, a specific number must be identified for the team. For instance, an EMS task force might be comprised of two ALS teams and three BLS teams and a supervisor.

Engine, Fire (Engine Company) Any ground vehicle providing specified levels of pumping, water, hose capacity, and staffed with a minimum number of personnel.

Engineering Services Depending on the type and magnitude of a disaster or terrorist incident, engineering service expertise will be used accordingly based on discipline specialization. In a general sense, the services that could be provided through engineering services include structural, electrical, civil, mechanical, architectural, geotechnical, and environmental/hazardous materials. Emergency management engineering service providers should posses indepth knowledge of damage assessment, safety evaluation, transportation infrastructure evaluation per Federal Highway Administration damage assessment procedures, cost recovery per the Stafford Act, and debris management. Additional skills of such engineering service providers should encompass evaluation of hazardous materials, traffic management, utility restoration, water and wastewater quality evaluations, telecommunications operations, and support for the FEMA Urban Search and Rescue Task Force. Engineering service providers should have the ability, experience, and knowledge to interact with the Army Corps of Engineers and other Federal agencies such as the Environmental Protection Agency, along with State, territorial, Tribal, or local building and utility inspectors. Other engineering services that can be provided should include strategic planning for technology, programs, concept development and requirements analysis, system design and integration, tests and evaluation, and integrated logistics support for emergency management.

EOC Finance/Administration Section Coordinator An EOC Finance/Administration Section Coordinator is an individual at the EOC responsible for tracking incident costs and reimbursement accounting, and coordinating/administering support for EOC personnel during disaster operations. This function is part of the standardized ICS structure per the National Incident Management System. If situation warrants, chief/coordinator oversees subunits of this function, including Compensation/Claims, Procurement, Cost, and Time.

EOC Operations Section Chief An EOC Operations Section Chief is an individual at the EOC responsible for managing tactical operations at the incident site directed toward reducing the immediate hazard, saving lives and property, establishing situation control, and restoring normal conditions; responsible for the delivery and coordination of disaster assistance programs and services, including emergency assistance, human services assistance, and infrastructure assistance; and oversight of subunits of Operations Section, including Branches (up to five), Division/Groups (up to 25) and Resources as warranted.

EOC Planning Section Chief The EOC Planning Section Chief is an individual at the EOC who oversees all incident-related data gathering and analysis regarding incident operations and assigned resources, develops alternatives for tactical operations, conducts planning meetings, and prepares the IAP for each operational period.

Equipment Transport (Heavy Equipment Transport) Any ground vehicle capable of transporting a dozer or tractor.

Evacuation Coordination Team An Evacuation Coordination Team provides support in State and local emergency response efforts by compiling, analyzing, and disseminating traffic-related information that can be used to facilitate the rapid, efficient, and safe evacuation of threatened populations. Primarily operates in the State or local EOC as an extension of Emergency Support Function (ESF) #1 – Transportation. The mission of the Evacuation Coordination Team is to provide for the protection of life and/or property by removing endangered persons and property form potential or actual disaster areas to areas of less danger through the successful execution of evacuation procedures.

Evacuation Liaison Team Team provides support in State and local emergency response efforts by compiling, analyzing, and disseminating traffic-related information that can be used to facilitate the rapid, efficient, and safe evacuation of threatened populations. Primarily operates in the State or local EOC as an extension of Emergency Support Function (ESF) #1 – Transportation.

Evidence Response Team (ERT) An Evidence Recovery Team (ERT) is capable of providing 24-hour access to specialized decontamination equipment for chemical release and advice to the On-Scene Coordinator in hazard evaluation; risk assessment; multimedia sampling and analysis; on-site safety, including development and implementation of plans; cleanup techniques and priorities; water supply decontamination and protection; application of dispersants; environmental assessment; degree of cleanup required; and disposal of contaminated material.

External Resources Resources that fall outside a team's particular agency, including other agency resources or commercially contracted resources.

Field Mobile Mechanic A motor-driven vehicle designed and constructed to provide specified level of equipment capacity and mechanically trained personnel.

Field Veterinary Medical Officer (Veterinary Medical Field Officer) A professional veterinarian who works to implement animal and poultry disease control programs. Duties can include supervising animal and poultry disease control and eradication services; contacting animal and poultry owners and organizations to explain disease control programs and to provide veterinary medicine advice; conducting epidemiologic investigation of disease outbreaks; inspecting health certificates, livestock auctions, and animal and poultry dealer records; monitoring animal and poultry production and marketing activities; and preparing surveys and reports of disease prevalence.

Flash Fire Protective Ensemble A compliant vapor-protective ensemble that is also certified as being compliant with the additional requirements for limited protection against chemical flash fire for escape only. (National Fire Protection Association [NFPA] Standard # 1991)

Flat Bed Trailer Truck Truck with a trailer attachment usually used for the transportation of goods and other commodities across long distances. Depending on the payload, some flat bed trucks have expandable tandems for meeting weight requirements. Flatbeds are usually a fifth-wheel mounted assembly. Payloads can be as much as 80,000 pounds and more if permitted.

Food Dispenser Unit (Food Dispenser) Any vehicle capable of dispensing food to incident personnel.

Generators Diesel-fueled engine generators are used to support electrical requirements at facilities of various sizes such as hospitals, housing, plants, and commercial stores. Units are usually mounted on tow behind or trailer mobilized equipment. Deployment and set up can be accomplished within hours.

Geographical Incident Management Teams, Firefighting A Geographical Incident Management Team is an interagency organization under the auspices of the Geographical Area Coordination Group composed of the Incident Commander (IC), and appropriate general and command staff personnel assigned to an incident, trained and certified to the Type II level. Type II level personnel may lack the degree of training and experience of Type I personnel in managing complex incidents at the type one level.

Ground Ambulance (Medical Transport) A ground transport vehicle configured, equipped, and staffed to respond to, care for, and transport patients.

Hazardous Materials (HazMat) Any material that is explosive, flammable, poisonous, corrosive, reactive, or radioactive, or any combination thereof, and requires special care in handling because of the hazards it poses to public health, safety, and/or the environment. Any hazardous substance under the Clean Water Act, or any element, compound, mixture, solution, or substance designated under the Comprehensive Environmental Response, Compensation, and Liability Act (CERCLA); any hazardous waste under the Resource Conservation and Recovery Act (RCRA); any toxic pollutant listed under pretreatment provisions of the Clean Water Act; any hazardous pollutant under Section 112 of the Clean Air Act; or any imminent hazardous chemical substance for which the administrator has taken action under the Toxic Substances Control Act (TSCA) Section 7. (Section 101[14] CERCLA)

Hazardous Material Response Team An organized group of individuals that is trained and equipped to perform work to control actual or potential leaks, spills, discharges, or releases of HazMat, requiring possible close approach to the material. The team/equipment may include external or contracted resources.

Hazardous Materials Company Any piece of equipment having the capabilities, personal protective equipment (PPE), equipment, and complement of personnel as specified in the Hazardous Materials Company types and minimum capabilities. The personnel complement will include one member who is trained to a minimum level of assistant safety officer – HazMat.

Hazardous Materials Incident Uncontrolled, unlicensed release of HazMat during storage or use from a fixed facility or during transport outside a fixed facility that may impact public health, safety, and/or the environment.

HazMat Task Force A group of resources with common communications and a leader. A HazMat Task Force may be pre-established and sent to an incident, or formed at the incident.

HazMat Trained and Equipped To the level of training and equipment defined by the Occupational Safety and Health Administration (OSHA) and the National Fire Protection Association (NFPA).

Helicopters, Firefighting (Helicopter or Copter) An aircraft that depends principally on the lift generated by one or more rotors for its support in flight. Capable of the delivery of firefighters, water, or chemical retardants (either a fixed tank or bucket system), and internal or external cargo.

Helitack Crew (Firefighting Crew) A crew of firefighters specially trained and certified in the tactical and logistical use of helicopters for fire suppression.

Helitanker A helicopter equipped with a fixed tank, Air Tanker Board certified, capable of delivering a minimum of 1,100 gallons of water, foam, or retardant (current model helicopter certified, Sikorsky S-64 Sky-Crane).

Helitanker (Firefighting Helicopter) A helicopter equipped with a fixed tank, Air Tanker Board certified, and capable of delivering a minimum of 1,100 gallons of water, retardant, or foam.

High-Angle Rope Rescue (Rope Rescue; Technical Rock) Rescue in which the load is predominately supported by the rope rescue system.

Hydraulic Excavator (Large Mass Excavation 13cy to 3cy Buckets) Track undercarriage construction equipment used to excavate and load earth, blasted rock, sands, and other types of aggregate, also used to load or handle demolition materials. Provides rapid excavation for construction and repair of runways, roads and trails, railroads, pipelines, waterways, and quarry operations. Larger hydraulic excavators may require some dismantling in meeting mobilization requirements. Dismantled pieces usually require additional mobilization support. Multiple accessories are available for varying tasks.

Hydraulic Excavator (Medium Mass Excavation 4cy to 1.75cy Buckets) Track undercarriage construction equipment that is a track-mounted, hydraulic-controlled, excavating system used to excavate and load earth, blasted rock, sands, and other types of aggregate, also used to load or handle demolition materials. Provides rapid excavation for construction and repair of runways, roads and trails, railroads, pipelines, waterways, and quarry operations. Slightly smaller than the larger hydraulic excavator category, these usually do not require dismantling for mobilization requirements. If dismantling is considered, it may require additional mobilization support. Multiple accessories are available for varying tasks.

Hydraulic Truck Cranes Highly flexible and mobile self-propelled cranes that can be deployed with ease. They usually do not require any setup or special mobilization consideration. Depending on the actual lifting requirements, these cranes come in various sizes and capabilities. Stabilizers include outrigger for stability.

Hyperspectral Imaging Support Team Civil Air Patrol (CAP) A CAP Hyperspectral Imaging Support Team provides specialized ground support to analyze and interpret data provided by CAP ARCHER Hyperspectral Imaging systems. ARCHER is an airborne reconnaissance asset that is only available through the CAP at the request of Federal, State, and local agencies.

Ice Search and Rescue Team (Water Rescue Team; Public Safety Dive Team) Team locates and rescues individuals trapped under ice-capped water.

Illumination Unit (Lighting Plant) A portable light-generating unit capable of providing three to six lights of 500 watts each with extension cords from 500 feet to 1,000 feet to provide specified level of illumination capacity.

Incident Management Team A command team comprised of the Incident Commander (IC), appropriate command, and general staff personnel assigned to an incident. (Source: FIRESCOPE)

Incident Management Team, Animal Protection An Animal Protection Incident Management Team, when deployed, will asses the emergency situation and determine the number of operational strike teams that will be required for rescuing, transporting, and sheltering of animals.

Incident Management Team, Firefighting An Incident Management Team is an interagency organization under the auspices of NWCG composed of the Incident Commander (IC) and appropriate general and command staff personnel assigned to an incident, trained and certified to the Type I level. Type I level personnel possess the highest level of training available and are experienced in the management of complex incidents.

Individual Assistance Disaster Assessment Team An Individual Assistance Disaster Assessment Team is responsible for providing expert assessments of the disaster situation pertaining to claims for individual assistance and other programs.

Individual Assistance Disaster Assessment Team Leader An Individual Assistance Disaster Assessment Team Leader is the individual responsible for leading the individual assistance disaster assessment team and possesses an administrative knowledge of Individual Assistance areas. (See Individual Assistance Disaster Assessment Team.)

In-House Assets or expertise specifically owned, possessed, directed, and/or controlled by the responding entity.

Instrument Flight Rules (IFR) Set of rules, guidelines, and procedures that the Federal Aviation Administration (FAA) has established for pilots to operate aircraft in marginal weather conditions, usually defined as ceilings below 1,000 feet/ visibility less than 3 miles.

Interagency Buying Team, Firefighting The Interagency Wildland Fire Community supports a Buying Team. A National Buying Team supports the procurement efforts through the local administrative staff and is authorized to procure a wide range of services, supplies, and land and equipment rentals. In addition, the buying team leader has the responsibility of coordinating property accountability with the supply unit leader.

International Medical Surgical Response Team (IMSuRT), National Disaster Medical System (NDMS) An IMSuRT is a volunteer group of medical and non-medical individuals, usually from the same State or region of a State, that has formed a response team under the guidance of the NDMS and the State Department, and whose personnel and equipment give it deployable medical and surgical treatment capability, worldwide. It is the only NDMS medical team with surgical operating room capability. Full team consists of roughly 26 personnel, which is a mix of physicians, nurses, medical technicians, and allied personnel.

Lattice Truck Cranes This is the larger of the wheel cranes. Usually used for long-term applications where significant weights and reaches are a factor. Stabilizers include outriggers for stability. Several mobilization units will be required to transport boom units and counterweights. Set-up time can be accomplished with relative ease and speed once all components are available for assembly.

Law Enforcement Aviation – Fixed-Wing Fixed-wing aircraft of various sizes used for surveillance, extraditions, personnel, and cargo transportation.

Law Enforcement Aviation – Helicopters – Patrol and Surveillance Helicopters of various sizes to provide multifunction aerial support for ground operations.

Law Enforcement Canine Teams – Cadaver-Detecting Dogs Patrol dogs trained to find and passively alert on decaying human tissues, bones, and fluids.

Law Enforcement Canine Teams – Explosive Detecting Dogs Patrol dogs trained to detect and passively alert on a variety of odors indicating the presence of explosive devices.

Law Enforcement Canine Teams – Narcotics Detecting Dogs Patrol dogs capable of finding and alerting on cocaine, marijuana, methamphetamines, heroin, and their derivatives.

Law Enforcement Canine Teams – Patrol Dogs (K-9s) Trained canine units providing law enforcement with a non-lethal means of apprehending dangerous criminal offenders; detecting intruders and alerting handlers to their presence; pursuing, attacking, and holding criminal offenders who resist apprehension; searching and clearing buildings and large open areas for criminals; tracking lost children or other persons; detecting the presence of certain narcotics, explosives, and tobacco products; locating deceased subjects, crime scenes, and minute physical evidence; and providing a strong psychological deterrent to certain types of criminal misconduct.

Law Enforcement Dive Teams – Evidence Recovery Underwater teams used to recover evidence.

Law Enforcement Dive Teams – Recovery Underwater teams used to recover drowning victims and lost vessels.

Liquid Splash-Protective Ensemble Multiple elements designed to provide a degree of protection for emergency response personnel from adverse exposure to the inherent risks of liquid-chemical exposure occurring during hazardous materials (HazMat) emergencies and similar operations. The liquid splash-protective ensemble is either an encapsulating or non-encapsulating ensemble. (National Fire Protection Association [NFPA] Standard # 1992)

Low-Angle Rope Rescue (Rope Rescue) Rescue in which the load is predominately supported by itself and not the rope rescue system.

Management Support Team (MST), National Disaster Medical System (NDMS) An MST is a command and control team that provides support and liaison functions for other NDMS teams in the field. MSTs are usually staffed by a mix of Federal employees and are constituted on an ad-hoc, missionspecific basis. An MST (perhaps as small as one or two individuals) always accompanies an NDMS unit on a deployment.

Mine and Tunnel Search and Rescue Team A specially trained and equipped team that searches for, rescues, and/or recovers individuals from working or abandoned mines and tunnels.

Mine Rescue Team (Confined Space Rescue) Team locates and rescues individuals lost or trapped in active or abandoned mine shafts or other below-ground entrapments.

Mobile Communications Center (Mobile Emergency Operations Center [EOC]; Mobile Command Center; Continuity of Operations Vehicle) A vehicle that serves as a self-sustaining mobile operations center capable of operating in an environment with little to no basic services, facilitating communications between multiple entities using an array of fixed and/or wireless communications equipment, providing appropriate work space for routine support functions, and providing basic services for personnel in short-term or long-term deployments.

Mobile Feeding Kitchen (Mobile Field Kitchen; Rapid Deployment Kitchen) A containerized kitchen that can be positioned forward in fulfillment of Emergency Support Function (ESF) #11 – Food and Water. The units are used to support feeding operations at emergency incidents.

Mobile Field Force (Crowd Control Teams; Riot Dispersal Team) Police units trained in handling large crowds and riot situations, including specialized training in crowd dispersal, tactics, and special weapons.

Mobile Kitchen Unit A unit designed and constructed to dispense food for incident personnel providing a specified level of capacity.

Mountain Search and Rescue Team (Wilderness Rescue Team) Team searches for and rescues people either above the timberline or in high-angle areas below the timberline, which can include glacier, crevasse, backcountry, alpine search and rescue, and other aspects of the environment.

National Strike Force, U.S. Coast Guard The U.S. Coast Guard National Strike Force was created in 1973 as a Coast Guard special force under the National Contingency Plan (NCP/see 40 CFR 300.145) to respond to oil and hazardous chemical incidents. The NSF consists of three interoperable regionally based Strike Teams: Atlantic, Gulf and Pacific, and the Public Information Assist Team (PIAT). The NSF supports USCG and EPA Federal On-Scene Coordinators (FOSCs) to protect public health, welfare, and the environment. In recent years, the capabilities have been expanded to include response to weapons of mass destruction (WMD) incidents, as well as incident management assistance.

National Urban Search and Rescue (US&R) Incident Support Team (IST) ISTs are components of ERT-As that provide Federal, State, and local officials with technical assistance in the acquisition and use of search and rescue resources through advice, Incident Command assistance, management, and coordination of US&R task forces and obtaining logistic support.

Occupational Health & Safety Specialists (Occupational Physicians; Occupational Health Nurses; Industrial Hygienists; Occupational Safety Specialists; Occupational Safety & Health Technicians; Health and Safety Inspectors; Industrial Hygienists) Personnel with specific training in occupational safety and health and topics such as workplace assessment or occupational medicine. Occupational health and safety specialists and technicians help keep workplaces safe and workers in good health unscathed. They promote occupational health and safety within organizations by developing safer, healthier, and more efficient ways of working. They analyze work environments and design programs to control, eliminate, and prevent disease or injury caused by chemical, physical, and biological agents or ergonomic factors. They may conduct inspections and enforce adherence to laws, regulations, or employer policies governing worker health and safety.

Paramedic A practitioner credentialed by a State to function at the advanced life support (ALS) level in the State Emergency Medical Services (EMS) system.

Personal Protective Equipment (PPE) Equipment and clothing required to shield or isolate personnel from the chemical, physical, thermal, and biological hazards that may be encountered at a hazardous materials (HazMat) incident. (National Fire Protection Association [NFPA] Standard # 472)

Public Assistance Coordinator (PAC) The Public Assistance Coordinator (PAC) is a subsection of the Public Assistance Team (PAT). The PAC is assigned to work with a Public Assistance (PA) applicant from declaration to funding approval. The PAC must possess an in-depth working knowledge of disaster relief laws, regulations, PA programs, and recovery roles of government and the private sector.

Public Safety Dive Team Team assists with location and recovery of drowning victims, evidence in criminal cases, and abandoned vehicles and provides safety divers for special events.

Public Safety Dive Team, Law Enforcement (Dive Team) A Law Enforcement Public Safety Dive Team is a group of law enforcement divers equipped and trained to perform a variety of functions, including evidence search and recovery.

Radio Direction Finding Team (Electronic Search Team) Teams use radio direction finding equipment to locate distress beacons (such as emergency locator transmitters, emergency position indicating radio beacons, and personal locator beacons). Beacons may be located in remote or populated areas, as teams can expect to work in varied localities, including airfields, marinas, and geographically secluded areas.

Radiological Material Any material that spontaneously emits ionizing radiation. (National Fire Protection Association [NFPA] Standard # 472)

Rapid Needs Assessment (RNA) Team Team provides a rapid assessment capability immediately following a major disaster or emergency. The RNA Team will collect and provide information to determine requirements for critical resources needed to support emergency response activities. The RNA Team is responsible for assessing both overall impact of a disaster event and determining Federal and/or State immediate response requirements.

Release Any spilling, leaking, pumping, pouring, emitting, emptying, discharging, injecting, escaping, leaching, dumping, or disposing into the environment (including the abandonment or discharging of barrels, containers, and other closed receptacles containing any hazardous substance or pollutant or contaminant). (Section 101[22] CERCLA)

Rescue To access, stabilize, and evacuate distressed or injured individuals by whatever means necessary to ensure their timely transfer to appropriate care or to a place of safety.

Rope Rescue (High-Angle Rescue; Low-Angle Rescue; Technical Rescue) To rescue through the use of rigging techniques, anchor systems, belays, mechanical advantages, subject extrication techniques, and low- and highangle rescue techniques.

Search To locate an overdue or missing individual, individuals, or objects.

Search Suit Suit made of Kevlar® and Nomex 3, often used by, but not limited to, bomb squad personnel, significantly lighter than bomb suits; allows user to conduct search with increased mobility.

Shelter Management Team Team provides managerial and operational support for a shelter during an emergency. Responsibilities of the team may include all or some of the following: operating the shelter; establishing security; ensuring the availability of adequate care, food, sanitation, and first aid; selecting and training personnel to perform operational tasks; monitoring contamination; performing decontamination; establishing exposure control and monitoring; monitoring overpressure and filtration systems; performing post-event reconnaissance; and directing egress.

Sheltering Team, Large Animal, Animal Protection An Animal Protection Large Animal Sheltering Team will deploy for a minimum of 7 days and will be responsible for advising and supporting local efforts in setting up a large animal shelter.

Sheltering Team, Small Animal, Animal Protection An Animal Protection Small Animal Sheltering Team will deploy for a minimum of 7 days and will be responsible for advising and supporting local efforts in setting up a small animal shelter.

Special-Needs Shelter A refuge specifically designed to accommodate individuals with special medical needs who are not ill enough to require hospitalization. These shelters are supported by volunteer doctors and nurses and often have backup electric capability to support those with medical equipment reliant on electricity.

Special Weapons and Tactics (SWAT)/Tactical Teams SWAT teams are specially trained to handle high-risk situations and specialized tactical needs. Team members have advanced skills beyond that of typical patrol officers.

Strike Team, Large Animal Rescue, Animal Protection An Animal Protection Large Animal Rescue Strike Team is a six-member team capable of completing an average of one rescue every 30 minutes in a suburban setting and one rescue every hour in rural settings.

Strike Team, Small Animal Rescue, Animal Protection An Animal Protection Small Animal Rescue Strike Team is a six-member team capable of completing an average of one rescue every 30 minutes in a suburban setting and one rescue every hour in rural settings.

Sustainability Ability to continue response operations for the prescribed duration necessary.

Swift Water Search and Rescue Team (Flood Search and Rescue; Water Rescue Team) Team conducts surface search and rescue operations on waterways where the water is moving fast enough to produce sufficient force to present a life and safety hazard to a person entering it.

Tender, Foam (Firefighting Foam Tender) The apparatus used to mix concentrate with water to make solution, pump, and mix air and solution to make foam, and transport and apply foam.

Tender, Fuel (Fuel Tender) Any vehicle capable of supplying fuel to ground or airborne equipment.

Tender, Helicopter (Helicopter Tender) A ground service vehicle capable of supplying fuel and support equipment to helicopters.

Total Containment Vessel (TCV) A TCV is designed to transport explosive or chemical devices, fully enclosed. Used for explosive and hazardous materials (HazMat).

Tractor Trailer Truck with a trailer attachment used for mobilization of various goods, supplies, and equipment. Predominately used for moving equipment, either long distances, overweight and over-width equipment, or equipment not permitted for over the road purposes, including track equipment. Trailers are either fifth-wheel mounted or tow behinds, depending on the size of the load. Also used for long- and short-haul needs, including smaller equipment. Loading and off-loading can be accomplished from either the front or the rear. Usually the rear loading will require ramps. If loading is done from the front, the trailer will be detached from the truck allowing use of the small ramps for loading purposes. Front-end loading using a detachable trailer is usually used for oversized equipment. Payloads can be as much as 80,000 pounds and more if permitted.

Transport Team, Large Animal, Animal Protection An Animal Protection Large Animal Transport Team will deploy for a minimum of 5 days and will be responsible for transporting large animals from a disaster site. All required vehicles will accompany team.

Transport Team, Small Animal, Animal Protection An Animal Protection Small Animal Transport Team will deploy for a minimum of 5 days and will be responsible for transporting large animals from a disaster site. All required vehicles will accompany team.

Tub Grinder Specialized equipment designed to grind heavy brush, pallets, demolition material, land-clearing debris, and yard waste. Units are equipped with hammer mills ranging from 26 inches to 36 inches that serve as steel fixed hammers or doubled-edged cutting tools. Tub grinders possess hydraulic tub tilt to provide safe access to the hammer mill during maintenance, and have a horsepower range from 157 to 1,050. Tub grinders shrink space requirement by a ratio of 10:1 yards. Feeding the equipment requires either a front-end loader or other hydraulic equipment such as an excavator with a thumb attachment or cherry picker. Processed materials can be stockpiled using conveyor systems or with stockpiled using a front-end loader. Depending on the size of the equipment's processing capabilities, it may be possible to feed and stockpile with one front-end loader. Equipment operations and controls are remotely managed, usually away from any potential flying debris. Mobilization is required, either with a tractor-trailer hook-up, fifth-wheel only, or pindle-hook option. The processing area should be firm soil with sufficient room for stockpiling pre- and post-products; however, track tub grinders are available for special processing needs. Over-width escort services would be used for wide loads.

Tug Boat Tugboats are commercial water vessels that move or assist in the movement of propelled and non-propelled water vessels, primarily with ship docking and barge towing. Ship-assist tugs are generally port or harbor related, while barge towing tugs are typically port-to-port transporters up and down rivers, inlets, and the coastline. With different sizes and modifications for varying tasks, tug boats require specially trained operators or captains licensed and subject to jurisdiction of the U.S. Coast Guard, and are also subject to random drug and alcohol testing procedures. Crew manifests generally range from 2 to 6+ individuals, including a captain and an inland waterways river pilot, required by law, who serves as servant to the vessel master. Docking pilots (specialists) should be used where possible, as they serve to enhance communications between the assisted ship and the tugboat in "unfamiliar waters." These crewmembers will, at times, live on the tug itself or on-call from nearby homes, and have a varying schedule dependent on the tug company. Tugboats also consist of model bows or pointed bows for towing while push tugs have square bows. Specially equipped tugboats can be specialized to serve as spray boats or firefighting boats for the purposes of emergency situations. Tugboats strongly rely on the need for communication as many assisted ships either originate in foreign countries or are unfamiliar with inland or harbor waters. In emergencies, the U.S. Coast Guard houses a master list of tug boats that can be contacted for assistance. Most tug boat owners and operators may belong to their trade association, the American Waterways Operators (AWO).

Urban Search and Rescue (US&R) US&R involves the location, rescue (extrication), and initial medical stabilization of victims trapped in confined spaces.

Urban Search and Rescue (US&R) Task Force (US&R Team) Federal asset that conducts physical search and rescue in collapsed buildings; provides emergency medical care to trapped victims; assesses and controls gas, electrical services, and hazardous materials (HazMat); and evaluates and stabilizes damaged structures.

Vapor Protective Ensemble A vapor protective ensemble or garment that is intended for use in an unknown threat atmosphere or for known high health risk atmospheres is vapor tight, and is in compliance with National Fire Protection Association (NFPA) Standard # 1991, "Standard on Vapor-Protective Ensembles for Hazardous Materials Emergencies."

Veterinary Epidemiologist A practitioner who studies factors influencing existence and spread of diseases among humans and animals, particularly those diseases transmissible from animals to humans. Required to hold degree of Doctor of Veterinary Medicine.

Veterinary Medical Assistance Team (VMAT), National Disaster Medical System (NDMS) VMATs are volunteer teams of veterinarians, technicians, and support personnel, usually from the same region, that have organized a response team under the guidance of the American Veterinary Medical Association and the NDMS, and whose personnel have specific training in responding to animal casualties and/or animal disease outbreaks during a disaster. They help assess medical needs of animals, and conduct animal disease surveillance, hazard mitigation, biological and chemical terrorism surveillance, and animal decontamination. Usually includes a mix of veterinarians, veterinary technicians, support personnel, microbiologists, epidemiologists, and veterinary pathologists.

Visual Flight Rules (VFR) Set of Federal Aviation Administration (FAA) rules, guidelines, and procedures that apply to aircraft when a pilot is conducting flight with visual reference to the ground.

Volcano Search and Rescue Team (Wilderness Rescue Team) Team provides technical rescue, avalanche rescue, and other aspects of mountain rescue services applicable for search and rescue operations in and around the surface of a volcano.

Volunteer Agency Liaison (VAL) The Volunteer Agency Liaison serves as the central point between government entities and volunteer organizations in the coordination of information and activities of VOADs (Volunteer Organizations Active in Disasters) responding in times of disaster.

Water Purification Team (Emergency Water Teams) A water purification team is a specialized team designed to support the Emergency Water Mission in support of the Federal Response Plan (FRP). Teams provide an emergency supply of potable water, both bottled and bulk, to include procurement, transportation, and distribution to impacted areas for usage by both the general public and response personnel. FEMA, who is the lead agency under the FRP for coordinating all Federal activities following a natural disaster or manmade emergency, assigned the Department of Defense (U.S. Army Corps of Engineers) as the lead agency in support of Emergency Support Function (ESF) #3 – Public Works and Engineering, that includes tasking of emergency potable water. Team members are fully trained and knowledgeable of water certification requirements and daily consumption rates, the procurement process including the Advanced Contracting Initiative (ACI) Water Contract, which is a supply and service contract for procuring bottled and bulk water, transportation, security measures, distribution processes, emergency management, and have previously worked with or able to build rapport with State and local governments. Teams coordinate with FEMA, State and local governments, and other ESF elements to scope the magnitude of the water mission. After mission scoping, teams assist FEMA in writing the mission assignment and tasks, estimating mission-funding requirements, and assessing when all emergency needs have been met and the water mission can be closed out. Emergency water teams are responsible for timely procurement and delivery of potable water to all Staging Areas and distribution sites. Teams are deployed on 30-day rotations, with 3 to 5-day transition periods, however, the average water mission only lasts about 2 to 3 weeks. In events with warning, such as hurricanes, emergency water teams are predeployed to the region and contract for the delivery of a small amount of potable water to predesignated Staging Areas so that water deliveries can begin immediately following the event. Following the event, the teams focus on meeting all post-declaration water mission mandates tasked by FEMA to ESF #3, including mass distribution at appropriate staging areas.

Water Search and Rescue Team Team conducts surface and subsurface search and rescue operations in all-water environments, including swift water and flood conditions. Water rescue teams come with all team equipment required to safely and effectively conduct operations. Water rescue teams can be assigned to special events to provide for the safety of citizens.

Water Truck A truck with a permanently mounted water tank with the capabilities of dispensing potable or nonpotable water. The dispensing is handled through gravity or pumped. For pumping action, the truck's engine or transmission is usually used to generate the requirement dispensing energy. Uses can range from delivering potable water to shelter locations, nonpotable form for irrigation, assisting in wildfire situations, dust control, compaction requirements, flushing of storm conveyance sanitary sewer lines, and washing areas of dirt, debris, and dust.

Weapons of Mass Destruction (WMD) (1) Any destructive device as defined in section 921 of this title ("destructive device" defined as any explosive, incendiary, or poison gas, bomb, grenade, rocket having a propellant charge of more than 4 ounces, missile having an explosive or incendiary charge of more than 1/4 ounce, mine or device similar to the above); (2) any weapon that is designed or intended to cause serious bodily injury through the release, dissemination, or impact of toxic or poisonous chemicals, or their precursors; (3) any weapon involving a disease organism; or (4) any weapon that is designed to release radiation or radioactivity at a level dangerous to human life. (United States Code, Title 18-Crimes and Criminal Procedure, Part I-Crimes, Chapter 113B-Terrorism, Sec. 2332a)

Wheel Dozer A wheel dozer is a rubber-tired piece of equipment used for spreading and compacting without vibratory means. This equipment can accomplish mass leveling tasks for agriculture, construction, forestry, heavy construction, industrial needs, open pit mining, and similar earth moving requirements. Rubber tires contribute by compacting the earth being moved during the process of leveling. Leveling in layers to maximize density requirements usually performs this action. Layered leveling limits will also be accommodated by the weight and size of the equipment being employed. Equipment can operate on slight slopes. Equipment capacities can vary from 100,000 lbs. at 33 yd^3 to 22,000 lbs. at 3.5 yd^3. Mobilization is usually required. A front-end loading detachable trailer is usually the preferred option. Over-width escort services would be used for wide loads.

Wheel Loaders (Large: 41cy to 8cy) Rubber-tired equipment used for moving and/or loading large masses of various aggregate materials or demolition debris. Materials are usually loaded into material carrying equipment, such as dump trucks or stockpiled, processed, and/or moved around onsite. Accessories are also available for handling bulky materials/waste.

A tractor-trailer unit usually handles the mobilization. Depending on the bucket size, dismantling is usually not an issue. Depending on the width, a transport permit may be required, along with escort services.

Wheel Loaders (Medium to Small: 7cy to 2cy) Rubber-tired equipment used for moving and/or loading small to large masses of various aggregate materials or demolition debris. Materials are usually loaded into material carrying equipment, such as dump trucks or stockpiled, processed, and/or moved around onsite. Accessories are also available for handling bulky materials/waste. A tractor-trailer unit usually handles the mobilization but is not necessary for some pieces of equipment. Mobilization without a transport usually requires an operator's license. Usually the width of this equipment does not require a transport permit but may still require an escort service.

Wilderness Search and Rescue Team (Ground Search and Rescue) Team provides response search and rescue services, including all-weather search and rescue of missing persons, search and rescue management capabilities, trained ground search teams of all levels, technical rescue specialists, specialized wilderness medical personnel, and safety and survival education.

Wilderness Search and Rescue Team (Ground Search and Rescue Team) Team provides ground search and rescue services, including all-weather search and rescue of missing persons, search and rescue management capabilities, evidence collection, trained ground search teams of all levels, technical rescue specialists, specialized wilderness medical personnel, and safety and survival education.

WMD Chem/Bio A shorthand phrase for "weapons of mass destruction, chemical/biological," in reference to those substances that were developed by military institutions to create widespread injury, illness, or death.

Zone, Contamination Reduction (Warm Zone) The area between the Exclusion Zone and the Support Zone. This zone contains the personnel decontamination station. This zone may require a lesser degree of personnel protection than the Exclusion Zone. This separates the contaminated area from the clean area and acts as a buffer to reduce contamination of the "clean" area. (U.S. Coast Guard Incident Management Handbook, 2001 edition)

Zone, Exclusion (Hot Zone) The area immediately around a spill or release and where contamination does or could occur. The innermost of the three zones of a hazardous substances/material incident. Special protection is required for all personnel while in this zone. (U.S. Coast Guard Incident Management Handbook, 2001 edition)

Zone, Support (Cold Zone) The "clean" area outside of the contamination control line. In this area, equipment and personnel are not expected to become contaminated. Special protective clothing is not required. This is the area where resources are assembled to support the hazardous substances/materials release operations. (U.S. Coast Guard Incident Management Handbook, 2001 edition)

DISASTER HOUSING STRATEGY

211 System A telephone service reference system for applicants and case managers. Similar to the 411 general information system, the 211 system expedites the process of searching for services by phone.

Applicant An individual or the head of a household who has applied for Federal disaster assistance. 44 CFR 206.111

Client An applicant that has registered with FEMA and determined eligible for Federal assistance by FEMA. This term is used in conjunction with disaster case management services.

Commercial Site A site customarily leased for a fee, which is fully equipped to accommodate a housing unit.

Community Site A site provided by the State or local government that accommodates two or more units and is complete with utilities.

Dependent Someone who is normally claimed as such on the Federal tax return of another, according to the Internal Revenue Code. It may also mean the minor children of a couple not living together, where the children live in the affected residence with the parent or guardian who does not actually claim them on the tax return. 44 CFR 206.111

Direct Assistance Assistance provided to disaster victims by the Federal Government in the form of physical resources; essentially all assistance that is not provided monetarily. This includes housing units that are acquired by purchase or lease, directly for individuals or households who, because of a lack of available housing resources, would be unable to make use of financial assistance as well as direct activities by the government to repair or rent units, such as contracting with a company to repair a rental property.

Duplication of Benefits Assistance provided from different sources for the same specific need.

Essential Services Services necessary to a basic standard of living and the general welfare of society. Services may include any of the following: electricity services, gas services, water and sewerage services, etc.

Existing Rental Property Property that has been used prior to a disaster as rental property. This includes mobile units, single family units, and multi-family units.

Fair Market Rent (FMR) An amount determined by the U.S. Department of Housing and Urban Development (HUD) to be the monthly cost of modest, non-luxury rental units in a specific market area, plus the cost of utilities, excluding telephone service.

Financial Assistance Monetary assistance provided to individuals and households to rent alternative housing accommodations, existing rental units, manufactured housing, recreational vehicles, or other readily fabricated dwellings. Such assistance may include the payment of the cost of utilities (excluding telephone service) or funds to be used for repair and replacement of housing and/or personal property.

Government-Owned Property Property that is owned by government for reasons including foreclosure and prior ownership. This applies to governments at all levels, including local, State and Federal, and applies to single family units as well as multi-family units.

Host State A State, territory, commonwealth, or tribe that, by agreement with an impact-State or the Federal Emergency Management Agency (FEMA), provides evacuation and sheltering support to individuals from another State that has received a Presidential emergency or major disaster declaration, due to an incident.

Household All residents of the pre-disaster residence who request temporary housing assistance, plus any additions during the temporary housing period, such as infants, spouses, or part-time residents who were not present at the time of the disaster but who are expected to return during the temporary housing period. 44 CFR 206.111

Individual with Disabilities Any person who has a physical or mental impairment that substantially limits one or more major life activities, has a record of such impairment, or is regarded as having such impairment. ADA definition

Interim Housing The intermediate period of housing assistance that covers the gap between sheltering and the return of disaster victims to permanent housing. Generally, this period may span from the day after the disaster is declared through up to 18 months.

Joint Field Office (JFO) A temporary Federal multi-agency coordination center established locally to facilitate field-level domestic incident management activities, and provides a central location for coordination of Federal, State, local, tribal, nongovernmental, and private-sector organizations with primary responsibility for activities associated with threat response and incident support.

Local Government (A) a county, municipality, city, town, township, local public authority, school district, special district, intrastate district, council of governments (regardless of whether the council of governments is incorporated as a nonprofit corporation under State law), regional or interstate government entity, or agency or instrumentality of a local government; (B) an Indian tribe or authorized tribal organization, or Alaska Native village or organization; and (C) a rural community, unincorporated town or village, or other public entity, for which an application for assistance is made by a State. 44 CFR 206.111

Long-Term Housing Safe, sanitary, and secure housing that can be sustained without continued disaster-related assistance.

Low Income Federal agencies and programs may-within the boundaries set by Federal law-establish their own guidelines for defining low-income populations. For the purposes of this document, low-income populations are defined as such by the agencies determining program eligibility:

- HUD. HUD defines a low-income household as a household whose total income does not exceed 80 percent of the median income for the area, as determined by HUD, with adjustments for smaller and larger families, except that HUD may establish income ceilings higher or lower than 80 percent of the median for the area on the basis of HUD's findings that such variations are necessary because of prevailing levels of construction costs or fair market rents, or unusually high or low family incomes. HUD income limits are updated annually and are available from local HUD offices for the appropriate jurisdictions.
- HHS. The Department of Health and Human Services (HHS) does not define "low-income," but it issues poverty guidelines in the Federal Register each year for use in determining eligibility for certain of its means-tested programs. These guidelines simplify poverty thresholds issued by the Census Bureau for use for administrative purposes such as determining financial eligibility for certain Federal programs. For example, the 2008 HHS poverty guidelines indicate that the poverty level for a family of four in the 48 contiguous States and the District of Columbia was $21,200.
- USDA. USDA Rural Development follows HUD's definition for a low-income household.

Major Disaster Any natural catastrophe (including any hurricane, tornado, storm, high water, winddriven water, tidal wave, tsunami, earthquake, volcanic eruption, landslide, mudslide, snowstorm, or drought), or, regardless of cause, any fire, flood, or explosion, in any part of the United States, which in the determination of the President causes damage of sufficient severity and magnitude to warrant major disaster assistance under this Act to supplement the efforts and available resources of States, local governments, and disaster relief organizations in alleviating the damage, loss, hardship, or suffering caused thereby. 44 CFR 206.111

Multi-Family Housing The definition of multi-family housing varies from agency to agency. The definitions include:
- DHS/FEMA. For the purposes of the Rental Repair Pilot, multi-family housing means a property consisting of more than four units (dwellings). The term includes apartments, cooperative buildings and condominium.
- HUD. A property consisting of five or more units, also including health care facilities.
- VA. A property consisting of two or more rental units.

National Emergency Management Information System (NEMIS) An integrated data management system that automates management of disaster response and recovery operations, including application registration, processing, and payment of assistance to disaster victims.

Nongovernmental Organization (NGO) An entity with an association that is based on interests of its members, individuals, or institutions. It is not created by a government, but it may work cooperatively with government. Such organizations serve a public purpose, not a private benefit. Examples of NGOs include faith-based charity organizations and the American Red Cross. NGOs, including voluntary and faith-based groups, provide relief services to sustain life, reduce physical and emotional distress, and promote the recovery of disaster victims. Often these groups provide specialized services that help individuals with disabilities. NGOs and voluntary organizations play a major role in assisting emergency managers before, during, and after an emergency.

Permanent Housing This refers to the state of "long-term housing."

Preliminary Damage Assessment (PDA) A joint assessment used to determine the magnitude and impact of an event's damage. A FEMA/State team will usually visit local applicants and view their damage first-hand to assess the scope of damage and estimate repair costs. The State uses the results of the PDA to determine if the situation is beyond the combined capabilities of the State and local resources and to verify the need for supplemental Federal assistance. The PDA also identifies any unmet needs that may require immediate attention.

Private Site A site provided or obtained by the applicant at no cost to the Federal Government. 44 CFR 206.111

Reasonable Commuting Distance A commuting distance that does not place undue hardship on an applicant. This also takes into consideration the traveling time involved due to road conditions, e.g., mountainous regions or bridges out, and the normal commuting patterns of the area. The US Census Bureau publishes the average travel time to work (in minutes) by State and county, as well as the percentage of residents who work within the county they live in as opposed to adjoining counties. The US Census Bureau is the preferred method of quantifying the "normal commuting patterns of the area" when attempting to determine the availability of housing resources.

Recertification The process for determining an applicant's need for continued temporary housing assistance.

Recovery Information Management System (RIMS) A web based information management system designed to expand disaster data access in order to increase data accuracy and streamline reporting processes.

Rehabilitation The return of infrastructure damaged by a major disaster to a safe and sanitary living or functioning condition. Specifically refers to returning infrastructure to a habitable condition.

Repair The return of infrastructure damaged by a major disaster to a safe and sanitary living or functioning condition.

Service Animals Any guide dog, signal dog, assistive dog, seizure dog, or other animal individually trained to do work or perform tasks for the benefit of an individual with a disability, including but not limited to guiding individuals with impaired vision, alerting individuals with impaired hearing to intruders or sounds, providing minimal protection or rescue work, pulling a wheelchair, or fetching dropped items. Service animals shall be treated as required by laws such as the Americans with Disabilities Act.

Shelter A place of refuge that provides life-sustaining services in a congregate facility for individuals who have been displaced by an emergency or a disaster.

Sheltering Housing that provides short-term refuge and life-sustaining services for disaster victims who have been displaced from their homes and are unable to meet their own immediate post-disaster housing needs.

Short-Term Housing This refers to the states of "sheltering" and "interim housing."

Social Services Services designated to provide meaningful opportunities for social and economic growth of the disadvantaged sector of the population in order to develop them into productive and self-reliant citizens and promote social equity. Basic social services of the government include self-employment assistance and practical skills development assistance.

Special Needs Populations As defined in the National Response Framework, special needs populations are those whose members may have additional needs before, during, and after an incident in functional areas, including but not limited to: maintaining independence, communication, transportation, supervision, and medical care. Individuals in need of additional response assistance may include those who have disabilities, live in institutionalized settings, are elderly, are children, are from diverse cultures, have limited English proficiency or are non-English speaking, or are transportation disadvantaged.

Temporary Housing Temporary accommodations provided by the Federal Government to individuals or families whose homes are made unlivable by an emergency or a major disaster. 44 CFR 206.111

Unmet Needs The deficit between verified disaster-caused damages and obtainable disaster aid, including insurance assistance, Federal and State assistance, and personal resources.

Very Low Income For federal housing programs, a household income of 50 percent of the area median by household size. HUD data is used to calculate very low-income limits.

Wrap-Around Services The delivery of infrastructure and additional essential services to address disaster-related needs of affected residents living in temporary housing sites. These services go beyond the physical need for housing or political subdivision of a State and typically include basic social services and access to utilities, transportation, grocery

FLOODING AND LEVEES

0.2-Percent-Annual-Chance Flood The flood that has a 0.2-percent chance of being equaled or exceeded in any given year (also known as the 500-year flood).

1-Percent-Annual-Chance Flood The flood that has a 1-percent chance of being equaled or exceeded in any given year (also known as the 100-year flood).

2-Percent-Annual-Chance Flood The flood that has a 2-percent chance of being equaled or exceeded in any given year (also known as the 50-year flood).

10-Percent-Annual-Chance Flood The flood that has a 10-percent chance of being equaled or exceeded in any given year (also known as the 10-year flood).

10-Year Flood See 10-Percent-Annual-Chance Flood.

44 CFR Section 6510 Requirements See Section 65.10 Requirements.

50-Year Flood See 2-Percent-Annual-Chance Flood.

100-Year Flood See 1-Percent-Annual-Chance Flood.

500-Year Flood See 0.2-Percent-Annual-Chance Flood.

Accredited Levee System A levee system that FEMA has shown on a Flood Insurance Rate Map (FIRM) or Digital Flood Insurance Rate Map (DFIRM) as providing protection from the 1-percent-annual-chance or greater flood. This determination is based on the submittal of data and documentation as required by Section 65.10 of the NFIP regulations. The impacted area landward of an accredited levee system is shown as Zone X (shaded) on the FIRM or DFIRM except for areas of residual flooding, such as ponding areas, which are shown as Special Flood Hazard Area.

Adequate Progress Determination A written determination issued by FEMA to the Chief Executive Officer of a community that has provided sufficient information for FEMA to determine that substantial completion of a flood protection system has been effected because: (1) 100 percent of the total financial project cost of the completed flood protection system has been authorized; (2) at least 60 percent of the total financial project cost of the completed flood protection system has been appropriated; (3) at least 50 percent of the total financial project cost of the completed flood protection system has been expended; (4) all critical features of the flood protection system, as identified by FEMA, are under construction, and each critical feature is 50 percent completed as measured by the actual expenditure of the estimated construction budget funds; and (5) The community has not been responsible for any delay in the completion of the system.

Appeal The formal objection to proposed and/or proposed modified Base Flood Elevations (BFEs) and/or base flood depths, submitted by a community official or an owner or lessee of real property within the community during the statutory 90-day appeal period. An appeal must be based on data that show the proposed or proposed modified BFEs or base flood depths are scientifically or technically incorrect.

Appeal Period The statutory period, beginning on the date of second publication of proposed BFEs, proposed modified BFEs, proposed base flood depths, or proposed modified base flood depths in the local newspaper, during which community officials or owners or lessees of real property within the community may appeal the proposed or proposed modified BFEs and/or base flood depths by submitting data to show those BFEs or base flood depths are scientifically or technically incorrect.

Application Forms The comprehensive, easy-to-use forms that were implemented by FEMA in October 1992 to facilitate the processing of requests for revisions or amendments to NFIP maps.

Approved Model A numerical computer model that has been accepted by FEMA for use in performing new or revised hydrologic or hydraulic analyses for NFIP purposes. All accepted models must meet the requirements set forth in Subparagraph 65.6(a)(6) of the NFIP regulations.

Approximate Study An engineering study that results in the delineation of floodplain boundaries for the 1-percent-annual-chance flood, but does not include the determination of BFEs or base flood depths.

As-Built A term used to describe mapping and mapping-related data that reflect conditions within a floodplain based on flood-control and other structures being completed.

Base Flood The flood that has a 1-percent chance of being equaled or exceeded in any given year.

Base Flood Elevation (BFE) The elevation of a flood having a 1-percent chance of being equaled or exceeded in any given year.

Berms Horizontal strips or shelves of material built contiguous to the base of either side of levee embankments for the purpose of providing protection from underseepage and erosion, thereby increasing the stability of the embankment or reducing seepage.

Breach See Levee Breach.

Building See Structure.

Channel A naturally or artificially created open conduit that periodically or continuously contains moving water or which forms a connecting link between two bodies of water.

Channel Capacity The maximum flow that can pass through a channel without overflowing the banks.

Chief Executive Officer (CEO) The official of a community who has the authority to implement and administer laws, ordinances, and regulations for that community.

Closure Devices Any movable and essentially watertight barriers, used during flood periods to close openings in levee systems, securing but not increasing the levee systems' design level of protection.

Coastal Flooding Flooding that occurs along the Great Lakes, the Atlantic and Pacific Oceans, and the Gulf of Mexico.

Coastal High Hazard Area An area of special flood hazard extending from offshore to the inland limit of a primary frontal dune along an open coast and any other area subject to high-velocity wave actions from storms or seismic sources.

Code of Federal Regulations (CFR) The codification of the general and permanent rules published in the FEDERAL REGISTER by the Executive Departments and agencies of the Federal Government. NFIP regulations are printed in Parts 59 through 77 of Title 44 of the CFR.

Community Any State or area or political subdivision thereof, or any Indian tribe or authorized tribal organization, or Alaska Native village or authorized native organization, which has the authority to adopt and enforce floodplain management regulations for the areas within its jurisdiction.

Community Assistance Call (CAC) A telephone call made by FEMA Regional Office staff or the State NFIP Coordinator to a community to supplement or replace a Community Assistance Visit.

Community Assistance Program (CAP) A FEMA program, funded by the NFIP, under which cost-shared funds are provided to States to provide technical assistance support to communities participating in the NFIP. The purpose of the CAP is to identify, prevent, and resolve floodplain management issues in NFIP participating communities before a flood occurs, or before poor performance or noncompliance warrant enforcement and intervention by FEMA.

Community Assistance Program State Support Services Element (CAP-SSSE) A FEMA program through which FEMA provides funding to States to provide technical assistance to communities in the NFIP and to evaluate community performance in implementing NFIP floodplain management activities.

Community Assistance Visit (CAV) A visit by FEMA Regional Office staff or the State NFIP Coordinator to a community to assess whether the community's floodplain management program meets NFIP participation requirements.

Community Coordination Meeting A meeting during which FEMA Regional Office staff, State NFIP Coordinators, community officials, and other project team members or stakeholders discuss scope and plans for a study/mapping project, interim results of a study/mapping project, and final results of a study/mapping project for a particular community or group of communities.

Community Rating System (CRS) A FEMA initiative, established under the National Flood Insurance Program, to recognize and reward communities that have implemented floodplain management measures beyond the minimum required by NFIP regulations. Under the CRS, those communities that choose to participate voluntarily may reduce the flood insurance premium rates for property owners in the community by taking these additional actions.

Compliance Period The period that begins with the issuance of a Letter of Final Determination and ends when a new or revised FIRM or DFIRM becomes effective. During the compliance period, a community must enact and adopt new or revised floodplain management ordinances required for participation in the NFIP.

Consultation Coordination Officer (CCO) The individual on the FEMA Regional Office staff who is responsible for coordinating with a community on activities related to the NFIP.

Cooperating Technical Partners (CTP) Program An innovative FEMA program to create partnerships between FEMA and participating NFIP communities, regional agencies, and State agencies that have the interest and capability to become more active participants in Flood Map Modernization.

Countywide Format A format used by FEMA to show flooding information for the entire geographic area of a county, including the incorporated communities in the county, on one map and in one report.

Crevasse See Levee Crevasse.

Critical Features Integral and readily identifiable parts of a levee or other flood protection system, without which the flood protection provided by the entire system would be compromised.

Cultural Features Railroads, airfields, streets, roads, highways, levees, dikes, seawalls, dams and other flood-control structures, and other prominent manmade features and landmarks shown on an NFIP map.

De-Accredited Levee System A levee system that was once shown on the FIRM or DFIRM as providing protection from the 1-percent-annual-chance or greater flood, but is no longer accredited with providing this protection because FEMA has not been provided with sufficient data and documentation to determine that the levee system continues to meet the NFIP regulatory requirements cited at 44 CFR Section 65.10. The impacted area landward of a de-accredited levee system is shown on a new DFIRM as a Special Flood Hazard Area, labeled Zone A or Zone AE, depending on the type of engineering study that was performed for the area.

Detailed Study An engineering study that, at a minimum, results in the delineation of floodplain boundaries for the 1-percent-annual-chance flood and the determination of BFEs and/or base flood depths.

Developed Area An area of a community that is:
(a) A primarily urbanized, built-up area that is a minimum of 20 contiguous acres, has basic urban infrastructure, including roads, utilities, communications, and public facilities, to sustain industrial, residential, and commercial activities, and (1) within which 75 percent or more of the parcels, tracts, or lots contain commercial, industrial, or residential structures or uses; or (2) Is a single parcel, tract, or lot in which 75 percent of the area contains existing commercial or industrial structures or uses; or (3) Is a subdivision developed at a density of at least two residential structures per acre within which 75 percent or more of the lots contain existing residential structures at the time the designation is adopted.

(b) Undeveloped parcels, tracts, or lots, the combination of which is less than 20 acres and contiguous on at least 3 sides to areas meeting the criteria of paragraph (a) at the time the designation is adopted.

(c) A subdivision that is a minimum of 20 contiguous acres that has obtained all necessary government approvals, provided that the actual "start of construction" of structures has occurred on at least 10 percent of the lots or remaining lots of a subdivision or 10 percent of the maximum building coverage or remaining building coverage allowed for a single lot subdivision at the time the designation is adopted and construction of structures is underway. Residential subdivisions must meet the density criteria in (a)(3) above.

Development Any manmade change to improved or unimproved real estate, including but not limited to buildings or other structures, mining, dredging, filling, grading, paving, excavation or drilling operations or storage of equipment or materials.

Digital Elevation Model (DEM) A file with terrain elevations recorded for the intersection of a fine-grained grid and organized by quadrangle as the digital equivalent of the elevation data on a topographic base map.

Digital Flood Insurance Rate Map (DFIRM) A FIRM that has been prepared as a digital product, which may involve converting an existing manually produced FIRM to digital format, or creating a product from new digital data sources using a Geographic Information System environment. The DFIRM product allows for the creation of interactive, multi-hazard digital maps. Links are built into an associated database to allow users options to access the engineering backup material used to develop the DFIRM, such as hydrologic and hydraulic models; Flood Profiles; data tables; DEMs; and structure-specific data, such as digital elevation certificates and digital photographs of bridges and culverts.

Digital Flood Insurance Rate Map (DFIRM) Spatial Database A database designed to facilitate collecting, storing, processing, and accessing data developed by FEMA, enabling Mapping Partners to share the data necessary for the DFIRM production and conversion process. Where possible, all mapping and engineering data elements are linked to physical geographic features and georeferenced. The use of a Geographic Information System as a component of the DFIRM spatial database provides the ability to georeference and overlay the mapping and engineering data, allowing the database to support a wide variety of existing and forthcoming FEMA engineering and mapping products.

Digital Orthophoto Quadrangle (DOQ) Photographic maps distributed by the U.S. Geological Survey. A DOQ is an aerial photograph that is adjusted to remove distortions caused by variations in terrain and the camera lens to produce a photograph that displays features in their planimetrically correct location. This term is sometimes used loosely to mean any photographic map produced by this process.

Digital Terrain Model (DTM) A land surface represented in digital form by an elevation grid or lists of three-dimensional coordinates.

Dikes Embankments constructed of earth or other suitable materials to protect land from overflows or to regulate water.

Dual Flood Zones Flood insurance risk zones shown on a FIRM or DFIRM when (1) a levee-impacted area that is labeled as Zone AR also is subject to 1-percent-annual-chance flooding from a flooding source other than the source on the riverward side of the levee that causes the Zone AR flooding; or (2) some residual 1-percent-annual-chance flooding from the flooding source that causes the Zone AR flooding will remain even after the restoration project is complete. The flood insurance risk zone designations for dual flood zones are AR/A1-30, AR/AE, AR/AH, AR/AO, and AR/A.

Effective Date The date on which the NFIP map for a community becomes effective and all sanctions of the NFIP apply.

Effective Map The NFIP map issued by FEMA that is in effect as of the date shown in the title block of the map as "Effective Date," "Revised," or "Map Revised."

Eligible Levee A levee categorized as "active" in the U.S. Army Corps of Engineers (USACE) Rehabilitation and Inspection Program (RIP), for which USACE can provide assistance under Public Law 84-99 to repair damage caused by a flood event.

Emergency Phase The phase of the NFIP that was implemented, on an emergency basis, to provide a first-layer amount of insurance on all insurable structures before the effective date of the initial FIRM/DFIRM.

Emergency Program See Emergency Phase

Encroachment Construction, placement of fill, or similar alteration of topography in the floodplain that reduces the area available to convey floodwaters.

Failure Breach See Levee Failure Breach.

Federal Emergency Management Agency (FEMA) The component of the U.S. Department of Homeland Security that oversees the administration of the NFIP.

Federal Register The document, published daily by the Federal Government, that presents regulation changes and legal notices issued by Federal agencies. FEMA publications in the Federal Register include Proposed, Interim, and Final Rules for BFE determinations; Compendium of Flood Map Changes, published twice each year; Final Rules concerning community eligibility for the sale of flood insurance; and Notices announcing clarifications of procedures and requirements.

Federally Authorized Levee System A levee system that was designed and built by the U.S. Army Corps of Engineers in cooperation with a local sponsor and then turned over to that local sponsor to operate and maintain.

FEMA Levee Inventory System (FLIS) A Web-based database and information retrieval system used by FEMA to collect and maintain information on structures shown on effective and soon-to-be-effective FIRMs/DFIRMs, including levees, dikes, floodwalls, and road and railroad embankments.

FEMA Map Assistance Center (FMAC) A FEMA customer service center staffed by Map Specialists that are specially trained to answer specific questions about NFIP mapping and related issues, including: levee resources; status of active and completed studies/mapping projects, conditional and final map revision requests, and conditional and final map amendment requests; technical and administrative support data available from the FEMA archives. FMAC Map Specialists will link callers with other FEMA service and fax numbers and the FEMA Web site and provide information regarding, or copies of, FEMA products, brochures, and publications.

Fill Soil that is brought in to raise the level of the ground. Depending on where the soil is placed, fill may change the flow of water or increase flood elevations. Fill may be used to elevate a building to meet NFIP requirements. Sometimes fill is combined with other methods of elevation such as pilings or foundation walls. Placement of fill requires a local permit from the community.

Fiscal Year The 12-month period that begins on October 1 and ends on September 30.

Flood A general and temporary condition of partial or complete inundation of normally dry land areas from (1) the overflow of inland or tidal waters or (2) the unusual and rapid accumulation or runoff of surface waters from any source.

Flood Elevation Determination Docket (FEDD) A file maintained by FEMA that includes all correspondence between FEMA and the community concerning a flood study; reports of meetings held among FEMA representatives, community representatives, the State NFIP Coordinator, private citizens, FEMA and community contractors, or other interested parties; relevant publications (e.g., newspaper notices, Federal Register notices); Letter of Final Determination; a copy of the Flood Insurance Study report; and a copy of the FIRM/DFIRM and Flood Boundary and Floodway Map.

Flood Fighting Actions taken immediately before or during a flood to protect human life and to reduce flood damages, such as evacuation, emergency sandbagging and diking, and providing assistance to flood victims.

Flood Hazard Boundary Map (FHBM) The initial insurance map issued by FEMA that identifies, based on approximate analyses, the areas of the 1-percent-annual-chance flood hazard within a community.

Flood Insurance Rate Map (FIRM) The insurance and floodplain management map produced by FEMA that identifies, based on detailed or approximate analyses, the areas subject to flooding during a 1-percent-annual-chance flood event in a community. Flood insurance risk zones, which are used to compute actuarial flood insurance rates, also are shown. In areas studied by detailed analyses, the FIRM shows BFEs and/or base flood depths to reflect the elevations of the 1-percent-annual-chance flood. For many communities, when detailed analyses are performed, the FIRM also may show areas inundated by 0.2-percent-annual-chance (500-year) flood and regulatory floodway areas.

Flood Insurance Rate Zones See Flood Insurance Risk Zones.

Flood Insurance Risk Zones The zones, also referred to as "risk premium rate zones" and "flood insurance rate zones," shown on a FIRM/DFIRM or FHBM that are used to determine flood insurance premium rates for properties in the community covered by the FIRM/DFIRM or FHBM. The flood insurance risk zones include Special Flood Hazard Areas (i.e., Zones A, A1-30, AE, A0, A99, AH, AR, AR/A, AR/A1-30, AR/AE, AR/A99, V, V1-30, VE, V0) and areas outside Special Flood Hazard Areas (i.e., Zones B, X, D, M, N, P, E).

Flood Insurance Study (FIS) Report A document, prepared and issued by FEMA, that documents the results of the detailed flood hazard assessment performed for a community. The primary components of the FIS report are text, data tables, photographs, and Flood Profiles.

Flood Map Modernization (Map Mod) The multi-year, congressionally supported initiative undertaken by FEMA to identify flood hazards, assess flood risks, and produce new or updated DFIRMs and FIS reports for floodprone communities throughout the United States.

Floodplain Any land area that is susceptible to being inundated by water from any source.

Floodplain Management The operation of a program of corrective and preventative measures for reducing flood damage, including, but not limited to, emergency preparedness plans, flood-control works, and floodplain management regulations.

Floodplain Management Regulations The zoning ordinances, subdivision regulations, building codes, health regulations, special-purpose ordinances, and other applications of enforcement used by a community to manage development in its floodplain areas.

Flood Profile A graph showing the relationship of water-surface elevation to location, with the latter generally expressed as distance above the mouth for a stream of water flowing in an open channel.

Floodprone Area See Floodplain.

Floodprone Community Any community that is subject to inundation by the 1-percent-annual-chance flood.

Floodproofing A process for reducing or eliminating flood damage to a structure and/or its contents.

Flood Protection Restoration Determination A written determination by FEMA, issued to the CEO of a community, that the community has provided the data and documentation required by Section 65.14 of the NFIP regulations to show that the community is in the process of restoring a flood protection system (i.e., a levee system) that was constructed using Federal funds, recognized as providing 1-percent-annual-chance flood protection on an effective FIRM or DFIRM, and decertified by a Federal agency responsible for flood protection design or construction. The determination informs the community that FEMA will revise the effective FIRM or DFIRM to designated areas impacted by the system as a Special Flood Hazard Area designated Zone AR.

Flood Protection Restoration Project A project undertaken by a community, alone or in cooperation with a sponsoring Federal agency, to restore a flood protection system (i.e., levee system) that was constructed using Federal funds, recognized as providing 1-percent-annual-chance flood protection on an effective FIRM or DFIRM, and decertified by a Federal agency responsible for flood protection design or construction. The intent of the completed project is to restore the system to providing at least a 1-percent-annual-chance level of flood protection.

Flood Protection System Those physical works for which funds have been authorized, appropriated, and expended and which have been constructed specifically to modify flooding in order to reduce the extent of the area subject to a "special flood hazard" and the extent of the depths of the associated flooding. Flood protection systems typically include hurricane tidal barriers, dams, reservoirs, levees, or dikes.

Floodwall Concrete wall constructed adjacent to streams for the purpose of reducing flooding of property on the landside of the wall. Floodwalls are normally constructed in lieu of or supplement levees where the land required for levee construction is too expensive or not available.

Floodway See Regulatory Floodway.

Floodway Fringe The portion of the 1-percent-annual-chance floodplain that is not within the regulatory floodway and in which development and other forms of encroachment may be permitted under certain circumstances.

Freeboard A factor of safety usually expressed in feet above a flood level for purposes of floodplain management.

Geographic Information System (GIS) A system of computer hardware, software, and procedures designed to support the capture, management, manipulation, analysis, modeling, and display of spatially referenced data for solving complex planning and management problems.

Gravity Outlets Culverts, conduits, or other similar conveyance openings through the line-of-protection that permit discharge of interior floodwaters through the line-of-protection by gravity when the exterior flood stages are relatively low. Gravity outlets are equipped with gates to prevent riverflows from entering the protected area during time of high exterior flood stages.

Hazard An event or physical condition that has the potential to cause fatalities, injuries, property damage, infrastructure damage, agricultural loss, damage to the environment, interruption of business, and other types of loss or harm.

Hazard Mitigation Grant Program (HMGP) The program, authorized under Section 404 of the Stafford Act, under which FEMA provides grants to States and local governments to implement long-term hazard mitigation measures after a presidential disaster declaration. The purpose of the HMGP is to reduce the loss of life and property due to natural disasters and to enable mitigation measures to be implemented during the immediate recovery from a presidentially declared disaster.

Head Pressure See Underseepage.

Headquarters (HQ) The FEMA office in Washington, DC.

Highest Adjacent Grade The highest natural elevation of the ground surface, prior to construction, next to the proposed walls of a structure.

Hydraulic Analysis An engineering analysis of a flooding source carried out to provide estimates of the elevations of floods of selected recurrence intervals

Hydraulic Computer Model A computer program that uses flood discharge values and floodplain characteristic data to simulate flow conditions and determine flood elevations.

Hydraulic Methodology Analytical methodology used for assessing the movement and behavior of floodwaters and determining flood elevations and regulatory floodway data.

Hydrograph A graph showing stage, flow, velocity, or other properties of water with respect to time.

Hydrologic Analysis An engineering analysis of a flooding source carried out to establish peak flood discharges and their frequencies of occurrence.

Hydrology The science encompassing the behavior of water as it occurs in the atmosphere, on the surface of the ground, and underground.

Indefinite Delivery/Indefinite Quantity Contractor (IDIQ) An architectural and engineering firm or a Federal, State, or local agency that performs flood hazard studies under contract with FEMA as part of Flood Map Modernization.

Interior Drainage Natural or modified outflow of streams within a levee-impacted area for the conveyance of runoff.

Interior Drainage Systems Systems associated with levee systems that usually include storage areas, gravity outlets, pumping stations, or a combination thereof.

Legally Defined Parcel of Land A parcel of land for which a metes and bounds description or a plat has been recorded. Structure may exist on legally defined parcels of land.

Letter of Final Determination (LFD) The letter in which FEMA announces its final determination regarding the flood hazard information, including (when appropriate) BFEs or base flood depths, presented on a new or revised DFIRM and FIS report. By issuing the LFD, FEMA begins the compliance period and establishes the effective date for the new or revised DFIRM and FIS report.

Letter of Map Change A collective term used to describe official amendments and revisions to National Flood Insurance maps that are accomplished by a cost-effective administrative procedure and disseminated by letter.

Levee A man-made structure, usually an earthen embankment, designed and constructed in accordance with sound engineering practices to contain, control, or divert the flow of water so as to provide protection from temporary flooding.

Levee Breach A rupture, break, or gap in a levee system that causes flooding in the adjacent area and whose cause has not been determined.

Levee Crevasse A crack or breach in a levee that causes flooding in the adjacent area.

Levee Failure Breach A rupture, break, or gap in a levee system that causes flooding in the adjacent area and for which a cause of failure is both known and occurred without overtopping. An investigation is usually required to determine the cause.

Levee-Impacted Area The floodplain area landward of a levee system for which the levee system provides some level of flood protection or risk reduction.

Levee Overtopping Floodwater levels that exceed the crest elevation of a levee system and flow into levee-impacted areas landward of the levee system.

Levee Overtopping Breach A rupture, break, or gap in a levee system that causes flooding in the adjacent area and whose cause is known to be a result of overtopping.

Levee Owner A Federal or State agency, a water management or flood control district, a local community, a levee district, a nonpublic organization, or an individual considered the proprietor of a levee.

Levee System A flood protection system that consists of a levee, or levees, and associated structures, such as closure and drainage devices, which are constructed and operated in accordance with sound engineering practices

Lines of Protection Locations of levees or walls that prevent floodwaters from entering an area.

Local Newspaper The community newspaper, identified by the Chief Executive Officer (CEO) or other designated community official, in which FEMA publishes notices at the beginning of a Mapping project, at the beginning of the appeal period, and at other times during the processing of a new or revised FIRM when required.

Local Sponsor See Public Sponsor.

Lot A parcel of land for which a metes and bounds description or a plat has been recorded and on which one or more structures may be built.

Lowest Adjacent Grade (LAG) The lowest natural elevation of the ground surface next to a structure.

Lowest Finished Floor Elevation (LFFE) The lowest floor of the lowest enclosed area (including basement) of a structure.

Maintenance Deficiency Correction Period – A one-time-only 1-year period granted to qualified levees that provides the time for levee owners/communities to correct maintenance deficiencies.

Map Amendment A change to an effective NFIP map that results in the exclusion from the SFHA of an individual structure or legally defined parcel of land that has been inadvertently included in the SFHA (i.e., no alterations of topography have occurred since the date of the first NFIP map that showed the structure or parcel to be within the SFHA.

Map Modernization See Flood Map Modernization.

Map Revision A change to an effective NFIP map that is accomplished by a LOMR or a Physical Map Revision (PMR).

Mapping Needs Update Support System (MNUSS) The computerized database system that is used by FEMA and its Flood Hazard Mapping Partners to compile information on mapping needs nationwide collected using the Mapping Needs Assessment Process.

Mapping Activity Statement (MAS) An agreement signed by FEMA and a participant (community, regional agency, or State agency) in the CTP Program under which the participant will complete specific mapping activities.

Mapping Project See Study/Mapping Project.

Mitigation A sustained action taken to reduce or eliminate long-term risk to people and property from flood hazards and their effects. Mitigation distinguishes actions that have a long-term impact from those are more closely associated with preparedness for, immediate response to, and short-term recovery from specific events.

Mitigation Directorate The component of FEMA that manages the NFIP and a range of other programs designed to reduce future losses to homes, businesses, schools, public buildings, and critical facilities from floods, earthquakes, tornadoes, and other natural disasters. The programs and initiatives managed by the Mitigation Directorate staff are: Map Mod and Risk Mapping, Analysis and Planning (RiskMAP), including the CTP Program; National Dam Safety Program; National Hurricane Program; Mitigation Planning; Hazard Mitigation Grant Program; Flood Mitigation Assistance Program; Pre-Disaster Mitigation Program; Severe Repetitive Loss Program; Repetitive Flood Claims Program; Community Rating System; and National Earthquake Hazards Reduction Program.

Mitigation Planning A process for State, local, and Indian Tribal governments to identify policies, activities, and tools to implement sustained actions to reduce or eliminate long-term risk to life and property from a hazard event. The mitigation planning process has four steps: (1) organizing resources; (2) assessing risks; (3) developing a mitigation plan; and (4) implementing the plan and monitoring progress.

National Flood Insurance Fund (NFIF) The fund used as the funding mechanism for the NFIP.

National Flood Insurance Program (NFIP) Federal Program under which flood-prone areas are identified and flood insurance is made available to the owners of the property in participating communities.

Non-Federal Levee System A levee system that was designed, built, operated, and maintained by an entity other than a Federal agency.

Non-Participating Community A community that has been identified by FEMA as being floodprone but has chosen not to participate in the NFIP.

Non-USACE Levee Systems Levee systems that are not authorized by the U.S. Congress or other Federal agency authority; levee systems built by other

Federal agencies and not incorporated into the USACE Federal system; locally built and maintained levee systems built by a local community; and levee systems that were privately built by a nonpublic organization or individuals and maintained by a local community.

Overtopping See Levee Overtopping.

Overtopping Breach See Levee Overtopping. Breach.

Participating Community Any community that voluntarily elects to participate in the NFIP by adopting and enforcing floodplain management regulations that are consistent with the standards of the NFIP.

Permanent Identifier (PID) The six-character alphanumeric code used by the National Geodetic Survey to identify control points and stations.

Ponding The result of runoff or flows collecting in a depression that may have no outlet, subterranean outlets, rim outlets, or manmade outlets such as culverts or pumping stations. Impoundments behind manmade obstructions are included in this type of shallow flooding as long as they are not backwater from a defined channel or do not exceed 3.0 feet in depth.

Pressure Conduits Closed conduits designed to convey interior flows through the line-of-protection under internal pressure. The inlet to a pressure conduit that discharges interior flows by force of gravity must be at a higher elevation than the river stage against which it functions. Some pressure conduits may serve as discharge conduits from pumping stations.

Procedure Memorandum (PM) A memorandum issued by FEMA to clarify mapping-related procedures, particularly procedures documented in FEMA's *Guidelines and Specifications for Flood Hazard Mapping Partners*.

Project Cost The total financial cost of a flood protection system (including design, land acquisition, construction, fees, overhead, and profits).

Proposed Base Flood Elevations/Depths and Proposed Modified Base Flood Elevations/Depths Those new and modified BFEs and base flood depths that FEMA publishes in a local newspaper and in the FEDERAL REGISTER at the start of the 90-day appeal period.

Protest An objection to any information, other than BFEs, shown on an NFIP map that is submitted by community officials or interested citizens through the community officials during the 90-day appeal period.

Provisionally Accredited Levee (PAL) A designation for a levee system that FEMA has previously accredited with providing 1-percent-annual-chance protection on an effective FIRM or DFIRM, and for which FEMA is awaiting data and/or documentation that will demonstrate the levee system's compliance with the NFIP regulatory criteria cited at 44 CFR Section 65.10. A PAL is shown on a DFIRM as providing 1-percent-annual-chance flood protection, and the area landward of the levee is shown as Zone X (shaded) except for areas of residual flooding, such as ponding areas, which will be shown as an SFHA

Provisionally Accredited Levee (PAL) Agreement A signed agreement stating that, to the best of the levee owner's knowledge, the levee that is the subject of the agreement meets the requirements of Title 44, Chapter 1, Section 65.10 of the Code of Federal Regulations and has been maintained in accordance with an adopted operation and maintenance plan as well as tests of any mechanized interior drainage systems.

Provisionally Accredited Levee (PAL) Progress Report A progress report due to FEMA within 12 months after initiation of the 24-month PAL period that reports progress toward obtaining 44 CFR Section 65.10-compliant data and documentation for a levee system.

Public Sponsor A public entity that is a legally constituted public body with full authority and capability to perform the terms of its agreement as the non-Federal partner of the U.S. Army Corps of Engineers for a project, and able to pay damages, if necessary, in the event of its failure to perform. A public sponsor may be a State, county, city, town, federally recognized Indian Tribe or tribal organization, Alaska Native Corporation, or any political subpart of a State or group of states that has the legal and financial authority and capability to provide the necessary cash contributions and lands, easements, rights-of-way, relocations, and borrow and dredged or excavated material disposal areas necessary for the project.

Pumping Stations Pumps located at or near the line-of-protection to discharge interior flows over or through the levees or floodwalls (or through pressure lines) when free outflow through gravity outlets is prevented by high exterior stages.

Regional Offices (ROs) The FEMA offices located in Boston, Massachusetts; New York, New York; Philadelphia, Pennsylvania; Atlanta, Georgia; Chicago, Illinois; Denton, Texas; Kansas City, Missouri; Denver, Colorado; San Francisco, California; and Bothell, Washington.

Regular Phase The phase of a community's participation in the NFIP when more comprehensive floodplain management requirements are imposed and higher amounts of insurance are available. The FIRM forms the basis for this phase of participation in the NFIP.

Regular Program See Regular Phase.

Regulatory Floodway A floodplain management tool that is the regulatory area defined as the channel of a stream, plus any adjacent floodplain areas, that must be kept free of encroachment so that the base flood discharge can be conveyed without increasing the BFEs more than a specified amount. The regulatory floodway is not an insurance rating factor.

Rehabilitation and Inspection Program (RIP) The Rehabilitation and Inspection Program is the U.S. Army Corps of Engineers' program that provides for inspection of flood control projects, the rehabilitation of damaged flood control projects, and the rehabilitation of federally authorized and constructed hurricane or shore protection projects.

Residual Flooding Area The area of 1-percent-annual-chance flooding that is shown an SFHA on a FIRM or DFIRM in the impacted area behind an accredited or provisionally accredited levee/levee system; the source of residual flooding is usually local drainage or flooding from a source that is controlled by the levee/levee system.

Ring Levees Levees that completely encircle or "ring" an area subject to inundation from all directions.

Risk Analysis Division The component of the Mitigation Directorate that applies engineering and planning practices in conjunction with advanced technology tools to identify hazards, assess vulnerabilities, and develop strategies to manage the risks associated with natural hazards.

Risk Insurance Division The component of the Mitigation Directorate that helps reduce flood losses by providing affordable flood insurance for property owners and by encouraging communities to adopt and enforce floodplain management regulations that mitigate the effects of flooding on new and improved structures.

Risk Reduction Division The component of the Mitigation Directorate that works to reduce risk to life and property through the use of land use controls, building practices, and other tools. These activities address risk in both the existing built environment and in future development, and they occur in both pre- and post-disaster environments.

Sand Boils The volcano-like cones of sand that that are formed on the landward side of a levee system when the upward pressure of water flowing through soil pores under a levee (underseepage) exceeds the downward pressure from the weight of the soil above it.

Secondary Levees L evees that are riverward of the main or principal levees. The level of protection of a secondary levee is always less than the level of protection provided by the main or principal levee.

Section 6510 Requirements The NFIP regulatory criteria for the evaluation and mapping of areas protected by levee systems, which are presented at Title 44, Chapter 1, Section 65.10 of the Code of Federal Regulations.

Sediment Fragmental material that originates from the weathering of rocks and is transported by, suspended in, or deposited by water or air or is accumulated in beds by other natural occurrence.

Setback Levees Levees that are built landward of existing levees, usually because the existing levees have suffered distress or are in some way being endangered, as by river or stream migration.

Scientifically Incorrect Base Flood Elevations/ Depths Those BFEs and base flood depths determined through analyses in which the methodologies used and/or assumptions made are inappropriate for the physical processes being evaluated or are otherwise erroneous.

Shallow Flooding Unconfined flows over broad, relatively low relief areas, such as alluvial plains; intermittent flows in arid regions that have not developed a system of well-defined channels; overbank flows that remain unconfined, such as on delta formations; overland flow in urban areas; and flows collecting in depressions to form ponding areas. For NFIP purposes, shallow flooding conditions are defined as flooding that is limited to 3.0 feet or less in depth where no defined channel exists.

Sheet Runoff The broad, relatively unconfined downslope movement of water across sloping terrain that results from many sources, including intense rainfall and/or snowmelt, overflow from a channel that crosses a drainage divide, and overflow from a perched channel onto deltas or plains of lower elevation. Sheet runoff is typical in areas of low topographic relief and poorly established drainage systems.

Special Flood Hazard Area (SFHA) The area delineated on an NFIP map (FHBM, FIRM, or DFIRM) as being subject to inundation by the 1-percent-annual-chance flood. SFHAs are determined using statistical analyses of records of riverflow, storm tides, and rainfall; information obtained through consultation with a community; floodplain topographic surveys; and hydrologic and hydraulic analyses.

Spur Levees Levees that project from main levees and serve to protect the main levees from the erosive action of stream currents. Spur levees are not true levees; they are training dikes.

State Any State, the District of Columbia, the territories and possessions of the United States, the Commonwealth of Puerto Rico, and the Trust Territory of the Pacific Islands.

State Coordinating Agency See State National Flood Insurance Program (NFIP) Coordinator.

State National Flood Insurance Program (NFIP) Coordinator The agency of the State government, or other office designated by the Governor of the State or by State statute at the request of FEMA to assist in the implementation of the NFIP in that State.

State Plane Coordinates A system of X,Y coordinates defined by the U.S. Geological Survey for each state. Locations are based on the distance from an origin within each State.

Stillwater Flood Elevation (SWEL) Projected elevation that flood waters would assume, referenced to National Geodetic Vertical Datum of 1929, North American Vertical Datum of 1988, or other datum, in the absence of waves resulting from wind or seismic effects.

Stillwater Flood Level (SWFL) Rise in the water surface above normal water level on the open coast due to the action of wind stress and atmospheric pressure on the water surface.

Stoplogs Logs, planks, cut timber, steel, or concrete beams fitting into end guides between walls or piers to close openings in levees, floodwalls, dams, or other hydraulic structures.

Street Gates Closure gates used during flood periods to close roadway openings through levees or floodwalls.

Structures For floodplain management purposes, walled and roofed buildings, including gas or liquid storage tanks that are principally above ground, as well as manufactured homes. For flood insurance purposes, walled and roofed buildings, other than a gas or liquid storage tanks, that are principally above ground and affixed to permanent sites, as well as a manufactured homes on a permanent foundation.

Study Contractor (SC) See Indefinite Delivery Indefinite Quantity Contractor (IDIQ).

Study/Mapping Project Any activity undertaken by FEMA, separately or in partnership with a mapping partner, to create a new or updated DFIRM, including detailed engineering studies, approximate engineering studies, and floodplain boundary redelineations based on updated topographic information.

Subcritical Flow Flow with a mean velocity that is less than the critical velocity; in other words, tranquil flow.

Sublevees Levees that are built for the purpose of underseepage control. Sublevees encircle areas impacted by the main levee that are subject, during high-water stages, to high uplift pressures and possibly the development of sand boils. Sublevees normally tie into the main levees, thus providing a basin that can be flooded during high-water stages. Sublevees are rarely employed as the use of relief wells or seepage berms make them unnecessary except in emergencies.

Substantial Improvement Any reconstruction, rehabilitation, addition, or other improvement of a structure, the cost of which equals or exceeds 50 percent of the market value of the structure before the start of the construction of the improvement.

Supercritical Flow Flow with a mean velocity that is greater than the critical velocity; in other words, rapid flow.

Technically Incorrect Base Flood Elevations/Depths Those BFEs and base flood depths determined through analyses in which the methodologies used have not been applied properly, are based on insufficient or poor-quality data, or do not account for the effects of physical changes that have occurred in the floodplain.

Temporary Bench Mark (TBM) Benchmark established for a particular mapping project or community.

Tieback Levees Levees that extend from the main levees along a river, lake, or coast to bluff line (high ground) and are part of the lines-of-protection.

Triangulated Irregular Network (TIN) A set of non-overlapping triangles developed from irregularly spaced points that are used to represent the facets of a surface.

USACE Levees Levees that are within the programs operated by the U.S, Army Corps of Engineers, including levees that were built by the USACE that were authorized for construction by the U.S. Congress or by USACE continuing authorities (e.g., Section 205); levee projects constructed by non-Federal interests or other (non-USACE) Federal agencies and incorporated into the USACE Federal system by specific congressional action; Federal projects that are either operated and maintained by the USACE or turned over to a local sponsor for operation and maintenance; and Non-Federal projects within the Rehabilitation and Inspection Program (RIP), Public Law 84-99).

Underseepage The upward pressure on the land behind a levee system that is exerted by groundwater, under pressure from the flooding source, when the elevation of the floodwaters are higher than the elevation of the land.

Unnumbered A Zones Flood insurance risk zones, designated "Zone A" on an FHBM, FIRM, or DFIRM, that are based on approximate studies.

Velocity Zone See Coastal High Hazard Area.

Violation The failure of a structure or other development to be fully compliant with a community's floodplain management regulations. A structure or other development without an Elevation Certificate, other certifications, or other evidence of compliance required in Section 60.3 of the NFIP regulations is presumed to be in violation until such time as that documentation is provided.

Watershed An area of land that drains into a single outlet and is separated from other drainage basins by a divide.

Water-Surface Elevations (WSELs) The heights of floods of various magnitudes and frequencies in the floodplains of coastal or riverine areas, in relation to a specified vertical datum.

Wave Height The vertical distance between the wave crest and the wave trough.

Wave Runup The rush of wave water up a slope or structure.

Wave Setup The increase in the still water surface near the shoreline, due to the presence of breaking waves.

Zone A99 Determination See Adequate Progress Determination.

Zone AR Determination See Flood Protection Restoration Determination.

Zone Gutter Boundary, shown on a FIRM or DFIRM, dividing SFHAs of different BFEs, base flood depths, flow velocities, or flood insurance risk zone designations.

INCIDENT COMMAND

Accessible Having the legally required features and/or qualities that ensure easy entrance, participation, and usability of places, programs, services, and activities by individuals with a wide variety of disabilities.

Acquisition Procedures A process used to obtain resources to support operational requirements.

Agency A division of government with a specific function offering a particular kind of assistance. In the Incident Command System, agencies are defined either as jurisdictional (having statutory responsibility for incident management) or as assisting or cooperating (providing resources or other assistance). Governmental organizations are most often in charge of an incident, though in certain circumstances private-sector organizations may be included. Additionally, nongovernmental organizations may be included to provide support.

Agency Administrator/Executive The official responsible for administering policy for an agency or jurisdiction. An Agency Administrator/Executive (or other public official with jurisdictional responsibility for the incident) usually makes the decision to establish an Area Command.

Agency Dispatch: The agency or jurisdictional facility from which resources are sent to incidents.

Agency Representative A person assigned by a primary, assisting, or cooperating Federal, State, tribal, or local government agency, or nongovernmental or private organization, that has been delegated authority to make decisions affecting that agency's or organization's participation in incident management activities following appropriate consultation with the leadership of that agency.

All-Hazards Describing an incident, natural or manmade, that warrants action to protect life, property, environment, and public health or safety, and to minimize disruptions of government, social, or economic activities.

Allocated Resource Resource dispatched to an incident.

Area Command An organization established to oversee the management of multiple incidents that are each being handled by a separate Incident Command System organization or to oversee the management of a very large or evolving incident that has multiple Incident Management Teams engaged. An Agency Administrator/Executive or other public official with jurisdictional responsibility for the incident usually makes the decision to establish an Area Command. An Area Command is activated only if necessary, depending on the complexity of the incident and incident management span-of-control considerations.

Assessment The process of acquiring, collecting, processing, examining, analyzing, evaluating, monitoring, and interpreting the data, information, evidence, objects, measurements, images, sound, etc., whether tangible or intangible, to provide a basis for decisionmaking.

Assigned Resource Resource checked in and assigned work tasks on an incident.

Assignment Task given to a personnel resource to perform within a given operational period that is based on operational objectives defined in the Incident Action Plan.

Assistant Title for subordinates of principal Command Staff positions. The title indicates a level of technical capability, qualifications, and responsibility subordinate to the primary positions. Assistants may also be assigned to Unit Leaders.

Assisting Agency An agency or organization providing personnel, services, or other resources to the agency with direct responsibility for incident management. See Supporting Agency.

Available Resource Resource assigned to an incident, checked in, and available for a mission assignment, normally located in a Staging Area.

Badging The assignment of physical incident-specific credentials to establish legitimacy and limit access to various incident sites.

Branch The organizational level having functional or geographical responsibility for major aspects of incident operations. A Branch is organizationally situated between the Section Chief and the Division or Group in the Operations Section, and between the Section and Units in the Logistics Section. Branches are identified by the use of Roman numerals or by functional area.

Cache A predetermined complement of tools, equipment, and/or supplies stored in a designated location, available for incident use.

Camp A geographical site within the general incident area (separate from the Incident Base) that is equipped and staffed to provide sleeping, food, water, and sanitary services to incident personnel.

Categorizing Resources The process of organizing resources by category, kind, and type, including size, capacity, capability, skill, and other characteristics. This makes the resource ordering and dispatch process within and across organizations and agencies, and between governmental and nongovernmental entities, more efficient, and ensures that the resources received are appropriate to their needs.

Certifying Personnel The process of authoritatively attesting that individuals meet professional standards for the training, experience, and performance required for key incident management functions.

Chain of Command The orderly line of authority within the ranks of the incident management organization.

Check-In The process through which resources first report to an incident. All responders, regardless of agency affiliation, must report in to receive an assignment in accordance with the procedures established by the Incident Commander.

Chief The Incident Command System title for individuals responsible for management of functional Sections: Operations, Planning, Logistics, Finance/Administration, and Intelligence/Investigations (if established as a separate Section).

Command The act of directing, ordering, or controlling by virtue of explicit statutory, regulatory, or delegated authority.

Command Staff The staff who report directly to the Incident Commander, including the Public Information Officer, Safety Officer, Liaison Officer, and other positions as required. They may have an assistant or assistants, as needed.

Common Operating Picture An overview of an incident by all relevant parties that provides incident information enabling the Incident Commander/Unified Command and any supporting agencies and organizations to make effective, consistent, and timely decisions.

Common Terminology Normally used words and phrases-avoiding the use of different words/phrases for same concepts-to ensure consistency and to allow diverse incident management and support organizations to work together across a wide variety of incident management functions and hazard scenarios.

Communications The process of transmission of information through verbal, written, or symbolic means.

Communications/Dispatch Center Agency or interagency dispatch centers, 911 call centers, emergency control or command dispatch centers, or any naming convention given to the facility and staff that handles emergency calls from the public and communication with emergency management/response personnel. The center can serve as a primary coordination and support element of the Multiagency Coordination System(s) (MACS) for an incident until other elements of the MACS are formally established.

Complex Two or more individual incidents located in the same general area and assigned to a single Incident Commander or to Unified Command.

Comprehensive Preparedness Guide 101 A guide designed to assist jurisdictions with developing operations plans. It promotes a common understanding of the fundamentals of planning and decisionmaking to help emergency planners examine a hazard and produce integrated, coordinated, and synchronized plans.

Continuity of Government A coordinated effort within the Federal Government's executive branch to ensure that National Essential Functions continue to be performed during a catastrophic emergency (as defined in National Security Presidential Directive 51/Homeland Security Presidential Directive 20).

Continuity of Operations An effort within individual organizations to ensure that Primary Mission Essential Functions continue to be performed during a wide range of emergencies.

Cooperating Agency An agency supplying assistance other than direct operational or support functions or resources to the incident management effort.

Coordinate To advance an analysis and exchange of information systematically among principals who have or may have a need to know certain information to carry out specific incident management responsibilities.

Corrective Actions The implementation of procedures that are based on lessons learned from actual incidents or from training and exercises.

Credentialing The authentication and verification of the certification and identity of designated incident managers and emergency responders.

Critical Infrastructure Assets, systems, and networks, whether physical or virtual, so vital to the United States that the incapacitation or destruction of such assets, systems, or networks would have a debilitating impact on security, national economic security, national public health or safety, or any combination of those matters.

Delegation of Authority A statement provided to the Incident Commander by the Agency Executive delegating authority and assigning responsibility. The delegation of authority can include objectives, priorities, expectations, constraints, and other considerations or guidelines, as needed. Many agencies require written delegation of authority to be given to the Incident Commander prior to assuming command on larger incidents. (Also known as Letter of Expectation.)

Demobilization The orderly, safe, and efficient return of an incident resource to its original location and status.

Department Operations Center (DOC) An Emergency Operations Center (EOC) specific to a single department or agency. The focus of a DOC is on internal agency incident management and response. DOCs are often linked to and, in most cases, are physically represented in a combined agency EOC by authorized agent(s) for the department or agency.

Deputy A fully qualified individual who, in the absence of a superior, can be delegated the authority to manage a functional operation or to perform a specific task. In some cases a deputy can act as relief for a superior, and therefore must be fully qualified in the position. Deputies generally can be assigned to the Incident Commander, General Staff, and Branch Directors.

Director The Incident Command System title for individuals responsible for supervision of a Branch.

Dispatch The ordered movement of a resource or resources to an assigned operational mission, or an administrative move from one location to another.

Division The organizational level having responsibility for operations within a defined geographic area. Divisions are established when the number of resources exceeds the manageable span of control of the Section Chief. See Group.

Emergency Any incident, whether natural or manmade, that requires responsive action to protect life or property. Under the Robert T. Stafford Disaster Relief and Emergency Assistance Act, an emergency means any occasion or instance for which, in the determination of the President, Federal assistance is needed to supplement State and local efforts and capabilities to save lives and to protect property and public health and safety, or to lessen or avert the threat of a catastrophe in any part of the United States.

Emergency Management Assistance Compact (EMAC) A congressionally ratified organization that provides form and structure to interstate mutual aid. Through EMAC, a disaster-affected State can request and receive assistance from other member States quickly and efficiently, resolving two key issues up front: liability and reimbursement.

Emergency Management/Response Personnel Includes Federal, State, territorial, tribal, substate regional, and local governments, NGOs, private sector-organizations, critical infrastructure owners and operators, and all other organizations and individuals who assume an emergency management role. (Also known as emergency responder).

Emergency Operations Center (EOC) The physical location at which the coordination of information and resources to support incident management (on-scene operations) activities normally takes place. An EOC may be a temporary facility or may be located in a more central or permanently established facility, perhaps at a higher level of organization within a jurisdiction. EOCs may be organized by major functional disciplines (e.g., fire, law enforcement, medical services), by jurisdiction (e.g., Federal, State, regional, tribal, city, county), or by some combination thereof.

Emergency Operations Plan An ongoing plan for responding to a wide variety of potential hazards.

Emergency Public Information Information that is disseminated primarily in anticipation of or during an emergency. In addition to providing situational information to the public, it frequently provides directive actions required to be taken by the general public.

Evacuation The organized, phased, and supervised withdrawal, dispersal, or removal of civilians from dangerous or potentially dangerous areas, and their reception and care in safe areas.

Event See Planned Event.

Federal Of or pertaining to the Federal Government of the United States of America.

Field Operations Guide Durable pocket or desk guides that contain essential information required to perform specific assignments or functions.

Finance/Administration Section The Incident Command System: Section responsible for all administrative and financial considerations surrounding an incident.

Function The five major activities in the Incident Command System: Command, Operations, Planning, Logistics, and Finance/Administration. A sixth function, Intelligence/Investigations, may be established, if required, to meet incident management needs. The term function is also used when describing the activity involved (e.g., the planning function).

General Staff A group of incident management personnel organized according to function and reporting to the Incident Commander. The General Staff normally consists of the Operations Section Chief, Planning Section Chief, Logistics Section Chief, and Finance/Administration Section Chief. An Intelligence/Investigations Chief may be established, if required, to meet incident management needs.

Group An organizational subdivision established to divide the incident management structure into functional areas of operation. Groups are composed of resources assembled to perform a special function not necessarily within a single geographic division. See Division.

Hazard Something that is potentially dangerous or harmful, often the root cause of an unwanted outcome.

Incident An occurrence, natural or manmade, that requires a response to protect life or property. Incidents can, for example, include major disasters, emergencies, terrorist attacks, terrorist threats, civil unrest, wildland and urban fires, floods, hazardous materials spills, nuclear accidents, aircraft accidents, earthquakes, hurricanes, tornadoes, tropical storms, tsunamis, war-related disasters, public health and medical emergencies, and other occurrences requiring an emergency response.

Incident Action Plan An oral or written plan containing general objectives reflecting the overall strategy for managing an incident. It may include the identification of operational resources and assignments. It may also include attachments that provide direction and important information for management of the incident during one or more operational periods.

Incident Base The location at which primary Logistics functions for an incident are coordinated and administered. There is only one Base per incident. (Incident name or other designator will be added to the term Base.) The Incident Command Post may be co-located with the Incident Base.

Incident Command The Incident Command System organizational element responsible for overall management of the incident and consisting of the Incident Commander (either single or unified command structure) and any assigned supporting staff.

Incident Commander (IC) The individual responsible for all incident activities, including the development of strategies and tactics and the ordering and release of resources. The IC has overall authority and responsibility for conducting incident operations and is responsible for the management of all incident operations at the incident site.

Incident Command Post (ICP) The field location where the primary functions are performed. The ICP may be co-located with the Incident Base or other incident facilities.

Incident Command System (ICS) A standardized on-scene emergency management construct specifically designed to provide an integrated organizational structure that reflects the complexity and demands of single or multiple incidents, without being hindered by jurisdictional boundaries. ICS is the combination of facilities, equipment, personnel, procedures, and communications operating within a common organizational structure, designed to aid in the management of resources during incidents. It is used for all kinds of emergencies and is applicable to small as well as large and complex incidents. ICS is used by various jurisdictions and functional agencies, both public and private, to organize field-level incident management operations.

Incident Management The broad spectrum of activities and organizations providing effective and efficient operations, coordination, and support applied at all levels of government, utilizing both governmental and nongovernmental resources to plan for, respond to, and recover from an incident, regardless of cause, size, or complexity.

Incident Management Team (IMT) An Incident Commander and the appropriate Command and General Staff personnel assigned to an incident. The level of training and experience of the IMT members, coupled with the identified formal response requirements and responsibilities of the IMT, are factors in determining "type," or level, of IMT.

Incident Objectives Statements of guidance and direction needed to select appropriate strategy(s) and the tactical direction of resources. Incident objectives are based on realistic expectations of what can be accomplished when all allocated resources have been effectively deployed. Incident objectives must be achievable and measurable, yet flexible enough to allow strategic and tactical alternatives.

Information Management The collection, organization, and control over the structure, processing, and delivery of information from one or more sources and distribution to one or more audiences who have a stake in that information.

Integrated Planning System A system designed to provide common processes for developing and integrating plans for the Federal Government to establish a comprehensive approach to national planning in accordance with the Homeland Security Management System as outlined in the National Strategy for Homeland Security.

Intelligence/Investigations An organizational subset within ICS. Intelligence gathered within the Intelligence/Investigations function is information that either leads to the detection, prevention, apprehension, and prosecution of criminal activities-or the individual(s) involved-including terrorist incidents or information that leads to determination of the cause of a given incident (regardless of the source) such as public health events or fires with unknown origins. This is different from the normal operational and situational intelligence gathered and reported by the Planning Section.

Interoperability Ability of systems, personnel, and equipment to provide and receive functionality, data, information and/or services to and from other systems, personnel, and equipment, between both public and private agencies, departments, and other organizations, in a manner enabling them to operate effectively together. Allows emergency management/response personnel and their affiliated organizations to communicate within and across agencies and jurisdictions via voice, data, or video-on-demand, in real time, when needed, and when authorized.

Job Aid Checklist or other visual aid intended to ensure that specific steps of completing a task or assignment are accomplished.

Joint Field Office (JFO) The primary Federal incident management field structure. The JFO is a temporary Federal facility that provides a central location for the coordination of Federal, State, tribal, and local governments and private-sector and nongovernmental organizations with primary responsibility for response and recovery. The JFO structure is organized, staffed, and managed in a manner consistent with National Incident Management System principles. Although the JFO uses an Incident Command System structure, the JFO does not manage on-scene operations. Instead, the JFO focuses on providing support to on-scene efforts and conducting broader support operations that may extend beyond the incident site.

Joint Information Center (JIC) A facility established to coordinate all incident-related public information activities. It is the central point of contact for all news media. Public information officials from all participating agencies should co-locate at the JIC.

Joint Information System (JIS) A structure that integrates incident information and public affairs into a cohesive organization designed to provide consistent, coordinated, accurate, accessible, timely, and complete information during crisis or incident operations. The mission of the JIS is to provide a structure and system for developing and delivering coordinated interagency messages; developing, recommending, and executing public information plans and strategies on behalf of the Incident Commander (IC); advising the IC concerning public affairs issues that could affect a response effort; and controlling rumors and inaccurate information that could undermine public confidence in the emergency response effort.

Jurisdiction A range or sphere of authority. Public agencies have jurisdiction at an incident related to their legal responsibilities and authority. Jurisdictional authority at an incident can be political or geographical (e.g., Federal, State, tribal, local boundary lines) or functional (e.g., law enforcement, public health).

Jurisdictional Agency The agency having jurisdiction and responsibility for a specific geographical area, or a mandated function.

Key Resource Any publicly or privately controlled resource essential to the minimal operations of the economy and government.

Letter of Expectation See Delegation of Authority.

Liaison A form of communication for establishing and maintaining mutual understanding and cooperation.

Liaison Officer A member of the Command Staff responsible for coordinating with representatives from cooperating and assisting agencies or organizations.

Local Government Public entities responsible for the security and welfare of a designated area as established by law. A county, municipality, city, town, township, local public authority, school district, special district, intrastate district, council of governments (regardless of whether the council of governments is incorporated as a nonprofit corporation under State law), regional or interstate government entity, or agency or instrumentality of a local government; an Indian tribe or authorized tribal entity, or in Alaska a Native Village or Alaska Regional Native Corporation; a rural community, unincorporated town or village, or other public entity. See Section 2 (10), Homeland Security Act of 2002, Pub. L. 107-296, 116 Stat. 2135 (2002).

Logistics The process and procedure for providing resources and other services to support incident management.

Logistics Section The Incident Command System Section responsible for providing facilities, services, and material support for the incident.

Management by Objectives A management approach that involves a five-step process for achieving the incident goal. The Management by Objectives approach includes the following: establishing overarching incident objectives; developing strategies based on overarching incident objectives; developing and issuing assignments, plans, procedures, and protocols; establishing specific, measurable tactics or tasks for various incident-management functional activities and directing efforts to attain them, in support of defined strategies; and documenting results to measure performance and facilitate corrective action.

Manager Individual within an Incident Command System organizational unit who is assigned specific managerial responsibilities (e.g., Staging Area Manager or Camp Manager).

Mitigation Activities providing a critical foundation in the effort to reduce the loss of life and property from natural and/or manmade disasters by avoiding or lessening the impact of a disaster and providing value to the public by creating safer communities. Mitigation seeks to fix the cycle of disaster damage, reconstruction, and repeated damage. These activities or actions, in most cases, will have a long-term sustained effect.

Mobilization The process and procedures used by all organizations-Federal, State, tribal, and local-for activating, assembling, and transporting all resources that have been requested to respond to or support an incident.

Mobilization Guide Reference document used by organizations outlining agreements, processes, and procedures used by all participating agencies/organizations for activating, assembling, and transporting resources.

Multiagency Coordination (MAC) Group A group of administrators or executives, or their appointed representatives, who are typically authorized to commit agency resources and funds. A MAC Group can provide coordinated decisionmaking and resource allocation among cooperating agencies, and may establish the priorities among incidents, harmonize agency policies, and provide strategic guidance and direction to support incident management activities. MAC Groups may also be known as multiagency committees, emergency management committees, or as otherwise defined by the Multiagency Coordination System.

Multiagency Coordination System (MACS) A system that provides the architecture to support coordination for incident prioritization, critical resource allocation, communications systems integration, and information coordination. MACS assist agencies and organizations responding to an incident. The elements of a MACS include facilities, equipment, personnel, procedures, and communications. Two of the most commonly used elements are Emergency Operations Centers and MAC Groups.

Multijurisdictional Incident An incident requiring action from multiple agencies that each have jurisdiction to manage certain aspects of an incident. In the Incident Command System, these incidents will be managed under Unified Command.

Mutual Aid Agreement or Assistance Agreement Written or oral agreement between and among agencies/organizations and/or jurisdictions that provides a mechanism to quickly obtain emergency assistance in the form of personnel, equipment, materials, and other associated services. The primary objective is to facilitate rapid, short-term deployment of emergency support prior to, during, and/or after an incident.

National Of a nationwide character, including the Federal, State, tribal, and local aspects of governance and policy.

National Essential Functions A subset of government functions that are necessary to lead and sustain the Nation during a catastrophic emergency and that, therefore, must be supported through continuity of operations and continuity of government capabilities.

National Incident Management System A set of principles that provides a systematic, proactive approach guiding government agencies at all levels, nongovernmental organizations, and the private sector to work seamlessly to prevent, protect against, respond to, recover from, and mitigate the effects of incidents, regardless of cause, size, location, or complexity, in order to reduce the loss of life or property and harm to the environment.

National Response Framework A guide to how the Nation conducts all-hazards response.

Nongovernmental Organization (NGO) An entity with an association that is based on interests of its members, individuals, or institutions. It is not created by a government, but it may work cooperatively with government. Such organizations serve a public purpose, not a private benefit. Examples of NGOs include faith-based charity organizations and the American Red Cross. NGOs, including voluntary and faith-based groups, provide relief services to sustain life, reduce physical and emotional distress, and promote the recovery of disaster victims. Often these groups provide specialized services that help individuals with disabilities. NGOs and voluntary organizations play a major role in assisting emergency managers before, during, and after an emergency.

Officer The Incident Command System title for a person responsible for one of the Command Staff positions of Safety, Liaison, and Public Information.

Operational Period The time scheduled for executing a given set of operation actions, as specified in the Incident Action Plan. Operational periods can be of various lengths, although usually they last 12 to 24 hours.

Operations Section The Incident Command System (ICS) Section responsible for all tactical incident operations and implementation of the Incident Action Plan. In ICS, the Operations Section normally includes subordinate Branches, Divisions, and/or Groups.

Organization Any association or group of persons with like objectives. Examples include, but are not limited to, governmental departments and agencies, nongovernmental organizations, and the private sector.

Personal Responsibility The obligation to be accountable for one's actions.

Personnel Accountability The ability to account for the location and welfare of incident personnel. It is accomplished when supervisors ensure that Incident Command System principles and processes are functional and that personnel are working within established incident management guidelines.

Plain Language Communication that can be understood by the intended audience and meets the purpose of the communicator. For the purpose of the National Incident Management System, plain language is designed to eliminate or limit the use of codes and acronyms, as appropriate, during incident response involving more than a single agency.

Planned Event A scheduled nonemergency activity (e.g., sporting event, concert, parade, etc.).

Planning Meeting A meeting held as needed before and throughout the duration of an incident to select specific strategies and tactics for incident control operations and for service and support planning. For larger incidents, the Planning Meeting is a major element in the development of the Incident Action Plan.

Planning Section The Incident Command System Section responsible for the collection, evaluation, and dissemination of operational information related to the incident, and for the preparation and documentation of the Incident Action Plan. This Section also maintains information on the current and forecasted situation and on the status of resources assigned to the incident.

Portability An approach that facilitates the interaction of systems that are normally distinct. Portability of radio technologies, protocols, and frequencies among emergency management/response personnel will allow for the successful and efficient integration, transport, and deployment of communications systems when necessary. Portability includes the standardized assignment of radio channels across jurisdictions, which allows responders to participate in an incident outside their jurisdiction and still use familiar equipment.

Preparedness A continuous cycle of planning, organizing, training, equipping, exercising, evaluating, and taking corrective action in an effort to ensure effective coordination during incident response. Within the National Incident Management System, preparedness focuses on the following elements: planning; procedures and protocols; training and exercises; personnel qualification and certification; and equipment certification.

Preparedness Organization An organization that provides coordination for emergency management and incident response activities before a potential incident. These organizations range from groups of individuals to small committees to large standing organizations that represent a wide variety of committees, planning groups, and other organizations (e.g., Citizen Corps, Local Emergency Planning Committees, Critical Infrastructure Sector Coordinating Councils).

Pre-Positioned Resource A resource moved to an area near the expected incident site in response to anticipated resource needs.

Prevention Actions to avoid an incident or to intervene to stop an incident from occurring. Prevention involves actions to protect lives and property. It involves applying intelligence and other information to a range of activities that may include such countermeasures as deterrence operations; heightened inspections; improved surveillance and security operations; investigations to determine the full nature and source of the threat; public health and agricultural surveillance and testing processes; immunizations, isolation, or quarantine; and, as appropriate, specific law enforcement operations aimed at deterring, preempting, interdicting, or disrupting illegal activity and apprehending potential perpetrators and bringing them to justice.

Primary Mission Essential Functions Government functions that must be performed in order to support or implement the performance of National Essential Functions before, during, and in the aftermath of an emergency.

Private Sector Organizations and individuals that are not part of any governmental structure. The private sector includes for-profit and not-for-profit organizations, formal and informal structures, commerce, and industry.

Protocol A set of established guidelines for actions (which may be designated by individuals, teams, functions, or capabilities) under various specified conditions.

Public Information Processes, procedures, and systems for communicating timely, accurate, and accessible information on an incident's cause, size, and current situation; resources committed; and other matters of general interest to the public, responders, and additional stakeholders (both directly affected and indirectly affected).

Public Information Officer A member of the Command Staff responsible for interfacing with the public and media and/or with other agencies with incident-related information requirements.

Publications Management Subsystem that manages the development, publication control, publication supply, and distribution of National Incident Management System materials.

Recovery The development, coordination, and execution of service- and site-restoration plans; the reconstitution of government operations and services; individual, private-sector, nongovernmental, and public assistance programs to provide housing and to promote restoration; long-term care and treatment of affected persons; additional measures for social, political, environmental, and economic restoration; evaluation of the incident to identify lessons learned; postincident reporting; and development of initiatives to mitigate the effects of future incidents.

Recovery Plan A plan developed to restore an affected area or community.

Reimbursement A mechanism to recoup funds expended for incident-specific activities.

Resource Management A system for identifying available resources at all jurisdictional levels to enable timely, efficient, and unimpeded access to resources needed to prepare for, respond to, or recover from an incident. Resource management under the National Incident Management System includes mutual aid agreements and assistance agreements; the use of special Federal, State, tribal, and local teams; and resource mobilization protocols.

Resource Tracking A standardized, integrated process conducted prior to, during, and after an incident by all emergency management/response personnel and their associated organizations.

Resources Personnel and major items of equipment, supplies, and facilities available or potentially available for assignment to incident operations and for which status is maintained. Resources are described by kind and type and may be used in operational support or supervisory capacities at an incident or at an Emergency Operations Center.

Response Activities that address the short-term, direct effects of an incident. Response includes immediate actions to save lives, protect property, and meet basic human needs. Response also includes the execution of emergency operations plans and of mitigation activities designed to limit the loss of life, personal injury, property damage, and other unfavorable outcomes. As indicated by the situation, response activities include applying intelligence and other information to lessen the effects or consequences of an incident; increased security operations; continuing investigations into nature and source of the threat; ongoing public health and agricultural surveillance and testing processes; immunizations, isolation, or quarantine; and specific law enforcement operations aimed at preempting, interdicting, or disrupting illegal activity, and apprehending actual perpetrators and bringing them to justice.

Retrograde To return resources back to their original location.

Safety Officer A member of the Command Staff responsible for monitoring incident operations and advising the Incident Commander on all matters relating to operational safety, including the health and safety of emergency responder personnel.

Section The Incident Command System organizational level having responsibility for a major functional area of incident management (e.g., Operations, Planning, Logistics, Finance/Administration, and Intelligence/Investigations (if established). The Section is organizationally situated between the Branch and the Incident Command.

Single Resource An individual, a piece of equipment and its personnel complement, or a crew/team of individuals with an identified work supervisor that can be used on an incident.

Situation Report Confirmed or verified information regarding the specific details relating to an incident.

Span of Control The number of resources for which a supervisor is responsible, usually expressed as the ratio of supervisors to individuals. (Under the National Incident Management System, an appropriate span of control is between 1:3 and 1:7, with optimal being 1:5, or between 1:8 and 1:10 for many large-scale law enforcement operations.)

Special Needs Population A population whose members may have additional needs before, during, and after an incident in functional areas, including but not limited to: maintaining independence, communication, transportation, supervision, and medical care. Individuals in need of additional response assistance may include those who have disabilities; who live in institutionalized settings; who are elderly; who are children; who are from diverse cultures, who have limited English proficiency, or who are non-English-speaking; or who are transportation disadvantaged.

Staging Area Temporary location for available resources. A Staging Area can be any location in which personnel, supplies, and equipment can be temporarily housed or parked while awaiting operational assignment.

Standard Operating Guidelines A set of instructions having the force of a directive, covering those features of operations which lend themselves to a definite or standardized procedure without loss of effectiveness.

Standard Operating Procedure A complete reference document or an operations manual that provides the purpose, authorities, duration, and details for the preferred method of performing a single function or a number of interrelated functions in a uniform manner.

State When capitalized, refers to any State of the United States, the District of Columbia, the Commonwealth of Puerto Rico, the Virgin Islands, Guam, American Samoa, the Commonwealth of the Northern Mariana Islands, and any possession of the United States. See Section 2 (14), Homeland Security Act of 2002, Pub. L. 107-296, 116 Stat. 2135 (2002).

Status Report Information specifically related to the status of resources (e.g., the availability or assignment of resources).

Strategy The general plan or direction selected to accomplish incident objectives.

Strike Team A set number of resources of the same kind and type that have an established minimum number of personnel, common communications, and a leader.

Substate Region A grouping of jurisdictions, counties, and/or localities within a State brought together for specified purposes (e.g., homeland security, education, public health), usually containing a governance structure.

Supervisor The Incident Command System title for an individual responsible for a Division or Group.

Supporting Agency An agency that provides support and/or resource assistance to another agency. See Assisting Agency.

Supporting Technology Any technology that may be used to support the National Incident Management System, such as orthophoto mapping, remote automatic weather stations, infrared technology, or communications.

System Any combination of facilities, equipment, personnel, processes, procedures, and communications integrated for a specific purpose.

Tactics The deployment and directing of resources on an incident to accomplish the objectives designated by strategy.

Task Force Any combination of resources assembled to support a specific mission or operational need. All resource elements within a Task Force must have common communications and a designated leader.

Technical Specialist Person with special skills that can be used anywhere within the Incident Command System organization. No minimum qualifications are prescribed, as technical specialists normally perform the same duties during an incident that they perform in their everyday jobs, and they are typically certified in their fields or professions.

Technology Standards Conditions, guidelines, or characteristics that may be required to facilitate the interoperability and compatibility of major systems across jurisdictional, geographic, and functional lines.

Technology Support Assistance that facilitates incident operations and sustains the research and development programs that underpin the long-term investment in the Nation's future incident management capabilities.

Terrorism As defined in the Homeland Security Act of 2002, activity that involves an act that is dangerous to human life or potentially destructive of critical infrastructure or key resources; is a violation of the criminal laws of the United States or of any State or other subdivision of the United States; and appears to be intended to intimidate or coerce a civilian population, to influence the policy of a government by intimidation or coercion, or to affect the conduct of a government by mass destruction, assassination, or kidnapping.

Threat Natural or manmade occurrence, individual, entity, or action that has or indicates the potential to harm life, information, operations, the environment, and/or property.

Tools Those instruments and capabilities that allow for the professional performance of tasks, such as information systems, agreements, doctrine, capabilities, and legislative authorities.

Tribal Referring to any Indian tribe, band, nation, or other organized group or community, including any Alaskan Native Village as defined in or established pursuant to the Alaskan Native Claims Settlement Act (85 Stat. 688) [43 U.S.C.A. and 1601 et seq.], that is recognized as eligible for the special programs and services provided by the United States to Indians because of their status as Indians.

Type An Incident Command System resource classification that refers to capability. Type 1 is generally considered to be more capable than Types 2, 3, or 4, respectively, because of size, power, capacity, or (in the case of Incident Management Teams) experience and qualifications.

Unified Approach The integration of resource management, communications and information management, and command and management in order to form an effective system.

Unified Area Command Version of command established when incidents under an Area Command are multijurisdictional. See Area Command.

Unified Command (UC) An Incident Command System application used when more than one agency has incident jurisdiction or when incidents cross political jurisdictions. Agencies work together through the designated members of the UC, often the senior persons from agencies and/or disciplines participating in the UC, to establish a common set of objectives and strategies and a single Incident Action Plan.

Unit The organizational element with functional responsibility for a specific incident planning, logistics, or finance/administration activity.

Unit Leader The individual in charge of managing Units within an Incident Command System (ICS) functional Section. The Unit can be staffed by a number of support personnel providing a wide range of services. Some of the support positions are preestablished within ICS (e.g., Base/Camp Manager), but many others will be assigned as technical specialists.

Unity of Command An Incident Command System principle stating that each individual involved in incident operations will be assigned to only one supervisor.

Vital Records The essential agency records that are needed to meet operational responsibilities under national security emergencies or other emergency or disaster conditions (emergency operating records), or to protect the legal and financial rights of the government and those affected by government activities (legal and financial rights records).

Volunteer For purposes of the National Incident Management System, any individual accepted to perform services by the lead agency (which has authority to accept volunteer services) when the individual performs services without promise, expectation, or receipt of compensation for services performed. See 16 U.S.C. 742f(c) and 29 CFR 553.10

NATIONAL RESPONSE FRAMEWORK

Accessible Having the legally required features and/or qualities that ensure entrance, participation, and usability of places, programs, services, and activities by individuals with a wide variety of disabilities.

Advanced Readiness Contracting A type of contracting that ensures contracts are in place before an incident for commonly needed commodities and services such as ice, water, plastic sheeting, temporary power, and debris removal.

Agency A division of government with a specific function offering a particular kind of assistance. In the Incident Command System, agencies are defined either as jurisdictional (having statutory responsibility for incident management) or as assisting or cooperating (providing resources or other assistance). Governmental organizations are most often in charge of an incident, though in certain circumstances private-sector organizations may be included. Additionally, nongovernmental organizations may be included to provide support.

Agency Representative A person assigned by a primary, assisting, or cooperating Federal, State, tribal, or local government agency or private organization that has been delegated authority to make decisions affecting that agency's or organization's participation in incident management activities following appropriate consultation with the leadership of that agency.

All-Hazards Describing an incident, natural or manmade, that warrants action to protect life, property, environment, and public health or safety, and to minimize disruptions of government, social, or economic activities.

Annexes See *Emergency Support Function Annexes*, *Incident Annexes*, and *Support Annexes*.

Area Command An organization established to oversee the management of multiple incidents that are each being handled by a separate Incident Command System organization or to oversee the management of a very large or evolving incident that has multiple incident management teams engaged. An agency administrator/executive or other public official with jurisdictional responsibility for the incident usually makes the decision to establish an Area Command. An Area Command is activated only if necessary, depending on the complexity of the incident and incident management span-of-control considerations.

Assessment The evaluation and interpretation of measurements and other information to provide a basis for decisionmaking.

Assignment A task given to a resource to perform within a given operational period that is based on operational objectives defined in the Incident Action Plan.

Attorney General The chief law enforcement officer of the United States. Generally acting through the Federal Bureau of Investigation, the Attorney General has the lead responsibility for criminal investigations of terrorist acts or terrorist threats by individuals or groups inside the United States or directed at U.S. citizens or institutions abroad, as well as for coordinating activities of the other members of the law enforcement community to detect, prevent, and disrupt terrorist attacks against the United States.

Branch The organizational level having functional or geographical responsibility for major aspects of incident operations. A Branch is organizationally situated between the Section Chief and the Division or Group in the Operations Section, and between the Section and Units in the Logistics Section. Branches are identified by the use of Roman numerals or by functional area.

Cache A predetermined complement of tools, equipment, and/or supplies stored in a designated location, available for incident use.

Catastrophic Incident Any natural or manmade incident, including terrorism, that results in extraordinary levels of mass casualties, damage, or disruption severely affecting the population, infrastructure, environment, economy, national morale, and/or government functions.

Chain of Command A series of command, control, executive, or management positions in hierarchical order of authority.

Chief The Incident Command System title for individuals responsible for management of functional Sections: Operations, Planning, Logistics, Finance/Administration, and Intelligence/Investigations (if established as a separate Section).

Chief Elected Official A mayor, city manager, or county manager.

Citizen Corps A community-level program, administered by the Department of Homeland Security, that brings government and private-sector groups together and coordinates the emergency preparedness and response activities of community members. Through its network of community, State, and tribal councils, Citizen Corps increases community preparedness and response capabilities through public education, outreach, training, and volunteer service.

Command The act of directing, ordering, or controlling by virtue of explicit statutory, regulatory, or delegated authority.

Command Staff An incident command component that consists of a Public Information Officer,

Safety Officer, Liaison Officer, and other positions as required, who report directly to the Incident Commander.

Common Operating Picture A continuously updated overview of an incident compiled throughout an incident's life cycle from data shared between integrated systems for communication, information management, and intelligence and information sharing. The common operating picture allows incident managers at all levels to make effective, consistent, and timely decisions. The common operating picture also helps ensure consistency at all levels of incident management across jurisdictions, as well as between various governmental jurisdictions and private-sector and nongovernmental entities that are engaged.

Comprehensive Preparedness Guide (CPG) 101 Producing Emergency Plans: A Guide for All-Hazard Emergency Operations Planning for State, Territorial, Local, and Tribal Governments Guide that describes the intersection of the Federal and State, tribal, and local plans and planning. Replaces State and Local Guide (SLG) 101.

Concept Plan (CONPLAN) A plan that describes the concept of operations for integrating and synchronizing Federal capabilities to accomplish critical tasks, and describes how Federal capabilities will be integrated into and support regional, State, and local plans to meet the objectives described in the Strategic Plan.

Coordinate To advance systematically an analysis and exchange of information among principals who have or may have a need to know certain information to carry out specific incident management responsibilities.

Corrective Actions Implementing procedures that are based on lessons learned from actual incidents or from training and exercises.

Counterterrorism Security Group (CSG) An interagency body convened on a regular basis to develop terrorism prevention policy and to coordinate threat response and law enforcement investigations associated with terrorism. This group evaluates various policy issues of interagency importance regarding counterterrorism and makes recommendations to senior levels of the policymaking structure for decision.

Critical Infrastructure Systems, assets, and networks, whether physical or virtual, so vital to the United States that the incapacity or destruction of such systems and assets would have a debilitating impact on security, national economic security, national public health or safety, or any combination of those matters.

Defense Coordinating Officer (DCO) Individual who serves as the Department of Defense (DOD)'s single point of contact at the Joint Field Office (JFO) for requesting assistance from DOD. With few exceptions, requests for Defense Support of Civil Authorities originating at the JFO are coordinated with and processed through the DCO. The DCO may have a Defense Coordinating Element consisting of a staff and military liaison officers to facilitate coordination and support to activated Emergency Support Functions.

Defense Support of Civil Authorities (DSCA) Support provided by U.S. military forces (Regular, Reserve, and National Guard), Department of Defense (DOD) civilians, DOD contract personnel, and DOD agency and component assets, in response to requests for assistance from civilian Federal, State, local, and tribal authorities for domestic emergencies, designated law enforcement support, and other domestic activities.

Demobilization The orderly, safe, and efficient return of a resource to its original location and status.

DHS Department of Homeland Security.

Director of National Intelligence Official who leads the Intelligence Community, serves as the President's principal intelligence advisor, and oversees and directs the implementation of the National Intelligence Program.

Disaster Recovery Center (DRC) A facility established in a centralized location within or near the disaster area at which disaster victims (individuals, families, or businesses) apply for disaster aid.

Division The partition of an incident into geographical areas of operation. Divisions are established when the number of resources exceeds the manageable span of control of the Operations Chief. A Division is located within the Incident Command System organization between the Branch and resources in the Operations Section.

DOD Department of Defense.

Domestic Readiness Group (DRG) An interagency body convened on a regular basis to develop and coordinate preparedness, response, and incident management policy. This group evaluates various policy issues of interagency importance regarding domestic preparedness and incident management and makes recommendations to senior levels of the policymaking structure for decision. During an incident, the DRG may be convened by the Department of Homeland Security to evaluate relevant interagency policy issues regarding response and develop recommendations as may be required.

Emergency Any incident, whether natural or manmade, that requires responsive action to protect life or property. Under the Robert T. Stafford Disaster Relief and Emergency Assistance Act, an emergency means any occasion or instance for which, in the determination of the President, Federal assistance is needed to supplement State and local efforts and capabilities to save lives and to protect property and public health and safety, or to lessen or avert the threat of a catastrophe in any part of the United States.

Emergency Management As subset of incident management, the coordination and integration of all activities necessary to build, sustain, and improve the capability to prepare for, protect against, respond to, recover from, or mitigate against threatened or actual natural disasters, acts of terrorism, or other manmade disasters.

Emergency Management Assistance Compact (EMAC) A congressionally ratified organization that provides form and structure to interstate mutual aid. Through EMAC, a disaster-affected State can request and receive assistance from other member States quickly and efficiently, resolving two key issues up front: liability and reimbursement.

Emergency Manager The person who has the day-to-day responsibility for emergency management programs and activities. The role is one of coordinating all aspects of a jurisdiction's mitigation, preparedness, response, and recovery capabilities.

Emergency Operations Center (EOC) The physical location at which the coordination of information and resources to support incident management (on-scene operations) activities normally takes place. An EOC may be a temporary facility or may be located in a more central or permanently established facility, perhaps at a higher level of organization within a jurisdiction. EOCs may be organized by major functional disciplines (e.g., fire, law enforcement, and medical services), by jurisdiction (e.g., Federal, State, regional, tribal, city, county), or some combination thereof.

Emergency Plan The ongoing plan maintained by various jurisdictional levels for responding to a wide variety of potential hazards.

Emergency Public Information Information that is disseminated primarily in anticipation of an emergency or during an emergency. In addition to providing situational information to the public, it also frequently provides directive actions required to be taken by the general public.

Emergency Support Function (ESF) Annexes Present the missions, policies, structures, and responsibilities of Federal agencies for coordinating resource and programmatic support to States, tribes, and other Federal agencies or other jurisdictions and entities when activated to provide coordinated Federal support during an incident.

Emergency Support Function (ESF) Coordinator The entity with management oversight for that particular ESF. The coordinator has ongoing responsibilities throughout the preparedness, response, and recovery phases of incident management.

Emergency Support Function (ESF) Primary Agency A Federal agency with significant authorities, roles, resources, or capabilities for a particular function within an ESF. A Federal agency designated as an ESF primary agency serves as a Federal executive agent under the Federal Coordinating Officer (or Federal Resource Coordinator for non-Stafford Act incidents) to accomplish the ESF mission.

Emergency Support Function (ESF) Support Agency An entity with specific capabilities or resources that support the primary agencies in executing the mission of the ESF.

Emergency Support Functions (ESFs) Used by the Federal Government and many State governments as the primary mechanism at the operational level to organize and provide assistance. ESFs align categories of resources and provide strategic objectives for their use. ESFs utilize standardized resource management concepts such as typing, inventorying, and tracking to facilitate the dispatch, deployment, and recovery of resources before, during, and after an incident.

External Affairs Organizational element that provides accurate, coordinated, and timely information to affected audiences, including governments, media, the private sector, and the local populace.

Evacuation Organized, phased, and supervised withdrawal, dispersal, or removal of civilians from dangerous or potentially dangerous areas, and their reception and care in safe areas.

Event See *Planned Event*.

FBI Federal Bureau of Investigation.

Federal Of or pertaining to the Federal Government of the United States of America.

Federal Coordinating Officer (FCO) The official appointed by the President to execute Stafford Act authorities, including the commitment of Federal Emergency Management Agency (FEMA) resources and mission assignment of other Federal departments or agencies. In all cases, the FCO represents the FEMA Administrator in the field to discharge all FEMA responsibilities for the response and recovery efforts underway. For Stafford Act events, the FCO is the primary Federal representative with whom the State Coordinating Officer and other State, tribal, and local response officials interface to determine the most urgent needs and set objectives for an effective response in collaboration with the Unified Coordination Group.

Federal Resource Coordinator (FRC) Official who may be designated by the Department of Homeland Security in non-Stafford Act situations when a Federal department or agency acting under its own authority has requested the assistance of the Secretary of Homeland Security to obtain support from other Federal departments and agencies. In these situations, the FRC coordinates support through interagency agreements and memorandums of understanding. The

FRC is responsible for coordinating timely delivery of resources to the requesting agency.

Federal-to-Federal Support Support that may occur when a Federal department or agency responding to an incident under its own jurisdictional authorities requests Department of Homeland Security coordination to obtain additional Federal assistance. As part of Federal-to-Federal support, Federal departments and agencies execute interagency or intra-agency reimbursable agreements, in accordance with the Economy Act or other applicable authorities.

FEMA Federal Emergency Management Agency.

FEMA Regional Offices FEMA has 10 regional offices, each headed by a Regional Administrator. The regional field structures are FEMA's permanent presence for communities and States across America.

Finance/Administration Section (1) Incident Command: Section responsible for all administrative and financial considerations surrounding an incident. (2) Joint Field Office (JFO): Section responsible for the financial management, monitoring, and tracking of all Federal costs relating to the incident and the functioning of the JFO while adhering to all Federal laws and regulations.

Function One of the five major activities in the Incident Command System: Command, Operations, Planning, Logistics, and Finance/Administration. The term function is also used when describing the activity involved (e.g., the planning function). A sixth function, Intelligence/Investigations, may be established, if required, to meet incident management needs.

Fusion Center Facility that brings together into one central location law enforcement, intelligence, emergency management, public health, and other agencies, as well as private-sector and nongovernmental organizations when appropriate, and that has the capabilities to evaluate and act appropriately on all available information.

General Staff A group of incident management personnel organized according to function and reporting to the Incident Commander. The General Staff normally consists of the Operations Section Chief, Planning Section Chief, Logistics Section Chief, and Finance/Administration Section Chief. An Intelligence/Investigations Chief may be established, if required, to meet incident management needs.

Governor's Authorized Representative An individual empowered by a Governor to: (1) execute all necessary documents for disaster assistance on behalf of the State, including certification of applications for public assistance; (2) represent the Governor of the impacted State in the Unified Coordination Group, when required; (3) coordinate and supervise the State disaster assistance program to include serving as its grant administrator; and (4) identify, in coordination with the State Coordinating Officer, the State's critical information needs for incorporation into a list of Essential Elements of Information.

Group Established to divide the incident management structure into functional areas of operation. Groups are composed of resources assembled to perform a special function not necessarily within a single geographic division. Groups, when activated, are located between Branches and resources in the Operations Section. See **Division**.

Hazard Something that is potentially dangerous or harmful, often the root cause of an unwanted outcome.

Hazard Identification and Risk Assessment (HIRA) A process to identify hazards and associated risk to persons, property, and structures and to improve protection from natural and human-caused hazards. HIRA serves as a foundation for planning, resource management, capability development, public education, and training and exercises.

Homeland Security Council (HSC) Entity that advises the President on national strategic and policy during large-scale incidents. Together with the National Security Council, ensures coordination for all homeland and national security-related activities among executive departments and agencies and promotes effective development and implementation of related policy.

Homeland Security Exercise and Evaluation Program (HSEEP) A capabilities and performance-based exercise program that provides a standardized methodology and terminology for exercise design, development, conduct, evaluation, and improvement planning.

Homeland Security Information Network (HSIN) The primary reporting method (common national network) for the Department of Homeland Security to reach departments, agencies, and operations centers at the Federal, State, local, and private-sector levels. HSIN is a collection of systems and communities of interest designed to facilitate information sharing, collaboration, and warnings.

HSPD-5 Homeland Security Presidential Directive 5, "Management of Domestic Incidents."

HSPD-7 Homeland Security Presidential Directive 7, "Critical Infrastructure, Identification, Prioritization, and Protection."

HSPD-8 Homeland Security Presidential Directive 8, "National Preparedness."

Hurricane Liaison Team (HLT) A small team designed to enhance hurricane disaster response by facilitating information exchange between the National Hurricane Center in Miami and other National Oceanic and Atmospheric Administration components, as well as Federal, State, tribal, and local government officials.

Incident An occurrence or event, natural or man-made, that requires a response to protect life or property. Incidents can, for example, include major disasters, emergencies, terrorist attacks, terrorist threats, civil unrest, wildland and urban fires, floods, hazardous materials spills, nuclear accidents, aircraft accidents, earthquakes, hurricanes, tornadoes, tropical storms, tsunamis, war-related disasters, public health and medical emergencies, and other occurrences requiring an emergency response.

Incident Action Plan (IAP) An oral or written plan containing general objectives reflecting the overall strategy for managing an incident. It may include the identification of operational resources and assignments. It may also include attachments that provide direction and important information for management of the incident during one or more operational periods.

Incident Annexes Describe the concept of operations to address specific contingency or hazard situations or an element of an incident requiring specialized application of the *National Response Framework*.

Incident Command Entity responsible for overall management of the incident. Consists of the Incident Commander, either single or unified command, and any assigned supporting staff.

Incident Command Post (ICP) The field location where the primary functions are performed. The ICP may be co-located with the incident base or other incident facilities.

Incident Command System (ICS) A standardized on-scene emergency management construct specifically designed to provide for the adoption of an integrated organizational structure that reflects the complexity and demands of single or multiple incidents, without being hindered by jurisdictional boundaries. ICS is a management system designed to enable effective incident management by integrating a combination of facilities, equipment, personnel, procedures, and communications operating within a common organizational structure, designed to aid in the management of resources during incidents. It is used for all kinds of emergencies and is applicable to small as well as large and complex incidents. ICS is used by various jurisdictions and functional agencies, both public and private, to organize field-level incident management operations.

Incident Commander The individual responsible for all incident activities, including the development of strategies and tactics and the ordering and the release of resources. The Incident Commander has overall authority and responsibility for conducting incident operations and is responsible for the management of all incident operations at the incident site.

Incident Management Refers to how incidents are managed across all homeland security activities, including prevention, protection, and response and recovery.

Incident Management Assistance Team (IMAT) An interagency national- or regional-based team composed of subject-matter experts and incident management professionals from multiple Federal departments and agencies.

Incident Management Team (IMT) An incident command organization made up of the Command and General Staff members and appropriate functional units of an Incident Command System organization. The level of training and experience of the IMT members, coupled with the identified formal response requirements and responsibilities of the IMT, are factors in determining the "type," or level, of IMT. IMTs are generally grouped in five types. Types I and II are national teams, Type III are State or regional, Type IV are discipline- or large jurisdiction-specific, and Type V are ad hoc incident command organizations typically used by smaller jurisdictions.

Incident Objectives Statements of guidance and direction needed to select appropriate strategy(s) and the tactical direction of resources. Incident objectives are based on realistic expectations of what can be accomplished when all allocated resources have been effectively deployed. Incident objectives must be achievable and measurable, yet flexible enough to allow strategic and tactical alternatives.

Indian Tribes The United States recognizes Indian tribes as domestic dependent nations under its protection and recognizes the right of Indian tribes to self-government. As such, tribes are responsible for coordinating tribal resources to address actual or potential incidents. When their resources are exhausted, tribal leaders seek assistance from States or even the Federal Government.

Infrastructure Liaison Individual assigned by the Department of Homeland Security Office of Infrastructure Protection who advises the Unified Coordination Group on regionally or nationally significant infrastructure and key resources issues.

Intelligence/Investigations Different from operational and situational intelligence gathered and reported by the Planning Section. Intelligence/investigations gathered within the Intelligence/Investigations function is information that either leads to the detection, prevention, apprehension, and prosecution of criminal activities (or the individual(s) involved), including terrorist incidents, or information that leads to determination of the cause of a given incident (regardless of the source) such as public health events or fires with unknown origins.

Interoperability The ability of emergency management/response personnel to interact and work well together. In the context of technology, interoperability also refers to having an emergency communications system that is the same or is linked to the same system that a jurisdiction uses for nonemergency procedures, and that effectively interfaces with national standards as they are developed. The system should allow the sharing of data with other jurisdictions and levels of government during planning and deployment.

Job Aid A checklist or other visual aid intended to ensure that specific steps for completing a task or assignment are accomplished.

Joint Field Office (JFO) The primary Federal incident management field structure. The JFO is a temporary Federal facility that provides a central location for the coordination of Federal, State, tribal, and local governments and private-sector and nongovernmental organizations with primary responsibility for response and recovery. The JFO structure is organized, staffed, and managed in a manner consistent with *National Incident Management System* principles and is led by the Unified Coordination Group. Although the JFO uses an Incident Command System structure, the JFO does not manage on-scene operations. Instead, the JFO focuses on providing support to on-scene efforts and conducting broader support operations that may extend beyond the incident site.

Joint Information Center (JIC) An interagency entity established to coordinate and disseminate information for the public and media concerning an incident. JICs may be established locally, regionally, or nationally depending on the size and magnitude of the incident.

Joint Information System (JIS) Mechanism that integrates incident information and public affairs into a cohesive organization designed to provide consistent, coordinated, accurate, accessible, timely, and complete information during crisis or incident operations. The mission of the JIS is to provide a structure and system for developing and delivering coordinated interagency messages; developing, recommending, and executing public information plans and strategies on behalf of the Incident Commander; advising the Incident Commander concerning public affairs issues that could affect a response effort; and controlling rumors and inaccurate information that could undermine public confidence in the emergency response effort.

Joint Operations Center (JOC) An interagency command post established by the Federal Bureau of Investigation to manage terrorist threats or incidents and investigative and intelligence activities. The JOC coordinates the necessary local, State, and Federal assets required to support the investigation, and to prepare for, respond to, and resolve the threat or incident.

Joint Task Force (JTF) Based on the complexity and type of incident, and the anticipated level of Department of Defense (DOD) resource involvement, DOD may elect to designate a JTF to command Federal (Title 10) military activities in support of the incident objectives. If a JTF is established, consistent with operational requirements, its command and control element will be co-located with the senior on-scene leadership at the Joint Field Office (JFO) to ensure coordination and unity of effort. The co-location of the JTF command and control element does not replace the requirement for a Defense Coordinating Officer (DCO)/Defense Coordinating Element as part of the JFO Unified Coordination Staff. The DCO remains the DOD single point of contact in the JFO for requesting assistance from DOD.

Joint Task Force (JTF) Commander Individual who exercises operational control of Federal military personnel and most defense resources in a Federal response. Some Department of Defense (DOD) entities, such as the U.S. Army Corps of Engineers, may respond under separate established authorities and do not provide support under the operational control of a JTF Commander. Unless federalized, National Guard forces remain under the control of a State Governor. Close coordination between Federal military, other DOD entities, and National Guard forces in a response is critical.

Jurisdiction A range or sphere of authority. Public agencies have jurisdiction at an incident related to their legal responsibilities and authority. Jurisdictional authority at an incident can be political or geographical (e.g., Federal, State, tribal, and local boundary lines) or functional (e.g., law enforcement, public health).

Jurisdictional Agency The agency having jurisdiction and responsibility for a specific geographical area, or a mandated function.

Key Resources Any publicly or privately controlled resources essential to the minimal operations of the economy and government.

Liaison Officer A member of the Command Staff responsible for coordinating with representatives from cooperating and assisting agencies or organizations.

Local Government A county, municipality, city, town, township, local public authority, school district, special district, intrastate district, council of governments (regardless of whether the council of governments is incorporated as a nonprofit corporation under State law), regional or interstate government entity, or agency or instrumentality of a local government; an Indian tribe or authorized tribal entity, or in Alaska a Native Village or Alaska Regional Native Corporation; a rural community, unincorporated town or village, or other public entity. See Section 2 (10), Homeland Security Act of 2002, P.L. 107–296, 116 Stat. 2135 (2002).

Logistics Section (1) Incident Command: Section responsible for providing facilities, services, and material support for the incident. (2) Joint Field Office (JFO): Section that coordinates logistics support to include control of and accountability for Federal supplies and equipment; resource ordering; delivery of equipment, supplies, and services to the JFO and other field locations; facility location, setup, space management, building services, and general facility operations; transportation coordination and fleet management services; information and technology systems services; administrative services such as mail management and reproduction; and customer assistance.

Long-Term Recovery A process of recovery that may continue for a number of months or years, depending on the severity and extent of the damage sustained. For example, long-term recovery may include the complete redevelopment of damaged areas.

Major Disaster Under the Robert T. Stafford Disaster Relief and Emergency Assistance Act, any natural catastrophe (including any hurricane, tornado, storm, high water, wind-driven water, tidal wave, tsunami, earthquake, volcanic eruption, landslide, mudslide, snowstorm, or drought) or, regardless of cause, any fire, flood, or explosion in any part of the United States that, in the determination of the President, causes damage of sufficient severity and magnitude to warrant major disaster assistance under the Stafford Act to supplement the efforts and available resources of States, local governments, and disaster relief organizations in alleviating the damage, loss, hardship, or suffering caused thereby.

Mission Assignment The mechanism used to support Federal operations in a Stafford Act major disaster or emergency declaration. It orders immediate, short-term emergency response assistance when an applicable State or local government is overwhelmed by the event and lacks the capability to perform, or contract for, the necessary work. See also **Pre-Scripted Mission Assignment.**

Mitigation Activities providing a critical foundation in the effort to reduce the loss of life and property from natural and/or manmade disasters by avoiding or lessening the impact of a disaster and providing value to the public by creating safer communities. Mitigation seeks to fix the cycle of disaster damage, reconstruction, and repeated damage. These activities or actions, in most cases, will have a long-term sustained effect.

Mobile Emergency Response Support (MERS) Response capability whose primary function is to provide mobile telecommunications capabilities and life, logistics, operational and power generation support required for the on-site management of disaster response activities. MERS support falls into three broad categories: (1) operational support elements; (2) communications equipment and operators; and (3) logistics support.

Mobilization The process and procedures used by all organizations—Federal, State, tribal, and local—for activating, assembling, and transporting all resources that have been requested to respond to or support an incident.

Multiagency Coordination (MAC) Group Typically, administrators/executives, or their appointed representatives, who are authorized to commit agency resources and funds, are brought together and form MAC Groups. MAC Groups may also be known as multiagency committees, emergency management committees, or as otherwise defined by the system. A MAC Group can provide coordinated decisionmaking and resource allocation among cooperating agencies, and may establish the priorities among incidents, harmonize agency policies, and provide strategic guidance and direction to support incident management activities.

Multiagency Coordination System(s) (MACS) Multiagency coordination systems provide the architecture to support coordination for incident prioritization, critical resource allocation, communications systems integration, and information coordination. The elements of multiagency coordination systems include facilities, equipment, personnel, procedures, and communications. Two of the most commonly used elements are emergency operations centers and MAC Groups. These systems assist agencies and organizations responding to an incident.

Multijurisdictional Incident An incident requiring action from multiple agencies that each have jurisdiction to manage certain aspects of the incident. In the Incident Command System, these incidents will be managed under Unified Command.

Mutual Aid and Assistance Agreement Written or oral agreement between and among agencies/organizations and/or jurisdictions that provides a mechanism to quickly obtain emergency assistance in the form of personnel, equipment, materials, and other associated services. The primary objective is to facilitate rapid, short-term deployment of emergency support prior to, during, and/or after an incident.

National Of a nationwide character, including the Federal, State, tribal, and local aspects of governance and policy.

National Counterterrorism Center (NCTC) The primary Federal organization for integrating and analyzing all intelligence pertaining to terrorism and counterterrorism and for conducting strategic operational planning by integrating all instruments of national power.

National Disaster Medical System (NDMS) A federally coordinated system that augments the Nation's medical response capability. The overall purpose of the NDMS is to establish a single, integrated national medical response capability for assisting

State and local authorities in dealing with the medical impacts of major peacetime disasters. NDMS, under Emergency Support Function #8 – Public Health and Medical Services, supports Federal agencies in the management and coordination of the Federal medical response to major emergencies and federally declared disasters.

National Exercise Program A Department of Homeland Security-coordinated exercise program based upon the National Planning Scenarios contained which are the *National Preparedness Guidelines*. This program coordinates and, where appropriate, integrates a 5-year homeland security exercise schedule across Federal agencies and incorporates exercises at the State and local levels.

National Incident Management System (NIMS) System that provides a proactive approach guiding government agencies at all levels, the private sector, and nongovernmental organizations to work seamlessly to prepare for, prevent, respond to, recover from, and mitigate the effects of incidents, regardless of cause, size, location, or complexity, in order to reduce the loss of life or property and harm to the environment.

National Infrastructure Coordinating Center (NICC) As part of the National Operations Center, monitors the Nation's critical infrastructure and key resources on an ongoing basis. During an incident, the NICC provides a coordinating forum to share information across infrastructure and key resources sectors through appropriate information-sharing entities.

National Infrastructure Protection Plan (NIPP) Plan that provides a coordinated approach to critical infrastructure and key resources protection roles and responsibilities for Federal, State, tribal, local, and private-sector security partners. The *NIPP* sets national priorities, goals, and requirements for effective distribution of funding and resources that will help ensure that our government, economy, and public services continue in the event of a terrorist attack or other disaster.

National Joint Terrorism Task Force (NJTTF) Entity responsible for enhancing communications, coordination, and cooperation among Federal, State, tribal, and local agencies representing the intelligence, law enforcement, defense, diplomatic, public safety, and homeland security communities by providing a point of fusion for terrorism intelligence and by supporting Joint Terrorism Task Forces throughout the United States.

National Military Command Center (NMCC) Facility that serves as the Nation's focal point for continuous monitoring and coordination of worldwide military operations. It directly supports combatant commanders, the Chairman of the Joint Chiefs of Staff, the Secretary of Defense, and the President in the command of U.S. Armed Forces in peacetime contingencies and war. Structured to support the President and Secretary of Defense effectively and efficiently, the NMCC participates in a wide variety of activities, ranging from missile warning and attack assessment to management of peacetime contingencies such as Defense Support of Civil Authorities activities. In conjunction with monitoring the current worldwide situation, the Center alerts the Joint Staff and other national agencies to developing crises and will initially coordinate any military response required.

National Operations Center (NOC) Serves as the primary national hub for situational awareness and operations coordination across the Federal Government for incident management. The NOC provides the Secretary of Homeland Security and other principals with information necessary to make critical national-level incident management decisions.

National Planning Scenarios Planning tools that represent a minimum number of credible scenarios depicting the range of potential terrorist attacks and natural disasters and related impacts facing our Nation. They form a basis for coordinated Federal planning, training, and exercises.

National Preparedness Guidelines Guidance that establishes a vision for national preparedness and provides a systematic approach for prioritizing preparedness efforts across the Nation. These *Guidelines* focus policy, planning, and investments at all levels of government and the private sector. The *Guidelines* replace the Interim National Preparedness Goal and integrate recent lessons learned.

National Preparedness Vision Provides a concise statement of the core preparedness goal for the Nation.

National Response Coordination Center (NRCC) As a component of the National Operations Center, serves as the Department of Homeland Security/Federal Emergency Management Agency primary operations center responsible for national incident response and recovery as well as national resource coordination. As a 24/7 operations center, the NRCC monitors potential or developing incidents and supports the efforts of regional and field components.

National Response Framework (NRF) Guides how the Nation conducts all-hazards response. The *Framework* documents the key response principles, roles, and structures that organize national response. It describes how communities, States, the Federal Government, and private-sector and nongovernmental partners apply these principles for a coordinated, effective national response. And it describes special circumstances where the Federal Government exercises a larger role, including incidents where Federal interests are involved and catastrophic incidents where a State would require significant support. It allows first responders, decisionmakers, and supporting entities to provide a unified national response.

National Security Council (NSC) Advises the President on national strategic and policy during large-scale incidents. Together with the Homeland Security Council, ensures coordination for all homeland and national security-related activities among executive departments and agencies and promotes effective development and implementation of related policy.

National Urban Search and Rescue (SAR) Response System Specialized teams that locate, rescue (extricate), and provide initial medical stabilization of victims trapped in confined spaces.

National Voluntary Organizations Active in Disaster (National VOAD) A consortium of more than 30 recognized national organizations active in disaster relief. Their organizations provide capabilities to incident management and response efforts at all levels. During major incidents, National VOAD typically sends representatives to the National Response Coordination Center to represent the voluntary organizations and assist in response coordination.

Nongovernmental Organization (NGO) An entity with an association that is based on interests of its members, individuals, or institutions. It is not created by a government, but it may work cooperatively with government. Such organizations serve a public purpose, not a private benefit. Examples of NGOs include faith-based charity organizations and the American Red Cross. NGOs, including voluntary and faith-based groups, provide relief services to sustain life, reduce physical and emotional distress, and promote the recovery of disaster victims. Often these groups provide specialized services that help individuals with disabilities. NGOs and voluntary organizations play a major role in assisting emergency managers before, during, and after an emergency.

Officer The ICS title for the personnel responsible for the Command Staff positions of Safety, Liaison, and Public Information.

Operations Section (1) Incident Command: Responsible for all tactical incident operations and implementation of the Incident Action Plan. In the Incident Command System, it normally includes subordinate Branches, Divisions, and/or Groups. (2) Joint Field Office: Coordinates operational support with on-scene incident management efforts. Branches, divisions, and groups may be added or deleted as required, depending on the nature of the incident. The Operations Section is also responsible for coordinating with other Federal facilities that may be established to support incident management activities.

Operations Plan (OPLAN) A plan developed by and for each Federal department or agency describing detailed resource, personnel, and asset allocations necessary to support the concept of operations detailed in the **Concept Plan**.

Other Senior Officials Representatives of other Federal departments and agencies; State, tribal, or local governments; and the private sector or nongovernmental organizations who may participate in a Unified Coordination Group.

Planned Event A planned, nonemergency activity (e.g., sporting event, concert, parade, etc).

Planning Section (1) Incident Command: Section responsible for the collection, evaluation, and dissemination of operational information related to the incident, and for the preparation and documentation of the Incident Action Plan. This Section also maintains information on the current and forecasted situation and on the status of resources assigned to the incident. (2) Joint Field Office: Section that collects, evaluates, disseminates, and uses information regarding the threat or incident and the status of Federal resources. The Planning Section prepares and documents Federal support actions and develops unified action, contingency, long-term, and other plans.

Preparedness Actions that involve a combination of planning, resources, training, exercising, and organizing to build, sustain, and improve operational capabilities. Preparedness is the process of identifying the personnel, training, and equipment needed for a wide range of potential incidents, and developing jurisdiction-specific plans for delivering capabilities when needed for an incident.

Pre-Positioned Resources Resources moved to an area near the expected incident site in response to anticipated resource needs.

Pre-Scripted Mission Assignment A mechanism used by the Federal Government to facilitate rapid Federal resource response. Pre-scripted mission assignments identify resources or capabilities that Federal departments and agencies, through various Emergency Support Functions (ESFs), are commonly called upon to provide during incident response. Pre-scripted mission assignments allow primary and supporting ESF agencies to organize resources that will be deployed during incident response.

Prevention Actions to avoid an incident or to intervene to stop an incident from occurring. Prevention involves actions to protect lives and property. It involves applying intelligence and other information to a range of activities that may include such countermeasures as deterrence operations; heightened inspections; improved surveillance and security operations; investigations to determine the full nature and source of the threat; public health and agricultural surveillance and testing processes; immunizations, isolation, or quarantine; and, as appropriate, specific law enforcement operations aimed at deterring, preempting, interdicting, or disrupting illegal activity and apprehending potential perpetrators and bringing them to justice.

Primary Agency See **Emergency Support Function (ESF) Primary Agency**.

Principal Federal Official (PFO) May be appointed to serve as the Secretary of Homeland Security's primary representative to ensure consistency of Federal support as well as the overall effectiveness of the Federal incident management for catastrophic or unusually complex incidents that require extraordinary coordination.

Private Sector Organizations and entities that are not part of any governmental structure. The private sector includes for-profit and not-for-profit organizations, formal and informal structures, commerce, and industry.

Protocol A set of established guidelines for actions (which may be designated by individuals, teams, functions, or capabilities) under various specified conditions.

Public Information Processes, procedures, and systems for communicating timely, accurate, accessible information on an incident's cause, size, and current situation; resources committed; and other matters of general interest to the public, responders, and additional stakeholders (both directly affected and indirectly affected).

Public Information Officer (PIO) A member of the Command Staff responsible for interfacing with the public and media and/or with other agencies with incident-related information requirements.

Recovery The development, coordination, and execution of service- and site-restoration plans; the reconstitution of government operations and services; individual, private-sector, nongovernmental, and public-assistance programs to provide housing and to promote restoration; long-term care and treatment of affected persons; additional measures for social, political, environmental, and economic restoration; evaluation of the incident to identify lessons learned; postincident reporting; and development of initiatives to mitigate the effects of future incidents.

Regional Response Coordination Centers (RRCCs) Located in each Federal Emergency Management Agency (FEMA) region, these multiagency agency coordination centers are staffed by Emergency Support Functions in anticipation of a serious incident in the region or immediately following an incident. Operating under the direction of the FEMA Regional Administrator, the RRCCs coordinate Federal regional response efforts and maintain connectivity with State emergency operations centers, State fusion centers, Federal Executive Boards, and other Federal and State operations and coordination centers that have potential to contribute to development of situational awareness.

Resource Management A system for identifying available resources at all jurisdictional levels to enable timely and unimpeded access to resources needed to prepare for, respond to, or recover from an incident. Resource management includes mutual aid and assistance agreements; the use of special Federal, State, tribal, and local teams; and resource mobilization protocols.

Resources Personnel and major items of equipment, supplies, and facilities available or potentially available for assignment to incident operations and for which status is maintained. Under the *National Incident Management System*, resources are described by kind and type and may be used in operational support or supervisory capacities at an incident or at an emergency operations center.

Response Immediate actions to save lives, protect property and the environment, and meet basic human needs. Response also includes the execution of emergency plans and actions to support short-term recovery.

Secretary of Defense Responsible for homeland defense and may also authorize Defense Support of Civil Authorities for domestic incidents as directed by the President or when consistent with military readiness operations and appropriate under the circumstances and the law. When Department of Defense military forces are authorized to support the needs of civil authorities, command of those forces remains with the Secretary of Defense.

Secretary of Homeland Security Serves as the principal Federal official for domestic incident management, which includes coordinating both Federal operations within the United States and Federal resources used in response to or recovery from terrorist attacks, major disasters, or other emergencies. The Secretary of Homeland Security is by Presidential directive and statutory authority also responsible for coordination of Federal resources utilized in the prevention of, preparation for, response to, or recovery from terrorist attacks, major disasters, or other emergencies, excluding law enforcement responsibilities otherwise reserved to the Attorney General.

Secretary of State Responsible for managing international preparedness, response, and recovery activities relating to domestic incidents and the protection of U.S. citizens and U.S. interests overseas.

Section The organizational level having responsibility for a major functional area of incident management (e.g., Operations, Planning, Logistics, Finance/Administration, and Intelligence/Investigations (if established)).

Senior Federal Law Enforcement Official (SFLEO) An official appointed by the Attorney General during an incident requiring a coordinated Federal response to coordinate all law enforcement, public safety, and security operations with intelligence or investigative law enforcement operations directly related to the incident. The SFLEO is a member of the Unified Coordination Group and, as such, is responsible to ensure that allocation of law enforcement requirements and resource allocations are coordinated as appropriate with all other members of the Group. In the event of a terrorist incident, the SFLEO will normally be a senior Federal Bureau of Investigation official who has coordinating authority over all law enforcement activities related to the incident, both those falling within the Attorney General's explicit authority as recognized in Homeland Security Presidential Directive 5 and those otherwise directly related to the incident itself.

Short-Term Recovery A process of recovery that is immediate and overlaps with response. It includes such actions as providing essential public health and safety services, restoring interrupted utility and other essential services, reestablishing transportation routes, and providing food and shelter for those displaced by a disaster. Although called "short term," some of these activities may last for weeks.

Situation Report Document that contains confirmed or verified information and explicit details (who, what, where, and how) relating to an incident.

Situational Awareness The ability to identify, process, and comprehend the critical elements of information about an incident.

Span of Control The number of resources for which a supervisor is responsible, usually expressed as the ratio of supervisors to individuals. (Under the *National Incident Management System*, an appropriate span of control is between 1:3 and 1:7, with optimal being 1:5).

Special Needs Populations Populations whose members may have additional needs before, during, and after an incident in functional areas, including but not limited to: maintaining independence, communication, transportation, supervision, and medical care. Individuals in need of additional response assistance may include those who have disabilities; who live in institutionalized settings; who are elderly; who are children; who are from diverse cultures; who have limited English proficiency or are non-English speaking; or who are transportation disadvantaged.

Stafford Act The Robert T. Stafford Disaster Relief and Emergency Assistance Act, P.L. 93-288, as amended. This Act describes the programs and processes by which the Federal Government provides disaster and emergency assistance to State and local governments, tribal nations, eligible private nonprofit organizations, and individuals affected by a declared major disaster or emergency. The Stafford Act covers all hazards, including natural disasters and terrorist events.

Staging Area Any location in which personnel, supplies, and equipment can be temporarily housed or parked while awaiting operational assignment.

Standard Operating Procedure (SOP) Complete reference document or an operations manual that provides the purpose, authorities, duration, and details for the preferred method of performing a single function or a number of interrelated functions in a uniform manner.

State When capitalized, refers to any State of the United States, the District of Columbia, the Commonwealth of Puerto Rico, the U.S. Virgin Islands, Guam, American Samoa, the Commonwealth of the Northern Mariana Islands, and any possession of the United States. See Section 2 (14), Homeland Security Act of 2002, P.L. 107–296, 116 Stat. 2135 (2002).

State Coordinating Officer (SCO) The individual appointed by the Governor to coordinate State disaster assistance efforts with those of the Federal Government. The SCO plays a critical role in managing the State response and recovery operations following Stafford Act declarations. The Governor of the affected State appoints the SCO, and lines of authority flow from the Governor to the SCO, following the State's policies and laws.

State Emergency Management Agency Director The official responsible for ensuring that the State is prepared to deal with large-scale emergencies and for coordinating the State response in any incident. This includes supporting local governments as needed or requested and coordinating assistance with other States and/or the Federal Government.

State Homeland Security Advisor Person who serves as counsel to the Governor on homeland security issues and may serve as a liaison between the Governor's office, the State homeland security structure, the Department of Homeland Security, and other organizations both inside and outside of the State.

Status Report Relays information specifically related to the status of resources (e.g., the availability or assignment of resources).

Strategic Guidance Statement and Strategic Plan Documents that together define the broad national strategic objectives; delineate authorities, roles, and responsibilities; determine required capabilities; and develop performance and effectiveness measures essential to prevent, protect against, respond to, and recover from domestic incidents.

Strategic Information and Operations Center (SIOC) The focal point and operational control center for all Federal intelligence, law enforcement, and investigative law enforcement activities related to domestic terrorist incidents or credible threats, including leading attribution investigations. The SIOC serves as an information clearinghouse to help collect, process, vet, and disseminate information relevant to law enforcement and criminal investigation efforts in a timely manner.

Strategy The general plan or direction selected to accomplish incident objectives.

Support Agency See **Emergency Support Function (ESF) Support Agency**.

Support Annexes Describe how Federal departments and agencies, the private sector, volunteer organizations, and nongovernmental organizations coordinate and execute the common support processes and administrative tasks required during an incident. The actions described in the Support Annexes are not limited to particular types of events, but are overarching in nature and applicable to nearly every type of incident.

Tactics Deploying and directing resources on an incident to accomplish the objectives designated by the strategy.

Target Capabilities List Defines specific capabilities that all levels of government should possess in order to respond effectively to incidents.

Task Force Any combination of resources assembled to support a specific mission or operational need. All resource elements within a Task Force must have common communications and a designated leader.

Territories Under the Stafford Act, U.S. territories are may receive federally coordinated response within the U.S. possessions, including the insular areas, and within the Federated States of Micronesia (FSM) and the Republic of the Marshall Islands (RMI). Stafford Act assistance is available to Puerto Rico, the U.S. Virgin Islands, Guam, American Samoa, and the Commonwealth of the Northern Mariana Islands, which are included in the definition of "State" in the Stafford Act. At present, Stafford Act assistance also is available to the FSM and the RMI under the compact of free association.

Terrorism As defined under the Homeland Security Act of 2002, any activity that involves an act dangerous to human life or potentially destructive of critical infrastructure or key resources; is a violation of the criminal laws of the United States or of any State or other subdivision of the United States in which it occurs; and is intended to intimidate or coerce the civilian population or influence or affect the conduct of a government by mass destruction, assassination, or kidnapping. See Section 2 (15), Homeland Security Act of 2002, P.L. 107–296, 116 Stat. 2135 (2002).

Threat An indication of possible violence, harm, or danger.

Tribal Referring to any Indian tribe, band, nation, or other organized group or community, including any Alaskan Native Village as defined in or established pursuant to the Alaskan Native Claims Settlement Act (85 Stat. 688) [43 U.S.C.A. and 1601 et seq.], that is recognized as eligible for the special programs and services provided by the United States to Indians because of their status as Indians.

Tribal Leader Individual responsible for the public safety and welfare of the people of that tribe.

Unified Area Command Command system established when incidents under an Area Command are multijurisdictional. See *Area Command*.

Unified Command (UC) An Incident Command System application used when more than one agency has incident jurisdiction or when incidents cross political jurisdictions. Agencies work together through the designated members of the UC, often the senior person from agencies and/or disciplines participating in the UC, to establish a common set of objectives and strategies and a single Incident Action Plan.

Unified Coordination Group Provides leadership within the Joint Field Office. The Unified Coordination Group is comprised of specified senior leaders representing State and Federal interests, and in certain circumstances tribal governments, local jurisdictions, the private sector, or nongovernmental organizations. The Unified Coordination Group typically consists of the Principal Federal Official (if designated), Federal Coordinating Officer, State Coordinating Officer, and senior officials from other entities with primary statutory or jurisdictional responsibility and significant operational responsibility for an aspect of an incident (e.g., the Senior Health Official, Department of Defense representative, or Senior Federal Law Enforcement Official if assigned). Within the Unified Coordination Group, the Federal Coordinating Officer is the primary Federal official responsible for coordinating, integrating, and synchronizing Federal response activities.

Unity of Command Principle of management stating that each individual involved in incident operations will be assigned to only one supervisor.

Universal Task List A menu of unique tasks that link strategies to prevention, protection, response, and recovery tasks for the major events represented by the National Planning Scenarios. It provides a common vocabulary of critical tasks that support development of essential capabilities among organizations at all levels. The List was used to assist in creating the Target Capabilities List.

Urban Search and Rescue (US&R) Task Forces A framework for structuring local emergency services personnel into integrated disaster response task forces. The 28 National US&R Task Forces, complete with the necessary tools, equipment, skills, and techniques, can be deployed by the Federal Emergency Management Agency to assist State and local governments in rescuing victims of structural collapse incidents or to assist in other search and rescue missions.

Volunteer Any individual accepted to perform services by the lead agency (which has authority to accept volunteer services) when the individual performs services without promise, expectation, or receipt of compensation for services performed. See 16 U.S.C. 742f(c) and 29 CFR 553.101.

NIMS

Accessible Having the legally required features and/or qualities that ensure easy entrance, participation, and usability of places, programs, services, and activities by individuals with a wide variety of disabilities.

Acquisition Procedures A process used to obtain resources to support operational requirements.

Agency A division of government with a specific function offering a particular kind of assistance. In the Incident Command System, agencies are defined either as jurisdictional (having statutory responsibility for incident management) or as assisting or cooperating (providing resources or other assistance). Governmental organizations are most often in charge of an incident, though in certain circumstances private-sector organizations may be included. Additionally, nongovernmental organizations may be included to provide support.

Agency Administrator/Executive The official responsible for administering policy for an agency or jurisdiction. An Agency Administrator/Executive (or other public official with jurisdictional responsibility for the incident) usually makes the decision to establish an Area Command.

Agency Dispatch The agency or jurisdictional facility from which resources are sent to incidents.

Agency Representative A person assigned by a primary, assisting, or cooperating Federal, State, tribal, or local government agency, or nongovernmental or private organization, that has been delegated authority to make decisions affecting that agency's or organization's participation in incident management activities following appropriate consultation with the leadership of that agency.

All-Hazards Describing an incident, natural or manmade, that warrants action to protect life, property, environment, and public health or safety, and to minimize disruptions of government, social, or economic activities.

Allocated Resource Resource dispatched to an incident.

Area Command An organization established to oversee the management of multiple incidents that are each being handled by a separate Incident Command System organization or to oversee the management of a very large or evolving incident that has multiple Incident Management Teams engaged. An Agency Administrator/Executive or other public official with jurisdictional responsibility for the incident usually makes the decision to establish an Area Command. An Area Command is activated only if necessary, depending on the complexity of the incident and incident management span-of-control considerations.

Assessment The process of acquiring, collecting, processing, examining, analyzing, evaluating, monitoring, and interpreting the data, information, evidence, objects, measurements, images, sound, etc., whether tangible or intangible, to provide a basis for decisionmaking.

Assigned Resource Resource checked in and assigned work tasks on an incident.

Assignment Task given to a personnel resource to perform within a given operational period that is based on operational objectives defined in the Incident Action Plan.

Assistant Title for subordinates of principal Command Staff positions. The title indicates a level of technical capability, qualifications, and responsibility subordinate to the primary positions. Assistants may also be assigned to Unit Leaders.

Assisting Agency An agency or organization providing personnel, services, or other resources to the agency with direct responsibility for incident management. See Supporting Agency.

Available Resource Resource assigned to an incident, checked in, and available for a mission assignment, normally located in a Staging Area.

Badging The assignment of physical incident-specific credentials to establish legitimacy and limit access to various incident sites.

Branch The organizational level having functional or geographical responsibility for major aspects of incident operations. A Branch is organizationally situated between the Section Chief and the Division or Group in the Operations Section, and between the Section and Units in the Logistics Section. Branches are identified by the use of Roman numerals or by functional area.

Cache A predetermined complement of tools, equipment, and/or supplies stored in a designated location, available for incident use.

Camp A geographical site within the general incident area (separate from the Incident Base) that is equipped and staffed to provide sleeping, food, water, and sanitary services to incident personnel.

Categorizing Resources The process of organizing resources by category, kind, and type, including size, capacity, capability, skill, and other characteristics. This makes the resource ordering and dispatch process within and across organizations and agencies, and between governmental and nongovernmental entities, more efficient, and ensures that the resources received are appropriate to their needs.

Certifying Personnel The process of authoritatively attesting that individuals meet professional standards for the training, experience, and performance required for key incident management functions.

Chain of Command The orderly line of authority within the ranks of the incident management organization.

Check-In The process through which resources first report to an incident. All responders, regardless of agency affiliation, must report in to receive an assignment in accordance with the procedures established by the Incident Commander.

Chief The Incident Command System title for individuals responsible for management of functional Sections: Operations, Planning, Logistics, Finance/Administration, and Intelligence/Investigations (if established as a separate Section).

Command The act of directing, ordering, or controlling by virtue of explicit statutory, regulatory, or delegated authority.

Command Staff The staff who report directly to the Incident Commander, including the Public Information Officer, Safety Officer, Liaison Officer, and other positions as required. They may have an assistant or assistants, as needed.

Common Operating Picture An overview of an incident by all relevant parties that provides incident information enabling the Incident Commander/Unified Command and any supporting agencies and organizations to make effective, consistent, and timely decisions.

Common Terminology Normally used words and phrases-avoiding the use of different words/phrases for same concepts-to ensure consistency and to allow diverse incident management and support organizations to work together across a wide variety of incident management functions and hazard scenarios.

Communications The process of transmission of information through verbal, written, or symbolic means.

Communications/Dispatch Center Agency or interagency dispatch centers, 911 call centers, emergency control or command dispatch centers, or any naming convention given to the facility and staff that handles emergency calls from the public and communication with emergency management/response personnel. The center can serve as a primary coordination and support element of the Multiagency Coordination System(s) (MACS) for an incident until other elements of the MACS are formally established.

Complex Two or more individual incidents located in the same general area and assigned to a single Incident Commander or to Unified Command.

Comprehensive Preparedness Guide 101 A guide designed to assist jurisdictions with developing operations plans. It promotes a common understanding of the fundamentals of planning and decision making to help emergency planners examine a hazard and produce integrated, coordinated, and synchronized plans.

Continuity of Government A coordinated effort within the Federal Government's executive branch to ensure that National Essential Functions continue to be performed during a catastrophic emergency (as defined in National Security Presidential Directive 51/Homeland Security Presidential Directive 20).

Continuity of Operations An effort within individual organizations to ensure that Primary Mission Essential Functions continue to be performed during a wide range of emergencies.

Cooperating Agency An agency supplying assistance other than direct operational or support functions or resources to the incident management effort.

Coordinate To advance an analysis and exchange of information systematically among principals who have or may have a need to know certain information to carry out specific incident management responsibilities.

Corrective Actions The implementation of procedures that are based on lessons learned from actual incidents or from training and exercises.

Credentialing The authentication and verification of the certification and identity of designated incident managers and emergency responders.

Critical Infrastructure Assets, systems, and networks, whether physical or virtual, so vital to the United States that the incapacitation or destruction of such assets, systems, or networks would have a debilitating impact on security, national economic security, national public health or safety, or any combination of those matters.

Delegation of Authority A statement provided to the Incident Commander by the Agency Executive delegating authority and assigning responsibility. The delegation of authority can include objectives, priorities, expectations, constraints, and other considerations or guidelines, as needed. Many agencies require written delegation of authority to be given to the Incident Commander prior to assuming command on larger incidents. (Also known as Letter of Expectation.)

Demobilization The orderly, safe, and efficient return of an incident resource to its original location and status.

Department Operations Center (DOC) An Emergency Operations Center (EOC) specific to a single department or agency. The focus of a DOC is on internal agency incident management and response. DOCs are often linked to and, in most cases, are physically represented in a combined agency EOC by authorized agent(s) for the department or agency.

Deputy A fully qualified individual who, in the absence of a superior, can be delegated the authority to manage a functional operation or to perform a specific task. In some cases a deputy can act as relief for a superior, and therefore must be fully qualified in the position. Deputies generally can be assigned to the Incident Commander, General Staff, and Branch Directors.

Director The Incident Command System title for individuals responsible for supervision of a Branch.

Dispatch The ordered movement of a resource or resources to an assigned operational mission, or an administrative move from one location to another.

Division The organizational level having responsibility for operations within a defined geographic area. Divisions are established when the number of resources exceeds the manageable span of control of the Section Chief. See Group.

Emergency Any incident, whether natural or manmade, that requires responsive action to protect life or property. Under the Robert T. Stafford Disaster Relief and Emergency Assistance Act, an emergency means any occasion or instance for which, in the determination of the President, Federal assistance is needed to supplement State and local efforts and capabilities to save lives and to protect property and public health and safety, or to lessen or avert the threat of a catastrophe in any part of the United States.

Emergency Management Assistance Compact (EMAC) A congressionally ratified organization that provides form and structure to interstate mutual aid. Through EMAC, a disaster-affected State can request and receive assistance from other member States quickly and efficiently, resolving two key issues up front: liability and reimbursement.

Emergency Management/Response Personnel Includes Federal, State, territorial, tribal, substate regional, and local governments, NGOs, private sector-organizations, critical infrastructure owners and operators, and all other organizations and individuals who assume an emergency management role. (Also known as emergency responder).

Emergency Operations Center (EOC) The physical location at which the coordination of information and resources to support incident management (on-scene operations) activities normally takes place. An EOC may be a temporary facility or may be located in a more central or permanently established facility, perhaps at a higher level of organization within a jurisdiction. EOCs may be organized by major functional disciplines (e.g., fire, law enforcement, medical services), by jurisdiction (e.g., Federal, State, regional, tribal, city, county), or by some combination thereof.

Emergency Operations Plan An ongoing plan for responding to a wide variety of potential hazards.

Emergency Public Information Information that is disseminated primarily in anticipation of or during an emergency. In addition to providing situational information to the public, it frequently provides directive actions required to be taken by the general public.

Evacuation The organized, phased, and supervised withdrawal, dispersal, or removal of civilians from dangerous or potentially dangerous areas, and their reception and care in safe areas.

Event See Planned Event.

Federal Of or pertaining to the Federal Government of the United States of America.

Field Operations Guide Durable pocket or desk guides that contain essential information required to perform specific assignments or functions.

Finance/Administration Section The Incident Command System Section responsible for all administrative and financial considerations surrounding an incident.

Function The five major activities in the Incident Command System Command, Operations, Planning, Logistics, and Finance/Administration. A sixth function, Intelligence/Investigations, may be established, if required, to meet incident management needs. The term function is also used when describing the activity involved (e.g., the planning function).

General Staff A group of incident management personnel organized according to function and reporting to the Incident Commander. The General Staff normally consists of the Operations Section Chief, Planning Section Chief, Logistics Section Chief, and Finance/Administration Section Chief. An Intelligence/Investigations Chief may be established, if required, to meet incident management needs.

Group An organizational subdivision established to divide the incident management structure into functional areas of operation. Groups are composed of resources assembled to perform a special function not necessarily within a single geographic division. See Division.

Hazard Something that is potentially dangerous or harmful, often the root cause of an unwanted outcome.

Incident An occurrence, natural or manmade, that requires a response to protect life or property. Incidents can, for example, include major disasters, emergencies, terrorist attacks, terrorist threats, civil unrest, wildland and urban fires, floods, hazardous materials spills, nuclear accidents, aircraft accidents, earthquakes, hurricanes, tornadoes, tropical storms, tsunamis, war-related disasters, public health and medical emergencies, and other occurrences requiring an emergency response.

Incident Action Plan An oral or written plan containing general objectives reflecting the overall strategy for managing an incident. It may include the identification of operational resources and assignments. It may also include attachments that provide direction and important information for management of the incident during one or more operational periods.

Incident Base The location at which primary Logistics functions for an incident are coordinated and administered. There is only one Base per incident. (Incident name or other designator will be added to the term Base.) The Incident Command Post may be co-located with the Incident Base.

Incident Command The Incident Command System organizational element responsible for overall management of the incident and consisting of the Incident Commander (either single or unified command structure) and any assigned supporting staff.

Incident Commander (IC) The individual responsible for all incident activities, including the development of strategies and tactics and the ordering and release of resources. The IC has overall authority and responsibility for conducting incident operations and is responsible for the management of all incident operations at the incident site.

Incident Command Post (ICP) The field location where the primary functions are performed. The ICP may be co-located with the Incident Base or other incident facilities.

Incident Command System (ICS) A standardized on-scene emergency management construct specifically designed to provide an integrated organizational structure that reflects the complexity and demands of single or multiple incidents, without being hindered by jurisdictional boundaries. ICS is the combination of facilities, equipment, personnel, procedures, and communications operating within a common organizational structure, designed to aid in the management of resources during incidents. It is used for all kinds of emergencies and is applicable to small as well as large and complex incidents. ICS is used by various jurisdictions and functional agencies, both public and private, to organize field-level incident management operations.

Incident Management The broad spectrum of activities and organizations providing effective and efficient operations, coordination, and support applied at all levels of government, utilizing both governmental and nongovernmental resources to plan for, respond to, and recover from an incident, regardless of cause, size, or complexity.

Incident Management Team (IMT) An Incident Commander and the appropriate Command and General Staff personnel assigned to an incident. The level of training and experience of the IMT members, coupled with the identified formal response requirements and responsibilities of the IMT, are factors in determining "type," or level, of IMT.

Incident Objectives Statements of guidance and direction needed to select appropriate strategy(s) and the tactical direction of resources. Incident objectives are based on realistic expectations of what can be accomplished when all allocated resources have been effectively deployed. Incident objectives must be achievable and measurable, yet flexible enough to allow strategic and tactical alternatives.

Information Management The collection, organization, and control over the structure, processing, and delivery of information from one or more sources and distribution to one or more audiences who have a stake in that information.

Integrated Planning System A system designed to provide common processes for developing and integrating plans for the Federal Government to establish a comprehensive approach to national planning in accordance with the Homeland Security Management System as outlined in the National Strategy for Homeland Security.

Intelligence/Investigations An organizational subset within ICS. Intelligence gathered within the Intelligence/Investigations function is information that either leads to the detection, prevention, apprehension, and prosecution of criminal activities-or the individual(s) involved-including terrorist incidents or information that leads to determination of the cause of a given incident (regardless of the source) such as public health events or fires with unknown origins. This is different from the normal operational and situational intelligence gathered and reported by the Planning Section.

Interoperability Ability of systems, personnel, and equipment to provide and receive functionality, data, information and/or services to and from other systems, personnel, and equipment, between both public and private agencies, departments, and other organizations, in a manner enabling them to operate effectively together. Allows emergency management/response personnel and their affiliated organizations to communicate within and across agencies and jurisdictions via voice, data, or video-on-demand, in real time, when needed, and when authorized.

Job Aid Checklist or other visual aid intended to ensure that specific steps of completing a task or assignment are accomplished.

Joint Field Office (JFO) The primary Federal incident management field structure. The JFO is a temporary Federal facility that provides a central location for the coordination of Federal, State, tribal, and local governments and private-sector and nongovernmental organizations with primary responsibility for response and recovery. The JFO structure is organized, staffed, and managed in a manner consistent with National Incident Management System principles. Although the JFO uses an Incident Command System structure, the JFO does not manage on-scene operations. Instead, the JFO focuses on providing support to on-scene efforts and conducting broader support operations that may extend beyond the incident site.

Joint Information Center (JIC) A facility established to coordinate all incident-related public information activities. It is the central point of contact for all news media. Public information officials from all participating agencies should co-locate at the JIC.

Joint Information System (JIS) A structure that integrates incident information and public affairs into a cohesive organization designed to provide consistent, coordinated, accurate, accessible, timely, and complete information during crisis or incident operations. The mission of the JIS is to provide a structure and system for developing and delivering coordinated interagency messages; developing, recommending, and executing public information plans and strategies on behalf of the Incident Commander (IC); advising the IC concerning public affairs issues that could affect a response effort; and controlling rumors and inaccurate information that could undermine public confidence in the emergency response effort.

Jurisdiction A range or sphere of authority. Public agencies have jurisdiction at an incident related to their legal responsibilities and authority. Jurisdictional authority at an incident can be political or geographical (e.g., Federal, State, tribal, local boundary lines) or functional (e.g., law enforcement, public health).

Jurisdictional Agency The agency having jurisdiction and responsibility for a specific geographical area, or a mandated function.

Key Resource Any publicly or privately controlled resource essential to the minimal operations of the economy and government.

Letter of Expectation See Delegation of Authority.

Liaison A form of communication for establishing and maintaining mutual understanding and cooperation.

Liaison Officer A member of the Command Staff responsible for coordinating with representatives from cooperating and assisting agencies or organizations.

Local Government Public entities responsible for the security and welfare of a designated area as established by law. A county, municipality, city, town, township, local public authority, school district, special district, intrastate district, council of governments (regardless of whether the council of governments is incorporated as a nonprofit corporation under State law), regional or interstate government entity, or agency or instrumentality of a local government; an Indian tribe or authorized tribal entity, or in Alaska a Native Village or Alaska Regional Native Corporation; a rural community, unincorporated town or village, or other public entity. See Section 2 (10), Homeland Security Act of 2002, Pub. L. 107-296, 116 Stat. 2135 (2002).

Logistics The process and procedure for providing resources and other services to support incident management.

Logistics Section The Incident Command System Section responsible for providing facilities, services, and material support for the incident.

Management by Objectives A management approach that involves a five-step process for achieving the incident goal. The Management by Objectives approach includes the following: establishing overarching incident objectives; developing strategies based on overarching incident objectives; developing and issuing assignments, plans, procedures, and protocols; establishing specific, measurable tactics or tasks for various incident-management functional activities and directing efforts to attain them, in support of defined strategies; and documenting results to measure performance and facilitate corrective action.

Manager Individual within an Incident Command System organizational unit who is assigned specific managerial responsibilities (e.g., Staging Area Manager or Camp Manager).

Mitigation Activities providing a critical foundation in the effort to reduce the loss of life and property from natural and/or manmade disasters by avoiding or lessening the impact of a disaster and providing value to the public by creating safer communities. Mitigation seeks to fix the cycle of disaster damage, reconstruction, and repeated damage. These activities or actions, in most cases, will have a long-term sustained effect.

Mobilization The process and procedures used by all organizations-Federal, State, tribal, and local-for activating, assembling, and transporting all resources that have been requested to respond to or support an incident.

Mobilization Guide Reference document used by organizations outlining agreements, processes, and procedures used by all participating agencies/organizations for activating, assembling, and transporting resources.

Multiagency Coordination (MAC) Group A group of administrators or executives, or their appointed representatives, who are typically authorized to commit agency resources and funds. A MAC Group can provide coordinated decisionmaking and resource allocation among cooperating agencies, and may establish the priorities among incidents, harmonize agency policies, and provide strategic guidance and direction to support incident management activities. MAC Groups may also be known as multiagency committees, emergency management committees, or as otherwise defined by the Multiagency Coordination System.

Multiagency Coordination System (MACS) A system that provides the architecture to support coordination for incident prioritization, critical resource allocation, communications systems integration, and information coordination. MACS assist agencies and organizations responding to an incident. The elements of a MACS include facilities, equipment, personnel, procedures, and communications. Two of the most commonly used elements are Emergency Operations Centers and MAC Groups.

Multijurisdictional Incident An incident requiring action from multiple agencies that each have jurisdiction to manage certain aspects of an incident. In the Incident Command System, these incidents will be managed under Unified Command.

Mutual Aid Agreement or Assistance Agreement Written or oral agreement between and among agencies/organizations and/or jurisdictions that provides a mechanism to quickly obtain emergency assistance in the form of personnel, equipment, materials, and other associated services. The primary objective is to facilitate rapid, short-term deployment of emergency support prior to, during, and/or after an incident.

National Of a nationwide character, including the Federal, State, tribal, and local aspects of governance and policy.

National Essential Functions A subset of government functions that are necessary to lead and sustain the Nation during a catastrophic emergency and that, therefore, must be supported through continuity of operations and continuity of government capabilities.

National Incident Management System A set of principles that provides a systematic, proactive approach guiding government agencies at all levels, nongovernmental organizations, and the private sector to work seamlessly to prevent, protect against, respond to, recover from, and mitigate the effects of incidents, regardless of cause, size, location, or complexity, in order to reduce the loss of life or property and harm to the environment.

National Response Framework A guide to how the Nation conducts all-hazards response.

Nongovernmental Organization (NGO) An entity with an association that is based on interests of its members, individuals, or institutions. It is not created by a government, but it may work cooperatively with government. Such organizations serve a public purpose, not a private benefit. Examples of NGOs include faith-based charity organizations and the American Red Cross. NGOs, including voluntary and faith-based groups, provide relief services to sustain life, reduce physical and emotional distress, and promote the recovery of disaster victims. Often these groups provide specialized services that help individuals with disabilities. NGOs and voluntary organizations play a major role in assisting emergency managers before, during, and after an emergency.

Officer The Incident Command System title for a person responsible for one of the Command Staff positions of Safety, Liaison, and Public Information.

Operational Period The time scheduled for executing a given set of operation actions, as specified in the Incident Action Plan. Operational periods can be of various lengths, although usually they last 12 to 24 hours.

Operations Section The Incident Command System (ICS) Section responsible for all tactical incident operations and implementation of the Incident Action Plan. In ICS, the Operations Section normally includes subordinate Branches, Divisions, and/or Groups.

Organization Any association or group of persons with like objectives. Examples include, but are not limited to, governmental departments and agencies, nongovernmental organizations, and the private sector.

Personal Responsibility The obligation to be accountable for one's actions.

Personnel Accountability The ability to account for the location and welfare of incident personnel. It is accomplished when supervisors ensure that Incident Command System principles and processes are functional and that personnel are working within established incident management guidelines.

Plain Language Communication that can be understood by the intended audience and meets the purpose of the communicator. For the purpose of the National Incident Management System, plain language is designed to eliminate or limit the use of codes and acronyms, as appropriate, during incident response involving more than a single agency.

Planned Event A scheduled nonemergency activity (e.g., sporting event, concert, parade, etc).

Planning Meeting A meeting held as needed before and throughout the duration of an incident to select specific strategies and tactics for incident control operations and for service and support planning. For larger incidents, the Planning Meeting is a major element in the development of the Incident Action Plan.

Planning Section The Incident Command System Section responsible for the collection, evaluation, and dissemination of operational information related to the incident, and for the preparation and documentation of the Incident Action Plan. This Section also maintains information on the current and forecasted situation and on the status of resources assigned to the incident.

Portability An approach that facilitates the interaction of systems that are normally distinct. Portability of radio technologies, protocols, and frequencies among emergency management/response personnel will allow for the successful and efficient integration, transport, and deployment of communications systems when necessary. Portability includes the standardized assignment of radio channels across jurisdictions, which allows responders to participate in an incident outside their jurisdiction and still use familiar equipment.

Pre-Positioned Resource A resource moved to an area near the expected incident site in response to anticipated resource needs.

Preparedness A continuous cycle of planning, organizing, training, equipping, exercising, evaluating, and taking corrective action in an effort to ensure effective coordination during incident response. Within the National Incident Management System, preparedness focuses on the following elements: planning; procedures and protocols; training and exercises; personnel qualification and certification; and equipment certification.

Preparedness Organization An organization that provides coordination for emergency management and incident response activities before a potential incident. These organizations range from groups of individuals to small committees to large standing organizations that represent a wide variety of committees, planning groups, and other organizations (e.g., Citizen Corps, Local Emergency Planning Committees, Critical Infrastructure Sector Coordinating Councils).

Prevention Actions to avoid an incident or to intervene to stop an incident from occurring. Prevention involves actions to protect lives and property. It involves applying intelligence and other information to a range of activities that may include such countermeasures as deterrence operations; heightened inspections; improved surveillance and security operations; investigations to determine the full nature and source of the threat; public health and agricultural surveillance and testing processes; immunizations, isolation, or quarantine; and, as appropriate, specific law enforcement operations aimed at deterring, pre-empting, interdicting, or disrupting illegal activity and apprehending potential perpetrators and bringing them to justice.

Primary Mission Essential Functions Government functions that must be performed in order to support or implement the performance of National Essential Functions before, during, and in the aftermath of an emergency.

Private Sector Organizations and individuals that are not part of any governmental structure. The private sector includes for-profit and not-for-profit organizations, formal and informal structures, commerce, and industry.

Protocol A set of established guidelines for actions (which may be designated by individuals, teams, functions, or capabilities) under various specified conditions.

Public Information Processes, procedures, and systems for communicating timely, accurate, and accessible information on an incident's cause, size, and current situation; resources committed; and other matters of general interest to the public, responders, and additional stakeholders (both directly affected and indirectly affected).

Public Information Officer A member of the Command Staff responsible for interfacing with the public and media and/or with other agencies with incident-related information requirements.

Publications Management Subsystem that manages the development, publication control, publication supply, and distribution of National Incident Management System materials.

Recovery The development, coordination, and execution of service- and site-restoration plans; the reconstitution of government operations and services; individual, private-sector, nongovernmental, and public assistance programs to provide housing and to promote restoration; long-term care and treatment of affected persons; additional measures for social, political, environmental, and economic restoration; evaluation of the incident to identify lessons learned; postincident reporting; and development of initiatives to mitigate the effects of future incidents.

Recovery Plan A plan developed to restore an affected area or community.

Reimbursement A mechanism to recoup funds expended for incident-specific activities.

Resource Management A system for identifying available resources at all jurisdictional levels to enable timely, efficient, and unimpeded access to resources needed to prepare for, respond to, or recover from an incident. Resource management under the National Incident Management System includes mutual aid agreements and assistance agreements; the use of special Federal, State, tribal, and local teams; and resource mobilization protocols.

Resource Tracking A standardized, integrated process conducted prior to, during, and after an incident by all emergency management/response personnel and their associated organizations.

Resources Personnel and major items of equipment, supplies, and facilities available or potentially available for assignment to incident operations and for which status is maintained. Resources are described by kind and type and may be used in operational support or supervisory capacities at an incident or at an Emergency Operations Center.

Response Activities that address the short-term, direct effects of an incident. Response includes immediate actions to save lives, protect property, and meet basic human needs. Response also includes the execution of emergency operations plans and of mitigation activities designed to limit the loss of life, personal injury, property damage, and other unfavorable outcomes. As indicated by the situation, response activities include applying intelligence and other information to lessen the effects or consequences of an incident; increased security operations; continuing investigations into nature and source of the threat; ongoing public health and agricultural surveillance and testing processes; immunizations, isolation, or quarantine; and specific law enforcement operations aimed at preempting, interdicting, or disrupting illegal activity, and apprehending actual perpetrators and bringing them to justice.

Retrograde To return resources back to their original location.

Safety Officer A member of the Command Staff responsible for monitoring incident operations and advising the Incident Commander on all matters relating to operational safety, including the health and safety of emergency responder personnel.

Section The Incident Command System organizational level having responsibility for a major functional area of incident management (e.g., Operations, Planning, Logistics, Finance/Administration, and Intelligence/Investigations (if established). The Section is organizationally situated between the Branch and the Incident Command.

Single Resource An individual, a piece of equipment and its personnel complement, or a crew/team of individuals with an identified work supervisor that can be used on an incident.

Situation Report Confirmed or verified information regarding the specific details relating to an incident.

Span of Control The number of resources for which a supervisor is responsible, usually expressed as the ratio of supervisors to individuals. (Under the National Incident Management System, an appropriate span of control is between 1:3 and 1:7, with optimal being 1:5, or between 1:8 and 1:10 for many large-scale law enforcement operations).

Special Needs Population A population whose members may have additional needs before, during, and after an incident in functional areas, including but not limited to: maintaining independence, communication, transportation, supervision, and medical care. Individuals in need of additional response assistance may include those who have disabilities; who live in institutionalized settings; who are elderly; who are children; who are from diverse cultures, who have limited English proficiency, or who are non-English-speaking; or who are transportation disadvantaged.

Staging Area Temporary location for available resources. A Staging Area can be any location in which personnel, supplies, and equipment can be temporarily housed or parked while awaiting operational assignment.

Standard Operating Guidelines A set of instructions having the force of a directive, covering those features of operations which lend themselves to a definite or standardized procedure without loss of effectiveness.

Standard Operating Procedure A complete reference document or an operations manual that provides the purpose, authorities, duration, and details for the preferred method of performing a single function or a number of interrelated functions in a uniform manner.

State When capitalized, refers to any State of the United States, the District of Columbia, the Commonwealth of Puerto Rico, the Virgin Islands, Guam, American Samoa, the Commonwealth of the Northern Mariana Islands, and any possession of the United States. See Section 2 (14), Homeland Security Act of 2002, Pub. L. 107-296, 116 Stat. 2135 (2002).

Status Report Information specifically related to the status of resources (e.g., the availability or assignment of resources).

Strategy The general plan or direction selected to accomplish incident objectives.

Strike Team A set number of resources of the same kind and type that have an established minimum number of personnel, common communications, and a leader.

Substate Region A grouping of jurisdictions, counties, and/or localities within a State brought together for specified purposes (e.g., homeland security, education, public health), usually containing a governance structure.

Supervisor The Incident Command System title for an individual responsible for a Division or Group.

Supporting Agency An agency that provides support and/or resource assistance to another agency. See Assisting Agency.

Supporting Technology Any technology that may be used to support the National Incident Management System, such as orthophoto mapping, remote automatic weather stations, infrared technology, or communications.

System Any combination of facilities, equipment, personnel, processes, procedures, and communications integrated for a specific purpose.

Tactics The deployment and directing of resources on an incident to accomplish the objectives designated by strategy.

Task Force Any combination of resources assembled to support a specific mission or operational need. All resource elements within a Task Force must have common communications and a designated leader.

Technical Specialist Person with special skills that can be used anywhere within the Incident Command System organization. No minimum qualifications are prescribed, as technical specialists normally perform the same duties during an incident that they perform in their everyday jobs, and they are typically certified in their fields or professions.

Technology Standards Conditions, guidelines, or characteristics that may be required to facilitate the interoperability and compatibility of major systems across jurisdictional, geographic, and functional lines.

Technology Support Assistance that facilitates incident operations and sustains the research and development programs that underpin the long-term investment in the Nation's future incident management capabilities.

Terrorism As defined in the Homeland Security Act of 2002, activity that involves an act that is dangerous to human life or potentially destructive of critical infrastructure or key resources; is a violation of the criminal laws of the United States or of any State or other subdivision of the United States; and appears to be intended to intimidate or coerce a civilian population, to influence the policy of a government by intimidation or coercion, or to affect the conduct of a government by mass destruction, assassination, or kidnapping.

Threat Natural or manmade occurrence, individual, entity, or action that has or indicates the potential to harm life, information, operations, the environment, and/or property.

Tools Those instruments and capabilities that allow for the professional performance of tasks, such as information systems, agreements, doctrine, capabilities, and legislative authorities.

Tribal Referring to any Indian tribe, band, nation, or other organized group or community, including any Alaskan Native Village as defined in or established pursuant to the Alaskan Native Claims Settlement Act (85 Stat. 688) [43 U.S.C.A. and 1601 et seq.], that is recognized as eligible for the special programs and services provided by the United States to Indians because of their status as Indians.

Type An Incident Command System resource classification that refers to capability. Type 1 is generally considered to be more capable than Types 2, 3, or 4, respectively, because of size, power, capacity, or (in the case of Incident Management Teams) experience and qualifications.

Unified Approach The integration of resource management, communications and information management, and command and management in order to form an effective system.

Unified Area Command Version of command established when incidents under an Area Command are multijurisdictional. See Area Command.

Unified Command (UC) An Incident Command System application used when more than one agency has incident jurisdiction or when incidents cross political jurisdictions. Agencies work together through the designated members of the UC, often the senior persons from agencies and/or disciplines participating in the UC, to establish a common set of objectives and strategies and a single Incident Action Plan.

Unit The organizational element with functional responsibility for a specific incident planning, logistics, or finance/administration activity.

Unit Leader The individual in charge of managing Units within an Incident Command System (ICS) functional Section. The Unit can be staffed by a number of support personnel providing a wide range of services. Some of the support positions are preestablished within ICS (e.g., Base/Camp Manager), but many others will be assigned as technical specialists.

Unity of Command An Incident Command System principle stating that each individual involved in incident operations will be assigned to only one supervisor.

Vital Records The essential agency records that are needed to meet operational responsibilities under national security emergencies or other emergency or disaster conditions (emergency operating records), or to protect the legal and financial rights of the government and those affected by government activities (legal and financial rights records).

Volunteer For purposes of the National Incident Management System, any individual accepted to perform services by the lead agency (which has authority to accept volunteer services) when the individual performs services without promise, expectation, or receipt of compensation for services performed. See 16 U.S.C. 742f(c) and 29 CFR 553.10.

DISASTER ACRONYMS

AFAA	Air Force Audit Agency
AAA	Army Audit Agency
ARC	Appalachian Regional Commission
CIA	Central Intelligence Agency
CNCS	Corporation for National and Community Service
DCAA	Defense Contract Audit Agency
DCIS	Defense Criminal Investigative Service

DHS	Department of Homeland Security	FMSHRC	Federal Mine Safety and Health Review Commission
DHS JFO	DHS Joint Field Office	FPS	Federal Protective Service
DHS OIG	DHS Office of Inspector General	GAO	Government Accountability Office
DHS OIG ISP	DHS OIG — Office of Inspection and Special Reviews	GSA	General Services Administration
DHS HSOC	DHS Homeland Security Operations Center	HAC	Housing Area Command
		HANO	Housing Authority of New Orleans
DISA	Defense Information Systems Agency	HHS	Department of Health and Human Services
DOC	Department of Commerce		
DOC EDA	DoC Economic Development Authority	HHS AOA	HHS Administration on Aging
DOC HCIC	DoC Hurricane Contracting Information Center	HHS ACF	HHS Administration for Children and Families
DOC MBDA	DoC Minority Business Development Agency	HHS CCB	HHS Child Care Bureau
		HHS CDCP	HHS Centers for Disease Control and Prevention
DOD	Department of Defense		
DODIG	Department of Defense Inspector General	HHS CMS	HHS Centers for Medicare and Medicaid Services
DOE	Department of Energy	HHS HSB	HHS Head Start Bureau
DOED	Department of Education	HHS HSRA	HHS Health Services Resource Administration
DOI	Department of Interior		
DOI BIA	DOI Bureau of Indian Affairs	HHS SAMHSA	HHS Substance Abuse and Mental Health Services Administration
DOI BUREC	DOI Bureau of Reclamation		
DOJ	Department of Justice	HHS OPHEP	HHS Office of Public Health Emergency Preparedness
DOJ BJA	DOJ Bureau of Justice Assistance		
DOJ BOP	DOJ Bureau of Prisons	HKFTF	Hurricane Katrina Fraud Task Force
DOJ OJP	Office of Justice Programs	HKFTFCC	Hurricane Katrina Fraud Task Force Command Center
DOL	Department of Labor		
DOL ETA	DOL Employment and Training Administration	HRRC	Hurricane Recovery and Response Center
DOL MBDA	DOL Minority Business Development Agency	HUD	Department of Housing and Urban Development
DOS	Department of State	HUD PHA	HUD Public Housing Agency
DOT	Department of Transportation	IRS	Internal Revenue Service
DOT	FAA DOT Federal Aviation Administration	IRS TAC	IRS Taxpayer Assistance Center
		LOLA	Louisiana Office of the Legislative Auditor
DOT FHA	DOT Federal Highway Administration		
DOT FRA	DOT Federal Railroad Administration	MDES	Mississippi Department of Employment Security
DOT FTA	DOT Federal Transit Administration		
DOT MARAD	DOT Maritime Administration	MSC	Military Sealift Command
ECIE	Executive Council on Integrity and Efficiency	MSPB	Merit Systems Protection Board
		NAR	National Association of Realtors
EDA	Economic Development Administration	NASA	National Aeronautics and Space Administration
EEOC	Equal Employment Opportunity Commission		
		NAS	Naval Audit Service
EOC	Emergency Operations Center	NCUA	National Credit Union Administration
EPA	Environmental Protection Agency	NIST	National Institute of Standards and Technology
ETA	Employment and Training Administration		
		NLRB	National Labor Relations Board
FBI	Federal Bureau of Investigation	NOAA	National Oceanographic and Atmospheric Administration
FCC	Federal Communications Commission		
FCSIC	Farm Credit System Insurance Corporation.	NRCS	Natural Resource Conservation Services
FDIC	Federal Deposit Insurance Corporation	NTIA	National Telecommunications and Information Administration
FEMA	Federal Emergency Management Agency	OI	Office of Investigations

OIG	Office of Inspector General	*CDP*	Office of Community Development
OMB	Office of Management and Budget	*COOP*	Continuity of Operations Plan (uSPS)
OPM	Office of Personnel Management	*COTR*	Contracting Officer Technical Representative
OSHA	Occupational Safety and Health Administration	*DAO*	Disaster Area Office (SbA)
OTS	Office of Thrift Supervision	*DBA*	Davis-Bacon Act
PCIE	President's Council on Integrity and Efficiency	*DCMS*	Disaster Credit Management System (SbA)
		DFA	Direct Federal Assistance
PCIE HSR	PCIE Homeland Security Roundtable	*DRC*	Disaster Relief Codes (TiGTA)
SBA	Small Business Administration	*DRF*	Disaster Relief Fund
SBA DAPDC	SBA Disaster Assistance Processing and Disbursement Center	*DUA*	Disaster Unemployment Assistance
		ECP	Emergency Conservation Program
SIG	Special Inspector General	*EO*	Exempt Organization (TIGTA)
SSA	Social Security Administration	*ERG*	Economic Recovery Grants
TIGTA	Treasury Inspector General for Tax Administration	*ESF*	Emergency Support Function
		EWP	Emergency Watershed Protection Program
TREAS	U.S. Treasury Department	*FAA AIG*	FAA Airport Improvement Grant
TVA	Tennessee Valley Authority	*FAG*	Family Assistance Grant
USA	U.S. Army	*FAR*	Federal Acquisition Regulation
USAF	U.S. Air Force	*FISCAM*	Federal Information System Controls Audit Manual
USACE	U.S. Army Corps of Engineers		
USDA	United States Department of Agriculture	*FPDS NG*	Federal Procurement Data System—Next Generation
USDA APHIS	USDA Animal and Plant Health Inspection Service		
		FSS	Federal Supply Schedule
USDA DFSP	USDA Disaster Food Stamp Program	*GAGAS*	Generally Accepted Government Auditing Standards
USDA ECP	USDA Emergency Conservation Program		
		FOS	Federal Operations Support
USDA EWP	USDA Emergency Watershed Protection Program	*GCHR*	Gulf Coast Hurricane Recovery
		HERA	Hurricane Education Recovery Act
USDA FNS	USDA Food and Nutrition Service	*HGJTG*	High-Growth Job Training Grants
USDA FS	USDA Forest Service	*HKFTF*	Hurricane Katrina Fraud Task Force
USDA FSA	USDA Farm Service Agency	*HOME*	Home Ownership Made Easy
USDA NRCS	USDA Natural Resources Conservation Service	*HSWG*	Homeland Security Working Group
		HTR	Hurricane Tax Relief (TiGTA)
DADDP	Dead Animal Debris Disposal Program	*IEMP*	Integrated Emergency Management Plan (USPS)
USDA RHS	USDA Rural Housing Service	*IG*	Inspector General
USDA RMA	USDA Risk Management Agency	*IH*	Individuals and Household
USMC	U.S. Marine Corps	*IHL*	Institutes of Higher Learning
USN	U.S. Navy	*IIMG*	Interagency Incident Management Group
USPHS	U.S. Public Health Service	*IMPAC*	International Merchant Purchase Authorization Card
USPS	United States Postal Service		
VA	Department of Veterans Affairs	*JAG*	Edward Byrne Memorial Justice Assistance Grants (DOJ)
VA-NPSC	Virginia National Processing Service Center		
		KDHAP	Katrina Disaster Housing Assistance Program

FEMA PROGRAMS

		LEA	Local Education Agency
BPA	Basic Purchasing Agreement	*LIHEAP*	Low Income Home Energy Assistance Program (HHS)
CAS	Customer Account Services	*MA*	Mission Assignments
CCC	Commodity Credit Corporation	*NDNH*	National Directory of New Hires
CCR	Central Contractor Registration	*NEG*	National Emergency Grant
CDBG	Community Development Block Grant	*NEMIS*	National Emergency Management Information System
		NFIP	National Flood Insurance Program

NRF	National Relief Fund
NRP	National Response Plan
ODA	Office of Disaster Assistance (SbA)
ONA	Other Needs Assistance
PHA	Public House Agency
PSE	Public Service Employment
RCG	Reintegration Counselor Grants
REO	Real Estate Owned
RFQ	Request for Quotation
SEA	State Education Agency
SSN	Social Security Number
START/ERRS	Superfund Technical Assessment and Response Team/Emergency and Rapid Response Services (EPA)
TA	Technical Assistance
TAC	Technical Assistance Contractor
UI	Unemployment Insurance
USF	Universal Service Fund
WIA NEG	Workforce Investment Act—National Emergency Grant

DHSS DISASTERS AND EMERGENCIES GLOSSARY

Adequate Denotes the quality or quantity of a system, process, procedure, or resource that will achieve the relevant incident response objective.

Area Command (Unified Area Command) An organization established (1) to oversee the management of multiple incidents that are each being handled by an ICS organization, or (2) to oversee the management of large or multiple incidents to which several Incident Management Teams have been assigned. Area Command has the responsibility to set overall strategy and priorities, allocate critical resources according to priorities, ensure that incidents are properly managed, and ensure that objectives are met and strategies followed. Area Command becomes Unified Area Command when incidents are multijurisdictional. (adapted from NIMS)

Assignments Tasks given to resources to perform within a given operational period that are based on operational objectives defined in the IAP. (adapted from NIMS)

Chief The Incident Command System (ICS) title for individuals responsible for command of the functional ICS Sections: Operations, Planning, Logistics, and Finance/Administration. This group is collectively referred to as the General Staff.

Command Staff In an incident management organization, the Command Staff consists of the Incident Command and the special staff positions of Public Information Officer, Safety Officer, Liaison Officer, and other positions as required (such as Senior Advisors). Special staff positions report directly to the Incident Commander and may have an assistant or assistants. (adapted from NIMS)

Complex Medical Incidents Events where the victims have unusual medical needs or require medical care that is not readily available. These medical needs may be very difficult to adequately define or address without specialized expertise, even with only a few casualties.

Contingency Plan Proposed strategy and tactics (often documented) to be used when a specific issue arises or event occurs during the course of emergency or disaster operations.

Disaster ("Major") As defined in the Robert T. Stafford Act, a "major disaster" is any natural catastrophe (including any hurricane, tornado, storm, high water, wind-driven water, tidal wave, tsunami, earthquake, volcanic eruption, landslide, mudslide, snowstorm, or drought), or, regardless of cause, any fire, flood, or explosion, in any part of the United States, which in the determination of the President causes damage of sufficient severity and magnitude to warrant major disaster assistance under this Act to supplement the efforts and available resources of States, local governments, and disaster relief organizations in alleviating the damage, loss, hardship, or suffering caused thereby.

Emergency (Federal) As defined in the Robert T. Stafford Act, any occasion or instance for which, in the determination of the President, Federal assistance is needed to supplement State and local efforts and capabilities to save lives and to protect property and public health and safety, or to lessen or avert the threat of a catastrophe in any part of the United States.

Emergency Management Describes the science of managing complex systems and multidisciplinary personnel to address emergencies or disasters, across all hazards, and through the phases of mitigation, preparedness, response, and recovery.

Emergency Management Program (EMP) A program that implements the organization's mission, vision, management framework, and strategic goals and objectives related to emergencies and disasters. It uses a comprehensive approach to emergency management as a conceptual framework, combining mitigation, preparedness, response, and recovery into a fully integrated set of activities. The "program" applies to all departments and organizational units within the organization that have roles in responding to a potential emergency. (adapted from NFPA 1600 and the VHA Guidebook, 2004)

Emergency Operations Center (EOC) The physical location from which the coordination of information and resources to support domestic incident management activities normally takes place. The use of EOCs is a standard practice in emergency management and is one type of Multiagency Coordination Center (MACC). The EOC is used in varying ways at all levels of government and within private industry to provide coordination, direction, control or support during emergencies.

Emergency Operations Plan (EOP) The "response" plan that an entity (organization, jurisdiction, State, etc.) maintains for responding to any hazard event. It provides action guidance for management and emergency response personnel, during the response phase of Comprehensive Emergency Management.

Emergency Support Function (ESF) As defined in the National Response Plan, an ESF refers to a group of capabilities of Federal departments and agencies to provide the support, resources, program implementation, and services that are most likely to be needed to save lives, protect property, restore essential services and critical infrastructure, and help victims return to normal following a national incident. An ESF represents the primary operational level mechanism to orchestrate activities to provide assistance to State, Tribal, or local governments, or to Federal departments or agencies conducting missions of primary Federal responsibility.

Exceptional Refers to unusual numbers or types of victims, impacted medical care systems, or other very adverse conditions.

Federal Of or pertaining to the Federal Government of the United States of America.

Finance/Administration The ICS functional area that addresses the financial, administrative, and legal/regulatory issues for the incident management system. It monitors costs related to the incident, and provides accounting, procurement, time recording, cost analyses, and overall fiscal guidance.

First Responder Refers to individuals who in the early stages of an incident are responsible for the protection and preservation of life, property, evidence, and the environment, including emergency response providers as defined in Section 2 of the Homeland Security Act of 2002 (6 U.S.C. 101). It includes emergency management, public health, clinical care, public works, and other skilled support personnel (e.g., equipment operators) that provide immediate support services during prevention, response, and recovery operations.

Function In the Incident Command System, refers to the five major activities (i.e., Command, Operations, Planning, Logistics, and Finance/Administration). Intelligence is not considered a separate function under traditional ICS but has been added for consideration as a possible separate function under NIMS. The term function is also used when describing the activity involved (e.g., the Planning function).

Functional Area A major grouping of the similar tasks that agencies perform in carrying out incident management activities. These are usually all or part of one of the five ICS sections (Command, Operations, Logistics, Planning, Administrative/Finance).

Hazard A potential or actual force, physical condition, or agent with the ability to cause human injury, illness, and/or death, and significant damage to property, the environment, critical infrastructure, agriculture and business operations, and other types of harm or loss.

Hazard Vulnerability Analysis (HVA) A systematic approach to identifying all hazards that may affect an organization, assessing the risk (probability of hazard occurrence and the consequence for the organization) associated with each hazard and analyzing findings to create a prioritized comparison of hazard vulnerabilities. The consequence, or vulnerability, is related to both the impact on organizational function and the likely service demands created by hazard impact.

Homeland Security Presidential Directive-5 (HSPD-5) A Presidential directive issued on February 28, 2003, and intended to enhance the ability of the United States to manage domestic incidents by establishing a single, comprehensive National Incident Management System.

Incident An actual or impending hazard impact, either human caused or by natural phenomena, that requires action by emergency personnel to prevent or minimize loss of life or damage to property and/or natural resources.

Incident Action Plan (IAP) The document in ICS that guides the response for that operational period. It contains the overall incident objectives and strategy, general tactical actions and supporting information to enable successful completion of objectives. The IAP may be oral or written. When written, the IAP may have a number of supportive plans and information as attachments (e.g., traffic plan, safety plan, communications plan, and maps). There is only one IAP at an incident. All other "action plans" are subsets of the IAP and their titles should be qualified accordingly. For example, the jurisdiction primarily impacted usually develops the IAP. Action plans developed below the level of the jurisdiction could be referred to as "Operations Plans" (e.g., Summary Hospital Operations Plans or Individual Hospital Operations Plans).

Incident Command Post (ICP) The physical location close to the incident site (or elsewhere for a diffuse incident or one with multiple sites), which serves as a base location for managing tactical or "field operations." Located within the ICP are designated representatives of the major response agencies for the incident, who fill positions in the incident command team. The ICP location is designated by the Incident Commander.

Incident Command System (ICS) The combination of facilities, equipment, personnel, procedures, and communications operating within a common organizational structure, designed to aid in the management of resources for emergency incidents. It may be used for all emergencies, and has been successfully employed by multiple response disciplines. ICS is used at all levels of government (local, State, Tribal, and Federal) to organize field level operations. (adapted from NIMS)

Incident Commander (IC) The individual responsible for all incident activities, including the development of strategies and tactics and the ordering and the releasWWe of resources. The IC has overall authority and responsibility for conducting incident operations and is responsible for the management of all incident operations at the incident site. (adapted from NIMS)

Incident Management Team (IMT) The Incident Commander, and appropriate Command and General Staff personnel assigned to an incident.

Incident Objectives Statements of guidance and direction necessary for selecting appropriate strategy(s) and the tactical direction of resources. Incident objectives are based on realistic expectations of what can be accomplished when allocated resources have been effectively deployed. Incident objectives must be achievable and measurable, yet flexible to allow for strategic and tactical alternatives. (adapted from NIMS)

Joint Information Center (JIC) A center established to coordinate the public information activities for a large incident. It is the central point of contact for all news media at the scene of the incident. Public information officials from all participating Federal agencies collaborate at the JIC, as well as public information officials from participating State and local agencies. (adapted from NIMS)

Jurisdiction A political subdivision (Federal, State, county, parish, and/or municipality) with the responsibility for ensuring public safety, health, and welfare within its legal authorities and geographic boundaries. In the context of this handbook, it refers to a geographic area's local government, which commonly has the primary role in emergency response.

Liaison In ICS, it is a position(s) assigned to establish and maintain direct coordination and information exchange with agencies and organizations outside of the specific incident's ICS structure. (adapted from NIMS)

Liaison Officer A member of the Command Staff responsible for filling the senior liaison function with representatives from cooperating and assisting agencies.

Local Government (HSPD-5 definition) A county, municipality, city, town, township, local public authority, school district, special district, intrastate district, council of governments (regardless of whether the council of governments is incorporated as a nonprofit corporation under State law), regional or interstate government entity, or agency or instrumentality of a local government; an Indian Tribe or authorized tribal organization, or in Alaska a Native Village or Alaska Regional Native Corporation; a rural community, unincorporated town or village, or other public entity. (As defined in Section 2 (10) of the Homeland Security Act of 2002, Pub. L. 107-296, 116 Stat. 2135, et seq. (2002).

Logistics The ICS functional section that provides resources and other support services to incident management, operations, and the other ICS sections. (adapted from NIMS)

Management by Objectives In the ICS, this is a proactive management activity that involves a four-step process to achieve the incident goal. The steps are: establishing the overarching incident objectives; developing and issuing assignments, plans, procedures, and protocols; establishing specific, measurable objectives for various incident command functional activities and directing efforts to fulfill them, in support of defined strategic objectives; and documenting results to measure performance and facilitate corrective action. (adapted from NIMS)

Management Meeting In the incident management process, the meeting that establishes (or revises) the incident goals and objectives and the makeup of the ICS structure. NIMS does not separate this meeting from the Planning meeting, although they are commonly separated in wildland fire and Urban Search and Rescue incident management.

Measures of Effectiveness Defined criteria for determining whether satisfactory progress is being accomplished toward achieving the incident objectives. Similarly, defined criteria can also be utilized to establish the effectiveness of the overall Emergency Management Program in meeting its defined goals across the four phases.

Medical Surge Describes the ability to provide adequate medical evaluation and care in events that severely challenge or exceed the normal medical infrastructure of an affected community (through numbers or types of patients).

Mission Assignment The vehicle used by DHS/FEMA to support Federal operations in a Robert T. Stafford Act major disaster or emergency declaration. It orders immediate, short-term emergency response assistance when an applicable State or local government is overwhelmed by the event and lacks the capability to perform, or contract for, the necessary work. (NRP definition)

Mitigation Activities designed to reduce or eliminate risks to persons or property or to lessen the actual or potential effects or consequences of a hazard. Mitigation involves ongoing actions to reduce exposure to, probability of, or potential loss from hazards. Examples include zoning and building codes, floodplain buyouts, and analysis of hazard-related data to determine where it is safe to build or locate temporary facilities. Mitigation can include efforts to educate governments, businesses and the public on measures they can take to reduce loss and injury. (adapted from NIMS)

Mobilization Activities and procedures carried out that ready an asset to perform incident operations according to the Emergency Operations Plan. During the response phase of Comprehensive Emergency Management, it is the stage that transitions functional elements from a state of inactivity or normal operations to their designated response state. This activity may occur well into the response phase, as additional assets are brought on line or as surge processes are instituted to meet demands.

Multijurisdiction Incident An incident that extends across political boundaries and/or response disciplines, requiring action from multiple governments and agencies to manage certain aspects of an incident. These incidents may best be managed under Unified Command. (adapted from NIMS)

Mutual Aid Agreement Written instrument between agencies and/or jurisdictions in which they agree to assist one another upon request, by furnishing personnel, equipment, supplies, and/or expertise in a specified manner. An "agreement" is generally more legally binding than an "understanding."

National Incident Management System (NIMS) A system mandated by HSPD-5 that provides a consistent nationwide approach for Federal, State, Tribal, and local governments, the private sector, and nongovernmental organizations to work effectively and efficiently together to prepare for, respond to, and recover from domestic incidents, regardless of cause, size, or complexity. To provide for interoperability and compatibility among Federal, State, and local capabilities, NIMS includes a core set of concepts, principles, and terminology. HSPD-5 identifies these as the Incident Command System; multiagency coordination systems; unified command; training; identification and management of resources (including systems for classifying types of resources); qualifications and certifications; and the collection, tracking, and reporting of incident information and incident resources. (adapted from NIMS)

National Response Plan (NRP) The NRP establishes a comprehensive all-hazards approach to enhance the ability of the United States to manage domestic incidents. The plan incorporates best practices and procedures from incident management disciplines—homeland security, emergency management, law enforcement, firefighting, public works, public health, responder and recovery worker health and safety, emergency medical services, and the private sector—and integrates them into a unified structure. It forms the basis of how the Federal government coordinates with State, local, and Tribal governments and the private sector during incidents.

Operations Section The ICS functional area responsible for all resources and activities that directly address the incident objectives. It develops all tactical operations at the incident, and in ICS, includes branches, divisions and/or groups, Task Forces, Strike Teams, Single Resources, and Staging Areas.

Planning (Incident Response): Activities that support the incident management process, including completing the incident action plan and support plans and accomplishing incident information processing. This is in contrast to preparedness planning, which is designed to ready a system for response.

Planning Meeting A meeting held as needed throughout the duration of an incident to select specific strategies and general tactics for incident operations, and for service and support planning. In the incident management process, the planning meeting establishes strategy and priorities based upon the goals and objectives developed in the management meeting. Remaining decisions for the action plan are achieved during this meeting. (adapted from NIMS)

Planning Section In ICS, this functional area is responsible for the collection, evaluation, and dissemination of operational information related to the incident, and for the preparation and documentation of the incident action plan and its support plans. The Planning Chief is responsible for running the management and planning meetings and the operations briefing, and the Planning Section supports these activities. The Planning Section also maintains information on the current and forecasted situation, the status of resources assigned to the incident, and other incident information. (adapted from NIMS)

Preparedness The range of deliberate, critical tasks and activities necessary to build, sustain, and improve the capability to protect against, respond to, and recover from hazard impacts. Preparedness is a continuous process. Within NIMS, preparedness involves efforts at all levels of government and the private sector to identify threats, to determine vulnerabilities, and to identify required response plans and resources. NIMS preparedness focuses on establishing guidelines, protocols, and standards for planning, training and exercise, personnel qualifications and certification, equipment certification, and publication management. (adapted from NIMS)

Prevention Actions to avoid a hazard occurrence, or to avoid or minimize the hazard impact (consequences) if it does occur. Prevention involves actions to protect lives and property. Under HSPD-5, it involves applying intelligence and other information to a range of activities that may include such countermeasures as deterrence operations; heightened inspections; improved surveillance and security operations; investigations to determine the full nature and source of the threat; public health and agricultural surveillance and testing processes; immunizations, isolation, or quarantine; and as appropriate specific law enforcement operations aimed at deterring, preempting, interdicting, or disrupting illegal activity, and apprehending potential perpetrators and bringing them to justice. (adapted from NIMS)

Private Sector Organizations and entities that are not part of any governmental structure. It includes for-profit and not-for-profit, and formal and informal structures, including commerce and industry, non-governmental organizations (NGO), and private voluntary organizations (PVO). (adapted from NIMS)

Processes Systems of operations that incorporate standardized procedures, methodologies, and functions necessary to effectively and efficiently accomplish objectives. (adapted from NIMS)

Public Health Emergency Defined by the Model State Emergency Health Powers Act (MSEHPA): An occurrence or imminent threat of an illness or health condition that is believed to be caused by: (1) bioterrorism; (2) the appearance of a novel or previously controlled or eradicated infectious agent or biological toxin; (3) a natural disaster; (4) a chemical attack or accidental release; or (5) a nuclear attack or accident. It must pose a high probability of a large number of deaths in the affected population, or a large number of serious or long-term disabilities in the affected population, or widespread exposure to an infectious or toxic agent that poses a significant risk of substantial future harm to a large number of people in the affected population. (Center for Law and the Public's Health at Georgetown and Johns Hopkins Universities)

Public Information Officer Official at headquarters or in the field responsible for preparing and coordinating the dissemination of public information in cooperation with other responding Federal, State, Tribal, and local agencies. In ICS, the term refers to a member of the Command Staff responsible for interfacing with the public and media and the Joint Information Center.

Recovery The phase of Comprehensive Emergency Management that encompasses activities and programs implemented during and after response that are designed to return the entity to its usual state or to a "new normal." For response organizations, this includes return-to-readiness activities.

Resiliency The ability of an individual or organization to quickly recover from change or misfortune.

Resources All personnel and major items of equipment, supplies, and facilities available, or potentially available, for assignment to incident or event tasks on which status is maintained.

Response Activities that address the direct effects of an incident. Response includes immediate actions to save lives, protect property, and meet basic human needs. Response also includes the execution of emergency operations plans as well as activities designed to limit the loss of life, personal injury, property damage, and other unfavorable outcomes. As indicated by the situation, response activities may include applying intelligence and other information to lessen the effects or consequences of an incident; increased security operations; continuing investigations into nature and source of the threat; ongoing public health and agricultural surveillance and testing processes; immunizations, isolation, or quarantine; and specific law enforcement operations aimed at preempting, interdicting, or disrupting illegal activity, and apprehending actual perpetrators and bringing them to justice. (adapted from NIMS)

Safety Officer A member of the Command Staff responsible for monitoring and assessing safety hazards or unsafe situations, and for developing measures for ensuring personnel safety. The Safety Officer may have assistants.

Span of Control The number of individuals a supervisor is responsible for, usually expressed as the ratio of supervisors to individuals (under NIMS, an appropriate span of control is between 1:3 and 1:7). (adapted from NIMS)

State When capitalized, refers to any State of the United States, the District of Columbia, the Commonwealth of Puerto Rico, the Virgin Islands, Guam, American Samoa, the Commonwealth of the Northern Mariana Islands, and any possession of the United States. (As defined in section 2 (14) of them Homeland Security Act of 2002, Pub. L. 107-296, 116 Stat. 2135, et seq.(2002).)

Strategic Strategic elements of incident management are characterized by continuous long-term, high-level planning by senior level organizations. They involve the adoption of long-range goals and objectives; the setting of priorities; the establishment of budgets and other fiscal decisions; policy development; and the application of measures of performance or effectiveness. (adapted from NIMS)

Surge Capability The ability to manage patients requiring unusual or very specialized medical evaluation and care. Requirements span the range of specialized medical and public health services (expertise, information, procedures, equipment, or personnel) that are not normally available at the location where they are needed. It also includes patient problems that require special intervention to protect medical providers, other patients, and the integrity of the health care organization.

Surge Capacity The ability to evaluate and care for a markedly increased volume of patients—one that challenges or exceeds normal operating capacity. Requirements may extend beyond direct patient care to include other medical tasks, such as extensive laboratory studies or epidemiologic investigations.

System A clearly described functional structure, including defined processes, that coordinates otherwise diverse parts to achieve a common goal.

Tactical Tactical elements of ICS are characterized by the execution of specific actions or plans in response to an actual incident or, prior to an incident, the implementation of individual or small unit activities, such as training or exercises.

Terrorism Any premeditated, unlawful act dangerous to human life or public welfare that is intended to intimidate or coerce civilian populations or governments (National Strategy for Homeland Security, July 2002). It includes activity potentially destructive of critical infrastructure or key resources. It is a violation of the criminal laws of the United States or of any State or other subdivision of the United States in which it occurs. It can include activities to affect the conduct of a government by mass destruction, assassination, or kidnapping (Section 2 (15), Homeland Security Act of 2002, Pub. L. 107-296, 116 Stat. 2135, (2002).

Threat An indication of possible violence, harm, or danger. (adapted from NIMS)

Unified Command An application of ICS used when there is more than one agency with incident jurisdiction. Agencies work together through their designated Incident Commanders or Managers at a single location to establish a common set of objectives and strategies, and a single incident action plan. (adapted from NIMS)

WIND AND HURRICANE TERMS

Basic Wind Speed A 3-second gust speed at 33 feet above the ground in Exposure C. (Exposure C is flat open terrain with scattered obstructions having heights generally less than 30 feet.) Note: Since 1995, ASCE 7 has used a 3-second peak gust measuring time. A 3-second peak gust is the maximum instantaneous speed with a duration of approximately 3 seconds. A 3-second peak gust speed could be associated with a given windstorm (e.g., a particular storm could have a 40-mile per hour peak gust speed), or a 3-second peak gust speed could be associated with a design-level event (e.g., the basic wind speed prescribed in ASCE 7).

Building, Enclosed A building that does not comply with the requirements for open or partially enclosed buildings.

Building, Open A building having each wall at least 80 percent open. This condition is expressed by an equation in ASCE 7.

Building, Partially Enclosed A building that complies with both of the following conditions:1. The total area of openings in a wall that receives positive external pressure exceeds the sum of the areas of openings in the balance of the building envelope (walls and roof) by more than 10 percent, and 2. The total area of openings in a wall that receives positive external pressure exceeds 4 square feet or 1 percent of the area of that wall, whichever is smaller, and the percentage of openings in the balance of the building envelope does not exceed 20 percent. These conditions are expressed by equations in ASCE 7.

Building, Regular Shaped A building having no unusual geometrical irregularity in spatial form.

Building, Simple Diaphragm An enclosed or partially enclosed building in which wind loads are transmitted through floor and roof diaphragms to the vertical main wind-force resisting system.

Components and Cladding Elements of the building envelope that do not qualify as part of the main wind-force resisting system.

Escarpment Also known as a scarp, with respect to topographic effects, a cliff or steep slope generally separating two levels or gently sloping areas.

Exposure The characteristics of the ground roughness and surface irregularities in the vicinity of a building. ASCE 7 defines three exposure categories—Exposures B, C, and D.

Glazing Glass or transparent or translucent plastic sheet used in windows, doors, and skylights.

Glazing, Impact-Resistant Glazing that has been shown by an approved test method to withstand the impact of wind-borne missiles likely to be generated in wind-borne debris regions during design winds.

Hill With respect to topographic effects, a land surface characterized by strong relief in any horizontal direction.

Hurricane-Prone Regions Areas vulnerable to hurricanes; in the U.S. and its territories defined as: 1. The U.S. Atlantic Ocean and Gulf of Mexico coasts where the basic wind speed is greater than 90 miles per hour, and 2. Hawaii, Puerto Rico, Guam, U.S. Virgin Islands, and American Samoa.

Impact-Resistant Covering A covering designed to protect glazing, which has been shown by an approved test method to withstand the impact of wind-borne missiles likely to be generated in wind-borne debris regions during design winds. Importance factor, I. A factor that accounts for the degree of hazard to human life and damage to property. The importance factor adjusts the mean recurrence interval. Importance factors are given in ASCE 7.

Main Wind-Force Resisting System An assemblage of structural elements assigned to provide support and stability for the overall structure. The system generally receives wind loading from more than one surface.

Mean Roof Height The average of the roof eave height and the height to the highest point on the roof surface, except that, for roof angles of less than or equal to 10 degrees, the mean roof height shall be the roof eave height.

Missiles Debris that became or could become ingested into the wind stream.

Openings Apertures or holes in the building envelope that allow air to flow through the building envelope and that are designed as "open" during design winds. A door that is intended to be in the closed position during a windstorm would not be considered an opening. Glazed openings are also not typically considered an opening. However, if the building is located in a wind-borne debris region and the glazing is not impact-resistant or protected with an impact-resistant covering, the glazing is considered an opening.

Ridge With respect to topographic effects, an elongated crest of a hill characterized by strong relief in two directions.

Wind-Borne Debris Regions Areas within hurricane-prone regions located: 1. Within 1 mile of the coastal mean high water line where the basic wind speed is equal to or greater than 110 mph and in Hawaii; or 2. In areas where the basic wind speed is equal to or greater than 120 mph.

FEMA ACRONYMS

AA&E	Arms, Ammunition, and Explosives
AAR	After Action Report
ACL	Access Control List
ACP	Access Control Point
ACS	Access Control System
ADA	Americans with Disabilities Act
ADAAG	Americans with Disabilities Act Accessibility Guidelines
AECS	Automated Entry Control System
AED	Automated External Defibrillator
AFJMAN	Air Force Joint Manual, also may be known as AFMAN (I) for Air Force Manual
AFMAN	Air Force Manual
ALERT	Automated Local Evaluation in Real Time
AMS	Aerial Measuring System
ANFO	Ammonium Nitrate and Fuel Oil
ANS	Alert and Notification System
ANSI	American National Standards Institute
ANSIR	Awareness of National Security Issues and Response Program
AOR	Area of Responsibility
AP	Armor Piercing
APHL	Agency for Public Health Laboratories
APS	Aapartment protected space
ARAC	Atmospheric Release Advisory Capability
ARC	American Red Cross
ARG	Accident Response Group
ARS	Agriculture Research Service
ASCE	American Society of Civil Engineers
ASHRAE	American Society of Heating, Refrigerating, and Air-Conditioning Engineers
ASTHO	Association for State and Territorial Health Officials
ASTM	American Society for Testing and Materials
ASZM-TEDA	Copper-Silver-Zinc-Molybdenum-Triethylenediamine
AT	Antiterrorism
ATC	Air Traffic Control
ATF	Bureau of Alcohol, Tobacco, and Firearms
ATSD(CS)	Assistant to the Secretary of Defense for Civil Support
ATSDR	Agency for Toxic Substances and Disease Registry
AWG	American Wire Gauge
BCA	Benefit/Cost Analysis
BCC	Backup Control Center
BCP	Business Continuity Plan
BDC	Bomb Data Center
BLASTOP	Blast-Resistant Window Program
BMS	Balanced Magnetic Switch
BPL	Bound with Pitch-Low
BW	Biological Warfare
CAMEO	Computer-Aided Management of Emergency Operations
CB	Citizens Band
CBIAC	Chemical and Biological Defense Information and Analysis Center
CBR	Chemical, Biological, or Radiological
CBRNE	Chemical, Biological, Radiological, Nuclear, or Explosive
CCTV	Closed Circuit Television
CDC	Centers for Disease Control and Prevention
CDR	Call Detail Report
CDRG	Catastrophic Disaster Response Group
CEO	Chief Executive Officer

CEPPO	Chemical Emergency Preparedness and Prevention Office	*CW/CBD*	Chemical Warfare/Contraband Detection
CERCLA	Comprehensive Environmental Response, Compensation, and Liability Act	*CWA*	Chemical Warfare Agent
		DBMS	Database Management System
		DBT	Design Basis Threat
		DBU	Dial Backup
CERT	Community Emergency Response Team	*DD*	Data Dictionary
		DES	Data Encryption Standard
CFD	Computational Fluid Dynamics	*DEST*	Domestic Emergency Support Team
CFM	Cubic Feet per Minute	*DFO*	Disaster Field Office
CFO	Chief Financial Officer	*DHS*	Department of Homeland Security
CFR	Code of Federal Regulations	*DISA*	Direct Inward System Access
CHEMTREC	Chemical Manufacturers' Association Chemical Transportation Emergency Center	*DMA*	Disaster Mitigation Act of 2000
		DMAT	Disaster Medical Assistance Team
		DMCR	Disaster Management Central Resource
CHPPM	Center for Health Promotion and Preventive Medicine	*DMORT*	Disaster Mortuary Operational Response Team
CIAO	Chief Infrastructure Assurance Office	*DOC*	Department of Commerce
CIAO	Critical Infrastructure Assurance Officer	*DoD*	Department of Defense
		DOE	Department of Energy
CICG	Critical Infrastructure Coordination Group	*DOJ*	Department of Justice
		DOS	Department of State
CIO	Chief Information Officer	*DOT*	Department of Transportation
CIP	Critical Infrastructure Protection	*DPP*	Domestic Preparedness Program
CIRG	Crisis Incident Response Group	*DRC*	Disaster Recovery Center
CJCS	Chairman of the Joint Chiefs of Staff	*DTCTPS*	Domestic Terrorism/Counterterrorism Planning Section (FBI HQ)
CM	Consequence Management		
CM	Crisis Management	*DTIC*	Defense Technical Information Center
CMS	Call Management System	*DTM*	Data-Transmission Media
CMU	Concrete Masonry Unit	*DWI*	Disaster Welfare Information
CMU	Crisis Management Unit (CIRG)	*EAS*	Emergency Alert System
COB	Continuity of Business	*ECL*	Emergency Classification Level
COBIT™	Control Objectives for Information Technology	*EECS*	Electronic Entry Control System
		EFR	Emergency First Responder
CO/DO	Central Office/Direct Outdial	*EM*	Emergency Management
CONEX	Container Express	*EMAC*	Emergency Medical Assistance Compact
CONOPS	Concept of Operations	*EMI*	Emergency Management Institute
COO	Chief Operating Officer	*EMP*	Electromagnetic Pulse
COOP	Continuity of Operations Plan	*EMS*	Emergency Medical Services
COR	Class of Restriction	*EOC*	Emergency Operations Center
COS	Class of Service	*EOD*	Explosive Ordnance Disposal
CPG	Civil Preparedness Guide	*EOP*	Emergency Operating Plan
CPR	Cardiopulmonary resuscitation	*EOP*	Emergency Operations Plan
CPTED	Crime Prevention Through Environmental Design	*EPA*	Environmental Protection Agency
		EPCRA	Emergency Planning and Community Right-to-Know Act
CPX	Command Post Exercise		
CRU	Crisis Response Unit	*EPG*	Emergency Planning Guide
CSEPP	Chemical Stockpile Emergency Preparedness Program	*EPI*	Emergency Public Information
		EP&R	Directorate of Emergency Preparedness and Response (DHS)
CSI	Construction Specifications Institute		
CSREES	Cooperative State Research, Education, and Extension Service	*EPZ*	Emergency Planning Zone
		ERP	Emergency Response Plan
CST	Civil Support Team	*ERT*	Emergency Response Team
CSTE	Council of State and Territorial Epidemiologists	*ERT-A*	Emergency Response Team Advance Element
CT	Counterterrorism	*ERT-N*	Emergency Response Team National

ERTU	Evidence Response Team Unit	HHS	Department of Health and Human Services
ESC	Expandable Shelter Container	HIRA	Hazard Identification and Risk Assessment
ESF	Emergency Support Function	HMRU	Hazardous Materials Response Unit
ESS	Electronic Security System	HQ	Headquarters
EST	Emergency Support Team	HRCQ	Highway Route Controlled Quantity
ETL	Engineering Technical Letter	HRT	Hostage Rescue Team (CIRG)
EU	Explosives Unit	HSO	Homeland Security Office
FAsT	Field Assessment Team	HTIS	Hazardous Technical Information Services (DoD)
FBI	Federal Bureau of Investigation		
FCC	Federal Communications Commission	HVAC	Heating, Ventilation, and Air Conditioning
FCC	Fire Control Center	IAQ	Indoor Air Quality
FCO	Federal Coordinating Officer	IC	Incident Commander
FEM	Finite Element	ICDDC	Interstate Civil Defense and Disaster Compact
FEMA	Federal Emergency Management Agency		
FEST	Foreign Emergency Support Team	ICP	Incident Command Post
FHBM	Flood Hazard Boundary Map	ICS	Incident Command System
FIA	Federal Insurance Administration	ID	Identification
FIPS	Federal Information Processing Standard	IDS	Intrusion Detection System
FIRM	Flood Insurance Rate Map	IED	Improvised Explosive Device
FIS	Flood Insurance Study	IEMS	Integrated Emergency Management System
FISCAM	Federal Information Systems Control Audit Manual	IESNA	Illuminating Engineering Society of North America
FMFIA	Federal Manager's Financial Integrity Act	IID	Improvised Incendiary Device
FNS	Food and Nutrition Service	IMS	Ion Mobility Spectrometry
FOIA	Freedom of Information Act	IMSion	Mobility spectrometry
FOUO	For Official Use Only	IND	Improvised Nuclear Device
FPEIS	Final Programmatic Environmental Impact Statement	IPL	Initial Program Load
		IR	Infrared
FPS	Floor Protected Space	IRZ	Immediate Response Zone
FRERP	Federal Radiological Emergency Response Plan	IS	Information System
		ISACF	Information Systems Audit and Control Foundation
FRF	Fragment Retention Film		
FRL	Facility Restriction Level	ISC	Interagency Security Committee
FRMAC	Federal Radiological Monitoring and Assessment Center	ISO	International Organization for Standardization
FRP	Federal Response Plan	ISP	Internet Service Provider
FS	Forest Service	IT	Information Technology
FSTFS	Frame-Supported Tensioned Fabric Structure	iwg	Inch Water Gauge
		JIC	Joint Information Center
FTP	File Transfer Protocol	JIISE	Joint Interagency Intelligence Support Element
FTX	Functional Training Exercise		
GAO	General Accounting Office	JIS	Joint Information System
GAR	Governor's Authorized Representative	JNACC	Joint Nuclear Accident Coordinating Center
GC/MS	Gas Chromatograph/Mass Spectrometer		
GIS	Geographic Information System	JOC	Joint Operations Center
GP	General Purpose	JSMG	Joint Service Materiel Group
GPS	Global Positioning System	JTF-CS	Joint Task Force for Civil Support
GSA	General Services Administration	JTTF	Joint Terrorism Task Force
HazMat	Hazardous Material	JTWG	Joint Terrorism Working Group
HAZUS	Hazards U.S.	kHz	Kilohertz
HEGA	High-Efficiency Gas Absorber	kPa	Kilo Pascal
HEPA	High Efficiency Particulate Air	LAN	Local Area Network
HEU	Highly Enriched Uranium	LAW	Light Antitank Weapon
HF	High Frequency	LBNL	Lawrence Berkley National Lab

LCM	Life-Cycle Management		*NOAA*	National Oceanic and Atmospheric Administration
LED	Light-Emitting Diode		*NRC*	National Response Center
LEED	Leadership in Energy and Environmental Design		*NRC*	Nuclear Regulatory Commission
LEPC	Local Emergency Planning Committee		*NRT*	National Response Team
LF	Low Frequency		*NSC*	National Security Council
LFA	Lead Federal Agency		*NTIS*	National Technical Information Service
LLNL	Lawrence Livermore National Laboratory		*NUREG*	Nuclear Regulation
LOP	Level of Protection		*NWS*	National Weather Service
LOS	Line of Sight		*OC*	Oleoresin capsicum
LPHA	Local Public Health Agency		*OCC*	Operational Control Center
LPHS	Local Public Health System		*ODP*	Office of Disaster Preparedness
MAC	Moves, Adds, Changes		*OEP*	Office of Emergency Preparedness
MEDCOM	Medical Command		*OES*	Office of Emergency Services
MEI	Minimum Essential Infrastructure		*OFCM*	Office of the Federal Coordinator for Meteorology
M/E/P	Mechanical/Electrical/Plumbing		*OHS*	Office of Homeland Security
MEP	Mission Essential Process		*OJP*	Office of Justice Programs
MERV	Minimum Efficiency Reporting Value		*O&M*	Operations and Maintenance
MMRS	Metropolitan Medical Response System		*OMB*	Office of Management and Budget
MOU/A	Memorandum of Understanding/Agreement		*OPA*	Oil Pollution Act
mph	Miles per Hour		*OSC*	On-Scene Coordinator
MPOP	Minimum-Points-of-Presence		*OSD*	Office of Secretary of Defense
Ms	Millisecond		*OSHA*	Occupational Safety and Health Administration
MSCA	Military Support to Civil Authorities		*OSLDPS*	Office for State and Local Domestic Preparedness Support
MSDS	Material Safety Data Sheet		*Pa*	Pascal
MSS	Medium Shelter System		*PA*	Public Address
MW	Medium Wave		*PAZ*	Protective Action Zone
NACCHO	National Association for County and City Health Officials		*PBX*	Public Branch Exchange
NACCT	National Advisory Committee on Children and Terrorism		*PC*	Personal Computer
			PCC	Policy Coordinating Committee
NAP	Nuclear Assessment Program		*PCCIP*	President's Commission on Critical Infrastructure Protection
NAVFAC	Naval Facilities Command			
NBC	Nuclear, Biological, and Chemical		*PCM*	Procedures Control Manual
NCJ	National Criminal Justice		*PDA*	Personal Data Assistant
NCP	National Contingency Plan (also known as National Oil and Hazardous Substances Pollution Contingency Plan)		*PDA*	Preliminary Damage Assessment
			PDD	Presidential Decision Directive
			PHS	Public Health Service
NDA	National Defense Area		*PIN*	Personal Identification Number
NDMS	National Disaster Medical System		*PIO*	Public Information Officer
NDPO	National Domestic Preparedness Office		*PL*	Public Law
NEST	Nuclear Emergency Search Team		*POC*	Point of Contact
NETC	National Emergency Training Center		*POD*	Probability of Detection
NFA	National Fire Academy		*POI*	Probability of Intrusion
NFIP	National Flood Insurance Program		*POL*	Petroleum, Oils, and Lubricants
NFPA	National Fire Protection Association		*POV*	Privately Owned Vehicle
NFPC	National Fire Protection Code		*PPA*	Performance Partnership Agreement
NIJ	National Institute of Justice		*Ppm*	Parts per Million
NIOSH	National Institute for Occupational Safety and Health		*PSE*	Particle Size Efficiency
			Psi	Pounds per Square Inch
NMRT	National Medical Response Team		*PT*	Preparedness, Training, and Exercises Directorate (FEMA)
NMS	Network Management System			

PTE	Potential Threat Element
PTZ	Pan-Tilt-Zoom (camera)
PVB	Polyvinyl Butyral
PZ	Precautionary Zone
RACES	Radio Amateur Civil Emergency Service
RAP	Radiological Assistance Program
RCRA	Research Conservation and Recovery Act
RDD	Radiological Dispersal Device
RDT&E	Research, Development, Test, and Evaluation
REACT	Radio Emergency Associated Communications Team
REAC/TS	Radiation Emergency Assistance Center /Training Site
REM	Roentgen Man Equivalent
REP	Radiological Emergency Preparedness Program
RF	Radio Frequency
ROC	Regional Operations Center
ROD	Record of Decision
RPG	Rocket Propelled Grenade
RRIS	Rapid Response Information System (FEMA)
RRP	Regional Response Plan
RRT	Regional Response Team
SAA	State Administrative Agency
SAC	Special Agent in Charge (FBI)
SAFEVU	Safety Viewport Analysis Code
SAME	Specific Area Message Encoder
SARA	Superfund Amendments and Reauthorization Act
SATCOM	Satellite Communications
SAW	Surface Acoustic Wave
SBCCOM	Soldier and Biological Chemical Command (U.S. Army)
SCADA	Supervisory, Control, and Data Acquisition
SCBA	Self-Contained Breathing Apparatus
SCC	Security Control Center
SCO	State Coordinating Officer
SDO	Single-degree-of-freedom
SEA	Southeast Asia
SEB	State Emergency Board
SEL	Standardized Equipment List
SEMA	State Emergency Management Agency
SERC	State Emergency Response Commission
SFO	Senior FEMA Official
SIOC	Strategic Information and Operations Center (FBI HQ)
SLA	Service Level Agreement
SLG	State and Local Guide
SNM	Special Nuclear Material
SOP	Standard Operating Procedure
SPCA	Society for the Prevention of Cruelty to Animals
SPSA	Super Power Small Arms
SRWF	Shatter-Resistant Window Film
SSS	Small Shelter System
STC	Sound Transmission Class
SWAT	Special Weapons and Tactics
TAC	Trunk Access Codes
TDR	Transferable Development Right
TEA	Threat Environment Assessment
TEDA	Triethylenediamine
TEMPER	Tent, Extendable, Modular, Personnel
TERC	Tribal Emergency Response Commission
TIA	Terrorist Incident Appendix
TIC	Toxic Industrial Chemical
TIM	Toxic Industrial Material
TM	Technical Manual
TNT	Trinitrotoluene
TRIS	Toxic Release Inventory System
TSC	Triple-Standard Concertina
TSO	Time Share Option
TTG	Thermally Tempered Glass
UC	Unified Command
UCS	Unified Command System
UFAS	Uniform Federal Accessibility Standards
UFC	Unified Facilities Criteria
UL	Underwriters Laboratories
ULPA	Ultra Low Penetration Air
UPS	Uninterrupted Power Supply
URV	UVGI Rating Values
US	United States
USA	United States Army
USACE	U.S. Army Corps of Engineers
USAF	United States Air Force
USC	U.S. Code
USDA	U.S. Department of Agriculture
USFA	U.S. Fire Administration
USGBC	U.S. Green Building Council
USGS	U.S. Geological Survey
US&R	Urban Search and Rescue
UV	Ultraviolet
UVGI	Ultraviolet germicidal irradiation
VA	Department of Veterans Affairs
VAP	Vulnerability Assessment Plan
VAV	Variable Air Volume
VDN	Vector Directory Number
VHF	Very High Frequency
VRU	Voice Response Unit
WAN	Wide Area Network
WG	Water Gauge
WINGARD	Window Glazing Analysis Response and Design
WINLAC	Window Lite Analysis Code
WMD	Weapons of Mass Destruction
WMD-CST	WMD Civil Support Tea
WMD	Weapons of Mass Destruction

DHHS DISASTER AND EMERGENCY ACRONYMS AND ABBREVIATIONS

AAFP	American Association of Family Practitioners
AAP	American Academy of Pediatrics
AAPA	American Academy of Physician Assistants
ACEP	American College of Emergency Physicians
ACF	Administration for Children and Families
ACIP	Advisory Committee on Immunization Practices
ACP	American College of Physicians
AERS	Adverse Events Reporting System
AFRIMS	Armed Forces Research Institute of Medical Sciences
AHA	American Hospital Association
AHRQ	Agency for Healthcare Research and Quality
AIM	Association of Immunization Managers
AMA	American Medical Association
AMDA	American Medical Directors Association
AMS	Advance Manifest System
ANA	American Nurses Association
AOA	Administration on Aging
APEC	Asia-Pacific Economic Cooperation
APHL	Association of Public Health Laboratories
APIC	Association for Practitioners in Infection Control and Epidemiology
APIS	Advance Passenger Information System
ASEAN	Association of Southeast Asian Nations
ASPHA	Assistant Secretary for Public Health Affairs
ASTHO	Association of State and Territorial Health Officials
ATA	Air Transportation Association of America, Inc.
BLA	Biological Licensing A
BRFSS	Behavioral Risk Factor Surveillance System
BSL	Bio-Safety Level
CBER	Center for Biologics Evaluation and Research, FDA
CBP	Customs and Border Protection
CBO	Community-Based Organization
CCID	Coordinating Center for Infectious Diseases, CDC
CDC	Centers for Disease Control and Prevention, HHS
CDER	Center for Drug Evaluation and Research, FDA
CEF	Chicken Embryo Fibroblasts
CERT	Center for Education and Research in Therapeutics
CMC	Chemistry, Manufacturing, and Controls
CMS	Centers for Medicare & Medicaid Services
CO	Commissioned Officer
COCA	Clinician Outreach and Communication Activity
COOP	Continuity of Operations Plan
CRA	Countermeasures and Response Administration
CRADA	Cooperative Research and Development Agreement
CSTE	Council of State and Territorial Epidemiologists
DEOC	Director's Emergency Operations Center
DHS	Department of Homeland Security
DMID	Division of Microbiology and Infectious Diseases
DOC	Department of Commerce
DOD	Department of Defense
DOD-GEIS	Department of Defense Global Emerging Infections System
DOI	Department of the Interior
DOJ	Department of Justice
DOL	Department of Labor
DOS	Department of State
DOT	Department of Transportation
DSNS	Division of Strategic National Stockpile
EARS	Early Aberration Reporting System
EC	European Community
ECS	Emergency Communications System (CDC)
ED	Emergency Department
EIP	Emerging Infections Program
EIS	Epidemic Intelligence Service
EML	Essential Material List
EMS	Emergency Medical Services
EOC	Emergency Operations Center
EPA	Environmental Protection Agency
EPI-X	Epidemic Information Exchange
ESAR-VHP	Emergency Systems for Advance Registration of Volunteer Health Professionals
ESF	Emergency Support Function
EUA	Emergency Use Authorization
EWORS	Early Warning Outbreak Recognition System
FAA	Federal Aviation Administration
FAO	United Nations Food and Agriculture Organization
FBO	Faith-Based Organization
FDA	Food and Drug Administration
FELTP	Field Epidemiology and Laboratory Training Program
FETP	Field Epidemiology Training Program
FDCA	Food, Drug, and Cosmetic Act
FMS	Federal Medical Station
FWS U.S.	Fish and Wildlife Service (DOI)

GBS	Guillain-Barré Syndrome
GCC	Government Coordinating Councils
GDD	Global Disease Detection
GEMS WHO	Global Event Management System
GHSAG	Global Health Security Action Group
GHSI	Global Health Security Initiative
GIS	Genome Institute of Singapore
GLP	Good Laboratory Practice
GOARN	Global Outbreak Alert Response Network (WHO)
HA	Haemagglutinin
HAN	Health Alert Network
HAvBED	Hospital Available Beds for Emergencies and Disasters
HHS	Department of Health and Human Services
HMO	Health Maintenance Organization
HPAI	Highly Pathogenic Avian Influenza
HRSA	Health Resources and Services Administration
HSC	Homeland Security Council
IATA	International Air Transport Association
IB	Influenza Branch, CDC
ICLN	Integrated Consortium of Laboratory Networks
ICAO	International Civil Aviation Organization
ICCL	International Council of Cruise Lines
ICD-9-CM	International Classification of Diseases, Ninth Revision, Clinical Modification
IDE	Investigational Device Exemption
IDSA	Infectious Disease Society of America
IEIP	International Emerging Infections Program
IHS	Indian Health Service
ILI	Influenza-Like Illness
IMO	International Maritime Organization
IMT	Incident Management Team
IND	Investigational New Drug
IPAPI	International Partnership on Avian and Pandemic Influenza
IRB	Institutional Review Board
IRCT	Incident Response Coordination Team
JCAHO	Joint Commission on Accreditation of Healthcare Organizations
LID	Laboratory of Infectious Diseases, NIAID
LRN	Laboratory Response Network
MDCK	Madin-Darby Canine Kidney Cell Line
MIDAS	Models of Infectious Disease Study (NIH)
MMWR	Morbidity and Mortality Weekly Report
MRC	Medical Reserve Corps
MOU	Memorandum of Understanding
NA	Neuraminidase
NACCHO	National Association of County and City Health Officials
NAHDO	National Association of Health Data Organizations
NAMRU-2	Naval Medical Research Unit 2 in Jakarta, Indonesia
NAMRU-3	Naval Medical Research Unit 3 in Cairo, Egypt
NBIS	National Biosurveillance Integration System
NCI	National Cancer Institute
NDA	New Drug Application
NDMS	National Disaster Medical System
NEC	National Economic Council
NEISS-CADE	National Electronic Injury Surveillance System Cooperative Adverse Drug Event
NGO	Non-Governmental Organization
NHSN	National Healthcare Safety Network
NIAID	National Institute of Allergy and Infectious Diseases
NIH	National Institutes of Health
NIMS	National Incident Management System
NIOSH	National Institute for Occupational Safety and Health, CDC
NIP	National Immunization Program
NREVSS	National Respiratory and Enteric Virus Surveillance System
NRP	National Response Plan NSC National Security Council
NVAC	National Vaccine Advisory Committee
NVPO	National Vaccine Program Office
NVSN	New Vaccine Surveillance Network
OCONUS	Outside Continental United States
OFRD	Office of Force Readiness and Deployment (HHS)
OIE	World Organization for Animal Health
OPDIV	Operational Division
OPHEP	Office of Public Health Emergency Preparedness
OPM	Office of Personnel Management
OS	Office of the Secretary, HHS
OSHA	Occupational Safety and Health Administration
PAPR	Powered Air Purifying Respirator
PCR	Polymerase Chain Reaction
PGO	Procurement and Grants Office
PER.C6	A Human Fetal Retinoblast Cell Line
PHIN	Public Health Information Network
PNR	Passenger Name Record
PPE	Personal Protective Equipment

RCA	Rapid Cycle Analysis Project	*SPN*	Sentinel Provider Network
REDI	Regional Emerging Diseases Intervention Center, Singapore	*SPP*	Security and Prosperity Partnership of North America
RT-PCR	Reverse Transcriptase-Polymerase Chain Reaction	*TIGR*	The Institute for Genomic Research
		TSA	Transportation Security Administration
SAMHSA	Substance Abuse and Mental Health Services Administration, HHS	*UN*	United Nations
		U.S.	United States
SARS	Severe Acute Respiratory Syndrome	*USAID*	United States Agency for International Development
SCC	Sector Coordinating Council		
SCHIP	State Children's Health Insurance Program	*USCG*	United States Coast Guard
		USDA	United States Department of Agriculture
SEARO WHO	Regional Office for South-East Asia	*USPHS*	United States Public Health Service
SHEA	Society for Healthcare Epidemiology of America	*USTR*	United States Trade Representative
		VA	Veterans Administration
SLEP	Shelf Life Extension Program	*VAERS*	Vaccine Adverse Event Reporting System
SLTT	State, Local, Territorial, and Tribal	*VSD*	Vaccine Safety Data
SNS	Strategic National Stockpile	*WHO*	World Health Organization

Drugs

Abbreviated New Drug Application (ANDA) An Abbreviated New Drug Application (ANDA) contains data that, when submitted to FDA's Center for Drug Evaluation and Research, Office of Generic Drugs, provides for the review and ultimate approval of a generic drug product. Generic drug applications are called "abbreviated" because they are generally not required to include preclinical (animal) and clinical (human) data to establish safety and effectiveness. Instead, a generic applicant must scientifically demonstrate that its product is bioequivalent (i.e., performs in the same manner as the innovator drug). Once approved, an applicant may manufacture and market the generic drug product to provide a safe, effective, low cost alternative to the American public.

Abbreviated New Drug Application (ANDA) Number This six-digit number is assigned by FDA staff to each application for approval to market a generic drug in the United States.

Active Ingredient An active ingredient is any component that provides pharmacological activity or other direct effect in the diagnosis, cure, mitigation, treatment, or prevention of disease, or to affect the structure or any function of the body of man or animals.

Application See New Drug Application (NDA), Abbreviated New Drug Application ANDA), or Biologic License Application (BLA).

Approval History The approval history is a chronological list of all FDA actions involving one drug product having a particular FDA Application number (NDA). There are over 50 kinds of approval actions including changes in the labeling, a new route of administration, and a new patient population for a drug product.

Approval Letter An official communication from FDA to a new drug application (NDA) sponsor that allows the commercial marketing of the product.

Application Number See FDA Application Number.

Biologic License Application (BLA) Biological products are approved for marketing under the provisions of the Public Health Service (PHS) Act. The Act requires a firm who manufactures a biologic for sale in interstate commerce to hold a license for the product. A biologics license application is a submission that contains specific information on the manufacturing processes, chemistry, pharmacology, clinical pharmacology and the medical affects of the biologic product. If the information provided meets FDA requirements, the application is approved and a license is issued allowing the firm to market the product.

Biological Product Biological products include a wide range of products such as vaccines, blood and blood components, allergenics, somatic cells, gene therapy, tissues, and recombinant therapeutic proteins. Biologics can be composed of sugars, proteins, or nucleic acids or complex combinations of these substances, or may be living entities such as cells and tissues. Biologics are isolated from a variety of natural sources — human, animal, or microorganism — and may be produced by biotechnology methods and other cutting-edge technologies. Gene-based and cellular biologics, for example, often are at the forefront of biomedical research, and may be used to treat a variety of medical conditions for which no other treatments are available.

Brand Name Drug A brand name drug is a drug marketed under a proprietary, trademark-protected name.

Chemical Type The Chemical Type represents the newness of a drug formulation or a new indication for an existing drug formulation. For example, Chemical Type 1 is assigned to an active ingredient that has never before been marketed in the United States in any form.

Company The company (also called applicant or sponsor) submits an application to FDA for approval to market a drug product in the United States.

Discontinued Drug Product Products listed in Drugs@FDA as "discontinued" are approved products that have never been marketed, have been discontinued from marketing, are for military use, are for export only, or have had their approvals withdrawn for reasons other than safety or efficacy after being discontinued from marketing.

Dosage Form A dosage form is the physical form in which a drug is produced and dispensed, such as a tablet, a capsule, or an injectable.

Drug A drug is defined as:

A substance recognized by an official pharmacopoeia or formulary.

A substance intended for use in the diagnosis, cure, mitigation, treatment, or prevention of disease.

A substance (other than food) intended to affect the structure or any function of the body.

A substance intended for use as a component of a medicine but not a device or a component, part or accessory of a device.

Biological products are included within this definition and are generally covered by the same laws and regulations, but differences exist regarding their manufacturing processes (chemical process versus biological process).

Drug Product The finished dosage form that contains a drug substance, generally, but not necessarily in association with other active or inactive ingredients.

FDA Action Date The action date tells when an FDA regulatory action, such as an original or supplemental approval, took place.

FDA Application Number This number, also known as the NDA (New Drug Application) number, is assigned by FDA staff to each application for approval to market a new drug in the United States. One drug can have more than one application number if it has different dosage forms or routes of administration.

Generic Drug A generic drug is the same as a brand name drug in dosage, safety, strength, how it is taken, quality, performance, and intended use. Before approving a generic drug product, FDA requires many rigorous tests and procedures to assure that the generic drug can be substituted for the brand name drug. The FDA bases evaluations of substitutability, or "therapeutic equivalence," of generic drugs on scientific evaluations. By law, a generic drug product must contain the identical amounts of the same active ingredient(s) as the brand name product. Drug products evaluated as "therapeutically equivalent" can be expected to have equal effect and no difference when substituted for the brand name product.

Label The FDA approved label is the official description of a drug product which includes indication (what the drug is used for); who should take it; adverse events (side effects); instructions for uses in pregnancy, children, and other populations; and safety information for the patient. Labels are often found inside drug product packaging.

Marketing Status Marketing status indicates how a drug product is sold in the United States. Drug products in Drugs@FDA are identified as: Prescription, Over the Counter, Discontinued or None (drug products that have been tentatively approved).

Medication Guide A medication guide contains information for patients on how to safely use a drug product.

NDA (see New Drug Application).

New Drug Application (NDA) When the sponsor of a new drug believes that enough evidence on the drug's safety and effectiveness has been obtained to meet FDA's requirements for marketing approval, the sponsor submits to FDA a new drug application (NDA). The application must contain data from specific technical viewpoints for review, including chemistry, pharmacology, medical, biopharmaceutics, and statistics. If the NDA is approved, the product may be marketed in the United States. For internal tracking purposes, all NDA's are assigned an NDA number.

New Drug Application (NDA) Number This six digit number is assigned by FDA staff to each application for approval to market a new drug in the United States. A drug can have more than one application number if it has different dosage forms or routes of administration. In Drugs@FDA, you can find the NDA number under the column named "FDA Application."

NME (see New Molecular Entity).

New Molecular Entity (NME) A New Molecular Entity is an active ingredient that has never before been marketed in the United States in any form.

Over-the-Counter Drugs (OTC) FDA defines OTC drugs as safe and effective for use by the general public without a doctor's prescription.

Patient Package Insert (PPI) A patient package insert contains information for patients' understanding of how to safely use a drug product.

Pharmaceutical Equivalents FDA considers drug products to be pharmaceutical equivalents if they meet these three criteria:

They contain the same active ingredient(s)

They are of the same dosage form and route of administration

They are identical in strength or concentration

Pharmaceutically equivalent drug products may differ in characteristics such as shape, release mechanism, labeling (to some extent), scoring and excipients (including colors, flavors, preservatives).

Prescription Drug Product A prescription drug product requires a doctor's authorization to purchase.

Product Number A product number is assigned to each drug product associated with an NDA (New Drug Application). If a drug product is available in multiple strengths, there are multiple product numbers.

Reference Listed Drug (see RLD).

Review A review is the basis of FDA's decision to approve an application. It is a comprehensive analysis of clinical trial data and other information prepared by FDA drug application reviewers. A review is divided into sections on medical analysis, chemistry, clinical pharmacology, biopharmaceutics, pharmacology, statistics, and microbiology.

Review Classification The NDA and BLA classification system provides a way of describing drug applications upon initial receipt and throughout the review process and prioritizing their review. (List of Review Classifications and their meanings)

RLD (Reference Listed Drug) A Reference Listed Drug (RLD) is an approved drug product to which new generic versions are compared to show that they are bioequivalent. A drug company seeking approval to market a generic equivalent must refer to the Reference Listed Drug in its Abbreviated New Drug Application (ANDA). By designating a single reference listed drug as the standard to which all generic versions must be shown to be bioequivalent, FDA hopes to avoid possible significant variations among generic drugs and their brand name counterpart.

Route A route of administration is a way of administering a drug to a site in a patient. A comprehensive list of specific routes of administration appears in the CDER Data Standards Manual.

Strength The strength of a drug product tells how much of the active ingredient is present in each dosage.

Supplement A supplement is an application to allow a company to make changes in a product that already has an approved new drug application (NDA). CDER must approve all important NDA changes (in packaging or ingredients, for instance) to ensure the conditions originally set for the product are still met.

Supplement Number A supplement number is associated with an existing FDA New Drug Application (NDA) number. Companies are allowed to make changes to drugs or their labels after they have been approved. To change a label, market a new dosage or strength of a drug, or change the way it manufactures a drug, a company must submit a supplemental new drug application (sNDA). Each sNDA is assigned a number which is usually, but not always, sequential, starting with 001.

Supplement Type Companies are allowed to make changes to drugs or their labels after they have been approved. To change a label, market a new dosage or strength of a drug, or change the way it manufactures a drug, a company must submit a supplemental new drug application (sNDA). The supplement type refers to the kind of change that was approved by FDA. This includes changes in manufacturing, patient population, and formulation.

Tentative Approval If a generic drug product is ready for approval before the expiration of any patents or exclusivities accorded to the reference listed drug product, FDA issues a tentative approval letter to the applicant. The tentative approval letter details the circumstances associated with the tentative approval. FDA delays final approval of the generic drug product until all patent or exclusivity issues have been resolved. A tentative approval does not allow the applicant to market the generic drug product.

Therapeutic Biological Product A therapeutic biological product is a protein derived from living material (such as cells or tissues) used to treat or cure disease.

Therapeutic Equivalence (TE) Drug products classified as therapeutically equivalent can be substituted with the full expectation that the substituted product will produce the same clinical effect and safety profile as the prescribed product. Drug products are considered to be therapeutically equivalent **only** if they meet these criteria:

They are pharmaceutical equivalents (contain the same active ingredient(s); dosage form and route of administration; and strength).

They are assigned by FDA the same therapeutic equivalence codes starting with the letter "A." To receive a letter "A," FDA designates a brand name drug or a generic drug to be the Reference Listed Drug (RLD).

Assigns therapeutic equivalence codes based on data that a drug sponsor submits in an ANDA to scientifically demonstrate that its product is bioequivalent (i.e., performs in the same manner as the Reference Listed Drug).

Therapeutic Equivalence (TE) Codes The coding system for therapeutic equivalence evaluations allows users to determine whether FDA has evaluated a particular approved product as therapeutically equivalent to other pharmaceutically equivalent products (first letter) and to provide additional information on the basis of FDA's evaluations (second letter). Sample TE codes: AA, AB, BC.

FDA assigns therapeutic equivalence codes to pharmaceutically equivalent drug products. A drug product is deemed to be therapeutically equivalent ("A" rated) only if:

A drug company's approved application contains adequate scientific evidence establishing through *in vivo* and/or *in vitro* studies the bioequivalence of the product to a selected reference listed drug.

Those active ingredients or dosage forms for which no *in vivo* bioequivalence issue is known or suspected.

Some drug products have more than one TE Code.

Those products which the FDA does not deem to be therapeutically equivalent are "B" rated.

ECONOMY (BUREAU OF ECONOMIC ANALYSIS)

AAR Annual Aid Review

Additive, additivity A characteristic of a measurement series whereby the summed components equal the aggregate. Related terms: chain-dollar estimate.

Advance estimate The first estimate of gross domestic product (GDP) and its components for a quarter. It is released 25–30 days after the end of the quarter and is based on source data that are incomplete and subject to revision. Related terms: preliminary estimate, final estimate.

AERO Automatic Earnings Reappraisal **Annual input-output (I-O) accounts** Set of I-O tables—make table, use table, direct requirements table, and total requirements tables—that are an update of the most recent benchmark I-O accounts. Annual tables are consistent with the gross domestic product (GDP)-by-industry accounts, but incorporate less comprehensive source data than those used for the benchmark I-O tables. Related terms: I-O accounts.*APEC* Asia Pacific Economic Corporation

Balance of payments Record of transactions between U.S. residents and foreign residents during a given time period. Includes transactions in goods, services, income, assets, and liabilities. It is broken down into the current account (international), capital account (international), and financial acount (international).

Balance on current account Record of net receipts or payments on goods, services, income, and unilateral current transfers. Current transfers include U.S. government grants to foreign countries, private remittances, and other current transfers. Related terms: balance on goods, balance on goods and services.

Balance on current account, national income and product accounts . Current receipts from the rest of the world less current payments to the rest of the world, formerly called "net foreign investment." Current receipts equal exports of goods and services plus income receipts from the rest of the world; current payments are the sum of imports of goods and services, income payments to the rest of the world, and current taxes and transfer payments to the rest of the world (net).

Balance on goods Record of the difference between exports of goods and imports of goods. Related terms: balance on current account, balance on goods and services.

Balance on goods and services Record of the difference between exports of goods and services and imports of goods and services. In the broad sense, this balance is conceptually equal to net exports of goods and services, which is a component of gross domestic product (GDP). Related terms: balance on current account, balance on goods.

Base period The period from which the weights for a measurement series are derived. The national income and product accounts (NIPAs) currently use the year 2000 as the base period. Related terms: chained-dollar estimate, Laspeyres price index, Paasche price index.

Benchmark input-output (I-O) accounts Statistical description–presented in a make table, use table, direct requirements table, and total requirements tables–of the production of goods and services and the transaction flows of goods and services between different industries and to different components of final uses. These accounts are prepared every five years, coinciding with economic census years. Related terms: I-O accounts, annual I-O accounts.

BOA Back office adjustment

BOP Balance of Payments

BPT Business, professional, and technical services

Business current transfer payments (net) Net payments by businesses to persons, government, and the rest of the world for which no current services are performed. Related terms: business current transfer payments to persons (net), business current transfer payments to government (net), business current transfer payments to the rest of the world (net).

Business current transfer payments to government (net) Consists of payments to the Federal government in the form of premiums for deposit insurance, fees for regulatory and inspection activities, and fines; payments to state and local governments in the form of fines, tobacco settlements, and donations; and net insurance settlements paid to governments as policyholders. Related terms: business current transfer payments (net), business current transfer payments to persons (net), business current transfer payments to the rest of the world (net).

Business current transfer payments to persons (net) Consists of net insurance settlements and income payments by businesses to persons for which no current services are performed. Related terms: business current transfer payments (net), business current transfer payments to government (net), business current transfer payments to the rest of the world (net).

Business current transfer payments to the rest of the world (net) Net insurance settlements paid to the rest of the world as policyholders. Excludes taxes paid by domestic corporations to foreign governments. Related terms: business current transfer payments (net), business current transfer payments to persons (net), business current transfer payments to government (net).

Business, professional, and technical services transactions (BPT) Transactions covering a wide range of private services sold to or purchased from foreigners, such as advertising, telecommunications, computer and data processing services, and accounting and legal services.

Business sector All corporate and noncorporate private entities organized for profit and certain other entities that are treated as businesses in the national income and product accounts (NIPAs), including mutual financial institutions, private noninsured pension funds, cooperatives, nonprofit organizations that primarily serve businesses, Federal Reserve banks, federally sponsored credit agencies, and government enterprises. Related terms: general government sector, households and institutions sector.

Capital account (international) Record of capital transfers between U.S. residents and foreign residents, such as debt forgiveness and migrants' transfers, and acquisitions and disposals of nonproduced nonfinancial assets between residents and nonresidents. Related terms: balance of payments, current account (international), financial account (international).

Capital consumption adjustment (CCAdj), (private) The difference between private capital consumption allowances (CCA) and private consumption of fixed capital (CFC).

Capital consumption allowance (CCA), (private) Consists of tax-return-based depreciation charges for corporations and nonfarm proprietorships and of historical-cost depreciation (calculated by BEA) for farm proprietorships, rental income of persons, and nonprofit institutions. Related terms: consumption of fixed capital (CFC), capital consumption adjustment (CCAdj).

Capital expenditures Expenditures made to acquire, add to, or improve property, plant, and equipment (PP&E). PP&E includes: land, timber, and minerals; structures, machinery, equipment, special tools, and other depreciable property; construction in progress; and tangible and intangible exploration and development costs. Changes in PP&E due to changes in entity—such as mergers, acquisitions, and divestitures—or to changes in accounting methods are excluded. Capital expenditures are measured on a gross basis; sales and other dispositions of fixed assets are not netted against them.

Capital flows table Table that expands the fixed investment component of the input-output (I-O) use table to show the types of new equipment, new structures, and software used by each industry. Related terms: input-output (I-O) accounts.

Capital transfers to the rest of the world (net) Cash or in-kind transfers to foreigners that are linked to the acquisition or disposition of a fixed asset.

CCAdj Capital consumption adjustment

Chained-dollar estimate A measure used to approximate the chain-type index level and is calculated by taking the current-dollar level of a series in the base period and multiplying it by the change in the chain-type quantity index number for the series since the base period. Chained-dollar estimates correctly show growth rates for a series, but are not additive in periods other than the base period. Related terms: chain-type index, current-dollar estimate.

Chained-type index Index that is based on the linking (chaining) of indexes to create a time series. Annual chain-type Fisher indices are used in BEA's national income and product accounts (NIPAs) whereby Fisher ideal price indices are calculated using the weights of adjacent years. Those annual changes are then multiplied (chained) together, forming the chain-type index time series. Related terms: chained-dollar estimate, current-dollar estimate.

Change in private inventories The change in the physical volume of inventories owned by private business, valued at the average prices of the period. It differs from the change in the book value of inventories reported by many businesses; the difference is the inventory valuation adjustment (IVA).

CMSA Consolidated metropolitan statistical area

Commodity flow method Method used to estimate purchases of a commodity by intermediate or final users. The method generally begins with an estimate of the total supply of a commodity available for domestic uses; it then either attributes a fixed percentage of supply to an intermediate or final use, or it adjusts for intermediate purchases and attributes the residual to final uses.

Compensation of employees (paid) Income accruing to employees as remuneration for their work for domestic production. It is the sum of wage and salary accruals and of supplements to wages and salaries. It includes compensation paid to the rest of the world and excludes compensation received from the rest of the world.

Compensation of employees (received) Wage and salary disbursements and supplements to wages and salaries received by U.S. residents, including wages and salaries received from the rest of the world.

Consumption of fixed capital (CFC) The charge for the using up of private and government fixed capital located in the United States. It is the decline in the value of the stock of fixed assets due to wear and tear, obsolescence, accidental damage, and aging. For general government and for nonprofit institutions that primarily serve individuals, CFC serves as a measure of the value of the current services of the fixed assets owned and used by these entities. Related terms: capital consumption adjustment (CCAdj), capital consumption allowance (CCA).

Contribution for government social insurance Employer contributions for government social insurance as well as payments by employees, the self-employed, and other individuals who participate in government social insurance programs.

Corporate profits with IVA and CCAdj This measure–profits from current production–is the income that arises from current production, measured before income taxes, of organizations treated as corporations in the national income and product accounts (NIPAS). With several differences, this income is measured as receipts less expenses as defined in Federal tax law. Among these differences are: Receipts exclude capital gains and dividends received; expenses exclude bad debt, depletion, and capital losses; inventory withdrawals are valued at current cost; and depreciation is on a consistent accounting basis and valued at current replacement cost. Related terms: inventory valuation adjustment (IVA), capital consumption adjustment (CCAdj).

Cross-border trade in services Transactions in services between the residents of one country and the residents of another country. From the U.S. viewpoint, it consists of exports and imports of services between U.S. residents and foreign residents. It includes both trade within multinational companies (intrafirm trade in services) and trade between unaffiliated parties. It is one of two channels of delivery of services in international markets; the other is sales of services through foreign affiliates of multinational companies.

Current account (international) Record of transactions in goods, services, income, and unilateral current transfers between residents and nonresidents. Related terms: balance of payments, capital account (international), financial account (international).

Current-dollar estimate The market value of an item. It reflects prices and quantities of the period being measured. Related terms: chained-dollar estimate.

Current payments to the rest of the world The sum of imports of goods and services, income payments to the rest of the world, and current taxes and transfer payments to the rest of the world.

Current receipts from the rest of the world The sum of exports of goods and services and income receipts from the rest of the world.

Current surplus of government enterprises The current operating revenue and subsidies received by government enterprises from other levels of government less the current expenses of government enterprises.

Current taxes and transfer payments to the rest of the world Payments consisting of business current transfer payments to the rest of the world (net), plus nonresident taxes paid by domestic corporations to foreign governments.

Current tax receipts Tax revenues received by government from all sources. It is the sum of personal current taxes, taxes on production and imports, taxes on corporate income, and taxes from the rest of the world.

Current transfer payments Payments consisting of government social benefits and other current transfer payments to the rest of the world.

Current transfer receipts Government net transfer receipts from businesses and from persons. These receipts largely consist of deposit insurance premiums, net insurance settlements, donations, fines, fees, certain penalty taxes, and excise taxes paid by nonprofit institutions serving households.

Direct investment Investment in which a resident of one country obtains a lasting interest in, and a degree of influence over, the management of a business enterprise in another country. In the United States, the criterion used to distinguish direct investment from other types of investment is ownership of at least 10 percent of the voting securities of an incorporated business enterprise or an equivalent ownership interest of an unincorporated business enterprise. Related terms: foreign direct investment in the United States, U.S. direct investment abroad.

Direct investment capital flows Funds that parent companies provide to their affiliates net of funds that affiliates provide to their parents. For U.S. direct investment abroad, capital flows also include funds that U.S. direct investors pay to unaffiliated foreign residents when foreign affiliates are acquired and funds that U.S. investors receive from them when foreign affiliates are sold. Similarly, for foreign direct investment in the United States, capital flows include funds that foreign direct investors pay to unaffiliated U.S. residents when U.S. affiliates are acquired and funds that foreign direct investors receive from them when U.S. affiliates are sold. Foreign direct investment in the United States capital flows also include debt and equity transactions between U.S. affiliates and members of their foreign parent groups other than their foreign parents. Direct investment capital flows consist of equity capital flows, intercompany debt, and reinvested earnings. Direct investment capital flows are components of the financial account (international). Related terms: direct investment, U.S. parent.

Direct investment income Return that direct investors receive on their investment in affiliates abroad. It consists of the direct investors' share in the earnings of the affiliates, plus net interest on intercompany debt.

Direct investment position The value of direct investors' equity in, and net outstanding loans to, their affiliates. The position may be viewed as the direct investors' net financial claims on their affiliates, whether in the form of equity (including retained earnings) or debt. Related terms: direct investment, direct investment position at historical cost, direct investment position at current cost, direct investment position at market value, foreign affiliate, U.S. affiliate.

Direct investment position at current cost A measure of the value of direct investors' equity in, and net outstanding loans to, their affiliates in which the equity portion of the position is valued based on the current cost of plant and equipment, land, and inventories. This measure values the direct investors' shares of the affiliates' investment in plant and equipment, using the current cost of capital equipment; in land, using general price indexes; and in inventories, using estimates of their replacement cost. Related terms: direct investment, direct investment position, direct investment position at historical cost, direct investment position at market value.

Direct investment position at historical cost A measure of the value of direct investors' equity in, and net outstanding loans to, their affiliates in which the direct investors' investment is valued at book value. It largely reflects prices at the time of the investment rather than prices of the current period and is not ordinarily adjusted to reflect the changes in the current costs or the replacement costs of tangible assets or in stock market valuations of firms. Related terms: direct investment, direct investment position, direct investment position at current cost, direct investment position at market value, foreign affiliate, U.S. affiliate.

Direct investment position at market value A measure of the value of direct investors' equity in, and net outstanding loans to, their affiliates, in which the equity portion of the position is valued at current stock market prices. This measure revalues direct investors' equity based on indexes of stock market prices. Related terms: direct investment, direct investment position, direct investment position at current cost, direct investment position at historical cost, foreign affiliate, U.S. affiliate.

Direct requirements table A table in the input-output (I-O) accounts that shows the input of commodities that an industry requires to produce a dollar of output. It also shows the value-added components that an industry requires to produce a dollar of output. The input coefficients are referred to as direct-requirements coefficients. Related terms: make table, use table, total requirements tables.

Directly estimated method Procedure for estimating Federal government purchases based on data from the budget and from the Monthly Treasury Statement.

Directly priced method Procedure for estimating Federal government purchases by multiplying the delivered quantity by the price paid.

Disposable personal income Total after-tax income received by persons; it is the income available to persons for spending or saving. Related terms: personal income, personal saving, personal consumption expenditures (PCE).

Dividend receipts from the rest of the world Receipts received by U.S. residents of dividends from foreign corporations plus earnings distributed by unincorporated foreign affiliates to their U.S. parents.

Dividends Payments in cash or other assets, excluding the corporation's own stock, made by corporations located in the United States and abroad to stockholders who are U.S. residents.

Double deflation Technique for estimating real value added by industry in the gross domestic product (GDP)-by-industry accounts. Under this procedure, an industry's gross output and its intermediate inputs are deflated separately–hence, the term "double deflation." Real value added is then estimated as the difference between deflated, or real, gross output and real intermediate inputs.

Durable goods Tangible products that can be stored or inventoried and that have an average life of at least three years. Related terms: nondurable goods, services, structures.

Employer contributions for employee pension and insurance funds Contributions consisting of employer payments (including payments-in-kind) to private pension and profit-sharing plans, publicly administered government employee retirement plans, private group health and life insurance plans, privately administered workers' compensation plans, and supplemental unemployment benefit plans, formerly called "other labor income."

Employer contributions for government social insurance Contributions consisting of employer payments under the following Federal Government and State and Local government programs: Old-age, survivors, and disability insurance (Social Security); hospital insurance; unemployment insurance; railroad retirement; pension benefit guaranty; veterans life insurance; publicly administered workers' compensation; military medical insurance and temporary disability insurance.

End-use A classification system for U.S. exported and imported merchandise based on principal use rather than the physical characteristics of the merchandise.

Enterprise A business, service, or membership organization consisting of one or more establishments under common, direct or indirect, ownership or control. It is the highest level of establishment aggregation. An enterprise may vary in composition, ranging from a single- establishment company to a complex family of parent and subsidiary companies (firms under common ownership or control).

Equipment and software Investment in equipment and software consists of capital account purchases of new machinery, equipment, furniture, vehicles, and computer software; dealers' margins on sales of used equipment; and net purchases of used equipment from government agencies, persons, and the rest of the world. Own-account production of computer software is also included. Related terms: nonresidential fixed investment, fixed investment.

Equity capital flows (direct investment) Equity capital increases and decreases. Equity capital increases consist of payments by parent companies to third parties abroad for the purchase of capital stock or other equity interests when they acquire an existing business, payments made to acquire additional ownership interests in their affiliates, and capital contributions to their affiliates. Equity capital decreases are funds that parent companies receive (except from distributions of earnings) when they reduce their equity interest in their affiliates. Related terms: direct investment capital flows.

Establishment An economic unit–business or industrial–at a single geographic location, where business is conducted or where services or industrial operations are performed. An establishment is not necessarily identical to an enterprise or company, which may consist of one or more establishments.

Exports of goods and services Goods and services sold by U.S. residents to foreign residents.

FAC Force-account compensation or force-account construction.

Factor income Labor and property earnings from current production. In national income, it is the incomes accruing to labor and property of U.S. residents, which include compensation of employees (received), proprietors' income, rental income of persons, and corporate profits.

FASB Financial accounting standards board.

FDIUS Foreign direct investment in the United States.

FIFO First in, first out.

Final demand Demand of final uses.

Final estimate The third estimate of gross domestic product (GDP) and its components for a quarter. It is released 85–90 days after the end of the quarter, and it is based on source data that are more detailed and comprehensive than the preliminary estimate. The final estimate is still subject to later revisions. Related terms: advanced estimate, preliminary estimate.

Final use(s) Final-demand components for goods and services, which consist of personal consumption expenditures (PCE); gross private fixed investment; change in private inventories; exports of goods and services; imports of goods and services; and government consumption expenditures and gross investment. Related terms: input-output (I-O) accounts.

Financial account (international) Record of transactions between U.S. residents and foreign residents resulting in changes in the level of international claims or liabilities, such as in deposits, ownership of portfolio investment securities, and direct investment. Related terms: balance of payments, current account (international), capital account (international).

Financial assets Deposits, stocks, bonds, notes, currencies, and other instruments that possess value and give rise to claims, liabilities, or equity investment. Financial assets include bank loans, direct investments, and official private holdings of debt and equity securities and other instruments. When the holder resides in a country that is different from the issuer of the instrument, it is included in the international investment position of both countries. Related terms: financial account (international), international investment position (IIP) of the United States.

Fisher ideal price index The geometric mean of the Laspeyres and Paasche price indexes. The Fisher index is superior to either the Laspeyres or the Paasche index if the structure of relative prices in the economy changes between the base period and the current period.

Fixed assets Produced assets that are used repeatedly, or continuously, in processes of production for an extended period of time. They consist of equipment and software and structures (including, by convention, owner-occupied housing), but exclude consumer durables.

Fixed investment Consists of purchases of residential and nonresidential structures and of equipment and software by private businesses, by nonprofit institutions, and by governments in the United States. (Owner-occupied housing is treated like a business in the NIPAs.) Related terms: nonresidential fixed investment, residential fixed investment.

Foreign affiliate A foreign business enterprise in which there is U.S. direct investment–that is, in which a U.S. person, or entity, owns or controls 10 percent or more of the voting securities of an incorporated foreign business enterprise or an equivalent interest in an unincorporated foreign business enterprise. Related terms: majority-owned foreign affiliate (MOFA), foreign parent, U.S. affiliate.

Foreign direct investment in the United States (FDIUS) Ownership or control, directly or indirectly, by one foreign person, or entity, of 10 percent or more of the voting securities of an incorporated U.S. business enterprise or an equivalent interest in an unincorporated U.S. business enterprise. Related terms: direct investment, U.S. affiliate, foreign parent.

Foreign parent The first person, or entity, outside the United States in a U.S. affiliate's ownership chain that has a direct investment interest in the affiliate. Related terms: foreign affiliate, U.S. affiliate, U.S. parent, ultimate beneficial owner (UBO), foreign parent group.

Foreign parent group Consists of the foreign parent and the ultimate beneficial owner (UBO) of a U.S. affiliate and other foreign companies affiliated with the foreign parent and ultimate beneficial owner. More specifically, the foreign parent group consists of (1) the foreign parent, (2) any foreign person, or entity, proceeding up the foreign parent's ownership chain, that owns or controls more than 50 percent of the person below it, up to and including the ultimate beneficial owner, and (3) any foreign person, or entity, proceeding down the ownership chain(s) of each of these members, that is owned more than 50 percent by the person above it.

Foreign residents Individuals, governments, business enterprises, trusts, associations, and nonprofit organizations that fulfill two criteria: (1) They have their center of economic interest outside the United States, and (2) they reside, or expect to reside, outside the United States for one year or more. Included in this definition are U.S. individuals living abroad for one year or more who are not employed by the U.S. government, foreigners residing in the United States for less than one year, and foreign affiliates of U.S. companies. In addition, foreign nationals employed in the United States by their home governments, foreign students enrolled at U.S. educational institutions, and international institutions located in the United States are also considered foreign residents.

FPG Foreign parent group.

General government sector Includes production by all Federal, state, and local government agencies except for government enterprises. Related terms: business sector, households and institutions sector.

GAAP Generally accepted accounting principles.

GBV Gross book value.

GDP Gross domestic product.

GNP Gross national product.

Government consumption expenditures Expenditures consisting of compensation of general government employees, consumption of fixed capital (CFC), and intermediate purchases of goods and services less sales to other sectors and own-account production of structures and software. It excludes current transactions of government enterprises, interest paid or received by government, and subsidies. Related terms: government consumption expenditures and gross investment.

Government consumption expenditures and gross investment The value of services produced by government, measured as the purchases made by government on inputs of labor, intermediate goods and services, and investment expenditures. It is the sum of government consumption expenditures and government gross investment.

Government current expenditures Expenditures consisting of government consumption expenditures, current transfer payments, interest payments, and subsidies.

Government current receipts Receipts consisting of current tax receipts, contributions for government social insurance, income receipts on assets, current transfer receipts from business and persons, and the current surplus of government enterprises.

Government enterprises Government agencies that cover a substantial portion of their operating costs by selling goods and services to the public and that maintain their own separate accounts.

Government gross investment Expenditures consisting of government purchases of structures, equipment, and own-account production of structures and software. It includes investment expenditures by both general government agencies and government enterprises.

Government social benefits Includes benefits from government social insurance funds and from certain other programs.

GPO Gross product originating, by industry.

Gross domestic income (GDI) The costs incurred and the incomes earned in the production of gross domestic product (GDP). In theory, GDI should equal GDP, but in practice they differ because their components are estimated using largely independent and less-than-perfect source data. The difference between the two is termed the statistical discrepancy.

Gross domestic investment The sum of gross private domestic fixed investment, the change in private inventories, and government gross investment.

Gross domestic product (GDP) The market value of goods and services produced by labor and property in the United States, regardless of nationality; GDP replaced gross national product (GNP) as the primary measure of U.S. production in 1991.

Gross domestic product (GDP)-by-industry accounts A set of accounts that present the contribution of each private industry and government to the Nation's gross domestic product (GDP). An industry's contribution is measured by its value added, which is equal to its gross output minus its intermediate purchases from domestic industries or from foreign sources. The GDP-by-industry accounts are consistent with the annual input-output (I-O) accounts.

Gross domestic product (GDP) price index Measures the prices paid for goods and services produced by the U.S. economy and is derived from the prices of personal consumption expenditures (PCE), gross private domestic investment, net exports of goods and services, and government consumption expenditures and gross investment. It differs from the gross domestic purchases price index in that it ignores price changes in imports of goods and services and includes price changes in exports of goods and services.

Gross domestic purchases The market value of goods and services purchased by U.S. residents, regardless of where those goods and services were produced. It is gross domestic product (GDP) minus net exports of goods and services. Equivalently, it is the sum of personal consumption expenditures (PCE), gross private domestic investment, and government consumption expenditures and gross investment.

Gross domestic purchases price index Measures the prices paid for goods and services purchased by U.S. residents. This index is derived from the prices of personal consumption expenditures (PCE), gross private domestic investment, and government consumption expenditures and gross investment. It differs from the gross domestic product (GDP) price index in that it excludes price changes in exports of goods and services and includes price changes in imports of goods and services.

Gross investment The sum of gross private domestic investment, government gross investment, and balance on current account, national income and product accounts.

Gross national product (GNP) The market value of goods and services produced by labor and property supplied by U.S. residents, regardless of where they are located. It was used as the primary measure of U.S. production prior to 1991, when it was replaced by gross domestic product (GDP).

Gross operating surplus Value derived as a residual for most industries after subtracting total intermediate inputs, compensation of employees, and taxes on production and imports less subsidies from total industry output. Gross operating surplus includes consumption of fixed capital (CFC), proprietors' income, corporate profits, and business current transfer payments (net). Prior to 2003, it was referred to as other value added or property-type income.

Gross output Consists of sales, or receipts, and other operating income, plus commodity taxes and changes in inventories.

Gross private domestic investment Private fixed investment and change in private inventories. It is measured without a deduction for consumption of fixed capital (CFC), includes replacements and additions to the capital stock, and excludes investment by U.S. residents in other countries. Related terms: gross investment, gross domestic investment.

Gross state product (GSP) A measurement of a state's output; it is the sum of value added from all industries in the state. GSP is the state counterpart to the Nation's gross domestic product (GDP).

GSP   Gross state product.
HS   Harmonized system.

Households and institutions sector Includes all production by households, which consists of families and unrelated individuals, and by nonprofit institutions that primarily serve households (NPISHs). Related terms: business sector, general government sector.

IIP   International investment position or imputed interest paid.
IMF   International Monetary Fund.

Implicit price deflator (IPD) The ratio of the current-dollar value of a series, such as gross domestic product (GDP), to its corresponding chained-dollar value, multiplied by 100.

Imports of goods and services Goods and services purchased by U.S. residents from foreign residents.

Imputations Estimates of the value of certain income and product flows that do not take measurable monetary form. In the national income and product accounts (NIPAs) for example, BEA imputes a rental value to owner-occupied housing and a value to services that banks and other depository institutions provide without charge.

Income payments on assets Payments that result from the ownership of assets. It includes interest payments, dividend payments, reinvested earnings on foreign direct investment in the United States, and rents and royalties paid by private enterprises to government. Related terms: income payments to the rest of the world, income receipts on assets.

Income payments to the rest of the world Consists of compensation paid to foreign residents, income payments on assets to the rest of the world (which includes interest and dividends paid to the rest of the world), and reinvested earnings on foreign direct investment in the United States.

Income receipts from the rest of the world Consists of compensation paid to U.S. residents by foreigners, income receipts on assets from the rest of the world (which includes interest and dividends received from the rest of the world), and reinvested earnings on U.S. direct investment abroad (USDIA).

Income receipts on assets For private businesses it consists of interest and dividend receipts from the rest of the world and reinvested earnings on U.S. direct investment abroad. For government, it consists of interest and miscellaneous receipts and dividends.

Input-output (I-O) accounts Show the relationships between all the industries in the economy and all the commodities that these industries produce and use. The estimates of purchases of commodities are shown in producers' prices. The I-O accounts consist of the make table, use table, direct requirements table, and total requirements tables. The make and use tables are prepared in two different ways. The first way uses the Standard Industrial Classification System (SIC) or the North American Industry Classification System (NAICS). The second way begins with the SIC or NAICS but includes adjustments (redefinitions and reclassifications) that move some secondary products from one industry to another to attain a common input structure for commodities produced by industries. The direct requirements table and total requirements tables are computed from the make and use tables with redefinition and reclassifications. Related terms: annual I-O accounts, benchmark I-O accounts.

Input-output (I-O) output multipliers Estimate of output required to satisfy a given level of final use. There are three I-O output multipliers, all of which correspond to the total requirements tables. The first shows the total commodity output required to deliver a dollar of a commodity to final uses. The second shows the total industry output required to deliver a dollar of a commodity to final uses. The third shows the total industry output required to deliver a dollar of an industry's output to final uses. Related terms: I-O accounts.

Intercompany debt flows (direct investment) Loans, trade credits, and other transactions in intercompany account payables or receivables between U.S. parent companies and their foreign affiliates, or between U.S. affiliates and their foreign parents or other members of their foreign parent groups.

Interest and miscellaneous payments Consist of interest paid by domestic private enterprises and rents and royalties paid by private enterprises to government.

Interest and miscellaneous receipts Includes rents and royalties received by government from private enterprises, including both monetary and imputed interest receipts.

Interest payments Government interest paid to persons.

Intermediate inputs Goods and services that are used in the production process of other goods and services and are not sold in final-demand markets. Related terms: final uses, intermediate purchases, input-output (I-O) accounts.

Intermediate purchases Purchases of intermediate inputs made by industries or government. Related terms: final uses, input-output (I-O) accounts.

International investment position (IIP) of the United States Value of accumulated stocks of U.S.-owned assets abroad and the accumulated values of foreign-owned assets in the United States at a point in time; the net IIP is the former minus the latter.

Intra-firm trade in services Receipts and payments between U.S. affiliates and their foreign parents, and between U.S. parents and their foreign affiliates, for services provided to one another. They consist of royalties and license fees for the use or sale of intangible property or rights (including patents, trademarks, and copyrights) and of receipts and payments for other private services (such as service charges, rentals for tangible property, and film and television tape rentals). Related terms: foreign parent, U.S. affiliate.

Inward investment Foreign residents' investment in U.S. assets.

Inventory valuation adjustment (IVA) An adjustment made in the national income and product accounts (NIPAs) to corporate profits and to proprietors' income in order to remove inventory "profits," which are more like a capital-gain than profits from current production.

I-O Input-output.
IPD Implicit price deflator.
IPF Indirect pricing factor.
IPS Interactive processing system.
IRP Information Returns Program adjustment.
ISI International Surveys Industry classification.
IVA Inventory valuation adjustment.

Laspeyres price index A fixed-weighted price index that is computed as the sum of base-period quantities valued at current-period prices divided by the sum of base-period quantities valued at base-period prices.

Leontief inversion approach A mathematical technique which is used at BEA to estimate the input-output (I-O) total requirement coefficients and RIMS II multipliers. Related terms: total requirements table (commodity-by-commodity), total requirements table (industry-by-commodity).

LIFO Last in, first out.

Local area personal income Income that is received by, or on behalf of, all persons who live in the local area. It is calculated as the sum of wage and salary disbursements, supplements to wages and salaries, proprietors' income with inventory valuation adjustment (IVA) and capital consumption adjustment (CCAdj), rental income of persons with CCAdj, personal dividend income, personal interest income, and personal current transfer receipts, less contributions for government social insurance. Estimates of local area personal income are presented by the place of residence of the income recipients. All estimates of local area personal income are in current dollars (not adjusted for inflation). Related terms: state personal income, personal income.

MAs Metropolitan areas.

Majority-owned foreign affiliate (MOFA) A foreign affiliate in which the combined ownership of all U.S. parents exceeds 50 percent. Related terms: foreign parent, U.S. affiliate.

Majority-owned U.S. affiliate A U.S. affiliate in which the combined ownership of all foreign parents exceeds 50 percent. Related terms: foreign affiliate, U.S. parent. Related terms: foreign affiliate, U.S. parent.

Make table A table in the input-output (I-O) accounts. The make table shows the production of commodities by industries. It shows the value, in producers' prices, of each commodity produced by each industry. In each row, one "diagonal" cell shows the value of the production of the commodity for which the industry has been designated the primary producer. The entries in the other cells in the row show the values of the production of commodities for which the industry is a secondary producer. The entries in each column of the make table represent the production by both primary and secondary producers of the commodity in the column. Related terms: use table, direct requirements table, total requirements tables.

MAPE Mean absolute percent error.

Margin, or margin costs The value of the trade services provided in delivering commodities from producers' establishments to purchasers, where the purchaser pays for the services. Related terms: input-output (I-O) accounts.

MINOFA Minority-owned foreign affiliate.

MINOUSA Minority-owned U.S. affiliate.

MNC Multi-national company.

MOFA Minority-owned foreign affiliate.

Monthly Treasury Statement Data series, released by the U.S. Treasury, which summarizes the financial activities of the federal government and off-budget Federal entities in accordance with the Budget of the U.S. Government. Related terms: directly estimated method.

MOUSA Majority-owned U.S. affiliate.

MSA Metropolitan statistical area.

NAC National Advisory Council on International Monetary and Financial Policies to the President and Congress

NAICS North American industry classification system.

National income (NI) The sum of all incomes, net of consumption of fixed capital (CFC), earned in production. Includes both factor incomes and nonfactor charges. It formerly excluded nonfactor charges.

National income and product accounts (NIPAs) BEA's economic accounts that display the value and composition of national output and the distribution of incomes generated in its production.

NESE National Economic, Social, and Environmental data bank

Net domestic product (NDP) The market value of the goods and services produced by labor and property in the United States less the value of the fixed capital used up in production; equal to gross domestic product (GDP) less consumption of fixed capital (CFC). NDP may be viewed as an estimate of sustainable product, which is a rough measure of the level of consumption that can be maintained while leaving capital assets intact.

Net exports of goods and services Exports of goods and services minus imports of goods and services.

Net government saving The difference between government current receipts and government current expenditures, formerly called current surplus or deficit (-), national income and product accounts.

Net gross receipts (NGR) A statistic tabulated from the tax returns of sole proprietors and partnerships; used in the estimation of nonfarm proprietors' income by state and county.

Net lending or net borrowing, national income and product accounts An indirect measure of the net acquisition of foreign assets by U.S. residents less the net acquisition of U.S. assets by foreign residents. It is equal to the balance on current account, national income and product accounts less capital transfers to the rest of the world (net).

Net national product (NNP) The market value of goods and services produced by labor and property supplied by U.S. residents, less the value of the fixed capital used up in production; equal to gross national product (GNP) less consumption of fixed capital (CFC).

Net operating surplus A profits-like measure that shows business income after subtracting the costs of compensation of employees (received), taxes on production and imports less subsidies, and consumption of fixed capital (CFC) from value added, but before subtracting financing costs and business transfer payments. Consists of the net operating surplus of private enterprises and the current surplus of government enterprises.

NGR Net gross receipts.

NI National income.

NIPAs National income and product accounts.

Nondurable goods Tangible products that can be stored or inventoried and that have an average life of less than three years. Related terms: durable goods, services, structures.

Nonfactor charges Income from current production not accruing to labor or capital. Includes business current transfer payments (net), taxes on production and imports, and the current surplus of government enterprises less subsidies. Related terms: factor income, national income.

Nonresidential fixed investment Consists of purchases of both nonresidential structures and equipment and software. Related terms: nonresidential structures, equipment and software, fixed investment.

Nonresidential structures Investment in nonresidential structures consists of new construction (including own-account production), improvements to existing structures, expenditures on new mobile structures, brokers' commissions on sales of structures, and net purchases of used structures by private businesses and by nonprofit institutions from government agencies. New construction includes hotels and motels and mining exploration, shafts, and wells. Nonresidential structures also includes equipment considered to be an integral part of a structure, such as plumbing, heating, and electrical systems. Related terms: nonresidential fixed investment, fixed investment.

North American Industry Classification System (NAICS) A classification system developed jointly by the U.S., Canada, and Mexico to provide improved comparability in industrial statistics across North America. NAICS replaced the U.S. Standard Industrial Classification (SIC) system.

NPLL Net profits less loss.

NTDB National Trade Data Bank.

ODA Official development assistance.

OECD Organization for Economic Co-operation and Development.

OLI Other labor income.

OOF Other official flows.

OPEC Organization of Petroleum Exporting Countries.

Other current transfer payments to the rest of the world Payments consisting of U.S. government military and nonmilitary grants-in-cash and grants-in-kind to foreign governments.

Outward investment U.S. residents' investment abroad.

Overseas adjustment An adjustment made to the national estimates of personal income to exclude the wages and salaries and related components of the income of U.S. residents employed abroad temporarily (e.g., military personnel stationed abroad). The adjusted national estimates are used in the estimation of state personal income.

Own-account production Production performed by a businesses or government for its own use.

Paasche price index A fixed-weighted price index that is computed as the sum of current-period quantities valued at current-period prices divided by the sum of current-period quantities valued at base-period prices.

PAT Profits after tax.

PBT Profits before tax.

PCE Personal consumption expenditure.

Persons In the national income and product accounts (NIPAs), persons consist of individuals, nonprofit institutions that primarily serve individuals, private noninsured welfare funds, and private trust funds. In the international accounts, persons refer to individuals, corporations, branches, partnerships, associated groups, associations, estates, trusts, organizations, or government entities.

Personal consumption expenditures (PCE) The goods and services purchased by persons.

Personal current taxes Includes taxes paid by persons on income, including realized net capital gains, and on personal property.

Personal current transfer payments Payments consisting of transfer payments by persons to government and to the rest of the world. Payments to government include donations, fees, and fines paid to Federal, state, and local governments, formerly classified as "personal nontax payments."

Personal current transfer receipts Consists of income payments to persons for which no current services are performed and net insurance settlements. It is the sum of government social benefits and net current transfer receipts from business.

Personal dividend income The dividend income received by persons.

Personal income Income received by persons from all sources. It includes income received from participation in production as well as from government and business transfer payments. It is the sum of compensation of employees (received), supplements to wages and salaries, proprietors' income with inventory valuation adjustment (IVA) and capital consumption adjustment (CCAdj), rental income of persons with CCAdj, personal income receipts on assets, and personal current transfer receipts, less contributions for government social insurance. Related terms: state personal income, local area personal income.

Personal income receipts on assets Personal interest income plus personal dividend income.

Personal interest income Interest income received by persons from all sources; includes both monetary and imputed interest.

Personal interest payments Non-mortgage interest paid by persons.

Personal outlays The sum of personal consumption expenditures (PCE), personal interest payments, and personal current transfer payments.

Personal saving Personal income less the sum of personal outlays and personal current taxes.

PMSA Primary metropolitan statistical area.

PP&E Plant, property & equipment.

Preliminary estimate The second estimate of gross domestic product (GDP) and its components for a quarter. It is released 55-60 days after the end of the quarter, and it is based on source data that are more complete than the advance estimate, though they are still subject to revision. Related terms: advance estimate, final estimate.

Primary inputs Capital and labor inputs to production; the related costs include, for example, compensation, profits, and depreciation.

Primary producer The industry that is the main producer of a particular good or service. Typically, this industry shares the same name as the good or service.

Primary product The principal good or service produced by an industry, which is used to classify establishments in the Standard Industrial Classification System (SIC) or the North American Industry Classification System (NAICS).

Private remittances Includes institutional and personal remittances between U.S. private residents and foreign residents. Institutional remittances includes funds transferred and goods shipped to foreign residents by U.S. religious, charitable, educational, scientific, and similar nonprofit organizations. Personal remittances include remittances in cash between U.S. private residents and foreign residents.

Producers' prices Commodity transactions in the input-output (I-O) accounts are valued in producers' prices in order to show the relationship between the production of commodities and their purchase by intermediate and final uses. These prices exclude wholesale and retail trade margins and transportation costs, but they include sales and excise taxes collected and remitted by producers. Transportation costs and wholesale and retail trade margins are treated separately as commodities that are produced by industries and purchased by intermediate and final users. Related terms: intermediate purchases.

Proprietors' income Current-production income of sole proprietorships, partnerships, and tax-exempt cooperatives. Excludes dividends, monetary interest received by nonfinancial business, and rental income received by persons not primarily engaged in the real estate business.

PurVal Purchaser's value.

RE Reinvested earnings or retained earnings.

Reclassification An adjustment made to the input-output (I-O) accounts when there are two or more industries whose primary activity is the production of similar commodities and the commodities differ only in the process used to produced them. The output of one commodity is moved ("reclassified") to be part of the output of the other, similar commodity. Total output for the affected industry remains unchanged; however, output for each affected commodity group changes.

Redefinition An adjustment made to the input-output (I-O) accounts when a secondary product is assumed to have very different inputs than the other products of the producing industry. The secondary product (output and inputs) is moved ("redefined") to the industry to which the product is primary. The adjustment is necessary to attain a homogenous input structure for the commodities produced by an I-O industry.

Reinvested earnings (direct investment) A parent company's claim on the current-period undistributed after-tax earnings of its affiliates. Related terms: direct investment capital flows.

Rental income of persons with capital consumption adjustment Earnings from the rental of real property by persons who are not primarily engaged in the real estate business. It also includes the imputed net rental income of owner-occupants and the royalties received by persons from patents, copyrights, and rights to natural resources.

Residential fixed investment Consists of purchases of private residential structures and residential equipment that is owned by landlords and rented to tenants. Related terms: residential structures, fixed investment.

Residential structures Investment in residential structures consists of new construction of permanent-site single-family and multi-family units, improvements (additions, alterations, and major structural replacements) to housing units, expenditures on manufactured homes, brokers' commissions on the sale of residential property, and net purchases of used structures from government agencies. Residential structures also include some types of equipment that are built into residential structures, such as heating and air-conditioning equipment. Related terms: residential fixed investment, fixed investment.

RIC Revision in change.

RIMS II or RIMS Regional input-output modeling system.

RIMS II multipliers Estimates of regional input-output multipliers for any state, county, or combination of states or counties. The multipliers estimate the impact from changes in final demand on one or more regional industries in terms of output, employment, and labor earnings. The multipliers are based on estimates of local area personal income and on the national input-output (I-O) accounts.

RLF Royalties and license fees.

RTL Revision to level.

Sales of services through foreign affiliates of multinational companies Sales of services through foreign affiliates of multinational companies. Services sold in international markets through the channel of direct investment. From the U.S. viewpoint, it consists of sales of services to foreigners by foreign affiliates of U.S. companies and U.S. purchases of services from other countries' U.S. affiliates. It is one of two channels in the delivery of services in international markets; the other is cross-border trade in services.

Secondary producer An industry that, in addition to producing its primary product, also produces other goods or services. These other goods or services are referred to as secondary products. Typically, the industry shares the same name as the primary product that it produces.

Secondary product Goods or services produced by an industry other than the primary product of that industry.

Services Products that cannot be stored and are consumed at the place and time of their purchase. Related terms: durable goods, nondurable goods, structures.

SIC Standard industrial classification.

SITC Standard international trade classification.

SNA System of national accounts.

Special drawing rights (SDR) Reserve assets created by the International Monetary Fund (IMF) and periodically allocated to IMF members in proportion to their respective quotas. The IMF determines the value of SDRs daily by summing, in U.S. dollars, the values–based on market exchange rates–of a weighted basket of currencies. SDRs can be used to acquire other members' currencies, to settle members' financial obligations, and to extend loans.

SSI Supplemental Security Income.

Standard Industrial Classification (SIC) A U.S. system for classifying economic activity; superceded by the North American Industry Classification System (NAICS).

Standard International Trade Classification (SITC) An internationally recognized foreign trade data classification system. This system, which was developed by the United Nations, provides the commodity aggregates needed for economic analysis and permits international comparisons of foreign trade data.

State personal income Income that is received by, or on behalf of, persons who live in the state. It is calculated as the sum of wage and salary disbursements, supplements to wages and salaries, proprietors' income with inventory valuation adjustment (IVA) and private capital consumption adjustment (CCAdj), rental income of persons with CCAdj, personal dividend income, personal interest income, and personal current transfer receipts, less contributions for government social insurance. Estimates of state personal income are presented by the place of residence of the income recipients. All estimates of state personal income are in current dollars (not adjusted for inflation). Related terms: local area personal income, personal income.

Statistical discrepancy The difference between gross domestic product (GDP) and gross domestic income (GDI).

Structures Products that are usually constructed at the location where they will be used and that typically have long economic lives. Related terms: durable goods, nondurable goods, services.

Subsidies The monetary grants paid by government agencies to private business or to government enterprises at another level of government.

Supplements to wages and salaries Consists of employer contributions for employee pension and insurance funds and employer contributions for government social insurance.

Taxes from the rest of the world Includes some taxes on production and some current transfers. The source data do not permit the reliable separation of the taxes on income.

Taxes on production and imports Consists of Federal excise taxes and customs duties, state and local sales taxes, property taxes (including residential real estate taxes), motor vehicle licenses, severance taxes, and special assessments.

TGFI Timeseries Generalized Fisher Ideal Index.

TIC Treasury international capital reporting system.

Top-down model A projections model that is used to force lower-level geographical or industry projections to higher-level totals.

Total requirements table A set of tables in the input-output (I-O) accounts calculated from the make table and use table. They show the inputs that are required directly and indirectly to deliver a dollar of output to final uses. There are three total requirements tables. In the commodity-by-commodity table, the column shows the commodity delivered to final uses and the rows show the total production of each commodity required to meet that demand. In the industry-by-commodity table, the column shows the commodity delivered to final uses and the rows show the total production of each industry required. In the industry-by-industry table, the column shows the industry output delivered to final uses and the rows show the total production required by each industry. Related terms: make table, use table, direct requirements table.

UBO Ultimate beneficial owner.

Ultimate beneficial owner (UBO) The person, or entity, that ultimately owns or controls a U.S. affiliate of a foreign company and that derives the benefits associated with ownership or control. The UBO of a U.S. affiliate is that person, or entity, proceeding up the affiliate's ownership chain beginning with the foreign parent, that is not owned more than 50 percent by another person, or entity. Unlike the foreign parent, the UBO of a U.S. affiliate may be located in the United States.

Undistributed profits The portion of corporate profits that remains after taxes and dividends have been paid.

Unilateral current transfers Recorded when transfers of resources that affect a nation's income or product in the current period occur without a quid pro quo; the country receiving the transfer neither provides nor promises to provide anything of economic value, measurable in monetary terms, in return. Related terms: current account (international), balance on current account.

U.S. affiliate A U.S. business enterprise in which there is foreign direct investment—that is, in which a single foreign person, or entity, owns or controls, directly or indirectly, 10 percent or more of the voting securities of an incorporated U.S. business enterprise or an equivalent interest in an unincorporated U.S. business enterprise. Related terms: majority-owned U.S. affiliate, foreign affiliate, foreign parent, U.S. parent.

U.S. direct investment abroad (USDIA) Ownership or control, directly or indirectly, by one U.S. person, or entity, of 10 percent or more of the voting securities of an incorporated foreign business enterprise or an equivalent interest in an unincorporated foreign business enterprise. Related terms: U.S. parent, foreign affiliate.

U.S. multinational company (MNC) U.S. parent and its foreign affiliates. (Usually defined as the U.S. parent and its majority-owned foreign affiliate).

U.S. parent A person, or entity, resident in the United States, that owns or controls 10 percent or more of the voting securities of an incorporated foreign business enterprise or an equivalent interest in an unincorporated foreign business enterprise. It comprises the domestic operations of a U.S. multinational company (MNC). Related terms: foreign affiliate, foreign parent, U.S. affiliate.

U.S. residents Individuals, governments, business enterprises, and nonprofit organizations that have their center of economic interest in the United States and that reside, or expect to reside, in the United States for one year or more. Related terms: foreign resident.

USDIA U.S. direct investment abroad.

Use table A table in the input-output (I-O) accounts that shows the consumption of commodities by industries, as well as the commodity composition of gross domestic product (GDP) and the industry distribution of value added. It shows the value, in producers' prices, of each commodity used by each industry or by each final use. It also shows detail on the components of value added and total intermediate inputs that are used by each industry to produce its output. The entry in each row shows the commodity that is used by the industry or final user in the column. Related terms: make table, direct requirements table, total requirements tables.

Value added The gross output of an industry or a sector less its intermediate inputs; the contribution of an industry or sector to gross domestic product (GDP). Value added by industry can also be measured as the sum of compensation of employees, taxes on production and imports less subsidies, and gross operating surplus.

VOD Value of dispersements.

Wage and salary accruals and disbursements The monetary remuneration of employees, including the compensation of corporate officers; commissions, tips, and bonuses; voluntary employee contributions to certain deferred compensation plans, such as 401(k) plans; and receipts in kind that represent income. Accruals and disbursements differ in the treatment of retroactive payments. In the national income and product accounts (NIPAs), wage and salary accruals is the appropriate measure for gross domestic income (GDI) and wage and salary disbursements is the appropriate measure for personal income.

WOPR Weapons and operations processing review.

Wpurval Wholesale purchaser's value.

Education

NO CHILD LEFT BEHIND

Accountability System Each state sets academic standards for what every child should know and learn. Student academic achievement is measured for every child, every year. The results of these annual tests are reported to the public.

Achievement Gap The difference between how well low-income and minority children perform on standardized tests as compared with their peers. For many years, low-income and minority children have been falling behind their white peers in terms of academic achievement.

Adequate Yearly Progress (AYP) An individual state's measure of yearly progress toward achieving state academic standards. "Adequate Yearly Progress" is the minimum level of improvement that states, school districts and schools must achieve each year.

Alternative Certification Most teachers are required to have both a college degree in education and a state certification before they can enter the classroom. No Child Left Behind encourages states to offer other methods of qualification that allow talented individuals to teach subjects they know.

Assessment Another word for "test." Under No Child Left Behind, tests are aligned with academic standards. Beginning in the 2002-03 school year, schools must administer tests in each of three grade spans: grades 3-5, grades 6-9, and grades 10-12 in all schools. Beginning in the 2005-06 school year, tests must be administered every year in grades 3 through 8 in math and reading. Beginning in the 2007-08 school year, science achievement must also be tested.

Charter School Charter schools are independent public schools designed and operated by educators, parents, community leaders, educational entrepreneurs, and others. They are sponsored by designated local or state educational organizations, who monitor their quality and effectiveness but allow them to operate outside of the traditional system of public schools.

Comprehension The ability to understand and gain meaning from what has been read.

Corrective Action When a school or school district does not make yearly progress, the state will place it under a "Corrective Action Plan." The plan will include resources to improve teaching, administration, or curriculum. If a school continues to be identified as in need of improvement, then the state has increased authority to make any necessary, additional changes to ensure improvement.

Disaggregated Data "Disaggregate" means to separate a whole into its parts. In education, this term means that test results are sorted into groups of students who are economically disadvantaged, from racial and ethnic minority groups, have disabilities, or have limited English fluency. This practice allows parents and teachers to see more than just the average score for their child's school. Instead, parents and teachers can see how each student group is performing.

Distinguished Schools Awards granted to schools when they make major gains in achievement.

Early Reading First A nationwide effort to provide funds to school districts and other public or private organizations that serve children from low-income families. The Department of Education will make competitive 6-year grants to local education agencies to support early language, literacy, and pre-reading development of preschool-age children, particularly those from low-income families.

Elementary and Secondary Education Act (ESEA) ESEA, which was first enacted in 1965, is the principal federal law affecting K-12 education. The No Child Left Behind Act is the most recent reauthorization of the ESEA.

Flexibility Refers to a new way of funding public education. The No Child Left Behind Act gives states and school districts unprecedented authority in the use of federal education dollars in exchange for strong accountability for results.

Fluency The capacity to read text accurately and quickly.

Local Education Agency (LEA) is a public board of education or other public authority within a State which maintains administrative control of public elementary or secondary schools in a city, county, township, school district, or other political subdivision of a state.

possible package of aid is one of the major responsibilities of a school's financial aid administrator.

Financial Need   In the context of student financial aid, financial need is equal to the cost of education (estimated costs for college attendance and basic living expenses) minus the expected family contribution (the amount a student's family is expected to pay, which varies according to the family's financial resources).

General Educational Development (GED) Diploma   The certificate students receive if they have passed a high school equivalency test. Students who don't have a high school diploma but who have a GED will still qualify for Federal student aid.

Grant   A grant is a sum of money given to a student for the purposes of paying at least part of the cost of college. A grant does not have to be repaid.

Individual Corporate Bonds or Stocks   A bond is a promise by a corporation to repay the face value of the bond, plus a fixed rate of interest, at a specific future date. Stock represents part ownership of a company. You make money on stocks either through the dividends you earn or by selling the stock at a price that is higher than the price for which you bought it. The prices of most stocks—and many bonds—are listed in major daily newspapers. Over longer periods, the price of the stock may increase or decrease. Stocks and bonds can be purchased from brokerage houses and through some banks.

Interest   This refers to the amount that your money earns when it is kept in a savings instrument.

Investment   In this guide, an investment refers to using your money to invest in something that will enable you to earn interest or dividends over time.

Liquidity   A term that refers to how quickly you can gain access to money that you invest or deposit in some kind of savings instrument.

Loan   A loan is a type of financial aid that is available to students and to the parents of students. An education loan must be repaid. In many cases, however, payments do not begin until the student finishes school.

Merit-based Financial Aid   This kind of financial aid is given to students who meet requirements not related to financial needs. Most merit-based aid is awarded on the basis of academic performance or potential and is given in the form of scholarships or grants.

Money Market Accounts/Money Market Mutual Funds   Money market accounts are savings accounts offered by banks, requiring a high minimum balance. Money market mutual funds are available from brokers, many banks, and directly by mail. The money that you deposit in these funds is invested in a wide variety of savings instruments.

Mutual Funds   These funds can be invested in U.S. Government securities or in stocks and bonds. You can purchase a mutual fund through an investment firm, brokerage house, many banks, or directly from the mutual fund by mail.

Need-based Financial Aid   This kind of financial aid is given to students who are determined to be in financial need of assistance based on their income and assets and their families' income and assets, as well as some other factors.

Open Admissions   This term means that a college admits most or all students who apply to the school. At some colleges it means that anyone who has a high school diploma or a GED can enroll. At other schools it means that anyone over 18 can enroll. "Open admissions," therefore, can mean slightly different things at different schools.

Pell Grants   These are federal need-based grants.

Perkins Loans   This is a federal financial aid program that consists of low-interest loans for undergraduates and graduate students with exceptional financial need. Loans are awarded by the school.

PLUS Loans   These federal loans allow parents to borrow money for their children's college education.

Postsecondary   This term means "after high school" and refers to all programs for high school graduates, including programs at two-and four-year colleges and vocational and technical schools.

Principal   This refers to the face value or the amount of money you place in a savings instrument on which interest is earned.

Proprietary   This is a term used to describe postsecondary schools that are private and are legally permitted to make a profit. Most proprietary schools offer technical and vocational courses.

PSAT/NMSQT   This stands for the Preliminary Scholastic Assessment Test/National Merit Scholarship Qualifying Test, a practice test that helps students prepare for the Scholastic Assessment Test (SAT I). The PSAT is usually administered to tenth or eleventh grade students. Although colleges do not see a student's PSAT/NMSQT score, a student who does very well on this test and who meets many other academic performance criteria may qualify for the National Merit Scholarship Program.

Return   Return refers to the amount of money you earn through a financial investment or savings instrument. You earn money on investments and savings instruments through interest earnings or dividends.

Risk   In reference to saving or investing, risk refers to the danger of losing money you set aside in some kind of savings plan.

ROTC   This stands for Reserve Officers Training Corps program, which is a scholarship program wherein the military covers the cost of tuition, fees, and textbooks and also provides a monthly allowance. Scholarship recipients participate in summer training while in college and fulfill a service commitment after college.

SAT This stands for the Scholastic Assessment Test, published by the College Board, a non-profit organization with headquarters in New York City. The SAT is a test that measures a student's mathematical and verbal reasoning abilities. Many colleges in the East and West require students to take the SAT and to submit their test scores when they apply for admission. Some colleges accept this test *or* the ACT. (See above for an explanation of the ACT.) Most students take the SAT or the ACT during their junior or senior year of high school.

SAT Subject Test SAT subject tests (also known as SAT II tests) are offered in many areas of study including English, mathematics, many sciences, history, and foreign languages. Some colleges require students to take one or more SAT subject tests when they apply for admission.

Savings Accounts Accounts at a bank, savings association, or credit union.

Savings Instrument Savings instrument refers to any kind of savings plan or mechanism you can use to save money over time. Examples of savings instruments are savings accounts, certificates of deposit (CDs), and money market accounts.

Scholarship A scholarship is a sum of money given to a student for the purposes of paying at least part of the cost of college. Scholarships can be awarded to students based on students' academic achievements or on many other factors.

SEOG (Supplemental Educational Opportunity Grant) This is a federal award that helps undergraduates with exceptional financial need, and is awarded by the school. The SEOG does not have to be paid back.

Stafford Loans These are student loans offered by the federal Government. There are two types of Stafford Loans: one need-based and another non-need-based. Under the Stafford Loan programs, students can borrow money to attend school and the federal Government will guarantee the loan in case of default.

Transcript This is a list of all the courses a student has taken with the grades that the student earned in each course. A college will often require a student to submit his or her high school transcript when the student applies for admission to the college.

Tuition This is the amount of money that colleges charge for classroom and other instruction and use of some facilities such as libraries. Tuition can range from a few hundred dollars per year to more than $20,000. A few colleges do not charge any tuition.

U.S. Government Securities The Treasury Department and Federal agencies issue different types of fixed-income investments such as short-term bills (13-, 26-, and 52-week bills), medium-term notes (2-10 years), and long-term bonds (over 10 years). These securities can be purchased directly from regional Federal Reserve banks, through regular banks, and through brokers. Because there are relatively large minimum purchase amounts, some people prefer to invest instead in mutual funds that invest only in U.S. Government securities.

U.S. Savings Bonds U.S. (EE) savings bonds are promises by the U.S. Treasury to repay the owner with interest when the bond is redeemed. Bonds earn interest for as long as 30 years. Bonds earn market-based rates right from the start. They can be purchased from banks and through employer payroll deduction plans in amounts as little as $50.

William D. Ford Federal Direct Loans Under this program, students may obtain federal loans directly from their college or university with funds provided by the U.S. Department of Education instead of a bank or other lender.

Work-Study Programs These programs are offered by many colleges. They allow students to work part time during the school year as part of their financial aid package. The jobs are usually on campus and the money earned is used to pay for tuition or other college charges.

STUDENT AID

Borrower Person responsible for repaying a loan who has signed and agreed to the terms in the promissory note.

Capitalization Adding unpaid interest to the loan principal. Capitalization increases the principal amount of the loan and its total cost.

Default Failure to repay a loan according to the terms of the promissory note. This failure must persist for 270 days.

Deferment A postponement of payment on a loan that is allowed under certain conditions and during which interest does not accrue for subsidized loans.

Dependent student A student who does not meet any of the criteria for an independent student (see below).

Disbursement A payment of loan money to the student or parent borrower.

Discharge The release of a borrower from the obligation to repay his or her loan.

Direct Loan Program The William D. Ford Federal Direct Loan Program provides loans to student and parent borrowers directly through the U.S. Department of Education rather than through a bank or other lender.

Direct Loan Servicing Center The U.S. Department of Education's agent contracted to collect Direct Loans and handle deferments, repayment options, and consolidation.

Direct Subsidized Stafford Loan A loan for students with financial need as determined by federal regulations. No interest is charged while you are in school at least half-time, during your grace period, and during deferment periods.

Direct Unsubsidized Stafford Loan A student loan that is not based on financial need. Interest is charged during all periods.

Expected Family Contribution (EFC) The EFC is a measure of the financial strength of a student's family. The U.S. Department of Education calculates a student's EFC based on information provided on the Free Application for Federal Student Aid (FAFSA).

Forbearance A postponement of payment on a loan, typically if the borrower doesn't qualify for a deferment and is unable to make payments for a reason such as poor health. Interest continues to accrue during forbearance.

Grace period A six-month period before the first payment must be made on a subsidized or unsubsidized Stafford loan. The grace period begins the day after the borrower ceases to be enrolled at least half time.

Independent student A student who is at least 24 years old, married, a graduate or professional student, a veteran or on active duty in the military for other than training or state purposes, an orphan, a ward of the court, or who has legal dependents other than a spouse.

Interest An expense of borrowing money that is calculated as a percentage of the amount borrowed.

Loan Money borrowed that must be repaid.

Loan fee An expense of borrowing deducted proportionately from each loan disbursement.

Principal balance The amount owed on a loan, which includes any capitalized interest.

Promissory note A legally binding contract between a lender and a borrower. The promissory note contains the terms and conditions of the loan, including how and when the loan must be repaid.

Repayment period The period during which a borrower is obligated to make payments on his or her loan(s).

Repayment schedule A statement provided by the Direct Loan Servicing Center to the borrower that lists the amount borrowed, the amount of monthly payments, and the date payments are due.

Variable interest Rate of interest on a loan that is tied to a stated index and changes annually every July 1 as the index changes.

PERFORMANCE AND ACCOUNTABILITY ACRONYMS

AARTS	Audit Accountability and Resolution Tracking System
ACSI	American Customer Satisfaction Index
AEFLA	Adult Education and Family Literacy Act
AGI	Adjusted Gross Income
APEB	Act to Promote the Education of the Blind
ASL	Accreditation and State Liaison
ATA	Assistive Technology Act
AYP	Adequate Yearly Progress
CFAA	Compact of Free Association Act, Amendments of 2003
CFDA	Catalogue of Federal Domestic Assistance
CHAFL	College Housing and Academic Facilities Loans
CHL	College Housing Loans
CIFMS	Continuous Improvement and Focused Monitoring System
CRA	Civil Rights Act
CSRS	Civil Service Retirement System
DCIA	Debt Collection Improvement Act
ED	Department of Education
EDA	Education of the Deaf Act of 1906
EDEN	Education Data Exchange Network
EDPAS	Education Department Performance Appraisal System
EFC	Expected Family Contribution
ESEA	Elementary and Secondary Education Act of 1965
ESRA	Education Sciences Reform Act of 2002
FAFSA	Free Application for Federal Student Aid
FASAB	Federal Accounting Standards Advisory Board
FBI	Federal Bureau of Investigation
FBCO	Faith-Based and Community Organizations
FECA	Federal Employees Compensation Act
FERS	Federal Employees Retirement System
FFB	Federal Financing Bank
FFEL	Federal Family Education Loan
FFMIA	Federal Financial Management Improvement Act
FISAP	Fiscal Operations Report and Application to Participate
FMFIA	Federal Managers' Financial Integrity Act of 1982
FP	Financial Partners Service
FPPS	Federal Personnel/Payroll System
FSA	Office of Federal Student Aid
FSEOG	Federal Supplemental Educational Opportunity Grant
FWS	Federal Work-Study
FY	Fiscal Year

GAAP	Generally Accepted Accounting Principles	OCFO	Office of the Chief Financial Officer
GAO	Government Accountability Office	OCR	Office for Civil Rights
GAPS	Grant Administration and Payment System	OELA	Office of English Language Acquisition
GED	General Educational Development	OESE	Office of Elementary and Secondary Education
GEAR-UP	Gaining Early Awareness and Readiness for Undergraduate Programs	OIG	Office of Inspector General
GPRA	Government Performance and Results Act of 1993	OMB	Office of Management and Budget
		OPE	Office of Postsecondary Education
GRS	Graduation Rate Survey	OPM	Office of Personnel Management
GSA	General Services Administration	ORNL	Oak Ridge National Laboratory
HBCUs	Historically Black Colleges and Universities	OSEP	Office of Special Education Programs
HEA	Higher Education Act of 1965	OSERS	Office of Special Education and Rehabilitative Services
HEFL	Higher Education Facilities Loans		
HEP	Higher Education Programs	OUS	Office of the Under Secretary
HKNCA	Helen Keller National Center Act	OVAE	Office of Vocational and Adult Education
HQT	Highly Qualified Teacher	PAR	Performance and Accountability Report
HSIs	Hispanic-Serving Institutions	PART	Program Assessment Rating Tool
IDEA	Individuals with Disabilities Education Act	PBDMI	Performance-Based Data Management Initiative
IG	Inspector General	PCP	Potomac Center Plaza
IP	Improper Payments	PMA	President's Management Agenda
IPA	Independent Public Accountants	RA	Rehabilitation Act of 1973
IPIA	Improper Payments Information Act of 2002	REAP	Rural Education Achievement Program
		RSA	Rehabilitation Services Administration
IRB	Investment Review Board	SAD	Single Audit Database
IRS	Internal Revenue Service	SAMHSA	Substance Abuse and Mental Health Services Administration
IT	Information Technology		
IUS	Internal Use Software	SES	Supplemental Educational Services
LEA	Local Educational Agency	SFA	Student Financial Assistance
LEP	Limited English Proficient	SFFAS	Statement of Federal Financial Accounting Standards
LVC	Loan Verification Certificate		
MECEA	Mutual Educational and Cultural Exchange Act of 1961	SLM	Student Loan Model
		SOF	Statement of Financing
MVHAA	McKinney-Vento Homeless Assistance Act	SY	School Year
NACSA	National Association of Charter School Authorizers	TASSIE	Title I Accountability Systems and School Improvement Efforts
NAEP	National Assessment of Educational Progress	TRIO	A group of grant programs under the HEA, originally three programs; not an acronym
NCER	National Center for Education Research		
NCES	National Center for Education Statistics	USC	United States Code
NCSER	National Center for Special Education Research	USDA	United States Department of Agriculture
		VTEA	Perkins Vocational and Technical Education Act
NLA	National Literacy Act of 1991		
NSLDS	National Student Loan Data System	YRBSS	Youth Risk Behavior Surveillance System

Energy

ACBM Acronym for "asbestos-containing building material."

Account classification The way in which suppliers of electricity, natural gas, or fuel oil classify and bill their customers. Commonly used account classifications are "Residential," "Commercial," "Industrial," and "Other." Suppliers' definitions of these terms vary from supplier to supplier. In addition, the same customer may be classified differently by each of its energy suppliers.

Account of others (natural gas) Natural gas deliveries for the account of others are deliveries to customers by transporters that do not own the natural gas but deliver it for others for a fee. Included are quantities covered by long-term contracts and quantities involved in short-term or spot market sales.

Accounting system A method of recording accounting data for a utility or company or a method of supplying accounting information for controlling, evaluating, planning and decisionmaking.

Acid mine drainage This refers to water pollution that results when sulfur-bearing minerals associated with coal are exposed to air and water and form sulfuric acid and ferrous sulfate. The ferrous sulfate can further react to form ferric hydroxide, or yellowboy, a yellow-orange iron precipitate found in streams and rivers polluted by acid mine drainage.

Acid rain Also called acid precipitation or acid deposition, acid rain is precipitation containing harmful amounts of nitric and sulfuric acids formed primarily by sulfur dioxide and nitrogen oxides released into the atmosphere when fossil fuels are burned. It can be wet precipitation (rain, snow, or fog) or dry precipitation (absorbed gaseous and particulate matter, aerosol particles or dust). Acid rain has a pH below 5.6. Normal rain has a pH of about 5.6, which is slightly acidic. The term pH is a measure of acidity or alkalinity and ranges from 0 to 14. A pH measurement of 7 is regarded as neutral. Measurements below 7 indicate increased acidity, while those above indicate increased alkalinity.

Acquisition (foreign crude oil) All transfers of ownership of foreign crude oil to a firm, irrespective of the terms of that transfer. Acquisitions thus include all purchases and exchange receipts as well as any and all foreign crude acquired under reciprocal buy-sell agreements or acquired as a result of a buy-back or other preferential agreement with a host government.

Acquisition (minerals) The procurement of the legal right to explore for and produce discovered minerals, if any, within a specific area; that legal right may be obtained by mineral lease, concession, or purchase of land and mineral rights or of mineral rights alone.

Acquisition costs, mineral rights Direct and indirect costs incurred to acquire legal rights to extract natural resources. Direct costs include costs incurred to obtain options to lease or purchase mineral rights and costs incurred for the actual leasing (e.g., lease bonuses) or purchasing of the rights. Indirect costs include such costs as brokers' commissions and expenses; abstract and recording fees; filing and patenting fees; and costs for legal examination of title and documents.

Acre-foot The volume of water that will cover an area of 1 acre to a depth of 1 foot.

Acreage An area, measured in acres, that is subject to ownership or control by those holding total or fractional shares of working interests. Acreage is considered developed when development has been completed. A distinction may be made between "gross" acreage and "net" acreage:
- Gross — All acreage covered by any working interest, regardless of the percentage of ownership in the interest.
- Net — Gross acreage adjusted to reflect the percentage of ownership in the working interest in the acreage.

Active power The component of electric power that performs work, typically measured in kilowatts (kW) or megawatts (MW). Also known as "real power." The terms "active" or "real" are used to modify the base term "power" to differentiate it from Reactive Power. See Apparent Power, Power, Reactive Power.

Active solar As an energy source, energy from the sun collected and stored using mechanical pumps or fans to circulate heat-laden fluids or air between solar collectors and a building.

Actual peak reduction The actual reduction in annual peak load (measured in kilowatts) achieved by customers that participate in a utility demand-side management (DSM) program. It reflects the changes in the demand for electricity resulting from a utility DSM program that is in effect at the same time the utility experiences its annual peak load, as opposed to the installed peak load reduction capability (i.e., potential peak reduction). It should account for the regular cycling of energy efficient units during the period of annual peak load.

Adequacy (electric) The ability of the electric system to supply the aggregate electrical demand and energy requirements of the end-use customers at all times, taking into account scheduled and reasonably expected unscheduled outages of system elements. (NERC definition)

Adjustable speed drives Drives that save energy by ensuring the motor's speed is properly matched to the load placed on the motor. Terms used to describe this category include polyphase motors, motor oversizing, and motor rewinding.

Adjusted electricity A measurement of electricity that includes the approximate amount of energy used to generate electricity. To approximate the adjusted amount of electricity, the site-value of the electricity is multiplied by a factor of 3. This conversion factor of 3 is a rough approximation of the Btu value of raw fuels used to generate electricity in a steam-generation power plant.

Adjustment bid A bid auction conducted by the independent system operator or power exchange to redirect supply or demand of electricity when congestion is anticipated.

Administrative and general expenses Expenses of an electric utility relating to the overall directions of its corporate offices and administrative affairs, as contrasted with expenses incurred for specialized functions. Examples include office salaries, office supplies, advertising, and other general expenses.

Advance royalty A royalty required to be paid in advanceof productlion from a mineral property that may or may not be recoverable from future production.

Advances from municipality The amount of loans and advances made by the municipality or its other departments to the utility department when such loans and advances are subject to repayment but not subject to current settlement.

Advances to municipality The amount of loans and advances made by the utility department to the municipality or its other departments when such loans or advances are subject to current settlement.

Adverse water conditions Reduced streamflow, lack of rain in the drainage basin, or low water supply behind a pondage or reservoir dam resulting in a reduced gross head that limits the production of hydroelectric power or forces restrictions to be placed on multipurpose reservoirs or other water uses.

Affiliate An entity which is directly or indirectly owned, operated, or controlled by another entity. See Firm.

Afforestation Planting of new forests on lands that have not been recently forested.

Aftermarket converted vehicle A standard conventionally fueled, factory-produced vehicle to which equipment has been added that enables the vehicle to operate on alternative fuel.

Aftermarket vehicle converter An organization or individual that modifies OEM vehicles after first use or sale to operate on a different fuel (or fuels).

Agglomerating character Agglomeration describes the caking properties of coal. Agglomerating character is determined by examination and testing of the residue when a small powdered sample is heated to 950 degrees Centigrade under specific conditions. If the sample is "agglomerating," the residue will be coherent, show swelling or cell structure, and be capable of supporting a 500-gram weight without pulverizing.

Aggregate ratio The ratio of two population aggregates (totals). For example, the aggregate expenditures per household is the ratio of the total expenditures in each category to the total number of households in the category.

Aggregator Any marketer, broker, public agency, city, county, or special district that combines the loads of multiple end-use customers in negotiating the purchase of electricity, the transmission of electricity, and other related services for these customers.

Agriculture An energy-consuming subsector of the industrial sector that consists of all facilities and equipment engaged in growing crops and raising animals.

Agriculture, mining, and construction (consumer category) Companies engaged in agriculture, mining (other than coal mining), or construction industries.

Air cleaner A device using filters or electrostatic precipitators to remove indoor-air pollutants such as tobacco smoke, dust, and pollen. Most portable units are 40 watts when operated on low speed and 100 watts on high speed.

Air collector A medium-temperature collector used predominantly in space heating, utilizing pumped air as the heat-transfer medium.

Air conditioning Cooling and dehumidifying the air in an enclosed space by use of a refrigeration unit powered by electricity or natural gas. *Note*: Fans, blowers, and evaporative cooling systems ("swamp coolers") that are not connected to a refrigeration unit are excluded.

Air conditioning intensity The ratio of air-conditioning consumption or expenditures to square footage of cooled floor space and cooling degree-days (base 65 degrees F). This intensity provides a way of comparing different types of housing units and households by controlling for differences in housing unit size and weather conditions. The square footage of cooled floor space is equal to the product of the total square footage times the ratio of the number of rooms that could be cooled to the total number of rooms. If the entire housing unit is cooled, the cooled floorspace is the same as the total floorspace. The ratio is calculated on a weighted, aggregate basis according to this formula:

Air-Conditioning Intensity = Btu for Air Conditioning/(Cooled Square Feet * Cooling Degree-Days)

Air pollution abatement equipment Equipment used to reduce or eliminate airborne pollutants, including particulate matter (dust, smoke, fly, ash, dirt, etc.), sulfur oxides, nitrogen oxides (NO_x), carbon monoxide, hydrocarbons, odors, and other pollutants. Examples of air pollution abatement structures and equipment include flue-gas particulate collectors, flue-gas desulfurization units and nitrogen oxide control devices.

Alcohol The family name of a group of organic chemical compounds composed of carbon, hydrogen, and oxygen. The series of molecules vary in chain length and are composed of a hydrocarbon plus a hydroxyl group; $CH(3)–(CH(2))_n–OH$ (e.g., methanol, ethanol, and tertiary butyl alcohol).

Alkylate The product of an alkylation reaction. It usually refers to the high-octane product from alkylation units. This alkylate is used in blending high octane gasoline.

Alkylation A refining process for chemically combining isobutane with olefin hydrocarbons (e.g., propylene, butylene) through the control of temperature and pressure in the presence of an acid catalyst, usually sulfuric acid or hydrofluoric acid. The product, alkylate, an isoparaffin, has high octane value and is blended with motor and aviation gasoline to improve the antiknock value of the fuel.

All-electric home A residence in which electricity is used for the main source of energy for space heating, water heating, and cooking. Other fuels may be used for supplementary heating or other purposes.

Alternate energy source for primary heater The fuel that would be used in place of the usual main heating fuel if the building had to switch fuels. (See Fuel-Switching Capability.)

Alternating current (AC) An electric current that reverses its direction at regularly recurring intervals.

Alternative fuel Alternative fuels, for transportation applications, include the following:
- methanol
- denatured ethanol, and other alcohols
- fuel mixtures containing 85 percent or more by volume of methanol, denatured ethanol, and other alcohols with gasoline or other fuels—natural gas
- liquefied petroleum gas (propane)
- hydrogen
- coal-derived liquid fuels
- fuels (other than alcohol) derived from biological materials (biofuels such as soy diesel fuel)
- electricity (including electricity from solar energy)

"... any other fuel the Secretary determines, by rule, is substantially not petroleum and would yield substantial energy security benefits and substantial environmental benefits." The term "alternative fuel" does not include alcohol or other blended portions of primarily petroleum-based fuels used as oxygenates or extenders, i.e. MTBE, ETBE, other ethers, and the 10-percent ethanol portion of gasohol.

Alternative-fuel vehicle (AFV) A vehicle designed to operate on an alternative fuel (e.g., compressed natural gas, methane blend, electricity). The vehicle could be either a dedicated vehicle designed to operate exclusively on alternative fuel or a nondedicated vehicle designed to operate on alternative fuel and/or a traditional fuel.

Alternative-fuel vehicle converter An organization (including companies, government agencies and utilities), or individual that performs conversions involving alternative alternative fuel vehicles. An AFV converter can convert (1) conventionally fueled vehicles to AFVs, (2) AFVs to conventionally fueled vehicles, or (3) AFVs to use another alternative fuel.

Alternative-rate DSM program assistance A DSM (demand-side management) program assistance that offers special rate structures or discounts on the consumer's monthly electric bill in exchange for participation in DSM programs aimed at cutting peak demands or changing load shape. These rates are intended to reduce consumer bills and shift hours of operation of equipment from on-peak to off-peak periods through the application of time-differentiated rates. For example, utilities often pay consumers several dollars a month (refund on their monthly electric bill) for participation in a load control program. Large commercial and industrial customers sometimes obtain interruptible rates, which provide a discount in return for the consumer's agreement to cut electric loads upon request from the utility (usually during critical periods, such as summer afternoons when the system demand approaches the utility's generating capability).

AMI Advanced Metering Infrastructure is a term denoting electricity meters that measure and record usage data at a minimum, in hourly intervals, and provide usage data to both consumers and energy companies at least once daily.

Amorphous silicon An alloy of silica and hydrogen, with a disordered, noncrystalline internal atomic arrangement, that can be deposited in thin-film layers (a few micrometers in thickness) by a number of deposition methods to produce thin-film photovoltaic cells on glass, metal, or plastic substrates.

Amortization The depreciation, depletion, or charge-off to expense of intangible and tangible assets over a period of time. In the extractive industries, the term is most frequently applied to mean either (1) the periodic charge-off to expense of the costs associated with nonproducing mineral properties incurred prior to the time when they are developed and entered into production or (2) the systematic charge-off to expense of those costs of productive mineral properties (including tangible and intangible costs of prospecting, acquisition, exploration, and development) that had been initially capitalized (or deferred) prior to the time the properties entered into production, and thereafter are charged off as minerals are produced.

Ampere The unit of measurement of electrical current produced in a circuit by 1 volt acting through a resistance of 1 Ohm.

AMR Automated Meter Reading is a term denoting electricity meters that collect data for billing purposes only and transmit this data one way, usually from the customer to the distribution utility.

Ancillary services Services that ensure reliability and support the transmission of electricity from generation sites to customer loads. Such services may include: load regulation, spinning reserve, non-spinning reserve, replacement reserve, and voltage support.

Annual operating factor The annual fuel consumption divided by the product of design firing rate and hours of operation per year.

Annual requirement The reporting company's best estimate of the annual requirement for natural gas to make direct sales or sales for resale under certificate authorizations and for company use and unaccounted-for gas during the year next following the current report year.

ANSI assembly identifier The serial numbering scheme adopted by the American National Standards Institute (ANSI) to ensure uniqueness of an assembly serial number.

Anthracite The highest rank of coal; used primarily for residential and commercial space heating. It is a hard, brittle, and black lustrous coal, often referred to as hard coal, containing a high percentage of fixed carbon and a low percentage of volatile matter. The moisture content of fresh-mined anthracite generally is less than 15 percent. The heat content of anthracite ranges from 22 to 28 million Btu per ton on a moist, mineral-matter-free basis. The heat content of anthracite coal consumed in the United States averages 25 million Btu per ton, on the as-received basis (i.e., containing both inherent moisture and mineral matter). *Note:* Since the 1980s, anthracite refuse or mine waste has been used for steam electric power generation. This fuel typically has a heat content of 15 million Btu per ton or less.

Anthropogenic Made or generated by a human or caused by human activity. The term is used in the context of global climate change to refer to gaseous emissions that are the result of human activities, as well as other potentially climate-altering activities, such as deforestation.

API The American Petroleum Institute, a trade association.

API gravity American Petroleum Institute measure of specific gravity of crude oil or condensate in degrees. An arbitrary scale expressing the gravity or density of liquid petroleum products. The measuring scale is calibrated in terms of degrees API; it is calculated as follows:

Degrees API = (141.5 / sp.gr.60 deg.F/60 deg.F) − 131.5

Apparent consumption, (coal) Coal production plus imports of coal, coke, and briquets minus exports of coal, coke, and briquets plus or minus stock changes. Note: The sum of "Production" and "Imports" less "Exports" may not equal "Consumption" due to changes in stocks, losses, unaccounted-for coal, and special arrangements such as the United States shipments of anthracite to United States Armed Forces in Europe.

Apparent consumption, natural gas (international) The total of an individual nation's dry natural gas production plus imports less exports.

Apparent consumption, petroleum (international) Consumption that includes internal consumption, refinery fuel and loss, and bunkering. For countries in the Organization for Economic Cooperation and Development (OECD), apparent consumption is derived from refined product output plus refined product imports minus refined product exports plus refined product stock changes plus other oil consumption (such as direct use of crude oil). For countries outside the OECD, apparent consumption is either a reported figure or is derived from refined product output plus refined product imports minus refined product exports, with stock levels assumed to remain the same. Apparent consumption also includes, where available, liquefied petroleum gases sold directly from natural gas processing plants for fuel or chemical uses.

Apparent power The product of the voltage (in volts) and the current (in amperes). It comprises both active and reactive power. It is measured in "volt-amperes" and often expressed in "kilovolt-amperes" (kVA) or "megavolt-amperes" (MVA). See Power, Reactive Power, Real Power.

Appliance A piece of equipment, commonly powered by electricity, used to perform a particular energy-driven function. Examples of common appliances are refrigerators, clothes washers and dishwashers, conventional ranges/ovens and microwave ovens, humidifiers and dehumidifiers, toasters, radios, and televisions. *Note:* Appliances are ordinarily self-contained with respect to their function. Thus, equipment such as central heating and air conditioning systems and water heaters, which are connected to distribution systems inherent to their purposes, are not considered appliances.

Appliance efficiency index A relative comparison of trends in new-model efficiencies for major appliances and energy-using equipment. The base year for relative comparisons was 1972 (1972 = 100). Efficiencies for each year were efficiencies of different model types that were weighted by their market shares.

Appliance efficiency standards The National Appliance Energy Conservation Act of 1987 established minimum efficiency standards for major home appliances, including furnaces, central and room air conditioners, refrigerators, freezers, water heaters, dishwashers, and heat pumps. Most of the standards took effect in 1990. The standards for clothes washers, dishwashers, and ranges took effect in 1988, because they required only minor changes in product design, such as eliminating pilot lights and requiring cold water rinse options. The standards for central air conditioners and furnaces took effect in 1992, because it took longer to redesign these products. Appliance efficiency standards for refrigerators took effect in 1993.

Aromatics Hydrocarbons characterized by unsaturated ring structures of carbon atoms. Commercial petroleum aromatics are benzene, toluene, and xylene (BTX).

Asbestos A group of naturally occurring minerals that separate into long, thin fibers. Asbestos was used for many years to insulate and fireproof buildings. In the 1989 CBECS, information on asbestos in buildings was collected (Section R of the Buildings Questionnaire) for the U.S. Environmental Protection Agency (EPA) Asbestos treatment methods include removal, encapsulation or sealing, and enclosure behind a permanent barrier.

Ash Impurities consisting of silica, iron, alumina, and other noncombustible matter that are contained in coal. Ash increases the weight of coal, adds to the cost of handling, and can affect its burning characteristics Ash content is measured as a percent by weight of coal on an "as received" or a "dry" (moisture-free, usually part of a laboratory analysis) basis.

Asphalt A dark brown-to-black cement-like material obtained by petroleum processing and containing bitumens as the predominant component; used primarily for road construction. It includes crude asphalt as well as the following finished products: cements, fluxes, the asphalt content of emulsions (exclusive of water), and petroleum distillates blended with asphalt to make cutback asphalts. *Note:* The conversion factor for asphalt is 5.5 barrels per short ton.

Asphalt (refined) See Asphalt above.

As received coal Coal in the condition as received by the user.

As-received condition or as-received basis (coal) Coal in the condition as received by the consumer or the laboratory analyzing the coal.

Assembly identifier A unique string of alphanumeric characters that identifies an assembly, bundle, or canister for a specific reactor in which it has been irradiated.

Assembly type Each assembly is characterized by a fabricator, rod-array size, and model type. An eight-digit assembly type code is assigned to each assembly type based on certain distinguishing characteristics, such as the number of rods per assembly, fuel rod diameter, cladding type, materials used in fabrication, and other design features.

Assessment work The annual or biennial work performed on a mining claim (or claims), after claim location and before patent, to benefit or develop the claim and to protect it from relocation by third parties.

Assistance for heating in winter Assistance from the Low-Income Home Energy Assistance Program (LIHEAP). The purpose of LIHEAP is to assist eligible households to meet the costs of home energy, i.e., a source of heating or cooling residential buildings.

Assistance for weatherization of residence The household received services free, or at a reduced cost, from the Federal, State, or local Government. Any of the following services could have been received:
- Insulation in the attic, outside wall, or basement/crawlspace below the floor of the house
- Insulation around the hot water heater
- Repair of broken windows or doors to keep out the cold or hot weather
- Weather stripping or caulking around any windows or doors to the outside
- Storm doors or windows added
- Repair of broken furnace
- Furnace tuneup and/or modifications
- Other home energy-saving devices

Associated-dissolved natural gas Natural gas that occurs in crude oil reservoirs either as free gas (associated) or as gas in solution with crude oil (dissolved gas). Also see Natural gas.

Associated natural gas See Associated-dissolved natural gas above and Natural gas.

ASTM The acronym for the American Society for Testing and Materials.

Atmospheric crude oil distillation The refining process of separating crude oil components at atmospheric pressure by heating to temperatures of about 600 degrees to 750 degrees Fahrenheit (depending on the nature of the crude oil and desired products) and subsequent condensing of the fractions by cooling.

at wt The abbreviation for atomic weight.

Auger mine A surface mine where coal is recovered through the use of a large-diameter drill driven into a coalbed exposed by surface mining excavations or in natural sloping terrain. It usually follows contour, area, or open-pit surface mining, particularly when the overburden becomes too thick for further economical excavation.

Authorized cash distribution to municipality The authorized cash distributions to the municipality from the earned surplus of the utility department.

Automatic set-back or clock thermostat A thermostat that can be set to turn the heating/cooling system off and on at certain predetermined times.

Automobile and truck classifications Vehicle classifications for automobiles and light duty trucks were obtained from the EPA (Environmental Protection Agency) mileage guide book. Almost every year there are small changes in the classifications, therefore the categories will change accordingly. The EPA mileage guide can be found at any new car dealership.

Auxiliary generator A generator at the electric plant site that provides power for the operation of the electrical generating equipment itself, including related demands such as plant lighting, during periods when the electric plant is not operating and power is unavailable from the grid. A black start generator used to start main central station generators is considered to be an auxiliary generator.

Available but not needed capability Net capability of main generating units that are operable but not considered necessary to carry load and cannot be connected to load within 30 minutes.

Average annual percent change (coal) The average annual percent change over a period of several years that is calculated by taking the nth root [where n is the number of years in the period of interest] of the result of the current year's value divided by the value of the first year of the period; this result then has 1 (one) subtracted from it and that result is then multiplied by 100.

$$(\sqrt[n]{V_n / V_0} - 1) \cdot 100$$

Where: V_0 = the value for the base period.
V_n = the value for the nth period.
n = the number of periods.

Average daily production The ratio of the total production at a mining operation to the total number of production days worked at the operation.

Average delivered price The weighted average of all contract price commitments and market price settlements in a delivery year.

Average household energy expenditures A ratio estimate defined as the total household energy expenditures divided by the total number of households.

Average mine price The ratio of the total value of the coal produced at the mine to the total production tonnage.

Average production per miner per day The product of the average production per miner per hour at a mining operation and the average length of a production shift at the operation.

Average production per miner per hour The ratio of the total production at a mining operation to the total direct labor hours worked at the operation.

Average revenue per kilowatthour The average revenue per kilowatthour of electricity sold by sector (residential, commercial, industrial, or other) and geographic area (State, Census division, and national) is calculated by dividing the total monthly revenue by the corresponding total monthly sales for each sector and geographic area.

Average stream flow The rate, usually expressed in cubic feet per second, at which water passes a given point in a stream over a set period of time.

Average vehicle fuel consumption A ratio estimate defined as total gallons of fuel consumed by all vehicles divided by: (1) the total number of vehicles (for average fuel consumption per vehicle) or (2) the total number of households (for average fuel consumption per household).

Average vehicle miles traveled A ratio estimate defined as total miles traveled by all vehicles, divided by: (1) the total number of vehicles (for average miles traveled per vehicle) or (2) the total number of households (for average miles traveled per household).

Average water conditions The amount and distribution of precipitation within a drainage basin and the run off conditions present as determined by reviewing the area water supply records over a long period of time.

Aviation gasoline (finished) A complex mixture of relatively volatile hydrocarbons with or without small quantities of additives, blended to form a fuel suitable for use in aviation reciprocating engines. Fuel specifications are provided in ASTM Specification D 910 and Military Specification MIL-G-5572. *Note:* Data on blending components are not counted in data on finished aviation gasoline.

Aviation gasoline blending components Naphthas that will be used for blending or compounding into finished aviation gasoline (e.g., straight run gasoline, alkylate, reformate, benzene, toluene, and xylene). Excludes oxygenates (alcohols, ethers), butane, and pentanes plus. Oxygenates are reported as other hydrocarbons, hydrogen, and oxygenates.

Backup fuel In a central heat pump system, the fuel used in the furnace that takes over the space heating when the outdoor temperature drops below that which is feasible to operate a heat pump.

Backup generator A generator that is used only for test purposes, or in the event of an emergency, such as a shortage of power needed to meet customer load requirements.

Backup power Electric energy supplied by a utility to replace power and energy lost during an unscheduled equipment outage.

Balancing authority (electric) The responsible entity that integrates resource plans ahead of time, maintains load-interchange-generation balance within a Balancing Authority Area, and supports Interconnection frequency in real time. (NERC definition)

Balancing item Represents differences between the sum of the components of natural gas supply and the sum of the components of natural gas disposition. These differences may be due to quantities lost or to the effects of data reporting problems. Reporting problems include differences due to the net result of conversions of flow data metered at varying temperature and pressure bases and converted to a standard temperature and pressure base; the effect of variations in company accounting and billing practices; differences between billing cycle and calendar period time frames; and imbalances resulting from the merger of data reporting systems that vary in scope, format, definitions, and type of respondents.

Barrel A unit of volume equal to 42 U.S. gallons.

Barrels per calendar day The amount of input that a distillation facility can process under usual operating conditions. The amount is expressed in terms of capacity during a 24-hour period and reduces the maximum processing capability of all units at the facility under continuous operation (see Barrels per Stream Day below) to account for the following limitations that may delay, interrupt, or slow down production.

1. the capability of downstream processing units to absorb the output of crude oil processing facilities of a given refinery. No reduction is necessary for intermediate streams that are distributed to other than downstream facilities as part of a refinery's normal operation;
2. the types and grades of inputs to be processed;
3. the types and grades of products expected to be manufactured;
4. the environmental constraints associated with refinery operations;
5. the reduction of capacity for scheduled downtime due to such conditions as routine inspection, maintenance, repairs, and turnaround; and
6. the reduction of capacity for unscheduled downtime due to such conditions as mechanical problems, repairs, and slowdowns.

Barrels per stream day The maximum number of barrels of input that a distillation facility can process within a 24-hour period when running at full capacity under optimal crude and product slate conditions with no allowance for downtime.

Base bill A charge calculated by taking the rate from the appropriate electric rate schedule and applying it to the level of consumption.

Base (cushion) gas The volume of gas needed as a permanent inventory to maintain adequate reservoir pressures and deliverability rates throughout the withdrawal season. All native gas is included in the base gas volume.

Base load The minimum amount of electric power delivered or required over a given period of time at a steady rate.

Base load capacity The generating equipment normally operated to serve loads on an around-the-clock basis.

Base load plant A plant, usually housing high-efficiency steam-electric units, which is normally operated to take all or part of the minimum load of a system, and which consequently produces electricity at an essentially constant rate and runs continuously. These units are operated to maximize system mechanical and thermal efficiency and minimize system operating costs.

Base period The period of time for which data used as the base of an index number, or other ratio, have been collected. This period is frequently one of a year but it may be as short as one day or as long as the average of a group of years. The length of the base period is governed by the nature of the material under review, the purpose for which the index number (or ratio) is being compiled, and the desire to use a period as free as possible from abnormal influences in order to avoid bias.

Base rate A fixed kilowatthour charge for electricity consumed that is independent of other charges and/or adjustments.

Baseboard heater As a type of heating equipment, a system in which either electric resistance coils or finned tubes carrying steam or hot water are mounted behind shallow panels along baseboards. Baseboards rely on passive convection to distribute heated air in the space. Electric baseboards are an example of an "Individual Space Heater." (Also see Individual Space Heater.)

bbl The abbreviation for barrel(s).

bbl/d The abbreviation for barrel(s) per day.

bbl/sd The abbreviation for barrel(s) per stream day

bcf The abbreviation for billion cubic feet.

Benzene (C₆H₆) An aromatic hydrocarbon present in small proportion in some crude oils and made commercially from petroleum by the catalytic reforming of naphthenes in petroleum naphtha. Also made from coal in the manufacture of coke. Used as a solvent in the manufacture of detergents, synthetic fibers, petrochemicals, and as a component of high-octane gasoline.

Bi-fuel vehicle A motor vehicle that operates on two different fuels, but not on a mixture of the fuels. Each fuel is stored in a separate tank.

Bilateral agreement A written statement signed by two parties that specifies the terms for exchanging energy.

Bilateral electricity contract A direct contract between an electric power producer and either a user or broker outside of a centralized power pool or power exchange.

Billing period The time between meter readings. It does not refer to the time when the bill was sent or when the payment was to have been received. In some cases, the billing period is the same as the billing cycle that corresponds closely (within several days) to meter-reading dates. For fuel oil and LPG, the billing period is the number of days between fuel deliveries.

Biodiesel A fuel typically made from soybean, canola, or other vegetable oils; animal fats; and recycled grease. It can serve as a substitute for petroleum-derived diesel or distillate fuel. For EIA reporting, it is a fuel composed of mono-alkyl esters of long chain fatty acids derived from vegetable oils or animal fats, designated B100, and meeting the requirements of ASTM (American Society for Testing & Materials) D 6751.

Biofuels Liquid fuels and blending components produced from biomass feedstocks, used primarily for transportation.

Biogenic Produced by biological processes of living organisms. Note: EIA uses the term "biogenic" to refer only to organic nonfossil material of biological origin.

Biomass Organic nonfossil material of biological origin constituting a renewable energy source.

Biomass-based diesel fuel Biodiesel and other renewable diesel fuel or diesel fuel blending components derived from biomass, but excluding renewable diesel fuel coprocessed with petroleum feedstocks.

Biomass gas A medium Btu gas containing methane and carbon dioxide, resulting from the action of microorganisms on organic materials such as a landfill.

Biomass waste Organic non-fossil material of biological origin that is a byproduct or a discarded product. "Biomass waste" includes municipal solid waste from biogenic sources, landfill gas, sludge waste, agricultural crop byproducts, straw, and other biomass solids, liquids, and gases; but excludes wood and wood-derived fuels (including black liquor), biofuels feedstock, biodiesel, and fuel ethanol. *Note*: EIA "biomass waste" data also include energy crops grown specifically for energy production, which would not normally constitute waste.

Bitumen A naturally occurring viscous mixture, mainly of hydrocarbons heavier than pentane, that may contain sulphur compounds and that, in its natural occurring viscous state, is not recoverable at a commercial rate through a well.

Bituminous coal A dense coal, usually black, sometimes dark brown, often with well-defined bands of bright and dull material, used primarily as fuel in steam-electric power generation, with substantial quantities also used for heat and power applications in manufacturing and to make coke. Bituminous coal is the most abundant coal in active U.S. mining regions. Its moisture content usually is less than 20 percent. The heat content of bituminous coal ranges from 21 to 30 million Btu per ton on a moist, mineral-matter-free basis. The heat content of bituminous coal consumed in the United States averages 24 million Btu per ton, on the as-received basis (i.e., containing both inherent moisture and mineral matter).

Black liquor A byproduct of the paper production process, alkaline spent liquor, that can be used as a source of energy. Alkaline spent liquor is removed from the digesters in the process of chemically pulping wood. After evaporation, the residual "black" liquor is burned as a fuel in a recovery furnace that permits the recovery of certain basic chemicals.

Black lung benefits In the content of the coal operation statement of income, this term refers to all payments, including taxes, made by the company attributable to Black Lung.

Blast furnace A furnace in which solid fuel (coke) is burned with an air blast to smelt ore.

Blast-furnace gas The waste combustible gas generated in a blast furnace when iron ore is being reduced with coke to metallic iron. It is commonly used as a fuel within steel works.

Blending components See Motor gasoline blending components.

Blending plant A facility that has no refining capability but is either capable of producing finished motor gasoline through mechanical blending or blends oxygenates with motor gasoline.

Block-rate structure An electric rate schedule with a provision for charging a different unit cost for various increasing blocks of demand for energy. A reduced rate may be charged on succeeding blocks.

BLS Bureau of Labor Statistics within the U.S. Department of Labor.

BOE The abbreviation for barrels of oil equivalent (used internationally).

Boiler A device for generating steam for power, processing, or heating purposes; or hot water for heating purposes or hot water supply. Heat from an external combustion source is transmitted to a fluid contained within the tubes found in the boiler shell. This fluid is delivered to an end-use at a desired pressure, temperature, and quality.

Boiler fuel An energy source to produce heat that is transferred to the boiler vessel in order to generate steam or hot water. Fossil fuel is the primary energy source used to produce heat for boilers.

Boiling-water reactor (BWR) A light-water reactor in which water, used as both coolant and moderator, is allowed to boil in the core. The resulting steam can be used directly to drive a turbine.

Bonded petroleum imports Petroleum imported and entered into Customs bonded storage. These imports are not included in the import statistics until they are: (1) withdrawn from storage free of duty for use as fuel for vessels and aircraft engaged in international trade; or (2) withdrawn from storage with duty paid for domestic use.

Bone coal Coal with a high ash content; it is dull in appearance, hard, and compact.

Book value The portion of the carrying value (other than the portion associated with tangible assets) prorated in each accounting period, for financial reporting purposes, to the extracted portion of an economic interest in a wasting natural resource.

Booked costs Costs allocated or assigned to interdepartmental or intracompany transactions, such as on-system or synthetic natural gas (SNG) production and company-owned gas used in gas operations and recorded in company books or records for accounting and/or regulatory purposes.

Borderline customer A customer located in the service area of one utility, but supplied by a neighboring utility through an arrangement between the utilities.

Bottled gas See Liquefied petroleum gases.

Bottled gas, LPG, or propane Any fuel gas supplied to a building in liquid form, such as liquefied petroleum gas, propane, or butane. It is usually delivered by tank truck and stored near the building in a tank or cylinder until used.

Bottom ash Residue mainly from the coal burning process that falls to the bottom of the boiler for removal and disposal.

Bottom-hole contribution A payment (either in cash or in acreage) that is required by agreement when a test well is drilled to a specified depth regardless of the outcome of the well and that is made in exchange for well and evaluation data.

Bottoming cycle A waste-heat recovery boiler recaptures the unused energy and uses it to produce steam to drive a steam turbine generator to produce electricity.

bp The abbreviation for boiling point.

Branded product A refined petroleum product sold by a refiner with the understanding that the purchaser has the right to resell the product under a trademark, trade name, service mark, or other identifying symbol or names owned by such refiner.

Break-even cutoff grade The lowest grade of material that can be mined and processed considering all applicable costs, without incurring a loss or gaining a profit.

Breccia A coarse-grained clastic rock, composed of angular broken rock fragments held together by a mineral cement or in a fine-grained matrix.

Breeder reactor A reactor that both produces and consumes fissionable fuel, especially one that creates more fuel than it consumes. The new fissionable material is created by a process known as breeding, in which neutrons from fission are captured in fertile materials.

Breeze The fine screenings from crushed coke. Usually breeze will pass through a 1/2-inch or 3/4-inch screen opening. It is most often used as a fuel source in the process of agglomerating iron ore.

British thermal unit The quantity of heat required to raise the temperature of 1 pound of liquid water by 1 degree Fahrenheit at the temperature at which water has its greatest density (approximately 39 degrees Fahrenheit).

Btu The abbreviation for British thermal unit(s).

Btu conversion factor A factor for converting energy data between one unit of measurement and British thermal units (Btu). Btu conversion factors are generally used to convert energy data from physical units of measure (such as barrels, cubic feet, or short tons) into the energy-equivalent measure of Btu. (See http://www.eia.doe.gov/emeu/mer/append_a.html for further information on Btu conversion factors.)

Btu per cubic foot The total heating value, expressed in Btu, produced by the combustion, at constant pressure, of the amount of the gas that would occupy a volume of 1 cubic foot at a temperature of 60 degrees F if saturated with water vapor and under a pressure equivalent to that of 30 inches of mercury at 32 degrees F and under standard gravitational force (980.665 cm. per sec. squared) with air of the same temperature and pressure as the gas, when the products of combustion are cooled to the initial temperature of gas and air when the water formed by combustion is condensed to the liquid state. (Sometimes called gross heating value or total heating value.)

BTX The acronym for the commercial petroleum aromatics—benzene, toluene, and xylene. See individual categories for definitions.

Budget plan An agreement between the household and the utility company or fuel supplier that allows the household to pay the same amount for fuel for each month for a number of months.

Building shell conservation feature A building feature designed to reduce energy loss or gain through the shell or envelope of the building. Data collected by EIA on the following specific building shell energy conservation features: roof, ceiling, or wall insulation; storm windows or double- or triple-paned glass (multiple glazing); tinted or reflective glass or shading films; exterior or interior shadings or awnings; and weather stripping or caulking. (See Roof or Ceiling Insulation, Wall Insulation, Reflective or Shading Glass or Film, Storm Windows or Triple-Paned Glass, Building Shell (Envelope), Exterior or Interior Shadings or Awnings, and Weather Stripping or Caulking.)

Building shell (envelope) DSM program A DSM program that promotes reduction of energy consumption through improvements to the building envelope. Includes installations of insulation, weatherstripping, caulking, window film, and window replacement. (Also see DSM, Demand-Side Management Programs.)

Built-in electric units An individual-resistance electric-heating unit that is permanently installed in the floors, walls, ceilings, or baseboards and is part of the electrical installation of the building. Electric-heating devices that are plugged into an electric socket or outlet are not considered built in. (Also see Heating Equipment.)

Bulk power transactions The wholesale sale, purchase, and interchange of electricity among electric utilities. Bulk power transactions are used by electric utilities for many different aspects of electric utility operations, from maintaining load to reducing costs.

Bulk sales Wholesale sales of gasoline in individual transactions which exceed the size of a truckload.

Bulk station A facility used primarily for the storage and/or marketing of petroleum products, which has a total bulk storage capacity of less than 50,000 barrels and receives its petroleum products by tank car or truck.

Bulk terminal A facility used primarily for the storage and/or marketing of petroleum products, which has a total bulk storage capacity of 50,000 barrels or more and/or receives petroleum products by tanker, barge, or pipeline.

Bundled utility service (electric) A means of operation whereby energy, transmission, and distribution services, as well as ancillary and retail services, are provided by one entity.

Bunker fuels Fuel supplied to ships and aircraft, both domestic and foreign, consisting primarily of residual and distillate fuel oil for ships and kerosene-based jet fuel for aircraft. The term "international bunker fuels" is used to denote the consumption of fuel for international transport activities. Note: For the purposes of greenhouse gas emissions inventories, data on emissions from combustion of international bunker fuels are subtracted from national emissions totals. Historically, bunker fuels have meant only ship fuel.

Burn days The number of days the station could continue to operate by burning coal already on hand assuming no additional deliveries of coal and an average consumption rate.

Burnup Amount of thermal energy generated per unit mass of fuel, expressed as Gigawatt-Days Thermal per Metric Ton of Initial Heavy Metal (GWDT/MTIHM), rounded to the nearest gigawatt day.

Bus An electrical conductor that serves as a common connection for two or more electrical circuits.

Butane (C_4H_{10}) A normally gaseous straight-chain or branch-chain hydrocarbon extracted from hydrocarbon extracted from natural gas or refinery gas streams. It includes isobutane and normal butane and is designated in ASTM Specification D1835 and Gas Processors Association Specifications for commercial butane.

Butylene (C_4H_8) An olefinic hydrocarbon recovered from refinery processes.

Buy-back oil Crude oil acquired from a host government whereby a portion of the government's ownership interest in the crude oil produced in that country may or should be purchased by the producing firm.

Bypassed footage Bypassed footage is the footage in that section of hole that is abandoned as the result of remedial sidetrack drilling operations.

Byproduct A secondary or additional product resulting from the feedstock use of energy or the processing of nonenergy materials. For example, the more common byproducts of coke ovens are coal gas, tar, and a mixture of benzene, toluene, and xylenes (BTX).

C_4H A mixture of light hydrocarbons that have the general formula C_4H_n, where **n** is the number of hydrogen atoms per molecule. Examples include butane (C_4H_{10}) and butylene (C_4H_8).

Calcination A process in which a material is heated to a high temperature without fusing, so that hydrates, carbonates, or other compounds are decomposed and the volatile material is expelled.

Calcium sulfate A white crystalline salt, insoluble in water. Used in Keene's cement, in pigments, as a paper filler, and as a drying agent.

Calcium sulfite A white powder, soluble in diluted sulfuric acid. Used in the sulfite process for the manufacture of wood pulp.

California Power Exchange A State-chartered, non-profit corporation which provides day-ahead and hour-ahead markets for energy and ancillary services in accordance with the power exchange tariff. The power exchange is a scheduling coordinator and is independent of both the independent system operator and all other market participants.

Canadian deuterium uranium reactor (CANDU) Uses heavy water or deuterium oxide (D_2O), rather than light water (H_2O), as the coolant and moderator. Deuterium is an isotope of hydrogen that has a different neutron absorption spectrum from that of ordinary hydrogen. In a deuterium-moderated-reactor, fuel made from natural uranium (0.71 U-235) can sustain a chain reaction.

Cannel coal A compact, tough variety of coal, originating from organic spore residues, that is non-caking, contains a high percentage of volatile matter, ignites easily, and burns with a luminous smoky flame.

Capable of being fueled A vehicle is capable of being fueled by a particular fuel(s) if that vehicle has the engine components in place to make operation possible on the fuel(s). The vehicle does not necessarily have to run on the fuel(s) in order for that vehicle to be considered capable of being fueled by the fuel(s). For example, a vehicle that is equipped to operate on either gasoline or natural gas but normally operates on gasoline is considered to be capable of being fueled by gasoline and natural gas.

Capacity See Generator capacity and Generator name plate capacity (installed).

Capacity (purchased) The amount of energy and capacity available for purchase from outside the system.

Capacity charge An element in a two-part pricing method used in capacity transactions (energy charge is the other element). The capacity charge, sometimes called *Demand Charge*, is assessed on the amount of capacity being purchased.

Capacity factor The ratio of the electrical energy produced by a generating unit for the period of time considered to the electrical energy that could have been produced at continuous full power operation during the same period.

Capacity transaction The acquisition of a specified quantity of generating capacity from another utility for a specified period of time. The utility selling the power is obligated to make available to the buyer a specified quantity of power.

Capacity utilization Capacity utilization is computed by dividing production by productive capacity and multiplying by 100.

Capital cost The cost of field development and plant construction and the equipment required for industry operations.

Capital stock Property, plant and equipment used in the production, processing and distribution of energy resources.

Captive coal Coal produced to satisfy the needs of the mine owner, or of a parent, subsidiary, or other affiliate of the mine owner (for example, steel companies and electricity generators), rather than for open market sale.

Captive refinery MTBE plants MTBE (methyl tertiary butyl ether) production facilities primarily located within refineries. These integrated refinery units produce MTBE from Fluid Cat Cracker isobutylene with production dedicated to internal gasoline blending requirements.

Captive refinery oxygenate plants Oxygenate production facilities located within or adjacent to a refinery complex.

Carbon black An amorphous form of carbon, produced commercially by thermal or oxidative decomposition of hydrocarbons and used principally in rubber goods, pigments, and printer's ink.

Carbon budget The balance of the exchanges (incomes and losses) of carbon between carbon sinks (e.g., atmosphere and biosphere) in the carbon cycle. Also see Carbon cycle and Carbon sink below.

Carbon cycle All carbon sinks and exchanges of carbon from one sink to another by various chemical, physical, geological, and biological processes. Also see Carbon sink below.

Carbon dioxide (CO_2) A colorless, odorless, non-poisonous gas that is a normal part of Earth's atmosphere. Carbon dioxide is a product of fossil-fuel combustion as well as other processes. It is considered a greenhouse gas as it traps heat (infrared energy) radiated by the Earth into the atmosphere and thereby contributes to the potential for global warming. The global warming potential (GWP) of other greenhouse gases is measured in relation to that of carbon dioxide, which by international scientific convention is assigned a value of one (1). Also see Global warming potential (GWP) and Greenhouse gases.

Carbon dioxide equivalent The amount of carbon dioxide by weight emitted into the atmosphere that would produce the same estimated radiative forcing as a given weight of another radiatively active gas. Carbon dioxide equivalents are computed by multiplying the weight of the gas being measured (for example, methane) by its estimated global warming potential (which is 21 for methane). "Carbon equivalent units" are defined as carbon dioxide equivalents multiplied by the carbon content of carbon dioxide (i.e., 12/44).

Carbon flux See Carbon budget above.

Carbon intensity The amount of carbon by weight emitted per unit of energy consumed. A common measure of carbon intensity is weight of carbon per British thermal unit (Btu) of energy. When there is only one fossil fuel under consideration, the carbon intensity and the emissions coefficient are identical. When there are several fuels, carbon intensity is based on their combined emissions coefficients weighted by their energy consumption levels. Also see Emissions coefficient and Carbon output rate.

Carbon output rate The amount of carbon by weight per kilowatthour of electricity produced.

Carbon sequestration The fixation of atmospheric carbon dioxide in a carbon sink through biological or physical processes.

Carbon sink A reservoir that absorbs or takes up released carbon from another part of the carbon cycle. The four sinks, which are regions of the Earth within which carbon behaves in a systematic manner, are the atmosphere, terrestrial biosphere (usually including freshwater systems), oceans, and sediments (including fossil fuels).

Carburetor A fuel delivery device for producing a proper mixture of gasoline vapor and air and for delivering it to the intake manifold of an internal combustion engine. Gasoline is gravity-fed from a reservoir bowl into a throttle bore, where it is allowed to evaporate into the stream of air being inducted by the engine. Also see Diesel Fuel System and Fuel Injection.

Carrying costs Costs incurred in order to retain exploration and property rights after acquisition but before production has occurred. Such costs include legal costs for title defense, ad valorem taxes on non-producing mineral properties, shut-in royalties, and delay rentals.

Cash and carry Kerosene, fuel oil, or bottled gas (tank or propane) purchased with cash, by check, or by credit card and taken home by the purchaser. The purchaser provides the container or pays extra for the container.

Casinghead gas (or oil well gas) Natural gas produced along with crude oil from oil wells. It contains either dissolved or associated gas or both.

Cast silicon Crystalline silicon obtained by pouring pure molten silicon into a vertical mold and adjusting the temperature gradient along the mold volume during cooling to obtain slow, vertically advancing crystallization of the silicon. The polycrystalline ingot thus formed is composed of large, relatively parallel, interlocking crystals. The cast ingots are sawed into wafers for further fabrication into photovoltaic cells. Cast silicon wafers and ribbon silicon sheets fabricated into cells are usually referred to as polycrystalline photovoltaic cells.

Catalyst coke In many catalytic operations (e.g., catalytic cracking), carbon is deposited on the catalyst, thus deactivating the catalyst. The catalyst is reactivated by burning off the carbon, which is used as a fuel in the refining process. This carbon or coke is not recoverable in a concentrated form.

Catalytic converter A device containing a catalyst for converting automobile exhaust into mostly harmless products.

Catalytic cracking The refining process of breaking down the larger, heavier, and more complex hydrocarbon molecules into simpler and lighter molecules. Catalytic cracking is accomplished by the use of a catalytic agent and is an effective process for increasing the yield of gasoline from crude oil. Catalytic cracking processes fresh feeds and recycled feeds.

Catalytic hydrocracking A refining process that uses hydrogen and catalysts with relatively low temperatures and high pressures for converting middle boiling or residual material to high octane gasoline, reformer charge stock, jet fuel, and/or high grade fuel oil. The process uses one or more catalysts, depending on product output, and can handle high sulfur feedstocks without prior desulfurization.

Catalytic hydrotreating A refining process for treating petroleum fractions from atmospheric or vacuum distillation units (e.g., naphthas, middle distillates, reformer feeds, residual fuel oil, and heavy gas oil) and other petroleum (e.g., cat cracked naphtha, coker naphtha, gas oil, etc.) in the presence of catalysts and substantial quantities of hydrogen. Hydrotreating includes desulfurization, removal of substances (e.g., nitrogen compounds) that deactivate catalysts, conversion of olefins to paraffins to reduce gum formation in gasoline, and other processes to upgrade the quality of the fractions.

Catalytic reforming A refining process using controlled heat and pressure with catalysts to rearrange certain hydrocarbon molecules, thereby converting paraffinic and naphthenic type hydrocarbons (e.g., low octane gasoline boiling range fractions) into petrochemical feedstocks and higher octane stocks suitable for blending into finished gasoline. Catalytic reforming is reported in two categories. They are:

- Low Pressure. A processing unit operating at less than 225 pounds per square inch gauge (PSIG) measured at the outlet separator.
- High Pressure. A processing unit operating at either equal to or greater than 225 pounds per square inch gauge (PSIG) measured at the outlet separator.

CDD See Cooling degree-days below.

Cells Refers to the un-encapsulated semiconductor components of the module that convert the solar energy to electricity.

Cells to OEM (non-PV) Cells shipped to non-photovoltaic original equipment manufacturers such as boat manufacturers, car manufacturers, etc.

Census division Any of nine geographic areas of the United States as defined by the U.S. Department of Commerce, Bureau of the Census. The divisions, each consisting of several States, are defined as follows:
- New England: Connecticut, Maine, Massachusetts, New Hampshire, Rhode Island, and Vermont;
- Middle Atlantic: New Jersey, New York, and Pennsylvania;
- East North Central: Illinois, Indiana, Michigan, Ohio, and Wisconsin;
- West North Central: Iowa, Kansas, Minnesota, Missouri, Nebraska, North Dakota, and South Dakota;
- South Atlantic: Delaware, District of Columbia, Florida, Georgia, Maryland, North Carolina, South Carolina, Virginia, and West Virginia;
- East South Central: Alabama, Kentucky, Mississippi, and Tennessee;
- West South Central: Arkansas, Louisiana, Oklahoma, and Texas;
- Mountain: Arizona, Colorado, Idaho, Montana, Nevada, New Mexico, Utah, and Wyoming;
- Pacific: Alaska, California, Hawaii, Oregon, and Washington.

Note: Each division is a sub-area within a broader Census Region. For the relationship between Regions and divisions, see Census Region/division below. In some cases, the Pacific division is subdivided into the Pacific Contiguous area (California, Oregon, and Washington) and the Pacific Noncontiguous area (Alaska and Hawaii).

Census Region Any of four geographic areas of the United States as defined by the U.S. Department of Commerce, Bureau of the Census. The Regions, each consisting of various States selected according to population size and physical location, are defined as follows:
- Northeast: Connecticut, Maine, Massachusetts, New Hampshire, New Jersey, New York, Pennsylvania, Rhode Island, and Vermont.
- South: Alabama, Arkansas, Delaware, District of Columbia, Florida, Georgia, Kentucky, Louisiana, Maryland, Mississippi, North Carolina, Oklahoma, South Carolina, Tennessee, Texas, Virginia, and West Virginia.
- Midwest: Illinois, Indiana, Iowa, Kansas, Michigan, Minnesota, Missouri, Nebraska, North Dakota, Ohio, South Dakota, and Wisconsin.
- West: Alaska, Arizona, California, Colorado, Hawaii, Idaho, Montana, Nevada, New Mexico, Oregon, Utah, Washington, and Wyoming.

Note: Each region comprises two or three sub-areas called Census divisions. For the relationship between Regions and divisions, see Census Region/division below.

Census Region/division An hierarchical organization of the **United States** according to geographic areas and sub-areas as follows:

Northeast Region
  New England division
  Middle Atlantic division
South Region
  South Atlantic division
  East South Central division
  West South Central division
Midwest Region
  East North Central division
  West North Central division
West Region
  Mountain division
  Pacific division

Note: In some cases, the Pacific division is subdivided into the Pacific Contiguous area (California, Oregon, and Washington) and the Pacific Noncontiguous area (Alaska and Hawaii).

Central chiller Any centrally located air conditioning system that produces chilled water in order to cool air. The chilled water or cold air is then distributed throughout the building, using pipes or air ducts or both. These systems are also commonly known as "chillers," "centrifugal chillers," "reciprocating chillers," or "absorption chillers." Chillers are generally located in or just outside the building they serve. Buildings receiving district chilled water are served by chillers located at central physical plants.

Central cooling Cooling of an entire building with a refrigeration unit to condition the air. Typically central chillers and ductwork are present in the centrally cooled building.

Central physical plant A plant owned by, and on the grounds of, a multibuilding facility that provides district heating, district cooling, or electricity to other buildings on the same facility. To qualify as a central plant it must provide district heat, district chilled water, or electricity to at least one other building. The central physical plant may be by itself in a separate building or may be located in a building where other activities occur.

Central warm air furnace A type of space heating equipment where a central combustor or resistance unit generally using gas, fuel oil, or electricity provides warm air through ducts leading to the various rooms. Heat pumps are not included in this category. A forced air furnace is one in which a fan is used to force the air through the ducts. In a gravity furnace, air is circulated by gravity, relying on the natural flow of warm air up and cold air down; the warm air rises through ducts and the cold air falls through ducts that return it to the furnace to be reheated and this completes the circulation cycle.

Centralized water heating system Equipment, to heat and store water for other than space heating purposes, which provides hot water from a single location for distribution throughout a building. A residential type tank water heater is a good example of a centralized water heater.

Certificate A type of permit for public convenience and necessity issued by a utility commission, which authorizes a utility or regulated company to engage in business, construct facilities, provide some services, or abandon service.

Certificate requirement The maximum annual volume allowed for sales to resale or direct sale customers under certificate authorizations by the Federal Energy Regulatory Commission.

Cesspool An underground reservoir for liquid waste, typically household sewage.

CFC See Chlorofluorocarbon below.

cfs Cubic feet per second.

Chained dollars A measure used to express real prices. Real prices are those that have been adjusted to remove the effect of changes in the purchasing power of the dollar; they usually reflect buying power relative to a reference year. Prior to 1996, real prices were expressed in constant dollars, a measure based on the weights of goods and services in a single year, usually a recent year. In 1996, the U.S. Department of Commerce introduced the chained-dollar measure. The new measure is based on the average weights of goods and services in successive pairs of years. It is "chained" because the second year in each pair, with its weights, becomes the first year of the next pair. The advantage of using the chained-dollar measure is that it is more closely related to any given period covered and is therefore subject to less distortion over time.

Characterization Sampling, monitoring, and analysis activities to determine the extent and nature of contamination at a facility or site. Characterization provides the necessary technical information to develop, screen, analyze, and select appropriate cleanup techniques.

Charge capacity The input (feed) capacity of the refinery processing facilities.

Chemical separation A process for extracting uranium and plutonium from dissolved spent nuclear fuel and irradiated targets. The fission products that are left behind are high-level waste. Chemical separation is also known as reprocessing.

Chlorofluorocarbon (CFC) Any of various compounds consisting of carbon, hydrogen, chlorine, and flourine used as refrigerants. CFCs are now thought to be harmful to the earth's atmosphere.

Christmas tree The valves and fittings installed at the top of a gas or oil well to control and direct the flow of well fluids.

CIF (cargo, insurance and freight) CIF refers to cargos for which the seller pays for the transportation and insurance up to the port of destination.

CIF (cost, insurance, freight) This term refers to a type of sale in which the buyer of the product agrees to pay a unit price that includes the f.o.b. value of the product at the point of origin plus all costs of insurance and transporation. This type of a transaction differs from a "delivered" purchase, in that the buyer accepts the quantity as determined at the loading port (as certified by the Bill of Lading and Quality Report) rather than pay based on the quantity and quality ascertained at the unloading port. It is similar to the terms of an f.o.b. sale, except that the seller, as a service for which he is compensated, arranges for transportation and insurance.

Circuit A conductor or a system of conductors through which electric current flows.

Circuit-mile The total length in miles of separate circuits regardless of the number of conductors used per circuit.

Citygate A point or measuring station at which a distributing gas utility receives gas from a natural gas pipeline company or transmission system.

Class rate schedule An electric rate schedule applicable to one or more specified classes of service, groups of businesses, or customer uses.

Classes of service Customers grouped by similar characteristics in order to be identified for the purpose of setting a common rate for electric service. Usually classified into groups identified as residential, commercial, industrial, and other.

Clean Development Mechanism (CDM) A Kyoto Protocol program that enables industrialized countries to finance emissions-avoiding projects in developing countries and receive credit for reductions achieved against their own emissions limitation targets. Also see Kyoto Protocol.

Climate change A term used to refer to all forms of climatic inconsistency, but especially to significant change from one prevailing climatic condition to another. In some cases, "climate change" has been used synonymously with the term "global warming"; scientists, however, tend to use the term in a wider sense inclusive of natural changes in climate, including climatic cooling.

Clinker Powdered cement, produced by heating a properly proportioned mixture of finely ground raw materials (calcium carbonate, silica, alumina, and iron oxide) in a kiln to a temperature of about 2,700 degrees Fahrenheit.

Cloud condensation nuclei Aerosol particles that provide a platform for the condensation of water vapor, resulting in clouds with higher droplet concentrations and increased albedo.

CO control period ("seasons") The portion of the year in which a CO nonattainment area is prone to high ambient levels of carbon monoxide. This portion of the year is to be specified by the Environmental Protection Agency but is to be not less than 4 months in length.

Coal A readily combustible black or brownish-black rock whose composition, including inherent moisture, consists of more than 50 percent by weight and more than 70 percent by volume of carbonaceous material. It is formed from plant remains that have been compacted, hardened, chemically altered, and metamorphosed by heat and pressure over geologic time.

Coal analysis Determines the composition and properties of coal so it can be ranked and used most effectively.

- **Proximate analysis** determines, on an as-received basis, the moisture content, volatile matter (gases released when coal is heated), fixed carbon (solid fuel left after the volatile matter is driven off), and ash (impurities consisting of silica, iron, alumina, and other incombustible matter). The moisture content affects the ease with which coal can be handled and burned. The amount of volatile matter and fixed carbon provides guidelines for determining the intensity of the heat produced. Ash increases the weight of coal, adds to the cost of handling, and can cause problems such as clinkering and slagging in boilers and furnaces.

- **Ultimate analysis** determines the amount of carbon, hydrogen, oxygen, nitrogen, and sulfur. Heating value is determined in terms of Btu, both on an as received basis (including moisture) and on a dry basis.

- **Agglomerating** refers to coal that softens when heated and forms a hard gray coke; this coal is called caking coal. Not all caking coals are coking coals. The agglomerating value is used to differentiate between coal ranks and also is a guide to determine how a particular coal reacts in a furnace.

- **Agglutinating** refers to the binding qualities of a coal. The agglutinating value is an indication of how well a coke made from a particular coal will perform in a blast furnace. It is also called a caking index.

- **Other tests** include the determination of the ash softening temperature, the ash fusion temperature (the temperature at which the ash forms clinkers or slag), the free swelling index (a guide to a coal's coking characteristics), the Gray King test (which determines the suitability of coal for making coke), and the Hardgrove grindability index (a measure of the ease with which coal can be pulverized). In a petrographic analysis, thin sections of coal or highly polished blocks of coal are studied with a microscope to determine the physical composition, both for scientific purposes and for estimating the rank and coking potential.

Coal bed A bed or stratum of coal. Also called a coal seam.

Coal bed degasification This refers to the removal of methane or coal bed gas from a coal mine before or during mining.

Coal bed methane Methane is generated during coal formation and is contained in the coal microstructure. Typical recovery entails pumping water out of the coal to allow the gas to escape. Methane is the principal component of natural gas. Coal bed methane can be added to natural gas pipelines without any special treatment.

Coal briquets Anthracite, bituminous, and lignite briquets comprise the secondary solid fuels manufactured from coal by a process in which the coal is partly dried, warmed to expel excess moisture, and then compressed into briquets, usually without the use of a binding substance. In the reduction of briquets to coal equivalent, different conversion factors are applied according to their origin from hard coal, peat, brown coal, or lignite.

Coal carbonized The amount of coal decomposed into solid coke and gaseous products by heating in a coke oven in a limited air supply or in the absence of air.

Coal chemicals Coal chemicals are obtained from the gases and vapor recovered from the manufacturing of coke. Generally, crude tar, ammonia, crude light oil, and gas are the basic products recovered. They are refined or processed to yield a variety of chemical materials.

Coal coke See Coke (coal) below.

Coal consumption The quantity of coal burned for the generation of electric power (in short tons), including fuel used for maintenance of standby service.

Coal delivered Coal which has been delivered from the coal supplier to any site belonging to the electric power company.

Coal exports Amount of U.S. coal shipped to foreign destinations, as reported in the U.S. Department of Commerce, Bureau of Census, "Monthly Report EM 545."

Coal face This is the exposed area from which coal is extracted.

Coal financial reporting regions A geographic classification of areas with coal resources which is used for financial reporting of coal statistics.

- Eastern Region. Consists of the Appalachian Coal Basin. The following comprise the Eastern Region: Alabama, eastern Kentucky, Georgia, Maryland, Mississippi, Ohio, Pennsylvania, Virginia, Tennessee, North Carolina, and West Virginia.
- Midwest Region. Consists of the Illinois and Michigan Coal Basins. The following comprise the Midwest Region: Illinois, Indiana, Michigan, and western Kentucky.
- Western Region. Consists of the Northern Rocky, Southern Rocky, West Coast Coal Basins and Western Interior. The following comprise the Western Region: Alaska, Arizona, Arkansas, California, Colorado, Idaho, Iowa, Kansas, Louisiana, Missouri, Montana, New Mexico, North Dakota, Oklahoma, Oregon, Texas, South Dakota, Utah, Washington, and Wyoming.

Coal fines Coal with a maximum particle size usually less than one-sixteenth inch and rarely above one-eighth inch.

Coal gas Substitute natural gas produced synthetically by the chemical reduction of coal at a coal gasification facility.

Coal gasification The process of converting coal into gas. The basic process involves crushing coal to a powder, which is then heated in the presence of steam and oxygen to produce a gas. The gas is then refined to reduce sulfur and other impurities. The gas can be used as a fuel or processed further and concentrated into chemical or liquid fuel.

Coal grade This classification refers to coal quality and use.

- *Briquettes* are made from compressed coal dust, with or without a binding agent such as asphalt.
- *Cleaned coal or prepared coal* has been processed to reduce the amount of impurities present and improve the burning characteristics.
- *Compliance coal* is a coal, or a blend of coal, that meets sulfur dioxide emission standards for air quality without the need for flue-gas desulfurization.
- *Culm and silt* are waste materials from preparation plants. In the anthracite region, culm consists of coarse rock fragments containing as much as 30 percent small-sized coal. Silt is a mixture of very fine coal particles (approximately 40 percent) and rock dust that has settled out from waste water from the plants. The terms culm and silt are sometimes used interchangeably and are sometimes called refuse. Culm and silt have a heat value ranging from 8 to 17 million Btu per ton.
- *Low-sulfur coal* generally contains 1 percent or less sulfur by weight. For air quality standards, "low sulfur coal" contains 0.6 pounds or less sulfur per million Btu, which is equivalent to 1.2 pounds of sulfur dioxide per million Btu.
- *Metallurgical coal (or coking coal)* meets the requirements for making coke. It must have a low ash and sulfur content and form a coke that is capable of supporting the charge of iron ore and limestone in a blast furnace. A blend of two or more bituminous coals is usually required to make coke.
- *Pulverized coal* is a coal that has been crushed to a fine dust in a grinding mill. It is blown into the combustion zone of a furnace and burns very rapidly and efficiently.
- *Slack coal* usually refers to bituminous coal one-half inch or smaller in size.
- *Steam coal* refers to coal used in boilers to generate steam to produce electricity or for other purposes.
- *Stoker coal* refers to coal that has been crushed to specific sizes (but not powdered) for burning on a grate in automatic firing equipment.

Coal imports Amount of foreign coal shipped to the United States, as reported in the U.S. Department of Commerce, Bureau of the Census, "Monthly Report IM 145."

Coal liquefaction A chemical process that converts coal into clean-burning liquid hydrocarbons, such as synthetic crude oil and methanol.

Coal mining productivity Coal mining productivity is calculated by dividing total coal production by the total direct labor hours worked by all mine employees.

Coal preparation The process of sizing and cleaning coal to meet market specifications by removing impurities such as rock, sulfur, etc. It may include crushing, screening, or mechanical cleaning.

Coal producing districts A classification of coal fields defined in the Bituminous Coal Act of 1937. The districts were originally established to aid in formulating minimum prices of bituminous and sub-bituminous coal and lignite. Because much statistical information was compiled in terms of these districts, their use for statistical purposes has continued since the abandonment of that legislation in 1943. District 24 was added for the anthracite-producing district in Pennsylvania.

Coal-Producing Regions A geographic classification of areas where coal is produced.

Appalachian Region Consists of Alabama, Eastern Kentucky, Maryland, Ohio, Pennsylvania, Tennessee, Virginia, and West Virginia.

Northern Appalachian Region Consists of Maryland, Ohio, Pennsylvania, and Northern West Virginia.

Central Appalachian Region Consists of Eastern Kentucky, Virginia, Southern West Virginia, and the Tennessee counties of: Anderson, Campbell, Claiborne, Cumberland, Fentress, Morgan, Overton, Pickett, Putnam, Roane, and Scott.

Southern Appalachian Region Consists of Alabama, and the Tennessee counties of: Bledsoe, Coffee, Franklin, Grundy, Hamilton, Marion, Rhea, Sequatchie, Van Buren, Warren, and White.

Interior Region (with Gulf Coast) Consists of Arkansas, Illinois, Indiana, Kansas, Louisiana, Mississippi, Missouri, Oklahoma, Texas, and Western Kentucky.

Illinois Basin Consists of Illinois, Indiana, and Western Kentucky.

Western Region Consists of Alaska, Arizona, Colorado, Montana, New Mexico, North Dakota, Utah, Washington, and Wyoming.

Powder River Basin Consists of the Montana counties of Big Horn, Custer, Powder River, Rosebud, and Treasure and the Wyoming counties of Campbell, Converse, Crook, Johnson, Natrona, Niobrara, Sheridan, and Weston.

Uinta Basin Consists of the Colorado counties of Delta, Garfield, Gunnison, Mesa, Moffat, Pitkin, Rio Blanco, Routt and the Utah counties of Carbon, Duchesne, Emery, Grand, Sanpete, Sevier, Uintah, Utah, and Wasatch.

Coal-Producing States The States where mined and/or purchased coal originates are defined as follows: Alabama, Alaska, Arizona, Arkansas, Colorado, Illinois, Indiana, Kansas, Kentucky Eastern, Kentucky Western, Louisiana, Maryland, Mississippi, Missouri, Montana, New Mexico, North Dakota, Ohio, Oklahoma, Pennsylvania anthracite, Pennsylvania bituminous, Tennessee, Texas, Utah, Virginia, Washington, West Virginia Northern, West Virginia Southern, and Wyoming.

The following coal-producing States are split in origin of coal, as defined by:

Kentucky, Eastern All mines in the following counties in Eastern Kentucky: Bell, Boyd, Breathitt, Carter, Clay, Clinton, Elliot, Estill, Floyd, Greenup, Harlan, Jackson, Johnson, Knott, Knox, Laurel, Lawrence, Lee, Leslie, Letcher, Lewis, Magoffin, Martin, McCreary, Menifee, Morgan, Owsley, Perry, Pike, Powell, Pulaski, Rockcastle, Rowan, Wayne, Whitley, and Wolfe.

Kentucky, Western All mines in the following counties in Western Kentucky: Breckinridge, Butler, Caldwell, Christian, Crittenden, Daviess, Edmonson, Grayson, Hancock, Hart, Henderson, Hopkins, Logan, McLean, Muhlenberg, Ohio, Todd, Union, Warren, and Webster.

Pennsylvania Anthracite All mines in the following counties: Carbon, Columbia, Dauphin, Lackawanna, Lebanon, Luzerne, Northumberland, Schuylkill, Sullivan, and Susquehanna. All anthracite mines in Bradford County.

Pennsylvania Bituminous All mines located in the following counties: Allegheny, Armstrong, Beaver, Bedford, Butler, Cambria, Clarion, Clearfield, Elk, Fayette, Greene, Indiana, Jefferson, Lawrence, Lycoming, Somerset, Venango, Washington, and Westmoreland, and all bituminous mines in Bradford County.

West Virginia, Northern All mines in the following counties (formerly defined as Coal-Producing Districts 1, 3, & 6): Barbour, Brooke, Braxton, Calhoun, Doddridge, Gilmer, Grant, Hancock, Harrison, Jackson, Lewis, Marion, Marshall, Mineral, Monongalia, Ohio, Pleasants, Preston, Randolph, Ritchie, Roane, Taylor, Tucker, Tyler, Upshur, Webster, Wetzel, Wirt, and Wood.

West Virginia, Southern All mines in the following counties (formerly Defined as Coal-Producing Districts 7 & 8): Boone, Cabell, Clay, Fayette, Greenbrier, Kanawha, Lincoln, Logan, Mason, McDowell, Mercer, Mingo, Nicholas, Pocahontas, Putnam, Raleigh, Summers, Wayne, and Wyoming.

Coal production The sum of sales, mine consumption, issues to miners, and issues to coke, briquetting, and other ancillary plants at mines. Production data include quantities extracted from surface and underground mines, and normally exclude wastes removed at mines or associated reparation plants.

Coal rank The classification of coals according to their degree of progressive alteration from lignite to anthracite. In the United States, the standard ranks of coal include lignite, subbituminous coal, bituminous coal, and anthracite and are based on fixed carbon, volatile matter, heating value, and agglomerating (or caking) properties.

Coal sampling The collection and proper storage and handling of a relatively small quantity of coal for laboratory analysis. Sampling may be done for a wide range of purposes, such as: coal resource exploration and assessment, characterization of the reserves or production of a mine, to characterize the results of coal cleaning processes, to monitor coal shipments or receipts for adherence to coal quality contract specifications, or to subject a coal to specific combustion or reactivity tests related to the customer's intended use.

During pre-development phases, such as exploration and resource assessment, sampling typically is from natural outcrops, test pits, old or existing mines in the region, drill cuttings, or drilled cores. Characterization of a mine's reserves or production may use sample collection in the mine, representative cuts from coal conveyors or from handling and loading equipment, or directly from stockpiles or shipments (coal rail cars or barges). Contract specifications rely on sampling from the production flow at the mining or coal handling facility or at the loadout, or from the incoming shipments at the receiver's facility. In all cases, the value of a sample taken depends on its being representative of the coal under consideration, which in turn requires that appropriate sampling procedures be carefully followed.

For coal resource and estimated reserve characterization, appropriate types of samples include:

- **Face channel or channel sample** a sample taken at the exposed coal in a mine by cutting away any loose or weathered coal then collecting on a clean surface a sample of the coal seam by chopping out a channel of uniform width and depth; a face channel or face sample is taken at or near the working face, the most freshly exposed coal where actual removal and loading of mined coal is taking place. Any partings greater than 3/8 inch and/or mineral concretions greater than 1/2 inch thick and 2 inches in maximum diameter are normally discarded from a channel sample so as better to represent coal that has been mined, crushed, and screened to remove at least gross non-coal materials.
- **Column sample** a channel or drill core sample taken to represent the entire geologic coalbed; it includes all partings and impurities that may exist in the coalbed.
- **Bench sample** a face or channel sample taken of just that contiguous portion of a coalbed that is considered practical to mine, also known as a "bench." For example, bench samples may be taken of minable coal where impure coal that makes up part of the geologic coalbed is likely to be left in the mine, or where thick partings split the coal into two or more distinct minable seams, or where extremely thick coalbeds cannot be recovered by normal mining equipment, so that the coal is mined in multiple passes, or benches, usually defined along natural bedding planes.
- **Composite sample** a recombined coalbed sample produced by averaging together thickness-weighted coal analyses from partial samples of the coalbed, such as from one or more bench samples, from one or more mine exposures or outcrops where the entire bed could not be accessed in one sample, or from multiple drill cores that were required to retrieve all local sections of a coal seam.

Coal stocks Coal quantities that are held in storage for future use and disposition. *Note:* When coal data are collected for a particular reporting period (month, quarter, or year), coal stocks are commonly measured as of the last day of this period.

Coal sulfur Coal sulfur occurs in three forms: organic, sulfate, and pyritic. Organic sulfur is an integral part of the coal matrix and cannot be removed by conventional physical separation. Sulfate sulfur is usually negligible. Pyritic sulfur occurs as the minerals pyrite and marcasite; larger sizes generally can be removed by cleaning the coal.

Coal Synfuel Coal-based solid fuel that has been processed by a coal synfuel plant; and coal-based fuels such as briquettes, pellets, or extrusions, which are formed from fresh or recycled coal and binding materials.

Coal type The classification is based on physical characteristics or microscopic constituents. Examples of coal types are banded coal, bright coal, cannel coal, and splint coal. The term is also used to classify coal according to heat and sulfur content. See **Coal grade** above.

Coal zone A series of laterally extensive and (or) lenticular coal beds and associated strata that arbitrarily can be viewed as a unit. Generally, the coal beds in a coal zone are assigned to the same geologic member or formation.

Cost-based rates (electric) A ratemaking concept used for the design and development of rate schedules to ensure that the filed rate schedules recover only the cost of providing the service. (FERC definition)

Code of Federal Regulations A compilation of the general and permanent rules of the executive departments and agencies of the Federal Government as published in the Federal Register. The code is divided into 50 titles that represent broad areas subject to Federal regulation. Title 18 contains the FERC regulations.

Cofiring The process of burning natural gas in conjunction with another fuel to reduce air pollutants.

Cogeneration The production of electrical energy and another form of useful energy (such as heat or steam) through the sequential use of energy.

Cogeneration system A system using a common energy source to produce both electricity and steam for other uses, resulting in increased fuel efficiency.

Cogenerator A generating facility that produces electricity and another form of useful thermal energy (such as heat or steam), used for industrial, commercial, heating, or cooling purposes. To receive status as a qualifying facility (QF) under the Public Utility Regulatory Policies Act (PURPA), the facility must produce electric energy and "another form of useful thermal energy through the sequential use of energy" and meet certain ownership, operating, and efficiency criteria established by the Federal Energy Regulatory Commission (FERC). (See the Code of Federal Regulations, Title 18, Part 292.)

Coincidental demand The sum of two or more demands that occur in the same time interval.

Coincidental peak load The sum of two or more peak loads that occur in the same time interval.

Coke (coal) A solid carbonaceous residue derived from low-ash, low-sulfur bituminous coal from which the volatile constituents are driven off by baking in an oven at temperatures as high as 2,000 degrees Fahrenheit so that the fixed carbon and residual ash are fused together. Coke is used as a fuel and as a reducing agent in smelting iron ore in a blast furnace. Coke from coal is grey, hard, and porous and has a heating value of 24.8 million Btu per ton.

Coke (petroleum) A residue high in carbon content and low in hydrogen that is the final product of thermal decomposition in the condensation process in cracking. This product is reported as marketable coke or catalyst coke. The conversion is 5 barrels (of 42 U.S. gallons each) per short ton. Coke from petroleum has a heating value of 6.024 million Btu per barrel.

Coke breeze The term refers to the fine sizes of coke, usually less than one-half inch, that are recovered from coke plants. It is commonly used for sintering iron ore.

Coke button A button-shaped piece of coke resulting from standard laboratory tests that indicates the coking or free-swelling characteristics of a coal; expressed in numbers and compared with a standard.

Coke oven gas The mixture of permanent gases produced by the carbonization of coal in a coke oven at temperatures in excess of 1,000 degrees Celsius.

Coke plants Plants where coal is carbonized for the manufacture of coke in slot or beehive ovens.

Coking Thermal refining processes used to produce fuel gas, gasoline blendstocks, distillates, and petroleum coke from the heavier products of atomspheric and vacuum distillation. Includes:

- *Delayed Coking* A process by which heavier crude oil fractions can be thermally decomposed under conditions of elevated temperatures and pressure to produce a mixture of lighter oils and petroleum coke. The light oils can be processed further in other refinery units to meet product specifications. The coke can be used either as a fuel or in other applications such as the manufacturing of steel or aluminum.
- *Flexicoking* A thermal cracking process which converts heavy hydrocarbons such as crude oil, tar sands bitumen, and distillation residues into light hydrocarbons. Feedstocks can be any pumpable hydrocarbons including those containing high concentrations of sulfur and metals.
- *Fluid Coking* A thermal cracking process utilizing the fluidized-solids technique to remove carbon (coke) for continuous conversion of heavy, low-grade oils into lighter products.

Coking coal Bituminous coal suitable for making coke. See **coke (coal)** above.

Cold-deck imputation A statistical procedure that replaces a missing value of an item with a constant value from an external source such as a value from a previous survey. See Imputation.

Combined cycle An electric generating technology in which electricity is produced from otherwise lost waste heat exiting from one or more gas (combustion) turbines. The exiting heat is routed to a conventional boiler or to a heat recovery steam generator for utilization by a steam turbine in the production of electricity. This process increases the efficiency of the electric generating unit.

Combined cycle unit An electric generating unit that consists of one or more combustion turbines and one or more boilers with a portion of the required energy input to the boiler(s) provided by the exhaust gas of the combustion turbine(s).

Combined heat and power (CHP) plant A plant designed to produce both heat and electricity from a single heat source. *Note:* This term is being used in place of the term "cogenerator" that was used by EIA in the past. CHP better describes the facilities because some of the plants included do not produce heat and power in a sequential fashion and, as a result, do not meet the legal definition of cogeneration specified in the Public Utility Regulatory Policies Act (PURPA).

Combined household energy expenditures The total amount of funds spent for energy consumed in, or delivered to, a housing unit during a given period of time and for fuel used to operate the motor vehicles that are owned or used on a regular basis by the household. The total dollar amount for energy consumed in a housing unit includes state and local taxes but excludes merchandise repairs or special service charges. Electricity, and natural gas expenditures are for the amount of those energy sources consumed. Fuel oil, kerosene, and LPG expenditures are for the amount of fuel purchased, which may differ from the amount of fuel consumed. The total dollar amount of fuel spent for vehicles is the product of fuel consumption and price.

Combined hydroelectric plant A hydroelectric plant that uses both pumped water and natural streamflow for the production of power.

Combined pumped-storage plant A pumped-storage hydroelectric power plant that uses both pumped water and natural streamflow to produce electricity.

Combustion Chemical oxidation accompanied by the generation of light and heat.

Combustion chamber An enclosed vessel in which chemical oxidation of fuel occurs.

Commercial building A building with more than 50 percent of its floor space used for commercial activities. Commercial buildings include, but are not limited to, stores, offices, schools, churches, gymnasiums, libraries, museums, hospitals, clinics, warehouses, and jails. Government buildings are included except for buildings on military bases or reservations.

Commercial facility An economic unit that is owned or operated by one person or organization and that occupies two or more commercial buildings at a single location. A university and a large hospital complex are examples of a commercial multi-building facility.

Commercial operation (nuclear) The phase of reactor operation that begins when power ascension ends and the operating utility formally declares the nuclear power plant to be available for the regular production of electricity. This declaration is usually related to the satisfactory completion of qualification tests on critical components of the unit.

Commercial sector An energy-consuming sector that consists of service-providing facilities and equipment of: businesses; Federal, State, and local governments; and other private and public organizations, such as religious, social, or fraternal groups. The commercial sector includes institutional living quarters. It also includes sewage treatment facilities. Common uses of energy associated with this sector include space heating, water heating, air conditioning, lighting, refrigeration, cooking, and running a wide variety of other equipment. *Note:* This sector includes generators that produce electricity and/or useful thermal output primarily to support the activities of the above-mentioned commercial establishments.

Commingling The mixing of one utility's generated supply of electric energy with another utility's generated supply within a transmission system.

Commissioned agent An agent who wholesales or retails a refined petroleum product under a commission arrangement. The agent does not take title to the product or establish the selling price, but receives a percentage of fixed fee for serving as an agent.

Common equity (book value) The retained earnings and common stock earnings plus the balances in common equity reserves and all other common stock accounts. This also includes the capital surplus, the paid-in surplus, the premium on common stocks, except those balances specifically related to preferred or preference stocks; less any common stocks held in the treasury.

Compact fluorescent bulbs These are also known as "screw-in fluorescent replacements for incandescent" or "screw-ins." Compact fluorescent bulbs combine the efficiency of fluorescent lighting with the convenience of a standard incandescent bulb. There are many styles of compact fluorescent, including exit light fixtures and floodlights (lamps containing reflectors). Many screw into a standard light socket, and most produce a similar color of light as a standard incandescent bulb. Compact fluorescent bulbs come with ballasts that are electronic (lightweight, instant, no-flicker starting, and 10 to 15% more efficient) or magnetic (much heavier and slower starting). Other types of compact fluorescent bulbs include adaptive circulation and PL and SL lamps and ballasts. Compact fluorescent bulbs are designed for residential uses; they are also used in table lamps, wall sconces, and hall and ceiling fixtures of hotels, motels, hospitals, and other types of commercial buildings with residential-type applications.

Company See Firm.

Company automotive (retail) outlet Any retail outlet selling motor fuel under the brand name of a company reporting in the EIA Financial Reporting System.

Company-lessee automotive outlet One of three types of company automotive (retail) outlets. This type of outlet is operated by an independent marketer who leases the station and land and has use of tanks, pumps, signs, etc. A lessee dealer typically has a supply agreement with a refiner or a distributor and purchases products at dealer tank wagon prices. The term includes outlets operated by commissioned agents and is limited to those dealers who are supplied directly by a refiner or any affiliate or subsidiary company of a refiner.

Company-open automotive outlet One of three types of company automotive (retail) outlets. This type of outlet is operated by an independent marketer who owns or leases (from a third party that is not a refiner) the station or land of a retail outlet and has use of tanks, pumps, signs, etc. An open dealer typically has a supply agreement with a refiner or a distributor and purchases products based on either rack or dealer tank wagon prices.

Company-operated automotive outlet One of three types of company automotive (retail) outlets. This type of outlet is operated by salaried or commissioned personnel paid by the reporting company.

Company-operated outlet See Company-operated retail outlet below.

Company-operated retail outlet Any retail outlet (i.e., service station) which sells motor vehicle fuels and is under the direct control of a firm that sets the retail product price and directly collects all or part of the retail margin. The category includes retail outlets operated by (1) salaried employees of the firm and/or its subsidiaries and affiliates, (2) licensed or commissioned agents, and/or (3) personnel services contracted by the firm.

Company outlet   See Company-operated automotive outlet above.

Competitive transition charge   A non-bypassable charge levied on each customer of the distribution utility, including those who are served under contracts with nonutility suppliers, for recovery of the utility's stranded costs that develop because of competition.

Completion (oil/gas production)   The term refers to the installation of permanent equipment for the production of oil or gas. If a well is equipped to produce only oil or gas from one zone or reservoir, the definition of a "well" (classified as an oil well or gas well) and the definition of a "completion" are identical. However, if a well is equipped to produce oil and/or gas separately from more than one reservoir, a "well" is not synonymous with a "completion." (See Well.)

Completion date (oil/gas production)   The date on which the installation of permanent equipment has been completed as reported to the appropriate regulatory agency. The date of completion of a dry hole is the date of abandonment as reported to the appropriate agency. The date of completion of a service well is the date on which the well is equipped to perform the service for which it was intended.

Compliance coal   A coal or a blend of coals that meets sulfur dioxide emission standards for air quality without the need for flue gas desulfurization.

Compressed natural gas (CNG)   Natural gas which is comprised primarily of methane, compressed to a pressure at or above 2,400 pounds per square inch and stored in special high-pressure containers. It is used as a fuel for natural gas powered vehicles.

Compressor station   Any combination of facilities that supply the energy to move gas in transmission or distribution lines or into storage by increasing the pressure.

Concentrating solar power or solar thermal power system   A solar energy conversion system characterized by the optical concentration of solar rays through an arrangement of mirrors to generate a high temperature working fluid. Also see Solar rough, Solar power tower, or Solar dish. Concentrating solar power (but not Solar thermal power) may also refer to a system that focuses solar rays on a photovoltaic cell to increase conversion efficiency.

Concentrator   A reflective or refractive device that focuses incident insolation onto an area smaller than the reflective or refractive surface, resulting in increased insolation at the point of focus.

Concession   The operating right to explore for and develop petroleum fields in consideration for a share of production in kind (equity oil).

Concessionary purchases   The quantity of crude oil exported during a reporting period, which was acquired from the producing government under terms that arise from the firm's participation in a concession. It includes preferential crude where the reporting firm's access to such crude is derived from a former concessionary relationship.

Condensate (lease condensate)   A natural gas liquid recovered from associated and nonassociated gas wells from lease separators or field facilities, reported in barrels of 42 U.S. gallons at atmospheric pressure and 60 degrees Fahrenheit.

Condenser cooling water   A source of water external to a boiler's feed system is passed through the steam leaving the turbine in order to cool and condense the steam. This reduces the steam's exit pressure and recaptures its heat, which is then used to preheat fluid entering the boiler, thereby increasing the plant's thermodynamic efficiency.

Conditional energy intensity   Total consumption of a particular energy source(s) or fuel(s) divided by the total floorspace of buildings that use the energy source(s) or fuel(s); i.e., the ratio of consumption to energy source-specific floorspace.

Conditionally effective rates   An electric rate schedule that has been put into effect by the FERC subject to refund pending final disposition or refiling.

Conductor   Metal wires, cables, and bus-bar used for carrying electric current. Conductors may be solid or stranded, that is, built up by a assembly of smaller solid conductors.

Conference of the Parties (COP)   The collection of nations that have ratified the Framework Convention on Climate Change (FCCC). The primary role of the COP is to keep implementation of the FCCC under review and make the decisions necessary for its effective implementation. Also see Framework Convention on Climate Change (FCCC).

Configuration maps   Geographic information containing transmission line, substation, and terminal information. It shows the normal operating voltages and includes information about other operational and political boundaries.

Congestion   A condition that occurs when insufficient transfer capacity is available to implement all of the preferred schedules for electricity transmission simultaneously.

Connected load   The sum of the continuous ratings or the capacities for a system, part of a system, or a customer's electric power consuming apparatus.

Connection   The physical connection (e.g., transmission lines, transformers, switch gear, etc.) between two electric systems permitting the transfer of electric energy in one or both directions.

CO nonattainment area Areas with carbon monoxide design values of 9.5 parts per million or more, generally based on data for 1988 and 1989.

Conservation and other DSM This Demand-Side Management category represents the amount of consumer load reduction at the time of system peak due to utility programs that reduce consumer load during many hours of the year. Examples include utility rebate and shared savings activities for the installation of energy efficient appliances, lighting and electrical machinery, and weatherization materials. In addition, this category includes all other Demand-Side Management activities, such as thermal storage, time-of-use rates, fuel substitution, measurement and evaluation, and any other utility-administered Demand-Side Management activity designed to reduce demand and/or electricity use.

Conservation feature A feature in the building designed to reduce the usage of energy.

Conservation program A program in which a utility company furnishes home weatherization services free or at reduced cost or provides free or low cost devices for saving energy, such as energy efficient light bulbs, flow restrictors, weather stripping, and water heater insulation.

Consolidated entity See Firm.

Consolidated Metropolitan Statistical Area (CMSA) An area that meets the requirements of a metropolitan statistical area, has a population of one million or more, and consists of two or more component parts that are recognized as primary metropolitan statistical areas.

Construction An energy-consuming subsector of the **industrial sector** that consists of all facilities and equipment used to perform land preparation and construct, renovate, alter, install, maintain, or repair major infrastructure or individual systems therein. Infrastructure includes buildings; industrial plants; and other major structures, such as tanks, towers, monuments, roadways, tunnels, bridges, dams, pipelines, and transmission lines.

Construction costs (of the electric power industry) All direct and indirect costs incurred in acquiring and constructing electric utility plant and equipment and proportionate shares of common utility plants. Included are the cost of land and improvements, nuclear fuel and spare parts, allowance for funds used during construction, and general overheads capitalized, less the cost of acquiring plant and equipment previously operated in utility service.

Construction expenditures (of the electric power industry) The gross expenditures for construction costs (including the cost of replacing worn out plants), and electric construction costs, and land held for future use.

Construction pipeline (of a nuclear reactor) The various stages involved in the acquisition of a nuclear reactor by a utility. The events that define these stages are the ordering of a reactor, the licensing process, and the physical construction of the nuclear generating unit. A reactor is said to be "in the pipeline" when the reactor is ordered and "out of the pipeline" when it completes low power testing and begins operation toward full power.

Construction work in progress (CWIP) The balance shown on a utility's balance sheet for construction work not yet completed but in process. This balance line item may or may not be included in the rate base.

Constructive surplus or deficit The amounts representing the exchange of services, supplies, etc., between the utility department and the municipality and its other departments without charge or at a reduced charge. Charges to this account include utility and other services, supplies, etc., furnished by the utility department to the municipality or its other departments without charge, or the amount of the reduction, if furnished at a reduced charge. Credits to the account consist of services, supplies, office space, etc., furnished by the municipality to the utility department without charge on the amount of the reduction, if furnished at a reduced charge.

Consumer (energy) Any individually metered dwelling, building, establishment, or location using natural gas, synthetic natural gas, and/or mixtures of natural and supplemental gas for feedstock or as fuel for any purpose other than in oil or gas lease operations; natural gas treating or processing plants; or pipeline, distribution, or storage compressors.

Consumer charge An amount charged periodically to a consumer for such utility costs as billing and meter reading, without regard to demand or energy consumption.

Consumer Price Index (CPI) These prices are collected in 85 urban areas selected to represent all urban consumers about 80 percent of the total U.S. population. The service stations are selected initially and on a replacement basis, in such a way that they represent the purchasing habits of the CPI population. Service stations in the current sample include those providing all types of service (i.e., full, mini, and self-service).

Consumption See Energy consumption.

Consumption per square foot The aggregate ratio of total consumption for a particular set of buildings to the total floorspace of those buildings.

Continuous delivery energy sources Those energy sources provided continuously to a building.

Continuous mining A form of room pillar mining in which a continuous mining machine extracts and removes coal from the working face in one operation; no blasting is required.

Contract price The delivery price determined when a contract is signed. It can be a fixed price or a base price escalated according to a given formula.

Contract receipts Purchases based on a negotiated agreement that generally covers a period of 1 or more years.

Contracted gas Any gas for which Interstate Pipeline has a contract to purchase from any domestic or foreign source that cannot be identified to a specific field or group. This includes tailgate plant purchases, single meter point purchases, pipeline purchases, natural gas imports, SNG purchases, and LNG purchases.

Contribution to net income The FRS (Financial Reporting System survey) segment equivalent to net income. However, some consolidated items of revenue and expense are not allocated to the segments, and therefore they are not equivalent in a strict sense. The largest item not allocated to the segments is interest expense since this is regarded as a corporate level item for FRS purposes.

Control Including the terms "controlling," "controlled by," and "under common control with," means the possession, direct or indirect, of the power to direct or cause the direction of the management and policies of a person, whether through the ownership of voting shares, by contract, or otherwise.

Control total The number of elements in the population or a subset of the population. The sample weights for the observed elements in a survey are adjusted so that they add up to the control total. The value of a control total is obtained from an outside source. The control totals are given by the number of households in one of the 12 cells by categorizing households by the four Census regions and by three categories of metropolitan status (Metropolitan Statistical Area central city, Metropolitan Statistical Area outside central city, and non Metropolitan Statistical Area). The control totals are obtained from the Current Population Survey.

Conventional blendstock for oxygenate blending (CBOB) Motor gasoline blending components intended for blending with oxygenates to produce finished conventional motor gasoline.

Conventional gasoline Finished motor gasoline not included in the oxygenated or reformulated gasoline categories. *Note:* This category excludes reformulated gasoline blendstock for oxygenate blending (RBOB) as well as other blendstock.

Conventional hydroelectric plant A plant in which all of the power is produced from natural streamflow as regulated by available storage.

Conventional mill (uranium) A facility engineered and built principally for processing of uraniferous ore materials mined from the earth and the recovery, by chemical treatment in the mill's circuits, of uranium and/or other valued coproduct components from the processed one.

Conventional mining The oldest form of room pillar mining, which consists of a series of operations that involve cutting the coal bed, so it breaks easily when blasted with explosives or high pressure air, and then loading the broken coal.

Conventional oil and natural gas production Crude oil and natural gas that is produced by a well drilled into a geologic formation in which the reservoir and fluid characteristics permit the oil and natural gas to readily flow to the wellbore.

Conventional thermal electricity generation Electricity generated by an electric power plant using coal, petroleum, or gas as its source of energy.

Conventionally fueled vehicle A vehicle that runs on petroleum-based fuels such as motor gasoline or diesel fuel.

Conversion company An organization that performs vehicle conversions on a commercial basis.

Conversion factor A factor for converting data between one unit of measurement and another (such as between short tons and British thermal units, or between barrels and gallons). (See http://www.eia.doe.gov/emeu/mer/append_a.html and http://www.eia.doe.gov/emeu/mer/append_b.html for further information on conversion factors.) See Btu Conversion Factor and Thermal Conversion Factor.

Converted (alternative-fuel) vehicle A vehicle originally designed to operate on gasoline/diesel that was modified or altered to run on an alternative fuel after its initial delivery to an end-user.

Cooling Conditioning of room air for human comfort by a refrigeration unit (such as an air conditioner or heat pump) or by circulating chilled water through a central cooling or district cooling system. Use of fans or blowers by themselves, without chilled air or water, is not included in this definition of cooling.

Cooling degree-days A measure of how warm a location is over a period of time relative to a base temperature, most commonly specified as 65 degrees Fahrenheit. The measure is computed for each day by subtracting the base temperature (65 degrees) from the average of the day's high and low temperatures, with negative values set equal to zero. Each day's cooling degree-days are summed to create a cooling degree-day measure for a specified reference period. Cooling degree-days are used in energy analysis as an indicator of air conditioning energy requirements or use.

Cooling pond A natural or man made body of water that is used for dissipating waste heat from power plants.

Cooling system An equipment system that provides water to the condensers and includes water intakes and outlets; cooling towers; and ponds, pumps, and pipes.

Cooperative electric utility An electric utility legally established to be owned by and operated for the benefit of those using its service. The utility company will generate, transmit, and/or distribute supplies of electric energy to a specified area not being serviced by another utility. Such ventures are generally exempt from Federal income tax laws. Most electric cooperatives have been initially financed by the Rural Utilities Service (prior Rural Electrification Administration), U.S. Department of Agriculture.

Coordination service The sale, exchange, or transmission of electricity between two or more electric utilities that typically have sufficient generation and transmission capacity to supply their load requirements under normal conditions.

Coordination service pricing The typical price components of a bulk power coordination sale are an energy charge, a capacity, or reservation charge, and an adder. The price for a particular sale may embody some or all of these components. The energy charge is made on a per-kilowatt basis and is intended to recover the seller's system incremental variable costs of making a sale. Because the nonfuel expenses are usually hard to quantify, and small relative to fuel expense, energy charges quoted are usually based on fuel cost. A capacity charge is set at a certain level per kilowatt and is normally paid whether or not energy is taken by the buyer. An adder is added to that energy charge to recover the hard quantify nonfuel variable costs. There are three types of adders: percentage, fixed, and split savings. A percentage adder increases the energy charge by a certain percentage. A fixed adder adds a fixed amount per kilowatthour to the energy charge. Split savings adders are used only in economy energy transactions. They split production costs savings between the seller and the buyer by adding one half of the savings to the energy cost.

Cord of wood A cord of wood measures 4 feet by 4 feet by 8 feet, or 128 cubic feet.

Correlation (statistical term) In its most general sense, correlation denotes the interdependence between quanitative or qualitative data. It would include the association of dichotomized attributes and the contingency of multiple classified attributes. The concept is quite general and may be extended to more than two variates. The word is most frequently used in a somewhat narrower sense to denote the relationship between measurable variates or ranks.

Cost, insurance, freight (CIF) A type of sale in which the buyer of the product agrees to pay a unit price that includes the f.o.b. value of the product at the point of origin plus all costs of insurance and transportation. This type of transaction differs from a "delivered" purchase in that the buyer accepts the quantity as determined at the loading port (as certified by the Bill of Loading and Quality Report) rather than pay on the basis of the quantity and quality ascertained at the unloading port. It is similar to the terms of an f.o.b. sale except that the seller, as a service for which he is compensated, arranges for transportation and insurance.

Cost model for undiscovered resources A computerized algorithm that uses the uranium endowment estimated for a given geological area and selected industry economic indexes to develop random variables that describe the undiscovered resources ultimately expected to be discovered in that area at chosen forward cost categories.

Cost of capital The rate of return a utility must offer to obtain additional funds. The cost of capital varies with the leverage ratio, the effective income tax rate, conditions in the bond and stock markets, growth rate of the utility, its dividend strategy, stability of net income, the amount of new capital required, and other factors dealing with business and financial risks. It is a omposite of the cost for debt interest, preferred stock dividends, and common stockholders' earnings that provide the facilities used in supplying utility service.

Cost of debt The interest rate paid on new increments of debt capital multiplied by 1 minus the tax rate.

Cost of preferred stock The preferred stock dividends divided by the net price of the preferred stock.

Cost of retained earnings The residual of an entity's earnings over expenditures, including taxes and dividends, that are reinvested in its business. The cost of these funds is always lower than the cost of new equity capital, due to taxes and transactions costs. Therefore, the cost of retained earnings is the yield that retained earnings accrue upon reinvestment.

Cost of service A ratemaking concept used for the design and development of rate schedules to ensure that the filed rate schedules recover only the cost of providing the electric service at issue. This concept attempts to correlate the utility's costs and revenue with the service provided to each of the various customer classes.

Cost-of-service regulation A traditional electric utility regulation under which a utility is allowed to set rates based on the cost of providing service to customers and the right to earn a limited profit.

Costs (imports of natural gas) All expenses incurred by an importer up to the U.S. point of delivery for the reported quantity (of natural gas) imported.

Criteria pollutant A pollutant determined to be hazardous to human health and regulated under EPA's National Ambient Air Quality Standards. The 1970 amendments to the Clean Air Act require EPA to describe the health and welfare impacts of a pollutant as the "criteria" for inclusion in the regulatory regime.

Crop residue Organic residue remaining after the harvesting and processing of a crop.

Crude oil A mixture of hydrocarbons that exists in liquid phase in natural underground reservoirs and remains liquid at atmospheric pressure after passing through surface separating facilities. Depending upon the characteristics of the crude stream, it may also include:

1. Small amounts of hydrocarbons that exist in gaseous phase in natural underground reservoirs but are liquid at atmospheric pressure after being recovered from oil well (casinghead) gas in lease separators and are subsequently commingled with the crude stream without being separately measured. Lease condensate recovered as a liquid from natural gas wells in lease or field separation facilities and later mixed into the crude stream is also included;
2. Small amounts of nonhydrocarbons produced with the oil, such as sulfur and various metals;
3. Drip gases, and liquid hydrocarbons produced from tar sands, oil sands, gilsonite, and oil shale.

Liquids produced at natural gas processing plants are excluded. Crude oil is refined to produce a wide array of petroleum products, including heating oils; gasoline, diesel and jet fuels; lubricants; asphalt; ethane, propane, and butane; and many other products used for their energy or chemical content.

Crude oil acquisitions (unfinished oil acquisitions) The volume of crude oil either
- acquired by the respondent for processing for his own account in accordance with accounting procedures generally accepted and consistently and historically applied by the refiner concerned, or
- in the case of a processing agreement, delivered to another refinery for processing for the respondent's own account.

Crude oil that has not been added by a refiner to inventory and that is thereafter sold or otherwise disposed of without processing for the account of that refiner shall be deducted from its crude oil purchases at the time when the related cost is deducted from refinery inventory in accordance with accounting procedures generally applied by the refiner concerned. Crude oil processed by the respondent for the account of another is not a crude oil acquisition.

Crude oil f.o.b. price The crude oil price actually charged at the oil producing country's port of loading. Includes deductions for any rebates and discounts or additions of premiums, where applicable. It is the actual price paid with no adjustment for credit terms.

Crude oil input The total crude oil put into processing units at refineries.

Crude oil landed cost The price of crude oil at the port of discharge, including charges associated with purchasing, transporting, and insuring a cargo from the purchase point to the port of discharge. The cost does not include charges incurred at the discharge port (e.g., import tariffs or fees, wharfage charges, and demurrage).

Crude oil less lease condensate A mixture of hydrocarbons that exists in liquid phase in natural underground reservoirs and remains liquid at atmospheric pressure after passing through surface separating facilities. Such hydrocarbons as lease condensate and natural gasoline recovered as liquids from natural gas wells in lease or field separation facilities and later mixed into the crude stream are excluded. Depending upon the characteristics of the crude stream, crude oil may also include:

1. Small amounts of hydrocarbons that exist in gaseous phase in natural underground reservoirs but are liquid at atmospheric pressure after being recovered from oil well (casinghead) gas in lease separators and are subsequently commingled with the crude stream without being separately measured;
2. Small amounts of nonhydrocarbons produced with the oil, such as sulfur and various metals.

Crude oil losses Represents the volume of crude oil reported by petroleum refineries as being lost in their operations. These losses are due to spills, contamination, fires, etc., as opposed to refining processing losses.

Crude oil production The volume of crude oil produced from oil reservoirs during given periods of time. The amount of such production for a given period is measured as volumes delivered from lease storage tanks (i.e., the point of custody transfer) to pipelines, trucks, or other media for transport to refineries or terminals with adjustments for (1) net differences between opening and closing lease inventories, and (2) basic sediment and water (BS&W).

Crude oil qualities Refers to two properties of crude oil, the sulfur content, and API gravity, which affect processing complexity and product characteristics.

Crude oil refinery input The total crude oil put into processing units at refineries.

Crude oil stocks Stocks of crude oil and lease condensate held at refineries, in pipelines, at pipeline terminals, and on leases.

Crude oil used directly Crude oil consumed as fuel by crude oil pipelines and on crude oil leases.

Crude oil, refinery receipts Receipts of domestic and foreign crude oil at a refinery. Includes all crude oil in transit except crude oil in transit by pipeline. Foreign crude oil is reported as a receipt only after entry through customs. Crude oil of foreign origin held in bonded storage is excluded.

Crystalline fully refined wax   A light colored paraffin wax having the following characteristics: viscosity at 210 degrees Fahrenheit (D88)-59.9 SUS (10.18 centistokes) maximum; oil content (D721)-0.5 percent maximum; other +20 color, Saybolt minimum.

Crystalline other wax   A paraffin wax having the following characteristics: viscosity at 210 deg. F(D88)-59.9 SUS (10.18 centistokes) maximum; oil content (D721)-0.51 percent minimum to 15 percent maximum.

Cubic foot (cf), natural gas   The amount of natural gas contained at standard temperature and pressure (60 degrees Fahrenheit and 14.73 pounds standard per square inch) in a cube whose edges are one foot long.

Cull wood   Wood logs, chips, or wood products that are burned.

Culm   Waste from Pennsylvania anthracite preparation plants, consisting of coarse rock fragments containing as much as 30 percent small sized coal; sometimes defined as including very fine coal particles called silt. Its heat value ranges from 8 to 17 million Btu per short ton.

Cultivar   A horticulturally or agriculturally derived variety of a plant.

Cumulative depletion   The sum in tons of coal extracted and lost in mining as of a stated date for a specified area or a specified coal bed.

Current (electric)   A flow of electrons in an electrical conductor. The strength or rate of movement of the electricity is measured in amperes.

Current assets   Cash and other assets that are expected to be turned into cash, sold, or exchanged within the normal operating cycle of the utility, usually one year. Current assets include cash, marketable securities, receivables, inventory, and current prepayments.

Current liabilities   A debt or other obligation that must be discharged within one year or the normal operating cycle of the utility by expending a current asset or the incurrence of another short-term obligation. Current liabilities include accounts payable, short-term notes payable, and accrued expenses payable such as taxes payable and salaries payable.

Current ratio   The ratio of current assets divided by current liabilities that shows the ability of a utility to pay its current obligations from its current assets. A measure of liquidity, the higher the ratio, the more assurance that current liabilities can be paid.

Customer choice   The right of customers to purchase energy from a supplier other than their traditional supplier or from more than one seller in the retail market.

Customs district (coal)   Customs districts, as defined by the Bureau of the Census, U.S. Department of Commerce, "Monthly Report EM 545," are as follows:

- *Eastern:* Bridgeport, CT, Washington, DC, Boston, MA, Baltimore, MD, Portland, ME, Buffalo, NY, New York City, NY, Ogdensburg, NY, Philadelphia, PA, Providence, RI, Norfolk, VA, St. Albans, VT.
- *Southern:* Mobile, AL, Savannah, GA, Miami, FL, Tampa, FL, New Orleans, LA, Wilmington, NC, San Juan, PR, Charleston, SC, Dallas-Fort Worth, TX, El Paso, TX, Houston-Galveston, TX, Laredo, TX, Virgin Islands.
- *Western:* Anchorage, AK, Nogales, AZ, Los Angeles, CA, San Diego, CA, San Francisco, CA, Honolulu, HI, Great Falls, MT, Portland, OR, Seattle, WA.
- *Northern*: Chicago, IL, Detroit, MI, Duluth, MN, Minneapolis, MN, St. Louis, MO, Pembina, ND, Cleveland, OH, Milwaukee, WI.

Customs import value (C.I.V.)   The price paid for merchandise when sold for exportation to the United States, excluding U.S. import duties, freight, insurance, and other charges incurred in bringing the merchandise to the United States.

Cut-off grade (uranium)   The lowest grade, in percent U_3O_8, of uranium ore at a minimum specified thickness that can be mined at a specified cost.

Cycle   The time period running from the startup of one reactor cycle to the startup of the following cycle.

Cycle/reactor history   A group of assemblies that have been irradiated in the same cycles in an individual reactor and are said to have the same cycle/reactor history.

Cycling (natural gas)   The practice of producing natural gas for the extraction of natural gas liquids, returning the dry residue to the producing reservoir to maintain reservoir pressure and increase the ultimate recovery of natural gas liquids. The reinjected gas is produced for disposition after cycling operations are completed.

Dam   A physical barrier constructed across a river or waterway to control the flow of or raise the level of water. The purpose of construction may be for flood control, irrigation needs, hydroelectric power production, and/or recreation usage.

Day-ahead and hour-ahead markets   Forward markets where electricity quantities and market clearing prices are calculated individually for each hour of the day on the basis of participant bids for energy sales and purchases.

Day-ahead schedule   A schedule prepared by a scheduling coordinator or the independent system operator before the beginning of a trading day. This schedule indicates the levels of generation and demand scheduled for each settlement period that trading day.

Daylighting controls A system of sensors that assesses the amount of daylight and controls lighting or shading devices to maintain a specified lighting level. The sensors are sometimes referred to as "photocells."

Deadweight tons The lifting capacity of a ship expressed in long tons (2,240 lbs.), including cargo, commodities, and crew.

Dealer tank wagon (DTW) sales Wholesale sales of gasoline priced on a delivered basis to a retail outlet.

Decatherm Ten therms or 1,000,000 Btu.

Decommissioning Retirement of a nuclear facility, including decontamination and/or dismantlement.

Decontamination Removal of unwanted radioactive or hazardous contamination by a chemical or mechanical process.

Dedicated reserves The volume of recoverable, salable gas reserves committed to, controlled by, or possessed by the reporting pipeline company and used for acts and services for which both the seller and the company have received certificate authorization from the Federal Energy Regulatory Commission (FERC). Reserves include both company-owned reserves (including owned gas in underground storage), reserves under contract from independent producers, and short-term and emergency supplies from the intrastate market. Gas volumes under contract from other interstate pipelines are not included as reserves, but may constitute part or all of a company's gas supply.

Dedicated vehicle A vehicle that operates only on an alternative fuel, as when a vehicle is configured to operate on compressed natural gas. *Note:* A vehicle powered by an electric motor is not to be treated as dedicated.

Deepest total depth The deepest total depth of a given well is the distance from a surface reference point (usually the Kelly bushing) to the point of deepest penetration measured along the well bore. If a well is drilled from a platform or barge over water, the depth of the water is included in the total length of the well bore.

Deferred cost An expenditure not recognized as a cost of operation of the period in which incurred, but carried forward to be written off in future periods.

Deferred fuel costs An expenditure for fuel that is not recognized for bookkeeping practices as a cost in the operating period incurred, but carried forward to be written off in future periods.

Deferred income tax (liability) A liability in the balance sheet representing the additional Federal income taxes that would have been due if a utility had not been allowed to compute tax expenses differently for income tax reporting purposes than for ratemaking purposes.

Deforestation The net removal of trees from forested land.

Degasification system The methods employed for removing methane from a coal seam that could not otherwise be removed by standard ventilation fans and thus would pose a substantial hazard to coal miners. These systems may be used prior to mining or during mining activities.

Degradable organic carbon The portion of organic carbon present in such solid waste as paper, food waste, and yard waste that is susceptible to biochemical decomposition.

Delayed coking A process by which heavier crude oil fractions can be thermally decomposed under conditions of elevated temperatures and pressure to produce a mixture of lighter oils and petroleum coke. The light oils can be processed further in other refinery units to meet product specifications. The coke can be used either as a fuel or in other applications such as the manufacturing of steel or aluminum.

Deliverability Represents the number of future years during which a pipeline company can meet its annual requirements for its presently certificated delivery capacity from presently committed sources of supply. The availability of gas from these sources of supply shall be governed by the physical capabilities of these sources to deliver gas by the terms of existing gas-purchase contracts, and by limitations imposed by State or Federal regulatory agencies.

Delivered cost The cost of fuel, including the invoice price of fuel, transportation charges, taxes, commissions, insurance, and expenses associated with leased or owned equipment used to transport the fuel.

Delivered energy The amount of energy delivered to the site (building); no adjustment is made for the fuels consumed to produce electricity or district sources. This is also referred to as net energy.

Delivered (gas) The physical transfer of natural, synthetic, and/or supplemental gas from facilities operated by the responding company to facilities operated by others or to consumers.

Deliveries (electric) Energy generated by one system and delivered to another system through one or more transmission lines.

Demand See Energy demand.

Demand bid A bid into the power exchange indicating a quantity of energy or an ancillary service that an eligible customer is willing to purchase and, if relevant, the maximum price that the customer is willing to pay.

Demand charge That portion of the consumer's bill for electric service based on the consumer's maximum electric capacity usage and calculated based on the billing demand charges under the applicable rate schedule.

Demand charge credit Compensation received by the buyer when the delivery terms of the contract cannot be met by the seller.

Demand indicator A measure of the number of energy-consuming units, or the amount of service or output, for which energy inputs are required.

Demand interval The time period during which flow of electricity is measured (usually in 15-, 30-, or 60-minute increments.)

Demand-metered Having a meter to measure peak demand (in addition to total consumption) during a billing period. Demand is not usually metered for other energy sources.

Demand-side management (DSM) The planning, implementation, and monitoring of utility activities designed to encourage consumers to modify patterns of electricity usage, including the timing and level of electricity demand. It refers to only energy and load-shape modifying activities that are undertaken in response to utility-administered programs. It does not refer to energy and load-shaped changes arising from the normal operation of the marketplace or from government-mandated energy-efficiency standards. Demand-Side Management covers the complete range of load-shape objectives, including strategic conservation and load management, as well as strategic load growth.

Demand-side management costs The costs incurred by the utility to achieve the capacity and energy savings from the Demand-Side Management Program. Costs incurred by customers or third parties are to be excluded. The costs are to be reported in thousands of dollars (nominal) in the year in which they are incurred, regardless of when the savings occur. The utility costs are all the annual expenses (labor, administrative, equipment, incentives, marketing, monitoring and evaluation, and other incurred by the utility for operation of the DSM Program), regardless of whether the costs are expensed or capitalized. Lump sum capital costs (typically accrued over several years prior to start up) are not to be reported. Program costs associated with strategic load growth activities are also to be excluded.

Demonstrated reserves See Energy reserves.

Demonstrated reserve base (coal) A collective term for the sum of coal in both measured and indicated resource categories of reliability, representing 100 percent of the in-place coal in those categories as of a certain date. Includes beds of bituminuous coal and anthracite 28 or more inches thick and beds of subbituminuous coal 60 or more inches thick that can occur at depths of up to 1,000 feet. Includes beds of lignite 60 or more inches thick that can be surface mined. Includes also thinner and/or deeper beds that presently are being mined or for which there is evidence that they could be mined commercially at a given time. Represents that portion of the identified coal resource from which reserves are calculated.

Demonstrated resources Same qualifications as identified resources, but include measured and indicated degrees of geologic assurance and excludes the inferred.

Demonstration and test vehicles Vehicles operated by a motor vehicle dealer solely for the purpose of promoting motor vehicle sales or permitting potential purchasers to drive the vehicle for pre-purchase or pre-lease evaluation; or a vehicle that is owned and operated by a motor vehicle manufacturer or motor vehicle component manufacturer, or owned or held by a university research department, independent testing laboratory, or other such evaluation facility, solely for the purpose of evaluating the performance of such vehicles for engineering, research and development, or quality control reasons.

Demurrage The charge paid to the vessel owner or operator for detention of a vessel at the port(s) beyond the time allowed, usually 72 hours, for loading and unloading.

Dependable capacity The load-carrying ability of a station or system under adverse conditions for a specified period of time.

Depletion (coal) The subtraction of both tonnage produced and the tonnage lost to mining from identified resources to determine the remaining tonnage as of a certain time.

Depletion allowance A term for either (1) a periodic assignment to expense of recorded amounts or (2) an allowable income tax deduction that is related to the exhaustion of mineral reserves. Depletion is included as one of the elements of amortization. When used in that manner, depletion refers only to book depletion.

> ***Book*** The portion of the carrying value (other than the portion associated with tangible assets) prorated in each accounting period, for financial reporting purposes, to the extracted portion of an economic interest in wasting natural resource.
>
> ***Tax-cost*** A deduction (allowance) under U.S. Federal income taxation normally calculated under a formula whereby the adjusted basis of the mineral property is multiplied by a fraction, the numerator of which is the number of units of minerals sold during the tax year and the denominator of which is the estimated number of units of unextracted minerals remaining at the end of the tax year plus the number of units of minerals sold during the tax year.
>
> ***Tax-percentage*** (for Statutory) A deduction (allowance) allowed to certain mineral producers under U.S. Federal income taxation calculated on the

basis of a specified percentage of gross revenue from the sale of minerals from each mineral property not to exceed the lesser of 50 percent of the taxable income from the property computed without allowance for depletion. (There are also other limits on percentage depletion on oil and gas production.) The taxpayer is entitled to a deduction representing the amount of tax-cost depletion or percentage (statutory) depletion, whichever is higher.

Excess statutory depletion The excess of estimated statutory depletion allowable as an income tax deduction over the amount of cost depletion otherwise allowable as a tax deduction, determined on a total enterprise basis.

Depleted resources Resources that have been mined; include coal recovered, coal lost in mining, and coal reclassified as subeconomic because of mining.

Depleted storage field A sub-surface natural geological reservoir, usually a depleted gas or oil field, used for storing natural gas.

Depletion factor The multiplier applied to the tonnage produced to compute depletion. This multiplier takes into account both the tonnage recovered and the tonnage lost due to mining. The depletion factor is the reciprocal of the recovery factor in relation to a given quantity of production.

Depreciation See definition for Amortization.

Depreciation and amortization of property, plant, and equipment The monthly provision for depreciation and amortization (applicable to utility property other than electric plant, electric plant in service, and equipment).

Depth of deepest production The depth of the deepest production is the length of the well bore measured (in feet) from the surface reference point to the bottom of the open hole or the deepest perforation in the casing of a producing well.

Deregulation The elimination of some or all regulations from a previously regulated industry or sector of an industry.

Design electrical rating (capacity) net The nominal net electrical output of a nuclear unit, as specified by the utility for the purpose of plant design.

Design head The achieved river, pondage, or reservoir surface height (forebay elevation) that provides the water level to produce the full flow at the gate of the turbine in order to attain the manufacturer's installed nameplate rating for generation capacity.

Desulfurization The removal of sulfur, as from molten metals, petroleum oil, or flue gases.

Development The preparation of a specific mineral deposit for commercial production; this preparation includes construction of access to the deposit and of facilities to extract the minerals. The development process is sometimes further distinguished between a preproduction stage and a current stage, with the distinction being made on the basis of whether the development work is performed before or after production from the mineral deposit has commenced on a commercial scale.

Development costs Costs incurred to obtain access to proved reserves and to provide facilities for extracting, treating, gathering, and storing the oil and gas. More specifically, development costs, depreciation and applicable operating costs of support equipment and facilities, and other costs of development activities, are costs incurred to:

- Gain access to and prepare well locations for drilling, including surveying well locations for the purpose of determing specific development drilling sites; clearing ground; draining; road building; and relocating public roads, gas lines, and power lines to the extent necessary in developing the proved reserves.
- Drill and equip development wells, development-type stratigraphic test wells, and service wells, including the costs of platforms and of well equipment such as casing, tubing, pumping equipment, and the wellhead assembly.
- Acquire, construct, and install production facilities such as lease flow lines, separators, treaters, heaters, manifolds, measuring devices, production storage tanks, natural gas cycling and processing plants, and utility waste disposal systems.
- Provide improved recovery systems.

Development drilling Drilling done to determine more precisely the size, grade, and configuration of an ore deposit subsequent to when the determination is made that the deposit can be commercially developed. Not included are: (1) secondary development drilling, (2) solution-mining drilling for production, or (3) production-related underground and openpit drilling done for control of mining operations.

Development well A well drilled within the proved area of an oil or gas reservoir to the depth of a stratigraphic horizon known to be productive. Also see Well.

Diesel-electric plant A generating station that uses diesel engines to drive its electric generators.

Diesel fuel A fuel composed of distillates obtained in petroleum refining operation or blends of such distillates with residual oil used in motor vehicles. The boiling point and specific gravity are higher for diesel fuels than for gasoline.

Diesel fuel system Diesel engines are internal combustion engines that burn diesel oil rather than gasoline. Injectors are used to spray droplets of diesel oil into the combustion chambers, at or near the top of the compression stroke. Ignition follows due to the very high temperature of the compressed intake air, or to the use of "glow plugs," which retain heat from previous ignitions (spark plugs are not used). Diesel engines are generally more fuel-efficient than gasoline engines but must be stronger and heavier because of high compression ratios.

Diffusive transport The process by which particles of liquids or gases move from an area of higher concentration to an area of lower concentration.

Direct access The ability of a retail customer to purchase electricity or other energy sources directly from a supplier other than their traditional supplier.

Direct control load management The magnitude of customer demand that can be interrupted at the time of the seasonal peak load by direct control of the system operator by interrupting power supply to individual appliances or equipment on customer premises. This type of control usually reduces the demand of residential customers.

Direct electricity load control The utility installs a radio-controlled device on the HVAC equipment. During periods of particulary heavy use of electricity, the utility will send a radio signal to the building in its service territory with this device and turn off the HVAC for a certain period.

Direct labor hours Direct labor hours worked by all mining employees at a mining operation during the year. Includes hours worked by those employees engaged in production, preparation, development, maintenance, repair, shop or yard work management, and technical or engineering work. Excludes office workers. Excludes vacation and leave hours.

Direct load control This Demand-Side Management category represents the consumer load that can be interrupted at the time of annual peak load by direct control of the utility system operator. Direct Load Control does not include Interruptible Load. This type of control usually involves residential consumers.

Direct milling cost Operating costs directly attributable to the processing of ores or other feed materials, including labor, supervision, engineering, power, fuel, supplies, reagents, and maintenance.

Direct mining cost Operating cost directly attributable to the mining of ore, including costs for labor, supervision, engineering, power, fuel, supplies, equipment replacement, maintenance, and taxes on production.

Direct nonprocess end use Those end uses that may be found on commercial, residential, or other sites, as well as at manufacturing establishments. They include heating, ventilation, and air conditioning (HVAC), facility lighting, facility support, onsite transportation, conventional electricity generation, and other nonprocess uses. "Direct" denotes that only the quantities of electricity or fossil fuel used in their original state (i.e., not transformed) are included in the estimates.

Direct process end use Those end uses that are specific to the carrying out of manufacturing. They include process heating, process cooling and refrigeration, machine drive, electrochemical processes, and other process uses. "Direct" denotes that only the quantities of electricity or fossil fuel used in their original state (i.e., not transformed) are included in the estimates.

Direct use Use of electricity that 1) is self-generated, 2) is produced by either the same entity that consumes the power or an affiliate, and 3) is used in direct support of a service or industrial process located within the same facility or group of facilities that house the generating equipment. Direct use is exclusive of station use.

Direct utility cost A utility cost that is identified with one of the DSM program categories (e.g., Energy Efficiency or Load Management).

Directional (deviated) well A well purposely deviated from the vertical, using controlled angles to reach an objective location other than directly below the surface location. A directional well may be the original hole or a directional "sidetrack" hole that deviates from the original bore at some point below the surface. The new footage associated with directional "sidetrack" holes should not be confused with footage resulting from remedial sidetrack drilling. If there is a common bore from which two or more wells are drilled, the first complete bore from the surface to the original objective is classified and reported as a well drilled. Each of the deviations from the common bore is reported as a separate well.

Discharged fuel Irradiated fuel removed from a nuclear reactor during refueling. Also see Spent Fuel.

Discrete-delivery energy sources Energy sources that must be delivered to a site.

Dispatching The operating control of an integrated electric system involving operations such as (1) the assignment of load to specific generating stations and other sources of supply to effect the most economical supply as the total or the significant area loads rise or fall (2) the control of operations and maintenance of high-voltage lines, substations, and equipment; (3) the operation of principal tie lines and switching; (4) the scheduling of energy transactions with connecting electric utilities.

Disposition, natural gas The removal of natural, synthetic, and/or supplemental gas, or any components or gaseous mixtures contained therein, from the responding company's facilities within the report State by any means or for any purpose, including the transportation of such gas out of the report State.

Disposition, petroleum A set of categories used to account for how crude oil and petroleum products are transferred, distributed, or removed from the supply stream. The categories include stock change, crude oil losses, refinery inputs, exports, and products supplied for domestic consumption.

Distillate fuel oil A general classification for one of the petroleum fractions produced in conventional distillation operations. It includes diesel fuels and fuel oils. Products known as No. 1, No. 2, and No. 4 diesel fuel are used in on-highway diesel engines, such as those in trucks and automobiles, as well as off-highway engines, such as those in railroad locomotives and agricultural machinery. Products known as No. 1, No. 2, and No. 4 fuel oils are used primarily for space heating and electric power generation.

No. 1 Distillate A light petroleum distillate that can be used as either a diesel fuel (see No. 1 Diesel Fuel) or a fuel oil. See No. 1 Fuel Oil.

- *No. 1 Diesel Fuel* A light distillate fuel oil that has distillation temperatures of 550 degrees Fahrenheit at the 90-percent point and meets the specifications defined in ASTM Specification D 975. It is used in high-speed diesel engines, such as those in city buses and similar vehicles. See No. 1 Distillate above.
- *No. 1 Fuel Oil* A light distillate fuel oil that has distillation temperatures of 400 degrees Fahrenheit at the 10-percent recovery point and 550 degrees Fahrenheit at the 90-percent point and meets the specifications defined in ASTM Specification D 396. It is used primarily as fuel for portable outdoor stoves and portable outdoor heaters. See No. 1 Distillate above.

No. 2 Distillate A petroleum distillate that can be used as either a diesel fuel (see No. 2 Diesel Fuel definition below) or a fuel oil. See No. 2 Fuel Oil below.

- *No. 2 Diesel Fuel* A fuel that has distillation temperatures of 500 degrees Fahrenheit at the 10-percent recovery point and 640 degrees Fahrenheit at the 90-percent recovery point and meets the specifications defined in ASTM Specification D 975. It is used in high-speed diesel engines, such as those in railroad locomotives, trucks, and automobiles. See **No. 2 Distillate** above.
- *Low Sulfur No. 2 Diesel Fuel* No. 2 diesel fuel that has a sulfur level no higher than 0.05 percent by weight. It is used primarily in motor vehicle diesel engines for on-highway use.
- *High Sulfur No. 2 Diesel Fuel* No. 2 diesel fuel that has a sulfur level above 0.05 percent by weight.
- *No. 2 Fuel oil (Heating Oil)* A distillate fuel oil that has distillation temperatures of 400 degrees Fahrenheit at the 10-percent recovery point and 640 degrees Fahrenheit at the 90-percent recovery point and meets the specifications defined in ASTM Specification D 396. It is used in atomizing type burners for domestic heating or for moderate capacity commercial/industrial burner units. See No. 2 Distillate above.

No. 4 Fuel A distillate fuel oil made by blending distillate fuel oil and residual fuel oil stocks. It conforms with ASTM Specification D 396 or Federal Specification VV-F-815C and is used extensively in industrial plants and in commercial burner installations that are not equipped with preheating facilities. It also includes No. 4 diesel fuel used for low- and medium-speed diesel engines and conforms to ASTM Specification D 975.

No. 4 Diesel Fuel and No. 4 Fuel Oil See No. 4 Fuel above.

Distillation unit (atmospheric) The primary distillation unit that processes crude oil (including mixtures of other hydrocarbons) at approximately atmospheric conditions. It includes a pipe still for vaporizing the crude oil and a fractionation tower for separating the vaporized hydrocarbon components in the crude oil into fractions with different boiling ranges. This is done by continuously vaporizing and condensing the components to separate higher oiling point material. The selected boiling ranges are set by the processing scheme, the properties of the crude oil, and the product specifications.

Distributed generator A generator that is located close to the particular load that it is intended to serve. General, but non-exclusive, characteristics of these generators include: an operating strategy that supports the served load; and interconnection to a distribution or sub-transmission system (138 kV or less).

Distributed/point-of-use water-heating system A system for heating hot water, for other than space heating purposes, which is located at more than one space within a building. A point-of-use water heater is located at the faucet and heats water only as required for immediate use. Because water is not heated until it is required, this equipment is more energy-efficient.

Distribution The delivery of energy to retail customers.

Distribution provider (electric) Provides and operates the "wires" between the transmission system and the end-use customer. For those end-use customers who are served at transmission voltages, the Transmission Owner also serves as the Distribution Provider. Thus, the Distribution Provider is not defined by a specific voltage, but rather as performing the Distribution function at any voltage. (NERC definition)

Distribution system The portion of the transmission and facilities of an electric system that is dedicated to delivering electric energy to an end-user.

Distribution use Natural gas used as fuel in the respondent's operations.

Distributor A company primarily engaged in the sale and delivery of natural and/or supplemental gas directly to consumers through a system of mains.

District chilled water Chilled water from an outside source used as an energy source for cooling in a building. The water is chilled in a central plant and piped into the building. Chilled water may be purchased from a utility or provided by a central physical plant in a separate building that is part of the same multibuilding facility (for example, a hospital complex or university).

District heat Steam or hot water from an outside source used as an energy source in a building The steam or hot water is produced in a central plant and piped into the building. The district heat may be purchased from a utility or provided by a physical plant in a separate building that is part of the same facility (for example, a hospital complex or university).

Diversity The electric utility system's load is made up of many individual loads that make demands upon the system usually at different times of the day. The individual loads within the customer classes follow similar usage patterns, but these classes of service place different demands upon the facilities and the system grid. The service requirements of one electrical system can differ from another by time-of-day usage, facility usage, and/or demands placed upon the system grid.

Diversity exchange An exchange of capacity or energy, or both, between systems whose peak loads occur at different times.

Divestiture The stripping off of one utility function from the others by selling (spinning-off) or in some other way changing the ownership of the assets related to that function. Stripping off is most commonly associated with spinning-off generation assets so they are no longer owned by the shareholders that own the transmission and distribution assets.

Docket A formal record of a Federal Energy Regulatory Commission proceeding. These records are available for inspection and copying by the public. Each individual case proceeding is identified by an assigned number.

DOE Department of Energy.

Domestic See United States.

Domestic inland consumption Domestic inland consumption is the sum of all refined petroleum products supplied for domestic use (excludes international marine bunkers). Consumption is calculated by product by adding production, imports, crude oil burned directly, and refinery fuel and losses, and then subtracting exports and charges in primary stocks (net withdrawals is a plus quantity and net additions is a minus quantity).

Domestic uranium industry Collectively, those businesses (whether U.S. or foreign-based) that operate under the laws and regulations pertaining to the conduct of commerce within the United States and its territories and possessions and that engage in activities within the United States, its territories, and possessions specifically directed toward uranium exploration, development, mining, and milling; marketing of uranium materials; enrichment; fabrication; or acquisition and management of uranium materials for use in commercial nuclear power plants.

Domestic vehicle producer An Original Vehicle Manufacturer that assembles vehicles in the United States for domestic use. The term "domestic" pertains to the fifty states, the District of Columbia, commonwealths, territories, and possessions of the United States.

Double circuit line A transmission line having two separate circuits. Because each carries three-phase power, at least six conductors, three per circuit, are required.

Drainage basin The land drained by a river system.

Drawdown The lowering of the water level of a reservoir as a result of withdrawing water.

Drawdown (maximum) The distance that the water surface of the reservoir is lowered from the normal full elevation to the lowest allowable elevation as the result of the withdrawal of water for the purposes of generating electricity.

Dredge mining A method of recovering coal from rivers or streams.

Drift mine A mine that opens horizontally into the coal bed or coal outcrop.

Drilling The act of boring a hole (1) to determine whether minerals are present in commercially recoverable quantities and (2) to accomplish production of the minerals (including drilling to inject fluids).

- Exploratory. Drilling to locate probable mineral deposits or to establish the nature of geological structures; such wells may not be capable of production if minerals are discovered.
- Developmental. Drilling to delineate the boundaries of a known mineral deposit to enhance the productive capacity of the producing mineral property.
- Directional. Drilling that is deliberately made to depart significantly from the vertical.

Drilling and equipping of wells The drilling and equipping of wells through completion of the "Christmas tree."

Drilling arrangement A contractual agreement under which a working interest owner (assignor) assigns a part of a working interest in a property to another party (the assignee) in exchange for which the assignee agrees to develop the property. The term may also be applied to an agreement under which an operator assigns fractional shares in production from a property to participants for cash considerations as a means of acquiring cash for developing the property. Under a "disproportionate cost" drilling arrangement, the participants normally pay a greater total share of costs than the total value of the fractional shares of the property received in the arrangement.

Dry bottom boiler No slag tanks at furnace throat area. The throat area is clear. Bottom ash drops through the throat to the bottom ash water hoppers. This design is used where the ash melting temperature is greater than the temperature on the furnace wall, allowing for relatively dry furnace wall conditions.

Dry (coal) basis Coal quality data calculated to a theoretical basis in which no moisture is associated with the sample. This basis is determined by measuring the weight loss of a sample when its inherent moisture is driven off under controlled conditions of low temperature air-drying followed by heating to just above the boiling point of water (104 to 110 degrees Centigrade).

Dry gas See Dry natural gas below.

Dry hole An exploratory or development well found to be incapable of producing either oil or gas in sufficient quantities to justify completion as an oil or gas well. Also see Well.

Dry hole charge The charge-off to expense of a previously capitalized cost upon the conclusion of an unsuccessful drilling effort.

Dry hole contribution A payment (either in cash or acreage) that is required by agreement only if a test well is unsuccessful and that is made in exchange for well test and evaluation data.

Dry natural gas Natural gas which remains after: 1) the liquefiable hydrocarbon portion has been removed from the gas stream (i.e., gas after lease, field, and/or plant separation); and 2) any volumes of nonhydrocarbon gases have been removed where they occur in sufficient quantity to render the gas unmarketable. Note: Dry natural gas is also known as consumer-grade natural gas. The parameters for measurement are cubic feet at 60 degrees Fahrenheit and 14.73 pounds per square inch absolute. Also see Natural gas.

Dry natural gas production The process of producing consumer-grade natural gas. Natural gas withdrawn from reservoirs is reduced by volumes used at the production (lease) site and by processing losses. Volumes used at the production site include (1) the volume returned to reservoirs in cycling, repressuring of oil reservoirs, and conservation operations; and (2) gas vented and flared. Processing losses include (1) nonhydrocarbon gases (e.g., water vapor, carbon dioxide, helium, hydrogen sulfide, and nitrogen) removed from the gas stream; and (2) gas converted to liquid form, such as lease condensate and plant liquids. Volumes of dry gas withdrawn from gas storage reservoirs are not considered part of production. Dry natural gas production equals marketed production less extraction loss.

Dry production See Dry natural gas production above.

Dual fuel vehicle (1) A motor vehicle that is capable of operating on an alternative fuel and on gasoline or diesel fuel. These vehicles have at least two separate fuel systems which inject each fuel simultaneously into the engine combustion chamber.

Dual fuel vehicle (2) A motor vehicle that is capable of operating on an alternative fuel and on gasoline or diesel fuel. This term is meant to represent all such vehicles whether they operate on the alternative fuel and gasoline/diesel simultaneously (e.g., flexible-fuel vehicles) or can be switched to operate on gasoline/diesel or an alternative fuel (e.g., bi-fuel vehicles).

Dual-fired unit A generating unit that can produce electricity using two or more input fuels. In some of these units, only the primary fuel can be used continuously; the alternate fuel(s) can be used only as a start-up fuel or in emergencies.

Dump energy Energy generated in a hydroelectric plant by water that cannot be stored or conserved and which energy is in excess of the needs of the system producing the energy.

E85 A fuel containing a mixture of 85 percent ethanol and 15 percent gasoline. (See motor gasoline (finished))

E95 A fuel containing a mixture of 95 percent ethanol and 5 percent gasoline

Economy of scale The principle that larger production facilities have lower unit costs than smaller facilities.

Effective full-power days The number of effective full-power days produced by a unit is a measure of the unit's energy generation. It is determined using the following ratio: Heat generation (planned or actual) in megawatt days thermal (MWdt)(divided by) Licensed thermal power in megawatts thermal (MWt)

EIA The Energy Information Administration. An independent agency within the U.S. Department of Energy that develops surveys, collects energy data, and analyzes and models energy issues. The Agency must meet the requests of Congress, other elements within the Department of Energy, Federal Energy Regulatory Commission, the Executive Branch, its own independent needs, and assist the general public, or other interest groups, without taking a policy position. See more information about EIA at http://tonto.eia.doe.gov/abouteia/

Electric baseboard An individual space heater with electric resistance coils mounted behind shallow panels along baseboards. Electric baseboards rely on passive convection to distribute heated air to the space.

Electric current The flow of electric charge. The preferred unit of measure is the ampere.

Electric energy The ability of an electric current to produce work, heat, light, or other forms of energy. It is measured in kilowatthours.

Electric expenses The cost of labor, material, and expenses incurred in operating a facility's prime movers, generators, auxiliary apparatus, switching gear, and other electric equipment for each of the points where electricity enters the transmission or distribution grid.

Electric generation See Gross generation and Net generation.

Electric generation industry Stationary and mobile generating units that are connected to the electric power grid and can generate electricity. The electric generation industry includes the "electric power sector" (utility generators and independent power producers) and industrial and commercial power generators, including combined-heat-and-power producers, but excludes units at single-family dwellings.

Electric generator A facility that produces only electricity, commonly expressed in kilowatthours (kWh) or megawatthours (MWh). Electric generators include electric utilities and independent power producers.

Electric hybrid vehicle An electric vehicle that either (1) operates solely on electricity, but contains an internal combustion motor that generates additional electricity (series hybrid); or (2) contains an electric system and an internal combustion system and is capable of operating on either system (parallel hybrid).

Electric industry reregulation The design and implementation of regulatory practices to be applied to the remaining traditional utilities after the electric power industry has been restructured. Reregulation applies to those entities that continue to exhibit characteristics of a natural monopoly. Reregulation could employ the same or different regulatory practices as those used before restructuring.

Electric industry restructuring The process of replacing a monopolistic system of electric utility suppliers with competing sellers, allowing individual retail customers to choose their supplier but still receive delivery over the power lines of the local utility. It includes the reconfiguration of vertically-integrated electric utilities.

Electric motor vehicle A motor vehicle powered by an electric motor that draws current from rechargeable storage batteries, fuel cells, photovoltaic arrays, or other sources of electric current.

Electric non-utility Any entity that generates, transmits, or sells electricity, or sells or trades electricity services and products, where costs are not established and recovered by regulatory authority. Examples of these entities include, but are not limited to, independent power producers, power marketers and aggregators (both wholesale and retail), merchant transmission service providers, self-generation entities, and cogeneration firms with Qualifying Facility Status.

Electric operating expenses Summation of electric operation-related expenses, such as operation expenses, maintenance expenses, depreciation expenses, amortization, taxes other than income taxes, Federal income taxes, other income taxes, provision for deferred income taxes, provision for deferred income-credit, and investment tax credit adjustment.

Electric plant (physical) A facility containing prime movers, electric generators, and auxiliary equipment for converting mechanical, chemical, and/or fission energy into electric energy.

Electric plant acquisition adjustment The difference between (a) the cost to the respondent utility of an electric plant acquired as an operating unit or system by purchase and (b) the depreciated original cost, estimated if not known, of such property.

Electric power The rate at which electric energy is transferred. Electric power is measured by capacity and is commonly expressed in megawatts (MW).

Electric power grid A system of synchronized power providers and consumers connected by transmission and distribution lines and operated by one or more control centers. In the continental United States, the electric power grid consists of three systems: the Eastern Interconnect, the Western Interconnect, and the Texas Interconnect. In Alaska and Hawaii, several systems encompass areas smaller than the State (e.g., the interconnect serving Anchorage, Fairbanks, and the Kenai Peninsula; individual islands).

Electric power plant A station containing prime movers, electric generators, and auxiliary equipment for converting mechanical, chemical, and/or fission energy into electric energy.

Electric power sector An energy-consuming sector that consists of electricity only and combined heat and power (CHP) plants whose primary business is to sell electricity, or electricity and heat, to the public—i.e., North American Industry Classification System 22 plants. See also Combined heat and power (CHP) plant and Electricity only plant.

Electric power system An individual electric power entity—a company; an electric cooperative; a public electric supply corporation as the Tennessee Valley Authority; a similar Federal department or agency such as the Bonneville Power Administration; the Bureau of Reclamation or the Corps of Engineers; a municipally owned electric department offering service to the public; or an electric public utility district (a "PUD"); also a jointly owned electric supply project such as the Keystone.

Electric pump for well water This pump forces the water from a well below ground level up into the water pipes that circulate through the house. When this pump is not working, there is a limited supply of running water in the house.

Electric rate The price set for a specified amount and type of electricity by class of service in an electric rate schedule or sales contract.

Electric rate schedule A statement of the electric rate and the terms and conditions governing its application, including attendant contract terms and conditions that have been accepted by a regulatory body with appropriate oversight authority.

Electric system loss Total energy loss from all causes for an electric utility.

Electric system reliability The degree to which the performance of the elements of the electrical system results in power being delivered to consumers within accepted standards and in the amount desired. Reliability encompasses two concepts, adequacy and security. Adequacy implies that there are sufficient generation and transmission resources installed and available to meet projected electrical demand plus reserves for contingencies. Security implies that the system will remain intact operationally (i.e., will have sufficient available operating capacity) even after outages or other equipment failure. The degree of reliability may be measured by the frequency, duration, and magnitude of adverse effects on consumer service.

Electric utility Any entity that generates, transmits, or distributes electricity and recovers the cost of its generation, transmission or distribution assets and operations, either directly or indirectly, through cost-based rates set by a separate regulatory authority (e.g., State Public Service Commission), or is owned by a governmental unit or the consumers that the entity serves. Examples of these entities include: investor-owned entities, public power districts, public utility districts, municipalities, rural electric cooperatives, and State and Federal agencies. Electric utilities may have Federal Energy Regulatory Commission approval for interconnection agreements and wholesale trade tariffs covering either cost-of-service and/or market-based rates under the authority of the Federal Power Act.

Electric utility company See Electric utility above.

Electric utility divestiture The separation of one electric utility function from others through the selling of the management and ownership of the assets related to that function. It is most commonly associated with selling generation assets so they are no longer owned or controlled by the shareholders that own the company's transmission and distribution assets.

Electric utility generator A generator that is owned by an electric utility, (see definition of electric utility) or a jointly owned generator with the greatest share of the generator being electric utility owned. Note: If two or more owners have equal shares of ownership in a generator, it is considered to be an electric utility generator if any one of the owners meets the definition of electric utility.

Electric utility restructuring The introduction of competition into at least the generation phase of electricity production, with a corresponding decrease in regulatory control.

Electric utility sector The electric utility sector consists of privately and publicly owned establishments that generate, transmit, distribute, or sell electricity primarily for use by the public and that meet the definition of an electric utility. Nonutility power producers are not included in the electric sector.

Electric zone A portion of the grid controlled by the independent system operator.

Electrical system energy losses The amount of energy lost during generation, transmission, and distribution of electricity, including plant and unaccounted for use.

Electricity A form of energy characterized by the presence and motion of elementary charged particles generated by friction, induction, or chemical change.

Electricity broker An entity that arranges the sale and purchase of electric energy, the transmission of electricity, and/or other related services between buyers and sellers but does not take title to any of the power sold.

Electricity congestion A condition that occurs when insufficient transmission capacity is available to implement all of the desired transactions simultaneously.

Electricity demand The rate at which energy is delivered to loads and scheduling points by generation, transmission, and distribution facilities.

Electricity demand bid A bid into the power exchange indicating a quantity of energy or an ancillary service that an eligible customer is willing to purchase and, if relevant, the maximum price that the customer is willing to pay.

Electricity generation The process of producing electric energy or the amount of electric energy produced by transforming other forms of energy, commonly expressed in kilowatthours (kWh) or megawatthours (MWh).

Electricity generation, gross See Gross generation.

Electricity generation, net See Net generation.

Electricity only plant A plant designed to produce electricity only. See also Combined heat and power (CHP) plant.

Electricity paid by household The household paid the electric utility company directly for all household uses of electricity (such as water heating, space heating, air-conditioning, cooking, lighting, and operating appliances.) Bills paid by a third party are not counted as paid by the household.

Electricity sales The amount of kilowatthours sold in a given period of time; usually grouped by classes of service, such as residential, commercial, industrial, and other. "Other" sales include sales for public street and highway lighting and other sales to public authorities, sales to railroads and railways, and interdepartmental sales.

Electrochemical process The direct process end use in which electricity is used to cause a chemical ransformation. Major uses of electrochemical process occur in the aluminum industry in which alumina is reduced to molten aluminum metal and oxygen, and in the alkalies and chlorine industry, in which brine is separated into caustic soda, chlorine, and hydrogen.

Elution Activities of removing "elutes" a material (uranium) adsorbed on ion exchange resin from the "eluant" solution.

Emergency The failure of an electric power system to generate or deliver electric power as normally intended, resulting in the cutoff or curtailment of service.

Emergency backup generation The use of electric generators only during interruptions of normal power supply.

Emergency energy Electric energy provided for a limited duration, intended only for use during emergency conditions.

Emissions Anthropogenic releases of gases to the atmosphere. In the context of global climate change, they consist of radiatively important greenhouse gases (e.g., the release of carbon dioxide during fuel combustion).

Emissions coefficient A unique value for scaling emissions to activity data in terms of a standard rate of emissions per unit of activity (e.g., pounds of carbon dioxide emitted per Btu of fossil fuel consumed).

End user A firm or individual that purchases products for its own consumption and not for resale (i.e., an ultimate consumer).

Ending stocks Primary stocks of crude oil and petroleum products held in storage as of 12 midnight on the last day of the month. Primary stocks include crude oil or petroleum products held in storage at (or in) leases, refineries, natural gas processing plants, pipelines, tank farms, and bulk terminals that can store at least 50,000 barrels of petroleum products or that can receive petroleum products by tanker, barge, or pipeline. Crude oil that is in-transit by water from Alaska or that is stored on Federal leases or in the Strategic Petroleum Reserve is included. Primary Stocks exclude stocks of foreign origin that are held in bonded warehouse storage.

Energy The capacity for doing work as measured by the capability of doing work (potential energy) or the conversion of this capability to motion (kinetic energy). Energy has several forms, some of which are easily convertible and can be changed to another form useful for work. Most of the world's convertible energy comes from fossil fuels that are burned to produce heat that is then used as a transfer medium to mechanical or other means in order to accomplish tasks. Electrical energy is usually measured in kilowatthours, while heat energy is usually measured in British thermal units (Btu).

Energy assistance program See Low-Income Home Energy Assistance Program.

Energy audit A program carried out by a utility company in which an auditor inspects a home and suggests ways energy can be saved.

Energy broker system Introduced into Florida by the Public Service Commission, the energy broker system is a system for exchanging information that allows utilities to efficiently exchange hourly quotations of prices at which each is willing to buy and sell electric energy. For the broker system to operate, utility systems must have in place bilateral agreements between all potential parties, must have transmission arrangements between all potential parties, and must have transmission arrangements that allow the exchanges to take place.

Energy charge That portion of the charge for electric service based upon the electric energy (kWh) consumed or billed.

Energy conservation features This includes building shell conservation features, HVAC conservation features, lighting conservation features, any conservation features, and other conservation features incorporated by the building. However, this category does not include any demand-side management (DSM) program participation by the building. Any DSM program participation is included in the DSM Programs.

Energy consumption The use of energy as a source of heat or power or as a raw material input to a manufacturing process.

Energy demand The requirement for energy as an input to provide products and/or services.

Energy deliveries Energy generated by one electric utility system and delivered to another system through one or more transmission lines.

Energy effects The changes in aggregate electricity use (measured in megawatthours) for consumers that participate in a utility DSM (demand-side management) program. Energy effects represent changes at the consumer's meter (i.e., exclude ransmission and distribution effects) and reflect only activities that are undertaken specifically in response to utility-administered programs, including those activities implemented by third parties under contract to the utility. To the extent possible, Energy effects should exclude non-program related effects such as changes in energy usage attributable to nonparticipants, government-mandated energy-efficiency standards that legislate improvements in building and appliance energy usage, changes in consumer behavior that result in greater energy use after initiation in a DSM program, the natural operations of the marketplace, and weather and business-cycle adjustments.

Energy efficiency, Electricity Refers to programs that are aimed at reducing the energy used by specific end-use devices and systems, typically without affecting the services provided. These programs reduce overall electricity consumption (reported in megawatthours), often without explicit consideration for the timing of program-induced savings. Such savings are generally achieved by substituting technologically more advanced equipment to produce the same level of end-use services (e.g. lighting, heating, motor drive) with less electricity. Examples include high-efficiency appliances, efficient lighting programs, high-efficiency heating, ventilating and air conditioning (HVAC) systems or control modifications, efficient building design, advanced electric motor drives, and heat recovery systems.

Energy-efficient motors Are also known as "high-efficiency motors" and "premium motors." They are virtually interchangeable with standard motors, but differences in construction make them more energy efficient.

Energy exchange Any transaction in which quantities of energy are received or given up in return for similar energy products. See exchange, electricity; exchange, petroleum; and exchange, natural gas (see definitions further below).

Energy expenditures The money directly spent by consumers to purchase energy. Expenditures equal the amount of energy used by the consumer multiplied by the price per unit paid by the consumer.

Energy information Includes (A) all information in whatever form on fuel reserves, extraction, and energy resources (including petrochemical feedstocks) wherever located; production, distribution, and consumption of energy and fuels wherever carried on; and (B) matters relating to energy and fuels, such as corporate structure and proprietary relationships, costs, prices, capital investment, and assets, and other matters directly related thereto, wherever they exist.

Energy Information Administration (EIA) An independent agency within the U.S. Department of Energy that develops surveys, collects energy data, and does analytical and modeling analyses of energy issues. The Agency must satisfy the requests of Congress, other elements within the Department of Energy, Federal Energy Regulatory Commission, the Executive Branch, its own independent needs, and assist the general public, or other interest groups, without taking a policy position.

Energy intensity Economy-wide energy intensity measures units of energy to units of gross domestic product (GDP). EIA uses energy consumption (measured in Btu) to the constant dollar value of the GDP. Energy intensity can also be measured at the sector level using sector-specific data. For example, energy intensity in the commercial sector is measured by the ratio of energy consumption measured in millions of Btu to square feet of commercial floor space.

Energy loss Deleted because there is no need for a general term to encompass all forms of energy loss. Terms referring to losses specific to particular energy sources are defined separately.

Energy loss (power) See Power loss.

Energy management and control system (EMCS) An energy conservation feature that uses mini/microcomputers, instrumentation, control equipment, and software to manage a building's use of energy for heating, ventilation, air conditioning, lighting, and/or business-related processes. These systems can also manage fire control, safety, and security. Not included as EMCS are time-clock thermostats.

Energy management practices Involvement, as a part of the building's normal operations, in energy efficiency programs that are designed to reduce the energy used by specific end-use systems. This includes the following: EMCS, DSM Program Participation, Energy Audit, and a Building Energy Manager.

Energy Policy Act of 1992 (EPACT) This legislation creates a new class of power generators, exempt wholesale generators, that are exempt from the provisions of the Public Holding Company Act of 1935 and grants the authority to the Federal Energy Regulatory Commission to order and condition access by eligible parties to the interconnected transmission grid.

Energy production See production terms associated with specific energy types.

Energy receipts Energy brought into a site from another location.

Energy reserves Estimated quantities of energy sources that are demonstrated to exist with reasonable certainty on the basis of geologic and engineering data (proved reserves) or that can reasonably be expected to exist on the basis of geologic evidence that supports projections from proved reserves (probable/indicated reserves). Knowledge of the location, quantity, and grade of probable/indicated reserves is generally incomplete or much less certain than it is for proved energy reserves. *Note:* This term is equivalent to "Demonstrated Reserves" as defined in the resource/reserve classification contained in the U.S. Geological Survey Circular 831, 1980. Demonstrated reserves include measured and indicated reserves but exclude inferred reserves.

Energy sale(s) The transfer of title of an energy commodity from a seller to a buyer for a price or the quantity transferred during a specified period.

Energy savings A reduction in the amount of electricity used by end users as a result of participation in energy efficiency programs and load management programs.

Energy service provider An energy entity that provides service to a retail or end-use customer.

Energy source Any substance or natural phenomenon that can be consumed or transformed to supply heat or power. Examples include petroleum, coal, natural gas, nuclear, biomass, electricity, wind, sunlight, geothermal, water movement, and hydrogen in fuel cells.

Energy supply Energy made available for future disposition. Supply can be considered and measured from the point of view of the energy provider or the receiver.

Energy supplier Fuel companies supplying electricity, natural gas, fuel oil, kerosene, or LPG (liquefied petroleum gas) to the household.

Energy used in the home For electricity or natural gas, the quantity is the amount used by the household during the 365- or 366-day period. For fuel oil, kerosene, and liquefied petroleum gas (LPG), the quantity consists of fuel purchased, not fuel consumed. If the level of fuel in the storage tank was the same at the beginning and end of the annual period, then the quantity consumed would be the same as the quantity purchased.

Energy-use sectors A group of major energy-consuming components of U.S. society developed to measure and analyze energy use. The sectors most commonly referred to in EIA are: residential, commercial, industrial, transportation, and electric power.

Energy-weighted industrial output The weighted sum of real output for all two-digit Standard Industrial Classification (SIC) manufacturing industries plus agriculture, construction, and mining. The weight for each industry is the ratio between the quantity of end-use energy consumption to the value of real output.

Engine size The total volume within all cylinders of an engine when pistons are at their lowest positions. The engine is usually measured in "liters" or "cubic inches of displacement (CID)." Generally, larger engines result in greater engine power, but less fuel efficiency. There are 61.024 cubic inches in a liter.

Enriched uranium Uranium in which the U-235 isotope concentration has been increased to greater than the 0.711 percent U-235 (by weight) present in natural uranium.

Enrichment feed deliveries Uranium that is shipped under contract to a supplier of enrichment services for use in preparing enriched uranium product to a specified U-235 concentration and that ultimately will be used as fuel in a nuclear reactor.

Enrichment tails assay A measure of the amount of fissile uranium (U-235) remaining in the waste stream from the uranium enrichment process. The natural uranium "feed" that enters the enrichment process generally contains 0.711 percent (by weight) U-235. The "product stream" contains enriched uranium (more than 0.711 percent U-235) and the "waste" or "tails" stream contains depleted uranium (less than 0.711 percent U-235). At the historical enrichment tails assay of 0.2 percent, the waste stream would contain 0.2 percent U-235. A higher enrichment tails assay requires more uranium feed (thus permitting natural uranium stockpiles to be decreased), while increasing the output of enriched material for the same energy expenditure.

Environmental impact statement A report that documents the information required to evaluate the environmental impact of a project. It informs decision-makers and the public of the reasonable alternatives that would avoid or minimize adverse impacts or enhance the quality of the environment.

Environmental Protection Agency (EPA) certification files Computer files produced by EPA for analysis purposes. For each vehicle make, model and year, the files contain the EPA test MPGs (city, highway, and 55/45 composite). These MPG's are associated with various combinations of engine and drive-train technologies (e.g., number of cylinders, engine size, gasoline or diesel fuel, and automatic or manual transmission). These files also contain information similar to that in the DOE/EPA Gas Mileage Guide, although the MPGs in that publication are adjusted for shortfall.

Environmental restoration Although usually described as "cleanup," this function encompasses a wide range of activities, such as stabilizing contaminated soil; treating ground water; decommissioning process buildings, nuclear reactors, chemical separations plants, and many other facilities; and exhuming sludge and buried drums of waste.

Environmental restrictions In reference to coal accessibility, land-use restrictions that constrain, postpone, or prohibit mining in order to protect environmental resources of an area; for example, surface- or groundwater quality, air quality affected by mining, or plants or animals or their habitats.

EPA certification A permanent label on fireplace inserts and freestanding wood stoves manufactured after July 1, 1988, indicating that the equipment meets EPA standards for clean burning.

EPA composite MPG The harmonic mean of the EPA city and highway MPG (miles per gallon), weighted under the assumption of 55 percent city driving and 45 percent highway driving.

Equilibrium cycle An analytical term that refers to fuel cycles that occur after the initial one or two cycles of a reactor's operation. For a given type of reactor, equilibrium cycles have similar fuel characteristics.

Equity (financial) Ownership of shareholders in a corporation represented by stock.

Equity capital The sum of capital from retained earnings and the issuance of stock.

Equity crude oil The proportion of production that a concession owner has the legal and contractual right to retain.

Equity in earnings of unconsolidated affiliates A company's proportional share (based on ownership) of the net earnings or losses of an unconsolidated affiliate.

Establishment An economic unit, generally, at a single physical location where business is conducted or where services or industrial operations are performed. However, "establishment" is not synonymous with "building."

Estimated additional resources (EAR) The uranium in addition to reasonable assured resources (RAR) that is expected to occur, mostly on the basis of direct geological evidence, in extensions of well-explored deposits, little-explored deposits, and undiscovered deposits believed to exist along a well-defined geologic trend with known deposits, such that the uranium can subsequently be recovered within the given cost ranges. Estimates of tonnage and grade are based on available sampling data and on knowledge of the deposit characteristics as determined in the best known parts of the deposit or in similar deposits. EAR correspond to DOE's Probable Potential Resource Category.

ETBE (ethyl tertiary butyl ether) $(CH_3)_3COC2H$: An oxygenate blend stock formed by the catalytic etherification of isobutylene with ethanol.

Ethane (C_2H_6) A normally gaseous straight-chain hydrocarbon. It is a colorless paraffinic gas that boils at a temperature of -127.48 degrees Fahrenheit. It is extracted from natural gas and refinery gas streams.

Ethanol (CH_3-CH_2OH) A clear, colorless, flammable oxygenated hydrocarbon. Ethanol is typically produced chemically from ethylene, or biologically from fermentation of various sugars from carbohydrates found in agricultural crops and cellulosic residues from crops or wood. It is used in the United States as a gasoline octane enhancer and oxygenate (blended up to 10 percent concentration). Ethanol can also be used in high concentrations (E85) in vehicles designed for its use. See Fuel ethanol and E85. *Note:* The lower heating value, equal to 76,000 Btu per gallon, is assumed for estimates in the *Renewables Energy Annual* report.

Ether A generic term applied to a group of organic chemical compounds composed of carbon, hydrogen, and oxygen, characterized by an oxygen atom attached to two carbon atoms (e.g., methyl tertiary butyl ether).

Ethylene An olefinic hydrocarbon recovered from refinery processes or petrochemical processes. Ethylene is used as a petrochemical feedstock for numerous chemical applications and the production of consumer goods.

Ethylene dichloride A colorless, oily liquid used as a solvent and fumigant for organic synthesis, and for ore flotation.

Eurasia The physical land mass containing the continents of Europe and Asia. For Energy Information Administration reporting, it includes the former parts of the Union of Soviet Socialist Republics (U.S.S.R.): Armenia, Azerbaijan, Belarus, Estonia, Georgia, Kazakhstan, Kyrgyzstan, Latvia, Lithuania, Moldova, Russia, Tajikistan, Turkmenistan, Ukraine, and Uzbekistan.

Evacuated-tube collector A collector in which solar thermal heat is captured by use of a collector fluid that flows through an absorber tube contained inside an evacuated glass tube.

Evaporation pond A containment pond (that preferably has an impermeable lining of clay or synthetic material such as hypalon) to hold liquid wastes and to concentrate the waste through evaporation.

Evaporative cooler (swamp cooler) An air-cooling unit that turns air into moist, cool air by saturating the air with water vapor. It does not cool air by use of a refrigeration unit.

Excess statutory depletion The excess of estimated statutory depletion allowable as an income tax deduction over the amount of cost depletion otherwise allowable as a tax deduction, determined on a total enterprise basis.

Exchange See energy exchange above.

Exchange agreement A contractual agreement in which quantities of crude oil, petroleum products, natural gas, or electricity are delivered, either directly or through intermediaries, from one company to another company, in exchange for the delivery by the second company to the first company of an equivalent volume or heat content. The exchange may take place at the same time and location or at different times and/or locations. Such agreements may also involve the payment of cash. *Note:* EIA excludes volumes sold through exchange agreements to avoid double counting of data. See energy exchange above.

Exchange, electricity A type of energy exchange in which one electric utility agrees to supply electricity to another. Electricity received is returned in kind at a later time or is accumulated as an energy balance until the end of a specified period, after which settlement may be made by monetary payment. *Note:* This term is also referred to as exchange energy.

Exchange energy See exchange, electricity above.

Exchange, natural gas A type of energy exchange in which one company agrees to deliver gas, either directly or through intermediaries, to another company at one location or in one time period in exchange for the delivery by the second company to the first company of an equivalent volume or heat content at a different location or time period. *Note:* Such agreements may or may not include the payment of fees in dollar or volumetric amounts.

Exchange, petroleum A type of energy exchange in which quantities of crude oil or any petroleum product(s) are received or given up in return for other crude oil or petroleum products. It includes reciprocal sales and purchases.

Exchange, power Delete in favor of the already-defined term exchange energy, which should be renamed exchange electricity or exchange, electricity.

Exempt wholesale generator (EWG) Wholesale generators created under the 1992 Energy Policy Act that are exempt from certain financial and legal restrictions stipulated in the Public Utilities Holding Company Act of 1935.

Exhaust fan Small fans located in the wall or ceiling that exhaust air, odors, and moisture from the bathroom, kitchen, or basement to the outside.

Expenditure The incurrence of a liability to obtain an asset or service.

Expenditures per million Btu The aggregate ratio of a group of buildings' total expenditures for a given fuel to the total consumption of that fuel.

Expenditures per square foot The aggregate ratio of a group of buildings' total expenditures for a given fuel to the total floor space in those buildings.

Exploration drilling Drilling done in search of new mineral deposits, on extensions of known ore deposits, or at the location of a discovery up to the time when the company decides that sufficient ore reserves are present to justify commercial exploration. Assessment drilling is reported as exploration drilling.

Exploratory well A hole drilled: a) to find and produce oil or gas in an area previously considered unproductive area; b) to find a new reservoir in a known field, i.e., one previously producing oil and gas from another reservoir, or c) to extend the limit of a known oil or gas reservoir.

Exports Shipments of goods from within the 50 States and the District of Columbia to U.S. possessions and territories or to foreign countries.

Extensions Any new reserves credited to a previously producing reservoir because of enlargement of its proved area. This enlargement in proved area is usually due to new well drilling outside of the previously known productive limits of the reservoir.

Extensions, discoveries, and other additions Additions to an enterprise's proved reserves that result from (1) extension of the proved acreage of previously discovered (old) reserves through additional drilling in periods subsequent to discovery and (2) discovery of new fields with proved reserves or of new reservoirs of proved reserves in old fields.

Externalities Benefits or costs, generated as a byproduct of an economic activity, that do not accrue to the parties involved in the activity. Environmental externalities are benefits or costs that manifest themselves through changes in the physical or biological environment.

Extraction loss The reduction in volume of natural gas due to the removal of natural gas liquid constituents such as ethane, propane, and butane at natural gas processing plants.

Extractive industries Industries involved in the activities of (1) prospecting and exploring for wasting (non-regenerative) natural resources, (2) acquiring them, (3) further exploring them, (4) developing them, and (5) producing (extracting) them from the earth. The term does not encompass the industries of forestry, fishing, agriculture, animal husbandry, or any others that might be involved with resources of a regenerative nature.

Extraordinary income deductions (electric utility) Those items related to transactions of a nonrecurring nature that are not typical or customary business activities of the utility and that would significantly distort the current year's net income if reported other than as extraordinary items.

Fabricated fuel Fuel assemblies composed of an array of fuel rods loaded with pellets of enriched uranium dioxide.

Facilities charge An amount to be paid by the customer in a lump sum, or periodically as reimbursement for facilities furnished. The charge may include operation and maintenance as well as fixed costs.

Facility An existing or planned location or site at which prime movers, electric generators, and/or equipment for converting mechanical, chemical, and/or nuclear energy into electric energy are situated or will be situated. A facility may contain more than one generator of either the same or different prime mover type. For a cogenerator, the facility includes the industrial or commercial process.

Fahrenheit A temperature scale on which the boiling point of water is at 212 degrees above zero on the scale and the freezing point is at 32 degrees above zero at standard atmospheric pressure.

Failure or hazard Any electric power supply equipment or facility failure or other event that, in the judgement of the reporting entity, constitutes a hazard to maintaining the continuity of the bulk electric power supply system such that a load reduction action may become necessary and reportable outage may occur. Types of abnormal conditions that should be reported include the imposition of a special operating procedure, the extended purchase of emergency power, other bulk power system actions that may be caused by a natural disaster, a major equipment failure that would impact the bulk power supply, and an environmental and/or regulatory action requiring equipment outages.

Farm out (in) arrangement An arrangement, used primarily in the oil and gas industry, in which the owner or lessee of mineral rights (the first party) assigns a working interest to an operator (the second party), the consideration for which is specified exploration and/or development activities. The first party retains an overriding royalty or other type of economic interest in the mineral production. The arrangement from the viewpoint of the second party is termed a "farm-in arrangement."

Farm use Energy use at establishments where the primary activity is growing crops and/or raising animals. Energy use by all facilities and equipment at these establishments is included, whether or not it is directly associated with growing crops and/or raising animals. Common types of energy-using equipment include tractors, irrigation pumps, crop dryers, smudge pots, and milking machines. Facility energy use encompasses all structures at the establishment, including the farm house.

f.a.s. See Free alongside ship (below).

f.a.s. value Free alongside ship value. The value of a commodity at the port of exportation, generally including the purchase price plus all charges incurred in placing the commodity alongside the carrier at the port of exportation in the country of exportation.

Fast breeder reactor (FBR) A reactor in which the fission chain reaction is sustained primarily by fast neutrons rather than by thermal or intermediate neutrons. Fast reactors require little or no moderator to slow down the neutrons from the speeds at which they are ejected from fissioning nuclei. This type of reactor produces more fissile material than it consumes.

Federal coal lease A lease granted to a mining company to produce coal from land owned and administered by the Federal Government in exchange for royalties and other revenues.

Federal electric utility A utility that is either owned or financed by the Federal Government.

Federal Energy Regulatory Commission (FERC) The Federal agency with jurisdiction over interstate electricity sales, wholesale electric rates, hydroelectric licensing, natural gas pricing, oil pipeline rates, and gas pipeline certification. FERC is an independent regulatory agency within the Department of Energy and is the successor to the Federal Power Commission.

Federal Power Act Enacted in 1920, and amended in 1935, the Act consists of three parts. The first part incorporated the Federal Water Power Act administered by the former Federal Power Commission, whose activities were confined almost entirely to licensing non-Federal hydroelectric projects. Parts II and III were added with the passage of the Public Utility Act. These parts extended the Act's jurisdiction to include regulating the interstate transmission of electrical energy and rates for its sale as wholesale in interstate commerce. The Federal Energy Regulatory Commission is now charged with the administration of this law.

Federal Power Commission (FPC) The predecessor agency of the Federal Energy Regulatory Commission. The Federal Power Commission was created by an Act of Congress under the Federal Water Power Act on June 10, 1920. It was charged originally with regulating the electric power and natural gas industries. It was abolished on September 30, 1977, when the Department of Energy was created. Its functions were divided between the Department of Energy and the Federal Energy Regulatory Commission, an independent regulatory agency.

Federal region In a Presidential directive issued in 1969, various Federal agencies (among them the currently designated Department of Health and Human Services, the Department of Labor, the Office of Economic Opportunity, and the Small Business Administration) were instructed to adopt a uniform field system of 10 geographic regions with common boundaries and headquarters cities. The action was taken to correct the evolution of fragmented Federal field organization structures that each agency or component created independently, usually with little reference to other agencies' arrangements. Most Federal domestic agencies or their components have completed realignments and relocations to conform to the Standard Federal Administration Regions (SFARs).

Fee interest The absolute, legal possession and ownership of land, property, or rights, including mineral rights. A fee interest can be sold (in its entirety or in part) or passed on to heirs or successors.

Feeder line An electrical line that extends radially from a distribution substation to supply electrical energy within an electric area or sub-area.

FERC The Federal Energy Regulatory Commission.

FERC guidelines A compilation of the Federal Energy Regulatory Commission's enabling statutes; procedural and program regulations; and orders, opinions, and decisions.

Fertile material Material that is not itself fissionable by thermal neutrons but can be converted to fissile material by irradiation. The two principal fertile materials are uranium-238 and thorium-232.

Field An area consisting of a single reservoir or multiple reservoirs all grouped on, or related to, the same individual geological structural feature and/or stratigraphic condition. There may be two or more reservoirs in a field that are separated vertically by intervening impervious strata or laterally by local geologic barriers, or by both.

Field area A geographic area encompassing two or more pools that have a common gathering and metering system, the reserves of which are reported as a single unit. This concept applies primarily to the Appalachian region.

Field discovery year The calendar year in which a field was first recognized as containing economically recoverable accumulations of oil and/or gas.

Field production Represents crude oil production on leases, natural gas liquids production at natural gas processing plants, new supply of other hydrocarbons/oxygenates and motor gasoline blending components, and fuel ethanol blended into finished motor gasoline.

Field separation facility A surface installation designed to recover lease condensate from a produced natural gas stream usually orginating from more than one lease and managed by the operator of one or more of these leases.

File rate schedule The rate for a particular electric service, including attendant contract terms and conditions, accepted for filing by a regulatory body with appropriate oversight authority.

Filing Any written application, complaint, declaration, petition, protest, answer, motion, brief, exception, rate schedule, or other pleading, amendment to a pleading, document, or similar paper that is submitted to a utility commission.

Final order A final ruling by FERC that terminates an action, decides some matter litigated by the petitioning parties, operates to some right, or completely disposes of the subject matter.

Financial Accounting Standards Board (FASB) An independent board responsible, since 1973, for establishing generally accepted accounting principles. Its official pronouncement are called "Statements of Financial Accounting Standards" and "Interpretations of Financial Accounting Standards."

Finished leaded gasoline Contains more than 0.05 gram of lead per gallon or more than 0.005 gram of phosphorus per gallon. Premium and regular grades are included, depending on the octane rating. Includes leaded gasohol. Blendstock is excluded until blending has been completed. Alcohol that is to be used in the blending of gasohol is also excluded.

Finished motor gasoline See motor gasoline (finished).

Firm An association, company, corporation, estate, individual, joint venture, partnership, or sole proprietorship, or any other entity, however organized, including: (a) charitable or educational institutions; (b) the Federal Government, including corporations, departments, Federal agencies, and other instrumentalities; and State and local governments. A firm may consist of (1) a parent entity, including the consolidated and unconsolidated entities (if any) that it directly or indirectly controls; (2) a parent and its consolidated entities only; (3) an unconsolidated entity; or (4) any part or combination of the above.

Firm power Power or power-producing capacity, intended to be available at all times during the period covered by a guaranteed commitment to deliver, even under adverse conditions.

First purchase (of crude oil) An equity (not custody) transaction commonly associated with a transfer of ownership of crude oil associated with the physical removal of the crude oil from a property for the first time (also referred to as a lease sale). A first purchase normally occurs at the time and place of ownership transfer where the crude oil volume sold is measured and recorded on a run ticket or other similar physical evidence of purchase. The volume purchased and the cost of such transaction shall not be measured farther from the wellhead than the point at which the value for landowner royalties is established, if there was a separate landowner.

First purchase price The price for domestic crude oil reported by the company that owns the crude oil the first time it is removed from the lease boundary.

Fiscal year The U.S. Government's fiscal year runs from October 1 through September 30. The fiscal year is designated by the calendar year in which it ends; e.g., fiscal year 2002 begins on October 1, 2001 and ends on September 30, 2002

Fissile material Material that can be caused to undergo atomic fission when bombarded by neutrons. The most important fissionable materials are uranium-235, plutonium-239, and uranium-233.

Fission The process whereby an atomic nucleus of appropriate type, after capturing a neutron, splits into (generally) two nuclei of lighter elements, with the release of substantial amounts of energy and two or more neutrons.

Fixed asset turnover A ratio of revenue to fixed assets which is a measure of the productivity and efficiency of property, plant, and equipment in generating revenue. A high turnover reflects positively on the entity's ability to utilize properly its fixed assets in business operations.

Fixed assets Tangible property used in the operations of an entity, but not expected to be consumed or converted into cash in the ordinary course of events. With a life in excess of one year, not intended for resale to customers, and subject to depreciation (with the exception of land), they are usually referred to as property, plant, and equipment.

Fixed carbon The nonvolatile matter in coal minus the ash. Fixed carbon is the solid residue other than ash obtained by prescribed methods of destructive distillation of a coal. Fixed carbon is the part of the total carbon that remains when coal is heated in a closed vessel until all matter is driven off.

Fixed charge coverage The ratio of earnings available to pay so-called fixed charges to such fixed charges. Fixed charges include interest on funded debt, including leases, plus the related amortizations of debt discount, premium, and expense. Earnings available for fixed charges may be computed before or after deducting income taxes. Occasionally credits for the "allowance for funds used during construction" are excluded from the earnings figures. The precise procedures followed in calculating fixed charge or interest coverages vary widely.

Fixed cost (expense) An expenditure or expense that does not vary with volume level of activity.

Fixed operating costs Costs other than those associated with capital investment that do not vary with the operation, such as maintenance and payroll.

Flared Gas disposed of by burning in flares usually at the production sites or at gas processing plants.

Flared natural gas See *flared* above.

Flat and meter rate schedule An electric rate schedule consisting of two components, the first of which is a service charge and the second a price for the energy consumed.

Flat demand rate schedule An electric rate schedule based on billing demand that provides no charge for energy.

Flat plate pumped A medium-temperature solar thermal collector that typically consists of a metal frame, glazing, absorbers (usually metal), and insulation and that uses a pumped liquid as the heat-transfer medium: predominant use is in water-heating applications.

Fleet vehicle Any motor vehicle a company owns or leases that is in the normal operations of a company. Vehicles which are used in the normal operation of a company, but are owned by company employees are not fleet vehicles. If a company provides services in addition to providing natural gas, only those vehicles that are used by the natural gas provider portion of a company should be counted as fleet vehicles. Vehicles that are considered "off-road" (e.g., farm or construction vehicles) or demonstration vehicles are not to be counted as fleet vehicles. Fleet vehicles include gasoline/diesel powered vehicles and alternative-fuel vehicles.

Flexible fuel vehicle A vehicle that can operate on (1) alternative fuels (such as M85 or E85), (2) 100-percent petroleum-based fuels, or (3) any mixture of an alternative fuel (or fuels) and a petroleum-based fuel. Flexible fuel vehicles have a single fuel system to handle alternative and petroleum-based fuels. Flexible fuel vehicle and variable fuel vehicle are synonymous terms.

Flexicoking A thermal cracking process which converts heavy hydrocarbons such as crude oil, tar sands bitumen, and distillation residues into light hydrocarbons. Feedstocks can be any pumpable hydrocarbons including those containing high concentrations of sulfur and metals.

Floor (coal) The upper surface of the stratum underlying a coal seam. In coals that were formed in persistent swamp environments, the floor is typically a bed of clay, known as "underclay," representing the soil in which the trees or other coal-forming swamp vegetation was rooted.

Floor price A price specified in a market-price contract as the lowest purchase price of the uranium, even if the market price falls below the specified price. The floor price may be related to the seller's production costs.

Floor space The area enclosed by exterior walls of a building, including parking areas, basements, or other floors below ground level. It is measured in square feet.

Floor, wall, or pipeless furnace Space-heating equipment consisting of a ductless combustor or resistance unit, having an enclosed chamber where fuel is burned or where electrical-resistance heat is generated to warm the rooms of a building. A floor furnace is located below the floor and delivers heated air to the room immediately above or (if under a partition) to the room on each side. A wall furnace is installed in a partition or in an outside wall and delivers heated air to the rooms on one or both sides of the wall. A pipeless furnace is installed in a basement and delivers heated air through a large register in the floor of the room or hallway immediately above.

Flow control The laws, regulations, and economic incentives or disincentives used by waste managers to direct waste generated in a specific geographic area to a designated landfill, recycling, or waste-to-energy facility.

Flue An enclosed passageway for directing products of combustion to the atmosphere.

Flue gas desulfurization Equipment used to remove sulfur oxides from the combustion gases of a boiler plant before discharge to the atmosphere. Also referred to as scrubbers. Chemicals such as lime are used as scrubbing media.

Flue-gas desulfurization unit (scrubber) Equipment used to remove sulfur oxides from the combustion gases of a boiler plant before discharge to the atmosphere. Chemicals such as lime are used as the scrubbing media.

Flue-gas particulate collector Equipment used to remove fly ash from the combustion gases of a boiler plant before discharge to the atmosphere. Particulate collectors include electrostatic precipitators, mechanical collectors (cyclones), fabric filters (baghouses), and wet scrubbers.

Fluid catalytic cracking The refining process of breaking down the larger, heavier, and more complex hydrocarbon molecules into simpler and lighter molecules. Catalytic cracking is accomplished by the use of a catalytic agent and is an effective process for increasing the yield of gasoline from crude oil. Catalytic cracking processes fresh feeds and recycled feeds.

Fluid coking A thermal cracking process utilizing the fluidized-solids technique to remove carbon (coke) for continuous conversion of heavy, low-grade oils into lighter products.

Fluidized-bed combustion A method of burning particulate fuel, such as coal, in which the amount of air required for combustion far exceeds that found in conventional burners. The fuel particles are continually fed into a bed of mineral ash in the proportions of 1 part fuel to 200 parts ash, while a flow of air passes up through the bed, causing it to act like a turbulent fluid.

Fluorescent lamp A glass enclosure in which light is produced when electricity is passed through mercury vapor inside the enclosure. The electricity creates a radiation discharge that strikes a coating on the inside surface of the enclosure, causing the coating to glow. *Note:* Traditional fluorescent lamps are usually straight or circular white glass tubes used in fixtures specially designed for them. A newer type of fluorescent lamp, the compact fluorescent lamp, takes up much less room, comes in many differently-shaped configurations, and is designed to be used in some fixtures originally intended to house incandescent lamps.

Fluorescent light bulbs These are usually long, narrow, white tubes made of glass coated on the inside with fluorescent material, which is connected to a fixture at both ends of the light bulb; some are circular tubes. The light bulb produces light by passing electricity through mercury vapor, which causes the fluorescent coating to glow or fluoresce.

Fluorescent lighting other than compact fluorescent bulbs In fluorescent lamps, energy is converted to light by using an electric charge to "excite" gaseous atoms within a fluorescent tube. Common types are "cool white," "warm white," etc. Special energy efficient fluorescent lights have been developed that produce the same amount of light while consuming less energy. *Note*: for definition of compact fluorescent bulbs, go to http://www.eia.doe.gov/glossary/glossary_c.htm#compact_bulbs.

Flux material A substance used to promote fusion, e.g., of metals or minerals.

Fly ash Particulate matter mainly from coal ash in which the particle diameter is less than 1×10^4 meter. This ash is removed from the flue gas using flue gas particulate collectors such as fabric filters and electrostatic precipitators.

FME Free Market Economies. Countries that are members of the Council for Mutual Economic Assistance (CMEA) are not included.

f.o.b. price The price actually charged at the producing country's port of loading. The reported price should be after deducting any rebates and discounts or adding premiums where applicable and should be the actual price paid with no adjustment for credit terms.

f.o.b. value (coal) Free-on-board value. This is the value of coal at the coal mine or of coke and breeze at the coke plant without any insurance or freight transportation charges added.

Footage drilled Total footage for wells in various categories, as reported for any specified period, includes (1) the deepest total depth (length of well bores) of all wells drilled from the surface, (2) the total of all bypassed footage drilled in connection with reported wells, and (3) all new footage drilled for directional sidetrack wells. Footage reported for directional sidetrack wells does not include footage in the common bore that is reported as footage for the original well. In the case of old wells drilled deeper, the reported footage is that which was drilled below the total depth of the old well.

Forced outage The shutdown of a generating unit, transmission line, or other facility for emergency reasons or a condition in which the generating equipment is unavailable for load due to unanticipated breakdown.

Foreign access Refers to proved reserves of crude, condensate, and natural gas liquids applicable to long-term supply agreements with foreign governments or authorities in which the company or one of its affiliates acts as producer.

Foreign-controlled firms (coal) Foreign-controlled firms are U.S. coal producers with more than 50 percent of their stock or assets owned by a foreign firm.

Foreign currency transaction gains and losses Gains or losses resulting from the effect of exchange rate changes on transactions denominated in currencies other than the functional currency (for example, a U.S. enterprise may borrow Swiss francs or a French subsidiary may have a receivable denominated in kroner from a Danish customer). Gains and losses on those foreign currency transactions are generally included in determining net income for the period in which exchange rates change unless the transaction hedges a foreign currency commitment or a net investment in a foreign entity. Intercompany transactions of a long-term investment nature are considered part of a parent's net investment and hence do not give rise to gains or losses.

Foreign currency translation effects Gains or losses resulting from the process of expressing amounts denominated or measured in one currency in terms of another currency by use of the exchange rate between the two currencies. This process is generally required to consolidate the financial statements of foreign affiliates into the total company financial statements and to recognize the conversion of foreign currency or the settlement of a receivable or payable denominated in foreign currency at a rate different from that at which the item is recorded. Translation adjustments are not included in determining net income, but are disclosed as separate components of consolidated equity.

Foreign operations These are operations that are located outside the United States. Determination of whether an enterprise's mobile assets, such as offshore drilling rigs or ocean-going vessels, constitute foreign operations should depend on whether such assets are normally identified with operations located outside the United States.

Forward cost (1) Forward costs are those operating and capital costs yet to be incurred at the time an estimate of reserves is made. Profits and "sunk" costs, such as past expenditures for property acquisition, exploration, and mine development, are not included. Therefore, the various forward-cost categories are independent of the market price at which uranium produced from the reserves would be sold.

Forward cost (2) The operating and capital costs still to be incurred in the production of uranium from in-place reserves. By using forward costing, estimates for reserves for ore deposits in differing geological settings and status of development can be aggregated and reported for selected cost categories. Included are costs for labor, materials, power and fuel, royalties, payroll taxes, insurance, and applicable general and administrative costs. Excluded from forward cost estimates are prior expenditures, if any, incurred for property acquisition, exploration, mine development, and mill construction, as well as income taxes, profit, and the cost of money. Forward costs are neither the full costs of production nor the market price at which the uranium, when produced, might be sold.

Forward coverage Amount of uranium required to assure uninterrupted operation of nuclear power plants.

Fossil fuel An energy source formed in the Earth's crust from decayed organic material. The common fossil fuels are petroleum, coal, and natural gas.

Fossil-fuel electric generation Electric generation in which the prime mover is a turbine rotated by high-pressure steam produced in a boiler by heat from burning fossil fuels.

Fossil fuel plant A plant using coal, petroleum, or gas as its source of energy.

Fossil fuel steam-electric power plant An electricity generation plant in which the prime mover is a turbine rotated by high-pressure steam produced in a boiler by heat from burning fossil fuels.

Foundry An operation where metal castings are produced, using coke as a fuel.

Foundry coke This is a special coke that is used in furnaces to produce cast and ductile iron products. It is a source of heat and also helps maintain the required carbon content of the metal product. Foundry coke production requires lower temperatures and longer times than blast furnace coke.

Fractionation The process by which saturated hydrocarbons are removed from natural gas and separated into distinct products, or "fractions," such as propane, butane, and ethane.

Framework Convention on Climate Change (FCCC) An agreement opened for signature at the "Earth Summit" in Rio de Janeiro, Brazil, on June 4, 1992, which has the goal of stabilizing greenhouse gas concentrations in the atmosphere at a level that would prevent significant anthropogenically forced climate change.

Free alongside ship (f.a.s.) The value of a commodity at the port of exportation, generally including the purchase price plus all charges incurred in placing the commodity alongside the carrier at the port of exportation.

Free on board (f.o.b.) A sales transaction in which the seller makes the product available for pick up at a specified port or terminal at a specified price and the buyer pays for the subsequent transportation and insurance.

Free well A well drilled and equipped by an assignee as consideration for the assignment of a fractional share of the working interest, commonly under a farm-out agreement.

Fresh feed input Represents input of material (crude oil, unfinished oils, natural gas liquids, other hydrocarbons and oxygenates or finished products) to processing units at a refinery that is being processed (input) into a particular unit for the first time. Examples:
(1) Unfinished oils coming out of a crude oil distillation unit which are input into a catalytic cracking unit are considered fresh feed to the catalytic cracking unit.
(2) Unfinished oils coming out of a catalytic cracking unit being looped back into the same catalytic cracking unit to be reprocessed are not considered fresh feed.

Fresh feeds Crude oil or petroleum distillates that are being fed to processing units for the first time.

FRS Financial Reporting System Survey (EIA survey).

Fuel Any material substance that can be consumed to supply heat or power. Included are petroleum, coal, and natural gas (the fossil fuels), and other consumable materials, such as uranium, biomass, and hydrogen.

Fuel cell A device capable of generating an electrical current by converting the chemical energy of a fuel (e.g., hydrogen) directly into electrical energy. Fuel cells differ from conventional electrical cells in that the active materials such as fuel and oxygen are not contained within the cell but are supplied from outside. It does not contain an intermediate heat cycle, as do most other electrical generation techniques.

Fuel cycle The entire set of sequential processes or stages involved in the utilization of fuel, including extraction, transformation, transportation, and combustion. Emissions generally occur at each stage of the fuel cycle.

Fuel efficiency See Miles per gallon.

Fuel emergencies An emergency that exists when supplies of fuels or hydroelectric storage for generation are at a level or estimated to be at a level that would threaten the reliability or adequacy of bulk electric power supply. The following factors should be taken into account to determine that a fuel emergency exists:
1. Fuel stock or hydroelectric project water storage levels are 50 percent or less of normal for that particular time of the year and a continued downward trend in fuel stock or hydroelectric project water storage level is estimated; or
2. Unscheduled dispatch or emergency generation is causing an abnormal use of a particular fuel type, such that the future supply of stocks of that fuel could reach a level that threatens the reliability or adequacy of bulk electric power supply.

Fuel ethanol (C_2H_5OH) An anhydrous alcohol (ethanol with less than 1% water) intended for gasoline blending as described in the Oxygenates definition.

Fuel expenses These costs include the fuel used in the production of steam or driving another prime mover for the generation of electricity. Other associated expenses include unloading the shipped fuel and all handling of the fuel up to the point where it enters the first bunker, hopper, bucket, tank, or holder in the boiler-house structure.

Fuel/fabricator assembly identifier Individual assembly identifier based on a numbering scheme developed by individual fuel fabricators. Most fuel fabricator assembly identifiers schemes closely match the scheme developed by the American National Standards Institute (ANSI) and are therefore unique.

Fuel injection A fuel delivery system whereby gasoline is pumped to one or more fuel injectors under high pressure. The fuel injectors are valves that, at the appropriate times, open to allow fuel to be sprayed or atomized into a throttle bore or into the intake manifold ports. The fuel injectors are usually solenoid operated valves under the control of the vehicle's on-board computer (thus the term "electronic fuel injection"). The fuel efficiency of fuel injection systems is less temperature-dependent than carburetor systems. Diesel engines always use injectors.

Fuel oil A liquid petroleum product less volatile than gasoline, used as an energy source. Fuel oil includes distillate fuel oil (No. 1, No. 2, and No. 4), and residual fuel oil (No. 5 and No. 6).

Fuel oil supplier See Energy supplier.

Fuel purchase agreement An agreement between a company and a fuel provider which stipulates that the company agrees to purchase its fuel from the fuel provider. If the company has a credit card for use at a fuel provider's locations, but is not bound by an additional agreement to purchase fuel from that provider, the credit card agreement alone is not considered a fuel purchase agreement.

Fuel ratio The ratio of fixed carbon to volatile matter in coal.

Fuel switching capability The short-term capability of a manufacturing establishment to have used substitute energy sources in place of those actually consumed. Capability to use substitute energy sources means that the establishment's combustors (for example, boilers, furnaces, ovens, and blast furnaces) had the machinery or equipment either in place or available for installation so that substitutions could actually have been introduced within 30 days without extensive modifications. Fuel-switching capability does not depend on the relative prices of energy sources; it depends only on the characteristics of the equipment and certain legal constraints.

Fuel-switching DSM program assistance DSM program assistance where the sponsor encourages consumers to change from one fuel to another for a particular end-use service. For example, utilities might encourage consumers to replace electric water heaters with gas units or encourage industrial consumers to use electric microwave heaters instead of natural gas-heaters.

Fuel wood Wood and wood products, possibly including scrubs and branches, etc, bought or gathered, and used by direct combustion.

Fuels solvent deasphalting A refining process for removing asphalt compounds from petroleum fractions, such as reduced crude oil. The recovered stream from this process is used to produce fuel products.

Fugitive emissions Unintended leaks of gas from the processing, transmission, and/or transportation of fossil fuels.

Full forced outage The net capability of main generating units that are unavailable for load for emergency reasons.

Full power day The equivalent of 24 hours of full power operation by a reactor. The number of full power days in a specific cycle is the product of the reactor's capacity factor and the length of the cycle.

Full power operation Operation of a unit at 100 percent of its design capacity. Full-power operation precedes commercial operation.

Full requirements consumer A wholesale consumer without other generating resources whose electric energy seller is the sole source of long-term firm power for the consumer's service area. The terms and conditions of sale are equivalent to the seller's obligations to its own retail service, if any.

Fumarole A vent from which gas or steam issue; a geyser or spring that emits gases.

Furnace The part of a boiler or warm-air space-heating plant in which combustion takes place.

Furnace coke plant A coke plant whose coke production is used primarily by the producing company.

Furnaces that heat directly, without using steam or hot water (similar to a residential furnace) Furnaces burn natural gas, fuel oil, propane/ butane (bottled gas), or electricity to warm the air. The warmed air is then distributed throughout the building through ducts. Many people use the words "boilers" and "furnaces" interchangeably. They are not the same. We mean that warm air is produced directly by burning some fuel.Warm-air furnaces typically rely on air ducts to carry the warm air throughout the building. Warm-air furnaces are often built in combination with central air-conditioning systems, so that they can use the same air ducts for both heating or air-conditioning (depending on the season).Other terms for describing this type of equipment include "central system," "split system," and "forced air/forces air furnace."

Futures market A trade center for quoting prices on contracts for the delivery of a specified quantity of a commodity at a specified time and place in the future.

GAAP See Generally accepted accounting principles below.

Gallon A volumetric measure equal to 4 quarts (231 cubic inches) used to measure fuel oil. One barrel equals 42 gallons.

Gas A non-solid, non-liquid combustible energy source that includes natural gas, coke-oven gas, blast-furnace gas, and refinery gas.

Gas-cooled fast breeder reactor (GCFB) A fast breeder reactor that is cooled by a gas (usually helium) under pressure.

Gas oil European and Asian designation for No. 2 heating oil and No. 2 diesel fuel.

Gas plant operator Any firm, including a gas plant owner, which operates a gas plant and keeps the gas plant records. A gas plant is a facility in which natural gas liquids are separated from natural gas or in which natural gas liquids are fractionated or otherwise separated into natural gas liquid products or both.

Gas processing unit A facility designed to recover natural gas liquids from a stream of natural gas that may or may not have passed through lease separators and/or field separation facilties. Another function of natural gas processing plants is to control the quality of the processed natural gas stream. Cycling plants are considered natural gas processing plants.

Gas to liquids (GTL) A process that combines the carbon and hydrogen elements in natural gas molecules to make synthetic liquid petroleum products, such as diesel fuel.

Gas turbine plant A plant in which the prime mover is a gas turbine. A gas turbine consists typically of an axial-flow air compressor and one or more combustion chambers where liquid or gaseous fuel is burned and the hot gases are passed to the turbine and where the hot gases expand drive the generator and are then used to run the compressor.

Gas well A well completed for production of natural gas from one or more gas zones or reservoirs. Such wells contain no completions for the production of crude oil.

Gas well productivity Derived annually by dividing gross natural gas withdrawals from gas wells by the number of producing gas wells on December 31 and then dividing the quotient by the number of days in the year.

Gasification A method for converting coal, petroleum, biomass, wastes, or other carbon-containing materials into a gas that can be burned to generate power or processed into chemicals and fuels.

Gasohol A blend of finished motor gasoline containing alcohol (generally ethanol but sometimes methanol) at a concentration between 5.7 percent and 10 percent by volume. Also see Oxygenates.

Gasoline See Motor gasoline (finished).

Gasoline blending components Naphthas which will be used for blending or compounding into finished aviation or motor gasoline (e.g., straight-run gasoline, alkylate, reformate, benzene, toluene, and xylene). Excludes oxygenates (alcohols, ethers), butane, and pentanes plus.

Gasoline grades The classification of gasoline by octane ratings. Each type of gasoline (conventional, oxygenated, and reformulated) is classified by three grades - Regular, Midgrade, and Premium. *Note:* Gasoline sales are reported by grade in accordance with their classification at the time of sale. In general, automotive octane requirements are lower at high altitudes. Therefore, in some areas of the United States, such as the Rocky Mountain States, the octane ratings for the gasoline grades may be 2 or more octane points lower.

- *Regular gasoline* Gasoline having an antiknock index, i.e., octane rating, greater than or equal to 85 and less than 88. *Note:* Octane requirements may vary by altitude.
- *Midgrade gasoline* Gasoline having an antiknock index, i.e., octane rating, greater than or equal to 88 and less than or equal to 90. Note: Octane requirements may vary by altitude.
- *Premium gasoline* Gasoline having an antiknock index, i.e., octane rating, greater than 90. *Note:* Octane requirements may vary by altitude. s or fluids at various depths beneath the surface of the earth. The energy is extracted by drilling and/or pumping.

Gasoline motor (leaded) Contains more than 0.05 grams of lead per gallon or more than 0.005 grams of phosphorus per gallon. The actual lead content of any given gallon may vary. Premium and regular grades are included, depending on the octane rating. Includes leaded gasohol. Blendstock is excluded until blending has been completed. Alcohol that is to be used in the blending of gasohol is also excluded.

Gasoline treated as blendstock (GTAB) Non-certified Foreign Refinery gasoline classified by an importer as blendstock to be either blended or reclassified with respect to reformulated or conventional gasoline. GTAB is classified as either reformulated or conventional quality based on emissions performance, formulation, and intended end use.

Gate station Location where the pressure of natural gas being transferred from the transmission system to the distribution system is lowered for transport through small diameter, low pressure pipelines.

Gatherer A company primarily engaged in the gathering of natural gas from well or field lines for delivery, for a fee, to a natural gas processing plant or central point. Gathering companies may also provide compression, dehydration, and/or treating services.

Generally accepted accounting principles (GAAP) Defined by the FASB as the conventions, rules, and procedures necessary to define accepted accounting practice at a particular time, includes both broad guidelines and relatively detailed practices and procedures.

Generating facility An existing or planned location or site at which electricity is or will be produced.

Generating station A station that consists of electric generators and auxiliary equipment for converting mechanical, chemical, or nuclear energy into electric energy.

Generating unit Any combination of physically connected generators, reactors, boilers, combustion turbines, and other prime movers operated together to produce electric power.

Generation The process of producing electric energy by transforming other forms of energy; also, the amount of electric energy produced, expressed in kilowatthours.

Generation company An entity that owns or operates generating plants. The generation company may own the generation plants or interact with the short-term market on behalf of plant owners.

Generator capacity The maximum output, commonly expressed in megawatts (MW), that generating equipment can supply to system load, adjusted for ambient conditions.

Generator nameplate capacity The maximum rated output of a generator under specific conditions designated by the manufacturer. Generator nameplate capacity is usually indicated in units of kilovolt-amperes (kVA) and in kilowatts (kW) on a nameplate physically attached to the generator.

Geologic assurance State of sureness, confidence, or certainty of the existence of a quantity of resources based on the distance from points where coal is measured or sampled and on the abundance and quality of geologic data as related to thickness of overburden, rank, quality, thickness of coal, areal extent, geologic history, structure, and correlations of coal beds and enclosing rocks. The degree of assurance increases as the nearness to points of control, abundance, and quality of geologic data increases.

Geologic considerations Conditions in the coal deposit or in the rocks in which it occurs that may complicate or preclude mining. Geologic considerations are evaluated in the context of the current state of technology and regulations, so the impact on mining may change with time.

Geological and geophysical (G&G) costs Costs incurred in making geological and geophysical studies, including, but not limited to, costs incurred for salaries, equipment, obtaining rights of access, and supplies for scouts, geologists, and geophysical crews.

Geological repository A mined facility for disposal of radioactive waste that uses waste packages and the natural geology as barriers to provide waste isolation.

Geopressured A type of geothermal resource occurring in deep basins in which the fluid is under very high pressure.

Geothermal energy Hot water or steam extracted from geothermal reservoirs in the earth's crust. Water or steam extracted from geothermal reservoirs can be used for geothermal heat pumps, water heating, or electricity generation.

Geothermal plant A plant in which the prime mover is a steam turbine. The turbine is driven either by steam produced from hot water or by natural steam that derives its energy from heat found in rock

Geyser A special type of thermal spring that periodically ejects water with great force.

GDP see gross domestic product (GDP)

Giga One billion.

Gigawatt (GW) One billion watts or one thousand megawatts.

Gigawatt-electric (GWe) One billion watts of electric capacity.

Gigawatthour (GWh) One billion watthours.

Gilsonite Trademark name for uintaite (or uintahite), a black, brilliantly lustrous natural variety of asphalt found in parts of Utah and western Colorado.

Global climate change See Climate change.

Global warming An increase in the near surface temperature of the Earth. Global warming has occurred in the distant past as the result of natural influences, but the term is today most often used to refer to the warming some scientists predict will occur as a result of increased anthropogenic emissions of greenhouse gases.

Global warming potential (GWP) An index used to compare the relative radiative forcing of different gases without directly calculating the changes in atmospheric concentrations. GWPs are calculated as the ratio of the radiative forcing that would result from the emission of one kilogram of a greenhouse gas to that from the emission of one kilogram of carbon dioxide over a fixed period of time, such as 100 years.

Government-owned stocks Oil stocks owned by the national government and held for national security. In the United States, these stocks are known as the Strategic Petroleum Reserve.

Greenhouse effect The result of water vapor, carbon dioxide, and other atmospheric gases trapping radiant (infrared) energy, thereby keeping the earth's surface warmer than it would otherwise be. Greenhouse gases within the lower levels of the atmosphere trap this radiation, which would otherwise escape into space, and subsequent re-radiation of some of this energy back to the Earth maintains higher surface temperatures than would occur if the gases were absent.

Greenhouse gases Those gases, such as water vapor, carbon dioxide, nitrous oxide, methane, hydrofluorocarbons (HFCs), perfluorocarbons (PFCs) and sulfur hexafluoride, that are transparent to solar (short-wave) radiation but opaque to long-wave (infrared) radiation, thus preventing long-wave radiant energy from leaving Earth's atmosphere. The net effect is a trapping of absorbed radiation and a tendency to warm the planet's surface.

Green pricing In the case of renewable electricity, green pricing represents a market solution to the various problems associated with regulatory valuation of the nonmarket benefits of renewables. Green pricing programs allow electricity customers to express their willingness to pay for renewable energy development through direct payments on their monthly utility bills.

Grid The layout of an electrical distribution system. See electric power grid.

Gross additions to construction work in progress for the month This amount should include the monthly gross additions for an electric plant in the process of construction.

Gross company-operated production Total production from all company-operated properties, including all working and nonworking interests.

Gross domestic product (GDP) The total value of goods and services produced by labor and property located in the United States. As long as the labor and property are located in the United States, the supplier (that is, the workers and, for property, the owners) may be either U.S. residents or residents of foreign countries.

Gross domestic product (GDP) implicit price deflator The implicit price deflator, published by the U.S. Department of Commerce, Bureau of Economic Analysis, is used to convert nominal figures to real figures.

Gross energy intensity Total consumption of a particular energy source(s) or fuel(s) by a group of buildings, divided by the total floor space of those buildings, including buildings and floor space where the energy source or fuel is not used, i.e., the ratio of consumption to gross floor space.

Gross gas withdrawal The full-volume of compounds extracted at the wellhead, including nonhydrocarbon gases and natural gas plant liquids.

Gross generation The total amount of electric energy produced by generating units and measured at the generating terminal in kilowatthours (kWh) or megawatthours (MWh).

Gross head A dam's maximum allowed vertical distance between the upstream's surface water (headwater) forebay elevation and the downstream's surface water (tailwater) elevation at the tail-race for reaction wheel dams or the elevation of the jet at impulse wheel dams during specified operation and water conditions.

Gross inputs The crude oil, unfinished oils, and natural gas plant liquids put into atmospheric crude oil distillation units.

Gross input to atmospheric crude oil distillation units Total input to atmospheric crude oil distillation units. Includes all crude oil, lease condensate, natural gas plant liquids, unfinished oils, liquefied refinery gases, slop oils, and other liquid hydrocarbons produced from tar sands, gilsonite, and oil shale.

Gross national product (GNP) The total value of goods and services produced by the nation's economy before deduction of depreciation charges and other allowances for capital consumption. It includes the total purchases of goods and services by private consumers and government, gross private domestic capital investment, and net foreign trade.

Gross vehicle weight rating (GVWR) Vehicle weight plus carrying capacity.

Gross withdrawals Full well stream volume, including all natural gas plant liquid and nonhydrocarbon gases, but excluding lease condensate. Also includes amounts delivered as royalty payments or consumed in field operations.

Gross working interest ownership basis Gross working interest ownership is the respondent's working interest in a given property plus the proportionate share of any royalty interest, including overriding royalty interest, associated with the working interest.

Group A group is a logical grouping of assemblies with similar characteristics. All assemblies in a group have the same initial average enrichment, the same cycle/reactor history, the same current location, the same burnup, the same owner, and the same assembly type.

Group name The DOE/EIA-assigned name identifying a composite supply source (i.e., commonly metered gas streams from more than one field), which is often the case in contract areas, field areas, and plants. A group name can also be a pipeline purchase (i.e., FERC Gas Tariff, Canadian Gas, Mexican Gas, and Algerian LNG). Emergency purchases and short term purchases are also group names. Group Code - The DOE/EIA-assigned code identifying a composite supply source.

Group quarters Living arrangement for institutional groups containing ten or more unrelated persons. Group quarters are typically found in hospitals, nursing or rest homes, military barracks, ships, halfway houses, college dormitories, fraternity and sorority houses, convents, monasteries, shelters, jails, and correctional institutions. Group quarters may also be found in houses or apartments shared by ten or more unrelated persons. Group quarters are often equipped with a dining area for residents.

GWe See Gigawatt-electric above.

Gypsum Calcium sulfate dihydrate ($C_aSO_4\ 2H_2O$) a sludge constituent from the conventional lime scrubber process, obtained as a byproduct of the dewatering operation and sold for commercial use.

Half-life The time it takes for an isotope to lose half of its radioactivity.

Halogen lamp A type of incandescent lamp that lasts much longer and is more efficient than the common incandescent lamp. The lamp uses a halogen gas, usually iodine or bromine, that causes the evaporating tungsten to be redeposited on the filament, thus prolonging its life. Also see Incandescent lamp.

Halogenated substances A volatile compound containing halogens, such as chlorine, fluorine or bromine.

Hand loading An underground loading method by which coal is removed from the working face by manual labor through the use of a shovel for conveyance to the surface. Though rapidly disappearing, it is still used in small-tonnage mines.

Haulage cost Cost of loading ore at a mine site and transporting it to a processing plant.

Head The product of the water's weight and a usable difference in elevation gives a measurement of the potential energy possessed by water.

Heap leach solutions The separation, or dissolving-out from mined rock of the soluble uranium constituents by the natural action of percolating a prepared chemical solution through mounded (heaped) rock material. The mounded material usually contains low grade mineralized material and/or waste rock produced from openpit or underground mines. The solutions are collected after percolation is completed and processed to recover the valued components.

Heat content The amount of heat energy available to be released by the transformation or use of a specified physical unit of an energy form (e.g., a ton of coal, a barrel of oil, a kilowatthour of electricity, a cubic foot of natural gas, or a pound of steam). The amount of heat energy is commonly expressed in British thermal units (Btu). Note: Heat content of combustible energy forms can be expressed in terms of either gross heat content (higher or upper heating value) or net heat content (lower heating value), depending upon whether or not the available heat energy includes or excludes the energy used to vaporize water (contained in the original energy form or created during the combustion process). The Energy Information Administration typically uses gross heat content values.

Heat pump Heating and/or cooling equipment that, during the heating season, draws heat into a building from outside and, during the cooling season, ejects heat from the building to the outside. Heat pumps are vapor-compression refrigeration systems whose indoor/outdoor coils are used reversibly as condensers or evaporators, depending on the need for heating or cooling.

Heat pump (air source) An air-source heat pump is the most common type of heat pump. The heat pump absorbs heat from the outside air and transfers the heat to the space to be heated in the heating mode. In the cooling mode the heat pump absorbs heat from the space to be cooled and rejects the heat to the outside air. In the heating mode when the outside air approaches 32o F or less, air-source heat pumps loose efficiency and generally require a back-up (resistance) heating system.

Heat pump (geothermal) A heat pump in which the refrigerant exchanges heat (in a heat exchanger) with a fluid circulating through an earth connection medium (ground or ground water). The fluid is contained in a variety of loop (pipe) configurations depending on the temperature of the ground and the ground area available. Loops may be installed horizontally or vertically in the ground or submersed in a body of water.

Heat pump efficiency The efficiency of a heat pump, that is, the electrical energy to operate it, is directly related to temperatures between which it operates. Geothermal heat pumps are more efficient than conventional heat pumps or air conditioners that use the outdoor air since the ground or ground water a few feet below the earth's surface remains relatively constant throughout the year. It is more efficient in the winter to draw heat from the relatively warm ground than from the atmosphere where the air temperature is much colder, and in summer transfer waste heat to the relatively cool ground than to hotter air. Geothermal heat pumps are generally more expensive ($2,000-$5,000) to install than outside air heat pumps. However, depending on the location geothermal heat pumps can reduce energy consumption (operating cost) and correspondingly, emissions by more than 20 percent compared to high-efficiency outside air heat pumps. Geothermal heat pumps also use the waste heat from air-conditioning to provide free hot water heating in the summer.

Heat rate A measure of generating station thermal efficiency commonly stated as Btu per kilowatthour. *Note:* Heat rates can be expressed as either gross or net heat rates, depending whether the electricity output is gross or net generation. Heat rates are typically expressed as net heat rates.

Heated floorspace The area within a buildingt hat is space heated.

Heating degree-days (HDD) A measure of how cold a location is over a period of time relative to a base temperature, most commonly specified as 65 degrees Fahrenheit. The measure is computed for each day by subtracting the average of the day's high and low temperatures from the base temperature (65 degrees), with negative values set equal to zero. Each day's heating degree-days are summed to create a heating degree-day measure for a specified reference period. Heating degree-days are used in energy analysis as an indicator of space heating energy requirements or use.

Heating equipment Any equipment designed and/or specifically used for heating ambient air in an enclosed space. Common types of heating equipment include: central warm air furnace, heat pump, plug-in or built-in room heater, boiler for steam or hot water heating system, heating stove, and fireplace. *Note:* A cooking stove in a housing unit is sometimes reported as heating equipment, even though it was built for preparing food.

Heating intensity The ratio of space-heating consumption or expenditures to square footage of heated floor space and heating degree-days (base 65 degrees Fahrenheit). This ratio provides a way of comparing different types of housing units and households by controlling for differences in housing unit size and weather conditions. The square footage of heated floor space is based on the measurements of the floor space that is heated. The ratio is calculated on a weighted, aggregate basis according to the following formula: Heating Intensity = Btu for Space Heating / (Heated Square Feet * Heating Degree-Days).

Heating stove burning wood, coal, or coke Any free-standing box or controlled-draft stove; or a stove installed in a fireplace opening, using the chimney of the fireplace. Stoves are made of cast iron, sheet metal, or plate steel. Free-standing fireplaces that can be detached from their chimneys are considered heating stoves.

Heating value The average number of British thermal units per cubic foot of natural gas as determined from tests of fuel samples.

Heavy gas oil Petroleum distillates with an approximate boiling range from 651degrees Fahrenheit to 1000 degrees Fahrenheit.

Heavy metals Metallic elements, including those required for plant and animal nutrition, in trace concentration but which become toxic at higher concentrations. Examples are mercury, chromium, cadmium, and lead.

Heavy rail An electric railway with the capacity for a "heavy volume" of traffic and characterized by exclusive rights-of-way, multi-car trains, high speed and rapid acceleration, sophisticated signaling, and high platform loading. Also known as "subway," elevated (railway), "metropolitan railway (metro)."

Heavy water Water containing a significantly greater proportion of heavy hydrogen (deuterium) atoms to ordinary hydrogen atoms than is found in ordinary (light) water. Heavy water is used as a moderator in some reactors because it slows neutrons effectively and also has a low cross section for absorption of neutrons.

Heavy-water-moderated reactor A reactor that uses heavy water as its moderator. Heavy water is an excellent moderator and thus permits the use of inexpensive natural (unenriched) uranium as fuel.

Hedging The buying and selling of futures contracts so as to protect energy traders from unexpected or adverse price fluctuations.

Hedging contracts Contracts which establish future prices and quantities of electricity independent of the short-term market. Derivatives may be used for this purpose.

Heliostat A mirror that reflects solar rays onto a central receiver. A heliostat automatically adjusts its position to track daily or seasonal changes in the sun's position. The arrangement of heliostats around a central receiver is also called a solar collector field.

Henry Hub A pipeline hub on the Louisiana Gulf coast. It is the delivery point for the natural gas futures contract on the New York Mercantile Exchange (NYMEX).

High-efficiency ballast A lighting conservation feature consisting of an energy-efficient version of a conventional electromagnetic ballast. The ballast is the transformer for fluorescent and high-intensity discharge (HID) lamps, which provides the necessary current, voltage, and wave-form conditions to operate the lamp. A high-efficiency ballast requires lower power input than a conventional ballast to operate HID and fluorescent lamps.

High-efficiency lighting Lighting provided by high-intensity discharge (HID) lamps and/or fluorescent lamps.

High-intensity discharge (HID) lamp A lamp that produces light by passing electricity through gas, which causes the gas to glow. Examples of HID lamps are mercury vapor lamps, metal halide lamps, and high-pressure sodium lamps. HID lamps have extremely long life and emit far more lumens per fixture than do fluorescent lights.

High-mileage households Households with estimated aggregate annual vehicle mileage that exceeds 12,000 miles.

High-temperature collector A solar thermal collector designed to operate at a temperature of 180 degrees Fahrenheit or higher.

Highwall The unexcavated face of exposed overburden and coal in a surface mine.

Hinshaw pipeline A pipeline or local distribution company that has received exemptions from regulations pursuant to the Natural Gas Act. These companies transport interstate natural gas not subject to regulations under NGA.

Holding company A company that confines its activities to owning stock in and supervising management of other companies. The Securities and Exchange Commission, as administrator of the Public Utility Holding Company Act of 1935, defines a holding company as "a company which directly or indirectly owns, controls or holds 10 percent or more of the outstanding voting securities of a holding company" (15 USC 79b, par. a (7)).

Holding pond A structure built to contain large volumes of liquid waste to ensure that it meets environmental requirements prior to release.

Horizontal axis wind turbine The most common type of wind turbine where the axis of rotation is oriented horizontally. Also see Wind turbine.

Horsepower A unit for measuring the rate of work (or power) equivalent to 33,000 foot-pounds per minute or 746 watts.

Host government The government (including any government-controlled firm engaged in the production, refining, or marketing of crude oil or petroleum products) of the foreign country in which the crude oil is produced.

Hot dry rock Heat energy residing in impermeable, crystalline rock. Hydraulic fracturing may be used to create permeability to enable circulation of water and removal of the heat.

Hot tub Water-filled wood, plastic, or ceramic container in which up to 12 people can lounge. Normally equipped with a heater that heats the water from 80 degrees to 106 degrees Fahrenheit. It may also have jets to bubble the water. The water is not drained after each use. An average-size hot tub holds 200 to 400 gallons of water. All reported hot tubs are assumed to include an electric pump. These are also called spas or jacuzzis.

Hours under load The hours the boiler is operating to drive the generator producing electricity.

Household A family, an individual, or a group of up to nine unrelated persons occupying the same housing unit. "Occupy" means that the housing unit is the person's usual or permanent place of residence.

Household energy expenditures The total amount of funds spent for energy consumed in, or delivered to, a housing unit during a given period of time.

Housing unit A house, an apartment, a group of rooms, or a single room if it is either occupied or intended for occupancy as separate living quarters by a family, an individual, or a group of one to nine unrelated persons. Separate living quarters means the occupants live and eat separately from other persons in the house or apartment and (2) have direct access from the outside of the buildings or through a common hall—that is, they can get to it without going through someone else's living quarters. Housing units do not include group quarters such as prisons or nursing homes where ten or more unrelated persons live. A common dining area used by residents is an indication of group quarters. Hotel and motel rooms are considered housing units if occupied as the usual or permanent place of residence.

Hub height In a horizontal-axis wind turbine, the distance from the turbine platform to the rotor shaft.

Humidifier A humidifier adds moisture to the air (often needed in winter when indoor air is very dry). It may be a portable unit or attached to the heating system.

Humidity The moisture content of air. Relative humidity is the ratio of the amount of water vapor actually present in the air to the greatest amount possible at the same temperature.

HVAC An abbreviation for the heating, ventilation, and air-conditioning system; the system or systems that condition air in a building.

HVAC conservation feature A building feature designed to reduce the amount of energy consumed by the heating, cooling, and ventilating equipment.

HVAC DSM program A DSM (demand-side management) program designed to promote the efficiency of the heating or cooling delivery system, including replacement. Includes ventilation (economizers; heat recovery from exhaust air), cooling (evaporative cooling, cool storage; heat recovery from chillers; high-efficiency air conditioning), heating, and automatic energy management systems.

Hybrid transmission line A double-circuit line that has one alternating current and one direct circuit. The AC circuit usually serves local loads along the line.

Hydraulic fracturing Fracturing of rock at depth with fluid pressure. Hydraulic fracturing at depth may be accomplished by pumping water into a well at very high pressures. Under natural conditions, vapor pressure may rise high enough to cause fracturing in a process known as hydrothermal brecciation.

Hydraulic head The distance between the respective elevations of the upstream water surface (headwater) above and the downstream surface water (tailwater) below a hydroelectric power plant.

Hydrocarbon An organic chemical compound of hydrogen and carbon in the gaseous, liquid, or solid phase. The molecular structure of hydrocarbon compounds varies from the simplest (methane, a constituent of natural gas) to the very heavy and very complex.

Hydrochlorofluorocarbons (HCFCs) Chemicals composed of one or more carbon atoms and varying numbers of hydrogen, chlorine, and fluorine atoms.

Hydrocracking See Catalytic hydrocracking.

Hydroelectric power The use of flowing water to produce electrical energy.

Hydrofluorocarbons (HFCs) A group of man-made chemicals composed of one or two carbon atoms and varying numbers of hydrogen and fluorine atoms. Most HFCs have 100-year Global Warming Potentials in the thousands.

Hydrogen The lightest of all gases, occurring chiefly in combination with oxygen in water; exists also in acids, bases, alcohols, petroleum, and other hydrocarbons.

Hydrotreating See Catalytic hydrotreating.

Hydroxyl radical (OH) An important chemical scavenger of many trace gases in the atmosphere that are greenhouse gases. Atmospheric concentrations of OH affect the atmospheric lifetimes of greenhouse gases, their abundance, and, ultimately, the effect they have on climate.

Hypothetical resources (coal) Undiscovered coal resources in beds that may reasonably be expected to exist in known mining districts under known geologic conditions. In general, hypothetical resources are in broad areas of coalfields where points of observation are absent and evidence is from distant outcrops, drill holes, or wells. Exploration that confirms their existence and better defines their quantity and quality would permit their reclassification as identified resources. Quantitative estimates are based on a broad knowledge of the geologic character of coalbed or region. Measurements of coal thickness are more than 6 miles apart. The assumption of continuity of coalbed is supported only by geologic evidence.

Identified resources Coal deposits whose location, rank, quality, and quantity are known from geologic evidence supported by engineering measurements. Included are beds of bituminous coal and anthracite (14 or more inches thick) and beds of subbituminous coal and lignite (30 or more inches thick) that occur at depths to 6,000 feet. The existence and quantity of these beds have been delineated within specified degrees of geologic assurance as measured, indicated, or inferred. Also included are thinner and/or deeper beds that presently are being mined or for which there is evidence that they could be mined commercially.

Idle capacity The component of operable capacity that is not in operation and not under active repair, but capable of being placed in operation within 30 days; and capacity not in operation but under active repair that can be completed within 90 days.

IEA International Energy Agency

Impedance The opposition to power flow in an AC circuit. Also, any device that introduces such opposition in the form of resistance, reactance, or both. The impedance of a circuit or device is measured as the ratio of voltage to current, where a sinusoidal voltage and current of the same frequency are used for the measurement; it is measured in ohms.

Implicit price deflator The implicit price deflator, published by the U.S. Department of Commerce, Bureau of Economic Analysis, is used to convert nominal figures to real figures.

Imported crude oil burned as fuel The amount of foreign crude oil burned as a fuel oil, usually as residual fuel oil, without being processed as such. Imported crude oil burned as fuel includes lease condensate and liquid hydrocarbons produced from tar sands, gilsonite, and oil shale.

Imported Refiners' Acquisition Cost (IRAC) The average price for imported oil paid by U.S. refiners.

Imports Receipts of goods into the 50 States and the District of Columbia from U.S. possessions and territories or from foreign countries.

Improved recovery Extraction of crude oil or natural gas by any method other than those that rely primarily on natural reservoir pressure, gas lift, or a system of pumps.

Inadvertent power exchange An unintended power exchange among utilities that is either not previously agreed upon or in an amount different from the amount agreed upon.

Incandescent lamp A glass enclosure in which light is produced when a tungsten filament is electrically heated so that it glows. Much of the energy is converted into heat; therefore, this class of lamp is a relatively inefficient source of light. Included in this category are the familiar screw-in light bulbs, as well as somewhat more efficient lamps, such as tungsten halogen lamps, reflector or r-lamps, parabolic aluminized reflector (PAR) lamps, and ellipsoidal reflector (ER) lamps.

Incandescent light bulbs, including regular or energy-efficient light bulbs An incandescent bulb is a type of electric light in which light is produced by a filament heated by electric current. The most common example is the type you find in most table and floor lamps. In commercial buildings, incandescent lights are used for display lights in retail stores, hotels and motels. This includes the very small, high-intensity track lights used to display merchandise or provide spot illumination in restaurants. Energy efficient light bulbs, known as "watt-savers," use less energy than a standard incandescent bulb. "Long-life" bulbs, bulbs that last longer than standard incandescent but produce considerably less light, are not considered energy-efficient bulbs. This category also includes halogen lamps. Halogen lamps are a special type of incandescent lamp containing halogen gas to produce a brighter, whiter light than standard incandescent. Halogen lamps come in three styles: bulbs, models with reflectors, and infrared models with reflectors. Halogen lamps are especially suited to recessed or "canned fixtures," track lights, and outdoor lights.

Incentives Demand-Side Management (DSM) program assistance This DSM program assistance offers monetary or non-monetary awards to encourage consumers to buy energy-efficient equipment and to participate in programs designed to reduce energy usage. Examples of incentives are zero or low-interest loans, rebates, and direct installation of low cost measures, such as water heater wraps or duct work for distributing the cool air; the units condition air only in the room or areas where they are located.

Incremental effects The annual changes in energy use (measured in megawatthours) and peak load (measured in kilowatts) caused by new participants in existing DSM (Demand-Side Management) programs and all participants in new DSM programs during a given year. Reported Incremental Effects are annualized to indicate the program effects that would have occurred had these participants been initiated into the program on January 1 of the given year. Incremental effects are not simply the Annual Effects of a given year minus the Annual Effects of the prior year, since these net effects would fail to account for program attrition, equipment degradation, building demolition, and participant dropouts. Please note that Incremental Effects are not a monthly disaggregate of the Annual Effects, but are the total year's effects of only the new participants and programs for that year.

Incremental energy costs The additional cost of producing and/or transmitting electric energy above some previously determined base cost.

Independent power producer A corporation, person, agency, authority, or other legal entity or instrumentality that owns or operates facilities for the generation of electricity for use primarily by the public, and that is not an *electric utility*.

Independent system operator (electric) An independent, Federally regulated entity established to coordinate regional transmission in a non-discriminatory manner and ensure the safety and reliability of the electric system. (FERC definition)

Indian coal lease A lease granted to a mining company to produce coal from Indian lands in exchange for royalties and other revenues; obtained by direct negotiation with Indian tribal authorities, but subject to approval and administration by the U.S. Department of the Interior.

Indicated reserves See Probable energy reserves.

Indicated resources, coal Coal for which estimates of the rank, quality, and quantity are based partly on sample analyses and measurements and partly on reasonable geologic projections. Indicated resources are computed partly from specified measurements and partly from projection of visible data for a reasonable distance on the basis of geologic evidence. The points of observation are 1/2 to 1-1/2 miles apart. Indicated coal is projected to extend as a 1/2-mile-wide belt that lies more than 1/4 mile from the outcrop, points of observation, or measurement.

Indirect cost Costs not directly related to mining or milling operations, such as overhead, insurance, security, office expenses, property taxes, and similar administrative expenses.

Indirect uses (end-use category) The end-use category that handles boiler fuel. Fuel in boilers is transformed into another useful energy source, steam or hot water, which is in turn used in other end uses, such as process or space heating or electricity generation. Manufacturers find measuring quantities of steam as it passes through to various end uses especially difficult because variations in both temperature and pressure affect energy content. Thus, the MECS (an EIA survey) does not present end-use estimates of steam or hot water and shows only the amount of the fuel used in the boiler to produce those secondary energy sources.

Indirect utility cost A utility cost that may not be meaningfully identified with any particular DSM program category. Indirect costs could be attributable to one of several accounting cost categories (i.e., Administrative, Marketing, Monitoring & Evaluation, Utility-Earned Incentives, Other). Accounting costs that are known DSM program costs should not be reported under Indirect Utility Cost; those costs should be reported as Direct Utility Costs under the appropriate DSM program category.

Industrial production The Federal Reserve Board calculates this index by compiling indices of physical output from a variety of agencies and trade groups, weighting each index by the Census' value added, and adding it to the cost of materials. When physical measures are not available, the Federal Reserve Board uses the number of production workers or amount of electricity consumed as the basis for the index. To convert industrial production into dollars, multiply by the "real value added" estimate used by the Federal Reserve Board.

Industrial restrictions (coal) Land-use restrictions that constrain, postpone, or prohibit mining in order to meet other industrial needs or goals; for example, resources not mined due to safety concerns or due to industrial or societal priorities, such as to preserve oil or gas wells that penetrate the coal reserves; to protect surface features such as pipelines, power lines, or company facilities; or to preserve public or private assets, such as highways, railroads, parks, or buildings.

Industrial sector An energy-consuming sector that consists of all facilities and equipment used for producing, processing, or assembling goods. The industrial sector encompasses the following types of activity: manufacturing (NAICS codes 31-33); agriculture, forestry, fishing and hunting (NAICS code 11); mining, including oil and gas extraction (NAICS code 21); and construction (NAICS code 23). Overall energy use in this sector is largely for process heat and cooling and powering machinery, with lesser amounts used for facility heating, air conditioning, and lighting. Fossil fuels are also used as raw material inputs to manufactured products. *Note:* This sector includes generators that produce electricity and/or useful thermal output primarily to support the above-mentioned industrial activities. Various EIA programs differ in sectoral coverage-for more information see http://www.eia.doe.gov/neic/datadefinitions/Guideforwebind.htm.

Inferred reserve base (coal) the resources in the inferred reliability category that meet the same criteria of bed thickness and depth from surface as the demonstrated reserve base.

Inferred resources Coal in unexplored extensions of demonstrated resources for which estimates of the quality and size are based on geologic evidence and projection. Quantitative estimates are based largely on broad knowledge of the geologic character of the bed or region and where few measurements of bed thickness are available. The estimates are based primarily on an assumed continuation from demonstrated coal for which there is geologic evidence. The points of observation are 1-1/2 to 6 miles apart. Inferred coal is projected to extend as a 2-1/4-mile wide belt that lies more than 3/4 mile from the outcrop, points of observation, or measurement.

In-house Demand-Side Management (DSM) program sponsor The building's owner or management encourages consumers in the building to improve energy efficiency, reduce energy costs, change timing or energy usage, or promote the use of a different energy source by sponsoring its own DSM programs.

Initial enrichment Average enrichment for a fresh fuel assembly as specified and ordered in fuel cycle planning. This average should include axial blankets and axially and radially zoned enrichments.

Initial operation First availability of a newly constructed unit to provide power to the grid. For a nuclear unit, this time is when the Full Power Operating License for the unit is received.

Injections Natural gas injected into storage reservoirs.

Inoperable capacity Generating capacity that is totally or partially out of service at the time of system peak load, either for scheduled outages (see GADS definition of "scheduled outages." These include both maintenance outages and planned outages.) or for reasons such as: environmental restrictions; extensive modifications or repair; or capacity specified as being in a mothballed state. This does not include derated portions of generating capacity.

In situ leach mining (ISL) The recovery, by chemical leaching, of the valuable components of a mineral deposit without physical extraction of the mineralized rock from the ground. Also referred to as "solution mining."

Installed nameplate capacity See Generator nameplate capacity (installed).

Instantaneous peak demand The maximum demand at the instant of greatest load.

Instantaneous water heater Also called a "tankless" or "point-of-use" water heater. The water is heated at the point of use as it is needed.

Institutional living quarters Space provided by a business or organization for long-term housing of individuals whose reason for shared residence is their association with the business or organization. Such quarters commonly have both individual and group living spaces, and the business or organization is responsible for some aspects of resident life beyond the simple provision of living quarters. Examples include prisons; nursing homes and other long-term medical care facilities; military barracks; college dormitories; and convents and monasteries.

Insulation Any material or substance that provides a high resistance to the flow of heat from one surface to another. The different types include blanket or batt, foam, or loose fill, which are used to reduce heat transfer by conduction. Dead air space is an insulating medium in storm windows and storms as it reduces passage of heat through conduction and convection. Reflective materials are used to reduce heat transfer by radiation.

Insulation around heating and/or cooling ducts Extra insulation around the heating and/or cooling ducts intended to reduce the loss of hot or cold air as it travels to different parts of the residence.

Insulation around hot-water pipes Wrapping of insulating material around hot-water pipes to reduce the loss of heat through the pipes.

Insulation around water heater Blanket insulation wrapped around the water heater to reduce loss of heat. To qualify under this definition, this wrapping must be in addition to any insulation provided by the manufacturer.

Insulator A material that is a very poor conductor of electricity. The insulating material is usually a ceramic or fiberglass when used in the transmission line and is designed to support a conductor physically and to separate it electrically from other conductors and supporting material.

Intangible drilling and development costs (IDC) Costs incurred in preparing well locations, drilling and deepening wells, and preparing wells for initial production up through the point of installing control valves. None of these functions, because of their nature, have salvage value. Such costs would include labor, transportation, consumable supplies, drilling tool rentals, site clearance, and similar costs.

Integral collector storage (ICS) A solar thermal collector in which incident solar radiation is absorbed directly by the storage medium.

Integrated demand The summation of the continuously varying instantaneous demand averaged over a specified interval of time. The information is usually determined by examining a demand meter.

Integrated gasification-combined cycle technology Coal, water, and oxygen are fed to gasifier, which produces syngas. This medium-Btu gas is cleaned (particulates and sulfur compounds removed) and is fed to a gas turbine. The hot exhaust of the gas turbine and heat recovered from the gasification process are routed through a heat-recovery routed through a heat-recovery generator to produce steam, which drives a steam turbine to produce electricity.

Intensity The amount of a quantity per unit floor space. This method adjusts either the amount of energy consumed or expenditures spent, for the effects of various building characteristics, such as size of the building, number of workers, or number of operating hours, to facilitate comparisons of energy across time, fuels, and buildings.

Intensity per hour Total consumption of a particular fuel(s) divided by the total floor space of buildings that use the fuel(s) divided by total annual hours of operation.

Interchange (electric) Energy transfers that cross Balancing Authority boundaries. (NERC definition)

Interchange authority (electric) The responsible entity that authorizes implementation of valid and balanced Interchange Schedules between Balancing

Authority Areas, and ensures communication of Interchange information for reliability assessment purposes. (NERC definition)

Interchange energy Kilowatthours delivered to or received by one electric utility or pooling system from another. Settlement may be payment, returned in kind at a later time, or accumulated as energy balances until the end of the stated period.

Interchange transaction (electric) An agreement to transfer energy from a seller to a buyer that crosses one or more Balancing Authority Area boundaries. (NERC definition)

Intercity bus A bus designed for high speed, long distance travel; equipped with front doors only, high backed seats, and usually restroom facilities.

Interconnected system A system consisting of two or more individual power systems normally operating with connecting tie lines.

Interconnection Two or more electric systems having a common transmission line that permits a flow of energy between them. The physical connection of the electric power transmission facilities allows for the sale or exchange of energy.

Interdepartmental sales Includes amounts charged by the electric department at tariff or other specified rates for electricity supplied by it to other utility departments.

Interdepartmental service (electric) Interdepartmental service includes amounts charged by the electric department at tariff or other specified rates for electricity supplied by it to other utility departments.

Interest coverage ratio The number of times that fixed interest charges were earned. It indicates the margin of safety of interest on fixed debt. The times-interest-earned ratio is calculated using net income before and after income taxes; and the credits of interest charged to construction being treated as other income. The interest charges include interest on long-term debt, interest on debt of associated companies, and other interest expenses.

Intergovernmental Panel on Climate Change (IPCC) A panel established jointly in 1988 by the World Meteorological Organization and the United Nations Environment Program to assess the scientific information relating to climate change and to formulate realistic response strategies.

Interlocking directorates The holding of a significant position in management or a position on the corporate board of a utility while simultaneously holding a comparable position with another utility, or with a firm doing business with the utility.

Intermediate grade gasoline A grade of unleaded gasoline with an octane rating intermediate between "regular" and "premium." Octane boosters are added to gasolines to control engine pre-ignition or "knocking" by slowing combustion rates.

Intermediate load (electric system) The range from base load to a point between base load and peak. This point may be the midpoint, a percent of the peak load, or the load over a specified time period.

Intermittent electric generator or intermittent resource An electric generating plant with output controlled by the natural variability of the energy resource rather than dispatched based on system requirements. Intermittent output usually results from the direct, non-stored conversion of naturally occurring energy fluxes such as solar energy, wind energy, or the energy of free-flowing rivers (that is, run-of-river hydroelectricity).

Internal Collector Storage (ICS) A solar thermal collector in which incident solar radiation is absorbed by the storage medium.

Internal combustion plant A plant in which the prime mover is an internal combustion engine. An internal combustion engine has one or more cylinders in which the process of combustion takes place, converting energy released from the rapid burning of a fuel-air mixture into mechanical energy. Diesel or gas-fired engines are the principal types used in electric plants. The plant is usually operated during periods of high demand for electricity.

International bunker fuels See Bunker fuels.

Interruptible gas Gas sold to customers with a provision that permits curtailment or cessation of service at the discretion of the distributing company under certain circumstances, as specified in the service contract.

Interruptible load or interruptible demand (electric) Demand that the end-use customer makes available to its Load-Serving Entity via contract or agreement for curtailment. (NERC definition)

Interruptible or curtailable rate A special electricity or natural gas arrangement under which, in return for lower rates, the customer must either reduce energy demand on short notice or allow the electric or natural gas utility to temporarily cut off the energy supply for the utility to maintain service for higher priority users. This interruption or reduction in demand typically occurs during periods of high demand for the energy (summer for electricity and winter for natural gas).

Interruptible power Power and usually the associated energy made available by one utility to another. This transaction is subject to curtailment or cessation of delivery by the supplier in accordance with a prior agreement with the other party or under specified conditions.

Interstate companies Natural gas pipeline companies subject to Federal Energy Regulatory Commission (FERC) jurisdiction.

Interstate pipeline Any person engaged in natural gas transportation subject to the jurisdiction of Federal Energy Regulatory Commission (FERC) under the Natural Gas Act.

Interstate pipeline purchase Any gas supply contracted from and volumes purchased from other interstate pipelines, overland natural gas import purchases, and LNG, SNG, or coal gas purchases from domestic or foreign sources. Purchases from intrastate pipelines to section 311 (b) of the NGPA of 1978 and from independent producers are not included with interstate pipelines purchase.

Intransit deliveries Redeliveries to a foreign country of foreign gas received for transportation across U.S. territory, and deliveries of U.S. gas to a foreign country for transportation across its territory and redelivery to the United States.

Intransit receipts Receipts of foreign gas for transportation across U.S. territory and redelivery to a foreign country, and redeliveries to the United States of U.S. gas transported across foreign territory.

Intrastate companies Companies not subject to Federal Energy Regulatory Commission (FERC) jurisdiction.

Intrastate pipeline Any person engaged in natural gas transportation (not including gathering) that is not subject to the jurisdiction of the Commission under the Natural Gas Act (other than any such pipeline that is not subject to the jurisdiction of the Commission soley by reason of Section 1(c) of the Natural Gas Act).

In-use (vehicles) Implies that a vehicle is:
1. Registered with the Government of one or more States, the District of Columbia, the Commonwealth of Puerto Rico, or the Virgin Islands; or
2. The vehicle is owned or operated by a Government or military organization within the United States that is not required to register vehicles with the Government agencies listed under 1 above. For example, civilian Federal vehicles are generally not required to register with the State Government in which they are assigned.

Investment of municipality The investment of the municipality in its utility department, when such investment is not subject to cash settlement on demand or at a fixed future time. Include the cost of debt-free utility plant constructed or acquired by the municipality and made available for the use of the utility department, cash transferred to the utility department for working capital, and other expenditures of an investment nature.

Investments and advances to unconsolidated affiliates The balance sheet account representing the cost of investments and advances to unconsolidated affiliates. Generally, affiliates that are less than 50-percent owned by a company may not be consolidated into the company's financial statements.

Investor-owned utility (IOU) A privately-owned electric utility whose stock is publicly traded. It is rate regulated and authorized to achieve an allowed rate of return.

Ion exchange Reversible exchange of ions adsorbed on a mineral or synthetic polymer surface with ions in solution in contact with the surface. A chemical process used for recovery of uranium from solution by the interchange of ions between a solution and a solid, commonly a resin.

Iron and steel industry Steel Works, Blast Furnaces (Including Coke Ovens), and Rolling Mills: Establishments primarily engaged in manufacturing hot metal, pig iron, and silvery pig iron from iron ore and iron and steel scrap; converting pig iron, scrap iron, and scrap steel into steel; and in hot-rolling iron and steel into basic shapes, such as plates, sheets, strips, rods, bars, and tubing.

Irradiated nuclear fuel Nuclear fuel that has been exposed to radiation in the reactor core at any power level.

Isobutane (C_4H_{10}) A normally gaseous branch-chain hydrocarbon. It is a colorless paraffinic gas that boils at a temperature of 10.9 degrees Fahrenheit. It is extracted from natural gas or refinery gas streams.

Isobutylene (C_4H_8) An olefinic hydrocarbon recovered from refinery processes or petrochemical processes.

Isohexane (C_6H_{14}) A saturated branch-chain hydrocarbon. It is a colorless liquid that boils at a temperature of 156.2 degrees Fahrenheit.

Isomerization A refining process that alters the fundamental arrangement of atoms in the molecule without adding or removing anything from the original material. Used to convert normal butane into isobutane (C_4), an alkylation process feedstock, and normal pentane and hexane into isopentane (C_5) and isohexane (C_6), high-octane gasoline components.

Isopach A line on a map drawn through points of equal thickness of a designated unit (such as a coal bed).

Isopentane A saturated branched-chain hydrocarbon (C_5H_{12}) obtained by fractionation of natural gasoline or isomerization of normal pentane.

Isotopes Forms of the same chemical element that differ only by the number of neutrons in their nucleus. Most elements have more than one naturally occurring isotope. Many isotopes have been produced in reactors and scientific laboratories.

Jacket The enclosure on a water heater, furnace, or boiler.

Jet fuel A refined petroleum product used in jet aircraft engines. It includes kerosene-type jet fuel and naphtha-type jet fuel.

Joint Implementation (JI) Agreements made between two or more nations under the auspices of the Framework Convention on Climate Change (FCCC) whereby a developed country can receive "emissions reduction units" when it helps to finance projects that reduce net emissions in another developed country (including countries with economies in transition).

Joint-use facility A multiple-purpose hydroelectric plant. An example is a dam that stores water for both flood control and power production.

Joule (J) The meter-kilogram-second unit of work or energy, equal to the work done by a force of one newton when its point of application moves through a distance of one meter in the direction of the force; equivalent to 107 ergs and one watt-second.

Joule's Law The rate of heat production by a steady current in any part of an electrical circuit that is proportional to the resistance and to the square of the current, or, the internal energy of an ideal gas depends only on its temperature.

Junction A region of transition between semiconductor layers, such as a p/n junction, which goes from a region that has a high concentration of acceptors (p-type) to one that has a high concentration of donors (n-type).

Jurisdictional utilities Utilities regulated by public laws.

Kaplan turbine A type of turbine that that has two blades whose pitch is adjustable. The turbine may have gates to control the angle of the fluid flow into the blades.

Kerosene A light petroleum distillate that is used in space heaters, cook stoves, and water heaters and is suitable for use as a light source when burned in wick-fed lamps. Kerosene has a maximum distillation temperature of 400 degrees Fahrenheit at the 10-percent recovery point, a final boiling point of 572 degrees Fahrenheit, and a minimum flash point of 100 degrees Fahrenheit. Included are No. 1-K and No. 2-K, the two grades recognized by ASTM Specification D 3699 as well as all other grades of kerosene called range or stove oil, which have properties similar to those of No. 1 fuel oil. Also see Kerosene-type jet fuel.

Kerosene-type jet fuel A kerosene-based product having a maximum distillation temperature of 400 degrees Fahrenheit at the 10-percent recovery point and a final maximum boiling point of 572 degrees Fahrenheit and meeting ASTM Specification D 1655 and Military Specifications MIL-T-5624P and MIL-T-83133D (Grades JP-5 and JP-8). It is used for commercial and military turbojet and turboprop aircraft engines.

- *Commercial* Kerosene-type jet fuel intended for use in commercial aircraft.
- *Military* Kerosene-type jet fuel intended for use in military aircraft.

Ketone-alcohol (cyclohexanol) An oily, colorless, hygroscopic liquid with a camphor-like odor. Used in soapmaking, dry cleaning, plasticizers, insecticides, and germicides.

Kilovolt-Ampere (kVa) A unit of apparent power, equal to 1,000 volt-amperes; the mathematical product of the volts and amperes in an electrical circuit.

Kilowatt (kW) One thousand watts.

Kilowatt-electric (kWe) One thousand watts of electric capacity.

Kilowatthour (kWh) A measure of electricity defined as a unit of work or energy, measured as 1 kilowatt (1,000 watts) of power expended for 1 hour. One kWh is equivalent to 3,412 Btu.

Kinetic energy Energy available as a result of motion that varies directly in proportion to an object's mass and the square of its velocity.

Kyoto Protocol The result of negotiations at the third Conference of the Parties (COP-3) in Kyoto, Japan, in December of 1997. The Kyoto Protocol sets binding greenhouse gas emissions targets for countries that sign and ratify the agreement. The gases covered under the Protocol include carbon dioxide, methane, nitrous oxide, hydrofluorocarbons (HFCs), perfluorocarbons (PFCs) and sulfur hexafluoride.

Lamp A term generally used to describe artificial light. The term is often used when referring to a "bulb" or "tube."

Land use The ultimate uses to be permitted for currently contaminated lands, waters, and structures at each Department of Energy installation. Land-use decisions will strongly influence the cost of environmental management.

Land-use restrictions Constraints placed upon mining by societal policies to protect surface features or entities that could be affected by mining. Because laws and regulations may be modified or repealed, the restrictions, including industrial and environmental restrictions, are subject to change.

Landfill gas Gas that is generated by decomposition of organic material at landfill disposal sites. The average composition of landfill gas is approximately 50 percent methane and 50 percent carbon dioxide and water vapor by volume. The methane percentage, however, can vary from 40 to 60 percent, depending on several factors including waste composition (e.g. carbohydrate and cellulose content). The methane in landfill gas may be vented, flared, combusted to generate electricity or useful thermal energy on-site, or injected into a pipeline for combustion off-site.

Langley A unit or measure of solar radiation; 1 calorie per square centimeter or 3.69 Btu per square foot.

Large passenger car A passenger car with more than 120 cubic feet of interior passenger and luggage volume.

Large pickup truck A pickup truck weighing between 4,500-8,500 lbs gross vehicle weight (GVW).

Latitude and longitude The distance on the earth's surface measured, respectively, north or south of the equator and east or west of the standard meridian, expressed in angular degrees, minutes, and seconds.

Leachate The liquid that has percolated through the soil or other medium.

Lead acid battery An electrochemical battery that uses lead and lead oxide for electrodes and sulfuric acid for the electrolyte.

Leaded gasoline A fuel that contains more than 0.05 gram of lead per gallon or more than 0.005 gram of phosphorus per gallon.

Leaded premium gasoline Gasoline having an antiknock index (R+M/2) greater than 90 and containing more than 0.05 grams of lead or 0.005 grams of phosphorus per gallon.

Leaded regular gasoline Gasoline having an antiknock index (R+M/2) greater than or equal to 87 and less than or equal to 90 and containing more than 0.05 grams of lead or 0.005 grams of phosphorus per gallon.

Leading edge In reference to a wind energy conversion system, the area of a turbine blade surface that first comes into contact with the wind.

Lease and plant fuel Natural gas used in well, field, and lease operations (such as gas used in drilling operations, heaters, dehydrators, and field compressors) and as fuel in natural gas processing plants.

Lease condensate A mixture consisting primarily of pentanes and heavier hydrocarbons which is recovered as a liquid from natural gas in lease separation facilities. This category excludes natural gas plant liquids, such as butane and propane, which are recovered at downstream natural gas processing plants or facilities.

Lease equipment All equipment located on the lease except the well to the point of the "Christmas tree."

Lease fuel Natural gas used in well, field, and lease operations, such as gas used in drilling operations, heaters, dehydrators, and field compressors.

Lease operations Any well, lease, or field operations related to the exploration for or production of natural gas prior to delivery for processing or transportation out of the field. Gas used in lease operations includes usage such as for drilling operations, heaters, dehydrators, field compressors, and net used for gas lift.

Lease separation facility (lease separator) A facility installed at the surface for the purpose of (a) separating gases from produced crude oil and water at the temperature and pressure conditions set by the separator and/or (b) separating gases from that portion of the produced natural gas stream that liquefies at the temperature and pressure conditions set by the separator.

Leasehold reserves Natural gas liquid reserves corresponding to the leasehold production defined above.

Lessee An independent marketer who leases the station and land and has use of tanks, pumps, signs, etc. A lessee dealer typically has a supply agreement with a refiner or distributor and purchases products at dealer tank-wagon prices. The term "lessee dealer" is limited to those dealers who are supplied directly by a refiner or any affiliate or subsidiary of the reporting company. "Direct supply" includes use of commission agent or common carrier delivery.

Levelized cost The present value of the total cost of building and operating a generating plant over its economic life, converted to equal annual payments. Costs are levelized in real dollars (i.e., adjusted to remove the impact of inflation).

Leverage ratio A measure that indicates the financial ability to meet debt service requirements and increase the value of the investment to the stockholders. (i.e. the ratio of total debt to total assets).

Liability An amount payable in dollars or by future services to be rendered.

Licensed site capacity Capacity (number of assemblies) for which the site is currently licensed.

Licensees Entity that has been granted permission to engage in an activity otherwise unlawful (i.e., hydropower project).

Life extension Restoration or refurbishment of a plant to its original performance without the installation of new combustion technologies. Life extension results in 10 to 20 years of plant life beyond the anticipated retirement date, but usually does not result in larger capacity.

Lift The force that pulls a wind turbine blade, as opposed to drag.

Lifting costs The costs associated with the extraction of a mineral reserve from a producing property.

Light bulbs A term generally used to describe a manmade source of light. The term is often used when referring to a "bulb" or "tube."

Light-duty vehicles Vehicles weighing less than 8,500 lbs (include automobiles, motorcycles, and light trucks).

Light gas oils Liquid petroleum distillates heavier than naphtha, with an approximate boiling range from 401 degrees to 650 degrees Fahrenheit.

Light rail An electric railway with a "light volume" traffic capacity compared to "heavy rail." Light rail may use exclusive or shared rights-of-way, high or low platform loading, and multi-car trains or single cars. Also known as "street car," "trolley car," and "tramway."

Light trucks All single unit two-axle, four-tire trucks, including pickup trucks, sports utility vehicles, vans, motor homes, etc. This is the Department of Transportation definition. The Energy Information Administration defined light truck as all trucks weighing 8,500 pounds or less.

Light water Ordinary water (H_2O), as distinguished from heavy water or deuterium oxide (D_2O).

Light water reactor (LWR) A nuclear reactor that uses water as the primary coolant and moderator, with slightly enriched uranium as fuel.

Lighting conservation feature A building feature or practice designed to reduce the amount of energy consumed by the lighting system.

Lighting Demand-Side Management (DSM) program A DSM program designed to promote efficient lighting systems in new construction or existing facilities. Lighting DSM programs can include: certain types of high-efficiency fluorescent fixtures including T-8 lamp technology, solid state electronic ballasts, specular reflectors, compact fluorescent fixtures, LED and electroluminescent Emergency Exist Signs, High Pressure Sodium with switchable ballasts, Compact Metal Halide, occupancy sensors, and daylighting controllers.

Lighting equipment These are light bulbs used to light the building's interior, such as incandescent light bulbs, fluorescent light bulbs, compact fluorescent light bulbs, and high-intensity discharge (HID) lights.

Lights All of the light bulbs controlled by one switch are counted as one light. For example, a chandelier with multiple lights controlled by one switch is counted as one light. A floor lamp with two separate globes or bulbs controlled by two separate switches would be counted as two lights. Indoor and outdoor lights were counted if they were under the control of the householder. This would exclude lights in the hallway of multifamily buildings.

Lignite The lowest rank of coal, often referred to as brown coal, used almost exclusively as fuel for steam-electric power generation. It is brownish-black and has a high inherent moisture content, sometimes as high as 45 percent The heat content of lignite ranges from 9 to 17 million Btu per ton on a moist, mineral-matter-free basis. The heat content of lignite consumed in the United States averages 13 million Btu per ton, on the as-received basis (i.e., containing both inherent moisture and mineral matter).

LIHEAP (Low-Income Home Energy Assistance Program) See definition further below.

Line loss Electric energy lost because of the transmission of electricity. Much of the loss is thermal in nature.

Line-miles of seismic exploration The distance along the Earth's surface that is covered by seismic surveying.

Liquefied natural gas (LNG) Natural gas (primarily methane) that has been liquefied by reducing its temperature to -260 degrees Fahrenheit at atmospheric pressure.

Liquefied petroleum gases A group of hydrocarbon-based gases derived from crude oil refining or natural gas fractionation. They include ethane, ethylene, propane, propylene, normal butane, butylene, isobutane, and isobutylene. For convenience of transportation, these gases are liquefied through pressurization.

Liquefied refinery gases (LRG) Liquefied petroleum gases fractionated from refinery or still gases. Through compression and/or refrigeration, they are retained in the liquid state. The reported categories are ethane/ethylene, propane/propylene, normal butane/butylene, and isobutane/isobutylene. Excludes **still gas**.

Liquid collector A medium-temperature solar thermal collector, employed predominantly in water heating, which uses pumped liquid as the heat-transfer medium.

Liquid fuels All petroleum products, natural gas liquids, biofuels, and liquids derived from other hydrocarbon sources (coal to liquids and gas to liquids). Not included are compressed natural gas (CNG), liquefied natural gas (LNG), and hydrogen.

Liquid metal fast breeder reactor A nuclear breeder reactor, cooled by molten sodium, in which fission is caused by fast neutrons.

LNG The abbreviation for Liquefied Natural Gas.

Load (electric) An end-use device or customer that receives power from the electric system. (NERC definition)

Load control program A program in which the utility company offers a lower rate in return for having permission to turn off the air conditioner or water heater for short periods of time by remote control. This control allows the utility to reduce peak demand.

Load curve The relationship of power supplied to the time of occurrence. Illustrates the varying magnitude of the load during the period covered.

Load diversity The difference between the peak of coincident and noncoincident demands of two or more individual loads.

Load factor The ratio of the average load to peak load during a specified time interval.

Load following Regulation of the power output of electric generators within a prescribed area in response to changes in system frequency, tieline loading, or the relation of these to each other, so as to maintain the scheduled system frequency and/or established interchange with other areas within predetermined limits.

Load leveling Any load control technique that dampens the cyclical daily load flows and increases baseload generation. Peak load pricing and time-of-day charges are two techniques that electric utilities use to reduce peak load and to maximize efficient generation of electricity.

Load loss (3 hours) Any significant incident on an electric utility system that results in a continuous outage of 3 hours or longer to more than 50,000 customers or more than one half of the total customers being served immediately prior to the incident, whichever is less.

Load management technique Utility demand management practices directed at reducing the maximum kilowatt demand on an electric system and/or modifying the coincident peak demand of one or more classes of service to better meet the utility system capability for a given hour, day, week, season, or year.

Load on equipment One hundred percent load is the maximum continuous net output of the unit at normal operating conditions during the annual peak load month. For example, if the equipment is capable of operating at 5% overpressure continuously, use this condition for 100% load.

Load reduction request The issuance of any public or private request to any customer or the general public to reduce the use of electricity for the reasons of maintaining the continuity of service of the reporting entity's bulk electric power supply system. Requests to a customer(s) served under provisions of an interruptible contract are not a reportable action unless the request is made for reasons of maintaining the continuity of service of the reporting entity's bulk electric power supply.

Load-Serving Entity (electric) Secures energy and transmission service (and related Interconnected Operations Services) to serve the electrical demand and energy requirements of its end-use customers. (NERC definition)

Load shape A method of describing peak load demand and the relationship of power supplied to the time of occurrence.

Load shedding Intentional action by a utility that results in the reduction of more than 100 megawatts (MW) of firm customer load for reasons of maintaining the continuity of service of the reporting entity's bulk electric power supply system. The routine use of load control equipment that reduces firm customer load is not considered to be a reportable action.

Local distribution company (LDC) A legal entity engaged primarily in the retail sale and/or delivery of natural gas through a distribution system that includes mainlines (that is, pipelines designed to carry large volumes of gas, usually located under roads or other major right-of-ways) and laterals (that is, pipelines of smaller diameter that connect the end user to the mainline). Since the restructuring of the gas industry, the sale of gas and/or delivery arrangements may be handled by other agents, such as producers, brokers, and marketers that are referred to as "non-LDC."

Long-term debt Debt securities or borrowings having a maturity of more than one year.

Long-term purchase A purchase contract under which at least one delivery of material is scheduled to occur during the second calendar year after the contract-signing year. Deliveries also can occur during the contract-signing year, during the first calendar year thereafter, or during any subsequent calendar year.

Long ton A unit that equals 20 long hundredweight or 2,240 pounds. Used mainly in England.

Longwall mining An automated form of underground coal mining characterized by high recovery and extraction rates, feasible only in relatively flat-lying, thick, and uniform coalbeds. A high-powered cutting machine is passed across the exposed face of coal, shearing away broken coal, which is continuously hauled away by a floor-level conveyor system. Longwall mining extracts all machine-minable coal between the floor and ceiling within a contiguous block of coal, known as a panel, leaving no support pillars within the panel area. Panel dimensions vary over time and with mining conditions but currently average about 900 feet wide (coal face width) and more than 8,000 feet long (the minable extent of the panel, measured in direction of mining). Longwall mining is done under movable roof supports that are advanced as the bed is cut. The roof in the mined-out area is allowed to fall as the mining advances.

Loop flow The movement of electric power from generator to load by dividing along multiple parallel paths; it especially refers to power flow along an unintended path that loops away from the most direct geographic path or contract path.

Loss of service (15 minutes) Any loss in service for greater than 15 minutes by an electric utility of firm loads totaling more than 200 MW, or 50 percent of the total load being supplied immediately prior to the incident, whichever is less. However, utilities with a peak load in the prior year of more than 3000 MW are only to report losses of service to firm loads totaling more than 300 MW for greater than 15 minutes. (The DOE shall be notified with service restoration and in any event, within three hours after the beginning of the interruption.)

Low Btu gas A fuel gas with a heating value between 90 and 200 Btu per cubic foot.

Low E glass Low-emission glass reflects up to 90% of long-wave radiation, which is heat, but lets in short-wave radiation, which is light. Windows are glazed with a coating that bonds a microscopic, transparent, metallic substance to the inside surface of the double-pane or triple-pane windows.

Low flush toilet A toilet that uses less water than a standard one during flushing, for the purpose of conserving water resources.

Low flow showerheads Reduce the amount of water flow through the showerhead from 5 to 6 gallons a minute to 3 gallons a minute.

Low head Vertical difference of 100 feet or less in the upstream surface water elevation (headwater) and the downstream surface water elevation (tailwater) at a dam.

Low Income Home Energy Assistance Program (LIHEAP) The purpose of LIHEAP is to assist eligible households to meet the cost of heating or cooling in residential dwellings. The Federal government provides the funds to the States that administer the program.

Low power testing The period of time between a plant's nuclear generating unit's initial fuel loading date and the issuance of its operating (full-power) license. The maximum level of operation during this period is 5 percent of the unit's thermal rating.

Low-pressure sodium lamp A type of lamp that produces light from sodium gas contained in a bulb operating at a partial pressure of 0.13 to 1.3 Pascal. The yellow light and large size make them applicable to lighting streets and parking lots.

Low sulfur diesel (LSD) fuel Diesel fuel containing more than 15 but less than 500 parts per million (ppm) sulfur.

Low temperature collectors Metallic or nonmetallic collectors that generally operate at temperatures below 110 degrees Fahrenheit and use pumped liquid or air as the heat transfer medium. They usually contain no glazing and no insulation, and they are often made of plastic or rubber, although some are made of metal.

Low volatile bituminous coal See Bituminous Coal.

Lubricants Substances used to reduce friction between bearing surfaces, or incorporated into other materials used as processing aids in the manufacture of other products, or used as carriers of other materials. Petroleum lubricants may be produced either from distillates or residues. Lubricants include all grades of lubricating oils, from spindle oil to cylinder oil to those used in greases.

Lumen An empirical measure of the quantity of light. It is based upon the spectral sensitivity of the photosensors in the human eye under high (daytime) light levels. Photometrically it is the luminous flux emitted with a solid angle (1 steradian) by a point source having a uniform luminous intensity of 1 candela.

Lumens/Watt (lpw) A measure of the efficacy (efficiency) of lamps. It indicates the amount of light (lumens) emitted by the lamp for each unit of electrical power (Watts) used.

Machine drive (motors) The direct process end use in which thermal or electric energy is converted into mechanical energy. Motors are found in almost every process in manufacturing. Therefore, when motors are found in equipment that is wholly contained in another end use (such as process cooling and refrigeration), the energy is classified there rather than in machine drive.

Made available (vehicle) A vehicle is considered "Made available" if it is available for delivery to dealers or users, whether or not it was actually delivered to them. To be "made available," the vehicle must be completed and available for delivery; thus, any conversion to be performed by an original equipment manufacturer (OEM) Vehicle Converter or Aftermarket Vehicle Converter must have been completed.

Magma Naturally occurring molten rock, generated within the earth and capable of intrusion and extrusion, from which igneous rocks are thought to have been derived through solidification and related processes. It may or may not contain suspended solids (such as crystals and rock fragments) and/or gas phases.

Main heating equipment Equipment primarily used for heating ambient air in the housing unit.

Main heating fuel The form of energy used most frequently to heat the largest portion of the floorspace of a structure. The energy source designated as the main heating fuel is the source delivered to the site for that purpose, not any subsequent form into which it is transformed on site to deliver the heat energy (e.g., for buildings heated by a steam boiler, the main heating fuel is the main input fuel to the boiler, not the steam or hot water circulated through the building.) *Note:* In commercial buildings, the heating must be to at least 50 degrees Fahrenheit.

Mains A system of pipes for transporting gas within a distributing gas utility's retail service area to points of connection with consumer service pipes.

Maintenance expenses That portion of operating expenses consisting of labor, materials, and other direct and indirect expenses incurred for preserving the operating efficiency and/or physical condition of utility plants used for power production, transmission, and distribution of energy.

Maintenance of boiler plant (expenses) The cost of labor, material, and expenses incurred in the maintenance of a steam plant. Includes furnaces; boilers; coal, ash-handling, and coal-preparation equipment; steam and feed water piping; and boiler apparatus and accessories used in the production of steam, mercury, or other vapor to be used primarily for generating electricity. The point at which an electric steam plant is distinguished from an electric plant is defined as follows:

1. Inlet flange of throttle valve on prime mover.
2. Flange of all steam extraction lines on prime mover.
3. Hotwell pump outlet on condensate lines.
4. Inlet flange of all turbine-room auxiliaries.
5. Connection to line side of motor starter for all boiler-plant equipment.

Maintenance of structures (expenses) The cost of labor, materials, and expenses incurred in maintenance of power production structures. Structures include all buildings and facilities to house, support, or safeguard property or persons.

Maintenance supervision and engineering expenses The cost of labor and expenses incurred in the general supervision and direction of the maintenance of power generation stations. The supervision and engineering included consists of the pay and expenses of superintendents, engineers, clerks, other employees, and consultants engaged in supervising and directing the maintenance of each utility function. Direct supervision and engineering of specific activities, such as fuel handling, boiler room operations, generator operations, etc., are charged to the appropriate accounts.

Major electric utility A utility that, in the last 3 consecutive calendar years, had sales or transmission services exceeding one of the following: (1) 1 million megawatthours of total annual sales; (2) 100 megawatthours of annual sales for resale; (3) 500 megawatthours of annual gross interchange out; or (4) 500 megawatthours of wheeling (deliveries plus losses) for others.

Major energy sources Fuels or energy sources such as: electricity, fuel oil, natural gas, district steam, district hot water, and district chilled water. District chilled water is not included in any totals for the sum of major energy sources or fuels; all other major fuels are included in these totals.

Major fuels Fuels or energy sources such as: electricity, fuel oil, liquefied petroleum gases, natural gas, district steam, district hot water, and district chilled water.

Major interstate pipeline company A company whose combined sales for resale, including gas transported interstate or stored for a fee, exceeded 50 million thousand cubic feet in the previous year.

Make-up air Air brought into a building from outside to replace exhaust air.

Manhattan Project The U.S. Government project that produced the first nuclear weapons during World War II. Started in 1942, the Manhattan Project formally ended in 1946. The Hanford Site, Oak Ridge Reservation, and Los Alamos National Laboratory were created for this effort. The project was named for the Manhattan Engineer District of the U.S. Army Corps of Engineers.

Manual dimmer switches These are like residential-style dimmer switches. They are not generally used with fluorescent and high-intensity discharge (HID) lamps.

Manufactured gas A gas obtained by destructive distillation of coal or by the thermal decomposition of oil, or by the reaction of steam passing through a bed of heated coal or coke. Examples are coal gases, coke oven gases, producer gas, blast furnace gas, blue (water) gas, carbureted water gas. Btu content varies widely.

Manufacturing An energy-consuming subsector of the industrial sector that consists of all facilities and equipment engaged in the mechanical, physical, chemical, or electronic transformation of materials, substances, or components into new products. Assembly of component parts of products is included, except for that which is included in construction.

Manufacturing division One of 10 fields of economic activity defined by the Standard Industrial Classification Manual. The manufacturing division includes all establishments engaged in the mechanical or chemical transformation of materials or substances into new products. The other divisions of the U.S. economy are agriculture, forestry, fishing, hunting, and trapping; mining; construction; transportation, communications, electric, gas, and sanitary services; wholesale trade; retail trade; finance, insurance, and real estate; personal, business, professional, repair, recreation, and other services; and public administration. The establishments in the manufacturing division constitute the universe for the MECS (an EIA survey).

Manufacturing establishment An economic unit at a single physical location where mechanical or chemical transformation of materials or substances into new products are performed.

Marginal cost The change in cost associated with a unit change in quantity supplied or produced.

Marine freight Freight transported over rivers, canals, the Great Lakes, and domestic ocean waterways.

Market clearing price The price at which supply equals demand for the Day-ahead or hour-ahead markets.

Market-based pricing Prices of electric power or other forms of energy determined in an open market system of supply and demand under which prices are set solely by agreement as to what buyers will pay and sellers will accept. Such prices could recover less or more than full costs, depending upon what the buyers and sellers see as their relevant opportunities and risks.

Market price contract A contract in which the price of uranium is not specifically determined at the time the contract is signed but is based instead on the prevailing market price at the time of delivery. A market price contract may include a floor price, that is, a lower limit on the eventual settled price. The floor price and the method of price escalation generally are determined when the contract is signed. The contract may also include a price ceiling or a discount from the agreed-upon market price reference.

Market price settlement (uranium) The price paid for uranium delivery under a market-price contract. The price is commonly (but not always) determined at or sometime before delivery and may be related to a floor price, ceiling price, or discount.

Marketed energy An energy source that is commercially traded. Typically, this energy is sold by a producer, such as a petroleum refiner, through a transmission and distribution network (e.g., pipelines and trucks) to an end-use consumer (e.g., gasoline sold at the pump).

Marketable coke Those grades of coke produced in delayed or fluid cokers that may be recovered as relatively pure carbon. This "green" coke may be sold as is or further purified by calcining.

Marketed production Gross withdrawals less gas used for repressuring, quantities vented and flared, and nonhydrocarbon gases removed in treating or processing operations. Includes all quantities of gas used in field and processing plant operations.

Masonry A general term covering wall construction using masonry materials such as brick, concrete block, stone, and tile that are set in mortar; also included is stucco. The category does not include concrete panels because concrete panels represent a different method of constructing buildings. Concrete panels are reported separately.

Masonry stove A type of heating appliance similar to a fireplace, but much more efficient and clean burning. They are made of masonry and have long channels through which combustion gases give up their heat to the heavy mass of the stove, which releases the heat slowly into a room. Often called Russian or Finnish fireplaces.

Mass burn facility A type of municipal solid waste (MSW) incineration facility in which MSW is burned with only minor presorting to remove oversize, hazardous, or explosive materials.

Master-metering Measurement of electricity or natural gas consumption of several tenants or housing units using a single meter. That is, one meter measures the energy usage for several households collectively.

Maximum deliverability The maximum deliverability rate (Mcf/d) estimated at the present developed maximum operating capacity.

Maximum demand The greatest of all demands of the load that has occurred within a specified period of time.

Maximum dependable capacity, net The gross electrical output measured at the output terminals of the turbine generator(s) during the most restrictive seasonal conditions, less the station service load.

Maximum established site capacity (reactors) The maximum established spent fuel capacity for the site is defined by DOE as the maximum number of intact assemblies that will be able to be stored at some point in the future (between the reporting date and the reactor's end of life) taking into account any established or current studies or engineering evaluations at the time of submittal for licensing approval from the NRC.

Maximum generator nameplate capacity The maximum rated output of a generator, prime mover, or other electric power production equipment under specific conditions designated by the manufacturer.

Maximum hourly load This is determined by the interval in which the 60-minute integrated demand is the greatest.

Maximum streamflow The maximum rate of water flow past a given point during a specified period.

Mcf One thousand cubic feet.

Mean indoor temperature The "usual" temperature. If different sections of the house are kept at different temperatures, the reported temperature is for the section where the people are. A thermostat setting is accepted if the temperature is not known.

Mean operating hours The arithmetic average number of operating hours per building is the weighted sum of the number of operating hours divided by the weighted sum of the number of buildings.

Mean power output (of a wind turbine) The average power output of a wind energy conversion system at a given mean wind speed based on a Raleigh frequency distribution.

Mean square feet per building The arithmetic average square feet per building is the weighted sum of the total square feet divided by the weighted sum of the number of buildings.

Measured heated area of residence The floor area of the housing unit that is enclosed from the weather and heated. Basements are included whether or not they contain finished space. Garages are included if they have a wall in common with the house. Attics that have finished space and attics that have some heated space are included. Crawl spaces are not included even if they are enclosed from the weather. Sheds and other buildings that are not attached to the house are not included. "Measured" area means the measurement of the dimensions of the home, using a metallic, retractable, 50-foot tape measure. "Heated area" is that portion of the measured area that is heated during most of the season. Rooms that are shut off during the heating season to save on fuel are not counted. Attached garages that are unheated and unheated areas in the attics and basements are also not counted.

Measured reserves See Proved energy reserves.

Measured resources, coal Coal resources for which estimates of the rank, quality, and quantity have been computed, within a margin of error of less than 20 percent, from sample analyses and measurements from closely spaced and geologically well known sample sites. Measured resources are computed from dimensions revealed in outcrops, trenches, mine workings, and drill holes. The points of observation and measurement are so closely spaced and the thickness and extent of coals are so well defined that the tonnage is judged to be accurate within 20 percent. Although the spacing of the points of observation necessary to demonstrate continuity of the coal differs from region to region, according to the character of the coalbeds, the point of observation are no greater than 1/2 mile apart. Measured coal is projected to extend as a belt 1/4 mile wide from the outcrop or points of observation or measurement.

Median The middle number of a data set when the measurements are arranged in ascending (or descending) order.

Median streamflow The middle rate of flow of water past a given point for which there have been several greater and lesser rates of flow occurring during a specified period.

Median water condition The middle precipitation and run-off condition for a distribution of water conditions that have happened over a long period of time. Usually determined by examining the water supply record of the period in question.

Medium pressure For valves and fittings, implies that they are suitable for working pressures between 125 to 175 pounds per square inch.

Medium-temperature collector A collector designed to operate in the temperature range of 140 degrees to 180 degrees Fahrenheit, but that can also operate at a temperature as low as 110 degrees Fahrenheit. The collector typically consists of a metal frame, metal absorption panels with integral flow channels (attached tubing for liquid collectors or integral ducting for air collectors), and glazing and insulation on the sides and back.

Medium-volatile bituminous coal See Bituminous coal.

Megavoltamperes (MVA) Millions of voltamperes, which are a measure of apparent power. (See definition for apparent power.)

Megawatt (MW) One million watts of electricity.

Megawatt electric (MWe) One million watts of electric capacity.

Megawatthour (MWh) One thousand kilowatt-hours or 1 million watt-hours.

Mercaptan An organic chemical compound that has a sulfur-like odor that is added to natural gas before distribution to the consumer, to give it a distinct, unpleasant odor (smells like rotten eggs). This serves as a safety device by allowing it to be detected in the atmosphere, in cases where leaks occur.

Merchant coke plant A coke plant where coke is produced primarily for sale on the commercial (open) market.

Merchant facilities High-risk, high-profit facilities that operate, at least partially, at the whims of the market, as opposed to those facilities that are constructed with close cooperation of municipalities and have significant amounts of waste supply guaranteed.

Merchant MTBE plants MTBE (methyl tertiary butyl ether) production facilities primarily located within petrochemical plants rather than refineries. Production from these units is sold under contract or on the spot market to refiners or other gasoline blenders.

Merchant oxygenate plants Oxygenate production facilities that are not associated with a petroleum refinery. Production from these facilities is sold under contract or on the spot market to refiners or other gasoline blenders.

Mercury vapor lamp A high-intensity discharge lamp that uses mercury as the primary light-producing element. Includes clear, phosphor coated, and self-ballasted lamps.

Merger A combining of companies or corporations into one, often by issuing stock of the controlling corporation to replace the greater part of that of the other.

Met An approximate unit of heat produced by a resting person, equal to about 18.5 Btu per square foot per hour.

Meta-anthracite See Anthracite.

Metal halide lamp A high-intensity discharge lamp type that uses mercury and several halide additives as light-producing elements. These lights have the best Color Rendition Index (CRI) of the high-intensity discharge lamps. They can be used for commercial interior lighting or for stadium lights.

Metallic The metallic material composition of the collector's absorber system.

Metallurgical coal Coking coal and pulverized coal consumed in making steel.

Metered data End-use data obtained through the direct measurement of the total energy consumed for specific uses within the individual household. Individual appliances can be submetered by connecting the recording meters directly to individual appliances.

Metered peak demand The presence of a device to measure the maximum rate of electricity consumption per unit of time. This device allows electric utility companies to bill their customers for maximum consumption, as well as for total consumption.

Methane A colorless, flammable, odorless hydrocarbon gas (CH_4) which is the major component of natural gas. It is also an important source of hydrogen in various industrial processes. Methane is a greenhouse gas. See also Greenhouse gases.

Methanogens Bacteria that synthesize methane, requiring completely anaerobic conditions for growth.

Methanol (CH_3OH) A light, volatile alcohol eligible for gasoline blending.

Methanol blend Mixtures containing 85 percent or more (or such other percentage, but not less than 70 percent) by volume of methanol with gasoline. Pure methanol is considered an "other alternative fuel."

Methanotrophs Bacteria that use methane as food and oxidize it into carbon dioxide.

Methyl chloroform (trichloroethane) An industrial chemical (CH_3CCl_3) used as a solvent, aerosol propellant, and pesticide and for metal degreasing.

Methylene chloride A colorless liquid, nonexplosive and practically nonflammable. Used as a refrigerant in centrifugal compressors, a solvent for organic materials, and a component in nonflammable paint removers.

Metric conversion factors (for floorspace) Floorspace estimates may be converted to metric units by using the relationship, 1 square foot is approximately equal to .0929 square meters. Energy estimates may be converted to metric units by using the relationship, 1 Btu is approximately equal to 1,055 joules. One kilowatthour is exactly 3,600,000 joules. One gigajoule is approximately 278 kilowatthours (kWh).

Metric ton A unit of weight equal to 2,204.6 pounds.

Metropolitan Located within the boundaries of a metropolitan area.

Metropolitan area A geographic area that is a metropolitan statistical area or a consolidated metropolitan statistical area as defined by the U.S. Office of Management and Budget.

Metropolitan statistical area (MSA) A county or group of contiguous counties (towns and cities in New England) that has (1) at least one city with 50,000 or more inhabitants; or (2) an urbanized area of 50,000 inhabitants and a total population of 100,000 or more inhabitants (75,000 in New England). These areas are defined by the U.S. Office of Management and Budget. The contiguous counties or other jurisdictions to be included in an MSA are those that, according to certain criteria, are essentially metropolitan in character and are socially and economically integrated with the central city or urbanized area.

Microcrystalline wax Wax extracted from certain petroleum residues having a finer and less apparent crystalline structure than paraffin wax and having the following physical characteristics: penetration at 77 degrees Fahrenheit (D1321)-60 maximum; viscosity at 210 degrees Fahrenheit in Saybolt Universal Seconds (SUS); (D88)-60 SUS (10.22 centistokes) minimum to 150 SUS (31.8 centistokes) maximum; oil content (D721)-5 percent minimum.

Microgroove A small groove scribed into the surface of a solar photovoltaic cell which is filled with metal for contacts.

Micrometer (or Micron) One-millionth of a meter. It can also be expressed as 10^{-6} meter.

Microwave oven A household cooking appliance consisting of a compartment designed to cook or heat food by means of microwave energy. It may also have a browning coil and convection heating as additional features.

Midgrade gasoline Gasoline having an antiknock index, i.e., octane rating, greater than or equal to 88 and less than or equal to 90. *Note:* Octane requirements may vary by altitude.

Mid-size passenger car A passenger car with between 110 and 119 cubic feet of interior passenger and luggage volume.

Middle distillates A general classification of refined petroleum products that includes distillate fuel oil and kerosene.

Middlings In coal preparation, this material called mid-coal is neither clean nor refuse; due to their intermediate specific gravity, middlings sink only partway in the washing vessels and are removed by auxiliary means.

Miles per gallon (MPG) A measure of vehicle fuel efficiency. Miles per gallon or MPG represents "Fleet Miles per Gallon." For each subgroup or "table cell," MPG is computed as the ratio of the total number of miles traveled by all vehicles in the subgroup to the total number of gallons consumed. MPGs are assigned to each vehicle using the EPA certification files and adjusted for on-road driving.

Military use Includes sales to the Armed Forces, including volumes sold to the Defense Fuel Supply Center (DFSC) for use by all branches of the Department of Defense (DOD).

Mill A monetary cost and billing unit used by utilities; it is equal to 1/1000 of the U.S. dollar (equivalent to 1/10 of 1 cent).

Mill capital Cost for transportation and equipping a plant for processing ore or other feed materials.

Mill feed Uranium ore supplied to a crusher or grinding mill in an ore-dressing process.

Milling The grinding or crushing of ore, concentration, and other benefication, including the removal of valueless or harmful constituents and preparation for market.

Milling capacity The maximum rate at which a mill is capable of treating ore or producing concentrate.

Milling of uranium The processing of uranium from ore mined by conventional methods, such as underground or openpit methods, to separate the uranium from the undesired material in the ore.

Million British Thermal Units MMBtu. See Btu

Minable Capable of being mined under current mining technology and environmental and legal restrictions, rules, and regulations.

Mine capital Cost for exploration and development, pre-mining stripping, shaft sinking, and mine development (including in situ leaching), as well as the mine plant and its equipment.

Mine count The number of mines, or mines collocated with preparation plants or tipples, located in a particular geographic area (state or region). If a mine is mining coal across two counties within a state, or across two states, then it is counted as two operations. This is done so that EIA can separate production by state and county.

Mineral Any of the various naturally occurring inorganic substances, such as metals, salt, sand, stone, sulfur, and water, usually obtained from the earth. Note: For reporting on the Financial Reporting System the term also includes organic non-renewable substances that are extracted from the earth such as coal, crude oil, and natural gas.

Mineral lease An agreement wherein a mineral interest owner (lessor) conveys to another party (lessee) the rights to explore for, develop, and produce specified minerals. The lessee acquires a working interest and the lessor retains a non-operating interest in the property, referred to as the royalty interest, each in proportions agreed upon.

Mineral-matter-free basis Mineral matter in coal is the parent material in coal from which ash is derived and which comes from minerals present in the original plant materials that formed the coal, or from extraneous sources such as sediments and precipitates from mineralized water. Mineral matter in coal cannot be analytically determined and is commonly calculated using data on ash and ash-forming constituents. Coal analyses are calculated to the mineral matter free basis by adjusting formulas used in calculations in order to deduct the weight of mineral matter from the total coal.

Mineral rights The ownership of the minerals beneath the earth's surface with the right to remove them. Mineral rights may be conveyed separately from surface rights.

Mining An energy-consuming subsector of the industrial sector that consists of all facilities and equipment used to extract energy and mineral resources.

Mini van Small van that first appeared with that designation in 1984. Any of the smaller vans built on an automobile-type frame. Earlier models such as the Volkswagen van are now included in this category.

Minimum streamflow The lowest rate of flow of water past a given point during a specified period.

Mining operation One mine and/or tipple at a single physical location.

Minority carrier A current carrier, either an electron or a hole, that is in the minority in a specific layer of a semiconductor material; the diffusion of minority carriers under the action of the cell junction voltage is the current in a photovoltaic device.

Miscellaneous petroleum products Includes all finished products not classified elsewhere (e.g., petrolatum lube refining byproducts (aromatic extracts and tars), absorption oils, ram-jet fuel, petroleum rocket fuels, synthetic natural gas feedstocks, and specialty oils).

Miscellaneous reserves A supply source having not more than 50 billion cubic feet of dedicated recoverable salable reserves and that falls within the definition of Supply Source.

Mixed waste Waste containing both radioactive and hazardous constituents.

MMbbl/d One million barrels of oil per day.

MMBtu One million British thermal units.

MMcf One million cubic feet.

MMgal/d One million gallons per day.

MMst One million short tons.

Mobile home A housing unit built on a movable chassis and moved to the site. It may be placed on a permanent or temporary foundation and may contain one room or more. If rooms are added to the structure, it is considered a single-family housing unit. A manufactured house assembled on site is a single-family housing unit, not a mobile home.

Moderator A material, such as ordinary water, heavy water, or graphite, used in a reactor to slow down high-velocity neutrons, thus increasing the likelihood of further fission.

Modules Photovoltaic cells or an assembly of cells into panels (modules) intended for and shipped for final consumption or to another organization for resale. When exported, incomplete modules and unencapsulated cells are also included. Modules used for space applications are not included.

Moist (coal) basis "Moist" coal contains its natural inherent or bed moisture, but does not include water adhering to the surface. Coal analyses expressed on a moist basis are performed or adjusted so as to describe the data when the coal contains only that moisture that exists in the bed in its natural state of deposition and when the coal has not lost any moisture due to drying.

Moisture content The water content of a substance (a solid fuel) as measured under specified conditions being the "dry basis," which equals the weight of the wet sample minus the weight of a (bone) dry sample divided by the weight of the dry sample times 100 (to get percent); "wet basis," which is equal to the weight of the wet sample minus the weight of the dry sample divided by the weight of the wet sample times 100.

Mole The quantity of a compound or element that has a weight in grams numerically equal to its molecular weight. Also referred to as "gram molecule" or "gram molecular weight."

Montreal Protocol The Montreal Protocol on Substances that Deplete the Ozone Layer (1987). An international agreement, signed by most of the industrialized nations, to substantially reduce the use of chlorofluorocarbons (CFCs). Signed in January 1989, the original document called for a 50-percent reduction in CFC use by 1992 relative to 1986 levels. The subsequent London Agreement called for a complete elimination of CFC use by 2000. The Copenhagen Agreement, which called for a complete phaseout by January 1, 1996, was implemented by the U.S. Environmental Protection Agency.

Motor gasoline blending Mechanical mixing of motor gasoline blending components, and oxygenates when required, to produce finished motor gasoline. Finished motor gasoline may be further mixed with other motor gasoline blending components or oxygenates, resulting in increased volumes of finished motor gasoline and/or changes in the formulation of finished motor gasoline (e.g., conventional motor gasoline mixed with MTBE to produce oxygenated motor gasoline).

Motor gasoline blending components Naphthas (e.g., straight-run gasoline, alkylate, reformate, benzene, toluene, xylene) used for blending or compounding into finished motor gasoline. These components include reformulated gasoline blendstock for oxygenate blending (RBOB) but exclude oxygenates (alcohols, ethers), butane, and pentanes plus. *Note:* Oxygenates are reported as individual components and are included in the total for other hydrocarbons, hydrogens, and oxygenates.

Motor gasoline (finished) A complex mixture of relatively volatile hydrocarbons with or without small quantities of additives, blended to form a fuel suitable for use in spark-ignition engines. Motor gasoline, as defined in ASTM Specification D 4814 or Federal Specification VV-G-1690C, is characterized as having a boiling range of 122 to 158 degrees Fahrenheit at the 10 percent recovery point to 365 to 374 degrees Fahrenheit at the 90 percent recovery point. Motor Gasoline includes conventional gasoline; all types of oxygenated gasoline, including gasohol; and reformulated gasoline, but excludes aviation gasoline. Volumetric data on blending components, such as oxygenates, are not counted in data on finished motor gasoline until the blending components are blended into the gasoline. *Note* E85 is included only in volumetric data on finished motor gasoline production and other components of product supplied.

Motor speed The number of revolutions that the motor turns in a given time period (i.e. revolutions per minute, rpm).

MPG Miles per gallon.

MPG shortfall The difference between actual on-road MPG and EPA laboratory test MPG. MPG shortfall is expressed as gallons per mile ratio (GPMR).

MSHA ID number Seven (7)-digit code assigned to a mining operation by the Mine Safety and Health Administration.

MTBE (methyl tertiary butyl ether) $(CH_3)_3COCH_3$ An ether intended for gasoline blending as described in "*Oxygenates.*"

Multiple completion well A well equipped to produce oil and/or gas separately from more than one reservoir. Such wells contain multiple strings of tubing or other equipment that permit production from the various completions to be measured and accounted for separately. For statistical purposes, a multiple completion well is reported as one well and classified as either an oil well or a gas well. If one of the several completions in a given well is an oil completion, the well is classified as an oil well. If all of the completions in a given well are gas completions, the well is classified as a gas well.

Multiple cropping A system of growing several crops on the same field in one year.

Multiple purpose project The development of hydroelectric facilities to serve more than one function. Some of the uses include hydroelectric power, irrigation, water supply, water quality control, and/or fish and wildlife enhancement.

Multiple purpose reservoir Stored water and its usage governed by advanced water resource conservation practices to achieve more than one water control objective. Some of the objectives include flood control, hydroelectric power development, irrigation, recreation usage, and wilderness protection.

Municipal solid waste Residential solid waste and some nonhazardous commercial, institutional, and industrial wastes.

Municipal waste As defined in the Energy Security Act (P.L. 96-294; 1980) as "any organic matter, including sewage, sewage sludge, and industrial or commercial waste, and mixtures of such matter and inorganic refuse from any publicly or privately operated municipal waste collection or similar disposal system, or from similar waste flows (other than such flows which constitute agricultural wastes or residues, or wood wastes or residues from wood harvesting activities or production of forest products)."

Municipal waste to energy project or plant A facility that produces fuel or energy from municipal solid waste.

Municipality A village town, city, county, or other political subdivision of a State.

NAICS (North American Industry Classification System) A coding system developed jointly by the United States, Canada, and Mexico to classify businesses and industries according to the type of economic activity in which they are engaged. NAICS replaces the Standard Industrial Classification (SIC) codes.

Name plate A metal tag attached to a machine or appliance that contains information such as brand name, serial number, voltage, power ratings under specified conditions, and other manufacturer supplied data.

Name plate capacity See Generator nameplate capacity (installed).

Naphtha A generic term applied to a petroleum fraction with an approximate boiling range between 122 degrees Fahrenheit and 400 degrees Fahrenheit.

Naphtha less than 401 degrees Fahrenheit See Petrochemical feedstocks.

Naphthas Refined or partly refined light distillates with an approximate boiling point range of 27 degrees to 221 degrees Centigrade. Blended further or mixed with other materials, they make high-grade motor gasoline or jet fuel. Also, used as solvents, petrochemical feedstocks, or as raw materials for the production of town gas.

Naphtha-type jet fuel A fuel in the heavy naphtha boiling range having an average gravity of 52.8 degrees API, 20 to 90 percent distillation temperatures of 290 degrees to 470 degrees Fahrenheit, and meeting Military Specification MIL-T-5624L (Grade JP-4). It is used primarily for military turbojet and turboprop aircraft engines because it has a lower freeze point than other aviation fuels and meets engine requirements at high altitudes and speeds. Note: Beginning with January 2004 data, naphtha-type jet fuel is included in Miscellaneous Products.

National Association of Regulatory Utility Commissioners (NARUC) An affiliation of the public service commissioners to promote the uniform treatment of members of the railroad, public utilities, and public service commissions of the 50 states, the District of Columbia, the Commonwealth of Puerto Rico, and the territory of the Virgin Islands.

National Defense Authorization Act The federal law, enacted in 1994 and amended in 1995, that required the Secretary of Energy to prepare the Baseline Report.

National priorities list The Environmental Protection Agency's list of the most serious uncontrolled or abandoned hazardous waste sites identified for possible long-term remedial action under the Comprehensive Environmental Response, Compensation, and Liability Act (CERCLA). The list is based primarily on the score a site receives from the Environmental Protection Agency Hazard Ranking System. The Environmental Protection Agency is required to update the National Priorities List at least once a year.

National Rural Electric Cooperative Association (NRECA) A national organization dedicated to representing the interests of cooperative electric utilities and the consumers they serve. Members come from the 46 states that have an electric distribution cooperative.

National uranium resource evaluation (NURE) A program begun by the U.S. Atomic Energy Commission (AEC) in 1974 to make a comprehensive evaluation of U.S. uranium resources and continued through 1983 by the AEC's successor agencies, the Energy Research and Development Administration (ERDA), and the Department of Energy (DOE). The NURE program included aerial radiometric and magnetic surveys, hydrogeochemical and stream sediment surveys, geologic drilling in selected areas, geophysical logging of selected boreholes, and geologic studies to identify and evaluate geologic environments favorable for uranium.

Native gas Gas in place at the time that a reservoir was converted to use as an underground storage reservoir in contrast to injected gas volumes.

Native load (electric) The end-use customers that the Load-Serving Entity is obligated to serve. (NERC definition)

Natural gas A gaseous mixture of hydrocarbon compounds, the primary one being methane. *Note*: The Energy Information Administration measures wet natural gas and its two sources of production, associated/dissolved natural gas and nonassociated natural gas, and dry natural gas, which is produced from wet natural gas.

Natural gas, "dry" See Dry natural gas.

Natural gas field facility A field facility designed to process natural gas produced from more than one lease for the purpose of recovering condensate from a stream of natural gas; however, some field facilities are designed to recover propane, normal butane, pentanes plus, etc., and to control the quality of natural gas to be marketed.

Natural gas gross withdrawals Full well-stream volume of produced natural gas, excluding condensate separated at the lease.

Natural gas hydrates Solid, crystalline, wax-like substances composed of water, methane, and usually a small amount of other gases, with the gases being trapped in the interstices of a water-ice lattice. They form beneath permafrost and on the ocean floor under conditions of moderately high pressure and at temperatures near the freezing point of water.

Natural gas liquids (NGL) Those hydrocarbons in natural gas that are separated from the gas as liquids through the process of absorption, condensation, adsorption, or other methods in gas processing or cycling plants. Generally such liquids consist of propane and heavier hydrocarbons and are commonly referred to as lease condensate, natural gasoline, and liquefied petroleum gases. Natural gas liquids include natural gas plant liquids (primarily ethane, propane, butane, and isobutane; see Natural Gas Plant Liquids) and lease condensate (primarily pentanes produced from natural gas at lease separators and field facilities; see **Lease Condensate**).

Natural gas liquids production The volume of natural gas liquids removed from natural gas in lease separators, field facilities, gas processing plants, or cycling plants during the report year.

Natural gas marketed production Gross withdrawals of natural gas from production reservoirs, less gas used for reservoir repressuring, nonhydrocarbon gases removed in treating and processing operations, and quantities vented and flared.

Natural gas marketer A company that arranges purchases and sales of natural gas. Unlike pipeline companies or local distribution companies, a marketer does not own physical assets commonly used in the supply of natural gas, such as pipelines or storage fields. A marketer may be an affiliate of another company, such as a local distribution company, natural gas pipeline, or producer, but it operates independently of other segments of the company. In States with residential choice programs, marketers serve as alternative suppliers to residential users of natural gas, which is delivered by a local distribution company.

Natural gas plant liquids Those hydrocarbons in natural gas that are separated as liquids at natural gas processing plants, fractionating and cycling plants, and, in some instances, field facilities. Lease condensate is excluded. Products obtained include ethane; liquefied petroleum gases (propane, butanes, propane-butane mixtures, ethane-propane mixtures); isopentane; and other small quantities of finished products, such as motor gasoline, special naphthas, jet fuel, kerosene, and distillate fuel oil.

Natural Gas Policy Act of 1978 (NGPA) Signed into law on November 9, 1978, the NGPA is a framework for the regulation of most facets of the natural gas industry.

Natural gas processing plant Facilities designed to recover natural gas liquids from a stream of natural gas that may or may not have passed through lease separators and/or field separation facilities. These facilities control the quality of the natural gas to be marketed. Cycling plants are classified as gas processing plants.

Natural gas production See Dry natural gas production.

Natural gas utility demand-side management (DSM) program sponsor A DSM (demand-side management) program sponsored by a natural gas utility that suggests ways to increase the energy efficiency of buildings, to reduce energy costs, to change the usage patterns, or to promote the use of a different energy source.

Natural gasoline A term used in the gas processing industry to refer to a mixture of liquid hydrocarbons (mostly pentanes and heavier hydrocarbons) extracted from natural gas. It includes isopentane.

Natural gasoline and isopentane A mixture of hydrocarbons, mostly pentanes and heavier, extracted from natural gas, that meets vapor pressure, endpoint, and other specifications for natural gasoline set by the Gas Processors Association. Includes isopentane which is a saturated branch-chain hydrocarbon, (C_5H_{12}), obtained by fractionation of natural gasoline or isomerization of normal pentane.

Natural reservoir pressure The energy within an oil or gas reservoir that causes the oil or gas to rise (unassisted by other forces) to the earth's surface when the reservoir is penetrated by an oil or gas well. The energy may be the result of "dissolved gas drive," "gas cap drive," or "water drive." Regardless of the type of drive, the principle is the same: the energy of the gas or water, creating a natural pressure, forces the oil or gas to the well bore.

Natural streamflow The rate of flow of water past a given point of an uncontrolled stream or regulated streamflow adjusted to eliminate the effects of reservoir storage or upstream diversions at a set time interval.

Natural uranium Uranium with the U-235 isotope present at a concentration of 0.711 percent (by weight), that is, uranium with its isotopic content exactly as it is found in nature.

NERC North American Electric Reliability Council. See definition further down on this page.

Net actual interchange (electric) The algebraic sum of all metered interchange over all interconnections between two physically Adjacent Balancing Authority Areas. (NERC definition)

Net cell shipments Represents the difference between cell shipments and cell purchases.

Net electricity consumption Consumption of electricity computed as generation, plus imports, minus exports, minus transmission and distribution losses.

Net energy for load (electric) Net Balancing Authority Area generation, plus energy received from other Balancing Authority Areas, less energy delivered to Balancing Authority Areas through interchange. It includes Balancing Authority Area losses but excludes energy required for storage at energy storage facilities. (NERC definition)

Net energy for system The sum of energy an electric utility needs to satisfy their service areas, including full and partial requirements consumers.

Net generation The amount of gross generation less the electrical energy consumed at the generating station(s) for station service or auxiliaries. *Note*: Electricity required for pumping at pumped-storage plants is regarded as electricity for station service and is deducted from gross generation.

Net head The gross head minus all hydraulic losses except those chargeable to the turbine.

Net income Operating income plus other income and extraordinary income less operating expenses, taxes, interest charges, other deductions, and extraordinary deductions.

Net interstate flow of electricity The difference between the sum of electricity sales and losses within a state and the total amount of electricity generated within that state. A positive number indicates that more electricity (including associated losses) came into the state than went out of the state during the year; conversely, a negative number indicates that more electricity (including associated losses) went out of the state than came into the state.

Net module shipments Represents the difference between module shipments and module purchases. When exported, incomplete modules and unencapsulated cells are also included.

Net operable capacity Total owned capacity less inoperable capacity.

Net photovoltaic module shipment The difference between photovoltaic module shipments and photovoltaic module purchases.

Net profits interest A contractual arrangement under which the beneficiary, in exchange for consideration paid, receives a stated percentage of the net profits. That type of arrangement is considered a nonoperating interest, as distinguished from a working interest, because it does not involve the rights and obligations of operating a mineral property (costs of exploration, development, and operation). The net profits interest does not bear any part of net losses.

Net receipts The difference between total movements into and total movements out of each PAD District by pipeline, tanker, and barge.

Net summer capacity The maximum output, commonly expressed in megawatts (MW), that generating equipment can supply to a system load, as demonstrated by a multi-hour test, adjusted to ambient weather conditions for summer peak demand (from June 1 through September 30). This output reflects a reduction in capacity attributed to station service or auxiliary equipment requirements.

Net winter capacity The maximum output, commonly expressed in megawatts (MW), that generating equipment can supply to a system load, as demonstrated by a multi-hour test, adjusted to the ambient weather conditions for winter peak demand (from December 1 through March 31). This output reflects a reduction in capacity attributed to station service or auxiliary equipment requirements.

Netback purchase Refers to a crude oil purchase agreement wherein the price paid for the crude is determined by sales prices of the types of products that are derivable from that crude as well as other considerations (e.g., transportation and processing costs). Typically, the price is calculated based on product prices extant on or near the cargo's date of importation.

New field A field discovered during the report year.

New field discoveries The volumes of proved reserves of crude oil, natural gas, and/or natural gas liquids discovered in new fields during the report year.

New reservoir A reservoir discovered during the report year.

Nitrogen dioxide A compound of nitrogen and oxygen formed by the oxidation of nitric oxide (NO) which is produced by the combustion of solid fuels.

Nitrogen oxides (NO_x) Compounds of nitrogen and oxygen produced by the burning of fossil fuels.

Nitrous oxide (N_2O) A colorless gas, naturally occurring in the atmosphere. Nitrous oxide has a 100-year Global Warming Potential of 310.

No. 1 diesel fuel A light distillate fuel oil that has a distillation temperature of 550 degrees Fahrenheit at the 90-percent recovery point and meets the specifications defined in ASTM Specification D 975. It is used in high speed diesel engines generally operated under frequent speed and load changes, such as those in city buses and similar vehicles. See No. 1 distillate below.

No. 1 distillate A light petroleum distillate that can be used as either a diesel fuel (see No. 1 diesel fuel above) or a fuel oil (see No. 1 fuel oil (below).

No. 1 fuel oil A light distillate fuel oil that has distillation temperatures of 400 degrees Fahrenheit at the 10-percent recovery point and 550 degrees Fahrenheit at the 90-percent recovery point and meets the specifications defined in ASTM Specification D 396. It is used primarily as fuel for portable outdoor stoves and portable outdoor heaters. See No. 1 distillate above.

No. 2 diesel fuel A distillate fuel oil that has a distillation temperature of 640 degrees Fahrenheit at the 90-percent recovery point and meets the specifications defined in ASTM Specification D 975. It is used in high-speed diesel engines that are generally operated under uniform speed and load conditions, such as those in railroad locomotives, trucks, and automobiles. See No. 2 distillate below.

No. 2 distillate A petroleum distillate that can be used as either a diesel fuel (see No. 2 diesel fuel above) or a fuel oil (see No. 2 fuel oil below).

No. 2 fuel oil (heating oil) A distillate fuel oil that has a distillation temperature of 640 degrees Fahrenheit at the 90-percent recovery point and meets the specifications defined in ASTM Specification D 396. It is used in atomizing type burners for domestic heating or for moderate capacity commercial/industrial burner units. See No. 2 distillate above.

No. 2 fuel oil and No. 2 diesel sold to consumers for all other end uses Those consumers who purchase fuel oil or diesel fuel for their own use including: commercial/institutional buildings (including apartment buildings), manufacturing and nonmanufacturing establishments, farms (including farm houses), motor vehicles, commercial or private boats, military, governments, electric utilities, railroads, construction, logging or any other nonresidential end-use purpose.

No. 2 fuel oil sold to private homes for heating Private household customers who purchase fuel oil for the specific purpose of heating their home, water heating, cooking, etc., excluding farm houses, farming and apartment buildings.

No. 4 fuel oil A distillate fuel oil made by blending distillate fuel oil and residual fuel oil stocks. It conforms with ASTM Specification D 396 or Federal Specification VV-F-815C and is used extensively in industrial plants and in commercial burner installations that are not equipped with preheating facilities. It also includes No. 4 diesel fuel used for low- and medium-speed diesel engines and conforms to ASTM Specification D 975.

No. 5 and no. 6 fuel oil sold directly to the ultimate consumer Includes ships, mines, smelters, manufacturing plants, electric utilities, drilling, railroad.

No. 5 and no. 6 fuel oil sold to refiners or other dealers who will resale the product Includes all volumes of No. 5 and No. 6 fuel oil purchased by a trade or business with the intent of reselling the product to the ultimate consumers.

NOAA National Oceanic and Atmospheric Administration.

NOAA division One of the 345 weather divisions designated by the National Oceanic and Atmospheric Administration (NOAA) encompassing the 48 contiguous states. These divisions usually follow county borders to encompass counties with similar weather conditions. The NOAA division does not follow county borders when weather conditions vary considerably within a county; such is likely to happen when the county borders the ocean or contains high mountains. A state contains an average of seven NOAA divisions; a NOAA division contains an average of nine counties.

Noload loss Power and energy lost by an electric system when not operating under demand.

Nominal dollars A measure used to express nominal price.

Nominal price The price paid for a product or service at the time of the transaction. Nominal prices are those that have not been adjusted to remove the effect of changes in the purchasing power of the dollar; they reflect buying power in the year in which the transaction occurred.

Nonassociated natural gas Natural gas that is not in contact with significant quantities of crude oil in the reservoir. See *natural gas* above.

Nonattainment area Any area that does not meet the national primary or secondary ambient air quality standard established by the Environmental Protection Agency for designated pollutants, such as carbon monoxide and ozone.

Non-biomass waste Material of non-biological origin that is a byproduct or a discarded product. "Non-biomass waste" includes municipal solid waste from non-biogenic sources, such as plastics, and tire-derived fuels.

Nonbranded product Any refined petroleum product that is not a branded product.

Noncoincident demand Sum of two or more demands on individual systems that do not occur in the same demand interval.

Noncoincidental peak load The sum of two or more peak loads on individual systems that do not occur in the same time interval. Meaningful only when considering loads within a limited period of time, such as a day, week, month, a heating or cooling season, and usually for not more than 1 year.

Nonconventional plant (uranium) A facility engineered and built principally for processing of uraniferous solutions that are produced during in situ leach mining, from heap leaching, or in the manufacture of other commodities, and the recovery, by chemical treatment in the plant's circuits, of uranium from the processing solutions.

Nondedicated vehicle A motor vehicle capable of operating on an alternative fuel and/or on either gasoline or diesel.

Nonfirm power Power or power-producing capacity supplied or available under a commitment having limited or no assured availability.

Nonfuel components Components that are not associated with a particular fuel. These include, but are not limited to, control spiders, burnable poison rod assemblies, control rod elements, thimble plugs, fission chambers, primary and secondary neutron sources, and BWR (boiling water reactor) channels.

Nonfuel use (of energy) Use of energy as feedstock or raw material input.

Nonfungible product A gasoline blend or blendstock that cannot be shipped via existing petroleum product distribution systems because of incompatibility problems. Gasoline/ethanol blends, for example, are contaminated by water that is typically present in petroleum product distribution systems.

Nonhydrocarbon gases Typical nonhydrocarbon gases that may be present in reservoir natural gas, such as carbon dioxide, helium, hydrogen sulfide, and nitrogen.

Nonmethane volatile organic compounds (NMVOC) Organic compounds, other than methane, that participate in atmospheric photochemical reactions.

Nonoperating interest Any mineral lease interest (e.g., royalty, production payment, net profits interest) that does not involve the rights and obligations of operating a mineral property.

Nonproducing reservoir Reservoir in which oil and/or gas proved reserves have been identified, but which did not produce during the report year to the owned or contracted interest of the reporting company regardless of the availability and/or operation of production, gathering, or transportation facilities.

Nonrenewable fuels Fuels that cannot be easily made or "renewed," such as oil, natural gas, and coal.

Nonrequirements consumer A wholesale consumer (unlike a full or partial requirements consumer) that purchases economic or coordination power to supplement their own or another system's energy needs.

Nonresidential building A building used for some purpose other than residential. Nonresidential buildings comprise three groups: commercial, manufacturing/industrial, and agricultural.

Nonroad alternative fuel vehicle (nonroad AFV) An alternative fuel vehicle designed for off-road operation and use for surface/air transportation, industrial, or commercial purposes. Nonroad AFVs include forklifts and other industrial vehicles, rail locomotives, self-propelled electric rail cars, aircraft, airport service vehicles, construction vehicles, agricultural vehicles, and marine vessels. Recreational AFVs (golf carts, snowmobiles, pleasure watercraft, etc.) are excluded from the definition.

Nonspinning reserve The generating capacity not currently running but capable of being connected to the bus and load within a specified time.

Nonutility generation Electric generation by end-users, or small power producers under the Public Utility Regulatory Policies Act, to supply electric power for industrial, commercial, and military operations, or sales to electric utilities.

Nonutility power producer A corporation, person, agency, authority, or other legal entity or instrumentality that owns or operates facilities for electric generation and is not an electric utility. Nonutility power producers include qualifying **cogenerators**, qualifying small power producers, and other nonutility generators (including independent power producers). Nonutility power producers are without a designated franchised service area and do not file forms listed in the Code of Federal Regulations, Title 18, Part 141.

Normal butane (C_4H_{10}) A normally gaseous straight chain hydrocarbon that is a colorless paraffinic gas which boils at a temperature of 31.1 degrees Fahrenheit.

North American Electric Reliability Council (NERC) A council formed in 1968 by the electric utility industry to promote the reliability and adequacy of bulk power supply in the electric utility systems of North America. NERC consists of regional reliability councils and encompasses essentially all the power regions of the contiguous United States, Canada, and Mexico. See the various NERC Regional Reliability Councils here: http://www.nerc.com/regional/

North American Industry Classification System (NAICS) A new classification scheme, developed by the Office of Management and Budget to replace the Standard Industrial Classification (SIC) System, that categorizes establishments according to the types of production processes they primarily use.

Nuclear electric power (nuclear power) Electricity generated by the use of the thermal energy released from the fission of nuclear fuel in a reactor.

Nuclear fuel Fissionable materials that have been enriched to such a composition that, when placed in a nuclear reactor, will support a self-sustaining fission chain reaction, producing heat in a controlled manner for process use.

Nuclear reactor An apparatus in which a nuclear fission chain reaction can be initiated, controlled, and sustained at a specific rate. A reactor includes fuel (fissionable material), moderating material to control the rate of fission, a heavy-walled pressure vessel to house reactor components, shielding to protect personnel, a system to conduct heat away from the reactor, and instrumentation for monitoring and controlling the reactor's systems.

Number of mines The number of mines, or mines collocated with preparation plants or tipples, located in a particular geographic area (State or region). If a mine is mining coal across two counties within a State, or across two States, then it is counted as two operations. This is done so that EIA can separate production by State and county.

Number of mining operations The number of mining operations includes preparation plants with greater than 5,000 total direct labor hours. Mining operations that consist of a mine and preparation plant, or a preparation plant only, will be counted as two operations if the preparation plant processes both underground and surface coal. Excluded are silt, culm, refuse bank, slurry dam, and dredge operations except for Pennsylvania anthracite. Excludes mines producing less than 10,000 short tons of coal during the year.

Occupancy sensors These are also known as "ultrasonic switchers." When movement is detected, the lights are turned on and remain on as long as there is movement in the room.

Ocean energy systems Energy conversion technologies that harness the energy in tides, waves, and thermal gradients in the oceans.

Ocean thermal energy conversion (OTEC) The process or technologies for producing energy by harnessing the temperature differences (thermal gradients) between ocean surface waters and that of ocean depths. Warm surface water is pumped through an evaporator containing a working fluid in a closed Rankine-cycle system. The vaporized fluid drives a turbine/generator.

Octane A flammable liquid hydrocarbon found in petroleum. Used as a standard to measure the antiknock properties of motor fuel.

Octane rating A number used to indicate gasoline's antiknock performance in motor vehicle engines. The two recognized laboratory engine test methods for determining the antiknock rating, i.e., octane rating, of gasolines are the Research method and the Motor method. To provide a single number as guidance to the consumer, the antiknock index $(R + M)/2$, which is the average of the Research and Motor octane numbers, was developed.

OEM Original equipment manufacturer.

Off-highway use Includes petroleum products sales for use in:
1. **Construction** Construction equipment including earthmoving equipment, cranes, stationary generators, air compressors, etc.
2. **Other** Sales for off-highway uses other than construction. Sales for logging are included in this category. Volumes for off-highway use by the agriculture industry are reported under "Farm Use" (which includes sales for use in tractors, irrigation pumps, other agricultural machinery, etc.)

Off-hours equipment reduction A conservation feature where there is a change in the temperature setting or reduction in the use of heating, cooling, domestic hot water heating, lighting or any other equipment either manually or automatically.

Off peak Period of relatively low system demand. These periods often occur in daily, weekly, and seasonal patterns; these off-peak periods differ for each individual electric utility.

Off-peak gas Gas that is to be delivered and taken on demand when demand is not at its peak.

Offshore That geographic area that lies seaward of the coastline. In general, the coastline is the line of ordinary low water along with that portion of the coast that is in direct contact with the open sea or the line marking the seaward limit of inland water. If a state agency uses a different basis for classifying onshore and offshore areas, the state classification should be used (e.g., Cook Inlet in Alaska is classified as offshore; for Louisiana, the coastline is defined as the Chapman Line, as modified by subsequent adjudication).

Offshore reserves and production Unless otherwise dedicated, reserves and production that are in either state or Federal domains, located seaward of the coastline.

Offsite-produced energy for heat, power, and electricity generation This measure of energy consumption, which is equivalent to purchased energy includes energy produced off-site and consumed onsite. It excludes energy produced and consumed onsite, energy used as raw material input, and electricity losses.

Off-system Any point not on, or directly interconnected with, a transportation, storage, and/or distribution system operated by a natural gas company within a state.

Off-system (natural gas) Natural gas that is transported to the end user by the company making final delivery of the gas to the end user. The end user purchases the gas from another company, such as a producer or marketer, not from the delivering company (typically a local distribution company or a pipeline company).

Ohm A measure of the electrical resistance of a material equal to the resistance of a circuit in which the potential difference of 1 volt produces a current of 1 ampere.

Ohm's law In a given electrical circuit, the amount of current in amperes is equal to the pressure in volts divided by the resistance, in ohms. The principle is named after the German scientist Georg Simon Ohm.

Oil A mixture of hydrocarbons usually existing in the liquid state in natural underground pools or reservoirs. Gas is often found in association with oil. Also see Petroleum.

Oil company use Includes sales to drilling companies, pipelines or other related oil companies not engaged in the selling of petroleum products. Includes fuel oil that was purchased or produced and used by company facilities for the operation of drilling equipment, other field or refinery operations, and space heating at petroleum refineries, pipeline companies, and oil-drilling companies. Oil used to bunker vessels is counted under vessel bunkering. Sales to other oil companies for field use are included, but sales for use as refinery charging stocks are excluded.

Oil shale A sedimentary rock containing kerogen, a solid organic material.

Oil stocks Oil stocks include crude oil (including strategic reserves), unfinished oils, natural gas plant liquids, and refined petroleum products.

Oil well A well completed for the production of crude oil from at least one oil zone or reservoir.

Oil well (casinghead) gas Associated and dissolved gas produced along with crude oil from oil completions.

Old field A field discovered prior to the report year.

Old reservoir A reservoir discovered prior to the report year.

On-highway use (diesel) Includes sales for use in motor vehicles. Volumes used by companies in the marketing and distribution of petroleum products are also included.

On peak Periods of relatively high system demand. These periods often occur in daily, weekly, and seasonal patterns; these on-peak periods differ for each individual electric utility.

On-system Any point on or directly interconnected with a transportation, storage, or distribution system operated by a natural gas company.

On-system sales Sales to customers where the delivery point is a point on, or directly interconnected with, a transportation, storage, and/or distribution system operated by the reporting company.

One sun Natural solar insulation falling on an object without concentration or diffusion of the solar rays.

One-time fee The fee assessed a nuclear utility for spent nuclear fuel (SNF) or solidified high-level radioactive waste derived from SNF, which fuel was used to generate electricity in a civilian nuclear power reactor prior to April 7, 1983, and which is assessed by applying industry-wide average dollar-per-kilogram charges to four distinct ranges of fuel burnup so that equivalent to an industry-wide average charge of 1.0 mill per kilowatthour.

Onsite transportation The direct nonprocess end use that includes energy used in vehicles and transportation equipment that primarily consume energy within the boundaries of the establishment. Energy used in vehicles that are found primarily offsite, such as delivery trucks, is not measured by the MECS (an EIA survey).

Onsystem (natural gas) Natural gas that is sold (and transported) to the end user by the company making final delivery of the gas to the end user. Companies that make final delivery of natural gas are typically local distribution companies or pipeline companies.

OPEC (Organization of the Petroleum Exporting Countries) An intergovernmental organization whose stated objective is to "coordinate and unify the petroleum policies of member countries." It was created at the Baghdad Conference on September 10–14, 1960. Current members (with years of membership) include Algeria (1969–present), Angola (2007–present), Ecuador (1973–1992 and 2007–present), Iran (1960–present), Iraq (1960–present), Kuwait (1960–present), Libya (1962–present), Nigeria (1971–present), Qatar (1961–present), Saudi Arabia (1960–present), United Arab Emirates (1967–present), and Venezuela (1960–present). Countries no longer members of OPEC include Gabon (1975–1994) and Indonesia (1962–2008).

Open access (electric) Federal Energy Regulatory Commission Order No. 888 requires public utilities to provide non-discriminatory transmission service over their transmission facilities to third parties to move bulk power from one point to another on a non-discriminatory basis for a cost-based fee. Order 890 expanded Open Access to cover the methodology for calculating available transmission transfer capability; improvements that opened a coordinated transmission planning processes; standardization of energy and generation imbalance charges; and other reforms regarding the designation and undesignation of transmission network resources. (NERC definition)

Open access transmission tariff (electric) Electronic transmission tariff accepted by the U.S. Federal Energy Regulatory Commission requiring the Transmission Service Provider to furnish to all shippers with non-discriminating service comparable to that provided by Transmission Owners to themselves. (NERC definition)

Open market coal Coal is sold in the open market, i.e., coal sold to companies other than the reporting company's parent company or an operating subsidiary of the parent company.

Open refrigeration unit Refrigeration in cabinets (units) without covers or with flexible covers made of plastic or some other material, hung in strips or curtains (fringed material, usually plastic, that push aside like a bead curtain). Flexible covers stop the flow of warm air into the refrigerated space.

Operable capacity The amount of capacity that, at the beginning of the period, is in operation; not in operation and not under active repair, but capable of being placed in operation within 30 days; or not in operation but under active repair that can be completed within 90 days. Operable capacity is the sum of the operating and idle capacity and is measured in barrels per calendar day or barrels per stream day.

Operable generators/units Electric generators or generating units that are available to provide power to the grid or generating units that have been providing power to the grid but are temporarily shut down. This includes units in standby status, units out of service for an indefinite period, and new units that have their construction complete and are ready to provide test generation. A nuclear unit is operable once it receives its Full Power Operating License.

Operable nuclear unit (U.S.) A U.S. nuclear generating unit that has completed low-power testing and is in possession of a full-power operating license issued by the Nuclear Regulatory Commission.

Operable nuclear unit (foreign) A nuclear generating unit outside the United States that generates electricity for a grid.

Operable refineries Refineries that were in one of the following three categories at the beginning of a given year: in operation; not in operation and not under active repair, but capable of being placed into operation within 30 days; or not in operation, but under active repair that could be completed within 90 days.

Operable unit A unit available to provide electric power to the grid. See definition for operating unit below.

Operable utilization rate Represents the use of the atmospheric crude oil distillation units. The rate is calculated by dividing the gross input to these units by the operable refining capacity of the units.

Operated Exercised management responsibility for the day-to-day operations of natural gas production, gathering, treating, processing, transportation, storage, and/or distribution facilities and/or a synthetic natural gas plant.

Operating capacity The component of operable capacity that is in operation at the beginning of the period.

Operating day A normal business day. Days when a company conducts business due to emergencies or other unexpected events are not included.

Operating expenses Segment expenses related both to revenue from sales to unaffiliated customers and revenue from intersegment sales or transfers, excluding loss on disposition of property, plant, and equipment; interest expenses and financial charges; foreign currency translation effects; minority interest; and income taxes.

Operating income Operating revenues less operating expenses. Excludes items of other revenue and expense, such as equity in earnings of unconsolidated affiliates, dividends, interest income and expense, income taxes, extraordinary items, and cumulative effects of accounting changes.

Operating revenues Segment revenues both from sales to unaffiliated customers (i.e., revenue from customers outside the enterprise as reported in the company's consolidated income statement) and from intersegment sales or transfers, if any, of product and services similar to those sold to unaffiliated customers, excluding equity in earnings of unconsolidated affiliates; dividend and interest income; gain on disposition of property, plant, and equipment; and foreign currency translation effects.

Operating subsidiary Company that operates a coal mining operation and is owned by another company (i.e., the parent company).

Operating unit A unit that is in operation at the beginning of the reporting period.

Operating utilization rate Represents the use of the atmospheric crude oil distillation units. The rate is calculated by dividing the gross input to these units by the operating refining capacity of the units.

Operator, gas plant The person responsible for the management and day-to-day operation of one or more natural gas processing plants as of December 31 of the report year. The operator is generally a working-interest owner or a company under contract to the working-interest owner(s). Plants shut down during the report year are also to be considered "operated" as of December 31.

Operator, oil and/or gas well The person responsible for the management and day-to-day operation of one or more crude oil and/or natural gas wells as of December 31 of the report year. The operator is generally a working-interest owner or a company under contract to the working-interest owner(s). Wells included are those that have proved reserves of crude oil, natural gas, and/or lease condensate in the reservoirs associated with them, whether or not they are producing. Wells abandoned during the report year are also to be considered "operated" as of December 31.

Optional delivery commitment A provision to allow the conditional purchase or sale of a specific quantity of material in addition to the firm quantity in the contract.

Order A ruling issued by a utility commission granting or denying an application in whole or in part. The order explains the basis for the decision, noting any dispute with the factual assertions of the applicant. Also applied to a final regulation of a utility commission.

Organic content The share of a substance that is of animal or plant origin.

Organic waste Waste material of animal or plant origin.

Organization for Economic Cooperation and Development (OECD) An international organization helping governments tackle the economic, social and governance challenges of a globalized economy. Its membership comprises about 30 member countries. With active relationships with some 70 other countries, NGOs and civil society, it has a global reach. For details about the organization, visit http://www.oecd.org.

Organization of the Petroleum Exporting Countries (OPEC) See "OPEC (Organization of the Petroleum Exporting Countries)"

Original cost The initial amount of money spent to acquire an asset. It is equal to the price paid, or present value of the liability incurred, or fair value of stock issued, plus normal incidental costs necessary to put the asset into its initial use.

Original equipment manufacturer (OEM) A company that provides the original design and materials for manufacture and engages in the assembly of vehicles. The OEM is directly responsible for manufacturing, marketing, and providing warranties for the finished product.

Original equipment manufacturer vehicle A vehicle produced and marketed by an original equipment manufacturer (OEM), including gasoline and diesel vehicles as well as alternative-fuel vehicles. A vehicle manufactured by an OEM but converted to an alternative-fuel vehicle before its initial delivery to an end-user (for example, through a contract between a conversion company and the OEM) is considered to be an OEM vehicle as long as that vehicle is still covered under the OEM's warranty.

Other The "other" category is defined as representing electricity consumers not elsewhere classified. This category includes public street and highway lighting service, public authority service to public authorities, railroad and railway service, and interdepartmental services.

Other capital costs Costs for items or activities not included elsewhere under capital-cost tabulations, such as for and decommissioning, dismantling, and reclamation.

Other demand-side management (DSM) assistance programs A DSM program assistance that includes alternative-rate, fuel-switching, and any other DSM assistance programs that are offered to consumers to encourage their participation in DSM programs.

Other end users For motor gasoline, all direct sales to end users other than those made through company outlets. For No. 2 distillate, all direct sales to end users other than residential, commercial/institutional, industrial sales, and sales through company outlets. Included in the "other end users" category are sales to utilities and agricultural users.

Other energy operations Energy operations not included under Petroleum or Coal. "Other energy" includes nuclear, oil shale, tar sands, coal liquefaction and gasification, geothermal, solar, and other forms of unconventional energy.

Other finished Motor gasoline not included in the oxygenated or reformulated gasoline categories.

Other gas Includes manufactured gas, coke-oven gas, blast-furnace gas, and refinery gas. Manufactured gas is obtained by distillation of coal, by the thermal decomposition of oil, or by the reaction of steam passing through a bed of heated coal or coke.

Other generation Electricity originating from these sources: biomass, fuel cells, geothermal heat, solar power, waste, wind, and wood.

Other industrial plant Industrial users, not including coke plants, engaged in the mechanical or chemical transformation of materials or substances into new products (manufacturing); and companies engaged in the agriculture, mining, or construction industries.

Other load management Demand-Side Management (DSM) program other than Direct Load Control and Interruptible Load that limits or shifts peak load from on-peak to off-peak time periods. It includes technologies that primarily shift all or part of a load from one time-of-day to another and secondarily may have an impact on energy consumption. Examples include space heating and water heating storage systems, cool storage systems, and load limiting devices in energy management systems. This category also includes programs that aggressively promote time-of-use rates and other innovative rates such as real time pricing. These rates are intended to reduce consumer bills and shift hours of operation of equipment from on-peak to off-peak periods through the application of time-differentiated rates.

Other oils equal to or greater than 401 degrees Fahrenheit Oils with a boiling range equal to or greater than 401 degrees Fahrenheit that are intended for use as a petrochemical feedstock.

Other operating costs Costs for other items or activities not included elsewhere in operating-cost tabulations, but required to support the calculation of a cutoff grade for ore reserves estimation.

Other oxygenates Other aliphatic alcohols and aliphatic ethers intended for motor gasoline blending (e.g., isopropyl ether (IPE) or n-propanol).

Other power producers Independent power producers that generate electricity and cogeneration plants that are not included in the other industrial, coke and commercial sectors.

Other refiners Refiners with a total refinery capacity in the United States and its possessions of less than 275,000 barrels per day as of January 1, 1982.

Other service to public authorities Electricity supplied to municipalities, divisions or agencies of state or Federal governments, under special contracts or agreements or service classifications applicable only to public authorities.

Other single-unit truck A motor vehicle consisting primarily of a single motorized device with more than two axles or more than four tires.

Other supply contracts Any contracted gas supply other than owned reserves, producer-contracted reserves, and interstate pipeline purchases that are used for acts and services for which the company has received certificate authorization from FERC. Purchases from intrastate pipelines pursuant to Section 311(b) of the NGPA of 1978 are included with other supply contracts.

Other trucks/vans Those trucks and vans that weigh more than 8,500 lbs GVW.

Other unavailable capability Net capability of main generating units that are unavailable for load for easons other than full-forced outage or scheduled maintenance. Legal restrictions or other causes make these units unavailable.

Outage The period during which a generating unit, transmission line, or other facility is out of service.

Outer Continental Shelf Offshore Federal domain.

Output The amount of power or energy produced by a generating unit, station, or system.

Oven An appliance that is an enclosed compartment supplied with heat and used for cooking food. Toaster ovens are not considered ovens. The range stove top or burners and the oven are considered two separate appliances, although they are often purchased as one appliance.

Overburden Any material, consolidated or unconsolidated, that overlies a coal deposit.

Overburden ratio Overburden ratio refers to the amount of overburden that must be removed to excavate a given quantity of coal. It is commonly expressed in cubic yards per ton of coal, but is sometimes expressed as a ratio comparing the thickness of the overburden with the thickness of the coalbed.

Overriding royalty A royalty interest, in addition to the basic royalty, created out of the working interest; it is, therefore, limited in its duration to the life of the lease under which it is created.

Owned reserves Any reserve of natural gas that the reporting company owns as a result of oil and gas leases, fee-mineral ownership, royalty reservations, or lease or royalty reservations and assignments committed to services under certificate authorizations by FERC. Company-owned recoverable natural gas in underground storage is classified as owned reserves.

Owned/rented (As used in EIA's consumption surveys.) The relationship of a housing unit's occupants to the structure itself, not the land on which the structure is located. "Owned" means the owner or co-owner is a member of the household and the housing unit is either fully paid for or mortgaged. A household is classified "rented" even if the rent is paid by someone not living in the unit. "Rent-free" means the unit is not owned or being bought and no money is paid or contracted for rent. Such units are usually provided in exchange for services rendered or as an allowance or favor from a relative or friend not living in the unit. Unless shown separately, rent-free households are grouped with rented households.

Owner occupied (As used in EIA's consumption surveys.) Having the owner or the owner's business represented at the site. A building is considered owner occupied if an employee or representative of the owner (such as a building engineer or building manager) maintains office space in the building. Similarly, a chain store is considered owner occupied even though the actual owner may not be in the building but headquartered elsewhere. Other examples of the owner's business occupying a building include State-owned university buildings, elementary and secondary schools owned by a public school district, and a post office where the building is owned by the U.S. Postal Service.

Owner's equity Interest of the owners in the assets of the business represented by capital contributions and retained earnings.

Ownership See Owned/rented above.

Ownership of building (As used in EIA's consumption surveys.) The individual, agency, or organization that owns the building. For certain EIA consumption surveys, building ownership is grouped into the following categories: Federal, State, or local government agency; a privately owned utility company; a church, synagogue, or other religious group; or any other type of individual or group.

Oxidize To chemically transform a substance by combining it with oxygen.

Oxygenated gasoline Finished motor gasoline, other than reformulated gasoline, having an oxygen content of 2.7percent or higher by weight and required by the U.S. Environmental Protection Agency (EPA) to be sold in areas designated by EPA as carbon monoxide (CO) nonattainment areas. See Nonattainment area. *Note* Oxygenated gasoline excludes oxygenated fuels program reformulated gasoline (OPRG) and reformulated gasoline blendstock for oxygenate blending (RBOB). Data on gasohol that has at least 2.7 percent oxygen, by weight, and is intended for sale inside CO nonattainment areas are included in data on oxygenated gasoline. Other data on gasohol (for use outside of nonattainment areas) are included in data on conventional gasoline.

Oxygenated gasoline (includes Gasohol) Finished motor gasoline, other than reformulated gasoline, having an oxygen content of 1.8 percent or higher by weight. This includes gasohol irrespective of where it is consumed. *Note*: Oxygenated gasoline excludes oxygenated fuels program reformulated gasoline (OPRG) and reformulated gasoline blendstock for oxygenate blending (RBOB).

Oxygenates Substances which, when added to gasoline, increase the amount of oxygen in that gasoline blend. Ethanol, Methyl Tertiary Butyl Ether (MTBE), Ethyl Tertiary Butyl Ether (ETBE), and methanol are common oxygenates.

Ozone A molecule made up of three atoms of oxygen. Occurs naturally in the stratosphere and provides a protective layer shielding the Earth from harmful ultraviolet radiation. In the troposphere, it is a chemical oxidant, a greenhouse gas, and a major component of photochemical smog.

Ozone precursors Chemical compounds, such as carbon monoxide, methane, nonmethane hydrocarbons, and nitrogen oxides, which in the presence of solar radiation react with other chemical compounds to form ozone.

Packaged air conditioning units Usually mounted on the roof or on a slab beside the building. (These are known as self-contained units, or Direct Expansion (DX). They contain air conditioning equipment as well as fans, and may or may not include heating equipment.) These are self-contained units that contain the equipment that generates cool air and the equipment that distributes the cooled air. These units commonly consume natural gas or electricity. The units are mounted on the rooftop, exposed to the elements. They typically blow cool air into the building through duct work, but other types of distribution systems may exist. The units usually serve more than one room. There are often several units on the roof of a single building. Also known as: Packaged Terminal Air Conditioners (PTAC). These packaged units are often constructed as a single unit for heating and for cooling.

Packaged units Units built and assembled at a factory and installed as a self-contained unit to heat or cool all or portions of a building. Packaged units are in contrast to engineer-specified units built up from individual components for use in a given building. Packaged Units can apply to heating equipment, cooling equipment, or combined heating and cooling equipment. Some types of electric packaged units are also called "Direct Expansion" or DX units.

PAD Districts or PADD See Petroleum Administration for Defense Districts (below).

Parabolic dish A high-temperature (above 180 degrees Fahrenheit) solar thermal concentrator, generally bowl-shaped, with two-axis tracking.

Parabolic trough A high-temperature (above 180 degrees Fahrenheit) solar thermal concentrator with the capacity for tracking the sun using one axis of rotation.

Paraffin (oil) A light-colored, wax-free oil obtained by pressing paraffin distillate.

Paraffin (wax) The wax removed from paraffin distillates by chilling and pressing. When separating from solutions, it is a colorless, more or less translucent, crystalline mass, without odor and taste, slightly greasy to touch, and consisting of a mixture of solid hydrocarbons in which the paraffin series predominates.

Paraffinic hydrocarbons Straight-chain hydrocarbon compounds with the general formula C_nH_{2n+2}.

Parent A firm that directly or indirectly controls another entity.

Parent company An affiliated company that exercises ultimate control over a business entity, either directly or indirectly, through one or more intermediaries.

Partial requirements consumer A wholesale consumer with generating resources insufficient to carry all its load and whose energy seller is a long-term firm power source supplemental to the consumer's own generation or energy received from others. The terms and conditions of sale are similar to those for a full equirements consumer.

Particulate A small, discrete mass of solid or liquid matter that remains individually dispersed in gas or liquid emissions. Particulates take the form of aerosol, dust, fume, mist, smoke, or spray. Each of these forms has different properties.

Passenger-miles traveled The total distance traveled by all passengers. It is calculated as the product of the occupancy rate in vehicles and the vehicle miles traveled.

Passive solar heating A solar heating system that uses no external mechanical power, such as pumps or blowers, to move the collected solar heat.

Payables to municipality The amounts payable by the utility department to the municipality or its other departments that are subject to current settlement.

Payment method for utilities The method by which fuel suppliers or utility companies are paid for all electricity, natural gas, fuel oil, kerosene, or liquefied petroleum gas used by a household. Households that pay the utility company directly are classified as "all paid by household." Households that pay directly for at least one but not all of their fuels used and that has at least one fuel charge included in the rent were classified as "some paid, some included in rent." Households for which all fuels used are included in rent were classified as "all included in rent." If the household did not fall into one of these categories, it was classified as "other." Examples of households falling into the "other" category are: (1) households for which fuel bills were paid by a social service agency or a relative, and (2) households that paid for some of their fuels used but paid for other fuels through another arrangement.

Peak day withdrawal The maximum daily withdrawal rate (Mcf/d) experienced during the reporting period.

Peak demand The maximum load during a specified period of time.

Peak kilowatt One thousand peak watts.

Peak load The maximum load during a specified period of time.

Peak load month The month of greatest plant electrical generation during the winter heating season (Oct-Mar) and summer cooling season (Apr-Sept), respectively.

Peak load plant A plant usually housing old, low-efficiency steam units, gas turbines, diesels, or pumped-storage hydroelectric equipment normally used during the peak-load periods.

Peak megawatt One million peak watts.

Peak watt A manufacturer's unit indicating the amount of power a photovoltaic cell or module will produce at standard test conditions (normally 1,000 watts per square meter and 25 degrees Celsius).

Peaking capacity Capacity of generating equipment normally reserved for operation during the hours of highest daily, weekly, or seasonal loads. Some generating equipment may be operated at certain times as peaking capacity and at other times to serve loads on an around-the-clock basis.

Peat Peat consists of partially decomposed plant debris. It is considered an early stage in the development of coal. Peat is distinguished from lignite by the presence of free cellulose and a high moisture content (exceeding 70 percent). The heat content of air-dried peat (about 50 percent moisture) is about 9 million Btu per ton. Most U.S. peat is used as a soil conditioner. The first U.S. electric power plant fueled by peat began operation in Maine in 1990.

Pentanes plus A mixture of hydrocarbons, mostly pentanes and heavier, extracted from natural gas. Includes isopentane, natural gasoline, and plant condensate.

Percent difference The relative change in a quantity over a specified time period. It is calculated as follows: the current value has the previous value subtracted from it; this new number is divided by the absolute value of the previous value; then this new number is multiplied by 100.

Percent utilization The ratio of total production to productive capacity, times 100.

Perfluorocarbons (PFCs) A group of man-made chemicals composed of one or two carbon atoms and four to six fluorine atoms, containing no chlorine. PFCs have no commercial uses and are emitted as a byproduct of aluminum smelting and semiconductor manufacturing. PFCs have very high 100-year Global Warming Potentials and are very long-lived in the atmosphere.

Perfluoromethane A compound (CF_4) emitted as a byproduct of aluminum smelting.

Permanently discharged fuel Spent nuclear fuel for which there are no plans for reinsertion in the reactor core.

Permeability The ease with which fluid flows through a porous medium.

Persian Gulf The countries that surround the Persian Gulf are: Bahrain, Iran, Iraq, Kuwait, Qatar, Saudi Arabia, and the United Arab Emirates. See http//:www.eia.doe.gov/emeu/cabs/pgulf.html for more information.

Person An individual, a corporation, a partnership, an association, a joint-stock company, a business trust, or an unincorporated organization.

Person-year One whole year, or fraction thereof, worked by an employee, including contracted manpower. Expressed as a quotient (to two decimal places) of the time units worked during a year (hours, weeks, or months) divided by the like total time units in a year. For example: 80 hours worked is 0.04 (rounded) of a person-year; 8 weeks worked is 0.15 (rounded) of a person-year; 12 months worked is 1.0 person-year. Contracted manpower includes survey crews, drilling crews, consultants, and other persons who worked under contract to support a firm's ongoing operations.

Personal computer A microcomputer for producing written, programmed, or coded material; playing games; or doing calculations. Laptop and notebook computers are excluded for the purposes of EIA surveys.

Petrochemical feedstocks Chemical feedstocks derived from petroleum principally for the manufacture of chemicals, synthetic rubber, and a variety of plastics.

Petrochemicals Organic and inorganic compounds and mixtures that include but are not limited to organic chemicals, cyclic intermediates, plastics and resins, synthetic fibers, elastomers, organic dyes, organic pigments, detergents, surface active agents, carbon black, and ammonia.

Petroleum A broadly defined class of liquid hydrocarbon mixtures. Included are crude oil, lease condensate, unfinished oils, refined products obtained from the processing of crude oil, and natural gas plant liquids. *Note:* Volumes of finished petroleum products include nonhydrocarbon compounds, such as additives and detergents, after they have been blended into the products.

Petroleum Administration for Defense District (PADD) A geographic aggregation of the 50 States and the District of Columbia into five Districts, with PADD I further split into three subdistricts. The PADDs include the States listed below:

PADD I (East Coast):
- PADD IA (New England): Connecticut, Maine, Massachusetts, New Hampshire, Rhode Island, and Vermont.
- PADD IB (Central Atlantic): Delaware, District of Columbia, Maryland, New Jersey, New York, and Pennsylvania.
- PADD IC (Lower Atlantic): Florida, Georgia, North Carolina, South Carolina, Virginia, and West Virginia.

PADD II (Midwest): Illinois, Indiana, Iowa, Kansas, Kentucky, Michigan, Minnesota, Missouri, Nebraska, North Dakota, Ohio, Oklahoma, South Dakota, Tennessee, and Wisconsin.

PADD III (Gulf Coast): Alabama, Arkansas, Louisiana, Mississippi, New Mexico, and Texas.

PADD IV (Rocky Mountain): Colorado, Idaho, Montana, Utah, and Wyoming.

PADD V (West Coast): Alaska, Arizona, California, Hawaii, Nevada, Oregon, and Washington.

Petroleum coke See Coke (petroleum).

Petroleum coke, catalyst The carbonaceous residue that is deposited on and deactivates the catalyst used in many catalytic operations (e.g., catalytic cracking). Carbon is deposited on the catalyst, thus deactivating the catalyst. The catalyst is reactivated by burning off the carbon, which is used as a fuel in the refining process. That carbon or coke is not recoverable in a concentrated form.

Petroleum coke, marketable Those grades of coke produced in delayed or fluid cokers that may be recovered as relatively pure carbon. Marketable petroleum coke may be sold as is or further purified by calcining.

Petroleum consumption See Products Supplied.

Petroleum imports Imports of petroleum into the 50 states and the District of Columbia from foreign countries and from Puerto Rico, the Virgin Islands, and other U.S. territories and possessions. Included are imports for the Strategic Petroleum Reserve and withdrawals from bonded warehouses for onshore consumption, offshore bunker use, and military use. Excluded are receipts of foreign petroleum into bonded warehouses and into U.S. territories and U.S. Foreign Trade Zones.

Petroleum jelly A semi-solid oily product produced from de-waxing lubricating oil basestocks.

Petroleum products Petroleum products are obtained from the processing of crude oil (including lease condensate), natural gas, and other hydrocarbon compounds. Petroleum products include unfinished oils, liquefied petroleum gases, pentanes plus, aviation gasoline, motor gasoline, naphtha-type jet fuel, kerosene-type jet fuel, kerosene, distillate fuel oil, residual fuel oil, petrochemical feedstocks, special naphthas, lubricants, waxes, petroleum coke, asphalt, road oil, still gas, and miscellaneous products.

Petroleum refinery An installation that manufactures finished petroleum products from crude oil, unfinished oils, natural gas liquids, other hydrocarbons, and alcohol.

Petroleum stocks, primary For individual products, quantities that are held at refineries, in pipelines and at bulk terminals that have a capacity of 50,000 barrels or more, or that are in transit thereto. Stocks held by product retailers and resellers, as well as tertiary stocks held at the point of consumption, are excluded. Stocks of individual products held at gas processing plants are excluded from individual product estimates but are included in other oils estimates and total.

pH A measure of acidity or alkalinity. A pH of 7 represents neutrality. Acid substances have lower pH. Basic substances have higher pH.

Photosynthesis The manufacture by plants of carbohydrates and oxygen from carbon dioxide and water in the presence of chlorophyll, with sunlight as the energy source. Carbon is sequestered and oxygen and water vapor are released in the process.

Photovoltaic and solar thermal energy (as used at electric utilities) Energy radiated by the sun as electromagnetic waves (electromagnetic radiation) that is converted at electric utilities into electricity by means of solar (photovoltaic) cells or concentrating (focusing) collectors.

Photovoltaic cell (PVC) An electronic device consisting of layers of semiconductor materials fabricated to form a junction (adjacent layers of materials with different electronic characteristics) and electrical contacts and being capable of converting incident light directly into electricity (direct current).

Photovoltaic cell net shipments Represents the difference between photovoltaic cell shipments and photovoltaic cell purchases.

Photovoltaic module An integrated assembly of interconnected photovoltaic cells designed to deliver a selected level of working voltage and current at its output terminals, packaged for protection against environmental degradation, and suited for incorporation in photovoltaic power systems.

Pig iron Crude, high-carbon iron produced by reduction of iron ore in a blast furnace.

Pipeline, distribution A pipeline that conveys gas from a transmission pipeline to its ultimate consumer.

Pipeline freight Refers to freight carried through pipelines, including natural gas, crude oil, and petroleum products (excluding water). Energy is consumed by various electrical components of the pipeline, including, valves, other, appurtenances attaches to the pipe, compressor units, metering stations, regulator stations, delivery stations, holders and fabricated assemblies.

Pipeline fuel Gas consumed in the operation of pipelines, primarily in compressors.

Pipeline, gathering A pipeline that conveys gas from a production well/field to a gas processing plant or transmission pipeline for eventual delivery to end-use consumers.

Pipeline (natural gas) A continuous pipe conduit, complete with such equipment as valves, compressor stations, communications systems, and meters for transporting natural and/or supplemental gas from one point to another, usually from a point in or beyond the producing field or processing plant to another pipeline or to points of utilization. Also refers to a company operating such facilities.

Pipeline (petroleum) Crude oil and product pipelines used to transport crude oil and petroleum products, respectively (including interstate, intrastate, and intracompany pipelines), within the 50 states and the District of Columbia.

Pipeline purchases Gas supply contracted from and volumes purchased from other natural gas companies as defined by the Natural Gas Act, as amended (52 Stat. 821), excluding independent producers, as defined in Paragraph 154.91(a), Chapter I, Title 18 of the Code of Federal Regulations.

Pipeline quality natural gas A mixture of hydrocarbon compounds existing in the gaseous phase with sufficient energy content, generally above 900 British thermal units, and a small enough share of impurities for transport through commercial gas pipelines and sale to end-users.

Pipeline, transmission A pipeline that conveys gas from a region where it is produced to a region where it is to be distributed.

Pipelines, rate regulated FRS (Financial Reporting System Survey) establishes three pipeline segments: crude/liquid (raw materials); natural gas; and refined products. The pipelines included in these segments are all federally or State rate-regulated pipeline operations, which are included in the reporting company's consolidated financial statements. However, at the reporting company's option, intrastate pipeline operations may be included in the U.S. Refining/Marketing Segment if: they would comprise less than 5 percent of U.S. Refining/Marketing Segment net PP&E, revenues, and earnings in the aggregate; and if the inclusion of such pipelines in the consolidated financial statements adds less than $100 million to the net PP&E reported for the U.S. Refining/Marketing Segment.

Pitcheblende Uranium oxide (U_3O_8). It is the main component of high-grade African or domestic uranium ore and also contains other oxides and sulfides, including radium, thorium, and lead components.

Place in service A vehicle is placed in service if that vehicle is new to the fleet and has not previously been in service for the fleet. These vehicles can be acquired as additional vehicles (increases the size of the company fleet), or as replacement vehicles to replace vehicles that are being retired from service (does not increase the size of the company fleet).

Planetary albedo The fraction of incident solar radiation that is reflected by the Earth-atmosphere system and returned to space, mostly by backscatter from clouds in the atmosphere.

Planned generator A proposal by a company to install electric generating equipment at an existing or planned facility or site. The proposal is based on the owner having obtained either (1) all environmental and regulatory approvals, (2) a signed contract for the electric energy, or (3) financial closure for the facility.

Planning Authority (electric) The responsible entity that coordinates and integrates transmission facility and service plans, resource plans, and protection systems. (NERC definition)

Plant A term commonly used either as a synonym for an industrial establishment or a generating facility or to refer to a particular process within an establishment.

Plant condensate One of the natural gas liquids, mostly pentanes and heavier hydrocarbons, recovered and separated as liquids at gas inlet separators or scrubbers in processing plants.

Plant hours connected to load The number of hours the plant is synchronized to load over a time interval usually of 1 year.

Plant liquids Those volumes of natural gas liquids recovered in natural gas processing plants.

Plant or gas processing plant A facility designated to achieve the recovery of natural gas liquids from the stream of natural gas, which may or may not have been processed through lease separators and field facilities, and to control the quality of the natural gas to be marketed.

Plant products Natural gas liquids recovered from natural gas processing plants (and in some cases from field facilities), including ethane, propane, butane, butane-propane mixtures, natural gasoline, plant condensate, and lease condensate.

Plant use The electric energy used in the operation of a plant. Included is the energy required for pumping at pump-storage plants.

Plant-use electricity The electric energy used in the operation of a plant. This energy total is subtracted from the gross energy production of the plant.

Plugged-back footage Under certain conditions, drilling operations may be continued to a greater depth than that at which a potentially productive formation is found. If production is not established at the greater depth, the well may be completed in the shallower formation. Except in special situations, the length of the well bore from the deepest depth at which the well is completed to the maximum depth drilled is defined as "plugged-back footage." Plugged-back footage is included in total footage drilled but is not reported separately.

Plutonium (Pu) A heavy, fissionable, radioactive, metallic element (atomic number 94) that occurs naturally in trace amounts. It can also result as a byproduct of the fission reaction in a uranium-fuel nuclear reactor and can be recovered for future use.

Pneumatic device A device moved or worked by air pressure.

Pole-mile A unit of measuring the simple length of an electric transmission/distribution line/feeder carrying electric conductors, without regard to the number of conductors carried.

Pole/Tower type The type of transmission line supporting structure.

Polystyrene A polymer of styrene that is a rigid, transparent thermoplastic with good physical and electrical insulating properties, used in molded products, foams, and sheet materials.

Polyvinyl chloride (PVC) A polymer of vinyl chloride. Tasteless. odorless, insoluble in most organic solvents. A member of the family vinyl resin, used in soft flexible films for food packaging and in molded rigid products, such as pipes, fibers, upholstery, and bristles.

Pondage The amount of water stored behind a hydroelectric dam of relatively small storage capacity; the dam is usually used for daily or weekly control of the flow of the river.

Pool In general, a reservoir. In certain situations, a pool may consist of more than one reservoir.

Pool site One or more spent fuel storage pools that has a single cask loading area. Each dry cask storage area is considered a separate site.

Population-weighted degree-days Heating or cooling degree-days weighted by the population of the area in which the degree-days are recorded. To compute national population-weighted degree-days, the Nation is divided into nine Census regions comprised of from three to eight states that are assigned weights based on the ratio of the population of the region to the total population of the Nation. Degree-day readings for each region are multiplied by the corresponding population weight for each region, and these products are then summed to arrive at the national population weighted degree-day figure.

Pore space The open spaces or voides of a rock taken collectively. It is a measure of the amount of liquid or gas that may be absorbed or yielded by a particular formation.

Portable electric heater A heater that uses electricity and that can be picked up and moved.

Portable fan Box fans, oscillating fans, table or floor fans, or other fans that can be moved.

Portable kerosene heater A heater that uses kerosene and that can be picked up and moved.

Post-mining emissions Emissions of methane from coal occurring after the coal has been mined, during transport or pulverization.

Potential consumption The total amount of consumption that would have occurred had the intensity of consumption remained the same over a period of time.

Potential peak reduction The potential annual peak load reduction (measured in kilowatts) that can be deployed from Direct Load Control, Interruptible Load, Other Load Management, and Other DSM Program activities. (Please note that Energy Efficiency and Load Building are not included in Potential Peak Reduction.) It represents the load that can be reduced either by the direct control of the utility system operator or by the consumer in response to a utility request to curtail load. It reflects the installed load reduction capability, as opposed to the Actual Peak Reduction achieved by participants, during the time of annual system peak load.

Pounds (district heat) A weight quantity of steam, also used to denote a quantity of energy in the form of steam. The amount of usable energy obtained from a pound of steam depends on its temperature and pressure at the point of consumption and on the drop in pressure after consumption.

Power The rate of producing, transferring, or using energy, most commonly associated with electricity. Power is measured in watts and often expressed in kilowatts (kW) or megawatts (mW). Also known as "real" or "active" power. See Active Power, Apparent Power, Reactive Power, Real Power

Power (electrical) An electric measurement unit of power called a voltampere is equal to the product of 1 volt and 1 ampere. This is equivalent to 1 watt for a direct current system, and a unit of apparent power is separated into real and reactive power. Real power is the work-producing part of apparent power that measures the rate of supply of energy and is denoted as kilowatts (kW). Reactive power is the portion of apparent power that does no work and is referred to as kilovars; this type of power must be supplied to most types of magnetic equipment, such as motors, and is supplied by generator or by electrostatic equipment. Voltamperes are usually divided by 1,000 and called kilovoltamperes (kVA). Energy is denoted by the product of real power and the length of time utilized; this product is expressed as kilowathours.

Power ascension The period of time between a plant's initial fuel loading date and its date of first commercial operation (including the low-power testing period). Plants in the first operating cycle (the time from initial fuel loading to the first refueling), which lasts approximately 2 years, operate at an average capacity factor of about 40 percent.

Power exchange An entity providing a competitive spot market for electric power through day- and/or hour-ahead auction of generation and demand bids.

Power exchange generation Generation scheduled by the power exchange. See definition for power exchange above.

Power exchange load Load that has been scheduled by the power exchange and is received through the use of transmission or distribution facilities owned by participating transmission owners.

Power factor The ratio of real power (kilowatt) to apparent power kilovolt-ampere for any given load and time.

Power loss The difference between electricity input and output as a result of an energy transfer between two points.

Power marketers Business entities engaged in buying and selling electricity. Power marketers do not usually own generating or transmission facilities. Power marketers, as opposed to brokers, take ownership of the electricity and are involved in interstate trade. These entities file with the Federal Energy Regulatory Commission (FERC) for status as a power marketer.

Power pool An association of two or more interconnected electric systems having an agreement to coordinate operations and planning for improved reliability and efficiencies.

Power production plant All the land and land rights, structures and improvements, boiler or reactor vessel equipment, engines and engine-driven generator, turbogenerator units, accessory electric equipment, and miscellaneous power plant equipment are grouped together for each individual facility.

Power transfer limit The maximum power that can be transferred from one electric utility system to another without overloading any facility in either system.

Powerhouse A structure at a hydroelectric plant site that contains the turbine and generator.

PP&E, additions to The current year's expenditures on property, plant, and equipment (PP&E). The amount is predicated upon each reporting company's accounting practice. That is, accounting practices with regard to capitalization of certain items may differ across companies, and therefore this figure in FRS (Financial Reporting System) will be a function of each reporting company's policy.

Prediscovery costs All costs incurred in an extractive industry operation prior to the actual discovery of minerals in commercially recoverable quantities; normally includes prospecting, acquisition, and exploration costs and may include some development costs.

Pregnant solution A solution containing dissolved extractable mineral that was leached from the ore; uranium leach solution pumped up from the underground ore zone though a production hole.

Preliminary permit (hydroelectric power) A single site permit granted by the FERC (Federal Energy Regulatory Commission), which gives the recipient priority over anyone else to apply for a hydroelectric license. The preliminary permit enables the recipient to prepare a license application and conduct various studies for economic feasibility and environmental impacts. The period for a preliminary permit may extend to 3 years.

Premium gasoline Gasoline having an antiknock index (R+M/2) greater than 90. Includes both leaded premium gasoline as well as unleaded premium gasoline.

Preparation plant A mining facility at which coal is crushed, screened, and mechanically cleaned.

Preproduction costs Costs of prospecting for, acquiring, exploring, and developing mineral reserves incurred prior to the point when production of commercially recoverable quantities of minerals commences.

Pressurized-water reactor (PWR) A nuclear reactor in which heat is transferred from the core to a heat exchanger via water kept under high pressure, so that high temperatures can be maintained in the primary system without boiling the water. Steam is generated in a secondary circuit.

Preventive maintenance program for heating and/or cooling equipment A HVAC conservation feature consisting of a program of routine inspection and service for the heating and/or cooling equipment. The inspection is performed on a regular basis, even if there are no apparent problems.

Price The amount of money or consideration-in-kind for which a service is bought, sold, or offered for sale.

Primary coal All coal milled and, when necessary, washed and sorted.

Primary energy Energy in the form that it is first accounted for in a statistical energy balance, before any transformation to secondary or tertiary forms of energy. For example, coal can be converted to synthetic gas, which can be converted to electricity; in this example, coal is primary energy, synthetic gas is secondary energy, and electricity is tertiary energy. See Primary energy production and Primary energy consumption.

Primary energy consumption Consumption of primary energy. (Energy sources that are produced from other energy sources—e.g., coal coke from coal—are included in primary energy consumption only if their energy content has not already been included as part of the original energy source. Thus, U.S. primary energy consumption does include net imports of coal coke, but not the coal coke produced from domestic coal.) The Energy Information Administration includes the following in U.S. primary energy consumption: coal consumption; coal coke net imports; petroleum consumption (petroleum products supplied, including natural gas plant liquids and crude oil burned as fuel); dry natural gas—excluding supplemental gaseous fuels—consumption; nuclear electricity net generation (converted to Btu using the nuclear plants heat rate); conventional hydroelectricity net generation (converted to Btu using the fossil-fueled plants heat rate); geothermal electricity net generation (converted to Btu using the geothermal plants heat rate), and geothermal heat pump energy and geothermal direct use energy; solar thermal and photovoltaic electricity net generation (converted to Btu using the fossil-fueled plants heat rate), and solar thermal direct use energy; wind electricity net generation (converted to Btu using the fossil-fueled plants heat rate); wood and wood-derived fuels consumption; biomass waste consumption; fuel ethanol and biodiesel consumption; losses and co-products from the production of fuel ethanol and biodiesel; and electricity net imports (converted to Btu using the electricity heat content of 3,412 Btu per kilowatthour).

Primary energy consumption expenditures Expenditures for energy consumed in each of the four major end-use sectors, excluding energy in the form of electricity, plus expenditures by the electric utilities sector for energy used to generate electricity. There are no fuel-associated expenditures for associated expenditures for hydroelectric power, geothermal energy, photovoltaic and solar energy, or wind energy. Also excluded are the quantifiable consumption expenditures that are an integral part of process fuel consumption.

Primary energy production Production of primary energy. The Energy Information Administration includes the following in U.S. primary energy production: coal production, waste coal supplied, and coal refuse recovery; crude oil and lease condensate production; natural gas plant liquids production; dry natural gas—excluding supplemental gaseous fuels—production; nuclear electricity net generation (converted to Btu using the nuclear plants heat rate); conventional hydroelectricity net generation (converted to Btu using the fossil-fueled plants heat rate); geothermal electricity net generation (converted to Btu using the geothermal plants heat rate), and geothermal heat pump energy and geothermal direct use energy; solar thermal and photovoltaic electricity net generation (converted to Btu using the fossil-fueled plants heat rate), and solar thermal direct use energy; wind electricity net generation (converted to Btu using the fossil-fueled plants heat rate); wood and wood-derived fuels consumption; biomass waste consumption; and biofuels feedstock.

Primary fuels Fuels that can be used continuously. They can sustain the boiler sufficiently for the production of electricity.

Primary metropolitan statistical area (PMSA) A component area of a Consolidated metropolitan statistical area consisting of a large urbanized county or cluster of counties (cities and towns in New England) that demonstrate strong internal economic and social links in addition to close ties with the central core of the larger area. To qualify, an area must meet specified statistical criteria that demonstrate these links and have the support of local opinion.

Primary recovery The crude oil or natural gas recovered by any method that may be employed to produce them where the fluid enters the well bore by the action of natural reservoir pressure (energy or gravity).

Primary transportation Conveyance of large shipments of petroleum raw materials and refined products usually by pipeline, barge, or ocean-going vessel. All crude oil transportation is primary, including the small amounts moved by truck. All refined product transportation by pipeline, barge, or ocean-going vessel is primary transportation.

Prime mover   The engine, turbine, water wheel, or similar machine that drives an electric generator; or, for reporting purposes, a device that converts energy to electricity directly (e.g., photovoltaic solar and fuel cells).

Prime supplier   A firm that produces, imports, or transports selected petroleum products across State boundaries and local marketing areas, and sells the product to local distributors, local retailers, or end users.

Private fueling facility   A fueling facility which normally services only fleets and is not open to the general public.

Privately owned electric utility   A class of ownership found in the electric power industry where the utility is regulated and authorized to achieve an allowed rate of return.

Probable energy reserves   Estimated quantities of energy sources that, on the basis of geologic evidence that supports projections from *proved reserves* (see definition below), can reasonably be expected to exist and be recoverable under existing economic and operating conditions. Site information is insufficient to establish with confidence the location, quality, and grades of the energy source. Note: This term is equivalent to "Indicated Reserves" as defined in the resource/reserve classification contained in the U.S. Geological Survey Circular 831, 1980. Measured and indicated reserves, when combined, constitute demonstrated reserves.

Probable (indicated) reserves, coal   Reserves or resources for which tonnage and grade are computed partly from specific measurements, samples, or production data and partly from projection for a reasonable distance on the basis of geological evidence. The sites available are too widely or otherwise inappropriately spaced to permit the mineral bodies to be outlined completely or the grade established throughout.

Process cooling and refrigeration   The direct process end use in which energy is used to lower the temperature of substances involved in the manufacturing process. Examples include freezing processed meats for later sale in the food industry and lowering the temperature of chemical feedstocks below ambient temperature for use in reactions in the chemical industries. Not included are uses such as air-conditioning for personal comfort and cafeteria refrigeration.

Process fuel   All energy consumed in the acquisition, processing, and transportation of energy. Quantifiable process fuel includes three categories: natural gas lease and plant operations, natural gas pipeline operations, and oil refinery operations.

Process heating or cooling demand-side management (DSM) program   A DSM program designed to promote increased electric energy efficiency applications in industrial process heating or cooling.

Process heating or cooling waste heat recovery   An energy conservation system whereby some space heating or water heating is done by actively capturing byproduct heat that would otherwise be ejected into the environment. In nonresidential buildings, sources of waste heat include refrigeration/air-conditioner compressors, manufacturing or other processes, data processing centers, lighting fixtures, ventilation exhaust air, and the occupants themselves. Not to be considered is the passive use of radiant heat from lighting, workers, motors, ovens, etc., when there are no special systems for collecting and redistributing heat.

Processed gas   Natural gas that has gone through a processing plant.

Processing   Uranium-recovery operations whether at a mill, an in situ leach, byproduct plant, or other ype of recovery operation.

Processing gain   The volumetric amount by which total output is greater than input for a given period of time. This difference is due to the processing of crude oil into products which, in total, have a lower specific gravity than the crude oil processed.

Processing loss   The volumetric amount by which total refinery output is less than input for a given period of time. This difference is due to the processing of crude oil into products which, in total, have a higher specific gravity than the crude oil processed.

Processing of uranium   The recovery of uranium produced by nonconventional mining methods, i.e., in situ leach mining, as a byproduct of copper or phosphate mining, or heap leaching.

Processing plant   A surface installation designed to separate and recover natural gas liquids from a stream of produced natural gas through the processes of condensation, absorption, adsorption, refrigeration, or other methods and to control the quality of natural gas marketed and/or returned to oil or gas reservoirs for pressure maintenance, repressuring, or cycling.

Producer   A company engaged in the production and sale of natural gas from gas or oil wells with delivery generally at a point at or near the wellhead, the field, or the tailgate of a gas processing plant. For the purpose of company classification, a company primarily engaged in the exploration for, development of, and/or production of oil and/or natural gas.

Producer and distributor coal stocks   Producer and distributor coal stocks consist of coal held in stock by producers/distributors at the end of a reporting period.

Producer contracted reserves The volume of recoverable salable gas reserves committed to or controlled by the reporting pipeline company as the buyer in gas purchase contracts with the independent producer as seller, including warranty contracts, and which are used for acts and services for which the company has received certificate authorization from the Federal Energy Regulatory Commission.

Producing property A term often used in reference to a property, well, or mine that produces wasting natural resources. The term means a property that produces in paying quantities (that is, one for which proceeds from production exceed operating expenses).

Production See production terms associated with specific energy types.

Production capacity The amount of product that can be produced from processing facilities.

Production costs Costs incurred to operate and maintain wells and related equipment and facilities, including depreciation and applicable operating costs of support equipment and facilities and other costs of operating and maintaining those wells and related equipment and facilities. They become part of the cost of oil and gas produced. The following are examples of production costs (sometimes called lifting costs): costs of labor to operate the wells and related equipment and facilities; repair and maintenance costs; the costs of materials, supplies, and fuels consumed and services utilized in operating the wells and related equipment and facilities; the costs of property taxes and insurance applicable to proved properties and wells and related equipment and facilities; the costs of severance taxes. Depreciation, depletion, and amortization (DD&A) of capitalized acquisition, exploration, and development costs are not production costs, but also become part of the cost of oil and gas produced along with production (lifting) costs identified above. Production costs include the following subcategories of costs: well workers and maintenance; operating fluid injections and improved recovery programs; operating gas processing plants; ad valorem taxes; production or severance taxes; other, including overhead.

Production, crude oil The volumes of crude oil that are extracted from oil reservoirs. These volumes are determined through measurement of the volumes delivered from lease storage tanks or at the point of custody transfer, with adjustment for (1) net differences between opening and closing lease inventories and (2) basic sediment and water. Crude oil used on the lease is considered production.

Production expenses Costs incurred in the production of electric power that conform to the accounting requirements of the Operation and Maintenance Expense Accounts of the FERC Uniform System of Accounts.

Production, lease condensate The volume of lease condensate produced. Lease condensate volumes include only those volumes recovered from lease or field separation facilities.

Production, natural gas The volume of natural gas withdrawn from reservoirs less (1) the volume returned to such reservoirs in cycling, repressuring of oil reservoirs, and conservation operations; less (2) shrinkage resulting from the removal of lease condensate; and less (3) nonhydrocarbon gases where they occur in sufficient quantity to render the gas unmarketable. Volumes of gas withdrawn from gas storage reservoirs and native gas, which has been transferred to the storage category, are not considered production. Flared and vented gas is also considered production. (This differs from "Marketed Production" which excludes flared and vented gas.)

Production, natural gas, dry The volume of natural gas withdrawn from reservoirs during the report year less (1) the volume returned to such reservoirs in cycling, repressuring of oil reservoirs, and conservation operations; less (2) shrinkage resulting from the removal of lease condensate and plant liquids; and less (3) nonhydrocarbon gases where they occur in sufficient quantity to render the gas unmarketable. Volumes of gas withdrawn from gas storage reservoirs and native gas, which has been transferred to the storage category, are not considered production. This is not the same as marketed production, because the latter also excludes vented and flared gas, but contains plant liquids.

Production, natural gas liquids Production of natural gas liquids is classified as follows:
- ***Contract Production*** Natural gas liquids accruing to a company because of its ownership of liquids extraction facilities that it uses to extract liquids from gas belonging to others, thereby earning a portion of the resultant liquids.
- ***Leasehold Production*** Natural gas liquids produced, extracted, and credited to a company's interest.
- ***Contract Reserves*** Natural gas liquid reserves corresponding to the contract production defined above.
- ***Leasehold Reserves*** Natural gas liquid reserves corresponding to leasehold production defined above.

Production, natural gas, wet after lease separation The volume of natural gas withdrawn from reservoirs less (1) the volume returned to such reservoirs in cycling, repressuring of oil reservoirs, and conservation operations; less (2) shrinkage resulting from the removal of lease condensate; and less (3) nonhydrocarbon gases where they occur in sufficient quantity to render the gas unmarketable. *Note:* Volumes of gas withdrawn from gas storage reservoirs and native gas that has been transferred to the storage category are not considered part of production. This production concept is not the same as marketed production, which excludes vented and flared gas.

Production, oil and gas The lifting of oil and gas to the surface and gathering, treating, field processing (as in the case of processing gas to extract liquid hydrocarbons), and field storage. The production function shall normally be regarded as terminating at the outlet valve on the lease or field production storage tank. If unusual physical or operational circumstances exist, it may be more appropriate to regard the production function as terminating at the first point at which oil, gas, or gas liquids are delivered to a main pipeline, a common carrier, a refinery, or a marine terminal.

Production payments A contractual arrangement providing a mineral interest that gives the owner a right to receive a fraction of production, or of proceeds from the sale of production, until a specified quantity of minerals (or a definite sum of money, including interest) has been received.

Production plant liquids The volume of liquids removed from natural gas in natural gas processing plants or cycling plants during the year.

Production, wet after lease separation See production, natural gas, wet after lease separation (above).

Productive capacity The maximum amount of coal that a mining operation can produce or process during a period with the existing mining equipment and/or preparation plant in place, assuming that the labor and materials sufficient to utilize the plant and equipment are available, and that the market exists for the maximum production.

Products supplied Approximately represents consumption of petroleum products because it measures the disappearance of these products from primary sources, i.e., refineries, natural gas-processing plants, blending plants, pipelines, and bulk terminals. In general, product supplied of each product in any given period is computed as follows: field production, plus refinery production, plus imports, plus unaccounted-for crude oil (plus net receipts when calculated on a PAD District basis) minus stock change, minus crude oil losses, minus refinery inputs, and minus exports.

Profit The income remaining after all business expenses are paid.

Program cost Utility costs that reflect the total cash expenditures for the year, reported in nominal dollars, that flowed out to support DSM (demand-side management) programs. They are reported in the year they are incurred, regardless of when the actual effects occur.

Propane (C_3H_8) A normally gaseous straight-chain hydrocarbon. It is a colorless paraffinic gas that boils at a temperature of -43.67 degrees Fahrenheit. It is extracted from natural gas or refinery gas streams. It includes all products designated in ASTM Specification D1835 and Gas Processors Association Specifications for commercial propane and HD-5 propane.

Propane air A mixture of propane and air resulting in a gaseous fuel suitable for pipeline distribution.

Propane, consumer grade A normally gaseous paraffinic compound (C_3H_8), which includes all products covered by Natural Gas Policy Act Specifications for commercial and HD-5 propane and ASTM Specification D 1835. Excludes: feedstock propanes, which are propanes not classified as consumer grade propanes, including the propane portion of any natural gas liquid mixes, i.e., butane-propane mix.

Proportional interest in investee reserves The proportional interest at the end of the year in the reserves of investees that are accounted for by the equity method.

Proposed rates New electric rate schedule proposed by an applicant to become effective at a future date.

Propylene (C_3H_6) (nonfuel use) Propylene intended for use in nonfuel applications such as petrochemical manufacturing. Nonfuel propylene includes chemical-grade propylene, polymer-grade propylene, and trace amounts of propane. Nonfuel propylene also includes the propylene component of propane/propylene mixes where the propylene will be separated from the mix in a propane/propylene splitting process. Nonfuel propylene excludes the propylene component of propane/propylene mixes where the propylene component of the mix is intended for use as fuel.

Prospecting The search for an area of probable mineralization; the search normally includes topographical, geological, and geophysical studies of relatively large areas undertaken in an attempt to locate specific areas warranting detailed exploration. Prospecting usually occurs prior to the acquisition of mineral rights.

Prospecting costs Direct and indirect costs incurred to identify areas of interest that may warrant detailed exploration. Such costs include those incurred for topographical, geological, and geophysical studies; rights of access to properties in order to conduct such studies, salaries, equipment, instruments, and supplies for geologists, including geophysical crews, and others conducting such studies; and overhead that can be identified with those activities.

Proved energy reserves Estimated quantities of energy sources that analysis of geologic and engineering data demonstrates with reasonable certainty are recoverable under existing economic and operating conditions. The location, quantity, and grade of the energy source are usually considered to be well established in such reserves. *Note:* This term is equivalent to "Measured

Reserves" as defined in the resource/reserve classification contained in the U.S. Geological Survey Circular 831, 1980. Measured and indicated reserves, when combined, constitute demonstrated reserves.

Proved (measured) reserves, coal Reserves or resources for which tonnage is computed from dimensions revealed in outcrops, trenches, workings, and drill holes and for which the grade is computed from the results of detailed sampling. The sites for inspection, sampling, and measurement are spaced so closely and the geologic character is so well defined that size, shape, and mineral content are well established. The computed tonnage and grade are judged to be accurate within limits that are stated, and no such limit is judged to be different from the computed tonnage or grade by more than 20 percent.

Public authorities Electricity supplied to municipalities, divisions, or agencies of state and Federal governments, usually under special contracts or agreements that are applicable only to public authorities.

Public authority service to public authorities Public authority service includes electricity supplied and services rendered to municipalities or divisions or agencies of State or Federal governments under special contracts, agreements, or service classifications applicable only to public authorities.

Public street and highway lighting Electricity supplied and services rendered for the purpose of lighting streets, highways, parks, and other public places; or for traffic or other signal system service, for municipalities or other divisions or agencies of State or Federal governments.

Public utility Enterprise providing essential public services, such as electric, gas, telephone, water, and sewer under legally established monopoly conditions.

Public utility district Municipal corporations organized to provide electric service to both incorporated cities and towns and unincorporated rural areas.

Public Utility Holding Company Act of 1935 (PUHCA) This act prohibits acquisition of any wholesale or retail electric business through a holding company unless that business forms part of an integrated public utility system when combined with the utility's other electric business. The legislation also restricts ownership of an electric business by non-utility corporations.

Public Utility Regulatory Policies Act (PURPA) of 1978 One part of the National Energy Act, PURPA contains measures designed to encourage the conservation of energy, more efficient use of resources, and equitable rates. Principal among these were suggested retail rate reforms and new incentives for production of electricity by cogenerators and users of renewable resources. The Commission has primary authority for implementing several key PURPA programs.

Publicly owned electric utility A class of ownership found in the electric power industry. This group includes those utilities operated by municipalities and State and Federal power agencies.

Pulp chips Timber or residues processed into small pieces of wood of more or less uniform dimensions with minimal amounts of bark.

Pulp wood Roundwood, whole-tree chips, or wood residues.

Pulping liquor (black liquor) The alkaline spent liquor removed from the digesters in the process of chemically pulping wood. After evaporation, the liquor is burned as a fuel in a recovery furnace that permits the recovery of certain basic chemicals.

Pumped-storage hydroelectric plant A plant that usually generates electric energy during peak load periods by using water previously pumped into an elevated storage reservoir during off-peak periods when excess generating capacity is available to do so. When additional generating capacity is needed, the water can be released from the reservoir through a conduit to turbine generators located in a power plant at a lower level.

Purchase-contract imports of uranium The amount of foreign-origin uranium material that enters the United States during a survey year as reported on the "Uranium Industry Annual Survey (UIAS)," Form EIA-858, as purchases of uranium ore, U3O8, natural UF6, or enriched UF6. The amount of foreign-origin uranium materials that enter the country during a survey year under other types of contracts, i.e., loans and exchanges, is excluded.

Purchased Receipts into transportation, storage, and/or distribution facilities within a state under gas purchase contracts or agreements whether or not billing or payment occurred during the report year.

Purchased power Power purchased or available for purchase from a source outside the system.

Purchased power adjustment A clause in a rate schedule that provides for adjustments to the bill when energy from another electric system is acquired and its cost varies from a specified unit base amount.

Pure pumped-storage hydroelectric plant A plant that produces power only from water that has previously been pumped to an upper reservoir.

PURPA The Public Utility Regulatory Policies Act of 1978, passed by the U.S. Congress. This statute requires States to implement utility conservation programs and create special markets for co-generators and small producers who meet certain standards, including the requirement that States set the prices and quantities of power the utilities must buy from such facilities.

PVCs that convert sunlight directly into energy A method for producing energy by converting sunlight using photovoltaic cells (PVCs) that are solid-state single converter devices. Although currently not in wide usage, commercial customers have a growing interest in usage and, therefore, DOE has a growing interest in the impact of PVCs on energy consumption. Economically, PVCs are competitive with other sources of electricity.

Pyrolysis The thermal decomposition of biomass at high temperatures (greater than 400° F, or 200° C) in the absence of air. The end product of pyrolysis is a mixture of solids (char), liquids (oxygenated oils), and gases (methane, carbon monoxide, and carbon dioxide) with proportions determined by operating temperature, pressure, oxygen content, and other conditions.

Quadrillion The quantity 1,000,000,000,000,000 (10 to the 15th power).

Qualifying facility (QF) A cogeneration or small power production facility that meets certain ownership, operating, and efficiency criteria established by the Federal Energy Regulatory Commission (FERC) pursuant to the Public Utility Regulatory Policies Act (PURPA).

Quality or grade (of coal) An informal classification of coal relating to its suitability for use for a particular purpose. Refers to individual measurements such as heat value, fixed carbon, moisture, ash, sulfur, major, minor, and trace elements, coking properties, petrologic properties, and particular organic constituents. The individual quality elements may be aggregated in various ways to classify coal for such special purposes as metallurgical, gas, petrochemical, and blending usages.

Quantity wires charge A fee for moving electricity over the transmission and/or distribution system that is based on the quantity of electricity that is transmitted.

R-value A measure of a material's resistance to heat flow in units of Fahrenheit degrees x hours x square feet per Btu. The higher the R-value of a material, the greater its insulating capability. The R-value of some insulating materials is 3.7 per inch for fiberglass and cellulose, 2.5 per inch for vermiculite, and more than 4 per inch for foam. All building materials have some R-value. For example, a 4-inch brick has an R-value of 0.8, and half-inch plywood has an R-value of 0.6. The below table converts the most common "R" values to inches. For other "R" values, divide the "R" value by 3 to get the number of inches.

Rack sales Wholesale truckload sales or smaller of gasoline where title transfers at a terminal.

Radiant barrier A thin, reflective foil sheet that exhibits low radiant energy transmission and under certain conditions can block radiant heat transfer; installed in attics to reduce heat flow through a roof assembly into the living space.

"R"-Value	Inches
3	1
11	3.5
19	6
52	18

Radiant ceiling panels Ceiling panels that contain electric resistance heating elements embedded within them to provide radiant heat to a room.

Radiant energy Energy that transmits away from its source in all directions.

Radiation The transfer of heat through matter or space by means of electromagnetic waves.

Radiative forcing A change in average net radiation at the top of the troposphere (known as the tropopause) because of a change in either incoming solar or exiting infrared radiation. A positive radiative forcing tends on average to warm the earth's surface; a negative radiative forcing on average tends to cool the earth's surface. Greenhouse gases, when emitted into the atmosphere, trap infrared energy radiated from the earth's surface and therefore tend to produce positive radiative forcing. Also see Greenhouse gases.

Radiatively active gases Gases that absorb incoming solar radiation or outgoing infrared radiation, affecting the vertical temperature profile of the atmosphere. Also see *Radiative forcing* above.

Radiator A heating unit usually exposed to view within the room or space to be heated; it transfers heat by radiation to objects within visible range and by conduction to the surrounding air, which in turn is circulated by natural convection; usually fed by steam or hot water.

Radioactive waste Materials left over from making nuclear energy. Radioactive waste can destroy living organisms if it is not stored safely.

Radioactivity The spontaneous emission of radiation from the nucleus of an atom. Radionuclides lose particles and energy through this process.

Radioisotope A radioactive isotope.

Radon A naturally occurring radioactive gas found in the United States in nearly all types of soil, rock, and water. It can migrate into most buildings. Studies have linked high concentrations of radon to lung cancer.

Rail (method of transportation to consumers) Shipments of coal moved to consumers by rail (private or public/commercial). Includes coal hauled to or away from a railroad siding by truck.

Railroad and railway electric service Electricity supplied to railroads and interurban and street railways, for general railroad use, including the propulsion of cars or locomotives, where such electricity is supplied under separate and distinct rate schedules.

Railroad locomotive Self-propelled vehicle that runs on rails and is used for moving railroad cars.

Railroad use Sales to railroads for any use, including that used for heating buildings operated by railroads.

Range top The range burners or stove top and the oven are considered two separate appliances. Counted also with range tops are stand-alone "cook tops."

Rankine cycle The thermodynamic cycle that is an ideal standard for comparing performance of heat-engines, steam power plants, steam turbines, and heat pump systems that use a condensable vapor as the working fluid. Efficiency is measured as work done divided by sensible heat supplied.

Rankine cycle engine The Rankine cycle system uses a liquid that evaporates when heated and expands to produce work, such as turning a turbine, which when connected to a generator, produces electricity. The exhaust vapor expelled from the turbine condenses and the liquid is pumped back to the boiler to repeat the cycle. The working fluid most commonly used is water, though other liquids can also be used. Rankine cycle design is used by most commercial electric power plants. The traditional steam locomotive is also a common form of the Rankine cycle engine. The Rankine engine itself can be either a piston engine or a turbine.

Rate base (electric) The value of property, upon which, a utility is permitted to earn a specified rate of return as established by a regulatory authority. (FERC definition)

Rate case A proceeding, usually before a regulatory commission, involving the rates to be charged for a public utility service.

Rate features Special rate schedules or tariffs offered to customers by electric and/or natural gas utilities.

Rate of return The ratio of net operating income earned by a utility is calculated as a percentage of its rate base.

Rate of return on rate base The ratio of net operating income earned by a utility, calculated as a percentage of its rate base.

Rate schedule (electric) The rates, charges, and provisions under which service is supplied to the designated class of customers. (FERC definition)

Ratemaking authority A utility commission's legal authority to fix, modify, approve, or disapprove rates as determined by the powers given the commission by a State or Federal legislature.

Rates The authorized charges per unit or level of consumption for a specified time period for any of the classes of utility services provided to a customer.

Rating A manufacturer's guaranteed performance of a machine, transmission line, or other electrical apparatus, based on design features and test data. The rating will specify such limits as load, voltage, temperature, and frequency. The rating is generally printed on a nameplate attached to equipment and is commonly referred to as the nameplate rating or nameplate capacity.

Ratio estimate The ratio of two population aggregates (totals). For example, "average miles traveled per vehicle" is the ratio of total miles driven by all vehicles, over the total number of vehicles, within any subgroup. There are two types of ratio estimates: those computed using aggregates for vehicles and those computed using aggregates for households.

Ratoon crop A crop cultivated from the shoots of a perennial plant.

Rayleigh frequency distribution A mathematical representation of the frequency or ratio that specific wind speeds occur within a specified time interval.

Reactance A phenomenon associated with AC power characterized by the existence of a time difference between voltage and current variations.

Reactive power The portion of electricity that establishes and sustains the electric and magnetic fields of alternating-current equipment. Reactive power must be supplied to most types of magnetic equipment, such as motors and transformers. Reactive power is provided by generators, synchronous condensers, or electrostatic equipment such as capacitors and directly influences electric system voltage. It is a derived value equal to the vector difference between the apparent power and the real power. It is usually expressed as kilovolt-amperes reactive (kVAR) or megavolt-ampere reactive (MVAR). See Apparent Power, Power, Real Power

Real dollars These are dollars that have been adjusted for inflation.

Real Power The component of electric power that performs work, typically measured in kilowatts (kW) or megawatts (MW)—sometimes referred to as Active Power. The terms "real" or "active" are often used to modify the base term "power" to differentiate it from Reactive Power and Apparent Power. See Apparent Power, Power, Reactive Power

Real price A price that has been adjusted to remove the effect of changes in the purchasing power of the dollar. Real prices, which are expressed in constant dollars, usually reflect buying power relative to a base year.

Reasonably assured resources (RAR) The uranium that occurs in known mineral deposits of such size, grade, and configuration that it could be recovered within the given production cost ranges, with currently proven mining and processing technology.

Estimates of tonnage and grade are based on specific sample data and measurements of the deposits and on knowledge of deposit characteristics. RAR correspond to DOE's Reserves category.

Rebate program A utility company-sponsored conservation program whereby the utility company returns a portion of the purchase price cost when a more energy-efficient refrigerator, water heater, air conditioner, or other appliance is purchased.

Reburn An advanced co-firing technique using natural gas to reduce pollution from electric power plants.

Receipts
- Deliveries of fuel to an electric plant
- Purchases of fuel
- All revenues received by an exporter for the reported quantity exported
- Also see Received (below)

Receivables from municipality All charges by the utility department against the municipality or its other departments that are subject to current settlement.

Received Gas (and other fuels) physically transferred into the responding company's transportation, storage, and/or distribution facilities.

Reclamation Process of restoring surface environment to acceptable pre-existing conditions. Includes surface contouring, equipment removal, well plugging, revegetation, etc.

Reclamation expenses In the context of the coal operation statement of income, refers to all payments made by the company attributable to reclamation, including taxes.

Recoverability In reference to accessible coal resources, the condition of being physically, technologically, and economically minable. Recovery rates and recovery factors may be determined or estimated for coal resources without certain knowledge of their economic minability; therefore, the availability of recovery rates or factors does not predict recoverability.

Recoverable coal Coal that is, or can be, extracted from a coal bed during mining.

Recoverable proved reserves The proved reserves of natural gas as of December 31 of any given year are the estimated quantities of natural gas which geological and engineering data demonstrates with reasonable certainty to be recoverable in the future from known natural oil and gas reservoirs under existing economic and operating conditions.

Recoverable reserves The amount of coal that can be recovered (mined) from the coal deposits at active producing mines as of the end of the year.

Recoverable reserves, estimated recoverable reserves (coal) Reserve estimates (broad meaning) based on a demonstrated reserve base adjusted for assumed accessibility factors and recovery factors. The term is used by EIA to distinguish estimated recoverable reserves, which are derived without specific economic feasibility criteria by factoring (downward) from a demonstrated reserve base for one or more study areas or regions, from recoverable reserves at active mines, which are aggregated (upward) from reserve estimates reported by currently active, economically viable mines on Form EIA-7A.

Recovery factor (coal) The percentage of total tons of coal estimated to be recoverable from a given area in relation to the total tonnage estimated to be in the demonstrated reserve base. The estimated recovery factors for the demonstrated reserve base generally are 50 percent for underground mining methods and 80 percent for surface mining methods. More precise recovery factors can be computed by determining the total coal in place and the total recoverable in any specific locale.

Recovery percentage (coal) The percentage of coal that can be recovered from the coal deposits at existing mines.

RECS See Residential Energy Consumption Survey below.

Rectifier A device for converting alternating current to direct current.

Recycled feeds Feeds that are continuously fed back for additional processing.

Recycling The process of converting materials that are no longer useful as designed or intended into a new product.

Redox potential A measurement of the state of oxidation of a system.

Redrill footage Occasionally, a hole is lost or junked and a second hole may be drilled from the surface in close proximity to the first. Footage drilled for the second hole is defined as "redrill footage." Under these circumstances, the first hole is reported as a dry hole (explanatory or developmental) and the total footage is reported as dry hole footage. The second hole is reported as an oil well, gas well, or dry hole according to the result. The redrill footage is included in the appropriate classification of total footage, but is not reported as a separate classification.

Reduced use-off hours A conservation feature consisting of manually or automatically reducing the amount of heating or cooling produced during the hours a building is not in full use.

Reference month The calendar month and year to which the reported cost, price, and volume information relates.

Reference year The calendar year to which the reported sales volume information relates.

Refined petroleum products Refined petroleum products include but are not limited to gasolines, kerosene, distillates (including No. 2 fuel oil), liquefied petroleum gas, asphalt, lubricating oils, diesel fuels, and residual fuels.

Refiner A firm or the part of a firm that refines products or blends and substantially changes products, or refines liquid hydrocarbons from oil and gas field gases, or recovers liquefied petroleum gases incident to petroleum refining and sells those products to resellers, retailers, reseller/retailers or ultimate consumers. "Refiner" includes any owner of products that contracts to have those products refined and then sells the refined products to resellers, retailers, or ultimate consumers.

Refiner acquisition cost of crude oil The cost of crude oil, including transportation and other fees paid by the refiner. The composite cost is the weighted average of domestic and imported crude oil costs. *Note:* The refiner acquisition cost does not include the cost of crude oil purchased for the Strategic Petroleum Reserve (SPR).

Refinery An installation that manufactures finished petroleum products from crude oil, unfinished oils, natural gas liquids, other hydrocarbons, and oxygenates.

Refinery and blender net inputs Raw materials, unfinished oils, and blending components processed at refineries, or blended at refineries or petroleum storage terminals to produce finished petroleum products. Included are gross inputs of crude oil, natural gas plant liquids, other hydrocarbon raw materials, hydrogen, oxygenates (excluding fuel ethanol), and renewable fuels (including fuel ethanol). Also included are net inputs of unfinished oils, motor gasoline blending components, and aviation gasoline blending components. Net inputs are calculated as gross inputs minus gross production. Negative net inputs indicate gross inputs are less than gross production. Examples of negative net inputs include reformulated gasoline blendstock for oxygenate blending (RBOB) produced at refineries for shipment to blending terminals, and unfinished oils produced and added to inventory in advance of scheduled maintenance of a refinery crude oil distillation unit.

Refinery and blender net production Liquefied refinery gases, and finished petroleum products produced at a refinery or petroleum storage terminal blending facility. Net production equals gross production minus gross inputs. Negative net production indicates gross production is less than gross inputs for a finished petroleum product. Examples of negative net production include reclassification of one finished product to another finished product, or reclassification of a finished product to unfinished oils or blending components.

Refinery capacity utilization Ratio of the total amount of crude oil, unfinished oils, and natural gas plant liquids run through crude oil distillation units to the operable capacity of these units.

Refinery fuel Crude oil and petroleum products consumed at the refinery for all purposes.

Refinery gas Noncondensate gas collected in petroleum refineries.

Refinery-grade butane A refinery produced stream that is composed predominantly of normal butane and/or isobutane and may also contain propane and/or natural gasoline. These streams may also contain significant levels of olefins and/or fluorides contamination.

Refinery input, crude oil Total crude oil (domestic plus foreign) input to crude oil distillation units and other refinery processing units (cokers, etc.).

Refinery input, total The raw materials and intermediate materials processed at refineries to produce finished petroleum products. They include crude oil, products of natural gas processing plants, unfinished oils, other hydrocarbons and oxygenates, motor gasoline and aviation gasoline blending components and finished petroleum products.

Refinery losses and gains Processing gain and loss that takes place during the refining process itself. Excludes losses that do not take place during the refining process, e.g., spills, fire losses, and contamination during blending, transportation, or storage.

Refinery output The total amount of petroleum products produced at a refinery. Includes petroleum consumed by the refinery.

Refinery production Petroleum products produced at a refinery or blending plant. Published production of these products equals refinery production minus refinery input. Negative production will occur when the amount of a product produced during the month is less than the amount that is reprocessed (input) or reclassified to become another product during the same month. Refinery production of unfinished oils and motor and aviation gasoline blending components appear on a net basis under refinery input.

Refinery utilization rate Represents the use of the atmospheric crude oil distillation units. The rate is calculated by dividing the gross input to these units by the operable refining capacity of the units.

Refinery yield Refinery yield (expressed as a percentage) represents the percent of finished product produced from input of crude oil and net input of unfinished oils. It is calculated by dividing the sum of crude oil and net unfinished input into the individual net production of finished products. Before calculating the yield for finished motor gasoline, the input of natural gas liquids, other hydrocarbons and oxygenates, and net input of motor gasoline blending components must be subtracted from the net production of finished aviation gasoline.

Reflective film Transparent covering for glass that helps keep out heat from the sun.

Reflectivity The ratio of the energy carried by a wave after reflection from a surface to its energy before reflection.

Reforestation Replanting of forests on lands that have recently been harvested or otherwise cleared of trees.

Reformulated blendstock for oxygenate blending (RBOB) Motor gasoline blending components intended for blending with oxygenates to produce finished reformulated gasoline.

Reformulated gasoline Finished gasoline formulated for use in motor vehicles, the composition and properties of which meet the requirements of the reformulated gasoline regulations promulgated by the U.S. Environmental Protection Agency under Section 211(k) of the Clean Air Act. It includes gasoline produced to meet or exceed emissions performance and benzene content standards of federal-program reformulated gasoline even though the gasoline may not meet all of the composition requirements (e.g. oxygen content) of federal-program reformulated gasoline. *Note:* This category includes Oxygenated Fuels Program Reformulated Gasoline (OPRG). Reformulated gasoline excludes Reformulated Blendstock for Oxygenate Blending (RBOB) and Gasoline Treated as Blendstock (GTAB).

Refrigeration unit Lowers the temperature through a mechanical process. In a typical refrigeration unit, electricity powers a motor that runs a pump to compress the refrigerant to maintain proper pressure. (A "refrigerant" is a substance that changes between liquid and gaseous states under desirable temperature and pressure conditions.) Heat from the compressed liquid is removed and discharged from the unit and the refrigerant then evaporates when pressure is reduced. The refrigerant picks up heat as it evaporates and it returns to the compressor to repeat the cycle. A few refrigeration units use gas (either natural gas or LPG) in an absorption process that does not use a compressor. The gas is burned to heat a chemical solution in which the refrigerant has been absorbed. Heating drives off the refrigerant which is later condensed. The condensed refrigerant evaporates by a release of pressure, and it picks up heat as it evaporates. The evaporated refrigerant is then absorbed back into the chemical solution, the heat is removed from the solution and discharged as waste heat, and the process repeats itself. By definition, refrigerators, freezers, and air-conditioning equipment all contain refrigeration units.

Refunding Retirement of one security issue with proceeds received from selling another. Refunding provides for retiring maturing debt by taking advantage of favorable money market conditions.

Refuse bank A repository for waste material generated by the coal cleaning process.

Refuse-derived fuel (RDF) A fuel produced by shredding municipal solid waste (MSW). Noncombustible materials such as glass and metals are generally removed prior to making RDF. The residual material is sold as-is or compressed into pellets, bricks, or logs. RDF processing facilities are typically located near a source of MSW, while the RDF combustion facility can be located elsewhere.

Refuse mine A surface mine where coal is recovered from previously mined coal. It may also be known as a silt bank, culm bank, refuse bank, slurry dam, or dredge operation.

Refuse recovery The recapture of coal from a refuse mine or the coal recaptured by that process. The resulting product has been cleaned to reduce the concentration of noncombustible materials.

Regional reserves, regional reserve estimates (coal) Same as reserves; alternative wording is used by EIA to distinguish regional reserves, which are derived by factoring (downward) from a demonstrated reserve base for one or more study areas or regions, from reserves at active mines, which are aggregated (upward) from reserve estimates reported by individual mines on Form EIA-7A.

Regional Transmission Group A utility industry concept that the Federal Energy Regulatory Commission (FERC) embraced for the certification of voluntary groups that would be responsible for transmission planning and use on a regional basis.

Regular grade gasoline A grade of unleaded gasoline with a lower octane rating (approximately 82) than other grades. Octane boosters are added to gasoline to control engine pre-ignition or "knocking" by slowing combustion rates.

Regulated entity For the purpose of EIA's data collection efforts, entities that either provide electricity within a designated franchised service area and/or file forms listed in the Code of Federal Regulations, Title 18, part 141 are considered regulated entities. This includes investor-owned electric utilities that are subject to rate regulation, municipal utilities, federal and state power authorities, and rural electric cooperatives. Facilities that qualify as cogenerators or small power producers under the Public Utility Regulatory Power Act (PURPA) are not considered regulated entities.

Regulated streamflow The rate of flow past a given point during a specified period that is controlled by reservoir water release operation.

Regulation The governmental function of controlling or directing economic entities through the process of rulemaking and adjudication.

Regulation, procedures, and practices A utility commission carries out its regulatory functions through rulemaking and adjudication. Under rulemaking, the utility commission may propose a general rule of regulation change. By law, it must issue a notice of the proposed rule and a request for comments is also made; the Federal Energy Regulatory Commission publishes this in the Federal Register. The final decision must be published. A utility commission may also work on a case-by-case basis from submissions from regulated companies or others. Objections to a proposal may come from the commission or intervenors, in which case the proposal must be presented to a hearing presided over by an administrative law judge. The judge's decision may be adopted, modified, or reversed by the utility commissioners, in which case those involved can petition for a rehearing and may appeal a decision through the courts system to the U.S. Supreme Court.

Reheating coils A part of some air-conditioning systems. Electric coils in air ducts used primarily to raise the temperature of circulated air after it was over-cooled to remove moisture. Some buildings have reheating coils as their sole heating source.

Reid Vapor Pressure (RVP) An indirect measure of the rate at which petroleum liquids evaporate. Its the absolute vapor pressure of a crude oil, or of single or mixed liquid petroleum products, as measured by the Reid Method (ASTM Method D 323).

Reinjected The forcing of gas under pressure into an oil reservoir in an attempt to increase recovery.

Reinserted fuel Irradiated fuel that is discharged in one cycle and inserted in the same reactor during a subsequent refueling. In a few cases, fuel discharged from one reactor has been used to fuel a different reactor.

Reinsertion The process of returning nuclear fuel that has been irradiated and then removed from a reactor back into a reactor for further irradiation. Reinserted assemblies are assemblies that have been irradiated in a cycle, were not in the core in the prior cycle (cycle N), and which are in the core in the current cycle (cycle N+1).

Reliability (electric system) A measure of the ability of the system to continue operation while some lines or generators are out of service. Reliability deals with the performance of the system under stress.

Reliability coordinator (electric) The entity that is the highest level of authority who is responsible for the reliable operation of the Bulk Electric System, has the Wide Area view of the Bulk Electric System, and has the operating tools, processes and procedures, including the authority to prevent or mitigate emergency operating situations in both next-day analysis and real-time operations. The Reliability Coordinator has the purview that is broad enough to enable the calculation of Interconnection Reliability Operating Limits, which may be based on the operating parameters of transmission systems beyond any Transmission Operator's vision. (NERC definition)

Relocation of tailings Relocation of tailings is sometimes necessary if the pile poses a threat to inhabitants or the environment, for example, through being situated too close to populated areas, on top of aquifers or other sources of water, or in unstable areas such as flood plains or faults near earthquake zones.

Remaining (resources/reserves) (coal) The amount of coal in the ground after some mining, excluding coal in the ground spoiled or left in place for which later recovery is not feasible.

Renewable diesel fuel (other) Diesel fuel and diesel fuel blending components produced from renewable sources that are coprocessed with petroleum feedstocks and meet requirements of advanced biofuels. *Note*: This category, "other," pertains to the petroleum supply data system.

Renewable energy resources Energy resources that are naturally replenishing but flow-limited. They are virtually inexhaustible in duration but limited in the amount of energy that is available per unit of time. Renewable energy resources include: biomass, hydro, geothermal, solar, wind, ocean thermal, wave action, and tidal action.

Renewable fuels (other) Fuels and fuel blending components, except biomass-based diesel fuel, renewable diesel fuel, and fuel ethanol, produced from renewable biomass. *Note*: This category "other" pertains to the petroleum supply data system.

Replacement energy source for primary heating For the CBECS (an EIA consumption survey), the heating energy source to which the building could switch within one week without major modifications to the main heating equipment, without substantially reducing the area heated, and without substantially reducing the temperature maintained in the heated area.

Replacement vehicle A vehicle which is acquired in order to take the place of a vehicle which is being retired from service. These acquisitions do not increase the size of the company fleet.

Report State The State, including adjacent offshore continental shelf areas in the Federal domain, in which a company operated natural gas gathering, transportation, storage, and/or distribution facilities or a synthetic natural gas plant covered by the individual report.

Report week   A calendar week beginning at 12:01 a.m. on Sunday and ending at midnight on Saturday.

Report year (calendar)   The 12-month period, January 1 through December 31.

Report year (fiscal)   A 12-month period for which an organization plans the use of its funds. The fiscal year is designated by the calendar year in which it ends.

Reporting   The average number of Btu per cubic foot of gas at 60 degrees Fahrenheit and 14.73 psia delivered directly to consumers. Where billing is on a thermal basis, the heat content values used for billing purposes are to be used to determine the annual average heat content.

Repowering   Refurbishment of a plant by replacement of the combustion technology with a new combustion technology, usually resulting in better performance and greater capacity.

Repressuring   The injection of gas into oil or gas formations to effect greater ultimate recovery.

Reprocessing   Synonymous with chemical separations.

Requirements power   The firm service needs required by designated load plus losses from the points of supply.

Reregulation   The design and implementation of regulatory practices to be applied to the remaining regulated entities after restructuring of the vertically-integrated electric utility. The remaining regulated entities would be those that continue to exhibit characteristics of a natural monopoly, where imperfections in the market prevent the realization of more competitive results, and where, in light of other policy considerations, competitive results are unsatisfactory in one or more respects. Regulation could employ the same or different regulatory practices as those used before restructuring.

Resale (wholesale) sales   Resale or wholesale sales are electricity sold (except under exchange agreements) to other electric utilities or to public authorities for resale distribution. (This includes sales to requirements and nonrequirements consumers.)

Research and development (R&D)   Basic and applied research in the sciences and engineering and the design and development of prototypes and processes, excluding quality control, routine product testing, market research, sales promotion, sales service, research in the social sciences or psychology, and other non-technological activities or technical services.

Reseller   A firm (other than a refiner) that is engaged in a trade or business that buys refined petroleum products and then sells them to a purchaser who is not the ultimate consumer of those refined products.

Reserve   That portion of the demonstrated reserve base that is estimated to be recoverable at the time of determination. The reserve is derived by applying a recovery factor to that component of the identified coal resource designated as the demonstrated reserve base.

Reserve additions   The estimated original, recoverable, salable, and new proved reserves credited to new fields, new reservoirs, new gas purchase contracts, amendments to old gas purchase contracts, or purchase of gas reserves in-place that occurred during the year and had not been previously reported. Reserve additions refer to domestic in-the-ground natural gas reserve additions and do not refer to interstate pipeline purchase agreements; contracts with foreign suppliers; coal gas, SNG, or LNG purchase arrangements.

Reserve cost categories of $15, $30, $50, and $100 per pound U_3O_8   Classification of uranium reserves estimated by using break-even cutoff grades that are calculated based on forward-operating costs of less than $15, $30, $50, and $100 per pound U_3O_8.

Reserve generating capacity   Amount of generating capacity available to meet peak or abnormally high demands for power and to generate power during scheduled or unscheduled outages.

Reserve margin (operating)   The amount of unused available capability of an electric power system (at peak load for a utility system) as a percentage of total capability.

Reserve revisions   Changes to prior year-end proved reserves estimates, either positive or negative, resulting from new information other than an increase in proved acreage (extension). Revisions include increases of proved reserves associated with the installation of improved recovery techniques or equipment. They also include correction of prior year arithmetical or clerical errors and adjustments to prior year-end production volumes to the extent that these alter reserves estimates.

Reserves, coal   Quantities of unextracted coal that comprise the demonstrated base for future production, including both proved and probable reserves. Also see Proved energy reserves; Probable energy reserves; Energy reserves; Proved (measured) reserves, coal; and Probable(indicated) reserves, coal.

Reserves, energy   See Proved energy reserves.

Reserves, net   Includes all proved reserves associated with the company's net working interests.

Reserves changes   Positive and negative revisions, extensions, new reservoir discoveries in old fields, and new field discoveries that occurred during the report year.

Reservoir   A porous and permeable underground formation containing an individual and separate natural accumulation of producible hydrocarbons (crude oil and/or natural gas) which is confined by impermeable rock or water barriers and is characterized by a single natural pressure system.

Reservoir capacity The present total developed capacity (base and working) of the storage reservoir, excluding contemplated future development.

Reservoir repressuring The injection of a pressurized fluid (such as air, gas, or water) into oil and gas reservoir formations to effect greater ultimate recovery.

Residential building A structure used primarily as a dwelling for one or more households.

Residential/commercial (consumer category) Housing units, wholesale or retail businesses (except coal wholesale dealers); health institutions (hospitals, social and educational institutions (schools and universities); and Federal, state, and local governments (military installations, prisons, office buildings, etc.). Excludes shipments to Federal power projects, such as TVA, and rural electrification cooperatives, power districts, and state power projects.

Residential consumers Consumers using gas for heating, air conditioning, cooking, water heating, and other residential uses in single and multi-family dwellings and apartments and mobile homes.

Residential energy consumption survey (RECS) A national multistage probability sample survey conducted by the Energy End Use Division of the Energy Information Administration. The RECS provides baseline information on how households in the United States use energy. The Residential Transportation Energy Consumption Survey (RTECS) sample is a subset of the RECS. Household demographic characteristics reported in the RTECS publication are collected during the RECS personal interview.

Residential heating oil price The price charged for home delivery of No. 2 heating oil, exclusive of any discounts such as those for prompt cash payment. Prices do not include taxes paid by the consumer.

Residential propane price The "bulk keep full" price for home delivery of consumer-grade propane intended for use in space heating, cooking, or hot water heaters in residences.

Residential sector An energy-consuming sector that consists of living quarters for private households. Common uses of energy associated with this sector include space heating, water heating, air conditioning, lighting, refrigeration, cooking, and running a variety of other appliances. The residential sector excludes institutional living quarters. *Note*: Various EIA programs differ in sectoral coverage. Click Here for further information on the variations of the residential sector used by EIA systems.

Residential type central air conditioner There are four basic parts to a residential central air-conditioning system: (1) a condensing unit, (2) a cooling coil, (3) ductwork, and (4) a control mechanism such as a thermostat. There are two basic configurations of residential central systems: (1) a "split system" where the condensing unit is located outside and the other components are inside, and (2) a packaged-terminal air-encased in one unit and is usually found in a "utility closet."

Residential vehicles Motorized vehicles used by U.S. households for personal transportation. Excluded are motorcycles, mopeds, large trucks, and buses. Included are automobiles, station wagons, passenger vans, cargo vans, motor homes, pickup trucks, and jeeps or similar vehicles. In order to be included (in the EIA survey), vehicles must be (1) owned by members of the household, or (2) company cars not owned by household members but regularly available to household members for their personal use and ordinarily kept at home, or (3) rented or leased for 1 month or more.

Residual fuel oil A general classification for the heavier oils, known as No. 5 and No. 6 fuel oils, that remain after the distillate fuel oils and lighter hydrocarbons are distilled away in refinery operations. It conforms to ASTM Specifications D 396 and D 975 and Federal Specification VV-F-815C. No. 5, a residual fuel oil of medium viscosity, is also known as Navy Special and is defined in Military Specification MIL-F-859E, including Amendment 2 (NATO Symbol F-770). It is used in steam-powered vessels in government service and inshore powerplants. No. 6 fuel oil includes Bunker C fuel oil and is used for the production of electric power, space heating, vessel bunkering, and various industrial purposes.

Residue gas Natural gas from which natural gas processing plant liquid products and, in some cases, nonhydrocarbon components have been extracted.

Residuum Residue from crude oil after distilling off all but the heaviest components, with a boiling range greater than 1,000 degrees Fahrenheit.

Resources (Coal) Naturally occurring concentrations or deposits of coal in the Earth's crust, in such forms and amounts that economic extraction is currently or potentially feasible.

Respondent A company or individual who completes and returns a report or survey form.

Restoration time The time when the major portion of the interrupted load has been restored and the emergency is considered to be ended. However, some of the loads interrupted may not have been restored due to local problems.

Restricted-universe census This is the complete enumeration of data from a specifically defined subset of entities including, for example, those that exceed a given level of sales or generator nameplate capacity.

Restructuring The process of replacing a monopoly system of electric utilities with competing sellers, allowing individual retail customers to choose their electricity supplier but still receive delivery over the power lines of the local utility. It includes the reconfiguration of the vertically-integrated electric utility.

Retail motor gasoline prices Motor gasoline prices calculated each month by the Bureau of Labor Statistics (BLS) in conjunction with the construction of the Consumer Price Index.

Retail wheeling The process of moving electric power from a point of generation across third-party-owned transmission and distribution systems to a retail customer.

Retail sales (electric) Sales made directly to the customer that consumes the energy product. (FERC definition)

Retailer A firm (other than a refiner, reseller, or reseller/retailer) that carries on the trade or business of purchasing refined petroleum products and reselling them to ultimate consumers without substantially changing their form.

Retained earnings The balance, either debit or credit, of appropriated or unappropriated retained earnings of the utility department arising from earnings.

Retire from service A vehicle is retired from service if that vehicle is placed out of service and there are no future plans to return that vehicle to service.

Retired hydropower plant sites The site of a plant that formerly produced electrical or mechanical power but is now out of service. Includes plants that have been abandoned, damaged by flood or fire, inundated by new reservoirs, or dismantled.

Return on common equity The net income less preferred stock dividends, divided by the average common stock equity.

Return on common stock equity An equity's earnings available for common stockholders calculated as a percentage of its common equity capital.

Revenue (electricity) The total amount of money received by an entity from sales of its products and/or services; gains from the sales or exchanges of assets, interest, and dividends earned on investments; and other increases in the owner's equity, except those arising from capital adjustments.

Revenue requirement The total revenue that the utility is authorized an opportunity to recover, which includes operating expenses and a reasonable return on rate base.

Reversible turbine A hydraulic turbine, normally installed in a pumped-storage plant, which can be used alternatively as a pump or as an engine, turbine, water wheel, or other apparatus that drives an electrical generator.

Revisions and additions (gross change in reserves) The difference (plus or minus) between the year-end reserves plus production for a given year and the year-end reserves for the previous year.

Ribbon silicon Crystalline silicon that is used in photovoltaic cells. Ribbon silicon is fabricated by a variety of solidification (crystallization) methods that withdraw thin silicon sheets from pools of relatively pure molten silicon.

Right-of-Way (ROW) (electric) A corridor of land on which electric lines may be located. The Transmission Owner may own the land in fee, own an easement, or have certain franchise, prescription, or license rights to construct and maintain lines. (NERC definition)

Rip rap Cobblestone or coarsely broken rock used for protection against erosion of embankment or gully.

River (method of transportation to consumers - coal) Shipments of coal moved to consumers via river by barge. Shipments to Great Lakes coal loading docks or Tidewater pier or coastal points are not included.

Road oil Any heavy petroleum oil, including residual asphaltic oil used as a dust pallative and surface treatment on roads and highways. It is generally produced in six grades, from 0, the most liquid, to 5, the most viscous.

Rodlet or GAD basket An open garbage and debris (GAD) basket that may have contain pieces of fuel rods, disassembled fuel rods, and other fuel and nonfuel components.

Roll front A type of uranium deposition localized as a roll or interface separating an oxidized interior from a reduced exterior. The reduced side of this interface is significantly enriched in uranium.

Roof (coal) The rock immediately above a coal seam. The roof is commonly a shale, often carbonaceous and softer than rocks higher up in the roof strata.

Roof insulation Insulating materials placed underneath the roof or on the roof (building).

Roof or ceiling insulation A building shell conservation feature consisting of insulation placed in the roof (below the waterproofing layer) or in the ceiling of the top floor in the building.

Roof or ceiling insulation, insulation in exterior walls Any material that when placed between the interior surface of the building and the exterior surface of the building, reduces the rate of heat loss to the environment or heat gain from the environment. Roof or ceiling insulation refers to insulation placed in the roof or ceiling of the top occupied floor in the building. Wall insulation refers to insulation placed between the exterior and interior walls of the building.

Roof pond A solar energy collection device consisting of containers of water located on a roof that absorb solar energy during the day so that the heat can be used at night or that cools a building by evaporation at night.

Room air conditioner Air-conditioning units that typically fit into the window or wall and are designed to cool only one room.

Room heater burning gas, oil, and kerosene Any of the following heating equipment: circulating heaters, convectors, radiant gas heaters, space heaters, or other nonportable room heaters that may or may not be connected to a flue, vent, or chimney.

Room-and-pillar mining The most common method of underground mining in which the mine roof is supported mainly by coal pillars left at regular intervals. Rooms are places where the coal is mined; pillars are areas of coal left between the rooms. Room-and-pillar mining is done either by conventional or continuous mining.

Rotary rig A machine used for drilling wells that employs a rotating tube attached to a bit for boring holes through rock.

Round test mesh A sieving screen with round holes, the dimensions of which are of specific sizes to allow certain sizes of coal to pass through while retaining other sizes.

Roundwood Wood cut specifically for use as a fuel.

Royalty A contractual arrangement providing a mineral interest that gives the owner a right to a fractional share of production or proceeds therefrom, that does not contain rights and obligations of operating a mineral property, and that is normally free and clear of exploration, developmental and operating costs, except production taxes.

Royalty cost A share of the profit or product reserved by the grantor of a mining lease, such as a royalty paid to a lessee.

Royalty interest An interest in a mineral property provided through a royalty contract.

Royalty interest (including overriding royalty) These interests entitle their owner(s) to a share of the mineral production from a property or to a share of the proceeds therefrom. They do not contain the rights and obligations of operating the property and normally do not bear any of the costs of exploration, development, and operation of the property.

Rulemaking (regulations) The authority delegated to administrative agencies by Congress or State legislative bodies to make rules that have the force of law. Frequently, statutory laws that express broad terms of a policy are implemented more specifically by administrative rules, regulations, and practices.

Run off That portion of the precipitation that flows over the land surface and ultimately reaches streams to complete the water cycle. Melting snow is an important source of this water as well as all amounts of surface water that move to streams or rivers through any given area of a drainage basin.

Run-of-mine coal Coal as it comes from the mine prior to screening or any other treatment.

Run-of-river hydroelectric plant A low-head plant using the flow of a stream as it occurs and having little or no reservoir capacity for storage.

Running and quick-start capability The net capability of generating units that carry load or have quick-start capability. In general, quick-start capability refers to generating units that can be available for load within a 30-minute period.

Rural Electrification Administration (REA) A lending agency of the U. S. Department of Agriculture, the REA makes self-liquidating loans to qualified borrowers to finance electric and telephone service to rural areas. The REA finances the construction and operation of generating plants, electric transmission and distribution lines, or systems for the furnishing of initial and continued adequate electric services to persons in rural areas not receiving central station service.

Salable coal The shippable product of a coal mine or preparation plant. Depending on customer specifications, salable coal may be run-of-mine, crushed-and-screened (sized) coal, or the clean coal yield from a preparation plant.

Salable natural gas Natural gas marketed under controlled quality conditions.

Sales See Energy sales.

Sales for Resale (electric) A type of wholesale sales covering energy supplied to other electric utilities, cooperatives, municipalities, and Federal and state electric agencies for resale to ultimate consumers. (FERC definition)

Sales to end users Sales made directly to the consumer of the product. Includes bulk consumers, such as agriculture, industry, and utilities, as well as residential and commercial consumers.

Sales type Sales categories of sales to end-users and sales for resale.

Sales volume (coal) The reported output from Federal and/or Indian lands, the basis of royalties. It is approximately equivalent to production, which includes coal sold, and coal added to stockpiles.

Salt dome A domical arch (anticline) of sedimentary rock beneath the earth's surface in which the layers bend downward in opposite directions from the crest and that has a mass of rock salt as its core.

Salt gradient solar ponds These consist of three main layers. The top layer is near ambient and has low salt content. The bottom layer is hot, typically 160° F to 212° F (71° C to 100° C), and is very salty. The important gradient zone separates these zones. The gradient zone acts as a transparent insulator, permitting the sunlight to be trapped in the hot bottom layer (from which useful heat is withdrawn). This is because the salt gradient, which increases the brine density with depth, counteracts the buoyancy effect of the warmer water below (which would otherwise rise to the surface and lose its heat to the air). An organic Rankine cycle engine is used to convert the thermal energy to electricity.

Sample (coal) A representative fraction of a coal bed collected by approved methods, guarded against contamination or adulteration, and analyzed to determine the nature; chemical, mineralogic, and (or) petrographic composition; percentage or parts-per-million content of specified constituents; heat value; and possibly the reactivity of the coal or its constituents.

Schedule A statement of the pricing format of electricity and the terms and conditions governing its applications.

Scheduled outage The shutdown of a generating unit, transmission line, or other facility for inspection or maintenance, in accordance with an advance schedule.

Scheduling coordinators Entities certified by the Federal Energy Regulatory Commission (FERC) that act on behalf of generators, supply aggregators (wholesale marketers), retailers, and customers to schedule the distribution of electricity.

Scoop loading An underground loading method by which coal is removed from the working face by a tractor unit equipped with a hydraulically operated bucket attached to the front; also called a front-end loader.

Screenings The undersized coal from a screening process, usually one-half inch or smaller.

Seam A bed of coal lying between a roof and floor. Equivalent term to bed, commonly used by industry.

Seasonal energy efficiency ratio (SEER) Ratio of the cooling output divided by the power consumption. It is the Btu of cooling output during its normal annual usage divided by the total electric energy input in watt hours during the same period. This is a measure of the cooling performance for rating central air conditioners and central heat pumps. The appliance standards required a minimum SEER of 10 for split-system central air conditioners and for split-system central heat pumps in 1992. (The average heat pump or central air conditioner sold in 1986 had an SEER of about 9.)

Seasonal pricing A special electric rate feature under which the price per unit of energy depends on the season of the year.

Seasonal rates Different seasons of the year are structured into an electric rate schedule whereby an electric utility provides service to consumers at different rates. The electric rate schedule usually takes into account demand based on weather and other factors.

Seasonal units Housing units intended for occupancy at only certain seasons of the year. Seasonal units include units intended only for recreational use, such as beach cottages and hunting cabins. It is not likely that this type of unit will be the usual residence for a household, because it may not be fit for living quarters for more than half of the year.

Seasoned wood Wood, used for fuel, that has been air dried so that it contains 15 to 20 percent moisture content (wet basis).

Secondary heating equipment Space-heating equipment used less often than the main space-heating equipment.

Secondary heating fuel Fuels used in secondary space-heating equipment.

Sector See Energy-use sectors.

Securitization A proposal for issuing bonds that would be used to buy down existing power contracts or other obligations. The bonds would be repaid by designating a portion of future customer bill payments. Customer bills would be lowered, since the cost of bond payments would be less than the power contract costs that would be avoided.

Securitize To aggregate contracts into one pool, which then offers shares for sale in the investment market. This strategy diversifies project risks from what they would be if each project were financed individually, thereby reducing the cost of financing.

Selective absorber A solar absorber surface that has high absorbtance at wavelengths corresponding to that of the solar spectrum and low emittance in the infrared range.

Self-generator A plant whose primary product is not electric power, but does generate electricity for its own use or for sale on the grid; for example, industrial combined heat and power plants.

Seller type Categories of major refiners and other refiners and gas plant operators.

Semianthracite See Anthracite.

Semiconductor Any material that has a limited capacity for conducting an electric current. Certain semiconductors, including silicon, gallium arsenide, copper indium diselenide, and cadmium telluride, are uniquely suited to the photovoltaic conversion process.

Separate metering Measurement of electricity or natural gas consumption in a building using a separate meter for each of several tenants or establishments in the building.

Separative work unit (SWU) The standard measure of enrichment services. The effort expended in separating a mass F of feed of assay x_f into a mass P of product assay x_p and waste of mass W and assay x_w is expressed in terms of the number of separative work units needed, given by the expression SWU = $WV(x_w)$

$+ PV(x_p) - FV(x_f)$, where $V(x)$ is the "value function," defined as $V(x) = (1 - 2x) \ln((1 - x)/x)$.

Septic tank A tank in which the solid matter of continuously flowing sewage is disintegrated by bacteria.

Series connection A way of joining photovoltaic cells by connecting positive leads to negative leads; such a configuration increases the voltage.

Series resistance Parasitic resistance to current flow in a cell due to mechanisms such as resistance from the bulk of the semiconductor material, metallic contacts, and interconnections.

Service area The territory in which a utility system or distributor is authorized to provide service to consumers.

Service provider See Energy service provider.

Service well A well drilled, completed, or converted for the purpose of supporting production in an existing field. Wells of this class also are drilled or converted for the following specific purposes: gas injection (natural gas, propane, butane or fuel-gas); water injection; steam injection; air injection; salt water disposal; water supply for injection; observation; and injection for in-situ combustion.

Shaft mine A mine that reaches the coal bed by means of a vertical shaft.

Shakes/shingles Flat pieces of weatherproof material laid with others in a series of overlapping rows as covering for roofs and sometimes the sides of buildings. Shakes are similar to wood shingles, but instead of having a cut and smoothly planed surface, shakes have textured grooves and a rough or "split" appearance to give a rustic feeling.

Shallow pitting Testing a potential mineral deposit by systematically sinking small shafts into the earth and analyzing the material recovered.

Shell storage capacity The design capacity of a petroleum storage tank which is always greater than or equal to working storage capacity.

Short circuit An electric current taking a shorter or different path than intended.

Short circuit current The current flowing freely through an external circuit that has no load or resistance; the maximum current possible.

Short purchases A single shipment of fuel or volumes of fuel purchased for delivery within 1 year. Spot purchases are often made by a user to fulfill a certain portion of energy requirements, to meet unanticipated energy needs, or to take advantage of low-fuel prices.

Short-term debt or borrowings Debt securities or borrowings having a maturity of less than one year.

Short-term purchase A purchase contract under which all deliveries of materials are scheduled to be completed by the end of the first calender year following the contract-signing year. Deliveries can be made during the contract year, but deliveries are not scheduled to occur beyond the first calendar year thereafter.

Short-term sales Any short-term purchase covering a time period of 2 years or less. Purchases from intrastate pipelines pursuant to Section 311(b) of the NGPA of 1978 are classified as short-term sales, regardless of the stated contract term.

Short ton A unit of weight equal to 2,000 pounds.

Shortwall mining A form of underground mining that involves the use of a continuous mining machine and movable roof supports to shear coal panels 150 to 200 feet wide and more than half a mile long. Although similar to longwall mining, shortwall mining is generally more flexible because of the smaller working area. Productivity is lower than with longwall mining because the coal is hauled to the mine face by shuttle cars as opposed to conveyors.

Shrinkage The volume of natural gas that is transformed into liquid products during processing, primarily at natural gas liquids processing plants.

Shut in Closed temporarily; wells and mines capable of production may be shut in for repair, cleaning, inaccessibility to a market, etc.

Shut-in royalty A royalty paid by a lessee as compensation for a lessor's loss of income because the lessee has deferred production from a property that is known to be capable of producing minerals. Shut in may be caused by a lack of a ready market, by a lack of transportation facilities, or by other reasons. A shut-in royalty may or may not be recoverable out of future production.

Shutdown date Month and year of shutdown for fuel discharge and refueling. The date should be the point at which the reactor became subcritical.

Sidetrack drilling This is a remedial operation that results in the creation of a new section of well bore for the purpose of (1) detouring around junk, (2) redrilling lost holes, or (3) straightening key seats and crooked holes. Directional "side-track" wells do not include footage in the common bore that is reported as footage for the original well.

Siding An exterior wall covering material made of wood, plastic (including vinyl), or metal. Siding is generally produced in the shape of boards and is applied to the outside of a building in overlapping rows.

Silicon A semiconductor material made from silica, purified for photovoltaic applications.

Silt Waste from Pennsylvania anthracite preparation plants, consisting of coarse rock fragments containing as much as 30 percent small-sized coal; sometimes defined as including very fine coal particles called silt. Its heat value ranges from 8 to 17 million Btu per short ton. Synonymous with culm.

Silt, culm, refuse bank, or slurry dam mining A mining operation producing coal from these sources of coal.

Single-circuit line A transmission line with one electric circuit. For three-phase supply, a single circuit requires at least three conductors, one per phase.

Single crystal silicon An extremely pure form of crystalline silicon produced by dipping a single crystal seed into a pool of molten silicon under high vacuum conditions and slowly withdrawing a solidifying single crystal boule (rod) of silicon. The boule is sawed into thin silicon wafers and fabricated into single-crystal photovoltaic cells.

Single crystal silicon (Czochralsky) Silicon cells with a well-ordered crystalline structure consisting of one crystal (usually obtained by means of the Czochralsky growth technique and involving ingot slicing), composing a module. Ribbon silicon is excluded.

Single-family housing unit See housing structure/housing unit, specifically under Residential Sector heading.

Single-purpose project A hydroelectric project constructed only to generate electricity.

Site characterization An onsite investigation at a known or suspected contaminated waste or release site to determine the extent and type(s) of contamination.

Site energy The Btu value of energy at the point it enters the home, sometimes referred to as "delivered" energy. The site value of energy is used for all fuels, including electricity.

Site energy consumption The Btu value of energy at the point it enters the home, building, or establishment, sometimes referred to as "delivered" energy.

Site-specific information DSM program assistance A DSM (demand-side management) assistance program that provides quidance on energy efficiency and load management options tailored to a particular customer'sfacility; it often involves an on-site inspection of the customer facility to identify cost-effective DSM actions that could be taken. They include audits, engineering design calculations on information provided about the building, and technical assistance to architects and engineers who design new facilities.

Sinter A chemical sedimentary rock deposited by precipitation from mineral waters, especially siliceous sinter and calcareous sinter.

Slope mine A mine that reaches the coal bed by means of an inclined opening.

Slot A physical position in a rack in a storage pool that is intended to be occupied by an intact assembly or equivalent (that is, a canister or an assembly skeleton).

Sludge A dense, slushy, liquid-to-semifluid product that accumulates as an end result of an industrial or technological process designed to purify a substance. Industrial sludges are produced from the processing of energy-related raw materials, chemical products, water, mined ores, sewerage, and other natural and man-made products. Sludges can also form from natural processes, such as the run off produced by rain fall, and accumulate on the bottom of bogs, streams, lakes, and tidelands.

Slurry A viscous liquid with a high solids content.

Slurry dam A repository for the silt or culm from a preparation plant.

Small pickup truck A pickup truck weighing under 4,500 lbs GVW.

Small power producer (SPP) Under the Public Utility Regulatory Policies Act (PURPA), a small power production facility (or small power producer) generates electricity using waste, renewable (biomass, conventional hydroelectric, wind and solar, and geothermal) energy as a primary energy source. Fossil fuels can be used, but renewable resource must provide at least 75 percent of the total energy input. (See Code of Federal Regulations, Title 18, Part 292.)

Sodium lights A type of high intensity discharge light that has the most lumens per watt of any light source.

Sodium silicate A grey-white powder soluble in alkali and water, insoluble in alcohol and acid. Used to fireproof textiles, in petroleum refining and corrugated paperboard manufacture, and as an egg preservative. Also referred to as liquid gas, silicate of soda, sodium metasilicate, soluble glass, and water glass.

Sodium tripolyphosphate A white powder used for water softening and as a food additive and texturizer.

Solar cell See Photovoltaic cell.

Solar constant The average amount of solar radiation that reaches the earth's upper atmosphere on a surface perpendicular to the sun's rays; equal to 1353 Watts per square meter or 492 Btu per square foot.

Solar cooling The use of solar thermal energy or solar electricity to power a cooling appliance. There are five basic types of solar cooling technologies: absorption cooling, which can use solar thermal energy to vaporize the refrigerant; desiccant cooling, which can use solar thermal energy to regenerate (dry) the desiccant; vapor compression cooling, which can use solar thermal energy to operate a Rankine-cycle heat engine; and evaporative coolers ("swamp" coolers), and heat-pumps and air conditioners that can by powered by solar photovoltaic systems.

Solar declination The apparent angle of the sun north or south of the earth's equatorial plane. The earth's rotation on its axis causes a daily change in the declination.

Solar dish See Parabolic dish.

Solar energy The radiant energy of the sun, which can be converted into other forms of energy, such as heat or electricity.

Solar pond A body of water that contains brackish (highly saline) water that forms layers of differing salinity (stratifies) that absorb and trap solar energy. Solar ponds can be used to provide heat for industrial or agricultural processes, building heating and cooling, and to generate electricity.

Solar power tower A solar energy conversion system that uses a large field of independently adjustable mirrors (heliostats) to focus solar rays on a near single point atop a fixed tower (receiver). The concentrated energy may be used to directly heat the working fluid of a Rankine cycle engine or to heat an intermediary thermal storage medium (such as a molten salt).

Solar radiation A general term for the visible and near visible (ultraviolet and near-infrared) electromagnetic radiation that is emitted by the sun. It has a spectral, or wavelength, distribution that corresponds to different energy levels; short wavelength radiation has a higher energy than long-wavelength radiation.

Solar spectrum The total distribution of electromagnetic radiation emanating from the sun. The different regions of the solar spectrum are described by their wavelength range. The visible region extends from about 390 to 780 nanometers (a nanometer is one billionth of one meter). About 99 percent of solar radiation is contained in a wavelength region from 300 nm (ultraviolet) to 3,000 nm (near-infrared). The combined radiation in the wavelength region from 280 nm to 4,000 nm is called the broadband, or total, solar radiation.

Solar thermal collector A device designed to receive solar radiation and convert it to thermal energy. Normally, a solar thermal collector includes a frame, glazing, and an absorber, together with appropriate insulation. The heat collected by the solar collector may be used immediately or stored for later use. Solar collectors are used for space heating; domestic hot water heating; and heating swimming pools, hot tubs, or spas.

Solar thermal collector, high-temperature A collector that generally operates at temperatures above 180 degrees Fahrenheit.

Solar thermal collector, low-temperature A collector that generally operates at temperatures below 110 degrees Fahrenheit. Typically, it has no glazing or insulation and is made of plastic or rubber, although some are made of metal.

Solar thermal collector, medium-temperature A collector that generally operates at temperatures of 140 degrees F to 180 degrees Fahrenheit, but can also operate at temperatures as low as 110 degrees Fahrenheit. Typically, it has one or two glazings, a metal frame, a metal absorption panel with integral flow channels or attached tubing (liquid collector) or with integral ducting (air collector) and insulation on the sides and back of the panel.

Solar thermal collector, special An evacuated tube collector or a concentrating (focusing) collector. Special collectors operate in the temperature range from just above ambient temperature (low concentration for pool heating) to several hundred degrees Fahrenheit (high concentration for air conditioning and specialized industrial processes).

Solar thermal panels A system that actively concentrates thermal energy from the sun by means of solar collector panels. The panels typically consist of fat, sun-oriented boxes with transparent covers, containing water tubes of air baffles under a blackened heat absorbent panel. The energy is usually used for space heating, for water heating, and for heating swimming pools.

Solar thermal parabolic dishes A solar thermal technology that uses a modular mirror system that approximates a parabola and incorporates two-axis tracking to focus the sunlight onto receivers located at the focal point of each dish. The mirror system typically is made from a number of mirror facets, either glass or polymer mirror, or can consist of a single stretched membrane using a polymer mirror. The concentrated sunlight may be used directly by a Stirling, Rankine, or Brayton cycle heat engine at the focal point of the receiver or to heat a working fluid that is piped to a central engine. The primary applications include remote electrification, water pumping, and grid-connected generation.

Solar trough or solar parabolic trough See Parabolic trough.

Source material The term "source material" means (1) uranium, thorium, or any other material that is determined by the Atomic Energy Commission pursuant to the provisions of section 61 of the Atomic Energy Act of 1954, as amended, to be source material; or (2) ores containing one or more of the foregoing materials, in such concentration as the Commission may by regulation determine from time to time.

Space heating The use of energy to generate heat for warmth in housing units using space-heating equipment. The equipment could be the main space-heating equipment or secondary space-heating equipment. It does not include the use of energy to operate appliances (such as lights, televisions, and refrigerators) that give off heat as a byproduct.

Special collector An evacuated tube collector or a concentrating (focusing) collector. Special collectors operate in the temperature range from just above ambient temperature (low concentration for pool heating) to several hundred degrees Fahrenheit (high concentration for air conditioning and specialized industrial processes).

Special contract rate schedule An electric rate schedule for an electric service agreement between a utility and another party in addition to, or independent of, any standard rate schedule.

Special naphthas All finished products within the naphtha boiling range that are used as paint thinners, cleaners, or solvents. These products are refined to a specified flash point. Special naphthas include all commercial hexane and cleaning solvents conforming to ASTM Specification D1836 and D484, respectively. Naphthas to be blended or marketed as motor gasoline or aviation gasoline, or that are to be used as petrochemical and synthetic natural gas (SNG) feedstocks are excluded.

Special nuclear material The term "special nuclear material" means (1) plutonium, uranium enriched in the isotope 233 or in the isotope 235, and any other material that the Atomic Energy Commission, pursuant to the provisions of section 51 of the Atomic Energy Act of 1954, as amended, determines to be special nuclear material, but does not include source material; or (2) any material artificially enriched by any of the foregoing, but does not include source material.

Special purpose rate schedule An electric rate schedule limited in its application to some particular purpose or process within one, or more than one, type of industry or business.

Specular reflectors Specular reflectors have mirrorlike characteristics (the word "specular" is derived from the Greek word meaning mirror). The most common materials used for ballasts, the devices that turn on and operate Fluorescent tubes, are aluminum and silver. Silver has the highest reflectivity; aluminum has the lowest cost. The materials and shape of the reflector are designed to reduce absorption of light within the fixture while delivering light in the desired angular pattern. Adding (or retrofitting) specular reflectors to an existing light fixture is frequently implemented as a conservation measure.

Speculative resources (coal) Undiscovered coal in beds that may occur either in known types of deposits in a favorable geologic setting where no discoveries have been made, or in deposits that remain to be recognized. Exploration that confirms their existence and better defines their quantity and quality would permit their reclassification as identified resources.

Speculative resources (uranium) Uranium in addition to Estimated Additional Resources (EAR) that is thought to exist, mostly on the basis of indirect evidence and geological extrapolations, in deposits discoverable with existing exploration techniques. The locations of deposits in this category can generally be specified only as being somewhere within given regions or geological trends. The existence and size of such deposits are speculative. The estimates in this category are less reliable than estimates of EAR. SR corresponds to DOE's Possible Potential Resources plus Speculative Potential Resources categories.

Spent fuel Irradiated fuel that is permanently discharged from a reactor. Except for possible reprocessing, this fuel must eventually be removed from its temporary storage location at the reactor site and placed in a permanent repository. Spent fuel is typically measured either in metric tons of heavy metal (i.e., only the heavy metal content of the spent fuel is considered) or in metric tons of initial heavy metal (essentially, the initial mass of the fuel before irradiation). The difference between these two quantities is the weight of the fission products.

Spent fuel disassembly hardware The skeleton of a fuel assembly after the fuel rods have been removed. Generally, SFD hardware for PWR assemblies includes guide tubes; instrument tubes, top and bottom nozzles; grid spacers; hold-down springs; and attachment components, such as nuts and locking caps. For BWR fuel assemblies, SFD hardware includes the top and bottom tie plates, compression springs for individual fuel rods, grid spacers, and water rods.

Spent liquor The liquid residue left after an industrial process; can be a component of waste materials used as fuel.

Spillway A passage for surplus water to flow over or around a dam.

Spinning reserve That reserve generating capacity running at a zero load and synchronized to the electric system.

Split system When applied to electric air-conditioning equipment, it means a two-part system—an indoor unit and an outdoor unit. The indoor unit is an evaporator coil mounted in the indoor circulating air system, and the outdoor unit is an air-cooled condensing unit containing an electric motor-driven compressor, a condenser fan, and a fan motor.

Split tails Use of one tails assay for transaction of enrichment services and a different tails assay for operation of the enrichment plant. This mode of operations typically increases the use of uranium, which is relatively inexpensive, while decreasing the use of separative work, which is expensive.

Spontaneous combustion, or self-heating, of coal A naturally occurring process caused by the oxidation of coal. It is most common in low-rank coals and is a potential problem in storing and transporting coal for extended periods. Factors involved in spontaneous combustion include the size of the coal (the smaller sizes are more susceptible), the moisture content, and the sulfur content. Heat buildup in stored coal can degrade the quality of coal, cause it to smolder, and lead to a fire.

Spot market (natural gas) A market in which natural gas is bought and sold for immediate or very near-term delivery, usually for a period of 30 days or less. The transaction does not imply a continuing arrangement between the buyer and the seller. A spot market is more likely to develop at a location with numerous pipeline interconnections, thus allowing for a large number of buyers and sellers. The Henry Hub in southern Louisiana is the best known spot market for natural gas.

Spot market (uranium) Buying and selling of uranium for immediate or very near-term delivery. It typically involves transactions for delivery of up to 500,000 pounds U_3O_8 within a year of contract execution.

Spot-market price See **spot price** below.

Spot price The price for a one-time open market transaction for near-term delivery of a specific quantity of product at a specific location where the commodity is purchased "on the spot" at current market rates. See also spot market terms associated with specific energy types.

Spot purchases A single shipment of fuel or volumes of fuel purchased for delivery within 1 year. Spot purchases are often made by a user to fulfill a certain portion of energy requirements, to meet unanticipated energy needs, or to take advantage of low-fuel prices.

SPR See **Strategic Petroleum Reserve** (below).

Stabilization lagoon A shallow artificial pond used for the treatment of wastewater. Treatment includes removal of solid material through sedimentation, the decomposition of organic material by bacteria, and the removal of nutrients by algae.

Stability (electric) The ability of an electric system to maintain a state of equilibrium during normal and abnormal conditions or disturbances. (NERC definition)

Stack A tall, vertical structure containing one or more flues used to discharge products of combustion to the atmosphere.

Stand-alone generator A power source/generator that operates independently of or is not connected to an electric transmission and distribution network; used to meet a load(s) physically close to the generator.

Standard contract The agreement between the Department of Energy (DOE) and the owners or generators of spent nuclear fuel and high-level radioactive waste, under which DOE will make available nuclear waste disposal services to those owners and generators.

Standard fluorescent A light bulb made of a glass tube coated on the inside with fluorescent material, which produces light by passing electricity through mercury vapor causing the fluorescent coating to glow or fluoresce.

Standard Industrial Classification (SIC) Replaced with North American Industry Classification System. See NAICS.

Standby charge A charge for the potential use of a utility service, usually done by an agreement with another electric utility service. These services include system backup support and other running and quick-start capabilities.

Standby electricity generation Involves use of generators during times of high demand on utilities to avoid extra "peak-demand" charges.

Standby facility A facility that supports a utility system and is generally running under no-load. It is available to replace or supplement a facility normally in service.

Standby heat loss A term used to describe heat energy lost from a water heater tank.

Standby service Support service that is available as needed to supplement a customer, a utility system, or another utility if a schedule or an agreement authorizes the transaction. The service is not regularly used.

Startup test phase of nuclear power plant A nuclear power plant that has been licensed by the Nuclear Regulatory Commission to operate but is still in the initial testing phase, during which the production of electricity may not be continuous. In general, when the electric utility is satisfied with the plant's performance, it formally accepts the plant from the manufacturer and places it in commercial operation status. A request is then submitted to the appropriate utility rate commission to include the power plant in the rate base calculation.

Startup/flame stabilization fuel Any fuel used to initiate or sustain combustion or used to stabilize the height of flames once combustion is underway.

State One of the 50 States, including adjacent outer continental shelf areas, or the District of Columbia.

State permit/license/mine number Code assigned to a mining operation by the state in which the operation is located.

State severance taxes Any severance, production, or similar tax, fee, or other levy imposed on the production of crude oil, natural gas, or coal by any State, local government acting under authority of State law, or by an Indian tribe recognized as eligible for services by the Secretary of the Interior.

Station (electric) A plant containing prime movers, electric generators, and auxiliary equipment for converting mechanical, chemical, and/or nuclear energy into electric energy.

Station use Energy that is used to operate an electric generating plant. It includes energy consumed for plant lighting, power, and auxiliary facilities, regardless of whether the energy is produced at the plant or comes from another source.

Steam Water in vapor form; used as the working fluid in steam turbines and heating systems. Also see District heat.

Steam (purchased) Steam, purchased for use by a refinery, that was not generated from within the refinery complex.

Steam boiler A type of furnace in which fuel is burned and the heat is used to produce steam.

Steam coal All nonmetallurgical coal.

Steam electric power plant (conventional) A plant in which the prime mover is a steam turbine. The steam used to drive the turbine is produced in a boiler where fossil fuels are burned.

Steam expenses The cost of labor, materials, fuel, and other expenses incurred in production of steam for electric generation.

Steam for heating/cooling Steam produced at a combined heat and power plant for the purpose of heating and/or cooling space, such as district heating systems.

Steam from other sources Steam purchased, transferred from another department of the utility, or acquired from others under a joint-facility operating agreement.

Steam or hot water radiators or baseboards A distribution system where steam or hot water circulates through cast-iron radiators or baseboards. Some other types of equipment in the building may be used to produce the steam or hot water or it may enter the building already heated as part of a district hot water system. Hot water does not include domestic hot water used for cooking and cleaning.

Steam or hot-water system Either of two types of a central space-heating system that supplies steam or hot water to radiators, convectors, or pipes. The more common type supplies either steam or hot water to conventional radiators, baseboard radiators, convectors, heating pipes embedded in the walls or ceilings, or heating coils or equipment that are part of a combined heating/ventilating or heating/air-conditioning system. The other type supplies radiant heat through pipes that carry hot water and are held in a concrete slab floor.

Steam transferred-credit The expenses of producing steam are charged to others or to other utility departments under a joint operating arrangement.

Steam turbine A device that converts high-pressure steam, produced in a boiler, into mechanical energy that can then be used to produce electricity by forcing blades in a cylinder to rotate and turn a generator shaft.

Still gas (refinery gas) Any form or mixture of gases produced in refineries by distillation, cracking, reforming, and other processes. The principal constituents are methane, ethane, ethylene, normal butane, butylene, propane, propylene, etc. Still gas is used as a refinery fuel and a petrochemical feedstock. The conversion factor is 6 million BTU's per fuel oil equivalent barrel.

Stock change The difference between stocks at the beginning of the reporting period and stocks at the end of the reporting period. *Note*: A negative number indicates a decrease (i.e., a drawdown) in stocks and a positive number indicates an increase (i.e., a buildup) in stocks during the reporting period.

Stocks Inventories of fuel stored for future use.

Storage additions Volumes of gas injected or otherwise added to underground natural gas reservoirs or liquefied natural gas storage.

Storage agreement Any contractual arrangement between the responding company and a storage operator under which gas was stored for, or gas storage service was provided to, the responding company by the storage operator, irrespective of any responding company ownership interest in either the storage facilities or stored gas.

Storage capacity The amount of energy an energy storage device or system can store.

Storage field capacity (underground gas storage) The presently developed maximum capacity of a field (as collected on EIA Survey Form 191).

Storage hydroelectric plant A hydroelectric plant with reservoir storage capacity for power use.

Storage site Spent nuclear fuel storage pool or dry cask storage facility, usually located at the reactor site, as licensed by (or proposed to be licensed by) the Nuclear Regulatory Commission (NRC).

Storage withdrawals Total volume of gas withdrawn from underground storage or from liquefied natural gas storage over a specified amount of time.

Storm door A second door installed outside or inside a prime door creating an insulating air space. Included are sliding glass doors made of double glass or of insulating glass such as thermopane and sliding glass doors with glass or Plexiglas placed on either the outside or inside of the door to create an insulating air space. Not included are doors or sliding glass doors covered by plastic sheets or doors with storm window covering on just the glass portion of the door.

Storm or multiple glazing A building shell conservation feature consisting of storm windows, storm doors, or double- or triple-paned glass that are placed on the exterior of the building to reduce the rate of heat loss.

Storm window A window or glazing material placed outside or inside a window creating an insulating air space. Plastic material over windows is counted a a storm window if the same plastic material can be used year after year or if the plastic is left in place year-round and is in good condition (no holes or tears). If the plastic material must be put up new each year, it is not counted as a storm window. It is counted as "plastic coverings." Glass or Plexiglas placed over windows on either the interior or exterior side is counted as storm windows.

Stranded benefits Benefits associated with regulated retail electric service which may be at risk under open market retail competition. Examples include conservation programs, fuel diversity, reliability of supply, and tax revenues based on utility revenues.

Stranded costs Costs incurred by a utility which may not be recoverable under market-based retail competition. Examples include undepreciated generating facilities, deferred costs, and long-term contract costs.

Strategic Petroleum Reserve (SPR) Petroleum stocks maintained by the Federal Government for use during periods of major supply interruption.

Stratigraphic test well A geologically directed drilling effort to obtain information pertaining to a specific geological condition that might lead toward the discovery of an accumulation of hydrocarbons. Such wells are customarily drilled without the intention of being completed for hydrocarbon production. This classification also includes tests identified as core tests and all types of expendable holes related to hydrocarbon exploration.

Stratosphere The region of the upper atmosphere extending from the tropopause (8 to 15 kilometers altitude) to about 50 kilometers. Its thermal structure, which is determined by its radiation balance, is generally very stable with low humidity.

Stream-flow The rate at which water passes a given point in a stream, usually expressed in cubic feet per second.

Strip mine An open cut in which the overburden is removed from a coal bed prior to the removal of coal.

Strip mining (surface) A method used on flat terrain to recover coal by mining long strips successively; the material excavated from the strip being mined is deposited in the strip previously mined.

Strip or stripping ratio The amount of overburden that must be removed to gain access to a unit amount of coal. A stripping ratio may be expressed as (1) thickness of overburden to thickness of coal, (2) volume of overburden to volume coal, (3) weight of overburden to weight of coal, or (4) cubic yards of overburden to tons of coal. A stripping ratio commonly is used to express the maximum thickness, volume, or weight of overburden that can be profitably removed to obtain a unit amount of coal.

Stripper well An oil or gas well that produces at relatively low rates. For oil, stripper production is usually defined as production rates of between 5 and 15 barrels of oil per day. Stripper gas production would generally be anything less than 60 thousand cubic feet per day.

Styrene A colorless, toxic liquid with a strong aromatic aroma. Insoluble in water, soluble in alcohol and ether; polymerizes rapidly; can become explosive. Used to make polymers and copolymers, polystyrene plastics, and rubber.

Subbituminous coal A coal whose properties range from those of lignite to those of bituminous coal and used primarily as fuel for steam-electric power generation. It may be dull, dark brown to black, soft and crumbly, at the lower end of the range, to bright, jet black, hard, and relatively strong, at the upper end. Subbituminous coal contains 20 to 30 percent inherent moisture by weight. The heat content of subbituminous coal ranges from 17 to 24 million Btu per ton on a moist, mineral-matter-free basis. The heat content of subbituminous coal consumed in the United States averages 17 to 18 million Btu per ton, on the as-received basis (i.e., containing both inherent moisture and mineral matter).

Subcompact/compact passenger car A passenger car containing less than 109 cubic feet of interior passenger and luggage volume.

Subdivision A prescribed portion of a given State or other geographical region.

Submetered data End-use consumption data obtained for individual appliances when a recording device has been attached to the appliance to measure the amount of energy consumed by the appliance.

Subsidiary An entity directly or indirectly controlled by a parent company which owns 50% or more of its voting stock.

Substation Facility equipment that switches, changes, or regulates electric voltage.

Subtransmission : A set of transmission lines of voltages between transmission voltages and distribution voltages. Generally, lines in the voltage range of 69 kV to 138 kV.

Sulfur A yellowish nonmetallic element, sometimes known as "brimstone." It is present at various levels of concentration in many fossil fuels whose combustion releases sulfur compounds that are considered harmful to the environment. Some of the most commonly used fossil fuels are categorized according to their sulfur content, with lower sulfur fuels usually selling at a higher price. *Note:* No. 2 Distillate fuel is currently reported as having either a 0.05 percent or lower sulfur level for on-highway vehicle use or a greater than 0.05 percent sulfur level for off-highway use, home heating oil, and commercial and industrial uses. Residual fuel, regardless of use, is classified as having either no more than 1 percent sulfur or greater than 1 percent sulfur. Coal is also classified as being low-sulfur at concentrations of 1 percent or less or high-sulfur at concentrations greater than 1 percent.

Sulfur dioxide (SO$_2$) A toxic, irritating, colorless gas soluble in water, alcohol, and ether. Used as a chemical intermediate, in paper pulping and ore refining, and as a solvent.

Sulfur hexafluoride (SF$_6$) A colorless gas soluble in alcohol and ether, and slightly less soluble in water. It is used as a dielectric in electronics. It possesses the highest 100-year Global Warming Potential of any gas (23,900).

Sulfur oxides (SO$_x$) Compounds containing sulfur and oxygen, such as sulfur dioxide (SO$_2$) and sulfur trioxide (SO$_3$).

Summer and winter peaking Having the annual peak demand reached both during the summer months (May through October) and during the winter months (November through April).

Sunk cost Part of the capital costs actually incurred up to the date of reserves estimation minus depreciation and amortization expenses. Items such as exploration costs, land acquisition costs, and costs of financing can be included.

Superconductivity The abrupt and large increase in electrical conductivity exhibited by some metals as the temperature approaches absolute zero.

Supervisory Control and Data Acquisition (electric) A system of remote control and telemetry used to monitor and control the transmission system. (NERC definition)

Supplemental gas Any gaseous substance introduced into or commingled with natural gas that increased the volume available for disposition. Such substances include, but are not limited to, propane-air, refinery gas, coke-oven gas, still gas, manufactured gas, biomass gas, or air or inerts added for Btu stabilization.

Supplemental gaseous fuels supplies Synthetic natural gas, propane-air, coke oven gas, refinery gas, biomass gas, air injected for Btu stabilization, and manufactured gas commingled and distributed with natural gas.

Supply The components of petroleum supply are field production, refinery production, imports, and net receipts when calculated on a PAD District basis.

Supply, petroleum A set of categories used to account for how crude oil and petroleum products are transferred, distributed, or placed into the supply stream. The categories include field production, refinery production, and imports. Net receipts are also included on a Petroleum Administration for Defense (PAD) District basis to account for shipments of crude oil and petroleum products across districts.

Supply source May be a single completion, a single well, a single field with one or more reservoirs, several fields under a single gas-purchase contract, miscellaneous fields, a processing plant, or a field area; provided, however, that the geographic area encompassed by a single supply source may not be larger than the state in which the reserves are reported.

Support equipment and facilities These include, but are not limited to, seismic equipment, drilling equipment, construction and grading equipment, vehicles, repair shops, warehouses, supply points, camps, and division, district, or field offices.

Supporting structure The main supporting unit (usually a pole or tower) for transmission line conductors, insulators, and other auxiliary line equipment.

Surface drilling expenses (uranium) These include drilling, drilling roads, site preparation, geological and other technical support, sampling, and drill-hole logging costs.

Surface mine A coal-producing mine that is usually within a few hundred feet of the surface. Earth above or around the coal (overburden) is removed to expose the coalbed, which is then mined with surface excavation equipment, such as draglines, power shovels, bulldozers, loaders, and augers. It may also be known as an area, contour, open-pit, strip, or auger mine.

Surface mining equipment
- An *Auger machine* is a large, horizontal drill, generally 3 feet or more in diameter and up to about 100 feet long. It can remove coal at a rate of more than 25 tons per minute.
- A *bucket-wheel* excavator is a continuous digging machine equipped with a broom on which is mounted a rotating wheel with buckets along its edge. The buckets scoop up material, then empty onto a conveyor leading to a spoil bank. It is best suited for removing overburden that does not require blasting. This excavator is not widely used in the United States.
- A *bulldozer* is a tractor with a movable steel blade mounted on the front. It can be used to remove overburden that needs little or no blasting.
- A *carryall scraper* (or **pan scraper**) is a self-loading machine, usually self-propelled, with a scraper-like retractable bottom. It is used to excavate and haul overburden.
- A *continuous surface miner*, used in some lignite mines, is equipped with crawlers, a rotating cutting head, and a conveyor. It travels over the bed, excavating a swath up to 13 feet wide and 2 feet deep.
- A *dragline excavator* removes overburden to expose the coal by means of a scoop bucket that is suspended from a long boom. The dragline digs by pulling the bucket toward the machine by means of a wire rope.

- A *walking dragline* is equipped with large outrigger platforms, or walking beams, instead of crawler tracks. It "walks" by the alternate movement of the walking beams.
- A *drilling rig* is used to determine the amount and type of overburden overlying a coal deposit and the extent of the deposit, to delineate major geologic features, and to drill holes for explosives to fragment the overburden for easier removal.
- A *front-end loader* is a tractor with a digging bucket mounted and operated on the front. It is often used to remove overburden in contour mining and to load coal.
- An *hydraulic shovel* excavates and loads by means of a bucket attached to a rigid arm that is hinged to a broom.
- A *power shovel* removes overburden and loads coal by means of a digging bucket mounted at the end of an arm suspended from a broom. The shovel digs by pushing the bucket forward and upward. It does not dig below the level at which it stands.
- A *thin-seam miner* resembles an auger machine but has a drum-type cutting head that cuts a rectangular cross section.

Surface mining methods
- *Auger mining* recovers coal through the use of a large-diameter drill driven into a coalbed in the side of a surface mine pit. It usually follows contour surface mining, particularly when the overburden is too costly to excavate.
- *Area mining* is practiced on relatively flat or gently rolling terrain and recovers coal by mining long strips successively; the material excavated from the strip being mined is deposited in the strip pit previously mined.
- *Contour mining* is practiced when the coal is mined on hillsides. The mining follows the contour of the hillside until the overburden becomes uneconomical to remove. This method creates a shelf, or bench, on the hillside. Several variations of contour mining have been developed to control environmental problems. These methods include slope reduction (overburden is spread so that the angle of the slope on the hillside is reduced), head-of-hollow fill (overburden is placed in narrow V-shaped valleys to control erosion), and block-cut (overburden from current mining is backfilled into a previously mined cut).
- *Explosives casting* is a technique designed to blast up to 65 percent of the overburden into the mine pit for easier removal. It differs from conventional overburden blasting, which only fractures the overburden before it is removed by excavating equipment.
- **Mountaintop mining** sometimes considered a variation of contour mining, refers to the mining of a coalbed that underlies the top of a mountain. The overburden, which is the mountaintop, is completely removed so that all of the coal can be recovered. The overburden material is later replaced in the mined-out area. This method leaves large plateaus of level land.
- **Open-pit** coal mining is essentially a combination of contour and area mining methods and is used to mine thick, steeply inclined coalbeds. The overburden is removed by power shovels and trucks.

Surface rights Fee ownership in surface areas of land. Also used to describe a lessee's right to use as much of the surface of the land as may be reasonably necessary for the conduct of operations under the lease.

Surplus energy Energy generated that is beyond the immediate needs of the producing system. This energy may be supplied by spinning reserve and sold on an interruptible basis.

Suspended rates New rates that have been accepted for review by a utility commission. When these rates are suspended, they do not go into effect for a designated period of time. Charges under the new rate may be refunded after the resolution of the rate proceeding.

Swamp coolers (evaporative coolers) Air-conditioning equipment that removes heat by evaporating water. Evaporative cooling techniques are most commonly found in warm, dry climates such as in the Southwest, although they are found throughout the country. They usually work by spraying cool water into the air ducts, cooling the air as the spray evaporates.

Switching station Facility equipment used to tie together two or more electric circuits through switches. The switches are selectively arranged to permit a circuit to be disconnected or to change the electric connection between the circuits.

Synthetic natural gas (SNG) (Also referred to as substitute natural gas) A manufactured product, chemically similar in most respects to natural gas, resulting from the conversion or reforming of hydrocarbons that may easily be substituted for or interchanged with pipeline-quality natural gas.

System (gas) An interconnected network of pipes, valves, meters, storage facilities, and auxiliary equipment used in the transportation, storage, and/or distribution of natural gas or commingled natural and supplemental gas.

System (electric) Physically connected generation, transmission, and distribution facilities operated as an integrated unit under one central management or operating supervision.

System interconnection A physical connection between two electric systems that permits the transfer of electric energy in either direction.

System Operator (electric) An individual at a control center (Balancing Authority, Transmission Operator, Generator Operator, Reliability Coordinator) whose responsibility it is to monitor and control that electric system in real time. (NERC definition)

Tailgate The outlet of a natural gas processing plant where dry residue gas is delivered or re-delivered for sale or transportation.

Tailings The remaining portion of a metal-bearing ore consisting of finely ground rock and process liquid after some or all of the metal, such as uranium, has been extracted.

Tall oil The oily mixture of rosin acids, fatty acids, and other materials obtained by acid treatment of the alkaline liquors from the digesting (pulping) of pine wood.

TAME See Tertiary amyl methyl ether below.

Tangible development costs Costs incurred during the development stage for access, mineral-handling, and support facilities having a physical nature. In mining, such costs would include tracks, lighting equipment, ventilation equipment, other equipment installed in the mine to facilitate the extraction of minerals, and supporting facilities for housing and care of work forces. In the oil and gas industry, tangible development costs would include well equipment (such as casing, tubing, pumping equipment, and well heads), as well as field storage tanks and gathering systems.

Tank farm An installation used by trunk and gathering pipeline companies, crude oil producers, and terminal operators (except refineries) to store crude oil.

Tanker and barge Vessels that transport crude oil or petroleum products. *Note* Data are reported for movements between PAD Districts; from a PAD District to the Panama Canal; or from the Panama Canal to a PAD District.

Tar sands Naturally occurring bitumen-impregnated sands that yield mixtures of liquid hydrocarbon and that require further processing other than mechanical blending before becoming finished petroleum products.

Tariff A published volume of rate schedules and general terms and conditions under which a product or service will be supplied.

Tax-cost A deduction (allowance) under U.S. Federal income taxation normally calculated under a formula whereby the adjusted basis of the mineral property is multiplied by a fraction, the numerator of which is the number of units of minerals sold during the tax year and the denominator of which is the estimated number of units of unextracted minerals remaining at the end of the tax year plus the number of units of minerals sold during the tax year.

Telemetering (electric) The process by which measurable electrical quantities from substations and generating stations are instantaneously transmitted to the control center, and, by which, operating commands from the control center are transmitted to the substations and generating stations. (NERC definition)

Temperature coefficient (of a solar photovoltaic cell) The amount that the voltage, current, and/or power output of a solar cell changes due to a change in the cell temperature.

Temporarily discharged fuel Fuel that was irradiated in the previous fuel cycle (cycle N) and not in the following fuel cycle (cycle N+1) and that will be irradiated in a subsequent fuel cycle.

Tennessee Valley Authority (TVA) A federal agency established in 1933 to develop the Tennessee river valley region of the southeastern U.S.

Terawatthour One trillion watthours.

Term agreement Any written or unwritten agreement between two parties in which one party agrees to supply a commodity on a continuing basis to a second party for a price or for other considerations.

Terminal location The physical location of one end of a transmission line segment.

Tertiary amyl methyl ether — $(CH_3)_2(C_2H_5)COCH_3$ An oxygenate blend stock formed by the catalytic etherification of isoamylene with methanol.

Tertiary butyl alcohol — $(CH_3)_3COH$ An alcohol primarily used as a chemical feedstock or a solvent or feedstock, for isobutylene production for MTBE (methyl tertiary butyl ether) and produced as a co-product of propylene oxide production or by direct hydration of isobutylene.

Test well contribution A payment made to the owner of an adjacent or nearby tract who has drilled an exploratory well on that tract in exchange for information obtained from the drilling effort.

Therm One hundred thousand (100,000) Btu.

Thermal A term used to identify a type of electric generating station, capacity, capability, or output in which the source of energy for the prime mover is heat.

Thermal conversion factor A factor for converting data between physical units of measure (such as barrels, cubic feet, or short tons) and thermal units of measure (such as British thermal units, calories, or joules); or for converting data between different thermal units of measure. See Btu conversion factor.

Thermal cracking A refining process in which heat and pressure are used to break down, rearrange, or combine hydrocarbon molecules. Thermal-cracking includes gas oil, visbreaking, fluid coking, delayed coking, and other thermal cracking processes (e.g., flexicoking).

Thermal efficiency A measure of the efficiency of converting a fuel to energy and useful work; useful work and energy output divided by higher heating value of input fuel times 100 (for percent).

Thermal energy storage The storage of heat energy during utility off-peak times at night, for use during the next day without incurring daytime peak electric rates.

Thermal limit The maximum amount of power a transmission line can carry without suffering heat-related deterioration of line equipment, particularly conductors.

Thermal Rating (electric) The maximum amount of electrical current that a transmission line or electrical facility can conduct over a specified time period before it sustains permanent damage by overheating or before it sags to the point that it violates public safety requirements. (NERC definition)

Thermal resistance (R-Value) This designates the resistance of a material to heat conduction. The greater the R-value the larger the number.

Thermal storage Storage of heat or heat sinks (coldness) for later heating or cooling. Examples are the storage of solar energy for night heating; the storage of summer heat for winter use; the storage of winter ice for space cooling in the summer; and the storage of electrically-generated heat or coolness when electricity is less expensive, to be released in order to avoid using electricity when the rates are higher. There are four basic types of thermal storage systems: ice storage; water storage; storage in rock, soil or other types of solid thermal mass; and storage in other materials, such as glycol (antifreeze).

Thermocouple A device consisting of two dissimilar conductors with their ends connected together. When the two junctions are at different temperatures, a small voltage is generated.

Thermodynamics A study of the transformation of energy from one form to another, and its practical application.

Thermophotovoltaic cell A device where sunlight concentrated onto a absorber heats it to a high temperature, and the thermal radiation emitted by the absorber is used as the energy source for a photovoltaic cell that is designed to maximize conversion efficiency at the wavelength of the thermal radiation.

Thermosiphon system A solar collector system for water heating in which circulation of the collection fluid through the storage loop is provided solely by the temperature and density difference between the hot and cold fluids.

Thermostat A device that adjusts the amount of heating and cooling produced and/or distributed by automatically responding to the temperature in the environment.

Third-party transactions Third-party transactions are arms-length transactions between nonaffiliated firms. Producing country-to-company transactions are not considered to be third-party transactions.

Third-party DSM program sponsor An energy service company (ESCO) which promotes a program sponsored by a manufacturer or distributor of energy products such as lighting or refrigeration whose goal is to encourage consumers to improve energy efficiency, reduce energy costs, change the time of usage, or promote the use of a different energy source.

Thorium An element that is a byproduct of the decay of uranium.

Three-phase power Power generated and transmitted from generator to load on three conductors.

Tidewater piers and coastal ports (method of transportation to consumers) Shipments of coal moved to tidewater piers and coastal ports for further shipments to consumers via coastal water or ocean.

Tie line (electric) A circuit connecting two Balancing Authority Areas. Also, describes circuits within an individual electrical system. (NERC definition)

Time clocks or timed switches Time clocks are automatic controls, which turn lights off and on at predetermined times.

Time-of-day lock-out or limit A special electric rate feature under which electricity usage is prohibited or restricted to a reduced level at fixed times of the day in return for a reduction in the price per kilowatthour.

Time-of-day pricing A special electric rate feature under which the price per kilowatthour depends on the time of day.

Time-of-day rate The rate charged by an electric utility for service to various classes of customers. The rate reflects the different costs of providing the service at different times of the day.

Timing differences Differences between the periods in which transactions affect taxable income and the periods in which they enter into the determination of pretax accounting income. Timing differences originate in one period and reverse or "turn around" in one or more subsequent periods. Some timing differences reduce income taxes that would otherwise be payable currently; others increase income taxes that would otherwise be payable currently.

Tinted or reflective glass or shading films Types of glass or a shading film applied to glass that, when installed on the exterior of a building, reduces the rates of solar penetration into the building. Includes Low E Glass.

Tipping fee Price charged to deliver municipal solid waste to a landfill, waste-to-energy facility, or recycling facility.

Tipple A central facility used in loading coal for transportation by rail or truck.

Tolling arrangement Contract arrangement under which a raw material or intermediate product stream from one company is delivered to the production facility of another company in exchange for the equivalent volume of finished products and payment of a processing fee.

Toluene ($C_6H_5CH_3$) Colorless liquid of the aromatic group of petroleum hydrocarbons, made by the catalytic reforming of petroleum naphthas containing methyl cyclohexane. A high-octane gasoline-blending agent, solvent, and chemical intermediate, and a base for TNT (explosive).

Ton mile The product of the distance that freight is hauled, measured in miles, and the weight of the cargo being hauled, measured in tons. Thus, moving one ton for one mile generates one ton mile.

Topping cycle A boiler produces steam to power a turbine-generator to produce electricity. The steam leaving the turbine is used in thermal applications such as space heating and/or cooling or delivered to other end user(s).

Total discoveries The sum of extensions, new reservoir discoveries in old fields, and new field discoveries, that occurred during the report year.

Total gas in storage The sum of base gas and working gas.

Total liquid hydrocarbon reserves The sum of crude oil and natural gas liquids reserves volumes.

Total operated basis The total reserves or production associated with the wells operated by an individual operator. This is also commonly known as the "gross operated" or "8/8ths" basis.

Transfer capability The overall capacity of inter-regional or international power lines, together with the associated electrical system facilities, to transfer power and energy from one electrical system to another.

Transfer price The monetary value assigned to products, services, or rights conveyed or exchanged between related parties, including those occurring between units of a consolidated entity.

Transformer An electrical device for changing the voltage of alternating current.

Transmission and distribution loss Electric energy lost due to the transmission and distribution of electricity. Much of the loss is thermal in nature.

Transmission (electric) An interconnected group of lines and associated equipment for the movement or transfer of electric energy between points of supply and points at which it is transformed for delivery to customers or is delivered to other electric systems. (NERC definition)

Transmission circuit A conductor used to transport electricity from generating stations to load.

Transmission constraint (electric) A limitation on one or more transmission elements that may be reached during normal or contingency system operations. (NERC definition)

Transmission line (electric) A system of structures, wires, insulators and associated hardware that carry electric energy from one point to another in an electric power system. Lines are operated at relatively high voltages varying from 69 kV up to 765 kV, and are capable of transmitting large quantities of electricity over long distances. (NERC definition)

Transmission network A system of transmission or distribution lines so cross-connected and operated as to permit multiple power supply to any principal point.

Transmission operator (electric) The entity responsible for the reliability of its localized transmission system, and that operates or directs the operations of the transmission facilities. (NERC definition)

Transmission owner (electric) The entity that owns and maintains transmission facilities. (NERC definition)

Transmission Service Provider (electric) The entity that administers the transmission tariff and provides Transmission Service to Transmission Customers under applicable transmission service agreements. (NERC definition)

Transmission system (electric) An interconnected group of electric transmission lines and associated equipment for moving or transferring electric energy in bulk between points of supply and points at which it is transformed for delivery over the distribution system lines to consumers or is delivered to other electric systems.

Transmission type (engine) The transmission is the part of a vehicle that transmits motive force from the engine to the wheels, usually by means of gears for different speeds using either a hydraulic "torque-converter" (automatic) or clutch assembly (manual). On front-wheel drive cars, the transmission is often called a "transaxle." Fuel efficiency is usually higher with manual rather than automatic transmissions, although modern, computer-controlled automatic transmissions can be efficient.

Transmitting utility A regulated entity which owns and may construct and maintain wires used to transmit wholesale power. It may or may not handle the power dispatch and coordination functions. It is regulated to provide non-discriminatory connections, comparable service, and cost recovery. According to the Energy Policy Act of 1992, it includes any electric utility, qualifying cogeneration facility, qualifying small power production facility, or Federal power marketing agency which owns or operates electric power transmission facilities which are used for the sale of electric energy at wholesale.

Transport Movement of natural, synthetic, and/or supplemental gas between points beyond the immediate vicinity of the field or plant from which produced except (1) for movements through well or field lines to a central point for delivery to a pipeline or processing plant within the same state or (2) movements from a citygate point of receipt to consumers through distribution mains.

Transportation agreement Any contractual agreement for the transportation of natural and/or supplemental gas between points for a fee.

Transportation energy expenditures See Vehicle fuel expenditures.

Transportation sector An energy-consuming sector that consists of all vehicles whose primary purpose is transporting people and/or goods from one physical location to another. Included are automobiles; trucks; buses; motorcycles; trains, subways, and other rail vehicles; aircraft; and ships, barges, and other waterborne vehicles. Vehicles whose primary purpose is not transportation (e.g., construction cranes and bulldozers, farming vehicles, and warehouse tractors and forklifts) are classified in the sector of their primary use. *Note*: Various EIA programs differ in sectoral coverage.

Transported gas Natural gas physically delivered to a building by a local utility, but not purchased from that utility. A separate transaction is made to purchase the volume of gas, and the utility is paid for the use of its pipeline to deliver the gas. Also called "Direct-Purchase Gas," "Spot Market Gas," "Spot Gas," "Gas for the Account of Others," and "Self-Help Gas."

Transporter The party or parties, other than buyer or seller, owning the facilities by which gas or LNG is physically transferred between buyer and seller.

Transshipment A method of ocean transportation whereby ships off-load their oil cargo to a deepwater terminal, floating storage facility, temporary storage, or to one or more smaller tankers from which or in which the oil is then transported to a market destination.

Treating plant A plant designed primarily to remove undesirable impurities from natural gas to render the gas marketable.

Trillion Btu Equivalent to 1,000,000,000,000 or 10 to the 12th power Btu.

Troposphere The inner layer of the atmosphere below about 15 kilometers, within which there is normally a steady decrease of temperature with increasing altitude. Nearly all clouds form and weather conditions manifest themselves within this region. Its thermal structure is caused primarily by the heating of the earth's surface by solar radiation, followed by heat transfer through turbulent mixing and convection.

Trough High-temperature (180+) concentrator with one axis-tracking.

Trunk line A main pipeline.

Turbine A machine for generating rotary mechanical power from the energy of a stream of fluid (such as water, steam, or hot gas). Turbines convert the kinetic energy of fluids to mechanical energy through the principles of impulse and reaction, or a mixture of the two.

Type of drive (vehicle) Refers to which wheels the engine power is delivered to, the so-called "drive wheels." Rear-wheel drive has drive wheels on the rear of the vehicle. Front-wheel drive, a newer technology, has drive wheels on the front of the vehicle. Four-wheel drive uses all four wheels as drive wheels and is found mostly on Jeep-like vehicles and trucks, though it is becoming increasingly more common on station wagons and vans.

Ultimate customer A customer that purchases electricity for its own use and not for resale.

Ultra-low sulfur diesel (ULSD) fuel Diesel fuel containing a maximum 15 parts per million (ppm) sulfur.

Ultraviolet Electromagnetic radiation in the wavelength range of 4 to 400 nanometers.

Unaccounted for (crude oil) Represents the arithmetic difference between the calculated supply and the calculated disposition of crude oil. The calculated supply is the sum of crude oil production plus imports minus changes in crude oil stocks. The calculated disposition of crude oil is the sum of crude oil input to refineries, crude oil exports, crude oil burned as fuel, and crude oil losses.

Unaccounted for (natural gas) Represents differences between the sum of the components of natural gas supply and the sum of components of natural gas disposition. These differences may be due to quantities lost or to the effects of data reporting problems. Reporting problems include differences due to the net result of conversions of flow data metered at varying temperatures and pressure bases and converted to a standard temperature and pressure base; the effect of variations in company accounting and billing practices; differences between billing cycle and calendar-period time frames; and imbalances resulting from the merger of data reporting systems that vary in scope, format, definitions, and type of respondents.

Unbundling Separating vertically integrated monopoly functions into their component parts for the purpose of separate service offerings.

Uncompleted wells, equipment, and facilities costs The costs incurred to (1) drill and equip wells that are not yet completed, and (2) acquire or construct equipment and facilities that are not yet completed and installed.

Unconsolidated entity A firm directly or indirectly controlled by a parent but not consolidated with the parent for purposes of financial statements prepared in accordance with generally accepted accounting principles. An unconsolidated entity includes any firm consolidated with the unconsolidated entity for purposes of financial statements prepared in accordance with generally accepted accounting principles historically and consistently applied. An individual shall be deemed to control a firm that is directly or indirectly controlled by him or by his father, mother, spouse, children, or grandchildren.

Unconventional oil and natural gas production An umbrella term for oil and natural gas that is produced by means that do not meet the criteria for conventional production. See Conventional oil and natural gas production. Note: What has qualified as "unconventional" at any particular time is a complex interactive function of resource characteristics, the available exploration and production technologies, the current economic environment, and the scale, frequency, and duration of production from the resource. Perceptions of these factors inevitably change over time and they often differ among users of the term. For these reasons, the scope of this term will be expressly stated in any EIA publication that uses it. For example, see International Energy Outlook, Table E4 for the list it currently uses for unconventional oil and natural gas production.

Underground gas storage The use of sub-surface facilities for storing gas that has been transferred from its original location. The facilities are usually hollowed-out salt domes, geological reservoirs (depleted oil or gas fields) or water-bearing sands topped by an impermeable cap rock (aquifer).

Underground gas storage reservoir capacity Interstate company reservoir capacities are those certificated by the Federal Energy Regulatory Commission. Independent producer and intrastate company reservoir capacities are reported as developed capacity.

Underground mine A mine where coal is produced by tunneling into the earth to the coalbed, which is then mined with underground mining equipment such as cutting machines and continuous, longwall, and shortwall mining machines. Underground mines are classified according to the type of opening used to reach the coal, i.e., drift (level tunnel), slope (inclined tunnel), or shaft (vertical tunnel).

Underground mining equipment

A *coal-cutting machine* is used in conventional mining to undercut, topcut, or shear the coal face so that coal can be fractured easily when blasted. It cuts 9 to 13 feet into the bed.

Continuous auger machine is used in mining coalbeds less than 3 feet thick. The auger has a cutting depth of about 5 feet and is 20 to 28 inches in diameter. Continuous auger mining usually uses a conveyor belt to haul the coal to the surface.

Continuous mining machine , used during continuous mining, cuts or rips coal from the face and loads it into shuttle cars or conveyors in one operation. It eliminates the use of blasting devices and performs many functions of other equipment such as drills, cutting machines, and loaders. A continuous mining machine typically has a turning "drum" with sharp bits that cut and dig out the coal for 16 to 22 feet before mining stops so that the mined area can be supported with roof bolts. This machine can mine coal at the rate of 8 to 15 tons per minute.

There are of two types of conveyor systems:
(1) A *mainline conveyor*, which is usually a permanent installation that carries coal to the surface.
(2) A *section conveyor*, which connects the working face to the mainline conveyor.

Face drill is used in conventional mining to drill shotholes in the coalbed for explosive charges.

Loading machine is used in conventional mining to scoop broken coal from the working area and load it into a shuttle car, which hauls the coal to mine cars or conveyors for delivery to the surface.

Longwall mining machine shears coal from a long straight coal face (up to about 700 feet) by working back and forth across the face under a movable, hydraulic-jack roof-support system. The broken coal is transported by converyor. Longwall machines can mine coal at the rate of 1,000 tons per shift.

Mine locomotive , operating on tracks, is used to haul mine cars containing coal and other material, and to move personnel in specially designed "mantrip" cars. Large locomotives can haul more than 20 tons at a speed of about 10 miles per hour. Most mine locomotives run on electricity provided by a trolley wire; some are battery-powered.

Ram car or shuttle ram is a rubber-tired haulage vehicle that is unloaded through the use of a movable steel plate located at the back of the haulage bed.

Roof-bolting machine, or roof bolter , is used to drill holes and place bolts to support the mine roof. Roof bolting units can be installed on a continuous mining machine.

Scoop is a rubber-tired haulage vehicle used in thin coalbeds.

Shortwall mining machine generally is a continuous-mining machine used with a powered, self-advancing roof support system. It shears coal from a short coal face (up to about 150 feet long). The broken coal is hauled by shuttle cars to a conveyor belt.

Shuttle car is a rubber-tired haulage vehicle that is unloaded by a built-in conveyor.

Underground mining methods
- A *drift mine* is driven horizontally into coal that is exposed or accessible in a hillside. In a hydraulic mine, high-pressure water jets break the coal from a steeply inclined, thick coalbed that would be difficult to mine with the usual underground methods. The coal is then transported to the surface by a system of flumes or by pipeline. Although currently not in commercial use in the United States, hydraulic mining is used in western Canada.
- A *punch mine* is a type of small drift mine used to recover coal from strip-mine highwalls or from small, otherwise uneconomical, coal deposits. A shaft mine is driven vertically to the coal deposit. A slope mine is driven at an angle to reach the coal deposit.
- In a *room-and-pillar mining* system, the most common method, the mine roof, is supported mainly by coal pillars left at regular intervals. Rooms are places where the coal is mined; pillars are areas of coal left between the rooms. Room-and-pillar mining is done either by 1) conventional mining, which involves a series of operations that require cutting the working face of the coalbed so that it breaks easily when blasted with explosives or high-pressure air, and then loading the broken coal or 2) continuous mining, in which a continuous mining machine extracts and removes coal from the working face in one operation. When a section of a mine has been fully developed, additional coal is extracted by mining the supportive pillars until the roof caves in; the procedure is called room-and-pillar retreat mining.
- In a *longwall mining* system, long sections of coal, up to about 700 feet, are removed and no pillars are left to support the mined-out areas. The working area is protected by a movable, powered roof support system. The caved area (gob) compacts and, after initial subsidence, supports the overlying strata. Longwall mining is used where the coalbed is thick and generally flat, where surface subsidence is acceptable.
- A *shortwall mining* system generally refers to the room-and-pillar mining in which the working face is wider than usual but smaller (less than 150 feet) than that in longwall mining.

Roof support and mine ventilation are paramount in all underground mining operations. Roof bolting is the principal method of supporting the mine roof. In roof bolting, long bolts, 2 to 10 feet long with an expansion shell or with resin grouting are placed in the mine roof. The bolts reinforce the roof by pulling together rock strata to make a strong beam or by fastening weak strata to strong strata. Mine ventilation, accomplished with fans, is essential to supply fresh air and to remove gases and dust from the mine. To reduce the possibility of coal dust explosions, rock dust is sprayed in an underground coal mine. Rock dust is a very fine noncombustible material (pulverized limestone).

Underground storage The storage of natural gas in underground reservoirs at a different location from which it was produced.

Underground storage injections Gas from extraneous sources put into underground storage reservoirs.

Underground storage withdrawals Gas removed from underground storage reservoirs.

Undifferentiated/unspecified reserves and production Reserves and production that are not separable by FERC production areas or by states. Undifferentiated and unspecified reserves consist only of company-owned gas in underground storage.

Undiscovered recoverable reserves (crude oil and natural gas) Those economic resources of crude oil and natural gas, yet undiscovered, that are estimated to exist in favorable geologic settings.

Undiscovered resources (coal) Unspecified bodies of coal surmised to exist on the basis of broad geologic knowledge and theory. Undiscovered resources include beds of bituminous coal and anthracite 14 inches or more thick and beds of subbituminous coal and lignite 30 inches or more thick that are presumed to occur in unmapped and unexplored areas to depths of 6,000 feet. The speculative and hypothetical resource categories comprise undiscovered resources.

Unfilled requirements Requirements not covered by usage of inventory or supply contracts in existence as of January 1 of the survey year.

Unfinished oils All oils requiring further processing, except those requiring only mechanical blending. Unfinished oils are produced by partial refining of crude oil and include naphthas and lighter oils, kerosene and light gas oils, heavy gas oils, and residuum.

Unfractionated streams Mixtures of unsegregated natural gas liquid components, excluding those in plant condensate. This product is extracted from natural gas.

Unglazed solar collector A solar thermal collector that has an absorber that does not have a glazed covering. Solar swimming pool heater systems usually use unglazed collectors because they circulate relatively large volumes of water through the collector and capture nearly 80 percent of the solar energy available.

Uniform system of accounts Prescribed financial rules and regulations established by the Federal Energy Regulatory Commission for utilities subject to its jurisdiction under the authority granted by the Federal Power Act.

Union of Soviet Socialist Republics (U.S.S.R.) A political entity that consisted of 15 constituent republics: Armenia, Azerbaijan, Belarus, Estonia, Georgia, Kazakhstan, Kyrgyzstan, Latvia, Lithuania, Moldova, Russia, Tajikistan, Turkmenistan, Ukraine, and Uzbekistan. The U.S.S.R. ceased to exist as of December 31, 1991.

Unit price Total revenue derived from the sale of product during the reference month divided by the total volume sold; also known as the weighted average price. Total revenue should exclude all taxes but include transportation costs that were paid as part of the purchase price.

Unit value, consumption Total price per specified unit, including all taxes, at the point of consumption.

Unit value, wellhead The wellhead sales price, including charges for natural gas plant liquids subsequently removed from the gas; gathering and compression charges; and state production, severance, and/or similar charges.

United States The 50 States and the District of Columbia. *Note*: The United States has varying degrees of jurisdiction over a number of territories and other political entities outside the 50 States and the District of Columbia, including Puerto Rico, the U.S. Virgin Islands, Guam, American Samoa, Johnston Atoll, Midway Islands, Wake Island, and the Northern Mariana Islands. EIA data programs may include data from some or all of these areas in U.S. totals. For these programs, data products will contain notes explaining the extent of geographic coverage included under the term "United States."

Unleaded midgrade gasoline See Gasoline grades.
Unleaded premium gasoline See Gasoline grades.
Unleaded regular gasoline See Gasoline grades.

Unprocessed gas Natural gas that has not gone through a processing plant.

Unregulated Entity For the purpose of EIA's data collection efforts, entities that do not have a designated franchised service area and that do not file forms listed in the Code of Federal Regulations, Title 18, Part 141, are considered unregulated entities. This includes qualifying cogenerators, qualifying small power producers, and other generators that are not subject to rate regulation, such as independent power producers.

Unscheduled outage service Power received by a system from another system to replace power from a generating unit forced out of service.

Uranium (U) A heavy, naturally radioactive, metallic element (atomic number 92). Its two principally occurring isotopes are uranium-235 and uranium-238. Uranium-235 is indispensable to the nuclear industry because it is the only isotope existing in nature, to any appreciable extent, that is fissionable by thermal neutrons. Uranium-238 is also important because it absorbs neutrons to produce a radioactive isotope that subsequently decays to the isotope plutonium-239, which also is fissionable by thermal neutrons.

Uranium concentrate A yellow or brown powder obtained by the milling of uranium ore, processing of in situ leach mining solutions, or as a byproduct of phosphoric acid production.

Uranium deposit A discrete concentration of uranium mineralization that is of possible economic interest.

Uranium endowment The uranium that is estimated to occur in rock with a grade of at least 0.01 percent U_3O_8. The estimate of the uranium endowment is made before consideration of economic availability of any associated uranium resources.

Uranium hexaflouride (UF_6) A white solid obtained by chemical treatment of U_3O_8 and which forms a vapor at temperatures above 56 degrees Centigrade. UF_6 is the form of uranium required for the enrichment process.

Uranium importation The actual physical movement of uranium from a location outside the United States to a location inside the United States.

Uranium mill A plant where uranium is separated from ore taken from mines.

Uranium mill tailings The sand-like materials left over from the separation of uranium from its ore. More than 99 percent of the ore becomes tailings.

Uranium Mill Tailings Radiation Control Act (UMTRA) of 1978 The act that directed the Department of Energy to provide for stabilization and control of the uranium mill tailings from inactive sites in a safe and environmentally sound manner to minimize radiation health hazards to the public. It authorized the Department to undertake remedial actions at 24 designated inactive uranium-processing sites and at an estimated 5,048 vicinity properties.

Uranium ore Rock containing uranium mineralization in concentrations that can be mined economically, typically one to four pounds of U_3O_8 per ton or 0.05 percent to 0.2 percent U_3O_8.

Uranium oxide Uranium concentrate or yellowcake. Abbreviated as U_3O_8.

Uranium property A specific piece of land with uranium reserves that is held for the ultimate purpose of economically recovering the uranium. The land can be developed for production or undeveloped.

Uranium reserves Estimated quantities of uranium in known mineral deposits of such size, grade, and configuration that the uranium could be recovered at or below a specified production cost with currently proven mining and processing technology and under current law and regulations. Reserves are based on direct radiometric and chemical measurements of drill holes and other types of sampling of the deposits. Mineral grades and thickness, spatial relationships, depths below the surface, mining and reclamation methods, distances to milling facilities, and amenability of ores to processing are considered in the evaluation. The amount of uranium in ore that could be exploited within the chosen forward-cost levels are estimated in accordance with conventional engineering practices.

Uranium resource categories (international) Three categories of uranium resources defined by the international community to reflect differing levels of confidence in the existence of the resources. Reasonably assured resources (RAR), estimated additional resources (EAR), and speculative resources (SR) are described below.

- *Reasonably assured resources (RAR)* Uranium that occurs in known mineral deposits of such size, grade, and configuration that it could be recovered within the given production cost ranges, with currently proven mining and processing technology. Estimates of tonnage and grade are based on specific sample data and measurements of the deposits and on knowledge of deposit characteristics. *Note*: RAR corresponds to DOE's uranium reserves category.

- *Estimated additional resources (EAR)* Uranium in addition to RAR that is expected to occur, mostly on the basis of geological evidence, in extensions of well-explored deposits, in little-explored deposits, and in undiscovered deposits believed to exist along well-defined geological trends with known deposits. This uranium can subsequently be recovered within the given cost ranges. Estimates of tonnage and grade are based on available sampling data and on knowledge of the deposit characteristics, as determined in the best-known parts of the deposit or in similar deposits. *Note*: EAR corresponds to DOE's probable potential resources category.

- *Speculative resources (SR)* Uranium in addition to EAR that is thought to exist, mostly on the basis of indirect evidence and geological extrapolations, in deposits discoverable with existing exploration techniques. The location of deposits in this category can generally be specified only as being somewhere within given regions or geological trends. The estimates in this category are less reliable than estimates of RAR and EAR. *Note*: SR corresponds to the combination of DOE's possible potential resources and speculative potential resources categories.

U.S. refiner acquisition cost of imported crude oil The average price paid by U.S. refiners for imported, that is, non-U.S., crude oil booked into their refineries in accordance with accounting procedures generally accepted and consistently and historically applied by the refiners concerned. The refiner acquisition cost of imported crude oil includes transportation and other fees paid by the refiner.

Useage agreement Contracts held by enrichment customers that allow feed material to be stored at the enrichment plant site in advance of need.

Used and useful A concept used by regulators to determine whether an asset should be included in the utility's rate base. This concept requires that an asset currently provide or be capable of providing a needed service to customers.

Useful thermal output The thermal energy made available in a combined-heat-and-power system for use in any industrial or commercial process, heating or cooling application, or delivered to other end users, i.e., total thermal energy made available for processes and applications other than electrical generation.

U.S.S.R. See Union of Soviet Socialist Republics (U.S.S.R.).

Utility See Electric utility.

Utility demand-side management costs The costs incurred by the utility to achieve the capacity and energy savings from the Demand-Side Management (DSM) Program. Costs incurred by consumers or third parties are to be excluded. The costs are to be reported in nominal dollars in the year in which they are incurred, regardless of when the savings occur. The utility costs are all the annual expenses (labor, administrative, equipment, incentives, marketing, monitoring and evaluation, and other) incurred by the utility for operation of the DSM Program, regardless of whether the costs are expensed or capitalized. Lump-sum capital costs (typically accrued over several years prior to start up) are not to be reported. Program costs associated with strategic load growth activities are also to be excluded.

Utility distribution companies The entities that will continue to provide regulated services for the distribution of electricity to customers and serve customers who do not choose direct access. Regardless of where a consumer chooses to purchase power, the customer's current utility, also known as the utility distribution company, will deliver the power to the consumer.

Utility generation Generation by electric systems engaged in selling electric energy to the public.

Utility-sponsored conservation program Any program sponsored by an electric and/or natural gas utility to review equipment and construction features in buildings and advise on ways to increase the energy efficiency of buildings. Also included are utility-sponsored programs to encourage the use of more energy-efficient equipment. Included are programs to improve the energy efficiency in the lighting system or building equipment or the thermal efficiency of the building shell. Also see Demand-side management.

Vacuum distillation Distillation under reduced pressure (less the atmospheric) which lowers the boiling temperature of the liquid being distilled. This technique with its relatively low temperatures prevents cracking or decomposition of the charge stock.

Value (of shipments) The value received for the complete systems at the company's net billing price, freight-on-board factory, including charges for cooperative advertising and warranties. This does not include excise taxes, freight or transportation charges, or installation charges.

Value added by manufacture A measure of manufacturing activity that is derived by subtracting the cost of materials (which covers materials, supplies, containers, fuel, purchased electricity, and contract work) from the value of shipments. This difference is then adjusted by the net change in finished goods and work-in-progress between the beginning- and end-of-year inventories.

Vapor displacement The release of vapors that had previously occupied space above liquid fuels stored in tanks. These releases occur when tanks are emptied and filled.

Vapor-dominated geothermal system A conceptual model of a hydrothermal system where steam pervades the rock and is the pressure-controlling fluid phase.

Vapor retarder A material that retards the movement of water vapor through a building element (walls, ceilings) and prevents insulation and structural wood from becoming damp and metals from corroding. Often applied to insulation batts or separately in the form of treated papers, plastic sheets, and metallic foils.

Variable air volume (VAV) system on the heating and cooling system A means of varying the amount of conditioned air to a space. A variable air volume system maintains the air flow at a constant temperature, but supplies varying quantities of conditioned air in different parts of the building according to the heating and cooling needs.

Variable fuel vehicle See Flexible fuel vehicle.

Variable-speed wind turbines Turbines in which the rotor speed increases and decreases with changing wind speed, producing electricity with a variable frequency.

Vehicle fuel consumption Vehicle fuel consumption is computed as the vehicle miles traveled divided by the fuel efficiency reported in miles per gallon (MPG). Vehicle fuel consumption is derived from the actual vehicle mileage collected and the assigned MPGs obtained from EPA certification files adjusted for on-road driving. The quantity of fuel used by vehicles.

Vehicle fuel efficiencies See Miles per gallon.

Vehicle fuel expenditures The cost, including taxes, of the gasoline, gasohol, or diesel fuel added to the vehicle's tank. Expenditures do not include the cost of oil or other items that may have been purchased at the same time as the vehicle fuel.

Vehicle identification number (VIN) A set of codes, usually alphanumeric characters, assigned to a vehicle at the factory and inscribed on the vehicle. When decoded, the VIN provides vehicle characteristics. The VIN is used to help match vehicles to the EPA certification file for calculating MPGs.

Vehicle importer An original vehicle manufacturer (of foreign or domestic ownership) that imports vehicles as finished products into the United States.

Vehicle miles traveled (VMT) The number of miles traveled nationally by vehicles for a period of 1 year. VMT is either calculated using two odometer readings or, for vehicles with less than two odometer readings, imputed using a regression estimate.

Vented Gas released into the air on the production site or at processing plants.

Vented natural gas See Vented above.

Vented/Flared Gas that is disposed of by releasing (venting) or burning (flaring).

Ventilation system A method for reducing methane concentrations in coal mines to non-explosive levels by blowing air across the mine face and using large exhaust fans to remove methane while mining operations proceed.

Vertical-axis wind turbine (VAWT) A type of wind turbine in which the axis of rotation is perpendicular to the wind stream and the ground.

Vertical integration The combination within a firm or business enterprise of one or more stages of production or distribution. In the electric industry, it refers to the historical arrangement whereby a utility owns its own generating plants, transmission system, and distribution lines to provide all aspects of electric service.

Vessel A ship used to transport crude oil, petroleum products, or natural gas products. Vessel categories are as follows: Ultra Large Crude Carrier (ULCC), Very Large Crude Carrier (VLCC), Other Tanker, and Specialty Ship (LPG/LNG). See Tanker and Barge.

Vessel bunkering Includes sales for the fueling of commercial or private boats, such as pleasure craft, fishing boats, tugboats, and ocean-going vessels, including vessels operated by oil companies. Excluded are volumes sold to the U.S. Armed Forces.

VIN (vehicle identification number) A set of about 17 codes, combining letters and numbers, assigned to a vehicle at the factory and inscribed on a small metal label attached to the dashboard and visible through the windshield. The VIN is a unique identifier for the vehicle and therefore is often found on insurance cards, vehicle registrations, vehicle titles, safety or emission certificates, insurance policies, and bills of sale. The coded information in the VIN describes characteristics of the vehicle such as engine size and weight.

Virgin coal Coal that has not been accessed by mining.

Visbreaking A thermal cracking process in which heavy atmospheric or vacuum-still bottoms are cracked at moderate temperatures to increase production of distillate products and reduce viscosity of the distillation residues.

Volatile matter Those products, exclusive of moisture, given off by a material as gas or vapor. Volatile matter is determined by heating the coal to 950 degrees Centigrade under carefully controlled conditions and measuring the weight loss, excluding weight of moisture driven off at 105 degrees Centigrade.

Volatile organic compounds (VOCs) Organic compounds that participate in atmospheric photochemical reactions.

Volatile solids A solid material that is readily decomposable at relatively low temperatures.

Volt (V) The volt is the International System of Units (SI) measure of electric potential or electromotive force. A potential of one volt appears across a resistance of one ohm when a current of one ampere flows through that resistance. Reduced to SI base units, $1\ V = 1$ kg times m^2 times s^{-3} times A^{-1} (kilogram meter squared per second cubed per ampere).

Voltage The difference in electrical potential between any two conductors or between a conductor and ground. It is a measure of the electric energy per electron that electrons can acquire and/or give up as they move between the two conductors.

Voltage reduction Any intentional reduction of system voltage by 3 percent or greater for reasons of maintaining the continuity of service of the bulk electric power supply system.

Volumetric wires charge See Quantity wires charge

Wafer A thin sheet of semiconductor (photovoltaic material) made by cutting it from a single crystal or ingot.

Walk-in refrigeration units Refrigeration/freezer units within a building that are large enough to walk into. They may be portable or permanent, such as a meat storage locker in a butcher store. Walk-in units may or may not have a door, plastic strips, or other flexible covers.

Wall insulation Insulating materials within or on the walls between heated areas of the building and unheated areas or the outside. The walls may separate air-conditioned areas from areas not air-conditioned.

Warm-air furnace See Furnace.

Warranty contracts Gas purchase agreements for the sale of natural gas by a producer to a pipeline company wherein the producer warrants it will have available sufficient gas supplies to meet its commitments over the life of the contract. Generally, the producer does not dedicate gas reserves underlying any specific acreage, lease, or fields to the agreement. Substitution of various sources of gas supply may be permitted according to the terms of the contract. Warranty contracts, by their terms, may vary from the above.

Waste coal: Usable material that is a byproduct of previous coal processing operations. Waste coal is usually composed of mixed coal, soil, and rock (mine waste). Most waste coal is burned as-is in unconventional fluidized-bed combustors. For some uses, waste coal may be partially cleaned by removing some extraneous noncombustible constituents. Examples of waste coal include fine coal, coal obtained from a refuse bank or slurry dam, anthracite culm, bituminous gob, and lignite waste.

Waste See Biomass waste and Non-biomass waste.

Waste heat boiler A boiler that receives all or a substantial portion of its energy input from the combustible exhaust gases from a separate fuel-burning process.

Waste heat recovery Any conservation system whereby some space heating or water heating is done by actively capturing byproduct heat that would otherwise be ejected into the environment. In commercial buildings, sources of water- heat recovery include refrigeration/air-conditioner compressors, manufacturing or other processes, data processing centers, lighting fixtures, ventilation exhaust air, and the occupants themselves. Not to be considered is the passive use of radiant heat from lighting, workers, motors, ovens, etc., when there are no special systems for collecting and redistributing heat.

Waste materials Otherwise discarded combustible materials that, when burned, produce energy for such purposes as space heating and electric power generation. The size of the waste may be reduced by shredders, grinders, or hammermills. Noncombustible materials, if any, may be removed. The waste may be dried and then burned, either alone or in combination with fossil fuels.

Waste oils and tar Petroleum-based materials that are worthless for any purpose other than fuel use.

Wastewater, domestic and commercial Wastewater (sewage) produced by domestic and commercial establishments.

Wastewater, industrial Wastewater produced by industrial processes.

Water bed heater An appliance that uses an electric resistance coil to maintain the temperature of the water in a water bed at a comfortable level.

Water conditions The status of the water supply and associated water in pondage and reservoirs at hydroelectric plants.

Water heated in furnace Some furnaces provide hot water as well as heat the home. The water is heated by a coil that is part of the furnace. There is no separate hot water tank.

Water heater An automatically controlled, thermally insulated vessel designed for heating water and storing heated water at temperatures less than 180 degrees Fahrenheit.

Water heating DSM programs These are demand-side management (DSM) programs designed to promote increased efficiency in water heating, including water heater insulation wraps.

Water heating equipment Automatically controlled, thermal insulated equipment designed for heating and storing heated water at temperatures less than 180 degrees Fahrenheit for other than space heating purposes.

Water pollution abatement equipment Equipment used to reduce or eliminate waterborne pollutants, including chlorine, phosphates, acids, bases, hydrocarbons, sewage, and other pollutants. Examples of water pollution abatement structures and equipment include those used to treat thermal pollution; cooling, boiler, and cooling tower blowdown water; coal pile runoff; and fly ash waste water. Water pollution abatement excludes expenditures for treatment of water prior to use at the plant.

Water pumping Photovoltaic modules/cells used for pumping water for agricultural, land reclamation, commercial, and other similar applications where water pumping is the main use.

Water reservoir A large inland body of water collected and stored above ground in a natural or artificial formation.

Water source heat pump A type of (geothermal) heat pump that uses well (ground) or surface water as a heat source. Water has a more stable seasonal temperature than air thus making for a more efficient heat source.

Water turbine A turbine that uses water pressure to rotate its blades; the primary types are the Pelton wheel, for high heads (pressure); the Francis turbine, for low to medium heads; and the Kaplan for a wide range of heads. Primarily used to power an electric generator.

Water vapor Water in a vaporous form, especially when below boiling temperature and diffused (e.g., in the atmosphere).

Water well A well drilled to (1) obtain a water supply to support drilling or plant operations, or (2) obtain a water supply to be used in connection with an improved recovery program.

Water wheel A wheel that is designed to use the weight and/or force of moving water to turn it, primarily to operate machinery or grind grain.

Waterway A river, channel, canal, or other navigable body of water used for travel or transport.

Watt (W) The unit of electrical power equal to one ampere under a pressure of one volt. A Watt is equal to 1/746 horsepower.

Watthour (Wh) The electrical energy unit of measure equal to one watt of power supplied to, or taken from, an electric circuit steadily for one hour.

Wattmeter A device for measuring power consumption.

Wax A solid or semi-solid material at 77°F consisting of a mixture of hydrocarbons obtained or derived from petroleum fractions, or through a Fischer-Tropsch type process, in which the straight chained paraffin series predominates. This includes all marketable wax, whether crude or refined, with a congealing point (ASTM D 938) between 80 (or 85) and 240°F and a maximum oil content (ASTM D 3235) of 50 weight percent.

Weather stripping or caulking Any of several kinds of crack-filling material around any windows or doors to the outside used to reduce the passage of air and moisture around moveable parts of a door or window. Weather stripping is available in strips or rolls of metal, vinyl, or foam rubber and can be applied on the inside or outside of a building.

Weir A dam in a waterway over which water flows and that serves to raise the water level or to direct or regulate flow.

Well A hole drilled in the earth for the purpose of (1) finding or producing **crude oil** or **natural gas**; or (2) producing services related to the production of crude or natural gas.

Well water for cooling A means of cooling that uses water from a well drilled specifically for that purpose. The subterranean temperature of the water stays at a relatively constant temperature. Where water is abundant, it provides a means of getting 55-degree Fahrenheit water with no mechanical cooling. Used usually for heat rejection in a water source heat pump.

Wellhead The point at which the crude (and/or natural gas) exits the ground. Following historical precedent, the volume and price for crude oil production are labeled as "wellhead," even though the cost and volume are now generally measured at the lease boundry. In the context of domestic crude price data, the term "wellhead" is the generic term used to reference the production site or lease property.

Wellhead price The value at the mouth of the well. In general, the wellhead price is considered to be the sales price obtainable from a third party in an arm's length transaction. Posted prices, requested prices, or prices as defined by lease agreements, contracts, or tax regulations should be used where applicable.

Wet bottom boiler Slag tanks are installed usually at the furnace throat to contain and remove molten ash.

Wet natural gas A mixture of hydrocarbon compounds and small quantities of various nonhydrocarbons existing in the gaseous phase or in solution with crude oil in porous rock formations at reservoir conditions. The principal hydrocarbons normally contained in the mixture are methane, ethane, propane, butane, and pentane. Typical nonhydrocarbon gases that may be present in reservoir natural gas are water vapor, carbon dioxide, hydrogen sulfide, nitrogen and trace amounts of helium. Under reservoir conditions, natural gas and its associated liquefiable portions occur either in a single gaseous phase in the reservoir or in solution with crude oil and are not distinguishable at the time as separate substances. *Note*: The Securities and Exchange Commission and the Financial Accounting Standards Board refer to this product as **natural gas**.

Wheeling charge An amount charged by one electrical system to transmit the energy of, and for, another system or systems.

Wheeling service The movement of electricity from one system to another over transmission facilities of interconnecting systems. Wheeling service contracts can be established between two or more systems.

White spirit A highly refined distillate with a boiling point range of about 150 degrees to 200 degrees Centigrade. It is used as a paint solvent and for dry-cleaning purposes.

Whole-house cooling fan A mechanical/electrical device used to pull air out of an interior space; usually located in the highest location of a building, in the ceiling, and venting to the attic or directly to the outside.

Wholesale competition A system whereby a distributor of power would have the option to buy its power from a variety of power producers, and the power producers would be able to compete to sell their power to a variety of distribution companies.

Wholesale electric power market The purchase and sale of electricity from generators to resellers (retailers), along with the ancillary services needed to maintain reliability and power quality at the transmission level.

Wholesale power market The purchase and sale of electricity from generators to resellers (who sell to retail customers), along with the ancillary services needed to maintain reliability and power quality at the transmission level.

Wholesale price The rack sales price charged for No. 2 heating oil; that is, the price charged customers who purchase No. 2 heating oil free-on-board at a supplier's terminal and provide their own transportation for the product.

Wholesale sales Energy supplied to other electric utilities, cooperatives, municipals, and Federal and state electric agencies for resale to ultimate consumers.

Wholesale transmission services The transmission of electric energy sold, or to be sold, in the wholesale electric power market.

Wholesale wheeling An arrangement in which electricity is transmitted from a generator to a utility through the transmission facilities of an intervening system.

Wind energy Kinetic energy present in wind motion that can be converted to mechanical energy for driving pumps, mills, and electric power generators.

Wind energy conversion system (WECS) or device An apparatus for converting the energy available in the wind to mechanical energy that can be used to power machinery (grain mills, water pumps) and to operate an electrical generator.

Wind farm See Wind power plant below.

Wind power plant A group of wind turbines interconnected to a common utility system through a system of transformers, distribution lines, and (usually) one substation. Operation, control, and maintenance functions are often centralized through a network of computerized monitoring systems, supplemented by visual inspection. This is a term commonly used in the United States. In Europe, it is called a generating station.

Wind turbine Wind energy conversion device that produces electricity; typically three blades rotating about a horizontal axis and positioned up-wind of the supporting tower.

Wires charge A broad term referring to fees levied on power suppliers or their customers for the use of the transmission or distribution wires.

Wood conversion to Btu Converting cords of wood into a Btu equivalent is an imprecise procedure. The number of cords each household reports having burned is inexact, even with the more precise drawings provided, because the estimate requires the respondent to add up the use of wood over a 12-month period during which wood may have been added to the supply as well as removed. Besides errors of memory inherent in this task, the estimates are subject to problems in definition and perception of what a cord is. The nominal cord as delivered to a suburban residential buyer may differ from the dimensions of the standard cord. This difference is possible because wood is most often cut in lengths that are longer than what makes a third of a cord (16 inches) and shorter than what makes a half cord (24 inches).

In other cases, wood is bought or cut in unusual units (for example, pickup-truck load, or trunk load). Finally, volume estimates are difficult to make when the wood is left in a pile instead of being stacked. Other factors that make it difficult to estimate the Btu value of the wood burned is that the amount of empty space between the stacked logs may vary from 12 to 40 percent of the volume. Moisture content may vary from 20 percent in dried wood to 50 percent in green wood. (Moisture reduces the useful Btu output because energy is used in driving off the moisture). Finally, some tree species contain twice the Btu content of species with the lowest Btu value. Generally, hard woods have greater Btu value than soft woods. Wood is converted to Btu at the rate of 20 million Btu per cord, which is a rough average that takes all these factors into account. Also see Btu conversion factors.

Wood energy Wood and wood products used as fuel, including round wood (cord wood), limb wood, wood chips, bark, sawdust, forest residues, charcoal, pulp waste, and spent pulping liquor.

Wood pellets Sawdust compressed into uniform diameter pellets to be burned in a heating stove.

Working (top storage) gas The volume of gas in the reservoir that is in addition to the cushion or base gas. It may or may not be completely withdrawn during any particular withdrawal season. Conditions permitting, the total working capacity could be used more than once during any season.

Working interest An interest in a mineral property that entitles the owner of that interest to all of share of the mineral production from the property, usually subject to a royalty. A working interest permits the owner to explore, develop, and operate the property. The working-interest owner bears the costs of exploration, development, and operation of the property and, in return, is entitled to a share of the mineral production from the property or to a share of the proceeds therefrom. It may be assigned to another party in whole or in part, or it may be divided into other special property interests.

Gross working interest. The reporting company's working interest plus the proportionate share of any basic royalty interest or overriding royalty interest related to the working interest.

Net working interest. The reporting company's working interest is not including any basic royalty or overriding royalty interests.

Working storage capacity The difference in volume between the maximum safe fill capacity and the quantity below which pump suction is ineffective (bottoms).

Xylene ($C_6H_4(CH_3)_2$) Colorless liquid of the aromatic group of hydrocarbons made the catalytic reforming of certain naphthenic petroleum fractions. Used as high-octane motor and aviation gasoline blending agents, solvents, chemical intermediates. Isomers are metaxylene, orthoxylene, paraxylene.

Yellowcake A natural uranium concentrate that takes its name from its color and texture. Yellowcake typically contains 70 to 90 percent U_3O_8 (uranium oxide) by weight. It is used as feedstock for uranium fuel enrichment and fuel pellet fabrication.

Environmental Health

Absorption The process of taking in. For a person or an animal, absorption is the process of a substance getting into the body through the eyes, skin, stomach, intestines, or lungs.

Acute Occurring over a short time [compare with chronic].

Acute exposure Contact with a substance that occurs once or for only a short time (up to 14 days) [compare with intermediate duration exposure and chronic exposure].

Additive effect A biologic response to exposure to multiple substances that equals the sum of responses of all the individual substances added together [compare with antagonistic effect and synergistic effect].

Adverse health effect A change in body function or cell structure that might lead to disease or health problems

Aerobic Requiring oxygen [compare with anaerobic].

Ambient Surrounding (for example, *ambient* air).

Anaerobic Requiring the absence of oxygen [compare with aerobic].

Analyte A substance measured in the laboratory. A chemical for which a sample (such as water, air, or blood) is tested in a laboratory. For example, if the analyte is mercury, the laboratory test will determine the amount of mercury in the sample.

Analytic epidemiologic study A study that evaluates the association between exposure to hazardous substances and disease by testing scientific hypotheses.

Antagonistic effect A biologic response to exposure to multiple substances that is *less* than would be expected if the known effects of the individual substances were added together [compare with additive effect and synergistic effect].

Background level An average or expected amount of a substance or radioactive material in a specific environment, or typical amounts of substances that occur naturally in an environment.

Biodegradation Decomposition or breakdown of a substance through the action of microorganisms (such as bacteria or fungi) or other natural physical processes (such as sunlight).

Biologic indicators of exposure study A study that uses (a) biomedical testing or (b) the measurement of a substance [an analyte], its metabolite, or another marker of exposure in human body fluids or tissues to confirm human exposure to a hazardous substance [also see exposure investigation].

Biologic monitoring Measuring hazardous substances in biologic materials (such as blood, hair, urine, or breath) to determine whether exposure has occurred. A blood test for lead is an example of biologic monitoring.

Biologic uptake The transfer of substances from the environment to plants, animals, and humans.

Biomedical testing Testing of persons to find out whether a change in a body function might have occurred because of exposure to a hazardous substance.

Biota Plants and animals in an environment. Some of these plants and animals might be sources of food, clothing, or medicines for people.

Body burden The total amount of a substance in the body. Some substances build up in the body because they are stored in fat or bone or because they leave the body very slowly.

CAP [See Community Assistance Panel.]

Cancer Any one of a group of diseases that occur when cells in the body become abnormal and grow or multiply out of control.

Cancer risk A theoretical risk for getting cancer if exposed to a substance every day for 70 years (a lifetime exposure). The true risk might be lower.

Carcinogen A substance that causes cancer.

Case study A medical or epidemiologic evaluation of one person or a small group of people to gather information about specific health conditions and past exposures.

Case-control study A study that compares exposures of people who have a disease or condition (cases) with people who do not have the disease or condition (controls). Exposures that are more common among the cases may be considered as possible risk factors for the disease.

CAS registry number A unique number assigned to a substance or mixture by the American Chemical Society Abstracts Service.

Central nervous system The part of the nervous system that consists of the brain and the spinal cord.

CERCLA [See Comprehensive Environmental Response, Compensation, and Liability Act of 1980.]

Chronic Occurring over a long time [compare with acute].

Chronic exposure Contact with a substance that occurs over a long time (more than 1 year) [compare with acute exposure and intermediate duration exposure].

Cluster investigation A review of an unusual number, real or perceived, of health events (for example, reports of cancer) grouped together in time and location. Cluster investigations are designed to confirm case reports; determine whether they represent an unusual disease occurrence; and, if possible, explore possible causes and contributing environmental factors.

Community Assistance Panel (CAP) A group of people from a community and from health and environmental agencies who work with ATSDR to resolve issues and problems related to hazardous substances in the community. CAP members work with ATSDR to gather and review community health concerns, provide information on how people might have been or might now be exposed to hazardous substances, and inform ATSDR on ways to involve the community in its activities.

Comparison value (CV) Calculated concentration of a substance in air, water, food, or soil that is unlikely to cause harmful (adverse) health effects in exposed people. The CV is used as a screening level during the public health assessment process. Substances found in amounts greater than their CVs might be selected for further evaluation in the public health assessment process.

Completed exposure pathway [See exposure pathway.]

Comprehensive Environmental Response, Compensation, and Liability Act of 1980 (CERCLA) CERCLA, also known as Superfund, is the federal law that concerns the removal or cleanup of hazardous substances in the environment and at hazardous waste sites. ATSDR, which was created by CERCLA, is responsible for assessing health issues and supporting public health activities related to hazardous waste sites or other environmental releases of hazardous substances. This law was later amended by the Superfund Amendments and Reauthorization Act (SARA).

Concentration The amount of a substance present in a certain amount of soil, water, air, food, blood, hair, urine, breath, or any other media.

Contaminant A substance that is either present in an environment where it does not belong or is present at levels that might cause harmful (adverse) health effects.

Delayed health effect A disease or an injury that happens as a result of exposures that might have occurred in the past.

Dermal Referring to the skin. For example, dermal absorption means passing through the skin.

Dermal contact Contact with (touching) the skin [see route of exposure].

Descriptive epidemiology The study of the amount and distribution of a disease in a specified population by person, place, and time.

Detection limit The lowest concentration of a chemical that can reliably be distinguished from a zero concentration.

Disease prevention Measures used to prevent a disease or reduce its severity.

Disease registry A system of ongoing registration of all cases of a particular disease or health condition in a defined population.

DOD United States Department of Defense.

DOE United States Department of Energy.

Dose (for chemicals that are not radioactive) The amount of a substance to which a person is exposed over some time period. Dose is a measurement of exposure. Dose is often expressed as milligram (amount) per kilogram (a measure of body weight) per day (a measure of time) when people eat or drink contaminated water, food, or soil. In general, the greater the dose, the greater the likelihood of an effect. An "exposure dose" is how much of a substance is encountered in the environment. An "absorbed dose" is the amount of a substance that actually got into the body through the eyes, skin, stomach, intestines, or lungs.

Dose (for radioactive chemicals) The radiation dose is the amount of energy from radiation that is actually absorbed by the body. This is not the same as measurements of the amount of radiation in the environment.

Dose-response relationship The relationship between the amount of exposure [dose] to a substance and the resulting changes in body function or health (response).

Environmental media Soil, water, air, biota (plants and animals), or any other parts of the environment that can contain contaminants.

Environmental media and transport mechanism Environmental media include water, air, soil, and biota (plants and animals). Transport mechanisms move contaminants from the source to points where human exposure can occur. The environmental media and transport mechanism is the second part of an exposure pathway.

EPA United States Environmental Protection Agency.

Epidemiologic surveillance [See Public health surveillance.]

Epidemiology The study of the distribution and determinants of disease or health status in a population; the study of the occurrence and causes of health effects in humans.

Exposure Contact with a substance by swallowing, breathing, or touching the skin or eyes. Exposure may be short-term [acute exposure], of intermediate duration, or long-term [chronic exposure].

Exposure assessment The process of finding out how people come into contact with a hazardous substance, how often and for how long they are in contact with the substance, and how much of the substance they are in contact with.

Exposure-dose reconstruction A method of estimating the amount of people's past exposure to hazardous substances. Computer and approximation methods are used when past information is limited, not available, or missing.

Exposure investigation The collection and analysis of site-specific information and biologic tests (when appropriate) to determine whether people have been exposed to hazardous substances.

Exposure pathway The route a substance takes from its source (where it began) to its end point (where it ends), and how people can come into contact with (or get exposed to) it. An exposure pathway has five parts: a source of contamination (such as an abandoned business); an environmental media and transport mechanism (such as movement through groundwater); a point of exposure (such as a private well); a route of exposure (eating, drinking, breathing, or touching), and a receptor population (people potentially or actually exposed). When all five parts are present, the exposure pathway is termed a completed exposure pathway.

Exposure registry A system of ongoing followup of people who have had documented environmental exposures.

Feasibility study A study by EPA to determine the best way to clean up environmental contamination. A number of factors are considered, including health risk, costs, and what methods will work well.

Geographic information system (GIS) A mapping system that uses computers to collect, store, manipulate, analyze, and display data. For example, GIS can show the concentration of a contaminant within a community in relation to points of reference such as streets and homes.

Grand rounds Training sessions for physicians and other health care providers about health topics.

Groundwater Water beneath the earth's surface in the spaces between soil particles and between rock surfaces [compare with surface water].

Half-life (t½) The time it takes for half the original amount of a substance to disappear. In the environment, the half-life is the time it takes for half the original amount of a substance to disappear when it is changed to another chemical by bacteria, fungi, sunlight, or other chemical processes. In the human body, the half-life is the time it takes for half the original amount of the substance to disappear, either by being changed to another substance or by leaving the body. In the case of radioactive material, the half life is the amount of time necessary for one half the initial number of radioactive atoms to change or transform into another atom (that is normally not radioactive). After two half lives, 25% of the original number of radioactive atoms remain.

Hazard A source of potential harm from past, current, or future exposures.

Hazardous Substance Release and Health Effects Database (HazDat) The scientific and administrative database system developed by ATSDR to manage data collection, retrieval, and analysis of site-specific information on hazardous substances, community health concerns, and public health activities.

Hazardous waste Potentially harmful substances that have been released or discarded into the environment.

Health consultation A review of available information or collection of new data to respond to a specific health question or request for information about a potential environmental hazard. Health consultations are focused on a specific exposure issue. Health consultations are therefore more limited than a public health assessment, which reviews the exposure potential of each pathway and chemical [compare with public health assessment].

Health education Programs designed with a community to help it know about health risks and how to reduce these risks.

Health investigation The collection and evaluation of information about the health of community residents. This information is used to describe or count the occurrence of a disease, symptom, or clinical measure and to evaluate the possible association between the occurrence and exposure to hazardous substances.

Health promotion The process of enabling people to increase control over, and to improve, their health.

Health statistics review The analysis of existing health information (i.e., from death certificates, birth defects registries, and cancer registries) to determine if there is excess disease in a specific population, geographic area, and time period. A health statistics review is a descriptive epidemiologic study.

Incidence The number of new cases of disease in a defined population over a specific time period [contrast with prevalence].

Indeterminate public health hazard The category used in ATSDR's public health assessment documents when a professional judgment about the level of health hazard cannot be made because information critical to such a decision is lacking.

Ingestion The act of swallowing something through eating, drinking, or mouthing objects. A hazardous substance can enter the body this way [see route of exposure].

Inhalation The act of breathing. A hazardous substance can enter the body this way [see route of exposure].

Intermediate duration exposure Contact with a substance that occurs for more than 14 days and less than a year [compare with acute exposure and chronic exposure].

In vitro In an artificial environment outside a living organism or body. For example, some toxicity testing is done on cell cultures or slices of tissue grown in the laboratory, rather than on a living animal [compare with in vivo].

In vivo Within a living organism or body. For example, some toxicity testing is done on whole animals, such as rats or mice [compare with in vitro].

Lowest-observed-adverse-effect level (LOAEL) The lowest tested dose of a substance that has been reported to cause harmful (adverse) health effects in people or animals.

Medical monitoring A set of medical tests and physical exams specifically designed to evaluate whether an individual's exposure could negatively affect that person's health.

Metabolism The conversion or breakdown of a substance from one form to another by a living organism.

Metabolite Any product of metabolism.

mg/kg Milligram per kilogram.

mg/cm² Milligram per square centimeter (of a surface).

mg/m³ Milligram per cubic meter; a measure of the concentration of a chemical in a known volume (a cubic meter) of air, soil, or water.

Migration Moving from one location to another.

Minimal risk level (MRL) An ATSDR estimate of daily human exposure to a hazardous substance at or below which that substance is unlikely to pose a measurable risk of harmful (adverse), noncancerous effects. MRLs are calculated for a route of exposure (inhalation or oral) over a specified time period (acute, intermediate, or chronic). MRLs should not be used as predictors of harmful (adverse) health effects [see reference dose].

Morbidity State of being ill or diseased. Morbidity is the occurrence of a disease or condition that alters health and quality of life.

Mortality Death. Usually the cause (a specific disease, a condition, or an injury) is stated.

Mutagen A substance that causes mutations (genetic damage).

Mutation A change (damage) to the DNA, genes, or chromosomes of living organisms.

National Priorities List for Uncontrolled Hazardous Waste Sites (National Priorities List or NPL) EPA's list of the most serious uncontrolled or abandoned hazardous waste sites in the United States. The NPL is updated on a regular basis.

National Toxicology Program (NTP) Part of the Department of Health and Human Services. NTP develops and carries out tests to predict whether a chemical will cause harm to humans.

No apparent public health hazard A category used in ATSDR's public health assessments for sites where human exposure to contaminated media might be occurring, might have occurred in the past, or might occur in the future, but where the exposure is not expected to cause any harmful health effects.

No-observed-adverse-effect level (NOAEL) The highest tested dose of a substance that has been reported to have no harmful (adverse) health effects on people or animals.

No public health hazard A category used in ATSDR's public health assessment documents for sites where people have never and will never come into contact with harmful amounts of site-related substances.

NPL [See National Priorities List for Uncontrolled Hazardous Waste Sites.]

Physiologically based pharmacokinetic model (PBPK model) A computer model that describes what happens to a chemical in the body. This model describes how the chemical gets into the body, where it goes in the body, how it is changed by the body, and how it leaves the body.

Pica A craving to eat nonfood items, such as dirt, paint chips, and clay. Some children exhibit pica-related behavior.

Plume A volume of a substance that moves from its source to places farther away from the source. Plumes can be described by the volume of air or water they occupy and the direction they move. For example, a plume can be a column of smoke from a chimney or a substance moving with groundwater.

Point of exposure The place where someone can come into contact with a substance present in the environment [see exposure pathway].

Population A group or number of people living within a specified area or sharing similar characteristics (such as occupation or age).

Potentially responsible party (PRP) A company, government, or person legally responsible for cleaning up the pollution at a hazardous waste site under Superfund. There may be more than one PRP for a particular site.

Ppb   Parts per billion.
Ppm   Parts per million.
Prevalence   The number of existing disease cases in a defined population during a specific time period [contrast with incidence].
Prevalence survey   The measure of the current level of disease(s) or symptoms and exposures through a questionnaire that collects self-reported information from a defined population.
Prevention   Actions that reduce exposure or other risks, keep people from getting sick, or keep disease from getting worse.
Public availability session   An informal, drop-by meeting at which community members can meet one-on-one with ATSDR staff members to discuss health and site-related concerns.
Public comment period   An opportunity for the public to comment on agency findings or proposed activities contained in draft reports or documents. The public comment period is a limited time period during which comments will be accepted.
Public health action   A list of steps to protect public health.
Public health advisory   A statement made by ATSDR to EPA or a state regulatory agency that a release of hazardous substances poses an immediate threat to human health. The advisory includes recommended measures to reduce exposure and reduce the threat to human health.
Public health assessment (PHA)   An ATSDR document that examines hazardous substances, health outcomes, and community concerns at a hazardous waste site to determine whether people could be harmed from coming into contact with those substances. The PHA also lists actions that need to be taken to protect public health [compare with health consultation].
Public health hazard   A category used in ATSDR's public health assessments for sites that pose a public health hazard because of long-term exposures (greater than 1 year) to sufficiently high levels of hazardous substances or radionuclides that could result in harmful health effects.
Public health hazard categories   Public health hazard categories are statements about whether people could be harmed by conditions present at the site in the past, present, or future. One or more hazard categories might be appropriate for each site. The five public health hazard categories are no public health hazard, no apparent public health hazard, indeterminate public health hazard, public health hazard, and urgent public health hazard.
Public health statement   The first chapter of an ATSDR toxicological profile. The public health statement is a summary written in words that are easy to understand. The public health statement explains how people might be exposed to a specific substance and describes the known health effects of that substance.
Public health surveillance   The ongoing, systematic collection, analysis, and interpretation of health data. This activity also involves timely dissemination of the data and use for public health programs.
Public meeting   A public forum with community members for communication about a site.
Radioisotope   An unstable or radioactive isotope (form) of an element that can change into another element by giving off radiation.
Radionuclide   Any radioactive isotope (form) of any element.
RCRA   [See Resource Conservation and Recovery Act (1976, 1984).]
Receptor population   People who could come into contact with hazardous substances [see exposure pathway].
Reference dose (RfD)   An EPA estimate, with uncertainty or safety factors built in, of the daily lifetime dose of a substance that is unlikely to cause harm in humans.
Registry   A systematic collection of information on persons exposed to a specific substance or having specific diseases [see exposure registry and disease registry].
Remedial investigation   The CERCLA process of determining the type and extent of hazardous material contamination at a site.
Resource Conservation and Recovery Act (1976, 1984) (RCRA)   This Act regulates management and disposal of hazardous wastes currently generated, treated, stored, disposed of, or distributed.
RFA   RCRA Facility Assessment. An assessment required by RCRA to identify potential and actual releases of hazardous chemicals.
RfD   [See reference dose.]
Risk   The probability that something will cause injury or harm.
Risk reduction   Actions that can decrease the likelihood that individuals, groups, or communities will experience disease or other health conditions.
Risk communication   The exchange of information to increase understanding of health risks.
Route of exposure   The way people come into contact with a hazardous substance. Three routes of exposure are breathing [inhalation], eating or drinking [ingestion], or contact with the skin [dermal contact].
Safety factor   [See uncertainty factor.]
SARA   [See Superfund Amendments and Reauthorization Act.]
Sample   A portion or piece of a whole. A selected subset of a population or subset of whatever is being studied. For example, in a study of people the sample

is a number of people chosen from a larger population [see population]. An environmental sample (for example, a small amount of soil or water) might be collected to measure contamination in the environment at a specific location.

Sample size The number of units chosen from a population or an environment.

Solvent A liquid capable of dissolving or dispersing another substance (for example, acetone or mineral spirits).

Source of contamination The place where a hazardous substance comes from, such as a landfill, waste pond, incinerator, storage tank, or drum. A source of contamination is the first part of an exposure pathway.

Special populations People who might be more sensitive or susceptible to exposure to hazardous substances because of factors such as age, occupation, sex, or behaviors (for example, cigarette smoking). Children, pregnant women, and older people are often considered special populations.

Stakeholder A person, group, or community who has an interest in activities at a hazardous waste site.

Statistics A branch of mathematics that deals with collecting, reviewing, summarizing, and interpreting data or information. Statistics are used to determine whether differences between study groups are meaningful.

Substance A chemical.

Substance-specific applied research A program of research designed to fill important data needs for specific hazardous substances identified in ATSDR's toxicological profiles. Filling these data needs would allow more accurate assessment of human risks from specific substances contaminating the environment. This research might include human studies or laboratory experiments to determine health effects resulting from exposure to a given hazardous substance.

Superfund [See Comprehensive Environmental Response, Compensation, and Liability Act of 1980 (CERCLA) and Superfund Amendments and Reauthorization Act (SARA).]

Superfund Amendments and Reauthorization Act (SARA) In 1986, SARA amended the Comprehensive Environmental Response, Compensation, and Liability Act of 1980 (CERCLA) and expanded the health-related responsibilities of ATSDR. CERCLA and SARA direct ATSDR to look into the health effects from substance exposures at hazardous waste sites and to perform activities including health education, health studies, surveillance, health consultations, and toxicological profiles.

Surface water Water on the surface of the earth, such as in lakes, rivers, streams, ponds, and springs [compare with groundwater].

Surveillance [See public health surveillance.]

Survey A systematic collection of information or data. A survey can be conducted to collect information from a group of people or from the environment. Surveys of a group of people can be conducted by telephone, by mail, or in person. Some surveys are done by interviewing a group of people [see prevalence survey].

Synergistic effect A biologic response to multiple substances where one substance worsens the effect of another substance. The combined effect of the substances acting together is greater than the sum of the effects of the substances acting by themselves [see additive effect and antagonistic effect].

Teratogen A substance that causes defects in development between conception and birth. A teratogen is a substance that causes a structural or functional birth defect.

Toxic agent Chemical or physical (for example, radiation, heat, cold, microwaves) agents that, under certain circumstances of exposure, can cause harmful effects to living organisms.

Toxicological profile An ATSDR document that examines, summarizes, and interprets information about a hazardous substance to determine harmful levels of exposure and associated health effects. A toxicological profile also identifies significant gaps in knowledge on the substance and describes areas where further research is needed.

Toxicology The study of the harmful effects of substances on humans or animals.

Tumor An abnormal mass of tissue that results from excessive cell division that is uncontrolled and progressive. Tumors perform no useful body function. Tumors can be either benign (not cancer) or malignant (cancer).

Uncertainty factor Mathematical adjustments for reasons of safety when knowledge is incomplete. For example, factors used in the calculation of doses that are not harmful (adverse) to people. These factors are applied to the lowest-observed-adverse-effect-level (LOAEL) or the no-observed-adverse-effect-level (NOAEL) to derive a minimal risk level (MRL). Uncertainty factors are used to account for variations in people's sensitivity, for differences between animals and humans, and for differences between a LOAEL and a NOAEL. Scientists use uncertainty factors when they have some, but not all, the information from animal or human studies to decide whether an exposure will cause harm to people [also sometimes called a safety factor].

Urgent public health hazard A category used in ATSDR's public health assessments for sites where short-term exposures (less than 1 year) to hazardous substances or conditions could result in harmful health effects that require rapid intervention.

Volatile organic compounds (VOCs) Organic compounds that evaporate readily into the air. VOCs include substances such as benzene, toluene, methylene chloride, and methyl chloroform.

Environmental Protection

Abandoned Well A well whose use has been permanently discontinued or which is in a state of such disrepair that it cannot be used for its intended purpose.

Abatement Reducing the degree or intensity of, or eliminating, pollution.

Abatement Debris Waste from remediation activities.

Absorbed Dose In exposure assessment, the amount of a substance that penetrates an exposed organism's absorption barriers (e.g. skin, lung tissue, gastrointestinal tract) through physical or biological processes. The term is synonymous with internal dose.

Absorption The uptake of water, other fluids, or dissolved chemicals by a cell or an organism (as tree roots absorb dissolved nutrients in soil.)

Absorption Barrier Any of the exchange sites of the body that permit uptake of various substances at different rates (e.g. skin, lung tissue, and gastrointestinal-tract wall)

Accident Site The location of an unexpected occurrence, failure or loss, either at a plant or along a transportation route, resulting in a release of hazardous materials.

Acclimatization The physiological and behavioral adjustments of an organism to changes in its environment.

Acid A corrosive solution with a pH less than 7.

Acid Aerosol Acidic liquid or solid particles small enough to become airborne. High concentrations can irritate the lungs and have been associated with respiratory diseases like asthma.

Acid Deposition A complex chemical and atmospheric phenomenon that occurs when emissions of sulfur and nitrogen compounds and other substances are transformed by chemical processes in the atmosphere, often far from the original sources, and then deposited on earth in either wet or dry form. The wet forms, popularly called "acid rain," can fall to earth as rain, snow, or fog. The dry forms are acidic gases or particulates.

Acid Mine Drainage Drainage of water from areas that have been mined for coal or other mineral ores. The water has a low pH because of its contact with sulfur-bearing material and is harmful to aquatic organisms.

Acid-Neutralizing Capacity Measure of ability of a base (e.g. water or soil) to resist changes in pH.

Acid Rain (See acid deposition.)

Acidic The condition of water or soil that contains a sufficient amount of acid substances to lower the pH below 7.0.

Action Levels 1. Regulatory levels recommended by EPA for enforcement by FDA and USDA when pesticide residues occur in food or feed commodities for reasons other than the direct application of the pesticide. As opposed to "tolerances" which are established for residues occurring as a direct result of proper usage, action levels are set for inadvertent residues resulting from previous legal use or accidental contamination. 2. In the Superfund program, the existence of a contaminant concentration in the environment high enough to warrant action or trigger a response under SARA and the National Oil and Hazardous Substances Contingency Plan. The term is also used in other regulatory programs. (See tolerances.)

Activated Carbon A highly adsorbent form of carbon used to remove odors and toxic substances from liquid or gaseous emissions. In waste treatment, it is used to remove dissolved organic matter from waste drinking water. It is also used in motor vehicle evaporative control systems.

Activated Sludge Product that results when primary effluent is mixed with bacteria-laden sludge and then agitated and aerated to promote biological treatment, speeding the breakdown of organic matter in raw sewage undergoing secondary waste treatment.

Activator A chemical added to a pesticide to increase its activity.

Active Ingredient In any pesticide product, the component that kills, or otherwise controls, target pests. Pesticides are regulated primarily on the basis of active ingredients.

Activity Plans Written procedures in a school's asbestos-management plan that detail the steps a Local Education Agency (LEA) will follow in performing the initial and additional cleaning, operation and maintenance-program tasks; periodic surveillance;

and reinspection required by the Asbestos Hazard Emergency Response Act (AHERA).

Acute Effect An adverse effect on any living organism which results in severe symptoms that develop rapidly; symptoms often subside after the exposure stops.

Acute Exposure A single exposure to a toxic substance which may result in severe biological harm or death. Acute exposures are usually characterized as lasting no longer than a day, as compared to longer, continuing exposure over a period of time.

Acute Toxicity The ability of a substance to cause severe biological harm or death soon after a single exposure or dose. Also, any poisonous effect resulting from a single short-term exposure to a toxic substance. (See chronic toxicity, toxicity.)

Adaptation Changes in an organism's physiological structure or function or habits that allow it to survive in new surroundings.

Add-on Control Device An air pollution control device such as carbon absorber or incinerator that reduces the pollution in an exhaust gas. The control device usually does not affect the process being controlled and thus is "add-on" technology, as opposed to a scheme to control pollution through altering the basic process itself.

Adequately Wet Asbestos containing material that is sufficiently mixed or penetrated with liquid to prevent the release of particulates.

Administered Dose In exposure assessment, the amount of a substance given to a test subject (human or animal) to determine dose-response relationships. Since exposure to chemicals is usually inadvertent, this quantity is often called potential dose.

Administrative Order A legal document signed by EPA directing an individual, business, or other entity to take corrective action or refrain from an activity. It describes the violations and actions to be taken, and can be enforced in court. Such orders may be issued, for example, as a result of an administrative complaint whereby the respondent is ordered to pay a penalty for violations of a statute.

Administrative Order on Consent A legal agreement signed by EPA and an individual, business, or other entity through which the violator agrees to pay for correction of violations, take the required corrective or cleanup actions, or refrain from an activity. It describes the actions to be taken, may be subject to a comment period, applies to civil actions, and can be enforced in court.

Administrative Procedures Act A law that spells out procedures and requirements related to the promulgation of regulations.

Administrative Record All documents which EPA considered or relied on in selecting the response action at a Superfund site, culminating in the record of decision for remedial action or, an action memorandum for removal actions.

Adsorption Removal of a pollutant from air or water by collecting the pollutant on the surface of a solid material; e.g., an advanced method of treating waste in which activated carbon removes organic matter from waste-water.

Adulterants Chemical impurities or substances that by law do not belong in a food, or pesticide.

Adulterated 1. Any pesticide whose strength or purity falls below the quality stated on its label. 2. A food, feed, or product that contains illegal pesticide residues.

Advanced Treatment A level of wastewater treatment more stringent than secondary treatment; requires an 85-percent reduction in conventional pollutant concentration or a significant reduction in non-conventional pollutants. Sometimes called tertiary treatment.

Advanced Wastewater Treatment Any treatment of sewage that goes beyond the secondary or biological water treatment stage and includes the removal of nutrients such as phosphorus and nitrogen and a high percentage of suspended solids. (See primary, secondary treatment.)

Adverse Effects Data FIFRA requires a pesticide registrant to submit data to EPA on any studies or other information regarding unreasonable adverse effects of a pesticide at any time after its registration.

Advisory A non-regulatory document that communicates risk information to those who may have to make risk management decisions.

Aerated Lagoon A holding and/or treatment pond that speeds up the natural process of biological decomposition of organic waste by stimulating the growth and activity of bacteria that degrade organic waste.

Aeration A process which promotes biological degradation of organic matter in water. The process may be passive (as when waste is exposed to air), or active (as when a mixing or bubbling device introduces the air).

Aeration Tank A chamber used to inject air into water.

Aerobic Life or processes that require, or are not destroyed by, the presence of oxygen. (See anaerobic.)

Aerobic Treatment Process by which microbes decompose complex organic compounds in the presence of oxygen and use the liberated energy for reproduction and growth. (Such processes include extended aeration, trickling filtration, and rotating biological contactors.)

Aerosol 1. Small droplets or particles suspended in the atmosphere, typically containing sulfur. They are usually emitted naturally (e.g. in volcanic eruptions) and as the result of anthropogenic (human) activities such as burning fossil fuels. 2. The pressurized gas used to propel substances out of a container.

Affected Landfill Under the Clean Air Act, landfills that meet criteria for capacity, age, and emissions rates set by the EPA. They are required to collect and combust their gas emissions.

Affected Public 1.The people who live and/or work near a hazardous waste site. 2. The human population adversely impacted following exposure to a toxic pollutant in food, water, air, or soil.

Afterburner In incinerator technology, a burner located so that the combustion gases are made to pass through its flame in order to remove smoke and odors. It may be attached to or be separated from the incinerator proper.

Age Tank A tank used to store a chemical solution of known concentration for feed to a chemical feeder. Also called a day tank.

Agent Any physical, chemical, or biological entity that can be harmful to an organism (synonymous with stressors).

Agent Orange A toxic herbicide and defoliant used in the Vietnam conflict, containing 2,4,5-trichlorophen-oxyacetic acid (2,4,5-T) and 2-4 dichlorophen-oxyacetic acid (2,4-D) with trace amounts of dioxin.

Agricultural Pollution Farming wastes, including runoff and leaching of pesticides and fertilizers; erosion and dust from plowing; improper disposal of animal manure and carcasses; crop residues, and debris.

Agricultural Waste Poultry and livestock manure, and residual materials in liquid or solid form generated from the production and marketing of poultry, livestock or fur-bearing animals; also includes grain, vegetable, and fruit harvest residue.

Agroecosystem Land used for crops, pasture, and livestock; the adjacent uncultivated land that supports other vegetation and wildlife; and the associated atmosphere, the underlying soils, groundwater, and drainage networks.

AHERA Designated Person (ADP) A person designated by a Local Education Agency to ensure that the AHERA requirements for asbestos management and abatement are properly implemented.

Air Binding Situation where air enters the filter media and harms both the filtration and backwash processes.

Air Changes per Hour (ACH) The movement of a volume of air in a given period of time; if a house has one air change per hour, it means that the air in the house will be replaced in a one-hour period.

Air Cleaning Indoor-air quality-control strategy to remove various airborne particulates and/or gases from the air. Most common methods are particulate filtration, electrostatic precipitation, and gas sorption.

Air Contaminant Any particulate matter, gas, or combination thereof, other than water vapor. (See air pollutant.)

Air Curtain A method of containing oil spills. Air bubbling through a perforated pipe causes an upward water flow that slows the spread of oil. It can also be used to stop fish from entering polluted water.

Air Exchange Rate The rate at which outside air replaces indoor air in a given space.

Air Gap Open vertical gap or empty space that separates drinking water supply to be protected from another water system in a treatment plant or other location. The open gap protects the drinking water from contamination by backflow or back siphonage.

Air Handling Unit Equipment that includes a fan or blower, heating and/or cooling coils, regulator controls, condensate drain pans, and air filters.

Air Mass A large volume of air with certain meteorological or polluted characteristics—e.g., a heat inversion or smogginess—while in one location. The characteristics can change as the air mass moves away.

Air Monitoring (See monitoring.)

Air/Oil Table The surface between the vadose zone and ambient oil; the pressure of oil in the porous medium is equal to atmospheric pressure.

Air Padding Pumping dry air into a container to assist with the withdrawal of liquid or to force a liquefied gas such as chlorine out of the container.

Air Permeability Permeability of soil with respect to air. Important to the design of soil-gas surveys. Measured in darcys or centimeters-per-second.

Air Plenum Any space used to convey air in a building, furnace, or structure. The space above a suspended ceiling is often used as an air plenum.

Air Pollutant Any substance in air that could, in high enough concentration, harm man, other animals, vegetation, or material. Pollutants may include almost any natural or artificial composition of airborne matter capable of being airborne. They may be in the form of solid particles, liquid droplets, gases, or in combination thereof. Generally, they fall into two main groups: (1) those emitted directly from identifiable sources and (2) those produced in the air by interaction between two or more primary pollutants, or by reaction with normal atmospheric constituents, with or without photoactivation. Exclusive of pollen, fog, and dust, which are of natural origin, about 100 contaminants have been identified. Air pollutants are often grouped in categories for ease in classification; some of the categories are solids, sulfur compounds, volatile organic chemicals, particulate matter, nitrogen compounds, oxygen compounds, halogen compounds, radioactive compound, and odors.

Air Pollution The presence of contaminants or pollutant substances in the air that interfere with human health or welfare, or produce other harmful environmental effects.

Air Pollution Control Device Mechanism or equipment that cleans emissions generated by a source (e.g. an incinerator, industrial smokestack, or an automobile exhaust system) by removing pollutants that would otherwise be released to the atmosphere.

Air Pollution Episode A period of abnormally high concentration of air pollutants, often due to low winds and temperature inversion, that can cause illness and death. (See episode, pollution.)

Air Quality Control Region An area, designated by the federal government, where communities share a common air pollution problem.

Air Quality Criteria The levels of pollution and lengths of exposure above which adverse health and welfare effects may occur.

Air Quality Standards The level of pollutants prescribed by regulations that are not be exceeded during a given time in a defined area.

Air Sparging Injecting air or oxygen into an aquifer to strip or flush volatile contaminants as air bubbles up through The ground water and is captured by a vapor extraction system.

Air Stripping A treatment system that removes volatile organic compounds (VOCs) from contaminated ground water or surface water by forcing an airstream through the water and causing the compounds to evaporate.

Air Toxics Any air pollutant for which a national ambient air quality standard (NAAQS) does not exist (i.e. excluding ozone, carbon monoxide, PM-10, sulfur dioxide, nitrogen oxide) that may reasonably be anticipated to cause cancer; respiratory, cardiovascular, or developmental effects; reproductive dysfunctions, neurological disorders, heritable gene mutations, or other serious or irreversible chronic or acute health effects in humans.

Airborne Particulates Total suspended particulate matter found in the atmosphere as solid particles or liquid droplets. Chemical composition of particulates varies widely, depending on location and time of year. Sources of airborne particulates include dust, emissions from industrial processes, combustion products from the burning of wood and coal, combustion products associated with motor vehicle or non-road engine exhausts, and reactions to gases in the atmosphere.

Airborne Release Release of any pollutant into the air.

Alachlor A herbicide, marketed under the trade name Lasso, used mainly to control weeds in corn and soybean fields.

Alar Trade name for daminozide, a pesticide that makes apples redder, firmer, and less likely to drop off trees before growers are ready to pick them. It is also used to a lesser extent on peanuts, tart cherries, concord grapes, and other fruits.

Aldicarb An insecticide sold under the trade name Temik. It is made from ethyl isocyanate.

Algae Simple rootless plants that grow in sunlit waters in proportion to the amount of available nutrients. They can affect water quality adversely by lowering the dissolved oxygen in the water. They are food for fish and small aquatic animals.

Algal Blooms Sudden spurts of algal growth, which can affect water quality adversely and indicate potentially hazardous changes in local water chemistry.

Algicide Substance or chemical used specifically to kill or control algae.

Aliquot A measured portion of a sample taken for analysis. One or more aliquots make up a sample. (See duplicate.)

Alkaline The condition of water or soil which contains a sufficient amount of alkali substance to raise the pH above 7.0.

Alkalinity The capacity of bases to neutralize acids. An example is lime added to lakes to decrease acidity.

Allergen A substance that causes an allergic reaction in individuals sensitive to it.

Alluvial Relating to and/or sand deposited by flowing water.

Alternate Method Any method of sampling and analyzing for an air or water pollutant that is not a reference or equivalent method but that has been demonstrated in specific cases-to EPA's satisfaction-to produce results adequate for compliance monitoring.

Alternative Compliance A policy that allows facilities to choose among methods for achieving emission-reduction or risk-reduction instead of command-and control regulations that specify standards and how to meet them. Use of a theoretical emissions bubble over a facility to cap the amount of pollution emitted while allowing the company to choose where and how (within the facility) it complies.(See bubble, emissions trading.)

Alternative Fuels Substitutes for traditional liquid, oil-derived motor vehicle fuels like gasoline and diesel. Includes mixtures of alcohol-based fuels with gasoline, methanol, ethanol, compressed natural gas, and others.

Alternative Remedial Contract Strategy Contractors Government contractors who provide project management and technical services to support remedial response activities at National Priorities List sites.

Ambient Air Any unconfined portion of the atmosphere: open air, surrounding air.

Ambient Air Quality Standards (See Criteria Pollutants and National Ambient Air Quality Standards.)

Ambient Measurement A measurement of the concentration of a substance or pollutant within the immediate environs of an organism; taken to relate it to the amount of possible exposure.

Ambient Medium Material surrounding or contacting an organism (e.g., outdoor air, indoor air, water, or soil, through which chemicals or pollutants can reach the organism. (See biological medium, environmental medium.)

Ambient Temperature Temperature of the surrounding air or other medium.

Amprometric Titration A way of measuring concentrations of certain substances in water using an electric current that flows during a chemical reaction.

Anaerobic A life or process that occurs in, or is not destroyed by, the absence of oxygen.

Anaerobic Decomposition Reduction of the net energy level and change in chemical composition of organic matter caused by microorganisms in an oxygen-free environment.

Animal Dander Tiny scales of animal skin, a common indoor air pollutant.

Animal Studies Investigations using animals as surrogates for humans with the expectation that the results are pertinent to humans.

Anisotropy In hydrology, the conditions under which one or more hydraulic properties of an aquifer vary from a reference point.

Annular Space, Annulus The space between two concentric tubes or casings, or between the casing and the borehole wall.

Antagonism Interference or inhibition of the effect of one chemical by the action of another.

Antarctic "Ozone Hole" Refers to the seasonal depletion of ozone in the upper atmosphere above a large area of Antarctica. (See Ozone Hole.)

Anti-Degradation Clause Part of federal air quality and water quality requirements prohibiting deterioration where pollution levels are above the legal limit.

Anti-Microbial An agent that kills microbes.

Applicable or Relevant and Appropriate Requirements (ARARs) Any state or federal statute that pertains to protection of human life and the environment in addressing specific conditions or use of a particular cleanup technology at a Superfund site.

Applied Dose In exposure assessment, the amount of a substance in contact with the primary absorption boundaries of an organism (e.g. skin, lung tissue, gastrointestinal track) and available for absorption.

Aqueous Something made up of water.

Aqueous Solubility The maximum concentration of a chemical that will dissolve in pure water at a reference temperature.

Aquifer An underground geological formation, or group of formations, containing water. Are sources of groundwater for wells and springs.

Aquifer Test A test to determine hydraulic properties of an aquifer.

Aquitard Geological formation that may contain groundwater but is not capable of transmitting significant quantities of it under normal hydraulic gradients. May function as confining bed.

Architectural Coatings Coverings such as paint and roof tar that are used on exteriors of buildings.

Area of Review In the UIC program, the area surrounding an injection well that is reviewed during the permitting process to determine if flow between aquifers will be induced by the injection operation.

Area Source Any source of air pollution that is released over a relatively small area but which cannot be classified as a point source. Such sources may include vehicles and other small engines, small businesses and household activities, or biogenic sources such as a forest that releases hydrocarbons.

Aromatics A type of hydrocarbon, such as benzene or toluene, with a specific type of ring structure. Aromatics are sometimes added to gasoline in order to increase octane. Some aromatics are toxic.

Arsenicals Pesticides containing arsenic.

Artesian (Aquifer or Well) Water held under pressure in porous rock or soil confined by impermeable geological formations.

Asbestos A mineral fiber that can pollute air or water and cause cancer or asbestosis when inhaled. EPA has banned or severely restricted its use in manufacturing and construction.

Asbestos Abatement Procedures to control fiber release from asbestos-containing materials in a building or to remove them entirely, including removal, encapsulation, repair, enclosure, encasement, and operations and maintenance programs.

Asbestos Assessment In the asbestos-in-schools program, the evaluation of the physical condition and potential for damage of all friable asbestos containing materials and thermal insulation systems.

Asbestos Program Manager A building owner or designated representative who supervises all aspects of the facility asbestos management and control program.

Asbestos-Containing Waste Materials (ACWM) Mill tailings or any waste that contains commercial asbestos and is generated by a source covered by the Clean Air Act Asbestos NESHAPS.

Asbestosis A disease associated with inhalation of asbestos fibers. The disease makes breathing progressively more difficult and can be fatal.

A-Scale Sound Level A measurement of sound approximating the sensitivity of the human ear, used to note the intensity or annoyance level of sounds.

Ash The mineral content of a product remaining after complete combustion.

Assay A test for a specific chemical, microbe, or effect.

Assessment Endpoint In ecological risk assessment, an explicit expression of the environmental value to be protected; includes both an ecological entity and specific attributed thereof. entity (e.g. salmon are a valued ecological entity; reproduction and population maintenance—the attribute—form an assessment endpoint).

Assimilation The ability of a body of water to purify itself of pollutants.

Assimilative Capacity The capacity of a natural body of water to receive wastewaters or toxic materials without deleterious effects and without damage to aquatic life or humans who consume the water.

Association of Boards of Certification An international organization representing boards which certify the operators of waterworks and wastewater facilities.

Attainment Area An area considered to have air quality as good as or better than the national ambient air quality standards as defined in the Clean Air Act. An area may be an attainment area for one pollutant and a non-attainment area for others.

Attenuation The process by which a compound is reduced in concentration over time, through absorption, adsorption, degradation, dilution, and/or transformation. an also be the decrease with distance of sight caused by attenuation of light by particulate pollution.

Attractant A chemical or agent that lures insects or other pests by stimulating their sense of smell.

Attrition Wearing or grinding down of a substance by friction. Dust from such processes contributes to air pollution.

Availability Session Informal meeting at a public location where interested citizens can talk with EPA and state officials on a one-to-one basis.

Available Chlorine A measure of the amount of chlorine available in chlorinated lime, hypochlorite compounds, and other materials used as a source of chlorine when compared with that of liquid or gaseous chlorines.

Avoided Cost The cost a utility would incur to generate the next increment of electric capacity using its own resources; many landfill gas projects' buy back rates are based on avoided costs.

Back Pressure A pressure that can cause water to backflow into the water supply when a user's waste water system is at a higher pressure than the public system.

Backflow/Back Siphonage A reverse flow condition created by a difference in water pressures that causes water to flow back into the distribution pipes of a drinking water supply from any source other than the intended one.

Background Level 1. The concentration of a substance in an environmental media (air, water, or soil) that occurs naturally or is not the result of human activities. 2. In exposure assessment the concentration of a substance in a defined control area, during a fixed period of time before, during, or after a data-gathering operation..

Backwashing Reversing the flow of water back through the filter media to remove entrapped solids.

Backyard Composting Diversion of organic food waste and yard trimmings from the municipal waste stream by composting hem in one's yard through controlled decomposition of organic matter by bacteria and fungi into a humus-like product. It is considered source reduction, not recycling, because the composted materials never enter the municipal waste stream.

Barrel Sampler Open-ended steel tube used to collect soil samples.

BACT — Best Available Control Technology An emission limitation based on the maximum degree of emission reduction (considering energy, environmental, and economic impacts) achievable through application of production processes and available methods, systems, and techniques. BACT does not permit emissions in excess of those allowed under any applicable Clean Air Act provisions. Use of the BACT concept is allowable on a case by case basis for major new or modified emissions sources in attainment areas and applies to each regulated pollutant.

Bacteria (Singular: bacterium) Microscopic living organisms that can aid in pollution control by metabolizing organic matter in sewage, oil spills or other pollutants. However, bacteria in soil, water or air can also cause human, animal and plant health problems.

Bactericide A pesticide used to control or destroy bacteria, typically in the home, schools, or hospitals.

Baffle A flat board or plate, deflector, guide, or similar device constructed or placed in flowing water or slurry systems to cause more uniform flow velocities to absorb energy and to divert, guide, or agitate liquids.

Baffle Chamber In incinerator design, a chamber designed to promote the settling of fly ash and coarse particulate matter by changing the direction and/or reducing the velocity of the gases produced by the combustion of the refuse or sludge.

Baghouse Filter Large fabric bag, usually made of glass fibers, used to eliminate intermediate and large (greater than 20 PM in diameter) particles. This device operates like the bag of an electric vacuum cleaner, passing the air and smaller particles while entrapping the larger ones.

Bailer A pipe with a valve at the lower end, used to remove slurry from the bottom or side of a well as it is being drilled, or to collect groundwater samples from wells or open boreholes. 2. A tube of varying length.

Baling Compacting solid waste into blocks to reduce volume and simplify handling.

Ballistic Separator A machine that sorts organic from inorganic matter for composting.

Band Application The spreading of chemicals over, or next to, each row of plants in a field.

Banking A system for recording qualified air emission reductions for later use in bubble, offset, or netting transactions. (See emissions trading.)

Bar Screen In wastewater treatment, a device used to remove large solids.

Barrier Coating(s) A layer of a material that obstructs or prevents passage of something through a surface that is to be protected; e.g., grout, caulk, or various sealing compounds; sometimes used with polyurethane membranes to prevent corrosion or oxidation of metal surfaces, chemical impacts on various materials, or, for example, to prevent radon infiltration through walls, cracks, or joints in a house.

Basal Application In pesticides, the application of a chemical on plant stems or tree trunks just above the soil line.

Basalt Consistent year-round energy use of a facility; also refers to the minimum amount of electricity supplied continually to a facility.

Bean Sheet Common term for a pesticide data package record.

Bed Load Sediment particles resting on or near the channel bottom that are pushed or rolled along by the flow of water.

BEN EPA's computer model for analyzing a violator's economic gain from not complying with the law.

Bench-scale Tests Laboratory testing of potential cleanup technologies. (See treatability studies.)

Benefit-Cost Analysis An economic method for assessing the benefits and costs of achieving alternative health-based standards at given levels of health protection.

Benthic/Benthos An organism that feeds on the sediment at the bottom of a water body such as an ocean, lake, or river.

Bentonite A colloidal clay, expansible when moist, commonly used to provide a tight seal around a well casing.

Beryllium An metal hazardous to human health when inhaled as an airborne pollutant. It is discharged by machine shops, ceramic and propellant plants, and foundries.

Best Available Control Measures (BACM) A term used to refer to the most effective measures (according to EPA guidance) for controlling small or dispersed particulates and other emissions from sources such as roadway dust, soot and ash from woodstoves and open burning of rush, timber, grasslands, or trash.

Best Available Control Technology (BACT) The most stringent technology available for controlling emissions; major sources are required to use BACT, unless it can be demonstrated that it is not feasible for energy, environmental, or economic reasons.

Best Demonstrated Available Technology (BDAT) As identified by EPA, the most effective commercially available means of treating specific types of hazardous waste. The BDATs may change with advances in treatment technologies.

Best Management Practice (BMP) Methods that have been determined to be the most effective, practical means of preventing or reducing pollution from non-point sources.

Bimetal Beverage containers with steel bodies and aluminum tops; handled differently from pure aluminum in recycling.

Bioaccumulants Substances that increase in concentration in living organisms as they take in contaminated air, water, or food because the substances are very slowly metabolized or excreted. (See biological magnification.)

Bioassay A test to determine te relative strength of a substance by comparing its effect on a test organism with that of a standard preparation.

Bioavailabiliity Degree of ability to be absorbed and ready to interact in organism metabolism.

Biochemical Oxygen Demand (BOD) A measure of the amount of oxygen consumed in the biological processes that break down organic matter in water. The greater the BOD, the greater the degree of pollution.

Bioconcentration The accumulation of a chemical in tissues of a fish or other organism to levels greater than in the surrounding medium.

Biodegradable Capable of decomposing under natural conditions.

Biodiversity Refers to the variety and variability among living organisms and the ecological complexes in which they occur. Diversity can be defined as the number of different items and their relative frequencies. For biological diversity, these items are organized at many levels, ranging from complete ecosystems to the biochemical structures that are the molecular basis of heredity. Thus, the term encompasses different ecosystems, species, and genes.

Biological Contaminants Living organisms or derivates (e.g. viruses, bacteria, fungi, and mammal and bird antigens) that can cause harmful health effects when inhaled, swallowed, or otherwise taken into the body.

Biological Control In pest control, the use of animals and organisms that eat or otherwise kill or out-compete pests.

Biological Integrity The ability to support and maintain balanced, integrated, functionality in the natural habitat of a given region. Concept is applied primarily in drinking water management.

Biological Magnification Refers to the process whereby certain substances such as pesticides or heavy metals move up the food chain, work their way into rivers or lakes, and are eaten by aquatic organisms such as fish, which in turn are eaten by large birds, animals or humans. The substances become concentrated in tissues or internal organs as they move up the chain. (See bioaccumulants.)

Biological Measurement A measurement taken in a biological medium. For exposure assessment, it is related to the measurement is taken to related it to the established internal dose of a compound.

Biological Medium One of the major component of an organism; e.g. blood, fatty tissue, lymph nodes or breath, in which chemicals can be stored or transformed. (See ambient medium, environmental medium.)

Biological Oxidation Decomposition of complex organic materials by microorganisms. Occurs in self-purification of water bodies and in activated sludge wastewater treatment.

Biological Oxygen Demand (BOD) An indirect measure of the concentration of biologically degradable material present in organic wastes. It usually reflects the amount of oxygen consumed in five days by biological processes breaking down organic waste.

Biological Pesticides Certain microorganism, including bacteria, fungi, viruses, and protozoa that are effective in controlling pests. These agents usually do not have toxic effects on animals and people and do not leave toxic or persistent chemical residues in the environment.

Biological Stressors Organisms accidentally or intentionally dropped into habitats in which they do not evolve naturally; e.g., gypsy moths, Dutch elm disease, certain types of algae, and bacteria.

Biological Treatment A treatment technology that uses bacteria to consume organic waste.

Biologically Effective Dose The amount of a deposited or absorbed compound reaching the cells or target sites where adverse effect occur, or where the chemical interacts with a membrane.

Biologicals Vaccines, cultures and other preparations made from living organisms and their products, intended for use in diagnosing, immunizing, or treating humans or animals, or in related research.

Biomass All of the living material in a given area; often refers to vegetation.

Biome Entire community of living organisms in a single major ecological area. (See biotic community.)

Biomonitoring 1. The use of living organisms to test the suitability of effluents for discharge into receiving waters and to test the quality of such waters downstream from the discharge. 2. Analysis of blood, urine, tissues, etc. to measure chemical exposure in humans.

Bioremediation Use of living organisms to clean up oil spills or remove other pollutants from soil, water, or wastewater; use of organisms such as nonharmful insects to remove agricultural pests or counteract diseases of trees, plants, and garden soil.

Biosensor Analytical device comprising a biological recognition element (e.g., enzyme, receptor, DNA, antibody, or microorganism) in intimate contact with an electrochemical, optical, thermal, or acoustic signal transducer that together permit analyses of chemical properties or quantities. Shows potential development in some areas, including environmental monitoring.

Biosphere The portion of Earth and its atmosphere that can support life.

Biostabilizer A machine that converts solid waste into compost by grinding and aeration.

Biota The animal and plant life of a given region.

Biotechnology Techniques that use living organisms or parts of organisms to produce a variety of products (from medicines to industrial enzymes) to improve plants or animals or to develop microorganisms to remove toxics from bodies of water, or act as pesticides.

Biotic Community A naturally occurring assemblage of plants and animals that live in the same environment and are mutually sustaining and interdependent. (See biome.)

Biotransformation Conversion of a substance into other compounds by organisms; includes biodegredation.

Blackwater Water that contains animal, human, or food waste.

Blood Products Any product derived from human blood, including but not limited to blood plasma, platelets, red or white corpuscles, and derived licensed products such as interferon.

Bloom A proliferation of algae and/or higher aquatic plants in a body of water; often related to pollution, especially when pollutants accelerate growth.

BOD5 The amount of dissolved oxygen consumed in five days by biological processes breaking down organic matter.

Body Burden The amount of a chemical stored in the body at a given time, especially a potential toxin in the body as the result of exposure.

Bog A type of wetland that accumulates appreciable peat deposits. Bogs depend primarily on precipitation for their water source, and are usually acidic and rich in plant residue with a conspicuous mat of living green moss.

Boiler A vessel designed to transfer heat produced by combustion or electric resistance to water. Boilers may provide hot water or steam.

Boom 1. A floating device used to contain oil on a body of water. 2. A piece of equipment used to apply pesticides from a tractor or truck.

Borehole Hole made with drilling equipment.

Botanical Pesticide A pesticide whose active ingredient is a plant-produced chemical such as nicotine or strychnine. Also called a plant-derived pesticide.

Bottle Bill Proposed or enacted legislation which requires a returnable deposit on beer or soda containers and provides for retail store or other redemption. Such legislation is designed to discourage use of throw-away containers.

Bottom Ash The non-airborne combustion residue from burning pulverized coal in a boiler; the material which falls to the bottom of the boiler and is removed mechanically; a concentration of non-combustible materials, which may include toxics.

Bottom Land Hardwoods Forested freshwater wetlands adjacent to rivers in the southeastern United States, especially valuable for wildlife breeding, nesting and habitat.

Bounding Estimate An estimate of exposure, dose, or risk that is higher than that incurred by the person in the population with the currently highest exposure, dose, or risk. Bounding estimates are useful in developing statements that exposures, doses, or risks are not greater than an estimated value.

Brackish Mixed fresh and salt water.

Breakpoint Chlorination Addition of chlorine to water until the chlorine demand has been satisfied.

Breakthrough A crack or break in a filter bed that allows the passage of floc or particulate matter through a filter; will cause an increase in filter effluent turbidity.

Breathing Zone Area of air in which an organism inhales.

Brine Mud Waste material, often associated with well-drilling or mining, composed of mineral salts or other inorganic compounds.

British Thermal Unit Unit of heat energy equal to the amount of heat required to raise the temperature of one pound of water by one degree Fahrenheit at sea level.

Broadcast Application The spreading of pesticides over an entire area.

Brownfields Abandoned, idled, or under used industrial and commercial facilities/sites where expansion or redevelopment is complicated by real or perceived environmental contamination. They can be in urban, suburban, or rural areas. EPA's Brownfields initiative helps communities mitigate potential health risks and restore the economic viability of such areas or properties.

Bubble A system under which existing emissions sources can propose alternate means to comply with a set of emissions limitations; under the bubble concept, sources can control more than required at one emission point where control costs are relatively low in return for a comparable relaxation of controls at a second emission point where costs are higher.

Bubble Policy (See emissions trading.)

Buffer A solution or liquid whose chemical makeup is such that it minimizes changes in pH when acids or bases are added to it.

Buffer Strips Strips of grass or other erosion-resisting vegetation between or below cultivated strips or fields.

Building Cooling Load The hourly amount of heat that must be removed from a building to maintain indoor comfort (measured in British thermal units (Btus).

Building Envelope The exterior surface of a building's construction—the walls, windows, floors, roof, and floor. Also called building shell.

Building Related Illness Diagnosable illness whose cause and symptoms can be directly attributed to a specific pollutant source within a building (e.g., Legionnaire's disease, hypersensitivity, pneumonitis). (See sick building syndrome.)

Bulk Sample A small portion (usually thumbnail size) of a suspect asbestos-containing building material collected by an asbestos inspector for laboratory analysis to determine asbestos content.

Bulky Waste Large items of waste materials, such as appliances, furniture, large auto parts, trees, stumps.

Burial Ground (Graveyard) A disposal site for radioactive waste materials that uses earth or water as a shield.

Buy-Back Center Facility where individuals or groups bring recyclables in return for payment.

By-product Material, other than the principal product, generated as a consequence of an industrial process or as a breakdown product in a living system.

Cadmium (Cd) A heavy metal that accumulates in the environment.

Cancellation Refers to Section 6 (b) of the Federal Insecticide, Fungicide and Rodenticide Act (FIFRA) which authorizes cancellation of a pesticide registration if unreasonable adverse effects to the environment and public health develop when a product is used according to widespread and commonly recognized practice, or if its labeling or other material required to be submitted does not comply with FIFRA provisions.

Cap A layer of clay, or other impermeable material installed over the top of a closed landfill to prevent entry of rainwater and minimize leachate.

Capacity Assurance Plan A statewide plan which supports a state's ability to manage the hazardous waste generated within its boundaries over a twenty-year period.

Capillary Action Movement of water through very small spaces due to molecular forces called capillary forces.

Capillary Fringe The porous material just above the water table which may hold water by capillarity (a property of surface tension that draws water upwards) in the smaller void spaces.

Capture Efficiency The fraction of organic vapors generated by a process that are directed to an abatement or recovery device.

Carbon Absorber An add-on control device that uses activated carbon to absorb volatile organic compounds from a gas stream. (The VOCs are later recovered from the carbon.)

Carbon Adsorption A treatment system that removes contaminants from ground water or surface water by forcing it through tanks containing activated carbon treated to attract the contaminants.

Carbon Monoxide (CO) A colorless, odorless, poisonous gas produced by incomplete fossil fuel combustion.

Carbon Tetrachloride (CC14) Compound consisting of one carbon atom ad four chlorine atoms, once widely used as a industrial raw material, as a solvent, and in the production of CFCs. Use as a solvent ended when it was discovered to be carcinogenic.

Carboxyhemoglobin Hemoglobin in which the iron is bound to carbon monoxide (CO) instead of oxygen.

Carcinogen Any substance that can cause or aggravate cancer.

Carrier 1. The inert liquid or solid material in a pesticide product that serves as a delivery vehicle for the active ingredient. Carriers do not have toxic properties of their own. 2. Any material or system that can facilitate the movement of a pollutant into the body or cells.

Carrying Capacity 1. In recreation management, the amount of use a recreation area can sustain without loss of quality. 2. In wildlife management, the maximum number of animals an area can support during a given period.

CAS Registration Number A number assigned by the Chemical Abstract Service to identify a chemical.

Case Study A brief fact sheet providing risk, cost, and performance information on alternative methods and other pollution prevention ideas, compliance initiatives, voluntary efforts, etc.

Cask A thick-walled container (usually lead) used to transport radioactive material. Also called a coffin.

Catalyst A substance that changes the speed or yield of a chemical reaction without being consumed or chemically changed by the chemical reaction.

Catalytic Converter An air pollution abatement device that removes pollutants from motor vehicle exhaust, either by oxidizing them into carbon dioxide and water or reducing them to nitrogen.

Catalytic Incinerator A control device that oxidizes volatile organic compounds (VOCs) by using a catalyst to promote the combustion process. Catalytic incinerators require lower temperatures than conventional thermal incinerators, thus saving fuel and other costs.

Categorical Exclusion A class of actions which either individually or cumulatively would not have a significant effect on the human environment and therefore would not require preparation of an environmental assessment or environmental impact statement under the National Environmental Policy Act (NEPA).

Categorical Pretreatment Standard A technology-based effluent limitation for an industrial facility discharging into a municipal sewer system. Analogous in stringency to Best Availability Technology (BAT) for direct dischargers.

Cathodic Protection A technique to prevent corrosion of a metal surface by making it the cathode of an electrochemical cell.

Cavitation The formation and collapse of gas pockets or bubbles on the blade of an impeller or the gate of a valve; collapse of these pockets or bubbles drives water with such force that it can cause pitting of the gate or valve surface.

Cells 1. In solid waste disposal, holes where waste is dumped, compacted, and covered with layers of dirt on a daily basis. 2. The smallest structural part of living matter capable of functioning as an independent unit.

Cementitious Densely packed and nonfibrous friable materials.

Central Collection Point Location were a generator of regulated medical waste consolidates wastes originally generated at various locations in his facility. The wastes are gathered together for treatment on-site or for transportation elsewhere for treatment and/or disposal. This term could also apply to community hazardous waste collections, industrial and other waste management systems.

Centrifugal Collector A mechanical system using centrifugal force to remove aerosols from a gas stream or to remove water from sludge.

CERCLIS The federal Comprehensive Environmental Response, Compensation, and Liability Information System is a database that includes all sites which have been nominated for investigation by the Superfund program.

Channelization Straightening and deepening streams so water will move faster, a marsh-drainage tactic that can interfere with waste assimilation capacity, disturb fish and wildlife habitats, and aggravate flooding.

Characteristic Any one of the four categories used in defining hazardous waste: ignitability, corrosivity, reactivity, and toxicity.

Characterization of Ecological Effects Part of ecological risk assessment that evaluates ability of a stressor to cause adverse effects under given circumstances.

Characterization of Exposure Portion of an ecological risk assessment that evaluates interaction of a stressor with one or more ecological entities.

Check-Valve Tubing Pump Water sampling tool also referred to as a water Pump.

Chemical Case For purposes of review and regulation, the grouping of chemically similar pesticide active ingredients (e.g., salts and esters of the same chemical) into chemical cases.

Chemical Compound A distinct and pure substance formed by the union or two or more elements in definite proportion by weight.

Chemical Element A fundamental substance comprising one kind of atom; the simplest form of matter.

Chemical Oxygen Demand (COD) A measure of the oxygen required to oxidize all compounds, both organic and inorganic, in water.

Chemical Stressors Chemicals released to the environment through industrial waste, auto emissions, pesticides, and other human activity that can cause illnesses and even death in plants and animals.

Chemical Treatment Any one of a variety of technologies that use chemicals or a variety of chemical processes to treat waste.

Chemnet Mutual aid network of chemical shippers and contractors that assigns a contracted emergency response company to provide technical support if a representative of the firm whose chemicals are involved in an incident is not readily available.

Chemosterilant A chemical that controls pests by preventing reproduction.

Chemtrec The industry-sponsored Chemical Transportation Emergency Center; provides information and/or emergency assistance to emergency responders.

Child-Resistant Packaging (CRP) Packaging that protects children or adults from injury or illness resulting from accidental contact with or ingestion of residential pesticides that meet or exceed specific toxicity levels. Required by FIFRA regulations. Term is also used for protective packaging of medicines.

Chiller A device that generates a cold liquid that is circulated through an air-handling unit's cooling coil to cool the air supplied to the building.

Chilling Effect The lowering of the Earth's temperature because of increased particles in the air blocking the sun's rays. (See greenhouse effect.)

Chisel Plowing Preparing croplands by using a special implement that avoids complete inversion of the soil as in conventional plowing. Chisel plowing can leave a protective cover or crops residues on the soil surface to help prevent erosion and improve filtration.

Chlorinated Hydrocarbons 1. Chemicals containing only chlorine, carbon, and hydrogen. These include a class of persistent, broad-spectrum insecticides that linger in the environment and accumulate in the food chain. Among them are DDT, aldrin, dieldrin, heptachlor, chlordane, lindane, endrin, Mirex, hexachloride, and toxaphene. Other examples include TCE, used as an industrial solvent. 2. Any chlorinated organic compounds including chlorinated solvents such as dichloromethane, trichloromethylene, chloroform.

Chlorinated Solvent An organic solvent containing chlorine atoms (e.g., methylene chloride and 1,1,1-trichloromethane). Uses of chlorinated solvents are include aerosol spray containers, in highway paint, and dry cleaning fluids.

Chlorination The application of chlorine to drinking water, sewage, or industrial waste to disinfect or to oxidize undesirable compounds.

Chlorinator A device that adds chlorine, in gas or liquid form, to water or sewage to kill infectious bacteria.

Chlorine-Contact Chamber That part of a water treatment plant where effluent is disinfected by chlorine.

Chlorofluorocarbons (CFCs) A family of inert, nontoxic, and easily liquefied chemicals used in refrigeration, air conditioning, packaging, insulation, or as solvents and aerosol propellants. Because CFCs are not destroyed in the lower atmosphere they drift into the upper atmosphere where their chlorine components destroy ozone. (See fluorocarbons.)

Chlorophenoxy A class of herbicides that may be found in domestic water supplies and cause adverse health effects.

Chlorosis Discoloration of normally green plant parts caused by disease, lack of nutrients, or various air pollutants.

Cholinesterase An enzyme found in animals that regulates nerve impulses by the inhibition of acetylcholine. Cholinesterase inhibition is associated with a variety of acute symptoms such as nausea, vomiting, blurred vision, stomach cramps, and rapid heart rate.

Chromium (See heavy metals.)

Chronic Effect An adverse effect on a human or animal in which symptoms recur frequently or develop slowly over a long period of time.

Chronic Exposure Multiple exposures occurring over an extended period of time or over a significant fraction of an animal's or human's lifetime (usually seven years to a lifetime).

Chronic Toxicity The capacity of a substance to cause long-term poisonous health effects in humans, animals, fish, and other organisms. (See acute toxicity.)

Circle of Influence The circular outer edge of a depression produced in the water table by the pumping of water from a well. (See cone of depression.)

Cistern Small tank or storage facility used to store water for a home or farm; often used to store rain water.

Clarification Clearing action that occurs during wastewater treatment when solids settle out. This is often aided by centrifugal action and chemically induced coagulation in wastewater.

Clarifier A tank in which solids settle to the bottom and are subsequently removed as sludge.

Class I Area Under the Clean Air Act. a Class I area is one in which visibility is protected more stringently than under the national ambient air quality standards; includes national parks, wilderness areas, monuments, and other areas of special national and cultural significance.

Class I Substance One of several groups of chemicals with an ozone depletion potential of 0.2 or higher, including CFCS, Halons, Carbon Tetrachloride, and Methyl Chloroform (listed in the Clean Air Act), and HBFCs and Ethyl Bromide (added by EPA regulations). (See Global warming potential.)

Class II Substance A substance with an ozone depletion potential of less than 0.2. All HCFCs are currently included in this classification. (See Global warming potential.)

Clay Soil Soil material containing more than 40 percent clay, less than 45 percent sand, and less than 40 percent silt.

Clean Coal Technology Any technology not in widespread use prior to the Clean Air Act Amendments of 1990. This Act will achieve significant reductions in pollutants associated with the burning of coal.

Clean Fuels Blends or substitutes for gasoline fuels, including compressed natural gas, methanol, ethanol, and liquified petroleum gas.

Cleaner Technologies Substitutes Assessment A document that systematically evaluates the relative risk, performance, and cost tradeoffs of technological alternatives; serves as a repository for all the technical data (including methodology and results) developed by a DfE or other pollution prevention or education project.

Cleanup Actions taken to deal with a release or threat of release of a hazardous substance that could affect humans and/or the environment. The term "cleanup" is sometimes used interchangeably with the terms remedial action, removal action, response action, or corrective action.

Clear Cut Harvesting all the trees in one area at one time, a practice that can encourage fast rainfall or snowmelt runoff, erosion, sedimentation of streams and lakes, and flooding, and destroys vital habitat.

Clear Well A reservoir for storing filtered water of sufficient quantity to prevent the need to vary the filtration rate with variations in demand. Also used to provide chlorine contact time for disinfection.

Climate Change (also referred to as "global climate change") The term "climate change" is sometimes used to refer to all forms of climatic inconsistency, but because the Earth's climate is never static, the term is more properly used to imply a significant change from one climatic condition to another. In some cases, "climate change" has been used synonymously with the term, "global warming"; scientists, however, tend to use the term in the wider sense to also include natural changes in climate. (See global warming.)

Cloning In biotechnology, obtaining a group of genetically identical cells from a single cell; making identical copies of a gene.

Closed-Loop Recycling Reclaiming or reusing wastewater for non-potable purposes in an enclosed process.

Closure The procedure a landfill operator must follow when a landfill reaches its legal capacity for solid ceasing acceptance of solid waste and placing a cap on the landfill site.

Coagulation Clumping of particles in wastewater to settle out impurities, often induced by chemicals such as lime, alum, and iron salts.

Coal Cleaning Technology A precombustion process by which coal is physically or chemically treated to remove some of its sulfur so as to reduce sulfur dioxide emissions.

Coal Gasification Conversion of coal to a gaseous product by one of several available technologies.

Coastal Zone Lands and waters adjacent to the coast that exert an influence on the uses of the sea and its ecology, or whose uses and ecology are affected by the sea.

Code of Federal Regulations (CFR) Document that codifies all rules of the executive departments and agencies of the federal government. It is divided into fifty volumes, known as titles. Title 40 of the CFR (referenced as 40 CFR) lists all environmental regulations.

Coefficient of Haze (COH) A measurement of visibility interference in the atmosphere.

Co-fire Burning of two fuels in the same combustion unit; e.g., coal and natural gas, or oil and coal.

Cogeneration The consecutive generation of useful thermal and electric energy from the same fuel source.

Coke Oven An industrial process which converts coal into coke, one of the basic materials used in blast furnaces for the conversion of iron ore into iron.

Cold Temperature CO A standard for automobile emissions of carbon monoxide (CO) emissions to be met at a low temperature (i.e. 20 degrees Fahrenheit). Conventional automobile catalytic converters are not efficient in cold weather until they warm up.

Coliform Index A rating of the purity of water based on a count of fecal bacteria.

Coliform Organism Microorganisms found in the intestinal tract of humans and animals. Their presence in water indicates fecal pollution and potentially adverse contamination by pathogens.

Collector Public or private hauler that collects nonhazardous waste and recyclable materials from residential, commercial, institutional and industrial sources. (See hauler.)

Collector Sewers Pipes used to collect and carry wastewater from individual sources to an interceptor sewer that will carry it to a treatment facility.

Colloids Very small, finely divided solids (that do not dissolve) that remain dispersed in a liquid for a long time due to their small size and electrical charge.

Combined Sewer Overflows Discharge of a mixture of storm water and domestic waste when the flow capacity of a sewer system is exceeded during rainstorms.

Combined Sewers A sewer system that carries both sewage and storm-water runoff. Normally, its entire flow goes to a waste treatment plant, but during a heavy storm, the volume of water may be so great as to cause overflows of untreated mixtures of storm water and sewage into receiving waters. Storm-water runoff may also carry toxic chemicals from industrial areas or streets into the sewer system.

Combustion 1. Burning, or rapid oxidation, accompanied by release of energy in the form of heat and light. 2. Refers to controlled burning of waste, in which heat chemically alters organic compounds, converting into stable inorganics such as carbon dioxide and water.

Combustion Chamber The actual compartment where waste is burned in an incinerator.

Combustion Product Substance produced during the burning or oxidation of a material.

Command Post Facility located at a safe distance upwind from an accident site, where the on-scene coordinator, responders, and technical representatives make response decisions, deploy manpower and equipment, maintain liaison with news media, and handle communications.

Command-and-Control Regulations Specific requirements prescribing how to comply with specific standards defining acceptable levels of pollution.

Comment Period Time provided for the public to review and comment on a proposed EPA action or rulemaking after publication in the Federal Register.

Commercial Waste All solid waste emanating from business establishments such as stores, markets, office buildings, restaurants, shopping centers, and theaters.

Commercial Waste Management Facility A treatment, storage, disposal, or transfer facility which accepts waste from a variety of sources, as compared to a private facility which normally manages a limited waste stream generated by its own operations.

Commingled Recyclables Mixed recyclables that are collected together.

Comminuter A machine that shreds or pulverizes solids to make waste treatment easier.

Comminution Mechanical shredding or pulverizing of waste. Used in both solid waste management and wastewater treatment.

Common Sense Initiative Voluntary program to simplify environmental regulation to achieve cleaner, cheaper, smarter results, starting with six major industry sectors.

Community In ecology, an assemblage of populations of different species within a specified location in space and time. Sometimes, a particular subgrouping may be specified, such as the fish community in a lake or the soil arthropod community in a forest.

Community Relations The EPA effort to establish two-way communication with the public to create understanding of EPA programs and related actions, to ensure public input into decision-making processes related to affected communities, and to make certain that the Agency is aware of and responsive to public concerns. Specific community relations activities are required in relation to Superfund remedial actions.

Community Water System A public water system which serves at least 15 service connections used by year-round residents or regularly serves at least 25 year-round residents.

Compact Fluorescent Lamp (CFL) Small fluorescent lamps used as more efficient alternatives to incandescent lighting. Also called PL, CFL, Twin-Tube, or BIAX lamps.

Compaction Reduction of the bulk of solid waste by rolling and tamping.

Comparative Risk Assessment Process that generally uses the judgement of experts to predict effects and set priorities among a wide range of environmental problems.

Complete Treatment A method of treating water that consists of the addition of coagulant chemicals, flash mixing, coagulation-flocculation, sedimentation, and filtration. Also called conventional filtration.

Compliance Coal Any coal that emits less than 1.2 pounds of sulfur dioxide per million Btu when burned. Also known as low sulfur coal.

Compliance Coating A coating whose volatile organic compound content does not exceed that allowed by regulation.

Compliance Cycle The 9-year calendar year cycle, beginning January 1, 1993, during which public water systems must monitor. Each cycle consists of three 3-year compliance periods.

Compliance Monitoring Collection and evaluation of data, including self-monitoring reports, and verification to show whether pollutant concentrations and loads contained in permitted discharges are in compliance with the limits and conditions specified in the permit.

Compliance Schedule A negotiated agreement between a pollution source and a government agency that specifies dates and procedures by which a source will reduce emissions and, thereby, comply with a regulation.

Composite Sample A series of water samples taken over a given period of time and weighted by flow rate.

Compost A humus or soil-like material created from aerobic, microbial decomposition of organic materials such as food scraps, yard trimmings, and manure

Composting The controlled biological decomposition of organic material in the presence of air to form a humus-like material. Controlled methods of composting include mechanical mixing and aerating, ventilating the materials by dropping them through a vertical series of aerated chambers, or placing the compost in piles out in the open air and mixing it or turning it periodically.

Composting Facilities 1. An offsite facility where the organic component of municipal solid waste is decomposed under controlled conditions; 2.an aerobic process in which organic materials are ground or shredded and then decomposed to humus in windrow piles or in mechanical digesters, drums, or similar enclosures.

Compressed Natural Gas (CNG) An alternative fuel for motor vehicles; considered one of the cleanest because of low hydrocarbon emissions and its vapors are relatively non-ozone producing. However, vehicles fueled with CNG do emit a significant quantity of nitrogen oxides.

Concentration The relative amount of a substance mixed with another substance. An example is five ppm of carbon monoxide in air or 1 mg/l of iron in water.

Condensate 1. Liquid formed when warm landfill gas cools as it travels through a collection system. 2. Water created by cooling steam or water vapor.

Condensate Return System System that returns the heated water condensing within steam piping to the boiler and thus saves energy.

Conditional Registration Under special circumstances, the Federal Insecticide, Fungicide, and Rodenticide Act (FIFRA) permits registration of pesticide products that is "conditional" upon the submission of additional data. These special circumstances include a finding by the EPA Administrator that a new product or use of an existing pesticide will not significantly increase the risk of unreasonable adverse effects. A product containing a new (previously unregistered) active ingredient may be conditionally registered only if the Administrator finds that such conditional registration is in the public interest, that a reasonable time for conducting the additional studies has not elapsed, and the use of the pesticide for the period of conditional registration will not present an unreasonable risk.

Conditionally Exempt Generators (CE) Persons or enterprises which produce less than 220 pounds of hazardous waste per month. Exempt from most regulation, they are required merely to determine whether their waste is hazardous, notify appropriate state or local agencies, and ship it by an authorized transporter to a permitted facility for proper disposal. (See small quantity generator.)

Conductance A rapid method of estimating the dissolved solids content of water supply by determining the capacity of a water sample to carry an electrical current. Conductivity is a measure of the ability of a solution to carry and electrical current.

Conductivity A measure of the ability of a solution to carry an electrical current.

Cone of Depression A depression in the water table that develops around a pumped well.

Cone of Influence The depression, roughly conical in shape, produced in a water table by the pumping of water from a well.

Cone Penterometer Testing (CPT) A direct push system used to measure lithology based on soil penetration resistance. Sensors in the tip of the cone of the DP rod measure tip resistance and side-wall friction, transmitting electrical signals to digital processing equipment on the ground surface. (See direct push.)

Confidential Business Information (CBI) Material that contains trade secrets or commercial or financial information that has been claimed as confidential by its source (e.g., a pesticide or new chemical formulation registrant). EPA has special procedures for handling such information.

Confidential Statement of Formula (CSF) A list of the ingredients in a new pesticide or chemical formulation. The list is submitted at the time for application for registration or change in formulation.

Confined Aquifer An aquifer in which ground water is confined under pressure which is significantly greater than atmospheric pressure.

Confluent Growth A continuous bacterial growth covering all or part of the filtration area of a membrane filter in which the bacteria colonies are not discrete.

Consent Decree A legal document, approved by a judge, that formalizes an agreement reached between EPA and potentially responsible parties (PRPs) through which PRPs will conduct all or part of a cleanup action at a Superfund site; cease or correct actions or processes that are polluting the environment; or otherwise comply with EPA initiated regulatory enforcement actions to resolve the contamination at the Superfund site involved. The consent decree describes the actions PRPs will take and may be subject to a public comment period.

Conservation Preserving and renewing, when possible, human and natural resources. The use, protection, and improvement of natural resources according to principles that will ensure their highest economic or social benefits.

Conservation Easement Easement restricting a landowner to land uses that that are compatible with long-term conservation and environmental values.

Constituent(s) of Concern Specific chemicals that are identified for evaluation in the site assessment process

Construction and Demolition Waste Waste building materials, dredging materials, tree stumps, and rubble resulting from construction, remodeling, repair, and demolition of homes, commercial buildings and other structures and pavements. May contain lead, asbestos, or other hazardous substances.

Construction Ban If, under the Clean Air Act, EPA disapproves an area's planning requirements for correcting nonattainment, EPA can ban the construction or modification of any major stationary source of the pollutant for which the area is in nonattainment.

Consumptive Water Use Water removed from available supplies without return to a water resources system, e.g., water used in manufacturing, agriculture, and food preparation.

Contact Pesticide A chemical that kills pests when it touches them, instead of by ingestion. Also, soil that contains the minute skeletons of certain algae that scratch and dehydrate waxy-coated insects.

Contaminant Any physical, chemical, biological, or radiological substance or matter that has an adverse effect on air, water, or soil.

Contamination Introduction into water, air, and soil of microorganisms, chemicals, toxic substances, wastes, or wastewater in a concentration that makes the medium unfit for its next intended use. Also applies to surfaces of objects, buildings, and various household and agricultural use products.

Contamination Source Inventory An inventory of contaminant sources within delineated State Water-Protection Areas. Targets likely sources for further investigation.

Contingency Plan A document setting out an organized, planned, and coordinated course of action to be followed in case of a fire, explosion, or other accident that releases toxic chemicals, hazardous waste, or radioactive materials that threaten human health or the environment. (See National Oil and Hazardous Substances Contingency Plan.)

Continuous Discharge A routine release to the environment that occurs without interruption, except for infrequent shutdowns for maintenance, process changes, etc.

Continuous Sample A flow of water, waste or other material from a particular place in a plant to the location where samples are collected for testing. May be used to obtain grab or composite samples.

Contour Plowing Soil tilling method that follows the shape of the land to discourage erosion.

Contour Strip Farming A kind of contour farming in which row crops are planted in strips, between alternating strips of close-growing, erosion-resistant forage crops.

Contract Labs Laboratories under contract to EPA, which analyze samples taken from waste, soil, air, and water or carry out research projects.

Control Technique Guidelines (CTG) EPA documents designed to assist state and local pollution authorities to achieve and maintain air quality standards for certain sources (e.g., organic emissions from solvent metal cleaning known as degreasing) through reasonably available control technologies (RACT).

Controlled Reaction A chemical reaction under temperature and pressure conditions maintained within safe limits to produce a desired product or process.

Conventional Filtration (See complete treatment.)

Conventional Pollutants Statutorily listed pollutants understood well by scientists. These may be in the form of organic waste, sediment, acid, bacteria, viruses, nutrients, oil and grease, or heat.

Conventional Site Assessment Assessment in which most of the sample analysis and interpretation of data is completed off-site; process usually requires repeated mobilization of equipment and staff in order to fully determine the extent of contamination.

Conventional Systems Systems that have been traditionally used to collect municipal wastewater in gravity sewers and convey it to a central primary or secondary treatment plant prior to discharge to surface waters.

Conventional Tilling Tillage operations considered standard for a specific location and crop and that tend to bury the crop residues; usually considered as a base for determining the cost effectiveness of control practices.

Conveyance Loss Water loss in pipes, channels, conduits, ditches by leakage or evaporation.

Cooling Electricity Use Amount of electricity used to meet the building cooling load. (See building cooling load.)

Cooling Tower A structure that helps remove heat from water used as a coolant; e.g., in electric power generating plants.

Cooperative Agreement An assistance agreement whereby EPA transfers money, property, services or anything of value to a state, university, non-profit, or not-for-profit organization for the accomplishment of authorized activities or tasks.

Core The uranium-containing heart of a nuclear reactor, where energy is released.

Core Program Cooperative Agreement An assistance agreement whereby EPA supports states or tribal governments with funds to help defray the cost of non-item-specific administrative and training activities.

Corrective Action EPA can require treatment, storage and disposal (TSDF) facilities handling hazardous waste to undertake corrective actions to clean up spills resulting from failure to follow hazardous waste management procedures or other mistakes. The process includes cleanup procedures designed to guide TSDFs toward in spills.

Corrosion The dissolution and wearing away of metal caused by a chemical reaction such as between water and the pipes, chemicals touching a metal surface, or contact between two metals.

Corrosive A chemical agent that reacts with the surface of a material causing it to deteriorate or wear away.

Cost/Benefit Analysis A quantitative evaluation of the costs which would have incurred by implementing an environmental regulation versus the overall benefits to society of the proposed action.

Cost-Effective Alternative An alternative control or corrective method identified after analysis as being the best available in terms of reliability, performance, and cost. Although costs are one important consideration, regulatory and compliance analysis does not require EPA to choose the least expensive alternative. For example, when selecting or approving a method for cleaning up a Superfund site, the Agency balances costs with the long-term effectiveness of the methods proposed and the potential danger posed by the site.

Cost Recovery A legal process by which potentially responsible parties who contributed to contamination at a Superfund site can be required to reimburse the Trust Fund for money spent during any cleanup actions by the federal government.

Cost Sharing A publicly financed program through which society, as a beneficiary of environmental protection, shares part of the cost of pollution control with those who must actually install the controls. In Superfund, for example, the government may pay part of the cost of a cleanup action with those responsible for the pollution paying the major share.

Cover Crop A crop that provides temporary protection for delicate seedlings and/or provides a cover canopy for seasonal soil protection and improvement between normal crop production periods.

Cover Material Soil used to cover compacted solid waste in a sanitary landfill.

Cradle-to-Grave or Manifest System A procedure in which hazardous materials are identified and followed as they are produced, treated, transported, and disposed of by a series of permanent, linkable, descriptive documents (e.g., manifests). Commonly referred to as the cradle-to-grave system.

Criteria Descriptive factors taken into account by EPA in setting standards for various pollutants. These factors are used to determine limits on allowable concentration levels, and to limit the number of violations per year. When issued by EPA, the criteria provide guidance to the states on how to establish their standards.

Criteria Pollutants The 1970 amendments to the Clean Air Act required EPA to set National Ambient Air Quality Standards for certain pollutants known to be hazardous to human health. EPA has identified and set standards to protect human health and welfare for six pollutants: ozone, carbon monoxide, total suspended particulates, sulfur dioxide, lead, and nitrogen oxide. The term, "criteria pollutants" derives from the requirement that EPA must describe the characteristics and potential health and welfare effects of these pollutants. It is on the basis of these criteria that standards are set or revised.

Critical Effect The first adverse effect, or its known precursor, that occurs as a dose rate increases. Designation is based on evaluation of overall database.

Crop Consumptive Use The amount of water transpired during plant growth plus what evaporated from the soil surface and foliage in the crop area.

Crop Rotation Planting a succession of different crops on the same land rea as opposed to planting the same crop time after time.

Cross-Connection Any actual or potential connection between a drinking water system and an unapproved water supply or other source of contamination.

Cross Contamination The movement of underground contaminants from one level or area to another due to invasive subsurface activities.

Crumb Rubber Ground rubber fragments the size of sand or silt used in rubber or plastic products, or processed further into reclaimed rubber or asphalt products.

Cryptosporidium A protozoan microbe associated with the disease cryptosporidiosis in man. The disease can be transmitted through ingestion of drinking water, person-to-person contact, or other pathways, and can cause acute diarrhea, abdominal pain, vomiting, fever, and can be fatal as it was in the Milwaukee episode.

Cubic Feet Per Minute (CFM) A measure of the volume of a substance flowing through air within a fixed period of time. With regard to indoor air, refers to the amount of air, in cubic feet, that is exchanged with outdoor air in a minute's time; i.e., the air exchange rate.

Cullet Crushed glass.

Cultural Eutrophication Increasing rate at which water bodies "die" by pollution from human activities.

Cultures and Stocks Infectious agents and associated biologicals including cultures from medical and pathological laboratories; cultures and stocks of infectious agents from research and industrial laboratories; waste from the production of biologicals; discarded live and attenuated vaccines; and culture dishes and devices used to transfer, inoculate, and mix cultures. (See regulated medical waste.)

Cumulative Ecological Risk Assessment Consideration of the total ecological risk from multiple stressors to a given eco-zone.

Cumulative Exposure The sum of exposures of an organism to a pollutant over a period of time.

Cumulative Working Level Months (CWLM) The sum of lifetime exposure to radon working levels expressed in total working level months.

Curb Stop A water service shutoff valve located in a water service pipe near the curb and between the water main and the building.

Curbside Collection Method of collecting recyclable materials at homes, community districts or businesses.

Cutie-Pie An instrument used to measure radiation levels.

Cuttings Spoils left by conventional drilling with hollow stem auger or rotary drilling equipment.

Cyclone Collector A device that uses centrifugal force to remove large particles from polluted air.

Data Call-In A part of the Office of Pesticide Programs (OPP) process of developing key required test data, especially on the long-term, chronic effects of existing pesticides, in advance of scheduled Registration Standard reviews. Data Call-In from manufacturers is an adjunct of the Registration Standards program intended to expedite re-registration.

Data Quality Objectives (DQOs) Qualitative and quantitative statements of the overall level of uncertainty that a decision-maker will accept in results or decisions based on environmental data. They provide the statistical framework for planning and managing environmental data operations consistent with user's needs.

Day Tank Another name for deaerating tank. (See age tank.)

DDT The first chlorinated hydrocarbon insecticide chemical name: Dichloro-Diphenyl-Trichloroethane. It has a half-life of 15 years and can collect in fatty tissues of certain animals. EPA banned registration and interstate sale of DDT for virtually all but emergency uses in the United States in 1972 because of its persistence in the environment and accumulation in the food chain.

Dead End The end of a water main which is not connected to other parts of the distribution system.

Deadmen Anchors drilled or cemented into the ground to provide additional reactive mass for DP sampling rigs.

Decant To draw off the upper layer of liquid after the heaviest material (a solid or another liquid) has settled.

Decay Products Degraded radioactive materials, often referred to as "daughters" or "progeny"; radon decay products of most concern from a public health standpoint are polonium-214 and polonium-218.

Dechlorination Removal of chlorine from a substance.

Decomposition The breakdown of matter by bacteria and fungi, changing the chemical makeup and physical appearance of materials.

Decontamination Removal of harmful substances such as noxious chemicals, harmful bacteria or other organisms, or radioactive material from exposed individuals, rooms and furnishings in buildings, or the exterior environment.

Deep-Well Injection Deposition of raw or treated, filtered hazardous waste by pumping it into deep wells, where it is contained in the pores of permeable subsurface rock.

Deflocculating Agent A material added to a suspension to prevent settling.

Defluoridation The removal of excess flouride in drinking water to prevent the staining of teeth.

Defoliant An herbicide that removes leaves from trees and growing plants.

Degasification A water treatment that removes dissolved gases from the water.

Degree-Day A rough measure used to estimate the amount of heating required in a given area; is defined as the difference between the mean daily temperature and 65 degrees Fahrenheit. Degree-days are also calculated to estimate cooling requirements.

Delegated State A state (or other governmental entity such as a tribal government) that has received authority to administer an environmental regulatory program in lieu of a federal counterpart. As used in connection with NPDES, UIC, and PWS programs, the term does not connote any transfer of federal authority to a state.

Delist Use of the petition process to have a facility's toxic designation rescinded.

Demand-side Waste Management Prices whereby consumers use purchasing decisions to communicate to product manufacturers that they prefer environmentally sound products packaged with the least amount of waste, made from recycled or recyclable materials, and containing no hazardous substances.

Demineralization A treatment process that removes dissolved minerals from water.

Denitrification The biological reduction of nitrate to nitrogen gas by denitrifying bacteria in soil.

Dense Non-Aqueous Phase Liquid (DNAPL) Non-aqueous phase liquids such as chlorinated hydrocarbon solvents or petroleum fractions with a specific gravity greater than 1.0 that sink through the water column until they reach a confining layer. Because they are at the bottom of aquifers instead of floating on the water table, typical monitoring wells do not indicate their presence.

Density A measure of how heavy a specific volume of a solid, liquid, or gas is in comparison to water, depending on the chemical.

Depletion Curve In hydraulics, a graphical representation of water depletion from storage-stream channels, surface soil, and groundwater. A depletion curve can be drawn for base flow, direct runoff, or total flow.

Depressurization A condition that occurs when the air pressure inside a structure is lower that the air pressure outdoors. Depressurization can occur when household appliances such as fireplaces or furnaces, that consume or exhaust house air, are not supplied with enough makeup air. Radon may be drawn into a house more rapidly under depressurized conditions.

Dermal Absorption/Penetration Process by which a chemical penetrates the skin and enters the body as an internal dose.

Dermal Exposure Contact between a chemical and the skin.

Dermal Toxicity The ability of a pesticide or toxic chemical to poison people or animals by contact with the skin. (See contact pesticide.)

DES A synthetic estrogen, diethylstilbestrol is used as a growth stimulant in food animals. Residues in meat are thought to be carcinogenic.

Desalination [Desalinization] (1) Removing salts from ocean or brackish water by using various technologies. (2) Removal of salts from soil by artificial means, usually leaching.

Desiccant A chemical agent that absorbs moisture; some desiccants are capable of drying out plants or insects, causing death.

Design Capacity The average daily flow that a treatment plant or other facility is designed to accommodate.

Design Value The monitored reading used by EPA to determine an area's air quality status; e.g., for ozone, the fourth highest reading measured over the most recent three years is the design value.

Designated Pollutant An air pollutant which is neither a criteria nor hazardous pollutant, as described in the Clean Air Act, but for which new source performance standards exist. The Clean Air Act does require states to control these pollutants, which include acid mist, total reduced sulfur (TRS), and fluorides.

Designated Uses Those water uses identified in state water quality standards that must be achieved and maintained as required under the Clean Water Act. Uses can include cold water fisheries, public water supply, and irrigation.

Designer Bugs Popular term for microbes developed through biotechnology that can degrade specific toxic chemicals at their source in toxic waste dumps or in ground water.

Destination Facility The facility to which regulated medical waste is shipped for treatment and destruction, incineration, and/or disposal.

Destratification Vertical mixing within a lake or reservoir to totally or partially eliminate separate layers of temperature, plant, or animal life.

Destroyed Medical Waste Regulated medical waste that has been ruined, torn apart, or mutilated through thermal treatment, melting, shredding, grinding, tearing, or breaking, so that it is no longer generally recognized as medical waste, but has not yet been treated (excludes compacted regulated medical waste).

Destruction and Removal Efficiency (DRE) A percentage that represents the number of molecules of a compound removed or destroyed in an incinerator relative to the number of molecules entering the system (e.g., a DRE of 99.99 percent means that 9,999 molecules are destroyed for every 10,000 that enter; 99.99 percent is known as "four nines." For some pollutants, the RCRA removal requirement may be as stringent as "six nines").

Destruction Facility A facility that destroys regulated medical waste.

Desulfurization Removal of sulfur from fossil fuels to reduce pollution.

Detectable Leak Rate The smallest leak (from a storage tank), expressed in terms of gallons- or liters-per-hour, that a test can reliably discern with a certain probability of detection or false alarm.

Detection Criterion A predetermined rule to ascertain whether a tank is leaking or not. Most volumetric tests use a threshold value as the detection criterion. (See volumetric tank tests.)

Detection Limit The lowest concentration of a chemical that can reliably be distinguished from a zero concentration.

Detention Time 1. The theoretical calculated time required for a small amount of water to pass through a tank at a given rate of flow. 2. The actual time that a small amount of water is in a settling basin, flocculating basin, or rapid-mix chamber. 3. In storage reservoirs, the length of time water will be held before being used.

Detergent Synthetic washing agent that helps to remove dirt and oil. Some contain compounds which kill useful bacteria and encourage algae growth when they are in wastewater that reaches receiving waters.

Development Effects Adverse effects such as altered growth, structural abnormality, functional deficiency, or death observed in a developing organism.

Dewater 1. Remove or separate a portion of the water in a sludge or slurry to dry the sludge so it can be handled and disposed of. 2. Remove or drain the water from a tank or trench.

Diatomaceous Earth (Diatomite) A chalk-like material (fossilized diatoms) used to filter out solid waste in wastewater treatment plants; also used as an active ingredient in some powdered pesticides.

Diazinon An insecticide. In 1986, EPA banned its use on open areas such as sod farms and golf courses because it posed a danger to migratory birds. The ban did not apply to agricultural, home lawn or commercial establishment uses.

Dibenzofurans A group of organic compounds, some of which are toxic.

Dicofol A pesticide used on citrus fruits.

Diffused Air A type of aeration that forces oxygen into sewage by pumping air through perforated pipes inside a holding tank.

Diffusion The movement of suspended or dissolved particles (or molecules) from a more concentrated to a less concentrated area. The process tends to distribute the particles or molecules more uniformly.

Digester In wastewater treatment, a closed tank; in solid-waste conversion, a unit in which bacterial action is induced and accelerated in order to break down organic matter and establish the proper carbon to nitrogen ratio.

Digestion The biochemical decomposition of organic matter, resulting in partial gasification, liquefaction, and mineralization of pollutants.

Dike A low wall that can act as a barrier to prevent a spill from spreading.

Diluent Any liquid or solid material used to dilute or carry an active ingredient.

Dilution Ratio The relationship between the volume of water in a stream and the volume of incoming water. It affects the ability of the stream to assimilate waste.

Dimictic Lakes and reservoirs that freeze over and normally go through two stratifications and two mixing cycles a year.

Dinocap A fungicide used primarily by apple growers to control summer diseases. EPA proposed restrictions on its use in 1986 when laboratory tests found it caused birth defects in rabbits.

Dinoseb A herbicide that is also used as a fungicide and insecticide. It was banned by EPA in 1986 because it posed the risk of birth defects and sterility.

Dioxin Any of a family of compounds known chemically as dibenzo-p-dioxins. Concern about them arises from their potential toxicity as contaminants in commercial products. Tests on laboratory animals indicate that it is one of the more toxic anthropogenic (man-made) compounds.

Direct Discharger A municipal or industrial facility which introduces pollution through a defined conveyance or system such as outlet pipes; a point source.

Direct Filtration A method of treating water which consists of the addition of coagulent chemicals, flash mixing, coagulation, minimal flocculation, and filtration. Sedimentation is not uses.

Direct Push Technology used for performing subsurface investigations by driving, pushing, and/ or vibrating small-diameter hollow steel rods into the ground/ Also known as direct drive, drive point, or push technology.

Direct Runoff Water that flows over the ground surface or through the ground directly into streams, rivers, and lakes.

Discharge Flow of surface water in a stream or canal or the outflow of ground water from a flowing artesian well, ditch, or spring. Can also apply tp discharge of liquid effluent from a facility or to chemical emissions into the air through designated venting mechanisms.

Disinfectant A chemical or physical process that kills pathogenic organisms in water, air, or on surfaces. Chlorine is often used to disinfect sewage treatment effluent, water supplies, wells, and swimming pools.

Disinfectant By-Product A compound formed by the reaction of a disinfenctant such as chlorine with organic material in the water supply; a chemical byproduct of the disinfection process..

Disinfectant Time The time it takes water to move from the point of disinfectant application (or the previous point of residual disinfectant measurement) to a point before or at the point where the residual disinfectant is measured. In pipelines, the time is calculated by dividing the internal volume of the pipe by he maximum hourly flow rate; within mixing basins and storage reservoirs it is determined by tracer studies of an equivalent demonstration.

Dispersant A chemical agent used to break up concentrations of organic material such as spilled oil.

Displacement Savings Saving realized by displacing purchases of natural gas or electricity from a local utility by using landfill gas for power and heat.

Disposables Consumer products, other items, and packaging used once or a few times and discarded.

Disposal Final placement or destruction of toxic, radioactive, or other wastes; surplus or banned pesticides or other chemicals; polluted soils; and drums containing hazardous materials from removal actions or accidental releases. Disposal may be accomplished through use of approved secure landfills, surface impoundments, land farming, deep-well injection, ocean dumping, or incineration.

Disposal Facilities Repositories for solid waste, including landfills and combustors intended for permanent containment or destruction of waste materials. Excludes transfer stations and composting facilities.

Dissolved Oxygen (DO) The oxygen freely available in water, vital to fish and other aquatic life and for the prevention of odors. DO levels are considered a most important indicator of a water body's ability to support desirable aquatic life. Secondary and advanced waste treatment are generally designed to ensure adequate DO in waste-receiving waters.

Dissolved Solids Disintegrated organic and inorganic material in water. Excessive amounts make water unfit to drink or use in industrial processes.

Distillation The act of purifying liquids through boiling, so that the steam or gaseous vapors condense to a pure liquid. Pollutants and contaminants may remain in a concentrated residue.

Disturbance Any event or series of events that disrupt ecosystem, community, or population structure and alters the physical environment.

Diversion 1. Use of part of a stream flow as water supply. 2. A channel with a supporting ridge on the lower side constructed across a slope to divert water at a non-erosive velocity to sites where it can be used and disposed of.

Diversion Rate The percentage of waste materials diverted from traditional disposal such as landfilling or incineration to be recycled, composted, or re-used.

DNA Hybridization Use of a segment of DNA, called a DNA probe, to identify its complementary DNA; used to detect specific genes.

Dobson Unit (DU) Units of ozone level measurement. measurement of ozone levels. If, for example, 100 DU of ozone were brought to the earth's surface they would form a layer one millimeter thick. Ozone levels vary geographically, even in the absence of ozone depletion.

Domestic Application Pesticide application in and around houses, office buildings, motels, and other living or working areas.(See residential use.)

Dosage/Dose 1. The actual quantity of a chemical administered to an organism or to which it is exposed. 2. The amount of a substance that reaches a specific tissue (e.g. the liver). 3. The amount of a substance available for interaction with metabolic processes after crossing the outer boundary of an organism. (See absorbed dose, administered dose, applied dose, potential dose.)

Dose Equivalent The product of the absorbed dose from ionizing radiation and such factors as account for biological differences due to the type of radiation and its distribution in the body in the body.

Dose Rate In exposure assessment, dose per time unit (e.g., mg/day), sometimes also called dosage.

Dose Response Shifts in toxicological responses of an individual (such as alterations in severity) or populations (such as alterations in incidence) that are related to changes in the dose of any given substance.

Dose-Response Assessment 1. Estimating the potency of a chemical. 2. In exposure assessment, the process of determining the relationship between the dose of a stressor and a specific biological response. 3. Evaluating the quantitative relationship between dose and toxicological responses.

Dose Response Curve Graphical representation of the relationship between the dose of a stressor and the biological response thereto.

Dose-Response Relationship The quantitative relationship between the amount of exposure to a substance and the extent of toxic injury or disease produced.

Dosimeter An instrument to measure dosage; many so-called dosimeters actually measure exposure rather than dosage. Dosimetry is the process or technology of measuring and/or estimating dosage.

DOT Reportable Quantity The quantity of a substance specified in a U.S. Department of Transportation regulation that triggers labeling, packaging and other requirements related to shipping such substances.

Downgradient The direction that groundwater flows; similar to "downstream" for surface water.

Downstream Processors Industries dependent on crop production (e.g. canneries and food processors).

DP Hole Hole in the ground made with DP equipment. (See direct push.)

Draft 1. The act of drawing or removing water from a tank or reservoir. 2. The water which is drawn or removed.

Draft Permit A preliminary permit drafted and published by EPA; subject to public review and comment before final action on the application.

Drainage Improving the productivity of agricultural land by removing excess water from the soil by such means as ditches or subsurface drainage tiles.

Drainage Basin The area of land that drains water, sediment, and dissolved materials to a common outlet at some point along a stream channel.

Drainage Well A well drilled to carry excess water off agricultural fields. Because they act as a funnel from the surface to the groundwater below. Drainage wells can contribute to groundwater pollution.

Drawdown 1. The drop in the water table or level of water in the ground when water is being pumped from a well. 2. The amount of water used from a tank or reservoir. 3. The drop in the water level of a tank or reservoir.

Dredging Removal of mud from the bottom of water bodies. This can disturb the ecosystem and causes silting that kills aquatic life. Dredging of contaminated muds can expose biota to heavy metals and other toxics. Dredging activities may be subject to regulation under Section 404 of the Clean Water Act.

Drilling Fluid Fluid used to lubricate the bit and convey drill cuttings to the surface with rotary drilling equipment. Usually composed of bentonite slurry or muddy water. Can become contaminated, leading to cross contamination, and may require special disposal. Not used with DP methods.

Drinking Water Equivalent Level Protective level of exposure related to potentially non-carcinogenic effects of chemicals that are also known to cause cancer.

Drinking Water State Revolving Fund The Fund provides capitalization grants to states to develop drinking water revolving loan funds to help finance system infrastructure improvements, assure source-water protection, enhance operation and management of drinking-water systems, and otherwise promote local water-system compliance and protection of public health.

Drive Casing Heavy duty steel casing driven along with the sampling tool in cased DP systems. Keeps the hole open between sampling runs and is not removed until last sample has been collected.

Drive Point Profiler An exposed groundwater DP system used to collect multiple depth-discrete groundwater samples. Ports in the tip of the probe connect to an internal stainless steel or teflon tube that extends to the surface. Samples are collected via suction or airlift methods. Deionized water is pumped down through the ports to prevent plugging while driving the tool to the next sampling depth.

Drop-off Recyclable materials collection method in which individuals bring them to a designated collection site.

Dual-Phase Extraction Active withdrawal of both liquid and gas phases from a well usually involving the use of a vacuum pump.

Dump A site used to dispose of solid waste without environmental controls.

Duplicate A second aliquot or sample that is treated the same as the original sample in order to determine the precision of the analytical method. (See aliquot.)

Dustfall Jar An open container used to collect large particles from the air for measurement and analysis.

Dynamometer A device used to place a load on an engine and measure its performance.

Dystrophic Lakes Acidic, shallow bodies of water that contain much humus and/or other organic matter; contain many plants but few fish.

Ecological Entity In ecological risk assessment, a general term referring to a species, a group of species, an ecosystem function or characteristic, or a specific habitat or biome.

Ecological/Environmental Sustainability Maintenance of ecosystem components and functions for future generations.

Ecological Exposure Exposure of a non-human organism to a stressor.

Ecological Impact The effect that a man-caused or natural activity has on living organisms and their non-living (abiotic) environment.

Ecological Indicator A characteristic of an ecosystem that is related to, or derived from, a measure of biotic or abiotic variable, that can provide quantitative information on ecological structure and function. An indicator can contribute to a measure of integrity and sustainability.

Ecological Integrity A living system exhibits integrity if, when subjected to disturbance, it sustains and organizes self-correcting ability to recover toward a biomass end-state that is normal for that system. End-states other than the pristine or naturally whole may be accepted as normal and good.

Ecological Risk Assessment The application of a formal framework, analytical process, or model to estimate the effects of human actions(s) on a natural resource and to interpret the significance of those effects in light of the uncertainties identified in each component of the assessment process. Such analysis includes initial hazard identification, exposure and dose-response assessments, and risk characterization.

Ecology The relationship of living things to one another and their environment, or the study of such relationships.

Economic Poisons Chemicals used to control pests and to defoliate cash crops such as cotton.

Ecosphere The "bio-bubble" that contains life on earth, in surface waters, and in the air. (See biosphere.)

Ecosystem The interacting system of a biological community and its non-living environmental surroundings.

Ecosystem Structure Attributes related to the instantaneous physical state of an ecosystem; examples include species population density, species richness or evenness, and standing crop biomass.

Ecotone A habitat created by the juxtaposition of distinctly different habitats; an edge habitat; or an ecological zone or boundary where two or more ecosystems meet.

Effluent Wastewater—treated or untreated—that flows out of a treatment plant, sewer, or industrial outfall. Generally refers to wastes discharged into surface waters.

Effluent Guidelines Technical EPA documents which set effluent limitations for given industries and pollutants.

Effluent Limitation Restrictions established by a state or EPA on quantities, rates, and concentrations in wastewater discharges.

Effluent Standard (See effluent limitation.)

Ejector A device used to disperse a chemical solution into water being treated.

Electrodialysis A process that uses electrical current applied to permeable membranes to remove minerals from water. Often used to desalinize salty or brackish water.

Electromagnetic Geophysical Methods Ways to measure subsurface conductivity via low-frequency electromagnetic induction.

Electrostatic Precipitator (ESP) A device that removes particles from a gas stream (smoke) after combustion occurs. The ESP imparts an electrical charge to the particles, causing them to adhere to metal plates inside the precipitator. Rapping on the plates causes the particles to fall into a hopper for disposal.

Eligible Costs The construction costs for wastewater treatment works upon which EPA grants are based.

EMAP Data Environmental monitoring data collected under the auspices of the Environmental Monitoring and Assessment Program. All EMAP data share the common attribute of being of known quality, having been collected in the context of explicit data quality objectives (DQOs) and a consistent quality assurance program.

Emergency and Hazardous Chemical Inventory An annual report by facilities having one or more extremely hazardous substances or hazardous chemicals above certain weight limits.

Emergency (Chemical) A situation created by an accidental release or spill of hazardous chemicals that poses a threat to the safety of workers, residents, the environment, or property.

Emergency Episode (See air pollution episode.)

Emergency Exemption Provision in FIFRA under which EPA can grant temporary exemption to a state or another federal agency to allow the use of a pesticide product not registered for that particular use. Such actions involve unanticipated and/or severe pest problems where there is not time or interest by a manufacturer to register the product for that use. (Registrants cannot apply for such exemptions.)

Emergency Removal Action 1. Steps take to remove contaminated materials that pose imminent threats to local residents (e.g., removal of leaking drums or the excavation of explosive waste). 2. The state record of such removals.

Emergency Response Values Concentrations of chemicals, published by various groups, defining acceptable levels for short-term exposures in emergencies.

Emergency Suspension Suspension of a pesticide product registration due to an imminent hazard. The action immediately halts distribution, sale, and sometimes actual use of the pesticide involved.

Emission Pollution discharged into the atmosphere from smokestacks, other vents, and surface areas of commercial or industrial facilities; from residential chimneys; and from motor vehicle, locomotive, or aircraft exhausts.

Emission Cap A limit designed to prevent projected growth in emissions from existing and future stationary sources from eroding any mandated reductions. Generally, such provisions require that any emission growth from facilities under the restrictions be offset by equivalent reductions at other facilities under the same cap. (See emissions trading.)

Emission Factor The relationship between the amount of pollution produced and the amount of raw material processed. For example, an emission factor for a blast furnace making iron would be the number of pounds of particulates per ton of raw materials.

Emission Inventory A listing, by source, of the amount of air pollutants discharged into the atmosphere of a community; used to establish emission standards.

Emission Standard The maximum amount of air polluting discharge legally allowed from a single source, mobile or stationary.

Emissions Trading The creation of surplus emission reductions at certain stacks, vents or similar emissions sources and the use of this surplus to meet or redefine pollution requirements applicable to other emissions sources. This allows one source to increase emissions when another source reduces them, maintaining an overall constant emission level. Facilities that reduce emissions substantially may "bank" their "credits" or sell them to other facilities or industries.

Emulsifier A chemical that aids in suspending one liquid in another. Usually an organic chemical in an aqueous solution.

Encapsulation The treatment of asbestos-containing material with a liquid that covers the surface with a protective coating or embeds fibers in an adhesive matrix to prevent their release into the air.

Enclosure Putting an airtight, impermeable, permanent barrier around asbestos-containing materials to prevent the release of asbestos fibers into the air.

End-of-the-pipe Technologies such as scrubbers on smokestacks and catalytic convertors on automobile tailpipes that reduce emissions of pollutants after they have formed.

End-use Product A pesticide formulation for field or other end use. The label has instructions for use or application to control pests or regulate plant growth. The term excludes products used to formulate other pesticide products.

End User Consumer of products for the purpose of recycling. Excludes products for re-use or combustion for energy recovery.

Endangered Species Animals, birds, fish, plants, or other living organisms threatened with extinction by anthropogenic (man-caused) or other natural changes in their environment. Requirements for declaring a species endangered are contained in the Endangered Species Act.

Endangerment Assessment A study to determine the nature and extent of contamination at a site on the National Priorities List and the risks posed to public health or the environment. EPA or the state conducts the study when a legal action is to be taken to direct potentially responsible parties to clean up a site or pay for it. An endangerment assessment supplements a remedial investigation.

Endrin A pesticide toxic to freshwater and marine aquatic life that produces adverse health effects in domestic water supplies.

Energy Management System A control system capable of monitoring environmental and system loads and adjusting HVAC operations accordingly in order to conserve energy while maintaining comfort.

Energy Recovery Obtaining energy from waste through a variety of processes (e.g., combustion).

Enforceable Requirements Conditions or limitations in permits issued under the Clean Water Act Section 402 or 404 that, if violated, could result in the issuance of a compliance order or initiation of a civil or criminal action under federal or applicable state laws. If a permit has not been issued, the term includes any requirement which, in the Regional Administrator's judgement, would be included in the permit when issued. Where no permit applies, the term includes any requirement which the RA determines is necessary for the best practical waste treatment technology to meet applicable criteria.

Enforcement EPA, state, or local legal actions to obtain compliance with environmental laws, rules, regulations, or agreements and/or obtain penalties or criminal sanctions for violations. Enforcement procedures may vary, depending on the requirements of different environmental laws and related implementing regulations. Under CERCLA, for example, EPA will seek to require potentially responsible parties to clean up a Superfund site, or pay for the cleanup, whereas under the Clean Air Act the Agency may invoke sanctions against cities failing to meet ambient air quality standards that could prevent certain types of construction or federal funding. In other situations, if investigations by EPA and state agencies uncover willful violations, criminal trials and penalties are sought.

Enforcement Decision Document (EDD) A document that provides an explanation to the public of EPA's selection of the cleanup alternative at enforcement sites on the National Priorities List. Similar to a Record of Decision.

Engineered Controls Method of managing environmental and health risks by placing a barrier between the contamination and the rest of the site, thus limiting exposure pathways.

Enhanced Inspection and Maintenance (I&M) An improved automobile inspection and maintenance program—aimed at reducing automobile emissions—that contains, at a minimum, more vehicle types and model years, tighter inspection, and better management practices. It may also include annual computerized or centralized inspections, under-the-hood inspection—for signs of tampering with pollution control equipment—and increased repair waiver cost.

Enrichment The addition of nutrients (e.g., nitrogen, phosphorus, carbon compounds) from sewage effluent or agricultural runoff to surface water, greatly increases the growth potential for algae and other aquatic plants.

Entrain To trap bubbles in water either mechanically through turbulence or chemically through a reaction.

Environment The sum of all external conditions affecting the life, development and survival of an organism.

Environmental Assessment An environmental analysis prepared pursuant to the National Environmental Policy Act to determine whether a federal action would significantly affect the environment and thus require a more detailed environmental impact statement.

Environmental Audit An independent assessment of the current status of a party's compliance with applicable environmental requirements or of a party's environmental compliance policies, practices, and controls.

Environmental/Ecological Risk The potential for adverse effects on living organisms associated with pollution of the environment by effluents, emissions, wastes, or accidental chemical releases; energy use; or the depletion of natural resources.

Environmental Equity/Justice Equal protection from environmental hazards for individuals, groups, or communities regardless of race, ethnicity, or economic status. This applies to the development, implementation, and enforcement of environmental laws, regulations, and policies, and implies that no population of people should be forced to shoulder a disproportionate share of negative environmental impacts of pollution or environmental hazard due to a lack of political or economic strength levels.

Environmental Exposure Human exposure to pollutants originating from facility emissions. Threshold levels are not necessarily surpassed, but low-level chronic pollutant exposure is one of the most common forms of environmental exposure (See threshold level).

Environmental Fate The destiny of a chemical or biological pollutant after release into the environment.

Environmental Fate Data Data that characterize a pesticide's fate in the ecosystem, considering factors that foster its degradation (light, water, microbes), pathways and resultant products.

Environmental Impact Statement A document required of federal agencies by the National Environmental Policy Act for major projects or legislative proposals significantly affecting the environment. A tool for decision making, it describes the positive and negative effects of the undertaking and cites alternative actions.

Environmental Indicator A measurement, statistic or value that provides a proximate gauge or evidence of the effects of environmental management programs or of the state or condition of the environment.

Environmental Justice The fair treatment of people of all races, cultures, incomes, and educational levels with respect to the development and enforcement of environmental laws, regulations, and policies.

Environmental Lien A charge, security, or encumbrance on a property's title to secure payment of cost or debt arising from response actions, cleanup, or other remediation of hazardous substances or petroleum products.

Environmental Medium A major environmental category that surrounds or contacts humans, animals, plants, and other organisms (e.g. surface water, ground water, soil or air) and through which chemicals or pollutants move. (See ambient medium, biological medium.)

Environmental Monitoring for Public Access and Community Tracking Joint EPA, NOAA, and USGS program to provide timely and effective communication of environmental data and information through improved and updated technology solutions that support timely environmental monitoring reporting, interpreting, and use of the information for the benefit of the public. (See real-time monitoring.)

Environmental Response Team EPA experts located in Edison, N.J., and Cincinnati, OH, who can provide around-the-clock technical assistance to EPA regional offices and states during all types of hazardous waste site emergencies and spills of hazardous substances.

Environmental Site Assessment The process of determining whether contamination is present on a parcel of real property.

Environmental Sustainability Long-term maintenance of ecosystem components and functions for future generations.

Environmental Tobacco Smoke Mixture of smoke from the burning end of a cigarette, pipe, or cigar and smoke exhaled by the smoker. (See passive smoking/secondhand smoke.)

Epidemiology Study of the distribution of disease, or other health-related states and events in human populations, as related to age, sex, occupation, ethnicity, and economic status in order to identify and alleviate health problems and promote better health.

Epilimnion Upper waters of a thermally stratified lake subject to wind action.

Episode (Pollution) An air pollution incident in a given area caused by a concentration of atmospheric pollutants under meteorological conditions that may result in a significant increase in illnesses or deaths. May also describe water pollution events or hazardous material spills.

Equilibrium In relation to radiation, the state at which the radioactivity of consecutive elements within a radioactive series is neither increasing nor decreasing.

Equivalent Method Any method of sampling and analyzing for air pollution which has been demonstrated to the EPA Administrator's satisfaction to be, under specific conditions, an acceptable alternative to normally used reference methods.

Erosion The wearing away of land surface by wind or water, intensified by land-clearing practices related to farming, residential or industrial development, road building, or logging.

Established Treatment Technologies Technologies for which cost and performance data are readily available. (See Innovative treatment technologies.)

Estimated Environmental Concentration The estimated pesticide concentration in an ecosystem.

Estuary Region of interaction between rivers and near-shore ocean waters, where tidal action and river flow mix fresh and salt water. Such areas include bays, mouths of rivers, salt marshes, and lagoons. These brackish water ecosystems shelter and feed marine life, birds, and wildlife. (See wetlands.)

Ethanol An alternative automotive fuel derived from grain and corn; usually blended with gasoline to form gasohol.

Ethylene Dibromide (EDB) A chemical used as an agricultural fumigant and in certain industrial processes. Extremely toxic and found to be a carcinogen in laboratory animals, EDB has been banned for most agricultural uses in the United States.

Eutrophic Lakes Shallow, murky bodies of water with concentrations of plant nutrients causing excessive production of algae. (See dystrophic lakes.)

Eutrophication The slow aging process during which a lake, estuary, or bay evolves into a bog or marsh and eventually disappears. During the later stages of eutrophication the water body is choked by abundant plant life due to higher levels of nutritive compounds such as nitrogen and phosphorus. Human activities can accelerate the process.

Evaporation Ponds Areas where sewage sludge is dumped and dried.

Evapotranspiration The loss of water from the soil both by evaporation and by transpiration from the plants growing in the soil.

Exceedance Violation of the pollutant levels permitted by environmental protection standards.

Exclusion In the asbestos program, one of several situations that permit a Local Education Agency (LEA) to delete one or more of the items required by the Asbestos Hazard Emergency Response Act (AHERA); e.g., records of previous asbestos sample collection and analysis may be used by the accredited inspector in lieu of AHERA bulk sampling.

Exclusionary Ordinance Zoning that excludes classes of persons or businesses from a particular neighborhood or area.

Exempt Solvent Specific organic compounds not subject to requirements of regulation because they are deemed by EPA to be of negligible photochemical reactivity.

Exempted Aquifer Underground bodies of water defined in the Underground Injection Control program as aquifers that are potential sources of drinking water though not being used as such, and thus exempted from regulations barring underground injection activities.

Exemption A state (with primacy) may exempt a public water system from a requirement involving a Maximum Contaminant Level (MCL), treatment technique, or both, if the system cannot comply due to compelling economic or other factors, or because the system was in operation before the requirement or MCL was instituted; and the exemption will not create a public health risk. (See variance.)

Exotic Species A species that is not indigenous to a region.

Experimental Use Permit Obtained by manufacturers for testing new pesticides or uses thereof whenever they conduct experimental field studies to support registration on 10 acres or more of land or one acre or more of water.

Explosive Limits The amounts of vapor in the air that form explosive mixtures; limits are expressed as lower and upper limits and give the range of vapor concentrations in air that will explode if an ignition source is present.

Exports In solid waste program, municipal solid waste and recyclables transported outside the state or locality where they originated.

Exposure The amount of radiation or pollutant present in a given environment that represents a potential health threat to living organisms.

Exposure Assessment Identifying the pathways by which toxicants may reach individuals, estimating how much of a chemical an individual is likely to be exposed to, and estimating the number likely to be exposed.

Exposure Concentration The concentration of a chemical or other pollutant representing a health threat in a given environment.

Exposure Indicator A characteristic of the environment measured to provide evidence of the occurrence or magnitude of a response indicator's exposure to a chemical or biological stress.

Exposure Level The amount (concentration) of a chemical at the absorptive surfaces of an organism.

Exposure Pathway The path from sources of pollutants via, soil, water, or food to man and other species or settings.

Exposure-Response Relationship The relationship between exposure level and the incidence of adverse effects.

Exposure Route The way a chemical or pollutant enters an organism after contact; i.e. by ingestion, inhalation, or dermal absorption.

Extraction Procedure (EP Toxic) Determining toxicity by a procedure which simulates leaching; if a certain concentration of a toxic substance can be leached from a waste, that waste is considered hazardous, i.e. "EP Toxic."

Extraction Well A discharge well used to remove groundwater or air.

Extremely Hazardous Substances Any of 406 chemicals identified by EPA as toxic, and listed under SARA Title III. The list is subject to periodic revision.

Fabric Filter A cloth device that catches dust particles from industrial emissions.

Facilities Plans Plans and studies related to the construction of treatment works necessary to comply with the Clean Water Act or RCRA. A facilities plan investigates needs and provides information on the cost-effectiveness of alternatives, a recommended plan, an environmental assessment of the recommendations, and descriptions of the treatment works, costs, and a completion schedule.

Facility Emergency Coordinator Representative of a facility covered by environmental law (e.g., a chemical plant) who participates in the emergency reporting process with the Local Emergency Planning Committee (LEPC).

Facultative Bacteria Bacteria that can live under aerobic or anaerobic conditions.

Feasibility Study 1. Analysis of the practicability of a proposal; e.g., a description and analysis of potential cleanup alternatives for a site such as one on the National Priorities List. The feasibility study usually recommends selection of a cost-effective alternative. It usually starts as soon as the remedial investigation is underway; together, they are commonly referred to as the "RI/FS." 2. A small-scale investigation of a problem to ascertain whether a proposed research approach is likely to provide useful data.

Fecal Coliform Bacteria Bacteria found in the intestinal tracts of mammals. Their presence in water or sludge is an indicator of pollution and possible contamination by pathogens.

Federal Implementation Plan Under current law, a federally implemented plan to achieve attainment of air quality standards, used when a state is unable to develop an adequate plan.

Federal Motor Vehicle Control Program All federal actions aimed at controlling pollution from motor vehicles by such efforts as establishing and enforcing tailpipe and evaporative emission standards for new vehicles, testing methods development, and guidance to states operating inspection and maintenance programs. Federally designated area that is required to meet and maintain federal ambient air quality standards. May include nearby locations in the same state or nearby states that share common air pollution problems.

Feedlot A confined area for the controlled feeding of animals. Tends to concentrate large amounts of animal waste that cannot be absorbed by the soil and, hence, may be carried to nearby streams or lakes by rainfall runoff.

Fen A type of wetland that accumulates peat deposits. Fens are less acidic than bogs, deriving most of their water from groundwater rich in calcium and magnesium. (See wetlands.)

Ferrous Metals Magnetic metals derived from iron or steel; products made from ferrous metals include appliances, furniture, containers, and packaging like steel drums and barrels. Recycled products include processing tin/steel cans, strapping, and metals from appliances into new products.

FIFRA Pesticide Ingredient An ingredient of a pesticide that must be registered with EPA under the Federal Insecticide, Fungicide, and Rodenticide Act. Products making pesticide claims must register under FIFRA and may be subject to labeling and use requirements.

Fill Man-made deposits of natural soils or rock products and waste materials.

Filling Depositing dirt, mud or other materials into aquatic areas to create more dry land, usually for agricultural or commercial development purposes, often with ruinous ecological consequences.

Filter Strip Strip or area of vegetation used for removing sediment, organic matter, and other pollutants from runoff and wastewater.

Filtration A treatment process, under the control of qualified operators, for removing solid (particulate) matter from water by means of porous media such as sand or a man-made filter; often used to remove particles that contain pathogens.

Financial Assurance for Closure Documentation or proof that an owner or operator of a facility such as a landfill or other waste repository is capable of paying the projected costs of closing the facility and monitoring it afterwards as provided in RCRA regulations.

Finding of No Significant Impact A document prepared by a federal agency showing why a proposed action would not have a significant impact on the environment and thus would not require preparation of an Environmental Impact Statement. An FNSI is based on the results of an environmental assessment.

Finished Water Water is "finished" when it has passed through all the processes in a water treatment plant and is ready to be delivered to consumers.

First Draw The water that comes out when a tap is first opened, likely to have the highest level of lead contamination from plumbing materials.

Fix a Sample A sample is "fixed" in the field by adding chemicals that prevent water quality indicators of interest in the sample from changing before laboratory measurements are made.

Fixed-Location Monitoring Sampling of an environmental or ambient medium for pollutant concentration at one location continuously or repeatedly.

Flammable Any material that ignites easily and will burn rapidly.

Flare A control device that burns hazardous materials to prevent their release into the environment; may operate continuously or intermittently, usually on top of a stack.

Flash Point The lowest temperature at which evaporation of a substance produces sufficient vapor to form an ignitable mixture with air.

Floc A clump of solids formed in sewage by biological or chemical action.

Flocculation Process by which clumps of solids in water or sewage aggregate through biological or chemical action so they can be separated from water or sewage.

Floodplain The flat or nearly flat land along a river or stream or in a tidal area that is covered by water during a flood.

Floor Sweep Capture of heavier-than-air gases that collect at floor level.

Flow Rate The rate, expressed in gallons -or liters-per-hour, at which a fluid escapes from a hole or fissure in a tank. Such measurements are also made of liquid waste, effluent, and surface water movement.

Flowable Pesticide and other formulations in which the active ingredients are finely ground insoluble solids suspended in a liquid. They are mixed with water for application.

Flowmeter A gauge indicating the velocity of wastewater moving through a treatment plant or of any liquid moving through various industrial processes.

Flue Gas The air coming out of a chimney after combustion in the burner it is venting. It can include nitrogen oxides, carbon oxides, water vapor, sulfur oxides, particles and many chemical pollutants.

Flue Gas Desulfurization A technology that employs a sorbent, usually lime or limestone, to remove sulfur dioxide from the gases produced by burning fossil fuels. Flue gas desulfurization is current state-of-the art technology for major SO_2 emitters, like power plants.

Fluidized A mass of solid particles that is made to flow like a liquid by injection of water or gas is said to have been fluidized. In water treatment, a bed of filter media is fluidized by backwashing water through the filter.

Fluidized Bed Incinerator An incinerator that uses a bed of hot sand or other granular material to transfer heat directly to waste. Used mainly for destroying municipal sludge.

Flume A natural or man-made channel that diverts water.

Fluoridation The addition of a chemical to increase the concentration of fluoride ions in drinking water to reduce the incidence of tooth decay.

Fluorides Gaseous, solid, or dissolved compounds containing fluorine that result from industrial processes. Excessive amounts in food can lead to fluorosis.

Fluorocarbons (FCs) Any of a number of organic compounds analogous to hydrocarbons in which one or more hydrogen atoms are replaced by fluorine. Once used in the United States as a propellant for domestic aerosols, they are now found mainly in coolants and some industrial processes. FCs containing chlorine are called chlorofluorocarbons (CFCs). They are believed to be modifying the ozone layer in the stratosphere, thereby allowing more harmful solar radiation to reach the Earth's surface.

Flush 1. To open a cold-water tap to clear out all the water which may have been sitting for a long time in the pipes. In new homes, to flush a system means to send large volumes of water gushing through the unused pipes to remove loose particles of solder and flux. 2. To force large amounts of water through a system to clean out piping or tubing, and storage or process tanks.

Flux 1. A flowing or flow. 2. A substance used to help metals fuse together.

Fly Ash Non-combustible residual particles expelled by flue gas.

Fogging Applying a pesticide by rapidly heating the liquid chemical so that it forms very fine droplets that resemble smoke or fog. Used to destroy mosquitoes, black flies, and similar pests.

Food Chain A sequence of organisms, each of which uses the next, lower member of the sequence as a food source.

Food Processing Waste Food residues produced during agricultural and industrial operations.

Food Waste Uneaten food and food preparation wastes from residences and commercial establishments such as grocery stores, restaurants, and produce stands, institutional cafeterias and kitchens, and industrial sources like employee lunchrooms.

Food Web The feeding relationships by which energy and nutrients are transferred from one species to another.

Formaldehyde A colorless, pungent, and irritating gas, CH20, used chiefly as a disinfectant and preservative and in synthesizing other compounds like resins.

Formulation The substances comprising all active and inert ingredients in a pesticide.

Fossil Fuel Fuel derived from ancient organic remains; e.g. peat, coal, crude oil, and natural gas.

Fracture A break in a rock formation due to structural stresses; e.g. faults, shears, joints, and planes of fracture cleavage.

Free Product A petroleum hydrocarbon in the liquid free or non aqueous phase. (See non-aqueous phase liquid.)

Freeboard 1. Vertical distance from the normal water surface to the top of a confining wall. 2. Vertical distance from the sand surface to the underside of a trough in a sand filter.

Fresh Water Water that generally contains less than 1,000 milligrams-per-liter of dissolved solids.

Friable Capable of being crumbled, pulverized, or reduced to powder by hand pressure.

Friable Asbestos Any material containing more than one-percent asbestos, and that can be crumbled or reduced to powder by hand pressure. (May include previously non-friable material which becomes broken or damaged by mechanical force.)

Fuel Economy Standard The Corporate Average Fuel Economy Standard (CAFE) effective in 1978. It enhanced the national fuel conservation effort imposing a miles-per-gallon floor for motor vehicles.

Fuel Efficiency The proportion of energy released by fuel combustion that is converted into useful energy.

Fuel Switching 1. A precombustion process whereby a low-sulfur coal is used in place of a higher sulfur coal in a power plant to reduce sulfur dioxide emissions. 2. Illegally using leaded gasoline in a motor vehicle designed to use only unleaded.

Fugitive Emissions Emissions not caught by a capture system.

Fume Tiny particles trapped in vapor in a gas stream.

Fumigant A pesticide vaporized to kill pests. Used in buildings and greenhouses.

Functional Equivalent Term used to describe EPA's decision-making process and its relationship to the environmental review conducted under the National Environmental Policy Act (NEPA). A review is considered functionally equivalent when it addresses the substantive components of a NEPA review.

Fungicide Pesticides which are used to control, deter, or destroy fungi.

Fungistat A chemical that keeps fungi from growing.

Fungus (Fungi) Molds, mildews, yeasts, mushrooms, and puffballs, a group of organisms lacking in chlorophyll (i.e. are not photosynthetic) and which are usually non-mobile, filamentous, and multicellular. Some grow in soil, others attach themselves to decaying trees and other plants whence they obtain nutrients. Some are pathogens, others stabilize sewage and digest composted waste.

Furrow Irrigation Irrigation method in which water travels through the field by means of small channels between each groups of rows.

Future Liability Refers to potentially responsible parties' obligations to pay for additional response activities beyond those specified in the Record of Decision or Consent Decree.

Game Fish Species like trout, salmon, or bass, caught for sport. Many of them show more sensitivity to environmental change than "rough" fish.

Garbage Animal and vegetable waste resulting from the handling, storage, sale, preparation, cooking, and serving of foods.

Gas Chromatograph/Mass Spectrometer Instrument that identifies the molecular composition and concentrations of various chemicals in water and soil samples.

Gasahol Mixture of gasoline and ethanol derived from fermented agricultural products containing at least nine percent ethanol. Gasohol emissions contain less carbon monoxide than those from gasoline.

Gasification Conversion of solid material such as coal into a gas for use as a fuel.

Gasoline Volatility The property of gasoline whereby it evaporates into a vapor. Gasoline vapor is a mixture of volatile organic compounds.

General Permit A permit applicable to a class or category of dischargers.

General Reporting Facility A facility having one or more hazardous chemicals above the 10,000 pound threshold for planning quantities. Such facilities must file MSDS and emergency inventory information with the SERC, LEPC, and local fire departments.

Generally Recognized as Safe (GRAS) Designation by the FDA that a chemical or substance (including certain pesticides) added to food is considered safe by experts, and so is exempted from the usual FFDCA food additive tolerance requirements.

Generator 1. A facility or mobile source that emits pollutants into the air or releases hazardous waste into water or soil. 2. Any person, by site, whose act or process produces regulated medical waste or whose act first causes such waste to become subject to regulation. Where more than one person (e.g. doctors with separate medical practices) are located in the same building, each business entity is a separate generator.

Genetic Engineering A process of inserting new genetic information into existing cells in order to modify a specific organism for the purpose of changing one of its characteristics.

Genotoxic Damaging to DNA; pertaining to agents known to damage DNA.

Geographic Information System (GIS) A computer system designed for storing, manipulating, analyzing, and displaying data in a geographic context.

Geological Log A detailed description of all underground features (depth, thickness, type of formation) discovered during the drilling of a well.

Geophysical Log A record of the structure and composition of the earth encountered when drilling a well or similar type of test hold or boring.

Geothermal/Ground Source Heat Pump These heat pumps are underground coils to transfer heat from the ground to the inside of a building. (See heat pump; water source heat pump.)

Germicide Any compound that kills disease-causing microorganisms.

Giardia Lamblia Protozoan in the feces of humans and animals that can cause severe gastrointestinal ailments. It is a common contaminant of surface waters.

Glass Containers For recycling purposes, containers like bottles and jars for drinks, food, cosmetics and other products. When being recycled, container glass is generally separated into color categories for conversion into new containers, construction materials or fiberglass insulation.

Global Warming An increase in the near surface temperature of the Earth. Global warming has occurred in the distant past as the result of natural influences, but the term is most often used to refer to the warming predicted to occur as a result of increased emissions of greenhouse gases. Scientists generally agree that the Earth's surface has warmed by about 1 degree Fahrenheit in the past 140 years. The Intergovernmental Panel on Climate Change (IPCC) recently concluded that increased concentrations of greenhouse gases are causing an increase in the Earth's surface temperature and that increased concentrations of sulfate aerosols have led to relative cooling in some regions, generally over and downwind of heavily industrialized areas. (See climate change.)

Global Warming Potential The ratio of the warming caused by a substance to the warming caused by a similar mass of carbon dioxide. CFC-12, for example, has a GWP of 8,500, while water has a GWP of zero. (See Class I Substance and Class II Substance.)

Glovebag A polyethylene or polyvinyl chloride bag-like enclosure affixed around an asbestos-containing source (most often thermal system insulation) permitting the material to be removed while minimizing release of airborne fibers to the surrounding atmosphere.

Gooseneck A portion of a water service connection between the distribution system water main and a meter. Sometimes called a pigtail.

Grab Sample A single sample collected at a particular time and place that represents the composition of the water, air, or soil only at that time and place.

Grain Loading The rate at which particles are emitted from a pollution source. Measurement is made by the number of grains per cubic foot of gas emitted.

Granular Activated Carbon Treatment A filtering system often used in small water systems and individual homes to remove organics. Also used by municipal water treatment plantsd. GAC can be highly effective in lowering elevated levels of radon in water.

Grasscycling Source reduction activities in which grass clippings are left on the lawn after mowing.

Grassed Waterway Natural or constructed watercourse or outlet that is shaped or graded and established in suitable vegetation for the disposal of runoff water without erosion.

Gray Water Domestic wastewater composed of wash water from kitchen, bathroom, and laundry sinks, tubs, and washers.

Greenhouse Effect The warming of the Earth's atmosphere attributed to a buildup of carbon dioxide or other gases; some scientists think that this build-up allows the sun's rays to heat the Earth, while making the infra-red radiation atmosphere opaque to infra-red radiation, thereby preventing a counterbalancing loss of heat.

Greenhouse Gas A gas, such as carbon dioxide or methane, which contributes to potential climate change.

Grinder Pump A mechanical device that shreds solids and raises sewage to a higher elevation through pressure sewers.

Gross Alpha/Beta Particle Activity The total radioactivity due to alpha or beta particle emissions as inferred from measurements on a dry sample.

Gross Power-Generation Potential The installed power generation capacity that landfill gas can support.

Ground Cover Plants grown to keep soil from eroding.

Ground-Penetrating Radar A geophysical method that uses high frequency electromagnetic waves to obtain subsurface information.

Ground Water The supply of fresh water found beneath the Earth's surface, usually in aquifers, which supply wells and springs. Because ground water is a major source of drinking water, there is growing concern over contamination from leaching agricultural or industrial pollutants or leaking underground storage tanks.

Ground-Water Discharge Ground water entering near coastal waters which has been contaminated by landfill leachate, deep well injection of hazardous wastes, septic tanks, etc.

Ground-Water Disinfection Rule A 1996 amendment of the Safe Drinking Water Act requiring EPA to promulgate national primary drinking water regulations requiring disinfection as for all public water systems, including surface waters and ground water systems.

Ground Water Under the Direct Influence (UDI) of Surface Water Any water beneath the surface of the ground with: 1. significant occurence of insects or other microorganisms, algae, or large-diameter pathogens; 2. significant and relatively rapid shifts in water characteristics such as turbidity, temperature, conductivity, or pH which closely correlate to climatological or surface water conditions. Direct influence is determined for individual sources in accordance with criteria established by a state.

Gully Erosion Severe erosion in which trenches are cut to a depth greater than 30 centimeters (a foot). Generally, ditches deep enough to cross with farm equipment are considered gullies.

Habitat The place where a population (e.g., human, animal, plant, microorganism) lives and its surroundings, both living and non-living.

Habitat Indicator A physical attribute of the environment measured to characterize conditions necessary to support an organism, population, or community in the absence of pollutants; e.g., salinity of estuarine waters or substrate type in streams or lakes.

Half-Life 1. The time required for a pollutant to lose one-half of its original coconcentrationor example, the biochemical half-life of DDT in the environment is 15 years. 2. The time required for half of the atoms of a radioactive element to undergo self-transmutation or decay (half-life of radium is 1620 years). 3. The time required for the elimination of half a total dose from the body.

Halogen A type of incandescent lamp with higher energy-efficiency that standard ones.

Halon Bromine-containing compounds with long atmospheric lifetimes whose breakdown in the stratosphere causes depletion of ozone. Halons are used in firefighting.

Hammer Mill A high-speed machine that uses hammers and cutters to crush, grind, chip, or shred solid waste.

Hard Water Alkaline water containing dissolved salts that interfere with some industrial processes and prevent soap from sudsing.

Hauler Garbage collection company that offers complete refuse removal service; many will also collect recyclables.

Hazard 1. Potential for radiation, a chemical or other pollutant to cause human illness or injury. 2. In the pesticide program, the inherent toxicity of a compound. Hazard identification of a given substances is an informed judgment based on verifiable toxicity data from animal models or human studies.

Hazard Assessment Evaluating the effects of a stressor or determining a margin of safety for an organism by comparing the concentration which causes toxic effects with an estimate of exposure to the organism.

Hazard Communication Standard An OSHA regulation that requires chemical manufacturers, suppliers, and importers to assess the hazards of the chemicals that they make, supply, or import, and to inform employers, customers, and workers of these hazards through MSDS information.

Hazard Evaluation A component of risk evaluation that involves gathering and evaluating data on the types of health injuries or diseases that may be produced by a chemical and on the conditions of exposure under which such health effects are produced.

Hazard Identification Determining if a chemical or a microbe can cause adverse health effects in humans and what those effects might be.

Hazard Quotient The ratio of estimated site-specific exposure to a single chemical from a site over a specified period to the estimated daily exposure level, at which no adverse health effects are likely to occur.

Hazard Ratio A term used to compare an animal's daily dietary intake of a pesticide to its LD 50 value. A ratio greater than 1.0 indicates that the animal is likely to consume an a dose amount which would kill 50 percent of animals of the same species. (See LD 50 /Lethal Dose.)

Hazardous Air Pollutants Air pollutants which are not covered by ambient air quality standards but which, as defined in the Clean Air Act, may present a threat of adverse human health effects or adverse environmental effects. Such pollutants include asbestos, beryllium, mercury, benzene, coke oven emissions, radionuclides, and vinyl chloride.

Hazardous Chemical An EPA designation for any hazardous material requiring an MSDS under OSHA's Hazard Communication Standard. Such substances are capable of producing fires and explosions or adverse health effects like cancer and dermatitis. Hazardous chemicals are distinct from hazardous waste.(See Hazardous Waste.)

Hazardous Ranking System The principal screening tool used by EPA to evaluate risks to public health and the environment associated with abandoned or uncontrolled hazardous waste sites. The HRS calculates a score based on the potential of hazardous substances spreading from the site through the air, surface water, or ground water, and on other factors such as density and proximity of human population. This score is the primary factor in deciding if the site should be on the National Priorities List and, if so, what ranking it should have compared to other sites on the list.

Hazardous Substance 1. Any material that poses a threat to human health and/or the environment. Typical hazardous substances are toxic, corrosive, ignitable, explosive, or chemically reactive. 2. Any substance designated by EPA to be reported if a designated quantity of the substance is spilled in the waters of the United States or is otherwise released into the environment.

Hazardous Waste By-products of society that can pose a substantial or potential hazard to human health or the environment when improperly managed. Possesses at least one of four characteristics (ignitability, corrosivity, reactivity, or toxicity), or appears on special EPA lists.

Hazardous Waste Landfill An excavated or engineered site where hazardous waste is deposited and covered.

Hazardous Waste Minimization Reducing the amount of toxicity or waste produced by a facility via source reduction or environmentally sound recycling.

Hazards Analysis Procedures used to (1) identify potential sources of release of hazardous materials from fixed facilities or transportation accidents; (2) determine the vulnerability of a geographical area to a release of hazardous materials; and (3) compare hazards to determine which present greater or lesser risks to a community.

Hazards Identification Providing information on which facilities have extremely hazardous substances, what those chemicals are, how much there is at each facility, how the chemicals are stored, and whether they are used at high temperatures.

Headspace The vapor mixture trapped above a solid or liquid in a sealed vessel.

Health Advisory Level A non-regulatory health-based reference level of chemical traces (usually in ppm) in drinking water at which there are no adverse health risks when ingested over various periods of time. Such levels are established for one day, 10 days, long-term and life-time exposure periods. They contain a wide margin of safety.

Health Assessment An evaluation of available data on existing or potential risks to human health posed by a Superfund site. The Agency for Toxic Substances and Disease Registry (ATSDR) of the Department of Health and Human Services (DHHS) is required to perform such an assessment at every site on the National Priorities List.

Heat Island Effect A "dome" of elevated temperatures over an urban area caused by structural and pavement heat fluxes, and pollutant emissions.

Heat Pump An electric device with both heating and cooling capabilities. It extracts heat from one medium at a lower (the heat source) temperature and transfers it to another at a higher temperature (the heat sink), thereby cooling the first and warming the second. (See geothermal, water source heat pump.)

Heavy Metals Metallic elements with high atomic weights; (e.g. mercury, chromium, cadmium, arsenic, and lead); can damage living things at low concentrations and tend to accumulate in the food chain.

Heptachlor An insecticide that was banned on some food products in 1975 and in all of them 1978. It was allowed for use in seed treatment until 1983. More recently it was found in milk and other dairy products in Arkansas and Missouri where dairy cattle were illegally fed treated seed.

Herbicide A chemical pesticide designed to control or destroy plants, weeds, or grasses.

Herbivore An animal that feeds on plants.

Heterotrophic Organisms Species that are dependent on organic matter for food.

High-Density Polyethylene A material used to make plastic bottles and other products that produces toxic fumes when burned.

High End Exposure (Dose) Estimate An estimate of exposure, or dose level received anyone in a defined population that is greater than the 90th percentile of all individuals in that population, but less than the exposure at the highest percentile in that population. A high end risk descriptor is an estimate of the risk level for such individuals. Note that risk is based on a combination of exposure and susceptibility to the stressor.

High Intensity Discharge A generic term for mercury vapor, metal halide, and high pressure sodium lamps and fixtures.

High-Level Nuclear Waste Facility Plant designed to handle disposal of used nuclear fuel, high-level radioactive waste, and plutonium waste.

High-Level Radioactive Waste (HLRW) Waste generated in core fuel of a nuclear reactor, found at nuclear reactors or by nuclear fuel reprocessing; is a serious threat to anyone who comes near the waste without shielding. (See low-level radioactive waste.)

High-Line Jumpers Pipes or hoses connected to fire hydrants and laid on top of the ground to provide emergency water service for an isolated portion of a distribution system.

High-Risk Community A community located within the vicinity of numerous sites of facilities or other potential sources of envienvironmental exposure/health hazards which may result in high levels of exposure to contaminants or pollutants.

High-to-Low-Dose Extrapolation The process of prediction of low exposure risk to humans and animals from the measured high-exposure-high-risk data involving laboratory animals.

Highest Dose Tested The highest dose of a chemical or substance tested in a study.

Holding Pond A pond or reservoir, usually made of earth, built to store polluted runoff.

Holding Time The maximum amount of time a sample may be stored before analysis.

Hollow Stem Auger Drilling Conventional drilling method that uses augurs to penetrate the soil. As the augers are rotated, soil cuttings are conveyed to the ground surface via augur spirals. DP tools can be used inside the hollow augers.

Homeowner Water System Any water system which supplies piped water to a single residence.

Homogeneous Area In accordance with Asbestos Hazard and Emergency Response Act (AHERA) definitions, an area of surfacing materials, thermal surface insulation, or miscellaneous material that is uniform in color and texture.

Hood Capture Efficiency Ratio of the emissions captured by a hood and directed into a control or disposal device, expressed as a percent of all emissions.

Host 1. In genetics, the organism, typically a bacterium, into which a gene from another organism is transplanted. 2. In medicine, an animal infected or parasitized by another organism.

Household Hazardous Waste Hazardous products used and disposed of by residential as opposed to industrial consumers. Includes paints, stains, varnishes, solvents, pesticides, and other materials or products containing volatile chemicals that can catch fire, react or explode, or that are corrosive or toxic.

Household Waste (Domestic Waste) Solid waste, composed of garbage and rubbish, which normally originates in a private home or apartment house. Domestic waste may contain a significant amount of toxic or hazardous waste.

Human Equivalent Dose A dose which, when administered to humans, produces an effect equal to that produced by a dose in animals.

Human Exposure Evaluation Describing the nature and size of the population exposed to a substance and the magnitude and duration of their exposure.

Human Health Risk The likelihood that a given exposure or series of exposures may have damaged or will damage the health of individuals.

Hydraulic Conductivity The rate at which water can move through a permeable medium (i.e., the coefficient of permeability).

Hydraulic Gradient In general, the direction of groundwater flow due to changes in the depth of the water table.

Hydrocarbons (HC) Chemical compounds that consist entirely of carbon and hydrogen.

Hydrogen Sulfide (H_2S) Gas emitted during organic decomposition. Also a by-product of oil refining and burning. Smells like rotten eggs and, in heavy concentration, can kill or cause illness.

Hydrogeological Cycle The natural process recycling water from the atmosphere down to (and through) the earth and back to the atmosphere again.

Hydrogeology The geology of ground water, with particular emphasis on the chemistry and movement of water.

Hydrologic Cycle Movement or exchange of water between the atmosphere and earth.

Hydrology The science dealing with the properties, distribution, and circulation of water.

Hydrolysis The decomposition of organic compounds by interaction with water.

Hydronic A ventilation system using heated or cooled water pumped through a building.

Hydrophilic Having a strong affinity for water.

Hydrophobic Having a strong aversion for water.

Hydropneumatic A water system, usually small, in which a water pump is automatically controlled by the pressure in a compressed air tank.

Hypersensitivity Diseases Diseases characterized by allergic responses to pollutants; diseases most clearly associated with indoor air quality are asthma, rhinitis, and pneumonic hypersensitivity.

Hypolimnion Bottom waters of a thermally stratified lake. The hypolimnion of a eutrophic lake is usually low or lacking in oxygen.

Hypoxia/Hypoxic Waters Waters with dissolved oxygen concentrations of less than 2 ppm, the level generally accepted as the minimum required for most marine life to survive and reproduce.

Identification Code or EPA I.D. Number The unique code assigned to each generator, transporter, and treatment, storage, or disposal facility by regulating agencies to facilitate identification and tracking of chemicals or hazardous waste.

Ignitable Capable of burning or causing a fire.

IM240 A high-tech, transient dynamometer automobile emissions test that takes up to 240 seconds.

Imhoff Cone A clear, cone-shaped container used to measure the volume of settleable solids in a specific volume of water.

Immediately Dangerous to Life and Health (IDLH) The maximum level to which a healthy individual can be exposed to a chemical for 30 minutes and escape without suffering irreversible health effects or impairing symptoms. Used as a "level of concern." (See level of concern.)

Imminent Hazard One that would likely result in unreasonable adverse effects on humans or the environment or risk unreasonable hazard to an endangered species during the time required for a pesticide registration cancellation proceeding.

Imminent Threat A high probability that exposure is occurring.

Immiscibility The inability of two or more substances or liquids to readily dissolve into one another, such as soil and water. Immiscibility The inability of two or more substances or liquids to readily dissolve into one another, such as soil and water.

Impermeable Not easily penetrated. The property of a material or soil that does not allow, or allows only with great difficulty, the movement or passage of water.

Imports Municipal solid waste and recyclables that have been transported to a state or locality for processing or final disposition (but that did not originate in that state or locality).

Impoundment A body of water or sludge confined by a dam, dike, floodgate, or other barrier.

In-Line Filtration Pre-treattment method in which chemicals are mixed by the flowing water; commonly used in pressure filtration installations. Eliminates need for flocculation and sedimentation.

In Situ In its original place; unmoved unexcavated; remaining at the site or in the subsurface.

In-Situ Flushing Introduction of large volumes of water, at times supplemented with cleaning compounds, into soil, waste, or ground water to flush hazardous contaminants from a site.

In-Situ Oxidation Technology that oxidizes contaminants dissolved in ground water, converting them into insoluble compounds.

In-Situ Stripping Treatment system that removes or "strips" volatile organic compounds from contaminated ground or surface water by forcing an airstream through the water and causing the compounds to evaporate.

In-Situ Vitrification Technology that treats contaminated soil in place at extremely high temperatures, at or more than 3000 degrees Fahrenheit.

In Vitro Testing or action outside an organism (e.g., inside a test tube or culture dish).

In Vivo Testing or action inside an organism.

Incident Command Post A facility located at a safe distance from an emergency site, where the incident commander, key staff, and technical representatives can make decisions and deploy emergency manpower and equipment.

Incident Command System (ICS) The organizational arrangement wherein one person, normally the Fire Chief of the impacted district, is in charge of an integrated, comprehensive emergency response organization and the emergency incident site, backed by an Emergency Operations Center staff with resources, information, and advice.

Incineration A treatment technology involving destruction of waste by controlled burning at high temperatures; e.g., burning sludge to remove the water and reduce the remaining residues to a safe, non-burnable ash that can be disposed of safely on land, in some waters, or in underground locations.

Incineration at Sea Disposal of waste by burning at sea on specially designed incinerator ships.

Incinerator A furnace for burning waste under controlled conditions.

Incompatible Waste A waste unsuitable for mixing with another waste or material because it may react to form a hazard.

Indemnification In the pesticide program, legal requirement that EPA pay certain end-users, dealers, and distributors for the cost of stock on hand at the time a pesticide registration is suspended.

Indicator In biology, any biological entity or processes, or community whose characteristics show the presence of specific environmental conditions. 2. In chemistry, a substance that shows a visible change, usually of color, at a desired point in a chemical reaction. 3.A device that indicates the result of a measurement; e.g. a pressure gauge or a moveable scale.

Indirect Discharge Introduction of pollutants from a non-domestic source into a publicly owned waste-treatment system. Indirect dischargers can be commercial or industrial facilities whose wastes enter local sewers.

Indirect Source Any facility or building, property, road or parking area that attracts motor vehicle traffic and, indirectly, causes pollution.

Indoor Air The breathable air inside a habitable structure or conveyance.

Indoor Air Pollution Chemical, physical, or biological contaminants in indoor air.

Indoor Climate Temperature, humidity, lighting, air flow and noise levels in a habitable structure or conveyance. Indoor climate can affect indoor air pollution.

Industrial Pollution Prevention Combination of industrial source reduction and toxic chemical use substitution.

Industrial Process Waste Residues produced during manufacturing operations.

Industrial Sludge Semi-liquid residue or slurry remaining from treatment of industrial water and wastewater.

Industrial Source Reduction Practices that reduce the amount of any hazardous substance, pollutant, or contaminant entering any waste stream or otherwise released into the environment. Also reduces the threat to public health and the environment associated with such releases. Term includes equipment or technology modifications, substitution of raw materials, and improvements in housekeeping, maintenance, training or inventory control.

Industrial Waste Unwanted materials from an industrial operation; may be liquid, sludge, solid, or hazardous waste.

Inert Ingredient Pesticide components such as solvents, carriers, dispersants, and surfactants that are not active against target pests. Not all inert ingredients are innocuous.

Inertial Separator A device that uses centrifugal force to separate waste particles.

Infectious Agent Any organism, such as a pathogenic virus, parasite, or or bacterium, that is capable of invading body tissues, multiplying, and causing disease.

Infectious Waste Hazardous waste capable of causing infections in humans, including contaminated animal waste; human blood and blood products; isolation waste, pathological waste; and discarded sharps (needles, scalpels or broken medical instruments).

Infiltration 1. The penetration of water through the ground surface into sub-surface soil or the penetration of water from the soil into sewer or other pipes through defective joints, connections, or manhole walls. 2. The technique of applying large volumes of waste water to land to penetrate the surface and percolate through the underlying soil. (See percolation.)

Infiltration Gallery A sub-surface groundwater collection system, typically shallow in depth, constructed with open-jointed or perforated pipes that discharge collected water into a watertight chamber from which the water is pumped to treatment facilities and into the distribution system. Usually located close to streams or ponds.

Infiltration Rate The quantity of water that can enter the soil in a specified time interval.

Inflow Entry of extraneous rain water into a sewer system from sources other than infiltration, such as basement drains, manholes, storm drains, and street washing.

Influent Water, wastewater, or other liquid flowing into a reservoir, basin, or treatment plant.

Information Collection Request (ICR) A description of information to be gathered in connection with rules, proposed rules, surveys, and guidance documents that contain information-gathering requirements. The ICR describes what information is needed, why it is needed, how it will be collected, and how much collecting it will cost. The ICR is submitted by the EPA to the Office of Management and Budget (OMB) for approval.

Information File In the Superfund program, a file that contains accurate, up-to-date documents on a Superfund site. The file is usually located in a public building (school, library, or city hall) convenient for local residents.

Inhalable Particles All dust capable of entering the human respiratory tract.

Initial Compliance Period (Water) The first full three-year compliance period which begins at least 18 months after promulgation.

Injection Well A well into which fluids are injected for purposes such as waste disposal, improving the recovery of crude oil, or solution mining.

Injection Zone A geological formation receiving fluids through a well.

Innovative Technologies New or inventive methods to treat effectively hazardous waste and reduce risks to human health and the environment.

Innovative Treatment Technologies Technologies whose routine use is inhibited by lack of data on performance and cost. (See Established treatment technologies.)

Inoculum 1. Bacteria or fungi injected into compost to start biological action. 2. A medium containing organisms, usually bacteria or a virus, that is introduced into cultures or living organisms.

Inorganic Chemicals Chemical substances of mineral origin, not of basically carbon structure.

Insecticide A pesticide compound specifically used to kill or prevent the growth of insects.

Inspection and Maintenance (I/M) 1. Activities to ensure that vehicles' emission controls work properly. 2. Also applies to wastewater treatment plants and other anti-pollution facilities and processes.

Institutional Waste Waste generated at institutions such as schools, libraries, hospitals, prisons, etc.

Instream Use Water use taking place within a stream channel; e.g., hydro-electric power generation, navigation, water quality improvement, fish propagation, recreation.

Integrated Exposure Assessment Cumulative summation (over time) of the magnitude of exposure to a toxic chemical in all media.

Integrated Pest Management (IPM) A mixture of chemical and other, non-pesticide, methods to control pests.

Integrated Waste Management Using a variety of practices to handle municipal solid waste; can include source reduction, recycling, incineration, and landfilling.

Interceptor Sewers Large sewer lines that, in a combined system, control the flow of sewage to the treatment plant. In a storm, they allow some of the sewage to flow directly into a receiving stream, thus keeping it from overflowing onto the streets. Also used in separate systems to collect the flows from main and trunk sewers and carry them to treatment points.

Interface The common boundary between two substances such as a water and a solid, water and a gas, or two liquids such as water and oil.

Interfacial Tension The strength of the film separating two immiscible fluids (e.g., oil and water) measured in dynes per, or millidynes per centimeter.

Interim (Permit) Status Period during which treatment, storage and disposal facilities coming under RCRA in 1980 are temporarily permitted to operate while awaiting a permanent permit. Permits issued under these circumstances are usually called "Part A" or "Part B" permits.

Internal Dose In exposure assessment, the amount of a substance penetrating the absorption barriers (e.g., skin, lung tissue, gastrointestinal tract) of an organism through either physical or biological processes. (See absorbed dose.)

Interstate Carrier Water Supply A source of water for drinking and sanitary use on planes, buses, trains, and ships operating in more than one state. These sources are federally regulated.

Interstate Commerce Clause A clause of the U.S. Constitution which reserves to the federal government the right to regulate the conduct of business across state lines. Under this clause, for example, the U.S. Supreme Court has ruled that states may not inequitably restrict the disposal of out-of-state wastes in their jurisdictions.

Interstate Waters Waters that flow across or form part of state or international boundaries; e.g., the Great Lakes, the Mississippi River, or coastal waters.

Interstitial Monitoring The continuous surveillance of the space between the walls of an underground storage tank.

Intrastate Product Pesticide products once registered by states for sale and use only in the state. All intrastate products have been converted to full federal registration or canceled.

Inventory (TSCA) Inventory of chemicals produced pursuant to Section 8 (b) of the Toxic Substances Control Act.

Inversion A layer of warm air that prevents the rise of cooling air and traps pollutants beneath it; can cause an air pollution episode.

Ion An electrically charged atom or group of atoms.

Ion Exchange Treatment A common water-softening method often found on a large scale at water purification plants that remove some organics and radium by adding calcium oxide or calcium hydroxide to increase the pH to a level where the metals will precipitate out.

Ionization Chamber A device that measures the intensity of ionizing radiation.

Ionizing Radiation Radiation that can strip electrons from atoms; e.g., alpha, beta, and gamma radiation.

IRIS EPA's Integrated Risk Information System, an electronic data base containing the Agency's latest descriptive and quantitative regulatory information on chemical constituents.

Irradiated Food Food subject to brief radioactivity, usually gamma rays, to kill insects, bacteria, and mold, and to permit storage without refrigeration.

Irradiation Exposure to radiation of wavelengths shorter than those of visible light (gamma, x-ray, or ultra-violet), for medical purposes, to sterilize milk or other foodstuffs, or to induce polymerization of monomers or vulcanization of rubber.

Irreversible Effect Effect characterized by the inability of the body to partially or fully repair injury caused by a toxic agent.

Irrigation Applying water or wastewater to land areas to supply the water and nutrient needs of plants.

Irrigation Efficiency The amount of water stored in the crop root zone compared to the amount of irrigation water applied.

Irrigation Return Flow Surface and subsurface water which leaves the field following application of irrigation water.

Irritant A substance that can cause irritation of the skin, eyes, or respiratory system. Effects may be acute from a single high level exposure, or chronic from repeated low-level exposures to such compounds as chlorine, nitrogen dioxide, and nitric acid.

Isoconcentration More than one sample point exhibiting the same isolate concentration.

Isopleth The line or area represented by an isoconcentration.

Isotope A variation of an element that has the same atomic number of protons but a different weight because of the number of neutrons. Various isotopes of the same element may have different radioactive behaviors, some are highly unstable.

Isotropy The condition in which the hydraulic or other properties of an aquifer are the same in all directions.

Jar Test A laboratory procedure that simulates a water treatment plant's coagulation/flocculation units with differing chemical doses, mix speeds, and settling times to estimate the minimum or ideal coagulant dose required to achieve certain water quality goals.

Joint and Several Liability Under CERCLA, this legal concept relates to the liability for Superfund site cleanup and other costs on the part of more than one potentially responsible party (i.e. if there were several owners or users of a site that became contaminated over the years, they could all be considered potentially liable for cleaning up the site).

Karst A geologic formation of irregular limestone deposits with sinks, underground streams, and caverns.

Kinetic Energy Energy possessed by a moving object or water body.

Kinetic Rate Coefficient A number that describes the rate at which a water constituent such as a biochemical oxygen demand or dissolved oxygen rises or falls, or at which an air pollutant reacts.

Laboratory Animal Studies Investigations using animals as surrogates for humans.

Lagoon 1. A shallow pond where sunlight, bacterial action, and oxygen work to purify wastewater; also used for storage of wastewater or spent nuclear fuel rods. 2. Shallow body of water, often separated from the sea by coral reefs or sandbars.

Land Application Discharge of wastewater onto the ground for treatment or reuse. (See irrigation.)

Land Ban Phasing out of land disposal of most untreated hazardous wastes, as mandated by the 1984 RCRA amendments.

Land Disposal Restrictions Rules that require hazardous wastes to be treated before disposal on land to destroy or immobilize hazardous constituents that might migrate into soil and ground water.

Land Farming (of Waste) A disposal process in which hazardous waste deposited on or in the soil is degraded naturally by microbes.

Landfills 1. Sanitary landfills are disposal sites for non-hazardous solid wastes spread in layers, compacted to the smallest practical volume, and covered by material applied at the end of each operating day. 2. Secure chemical landfills are disposal sites for hazardous waste, selected and designed to minimize the chance of release of hazardous substances into the environment.

Landscape The traits, patterns, and structure of a specific geographic area, including its biological composition, its physical environment, and its anthropogenic or social patterns. An area where interacting ecosystems are grouped and repeated in similar form.

Landscape Characterization Documentation of the traits and patterns of the essential elements of the landscape.

Landscape Ecology The study of the distribution patterns of communities and ecosystems, the ecological processes that affect those patterns, and changes in pattern and process over time.

Landscape Indicator A measurement of the landscape, calculated from mapped or remotely sensed data, used to describe spatial patterns of land use and land cover across a geographic area. Landscape indicators may be useful as measures of certain kinds of environmental degradation such as forest fragmentation.

Langelier Index (LI) An index reflecting the equilibrium pH of a water with respect to calcium and alkalinity; used in stabilizing water to control both corrosion and scale deposition.

Large Quantity Generator Person or facility generating more than 2200 pounds of hazardous waste per month. Such generators produce about 90 percent of the nation's hazardous waste, and are subject to all RCRA requirements.

Large Water System A water system that services more than 50,000 customers.

Laser-Induced Fluorescence A method for measuring the relative amount of soil and/or groundwater with an in-situ sensor.

Latency Time from the first exposure of a chemical until the appearance of a toxic effect.

Lateral Sewers Pipes that run under city streets and receive the sewage from homes and businesses, as opposed to domestic feeders and main trunk lines.

Laundering Weir Sedimention basin overflow weir.

LC 50/Lethal Concentration Median level concentration, a standard measure of toxicity. It tells how much of a substance is needed to kill half of a group of experimental organisms in a given time. (See LD 50.)

LD 50/ Lethal Dose The dose of a toxicant or microbe that will kill 50 percent of the test organisms within a designated period. The lower the LD 50, the more toxic the compound.

Ldlo Lethal dose low; the lowest dose in an animal study at which lethality occurs.

Leachate Water that collects contaminants as it trickles through wastes, pesticides or fertilizers. Leaching may occur in farming areas, feedlots, and landfills, and may result in hazardous substances entering surface water, ground water, or soil.

Leachate Collection System A system that gathers leachate and pumps it to the surface for treatment.

Leaching The process by which soluble constituents are dissolved and filtered through the soil by a percolating fluid. (See leachate.)

Lead (Pb) A heavy metal that is hazardous to health if breathed or swallowed. Its use in gasoline, paints, and plumbing compounds has been sharply restricted or eliminated by federal laws and regulations. (See heavy metals.)

Lead Service Line A service line made of lead which connects the water to the building inlet and any lead fitting connected to it.

Legionella A genus of bacteria, some species of which have caused a type of pneumonia called Legionaires Disease.

Lethal Concentration 50 Also referred to as LC50, a concentration of a pollutant or effluent at which 50 percent of the test organisms die; a common measure of acute toxicity.

Lethal Dose 50 Also referred to as LD50, the dose of a toxicant that will kill 50 percent of test organisms within a designated period of time; the lower the LD 50, the more toxic the compound.

Level of Concern (LOC) The concentration in air of an extremely hazardous substance above which there may be serious immediate health effects to anyone exposed to it for short periods

Life Cycle of a Product All stages of a product's development, from extraction of fuel for power to production, marketing, use, and disposal.

Lifetime Average Daily Dose Figure for estimating excess lifetime cancer risk.

Lifetime Exposure Total amount of exposure to a substance that a human would receive in a lifetime (usually assumed to be 70 years).

Lift In a sanitary landfill, a compacted layer of solid waste and the top layer of cover material.

Lifting Station (See pumping station.)

Light Non-Aqueous Phase Liquid (LNAPL) A non-aqueous phase liquid with a specific gravity less than 1.0. Because the specific gravity of water is 1.0, most LNAPLs float on top of the water table. Most common petroleum hydrocarbon fuels and lubricating oils are LNAPLs.

Light-Emitting Diode A long-lasting illumination technology used for exit signs which requires very little power

Limestone Scrubbing Use of a limestone and water solution to remove gaseous stack-pipe sulfur before it reaches the atmosphere.

Limit of Detection (LOD) The minimum concentration of a substance being analyzed test that has a 99 percent probability of being identified.

Limited Degradation An environmental policy permitting some degradation of natural systems but terminating at a level well beneath an established health standard.

Limiting Factor A condition whose absence or excessive concentration, is incompatible with the needs or tolerance of a species or population and which may have a negative influence on their ability to thrive.

Limnology The study of the physical, chemical, hydrological, and biological aspects of fresh water bodies.

Lindane A pesticide that causes adverse health effects in domestic water supplies and is toxic to freshwater fish and aquatic life.

Liner 1. A relatively impermeable barrier designed to keep leachate inside a landfill. Liner materials include plastic and dense clay. 2. An insert or sleeve for sewer pipes to prevent leakage or infiltration.

Lipid Solubility The maximum concentration of a chemical that will dissolve in fatty substances. Lipid soluble substances are insoluble in water. They will very selectively disperse through the environment via uptake in living tissue.

Liquefaction Changing a solid into a liquid.

Liquid Injection Incinerator Commonly used system that relies on high pressure to prepare liquid wastes for incineration by breaking them up into tiny droplets to allow easier combustion.

List Shorthand term for EPA list of violating facilities or firms debarred from obtaining government contracts because they violated certain sections of the Clean Air or Clean Water Acts. The list is maintained by The Office of Enforcement and Compliance Monitoring.

Listed Waste Wastes listed as hazardous under RCRA but which have not been subjected to the Toxic Characteristics Listing Process because the dangers they present are considered self-evident.

Lithology Mineralogy, grain size, texture, and other physical properties of granular soil, sediment, or rock.

Litter 1. The highly visible portion of solid waste carelessly discarded outside the regular garbage and trash collection and disposal system. 2. leaves and twigs fallen from forest trees.

Littoral Zone 1. That portion of a body of fresh water extending from the shoreline lakeward to the limit of occupancy of rooted plants. 2. A strip of land along the shoreline between the high and low water levels.

Local Education Agency (LEA) In the asbestos program, an educational agency at the local level that exists primarily to operate schools or to contract for educational services, including primary and secondary public and private schools. A single, unaffiliated school can be considered an LEA for AHERA purposes.

Local Emergency Planning Committee (LEPC) A committee appointed by the state emergency response commission, as required by SARA Title III, to formulate a comprehensive emergency plan for its jurisdiction.

Low Density Polyethylene (LOPE) Plastic material used for both rigid containers and plastic film applications.

Low Emissivity (low-E) Windows New window technology that lowers the amount of energy loss through windows by inhibiting the transmission of radiant heat while still allowing sufficient light to pass through.

Low-Level Radioactive Waste (LLRW) Wastes less hazardous than most of those associated with a nuclear reactor; generated by hospitals, research laboratories, and certain industries. The Department of Energy, Nuclear Regulatory Commission, and EPA share responsibilities for managing them. (See high-level radioactive wastes.)

Low NO$_x$ Burners One of several combustion technologies used to reduce emissions of Nitrogen Oxides (NOx).

Lower Detection Limit The smallest signal above background noise an instrument can reliably detect.

Lower Explosive Limit (LEL) The concentration of a compound in air below which the mixture will not catch on fire.

Lowest Acceptable Daily Dose The largest quantity of a chemical that will not cause a toxic effect, as determined by animal studies.

Lowest Achievable Emission Rate Under the Clean Air Act, the rate of emissions that reflects (1) the most stringent emission limitation in the implementation plan of any state for such source unless the owner or operator demonstrates such limitations are not achievable; or (2) the most stringent emissions limitation achieved in practice, whichever is more stringent. A proposed new or modified source may not emit pollutants in excess of existing new source standards.

Lowest Observed Adverse Effect Level (LOAEL) The lowest level of a stressor that causes statistically and biologically significant differences in test samples as compared to other samples subjected to no stressor.

Macropores Secondary soil features such as root holes or desiccation cracks that can create significant conduits for movement of NAPL and dissolved contaminants, or vapor-phase contaminants.

Magnetic Separation Use of magnets to separate ferrous materials from mixed municipal waste stream.

Major Modification This term is used to define modifications of major stationary sources of emissions with respect to Prevention of Significant Deterioration and New Source Review under the Clean Air Act.

Major Stationary Sources Term used to determine the applicability of Prevention of Significant Deterioration and new source regulations. In a nonattainment area, any stationary pollutant source with potential to emit more than 100 tons per year is considered a major stationary source. In PSD areas the cutoff level may be either 100 or 250 tons, depending upon the source.

Majors Larger publicly owned treatment works (POTWs) with flows equal to at least one million gallons per day (mgd) or servicing a population equivalent to 10,000 persons; certain other POTWs having significant water quality impacts. (See minors.)

Man-Made (Anthropogenic) Beta Particle and Photon Emitters All radionuclides emitting beta particles and/or photons listed in Maximum Permissible Body Burdens and Maximum Permissible Concentrations of Radonuclides in Air and Water for Occupational Exposure.

Management Plan Under the Asbestos Hazard Emergency Response Act (AHERA), a document that each Local Education Agency is required to prepare, describing all activities planned and undertaken by a school to comply with AHERA regulations, including building inspections to identify asbestos-containing materials, response actions, and operations and maintenance programs to minimize the risk of exposure.

Managerial Controls Methods of nonpoint source pollution control based on decisions about managing agricultural wastes or application times or rates for agrochemicals.

Mandatory Recycling Programs which by law require consumers to separate trash so that some or all recyclable materials are recovered for recycling rather than going to landfills.

Manifest A one-page form used by haulers transporting waste that lists EPA identification numbers, type and quantity of waste, the generator it originated from, the transporter that shipped it, and the storage or disposal facility to which it is being shipped. It includes copies for all participants in the shipping process.

Manifest System Tracking of hazardous waste from "cradle-to-grave" (generation through disposal) with accompanying documents known as manifests. (See cradle to grave.)

Manual Separation Hand sorting of recyclable or compostable materials in waste.

Manufacturer's Formulation A list of substances or component parts as described by the maker of a coating, pesticide, or other product containing chemicals or other substances.

Manufacturing Use Product Any product intended (labeled) for formulation or repackaging into other pesticide products.

Margin of Safety Maximum amount of exposure producing no measurable effect in animals (or studied humans) divided by the actual amount of human exposure in a population.

Margin of Exposure (MOE) The ratio of the no-observed adverse-effect-level to the estimated exposure dose.

Marine Sanitation Device Any equipment or process installed on board a vessel to receive, retain, treat, or discharge sewage.

Marsh A type of wetland that does not accumulate appreciable peat deposits and is dominated by herbaceous vegetation. Marshes may be either fresh or saltwater, tidal or non-tidal. (See wetlands.)

Material Category In the asbestos program, broad classification of materials into thermal surfacing insulation, surfacing material, and miscellaneous material.

Material Safety Data Sheet (MSDS) A compilation of information required under the OSHA Communication Standard on the identity of hazardous chemicals, health, and physical hazards, exposure limits, and precautions. Section 311 of SARA requires facilities to submit MSDSs under certain circumstances.

Material Type Classification of suspect material by its specific use or application; e.g., pipe insulation, fireproofing, and floor tile.

Materials Recovery Facility (MRF) A facility that processes residentially collected mixed recyclables into new products available for market.

Maximally (or Most) Exposed Individual The person with the highest exposure in a given population.

Maximum Acceptable Toxic Concentration For a given ecological effects test, the range (or geometric mean) between the No Observable Adverse Effect Level and the Lowest Observable Adverse Effects Level.

Maximum Available Control Technology (MACT) The emission standard for sources of air pollution requiring the maximum reduction of hazardous emissions, taking cost and feasibility into account. Under the Clean Air Act Amendments of 1990, the MACT must not be less than the average emission level achieved by controls on the best performing 12 percent of existing sources, by category of industrial and utility sources.

Maximum Contaminant Level The maximum permissible level of a contaminant in water delivered to any user of a public system. MCLs are enforceable standards.

Maximum Contaminant Level Goal (MCLG) Under the Safe Drinking Water Act, a non-enforceable concentration of a drinking water contaminant, set at the level at which no known or anticipated adverse effects on human health occur and which allows an adequate safety margin. The MCLG is usually the starting point for determining the regulated Maximum Contaminant Level. (See maximum contaminant level.)

Maximum Exposure Range Estimate of exposure or dose level received by an individual in a defined population that is greater than the 98th percentile dose for all individuals in that population, but less than the exposure level received by the person receiving the highest exposure level.

Maximum Residue Level Comparable to a U.S. tolerance level, the Maximum Residue Level the enforceable limit on food pesticide levels in some countries. Levels are set by the Codex Alimentarius Commission, a United Nations agency managed and funded jointly by the World Health Organization and the Food and Agriculture Organization.

Maximum Tolerated Dose The maximum dose that an animal species can tolerate for a major portion of its lifetime without significant impairment or toxic effect other than carcinogenicity.

Measure of Effect/Measurement Endpoint A measurable characteristic of ecological entity that can be related to an assessment endpoint; e.g. a laboratory test for eight species meeting certain requirements may serve as a measure of effect for an assessment endpoint, such as survival of fish, aquatic, invertebrate or algal species under acute exposure.

Measure of Exposure A measurable characteristic of a stressor (such as the specific amount of mercury in a body of water) used to help quantify the exposure of an ecological entity or individual organism.

Mechanical Aeration Use of mechanical energy to inject air into water to cause a waste stream to absorb oxygen.

Mechanical Separation Using mechanical means to separate waste into various components.

Mechanical Turbulence Random irregularities of fluid motion in air caused by buildings or other non-thermal, processes.

Media Specific environments—air, water, soil—which are the subject of regulatory concern and activities.

Medical Surveillance A periodic comprehensive review of a worker's health status; acceptable elements of such surveillance program are listed in the Occupational Safety and Health Administration standards for asbestos.

Medical Waste Any solid waste generated in the diagnosis, treatment, or immunization of human beings or animals, in research pertaining thereto, or in the production or testing of biologicals, excluding hazardous waste identified or listed under 40 CFR Part 261 or any household waste as defined in 40 CFR Sub-section 261.4 (b)(1).

Medium-Size Water System A water system that serves 3,300 to 50,000 customers.

Meniscus The curved top of a column of liquid in a small tube.

Mercury (Hg) Heavy metal that can accumulate in the environment and is highly toxic if breathed or swallowed. (See heavy metals.)

Mesotrophic Reservoirs and lakes which contain moderate quantities of nutrients and are moderately productive in terms of aquatic animal and plant life.

Metabolites Any substances produced by biological processes, such as those from pesticides.

Metalimnion The middle layer of a thermally stratified lake or reservoir. In this layer there is a rapid decrease in temperature with depth. Also called thermocline.

Methane A colorless, nonpoisonous, flammable gas created by anaerobic decomposition of organic compounds. A major component of natural gas used in the home.

Methanol An alcohol that can be used as an alternative fuel or as a gasoline additive. It is less volatile than gasoline; when blended with gasoline it lowers the carbon monoxide emissions but increases hydrocarbon emissions. Used as pure fuel, its emissions are less ozone-forming than those from gasoline. Poisonous to humans and animals if ingested.

Method 18 An EPA test method which uses gas chromatographic techniques to measure the concentration of volatile organic compounds in a gas stream.

Method 24 An EPA reference method to determine density, water content and total volatile content (water and VOC) of coatings.

Method 25 An EPA reference method to determine the VOC concentration in a gas stream.

Method Detection Limit (MDL) See limit of detection.

Methoxychlor Pesticide that causes adverse health effects in domestic water supplies and is toxic to freshwater and marine aquatic life.

Methyl Orange Alkalinity A measure of the total alkalinity in a water sample in which the color of methyl orange reflects the change in level.

Microbial Growth The amplification or multiplication of microorganisms such as bacteria, algae, diatoms, plankton, and fungi.

Microbial Pesticide A microorganism that is used to kill a pest, but is of minimum toxicity to humans.

Microclimate 1. Localized climate conditions within an urban area or neighborhood. 2. The climate around a tree or shrub or a stand of trees.

Microenvironmental Method A method for sequentially assessing exposure for a series of microenvironments that can be approximated by constant concentrations of a stressor.

Microenvironments Well-defined surroundings such as the home, office, or kitchen that can be treated as uniform in terms of stressor concentration.

Million-Gallons Per Day (MGD) A measure of water flow.

Minimization A comprehensive program to minimize or eliminate wastes, usually applied to wastes at their point of origin. (See waste minimization.)

Mining of an Aquifer Withdrawal over a period of time of ground water that exceeds the rate of recharge of the aquifer.

Mining Waste Residues resulting from the extraction of raw materials from the earth.

Minor Source New emissions sources or modifications to existing emissions sources that do not exceed NAAQS emission levels.

Minors Publicly owned treatment works with flows less than 1 million gallons per day. (See majors.)

Miscellaneous ACM Interior asbestos-containing building material or structural components, members or fixtures, such as floor and ceiling tiles; does not include surfacing materials or thermal system insulation.

Miscellaneous Materials Interior building materials on structural components, such as floor or ceiling tiles.

Miscible Liquids Two or more liquids that can be mixed and will remain mixed under normal conditions.

Missed Detection The situation that occurs when a test indicates that a tank is "tight" when in fact it is leaking.

Mist Liquid particles measuring 40 to 500 micrometers (pm), are formed by condensation of vapor. By comparison, fog particles are smaller than 40 micrometers (pm).

Mitigation Measures taken to reduce adverse impacts on the environment.

Mixed Funding Settlements in which potentially responsible parties and EPA share the cost of a response action.

Mixed Glass Recovered container glass not sorted into categories (e.g., color, grade).

Mixed Liquor A mixture of activated sludge and water containing organic matter undergoing activated sludge treatment in an aeration tank.

Mixed Metals Recovered metals not sorted into categories such as aluminum, tin, or steel cans or ferrous or non-ferrous metals.

Mixed Municipal Waste Solid waste that has not been sorted into specific categories (such as plastic, glass, yard trimmings, etc.)

Mixed Paper Recovered paper not sorted into categories such as old magazines, old newspapers, old corrugated boxes, etc.

Mixed Plastic Recovered plastic unsorted by category.

Mobile Incinerator Systems Hazardous waste incinerators that can be transported from one site to another.

Mobile Source Any non-stationary source of air pollution such as cars, trucks, motorcycles, buses, airplanes, and locomotives.

Model Plant A hypothetical plant design used for developing economic, environmental, and energy impact analyses as support for regulations or regulatory guidelines; first step in exploring the economic impact of a potential NSPS.

Modified Bin Method Way of calculating the required heating or cooling for a building based on determining how much energy the system would use if outdoor temperatures were within a certain temperature interval and then multiplying the energy use by the time the temperature interval typically occurs.

Modified Source The enlargement of a major stationary pollutant sources is often referred to as modification, implying that more emissions will occur.

Moisture Content 1.The amount of water lost from soil upon drying to a constant weight, expressed as the weight per unit of dry soil or as the volume of water per unit bulk volume of the soil. For a fully saturated medium, moisture content indicates the porosity. 2. Water equivalent of snow on the ground; an indicator of snowmelt flood potential.

Molecule The smallest division of a compound that still retains or exhibits all the properties of the substance.

Molten Salt Reactor A thermal treatment unit that rapidly heats waste in a heat-conducting fluid bath of carbonate salt.

Monitoring Periodic or continuous surveillance or testing to determine the level of compliance with statutory requirements and/or pollutant levels in various media or in humans, plants, and animals.

Monitoring Well 1. A well used to obtain water quality samples or measure groundwater levels. 2. A well drilled at a hazardous waste management facility or Superfund site to collect ground-water samples for the purpose of physical, chemical, or biological analysis to determine the amounts, types, and distribution of contaminants in the groundwater beneath the site.

Monoclonal Antibodies (Also called MABs and MCAs) 1. Man-made (anthropogenic) clones of a molecule, produced in quantity for medical or research purposes. 2. Molecules of living organisms that selectively find and attach to other molecules to which their structure conforms exactly. This could also apply to equivalent activity by chemical molecules.

Monomictic Lakes and reservoirs which are relatively deep, do not freeze over during winter, and undergo a single stratification and mixing cycle during the year (usually in the fall).

Montreal Protocol Treaty, signed in 1987, governs stratospheric ozone protection and research, and the production and use of ozone-depleting substances. It provides for the end of production of ozone-depleting substances such as CFCS. Under the Protocol, various research groups continue to assess the ozone layer. The Multilateral Fund provides resources to developing nations to promote the transition to ozone-safe technologies.

Moratorium During the negotiation process, a period of 60 to 90 days during which EPA and potentially responsible parties may reach settlement but no site response activities can be conducted.

Morbidity Rate of disease incidence.

Mortality Death rate.

Most Probable Number An estimate of microbial density per unit volume of water sample, based on probability theory.

Muck Soils Earth made from decaying plant materials.

Mudballs Round material that forms in filters and gradually increases in size when not removed by backwashing.

Mulch A layer of material (wood chips, straw, leaves, etc.) placed around plants to hold moisture, prevent weed growth, and enrich or sterilize the soil.

Multi-Media Approach Joint approach to several environmental media, such as air, water, and land.

Multiple Chemical Sensitivity A diagnostic label for people who suffer multi-system illnesses as a result of contact with, or proximity to, a variety of airborne agents and other substances.

Multiple Use Use of land for more than one purpose; e.g., grazing of livestock, watershed and wildlife protection, recreation, and timber production. Also applies to use of bodies of water for recreational purposes, fishing, and water supply.

Multistage Remote Sensing A strategy for landscape characterization that involves gathering and analyzing information at several geographic scales, ranging from generalized levels of detail at the national level through high levels of detail at the local scale.

Municipal Discharge Discharge of effluent from waste water treatment plants which receive waste water from households, commercial establishments, and industries in the coastal drainage basin. Combined sewer/separate storm overflows are included in this category.

Municipal Sewage Wastes (mostly liquid) orginating from a community; may be composed of domestic wastewaters and/or industrial discharges.

Municipal Sludge Semi-liquid residue remaining from the treatment of municipal water and wastewater.

Municipal Solid Waste Common garbage or trash generated by industries, businesses, institutions, and homes.

Mutagen/Mutagenicity An agent that causes a permanent genetic change in a cell other than that which occurs during normal growth. Mutagenicity is the capacity of a chemical or physical agent to cause such permanent changes.

National Ambient Air Quality Standards (NAAQS) Standards established by EPA that apply for outdoor air throughout the country. (See criteria pollutants, state implementation plans, emissions trading.)

National Emissions Standards for Hazardous Air Pollutants (NESHAPS) Emissions standards set by EPA for an air pollutant not covered by NAAQS that may cause an increase in fatalities or in serious, irreversible, or incapacitating illness. Primary standards are designed to protect human health, secondary standards to protect public welfare (e.g., building facades, visibility, crops, and domestic animals).

National Environmental Performance Partnership Agreements System that allows states to assume greater responsibility for environmental programs based on their relative ability to execute them.

National Estuary Program A program established under the Clean Water Act Amendments of 1987 to develop and implement conservation and management plans for protecting estuaries and restoring and maintaining their chemical, physical, and biological integrity, as well as controlling point and nonpoint pollution sources.

National Municipal Plan A policy created in 1984 by EPA and the states in 1984 to bring all publicly owned treatment works (POTWs) into compliance with Clean Water Act requirements.

National Oil and Hazardous Substances Contingency Plan (NOHSCP/NCP) The federal regulation that guides determination of the sites to be corrected under both the Superfund program and the program to prevent or control spills into surface waters or elsewhere.

National Pollutant Discharge Elimination System (NPDES) A provision of the Clean Water Act which prohibits discharge of pollutants into waters of the United States unless a special permit is issued by EPA, a state, or, where delegated, a tribal government on an Indian reservation.

National Priorities List (NPL) EPA's list of the most serious uncontrolled or abandoned hazardous waste sites identified for possible long-term remedial action under Superfund. The list is based primarily on the score a site receives from the Hazard Ranking System. EPA is required to update the NPL at least once a year. A site must be on the NPL to receive money from the Trust Fund for remedial action.

National Response Center The federal operations center that receives notifications of all releases of oil and hazardous substances into the environment; open 24 hours a day, is operated by the U.S. Coast Guard, which evaluates all reports and notifies the appropriate agency.

National Response Team (NRT) Representatives of 13 federal agencies that, as a team, coordinate federal responses to nationally significant incidents of pollution—an oil spill, a major chemical release, or a - superfund response action—and provide advice and technical assistance to the responding agency(ies) before and during a response action.

National Secondary Drinking Water Regulations Commonly referred to as NSDWRs.

Navigable Waters Traditionally, waters sufficiently deep and wide for navigation by all, or specified vessels; such waters in the United States come under federal jurisdiction and are protected by certain provisions of the Clean Water Act.

Necrosis Death of plant or animal cells or tissues. In plants, necrosis can discolor stems or leaves or kill a plant entirely.

Negotiations (Under Superfund) After potentially responsible parties are identified for a site, EPA coordinates with them to reach a settlement that will result in the PRP paying for or conducting the cleanup under EPA supervision. If negotiations fail, EPA can order the PRP to conduct the cleanup or EPA can pay for the cleanup using Superfund monies and then sue to recover the costs.

Nematocide A chemical agent which is destructive to nematodes.

Nephelometric Method of of measuring turbidity in a water sample by passing light through the sample and measuring the amount of the light that is deflected.

Netting A concept in which all emissions sources in the same area that owned or controlled by a single company are treated as one large source, thereby allowing flexibility in controlling individual sources in order to meet a single emissions standard. (See bubble.)

Neutralization Decreasing the acidity or alkalinity of a substance by adding alkaline or acidic materials, respectively.

New Source Any stationary source built or modified after publication of final or proposed regulations that prescribe a given standard of performance.

New Source Performance Standards (NSPS) Uniform national EPA air emission and water effluent standards which limit the amount of pollution allowed from new sources or from modified existing sources.

New Source Review (NSR) A Clean Air Act requirement that State Implementation Plans must include a permit review that applies to the construction and operation of new and modified stationary sources in nonattainment areas to ensure attainment of national ambient air quality standards.

Nitrate A compound containing nitrogen that can exist in the atmosphere or as a dissolved gas in water and which can have harmful effects on humans and animals. Nitrates in water can cause severe illness in infants and domestic animals. A plant nutrient and inorganic fertilizer, nitrate is found in septic systems, animal feed lots, agricultural fertilizers, manure, industrial waste waters, sanitary landfills, and garbage dumps.

Nitric Oxide (NO) A gas formed by combustion under high temperature and high pressure in an internal combustion engine; it is converted by sunlight and photochemical processes in ambient air to nitrogen oxide. NO is a precursor of ground-level ozone pollution, or smog..

Nitrification The process whereby ammonia in wastewater is oxidized to nitrite and then to nitrate by bacterial or chemical reactions.

Nitrilotriacetic Acid (NTA) A compound now replacing phosphates in detergents.

Nitrite 1. An intermediate in the process of nitrification. 2. Nitrous oxide salts used in food preservation.

Nitrogen Dioxide (NO$_2$) The result of nitric oxide combining with oxygen in the atmosphere; major component of photochemical smog.

Nitrogen Oxide (NO$_x$) The result of photochemical reactions of nitric oxide in ambient air; major component of photochemical smog. Product of combustion from transportation and stationary sources and a major contributor to the formation of ozone in the troposphere and to acid deposition.

Nitrogenous Wastes Animal or vegetable residues that contain significant amounts of nitrogen.

Nitrophenols Synthetic organopesticides containing carbon, hydrogen, nitrogen, and oxygen.

No Further Remedial Action Planned Determination made by EPA following a preliminary assessment that a site does not pose a significant risk and so requires no further activity under CERCLA.

No Observable Adverse Effect Level (NOAEL) An exposure level at which there are no statistically or biologically significant increases in the frequency or severity of adverse effects between the exposed population and its appropriate control; some effects may be produced at this level, but they are not considered as adverse, or as precursors to adverse effects. In an experiment with several NOAELs, the regulatory focus is primarily on the highest one, leading to the common usage of the term NOAEL as the highest exposure without adverse effects.

No Till Planting crops without prior seedbed preparation, into an existing cover crop, sod, or crop residues, and eliminating subsequent tillage operations.

No-Observed-Effect-Level (NOEL) Exposure level at which there are no statistically or biological significant differences in the frequency or severity of any effect in the exposed or control populations.

Noble Metal Chemically inactive metal such as gold; does not corrode easily.

Noise Product-level or product-volume changes occurring during a test that are not related to a leak but may be mistaken for one.

Non-Aqueous Phase Liquid (NAPL) Contaminants that remain undiluted as the original bulk liquid in the subsurface, e.g. spilled oil. (See fee product.)

Non-Attainment Area Area that does not meet one or more of the National Ambient Air Quality Standards for the criteria pollutants designated in the Clean Air Act.

Non-Binding Allocations of Responsibility (NBAR) A process for EPA to propose a way for potentially responsible parties to allocate costs among themselves.

Non-Community Water System A public water system that is not a community water system; e.g. the water supply at a camp site or national park.

Non-Compliance Coal Any coal that emits greater than 3.0 pounds of sulfur dioxide per million BTU when burned. Also known as high-sulfur coal.

Non-Contact Cooling Water Water used for cooling which does not come into direct contact with any raw material, product, byproduct, or waste.

Non-Conventional Pollutant Any pollutant not statutorily listed or which is poorly understood by the scientific community.

Non-Degradation An environmental policy which disallows any lowering of naturally occurring quality regardless of preestablished health standards.

Nondischarging Treatment Plant A treatment plant that does not discharge treated wastewater into any stream or river. Most are pond systems that dispose of the total flow they receive by means of evaporation or percolation to groundwater, or facilities that dispose of their effluent by recycling or reuse (e.g. spray irrigation or groundwater discharge).

Non-Ferrous Metals Nonmagnetic metals such as aluminum, lead, and copper. Products made all or in part from such metals include containers, packaging, appliances, furniture, electronic equipment and aluminum foil.

Nonfriable Asbestos-Containing Materials Any material containing more than one percent asbestos (as determined by Polarized Light Microscopy) that, when dry, cannot be crumbled, pulverized, or reduced to powder by hand pressure.

Nonhazardous Industrial Waste Industrial process waste in wastewater not considered municipal solid waste or hazardous waste under RARA.

Non-Ionizing Electromagnetic Radiation 1. Radiation that does not change the structure of atoms but does heat tissue and may cause harmful biological effects. 2. Microwaves, radio waves, and low-frequency electromagnetic fields from high-voltage transmission lines.

Non-Methane Hydrocarbon (NMHC) The sum of all hydrocarbon air pollutants except methane; significant precursors to ozone formation.

Non-Methane Organic Gases (NMOG) The sum of all organic air pollutants. Excluding methane; they account for aldehydes, ketones, alcohols, and other pollutants that are not hydrocarbons but are precursors of ozone.

Non-Point Sources Diffuse pollution sources (i.e. without a single point of origin or not introduced into a receiving stream from a specific outlet). The pollutants are generally carried off the land by storm water. Common non-point sources are agriculture, forestry, urban, mining, construction, dams, channels, land disposal, saltwater intrusion, and city streets.

Non-Potable Water that is unsafe or unpalatable to drink because it contains pollutants, contaminants, minerals, or infective agents.

Non-Road Emissions Pollutants emitted by combustion engines on farm and construction equipment, gasoline-powered lawn and garden equipment, and power boats and outboard motors.

Non-Transient Non-Community Water System A public water system that regularly serves at least 25 of the same non-resident persons per day for more than six months per year.

Notice of Deficiency An EPA request to a facility owner or operator requesting additional information before a preliminary decision on a permit application can be made.

Notice of Intent to Cancel Notification sent to registrants when EPA decides to cancel registration of a product containing a pesticide.

Notice of Intent to Deny Notification by EPA of its preliminary intent to deny a permit application.

Notice of Intent to Suspend Notification sent to a pesticide registrant when EPA decides to suspend product sale and distribution because of failure to submit requested data in a timely and/or acceptable manner, or because of imminent hazard. (See emergency suspension.)

Nuclear Reactors and Support Facilities Uranium mills, commercial power reactors, fuel reprocessing plants, and uranium enrichment facilities.

Nuclear Winter Prediction by some scientists that smoke and debris rising from massive fires of a nuclear war could block sunlight for weeks or months, cooling the earth's surface and producing climate changes that could, for example, negatively affect world agricultural and weather patterns.

Nuclide An atom characterized by the number of protons, neturons, and energy in the nucleus.

Nutrient Any substance assimilated by living things that promotes growth. The term is generally applied to nitrogen and phosphorus in wastewater, but is also applied to other essential and trace elements.

Nutrient Pollution Contamination of water resources by excessive inputs of nutrients. In surface waters, excess algal production is a major concern.

Ocean Discharge Waiver A variance from Clean Water Act requirements for discharges into marine waters.

Odor Threshold The minimum odor of a water or air sample that can just be detected after successive dilutions with odorless water. Also called threshold odor.

OECD Guidelines Testing guidelines prepared by the Organization of Economic and Cooperative Development of the United Nations. They assist in preparation of protocols for studies of toxicology, environmental fate, etc.

Off-Site Facility A hazardous waste treatment, storage or disposal area that is located away from the generating site.

Office Paper High grade papers such as copier paper, computer printout, and stationary almost entirely made of uncoated chemical pulp, although some ground wood is used. Such waste is also generated in homes, schools, and elsewhere.

Offsets A concept whereby emissions from proposed new or modified stationary sources are balanced by reductions from existing sources to stabilize total emissions. (See bubble, emissions trading, netting.)

Offstream Use Water withdrawn from surface or groundwater sources for use at another place.

Oil and Gas Waste Gas and oil drilling muds, oil production brines, and other waste associated with exploration for, development and production of crude oil or natural gas.

Oil Desulfurization Widely used precombustion method for reducing sulfur dioxide emissions from oil-burning power plants. The oil is treated with hydrogen, which removes some of the sulfur by forming hydrogen sulfide gas.

Oil Fingerprinting A method that identifies sources of oil and allows spills to be traced to their source.

Oil Spill An accidental or intentional discharge of oil which reaches bodies of water. Can be controlled by chemical dispersion, combustion, mechanical containment, and/or adsorption. Spills from tanks and pipelines can also occur away from water bodies, contaminating the soil, getting into sewer systems and threatening underground water sources.

Oligotrophic Lakes Deep clear lakes with few nutrients, little organic matter and a high dissolved-oxygen level.

On-Scene Coordinator (OSC) The predesignated EPA, Coast Guard, or Department of Defense official who coordinates and directs Superfund removal actions or Clean Water Act oil- or hazardous-spill response actions.

On-Site Facility A hazardous waste treatment, storage or disposal area that is located on the generating site.

Onboard Controls Devices placed on vehicles to capture gasoline vapor during refueling and route it to the engines when the vehicle is starting so that it can be efficiently burned.

Onconogenicity The capacity to induce cancer.

One-Hit Model A mathematical model based on the biological theory that a single "hit" of some minimum critical amount of a carcinogen at a cellular target such as DNA can start an irreversible series events leading to a tumor.

Opacity The amount of light obscured by particulate pollution in the air; clear window glass has zero opacity, a brick wall is 100 percent opaque. Opacity is an indicator of changes in performance of particulate control systems.

Open Burning Uncontrolled fires in an open dump.

Open Dump An uncovered site used for disposal of waste without environmental controls. (See dump.)

Operable Unit Term for each of a number of separate activities undertaken as part of a Superfund site cleanup. A typical operable unit would be removal of drums and tanks from the surface of a site.

Operating Conditions Conditions specified in a RCRA permit that dictate how an incinerator must operate as it burns different waste types. A trial burn is used to identify operating conditions needed to meet specified performance standards.

Operation and Maintenance 1. Activities conducted after a Superfund site action is completed to ensure that the action is effective. 2. Actions taken after construction to ensure that facilities constructed to treat waste water will be properly operated and maintained to achieve normative efficiency levels and prescribed effluent limitations in an optimum manner. 3. On-going asbestos management plan in a school or other public building, including regular inspections, various methods of maintaining asbestos in place, and removal when necessary.

Operator Certification Certification of operators of community and nontransient noncommunity water systems, asbestos specialists, pesticide applicators, hazardous waste transporter, and other such specialists as required by the EPA or a state agency implementing an EPA-approved environmental regulatory program.

Optimal Corrosion Control Treatment An erosion control treatment that minimizes the lead and copper concentrations at users' taps while also ensuring that the treatment does not cause the water system to violate any national primary drinking water regulations.

Oral Toxicity Ability of a pesticide to cause injury when ingested.

Organic 1. Referring to or derived from living organisms. 2. In chemistry, any compound containing carbon.

Organic Chemicals/Compounds Naturally occurring (animal or plant-produced or synthetic) substances containing mainly carbon, hydrogen, nitrogen, and oxygen.

Organic Matter Carbonaceous waste contained in plant or animal matter and originating from domestic or industrial sources.

Organism Any form of animal or plant life.

Organophosphates Pesticides that contain phosphorus; short-lived, but some can be toxic when first applied.

Organophyllic A substance that easily combines with organic compounds.

Organotins Chemical compounds used in antifoulant paints to protect the hulls of boats and ships, buoys, and pilings from marine organisms such as barnacles.

Original AHERA Inspection/Original Inspection/Inspection Examination of school buildings arranged by Local Education Agencies to identify asbestos-containing-materials, evaluate their condition, and take samples of materials suspected to contain asbestos; performed by EPA-accredited inspectors.

Original Generation Point Where regulated medical or other material first becomes waste.

Osmosis The passage of a liquid from a weak solution to a more concentrated solution across a semipermeable membrane that allows passage of the solvent (water) but not the dissolved solids.

Other Ferrous Metals Recyclable metals from strapping, furniture, and metal found in tires and consumer electronics but does not include metals found in construction materials or cars, locomotives, and ships. (See ferrous metals.)

Other Glass Recyclable glass from furniture, appliances, and consumer electronics. Does not include glass from transportation products (cars trucks or shipping containers) and construction or demolition debris. (See glass.)

Other Nonferrous Metals Recyclable nonferrous metals such as lead, copper, and zinc from appliances, consumer electronics, and nonpackaging aluminum products. Does not include nonferrous metals from industrial applications and construction and demolition debris. (See nonferrous metals.)

Other Paper For Recyclable paper from books, third-class mail, commercial printing, paper towels, plates and cups; and other nonpackaging paper such as posters, photographic papers, cards and games, milk cartons, folding boxes, bags, wrapping paper, and paperboard. Does not include wrapping paper or shipping cartons.

Other Plastics Recyclable plastic from appliances, eating utensils, plates, containers, toys, and various kinds of equipment. Does not include heavy-duty plastics such as yielding materials.

Other Solid Waste Recyclable nonhazardous solid wastes, other than municipal solid waste, covered under Subtitle D of RARA. (See solid waste.)

Other Wood Recyclable wood from furniture, consumer electronics cabinets, and other nonpackaging wood products. Does not include lumber and tree stumps recovered from construction and demolition activities, and industrial process waste such as shavings and sawdust.

Outdoor Air Supply Air brought into a building from outside.

Outfall The place where effluent is discharged into receiving waters.

Overburden Rock and soil cleared away before mining.

Overdraft The pumping of water from a groundwater basin or aquifer in excess of the supply flowing into the basin; results in a depletion or "mining" of the groundwater in the basin. (See groundwater mining.)

Overfire Air Air forced into the top of an incinerator or boiler to fan the flames.

Overflow Rate One of the guidelines for design of the settling tanks and clarifers in a treatment plant; used by plant operators to determine if tanks and clarifiers are over or under-used.

Overland Flow A land application technique that cleanses waste water by allowing it to flow over a sloped surface. As the water flows over the surface, contaminants are absorbed and the water is collected at the bottom of the slope for reuse.

Oversized Regulated Medical Waste Medical waste that is too large for plastic bags or standard containers.

Overturn One complete cycle of top to bottom mixing of previously stratified water masses. This phenomenon may occur in spring or fall, or after storms, and results in uniformity of chemical and physical properties of water at all depths.

Oxidant A collective term for some of the primary constituents of photochemical smog.

Oxidation Pond A man-made (anthropogenic) body of water in which waste is consumed by bacteria, used most frequently with other waste-treatment processes; a sewage lagoon.

Oxidation The chemical addition of oxygen to break down pollutants or organizac waste; e.g., destruction of chemicals such as cyanides, phenols, and organic sulfur compounds in sewage by bacterial and chemical means.

Oxidation-Reduction Potential The electric potential required to transfer electrons from one compound or element (the oxidant) to another compound (the reductant); used as a qualitative measure of the state of oxidation in water treatment systems.

Oxygenated Fuels Gasoline which has been blended with alcohols or ethers that contain oxygen in order to reduce carbon monoxide and other emissions.

Oxygenated Solvent An organic solvent containing oxygen as part of the molecular structure. Alcohols and ketones are oxygenated compounds often used as paint solvents.

Ozonation/Ozonator Application of ozone to water for disinfection or for taste and odor control. The ozonator is the device that does this.

Ozone (O_3) Found in two layers of the atmosphere, the stratosphere and the troposphere. In the stratosphere (the atmospheric layer 7 to 10 miles or more above the earth's surface) ozone is a natural form of oxygen that provides a protective layer shielding the earth from ultraviolet radiation.In the troposphere (the layer extending up 7 to 10 miles from the earth's surface), ozone is a chemical oxidant and major component of photochemical smog. It can seriously impair the respiratory system and is one of the most wide- spread of all the criteria pollutants for which the Clean Air Act required EPA to set standards. Ozone in the troposphere is produced through complex chemical reactions of nitrogen oxides, which are among the primary pollutants emitted by combustion sources; hydrocarbons, released into the atmosphere through the combustion, handling and processing of petroleum products; and sunlight.

Ozone Depletion Destruction of the stratospheric ozone layer which shields the earth from ultraviolet radiation harmful to life. This destruction of ozone is caused by the breakdown of certain chlorine and/or bromine containing compounds (chlorofluorocarbons or halons), which break down when they reach the stratosphere and then catalytically destroy ozone molecules.

Ozone Hole A thinning break in the stratospheric ozone layer. Designation of amount of such depletion as an "ozone hole" is made when the detected amount of depletion exceeds fifty percent. Seasonal ozone holes have been observed over both the Antarctic and Arctic regions, part of Canada, and the extreme northeastern United States.

Ozone Layer The protective layer in the atmosphere, about 15 miles above the ground, that absorbs some of the sun's ultraviolet rays, thereby reducing the amount of potentially harmful radiation that reaches the earth's surface.

Packaging The assembly of one or more containers and any other components necessary to ensure minimum compliance with a program's storage and shipment packaging requirements. Also, the containers, etc. involved.

Packed Bed Scrubber An air pollution control device in which emissions pass through alkaline water to neutralize hydrogen chloride gas.

Packed Tower A pollution control device that forces dirty air through a tower packed with crushed rock or wood chips while liquid is sprayed over the packing material. The pollutants in the air stream either dissolve or chemically react with the liquid.

Packer An inflatable gland, or balloon, used to create a temporary seal in a borehole, probe hole, well, or drive casing. It is made of rubber or non-reactive materials.

Palatable Water Water, at a desirable temperature, that is free from objectionable tastes, odors, colors, and turbidity.

Pandemic A widespread epidemic throughout an area, nation or the world.

Paper In the recycling business, refers to products and materials, including newspapers, magazines, office papers, corrugated containers, bags and some paperboard packaging that can be recycled into new paper products.

Paper Processor/Plastics Processor Intermediate facility where recovered paper or plastic products and materials are sorted, decontaminated, and prepared for final recycling.

Parameter A variable, measurable property whose value is a determinant of the characteristics of a system; e.g. temperature, pressure, and density are parameters of the atmosphere.

Paraquat A standard herbicide used to kill various types of crops, including marijuana. Causes lung damage if smoke from the crop is inhaled..

Parshall Flume Device used to measure the flow of water in an open channel.

Part A Permit, Part B Permit (See Interim Permit Status.)

Participation Rate Portion of population participating in a recycling program.

Particle Count Results of a microscopic examination of treated water with a special "particle counter" that classifies suspended particles by number and size.

Particulate Loading The mass of particulates per unit volume of air or water.

Particulates 1. Fine liquid or solid particles such as dust, smoke, mist, fumes, or smog, found in air or emissions. 2. Very small solids suspended in water; they can vary in size, shape, density and electrical charge and can be gathered together by coagulation and flocculation.

Partition Coefficient Measure of the sorption phenomenon, whereby a pesticide is divided between the soil and water phase; also referred to as adsorption partition coefficient.

Parts per Billion (ppb)/Parts per Million (ppm) Units commonly used to express contamination ratios, as in establishing the maximum permissible amount of a contaminant in water, land, or air.

Passive Smoking/Secondhand Smoke Inhalation of others' tobacco smoke.

Passive Treatment Walls Technology in which a chemical reaction takes place when contaminated ground water comes in contact with a barrier such as limestone or a wall containing iron filings.

Pathogens Microorganisms (e.g., bacteria, viruses, or parasites) that can cause disease in humans, animals and plants.

Pathway The physical course a chemical or pollutant takes from its source to the exposed organism.

Pay-as-You-Throw/Unit-Based Pricing Systems under which residents pay for municipal waste management and disposal services by weight or volume collected, not a fixed fee.

Peak Electricity Demand The maximum electricity used to meet the cooling load of a building or buildings in a given area.

Peak Levels Levels of airborne pollutant contaminants much higher than average or occurring for short periods of time in response to sudden releases.

Percent Saturation The amount of a substance that is dissolved in a solution compared to the amount that could be dissolved in it.

Perched Water Zone of unpressurized water held above the water table by impermeable rock or sediment.

Percolating Water Water that passes through rocks or soil under the force of gravity.

Percolation 1. The movement of water downward and radially through subsurface soil layers, usually continuing downward to ground water. Can also involve upward movement of water. 2. Slow seepage of water through a filter.

Performance Bond Cash or securities deposited before a landfill operating permit is issued, which are held to ensure that all requirements for operating ad subsequently closing the landfill are faithful performed. The money is returned to the owner after proper closure of the landfill is completed. If contamination or other problems appear at any time during operation, or upon closure, and are not addressed, the owner must forfeit all or part of the bond which is then used to cover clean-up costs.

Performance Data (For Incinerators) Information collected, during a trial burn, on concentrations of designated organic compounds and pollutants found in incinerator emissions. Data analysis must show that the incinerator meets performance standards under operating conditions specified in the RCRA permit. (See trial burn; performance standards.)

Performance Standards 1. Regulatory requirements limiting the concentrations of designated organic compounds, particulate matter, and hydrogen chloride in emissions from incinerators. 2. Operating standards established by EPA for various permitted pollution control systems, asbestos inspections, and various program operations and maintenance requirements.

Periphyton Microscopic underwater plants and animals that are firmly attached to solid surfaces such as rocks, logs, and pilings.

Permeability The rate at which liquids pass through soil or other materials in a specified direction.

Permissible Dose The dose of a chemical that may be received by an individual without the expectation of a significantly harmful result.

Permissible Exposure Limit Also referred to as PEL, federal limits for workplace exposure to contaminants as established by OSHA.

Permit An authorization, license, or equivalent control document issued by EPA or an approved state agency to implement the requirements of an environmental regulation; e.g., a permit to operate a wastewater treatment plant or to operate a facility that may generate harmful emissions.

Persistence Refers to the length of time a compound stays in the environment, once introduced. A compound may persist for less than a second or indefinitely.

Persistent Pesticides Pesticides that do not break down chemically or break down very slowly and remain in the environment after a growing season.

Personal Air Samples Air samples taken with a pump that is directly attached to the worker with the collecting filter and cassette placed in the worker's breathing zone (required under OSHA asbestos standards and EPA worker protection rule).

Personal Measurement A measurement collected from an individual's immediate environment.

Personal Protective Equipment Clothing and equipment worn by pesticide mixers, loaders and applicators and re-entry workers, hazmat emergency responders, workers cleaning up Superfund sites, et. al., which is worn to reduce their exposure to potentially hazardous chemicals and other pollutants.

Pest An insect, rodent, nematode, fungus, weed or other form of terrestrial or aquatic plant or animal life that is injurious to health or the environment.

Pest Control Operator Person or company that applies pesticides as a business (e.g., exterminator); usually describes household services, not agricultural applications.

Pesticide Substances or mixture there of intended for preventing, destroying, repelling, or mitigating any pest. Also, any substance or mixture intended for use as a plant regulator, defoliant, or desiccant.

Pesticide Regulation Notice Formal notice to pesticide registrants about important changes in regulatory policy, procedures, regulations.

Pesticide Tolerance The amount of pesticide residue allowed by law to remain in or on a harvested crop. EPA sets these levels well below the point where the compounds might be harmful to consumers.

PETE (Polyethylene Terepthalate) Thermoplastic material used in plastic soft drink and rigid containers.

Petroleum Crude oil or any fraction thereof that is liquid under normal conditions of temperature and pressure. The term includes petroleum-based substances comprising a complex blend of hydrocarbons derived from crude oil through the process of separation, conversion, upgrading, and finishing, such as motor fuel, jet oil, lubricants, petroleum solvents, and used oil.

Petroleum Derivatives Chemicals formed when gasoline breaks down in contact with ground water.

pH An expression of the intensity of the basic or acid condition of a liquid; may range from 0 to 14, where 0 is the most acid and 7 is neutral. Natural waters usually have a pH between 6.5 and 8.5.

Pharmacokinetics The study of the way that drugs move through the body after they are swallowed or injected.

Phenolphthalein Alkalinity The alkalinity in a water sample measured by the amount of standard acid needed to lower the pH to a level of 8.3 as indicated by the change of color of the phenolphthalein from pink to clear.

Phenols Organic compounds that are byproducts of petroleum refining, tanning, and textile, dye, and resin manufacturing. Low concentrations cause taste and odor problems in water; higher concentrations can kill aquatic life and humans.

Phosphates Certain chemical compounds containing phosphorus.

Phosphogypsum Piles (Stacks) Principal byproduct generated in production of phosphoric acid from phosphate rock. These piles may generate radioactive radon gas.

Phosphorus An essential chemical food element that can contribute to the eutrophication of lakes and other water bodies. Increased phosphorus levels result from discharge of phosphorus-containing materials into surface waters.

Phosphorus Plants Facilities using electric furnaces to produce elemental phosphorous for commercial use, such as high grade phosphoric acid, phosphate-based detergent, and organic chemicals use.

Photochemical Oxidants Air pollutants formed by the action of sunlight on oxides of nitrogen and hydrocarbons.

Photochemical Smog Air pollution caused by chemical reactions of various pollutants emitted from different sources. (See photochemical oxidants.)

Photosynthesis The manufacture by plants of carbohydrates and oxygen from carbon dioxide mediated by chlorophyll in the presence of sunlight.

Physical and Chemical Treatment Processes generally used in large-scale wastewater treatment facilities. Physical processes may include air-stripping or filtration. Chemical treatment includes coagulation, chlorination, or ozonation. The term can also refer to treatment of toxic materials in surface and ground waters, oil spills, and some methods of dealing with hazardous materials on or in the ground.

Phytoplankton That portion of the plankton community comprised of tiny plants; e.g. algae, diatoms.

Phytoremediation Low-cost remediation option for sites with widely dispersed contamination at low concentrations.

Phytotoxic Harmful to plants.

Phytotreatment The cultivation of specialized plants that absorb specific contaminants from the soil through their roots or foliage. This reduces the concentration of contaminants in the soil, but incorporates them into biomasses that may be released back into the environment when the plant dies or is harvested.

Picocuries per Liter (pCi/L) A unit of measure for levels of radon gas; becquerels per cubic meter is metric equivalent.

Piezometer A nonpumping well, generally of small diameter, for measuring the elevation of a water table.

Pilot Tests Testing a cleanup technology under actual site conditions to identify potential problems prior to full-scale implementation.

Plankton Tiny plants and animals that live in water.

Plasma Arc Reactors Devices that use an electric arc to thermally decompose organic and inorganic materials at ultra-high temperatures into gases and a vitrified slag residue. A plasma arc reactor can operate as any of the following:
- integral component of chemical, fuel, or electricity production systems, processing high or medium value organic compounds into a synthetic gas used as a fuel
- materials recovery device, processing scrap to recover metal from the slag
- destruction or incineration system, processing waste materials into slag and gases ignited inside of a secondary combustion chamber that follows the reactor

Plasmid A circular piece of DNA that exists apart from the chromosome and replicates independently of it. Bacterial plasmids carry information that renders the bacteria resistant to antibiotics. Plasmids are often used in genetic engineering to carry desired genes into organisms.

Plastics Non-metallic chemoreactive compounds molded into rigid or pliable construction materials, fabrics, etc.

Plate Tower Scrubber An air pollution control device that neutralizes hydrogen chloride gas by bubbling alkaline water through holes in a series of metal plates.

Plug Flow Type of flow the occurs in tanks, basins, or reactors when a slug of water moves through without ever dispersing or mixing with the rest of the water flowing through.

Plugging Act or process of stopping the flow of water, oil, or gas into or out of a formation through a borehole or well penetrating that formation.

Plume 1. A visible or measurable discharge of a contaminant from a given point of origin. Can be visible or thermal in water, or visible in the air as, for example, a plume of smoke. 2 The area of radiation leaking from a damaged reactor. 3. Area downwind within which a release could be dangerous for those exposed to leaking fumes.

Plutonium A radioactive metallic element chemically similar to uranium.

PM-10/PM-2.5 PM 10 is measure of particles in the atmosphere with a diameter of less than ten or equal to a nominal 10 micrometers. PM-2.5 is a measure of smaller particles in the air. PM-10 has been the pollutant particulate level standard against which EPA has been measuring Clean Air Act compliance. On the basis of newer scientific findings, the Agency is considering regulations that will make PM-2.5 the new "standard."

Pneumoconiosis Health conditions characterized by permanent deposition of substantial amounts of particulate matter in the lungs and by the tissue reaction to its presence; can range from relatively harmless forms of sclerosis to the destructive fibrotic effect of silicosis.

Point Source A stationary location or fixed facility from which pollutants are discharged; any single identifiable source of pollution; e.g. a pipe, ditch, ship, ore pit, factory smokestack.

Point-of-Contact Measurement of Exposure Estimating exposure by measuring concentrations over time (while the exposure is taking place) at or near the place where it is occurring.

Point-of-Disinfectant Application The point where disinfectant is applied and water downstream of that point is not subject to recontamination by surface water runoff.

Point-of-Use Treatment Device Treatment device applied to a single tap to reduce contaminants in the drinking water at the one faucet.

Pollen The fertilizing element of flowering plants; background air pollutant.

Pollutant Generally, any substance introduced into the environment that adversely affects the usefulness of a resource or the health of humans, animals, or ecosystems..

Pollutant Pathways Avenues for distribution of pollutants. In most buildings, for example, HVAC systems are the primary pathways although all building components can interact to affect how air movement distributes pollutants.

Pollutant Standard Index (PSI) Indicator of one or more pollutants that may be used to inform the public about the potential for adverse health effects from air pollution in major cities.

Pollution Generally, the presence of a substance in the environment that because of its chemical composition or quantity prevents the functioning of natural processes and produces undesirable environmental and health effects. Under the Clean Water Act, for example, the term has been defined as the man-made or man-induced alteration of the physical, biological, chemical, and radiological integrity of water and other media.

Pollution Prevention 1. Identifying areas, processes, and activities which create excessive waste products or pollutants in order to reduce or prevent them through, alteration, or eliminating a process. Such activities, consistent with the Pollution Prevention Act of 1990, are conducted across all EPA programs and can involve cooperative efforts with such agencies as the Departments of Agriculture and Energy. 2. EPA has initiated a number of voluntary programs in which industrial, or commercial or "partners" join with EPA in promoting activities that conserve energy, conserve and protect water supply, reduce emissions or find ways of utilizing them as energy resources, and reduce the waste stream.

Among these are: Agstar, to reduce methane emissions through manure management. Climate Wise, to lower industrial greenhouse-gas emissions and energy costs. Coalbed Methane Outreach, to boost methane recovery at coal mines. Design for the Environment, to foster including environmental considerations in product design and processes. Energy Star programs, to promote energy efficiency in commercial and residential buildings, office equipment, transformers, computers, office equipment, and home appliances. Environmental Accounting, to help businesses identify environmental costs and factor them into management decision making. Green Chemistry, to promote and recognize cost-effective breakthroughs in chemistry that prevent pollution. Green Lights, to spread the use of energy-efficient lighting technologies. Indoor Environments, to reduce risks from indoor-air pollution. Landfill Methane Outreach, to develop landfill gas-to-energy projects. Natural Gas Star, to reduce methane emissions from the natural gas industry. Ruminant Livestock Methane, to reduce methane emissions from ruminant livestock. Transportation Partners, to reduce carbon dioxide emissions from the transportation sector. Voluntary Aluminum Industrial Partnership, to reduce perfluorocarbon emissions from the primary aluminum industry. WAVE, to promote efficient water use in the lodging industry. Wastewi$e, to reduce business-generated solid waste through prevention, reuse, and recycling. (See Common Sense Initiative and Project XL.)

Polychlorinated Biphenyls A group of toxic, persistent chemicals used in electrical transformers and capacitors for insulating purposes, and in gas pipeline systems as lubricant. The sale and new use of these chemicals, also known as PCBs, were banned by law in 1979.

Portal-of-Entry Effect A local effect produced in the tissue or organ of first contact between a toxicant and the biological system.

Polonium A radioactive element that occurs in pitchblende and other uranium-containing ores.

Polyelectrolytes Synthetic chemicals that help solids to clump during sewage treatment.

Polymer A natural or synthetic chemical structure where two or more like molecules are joined to form a more complex molecular structure (e.g., polyethylene in plastic).

Polyvinyl Chloride (PVC) A tough, environmentally indestructible plastic that releases hydrochloric acid when burned.

Population A group of interbreeding organisms occupying a particular space; the number of humans or other living creatures in a designated area.

Population at Risk A population subgroup that is more likely to be exposed to a chemical, or is more sensitive to the chemical, than is the general population.

Porosity Degree to which soil, gravel, sediment, or rock is permeated with pores or cavities through which water or air can move.

Post-Chlorination Addition of chlorine to plant effluent for disinfectant purposes after the effluent has been treated.

Post-Closure The time period following the shutdown of a waste management or manufacturing facility; for monitoring purposes, often considered to be 30 years.

Post-Consumer Materials/Waste Materials or finished products that have served their intended use and have been diverted or recovered from waste destined for disposal, having completed their lives as consumer items. Postconsumer materials are part of the broader category of recovered materials.

Post-Consumer Recycling Use of materials generated from residential and consumer waste for new or similar purposes; e.g., converting wastepaper from offices into corrugated boxes or newsprint.

Potable Water Water that is safe for drinking and cooking.

Potential Dose The amount of a compound contained in material swallowed, breathed, or applied to the skin.

Potentially Responsible Party (PRP) Any individual or company—including owners, operators, transporters or generators—potentially responsible for, or contributing to a spill or other contamination at a Superfund site. Whenever possible, through administrative and legal actions, EPA requires PRPs to clean up hazardous sites they have contaminated.

Potentiation The ability of one chemical to increase the effect of another chemical.

Potentiometric Surface The surface to which water in an aquifer can rise by hydrostatic pressure.

Precautionary Principle When information about potential risks is incomplete, basing decisions about the best ways to manage or reduce risks on a preference for avoiding unnecessary health risks instead of on unnecessary economic expenditures.

Prechlorination The addition of chlorine at the headworks of a treatment plant prior to other treatment processes. Done mainly for disinfection and control of tastes, odors, and aquatic growths, and to aid in coagulation and settling,

Precipitate A substance separated from a solution or suspension by chemical or physical change.

Precipitation Removal of hazardous solids from liquid waste to permit safe disposal; removal of particles from airborne emissions as in rain (e.g., acid precipitation).

Precipitator Pollution control device that collects particles from an air stream.

Pre-Consumer Materials/Waste Materials generated in manufacturing and converting processes such as manufacturing scrap and trimmings and cuttings. Includes print overruns, overissue publications, and obsolete inventories.

Precursor In photochemistry, a compound antecedent to a pollutant. For example, volatile organic compounds (VOCs) and nitric oxides of nitrogen react in sunlight to form ozone or other photochemical oxidants. As such, VOCs and oxides of nitrogen are precursors.

Pre-Harvest Interval The time between the last pesticide application and harvest of the treated crops.

Preliminary Assessment The process of collecting and reviewing available information about a known or suspected waste site or release.

Prescriptive Water rights which are acquired by diverting water and putting it to use in accordance with specified procedures; e.g., filing a request with a state agency to use unused water in a stream, river, or lake.

Pressed Wood Products Materials used in building and furniture construction that are made from wood veneers, particles, or fibers bonded together with an adhesive under heat and pressure.

Pressure Sewers A system of pipes in which water, wastewater, or other liquid is pumped to a higher elevation.

Pressure, Static In flowing air, the total pressure minus velocity pressure, pushing equally in all directions.

Pressure, Total In flowing air, the sum of the static and velocity pressures.

Pressure, Velocity In flowing air, the pressure due to velocity and density of air.

Pretreatment Processes used to reduce, eliminate, or alter the nature of wastewater pollutants from non-domestic sources before they are discharged into publicly owned treatment works (POTWs).

Prevalent Level Samples Air samples taken under normal conditions (also known as ambient background samples).

Prevalent Levels Levels of airborne contaminant occurring under normal conditions.

Prevention of Significant Deterioration (PSD) EPA program in which state and/or federal permits are required in order to restrict emissions from new or modified sources in places where air quality already meets or exceeds primary and secondary ambient air quality standards.

Primacy Having the primary responsibility for administering and enforcing regulations.

Primary Drinking Water Regulation Applies to public water systems and specifies a contaminant level, which, in the judgment of the EPA Administrator, will not adversely affect human health.

Primary Effect An effect where the stressor acts directly on the ecological component of interest, not on other parts of the ecosystem. (See secondary effect.)

Primary Standards National ambient air quality standards designed to protect human health with an adequate margin for safety. (See National Ambient Air Quality Standards, secondary standards.)

Primary Treatment First stage of wastewater treatment in which solids are removed by screening and settling.

Primary Waste Treatment First steps in wastewater treatment; screens and sedimentation tanks are used to remove most materials that float or will settle. Primary treatment removes about 30 percent of carbonaceous biochemical oxygen demand from domestic sewage.

Principal Organic Hazardous Constituents (POHCs) Hazardous compounds monitored during an incinerator's trial burn, selected for high concentration in the waste feed and difficulty of combustion.

Prions Microscopic particles made of protein that can cause disease.

Prior Appropriation A doctrine of water law that allocates the rights to use water on a first-come, first-served basis.

Probability of Detection The likelihood, expressed as a percentage, that a test method will correctly identify a leaking tank.

Process Variable A physical or chemical quantity which is usually measured and controlled in the operation of a water treatment plant or industrial plant.

Process Verification Verifying that process raw materials, water usage, waste treatment processes, production rate and other facts relative to quantity and quality of pollutants contained in discharges are substantially described in the permit application and the issued permit.

Process Wastewater Any water that comes into contact with any raw material, product, byproduct, or waste.

Process Weight Total weight of all materials, including fuel, used in a manufacturing process; used to calculate the allowable particulate emission rate.

Producers Plants that perform photosynthesis and provide food to consumers.

Product Level The level of a product in a storage tank.

Product Water Water that has passed through a water treatment plant and is ready to be delivered to consumers.

Products of Incomplete Combustion (PICs) Organic compounds formed by combustion. Usually generated in small amounts and sometimes toxic, PICs are heat-altered versions of the original material fed into the incinerator (e.g., charcoal is a P.I.C. from burning wood).

Project XL An EPA initiative to give states and the regulated community the flexibility to develop comprehensive strategies as alternatives to multiple current regulatory requirements in order to exceed compliance and increase overall environmental benefits.

Propellant Liquid in a self-pressurized pesticide product that expels the active ingredient from its container.

Proportionate Mortality Ratio (PMR) The number of deaths from a specific cause in a specific period of time per 100 deaths from all causes in the same time period.

Proposed Plan A plan for a site cleanup that is available to the public for comment.

Proteins Complex nitrogenous organic compounds of high molecular weight made of amino acids; essential for growth and repair of animal tissue. Many, but not all, proteins are enzymes.

Protocol A series of formal steps for conducting a test.

Protoplast A membrane-bound cell from which the outer wall has been partially or completely removed. The term often is applied to plant cells.

Protozoa One-celled animals that are larger and more complex than bacteria. May cause disease.

Public Comment Period The time allowed for the public to express its views and concerns regarding an action by EPA (e.g., a Federal Register Notice of proposed rule-making, a public notice of a draft permit, or a Notice of Intent to Deny).

Public Health Approach Regulatory and voluntary focus on effective and feasible risk management actions at the national and community level to reduce human exposures and risks, with priority given to reducing exposures with the biggest impacts in terms of the number affected and severity of effect.

Public Health Context The incidence, prevalence, and severity of diseases in communities or populations and the factors that account for them, including infections, exposure to pollutants, and other exposures or activities.

Public Hearing A formal meeting wherein EPA officials hear the public's views and concerns about an EPA action or proposal. EPA is required to consider such comments when evaluating its actions. Public hearings must be held upon request during the public comment period.

Public Notice 1. Notification by EPA informing the public of Agency actions such as the issuance of a draft permit or scheduling of a hearing. EPA is required to ensure proper public notice, including publication in newspapers and broadcast over radio and television stations. 2. In the safe drinking water program, water suppliers are required to publish and broadcast notices when pollution problems are discovered.

Public Water System A system that provides piped water for human consumption to at least 15 service connections or regularly serves 25 individuals.

Publicly Owned Treatment Works (POTWs) A waste-treatment works owned by a state, unit of local government, or Indian tribe, usually designed to treat domestic wastewaters.

Pumping Station Mechanical device installed in sewer or water system or other liquid-carrying pipelines to move the liquids to a higher level.

Pumping Test A test conducted to determine aquifer or well characteristics.

Purging Removing stagnant air or water from sampling zone or equipment prior to sample collection.

Putrefaction Biological decomposition of organic matter; associated with anaerobic conditions.

Putrescible Able to rot quickly enough to cause odors and attract flies.

Pyrolysis Decomposition of a chemical by extreme heat.

Qualitative Use Assessment Report summarizing the major uses of a pesticide including percentage of crop treated, and amount of pesticide used on a site.

Quality Assurance/Quality Control A system of procedures, checks, audits, and corrective actions to ensure that all EPA research design and performance, environmental monitoring and sampling, and other technical and reporting activities are of the highest achievable quality.

Quench Tank A water-filled tank used to cool incinerator residues or hot materials during industrial processes.

Real-Time Monitoring Monitoring and measuring environmental developments with technology and communications systems that provide time-relevant information to the public in an easily understood format people can use in day-to-day decision-making about their health and the environment.

Reasonable Further Progress Annual incremental reductions in air pollutant emissions as reflected in a State Implementation Plan that EPA deems sufficient to provide for the attainment of the applicable national ambient air quality standards by the statutory deadline.

Reasonable Maximum Exposure The maximum exposure reasonably expected to occur in a population.

Reasonable Worst Case An estimate of the individual dose, exposure, or risk level received by an individual in a defined population that is greater than the 90th percentile but less than that received by anyone in the 98th percentile in the same population.

Reasonably Available Control Measures (RACM) A broadly defined term referring to technological and other measures for pollution control.

Reasonably Available Control Technology (RACT) Control technology that is reasonably available, and both technologically and economically feasible. Usually applied to existing sources in nonattainment areas; in most cases is less stringent than new source performance standards.

Recarbonization Process in which carbon dioxide is bubbled into water being treated to lower the pH.

Receiving Waters A river, lake, ocean, stream or other watercourse into which wastewater or treated effluent is discharged.

Receptor Ecological entity exposed to a stressor.

Recharge The process by which water is added to a zone of saturation, usually by percolation from the soil surface; e.g., the recharge of an aquifer.

Recharge Area A land area in which water reaches the zone of saturation from surface infiltration, e.g., where rainwater soaks through the earth to reach an aquifer.

Recharge Rate The quantity of water per unit of time that replenishes or refills an aquifer.

Reclamation (In recycling) Restoration of materials found in the waste stream to a beneficial use which may be for purposes other than the original use.

Recombinant Bacteria A microorganism whose genetic makeup has been altered by deliberate introduction of new genetic elements. The offspring of these altered bacteria also contain these new genetic elements; i.e. they "breed true."

Recombinant DNA The new DNA that is formed by combining pieces of DNA from different organisms or cells.

Recommended Maximum Contaminant Level (RMCL) The maximum level of a contaminant in drinking water at which no known or anticipated adverse effect on human health would occur, and that includes an adequate margin of safety. Recommended levels are nonenforceable health goals. (See maximum contaminant level.)

Reconstructed Source Facility in which components are replaced to such an extent that the fixed capital cost of the new components exceeds 50 percent of the capital cost of constructing a comparable brand-new facility. New-source performance standards may be applied to sources reconstructed after the proposal of the standard if it is technologically and economically feasible to meet the standards.

Reconstruction of Dose Estimating exposure after it has occurred by using evidence within an organism such as chemical levels in tissue or fluids.

Record of Decision (ROD) A public document that explains which cleanup alternative(s) will be used at National Priorities List sites where, under CERCLA, Trust Funds pay for the cleanup.

Recovery Rate Percentage of usable recycled materials that have been removed from the total amount of municipal solid waste generated in a specific area or by a specific business.

Recycle/Reuse Minimizing waste generation by recovering and reprocessing usable products that might otherwise become waste (i.e., recycling of aluminum cans, paper, and bottles, etc.).

Recycling and Reuse Business Assistance Centers Located in state solid-waste or economic-development agencies, these centers provide recycling businesses with customized and targeted assistance.

Recycling Economic Development Advocates Individuals hired by state or tribal economic development offices to focus financial, marketing, and permitting resources on creating recycling businesses.

Recycling Mill Facility where recovered materials are remanufactured into new products.

Recycling Technical Assistance Partnership National Network A national information-sharing resource designed to help businesses and manufacturers increase their use of recovered materials.

Red Bag Waste (See infectious waste.)

Red Border An EPA document undergoing review before being submitted for final management decision-making.

Red Tide A proliferation of a marine plankton toxic and often fatal to fish, perhaps stimulated by the addition of nutrients. A tide can be red, green, or brown, depending on the coloration of the plankton.

Redemption Program Program in which consumers are monetarily compensated for the collection of recyclable materials, generally through prepaid deposits or taxes on beverage containers. In some states or localities legislation has enacted redemption programs to help prevent roadside litter. (See bottle bill.)

Reduction The addition of hydrogen, removal of oxygen, or addition of electrons to an element or compound.

Reentry Interval The period of time immediately following the application of a pesticide during which unprotected workers should not enter a field.

Reference Dose (RfD) The RfD is a numerical estimate of a daily oral exposure to the human population, including sensitive subgroups such as children, that is not likely to cause harmful effects during a lifetime. RfDs are generally used for health effects that are thought to have a threshold or low dose limit for producing effects.

Reformulated Gasoline Gasoline with a different composition from conventional gasoline (e.g., lower aromatics content) that cuts air pollutants.

Refueling Emissions Emissions released during vehicle re-fueling.

Refuse (See solid waste.)

Refuse Reclamation Conversion of solid waste into useful products; e.g., composting organic wastes to make soil conditioners or separating aluminum and other metals for recycling.

Regeneration Manipulation of cells to cause them to develop into whole plants.

Regional Response Team (RRT) Representatives of federal, local, and state agencies who may assist in coordination of activities at the request of the On-Scene Coordinator before and during a significant pollution incident such as an oil spill, major chemical release, or Superfund response.

Registrant Any manufacturer or formulator who obtains registration for a pesticide active ingredient or product.

Registration Formal listing with EPA of a new pesticide before it can be sold or distributed. Under the Federal Insecticide, Fungicide, and Rodenticide Act, EPA is responsible for registration (pre-market licensing) of pesticides on the basis of data demonstrating no unreasonable adverse effects on human health or the environment when applied according to approved label directions.

Registration Standards Published documents which include summary reviews of the data available on a pesticide's active ingredient, data gaps, and the Agency's existing regulatory position on the pesticide.

Regulated Asbestos-Containing Material (RACM) Friable asbestos material or nonfriable ACM that will be or has been subjected to sanding, grinding, cutting, or abrading or has crumbled, or been pulverized or reduced to powder in the course of demolition or renovation operations.

Regulated Medical Waste Under the Medical Waste Tracking Act of 1988, any solid waste generated in the diagnosis, treatment, or immunization of human beings or animals, in research pertaining thereto, or in the production or testing of biologicals. Included are cultures and stocks of infectious agents; human blood and blood products; human pathological body wastes from surgery and autopsy; contaminated animal carcasses from medical research; waste from patients with communicable diseases; and all used sharp implements, such as needles and scalpels, and certain unused sharps. (See treated medical waste; untreated medical waste; destroyed medical waste.)

Relative Ecological Sustainability Ability of an ecosystem to maintain relative ecological integrity indefinitely.

Relative Permeability The permeability of a rock to gas, NAIL, or water, when any two or more are present.

Relative Risk Assessment Estimating the risks associated with different stressors or management actions.

Release Any spilling, leaking, pumping, pouring, emitting, emptying, discharging, injecting, escaping, leaching, dumping, or disposing into the environment of a hazardous or toxic chemical or extremely hazardous substance.

Remedial Action (RA) The actual construction or implementation phase of a Superfund site cleanup that follows remedial design.

Remedial Design A phase of remedial action that follows the remedial investigation/feasibility study and includes development of engineering drawings and specifications for a site cleanup.

Remedial Investigation An in-depth study designed to gather data needed to determine the nature and extent of contamination at a Superfund site; establish site cleanup criteria; identify preliminary alternatives for remedial action; and support technical and cost analyses of alternatives. The remedial investigation is usually done with the feasibility study. Together they are usually referred to as the "RI/FS."

Remedial Project Manager (RPM) The EPA or state official responsible for overseeing on-site remedial action.

Remedial Response Long-term action that stops or substantially reduces a release or threat of a release of hazardous substances that is serious but not an immediate threat to public health.

Remediation 1. Cleanup or other methods used to remove or contain a toxic spill or hazardous materials from a Superfund site; 2. for the Asbestos Hazard Emergency Response program, abatement methods including evaluation, repair, enclosure, encapsulation, or removal of greater than 3 linear feet or square feet of asbestos-containing materials from a building.

Remote Sensing The collection and interpretation of information about an object without physical contact with the object; e.g., satellite imaging, aerial photography, and open path measurements.

Removal Action Short-term immediate actions taken to address releases of hazardous substances that require expedited response. (See cleanup.)

Renewable Energy Production Incentive (REPI) Incentive established by the Energy Policy Act available to renewable energy power projects owned by a state or local government or nonprofit electric cooperative.

Repeat Compliance Period Any subsequent compliance period after the initial one.

Reportable Quantity (RQ) Quantity of a hazardous substance that triggers reports under CERCLA. If a substance exceeds its RQ, the release must be reported to the National Response Center, the SERC, and community emergency coordinators for areas likely to be affected.

Repowering Rebuilding and replacing major components of a power plant instead of building a new one.

Representative Sample A portion of material or water that is as nearly identical in content and consistency as possible to that in the larger body of material or water being sampled.

Reregistration The reevaluation and relicensing of existing pesticides originally registered prior to current scientific and regulatory standards. EPA reregisters pesticides through its Registration Standards Program.

Reserve Capacity Extra treatment capacity built into solid waste and wastewater treatment plants and interceptor sewers to accommodate flow increases due to future population growth.

Reservoir Any natural or artificial holding area used to store, regulate, or control water.

Residential Use Pesticide application in and around houses, office buildings, apartment buildings, motels, and other living or working areas.

Residential Waste Waste generated in single and multi-family homes, including newspapers, clothing, disposable tableware, food packaging, cans, bottles, food scraps, and yard trimmings other than those that are diverted to backyard composting. (See Household hazardous waste.)

Residual Amount of a pollutant remaining in the environment after a natural or technological process has taken place; e.g., the sludge remaining after initial wastewater treatment, or particulates remaining in air after it passes through a scrubbing or other process.

Residual Risk The extent of health risk from air pollutants remaining after application of the Maximum Achievable Control Technology (MACT).

Residual Saturation Saturation level below which fluid drainage will not occur.

Residue The dry solids remaining after the evaporation of a sample of water or sludge.

Resistance For plants and animals, the ability to withstand poor environmental conditions or attacks by chemicals or disease. May be inborn or acquired.

Resource Recovery The process of obtaining matter or energy from materials formerly discarded.

Response Action 1. Generic term for actions taken in response to actual or potential health-threatening environmental events such as spills, sudden releases, and asbestos abatement/management problems. 2. A CERCLA-authorized action involving either a short-term removal action or a long-term removal response. This may include but is not limited to removing hazardous materials from a site to an EPA-approved hazardous waste facility for treatment, containment or treating the waste on-site, identifying and removing the sources of ground-water contamination and halting further migration of contaminants. 3. Any of the following actions taken in school buildings in response to AHERA to reduce the risk of exposure to asbestos: removal, encapsulation, enclosure, repair, and operations and maintenance. (See cleanup.)

Responsiveness Summary A summary of oral and/or written public comments received by EPA during a comment period on key EPA documents, and EPA's response to those comments.

Restoration Measures taken to return a site to pre-violation conditions.

Restricted Entry Interval The time after a pesticide application during which entry into the treated area is restricted.

Restricted Use A pesticide may be classified (under FIFRA regulations) for restricted use if it requires special handling because of its toxicity, and, if so, it may be applied only by trained, certified applicators or those under their direct supervision.

Restriction Enzymes Enzymes that recognize specific regions of a long DNA molecule and cut it at those points.

Retrofit Addition of a pollution control device on an existing facility without making major changes to the generating plant. Also called backfit.

Reuse Using a product or component of municipal solid waste in its original form more than once; e.g., refilling a glass bottle that has been returned or using a coffee can to hold nuts and bolts.

Reverse Osmosis A treatment process used in water systems by adding pressure to force water through a semi-permeable membrane. Reverse osmosis removes most drinking water contaminants. Also used in wastewater treatment. Large-scale reverse osmosis plants are being developed.

Reversible Effect An effect which is not permanent; especially adverse effects which diminish when exposure to a toxic chemical stops.

Ribonucleic Acid (RNA) A molecule that carries the genetic message from DNA to a cellular protein-producing mechanism.

Rill A small channel eroded into the soil by surface runoff; can be easily smoothed out or obliterated by normal tillage.

Ringlemann Chart A series of shaded illustrations used to measure the opacity of air pollution emissions, ranging from light grey through black; used to set and enforce emissions standards.

Riparian Habitat Areas adjacent to rivers and streams with a differing density, diversity, and productivity of plant and animal species relative to nearby uplands.

Riparian Rights Entitlement of a land owner to certain uses of water on or bordering the property, including the right to prevent diversion or misuse of upstream waters. Generally a matter of state law.

Risk A measure of the probability that damage to life, health, property, and/or the environment will occur as a result of a given hazard.

Risk (Adverse) for Endangered Species Risk to aquatic species if anticipated pesticide residue levels equal one-fifth of LD10 or one-tenth of LC50; risk to terrestrial species if anticipated pesticide residue levels equal one-fifth of LC10 or one-tenth of LC50.

Risk Assessment Qualitative and quantitative evaluation of the risk posed to human health and/or the environment by the actual or potential presence and/or use of specific pollutants.

Risk-Based Targeting The direction of resources to those areas that have been identified as having the highest potential or actual adverse effect on human health and/or the environment.

Risk Characterization The last phase of the risk assessment process that estimates the potential for adverse health or ecological effects to occur from exposure to a stressor and evaluates the uncertainty involved.

Risk Communication The exchange of information about health or environmental risks among risk assessors and managers, the general public, news media, interest groups, etc.

Risk Estimate A description of the probability that organisms exposed to a specific dose of a chemical or other pollutant will develop an adverse response, e.g., cancer.

Risk Factor Characteristics (e.g., race, sex, age, obesity) or variables (e.g., smoking, occupational exposure level) associated with increased probability of a toxic effect.

Risk for Non-Endangered Species Risk to species if anticipated pesticide residue levels are equal to or greater than LC50.

Risk Management The process of evaluating and selecting alternative regulatory and non-regulatory responses to risk. The selection process necessarily requires the consideration of legal, economic, and behavioral factors.

Risk-Specific Dose The dose associated with a specified risk level.

River Basin The land area drained by a river and its tributaries.

Rodenticide A chemical or agent used to destroy rats or other rodent pests, or to prevent them from damaging food, crops, etc.

Rotary Kiln Incinerator An incinerator with a rotating combustion chamber that keeps waste moving, thereby allowing it to vaporize for easier burning.

Rough Fish Fish not prized for sport or eating, such as gar and suckers. Most are more tolerant of changing environmental conditions than are game or food species.

Route of Exposure The avenue by which a chemical comes into contact with an organism, e.g., inhalation, ingestion, dermal contact, injection.

Rubbish Solid waste, excluding food waste and ashes, from homes, institutions, and workplaces.

Run-Off That part of precipitation, snow melt, or irrigation water that runs off the land into streams or other surface-water. It can carry pollutants from the air and land into receiving waters.

Running Losses Evaporation of motor vehicle fuel from the fuel tank while the vehicle is in use.

Sacrifical Anode An easily corroded material deliberately installed in a pipe or intake to give it up (sacrifice it) to corrosion while the rest of the water supply facility remains relatively corrosion-free.

Safe Condition of exposure under which there is a practical certainty that no harm will result to exposed individuals.

Safe Water Water that does not contain harmful bacteria, toxic materials, or chemicals, and is considered safe for drinking even if it may have taste, odor, color, and certain mineral problems.

Safe Yield The annual amount of water that can be taken from a source of supply over a period of years without depleting that source beyond its ability to be replenished naturally in "wet years."

Safener A chemical added to a pesticide to keep it from injuring plants.

Salinity The percentage of salt in water.

Salt Water Intrusion The invasion of fresh surface or ground water by salt water. If it comes from the ocean it may be called sea water intrusion.

Salts Minerals that water picks up as it passes through the air, over and under the ground, or from households and industry.

Salvage The utilization of waste materials.

Sampling Frequency The interval between the collection of successive samples.

Sanctions Actions taken by the federal government for failure to provide or implement a State Implementation Plan (SIP). Such action may include withholding of highway funds and a ban on construction of new sources of potential pollution.

Sand Filters Devices that remove some suspended solids from sewage. Air and bacteria decompose additional wastes filtering through the sand so that cleaner water drains from the bed.

Sanitary Landfill (See landfills.)

Sanitary Sewers Underground pipes that carry off only domestic or industrial waste, not storm water.

Sanitary Survey An on-site review of the water sources, facilities, equipment, operation and maintenance of a public water system to evaluate the adequacy of those elements for producing and distributing safe drinking water.

Sanitary Water (Also known as gray water) Water discharged from sinks, showers, kitchens, or other non-industrial operations, but not from commodes.

Sanitation Control of physical factors in the human environment that could harm development, health, or survival.

Saprolite A soft, clay-rich, thoroughly decomposed rock formed in place by chemical weathering of igneous or metamorphic rock. Forms in humid, tropical, or subtropical climates.

Saprophytes Organisms living on dead or decaying organic matter that help natural decomposition of organic matter in water.

Saturated Zone The area below the water table where all open spaces are filled with water under pressure equal to or greater than that of the atmosphere.

Saturation The condition of a liquid when it has taken into solution the maximum possible quantity of a given substance at a given temperature and pressure.

Science Advisory Board (SAB) A group of external scientists who advise EPA on science and policy.

Scrap Materials discarded from manufacturing operations that may be suitable for reprocessing.

Scrap Metal Processor Intermediate operating facility where recovered metal is sorted, cleaned of contaminants, and prepared for recycling.

Screening Use of screens to remove coarse floating and suspended solids from sewage.

Screening Risk Assessment A risk assessment performed with few data and many assumptions to identify exposures that should be evaluated more carefully for potential risk.

Scrubber An air pollution device that uses a spray of water or reactant or a dry process to trap pollutants in emissions.

Secondary Drinking Water Regulations Non-enforceable regulations applying to public water systems and specifying the maximum contamination levels that, in the judgment of EPA, are required to protect the public welfare. These regulations apply to any contaminants that may adversely affect the odor or appearance of such water and consequently may cause people served by the system to discontinue its use.

Secondary Effect Action of a stressor on supporting components of the ecosystem, which in turn impact the ecological component of concern. (See primary effect.)

Secondary Materials Materials that have been manufactured and used at least once and are to be used again.

Secondary Standards National ambient air quality standards designed to protect welfare, including effects on soils, water, crops, vegetation, man-made (anthropogenic) materials, animals, wildlife, weather, visibility, and climate; damage to property; transportation hazards; economic values, and personal comfort and well-being.

Secondary Treatment The second step in most publicly owned waste treatment systems in which bacteria consume the organic parts of the waste. It is accomplished by bringing together waste, bacteria, and oxygen in trickling filters or in the activated sludge process. This treatment removes floating and settleable solids and about 90 percent of the oxygen-demanding substances and suspended solids. Disinfection is the final stage of secondary treatment. (See primary, tertiary treatment.)

Secure Chemical Landfill (See landfills.)

Secure Maximum Contaminant Level Maximum permissible level of a contaminant in water delivered to the free flowing outlet of the ultimate user, or of contamination resulting from corrosion of piping and plumbing caused by water quality.

Sediment Topsoil, sand, and minerals washed from the land into water, usually after rain or snow melt.

Sediment Yield The quantity of sediment arriving at a specific location.

Sedimentation Letting solids settle out of wastewater by gravity during treatment.

Sedimentation Tanks Wastewater tanks in which floating wastes are skimmed off and settled solids are removed for disposal.

Sediments Soil, sand, and minerals washed from land into water, usually after rain. They pile up in reservoirs, rivers and harbors, destroying fish and wildlife habitat, and clouding the water so that sunlight cannot reach aquatic plants. Careless farming, mining, and building activities will expose sediment materials, allowing them to wash off the land after rainfall.

Seed Protectant A chemical applied before planting to protect seeds and seedlings from disease or insects.

Seepage Percolation of water through the soil from unlined canals, ditches, laterals, watercourses, or water storage facilities.

Selective Pesticide A chemical designed to affect only certain types of pests, leaving other plants and animals unharmed.

Semi-Confined Aquifer An aquifer partially confined by soil layers of low permeability through which recharge and discharge can still occur.

Semivolatile Organic Compounds Organic compounds that volatilize slowly at standard temperature (20 degrees C and 1 atm pressure).

Senescence The aging process. Sometimes used to describe lakes or other bodies of water in advanced stages of eutrophication. Also used to describe plants and animals.

Septic System An on-site system designed to treat and dispose of domestic sewage. A typical septic system consists of tank that receives waste from a residence or business and a system of tile lines or a pit for disposal of the liquid effluent (sludge) that remains after decomposition of the solids by bacteria in the tank and must be pumped out periodically.

Septic Tank An underground storage tank for wastes from homes not connected to a sewer line. Waste goes directly from the home to the tank. (See septic system.)

Service Connector The pipe that carries tap water from a public water main to a building.

Service Line Sample A one-liter sample of water that has been standing for at least 6 hours in a service pipeline and is collected according to federal regulations.

Service Pipe The pipeline extending from the water main to the building served or to the consumer's system.

Set-Back Setting a thermometer to a lower temperature when the building is unoccupied to reduce consumption of heating energy. Also refers to setting the thermometer to a higher temperature during unoccupied periods in the cooling season.

Settleable Solids Material heavy enough to sink to the bottom of a wastewater treatment tank.

Settling Chamber A series of screens placed in the way of flue gases to slow the stream of air, thus helping gravity to pull particles into a collection device.

Settling Tank A holding area for wastewater, where heavier particles sink to the bottom for removal and disposal.

7Q10 Seven-day, consecutive low flow with a ten-year return frequency; the lowest stream flow for seven consecutive days that would be expected to occur once in ten years.

Sewage The waste and wastewater produced by residential and commercial sources and discharged into sewers.

Sewage Lagoon (See lagoon.)

Sewage Sludge Sludge produced at a Publicly Owned Treatment Works, the disposal of which is regulated under the Clean Water Act.

Sewer A channel or conduit that carries wastewater and storm-water runoff from the source to a treatment plant or receiving stream. "Sanitary" sewers carry household, industrial, and commercial waste. "Storm" sewers carry runoff from rain or snow. "Combined" sewers handle both.

Sewerage The entire system of sewage collection, treatment, and disposal.

Shading Coefficient The amount of the sun's heat transmitted through a given window compared with that of a standard 1/8- inch-thick single pane of glass under the same conditions.

Sharps Hypodermic needles, syringes (with or without the attached needle), Pasteur pipettes, scalpel blades, blood vials, needles with attached tubing, and culture dishes used in animal or human patient care or treatment, or in medical, research or industrial laboratories. Also included are other types of broken or unbroken glassware that were in contact with infectious agents, such as used slides and cover slips, and unused hypodermic and suture needles, syringes, and scalpel blades.

Shock Load The arrival at a water treatment plant of raw water containing unusual amounts of algae, colloidal matter. color, suspended solids, turbidity, or other pollutants.

Short-Circuiting When some of the water in tanks or basins flows faster than the rest; may result in shorter contact, reaction, or settling times than calculated or presumed.

Sick Building Syndrome Building whose occupants experience acute health and/or comfort effects that appear to be linked to time spent therein, but where no specific illness or cause can be identified. Complaints may be localized in a particular room or zone, or may spread throughout the building. (See building-related illness.)

Signal The volume or product-level change produced by a leak in a tank.

Signal Words The words used on a pesticide label—Danger, Warning, Caution—to indicate level of toxicity.

Significant Deterioration Pollution resulting from a new source in previously "clean" areas. (See prevention of significant deterioration.)

Significant Municipal Facilities Those publicly owned sewage treatment plants that discharge a million gallons per day or more and are therefore considered by states to have the potential to substantially affect the quality of receiving waters.

Significant Non-Compliance (See significant violations.)

Significant Potential Source of Contamination A facility or activity that stores, uses, or produces compounds with potential for significant contaminating impact if released into the source water of a public water supply.

Significant Violations Violations by point source dischargers of sufficient magnitude or duration to be a regulatory priority.

Silt Sedimentary materials composed of fine or intermediate-sized mineral particles.

Silviculture Management of forest land for timber.

Single-Breath Canister Small one-liter canister designed to capture a single breath. Used in air pollutant ingestion research.

Sink Place in the environment where a compound or material collects.

Sinking Controlling oil spills by using an agent to trap the oil and sink it to the bottom of the body of water where the agent and the oil are biodegraded.

SIP Call EPA action requiring a state to resubmit all or part of its State Implementation Plan to demonstrate attainment of the require national ambient air quality standards within the statutory deadline. A SIP Revision is a revision of a SIP altered at the request of EPA or on a state's initiative. (See State Implementation Plan.)

Site An area or place within the jurisdiction of the EPA and/or a state.

Site Assessment Program A means of evaluating hazardous waste sites through preliminary assessments and site inspections to develop a Hazard Ranking System score.

Site Inspection The collection of information from a Superfund site to determine the extent and severity of hazards posed by the site. It follows and is more extensive than a preliminary assessment. The purpose is to gather information necessary to score the site, using the Hazard Ranking System, and to determine if it presents an immediate threat requiring prompt removal.

Site Safety Plan A crucial element in all removal actions, it includes information on equipment being used, precautions to be taken, and steps to take in the event of an on-site emergency.

Siting The process of choosing a location for a facility.

Skimming Using a machine to remove oil or scum from the surface of the water.

Slow Sand Filtration Passage of raw water through a bed of sand at low velocity, resulting in substantial removal of chemical and biological contaminants.

Sludge A semi-solid residue from any of a number of air or water treatment processes; can be a hazardous waste.

Sludge Digester Tank in which complex organic substances like sewage sludges are biologically dredged. During these reactions, energy is released and much of the sewage is converted to methane, carbon dioxide, and water.

Slurry A watery mixture of insoluble matter resulting from some pollution control techniques.

Small Quantity Generator (SQG-sometimes referred to as "Squeegee") Persons or enterprises that produce 220-2200 pounds per month of hazardous waste; they are required to keep more records than conditionally exempt generators. The largest category of hazardous waste generators, SQGs, include automotive shops, dry cleaners, photographic developers, and many other small businesses. (See conditionally exempt generators.)

Smelter A facility that melts or fuses ore, often with an accompanying chemical change, to separate its metal content. Emissions cause pollution. "Smelting" is the process involved.

Smog Air pollution typically associated with oxidants. (See photochemical smog.)

Smoke Particles suspended in air after incomplete combustion.

Soft Detergents Cleaning agents that break down in nature.

Soft Water Any water that does not contain a significant amount of dissolved minerals such as salts of calcium or magnesium.

Soil Adsorption Field A sub-surface area containing a trench or bed with clean stones and a system of piping through which treated sewage may seep into the surrounding soil for further treatment and disposal.

Soil and Water Conservation Practices Control measures consisting of managerial, vegetative, and structural practices to reduce the loss of soil and water.

Soil Conditioner An organic material like humus or compost that helps soil absorb water, build a bacterial community, and take up mineral nutrients.

Soil Erodibility An indicator of a soil's susceptibility to raindrop impact, runoff, and other erosive processes.

Soil Gas Gaseous elements and compounds in the small spaces between particles of the earth and soil. Such gases can be moved or driven out under pressure.

Soil Moisture The water contained in the pore space of the unsaturated zone.

Soil Sterilant A chemical that temporarily or permanently prevents the growth of all plants and animals,

Solder Metallic compound used to seal joints between pipes. Until recently, most solder contained 50 percent lead. Use of solder containing more than 0.2 percent lead in pipes carrying drinking water is now prohibited.

Sole-Source Aquifer An aquifer that supplies 50-percent or more of the drinking water of an area.

Solid Waste Non-liquid, non-soluble materials ranging from municipal garbage to industrial wastes that contain complex and sometimes hazardous substances. Solid wastes also include sewage sludge, agricultural refuse, demolition wastes, and mining residues. Technically, solid waste also refers to liquids and gases in containers.

Solid Waste Disposal The final placement of refuse that is not salvaged or recycled.

Solid Waste Management Supervised handling of waste materials from their source through recovery processes to disposal.

Solidification and Stabilization Removal of wastewater from a waste or changing it chemically to make it less permeable and susceptible to transport by water.

Solubility The amount of mass of a compound that will dissolve in a unit volume of solution. Aqueous Solubility is the maximum concentration of a chemical that will dissolve in pure water at a reference temperature.

Soot Carbon dust formed by incomplete combustion.

Sorption The action of soaking up or attracting substances; process used in many pollution control systems.

Source Area The location of liquid hydrocarbons or the zone of highest soil or groundwater concentrations, or both, of the chemical of concern.

Source Characterization Measurements Measurements made to estimate the rate of release of pollutants into the environment from a source such as an incinerator, landfill, etc.

Source Reduction Reducing the amount of materials entering the waste stream from a specific source by redesigning products or patterns of production or consumption (e.g., using returnable beverage containers). Synonymous with waste reduction.

Source Separation Segregating various wastes at the point of generation (e.g., separation of paper, metal and glass from other wastes to make recycling simpler and more efficient).

Source-Water Protection Area The area delineated by a state for a Public Water Supply or including numerous such suppliers, whether the source is ground water or surface water or both.

Sparge or Sparging Injection of air below the water table to strip dissolved volatile organic compounds and/or oxygenate ground water to facilitate aerobic biodegradation of organic compounds.

Special Local-Needs Registration Registration of a pesticide product by a state agency for a specific use that is not federally registered. However, the active ingredient must be federally registered for other uses. The special use is specific to that state and is often minor, thus may not warrant the additional cost of a full federal registration process. SLN registration cannot be issued for new active ingredients, food-use active ingredients without tolerances, or for a canceled registration. The products cannot be shipped across state lines.

Special Review Formerly known as Rebuttable Presumption Against Registration (RPAR), this is the regulatory process through which existing pesticides suspected of posing unreasonable risks to human health, non-target organisms, or the environment are referred for review by EPA. Such review requires an intensive risk/benefit analysis with opportunity for public comment. If risk is found to outweigh social and economic benefits, regulatory actions can be initiated, ranging from label revisions and use-restriction to cancellation or suspended registration.

Special Waste Items such as household hazardous waste, bulky wastes (refrigerators, pieces of furniture, etc.) tires, and used oil.

Species 1. A reproductively isolated aggregate of interbreeding organisms having common attributes and usually designated by a common name. 2. An organism belonging to belonging to such a category.

Specific Conductance Rapid method of estimating the dissolved solid content of a water supply by testing its capacity to carry an electrical current.

Specific Yield The amount of water a unit volume of saturated permeable rock will yield when drained by gravity.

Spill Prevention, Containment, and Countermeasures Plan (SPCP) Plan covering the release of hazardous substances as defined in the Clean Water Act.

Spoil Dirt or rock removed from its original location—destroying the composition of the soil in the process—as in strip-mining, dredging, or construction.

Sprawl Unplanned development of open land.

Spray Tower Scrubber A device that sprays alkaline water into a chamber where acid gases are present to aid in neutralizing the gas.

Spring Ground water seeping out of the earth where the water table intersects the ground surface.

Spring Melt/Thaw The process whereby warm temperatures melt winter snow and ice. Because various forms of acid deposition may have been stored in the frozen water, the melt can result in abnormally large amounts of acidity entering streams and rivers, sometimes causing fish kills.

Stabilization Conversion of the active organic matter in sludge into inert, harmless material.

Stabilization Ponds (See lagoon.)

Stable Air A motionless mass of air that holds, instead of dispersing, pollutants.

Stack A chimney, smokestack, or vertical pipe that discharges used air.

Stack Effect Flow of air resulting from warm air rising, creating a positive pressure area at the top of a building and negative pressure area at the bottom. This effect can overpower the mechanical system and disrupt building ventilation and air circulation.

Stack Gas (See flue gas.)

Stage II Controls Systems placed on service station gasoline pumps to control and capture gasoline vapors during refuelling.

Stagnation Lack of motion in a mass of air or water that holds pollutants in place.

Stakeholder Any organization, governmental entity, or individual that has a stake in or may be impacted by a given approach to environmental regulation, pollution prevention, energy conservation, etc.

Standard Industrial Classification Code Also known as SIC Codes, a method of grouping industries with similar products or services and assigning codes to these groups.

Standard Sample The part of finished drinking water that is examined for the presence of coliform bacteria.

Standards Norms that impose limits on the amount of pollutants or emissions produced. EPA establishes minimum standards, but states are allowed to be stricter.

Start of a Response Action The point in time when there is a guarantee or set-aside of funding by EPA, other federal agencies, states or Principal Responsible Parties in order to begin response actions at a Superfund site.

State Emergency Response Commission (SERC) Commission appointed by each state governor according to the requirements of SARA Title III. The SERCs designate emergency planning districts, appoint local emergency planning committees, and supervise and coordinate their activities.

State Environmental Goals and Indication Project Program to assist state environmental agencies by providing technical and financial assistance in the development of environmental goals and indicators.

State Implementation Plans (SIP) EPA approved state plans for the establishment, regulation, and enforcement of air pollution standards.

State Management Plan Under FIFRA, a state management plan required by EPA to allow states, tribes, and U.S. territories the flexibility to design and implement ways to protect ground water from the use of certain pesticides.

Static Water Depth The vertical distance from the centerline of the pump discharge down to the surface level of the free pool while no water is being drawn from the pool or water table.

Static Water Level 1. Elevation or level of the water table in a well when the pump is not operating. 2. The level or elevation to which water would rise in a tube connected to an artesian aquifer or basin in a conduit under pressure.

Stationary Source A fixed-site producer of pollution, mainly power plants and other facilities using industrial combustion processes. (See point source.)

Sterilization The removal or destruction of all microorganisms, including pathogenic and other bacteria, vegetative forms, and spores.

Sterilizer One of three groups of anti-microbials registered by EPA for public health uses. EPA considers an antimicrobial to be a sterilizer when it destroys or eliminates all forms of bacteria, viruses, and fungi and their spores. Because spores are considered the most difficult form of microorganism to destroy, EPA considers the term sporicide to be synonymous with sterilizer.

Storage Temporary holding of waste pending treatment or disposal, as in containers, tanks, waste piles, and surface impoundments.

Storm Sewer A system of pipes (separate from sanitary sewers) that carries water runoff from buildings and land surfaces.

Stratification Separating into layers.

Stratigraphy Study of the formation, composition, and sequence of sediments, whether consolidated or not.

Stratosphere The portion of the atmosphere 10-to-25 miles above the earth's surface.

Stressors Physical, chemical, or biological entities that can induce adverse effects on ecosystems or human health.

Strip-Cropping Growing crops in a systematic arrangement of strips or bands that serve as barriers to wind and water erosion.

Strip-Mining A process that uses machines to scrape soil or rock away from mineral deposits just under the earth's surface.

Structural Deformation Distortion in walls of a tank after liquid has been added or removed.

Subchronic Of intermediate duration, usually used to describe studies or periods of exposure lasting between 5 and 90 days.

Subchronic Exposure Multiple or continuous exposures lasting for approximately ten percent of an experimental species lifetime, usually over a three-month period.

Submerged Aquatic Vegetation Vegetation that lives at or below the water surface; an important habitat for young fish and other aquatic organisms.

Subwatershed Topographic perimeter of the catchment area of a stream tributary.

Sulfur Dioxide (SO2) A pungent, colorless, gas-formed primarily by the combustion of fossil fuels; becomes a pollutant when present in large amounts.

Sump A pit or tank that catches liquid runoff for drainage or disposal.

Superchlorination Chlorination with doses that are deliberately selected to produce water free of combined residuals so large as to require dechlorination.

Supercritical Water A type of thermal treatment using moderate temperatures and high pressures to enhance the ability of water to break down large organic molecules into smaller, less toxic ones. Oxygen injected during this process combines with simple organic compounds to form carbon dioxide and water.

Superfund The program operated under the legislative authority of CERCLA and SARA that funds and carries out EPA solid waste emergency and long-term removal and remedial activities. These activities include establishing the National Priorities List, investigating sites for inclusion on the list, determining their priority, and conducting and/or supervising cleanup and other remedial actions.

Superfund Innovative Technology Evaluation (SITE) Program EPA program to promote development and use of innovative treatment and site characterization technologies in Superfund site cleanups.

Supplemental Registration An arrangement whereby a registrant licenses another company to market its pesticide product under the second company's registration.

Supplier of Water Any person who owns or operates a public water supply.

Surface Impoundment Treatment, storage, or disposal of liquid hazardous wastes in ponds.

Surface Runoff Precipitation, snow melt, or irrigation water in excess of what can infiltrate the soil surface and be stored in small surface depressions; a major transporter of non-point source pollutants in rivers, streams, and lakes.

Surface Uranium Mines Strip mining operations for removal of uranium-bearing ore.

Surface Water All water naturally open to the atmosphere (rivers, lakes, reservoirs, ponds, streams, impoundments, seas, estuaries, etc.).

Surface-Water Treatment Rule Rule that specifies maximum contaminant level goals for Giardia lamblia, viruses, and Legionella and promulgates filtration and disinfection requirements for public water systems using surface-water or ground-water sources under the direct influence of surface water. The regulations also specify water quality, treatment, and watershed protection criteria under which filtration may be avoided.

Surfacing ACM Asbestos-containing material that is sprayed or troweled on or otherwise applied to surfaces, such as acoustical plaster on ceilings and fireproofing materials on structural members.

Surfacing Material Material sprayed or troweled onto structural members (beams, columns, or decking) for fire protection; or on ceilings or walls for fireproofing, acoustical or decorative purposes. Includes textured plaster, and other textured wall and ceiling surfaces.

Surfactant A detergent compound that promotes lathering.

Surrogate Data Data from studies of test organisms or a test substance that are used to estimate the characteristics or effects on another organism or substance.

Surveillance System A series of monitoring devices designed to check on environmental conditions.

Susceptibility Analysis An analysis to determine whether a Public Water Supply is subject to significant pollution from known potential sources.

Suspect Material Building material suspected of containing asbestos; e.g., surfacing material, floor tile, ceiling tile, thermal system insulation.

Suspended Loads Specific sediment particles maintained in the water column by turbulence and carried with the flow of water.

Suspended Solids Small particles of solid pollutants that float on the surface of, or are suspended in, sewage or other liquids. They resist removal by conventional means.

Suspension Suspending the use of a pesticide when EPA deems it necessary to prevent an imminent hazard resulting from its continued use. An emergency suspension takes effect immediately; under an ordinary suspension a registrant can request a hearing before the suspension goes into effect. Such a hearing process might take six months.

Suspension Culture Cells growing in a liquid nutrient medium.

Swamp A type of wetland dominated by woody vegetation but without appreciable peat deposits. Swamps may be fresh or salt water and tidal or nontidal. (See wetlands.)

Synergism An interaction of two or more chemicals that results in an effect greater than the sum of their separate effects.

Synthetic Organic Chemicals (SOCs) Man-made (anthropogenic) organic chemicals. Some SOCs are volatile; others tend to stay dissolved in water instead of evaporating.

System with a Single Service Connection A system that supplies drinking water to consumers via a single service line.

Systemic Pesticide A chemical absorbed by an organism that interacts with the organism and makes the organism toxic to pests.

Tail Water The runoff of irrigation water from the lower end of an irrigated field.

Tailings Residue of raw material or waste separated out during the processing of crops or mineral ores.

Tailpipe Standards Emissions limitations applicable to mobile source engine exhausts.

Tampering Adjusting, negating, or removing pollution control equipment on a motor vehicle.

Technical Assistance Grant (TAG) As part of the Superfund program, Technical Assistance Grants of up to $50,000 are provided to citizens' groups to obtain assistance in interpreting information related to clean-ups at Superfund sites or those proposed for the National Priorities List. Grants are used by such groups to hire technical advisors to help them understand the site-related technical information for the duration of response activities.

Technical-Grade Active Ingredient (TGA) A pesticide chemical in pure form as it is manufactured prior to being formulated into an end-use product (e.g. wettable powders, granules, emulsifiable concentrates). Registered manufactured products composed of such chemicals are known as Technical Grade Products.

Technology-Based Limitations Industry-specific effluent limitations based on best available preventive technology applied to a discharge when it will not cause a violation of water quality standards at low stream flows. Usually applied to discharges into large rivers.

Technology-Based Standards Industry-specific effluent limitations applicable to direct and indirect sources which are developed on a category-by-category basis using statutory factors, not including water-quality effects.

Teratogen A substance capable of causing birth defects.

Teratogenesis The introduction of nonhereditary birth defects in a developing fetus by exogenous factors such as physical or chemical agents acting in the womb to interfere with normal embryonic development.

Terracing Dikes built along the contour of sloping farm land that hold runoff and sediment to reduce erosion.

Tertiary Treatment Advanced cleaning of wastewater that goes beyond the secondary or biological stage, removing nutrients such as phosphorus, nitrogen, and most BOD and suspended solids.

Theoretical Maximum Residue Contribution The theoretical maximum amount of a pesticide in the daily diet of an average person. It assumes that the diet is composed of all food items for which there are tolerance-level residues of the pesticide. The TMRC is expressed as milligrams of pesticide/kilograms of body weight/day.

Therapeutic Index The ratio of the dose required to produce toxic or lethal effects to the dose required to produce nonadverse or therapeutic response.

Thermal Pollution Discharge of heated water from industrial processes that can kill or injure aquatic organisms.

Thermal Stratification The formation of layers of different temperatures in a lake or reservoir.

Thermal System Insulation (TSI) Asbestos-containing material applied to pipes, fittings, boilers, breeching, tanks, ducts, or other interior structural components to prevent heat loss or gain or water condensation.

Thermal Treatment Use of elevated temperatures to treat hazardous wastes. (See incineration; pyrolysis.)

Thermocline The middle layer of a thermally stratified lake or reservoir. In this layer, there is a rapid decrease in temperatures in a lake or reservoir.

Threshold The dose or exposure level below which a significant adverse effect is not expected.

Threshold Level Time-weighted average pollutant concentration values, exposure beyond which is likely to adversely affect human health. (See environmental exposure.)

Threshold Limit Value (TLV) The concentration of an airborne substance to which an average person can be repeatedly exposed without adverse effects. TLVs may be expressed in three ways: (1) TLV-TWA—Time weighted average, based on an allowable exposure averaged over a normal 8-hour workday or 40-hour work-week; (2) TLV-STEL—Short-term exposure limit or maximum concentration for a brief specified period of time, depending on a specific chemical (TWA must still be met); and (3) TLV-C—Ceiling Exposure Limit or maximum exposure concentration not to be exceeded under any circumstances. (TWA must still be met.)

Threshold Odor (See Odor threshold.)

Threshold Planning Quantity A quantity designated for each chemical on the list of extremely hazardous substances that triggers notification by facilities to the State Emergency Response Commission that such facilities are subject to emergency planning requirements under SARA Title III.

Thropic Levels A functional classification of species that is based on feeding relationships (e.g., generally aquatic and terrestrial green plants comprise the first thropic level, and herbivores comprise the second).

Tidal Marsh Low, flat marshlands traversed by channels and tidal hollows, subject to tidal inundation; normally, the only vegetation present is salt-tolerant bushes and grasses. (See wetlands.)

Tillage Plowing, seedbed preparation, and cultivation practices.

Time-weighted Average (TWA) In air sampling, the average air concentration of contaminants during a given period.

Tire Processor Intermediate operating facility where recovered tires are processed in preparation for recycling.

Tires As used in recycling, passenger car and truck tires (excludes airplane, bus, motorcycle and special service military, agricultural, off-the-road and slow speed industrial tires). Car and truck tires are recycled into rubber products such as trash cans, storage containers, rubberized asphalt or used whole for playground and reef construction.

Tolerance Petition A formal request to establish a new tolerance or modify an existing one.

Tolerances Permissible residue levels for pesticides in raw agricultural produce and processed foods. Whenever a pesticide is registered for use on a food or a feed crop, a tolerance (or exemption from the tolerance requirement) must be established. EPA establishes the tolerance levels, which are enforced by the Food and Drug Administration and the Department of Agriculture.

Tonnage The amount of waste that a landfill accepts, usually expressed in tons per month. The rate at which a landfill accepts waste is limited by the landfill's permit.

Topography The physical features of a surface area including relative elevations and the position of natural and man-made (anthropogenic) features.

Total Dissolved Phosphorous The total phosphorous content of all material that will pass through a filter, which is determined as orthophosphate without prior digestion or hydrolysis. Also called soluble P. or ortho P.

Total Dissolved Solids (TDS) All material that passes the standard glass river filter; now called total filtrable residue. Term is used to reflect salinity.

Total Maximum Daily Load (TMDL) A calculation of the highest amount of a pollutant that a water body can receive and safely meet water quality standards set by the state, territory, or authorized tribe.

Total Petroleum Hydrocarbons (TPH) Measure of the concentration or mass of petroleum hydrocarbon constituents present in a given amount of soil or water. The word "total" is a misnomer—few, if any, of the procedures for quantifying hydrocarbons can measure all of them in a given sample. Volatile ones are usually lost in the process and not quantified and non-petroleum hydrocarbons sometimes appear in the analysis.

Total Recovered Petroleum Hydrocarbon A method for measuring petroleum hydrocarbons in samples of soil or water.

Total Suspended Particles (TSP) A method of monitoring airborne particulate matter by total weight.

Total Suspended Solids (TSS) A measure of the suspended solids in wastewater, effluent, or water bodies, determined by tests for "total suspended non-filterable solids." (See suspended solids.)

Toxaphene Chemical that causes adverse health effects in domestic water supplies and is toxic to fresh water and marine aquatic life.

Toxic Chemical Any chemical listed in EPA rules as "Toxic Chemicals Subject to Section 313 of the Emergency Planning and Community Right-to-Know Act of 1986."

Toxic Chemical Release Form Information form required of facilities that manufacture, process, or use (in quantities above a specific amount) chemicals listed under SARA Title III.

Toxic Chemical Use Substitution Replacing toxic chemicals with less harmful chemicals in industrial processes.

Toxic Cloud Airborne plume of gases, vapors, fumes, or aerosols containing toxic materials.

Toxic Concentration The concentration at which a substance produces a toxic effect.

Toxic Dose The dose level at which a substance produces a toxic effect.

Toxic Pollutants Materials that cause death, disease, or birth defects in organisms that ingest or absorb them. The quantities and exposures necessary to cause these effects can vary widely.

Toxic Release Inventory Database of toxic releases in the United States compiled from SARA Title III Section 313 reports.

Toxic Substance A chemical or mixture that may present an unreasonable risk of injury to health or the environment.

Toxic Waste A waste that can produce injury if inhaled, swallowed, or absorbed through the skin.

Toxicant A harmful substance or agent that may injure an exposed organism.

Toxicity The degree to which a substance or mixture of substances can harm humans or animals. *Acute toxicity* involves harmful effects in an organism through a single or short-term exposure. *Chronic toxicity* is the ability of a substance or mixture of substances to cause harmful effects over an extended period, usually upon repeated or continuous exposure sometimes lasting for the entire life of the exposed organism. *Subchronic toxicity* is the ability of the substance to cause effects for more than one year but less than the lifetime of the exposed organism.

Toxicity Assessment Characterization of the toxicological properties and effects of a chemical, with special emphasis on establishment of dose-response characteristics.

Toxicity Testing Biological testing (usually with an invertebrate, fish, or small mammal) to determine the adverse effects of a compound or effluent.

Toxicological Profile An examination, summary, and interpretation of a hazardous substance to determine levels of exposure and associated health effects.

Transboundary Pollutants Air pollution that travels from one jurisdiction to another, often crossing state or international boundaries. Also applies to water pollution.

Transfer Station Facility where solid waste is transferred from collection vehicles to larger trucks or rail cars for longer distance transport.

Transient Water System A non-community water system that does not serve 25 of the same nonresidents per day for more than six months per year.

Transmission Lines Pipelines that transport raw water from its source to a water treatment plant, then to the distribution grid system.

Transmissivity The ability of an aquifer to transmit water.

Transpiration The process by which water vapor is lost to the atmosphere from living plants. The term can also be applied to the quantity of water thus dissipated.

Transportation Control Measures (TCMs) Steps taken by a locality to reduce vehicular emission and improve air quality by reducing or changing the flow of traffic; e.g. bus and HOV lanes, carpooling and other forms of ride-sharing, public transit, bicycle lanes.

Transporter Hauling firm that picks up properly packaged and labeled hazardous waste from generators and transports it to designated facilities for treatment, storage, or disposal. Transporters are subject to EPA and DOT hazardous waste regulations.

Trash Material considered worthless or offensive that is thrown away. Generally defined as dry waste material, but in common usage it is a synonym for garbage, rubbish, or refuse.

Trash-to-Energy Plan Burning trash to produce energy.

Treatability Studies Tests of potential cleanup technologies conducted in a laboratory (See bench-scale tests.)

Treated Regulated Medical Waste Medical waste treated to substantially reduce or eliminate its pathogenicity, but that has not yet been destroyed.

Treated Wastewater Wastewater that has been subjected to one or more physical, chemical, and biological processes to reduce its potential of being health hazard.

Treatment (1) Any method, technique, or process designed to remove solids and/or pollutants from solid waste, waste-streams, effluents, and air emissions. (2) Methods used to change the biological character or composition of any regulated medical waste so as to substantially reduce or eliminate its potential for causing disease.

Treatment Plant A structure built to treat wastewater before discharging it into the environment.

Treatment, Storage, and Disposal Facility Site where a hazardous substance is treated, stored, or disposed of. TSD facilities are regulated by EPA and states under RCRA.

Tremie Device used to place concrete or grout under water.

Trial Burn An incinerator test in which emissions are monitored for the presence of specific organic compounds, particulates, and hydrogen chloride.

Trichloroethylene (TCE) A stable, low boiling-point colorless liquid, toxic if inhaled. Used as a solvent or metal degreasing agent, and in other industrial applications.

Trickle Irrigation Method in which water drips to the soil from perforated tubes or emitters.

Trickling Filter A coarse treatment system in which wastewater is trickled over a bed of stones or other material covered with bacteria that break down the organic waste and produce clean water.

Trihalomethane (THM) One of a family of organic compounds named as derivative of methane. THMs are generally by-products of chlorination of drinking water that contains organic material.

Troposhpere The layer of the atmosphere closest to the earth's surface.

Trust Fund (CERCLA) A fund set up under the Comprehensive Environmental Response, Compensation and Liability Act (CERCLA) to help pay for cleanup of hazardous waste sites and for legal action to force those responsible for the sites to clean them up.

Tube Settler Device using bundles of tubes to let solids in water settle to the bottom for removal by conventional sludge collection means; sometimes used in sedimentation basins and clarifiers to improve particle removal.

Tuberculation Development or formation of small mounds of corrosion products on the inside of iron pipe. These tubercules roughen the inside of the pipe, increasing its resistance to water flow.

Tundra A type of treeless ecosystem dominated by lichens, mosses, grasses, and woody plants. Tundra is found at high latitudes (arctic tundra) and high altitudes (alpine tundra). Arctic tundra is underlain by permafrost and is usually water saturated. (See wetlands.)

Turbidimeter A device that measures the cloudiness of suspended solids in a liquid; a measure of the quantity of suspended solids.

Turbidity 1. Haziness in air caused by the presence of particles and pollutants. 2. A cloudy condition in water due to suspended silt or organic matter.

Ultra Clean Coal (UCC) Coal that is washed, ground into fine particles, then chemically treated to remove sulfur, ash, silicone, and other substances; usually briquetted and coated with a sealant made from coal.

Ultraviolet Rays Radiation from the sun that can be useful or potentially harmful. UV rays from one part of the spectrum (UV-A) enhance plant life. UV rays from other parts of the spectrum (UV-B) can cause skin cancer or other tissue damage. The ozone layer in the atmosphere partly shields us from ultraviolet rays reaching the earth's surface.

Uncertainty Factor One of several factors used in calculating the reference dose from experimental data. UFs are intended to account for (1) the variation in sensitivity among humans; (2) the uncertainty in extrapolating animal data to humans; (3) the uncertainty in extrapolating data obtained in a study that covers less than the full life of the exposed animal or human; and (4) the uncertainty in using LOAEL data rather than NOAEL data.

Unconfined Aquifer An aquifer containing water that is not under pressure; the water level in a well is the same as the water table outside the well.

Underground Injection Control (UIC) The program under the Safe Drinking Water Act that regulates the use of wells to pump fluids into the ground.

Underground Injection Wells Steel- and concrete-encased shafts into which hazardous waste is deposited by force and under pressure.

Underground Sources of Drinking Water Aquifers currently being used as a source of drinking water or those capable of supplying a public water system. They have a total dissolved solids content of 10,000 milligrams per liter or less, and are not "exempted aquifers." (See exempted aquifer.)

Underground Storage Tank (UST) A tank located at least partially underground and designed to hold gasoline or other petroleum products or chemicals.

Unreasonable Risk Under the Federal Insecticide, Fungicide, and Rodenticide Act (FIFRA), "unreasonable adverse effects" means any unreasonable risk to man or the environment, taking into account the medical, economic, social, and environmental costs and benefits of any pesticide.

Unsaturated Zone The area above the water table where soil pores are not fully saturated, although some water may be present.

Upper Detection Limit The largest concentration that an instrument can reliably detect.

Uranium Mill Tailings Piles Former uranium ore processing sites that contain leftover radioactive materials (wastes), including radium and unrecovered uranium.

Uranium Mill-Tailings Waste Piles Licensed active mills with tailings piles and evaporation ponds created by acid or alkaline leaching processes.

Urban Runoff Storm water from city streets and adjacent domestic or commercial properties that carries pollutants of various kinds into the sewer systems and receiving waters.

Urea-Formaldehyde Foam Insulation A material once used to conserve energy by sealing crawl spaces, attics, etc.; no longer used because emissions were found to be a health hazard.

Use Cluster A set of competing chemicals, processes, and/or technologies that can substitute for one another in performing a particular function.

Used Oil Spent motor oil from passenger cars and trucks collected at specified locations for recycling (not included in the category of municipal solid waste).

User Fee Fee collected from only those persons who use a particular service, as compared to one collected from the public in general.

Utility Load The total electricity demand for a utility district.

Vadose Zone The zone between land surface and the water table within which the moisture content is less than saturation (except in the capillary fringe) and pressure is less than atmospheric. Soil pore space also typically contains air or other gases. The capillary fringe is included in the vadose zone. (See Unsaturated Zone.)

Valued Environmental Attributes/Components Those aspects(components/processes/functions) of ecosystems, human health, and environmental welfare considered to be important and potentially at risk from human activity or natural hazards. Similar to the term "valued environmental components" used in environmental impact assessment.

Vapor The gas given off by substances that are solids or liquids at ordinary atmospheric pressure and temperatures.

Vapor Capture System Any combination of hoods and ventilation system that captures or contains organic vapors so they may be directed to an abatement or recovery device.

Vapor Dispersion The movement of vapor clouds in air due to wind, thermal action, gravity spreading, and mixing.

Vapor Plumes Flue gases visible because they contain water droplets.

Vapor Pressure A measure of a substance's propensity to evaporate, vapor pressure is the force per unit area exerted by vapor in an equilibrium state with surroundings at a given pressure. It increases exponentially with an increase in temperature. A relative measure of chemical volatility, vapor pressure is used to calculate water partition coefficients and volatilization rate constants.

Vapor Recovery System A system by which the volatile gases from gasoline are captured instead of being released into the atmosphere.

Variance Government permission for a delay or exception in the application of a given law, ordinance, or regulation.

Vector 1. An organism, often an insect or rodent, that carries disease. 2. Plasmids, viruses, or bacteria used to transport genes into a host cell. A gene is placed in the vector; the vector then "infects" the bacterium.

Vegetative Controls Non-point source pollution control practices that involve vegetative cover to reduce erosion and minimize loss of pollutants.

Vehicle Miles Travelled (VMT) A measure of the extent of motor vehicle operation; the total number of vehicle miles travelled within a specific geographic area over a given period of time.

Ventilation Rate The rate at which indoor air enters and leaves a building. Expressed as the number of changes of outdoor air per unit of time (air changes per hour (ACH), or the rate at which a volume of outdoor air enters in cubic feet per minute (CFM).

Ventilation/Suction The act of admitting fresh air into a space in order to replace stale or contaminated air; achieved by blowing air into the space. Similarly, suction represents the admission of fresh air into an interior space by lowering the pressure outside of the space, thereby drawing the contaminated air outward.

Venturi Scrubbers Air pollution control devices that use water to remove particulate matter from emissions.

Vinyl Chloride A chemical compound, used in producing some plastics, that is believed to be oncogenic.

Virgin Materials Resources extracted from nature in their raw form, such as timber or metal ore.

Viscosity The molecular friction within a fluid that produces flow resistance.

Volatile Any substance that evaporates readily.

Volatile Liquids Liquids which easily vaporize or evaporate at room temperature.

Volatile Organic Compound (VOC) Any organic compound that participates in atmospheric photochemical reactions except those designated by EPA as having negligible photochemical reactivity.

Volatile Solids Those solids in water or other liquids that are lost on ignition of the dry solids at 550° centigrade.

Volatile Synthetic Organic Chemicals Chemicals that tend to volatilize or evaporate.

Volume Reduction Processing waste materials to decrease the amount of space they occupy, usually by compacting, shredding, incineration, or composting.

Volumetric Tank Test One of several tests to determine the physical integrity of a storage tank; the volume of fluid in the tank is measured directly or calculated from product-level changes. A marked drop in volume indicates a leak.

Vulnerability Analysis Assessment of elements in the community that are susceptible to damage if hazardous materials are released.

Vulnerable Zone An area over which the airborne concentration of a chemical accidentally released could reach the level of concern.

Xenobiota Any biotum displaced from its normal habitat; a chemical foreign to a biological system.

Yard Waste The part of solid waste composed of grass clippings, leaves, twigs, branches, and other garden refuse.

Yellow-Boy Iron oxide flocculant (clumps of solids in waste or water); usually observed as orange-yellow deposits in surface streams with excess iron content. (See floc, flocculation.)

Yield The quantity of water (expressed as a rate of flow or total quantity per year) that can be collected for a given use from surface or groundwater sources.

Zero Air Atmospheric air purified to contain less than 0.1 ppm total hydrocarbons.

Zooplankton Small (often microscopic) free-floating aquatic plants or animals.

Zone of Saturation The layer beneath the surface of the land containing openings that may fill with water.

ACRONYMS

A&I	Alternative and Innovative (Wastewater Treatment System)
AA	Accountable Area; Adverse Action; Advices of Allowance; Assistant Administrator; Associate Administrator; Atomic Absorption
AAEE	American Academy of Environmental Engineers
AANWR	Alaskan Arctic National Wildlife Refuge
AAP	Asbestos Action Program
AAPCO	American Association of Pesticide Control Officials
AARC	Alliance for Acid Rain Control
ABEL	EPA's computer model for analyzing a violator's ability to pay a civil penalty.
ABES	Alliance for Balanced Environmental Solutions
AC	Actual Commitment. Advisory Circular
A&C	Abatement and Control
ACA	American Conservation Association
ACBM	Asbestos-Containing Building Material
ACE	Alliance for Clean Energy
ACE	Any Credible Evidence
ACEEE	American Council for an Energy Efficient Economy
ACFM	Actual Cubic Feet per Minute
ACL	Alternate Concentration Limit. Analytical Chemistry Laboratory
ACM	Asbestos-Containing Material
ACP	Agriculture Control Program (Water Quality Management); Air Carcinogen Policy
ACQUIRE	Aquatic Information Retrieval
ACQR	Air Quality Control Region
ACS	American Chemical Society; Annual Commitment System
ACT	Action
ACTS	Asbestos Contractor Tracking System
ACWA	American Clean Water Association
ACWM	Asbestos-Containing Waste Material
ADABA	Acceptable Data Base
ADB	Applications Data Base
ADI	Acceptable Daily Intake
ADP	AHERA Designated Person; Automated Data Processing
ADQ	Audits of Data Quality
ADR	Alternate Dispute Resolution
ADSS	Air Data Screening System
ADT	Average Daily Traffic
AEA	Atomic Energy Act
AEC	Associate Enforcement Counsels
AEE	Alliance for Environmental Education
AEERL	Air and Energy Engineering Research Laboratory
AEM	Acoustic Emission Monitoring
AERE	Association of Environmental and Resource Economists
AES	Auger Electron Spectrometry
AFA	American Forestry Association
AFCA	Area Fuel Consumption Allocation
AFCEE	Air Force Center for Environmental Excellence
AFS	AIRS Facility Subsystem; Air Facility System
AFSICR	Air Facilities System — Information Collection Request
AFUG	AIRS Facility Users Group
AH	Allowance Holders

AHERA	Asbestos Hazard Emergency Response Act	AQCR	Air-Quality Control Region
AHU	Air Handling Unit	AQD	Air-Quality Digest
AI	Active Ingredient	AQDHS	Air-Quality Data Handling System
AIC	Active to Inert Conversion	AQDM	Air-Quality Display Model
AICUZ	Air Installation Compatible Use Zones	AQMA	Air-Quality Maintenance Area
AID	Agency for International Development	AQMD	Air Quality Management District
AIHC	American Industrial Health Council	AQMP	Air-Quality Maintenance Plan; Air-Quality Management Plan
AIP	Auto Ignition Point	AQSM	Air-Quality Simulation Model
AIRMON	Atmospheric Integrated Research Monitoring Network	AQTAD	Air-Quality Technical Assistance Demonstration
AIRS	Aerometric Information Retrieval System	AR	Administrative Record
AL	Acceptable Level	A&R	Air and Radiation
ALA	Delta-Aminolevulinic Acid	ARA	Assistant Regional Administrator; Associate Regional Administrator
ALA-O	Delta-Aminolevulinic Acid Dehydrates	ARAC	Acid Rain Advisory Committee
ALAPO	Association of Local Air Pollution Control Officers	ARAR	Applicable or Relevant and Appropriate Standards, Limitations, Criteria, and Requirements
ALARA	As Low As Reasonably Achievable		
ALC	Application Limiting Constituent		
ALJ	Administrative Law Judge	ARB	Air Resources Board
ALMS	Atomic Line Molecular Spectroscopy	ARC	Agency Ranking Committee
ALR	Action Leakage Rate	ARCC	American Rivers Conservation Council
AMBIENS	Atmospheric Mass Balance of Industrially Emitted and Natural Sulfur	ARCS	Alternative Remedial Contract Strategy
		ARG	American Resources Group
AMOS	Air Management Oversight System	ARIP	Accidental Release Information Program
AMPS	Automatic Mapping and Planning System	ARL	Air Resources Laboratory
AMSA	Association of Metropolitan Sewer Agencies	ARM	Air Resources Management
		ARNEWS	Acid Rain National Early Warning Systems
ANC	Acid Neutralizing Capacity		
ANPR	Advance Notice of Proposed Rulemaking	ARO	Alternate Regulatory Option
ANRHRD	Air, Noise, & Radiation Health Research Division/ORD	ARRP	Acid Rain Research Program
		ARRPA	Air Resources Regional Pollution Assessment Model
ANSS	American Nature Study Society		
AO	Administrative Orders	ARS	Agricultural Research Service
AOAC	Association of Official Analytical Chemists	ARZ	Auto Restricted Zone
		AS	Area Source
AOC	Abnormal Operating Conditions	ASC	Area Source Category
AOD	Argon-Oxygen Decarbonization	ASDWA	Association of State Drinking Water Administrators
AOML	Atlantic Oceanographic and Meteorological Laboratory		
		ASHAA	Asbestos in Schools Hazard Abatement Act
AP	Accounting Point		
APA	Administrative Procedures Act	ASHRAE	American Society of Heating, Refrigerating, and Air-Conditioning Engineers
APCA	Air Pollution Control Association		
APCD	Air Pollution Control District	ASIWCPA	Association of State and Interstate Water Pollution Control Administrators
APDS	Automated Procurement Documentation System		
		ASMDHS	Airshed Model Data Handling System
APHA	American Public Health Association	ASRL	Atmospheric Sciences Research Laboratory
APRAC	Urban Diffusion Model for Carbon Monoxide from Motor Vehicle Traffic	AST	Advanced Secondary (Wastewater) Treatment; Above Ground Storage Tank
APTI	Air Pollution Training Institute	ASTHO	Association of State and Territorial Health Officers
APWA	American Public Works Association		
AQ-7	Non-reactive Pollutant Modelling	ASTM	American Society for Testing and Materials
AQCCT	Air-Quality Criteria and Control Techniques		
		ASTSWMO	Association of State and Territorial Solid Waste Management Officials
AQCP	Air Quality Control Program		

AT	Advanced Treatment. Alpha Track Detection	BOP	Basic Oxygen Process; Bureau of Prisons
ATERIS	Air Toxics Exposure and Risk Information System	BOPF	Basic Oxygen Process Furnace
		BOYSNC	Beginning of Year Significant Non-Compliers
ATS	Action Tracking System; Allowance Tracking System	BP	Boiling Point
		BPJ	Best Professional Judgment
ATSDR	Agency for Toxic Substances and Disease Registry	BPT	Best Practicable Technology. Pest Practicable Treatment
ATTF	Air Toxics Task Force	BPWTT	Best Practical Wastewater Treatment Technology
AUSM	Advanced Utility Simulation Model		
A/WPR	Air/Water Pollution Report	BRI	Building-Related Illness
AWRA	American Water Resources Association	BRS	Bibliographic Retrieval Service
AWT	Advanced Wastewater Treatment	BSI	British Standards Institute
AWWA	American Water Works Association	BSO	Benzene Soluble Organics
AWWARF	American Water Works Association Research Foundation.	BTZ	Below the Treatment Zone
		BUN	Blood Urea Nitrogen
BAA	Board of Assistance Appeals	CA	Citizen Act. Competition Advocate. Cooperative Agreements. Corrective Action, Compliance Assistance
BAC	Bioremediation Action Committee; Biotechnology Advisory Committee		
BACM	Best Available Control Measures	CAA	Clean Air Act; Compliance Assurance Agreement
BACT	Best Available Control Technology		
BADT	Best Available Demonstrated Technology	CAAA	Clean Air Act Amendments
		CAC	Compliance Assistance Coordinator
BAF	Bioaccumulation Factor	CACDS	Compliance Assistance Conclusion Data Sheet
BaP	Benzo(a)Pyrene		
BAP	Benefits Analysis Program	CAER	Community Awareness and Emergency Response
BART	Best Available Retrofit Technology		
BASIS	Battelle's Automated Search Information System	CAFE	Corporate Average Fuel Economy
		CAFO	Concentrated Animal Feedlot; Consent Agreement/Final Order
BAT	Best Available Technology		
BATEA	Best Available Treatment Economically Achievable	CAG	Carcinogenic Assessment Group
		CAIR	Clean Air Interstate Rule; Comprehensive Assessment of Information Rule
BCPCT	Best Conventional Pollutant Control Technology		
		CALINE	California Line Source Model
BCT	Best Control Technology	CAM	Compliance Assurance Monitoring rule; Compliance Assurance Monitoring
BDAT	Best Demonstrated Achievable Technology		
		CAMP	Continuous Air Monitoring Program
BDCT	Best Demonstrated Control Technology	CAN	Common Account Number
BDT	Best Demonstrated Technology	CAO	Corrective Action Order
BEJ	Best Engineering Judgement. Best Expert Judgment	CAP	Corrective Action Plan. Cost Allocation Procedure. Criteria Air Pollutant
BF	Bonafide Notice of Intent to Manufacture or Import (IMD/OTS)	CAPMoN	Canadian Air and Precipitation Monitoring Network
BIA	Bureau of Indian Affairs	CAR	Corrective Action Report
BID	Background Information Document. Buoyancy Induced Dispersion	CAS	Center for Automotive Safety; Chemical Abstract Service
BIOPLUME	Model to Predict the Maximum Extent of Existing Plumes	CASAC	Clean Air Scientific Advisory Committee
		CASLP	Conference on Alternative State and Local Practices
BMP	Best Management Practice(s)		
BMR	Baseline Monitoring Report	CASTNet	Clean Air Status and Trends Network
BO	Budget Obligations	CATS	Corrective Action Tracking System
BOA	Basic Ordering Agreement (Contracts)	CAU	Carbon Adsorption Unit; Command Arithmetic Unit
BOD	Biochemical Oxygen Demand. Biological Oxygen Demand		
		CB	Continuous Bubbler
BOF	Basic Oxygen Furnace		

CBA	Chesapeake Bay Agreement, Cost Benefit Analysis
CBD	Central Business District
CBEP	Community Based Environmental Project
CBI	Compliance Biomonitoring Inspection; Confidential Business Information
CBOD	Carbonaceous Biochemical Oxygen Demand
CBP	Chesapeake Bay Program; County Business Patterns; Bureau of Customs and Border Protection
CCA	Competition in Contracting Act
CCAA	Canadian Clean Air Act
CCAP	Center for Clean Air Policy; Climate Change Action Plan
CCDS	Case Conclusion Data Sheet
CCEA	Conventional Combustion Environmental Assessment
CCHW	Citizens Clearinghouse for Hazardous Wastes
CCID	Confidential Chemicals Identification System
CCMS/NATO	Committee on Challenges of a Modern Society/North Atlantic Treaty Organization
CCP	Composite Correction Plan
CC/RTS	Chemical Collection/ Request Tracking System
CCTP	Clean Coal Technology Program
CD	Climatological Data
CDB	Consolidated Data Base
CDBA	Central Data Base Administrator
CDBG	Community Development Block Grant
CDD	Chlorinated dibenzo-p-dioxin
CDF	Chlorinated dibenzofuran
CDHS	Comprehensive Data Handling System
CDI	Case Development Inspection
CDM	Climatological Dispersion Model; Comprehensive Data Management
CDMQC	Climatological Dispersion Model with Calibration and Source Contribution
CDNS	Climatological Data National Summary
CDP	Census Designated Places
CDS	Compliance Data System
CE	Categorical Exclusion. Conditionally Exempt Generator
CEA	Cooperative Enforcement Agreement; Cost and Economic Assessment
CEARC	Canadian Environmental Assessment Research Council
CEAT	Contractor Evidence Audit Team
CEB	Chemical Element Balance
CEC	Commission for Environmental Cooperation
CECATS	CSB Existing Chemicals Assessment Tracking System
CEE	Center for Environmental Education
CEEM	Center for Energy and Environmental Management
CEI	Compliance Evaluation Inspection
CELRF	Canadian Environmental Law Research Foundation
CEM	Continuous Emission Monitoring
CEMS	Continuous Emission Monitoring System
CEPA	Canadian Environmental Protection Act
CEPP	Chemical Emergency Preparedness Plan
CEQ	Council on Environmental Quality
CERCLA	Comprehensive Environmental Response, Compensation, and Liability Act (1980)
CERCLIS	Comprehensive Environmental Response, Compensation, and Liability Information System
CERT	Certificate of Eligibility
CESQG	Conditionally Exempt Small Quantity Generator
CEST	Community Environmental Service Teams
CF	Conservation Foundation
CFC	Chlorofluorocarbons
CFM	Chlorofluoromethanes
CFR	Code of Federal Regulations
CHABA	Committee on Hearing and Bio-Acoustics
CHAMP	Community Health Air Monitoring Program
CHEMNET	Chemical Industry Emergency Mutual Aid Network
CHESS	Community Health and Environmental Surveillance System
CHIP	Chemical Hazard Information Profiles
CI	Compression Ignition. Confidence Interval
CIAQ	Council on Indoor Air Quality
CIBL	Convective Internal Boundary Layer
CICA	Competition in Contracting Act
CICIS	Chemicals in Commerce Information System
CID	Criminal Investigations Division
CIDRS	Cascade Impactor Data Reduction System
CIMI	Committee on Integrity and Management Improvement
CIP	Compliance Incentive Programs

CIS	Chemical Information System; Contracts Information System	CVS	Constant Volume Sampler
CKD	Cement Kiln Dust	CW	Continuous working-level monitoring
CKRC	Cement Kiln Recycling Coalition	CWA	Clean Water Act (aka FWPCA)
CLC	Capacity Limiting Constituents	CWAP	Clean Water Action Project
CLEANS	Clinical Laboratory for Evaluation and Assessment of Toxic Substances	CWTC	Chemical Waste Transportation Council
		CZARA	Coastal Zone Management Act Reauthorization Amendments
CLEVER	Clinical Laboratory for Evaluation and Validation of Epidemiologic Research	CZMA	Coastal Zone Management Act
		DAPSS	Document and Personnel Security System (IMD)
CLF	Conservation Law Foundation		
CLI	Consumer Labelling Initiative	DBP	Disinfection By-Product
CLIPS	Chemical List Index and Processing System	DCI	Data Call-In
CLP	Contract Laboratory Program	DCO	Delayed Compliance Order
CM	Corrective Measure	DCO	Document Control Officer
CMA	Chemical Manufacturers Association	DDT	DichloroDiphenylTrichloroethane
CMB	Chemical Mass Balance	DERs	Data Evaluation Records
CME	Comprehensive Monitoring Evaluation	DES	Diethylstilbesterol
CMEL	Comprehensive Monitoring Evaluation Log	DfE	Design for the Environment
		DI	Diagnostic Inspection
CMEP	Critical Mass Energy Project	DMR	Discharge Monitoring Report
CMS	Compliance Monitoring Strategy	DNA	Deoxyribonucleic acid
CNG	Compressedd Natural Gas	DNAPL	Dense Non-Aqueous Phase Liquid
COCO	Contractor-Owned/ Contractor-Operated	DO	Dissolved Oxygen
COD	Chemical Oxygen Demand	DOW	Defenders Of Wildlife
COH	Coefficient of Haze	DPA	Deepwater Ports Act
CPDA	Chemical Producers and Distributor Association	DPD	Method of Measuring Chlorine Residual in Water
CPF	Carcinogenic Potency Factor	DQO	Data Quality Objective
CPO	Certified Project Officer	DRE	Destruction and Removal Efficiency
CQA	Construction Quality Assurance	DRES	Dietary Risk Evaluation System
CR	Continuous Radon Monitoring	DRMS	Defense Reutilization and Marketing Service
CROP	Consolidated Rules of Practice	DRR	Data Review Record
CRP	Child-Resistant Packaging; Conservation Reserve Program	DS	Dichotomous Sampler
		DSAP	Data Self Auditing Program
CRR	Center for Renewable Resources	DSCF	Dry Standard Cubic Feet
CRSTER	Single Source Dispersion Model	DSCM	Dry Standard Cubic Meter
CSCT	Committee for Site Characterization	DSS	Decision Support System; Domestic Sewage Study
CSGWPP	Comprehensive State Ground Water Protection Program		
		DT	Detectors (radon) damaged or lost; Detention Time
CSI	Common Sense Initiative; Compliance Sampling Inspection		
		DU	Decision Unit; Ducks Unlimited; Dobson Unit
CSIN	Chemical Substances Information Network		
CSMA	Chemical Specialties Manufacturers Association	DUC	Decision Unit Coordinator
		DWEL	Drinking Water Equivalent Level
CSO	Combined Sewer Overflow	DWS	Drinking Water Standard
CSPA	Council of State Planning Agencies	DWSRF	Drinking Water State Revolving Fund
CSRL	Center for the Study of Responsive Law	EA	Endangerment Assessment; Enforcement Agreement; Environmental Action; Environmental Assessment; Environmental Audit
CSS	Combined Sewer Systems		
CTARC	Chemical Testing and Assessment Research Commission		
		EAF	Electric Arc Furnaces
CTG	Control Techniques Guidelines	EAG	Exposure Assessment Group
CTSA	Cleaner Technologies Substitutess Assessment	EAO	Emergency Administrative Order
		EAP	Environmental Action Plan
CUPA	Certified Unified Program Agencies	EAR	Environmental Auditing Roundtable
CV	Chemical Vocabulary		

EASI	Environmental Alliance for Senior Involvement	EJSEAT	Environmental Justice Strategic Enforcement Assessment Tool
EB	Emissions Balancing	EKMA	Empirical Kinetic Modeling Approach
EC	Emulsifiable Concentrate; Environment Canada; Effective Concentration	EL	Exposure Level
		ELI	Environmental Law Institute
ECA	Economic Community for Africa	ELR	Environmental Law Reporter
ECAP	Employee Counselling and Assistance Program	EM	Electromagnetic Conductivity
		EMAP	Environmental Mapping and Assessment Program
ECD	Electron Capture Detector		
ECHH	Electro-Catalytic Hyper-Heaters	EMAS	Enforcement Management and Accountability System
ECHO	Enforcement and Compliance History Online		
ECL	Environmental Chemical Laboratory	EMP	Environmental Management Practices
ECOS	Environmental Council of the States	EMR	Environmental Management Report; Environmental Management Reviews
ECR	Enforcement Case Review		
ECRA	Economic Cleanup Responsibility Act	EMS	Enforcement Management System; Environmental Management System
ED	Effective Dose		
EDA	Emergency Declaration Area	EMSL	Environmental Monitoring Support Systems Laboratory
EDB	Ethylene Dibromide		
EDC	Ethylene Dichloride	EMTS	Environmental Monitoring Testing Site; Exposure Monitoring Test Site
EDD	Enforcement Decision Document		
EDF	Environmental Defense Fund	EnPA	Environmental Performance Agreement
EDRS	Enforcement Document Retrieval System	EO	Ethylene Oxide
EDS	Electronic Data System; Energy Data System	EOC	Emergency Operating Center
		EOF	Emergency Operations Facility (RTP)
EDTA	Ethylene Diamine Triacetic Acid	EOP	End of Pipe
EDX	Electronic Data Exchange	EOT	Emergency Operations Team
EDZ	Emission Density Zoning	EP	Earth Protectors; Environmental Profile; End-use Product; Experimental Product; Extraction Procedure
EEA	Energy and Environmental Analysis		
EECs	Estimated Environmental Concentrations		
EER	Excess Emission Report		
EERL	Eastern Environmental Radiation Laboratory	EPAA	Environmental Programs Assistance Act
		EPA	Environmental Protection Agency
EERU	Environmental Emergency Response Unit	EPAAR	EPA Acquisition Regulations
EESI	Environment and Energy Study Institute	EPCA	Energy Policy and Conservation Act
EESL	Environmental Ecological and Support Laboratory	EPACT	Environmental Policy Act
		EPACASR	EPA Chemical Activities Status Report
EETFC	Environmental Effects, Transport, and Fate Committee	EPCRA	Emergency Planning and Community Right to Know Act
EF	Emission Factor	EPD	Emergency Planning District
EFO	Equivalent Field Office	EPI	Environmental Policy Institute
EFTC	European Fluorocarbon Technical Committee	EPIC	Environmental Photographic Interpretation Center
EGR	Exhaust Gas Recirculation		
EH	Redox Potential	EPNL	Effective Perceived Noise Level
EHC	Environmental Health Committee	EPRI	Electric Power Research Institute
EHS	Extremely Hazardous Substance	EPTC	Extraction Procedure Toxicity Characteristic
EI	Emissions Inventory	EQIP	Environmental Quality Incentives Program
EIA	Environmental Impact Assessment. Economic Impact Assessment		
		ER	Ecosystem Restoration; Electrical Resistivity
EIL	Environmental Impairment Liability		
EIR	Endangerment Information Report; Environmental Impact Report	ERA	Economic Regulatory Agency
		ERAMS	Environmental Radiation Ambient Monitoring System
EIS	Environmental Impact Statement; Environmental Inventory System		
		ERC	Emergency Response Commission. Emissions Reduction Credit, Environmental Research Center
EIS/AS	Emissions Inventory System/Area Source		
EIS/PS	Emissions Inventory System/Point Source		
EJ	Environmental Justice		
EJAC	Environmental Justice Areas of Concern	ERCS	Emergency Response Cleanup Services

ERDA	Energy Research and Development Administration	FEMA	Federal Emergency Management Agency
ERD&DAA	Environmental Research, Development and Demonstration Authorization Act	FEPCA	Federal Environmental Pesticide Control Act; enacted as amendments to FIFRA.
ERL	Environmental Research Laboratory	FERC	Federal Energy Regulatory Commission
ERNS	Emergency Response Notification System	FES	Factor Evaluation System
ERP	Enforcement Response Policy; Environmental Results Program	FEV	Forced Expiratory Volume
		FEV1	Forced Expiratory Volume—one second; Front End Volatility Index
ERT	Emergency Response Team	FF	Federal Facilities
ERTAQ	ERT Air Quality Model	FFAR	Fuel and Fuel Additive Registration
ES	Enforcement Strategy	FFDCA	Federal Food, Drug, and Cosmetic Act
ESA	Endangered Species Act. Environmentally Sensitive Area	FFEO	Federal Facilities Enforcement Office
		FFF	Firm Financial Facility
ESC	Endangered Species Committee	FFFSG	Fossil-Fuel-Fired Steam Generator
ESCA	Electron Spectroscopy for Chemical Analysis	FFIS	Federal Facilities Information System
		FFP	Firm Fixed Price
ESCAP	Economic and Social Commission for Asia and the Pacific	FGD	Flue-Gas Desulfurization
		FID	Flame Ionization Detector
ESD	Explanations of Significant Differences	FIFRA	Federal Insecticide, Fungicide, and Rodenticide Act
ESECA	Energy Supply and Environmental Coordination Act		
		FIM	Friable Insulation Material
ESH	Environmental Safety and Health	FINDS	Facility Index System
ESP	Electrostatic Precipitators	FIP	Final Implementation Plan
ET	Emissions Trading	FIPS	Federal Information Procedures System
ETI	Environmental Technology Initiative	FIT	Field Investigation Team
ETP	Emissions Trading Policy	FLETC	Federal Law Enforcement Training Center
ETS	Emissions Tracking System; Environmental Tobacco Smoke	FLM	Federal Land Manager
		FLP	Flash Point
ETV	Environmental Technology Verification Program	FLPMA	Federal Land Policy and Management Act
		F/M	Food to Microorganism Ratio
EUP	End-Use Product; Experimental Use Permit	FMAP	Financial Management Assistance Project
		FML	Flexible Membrane Liner
EWCC	Environmental Workforce Coordinating Committee	FMP	Facility Management Plan
		FMP	Financial Management Plan
EXAMS	Exposure Analysis Modeling System	FMS	Financial Management System
ExEx	Expected Exceedance	FMVCP	Federal Motor Vehicle Control Program
FACA	Federal Advisory Committee Act	FOE	Friends of the Earth
FAN	Fixed Account Number	FOIA	Freedom of Information Act
FATES	FIFRA and TSCA Enforcement System	FOISD	Fiber Optic Isolated Spherical Dipole Antenna
FBC	Fluidized Bed Combustion		
FCC	Fluid Catalytic Converter	FONSI	Finding Of No Significant Impact
FCCC	Framework Convention on Climate Change	FORAST	Forest Response to Anthropogenic Stress
		FP	Fine Particulate
FCCU	Fluid Catalytic Cracking Unit	FPA	Federal Pesticide Act
FCE	Full Compliance Evaluation	FPAS	Foreign Purchase Acknowledgement Statements
FCO	Federal Coordinating Officer (in disaster areas); Forms Control Officer		
		FPD	Flame Photometric Detector
FDF	Fundamentally Different Factors	FPEIS	Fine Particulate Emissions Information System
FDL	Final Determination Letter		
FDO	Fee Determination Official	FPM	Federal Personnel Manual
FE	Fugitive Emissions	FPPA	Federal Pollution Prevention Act
FEDS	Federal Energy Data System	FPR	Federal Procurement Regulation
FEFx	Forced Expiratory Flow	FPRS	Federal Program Resources Statement; Formal Planning and Supporting System
FEIS	Fugitive Emissions Information System		
FEL	Frank Effect Level	FQPA	Food Quality Protection Act

FR	Federal Register; Final Rulemaking	GLWQA	Great Lakes Water Quality Agreement
FRA	Federal Register Act	GMCC	Global Monitoring for Climatic Change
FREDS	Flexible Regional Emissions Data System	GME	Groundwater Monitoring Evaluation
FRES	Forest Range Environmental Study	G/MI	Grams per Mile
FRM	Federal Reference Methods	GOCO	Government-Owned/ Contractor-Operated
FRN	Federal Register Notice; Final Rulemaking Notice	GOGO	Government-Owned/ Government-Operated
FRP	Facility Response Plan	GOP	General Operating Procedures
FRS	Formal Reporting System	GOPO	Government-Owned/ Privately-Operated
FS	Feasibility Study		
FSA	Food Security Act	GPAD	Gallons-per-Acre per-Day
FSS	Facility Status Sheet; Federal Supply Schedule	GPG	Grams-per-Gallon
		GPR	Ground-Penetrating Radar
FTE	Full-Time Equivalent	GPRA	Government Performance and Results Act
FTP	Federal Test Procedure (for motor vehicles)	GPS	Groundwater Protection Strategy
		GR	Grab Radon Sampling
FTS	File Transfer Service	GRAS	Generally Recognized as Safe
FTTS	FIFRA/TSCA Tracking System	GRCDA	Government Refuse Collection and Disposal Association
FUA	Fuel Use Act		
FURS	Federal Underground Injection Control Reporting System	GRGL	Groundwater Residue Guidance Level
		GT	Gas Turbine
FVMP	Federal Visibility Monitoring Program	GTN	Global Trend Network
FWCA	Fish and Wildlife Coordination Act	GTR	Government Transportation Request
FWPCA	Federal Water Pollution and Control Act (aka CWA); Federal Water Pollution and Control Administration	GVP	Gasoline Vapor Pressure
		GVW	Gross Vehicle Weight
		GVWR	Gross Vehicle Weight Rating
FY	Fiscal Year	GW	Grab Working-Level Sampling; Groundwater
GAAP	Generally Accepted Accounting Principles		
GAC	Granular Activated Carbon	GWDR	Ground Water Disinfection Rule
GACT	Granular Activated Carbon Treatment	GWM	Groundwater Monitoring
GAO	Government Accountability Office	GWP	Global Warming Potential
GAW	Global Atmospheric Watch	GWPC	Ground Water Protection Council
GCC	Global Climate Convention	GWPS	Groundwater Protection Standard; Groundwater Protection Strategy
GC/MS	Gas Chromatograph/ Mass Spectograph		
GCVTC	Grand Canyon Visibility Transport Commission	HA	Health Advisory
		HAD	Health Assessment Document
GCWR	Gross Combination Weight Rating	HAP	Hazardous Air Pollutant
GDE	Generic Data Exemption	HAPEMS	Hazardous Air Pollutant Enforcement Management System
GEI	Geographic Enforcement Initiative		
GEMI	Global Environmental Management Initiative	HAPPS	Hazardous Air Pollutant Prioritization System
GEMS	Global Environmental Monitoring System; Graphical Exposure Modeling System	HATREMS	Hazardous and Trace Emissions System
		HAZMAT	Hazardous Materials
GEP	Good Engineering Practice	HAZOP	Hazard and Operability Study
GFF	Glass Fiber Filter	HBFC	Hydrobromofluorocarbon
GFO	Grant Funding Order	HC	Hazardous Constituents; Hydrocarbon
GFP	Government-Furnished Property	HCCPD	Hexachlorocyclo-pentadiene
GICS	Grant Information and Control System	HCFC	Hydrochlorofluorocarbon
GIS	Geographic Information Systems; Global Indexing System	HCP	Hypothermal Coal Process
		HDD	Heavy-Duty Diesel
GLC	Gas Liquid Chromatography	HDDT	Heavy-Duty Diesel Truck
GLERL	Great Lakes Environmental Research Laboratory	HDDV	Heavy-Duty Diesel Vehicle
		HDE	Heavy-Duty Engine
GLNPO	Great Lakes National Program Office	HDG	Heavy-Duty Gasoline-Powered Vehicle
GLP	Good Laboratory Practices		

HDGT	Heavy-Duty Gasoline Truck	HWRTF	Hazardous Waste Restrictions Task Force
HDGV	Heavy-Duty Gasoline Vehicle	HWTC	Hazardous Waste Treatment Council
HDPE	High Density Polyethylene	I/A	Innovative/Alternative
HDT	Highest Dose Tested in a study. Heavy-Duty Truck	IA	Interagency Agreement
HDV	Heavy-Duty Vehicle	IAAC	Interagency Assessment Advisory Committee
HEAL	Human Exposure Assessment Location	IAC	Innovative Action Council
HECC	House Energy and Commerce Committee	IADN	Integrated Atmospheric Deposition Network
HEI	Health Effects Institute	IAG	Interagency Agreement
HEM	Human Exposure Modeling	IAP	Incentive Awards Program. Indoor Air Pollution
HEPA	High-Efficiency Particulate Air	IAQ	Indoor Air Quality
HEPA	Highly Efficient Particulate Air Filter	IARC	International Agency for Research on Cancer
HERS	Hyperion Energy Recovery System	IATDB	Interim Air Toxics Data Base
HFC	Hydrofluorocarbon	IBSIN	Innovations in Building Sustainable Industries
HHDDV	Heavy Heavy-Duty Diesel Vehicle	IBT	Industrial Biotest Laboratory
HHE	Human Health and the Environment	IC	Internal Combustion
HHV	Higher Heating Value	ICAIR	Interdisciplinary Planning and Information Research
HI	Hazard Index	ICAP	Inductively Coupled Argon Plasma
HI-VOL	High-Volume Sampler	ICB	Information Collection Budget
HIWAY	A Line Source Model for Gaseous Pollutants	ICBN	International Commission on the Biological Effects of Noise
HLRW	High Level Radioactive Waste	ICCP	International Climate Change Partnership
HMIS	Hazardous Materials Information System	ICDS	Inspection Conclusion Data Sheet
HMS	Highway Mobile Source	ICE	Industrial Combustion Emissions Model. Internal Combustion Engine
HMTA	Hazardous Materials Transportation Act	ICIS	Integrated Compliance Information System
HMTR	Hazardous Materials Transportation Regulations	ICIS - NPDES	Integrated Compliance Information System – National Pollutant Discharge Elimination System
HOC	Halogenated Organic Carbons	ICP	Inductively Coupled Plasma
HON	Hazardous Organic NESHAP	ICR	Information Collection Request
HOV	High-Occupancy Vehicle	ICRE	Ignitability, Corrosivity, Reactivity, Extraction
HP	Horse Power	ICRP	International Commission on Radiological Protection
HPLC	High-Performance Liquid Chromatography	ICRU	International Commission of Radiological Units and Measurements
HPMS	Highway Performance Monitoring System	ICS	Incident Command System. Institute for Chemical Studies; Intermittent Control Strategies.; Intermittent Control System
HPV	High Priority Violator		
HQ	Headquarters		
HQCDO	Headquarters Case Development Officer		
HRS	Hazardous Ranking System		
HRUP	High-Risk Urban Problem	ICWM	Institute for Chemical Waste Management
HSDB	Hazardous Substance Data Base		
HSL	Hazardous Substance List	IDEA	Integrated Data for Enforcement Analysis
HSWA	Hazardous and Solid Waste Amendments		
HT	Hypothermally Treated	IDLH	Immediately Dangerous to Life and Health
HTP	High Temperature and Pressure		
HUD	Housing and Urban Development		
HVAC	Heating, Ventilation, and Air-Conditioning system		
HVIO	High Volume Industrial Organics		
HW	Hazardous Waste		
HWDMS	Hazardous Waste Data Management System		
HWGTF	Hazardous Waste Groundwater Task Force; Hazardous Waste Groundwater Test Facility		
HWIR	Hazardous Waste Identification Rule		
HWLT	Hazardous Waste Land Treatment		
HWM	Hazardous Waste Management		

IEB	International Environment Bureau	IRR	Institute of Resource Recovery
IEMP	Integrated Environmental Management Project	IRS	International Referral Systems
		IS	Interim Status
IES	Institute for Environmental Studies	ISAM	Indexed Sequential File Access Method
IFB	Invitation for Bid	ISC	Industrial Source Complex
IFCAM	Industrial Fuel Choice Analysis Model	ISCL	Interim Status Compliance Letter
IFCS	International Forum on Chemical Safety	ISCLT	Industrial Source Complex Long Term Model
IFIS	Industry File Information System		
IFMS	Integrated Financial Management System	ISCST	Industrial Source Complex Short Term Model
IFPP	Industrial Fugitive Process Particulate	ISD	Interim Status Document
IG	Inspector General	ISE	Ion-specific electrode
IGCC	Integrated Gasification Combined Cycle	ISMAP	Indirect Source Model for Air Pollution
IGCI	Industrial Gas Cleaning Institute	ISO	International Organization for Standardization
IINERT	In-Place Inactivation and Natural Restoration Technologies	ISPF	(IBM) Interactive System Productivity Facility
IIS	Inflationary Impact Statement	ISS	Interim Status Standards
IJC	International Joint Commission (on Great Lakes)	ITC	Innovative Technology Council
		ITC	Interagency Testing Committee
I/M	Inspection/Maintenance	ITRC	Interstate Technology Regulatory Coordination
IMM	Intersection Midblock Model	ITRD	Innovative Treatment Remediation Demonstration
IMPACT	Integrated Model of Plumes and Atmosphere in Complex Terrain		
		IU	Industrial Users (non-domestic)
IMPROVE	Interagency Monitoring of Protected Visual Environment	IUP	Intended Use Plan
		IUR	Inventory Update Rule
INECE	International Network for Environmental Compliance and Enforcement	IWC	In-Stream Waste Concentration
		IWS	Ionizing Wet Scrubber
INPUFF	Gaussian Puff Dispersion Model	JAPCA	Journal of Air Pollution Control Association
INT	Intermittent	JCL	Job Control Language
IOB	Iron Ore Beneficiation	JEC	Joint Economic Committee
IOU	Input/Output Unit	JECFA	Joint Expert Committee of Food Additives
IPCS	International Program on Chemical Safety	JEIOG	Joint Emissions Inventory Oversight Group
		JLC	Justification for Limited Competition
IP	Inhalable Particles	JMPR	Joint Meeting on Pesticide Residues
IPCC	Intergovernmental Panel on Climate Change	JNCP	Justification for Non-Competitive Procurement
IPM	Inhalable Particulate Matter; Integrated Pest Management	JOFOC	Justification for Other Than Full and Open Competition
IPOD	ICIS Policy on Demand	JPA	Joint Permitting Agreement
IPP	Implementation Planning Program. Integrated Plotting Package; Inter-media Priority Pollutant (document); Independent Power Producer	JSD	Jackson Structured Design
		JSP	Jackson Structured Programming
		JTU	Jackson Turbidity Unit
		LAA	Lead Agency Attorney
IRG	Interagency Review Group	LADD	Lifetime Average Daily Dose; Lowest Acceptable Daily Dose
IRIS	Instructional Resources Information System; Integrated Risk Information System		
		LAER	Lowest Achievable Emission Rate
IRLG	Interagency Regulatory Liaison Group (Composed of EPA, CPSC, FDA, and OSHA)	LAI	Laboratory Audit Inspection
		LAMP	Lake Acidification Mitigation Project
		LBP	Lead-Based Paint
IRM	Intermediate Remedial Measures	LC	Lethal Concentration. Liquid Chromatography
IRMC	Inter-Regulatory Risk Management Council		
		LCA	Life Cycle Assessment
IRP	Installation Restoration Program	LCD	Local Climatological Data
IRPTC	International Register of Potentially Toxic Chemicals	LCL	Lower Control Limit
		LCM	Life Cycle Management

LCRS	Leachate Collection and Removal System	MEC	Model Energy Code
LD	Land Disposal. Light Duty	MEI	Maximally (or most) Exposed Individual
LD L0	The lowest dosage of a toxic substance that kills test organisms.	MEP	Multiple Extraction Procedure
LDAR	Leak Detection and Repair	MHDDV	Medium Heavy-Duty Diesel Vehicle
LDC	London Dumping Convention	MOA	Memorandum of Agreement
LDCRS	Leachate Detection, Collection, and Removal System	MOBILE5A	Mobile Source Emission Factor Model
LDD	Light-Duty Diesel	MOE	Margin of Exposure
LDDT	Light-Duty Diesel Truck	MOS	Margin of Safety
LDDV	Light-Duty Diesel Vehicle	MP	Manufacturing-Use Product; Melting Point
LDGT	Light-Duty Gasoline Truck	MPCA	Microbial Pest Control Agent
LDIP	Laboratory Data Integrity Program	MPI	Maximum Permitted Intake
LDR	Land Disposal Restrictions	MPN	Maximum Possible Number
LDRTF	Land Disposal Restrictions Task Force	MPWC	Multiprocess Wet Cleaning
LDS	Leak Detection System	MRBMA	Mercury-Containing and Rechargeable Battery Management Act
LDT	Lowest Dose Tested. Light-Duty Truck	MRF	Materials Recovery Facility
LDV	Light-Duty Vehicle	MRID	Master Record Identification number
LEA	Local Education Authority	MRL	Maximum-Residue Limit (Pesticide Tolerance)
LEL	Lowest Effect Level. Lower Explosive Limit	MS4	Municipal Separate Storm Sewer System
LEP	Laboratory Evaluation Program	MSW	Municipal Solid Waste
LEPC	Local Emergency Planning Committee	MTBE	Methyl tertiary butyl ether
LERC	Local Emergency Response Committee	MTD	Maximum Tolerated Dose
LEV	Low Emissions Vehicle	MUP	Manufacturing-Use Product
LFG	Landfill Gas	MUTA	Mutagenicity
LFL	Lower Flammability Limit	MWC	Machine Wet Cleaning
LGEAN	Local Government Environmental Assistance Network	NAA	Nonattainment Area
LGR	Local Governments Reimbursement Program	NAAEC	North American Agreement on Environmental Cooperation
LHDDV	Light Heavy-Duty Diesel Vehicle	NAAQS	National Ambient Air Quality Standards
LI	Langelier Index	NACA	National Agricultural Chemicals Association
LIDAR	Light Detection and Ranging	NACEPT	National Advisory Council for Environmental Policy and Technology
LIMB	Limestone-Injection Multi-Stage Burner	NADP/NTN	National Atmospheric Deposition Program/National Trends Network
LLRW	Low Level Radioactive Waste	NAMS	National Air Monitoring Stations
LMFBR	Liquid Metal Fast Breeder Reactor	NAPAP	National Acid Precipitation Assessment Program
LMOP	Landfill Methane Outreach Program	NAPL	Non-Aqueous Phase Liquid
LNAPL	Light Non-Aqueous Phase Liquid	NAPS	National Air Pollution Surveillance
LOAEL	Lowest-Observed-Adverse-Effect-Level	NARA	National Agrichemical Retailers Association
LOD	Limit of Detection	NARSTO	North American Research Strategy for Tropospheric Ozone
LQER	Lesser Quantity Emission Rates	NAS	National Academy of Sciences
LQG	Large Quantity Generator	NASA	National Aeronautics and Space Administration
LRTAP	Long Range Transboundary Air Pollution	NASDA	National Association of State Departments of Agriculture
LUIS	Label Use Information System	NCAMP	National Coalition Against the Misuse of Pesticides
MAC	Mobile Air Conditioner		
MACT	Maximum Achievable Control Technology		
MAPSIM	Mesoscale Air Pollution Simulation Model		
MATC	Maximum Acceptable Toxic Concentration		
MBAS	Methylene-Blue-Active Substances		
MCL	Maximum Contaminant Level		
MCLG	Maximum Contaminant Level Goal		
MCS	Multiple Chemical Sensitivity		
MDL	Method Detection Limit		
MDR	Minimum Data Requirements		

NCEPI	National Center for Environmental Publications and Information	NRC	National Response Center
NCWS	Non-Community Water System	NRD	Natural Resource Damage
NEDS	National Emissions Data System	NRDC	Natural Resources Defense Council
NEIC	National Enforcement Investigations Center	NSDWR	National Secondary Drinking Water Regulations
NEJAC	National Environmental Justice Advisory Council	NSEC	National System for Emergency Coordination
NEPA	National Environmental Policy Act	NSEP	National System for Emergency Preparedness
NEPI	National Environmental Policy Institute	NSPS	New Source Performance Standards
NEPPS	National Environmental Performance Partnership System	NSR	New Source Review
NESHAP	National Emission Standard for Hazardous Air Pollutants	NSR/PSD	National Source Review/Prevention of Significant Deterioration
NIEHS	National Institute for Environmental Health Sciences	NTI	National Toxics Inventory
		NTIS	National Technical Information Service
NETA	National Environmental Training Association	NTNCWS	Non-Transient Non-Community Water System
NETI	National Enforcement Training Institute	NTP	National Toxicology Program; National Training Plan
NFRAP	No Further Remedial Action Planned		
NICT	National Incident Coordination Team	NTU	Nephlometric Turbidity Unit
NIOSH	National Institute of Occupational Safety and Health	O_3	Ozone
		OAM	Operation and Maintenance
NIPDWR	National Interim Primary Drinking Water Regulations	OAP	Office of Administration and Policy
		OAQPS	Office of Air Quality Planning and Standards
NISAC	National Industrial Security Advisory Committee	OC	Office of Compliance
NMHC	Nonmethane Hydrocarbons	OCD	Offshore and Coastal Dispersion
NMOC	Non-Methane Organic Component	OCE	Office of Civil Enforcement
NMVOC	Non-methane Volatile Organic Chemicals	OCEFT	Office of Criminal Enforcement, Forensics and Training
NO	Nitric Oxide		
NO_2	Nitrogen Dioxide	OCFO	Office of Chief Financial Officer
NOA	Notice of Arrival	OCIR	Office of Congressional and Intergovernmental Relations
NOAA	National Oceanographic and Atmospheric Agency		
		ODP	Ozone-Depleting Potential
NOAC	Nature of Action Code	ODS	Ozone-Depleting Substances
NOAEL	No Observable Adverse Effect Level	OECA	Office of Enforcement and Compliance Assurance
NOEL	No Observable Effect Level		
NOIC	Notice of Intent to Cancel	OECD	Organization for Economic Cooperation and Development
NOIS	Notice of Intent to Suspend		
N_2O	Nitrous Oxide	OEJ	Office of Environmental Justice
NOV	Notice of Violation	OF	Optional Form
NO_x	Nitrogen Oxides	OGD	Office of Grants and Disbarment
NORM	Naturally Occurring Radioactive Material	OI	Order for Information
NPCA	National Pest Control Association>	OIG	Office of the Inspector General
NPDES	National Pollutant Discharge Elimination System	OLC	Office of Legal Counsel
		OLTS	On-Line Tracking System
NPHAP	National Pesticide Hazard Assessment Program	O&M	Operations and Maintenance
		OMB	Office of Management and Budget
NPIRS	National Pesticide Information Retrieval System	OPP	Office of Pesticide Programs
		OPPTS	Office of Prevention, Pesticides, and Toxic Substances
NPL	National Priorities List		
NPM	National Program Manager	ORE	Office of Regulatory Enforcement
NPMS	National Performance Measures Strategy	ORM	Other Regulated Material
NPTN	National Pesticide Telecommunications Network	ORP	Oxidation-Reduction Potential
		OTAG	Ozone Transport Assessment Group

OTC	Ozone Transport Commission
OTIS	Online Tracking Information System
OTR	Ozone Transport Region
P2	Pollution Prevention
PAG	Pesticide Assignment Guidelines
PAH	Polynuclear Aromatic Hydrocarbons
PAI	Performance Audit Inspection (CWA); Pure Active Ingredient compound
PAM	Pesticide Analytical Manual
PAMS	Photochemical Assessment Monitoring Stations
PAT	Permit Assistance Team (RCRA)
PATS	Pesticide Action Tracking System; Pesticides Analytical Transport Solution
Pb	Lead
PBA	Preliminary Benefit Analysis (BEAD)
PBT	Persistent Bio-Accumulative Toxics
PCA	Principle Component Analysis
PCB	Polychlorinated Biphenyl
PCE	Perchloroethylene; Partial Compliance Evaluation
PCM	Phase Contrast Microscopy
PCN	Policy Criteria Notice
PCO	Pest Control Operator
PCS	Permit Compliance System
PCSD	President's Council on Sustainable Development
PDCI	Product Data Call-In
PEI	Production Establishment Inspections
PFA	Preliminary Financial Assessments
PFC	Perfluorated Carbon
PFCRA	Program Fraud Civil Remedies Act
PHC	Principal Hazardous Constituent
PHI	Pre-Harvest Interval
PHSA	Public Health Service Act
PI	Preliminary Injunction. Program Information
PIC	Products of Incomplete Combustion
PIGS	Pesticides in Groundwater Strategy
PIMS	Pesticide Incident Monitoring System
PIN	Pesticide Information Network
PIN	Procurement Information Notice
PIP	Public Involvement Program
PIPQUIC	Program Integration Project Queries Used in Interactive Command
PIRG	Public Interest Research Group
PIRT	Pretreatment Implementation Review Task Force
PIT	Permit Improvement Team
PITS	Project Information Tracking System
PLIRRA	Pollution Liability Insurance and Risk Retention Act
PLM	Polarized Light Microscopy
PLUVUE	Plume Visibility Model
PM	Particulate Matter
PMAS	Photochemical Assessment Monitoring Stations
PM2.5	Particulate Matter Smaller than 2.5 Micrometers in Diameter
PM10	Particulate Matter (nominally 10m and less)
PM15	Particulate Matter (nominally 15m and less)
PMEL	Pacific Marine Environmental Laboratory
PMN	Premanufacture Notification
PMNF	Premanufacture Notification Form
PMR	Pollutant Mass Rate
PMR	Proportionate Mortality Ratio
PMRS	Performance Management and Recognition System
PMS	Program Management System
PNA	Polynuclear Aromatic Hydrocarbons
PO	Project Officer
POC	Point Of Compliance
POE	Point Of Exposure
POGO	Privately-Owned/ Government-Operated
POHC	Principal Organic Hazardous Constituent
POI	Point Of Interception
POLREP	Pollution Report
POM	Particulate Organic Matter. Polycyclic Organic Matter
POP	Persistent Organic Pollutant
POR	Program of Requirements
POTW	Publicly Owned Treatment Works
POV	Privately Owned Vehicle
PP	Program Planning
PPA	Planned Program Accomplishment; Performance Partnership Agreement
PPB	Parts Per Billion
PPE	Personal Protective Equipment
PPG	Performance Partnership Grant
PPIC	Pesticide Programs Information Center
PPIS	Pesticide Product Information System; Pollution Prevention Incentives for States
PPMAP	Power Planning Modeling Application Procedure
PPM/PPB	Parts per million/ parts per billion
PPSP	Power Plant Siting Program
PPT	Parts Per Trillion
PPTH	Parts Per Thousand
PQUA	Preliminary Quantitative Usage Analysis
PR	Pesticide Regulation Notice; Preliminary Review
PRA	Paperwork Reduction Act; Planned Regulatory Action
PRATS	Pesticides Regulatory Action Tracking System
PRC	Planning Research Corporation
PRI	Periodic Reinvestigation
PRM	Prevention Reference Manuals

PRN	Pesticide Registration Notice	RACM	Reasonably Available Control Measures
PRP	Potentially Responsible Party	RACT	Reasonably Available Control Technology
PRZM	Pesticide Root Zone Model	RAD	Radiation Adsorbed Dose (unit of measurement of radiation absorbed by humans)
PS	Point Source		
PSAM	Point Source Ambient Monitoring		
PSC	Program Site Coordinator	RADM	Random Walk Advection and Dispersion Model; Regional Acid Deposition Model
PSD	Prevention of Significant Deterioration		
PSES	Pretreatment Standards for Existing Sources	RAM	Urban Air Quality Model for Point and Area Source in EPA UNAMAP Series
PSI	Pollutant Standards Index; Pounds Per Square Inch; Pressure Per Square Inch		
		RAMP	Rural Abandoned Mine Program
PSIG	Pressure Per Square Inch Gauge	RAMS	Regional Air Monitoring System
PSM	Point Source Monitoring	RAP	Radon Action Program; Registration Assessment Panel; Remedial Accomplishment Plan; Response Action Plan
PSNS	Pretreatment Standards for New Sources		
PSU	Primary Sampling Unit		
PTDIS	Single Stack Meteorological Model in EPA UNAMAP Series	RAPS	Regional Air Pollution Study
		RARG	Regulatory Analysis Review Group
PTE	Potential to Emit	RAS	Routine Analytical Service
PTFE	Polytetrafluoroethylene (Teflon)	RAT	Relative Accuracy Test
PTMAX	Single Stack Meteorological Model in EPA UNAMAP series	RB	Request for Bid
		RBAC	Re-use Business Assistance Center
PTPLU	Point Source Gaussian Diffusion Model	RBC	Red Blood Cell
PUC	Public Utility Commission	RC	Responsibility Center
PV	Project Verification	RCC	Radiation Coordinating Council
PVC	Polyvinyl Chloride	RCDO	Regional Case Development Officer
PWB	Printed Wiring Board	RCO	Regional Compliance Officer
PWS	Public Water Supply/ System	RCP	Research Centers Program
PWSS	Public Water Supply System; Public Water System Supervision	RCRA	Resource Conservation and Recovery Act
QAC	Quality Assurance Coordinator	RCRAInfo	Resource Conservation and Recovery Act Information
QA/QC	Quality Assistance/ Quality Control		
QAMIS	Quality Assurance Management and Information System	RCRIS	Resource Conservation and Recovery Information System
QAO	Quality Assurance Officer	RD/RA	Remedial Design/ Remedial Action
QAPP	Quality Assurance Program (or Project) Plan	R&D	Research and Development
		RD&D	Research, Development and Demonstration
QAT	Quality Action Team		
QBTU	Quadrillion British Thermal Units	RDF	Refuse-Derived Fuel
QC	Quality Control	RDNA	Recombinant DNA
QCA	Quiet Communities Act	RDU	Regional Decision Units
QCI	Quality Control Index	RDV	Reference Dose Values
QCP	Quiet Community Program	RE	Reasonable Efforts; Reportable Event
QL	Quantification Limit	REAP	Regional Enforcement Activities Plan
QNCR	Quarterly Noncompliance Report	RECAP	Regional Enforcement and Compliance Assurance Program
QUA	Qualitative Use Assessment		
QUIPE	Quarterly Update for Inspector in Pesticide Enforcement	RECLAIM	Regional Clean Air Initiatives Marker
		RED	Reregistration Eligibility Decision Document
RA	Reasonable Alternative; Regulatory Alternatives; Regulatory Analysis; Remedial Action; Resource Allocation; Risk Analysis; Risk Assessment		
		REDA	Recycling Economic Development Advocate
		REE	Rare Earth Elements
RAATS	RCRA Administrate Action Tracking System	REEP	Review of Environmental Effects of Pollutants
		ReFIT	Reinvention for Innovative Technologies
RAC	Radiation Advisory Committee. Raw Agricultural Commodity; Regional Asbestos Coordinator. Response Action Coordinator	REI	Restricted Entry Interval
		REM	Roentgen Equivalent Man

REM/FIT	Remedial/Field Investigation Team	ROP	Rate of Progress; Regional Oversight Policy
REMS	RCRA Enforcement Management System	ROPA	Record Of Procurement Action
REP	Reasonable Efforts Program	ROSA	Regional Ozone Study Area
REPS	Regional Emissions Projection System	RP	Radon Progeny Integrated Sampling; Respirable Particulates; Responsible Party
RESOLVE	Center for Environmental Conflict Resolution	RPAR	Rebuttable Presumption Against Registration
RF	Response Factor		
RFA	Regulatory Flexibility Act	RPM	Reactive Plume Model; Remedial Project Manager
RFB	Request for Bid		
RfC	Reference Concentration	RQ	Reportable Quantities
RFD	Reference Dose Values	RRC	Regional Response Center
RFI	Remedial Field Investigation	RR+P	Renovation, Repair and Painting
RFP	Reasonable Further Programs; Request for Proposal	RRT	Regional Response Team; Requisite Remedial Technology
RHRS	Revised Hazard Ranking System	RS	Registration Standard
RI	Reconnaissance Inspection	RSCC	Regional Sample Control Center
RI	Remedial Investigation	RSD	Risk-Specific Dose
RIA	Regulatory Impact Analysis; Regulatory Impact Assessment	RSE	Removal Site Evaluation
		RTCM	Reasonable Transportation Control Measure
RIC	Radon Information Center		
RICC	Retirement Information and Counseling Center	RTDF	Remediation Technologies Development Forum
RICO	Racketeer Influenced and Corrupt Organizations Act	RTDM	Rough Terrain Diffusion Model
		RTECS	Registry of Toxic Effects of Chemical Substances
RI/FS	Remedial Investigation/ Feasibility Study	RTM	Regional Transport Model
RIM	Regulatory Interpretation Memorandum	RTP	Research Triangle Park
		RUP	Restricted Use Pesticide
RIN	Regulatory Identifier Number	RVP	Reid Vapor Pressure
RIP	RCRA Implementation Plan	RWC	Residential Wood Combustion
RISC	Regulatory Information Service Center	S&A	Sampling and Analysis; Surveillance and Analysis
RJE	Remote Job Entry	SAAP	Special Appropriations Act Projects
RLL	Rapid and Large Leakage (Rate)	SAB	Science Advisory Board
RMCL	Recommended Maximum Contaminant Level (this phrase being discontinued in favor of MCLG)	SAC	Suspended and Cancelled Pesticides; Special Agent-in-Charge
		SAEWG	Standing Air Emissions Work Group
RMDHS	Regional Model Data Handling System	SAIC	Special-Agents-In-Charge
		SAIP	Systems Acquisition and Implementation Program
RMIS	Resources Management Information System		
		SAMI	Southern Appalachian Mountains Initiative
RMP	Risk Management Plan		
RNA	Ribonucleic Acid	SAMWG	Standing Air Monitoring Work Group
ROADCHEM	Roadway Version that Includes Chemical Reactions of BI, NO_2, and O_3	SANE	Sulfur and Nitrogen Emissions
		SANSS	Structure and Nomenclature Search System
ROADWAY	A Model to Predict Pollutant Concentrations Near a Roadway	SAP	Scientific Advisory Panel
ROC	Record Of Communication	SAR	Start Action Request; Structural Activity Relationship (of a qualitative assessment)
RODS	Records Of Decision System		
ROG	Reactive Organic Gases	SARA	Superfund Amendments and Reauthorization Act of 1986
ROLLBACK	A Proportional Reduction Model		
ROM	Regional Oxidant Model	SAROAD	Storage and Retrieval Of Aerometric Data
ROMCOE	Rocky Mountain Center on Environment	SAS	Special Analytical Service; Statistical Analysis System

SASS	Source Assessment Sampling System
SAV	Submerged Aquatic Vegetation
SBC	Single Breath Cannister
SC	Sierra Club
SCAP	Superfund Consolidated Accomplishments Plan
SCBA	Self-Contained Breathing Apparatus
SCC	Source Classification Code
SCD/SWDC	Soil or Soil and Water Conservation District
SCFM	Standard Cubic Feet Per Minute
SCLDF	Sierra Club Legal Defense Fund
SCR	Selective Catalytic Reduction
SCRAM	State Consolidated RCRA Authorization Manual
SCRC	Superfund Community Relations Coordinator
SCS	Supplementary Control Strategy/System
SCSA	Soil Conservation Society of America
SCSP	Storm and Combined Sewer Program
SCW	Supercritical Water Oxidation
SDC	Systems Decision Plan
SDWA	Safe Drinking Water Act
SDWIS	Safe Drinking Water Information System
SDWIS/ODS	Safe Drinking Water Information System/Operational Data System
SBS	Sick Building Syndrome
SEA	State Enforcement Agreement
SEA	State/EPA Agreement
SEAM	Surface, Environment, and Mining
SEAS	Strategic Environmental Assessment System
SEC	Securities and Exchange Commission
SEDS	State Energy Data System
SEE	Senior Environmental Employment
SEGIP	State Environmental Goals and Improvement Project
SEIA	Socioeconomic Impact Analysis
SEM	Standard Error of the Means
SEP	Standard Evaluation Procedures; Supplementary Environmental Project
SEPWC	Senate Environment and Public Works Committee
SERC	State Emergency Planning Commission
SES	Secondary Emissions Standard
SETAC	Society for Environmental Toxicology and Chemistry
SETS	Site Enforcement Tracking System
SF	Standard Form. Superfund
SFA	Spectral Flame Analyzers
SFDS	Sanitary Facility Data System
SFFAS	Superfund Financial Assessment System
SFIP	Sector Facility Indexing Project
SFIREG	State FIFRA Issues Research and Evaluation Group
SFS	State Funding Study
SGTM	State Grant Template Measures
SHORTZ	Short-Term Terrain Model
SHWL	Seasonal High Water Level
SI	International System of Units. Site Inspection. Surveillance Index. Spark Ignition
SIC	Standard Industrial Classification
SICEA	Steel Industry Compliance Extension Act
SIMS	Secondary Ion-Mass Spectrometry
SIP	State Implementation Plan
SITE	Superfund Innovative Technology Evaluation
SITS	Strategy Implementation Teams
SJVAPCD	San Joaquin Valley Air Pollution Control District
SLAMS	State/Local Air Monitoring Station
SLN	Special Local Need
SLPD	Special Litigation and Projects Division
SLSM	Simple Line Source Model
SM	Synthetic Minor
SMART	Simple Maintenance of ARTS
SMCL	Secondary Maximum Contaminant Level
SMCRA	Surface Mining Control and Reclamation Act
SME	Subject Matter Expert
SMO	Sample Management Office
SMOA	Superfund Memorandum of Agreement
SMP	State Management Plan
SMR	Standardized Mortality Ratio
SMSA	Standard Metropolitan Statistical Area
SNA	System Network Architecture
SNAAQS	Secondary National Ambient Air Quality Standards
SNAP	Significant New Alternatives Project; Significant Noncompliance Action Program
SNARL	Suggested No Adverse Response Level
SNC	Significant Noncompliers; Significant Noncompliance
SNUR	Significant New Use Rule
SNY	SNC Yes
SO_2	Sulfur Dioxide
SOC	Synthetic Organic Chemicals; Significant Operational Compliance
SOCMI	Synthetic Organic Chemicals Manufacturing Industry
SOFC	Solid Oxide Fuel Cell
SOTDAT	Source Test Data
SOW	Scope Of Work
SPAR	Status of Permit Application Report
SPCC	Spill Prevention, Containment, and Countermeasure
SPE	Secondary Particulate Emissions

SPF	Structured Programming Facility	STP	Sewage Treatment Plant; Standard Temperature and Pressure
SPI	Strategic Planning Initiative		
SPLMD	Soil-pore Liquid Monitoring Device	STTF	Small Town Task Force (EPA)
SPMS	Strategic Planning and Management System; Special Purpose Monitoring Stations	SUP	Standard Unit of Processing
		SURE	Sulfate Regional Experiment Program
		SV	Sampling Visit; Significant Violater
SPOC	Single Point Of Contact	SW	Slow Wave
SPS	State Permit System	SWAP	Source Water Assessment Program
SPSS	Statistical Package for the Social Sciences	SWARF	Waste from Metal Grinding Process
		SWC	Settlement with Conditions
SPUR	Software Package for Unique Reports	SWDA	Solid Waste Disposal Act
SQBE	Small Quantity Burner Exemption	SWIE	Southern Waste Information Exchange
SQG	Small Quantity Generator	SWMU	Solid Waste Management Unit
SR	Special Review	SWPA	Source Water Protection Area
SRAP	Superfund Remedial Accomplishment Plan	SWPPP	Stormwater Pollution Prevention Plan
		SWQPPP	Source Water Quality Protection Partnership Petitions
SRC	Solvent-Refined Coal		
SRF	State Revolving Fund; State Review Framework	SWTR	Surface Water Treatment Rule
		SYSOP	Systems Operator
SRM	Standard Reference Method	TAD	Technical Assistance Document
SRP	Special Review Procedure	TAG	Technical Assistance Grant
SRR	Second Round Review; Submission Review Record	TALMS	Tunable Atomic Line Molecular Spectroscopy
SRTS	Service Request Tracking System	TAMS	Toxic Air Monitoring System
SS	Settleable Solids; Superfund Surcharge; Suspended Solids	TAMTAC	Toxic Air Monitoring System Advisory Committee
SSA	Sole Source Aquifer	TAP	Technical Assistance Program
SSAC	Soil Site Assimilated Capacity	TAPDS	Toxic Air Pollutant Data System
SSC	State Superfund Contracts	TAS	Tolerance Assessment System
SSD	Standards Support Document	TBT	Tributyltin
SSEIS	Standard Support and Environmental Impact Statement; Stationary Source Emissions and Inventory System	TC	Target Concentration; Technical Center. Toxicity Characteristics; Toxic Concentration
SSI	Size Selective Inlet	TCDD	Dioxin (Tetrachlorodibenzo-p-dioxin)
SSMS	Spark Source Mass Spectrometry	TCDF	Tetrachlorodi-benzofurans
SSO	Sanitary Sewer Overflow; Source Selection Official	TCE	Trichloroethylene
		TCF	Total Chlorine Free
SSRP	Source Reduction Review Project	TCLP	Total Concentrate Leachate Procedure; Toxicity Characteristic Leachate Procedure
SSTS	Section Seven Tracking System		
SSURO	Stop Sale, Use and Removal Order	TCM	Transportation Control Measure
STAG	State and Tribal Assistance Grant	TCP	Transportation Control Plan; Trichloropropane;
STALAPCO	State and Local Air-Pollution Control Officials		
		TCRI	Toxic Chemical Release Inventory
STAPPA	State and Territorial Air Pollution	TD	Toxic Dose
STAR	Stability Wind Rose; State Acid Rain Projects	TDS	Total Dissolved Solids
		TEAM	Total Exposure Assessment Model
STARS	Strategic Targeted Activities for Results System	TEC	Technical Evaluation Committee
		TED	Turtle Excluder Devices
STEL	Short Term Exposure Limit	TEG	Tetraethylene Glycol
STEM	Scanning Transmission-Electron Microscope	TEGD	Technical Enforcement Guidance Document
STN	Scientific and Technical Information Network	TEL	Tetraethyl Lead
		TEM	Texas Episodic Model
STORET	Storage and Retrieval of Water-Related Data	TEP	Typical End-Use Product; Technical Evaluation Panel

TERA	TSCA Environmental Release Application
TES	Technical Enforcement Support
TEXIN	Texas Intersection Air Quality Model
TGO	Total Gross Output
TGAI	Technical Grade of the Active Ingredient
TGP	Technical Grade Product
THC	Total Hydrocarbons
THM	Trihalomethane
TI	Temporary Intermittent
TI	Therapeutic Index
TIBL	Thermal Internal Boundary Layer
TIC	Technical Information Coordinator. Tentatively Identified Compounds
TIM	Technical Information Manager
TIP	Technical Information Package
TIP	Transportation Improvement Program
TIS	Tolerance Index System
TISE	Take It Somewhere Else
TITC	Toxic Substance Control Act Interagency Testing Committee
TLV	Threshold Limit Value
TLV-C	TLV-Ceiling
TLV-STEL	TLV-Short Term Exposure Limit
TLV-TWA	TLV-Time Weighted Average
TMDL	Total Maximum Daily Limit; Total Maximum Daily Load
TMRC	Theoretical Maximum Residue Contribution
TNCWS	Transient Non-Community Water System
TNT	Trinitrotoluene
TO	Task Order
TOA	Trace Organic Analysis
TOC	Total Organic Carbon/Compound
TOX	Tetradichloroxylene
TP	Technical Product; Total Particulates
TPC	Testing Priorities Committee
TPI	Technical Proposal Instructions
TPQ	Threshold Planning Quantity
TPSIS	Transportation Planning Support Information System
TPTH	Triphenyltinhydroxide
TPY	Tons Per Year
TQM	Total Quality Management
T-R	Transformer-Rectifier
TRC	Technical Review Committee
TRD	Technical Review Document
TRI	Toxic Release Inventory
TRIP	Toxic Release Inventory Program
TRIS	Toxic Chemical Release Inventory System
TRLN	Triangle Research Library Network
TRO	Temporary Restraining Order
TSA	Technical Systems Audit
TSCA	Toxic Substances Control Act
TSCATS	TSCA Test Submissions Database
TSCC	Toxic Substances Coordinating Committee
TSD	Technical Support Document; Treatment, Storage and Disposal
TSDF	Treatment, Storage, and Disposal Facility
TSDG	Toxic Substances Dialogue Group
TSI	Thermal System Insulation
TSM	Transportation System Management
TSO	Time Sharing Option
TSP	Total Suspended Particulates
TSS	Total Suspended (non-filterable) Solids
TTFA	Target Transformation Factor Analysis
TTHM	Total Trihalomethane
TTN	Technology Transfer Network
TTO	Total Toxic Organics
TTY	Teletypewriter
TVA	Tennessee Valley Authority
TVOC	Total Volatile Organic Compounds
TWA	Time Weighted Average
TWS	Transient Water System
UAC	User Advisory Committee
UAM	Urban Airshed Model
UAO	Unilateral Administrative Order
UAPSP	Utility Acid Precipitation Study Program
UAQI	Uniform Air Quality Index
UARG	Utility Air Regulatory Group
UCC	Ultra Clean Coal
UCCI	Urea-Formaldehyde Foam Insulation
UCL	Upper Control Limit
UDMH	Unsymmetrical Dimethyl Hydrazine
UEL	Upper Explosive Limit
UF	Uncertainty Factor
UFL	Upper Flammability Limit
$\mu g/m^3$	Micrograms Per Cubic Meter
UIC	Underground Injection Control
ULEV	Ultra Low Emission Vehicles
UMTRCA	Uranium Mill Tailings Radiation Control Act
UNAMAP	Users' Network for Applied Modeling of Air Pollution
UNECE	United Nations Economic Commission for Europe
UNEP	United Nations Environment Program
UNICOR	trade name of Federal Prison Industries
UPDS	Unified Program Database System
USC	Unified Soil Classification
USDA	United States Department of Agriculture
USDW	Underground Sources of Drinking Water
USFS	United States Forest Service
UST	Underground Storage Tank
UTM	Universal Transverse Mercator
UTP	Urban Transportation Planning
UV	Ultraviolet

UVA, UVB, UVC	Ultraviolet Radiation Bands	WERL	Water Engineering Research Laboratory
UZM	Unsaturated Zone Monitoring	WET	Whole Effluent Toxicity test
VALLEY	Meteorological Model to Calculate Concentrations on Elevated Terrain	WHO	World Health Organization
		WHP	Wellhead Protection Program
VCM	Vinyl Chloride Monomer	WHPA	Wellhead Protection Area
VCP	Voluntary Cleanup Program	WHWT	Water and Hazardous Waste Team
VE	Visual Emissions	WICEM	World Industry Conference on Environmental Management
VEO	Visible Emission Observation		
VHS	Vertical and Horizontal Spread Model	WL	Warning Letter; Working Level (radon measurement)
VHT	Vehicle-Hours of Travel	WLA/TMDL	Wasteload Allocation/Total Maximum Daily Load
VISTTA	Visibility Impairment from Sulfur Transformation and Transport in the Atmosphere	WLM	Working Level Months
		WMO	World Meteorological Organization
VKT	Vehicle Kilometers Traveled	WP	Wettable Powder
VMT	Vehicle Miles Traveled	WPCF	Water Pollution Control Federation
VOC	Volatile Organic Compounds	WQS	Water Quality Standard
VOS	Vehicle Operating Survey	WRC	Water Resources Council
VOST	Volatile Organic Sampling Train	WRDA	Water Resources Development Act
VP	Vapor Pressure	WRI	World Resources Institute
VSD	Virtually Safe Dose	WS	Work Status
VSI	Visual Site Inspection	WSF	Water Soluble Fraction
VSS	Volatile Suspended Solids	WSRA	Wild and Scenic Rivers Act
WA	Work Assignment	WSTB	Water Sciences and Technology Board
WADTF	Western Atmospheric Deposition Task Force	WSTP	Wastewater Sewage Treatment Plant
		WW	Wet Weather
WAP	Waste Analysis Plan	WWEMA	Waste and Wastewater Equipment Manufacturers Association
WAVE	Water Alliances for Environmental Efficiency		
		WWF	World Wildlife Fund
WB	Wet Bulb	WWTP	Wastewater Treatment Plant
WCED	World Commission on Environment and Development	WWTU	Wastewater Treatment Unit
		ZEV	Zero Emissions Vehicle
WDROP	Distribution Register of Organic Pollutants in Water	ZHE	Zero Headspace Extractor
		ZOI	Zone Of Incorporation
WENDB	Water Enforcement National Data Base	ZRL	Zero Risk Level

Equal Opportunities

Administrative Support Workers See "Occupational Categories."

ADR Election Rate Of the total counselings or complaints that received an ADR offer, the election rate represents the percentage that participated in the ADR process.

ADR Offer Rate The percentage of the total counselings or complaints that received an ADR offer.

ADR Participation Rate The percentage of completed counselings or complaints workload where both parties agreed to participate in ADR.

ADR Resolution Rate The percentage of ADR closures that were resolved by either settlement or withdrawal from the EEO process.

Agency Executive agencies as defined in Section 102 of Title 5, U.S. Code (including those with employees and applicants for employment who are paid from nonappropriated funds), the United States Postal Service, the Postal Rate Commission, and those units of the legislative and judicial branches of the Federal government having positions in the competitive service.

Annual Reports Reports required to be submitted to EEOC on agencies affirmative employment program accomplishments pursuant to EEOC Management Directives 715.

Blue Collar Occupational Category Occupations that OPM defines as comprising the trades, crafts, and manual labor (unskilled, semi-skilled, or skilled), including foremen and supervisory positions entailing trade, craft, or laboring experience and knowledge as the paramount requirement.

Central Personnel Data File (CPDF) This is a computer file created and maintained by the OPM. The file is based on personnel action information submitted directly to the OPM by federal agency appointing offices, and is updated monthly. The following agencies do not submit data to the CPDF: the Tennessee Valley Authority, United States Postal Service, Army and Air Force Exchange Service, Central Intelligence Agency, Defense Intelligence Agency, National Imagery and Mapping Agency, and the National Security Agency.

Civilian Labor Force (CLF) Data derived from the decennial census reflecting persons, 16 years of age or older who were employed or seeking employment, excluding those in the Armed Services. CLF data used in this report is based on the 2000 Census.

Craft Workers (skilled) See "Occupational Categories." Data from 2000 Census Special EEO File - Data derived from the 2000 decennial census (www.census.gov/eeo2000/).

Disability A physical or mental impairment that substantially limits one or more major life activities.

Federal Wage System Positions Positions OPM classifies as those whose primary duty involves the performance of physical work which requires a knowledge or experience of a trade, craft, or manual-labor work.

General Schedule Positions Positions OPM classifies as those whose primary duty requires knowledge or experience of an administrative, clerical, scientific, artistic, or technical nature.

Laborers (unskilled) See "Occupational Categories."

Lump Sum Payment A single payment made in a settlement which does not identify the portion of the amount paid for backpay, compensatory damages, attorney fees, etc.

Major Occupations The most populous occupations in the Professional and the Administrative categories in an agency.

Merit Decision A decision determining whether or not discrimination occurred.

MD-110 EEO Management Directive 110 provides policies, procedures and guidance relating to the processing of employment discrimination complaints governed by the Commission's regulations in 29 CFR Part 1614.

MD-715 A document describing program responsibilities and reporting requirements relating to agencies' EEO programs.

Occupational Categories The occupational categories for the EEO-9 are as follows:

- **Administrative Support Workers** Includes all clerical-type work regardless of level of difficulty, where the activities are predominantly non-manual though some manual work not directly involved with altering or transporting the products is included. Includes: bookkeepers,

collectors (bills and accounts), messengers and office helpers, office machine operators (including computer), shipping and receiving clerks, stenographers, typists and secretaries, telegraph and telephone operators, legal assistants, and kindred workers.
- **Craft Workers (skilled)** Manual workers of relatively high skill level having a thorough and comprehensive knowledge of the processes involved in their work. Exercise considerable independent judgment and usually receive an extensive period of training. Includes: the building trades, hourly paid supervisors and lead operators who are not members of management, mechanics and repairers, skilled machining occupations, compositors and typesetters, electricians, engravers, painters (construction and maintenance), motion picture projectionists, pattern and model makers, stationary engineers, tailors, arts occupations, hand painters, coaters, bakers, decorating occupations, and kindred workers.
- **Laborers (unskilled)** Workers in manual occupations which generally require no special training who perform elementary duties that may be learned in a few days and require the application of little or no independent judgment. Includes: garage laborers, car washers and greasers, grounds keepers and gardeners, farm workers, stevedores, wood choppers, laborers performing lifting, digging, mixing, loading and pulling operations, and kindred workers.
- **Officials and Managers** Occupations requiring administrative and managerial personnel who set broad policies, exercise overall responsibility for execution of these policies, and direct individual offices, programs, divisions or other units or special phases of an agency's operations. In the federal sector, this category is further broken out into four sub-categories: (1) Executive/Senior Level - includes those at the GS-15 grade or in the Senior Executive Service, (2) Mid-Level - includes those at the GS-13 or 14 grade, (3) First-Level - includes those at or below the GS-12 grade and (4) Other - includes employees in a number of different occupations which are primarily business, financial and administrative in nature, and do not have supervisory or significant policy responsibilities, such as Administrative Officers.
- **Operatives (semiskilled)** Workers who operate machine or processing equipment or perform other factory-type duties of intermediate skill level which can be mastered in a few weeks and require only limited training. Includes: apprentices (auto mechanics, plumbers, bricklayers, carpenters, electricians, machinists, mechanics, building trades, printing trades, etc.), operatives, attendants (auto service and parking), blasters, chauffeurs, delivery workers, sewers and stitchers, dryers, furnace workers, heaters, laundry and dry cleaning operatives, milliners, mine operatives and laborers, motor operators, oilers and greasers (except auto), painters (manufactured articles), photographic process workers, truck and tractor drivers, knitting, looping, taping and weaving machine operators, welders and flame cutters, electrical and electronic equipment assemblers, butchers and meat cutters, inspectors, testers and graders, hand packers and packagers, and kindred workers.
- **Professionals** Occupations requiring either college graduation or experience of such kind and amount as to provide a comparable background.
- **Technicians** Occupations requiring a combination of basic scientific knowledge and manual skill which can be obtained through 2 years of post high school education, such as is offered in many technical institutes and junior colleges, or through equivalent on-the- job training.
- **Sales** Occupations engaging wholly or primarily in direct selling.
- **Service Workers** Workers in both protective and non-protective service occupations.

Office and clerical See "Occupational Categories."

Officials and Managers See "Occupational Categories."

Operatives (semiskilled) See "Occupational Categories."

Participation Rate The extent to which members of a specific demographic group participate in an agency's work force.

Permanent Work Force Full-time, part-time and intermittent employees of a particular agency. For purposes of this Report, those persons employed as of September 30, 2003.

Professionals See "Occupational Categories."

Race/Ethnicity
- **White (Not of Hispanic Origin)** All persons having origins in any of the original peoples of Europe, North Africa, or the Middle East.
- **Black (Not of Hispanic Origin)** All persons having origins in any of the black racial groups of Africa.
- **Hispanic** All persons of Mexican, Puerto Rican, Cuban, Central or South American, or other Spanish culture or origin, regardless of race.
- **Asian/Pacific Islander** All persons having origins in any of the original peoples of the Far East, Southeast Asia, the Indian subcontinent, or the

Pacific Islands. This area includes, for example, China, Japan, Korea, the Philippine Islands and Samoa.
- **American Indian/Alaskan Native** All persons having origins in any of the original peoples of North America, and who maintain cultural identification through tribal affiliation or community recognition.

Reportable Disability Any self-identified disability reported by an employee to the employing agency.

Sales Workers See "Occupational Categories."

Second-Level Reporting Component A subordinate component of a Federal agency which has 1,000 or more employees and which is required to file EEOC FORM 715-01 with the EEOC. While many Federal agencies have subordinate components, not every subordinate component is a Second Level Reporting Component for purposes of filing EEOC FORM 715-01. A list of Federal agencies and departments covered by MD-715 and Second Level Reporting Components is posted on EEOC's website at: http://www.eeoc.gov/federal/715instruct/agencylist.html.

Senior Pay Level Civil Service positions above GS 15.

Service Workers See "Occupational Categories."

Targeted Disabilities Those disabilities that the federal government, as a matter of policy, has identified for special emphasis. The targeted disabilities (and the codes that represent them on the Office of Personnel Management's Standard Form 256) are: deafness (16 and 17); blindness (23 and 25); missing extremities (28 and 32 through 38); partial paralysis (64 through 68); complete paralysis (71 through 78); convulsive disorders (82); mental retardation (90); mental illness (91); and distortion of limb and/or spine (92).

Technicians See "Occupational Categories."

Total Work Force All employees of an agency subject to 29 C.F.R. Part 1614 regulations, including temporary, seasonal and permanent employees.

White Collar Employees Those workers in grade levels GS 1 through GS 15 and the Senior Pay Level. This category does not include Blue Collar (Wage Grade) workers.

ACRONYMS

ADA	Americans with Disabilities Act of 1990
ADEA	Age Discrimination in Employment Act of 1967
ADR	Alternate Dispute Resolution
AJ	Administrative Judge
EEO	Equal Employment Opportunity
EEOC	Equal Employment Opportunity Commission
FEPA	Fair Employment Practice Agencies
FLSA	Fair Labor Standards Act
IFMS	Integrated Financial Management System
IMS	Integrated Management System
MDI	Management Development Institute
NFI	New Freedom Initiative
NUAM	National Universal Agreements to Mediate
PMA	President's Management Agenda
TERO	Tribal Employment Rights Offices
UAM	Universal Agreements to Mediate

Family Violence

ABA	American Bar Association	*HIPPA*	Health Insurance Portability Accountability Act of 1996
ACF	Administration for Children and Families	*HHS*	U.S. Department of Health and Human Services
ACYF	Administration on Children, Youth and Families	*ICWA*	Indian Child Welfare Act
ADA	Americans with Disabilities Act	*IDVAAC*	Institute on Domestic Violence in the African American Community
AG	Attorney General	*IPV*	Intimate Partner Violence
APS	Adult Protective Services	*LAV*	Legal Assistance to Victims (Grant Program)
ASFA	Adoption and Safe Families Act		
BIP	Batterer Intervention Program	*LGBT*	Lesbian, Gay, Bi-Sexual, and Transgender (Community)
BJA	Bureau of Justice Assistance		
BJS	Bureau of Justice Statistics	*LE*	Law Enforcement
BWJP	Battered Women's Justice Project	*LEP*	Limited English Proficiency
CAC	Child Advocacy Center	*MOU*	Memorandum of Understanding
CASA	Court Appointed Special Advocate	*NAESV*	National Alliance to End Sexual Violence
CCR	Coordinated Community Response	*NCADV*	National Coalition Against Domestic Violence
CDC	Centers for Disease Control and Prevention		
CFDA	Catalog of Federal Domestic Assistance	*NCJFCJ*	National Council of Juvenile and Family Court Judges
CFR	Code of Federal Regulations		
CPS	Child Protective Services	*NCVC*	National Center for Victims of Crime
DA	District Attorney	*NDVH*	National Domestic Violence Hotline
DELTA	Domestic Violence Prevention Enhancement and Leadership Through Alliances	*NIJ*	National Institute of Justice
		NNEDV	National Network to End Domestic Violence
DFCS	Department of Family and Children's Services		
		NRCDV	National Resource Center on Domestic Violence
DOJ	Department of Justice		
DUNS	Data Universal Numbering System	*OCVA*	Office for Crime Victims Advocacy
DV	Domestic Violence	*OGM*	Office of Grants Management
DVRN	Domestic Violence Resource Network	*OJP*	Office of Justice Programs
ED	Executive Director	*OLDC*	Online Data Collection
EIN	Employer Identification Number	*OMB*	Office of Management and Budget
FFR	Federal Financial Report	*OOP*	Order of Protection
FLSA	Fair Labor Standards Act	*OVC*	Office of Victims of Crime
FOIA	Freedom of Information Act	*OVW*	Office on Violence Against Women
FSR	Financial Status Report	*PO*	Protection Order
FVPSA	Family Violence Prevention and Services Act	*PPR*	Performance Progress Report
		PTSD	Post Traumatic Stress Disorder
FVPSP	Family Violence Prevention and Services Program	*RAINN*	Rape, Abuse and Incest National Network
FY	Fiscal Year	*RFP*	Request for Proposals
FYSB	Family and Youth Services Bureau	*RPE*	Rape Prevention and Education
GAL	Guardian ad Litem	*SA*	Sexual Assault
GAO	Government Accountability Office	*SASP*	Sexual Assault Services Program
GMS	Grants Management System	*SF*	Standard Form
GPO	Government Printing Office		
GPS	Grant Policy Statement		

STOP   Services–Training–Officers–Prosecutors Violence Against Women Formula Grant Program
SV   Sexual Violence
TA   Technical Assistance
TANF   Temporary Aid to Needy Families
TDM   Team Decision-Making
VAWA   Violence Against Women Act
VAWnet   National Online Resource Center on Violence Against Women
VOCA   Victims of Crime Act

Abuse Another term for domestic violence or intimate partner violence. Abuse can also mean child or elder abuse.

Abuser Another term for Batterer or Perpetrator.

Advocate A person who provides advocacy, support, options, resources, and referrals for victims/survivors. Advocates also work on a community and system-level identifying and promoting changes that will improve responses to victims/survivors and their children.

Advocacy For purposes of FVPSA, advocacy is considered any individual or group supportive services provided to adults or children which extend beyond a brief, isolated contact, e.g., crisis intervention, safety planning, individual counseling, peer counseling, educational services. This activity is reported by states on the FVPSA performance progress report.

Allowable Cost A permitted expenditure under the grant funds usually set by Congress or the granting agency (funder). Additionally, the cost must be reasonable for the performance of the award, in conformity with the law, and included in the grant budget.

Application A formal request for financial support of a project, program, or activity submitted on specified forms and in accordance with grant instructions. Sometimes called a grant proposal.

Approved Budget The financial expenditure plan, including any revisions approved by the awarding party for the grant-supported project or activity. The approved budget consists of federal grant funds and non-federal participation and will be specified on the Notice of Grant Award and on any subsequent revised or amended award notice.

Assurances Written and signed agreement(s) that grantee will comply with federal grant requirements if awarded the grant. Assurances are often required to be included with the application.

Authorization Legislation enacted by Congress that establishes or continues the operation of a federal program or authorizes expenditures. Such legislation is normally a prerequisite for subsequent appropriations or other kinds of budget authority to be contained in appropriation acts.

Batterer The person who engages in acts of domestic violence against another person. A batterer is someone who uses physical, emotional, psychological, sexual, and economic abuse and other tactics in order to maintain power and control over their intimate partner.

Batterer Intervention Program (BIP) A program designed to hold people who use violence against their partners accountable for their behavior with the goal of changing the behavior. BIPs are grounded in the understanding of the dynamics of intimate partner violence as opposed to anger management programming, and are considered an important component of an effective community response effort.

Best Practices A standard, technique, or methodology that through research and replication, has been proven valid and reliable. A commitment to using the best practices in any field is a commitment to using all the knowledge and technology at one's disposal to ensure success.

Block Grant For FVPSA, typically an award made by the state to a subgrantee where the dollar amount is set/pre-established and the funds are generally paid on a quarterly, monthly or annual basis.

Budget Period The intervals of time (usually 12 months each) into which a project period is divided for budgetary and funding purposes. Funding of individual budget periods sometimes is referred to as "incremental funding."

Carryover Unobligated federal funds remaining at the end of any budget period that may be carried forward to another budget period to cover allowable costs of that budget period (whether as an offset or additional authorization).

Certifications Documents that confirm certain facts or statements that are signed by an individual with the authority to attest to their truthfulness. For federal funding streams, different certifications are required most often pertaining to lobbying and workplace requirements.

Child Anyone under the age of 18, unless legally emancipated.

Children's Activities A type of activity that states are required to keep count of for FVPSA performance progress reports. Under FVPSA, children's activities are defined as any activity that falls outside of child advocacy, including unplanned/ unstructured contacts such as mentoring, recreational activities, childcare, etc.

Closeout When all administrative actions have been completed, all disputes settled, and final payment has been made under the grant.

Contract A written agreement between a recipient and a third party to acquire commercial goods or services.

Collaborate The process in which individuals and/or organizations share resources and responsibilities jointly to plan, implement, and evaluate programs to achieve common goals. The emphasis is on fundamentally altering traditional agency relationships. Formal collaboration requires individual agencies to commit considerable amounts of resources on behalf of individual agencies. The relationship includes a commitment to mutual relationships and goals; a jointly developed structure and shared responsibility; mutual authority and accountability for success, and sharing of resources and rewards. Such relationships require comprehensive planning and well-defined communication channels operating on many levels.

Competence Acquisition of knowledge, skills, and experience necessary for the development and implementation of services to different groups served.

Community Education Any presentations or training related to intimate partner violence including what resources and services are available to families experiencing domestic violence.

Confidentiality The process of ensuring that information is accessible only to those authorized to have access. Strict confidentiality requirements have been created under VAWA and apply to programs receiving funds authorized under VAWA funds.

Consultant An individual who provides professional advice or services for a fee, but normally not as an employee of the engaging party. The term "consultant" also includes a firm that provides paid professional advice or services.

Co-Occurrence When a child is independently abused or neglected in a family where domestic violence is also occurring. The abuse or neglect may or may not be related to the domestic violence.

Cooperation Cooperation is characterized by informal relationships that exist without any commonly defined mission, structure, or planning efforts. Information is shared as needed, and authority is retained by each organization so there is virtually no risk. Resources are separate as are rewards.

Cooperative Agreement Where money is awarded from the federal government, but such award is made with the understanding that there will be substantial involvement of the federal government in the implementation of the award. The recipient can expect substantial collaboration, participation, and/or intervention in the management of the grant project.

Coordinate To bring entities into causal, complementary, parallel, or reciprocal relationship; to harmonize. Coordination is characterized by formal relationships and understanding of compatible missions. Some planning and division of roles are required, and communication channels are established. Authority still rests with individual organizations, but resources are available to participants and rewards are mutually acknowledged.

Culture The shared values, traditions, norms, customs, arts, history, folklore, and institutions of a group of people that are unified by race, ethnicity, language, nationality, or religion.

Crisis Line /Hotline A dedicated line where calls are received by those who have experience dealing with domestic violence. Under FVPSA, all calls received on an agency line that relate to an individual or family in need of some kind of service are to be counted and included on FVPSA grant reports.

Cultural Competency The ability of practitioners to function effectively in the context of racial, ethnic, religious, or cultural differences by responding to the unique strengths and concerns of families.

Cultural Diversity Differences in race, ethnicity, language, nationality, or religion among various groups within a community. A community is said to be culturally diverse if its residents include members of different groups.

Cultural Sensitivity An awareness of the nuances of one's own and other cultures.

Dating Violence Violence committed by a person: (A) Who is or has been in a social relationship of a romantic or intimate nature with the victim; and (B) Where the existence of such a relationship shall be determined based on a consideration of the following factors: (i) The length of the relationship (ii) The type of relationship (iii) The frequency of interaction between the persons involved in the relationship.

DELTA Domestic Violence Prevention Enhancement and Leadership Through Alliances is a prevention program that seeks to reduce the incidence of intimate partner violence by addressing the entire continuum of IPV.

Deobligation Deobligation occurs when unspent funds remain at the end of the fiscal year and the federal agency takes repossession of these funds.

Disability A person is considered to have a disability under federal law if he/she has a physical or mental impairment which substantially limits one or more major life activities even with the help of medication or aids/devices. Some examples include AIDS, alcoholism, heart disease, and mental illness.

Discretionary Unlike a formula grant, a discretionary grant awards funds on the basis of a competitive process. The department reviews applications, in part through a formal review process, in light of the legislative and regulatory requirements and published selection criteria established for a program. The review process gives the department discretion to determine which applications best address the program requirements and are, therefore, most worthy of funding.

Domestic Violence Each state has its own definition for civil and criminal proceedings but generally, domestic violence is a pattern of assaultive and coercive behaviors, including physical, sexual, and psychological attacks, as well as economic coercion, that adults or adolescents use against their intimate partners where the perpetrator and victim are currently or have been previously dating, cohabiting, married, or divorced. Under FVPSA, domestic violence includes felony or misdemeanor crimes of violence committed by a current or former spouse of the victim, by a person with whom the victim shares a child in common, by a person who is cohabiting with or has cohabited with the victim as a spouse, by a person similarly situated to a spouse of the victim under the domestic or family violence laws of the jurisdiction receiving grant monies, or by any other person against an adult or youth victim who is protected from that person's acts under the domestic or family violence laws of the jurisdiction. Immediate Family Member means: (A) a spouse, parent, brother, sister, or child of that person, or an individual to whom that person stands in loco parentis; or (B) any other person living in the household of that person and related to that person by blood or marriage.

Domestic Violence Coalition A statewide nongovernmental nonprofit private domestic violence organization that: (A) Has a membership that includes a majority of the primary-purpose domestic violence service providers in the State; (B) Has a board membership that is representative of primary-purpose domestic violence service providers, and which may include representatives of the communities in which the services are being provided in the State; (C) Has as its purpose to provide education, support, and technical assistance to such service providers to enable the providers to establish and maintain shelter and supportive services for victims of domestic violence and their dependents; and (D) Serves as an information clearinghouse, primary point of contact, and resource center on domestic violence for the State and supports the development of policies, protocols, and procedures to enhance domestic violence intervention and prevention in the State.

DUNS A unique nine-digit number issued to businesses by Dun & Bradstreet. A Data Universal Numbering System number is required when applying for federal grants.

DVRN The Domestic Violence Resource Network is funded by the U.S. Department of Health and Human Services to inform and strengthen domestic violence intervention and prevention efforts at the individual, community, and societal levels. The DVRN includes two national resource centers, three special issue resource centers, five culturally specific Institutes, the National Center on Domestic Violence, Trauma & Mental Health, the National Network to End Domestic Violence, and the National Domestic Violence Hotline.

Economic Abuse Any action by one person that limits their partner's ability to earn, have access to, or manage the economic resources in their life.

EIN An Employer Identification Number is also known as a Federal Tax Identification Number, and is used to identify a business entity. It is issued by the Internal Revenue Service.

Emotional Abuse Any statements, actions, or lack of action intended to or resulting in one's partner experiencing any emotional or psychological injury. Also known as psychological abuse.

Expenditure Period The calendar period during which grant funds can be used. FVPSA funds may be spent on and after October 1 of each fiscal year for which they are granted, and will be available for expenditure through September 30 of the following fiscal year.

Family Violence A broader concept than domestic violence that can include child abuse and neglect, child-to-parent violence, or sibling violence. Under FVPSA legislation it is defined as: "Any act or threatened act of violence, including any forceful detention of an individual, that: (a) results or threatens to result in physical injury; and (b) is committed by a person against another individual (including an elderly person) to whom such person is or was related by blood or marriage or otherwise legally related or with whom such person is or was lawfully residing."

Fee for Service The amount of payment agreed upon for the delivery of a service rendered.

Federal Appropriation A formal approval to draw funds from the federal treasury for specific purposes.

Federal Budget The president's annual proposal to Congress, usually submitted in January, for federal expenditures and revenues for the coming fiscal year (which starts October 1).

Federal Grant An award of financial assistance from a federal agency to a recipient to carry out a public purpose of support or stimulation authorized by a law of the United States. Federal grants are not federal assistance or loans to individuals.

Federal Register Published by the Office of the Federal Register, National Archives and Records Administration (NARA), the Federal Register is the official daily publication for rules, proposed rules, and notices of Federal agencies and organizations, as well as executive orders and other presidential documents. It is updated daily by 6 a.m. and is published Monday through Friday, except Federal holidays.

Financial Status Report A standard federal form that shows the status of funds and is used to monitor the financial progress of awards. The form requires information on total outlays (federal and recipient shares) and unobligated balances of federal funds. The form used for FVPSA is the Federal Financial Report SF-425.

Fiscal Year A fiscal year (or financial year, or sometimes budget year) is a period used for calculating annual ("yearly") financial statements in businesses and other organizations. The federal government's fiscal year begins on October 1 of the previous calendar year and ends on September 30 of the year with which it is numbered. For example, FY2010 runs from October 1, 2009 and ends September 30, 2010.

Flow-Down/Through Provisions The rules governing whether, and how, grant terms apply to subawards or contracts under grants.

Formula Grant Noncompetitive grants given to eligible agencies where awards are based on a predetermined formula. May also be called a mandatory grant.

Grantee The recipient of a grant. The organizational entity or individual to which a grant (or cooperative agreement) is awarded and which is responsible and accountable both for the use of the funds provided and for the performance of the grant-supported project or activities. The grantee is the entire legal entity even if only a particular component is designated in the award document.

Grantor The entity that makes/awards a grant.

Grants.gov Grants.gov was established as a governmental resource named the E-Grants Initiative, part of the President's 2002 Fiscal Year Management Agenda to improve government services to the public.

Human Trafficking Trafficking involves forcible movement of a person from one place to another and forcible utilization of their services with the intention of inducting them into trade for commercial gains. The word 'forcible' signifies that the action is against the person's will or that consent has been obtained by making deceptive claims and false allurements.

Informed Consent Informed consent is a phrase to indicate that the consent a person gives meets certain minimum, legally required standards. The person consenting must have a clear appreciation and understanding of all the facts, implications, and future consequences of an action. Additionally, the person consenting must have adequate reasoning faculties, be provided with all the relevant facts at the time consent is given, and indicate the consent in writing.

Intimate Partner Violence Intimate Partner Violence (IPV) is another term for domestic violence.

Intimate Partners Intimate partners include current and former spouses and dating partners (sexual activity does not need to be occurring to be considered an intimate partner). Intimate partners include same-sex and opposite-sex relationships.

Linguistically and Culturally Relevant Services Community-based services that offer full linguistic access and culturally specific services and resources, including outreach, collaboration, and support mechanisms primarily directed toward underserved communities.

Liquidate To liquidate funds means to use the grant funds, i.e., they have been spent

Mandated Reporter Certain professionals are required by law to report (or cause a report to be made) whenever financial, physical, sexual or other types of abuse have been observed or are suspected, or when there is evidence of neglect, knowledge of an incident, or an imminent risk of serious harm. These professionals tend to be physicians, social workers, and other providers who have contact with children or vulnerable adults.

Mandatory Grants Those grants that a federal agency is required by statute to award if the recipient, usually a state, submits an acceptable State Plan or application and meets the eligibility and compliance requirements of the statutory and regulatory provisions of the grant program.

Match Contributions made by a third party to support the overall costs of a project; often a requirement of federal grants. There can be a cash match or an in-kind match; the latter refers to goods and services.

Monitoring A process in which a grant's programmatic performance and business management performance are assessed by reviewing information gathered from various required reports, audits, site visits, and other sources. Monitoring can be accomplished through several different mechanisms, such as onsite or desk monitoring.

National Domestic Violence Hotline The hotline was established in 1996 as a component of the Violence Against Women Act (VAWA) and receives its core funding through FVPSA. It is a nonprofit organization that provides crisis intervention, information, and referrals to victims of domestic violence, perpetrators, friends, and families. The hotline is a resource for domestic violence advocates, government officials, law enforcement agencies, and the general public.

NCADV The National Coalition Against Domestic Violence, whose work includes coalition building at the local, state, regional, and national levels; support for the provision of community-based, non-violent alternatives - such as safe home and shelter programs - for battered women and their children; public education and technical assistance; policy development and innovative legislation; focus on the leadership of NCADV's caucuses developed to represent the concerns of organizationally underrepresented groups; and efforts to eradicate social conditions which contribute to violence against women and children.

NNEDV The National Network to End Domestic Violence, which serves as the membership organization for the state-level domestic violence coalitions. As a social change organization, it is dedicated to creating a social, political, and economic environment in which violence against women no longer exists. It addresses public policy nationally, offers training and technical assistance to coalitions, lobbies for funding, and offers a range of programs and initiatives to address the complex causes and far-reaching consequences of domestic violence.

Obligate To obligate funds means to have incurred an expense where the intention is to use grant funds to pay for that cost.

OMB The United States Office of Management and Budget is the White House office responsible for devising and submitting the president's annual budget proposal to Congress.

OMB Circulars, instructions, or information issued by OMB to federal agencies. Circulars that pertain to the FVPSA program include: OMB Circular A-87, 2 CFR 225 Cost Principles for State, Local and Indian Tribal Governments OMB Circular A-133 Audits of States, Local Governments, and Non-Profits Organizations OMB Circular A-122 Cost Principles for Non-Profit Organizations OMB Circular A-110 Uniform Administrative Requirements for Grants and Agreements With Institutions of Higher Education, Hospitals, and Other Non-Profit Organizations

OVW Created in 1995, the Office on Violence Against Women administers financial and technical assistance to communities across the country that are developing programs, policies, and practices aimed at ending domestic violence, dating violence, sexual assault, and stalking. Currently, OVW administers two formula grant programs and 17 discretionary grant programs, which were established under VAWA and subsequent legislation.

Outcome An outcome is a change in knowledge, attitude, skill, behavior, expectation, emotional status, or life circumstance due to the service being provided. Also known as an outcome measure.

Outcome Evaluation An outcome evaluation involves examining change that has occurred because a specific service has been provided.

Outlays Another term for expenditures. The charges made to the federally sponsored project or program. They may be reported on a cash or accrual basis.

OVC The Office for Victims of Crime was established by the 1984 Victims of Crime Act (VOCA) to oversee diverse programs that benefit victims of crime. OVC provides substantial funding to state victim assistance and compensation programs– the lifeline services that help victims to heal. The agency supports trainings designed to educate criminal justice and allied professionals regarding the rights and needs of crime victims.

Peer Review Peer review is the evaluation of creative work or performance by other people in the same field in order to maintain or enhance the quality of the work or performance in that field. Peer review utilizes the independence, and in some cases the anonymity, of the reviewers in order to discourage cronyism (i.e., favoritism shown to relatives and friends) and obtain an unbiased evaluation.

Performance Progress Report The PPR is the annual report submitted by the state to assess progress. It describes the activities carried out and includes an assessment of the effectiveness of those activities in achieving the purpose of the grant.

Perpetrator Another word for batterer or abuser.

Personally Identifying Information Individually identifying information for or about an individual including information likely to disclose the location of a victim of domestic violence, dating violence, sexual assault, or stalking, including: (A) A first and last name; (B) A home or other physical address; (C) Contact information (including a postal, e-mail or Internet protocol address, or telephone or facsimile number); (D) A Social Security number; and (E) Any other information, including date of birth, racial or ethnic background, or religious affiliation, that, in combination with any of subparagraphs (A) through (D), would serve to identify any individual.

Physical Abuse Any unwanted physical contact, especially that which may cause fear, pain or injury, whether done directly or indirectly.

Post-Separation Violence Any type of behavior that would qualify as domestic violence that occurs after two people have ended their intimate partner relationship. This type of violence can take many forms, including physical or sexual assault, threats of abuse or violence, stalking, harassment, and threats related to taking custody of the children, refusing child support or threatening to harm the children.

Primary Victim The person to whom the abuse is directed.

Privilege Also known as a privileged communication, privilege is a legal term describing certain specific types of relationships that enjoy protection from disclosure in legal proceedings Privilege is granted by law and belongs to the client in the relationship. It can either be absolute or qualified, each affording a different level of protection. Privileged relationships vary by state law.

Project Period The length of time the entire grant runs. FVPSA has three-year project periods.

Protection Order A legal order that is issued by the court at the request of the victim (petitioner) against the batterer (respondent) to prevent violent or threatening acts or harassment against; contact or communication with; or physical proximity to, the victim. A protection order (in some places called a restraining order) can provide legal protection but not necessarily physical protection.

Rape Although the legal definition of rape varies from state to state, rape is generally defined as forced or non-consensual sexual contact.

Reimbursement Compensation paid to an entity for monies already spent. Typically there is a formal request made for reimbursement.

Related Assistance This term is no longer used. See Supportive Services.

Release of Information A form that is signed by a client or the client's guardian and gives permission to an entity or agency to release certain personal information or documentation about that client. There are many requirements for a valid release.

RFP A Request for Proposals (RFP) is a process where proposals are solicited for contracts under the negotiated procurement method.

Risk Assessment A tool used to identify how much danger a victim is in for serious harm or even death from a batterer. Risk assessments are complex and should not be considered foolproof.

Safety Condition of being safe; freedom from danger or hazard.

Safe Homes Residences of volunteers who offer their private homes for short-term crisis situations or other temporary housing that a program arranges.

Safety Planning A process where victims of domestic violence explore and evaluate strategies to safeguard themselves and their children in different situations that may bring about safety concerns. The philosophy is to have decisions made in advance so if an emergency arises, there are concrete plans in place to achieve, eliminate, or manage a safety threat.

Sexual Assault Any contact, statements, or actions that are intended to cause or result in physical, emotional, or psychological sexual injury to another person. Sexual assault takes many forms, including attacks such as rape or attempted rape, as well as any unwanted sexual contact or threats. Usually a sexual assault occurs when someone touches any part of another person's body in a sexual way, even through clothes, without that person's consent. Some types of sexual acts which fall under the category of sexual assault include forced sexual intercourse (rape), sodomy (oral or anal sexual acts), child molestation, incest, fondling, and attempted rape.

Shelter In general, refers to safe and confidential emergency housing provided to victims and their children who are fleeing their homes due to domestic violence. Shelters are often run by domestic violence organizations that offer a continuum of services. Under FVPSA, a shelter is the provision of temporary refuge and supportive services in compliance with applicable State law (including regulation) governing the provision, on a regular basis, of shelter, safe homes, meals, and supportive services to victims of family violence, domestic violence, or dating violence, and their dependents.

Shelter Night Any night a victim of domestic violence spends in an onsite shelter managed by the domestic violence program, program-sponsored hotel rooms, and safe houses, or other temporary housing that a program arranges.

SMARTLINK A payment management system used by HHS for grantees to request payments.

Special Conditions Specific conditions placed on the grantee if awarded the grant, as found in the grant solicitation or included in the grant award.

Stalking The exact definition varies by state, but in general it is a pattern of repeated, unwanted attention, harassment, and contact which reasonably alarms, torments, or terrorizes the person being stalked.

State Government The government of any state of the United States, the District of Columbia, the Commonwealth of Puerto Rico, any U.S. territory or possession, and, except as otherwise provided, Guam, American Samoa, the United States Virgin Islands, and the Commonwealth of the Northern Mariana Islands, or any agency or instrumentality of a State exclusive of local governments. State institutions of higher education and state hospitals are not considered state governments for purposes of the HHS general administrative requirements for grants.

State Plan A state plan is required to receive FVPSA funds. It is a document that outlines the state's plan to address domestic violence, the resources necessary to support that plan, a description of how and for what purposes the resources are to be used, and a projection of the effects of the programs on people and the environment.

State Population The number of people living in the state as determined by the most recent U.S. Census data available.

STOP The Service, Training, Officers, Prosecutors grant program funds coordinated community responses supporting police officers, prosecutors, courts, and victim services. It is the largest source of VAWA funding for states to combat domestic and sexual violence.

Subgrantee A recipient of grant funds from the grantee and not directly from the original grantor. A subgrantee is held to all of the regulations of the original grant plus any conditions added by the subgrantor.

Supplant Supplanting funds are loosely defined as using federal grant money to "replace" or "take the place of" existing local funding.

Supportive Services Services for adult and youth victims of family violence, domestic violence or dating violence, and dependents exposed to family violence, domestic violence or dating violence that are designed to: (A) Meet the needs of victims of family violence, domestic violence, or dating violence, and their dependents, for short-term, transitional, or long-term safety; and (B) Provide counseling, advocacy, or assistance for victims of family violence, domestic violence, or dating violence, and their dependents. Supportive services include: 1. Prevention services such as outreach, parenting, employment training, educational services, promotion of good nutrition, disease prevention, and substance abuse prevention; 2. Counseling with respect to family violence, counseling or other supportive services provided by peers, either individually or in groups, and referral to community social services; 3. Transportation and technical assistance with respect to obtaining financial assistance under Federal and State programs, and referrals for appropriate health-care services (including alcohol and drug abuse treatment), but shall not include reimbursement for any health-care services; 4. Legal advocacy to provide victims with information and assistance through the civil and criminal courts, and legal assistance; 5. Children's counseling and support services, and child care services for children who are victims of family violence of the dependents of such victims, and children who witness domestic violence.

Survivor Someone who has experienced any form of intimate partner violence. Some advocates assert a survivor is someone who has overcome the domestic violence, or who has escaped an abusive relationship. Other advocates say that simply the experience of domestic violence makes a person a "survivor." Another word for victim.

Underserved Populations These are populations that experience barriers related to access to prevention and intervention resources and services. The term "underserved populations" includes populations underserved because of geographic location, underserved racial and ethnic populations, populations underserved because of special needs (such as language barriers, disabilities, alien status, or age), and any other population determined to be underserved by the U.S. Secretary of Health and Human Services.

Unduplicated Count Number of primary victims served (adult and youth). Instructions on how to count shelter and non-shelter services are provided with the reporting forms. A client can only be counted once by a program but a separate program who also served that client can also count that client.

Vendor An organization/company that provides goods and services in a competitive environment to many different purchasers. Such goods and services are ancillary to the operation of the federal program and not subject to compliance requirements of the federal program.

Victim Someone who has experienced any form of intimate partner violence. Another term for survivor.

VOCA The Victims of Crime Act is a key funding source for services that help victims of sexual assault, domestic violence, child abuse, and other offenses to cope with the trauma and aftermath of crime. This fund is not from taxpayer money but rather consists of funds and penalties collected from federal offenders.

Youth IPV Victim Youth under the age of 18 who are victims of intimate partner violence (e.g., teen dating violence, including sexual assault).

Federal Aviation Administration

ACRONYMS

A/C	Aircraft
A/G	Air to Ground
A/H	Altitude/Height
AAC	Mike Monroney Aeronautical Center
AAF	Army Air Field
AAI	Arrival Aircraft Interval
AAP	Advanced Automation Program
AAR	Airport Acceptance Rate
ABDIS	Automated Data Interchange System Service B
ACAIS	Air Carrier Activity Information System
ACAS	Aircraft Collision Avoidance System
ACC	Airports Consultants Council
ACC	Area Control Center
ACCT	Accounting Records
ACD	Automatic Call Distributor
ACDO	Air Carrier District Office
ACF	Area Control Facility
ACFO	Aircraft Certification Field Office
ACFT	Aircraft
ACI-NA	Airports Council International-North America
ACID	Aircraft Identification
ACIP	Airport Capital Improvement Plan
ACLS	Automatic Carrier Landing System
ACLT	Actual Landing Time Calculated
ACO	Office of Airports Compliance and Field Operations; Aircraft Certification Office
ACRP	Airport Cooperative Research Program
ADA	Air Defense Area
ADAP	Airport Development Aid Program
ADAS	AWOS Data Acquisition System
ADCCP	Advanced Data Communications Control Procedure
ADDA	Administrative Data
ADF	Automatic Direction Finding
ADI	Automatic De-Ice and Inhibitor
ADIN	AUTODIN Service
ADIZ	Air Defense Identification Zone
ADL	Aeronautical Data-Link
ADLY	Arrival Delay
ADO	Airline Dispatch Office
ADP	Automated Data Processing
ADS	Automatic Dependent Surveillance
ADSIM	Airfield Delay Simulation Model
ADSY	Administrative Equipment Systems
ADTN	Administrative Data Transmission Network
ADTN2000	Administrative Data Transmission Network 2000
ADVO	Administrative Voice
AEG	Aircraft Evaluation Group
AERA	Automated En-Route Air Traffic Control
AEX	Automated Execution
AF	Airway Facilities
AFB	Air Force Base
AFIS	Automated Flight Inspection System
AFP	Area Flight Plan
AFRES	Air Force Reserve Station
AFS	Airways Facilities Sector
AFSFO	AFS Field Office
AFSFU	AFS Field Unit
AFSOU	AFS Field Office Unit (Standard is AFSFOU)
AFSS	Automated Flight Service Station
AFTN	Automated Fixed Telecommunications Network
AGL	Above Ground Level
AID	Airport Information Desk
AIG	Airbus Industries Group
AIM	Airman's Information Manual
AIP	Airport Improvement Plan
AIRMET	Airmen's Meteorological Information
AIRNET	Airport Network Simulation Model
AIS	Aeronautical Information Service
AIT	Automated Information Transfer
ALP	Airport Layout Plan
ALS	Approach Lighting System
ALSF1	ALS with Sequenced Flashers I
ALSF2	ALS with Sequenced Flashers II
ALSIP	Approach Lighting System Improvement Plan
ALTRV	Altitude Reservation
AMASS	Airport Movement Area Safety System

AMCC	ACF/ARTCC Maintenance Control Center	*ATCBI*	Air Traffic Control Beacon Indicator
AMOS	Automated Meteorological Observation Station	*ATCCC*	Air Traffic Control Command Center
		ATCO	Air Taxi Commercial Operator
AMP	ARINC Message Processor (OR) Airport Master Plan	*ATCRB*	Air Traffic Control Radar Beacon
		ATCRBS	Air Traffic Control Radar Beacon System
AMVER	Automated Mutual Assistance Vessel Rescue System	*ATCSCC*	Air Traffic Control Systems Command Center
ANC	Alternate Network Connectivity	*ATCT*	Airport Traffic Control Tower
ANCA	Airport Noise and Capacity Act	*ATIS*	Automated Terminal Information Service
ANG	Air National Guard		
ANGB	Air National Guard Base	*ATISR*	ATIS Recorder
ANMS	Automated Network Monitoring System	*ATM*	Air Traffic Management; Asynchronous Transfer Mode
ANSI	American National Standards Group	*ATMS*	Advanced Traffic Management System
AOA	Air Operations Area		
AP	Acquisition Plan	*ATN*	Aeronautical Telecommunications Network
APP	Approach		
APS	Airport Planning Standard	*ATODN*	AUTODIN Terminal (FUS)
AQAFO	Aeronautical Quality Assurance Field Office	*ATOMS*	Air Traffic Operations Management System
ARAC	Army Radar Approach Control (AAF)	*ATOVN*	AUOTVON (Facility)
ARAC	Aviation Rulemaking Advisory Committee	*ATS*	Air Traffic Service
		ATSCCP	ATS Contingency Command Post
ARCTR	FAA Aeronautical Center or Academy	*AT&T*	American Telephone and Telegraph
ARF	Airport Reservation Function	*AT&TASDC*	AT&T Agency Service Delivery Center
ARFF	Aircraft Rescue and Fire Fighting	*AT&TCSA*	AT&T Customer Support Associate
ARINC	Aeronautical Radio, Inc.	*ATTIS*	AT&T Information Systems
ARLNO	Airline Office	*AUTODIN*	DoD Automatic Digital Network
ARO	Airport Reservation Office	*AUTOVON*	DoD Automatic Voice Network
ARP	Airport Reference Point	*AVON*	AUTOVON Service
ARRA	American Recovery and Reinvestment Act of 2009	*AVN*	Aviation Standards National Field Office, Oklahoma City
ARSA	Airport Service Radar Area	*AWIS*	Airport Weather Information
ARSR	Air Route Surveillance Radar	*AWOS*	Automated Weather Observation System
ARTCC	Air Route Traffic Control Center		
ARTS	Automated Radar Terminal System	*AWP*	Aviation Weather Processor
ASAS	Aviation Safety Analysis System	*AWPG*	Aviation Weather Products Generator
ASC	AUTODIN Switching Center	*AWS*	Air Weather Station
ASCP	Aviation System Capacity Plan	*BANS*	BRITE Alphanumeric System
ASD	Aircraft Situation Display	*BART*	Billing Analysis Reporting Tool (GSA software tool)
ASDA	Accelerate Stop Distance Available		
ASLAR	Aircraft Surge Launch And Recovery	*BASIC*	Basic Contract Observing Station
ASM	Available Seat Mile	*BASOP*	Military Base Operations
ASOS	Automatic Surface Observation System	*BCA*	Benefit/Cost Analysis
ASP	Arrival Sequencing Program	*BCR*	Benefit/Cost Ratio
ASQP	Airline Service Quality Performance	*BDAT*	Digitized Beacon Data
ASR	Airport Surveillance Radar	*BMP*	Best Management Practices
ASTA	Airport Surface Traffic Automation	*BOC*	Bell Operating Company
ASV	Airline Schedule Vendor	*bps*	bits per second
AT	Air Traffic	*BRI*	Basic Rate Interface
ATA	Air Transport Association of America	*BRITE*	Bright Radar Indicator Terminal Equipment
ATAS	Airspace and Traffic Advisory Service		
ATC	Air Traffic Control	*BRL*	Building Restriction Line
ATCAA	Air Traffic Control Assigned Airspace	*BUEC*	Back-up Emergency Communications

BUECE	Back-up Emergency Communications Equipment	CSIS	Centralized Storm Information System
CAA	Civil Aviation Authority; Clean Air Act	CSO	Customer Service Office
CAB	Civil Aeronautics Board	CSR	Communications Service Request
CARF	Central Altitude Reservation Facility	CSS	Central Site System
CASFO	Civil Aviation Security Office	C/S/S/N	Capacity/Safety/Security/Noise
CAT	Category; Clear Air Turbulence	CTA	Controlled Time of Arrival; Control Area
CAU	Crypto Ancillary Unit	CTAF	Common Traffic Advisory Frequency
CBI	Computer Based Instruction	CTA/FIR	Control Area/Flight Information Region
CCC	Communications Command Center	CTAS	Center Tracon Automation System
CCCC	Staff Communications	CTMA	Center Traffic Management Advisor
CCCH	Central Computer Complex Host	CUPS	Consolidated Uniform Payroll System
CC&O	Customer Cost and Obligation	CVFR	Controlled Visual Flight Rules
CCS7-NI	Communication Channel Signal-7 Network Interconnect	CVTS	Compressed Video Transmission Service
CCSD	Command Communications Service Designator	CW	Continuous Wave
		CWSU	Central Weather Service Unit
CCU	Central Control Unit	CWY	Clearway
CD	Common Digitizer	DA	Direct Access; Decision Altitude/Decision Height; Descent Advisor
CDR	Cost Detail Report		
CDT	Controlled Departure Time	DABBS	DITCO Automated Bulletin Board System
CDTI	Cockpit Display of Traffic Information		
CENTX	Central Telephone Exchange	DAIR	Direct Altitude and Identity Readout
CEP	Capacity Enhancement Program	DAR	Designated Agency Representative
CEQ	Council on Environmental Quality	DARC	Direct Access Radar Channel
CERAP	Central Radar Approach	dBA	Decibels A-weighted
CFC	Central Flow Control	DBCRC	Defense Base Closure and Realignment Commission
CFCF	Central Flow Control Facility		
CFCS	Central Flow Control Service	DBE	Disadvantaged Business Enterprise
CFR	Code of Federal Regulations	DBMS	Data Base Management System
CFWP	Central Flow Weather Processor	DBRITE	Digital Bright Radar Indicator Tower Equipment
CFWU	Central Flow Weather Unit		
CGAS	Coast Guard Air Station	DCA	Defense Communications Agency
CLC	Course Line Computer	DCAA	Dual Call, Automatic Answer Device
CLIN	Contract Line Item	DCCU	Data Communications Control Unit
CLT	Calculated Landing Time	DCE	Data Communications Equipment
CM	Commercial Service Airport	DDA	Dedicated Digital Access
CNMPS	Canadian Minimum Navigation Performance Specification Airspace	DDD	Direct Distance Dialing
		DDM	Difference in Depth of Modulation
CNS	Consolidated NOTAM System	DDS	Digital Data Service
CNSP	Consolidated NOTAM System Processor	DEA	Drug Enforcement Agency
		DEDS	Data Entry and Display System
CO	Central Office	DEIS	Draft Environmental Impact Statement
COE	U.S. Army Corps of Engineers	DEP	Departure
COMCO	Command Communications Outlet	DEWIZ	Distance Early Warning Identification Zone
CONUS	Continental United States		
CORP	Private Corporation other than ARINC or MITRE	DF	Direction Finder
		DFAX	Digital Facsimile
CPE	Customer Premise Equipment	DFI	Direction Finding Indicator
CPMIS	Consolidated Personnel Management Information System	DGPS	Differential Global Positioning Satellite (System)
CRA	Conflict Resolution Advisory	DH	Decision Height
CRDA	Converging Runway Display Aid	DID	Direct Inward Dial
CRT	Cathode Ray Tube	DIP	Drop and Insert Point
CSA	Communications Service Authorization	DIRF	Direction Finding

DITCO	Defense Information Technology Contracting Office Agency	ETA	Estimated Time of Arrival
DME	Distance Measuring Equipment	ETE	Estimated Time En Route
DME/P	Precision Distance Measuring Equipment	ETG	Enhanced Target Generator
		ETMS	Enhanced Traffic Management System
DMN	Data Multiplexing Network	ETN	Electronic Telecommunications Network
DNL	Day-Night Equivalent Sound Level (Also called Ldn)	EVAS	Enhanced Vortex Advisory System
		EVCS	Emergency Voice Communications System
DOD	Direct Outward Dial		
DOD	Department of Defense	FAA	Federal Aviation Administration
DOI	Department of Interior	FAAAC	FAA Aeronautical Center
DOS	Department of State	FAACIS	FAA Communications Information System
DOT	Department of Transportation		
DOTCC	Department of Transportation Computer Center	FAATC	FAA Technical Center
		FAATSAT	FAA Telecommunications Satellite
DOTS	Dynamic Ocean Tracking System	FAC	Facility
DSCS	Digital Satellite Compression Service	FAF	Final Approach Fix
DSUA	Dynamic Special Use Airspace	FAP	Final Approach Point
DTS	Dedicated Transmission Service	FAPM	FTS2000 Associate Program Manager
DUAT	Direct User Access Terminal	FAR	Federal Aviation Regulation
DVFR	Defense Visual Flight Rules	FAST	Final Approach Spacing Tool
DVFR	Day Visual Flight Rules	FAX	Facsimile Equipment
DVOR	Doppler Very High Frequency Omni-Directional Range	FBO	Fixed Base Operator
		FBS	Fall Back Switch
DYSIM	Dynamic Simulator	FCC	Federal Communications Commission
E-MSAW	En-Route Automated Minimum Safe Altitude Warning	FCLT	Freeze Calculated Landing Time
		FCOM	FSS Radio Voice Communications
EA	Environmental Assessment	FCPU	Facility Central Processing Unit
EARTS	En Route Automated Radar Tracking System	FDAT	Flight Data Entry and Printout (FDEP) and Flight Data Service
ECOM	En Route Communications	FDE	Flight Data Entry
ECVFP	Expanded Charted Visual Flight Procedures	FDEP	Flight Data Entry and Printout
		FDIO	Flight Data Input/Output
EDCT	Expedite Departure Path	FDIOC	Flight Data Input/Output Center
EFAS	En Route Flight Advisory Service	FDIOR	Flight Data Input/Output Remote
EFC	Expect Further Clearance	FDM	Frequency Division Multiplexing
EFIS	Electronic Flight Information Systems	FDP	Flight Data Processing
EIAF	Expanded Inward Access Features	F&E	Facility and Equipment
EIS	Environmental Impact Statement	FED	Federal
ELT	Emergency Locator Transmitter	FEIS	Final Environmental Impact Statement
ELWRT	Electrowriter	FEP	Front End Processor
EMAS	Engineered Materials Arresting System	FFAC	From Facility
EMPS	En Route Maintenance Processor System	FIFO	Flight Inspection Field Office
		FIG	Flight Inspection Group
EMS	Environmental Management System	FINO	Flight Inspection National Field Office
ENAV	En Route Navigational Aids	FIPS	Federal Information Publication Standard
EPA	Environmental Protection Agency		
EPS	Engineered Performance Standards	FIR	Flight Information Region
EOF	Emergency Operating Facility	FIRE	Fire Station
EPSS	Enhanced Packet Switched Service	FIRMR	Federal Information Resource Management Regulation
ERAD	En Route Broadband Radar		
ESEC	En Route Broadband Secondary Radar	FL	Flight Level
ESF	Extended Superframe Format	FLOWSIM	Traffic Flow Planning Simulation
ESP	En Route Spacing Program	FMA	Final Monitor Aid
ESYS	En Route Equipment Systems	FMF	Facility Master File

FMIS	FTS2000 Management Information System	*HDQ*	FAA Headquarters
FMS	Flight Management System	*HELI*	Heliport
FNMS	FTS2000 Network Management System	*HF*	High Frequency
FOIA	Freedom of Information Act	*HH*	NDB, 2kw or More
FONSI	Finding of No Significant Impact	*HI-EFAS*	High Altitude EFAS
FP	Flight Plan	*HOV*	High Occupancy Vehicle
FRC	Request Full Route Clearance	*HSI*	Horizontal Situation Indicators
FSAS	Flight Service Automation System	*HUD*	Housing and Urban Development
FSDO	Flight Standards District Office	*HWAS*	Hazardous In-Flight Weather Advisory
FSDPS	Flight Service Data Processing System	*Hz*	HERTZ
FSEP	Facility/Service/Equipment Profile	*IA*	Indirect Access
FSP	Flight Strip Printer	*IAF*	Initial Approach Fix
FSPD	Freeze Speed Parameter	*I/AFSS*	International AFSS
FSS	Flight Service Station	*IAP*	Instrument Approach Procedures
FSSA	Flight Service Station Automated Service	*IAPA*	Instrument Approach Procedures Automation
FSTS	Federal Secure Telephone Service	*IBM*	International Business Machines
FSYS	Flight Service Station Equipment Systems	*IBP*	International Boundary Point
		IBR	Intermediate Bit Rate
FTS	Federal Telecommunications System	*ICAO*	International Civil Aviation Organization
FTS2000	Federal Telecommunications System 2000	*ICSS*	International Communications Switching Systems
FUS	Functional Units or Systems	*IDAT*	Interfacility Data
FWCS	Flight Watch Control Station	*IF*	Intermediate Fix
GA	General Aviation	*IFCP*	Interfacility Communications Processor
GAA	General Aviation Activity	*IFDS*	Interfacility Data System
GAAA	General Aviation Activity and Avionics	*IFEA*	In-Flight Emergency Assistance
GADO	General Aviation District Office	*IFO*	International Field Office
GCA	Ground Control Approach	*IFR*	Instrument Flight Rules
GNAS	General National Airspace System	*IFSS*	International Flight Service Station
GNSS	Global Navigation Satellite System	*ILS*	Instrument Landing System
GOES	Geostationary Operational Environmental Satellite	*IM*	Inner Marker
		IMC	Instrument Meteorological Conditions
GOESF	GOES Feed Point	*INM*	Integrated Noise Model
GOEST	GOES Terminal Equipment	*INS*	Inertial Navigation System
GPRA	Government Performance Results Act	*IRMP*	Information Resources Management Plan
GPS	Global Positioning Satellite		
GPWS	Ground Proximity Warning System	*ISDN*	Integrated Services Digital Network
GRADE	Graphical Airspace Design Environment	*ISMLS*	Interim Standard Microwave Landing System
GS	Glide Slope Indicator	*ITI*	Interactive Terminal Interface
GSA	General Services Administration	*IVRS*	Interim Voice Response System
GSE	Ground Support Equipment	*IW*	Inside Wiring
H	Non-Directional Radio Homing Beacon (NDB)	*Kbps*	Kilobits Per Second
		Khz	Kilohertz
HAA	Height Above Airport	*KVDT*	Keyboard Video Display Terminal
HAL	Height Above Landing	*LAA*	Local Airport Advisory
HARS	High Altitude Route System	*LAAS*	Low Altitude Alert System
HAT	Height Above Touchdown	*LABS*	Leased A B Service
HAZMAT	Hazardous Materials	*LABSC*	LABS GS-200 Computer
HCAP	High Capacity Carriers	*LABSR*	LABS Remote Equipment
HLDC	High Level Data Link Control	*LABSW*	LABS Switch System
HDME	NDB with Distance Measuring Equipment	*LAHSO*	Land and Hold Short Operation
		LAN	Local Area Network

LATA	Local Access and Transport Area	MIDO	Manufacturing Inspection District Office
LAWRS	Limited Aviation Weather Reporting System	MIS	Meteorological Impact Statement
LCF	Local Control Facility	MISC	Miscellaneous
LCN	Local Communications Network	MISO	Manufacturing Inspection Satellite Office
LDA	Localizer Directional Aid		
LDA	Landing Directional Aid	MIT	Miles In Trail
LDIN	Lead-in Lights	MITRE	Mitre Corporation
LEC	Local Exchange Carrier	MLS	Microwave Landing System
LF	Low Frequency	MM	Middle Marker
LINCS	Leased Interfacility NAS Communications System	MMC	Maintenance Monitoring Console
		MMS	Maintenance Monitoring System
LIS	Logistics and Inventory System	MNPS	Minimum Navigation Performance Specification
LLWAS	Low Level Wind Shear Alert System		
LMM	Locator Middle Marker	MNPSA	Minimum Navigation Performance Specifications Airspace
LM/MS	Low/Medium Frequency		
LMS	LORAN Monitor Site	MOA	Memorandum of Agreement; Military Operations Area
LOC	Localizer		
LOCID	Location Identifier	MOCA	Minimum Obstruction Clearance Altitude
LOI	Letter of Intent		
LOM	Compass Locator at Outer Marker	MODEC	Altitude-Encoded Beacon Reply; Altitude Reporting Mode of Secondary Radar
LORAN	Long Range Aid to Navigation		
LPV	Lateral Precision Performance with Vertical Guidance		
		MODES	Mode Select Beacon System
LRCO	Limited Remote Communications Outlet	MOU	Memorandum of Understanding
		MPO	Metropolitan Planning Organization
LRNAV	Long Range Navigation	MPS	Maintenance Processor Subsystem (OR) Master Plan Supplement
LRR	Long Range Radar		
MAA	Maximum Authorized Altitude	MRA	Minimum Reception Altitude
MALS	Medium Intensity Approach Lighting System	MRC	Monthly Recurring Charge
		MSA	Minimum Safe Altitude
MALSF	MALS with Sequenced Flashers	MSAW	Minimum Safe Altitude Warning
MALSR	MALS with Runway Alignment Indicator Lights	MSL	Mean Sea Level
		MSN	Message Switching Network
MAP	Maintenance Automation Program; Military Airport Program; Missed Approach Point; Modified Access Pricing	MTCS	Modular Terminal Communications System
		MTI	Moving Target Indicator
		MUX	Multiplexor
Mbps	Megabits Per Second	MVA	Minimum Vectoring Altitude
MCA	Minimum Crossing Altitude	MVFR	Marginal Visual Flight Rules
MCAS	Marine Corps Air Station	NAAQS	National Ambient Air Quality Standards
MCC	Maintenance Control Center		
MCL	Middle Compass Locater	NADA	NADIN Concentrator
MCS	Maintenance and Control System	NADIN	National Airspace Data Interchange Network
MDA	Minimum Descent Altitude		
MDT	Maintenance Data Terminal	NADSW	NADIN Switches
MEA	Minimum En Route Altitude	NAILS	National Airspace Integrated Logistics Support
METI	Meteorological Information		
MF	Middle Frequency	NAMS	NADIN IA
MFJ	Modified Final Judgment	NAPRS	National Airspace Performance Reporting System
MFT	Meter Fix Crossing Time/Slot Time		
MHA	Minimum Holding Altitude	NAS	National Airspace System or Naval Air Station
Mhg	MegHERTZ		
MIA	Minimum IFR Altitudes	NASDC	National Aviation Safety Data
		NASP	National Airspace System Plan

NASPAC	National Airspace System Performance Analysis Capability	NTAP	Notices To Airmen Publication
NATCO	National Communications Switching Center	NTP	National Transportation Policy
		NTSB	National Transportation Safety Board
NAVAID	Navigation Aid	NTZ	No Transgression Zone
NAVMN	Navigation Monitor and Control	NWS	National Weather Service
NAWAU	National Aviation Weather Advisory Unit	NWSR	NWS Weather Excluding NXRD
		NWSRH	NWS Regional Headquarters
NAWPF	National Aviation Weather Processing Facility	NXRD	Advanced Weather Radar System
		OAG	Official Airline Guide
		OALT	Operational Acceptable Level of Traffic
NCAR	National Center for Atmospheric Research; Boulder, CO	OAW	Off-Airway Weather Station
		ODAL	Omnidirectional Approach Lighting System
NCF	National Control Facility		
NCIU	NEXRAD Communications Interface Unit	ODAPS	Oceanic Display and Processing Station
		OEP	Operational Evolution Plan / Partnership
NCP	Noise Compatibility Program		
NCS	National Communications System	OFA	Object Free Area
NDB	Non-Directional Radio Homing Beacon	OFDPS	Offshore Flight Data Processing System
NDNB	NADIN II	OFT	Outer Fix Time
NEM	Noise Exposure Map	OFZ	Obstacle Free Zone
NEPA	National Environmental Policy Act	OM	Outer Marker
NEXRAD	Next Generation Weather Radar	OMB	Office of Management and Budget
NFAX	National Facsimile Service	ONER	Oceanic Navigational Error Report
NFDC	National Flight Data Center	OPLT	Operational Acceptable Level of Traffic
NFIS	NAS Facilities Information System	OPSW	Operational Switch
NI	Network Interface	OPX	Off Premises Exchange
NICS	National Interfacility Communications System	ORD	Operational Readiness Demonstration
		OTR	Oceanic Transition Route
NPE	Non-primary Airport Entitlement	OTS	Organized Track System
NPIAS	National Plan of Integrated Airport Systems	PABX	Private Automated Branch Exchange
		PAD	Packet Assembler/Disassembler
NM	Nautical Mile	PAM	Peripheral Adapter Module
NMAC	Near Mid Air Collision	PAPI	Precision Approach Path Indicator
NMC	National Meteorological Center	PAR	Precision Approach Radar; Preferential Arrival Route
NMCE	Network Monitoring and Control Equipment		
		PATWAS	Pilots Automatic Telephone Weather Answering Service
NMCS	Network Monitoring and Control System		
		PBCT	Proposed Boundary Crossing Time
NOAA	National Oceanic and Atmospheric Administration	PBRF	Pilot Briefing
		PBX	Private Branch Exchange
NOC	Notice of Completion	PCA	Positive Control Airspace
NOTAM	Notice to Airmen	PCM	Pulse Code Modulation
NPDES	National Pollutant Discharge Elimination System	PDAR	Preferential Arrival and Departure Route
NPIAS	National Plan of Integrated Airport Systems	PDC	Pre-Departure Clearance; Program Designator Code
		PDN	Public Data Network
NRC	Non-Recurring Charge	PDR	Preferential Departure Route
NRCS	National Radio Communications Systems	PFC	Passenger Facility Charge
		PGP	Planning Grant Program
NSAP	National Service Assurance Plan	PIC	Principal Interexchange Carrier
NSRCATN	National Strategy to Reduce Congestion on America's Transportation Network	PIDP	Programmable Indicator Data Processor
		PIREP	Pilot Weather Report
NSSFC	National Severe Storms Forecast Center	PMS	Program Management System
NSSL	National Severe Storms Laboratory; Norman, OK	POLIC	Police Station

POP	Point of Presence	ROD	Record of Decision
POT	Point of Termination	ROSA	Report of Service Activity
PPIMS	Personal Property Information Management System	ROT	Runway Occupancy Time
		RP	Restoration Priority
PR	Primary Commercial Service Airport	RPC	Restoration Priority Code
PRI	Primary Rate Interface	RPG	Radar Processing Group
PRM	Precision Runway Monitor	RPZ	Runway Protection Zone
PSDN	Public Switched Data Network	RRH	Remote Reading Hygrothermometer
PSN	Packet Switched Network	RRHS	Remote Reading Hydrometer
PSS	Packet Switched Service	RRWDS	Remote Radar Weather Display
PSTN	Public Switched Telephone Network	RRWSS	RWDS Sensor Site
PTC	Presumed-to-Conform	RSA	Runway Safety Area
PUB	Publication	RSAT	Runway Safety Action Team
PUP	Principal User Processor	RSS	Remote Speaking System
PVC	Permanent Virtual Circuit	RT	Remote Transmitter
PVD	Plan View Display	RTAD	Remote Tower Alphanumerics Display
RAIL	Runway Alignment Indicator Lights	RT& BTL	Radar Tracking and Beacon Tracking Level
RAPCO	Radar Approach Control (USAF)		
RAPCON	Radar Approach Control (FAA)	RTCA	Radio Technical Commission for Aeronautics
RATCC	Radar Air Traffic Control Center		
RATCF	Radar Air Traffic Control Facility (USN)	RTP	Regional Transportation Plan
RBC	Rotating Beam Ceilometer	RTR	Remote Transmitter/Receiver
RBDPE	Radar Beacon Data Processing Equipment	RTRD	Remote Tower Radar Display
		RVR	Runway Visual Range
RBSS	Radar Bomb Scoring Squadron	RW	Runway
RCAG	Remote Communications Air/Ground	RWDS	Same as RRWDS
RCC	Rescue Coordination Center	RWP	Real-time Weather Processor
RCCC	Regional Communications Control Centers	SAC	Strategic Air Command
		SAFI	Semi Automatic Flight Inspection
RCF	Remote Communication Facility	SALS	Short Approach Lighting System
RCIU	Remote Control Interface Unit	SATCOM	Satellite Communications
RCL	Radio Communications Link	SAWRS	Supplementary Aviation Weather Reporting System
RCLR	RCL Repeater		
RCLT	RCL Terminal	SBGP	State Block Grant Program
RCO	Remote Communications Outlet	SCC	System Command Center
RCU	Remote Control Unit	SCVTS	Switched Compressed Video Telecommunications Service
RDAT	Digitized Radar Data		
RDP	Radar Data Processing	SDF	Simplified Direction Finding; Software Defined Network
RDSIM	Runway Delay Simulation Model		
REIL	Runway End Identification Lights	SDIS	Switched Digital Integrated Service
RF	Radio Frequency	SDP	Service Delivery Point
RL	General Aviation Reliever Airport	SDS	Switched Data Service
RMCC	Remote Monitor Control Center	SEL	Single Event Level
RMCF	Remote Monitor Control Facility	SELF	Simplified Short Approach Lighting System with Sequenced Flashing Lights
RML	Radio Microwave Link		
RMLR	RML Repeater		
RMLT	RML Terminal	SFAR-38	Special Federal Aviation Regulation 38
RMM	Remote Maintenance Monitoring	SHPO	State Historic Preservation Officer
RMMS	Remote Maintenance Monitoring System	SIC	Service Initiation Charge
		SID	Station Identifier; Standard Instrument Departure
RMS	Remote Monitoring Subsystem		
RMSC	Remote Monitoring Subsystem Concentrator	SIGMET	Significant Meteorological Information
		SIMMOD	Airport and Airspace Simulation Model
RNAV	Area Navigation	SIP	State Implementation Plan
RNP	Required Navigation Performance	SM	Statute Miles

SMGC	Surface Movement Guidance and Control	TCLT	Tentative Calculated Landing Time
SMPS	Sector Maintenance Processor Subsystem	TCO	Telecommunications Certification Officer
SMS	Safety Management System; Simulation Modeling System	TCOM	Terminal Communications
		TCS	Tower Communications System
SNR	Signal-to-Noise Ratio, also: S/N	TDLS	Tower Data-Link Services
SOAR	System of Airports Reporting	TDMUX	Time Division Data Multiplexer
SOC	Service Oversight Center	TDWR	Terminal Doppler Weather Radar
SOIR	Simultaneous Operations on Intersecting Runways	TELCO	Telephone Company
		TELMS	Telecommunications Management System
SOIWR	Simultaneous Operations on Intersecting Wet Runways	TERPS	Terminal Instrument Procedures
		TFAC	To Facility
SRAP	Sensor Receiver and Processor	TH	Threshold
S/S	Sector Suite	TIMS	Telecommunications Information Management System
SSALF	SSALS with Sequenced Flashers		
SSALR	Simplified Short Approach Lighting System	TIPS	Terminal Information Processing System
SSB	Single Side Band	TL	Taxilane
STAR	Standard Terminal Arrival Route	TMA	Traffic Management Advisor
STD	Standard	TMC	Traffic Management Coordinator
STMUX	Statistical Data Multiplexer	TMC/MC	Traffic Management Coordinator/Military Coordinator
STOL	Short Takeoff and Landing		
SURPIC	Surface Picture	TMCC	Terminal Information Processing System; Traffic Management Computer Complex
SVCA	Service A		
SVCB	Service B		
SVCC	Service C	TMF	Traffic Management Facility
SVCO	Service O	TML	Television Microwave Link
SVFO	Interphone Service F (A)	TMLI	Television Microwave Link Indicator
SVFB	Interphone Service F (B)	TMLR	Television Microwave Link Repeater
SVFC	Interphone Service F (C)	TMLT	Television Microwave Link Terminal
SVFD	Interphone Service F (D)	TM&O	Telecommunications Management and Operations
SVFR	Special Visual Flight Rules		
T1MUX	T1 Multiplexer	TMP	Traffic Management Processor
TAAS	Terminal Advance Automation System	TMS	Traffic Management System
TACAN	Tactical Aircraft Control and Navigation	TMSPS	Traffic Management Specialists
		TMU	Traffic Management Unit
TACR	TACAN at VOR, TACAN only	TODA	Takeoff Distance Available
TAF	Terminal Area Forecast	TOF	Time of Flight
TARS	Terminal Automated Radar Service	TOFMS	Time of Flight Mass Spectrometer
TAS	True Air Speed	TOPS	Telecommunications Ordering and Pricing System (GSA software tool)
TATCA	Terminal Air Traffic Control Automation		
		TORA	Take-off Run Available
TAVT	Terminal Airspace Visualization Tool	TNAV	Terminal Navigational Aids
TCA	Traffic Control Airport or Tower Control Airport	TR	Telecommunications Request
		TRACAB	Terminal Radar Approach Control in Tower Cab
TCA	Terminal Control Area		
TCACCIS	Transportation Coordinator Automated Command and Control Information System	TRACON	Terminal Radar Approach Control Facility
		TRAD	Terminal Radar Service
		TRB	Transportation Research Board
TCAS	Traffic Alert and Collision Avoidance System	TRNG	Training
		TSA	Taxiway Safety Area
TCC	DOT Transportation Computer Center	TSEC	Terminal Secondary Radar Service
TCCC	Tower Control Computer Complex	TSP	Telecommunications Service Priority
TCE	Tone Control Equipment	TSR	Telecommunications Service Request

TSYS	Terminal Equipment Systems	*VOR*	VHF Omnidirectional Range
TTMA	TRACON Traffic Management Advisor	*VOR/DME*	VHF Omnidirectional Range/Distance Measuring Equipment
TTY	Teletype		
TVOR	Terminal VHF Omnidirectional Range	*VORTAC*	VOR collocated with TACAN
TW	Taxiway	*VOT*	VOR Test Facility
TWEB	Transcribed Weather Broadcast	*VP/D*	Vehicle/Pedestrian Deviation
TWR	Tower (non-controlled)	*VRS*	Voice Recording System
TY	Type (FAACIS)	*VSCS*	Voice Switching and Control System
UAS	Uniform Accounting System	*VTA*	Vertex Time of Arrival
UHF	Ultra High Frequency	*VTAC*	VOR collocated with TACAN
URA	Uniform Relocation Assistance and Real Property Acquisition Policies Act of 1970	*VTOL*	Vertical Takeoff and Landing
		VTS	Voice Telecommunications System
		WAAS	Wide Area Augmentation System
USAF	United States Air Force	*WAN*	Wide Area Network
USC	United States Code	*WC*	Work Center
USOC	Uniform Service Order Code	*WCP*	Weather Communications Processor
VALE	Voluntary Airport Low Emission	*WECO*	Western Electric Company
VASI	Visual Approach Slope Indicator	*WESCOM*	Western Electric Satellite Communications
VDME	VOR with Distance Measuring Equipment	*WMSC*	Weather Message Switching Center
		WMSCR	Weather Message Switching Center Replacement
VF	Voice Frequency		
VFR	Visual Flight Rules	*WSCMO*	Weather Service Contract Meteorological Observatory
VHF	Very High Frequency		
VLF	Very Low Frequency	*WSFO*	Weather Service Forecast Office
VMC	Visual Meteorological Conditions	*WSMO*	Weather Service Meteorological Observatory
VNAV	Visual Navigational Aids		
VNTSC	Volpe National Transportation System Center	*WSO*	Weather Service Office
		WTHR	Weather
VON	Virtual On-net	*WX*	Weather

Federal Budget

Account A separate financial reporting unit for budget, management, and/or accounting purposes. All budgetary transactions are recorded in accounts, but not all accounts are budgetary in nature. Some accounts do not directly affect the budget but are used purely for accounting purposes. Budget accounts are used to record all transfers within the budget, whereas other accounts (such as deposit fund, credit financing, and foreign currency accounts) are used for accounting purposes connected with funds that are nonbudgetary in nature. The Office of Management and Budget (OMB), in consultation with the Department of the Treasury (Treasury), assigns account identification codes reflecting appropriations as enacted in appropriations laws. Treasury establishes and maintains a system of accounts that provides the basic structure for the U.S. Standard General Ledger Chart of Accounts

Account in the President's Budget: Expenditure/ Appropriation and Receipt Accounts Classified by Fund Types Accounts used by the federal government to record outlays (expenditure accounts) and income (receipt accounts) primarily for budgeting or management information purposes but also for accounting purposes. All budget (and off-budget) accounts are classified as being either expenditure or receipt (including offsetting receipt) accounts and by fund group. Budget (and off-budget) transactions fall within either of two fund groups: (1) federal funds and (2) trust funds. All federal fund and trust fund accounts are included within the budget (that is, they are on-budget) unless they are excluded from the budget by law. Federal and trust funds excluded from the budget by law are classified as being off-budget. The term off-budget differs from the term nonbudgetary. Nonbudgetary refers to activities (such as the credit financing accounts) that do not belong in the budget under existing concepts, while off-budget refers to accounts that belong on-budget under budget concepts but that are excluded from the budget under terms of law.

Accounts Payable Amounts owed by a federal agency for goods and services received from, progress in contract performance made by, and rents due to other entities. This is a proprietary (or financial) accounting term. For balance sheet reporting purposes, according to OMB Circular No. A-11 "accounts payable" consists of the amount owed by the reporting entity for goods and services received from other entities, progress in contract performance made by other entities, and rents due to other entities.

Accounts Receivable Amounts due from others for goods furnished and services rendered. Such amounts include reimbursements earned and refunds receivable. This is a proprietary (or financial) accounting and not a budget term. Accounts receivable do not constitute budget authority against which an agency may incur an obligation. For federal proprietary accounting, accounts receivable are assets that arise from specifically identifiable, legally enforceable claims to cash or other assets through an entity's established assessment processes or when goods or services are provided.

Accrual Accounting A system of accounting in which revenues are recorded when earned and expenses are recorded when goods are received or services are performed, even though the actual receipt of revenues and payment for goods or services may occur, in whole or in part, at a different time.

Administrative Division or Subdivision of Funds Any apportionment or other distribution of an appropriation or fund made pursuant to the Antideficiency Act (31 U.S.C. §§ 1511-1519). The appropriation may be divided or subdivided administratively within the limits of the apportionment (31 U.S.C. § 1513(d)). The expenditure or obligation of the divided or subdivided appropriation or fund may not exceed the apportionment (31 U.S.C. § 1517(a)).

Accrual Basis The basis whereby transactions and events are recognized when they occur, regardless of when cash is received or paid. (See also Accrual Accounting.)

Administrative Expense The cost that is directly related to credit program operations, including payments to contractors. The Federal Credit Reform Act of 1990 (FCRA) requires that administrative expenses for both direct loans and loan guarantees be included in program accounts. Administrative expenses are not included in subsidy costs appropriations but are separately appropriated.

Advance Appropriation Budget authority provided in an appropriation act that becomes available 1 or more fiscal years after the fiscal year for which the appropriation act was enacted. For example, a fiscal year 2015 appropriation act could provide that the budget authority for a specified activity would not become available until October 1, 2015 (the start of fiscal year 2016), or later. The amount is not included in the budget totals of the year for which the appropriation act is enacted but rather in those for the fiscal year in which the amount will become available for obligation. In the example above, the budget authority would be recorded in fiscal year 2016. (For a distinction, see Advance Funding; Forward Funding; Multiple-Year Authority under Duration under Budget Authority.)

Advance Funding Budget authority provided in an appropriation act to obligate and disburse (outlay) in the current fiscal year funds from a succeeding year's appropriation. Advance funding is a means to avoid making supplemental requests late in the fiscal year for certain entitlement programs in cases where the appropriations for the current year prove to be insufficient. When such budget authority is used (i.e., funds obligated), the budget records an increase in the budget authority for the fiscal year in which it is used and a reduction in the budget authority for the following fiscal year. (For a distinction, see Advance Appropriation; Multiple-Year Authority under Duration under Budget Authority; Forward Funding.)

Advance Payment An amount paid prior to the later receipt of goods, services, or other assets. Advances are ordinarily made only to payees to whom an agency has an obligation, and they do not exceed the amount of the obligation.

Agency No one definition of this term has general, government wide applicability. "Agency" and related terms, like "executive agency" or "federal agency," are defined in different ways in different laws and regulations. For example, the provisions of the Budget and Accounting Act of 1921 relating to the preparation of the President's budget specifically define "agency" to include the District of Columbia government but exclude the legislative branch or the Supreme Court (31 U.S.C. § 1101).

Agency Debt That portion of the gross federal debt incurred when a federal agency other than the Department of the Treasury (Treasury) is authorized by law to issue debt securities directly to the public or to another government account. While an agency may have authority to borrow directly from the public, agencies usually borrow from Treasury's Federal Financing Bank (FFB). Since Treasury borrowing required to obtain the money to lend to the agency through FFB is already part of the gross federal debt, to avoid double counting, agency borrowing from FFB is not included in the gross federal debt. In addition, federal fund advances from Treasury to trust funds are not included in the gross federal debt to avoid double counting. Debt of government-sponsored, privately owned enterprises, such as the Federal National Mortgage Association, is not included in the federal debt.

Agency Mission Term used in section 1105(a)(22) of title 31 of the United States Code, which outlines content requirements for the President's budget submission to Congress. Section 1105 requires that the President's budget contain a statement of agency budget authority in terms of agency missions, but this section offers no definition. The term is generally accepted to refer to the purpose of the programs of the agency and its component organizations. In the Office of Management and Budget's (OMB) budget functional classification system, agency missions are distinguished from national needs. National needs are generally described as major functions, while agency missions are generally described in the context of subfunctions. (See also Functional Classification.)

Allocation For the purposes of budgeting, an allocation means a delegation, authorized in law, by one agency of its authority to obligate budget authority and outlay funds to another agency. (The appropriation or fund from which the allocation is made is generally referred to as the parent appropriation or fund.) An allocation is made when one or more agencies share the administration of a program for which appropriations are made to only one of the agencies or to the President. When an allocation occurs, the Department of the Treasury establishes a subsidiary account called a "transfer appropriation account," and the agency receiving the allocation may obligate up to the amount included in the account. The budget does not show the transfer appropriation account separately. Transactions involving allocation accounts appear in the Object Classification Schedule, with the corresponding Program and Financing Schedule, in the President's budget. For an illustration of the treatment of Object Classification--With Allocation Accounts, see OMB Circular No. A-11. (See also Object Classification; Transfer; Transfer Appropriation (Allocation) Accounts under Account for Purposes Other Than Budget Presentation.) For purposes of section 302(a) of the Congressional Budget and Impoundment Control Act of 1974 (2 U.S.C. § 633(a)), an allocation is the distribution of spending authority and outlays to relevant committees based on the levels contained in a concurrent resolution on the budget. (See also Committee Allocation.) For purposes of section 302(b) of the Congressional Budget and Impoundment Control Act of 1974 (2 U.S.C. § 633(b)), an allocation is the distribution of spending authority and outlays to relevant subcommittees based on the levels contained in the concurrent resolution on the budget. (See also Subcommittee Allocation.) For funds control purposes, an allocation is a further subdivision of an apportionment.

Allotment An authorization by either the agency head or another authorized employee to his/her subordinates to incur obligations within a specified amount. Each agency makes allotments pursuant to specific procedures it establishes within the general apportionment requirements stated in OMB Circular No. A-11. The amount allotted by an agency cannot exceed the amount apportioned by the Office of Management and Budget (OMB). An allotment is part of an agency system of administrative control of funds whose purpose is to keep obligations and expenditures from exceeding apportionments and allotments. (See also Administrative Division or Subdivision of Funds; Apportionment; Reapportionment.)

Allowance An amount included in the President's budget request or included in a projection in a congressional resolution on the budget to cover possible additional proposals, such as contingencies for programs whose expenditures are controllable only by statutory change and other requirements. As used by Congress in the concurrent resolutions on the budget, an allowance represents a special functional classification designed to include an amount to cover possible requirements. An allowance remains undistributed until the contingency on which it is based occurs; then it is distributed to the appropriate functional classification. For agency budgetary accounting and fund control purposes, an allowance is a subdivision of an allotment. For treatment of undistributed allowances, see function 920 in the table "Outlays by Function and Subfunction" in the Historical Tables of the President's budget. (For more details on the government accounting definition, see Standard General Ledger Chart of Accounts.) For federal proprietary accounting, an allowance also represents the estimated uncollectible amount of accounts receivable.

Antideficiency Act Federal law that:* prohibits the making of expenditures or the incurring of obligations in advance of an appropriation; * prohibits the incurring of obligations or the making of expenditures in excess of amounts available in appropriation or fund accounts unless specifically authorized by law (31 U.S.C. § 1341(a)); * prohibits the acceptance of voluntary or personal services unless authorized by law (31 U.S.C. § 1342); * requires the Office of Management and Budget (OMB), via delegation from the President, to apportion appropriated funds and other budgetary resources for all executive branch agencies (31 U.S.C. § 1512); * requires a system of administrative controls within each agency (see 31 U.S.C. § 1514 for the administrative divisions established); * prohibits incurring any obligation or making any expenditure in excess of an apportionment or reapportionment or in excess of other subdivisions established pursuant to sections 1513 and 1514 of title 31 of the United States Code (31 U.S.C. § 1517); and: * specifies penalties for deficiencies (see Antideficiency Act Violation). The act permits agencies to reserve funds (that is, withhold them from obligation) under certain circumstances. (See also Administrative Division or Subdivision of Funds; Antideficiency Act Violation; Apportionment; Budgetary Reserves; Deferral of Budget Authority; Deficiency Apportionment; Deficiency Appropriation; Expenditure; Fund Accounting; Congressional Budget and Impoundment Control Act of 1994; Outlay.)

Antideficiency Act Violation Occurs when one or more of the following happens: * overobligation or overexpenditure of an appropriation or fund account (31 U.S.C. § 1341(a)); * entering into a contract or making an obligation in advance of an appropriation, unless specifically authorized by law (31 U.S.C. § 1341(a)); * acceptance of voluntary service, unless authorized by law (31 U.S.C. § 1342); or: * overobligation or overexpenditure of (1) an apportionment or reapportionment or (2) amounts permitted by the administrative control of funds regulations (31 U.S.C. § 1517(a)). Once it has been determined that there has been a violation of the Antideficiency Act, the agency head must report all relevant facts and a statement of actions taken to the President and Congress and submit a copy of the report to the Comptroller General. Penalties for Antideficiency Act violations include administrative discipline, such as suspension from duty without pay or removal from office. In addition, an officer or employee convicted of willfully and knowingly violating the law shall be fined not more than $5,000, imprisoned for not more than 2 years, or both (31 U.S.C. §§ 1349, 1350, 1518, and 1519). (See also Administrative Division or Subdivision of Funds; Antideficiency Act; Expenditure.)

Apportionment The action by which the Office of Management and Budget (OMB) distributes amounts available for obligation, including budgetary reserves established pursuant to law, in an appropriation or fund account. An apportionment divides amounts available for obligation by specific time periods (usually quarters), activities, projects, objects, or a combination thereof. The amounts so apportioned limit the amount of obligations that may be incurred. An apportionment may be further subdivided by an agency into allotments, suballotments, and allocations. In apportioning any account, some funds may be reserved to provide for contingencies or to effect savings made possible pursuant to the Antideficiency

Act. Funds apportioned to establish a reserve must be proposed for deferral or rescission pursuant to the Impoundment Control Act of 1974 (2 U.S.C. §§ 681-688). The apportionment process is intended to (1) prevent the obligation of amounts available within an appropriation or fund account in a manner that would require deficiency or supplemental appropriations and (2) achieve the most effective and economical use of amounts made available for obligation. (See also Administrative Division or Subdivision of Funds; Allotment; Antideficiency Act; Appropriated Entitlement; Budgetary Reserves; Deferral of Budget Authority; Deficiency Apportionment; Deficiency Appropriation; Limitation; Reapportionment; Rescission; Supplemental Appropriation.)

Appropriated Entitlement An entitlement whose source of funding is in an annual appropriation act. However, because the entitlement is created by operation of law, if Congress does not appropriate the money necessary to fund the payments, eligible recipients may have legal recourse. Veterans' compensation and Medicaid are examples of such appropriated entitlements. (See also Entitlement Authority.)

Appropriation Account The basic unit of an appropriation generally reflecting each unnumbered paragraph in an appropriation act. An appropriation account typically encompasses a number of activities or projects and may be subject to restrictions or conditions applicable to only the account, the appropriation act, titles within an appropriation act, other appropriation acts, or the government as a whole.

Appropriation Act A statute, under the jurisdiction of the House and Senate Committees on Appropriations, that generally provides legal authority for federal agencies to incur obligations and to make payments out of the Treasury for specified purposes. An appropriation act fulfills the requirement of Article I, Section 9, of the U.S. Constitution, which provides that "no money shall be drawn from the Treasury, but in Consequence of Appropriations made by Law." Under the rules of both houses, an appropriation act should follow enactment of authorizing legislation. (See also Appropriations under Forms of Budget Authority under Budget Authority; Authorizing Legislation; Limitation.) Major types of appropriation acts are regular, supplemental, deficiency, and continuing. Regular appropriation acts are all appropriation acts that are not supplemental, deficiency, or continuing. Currently, regular annual appropriation acts that provide funding for the continued operation of federal departments, agencies, and various government activities are considered by Congress annually. From time to time, supplemental appropriation acts are also enacted. When action on regular appropriation bills is not completed before the beginning of the fiscal year, a continuing resolution (often referred to simply as "CR") may be enacted in a bill or joint resolution to provide funding for the affected agencies for the full year, up to a specified date, or until their regular appropriations are enacted. A deficiency appropriation act provides budget authority to cover obligations incurred in excess of available budget authority. (See also Continuing Appropriation/Continuing Resolution; Supplemental Appropriation; Deficiency Appropriation.)

Appropriation Rider Sometimes used to refer to (1) a provision that is not directly related to the appropriation to which it is attached or (2) a limitation or requirement in an appropriation act. (See also Limitation.)

Appropriations Budget authority to incur obligations and to make payments from the Treasury for specified purposes. An appropriation act is the most common means of providing appropriations; however, authorizing and other legislation itself may provide appropriations. (See also Backdoor Authority/Backdoor Spending.) Appropriations do not represent cash actually set aside in the Treasury for purposes specified in the appropriation act; they represent amounts that agencies may obligate during the period of time specified in the respective appropriation acts. An appropriation may make funds available from the general fund, special funds, or trust funds. Certain types of appropriations are not counted as budget authority because they do not provide authority to incur obligations. Among these are appropriations to liquidate contract authority (legislation to provide funds to pay obligations incurred against contract authority), to redeem outstanding debt (legislation to provide funds for debt retirement), and to refund receipts. Sometimes appropriations are contingent upon the occurrence of some other action specified in the appropriation law, such as the enactment of a subsequent authorization or the fulfillment of some action by the executive branch. (See also Appropriation Act; Discretionary; Expired Budget Authority under Availability for New Obligations under Budget Authority; Mandatory.)

Asset Tangible or intangible items owned by the federal government, which would have probable economic benefits that can be obtained or controlled by a federal government entity. (See also Liability.)

Asset Sale The sale of a physical or financial asset owned in whole or in part by the federal government to the public. Asset sales are typically large-dollar transactions ($50 million or more) for which advance notification must be provided to the Department of the Treasury. Revenue from the sale of assets is accounted for in the budget as offsetting receipts or collections. In general, asset sales increase current cash payments received by the government at the expense of a stream of future income that the government would otherwise receive. (See also Direct Loan under Federal Credit.)

Authorizing Committee A standing committee of the House or Senate with legislative jurisdiction over the establishment, continuation, and operations of federal programs or agencies. The jurisdiction of such committees extends, in addition to program legislation, to authorization of appropriations legislation. (Normally, authorization of appropriations legislation is a prerequisite for making appropriations for the given programs or agencies). An authorizing committee also has jurisdiction in those instances where backdoor authority is provided in the substantive legislation. For further discussion, see the current rules Legislation; Backdoor Authority/Backdoor of the House of Representatives and the Senate. (See also Authorizing Spending; Oversight Committee; Spending Committee.)

Authorizing Legislation Substantive legislation, proposed by a committee of jurisdiction other than the House or Senate Appropriations Committees, that establishes and continues the operation of a federal program or agency either indefinitely or for a specific period or that sanctions a particular type of obligation or expenditure within a program. This term is used in two different ways: (1) to describe legislation enacting new program authority, that is, authorizing the program, and (2) to describe legislation authorizing an appropriation. Authorization of appropriations legislation authorizes the enactment of appropriations of specific amounts for specific programs and activities to be provided in an appropriation act. An authorization of appropriations is, under congressional rules, a prerequisite for such an appropriation. Thus, for example, a point of order may be raised in either house objecting to an appropriation in an appropriation act that is not previously authorized by law. An authorization of appropriations may be part of the organic legislation for the agency or program or it may be separate legislation. Oftentimes, the authorization of appropriation may be inferred from an appropriation provided in an appropriation act. The authorization of appropriation may specify the amount of budget authority to be included in the appropriation act or it may authorize the appropriation of "such sums as may be necessary." In some instances, authorizing legislation may contain an appropriation or provide other forms of budget authority, such as contract authority, borrowing authority, or entitlement authority. (See also Appropriation Act; Backdoor Authority/Backdoor Spending; Entitlement Authority; Limitation; Point of Order; Reauthorization.)

Backdoor Authority/Backdoor Spending A colloquial phrase for budget authority provided in laws other than appropriations acts, including contract authority and borrowing authority, as well as entitlement authority and the outlays that result from that budget authority. (See also Appropriations and Contract Authority under Forms of Budget Authority under Budget Authority; Authorizing Legislation; Entitlement Authority; Spending Committee.)

Balanced Budget A budget in which receipts equal outlays. (See also Deficit; Surplus.)

Balanced Budget and Emergency Deficit Control Act of 1985 Also known as the Deficit Control Act, originally known as Gramm-Rudman-Hollings. Among other changes to the budget process, the law established "maximum deficit amounts" and a sequestration procedure to reduce spending if those targets were exceeded. The Deficit Control Act has been amended and extended several times—most significantly by the Budget Enforcement Act (BEA) of 1990. The sequestration and enforcement mechanisms expired or became ineffective at the end of fiscal year 2002. (See also Budget Enforcement Act; Gramm-Rudman-Hollings.)

Balanced Budget and Emergency Deficit Control Reaffirmation Act of 1987 Amended the Balanced Budget and Emergency Deficit Control Act of 1985 (Gramm-Rudman-Hollings) to extend the date for achieving the goal of a balanced budget until fiscal year 1993, revise sequestration procedures, and require the Director of the Office of Management and Budget (OMB) to determine whether a sequester is necessary. (See also Budget and Accounting Act of 1921; Budget Enforcement Act; Gramm-Rudman-Hollings; Sequestration.)

Baseline An estimate of spending, revenue, the deficit or surplus, and the public debt expected during a fiscal year under current laws and current policy. The baseline is a benchmark for measuring the budgetary effects of proposed changes in revenues and spending. It assumes that receipts and mandatory spending will continue or expire in the future as required by law and that the future funding for discretionary programs will equal the most recently enacted appropriation, adjusted for inflation. Under the Budget Enforcement Act (BEA), the baseline is defined as the projection of current-year levels of new budget authority, outlays, revenues, and the surplus or deficit into the budget year and outyears based on laws enacted through the applicable date. (See also Projections.)

Bases of Budgeting Methods for calculating budget figures. Not all methods are mutually exclusive. For example, the federal budget includes both net and gross figures and reports both obligations and cash or cash equivalent spending. As a general rule, budget receipts and outlays are on a cash or cash equivalent basis; however, interest on public issues of public debt is recorded on an accrual basis. Under credit reform, the subsidy cost of both direct loans and guaranteed loans is included in the budget (i.e., the budget records the net present value of the estimated cash flows of direct loans and loan guarantees as outlays). (See also Capital Budget; Direct Loan and Guaranteed Loan under Federal Credit. For a more detailed presentation of this subject, see app. III.)

Biennial Budget A budget covering a period of 2 years. The federal government has an annual budget, but there have been proposals to shift to a biennial budget. The 2-year period can apply to the budget presented to Congress by the President, to the budget resolution adopted by Congress, or to the frequency and period covered by appropriations acts. The Department of Defense Authorization Act, 1986, Pub. L. No. 99-145, required the Department of Defense to submit 2-year budgets beginning with the budgets for 1988 and 1989. However, to date, appropriations have been made on an annual basis.

Borrowing Authority Budget authority enacted to permit an agency to borrow money and then to obligate against amounts borrowed. It may be definite or indefinite in nature. Usually the funds are borrowed from the Treasury, but in a few cases agencies borrow directly from the public. (See also Debt, Federal.)

Budget A detailed statement of anticipated revenues and expenditures during an accounting period. For the federal government, the term "budget" often refers to the President's budget submission to Congress early each calendar year in accordance with the Budget and Accounting Act of 1921, as amended, and represents proposals for congressional consideration. The President's budget includes requests for budget authority for federal programs and estimates of revenues and outlays for the upcoming fiscal year and, with respect to budget authority requests in some cases, for future fiscal years. By law, elements of the budget, such as the estimates for the legislative branch and the judiciary, must be included without review by the Office of Management and Budget (OMB) or approval by the President. In the context of individual federal agencies and their programs, the term "budget" also may be used to refer to their budget submissions or, in response to Congress passing laws providing budget authority, the agencies' plans for spending the funds they were provided. (See also President's Budget; app. I.)

Budget Act The common name of the Congressional Budget and Impoundment Control Act of 1974. (See under Congressional Budget and Impoundment Control Act of 1974.)

Budget Activity A specific and distinguishable line of work performed by a governmental unit to discharge a function or subfunction for which the governmental unit is responsible. Activities within most accounts identify the purposes, projects, or types of activities financed. For example, food inspection is an activity performed in the discharge of the health function. A budget activity is presented in the Program by Activities section in the Program and Financing Schedule for each account in the President's budget. (See also Functional Classification; for a partial distinction, see Program, Project, or Activity.)

Budget Amendment A revision to a pending budget request that the President submits to Congress before Congress completes appropriations action.

Budget and Accounting Act of 1921 Enhanced budgetary efficiency and aided in the performance of constitutional checks and balances through the budget process. It required the President to submit a national budget each year and restricted the authority of the agencies to present their own proposals. (See 31 U.S.C. §§ 1104, 1105.) With this centralization of authority for the formulation of the executive branch budget in the President and the newly established Bureau of the Budget (now the Office of Management and Budget (OMB)), Congress also took steps to strengthen its oversight of fiscal matters by establishing the General Accounting Office, renamed the Government Accountability Office (GAO) in 2004.

Budget Authority Authority provided by federal law to enter into financial obligations that will result in immediate or future outlays involving federal government funds. The basic forms of budget authority include (1) appropriations, (2) borrowing authority, (3) contract authority, and (4) authority to obligate and expend offsetting receipts and collections. Budget authority includes the credit subsidy cost for direct loan and loan guarantee programs, but does not include the underlying authority to insure or guarantee the repayment of indebtedness incurred by another person or government. Budget authority may be classified by its duration (1-year, multiple-year, or no-year), by the timing provided in the legislation (current or permanent), by the manner of determining the amount available (definite or indefinite), or by its availability for new obligations. (See also Current Level Estimate; Credit Subsidy Cost, Direct Loan, and Guaranteed Loan under Federal Credit; Offsetting Collections under Collections.)

Budget Deficit The amount by which the government's budget outlays exceed its budget receipts for a given period, usually a fiscal year. (See also Budget Surplus under Surplus.)

Budget Enforcement Act (BEA) First enacted as Title XIII of the Omnibus Budget Reconciliation Act of 1990. BEA amended the Balanced Budget and

Emergency Deficit Control Act of 1985 and related amendments (Gramm-Rudman-Hollings) and the Congressional Budget and Impoundment Control Act of 1974. BEA modified procedures and definitions for sequestration and deficit reduction, reformed budgetary credit accounting, maintained the off-budget status of the Old-Age and Survivors Insurance and Disability Insurance Trust Funds, and removed Social Security trust fund receipts and outlays from deficit and sequestration calculations.

Budget Estimates Estimates of budget authority, outlays, receipts, budget amendments, supplemental requests from the President, or other budget measures that cover the current, budget, and future years, as reflected in the President's budget and budget updates. (See also Budget Update.)

Budget Update A revised estimate of budget authority, receipts, and outlays issued subsequent to the issuance of the President's budget. The President is required by provisions of the Congressional Budget and Impoundment Control Act of 1974 (see provisions of 31 U.S.C. §§ 1105(d), 1106) to transmit such statements to Congress by July 15 of each year; however, the President may also submit budget updates.

Budget Year A term used in the budget formulation process to refer to the fiscal year for which the budget is being considered, that is, with respect to a session of Congress, the fiscal year of the government that starts on October 1 of the calendar year in which that session of Congress begins.

Budgetary Reserves Portions of budgetary resources set aside (withheld through apportionment) by the Office of Management and Budget (OMB) by authority of the Antideficiency Act (31 U.S.C. § 1512) solely to provide for contingencies or to effect savings. Such savings are made possible through changes in requirements or through greater efficiency of operations. Budgetary resources may also be set aside if specifically provided for by particular appropriation acts or other laws at other times during the fiscal year. (See also Budget Estimates.) Except as specifically provided by law, no reserves shall be established other than as authorized under the Antideficiency Act (31 U.S.C. § 1512). Reserves established are reported to Congress in accordance with provisions of the Impoundment Control Act of 1974 (2 U.S.C. §§ 681-688). (See also Antideficiency Act; Apportionment; Deferral of Budget Authority; Rescission.)

Budgetary Resources An amount available to enter into new obligations and to liquidate them. Budgetary resources are made up of new budget authority (including direct spending authority provided in existing statute and obligation limitations) and unobligated balances of budget authority provided in previous years. (See also Budget Authority.)

Buyback In the context of federal debt, the Department of the Treasury's purchases of marketable Treasury securities from the public prior to their maturity through competitive redemption processes (as opposed to redemptions prior to maturity under call provisions) are often referred to as "debt buybacks." The budget records buyback premiums and discounts as means of financing a surplus or deficit, rather than as outlays or offsetting collections or receipts. The buyback premium or discount is the difference between the reacquisition price of a security and its book value. (See also Means of Financing.)

Byrd Rule A rule of the Senate that allows a senator to strike extraneous material in, or proposed to be in, reconciliation legislation or the related conference report. The rule defines six provisions that are "extraneous," including a provision that does not produce a change in outlays or revenues and a provision that produces changes in outlays or revenues that are merely incidental to the nonbudgetary components of the provision. The Byrd Rule was first enacted as section 20001 of the Consolidated Omnibus Budget Reconciliation Act of 1985 and later transferred in 1990 to section 313 of the Congressional Budget Act (2 U.S.C. § 644). The rule is named after its primary sponsor, Senator Robert C. Byrd. (See also Reconciliation; Reconciliation Bill; Reconciliation Instruction; Reconciliation Resolution.)

Capital Has different meanings depending on the context in which it is used. Physical capital is land and the stock of products set aside to support future production and consumption. In the National Income and Product Accounts, private capital consists of business inventories, producers' durable equipment, and residential and nonresidential structures. (See National Income and Product Accounts.) Financial capital is funds raised by governments, individuals, or businesses by incurring liabilities such as bonds, mortgages, or stock certificates. Human capital is the education, training, work experience, and other attributes that enhance the ability of the labor force to produce goods and services. Capital assets are land, structures, equipment, intellectual property (e.g., software), and information technology (including information technology service contracts) that are used by the federal government and have an estimated useful life of 2 years or more. Capital assets may be acquired in different ways: through purchase, construction, or manufacturing; through a lease-purchase or other capital lease (regardless of whether title has passed to the federal government); through an operating lease for an asset with an estimated useful life of 2 years or more; or through exchange. Capital assets may or may not be recorded in an entity's balance sheet under federal accounting standards. Capital assets do not include grants to state and local governments or other entities for acquiring capital assets (such as National Science Foundation grants to universities or Department of Transportation grants to Amtrak), intangible assets (such as the knowledge resulting from research and development), or the human capital resulting from education and training. For more on capital assets, consult the Capital Programming Guide (June 1997), a supplement to OMB Circular No. A-11.

Capital Budget A budget that segregates capital investments from the operating budget's expenditures. In such a budget, the capital investments that are excluded from the operating budget do not count toward calculating the operating budget's surplus or deficit at the time the investment is made. States that use capital budgets usually include only part of their capital expenditures in that budget and normally finance the capital investment from borrowing and then charge amortization (interest and debt repayment) to the operating budget.

Capital Lease A lease other than a lease-purchase that transfers substantially all the benefits and risks of ownership to the lessee and does not meet the criteria of an operating lease. (See also Operating Lease.)

Cash or Cash Equivalent Basis The basis whereby receipts are recorded when received and expenditures are recorded when paid, without regard to the accounting period in which the receipts are earned or the costs are incurred. "Cash" generally refers to payment by cash, checks, or electronic funds transfers. "Cash equivalent" refers to the use of an instrument or process that creates a substitute for cash. For example, when the government issues a debt instrument of any kind in satisfaction of claims, the transaction is recorded as simultaneous outlays and borrowing--the outlays when the debt instrument is issued, not when it is redeemed.

Cash Accounting A system of accounting in which revenues are recorded when cash is actually received and expenses are recorded when payment is made without regard to the accounting period in which the revenues were earned or costs were incurred. (See also Accrual Accounting; app. III.)

CBO Baseline Projected levels of governmental receipts (revenues), budget authority, and outlays for the budget year and subsequent fiscal years, assuming generally that current policies remain the same, except as directed by law. The baseline is described in the Congressional Budget Office's (CBO) annual report for the House and Senate Budget Committees, The Budget and Economic Outlook, which is published in January. The baseline, by law, includes projections for 5 years, but at the request of the Budget Committees, CBO has provided such projections for 10 years. In most years the CBO baseline is revised in conjunction with CBO's analysis of the President's budget, which is usually issued in March, and again during the summer. The "March" baseline is the benchmark for measuring the budgetary effects of proposed legislation under consideration by Congress.

Chain Price Indexes (Economics Term) Index calculated by linking (chaining) of price indexes based on changing weights to create a time series. Chain-type indexes are used in the Bureau of Economic Analysis National Income and Product Accounts (NIPA). (See also Chained Dollars; Real Dollar.)

Chained Dollars Dollar values calculated by taking the current dollar level of a series in the base period (or period from which the weights for a measurement series are derived) and multiplying it by the change in the chain quantity index number for the series (calculated using chained weights) since the base period. Chained-dollar estimates correctly show growth rates for a series, but the summed components do not equal the aggregate in periods other than the period from which the weights for a measurement series are derived. (See also Chain Price Indexes; Real Dollar.)

Clearing Accounts Accounts that temporarily hold general, special, or trust fund federal government collections or disbursements pending clearance to the applicable receipt or expenditure accounts.

Closed (Canceled) Account An appropriation account whose balance has been canceled. Once balances are canceled, the amounts are not available for obligation or expenditure for any purpose. An account available for a definite period (fixed appropriation account) is canceled 5 fiscal years after the period of availability for obligation ends. An account available for an indefinite period (no-year account) is canceled if (1) the head of the agency concerned or the President determines that the purposes for which the appropriation was made have been carried out and (2) no disbursement has been made against the appropriation for 2 consecutive fiscal years. (See also Expired Account; Obligational Authority.)

Cohort All direct loans or loan guarantees of a program for which a subsidy appropriation is provided for a given fiscal year, even when disbursements occur in subsequent fiscal years. For direct loans and loan guarantees that receive multiyear or no-year appropriations, the cohort is defined by the year of obligation. Pre-1992 direct loans that are modified will constitute a single cohort. Likewise, pre-1992 loan guarantees that are modified constitute a cohort. (See also Direct Loan and Guaranteed Loan under Federal Credit.)

Collections Amounts received by the federal government during the fiscal year. Collections are classified into three major categories: (1) governmental receipts (also called budget receipts or federal receipts), (2) offsetting collections, and (3) offsetting receipts. Governmental receipts result from the exercise of the government's sovereign powers. Offsetting collections and receipts result from businesslike transactions with the public or transactions between appropriated activities. Offsetting collections and offsetting receipts are recorded as offsets to spending. They are offsetting collections when the collections are authorized by law to be credited to expenditure accounts. Otherwise, they are deposited in receipt accounts and called offsetting receipts.

Commitment An administrative reservation of allotted funds, or of other funds, inanticipation of their obligation. For federal proprietary accounting, a commitment may also manifest an intent to expend assets (e.g., to provide government social insurance benefits). See Statement of Federal Financial Accounting Standards (SFFAS) No. 25, Basis for Conclusions, para. 8, and SFFAS No. 17, Basis for Conclusions, paras. 65 and 94. (See also Allotment; Loan Guarantee Commitment under Federal Credit; Obligation.)

Committee Allocation The distribution of total proposed new budget authority and outlays, as set forth in the concurrent resolution on the budget, among the congressional committees according to their jurisdictions. The allocations are set forth in the joint explanatory statement of managers included in the conference report on the congressional budget resolution. House and Senate committees receive allocations of total new budget authority and total outlays. House committees also receive allocations of total entitlement authority, and Senate committees also receive allocations of Social Security outlays. Allocations are committee specific, but not program specific. Under section 302(a) of the Congressional Budget and Impoundment Control Act of 1974 (2 U.S.C. § 633(a)), committee allocations are limits, not simply recommendations. (See also Allocation; Concurrent Resolution on the Budget; Entitlement Authority.)

Comparative Statement of New Budget Authority A table accompanying a regular or supplemental appropriations act in the report of the House or Senate Appropriations Committee. It compares the appropriation recommended for each account in that act with the amount requested by the President in the budget submission and the amount enacted in the preceding fiscal year. In some cases, such as when a continuing appropriations act is considered, the statement may be inserted into the Congressional Record.

Concurrent Resolution on the Budget A concurrent resolution adopted by both houses of Congress as part of the annual budget and appropriations process, setting forth an overall budget plan for Congress against which individual appropriations bills, other appropriations, and revenue measures are to be evaluated. As a plan for Congress, the resolution is not presented to the President for signature and does not have the force of law. Pursuant to section 301 of the Congressional Budget Act, as amended (2 U.S.C. § 632), the resolution is expected to establish, for at least 5 fiscal years beginning on October 1 of the year of the resolution, appropriate levels for the following: * totals of new budget authority and outlays, * total federal revenues, * the surplus or deficit in the budget, * new budget authority and outlays for each major functional category, * the public debt, and: * outlays and revenues for Social Security insurance programs. The concurrent resolution generally contains budget levels for the 5 fiscal years and may contain reconciliation instructions to specified committees. The concurrent resolution most recently adopted may be revised or affirmed before the end of the year to which it applies, as provided in section 304 of the Congressional Budget Act, as amended (2 U.S.C. § 635). (See also Congressional Budget and Impoundment Control Act of 1974).

Congressional Budget The Concurrent Resolution on the Budget is oftentimes referred to as the Congressional Budget. (See Concurrent Resolution on the Budget.)

Congressional Budget Act Titles I-IX of the Congressional Budget and Impoundment Control Act of 1974, as amended (2 U.S.C. §§ 601-661), are commonly referred to as the Congressional Budget Act. (See also Congressional Budget and Impoundment Control Act of 1974. For an overview of the federal budget process, see app. I.)

Congressional Budget and Impoundment Control Act of 1974 Established a process through which Congress could systematically consider the total spending policy of the United States and determine priorities for allocating budgetary resources. The process calls for procedures for coordinating congressional revenue and spending decisions made in separate tax, appropriations, and legislative measures. It established the House and Senate Budget Committees, the Congressional Budget Office (CBO), and the procedures for congressional review of impoundments in the form of rescissions and deferrals proposed by the President. (See also Budget Enforcement Act; Deferral of Budget Authority; Gramm-Rudman-Hollings; Impoundment; Rescission.)

Consolidated Financial Statement The financial statements of a parent and its subsidiary or component entities, presented as if the group were a single entity. In the U.S. government, there is a consolidated financial statement for the federal government that encompasses the executive, legislative, and judicial branches as well as consolidated statements for agencies that encompass all their offices, bureaus, and activities.

Consolidated Working Fund Accounts A subset of management funds. These are special working funds established under the authority of Section 601 of the Economy Act (31 U.S.C. §§ 1535, 1536) to receive advance payments from other agencies or accounts. Consolidated working fund accounts are not used to finance the work directly but only to reimburse the appropriation or fund account that will finance the work to be performed. Amounts in consolidated working fund accounts are available for the same periods as those of the accounts advancing the funds. Consolidated working fund accounts are shown as separate accounts on the books of Treasury but are not separately identified in the President's budget. Transactions of these accounts are included in the presentation of the appropriation or fund account

Consumer Price Index (CPI) A measure of the average change over time in the prices paid by urban consumers for a market basket of consumer goods and services commonly referred to as "inflation." Measures for two population groups are currently published, CPI-U and CPI-W. CPI-U is based on a market basket determined by expenditure patterns of all urban households, while the market basket for CPI-W is determined by expenditure patterns of only urban wage-earner and clerical-worker families. The urban wage-earner and clerical-worker population consists of clerical workers, sales workers, craft workers, operatives, service workers, and laborers. Both indexes are published monthly by the Bureau of Labor Statistics. The CPI is used to adjust for inflation, the income payments of Social Security beneficiaries, and payments made by other programs. In addition, the CPI is used to adjust certain amounts defined by the tax code, such as personal exemptions and the tax brackets.

Contingent Liability An existing condition, situation, or set of circumstances that poses the possibility of a loss to an agency that will ultimately be resolved when one or more events occur or fail to occur. Contingent liabilities may lead to outlays. Contingent liabilities may arise, for example, with respect to unadjudicated claims, assessments, loan guarantee programs, and federal insurance programs. Contingent liabilities are normally not covered by budget authority in advance. However, credit reform changed the normal budgetary treatment of loans and loan guarantees by establishing that for most programs, loan guarantee commitments cannot be made unless Congress has made appropriations of budget authority to cover the credit subsidy cost in advance in annual appropriations acts. (See also Credit Subsidy Cost under Federal Credit; Liability.)

Continuing Appropriation/Continuing Resolution (often referred to simply as "CR"): An appropriation act that provides budget authority for federal agencies, specific activities, or both to continue in operation when Congress and the President have not completed action on the regular appropriation acts by the beginning of the fiscal year. Enacted in the form of a joint resolution, a continuing resolution is passed by both houses of Congress and signed into law by the President. A continuing resolution may be enacted for the full year, up to a specified date, or until regular appropriations are enacted. A continuing resolution usually specifies a maximum rate at which the obligations may be incurred based on levels specified in the resolution. For example, the resolution may state that obligations may not exceed the current rate or must be the lower of the amounts provided in the appropriation bills passed in the House or Senate. If enacted to cover the entire fiscal year, the resolution will usually specify amounts provided for each appropriation account. (See also Appropriation Act; Current Rate; Joint Resolution; Seasonal Rate; Supplemental Appropriation.)

Contract Authority Budget authority that permits an agency to incur obligations in advance of appropriations, including collections sufficient to liquidate the obligation or receipts. Contract authority is unfunded, and a subsequent appropriation or offsetting collection is needed to liquidate the obligations. The Food and Forage Act (41 U.S.C. § 11) and the Price Anderson Act (42 U.S.C. § 2210) are examples of such authority. (See also Backdoor Authority/Backdoor Spending.)

Cost The price or cash value of the resources used to produce a program, project, or activity. This term is used in many different contexts. When used in connection with federal credit programs, the term means the estimated long-term cost to the government of a direct loan or loan guarantee, calculated on a net present value basis over the life of the loan, excluding administrative costs and any incidental effects on governmental receipts or outlays. (See also Credit Subsidy Cost under Federal Credit; Expense.) For federal proprietary accounting, the monetary value of resources used or sacrificed or the liabilities incurred to achieve an objective. In economic terms, it is a measure of what must be given up in order to obtain something, whether by purchase, exchange, or production. Economists generally use the concept of opportunity cost, which is the value of all of the things that must be forgone or given up in obtaining something. The opportunity cost measure may, but will not always, equal the money outlays used to measure accounting costs. Economists sometimes distinguish between the private costs of a good or activity to the consumer or producer and the social costs imposed on the community as a whole.

Cost-Benefit Analysis An analytic technique that compares the costs and benefits of investments, programs, or policy actions in order to determine which alternative or alternatives maximize net benefits (economic efficiency). Cost-benefit analysis attempts to consider all costs and benefits to whomever they accrue, regardless of whether they are reflected in market transactions. The costs and benefits included depend upon the scope of the analysis, although the standard federal analysis is national in scope. Net benefits of an alternative are determined by subtracting the present value of costs from the present value of benefits. (See also Present Value.)

Cost Estimates Under the Congressional Budget Act of 1974, estimates of the impact legislation under consideration by Congress would have on the federal budget if the legislation became law. Cost estimates are provided by the Congressional Budget Office (CBO) on all legislation of a public character reported by a congressional committee and are, typically, published in the report accompanying that legislation.

Countercyclical Policy Policy aimed at reducing the size and duration of swings in economic activity in order to keep economic growth closer to a pace consistent with low inflation and high employment. It includes monetary and fiscal policies affecting the level of interest rates, money supply, taxes, and government spending.

Credit Program Account A budget account that receives and obligates appropriations to cover the subsidy cost (on a net present value basis) of a direct loan or loan guarantee and disburses the subsidy cost to the financing account. Usually, a separate amount is also appropriated in the program account for administrative expenses that are directly related to credit program operations. (See also Present Value.)

Credit Reestimates Recalculation of the estimated cost to the government of a group of direct loans or loan guarantees. After new direct loans or loan guarantees are made, the Federal Credit Reform Act of 1990 (FCRA) requires periodic revisions of the subsidy cost estimate of a cohort (or risk category) based on information about the actual performance, estimated changes in future cash flows of the cohort, or both. Reestimates must generally be made annually (with an associated recalculation of applicable cumulative interest), as long as any loans in the cohort are outstanding. These reestimates represent additional costs or savings to the government and are recorded in the budget. An upward reestimate indicates that insufficient funds had been paid to the financing account, so the increase (plus interest on reestimates) is paid from the program account to the financing account to make it whole. Permanent indefinite budget authority is available for this purpose. A downward reestimate indicates that too much subsidy had been paid to the financing account. The excess identified in a downward reestimate (plus interest) may be credited directly to the program account as offsetting collections for programs classified as mandatory or to a downward reestimate receipt account for programs classified as discretionary.

Credit Reform The method of controlling and accounting for credit programs in the federal budget after fiscal year 1991. The Federal Credit Reform Act of 1990 (FCRA) added title V to the Congressional Budget Act of 1974. It requires that the credit subsidy cost be financed from new budget authority and be recorded as budget outlays at the time the direct or guaranteed loans are disbursed. In turn, it authorizes the creation of nonbudgetary financing accounts to receive this subsidy cost payment. Agencies must have appropriations for the subsidy cost before they can enter into direct loan obligations or loan guarantee commitments. (See also Credit Subsidy Cost, Direct Loan Obligation, Discount Rate, and Loan Guarantee Commitment under Federal Credit; Present Value.)

Credit Subsidy Cost The estimated long-term cost to the government of a direct loan or loan guarantee, calculated on a net present value basis and excluding administrative costs.

Current Authority Budget authority made available by Congress for the fiscal year or years during which the funds are available for obligation.

Current Dollar "In current dollars" means valued in the prices of the current year. The current dollar value of a good or service is its value in terms of prices current at the time the good or service is acquired or sold.

Current Level Estimate An estimate of the amounts of new budget authority, outlays, and revenues for a full fiscal year, based upon enacted law. Current level estimates used by Congress do not take into account the potential effects of pending legislation. Current level estimates include a tabulation comparing estimates with the aggregates approved in the most recent budget resolution, and they are consistent with the technical and economic assumptions in that resolution. This means that the current level is not only compared to the resolution, but the current level estimate's framework is consistent with the resolution. Section 308(b) of the Congressional Budget and Impoundment Control Act of 1974, as amended (2 U.S.C. § 639(b)), requires the House and Senate Budget Committees to make this tabulation at least once a month. The Congressional Budget Office (CBO) assists these committees by regularly submitting reports of the budgetary impact of congressional actions. (See also Budget Authority; Committee Allocation; Congressional Budget Act; Scorekeeping.)

Current Rate Used in a continuing resolution, the total amount of budget authority that was available for obligation for an activity during the fiscal year immediately prior to the one for which the continuing resolution is enacted. Congress often uses the "current rate" as part of a formula to indicate a level of spending that it desires for a program for the duration of the continuing resolution. The current rate does not allow agencies to fund new initiatives, programs, or both requested for the current year unless Congress specifically authorizes them to be funded. (See also Continuing Appropriation/Continuing Resolution; Seasonal Rate.)

Current Services Estimates Estimates submitted by the President of the levels of budget authority and outlays for the ensuing fiscal year based on the continuation of existing levels of service. These estimates reflect the anticipated costs of continuing federal programs and activities at present levels without policy changes. Such estimates ignore all new presidential or congressional initiatives, including reductions or increases that are not yet law. With the proposed budget each year, the President must transmit current services estimates and the economic assumptions upon which they are based. Updated current services estimates are also included in the Mid-Session Review of the President's budget, but are not identified by that title and are confined to those programs that are essentially automatic (that is, they exclude programs controlled through annual appropriations). The current services data in the Mid-Session Review are identified as being for "mandatory and related programs under current law." The Congressional Budget Office (CBO) also prepares similar estimates.

Current Year A term used in the budget formulation process to refer to the fiscal year immediately preceding the budget year under consideration.

Cyclical Surplus/Deficit The part of the federal budget surplus or deficit that results from cyclical factors rather than from underlying fiscal policy. This cyclical component reflects the way in which the surplus or deficit automatically increases or decreases during economic booms or recessions.

Cyclically Adjusted Surplus or Deficit The portion of surplus or deficit remaining after the impact of the business cycle has been removed.

Debt, Federal Generally, the amount borrowed by the government from the public or from government accounts. Four ways that federal debt may be categorized for reporting purposes are (1) gross federal debt, (2) debt held by the public, (3) debt held by government accounts, and (4) debt subject to statutory debt limit.

Debt Held by Government Accounts (Intragovernmental Debt) Federal debt owed by the federal government to itself. Most of this debt is held by trust funds, such as Social Security and Medicare. The Office of Management and Budget (OMB) contrasts it to debt held by the public by noting that it is not a current transaction of the government with the public; it is not financed by private saving and thus does not compete with the private sector for available funds in the credit market; and it does not represent an obligation to make payments to the public.

Debt Held by the Public That portion of the gross federal debt held outside of the federal government. This includes any federal debt held by individuals, corporations, state or local governments, the Federal Reserve System, and foreign governments and central banks. Debt held by government accounts (intragovernmental debt) is excluded from debt held by the public. Debt held by the public is not the same as public debt or Treasury debt.

Debt Service Payment of interest on, and repayment of principal on, borrowed funds. The term may also be used to refer to payment of interest alone. (See also Means of Financing.) As used in the Congressional Budget Office's (CBO) Budget and Economic Outlook, debt service refers to a change in interest payments resulting from a change in estimates of the surplus or the deficit.

Deeming Resolution An informal term that refers to a resolution or bill passed by one or both houses of Congress that in the absence of a concurrent resolution, serves for the chamber passing it as an annual budget resolution for purposes of establishing enforceable budget levels for a budget cycle. The Congressional Budget and Impoundment Control Act of 1974 requires the adoption each year of a concurrent resolution on the budget. (See Concurrent Resolution on the Budget.) At a minimum, deeming resolutions provide new spending allocations to the appropriations committees, but they also may set new aggregate budget levels, provide revised spending allocations to other House and Senate committees, or provide for other related purposes. A deeming resolution may even declare that a budget resolution (in its entirety), passed earlier in the session by one house is deemed to have the force and effect as if adopted by both houses.

Deferral of Budget Authority Temporary withholding or delaying of the obligation or expenditure of budget authority or any other type of executive action, which effectively precludes the obligation or expenditure of budget authority. A deferral is one type of impoundment. Under the Impoundment Control Act of 1974 (2 U.S.C. § 684), budget authority may only be deferred to provide for contingencies, to achieve savings or greater efficiency in the operations of the government, or as otherwise specifically provided by law. Budget authority may not be deferred for policy or any other reason. Deferrals may be proposed by agencies but must be communicated to Congress by the President in a special message. Deferred budget authority may be withheld without further action by Congress. Congress may disapprove a deferral by law. A deferral may not extend beyond the end of the fiscal year of the budget authority's availability. However, for multiyear funds, the President may re-report the deferral the next fiscal year. Deferred budget authority that is disapproved by Congress must be made available immediately. Agencies must release all other deferred budget authority with sufficient time remaining in the fiscal year to prudently obligate that budget authority before the end of the fiscal year. (See also Apportionment; Budgetary Reserves; Impoundment; Rescission.)

Deficiency Apportionment As provided for in the Antideficiency Act (31 U.S.C. § 1515) an apportionment by the Office of Management and Budget (OMB) indicating the need for supplemental budget authority to permit payment of pay increases to civilian and military employees and military retirees as required by law. In addition, the head of an executive branch agency may request a deficiency apportionment if (1) a new law is enacted requiring unanticipated expenditures beyond administrative control or (2) an emergency arises involving the safety of human life or the protection of property. Approval for requests for such an apportionment does not authorize agencies to exceed available resources within an account. (See also Antideficiency Act; Apportionment; Deficiency Appropriation; Supplemental Appropriation.)

Deficiency Appropriation An appropriation made to pay obligations for which sufficient funds are not available. The need often results from violations of the Antideficiency Act. Though technically distinct from a supplemental appropriation, Congress has stopped passing separate deficiency appropriations and the distinction therefore has become obscured since the 1960s.

Deficit The amount by which the government's spending exceeds its revenues for a given period, usually a fiscal year (opposite of surplus).

Definite Authority Budget authority that is stated as a specified sum at the time the authority is enacted. This type of authority, whether in an appropriation act or other law, includes authority stated as "not to exceed" a specified amount.

Deflation A sustained decrease in the general price level.

Deflator An index used to adjust a current dollar amount to its real dollar counterpart, that is, to remove the effects of inflation. (See also Inflator.)

Deobligation An agency's cancellation or downward adjustment of previously incurred obligations. Deobligated funds may be reobligated within the period of availability of the appropriation. For example, annual appropriated funds may be reobligated in the fiscal year in which the funds were appropriated, while multiyear or no-year appropriated funds may be reobligated in the same or subsequent fiscal years. (See Reobligation.)

Deposit Fund Accounts Nonbudgetary accounts established to account for collections that are either (1) held temporarily and later refunded or paid upon administrative or legal determination as to the proper disposition thereof or (2) held by the government, which acts as banker or agent for others, and paid out at the direction of the depositor. Examples include savings accounts for military personnel, state and local income taxes withheld from federal employees' salaries, and payroll deductions for the purchase of savings bonds by civilian employees of the government. Deposit fund balances are accounted for as liabilities of the federal government. These accounts are not included in the budget totals because the amounts are not owned by the government. Therefore, the budget records transactions between deposit funds and budgetary accounts as transactions with the public. Deposit fund balances may be held in the form of either invested or uninvested balances. However, since the cash in the accounts is used by the Department of the Treasury to satisfy immediate cash requirements of the government, to the extent that they are not invested in federal debt, changes in uninvested deposit fund balances are shown as a means of financing the deficit in the budget.

Depreciation The systematic and rational allocation of the acquisition cost of an asset, less its estimated salvage or residual value, over its estimated useful life. Depreciation reflects the use of the asset(s) during specific operating periods in order to match costs with related revenues in measuring income or determining the costs of carrying out program activities.

Direct Loan A disbursement of funds by the government to a nonfederal borrower under a contract that requires the repayment of such funds either with or without interest. The term includes the purchase of or the participation in a loan made by a lender; financing arrangements that defer payment for more than 90 days, including the sale of a government asset on credit terms; and loans financed by the Federal Financing Bank (FFB) pursuant to agency loan guarantee authority. It does not include the acquisition of federally guaranteed loans in satisfaction of default or other price support loans of the Commodity Credit Corporation. Under credit reform, the budget records the credit subsidy cost of direct loans as outlays. The subsidies are paid to the direct loan financing accounts, which, in turn, make the loans to the public.

Direct Loan Obligation A binding agreement by a federal agency to make a direct loan when the borrower fulfills specified conditions. Under credit reform, direct loan obligations are composed of obligations for both the credit subsidy cost and the unsubsidized amounts of the loan. When an agency enters into a direct loan obligation, it obligates itself to pay the credit subsidy cost to the direct loan financing account, and the financing account is committed to make the loan to the borrower. Only the credit subsidy cost is recorded as a budgetary obligation. (See also Direct Loan under Federal Credit.)

Direct Loan Subsidy Cost The estimated long-term cost to the government of a direct loan, excluding administrative costs. Specifically, the subsidy cost of a direct loan is the net present value, at the time when the direct loan is disbursed from the financing account, of the estimated loan disbursements, repayments of principal, payments of interest, recoveries or proceeds of asset sales, and other payments by or to the government over the life of the loan. These estimated cash flows include the effects of estimated defaults, prepayments, fees, penalties, and expected actions by the government and the borrower within the terms of the loan contract.

Direct Spending As defined by the Balanced Budget and Emergency Deficit Control Act of 1985, entitlement authority, the Food Stamp Program, and budget authority provided by law other than appropriations acts. Direct spending may be temporary or permanent, definite or indefinite (as to amount) but it is an appropriation or other budget authority made available to agencies in an act other than an appropriation act. Under expired Budget Enforcement Act (BEA) provisions, new direct spending was subject to pay-as-you-go (PAYGO) requirements. (See also Balanced Budget and Emergency Deficit Control Act of 1985; Entitlement Authority; Mandatory; Pay-as-You-Go. For a distinction, see Discretionary.)

Disbursements Amounts paid by federal agencies, by cash or cash equivalent, during the fiscal year to liquidate government obligations. "Disbursement" is used interchangeably with the term "outlay." In budgetary usage, gross disbursements represent the amount of checks issued and cash or other payments made, less refunds received. Net disbursements represent gross disbursements less income collected and credited to the appropriation or fund account, such as amounts received for goods and services provided. (See also Outlay; Expenditure.)

Discount Rate The interest rate used to determine the present value of a future stream of receipts and outlays, or in cost-benefit analysis, of benefits and costs. This use of the term is completely distinct from that in monetary policy, and the interest rates involved are generally not those charged by Federal Reserve Banks. Discount rate policies of the three major oversight and budget agencies—the Government Accountability Office (GAO), the Office of Management and Budget (OMB), and the Congressional Budget Office (CBO) -are consistent with basic economic principles but vary significantly in their formulations for different analyses In estimating net present values under credit reform, discount rate represents the average interest rate on marketable Treasury securities of similar maturity to the cash flows of the direct loan or loan guarantee for which the estimate is being made. (See Credit Subsidy Cost under Federal Credit.)

Discretionary A term that usually modifies either "spending," "appropriation," or "amount." "Discretionary spending" refers to outlays from budget authority that is provided in and controlled by appropriation acts. "Discretionary appropriation" refers to those budgetary resources that are provided in appropriation acts, other than those that fund mandatory programs. "Discretionary amount" refers to the level of budget authority, outlays, or other budgetary resources (other than those which fund mandatory programs) that are provided in, and controlled by, appropriation acts. (See also Appropriation Act; Appropriations under Forms of Budget Authority under Budget Authority; One-Year Authority under Duration under Budget Authority; Gramm-Rudman-Hollings. For a contrast, see Entitlement Authority; Mandatory.)

Duration One-Year Authority. Budget authority available for obligation only during a specific fiscal year that expires at the end of that fiscal year. It is also known as "fiscal year" or "annual" budget authority.

Earmarking (1) Dedicating collections by law for a specific purpose or program. Earmarked collections include trust fund receipts, special fund receipts, intragovernmental receipts, and offsetting collections credited to appropriation accounts. These collections may be classified as budget receipts, proprietary receipts, or reimbursements to appropriations. (2) Designating any portion of a lump-sum amount for particular purposes by means of legislative language. Sometimes "earmarking" is colloquially used to characterize directions included in congressional committee reports but not in the legislation itself. (See also Special Fund Accounts under Federal Fund Accounts under Account in the President's Budget; Trust Fund Accounts under Account in the President's Budget; Offsetting Collections under Collections; Proprietary Receipts from the Public under Offsetting Receipts under Collections; Committee Allocation.)

Economy Act A common reference to section 1535 of title 31 of the United States Code that provides general authority for one agency or unit thereof to obtain goods and services from another agency or unit. Payment may be made in advance or upon the provision of the goods and services ordered.

Emergency A term that usually modifies "appropriation," "legislation," or "supplemental." Under procedures typically prescribed in concurrent resolutions on the budget, the House or the Senate, or their respective committees of jurisdiction, may designate proposed appropriations or other legislation as "emergency legislation" and thereby exempt any new budget authority, outlays, or receipts resulting from such legislation from specified enforcement provisions in the Congressional Budget Act, the concurrent resolution itself, or both. (See also Appropriations under Forms of Budget Authority under Budget Authority.) Acts appropriating funds for national or international emergencies such as natural disasters or urgent national security events are typically designated "emergency supplemental." (See also Supplemental Appropriation.)

Enhanced Rescission Legislative initiatives, proposed over the years, that would allow the President to withhold funds from obligation upon proposing a rescission and to continue withholding the funds unless and until Congress acts to disapprove the presidential proposal to rescind funds. The President could then veto the disapproval bill, forcing each house to muster a two-thirds majority to override the veto. This would be a reversal of current Impoundment Control Act procedures that require funds proposed for rescission to be released unless Congress approves, by law, all or part of the amount proposed to be rescinded by the President. In 1996, Congress enacted a form of enhanced rescission authority in the Line Item Veto Act, which authorized the President, after signing a bill into law, to cancel in whole any dollar amount of discretionary budget authority, any item of new direct spending, or any limited tax benefit if the President made certain determinations. The act provided that the cancellation was effective unless Congress enacted a disapproval bill into law to void the cancellation. In 1998, the United States Supreme Court in Clinton v. City of New York, 524 U.S. 417 (1998), held that the Line Item Veto Act violated the Presentment Clause, Article 1, Section 7, of the U.S. Constitution. (See also Impoundment; Line Item Veto; Rescission.)

Entitlement Authority Authority to make payments (including loans and grants) for which budget authority is not provided in advance by appropriation acts to any person or government if, under the provisions of the law containing such authority, the U.S. government is legally required to make the payments to persons or governments that meet the requirements established by law (2 U.S.C. § 622(9)). Under the Budget Enforcement Act (BEA), new entitlement authority was defined as direct spending and was subject to the pay-as-you-go (PAYGO) provisions. (See also Appropriated Entitlement; Authorizing Legislation; Backdoor Authority/Backdoor Spending; Budget Enforcement Act; Mandatory; Pay-as-You-Go.)

Expedited Rescission Legislative proposals designed to ensure rapid and formal congressional consideration of rescissions proposed by the President. An essential element of an expedited rescission procedure is a prompt up-or-down vote in Congress on the President's proposals to reduce enacted spending authority. This would prevent rescissions from being enacted solely due to absence of action. While such legislation has been proposed at various times in the past, Congress has not enacted expedited rescission procedures. (See also Impoundment; Line Item Veto; Rescission.)

Expenditure The actual spending of money; an outlay.

Expenditure Transfer For accounting and reporting purposes, a transaction between appropriation and fund accounts, which represents payments, repayments or receipts for goods or services furnished or to be furnished. Where the purpose is to purchase goods or services or otherwise benefit the transferring account, an expenditure transfer/transaction is recorded as an obligation/outlay in the transferring account and an offsetting collection in the receiving account. If the receiving account is a general fund appropriation account or a revolving fund account, the offsetting collection is credited to the appropriation or fund account. If the receiving account is a special fund or trust account, the offsetting collection is usually credited to a receipt account of the fund. All transfers between federal funds (general, special, and nontrust revolving funds) and trust funds are also treated as expenditure transfers.

Expense Outflow or other depletion of assets or incurrences of liabilities (or a combination of both) during some period as a result of providing goods, rendering services, or carrying out other activities related to an entity's programs and missions, the benefits from which do not extend beyond the present operating period.

Expired Account An account within the Department of the Treasury to hold expired budget authority. The expired budget authority retains its fiscal year (or multiyear) identity for an additional 5 fiscal years. After the 5-year period has elapsed, all obligated and unobligated balances are canceled, the expired account is closed, and all remaining funds are returned to the general fund of the Treasury and are thereafter no longer available for any purpose. (See Expired Budget

Authority under Availability for New Obligations under Budget Authority.)

Expired Budget Authority Budget authority that is no longer available to incur new obligations but is available for an additional 5 fiscal years for disbursement of obligations properly incurred during the budget authority's period of availability. Unobligated balances of expired budget authority remain available for 5 years to cover legitimate obligation adjustments or for obligations properly incurred during the budget authority's period of availability that the agency failed to record. (See 31 U.S.C. §§ 1552(a), 1553(a).) (See also Expired Account; Unobligated Balance under Obligational Authority; Warrant.)

Federal Accounting Standards Advisory Board (FASAB) Sponsored under an agreement between the Department of the Treasury, the Office of Management and Budget (OMB), and Government Accountability Office (GAO). FASAB promulgates Statements of Federal Financial Accounting Standards (SFFAS) after considering the financial and budgetary information needs of citizens, congressional oversight groups, executive agencies, and other users of federal financial information.

Federal Credit Defined by the Federal Credit Reform Act of 1990 (FCRA) as federal direct loans and federal loan guarantees.

Federal Financing Bank (FFB) A government corporation created by the Federal Financing Bank Act of 1973 under the general supervision of the Secretary of the Treasury. FFB was established to (1) finance federal and federally assisted borrowings in ways that least disrupt private markets, (2) coordinate such borrowing programs with the government's overall fiscal policy, and (3) reduce the costs of such borrowing from the public. FFB provides financial assistance to or on behalf of federal agencies by (1) making direct loans to federal agencies to help them fund their programs, (2) purchasing loan assets from federal agencies, and (3) making direct loans to nonfederal borrowers (including foreign governments) that are secured by federal agency guarantees against risk of default by borrowers on loan principal and interest payments. FFB obtains funds by borrowing from the Department of the Treasury.

Federal Fund Accounts Budgetary accounts composed of moneys collected and spent by the federal government other than those designated as trust funds. Federal fund accounts include general, special, public enterprise, and intragovernmental fund accounts.

Feeder Account Appropriation and revolving fund accounts whose resources are available only for transfer to other specified appropriation or revolving fund accounts.

Financial Statements A document that describes an entity's financial activity and status for a specified period. Under federal law and applicable accounting standards, the financial statements for a federal agency usually include a balance sheet, statement of net cost, statement of changes in net position, statement of budgetary resources, and statement of financing.

Financing Account A nonbudgetary account (or accounts) associated with each credit program account that holds balances, receives the subsidy cost payment from the credit program account, and includes all other cash flows to and from the government resulting from direct loan obligations or loan guarantee commitments made on or after October 1, 1991. It disburses loans, collects repayments and fees, makes claim payments, holds balances, borrows from the Department of the Treasury, earns or pays interest, and receives the subsidy cost payment from the credit program account.

Fiscal Policy Federal government policies with respect to taxes and spending that affect the level, composition, and distribution of national income and output. The budget process is a major vehicle for determining and implementing federal fiscal policy. Many summary indicators of fiscal policy exist. Some, such as the budget surplus or deficit, are narrowly budgetary. Others attempt to reflect aspects of how fiscal policy affects the economy.

Fiscal Year Any yearly accounting period, regardless of its relationship to a calendar year. The fiscal year for the federal government begins on October 1 of each year and ends on September 30 of the following year; it is designated by the calendar year in which it ends.

Fixed Appropriation Account An account in which appropriations are available for obligation for a definite period. A fixed appropriation account can receive appropriations available for obligation for 1 year (an annual account) or for a specified number of years (a multiyear account). (For a distinction, see No-Year Authority under Duration under Budget Authority.)

Foreign Currency Fund Accounts Accounts established in the Department of the Treasury for foreign currency that is acquired without payment of U.S. dollars. Examples of such accounts are those set up through the Agricultural Trade Development and Assistance Act (7 U.S.C. §§ 1691-1736g).

Forward Funding Budget authority that is made available for obligation beginning in the last quarter of the fiscal year for the financing of ongoing activities (usually grant programs) during the next fiscal year. This funding is used mostly for education programs, so that obligations for grants can be made prior to the beginning of the next school year. (For a distinction, see Advance Appropriation; Advance Funding; Multiple-Year Authority under Duration under Budget Authority.)

Franchise Fund A type of intragovernmental revolving fund that operates as a self-supporting entrepreneurial entity to provide common administrative services benefiting other federal entities. These funds function entirely from the fees charged for the services they provide consistent with their statutory authority. (See also Intragovermental Revolving Fund Account under Intragovernmental Fund Account under Federal Fund Accounts under Account in the President's Budget.)

FTE (Full-Time Equivalent) Reflects the total number of regular straight-time hours (i.e., not including overtime or holiday hours) worked by employees divided by the number of compensable hours applicable to each fiscal year. Annual leave, sick leave, and compensatory time off and other approved leave categories are considered to be "hours worked" for purposes of defining FTE employment.

Full Funding The provision of budgetary resources to cover the total estimated cost of a program or project at the time it is undertaken (regardless of when the funds will actually be obligated). Full funding generally pertains to the acquisition of capital assets, such as the construction of Navy ships or buildings to house federal agencies. (For a distinction, see Incremental Funding. See also Multiple-Year Authority under Duration under Budget Authority; Multiyear Budget Planning.) The term full funding can sometimes refer to the appropriation of the total amount authorized by law. A program is said to be "fully funded" when the appropriation equals the authorized level or when appropriations are sufficient to cover service for all eligible persons or organizations.

Functional Classification A system of classifying budget authority, outlays, receipts, and tax expenditures according to the national needs being addressed. Each concurrent resolution on the budget allocates budget authority and outlays among the various functions.

Fund Accounting Commonly used to refer to the administrative system of funds control that each agency establishes to ensure compliance with federal fiscal laws. The statutory basis for fund accounting is found primarily in the requirement of the Antideficiency Act that the head of each agency prescribe, by regulation, a system of funds control (31 U.S.C. § 1514(a)). (See also Antideficiency Act.)

GDP (Gross Domestic Product) The value of all final goods and services produced within the borders of a country such as the United States in a given period, whether produced by residents or nonresidents. The components of GDP are personal consumption expenditures, gross private domestic investment, net exports of goods and services, and government consumption expenditures and gross investment. That value is conceptually equal to the sum of incomes generated within the borders of the country in the same time period. (See also GNP; National Income and Product Accounts.)

GDP Price Index A measure of the price level for the whole economy covering the prices of goods and services produced in a country such as the United States.

General Fund Accounts. Accounts in the U.S. Treasury holding all federal money not allocated by law to any other fund account.

General Fund Expenditure Account An appropriation account established to record amounts appropriated by law for the general support of federal government activities and the subsequent expenditure of these funds. It includes spending from both annual and permanent appropriations.

General Fund Receipt Account A receipt account credited with all collections that are not earmarked by law for another account for a specific purpose. These collections are presented in the President's budget as either governmental (budget) receipts or offsetting receipts. These include taxes, customs duties, and miscellaneous receipts.

Generational Accounting Estimates who pays for all that the government buys. Generational accounts estimate the real (inflation-adjusted) net taxes to be paid by the average member of each generation (today's newborns, 1-year-olds, and so on). They also estimate the net taxes of the average member of the representative future generation (those not yet born). The accounts project government purchases and net taxes of current generations and calculate their present values. Generational accounts do not try to estimate who benefits from what the government buys, only who pays for it with their net taxes. They do not try to predict the actual course of policy. Generational accounts act as a gauge, not a predictor or goal. They do not try to say how policy will actually evolve. And they cannot say what distributions are fair; that is a matter of policy, not analysis. The accounts serve only as a norm by which to evaluate prevailing policy and compare alternative policies.

GNP (Gross National Product) The value of all final goods and services produced by labor and capital supplied by residents of a country such as the United States in a given period, whether or not the residents are located within the country. That value is conceptually equal to the sum of incomes accruing to residents of the country in the same time period. GNP differs from GDP in that GNP includes net receipts of income from the rest of the world while GDP excludes them. (See also GDP; National Income and Product Accounts.)

Government Performance and Results Act (GPRA) The Government Performance and Results Act of 1993. GPRA, also known as the Results Act, intends to improve the efficiency and effectiveness of federal programs by requiring federal agencies to develop strategic plans, annual performance plans, and annual program performance reports.

Government-Sponsored Enterprise (GSE) A privately owned and operated federally chartered financial institution that facilitates the flow of investment funds to specific economic sectors. GSEs, acting as financial intermediaries, provide these sectors access to national capital markets. The activities of GSEs are not included in the federal budget's totals because they are classified as private entities. However, because of their relationship to the government, detailed statements of financial operations and conditions are presented as supplementary information in the budget document. For the purposes of the Congressional Budget Act of 1974, as amended (2 U.S.C. § 622(8)), an entity must meet certain criteria to qualify as a GSE. (For distinctions, see Mixed-Ownership Government Corporation; Off-Budget; Wholly-Owned Government Corporation.)

Governmental Receipt Collections from the public based on the government's exercise of its sovereign powers, including individual and corporate income taxes and social insurance taxes, excise taxes, duties, court fines, compulsory licenses, and deposits of earnings by the Federal Reserve System. Gifts and contributions (as distinguished from payments for services or cost-sharing deposits by state and local governments) are also counted as governmental receipts. Total governmental receipts include those specifically designated as off-budget by provisions of law. Total governmental receipts are compared with total outlays in calculating the budget surplus or deficit. (See also Federal Fund Accounts under Account in the President's Budget; Gross Basis and Net Basis under Budgeting in Relation to Totals under Bases of Budgeting; Off-Budget; On-Budget.)

GPRA See under Government Performance and Results Act.

Gramm-Rudman-Hollings (GRH) The popular name of the Balanced Budget and Emergency Deficit Control Act of 1985, so named for the Senate sponsors: Senators Phil Gramm, Warren Rudman, and Ernest F. Hollings. The act, a mechanism for reducing the federal deficit, set declining deficit targets for the federal government and established an automatic enforcement mechanism called sequestration. GRH has been amended several times, most significantly by the Budget Enforcement Act of 1990 (BEA) and the Balanced Budget Act of 1997. (See also Budget Enforcement Act; Discretionary; Limitation; Mandatory; Sequestration.)

Grant A federal financial assistance award making payment in cash or in kind for a specified purpose. The federal government is not expected to have substantial involvement with the state or local government or other recipient while the contemplated activity is being performed. The term "grant" is used broadly and may include a grant to nongovernmental recipients as well as one to a state or local government, while the term "grant-in-aid" is commonly used to refer only to a grant to a state or local government. (For a more detailed description, see the Federal Grant and Cooperative Agreement Act of 1977, 31 U.S.C. §§ 6301- 6308.) The two major forms of federal grants-in-aid are block and categorical. Block grants are given primarily to general purpose governmental units in accordance with a statutory formula. Such grants can be used for a variety of activities within a broad functional area. Examples of federal block grant programs are the Omnibus Crime Control and Safe Streets Act of 1968, the Housing and Community Development Act of 1974, and the grants to states for social services under title XX of the Social Security Act. Categorical grants can be used only for specific programs or for narrowly defined activities. They may be formula or project grants. Formula grants allocate federal funds to states or their subdivisions in accordance with a distribution formula prescribed by law or administrative regulation. Project grants provide federal funding for fixed or known periods for specific projects or the delivery of specific services or products.

Gross Basis Budgetary totals from which offsetting collections have not been deducted. In customary use, "gross" refers to the sum or total value of a transaction before reduction by applicable offsets. Under this display, totals include obligations and expenditures from offsetting collections and governmental receipts rather than as offsets to outlays. (See also Offsetting Collections and Offsetting Receipts under Collections.)

Gross Federal Debt The total amount of federal government debt comprising debt securities issued by the Department of the Treasury (including securities issued by the Federal Financing Bank (FFB) under section 9(a) of the Federal Financing Bank Act of 1973 (12 U.S.C. § 2888(a)) and other government agencies. Gross federal debt is the sum of debt held by the public and debt held by government accounts (intragovernmental debt).

Guaranteed Loan A nonfederal loan to which a federal guarantee is attached. The loan principal is recorded as a guaranteed loan regardless of whether the federal guarantee is full or partial. For the purposes of the Federal Credit Reform Act of 1990

(FCRA), a loan guarantee is defined as any guarantee, insurance, or other pledge with respect to the payment of all or a part of the principal or interest on any debt obligation of a nonfederal borrower to a nonfederal lender, but does not include the insurance of deposits, shares, or other withdrawable accounts in financial institutions. Under credit reform, the budget records the credit subsidy cost of guaranteed loans as outlays. The subsidies are paid to the guaranteed loan financing accounts, which hold these uninvested funds to serve as a reserve against future loan defaults or other payments to lenders. (See also Credit Reform, Direct Loan, and Loan Guarantee Commitment under Federal Credit.)

Guaranteed Loan Subsidy Cost The estimated long-term cost to the government of a loan guarantee, excluding administrative costs. The Federal Credit Reform Act of 1990 (FCRA) specifies that the credit subsidy cost of a loan guarantee is the net present value, at the time a guaranteed loan is disbursed by the lender, of the following cash flows: (1) estimated payments by the government to cover defaults, delinquencies, interest subsidies, or other payments and (2) the estimated payments to the government, including origination and other fees, penalties, and recoveries.

Identification Code Each appropriation or fund account in the President's budget carries an 11-digit code that identifies (1) the agency, (2) the account, (3) the nature or timing of the transmittal to Congress (for example, regular budget cycle or supplemental), (4) the type of fund, and (5) the account's functional and subfunctional classifications.

Implicit Price Deflator Weighted averages of the most detailed price indexes used in estimating real output. Before 1995, implicit price deflators were calculated as the ratio of current-to constant-dollar output multiplied by 100. Since 1995, implicit price deflators have been calculated as the ratio of current-to chained-dollar output multiplied by 100. For all but the most recent estimates, the implicit price deflators are identical to the chain-type price indexes because the weights used to aggregate the detailed prices for the two measures are the same. Implicit price deflators are used in the National Income and Product Accounts (NIPA). (See also Chain Price Indexes; Chained Dollars.)

Impoundment Any action or inaction by an officer or employee of the federal government that precludes obligation or expenditure of budget authority. There are two types of impoundments: deferrals and proposed rescissions. Not all delays in obligating funds are deferrals. Sometimes obligation delays are due to legitimate programmatic reasons or the result of outside forces not under the agency's control; for example, an agency administering a grant program receives no grant applications so no grants can be made. (See also Congressional Budget and Impoundment Control Act of 1974; Deferral of Budget Authority; Rescission.)

Incremental Funding The provision or recording of budgetary resources for a program or project based on obligations estimated to be incurred within a fiscal year when such budgetary resources are provided for only part of the estimated cost of the acquisition. (For a distinction, see Full Funding.)

Indefinite Authority Budget authority that, at time of enactment, is for an unspecified amount. Indefinite budget authority may be appropriated as all or part of the amount of proceeds from the sale of financial assets, the amount necessary to cover obligations associated with payments, the receipts from specified sources—the exact amount of which is determinable only at some future date—or it may be appropriated as "such sums as may be necessary" for a given purpose.

Inflation A rise in the general price level.

Inflator An index used to express a current dollar amount in prices of another period.

Internal Control An integral component of an organization's management that provides reasonable assurance that the following objectives are being achieved: (1) effectiveness and efficiency of operations, (2) reliability of financial reporting, and (3) compliance with applicable laws and regulations. Safeguarding of assets is a subset of all three of these objectives.

Intragovernmental Fund Accounts Expenditure accounts authorized by law to facilitate financing transactions primarily within and between federal agencies.

Intragovernmental Revolving Fund Account An appropriation account authorized to be credited with collections from other federal agencies' accounts that are earmarked to finance a continuing cycle of business-type operations, including working capital funds, industrial funds, stock funds, and supply funds. According to the Office of Management and Budget (OMB), collections of intragovernmental revolving fund accounts are derived primarily from within the government. For example, the franchise fund operations within several agencies provide common administrative services to federal agencies on a fee-for-service basis.

Intragovernmental Transfers Collections from other federal government accounts, often as payment for goods or services provided. Most offsetting receipts from intragovernmental transfers are offset against budget authority and outlays of the agency or subfunction that produced the goods or services. However, two intragovernmental transfers are classified as undistributed offsetting receipts: (1) agency payments as employers into employee retirement trust funds and (2) interest received by trust funds. These offsetting receipts appear as offsets to budget authority and outlays for the government as a whole, rather than at the agency level. Intragovernmental transfers may be (1) intrabudgetary (on-budget), (2) off-budget, or (3) transfers between on-budget and off-budget accounts. Intrabudgetary transfers are further subdivided into three categories: (1) interfund transfers, where the payment is from one fund group, either federal or trust, to a receipt account in the other fund group; (2) federal intrafund transfers, where the payment and receipt both occur within the federal fund group; and (3) trust intrafund transfers, where the payment and receipt both occur within the trust fund group.

Joint Resolution A form of legislation (designated with S.J. Res. or H.J. Res.) that is either: (1) A congressional action typically used in dealing with matters such as a single appropriation for a specific purpose, increasing the statutory limit on the public debt, or continuing appropriations. There is no real difference between a bill and a joint resolution; both require a majority vote and become law in the same manner, that is, by bicameral enactment and signature of the President. (2) A congressional action used to propose amendments to the Constitution. Adoption of a joint resolution to propose a constitutional amendment requires a two-thirds majority vote by both the Senate and the House and is not presented to the President for approval. A proposed amendment becomes effective only when ratified by three-fourths of the states.

Justification The documents an agency submits to the appropriations committees in support of its budget request. The Office of Management and Budget (OMB) prescribes justification materials, which typically explain changes between the current appropriation and the amounts requested for the next fiscal year.

Lease-Purchase An agreement between a lessor and lessee in which the lessee agrees to lease a building or other property for a specified length of time and then takes title to the building or other property at the end of the lease period. (See also Capital Lease; Operating Lease.)

Liability Defined differently for obligational (or budgetary) and proprietary (or financial) accounting purposes. Obligational (or budgetary) accounting, designed to ensure compliance with fiscal laws, is based on the concept of legal liability. A legal liability is a claim that may be legally enforced against the government. It may be created in a variety of ways, such as by signing a contract, grant, or cooperative agreement or by operation of law. (See also Obligation.) Proprietary (or financial) accounting, designed to generate data for financial statement purposes, is based on the concept of accounting liability. For federal financial accounting purposes, a liability is a probable future outflow or other sacrifice of resources as a result of past transactions or events. Generally, liabilities are thought of as amounts owed for items or services received, assets acquired, construction performed (regardless of whether invoices have been received), an amount received but not yet earned, or other expenses incurred. (See also Contingent Liability.)

Life-Cycle Costs The overall estimated cost, both government and contractor, for a particular program alternative over the time period corresponding to the life of the program, including direct and indirect initial costs plus any periodic or continuing costs of operation and maintenance.

Limitation A restriction on the amount, purpose, or period of availability of budget authority. While limitations are most often established through appropriations acts, they may also be established through authorization legislation. Limitations may be placed on the availability of funds for program levels, administrative expenses, direct loan obligations, loan guarantee commitments, or other purposes. (See also Administrative Division or Subdivision of Funds; Apportionment; Appropriation Act; Appropriation Rider; Authorizing Legislation; Duration under Budget Authority.)

Line Item In executive budgeting, a particular expenditure, such as program, subprogram, or object class. For purposes of the concurrent budget resolution, it usually refers to assumptions about particular programs or accounts implicit but not explicit in the budget resolution. In appropriation acts, it usually refers to an individual account or part of an account for which a specific amount is available. (See also Line Item Veto; Obligated Balance under Obligational Authority; Appropriation Rider.)

Line Item Veto A phrase used to describe an executive power to veto or "cross out" only certain parts of legislation while allowing the rest of the legislation to become law. At the federal level, legislation granting the President a line item veto has been declared unconstitutional. The line item veto exists at the state level because their constitutions grant the power to the governors in forms that vary from state to state. Some states only permit line item vetoes in bills appropriating money.

Liquidating Appropriation An appropriation to pay obligations incurred pursuant to substantive legislation, usually contract authority. A liquidating appropriation is not recorded as budget authority.

Liquidating Account A budget account that includes all cash flows to and from the government resulting from direct loan obligations or loan guarantee commitments made prior to October 1, 1991. The Federal Credit Reform Act of 1990 (FCRA) requires that such accounts be shown in the budget on a cash basis. Agencies are required to transfer end-of-year unobligated balances in these accounts to the general fund as soon as practicable after the close of the fiscal year.

Loan Guarantee Commitment A binding agreement by a federal agency to make a loan guarantee when specified conditions are fulfilled by the borrower, the lender, or any other party to the guarantee agreement. (See also Commitment; Credit Reform and Guaranteed Loan under Federal Credit.)

Lockbox In the budget context, any of several legislative mechanisms that attempt to isolate, or "lock away," funds of the federal government for purposes such as reducing federal spending, preserving surpluses, or protecting the solvency of trust funds.

Management Fund Account An account established by the Department of the Treasury (Treasury) that is authorized by law to credit collections from two or more appropriations to finance activity not involving a continuing cycle of business-type operations. Such accounts do not generally own a significant amount of assets, such as supplies, equipment, or loans, nor do they have a specified amount of capital provided--a corpus. The Navy Management Fund is an example of such an account.

Mandatory A term that usually modifies either "spending" or "amount." "Mandatory spending," also known as "direct spending," refers to budget authority that is provided in laws other than appropriation acts and the outlays that result from such budget authority. Mandatory spending includes entitlement authority (for example, the Food Stamp, Medicare, and veterans' pension programs), payment of interest on the public debt, and nonentitlements such as payments to states from Forest Service receipts. By defining eligibility and setting the benefit or payment rules, Congress controls spending for these programs indirectly rather than directly through appropriations acts. "Mandatory amount" refers to the level of budget authority, outlays, or other budgetary resources that are controlled by laws other than appropriations acts. Budget authority provided in annual appropriations acts for certain programs is treated as mandatory because the authorizing legislation entitles beneficiaries to receive payment or otherwise obligates the government to make payment. (See also Appropriated Entitlement; Appropriations under Forms of Budget Authority under Budget Authority; Multiple-Year Authority and No-Year Authority under Duration under Budget Authority; Committee Allocation; Direct Spending Authority; Discretionary; Entitlement Authority; Gramm-Rudman-Hollings.)

Mark-Up Meetings where congressional committees work on language of bills or resolutions. For example, at Budget Committee mark-ups, the House and Senate Budget Committees work on the language and numbers contained in budget resolutions and legislation affecting the congressional budget process.

Means of Financing Ways in which a budget deficit is financed or a budget surplus is used. A budget deficit may be financed by the Department of the Treasury (Treasury) (or agency) borrowing, by reducing Treasury cash balances, by the sale of gold, by seigniorage, by net cash flows resulting from transactions in credit financing accounts, by allowing certain unpaid liabilities to increase, or by other similar transactions. It is customary to separate total means of financing into "change in debt held by the public" (the government's debt, which is the primary means of financing) and "other means of financing" (seigniorage, change in cash balances, transactions of credit financing accounts, etc.) (See also Debt, Federal; Debt Service; Financing Account under Credit Reform Accounts under Federal Credit; Seigniorage.)

Mid-Session Review of the Budget A supplemental summary and update of the budget that the President submitted to Congress in January or February of that year. Section 1106 of title 31 of the United States Code requires the mid-session review to contain revised estimates of budget receipts, outlays, and budget authority and other summary information and that it be issued by July 15 of each year. (See also Budget Update.)

Mixed-Ownership Government Corporation An enterprise or business activity designated by the Government Corporation Control Act (31 U.S.C. § 9101) or some other statute as a mixed-ownership government corporation. The fiscal activities of some mixed-ownership government corporations appear in the budget. The Federal Deposit Insurance Corporation (FDIC) is an example of such a corporation. (For distinctions, see Government-Sponsored Enterprise; Off-Budget; Wholly-Owned Government Corporation.)

Monetary Policy A policy affecting the money supply, interest rates, and credit availability that is intended to achieve maximum sustainable output and employment and to promote stable prices (interpreted as a low-inflation environment in practice). Monetary policy is directed by the Federal Reserve System. It functions by influencing the cost and availability of bank reserves through (1) open-market operations (the purchase and sale of securities, primarily Treasury securities), (2) changes in the ratio of reserves to deposits that commercial banks are required to maintain, (3) changes in the discount rate, and (4) changes in the federal fund rate. (See also Discount Rate; Fiscal Policy.)

Money Supply Anything that is generally accepted in payment for goods and services or in the repayment of debt. Narrow definitions of the money supply include currency and checking accounts, while broader definitions include other types of assets, such as savings deposits and money market mutual funds.

Monthly Treasury Statement (MTS) A summary statement prepared from agency accounting reports and issued by the Department of the Treasury (Treasury). The MTS presents the receipts, outlays, resulting budget surplus or deficit, and federal debt for the month and the fiscal year to date and a comparison of those figures to those of the same period in the previous year. Treasury also issues the Daily Treasury Statement (DTS), which is published every working day of the federal government. It provides data on Treasury's cash and debt operations.

Multiple-Year Authority (Multiyear) Budget authority available for a fixed period of time in excess of 1 fiscal year. This authority generally takes the form of 2-year, 3-year, and so forth, availability but may cover periods that do not coincide with the start or end of a fiscal year. For example, the authority may be available from July 1 of one fiscal year through September 30 of the following fiscal year, a period of 15 months. This latter type of multiple-year authority is sometimes referred to as "forward funding." (For a distinction, see Advance Appropriation; Advance Funding. See also Full Funding).

Multiyear Budget Planning A process--such as the one used to develop the President's budget and the congressional budget resolution--designed to ensure that the longer range consequences of budget decisions are identified and reflected in the budget totals. The President's (or executive) budget includes multiyear planning estimates for budget authority, outlays, and receipts for 4 years beyond the budget year. As of the date of this glossary, the congressional budget resolution provided budget totals for the budget year and, at least, each of the 4 succeeding fiscal years. This process provides a structure for the review and analysis of long-term program and tax policy choices.

National Income and Product Accounts (NIPA) The comprehensive set of accounts prepared and published by the Department of Commerce that measures the total value of goods and services (gross domestic product, or GDP) produced by the U.S. economy and the total income earned in producing that output.

Negative Subsidy Receipt Account A budget account for the receipt of amounts paid from the financing account when there is a negative subsidy for the original estimate. In most cases, the receipt account is a general fund receipt account and amounts are not earmarked for the credit program. They are available for appropriation only in the sense that all general fund receipts are available for appropriation. Separate downward reestimate receipt accounts are used to record amounts paid from the financing account for downward reestimates.

Net Basis The use of budgetary totals from which offsetting collections have been deducted. Under this display, budgetary totals include offsetting collections as offsets to obligations and outlays rather than as receipts. (See also Offsetting Collections under Collections.)

Net Present Value The present value of the estimated future cash inflows minus the present value of the cash outflows.

Nominal Dollar See under Current Dollar.

Nonbudgetary A term used to refer to transactions of the government that do not belong within the budget. Nonbudgetary transactions (such as deposit funds, direct loan and loan guarantee financing accounts, and seigniorage) do not belong in the budget because they do not represent net budget authority or outlays, but rather are means of financing. This contrasts with "off-budget," which refers to activities that are budgetary in nature but are required by law to be excluded from the budget. (See Off-Budget; Means of Financing.)

Nonexpenditure Transfer For accounting and reporting purposes, a transaction between appropriation and fund accounts that does not represent payments for goods and services received or to be received but rather serves only to adjust the amounts available in the accounts for making payments. However, transactions between budget accounts and deposit funds will always be treated as expenditure transactions since the deposit funds are outside the budget. Nonexpenditure transfers also include allocations. These transfers may not be recorded as obligations or outlays of the transferring accounts or as reimbursements or receipts of the receiving accounts. For example, the transfer of budget authority from one account to another to absorb the cost of a federal pay raise is a nonexpenditure transfer. (See Allocation; see also Transfer Appropriation (Allocation) Accounts under Accounts for Purposes Other Than Budget Presentation.)

No-Year Authority Budget authority that remains available for obligation for an indefinite period of time. A no-year appropriation is usually identified by language such as "to remain available until expended."

Object Classification A uniform classification identifying the obligations of the federal government by the types of goods or services purchased (such as personnel compensation, supplies and materials, and equipment) without regard to the agency involved or the purpose of the programs for which they are used. If the obligations are in a single object classification category, the classification is identified in the Program and Financing Schedule in the President's budget. For the activities distributed among two or more object classification categories, the budget has a separate object classification schedule to show the distribution of the obligations by object classification.

Obligated Balance The amount of obligations already incurred for which payment has not yet been made. Technically, the obligated balance is the unliquidated obligations. Budget authority that is available for a fixed period expires at the end of its period of availability, but the obligated balance of the budget authority remains available to liquidate obligations for 5 additional fiscal years. At the end of the fifth fiscal year, the account is closed and any remaining balance is canceled. Budget authority available for an indefinite period may be canceled, and its account closed if (1) it is specifically rescinded by law or (2) the head of the agency concerned or the President determines that the purposes for which the appropriation was made have been carried out and disbursements have not been made from the appropriation for 2 consecutive years. (See also Duration under Budget Authority; Fixed Appropriation Account.)

Obligation A definite commitment that creates a legal liability of the government for the payment of goods and services ordered or received, or a legal duty on the part of the United States that could mature into a legal liability by virtue of actions on the part of the other party beyond the control of the United States. Payment may be made immediately or in the future. An agency incurs an obligation, for example, when it places an order, signs a contract, awards a grant, purchases a service, or takes other actions that require the government to make payments to the public or from one government account to another. The standards for the proper reporting of obligations are found in section 1501(a) of title 31 of the United States Code. See also OMB Circular No. A-11.

Obligational Accounting The accounting systems, processes, and people involved in collecting financial information necessary to control, monitor, and report on all funds made available to federal entities by legislation, including permanent, indefinite appropriations as well as appropriations enacted in annual and supplemental appropriations laws that may be available for one or multiple fiscal years. It is through obligational accounting that agencies ensure compliance with fiscal laws, including the Antideficiency Act and statutes related to the purpose and period of availability of appropriations. Obligational accounting rests on the central concepts of the "obligation" and "disbursement" of public funds, as those terms are defined in this glossary. The Antideficiency Act, codified in part at sections 1341, 1514, and 1517, and the provisions of section 1501 (commonly referred to as the recording statute) of the United States Code provide the fundamental components of obligational accounting. Obligational accounting is sometimes also referred to as "fund control accounting," "appropriation accounting," and "budgetary accounting."

Obligational Authority The sum of (1) budget authority enacted for a given fiscal year, (2) unobligated balances of amounts that have not expired brought forward from prior years, (3) amounts of offsetting collections to be credited and available to specific funds or accounts during that year, and (4) budget authority transferred from other funds or accounts. The balance of obligational authority is an amount carried over from one year to the next if the budget authority is available for obligation in the next fiscal year. Not all obligational authority that becomes available in a fiscal year is obligated and paid out in that same year. Balances are described as (1) obligated, (2) unobligated, or (3) unexpended.

Obligations Basis The basis whereby financial transactions involving the use of funds are recorded in the accounts primarily when goods and services are ordered, regardless of when the resources acquired are to be received or consumed or when cash is received or paid. (See also Liability; Obligation.)

Off-Budget Those budgetary accounts (either federal or trust funds) designated by law as excluded from budget totals. As of the date of this glossary, the revenues and outlays of the two Social Security trust funds (the Old-Age and Survivors Insurance Trust Fund and the Disability Insurance Trust Fund) and the transactions of the Postal Service are the only off-budget accounts. The budget documents routinely report the on- budget and off-budget amounts separately and then add them together to arrive at the consolidated government totals. (See also Nonbudgetary; On-Budget; Outlay; Trust Fund Expenditure Account under Trust Fund Accounts under Account in the President's Budget; Unified Budget.)

Offsetting Collections Collections authorized by law to be credited to appropriation or fund expenditure accounts. They result from (1) businesslike transaction market-oriented activities with the public, (2) intragovernmental transfers, and (3) collections from the public that are governmental in nature but required by law to be classified as offsetting. Collections resulting from businesslike transactions with the public and other government accounts are also known as reimbursements. Laws authorizing offsetting collections make them available for obligation to meet the account's purpose without further legislative action. However, it is not uncommon for annual appropriation acts to include limitations on the obligations to be financed by these collections. The authority to obligate and spend offsetting collections is a form of budget authority. The Congressional Budget Act of

1974, as amended by the Budget Enforcement Act (BEA) of 1990, defines offsetting collections as negative budget authority and the reductions to it as positive budget authority. Offsetting collections include reimbursements, transfers between federal and trust fund accounts, offsetting governmental collections, and refunds.

Offsetting Governmental Collections A term used by the Office of Management and Budget (OMB) to designate offsetting collections from nonfederal sources that are governmental in nature but are required by law to be credited to expenditure accounts.

Offsetting Governmental Receipts A term used by the Office of Management and Budget (OMB) to designate receipts that are governmental in nature (e.g., tax receipts, regulatory fees, and compulsory user charges) but are required by law to be classified as offsetting.

Offsetting Receipts Collections that are offset against gross outlays but are not authorized to be credited to expenditure accounts. Offsetting receipts are deposited in receipt accounts. Like offsetting collections, they result from (1) businesslike transactions or market-oriented activities with the public, (2) intragovernmental transfers, and (3) collections from the public that are governmental in nature but required by law to be classified as offsetting receipts. Offsetting receipts are offsets to gross budget authority and outlays, usually at the agency or subfunction level, but some are undistributed and are offsets to budget authority and outlays in the aggregate. (See also Undistributed Offsetting Receipts.) Unlike offsetting collections, offsetting receipts cannot be used without being appropriated. Trust fund offsetting receipts are permanently appropriated and, therefore, can be used without subsequent annual appropriation legislation. (See Permanent Authority under Timing of Legislative Action under Budget Authority; Trust Fund Receipt Account under Trust Fund Accounts under Account in the President's Budget.) The Congressional Budget Act of 1974, as amended by the Budget Enforcement Act (BEA) of 1990, defines offsetting receipts and collections as negative budget authority and the reductions to it as positive budget authority. (See also Earmarking; Reimbursement.)

Offsetting Receipts and Collections A form of budget authority that permits agencies to obligate and expend the proceeds of offsetting receipts and collections. The Congressional Budget Act of 1974, as amended by the Budget Enforcement Act (BEA) of 1990, defines offsetting receipts and collections as negative budget authority and the reductions to it as positive budget authority. In the President's budget, the Office of Management and Budget (OMB) reports offsetting receipts as appropriations.

OMB Circular No. A-11 Document that provides detailed guidance to executive departments and establishments by the Office of Management and Budget (OMB) for preparing and submitting the President's budget and executing the budget.

On-Budget All budgetary accounts other than those designated by law as off-budget. (See also Off-Budget.)

Operating Budget A detailed projection of all estimated income and expenses during a given future period.

Operating Lease An agreement conveying the right to use property for a limited time in exchange for periodic payments. Operating lease criteria are ownership of the asset remains with lessor, the lease does not contain a bargain-price purchase option, the lease term does not exceed 75 percent of the estimated economic life of the asset, the present value of the minimum lease payments over the life of the lease does not exceed 90 percent of the fair market value of the asset at the beginning of the lease term, the asset is a general purpose asset rather than being for a special purpose of the government and is not built to the unique specification of the government as lessee, and there is a private sector market for the asset. (See also Capital Lease.)

Outlay The issuance of checks, disbursement of cash, or electronic transfer of funds made to liquidate a federal obligation. Outlays also occur when interest on the Treasury debt held by the public accrues and when the government issues bonds, notes, debentures, monetary credits, or other cash-equivalent instruments in order to liquidate obligations. Also, under credit reform, the credit subsidy cost is recorded as an outlay when a direct or guaranteed loan is disbursed. An outlay is not recorded for repayment of debt principal, disbursements to the public by federal credit programs for direct loan obligations and loan guarantee commitments made in fiscal year 1992 or later, disbursements from deposit funds, and refunds of receipts that result from overpayments. Outlays during a fiscal year may be for payment of obligations incurred in prior years (prior-year obligations) or in the same year. Outlays, therefore, flow in part from unexpended balances of prior-year budgetary resources and in part from budgetary resources provided for the year in which the money is spent. Outlays are stated both gross and net of offsetting collections. (See Offsetting Collections under Collections.) Total government outlays include outlays of off-budget federal entities. (See also Expenditure; Expense.)

Output Goal A description of the level of activity or effort that will be produced or provided over a period or by a specified date, including a description of the characteristics and attributes (e.g., timeliness) established as standards in the course of conducting the activity or effort.

Output Measure The level of activity or effort of a program (i.e., the products and services delivered) over a period that can be expressed quantitatively or qualitatively.

Outyear In the Concurrent Resolution on the Budget, or in the President's budget submission, any fiscal year (or years) beyond the budget year for which projections are made.

Oversight Committee The congressional committee charged with general oversight of an agency's or program's operations. In most cases, the oversight committee for an agency or program is also its authorizing committee. The Senate Committee on Homeland Security and Governmental Affairs and the House Committee on Government Reform also have general oversight on budget and accounting measures other than appropriations, except as provided in the Congressional Budget Act of 1974. (See also Authorizing Committee.)

Pay-as-You-Go (PAYGO) A budgetary enforcement mechanism originally set forth in the Budget Enforcement Act (BEA), which effectively expired at the end of fiscal year 2002. Under this mechanism, proposed changes in, or new permanent, law were expected to be deficit neutral in the aggregate in the fiscal year of enactment or in a period of years. PAYGO was intended to control growth in direct spending and tax legislation. The Senate, in the concurrent resolution on the budget, has established an internal rule enforcing a requirement that direct spending or receipts legislation under consideration in the Senate be deficit neutral over certain periods of time. This Senate PAYGO rule is enforced by points of order. (See also Point of Order; Sequestration.)

Performance and Accountability Report (PAR) Provides financial and performance information that enables Congress, the President, and the public to assess the performance of an organization relative to its mission and for management to be accountable for its actions and resources. The Office of Management and Budget (OMB) provides guidance on the contents of the PARs, which integrate the reporting requirements of several laws, including (1) the Chief Financial Officers Act of 1990, (2) the Federal Managers' Financial Integrity Act of 1982, (3) the Government Management Reform Act of 1994, (4) the Government Performance and Results Act (GPRA) of 1993, and (5) the Reports Consolidation Act of 2000.

Performance Budget A presentation that links strategic goals with related long-term and annual performance goals and with the costs of specific activities that contribute to the achievement of those goals.

Performance Budgeting Generally understood to refer to the infusion of performance information into the resource allocation process used to develop budget proposals or to execute an agreed-upon budget. Also known as results-based budgeting. (See Government Performance and Results Act.)

Performance Goal A target level of performance expressed as a tangible, measurable objective, against which actual achievement can be compared, including a goal expressed as a quantitative standard, value, or rate.

Performance Measure/Performance Indicator A particular value or characteristic used to measure output, outcome, or efficiency of an organization or program. Performance measures are associated with performance goals in the annual performance plan.

Performance Measurement The ongoing monitoring and reporting of program accomplishments, particularly progress toward preestablished goals. It is typically conducted by program or agency management. Performance measures may address the type or level of program activities conducted (process), the direct products and services delivered by a program (outputs), or the results of those products and services (outcomes).

Performance Plan A plan that covers each program activity set forth in an agency's budget. It establishes performance goals to define the level of performance to be achieved by a program activity; expresses such goals in an objective, quantifiable, and measurable form; briefly describes the operational processes, skills, technology, and resources required to meet the performance goals; establishes performance indicators to be used in measuring or assessing the relevant outputs, service levels, and outcomes of each program activity; provides a basis for comparing actual program results with the established performance goals; and describes the means to be used to verify and validate measured values.

Performance Report A report that sets forth the performance indicators established in the agency performance plan under the Government Performance and Results Act (GPRA) of 1993, along with the actual program performance achieved compared with the performance goals expressed in the plan for that fiscal year.

Permanent Authority Budget authority that is available as the result of previously enacted legislation and is available without further legislative action. For example, authority to retain and use offsetting receipts tends to be permanent authority. Such budget authority can be the result of substantive legislation or appropriation acts.

Point of Order An objection raised on the House or Senate floor or in committees to an action being taken as contrary to that body's rules. In the House, for example, a point of order may be raised under Rule

XXI objecting to an appropriation in an appropriation bill that was not previously authorized by law. Many of the rules established in the Congressional Budget Act and related rules preclude the consideration of legislation that would violate totals in the budget resolutions, spending limits, or committee allocations. These rules are typically enforced through points of order. Points of order may be waived by a majority vote in the House. In the Senate, only points of order under the Budget Act may be waived (not points of order against actions that violate the Senate's standing rules), but the waiver generally requires a three-fifths vote. (See also Concurrent Resolution on the Budget; Congressional Budget Act.)

Present Value The worth of a future stream of returns or costs in terms of money paid immediately (or at some designated date). (Differs from Net Present Value.) A dollar available at some date in the future is worth less than a dollar available today because the latter could be invested at interest in the interim. In calculating present value, prevailing interest rates provide the basis for converting future amounts into their "money now" equivalents. (See also Discount Rate; Net Present Value.)

President's Budget The document sent to Congress by the President in January or February of each year, as required by law (31 U.S.C. § 1105), requesting new budget authority for federal programs and estimating federal revenues and outlays for the upcoming fiscal year and 4 subsequent outyears. Although the title of the document is Budget of the U.S. Government, it represents proposals for congressional consideration.

Prior Year The fiscal year immediately preceding the current year.

Program Generally, an organized set of activities directed toward a common purpose or goal that an agency undertakes or proposes to carry out its responsibilities. Because the term has many uses in practice, it does not have a well-defined, standard meaning in the legislative process. It is used to describe an agency's mission, functions, activities, services, projects, and processes. (See also Program, Project, or Activity.)

Program Account See under Credit Program Account under Credit Reform Act Accounts under Federal Credit.

Program Activity A specific activity or project as listed in the program and financing schedules of the President's budget.

Program and Financing Schedule A schedule published in the President's budget "Detailed Budget Estimates" presenting budget data by each appropriation or fund account. The schedule consists of eight sections: (1) obligations by program activity; (2) budgetary resources available for obligation; (3) new budget authority (gross), detail; (4) change in obligated balances; (5) outlays (gross), detail; (6) offsets to gross budget authority and outlays; (7) net budget authority and outlays; (8) and memorandum (non add) entries.

Program Evaluation An individual systematic study conducted periodically or on an ad hoc basis to assess how well a program is working. It is often conducted by experts external to the program, either inside or outside the agency, as well as by program managers. A program evaluation typically examines achievement of program objectives in the context of other aspects of program performance or in the context in which it occurs. (See also Performance Budgeting; Performance and Accountability Report under Performance Budgeting; Government Performance and Results Act.)

Program, Project, or Activity (PPA) An element within a budget account. For annually appropriated accounts, the Office of Management and Budget (OMB) and agencies identify PPAs by reference to committee reports and budget justifications; for permanent appropriations, OMB and agencies identify PPAs by the program and financing schedules that the President provides in the "Detailed Budget Estimates" in the budget submission for the relevant fiscal year. Program activity structures are intended to provide a meaningful representation of the operations financed by a specific budget account- usually by project, activity, or organization.

Program Year Describes the authorized operating period of a particular program. The term is usually used to distinguish the program's operating period from the federal government's fiscal year. For example, a program year may begin on July 1 of a year and end on June 30 of the following year.

Projections Estimates of budget authority, outlays, receipts, or other budget amounts extending several years into the future. Projections are generally intended to indicate the budgetary implications of existing or proposed programs and legislation. Projections may include alternative program and policy strategies and ranges of possible budget amounts. Projections are not firm estimates of what will occur in future years, nor are they intended to be recommendations for future budget decisions.

Proprietary Accounting Involves federal entities recording and accumulating financial information on transactions and balances for purposes of reporting both internally to management and externally in an entity's financial statements. "Proprietary accounting" is also referred to as "financial accounting" and is usually based on generally accepted accounting principles (GAAP), which follow established conventions, such as the recognition of the depreciation of capital assets over time as expenses, instead of recognition on the basis of strict association with the obligation or expenditure of appropriated funds. Most federal entities are subject to proprietary accounting standards promulgated through the Federal Accounting Standards Advisory Board (FASAB).

Proprietary Accounts See under Standard General Ledger (SGL) Chart of Accounts.

Proprietary Receipts from the Public Collections from outside the government that are deposited in receipt accounts that arise as a result of the government's business-type or market-oriented activities. Among these are interest received, proceeds from the sale of property and products, charges for nonregulatory services, and rents and royalties. Such collections may be credited to general fund, special fund, or trust fund receipt accounts and are offset against budget authority and outlays. In most cases, such offsets are by agency and by subfunction, but some proprietary receipts are deducted from total budget authority and outlays for the government as a whole. An example of the latter is rents and royalties on the Outer Continental Shelf. (See Subfunction 953 in app. IV. See also Earmarking.)

Public Enterprise Revolving Fund Account A type of revolving fund that conducts cycles of businesslike operations, mainly with the public, in which it charges for the sale of products or services and uses the proceeds to finance its spending, usually without requirement for annual appropriations. Most government corporations are financed by public enterprise funds.

Public-Private Partnership An arrangement between a public agency (federal, state, or local) and a for-profit corporation. Each sector (public and private) contributes skills and assets in delivering a service or facility for the use of the general public or the parties to the partnership.

Real Dollar A dollar value adjusted to remove the effects of inflation by dividing the nominal value (also called the current dollar value) by the appropriate price index. The resulting amount can be labeled real or inflation adjusted. Real dollar values can reflect a measure of purchasing power, such as real income, or a measure of quantity, such as real GDP. Real dollar is frequently called constant dollar when referring to measures of purchasing power.

Real Economic Growth The increase in GDP, adjusted for inflation.

Real Interest Rate A measure of an interest rate adjusted to remove the effects of expected general inflation.

Real Measures Measures of interest rates and prices for specific commodities adjusted to remove the effects of general inflation (i.e., real interest rates and real prices).

Reapportionment A revision of a previous apportionment of budgetary resources for an appropriation or fund account. The Office of Management and Budget (OMB) reapportions just as it apportions. Agencies usually submit requests for reapportionment to OMB as soon as a change becomes necessary due to changes in amounts available, program requirements, or cost factors. For exceptions, see OMB Circular No. A-11, sec. 120. This approved revision would ordinarily cover the same period, project, or activity covered in the original apportionment. (See also Allotment; Apportionment.)

Reappropriation Legislation permitting an agency to obligate, whether for the same or different purposes, all or part of the unobligated portion of budget authority that has expired or would otherwise expire if not reappropriated. In the President's budget, reappropriations of expired balances are counted as new budget authority or balance transfers depending on the year for which the amounts are reappropriated.

Reauthorization Legislation that renews an expiring or expired authorization that was in effect for a fixed period, with or without substantive change. (See also Authorizing Legislation.)

Receipts See under Governmental Receipts under Collections.

Recession A pervasive, substantial decline in overall business activity that is of at least several months' duration. The National Bureau of Economic Research identifies recessions on the basis of several indicators. As a rule of thumb, recessions are commonly identified by a decline in real GDP for at least two consecutive quarters.

Reconciliation A process Congress uses to reconcile amounts determined by tax, spending, credit, and debt legislation for a given fiscal year with levels set in the concurrent resolution on the budget for the year. Section 310 of the Congressional Budget and Impoundment Control Act of 1974 (2 U.S.C. § 641) provides that the resolution may direct committees to determine and recommend changes to laws and pending legislation as required to conform to the resolution's totals for budget authority, revenues, and the public debt. Such changes are incorporated into either a reconciliation resolution or a reconciliation bill. (See also Concurrent Resolution on the Budget; Congressional Budget Act.)

Reconciliation Bill A bill reported pursuant to reconciliation instructions in a congressional budget resolution proposing changes in laws that if enacted, would achieve the budgetary goals set forth in the budget resolution. (See also Congressional Budget Act.)

Reconciliation Instruction A provision in a concurrent budget resolution directing one or more committees to report (or submit to the House and Senate Budget Committees) legislation changing existing laws or pending legislation in order to bring spending, revenues, or debt limit into conformity with the budget resolution. The instructions specify the committees to which they apply, indicate the appropriate total dollar changes to be achieved, and usually provide a deadline by which the legislation is to be reported or submitted.

Reconciliation Resolution A concurrent resolution (i.e., a resolution that the President does not sign) reported pursuant to reconciliation instructions in a congressional budget resolution directing the Clerk of the House of Representatives or the Secretary of the Senate to make specified changes in bills and joint resolutions that have not been enrolled to bring direct spending or revenue laws into conformity with the budget resolution.

Reduction Cancellation of the availability of budgetary resources previously provided by law before the authority would otherwise lapse. Reductions can be account specific and across-the-board. (See also Rescission; Sequestration.)

Refunds Payments returned to the government that were made in error. They are credited to the appropriation originally charged. (See also Offsetting Collections under Collections.)

Reimbursements When authorized by law, amounts collected for materials or services furnished to the public or other government accounts. (For accounting purposes, earned reimbursements are also known as revenues.) These offsetting collections are netted against gross outlays in determining net outlays from such appropriations. (See also Unfilled Customer Orders.)

Reobligation Obligation of deobligated funds for a different authorized use. (See also Deobligation.)

Reprogramming Shifting funds within an appropriation or fund account to use them for purposes other than those contemplated at the time of appropriation; it is the shifting of funds from one object class to another within an appropriation or from one program activity to another. While a transfer of funds involves shifting funds from one account to another, reprogramming involves shifting funds within an account. (For a distinction, see Transfer.) Generally agencies may shift funds within an appropriation or fund account as part of their duty to manage their funds. Unlike transfers, agencies may reprogram without additional statutory authority. Nevertheless, reprogramming often involves some form of notification to the congressional appropriations committees, authorizing committees, or both. Sometimes committee oversight of reprogramming actions is prescribed by statute and requires formal notification of one or more committees before a reprogramming action may be implemented.

Rescission Legislation enacted by Congress that cancels the availability of budget authority previously enacted before the authority would otherwise expire. The Impoundment Control Act of 1974 (2 U.S.C. § 683) provides for the President to propose rescissions whenever the President determines that all or part of any budget authority will not be needed to carry out the full objectives or scope of programs for which the authority was provided. Rescissions of budget authority may be proposed for fiscal policy or other reasons. All funds proposed for rescission must be reported to Congress in a special message. Amounts proposed for rescission may be withheld for up to 45 calendar days of continuous session while Congress considers the proposals. If both houses have not completed action on a rescission bill rescinding all or part of the amount proposed by the President for rescission in his special message within 45 calendar days of continuous session, any funds being withheld must be made available for obligation. Congress may also initiate rescissions. Such congressional action occurs for various reasons, including changing priorities, program terminations, excessive unobligated balances, offsets, and program slippage. (See also Apportionment; Budgetary Reserves; Deferral of Budget Authority; Impoundment; Reduction; Rescission Bill under Rescission.)

Rescission Bill A bill or joint resolution to cancel, in whole or in part, budget authority previously enacted by law. Rescissions proposed by the President must be transmitted in a special message to Congress. Under section 1012 of the Impoundment Control Act of 1974 (2 U.S.C. § 683), unless both houses of Congress complete action on a rescission bill within 45 calendar days of continuous session after receipt of the proposal, the budget authority must be made available for obligation. (See also Rescission.)

Revenue (1) As used in the congressional budget process, a synonym for governmental receipts. Revenues result from amounts that result from the government's exercise of its sovereign power to tax or otherwise compel payment or from gifts to the government. Article I, Section 7, of the U.S. Constitution requires that revenue bills originate in the House of Representatives. (2) As used in federal proprietary accounting, an inflow of resources that the government demands, earns, or receives by donation. Revenue comes from two sources: exchange transactions and nonexchange transactions. Exchange revenues arise when a government entity provides goods and services to the public or to another government entity for a price. Another term for exchange revenue is "earned revenue." Nonexchange revenues arise primarily from exercise of the government's power to demand payments from the public (e.g., taxes, duties, fines, and penalties) but also include donations. The term "revenue" does not encompass all financing sources of government reporting entities, such as most of the appropriations they receive. Revenues result from (1) services performed by the federal government and (2) goods and other property delivered to purchasers. (See also Collections.)

Revolving Fund A fund established by Congress to finance a cycle of businesslike operations through amounts received by the fund. A revolving fund charges for the sale of products or services and uses the proceeds to finance its spending, usually on a self-sustaining basis. Instead of recording the collections in receipt accounts, the budget records the collections and the outlays of revolving funds in the same account. A revolving fund is a form of permanent appropriation. (See also Account.)

Rollover Instead of paying off a loan when due, the principal and sometimes accrued interest outstanding of a borrower is refinanced (rolled over) as a new loan with a new maturity date. (See also Federal Credit.)

Scorekeeping The process of estimating the budgetary effects of pending legislation and comparing them to a baseline, such as a budget resolution, or to any limits that may be set in law. Scorekeeping tracks data such as budget authority, receipts, outlays, the surplus or deficit, and the public debt limit. The process allows Congress to compare the cost of proposed budget policy changes to existing law and to enforce spending and revenue levels agreed upon in the budget resolution. Budget Committees and the Congressional Budget Office (CBO) score legislation in relation to the levels set by Congress in concurrent budget resolutions.

Scorekeeping Rules Guidelines established for use by the Office of Management and Budget (OMB), the Congressional Budget Office (CBO), and the Committees on Budget and Appropriations in the House of Representatives and the Senate in measuring compliance with the Balanced Budget and Emergency Deficit Control Act, as amended by the Budget Enforcement Act (BEA), and with the congressional budget process. Though the enforcement mechanisms of BEA expired, or became ineffective, at the end of fiscal year 2002, OMB continues to use the same scorekeeping rules developed for use with BEA for purposes of budget execution. Scorekeepers (OMB, CBO, and budget committees) have an ongoing dialogue and may revise rules, as required.

Scoring See under Scorekeeping.

Seasonal Rate The average commitments, obligations, and expenses of 1 or more of the last 5 fiscal years used to determine funding under a continuing resolution. (See also ContinuingAppropriation/Continuing Resolution; Current Rate.)

Seigniorage The difference between the face value of minted circulating coins and the cost of their production, including the cost of metal used in the minting and the cost of transporting the coins to Federal Reserve Banks for distribution to the public. Seigniorage reflects an increase in the value of government assets when coinage metal is converted to a coin whose face value is higher than the cost of the metal. Seigniorage arises from the government's exercise of its monetary powers. In contrast to receipts from the public, seigniorage involves no corresponding payment by another party. For budget reporting purposes, seigniorage is excluded from receipts and treated as a means of financing a deficit—other than borrowing from the public—or as a supplementary amount that can be applied to reduce debt or to increase the Treasury's cash. The budget includes an estimate of receipts (offsetting collections) equal to the cost of manufacturing and distributing circulating coins, including a charge for capital. (See also Means of Financing.)

Separate Enrollment A procedure that would require that once an appropriation bill is passed by Congress, each provision of funding would be separately enrolled as a discrete "bill." An enrolled bill is the final, official copy of a bill or joint resolution that both houses have passed in identical form to present to the President for signature. Each separately enrolled provision would be presented independently to the President for signature, allowing the veto of some "bills" with spending provisions to which the President objects while allowing signing the others. While such legislation has been proposed at various times in the past as a way of providing the President with something like a line item veto, Congress has not enacted separate enrollment procedures. (See also Impoundment; Line Item Veto; Rescission.)

Sequestration which expired in 2002, the cancellation of budgetary resources provided by discretionary appropriations or direct spending laws. New budget authority, unobligated balances, direct spending authority, and obligation limitations were "sequestrable" resources; that is, they were subject to reduction or cancellation under a presidential sequester order. (See also Budgetary Resources; Entitlement Authority; Gramm-Rudman-Hollings; Impoundment; Rescission.)

Special Fund Accounts Federal fund accounts earmarked by law for a specific purpose.

Special Fund Expenditure Account An appropriation account established to record appropriations, obligations, and outlays financed by the proceeds of special fund receipts.

Special Fund Receipt Account A receipt account credited with collections that are earmarked by law but included in the federal funds group rather than classified as trust fund collections. These collections are presented in the President's budget as either governmental (budget) receipts or offsetting receipts.

Spending Caps Overall limits on discretionary spending, which were originally set in the Budget Enforcement Act (BEA) and the enforcement of which expired at the end of fiscal year 2002. Congress, however, continues to set limits on discretionary spending, typically in concurrent budget resolutions, which are enforceable during the congressional budget process. (See also Discretionary; Concurrent Resolution on the Budget.)

Spending Committee A standing committee of the House or Senate with jurisdiction over legislation permitting the obligation of funds. The House and Senate Appropriations Committees are spending committees for discretionary programs. For other programs, the authorizing legislation itself permits the obligation of funds (backdoor authority). In that case, the authorizing committees are the spending committees. (See also Authorizing Committee; Backdoor Authority/Backdoor Spending.)

Spendout Rate/Outlay Rate The rate at which budget authority becomes outlays in a fiscal year. It is usually presented as an annual percentage.

Standard General Ledger (SGL) Chart of Accounts A chart of accounts (and technical guidance) established to support the consistent recording of financial events as well as the preparation of standard external reports required by the Office of Management and Budget (OMB) and the Department of the Treasury. Agencies are required by law (31 U.S.C. § 3512) to "implement and maintain financial management systems that comply substantially with," among other things, the Standard General Ledger. It contains two complete and separate, but integrated, self-balancing sets of accounts—budgetary and proprietary. Budgetary accounts are used to recognize and track budget approval and execution, whereas proprietary accounts are used to recognize and track assets, liabilities, revenues, and expenses. The Standard General Ledger is reproduced in the Treasury Financial Manual "Standard General Ledger Supplement."

Statement of Federal Financial Accounting Standards (SFFAS) See under Federal Accounting Standards Advisory Board.

Statutory Debt Limit The ceiling on the amount of most Treasury and agency debt established by section 3101 of title 31 of the United States Code, sometimes referred to as the public debt ceiling or the public debt limit.

Strategic Goal/Strategic Objective A statement of aim or purpose included in a strategic plan (required under the Government Performance and Results Act (GPRA) of 1993) that defines how an agency will carry out a major segment of its mission over a certain period. The goal is expressed in a manner that allows a future assessment to be made of whether the goal was or is being achieved. In a performance budget/performance plan, strategic goals should be used to group multiple program outcome goals; the program outcome goals should relate to and in the aggregate be sufficient to influence the strategic goals or objectives and their performance measures.

Strategic Plan Federal agency plan containing the organization's comprehensive mission statement, general goals and objectives, description of how the goals and objectives are to be achieved, description of how performance goals are related to the general goals and objectives, identification of key external factors, and description of program evaluations used to establish the general goals and objectives. Strategic plans must cover a period of not less than 5 years and must be updated and revised at least every 3 years.

Structural/Standardized Budget Surplus/Deficit A concept adjusting the surplus/deficit for the effects of the business cycle and other temporary factors such as sales and spectrum auctions.

Structural Surplus/Deficit See under Cyclically Adjusted Surplus or Deficit.

Subcommittee Allocation As required by section 302(b) of the Congressional Budget and Impoundment Control Act of 1974 (2 U.S.C. § 633(b)), the distribution of spending authority and outlays by the appropriations committees of each house of Congress to their relevant appropriations subcommittees of jurisdiction based on the levels contained in the concurrent resolution on the budget.

Subfunction A subdivision of a budget function. For example, health care services and health research are subfunctions of the health budget function.

Subsidy Generally, a payment or benefit made by the federal government where the benefit exceeds the cost to the beneficiary. Subsidies are designed to support the conduct of an economic enterprise or activity, such as ship operations. They may also refer to (1) provisions in the tax laws for certain tax expenditures and (2) the provision of loans, goods, and services to the public at prices lower than market value. These include interest subsidies. Under credit reform, subsidy means the estimated long-term cost to the government of a direct loan or loan guarantee, calculated on a net present value basis over the life of the loan, excluding administrative costs and any incidental effects on governmental receipts or outlays. (See also

Credit Reform and Credit Subsidy Cost under Federal Credit; Tax Expenditure.)

Subsidy Cost See under Credit Subsidy Cost under Federal Credit.

Supplemental Appropriation An act appropriating funds in addition to those already enacted in an annual appropriation act. Supplemental appropriations provide additional budget authority usually in cases where the need for funds is too urgent to be postponed until enactment of the regular appropriation bill. Supplementals may sometimes include items not appropriated in the regular bills for lack of timely authorizations.

Surplus The amount by which the government's budget receipts exceed its budget outlays for a given period, usually a fiscal year. Sometimes a deficit is called a negative surplus and is shown in parentheses in budget tables.

Suspense Accounts Combined receipt and expenditure accounts established to temporarily hold funds that are later refunded or paid into another government fund when an administrative or final determination as to the proper disposition is made.

Tax A sum that legislation imposes upon persons (broadly defined to include individuals, trusts, estates, partnerships, associations, companies, and corporations), property, or activities to pay for government operations. The power to impose and collect federal taxes is given to Congress in Article I, Section 8, of the U.S. Constitution. Collections that arise from the sovereign powers of the federal government constitute the bulk of governmental receipts, which are compared with budget outlays in calculating the budget surplus or deficit. (See also Government Receipts under Collections; Revenue.)

Tax Credit An amount that offsets or reduces tax liability. When the allowable tax credit amount exceeds the tax liability and the difference is paid to the taxpayer, the credit is considered refundable and is considered an increase in outlays in the federal budget. Otherwise, the difference can be (1) allowed as a carryforward against future tax liability, (2) allowed as a carryback against taxes paid, or (3) lost as a tax benefit. (See also Tax Expenditure.)

Tax Deduction An amount that is subtracted from the tax base before tax liability is calculated.

Tax Expenditure A revenue loss attributable to a provision of the federal tax laws that (1) allows a special exclusion, exemption, or deduction from gross income or (2) provides a special credit, preferential tax rate, or deferral of tax liability. Tax expenditures are subsidies provided through the tax system. Rather than transferring funds from the government to the private sector, the U.S. government forgoes some of the receipts that it would have collected, and the beneficiary taxpayers pay lower taxes than they would have had to pay. The Congressional Budget Act requires that a list of "tax expenditures" be included in the President's budget. Examples include tax expenditures for child care and the exclusion of fringe benefits, such as employer-provided health insurance, from taxation.

Technical and Economic Assumptions Assumptions about factors affecting estimations of future outlays and receipts that are not a direct function of legislation. Economic assumptions involve such factors as the future inflation and interest rates. Technical assumptions involve all other nonpolicy factors. For example, in the Medicare program, estimations regarding demography, hospitalization versus outpatient treatment, and morbidity all affect estimations of future outlays.

Transfer Shifting of all or part of the budget authority in one appropriation or fund account to another. Agencies may transfer budget authority only as specifically authorized by law. For accounting purposes, the nature of the transfer determines whether the transaction is treated as an expenditure or a nonexpenditure transfer. (See also Allocation. For a distinction, see Reprogramming.)

Transfer Appropriation (Allocation) Accounts Accounts established to receive and disburse allocations. Such allocations and transfers are not adjustments to budget authority or balances of budget authority. Rather, the transactions and any adjustments therein are treated as nonexpenditure transfers at the time the allocations are made. The accounts carry symbols that identify the original appropriation from which moneys have been advanced. Transfer appropriation accounts are symbolized by adding the receiving agency's department prefix to the original appropriation or fund account symbol. In some cases, a bureau suffix is added to show that the transfer is being made to a particular bureau within the receiving department. For budget purposes, transactions in the transfer accounts are reported with the transactions in the parent accounts.

Transfer Authority Statutory authority provided by Congress to transfer budget authority from one appropriation or fund account to another.

Transfer Payment A payment made for which no current or future goods or services are required in return. Government transfer payments include Social Security benefits, unemployment insurance benefits, and welfare payments. Taxes are considered transfer payments. Governments also receive transfer payments in the form of fees, fines, and donations from businesses and persons. (See also National Income and Product Accounts.)

Transfers between Federal and Trust Fund Accounts Transfers of resources between federal and trust fund accounts are treated as expenditure transfers regardless of the nature of the transaction. The receiving account reports offsetting collections from federal sources (for offsetting collections) or intragovernmental receipts (for offsetting receipts).

Treasury Bill The shortest term federal debt instrument or security. Treasury bills mature within 1 year after the date of issue.

Treasury Bond A federal debt instrument with a maturity of more than 10 years.

Treasury Debt/Public Debt That portion of the gross federal debt issued by the Department of the Treasury to the public or to government accounts (including securities issued by the Federal Financing Bank (FFB) under section 9(a) of the Federal Financing Bank Act of 1973 (12 U.S.C. § 2888(a)). (See also Debt Held by Government Accounts under Debt, Federal.)

Treasury Note A federal debt instrument with a maturity of at least 1 year but not more than 10 years.

Treasury Security A debt instrument of the U.S. Treasury issued to finance the operations of the government or refinance the government's debt.

Trust Fund Accounts Accounts designated as "trust funds" by law, regardless of any other meaning of the term "trust fund." A trust fund account is usually either a receipt, an expenditure, or a revolving fund account. Except in rare circumstances (for example, Indian Trust Funds), a trust fund account imposes no fiduciary responsibility on the federal government.

Trust Fund Expenditure Account An appropriation account established to record appropriated amounts of trust fund receipts used to finance specific purposes or programs under a trust agreement or statute.

Trust Fund Receipt Account A receipt account credited with collections classified as trust fund collections. These collections are recorded as either governmental receipts or offsetting receipts.

Trust Revolving Fund Account A trust fund expenditure account that is an appropriation account authorized to be credited with collections used, without further appropriation action, to carry out a cycle of business-type operations in accordance with statute.

Uncollected Customer Payments from Federal Sources Orders on hand from other federal government accounts that are recorded as valid obligations of the ordering account and for which funds or noncash resources have not yet been collected. The amount represents both accounts receivable from federal sources and unpaid, unfilled orders from federal sources.

Undelivered Orders The value of goods and services ordered and obligated that have not been received. This amount includes any orders for which advance payment has been made but for which delivery or performance has not yet occurred. (See also Advance Payments; Unliquidated Obligations.)

Undistributed Offsetting Receipts Offsetting receipts that are deducted from totals for the government as a whole rather than from a single agency or subfunction in order to avoid distortion of agency or subfunction totals. Offsetting receipts that are undistributed in both agency and functional tables are the collections of employer share of employee retirement payments, rents, and royalties on the Outer Continental Shelf, and the sales of major assets. Interest received by trust funds is undistributed offsetting receipts in the agency tables, but is distributed by function (i.e., subfunction 950 in functional tables).

Unemployment Rate As defined by the Bureau of Labor Statistics (BLS), the number of people who do not have jobs but have actively looked for work in the prior 4 weeks and are currently available for work, expressed as a percentage of the civilian labor force.

Unexpended Balance The sum of the obligated and unobligated balances.

Unexpired Budget Authority Budget authority that is available for incurring new obligations.

Unfilled Customer Orders The dollar amount of orders accepted from other accounts within the government for goods and services to be furnished on a reimbursable basis. In the case of transactions with the public, these orders are amounts advanced or collected for which the account or fund has not yet performed the service or incurred its own obligations for that purpose. (See also Reimbursements under Offsetting Collections under Collections.)

Unfunded Mandate Federal statutes and regulations that require state, local, or tribal governments or the private sector to expend resources to achieve legislative goals without being provided federal funding to cover the costs. The Unfunded Mandates Reform Act of 1995, Pub. L. No. 104-4 (2 U.S.C. §§ 658-658g), generally defines intergovernmental and private sector mandates as "any provision in legislation, statute, or regulation that imposes an enforceable duty" but excludes "conditions of federal assistance" and "duties that arise from participation in a voluntary federal program," among others. The Congressional Budget Office (CBO) is required to determine whether the costs to the states or private sector of a mandate in legislation reported from a congressional committee exceeds certain statutory thresholds. This determination is included in the cost estimate provided to Congress on that legislation. The act also contains procedures for congressional consideration of proposed legislation that contains mandates whose costs are estimated to be over the thresholds unless the legislation also provides funding to cover those costs.

Unified Budget Under budget concepts set forth in the Report of the President's Commission on Budget Concepts, a comprehensive budget in which receipts and outlays from federal and trust funds are consolidated. When these fund groups are consolidated to display budget totals, transactions that are outlays of one fund group for payment to the other fund group (that is, interfund transactions) are deducted to avoid double counting. The unified budget should, as conceived by the President's Commission, take in the full range of federal activities. By law, budget authority, outlays, and receipts of off-budget programs (currently only the Postal Service and Social Security) are excluded from the current budget, but data relating to off-budget programs are displayed in the budget documents. However, the most prominent total in the budget is the unified total, which is the sum of the on-and off- budget totals. (See also Nonbudgetary; Off-Budget; On-Budget.)

Unified Deficit/Total Deficit The amount by which the government's on-budget and off-budget outlays exceed the sum of its on-budget and off-budget receipts for a given period, usually a fiscal year. (See also Budget Surplus under Surplus; Off-Budget.)

Unified Surplus/Total Surplus Used interchangeably to refer to the amount by which the sum of the government's on-budget and off-budget receipts exceed the sum of its on-budget and off-budget outlays for a given period, usually a fiscal year. (See also Unified Deficit/Total Deficit under Deficit.)

Unliquidated Obligations The amount of outstanding obligations or liabilities. (See also Obligation; Undelivered Orders.)

Unobligated Balance The portion of obligational authority that has not yet been obligated. For an appropriation account that is available for a fixed period, the budget authority expires after the period of availability ends but its unobligated balance remains available for 5 additional fiscal years for recording and adjusting obligations properly chargeable to the appropriations period of availability. For example, an expired, unobligated balance remains available until the account is closed to record previously unrecorded obligations or to make upward adjustments in previously underrecorded obligations, such as contract modifications properly within scope of the original contract. At the end of the fifth fiscal year, the account is closed and any remaining balance is canceled. For a no-year account, the unobligated balance is carried forward indefinitely until (1) specifically rescinded by law or (2) the head of the agency concerned or the President determines that the purposes for which the appropriation was made have been carried out and disbursements have not been made from the appropriation for 2 consecutive years. (See also Duration under Budget Authority; Expired Account; Expired Budget Authority under Availability for New Obligations under Budget Authority; Fixed Appropriation Account).

User Fee/User Charge A fee assessed to users for goods or services provided by the federal government. User fees generally apply to federal programs or activities that provide special benefits to identifiable recipients above and beyond what is normally available to the public. User fees are normally related to the cost of the goods or services provided. Once collected, they must be deposited into the general fund of the Treasury, unless the agency has specific authority to deposit the fees into a special fund of the Treasury. An agency may not obligate against fees collected without specific statutory authority. An example of a user fee is a fee for entering a national park. From an economic point of view, user fees may also be collected through a tax such as an excise tax. Since these collections result from the government's sovereign powers, the proceeds are recorded as governmental receipts, not as offsetting receipts or offsetting collections. In the narrow budgetary sense, a toll for the use of a highway is considered a user fee because it is related to the specific use of a particular section of highway. Such a fee would be counted as an offsetting receipt or collection and might be available for use by the agency. Alternatively, highway excise taxes on gasoline are considered a form of user charge in the economic sense, but since the tax must be paid regardless of how the gasoline is used and since it is not directly linked with the provision of the specific service, it is considered a tax and is recorded as a governmental receipt in the budget. (See also Offsetting Collections under Collections; Tax).

Views and Estimates Report A report that the Congressional Budget Act of 1974 requires each House and Senate committee with jurisdiction over federal programs to submit to its respective budget committees each year within 6 weeks of the submission of the President's budget, in advance of the House and Senate Budget Committees' drafting of a concurrent resolution on the budget. Each report contains a committee's comments or recommendations on budgetary matters within its jurisdiction. (See also Concurrent Resolution on the Budget).

Warrant An official document that the Secretary of the Treasury issues upon enactment of an appropriation that establishes the amount of moneys authorized to be withdrawn from the central accounts that the Department of the Treasury maintains. Warrants for currently unavailable special and trust fund receipts are issued when requirements for their availability have been met. (For a discussion of availability, see Availability for New Obligations under Budget Authority).

Wholly Owned Government Corporation An enterprise or business activity designated by the Government Corporation Control Act of 1945 (31 U.S.C. § 9101) or some other statute as a wholly-owned government corporation. Each such corporation is required to submit an annual business-type statement to the Office of Management and Budget (OMB). Wholly-owned government corporations are audited by Government Accountability Office (GAO) as required by the Government Corporation Control Act, as amended (31 U.S.C. § 9105), and other laws. The Pension Benefit Guaranty Corporation is an example of a wholly-owned government corporation. Budget concepts call for any corporation that is wholly owned by the government to be included on-budget. (For distinctions, see Government-Sponsored Enterprise; Mixed-Ownership Government Corporation; Off-Budget).

Working Capital Fund A type of intragovernmental revolving fund that operates as a self-supporting entity that conducts a regular cycle of businesslike activities. These funds function entirely from the fees charged for the services they provide consistent with their statutory authority. (See also Intragovernmental Revolving Fund Account under Intragovernmental Fund Accounts under Federal Fund Accounts under Account in the President's Budget.)

Federal Highway Administration

1-Hour Ozone NAAQS The 1-hour ozone national ambient air quality standard codified at 40 CFR 50.9.

23 CFR 420 Planning and Research Program Administration

23 CFR 450 Planning Assistance and Standards

23 CFR 460 Public Road Mileage for Apportionment of Highway Safety Funds

23 CFR 470 Highway Systems

23 CFR 500 Management and Monitoring Systems

23 CFR 652 Pedestrian and Bicycle Accomodations and Projects

23 CFR 710 Right-of-way and Real Estate

23 CFR 750 Highway Beautification

23 CFR 751 Junkyard control and acquisition

23 CFR 752 Landscape and Roadside Development

23 CFR 771 Environmental Impact and Related Procedures

23 CFR 772 Procedures for Abatement of Highway Traffic Noise and Construction Noise

23 CFR 777 Mitigation of Impacts to Wetlands and Natural Habitat

23 CFR 940 Intelligent Transportation System Architecture and Standards

23 USC 134 Metropolitan Planning

23 USC 135 Statewide Planning

23 USC 149 Congestion Mitigation and Air Quality Improvement Program

23 USC 162 National Scenic Byways Program

23 USC 202 Allocation of Highway Trust Funds for the Federal Lands Highway Program including the IRR Program.

23 USC 204 The administration of the Federal Lands Highway Program including the IRR Program.

23 USC 206 Recreational trails Program

23 USC 217 Bicycle Transportation and Pedestrian Walkways

23 USC 505 State Planning and Research

25 CFR 170 The rules for the administration of the IRR Program by the Bureau of Indian Affairs (BIA).

40 CFR 51 Requirements for Preparation, Adoption, and Submittal of Implementation Plans; Subpart T-Conformity to State or Federal Implementation Plans of Transportation Plans, Programs, and Projects Developed, Funded or Approved Under Title 23 U.S.C. or the Federal Transit Laws; Section 51.390, Implementation Plan Revision

40 CFR 52 Approval and Promulgation of Implementation Plans; Sections 5230-5234, Sanctions

40 CFR 93 Determining Conformity of Federal Actions to State or Federal Implementation Plans

42 USC 61 The Uniform Relocation Assistance and Real Property Acquisition Policies for Federal and Federally Assisted Programs

42 USC 85 Law regarding Air Pollution Prevention and Control

49 CFR 17 Intergovernmental Review of Department of Transportation Programs and Activities

49 CFR 18 Uniform Administrative Requirements for Grants and Cooperative Agreements to State and Local Governments

49 CFR 19 Uniform Administrative Requirements for Grants and Agreements with Institutions of Higher Education, Hospitals and Other Non-Profit Organizations

49 CFR 20 New Restrictions on Lobbying

49 CFR 21 Nondiscrimination in Federally-Assisted Programs of the Department of Transportation–Effectuation of Title VI of the Civil Rights Act of 1964

49 CFR 24 Uniform Relocation and Real Property Acquisition for Federal and Federally Assisted Programs

49 CFR 26 Participation by Disadvantaged Business Enterprises in Department of Transportation Financial Assistance Programs

49 CFR 27 Nondiscrimination on the Basis of Disability in Programs or Activities Receiving Federal Financial Assistance

49 CFR 29 Government Wide Debarment and Suspension (Nonprocurement)

49 CFR 32 Government wide Requirements for Drug-Free Workplace (Financial Assistance)

49 USC 53 Law regarding Mass Transportation

8-Hour Ozone NAAQS The 8-hour ozone national ambient air quality standard codified at 40 CFR 50.10.

Accident An incident involving a moving vehicle. Includes collisions with a vehicle, object, or person (except suicides) and derailment/left roadway. (FTA2) Occurrence in a sequence of events that produces unintended injury, death or property damage. Accident refers to the event, not the result of the event. (NSC1)

Accident (Aircraft) As defined by the National Transportation Safety Board, an occurrence incidental to flight in which, as a result of the operation of an aircraft, any person (occupant or nonoccupant) receives fatal or serious injury or any aircraft receives substantial damage.

Air Carrier The commercial system of air transportation comprising large certificated air carriers, small certificated air carriers, commuter air carriers, on-demand air taxis, supplemental air carriers, and air travel clubs.

Air Quality Conformity The link between air quality planning and transportation planning.

Airplane An engine-driven fixed-wing aircraft heavier than air, that is supported in flight by the dynamic reaction of the air against its wings. (14CFR1)

Airport A landing area regularly used by aircraft for receiving or discharging passengers or cargo.

Airship An engine-driven lighter-than-air aircraft that can be steered. (14CFR1)

Alcohol Concentration (AC) The concentration of alcohol in a person's blood or breath. When expressed as a percentage it means grams of alcohol per 100 milliliters of blood or grams of alcohol per 210 liters of breath. (49CFR383)

Allocation An administrative distribution of funds for programs that do not have statutory distribution formulas.

Alternative Fuels The Energy Policy Act of 1992 defines alternative fuels as methanol, denatured ethanol, and other alcohol; mixtures containing 85 percent or more (but not less than 70 percent as determined by the Secretary of Energy by rule to provide for requirements relating to cold start, safety, or vehicle functions) by volume of methanol, denatured ethanol, and other alcohols with gasoline or other fuels. Includes compressed natural gas, liquid petroleum gas, hydrogen, coal-derived liquid fuels, fuels other than alcohols derived from biological materials, electricity, or any other fuel the Secretary of Energy determines by rule is substantially not petroleum and would yield substantial energy security and environmental benefits.

Altitude The vertical distance of a level, a point or an object considered as a point measured in feet Above Ground Level (AGL) or from Mean Sea Level (MSL). 1) MSL Altitude. Altitude expressed in feet measured from mean sea level. 2) AGL Altitude. Altitude expressed in feet measured above ground level. 3) Indicated Altitude. The altitude as shown by an altimeter. On a pressure or barometric altimeter it is altitude as shown uncorrected for instrument error and uncompensated for variation from standard atmospheric conditions. (FAA4)

American Association of State Highway & Transportation Officials (AASHTO) A nonprofit, nonpartisan association representing highway and transportation departments in the 50 states, the District of Columbia and Puerto Rico. It represents all five transportation modes: air, highways, public transportation, rail and water. Its primary goal is to foster the development, operation and maintenance of an integrated national transportation system.

American Institute of Certified Planners (AICP) The American Planning Association's professional institute that provides recognized leadership nationwide in the certification of professional planners, ethics, professional development, planning education, and the standards of planning practice.

American Planning Association (APA) A nonprofit public interest and research organization committed to urban, suburban, regional, and rural planning. APA and its professional institute, the American Institute of Certified Planners, advance the art and science of planning to meet the needs of people and society.

American Public Transportation Association (APTA) Acting as a leading force in advancing public transportation, APTA serves and leads its diverse membership through advocacy, innovation, and information sharing to strengthen and expand public transportation.

Americans with Disabilities Act (ADA) The legislation defining the responsibilities of and requirements for transportation providers to make transportation accessible to individuals with disabilities. (FTA1)

Amtrak Operated by the National Railroad Passenger Corporation, this rail system was created by the Rail Passenger Service Act of 1970 (Public Law 91-518, 84 Stat. 1327) and given the responsibility for the operation of intercity, as distinct from suburban, passenger trains between points designated by the Secretary of Transportation.

Analysis of Alternatives Understanding how the transportation system and its components work such as information on the costs, benefits and impacts of potential chances to the system.

Annual Funding Agreement A negotiated annual written funding agreement between a Self-Governance Indian Tribal Government (ITG) and the Secretary of the Interior, authorizing the ITG to plan, conduct, consolidate, and administer programs, services, functions, and activities or portions thereof previously administered by the Department of the Interior through the BIA, and other programs for which appropriations are made available for the ITG through the Secretary of the Interior from agencies other than Department of the Interior (DOI).

Apportionment 1) A term that refers to a statutorily prescribed division or assignment of funds. An apportionment is based on prescribed formulas in the law and consists of dividing authorized obligation authority for a specific program among the States. 2) The distribution of funds as prescribed by a statutory formula.

Appropriation Authorization of funding expenditures from Congress.

Appropriations Act Action of a legislative body that makes funds available for expenditure with specific limitations as to amount, purpose, and duration. In most cases, it permits money previously authorized to be obligated and payments made, but for the highway program operating under contract authority, the appropriations act specifies amounts of funds that Congress will make available for the fiscal year to liquidate obligations.

Area Source Small stationary and non-transportation pollution sources that are too small and/or numerous to be included as point sources but may collectively contribute significantly to air pollution (e.g., dry cleaners).

Areawide Control Schedule An accounting and project management tool that is developed from tribal Transportation Improvement Programs, tribal control schedules, and tribal priority lists to identify detailed project information for the expenditure of IRR funds for the current and next four fiscal years.

Arterial A class of roads serving major traffic movements (high-speed, high volume) for travel between major points.

Arterial Highway A major highway used primarily for through traffic.

Arterial Street A class of street serving major traffic movements (high-speed, high volume) for travel between major points.

Asphalt A dark brown to black cement-like material containing bitumen as the predominant constituent. The definition includes crude asphalt and finished products such as cements, fluxes, the asphalt content of emulsions, and petroleum distillates blended with asphalt to make cutback asphalt. Asphalt is obtained by petroleum processing.

Association of Metropolitan Planning Organizations (AMPO) AMPO is a nonprofit, membership organization established in 1994 to serve the needs and interests of "metropolitan planning organizations (MPOs)" nationwide. AMPO offers its member MPOs technical assistance and training, conferences and workshops, frequent print and electronic communications, research, a forum for transportation policy development and coalition building, and a variety of other services.

Attainment Area An area considered to have air quality that meets or exceeds the U.S. Environmental Protection Agency (EPA) health standards used in the Clean Air Act. Nonattainment areas are areas considered not to have met these standards for designated pollutants. An area may be an attainment area for one pollutant and a nonattainment area for others.

Audit Periodic investigation of financial statements and their relationships to planned or permitted expenditures.

Authorization Basic substantive legislation or that which empowers an agency to implement a particular program and also establishes an upper limit on the amount of funds that can be appropriated for that program.

Authorization Act Basic substantive legislation that establishes or continues Federal programs or agencies and establishes an upper limit on the amount of funds for the program(s). The current authorization act for surface transportation programs is the Transportation Equity Act for the 21st Century (TEA-21).

Auto Inspection and Maintenance (IM) Programs require the testing of motor vehicles in parts of the country with unhealthy air and the repair of those that do not meet standards.

Automobile A privately owned and/or operated licensed motorized vehicle including cars, jeeps and station wagons. Leased and rented cars are included if they are privately operated and not used for picking up passengers in return for fare. (FHWA3)

Average Annual Daily Traffic (AADT) The total volume of traffic on a highway segment for one year, divided by the number of days in the year.

Average Annual Daily Truck Traffic (AADTT) The total volume of truck traffic on a highway segment for one year, divided by the number of days in the year.

Average Haul The average distance, in miles, one ton is carried. It is computed by dividing ton-miles by tons of freight originated.

Average Passenger Trip Length (Bus/Rail) Calculated by dividing revenue passenger-miles by the number of revenue passengers.

BIA Area Certification Acceptance Plan A plan prepared by a specific area office which delineates how it will meet certification acceptance requirements under 23 U.S.C., Section 117(a). {This section of law was deleted in the Transportation Equity Act for the 21st Century. CA is being replaced by Stewardship Agreements}.

BIA Atlas Map A series of maps which depict the IRR/BIA road system by reservation and jurisdictions.

BIA Classification of Roads An identification of specific roads or trails that take into account current and future traffic generators, and relationships to connecting or adjacent BIA, State, county, Federal, and/or local roads.

BIA Roads System Those existing and proposed roads for which the BIA has or plans to obtain legal right(s)-of-way. This includes only roads for which the BIA has the primary responsibility to construct, improve, and maintain. Any additions or deletions to this system must be supported by resolution from the ITG.

BIA/FHWA Memorandum of Agreement An agreement between the BIA and the FHWA which contains mutually agreeable roles and responsibilities for the administration of the IRR and Highway Bridge Replacement and Rehabilitation programs.

Bicycle A vehicle having two tandem wheels, propelled solely by human power, upon which any person or persons may ride. (23CFR217)

Bikeway 1) Any road, path, or way which in some manner is specifically designated as being open to bicycle travel, regardless of whether such facilities are designated for the exclusive use of bicycles or are to be shared with other transportation modes. (23CFR217) 2) A facility designed to accommodate bicycle travel for recreational or commuting purposes. Bikeways are not necessarily separated facilities; they may be designed and operated to be shared with other travel modes.

Blind Spot An area from which radio transmissions and/or radar echoes cannot be received. The term is also used to describe portions of the airport not visible from the control tower. (FAA4)

Blood Alcohol Concentration (BAC) Is measured as a percentage by weight of alcohol in the blood (grams/deciliter). A positive BAC level (0.01 g/dl and higher) indicates that alcohol was consumed by the person tested. A BAC level of 0.10 g/dl or more indicates that the person was intoxicated. (NHTSA3)

Blood Alcohol Concentration (Highway) A measurement of the percentage of alcohol in the blood by grams per deciliter.

Bodily Injury Injury to the body, sickness, or disease including death resulting from any of these. (49CFR387)

Bow The front of a vessel. (MARAD2)

Brake An energy conversion mechanism used to stop, or hold a vehicle stationary. (49CFR393)

Bridge Management System (BMS) A systematic process that provides, analyzes, and summarizes bridge information for use in selecting and implementing cost-effective bridge construction, rehabilitation, and maintenance programs.

Budget Authority Empowerment by Congress that allows Federal agencies to incur obligations that will result in the outlay of funds. This empowerment is generally in the form of appropriations. However, for most of the highway programs, it is in the form of contract authority.

Budget Resolution A concurrent resolution passed by Congress presenting the Congressional Budget for each of the succeeding 5 years. A concurrent resolution does not require the signature of the President.

Bulk Carrier (Water) A ship with specialized holds for carrying dry or liquid commodities, such as oil, grain, ore, and coal, in unpackaged bulk form. Bulk carriers may be designed to carry a single bulk product (crude oil tanker) or accommodate several bulk product types (ore/bulk/oil carrier) on the same voyage or on a subsequent voyage after holds are cleaned.

Bureau of Economic Analysis (BEA) The Bureau of Economic Analysis is an agency of the U.S. Department of Commerce

Bureau of Labor Statistics (BLS) The Bureau of Labor Statistics (BLS) is the principal fact-finding agency for the Federal Government in the broad field of labor economics and statistics. The BLS is an independent national statistical agency that collects, processes, analyzes, and disseminates essential statistical data to the American public, the U.S. Congress, other Federal agencies, State and local governments, business, and labor. The BLS also serves as a statistical resource to the Department of Labor. BLS data must satisfy a number of criteria, including relevance to current social and economic issues, timeliness in reflecting today's rapidly changing economic conditions, accuracy and consistently high statistical quality, and impartiality in both subject matter and presentation.

Bureau of Transportation Statistics (BTS) The Bureau was organized pursuant to section 6006 of the Intermodal Surface Transportation Efficiency Act (ISTEA) of 1991 (49 U.S.C. 111), and was formally established by the Secretary of Transportation on December 16, 1992. BTS has an intermodal transportation focus whose missions are to compile, analyze and make accessible information on the Nation's transportation systems; to collect information on intermodal transportation and other areas; and to enhance the quality and effectiveness of DOT's statistical programs through research, the development of guidelines, and the promotion of improvements in data acquisition and use. The programs of BTS are organized in six functional areas and are mandated by ISTEA to 1) Compile, analyze, and publish statistics 2) Develop a long-term data collection program 3) Develop guidelines to improve the credibility and effectiveness of the Department's statistics 4) Represent transportation interests in the statistical community 5) Make statistics accessible and understandable and 6) Identify data needs. (OFR1)

Bus Large motor vehicle used to carry more than 10 passengers, including school buses, intercity buses, and transit buses.

Bus Lane 1) A street or highway lane intended primarily for buses, either all day or during specified periods, but sometimes also used by carpools meeting requirements set out in traffic laws. (APTA1) 2) A lane reserved for bus use only. Sometimes also known as a "diamond lane."

Caboose A car in a freight train intended to provide transportation for crew members. (49CFR223)

Calendar Year The period of time between January 1 and December 31 of any given year. (DOE6)

Capacity A transportation facility's ability to accommodate a moving stream of people or vehicles in a given time period.

Capital Gains or Losses, Other Gains or losses on no operating assets, investments in other than marketable equity securities, and troubled debt restructuring. (BTS4)

Capital Program Funds Financial assistance from the Capital Program of 49 U.S.C. This program enables the Secretary of Transportation to make discretionary capital grants and loans to finance public transportation projects divided among fixed guideway (rail) modernization; construction of new fixed guideway systems and extensions to fixed guideway systems; and replacement, rehabilitation, and purchase of buses and rented equipment, and construction of bus-related facilities.

Carbon Dioxide (CO2) 1) A fluid consisting of more than 90 percent carbon dioxide molecules compressed to a supercritical state. (49CFR195) 2) A colorless, odorless gas. It is not a liquid under standard temperature and pressure.

Carbon Monoxide (CO) A colorless, odorless, highly toxic gas that is a normal by-product of incomplete fossil fuel combustion. Carbon monoxide, one of the major air pollutants, can be harmful in small amounts if breathed over a certain period of time. (DOE6)

Carpool An arrangement where two or more people share the use and cost of privately owned automobiles in traveling to and from pre-arranged destinations together. (ATPA1)

Census The complete enumeration of a population or groups at a point in time with respect to well-defined characteristics for example, population, production, traffic on particular roads. In some connection the term is associated with the data collected rather than the extent of the collection so that the term sample census has a distinct meaning. The partial enumeration resulting from a failure to cover the whole population, as distinct from a designed sample enquiry, may be referred to as an "incomplete census." (DOE5)

Census Division A geographic area consisting of several States defined by the U.S. Department of Commerce, Bureau of the Census. The States are grouped into nine divisions and four regions. (DOE4)

Certification Acceptance ((CA)) A procedure authorized by 23 U.S.C. 117(a) wherein the FHWA can delegate any of the 23 U.S.C. responsibilities for planning, design, and construction of projects, not on the Interstate System, to other qualified governmental entities. {This section of law was deleted in the Transportation Equity Act for the 21st Century. CA is being replaced by Stewardship Agreements. BIA area offices and ITGs may apply for Stewardship Agreements}.

Certification of Public Road Mileage An annual document (certification) that must be furnished by each state to Federal Highway Administration (FHWA) certifying the total public road mileage (kilometers) in the state as of December 31 of the preceding year. (FHWA2)

Certified Capacity The capability of a pipeline project to move gas volumes on a given day, based on a specific set of flowing parameters (operating pressures, temperature, efficiency, and fluid properties) for the pipeline system as stated in the dockets filed (and subsequently certified) in the application for the Certificate of Public Convenience and Necessity at the Federal Energy Regulatory Commission. Generally, the certificated capacity represents a level of service that can be maintained over an extended period of time and may not represent the maximum throughput capability of the system on any given day. (DOE1)

Charter Bus A bus transporting a group of persons who pursuant to a common purpose, and under a single contract at a fixed price, have acquired the exclusive use of a bus to travel together under an itinerary. (APTA1)

Class 1) With respect to the certification, ratings, privileges, and limitations of airmen, means a classification of aircraft within a category having similar operating characteristics. Examples include single engine; multiengine; land; water; gyroplane; helicopter; airship; and free balloon; and 2) With respect to the certification of aircraft, means a broad grouping of aircraft having similar characteristics of propulsion, flight, or landing. Examples include airplane; rotorcraft; glider; balloon; landplane; and seaplane. (14CFR1)

Class 1 Road Hard surface highways including Interstate and U.S. numbered highways (including alternates), primary State routes, and all controlled access highways. (DOI3)

Class 2 Road Hard surface highways including secondary State routes, primary county routes, and other highways that connect principal cities and towns, and link these places with the primary highway system. (DOI3)

Class 3 Road Hard surface roads not included in a higher class and improved, loose surface roads passable in all kinds of weather. These roads are adjuncts to the primary and secondary highway systems. Also included are important private roads such as main logging or industrial roads which serve as connecting links to the regular road network. (DOI3)

Class 4 Road Unimproved roads which are generally passable only in fair weather and used mostly for local traffic. Also included are driveways, regardless of construction. (DOI3)

Class 5 Road Unimproved roads passable only with 4 wheel drive vehicles. (DOI3)

Class I Railroad Railroad with an annual operating revenue of at least $266.7 million.

Clean Air Act Amendments (CAAA) The original Clean Air Act was passed in 1963, but the national air pollution control program is actually based on the 1970 version of the law. The 1990 Clean Air Act Amendments are the most far-reaching revisions of the 1970 law. The 1990 Clean Air Act is the most recent version of the 1970 version of the law. The 1990 amendments made major changes in the Clean Air Act.

Code of Federal Regulations (CFR) A compilation of the general and permanent rules of the executive departments and agencies of the Federal Government as published in the Federal Register. The code is divided into 50 titles that represent broad areas subject to Federal regulation. (DOE5)

Collector (Highway) In rural areas, routes that serve intracounty rather than statewide travel. In urban areas, streets that provide direct access to neighborhoods and arterials.

Combination Truck A power unit (truck tractor) and one or more trailing units (a semitrailer or trailer).

Commercial Bus Any bus used to carry passengers at rates specified in tariffs; charges may be computed per passenger (as in regular route service) or per vehicle (as in charter service).

Commercial Driver's License (CDL) A license issued by a State or other jurisdiction, in accordance with the standards contained in 49 CFR 383, to an individual which authorizes the individual to operate a class of a commercial motor vehicle. (49CFR383)

Commercial Service Airport Airport receiving scheduled passenger service and having 2,500 or more enplaned passengers per year.

Commute Regular travel between home and a fixed location (e.g., work, school). (TRB1)

Commuter A person who travels regularly between home and work or school. (APTA1)

Commuter Air Carrier Different definitions are used for safety purposes and for economic regulations and reporting. For safety analysis, commuter carriers are defined as air carriers operating under 14 CFR 135 that carry passengers for hire or compensation on at least five round trips per week on at least one route between two or more points according to published flight schedules, which specify the times, days of the week, and points of service. On March 20, 1997, the size of the aircraft subject to 14 CFR 135 was reduced from 30 to fewer than 10 passenger seats. (Larger aircraft are subject to the more stringent regulations of 14 CFR 121.) Helicopters carrying passengers or cargo for hire, however, are regulated under CFR 135 whatever their size. Although, in practice, most commuter air carriers operate aircraft that are regulated for safety purposes under 14 CFR 135 and most aircraft that are regulated under 14 CFR 135 are operated by commuter air carriers, this is not necessarily the case. For economic regulations and reporting requirements, commuter air carriers are those carriers that operate aircraft of 60 or fewer seats or a maximum payload capacity of 18,000 pounds or less. These carriers hold a certificate issued under section 298C of the Federal Aviation Act of 1958, as amended.

Commuter Lane Another name for "High-Occupancy Vehicle Lane." (APTA1)

Commuter Rail Long-haul passenger service operating between metropolitan and suburban areas, whether within or across the geographical boundaries of a state, usually characterized by reduced fares for multiple rides, and commutation tickets for regular, recurring riders. (FTA1)

Commuter Rail (Transit) Urban passenger train service for short-distance travel between a central city and adjacent suburb. Does not include rapid rail transit or light rail service.

Compressed Natural Gas Natural gas compressed to a volume and density that is practical as a portable fuel supply. It is used as a fuel for natural gas-powered vehicles.

Conformity Process to assess the compliance of any transportation plan, program, or project with air quality implementation plans. The conformity process is defined by the Clean Air Act.

Congestion Management System (CMS) Systematic process for managing congestion. Provides information on transportation system performance and finds alternative ways to alleviate congestion and enhance the mobility of people and goods, to levels that meet state and local needs.

Congestion Mitigation & Air Quality Improvement Program (CMAQ) A categorical Federal-aid funding program created with the ISTEA. Directs funding to projects that contribute to meeting National air quality standards. CMAQ funds generally may not be used for projects that result in the construction of new capacity available to SOVs (single-occupant vehicles).

Constant Dollars Dollar value adjusted for changes in the average price level by dividing a current dollar amount by a price index. See also Chained Dollar and Current Dollar.

Containerized Cargo Cargo that is transported in containers that can be transferred easily from one transportation mode to another.

Contract Authority (CA) A form of Budget Authority that permits obligations to be made in advance of appropriations. Most of the programs under the Federal-Aid Highway Program operate under Contract Authority.

Contract Carrier Carrier engaged in interstate transportation of persons/ property by motor vehicle on a for-hire basis, but under continuing contract with one or a limited number of cus-tomers to meet specific needs.

Control Strategy Implementation Plan Revision The implementation plan which contains specific strategies for controlling the emissions of and reducing ambient levels of pollutants in order to satisfy CAA requirements for demonstrations of reasonable further progress and attainment (including implementation plan revisions submitted to satisfy CAA sections 172(c), 182(b)(1), 182(c)(2)(A), 182(c)(2)(B), 187(a)(7), 187(g), 189(a)(1)(B), 189(b)(1)(A), and 189(d); sections 192(a) and 192(b), for nitrogen dioxide; and any other applicable CAA provision requiring a demonstration of reasonable further progress or attainment).

Corporate Average Fuel Economy Standards (CAFÉ) Originally established by Congress for new automobiles and later for light trucks. This law requires automobile manufacturers to produce vehicle fleets with a composite sales-weighted fuel economy not lower than the CAFE standards in a given year. For every vehicle that does not meet the standard, a fine is paid for every one-tenth of a mile per gallon that vehicle falls below the standard.

Corridor A broad geographical band that follows a general directional flow connecting major sources of trips that may contain a number of streets, highways and transit route alignments. (APTA1)

Crash (Highway) An event that produces injury and/or property damage, involves a motor vehicle in transport, and occurs on a traffic way or while the vehicle is still in motion after running off the traffic way.

Cubic Foot Conversion equivalents 1,728 cubic inches, 60 pints, 8/10 bushel, 0.028 cubic meter, 28.32 liters.

Current Assets Cash and cash equivalents, as well as current receivables and short-term investments, deposits and inventories.

Current Flight Plan The flight plan, including changes, if any, brought about by subsequent clearances. (FAA4)

Current Liabilities Current portion of long-term debt and of capital leases, air travel liabilities and other short-term trade accounts payable. (BTS4)

Dedicated Funds Any funds raised specifically for transit purposes and which are dedicated at their source (e.g., sales taxes, gasoline taxes, and property taxes), rather than through an allocation from the pool of general funds. (FTA1)

Degree of (Critical) Hazard A situation in which collision avoidance was due to chance rather than an act on the part of the pilot. Less than 100 feet of aircraft separation would be considered critical.

Degree of (No Hazard) Hazard A situation in which direction and altitude would have made a mid-air collision improbable regardless of evasive action taken. (FAA10)

Degree of (Potential) Hazard An incident which would have resulted in a collision if no action had been taken by either pilot. Closest proximity of less than 500 feet would usually be required in this case. (FAA10)

Demand-Responsive Vehicle (Transit) A non-fixed-route, nonfixed-schedule vehicle that operates in response to calls from passengers or their agents to the transit operator or dispatcher.

Demand-Responsive Descriptive term for a service type, usually considered paratransit, in which a user can access transportation service that can be variably routed and timed to meet changing needs on an as-needed basis.

Department of Energy (DOE) The Department of Energy's overarching mission is to advance the national , economic and energy security of the United States; to promote scientific and technological innovation in support of that mission; and to ensure the environmental cleanup of the national nuclear weapons complex. The Department has four strategic goals toward achieving the mission: Defense Strategic Goal: To protect our national security by applying advanced science and nuclear technology to the Nation's defense; Energy Strategic Goal: To protect our national and economic security by promoting a diverse supply and delivery of reliable, affordable, and environmentally sound energy; Science Strategic Goal: To protect our national and economic security by providing world-class scientific research capacity and advancing scientific knowledge; and Environment Strategic Goal: To protect the environment by providing a responsible resolution to the environmental legacy of the Cold War and by providing for the permanent disposal of the Nation's high-level radioactive waste.

Department of Health and Human Services (HHS) The Department of Health and Human Services is the United States government's principal agency for protecting the health of all Americans and providing essential human services, especially for those who are least able to help themselves.

Department of Housing and Urban Development (HUD) HUD's mission is to increase homeownership, support community development and increase access to affordable housing free from discrimination. To fulfill this mission, HUD will embrace high standards of ethics, management and accountability and forge new partnerships–particularly with faith-based and community organizations–that leverage resources and improve HUD's ability to be effective on the community level.

Department of Transportation (DOT) Establishes the nation's overall transportation policy. Under its umbrella there are ten administrations whose jurisdictions include highway planning, development and construction; urban mass transit; railroads; aviation; and the safety of waterways, ports, highways, and oil and gas pipelines. The Department of Transportation (DOT) was established by act of October 15, 1966, as amended (49 U.S.C. 102 and 102 note), "to assure the coordinated, effective administration of the transportation programs of the Federal Government" and to develop "national transportation policies and programs conducive to the provision of fast, safe, efficient, and convenient transportation at the lowest cost consistent therewith." (OFR1)

Depreciation and Amortization All depreciation and amortization expenses applicable to owned or leased property and equipment including that categorized as flight equipment or ground property and equipment. (BTS4)

Deregulation Revisions or complete elimination of economic regulations controlling transportation. For example, the Motor Carrier Act of 1980 and the Staggers Act of 1980 revised the economic controls over motor carriers and railroads. (MARAD1)

Dial-a-Ride Term for demand-responsive systems usually delivering door-to-door service to clients, who make request by telephone on an as-needed reservation or subscription basis.

Direct Funding Funds transferred directly from the Secretary of the Interior to the ITG upon request for programs contracted or compacted under P.L. 93-638 as amended.

Direct Service Tribes ITGs that receive services directly from the BIA.

Domestic Produced in the United States, including the Outer Continental Shelf (OCS). (DOE5)

Domestic Freight (Water) All waterborne commercial movement between points in the United States, Puerto Rico, and the Virgin Islands, excluding traffic with the Panama Canal Zone. Cargo moved for the military in commercial vessels is reported as ordinary commercial cargo; military cargo moved in military vessels is omitted.

Domestic Operations (Air Carrier) All air carrier operations having destinations within the 50 United States, the District of Columbia, the Commonwealth of Puerto Rico, and the U.S. Virgin Islands.

Donut Areas Geographic areas outside a metropolitan planning area boundary, but inside the boundary of a nonattainment or maintenance area that contains any part of a metropolitan area(s). These areas are not isolated rural nonattainment and maintenance areas.

Driver 1) A person who operates a motorized vehicle. If more than one person drives on a single trip, the person who drives the most miles is classified as the principal driver. 2) An occupant of a vehicle who is in physical control of a motor vehicle in transport or, for an out of-control vehicle, an occupant who was in control until control was lost. (FHWA3) (NHTSA3)

Driver's License A license issued by a State or other jurisdiction, to an individual which authorizes the individual to operate a motor vehicle on the highways. (49CFR383)

Driving Under the Influence (DUI) The driving or operating of any vehicle or common carrier while drunk or under the influence of liquor or narcotics. (FTA1)

Emergency Preparedness Plan A comprehensive plan which identifies potential emergencies and their impact on the community, and identifies operating procedures and actions to put in place during actual emergencies.

Emissions Budget The part of the State Implementation Plan (SIP) that identifies the allowable emissions levels, mandated by the National Ambient Air Quality Standards (NAAQS), for certain pollutants emitted from mobile, stationary, and area sources. The emissions levels are used for meeting emission reduction milestones, attainment, or maintenance demonstrations.

Emissions Inventory A complete list of sources and amounts of pollutant emissions within a specific area and time interval.

Energy Efficiency The ratio of energy inputs to outputs from a process, for example, miles traveled per gallon of fuel (mpg).

Energy Information Administration (EIA) An independent agency within the U.S. Department of Energy that develops surveys, collects energy data, and analyzes and models energy issues. The Agency must meet the requests of Congress, other elements within the Department of Energy, Federal Energy Regulatory Commission, the Executive Branch, its own independent needs, and assist the general public, or other interest groups, without taking a policy position. (DOE5)

Enhancement Activities Refers to activities related to a particular transportation project that "enhance" or contribute to the existing or proposed project. Examples of such activities include provision of facilities for pedestrians or cyclists, landscaping or other scenic beautification projects, historic preservation, control and removal of outdoor advertising, archaeological planning and research, and mitigation of water pollution due to highway runoff.

Environmental Impact Statement (EIS) Report developed as part of the National Environmental Policy Act requirements, which details any adverse economic, social, and environmental effects of a proposed transportation project for which Federal funding is being sought. Adverse effects could include air, water, or noise pollution; destruction or disruption of natural resources; adverse employment effects; injurious displacement of people or businesses; or disruption of desirable community or regional growth.

Environmental Justice (EJ) Environmental justice assures that services and benefits allow for meaningful participation and are fairly distributed to avoid discrimination.

Environmental Protection Agency (EPA) The federal regulatory agency responsible for administering and enforcing federal environmental laws, including the Clean Air Act, the Clean Water Act, the Endangered Species Act, and others.

Environmental Restoration Re-establishment (including all site preparation activities) of natural habitats or other environmental resources on a site where they formerly existed or currently exist in a substantially degraded state. This can include the restitution for the loss, damage, or destruction of natural resources arising out of the accidental discharge, dispersal, release or escape into or upon the land, atmosphere, watercourse, or body of water of any commodity transported by a motor carrier. This also may include the on-site or offsite replacement of wetlands and other natural habitats lost through development activities. (49CFR387 and 23CFR 777)

Environmentally Sensitive Area An area of environmental importance having natural resources which if degraded may lead to significant adverse, social, economic or ecological consequences. These could be areas in or adjacent to aquatic ecosystems, drinking water sources, unique or declining species habitat, and other similar sites. (49CFR194)

Ethanol A clear, colorless, flammable oxygenated hydrocarbon with a boiling point of 78.5 °C in the anhydrous state. It is used in the United States as a gasoline octane enhancer and oxygenate (10 percent concentration). Ethanol can be used in high concentrations in vehicles optimized for its use. Otherwise known as ethyl alcohol, alcohol, or grain-spirit.

Evaluation of Alternatives A synthesis of the information generated by an analysis in which judgments are made on the relative merits of alternative actions.

Expenditures 1) Actual cash (or electronic transfer) payments made to the States or other entities. Outlays are provided as reimbursement for the Federal share for approved highway program activities. 2) A term signifying disbursement of funds for repayment of obligations incurred. An electronic transfer of funds, or a check sent to a State highway or transportation agency for voucher payment, is an expenditure or outlay.

Expressway A controlled access, divided arterial highway for through traffic, the intersections of which are usually separated from other roadways by differing grades.

Fatality For purposes of statistical reporting on transportation safety, a fatality is considered a death due to injuries in a transportation crash, accident, or incident that occurs within 30 days of that occurrence.

Federal Aviation Administration (FAA) FAA provides a safe, secure, and efficient global aerospace system that contributes to national security and the promotion of US aerospace safety. As the leading authority in the international aerospace community, FAA is responsive to the dynamic nature of customer needs, economic conditions, and environmental concerns.

Federal Aviation Administration (FAA) Formerly the Federal Aviation Agency, the Federal Aviation Administration was established by the Federal Aviation Act of 1958 (49 U.S.C. 106) and became a component of the Department of Transportation in 1967 pursuant to the Department of Transportation

Federal Aviation Regulations (FAR) The set of regulatory obligations contained in Title 14 of the Code of Federal Regulations which FAA is charged to enforce in order to promote the safety of civil aviation both domestically and internationally. (FAA1)

Federal Energy Regulatory Commission (FERC) The federal agency with jurisdiction over, among other things, gas pricing, oil pipeline rates, and gas pipeline certification.

Federal Finance System (FFS) An automated accounting system used by the DOI for tracking obligations and expenditures.

Federal Highway Administration (FHWA) A branch of the US Department of Transportation that administers the federal-aid Highway Program, providing financial assistance to states to construct and improve highways, urban and rural roads, and bridges. The FHWA also administers the Federal Lands Highway Program, including survey, design, and construction of forest highway system roads, parkways and park roads, Indian reservation roads, defense access roads, and other Federal lands roads. The Federal agency within the U.S. Department of Transportation responsible for administering the

Federal-Aid Highway Program. Became a component of the Department of Transportation in 1967 pursuant to the Department of Transportation Act (49 U.S.C. app. 1651 note). It administers the highway transportation programs of the Department of Transportation under pertinent legislation

Federal Lands Highway Program (FLHP) Provides funds to construct roads and trails within (or, in some cases, providing access to) Federal lands. There are four categories of FLHP funds: Indian Reservation Roads, Public Lands Highways, Park Roads and Parkways, and Refuge Roads. Funds available to the US Forest Service may be used for forest development roads and trails. To be eligible for funding, projects must be open to the public and part of an approved Federal land management agency general management plan. 23 U.S.C. 204.

Federal Motor Carrier Safety Regulations (FMCSR) The regulations are contained in the Code of Federal Regulations, Title 49, Chapter III, Subchapter B. (FHWA2) (FHWA4)

Federal Railroad Administration (FRA) The purpose of the Federal Railroad Administration is to promulgate and enforce rail safety regulations, administer railroad financial assistance programs, conduct research and development in support of improved railroad safety and national rail transportation policy, provide for the rehabilitation of Northeast corridor rail passenger service, and consolidate government support of rail transportation activities. The FRA was created pursuant to section 3(e)(1) of the Department of Transportation Act of 1966 (49 U.S.C. app. 1652). (OFR1)

Federal Register Daily publication which provides a uniform system for making regulations and legal notices issued by the Executive Branch and various departments of the Federal government available to the public. (USCG1)

Federal Transit Administration (FTA) A branch of the US Department of Transportation that is the principal source of federal financial assistance to America's communities for planning, development, and improvement of public or mass transportation systems. FTA provides leadership, technical assistance, and financial resources for safe, technologically advanced public transportation to enhance mobility and accessibility, to improve the Nation's communities and natural environment, and to strengthen the national economy. (Formerly the Urban Mass Transportation Administration) operates under the authority of the Federal Transit Act, as amended (49 U.S.C. app. 1601 et seq.). The Federal Transit Act was repealed on July 5, 1994, and the Federal transit laws were codified and re-enacted as chapter 53 of Title 49, United States Code. The Federal Transit Administration was established as a component of the Department of Transportation by section 3 of Reorganization Plan No. 2 of 1968 (5 U.S.C. app.), effective July 1, 1968. The missions of the Administration are 1) to assist in the development of improved mass transportation facilities, equipment, techniques, and methods, with the cooperation of mass transportation companies both public and private. 2) to encourage the planning and establishment of area wide urban mass transportation systems needed for economical and desirable urban development, with the cooperation of mass transportation companies both public and private. and 3) to provide assistance to State and local governments and their instrumentalities in financing such systems, to be operated by public or private mass transportation companies as determined by local needs; and 4) to provide financial assistance to State and local governments to help implement national goals relating to mobility for elderly persons, persons with disabilities, and economically disadvantaged persons. (OFR1)

Federal-Aid Highway Program (FAHP) An umbrella term for most of the Federal programs providing highway funds to the States. This is not a term defined in law. As used in this document, FAHP is comprised of those programs authorized in Titles I and V of TEA-21 that are administered by FHWA.

Federal-Aid Highways Those highways eligible for assistance under Title 23 U.S.C. except those functionally classified as local or rural minor collectors. (23CFR500)

Ferry Boat A boat providing fixed-route service across a body of water. (APTA1)

Ferryboat (Transit) Vessels that carry passengers and/or vehicles over a body of water. Generally steam or diesel-powered, ferryboats may also be hovercraft, hydrofoil, and other high-speed vessels. The vessel is limited in its use to the carriage of deck passengers or vehicles or both, operates on a short run on a frequent schedule between two points over the most direct water routes other than in ocean or coastwise service, and is offered as a public service of a type normally attributed to a bridge or tunnel.

Financial Analysis Estimating costs, establishing a revenue baseline, comparing revenues with costs and evaluating new revenue sources.

Financial Capacity Refers to the ISTEA requirement that an adequate financial plan for funding and sustaining transportation improvements be in place prior to programming Federally-funded projects. Generally refers to the stability and reliability of revenue in meeting proposed costs.

Financial Planning The process of defining and evaluating funding sources, sharing the information, and deciding how to allocate the funds.

Financial Programming A short-term commitment of funds to specific projects identified in the regional Transportation Improvement Program (see TIP).

Fine Particulates Particulate matter less than 2.5 microns in size (PM-2.5). A micron is one millionth of a meter. See "Particulate matter" below.

Fiscal Constraint Making sure that a given program or project can reasonably expect to receive funding within the time allotted for its implementation.

Fiscal Year (FY) The yearly accounting period beginning October 1 and ending September 30 of the subsequent calendar year. Fiscal years are denoted by the calendar year in which they end (e.g., FY 1991 began October 1, 1990, and ended September 30, 1991).

Fixed-Route Term applied to transit service that is regularly scheduled and operates over a set route; usually refers to bus service.

For Hire Carrier Carrier that provides transportation service to the public on a fee basis.

Formula Capital Grants Federal transit funds for transit operators; allocation of funds overseen by FTA.

Freedom of Information Act (FOIA) Allows all U.S. citizens and residents to request any records in possession of the executive branch of the federal government. The term "records" includes documents, papers, reports, letters, films, photographs, sound recordings, computer tapes and disks.

Freeway A divided arterial highway designed for the unimpeded flow of large traffic volumes. Access to a freeway is rigorously controlled and intersection grade separations are required.

Freight Revenue (Rail) Revenue from the transportation of freight and from the exercise of transit, stopoff, diversion, and reconsignment privileges as provided for in tariffs.

Future Needs Represents the gap between the vision and the current or porjected performance of the system.

Gasohol A blend of finished motor gasoline (leaded or unleaded) and alcohol (generally ethanol but sometimes methanol) limited to 10 percent by volume of alcohol.

Gasoline A complex mixture of relatively volatile hydrocarbons, with or without small quantities of additives that have been blended to produce a fuel suitable for use in spark ignition engines. Motor gasoline includes both leaded or unleaded grades of finished motor gasoline, blending components, and gasohol. Leaded gasoline is no longer used in highway motor vehicles in the United States.

General Accounting Office (GAO) The General Accounting Office is the audit, evaluation, and investigative arm of Congress. GAO exists to support the Congress in meeting its Constitutional responsibilities and to help improve the performance and ensure the accountability of the federal government for the American people. GAO examines the use of public funds, evaluates federal programs and activities, and provides analyses, options, recommendations, and other assistance to help the Congress make effective oversight, policy, and funding decisions. In this context, GAO works to continuously improve the economy, efficiency, and effectiveness of the federal government through financial audits, program reviews and evaluations, analyses, legal opinions, investigations, and other services. GAO's activities are designed to ensure the executive branch's accountability to the Congress under the Constitution and the government's accountability to the American people. GAO is dedicated to good government through its commitment to the core values of accountability, integrity, and reliability.

General Aviation 1) All civil aviation operations other than scheduled air services and nonscheduled air transport operations for taxis, commuter air carriers, and air travel clubs that do not hold Certificates of Public Convenience and Necessity. 2) All civil aviation activity except that of air carriers certificated in accordance with Federal Aviation Regulations, Parts 121, 123, 127, and 135. The types of aircraft used in general aviation range from corporate multiengine jet aircraft piloted by professional crews to amateur-built single-engine piston-driven acrobatic planes to balloons and dirigibles.

Geographic Information System (GIS) 1) Computerized data management system designed to capture, store, retrieve, analyze, and display geographically referenced information. 2) A system of hardware, software, and data for collecting, storing, analyzing, and disseminating information about areas of the Earth. For Highway Performance Monitoring System (HPMS) purposes, Geographical Information System (GIS) is defined as a highway network (spatial data which graphically represents the geometry of the highways, an electronic map) and its geographically referenced component attributes (HPMS section data, bridge data, and other data including socioeconomic data) that are integrated through GIS technology to perform analyses. From this, GIS can display attributes and analyze results electronically in map form. (FHWA2)

Goals Generalized statements which broadly relate to the physical environment to values.

Grants A federal financial assistance award making payment in cash or in kind for a specified purpose. The federal government is not expected to have substantial involvement with the state or local government or other recipient while the contemplated activity is being performed. The term "grants-in-aid" is commonly restricted to grants to states and local governments. (BTS3)

Gross Domestic Product (GDP) 1) The total value of goods and services produced by labor and property located in the United States. As long as the labor and property are located in the United States, the supplier (that is, the workers and, for property, the owners) may be either U.S. residents or residents of foreign countries. (DOE3) 2) The total output of goods and services produced by labor and property located in the United States, valued at market prices. As long as the labor and property are located in the United States, the suppliers (workers and owners) may be either U.S. residents or residents of foreign countries.

Gross National Product (GNP) A measure of monetary value of the goods and services becoming available to the nation from economic activity. Total value at market prices of all goods and services produced by the nation's economy. Calculated quarterly by the Department of Commerce, the Gross National Product is the broadest available measure of the level of economic activity. (DOE6)

Gross Vehicle Weight (GVW) The combined total weight of a vehicle and its freight.

Gross Vehicle Weight Rating (Truck) The maximum rated capacity of a vehicle, including the weight of the base vehicle, all added equipment, driver and passengers, and all cargo.

Hazardous Material Any toxic substance or explosive, corrosive, combustible, poisonous, or radioactive material that poses a risk to the public's health, safety, or property, particularly when transported in commerce.

Heavy Rail (Transit) An electric railway with the capacity to transport a heavy volume of passenger traffic and characterized by exclusive rights-of-way, multicar trains, high speed, rapid acceleration, sophisticated signaling, and high-platform loading. Also known as: Subway, Elevated (railway), or Metropolitan railway (metro).

High Occupancy Vehicle (HOV) Vehicles carrying two or more people. The number that constitutes an HOV for the purposes of HOV highway lanes may be designated differently by different transportation agencies.

High Occupancy Vehicle Lane Exclusive road or traffic lane limited to buses, vanpools, carpools, and emergency vehicles. (APTA1)

Highway Is any road, street, parkway, or freeway/expressway that includes rights-of-way, bridges, railroad-highway crossings, tunnels, drainage structures, signs, guardrail, and protective structures in connection with highways. The highway further includes that portion of any interstate or international bridge or tunnel and the approaches thereto (23 U.S.C. 101a). (FHWA2)

Highway Bridge Replacement and Rehabilitation Program (HBRRP) Established under 23 U.S.C., Section 144, to enable the several states to replace and rehabilitate highway bridges when it is determined that the bridge is unsafe because of structural deficiencies, physical deterioration, or functional obsolescence.

Highway-Rail Grade Crossing (Rail) A location where one or more railroad tracks are crossed by a public highway, road, street, or a private roadway at grade, including sidewalks and pathways at or associated with the crossing.

Highway Trust Fund (HTF) An account established by law to hold Federal highway user taxes that are dedicated for highway and transit related purposes. The HTF has two accounts: the Highway Account, and the Mass Transit Account.

Highway-User Tax A charge levied on persons or organizations based on their use of public roads. Funds collected are usually applied toward highway construction, reconstruction, and maintenance.

Historic Preservation Protection and treatment of the nation's significant historic buildings, landmarks, landscapes, battlefields, tribal communities, and archeological sites; prominent federally-owned buildings; and State and privately-owned properties. [National Park Service, Historic Preservation Services]

Hydrocarbons (HC) Colorless gaseous compounds originating from evaporation and the incomplete combustion of fossil fuels.

Imports Receipts of goods into the 50 States and the District of Columbia from foreign countries and from Puerto Rico, the Virgin Islands, and other U.S. possessions and territories. (DOE3)

Indian Lands Indian reservation or Indian trust land or restricted Indian land which is not subject to fee title alienation without the approval of the Federal Government, or Indian and Alaska Native villages, group, or communities in which Indians and Alaskan Natives reside, whom the Secretary of the Interior has determined are eligible for services generally available to Indians under Federal laws specifically applicable to Indians.

Indian Reservation Roads (IRR) Public roads that are located within or provide access to an Indian reservation or Indian trust land or restricted Indian land which is not subject to fee title alienation without the approval of the Federal Government, or Indian and Alaska Native villages, group, or communities in which Indians and Alaskan Natives reside, whom the Secretary of the Interior has determined are eligible for services generally available to Indians under Federal laws specifically applicable to Indians. Roads on the BIA Road System are also IRR roads.

Indian Tribal Government (ITG) Duly formed governing body of an Indian Tribe.

Indian Tribe Means any Indian or Alaska Native tribe, band, nation, pueblo, village, or community that the Secretary of the Interior acknowledges to exist as an Indian tribe pursuant to the Federally Recognized Indian Tribe List Act of 1994, 25 U.S.C. 479a.

Infrastructure 1) In transit systems, all the fixed components of the transit system, such as rights-of-way, tracks, signal equipment, stations, park-and-ride lots, but stops, maintenance facilities. 2) In transportation planning, all the relevant elements of the environment in which a transportation system operates. (TRB1) 3) A term connoting the physical underpinnings of society at large, including, but not limited to, roads, bridges, transit, waste systems, public housing, sidewalks, utility installations, parks, public buildings, and communications networks.

Inland and Coastal Channels Includes the Atlantic Coast Waterways, the Atlantic Intracoastal Waterway, the New York State Barge Canal System, the Gulf Coast Waterways, the Gulf Intracoastal Waterway, the Mississippi River System (including the Illinois Waterway), the Pacific Coast Waterways, the Great Lakes, and all other channels (waterways) of the United States, exclusive of Alaska, that are usable for commercial navigation.

Inspection and Maintenance (I/M) An emissions testing and inspection program implemented by States in nonattainment areas to ensure that the catalytic or other emissions control devices on in-use vehicles are properly maintained.

The Institute of Transportation Engineers (ITE) An international individual member educational and scientific association, is one of the largest and fastest-growing multimodal professional transportation organizations in the world. ITE members are traffic engineers, transportation planners and other professionals who are responsible for meeting society's needs for safe and efficient surface transportation through planning, designing, implementing, operating and maintaining surface transportation systems worldwide.

Intelligent Transportation Systems (ITS) The application of advanced technologies to improve the efficiency and safety of transportation systems.

Intercity Class I Bus As defined by the Bureau of Transportation Statistics, an interstate motor carrier of passengers with an average annual gross revenue of at least $1 million.

Intercity Truck A truck that carries freight beyond local areas and commercial zones.

Intermodal The ability to connect, and the connections between, modes of transportation.

Intermodal Surface Transportation Efficiency Act of 1991 (ISTEA) Legislative initiative by the U.S. Congress that restructured funding for transportation programs. ISTEA authorized increased levels of highway and transportation funding from FY92-97 and increased the role of regional planning commissions/MPOs in funding decisions. The Act also required comprehensive regional and Statewide long-term transportation plans and places an increased emphasis on public participation and transportation alternatives.

International Airport 1) Any airport designated by the Contracting State in whose territory it is situated as an airport of entry and departure for international air traffic. 2) An airport of entry which has been designated by the Secretary of Treasury or Commissioner of Customs as an international airport for customs service. 3) A landing rights airport at which specific permission to land must be obtained from customs authorities in advance of contemplated use. 4) Airports designated under the Convention on International Civil Aviation as an airport for use by international commercial air transport and/or international general aviation. (FAA4)

International Passenger Any person traveling on a waterborne public conveyance between the United States and foreign countries and between Puerto Rico and the Virgin Islands and foreign countries. (TNDOT1)

International Transportation Transportation between any place in the United States and any place in a foreign country; between places in the United States through a foreign country; or between places in one or more foreign countries through the United States. (49CFR171)

Intersection 1) A point defined by any combination of courses, radials, or bearings of two or more navigational aids. 2). Used to describe the point where two runways, a runway and a taxiway, or two taxiways cross or meet. (FAA4)

Interstate Limited access divided facility of at least four lanes designated by the Federal Highway Administration as part of the Interstate System. (NHTSA3)

Interstate Commerce Trade, traffic, or transportation in the United States which is between a place in a State and a place outside of such State (including a place outside of the United States) or is between two places in a State through another State or a place outside of the United States. (49CFR390)

Interstate Highway Limited access, divided highway of at least four lanes designated by the Federal Highway Administration as part of the Interstate System.

Interstate Highway (Freeway or Expressway) A divided arterial highway for through traffic with full or partial control of access and grade separations at major intersections. (FHWA3)

Interstate Highway System (IHS) The system of highways that connects the principal metropolitan areas, cities, and industrial centers of the United

States. Also connects the US to internationally significant routes in Canada and Mexico.

Interstate Maintenance (IM) The Interstate Maintenance (IM) program provides funding for resurfacing, restoring, rehabilitating and reconstructing (4R) most routes on the Interstate System.

Intrastate Travel within the same state. (BOC3)

Intrastate Commerce Any trade, traffic, or transportation in any State which is not described in the term "interstate commerce." (49CFR390)

IRR Inventory An inventory of roads which meet the following criteria: a) public roads strictly within reservation boundaries, b) public roads that provide access to lands, to groups, villages, and communities in which the majority of residences are Indian, c) public roads that serve Indian lands not within reservation boundaries, and d) public roads that serve recognized Indian groups, villages, and isolated communities not located within a reservation.

IRR Program Stewardship Plan The plan which details the roles and responsibilities of the BIA, FHWA and ITGs in the administration and operation of the IRR Program.

IRR Road/Bridge Inventory An inventory of BIA owned IRR and bridges.

IRR TIP A multi-year listing of road improvement projects programmed for construction by a BIA area office, with IRR Program funds, for the next 3-5 years. A separate IRR TIP is prepared for each State within the area office's jurisdiction.

IRR Transportation Planning Funds Funds provided under 23 U.S.C., Section 204 (j), for transportation planning by ITGs.

Isolated Rural Nonattainment and Maintenance Areas Areas that do not contain or are not part of any metropolitan planning area as designated under the transportation planning regulations. Isolated rural areas do not have Federally required metropolitan transportation plans or TIPs and do not have projects that are part of the emissions analysis of any MPO's metropolitan transportation plan or TIP. Projects in such areas are instead included in statewide transportation improvement programs. These areas are not donut areas.

Just in Time (JIT) Cargo or components that must be at a destination at the exact time needed. The container or vehicle is the movable warehouse.

Land Use Refers to the manner in which portions of land or the structures on them are used, i.e., commercial, residential, retail, industrial, etc.

Land Use Plan A plan which establishes strategies for the use of land to meet identified community needs.

Large Regionals (Air) Air carrier groups with annual operating revenues between $20 million and $99,999,999.

Large Truck Trucks over 10,000 pounds gross vehicle weight rating, including single-unit trucks and truck tractors.

Level of Service (LOS) 1) A qualitative assessment of a road's operating conditions. For local government comprehensive planning purposes, level of service means an indicator of the extent or degree of service provided by, or proposed to be provided by, a facility based on and related to the operational characteristics of the facility. Level of service indicates the capacity per unit of demand for each public facility. 2) This term refers to a standard measurement used by transportation officials which reflects the relative ease of traffic flow on a scale of A to F, with free-flow being rated LOS-A and congested conditions rated as LOS-F.

Light Rail A streetcar-type vehicle operated on city streets, semi-exclusive rights-of-way, or exclusive rights-of-way. Service may be provided by step-entry vehicles or by level boarding.

Light Truck Trucks of 10,000 pounds gross vehicle weight rating or less, including pickups, vans, truck-based station wagons, and sport utility vehicles.

Light-Duty Vehicle A vehicle category that combines light automobiles and trucks.

Limitation on Obligations Any action or inaction by an officer or employee of the United States that limits the amount of Federal assistance that may be obligated during a specified time period. A limitation on obligations does not affect the scheduled apportionment or allocation of funds, it just controls the rate at which these funds may be used.

Limited Maintenance Plan A maintenance plan that EPA has determined meets EPA's limited maintenance plan policy criteria for a given NAAQS and pollutant. To qualify for a limited maintenance plan, for example, an area must have a design value that is significantly below a given NAAQS, and it must be reasonable to expect that a NAAQS violation will not result from any level of future motor vehicle emissions growth.

Liquefied Natural Gas (LNG) Natural gas, primarily methane, that has been liquefied by reducing its temperature to -260 °F at atmospheric pressure.

Liquefied Petroleum Gas (LPG) Pro-pane, propylene, normal butane, butylene, isobutane, and isobutylene produced at refineries or natural gas processing plants, including plants that fractionate new natural gas plant liquids.

Local Street A street intended solely for access to adjacent properties.

Local Technical Assistance Program Center These Centers are responsible for providing transportation assistance to State and local governments that includes, but is not limited to, circuit rider programs, providing training on intergovernmental transportation planning and project selection, and tourism recreation travel.

Locomotive Railroad vehicle equipped with flanged wheels for use on railroad tracks, powered directly by electricity, steam, or fossil fuel, and used to move other railroad rolling equipment.

Logistics All activities involved in the management of product movement; delivering the right product from the right origin to the right destination, with the right quality and quantity, at the right schedule and price.

Long Range Transportation Plan (LRTP) A document resulting from regional or statewide collaboration and consensus on a region or state's transportation system, and serving as the defining vision for the region's or state's transportation systems and services. In metropolitan areas, the plan indicates all of the transportation improvements scheduled for funding over the next 20 years.

Long Term In transportation planning, refers to a time span of, generally, 20 years. The transportation plan for metropolitan areas and for States should include projections for land use, population, and employment for the 20-year period.

Maintenance Area Maintenance area is any geographic region of the United States previously designated nonattainment pursuant to the CAA Amendments of 1990 and subsequently redesignated to attainment subject to the requirement to develop a maintenance plan under section 175A of the CAA, as amended.

Majors (Air) Air carrier groups with annual operating revenues exceeding $1 billion.

Management Systems (1) Systems to improve identification of problems and opportunities throughout the entire surface transportation network, and to evaluate and prioritize alternative strategies, actions and solutions. (2) A systematic process, designed to assist decisionmakers in selecting cost-effective strategies/actions to improve the efficiency and safety of, and protect the investment in, the nation's transportation infrastructure.

Maritime Business pertaining to commerce or navigation transacted upon the sea or in seaports in such matters as the court of admiralty has jurisdiction. (MARAD2)

Maritime Administration (MARAD) The Maritime Administration was established by Reorganization Plan No. 21 of 1950 (5 U.S.C. app.) effective May 24, 1950. The Maritime Act of 1981 (46 U.S.C. 1601) transferred the Maritime Administration to the Department of Transportation, effective Aug.

Mass Transportation Another name for public transportation. (APTA1)

Mass Transportation Agency An agency authorized to transport people by bus, rail, or other conveyance, either publicly or privately owned, and providing to the public general or special service (but not including school, charter or sightseeing service) on a regular basis. (FTA1)

Measures of Effectiveness Measures or tests which reflect the degree of attainment of particular objectives.

Memorandum of Understanding (MOU) A document providing a general description of the responsibilities that are to be assumed by two or more parties in their pursuit of some goal(s). More specific information may be provided in an associated SOW.

Methanol A light, volatile alcohol produced commercially by the catalyzed reaction of hydrogen and carbon monoxide. Methanol is blended with gasoline to improve its operational efficiency.

Methyl-Tertiary-Butyl-Ether (MTBE) A colorless, flammable, liquid oxygenated hydrocarbon that contains 18.15 percent oxygen. It is a fuel oxygenate produced by reacting methanol with isobutylene.

Metropolitan Planning Area The geographic area in which the metropolitan transportation planning process required by 23 U.S.C. 134 and section 8 of the Federal Transit Act (49 U.S.C. app. 1607) must be carried out. (23CFR420)

Metropolitan Planning Organization (MPO) 1) Regional policy body, required in urbanized areas with populations over 50,000, and designated by local officials and the governor of the state. Responsible in cooperation with the state and other transportation providers for carrying out the metropolitan transportation planning requirements of federal highway and transit legislation. 2) Formed in cooperation with the state, develops transportation plans and programs for the metropolitan area. For each urbanized area, a Metropolitan Planning Organization (MPO) must be designated by agreement between the Governor and local units of government representing 75% of the affected population (in the metropolitan area), including the central cities or cities as defined by the Bureau of the Census, or in accordance with procedures established by applicable State or local law (23 U.S.C. 134(b)(1)/Federal Transit Act of 1991 Sec. 8(b)(1)). (FHWA2)

Metropolitan Statistical Area (MSA) Areas defined by the U.S. Office of Management and Budget. A Metropolitan Statistical Area (MSA) is 1) A county or a group of contiguous counties that contain at least one city of 50,000 inhabitants or more, or 2) An urbanized area of at least 50,000 inhabitants and a total MSA population of at least 100,000 (75,000 in New England). The contiguous counties are included in an MSA if, according to certain criteria, they are essentially metropolitan in character and are socially and economically integrated with the central city. In New England,

MSAs consist of towns and cities rather than counties. (DOE4) (DOE5) (FHWA3)

Metropolitan Status A building classification referring to the location of the building either located within a Metropolitan Statistical Area (MSA) or outside a MSA. (DOE5)

Metropolitan Transportation Plan (MTP) The official intermodal transportation plan that is developed and adopted through the metropolitan transportation planning process for the metropolitan planning area, in accordance with 23 U.S.C. 134, 23 USC 135 and 49 U.S.C. 5303.

Mile A statute mile (5,280 feet). All mileage computations are based on statute miles. (BTS5) (BTS6)

Miles per Gallon (MPG) A measure of vehicle fuel efficiency. Miles Per Gallon (MPG) represents "Fleet Miles per Gallon." For each subgroup or "table cell," MPG is computed as the ratio of the total number of miles traveled by all vehicles in the subgroup to the total number of gallons consumed. MPGs are assigned to each vehicle using the Environmental Protection Agency (EPA) certification files and adjusted for on-road driving. (DOE4) (DOE5)

Milestone The meaning given in CAA sections 182(g)(1) and 189(c) for serious and above ozone nonattainment areas and PM10 nonattainment areas, respectively. For all other nonattainment areas, a milestone consists of an emissions level and the date on which that level is to be achieved as required by the applicable CAA provision for reasonable further progress towards attainment.

Minor Arterials (Highway) Roads linking cities and larger towns in rural areas. In urban areas, roads that link but do not penetrate neighborhoods within a community.

Mobile Source 1) The mobile source-related pollutants are carbon monoxide (CO), hydrocarbons (HC), nitrogen oxides (NOx), and particulate matter (PM-10 and PM 2.5). 2) Mobile sources include motor vehicles, aircraft, seagoing vessels, and other transportation modes. The mobile source related pollutants are carbon monoxide (CO), hydrocarbons (HC) or volatile organic compounds (VOCs), nitrogen oxides (NOx), and small particulate matter (PM-10).

Mobile Source Air Toxics (MSATS) Identified by the EPA, MSATs are the 21 hazardous air pollutants generated in large part by transportation sources.

Mobility The ability to move or be moved from place to place.

Mode A specific form of transportation, such as automobile, subway, bus, rail, or air.

Motor Carrier Safety Administration (FMCS) The Federal Motor Carrier Safety Administration (FMCSA) was established as a separate administration within the U.S. Department of Transportation on January 1, 2000, pursuant to the Motor Carrier Safety Improvement Act of 1999. The primary mission of FMCS is to reduce crashes, injuries, and fatalities involving large trucks and buses . FMCSA is headquartered in Washington, DC. We employ more than 1,000 individuals, in all 50 States and the District of Columbia, dedicated to improving bus and truck safety and saving lives.

Motor Vehicle Emissions Budget The portion of the total allowable emissions defined in the submitted or approved control strategy implementation plan revision or maintenance plan for a certain date for the purpose of meeting reasonable further progress milestones or demonstrating attainment or maintenance of the NAAQS, for any criteria pollutant or its precursors, allocated to highway and transit vehicle use and emissions.

Motorbus (Transit) A rubber-tired, self-propelled, manually steered bus with a fuel supply onboard the vehicle. Motorbus types include intercity, school, and transit.

Motorcycle A two- or three-wheeled motor vehicle designed to transport one or two people, including motor scooters, minibikes, and mopeds.

Motorized Vehicle Includes all vehicles that are licensed for highway driving. Specifically excluded are snow mobiles and minibikes. (FHWA3)

Multimodal The availability of transportation options using different modes within a system or corridor.

Multimodal Transportation Often used as a synonym for intermodalism. Congress and others frequently use the term intermodalism in its broadest interpretation as a synonym for multimodal transportation. Most precisely, multimodal transportation covers all modes without necessarily including a holistic or integrated approach. (BTS2)

National Airspace System (NAS) The common network of U.S. airspace; air navigation facilities, equipment, and services; airports or landing areas; aeronautical charts, information, and services; rules, regulations, and procedures; technical information, manpower, and material. Included are system components shared jointly with the military. (FAA4) (FAA8)

National Ambient Air Quality Standards (NAAQS) Federal standards that set allowable concentrations and exposure limits for various pollutants. The EPA developed the standards in response to a requirement of the CAA. Air quality standards have been established for the following six criteria pollutants: ozone (or smog), carbon monoxide, particulate matter, nitrogen dioxide, lead, and sulfur dioxide.

National Cooperative Highway Research Program (NCHRP) The cooperative research, development, and technology transfer (RD&T) program directed toward solving problems of national or regional significance identified by States and the FHWA, and administered by the Transportation Research Board, National Academy of Sciences. (23CFR420)

National Cooperative Transit Research and Development Program A program established under Section 6a) of the Urban Mass Transportation Act of 1964, as amended, to provide a mechanism by which the principal client groups of the Urban Mass Transportation Administration can join cooperatively in an attempt to resolve near-term public transportation problems through applied research, development, testing, and evaluation. NCTRP is administered by the Transportation Research Board. (TRB1)

National Environmental Policy Act of 1969 (NEPA) Established a national environmental policy requiring that any project using federal funding or requiring federal approval, including transportation projects, examine the effects of proposed and alternative choices on the environment before a federal decision is made.

National Highway System (NHS) This system of highways designated and approved in accordance with the provisions of 23 U.S.C. 103b). (23CFR500)

National Highway Traffic Safety Administration (NHTSA) The Administration was established by the Highway Safety Act of 1970 (23 U.S.C. 401 note). The Administration was established to carry out a congressional mandate to reduce the mounting number of deaths, injuries, and economic losses resulting from motor vehicle crashes on the Nation's highways and to provide motor vehicle damage susceptibility and ease of repair information, motor vehicle inspection demonstrations and protection of purchasers of motor vehicles having altered odometers, and to provide average standards for greater vehicle mileage per gallon of fuel for vehicles under 10,000 pounds (gross vehicle weight). (OFR1)

National Historic Trail (NHT) A historic or prehistoric route of travel of significance to the entire Nation. It must meet three criteria listed in Section 5(b)(11) of the National Trails System Act, and be established by Act of Congress. 16 U.S.C. 1241-51.

National ITS Architecture A systems framework to guide the planning and deployment of ITS infrastructure. The national ITS architecture is a blueprint for the coordinated development of ITS technologies in the U.S. It is unlikely that any single metropolitan area or state would plan to implement the entire national ITS architecture.

National Scenic Byways Program (NSBP) Designates roads that have outstanding scenic, historic, cultural, natural, recreational, and archaeological qualities as All-American Roads or National Scenic Byways, and provides grants for scenic byway projects. 23 U.S.C. 162

National Scenic Trail (NST) A continuous, primarily nonmotorized route of outstanding recreation opportunity, established by Act of Congress. 16 U.S.C. 1241-51.

National Trails System (NTS) The network of scenic, historic, and recreation trails created by the National Trails System Act of 1968. These trails provide for outdoor recreation needs, promote the enjoyment, appreciation, and preservation of open-air, outdoor areas and historic resources, and encourage public access and citizen involvement. 16 U.S.C. 1241-51.

Native American Local Technical Assistance Programs Primarily responsible for transportation related technology transfer to Native Americans through Tribal Technical Assistance Program (TTAP) Centers.

Natural Gas A naturally occurring mixture of hydrocarbon and nonhydrocarbon gases found in porous geologic formations beneath the Earth's surface, often in association with petroleum. The principal constituent is methane.

Natural Gas Policy Act of 1978 (NGPA) Section 311 Construction, allows an interstate pipeline company to transport gas "on behalf of" any intrastate pipeline or local distribution company. Pipeline companies may expand or construct facilities used solely to enable this transportation service, subject to certain conditions and reporting requirements. (DOE1)

Nitrogen Oxide Emissions Nitrogen oxides (NOx), the term used to describe the sum of nitric oxide (NO), nitrogen dioxide (N02) and other oxides of nitrogen, play a major role in the formation of ozone. The major sources of manmade NOx emissions are high-temperature combustion processes, such as those occurring in automobiles and power plants.

Nitrogen Oxides A product of combustion of fossil fuels whose production increases with the temperature of the process. It can become an air pollutant if concentrations are excessive. (DOE6)

Noise Standards 23 U.S.C. 109(i)

Nonattainment Area (NAA) Any geographic area that has not met the requirements for clean air as set out in the Clean Air Act of 1990.

Noncompliance Failure to comply with a standard or regulation issued under 46 U.S.C. Chapter 43, or with a section of the statutes. (USCG1)

Noncurrent Liabilities Non-current portion of long-term debt and of capital leases, advances to associated companies and other liabilities not due during the normal business cycle. (BTS4)

Nonoccupant (Automobile) Any person who is not an occupant of a motor vehicle in transport (e.g., bystanders, pedestrians, pedal cyclists, or an occupant of a parked motor vehicle).

Nonresident Commercial Driver's License A commercial driver's license (CDL) issued by a State to an individual domiciled in a foreign country. (49CFR383)

Notice of Funding Availability Written notice to the respective area tribes that the BIA area office has received contractible program funds.

Objectives Specific, measurable statements related to the attainment of goals.

Obligation The Federal government's legal commitment (promise) to pay or reimburse the States or other entities for the Federal share of a project's eligible costs.

Obligation Limitation A restriction, or "ceiling" on the amount of Federal assistance that may be promised (obligated) during a specified time period. This is a statutory budgetary control that does not affect the apportionment or allocation of funds. Rather, it controls the rate at which these funds may be used.

Obligational Authority (OA) The total amount of funds that may be obligated in a year. For the Federal-Aid Highway Program this is comprised of the obligation limitation amount plus amounts for programs exempt from the limitation.

Occupancy The number of persons, including driver and passenger(s) in a vehicle. Nationwide Personal Transportation Survey (NPTS) occupancy rates are generally calculated as person miles divided by vehicle miles. (FHWA3)

Occupant Any person who is in or upon a motor vehicle in transport. Includes the driver, passengers, and persons riding on the exterior of a motor vehicle (e.g., a skateboard rider who is set in motion by holding onto a vehicle). (NHTSA3)

Occupant (Highway) Any person in or on a motor vehicle in transport. Includes the driver, passengers, and persons riding on the exterior of a motor vehicle (e.g., a skateboard rider holding onto a moving vehicle). Excludes occupants of parked cars unless they are double parked or motionless on the roadway.

Office of Management and Budget (OMB) OMB's predominant mission is to assist the President in overseeing the preparation of the federal budget and to supervise its administration in Executive Branch agencies. In helping to formulate the President's spending plans, OMB evaluates the effectiveness of agency programs, policies, and procedures, assesses competing funding demands among agencies, and sets funding priorities. OMB ensures that agency reports, rules, testimony, and proposed legislation are consistent with the President's Budget and with Administration policies. In addition, OMB oversees and coordinates the Administration's procurement, financial management, information, and regulatory policies. In each of these areas, OMB's role is to help improve administrative management, to develop better performance measures and coordinating mechanisms, and to reduce any unnecessary burdens on the public.

Other 2-Axle 4-Tire Vehicles (Truck) Includes vans, pickup trucks, and sport utility vehicles.

Other Freeways And Expressways (Highway) All urban principal arterials with limited access but not part of the Interstate system.

Other Principal Arterials (Highway) Major streets or highways, many of multi-lane or freeway design, serving high-volume traffic corridor movements that connect major generators of travel.

Other Revenue Vehicles (Transit) Other revenue-generating modes of transit service, such as cable cars, personal rapid transit systems, monorail vehicles, inclined and railway cars, not covered otherwise.

Outlays Actual cash (or electronic transfer) payments made to the States or other entities. Outlays are provided as reimbursement for the Federal share for approved highway program activities.

Oxygenated gasoline Gasoline enriched with oxygen bearing liquids to reduce CO production by permitting more complete combustion.

Oxygenates Any substance that when added to motor gasoline increases the amount of oxygen in that gasoline blend. Includes oxygen-bearing compounds such as ethanol, methanol, and methyl-tertiary-butyl-ether. Oxygenated fuel tends to give a more complete combustion of carbon into carbon dioxide (rather than monoxide), thereby reducing air pollution from exhaust emissions.

Ozone 03 Ozone is a colorless gas with a sweet odor. Ozone is not a direct emission from transportation sources. It is a secondary pollutant formed when VOCs and NOx combine in the presence of sunlight. Ozone is associated with smog or haze conditions. Although the ozone in the upper atmosphere protects us from harmful ultraviolet rays, ground-level ozone produces an unhealthy environment in which to live. Ozone is created by human and natural sources.

P.L. 93-638 — Indian Self-Determination and Education Assistance Act, as amended The response by Congress, in recognition of the unique obligation of the United States, to the strong expression of the Indian people for self-determination, assuring maximum Indian participation in the direction of education as well as other Federal services for Indian communities so as to render such programs and services more responsive to the needs and desires of Indian communities.

Paratransit 1) Comparable transportation service required by the American Disabilities Act (ADA) for individuals with disabilities who are unable to use fixed route transportation systems. (49CFR37)(APTA1) 2) A variety of smaller, often flexibly scheduled-and-routed transportation services using low-capacity vehicles, such as vans, to operate within normal urban transit corridors or rural areas. These services usually serve the needs of persons that standard mass-transit services would serve with difficulty, or not at all. Often, the patrons include the elderly and persons with disabilities.

Park A place or area set aside for recreation or preservation of a cultural or natural resource. (DOI4)

Parking Area An area set aside for the parking of motor vehicles. (DOI4)

Parkway A highway that has full or partial access control, is usually located within a park or a ribbon of park-like developments, and prohibits commercial vehicles. Buses are not considered commercial vehicles in this case. (FHWA2)

Participating Agency A federal department or agency which transferred (consolidated) vehicles to the Interagency Fleet Management System (IFMS). (GSA2)

Particulate Matter (PM10 and PM2.5) Particulate matter consists of airborne solid particles and liquid droplets. Particulate matter may be in the form of fly ash, soot, dust, fog, fumes, etc. These particles are classified as "coarse" if they are smaller than 10 microns, or "fine" if they are smaller than 2.5 microns. Coarse airborne particles are produced during grinding operations, or from the physical disturbance of dust by natural air turbulence processes, such as wind. Fine particles can be a by-product of fossil fuel combustion, such as diesel and bus engines. Fine particles can easily reach remote lung areas, and their presence in the lungs is linked to serious respiratory ailments such as asthma, chronic bronchitis and aggravated coughing. Exposure to these particles may aggravate other medical conditions such as heart disease and emphysema and may cause premature death. In the environment, particulate matter contributes to diminished visibility and particle deposition (soiling).

Particulate Matter Emissions (PM) Particulate matter (PM) is the general term used for a mixture of solid particles and liquid droplets found in the air. They originate from many differ-ent stationary and mobile sources as well as from natural sources, including fuel combustion from motor vehicles, power generation, and industrial facilities, as well as from residential fire-places and wood stoves. Fine particles are most closely associated with such health effects as increased hospital admissions and emergency room visits for heart and lung disease, increased respiratory symptoms and disease, decreased lung function, and even premature death.

Parts per Million (PPM) A measure of air pollutant concentrations.

Passenger Car A motor vehicle designed primarily for carrying passengers on ordinary roads, includes convertibles, sedans, and stations wagons.

Passenger Mile 1) One passenger transported one mile. Total passenger miles are computed by summation of the products of the aircraft miles flown on each inter-airport flight stage multiplied by the number of passengers carried on that flight stage. (AIA1) (FAA11) (NTSB1) 2) The cumulative sum of the distances ridden by each passenger. (FTA1)

Passenger Revenue 1) Rail Revenue from the sale of tickets. 2) Air Revenues from the transport of passengers by air. 3) Transit Fares, transfer, zone, and park-an

Passenger Service Both intercity rail passenger service and commuter rail passenger service. (49CFR245)

Passenger Vessels (Water) A vessel designed for the commercial transport of passengers.

Pavement Management System A systematic process that provides, analyzes, and summarizes pavement information for use in selecting and implementing cost-effective pavement construction, rehabilitation, and maintenance programs. Pavement includes all road surface types including paved, gravel, and improved or unimproved earth.

Pedestrian Any person not in or on a motor vehicle or other vehicle. Excludes people in buildings or sitting at a sidewalk cafe. The National Highway Traffic Safety Administration also uses another pedestrian category to refer to pedestrians using conveyances and people in buildings. Examples of pedestrian conveyances include skateboards, nonmotorized wheelchairs, rollerskates, sleds, and transport devices used as equipment.

Pedestrian Walkway (or Walkway) A continuous way designated for pedestrians and separated from the through lanes for motor vehicles by space or barrier. (23CFR217)

Performance Measures Indicators of how well the transportation system is performing with regard to such things as average speed, reliability of travel, and accident rates. Used as feedback in the decisionmaking process.

Person-Miles An estimate of the aggregate distances traveled by all persons on a given trip based on the estimated transportation-network-miles traveled on that trip.

Person Trip A trip taken by an individual. For example, if three persons from the same household travel together, the trip is counted as one household trip and three person trips.

Petroleum (Oil) A generic term applied to oil and oil products in all forms, such as crude oil, lease condensate, unfinished oils, petroleum products, natural gas plant liquids, and nonhydrocarbon compounds blended into finished petroleum products.

Planning Funds (PL) Primary source of funding for metropolitan planning designated by the FHWA.

Port 1) Harbor with piers or docks ; 2) left side of ship when facing forward ; 3) opening in a ship's side for handling freight. (MARAD2)

Possible Injury Any injury reported or claimed that is not evident. Includes, among others, momentary unconsciousness, claim of injuries not obvious, limping, complaint of pain, nausea, and hysteria.

Private Carrier A carrier that provides transportation service to the firm that owns or leases the vehicles and does not charge a fee.

Privately Owned Vehicle (POV) 1) A privately-owned vehicle or privately-operated vehicle. 2) Employee's own vehicle used on official business for which the employee is reimbursed by the government on the basis of mileage. (GSA1)

Problem Identification An element in the planning process which represents the gap between the desired vision, goals and objectives and the current or projected performance of the system.

Program Development An element in the planning process in which improvements are formalized in the transportation improvement program and provides more detailed strategies.

Programming Prioritizing proposed projects and matching those projects with available funds to accomplish agreed upon, stated needs.

Project A locally sponsored, coordinated, and administered program, or any part thereof, to plan, finance, construct, maintain, or improve an intermodal passenger terminal, which may incorporate civic or cultural activities where feasible in an architecturally or historically distinctive railroad passenger terminal. (49CFR256)

Property Damage (Transit) The dollar amount required to repair or replace transit property (including stations, right-of-way, bus stops, and maintenance facilities) damaged during an incident.

Public Authority A Federal, State, county, town or township, Indian tribe, municipal or other local government or instrumentality thereof, with authority to finance, build, operate, or maintain highway facilities, either as toll or toll- free highway facilities. (23CFR460)

Public Crossing A location open to public travel where railroad tracks intersect a roadway that is under the jurisdiction and maintenance of a public authority. (FRA3)

Public Entity 1) Any state or local government; 2) Any department, agency, special purpose district, or other instrumentality of one or more state or local governments; and 3) The National Railroad Passenger Corporation (Amtrak) and any commuter authority. (49CFR37)

Public Hearings 23 U.S.C. 128

Public Liability Liability for bodily injury or property damage and includes liability for environmental restoration. (49CFR387)

Public Meeting or Hearing A public gathering for the express purpose of informing and soliciting input from interested individuals regarding transportation issues.

Public Participation The active and meaningful involvement of the public in the development of transportation plans and programs.

Public Road Any road under the jurisdiction of and maintained by a public authority (federal, state, county, town or township, local government, or instrumentality thereof) and open to public travel.

Public Transit Passenger transportation services, usually local in scope, that is available to any person who pays a prescribed fare. It operates on established schedules along designated routes or lines with specific stops and is designed to move relatively large numbers of people at one time. (TRB1)

Public Transit Agencies A public entity responsible for administering and managing transit activities and services. Public transit agencies can directly operate transit service or contract out for all or part of the total transit service provided. (FTA1)

Public Transit System An organization that provides transportation services owned, operated, or subsidized by any municipality, county, regional authority, state, or other governmental agency, including those operated or managed by a private management firm under contract to the government agency owner. (APTA1)

Public Transportation Transportation by bus, rail, or other conveyance, either publicly or privately owned, which provides to the public general or special service on a regular and continuing basis. Also known as "mass transportation," "mass transit" and "transit." (APTA1)

Rail A rolled steel shape laid in two parallel lines to form a track for carrying vehicles with flanged steel wheels. (TRB1)

Rapid Rail Transit Transit service using railcars driven by electricity usually drawn from a third rail, configured for passenger traffic, and usually operated on exclusive rights-of-way. It generally uses longer trains and has longer station spacing than light rail.

Recreational Trails Program (RTP) Provides funds to the States to develop and maintain recreational trails and trail-related facilities for motorized and nonmotorized recreational trail uses. 23 U.S.C. 206.

Reformulated Gasoline 1) Gasoline whose composition has been changed to meet performance specifications regarding ozone-forming tendencies and release of toxic substances into the air from both evaporation and tailpipe emissions. Reformulated gasoline includes oxygenates and, compared with gasoline sold in 1990, has a lower content of olefins, aromatics, volatile components, and heavy hydrocarbons. 2) Gasoline specifically developed to reduce undesirable combustion products.

Regional Planning Organization (RPO) An organization that performs planning for multi-jurisdictional areas. MPOs, regional councils, economic development associations, rural transportation associations are examples of RPOs.

Regional Railroad Railroad defined as line haul railroad operating at least 350 miles of track and/or earns revenue between $40 million and $266.7 million.

Regionally Significant Project A project that is on a facility which serves regional transportation needs.

Relative Need Formula An allocation formula used by BIADOT to distribute construction funds to the 12 BIA area offices.

Reliability Refers to the degree of certainty and predictability in travel times on the transportation system. Reliable transportation systems offer some assurance of attaining a given desti-nation within a reasonable range of an expected time. An unreliable transportation system is subject to unexpected delays, increasing costs for system users

Remote Areas Sparsely populated areas such as mountains, swamps, and large bodies of water. (FAA8)

Research Investigation or experimentation aimed at the discovery of new theories or laws and the discovery and interpretation of facts or revision of accepted theories or laws in the light of new facts. (49CFR171)

Research and Special Programs Administration (RSPA) The Administration was established formally on September 23, 1977. It is responsible for hazardous materials transportation and pipeline safety, transportation emergency preparedness, safety training, multimodal transportation research and development activities, and collection and dissemination of air carrier economic data. It includes the Office of Hazardous Materials Safety; the Office of Pipeline Safety; the Office of Research Technology, and Analysis; the Office of University Research and Education; the Office of Automated Tariffs; the Office of Research Policy and Technology Transfer; the Volpe National Transportation Systems Center; and the Transportation Safety Institute. (OFR1)

Restricted Area Airspace designated under Federal Aviation Regulations (FAR), Part 73, within which the flight of aircraft, while not wholly prohibited, is subject to restriction. Most restricted areas are designated joint use and Intermediate Fix/Visual Flight Rules IF/VFR operations in the area may be authorized by the controlling Air Traffic Control (ATC) facility when it is not being utilized by the using agency. Restricted areas are depicted on en route charts. Where joint use is authorized, the name of the ATC controlling facility is also shown. (FAA8)

Restricted Road Public road with restricted public use. (DOI3)

Revenue Remuneration received by carriers for transportation activities.

Revenue Aligned Budget Authority (RABA) The adjustment in funding made annually to the highway program, beginning in FY 2000, as a result of the adjustment in the firewall level for highways. The firewall level is adjusted to reflect revised receipt estimates for the Highway Account of the Highway Trust Fund. Then, adjustments equal to the firewall adjustment-are made to Federal-Aid highway authorizations and obligation limitation for the fiscal year.

Revenue Passenger-Mile One revenue passenger transported one mile.

Revenue Ton-Mile One short ton of freight transported one mile.

Revenue Vehicle-Miles (Transit) One vehicle (bus, trolley bus, or streetcar) traveling one mile, while revenue passengers are on board, generates one revenue vehicle-mile. Revenue vehicle-miles reported represent the total mileage traveled by vehicles in scheduled or unscheduled revenue-producing services.

Right of Way The land (usually a strip) acquired for or devoted to highway transportation purposes. (FHWA2)

Road An open way for the passage of vehicles, persons, or animals on land. (DOI4)

Road Class The category of roads based on design, weatherability, their governmental designation, and the Department of Transportation functional classification system. (DOI3)

Road Functional Classification The classification of a road in accordance with the Bureau of Land Management (BLM) 9113.16. Code as follows C-collector, L-local, R-resource. (DOI2)

Rural Highway Any highway, road, or street that is not an urban highway.

Rural Mileage (Highway) Roads outside city, municipal district, or urban boundaries.

Safety Management System A systematic process that has the goal of reducing the number and severity of transportation related accidents by ensuring that all opportunities to improve safety are identified, considered and implemented as appropriate.

School Bus A passenger motor vehicle that is designed or used to carry more than 10 passengers, in addition to the driver, and, as determined by the Secretary of Transportation, is likely to be significantly used for the purpose of transporting pre-primary, primary, or secondary school students between home and school.

Self-Propelled Vessel A vessel that has its own means of propulsion. Includes tankers, containerships, dry bulk cargo ships, and general cargo vessels.

Serious Injury (Air Carrier/General Aviation) An injury that requires hospitalization for more than 48 hours, commencing within 7 days from the date when the injury was received; results in a bone fracture (except simple fractures of fingers, toes, or nose); involves lacerations that cause severe hemorrhages, or nerve, muscle, or tendon damage; involves injury to any internal organ; or involves second- or third-degree burns or any burns affecting more than 5 percent of the body surface.

Shortline Railroad Freight railroads which are not Class I or Regional Railroads, that operate less than 350 miles of track and earn less than $40 million.

Small Particulate Matter (PM-10) Particulate matter which is less than 10 microns in size. A micron is one millionth of a meter. Particulate matter this size is too small to be filtered by the nose and lungs.

Smart Growth A set of policies and programs design to protect, preserve, and economically develop established communities and valuable natural and cultural resources.

Sources Refers to the origin of air contaminants. Can be point (coming from a defined site) or non-point (coming from many diffuse sources).[Stationary sources include relatively large, fixed facilities such as power plants, chemical process industries, and petroleum refineries. Area sources are small, stationary, non-transportation sources that collectively contribute to air pollution, and include such sources as dry cleaners and bakeries, surface coating operations, home furnaces, and crop burning. Mobile sources include on-road vehicles such as cars, trucks, and buses; and off-road sources such as trains, ships, airplanes, boats, lawnmowers, and construction equipment.

Sponsor Any private owner of a public-use airport or any public agency (either individually or jointly with other public agencies) that submit to the Secretary of Transportation, in accordance with the Airport & Airway Improvement Act of 1982, an application for financial assistance. (FAA2)

Sprawl Urban form that connotatively depicts the movement of people from the central city to the suburbs. Concerns associated with sprawl include loss of farmland and open space due to low-density land development, increased public service costs, and environmental degradation as well as other concerns associated with transportation.

Stakeholders Individuals and organizations involved in or affected by the transportation planning process. Include federal/state/local officials, MPOs, transit operators, freight companies, shippers, and the general public.

State As defined in chapter 1 of Title 23 of the United States Code, any of the 50 States, comprising the United States, plus the District of Columbia and the Commonwealth of Puerto Rico. However, for some purposes (e.g., highway safety programs under 23 U.S.C. 402), the term may also include the Territories (the U.S. Virgin Islands, Guam, American Samoa, and the Northern Mariana Islands) and the Secretary of the Interior (for Indian Reservations). For the purposes of apportioning funds under sections 104, 105, 144, and 206 of Title 23, United States Code, the term "State" is defined by section 1103(n) of the TEA-21 to mean any of the 50 States and the District of Columbia.

State-Designated Route A preferred route selected in accordance with U.S. DOT "Guidelines for Selecting Preferred Highway Routes for Highway Route Controlled Quantities of Radioactive Materials" or an equivalent routing analysis which adequately considers overall risk to the public. (49CFR171)

State Implementation Plan (SIP) Produced by the state environmental agency, not the MPO. A plan mandated by the CAA that contains procedures to monitor, control, maintain, and enforce compliance with the NAAQS. Must be taken into account in the transportation planning process.

State Infrastructure Bank (SIB) A revolving fund mechanism for financing a wide variety of highway and transit projects through loans and credit enhancement. SIBs are designed to complement traditional Federal-aid highway and transit grants by providing States increased flexibility for financing infrastructure investments.

State Planning and Research Funds (SPR) Primary source of funding for statewide long-range planning.

State Routing Agency An entity (including a common agency of more than one state such as one established by Interstate compact) which is authorized to use state legal process pursuant to 49 CFR 177.825 to impose routing requirements, enforceable by State agencies, on carriers of radioactive materials without regard to intrastate jurisdictional boundaries. This term also includes Indian tribal authorities which have police powers to regulate and enforce highway routing requirements within their lands. (49CFR171)

State Transportation Agency The State highway department, transportation department, or other State transportation agency to which Federal-aid highway funds are apportioned. (23CFR420)

State Transportation Improvement Program (STIP) A staged, multi-year, statewide, intermodal program of transportation projects, consistent with the statewide transportation plan and planning processes as well as metropolitan plans, TIPs, and processes.

Statewide Comprehensive Outdoor Recreation Plan (SCORP) A statewide recreation plan required by the Land and Water Conservation Fund Act of 1965. Addresses the demand for and supply of recreation resources (local, State, and Federal) within a State, identifies needs and new opportunities for recreation improvements, and sets forth an implementation program to meet the goals identified by its citizens and elected leaders. [National Park Service] NOTE: Metropolitan and statewide transportation plans should be coordinated with SCORPs.

Statewide Transportation Plan The official statewide intermodal transportation plan that is developed through the statewide transportation planning process.

Stationary Source Relatively large, fixed sources of emissions (i.e., chemical process industries, petroleum refining and petrochemical operations, or wood processing).

Streetcars Relatively lightweight passenger railcars operating singly or in short trains, or on fixed rails in rights-of-way that are not always separated from other traffic. Streetcars do not necessarily have the right-of-way at grade crossings with other traffic.

Sub-Allocation An administrative distribution of funds from BIA Central Office down to the BIA area.

Surface Transportation Program (STP) Federal-aid highway funding program that funds a broad range of surface transportation capital needs, including many roads, transit, sea and airport access, vanpool, bike, and pedestrian facilities.

Tanker An oceangoing ship designed to haul liquid bulk cargo in world trade.

Telecommuting Communicating electronically (by telephone, computer, fax, etc.) with an office, either from home or from another site, instead of traveling to it physically.

Third-Party Logistics (3PL) Provider. A specialist in logistics who may provide a variety of transportation, warehousing, and logistics related services to buyers or sellers. These tasks were previously performed in house by the customer.

Throughput Total amount of freight imported or exported through a seaport measured in tons or TEUs.

Title VI Title VI of the Civil Rights Act of 1964. Prohibits discrimination in any program receiving federal assistance.

Ton Mile A measure of output for freight transportation; reflects weight of shipment and the distance it is hauled; a multiplication of tons hauled by the distance traveled.

Ton-Mile (Water) The movement of one ton of cargo the distance of one statute mile. Domestic ton-miles are calculated by multiplying tons moved by the number of statute miles moved on the water (e.g., 50 short tons moving 200 miles on a waterway would yield 10,000 ton-miles for that waterway). Ton-miles are not computed for ports. For coastwise traffic, the shortest route that safe navigation permits between the port of origin and destination is used to calculate ton-miles.

Total Benefit/Cost Ratio The sum of five categories of quantifiable project benefits divided by the annualized cost of the project.

Trafficway (Highway) Any right-of-way open to the public as a matter of right or custom for moving persons or property from one place to another, including the entire width between property lines or other boundaries.

Train Line Mileage The aggregate length of all line-haul railroads. It does not include the mileage of yard tracks or sidings, nor does it reflect the fact that a mile of railroad may include two or more parallel tracks. Jointly-used track is counted only once.

Train-Mile The movement of a train, which can consist of many cars, the distance of one mile. A train-mile differs from a vehicle-mile, which is the movement of one car (vehicle) the distance of one mile. A 10-car (vehicle) train traveling 1 mile is measured as 1 train-mile and 10 vehicle-miles. Caution should be used when comparing train-miles to vehicle-miles.

Transit Vehicle Includes light, heavy, and commuter rail; motorbus; trolley bus; van pools; automated guideway; and demand responsive vehicles.

Transport Movement of natural, synthetic, and/or supplemental gas between points beyond the immediate vicinity of the field or plant from which produced except 1) For movements through well or field lines to a central point for delivery to a pipeline or processing plant within the same state or 2) Movements from a citygate point of receipt to consumers through distribution mains. (DOE5)

Transportation Administration and Support All activities associated with transportation administration, revenue vehicle movement control and scheduling including supervision and clerical support. (FTA1)

Transportation Agreement Any contractual agreement for the transportation of natural and/or supplemental gas between points for a fee. (DOE5)

Transportation Bill The bill refers to the market value of all purchases of transportation services and facilities; it includes all domestic expenditures made by an economy for transportation purposes. Although the transportation bill does not reflect several significant non-market costs, it is a useful indicator of a country's transportation expenditures, and transportation analysts closely follow changes in the bill and its components. (BTS1)

Transportation Conformity Process to assess the compliance of any transportation plan, program, or project with air quality implementation plans. The conformity process is defined by the Clean Air Act.

Transportation Control Measures (TCM) Transportation strategies that affect traffic patterns or reduce vehicle use to reduce air pollutant emissions. These may include HOV lanes, provision of bicycle facilities, ridesharing, telecommuting, etc. Such actions may be included in a SIP if needed to demonstrate attainment of the NAAQS.

Transportation Demand Management (TDM) Programs designed to reduce demand for transportation through various means, such as the use of transit and of alternative work hours.

Transportation Enhancement Activities (TE) Provides funds to the States for safe bicycle and pedestrian facilities, scenic routes, beautification, restoring historic buildings, renovating streetscapes, or providing transportation museums and visitors centers. 23 U.S.C. 101(a) and 133(b)(8).

Transportation Equity Act for the 21st Century (TEA-21) Authorized in 1998, TEA-21 authorized federal funding for transportation investment for fiscal years 1998-2003. Approximately $217 billion in funding was authorized, which was used for highway, transit, and other surface transportation programs.

Transportation Improvement Program (TIP) A document prepared by a metropolitan planning organization that lists projects to be funded with FHWA/FTA funds for the next one- to three-year period.

Transportation Infrastructure A federal credit program under which the USDOT may provide three forms of credit assistance—secured (direct) loans, loan guarantees, and standby lines of credit—for surface transportation projects of national or regional significance. The fundamental goal is to leverage federal funds by attracting substantial private and non-federal co-investment in critical improvements to the nation's surface transportation system.

Transportation Management Area (TMA) 1) All urbanized areas over 200,000 in population, and any other area that requests such designation. 2) An urbanized area with a population over 200,000 (as determined by the latest decennial census) or other area when TMA designation is requested by the Governor and the MPO (or affect local officials), and officially designated by the Administrators of the FHWA and the FTA. The TMA designation applies to the entire metropolitan planning area(s). (23CFR500)

Transportation Research Information Services (TRIS) The Transportation Research Board-maintained computerized storage and retrieval system for abstracts of ongoing and completed research, development, and technology transfer (RD&T) activities, including abstracts of RD&T reports and articles. (23CFR420)

Travel Advisory Program The Department of State manages a travel advisory program which publicizes 1) Travel warnings which are issued when State decides to recommend that Americans avoid travel to a certain country and 2) Consular information sheets, issued for every country, which advise travelers of health concerns, immigration and currency regulations, crime and security conditions, areas of unrest or instability, and the location of U.S. embassies or consulates. (USTTA1)

Travel Agencies Establishments primarily engaged in furnishing travel information and acting as agents in arranging tours, transportation, rental of cars, and lodging for travelers. (BOC1)

Travel Model Improvement Program (TMIP) TMIP supports and empowers planning agencies through leadership, innovation and support of planning analysis improvements to provide better information to support transportation and planning decisions.

Tribal Control Schedule The implementing document for the Tribal TIP. The ITG may elect to develop the tribal control schedule under Self-Governance compact or Indian Self-Determination contract. The tribal control schedule is an accounting and project management tool that is developed from the tribal TIP. It contains detailed project and tasks information for all projects identified in the tribal TIP. Project information is included in the areawide control schedule without changing the total dollar amounts.

Tribal Lands Land held in trust for Indian people, restricted Indian land which is not subject to fee title alienation without the approval of the Federal Government, and fee lands owned by tribal governments.

Tribal Priority List A list of transportation projects which the ITG considers a high priority.

Tribal Technical Assistance Program Center (TTAP) These centers are responsible for providing transportation assistance to native Americans that includes, but is not limited to, circuit rider programs, providing training on intergovernmental transportation planning and project selection, and tourism recreation travel.

Tribal TIP A multi-year, financially constrained, list of proposed transportation projects to be implemented within or providing access to Indian country during the next 3-5 years. It is developed from the tribal priority list.

Trolley Bus Rubber-tired electric transit vehicle, manually steered and propelled by a motor drawing current, normally through overhead wires, from a central power source.

Truckload (TL) Quantity of freight required to fill a truck, or at a minimum, the amount required to qualify for a truckload rate.

Trust Fund A fund credited with receipts that are held in trust by the government and earmarked by law for use in carrying out specific purposes and programs in accordance with an agreement or a statute.

Tug Boat A powered vessel designed for towing or pushing ships, dumb barges, pushed-towed barges, and rafts, but not for the carriage of goods.

Turner-Fairbank Highway Research Center (TFHRC) TFHRC provides FHWA and the world highway community with the most advanced research and development related to new highway technologies. The research focuses on providing solutions to complex technical problems through the development of more economical, environmentally sensitive designs; more efficient, quality controlled constructions practices; and more durable materials. The end result is a safer, more reliable highway transportation system.

Twenty-Foot Equivalent Unit (TEU) The 8 foot by 8 foot by 20 foot intermodal container is used as a basic measure in many statistics and is the standard measure used for containerized cargo.

Unified Planning Work Program (UPWP) The management plan for the (metropolitan) planning program. Its purpose is to coordinate the planning activities of all participants in the planning process.

Union of Soviet Socialist Republic (U.S.S.R) Consisted of 15 constituent republics Armenia, Azerbaijan, Belarus, Estonia, Georgia, Kazakhstan, Kyrgystan, Latvia, Lithuania, Moldava, Russia, Tajikistan, Turkmenistan, Ukraine, and Uzbekistan. As a political entity, the U.S.S.R. ceased to exist as of December 31, 1991. (DOE3)

United States (U.S.) Territories Include Samoa, Guam, the Northern Marianas, Puerto Rico and the Virgin Islands. (FHWA2)

United States Code Contains a consolidation and codification of all general and permanent laws of the *U.S. (USCG1)* United States Travel and Tourism Administration (USTTA)

An agency in the Commerce Department; its principal mission is to implement broad tourism policy initiatives for the development of international travel to the U.S. as a stimulus for economic stability.

Unlinked Passenger Trips (Transit) The number of passengers boarding public transportation vehicles. A passenger is counted each time he/she boards a vehicle even if the boarding is part of the same journey from origin to destination.

Unpaved Road Surface Gravel/soil and unimproved roads and streets (Surface/Pavement Type Codes 20, 30 and 40). (FHWA2)

Urban Highway Any road or street within the boundaries of an urban area. An urban area is an area including and adjacent to a municipality or urban place with a population of 5,000 or more. The boundaries of urban areas are fixed by state highway departments, subject to the approval of the Federal Highway Administration, for purposes of the Federal-Aid Highway Program.

Urbanized Area Area that contains a city of 50,000 or more population plus incorporated surrounding areas meeting size or density criteria as defined by the U.S. Census.

U.S. Flag Carrier or American Flag Carrier (Air) One of a class of air carriers holding a Certificate of Public Convenience and Necessity, issued by the U.S. Department of Transportation and approved by the President, authorizing scheduled operations over specified routes between the United States (and/or its territories) and one or more foreign countries.

Vanpool (Transit) Public-sponsored commuter service operating under prearranged schedules for previously formed groups of riders in 8- to 18-seat vehicles. Drivers are also commuters who receive little or no compensation besides the free ride.

Vehicle Identification Number (VIN) A set of about 17 codes, combining letters and numbers, assigned to a vehicle at the factory and inscribed on a small metal label attached to the dashboard and visible through the windshield. The vehicle identification number (VIN) is a unique identifier for the vehicle and therefore is often found on insurance cards, vehicle registrations, vehicle titles, safety or emission certificates, insurance policies, and bills of sale. The coded information in the VIN describes characteristics of the vehicle such as engine size and weight. (DOE4) (DOE5)

Vehicle Miles of Travel (VMT) The number of miles traveled nationally by vehicles for a period of 1 year. VMT is either calculated using 2 odometer readings or, for vehicles with less than 2 odometer readings, imputed using a regression estimate. (DOE5)

Vehicle-Miles (Highway) Miles of travel by all types of motor vehicles as determined by the states on the basis of actual traffic counts and established estimating procedures.

Vehicle-Miles (Transit) The total number of miles traveled by transit vehicles. Commuter rail, heavy rail, and light rail report individual car-miles, rather than train-miles for vehicle-miles.

Visioning A variety of techniques that can be used to identify goals.

Volatile Organic Compounds (VOCs) VOCs come from vehicle exhaust, paint thinners, solvents, and other petroleum-based products. A number of exhaust VOCs are also toxic, with the potential to cause cancer.

Waterborne Transportation Transport of freight and/or people by commercial vessels under U.S. Coast Guard jurisdiction.

Waybill A document that lists goods and shipping instructions relative to a shipment.

Zone The smallest geographically designated area for analysis of transportation activity. A zone can be from one to ten square miles in area. Average zone size depends on the total size of study area.

Food Safety

Absorbent Packing Material within a package which absorbs liquids from product; pad in meat trays is made from paper and has a plastic liner.

Acceptable Daily Intake (ADI) An estimate by the Joint Food and Agricultural Organization (United Nations)/World Health Organization Expert Committee on Food Additives (JECFA) of the amount of a veterinary drug, expressed on a body weight basis, that can be ingested daily over a lifetime without appreciable health risk (standard man=60 kg).

Accredited Laboratory Program (ALP) The Accredited Laboratory Program accredits nonfederal analytical chemistry laboratories to analyze meat and poultry food products for moisture, protein, fat, and salt (MPFS) content, and/or certain specific classes of chemical residues. Currently the specific chemical residues are chlorinated hydrocarbons (CHC), polychlorinated biphenyls (PCB), sulfonamides, nitrosamines, and arsenic.

Advanced Meat Recovery (AMR) Product derived from AMR systems is defined as "meat." AMR is a process that uses machinery to separate edible meat from bones by scraping, shaving, or pressing the meat from the bone. AMR machinery is not permitted to break, grind, crush, or pulverize bones to separate meat, and bones must emerge intact and in natural physical conformation. Meat produced using this method is comparable in appearance, texture, and composition to meat trimmings and similar meat products derived by hand trimming of bones. Product derived from AMR systems cannot contain spinal cord tissue. FSIS verifies that establishments using AMR systems do not incorporate spinal cord tissue into the products as a consequence of the pressure used to force meat tissue from the bone. Questionable products may be sampled by FSIS for analytical testing for the presence of spinal cord.

Adulterated Food Generally, impure, unsafe, or unwholesome; however, the Federal Food, Drug, and Cosmetic Act, the Federal Meat Inspection Act, the Poultry Products Inspection Act, and the Egg Products Inspection Act contain separate language defining in very specific (and lengthy) terms how the term "adulterated" will be applied to the foods each of these laws regulates. Products found to be adulterated under these laws cannot enter into commerce for human food use.

Aged See Dry Aged.

Agricultural Marketing Service (AMS) USDA agency that establishes standards for grades of cotton, tobacco, meat, dairy products, eggs, fruits, and vegetables. It also operates inspection, grading, and market news services, and provides supervisory administration for federal marketing orders.

Agricultural Research Service (ARS) USDA agency employing federal scientists to conduct basic, applied, and developmental research in the following fields: livestock; plants; soil, water and air quality; energy; food safety and quality; nutrition; food processing, storage, and distribution efficiency; non-food agricultural products; and international development.

Amenable Animals subject to the Federal Meat Inspection Act or the Poultry Products Inspection Act's mandatory inspection requirements. USDA exempts from its inspection foods containing three percent or less raw (or less than two percent cooked) red meat or other edible portions of a carcass, or products which historically have not been considered by consumers as products of the meat industry. For poultry products, see 9 CFR §381.15.

Animal and Plant Health Inspection Service (APHIS) USDA agency established to conduct inspections and regulatory and control programs to protect animal and plant health. It utilizes border inspections to prevent international transmission of pests and disease, administers quarantine and eradication programs, and certifies that U.S. exports meet importing countries' animal and plant health standards.

Animal Disposition Reporting System (ADRS) The Animal Disposition Reporting System contains slaughter totals and disposition summaries for federally inspected livestock and poultry slaughter establishments. Each animal carcass is inspected for diseases and other conditions, which if present, may result in the animal being condemned as unfit for human consumption. If a carcass is condemned, the reason for condemnation, also referred to as the disposition, is recorded in the ADRS database.

Animal (Veterinary) Drugs Drugs intended for use in the diagnosis, cure, mitigation, treatment, or prevention of disease in animals. The Food and Drug Administration (FDA) has the broad mandate under the Federal Food, Drug, and Cosmetic Act to assure the safety and effectiveness of animal drugs and their use in all animals, including farm animals. Before FDA formally approves an animal drug, the sponsor or manufacturer of the drug must show in its premarket approval application that the drug is "safe and effective" in scientific testing. Such testing data, included with the application, must demonstrate a methodology to detect and measure any residue left in edible animal products and show that edible animal products when ready-to-eat are free from unsafe residues. Farmers and veterinarians treating farm animals must adhere to any restrictions about withdrawal times, or any warning or use constraints stated on the drug label.

Animal Food Any article intended for use as food for dogs, cats, or other animals derived wholly, or in part, from the carcass or parts or products of the carcass of any livestock, except that the term animal food as used herein does not include:
1. Processed dry animal food or
2. Livestock or poultry feeds manufactured from processed livestock byproducts (such as meat-meal tankage, meat and bonemeal, bloodmeal, and feed grade animal fat).

Animal Food Manufacturer Any person engaged in the business of manufacturing or processing animal food.

Animal Identification and Traceback Currently, the private marketing system, assisted by computerization of records, generally can trace products back to their original suppliers, although not necessarily all the way to the farm. It has been suggested that a type of traceback program might be formalized to monitor and contain outbreaks of foodborne illness better. USDA has called "animal identification" an important element of any traceback system. Many livestock producers currently identify their animals using backtags, ear tags, tattoos, and other devices, so incorporating animal identification into a traceback program might not be difficult.

ANPR Advance notice of proposed rulemaking.

Antemortem Inspection As used in the meat and poultry inspection program, the term refers to the examination that USDA meat and poultry inspectors are required to conduct of all live animals prior to slaughter.

Anthrax A disease of mammals and humans caused by a spore-forming bacterium called *Bacillus anthracis*. Anthrax has an almost worldwide distribution and is a zoonotic disease, meaning it may spread from animals to humans. All mammals appear to be susceptible to anthrax to some degree, but ruminants such as cattle, sheep, and goats are the most susceptible and commonly affected, followed by horses, and then swine.

Antibiotics Chemical substances produced by microorganisms or synthetically that inhibit the growth of, or destroy, bacteria. Rules guiding the use of veterinary drugs and medicated animal feeds, including tolerance levels for drug residues in meats for human consumption, are set by the Center for Veterinary Medicine of the Food and Drug Administration (FDA). The Food Safety and Inspection Service (FSIS) enforces the FDA rules through a sampling and testing program that is part of its overall meat and poultry inspection program.

Antibiotic Resistance Action Plan Public health action plan developed by an Interagency Task Force on Antimicrobial Resistance that was created in 1999 to combat antimicrobial resistance. The task force is co-chaired by the Centers for Disease Control and Prevention, Food and Drug Administration, National Institutes of Health, Agency for Healthcare Research and Quality, Center for Medicaid and Medicare Services, U.S. Department of Agriculture, Department of Defense, Department of Veterans Affairs, Environmental Protection Agency, and Health Resources and Services Administration.

Antimicrobial Resistance Bacteria and other disease-causing organisms have a remarkable ability to mutate and acquire resistance genes from other organisms and thereby develop resistance to antimicrobial drugs. When an antimicrobial drug is used, the selective pressure exerted by the drug favors the growth of organisms that are resistant to the drug's action.

Antioxidant Substance added to food to prevent the oxygen present in the air from causing undesirable changes in flavor color. BHA, BHT, and tocopherols are examples of antioxidants.

Artificial Coloring A coloring containing any dye or pigment manufactured by a process of synthesis or other similar artifice, or a coloring which was manufactured by extracting naturally produced dyes or pigments from a plant or other material.

Artificial Flavoring Artificial flavors are restricted to an ingredient which was manufactured by a process of synthesis or similar process. The principal components of artificial flavors usually are esters, ketones, and aldehyde groups. These ingredients are declared in the ingredients statement as "Artificial Flavors" without naming the individual components. See 9 CFR 317.2(j)(3) and 381.119.

Aseptic Packaging Technique for creating a shelf-stable container by placing a commercially sterile product into a commercially sterile container in a commercially sterile environment. The sealed container is designed to maintain product sterility until the seal is broken.

Automated Import Information System (AIIS) A centralized FSIS database that stores inspection results and provides a record of how each exporting country maintains inspection controls.

Bacon The cured belly of a swine carcass. If meat from other portions of the carcass is used, the product name must be qualified to identify the portions, e.g., "Pork Shoulder Bacon." "Certified" refers to products that have been treated for trichinae.

Bacteria Living single-cell organisms. Bacteria can be carried by water, wind, insects, plants, animals, and people and survive well on skin and clothes and in human hair. They also thrive in scabs, scars, the mouth, nose, throat, intestines, and room-temperature foods. Often bacteria are maligned as the causes of human and animal disease, but there are certain types which are beneficial for all types of living matter.

Baste To moisten meat or other food while cooking. Melted butter or other fat, meat drippings, or liquid such as stock is spooned or brushed on food as it cooks to moisten it.

Basted or Self-Basted Bone-in poultry products that are injected or marinated with a solution containing butter or other edible fat, broth, stock or water plus spices, flavor enhancers and other approved substances must be labeled as basted or self basted. The maximum added weight of approximately 3% solution before processing is included in the net weight on the label. Label must include a statement identifying the total quantity and common or usual name of all ingredients in the solution, e.g., "Injected with approximately 3% of a solution of _____ (list of ingredients)." Use of terms "basted" or "self-basted" on boneless poultry products is limited to 8% of the weight of the raw poultry before processing.

Beef Meat from full-grown cattle about two years old. "Baby beef" and "calf" are interchangeable terms used to describe young cattle weighing about 700 pounds that have been raised mainly on milk and grass.

Beef Patties "Beef Patties" shall consist of chopped fresh and/or frozen beef with or without the addition of beef fat and/or seasonings.

Beef Suet Hard fat from kidneys and loin, mainly used for tallow. May be labeled as "Beef Fat" or "Beef Suet."

Biosecurity Biosecurity refers to policies and measures taken to protect this nation's food supply and agricultural resources from both accidental contamination and deliberate attacks of bioterrorism. Now viewed as an emerging threat, bioterrorism might include such acts as introducing pests intended to kill U.S. food crops; spreading a virulent disease among animal production facilities; and poisoning air, water, food, and blood supplies. The federal government is now increasing its efforts to improve biosecurity to lessen the vulnerabilities to bioterrorism threats.

Biotechnology Agricultural biotechnology is a collection of scientific techniques, including genetic engineering, that are used to create, improve, or modify plants, animals, and microorganisms. Using conventional techniques, such as selective breeding, scientists have been working to improve plants and animals for human benefit for hundreds of years. Modern techniques now enable scientists to move genes (and therefore desirable traits) in ways they could not before—and with greater ease and precision.

Bioterrorism Intentional use of biological agents or toxins to cause a public health emergency or to threaten the integrity of the food and agricultural system.

Bison The National Bison Association encourages the name bison to differentiate the American buffalo from the Asian Water buffalo and African Cape buffalo. The American buffalo is not a true buffalo. Its scientific name is Bison and it belongs to the bovine family along with domestic cattle.

Botulism A rare but serious paralytic illness caused by a nerve toxin that is produced by the bacterium Clostridium botulinum. There are three main kinds of botulism, one of which is foodborne botulism caused by eating foods that contain the botulism toxin. Foodborne botulism can be especially dangerous because many people can be poisoned by eating a contaminated food. All forms of botulism can be fatal and are considered medical emergencies. Good supportive care in a hospital is the mainstay of therapy for all forms of botulism.

Bovine Spongiform Encephalopathy (BSE) Commonly known as "mad cow disease," BSE is a slowly progressive, incurable disease affecting the central nervous system of cattle, first diagnosed in the United Kingdom in 1986. BSE belongs to a family of diseases known as the transmissible spongiform encephalopathies (TSEs). Consumption by cattle of animal feed containing TSE-contaminated ruminant protein has been cited as one possible means of transmission. Scientific evidence supports a causal relationship between BSE outbreaks in Europe and more than 120 recent European cases of a human TSE, variant Creutzfeldt-Jakob Disease (vCJD). TSE animal diseases are found in the United States, including scrapie in sheep and goats and chronic wasting disease in deer and elk. Since 1989, USDA has prohibited the importation of live ruminants from countries where BSE is known to exist in native cattle. In 1997, the Food and Drug Administration (FDA) prohibited the use of most mammalian protein in ruminant feeds.

Brine (Verb) To treat with or steep in brine. (Noun) A strong solution of water and salt, and a sweetener such as sugar, molasses, honey, or corn syrup may be added to the solution for flavor and to improve browning.

Brine Curing Brine curing (or wet curing) is the most popular way of producing hams. It is a wet cure whereby fresh meat is injected with a curing solution before cooking. Brining ingredients can be salt, sugar, sodium nitrite, sodium nitrate, sodium erythorbate, sodium phosphate, potassium chloride, water and flavorings. Smoke flavoring (liquid smoke) may also be injected with brine solution. Cooking may occur during this process.

Broiler or Fryer A broiler or fryer is a young chicken, usually under 13 weeks of age, of either sex, that is tender-meated with soft, pliable, smooth-textured skin and flexible breastbone cartilage.

Byproduct See Meat Byproduct.

Campylobacter *Campylobacter* is a bacterium that is commonly found in the intestinal tracts of cats, dogs, poultry, cattle, swine, rodents, monkeys, wild birds, and some humans. The bacteria pass through feces to cycle through the environment and are also in untreated water. *Campylobacter jejuni (C. jejuni)*, the strain associated with most reported human infections, may be present in the body without causing illness.

Campylobacteriosis A diarrheal disease often caused by the type of bacteria known as *Campylobacter jejuni (C. jejuni)* associated with poultry, raw milk, and water. There are an estimated 2.5 million cases annually in the United States with 200 to 730 deaths. Campylobacteriosis has been linked to Guillain-Barre syndrome (a disease which paralyzes limbs and breathing muscles) as well as Epstein-Barr, Cytomegalovirus, and other viruses. USDA has estimated that this disease costs the United States between $1.2 to $1.4 billion annually in medical costs, productivity losses, and residential care.

Can A receptacle generally having less than 10 gallon capacity (consumer or institutional sizes); also means to pack a product in a can or a wide-mouth glass container for processing, shipping or storage.

Capacolla Boneless pork shoulder butts which are dry cured; not necessarily cooked.

Capon A surgically unsexed male chicken, usually under eight months of age, that is tender-meated with soft, pliable, smooth-textured skin.

Captive Bolt An instrument used to stun cattle prior to slaughter. The bolt is driven into the animal's brain, rendering it unconscious.

Carcass All parts of any slaughtered livestock.

Casing A membranous case for processed meat.

Center for Food Safety and Applied Nutrition (CFSAN) The agency within the Food and Drug Administration responsible for developing and overseeing enforcement of food safety and quality regulations. CFSAN coordinates surveillance and compliance with FDA and other states' surveillance and compliance programs. FDA's roughly 800 field inspectors (located administratively within FDA's Office of Regulatory Affairs)enforce CFSAN's food safety regulations at 53,000 processing facilities.

Center for Veterinary Medicine (CVM) An agency within the Food and Drug Administration that is responsible for assuring that all animal drugs, feeds (including pet foods), and veterinary devices are safe for animals, properly labeled, and produce no human health hazards when used in food-producing animals.

Centers for Disease Control (CDC) and Prevention An agency within the U.S. Department of Health and Human Services that monitors and investigates food borne disease outbreaks and compiles baseline data against which to measure the success of changes in food safety programs.

Certified The term *"certified"* implies that the USDA's Food Safety and Inspection Service and the Agriculture Marketing Service have officially evaluated a meat product for class, grade, or other quality characteristics (e.g., "Certified Angus Beef"). When used under other circumstances, the term must be closely associated with the name of the organization responsible for the *"certification"* process, e.g., "XYZ Company's Certified Beef."

Chronic Wasting Disease Chronic wasting disease (CWD) is a transmissible spongiform encephalopathy (TSE) of deer and elk. To date, this disease has been found only in cervids (members of the deer family) in North America. First recognized as a clinical "wasting" syndrome in 1967 in mule deer in a wildlife research facility in northern Colorado, it was identified as a TSE in 1978. CWD is typified by chronic weight loss leading to death. There is no known relationship between CWD and any other TSE of animals or people.

Chemical Preservative Any chemical that, when added to a meat or meat food product, tends to prevent or retard deterioration thereof, but does not include common salt, sugars, vinegars, spices, or oils extracted from spices or substances added to meat and meat food products by exposure to wood smoke.

Chevon (FR) Goat meat used for food.

Chub An acceptable name to denote a short, usually plump meat food product, unsliced in casing.

Clostridium botulinum The name of a group of bacteria commonly found in soil. These rod-shaped organisms grow best in low oxygen conditions. The bacteria form spores which allow them to survive in a dormant state until exposed to conditions that can support their growth. *Clostridium botulinum* is the bacterium that produces the nerve toxin that causes botulism.

Cock or Rooster A mature male chicken with coarse skin, toughened and darkened meat, and hardened breastbone tip.

Code of Federal Regulations (CFR) The codification of the general and permanent rules published in the Federal Register by the Executive departments and agencies of the federal government. The Code is divided into 50 titles that represent broad areas subject to regulation. Most regulations directly related to agriculture are in Title 7. Each title is divided into chapters that usually bear the name of the issuing agency, followed by subdivisions into parts covering specific regulatory areas. Title 9, Chapter III covers the Food Safety and Inspection Service.

Codex Alimentarius Commission A joint commission of the Food and Agriculture Organization (FAO) and the World Health Organization, comprised of some 146 member countries, created in 1962 to ensure consumer food safety, establish fair practices in food trade, and promote the development of international food standards. The Commission drafts nonbinding standards for food additives, veterinary drugs, pesticide residues, and other substances that affect consumer food safety. It publishes these standards in a listing called the "Codex Alimentarius."

Consumer Safety Officer The Consumer Safety Officer (CSO), a professional position created by FSIS in 2001, serves as a representative of a district office within the agency. The CSO's duties include focusing on in-plant inspection activities, serving on in-depth verification reviews, investigations, and other Agency reviews to assess the effectiveness of a plant's food safety control systems. In addition, a key responsibility of the CSO will be to assist with activities associated with the Small Business Regulatory Enforcement Fairness Act (SBREFA) which supports in-plant food safety inspection activities and helps small and very small establishments identify resources for the design and implementation of HACCP plans, SSOPs, *E. coli* testing plans, and microbiological control strategies.

Continuous Inspection USDA's meat and poultry inspection system is often called "continuous" because no animal destined for human food may be slaughtered or dressed unless an inspector is present to examine it before slaughter (antemortem inspection), and its carcass and parts after slaughter (postmortem inspection). In processing plants, as opposed to slaughter plants, inspectors need not be present at all times, but they do visit at least once daily. Processing inspection is also considered continuous.

Controlled Atmosphere Packaging (CAP) Packaging method in which selected atmospheric concentrations of gases are maintained throughout storage in order to extend product shelf life. Gas may either be evacuated or introduced to achieve the desired atmosphere. Normally used for fruits and vegetables, not meat products.

Corned Beef Corning is a form of curing one of the several less-tender cuts of beef like the brisket, rump or round. It has nothing to do with corn. The name comes from Anglo-Saxon times before refrigeration. In those days, the meat was dry-cured in coarse "corns" of salt. Pellets of salt, some the size of kernels of corn, were rubbed into the beef to keep it from spoiling and to preserve it. Today, brining has replaced the dry salt cure, but the name "corned beef" is still used, rather than "brined" or "pickled" beef. Commonly used spices that give corned beef its distinctive flavor are peppercorns and bay leaf.

(Rock) Cornish Game Hen A Rock Cornish game hen or Cornish game hen is a young immature chicken (usually five to six weeks of age) weighing not more than two pounds ready-to-cook weight, which was prepared from a Cornish chicken or the progeny of a Cornish chicken crossed with another breed of chicken.

(Rock) Cornish Fryer, Roaster, or Hen A Rock Cornish fryer, roaster, or hen is the progeny of a cross between a purebred Cornish and a purebred Rock chicken, without regard to the weight of the carcass involved; however, the term "fryer," "roaster," or "hen" shall apply only if the carcasses are from birds with ages and characteristics of a "broiler or fryer" or "roaster or roasting chicken."

Cottage Ham A ham made from the shoulder butt end.

Country Ham Uncooked, cured, dried, smoked-or-unsmoked meat products made from a single piece of meat from the hind leg of a hog or from a single piece of meat from a pork shoulder.

Country-of-origin Labeling Under Section 304 of the Tariff Act of 1930, as amended, most products entering the United States must be clearly marked so that the "ultimate purchaser" can identify the country of origin. Imported meat products are subject to this requirement: imported carcasses and parts of carcasses must be labeled, and individual retail (consumer-ready) packages also must be labeled. Imported carcasses or parts generally go to U.S. plants for further processing. The labeling policy considers these plants as the "ultimate purchasers." Therefore, any products these plants make from the imported meat (for example, ground beef patties made in the United States from beef that originated in Canada or elsewhere) do not have to bear country-of-origin labels. A number of other agricultural articles are exempt from the basic country-of-origin labeling requirements: eggs, livestock and other animals, live or dead; and other "natural products" such as fruits, vegetables, nuts and berries. (However, the outermost containers used to bring these articles into the United States must indicate the country of origin.) On May 13, 2002, President Bush signed into law the Farm Security and Rural Investment Act of 2002, which requires beef, lamb, pork, farm-raised fish, wild fish, perishable agricultural commodities, and peanuts to bear Country-of-origin labeling at the point of retail sale.

Creutzfeldt-Jacob Disease (CJD) A sporadic and rare, but fatal human disease that usually strikes people over 65. It occurs worldwide at an estimated rate of one case per million population. About 10-15% of CJD cases are inherited. A small number of cases occurred as the result of various medical treatments or procedures which inadvertently transferred the CJD agent. In March 1996, the British government announced a possible link between bovine spongiform encephalopathy (BSE) and CJD. The announcement was prompted by the discovery of several atypical cases of CJD in Great Britain.

Critical Control Point An operation (practice, procedure, process, or location) at or by which preventive or control measures can be exercised that will eliminate, prevent, or minimize one or more hazards. Critical control points are fundamental to Hazard Analysis and Critical Control Point (HACCP) systems.

Cross-Contamination The transfer of harmful substances or disease-causing microorganisms to food by hands, food-contact surfaces, sponges, cloth towels and utensils that touch raw food, are not cleaned, and then touch ready-to-eat foods. Cross contamination can also occur when raw food touches or drips onto cooked or ready-to-eat foods.

Cure A chemical agent placed in or on meat or poultry for use in preservation, flavor, or color.

Curing Curing is the addition of salt, sodium nitrate (or saltpeter), nitrites and sometimes sugars, seasonings, phosphates and ascorbates to pork for preservation, color development and flavor enhancement.

Custom Exempt Custom exempt establishments are slaughter and processing establishments which are not subject to the routine inspection requirements of the Federal Meat Inspection Act and Poultry Products Inspection Act, provided the specified operations meet the exemption requirements of Section 23 of the FMIA and section 15 of the PIA.

Cutting Up Any division of any carcass or part thereof, except that the trimming of carcasses or parts thereof to remove surface contaminants is not considered as cutting up.

Dead Livestock The body (cadaver) of livestock which has died otherwise than by slaughter.

Delaney Clause The Delaney Clause in the Federal Food, Drug, and Cosmetic Act (FFDCA) states that no additive shall be deemed to be safe for human food if it is found to induce cancer in man or animals. It is an example of the zero tolerance concept in food safety policy. The Delaney prohibition appears in three separate parts of the FFDCA: Section 409 on food additives; Section 512, relating to animal drugs in meat and poultry; and Section 721 on color additives. The Section 409 prohibition applied to many pesticide residues until enactment of the Food Quality Protection Act of 1996 (P.L. 104-170, August 3, 1996). This legislation removed pesticide residue tolerances from Delaney Clause constraints.

Deli or Delicatessen Style This terminology has been permitted on labeling for ready-to-eat meat food products that consumers would normally expect to find in a delicatessen.

Diglycerides, Monoglycerides Emulsifying agents for rendered fats.

Dioxins A group of chemical compounds that share certain similar chemical structures and biological characteristics. Dioxins are present in the environment all over the world. Within animals, dioxins tend to accumulate in fat. About 95% of the average person's exposure to dioxins occurs through consumption of food, especially food containing animal fat. Scientists and health experts are concerned about dioxins because studies have shown that exposure may cause a number of adverse health effects.

Disposition A food manufacturer's action to correct a situation leading to a recall such as relabeling, reworking, or destroying product.

Downer (or downed animals) Commonly used term for an animal that is unable to rise and walk.

Dry Aged Fresh Meat is held (without vacuum packing) for various periods of time (usually 10 days to 6 weeks) under controlled temperatures (34°F to 38°F), humidity, and airflow to avoid spoilage and ensure flavor enhancement, tenderness, and palatability.

Dry Curing Dry curing is the process used to make country hams and prosciutto. Fresh meat is rubbed with a dry cure mixture of salt and other ingredients. Dry curing produces a salty product. In 1992, FSIS approved a trichina treatment method that permits substituting up to half of the sodium chloride with potassium chloride to result in lower sodium levels. Since dry curing draws out moisture, it reduces ham weight by at least 18%—usually 20 to 25%; this results in a more concentrated ham flavor.

Dying, Diseased, or Disabled Livestock Livestock which has or displays symptoms of having any of the following:

1. Central nervous system disorder;
2. Abnormal temperature (high or low);
3. Difficult breathing;
4. Abnormal swellings;
5. Lack of muscular coordination;
6. Inability to walk normally or stand;
7. Any of the conditions for which livestock is required to be condemned on ante-mortem inspection in accordance with the regulations

E. coli O157:H7 (Escherichia Coli O157:H7) A bacterium that lives harmlessly in the intestines of animals such as cattle, reptiles, and birds. However, in humans the bacterium, which can be transmitted by foods, animal contact, and drinking water, can cause bloody diarrhea, and also lead to hemolytic uremic syndrome (HUS), a life threatening disease. Although other generic strains of E. coli are thought to be harmless to humans, the O157:H7 strain is particularly virulent and dangerous. USDA began an E. coli O157:H7 testing plan in 1994. As part of the Hazard Analysis and Critical Control Point (HACCP) rule,all meat and poultry slaughter plants are required to test carcasses regularly for generic E. coli in order to verify that their sanitary systems are effectively controlling fecal contamination.

Economic Research Service (ERS) The Economic Research Service (ERS) is the main source of economic information and research from the U.S. Department of Agriculture. The mission of ERS is to inform and enhance public and private decision making on economic and policy issues related to agriculture, food, natural resources, and rural development. To accomplish this mission, highly trained economists and social scientists develop and distribute a broad range of economic and other social science information and analyses.

Edible Intended for use as human food.

Egg Products Eggs that are removed from their shells for processing. The processing of egg products includes breaking eggs, filtering, mixing, stabilizing, blending, pasteurizing, cooling, freezing or drying, and packaging. Egg products include whole eggs, whites, yolks and various blends with or without non-egg ingredients that are processed and pasteurized and may be available in liquid, frozen, and dried forms. FSIS is responsible for inspecting egg products and enforcing the Egg Products Inspection Act (EPIA).

Egg Products Inspection Act (EPIA) The Egg Products Inspection Act (EPIA), passed by Congress in 1970, provides for the mandatory continuous inspection of the processing of liquid, frozen, and dried egg products.

Emulsifier A substance added to products, such as meat spreads, to prevent separation of product components to ensure consistency. Examples of these types of additives include lecithin, and mono- and diglycerides.

Environmental Protection Agency (EPA) The Federal Agency whose mission is to protect human health and to safeguard the natural environment &151; air, water, and land &151; upon which life depends. EPA provides leadership in the nation's environmental science, research, education and assessment efforts. EPA works closely with other federal agencies, state and local governments, and Indian tribes to develop and enforce regulations under existing environmental laws. EPA is responsible for researching and setting national standards for a variety of environmental programs and delegates to states and tribes responsibility for issuing permits, and monitoring and enforcing compliance.

Epidemiology Study of the distribution of disease, or other health-related conditions and events in human or animal populations, in order to identify health problems and possible causes.

Equivalence A term applied by the Uruguay Round Agreement on the Application of Sanitary and Phytosanitary (SPS) Measures. WTO Member countries shall accord acceptance to the SPS measures of other countries (even if those measures differ from their own or from those used by other Member countries trading in the same product) if the exporting country demonstrates to the importing country that its measures achieve the importer's appropriate level of sanitary and phytosanitary protection.

Establishment or Official Establishment Any slaughtering, cutting, boning, meat canning, curing, smoking, salting, packing, rendering, or similar facility at which inspection is maintained under regulations of the Federal Meat Inspection Act, Poultry Products Inspection Act, Egg Products Inspection Act, and the Humane Methods of Slaughter Act.

Exotic Newcastle Disease A contagious and fatal viral disease affecting all species of birds. Exotic Newcastle disease is one of the most infectious diseases of poultry in the world. A death rate of almost 100 percent can occur in unvaccinated poultry flocks.

Experimental Animal Any animal used in any research investigation involving the feeding or other administration of, or subjection to, an experimental biological product, drug, or chemical or any nonexperimental biological product, drug, or chemical used in a manner for which it was not intended.

Fabricated Steak Fabricated beef steaks, veal steaks, beef and veal steaks, or veal and beef steaks, and similar products, such as those labeled "Beef Steak, Chopped, Shaped, Frozen," "Minute Steak, Formed, Wafer Sliced, Frozen," "Veal Steaks, Beef Added, Chopped-Molded-Cubed-Fro-Flavoring" shall be prepared by comminuting and forming the product from fresh and/or frozen meat, with or without added fat, of the species indicated on the label. Such products shall not contain more than 30 percent fat and shall not contain added water, binders or extenders.

Farm Bill A phrase that refers to a multi-year, multi-commodity federal support law. It usually amends some and suspends many provisions of permanent law, reauthorizes, amends, or repeals provisions of preceding temporary agricultural acts, and puts forth new policy provisions for a limited time into the future. Beginning in 1973, farms bills have included titles on commodity programs, trade, rural development, farm credit, conservation, agricultural research, food and nutrition programs, marketing, etc. These are referred to as omnibus farm bills. The following is a generally agreed chronological list of farm bills: (1) Food and Agriculture Act of 1965, P.L. 89-321; (2) Agricultural Act of 1970, P.L. 91-524; (3) Agriculture and Consumer Protection Act of 1973, P.L. 93-86; (4) Food and Agriculture Act of 1977, P.L. 95-113; (5) Agriculture and Food Act of 1981, P.L. 97-98; (6) Food Security Act of 1985, P.L. 99-198; (7) Food, Agriculture, Conservation, and Trade Act of 1990, P.L. 101-624; (8) Federal Agricultural Improvement and Reform Act of 1996, P.L. 104-127, Farm Security and Rural Investment Act of 2002.

Farm-to-Table Continuum A multi-step journey that food travels before it is consumed.

Federal Food, Drug, and Cosmetic Act (FFDCA) of 1938 P.L. 75-717 (June 25, 1938) is the basic authority intended to ensure that foods are pure and wholesome, safe to eat, and produced under sanitary conditions; that drugs and devices are safe and effective for their intended uses; that cosmetics are safe and made from appropriate ingredients; and that all labeling and packaging is truthful, informative, and not deceptive. The Food and Drug Administration is primarily responsible for enforcing the FFDCA, although USDA also has some enforcement responsibility. The Environmental Protection Agency establishes limits for concentrations of pesticide residues on food under this Act.

Federal Meat Inspection Act of 1906 (FMIA) Enacted June 30, 1906, as chapter 3913, 34 Stat. 674, and substantially amended by the Wholesome Meat Act 1967 (P.L. 90-201), requires USDA to inspect all cattle, sheep, swine, goats, and horses when slaughtered and processed into products for human consumption. The primary goals of the law are to prevent adulterated or misbranded livestock and products from being sold as food, and to ensure that meat and meat products are slaughtered and processed under sanitary conditions. These requirements apply to animals and their products produced and sold within states as well as to imports, which must be inspected under equivalent foreign standards. The Food and Drug Administration is responsible for all meats considered "exotic" at this time, including venison and buffalo.

Federal Register A federal document containing current Presidential orders or directives, agency regulations, proposed agency rules, notices and other documents that are required by statute to be published for wide public distribution. The Federal Register is published each federal working day. USDA publishes its rules, notices and other documents in the Federal Register. Final regulations are organized by agency and programs in the Code of Federal Regulations.

Fight Bac!® Campaign A national public education project by the Partnership for Food Safety Education, which bring together industry, government, and consumer groups to educate Americans about the importance of using safe food-handling practices. The campaign focuses on the "4 Cs" of food safety the four simple steps people can take to fight foodborne bacteria and reduce the risk of foodborne illness. The four simple steps are Clean, Cook, Separate, and Chill.

Flash Pasteurization A pasteurization process which involves a high temperature, short-time treatment in which pourable products, such as juices, are heated for three to 15 seconds to a temperature that destroys harmful micro-organisms.

Food Additive Any substance or mixture of substances other than the basic foodstuff present in a food as a result of any phase of production, processing, packaging, storage, transport or handling. USDA allows food additives in meat, poultry and egg products only after they have received Food and Drug Administration safety approval. Food additives are regulated under the authority of the Federal Food Drug and Cosmetic Act and are subject to the Delaney Clause.

Food and Agriculture Organization of the United Nations (FAO) A UN organization, founded in 1945, that collects and disseminates information about world agriculture. FAO also provides technical assistance to developing countries in agricultural production and distribution, food processing, nutrition, fisheries, and forestry.

Food and Drug Administration (FDA) An agency within the Public Health Service of the Department of Health and Human Services. FDA is a public health agency, charged with protecting consumers by enforcing the Federal Food, Drug, and Cosmetic Act and several related public health laws. Importantly for agriculture, a major FDA mission is to protect the safety and wholesomeness of food. In this regard, its scientists test samples to see if any substances, such as pesticide residues, are present in unacceptable amounts, it sets food labeling standards, and it sees that medicated feeds and other drugs given to animals raised for food are not threatening to the consumer's health.

Food and Nutrition Service (FNS) The USDA agency whose goals are to provide needy people with access to a more nutritious diet, to improve the eating habits of the nation's children, and to stabilize farm prices through the distribution of surplus foods. It administers 15 domestic food assistance programs (including the food stamp program, child nutrition programs [e.g., school feeding programs], and the Special Supplemental Nutrition Program for Women, Infants and Children [WIC]). FNS works in partnership with the states and reimburses most of the administrative costs the states incur for carrying out local program administration.

Food Biosecurity Action Team (F-BAT) The USDA Under Secretary for Food Safety formed the Food Biosecurity Action Team (F-BAT) to coordinate and facilitate all activities pertaining to biosecurity, countering terrorism, and emergency preparedness with FSIS. F-BAT also serves as FSIS' voice with other governmental agencies and internal and external constituents on biosecurity issues.

Food Code The code, published by the Food and Drug Administration, consists of model requirements for safeguarding public health that may be adopted and used by various parts of local, state, and federal governments, if desired. It is used by officials who have compliance responsibilities for food service, retail food stores, or food vending operations.

Food Isolate A microorganism that is derived from food for the purpose of identifying or characterizing it.

Food Safety and Inspection Service (FSIS) The Food Safety and Inspection Service (FSIS) is the public health agency in the U.S. Department of Agriculture responsible for ensuring that the nation's commercial supply of meat, poultry, and egg products is safe, wholesome, and correctly labeled and packaged, as required by the Federal Meat Inspection Act, the Poultry Products Inspection Act, and the Egg Products Inspection Act.

The Food Safety Educator The Food Safety Educator was a free quarterly newsletter published by FSIS' Food Safety Education Staff that reports on new food safety educational programs and materials as well as emerging science concerning food safety risks. (It is no longer published.)

(National) Food Safety Initiative A 1997 interagency initiative among the Food and Drug Administration, Center for Disease Control, Environmental Protection Agency, and U.S. Department of Agriculture to implement a series of coordinated efforts to reduce the annual incidence of foodborne illness and resultant economic losses to consumers and industry by enhancing the safety of the U.S. food supply.

Food Security Access by all people at all times to enough food for an active healthy life. Food security at a minimum includes the ready availability of nutritionally adequate and safe food, and an assured ability to acquire acceptable foods in socially acceptable ways, that is, without having to resort to emergency food supplies, scavenging, stealing, or other coping strategies. Causes of food insecurity may include poverty, civil conflict, governmental corruption, environmental degradation, and natural disasters.

Food Thermometer A special device that measures the internal temperature of cooked foods, such as meat, poultry, and any combination dishes to ensure that a safe food temperature is reached.

Food Threat Preparedness Network See PrepNet.

Foodborne Illnesses Illnesses caused by pathogens that enter the human body through foods.

Foodborne Outbreak The occurrence of two or more people experiencing the same illness after eating the same food.

Foodborne Pathogens Disease-causing microorganisms found in food, usually bacteria, fungi, parasites, protozoans, and viruses. The top ten pathogens are: *Salmonella*; *Staphylococcus Aureus*; *Campylobacter jejuni*; *Yersinia enerocolitica*; *Listeria monocytogenes*; *Vibro cholerae non-01*; *Vibrio Parahemolyticus*; *Bacillus cereus*; *Escherichia coli*—enteropathogenic; and *Shigella*. Many of these pathogens may be found in contaminated meat, poultry, shell eggs, dairy products, and seafood.

FoodNet The Foodborne Diseases Active Surveillance Network (FoodNet) is the principal foodborne disease component of CDC's Emerging Infections Program (EIP). FoodNet is a collaborative project of the CDC, nine EIP sites (California, Colorado, Connecticut, Georgia, New York, Maryland, Minnesota, Oregon and Tennessee), the USDA, and the FDA. The project consists of active surveillance for foodborne diseases and related epidemiologic studies designed to help public health officials better understand the epidemiology of foodborne diseases in the United States. FoodNet provides a network for responding to new and emerging foodborne diseases of national importance, monitoring the burden of foodborne diseases, and identifying the sources of specific foodborne diseases.

Foot and Mouth Disease (FMD) a highly contagious viral disease of cattle and swine, as well as sheep, goats, deer, and other cloven-hoofed ruminants. Although rarely transmissible to humans, FMD is devastating to livestock and has critical economic consequences with potentially severe losses in the production and marketing of meat and milk.

Foreign Agricultural Service (FAS) USDA agency that administers agricultural export and food aid programs. FAS is also responsible for formulating agricultural trade policy, negotiating to reduce foreign agricultural trade barriers, and carrying out programs of international cooperation and technical assistance. The agency maintains a global network of agricultural officers (counselors and attaches) as well as a Washington-based staff to analyze and disseminate information on world agricultural trade policy interests of U.S. producers in multilateral forums.

Frankfurters (a.k.a., hot dogs, wieners, or bologna) Cooked and/or smoked sausages prepared according to the Federal standards of identity. Federal standards of identity describe the requirements for processors to follow in formulating and marketing meat, poultry, and egg products produced in the United States for sale in this country and in foreign commerce. The standard also requires that they be comminuted (reduced to minute particles), semisolid products made from one or more kinds of raw skeletal muscle from livestock (like beef or pork) and may contain poultry meat. Smoking and curing ingredients contribute to flavor, color, and preservation of the product. They are link-shaped and come in all sizes—short, long, thin, and chubby.

Free Range or Free Roaming Livestock or poultry has been allowed access to the outside.

Fresh (Poultry) Poultry whose internal temperature has never been below 26°F.

Fresh Ham The uncured leg of pork. Since the meat is not cured or smoked, it has the flavor of a fresh pork loin roast or pork chops. Its raw color is pinkish red and after cooking, greyish white.

Fryer-Roaster Turkey A young immature turkey, usually under 16 weeks of age, of either sex, that is tender-meated with soft, pliable, smooth-textured skin, and flexible breastbone cartilage.

Fully Cooked Fully cooked product needs no further cooking. The product is fully cooked in the plant, and it can be reheated or eaten directly from the package. Also known as ready-to-eat.

Further Processing Smoking, cooking, canning, curing, refining, or rendering in an official establishment of product previously prepared in official establishments.

Gelatin Thickener from collagen which is derived from the skin, tendons, ligaments, or bones of livestock. It may be used in canned hams or jellied meat products, as well as non-food products such as photography and medicine.

Giblets Giblets are the heart, liver, and gizzard of a poultry carcass. Although often packaged with them, the neck of the bird is not a giblet. Giblets are not packaged with the original bird; however, they are inspected by FSIS inspectors.

Gizzard The gizzard is the mechanical "stomach" of a bird. It is located just after the true or glandular stomach in the gastrointestinal system. Since poultry have no teeth and swallow feed whole, this muscular organ, sometimes called "hen's teeth," mechanically grinds and mixes the bird's feed.

Grade, Grading The inspection and grading of meat and poultry are two separate programs within the U.S. Department of Agriculture. Inspection for wholesomeness is mandatory and is paid for out of tax dollars. Grading for quality is voluntary, and the service is requested and paid for by meat and poultry producers/processors.

Ground Beef "Ground Beef" or "Chopped Beef" shall consist of chopped fresh and/or frozen beef with or without seasoning and without the addition of beef fat as such, shall not contain more than 30 percent fat, and shall not contain added water, phosphates, binders, or extenders.

Halal and Zabiah Halal Products prepared by federally inspected meat packing plants identified with labels bearing references to *"Halal"* or *"Zabiah Halal"* must be handled according to Islamic law and under Islamic authority.

Ham Ham means pork which comes from the hind leg of a hog. Ham made from the front leg of a hog will be labeled "pork shoulder picnic." Hams may be fresh, cured, or cured-and-smoked. The usual color for cured ham is deep rose or pink; fresh ham (which is not cured) has the pale pink or beige color of fresh pork roast; country hams and prosciutto (which are dry cured) range from pink to mahogany color. "Turkey ham" must be made from the thigh meat of turkey.

Ham Steak Another name for center cut ham slices.

Hamburger "Hamburger" shall consist of chopped fresh and/or frozen beef with or without the addition of beef fat as such and/or seasoning, shall not contain more than 30 percent fat, and shall not contain added water, phosphates, binders, or extenders.

Hazard A biological, physical, or chemical property that may cause a food to be unsafe for human consumption.

Hazard Analysis And Critical Control Points (HACCP) A production quality control system now being adopted throughout much of the food industry as a method for minimizing the entry of foodborne pathogens into the food supply in order to protect human health. Under a HACCP (pronounced *Ha-sip*) system, potential hazards are identified and risks are analyzed in each phase of production; critical control points for preventing such hazards are identified and constantly monitored; and corrective actions are taken when necessary. Record keeping and verification procedures are used to ensure that the system is working. HACCP is one of the major elements of regulations, issued by USDA in July 1996 to control pathogens in meat and poultry products. Under the rules, all meat and poultry slaughter and processing plants with 500 or more employees had to develop and implement, by January 1998, a USDA-approved HACCP plan for each of their processes and products. Plants with 10 to 500 employees implemented HACCP by January 1999, and plants with less than 10 employees implemented the system by January 2000. Under separate rules issued by the Food and Drug Administration on December 5, 1995, seafood processors and importers also were required to implement HACCP plans and be in full compliance by December 1997.

Headcheese A jellied product consisting predominantly of pork byproducts and seasoning ingredients. It must contain some product from the head.

Hen, Fowl (Baking or Stewing) A bird of this class is a mature female chicken, usually more than 10 months of age, with meat less tender than that of a roaster, or roasting chicken and nonflexible breastbone tip.

Hickory-Smoked Ham A cured ham which has been smoked by hanging over burning hickory wood chips in a smokehouse. The ham may not be labeled "hickory smoked" unless hickory wood has been used.

HIMP or HACCP-Based Inspection Models Project HIMP is an effort to determine how FSIS can improve the use of its online slaughter inspectors and continue to ensure the reduction and/or elimination of defects that pass through traditional inspection. Under this project, FSIS has established performance standards for food safety and non-food safety defects (also known as "other consumer protections" or OCP) found in young chickens, hogs, and turkeys. The food safety performance standards are set at zero to protect consumers from conditions that may be harmful. The OCP performance standards are more stringent than current standards and thus require improved plant performance. Participating plants must revise their HACCP systems to meet these food safety performance standards and establish process control systems to address the OCP concerns. Under this project, FSIS conducts continuous inspection with verification to ensure that performance standards are met.

Honey-Cured Honey-cured may be shown on the labeling of a cured product if honey is the only sweetening ingredient or is at least half the sweetening ingredients used, and if the honey is used in an amount sufficient to flavor and/or affect the appearance of the finished product.

Humane Methods of Slaughter Act This Act amended the FMIA by requiring that all meat inspected at Federal establishments by FSIS for use as human food be produced from livestock slaughtered by humane methods in accordance with the Humane Slaughter Act of 1958. The 1958 Act required all livestock in the United States be slaughtered humanely, except for Kosher, Halal, and other religious slaughter.

Humectant A substance added to foods to help retain moisture and soft texture. An example is glycerine, which may be used in dried meat snacks.

Hydrolyzed (Source) Protein Flavor enhancers that can be used in meat and poultry products. They are made from protein obtained from a plant source such as soy or wheat, or from an animal source, such as milk. The source used must be identified on the label.

Incidental Additives As defined in the Food and Drug Administration regulations (21 CFR 101.100(a)(3)), incidental additives are substances present in foods at insignificant levels that do not serve a technical or functional effect in that food.

Inedible Adulterated, uninspected, or not intended for use as human food.

Inhumane Slaughter Slaughter of livestock that is not in accordance with the Humane Methods of Slaughter Act of 1978 and FSIS regulations promulgated to enforce the Act. Inadequate methods to prevent pain and suffering of animals presented for slaughter.

"Inspected and Passed" or "U.S. Inspected and Passed" or "U.S. Inspected and Passed by Department of Agriculture" (or any authorized abbreviation thereof) This term means that the product so identified has been inspected and passed under the regulations in CFR, and at the time it was inspected, passed, and identified, it was found to be not adulterated.

Inspector An inspector of the Program.

Inspector in Charge A designated program employee who is in charge of one or more official establishments within a circuit and is responsible to the circuit supervisor or his/her designee.

Internal Temperature The temperature of the internal portion of a food product.

Irradiation The process where foods, such as poultry, red meat, spices, and fruits and vegetables, are subjected to small amounts of radiant energy including gamma rays, electron beams, and x-rays in amounts approved by the Food and Drug Administration. USDA's Food Safety and Inspection Service oversees the irradiation of meat and poultry.

ISO Accreditation Accreditation by the International Organization for Standardization (ISO), which develops international agreements on standards for various industries.

Jerky This product is a nutrient-dense meat that has been made lightweight by drying. Products may be cured or uncured, dried, and may be smoked or unsmoked, air or oven dried.

Kosher Kosher may be used only on the labels of meat and poultry products prepared under Rabbinical supervision.

Label A display of written, printed, or graphic matter upon the immediate container (not including package liners) of any food product.

Lamb Meat from sheep less than one year old. If the phrase "Spring Lamb" is on a meat label, it means the lamb was produced between March and October.

Lard Lard is the fat rendered from clean and sound edible tissues from swine.

Listeria Listeria monocytogenes, a pathogenic bacterium that can be carried in a variety of foods such as dairy products, red meat, poultry, seafood, and vegetables.

Livestock Cattle, sheep, swine, goat, horse, mule, or other equine.

Log Reduction "Log" stands for logarithm, which is the exponent of 10. For example, log2 represents 102 or 10 x 10 or 100. Log reduction stands for a 10-fold or one decimal or 90% reduction in numbers of recoverable bacteria in a test food vehicle. Another way to look at it is: 1 log reduction would reduce the number of bacteria 90%. This means, for example, that 100 bacteria would be reduced to 10 or 10 reduced to 1.

Mad Cow Disease The common term used for Bovine Spongiform Encephalopathy (BSE).

Market Withdrawal A firm's removal or correction by its own volition of a distributed product that involves a minor infraction that would not warrant legal action by FSIS, or that involves no violation of the FMIA or the PPIA, or no health hazard.

Marinate To steep food in a marinade.

Marinade A savory acidic sauce in which a food is soaked to enrich its flavor or to tenderize it. Marinade consists of a cooking oil, an acid (vinegar, lemon juice, wine), and spices. As the food stands in the mixture, the acid and the oil impart the savory flavors of the spices to the food. The acid also has a tenderizing action.

MDM Mechanically deboned meat.

Meat The flesh of animals used as food including the dressed flesh of cattle, swine, sheep, or goats and other edible animals, except fish, poultry, and wild game animals.

Meat Base A granular, paste-like product which is shelf-stable primarily because of its high salt content (30-40%).

1. Beef Base - 15% beef or 10.5% cooked beef.
2. Pork Base - 15% pork or 10.5% cooked pork.
3. Ham Base - 18% ham.

Meat Broker Any person engaged in the business of buying or selling carcasses, parts of carcasses, meat or meat food products of livestock on commission, or otherwise negotiating purchases or sales of such articles other than for his/her own account or as an employee of another person.

Meat Byproduct Any part capable of use as human food, other than meat, which has been derived from one or more cattle, sheep, swine, or goats. This term, as applied to products of equines, shall have a meaning comparable to that provided in this paragraph with respect to cattle, sheep, swine, and goats.

Mechanically Separated Poultry Mechanically separated poultry (i.e., chicken, turkey) is a paste-like and batter-like product produced by forcing the bones and attached edible tissue through a sieve or similar device to separate the bone from the edible poultry tissue. This product is intended for use in the formulation of other poultry products. During this process, it is possible for bones to be crushed or pulverized, resulting in a limited amount of bone particles. Because it may contain some bone particles, any product that has been produced using the mechanical separation process cannot, by definition, be labeled as "poultry." Instead, it must be labeled appropriately as "mechanically separated chicken" (or turkey) on the product's label. Mechanically separated chicken and turkey are used in products such as chicken and turkey franks, bologna, nuggets, and patties.

Mechanically Separated (Species) Mechanically separated meat (i.e., beef, veal, pork, lamb)also known as mechanically separated (species) or MS(S)is a paste-like and batter-like product produced by forcing the bones and attached edible tissue through a sieve or similar device to separate the bone from the edible meat tissue. This product is intended for use in the formulation of other meat products. During this process, it is possible for bones to be crushed or pulverized, resulting in a limited amount of bone particles. Because it may contain some bone particles, any product that has been produced using the mechanical separation process cannot, by definition, be labeled as "meat." Instead, it must be labeled appropriately as "mechanically separated beef" (or other species). The manufacture and sale of mechanically separated beef, veal, pork, or lamb in the United States is not common, but a small amount is exported.

Memorandum of Agreement (MOA) An agreement between federal agencies, or divisions/units within an agency or department, or between federal and state agencies, which delineate tasks, jurisdiction, standard operating procedures or other matters which the agencies or units are duly authorized and directed to conduct. Sometimes referred to as a memorandum of understanding (MOU).

Microorganism A form of life that can be seen only with a microscope; including bacteria, viruses, yeast, and single-celled animals.

Migration Transfer of a component of a packaging material into the product contained, or loss of a component of the product into the packaging material.

Misbranded This term applies to any carcass, part thereof, meat or meat food product under one or more of the following circumstances: 1) If its labeling is false or misleading in any particular; 2) If it is offered for sale under the name of another food; 3) If it is an imitation of another food, unless its label bears, in type of uniform size and prominence, the word "imitation" and immediately thereafter, the name of the food imitated; 4) If its container is so made, formed, or filled as to be misleading; 5) If in a package or other container unless it bears a label showing: a.) the name and place of business of the manufacturer, packer, or distributor; and b.) an accurate statement of the quantity of the contents in terms of weight, measure, or numerical count; except as otherwise provided.

Modified Atmosphere Packaging (MAP) Packaging method in which a combination of gases such as oxygen, carbon dioxide and nitrogen is introduced into the package at the time of closure. The purpose is to extend shelf life of the product packaged.

Modified Food Starch Starch that has been chemically altered to improve its thickening properties. Before the starch is modified, it is separated from the protein through isolation techniques; therefore, the source of the starch used is not required on the label.

Monosodium Glutamate (MSG) MSG is a flavor enhancer. It comes from a common amino acid, glutamic acid, and must be declared as monosodium glutamate on meat and poultry labels.

MOU Memorandum of Understanding (MOU), the same as a memorandum of agreement (MOA).

Mutton Meat from sheep more than one year old.

NACMCF National Advisory Committee on Microbiological Criteria for Foods. The purpose of the Committee is to provide impartial, scientific advice to Federal food safety agencies for use in the development of an integrated national food safety systems approach from farm to final consumption to assure the safety of domestic, imported, and exported foods.

NACMPI National Advisory Committee on Meat and Poultry Inspection. Congress established the National Advisory Committee on Meat and Poultry Inspection in 1971 under authority of the Federal Meat and Inspection Act (FMIA) and the Poultry Products Inspection Acts (PPIA). Both acts require the Secretary of Agriculture to consult with an advisory committee before issuing product standards and labeling changes or any matters affecting federal and state program activities. Membership in the committee includes representatives from industry, consumer interests, and state agencies.

National Academy of Sciences (NAS) An institution created by Congress in 1863 to provide science-based advice to the government. The sister organizations associated with the Academy are the National Academy of Engineers, Institute of Medicine, and the National Research Council. The Academies and the Institute are honorary societies that elect new members to their ranks each year. The bulk of the institutions' science-policy and technical work is conducted by the National Research Council (NRC), created expressly for that purpose. The NRC's Board on Agriculture addresses issues confronting agriculture, food, and related environmental topics.

National Agricultural Library (NAL) A national depository of scientific and popular agricultural information located at the Agricultural Research Service's research center in Beltsville, Maryland. NAL's administration was merged with ARS in 1994.

National Agricultural Statistics Service (NASS) USDA agency that collects and publishes statistics on the U.S. food and fiber system, with offices located in each state's department of agriculture.

National Antimicrobial Resistance Monitoring System (NARMS) A collaborative agreement established in 1996 with the U.S. Department of Agriculture (USDA), Food and Drug Administration, and the Center for Disease Control and Prevention (CDC). The NARMS program is a national surveillance program that monitors changes in susceptibilities of human and animal enteric bacteria to 17 antimicrobial drugs. The program provides baseline information on prevalence of resistance, allows for detection of small decreases in susceptibility, and predicts trends in time to allow for mitigation.

National Early Warning System A program run by the Centers for Disease Control and Prevention to increase federal support to state health departments to detect foodborne diseases by increasing the number of scientists available to investigate food borne outbreaks and by enhancing laboratory-based surveillance of important foodborne pathogens.

Natural A product containing no artificial ingredient or added color that is only minimally processed (a process which does not fundamentally alter the raw product) may be labeled natural. The label must explain the use of the term natural (such as no added colorings or artificial ingredients; minimally processed.)

Netting (plastic) Continuous extruded net of flexible plastic material, most commonly polyethylene, which can be made into bags, sleeves or wraps (example: net over a frozen turkey package).

Nitrite See Sodium Nitrite.

No Roll The term "No Roll" is permitted on marking devices and labels for single ingredient red meats (carcasses, primal and retail cuts) provided the term is not accompanied with an official grade name (e.g., "No Roll Choice").

Nutrition Labeling Identification of the nutritional components of a food product. The Nutrition Labeling and Education Act of 1990 required nutrition labeling of most foods regulated by the Food and Drug Administration. On January 6, 1993, FSIS published final regulations requiring comparable nutrition labeling requirements, with certain exemptions, for multi-ingredient and heat processed meat and poultry products such as hot dogs and luncheon meats. FSIS also established guidelines for voluntary nutrition labeling of single-ingredient, raw meat and poultry products, including those that are ground and chopped. Retailers and manufacturers voluntarily provide nutrition information on the labels of these products or at their point-of-purchase.

Occupational Safety and Health Administration (OSHA) The U.S. Department of Labor agency responsible for administering the Occupational Safety and Health Act (P.L. 91-596). According to OSHA, farming is the nation's most hazardous occupation. Agriculture is the largest occupational group in the United States, with some 10 to 20 million people depending upon one's criteria of "agriculture." The intrinsically seasoned nature of many segments of agriculture not only causes the size of this workforce to vary temporally and often geographically via migrant work groups, but usually also has major effects on the nature and intensity of the work itself. OSHA has issued safety standards relating to agricultural operations.

Office of Homeland Security The Office of Homeland Security was established on October 8, 2001 by President George W. Bush to develop and coordinate the implementation of a comprehensive national strategy to secure the United States from terrorist threats or attacks. The Office coordinates the executive branch's efforts to detect, prepare for, prevent, protect against, respond to, and recover from terrorist attacks within the United States. These efforts include working with executive departments and agencies, State and local governments, and private entities to ensure the adequacy of the national strategy.

Official Mark The official inspection legend or any other symbol prescribed by FSIS regulations to identify the status of any article or animal under the Federal Meat Inspection Act.

Organic Chemically, a compound or molecule containing carbon bound to hydrogen. Organic compounds make up all living matter. The term organic frequently is used to distinguish "natural" products or processes from man-made "synthetic" ones. Thus natural fertilizers include manures or rock phosphate, as opposed to fertilizers synthesized from chemical feedstocks. Likewise, in organic farming pests are controlled by cultivation techniques and the use of pesticides derived from natural sources (e.g., rotenone and pyrethrins, both from plants) and the use of natural fertilizers (e.g., manure and compost). Some consumers, alleging risks from synthetic chemicals, prefer organic food products. The FACT Act of 1990 required USDA to define organic foods for marketing purposes and implement a National Organic Program.

Organic Farming An approach to farming based on biological methods that avoid the use of synthetic crop or livestock production inputs; also a broadly defined philosophical approach to farming that puts value on ecological harmony, resource efficiency, and non-intensive animal husbandry practices. Farmers who wish to have their operations certified as organic so that they can label their products as organically produced currently follow standards and submit to inspection by private or state certification organizations.

Organic Foods Food products produced by organic farming practices and handled or processed under organic handling and manufacturing processes as defined by several private and state organic certifying agencies.

Organoleptic Related to or perceived by a sensory organ.

Oven Ready Product is ready to cook.

Parasites Organisms that derive nourishment and protection from other living organisms known as hosts. They may be transmitted from animals to humans, from humans to humans, or from humans to animals. Several parasites have emerged as significant causes of foodborne and waterborne disease. These organisms live and reproduce within the tissues and organs of infected human and animal hosts, and are often excreted in feces. Some common parasites are *Giardia duodenalis, Cryptosporidium parvum, Cyclospora cayetanensis, Toxoplasma gondii, Trichinella spiralis, Taenia saginata* (beef tapeworm), and *Taenia solium* (pork tapeworm).

Parma Ham Parma Ham is prosciutto from the Parma locale in Italy. These hams tend to be larger than the U.S. produced product, as Italian hogs are larger at slaughter.

Partially Defatted (Beef or Pork) Fatty Tissue These are byproducts produced from fatty trimmings containing less than 12% lean meat. These ingredients may be used in meat products in which byproducts are acceptable.

Partnership for Food Safety Education A public-private coalition formed in 1977, which is dedicated to educating the public about safe food handling to help reduce foodborne illnesses. The partnership is comprised of industry, government and consumer groups and has developed a far-reaching, ambitious and consumer-friendly public education campaign focused on safe food handling.

Pasteurization The process of destroying microorganisms that could disease. This is usually done by applying heat to food. Three processes used to pasteurize foods are flash pasteurization, steam pasteurization, and irradiation pasteurization.

Pathogen A microorganism (bacteria, parasites, viruses, or fungi) that is infectious and causes disease.

Performance-Based Inspection System (PBIS) A computer-based system used by USDA's Food Safety and Inspection Service. The system organizes inspection requirements, schedules inspection activities, and maintains records of findings for meat and poultry processing operations under federal inspection.

Perishable Food that is subject to decay, spoilage, or bacteria unless it is properly refrigerated or frozen.

Pesticide A substance used to kill, control, repel, or mitigate any pest. Insecticides, fungicides, rodenticides, herbicides, and germicides are all pesticides. Environmental Protection Agency (EPA) regulates pesticides under authority of the Federal Insecticide, Fungicide, and Rodenticide Act (FIFRA). In addition, under FIFRA, a substance used as a plant regulator, defoliant, desiccant is defined as a pesticide and regulated accordingly. All pesticides must be registered and carry a label approved by EPA.

Pesticide Data Program (PDP) A program initiated in 1991 by the Agricultural Marketing Service to collect pesticide residue data on selected food commodities, primarily fruits and vegetables. PDP data are used by the Environmental Protection Agency to support its dietary risk assessment process and pesticide registration process, by the Food and Drug Administration to refine sampling for enforcement of tolerances, by the Foreign Agricultural Service, to support export of U.S. commodities in a competitive global market, by the Economic Research Service to evaluate pesticide alternatives, and by the public sector to address food safety issues.

PFF Protein Fat Free.

Plasticizer Material added during the manufacturing process to increase flexibility; for example, the plasticizer ATBC (acetyl tributyl citrate), used in such DowBrands™ as Saran™ and Handiwrap™, is made from citric acid which is commonly present in citrus fruit.

Pork The meat from hogs, or domestic swine. Much of a hog is cured and made into ham, bacon, and sausage. Uncured meat is called "fresh pork."

Pork Bellies One of the major cuts of the hog carcass that, when cured, becomes bacon.

Pork Shoulder Picnic A front shoulder cut of pork which has been cured in the same manner as ham.

Postmortem Inspection As used in the meat and poultry inspection program, the phrase refers to the inspection that Food Safety and Inspection Service inspectors are required to conduct of all animal carcasses immediately after they are killed.

Potentially Hazardous Foods A food that is natural or synthetic and that requires temperature control because it is in a form capable of supporting the rapid and progressive growth of infectious or toxigenic microorganisms.

Poultry Products Inspection Act of 1957 (PPIA) P.L. 85-172 (August 28, 1957), as amended by the Wholesome Poultry Products Act of 1968 (P.L. 90-492, August 18, 1968), requires USDA to inspect all "domesticated birds" when slaughtered and processed into products for human consumption. The USDA has defined, by regulation, domesticated birds as chickens, turkeys, ducks, geese, and guineas. The primary goals of the law are to prevent adulterated or misbranded poultry and products from being sold as food, and to ensure that poultry, poultry products, ratites, and squabs are slaughtered and processed under sanitary conditions. These requirements also apply to products produced and sold within states as well as to imports, which must be inspected under equivalent foreign standards.

Poultry, Product Classes Standards for kinds and classes, and for cuts of raw poultry are discussed in 9 CFR 381.170.

PrepNet The Food Threat Preparedness Network (PrepNet) functions across Federal departments to ensure effective coordination of food security efforts throughout the Government. PrepNet is co-chaired by the Administrator of FSIS and the Director of the Center for Food Safety and Applied Nutrition at the U.S. Food and Drug Administration (FDA). Other members include the Centers for Disease Control and Prevention (CDC), the USDA Animal and Plant Health Inspection Service (APHIS), the Department of Defense (DOD), and the Environmental Protection Agency (EPA). The focus of this group is on preventive activities to protect the food supply proactively, as well as on rapid response. PrepNet, which works in conjunction with the Office of Homeland Security, is reviewing each agency's statutory authorities and conducting an assessment of needs, with plans to fill the statutory gaps. PrepNet members share scientific and laboratory assets.

Prepared Slaughtered, canned, salted, rendered, boned, cut up, or otherwise manufactured or processed.

Preservation A variety of methods used at the processing stage and at home to keep food safe from harmful bacteria and extend the storage life of food.

Product Any carcass, meat, meat by-product, or meat food product, capable of use as human food.

Prosciutto Ham An Italian-style dry cured raw ham; not smoked; often coated with pepper. Prosciutto can be eaten raw because of the way it is processed.

Public Health The science and the art of 1) preventing disease; 2) prolonging life; and organized community efforts for a) the sanitation of the environment; b) the control of communicable infections; c) the education of the individual in personal hygiene; d) the organization of medical and nursing devices for the early diagnosis and preventive treatment of disease; and e) the development of the social machinery to ensure everyone a standard of living adequate for the maintenance of health, so organizing these benefits as to enable every citizen to realize his/her birthright of health and longevity.

Pulse-Field Gel Electrophorsis (PFGE) The DNA fingerprinting method that scientists use to determine the source of bacteria in foods.

PulseNet FSIS participates in PulseNet, a national network of public health laboratories directed by the Centers for Disease Control and Prevention (CDC). PulseNet performs DNA fingerprinting on foodborne bacteria and assists in the detection of foodborne illness outbreaks and traceback to their sources, including detection of a linkage among sporadic cases. PulseNet, combined with epidemiology, has been key in enabling Federal agencies to detect and control outbreaks of foodborne illness rapidly.

Qualitative Analysis The process of testing for a substance to determine what it is and what its components are. The results are reported in terms of the presence or absence of particular components, based on the size of the sample used in the analysis, the number of samples analyzed, and the testing method. An example of qualitative analysis would be testing for the presence of the bacterial pathogen *Listeria monocytogenes* in a specific food.

Qualitative Risk Assessment A risk assessment that is based on qualitative data or giving a qualitative result. The results are often stated in an estimated range, such as "there is a moderate to high risk of a certain outcome occurring"

Quantitative Analysis The process of testing for a substance to determine how much of it there is and the numerical value of each of its components. An example would be testing for the amount or concentration of a certain chemical or microorganism, such as *E. coli*, in a food.

Quantitative Risk Assessment A risk assessment that uses modeling to determine the probability(s) of what can go wrong, how likely it is to happen, and how severe is the health impact. The results are stated in numerical terms, such as there is a 42% probability that one illness may occur from eating a serving of X food with a certain health outcome.

Rancid/Rancidity Oxidation/breakdown of fat that occurs naturally, causing undesirable smell and taste.

Ratites A family of large flightless birds that include ostriches, emus, and rheas, which U.S. farmers are beginning to domesticate and raise for food. On April 26, 2001, FSIS mandated the inspection of ratites. As a result of this action U.S. establishments slaughtering or processing ratites for distribution into commerce as human food are now subject to mandatory requirements of the Poultry Products Inspection Act and no longer pay a fee for inspection. Previously, some ratites had been inspected under the Agency's voluntary poultry inspection program, which requires establishments to pay a fee for inspection services.

Ready-to-Eat Food that is in a form that is edible without washing, cooking, or additional preparation by the food establishment or consumer and that is reasonably expected to be consumed in that form.

Recall Recalls are voluntary actions carried out by a food manufacturer or distributor in cooperation with Federal and State agencies. Products are recalled when found to be contaminated, adulterated, or misbranded. Even when the food has been previously inspected and passed by FSIS, a recall is necessary when new information becomes available indicating a possible public health issue. A recall does not include a market withdrawal or stock recovery.

Recall Classifications FSIS assesses the public health concern or hazard presented by a product being recalled, or considered for recall, whether firm-initiated or requested by FSIS, and classifies the concern as one of the following:

1. Class I. This is a health hazard situation where there is a reasonable probability that the use of the product will cause serious, adverse health consequences or death. For example, the presence of pathogens in ready-to-eat product or the presence of *E. coli* O157:H7 in ground beef.
2. Class II. This is a health hazard situation where there is a remote probability of adverse health consequences from the use of the product. For example, the presence of undeclared allergens such as milk or soy products.
3. Class III. This is a situation where the use of the product will not cause adverse health consequences. For example, the presence of undeclared generally recognized as safe non-allergen substances, such as excess water.

Recall, Depth of The level of product distribution to which the recall is to extend:

1. Consumer—This includes household consumers as well as all other levels of distribution.
2. Retail Level—The level that includes all retail sales of the recalled product.
3. User Level—This level includes hotels, restaurants, and other food service institutional consignees.
4. Wholesale Level—The distribution level between the manufacturer and the retailer. This level may not be encountered in every recall situation (i.e., the recalling firm may sell directly to the retail or consumer level).

Recall Scope This defines the amount and kind of product in question. For example, all products produced under a single HACCP plan between performance of complete cleaning and sanitation procedures (clean up to clean up).

Renderer A business engaged in the separation of fats from animal tissue by heating.

Residue Any substance, including metabolites, remaining in livestock at time of slaughter or in carcass tissues after slaughter as the result of treatment or exposure of the livestock to a pesticide, organic or inorganic compound, hormone, hormone like substance, growth promoter, antibiotic, anthelmintic, tranquilizer, or other therapeutic or prophylactic agent.

Risk Analysis The assessment and management of hazards that cause harm (risk) to human health and the communication of how those hazards can be controlled, reduced or eliminated.

Risk Assessment The process of estimating the severity and likelihood of harm to human health or the environment occurring from exposure to a substance or activity that, under plausible circumstances, can cause harm to human health or the environment.

Risk Communication Exchanges of information among risk assessors, risk managers, other stakeholders, and the public about levels of health or environmental risk, the significance and meaning of those risks, and the decisions, actions, or policies aimed at managing or controlling the risks.

Risk Management The process of evaluating policy alternatives in view of the results of risk assessment and selecting and implementing appropriate options to protect public health. Risk management determines what action to take to reduce, eliminate, or control risks. This includes establishing risk assessment policies, regulations, procedures, and a framework for decision making based on risk.

Roaster or Roasting Chicken A bird of this class is a young chicken, usually three to five months of age, of either sex, that is tender-meated with soft, pliable, smooth-textured skin and breastbone cartilage that may be somewhat less flexible than that of a broiler or fryer.

Roaster Duckling A young duck, usually under 16 weeks of age, of either sex, that is tender-meated and has a bill that is not completely hardened and a windpipe that is easily dented.

Ruminant An animal with a stomach that has four compartments, and a more complex digestive system than other mammals. Ruminants include cattle, sheep, goats, deer, bison, elk, and camels. Swine, dogs, and humans are examples of nonruminants.

Salmonella A pathogenic, diarrhea-producing bacterium that is the leading cause of human foodborne illness among intestinal pathogens. It is commonly found in raw meats, poultry, milk, and eggs, but other foods can carry it. Under 1996 rules published by USDA to control pathogens in meat and poultry, all plants that slaughter food animals and produce raw ground meat products must meet established pathogen reduction performance standards for *salmonella* contamination. The standards, which took effect in January 1998, vary by product. Plants where USDA testing indicates contamination rates are above the national standard will be required to take remedial actions.

Sample A specimen that is taken from food and tested for the purpose of identifying a foodborne pathogen or various kinds of chemical contaminants in food.

Sanitation The act of maintaining a clean condition in a food-handling situation in order to prevent disease and other potentially harmful contaminants.

Sanitation Standard Operating Procedures (SSOPs) Refers to the sanitation procedures that meat and poultry plants use, both before and during production, to prevent contamination of products. Site-specific SSOPs were required to be implemented in January 1997 by all slaughter and processing plants, under the comprehensive pathogen reduction regulations issued by USDA in July 1996.

Sanitizer Chemical or physical agents that reduce microorganism contamination levels present on inanimate environmental surfaces.

Scrapie A fatal, degenerative neurological disease of sheep and goats. Belonging to a family of diseases known as transmissible spongiform encephalopathies (TSEs), scrapie is similar to bovine spongiform encephalopathy (BSE) (mad cow), a disease of cattle. There is no scientific evidence to indicate that scrapie poses a risk to human health. The Animal and Plant Health Inspection Service conducts a Scrapie Flock Certification Program to certify scrapie-free herds and a Scrapie Eradication Program to accelerate the eradication of scrapie from the United States.

Sectioned and Formed (or Chunked and Formed) A boneless ham that is made from different cuts, tumbled or massaged and reassembled into a casing or mold and fully cooked. During this process it is usually thoroughly defatted.

"Sell By" Date A calendar date on the packaging of a food product that indicates the last day the product can be sold.

Shigella A bacterium carried only by humans and causes an estimated 300,000 cases of diarrheal illnesses in the United States per year. Poor hygiene, especially poor hand washing, causes *Shigella* to be passed easily from person to person via food. Once it is in food, it multiplies rapidly at room temperature.

Shrink Wrapping Plastic film that shrinks when heated, producing a tight, neat fit; the most popular form of grocery store meat packaging is PVC wrapping with foam trays.

Smoke Flavoring After curing, some hams are smoked. Smoke flavoring (or smoked) is a process by which ham is hung in a smokehouse and allowed to absorb smoke from smoldering fires. This gives added flavor and color to meat and slows the development of rancidity.

Sodium Nitrite Used alone or in conjunction with sodium nitrate as a color fixative in cured meat and poultry products (bologna, hot dogs, bacon). Sodium Nitrate helps prevent the growth of *Clostridium botulinum*, which can cause botulism in humans.

Souse Seasoned and chopped pork trimmings.

Squab A squab is a fledging pigeon, of either sex that has not flown yet. Effective April 26, 2001, establishments processing squabs will be inspected pursuant to the Poultry Products Inspection Act.

Standards of Identity for Food Mandatory, federally set requirements that determine what a food product must contain in order to be marketed under a certain name in interstate commerce. Mandatory standards (which differ from voluntary grades and standards applied to agricultural commodities) protect the consumer by ensuring that a label accurately reflects what is inside (for example, that "mayonnaise" is not an imitation spread, or that "ice cream" is not a similar, but different, frozen dessert).

State Inspection Program Often refers to the state-run meat and poultry inspection programs to which USDA contributes 50% of the cost. State programs (about half the states use them) must be certified by USDA to be at least equal to federal inspection requirements. However, products from state-inspected plants (most of them are relatively smaller operations) cannot be sold outside of the state. Small plants and many state officials have endorsed bills in Congress that would permit state-inspected products to be sold into interstate and foreign commerce, but large meat and poultry companies (most of them already under federal inspection) generally oppose such a change.

Steam Pasteurization A technology that uses heat to control or reduce harmful microorganisms in beef. This system passes freshly slaughtered beef carcasses that are already inspected, washed, and trimmed, through a chamber that exposes the beef to pressurized steam for approximately 6 to 8 seconds. The steam raises the surface temperature of the carcasses to 190° to 200° F (88° to 93° C). The carcasses are then cooled with a cold water spray. This process has proven to be successful in reducing pathogenic bacteria, such as *E. coli* O157:H7, *Salmonella*, and *Listeria*, without the use of any chemicals.

Stock Recovery A firm's removal or correction of product that has not been marketed or that has not left the direct control of the firm. For example, product is located on premises owned by, or under the control of, the firm, and no portion of the lot has been released for sale or use.

Sugar Cured A term that may appear on ham labels if cane or beet sugar is at least half the sweetening ingredients used and if the sugar is used in an amount sufficient to flavor and/or affect the appearance of the finished product. Most hams contain sugar in the curing mixture.

Surveillance A system of monitoring the health of the population, which is used to prevent foodborne illness outbreaks from increasing.

Survey A tool used by epidemiologists to understand the state of health of the population or to identify the source of a foodborne outbreak.

Tallow The white nearly tasteless solid rendered fat of cattle and sheep used chiefly in soap, candles, and lubricants.

Thermy! ™ The messenger, developed by FSIS, of a national consumer education campaign designed to promote the use of food thermometers.

Tolerance, pesticide residue The amount of pesticide residue allowed by regulation to remain in or on a food sold in interstate commerce. Whenever a pesticide is registered for use on a food or a feed crop, a tolerance (or exemption from the tolerance requirement) must be established. The Environmental Protection Agency establishes the tolerance levels, which are enforced by the Food and Drug Administration and verified by USDA.

Toxic Substances Control Act (TSCA) P.L. 94-469 (October 11, 1976) authorizes the Environmental Protection Agency to regulate toxic substances (any chemical that may present a risk of unreasonable harm to man or the environment). By definition, however, the Act excludes from EPA regulation under TSCA certain substances, including pesticides (as defined by and regulated under the Federal Insecticide, Fungicide, and Rodenticide Act), tobacco or tobacco products, and any food or food additive (as defined by and regulated under the Poultry Products Inspection Act, the Federal Meat Inspection Act, the Egg Products Inspection Act, or the Federal Food, Drug, and Cosmetic Act).

Toxin A poisonous substance that may be found in food.

Transmissible Spongiform Encephalopathy (TSE) A family of diseases sharing some common characteristics, including a prolonged incubation period ranging from a few months to years and progressively debilitating neurological illnesses, which are always fatal. Examples of other TSEs include scrapie (sheep and goats), chronic wasting disease (deer and elk), feline spongiform encephalopathy (cats), kuru (humans), Creutzfeldt-Jakob Disease (humans), and variant Creutzfeldt-Jakob Disease (humans).

Transparency A World Trade Organization principle stipulating that a country's policies and regulations affecting foreign trade should be clearly communicated to its trading partners. For example, out of recognition that sanitary and phytosanitary measures may (sometimes deliberately) be unclear, arbitrary, or capricious, recent international trading agreements have provisions calling on countries to notify others, in advance, about any measures that could affect trade, to explain them fully, and to provide a means for commenting on them.

United States Code (USC) The consolidation and codification of all the general and permanent laws of the United States. The U.S. Code is divided into 50 titles that represent broad subject areas. Title 7 is Agriculture. Each title is divided into chapters followed by subdivisions into parts covering specific areas. For example, 7 USC Chapter 45 Subchapter III deals with the Conservation Reserve Program. Regulations issued to administer the laws are first published in the Federal Register and then in the Code of Federal Regulations.

U.S. Condemned This term means that the livestock so identified has been inspected and found to be in a dying condition, or to be affected with any other condition or disease that would require condemnation of its carcass.

U.S. Passed for Cooking This term means that the meat or meat byproduct so identified has been inspected and passed on condition that it be cooked.

U.S. Passed for Refrigeration This term means that the meat or meat byproduct so identified has been inspected and passed on condition that it be refrigerated.

U.S. Retained This term means that the carcass, viscera, other part of carcass, or other product, or article so identified is held for further examination by an inspector to determine its disposal.

U.S. Suspect This term means that the livestock so identified is suspected of being affected with a disease or condition which may require its condemnation, in whole or in part, when slaughtered, and is subject to further examination by an inspector to determine its disposal.

USDA U.S. Department of Agriculture. The department of the Federal government responsible for enhancing the quality of life for the American people by supporting the production of Agriculture. This mission is achieved through: 1) ensuring a safe, affordable, nutritious and accessible food supply; 2) caring for agricultural, forests, and range lands; 3) supporting sound development of rural communities; 4) providing economic opportunities for farm and rural residents; 5) expanding global markets for agricultural and forest products and services; and 6) working to reduce hunger in America and throughout the world.

USDA Homeland Security Council The USDA Homeland Security Council is an internal organization designed to work in partnership with the Office of Homeland Security, the National Security Council, and other Departments. The Council is responsible for establishing overall USDA Homeland Security policy, coordinating department- wide homeland security issues, tracking USDA progress on homeland security objectives, and appointing a representative to interagency or other external groups. The Council also ensures that information, research, and resources are shared and activities are coordinated with other Federal agencies.

User Fees Any of various charges and assessments levied on a specifically delineated group that is directly subject to a particular government service, program, or activity; such fees are not levied on the general public. User fees are intended to be used solely to support that service, program, or activity. For example, about 75% of the $225 million budget of the Agricultural Marketing Service, which provides a variety of inspection and grading, market news reporting, and other services to the agricultural community, comes from user fees; the other 25% is appropriated funds. Similarly, grain inspection is paid for through user fees.

Vacuum Packaging Rigid or flexible containers from which substantially all air has been removed before sealing. Carbon dioxide or nitrogen may be introduced into the container. This process prolongs shelf life, preserves the flavors and retards bacterial growth.

Variant Creutzfeldt-Jakob Disease (vCJD) vCJD is a variant of the most commonly identified TSE in humans, classic (sporadic) Creutzfeldt-Jakob Disease (CJD). Scientific evidence supports a causal relationship between BSE outbreaks in Europe and vCJD. The disease vCJD is most likely caused by the ingestion of products contaminated with the BSE agent. There has never been a case of vCJD that did not have a history of exposure within a country where BSE was occurring. Patients with vCJD have primarily been younger and exhibit clinical signs of the disease longer than patients with classic CJD.

Veal The meat from a calf or young beef animal. Male dairy calves are used in the veal industry. Dairy cows must give birth to continue producing milk, but male dairy calves are of little or no value to the dairy farmer. A small percentage are raised to maturity and used for breeding.

Veal Calf A calf is a young bovine of either sex that has not reached puberty (up to about nine months of age), and has a maximum live weight of 750 pounds.

Veal, "Bob" About fifteen percent of veal calves are marketed up to three weeks of age or at a weight of 150 pounds. These are called Bob Calves.

Veal, "Special-Fed" The majority of veal calves are "special-fed." A veal calf is raised until about 16 to 18 weeks of age, weighing up to 450 pounds. They are raised in specially designed facilities where they can be cared for and monitored. Special, milk fed, and formula fed are the names given to nutritionally balanced milk or soy based diets fed to calves. These diets contain iron and 40 other essential nutrients, including amino acids, carbohydrates, fats, minerals and vitamins.

Verification The use of methods, procedures, or tests by supervisors, designated personnel, or regulators to determine if the food safety system based on the HACCP principles is working to control identified hazards or if modifications need to be made.

Vertical Coordination The process of ensuring that each successive stage in the production, processing, and marketing of a product is appropriately managed and interrelated to the next, so that decisions about what to produce, and how much, are communicated as efficiently as possible from the consumer to the producer. Agricultural economists believe that vertical coordination of markets is particularly important in the food industry because of its complexity, the large number of firms that participate in one or more stages, and the relative perishability of the products involved. Vertical integration is a type of vertical coordination, but the latter does not necessarily require that a single organization own or control all of the stages. For example, the use of contracts and marketing agreements between buyers and sellers, and the availability of timely, accurate price and other market information are methods for achieving vertical coordination.

Vertical Integration The integrating of successive stages of the production and marketing functions under the ownership or control of a single management organization. For example, much of the broiler industry is highly vertically integrated in that processing companies own or control the activities from production and hatching of eggs, through the growth and feeding of the chickens, to slaughter, processing, and wholesale marketing.

Veterinary Biologics Vaccines, antigens, antitoxins and other preparations made from living organisms (or genetically engineered) and intended for use in diagnosing, treating, or immunizing animals. Unlike some pharmaceutical products, such as antibiotics, most biologics leave no residues in animals. Veterinary biologics are regulated by the Animal and Plant Health Inspection Service, which licenses the facilities that produce them and conducts a program to ensure that animal vaccines and other veterinary biologics are safe, pure, potent, and effective.

Veterinary Equivalency The mutual recognition by two or more countries that each party's safety and sanitation standards for animal products, even where not identical, provide an equivalent level of protection to public and animal health. Aimed at facilitating trade, the practical effect of veterinary equivalency is that each country's individual products and facilities will not have to submit to the separate standards of importing countries and to cumbersome and costly inspections by foreign reviewers. Veterinary equivalency has been a contentious issue for the United States and European Union (EU); the two parties in 1997 agreed in principle to an agreement recognizing each other's standards.

Viscus (Plural, viscera) An internal organ of a human or animal.

Voluntary Inspection Under the authority of the Agricultural Marketing Act of 1946, as amended (7 U.S.C. 1621 et seq.), FSIS provides voluntary inspection of exotic animal products. Voluntary inspection is conducted by USDA inspectors who must have knowledge about each particular species they inspect. Under the FSIS voluntary inspection program, establishments are required to pay a fee for inspection services.

Westphalian Ham A German-style dry cured ham that is similar to Prosciutto; smoked, sometimes with juniper berries. Also called Westfalischer Schinken.

Withdrawal Time A "withdrawal" period is required from the time antibiotics are administered until it is legal to slaughter the animal. This is so residues can exit the animal's system.

World Trade Organization (WTO) The international organization established by the Uruguay Round of multilateral trade negotiations to oversee implementation of the General Agreement on Tariffs and Trade and the agreements arising from the Uruguay Round, including the Uruguay Round Agreement on Agriculture.

Yearling Turkey A fully matured turkey, usually under 15 months of age that is reasonably tender-meated and with reasonably smooth-textured skin.

Yersinia enterocolita A pathogen which causes yersiniosis, a disease characterized by diarrhea and/or vomiting. *Yersinia* is found in raw meat, seafood, dairy products, produce, and untreated water.

Young Turkey A turkey, usually under eight months of age, that is tender-meated with soft, pliable, smooth-textured skin, and breastbone cartilage that is somewhat less flexible than in a fryer-roaster turkey.

Zero Tolerance In food safety policy, a "zero tolerance" standard generally means that if a potentially dangerous substance (whether microbiological, chemical, or other) is present in or on a product, that product will be considered adulterated and unfit for human consumption. In the meat and poultry inspection program, "zero tolerance" usually refers to USDA's rule that permits no visible signs of fecal contamination (feces) on meat and poultry carcasses.

Zoonotic Diseases Diseases that under natural conditions are communicable from animals to humans. Anthrax, Brucellosis, Psittacosis, Rabies, Tuberculosis, and Tularemia are example of zoonotic diseases. Brucellosis in livestock becomes undulant fever in humans.

Health and Human Services

ACRONYMS

ACF	Administration for Children and Families
ADD	Attention Deficit Disorder
AHM	American Healthcare Management
AHRQ	Agency for Healthcare Research and Quality
AIDS	Acquired Immunodeficiency Syndrome
AMP	Average Manufacturer Price
AoA	Administration on Aging
ASAM	Assistant Secretary for Management and Administration
ASP	Average Sale Price
ASPR	Assistant Secretary for Preparedness and Response
ATSDR	Agency for Toxic Substances and Disease Registry
AWP	Average Wholesale Price
BBA	Balanced Budget Act of 1997
BIMO	Bioresearch Monitoring
CARE	Comprehensive AIDS Resources Emergency
CCDF	Child Care Development Fund
CDC	Centers for Disease Control and Prevention
CEO	Chief Executive Officer
CERT	Comprehensive Error Rate Testing
CFR	Code of Federal Regulations
CIA	Corporate Integrity Agreement
CMP	Civil Monetary Penalties
CMS	Centers for Medicare & Medicaid Services
CMSO	Center for Medicaid and State Operations
COLA	Cost of Living Adjustment
CoP	Conditions of Participation
COTS	Commercial-off-the-shelf
CPI	Consumer Price Index
CPIM	Consumer Price Index Medical
CSRS	Civil Service Retirement System
CY	Calendar Year (or Current Year in IPIA Tables)
DAEO	Designated Agency Ethics Officer
DC	District of Columbia
DECs	Deputy Ethics Counselors
DME	Durable Medical Equipment
DMEPOS	Durable Medical Equipment, Prosthetics, Orthotics, and Supplies
DMERC	Durable Medical Equipment Regional
DOJ	Department of Justice
DOL	Department of Labor
DRA	Deficit Reduction Act
DSH	Disproportionate Share Hospital
EBDP	Entitlement Benefits Due and Payable
ERRP	Error Rate Reduction Plan
e-Gov	Electronic Government
EPA	Environmental Protection Agency
FASAB	Federal Accounting Standards Advisory Board
FBWT	Fund Balance with Treasury
FCRA	Federal Credit Reform Act
FDA	Food and Drug Administration
FECA	Federal Employees' Compensation Act
FERS	Federal Employees Retirement System
FFMIA	Federal Financial Management Improvement Act of 1996
FFS	Fee-for-Service
FI	Fiscal Intermediary
FICA	Federal Insurance Contribution Act
FISMA	Federal Information Security Management Act of 2002
FMFIA	Federal Managers' Financial Integrity Act of 1982
FUL	Federal Upper Limit
FY	Fiscal Year
GAAP	Generally Accepted Accounting Principles
GAO	U.S. Government Accountability Office
GDP	Gross Domestic Product
GPRA	Government Performance and Results Act of 1993
GSA	General Services Administration
HEAL	Health Education Assistance Loans
HEW	Department of Health, Education and Welfare (now HHS)
HHS	Department of Health and Human Services
HI	Hospital Insurance
HIE	Health Information Exchange

HIGLAS	Healthcare Integrated General Ledger Accounting System
HIPAA	Health Insurance Portability and Accountability Act of 1996
HIV	Human Immunodeficiency Virus
HPMP	Hospital Payment Monitoring Program
HRSA	Health Resources and Services Administration
HSP/BIMO	Human Subject Protection/Bioresearch Monitoring
IBNR	Incurred But Not Reported
IG	Inspector General
IGT	Intergovernmental Transfers
IHS	Indian Health Service
IP	Improper Payment
IPIA	Improper Payments Information Act
IT	Information Technology
J3	Jurisdiction 3
LLP	Limited Liability Partnership
MA	Medicare Advantage
MACs	Medicare Administrative Contractors
MC	Managed Care
MEDIC	Medicare Drug Integrity Contractor
MITA	Medicaid Information Technology Architecture
MK	Non-Marketable Market Based
MMA	Medicare Prescription Drug, Improvement and Modernization Act 0f 2003
MPDB	Medicare Prescription Drug Benefit
N/A	Not Applicable
NCI	National Cancer Institute
NHIN	National Health Information Network
NIH	National Institutes of Health
NRS	National Reporting System
OACT	Office of the Actuary
OGE	Office of Government Ethics
OHRP	Office of Human Research Protection
OIG	Office of Inspector General
OMB	Office of Management and Budget
ONC	Office of the National Coordinator (for Health Information Technology)
OnePI	One Program Integrity System Integrator
OPD	Orphan Products Development
OPDIV	Operating Division
OS	Office of the Secretary
PAHPA	Pandemic and All-Hazards Preparedness Act
PAM	Payment Accuracy Measurement
PAR	Performance and Accountability Report
PARIS	Public Assistance Reporting Information System
PART	Program Assessment Rating Tool
PDP	Prescription Drug Plan
PERM	Payment Error Rate Measurement
PHIN	Public Health Information Network
PHS	Public Health Service
PL	Public Law
PMA	President's Management Agenda
PMCs	Postmarketing Study Commitments
PMS	Payment Management System
PNS	Projects of National Significance
PP&E	Property, Plant and Equipment
PPS	Prospective Payment System
PRRB	Provider Reimbursement Review Board
PSC	Program Support Center
PSCD	Payment System Calculation Discrepancies
PUR	Period Under Review
PwC	PricewaterhouseCoopers
PY	Prior Year
QIO	Quality Improvement Organization
RACs	Recovery Audit Contractors
R&D	Research and Development
RDS	Retiree Drug Subsidy
RRB	Railroad Retirement Board
RSI	Required Supplementary Information
RSSI	Required Supplementary Stewardship Information
SAMHS	A Substance Abuse and Mental Health Services Administration
SAS	Statement of Auditing Standards
SBR	Statement of Budgetary Resources
SCHIP	State Children's Health Insurance Program
SECA	Self-Employment Contribution Act of 1954
SFFAS	Statement of Federal Accounting Standards
SIU	Special Investigations Unit
SMI	Supplementary Medical Insurance
SOSI	Statement of Social Insurance
SSA	Social Security Administration
TANF	Temporary Assistance for Needy Families
Treasury	Department of the Treasury
TrOOP	True Out-of-Pocket (cost)
TROR	Treasury Report on Receivables
UFMS	Unified Financial Management System
UPL	Upper Payment Limit
US	United States
VICP	Vaccine Injury Compensation Program
WAC	Wholesale Acquisition Cost

IMMUNIZATION

Adjuvant A substance that is used in a vaccine to improve the immune response so that less vaccine is needed to produce a non-specific stimulator of the immune response.

Adult Immunizations Vaccinations that are given to people over 18 years of age (i.e., booster tetanus shots, annual influenza shots, and pneumococcal or pneumonia vaccine).

Adverse Event Any undesirable side effect that may result from a vaccination.

Agammaglobulinemia A rare disease in which the body is not able to produce immune antibodies due to a lack of gamma globulin (a type of immunoglobulin) in the blood.

Anaphylaxis An immediate and severe allergic response; a shock reaction to a substance. This can result in sudden severe breathing difficulty, severe drop in blood pressure, and/or loss of consciousness. Anaphylactic shock can kill if not treated promptly. Common causes of anaphylaxis *include* bee stings in people that are allergic to bees, ingestion of certain foods by people that are allergic to those foods, and drug reactions.

Antimicrobial Agents A general term for the drugs, chemicals, or other substances that kill microbes (tiny organisms that cause disease). Among the antimicrobial agents in use today *are* antibacterial drugs (kill bacteria); antiviral agents (kill viruses); antifungal agents (kill fungi); and antiparisitic drugs (kill parasites).

Attenuated To be weakened. An attenuated vaccine is one that has been weakened by chemicals, or other processes so that it will produce an adequate immune response without causing the serious effects of an infection.

Bacteria (*Plural for bacterium*). Tiny microorganisms that reproduce by cell division and usually have a cell wall. Bacteria can be shaped like a sphere, rod, or spiral and can be found in virtually any environment.

Booster Administration of an additional vaccination to help increase or speed the immune response to a previous vaccination.

Childhood Immunizations A series of immunizations that are given to prevent diseases that pose a threat to children. The immunizations in the United States currently *include* Hepatitis B, Diphtheria, Tetanus, Acellular Pertussis, *Haemophilus Influenzae* type b, Inactivated Polio, Pneumococcal Conjugate, Measles, Mumps, Rubella, Varicella, and Hepatitis A.

Combination Vaccine A combination of two or more vaccines (i.e., the diphtheria/tetanus/pertussis vaccine). Like the individual vaccines, combination vaccines are developed through scientific research. They are also tested through clinical trials for appropriateness, safety, and effectiveness before they are licensed and released for use by the public.

Community Immunity A concept of protecting a community against certain diseases by having a high percentage of the community's population immunized. (Sometimes referred to as "herd" immunity). Even if a few members of the community are unable to be immunized, the entire community will be indirectly protected because the disease has little opportunity for an outbreak. However, with a low percentage of population immunity, the disease would have great opportunity for an outbreak.

Examples of the key role of community immunity include being vaccinated with Hepatitis B, Diphtheria, Acellular Pertussis, *Haemophilus Influenzae* type b, Inactivated Polio, Pneumococcal Conjugate, Measles, Mumps, Rubella, Varicella, and Hepatitis A because these are diseases that can spread through person-to-person transmission. Tetanus, on the other hand, cannot be spread through person-to-person transmission. It is transmitted through skin wounds. For example, if a person steps on a nail or sustains some kind of penetrating injury from something that has been contaminated with Tetanus spores, there is significant risk for a life-threatening Tetanus infection. The level of community immunity would have no impact on this risk.

Conjugate Vaccines A vaccine in which a polysaccharide antigen is chemically joined with a protein molecule to improve the immunogenicity of the polysaccharide.

Conjunctivitis Inflammation of the eyelid. Sometimes this condition occurs independently, but it can also occur with other illnesses (i.e., measles).

Contraindication Any condition (especially of disease), which renders some particular line of treatment improper or undesirable.

Disease Sickness; illness; an interruption, or disturbance of the bodily functions or organs, which causes or threatens pain and weakness.

Encephalitis Inflammation of the brain and central nervous system.

Epidemic An outbreak of disease that spreads within a specific region and/or country.

Hib Disease Disease caused by Haemophilus Influenzae type b. Until recently, this disease was the most common cause of deadly bacterial meningitis in children. It can also cause infection of the bloodstream, pneumonia, epiglottis, and otitis media, among other conditions.

Hypogammaglobulinemia Abnormally low levels of all classes of immunoglobulins.

Immune A state of being protected against infectious diseases by either specific or non-specific mechanisms (i.e., immunization, previous natural infection, inoculation, or transfer of protective antibodies). For certain diseases, immune mothers may temporarily transfer protective antibodies to their newborns through the placenta. Protection can result from this placental transfer for up to 4-6 months.

Immune System The body's very complex system (made of many organs and cells), which defends the body against infection, disease, and foreign substances.

Immunity The condition of being immune or protected against infection, disease, and foreign substances.

Immunization A process or procedure that increases an organism's reaction to antigens, thereby, improving its ability to resist or overcome infection.

Immunoglobulins A specific protein substance, produced by plasma cells to help fight infection.

Inoculation Introduction of material (i.e., vaccine, bacteria) into the body's tissues.font>

International Importation of Disease Transmission of a disease from one country to another by way of an outside source (i.e., infected person or insect); or because a pathogen (bacterium or virus) has changed in a way that has either enabled it to avoid the immune system, or has made it stronger and more aggressive.

Live Vaccine A vaccine that contains a living, yet weakened organism or virus.

Microorganism Living organisms or living things (plants or animals) so small in size that they are only visible by the aid of a microscope.

Multi-Drug Resistance The ability to withstand many antimicrobial drugs. For example, a new strain of pathogen may be resistant to many or all of the drugs that previously worked against the disease caused by the pathogen.

Outbreak Spread of disease, which occurs in a short period of time and in a limited geographic location (i.e., neighborhood, community, school, or hospital).

Pandemic An outbreak of disease that spreads throughout the world.

Pathogen Bacteria, viruses, parasites, or fungi that have the capability to cause disease in humans.

Quarantine To isolate an individual who has or is suspected of having a disease, in order to prevent spreading the disease to others; alternatively, to isolate a person who does not have a disease during a disease outbreak, in order to prevent that person from catching the disease. Quarantine can be voluntary or ordered by public health officials in times of emergency.

SSPE, or Subacute Sclerosing Pan-Encephalitis Progressive, fatal destruction of nerve cells in the brain, which results in progressive deterioration of the personality, behavior, and intellectual abilities; seizures; coma, and death. For example, when measles or rubella virus infects brain cells, the immune system responds by attacking the virus. SSPE is the result of the immune system's activity.

Strain A specific biologic version of a microorganism (i.e., bacterium or virus). The identity of a strain is defined by its genetic makeup, or code; changing just one piece of the code produces a new strain.

Traveler's Immunizations A vaccination or series of vaccinations designed for people who travel to countries where certain diseases can be acquired. (www.cdc.gov/travel).

Vaccination Injection of a weakened or killed microorganism (bacterium or virus) given for the prevention or treatment of infectious diseases.

Vaccine A product of weakened or killed microorganism (bacterium or virus) given for the prevention or treatment of infectious diseases.

Vaccine Schedule A chart or plan of vaccinations that are recommended for specific ages and/or circumstances.

Virus A tiny parasite that grows and reproduces in living cells. Vaccines prevent illnesses caused by the following *viruses* Hepatitis B, Polio, Measles, Mumps, Rubella, Varicella, and Hepatitis A.

INSTITUTIONAL REVIEW BOARD

Abuse-Liable Pharmacological substances that have the potential for creating abusive dependency. Abuse-liable substances can include both illicit drugs (*e.g.*, heroine) and licit drugs (*e.g.*, methamphetamines).

ADAMHA Alcohol, Drug Abuse, and Mental Health Administration; reorganized in October 1992 as the Substance Abuse and Mental Health Services Administration (SAMHSA). ADAMHA included the National Institute of Mental Health (NIMH), the National Institute on Alcohol Abuse and Alcoholism (NIAAA), the National Institute on Drug Abuse (NIDA), the Office for Substance Abuse Prevention (OSAP), and the Office for Treatment Intervention (OTI). NIMH, NIAAA, and NIDA are now part of the National Institutes of Health (NIH). (*See also SAMHSA*).

Adjuvant Therapy Therapy provided to enhance the effect of an primary therapy; auxiliary therapy.

Adverse Effect An undesirable and unintended, although not necessarily unexpected, result of therapy or other intervention (*e.g.*, headache following spinal tap or intestinal bleeding associated with aspirin therapy).

Assent Agreement by an individual not competent to give legally valid informed consent (*e.g.*, a child or cognitively impaired person) to participate in research.

Assurance A formal written, binding commitment that is submitted to a federal agency in which an institution promises to comply with applicable regulations governing research with human subjects and stipulates the procedures through which compliance will be achieved.

Authorized Institutional Official An officer of an institution with the authority to speak for and legally commit the institution to adherence to the requirements of the federal regulations regarding the involvement of human subjects in biomedical and behavioral research.

Autonomy Personal capacity to consider alternatives, make choices, and act without undue influence or interference of others.

Autopsy Examination by dissection of the body of an individual to determine cause of death and other medically relevant facts.

Belmont Report A statement of basic ethical principles governing research involving human subjects issued by the National Commission for the Protection of Human Subjects in 1978.

Beneficence An ethical principle discussed in the Belmont Report that entails an obligation to protect persons from harm. The principle of beneficence can be expressed in two general *rules* (1) do not harm; and (2) protect from harm by maximizing possible benefits and minimizing possible risks of harm.

Benefit A valued or desired outcome; an advantage.

Biologic Any therapeutic serum, toxin, antitoxin, or analogous microbial product applicable to the prevention, treatment, or cure of diseases or injuries.

Blind Study Designs See Masked Study Designs; Double-Masked Design; and Single-Masked Design.

Cadaver The body of a deceased person.

Case-Control Study A study comparing persons with a given condition or disease (the cases) and persons without the condition or disease (the controls) with respect to antecedent factors. (*See also* Retrospective Studies.)

CAT Scan Abbreviation for Computerized Axial Tomography, an X-ray technique for producing images of internal bodily structures through the assistance of a computer.

Children Persons who have not attained the legal age for consent to treatment or procedures involved in the research, as determined under the applicable law of the jurisdiction in which the research will be conducted [45 CFR 46.401(a)].

CDC Centers for Disease Control and Prevention; an agency within the Public Health Service, Department of Health and Human Services.

Class I, II, III Devices Classification by the Food and Drug Administration of medical devices according to potential risks or hazards.

Clinical Trial A controlled study involving human subjects, designed to evaluate prospectively the safety and effectiveness of new drugs or devices or of behavioral interventions.

Cognitively Impaired Having either a psychiatric disorder (*e.g.,* psychosis, neurosis, personality or behavior disorders, or dementia) or a developmental disorder (*e.g.,* mental retardation) that affects cognitive or emotional functions to the extent that capacity for judgment and reasoning is significantly diminished. Others, including persons under the influence of or dependent on drugs or alcohol, those suffering from degenerative diseases affecting the brain, terminally ill patients, and persons with severely disabling physical handicaps, may also be compromised in their ability to make decisions in their best interests.

Cohort A group of subjects initially identified as having one or more characteristics in common who are followed over time. In social science research, this term may refer to any group of persons who are born at about the same time and share common historical or cultural experiences.

Compensation Payment or medical care provided to subjects injured in research; does not refer to payment (remuneration) for participation in research. (*Compare Remuneration.*)

Competence Technically, a legal term, used to denote capacity to act on one's own behalf; the ability to understand information presented, to appreciate the consequences of acting (or not acting) on that information, and to make a choice. (*See also* Incompetence, Incapacity).

Confidentiality Pertains to the treatment of information that an individual has disclosed in a relationship of trust and with the expectation that it will not be divulged to others without permission in ways that are inconsistent with the understanding of the original disclosure.

Consent See Informed Consent.

Contract An agreement; as used here, an agreement that a specific research activity will be performed at the request, and under the direction, of the agency providing the funds. Research performed under contract is more closely controlled by the agency than research performed under a grant. (*Compare Grant.*)

Control (Subjects) or *Controls* Subject(s) used for comparison who are not given a treatment under study or who do not have a given condition, background, or risk factor that is the object of study. Control conditions may be concurrent (occurring more or less simultaneously with the condition under study) or historical (preceding the condition under study). When the present condition of subjects is compared with their own condition on a prior regimen or treatment, the study is considered historically controlled.

Contraindicated Disadvantageous, perhaps dangerous; a treatment that should not be used in certain individuals or conditions due to risks (*e.g.*, a drug may be contraindicated for pregnant women and persons with high blood pressure).

Correlation Coefficient A statistical index of the degree of relationship between two variables. Values of correlation coefficients range from -1.00 through zero to +1.00. A correlation coefficient of 0.00 indicates no relationship between the variables. Correlations approaching -1.00 or +1.00 indicate strong relationships between the variables. However, causal inferences about the relationship between two variables can never be made on the basis of correlation coefficients, no matter how strong a relationship is indicated.

Cross-Over Design A type of clinical trial in which each subject experiences, at different times, both the experimental and control therapy. For example, half of the subjects might be randomly assigned first to the control group and then to the experimental intervention, while the other half would have the sequence reversed.

Data and Safety Monitoring Board A committee of scientists, physicians, statisticians, and others that collects and analyzes data during the course of a clinical trial to monitor for adverse effects and other trends (such as an indication that one treatment is significantly better than another, particularly when one arm of the trial involves a placebo control) that would warrant modification or termination of the trial or notification of subjects about new information that might affect their willingness to continue in the trial.

Dead Fetus An expelled or delivered fetus that exhibits no heartbeat, spontaneous respiratory activity, spontaneous movement of voluntary muscles, or pulsation of the umbilical cord (if still attached) [45 CFR 46.203(f)]. Generally, some organs, tissues, and cells (referred to collectively as fetal tissue) remain alive for varying periods of time after the total organism is dead.

Debriefing Giving subjects previously undisclosed information about the research project following completion of their participation in research. (Note that this usage, which occurs within the behavioral sciences, departs from standard English, in which debriefing is obtaining rather than imparting information.)

Declaration of Helsinki A code of ethics for clinical research approved by the World Medical Association in 1964 and widely adopted by medical associations in various countries. It was revised in 1975 and 1989.

Dependent Variables The outcomes that are measured in an experiment. Dependent variables are expected to change as a result of an experimental manipulation of the independent variable(s).

Descriptive Study Any study that is not truly experimental (*e.g.*, quasi-experimental studies, correlational studies, record reviews, case histories, and observational studies.)

Device (Medical) See *Medical Device.*

DHEW A federal agency U.S. Department of Health, Education and Welfare; reorganized in 1980 as the Department of Health and Human Services (DHHS) and the Department of Education.

DHHS A federal agency U.S. Department of Health and Human Services; formerly the Department of Health, Education and Welfare (DHEW).

Diagnostic (Procedure) Tests used to identify a disorder or disease in a living person.

Double-Masked Design A study design in which neither the investigators nor the subjects know the treatment group assignments of individual subjects. Sometimes referred to as "double-blind."

Drug Any chemical compound that may be used on or administered to humans as an aid in the diagnosis, treatment, cure, mitigation, or prevention of disease or other abnormal conditions.

Emancipated Minor A legal status conferred upon persons who have not yet attained the age of legal competency as defined by state law (for such purposes as consenting to medical care), but who are entitled to treatment as if they had by virtue of assuming adult responsibilities such as being self-supporting and not living at home, marriage, or procreation. (*See also Mature Minor.*)

Embryo Early stages of a developing organism, broadly used to refer to stages immediately following fertilization of an egg through implantation and very early pregnancy (*i.e.*, from conception to the eighth week of pregnancy). (*See also Fetus.*)

Epidemiology A scientific discipline that studies the factors determining the causes, frequency, and distribution of diseases in a community or given population.

Equitable Fair or just; used in the context of selection of subjects to indicate that the benefits and burdens of research are fairly distributed.

Ethics Advisory Board An interdisciplinary group that advises the Secretary, HHS, on general policy matters and on research proposals (or classes of proposals) that pose ethical problems.

Ethnographic Research Ethnography is the study of people and their culture. Ethnographic research, also called fieldwork, involves observation of and interaction with the persons or group being studied in the group's own environment, often for long periods of time. (*See also Fieldwork.*)

Expanded Availability Policy and procedure that permits individuals who have serious or life-threatening diseases for which there are no alternative therapies to have access to investigational drugs and devices that may be beneficial to them. Examples of expanded availability mechanisms include Treatment INDs, Parallel Track, and open study protocols.

Expedited Review   Review of proposed research by the IRB chair or a designated voting member or group of voting members rather than by the entire IRB. Federal rules permit expedited review for certain kinds of research involving no more than minimal risk and for minor changes in approved research.

Experimental   Term often used to denote a therapy (drug, device, procedure) that is unproven or not yet scientifically validated with respect to safety and efficacy. A procedure may be considered "experimental" without necessarily being part of a formal study (research) to evaluate its usefulness. (*See also Research.*)

Experimental Study   A true experimental study is one in which subjects are randomly assigned to groups that experience carefully controlled interventions manipulated by the experimenter according to a strict logic allowing causal inference about the effects of the interventions under investigation. (*See also Quasi-Experimental Study.*)

False Negative   When a test wrongly shows an effect or condition to be absent (*e.g.*, that a woman is not pregnant when, in fact, she is).

False Positive   When a test wrongly shows an effect or condition to be present (*e.g.*, that is woman is pregnant when, in fact, she is not).

FDA   Food and Drug Administration; an agency of the federal government established by Congress in 1912 and presently part of the Department of Health and Human Services.

Federal Policy (The)   The federal policy that provides regulations for the involvement of human subjects in research. The Policy applies to all research involving human subjects conducted, supported, or otherwise subject to regulation by any federal department or agency that takes appropriate administrative action to make the Policy applicable to such research. Currently, sixteen federal agencies have adopted the Federal Policy. (Also known as the "Common Rule.")

Fetal Material   The placenta, amniotic fluid, fetal membranes, and umbilical cord.

Fetus   The product of conception from the time of implantation until delivery. If the delivered or expelled fetus is viable, it is designated an infant [45 CFR 46.203(c)]. The term "fetus" generally refers to later phases of development; the term "embryo" is usually used for earlier phases of development. (*See also Embryo.*)

Fieldwork   Behavioral, social, or anthropological research involving the study of persons or groups in their own environment and without manipulation for research purposes (distinguished from laboratory or controlled settings). (*See also Ethnographic Research*).

510(K) Device   A medical device that is considered substantially equivalent to a device that was or is being legally marketed. A sponsor planning to market such a device must submit notification to the FDA 90 days in advance of placing the device on the market. If the FDA concurs with the sponsor, the device may then be marketed. 510(k) is the section of the Food, Drug and Cosmetic Act that describes premarket notification; hence the designation "510(k) device."

Full Board Review   Review of proposed research at a convened meeting at which a majority of the membership of the IRB are present, including at least one member whose primary concerns are in nonscientific areas. For the research to be approved, it must receive the approval of a majority of those members present at the meeting.

Gene Therapy   The treatment of genetic disease accomplished by altering the genetic structure of either somatic (nonreproductive) or germline (reproductive) cells.

General Assurance   Obsolete term, previously used to denote an institutional assurance covering multiple research projects. (*See also Assurance.*)

General Controls   Certain FDA statutory provisions designed to control the safety of marketed drugs and devices. The general controls include provisions on adulteration, misbranding, banned devices, good manufacturing practices, notification and record keeping, and other sections of the Medical Device Amendments to the Food, Drug and Cosmetic Act [21 U.S. Code 360(c) (Food, Drug and Cosmetic Act 513)].

Genetic Screening   Tests to identify persons who have an inherited predisposition to a certain phenotype or who are at risk of producing offspring with inherited diseases or disorders.

Genotype   The genetic constitution of an individual.

Grant   Financial support provided for research study designed and proposed by the principal investigator(s). The granting agency exercises no direct control over the conduct of approved research supported by a grant. (*Compare Contract.*)

Guardian   An individual who is authorized under applicable state or local law to give permission on behalf of a child to general medical care [45 CFR 46.402(3)].

Helsinki Declaration   See   *Declaration of Helsinki.*

Historical Controls   Control subjects (followed at some time in the past or for whom data are available through records) who are used for comparison with subjects being treated concurrently. The study is considered historically controlled when the present condition of subjects is compared with their own condition on a prior regimen or treatment.

Human in Vitro Fertilization Any fertilization involving human sperm and ova that occurs outside the human body.

Human Subjects Individuals whose physiologic or behavioral characteristics and responses are the object of study in a research project. Under the federal regulations, human subjects are defined *as* living individual(s) about whom an investigator conducting research *obtains* (1) data through intervention or interaction with the individual; or (2) identifiable private information.

IDE See Investigational Device Exemptions.

Incapacity Refers to a person's mental status and means inability to understand information presented, to appreciate the consequences of acting (or not acting) on that information, and to make a choice. Often used as a synonym for incompetence. (*See also Incompetence*).

Incompetence Technically, a legal term meaning inability to manage one's own affairs. Often used as a synonym for incapacity. (*See also Incapacity.*)

IND See Investigational New Drug.

Independent Variables The conditions of an experiment that are systematically manipulated by the investigator.

Informed Consent A person's voluntary agreement, based upon adequate knowledge and understanding of relevant information, to participate in research or to undergo a diagnostic, therapeutic, or preventive procedure. In giving informed consent, subjects may not waive or appear to waive any of their legal rights, or release or appear to release the investigator, the sponsor, the institution or agents thereof from liability for negligence [Federal Policy—116; 21 CFR 50.20 and 50.25].

Institution (1) Any public or private entity or agency (including federal, state, and local agencies). (2) A residential facility that provides food, shelter, and professional services (including treatment, skilled nursing, intermediate or long-term care, and custodial or residential care). Examples include general, mental, or chronic disease hospitals; inpatient community mental health centers; halfway houses and nursing homes; alcohol and drug addiction treatment centers; homes for the aged or dependent, residential schools for the mentally or physically handicapped; and homes for dependent and neglected children.

Institutional Review Board A specially constituted review body established or designated by an entity to protect the welfare of human subjects recruited to participate in biomedical or behavioral research.

Institutionalized Confined, either voluntarily or involuntarily (*e.g.*, a hospital, prison, or nursing home).

Institutionalized Cognitively Impaired Persons who are confined, either voluntarily or involuntarily, in a facility for the care of the mentally or otherwise disabled (*e.g.*, a psychiatric hospital, home, or school for the retarded).

Investigational Device Exemptions (IDE) Exemptions from certain regulations found in the Medical Device Amendments that allow shipment of unapproved devices for use in clinical investigations [21 CFR 812.20].

Investigational New Drug or Device A drug or device permitted by FDA to be tested in humans but not yet determined to be safe and effective for a particular use in the general population and not yet licensed for marketing.

Investigator In clinical trials, an individual who actually conducts an investigation [21 CFR 312.3]. Any interventions (*e.g.*, drugs) involved in the study are administered to subjects under the immediate direction of the investigator. (*See also Principal Investigator.*)

In Vitro Literally, "in glass" or "test tube"; used to refer to processes that are carried out outside the living body, usually in the laboratory, as distinguished from in vivo.

In Vivo Literally, "in the living body"; processes, such as the absorption of a drug by the human body, carried out in the living body rather than in a laboratory (in vitro).

IRB See Institutional Review Board.

Justice An ethical principle discussed in the Belmont Report requiring fairness in distribution of burdens and benefits; often expressed in terms of treating persons of similar circumstances or characteristics similarly.

Lactation The period of time during which a woman is providing her breast milk to an infant or child.

Legally Authorized Representative A person authorized either by statute or by court appointment to make decisions on behalf of another person. In human subjects research, an individual or judicial or other body authorized under applicable law to consent on behalf of a prospective subject to the subject's participation in the procedure(s) involved in the research.

LOD Score An expression of the probability that a gene and a marker are linked.

Longitudinal Study A study designed to follow subjects forward through time.

Masked Study Designs Study designs comparing two or more interventions in which either the investigators, the subjects, or some combination thereof do not know the treatment group assignments of individual subjects. Sometimes called "blind" study designs. (*See also* Double-Masked Design; Single-Masked Design).

Mature Minor Someone who has not reached adulthood (as defined by state law) but who may be treated as an adult for certain purposes (*e.g.*, consenting to medical care). Note that a mature minor is not necessarily an emancipated minor. (*See* **also** *Emancipated Minor*).

Medical Device A diagnostic or therapeutic article that does not achieve any of its principal intended purpose through chemical action within or on the body. Such devices include diagnostic test kits, crutches, electrodes, pacemakers, arterial grafts, intraocular lenses, and orthopedic pins or other orthopedic equipment.

Medical Device Amendments (MDA) Amendments to the Federal Food, Drug and Cosmetic Act passed in 1976 to regulate the distribution of medical devices and diagnostic products.

Mentally Disabled *See Cognitively Impaired.*

Metabolism (of a Drug) The manner in which a drug is acted upon (taken up, converted to other substances, and excreted) by various organs of the body.

Minimal Risk A risk is minimal where the probability and magnitude of harm or discomfort anticipated in the proposed research are not greater, in and of themselves, than those ordinarily encountered in daily life or during the performance of routine physical or psychological examinations or tests. For example, the risk of drawing a small amount of blood from a healthy individual for research purposes is no greater than the risk of doing so as part of routine physical examination.

The definition of minimal risk for research involving prisoners differs somewhat from that given for noninstitutionalized adults. [*See 45 CFR 46.303(d) and Guidebook Chapter 6, Section E, "Prisoners."*]

Monitoring The collection and analysis of data as the project progresses to assure the appropriateness of the research, its design and subject protections.

National Commission National Commission for the Protection of Human Subjects of Biomedical and Behavioral Research. An interdisciplinary advisory body, established by Congressional legislation in 1974, which was in existence until 1978, and which issued a series of reports and recommendations on ethical issues in research and medicine, many of which are now embodied in federal regulations.

NDA *See New Drug Application.*

New Drug Application Request for FDA approval to market a new drug.

NIAAA National Institute on Alcohol Abuse and Alcoholism; an institute in NIH.

NIDA National Institute on Drug Abuse; an institute in NIH.

NIH National Institutes of **Health** a federal agency within the Public Health Service, DHHS, comprising 21 institutes and centers. It is responsible for carrying out and supporting biomedical and behavioral research.

NIMH National Institute of Mental Health; an institute in NIH.

Nonaffiliated Member Member of an Institutional Review Board who has no ties to the parent institution, its staff, or faculty. This individual is usually from the local community (*e.g.*, minister, business person, attorney, teacher, homemaker).

Nonsignificant Risk Device An investigational medical device that does not present significant risk to the patient. (*See also Significant Risk Device.*)

Nontherapeutic Research Research that has no likelihood or intent of producing a diagnostic, preventive, or therapeutic benefit to the current subjects, although it may benefit subjects with a similar condition in the future.

Nonviable Fetus An expelled or delivered fetus which, although it is living, cannot possibly survive to the point of sustaining life independently, even with the support of available medical therapy [45 CFR 46.203 (d) and (e)]. Although it may be presumed that an expelled or delivered fetus is nonviable at a gestational age less than 20 weeks and weight less than 500 grams [Federal Register 40 (August 8, 1975): 33552], a specific determination as to viability must be made by a physician in each instance. (*See also Viable Infant.*)

Normal Volunteers Volunteer subjects used to study normal physiology and behavior or who do not have the condition under study in a particular protocol, used as comparisons with subjects who do have the condition. "Normal" may not mean normal in all respects. For example, patients with broken legs (if not on medication that will affect the results) may serve as normal volunteers in studies of metabolism, cognitive development, and the like. Similarly, patients with heart disease but without diabetes may be the "normals" in a study of diabetes complicated by heart disease.

Null Hypothesis The proposition, to be tested statistically, that the experimental intervention has "no effect," meaning that the treatment and control groups will not differ as a result of the intervention. Investigators usually hope that the data will demonstrate some effect from the intervention, thereby allowing the investigator to reject the null hypothesis.

Nuremberg Code A code of research ethics developed during the trials of Nazi war criminals following World War II and widely adopted as a standard during the 1950s and 1960s for protecting human subjects.

Office for Protection from Research Risks (OPRR) The office within the National Institutes of Health, an agency of the Public Health Service, Department of Health and Human Services, responsible for implementing DHHS regulations (45 CFR Part 46) governing research involving human subjects.

Open Design An experimental design in which both the investigator(s) and the subjects know the treatment group(s) to which subjects are assigned.

OPRR See Office for Protection from Research Risks.

Paternalism Making decisions for others against or apart from their wishes with the intent of doing them good.

Permission The agreement of parent(s) or guardian to the participation of their child or ward in research [45 CFR 46.402(c)].

Pharmacology The scientific discipline that studies the action of drugs on living systems (animals or human beings).

Phase 1, 2, 3, 4 Drug Trials Different stages of testing drugs in humans, from first application in humans (Phase 1) through limited and broad clinical tests (Phase 3), to postmarketing studies (Phase 4).

- *Phase 1 Drug Trial* Phase 1 trials include the initial introduction of an investigational new drug into humans. These studies are typically conducted with healthy volunteers; sometimes, where the drug is intended for use in patients with a particular disease, however, such patients may participate as subjects. Phase 1 trials are designed to determine the metabolic and pharmacological actions of the drug in humans, the side effects associated with increasing doses (to establish a safe dose range), and, if possible, to gain early evidence of effectiveness; they are typically closely monitored. The ultimate goal of Phase 1 trials is to obtain sufficient information about the drug's pharmacokinetics and pharmacological effects to permit the design of well-controlled, sufficiently valid Phase 2 studies. Other examples of Phase 1 studies include studies of drug metabolism, structure-activity relationships, and mechanisms of actions in humans, as well as studies in which investigational drugs are used as research tools to explore biological phenomena or disease processes. The total number of subjects involved in Phase 1 investigations is generally in the range of 20-80.

- *Phase 2 Drug Trial* Phase 2 trials include controlled clinical studies conducted to evaluate the drug's effectiveness for a particular indication in patients with the disease or condition under study, and to determine the common short-term side effects and risks associated with the drug. These studies are typically well-controlled, closely monitored, and conducted with a relatively small number of patients, usually involving no more than several hundred subjects.

- *Phase 3 Drug Trial* Phase 3 trials involve the administration of a new drug to a larger number of patients in different clinical settings to determine its safety, efficacy, and appropriate dosage. They are performed after preliminary evidence of effectiveness has been obtained, and are intended to gather necessary additional information about effectiveness and safety for evaluating the overall benefit-risk relationship of the drug, and to provide and adequate basis for physician labeling. In Phase 3 studies, the drug is used the way it would be administered when marketed. When these studies are completed and the sponsor believes that the drug is safe and effective under specific conditions, the sponsor applies to the FDA for approval to market the drug. Phase 3 trials usually involve several hundred to several thousand patient-subjects.

- *Phase 4 Drug Trial* Concurrent with marketing approval, FDA may seek agreement from the sponsor to conduct certain postmarketing (Phase 4) studies to delineate additional information about the drug's risks, benefits, and optimal use. These studies could include, but would not be limited to, studying different doses or schedules of administration than were used in Phase 2 studies, use of the drug in other patient populations or other stages of the disease, or use of the drug over a longer period of time [21 CFR—312.85].

Phenotype The physical manifestation of a gene function.

PHS Public Health Service. Part of the U.S. Department of Health and Human Services, it includes FDA, NIH, CDC, SAMHSA, and HRSA.

Placebo A chemically inert substance given in the guise of medicine for its psychologically suggestive effect; used in controlled clinical trials to determine whether improvement and side effects may reflect imagination or anticipation rather than actual power of a drug.

Postamendments Devices Medical devices marketed after enactment of the 1976 Medical Device Amendments.

Preamendments Devices Medical devices marketed before enactment of the 1976 Medical Device Amendments.

Preclinical Investigations Laboratory and animal studies designed to test the mechanisms, safety, and efficacy of an intervention prior to its applications to humans.

Predicate Devices Currently legally marketed devices to which new devices may be found substantially equivalent under the 510(k) process.

Pregnancy The period of time from confirmation of implantation of a fertilized egg within the uterus until the fetus has entirely left the uterus (*i.e.*, has been delivered). Implantation is confirmed through a presumptive sign of pregnancy such as missed menses or a positive pregnancy test [45 CFR 46.203(b)]. This "confirmation" may be in error, but, for research purposes, investigators would presume that a living fetus was present until evidence to the contrary was clear. Although fertilization occurs a week or more before implantation, the current inability to detect the fertilization event or the presence of a newly fertilized egg makes a definition of pregnancy based on implantation necessary.

Premarket Approval Process of scientific and regulatory review by the FDA to ensure the safety and effectiveness of Class III devices.

President's Commission President's Commission for the Study of Ethical Problems in Medicine and Biomedical and Behavioral Research. An interdisciplinary advisory group, established by congressional legislation in 1978, which was in existence until 1983, and which issued reports on ethical problems in health care and in research involving human subjects.

Principal Investigator The scientist or scholar with primary responsibility for the design and conduct of a research project. (See *also* Investigator).

Prisoner An individual involuntarily confined in a penal institution, including *persons* (1) sentenced under a criminal or civil statue; (2) detained pending arraignment, trial, or sentencing; and (3) detained in other facilities (*e.g.*, for drug detoxification or treatment of alcoholism) under statutes or commitment procedures providing such alternatives to criminal prosecution or incarceration in a penal institution [45 CFR 46.303(c)].

Privacy Control over the extent, timing, and circumstances of sharing oneself (physically, behaviorally, or intellectually) with others.

Proband The person whose case serves as the stimulus for the study of other members of the family to identify the possible genetic factors involved in a given disease, condition, or characteristic.

Prophylactic Preventive or protective; a drug, vaccine, regimen, or device designed to prevent, or provide protection against, a given disease or disorder.

Prospective Studies Studies designed to observe outcomes or events that occur subsequent to the identification of the group of subjects to be studied. Prospective studies need not involve manipulation or intervention but may be purely observational or involve only the collection of data.

Protocol The formal design or plan of an experiment or research activity; specifically, the plan submitted to an IRB for review and to an agency for research support. The protocol includes a description of the research design or methodology to be employed, the eligibility requirements for prospective subjects and controls, the treatment regimen(s), and the proposed methods of analysis that will be performed on the collected data.

Purity The relative absence of extraneous matter in a drug or vaccine that may or may not be harmful to the recipient or deleterious to the product.

Quasi-Experimental Study A study that is similar to a true experimental study except that it lacks random assignments of subjects to treatment groups. (*See also Experimental Study*.)

Radioactive Drug Any substance defined as a drug in 201(b)(1) of the Federal Food, Drug and Cosmetic Act that exhibits spontaneous disintegration of unstable nuclei with the emission of nuclear particles or photons [21 CFR 310.3(n)]. Included are any non-radioactive reagent kit or nuclide generator that is intended to be used in the preparation of a radioactive drug and "radioactive biological products," as defined in 21 CFR 600.3(ee). Drugs such as carbon-containing compounds or potassium-containing salts containing trace quantities of naturally occurring radionuclides are not considered radioactive drugs.

Radioactive Drug Research Committee (RDRC) An institutional committee responsible for the use of radioactive drugs in human subjects for research purposes. Research involving human subjects that proposes to use radioactive drugs must meet various FDA requirements, including limitations on the pharmacological dose and the radiation dose. Furthermore, the exposure to radiation must be justified by the quality of the study and the importance of the information it seeks to obtain. The committee is also responsible for continuing review of the drug use to ensure that the research continues to comply with FDA requirements, including reporting obligations. The committee must include experts in nuclear medicine and the use of radioactive drugs, as well as other medical and scientific members [21 CFR 36.1].

Radiopaque Contrast Agents Materials that stop or attenuate radiation that is passed through the body, creating an outline on film of the organ(s) being examined. Contrast agents, sometimes called "dyes," do not contain radioisotopes. When such agents are used, exposure to radiation results only from the X-ray equipment used in the examination. The chemical structure of radiopaque contrast agents can produce a variety of adverse reactions, some of which may be severe—and possibly life-threatening—in certain individuals.

Radiopharmaceuticals Drugs (compounds or materials) that may be labeled or tagged with a radioisotope. These materials are largely physiological or subpharmacological in action, and, in many cases, function much like materials found in the body. The principal risk associated with these materials is the consequent radiation exposure to the body or to specific organ systems when they are injected into the body.

Random, Random Assignment, Randomization, Randomized Assignment of subjects to different treatments, interventions, or conditions according to chance rather than systematically (*e.g.*, as dictated by the standard or usual response to their condition, history, or prognosis, or according to demographic characteristics). Random assignment of subjects to conditions is an essential element of experimental research because it makes more likely the probability that differences observed between subject groups are the result of the experimental intervention.

Recombinant Dna Technology "The ability to chop up DNA, the stuff of which genes are made, and move the pieces, [which] permits the direct examination of the human genome," and the identification of the genetic components of a wide variety of disorders [Holtzman (1989), p. 1]. Recombinant DNA technology is also used to develop diagnostic screens and tests, as well as drugs and biologics for treating diseases with genetic components. See Guidebook Chapter 5, Section H, "Human Genetic Research."

REM Acronym for Roentgen Equivalent in Man; the unit of measurement for a dose of an ionizing radiation that produces the same biological effect as a unit of absorbed does (1 rad) of ordinary X-rays. One millirem is equal to 1/1000 of a rem.

Remission A period in which the signs and symptoms of a disease are diminished or in abeyance. The term "remission" is used when one cannot say with confidence that the disease has been cured.

Remuneration Payment for participation in research. (*NOTE* It is wise to confine use of the term "compensation" to payment or provision of care for research-related injuries). (*Compare Compensation*.)

Research A systematic investigation (*i.e.*, the gathering and analysis of information) designed to develop or contribute to generalizable knowledge.

Respect for Persons An ethical principle discussed in the Belmont Report requiring that individual autonomy be respected and that persons with diminished autonomy be protected.

Retrospective Studies Research conducted by reviewing records from the past (*e.g.*, birth and death certificates, medical records, school records, or employment records) or by obtaining information about past events elicited through interviews or surveys. Case control studies are an example of this type of research.

Review (of Research) The concurrent oversight of research on a periodic basis by an IRB. In addition to the at least annual reviews mandated by the federal regulations, reviews may, if deemed appropriate, also be conducted on a continuous or periodic basis.

Risk The probability of harm or injury (physical, psychological, social, or economic) occurring as a result of participation in a research study. Both the probability and magnitude of possible harm may vary from minimal to significant. Federal regulations define only "minimal risk." (*See also Minimal Risk*.)

SAMHSA Substance Abuse and Mental Health Services Administration; includes the Center for Substance Abuse Prevention, the Center for Substance Abuse Treatment and the Center on Mental Health Services. Previously the Alcohol, Drug Abuse, and Mental Health Administration (ADAMHA). (*See also ADAMHA*.)

Scientific Review Group A group of highly regarded experts in a given field, convened by NIH to advise NIH on the scientific merit of applications for research grants and contracts. Scientific review groups are also required to review the ethical aspects of proposed involvement of human subjects. Various kinds of scientific review groups exist, and are known by different names in different institutes of the NIH (*e.g.*, Study Sections, Initial Review Groups, Contract Review Committees, or Technical Evaluation Committees).

Secretary A U.S. Cabinet Officer. In the context of DHHS-conducted or -supported research, usually refers to the Secretary of Health and Human Services.

Significant Risk Device An investigational medical device that presents a potential for serious risk to the health, safety, or welfare of the subject.

Single-Masked Design Typically, a study design in which the investigator, but not the subject, knows the identity of the treatment assignment. Occasionally the subject, but not the investigator, knows the assignment. Sometimes called "single-blind design."

Site Visit A visit by agency officials, representatives, or consultants to the location of a research activity to assess the adequacy of IRB protection of human subjects or the capability of personnel to conduct the research.

Social Experimentation Systematic manipulation of, or experimentation in, social or economic systems; used in planning public policy.

Sponsor (of a Drug Trial) A person or entity that initiates a clinical investigation of a drug - usually the drug manufacturer or research institution that developed the drug. The sponsor does not actually conduct the investigation, but rather distributes the new drug to investigators and physicians for clinical trials. The drug is administered to subjects under the immediate direction of an investigator who is not also a sponsor. A clinical investigator may, however, serve as a sponsor-investigator. The sponsor assumes responsibility for investigating the new drug, including responsibility for compliance with applicable laws and regulations. The sponsor, for example, is responsible for obtaining FDA approval to conduct a trial and for reporting the results of the trial to the FDA.

Sponsor-Investigator An individual who both initiates and actually conducts, alone or with others, a clinical investigation. Corporations, agencies, or other institutions do not qualify as sponsor-investigators.

Statistical Significance A determination of the probability of obtaining the particular distribution of the data on the assumption that the null hypothesis is true. Or, more simply put, the probability of coming to a false positive conclusion. [*See McLarty (1987), p. 2.*] If the probability is less than or equal to a predetermined value (*e.g.*, 0.05 or 0.01), then the null hypothesis is rejected at that significance level (0.05 or 0.01).

Sterility (1) The absence of viable contaminating microorganisms; aseptic state. (2) The inability to procreate; the inability to conceive or induce conception.

Study Section See Scientific Review Group.

Subjects (Human) See Human Subjects.

Surveys Studies designed to obtain information from a large number of respondents through written questionnaires, telephone interviews, door-to-door canvassing, or similar procedures.

Therapeutic Intent The research physician's intent to provide some benefit to improving a subject's condition (*e.g.*, prolongation of life, shrinkage of tumor, or improved quality of life, even though cure or dramatic improvement cannot necessarily be effected). This term is sometimes associated with Phase 1 drug studies in which potentially toxic drugs are given to an individual with the hope of inducing some improvement in the patient's condition as well as assessing the safety and pharmacology of a drug.

Therapy Treatment intended and expected to alleviate a disease or disorder.

Uniform Anatomical Gift Act Legislation adopted by all 50 States and the District of Columbia that indicates procedures for donation of all or part of a decedent's body for such activities as medical education, scientific research, and organ transplantation.

Vaccine A biologic product generally made from an infectious agent or its components—a virus, bacterium, or other microorganism—that is killed (inactive) or live-attenuated (active, although weakened). Vaccines may also be biochemically synthesized or made through recombinant DNA techniques.

Variable (Noun) An element or factor that the research is designed to study, either as an experimental intervention or a possible outcome (or factor affecting the outcome) of that intervention.

Viable Infant When referring to a delivered or expelled fetus, the term "viable infant" means likely to survive to the point of sustaining life independently, given the benefit of available medical therapy [45 CFR 46.203(d)]. This judgment is made by a physician. In accordance with DHHS regulations, the Secretary, HHS, may publish guidelines to assist in the determination of viability. Such guidelines were published in 1975, and specify an estimated gestational age of 20 weeks or more and a body weight of 500 grams or more as indices of fetal viability [Federal Register 40 (August 8, 1975): 33552]. These indices depend on the state of present technology and may be revised periodically. (*See also Nonviable Fetus.*)

Voluntary Free of coercion, duress, or undue inducement. Used in the research context to refer to a subject's decision to participate (or to continue to participate) in a research activity.

MEDICARE HEARINGS AND APPEALS (OMHA)

Adjudicator The person who makes the decision in a beneficiary's case. There is an adjudicator at each of the five levels of Medicare appeals. In OMHA, the adjudicator of an appeal is the Administrative Law Judge (ALJ).

Adjusted annually A change that occurs on a yearly basis.

Administrative Law Judge (ALJ) An Administrative Law Judge (ALJ) is an independent decision-maker who is authorized to preside over hearings and render legally binding decisions. In the Medicare appeals process the ALJ is the adjudicator at OMHA, the third level of the claim appeals process. At OMHA, the ALJ presides over the hearing by administering oaths, taking testimony, ruling on questions of evidence and making factual and legal determinations. In issuing his or her decision, the OMHA ALJ is bound by the Administrative Procedure Act, Medicare statutes and regulations and national coverage determinations issued by Centers for Medicare and Medicaid Services (CMS).

Advance Beneficiary Notice (ABN) An Advance Beneficiary Notice (ABN) is a letter officially informing you that your health care provider or supplier believes that Medicare will not cover an item(s) and/or service(s). The ABN helps you make an informed choice about whether or not you want to receive the item(s) and/or service(s) knowing that you may be responsible for payment. Remember, if you decide to receive the item(s) and/or services, you may be financially responsible for those charges.

ALJ hearing An ALJ hearing is an official proceeding for an administrative appeal. For Medicare, an ALJ hearing takes place at the third level of appeal where the ALJ hears arguments and takes testimony to determine if a medical service or item is covered by Medicare or an individual is entitled to Medicare benefits. In the Medicare appeals process, an ALJ hearing can only take place after the first two levels of appeals have been completed.

Amount in Controversy The threshold dollar amount that is required for an ALJ hearing at Level 3 of the Medicare appeals process, which is $120 for 2008. The threshold dollar amount for subsequent court review at Level 5 of the Medicare appeals process is $1,130.

Appeal For Medicare purposes, an appeal is the process used when a party, e.g., beneficiary, provider or supplier, disagrees with a decision to deny or stop payment for health care items or services or a decision denying an individual's enrollment in the Medicare program.

Appellant A beneficiary, provider, supplier or other entity that submits an appeal of a particular Medicare initial determination. Designation as an appellant does not in itself convey standing to appeal the determination in question.

Appointed Representative An individual a party selects to assist in pursuing a Medicare claim or appeal. An appointed representative can include the beneficiary's family member, friend, lawyer or the provider or supplier that furnished the Medicare items or services.

Authorized Representative An individual authorized under State or other applicable law to act on behalf of a beneficiary or other party involved in the appeal. An authorized representative has all the rights and responsibilities of a beneficiary or party, as applicable, throughout the appeals process. Examples of an "authorized representative" include a court-appointed guardian, an individual with durable power of attorney, and an individual designated under a State health care consent statute.

Beneficiary An individual who is enrolled to receive benefits under the Medicare program. See 42 C.F.R. 405.902.

Carrier A private company that has a contract with the Centers for Medicare and Medicaid Services (CMS) to determine and make Medicare payment for Part B items and services. As part of the mandatory Medicare Contract Reform, CMS is currently replacing Medicare Carriers with Medicare Administrative Contractors. (See also "Medicare Administrative Contractors.")

Centers for Medicare and Medicaid Services (CMS) The federal agency within the Department of Health and Human Services (DHHS) that administers the Medicare program. Among its responsibilities, CMS oversees the Medicare Administrative Contractors involved in the processing and review of Medicare claims at the first and second level of appeals.

Chief Administrative Law Judge The Chief Administrative Law Judge is the head official of OMHA and oversees all OMHA operations and personnel.

Claim A claim is a request for payment for items and services billed under the Medicare program.

Coverage Determination A decision by a Medicare Part D plan sponsor not to provide or pay for a Part D drug that the enrollee believes may be covered by the plan. See 42 C.F.R. 423.566.

Departmental Appeals Board (DAB) A Board established in the Office of the Secretary of DHHS whose members act in panels to provide impartial review of disputed decisions made by operating components of the Department or by ALJs. The Medicare Appeals Council is a division of the DAB. Note, this is the regulatory definition. See 42 C.F.R. 400.202.

Enrollee An individual who is eligible and has elected or has enrolled in a Medicare Part D Prescription Drug plan.

Entitlement Appeals The process pertaining to an individual's application to enroll in the Medicare program and receive Medicare benefits.

Evidence Information presented throughout the appeals process for the purpose of establishing the truth or falsity of an alleged matter of fact. This may include the testimony of witnesses, records, documents or objects.

Fiscal Intermediary A private company that has a contract with CMS to determine and make Medicare payment for Part A benefits and certain Part B benefits. As part of the mandatory Medicare Contract Reform, CMS is currently replacing Fiscal Intermediaries with Medicare Administrative Contractors. (See Medicare Administrative Contractors). See 42 C.F.R. § 405.902.

Hearing See "ALJ Hearing."

Health Insurance Claims Number (HICN) The number assigned by the Social Security Administration to an individual identifying him/her as a Medicare beneficiary. This number is shown on the beneficiary's insurance card and is used in processing Medicare claims for that beneficiary.

Hospital Insurance Benefits (Medicare Part A) The Hospital Insurance benefits help pay for inpatient hospital services, post hospital skilled nursing facility care, home health services and hospice care.

Income-Related Monthly Adjustment Amount (IRMAA) The additional amount of premium that a beneficiary will pay for Medicare Part B coverage based on income above a certain threshold. The income-related monthly adjustment amount is based on a beneficiary's modified adjusted gross income.

Initial Determination (Entitlement Appeals) A determination made by the Social Security Administration (SSA) pertaining to an individual's application for Medicare benefits and/or entitlement to receive Medicare benefits under Part A and/or Part B of the Medicare program.

Initial Determination (Claim Appeals) Following a receipt of a claim for payment, a determination issued by the Medicare Administrative Contractor indicating whether the item or service is covered and otherwise reimbursable under the Medicare program, and the amount of payment due.

Managing Administrative Law Judge (MALJ) In OHMA, a Managing Administrative Law Judge (MALJ) is responsible for and leads a field office. The MALJ report to the Chief Administrative Law Judge and supervises the Administrative Law Judges within his or her respective field office.

Medicare Advantage Plan (MA Plan) Health benefits coverage offered under a policy or contract by an MS organization that includes a specific set of health benefits offered at a uniform premium and uniform level of cost-sharing to all Medicare beneficiaries residing in the service area of the MA plan.

Medicare Advantage Program (Part C) The program under Part C which provides all Part A and Part B services as well as additional services in some cases through Medicare Advantage health plans.

Medicare Administrative Contractor The entity contracted with CMS that is responsible for the receipt, processing and payment of Medicare service claims under the Original Medicare Part A and Part B programs. In addition to providing claims processing, these contractors will be the primary contact for physicians and perform functions related *to* Appeals, Provider Outreach and Education, Financial Management, Provider Enrollment, Reimbursement, Payment Safeguards, and Information Systems Security. As part of the Medicare Contract Reform, CMS is currently replacing the fiscal intermediaries and carriers with Medicare Administrative Contractors.

Medicare Appeals Council A division within HHS Departmental Appeals Board that reviews and hears cases following an Administrative Law Judge decision pertaining to Medicare claims and entitlement appeals.

Medicare Prescription Drug Plan A prescription drug plan offering qualified prescription drug coverage, or a cost plan offering qualified prescription drug coverage. See 42 C.F.R. § 423.4.

Medicare Prescription Drug Program (Part D) The program under Part D of the Medicare statute that helps pay for medications doctors prescribe for treatment. Beneficiaries obtain prescription drugs through Medicare Prescription Drug Plans

Medicare Prescription Drug, Improvement, and Modernization Act of 2003 (MMA) This 2003 legislation provided Medicare eligible seniors and individuals with disabilities with a prescription drug benefit. The MMA also authorized OMHA's creation.

Notice of Administrative Law Judge (ALJ) decision A document that notifies the parties of the written decision of the ALJ. The notice of decision gives findings of fact, conclusions of law and the reasons for the decision. The notice of decision also provides information about the right to appeal the decision to the MAC. See 42 C.F.R. 405.1046.

On-the-Record An appeal in which the issues are decided based solely on the documentary evidence and without an oral hearing. In OMHA, a party can waive its right to an oral hearing and request the case be decided on- the- record. An ALJ may decide a case on-the-record when all parties indicate in writing that they do not wish to appear at an oral hearing. The ALJ may also decide a case on-the-record when the documentary evidence supports a finding fully favorable to the appellant(s). See 42 C.F.R. 405.1038.

Organization Determination A determination regarding the benefits an enrollee is entitled to receive under a MA plan. The organization determination is made by MA plan under Part C of the Medicare program. See 42 C.F.R. 422.566.

Original Medicare Health insurance available under Medicare Part A and Part B through the traditional fee for service payment system.

Party An individual or entity listed in 42 C.F.R. § 405.906 that has standing to appeal an initial determination and/or a subsequent administrative appeal determination. This can include a beneficiary, a provider, a supplier, or a Medicaid State agency.

Provider A hospital, critical access hospital, skilled nursing facility, comprehensive outpatient rehabilitation facility, home health agency, or hospice that has in effect an agreement to participate in Medicare, or clinic, rehabilitation agency or public health agency that has in effect a similar agreement, but only to furnish outpatient physical therapy or speech pathology services, or a community mental health center that has in effect a similar agreement but only to furnish partial hospitalization services. See 42 C.F.R. § 405.902.

Qualified Independent Contractor (QIC) An entity that has a contract with the Centers for Medicare and Medicaid Services (CMS) to review appeals following a redetermination by a Medicare Administrative Contractor (e.g., fiscal intermediary, carrier) and reconsiderations issued by Quality Improvement Organizations. QICs issue reconsiderations and represent level 2 of the Medicare appeals process.

Quality Improvement Organization (QIO) An entity that has a contract with CMS to monitor the appropriateness, effectiveness and quality of care furnished to Medicare beneficiaries. QIOs makes determinations as to whether the services provided were medically necessary and responses to beneficiary's complaints about the quality of care provided.

Reconsideration The decision made in the second level of the Medicare appeals process. A reconsideration consists of an independent on-the-record review of an initial determination, including the redetermination and all issues related to payment of the claim. A reconsideration is conducted by a QIC under Medicare Parts A and B or an Independent Review Entity under Part D.

Reconsidered Determination In Part C cases, an on-the-record decision issued by an Independent Outside Entity following an adverse reconsideration, in whole or in part, by a MA organization.

Redetermination An independent review of an initial determination. A redetermination is conducted by the same Medicare contractor that issued the initial determination and refers to the decision made in the first level of the Medicare appeals process.

Regulation A rule or order established by a government agency in accordance with the Administrative Procedure Act.

Supplementary Medicare Insurance Program (Part B) The Medicare program that pays for a portion of the costs related to physicians' services, outpatient hospital services, ambulance services, laboratory tests, wheelchairs, hospital beds and other medical and health related services not covered by Medicare Part A for voluntarily insured aged and disabled individuals.

Supplier A physician or other practitioner, a facility or other entity (other than a provider of services) that furnishes items or services under Medicare. See 42 C.F.R. § 405.902.

Video Teleconference (VTC) A meeting where those attending view and hear each other with the use of video cameras and televisions from different locations.

Witness A person who testifies under oath at a hearing and who provides firsthand or expert evidence.

PERSONALIZED HEALTH CARE

Biomarkers The biological parameters associated with the presence and severity of specific disease states. Biomarkers are detectable and measurable by a variety of methods including physical examination, laboratory assays and medical imaging.

Genetic testing examines a person's genetic code, using a sample of blood or other body fluids/tissues, for health or medical identification purposes.

The *Genome* is all the genetic information possessed by an organism. *Genomics* is the study of this genetic information. A *Genotype* is the genetic identity of an organism.

Genome Wide Association Studies An approach that involves rapidly scanning markers across an individual's genome, to find genetic variations associated with a particular disease. Once new genetic targets are identified, researchers can use the information to develop better strategies to detect, treat and prevent the disease.

Health informatics or *medical informatics* is the intersection of information science, medicine and health care. It deals with the resources, devices and methods required to optimize the acquisition, storage, indexing, retrieval and use of information in health and biomedicine. Health informatics tools include not only computers but also clinical guidelines, formal medical terminologies, and information and communication systems.

Micro array technology A new way of studying how large numbers of genes interact with each other and how a cell's regulatory networks control vast batteries of genes simultaneously.

Personalized health care describes medical practices that are targeted to individuals based on their specific genetic code in order to provide a tailored approach. These practices use preventive, diagnostic, and therapeutic interventions that are based on genetic tests and family history information. The goal of personalized health care is to improve health outcomes and the health care delivery system, as well as the quality of life of patients everywhere.

Phenotype The observable traits or characteristics of an organism, for example hair color, weight, or the presence or absence of a disease. Phenotypic traits are not necessarily genetic.

Pharmacogenomics The study of how variations in the human genome affect an individual's response to medications.

RECORD KEEPING

Accession The transfer of the legal and physical custody of records from an agency to an archival agency or a records center. The agency retains legal custody of the records when transferred for temporary storage at a records center.

Accession Number A number assigned to identify shipments of records in the records center.

Adequacy of Documentation A standard of sufficiently and properly recorded actions and/or decisions. Derives from the legal requirement that agency heads "make and preserve records containing adequate and proper documentation of the organizations, functions, policies, decisions, procedures, and essential transactions of the agency and designed to furnish the information necessary to protect the legal and financial rights of the Government and of persons directly affected by the agency's activities" (U.S.C. 3101).

Agency Records (FOIA Records) The Supreme Court has articulated a basic, two-part test for determining what constitutes "agency records" under the FOIA: "Agency records" are records that are (1) either created or obtained by an agency, and (2) under agency control at the time of the FOIA request. Inasmuch as the "agency record" analysis usually hinges upon whether an agency has sufficient "control" over a record, courts have identified four relevant factors for an agency to consider when making such a *determination* the intent of the record's creator to retain or relinquish control over the record; the ability of the agency to use and dispose of the record as it sees fit; the extent to which agency personnel have read or relied upon the record; and the degree to which the record was integrated into the agency's recordkeeping system or files. Agency "control" is also the predominant consideration in determining the "agency record" status of records that are either generated or maintained by a government contractor.

Alphabetic-Subject Filing System A classification system in which subjects are arranged in alphabetical order regardless of their relationship to one another. For example, the subject "adrenalin" might immediately follow the subject "administration."

Appraisal The process of determining the value, and thus the final disposition of records, making them either temporary or permanent.

Archives The noncurrent records of an organization, preserved because of their continuing or enduring value.

Audiovisual Records Records in pictorial or audio form, regardless of format. Includes still photographs or still pictures, graphic arts (posters and original art), motion pictures, video recordings, audio (or sound) recordings, and related records.

Block A chronological grouping of records consisting of one or more segments of cutoff records, that belong to the same series and are dealt with as a unit for purposes of their sufficient transfer, especially the transfer of permanent records to the National Archives. For example, the records schedule may direct a transfer of permanent records in 5-year blocks. In electronic recordkeeping, a grouping of data stored as a unit on an external storage medium and dealt with as a unit by the computer for input or output.

Cartographic Records Graphic representations at reduced scale of selected physical and cultural features of the surface of the earth and other planets. Includes maps, charts (hydrographic/nautical, weather, and aeronautical), photomaps, atlases, cartograms, globes, relief models, and related records, such as field survey notes, map history case files, and finding aids. Also includes geographic information system records, or digital cartographic records, which are managed like other electronic records.

Central Files Files accumulated by several offices organizational units, and maintained and supervised in one location; also called centralized files. This arrangement is most effective in small organizations.

Charge Out The act and result of recording the removal and loan of a document or a file, from the main filing system, to include its location. Usually involves the use of a form, such as OF-23, Charge out Record.

Classification The process of determining the sequence or order in which to arrange documents.

Classified Information Records or information requiring, for national security reasons, safeguards against unauthorized disclosure.

Closed File A file unit or series containing documents, on which action has been completed and to which more documents are not likely to be added. A file unit or series to which access is limited or denied.

Contingent Records Records scheduled for final disposition after the occurrence of an event at some unspecified future time, such as an internal audit.

Continuity Reference A reference form used to replace material withdrawn for consolidation with more up-to-date material.

Current Records (Also referred to as "active records.") Records that are necessary for conducting the current business of an office and must be maintained in office space and equipment.

Costing The calculated financial cost of storing 1 cubic foot of records both on and off site for a government facility.

Cut-Off Breaking or ending files at regular intervals, usually at the close of a fiscal or calendar year, to permit their disposal or transfer in complete blocks and to permit the establishment of new files. (Also called file cutoff or file break).

Decentralized Files Files accumulated by each principal element of an agency and maintained at the point of reference.

Disposal The actions taken regarding temporary or nonpermanent records after their retention periods expire, and including either destruction or, in rare instances, donation. Also, when so specified, the actions taken regarding non-record materials when no longer needed, especially their destruction.

Disposal Authority Legal approval empowering an agency to transfer permanent records to the National Archives or carrying out the disposal of temporary records. Must be obtained from the National Archives and Records Administration and also, for certain records proposed as temporary, from the General Accounting Office. The agency's approval of disposition instructions for non-record material.

Dispose To carry out disposal, which includes either the destruction or the donation of temporary records, but not the transfer of permanent records to the National Archives.

Disposition Schedule A document providing authority for the final disposition of recurring or nonrecurring records. Also called records disposition schedule, records control schedule, records retention schedule, or schedule. Includes the SF-115, Requests for Records Disposition Authority, the General Records Schedules, and the agency records schedule, which when completed becomes a comprehensive records schedule that also contains agency disposition instructions for non-record materials.

E-discovery An abbreviated term for electronic discovery, is the obligation of parties to a lawsuit to exchange documents that exist only in electronic form. Amendments to the Federal Rules of Civil Procedure, enacted in late 2006, now compel include civil litigants to preserve and produce electronic evidence. Examples of electronic documents and data subject to e-discovery are e-mails, voicemails, instant messages, e-calendars, audio files, data on handheld devices, animation, metadata, graphics, photographs, spreadsheets, websites, drawings and other types of digital data.

Electronic Mail System A computer application used to create, receive, and transmit messages and other documents or create calendars that can be used by multiple staff members. Excluded from this definition are file transfer utilities (software that transmits files between users but does not retain any transmission data), data systems used to collect and process data that have been organized into data files or databases on either personal computers or mainframe computers, and word processing documents not transmitted on an E-mail system.

Electronic Record Numeric, graphic, text, and any other information recorded on any medium that can be read using a computer and satisfies the definition of a Federal record in 44 U.S.C. 3301. This includes, but is not limited to, both on-line storage and off-line media such as tapes, disks, and optical disks. [36 CFR 1234.1]

Electronic Mail Message A document created or received on an E-mail system, including brief notes, substantive documents, and any attachments which may be transmitted with the message.

Emergency-Operating Records Vital records essential to the continued functioning or reconstitution of an organization during and after an emergency.

Federal Records Center A storage facility operated by the National Archives and Records Administration.

File Plan A listing of the files (not necessarily records) contained in a specified location. An inventory is a descriptive listing of each record series or system and other pertinent data.

Files A collective term usually applied to all records and non-record materials of an office or agency.

Files Custodian The individual or office in charge of agency files. Often used interchangeably with records custodian.

Filing System A set of policies and procedures for organizing and identifying files or documents to speed their retrieval, use, and disposition. (Sometimes called recordkeeping system).

Finding Aids Indexes or other lists, manual or automated, that are designed to make it easier to locate relevant files.

Fiscal Value The usefulness of records in documenting an agency's financial transactions and obligations.

FOIA Records (Agency Records) The Supreme Court has articulated a basic, two-part test for determining what constitutes "agency records" under the FOIA: "Agency records" are records that are (1) either created or obtained by an agency, and (2) under agency control at the time of the FOIA request. Inasmuch as the "agency record" analysis usually hinges upon whether an agency has sufficient "control" over a record, courts have identified four relevant factors for an agency to consider when making such a determination: the intent of the record's creator to retain or relinquish control over the record; the ability of the agency to use and dispose of the record as it sees fit; the extent to which agency personnel have read or relied upon the record; and the degree to which the record was integrated into the agency's recordkeeping system or files. Agency "control" is also the predominant consideration in determining the "agency record" status of records that are either generated or maintained by a government contractor.

Frozen Records In records disposition, those temporary records that cannot be destroyed on schedule because special circumstances, such as a court order, require a temporary extension of the approved retention period. Also see Litigation Hold.

General Records Schedule Schedules authorizing the disposal, after the lapse of specified periods of time, of records common to several or all agencies, if such records will not, at the end of the periods specified, have sufficient administrative, legal, research, or other value to warrant their further preservation by the United States Government. [44 U.S.C. 3303A(d)]

Inactive or Noncurrent Records Records no longer required to conduct agency business and therefore ready for final disposition.

Information Technology (IT) System A discrete set of information resources organized for the collection, processing, maintenance, transmission, and dissemination of information, in accordance with defined procedures, whether automated or manual to support HHS' or OPDIV's mission. An interconnected set of information resources under the same direct management control, which shares common functionality. A system normally includes hardware, software, information, data, applications, communications, and people. Refers to a set of information resources under the same management control that share common functionality and require the same level of security controls.

Intrinsic Value In archives administration, the value of those permanent records that should be preserved in their original form rather than as copies.

Inventory A survey of agency records and nonrecord materials taken before developing schedules. A File Plan is a listing of the files (not necessarily records) contained in a specified location. An inventory is a descriptive listing of each record series or system and other pertinent data.

Item A separately numbered entry describing records on Form SF-115, Request for Records Disposition Authority. Usually consists of a record series or part of an information system. A document.

Legal Custody Guardianship, or control, of records, including both physical possession (physical custody) and legal responsibility (legal custody), unless one or the other is specified.

Legal Value The usefulness of records in documenting legally enforceable rights or obligations, both those of the Federal Government and those of persons directly affected by the agency's activities.

Life Cycle of Records The concept that records pass through three main stages: creation, maintenance and use, and disposition.

Litigation Hold Within the context of records management, a "hold" is an agency's temporary suspension of disposition action(s) because of legal, audit, or investigative needs. When a hold is initiated, documentary materials, regardless of physical location, are required to be kept for as long as the hold is in place. Because this category of records potentially could affect multiple OPDIVs, it is imperative that all potential holders of the information be informed to preserve and not destroy or alter any documents of any type, including hard copy, electronic format, and e-mails. Also see Frozen Records.

Mnemonic Filing System A classification system in which records are coded by symbols that remind the user of the subjects; for example, ADM for administration and PER for personnel. These symbols are usually arranged alphabetically.

National Archives The organization or agency responsible for appraising, accessioning, preserving, and making available permanent records.

National Archives and Records Administration (NARA) The agency having overall responsibility for the records management program throughout the Federal Government. When permanent records are transferred to the National Archives, they are placed in the custody of NARA's Office of the National Archives.

Nonrecord U.S. Government-owned informational materials excluded from the legal definition of records. Consists of extra copies of documents kept only for convenience of reference, stocks of publications and of processed documents, and library or museum material intended solely for reference or exhibition.

Numeric-Alphabetic Filing System A classification system in which numbers are assigned to main divisions, and letters and numbers to succeeding subdivisions, and the records are arranged accordingly. For example, "ADM" might stand for "Administrative Management," and "1" for the subdivision "Policy." "ADM 2" might stand for "Reports and Statistics," and further subdivided under this subject may be "ADM 2-1, Activity Reports."

Office of Primary Responsibility (OPR) The office delegated responsibility for a specific function. This office normally maintains the official agency record, including the yellow copy and related incoming correspondence. The OPR may designate other offices to maintain the official agency record copy for that function.

Official File Station Any location in an organization at whichrecords are maintained for current use.

Official Record Copy The yellow file or otherwise designated copy maintained by the originating office. Also includes incoming correspondence used to document a specific function.

Permanent Records Records appraised by the National Archives and Records Administration as having sufficient historical or other value to warrant continued preservation by the Federal Government, beyond the time they are needed for administrative, legal, or fiscal purposes. Sometimes called "archival records."

Personal Papers Nonofficial or private papers, relating solely to an individual's own affairs. Must be clearly designated as such and kept separate from the agency's records. Also called "personal files" or "personal records."

Preserved Record Documentary materials that have been deliberately filed, stored, or otherwise systematically maintained as evidence of the organization, functions, policies, decisions, procedures, operations, or other activities of the Government, or because of the informational value of the data. This applies to documentary materials in a file or other storage system, including electronic files and systems, and those temporarily removed from the files or other storage systems.

Program Records Records documenting the unique, substantive functions for which an agency is responsible, in contrast to administrative records.

Public Records In general usage, records accumulated by Government agencies. Records open to public inspection by law or custom.

Reading Files Outgoing correspondence records arranged chronologically, in contrast to those arranged by subject. (Chronological (chron) or day files).

Record Group A body of organizationally related records, established by an archival agency after considering the organization's administrative history and complexity and the volume of its records. National Archives and Records Administration uses record group numbers to keep track of agency records during and after the scheduling process, including those transferred to a Federal Records Center and/or the National Archives.

Record Series File units or documents arranged according to a filing system, or kept together because they relate to a particular subject or function, result from the same activity, document a specific kind of transaction, take a particular physical form, or have some other relationship arising out of their creation, receipt, or use, such as restrictions on access and use.

Recordkeeping System A system for collecting, organizing, and storing records to facilitate their preservation, retrieval, use, and disposition, and to fulfill recordkeeping requirements.

Records According to 44 U.S.C. 3301, the term "includes all books, papers, maps, photographs, machine-readable materials, or other documentary materials, regardless of physical form or characteristics, made or received by an agency of the United States Government under Federal law or in connection with the transaction of public business and preserved or appropriate for preservation by that agency or its legitimate successor as evidence of the organization, functions, policies, decisions, procedures, operations, or other activities of the Government or because of the informational value of data in them. Library and museum material made or acquired and preserved solely for reference or exhibition purposes, extra copies of documents preserved only for convenience of reference, and stocks of publications and of processed documents are not included." A more simple, working definition: Official Federal Government records include documentary material that you create, or that you receive from outside of AMS.

Records Maintenance and Use Any action involving the location of Federal agency records or the storage, retrieval, and handling of records kept at office file locations by, or for, a Federal agency. This is the second stage of the records life cycle.

Records Maintenance System (Centralized) A centralized records maintenance system is one in which all records accumulating in an organization unit are centralized in one location, and designated personnel are assigned the responsibility to properly manage the organization's records. As technology advances and the need for information grows, a centralized records maintenance system may prove to be more cost effective and achieve greater benefits than those associated with a decentralized system.

Records Maintenance System (Decentralized) A decentralized records maintenance system is one in which accumulating records are maintained by the individuals performing the agency's functions, or the originators.

Records Management The planning, controlling, directing, organizing, training, promoting, and other managerial activities involved with respect to records creation, records maintenance and use, and records disposition in order to achieve adequate and proper documentation of the policies and transactions of the Federal Government and effective and economical management of agency operations. [36 CFR 1220.14]

Records Management Program A planned, coordinated set of policies, procedures, and activities needed to manage an agency's recorded information. Encompasses the creation, maintenance and use, and disposition of records, regardless of media. Essential elements include issuing up-to-date program directives, properly training those responsible for implementation, and carefully evaluating the results to ensure adequacy, effectiveness, and efficiency.

Records Officer The person assigned responsibility by the agency head for overseeing an agency-wide records management program. A person assigned a Record Group.

Records Schedule A document describing, providing instructions for, and approving the disposition of specified Federal records. It consists of one of the following:

a. An SF-115, Request for Records Disposition Authority, which the National Archives and Records Administration (NARA) has approved to authorize the disposition of Federal records;
b. the General Records Schedules (GRS) issued by NARA; or
c. a printed agency manual or directive containing the records descriptions and disposition instructions approved by NARA on one or more SF-115's or issued by NARA in the GRS. [36 CFR 1220.14]

Retention Period The length of time that records are to be kept.

Retirement The sending of inactive records to the Federal Records Center or to the National Archives, either for storage until time for disposal (destruction) for permanent retention.

Rights-and-Interests Records Vital records essential to protecting the rights and interests of an organization and of the individuals directly affected by its activities.

Screening Reviewing files to apply access restrictions. Examining files to identify and remove documents of short-term value, especially those eligible for immediate destruction. Also called weeding or purging.

Security Backup Copy of a record in any medium created to provide a means of ensuring retention and access in the event the original record is destroyed, inaccessible, or corrupted.

Special Records Types of records maintained separately from textual/paper records because their physical form or characteristics require unusual care, and/or because they have nonstandard sizes. Includes electronic, audiovisual, microform, cartographic and remote-sensing imagery, architectural and engineering, printed, and card records.

Standard Form 115, Request for Records Disposition Authority The form used by Federal agencies to obtain disposition authority from the National Archives and Records Administration for records which the General Records Schedules are inapplicable.

Standard Form 135, Records Transmittal and Receipt The form to be submitted by Federal agencies before transferring records to a Federal Records Center. Sometimes referred to as "shelf lists."

Subject Files Records arranged and filed according to their general informational or subject content. Mainly letters and memorandums, but also forms, reports, and other material, all relating to program and administrative functions, not to specific cases.

Subject-Numeric Filing System A subject classification system in which the main topics are arranged alphabetically and the subdivisions, i.e., secondary (second) and tertiary (third) are coded numerically. For example, "Personnel 8" might stand for "Hours of Duty." This system may be modified by combining it with the mnemonic filing system so that, for example, "Personnel 8" would become "PER 8."
a. Primary Subjects are the prime or major subject designations that identify and describe groups of related records.
b. Secondary Subjects are one or more related subjects that have been created or established by the division of a primary subject.

System of Records System of Records is used to identify records that contain information covered under the Privacy Act.

System Top-up Copy of off-line storage media of software and data stored on direct access storage devices in a computer system, used to recreate a system and its data in case of unintentional loss of data or software.

Tertiary Subjects One or more related subjects that have been created or established by the division of a secondary subject.

Technical Reference Files Non-record copies of articles, periodicals, reports, studies, vendor catalogs, and similar materials that are needed for reference and information but are not properly part of the office's records.

Temporary Records Any Federal record that the Archivist of the United States has determined to have insufficient value to warrant its preservation by the National Archives and Records Administration. [36 CFR 1220.14]

Transmission and Receipt Data
a. Transmission Data. Information in E-mail systems regarding the identities of sender and addressee(s), and the date and time messages were sent.
b. Receipt Data. Information in E-mail systems regarding date and time of receipt of a message, and/or acknowledgement of receipt or access by addressee(s).

Unscheduled Records Records for which no ultimate disposition has been determined.

Vital Records Records essential to the continued functioning or reconstitution of an organization during and after an emergency; also, those records essential to protecting the rights and interests of that organization and of the individuals directly affected by its activities. Sometimes called essential records. Include both emergency-operating and rights-and-interests records. Vital record considerations are part of an agency's records disaster prevention and recovery program.

Washington National Records Center The Federal Records Center for the inactive permanent records (except those located in the National Archives) and temporary Federal records for offices located in the Washington metropolitan area.

RISK TERMS

Accidental Hazard

Definition source of harm or difficulty created by negligence, error, or unintended failure
Example The chemical storage tank in the loading area without a concrete barrier may present an accidental hazard.

Adversary

Definition individual, group, organization, or government that conducts or has the intent to conduct detrimental activities *Example* Al-Qaeda is considered an adversary of the United States. *Annotation*
1) An adversary can be hypothetical for the purposes of training, exercises, red teaming, and other activities. 2) An adversary differs from a threat in that an adversary may have the intent, but not the capability, to conduct detrimental activities, while a threat possesses both intent and capability.

Asset

Definition person, structure, facility, information, material, or process that has value
Example Some organizations use an asset inventory to plan protective security activities.
Extended Definition includes contracts, facilities, property, records, unobligated or unexpended balances of appropriations, and other funds or resources, personnel, intelligence, technology, or physical infrastructure, or anything useful that contributes to the success of something, such as an organizational mission; assets are things of value or properties to which value can be assigned; from an intelligence standpoint, includes any resource—person, group, relationship, instrument, installation, or supply—at the disposal of an intelligence organization for use in an operational or support role
Annotation In some domains, capabilities and activities may be considered assets as well. In the context of the National Infrastructure Protection Plan, people are not considered assets.

Attack Method

Definition manner and means, including the weapon and delivery method, an adversary may use to cause harm on a target
Example Analysts have identified weaponization of an aircraft as an attack method that terrorists may use.
Annotation Attack method and attack mode are synonymous.

Attack Path

Definition steps that an adversary takes or may take to plan, prepare for, and execute an attack
Example Part of the attack path for the car bombing involved dozens of individuals moving money, arms and operatives from the terrorist safe haven to the target area.
Annotation An attack path may include recruitment, radicalization, and training of operatives, selection and surveillance of the target, construction or procurement of weapons, funding, deployment of operatives to the target, execution of the attack, and related post-attack activities.

Capability

Definition means to accomplish a mission, function, or objective
Example Counterterrorism operations are intended to reduce the capability of terrorist groups.
Annotation Adversary capability is one of two elements, the other being adversary intent, that is commonly considered when estimating the likelihood of terrorist attacks. Adversary capability is the ability of an adversary to attack with a particular attack method. Other communities of interest may use capability to refer to any organization's ability to perform its mission, activities, and functions.

Consequence

Definition effect of an event, incident, or occurrence
Example One consequence of the explosion was the loss of over 50 lives.
Annotation Consequence is commonly measured in four *ways* human, economic, mission, and psychological, but may also include other factors such as impact on the environment.
See Also human consequence, economic consequence, mission consequence, psychological consequence.

Consequence Assessment

Definition process of identifying or evaluating the potential or actual effects of an event, incident, or occurrence
Example The consequence assessment for the hurricane included estimates for human casualties and property damage caused by the landfall of the hurricane and cascading effects.

Countermeasure

Definition action, measure, or device that reduces an identified risk

Example Some facilities employ surveillance cameras as a countermeasure.
Annotation A countermeasure can reduce any component of risk, threat, vulnerability, or consequence.

Deterrent

Definition measure that discourages an action or prevents an occurrence by instilling fear, doubt, or anxiety
Example Fear of lethal retaliation can serve as a deterrent to some adversaries.
Annotation A deterrent reduces threat by decreasing the likelihood of an attempted attack.

Economic Consequence

Definition effect of an incident, event, or occurrence on the value of property or on the production, trade, distribution, or use of income, wealth, or commodities
Example The loss of the company's entire trucking fleet was an economic consequence of the tornado.
Annotation When measuring economic consequence in the context of homeland security risk, consequences are usually assessed as negative and measured in monetary units.

Evaluation

Definition process of examining, measuring and/or judging how well an entity, procedure, or action has met or is meeting stated objectives
Example After increasing the number of sensors at the port, the team conducted an evaluation to determine how the sensors reduced risks to the facility.
Annotation Evaluation is the step in the risk management cycle that measures the effectiveness of an implemented risk management option.

Function

Definition service, process, capability, or operation performed by an asset, system, network, or organization
Example A primary function of the aviation industry is the transportation of people and cargo over long distances.

Hazard

Definition natural or man-made source or cause of harm or difficulty
Example Improperly maintained or protected chemical storage tanks present a potential hazard.
Annotation
1. A hazard differs from a threat in that a threat is directed at an entity, asset, system, network, or geographic area, while a hazard is not directed.
2. A hazard can be actual or potential.

Human Consequence

Definition effect of an incident, event, or occurrence that results in injury, illness, or loss of life
Example The human consequence of the attack was 20 fatalities and 50 injured persons.
Annotation When measuring human consequence in the context of homeland security risk, consequence is assessed as negative and can include loss of life or limb, or other short-term or long-term bodily harm or illness.

Implementation

Definition act of putting a procedure or course of action into effect to support goals or achieve objectives
Example The implementation of the emergency evacuation plan involved the activation of additional response personnel.
Annotation Implementation is one of the stages of the risk management cycle and involves the act of executing a risk management strategy.

Incident

Definition occurrence, caused by either human action or natural phenomena, that may cause harm and that may require action
Example The Department of Homeland Security plays a role in reducing the risk of a catastrophic incident in the United States.
Annotation
1. Homeland security incidents can include major disasters, emergencies, terrorist attacks, terrorist threats, wildland and urban fires, floods, hazardous materials spills, nuclear accidents, aircraft accidents, earthquakes, hurricanes, tornadoes, tropical storms, war-related disasters, public health and medical emergencies, law enforcement encounters and other occurrences requiring a mitigating response.
2. Harm can include human casualties, destruction of property, adverse economic impact, and/or damage to natural resources.

Integrated Risk Management

Definition incorporation and coordination of strategy, capability, and governance to enable risk-informed decision making
Example DHS uses a framework of integrated risk management to ensure a unified approach to managing all homeland security risks.

Intent

Definition determination to achieve an objective
Example The content of domestic extremist websites may demonstrate an intent to conduct acts of terrorism.
Annotation
1. Adversary intent is the desire or design to conduct a type of attack or to attack a type of target.
2. Adversary intent is one of two elements, along with adversary capability, that is commonly considered when estimating the likelihood of terrorist attacks and often refers to the likelihood that an adversary will execute a chosen course of action or attempt a particular type of attack.

Intentional Hazard

Definition source of harm, duress, or difficulty created by a deliberate action or a planned course of action
Example Cyber-attacks are an intentional hazard that DHS works to prevent.

Likelihood

Definition estimate of the potential of an incident or event's occurrence
Example The likelihood of natural hazards can be estimated through the examination of historical data.
Annotation
1. Qualitative and semi-quantitative risk assessments can use qualitative estimates of likelihood such as high, medium, or low, which may be represented numerically but not mathematically. Quantitative assessments use mathematically derived values to represent likelihood.
2. The likelihood of a successful attack occurring is typically broken into two related quantities: the likelihood that an attack occurs (which is a common mathematical representation of threat), and the likelihood that the attack succeeds, given that it is attempted (which is a common mathematical representation of vulnerability). In the context of natural hazards, likelihood of occurrence is typically informed by the frequency of past incidents or occurrences.
3. The intelligence community typically estimates likelihood in bins or ranges such as "remote," "unlikely," "even chance," "probable/likely," or "almost certain."
4. Probability is a specific type of likelihood. Likelihood can be communicated using numbers (e.g., 0-100, 1-5) or phrases (e.g., low, medium, high), while probabilities must meet more stringent conditions. See Also Probability (Mathematical).

Mission Consequence

Definition effect of an incident, event, operation, or occurrence on the ability of an organization or group to meet a strategic objective or perform a function
Example The city government's inability to ensure the public's access to clean drinking water was a mission consequence of the earthquake.
Annotation Valuation of mission consequence should exclude other types of consequences (e.g., human consequence, economic consequence, etc). if they are evaluated separately in the assessment.

Model

Definition approximation, representation, or idealization of selected aspects of the structure, behavior, operation, or other characteristics of a real-world process, concept, or system
Example To assess risk for over 400 events, analysts created a model based on only the most important factors.
Annotation See Also simulation.

Natural Hazard

Definition source of harm or difficulty created by a meteorological, environmental, or geological phenomenon or combination of phenomena
Example A natural hazard, such as an earthquake, can occur without warning.

Network

Definition group of components that share information or interact with each other in order to perform a function
Example Power plants, substations, and transmission lines constitute a network that creates and distributes electricity.
Annotation Network is used across DHS to explain the joining of physical, cyber, and other entities for a particular purpose or function.

Probabilistic Risk Assessment

Definition type of quantitative risk assessment that considers possible combinations of occurrences with associated consequences, each with an associated probability or probability distribution
Example The engineers conducted a probabilistic risk assessment to determine the risk of a meltdown resulting from a series of compounding failures.
Annotation Probabilistic risk assessments are typically performed on complex technological systems with tools such as fault and event trees, and Monte Carlo simulations to evaluate security risks and/or accidental failures.

Probability (Mathematical)

Definition likelihood that is expressed as a number between 0 and 1, where 0 indicates that the occurrence is impossible and 1 indicates definite knowledge that the occurrence has happened or will happen, where the ratios between numbers reflect and maintain quantitative relationships
Example The probability of a coin landing on "heads" is 1/2.
Annotation
1. Probability (mathematical) is a specific type of likelihood estimate that obeys the laws of probability theory.
2. Probability is used colloquially as a synonym for likelihood.

Psychological Consequence

Definition effect of an incident, event, or occurrence on the mental or emotional state of individuals or groups resulting in a change in perception and/or behavior
Example A psychological consequence of the disease outbreak could include the reluctance of the public to visit hospitals for fear of infection, which may make it more difficult for experts to control the outbreak.
Annotation In the context of homeland security, psychological consequences are negative and refer to the impact of an incident, event, or occurrence on the behavior or emotional and mental state of an affected population.

Qualitative Risk Assessment Methodology

Definition set of methods, principles, or rules for assessing risk based on non-numerical categories or levels
Example The qualitative risk assessment methodology allows for categories of "low risk," "medium risk," and "high risk."

Quantitative Risk Assessment Methodology

Definition set of methods, principles, or rules for assessing risks based on the use of numbers where the meanings and proportionality of values are maintained inside and outside the context of the assessment
Example Engineers at the nuclear power plant used a quantitative risk assessment methodology to assess the risk of reactor failure.
Annotation While a semi-quantitative methodology also involves the use of numbers, only a purely quantitative methodology uses numbers in a way that allows for the consistent use of values outside the context of the assessment.

Redundancy

Definition additional or alternative systems, sub-systems, assets, or processes that maintain a degree of overall functionality in case of loss or failure of another system, sub-system, asset, or process
Example A lack of redundancy in access control mechanisms is a vulnerability that can result in a higher likelihood of a successful attack.

Residual Risk

Definition risk that remains after risk management measures have been implemented
Example While increased patrols lessened the likelihood of trespassers, residual risk remained due to the unlocked exterior doors.

Resilience

Definition ability to resist, absorb, recover from or successfully adapt to adversity or a change in conditions
Example The county was able to recover quickly from the disaster because of the resilience of governmental support systems.
Extended Definition
1. ability of systems, infrastructures, government, business, and citizenry to resist, absorb recover from, or adapt to an adverse occurrence that may cause harm, destruction, or loss of national significance
2. capacity of an organization to recognize threats and hazards and make adjustments that will improve future protection efforts and risk reduction measures

Annotation Resilience can be factored into vulnerability and consequence estimates when measuring risk.

Return On Investment (Risk)

Definition calculation of the value of risk reduction measures in the context of the cost of developing and implementing those measures
Example Although the installation of new detection equipment was expensive, the team concluded that the return on investment for the new equipment was positive because of the significant reduction in risk.

Risk

Definition potential for an unwanted outcome resulting from an incident, event, or occurrence, as determined by its likelihood and the associated consequences

Example The team calculated the risk of a terrorist attack after analyzing intelligence reports, vulnerability assessments, and consequence models.
Extended Definition potential for an adverse outcome assessed as a function of threats, vulnerabilities, and consequences associated with an incident, event, or occurrence
Annotation
1) Risk is defined as the potential for an unwanted outcome. This potential is often measured and used to compare different future situations.
2) Risk may manifest at the strategic, operational, and tactical levels.

Risk Acceptance

Definition explicit or implicit decision not to take an action that would affect all or part of a particular risk
Example After determining that the cost of mitigation measures was higher than the consequence estimates, the organization decided on a strategy of risk acceptance.
Annotation Risk acceptance is one of four risk management strategies, along with risk avoidance, risk control, and risk transfer.

Risk Analysis

Definition systematic examination of the components and characteristics of risk
Example Using risk analysis, the community identified the potential consequences from flooding.
Annotation In practice, risk analysis is generally conducted to produce a risk assessment. Risk analysis can also involve aggregation of the results of risk assessments to produce a valuation of risks for the purpose of informing decisions. In addition, risk analysis can be done on proposed alternative risk management strategies to determine the likely impact of the strategies on the overall risk.

Risk Assessment

Definition product or process which collects information and assigns values to risks for the purpose of informing priorities, developing or comparing courses of action, and informing decision making
Example The analysts produced a risk assessment outlining risks to the aviation industry.
Extended Definition appraisal of the risks facing an entity, asset, system, network, geographic area or other grouping
Annotation A risk assessment can be the resulting product created through analysis of the component parts of risk.

Risk Assessment Methodology

Definition set of methods, principles, or rules used to identify and assess risks and to form priorities, develop courses of action, and inform decision-making
Example The Maritime Security Risk Analysis Model (MSRAM) is a risk assessment methodology used to assess risk at our Nation's ports.

Risk Assessment Tool

Definition activity, item, or program that contributes to determining and evaluating risks
Example A checklist is a common risk assessment tool that allows users to easily execute risk assessments in a consistent way.
Annotation Tools can include computer software and hardware or standard forms or checklists for recording and displaying risk assessment data.

Risk Avoidance

Definition strategies or measures taken that effectively remove exposure to a risk
Example He exercised a strategy of risk avoidance by refusing to live in an area prone to tornados.
Annotation Avoidance is one of a set of four commonly used risk management strategies, along with risk control, risk acceptance, and risk transfer.

Risk Communication

Definition exchange of information with the goal of improving risk understanding, affecting risk perception and/or equipping people or groups to act appropriately in response to an identified risk
Annotation Risk communication is practiced for both non-hazardous conditions and during incidents. During an incident, risk communication is intended to provide information that fosters trust and credibility in government and empowers partners, stakeholders, and the public to make the best possible decisions under extremely difficult time constraints and circumstances.
Example As part of risk communication efforts, DHS provides information regarding the current threat level to the public.

Risk Control

Definition deliberate action taken to reduce the potential for harm or maintain it at an acceptable level
Example As a risk control measure, security guards screen suitcases and other packages to reduce the likelihood of dangerous articles getting inside of office buildings.

Risk Identification

Definition process of finding, recognizing, and describing potential risks
Example During the initial risk identification for the facility's risk assessment, explosives and seismic events were chosen as scenarios to consider because of their potentially high consequences.

Risk Management

Definition process of identifying, analyzing, assessing, and communicating risk and accepting, avoiding, transferring or controlling it to an acceptable level at an acceptable cost
Annotation The primary goal of risk management is to reduce or eliminate risk through mitigation measures (avoiding the risk or reducing the negative effect of the risk), but also includes the concepts of acceptance and/or transfer of responsibility for the risk as appropriate. Risk management principles acknowledge that, while risk often cannot be eliminated, actions can usually be taken to reduce risk.

Risk Management Alternatives Development

Definition process of systematically examining risks to develop a range of options and their anticipated effects for decision makers
Example After completing the risk management alternatives development step, the analysis team presented the mayor with a list of risk management options.
Annotation The risk management alternatives development step of the risk management process generates options for decision-makers to consider before deciding on which option to implement.

Risk Management Cycle

Definition sequence of steps that are systematically taken and revisited to manage risk
Example Using the risk management cycle, the organization was able to understand and measurably decrease the risks it faced.

Risk Management Methodology

Definition set of methods, principles, or rules used to identify, analyze, assess, and communicate risk, and mitigate, accept, or control it to an acceptable level at an acceptable cost
Example The risk management methodology recommended by the Government Accountability Office consists of five steps.

Risk Management Plan

Definition document that identifies risks and specifies the actions that have been chosen to manage those risks
Example Businesses often have a risk management plan to address the potential risks that they might encounter.

Risk Management Strategy

Definition course of action or actions to be taken in order to manage risks
Example Mutual Aid Agreements are a risk management strategy used by some emergency response authorities to increase their capacity to respond to large scale incidents.
Extended Definition proactive approach to reduce the usually negative impacts of various risks by choosing within a range of options that include complete avoidance of any risk that would cause harm or injury, accepting the risk, controlling the risk by employing risk mitigation options to reduce impacts, or transferring some or all of the risk to another entity based on a set of stated priorities

Risk Matrix

Definition tool for ranking and displaying components of risk in an array
Example The security staff devised a risk matrix with the likelihoods of various threats to the subway system in the rows and corresponding consequences in the columns.
Annotation A risk matrix is typically displayed in a graphical format to show the relationship between risk components.

Risk Mitigation

Definition application of measure or measures to reduce the likelihood of an unwanted occurrence and/or its consequences
Example Through risk mitigation, the potential impact of the tsunami on the local population was greatly reduced.
Annotation Measures may be implemented prior to, during, or after an incident, event, or occurrence.

Risk Mitigation Option

Definition measure, device, policy, or course of action taken with the intent of reducing risk
Example Medical professionals advised the risk mitigation option of inoculations to reduce the risk of a disease outbreak.

Risk Perception

Definition subjective judgment about the characteristics and/or severity of risk
Example The fear of terrorist attacks may create a skewed risk perception.
Annotation Risk perception may be driven by sense, emotion, or personal experience.

Risk Profile

Definition description and/or depiction of risks to an asset, system, network, geographic area or other entity
Example A risk profile for a hydroelectric plant may address risks such as structural failure, mechanical malfunction, sabotage, and terrorism.
Annotation A risk profile can be derived from a risk assessment; it is often used as a presentation tool to show how risks vary across comparable entities.

Risk Reduction

Definition decrease in risk through risk avoidance, risk control or risk transfer
Example By placing vehicle barriers outside the facility, the security team achieved a significant risk reduction.
Annotation Risk reduction may be estimated both during the decision and evaluation phases of the risk management cycle.

Risk Score

Definition numerical result of a semi-quantitative risk assessment methodology
Example By installing a surveillance system, the chemical plant was able to reduce its risk score when the next assessment was conducted.
Extended Definition numerical representation that gauges the combination of threat, vulnerability, and consequence at a specific moment
Annotation The application of risk management alternatives may result in a change of risk score.

Risk Tolerance

Definition degree to which an entity is willing to accept risk
Example After a major disaster, a community's risk tolerance may decrease significantly.

Risk Transfer

Definition action taken to manage risk that shifts some or all of the risk to another entity, asset, system, network, or geographic area
Example A risk transfer may occur after increasing security at one facility because it might make an alternate facility a more attractive target.
Annotation Risk transfer may refer to transferring the risk from asset to asset, asset to system, or some other combination, or shifting the responsibility for managing the risk from one authority to another (for example, responsibility for economic loss could be transferred from a homeowner to an insurance company).

Risk-Based Decision Making

Definition determination of a course of action predicated primarily on the assessment of risk and the expected impact of that course of action on that risk
Example After reading about threats and vulnerabilities associated with vehicle explosives downtown, the Mayor practiced risk-based decision making by authorizing the installation of vehicle barriers.
Annotation Risk-based decision making uses the assessment of risk as the primary decision driver, while risk-informed decision making may account for multiple sources of information not included in the assessment of risk as significant inputs to the decision process in addition to risk information. Risk-based decision making has often been used interchangeably with risk-informed decision making.

Risk-Informed Decision Making

Definition determination of a course of action predicated on the assessment of risk, the expected impact of that course of action on that risk, as well as other relevant factors
Example The Mayor practiced risk-informed decision making in planning event security by considering both the results of the risk assessment and logistical constraints.
Annotation Risk-informed decision making may take into account multiple sources of information not included specifically in the assessment of risk as inputs to the decision process in addition to risk information, while risk-based decision making uses the assessment of risk as the primary decision driver.

Scenario (Risk)

Definition hypothetical situation comprised of a hazard, an entity impacted by that hazard, and associated conditions including consequences when appropriate
Example The team designed a scenario involving a car bomb at the power plant to help assess the risk of vehicle-borne improvised explosive devices.

Annotation A scenario can be created and used for the purposes of training, exercise, analysis, or modeling as well as for other purposes. A scenario that has occurred or is occurring is an incident.

Semi-Quantitative Risk Assessment Methodology

Definition set of methods, principles, or rules to assess risk that uses bins, scales, or representative numbers whose values and meanings are not maintained in other contexts

Example By giving the "low risk," "medium risk," and "high risk" categories corresponding numerical values, the assessor used a semi-quantitative risk assessment methodology.

Annotation While numbers may be used in a semi-quantitative methodology, the values are not applicable outside of the methodology, and numerical results from one methodology cannot be compared with those from other methodologies.

Sensitivity Analysis

Definition process to determine how outputs of a methodology differ in response to variation of the inputs or conditions

Example The sensitivity analysis showed that the population variable had the largest effect on the output of the model.

Annotation
1. When a factor considered in a risk assessment has uncertainty, sensitivity analysis examines the effect that the uncertainty has on the results.
2. A sensitivity analysis can be used to examine how individual variables can affect the outputs of risk assessment methodologies.
3. Alternatively, sensitivity analysis can show decision makers or evaluators the impact or predicted impact of risk management alternatives.

Simulation

Definition model that behaves or operates like a given process, concept, or system when provided a set of controlled inputs

Example The scientists designed a simulation to see how weather impacted the plume of smoke.

Annotation See Also model.

Subject Matter Expert

Definition individual with in-depth knowledge in a specific area or field

Example A subject matter expert was consulted to inform team members on improvised nuclear devices.

Annotation Structured techniques for the elicitation of expert judgment are key tools for risk assessment. Subject matter experts are also used to supplement empirical data when needed, or to provide input on specialized subject areas for the purposes of designing and executing risk assessments.

System

Definition any combination of facilities, equipment, personnel, procedures, and communications integrated for a specific purpose

Example The collection of roads, tunnels, and bridges provided the country with the foundation for a useful transit system.

Target

Definition asset, network, system or geographic area chosen by an adversary to be impacted by an attack

Example Analysts identified mass gatherings as one potential target of an attack.

Threat

Definition natural or man-made occurrence, individual, entity, or action that has or indicates the potential to harm life, information, operations, the environment and/or property

Example Intelligence suggested that the greatest threat to the building was from explosives concealed in a vehicle.

Annotation Threat as defined refers to an individual, entity, action, or occurrence; however, for the purpose of calculating risk, the threat of an intentional hazard is generally estimated as the likelihood of an attack (that accounts for both the intent and capability of the adversary) being attempted by an adversary; for other hazards, threat is generally estimated as the likelihood that a hazard will manifest.

Threat Assessment

Definition process of identifying or evaluating entities, actions, or occurrences, whether natural or man-made, that have or indicate the potential to harm life, information, operations and/or property

Example Analysts produced a threat assessment detailing the capabilities of domestic and foreign terrorist organizations to threaten particular infrastructure sectors.

Uncertainty

Definition degree to which a calculated, estimated, or observed value may deviate from the true value
Example The uncertainty in the fatality estimate for the chemical attack was due to the unpredictable wind direction in the affected area.
Annotation
1) Uncertainty may stem from many causes, including the lack of information.
2) The concept of uncertainty is useful in understanding that likelihoods and consequences can oftentimes not be predicted with a high degree of precision or accuracy.

Vulnerability

Definition physical feature or operational attribute that renders an entity open to exploitation or susceptible to a given hazard
Example Installation of vehicle barriers may remove a vulnerability related to attacks using vehicle-borne improvised explosive devices.
Extended Definition characteristic of design, location, security posture, operation, or any combination thereof, that renders an asset, system, network, or entity susceptible to disruption, destruction, or exploitation
Annotation In calculating risk of an intentional hazard, the common measurement of vulnerability is the likelihood that an attack is successful, given that it is attempted.

Vulnerability Assessment

Definition process for identifying physical features or operational attributes that render an entity, asset, system, network, or geographic area susceptible or exposed to hazards
Example The team conducted a vulnerability assessment on the ship to determine how it might be exploited or attacked by an adversary.
Annotation Vulnerability assessments can produce comparable estimates of vulnerabilities across a variety of hazards or assets, systems or networks.

VACCINES AND VACCINATION

Acellular vaccine A vaccine containing partial cellular material as opposed to complete cells.

Acquired Immune Deficiency Syndrome (AIDS) A medical condition where the immune system cannot function properly and protect the body from disease. As a result, the body cannot defend itself against infections (like pneumonia). AIDS is caused by the Human Immunodeficiency Virus (HIV). This virus is spread through direct contact with the blood and body fluids of an infected individual. High risk activities include unprotected sexual intercourse and intravenous drug use (sharing needles). There is no cure for AIDS, however, research efforts are on-going to develop a vaccine.

Active immunity The production of antibodies against a specific disease by the immune system. Active immunity can be acquired in two ways, either by contracting the disease or through vaccination. Active immunity is usually permanent, meaning an individual is protected from the disease for the duration of their lives.

Acute A short-term, intense health effect.

Adjuvant A substance (e.g., aluminum salt) that is added during production to increase the body's immune response to a vaccine.

Adverse events Undesirable experiences occurring after immunization that may or may not be related to the vaccine.

Advisory Committee on Immunization Practices (ACIP) A panel of 10 experts who make recommendations on the use of vaccines in the United States. The panel is advised on current issues by representatives from the Centers for Disease Control and Prevention, Food and Drug Administration, National Institutes of Health, American Academy of Pediatrics, American Academy of Family Physicians, American Medical Association and others. The recommendations of the ACIP guide immunization practice at the federal, state and local level.

Allergy A condition in which the body has an exaggerated response to a substance (e.g., food or drug). Also known as hypersensitivity.

Anaphylaxis An immediate and severe allergic reaction to a substance (e.g., food or drugs). Symptoms of anaphylaxis include breathing difficulties, loss of consciousness and a drop in blood pressure. This condition can be fatal and requires immediate medical attention.

Anthrax An acute infectious disease caused by the spore-forming bacterium *Bacillus anthracis*. Anthrax most commonly occurs in hoofed mammals and can also infect humans.

Antibiotic A substance that fights bacteria.

Antibody A protein found in the blood that is produced in response to foreign substances (e.g., bacteria or viruses) invading the body. Antibodies protect the body from disease by binding to these organisms and destroying them.

Antigens Foreign substances (e.g., bacteria or viruses) in the body that are capable of causing disease. The presence of antigens in the body triggers an immune response, usually the production of antibodies.

Antitoxin Antibodies capable of destroying microorganisms including viruses and bacteria.

Antiviral Literally "against-virus"—any medicine capable of destroying or weakening a virus.

Arthralgia Joint pain.

Arthritis A medical condition characterized by inflammation of the joints which results in pain and difficulty moving.

Association The degree to which the occurrence of two variables or events is linked. Association describes a situation where the likelihood of one event occurring depends on the presence of another event or variable. However, an association between two variables does not necessarily imply a cause and effect relationship. The term association and relationship are often used interchangeably. See causal and temporal association.

Asthma A chronic medical condition where the bronchial tubes (in the lungs) become easily irritated. This leads to constriction of the airways resulting in wheezing, coughing, difficulty breathing and production of thick mucus. The cause of asthma is not yet known but environmental triggers, drugs, food allergies, exercise, infection and stress have all been implicated.

Asymptomatic infection The presence of an infection without symptoms. Also known as inapparent or subclinical infection.

Attenuated vaccine A vaccine in which live virus is weakened through chemical or physical processes in order to produce an immune response without causing the severe effects of the disease. Attenuated vaccines currently licensed in the United States include measles, mumps, rubella, polio, yellow fever and varicella. Also known as a live vaccine.

Autism A chronic developmental disorder usually diagnosed between 18 and 30 months of age. Symptoms include problems with social interaction and communication as well as repetitive interests and activities. At this time, the cause of autism is not known although many experts believe it to be a genetically based disorder that occurs before birth.

B cells Small white blood cells that help the body defend itself against infection. These cells are produced in bone marrow and develop into plasma cells which produce antibodies. Also known as B lymphocytes.

Bacteria Tiny one-celled organisms present throughout the environment that require a microscope to be seen. While not all bacteria are harmful, some cause disease. Examples of bacterial disease include diphtheria, pertussis, tetanus, Haemophilus influenza, and pneumococcus (pneumonia).

Bias Flaws in the collection, analysis or interpretation of research data that lead to incorrect conclusions.

Biological plausibility A causal association (or relationship between two factors) is consistent with existing medical knowledge.

Bone marrow Soft tissue located within bones that produce all blood cells, including the ones that fight infection.

Booster shots Additional doses of a vaccine needed periodically to "boost" the immune system. For example, the tetanus and diphtheria (Td) vaccine which is recommended for adults every ten years.

Brachial neuritis Inflammation of nerves in the arm causing muscle weakness and pain.

Breakthrough infection Development of a disease despite a person's having responded to a vaccine.

Causal association The presence or absence of a variable (e.g., smoking) is responsible for an increase or decrease in another variable (e.g., cancer). A change in exposure leads to a change in the outcome of interest.

Chronic health condition A health-related state that lasts for a long period of time (e.g., cancer, asthma).

Combination vaccine Two or more vaccines administered at once in order to reduce the number of shots given. For example, the MMR (measles, mumps, rubella) vaccine.

Communicable Capable of spreading disease. Also known as infectious.

Community immunity Having a large percentage of the population vaccinated in order to prevent the spread of certain infectious diseases. Even individuals not vaccinated (such as newborns and those with chronic illnesses) are offered some protection because the disease has little opportunity to spread within the community. Also known as herd immunity.

Conjugate vaccine The joining together of two compounds (usually a protein and polysaccharide) to increase a vaccine's effectiveness.

Conjunctivitis Inflammation of the mucous membranes surrounding the eye causing the area to become red and irritated. The membranes may be irritated because of exposure to heat, cold or chemicals. This condition is also caused by viruses, bacteria or allergies.

Contraindication A condition in a recipient which is likely to result in a life-threatening problem if a vaccine were given.

Convulsion See Seizure.

Crib or Cot Death See Sudden Infant Death Syndrome (SIDS).

Crohn's disease A chronic medical condition characterized by inflammation of the bowel. Symptoms include abdominal pain, diarrhea, fever, loss of appetite and weight loss. The cause of Crohn's disease is not yet known, but genetic, dietary, and infectious factors may play a part.

Deltoid A muscle in the upper arm where shots are usually given.

Demyelinating disorders A medical condition where the myelin sheath is damaged. The myelin sheath surrounds nerves and is responsible for the transmission of impulses to the brain. Damage to the myelin sheath results in muscle weakness, poor coordination and possible paralysis. Examples of demyelinating disorders include Multiple Sclerosis (MS), optic neuritis, transverse neuritis and Guillain-Barré Syndrome (GBS).

Diabetes A chronic health condition where the body is unable to produce insulin and properly breakdown sugar (glucose) in the blood. Symptoms include hunger, thirst, excessive urination, dehydration and weight loss. The treatment of diabetes requires daily insulin injections, proper nutrition and regular exercise. Complications can include heart disease, stroke, neuropathy, poor circulation leading to loss of limbs, hearing impairment, vision problems and death.

Diphtheria A bacterial disease marked by the formation of a false membrane, especially in the throat, which can cause death.

Disease Sickness, illness or loss of health.

Efficacy rate A measure used to describe how good a vaccine is at preventing disease.

Encephalitis Inflammation of the brain caused by a virus. Encephalitis can result in permanent brain damage or death.

Encephalopathy A general term describing brain dysfunction. Examples include encephalitis, meningitis, seizures and head trauma.

Endemic The continual, low-level presence of disease in a community

Epidemic The occurrence of disease within a specific geographical area or population that is in excess of what is normally expected.

Erythema Multiforme A medical condition characterized by inflammation of the skin or mucous membranes (including the mouth, throat and eyes). Erthema Multiforme has been reported following infection. Symptoms persist anywhere from 2 days to 4 weeks and include skin lesions, blisters, itching, fatigue, joint pain and fever.

Etiology The cause of.

Exposure Contact with infectious agents (bacteria or viruses) in a manner that promotes transmission and increases the likelihood of disease.

Febrile Relating to fever; feverish.

Guillain-Barré Syndrome (GBS) A rare neurological disease characterized by loss of reflexes and temporary paralysis. Symptoms include weakness, numbness, tingling and increased sensitivity that spreads over the body. Muscle paralysis starts in the feet and legs and moves upwards to the arms and hands. Sometimes paralysis can result in the respiratory muscles causing breathing difficulties. Symptoms usually appear over the course of one day and may continue to progress for 3 or 4 days up to 3 or 4 weeks. Recovery begins within 2-4 weeks after the progression stops. While most patients recover, approximately 15%-20% experience persistent symptoms. GBS is fatal in 5% of cases.

Haemophilus influenzae type B (Hib) A bacterial infection that may result in severe respiratory infections, including pneumonia, and other diseases such as meningitis.

Hepatitis A A minor viral disease, that usually does not persist in the blood; transmitted through ingestion of contaminated food or water.

Hepatitis B A viral disease transmitted by infected blood or blood products, or through unprotected sex with someone who is infected.

Hepatitis C is a liver disease caused by the Hepatitis C virus (HCV), which is found in the blood of persons who have the disease. HCV is spread by contact with the blood of an infected person.

Hepatitis D is a defective virus that needs the hepatitis B virus to exist. Hepatitis D virus (HDV) is found in the blood of persons infected with the virus.

Hepatitis E is a virus (HEV) transmitted in much the same way as hepatitis A virus. Hepatitis E, however, does not often occur in the United States.

Herd immunity See Community immunity.

Herpes Zoster A disease characterized by painful skin lesions that occur mainly on the trunk (back and stomach) of the body but which can also develop on the face and in the mouth. Complications include headache, vomiting, fever and meningitis. Recovery may take up to 5 weeks. Herpes Zoster is caused by the same virus that is responsible for chickenpox. Most people are exposed to this virus during childhood. After the primary infection (chickenpox), the virus becomes dormant, or inactivated. In some people the virus reactivates years, or even decades, later and causes herpes zoster. Also known as the shingles.

Hives The eruption of red marks on the skin that are usually accompanied by itching. This condition can be caused by an allergy (e.g., to food or drugs), stress, infection or physical agents (e.g., heat or cold). Also known as uticaria.

Hypersensitivity A condition in which the body has an exaggerated response to a substance (e.g., food or drug). Also known as an allergy.

Hyposensitivity A condition in which the body has a weakened or delayed reaction to a substance.

Immune globulin A protein found in the blood that fights infection. Also known as gamma globulin.

Immune system The complex system in the body responsible for fighting disease. Its primary function is to identify foreign substances in the body (bacteria, viruses, fungi or parasites) and develop a defense against them. This defense is known as the immune response. It involves production of protein molecules called antibodies to eliminate foreign organisms that invade the body.

Immunity Protection against a disease. There are two types of immunity, passive and active. Immunity is indicated by the presence of antibodies in the blood and can usually be determined with a laboratory test. See active and passive immunity.

Immunization The process by which a person or animal becomes protected against a disease. This term is often used interchangeably with vaccination or inoculation.

Immunosupression When the immune system is unable to protect the body from disease. This condition can be caused by disease (like HIV infection or cancer) or by certain drugs (like those used in chemotherapy). Individuals whose immune systems are compromised should not receive live, attenuated vaccines.

Inactive vaccine A vaccine made from viruses and bacteria that have been killed through physical or chemical processes. These killed organisms cannot cause disease.

Inapparent infection The presence of infection without symptoms. Also known as subclinical or asymptomatic infection.

Incidence The number of new disease cases reported in a population over a certain period of time.

Incubation period The time from contact with infectious agents (bacteria or viruses) to onset of disease.

Infectious Capable of spreading disease. Also known as communicable.

Infectious agents Organisms capable of spreading disease (e.g., bacteria or viruses).

Inflammation Redness, swelling, heat and pain resulting from injury to tissue (parts of the body underneath the skin). Also known as swelling.

Inflammatory bowel disease (IBD) A general term for any disease characterized by inflammation of the bowel. Examples include colitis and Crohn's disease. Symptoms include abdominal pain, diarrhea, fever, loss of appetite and weight loss.

Influenza A highly contagious viral infection characterized by sudden onset of fever, severe aches and pains, and inflammation of the mucous membrane.

Investigational vaccine A vaccine that has been approved by the Food and Drug Administration (FDA) for use in clinical trials on humans. However, investigational vaccines are still in the testing and evaluation phase and are not licensed for use in the general public.

Jaundice Yellowing of the eyes. This condition is often a symptom of hepatitis infection.

Lesion An abnormal change in the structure of an organ, due to injury or disease.

Live vaccine A vaccine in which live virus is weakened through chemical or physical processes in order to produce an immune response without causing the severe effects of the disease. Attenuated vaccines currently licensed in the United States include measles, mumps, rubella, polio, yellow fever and varicella. Also known as an attenuated vaccine.

Lupus A disease characterized by inflammation of the connective tissue (which supports and connects all parts of the body). Chronic swelling of the connective tissue causes damage to the skin, joints, kidneys, nervous system, and mucous membranes. The disease begins with fever, joint pain, and fatigue. Additional symptoms continue to develop over the years including nausea, fatigue, weight loss, arthritis, headaches, and epilepsy. Problems with heart, lung, and kidney function may also result. This condition is diagnosed most frequently in young women but also occurs in children.

Lyme disease A bacterial disease transmitted by infected ticks. Human beings may come into contact with infected ticks during outdoor activities (camping, hiking). Symptoms include fatigue, chills, fever, headache, joint and muscle pain, swollen lymph nodes, and a skin rash (in a circular pattern). Long-term problems include arthritis, nervous system abnormalities, irregular heart rhythm, and meningitis. Lyme disease can be treated with antibiotics. A vaccine was available from 1998 to 2002.

Lymphocytes Small white blood cells that help the body defend itself against infection. These cells are produced in bone marrow and develop into plasma cells which produce antibodies. Also known as B cells.

Macrophage A large cell that helps the body defend itself against disease by surrounding and destroying foreign organisms (viruses or bacteria).

Macular Skin lesions, normally red-colored.

Measles A contagious viral disease marked by the eruption of red circular spots on the skin.

Memory cell A group of cells that help the body defend itself against disease by remembering prior exposure to specific organisms (e.g., viruses or bacteria). Therefore these cells are able to respond quickly when these organisms repeatedly threaten the body.

Meningitis Inflammation of the brain and spinal cord that can result in permanent brain damage and death.

Meningoenephalitis ["men in joe en sef uh LIGHT iss"]—inflammation of the brain and meninges (membranes) that involves the encephalon (area inside the skull) and spinal column.

Microbes Tiny organisms (including viruses and bacteria) that can only be seen with a microscope.

Mucosal membranes The soft, wet tissue that lines body openings specifically the mouth, nose, rectum and vagina.

Multiple sclerosis Multiple sclerosis is a disease of the central nervous system characterized by the destruction of the myelin sheath surrounding neurons, resulting in the formation of "plaques." MS is a progressive and usually fluctuating disease with exacerbations (patients feeling worse) and remissions (patients feeling better) over many decades. Eventually, in most patients, remissions do not reach baseline levels and permanent disability and sometimes death occurs. The cause of MS is unknown. The most widely held hypothesis is that MS occurs in patients with a genetic susceptibility and that some environmental factors "trigger" exacerbations. MS is 3 times more common in women than men, with diagnosis usually made as young adults. Also see demyelinating disorders.

Mumps Acute contagious viral illness marked by swelling, especially of the parotid glands.

Neuritis Inflammation of the nerves.

Neuropathy A general term for any dysfunction in the peripheral nervous system. Symptoms include pain, muscle weakness, numbness, loss of coordination and paralysis. This condition may result in permanent disability.

Optic neuritis A medical condition where vision deteriorates rapidly over hours or days. One or both eyes may be affected. This condition results for the demyelination of optic nerves. In most cases, the cause of optic neuritis is unknown. Patients may regain their vision or be left with permanent impairment. Also see demyelinating disorders.

Orchitis A complication of mumps infection occurring in males (who are beyond puberty). Symptoms begin 7-10 days after onset of mumps and include inflammation of the testicles, headache, nausea, vomiting, pain and fever. Most patients recover but in rare cases sterility occurs.

Otitis media A viral or bacterial infection that leads to inflammation of the middle ear. This condition usually occurs along with an upper respiratory infection. Symptoms include earache, high fever, nausea, vomiting and diarrhea. In addition, hearing loss, facial paralysis and meningitis may result.

Outbreak Sudden appearance of a disease in a specific geographic area (e.g., neighborhood or community) or population (e.g., adolescents).

Pandemic An epidemic occurring over a very large area.

Papular Marked by small red-colored elevation of the skin.

Passive immunity Protection against disease through antibodies produced by another human being or animal. Passive immunity is effective, but protection is generally limited and diminishes over time (usually a few weeks or months). For example, maternal antibodies are passed to the infant prior to birth. These antibodies temporarily protect the baby for the first 4-6 months of life.

Pathogens Organisms (e.g., bacteria, viruses, parasites and fungi) that cause disease in human beings.

Pertussis (whooping cough) Bacterial infectious disease marked by a convulsive spasmodic cough, sometimes followed by a crowing intake of breath.

Petechiae ["pe TEEK ee ay"]—a tiny reddish or purplish spot on the skin or mucous membrane, commonly part of infectious diseases such as typhoid fever.

Placebo A substance or treatment that has no effect on human beings.

Pneumonia Inflammation of the lungs characterized by fever, chills, muscle stiffness, chest pain, cough, shortness of breath, rapid heart rate and difficulty breathing.

Poliomyelitis (polio) An acute infectious viral disease characterized by fever, paralysis, and atrophy of skeletal muscles.

Polysaccharide vaccines Vaccines that are composed of long chains of sugar molecules that resemble the surface of certain types of bacteria. Polysaccharide vaccines are available for pneumococcal disease, meningococcal disease and *Haemophilus Influenzae* type B.

Potency A measure of strength.

Precaution A condition in a recipient which may result in a life-threatening problem if the vaccine is given, or a condition which could compromise the ability of the vaccine to produce immunity.

Prevalence The number of disease cases (new and existing) within a population over a given time period.

Prodromal An early symptom indicating the onset of an attack or a disease.

Quarantine The isolation of a person or animal who has a disease (or is suspected of having a disease) in order to prevent further spread of the disease.

Recombinant Of or resulting from new combinations of genetic material or cells; the genetic material produced when segments of DNA from different sources are joined to produce recombinant DNA.

Reye syndrome Encephalopathy (general brain disorder) in children following an acute illness such as influenza or chickenpox. Symptoms include vomiting, agitation and lethargy. This condition may result in coma or death.

Residual seizure disorder (RSD)   See seizures.

Risk   The likelihood that an individual will experience a certain event.

Rotavirus   A group of viruses that cause diarrhea in children.

Rubella   (German measles) Viral infection that is milder than normal measles but as damaging to the fetus when it occurs early in pregnancy.

Rubeola   See Measles.

Seroconversion   Development of antibodies in the blood of an individual who previously did not have detectable antibodies.

Serology   Measurement of antibodies, and other immunological properties, in the blood serum.

Serosurvey   Study measuring a person's risk of developing a particular disease.

Seizure   The sudden onset of a jerking and staring spell usually caused by fever. Also known as convulsions.

Shingles   See herpes zoster.

Side Effect   Undesirable reaction resulting from immunization.

Smallpox   An acute, highly infectious, often fatal disease caused by a poxvirus and characterized by high fever and aches with subsequent widespread eruption of pimples that blister, produce pus, and form pockmarks. Also called *variola*.

Strain   A specific version of an organism. Many diseases, including HIV/AIDS and hepatitis, have multiple strains.

Subclinical infection   The presence of infection without symptoms. Also known as inapparent or asymptomatic infection.

Sudden infant death syndrome (SIDS)   The sudden and unexpected death of a healthy infant under 1 year of age. A diagnosis of SIDS is made when an autopsy cannot determine another cause of death. The cause of SIDS is unknown. Also known as "crib" or "cot" death.

Susceptible   Unprotected against disease.

Temporal association   Two or more events that occur around the same time but are unrelated, chance occurrences.

Teratogenic   Of, relating to, or causing developmental malformations.

Tetanus   Toxin-producing bacterial disease marked by painful muscle spasms.

Thimerosal   Thimerosal is a mercury-containing preservative that has been used in some vaccines and other products since the 1930's. There is no evidence that the low concentrations of thimerosal in vaccines have caused any harm other than minor reactions like redness or swelling at the injection site. However, in July 1999 the U.S. Public Health Service, the American Academy of Pediatrics, and vaccine manufacturers agreed that thimerosal should be reduced or eliminated from vaccines as a precautionary measure. Today, all routinely recommended childhood vaccines manufactured for the U.S. market contain either no thimerosal or only trace amounts.

Titer   The detection of antibodies in blood through a laboratory test.

Transverse myelitis   The sudden onset of spinal cord disease. Symptoms include general back pain followed by weakness in the feet and legs that moves upward. There is no cure and many patients are left with permanent disabilities or paralysis. Transverse myelitis is a demyelinating disorder that may be associated with multiple sclerosis (MS). Also see demyelinating disorders.

Urticaria   The eruption of red marks on the skin that are usually accompanied by itching. This condition can be caused by an allergy (e.g., to food or drugs), stress, infection or physical agents (e.g., heat or cold). Also known as hives.

Vaccination   Injection of a killed or weakened infectious organism in order to prevent the disease.

Vaccine   A product that produces immunity therefore protecting the body from the disease. Vaccines are administered through needle injections, by mouth and by aerosol.

Vaccine Adverse Event Reporting System (VAERS)   A database managed by the Centers for Disease Control and Prevention and the Food and Drug Administration. VAERS provides a mechanism for the collection and analysis of adverse events associated with vaccines currently licensed in the United States. Reports to VAERS can be made by the vaccine manufacturer, recipient, their parent/guardian or health care provider. For more information on VAERS, call (800) 822-7967 / (800) 822-7967.

Vaccine Safety Datalink Project (VSD)   In order to increase knowledge about vaccine adverse events, the Centers for Disease Control and Prevention have formed partnerships with eight large health Management Organizations (HMOs) to continually evaluate vaccine safety. The project contains data on more than 6 million people. Medical records are monitored for potential adverse events following immunization. The VSD project allows for planned vaccine safety studies as well as timely investigations of hypothesis.

Varicella   (Chickenpox) An acute contagious disease characterized by papular and vesicular lesions.

Variola See smallpox.

Vesicular Characterized by small elevations of the skin containing fluid (blisters).

Viremia The presence of a virus in the blood.

Virulence The relative capacity of a pathogen to overcome body defenses.

Virus A tiny organism that multiplies within cells and causes disease such as chickenpox, measles, mumps, rubella, pertussis and hepatitis. Viruses are not affected by antibiotics, the drugs used to kill bacteria.

Waning immunity The loss of protective antibodies over time.

Whooping cough See *Pertussis*.

Health—Long-Term Care

Advocacy and Assertion Techniques for intervening when your viewpoint does not match that of the decisionmaker.

Adaptability The ability to adjust strategies and alter a course of action in response to changing conditions (internal or external).

Brief Discussion prior to start that assigns essential roles, establishes expectations, identifies anticipated outcomes, and identifies likely contingencies.

Call-Out A tactic used to communicate critical information during an emergent event. Call-outs help the team prepare for vital next steps in resident care.

Check-Back A communication strategy that requires verification of information. The sender initiates the message; the receiver accepts it and restates the message. In return, the sender verifies that the restatement of the original message is correct or amends it if not.

Checklist A list of items to be noted, checked, or remembered.

Closed-Loop Communication/Information Exchange The initiation of a message by a sender, the receipt and verbal acknowledgment of the message by the receiver, and the verification of the message by the initial sender.

Coaching The process of helping someone else expand and apply his or her skills, knowledge, and abilities. Generally takes place within a defined context, such as a specific task, skill, or responsibility.

Collaboration An approach to manage conflict that results in a mutually satisfying solution that is in the resident's best interest.

Communication The process by which information is clearly and accurately exchanged among team members.

Crew Resource Management (CRM) Encompasses a wide range of knowledge, skills, and attitudes, including communications, situational awareness, problem solving, decisionmaking, and teamwork, making optimum use of all available resources (e.g., equipment, procedures, and people) to promote and enhance efficiency of operations.

Cross-Monitoring The process of monitoring other team members' actions against the standard or shared plan of care for the purpose of sharing workload and reducing or avoiding errors.

CUS Signal phrases that denote "I am Concerned. I am Uncomfortable. This is a Safety Issue." When these phrases are used, all team members will understand clearly not only the issue but also the magnitude of the issue.

Debrief Brief, informal information exchange session designed to improve team performance and effectiveness; after action review.

DESC Script A technique for managing and resolving conflict.

Feedback The transmission of evaluative or corrective information.

Handoff The transfer of information/knowledge along with authority and responsibility among care providers at all levels of care transitions and across the continuum of care.

Huddle Ad hoc planning to reestablish situation awareness; designed to reinforce plans already in place and assess the need to adjust the plan.

Human Factors Human capabilities and limitations to the design and organization of the work environment. Primarily attributed to errors but also a consideration in the design of workflow and processes. The study of human factors can help identify operations susceptible to human error and improve working conditions to reduce fatigue and inattention.

I PASS the BATON A mnemonic used during handoffs to facilitate a structured transition in care.

I'M SAFE Checklist A simple checklist that should be used daily to determine both your co-workers' and your own ability to perform safely.

Leadership The ability to coordinate the activities of team members and teams by managing the resources available to team members and facilitating team performance by communicating plans, providing information about team performance through debriefs, and providing support to team members when needed.

Mutual Support Assessing and anticipating other team members' needs through accurate knowledge about their responsibilities, task load, and core capabilities and responding by shifting the workload among members to achieve balance during high or low periods of workload or pressure.

Mutual Trust The shared belief that team members will perform their roles and protect the interests of their teammates.

Obstacles Human behaviors that result from both personality and attitude that prevent effective job performance. Obstacles are ever present, requiring vigilant awareness to overcome them. Some examples of obstacles include:

- *Excessive Professional Courtesy* Giving someone of higher rank or status too much respect or deference so that it affects the level of health care they receive as patients. May also occur among team members having higher rank or status, resulting in a hesitancy of team members to point out deficiencies in performance.
- *Halo Effect* Occurs when someone else's "great" reputation or extensive experience clouds our judgment.
- *Passenger Syndrome* Team members experience "Passenger Syndrome" ("just along for the ride") when they abdicate responsibility, believing someone else is in charge.
- *Hidden Agenda* When a team member makes suggestions or decisions on information or desires of which the rest of the team may be unaware. An example of hidden agenda is a strong desire to get off work early or avoid a procedure in which they are poorly trained.
- *Complacency* When individuals or teams become comfortable with the most routine to the most difficult or critical tasks. Becomes a hazard when individuals and teams lose their vigilance and situational awareness.
- *High-Risk Phase* A procedure or time in which a medical mishap is likely to happen (e.g., shift change).
- *Task (Target) Fixation* A condition in which an individual's or team's focus on a task may impair their decisionmaking or make them oblivious to "the big picture." It is generally precipitated by real or perceived pressure to perform or by workload or stressrelated issues.
- *Strength of an Idea* An unconscious attempt to make available evidence fit a preconceived situation. Once people get a certain idea in their head, it can be difficult or impossible for them to alter that idea no matter how much conflicting information is received.
- *Hazardous Attitudes* Ways of thinking and viewing the world (e.g., antiauthority, impulsiveness, invulnerability, machismo, or resignation).

Performance Monitoring The ability of team members to monitor each other's task execution and give feedback during task execution.

Resident Care Team Composed of the resident, caregivers, and all staff within the nursing home.

Resident-Centered Care Also known as person-centered care, a philosophy that puts the needs, interests, and choices of residents at the center of care. It allows residents to exercise control and autonomy over their own lives, to the fullest extent possible. Evidence shows that giving residents a greater role in their care can improve their health.

Root Cause Analysis (RCA) A structured approach to investigation of undesirable events or outcomes to determine all the underlying causes of the event so that effective corrective or preventive actions may be developed. RCA focuses on weaknesses in systems and processes that may have diminished human performance.

SBAR A framework for team members to structure information when communicating with each other (physician to physician, nurse to physician, nurse to nurse, nurse to staff, nurse to resident).

Shared Mental Model An organizing knowledge structure of relevant facts and relationships about a task or situation that are commonly held by members of a team.

Situation Awareness The ability to identify, process, and comprehend the critical elements of information about what is happening to the team with regard to the mission (plan of care). Simply put, it is knowing what is going on around you and what is likely to happen next, maintaining mindfulness at all times.

Situation Monitoring The process of actively scanning and assessing elements of the situation to gain information or maintain an accurate awareness or understanding of the situation in which the team functions.

STEP A tool for monitoring the following elements of the situation: Status of the resident, Team members, Environment, and Progress toward the goal.

Task Assistance A form of mutual support, a team behavior that protects individual members from work overload situations that may reduce effectiveness and increase the risk of error.

Team (Multi-Team System) Each team within a multi-team system is responsible for various aspects of resident care, requiring coordination among them all to ensure quality resident care. A multi-team system is composed of the following teams:

- *Core Team* A group of caregivers who work interdependently to manage a set of assigned residents from point of assessment to disposition.
- *Coordinating Team* Members of a department/unit responsible for managing the operational environment that supports the Core Team.

- *Contingency Team* A time-limited team formed for emergent or specific events and composed of members from various teams.
- *Ancillary Services* Primarily a service delivery team whose mission is to support the core team (e.g., lab, pharmacy).
- *Support Services* Primarily a service-focused team whose mission is to create efficient, safe, comfortable, and clean health care environment (e.g., housekeeping).
- *Administration* Includes executive leadership of a unit or facility. They have overall responsibility and accountability for the nursing home. They create the climate and culture in which a teamwork system functions.

Team Competencies The attributes team members need to perform successfully as a team. The three types of competencies that are critical for effective teamwork include:

- *Team Knowledge Competencies* The principles and concepts that underlie a team's effective task performance. To function effectively in a team, team members should know what team skills are required, when particular team behaviors are appropriate, and how to manifest these skills and behaviors in a team setting. Team members should also know the team's mission and goals and be aware of one another's roles and responsibilities in achieving them.
- *Team Skill Competencies* A learned capacity to interact with other team members at some minimal proficiency.
- *Team Attitude Competencies* Internal states that influence a team member's choices or decisions to act in a particular way. Positive attitudes toward teamwork, a collective orientation, and mutual trust among team members are critical to a successful team process.

Team Orientation The propensity to take others' behavior into account during group interaction and the belief in the importance of team goals over individual member goals.

Team Self-Correction The process in which team members engage in evaluating their performance and in determining the strategies after task execution.

Team Structure The delineation of fundamentals (e.g., team size, team membership, team leadership, team identification, and team distribution).

Transformational Change The movement to place the needs, interests, and choices of residents at the center of care practices, which is also known as "culture change," "resident-centered care," "resident-directed care," and "person-centered care."

Two-Challenge Rule A strategy for asserting a concern that results when clinical actions or a course of care differ from the agreed-on plan or usual procedure for the presenting event. The Two-Challenge rule involves asserting the concern at least two times to ensure that it has been heard. State the concern (first challenge), and if no response or discussion occurs, rephrase and restate the concern (second challenge) to be certain the challenge has been both heard and understood.

Health—Medicare

Advance Beneficiary Notice (ABN) In original Medicare, a notice that a doctor, supplier, or provider gives a Medicare beneficiary before furnishing an item or service if the doctor, supplier, or provider believes that Medicare may deny payment. In this situation, if you aren't given an ABN before you get the item or service, and Medicare denies payment, then you may not have to pay for it. If you are given an ABN, and you sign it, you will probably have to pay for the item or service if Medicare denies payment.

Advance Coverage Decision A notice you get from a Medicare Advantage Plan letting you know in advance whether it will cover a particular service.

Advance Directive A written document stating how you want medical decisions to be made if you lose the ability to make them for yourself. It may include a living will and a durable power of attorney for health care.

ALS Amyotrophic lateral sclerosis, also known as Lou Gehrig's disease.

Ambulatory Surgical Center A facility where simpler surgeries are performed for patients who aren't expected to need more than 24 hours of care.

Appeal An appeal is the action you can take if you disagree with a coverage or payment decision made by Medicare, your Medicare health plan, or your Medicare Prescription Drug Plan. You can appeal if Medicare or your plan denies one of the following: your request for a health care service, supply or prescription that you think you should be able to get; your request for payment for health care or a prescription drug you already got; your request to change the amount you must pay for a prescription drug; you can also appeal of you're already getting coverage and Medicare or your plan stops paying.

Assignment An agreement by your doctor or other supplier to be paid directly by Medicare, to accept the payment amount Medicare approves for the service, and not to bill you for any more than the Medicare deductible and coinsurance.

Benefit Period The way that Original Medicare measures your use of hospital and skilled nursing facility (SNF) services. A benefit period begins the day you're admitted as an inpatient in a hospital or skilled nursing facility. The benefit period ends when you haven't received any inpatient hospital care (or skilled care in a SNF) for 60 days in a row. If you go into a hospital or a skilled nursing facility after one benefit period has ended, a new benefit period begins. You must pay the inpatient hospital deductible for each benefit period. There is no limit to the number of benefit periods.

Certified (certification) See "Medicare-certified provider" Claim A request for payment that you submit to Medicare or other health insurance when you get items and services that you think are covered.

Clinical Breast Exam An exam by your doctor or other health care provider to check for breast cancer by feeling and looking at your breasts. This exam isn't the same as a mammogram and is usually done in the doctor's office during your Pap test and pelvic exam.

Coinsurance An amount you may be required to pay as your share of the cost for services after you pay any deductibles. Coinsurance is usually a percentage (for example, 20%). Comprehensive outpatient rehabilitation facility A facility that provides a variety of services on an outpatient basis, including physicians' services, physical therapy, social or psychological services, and rehabilitation.

Copayment An amount you may be required to pay as your share of the cost for a medical service or supply, like a doctor's visit, hospital outpatient visit, or prescription. A copayment is usually a set amount, rather than a percentage. For example, you might pay $10 or $20 for a doctor's visit or prescription.

Coverage Determination (Part D) The first decision made by your Medicare drug plan (not the pharmacy) about your drug benefits, including the following: Whether a particular drug is covered • Whether you've met all the requirements for getting a requested drug • How much you're required to pay for a drug • Whether to make an exception to a plan rule when you request it. If the drug plan doesn't give you a prompt decision and you can show that the delay would affect your health, the plan's failure to act is considered to be a coverage determination. If you disagree with the coverage determination, the next step is an appeal.

Coverage Gap (Medicare prescription drug coverage) A period of time in which you pay higher cost sharing for prescription drugs until you spend enough to qualify for catastrophic coverage. The coverage gap (also called the "donut hole") starts when you and your plan have paid a set dollar amount for prescription drugs during that year.

Creditable Coverage See "creditable coverage (Medigap)" or "creditable prescription drug coverage" Creditable coverage (Medigap) Previous health insurance coverage that can be used to shorten a pre-existing condition waiting period under a Medigap policy.

Creditable Prescription Drug Coverage Prescription drug coverage (for example, from an employer or union) that's expected to pay, on average, at least as much as Medicare's standard prescription drug coverage. People who have this kind of coverage when they become eligible for Medicare can generally keep that coverage without paying a penalty, if they decide to enroll in Medicare prescription drug coverage later.

Critical Access Hospital (CAH) A small facility that provides outpatient services, as well as inpatient services on a limited basis, to people in rural areas.

Custodial Care Non-skilled personal care, such as help with activities of daily living like bathing, dressing, eating, getting in or out of a bed or chair, moving around, and using the bathroom. It may also include the kind of health-related care that most people do themselves, like using eye drops. In most cases, Medicare doesn't pay for custodial care.

Deductible The amount you must pay for health care or prescriptions before Original Medicare, your prescription drug plan, or your other insurance begins to pay.

Demonstrations Special projects, sometimes called "pilot programs" or "research studies," that test improvements in Medicare coverage, payment, and quality of care. They usually operate only for a limited time, for a specific group of people, and in specific areas.

Diethylstilbestrol (DES) A drug given to pregnant women from the early 1940s until 1971 to help with common problems during pregnancy. The drug has been linked to cancer of the cervix or vagina in women whose mother took the drug while pregnant.

Drug List A list of prescription drugs covered by a prescription drug plan or another insurance plan offering prescription drug benefits. This list is also called a formulary.

Durable Medical Equipment Certain medical equipment, such as a walker, wheelchair, or hospital bed, that's ordered by your doctor for use in the home.

Durable Power of Attorney A legal document that enables you to designate another person to act on your behalf in the event you become disabled or incapacitated.

End-Stage Renal Disease (ESRD) Permanent kidney failure that requires a regular course of dialysis or a kidney transplant.

Exception A type of Medicare prescription drug coverage determination. A formulary exception is a drug plan's decision to cover a drug that's not on its drug list or to waive a coverage rule. A tiering exception is a drug plan's decision to charge a lower amount for a drug that's on its non-preferred drug tier. You must request an exception, and your doctor or other prescriber must send a supporting statement explaining the medical reason for the exception.

Excess Charge If you have Original Medicare, and the amount a doctor or other health care provider is legally permitted to charge is higher than the Medicare approved amount, the difference is called the excess charge.

Extra Help A Medicare program to help people with limited income and resources pay Medicare prescription drug program costs, such as premiums, deductibles, and coinsurance.

Formulary A list of prescription drugs covered by a prescription drug plan or another insurance plan offering prescription drug benefits.

Grievance A complaint about the way your Medicare health plan or Medicare drug plan is giving care. For example, you may file a grievance if you have a problem calling the plan or if you're unhappy with the way a staff person at the plan has behaved towards you. However, if you have a complaint about a plan's refusal to cover a service, supply, or prescription, you file an appeal.

Group Health Plan In general, a health plan offered by an employer or employee organization that provides health coverage to employees, former employees, and their families.

Guaranteed Issue Rights (also called "Medigap protections") Rights you have in certain situations when insurance companies are required by law to sell or offer you a Medigap policy. In these situations, an insurance company can't deny you a Medigap policy, or place conditions on a Medigap policy, such as exclusions for pre-existing conditions, and can't charge you more for a Medigap policy because of a past or present health problem.

Guaranteed Renewable Policy An insurance policy that can't be terminated by the insurance company unless you make untrue statements to the insurance company, commit fraud, or don't pay your premiums. All Medigap policies issued since 1992 are guaranteed renewable.

Health Care Provider A person or organization that's licensed to give health care. Doctors, nurses, and hospitals are examples of health care providers.

Home Health Agency An organization that provides home health care.

Home Health Care Health care services and supplies a doctor decides you may receive in your home under a plan of care established by your doctor. Medicare only covers home health care on a limited basis as ordered by your doctor.

Hospice A special way of caring for people who are terminally ill. Hospice care involves a team-oriented approach that addresses the medical, physical, social, emotional, and spiritual needs of the patient. Hospice also provides support to the patient's family or caregiver.

Independent Reviewer An organization (sometimes called an Independent Review Entity or IRE) that has no connection to your Medicare health plan or Medicare Prescription Drug Plan. Medicare contracts with the IRE to review your case if you appeal your plan's payment or coverage decision or if your plan doesn't make a timely appeals decision.

Inpatient Rehabilitation Facility A hospital, or part of a hospital, that provides an intensive rehabilitation program to inpatients.

Large Group Health Plan In general, a group health plan that covers employees of either an employer or employee organization that has 100 or more employees.

Lifetime Reserve Days In Original Medicare, these are additional days that Medicare will pay for when you're in a hospital for more than 90 days. You have a total of 60 reserve days that can be used during your lifetime. For each lifetime reserve day, Medicare pays all covered costs except for a daily coinsurance.

Limiting Charge In Original Medicare, the highest amount of money you can be charged for a covered service by doctors and other health care suppliers who don't accept assignment. The limiting charge is 15% over Medicare's approved amount. The limiting charge only applies to certain services and doesn't apply to supplies or equipment.

Living Will A legal document also known as a medical directive or advance directive. It states your wishes regarding life-support or other medical treatment in certain circumstances, usually when death is imminent.

Long-Term Care A variety of services that help people with their medical and non-medical needs over a period of time. Long-term care can be provided at home, in the community, or in various types of facilities, including nursing homes and assisted living facilities. Most long-term care is custodial care. Medicare doesn't pay for this type of care if this is the only kind of care you need.

Long-Term Care Hospital Acute care hospitals that provide treatment for patients who stay, on average, more than 25 days. Most patients are transferred from an intensive or critical care unit. Services provided include comprehensive rehabilitation, respiratory therapy, head trauma treatment, and pain management.

Long-Term Care Ombudsman An independent advocate (supporter) for nursing home and assisted living facility residents who works to solve problems between residents and nursing homes or assisted living facilities. They may be able to provide information about home health agencies in their area.

Medicaid A joint federal and state program that helps with medical costs for some people with limited income and resources. Medicaid programs vary from state to state, but most health care costs are covered if you qualify for both Medicare and Medicaid.

Medicaid-Certified Provider A health care provider (like a home health agency, hospital, nursing home, or dialysis facility) that has been approved by Medicaid. Providers are approved or "certified" if they have passed an inspection conducted by a state government agency.

Medical Underwriting The process that an insurance company uses to decide, based on your medical history, whether to take your application for insurance, whether to add a waiting period for pre-existing conditions (if your state law allows it), and how much to charge you for that insurance.

Medically Necessary Services or supplies that are needed for the diagnosis or treatment of your medical condition and meet accepted standards of medical practice.

Medicare The federal health insurance program for people who are age 65 or older, certain younger people with disabilities, and people with End-Stage Renal Disease (permanent kidney failure requiring dialysis or a transplant, sometimes called ESRD).

Medicare Advantage Plan (Part C) A type of Medicare health plan offered by a private company that contracts with Medicare to provide you with all your Part A and Part B benefits. Medicare Advantage Plans include Health Maintenance Organizations, Preferred Provider Organizations, Private Fee-for-Service Plans, Special Needs Plans, and Medicare Medical Savings Account Plans. If you're enrolled in a Medicare Advantage Plan, Medicare services are covered through the plan and aren't paid for under Original Medicare. Most Medicare Advantage Plans offer prescription drug coverage.

Medicare Approved Amount In Original Medicare, this is the amount a doctor or supplier that accepts assignment can be paid. It may be less than the actual amount a doctor or supplier charges. Medicare pays part of this amount and you're responsible for the difference.

Medicare-Certified Provider A health care provider (like a home health agency, hospital, nursing home, or dialysis facility) that has been approved by Medicare. Providers are approved or "certified" by Medicare if they have passed an inspection conducted by a state government agency. Medicare only covers care given by providers who are certified.

Medicare Coordination of Benefits Contractor The company that acts on behalf of Medicare to collect and manage information on other types of insurance or coverage that a person with Medicare may have, and determine whether the coverage pays before or after Medicare.

Medicare Cost Plan A type of Medicare health plan available in some areas. In a Medicare Cost Plan, if you get services outside of the plan's network without a referral, your Medicare-covered services will be paid for under Original Medicare (your Cost Plan pays for emergency services or urgently needed services).

Medicare Health Maintenance Organization (HMO) Plan A type of Medicare Advantage Plan (Part C) available in some areas of the country. In most HMOs, you can only go to doctors, specialists, or hospitals on the plan's list except in an emergency. Most HMOs also require you to get a referral from your primary care physician.

Medicare Health Plan A plan offered by a private company that contracts with Medicare to provide Part A and Part B benefits to people with Medicare who enroll in the plan. Medicare health plans include all Medicare Advantage Plans, Medicare Cost Plans, Demonstration/Pilot Programs, and Programs of Allinclusive Care for the Elderly (PACE).

Medicare Medical Savings Account (MSA) Plan MSA Plans combine a high deductible Medicare Advantage Plan and a bank account. The plan deposits money from Medicare into the account. You can use the money in this account to pay for your health care costs, but only Medicare-covered expenses count toward your deductible. The amount deposited is usually less than your deductible amount so you generally will have to pay out-of-pocket before your coverage begins.

Medicare Part A (Hospital Insurance) Coverage for inpatient hospital stays, care in a skilled nursing facility, hospice care, and some home health care. Medicare Part B (medical insurance) Coverage for certain doctors' services, outpatient care, medical supplies, and preventive services.

Medicare Plan Any way other than Original Medicare that you can get your Medicare health or prescription drug coverage. This term includes all Medicare health plans and Medicare Prescription Drug Plans.

Medicare Preferred Provider Organization (PPO) Plan A type of Medicare Advantage Plan (Part C) available in some areas of the country in which you pay less if you use doctors, hospitals, and other health care providers that belong to the plan's network. You can use doctors, hospitals, and providers outside of the network for an additional cost.

Medicare Prescription Drug Coverage (Part D) Optional benefits for prescription drugs available to all people with Medicare for an additional charge. This coverage is offered by insurance companies and other private companies approved by Medicare.

Medicare Prescription Drug Plan (Part D) A stand-alone drug plan that adds prescription drug coverage to Original Medicare, some Medicare Cost Plans, some Medicare Private-Fee-for-Service Plans, and Medicare Medical Savings Account Plans. These plans are offered by insurance companies and other private companies approved by Medicare. Medicare Advantage Plans may also offer prescription drug coverage that follows the same rules as Medicare Prescription Drug Plans.

Medicare Private Fee-for-Service (PFFS) Plan A type of Medicare Advantage Plan (Part C) in which you can generally go to any doctor or hospital you could go to if you had Original Medicare, if the doctor or hospital agrees to treat you. The plan determines how much it will pay doctors and hospitals, and how much you must pay when you get care. A Private Fee-For-Service Plan is very different than Original Medicare, and you must follow the plan rules carefully when you go for health care services. When you're in a Private Fee-For-Service Plan, you may pay more or less for Medicare-covered benefits than in Original Medicare.

Medicare Savings Program A Medicaid program that helps people with limited income and resources pay some or all of their Medicare premiums, deductibles, and coinsurance.

Medicare SELECT A type of Medigap policy that may require you to use hospitals and, in some cases, doctors within its network to be eligible for full benefits.

Medicare Special Needs Plan (SNP) A special type of Medicare Advantage Plan (Part C) that provides more focused and specialized health care for specific groups of people, such as those who have both Medicare and Medicaid, who live in a nursing home, or have certain chronic medical conditions.

Medicare Summary Notice (MSN) A notice you get after the doctor or provider files a claim for Part A or Part B services in Original Medicare. It explains what the doctor or provider billed for, the Medicare-approved amount, how much Medicare paid, and what you must pay.

Medigap Open Enrollment Period A one-time-only, 6-month period when federal law allows you to buy any Medigap policy you want that's sold in your state. It starts in the first month that you're covered under Part B and you're age 65 or older. During this period, you can't be denied a Medigap policy or charged more due to past or present health problems. Some states may have additional open enrollment rights under state law.

Medigap Policy Medicare Supplement Insurance sold by private insurance companies to fill "gaps" in Original Medicare coverage.

Multi-Employer Plan In general, a group health plan that's sponsored jointly by 2 or more employers.

Original Medicare Original Medicare is fee-for-service coverage under which the government pays your health care providers directly for your Part A and/or Part B benefits.

Out-of-Pocket Costs Health or prescription drug costs that you must pay on your own because they aren't covered by Medicare or other insurance.

Pap Test A test to check for cancer of the cervix, the opening to a woman's uterus. It's done by removing cells from the cervix. The cells are then prepared so they can be seen under a microscope.

Pelvic Exam An exam to check if internal female organs are normal by feeling their shape and size.

Penalty An amount added to your monthly premium for Part B or a Medicare drug plan (Part D) if you don't join when you're first eligible. You pay this higher amount as long as you have Medicare. There are some exceptions.

Pilot Programs See "demonstrations."

Point-of-Service Option In a Health Maintenance Organization (HMO), this option lets you use doctors and hospitals outside the plan for an additional cost.

Power of Attorney A medical power of attorney is a document that lets you appoint someone you trust to make decisions about your medical care. This type of advance directive also may be called a health care proxy, appointment of health care agent, or a durable power of attorney for health care.

Pre-Existing Condition A health problem you had before the date that a new insurance policy starts.

Premium The periodic payment to Medicare, an insurance company, or a health care plan for health or prescription drug coverage.

Preventive Services Health care to prevent illness or detect illness at an early stage, when treatment is likely to work best (for example, preventive services include Pap tests, flu shots, and screening mammograms).

Primary Care Doctor The doctor you see first for most health problems. He or she makes sure you get the care you need to keep you healthy. He or she also may talk with other doctors and health care providers about your care and refer you to them. In many Medicare Advantage Plans, you must see your primary care doctor before you see any other health care provider.

Programs of All-Inclusive Care for the Elderly (PACE) A special type of health plan that provides all the care and services covered by Medicare and Medicaid as well as additional medically-necessary care and services based on your needs as determined by an interdisciplinary team. PACE serves frail older adults who need nursing home services but are capable of living in the community. PACE combines medical, social, and longterm care services and prescription drug coverage.

Quality Improvement Organization (QIO) A group of practicing doctors and other health care experts paid by the federal government to check and improve the care given to people with Medicare.

Recovery Contractor A company that acts on behalf of Medicare to obtain repayment when Medicare makes a conditional payment and the other payer is determined to be primary.

Referral A written order from your primary care doctor for you to see a specialist or get certain medical services. In many Health Maintenance Organizations (HMOs), you need to get a referral before you can get medical care from anyone except your primary care doctor. If you don't get a referral first, the plan may not pay for the services.

Rehabilitation Services Services that help you regain abilities, such as speech or walking, that have been impaired by an illness or injury. These services are given by nurses, and physical, occupational and speech therapists. Examples include working with a physical therapist to help you walk and with an occupational therapist to help you get dressed.

Religious Nonmedical Health Care Institution A facility that provides nonmedical health care items and services to people who need hospital or skilled nursing facility care, but for whom that care would be inconsistent with their religious beliefs.

Respite Care Temporary care provided in a nursing home, hospice inpatient facility, or hospital so that a family member or friend who is the patient's caregiver can rest or take some time off.

Secondary Payer The insurance policy, plan, or program that pays second on a claim for medical care. This could be Medicare, Medicaid, or other insurance depending on the situation.

Service Area A geographic area where a health insurance plan accepts members if it limits membership based on where people live. For plans that limit which doctors and hospitals you may use, it's also generally the area where you can get routine (non-emergency) services. The plan may disenroll you if you move out of the plan's service area.

Skilled Nursing Care Care such as intravenous injections that can only be given by a registered nurse or doctor.

Skilled Nursing Facility (SNF) A nursing facility with the staff and equipment to give skilled nursing care and, in most cases, skilled rehabilitative services and other related health services.

Skilled Nursing Facility (SNF) Care Skilled nursing care and rehabilitation services provided on a continuous, daily basis, in a skilled nursing facility. Examples of skilled nursing facility care include physical therapy or intravenous injections that can only be given by a registered nurse or doctor.

State Health Insurance Assistance Program (SHIP) A state program that gets money from the federal government to give free local health insurance counseling to people with Medicare.

State Insurance Department A state agency that regulates insurance and can provide information about Medigap policies and other private health insurance.

State Medical Assistance Office A state agency that's in charge of the State's Medicaid program and can give information about programs that help pay medical bills for people with limited income and resources.

State Pharmacy Assistance Program (SPAP) A state program that provides help paying for drug coverage based on financial need, age, or medical condition.

State Survey Agency A state agency that oversees health care facilities that participate in the Medicare and/or Medicaid programs. The State Survey Agency inspects health care facilities and investigates complaints to ensure that health and safety standards are met.

Supplemental Security Income (SSI) A monthly benefit paid by Social Security to people with limited income and resources who are disabled, blind, or age 65 or older. SSI benefits aren't the same as Social Security retirement or disability benefits.

Supplier Generally, any company, person, or agency that gives you a medical item or service, except when you're an inpatient in a hospital or skilled nursing facility.

Telemedicine Medical or other health services given to a patient using a communications system (like a computer, telephone, or television) by a practitioner in a location different than the patient's.

TTY A teletypewriter (TTY) is a communication device used by people who are deaf, hard-of-hearing, or have a severe speech impairment. People who don't have a TTY can communicate with a TTY user through a message relay center (MRC). An MRC has TTY operators available to send and interpret TTY messages.

Urgently Needed Care Care that you get outside of your Medicare health plan's service area for a sudden illness or injury that needs medical care right away but isn't life threatening. If it's not safe to wait until you get home to get care from a plan doctor, the health plan must pay for the care.

Workers' Compensation A plan that employers are required to have to cover employees who get sick or injured on the job.

Homeland Security

ACQUISITION GLOSSARY

Acquisition means the acquiring by contract with appropriated funds of supplies or services (including construction) by and for the use of the Federal Government through purchase or lease, whether the supplies or services are already in existence or must be created, developed, demonstrated, and evaluated. Acquisition begins at the point when agency needs are established and includes the description of requirements to satisfy agency needs, solicitation and selection of sources, award of contracts, contract financing, contract performance, contract administration, and those technical and management functions directly related to the process of fulfilling agency needs by contract (see FAR 2.101).

Acquisition Cost means the amount that the contractor will receive for successfully completing the contract action.

Acquisition Planning means the process by which the efforts of all personnel responsible for an acquisition are coordinated and integrated through a comprehensive plan for fulfilling the agency need in a timely manner and at a reasonable cost. It includes developing the overall strategy for managing the acquisition (see FAR 2.101).

Acquisition Program Baseline (APB) is a program document required for all programs that are reviewed and or approved by DHS headquarters. The APB establishes the program's performance requirements, schedule requirements and estimate of total acquisition cost of the entire program (rather than each acquisition).

Acquisition Strategy includes: the proposed contract type, terms and conditions, and acquisition planning schedules; the feasibility of the requirement, including performance requirements, statements of work, and data requirements; the suitability of the proposal instructions and evaluation criteria, including the approach for assessing past performance information; and related program documents (see FAR 15.201). For Major Systems the Acquisition Strategy is the program manager's overall plan for satisfying the mission need in the most effective, economical, and timely manner. The strategy shall be in writing and prepared in accordance with the requirements of FAR 7.1 (also see FAR 34.004, HSAR 3007, HSAM 3007 and Template for Acquisition Strategies).

Acquisition Streamlining means any effort that results in more efficient and effective use of resources to design and develop, or produce quality systems. This includes ensuring that only necessary and cost-effective requirements are included, at the most appropriate time in the acquisition cycle, in solicitations and resulting contracts for the design, development, and production of new systems, or for modifications to existing systems that involve redesign of systems or subsystems (see FAR 7.101).

Advanced Acquisition Plan (AAP) means a plan of all anticipated procurements, including interagency agreements, blanket purchase agreements and task orders over $100,000 for the forthcoming fiscal year. This does not include interagency agreements where DHS is acting as the serving activity (see HSAM 3007.102 and HSAM 3007.172).

Bundling or Bundled Contract means consolidating two or more requirements for supplies or services, previously provided or performed under separate smaller contracts, orders, into a solicitation for a single contract or order that is likely to be unsuitable for award to a small business concern due to—
   i. The diversity, size, or specialized nature of the elements of the performance specified;
   ii. The aggregate dollar value of the anticipated award;
   iii. The geographical dispersion of the contract performance sites; or
   iv. Any combination of the factors described in paragraphs (1)(i), (ii), and (iii) of this definition (see FAR 2.101).

Commercial Item means a supply or service that is commonly available to the public. All items purchased under FAR Part 12 or under FAR 8.4 must be commercial items.

Contractual Actions means any contract purchase order project order, delivery or task order, interagency agreement, memorandum of agreement, memorandum of understanding to obtain anything of value (supply or service) in exchange for money.

Design-to-Cost means a concept that establishes cost elements as management goals to achieve the best balance between life-cycle cost, acceptable performance, and schedule. Under this concept, cost is a design constraint during the design and development phases and a management discipline throughout the acquisition and operation of the system or equipment (see FAR 2.101).

Life-Cycle Cost means the total cost to the Government of acquiring, operating, supporting, and (if applicable) disposing of the items being acquired (see FAR 7.101).

Major System means that combination of elements that will function together to produce the capabilities required to fulfill a mission need. The elements may include hardware, equipment, software, or any combination thereof, but exclude construction or other improvements to real property. A system is a major system if the total expenditures for the system are estimated to exceed $750,000 (based on fiscal year 1980 constant dollars) or the dollar threshold for a "major system" established Management Directive MD 1400; or the system is designated a "major system" by DHS (see 10 U.S.C. 2302, 41 U.S.C. 403, FAR 2.101 and HSAR 3002.101).

Multi-Year Contract means a contract for the purchase of supplies or services for more than 1, but not more than 5, program years. A multi-year contract may provide that performance under the contract during the second and subsequent years of the contract is contingent upon the appropriation of funds, and (if it does so provide) may provide for a cancellation payment to be made to the contractor if appropriations are not made. A multi-year contract, defined in the statutes cited at FAR 17.101, buys more than 1 year's requirement (of a product or service) without establishing and having to exercise an option for each program year after the first (see FAR 17.103).

Multiple Year Contract means a contract that buys more than 1 year's requirement (of a product or service) using options for each program year after the first (see FAR 17.103).

Order means an order placed under a Federal Supply Schedule contract; or a task order contract or delivery-order contract awarded by another agency, (*i.e.*, Government wide acquisition contract or multi-agency contract, see FAR 7.101).

Performance-Based Contracting means structuring all aspects of an acquisition around the purpose of the work to be performed with the contract requirements set forth in clear, specific and objective terms with measurable outcomes as opposed to either the manner by which the work is to be performed or broad and imprecise statements of work (see FAR 2.101).

Value of the Acquisition means the maximum monetary amount that the government could obligate against a contractual action including all options, incentives, award fees and cancellation fees.

BIO AND AGRO-DEFENSE TERMS

Biological Safety Cabinets (BSCs) The most effective and the most commonly used primary containment devices in laboratories working with infectious agents. There are three general types available (Class I, II, III). Properly maintained Class I and II BSCs, when used in conjunction with good microbiological techniques, provide an effective containment system for safe manipulation of moderate and high-risk microorganisms(biosafety level 2 and 3 microorganisms). Class II BSCs also protect the research material itself through high-efficiency particulate air filtration (HEPA filtration) of the air flow down across the work surface. Class III cabinets offer the maximum protection to laboratory personnel because all hazardous materials are contained in a totally enclosed cabinet.

Biosafety Levels (BSLs) There are four levels of biosafety used to designate and regulate lab work with microorganisms. The range is BSL-1 in which the microorganisms are not known to cause disease in healthy adult human beings to BSL-4 in which the microorganisms pose a risk of life-threatening disease and for which there is no known vaccine or therapy. BSL-3Ag refers to research involving large agricultural animals. There are guidelines in place to ensure safe work sites through a combination of engineering controls, management policies, work practices, and procedures. Increasing levels of personnel and environmental protection are provided for by the different biosafety levels used in microbiological/biomedical laboratories. The higher the level of the biosafety lab, the more stringent the level of protection.

Countermeasures A collective term used in biocontainment laboratories to include vaccines, biotherapeutics, diagnostic assays, therapies, and vector control.

Diagnostic Assay A test to determine presence or absence of infectious agents or antibodies to determine if an animal has or has been exposed to an agent.

Environmental Impact Statement A document required of federal agencies by the National Environmental Policy Act for major federal actions that may significantly affect the quality of the environment. A tool for decisionmaking, it describes, analyzes, and compares the potential environmental impacts of the alternatives to accomplish the purpose and need to which the agency is responding.

Glovebox A sealed container designed to allow a trained scientist to manipulate microorganisms while being in a different containment level than that of the agent they are manipulating. Built into the sides of the glovebox are two glove ports arranged in such a way that one can place their hands into the ports, into gloves and perform tasks inside the box without breaking the seal. There are three general types available (Class I, II, III) based on the material the box and gloves are made of.

High-Consequence Foreign Animal Diseases (FADs) Diseases not present in the United States that are capable of rapidly spreading and causing high numbers of deaths and/or devastating economic consequences (e.g., foot and mouth disease).

Homeland Security Presidential Directives 9 and 10 These directives established a national goal to protect agricultural infrastructure to ensure our livestock and food safety and security.

Host In biology, a host is an organism that harbors a virus or parasite, typically providing nourishment and shelter.

National Bio and Agro-Defense Facility (NBAF) Proposed facility that would address both current and future requirements in research, diagnostics, and training for combating high-consequence agricultural threats. Research would focus on early development and discovery of vaccines and diagnostic tests for these important agricultural diseases.

National Environmental Policy Act (NEPA) Requires the preparation of an environmental impact statement (EIS) for major federal actions that may significantly affect the quality of the environment. In NEPA, the term "environment" encompasses the natural and physical environment (i.e., air, water, geography, and geology), as well as the relationship of people with that environment (i.e., health and safety, socioeconomic conditions, cultural resources, noise, and aesthetics).

Natural Reservoir Refers to the long-term host of the pathogen of an infectious disease. It is often the case that hosts do not get severely ill.

Pathogen or Infectious Agent A biological agent that causes disease or illness to its host. The term is most often used for agents that disrupt the normal physiology of an animal or person.

Plum Island Animal Disease Center (PIADC) U.S. laboratory for the diagnosis, research, and training for foreign animal diseases. The U.S. Department of Agriculture (USDA) Animal and Plant Health Inspection Service (APHIS) Foreign Animal Disease Diagnostic Laboratory is located at PIADC. This laboratory has the capability of diagnosing over 30 foreign animal diseases and is responsible for educating veterinarians in the recognition and diagnosis of these diseases. The USDA Agricultural Research Service (ARS) operates a program focused on basic discovery and research of foreign animal diseases. The DHS scientific program focuses primarily on the advanced development of vaccines and other countermeasures.

Wildlife Reservoir Wildlife are normally defined as wild, free-roaming animals (e.g., mammals, birds, fish, reptiles, and amphibians); therefore, this refers to a wild animal as long-term host of the pathogen of an infectious disease. It is often the case that hosts do not get the disease carried by the pathogen or it does not show symptoms of the disease and is non-lethal.

Zoonotic A term for diseases transmitted by animals to humans.

ACRONYMS AND ABBREVIATIONS

AA	Alternatives Analysis
ACE	Automated Commercial Environment
ADASP	Aviation Direct Access Screening Program
ADD	Automated Deployment Database
ADVISE	Analysis, Dissemination, Visualization, Insight, and Semantic Enhancement
AFG	Assistance to Firefighters Grants
AFR	Annual Financial Report
AMSC	Area Maritime Security Committee
AMSP	Area Maritime Security Plan
AOR	Area of Responsibility
APIS	Advance Passenger Information System
APL	Acquisition Policy & Legislation
APR	Annual Performance Report
ARC	American Red Cross
ASAP	Aviation Screening Assessment Program
ASGB	Acquisition Systems Governance Board
ASI	Aviation Security Inspectors
ATO	Authority to Operate
ATS	Automated Targeting System
ATSA	Aviation and Transportation Security Act
BAO	Bomb Appraisal Officer
BDO	Behavior Detection Officer
BPD	Bureau of Public Debt
B&SA	Bureau & Statistical Agent
BZPP	Buffer Zone Protection Plan
C4ISR	Command, Control, Communications, Computers, Intelligence, and Reconnaissance
C4IT	Command, Control, Communications, Computers, and Information Technology
C&A	Certification and Accreditation
CAO	Chief of Administrative Services
CBJ	Congressional Budget Justification

CBP	Customs and Border Protection
CDC	Certain Dangerous Cargo
CDL	Community Disaster Loan
CDSOA	Continued Dumping & Subsidy Offset Account
CERTS	Cargo Enforcement Reporting and Tracking System
CFO	Chief Financial Officer
C.F.R.	Code of Federal Regulations
CIA	Central Intelligence Agency
CIIN	Critical Infrastructure Information Notices
CI-KR	Critical Infrastructure and Key Resources
CIO	Chief Information Officer
CIS	Community Information System
CISO	Chief Information Security Officer
COBRA	Consolidated Omnibus Budget Reconciliation Act
COE	U.S. Army Corps of Engineers
CONOPS	Concept of Operations
COP	Common Operating Picture
COTR	Contracting Officer Technical Representative
COTS	Commercial Off-the-Shelf Software
CPIC	Capital Planning Investment Control
CS&C	Cyber Security and Communications
CSI	Container Security Initiative
CSRS	Civil Service Retirement System
C-TPAT	Customs-Trade Partnership Against Terrorism
CY	Current Year
DADLP	Disaster Assistance Direct Loan Program
DAU	Defense Acquisition University's
DAWIA	Defense Acquisition Workforce Improvement Act
DCIA	Debt Collection Improvement Act
DCMA	Defense Contract Management Agency
DHS	Department of Homeland Security
DM	Disaster Management
DNDO	Domestic Nuclear Detection Office
DOC	Department of Commerce
DOD	Department of Defense
DOE	Department of Energy
DOI	Department of Interior
DOJ	Department of Justice
DOL	Department of Labor
DOS	Department of State
DRF	Disaster Relief Fund
DRO	Detention and Removal Operations
EA	Enterprise Architecture; Environmental Assessment
EASI	Enterprise Acquisition System Initiative
EFS	Electronic Fingerprint System
EHC	Especially Hazardous Cargo
EMIMS	Emergency Management Information Management System
EMS	Executive Management System
EPI	Enterprise PRISM Instance
ER	Expedited Removal
ESC	Executive Steering Committee
ESRI	Environmental Systems Research Institute
EVM	Earned Value Management
FAA	Financial Accountability Act
FAMS	Federal Air Marshal Service
FAR	Federal Acquisition Regulation
FASAB	Federal Accounting Standards Advisory Board
FBI	Federal Bureau of Investigation
FBwT	Fund Balance with Treasury
FCRA	Federal Credit Reform Act of 1990
FECA	Federal Employees Compensation Act
FEGLI	Federal Employees Group Life Insurance Program
FEHB	Federal Employees Health Benefits Program
FEMA	Federal Emergency Management Agency
FFMIA	Federal Financial Management Improvement Act
FERS	Federal Employees Retirement System
FIN	Federal Information Notice
FIRA	Flood Insurance Reform Act
FISCAM	Federal Information System Controls Audit Manual
FISMA	Federal Information Security Management Act
FLETC	Federal Law Enforcement Training Center
FMA	Flood Mitigation Assistance
FMFIA	Federal Managers' Financial Integrity Act
FOC	Full Operating Capability
FPDS	Federal Procurement Data System
FPDS-NG	Federal Procurement Data System-Next Generation
FPS	Federal Protective Service
FSD	Federal Security Director
FSIO	Financial Systems Integration Office
FY	Fiscal Year
FYHSP	Future Years Homeland Security Program

GAAP	Generally Accepted Accounting Principles	ISGB	Information Sharing Governance Board
GAO	Government Accountability Office	ISIS	Integrated Surveillance Intelligence System
GIS	Geographic Information System		
GMS	Grants Management Specialist	ISSO	Information System Security Officer
GOTS	Government Off-the-Shelf	IT	Information Technology
GPEA	Government Paper Elimination Act	ITSD	Information Technology Services Division
GPRA	Government Performance and Results Act	IWN	Integrated Wireless Network
GSA	General Services Administration	JPO	Joint Program Office
G&T	Grants and Training	LAN	Local Area Network
HHS	Department of Health and Human Services	LIMS	Logistics Inventory Management System
HQ	Headquarters	MAST	Mitigation Advisors Statistical Tracker
HSA	Homeland Security Act		
HSAM	Homeland Security Acquisition Manual	MD&A	Management's Discussion and Analysis
HSAR	Homeland Security Acquisition Regulation	MDP	Milestone Decision Point
		MFPU	Maritime Force Protection Unit
HSDN	Homeland Secure Data Network	MGMT	Management Directorate
HSGP	Homeland Security Grant Program	MOA	Memorandum of Agreement
HSIN	Homeland Security Information Network	MOU	Memorandum of Understanding
		MRS	Military Retirement System
HUD	Department of Housing and Urban Development	MSAM	Major Systems Acquisition Manual
		MSRAM	Maritime Security Risk Analysis Model
I&A	Intelligence and Analysis		
IAA	Interagency Acquisition	MTS	Marine Transportation System
iCAV	Infrastructure Critical Asset Viewer	MTS	Metric Tracking System
ICCB	Internal Control Coordination Board	NADB	National Asset Database
ICE	U.S. Immigration and Customs Enforcement	NAVICP	Navy Inventory Control Point
		NBIS	National Bio-Surveillance Integration System
ICOFR	Internal Controls Over Financial Reporting		
		NCA	National Capital Area
IDI	Injured Domestic Industries	NCAS	National Cyber Alert System
IDS	Integrated Deepwater System	NCCIPS	National Center for Critical Information Processing and Storage
IEFA	Immigration Examination Fee Account		
		NCSD	National Cyber Security Division
IFMIS	Integrated Financial Management Information System	NDMS	National Disaster Medical Systems
		NEMIS	National Emergency Management Information System
IHP	Individuals and Households Program		
		NFIP	National Flood Insurance Program
IHS	Internet Health System	NGA	National Geospatial-Intelligence Agency
INA	Immigration and Nationality Act		
IP	Improper Payment	NICC	National Infrastructure Coordination Center
IPA	Independent Public Accountant		
IPIA	Improper Payments Information Act	NIMS	National Incident Management System
IPP	Infrastructure Protection Program		
IPT	Integrated Product Teams	NIPP	National Infrastructure Protection Plan
ISAA	Information Sharing and Access Agreement		
		NIST	National Institute of Standards and Technology
ISAC	Information and Analysis Center		
ISCC	Information Sharing Coordinating Council	NMSRA	National Maritime Strategic Risk Assessment
ISDC	Interagency Suspension and Debarment Committee	NMSZ	New Madrid Seismic Zone
		NOC	National Operations Center

NPPD	National Protection and Programs Directorate	PY	Prior Year
		QASP	Quality Assurance Surveillance Plan
NRCC	National Response Coordination Center	RAP	Resource Allocation Plan
		REPP	Radiological Emergency Preparedness Program
NRF	National Response Framework		
NRP	National Response Plan	RFC	Repetitive Flood Claim
NSA	National Security Agency	RND	Results Not Demonstrated
NSVSS	National Small Vessel Security Summit	RSSI	Required Supplementary Stewardship Information
NVD	National Vulnerability Database	SAFETEA-LU	Safe, Accountable, Flexible, and Efficient Transportation Equity Act: A Legacy for Users
OASISS	Operation Against Smugglers Initiative for Safety and Security		
OCPO	Office of the Chief Procurement Officer	SAP	Systems Applications Products
		SAT	Senior Assessment Team
OEC	Office of Emergency Communications	SBA	Small Business Administration
		SBI	Secure Border Initiative
OFPP	Office of Federal Procurement Policy	SBInet	Secure Border Initiative Network
OHA	Office of Health Affairs	SCIP	Statewide Communications Interoperability Plan
OHC	Office of Human Capital		
OI&A	Office of Intelligence and Analysis	SCNP	Statement of Changes in Net Position
OIG	Office of Inspector General	SCSS	Supply Chain Security Specialists
OJS	Operation Jump Start	SDLC	System Development Life Cycle
O&M	Operations and Management	SES	Senior Executive Service
OMB	Office of Management and Budget	SFFAS	Statements of Federal Financial Accounting Standards
OM&S	Operating Supplies and Materials		
OPEB	Other Post Employment Benefits	SFI	Secure Freight Initiative
OPM	Office of Personnel Management	SFRBTF	Sport Fish Restoration and Boating Trust Fund
OPO	Office of Procurement Operations		
ORB	Other Retirement Benefits	SIPRNet	Secret Internet Protocol Router Network
OSEM	Office of the Secretary Executive Management		
		SLFC	State and Local Fusion Centers
OTM	Other than Mexican	SMC	Senior Management Council
PA&E	Performance Analysis and Evaluation	SME	Subject Matter Expert
		SOC	Security Operations Center
PAR	Performance and Accountability Report	SOP	Standard Operating Procedure
		SRL	Severe Repetitive Loss
PART	Program Assessment Rating Tool	SRM	Stakeholder Relationship Management
PASS	People Access Security Service		
PBA	Performance-Based Acquisition	SSP	Strategic Sourcing Program
PCIS	Partnership for Critical Infrastructure Security	S&T	Science and Technology
		ST&E	System Tests and Evaluations
PII	Personally Identifiable Information	TAI	TSA Approved Instructor
PKEMR	Post Katrina Emergency Management Reform Act	TASC	Transformation and Systems Consolidation
PL	Public Law	TAV	Total Asset Visibility
PM	Program Manager	TDL	Test Development Laboratory
PMA	President's Management Agenda	TFS	Treasury Fund Symbol
POA&M	Plans of Action and Milestones	T&M	Time and Material
PPBE	Planning, Programming, Budgeting, and Execution	TOD	Test of Design
		TOE	Test of Operating Effectiveness
PP&E	Property, Plant, and Equipment	TPO	Transformation Program Office
PREP	Preparedness Directorate	TRM	Technology Reference Model
PRM	Performance Reference Model	TSA	Transportation Security Administration
PWCS	Ports, Waterways, and Coastal Security		
		TSI	Transportation Security Inspector

TSO	Transportation Security Officer	*US-VISIT*	U.S. Visitor and Immigrant Status Indicator Technology
U.S.C.	United States Code		
US-CERT	United States Computer Emergency Readiness Team	*UTPP*	Underwater Terrorism Preparedness Plan
USCG	U.S. Coast Guard	*VA*	Vulnerability Assessment
USCIS	U.S. Citizenship and Immigration Services	*VIPR*	Visible Intermodal Protection and Response
USGS	U.S. Geological Survey	*VoIP*	Voice over Internet Protocol
USPS	U.S. Postal Service	*VTC*	Video Teleconference
USSGL	United States Standard General Ledger	*WHTI*	Western Hemisphere Travel Initiative
		WYO	Write Your Own
USSS	U.S. Secret Service		

Housing and Urban Development

203(b) FHA's single family program which provides mortgage insurance to lenders to protect against the borrower defaulting; 203(b) is used to finance the purchase of new or existing one to four family housing; 203(b) insured loans are known for requiring a low down payment, flexible qualifying guidelines, limited fees, and a limit on maximum loan amount.

203(k) this FHA mortgage insurance program enables homebuyers to finance both the purchase of a house and the cost of its rehabilitation through a single mortgage loan.

"A" Loan or "A" Paper a credit rating where the FICO score is 660 or above. There have been no late mortgage payments within a 12-month period. This is the best credit rating to have when entering into a new loan.

Abstract of Title documents recording the ownership of property throughout time.

Acceleration the right of the lender to demand payment on the outstanding balance of a loan.

Acceptance the written approval of the buyer's offer by the seller.

Additional Principal Payment money paid to the lender in addition to the established payment amount used directly against the loan principal to shorten the length of the loan.

Adjustable-Rate Mortgage (ARM) a mortgage loan that does not have a fixed interest rate. During the life of the loan the interest rate will change based on the index rate. Also referred to as adjustable mortgage loans (AMLs) or variable-rate mortgages (VRMs).

Adjustment Date the actual date that the interest rate is changed for an ARM.

Adjustment Index the published market index used to calculate the interest rate of an ARM at the time of origination or adjustment.

Adjustment Interval the time between the interest rate change and the monthly payment for an ARM. The interval is usually every one, three or five years depending on the index.

Affidavit a signed, sworn statement made by the buyer or seller regarding the truth of information provided.

Amenity a feature of the home or property that serves as a benefit to the buyer but that is not necessary to its use; may be natural (like location, woods, water) or man-made (like a swimming pool or garden).

American Society of Home Inspectors the American Society of Home Inspectors is a professional association of independent home inspectors. Phone: (800) 743-2744 / (800) 743-2744.

Amortization a payment plan that enables you to reduce your debt gradually through monthly payments. The payments may be principal and interest, or interest-only. The monthly amount is based on the schedule for the entire term or length of the loan.

Annual Mortgagor Statement yearly statement to borrowers detailing the remaining principal and amounts paid for taxes and interest.

Annual Percentage Rate (APR) a measure of the cost of credit, expressed as a yearly rate. It includes interest as well as other charges. Because all lenders, by federal law, follow the same rules to ensure the accuracy of the annual percentage rate, it provides consumers with a good basis for comparing the cost of loans, including mortgage plans. APR is a higher rate than the simple interest of the mortgage.

Application the first step in the official loan approval process; this form is used to record important information about the potential borrower necessary to the underwriting process.

Application Fee a fee charged by lenders to process a loan application.

Appraisal a document from a professional that gives an estimate of a property's fair market value based on the sales of comparable homes in the area and the features of a property; an appraisal is generally required by a lender before loan approval to ensure that the mortgage loan amount is not more than the value of the property.

Appraisal Fee fee charged by an appraiser to estimate the market value of a property.

Appraised Value an estimation of the current market value of a property.

Appraiser a qualified individual who uses his or her experience and knowledge to prepare the appraisal estimate.

Appreciation an increase in property value.

Arbitration a legal method of resolving a dispute without going to court.

ARM Adjustable Rate Mortgage; a mortgage loan subject to changes in interest rates; when rates change, ARM monthly payments increase or decrease at intervals determined by the lender; the change in monthly payment amount, however, is usually subject to a cap.

As-is Condition the purchase or sale of a property in its existing condition without repairs.

Asking Price a seller's stated price for a property.

Assessed Value the value that a public official has placed on any asset (used to determine taxes).

Assessments the method of placing value on an asset for taxation purposes.

Assessor a government official who is responsible for determining the value of a property for the purpose of taxation.

Assets any item with measurable value.

Assumable Mortgage when a home is sold, the seller may be able to transfer the mortgage to the new buyer. This means the mortgage is assumable. Lenders generally require a credit review of the new borrower and may charge a fee for the assumption. Some mortgages contain a due-on-sale clause, which means that the mortgage may not be transferable to a new buyer. Instead, the lender may make you pay the entire balance that is due when you sell the home. An assumable mortgage can help you attract buyers if you sell your home.

Assumption Clause a provision in the terms of a loan that allows the buyer to take legal responsibility for the mortgage from the seller.

Automated Underwriting loan processing completed through a computer-based system that evaluates past credit history to determine if a loan should be approved. This system removes the possibility of personal bias against the buyer.

Average Price determining the cost of a home by totaling the cost of all houses sold in one area and dividing by the number of homes sold.

"B" Loan or "B" Paper FICO scores from 620–659. Factors include two 30 day late mortgage payments and two to three 30 day late installment loan payments in the last 12 months. No delinquencies over 60 days are allowed. Should be two to four years since a bankruptcy. Also referred to as Sub-Prime.

Back End Ratio (debt ratio) a ratio that compares the total of all monthly debt payments (mortgage, real estate taxes and insurance, car loans, and other consumer loans) to gross monthly income.

Back-to-Back Escrow arrangements that an owner makes to oversee the sale of one property and the purchase of another at the same time.

Balance Sheet a financial statement that shows the assets, liabilities and net worth of an individual or company.

Balloon Loan or Mortgage a mortgage that typically offers low rates for an initial period of time (usually 5, 7, or 10) years; after that time period elapses, the balance is due or is refinanced by the borrower.

Balloon Payment the final lump sum payment due at the end of a balloon mortgage.

Bankruptcy a federal law whereby a person's assets are turned over to a trustee and used to pay off outstanding debts; this usually occurs when someone owes more than they have the ability to repay.

Biweekly Payment Mortgage a mortgage paid twice a month instead of once a month, reducing the amount of interest to be paid on the loan.

Borrower a person who has been approved to receive a loan and is then obligated to repay it and any additional fees according to the loan terms.

Bridge Loan a short-term loan paid back relatively fast. Normally used until a long-term loan can be processed.

Broker a licensed individual or firm that charges a fee to serve as the mediator between the buyer and seller. Mortgage brokers are individuals in the business of arranging funding or negotiating contracts for a client, but who does not loan the money. A real estate broker is someone who helps find a house.

Building Code based on agreed upon safety standards within a specific area, a building code is a regulation that determines the design, construction, and materials used in building.

Budget a detailed record of all income earned and spent during a specific period of time.

Buy Down the seller pays an amount to the lender so the lender provides a lower rate and lower payments many times for an ARM. The seller may increase the sales price to cover the cost of the buy down.

"C" Loan or "C" Paper FICO scores typically from 580 to 619. Factors include three to four 30 day late mortgage payments and four to six 30 day late installment loan payments or two to four 60 day late payments. Should be one to two years since bankruptcy. Also referred to as Sub - Prime.

Callable Debt a debt security whose issuer has the right to redeem the security at a specified price on or after a specified date, but prior to its stated final maturity.

Cap a limit, such as one placed on an adjustable rate mortgage, on how much a monthly payment or interest rate can increase or decrease, either at each adjustment period or during the life of the mortgage. Payment caps do not limit the amount of interest the lender is earning, so they may cause negative amortization.

Capacity The ability to make mortgage payments on time, dependant on assets and the amount of income each month after paying housing costs, debts and other obligations.

Capital Gain the profit received based on the difference of the original purchase price and the total sale price.

Capital Improvements property improvements that either will enhance the property value or will increase the useful life of the property.

Capital or Cash Reserves an individual's savings, investments, or assets.

Cash-Out Refinance when a borrower refinances a mortgage at a higher principal amount to get additional money. Usually this occurs when the property has appreciated in value. For example, if a home has a current value of $100,000 and an outstanding mortgage of $60,000, the owner could refinance $80,000 and have additional $20,000 in cash.

Cash Reserves a cash amount sometimes required of the buyer to be held in reserve in addition to the down payment and closing costs; the amount is determined by the lender.

Casualty Protection property insurance that covers any damage to the home and personal property either inside or outside the home.

Certificate of Title a document provided by a qualified source, such as a title company, that shows the property legally belongs to the current owner; before the title is transferred at closing, it should be clear and free of all liens or other claims.

Chapter 7 Bankruptcy a bankruptcy that requires assets be liquidated in exchange for the cancellation of debt.

Chapter 13 Bankruptcy this type of bankruptcy sets a payment plan between the borrower and the creditor monitored by the court. The homeowner can keep the property, but must make payments according to the court's terms within a 3 to 5 year period.

Charge-Off the portion of principal and interest due on a loan that is written off when deemed to be uncollectible.

Clear Title a property title that has no defects. Properties with clear titles are marketable for sale.

Closing the final step in property purchase where the title is transferred from the seller to the buyer. Closing occurs at a meeting between the buyer, seller, settlement agent, and other agents. At the closing the seller receives payment for the property. Also known as settlement.

Closing Costs fees for final property transfer not included in the price of the property. Typical closing costs include charges for the mortgage loan such as origination fees, discount points, appraisal fee, survey, title insurance, legal fees, real estate professional fees, prepayment of taxes and insurance, and real estate transfer taxes. A common estimate of a Buyer's closing costs is 2 to 4 percent of the purchase price of the home. A common estimate for Seller's closing costs is 3 to 9 percent.

Cloud on the Title any condition which affects the clear title to real property.

Co-Borrower an additional person that is responsible for loan repayment and is listed on the title.

Co-Signed Account an account signed by someone in addition to the primary borrower, making both people responsible for the amount borrowed.

Co-Signer a person that signs a credit application with another person, agreeing to be equally responsible for the repayment of the loan.

Collateral security in the form of money or property pledged for the payment of a loan. For example, on a home loan, the home is the collateral and can be taken away from the borrower if mortgage payments are not made.

Collection Account an unpaid debt referred to a collection agency to collect on the bad debt. This type of account is reported to the credit bureau and will show on the borrower's credit report.

Commission an amount, usually a percentage of the property sales price that is collected by a real estate professional as a fee for negotiating the transaction. Traditionally the home seller pays the commission. The amount of commission is determined by the real estate professional and the seller and can be as much as 6% of the sales price.

Common Stock a security that provides voting rights in a corporation and pays a dividend after preferred stock holders have been paid. This is the most common stock held within a company.

Comparative Market Analysis (COMPS) a property evaluation that determines property value by comparing similar properties sold within the last year.

Compensating Factors factors that show the ability to repay a loan based on less traditional criteria, such as employment, rent, and utility payment history.

Condominium a form of ownership in which individuals purchase and own a unit of housing in a multi-unit complex. The owner also shares financial responsibility for common areas.

Conforming Loan is a loan that does not exceed Fannie Mae's and Freddie Mac's loan limits. Freddie Mac and Fannie Mae loans are referred to as conforming loans.

Consideration an item of value given in exchange for a promise or act.

Construction Loan a short-term, to finance the cost of building a new home. The lender pays the builder based on milestones accomplished during the building process. For example, once a sub-contractor pours the foundation and it is approved by inspectors the lender will pay for their service.

Contingency a clause in a purchase contract outlining conditions that must be fulfilled before the contract is executed. Both, buyer or seller may include contingencies in a contract, but both parties must accept the contingency.

Conventional Loan a private sector loan, one that is not guaranteed or insured by the U.S. government.

Conversion Clause a provision in some ARMs allowing it to change to a fixed-rate loan at some point during the term. Usually conversions are allowed at the end of the first adjustment period. At the time of the conversion, the new fixed rate is generally set at one of the rates then prevailing for fixed rate mortgages. There may be additional cost for this clause.

Convertible ARM an adjustable-rate mortgage that provides the borrower the ability to convert to a fixed-rate within a specified time.

Cooperative (Co-op) residents purchase stock in a cooperative corporation that owns a structure; each stockholder is then entitled to live in a specific unit of the structure and is responsible for paying a portion of the loan.

Cost of Funds Index (COFI) an index used to determine interest rate changes for some adjustable-rate mortgages.

Counter Offer a rejection to all or part of a purchase offer that negotiates different terms to reach an acceptable sales contract.

Covenants legally enforceable terms that govern the use of property. These terms are transferred with the property deed. Discriminatory covenants are illegal and unenforceable. Also known as a condition, restriction, deed restriction or restrictive covenant.

Credit an agreement that a person will borrow money and repay it to the lender over time.

Credit Bureau an agency that provides financial information and payment history to lenders about potential borrowers. Also known as a National Credit Repository.

Credit Counseling education on how to improve bad credit and how to avoid having more debt than can be repaid.

Credit Enhancement a method used by a lender to reduce default of a loan by requiring collateral, mortgage insurance, or other agreements.

Credit Grantor the lender that provides a loan or credit.

Credit History a record of an individual that lists all debts and the payment history for each. The report that is generated from the history is called a credit report. Lenders use this information to gauge a potential borrower's ability to repay a loan.

Credit Loss Ratio the ratio of credit-related losses to the dollar amount of MBS outstanding and total mortgages owned by the corporation.

Credit-Related Expenses foreclosed property expenses plus the provision for losses.

Credit-Related Losses foreclosed property expenses combined with charge-offs.

Credit Repair Companies Private, for-profit businesses that claim to offer consumers credit and debt repayment difficulties assistance with their credit problems and a bad credit report.

Credit Report a report generated by the credit bureau that contains the borrower's credit history for the past seven years. Lenders use this information to determine if a loan will be granted.

Credit Risk a term used to describe the possibility of default on a loan by a borrower.

Credit Score a score calculated by using a person's credit report to determine the likelihood of a loan being repaid on time. Scores range from about 360 to 840: a lower score meaning a person is a higher risk, while a higher score means that there is less risk.

Credit Union a non-profit financial institution federally regulated and owned by the members or people who use their services. Credit unions serve groups that hold a common interest and you have to become a member to use the available services.

Creditor the lending institution providing a loan or credit.

Creditworthiness the way a lender measures the ability of a person to qualify and repay a loan.

Debtor The person or entity that borrows money. The term debtor may be used interchangeably with the term borrower.

Debt-to-Income Ratio a comparison or ratio of gross income to housing and non-housing expenses; With the FHA, the-monthly mortgage payment should be no more than 29% of monthly gross income (before taxes) and the mortgage payment combined with non-housing debts should not exceed 41% of income.

Debt Security a security that represents a loan from an investor to an issuer. The issuer in turn agrees to pay interest in addition to the principal amount borrowed.

Deductible the amount of cash payment that is made by the insured (the homeowner) to cover a portion of a damage or loss. Sometimes also called "out-of-pocket expenses." For example, out of a total damage claim of $1,000, the homeowner might pay a $250 deductible toward the loss, while the insurance company pays $750 toward the loss. Typically, the higher the deductible, the lower the cost of the policy.

Deed a document that legally transfers ownership of property from one person to another. The deed is recorded on public record with the property description and the owner's signature. Also known as the title.

Deed-in-Lieu to avoid foreclosure ("in lieu" of foreclosure), a deed is given to the lender to fulfill the obligation to repay the debt; this process does not allow the borrower to remain in the house but helps avoid the costs, time, and effort associated with foreclosure.

Default the inability to make timely monthly mortgage payments or otherwise comply with mortgage terms. A loan is considered in default when payment has not been paid after 60 to 90 days. Once in default the lender can exercise legal rights defined in the contract to begin foreclosure proceedings.

Delinquency failure of a borrower to make timely mortgage payments under a loan agreement. Generally after fifteen days a late fee may be assessed.

Deposit (Earnest Money) money put down by a potential buyer to show that they are serious about purchasing the home; it becomes part of the down payment if the offer is accepted, is returned if the offer is rejected, or is forfeited if the buyer pulls out of the deal. During the contingency period the money may be returned to the buyer if the contingencies are not met to the buyer's satisfaction.

Depreciation a decrease in the value or price of a property due to changes in market conditions, wear and tear on the property, or other factors.

Derivative a contract between two or more parties where the security is dependent on the price of another investment.

Disclosures the release of relevant information about a property that may influence the final sale, especially if it represents defects or problems. "Full disclosure" usually refers to the responsibility of the seller to voluntarily provide all known information about the property. Some disclosures may be required by law, such as the federal requirement to warn of potential lead-based paint hazards in pre-1978 housing. A seller found to have knowingly lied about a defect may face legal penalties.

Discount Point normally paid at closing and generally calculated to be equivalent to 1% of the total loan amount, discount points are paid to reduce the interest rate on a loan. In an ARM with an initial rate discount, the lender gives up a number of percentage points in interest to give you a lower rate and lower payments for part of the mortgage term (usually for one year or less). After the discount period, the ARM rate will probably go up depending on the index rate.

Document Recording after closing on a loan, certain documents are filed and made public record. Discharges for the prior mortgage holder are filed first. Then the deed is filed with the new owner's and mortgage company's names.

Down Payment the portion of a home's purchase price that is paid in cash and is not part of the mortgage loan. This amount varies based on the loan type, but is determined by taking the difference of the sale price and the actual mortgage loan amount. Mortgage insurance is required when a down payment less than 20 percent is made.

Due on Sale Clause a provision of a loan allowing the lender to demand full repayment of the loan if the property is sold.

Duration the number of years it will take to receive the present value of all future payments on a security to include both principal and interest.

Earnest Money (Deposit) money put down by a potential buyer to show that they are serious about purchasing the home; it becomes part of the down payment if the offer is accepted, is returned if the offer is rejected, or is forfeited if the buyer pulls out of the deal. During the contingency period the money may be returned to the buyer if the contingencies are not met to the buyer's satisfaction.

Earnings Per Share (EPS) a corporation's profit that is divided among each share of common stock. It is determined by taking the net earnings divided by the number of outstanding common stocks held. This is a way that a company reports profitability.

Easements the legal rights that give someone other than the owner access to use property for a specific purpose. Easements may affect property values and are sometimes a part of the deed.

EEM Energy Efficient Mortgage; an FHA program that helps homebuyers save money on utility bills by enabling them to finance the cost of adding energy efficiency features to a new or existing home as part of the home purchase

Eminent Domain when a government takes private property for public use. The owner receives payment for its fair market value. The property can then proceed to condemnation proceedings.

Encroachments a structure that extends over the legal property line on to another individual's property. The property surveyor will note any encroachment on the lot survey done before property transfer. The person who owns the structure will be asked to remove it to prevent future problems.

Encumbrance anything that affects title to a property, such as loans, leases, easements, or restrictions.

Equal Credit Opportunity Act (ECOA) a federal law requiring lenders to make credit available equally without discrimination based on race, color, religion, national origin, age, sex, marital status, or receipt of income from public assistance programs.

Equity an owner's financial interest in a property; calculated by subtracting the amount still owed on the mortgage loon(s)from the fair market value of the property.

Escape Clause a provision in a purchase contract that allows either party to cancel part or the entire contract if the other does not respond to changes to the sale within a set period. The most common use of the escape clause is if the buyer makes the purchase offer contingent on the sale of another house.

Escrow funds held in an account to be used by the lender to pay for home insurance and property taxes. The funds may also be held by a third party until contractual conditions are met and then paid out.

Escrow Account a separate account into which the lender puts a portion of each monthly mortgage payment; an escrow account provides the funds needed for such expenses as property taxes, homeowners insurance, mortgage insurance, etc.

Estate the ownership interest of a person in real property. The sum total of all property, real and personal, owned by a person.

Exclusive Listing a written contract giving a real estate agent the exclusive right to sell a property for a specific timeframe.

Fair Credit Reporting Act federal act to ensure that credit bureaus are fair and accurate protecting the individual's privacy rights enacted in 1971 and revised in October 1997.

Fair Housing Act a law that prohibits discrimination in all facets of the home buying process on the basis of race, color, national origin, religion, sex, familial status, or disability.

Fair Market Value the hypothetical price that a willing buyer and seller will agree upon when they are acting freely, carefully, and with complete knowledge of the situation.

Familial Status HUD uses this term to describe a single person, a pregnant woman or a household with children under 18 living with parents or legal custodians who might experience housing discrimination.

Fannie Mae Federal National Mortgage Association (FNMA); a federally-chartered enterprise owned by private stockholders that purchases residential mortgages and converts them into securities for sale to investors; by purchasing mortgages, Fannie Mae supplies funds that lenders may loan to potential homebuyers. Also known as a Government Sponsored Enterprise (GSE).

FHA Federal Housing Administration; established in 1934 to advance homeownership opportunities for all Americans; assists homebuyers by providing mortgage insurance to lenders to cover most losses that may occur when a borrower defaults; this encourages lenders to make loans to borrowers who might not qualify for conventional mortgages.

FICO Score FICO is an abbreviation for Fair Isaac Corporation and refers to a person's credit score based on credit history. Lenders and credit card companies use the number to decide if the person is likely to pay his or her bills. A credit score is evaluated using information from the three major credit bureaus and is usually between 300 and 850.

First Mortgage the mortgage with first priority if the loan is not paid.

Fixed Expenses payments that do not vary from month to month.

Fixed-Rate Mortgage a mortgage with payments that remain the same throughout the life of the loan because the interest rate and other terms are fixed and do not change.

Fixture personal property permanently attached to real estate or real property that becomes a part of the real estate.

Float the act of allowing an interest rate and discount points to fluctuate with changes in the market.

Flood Insurance insurance that protects homeowners against losses from a flood; if a home is located in a flood plain, the lender will require flood insurance before approving a loan.

Forbearance a lender may decide not to take legal action when a borrower is late in making a payment. Usually this occurs when a borrower sets up a plan that both sides agree will bring overdue mortgage payments up to date.

Foreclosure a legal process in which mortgaged property is sold to pay the loan of the defaulting borrower. Foreclosure laws are based on the statutes of each state.

Freddie Mac Federal Home Loan Mortgage Corporation (FHLM); a federally chartered corporation that purchases residential mortgages, securitizes them, and sells them to investors; this provides lenders with funds for new homebuyers. Also known as a Government Sponsored Enterprise (GSE).

Front End Ratio a percentage comparing a borrower's total monthly cost to buy a house (mortgage principal and interest, insurance, and real estate taxes) to monthly income before deductions.

FSBO (For Sale by Owner) a home that is offered for sale by the owner without the benefit of a real estate professional.

GSE abbreviation for government sponsored enterprises: a collection of financial services corporations formed by the United States Congress to reduce interest rates for farmers and homeowners. Examples include Fannie Mae and Freddie Mac.

Ginnie Mae Government National Mortgage Association (GNMA); a government-owned corporation overseen by the U.S. Department of Housing and Urban Development, Ginnie Mae pools FHA-insured and VA-guaranteed loans to back securities for private investment; as With Fannie Mae and Freddie Mac, the investment income provides funding that may then be lent to eligible borrowers by lenders.

Global Debt Facility   designed to allow investors all over the world to purchase debt (loans) of U.S. dollar and foreign currency through a variety of clearing systems.

Good Faith Estimate   an estimate of all closing fees including pre-paid and escrow items as well as lender charges; must be given to the borrower within three days after submission of a loan application.

Graduated Payment Mortgages   mortgages that begin with lower monthly payments that get slowly larger over a period of years, eventually reaching a fixed level and remaining there for the life of the loan. Graduated payment loans may be good if you expect your annual income to increase.

Grantee   an individual to whom an interest in real property is conveyed.

Grantor   an individual conveying an interest in real property.

Gross Income   money earned before taxes and other deductions. Sometimes it may include income from self-employment, rental property, alimony, child support, public assistance payments, and retirement benefits.

Guaranty Fee   payment to Fannie Mae from a lender for the assurance of timely principal and interest payments to MBS (Mortgage Backed Security) security holders.

Hazard Insurance   protection against a specific loss, such as fire, wind etc., over a period of time that is secured by the payment of a regularly scheduled premium.

HECM (Reverse Mortgage)   the reverse mortgage is used by senior homeowners age 62 and older to convert the equity in their home into monthly streams of income and/or a line of credit to be repaid when they no longer occupy the home. A lending institution such as a mortgage lender, bank, credit union or savings and loan association funds the FHA insured loan, commonly known as HECM.

HELP   Homebuyer Education Learning Program; an educational program from the FHA that counsels people about the home buying process; HELP covers topics like budgeting, finding a home, getting a loan, and home maintenance; in most cases, completion of the program may entitle the homebuyer to a reduced initial FHA mortgage insurance premium-from 2.25% to 1.75% of the home purchase price.

Home Equity Line of Credit   a mortgage loan, usually in second mortgage, allowing a borrower to obtain cash against the equity of a home, up to a pre-determined amount.

Home Equity Loan   a loan backed by the value of a home (real estate). If the borrower defaults or does not pay the loan, the lender has some rights to the property. The borrower can usually claim a home equity loan as a tax deduction.

Home Inspection   an examination of the structure and mechanical systems to determine a home's quality, soundness and safety; makes the potential homebuyer aware of any repairs that may be needed. The homebuyer generally pays inspection fees.

Home Warranty   offers protection for mechanical systems and attached appliances against unexpected repairs not covered by homeowner's insurance; coverage extends over a specific time period and does not cover the home's structure.

Homeowner's Insurance   an insurance policy, also called hazard insurance, that combines protection against damage to a dwelling and its contents including fire, storms or other damages with protection against claims of negligence or inappropriate action that result in someone's injury or property damage. Most lenders require homeowners insurance and may escrow the cost. **Flood insurance is generally not included in standard policies and must be purchased separately.**

Homeownership Education Classes   classes that stress the need to develop a strong credit history and offer information about how to get a mortgage approved, qualify for a loan, choose an affordable home, go through financing and closing processes, and avoid mortgage problems that cause people to lose their homes.

Homestead Credit   property tax credit program, offered by some state governments, that provides reductions in property taxes to eligible households.

Housing Counseling Agency   provides counseling and assistance to individuals on a variety of issues, including loan default, fair housing, and home buying.

HUD   the U.S. Department of Housing and Urban Development; established in 1965, HUD works to create a decent home and suitable living environment for all Americans; it does this by addressing housing needs, improving and developing American communities, and enforcing fair housing laws.

HUD1 Statement   also known as the "settlement sheet," or "closing statement" it itemizes all closing costs; must be given to the borrower at or before closing. Items that appear on the statement include real estate commissions, loan fees, points, and escrow amounts.

HVAC   Heating, Ventilation and Air Conditioning; a home's heating and cooling system.

Indemnification   to secure against any loss or damage, compensate or give security for reimbursement for loss or damage incurred. A homeowner should negotiate for inclusion of an indemnification provision in a contract with a general contractor or for a separate indemnity agreement protecting the homeowner from harm, loss or damage caused by actions or omissions of the general (and all sub) contractor.

Index the measure of interest rate changes that the lender uses to decide how much the interest rate of an ARM will change over time. No one can be sure when an index rate will go up or down. If a lender bases interest rate adjustments on the average value of an index over time, your interest rate would not be as volatile. You should ask your lender how the index for any ARM you are considering has changed in recent years, and where it is reported.

Inflation the number of dollars in circulation exceeds the amount of goods and services available for purchase; inflation results in a decrease in the dollar's value.

Inflation Coverage endorsement to a homeowner's policy that automatically adjusts the amount of insurance to compensate for inflationary rises in the home's value. This type of coverage does not adjust for increases in the home's value due to improvements.

Inquiry a credit report request. Each time a credit application is completed or more credit is requested counts as an inquiry. A large number of inquiries on a credit report can sometimes make a credit score lower.

Interest a fee charged for the use of borrowing money.

Interest Rate the amount of interest charged on a monthly loan payment, expressed as a percentage.

Interest Rate Swap a transaction between two parties where each agrees to exchange payments tied to different interest rates for a specified period of time, generally based on a notional principal amount.

Intermediate Term Mortgage a mortgage loan with a contractual maturity from the time of purchase equal to or less than 20 years.

Insurance protection against a specific loss, such as fire, wind etc., over a period of time that is secured by the payment of a regularly scheduled premium.

Joint Tenancy (with Rights of Survivorship) two or more owners share equal ownership and rights to the property. If a joint owner dies, his or her share of the property passes to the other owners, without probate. In joint tenancy, ownership of the property cannot be willed to someone who is not a joint owner.

Judgment a legal decision; when requiring debt repayment, a judgment may include a property lien that secures the creditor's claim by providing a collateral source.

Jumbo Loan or non-conforming loan, is a loan that exceeds Fannie Mae's and Freddie Mac's loan limits. Freddie Mac and Fannie Mae loans are referred to as conforming loans.

Late Payment Charges the penalty the homeowner must pay when a mortgage payment is made after the due date grace period.

Lease a written agreement between a property owner and a tenant (resident) that stipulates the payment and conditions under which the tenant may occupy a home or apartment and states a specified period of time.

Lease Purchase (Lease Option) assists low to moderate income homebuyers in purchasing a home by allowing them to lease a home with an option to buy; the rent payment is made up of the monthly rental payment plus an additional amount that is credited to an account for use as a down payment.

Lender A term referring to an person or company that makes loans for real estate purchases. Sometimes referred to as a loan officer or lender.

Lender Option Commitments an agreement giving a lender the option to deliver loans or securities by a certain date at agreed upon terms.

Liabilities a person's financial obligations such as long-term / short-term debt, and other financial obligations to be paid.

Liability Insurance insurance coverage that protects against claims alleging a property owner's negligence or action resulted in bodily injury or damage to another person. It is normally included in homeowner's insurance policies.

Lien a legal claim against property that must be satisfied when the property is sold. A claim of money against a property, wherein the value of the property is used as security in repayment of a debt. Examples include a mechanic's lien, which might be for the unpaid cost of building supplies, or a tax lien for unpaid property taxes. A lien is a defect on the title and needs to be settled before transfer of ownership. A lien release is a written report of the settlement of a lien and is recorded in the public record as evidence of payment.

Lien Waiver A document that releases a consumer (homeowner) from any further obligation for payment of a debt once it has been paid in full. Lien waivers typically are used by homeowners who hire a contractor to provide work and materials to prevent any subcontractors or suppliers of materials from filing a lien against the homeowner for nonpayment.

Life Cap a limit on the range interest rates can increase or decrease over the life of an adjustable-rate mortgage (ARM).

Line of Credit an agreement by a financial institution such as a bank to extend credit up to a certain amount for a certain time to a specified borrower.

Liquid Asset a cash asset or an asset that is easily converted into cash.

Listing Agreement a contract between a seller and a real estate professional to market and sell a home. A listing agreement obligates the real estate professional (or his or her agent) to seek qualified buyers, report all purchase offers and help negotiate the highest possible price and most favorable terms for the property seller.

Loan money borrowed that is usually repaid with interest.

Loan Acceleration an acceleration clause in a loan document is a statement in a mortgage that gives the lender the right to demand payment of the entire outstanding balance if a monthly payment is missed.

Loan Fraud purposely giving incorrect information on a loan application in order to better qualify for a loan; may result in civil liability or criminal penalties.

Loan Officer a representative of a lending or mortgage company who is responsible for soliciting homebuyers, qualifying and processing of loans. They may also be called lender, loan representative, account executive or loan rep.

Loan Origination Fee a charge by the lender to cover the administrative costs of making the mortgage. This charge is paid at the closing and varies with the lender and type of loan. A loan origination fee of 1 to 2 percent of the mortgage amount is common.

Loan Servicer the company that collects monthly mortgage payments and disperses property taxes and insurance payments. Loan servicers also monitor nonperforming loans, contact delinquent borrowers, and notify insurers and investors of potential problems. Loan servicers may be the lender or a specialized company that just handles loan servicing under contract with the lender or the investor who owns the loan.

Loan-to-Value (LTV) Ratio a percentage calculated by dividing the amount borrowed by the price or appraised value of the home to be purchased; the higher the LTV, the less cash a borrower is required to pay as down payment.

Lock-In since interest rates can change frequently, many lenders offer an interest rate lock-in that guarantees a specific interest rate if the loan is closed within a specific time.

Lock-In Period the length of time that the lender has guaranteed a specific interest rate to a borrower.

Loss Mitigation a process to avoid foreclosure; the lender tries to help a borrower who has been unable to make loan payments and is in danger of defaulting on his or her loan

Mandatory Delivery Commitment an agreement that a lender will deliver loans or securities by a certain date at agreed-upon terms.

Margin the number of percentage points the lender adds to the index rate to calculate the ARM interest rate at each adjustment.

Market Value the amount a willing buyer would pay a willing seller for a home. An appraised value is an estimate of the current fair market value.

Maturity the date when the principal balance of a loan becomes due and payable.

Median Price the price of the house that falls in the middle of the total number of homes for sale in that area.

Medium Term Notes unsecured general obligations of Fannie Mae with maturities of one day or more and with principal and interest payable in U.S. dollars.

Merged Credit Report raw data pulled from two or more of the major credit-reporting firms.

Mitigation term usually used to refer to various changes or improvements made in a home; for instance, to reduce the average level of radon.

Modification when a lender agrees to modify the terms of a mortgage without refinancing the loan.

Mortgage a lien on the property that secures the Promise to repay a loan. A security agreement between the lender and the buyer in which the property is collateral for the loan. The mortgage gives the lender the right to collect payment on the loan and to foreclose if the loan obligations are not met.

Mortgage Acceleration Clause a clause allowing a lender, under certain circumstances, demand the entire balance of a loan is repaid in a lump sum. The acceleration clause is usually triggered if the home is sold, title to the property is changed, the loan is refinanced or the borrower defaults on a scheduled payment.

Mortgage-Backed Security (MBS) a Fannie Mae security that represents an undivided interest in a group of mortgages. Principal and interest payments from the individual mortgage loans are grouped and paid out to the MBS holders.

Mortgage Banker a company that originates loans and resells them to secondary mortgage lenders like Fannie Mae or Freddie Mac.

Mortgage Broker a firm that originates and processes loans for a number of lenders.

Mortgage Life and Disability Insurance term life insurance bought by borrowers to pay off a mortgage in the event of death or make monthly payments in the case of disability. The amount of coverage decreases as the principal balance declines. There are many different terms of coverage determining amounts of payments and when payments begin and end.

Mortgage Insurance a policy that protects lenders against some or most of the losses that can occur when a borrower defaults on a mortgage loan; mortgage insurance is required primarily for borrowers with a down payment of less than 20 percent of the home's purchase price. Insurance purchased by the buyer to protect the lender in the event of default. Typically purchased for loans with less than 20 percent down payment. The cost of mortgage insurance is usually added to the monthly payment. Mortgage insurance is maintained on conventional loans until the outstanding amount of the loan is less than 80 percent of the value of the house or for a set period of time (7 years is common). Mortgage insurance also is available through a government agency, such as the Federal Housing Administration (FHA) or through companies (Private Mortgage Insurance or PMI).

Mortgage Insurance Premium (MIP) a monthly payment—usually part of the mortgage payment—paid by a borrower for mortgage insurance.

Mortgage Interest Deduction the interest cost of a mortgage, which is a tax-deductible expense. The interest reduces the taxable income of taxpayers.

Mortgage Modification a loss mitigation option that allows a borrower to refinance and/or extend the term of the mortgage loan and thus reduce the monthly payments.

Mortgage Note a legal document obligating a borrower to repay a loan at a stated interest rate during a specified period; the agreement is secured by a mortgage that is recorded in the public records along with the deed.

Mortgage Qualifying Ratio Used to calculate the maximum amount of funds that an individual traditionally may be able to afford. A typical mortgage qualifying ratio is 28:36.

Mortgage Score a score based on a combination of information about the borrower that is obtained from the loan application, the credit report, and property value information. The score is a comprehensive analysis of the borrower's ability to repay a mortgage loan and manage credit.

Mortgagee the lender in a mortgage agreement.

Mortgagor the borrower in a mortgage agreement

Multifamily Housing a building with more than four residential rental units.

Multiple Listing Service (MLS) within the Metro Columbus area, Realtors submit listings and agree to attempt to sell all properties in the MLS. The MLS is a service of the local Columbus Board of Realtors®. The local MLS has a protocol for updating listings and sharing commissions. The MLS offers the advantage of more timely information, availability, and access to houses and other types of property on the market.

National Credit Repositories currently, there are three companies that maintain national credit-reporting databases. These are Equifax, Experian, and Trans Union, referred to as Credit Bureaus.

Negative Amortization amortization means that monthly payments are large enough to pay the interest and reduce the principal on your mortgage. Negative amortization occurs when the monthly payments do not cover all of the interest cost. The interest cost that isn't covered is added to the unpaid principal balance. This means that even after making many payments, you could owe more than you did at the beginning of the loan. Negative amortization can occur when an ARM has a payment cap that results in monthly payments not high enough to cover the interest due.

Net Income Your take-home pay, the amount of money that you receive in your paycheck after taxes and deductions.

No Cash Out Refinance a refinance of an existing loan only for the amount remaining on the mortgage. The borrower does not get any cash against the equity of the home. Also called a "rate and term refinance."

No Cost Loan there are many variations of a no cost loan. Generally, it is a loan that does not charge for items such as title insurance, escrow fees, settlement fees, appraisal, recording fees or notary fees. It may also offer no points. This lessens the need for upfront cash during the buying process however no cost loans have a higher interest rate.

Non-Conforming Loan a loan that exceeds Fannie Mae's and Freddie Mac's loan limits. Freddie Mac and Fannie Mae loans are referred to as conforming loans.

Nonperforming Asset an asset such as a mortgage that is not currently accruing interest or which interest is not being paid.

Notary Public a person who serves as a public official and certifies the authenticity of required signatures on a document by signing and stamping the document.

Note a legal document obligating a borrower to repay a mortgage loan at a stated interest rate over a specified period of time.

Note Rate the interest rate stated on a mortgage note.

Notice of Default a formal written notice to a borrower that there is a default on a loan and that legal action is possible.

Notional Principal Amount the proposed amount which interest rate swap payments are based but generally not paid or received by either party.

Offer indication by a potential buyer of a willingness to purchase a home at a specific price; generally put forth in writing.

Original Principal Balance the total principal owed on a mortgage prior to any payments being made.

Origination the process of preparing, submitting, and evaluating a loan application; generally includes a credit check, verification of employment, and a property appraisal.

Origination Fee the charge for originating a loan; is usually calculated in the form of points and paid at closing. One point equals one percent of the loan amount. On a conventional loan, the loan origination fee is the number of points a borrower pays.

Owner Financing a home purchase where the seller provides all or part of the financing, acting as a lender.

Ownership ownership is documented by the deed to a property. The type or form of ownership is important if there is a change in the status of the owners or if the property changes ownership.

Owner's Policy the insurance policy that protects the buyer from title defects.

Partial Claim a loss mitigation option offered by the FHA that allows a borrower, with help from a lender, to get an interest-free loan from HUD to bring their mortgage payments up to date.

Partial Payment a payment that is less than the total amount owed on a monthly mortgage payment. Normally, lenders do not accept partial payments. The lender may make exceptions during times of difficulty. Contact your lender prior to the due date if a partial payment is needed.

Payment Cap a limit on how much an ARM's payment may increase, regardless of how much the interest rate increases.

Payment Change Date the date when a new monthly payment amount takes effect on an adjustable-rate mortgage (ARM) or a graduated-payment mortgage (GPM). Generally, the payment change date occurs in the month immediately after the interest rate adjustment date.

Payment Due Date Contract language specifying when payments are due on money borrowed. The due date is always indicated and means that the payment must be received on or before the specified date. Grace periods prior to assessing a late fee or additional interest do not eliminate the responsibility of making payments on time.

Perils for homeowner's insurance, an event that can damage the property. Homeowner's insurance may cover the property for a wide variety of perils caused by accidents, nature, or people.

Personal Property any property that is not real property or attached to real property. For example furniture is not attached however a new light fixture would be considered attached and part of the real property.

PITI (Principal, Interest, Taxes, and Insurance) the four elements of a monthly mortgage payment; payments of principal and interest go directly towards repaying the loan while the portion that covers taxes and insurance (homeowner's and mortgage, if applicable) goes into an escrow account to cover the fees when they are due.

PITI Reserves a cash amount that a borrower must have on hand after making a down payment and paying all closing costs for the purchase of a home. The principal, interest, taxes, and insurance (PITI) reserves must equal the amount that the borrower would have to pay for PITI for a predefined number of months.

Planned Unit Development (PUD) a development that is planned, and constructed as one entity. Generally, there are common features in the homes or lots governed by covenants attached to the deed. Most planned developments have common land and facilities owned and managed by the owner's or neighborhood association. Homeowners usually are required to participate in the association via a payment of annual dues.

PMI Private Mortgage Insurance; privately-owned companies that offer standard and special affordable mortgage insurance programs for qualified borrowers with down payments of less than 20% of a purchase price.

Points a point is equal to one percent of the principal amount of your mortgage. For example, if you get a mortgage for $95,000, one point means you pay $950 to the lender. Lenders frequently charge points in both fixed-rate and adjustable-rate mortgages in order to increase the yield on the mortgage and to cover loan closing costs. These points usually are collected at closing and may be paid by the borrower or the home seller, or may be split between them.

Power of Attorney a legal document that authorizes another person to act on your behalf. A power of attorney can grant complete authority or can be limited to certain acts or certain periods of time or both.

Pre-Approval a lender commits to lend to a potential borrower a fixed loan amount based on a completed loan application, credit reports, debt, savings and has been reviewed by an underwriter. The commitment remains as long as the borrower still meets the qualification requirements at the time of purchase. This does not guaranty a loan until the property has passed inspections underwriting guidelines.

Predatory Lending abusive lending practices that include a mortgage loan to someone who does not have the ability to repay. It also pertains to repeated refinancing of a loan charging high interest and fees each time.

Predictive Variables The variables that are part of the formula comprising elements of a credit-scoring model. These variables are used to predict a borrower's future credit performance.

Preferred Stock stock that takes priority over common stock with regard to dividends and liquidation rights. Preferred stockholders typically have no voting rights.

Pre-Foreclosure Sale a procedure in which the borrower is allowed to sell a property for an amount less than what is owed on it to avoid a foreclosure. This sale fully satisfies the borrower's debt.

Prepayment any amount paid to reduce the principal balance of a loan before the due date or payment in full of a mortgage. This can occur with the sale of the property, the pay off the loan in full, or a foreclosure. In each case, full payment occurs before the loan has been fully amortized.

Premium an amount paid on a regular schedule by a policyholder that maintains insurance coverage.

Prepayment payment of the mortgage loan before the scheduled due date; may be subject to a prepayment penalty.

Prepayment Penalty a fee charged to a homeowner who pays one or more monthly payments before the due date. It can also apply to principal reduction payments.

Prepayment Penalty Mortgage (PPM) a type of mortgage that requires the borrower to pay a penalty for prepayment, partial payment of principal or for repaying the entire loan within a certain time period. A partial payment is generally defined as an amount exceeding 20% of the original principal balance.

Pre-Qualify a lender informally determines the maximum amount an individual is eligible to borrow. This is not a guaranty of a loan.

Price Range the high and low amount a buyer is willing to pay for a home.

Prime Rate the interest rate that banks charge to preferred customers. Changes in the prime rate are publicized in the business media. Prime rate can be used as the basis for adjustable rate mortgages (ARMs) or home equity lines of credit. The prime rate also affects the current interest rates being offered at a particular point in time on fixed mortgages. Changes in the prime rate do not affect the interest on a fixed mortgage.

Principal the amount of money borrowed to buy a house or the amount of the loan that has not been paid back to the lender. This does not include the interest paid to borrow that money. The principal balance is the amount owed on a loan at any given time. It is the original loan amount minus the total repayments of principal made.

Principal, Interest, Taxes, and Insurance (PITI) the four elements of a monthly mortgage payment; payments of principal and interest go directly towards repaying the loan while the portion that covers taxes and insurance (homeowner's and mortgage, if applicable) goes into an escrow account to cover the fees when they are due.

Private Mortgage Insurance (PMI) insurance purchased by a buyer to protect the lender in the event of default. The cost of mortgage insurance is usually added to the monthly payment. Mortgage insurance is generally maintained until over 20 Percent of the outstanding amount of the loan is paid or for a set period of time, seven years is normal. Mortgage insurance may be available through a government agency, such as the Federal Housing Administration (FHA) or the Veterans Administration (VA), or through private mortgage insurance companies (PMI).

Promissory Note a written promise to repay a specified amount over a specified period of time.

Property (Fixture and Non-Fixture) in a real estate contract, the property is the land within the legally described boundaries and all permanent structures and fixtures. Ownership of the property confers the legal right to use the property as allowed within the law and within the restrictions of zoning or easements. Fixture property refers to those items permanently attached to the structure, such as carpeting or a ceiling fan, which transfers with the property.

Property Tax a tax charged by local government and used to fund municipal services such as schools, police, or street maintenance. The amount of property tax is determined locally by a formula, usually based on a percent per $1,000 of assessed value of the property.

Property Tax Deduction the U.S. tax code allows homeowners to deduct the amount they have paid in property taxes from there total income.

Public Record Information Court records of events that are a matter of public interest such as credit, bankruptcy, foreclosure and tax liens. The presence of public record information on a credit report is regarded negatively by creditors.

Punch List a list of items that have not been completed at the time of the final walk through of a newly constructed home.

Purchase Offer A detailed, written document that makes an offer to purchase a property, and that may be amended several times in the process of negotiations. When signed by all parties involved in the sale, the purchase offer becomes a legally binding contract, sometimes called the Sales Contract.

Qualifying Ratios guidelines utilized by lenders to determine how much money a homebuyer is qualified to borrow. Lending guidelines typically include a maximum housing expense to income ratio and a maximum monthly expense to income ratio.

Quitclaim Deed a deed transferring ownership of a property but does not make any guarantee of clear title.

Radon a radioactive gas found in some homes that, if occurring in strong enough concentrations, can cause health problems.

Rate Cap a limit on an ARM on how much the interest rate or mortgage payment may change. Rate caps limit how much the interest rates can rise or fall on the adjustment dates and over the life of the loan.

Rate Lock a commitment by a lender to a borrower guaranteeing a specific interest rate over a period of time at a set cost.

Real Estate Agent an individual who is licensed to negotiate and arrange real estate sales; works for a real estate broker.

Real Estate Mortgage Investment Conduit (REMIC) a security representing an interest in a trust having multiple classes of securities. The securities of each class entitle investors to cash payments structured differently from the payments on the underlying mortgages.

Real Estate Property Tax Deduction a tax deductible expense reducing a taxpayer's taxable income.

Real Estate Settlement Procedures Act (RESPA) a law protecting consumers from abuses during the residential real estate purchase and loan process by requiring lenders to disclose all settlement costs, practices, and relationships

Real Property land, including all the natural resources and permanent buildings on it.

REALTOR® a real estate agent or broker who is a member of the NATIONAL ASSOCIATION OF REALTORS, and its local and state associations.*Recorder* the public official who keeps records of transactions concerning real property. Sometimes known as a "Registrar of Deeds" or "County Clerk."

Recording the recording in a registrar's office of an executed legal document. These include deeds, mortgages, satisfaction of a mortgage, or an extension of a mortgage making it a part of the public record.

Recording Fees charges for recording a deed with the appropriate government agency.

Refinancing paying off one loan by obtaining another; refinancing is generally done to secure better loan terms (like a lower interest rate).

Rehabilitation Mortgage a mortgage that covers the costs of rehabilitating (repairing or Improving) a property; some rehabilitation mortgages - like the FHA's 203(k) - allow a borrower to roll the costs of rehabilitation and home purchase into one mortgage loan.

Reinstatement Period a phase of the foreclosure process where the homeowner has an opportunity to stop the foreclosure by paying money that is owed to the lender.

Remaining Balance the amount of principal that has not yet been repaid.

Remaining Term the original amortization term minus the number of payments that have been applied.

Repayment Plan an agreement between a lender and a delinquent borrower where the borrower agrees to make additional payments to pay down past due amounts while making regularly scheduled payments.

RESPA Real Estate Settlement Procedures Act; a law protecting consumers from abuses during the residential real estate purchase and loan process by requiring lenders to disclose all settlement costs, practices, and relationships

Return on Average Common Equity net income available to common stockholders, as a percentage of average common stockholder equity.

Reverse Mortgage (HECM) the reverse mortgage is used by senior homeowners age 62 and older to convert the equity in their home into monthly streams of income and/or a line of credit to be repaid when they no longer occupy the home. A lending institution such as a mortgage lender, bank, credit union or savings and loan association funds the FHA insured loan, commonly known as HECM.

Right of First Refusal a provision in an agreement that requires the owner of a property to give one party an opportunity to purchase or lease a property before it is offered for sale or lease to others.

Risk-Based Capital an amount of capital needed to offset losses during a ten-year period with adverse circumstances.

Risk-Based Pricing Fee structure used by creditors based on risks of granting credit to a borrower with a poor credit history.

Risk Scoring an automated way to analyze a credit report verses a manual review. It takes into account late payments, outstanding debt, credit experience, and number of inquiries in an unbiased manner.

Sale Leaseback when a seller deeds property to a buyer for a payment, and the buyer simultaneously leases the property back to the seller.

Second Mortgage an additional mortgage on property. In case of a default the first mortgage must be paid before the second mortgage. Second loans are more risky for the lender and usually carry a higher interest rate.

Secondary Mortgage Market the buying and selling of mortgage loans. Investors purchase residential mortgages originated by lenders, which in turn provides the lenders with capital for additional lending.

Secured Loan a loan backed by collateral such as property.

Security the property that will be pledged as collateral for a loan.

Seller Take Back an agreement where the owner of a property provides second mortgage financing. These are often combined with an assumed mortgage instead of a portion of the seller's equity.

Serious Delinquency a mortgage that is 90 days or more past due.

Servicer a business that collects mortgage payments from borrowers and manages the borrower's escrow accounts.

Servicing the collection of mortgage payments from borrowers and related responsibilities of a loan servicer.

Setback the distance between a property line and the area where building can take place. Setbacks are used to assure space between buildings and from roads for a many of purposes including drainage and utilities.

Settlement another name for closing.

Settlement Statement a document required by the Real Estate Settlement Procedures Act (RESPA). It is an itemized statement of services and charges relating to the closing of a property transfer. The buyer has the right to examine the settlement statement 1 day before the closing. This is called the HUD 1 Settlement Statement.

Special Forbearance a loss mitigation option where the lender arranges a revised repayment plan for the borrower that may include a temporary reduction or suspension of monthly loan payments.

Stockholders' Equity the sum of proceeds from the issuance of stock and retained earnings less amounts paid to repurchase common shares.

Stripped MBS (SMBS) securities created by "stripping" or separating the principal and interest payments from the underlying pool of mortgages into two classes of securities, with each receiving a different proportion of the principal and interest payments.

Subordinate to place in a rank of lesser importance or to make one claim secondary to another.

Sub-Prime Loan "B" Loan or "B" paper with FICO scores from 620 to 659. "C" Loan or "C" Paper with FICO scores typically from 580 to 619. An industry term to used to describe loans with less stringent lending and underwriting terms and conditions. Due to the higher risk, sub-prime loans charge higher interest rates and fees.

Survey a property diagram that indicates legal boundaries, easements, encroachments, rights of way, improvement locations, etc. Surveys are conducted by licensed surveyors and are normally required by the lender in order to confirm that the property boundaries and features such as buildings, and easements are correctly described in the legal description of the property.

Sweat Equity using labor to build or improve a property as part of the down payment

Terms The period of time and the interest rate agreed upon by the lender and the borrower to repay a loan.

Third-Party Origination a process by which a lender uses another party to completely or partially originate, process, underwrite, close, fund, or package the mortgages it plans to deliver to the secondary mortgage market.

Title a legal document establishing the right of ownership and is recorded to make it part of the public record. Also known as a Deed.

Title 1 an FHA-insured loan that allows a borrower to make non-luxury improvements (like renovations or repairs) to their home; Title I loans less than $7,500 don't require a property lien.

Title Company a company that specializes in examining and insuring titles to real estate.

Title Defect an outstanding claim on a property that limits the ability to sell the property. Also referred to as a cloud on the title.

Title Insurance insurance that protects the lender against any claims that arise from arguments about ownership of the property; also available for homebuyers. An insurance policy guaranteeing the accuracy of a title search protecting against errors. Most lenders require the buyer to purchase title insurance protecting the lender against loss in the event of a title defect. This charge is included in the closing costs. A policy that protects the buyer from title defects is known as an owner's policy and requires an additional charge.

Title Search a check of public records to be sure that the seller is the recognized owner of the real estate and that there are no unsettled liens or other claims against the property.

Transfer Agent a bank or trust company charged with keeping a record of a company's stockholders and canceling and issuing certificates as shares are bought and sold.

Transfer of Ownership any means by which ownership of a property changes hands. These include purchase of a property, assumption of mortgage debt, exchange of possession of a property via a land sales contract or any other land trust device.

Transfer Taxes State and local taxes charged for the transfer of real estate. Usually equal to a percentage of the sales price.

Treasury Index can be used as the basis for adjustable rate mortgages (ARMs) It is based on the results of auctions that the U.S. Treasury holds for its Treasury bills and securities.

Truth-in-Lending a federal law obligating a lender to give full written disclosure of all fees, terms, and conditions associated with the loan initial period and then adjusts to another rate that lasts for the term of the loan.

Two-Step Mortgage an adjustable-rate mortgage (ARM) that has one interest rate for the first five to seven years of its term and a different interest rate for the remainder of the term.

Trustee a person who holds or controls property for the benefit of another.

Underwriting the process of analyzing a loan application to determine the amount of risk involved in making the loan; it includes a review of the potential borrower's credit history and a judgment of the property value.

Up Front Charges the fees charged to homeowners by the lender at the time of closing a mortgage loan. This includes points, broker's fees, insurance, and other charges.

VA (Department of Veterans Affairs) a federal agency, which guarantees loans made to veterans; similar to mortgage insurance, a loan guarantee protects lenders against loss that may result from a borrower default.

VA Mortgage a mortgage guaranteed by the Department of Veterans Affairs (VA).

Variable Expenses Costs or payments that may vary from month to month, for example, gasoline or food.

Variance a special exemption of a zoning law to allow the property to be used in a manner different from an existing law.

Vested a point in time when you may withdraw funds from an investment account, such as a retirement account, without penalty.

Walk Through the final inspection of a property being sold by the buyer to confirm that any contingencies specified in the purchase agreement such as repairs have been completed, fixture and nonfixture property is in place and confirm the electrical, mechanical, and plumbing systems are in working order.

Warranty Deed a legal document that includes the guarantee the seller is the true owner of the property, has the right to sell the property and there are no claims against the property.

Zoning local laws established to control the uses of land within a particular area. Zoning laws are used to separate residential land from areas of nonresidential use, such as industry or businesses. Zoning ordinances include many provisions governing such things as type of structure, setbacks, lot size, and uses of a building.

Information Technology

Adaptation See Maintenance (Adaptive).

Application A set of software that provides functionality to the business process or is necessary to operate and maintain the automated information systems

Application Architecture The model(s) that describes how a set of applications will be structured and the interfaces and design rules for each of its parts (e.g., isolating graphical user interface code from business logic).

Application Platform A collection of tightly integrated computing hardware, peripherals, operating system, and middleware upon which an application is built. The application provides some of its functionality by accessing services residing on the application platform through an Application Program Interface.

Application Platform Entity The set of resources, including hardware and software, that provides all the services to application software executing on that platform, including the ability to have application-to-application services.

Application Portfolio The aggregation of applications required to support the Agency.

Application Service Provider Organizations that provide application programs or services for a fee over the Internet. These programs or services were previously made available from the Enterprise's server or personal computers.

Automated Information System A combination of computer hardware and software, data, and telecommunications that performs functions for an organization.

Baseline A set of items that have been formally reviewed and agreed upon. The agreement is between key stakeholders, such as the item's producer and consumer (user). A baseline establishes a fixed point for further development or use. Items in a baseline can be modified only through formal change control procedures in which the stakeholders participate.

Baseline Data Initial collection of data to establish a basis for comparison. (National Performance Review)

Benchmark A standard or point of reference used in measuring and/or judging quality or value. (National Performance Review)

Business Any Enterprise that provides a type of offering. The organizational entity being studied, regardless of its size or purpose either private or public sector.

Business Process A set of interacting activities and decisions that produce one or more products or services for customers of the business Enterprise.

Business Process Reengineering The significant redesign and restructuring of an organization's business operations and management practices to achieve a significant change in performance, such as cost, cycle time, service, and quality. Traditional organizational boundaries are eliminated and replaced by an emphasis on core business processes.

Business Rule An expression of the business policies and procedures (e.g, Agency or Program), often embedded within the logic of an application program.

Capacity A measure of an organization's output, for example participation rates in an program or other Federal reporting requirements. For the IT organization, this may resolve into measures of efficiency or effectiveness of meeting IT evolving needs.

Component A software item that can be independently developed, distributed (provided and/or sold), and used in its binary form separable from the original context. Components can be used to develop distributed applications in which the components can communicate with one another. A component is based on a component model, such as COM or JavaBeans. Component models support runtime interface exposure and discovery, component properties, persistence, event handling, application builder support, distribution (location transparency), and component packaging. Components have two distinct parts: specifications (or interfaces) and implementations. Components are typically generated with object-oriented approaches, but this is not essential, as long as they can be used as objects.

Core Competency A bundle of skill sets or capabilities that significantly contribute to an organization's ability to satisfy the customer, offer unique services, or have future value.

Core Process The fundamental activities, or group of activities, so critical to an organization's success that failure to perform them in an exemplary manner will result in deterioration of the organization's mission.

Critical Success Factors Those few areas where things must go right for the Enterprise to be considered successful in achieving its mission. CSFs are internal and external states and events that can have significant impact on perceived results.

Cultural Filter A concept that describes how one delivers, views, or interprets information in different regions. For instance, telephone interviews or face-to-face interviews may be necessary given the interviewee's circumstances.

Culture The sum of individual opinions, shared mindsets, values, and norms.

Data Information absent its context. A representation of facts, concepts, and instructions in a defined format and structure that permits the processing of interpretation by humans or machines.

Environment Circumstances and conditions that interact with and affect an organization. These can include economic, political, cultural, and physical conditions inside or outside of the organization. See the Roles for additional information. (National Performance Review).

Enterprise The whole (or portion) of the State Agency (or additional Agencies) that is affected by change in the IT infrastructure. This scope is necessary to establish the boundaries, within which the Agency decision makers can manage the interoperability and integration within and across this boundary.

Enterprise Application Integration The application of technology to consolidate and coordinate disparate legacy applications and databases to extend their useful lifetime across the enterprise. The interoperability generally relies on message-oriented middleware with adaptors and or connectors that allow for existing applications to interact by moving, routing, and transforming data between them in real time.

Entity A discrete, identifiable element of technology. An entity may be made up of subsidiary entities and also may be part of a larger entity. As an element of technology, an entity is "thing" and can be characterized in part by the technology used to implement it. For example, a candle and a light bulb are both implementations of a "light source" entity.

Function (business) A collection of resources (equipment, networking, individuals) in a single area of operations, such as finance, accounting, personnel, production, engineering, operations, development, or support.

Goal A general target the Agency or organization wishes to reach in a specific area. It is a broad direction for managerial decision making, often stated in terms of qualitative measures. Goals need to be achieved for the Agency or organization to achieve its mission.

Guiding Principles The shared values and management or technical style of the Enterprise. They articulate the ethical standards by which the organization makes decisions and conducts activities.

Information Data that has been given meaning by human reference. Data becomes information only when it is placed into a meaningful context or relationship.

Information Appliance Combines the application software and application platform entities into one entity. This term is used when the presence of configurable and/or separately procurable software is not visible to the user of a particular information technology. Examples: set-top cable TV boxes, video cassette recorders, television sets, fax machines, cell phones.

Information Technology The processing equipment, interconnecting (networking) equipment, and the software entities that operate within this equipment.

Integration Combining separately developed parts into a whole so that they work together. The means of integration may vary, from simply mating the parts together at an interface, to radically altering the parts or providing something to mediate between them.

Interface A boundary between two or more entities such as human-computer or application program to application.

Interoperability The ability of independently developed and fielded applications that execute on heterogeneous computer platforms to communicate with one another and to exchange and use information (content, format, and semantics).

Legacy System Jargon for an AIS (or set of applications) that is currently in use, and initially deployed many years ago, using a computing infrastructure that is several generations old. These systems tend to be critical to the business and cannot be easily replaced or cost-effectively maintained. They are approaching or have reached the end of their practical operational life span.

Maintenance The process of modifying a system or component after delivery to correct faults, improve performance or other attributes, or adapt to a changed environment, with the purpose of maintaining the value of the existing system.

Maintenance (Adaptive) Maintenance performed to make a system usable in a changing environment. Adaptation refers to evolutionary changes (usually involves a progressive modification of some structure or structures), which a system makes in order to cope with the changes in the environment, while still keeping the essential attributes of the system's structure and processes constant. For example: responding to increased enrollment by hiring more teachers; adjusting the clothing to suit the weather.

Maintenance (Corrective) Maintenance performed to correct faults (defects) in hardware or software.

Maintenance (Perfective) Maintenance performed to improve the performance, maintainability, or other attributes of a system.

Measure One of several measurable values that contribute to the understanding and quantification of a key performance indicator.

Metrics The elements of a measurement system consisting of key performance indicators, measures, and measurement methodologies.

Migration The process of transferring all or part of an AIS's functionality, data, or communications to another technical infrastructure. The original application code may be ported or replaced. The business data (and its schema) is usually retained in a significant way.

Mission An enduring statement of purpose; the organization's reason for existence. The mission describes what the organization does, who it does it for, and how it does it. (National Performance Review)

Noncompliance An instance where performance of a task or a resultant work product does not follow the agreed upon procedures, descriptions, standards, or other requirements. A noncompliance is generally found through QA reviews and audits and formally tracked until it is resolved.

Objective A broad, general direction or intent.

Open system (environment) An AIS that is built to a set of specifications that are nonproprietary, allowing the system to better interoperate, scale, or allow for porting of applications across heterogeneous, multivendor computing platforms.

Organization A logical grouping of people and resources (including information) for accomplishing some aspect of the mission of an Enterprise. See the Roles for the generic organizational entities assumed by the guides.

Packaged Solution An integrated collection of software, hardware, or other parts provided by vendors as a basis for developing solutions to common business domain functions. A packaged solution is often highly tailorable at the design level to meet Enterprise-unique needs. Systems transferred from one State and adapted for another are also in this category.

Performance Measure A quantitative or qualitative characterization of performance. (National Performance Review)

Plateau (Evolution Planning) An incremental level of capability at which the Agency operates, as it moves to achieve its vision in accordance with the strategy. It is a point where the Agency can reevaluate the progress being made; note significant changes in the Agency's external, internal, or IT Division conditions; and readjust plans. Plateaus can be represented in the IT Evolution Plan as intermediate milestones.

Platform See Application platform.

Plug-In A program that can be downloaded and installed on demand to be used as part of a Web browser. A plug-in is generally a small program that is activated by the Web browser to perform special processing of objects within the HTML document, such as viewing Portable Document Format (PDF) or streaming video objects.

Portability (Porting) Portability is a characteristic of a system (or part) that describes the ease with which the system (or part) can run on multiple, heterogeneous platforms. There are two general levels of portability: the binary-program level and the source-code level. Binary portability is exemplified by the Java language, whose byte codes are capable of executing on any computer that supports its runtime environment (Java Virtual Machine). Source code portability is generally achieved by coding to a recognized standard (e.g., ANSI C++) and APIs to facilitate program compilation in multiple target environments.

Portal A (Web) application that provides a single means of access to many information sources and applications. Portals typically provide personalization, collaboration, content management, security, and other services to users. A portal may serve one or more types of users within or across Agency boundaries, such as clients, case workers, or service providers.

Process A sequence of activities that transforms or uses inputs to produce outputs.

Profile A profile is a collection of specifications developed to meet a set of requirements. Elements of a profile may consist of either formal standards (i.e., those developed within a voluntary standards organization such as ANSI or IEEE) or de facto standards (i.e., those accepted within the marketplace). Each element of a profile may be a specification in its entirety or a specification with certain options or parameters to be chosen. The NIST APP organizes the standards into several services areas: Operating System, Human Computer Interface, Software Engineering, Data Management, Data Interchange, Graphics, and Network Services.

Program An organizational structure within an Enterprise. The program maintains expertise and resources in a particular area (e.g., the TANF program) and may allocate these resources to specific projects. The program exists for a significant period of time because it is associated with a business or other long-term and evolving objective. The program may be part or all of an Agency department, center, or IT Division.

Project An effort, directed toward achieving a specific goal, that has been assigned specific resources and duration (for contrast, see Program). Projects are the context in which all development work is done for the program.

Quality Assurance A planned and systematic set of actions to provide adequate confidence that work products and the processes used to produce them conform to established requirements.

Reengineering The examination of a system to extract inherent knowledge and functionality followed by the implementation of equivalent capability in a new system. The new implementation may include modifications for changed requirements not part of the original system. Also known as renovation and reclamation.

Resource That which is used or consumed by the Enterprise in fulfillment of its objectives.

Restructuring A process to reorganize a system in another form, preserving the original system's external behavior (functional and semantics).

Return on Investment (IT) The gains achieved from spending on IT for the Agency.

Reverse Engineering The examination of a system to extract inherent knowledge and functionality with the express purpose of creating an abstract model or specification of the system (does not involve changing the subject system).

Role A unit of defined responsibility that may be assumed by one or more individuals (e.g., a team that fulfills the planner responsibilities). Roles are defined for the framework in a Role model.

Scalable A scalable application system is one that can increase its throughput without significantly increasing its cost per user (or cost per transaction). The system should also be able to scale down as well.

Service A capability that a provider entity makes available to a user entity at the interface between those entities (e.g., a Web service)

Standard A special case, or type of specification, that has been through a formal ballot in a group open to wide participation, and have a known community of consensus. These formal standards may be considered U.S. national standards.

Standard (De Facto) A proprietary specification that becomes widely adopted in the marketplace based on marketplace success, made available by the developer of the technology in a public or private domain (e.g., for a fee).

Standard (Formal) Standards that have been agree upon by a group open to wide participation. These standards have been through a defined balloting process.

Standard (International) A standard developed and successfully balloted outside the U.S., using an approach that may vary greatly from the U.S. approach. The scope of ballot is global (e.g., ISO/IEC).

Standard (Private or Proprietary) Specification developed within an organization; may be protected by intellectual property restrictions or agreement prior to use.

Standard (Public) Any specification that has established some consensus but has not been formally balloted. Usually a proprietary specification that became widely adopted in the marketplace.

Standard (Regional) A standard developed and successfully balloted outside the U.S., using an approach that may vary greatly from the U.S. approach. Regional is when the scope of ballot is limited to a specific part of the world (e.g., European, Pacific Rim, or North American) as opposed to international.

Standard (U.S. National) A standard developed and successfully balloted inside the U.S., usually by a voluntary standards organization subject to basic ANSI guidelines.

Strategic Planning Those actions that lead to the definition of the IT organization's mission, the formulation of its goals, and the definition of the essential action to be implemented to meet those goals.

Strategy Strategies are the "hows" of pursuing a mission and achieving goals. A strategy is a managerial action plan for achieving targeted outcomes, mirrored in the pattern of moves and approaches devised to produce desired results.

Strategy Project A managed set of activities that generate the IT Strategic Plan.

System Architecture The model(s) that describes how the major IT elements (equipment, data sources, applications, and networking) are arranged to provide or exchange services between the elements and external entities (people or automated systems).

Target Application Platform A Target Application Platform is the realization of an application platform described in the Target Architecture, using appropriately adapted custom or vendor provided frameworks (software and hardware products). The Target Application Platform is the physical environment upon which the applications for an AIS are built, executed, and maintained.

Target Architecture The Target Architecture is the design for an instance of elements defined in the Technical Architecture. A Target Architecture elaborates the Technical Architecture by binding specific versions of software, hardware, data stores, and networking implementations to abstract Technical Architecture descriptions. A target Application Platform, for example, is a realization of an application platform described in the Technical Architecture, using appropriately adapted vendor provided frameworks (software and hardware products).

Task In the context of project management, this is a well defined unit of work that can be assigned to individuals to perform, and tracked to completion.

Technical Architecture A Technical Architecture identifies and describes the types of applications, platforms, and external entities; their interfaces; and their services; as well as the context within which the entities interoperate. A Technical Architecture is based on a Technical Reference Model (TRM) and the selected standards that further describe the TRM elements (the profile). The Technical Architecture is the basis for selecting and implementing the infrastructure to establish the target architecture.

Technical Reference Model A taxonomy of services arranged according to a conceptual model, such as the Open System Environment model. The enumerated services are specific to those needed to support the technology computing style (e.g., distributed object computing) and the industry/business application needs (e.g., Human Services, financial).

Tier (n-Tier) A physical partitioning of an application across three or more networked computer platforms, such as user interface, business logic, and data access and storage functions.

Transcoding The process of dynamically transforming data as it is delivered so that it is optimally formatted for the destination environment. Transcoding can be applied in many situations: character encoding (internationalization), addressing differences in link speed or display screen form factors (wireless), or converting between video compression formats.

Value Chain The collection of activities within a company that allow it to compete within an industry. The activities in a value chain can be grouped into two categories: primary activities, which include inbound logistics, outbound logistics and after-sales service, and support activities, which include human resources management, Agency infrastructure, procurement, and technology development.

Vision A guiding theme that articulates the nature of the organization's operation (business) and the intent for its future. It is a description of what senior management wants to achieve, usually refers to the mid- to long-term, and often is expressed in terms of a series of goals.

Web Service A unit of application logic providing data and services to other applications via ubiquitous Web protocols and data formats such as HTTP, XML, and SOAP. The service implementation (and physical location) is generally hidden from the user of the service.

Immigration and Naturalization

Adoption See Orphan.

Adjustment to Immigrant Status Procedure allowing certain aliens already in the United States to apply for immigrant status. Aliens admitted to the United States in a nonimmigrant, refugee, or parolee category may have their status changed to that of lawful permanent resident if they are eligible to receive an immigrant visa and one is immediately available. In such cases, the alien is counted as an immigrant as of the date of adjustment, even though the alien may have been in the United States for an extended period of time.

Aggravated Felony Usually refers to particularly serious crimes. If you have committed an aggravated felony, you may be permanently ineligible for naturalization. The Immigration and Nationality Act and the laws in each State determine what is considered an aggravated felony

Agricultural Worker As a nonimmigrant class of admission, an alien coming temporarily to the United States to perform agricultural labor or services, as defined by the Secretary of Labor.

Alien Any person not a citizen or national of the United States.

Amerasian Act Public Law 97-359 (Act of 10/22/82) provides for the immigration to the United States of certain Amerasian children. In order to qualify for benefits under this law, an alien must have been born in Cambodia, Korea, Laos, Thailand, or Vietnam after December 31, 1950, and before October 22, 1982, and have been fathered by a U.S. citizen.

Amerasian (Vietnam) Immigrant visas are issued to Amerasians under Public Law 100-202 (Act of 12/22/87), which provides for the admission of aliens born in Vietnam after January 1, 1962, and before January 1, 1976, if the alien was fathered by a U.S. citizen. Spouses, children, and parents or guardians may accompany the alien.

Application Support Center (ASC) USCIS offices where applicants usually have their fingerprints taken. Once you have filed your application with USCIS, you will receive a notice telling you which ASC serves your area.

Apprehension The arrest of a removable alien by the Department of Homeland Security. Each apprehension of the same alien in a fiscal year is counted separately.

AR-11, "Alien's Change of Address Card" This is the form you use to tell USCIS when you have moved to a new address. The AR-11 is pre-printed with USCIS' address. It is very important to tell USCIS when your address changes. This way, you will receive any information USCIS sends you, including interview notices and requests for additional documents.

Asylee An alien in the United States or at a port of entry who is found to be unable or unwilling to return to his or her country of nationality, or to seek the protection of that country because of persecution or a well-founded fear of persecution. Persecution or the fear thereof must be based on the alien's race, religion, nationality, membership in a particular social group, or political opinion. For persons with no nationality, the country of nationality is considered to be the country in which the alien last habitually resided. Asylees are eligible to adjust to lawful permanent resident status after one year of continuous presence in the United States. These immigrants are limited to 10,000 adjustments per fiscal year B.

Beneficiaries Aliens on whose behalf a U.S. citizen, lawful permanent resident, or employer have filed a petition for such aliens to receive immigration benefits from the U.S. Department of Homeland Security. Beneficiaries generally receive a lawful status as a result of their relationship to a U.S. citizen, lawful permanent resident, or U.S. employer.

Border Crosser An alien resident of the United States reentering the country after an absence of less than six months in Canada or Mexico, or a nonresident alien entering the United States across the Canadian border for stays of no more than six months or across the Mexican border for stays of no more than 72 hours.

Border Patrol Sector Any one of 21 geographic areas into which the United States is divided for the Department of Homeland Security's Border Patrol activities.

Business Nonimmigrant An alien coming temporarily to the United States to engage in commercial transactions which do not involve gainful employment in the United States, i.e., engaged in international commerce on behalf of a foreign firm, not employed in the U.S. labor market, and receives no salary from U.S. sources.

Cancellation of Removal A discretionary benefit adjusting an alien's status from that of deportable alien to one lawfully admitted for permanent residence. Application for cancellation of removal is made during the course of a hearing before an immigration judge.

Certificate of Citizenship Identity document proving U.S. citizenship. Certificates of citizenship are issued to derivative citizens and to persons who acquired U.S. citizenship (see definitions for Acquired and Derivative Citizenship).

Certificate of Naturalization A certificate given at the oath ceremony. It serves as evidence of your citizenship. USCIS also recommends getting a United States passport as evidence that you are a U.S. citizen.

Child Generally, an unmarried person under 21 years of age who is: a child born in wedlock; a stepchild, provided that the child was under 18 years of age at the time that the marriage creating the stepchild relationship occurred; a legitimated child, provided that the child was legitimated while in the legal custody of the legitimating parent; a child born out of wedlock, when a benefit is sought on the basis of its relationship with its mother, or to its father if the father has or had a bona fide relationship with the child; a child adopted while under 16 years of age who has resided since adoption in the legal custody of the adopting parents for at least 2 years; or an orphan, under 16 years of age, who has been adopted abroad by a U.S. citizen or has an immediate-relative visa petition submitted in his/her behalf and is coming to the United States for adoption by a U.S. citizen.

Community-Based Organization (CBO) Organizations that assist immigrants who are new to the United States or who are going through the naturalization process.

Many CBOs will help you complete your application and guide you through the naturalization process. CBOs may charge a fee or offer their services free of charge.

Continued One of three things that may happen to your case after your interview (granted, denied, or continued). If your case is continued, it is put on hold until further action is taken by you or USCIS. If your case is continued, USCIS may ask you to provide more documents or to come to an additional interview.

Continuous Residence An important requirement for naturalization. Continuous residence may be broken if you take a single trip out of the country that lasts for 6 months or more.

Country of Birth The country in which a person is born.

Chargeability: The independent country to which an immigrant entering under the preference system is accredited for purposes of numerical limitations.

Citizenship: The country in which a person is born (and has not renounced or lost citizenship) or naturalized and to which that person owes allegiance and by which he or she is entitled to be protected. Former Allegiance: The previous country of citizenship of a naturalized U.S. citizen or of a person who derived U.S. citizenship. (Last) Residence: The country in which an alien habitually resided prior to entering the United States.

Nationality: The country of a person's citizenship or country in which the person is deemed a national.

Crewman A foreign national serving in a capacity required for normal operations and service on board a vessel or aircraft. Crewmen are admitted for twenty-nine days, with no extensions. Two categories of crewmen are defined in the INA: D1, departing from the United States with the vessel or aircraft on which he arrived or some other vessel or aircraft; and D2, departing from Guam with the vessel on which he arrived.

Criminal Removal The deportation, exclusion, or removal of an alien who has 1) been charged under a section of the Immigration and Nationality Act that requires a criminal conviction and that charge is the basis for the removal or 2) a criminal conviction noted in the Deportable Alien Control System (DACS) for a crime that renders the alien removable. An alien with an appropriate criminal conviction is considered a criminal alien regardless of the section of law under which the alien was removed.

Cuban/Haitian Entrant Status accorded 1) Cubans who entered illegally or were paroled into the United States between April 15, 1980, and October 10, 1980, and 2) Haitians who entered illegally or were paroled into the country before January 1, 1981. Cubans and Haitians meeting these criteria who have continuously resided in the United States since before January 1, 1982, and who were known to the INS before that date, may adjust to permanent residence under a provision of the Immigration Control and Reform Act of 1986.

Deferred Inspection See Parolee.

Denied One of three things that may happen to your case after your interview (granted, denied, or continued). If your application is denied, USCIS has determined that you have not met the eligibility requirements for naturalization.

Departure Under Safeguards The departure of an illegal alien from the United States which is physically observed by a Department of Homeland Security official.

Deportable Alien An alien in and admitted to the United States subject to any grounds of removal specified in the Immigration and Nationality Act. This includes any alien illegally in the United States, regardless of whether the alien entered the country by fraud or misrepresentation or entered legally but subsequently lost legal status.

Deportation The formal removal of an alien from the United States when the alien has been found removable for violating the immigration laws. Deportation is ordered by an immigration judge without any punishment being imposed or contemplated. Prior to April 1997 deportation and exclusion were separate removal procedures. The Illegal Immigration Reform and Immigrant Responsibility Act of 1996 consolidated these procedures. After April 1, 1997, aliens in and admitted to the United States may be subject to removal based on deportability.

Derivative Citizenship Citizenship conveyed to children through the naturalization of parents or, under certain circumstances, to foreign-born children adopted by U.S. citizen parents, provided certain conditions are met.

Districts The geographic divisions of the United States used by USCIS.

Diversity A category of immigrants replacing the earlier categories for nationals of underrepresented countries and countries adversely "affected" by the Immigration and Nationality Act Amendments of 1965 (P.L. 89-236). The annual limit on diversity immigration was 40,000 during fiscal years 1992–94, under a transitional diversity program, and 55,000 beginning in fiscal year 1995, under a permanent diversity program.

Docket Control The DHS mechanism for tracking the case status of potentially removable aliens.

Employer Sanctions The employer sanctions provision of the Immigration Reform and Control Act of 1986 prohibits employers from hiring, recruiting, or referring for a fee aliens known to be unauthorized to work in the United States. Violators of the law are subject to a series of civil fines for violations or criminal penalties when there is a pattern or practice of violations.

Exchange Visitor An alien coming temporarily to the United States as a participant in a program approved by the Secretary of State for the purpose of teaching, instructing or lecturing, studying, observing, conducting research, consulting, demonstrating special skills, or receiving training.

Exclusion Prior to the Illegal Immigration Reform and Immigrant Responsibility Act of 1996, exclusion was the formal term for denial of an alien's entry into the United States. The decision to exclude an alien was made by an immigration judge after an exclusion hearing. Since April 1, 1997, the process of adjudicating inadmissibility may take place in either an expedited removal process or in removal proceedings before an immigration judge.

Expedited Removal The Illegal Immigration Reform and Immigrant Responsibility Act of 1996 authorized the DHS to quickly remove certain inadmissible aliens from the United States. The authority covers aliens who are inadmissible because they have no entry documents or because they have used counterfeit, altered, or otherwise fraudulent or improper documents. The authority covers aliens who arrive in, attempt to enter, or have entered the United States without having been admitted or paroled by an immigration officer at a port-of-entry. The DHS has the authority to order the removal, and the alien is not referred to an immigration judge except under certain circumstances after an alien makes a claim to lawful status in the United States or demonstrates a credible fear of persecution if returned to his or her home country.

Fiance(e)s of U.S. Citizen A nonimmigrant alien coming to the United States to conclude a valid marriage with a U.S. citizen within ninety days after entry.

Fiscal Year Currently, the twelve-month period beginning October 1 and ending September 30. Historically, until 1831 and from 1843–49, the twelve-month period ending September 30 of the respective year; from 1832–42 and 1850–67, ending December 31 of the respective year; from 1868-1976, ending June 30 of the respective year. The transition quarter (TQ) for 1976 covers the three-month period, July-September 1976.

Foreign Government Official As a nonimmigrant class of admission, an alien coming temporarily to the United States who has been accredited by a foreign government to function as an ambassador, public minister, career diplomatic or consular officer, other accredited official, or an attendant, servant or personal employee of an accredited official, and all above aliens' spouses and unmarried minor (or dependent) children.

Foreign Information Media Representative As a nonimmigrant class of admission, an alien coming temporarily to the United States as a bona fide representative of foreign press, radio, film, or other foreign information media and the alien's spouse and unmarried minor (or dependent) children.

Foreign State of Chargeability The independent country to which an immigrant entering under the preference system is accredited. No more than 7 percent of the family-sponsored and employment-based visas may be issued to natives of any one independent country in a fiscal year. No one dependency of any independent country may receive more than 2 percent of the family-sponsored and employment-based visas issued. Since these limits are based on visa issuance rather than entries into the United States, and immigrant visas are valid for 6 months, there is not total correspondence between these two occurrences. Chargeability is usually determined by country of birth. Exceptions are made to prevent the separation of family members when the limitation for the country of birth has been met.

G-28, "Notice of Entry of Appearance as Attorney or Representative" The form you must file with your Form N-400 if you wish to bring a representative with you to your USCIS interview.

General Naturalization Provisions The basic requirements for naturalization that every applicant must meet, unless a member of a special class. General provisions require an applicant to be at least 18 years of age and a lawful permanent resident with five years of continuous residence in the United States, have been physically present in the country for half that period, and have established good moral character for at least that period.

Geographic Area of Chargeability Any one of five regions-Africa, East Asia, Latin America and the Caribbean, Near East and South Asia, and the former Soviet Union and Eastern Europe-into which the world is divided for the initial admission of refugees to the United States. Annual consultations between the Executive Branch and the Congress determine the ceiling on the number of refugees who can be admitted to the United States from each area. Beginning in fiscal year 1987, an unallocated reserve was incorporated into the admission ceilings.

Good Moral Character Good moral character is an important eligibility requirement for naturalization. When determining if an applicant has good moral character, USCIS considers such things as honesty and criminal records.

Granted One of three things that may happen to your case after your interview (granted, denied, or continued). If USCIS determines that you are eligible, your application will be approved or "granted." After you take the Oath of Allegiance, you will be a United States citizen.

H-1B Beneficiary 1) the approved petition associated with a specialty worker admitted on the basis of professional education, skills, and/or equivalent experience (the H-1B subsection uses this definition); 2) a specialty worker whose petition to work temporarily in the United States has been approved by the Department of Homeland Security.

H-1B Petition An application form used by employers seeking permission for an alien to work temporarily in the United States. An H-1B petition must be approved by the Department of Homeland Security before an alien specialty worker is authorized to begin or continue working in the United States. This requirement is true regardless of whether the alien is residing overseas or within the United States at the time of application. After a petition is approved, an H-1B worker is said to be a beneficiary.

Hemispheric Ceilings Statutory limits on immigration to the United States in effect from 1968 to October 1978. Mandated by the Immigration and Nationality Act Amendments of 1965, the ceiling on immigration from the Eastern Hemisphere was set at 170,000, with a per-country limit of 20,000. Immigration from the Western Hemisphere was held to 120,000, without a per-country limit until January 1, 1977. The Western Hemisphere was then made subject to a 20,000 per country limit. Effective October 1978, the separate hemisphere limits were abolished in favor of a worldwide limit.

Immediate Relatives Certain immigrants who because of their close relationship to U.S. citizens are exempt from the numerical limitations imposed on immigration to the United States. Immediate relatives are: spouses of citizens, children (under 21 years of age and unmarried) of citizens, and parents of citizens 21 years of age or older.

Immigrant See Permanent Resident Alien.

Immigration Act of 1990 Public Law 101-649 (Act of November 29, 1990), increased the limits on lawful immigration to the United States, revised all grounds for exclusion and deportation, authorized temporary protected status to aliens of designated countries, revised and established new nonimmigrant admission categories, revised and extended the Visa Waiver Pilot Program, and revised naturalization authority and requirements.

Immigration Judge An attorney appointed by the Attorney General to act as an administrative judge within the Executive Office for Immigration Review. They are qualified to conduct specified classes of proceedings, including removal proceedings.

INA See Immigration and Nationality Act.

Immigration and Nationality Act The Act (INA), which, along with other immigration laws, treaties, and conventions of the United States, relates to the immigration, temporary admission, naturalization, and removal of aliens.

Immigration Marriage Fraud Amendments of 1986 Public Law 99-639 (Act of 11/10/86), was passed in order to deter immigration-related marriage fraud. Its major provision stipulates that aliens deriving their immigrant status based on a marriage of less than two years are conditional immigrants. To remove their conditional status the immigrants must apply at an Department of Homeland Security office during the

90-day period before their second-year anniversary of receiving conditional status. If the aliens cannot show that the marriage through which the status was obtained was and is a valid one, their conditional immigrant status may be terminated and they may become deportable.

Immigration Reform and Control Act (IRCA) of 1986 Public Law 99-603 (Act of 11/6/86), was passed in order to control and deter illegal immigration to the United States. Its major provisions stipulate legalization of undocumented aliens who had been continuously unlawfully present since 1982, legalization of certain agricultural workers, sanctions for employers who knowingly hire undocumented workers, and increased enforcement at U.S. borders.

Inadmissible An alien seeking admission at a port of entry who does not meet the criteria in the INA for admission. The alien may be placed in removal proceedings or, under certain circumstances, allowed to withdraw his or her application for admission. Industrial Trainee See Temporary Worker.

International Representative As a nonimmigrant class of admission, an alien coming temporarily to the United States as a principal or other accredited representative of a foreign government (whether officially recognized or not recognized by the United States) to an international organization, an international organization officer or employee, and all above aliens' spouses and unmarried minor (or dependent) children.

Intracompany Transferee An alien, employed for at least one continuous year out of the last three by an international firm or corporation, who seeks to enter the United States temporarily in order to continue to work for the same employer, or a subsidiary or affiliate, in a capacity that is primarily managerial, executive, or involves specialized knowledge, and the alien's spouse and minor unmarried children.

IRCA See Immigration Reform and Control Act of 1986.

Irish Peace Process Cultural and Training Program Act of 1998 Amended the INA to establish new nonimmigrant classes (Q2 and Q3) to allow temporary admission to young people (and their spouses and minor children) of disadvantaged areas in Northern Ireland and certain counties of the Republic of Ireland for the purpose of developing job skills and conflict resolution abilities, so that those young people can return to their homes better able to contribute toward economic regeneration and the Irish peace process. Period of temporary admission not to exceed 36 months; program repealed,

Labor Certification Requirement for U.S. employers seeking to employ certain persons whose immigration to the United States is based on job skills or nonimmigrant temporary workers coming to perform services for which qualified authorized workers are unavailable in the United States. Labor certification is issued by the Secretary of Labor and contains attestations by U.S. employers as to the numbers of U.S. workers available to undertake the employment sought by an applicant, and the effect of the alien's employment on the wages and working conditions of U.S. workers similarly employed. Determination of labor availability in the United States is made at the time of a visa application and at the location where the applicant wishes to work.

Legal Immigration Family Equity (LIFE) Act of 2000 Public Law 106-553 (Act of 12/21/2000) temporarily reinstated Section 245(i) of the INA to allow persons who were qualified for permanent resident status but had immigration status violations to pay a penalty fee and apply for adjustment of status at an INS office; these persons were required to have been beneficiaries of an immigrant petition or labor certification filed no later than April 30, 2001. Application for adjustment of status was also allowed for certain persons who had filed for class membership in one of three lawsuits challenging the implementation of IRCA legalization by INS. The Act also created nonimmigrant classes of admission allowing entry of spouses and children (and dependent children of spouses and children) of U.S. citizens and permanent resident aliens who had had petitions for immigrant visas pending for three years or more; adjustment to permanent resident status is afforded when the immigrant visa has been approved.

Legalization Dependents A maximum of 55,000 visas were issued to spouses and children of aliens legalized under the provisions of the Immigration Reform and Control Act of 1986 in each of fiscal years 1992-94.

Legalized Aliens Certain illegal aliens who were eligible to apply for temporary resident status under the legalization provision of the Immigration Reform and Control Act of 1986. To be eligible, aliens must have continuously resided in the United States in an unlawful status since January 1, 1982, not be excludable, and have entered the United States either 1) illegally before January 1, 1982, or 2) as temporary visitors before January 1, 1982, with their authorized stay expiring before that date or with the Government's knowledge of their unlawful status before that date. Legalization consists of two stages-temporary and then permanent residency. In order to adjust to permanent status aliens must have had continuous residence in the United States, be admissible as an immigrant, and demonstrate at least a minimal understanding and knowledge of the English language and U.S. history and government.

Medical and Legal Parolee   See Parolee.

Metropolitan Statistical Areas (MSAs)   MSAs consist of a core area with a large population and adjacent communities having a high degree of social and economic integration with the core. They are defined by the U.S. Office of Management and Budget (OMB). MSAs are generally counties (cities and towns in New England) containing at least one city or urbanized area with a population of at least 50,000 and a total metropolitan population of at least 100,000 (75,000 in New England). MSAs of one million or more population may be recognized as Consolidated Metropolitan Statistical Areas (CMSAs). Primary Metropolitan Statistical Areas (PSMAs) are component areas within MSAs. New England County Metropolitan Areas (NECMAs) are the county based metropolitan alternative of the New England states for the city and town based MSAs and CMSAs.

Migrant   A person who leaves his/her country of origin to seek residence in another country.

N-400, "Application for Naturalization"   The N-400 is the form that all people 18 years of age or older use to apply for naturalization.

N-445, "Notice of Naturalization Oath Ceremony"   If you are approved for naturalization, you will receive an N-445 telling you when and where to attend your oath ceremony. On the back of the form will be several questions that you must answer before you check in at the ceremony.

N-470, "Application to Preserve Residence for Naturalization Purposes"   The N-470 is a form that certain types of applicants who plan to remain longer than a year outside the United States may file to preserve "continuous residence" status.

N-565, "Application for Replacement Naturalization/Citizenship Document"   If you lose your Certificate of Naturalization, or your Certificate of Citizenship, you may file an N-565 to get a replacement. USCIS advises naturalized citizens to also obtain a United States passport as evidence of their U.S. citizenship.

N-600, "Application for Certificate of Citizenship"   Qualified U.S. residents born outside the United States to U.S. citizen parents, or parents who became citizens, may file a Form N-600 to get a Certificate of Citizenship.

N-600K, "Application for Citizenship and Issuance of Certificate under Section 322"   Qualified children born to U.S. citizen parents, and currently residing outside the United States, may obtain naturalization and a Certificate of Citizenship by filing Form N-600K.

N-648, "Medical Certification for Disability Exceptions"   The form used to apply for a disability exemption. If you have a qualifying medical disability that prevents you from fulfilling the English and civics requirement, you must have a licensed medical or osteopathic doctor, or licensed clinical psychologist complete and sign an N-648. Applicants are encouraged, but not required, to submit the N-648 at the time of filing the N-400 to ensure timely adjudication of both applications

NACARA   Nicaraguan Adjustment and Central American Relief Act, Public Law 105-100 (Act of 11/19/97). Pertains to certain Central American and other aliens who were long-term illegal residents in the United States when hardship relief rules were made more stringent by the Illegal Immigration Reform and Immigrant Responsibility Act (IIRIRA). Provisions: 1) allowed approximately 150,000 Nicaraguans and 5,000 Cubans adjustment to permanent resident status without having to make any hardship showing; 2) allowed approximately 200,000 Salvadorans and 50,000 Guatemalans as well as certain aliens from the former Soviet Union to seek hardship relief under more lenient hardship rules than existed prior to IIRIRA amendments.

National   A person owing permanent allegiance to a state.

NATO Official   As a nonimmigrant class of admission, an alien coming temporarily to the United States as a member of the armed forces or as a civilian employed by the armed forces on assignment with a foreign government signatory to NATO (North Atlantic Treaty Organization), and the alien's spouse and unmarried minor (or dependent) children.

Naturalization   The conferring, by any means, of citizenship upon a person after birth.

Naturalization Application   The form used by a lawful permanent resident to apply for U.S. citizenship. The application is filed with the Department of Homeland Security at the Service Center with jurisdiction over the applicant's place of residence.

Naturalization Eligibility Worksheet   A worksheet that you may use as a tool to determine whether you are eligible for naturalization.

Nonimmigrant   An alien who seeks temporary entry to the United States for a specific purpose. The alien must have a permanent residence abroad (for most classes of admission) and qualify for the nonimmigrant classification sought. The nonimmigrant classifications include: foreign government officials, visitors for business and for pleasure, aliens in transit through the United States, treaty traders and investors, students, international representatives, temporary workers and trainees, representatives of foreign information media, exchange visitors, fiance(e)s of U.S. citizens, intracompany transferees, NATO officials, religious workers, and some others. Most nonimmigrants can be accompanied or joined by spouses and unmarried minor (or dependent) children.

Nonpreference Category Nonpreference visas were available to qualified applicants not entitled to a visa under the preferences until the category was eliminated by the Immigration Act of 1990. Nonpreference visas for persons not entitled to the other preferences had not been available since September 1978 because of high demand in the preference categories. An additional 5,000 nonpreference visas were available in each of fiscal years 1987 and 1988 under a provision of the Immigration Reform and Control Act of 1986. This program was extended into 1989, 1990, and 1991 with 15,000 visas issued each year. Aliens born in countries from which immigration was adversely affected by the Immigration and Nationality Act Amendments of 1965 (Public Law 89-236) were eligible for the special nonpreference visas.

North American Free-Trade Agreement (NAFTA) Public Law 103-182 (Act of 12/8/93), superseded the United States-Canada Free-Trade Agreement as of 1/1/94. It continues the special, reciprocal trading relationship between the United States and Canada (see United States-Canada Free-Trade Agreement), and establishes a similar relationship with Mexico.

Numerical Limit, Exempt from Those aliens accorded lawful permanent residence who are exempt from the provisions of the flexible numerical limit of 675,000 set by the Immigration Act of 1990. Exempt categories include immediate relatives of U.S. citizens, refugees, asylees (limited to 10,000 per year by section 209(b) of the Immigration and Nationality Act), Amerasians, aliens adjusted under the legalization provisions of the Immigration Reform and Control Act of 1986, and certain parolees from the former Soviet Union and Indochina.

Nursing Relief Act of 1989 Public Law 101-238 (Act of 12/18/89), provides for the adjustment to permanent resident status of certain nonimmigrants who as of September 1, 1989, had H-1 nonimmigrant status as registered nurses; who had been employed in that capacity for at least 3 years; and whose continued nursing employment meets certain labor certification requirements.

Nursing Relief for Disadvantaged Areas Act of 1999 Public Law 106-95 (Act of 11/12/1999), enacted as a short-term solution for nursing shortages in a limited number of medically underserved areas. Established a new nonimmigrant class of admission (H-1C) for temporary admission of 500 nurses annually for 4 years in health professional shortage areas. Sets forth admission requirements, including a maximum 3-year stay. Petitioning hospitals have to be in shortage areas defined by the Department of Health and Human Services, have at least 190 acute care beds, and have specified percentages of Medicare and Medicaid patients. Subject to fewer restrictions than the previous, expired H-1A provisions.

Oath Ceremony To become a naturalized citizen of the United States, you must attend an oath ceremony where you take the Oath of Allegiance to the United States.

Oath of Allegiance to the United States The Oath you take to become a U.S. citizen. When you take the Oath of Allegiance to the United States, you are promising to give up your allegiance to other countries and to support and defend the United States and its constitution and laws. Ability to take and understand the Oath of Allegiance is a normal requirement for becoming a naturalized U.S. citizen.

Occupation For an alien entering the United States or adjusting without a labor certification, occupation refers to the employment held in the country of last lawful residence or in the United States. For an alien with a labor certification, occupation is the employment for which certification has been issued.

Orphan For immigration purposes, a child whose parents have died or disappeared, or who has been abandoned or otherwise separated from both parents. An orphan may also be a child whose sole or surviving parent is incapable of providing that child with proper care and who has, in writing, irrevocably released the child for emigration and adoption. In order to qualify as an immediate relative, the orphan must be under the age of sixteen at the time a petition is filed on his or her behalf. To enter the United States, an orphan must have been adopted abroad by a U.S. citizen (and spouse, if married) or be coming to the United States for adoption by a citizen.

Outlying Possessions The current outlying possessions of the United States are American Samoa and Swains Island.

Panama Canal Act Immigrants Three categories of special immigrants established by Public Law 96-70 (Act of 9/27/79): 1) certain former employees of the Panama Canal Company or Canal Zone Government, their spouses and accompanying children; 2) certain former employees of the U.S. Government in the Panama Canal Zone who are Panamanian nationals, their spouses and children; and 3) certain former employees of the Panama Canal Company or Canal Zone Government on April 1, 1979, their spouses and children. The Act provides for admission of a maximum of 15,000 immigrants, at a rate of no more than 5,000 each year.

Parolee A parolee is an alien, appearing to be inadmissible to the inspecting officer, allowed into the United States for urgent humanitarian reasons or when that alien's entry is determined to be for significant public benefit. Parole does not constitute a formal admission to the United States and confers temporary status only, requiring parolees to leave when the conditions

supporting their parole cease to exist. Types of parolees include:
1. Deferred inspection: authorized at the port upon alien's arrival; may be conferred by an immigration inspector when aliens appear at a port of entry with documentation, but after preliminary examination, some question remains about their admissibility which can best be answered at their point of destination.
2. Advance parole: authorized at an DHS District office in advance of alien's arrival; may be issued to aliens residing in the United States in other than lawful permanent resident status who have an unexpected need to travel and return, and whose conditions of stay do not otherwise allow for readmission to the United States if they depart.
3. Port-of-entry parole: authorized at the port upon alien's arrival; applies to a wide variety of situations and is used at the discretion of the supervisory immigration inspector, usually to allow short periods of entry. Examples include allowing aliens who could not be issued the necessary documentation within the required time period, or who were otherwise inadmissible, to attend a funeral and permitting the entry of emergency workers, such as fire fighters, to assist with an emergency.
4. Humanitarian parole: authorized at DHS headquarters for "urgent humanitarian reasons" specified in the law. It is used in cases of medical emergency and comparable situations.
5. Public interest parole: authorized at DHS headquarters for "significant public benefit" specified in the law. It is generally used for aliens who enter to take part in legal proceedings.
6. Overseas parole: authorized at an DHS District or suboffice while the alien is still overseas; designed to constitute long-term admission to the United States. In recent years, most of the aliens the DHS has processed through overseas parole have arrived under special legislation or international migration agreements.

Per-Country Limit The maximum number of family-sponsored and employment-based preference visas that can be issued to citizens of any country in a fiscal year. The limits are calculated each fiscal year depending on the total number of family-sponsored and employment-based visas available. No more than 7 percent of the visas may be issued to natives of any one independent country in a fiscal year; no more than 2 percent may issued to any one dependency of any independent country. The per-country limit does not indicate, however, that a country is entitled to the maximum number of visas each year, just that it cannot receive more than that number. Because of the combined workings of the preference system and per-country limits, most countries do not reach this level of visa issuance.

Permanent Resident A Permanent Resident is a person who has been granted permanent resident status in the United States and has (or is waiting for) a Permanent Resident Card.

Permanent Resident Alien An alien admitted to the United States as a lawful permanent resident. Permanent residents are also commonly referred to as immigrants; however, the Immigration and Nationality Act (INA) broadly defines an immigrant as any alien in the United States, except one legally admitted under specific nonimmigrant categories (INA section 101(a)(15)). An illegal alien who entered the United States without inspection, for example, would be strictly defined as an immigrant under the INA but is not a permanent resident alien. Lawful permanent residents are legally accorded the privilege of residing permanently in the United States. They may be issued immigrant visas by the Department of State overseas or adjusted to permanent resident status by the Department of Homeland Security in the United States.

Permanent Resident Card The Permanent Resident Card is a USCIS document that identifies a person as a Permanent Resident. The Permanent Resident Card may be identified as Form I-551. The Permanent Resident Card used to be known as the Alien Registration Card and/or "Green Card."

Physical Presence Physical presence in the United States is an important eligibility requirement. Most naturalization applicants must spend a specified amount of time in the United States in order to meet the physical presence requirement for naturalization. Except in a few cases, time spent outside of the United States, even brief trips to Canada and Mexico, does not count toward your "physical presence."

Port of Entry Any location in the United States or its territories that is designated as a point of entry for aliens and U.S. citizens. All district and files control offices are also considered ports, since they become locations of entry for aliens adjusting to immigrant status.

Pre-Inspection Complete immigration inspection of airport passengers before departure from a foreign country. No further immigration inspection is required upon arrival in the United States other than submission of Form I-94 for nonimmigrant aliens.

Preference System (prior to fiscal year 1992) The six categories among which 270,000 immigrant visa numbers were distributed each year during the period 1981-91. This preference system was amended by the Immigration Act of 1990, effective fiscal year 1992.

(see Preference System-Immigration Act of 1990). The six categories were: 1) unmarried sons and daughters (over 21 years of age) of U.S. citizens (20 percent); 2) spouses and unmarried sons and daughters of aliens lawfully admitted for permanent residence (26 percent); 3) members of the professions or persons of exceptional ability in the sciences and arts (10 percent); 4) married sons and daughters of U.S. citizens (10 percent); 5) brothers and sisters of U.S. citizens over 21 years of age (24 percent); and 6) needed skilled or unskilled workers (10 percent). A nonpreference category, historically open to immigrants not entitled to a visa number under one of the six preferences just listed, had no numbers available beginning in September 1978.

Preference System (Immigration Act of 1990) The nine categories since fiscal year 1992 among which the family-sponsored and employment-based immigrant preference visas are distributed. The family-sponsored preferences are: 1) unmarried sons and daughters of U.S. citizens; 2) spouses, children, and unmarried sons and daughters of permanent resident aliens; 3) married sons and daughters of U.S. citizens; 4) brothers and sisters of U.S. citizens. The employment-based preferences are: 1) priority workers (persons of extraordinary ability, outstanding professors and researchers, and certain multinational executives and managers); 2) professionals with advanced degrees or aliens with exceptional ability; 3) skilled workers, professionals (without advanced degrees), and needed unskilled workers; 4) special immigrants; and 5) employment creation immigrants (investors).

Principal Alien The alien who applies for immigrant status and from whom another alien may derive lawful status under immigration law or regulations (usually spouses and minor unmarried children).

Refugee Any person who is outside his or her country of nationality who is unable or unwilling to return to that country because of persecution or a well-founded fear of persecution. Persecution or the fear thereof must be based on the alien's race, religion, nationality, membership in a particular social group, or political opinion. People with no nationality must generally be outside their country of last habitual residence to qualify as a refugee. Refugees are subject to ceilings by geographic area set annually by the President in consultation with Congress and are eligible to adjust to lawful permanent resident status after one year of continuous presence in the United States.

Refugee Approvals The number of refugees approved for admission to the United States during a fiscal year. Department of Homeland Security officers in overseas offices make refugee approvals.

Refugee Arrivals The number of refugees the Department of Homeland Security initially admits to the United States through ports of entry during a fiscal year.

Refugee Authorized Admissions The maximum number of refugees allowed to enter the United States in a given fiscal year. As set forth in the Refugee Act of 1980 (Public Law 96-212) the President determines the annual figure after consultations with Congress.

Refugee-Parolee A qualified applicant for conditional entry, between February 1970 and April 1980, whose application for admission to the United States could not be approved because of inadequate numbers of seventh preference visas. As a result, the applicant was paroled into the United States under the parole authority granted the Attorney General.

Registry Date Aliens who have continuously resided in the United States since January 1, 1972, are of good moral character, and are not inadmissible, are eligible to adjust to lawful permanent resident status under the registry provision. Before the Immigration Reform and Control Act of 1986 amended the date, aliens had to have been in the country continuously since June 30, 1948, to qualify.

Removal The expulsion of an alien from the United States. This expulsion may be based on grounds of inadmissibility or deportability.

Required Departure See Voluntary Departure.

Resettlement Permanent relocation of refugees in a place outside their country of origin to allow them to establish residence and become productive members of society there. Refugee resettlement is accomplished with the direct assistance of private voluntary agencies working with the Department of Health and Human Services Office of Refugee Resettlement.

Safe Haven Temporary refuge given to migrants who have fled their countries of origin to seek protection or relief from persecution or other hardships, until they can return to their countries safely or, if necessary until they can obtain permanent relief from the conditions they fled.

Selective Service The Selective Service System is the Federal agency responsible for providing manpower to the U.S. Armed Forces in an emergency. Male applicants generally are required to have registered with the Selective Service before applying for naturalization.

Service Centers Five offices established to handle the filing, data entry, and adjudication of certain applications for immigration services and benefits. The applications are mailed to DHS Service Centers-Service Centers are not staffed to receive walk-in applications or questions.

Special Agricultural Workers (SAW) Aliens who performed labor in perishable agricultural commodities for a specified period of time and were admitted for temporary and then permanent residence under a provision of the Immigration Reform and Control Act of 1986. Up to 350,000 aliens who worked at least 90 days in each of the 3 years preceding May 1, 1986 were eligible for Group I temporary resident status. Eligible aliens who qualified under this requirement but applied after the 350,000 limit was met and aliens who performed labor in perishable agricultural commodities for at least 90 days during the year ending May 1, 1986 were eligible for Group II temporary resident status. Adjustment to permanent resident status is essentially automatic for both groups; however, aliens in Group I were eligible on December 1, 1989 and those in Group II were eligible one year later on December 1, 1990.

Special Immigrants Certain categories of immigrants who were exempt from numerical limitation before fiscal year 1992 and subject to limitation under the employment-based fourth preference beginning in 1992; persons who lost citizenship by marriage; persons who lost citizenship by serving in foreign armed forces; ministers of religion and other religious workers, their spouses and children; certain employees and former employees of the U.S. Government abroad, their spouses and children; Panama Canal Act immigrants; certain foreign medical school graduates, their spouses and children; certain retired employees of international organizations, their spouses and children; juvenile court dependents; and certain aliens serving in the U.S. Armed Forces, their spouses and children.

Special Naturalization Provisions Provisions covering special classes of persons whom may be naturalized even though they do not meet all the general requirements for naturalization. Such special provisions allow: 1) wives or husbands of U.S. citizens to file for naturalization after three years of lawful permanent residence instead of the prescribed five years; 2) a surviving spouse of a U.S. citizen who served in the armed forces to file his or her naturalization application in any district instead of where he/she resides; and 3) children of U.S. citizen parents to be naturalized without meeting certain requirements or taking the oath, if too young to understand the meaning. Other classes of persons who may qualify for special consideration are former U.S. citizens, servicemen, seamen, and employees of organizations promoting U.S. interests abroad.

Stateless Having no nationality.

Stowaway An alien coming to the United States surreptitiously on an airplane or vessel without lawful status of admission. Such an alien is subject to denial of formal admission and return to the point of embarkation by the transportation carrier.

Student As a nonimmigrant class of admission, an alien coming temporarily to the United States to pursue a full course of study in an approved program in either an academic (college, university, seminary, conservatory, academic high school, elementary school, other institution, or language training program) or a vocational or other recognized nonacademic institution.

Subject to the Numerical Limit Categories of lawful immigrants subject to annual limits under the provisions of the flexible numerical limit of 675,000 set by the Immigration Act of 1990. The largest categories are: family-sponsored preferences; employment-based preferences; and diversity immigrants.

Temporary Protected Status (TPS) Establishes a legislative basis for allowing a group of persons temporary refuge in the United States. Under a provision of the Immigration Act of 1990, the Attorney General may designate nationals of a foreign state to be eligible for TPS with a finding that conditions in that country pose a danger to personal safety due to ongoing armed conflict or an environmental disaster. Grants of TPS are initially made for periods of 6 to 18 months and may be extended depending on the situation. Removal proceedings are suspended against aliens while they are in Temporary Protected Status.

Temporary Resident See Nonimmigrant.

Temporary Worker An alien coming to the United States to work for a temporary period of time. The Immigration Reform and Control Act of 1986 and the Immigration Act of 1990, as well as other legislation, revised existing classes and created new classes of nonimmigrant admission. Nonimmigrant temporary worker classes of admission are as follows:

1. H-1A-registered nurses (valid from 10/1/1990 through 9/30/1995);
2. H-1B-workers with "specialty occupations" admitted on the basis of professional education, skills, and/or equivalent experience;
3. H-1C-registered nurses to work in areas with a shortage of health professionals under the Nursing Relief for Disadvantaged Areas Act of 1999;
4. H-2A-temporary agricultural workers coming to the United States to perform agricultural services or labor of a temporary or seasonal nature when authorized workers are unavailable in the United States;
5. H-2B-temporary non-agricultural workers coming to the United States to perform temporary services or labor if unemployed persons capable of performing the service or labor cannot be found in the United States;
6. H-3-aliens coming temporarily to the United States as trainees, other than to receive graduate medical education or training;
7. O-1, O-2, O-3-temporary workers with extraordinary ability or achievement in the sciences, arts, education, business, or athletics; those entering

solely for the purpose of accompanying and assisting such workers; and their spouses and children;

8. P-1, P-2, P-3, P-4-athletes and entertainers at an internationally recognized level of performance; artists and entertainers under a reciprocal exchange program; artists and entertainers under a program that is "culturally unique"; and their spouses and children;
9. Q-1, Q-2, Q-3-participants in international cultural exchange programs; participants in the Irish Peace Process Cultural and Training Program; and spouses and children of Irish Peace Process participants;
10. R-1, R-2-temporary workers to perform work in religious occupations and their spouses and children.

See other sections of this Glossary for definitions of Exchange Visitor, Intracompany Transferee, and U.S.-Canada or North American Free-Trade Agreement classes of nonimmigrant admission.

Transit Alien An alien in immediate and continuous transit through the United States, with or without a visa, including, 1) aliens who qualify as persons entitled to pass in transit to and from the United Nations Headquarters District and foreign countries and 2) foreign government officials and their spouses and unmarried minor (or dependent) children in transit.

Transition Quarter The three-month period— July 1 through September 30, 1976—between fiscal year 1976 and fiscal year 1977. At that time, the fiscal year definition shifted from July 1-June 30 to October 1-September 30.

Transit Without Visa (TWOV) A transit alien traveling without a nonimmigrant visa under section 233 of the INA. An alien admitted under agreements with a transportation line, which guarantees his immediate and continuous passage to a foreign destination. The TWOV program was suspended on August 2, 2003 based on credible intelligence concerning a specific threat of exploitation of the TWOV program by terrorist organizations. (See Transit Alien).

Treaty Trader or Investor As a nonimmigrant class of admission, an alien coming to the United States, under the provisions of a treaty of commerce and navigation between the United States and the foreign state of such alien, to carry on substantial trade or to direct the operations of an enterprise in which he/she has invested a substantial amount of capital, and the alien's spouse and unmarried minor children.

Underrepresented Countries, Natives of The Immigration Amendments of 1988, Public Law 101-658 (Act of 11/5/88) allowed for 10,000 visas to be issued to natives of underrepresented countries in each of fiscal years 1990 and 1991. Under-represented countries are defined as countries that received less than 25 percent of the maximum allowed under the country limitations (20,000 for independent countries and 5,000 for dependencies) in fiscal year 1988. (See Diversity.)

United States-Canada Free-Trade Agreement Public Law 100-449 (Act of 9/28/88) established a special, reciprocal trading relationship between the United States and Canada. It provided two new classes of nonimmigrant admission for temporary visitors to the United States-Canadian citizen business persons and their spouses and unmarried minor children. Entry is facilitated for visitors seeking classification as visitors for business, treaty traders or investors, intracompany transferees, or other business people engaging in activities at a professional level. Such visitors are not required to obtain nonimmigrant visas, prior petitions, labor certifications, or prior approval but must satisfy the inspecting officer they are seeking entry to engage in activities at a professional level and that they are so qualified. The United States-Canada Free-Trade Agreement was superseded by the North American Free-Trade Agreement (NAFTA) as of 1/1/94.

United States Passport A U.S. passport is an official document that identifies you as a U.S. citizen. All naturalized citizens are encouraged to get a passport as soon as possible after they are naturalized.

USCIS Forms Line The USCIS Forms Line distributes all forms for immigration and naturalization.

USCIS Information Counter USCIS offices have information counters staffed by USCIS employees called Immigration Information Officers (IIOs). IIOs are available to answer questions about naturalization.

USCIS Lockbox Facility There are four Lockbox Facilities in the United States that handle the receipting of applications for immigration services and benefits.

U.S. National (but not U.S. Citizen) A person who, because of his or her birth in American Samoa or on Swains Island, owes permanent allegiance to the United States, and who may naturalize based on residence in an outlying possession of the United States.

Victims of Trafficking and Violence Protection Act of 2000 Public Law 106-386 (Act of 10/28/2000), enacted to combat trafficking in persons, especially into the sex trade, slavery, and involuntary servitude, and to reauthorize certain Federal programs to prevent violence against immigrant women and children. Created nonimmigrant classes of admission allowing temporary status to individuals (and spouses, children, and parents) in the United States who are or have been victims of a severe form of trafficking or who have suffered substantial physical or mental abuse as victims of criminal activity. Afforded the same immigrant benefits as refugees, with allowance for adjustment to permanent resident status.

Visa Waiver Program Allows citizens of certain selected countries, traveling temporarily to the United States under the nonimmigrant admission classes of visitors for pleasure and visitors for business, to enter the United States without obtaining nonimmigrant visas. Admission is for no more than 90 days. The program was instituted by the Immigration Reform and Control Act of 1986 (entries began 7/1/88). Under the Guam Visa Waiver Program, certain visitors from designated countries may visit Guam only for up to 15 days without first having to obtain nonimmigrant visitor visas. The Visa Waiver Program was made permanent in 2000.

Voluntary Departure The departure of an alien from the United States without an order of removal. The departure may or may not have been preceded by a hearing before an immigration judge. An alien allowed to voluntarily depart concedes removability but does not have a bar to seeking admission at a port-of-entry at any time. Failure to depart within the time granted results in a fine and a ten-year bar to several forms of relief from deportation.

Withdrawal An arriving alien's voluntary retraction of an application for admission to the United States in lieu of a removal hearing before an immigration judge or an expedited removal. Withdrawals are not included in nonimmigrant admission data.

Internal Revenue Service

AUDITS

ATAT—Abusive Tax Avoidance Transaction The IRS is engaged in extensive efforts to curb abusive tax shelter schemes and transactions. The Tax Exempt and Governmental Entities Division of the IRS, including the office of Employee Plans, participates in this IRS-wide effort by devoting substantial resources to the identification, analysis, and examination of abusive tax shelter schemes and promotions.

CAP—Closing Agreement Program If a failure (other than a failure corrected through SCP or VCP) is identified on audit, the Plan Sponsor may correct the failure and pay a sanction. The sanction imposed will bear a reasonable relationship to the nature, extent, and severity of the failure, taking into account the extent to which correction occurred before audit.

CIS—Case Identification Specialist This person is responsible for identifying the EPTA universe of cases to be reviewed by the CSC as part of the case selection process.

CSC—Case Selection Committee This committee is composed of three Area Managers, three EPTA Group Managers and the EPTA National Coordinator. The CSC uses a three-step process to select the cases that will be examined by the EPTA groups.

EO—Exempt Organizations The office of Exempt Organizations ensures religious, charitable, social, educational, political and other not-for-profit organizations meet and maintain compliance with the complex requirements for tax-exempt status.

EP—Employee Plans The office of Employee Plans serves the market of qualified pension benefit plans. Currently there are nearly one million plans that must file annual returns for group pension, profit sharing, 401(k), employee stock ownership (ESOP), and stock bonus plans. Simplified Employee Pensions (SEPs), SIMPLE plans, 403(b) tax-sheltered annuities, and IRC 457 government deferred compensation plans are generally not required to file returns.

EPCU—Employee Plans Compliance Unit This is a newly established unit that will focus on data mining, emerging tax issues, EPCRS resolution compliance checks, funding deficiencies and non-filers.

EPCRS—Employee Plans Compliance Resolution System EPCRS is a comprehensive system of correction programs for sponsors of retirement plans that are intended to satisfy the requirements of sections 401(a), 403(a) or 403(b) of the Internal Revenue Code, but which have not met these requirements for a period of time.

EPTA—Employee Plans Team Audit This is an audit involving some or all of the plans of a plan sponsor that warrants application of team examination procedures and is selected by the EPTA Case Selection Committee.

EPTA Plan Sponsor This refers to any entity sponsoring a pension plan or plans with an aggregate plan population of 2,500 or more. This would include multi-employer/multiple employer (MAP) and IRC section 403(b)/457 plans for which EPTA has examination responsibility.

EPTA Team The EPTA Team consists of EPTA specialist(s), Computer Audit Specialist (CAS), actuary, attorney and other specialist/revenue agents working under the direction of the EPTA Case Manager.

EPTA Team Coordinator The Team Coordinator is a Team Member who, in addition to being responsible for a specific examination assignment, performs coordinating duties in planning and executing a team examination.

ESOP—Employee Stock Ownership Plan An ESOP is essentially a defined contribution plan whose funds must be invested primarily in employer securities. An ESOP may borrow from the employer or use the employer's credit to acquire employer securities.

GE—Government Entities The office of Government Entities encompasses three distinct types of customers, Federal State and Local Governments (FSLG), Indian Tribal Governments (ITG) and Tax Exempt Bonds (TEB). Although not subject to Federal income tax, these governments are responsible for income tax withholding and paying employment taxes.

IDR—Information Document Request The Information Document Request (Form 4564) is the form used by EPTA team members to request information and documentation from the plan sponsor.

IDRS—Information Document Retrieval System The Information Document Retrieval System is an IRS system containing plan sponsor return information that can be accessed by IRS employees.

Listed Transactions These transactions involve abusive tax avoidance transactions that must be disclosed pursuant to I.T. Regulation 1.6011-4. In addition, registration and record keeping rules are applicable to organizers and promoters of these transactions.

LMSB—Large and Mid-Size Business Division LMSB serves corporations, subchapter S corporations, and partnerships with assets greater than $10 million. These businesses employ a large number of employees, deal with complicated issues involving tax law and accounting principles, and conduct business in an expanding global environment.

MAP—Multi-Employer Plan This is a plan established under a collective bargaining agreement that is maintained by two or more unrelated employers. These plans are commonly referred to as Taft-Hartley Plans.

NOPA—Notice of Proposed Adjustment The NOPA (Form 5701) is used by the EPTA team to formally notify the plan sponsor of a proposed adjustment and/or plan failure.

Post-Examination Critique This consists of a meeting held among EPTA personnel and a separate meeting among EPTA and Plan Sponsor personnel to discuss the examination process and determine or identify opportunities for improvements.

Pre-Examination This is the process involving a review of all returns, the planning file, commercial services, public records, etc. It is recorded in the form of a general outline of observations regarding size, dispersion, and diversification of the case, probable examination expertise and staffing requirements, and matters to be discussed or clarified at the pre-examination conference. When supplemented by information gained at the pre-examination conference it will form the basis for construction of the examination plan. It initially establishes the scope and depth of the examination.

SCP—Self-Correction Program A Plan Sponsor that has established compliance practices and procedures may, at any time without paying any fee or sanction, correct insignificant Operational Failures.

Support Specialists This refers to the specialists assigned to the case. Generally, they may be actuaries, commodity and financial products agents, engineers, excise tax agents, economists, international examiners, computer audit specialists, exempt organization agents, tax-exempt bonds agents, Indian tribal government specialists and any other revenue agent specialists who may be assigned to the EPTA Team.

TE/GE—Tax Exempt Government Entities The Tax Exempt and Government Entities Division was established to improve the Service's ability to meet the special needs of pension plans, exempt organizations, and government entities in complying with the tax laws. TE/GE provides end-to-end service and accountability to its unique customer base. TE/GE's three major business units—Exempt Organizations (EO), Employee Plans (EP), and Government Entities (GE)—oversee a diverse range of customers, from small volunteer community organizations to sovereign Indian tribes to large pension funds. While these entities are not subject to Federal income tax, they nonetheless represent a significant aspect of tax administration.

VCP—Voluntary Compliance Program A Plan Sponsor, at any time before audit, may pay a limited fee and receive the Service's approval for correction of a qualified plan, 403(b) plan, SEP or SIMPLE IRA plan. Under VCP, there are special procedures for anonymous submissions and group submissions.

ELECTRONIC FILING

Acceptance Letter Correspondence issued by the IRS to applicants confirming they may participate in IRS e-file. See also Credentials.

Acceptance or Assurance Testing (ATS) Required testing for Software Developer that participate in IRS e-file to assess their software and transmission capability with the IRS, prior to live processing. PATS, BATS and CATS are acceptance or assurance testing specific to certain form types.

Acknowledgment (ACK) A report generated by the IRS to a Transmitter that indicates receipt of all transmissions. An ACK Report identifies the returns in each transmission that are accepted or rejected for specific reasons.

Administrative Review Process The process by which a denied applicant or sanctioned Authorized IRS e-file Provider may appeal the IRS' denial or sanction.

Adoption Taxpayer Identification Number (ATIN) A tax processing number issued by the IRS as a temporary taxpayer identification number for a child in the domestic adoption process who is not yet eligible for a Social Security number (SSN). An ATIN is not a permanent identification number and is only intended for temporary use. To obtain an ATIN, complete IRS Form W-7A, Application for Taxpayer Identification Number for Pending U.S. Adoptions.

Authorized IRS e-file Provider (Provider) A firm accepted to participant in IRS e-file.

Automated Clearing House (ACH) A system that administers electronic funds transfers (EFTs) among participating financial institutions. An example of such a transfer is Direct Deposit of a tax refund from IRS into a taxpayer's account at a financial institution.

Batch A single transmission consisting of the electronic data from single or multiple tax returns.

Business Rules (BR) Error codes included on an Acknowledgement (Ack) for returns that the IRS rejected. The IRS publishes explanations prior to the filing season on IRS.gov. Providers can locate these on the Schemas and Business Rules for Forms 1040/4868 Modernized e-File (MeF).

Communications Testing Required test for all Transmitters using accepted IRS e-file software to assess their transmission capability with the IRS prior to live processing.

Credentials Documentation issued by the IRS which indicates qualification of an Authorized IRS e-file Providers to participate in the IRS e-file Program. The documentation consists of identification numbers and acceptance letters.

Debt Indicator (DI) The Debt Indicator is a field on an ACK Report. It only indicates whether a debt offset of a taxpayer's refund occurs. It does not indicate how much the offset is. Offsets taken by IRS may be for current and prior year tax obligations. Offsets taken by the Financial Management Service (FMS) are for past due student loans, child support, federal taxes, state taxes, or other governmental agency debts.

Declaration Control Number (DCN) A unique 14-digit number assigned by the ERO (or Transmitter, in the case of Online Filing), to each electronically filed tax return.

Denied Applicant An applicant that the IRS does not accept to participate in IRS e-file. An applicant that the IRS denies from participation in IRS e-file has the right to an administrative review.

Depositor Account Number (DAN) The financial institution account to which a Direct Deposit refund is to be routed.

Direct Deposit An electronic transfer of a refund into a taxpayer's financial institution account.

Direct Filer See "Transmitter."

Drain The IRS scheduled time for processing electronically filed return data.

Drop or Dropped An EFIN that is no longer valid due to inactivity or other administrative action.

Due Diligence Due Diligence, when used in context with the Earned Income Tax Credit (EITC), refers to requirements that income tax return preparers must follow when preparing returns or refund claims that involve EITC.

Earned Income Tax Credit (EITC) The Earned Income Tax Credit is a refundable individual income tax credit for certain persons who work.

EITC Recertification A requirement for a taxpayer previously denied EITC to provide additional information on Form 8862, Information to Claim Earned Income Tax Credit After Disallowance, when they file a similar EITC claim on a subsequent return.

Electronic Federal Tax Payment System (EFTPS) A free service from the U.S. Treasury through which federal taxes may be paid. The taxpayer can pay taxes via the Internet, by phone or through a service provider. After authorization, EFTPS electronically transfers payments from the authorized bank account to the Treasury's general account.

Electronic Filing Identification Number (EFIN) An identification number assigned by the IRS to accepted applicants for participation in IRS e-file.

Electronic Funds Transfer (EFT) The process through which Department of the Treasury transmits Direct Deposit refunds from the government to the taxpayer's account at a financial institution.

Electronic Funds Withdrawal (EFW) A payment method which allows the taxpayer to authorize the U.S. Treasury to electronically withdraw funds from their checking or savings account.

Electronic Management System (EMS) front-end processing system for electronic information exchange between the Internal Revenue Service (IRS) and Authorized IRS e-file Providers (Providers), to a designated Submission Processing Campus. EMS receives returns from Transmitters, acknowledges the receipt of the information and prepares the information for mainframe processing.

Electronic Postmark The Electronic Postmark is the date and time the Transmitter first receives the electronic return on its host computer in the Transmitter's time zone. The taxpayer adjusts the time to their time zone to determine timeliness.

Electronic Return Originator (ERO) An Authorized IRS e-file Provider that originates the electronic submission of returns to the IRS.

Electronic Signature Method of signing a return electronically through use of a Personal Identification Number (PIN). See also Self-Select PIN Method and Practitioner PIN Method.

Electronic Tax Administration and Refundable Credits (ETARC) The office within IRS with management oversight of the IRS' electronic commerce initiatives. The mission of ETARC is to revolutionize how taxpayers transact and communicate with the IRS.

Electronic Tax Administration Advisory Committee (ETAAC) An advisory group established by the IRS Restructuring and Reform Act of 1998 to provide an organized public forum for discussion of ETARC issues in support of the overriding goal that paperless filing should be the preferred and most convenient method of filing tax and information returns.

Electronic Transmitter Identification Number (ETIN) An identification number assigned by the IRS to a participant in IRS e-file that performs activity of transmission and/or software development.

Electronically Transmitted Documents (ETD) A system created to process electronic documents that a Provider does not attach to a tax return and the taxpayer files separately from the tax return.

Error Reject Code (ERC) Codes included on an Acknowledgment (ACK) Report for returns that the IRS rejected. The IRS publishes explanations prior to the filing season on IRS.gov. Providers can locate these on the e-file for Tax Professionals page titled 2008 Tax Year IRS e-file for Individual Income Tax Returns. In addition, the IRS also provides these in Publication 1346, Electronic Return File Specifications and Record Layouts for Individual Income Tax Returns.

Federal/State e-File The Federal/State e-file option allows taxpayers to file federal and state income tax returns electronically in a single transmission to the IRS.

Financial Institution For the purpose of Direct Deposit of tax refunds, the IRS defines a financial institution as a state or national bank, savings and loan association, mutual savings bank or credit union. Only certain financial institutions and certain kinds of accounts are eligible to receive Direct Deposits of tax refunds.

Financial Management Service (FMS) The agency of the Department of the Treasury through which payments to and from the government, such as Direct Deposits of refunds, are processed.

Form Field Number or Form Sequence (SEQ) Number The identifier of specific data on an electronic tax return record layout as defined in Publication 1346, Electronic Return File Specifications and Record Layouts for Individual Income Tax Returns.

Fraudulent Return A "fraudulent return" is a return in which the individual is attempting to file using someone's name or SSN on the return or where the taxpayer is presenting documents or information that have no basis in fact. *Note*: Taxpayers should not file fraudulent returns with the IRS.

Indirect Filer An Authorized IRS e-file Provider who submits returns to IRS via the services of a Transmitter.

Individual Taxpayer Identification Number (ITIN) A tax processing number that became available on July 1, 1996, for certain nonresident and resident aliens, their spouses and dependents. The ITIN is only available from IRS for those individuals who cannot obtain a Social Security number (SSN). To obtain an ITIN, complete IRS Form W-7, Application for IRS Individual Identification Number.

Intermediate Service Provider An Authorized IRS e-file Provider that receives electronic tax return information from an ERO or a taxpayer who files electronically using a personal computer and commercial tax preparation software, that processes the electronic tax return information and either forwards the information to a Transmitter or sends the information back to the ERO or taxpayer.

Internet Protocol (IP) Information The IP address, date, time and time zone of the origination of a tax return filed through Online Filing via the Internet. IRS requires Transmitters that provide Online Services via the Internet to capture the Internet Protocol Information of Online returns. By capturing this information, it transmits the location of the return's originator with the individual's electronic return. See Publication 1346 for additional Information.

IRS e-File The brand name of the electronic filing method established by the IRS.

IRS e-File Marketing Tool Kit A specially designed kit containing professionally developed material that EROs may customize for use in advertising campaigns and promotional efforts.

IRS Master File A centralized IRS database containing taxpayers' personal return information.

Levels of Infractions (LOI) Categories of infractions of IRS e-file rules based on the seriousness of the infraction with specified sanctions associated with each level. Level One is the least serious, Level Two is moderately serious and Level Three is the most serious.

Memorandum of Agreement (MOA) & Memorandum of Understanding (MOU) The implementing document containing the set of rules established by the IRS for participating in IRS pilot programs.

Modernized e-File (MeF) The Modernized e-File (MeF) system is an internet-based electronic filing platform. It is a transaction-based system that allows tax return originators to transmit returns electronically to the IRS in real-time. MeF improves the response time required to issue an acknowledgement file to the transmitter that indicates whether the return was accepted or rejected for downstream processing.

Monitoring Activities the IRS performs in order to ensure that Authorized IRS e-file Providers are in compliance with the IRS e-file requirements. Monitoring may include, but is not limited to, reviewing IRS e-file submissions, investigating complaints, scrutinizing advertising material, checking signature form submissions and/or recordkeeping, examining records, observing office procedures and conducting periodic suitability checks. IRS personnel perform these activities at IRS offices and at the offices of Providers.

Name Control The first four significant letters of a taxpayer's last name that the IRS uses in connection with the taxpayer SSN to identify the taxpayer, spouse and dependents.

Nonsubstantive Change A correction or change limited to a transposition error, misplaced entry, spelling error or arithmetic correction which does not require new signatures or authorizations to be transmitted or retransmitted.

Originate or Origination Origination of an electronic tax return submission occurs when an ERO either: directly transmits electronic returns to the IRS, sends electronic returns to a Transmitter or provides tax return data to an Intermediate Service Provider.

Participants Acceptance Testing (PATS) Required testing for all Software Developers that participate in IRS e-file of individual income tax returns to assess their software and transmission capability with the IRS prior to live processing. See also Acceptance or Assurance Testing.

PATS Communications Test Required for all Transmitters using accepted IRS e-file software for individual income tax returns to assess their transmission capability with the IRS prior to live processing.

Pilot Programs An approach that the IRS uses to improve and simplify IRS e-file. The IRS usually conducts pilot programs within a limited geographic area or within a limited taxpayer or practitioner community. The IRS embodies rules for participating in pilot programs in an implementing document typically referred to as a "Memorandum of Understanding" (MOU) or "Memorandum of Agreement" (MOA). Pilot participants must agree to the provisions of the implementing document in order to participate in the pilot program.

Potentially Abusive Return A "potentially abusive return" is a return that is not a fraudulent return; that the taxpayer is required to file; or that may contain inaccurate information that may lead to an understatement of a liability or an overstatement of a credit resulting in production of a refund to which the taxpayer may not be entitled. *Note*: The decision not to provide a RAL or other bank product does not necessarily make it an abusive return.

Practitioner PIN Method An electronic signature option for taxpayers who use an ERO to e-file. This method requires the taxpayer to create a five-digit Personal Identification Number (PIN) to use as the signature on the e-filed return. *Note*: Requires Form 8879 to be completed.

Preparer's Tax Identification Number (PTIN) An identification number issued by the IRS which paid tax return preparers may use in lieu of disclosing their Social Security number (SSN) on returns that they prepared. A PTIN meets the requirements under section 6109(a)(4) of furnishing a paid tax return preparer's identifying number on returns that he or she prepares. Click here obtain a PTIN.

Refund Anticipation Loan (RAL) A Refund Anticipation Loan is money borrowed by a taxpayer that lender bases on a taxpayer's anticipated income tax refund. The IRS has no involvement in RALs. A RAL is a contract between the taxpayer and the lender. A lender may market a RAL under various commercial or financial product names.

Refund Cycle The anticipated date that the IRS would issue a refund either by Direct Deposit or by mail to a taxpayer for a return included within a specific "drain." However, neither the IRS nor FMS guarantees the specific date that Department of the Treasury mails a refund or deposits it into a taxpayer's financial institution account.

Request for Agreement (RFA) A solicitation, normally a written document, used in establishing nonmonetary memoranda of agreement. RFAs are not "acquisitions" as defined by the Federal Acquisition Regulations (FAR).

Request for Procurement (RFP) A solicitation, normally a written document, used in negotiated acquisitions estimated over $100,000 (as opposed to sealed bids) to communicate government requirements to prospective contractors and to solicit proposals to perform contracts.

Responsible Official An individual with authority over the IRS e-file operation of the office(s) of an Authorized IRS e-file Provider, who is the first point of contact with the IRS and has authority to sign revised IRS e-file applications. A Responsible Official is responsible for ensuring that the Authorized IRS e-file Provider adheres to the provisions of the Revenue Procedure and the publications and notices governing IRS e-file.

Revenue Protection A series of compliance programs designed to ensure that the revenue the government collects and/or disburses in the form of refunds is accurate and timely, and that it issues disbursement of revenue only to entitled taxpayers.

Routing Transit Number (RTN) A number assigned by the Federal Reserve to each financial institution.

Sanction An action taken by the IRS to reprimand, suspend or expel from participation in IRS e-file, an Authorized IRS e-file Provider based on the level of infraction. See also Level of Infraction.

Self-Select PIN Method An electronic signature option for taxpayers who e-file using either a personal computer or an ERO. This method requires the taxpayer to create a five-digit Personal Identification Number (PIN) to use as the signature on the e-file return and to submit authentication information to the IRS with the e-file return.

Software Developer An Authorized IRS e-file Provider that develops software for the purposes of (a) formatting the electronic portions of returns according to Publication 1346 and/or (b) transmitting the electronic portion of returns directly to the IRS. A Software Developer may also sell its software.

Stockpiling Stockpiling is waiting more than three calendar days to submit returns to the IRS after the Provider has all necessary information for origination of the electronic return or collecting e-file returns prior to official acceptance for participation in IRS e-file. The IRS does not consider collecting tax returns for IRS e-file prior to the startup of IRS e-file as stockpiling. However, Providers must advise taxpayers that it can not transmit the returns to the IRS prior to the startup date.

Submission Identification Number (SID) A submission identifier (ID) uniquely identifies a submission. A submission ID is present in all attachment files and many request and response messages. The first six digits (003497) contain the Electronic Filer Identification Number (EFIN), the next four digits (2006) contain the year, the next three digits (073) contain the Julian date, and the last seven digits (1234567) contain a sequence number to uniquely identify messages sent within a day with the given EFIN: EFIN + ccyyddd + xxxxxxx. The total number of characters of the submission ID is twenty.

Suitability A check conducted on all firms and the Principals and Responsible Officials of firms when an application is initially processed, and on a regular basis thereafter. The suitability check includes a background check conducted by the IRS to ensure the firm and individuals are eligible for participation in IRS e-file.

Suspension A sanction revoking an Authorized IRS e-file Provider's privilege to participate in IRS e-file.

Transmitter An Authorized IRS e-file Provider that transmits the electronic portion of a return directly to the IRS. An entity that provides a "bump-up" service is also a Transmitter. A bump-up service provider increases the transmission rate or line speed of formatted or reformatted information that it is sending to the IRS via a public switched telephone network.

Treasury Offset Program (TOP) Public Law that established the Tax Refund Offset Program which permits the government to offset overpayments against delinquent child support obligations as well as debts owed to participating federal and state agencies. Treasury's Financial Management Service (FMS) office assumes responsibility and oversight for TOP.

Warning Written notice given by the IRS to an Authorized IRS e-file Provider requesting specific corrective action be taken to avoid future sanctioning.

Written Reprimand A sanction for a level one infraction of the IRS e-file rules. It reprimands a Provider for an infraction but does not restrict or revoke participation in IRS e-file.

Justice

DNA TESTING

2p rule The NRCII report recommends using this approach for dealing with homozygotes.

A.F.I.S. Automated Fingerprint Identification System

ABO blood typing A commonly used genetic typing test that uses antibodies to detect variations on the surface of human red blood cells. Individuals are typed as having A, B, O, or AB type blood by testing liquid or stains from body fluids (e.g., blood, saliva, vaginal secretions). One out of every three randomly selected pairs of people have the same ABO blood type.

Adenosine triphosphate (ATP) Main source of energy for biochemical reactions within the cell.

Allele A different form of a gene at a particular locus. The characteristics of a single copy of a specific gene, or of a single copy of a specific location on a chromosome. For example, one copy of a specific short tandem repeat (STR) region might have 10 repeats, while the other copy might have 11 repeats. These would represent two alleles of that STR region.

Allele frequencies Term used to characterize genetic variation of a species population.

Allelic dropout Failure to detect an allele within a sample or failure to amplify an allele during PCR.

Allelic ladder Comprised of DNA fragments that represent common alleles at a locus.

Alternate light source (ALS) Equipment used to produce visible and invisible light at various wavelengths to enhance or visualize items of evidence (fluids, fingerprints, clothing fibers, etc.). The light will cause possible biological stains to change color or fluoresce, assisting in the location process.

Alu Non-coding regions of DNA containing a restriction site for the enzyme Alu 1. The sequences are about 300 base pairs long and are repeated several thousand times throughout the genome.

Amelogenin A gene present on the X and Y sex chromosomes that is used in DNA identification testing to determine the gender of the donor of the DNA in a biological sample.

Amorphous medulla An amorphous medulla has no distinct form, pattern, or shape when viewed with a transmitted light microscope

Amplicons Amplified DNA fragments.

Amplification Producing multiple copies of a chosen DNA region, usually by PCR (Polymerase Chain Reaction).

Amplified fragment length polymorphisms (AFLP or AmpFLP) A highly sensitive method for detecting polymorphisms in DNA. DNA first undergoes restriction enzyme digestion, and a subset of DNA fragments is then selected for PCR amplification and visualization.

Anagen The anagen root is the active growth phase of a hair follicle in the hair growth cycle

Analytical threshold An acceptable "Relative Fluorescence Units" (RFU) level determined to be appropriate for use in the PCR/STR DNA typing process. A minimum threshold for data comparison is identified by the specific forensic laboratory doing the testing through independent validation studies.

Angular aperture The angle (or cone) of light rays capable of entering the front lens of the objective from a point in the object. If the angular aperture of an objective is increased, more light rays from the specimen can be taken in by the lens, increasing the resolving power.

Annealing temperature (Ta) An annealing temperature is approximately 5°C below the lowest melting temperature (Tm) of the pair of primers used.

Anode A positively charged electrode.

Artifact Any non-allelic product of the amplification process (Stutter or Minus A) or anomaly of the detection process (Pull-up or Spike).

ASCLD American Society of Crime Lab Directors

ASCLD-LAB The American Society of Crime Lab Directors–Laboratory Accreditation Board. ASCLD-LAB is a crime lab accreditation program organized to review and inspect the quality assurance of forensic laboratories and insure that specified standards are followed. Accreditation is only available to forensic laboratories that perform casework.

Autosomal Chromosomes which are not sex chromosomes.

Base pairing A,T,C and G are molecular building blocks of DNA that only continue in specific "base" pairs, e.g., A only pairs with T, and C only pairs with G

Baseline Residual signal associated with an instrument's blank response.

Bases The four building blocks of DNA are called bases. The building blocks are Cytosine, Guanine, Thymine, Adenine and are commonly referred to as C, G, T, A.

Bayesian probability System of probability based on beliefs in which the measure of probability is continuously revised as available information changes.

Bench notes A laboratory analyst's recorded notes.

Biallelic Pertaining to both alleles, e.g., single nucleotide polymorphisms display two alternate forms and are biallelic.

Bindle paper Clean paper folded for the containment of trace evidence, sometimes included as part of the packaging for collecting trace evidence.

Biohazard bag A container for materials that have been exposed to blood or other biological fluids and have the potential to be contaminated with hepatitis, AIDS, or other contagions.

Biological Evidence Evidence commonly recovered from crime scenes in the form of hair, tissue, bones, teeth, blood or other bodily fluids.

Biological fluids Fluids that have human or animal origin, most commonly encountered at crime scenes (e.g., blood, mucous, perspiration, saliva, semen, vaginal fluid, and urine).

Blind testing In a blind test, analysts do not know they are being tested. In most forensic DNA laboratories, blind tests are not used. In practice, it is almost impossible to design and implement an effective blind PT (proficiency test) program in forensic science. Most attempts have failed because they could not produce an effective case scenario with realistic representation of the pre-laboratory steps. Others failed because the analyst recognized that the supposed "evidence" was a manufactured artifact. Overall, it has proven impossible to realize the theoretical extra benefits of blind testing, and resources have been devoted to promoting better quality external open tests.

Bloodborne pathogens Disease-causing microorganisms that are present in blood and can cause disease in humans. Pathogens include, but are not limited to, hepatitis B virus (HBV) and human immunodeficiency virus (HIV).

Boundaries The perimeter or border surrounding potential physical evidence related to the crime.

Bovine serum albumin (BSA) Protein fraction of serum isolated from the bovine family (i.e., cow, ox, buffalo).

Buckling Buckling is a disruption of the hair shaft demonstrating itself as an abrupt change in direction with or without a slight twist. This feature may be due to genetic factors, or it may result from damage (i.e., hair treatments).

Buffer Chemical solution that maintains a relatively constant pH even with the addition of strong acids or bases.

Cambridge Reference Sequence (CRS) A "master template" of the HVR-1 region of mitochondrial DNA.

Cambridge Reference Sequence, revised (rCRS) The rCRS sequence is a modified version of the original Cambridge Reference Sequence (GenBank #J01415.0 gi:337188) of Anderson et al (1981).

Capillary electrophoresis (CE) The platform for CE uses narrow silica capillaries (or tubes) containing a polymer solution through which the negatively charged DNA molecules migrate under the influence of a high voltage electric field. Important advantages of the CE technique, compared to slab gel electrophoresis, include quicker and more easily automated analyses

Cartilage hair hypoplasis A hair disorder that results in abnormally fine, sparse, and lightly colored hair that is usually short.

Case file The collection of documents comprising information concerning a particular investigation. (This collection may be kept in case jackets, file folders, ring binders, boxes, file drawers, file cabinets, or rooms. Sub-files are often used within case files to segregate and group interviews, media coverage, laboratory requests and reports, evidence documentation, photographs, videotapes, audiotapes, and other documents.)

Case identifier The alphabetic and/or numeric characters assigned to identify a particular case.

Catagen The catagen phase is the transitional phase of the hair follicle from the active growth phase (anagen) to the resting growth phase (telogen) in the hair growth cycle.

Cathode A negatively charged electrode.

Cation Positively charged ion. (e.g., K+, Na+, NH4+)

Caucasoid Caucasoid is an archaic anthropological term designating the peoples originating from Europe and the Indian subcontinent.

Cell The smallest component of life capable of independent reproduction and from which DNA is isolated for forensic analysis.

Central distribution (pigment) The distribution and concentration of the pigment in the center of the cortex.

Chain of custody A record of individuals who have had physical possession of the evidence and the process used to maintain and document the chronological history of the evidence. (Documents can include, but are not limited to, name or initials of the individual collecting the evidence; each person or entity subsequently having physical possession of it; dates the items were collected or transferred; from where the item(s) were collected; agency and case number; victim's or suspect's name (if known); and a brief description of the item.)

Chaotropic Property of certain substances to disrupt the structure of water. Promotes the solubility of non-polar substances and the elution from or movement through a chromatographic medium of an otherwise tightly bound substance.

Chemiluminescence The release of light (photons) as the result of a chemical reaction.

Chi-squared test of association Comparison of the observed frequencies with the frequencies that would be expected if the null hypothesis of no association were true.

Chloroform A chemical used in organic extraction. When used with phenol, promotes a sharp interface between the organic and aqueous layers.

Chromosome The biological structure by which hereditary information is physically transmitted from one generation to the next. Located in the cell nucleus, it consists of a tightly coiled thread of DNA with associated proteins and RNA. The genes are arranged in linear order along the DNA.

Clean/sanitize The process of removing biological and/or chemical contaminants from tools and/or equipment.

CODIS Combined DNA Index System A collection of databases of DNA profiles obtained from evidence samples from unsolved crimes and from known individuals convicted of particular crimes. Contributions to this database are made through State crime laboratories and the data are maintained by the FBI. Learn more about CODIS on the FBI's Web site.

CODIS core loci Thirteen STR (short tandem repeat) sequences that have been selected for the Combined DNA Index System (CODIS).

Cold hit When CODIS recognizes a match between an offender and forensic profile, it is referred to as a "cold hit."

Collect/collection The process of identifying, documenting, gathering, and packaging or retaining physical evidence.

Combined Paternity Index (CPI) Odds ratio that depicts the likelihood of the alleged father being the biological father, in comparison to the likelihood of a random unrelated man in the population being the biological father.

Comparison microscope Two microscopes joined by an optical bridge to present a split-view, side-by-side comparison of two specimens; for example, two hairs on separate slides.

Competency The combination of demonstrated knowledge, skills, and abilities.

Competency test A test given during training to assess the ability of a trainee.

Concave Lenses or mirrors which bow in.

Confidence interval Estimated range of values (calculated from a given set of sample data) that is likely to include an unknown population parameter.

Confirmatory test A simplistic method for estimating genotype frequency by direct counting of the number of times a genotype is observed in a database.

Contamination The undesirable transfer of material to physical evidence (DNA) from another source.

Continuous (medulla) A form of hair medullation where the visible medulla extends uninterrupted along a length of hair shaft.

Control samples Cuttings, swabbings, etc., from unstained adjacent material. A control sample is material of a known source that presumably was uncontaminated during the commission of the crime (e.g., a sample to be used in laboratory testing to ensure that the surface on which the sample is deposited does not interfere with testing. For example, when a bloodstain is collected from a carpet, a segment of unstained carpet must be collected). The control sample should be taken adjacent to the biological stain being collected.

Controls Tests designed to demonstrate that a procedure worked correctly and performed in parallel with experimental samples.

Convex Lenses or mirrors that bow out.

Convolution A convolution is an abrupt rotation of the hair shaft that can occur naturally, from disease, or as a result of mechanical force.

Cortex The cortex is the primary anatomical region of a hair between the cuticle region and the medullary region composed of elongated and fusiform cells.

Cortical fusi Cortical fusi are the small spaces within the hair shaft that appear as microscopic dark structures, commonly at the proximal end of hairs; they can be filled with air or liquid.

Cross contamination The undesirable transfer of material between two or more sources of physical evidence.

Cross projection sketch Also commonly referred to as an Exploded View Sketch. This type of sketch views the scene from above similar to a bird's-eye view but with the walls folded down. This sketch is used to show evidence on the walls such as blood spatter and bullet holes.

Cross-sectional shape The cross-sectional shape is the shape of a hair shaft cut and viewed at a right angle to its longitudinal axis.

Curled A hair shaft form that is bent into or towards a spiral form.

Curved A hair shaft form with slight curvature but does not exhibit waviness or does not curl back upon itself to form a circle.

Cuticle The cuticle is the outermost region of a hair and is composed of layers of overlapping scales.

Cycle threshold (CT) Cycle number (in qPCR) at which the fluorescence generated within a reaction well exceeds the defined threshold. The threshold is arbitrarily defined by the manufacturer to reflect the point during the reaction at which a sufficient number of amplicons have accumulated.

Cytoplasm The viscid, semifluid matter contained within the plasma membrane of a cell, excluding the nucleus.

Degenerate primer A PCR primer sequence is called degenerate if some of its positions have several possible bases.

Degradation The fragmenting, or breakdown, of DNA by chemical or physical means.

Denaturation Separation of the two strands of a DNA double helix.

Deposition The taking and recording of testimony of a witness under oath before a court reporter in a place away from the courtroom before trial.

Depth of field Axial resolving power of an objective, which is measured parallel to the optical axis.

Depth of focus The range of distances between a lens and image plane for which the image formed by the lens at a given setting is clearly focused. With a high numerical aperture microscope objective, the depth of field is very shallow, but the depth of focus can be quite deep and reach several millimeters.

Dermal papilla Connective living tissue from which hair is generated from the follicle in the thick layer of the skin below the epidermis

Dideoxy sequencing Dideoxynucleotide sequencing, also known as the "Sanger method," is a technique which uses dideoxyribose instead of deoxyribose to stop the synthesis of a complementary DNA strand at various points when sequencing.

Differential extraction A procedure in which sperm cells are separated, or extracted, from all other cells in a sample.

Diffuse light light reflected uniformly in all directions regardless of what angle the light comes in at.

Discontinuous (medulla) A form of hair medullation where the visible medulla is interrupted or fragmented along a length of hair shaft.

Discriminating power The ability of a blood grouping technique to differentiate between individuals selected at random. This can also be applied to other analytical techniques in forensic science.

Disposable instruments Items that will be used only once to collect evidence, such as biological samples, then discarded to minimize contamination (e.g., tweezers, scalpel blades, droppers).

Dissimilar Not similar or alike; different in appearance, properties, or nature; unlike.

Distal end The end of the hair away from the root; towards the tip.

Dithiothreitol (DTT) Reducing or deprotecting agent for thiolated DNA. (1,4-Dicaptomercapto-2,3-butanediol; formula is $C_4H_{10}O_2S_2$)

DNA (Deoxyribonucleic acid) Often referred to as the "blueprint of life," DNA is the genetic material present in the nucleus of cells which is inherited half from each biological parent. DNA is a chemical substance contained in cells, which determines each person's individual characteristics. An individual's DNA is unique except in cases of identical twins.

DNA analysis The process of testing to identify DNA patterns or types. In the forensic setting, this testing is used to exclude or include individuals as possible sources of body fluid stains (blood, saliva, semen) and other biological evidence (bones, teeth, hair). This testing can also be used to indicate parentage.

DNA fingerprinting Analyses of the lengths of the fragments reveal that when looking at multiple VNTRs (variable number of tandem repeats) within and between individuals, no two people have the same assortment of lengths. This technique became known to the public as "DNA fingerprinting" because of its powerful ability to discriminate between unrelated individuals.

DNA mixtures A sample that contains the DNA of more than one individual.

DNA profile The result of determining the relative positions of DNA sequences at several locations on the molecule. Each person (except identical twins) has a unique DNA profile when used in the context of the CODIS database, which evaluates 13 specific DNA locations.

Documentation Written notes, audio/videotapes, printed forms, sketches, and/or photographs that form a detailed record of the scene, evidence recovered, and actions taken during the search of the crime scene, including chain of custody information.

Double helix The shape the DNA assumes after it replicates during cell life.

Electropherogram The graphic representation of the separation of molecules by electrophoresis or other means of separation.

Electrophoresis A method of separating large molecules (such as DNA fragments) from a mixture of similar molecules. An electric current is passed through a medium at a different rate, depending on its electrical charge and size. Separation of DNA markers is based on these differences.

Elimination/reference samples A term used to describe a sample of known source taken for comparison purposes.

Example: An elimination sample is one of known source taken from a person who had lawful access to the crime scene (e.g., blood or cheek [buccal] swabs for DNA analysis, fingerprints from occupants, tire tread impressions from police vehicles, footwear impressions from emergency medical personnel) to be used for comparison with evidence of the same type.

A reference sample is material of a verifiable/documented source which, when compared with evidence of an unknown source, shows whether an association or linkage exists between an offender, crime scene and/or victim (e.g., a carpet cutting taken from a location suspected as the point of transfer for comparison with the fibers recovered from the suspect's shoes, a sample of paint removed from a suspect's vehicle to be compared with paint found on a victim's vehicle following an accident, or a sample of the suspect's and/or victim's blood submitted for comparison with a bloodstained shirt recovered as evidence).

Ethnicity Property of a culture or subculture whose members are readily distinguishable based on traits originating from a common source (e.g. racial, national, linguistic, etc.). Members of an ethnic group are often presumed to be culturally or genetically similar; this is not necessarily true.

Evidence Something that can help identify the responsible persons, establish an element of crime, reconstruct crime events or link crimes.

Evidentiary samples A generic term used to describe physical material/evidence discovered at crime scenes that may be compared with samples from persons, tools, and physical locations.

Excluded Two samples cannot have come from the same source.

Exclusion A DNA test result indicating that an individual is excluded as the source of the DNA evidence. In a criminal case, "exclusion" does not necessarily equate to "innocence." This occurs when one or more types from a specific location in the DNA of a known individual are not present in the type(s) for that specific location in the DNA obtained from an evidence sample.

Exogenous DNA DNA originating outside an organism that has been introduced into the organism.

Exonuclease An enzyme that cleaves nucleotides one at a time from an end of a polynucleotide chain. An enzyme that hydrolyzes phosphodiester bonds from either the 3' or 5' terminus of a polynucleotide molecules.

Expected heterozygosity Mean value of all the expected values found for all loci in a sample.

Expert system A software program or set of software programs designed to rapidly process data without human intervention.

External testing An external test is one that is created and administered by an outside agency.

First responder The initial responding law enforcement officer and/or other public safety official or service provider arriving at the scene prior to the arrival of the investigators in charge.

Focal plane A plane that is perpendicular to the axis of a lens or mirror and passes through the focus.

Forensic hit A CODIS match between two or more crime scene profiles.

Forensic index DNA profiles developed from crime scene evidence and uploaded into CODIS are maintained in the forensic index of the database.

Forensic science The application of science to analyze evidence involved in criminal and civil litigation.

Forensic unknowns DNA profiles obtained from crime scene evidence samples that are unmatched to a known individual.

Fractions The result of the differential extraction; separating sperm cells from all other DNA material.

Fragile evidence Evidence that will lose its evidentiary value if not preserved and protected, either because of its nature or the conditions at the scene (e.g., blood in the rain).

Fusiform Spindle-shaped; tapering from the middle towards each end. This shape is commonly seen in cortical cells and cortical fusi.

Gene The basic unit of heredity; a functional sequence of DNA in a chromosome.

Genetic loci Places in the genetic material of an organism where specific DNA sequences can be found.

Genetics The study of the patterns of inheritance of specific traits.

Genome All the genetic material in the chromosomes of a particular organism; its size is generally given as its total number of base pairs.

Genotype The genetic constitution of an organism, as distinguished from its physical appearance (its phenotype). The designation of two alleles at a particular locus is a genotype.

Hair One of the numerous fine and generally cylindrical filaments that grow from the skin or integument of animals, esp. of most mammals, of which they form the characteristic coat; applied also to similar-looking filamentous outgrowths from the body of insects and other invertebrates. These are usually of different structures.

Hair cuticular cast A freely movable, firm yellowish-white material ensheathing scalp hairs resulting from scalp disorders such as psoriasis or seborrhoeic dermatitis.

Haplotype A way of denoting the collective genotype of a number of closely linked loci on a chromosome.

Haptoglobin A protein present in blood serum that combines with hemoglobin to form a complex that is rapidly removed from the circulation by the liver.

Hardy-Weinberg (Equilibrium) In a large random intrabreeding population, not subjected to excessive selection or mutation, the gene and genotype frequencies will remain constant overt time. The sum of $p^2+2pq+q^2$ applies at equilibrium for a single allele pair where p is the frequency of the allele A, q is the frequency of a, p^2 is the frequency of genotype AA, q^2 is the frequency of aa, and 2pq is the frequency of Aa.

Heme The deep red, non-protein, ferrous component of hemoglobin. $C_{34}H_{32}FeN_4O_4$

Heredity The transmission of characteristics from one generation to the next.

Heteroplasmy The presence of more than one mtDNA type within a single individual.

Heterozygosity The probability that a given loci will be heterozygous in a randomly selected individual; having two different alleles at one locus.

Heterozygous If two alleles are different at one locus, the person is heterozygous at that genetic location.

HIPAA Health Insurance Portability and Accountability Act of 1996.

Histone A type of basic protein that forms the unit around which DNA is coiled in the nucleosomes of eukaryotic chromosomes. Arginine- and lysine-rich basic proteins making up a substantial portion of eukaryotic nucleoprotein.

HLA DQ-alpha A polymorphic gene in the Human Leukocyte Antigen (HLA) region of chromosome 6 that has been well studied and analyzed for many purposes including paternity testing, transplantation biology, and human DNA identification testing.

Homozygous If two alleles at a locus that are indistinguishable, the person is homozygous at that genetic location.

Humic An organic residue of decaying organic matter.

Hydroxyquinoline A bicyclic aromatic compound, which when added to phenol turns the aqueous phase orange, making it easier to differentiate in the organic extraction. See figure to the right.

Hypervariable An area on the DNA which can have many different alleles in differing sequences.

Hypervariable control region The D-loop of mitochondrial DNA in which base pairs of nucleotides repeat.

Immunoglobulin A general term for the kind of globular blood proteins that constitute antibodies. A tetrameric protein composed of two identical light chains and two identical heavy chains. Specific proteins produced by derivatives of B lymphocytes that interact with and help protect an organism from specific antigens.

Included Two samples could have come from the same source.

Inclusion (Failure to Exclude) The inability to exclude an individual as a possible source of a biological sample. This occurs when all types from a specific location in the DNA of a known individual are also present in the types for that specific location in the DNA obtained from an evidence sample.

Inconclusive A situation in which no conclusion can be reached regarding testing done due to one of many possible reasons (e.g., no results obtained, uninterpretable results obtained, no exemplar/standard available for testing).

Indigo dye A blue-colored dye that is derived from several plant species and commonly used to dye denim for blue jeans. A known PCR inhibitor.

Individualization In forensic science, the process of attempting to associate an item of evidence with one and only one source.

Inhibitors A substance that interferes with or prevents the polymerase chain reaction.

Inner cuticle margin The border between the cuticle and the cortex.

Intercalating dye A chemical that can insert itself between the stacked bases at the center of the DNA double helix, possibly causing a frameshift mutation.

Internal size standard (ISS) Specific DNA fragments of known sizes which are defined and used to size unknown fragments.

Internal testing An internal test is one that is created and administered by the laboratory itself.

Intimate sample An intimate sample is generally referred to a biological sample obtained from a source other than the mouth (saliva) and head (hair).

Irresolvable mixture A DNA profile where multiple individuals have contributed biological material and no profile is more or less apparent than any other and the developed alleles cannot be isolated to a single source.

Isoamyl alcohol A chemical used in organic extractions to reduce the foaming of reagents, making it easier to detect the interface between the organic and aqueous phases.

Isoenzyme Multiple forms of enzymes arising from genetically determined differences in primary structure. The term does not apply to those derived by modification of the same primary sequence.

John Doe warrant A warrant used when crime scene evidence yields a DNA profile but the individual corresponding to the DNA profile is unknown. In lieu of the suspect's name, the warrant will be filed as "John Doe" and cite the DNA profile.

Junk DNA Stretches of DNA that do not code for genes; "most of the genome consists of junk DNA."

Keratin Any of the various sulphur-containing fibrous proteins that form chemical basis for keratinized epidermal tissues such as hair, nails, feathers, and horns of animals.

Kinked Hair that is closely curled or twisted.

Known samples A DNA sample for which the source is known. These samples are generally obtained from the victim and/or suspected perpetrator of a crime, as well as from other persons whose DNA might be reflected when samples of the evidence are analyzed (could include a boyfriend, husband, or other third-party). These samples are also referred to as reference samples, since they serve as a reference to which the unknown DNA samples are compared with the goal of identifying the source of the unknown DNA samples.

Lanugo The fine hairs found on the human fetus.

Latent print A print impression that is not readily visible, made by contact with a surface.

LDIS The Local DNA Index System of CODIS, which uploads forensic and offender DNA profiles to the State DNA Index System, or SDIS.

Length heteroplasmy The presence of mtDNA molecules that differ in length.

Likelihood ratio The ratio of two probabilities of the same event under different hypotheses. In DNA testing often expressed as the ratio between the likelihood that a given profile came from a particular individual and the likelihood that it came from a random unrelated person. Note that in this case the likelihood of each event does not add to give 1 (100% likelihood) as it does not incorporate the possibility of error or that the profiles came from twins or other near relatives.

Linkage equilibrium When two or more genetic loci appear to segregate randomly in a given population. The genotypes appear randomly with respect to each other.

Lipopolysaccharides A large molecule containing a lipid and a carbohydrate. Locard's Exchange Principal States that every time someone enters an environment, something is added to and removed from it. The principle is sometimes stated as "every contact leaves a trace," and applies to contact between individuals as well as between individuals and a physical environment. Local (LDIS) The Local DNA Index System of CODIS which uploads forensic and offender DNA profiles to the State DNA Index System, or SDIS.

Locus (pl. loci) The specific physical location of a gene on a chromosome.

Looped cuticle A looped cuticle is a condition in which the distal edges of the cuticle scales are curved from or cup toward the hair shaft.

Low copy number Refers to examination of less than 100pg (picograms) of input DNA.

Macroscopic A term that describes characteristics large enough to be perceived without magnification; in forensic hair examination, this typically applies to unmounted hairs.

Magnification The height of the image divided by the height of the object. The apparent enlargement of an object by an optical instrument.

Major contributor profile A DNA profile where multiple individuals have contributed biologic material and one individual's DNA profile is more apparent.

Marker Pieces of DNA sequence of known locations on chromosomes that are used to identify the specific genetic variations an individual possesses.

Match Genetic profiles are said to "match" when they have the same allele designations at every loci.

Mean The mean of sample is calculated by taking the sum of all data values and dividing by the total number of data values.

Measurement scale An object showing standard units of length (e.g., ruler) used in photographic documentation of an item of evidence.

Medial Towards the long axis of the hair.

Medulla A series of air- or fluid-filled cells along the central axis of the hair.

Medullary continuity The continuous or discontinuous nature of the medulla.

Melanin The pigment occurring in plants, animals, and protista. It is responsible for skin and hair pigmentation. Two forms of melanin, eumelanin and phaeomelanin, determine the color of human hair.

Melting temperature (Tm) The temperature at which one-half of a particular DNA duplex will dissociate and become single strand DNA.

Microbial epidemiology microbial: relating to a microbe or microbes; epidemiology: the study or the distribution and determinants of health-related states or events in specified populations, and the application of this study to control health problems.

Microscope An instrument consisting essentially of a tube 160 mm long, with an objective lens at the distant end and an eyepiece at the near end. The objective forms a real aerial image of the object in the focal plane of the eyepiece where it is observed by the eye.

Microscopic A term for objects which are too small to be resolved by the unaided eye.

Midshaft region The region of the hair between the proximal and distal ends.

Minisatellite variant repeat (MVR) Tandem repeats of a short (10- to 100-bp) DNA fragments spanning several hundred to several thousand base pairs.

Mitochondrial DNA (mtDNA) The DNA found in the many mitochondria found in each cell of a body. The sequencing of mitochondrial DNA can link individuals descended from a common female ancestor.

Mongoloid An archaic anthropological term designating peoples originating from Asia, excluding the Indian subcontinent but including the Native Americans.

Monilethrix Monilethrix is a hair disorder that results in periodic nodes or beading along the length of the hair with intervening, tapering constrictions that are not medullated.

Morphology Shape, form, external structure, or arrangement, especially as an object of study or classification

mtDNA types A mtDNA type is the sequence of a region of mtDNA. Common sources of mtDNA are hairs, skeletal remains, and teeth.

Multiplexed A system for analyzing several loci at once.

Mutation Damaged or changed DNA anywhere along the DNA strand.

National DNA Index System (NDIS) Authorized by the DNA Identification Act of 1994, the FBI administers this national index. NDIS compares DNA profiles associated with a crime scene to DNA profiles collected from known convicted offenders, as well as to other crime scene profiles. When the DNA profiles are uploaded to NDIS, they are searched against the other DNA profiles submitted by other participating states.

National Research Council (NRC) The National Research Council was convened in 1989. In 1996 the NRC filed the report The Evaluation of Forensic DNA Evidence (referred to as NRC II). This document revised and expanded the initial report written in 1992 (NRC I). These recommendations are recognized by U.S. courts.

Negroid An archaic anthropological term designating most of the peoples originating from Africa.

No results A situation in which no interpretable results are obtained from testing a DNA sample. A finding of no results can be due to the absence of DNA, insufficient DNA, or substances that inhibit the PCR process, among others.

Nonconformances Inconsistencies in laboratory practices that do not meet accreditation standards.

Nonmatch An individual is eliminated as the source of a biological sample. This occurs when one or more types from a specific location in the DNA of a known individual are not present in the type(s) for that specific location in the DNA obtained from an evidence sample.

Nonporous container Packaging through which liquids or vapors cannot pass (e.g., glass jars or metal cans).

Nuclear DNA The DNA found in the nucleus of a cell.

Nucleases One of the several classes of enzymes that degrade nucleic acid. An enzyme that can degrade DNA or RNA by breaking phosphodiester bonds.

Nucleated A nucleus or occurring in the nucleus.

Nucleus The cellular organelle that contains most of the genetic material.

Numerical aperture A measure of the information-collecting ability of a microscope optic. The greater the NA, the better the resolving ability. It is a measure of the light-gathering capacity of the lens system and determines its resolving power and depth of field.

Objective test A test which having been documented and validated is under control so that it can be demonstrated that all appropriately trained staff will obtain the same results within defined limits. These defined limits relate to expressions of degrees of probability as well as numerical values.

Off ladder (OL) alleles Alleles that size outside allele categories represented in the ladder.

Offender hit A CODIS match between a crime scene profile and an offender profile.

Offender index DNA profiles developed from qualifying offenders and uploaded into CODIS are maintained in the offender index of the database.

Ohm's law The amount of current flowing in a circuit made up of pure resistances is directly proportional to the electromotive forces impressed on the circuit and inversely proportional to the total resistance of the circuit.

Oligonucleotides A molecule usually composed of 25 or fewer nucleotides; used as a DNA synthesis primer.

Optical density (OD) Synonymous with absorbance. Absorbance is the logarithm of the ratio of incident to transmitted radiant power through a sample.

Outer cuticle margin The border of the outermost edge of the cuticle.

Ovoid bodies Oval-shaped heavily pigmented bodies that may occur in the hair cortex.

Partial profile DNA evidence that does not yield identifiable results in all 13 core loci.

Partially degraded DNA Forensic DNA evidence exposed to environmental conditions that may prevent it from yielding a usable profile.

Paternal inheritance Genetic material which is inherited from one's father; for example, the possibility that mtDNA can be inherited from one's father.

Paternity or System Index (PI or SI) A statistic that compares the likelihood that a genetic marker (allele) that the alleged father passed to the child to the probability that a randomly selected unrelated man of similar ethnic background could pass the allele to the child.

PCR Inhibitors A substance that interferes with the Polymerase Chain Reaction (PCR) process. Examples of PCR inhibitors include dyes, soil, chemicals, and heme (hemoglobin).

Peripheral region The peripheral region is the portion of the hair toward the outermost areas of the hair, including the cuticle and the outer areas of the cortex, distant from the medullary or central region.

Personal protective equipment (PPE) Articles such as disposable (latex) gloves, masks, shoe covers, and eye protection that are utilized to provide a barrier to keep biological or chemical hazards from contacting the skin, eyes, and mucous membranes and to avoid contamination of the crime scene.

Phenol A chemical used in organic extraction. Polysaccharides and proteins are soluble in phenol, allowing for their separation from DNA. C6H5OH. See figure to the right.

Phenotype The detectable outward manifestations of a specific genotype; the physical characteristics of a living object.

Pigmentation Coloration or discoloration by formation or deposition of pigment in the tissues. In a forensic hair examination, the description of the aggregation, distribution, and density of pigment granules.

Pili annulati Pili annulati is a hair disorder that results in ringed or banded hair, alternating bright and dark bands in the hair shaft. The dark bands are a manifestation of the abnormal air spaces in the cortex.

Pili bifurcati A genetic hair disorder characterized by two hairs joined at the shaft along their entire length.

Pili torti A genetic hair disorder characterized by the hair shaft being flattened and twisted 180 degrees numerous times along its axis. It is usually found at irregular intervals along the shaft.

Polymerase chain reaction (PCR) A process used in DNA identification testing in which one or more specific small regions of the DNA are copied using a DNA polymerase enzyme so that a sufficient amount of DNA is generated for analysis.

Polymorphic Variable, more than one kind.

Polymorphism Variations in DNA sequences in a population that are detected in human DNA identification testing.

Polypurine A stretch of adenine and/or guanine.

Polypyrimidine A stretch of cytosine and/or thyamine.

PopStats FBI CODIS software program used to perform statistical DNA match estimates.

Population genetics The study of the distribution of genes in populations and of how the frequencies of genes and genotypes are maintained or changed.

Postmortem root banding An opaque ellipsoidal band, composed of parallel elongated air spaces, which appear on the proximal portion of hair shafts from postmortem hairs, likely to be in the anagen growth phase.

Preferential amplification Imbalanced amplification or lack of amplification at a locus.

Presumptive test A screening test used to indicate the possible presence of the named body fluid.

Primer A segment of DNA or RNA that is complementary to a given DNA sequence and that is needed to initiate replication by DNA polymerase.

Primer dimer Formed by intermolecular interactions between the two primers (i.e., self-dimers and cross-dimers).

Probability The chance of observing a particular future event; a simple ratio of the number of observed events divided by the total number of possible events.

Probability calculations Predictions based on small sampling of a larger population.

Probability of exclusion The probability that a random individual would be excluded as the source of analyzed DNA evidence.

Probability of inclusion The probability that a random individual would be included as a potential source of analyzed DNA evidence.

Probability of paternity A formula that tests the hypothesis that the accused is the biological father of the child.

Probe Defined nucleic acid (DNA or RNA) that can be used to identify, usually through autoradiography, specific DNA or RNA molecules bearing the complementary sequence.

Product rule The product rule calculates the expected chance of finding a given STR (short tandem repeat) profile within a population by multiplying the frequency of occurrence of the combination of alleles (genotype) found at a single locus, by the frequency of occurrence of the genotype found at the second locus, by the frequency of occurrence, in turn, of each of the other genotypes at the remaining STR loci.

Proficiency test A proficiency test is a quality assurance measure used to monitor performance of an examiner.

Proficiency testing A DNA proficiency test uses biological samples to assess a lab analyst's ongoing competency and the laboratory's ability to produce accurate results.

Protamine Protein that binds DNA in sperm, replacing histones and allowing chromosomes to become more highly condensed than possible with histones.

Proteinase K An endolytic protease that cleaves peptide bonds at the carboxylic sides of aliphatic, aromatic, or hydrophobic amino acids. Proteinase K in the extraction buffer inactivates nucleases and aids in lysis of epithelial and white blood cells to free nuclear DNA.

Proximal end The portion of the hair towards the root.

Pull-up Specifically related to ABI Gene Scan® software, a peak seen in one color that is not due to the presence of DNA, but to incorrect compensation for the spectral overlap of the four dyes used in detecting multiple loci in one reaction. See also: Artifact Q

Quality assurance (QA) A program conducted by a laboratory to ensure accuracy and reliability of tests performed.

Quality assurance standards The standards originated from the DNA Advisory Board and are maintained by the FBI; they place specific requirements on labs involved in forensic DNA analysis, both casework and convicted offender databasing. See the FBI's QAS for Forensic DNA Testing Laboratories and QAS for DNA Databasing Laboratories

Quantitation Method used to determine the quantity of "x" in a given sample. In this context, it refers to the quantity of DNA in a sample and is usually reported as ng/μl.

Quantitative PCR (qPCR) Sometimes referred to in forensic science as real-time PCR. An amplification process that detects and measures the accumulation of fluorescent dyes as the reaction progresses. The initial quantity of DNA in the sample is detected by monitoring the exponential growth phase of the reaction and measuring the cycle number at which the fluorescent intensity of the sample overcomes the background noise or threshold.

Questioned sample A sample recovered or collected, about which there are questions, for a forensic examination.

Racial group A group of people defined by race, color, nationality, and ethnic or national origins.

Random match probability The probability that the DNA in a random sample from the population has the same profile as the DNA in the evidence sample.

Randomly amplified polymorphic DNA markers Random amplification of polymorphic DNA. A method for identifying differences between genomes of different individuals by PCR with a single short (usually 10-base) primer, which will anneal with complementary sequence at undetermined positions in the genome.

Reciprocal discovery Some jurisdictions enable a prosecutor by motion to request that the defense provide specific discovery material to the prosecution.

Recombinant DNA Altered DNA resulting from the insertion into the chain, by chemical, enzymatic, or other biological means, of a sequence (a whole or partial chain of DNA) not originally (biologically) present in that chain.

Recombination The reversal of coupling phase I meiosis as gauged by the resulting phenotype. See also Recombinant DNA above.

Reference samples A standard/reference sample is material of a verifiable/documented source which, when compared with evidence of an unknown source, shows an association or linkage between an offender, crime scene, and/or victim (e.g., a carpet cutting taken from a location suspected as the point of transfer for comparison with the fibers recovered from the suspect's shoes, a sample of paint removed from a suspect vehicle to be compared with paint found on a victim's vehicle following an accident, or a sample of the suspect's and/or victim's blood submitted for comparison with a bloodstained shirt recovered as evidence).

Reflected light Incident illumination (cf. transmitted light).

Reflection When light strikes a surface and then leaves at the same angle. Angle in=angle out. The production of an image by or as if by a mirror.

Relative fluorescence unit (RFU) a unit of measurement used in electrophoreses methods employing fluorescence detection. Fluorescence is detected on the CCD array as the labeled fragments, separated in the capillary by electrophoresis, and excited by the laser, pass the detection window. The software interprets the results, calculating the size or quantity of the fragments from the fluorescence intensity at each data point.

Refraction The deflection from a straight path undergone by a light ray or energy wave in passing obliquely from one medium (as air) into another (as glass) in which its velocity is different, or the action of distorting an image by viewing through a medium.

Representative sample A collection of hairs from a specific body area that encompasses the characteristics expressed in an individual's hair.

Resolution A measurement of how well the smallest details of an image can be discerned. The process or capability of making distinguishable the individual parts of an object, closely adjacent optical images, or sources of light.

Restriction enzyme A protein harnessed from bacteria that recognizes specific, short nucleotide sequences and cuts DNA at those sites.

Restriction fragment length polymorphism Variation in the length of a stretch of DNA; abbreviated RFLP.

Root The root is the structure at the proximal end of a hair.

Sanger sequencing A widely used method of determining the order of bases in DNA.

Sarkosyl Also known as sodium lauroylsarcosine. A detergent used in DNA extraction.

Scales Scales are plate-like structures composed of keratin that overlap to form the cuticle.

SDIS State DNA Index System containing the state-level DNA records uploaded from local laboratory sites within the state. SDIS is the state's repository of DNA identification records and is under the control of state authorities. The SDIS laboratory serves as the central point of contact for access to the National DNA Index System (NDIS). The DNA Analysis Unit I (DNAUI) serves as the SDIS laboratory for the FBI.

Semen The fluid (ejaculate) that is released through the penis during orgasm. Semen is made up of sperm from the testicles and other fluid from other sex glands.

Sequence (or site) heteroplasmy Presence of mtDNA molecules that have different nucleotides at the same address.

Sequencing Determination of the order of base sequences in a DNA molecule.

Shaft The portion of a hair between the root and the tip.

Short tandem repeat (STR) typing DNA analysis method which targets regions on the chromosome which contain multiple copies of an identical DNA sequence in succession.

Short tandem repeats (STR) Multiple copies of a short identical DNA sequence arranged in direct succession in particular regions of chromosomes.

Shouldering An asymmetrical cross-section.

Signal-to-noise ratio A measure of signal strength relative to background noise.

Similar Of the same substance or structure throughout; homogeneous; having a marked resemblance or likeness; of a like nature or kind.

Simple sequence repeats (SSR) A sequence consisting largely of a tandem repeat of a specific k-mer (such as (CA)15). Many SSRs are polymorphic and have been widely used in genetic mapping.

SINE (Short INterspersed Element) A type of small dispersed repetitive DNA sequence (e.g., Alu family in the human genome) found throughout a eukaryotic genome.

Single nucleotide polymorphisms (SNPs) DNA sequence variations that occur at a single nucleotide (A, T, C, or G).

Single source profile A DNA profile where only one individual has contributed biologic material.

Single-use equipment Items that will be used only once to collect evidence, such as biological samples, then discarded to minimize contamination (e.g., tweezers, scalpel blades, droppers).

Slot blot A technique for measuring the amount DNA or RNA. Samples are placed onto a hybridization membrane, fixed, and hybridized with a probe. Visualization techniques include use of a radioactive probe, chemiluminescence, or colorimetric based systems. The concentration of the samples is determined by comparing to standards of known concentrations.

Sodium dodecyl sulfate (SDS) Also known as sodium lauryl sulfate (SLS). A detergent used in DNA extraction.

Somatic Referring to an area of the body.

Spectrophotometry The determination of the structure or quantity of substances by measuring their capacity to absorb light of various wavelengths.

Spermidine Polyamines originally isolated from semen and can inhibit PCR. Found in ribosomes and living tissues.

Spermine Polyamines originally isolated from semen and can inhibit PCR. Found in ribosomes and living tissues.

Standard operation procedures (SOP) A prescribed procedure to be followed routinely.

State (SDIS) State DNA Index System containing the state-level DNA records uploaded from local laboratory sites within the state. SDIS is the state's repository of DNA identification records and is under the control of state authorities. The SDIS laboratory serves as the central point of contact for access to NDIS. The DNA Analysis Unit I (DNAUI) serves as the SDIS laboratory for the FBI.

Stochastic effects Being or having a random variable.

Stutter A minor band or peak appearing one repeat unit smaller than a primary STR (short tandem repeat) allele. Occasionally, the repeat unit is larger than the primary allele.

Substrate Any background material upon which biological sample has been deposited (e.g., clothing, glass, wood, upholstery).

Supernatant Liquid portion remaining after centrifugation or precipitation of a sample.

SWGDAM Scientific Working Group of DNA Analysis and Methods, formerly called TWGDAM (Technical Working Group on DNA Analysis and Methods).

Tannic acid A naturally occurring compound used for tanning animal hides into leather. A known PCR inhibitor.

Taq polymerase A heat-stable DNA polymerase isolated from the bacterium Thermus aquaticus, used in PCR.

TE buffer A commonly used buffer in Molecular Biology, especially in procedures involving DNA. It is called "TE" buffer because it contains Tris and EDTA.

Telogen The last phase of the hair growth cycle when the hair root becomes a bulbous shaped root.

Terminal hair Long, coarse, generally pigmented hairs, sometimes with medullation, representing the final state of differentiation of human hair. (cf. vellus, lanugo)

Thermal cycler An instrument used to perform the polymerase chain reaction (PCR).

Theta correction A theta adjustment is a mathematical correction applied to a frequency calculation when both alleles at a locus are the same (known as a homozygous state). It is not applied when alleles are different at a locus (known as a heterozygous state). This correction adjusts the frequency slightly upwards to account for the presence of subpopulations in a general population database that might otherwise cause the genotype frequency to be underestimated at that locus.

Third-party defense motion A motion filed by the prosecution to preclude the defense from asserting that DNA evidence is derived from a third party, possibly a relative of the accused.

Threshold The point that must be exceeded to begin producing a given effect or result or to elicit a response.

Threshold value A relative fluorescent unit (RFU) value that must be exceeded to make an allele call. This value will vary among laboratories.

Tip The most distal end of a hair's shaft.

Trace evidence Physical evidence that results from the transfer of small quantities of materials (e.g., hair, textile fibers, paint chips, glass fragments, gunshot residue particles).

Translucent Allowing the passage of light, yet diffusing it so as not to render bodies lying beyond clearly visible; semi-transparent.

Transmitted light Illumination which passes through a medium.

Transparent Having the property of transmitting light, so as to render bodies lying beyond completely visible.

Trichology The study of the structure, functions, and diseases of the hair.

Trichonodosis A condition characterized by apparent or actual knotting of the hair.

Trichoptilosis A disease condition characterized by longitudinal splitting or fraying of the hair shaft.

Trichorrhexis invaginati A genetic disease characterized by a segment of bulbous, dilated hair being enfolded into a concave hair terminal, recalling the appearance of a bamboo node. If the hair breaks at the bulbous end, the hair has a "golf tee cup" end.

Trichorrhexis nodosa A condition characterized by the formation of nodes, and in extreme cases, the hair is weaker at the node and is subject to breakage.

Trichoschisis A condition characterized by brittle hair with a transverse crack or a clean break.

Tris An abbreviation for tris (hydroxymethyl) methylamine, also known as tris(hydroxymethyl)aminomethane. It is widely used in biochemistry as a buffer salt.

Ubiquitous Existing or being everywhere, widespread

Undulated Changes in diameter along the length of the hair shaft that result from changes in cross-sectional area. This can give the hair a wavy appearance.

Uninterpretable Results which might be reported by the laboratory when alleles can not be interpreted.

Upper bound frequency estimates an estimate of the percentage of individuals who could be potential contributors of a mtDNA profile.

UV light source Use of an ultraviolet light source to enhance or visualize potential items of evidence (fluids, fingerprints, clothing fibers, etc.). The light will cause possible biological stains to change color or fluoresce, assisting in the location process.

Validation The process of extensive and rigorous evaluation of DNA methods before acceptance for routine use.

Variable number of tandem repeats (VNTRs) Repeating units of a DNA sequence; a class of RFLPs (restriction fragment length polymorphism); abbreviated VNTR.

Variance A measure of the spread of a distribution about its average value.

Variant A dissimilarity in the commonly occuring sequence of a gene.

Vellus Short, fine, unmedullated hairs spread more or less uniformly over the body.

Virtual Image An image (as seen in a plane mirror) formed of points from which divergent rays (as of light) seem to emanate without actually doing so. It does not exist physically.

Walk-through An initial assessment conducted by carefully walking through the scene to evaluate the situation, identify potential evidence, and determine resources required. It can also be a final survey conducted to ensure the scene has been effectively and completely processed.

Waved A hair shaft form with curvature that changes its direction to produce a sinuous wave form and does not curve back upon itself to form a circle.

Working distance Distance between the front vertex of a lens and the object.

Y-STR Short tandem repeats located on the Y chromosome.

Justice—U.S. Courts

Acquittal A jury verdict that a criminal defendant is not guilty, or the finding of a judge that the evidence is insufficient to support a conviction.

Active judge A judge in the full-time service of the court. Compare to senior judge.

Administrative Office of the United States Courts (AO) The federal agency responsible for collecting court statistics, administering the federal courts' budget, and performing many other administrative and programmatic functions, under the direction and supervision of the Judicial Conference of the United States.

Admissible A term used to describe evidence that may be considered by a jury or judge in civil and criminal cases.

Adversary proceeding A lawsuit arising in or related to a bankruptcy case that begins by filing a complaint with the court, that is, a "trial" that takes place within the context of a bankruptcy case.

Affidavit A written or printed statement made under oath.

Affirmed In the practice of the court of appeals, it means that the court of appeals has concluded that the lower court decision is correct and will stand as rendered by the lower court.

Alternate juror A juror selected in the same manner as a regular juror who hears all the evidence but does not help decide the case unless called on to replace a regular juror.

Alternative dispute resolution (ADR) A procedure for settling a dispute outside the courtroom. Most forms of ADR are not binding, and involve referral of the case to a neutral party such as an arbitrator or mediator.

Amicus curiae Latin for "friend of the court." It is advice formally offered to the court in a brief filed by an entity interested in, but not a party to, the case.

Answer The formal written statement by a defendant in a civil case that responds to a complaint, articulating the grounds for defense.

Appeal A request made after a trial by a party that has lost on one or more issues that a higher court review the decision to determine if it was correct. To make such a request is "to appeal" or "to take an appeal." One who appeals is called the "appellant"; the other party is the "appellee."

Appellant The party who appeals a district court's decision, usually seeking reversal of that decision.

Appellate About appeals; an appellate court has the power to review the judgment of a lower court (trial court) or tribunal. For example, the U.S. circuit courts of appeals review the decisions of the U.S. district courts.

Appellee The party who opposes an appellant's appeal, and who seeks to persuade the appeals court to affirm the district court's decision.

Arraignment A proceeding in which a criminal defendant is brought into court, told of the charges in an indictment or information, and asked to plead guilty or not guilty.

Article III judge A federal judge who is appointed for life, during "good behavior," under Article III of the Constitution. Article III judges are nominated by the President and confirmed by the Senate.

Assets Property of all kinds, including real and personal, tangible and intangible.

Assume An agreement to continue performing duties under a contract or lease.

Automatic stay An injunction that automatically stops lawsuits, foreclosures, garnishments, and most collection activities against the debtor the moment a bankruptcy petition is filed.

Bail The release, prior to trial, of a person accused of a crime, under specified conditions designed to assure that person's appearance in court when required. Also can refer to the amount of bond money posted as a financial condition of pretrial release.

Bankruptcy A legal procedure for dealing with debt problems of individuals and businesses; specifically, a case filed under one of the chapters of title 11 of the United States Code (the Bankruptcy Code).

Bankruptcy administrator An officer of the Judiciary serving in the judicial districts of Alabama and North Carolina who, like the United States trustee, is responsible for supervising the administration of bankruptcy cases, estates, and trustees; monitoring plans and disclosure statements; monitoring creditors' committees; monitoring fee applications; and performing other statutory duties.

Bankruptcy code The informal name for title 11 of the United States Code (11 U.S.C. §§ 101-1330), the federal bankruptcy law.

Bankruptcy court The bankruptcy judges in regular active service in each district; a unit of the district court.

Bankruptcy estate All interests of the debtor in property at the time of the bankruptcy filing. The estate technically becomes the temporary legal owner of all of the debtor's property.

Bankruptcy judge A judicial officer of the United States district court who is the court official with decision-making power over federal bankruptcy cases.

Bankruptcy petition A formal request for the protection of the federal bankruptcy laws. (There is an official form for bankruptcy petitions.)

Bankruptcy trustee A private individual or corporation appointed in all Chapter 7 and Chapter 13 cases to represent the interests of the bankruptcy estate and the debtor's creditors.

Bench trial A trial without a jury, in which the judge serves as the fact-finder.

Brief A written statement submitted in a trial or appellate proceeding that explains one side's legal and factual arguments.

Burden of proof The duty to prove disputed facts. In civil cases, a plaintiff generally has the burden of proving his or her case. In criminal cases, the government has the burden of proving the defendant's guilt. (See standard of proof.)

Business bankruptcy A bankruptcy case in which the debtor is a business or an individual involved in business and the debts are for business purposes.

Capital offense A crime punishable by death.

Case file A complete collection of every document filed in court in a case.

Case law The law as established in previous court decisions. A synonym for legal precedent. Akin to common law, which springs from tradition and judicial decisions.

Caseload The number of cases handled by a judge or a court.

Cause of action A legal claim.

Chambers The offices of a judge and his or her staff.

Chapter 11 A reorganization bankruptcy, usually involving a corporation or partnership. A Chapter 11 debtor usually proposes a plan of reorganization to keep its business alive and pay creditors over time. Individuals or people in business can also seek relief in Chapter 11.

Chapter 12 The chapter of the Bankruptcy Code providing for adjustment of debts of a "family farmer" or "family fisherman," as the terms are defined in the Bankruptcy Code.

Chapter 13 The chapter of the Bankruptcy Code providing for the adjustment of debts of an individual with regular income, often referred to as a "wage-earner" plan. Chapter 13 allows a debtor to keep property and use his or her disposable income to pay debts over time, usually three to five years.

Chapter 13 trustee A person appointed to administer a Chapter 13 case. A Chapter 13 trustee's responsibilities are similar to those of a Chapter 7 trustee; however, a Chapter 13 trustee has the additional responsibilities of overseeing the debtor's plan, receiving payments from debtors, and disbursing plan payments to creditors.

Chapter 15 The chapter of the Bankruptcy Code dealing with cases of cross-border insolvency.

Chapter 7 The chapter of the Bankruptcy Code providing for "liquidation," that is, the sale of a debtor's nonexempt property and the distribution of the proceeds to creditors. In order to be eligible for Chapter 7, the debtor must satisfy a "means test." The court will evaluate the debtor's income and expenses to determine if the debtor may proceed under Chapter 7.

Chapter 7 trustee A person appointed in a Chapter 7 case to represent the interests of the bankruptcy estate and the creditors. The trustee's responsibilities include reviewing the debtor's petition and schedules, liquidating the property of the estate, and making distributions to creditors. The trustee may also bring actions against creditors or the debtor to recover property of the bankruptcy estate.

Chapter 9 The chapter of the Bankruptcy Code providing for reorganization of municipalities (which includes cities and towns, as well as villages, counties, taxing districts, municipal utilities, and school districts).

Chief judge The judge who has primary responsibility for the administration of a court; chief judges are determined by seniority

Claim A creditor's assertion of a right to payment from a debtor or the debtor's property.

Class action A lawsuit in which one or more members of a large group, or class, of individuals or other entities sue on behalf of the entire class. The district court must find that the claims of the class members contain questions of law or fact in common before the lawsuit can proceed as a class action.

Clerk of court The court officer who oversees administrative functions, especially managing the flow of cases through the court. The clerk's office is often called a court's central nervous system.

Collateral Property that is promised as security for the satisfaction of a debt.

Common law The legal system that originated in England and is now in use in the United States, which relies on the articulation of legal principles in a historical succession of judicial decisions. Common law principles can be changed by legislation.

Community service A special condition the court imposes that requires an individual to work—without pay—for a civic or nonprofit organization.

Complaint A written statement that begins a civil lawsuit, in which the plaintiff details the claims against the defendant.

Concurrent sentence Prison terms for two or more offenses to be served at the same time, rather than one after the other. Example: Two five-year sentences and one three-year sentence, if served concurrently, result in a maximum of five years behind bars.

Confirmation Approval of a plan of reorganization by a bankruptcy judge.

Consecutive sentence Prison terms for two or more offenses to be served one after the other. Example: Two five-year sentences and one three-year sentence, if served consecutively, result in a maximum of 13 years behind bars.

Consumer bankruptcy A bankruptcy case filed to reduce or eliminate debts that are primarily consumer debts.

Consumer debts Debts incurred for personal, as opposed to business, needs.

Contingent claim A claim that may be owed by the debtor under certain circumstances, e.g., where the debtor is a cosigner on another person's loan and that person fails to pay.

Contract An agreement between two or more people that creates an obligation to do or not to do a particular thing.

Conviction A judgment of guilt against a criminal defendant.

Counsel Legal advice; a term also used to refer to the lawyers in a case.

Count An allegation in an indictment or information, charging a defendant with a crime. An indictment or information may contain allegations that the defendant committed more than one crime. Each allegation is referred to as a count.

Court Government entity authorized to resolve legal disputes. Judges sometimes use "court" to refer to themselves in the third person, as in "the court has read the briefs."

Court reporter A person who makes a word-for-word record of what is said in court, generally by using a stenographic machine, shorthand or audio recording, and then produces a transcript of the proceedings upon request.

Credit counseling Generally refers to two events in individual bankruptcy cases: (1) the "individual or group briefing" from a nonprofit budget and credit counseling agency that individual debtors must attend prior to filing under any chapter of the Bankruptcy Code; and (2) the "instructional course in personal financial management" in chapters 7 and 13 that an individual debtor must complete before a discharge is entered. There are exceptions to both requirements for certain categories of debtors, exigent circumstances, or if the U.S. trustee or bankruptcy administrator have determined that there are insufficient approved credit counseling agencies available to provide the necessary counseling.

Creditor A person to whom or business to which the debtor owes money or that claims to be owed money by the debtor.

Damages Money that a defendant pays a plaintiff in a civil case if the plaintiff has won. Damages may be compensatory (for loss or injury) or punitive (to punish and deter future misconduct).

De facto Latin, meaning "in fact" or "actually." Something that exists in fact but not as a matter of law.

De jure Latin, meaning "in law." Something that exists by operation of law.

De novo Latin, meaning "anew." A trial de novo is a completely new trial. Appellate review de novo implies no deference to the trial judge's ruling.

Debtor A person who has filed a petition for relief under the Bankruptcy Code.

Debtor's plan A debtor's detailed description of how the debtor proposes to pay creditors' claims over a fixed period of time.

Declaratory judgment A judge's statement about someone's rights. For example, a plaintiff may seek a declaratory judgment that a particular statute, as written, violates some constitutional right.

Default judgment A judgment awarding a plaintiff the relief sought in the complaint because the defendant has failed to appear in court or otherwise respond to the complaint.

Defendant An individual (or business) against whom a lawsuit is filed.

Defendant In a civil case, the person or organization against whom the plaintiff brings suit; in a criminal case, the person accused of the crime.

Deposition An oral statement made before an officer authorized by law to administer oaths. Such statements are often taken to examine potential witnesses, to obtain discovery, or to be used later in trial. See discovery.

Discharge A release of a debtor from personal liability for certain dischargeable debts. Notable exceptions to dischargeability are taxes and student loans. A discharge releases a debtor from personal liability for certain debts known as dischargeable debts and prevents the creditors owed those debts from taking any action against the debtor or the debtor's property to collect the debts. The discharge also prohibits creditors from communicating with the debtor regarding the debt, including through telephone calls, letters, and personal contact.

Dischargeable debt A debt for which the Bankruptcy Code allows the debtor's personal liability to be eliminated.

Disclosure statement A written document prepared by the Chapter 11 debtor or other plan proponent that is designed to provide "adequate information" to creditors to enable them to evaluate the Chapter 11 plan of reorganization.

Discovery Procedures used to obtain disclosure of evidence before trial.

Dismissal with prejudice Court action that prevents an identical lawsuit from being filed later.

Dismissal without prejudice Court action that allows the later filing.

Disposable income Income not reasonably necessary for the maintenance or support of the debtor or dependents. If the debtor operates a business, disposable income is defined as those amounts over and above what is necessary for the payment of ordinary operating expenses.

Docket A log containing the complete history of each case in the form of brief chronological entries summarizing the court proceedings.

Due process In criminal law, the constitutional guarantee that a defendant will receive a fair and impartial trial. In civil law, the legal rights of someone who confronts an adverse action threatening liberty or property.

En banc French, meaning "on the bench." All judges of an appellate court sitting together to hear a case, as opposed to the routine disposition by panels of three judges. In the Ninth Circuit, an en banc panel consists of 11 randomly selected judges.

Equitable Pertaining to civil suits in "equity" rather than in "law." In English legal history, the courts of "law" could order the payment of damages and could afford no other remedy (see damages). A separate court of "equity" could order someone to do something or to cease to do something (e.g., injunction). In American jurisprudence, the federal courts have both legal and equitable power, but the distinction is still an important one. For example, a trial by jury is normally available in "law" cases but not in "equity" cases.

Equity The value of a debtor's interest in property that remains after liens and other creditors' interests are considered. (Example: If a house valued at $60,000 is subject to a $30,000 mortgage, there is $30,000 of equity.)

Evidence Information presented in testimony or in documents that is used to persuade the fact finder (judge or jury) to decide the case in favor of one side or the other.

Ex parte A proceeding brought before a court by one party only, without notice to or challenge by the other side.

Exclusionary rule Doctrine that says evidence obtained in violation of a criminal defendant's constitutional or statutory rights is not admissible at trial.

Exculpatory evidence Evidence indicating that a defendant did not commit the crime.

Executory contracts Contracts or leases under which both parties to the agreement have duties remaining to be performed. If a contract or lease is executory, a debtor may assume it (keep the contract) or reject it (terminate the contract).

Exempt assets Property that a debtor is allowed to retain, free from the claims of creditors who do not have liens on the property.

Exemptions, exempt property Certain property owned by an individual debtor that the Bankruptcy Code or applicable state law permits the debtor to keep from unsecured creditors. For example, in some states the debtor may be able to exempt all or a portion of the equity in the debtor's primary residence (homestead exemption), or some or all "tools of the trade" used by the debtor to make a living (i.e., auto tools for an auto mechanic or dental tools for a dentist). The availability and amount of property the debtor may exempt depends on the state the debtor lives in.

Face sheet filing A bankruptcy case filed either without schedules or with incomplete schedules listing few creditors and debts. (Face sheet filings are often made for the purpose of delaying an eviction or foreclosure

Family farmer An individual, individual and spouse, corporation, or partnership engaged in a farming operation that meets certain debt limits and other statutory criteria for filing a petition under Chapter 12.

Federal public defender An attorney employed by the federal courts on a full-time basis to provide legal defense to defendants who are unable to afford counsel. The judiciary administers the federal defender program pursuant to the Criminal Justice Act.

Federal public defender organization As provided for in the Criminal Justice Act, an organization established within a federal judicial circuit to represent criminal defendants who cannot afford an adequate defense. Each organization is supervised by a federal public defender appointed by the court of appeals for the circuit.

Federal question jurisdiction Jurisdiction given to federal courts in cases involving the interpretation and application of the U.S. Constitution, acts of Congress, and treaties.

Felony A serious crime, usually punishable by at least one year in prison.

File To place a paper in the official custody of the clerk of court to enter into the files or records of a case.

Fraudulent transfer A transfer of a debtor's property made with intent to defraud or for which the debtor receives less than the transferred property's value.

Fresh start The characterization of a debtor's status after bankruptcy, i.e., free of most debts. (Giving debtors a fresh start is one purpose of the Bankruptcy Code.)

Grand jury A body of 16-23 citizens who listen to evidence of criminal allegations, which is presented by the prosecutors, and determine whether there is probable cause to believe an individual committed an offense. See also indictment and U.S. attorney.

Habeas corpus Latin, meaning "you have the body." A writ of habeas corpus generally is a judicial order forcing law enforcement authorities to produce a prisoner they are holding, and to justify the prisoner's continued confinement. Federal judges receive petitions for a writ of habeas corpus from state prison inmates who say their state prosecutions violated federally protected rights in some way.

Hearsay Evidence presented by a witness who did not see or hear the incident in question but heard about it from someone else. With some exceptions, hearsay generally is not admissible as evidence at trial

Home confinement A special condition the court imposes that requires an individual to remain at home except for certain approved activities such as work and medical appointments. Home confinement may include the use of electronic monitoring equipment—a transmitter attached to the wrist or the ankle—to help ensure that the person stays at home as required.

Impeachment 1. The process of calling a witness's testimony into doubt. For example, if the attorney can show that the witness may have fabricated portions of his testimony, the witness is said to be "impeached"; 2. The constitutional process whereby the House of Representatives may "impeach" (accuse of misconduct) high officers of the federal government, who are then tried by the Senate.

In camera Latin, meaning in a judge's chambers. Often means outside the presence of a jury and the public. In private.

In forma pauperis "In the manner of a pauper." Permission given by the court to a person to file a case without payment of the required court fees because the person cannot pay them.

Inculpatory evidence Evidence indicating that a defendant did commit the crime.

Indictment The formal charge issued by a grand jury stating that there is enough evidence that the defendant committed the crime to justify having a trial; it is used primarily for felonies. See also information.

Information A formal accusation by a government attorney that the defendant committed a misdemeanor. See also indictment.

Injunction A court order preventing one or more named parties from taking some action. A preliminary injunction often is issued to allow fact-finding, so a judge can determine whether a permanent injunction is justified.

Insider (of corporate debtor) A director, officer, or person in control of the debtor; a partnership in which the debtor is a general partner; a general partner of the debtor; or a relative of a general partner, director, officer, or person in control of the debtor.

Insider (of individual debtor) Any relative of the debtor or of a general partner of the debtor; partnership in which the debtor is a general partner; general partner of the debtor; or corporation of which the debtor is a director, officer, or person in control.

Interrogatories A form of discovery consisting of written questions to be answered in writing and under oath.

Issue 1. The disputed point between parties in a lawsuit; 2. To send out officially, as in a court issuing an order.

Joint administration A court-approved mechanism under which two or more cases can be administered together. (Assuming no conflicts of interest, these separate businesses or individuals can pool their resources, hire the same professionals, etc.)

Joint petition One bankruptcy petition filed by a husband and wife together.

Judge An official of the Judicial branch with authority to decide lawsuits brought before courts. Used generically, the term judge may also refer to all judicial officers, including Supreme Court justices.

Judgeship The position of judge. By statute, Congress authorizes the number of judgeships for each district and appellate court.

Judgment The official decision of a court finally resolving the dispute between the parties to the lawsuit.

Judicial Conference of the United States The policy-making entity for the federal court system. A 27-judge body whose presiding officer is the Chief Justice of the United States.

Jurisdiction The legal authority of a court to hear and decide a certain type of case. It also is used as a synonym for venue, meaning the geographic area over which the court has territorial jurisdiction to decide cases.

Jurisprudence The study of law and the structure of the legal system

Jury The group of persons selected to hear the evidence in a trial and render a verdict on matters of fact. See also grand jury.

Jury instructions A judge's directions to the jury before it begins deliberations regarding the factual questions it must answer and the legal rules that it must apply.

Lawsuit A legal action started by a plaintiff against a defendant based on a complaint that the defendant failed to perform a legal duty which resulted in harm to the plaintiff.

Lien A charge on specific property that is designed to secure payment of a debt or performance of an obligation. A debtor may still be responsible for a lien after a discharge.

Liquidated claim A creditor's claim for a fixed amount of money.

Liquidation The sale of a debtor's property with the proceeds to be used for the benefit of creditors.

Litigation A case, controversy, or lawsuit. Participants (plaintiffs and defendants) in lawsuits are called litigants.

Magistrate judge A judicial officer of a district court who conducts initial proceedings in criminal cases, decides criminal misdemeanor cases, conducts many pretrial civil and criminal matters on behalf of district judges, and decides civil cases with the consent of the parties.

Means test Section 707(b)(2) of the Bankruptcy Code applies a "means test" to determine whether an individual debtor's Chapter 7 filing is presumed to be an abuse of the Bankruptcy Code requiring dismissal or conversion of the case (generally to Chapter 13). Abuse is presumed if the debtor's aggregate current monthly income (see definition above) over 5 years, net of certain statutorily allowed expenses is more than (i) $10,000, or (ii) 25% of the debtor's nonpriority unsecured debt, as long as that amount is at least $6,000. The debtor may rebut a presumption of abuse only by a showing of special circumstances that justify additional expenses or adjustments of current monthly income.

Mental health treatment Special condition the court imposes to require an individual to undergo evaluation and treatment for a mental disorder. Treatment may include psychiatric, psychological, and sex offense-specific evaluations, inpatient or outpatient counseling, and medication.

Misdemeanor An offense punishable by one year of imprisonment or less. See also felony.

Mistrial An invalid trial, caused by fundamental error. When a mistrial is declared, the trial must start again with the selection of a new jury.

Moot Not subject to a court ruling because the controversy has not actually arisen, or has ended

Motion A request by a litigant to a judge for a decision on an issue relating to the case.

Motion in Limine A pretrial motion requesting the court to prohibit the other side from presenting, or even referring to, evidence on matters said to be so highly prejudicial that no steps taken by the judge can prevent the jury from being unduly influenced.

Motion to lift the automatic stay A request by a creditor to allow the creditor to take action against the debtor or the debtor's property that would otherwise be prohibited by the automatic stay.

No-asset case A Chapter 7 case in which there are no assets available to satisfy any portion of the creditors' unsecured claims.

Nolo contendere No contest. A plea of nolo contendere has the same effect as a plea of guilty, as far as the criminal sentence is concerned, but may not be considered as an admission of guilt for any other purpose.

Nondischargeable debt A debt that cannot be eliminated in bankruptcy. Examples include a home mortgage, debts for alimony or child support, certain taxes, debts for most government funded or guaranteed educational loans or benefit overpayments, debts arising from death or personal injury caused by driving while intoxicated or under the influence of drugs, and debts for restitution or a criminal fine included in a sentence on the debtor's conviction of a crime. Some debts, such as debts for money or property obtained by false pretenses and debts for fraud or defalcation while acting in a fiduciary capacity may be declared nondischargeable only if a creditor timely files and prevails in a nondischargeability action.

Nonexempt assets Property of a debtor that can be liquidated to satisfy claims of creditors.

Objection to dischargeability A trustee's or creditor's objection to the debtor being released from personal liability for certain dischargeable debts. Common reasons include allegations that the debt to be discharged was incurred by false pretenses or that debt arose because of the debtor's fraud while acting as a fiduciary.

Objection to exemptions A trustee's or creditor's objection to the debtor's attempt to claim certain property as exempt from liquidation by the trustee to creditors.

Opinion A judge's written explanation of the decision of the court. Because a case may be heard by three or more judges in the court of appeals, the opinion in appellate decisions can take several forms. If all the judges completely agree on the result, one judge will write the opinion for all. If all the judges do not agree, the formal decision will be based upon the view of the majority, and one member of the majority will write the opinion. The judges who did not agree with the majority may write separately in dissenting or concurring opinions to present their views. A dissenting opinion disagrees with the majority opinion because of the reasoning and/or the principles of law the majority used to decide the case. A concurring opinion agrees with the decision of the majority opinion, but offers further comment or clarification or even an entirely different reason for reaching the same result. Only the majority opinion can serve as binding precedent in future cases. See also precedent.

Oral argument An opportunity for lawyers to summarize their position before the court and also to answer the judges' questions.

Panel 1. In appellate cases, a group of judges (usually three) assigned to decide the case; 2. In the jury selection process, the group of potential jurors; 3. The list of attorneys who are both available and qualified to serve as court-appointed counsel for criminal defendants who cannot afford their own counsel.

Parole The release of a prison inmate—granted by the U.S. Parole Commission—after the inmate has completed part of his or her sentence in a federal prison. When the parolee is released to the community, he or she is placed under the supervision of a U.S. probation officer.

The Sentencing Reform Act of 1984 abolished parole in favor of a determinate sentencing system in which the sentence is set by sentencing guidelines. Now, without the option of parole, the term of imprisonment the court imposes is the actual time the person spends in prison.

Party in interest A party who has standing to be heard by the court in a matter to be decided in the bankruptcy case. The debtor, U.S. trustee or bankruptcy administrator, case trustee, and creditors are parties in interest for most matters.

Per curiam Latin, meaning "for the court." In appellate courts, often refers to an unsigned opinion.

Peremptory challenge A district court may grant each side in a civil or criminal trial the right to exclude a certain number of prospective jurors without cause or giving a reason.

Petit jury (or trial jury) A group of citizens who hear the evidence presented by both sides at trial and determine the facts in dispute. Federal criminal juries consist of 12 persons. Federal civil juries consist of at least six persons.

Petition The document that initiates the filing of a bankruptcy proceeding, setting forth basic information regarding the debtor, including name, address, chapter under which the case is filed, and estimated amount of assets and liabilities.

Petition preparer A business not authorized to practice law that prepares bankruptcy petitions.

Petty offense A federal misdemeanor punishable by six months or less in prison.

Plaintiff A person or business that files a formal complaint with the court.

Plan A debtor's detailed description of how the debtor proposes to pay creditors' claims over a fixed period of time.

Plea In a criminal case, the defendant's statement pleading "guilty" or "not guilty" in answer to the charges. See also nolo contendere.

Pleadings Written statements filed with the court that describe a party's legal or factual assertions about the case.

Postpetition transfer A transfer of the debtor's property made after the commencement of the case.

Prebankruptcy planning The arrangement (or rearrangement) of a debtor's property to allow the debtor to take maximum advantage of exemptions. (Prebankruptcy planning typically includes converting nonexempt assets into exempt assets.)

Precedent A court decision in an earlier case with facts and legal issues similar to a dispute currently before a court. Judges will generally "follow precedent"—meaning that they use the principles established in earlier cases to decide new cases that have similar facts and raise similar legal issues. A judge will disregard precedent if a party can show that the earlier case was wrongly decided, or that it differed in some significant way from the current case.

Preferential debt payment A debt payment made to a creditor in the 90-day period before a debtor files bankruptcy (or within one year if the creditor was an insider) that gives the creditor more than the creditor would receive in the debtor's Chapter 7 case.

Presentence report A report prepared by a court's probation officer, after a person has been convicted of an offense, summarizing for the court the background information needed to determine the appropriate sentence.

Pretrial conference A meeting of the judge and lawyers to plan the trial, to discuss which matters should be presented to the jury, to review proposed evidence and witnesses, and to set a trial schedule. Typically, the judge and the parties also discuss the possibility of settlement of the case.

Pretrial services A function of the federal courts that takes place at the very start of the criminal justice process—after a person has been arrested and charged with a federal crime and before he or she goes to trial. Pretrial services officers focus on investigating the backgrounds of these persons to help the court determine whether to release or detain them while they await trial. The decision is based on whether these individuals are likely to flee or pose a threat to the community. If the court orders release, a pretrial services officer supervises the person in the community until he or she returns to court.

Priority The Bankruptcy Code's statutory ranking of unsecured claims that determines the order in which unsecured claims will be paid if there is not enough money to pay all unsecured claims in full.

Priority claim An unsecured claim that is entitled to be paid ahead of other unsecured claims that are not entitled to priority status. Priority refers to the order in which these unsecured claims are to be paid.

Pro per A slang expression sometimes used to refer to a pro se litigant. It is a corruption of the Latin phrase "in propria persona."

Pro se Representing oneself. Serving as one's own lawyer.

Pro tem Temporary.

Probation Sentencing option in the federal courts. With probation, instead of sending an individual to prison, the court releases the person to the community and orders him or her to complete a period of supervision monitored by a U.S. probation officer and to abide by certain conditions.

Probation officer Officers of the probation office of a court. Probation officer duties include conducting presentence investigations, preparing presentence reports on convicted defendants, and supervising released defendants.

Procedure The rules for conducting a lawsuit; there are rules of civil procedure, criminal procedure, evidence, bankruptcy, and appellate procedure.

Proof of claim A written statement describing the reason a debtor owes a creditor money, which typically sets forth the amount of money owed. (There is an official form for this purpose.)

Property of the estate All legal or equitable interests of the debtor in property as of the commencement of the case.

Prosecute To charge someone with a crime. A prosecutor tries a criminal case on behalf of the government

Reaffirmation agreement An agreement by a debtor to continue paying a dischargeable debt after the bankruptcy, usually for the purpose of keeping collateral or mortgaged property that would otherwise be subject to repossession.

Record A written account of the proceedings in a case, including all pleadings, evidence, and exhibits submitted in the course of the case.

Redemption A procedure in a Chapter 7 case whereby a debtor removes a secured creditor's lien on collateral by paying the creditor the value of the property. The debtor may then retain the property.

Remand Send back.

Reverse The act of a court setting aside the decision of a lower court. A reversal is often accompanied by a remand to the lower court for further proceedings.

Sanction A penalty or other type of enforcement used to bring about compliance with the law or with rules and regulations.

Schedules Lists submitted by the debtor along with the petition (or shortly thereafter) showing the debtor's assets, liabilities, and other financial information. (There are official forms a debtor must use.)

Secured creditor A secured creditor is an individual or business that holds a claim against the debtor that is secured by a lien on property of the estate. The property subject to the lien is the secured creditor's collateral.

Secured debt Debt backed by a mortgage, pledge of collateral, or other lien; debt for which the creditor has the right to pursue specific pledged property upon default. Examples include home mortgages, auto loans and tax liens.

Senior judge A federal judge who, after attaining the requisite age and length of judicial experience, takes senior status, thus creating a vacancy among a court's active judges. A senior judge retains the judicial office and may cut back his or her workload by as much as 75 percent, but many opt to keep a larger caseload.

Sentence The punishment ordered by a court for a defendant convicted of a crime.

Sentencing guidelines A set of rules and principles established by the United States Sentencing Commission that trial judges use to determine the sentence for a convicted defendant.

Sequester To separate. Sometimes juries are sequestered from outside influences during their deliberations.

Service of process The delivery of writs or summonses to the appropriate party.

Settlement Parties to a lawsuit resolve their dispute without having a trial. Settlements often involve the payment of compensation by one party in at least partial satisfaction of the other party's claims, but usually do not include the admission of fault.

Small business case A special type of Chapter 11 case in which there is no creditors' committee (or the creditors' committee is deemed inactive by the court) and in which the debtor is subject to more oversight by the U.S. trustee than other Chapter 11 debtors. The Bankruptcy Code contains certain provisions designed to reduce the time a small business debtor is in bankruptcy.

Standard of proof Degree of proof required. In criminal cases, prosecutors must prove a defendant's guilt "beyond a reasonable doubt." The majority of civil lawsuits require proof "by a preponderance of the evidence" (50 percent plus), but in some the standard is higher and requires "clear and convincing" proof.

Statement of financial affairs A series of questions the debtor must answer in writing concerning sources of income, transfers of property, lawsuits by creditors, etc. (There is an official form a debtor must use.)

Statement of intention   A declaration made by a Chapter 7 debtor concerning plans for dealing with consumer debts that are secured by property of the estate.

Statute   A law passed by a legislature.

Statute of limitations   The time within which a lawsuit must be filed or a criminal prosecution begun. The deadline can vary, depending on the type of civil case or the crime charged.

Sua sponte   Latin, meaning "of its own will." Often refers to a court taking an action in a case without being asked to do so by either side.

Subordination   The act or process by which a person's rights or claims are ranked below those of others.

Subpoena   A command, issued under a court's authority, to a witness to appear and give testimony.

Subpoena duces tecum   A command to a witness to appear and produce documents.

Temporary restraining order   Akin to a preliminary injunction, it is a judge's short-term order forbidding certain actions until a full hearing can be conducted. Often referred to as a TRO.

Testimony   Evidence presented orally by witnesses during trials or before grand juries.

Toll   See statute of limitations.

Tort   A civil, not criminal, wrong. A negligent or intentional injury against a person or property, with the exception of breach of contract.

Transcript   A written, word-for-word record of what was said, either in a proceeding such as a trial, or during some other formal conversation, such as a hearing or oral deposition

Transfer   Any mode or means by which a debtor disposes of or parts with his/her property.

Trustee   The representative of the bankruptcy estate who exercises statutory powers, principally for the benefit of the unsecured creditors, under the general supervision of the court and the direct supervision of the U.S. trustee or bankruptcy administrator. The trustee is a private individual or corporation appointed in all Chapter 7, Chapter 12, and Chapter 13 cases and some Chapter 11 cases. The trustee's responsibilities include reviewing the debtor's petition and schedules and bringing actions against creditors or the debtor to recover property of the bankruptcy estate. In Chapter 7, the trustee liquidates property of the estate, and makes distributions to creditors. Trustees in Chapters 12 and 13 have similar duties to a Chapter 7 trustee and the additional responsibilities of overseeing the debtor's plan, receiving payments from debtors, and disbursing plan payments to creditors.

Typing service   A business not authorized to practice law that prepares bankruptcy petitions.

U.S. attorney   A lawyer appointed by the President in each judicial district to prosecute and defend cases for the federal government. The U.S. Attorney employs a staff of Assistant U.S. Attorneys who appear as the government's attorneys in individual cases.

U.S. trustee   An officer of the U.S. Department of Justice responsible for supervising the administration of bankruptcy cases, estates, and trustees; monitoring plans and disclosure statements; monitoring creditors' committees; monitoring fee applications; and performing other statutory duties.

Undersecured claim   A debt secured by property that is worth less than the amount of the debt.

Undue hardship   The most widely used test for evaluating undue hardship in the dischargeability of a student loan includes three conditions: (1) the debtor cannot maintain—based on current income and expenses—a minimal standard of living if forced to repay the loans; (2) there are indications that the state of affairs is likely to persist for a significant portion of the repayment period; and (3) the debtor made good faith efforts to repay the loans.

Unlawful detainer action   A lawsuit brought by a landlord against a tenant to evict the tenant from rental property—usually for nonpayment of rent.

Unliquidated claim   A claim for which a specific value has not been determined.

Unscheduled debt   A debt that should have been listed by the debtor in the schedules filed with the court but was not. (Depending on the circumstances, an unscheduled debt may or may not be discharged.)

Unsecured claim   A claim or debt for which a creditor holds no special assurance of payment, such as a mortgage or lien; a debt for which credit was extended based solely upon the creditor's assessment of the debtor's future ability to pay.

Uphold   The appellate court agrees with the lower court decision and allows it to stand. See affirmed.

Venue   The geographic area in which a court has jurisdiction. A change of venue is a change or transfer of a case from one judicial district to another.

Verdict   The decision of a trial jury or a judge that determines the guilt or innocence of a criminal defendant, or that determines the final outcome of a civil case.

Voir dire   Jury selection process of questioning prospective jurors, to ascertain their qualifications and determine any basis for challenge.

Voluntary transfer   A transfer of a debtor's property with the debtor's consent.

Wage garnishment   A nonbankruptcy legal proceeding whereby a plaintiff or creditor seeks to subject to his or her claim the future wages of a debtor. In other words, the creditor seeks to have part of the debtor's future wages paid to the creditor for a debt owed to the creditor.

Warrant Court authorization, most often for law enforcement officers, to conduct a search or make an arrest.

Witness A person called upon by either side in a lawsuit to give testimony before the court or jury.

Writ A written court order directing a person to take, or refrain from taking, a certain act.

Writ of certiorari An order issued by the U.S. Supreme Court directing the lower court to transmit records for a case which it will hear on appeal.

Labor—Employment Benefits

Absence rate (Current Population Survey) The ratio of workers with absences to total full-time wage and salary employment. Absences are defined as instances when persons who usually work 35 or more hours per week worked less than 35 hours during the reference week for one of the following reasons: own illness, injury, or medical problems; childcare problems; other family or personal obligations; civic or military duty; and maternity or paternity leave.

Accidental death and dismemberment (National Compensation Survey—Benefits) A term used to describe a policy that pays additional benefits to the beneficiary if the cause of death is due to a non-work-related accident. Fractional amounts of the policy will be paid out if the covered employee loses a bodily appendage or sight because of an accident.

All other occupational illnesses Illnesses other than skin diseases or disorders, respiratory conditions, or poisoning. Examples include anthrax, brucellosis, infectious hepatitis, malignant and benign tumors, food poisoning, histoplasmosis, coccidioidomycosis.

Alternative employment arrangements (Current Population Survey) BLS has collected data for workers in four types of alternative employment arrangements: 1) independent contractors, 2) on-call workers, 3) temporary help agency workers, and 4) workers provided by contract firms.

Average hours per day (American Time Use Survey) This term refers to the average number of hours spent in a 24-hour day (between 4 a.m. on the diary day and 4 a.m. on the interview day) doing a specified activity.

Average hours per day, population (American Time Use Survey) The average number of hours per day is computed using all responses from a given population, including respondents who did not do a particular activity on their diary day.

Average hours per day, persons reporting the activity on the diary day (American Time Use Survey) The average number of hours per day is computed using only responses from those who engaged in a particular activity on their diary day.

Base period A point in time used as a reference point for comparison with some later period.

Benefit incidence A measure of the availability of a benefit. The National Compensation Survey (NCS) presents data on the percent of workers with access to, and who participate in, employee benefits. Access is defined as the percent of workers in an occupation who are offered a benefit. For example, an employee may have access to an employer-sponsored fitness center, but may or may not use it. Employees in contributory plans are counted as participating in an insurance plan or a retirement plan if they have paid required contributions and met any applicable service requirements. Employees in noncontributory plans are counted as participating regardless of whether they have fulfilled their service requirements.

Benefits Nonwage compensation provided to employees. The National Compensation Survey groups benefits into five categories: paid leave (vacations, holidays, sick leave); supplementary pay (premium pay for overtime and work on holidays and weekends, shift differentials, nonproduction bonuses); retirement (defined benefit and defined contribution plans); insurance (life insurance, health benefits, short-term disability, and long-term disability insurance) and legally required benefits (Social Security and Medicare, Federal and State unemployment insurance taxes, and workers' compensation).

Blue-collar and service occupations (National Compensation Survey) Includes precision production, craft, and repair occupations; machine operators and inspectors; transportation and moving occupations; handlers, equipment cleaners, helpers, and laborers; and service occupations.

Business sector (Productivity and Costs) The business sector is a subset of the domestic economy and excludes the economic activities of the following: general government, private households, and nonprofit organizations serving individuals. The business sector accounted for about 78 percent of the value of gross domestic product (GDP) in 2000.

Capital services A chain-type index of service flows derived from the stock of physical assets and software. Assets include equipment and software, structures, land, and inventories. Capital services are estimated as a capital-income weighted average of the growth rates of each asset. Capital services differ from capital stocks because short-lived assets such as equipment and software provide more services per unit of stock than long-lived assets such as land.

Civilian noninstitutional population (Current Population Survey) Included are persons 16 years of age and older residing in the 50 States and the District of Columbia who are not inmates of institutions (for example, penal and mental facilities, homes for the aged), and who are not on active duty in the Armed Forces.

Civilian workers (National Compensation Survey) The National Compensation Survey defines Civilian Workers as the sum of all private industry and State and local government workers. Federal Government, military and agricultural workers are excluded.

Cohort (National Longitudinal Surveys) A cohort in the BLS National Longitudinal Surveys (NLS) program is a group of people, defined by year of birth, that make up a particular study. For example, the National Longitudinal Survey of Youth 1979 (NLSY79) cohort consists of people born between January 1, 1957, and December 31, 1964.

Collective bargaining Method whereby representatives of employees (unions) and employers negotiate the conditions of employment, normally resulting in a written contract setting forth the wages, hours, and other conditions to be observed for a stipulated period (e.g., 3 years). The term also applies to union-management dealings during the term of the agreement.

Comparative advantage When one nation's opportunity cost of producing an item is less than another nation's opportunity cost of producing that item. A good or service with which a nation has the largest absolute advantage (or smallest absolute disadvantage) is the item for which they have a comparative advantage.

Compensation (National Compensation Survey) A term used to encompass the entire range of wages and benefits, both current and deferred, that employees receive in return for their work. In the Employment Cost Index (ECI), compensation includes the employer's cost of wages and salaries, plus the employer's cost of providing employee benefits.

Complete income reporters (Consumer Expenditure Survey) The distinction between complete and incomplete income reporters generally is based on whether the respondent provided values for major sources of income, such as wages and salaries, self-employment income, and Social Security income. Even complete income reporters may not have provided a full accounting of all income from all sources. In the current survey, across-the-board zero income reporting was designated as invalid, and the consumer unit was categorized as an incomplete reporter. In all tables, income data are for complete income reporters only.

Computer-assisted telephone interviewing (CATI) A structured system of microdata collection by telephone that speeds up the collection and editing of microdata; it also permits the interviewer to educate the respondents on the importance of timely and accurate data.

Consumer unit (Consumer Expenditure Survey) A consumer unit is defined as either (1) all members of a particular household who are related by blood, marriage, adoption, or other legal arrangements; (2) a person living alone or sharing a household with others or living as a roomer in a private home or lodging house or in permanent living quarters in a hotel or motel, but who is financially independent; or (3) two or more persons living together who pool their income to make joint expenditure decisions. Financial independence is determined by the three major expense categories: housing, food, and other living expenses. To be considered financially independent, a respondent must provide at least two of the three major expense categories.

Contingent workers (Current Population Survey) Workers who do not have an implicit or explicit contract for long-term employment. BLS uses three alternative measures of contingent workers that vary in scope.

Contract escalation Producer Price Index (PPI) data are commonly used in escalating purchase and sales contracts. These contracts typically specify dollar amounts to be paid at some point in the future. It is often desirable to include an escalation clause that accounts for changes in input prices. For example, a long-term contract for bread may be escalated for changes in wheat prices by applying the percent change in the PPI for wheat to the contracted price for bread. Consumer Price Index (CPI) data can also be used in escalation. For example, the CPI may be used to escalate lease payments or child support payments.

Cost-of-living index A cost-of-living index measures differences in the price of goods and services, and allows for substitutions to other items as prices change. A consumer price index measures a price change for a constant market basket of goods and services from one period to the next within the same city (or in the Nation). The CPIs are not true cost-of-living indexes and should not be used for place-to-place comparisons.

Defined benefit pension plan A retirement plan that uses a specific predetermined formula to calculate the amount of an employee's future benefit. The most common type of formula is based on the employee's terminal earnings. Under this formula, benefits are based on a percentage of average earnings during a specified number of years at the end of a worker's career—for example, the highest 5 out of the last 10 years—multiplied by the maximum number of years of credited service under the plan. In recent years, a new type of defined benefit plan, a cash balance plan, has become more prevalent. Under this type of plan, benefits are computed as a percentage of each employee's account balance. Employers specify a contribution—usually based on a percentage of the employee's earnings—and a rate of interest on that contribution that will provide a predetermined amount at retirement, usually in the form of a lump sum. In the private sector, defined benefit plans are typically funded exclusively by employer contributions. In the public sector, defined benefit plans often require employee contributions.

Defined contribution plan A retirement plan in which the amount of the employer's annual contribution is specified. Individual accounts are set up for participants and benefits are based on the amounts credited to these accounts (through employer contributions and, if applicable, employee contributions) plus any investment earnings on the money in the account. Only employer contributions to the account are guaranteed, not the future benefits. In defined contribution plans, future benefits fluctuate on the basis of investment earnings. The most common type of defined contribution plan is a savings and thrift plan. Under this type of plan, the employee contributes a predetermined portion of his or her earnings (usually pretax) to an individual account, all or part of which is matched by the employer.

Deflator A value that allows data to be measured over time in terms of some base period; or, in more obscure terms, an implicit or explicit price index used to distinguish between those changes in the money value of gross national product which result from a change in prices and those which result from a change in physical output. The import and export price indexes produced by the International Price Program are used as deflators in the U.S. national accounts. For example, the Gross Domestic Product (GDP) equals consumption expenditures plus net investment plus government expenditures plus exports minus imports. Various price indexes are used to "deflate" each component of the GDP in order to make the GDP figures comparable over time. Import price indexes are used to deflate the import component (i.e., import volume is divided by the Import Price index) and the export price indexes are used to deflate the export component (i.e., export volume is divided by the Export Price index).

Demand for additional workers (Employment Projections) Job openings resulting from employment growth and the need to replace workers who leave an occupation.

Designated person (American Time Use Survey) One individual age 15 or older who is randomly selected from each sampled household to participate in the American Time Use Survey. The designated person is interviewed by telephone once about only his or her activities on the day before the interview. No other household member may respond for the designated person.

Diary day (American Time Use Survey) The diary day is the day about which the designated person reports his or her activities for the American Time Use Survey. For example, the diary day of a designated person interviewed on Tuesday is Monday.

Disability insurance Includes paid sick leave, short-term disability benefits, and long-term disability benefits.

Discharge (Job Openings and Labor Turnover Survey) A separation of an employee from an establishment that is initiated by the employer; an involuntary separation

Discouraged workers (Current Population Survey) Persons not in the labor force who want and are available for a job and who have looked for work sometime in the past 12 months (or since the end of their last job if they held one within the past 12 months), but who are not currently looking because they believe there are no jobs available or there are none for which they would qualify.

Displaced workers (Current Population Survey) Persons 20 years and over who lost or left jobs because their plant or company closed or moved, there was insufficient work for them to do, or their position or shift was abolished.

Division, geographic or census One of nine geographic areas of the United States defined by the Census Bureau and widely used by BLS for presenting regional data.

Duration of unemployment (Current Population Survey) The length of time in weeks (through the current reference week) that persons classified as unemployed had been looking for work. For persons on layoff who are counted as unemployed, duration of unemployment represents the number of full weeks they had been on layoff. The data do not represent completed spells of unemployment.

Earnings Remuneration (pay, wages) of a worker or group of workers for services performed during a specific period of time. The term usually carries a defining word or phrase, such as straight-time average hourly earnings. Because a statistical concept is usually involved in the term and its variations, the producers and users of earnings data should define them clearly. In the absence of such definitions, the following may serve as rough guidelines:

- Hourly, daily, weekly, annual: period of time to which earnings figures, as stated or computed, relate. The context in which annual earnings (sometimes weekly earnings) are used may indicate whether the reference includes earnings from one employer only or from all employment plus other sources of income.
- Average: usually refers to the arithmetic mean; that is, total earnings (as defined) of a group of workers (as identified) divided by the number of workers in the group.
- Gross: usually refers to total earnings, before any deductions (such as tax withholding) including, where applicable, overtime payments, shift differentials, production bonuses, cost-of-living allowances, commissions, etc.
- Straight-time: usually refers to gross earnings excluding overtime payments and (with variations at this point) shift differentials and other monetary payments.

Educational attainment cluster (Employment Projections) Six clusters are defined based on the distribution of educational attainment across occupations. The clusters are as follows: high school occupations, high school/some college occupations, some college occupations, high school/some college/college occupations, some college/college occupations, and college occupations.

Educational attainment The highest diploma or degree, or level of work towards a diploma or degree, an individual has completed.

Employed persons (American Time Use Survey) Same as definition for Employed persons (Current Population Survey), EXCEPT that in the American Time Use Survey, the definition includes persons 15 years and over and the reference period is the last 7 days prior to the American Time Use Survey interview.

Employed persons (Current Population Survey) Persons 16 years and over in the civilian noninstitutional population who, during the reference week, (a) did any work at all (at least 1 hour) as paid employees; worked in their own business, profession, or on their own farm, or worked 15 hours or more as unpaid workers in an enterprise operated by a member of the family; and (b) all those who were not working but who had jobs or businesses from which they were temporarily absent because of vacation, illness, bad weather, childcare problems, maternity or paternity leave, labor-management dispute, job training, or other family or personal reasons, whether or not they were paid for the time off or were seeking other jobs. Each employed person is counted only once, even if he or she holds more than one job. Excluded are persons whose only activity consisted of work around their own house (painting, repairing, or own home housework) or volunteer work for religious, charitable, and other organizations.

Employer (Quarterly Census of Employment and Wages) A person or business employing one or more persons for wages or salary; the legal entity responsible for payment of quarterly unemployment insurance taxes or for reimbursing the State fund for unemployment insurance benefits costs in lieu of paying the quarterly taxes.

Employer costs for employee compensation (National Compensation Survey) The Employer Costs for Employee Compensation (ECEC) series shows employer costs per hour worked for wages and salaries and individual benefits. Cost data are presented in both dollar amounts and as percentages of compensation.

Employment Cost Index (National Compensation Survey) The Employment Cost Index (ECI) is a measure of the change in the cost of labor, free from the influence of employment shifts among occupations and industries. The series measures changes in compensation costs (wages and salaries and employer costs for employee benefits).

Employment-population ratio (Current Population Survey) The proportion of the civilian noninstitutional population aged 16 years and over that is employed.

Establishment The physical location of a certain economic activity—for example, a factory, mine, store, or office. A single establishment generally produces a single good or provides a single service. An enterprise (a private firm, government, or nonprofit organization) can consist of a single establishment or multiple establishments. All establishments in an enterprise may be classified in one industry (e.g., a chain), or they may be classified in different industries (e.g., a conglomerate).

Event or exposure (Safety and Health Statistics) Signifies the manner in which an occupational injury or illness was produced or inflicted—for example, overexertion while lifting, or a fall from a ladder.

Expenditure shares (Consumer Expenditure Survey) Expenditure shares are the portions of total expenditures (as percentages) allotted to each expenditure category. Tables organized by various demographic characteristics are available.

Expenditures (Consumer Expenditure Survey) Expenditures consist of the transaction costs, including excise and sales taxes, of goods and services acquired during the interview or recordkeeping period. Expenditure estimates include expenditures for gifts, but exclude purchases or portions of purchases directly assignable to business purposes. Also excluded are periodic credit or installment payments on goods or services already acquired. The full cost of each purchase is recorded even though full payment may not have been made at the date of purchase. Expenditure categories include food, alcoholic beverages, housing, apparel and services, transportation, health care, entertainment, personal care products and services, reading, education, tobacco products and smoking supplies, cash contributions, personal insurance and pensions, and miscellaneous).

Export A domestic good or service that is sold to a foreign resident from a U.S. resident. Exports include government and nongovernment goods and services; however they exclude goods and services sold to the U.S. military and diplomatic and consular institutions abroad. Exports do include goods and services that were previously imported.

Extended mass layoff Layoff of at least 31 days in duration and involving 50 or more individuals from a single establishment filing initial claims for unemployment insurance during a consecutive 5-week period.

Fatality rate (Safety and Health Statistics) Represents the number of fatal injuries per 100,000 workers, calculated as follows: (N/W) × 100,000, where N = number of fatal injuries, W = number of workers employed, and 100,000 = base to express the fatality rate per 100,000 workers.

Federal Information Processing Standards (FIPS) Standards for information processing issued by the National Institute of Standards and Technology of the U.S. Department of Commerce; includes a numeric designation for geographic areas such as States, counties, and metropolitan areas.

Flexible benefits A type of plan under Section 125 of the Internal Revenue Code that provides employees a choice between permissible taxable benefits, including cash, and nontaxable benefits such as life and health insurance, vacations, retirement plans, and child care. Although a common core of benefits may be required, the employee can determine how his or her remaining benefit dollars are to be allocated for each type of benefit from the total amount promised by the employer.

Full-time employees (National Compensation Survey) Employees are classified as full time or part time as defined by their employer.

Full-time workers (Current Population Survey and American Time Use Survey) Persons who work 35 hours or more per week.

Goods-producing industries (Standard Industrial Classification) Includes manufacturing, mining, and construction.

Goods-producing industries (North American Industry Classification System) Includes manufacturing, construction, and natural resources and mining.

Health insurance plan Insurance plans that include coverage for one or more of the following: medical care, dental care, and vision care.

Hire (Job Openings and Labor Turnover Survey) Any addition to an establishment's payroll, including newly hired and rehired employees.

Hires rate (Job Openings and Labor Turnover Survey) The number of hires during the month divided by the number of employees who worked during or received pay for the pay period that includes the 12th of the month.

Hispanic or Latino ethnicity Refers to persons who identified themselves in the enumeration process as being Spanish, Hispanic, or Latino. Persons of Hispanic or Latino ethnicity may be of any race.

Hourly compensation (Productivity and Costs) Compensation costs are defined as the sum of wage and salary accruals and supplements to wages and salaries. Wage and salary accruals consist of the monetary remuneration of employees, including the compensation of corporate officers; commissions, tips, and bonuses; voluntary employee contributions to certain deferred compensation plans, such as 401(k) plans; employee gains from exercising nonqualified stock options; and receipts in kind that represent income. Supplements to wages and salaries consist of employer contributions for social insurance and employer payments (including payments in kind) to private pension and profit-sharing plans, group health and life insurance plans, privately administered workers' compensation plans. For employees (wage and salary workers), hourly compensation is measured relative to hours at work and includes payments made by employers for time not at work, such as vacation, holiday, and sick pay. Because compensation costs for the business and nonfarm business sectors would otherwise be severely understated, an estimate of the hourly compensation of proprietors of unincorporated businesses is made by assuming that their hourly compensation is equal to that of employees in the same sector.

Hourly compensation costs (International Labor Comparisons) Hourly compensation costs, as measured in the BLS international comparison series, are defined as (1) all payments made directly to workers—pay for time worked (basic time and piece rates plus overtime premiums, shift differentials, other premiums and bonuses paid regularly each pay period, and cost-of-living adjustments), pay for time not worked (such as for vacations and holidays), seasonal or irregular bonuses and other special payments, selected social allowances, and the cost of payments in kind—before payroll deductions of any kind, and (2) employer expenditures for legally required insurance programs and contractual and private benefit plans (such as retirement plans, health insurance, unemployment insurance, and family allowances). In addition, for some countries, compensation is adjusted for other taxes on payrolls or employment (or reduced to reflect subsidies), even if they do not finance programs that directly benefit workers, because such taxes are regarded as labor costs. The BLS definition of hourly compensation costs used in its international comparisons series is based on the International Labour Office standard definition of total labor costs. However, it does not include all items of total labor costs; the items excluded are the costs of recruitment, employee training, and plant facilities and services, such as cafeterias and medical clinics. Hourly compensation costs include all the items of compensation covered in the BLS series Employer Costs for Employee Compensation, the Employment Cost Index, and the index of hourly compensation (published with the index of labor productivity); hourly compensation costs also include the costs of payments in kind and other taxes and subsidies, which may not be included in the other BLS compensation series. The classification of the compensation items and the terminology used in the definitions differ among the series.

Hours at work (Productivity and Costs) For productivity measurement, the proper measure of hours is "hours at work," which include paid time working, traveling between job sites, coffee breaks, and machine downtime. Hours at work, however, exclude hours for which employees are paid but not at work (examples: vacation time, holidays, and paid sick leave).

Hours worked (Current Population Survey) There are two different hours concepts measured in the CPS: usual hours and actual hours at work. Usual hours refer to a person's normal work schedule versus their actual hours at work during the survey reference week. For example, a person who normally works 40 hours per week, but was off for a 1-day holiday during the reference week, would report his or her usual hours as 40 but actual hours at work for the reference week as 32.

Import A good or service that is sold to a U.S. resident from a foreign resident. Imports include government and nongovernment goods and services; however they exclude goods and services to the U.S. military, diplomatic, and consular institutions abroad. Imports do include goods and services that were previously exported.

Incidence rate (Safety and Health Statistics) Represents the number of injuries and/or illnesses per 100 full-time workers, calculated as follows: (N/EH) × 200,000, where: N = number of injuries and/or illnesses, EH = total hours worked by all employees during the calendar year, and 200,000 = base for 100 full-time equivalent workers (working 40 hours per week, 50 weeks per year).

Income before taxes (Consumer Expenditure Survey) Income before taxes is the total money earnings and selected money receipts of all consumer unit members aged 14 years or older during the 12 months prior to the interview date. It includes the following components: wages and salaries; self-employment income; Social Security, private and government retirement; interest, dividends, rental income, and other property income; unemployment, workers' compensation and veteran's benefits; public assistance, supplemental security income, and food stamps; regular contributions for support (including alimony and child support); other income (including cash scholarships, fellowships or stipends not based on working, and meals and rent as pay).

Industry A group of establishments that produce similar products or provide similar services. For example, all establishments that manufacture automobiles are in the same industry. A given industry, or even a particular establishment in that industry, might have employees in dozens of occupations. The North American Industry Classification System (NAICS) groups similar establishments into industries. NAICS is replacing the former Standard Industrial Classification (SIC) system.

Inflation Inflation has been defined as a process of continuously rising prices, or equivalently, of a

Initial claimant A person who files any notice of unemployment to initiate a request either for a determination of entitlement to and eligibility for compensation, or for a subsequent period of unemployment within a benefit year or period of eligibility.

Item specification The description of a good or service that includes all price-determining characteristics and any other information necessary to distinguish the item from all others.

Job leavers (Current Population Survey) Unemployed persons who quit or otherwise terminated their employment voluntarily and immediately began looking for work.

Job losers (Current Population Survey) Unemployed persons who involuntarily lost their last job or who had completed a temporary job. This includes persons who were on temporary layoff expecting to return to work, as well as persons not on temporary layoff. Those not on temporary layoff include permanent job losers and persons whose temporary jobs had ended.

Job opening (Job Openings and Labor Turnover Survey) A specific position of employment to be filled at an establishment; conditions include the following: there is work available for that position, the job could start within 30 days, and the employer is actively recruiting for the position.

Job openings rate (Job Openings and Labor Turnover Survey) The number of job openings on the last business day of the month divided by the sum of the number of employees who worked during or received pay for the pay period that includes the 12th of the month and the number of job openings on the last business day of the month.

Job tenure (Current Population Survey) The length of time an employee has worked for his or her current employer. The data do not represent completed spells of tenure.

Labor dispute See Labor Management Dispute.

Labor force (Current Population Survey) The labor force includes all persons classified as employed or unemployed in accordance with the definitions contained in this glossary.

Labor force participation rate The labor force as a percent of the civilian noninstitutional population.

Labor management dispute A conflict between employees, typically represented by a union, and management or the employer. This general term covers all types of conflicts from a grievance to a strike or a lockout. Labor management disputes are more common during collective bargaining or union contract negotiations.

Labor productivity Labor productivity refers to the relationship between output and the labor time used in generating that output. It is the ratio of output per hour.

Laspeyres index Sum(p2q1)/Sum(p1q1): A weighted aggregative index showing the ratio of expenditures in the current period (p2q1, where p2 is the current period price and q1 is the base period quantity) to the expenditure in the base period (p1q1, where p1 is the base period price and q1 is the base period quantity) to purchase the identical market basket of items. It answers the question "How much more or less does it cost now to purchase the same items as in the base period?" The main shortcoming of the Laspeyres index is that it does not track actual expenditures because consumers adjust their buying in response to changes in relative price, which changes the composition of the market basket. This invalid assumption that consumer demand is totally price inelastic causes the index to overstate the actual effect on consumers when there is a change in prices.

Layoff (Job Openings and Labor Turnover Survey) A separation of an employee from an establishment that is initiated by the employer; an involuntary separation; a period of forced unemployment

Layoff and discharges rate (Job Openings and Labor Turnover Survey) The number of layoffs and discharges during the month divided by the number of employees who worked during or received pay for the pay period that includes the 12th of the month.

Legally required benefits (National Compensation Survey) Legally required benefits include the employer's costs for Social Security, Medicare, Federal and State unemployment insurance, and workers' compensation.

Life insurance A contract that pays the beneficiary a set sum of money upon the death of the policyholder. These plans pay benefits usually in the form of a lump sum, but they may be distributed as an annuity.

Locality of origin indexes U.S. import price indexes based on country or region, rather than product type.

Location quotient Ratio that compares the concentration of a resource or activity, such as employment, in a defined area to that of a larger area or base. For example, location quotients can be used to compare State employment by industry to that of the nation.

Lockout A temporary withholding or denial of employment during a labor dispute in order to enforce terms of employment upon a group of employees. A lockout is initiated by the management of an establishment.

Long-term disability insurance (National Compensation Survey—benefits) Provides a monthly benefit to employees who, due to a non-work-related injury or illness, are unable to perform the duties of their normal occupation or any other, for periods of time extending beyond their short-term disability or sickness and accident insurance.

Longitudinal data (National Longitudinal Surveys and Business Employment Dynamics) Data in which the same units are observed over multiple time periods. Another term for longitudinal data is panel data. For example, the BLS National Longitudinal Surveys (NLS) program collects data from several groups of individuals over many years on an annual or biennial basis.

Lost-worktime cases (Safety and Health Statistics) Cases involving days away from work, or days of restricted work activity, or both.

Lost-worktime cases involving days away from work (Safety and Health Statistics) Cases resulting in days away from work, or a combination of days away from work and days of restricted work activity.

Lost-worktime cases involving restricted work activity (Safety and Health Statistics) Cases resulting in restricted work activity only.

Lost-worktime rate (Current Population Survey) Hours absent as a percent of hours usually worked. Absences are defined as instances when persons who usually work 35 or more hours per week worked less than 35 hours during the reference week for one of the following reasons: own illness, injury, or medical problems; childcare problems; other family or personal obligations; civic or military duty; and maternity or paternity leave.

Lump-sum payments (National Compensation Survey) Payments made to employees in lieu of a general wage rate increase. The payment may be a fixed amount as set forth in a labor agreement or an amount determined by a formula—for example, 2.5 percent of an employee's earnings during the prior year. Lump-sum payments are not incorporated into an employee's base pay rate or salary, but are considered as nonproduction bonuses in the Employment Cost Index and Employer Costs for Employee Compensation series.

Marginally attached workers (Current Population Survey) Persons not in the labor force who want and are available for work, and who have looked for a job sometime in the prior 12 months (or since the end of their last job if they held one within the past 12 months), but were not counted as unemployed because they had not searched for work in the 4 weeks preceding the survey. Discouraged workers are a subset of the marginally attached.

Market basket (Consumer Price Index) The market basket is a package of goods and services that consumers purchase for day-to-day living. The weight of each item is based on the amount of expenditure reported by a sample of households.

Mass layoff A situation in which 50 or more persons have filed initial claims for unemployment insurance benefits against an establishment during a consecutive 5-week period.

Mean wage (Occupational Employment Statistics) An average wage; an occupational mean wage estimate is calculated by summing the wages of all the employees in a given occupation and then dividing the total wages by the number of employees.

Median days away from work (Safety and Health Statistics) The measure used to summarize the varying lengths of absences from work among the cases with days away from work. The median is the point at which half of the cases involved more days away from work and half involved less days away from work.

Median wage An occupational median wage estimate is the boundary between the highest paid 50 percent and the lowest paid 50 percent of workers in that occupation. Half of the workers in a given occupation earn more than the median wage, and half the workers earn less than the median wage.

Medical care coverage A type of insurance coverage that provides for the payment of benefits as a result of sickness or injury. Medical care coverage can be provided in a hospital or a doctor's office. There are two main types of medical care plans. An indemnity plan—also called a fee-for-service plan— reimburses the patient or the provider as expenses are incurred. The most common type of indemnity plan is a preferred provider organization (PPO). A PPO provides coverage to the enrollee through a network of selected health care providers (such as hospitals and physicians). Enrollees may go outside the network, but would incur higher costs in the form of higher deductibles and higher coinsurance rates than if they stayed within the network. The second type of medical care plan is called a prepaid plan—also called a health maintenance organization. A prepaid plan assumes both the financial risks associated with providing comprehensive medical services and the responsibility for health care delivery in a particular geographic area, usually in return for a fixed prepaid fee from its members.

Metropolitan statistical areas (MSAs) The general concept of an MSA is one of a large population nucleus, together with adjacent communities which have a high degree of economic and social integration with that nucleus. These are defined by the Office of Management and Budget as a standard for Federal agencies in the preparation and publication of statistics relating to metropolitan areas.

Most significant source of postsecondary education or training (Employment Projections) An occupation is classified into 1 of 11 categories that best describes the postsecondary education or training needed by most workers to become fully qualified in the occupation. The categories are as follows: first professional degree; doctoral degree; master's degree; bachelor's or higher degree, plus work experience; bachelor's degree; associate degree; postsecondary vocational award; work experience in a related occupation; long-term on-the-job training; moderate-term on-the-job training; and short-term on-the-job training.

Multifactor productivity For the *private business and private nonfarm business* sectors, the growth rate of multifactor productivity is measured as the growth rate of output less the growth rate of combined inputs of labor and capital. Labor is measured by a weighted average of the number of hours worked classified by education, work experience, and gender. Capital services measure the flow of services from the stocks of equipment and software, structures, land, and inventories. For the *manufacturing* sector, multifactor productivity is the growth rate of output less the combined inputs of labor, capital, and intermediate purchases. Labor is measured by the number of hours worked. Capital services measure the flow of services from the stocks of equipment and software, structures, land, and inventories. Intermediate purchases are composed of materials, fuels, electricity, and purchased services.

Multiple jobholders (Current Population Survey and American Time Use Survey) Employed persons who, during the reference week, either had two or more jobs as a wage and salary worker, were self-employed and also held a wage and salary job, or worked as an unpaid family worker and also held a wage and salary job. Excluded are self-employed persons with multiple businesses and persons with multiple jobs as unpaid family workers.

Nature of injury or illness Names the principal physical characteristic of a disabling condition, such as sprain/strain, cut/laceration, or carpal tunnel syndrome.

New entrants (Current Population Survey) Unemployed persons who never worked before and who are entering the labor force for the first time.

Nonfarm business sector (Productivity and Costs) The nonfarm business sector is a subset of the domestic economy and excludes the economic activities of the following: general government, private households, nonprofit organizations serving individuals, and farms.

Nonfinancial corporations (Productivity and Costs) The nonfinancial corporate business sector is a subset of the domestic economy and excludes the economic activities of the following: general government, private households, nonprofit organizations serving individuals, and those corporations classified as offices of bank holding companies, offices of other holding companies, or offices in the finance and insurance sector.

Nonlabor payments (Productivity and Costs) These payments include profits, consumption of fixed capital, taxes on production and imports less subsidies, net interest and miscellaneous payments, business current transfer payments, rental income of persons, and the current surplus of government enterprises.

North American Industry Classification System (NAICS) The successor to the Standard Industrial Classification (SIC) system; this system of classifying business establishments is being adopted by the United States, Canada, and Mexico.

Not employed (American Time Use Survey) The term refers to persons who are classified as unemployed as well as those classified as not in the labor force (using Current Population Survey definitions).

Not in the labor force (Current Population Survey) Includes persons aged 16 years and older in the civilian noninstitutional population who are neither employed nor unemployed in accordance with the definitions contained in this glossary. Information is collected on their desire for and availability for work, job search activity in the prior year, and reasons for not currently searching

Not seasonally adjusted This term is used to describe data series that have not been subjected to the seasonal adjustment process. In other words, the effects of regular or seasonal patterns have not been removed from these series.

Occupation A set of activities or tasks that employees are paid to perform. Employees that perform essentially the same tasks are in the same occupation, whether or not they work in the same industry. Some occupations are concentrated in a few particular industries; other occupations are found in many industries.

Occupational groups A group of related occupations; examples: sales occupations and service occupations.

Occupational illness Any abnormal condition or disorder, other than one resulting from an occupational injury, caused by exposure to factors associated with employment. It includes acute and chronic illnesses or diseases which may be caused by inhalation, absorption, ingestion, or direct contact.

Occupational injury Any injury such as a cut, fracture, sprain, amputation, etc., which results from a work-related event or from a single instantaneous exposure in the work environment.

Occupational Injury and Illness Classification System (Safety and Health Statistics) Defines many of the data elements—such as nature, part, event, and source—that are used in the production of safety and health statistics by BLS.

On-call employees Employees who are not permanent, but are called to work as needed, often on short notice, although they can be scheduled to work for several days or weeks in a row.

Other separation (Job Openings and Labor Turnover Survey) A separation of an employee from an establishment for miscellaneous reasons, including retirement, death, separation due to employee disability, or transfer to another location of the enterprise.

Other separations rate (Job Openings and Labor Turnover Survey) The number of other separations during the month divided by the number of employees who worked during or received pay for the pay period that includes the 12th of the month.

Paid leave (National Compensation Survey) Paid leave includes vacations, holidays, sick leave, and other leave with pay.

Panel data (National Longitudinal Surveys and Business Employment Dynamics) See Longitudinal data.

Part of body affected (Safety and Health Statistics) Directly linked to the nature of injury or illness cited, such as back, finger, or eye.

Part-time workers (Current Population Survey and American Time Use Survey) Persons who work less than 35 hours per week.

Pay period that includes the 12th of the month Standard measurement period for all Federal agencies collecting employment data from business establishments; time unit that employers use to pay employees that overlaps the 12th of the month; length of the pay period does not matter, as long as the 12th of the month is included in the pay period: For establishments with a Monday-through-Friday pay period, if the 12th of the month falls on a Saturday, it should be taken as the last day of the requested pay period, and if the 12th of the month falls on a Sunday, it should be taken as the first day of the requested pay period.

Payroll employment (Current Employment Statistics) Employment is the total number of persons on establishment payrolls employed full or part time who received pay for any part of the pay period which includes the 12th day of the month. Temporary and intermittent employees are included, as are any workers who are on paid sick leave, on paid holiday, or who work during only part of the specified pay period. A striking worker who only works a small portion of the survey period, and is paid, would be included as employed under the CES definitions. Persons on the payroll of more than one establishment are counted in each establishment. Data exclude proprietors, self-employed, unpaid family or volunteer workers, farm workers, and domestic workers. Persons on layoff the entire pay period, on leave without pay, on strike for the entire period or who have not yet reported for work are not counted as employed. Government employment covers only civilian workers. With the release of NAICS-based estimates in June 2003, the scope and definition of Federal Government employment estimates changed due to a change in source data and estimation methods. The previous series was an end-of-month federal employee count produced by the Office of Personnel Management, and it excluded some workers, mostly employees who work in Department of Defense-owned establishments such as military base commissaries. Beginning in June 2003, the CES national series began to include these workers. Also, Federal Government employment is now estimated from a sample of Federal establishments, is benchmarked annually to counts from unemployment insurance tax records, and reflects employee counts as of the pay period including the 12th of the month, consistent with other CES industry series. The historical time series for Federal Government employment was revised to reflect these changes.

Percentile wage estimate Shows what percentage of workers in an occupation earn less than a given wage and what percentage earn more. For example, a 25th percentile wage of $15.00 indicates that 25% of workers (in a given occupation in a given area) earn less than $15.00; therefore 75% of workers earn more than $15.00.

Permanent job losers (Current Population Survey) Unemployed persons whose employment ended involuntarily and who began looking for work.

Primary activity (American Time Use Survey) A primary activity is the main activity a respondent was doing at a specified time. Most published time use estimates reflect time spent in primary activities only.

Price index A price index is a tool that simplifies the measurement of price movements in a numerical series. Movements are measured with respect to the base period, when the index is set to 100.

Producer Price Index (PPI) A family of indexes that measure the average change over time in selling prices received by domestic producers of goods and services. PPIs measure price change from the perspective of the seller. This contrasts with other measures that measure price change from the purchaser's perspective, such as the Consumer Price Index (CPI). Sellers' and purchasers' prices may differ due to government subsidies, sales and excise taxes, and distribution costs.

Productivity A measure of economic efficiency that shows how effectively economic inputs are converted into output. Productivity is measured by comparing the amount of goods and services produced with the inputs that were used in production.

Professional employer organization (PEO) A business that supplies management and administrative services with regard to human resource responsibilities for employers; it serves as the co-employer of the client's employees for payroll, benefits, and related purposes. PEOs are referred to as "employee leasing companies" in the Standard Industrial Classification Manual.

Quit (Job Openings and Labor Turnover Survey) A separation of an employee from an establishment that is initiated by the employee; a voluntary separation; a resignation from a job or position.

Quits rate (Job Openings and Labor Turnover Survey) The number of quits during the month divided by the number of employees who worked during or received pay for the pay period that includes the 12th of the month.

Race (Current Population Survey) The CPS provides data by race, with the race given by the household respondent. Since 2003, respondents are allowed to choose more than one race; previously, multiracial persons were required to select a single primary race. Persons who select more than one race are classified separately in the category "two or more races." Persons who select one race only are classified in one of the following five categories: 1) white, 2) black or African American, 3) Asian, 4) Native Hawaiian and other Pacific Islander, and 5) American Indian or Alaska Native. Only data for whites, blacks, and Asians are currently published because the number of survey respondents for the other racial categories is not large enough to produce statistically reliable estimates.

Recordable injuries and illnesses (Safety and Health statistics) Recordable cases include work-related injuries and illnesses that result in one or more of the following: death, loss of consciousness, days away from work, restricted work activity or job transfer, medical treatment (beyond first aid), significant work-related injuries or illnesses that are diagnosed by a physician or other licensed heath care professional (these include any work-related case involving cancer, chronic irreversible disease, a fracture or cracked bone, or a punctured eardrum); additional criteria include any needle-stick injury or cut from a sharp object that is contaminated with another person's blood or other potentially infectious material, any case requiring an employee to be medically removed under the requirements of an OSHA health standard, tuberculosis infection as evidenced by a positive skin test or diagnosis by a physician or other licensed health care professional after exposure to a known case of active tuberculosis.

Reentrants (Current Population Survey) Unemployed persons who previously worked but were out of the labor force prior to beginning their job search.

Reference person (Consumer Expenditure Survey) The first member mentioned by the respondent when asked to "Start with the name of the person or one of the persons who owns or rents the home." It is with respect to this person that the relationship of the other consumer unit members is determined.

Region—Midwest Illinois, Indiana, Iowa, Kansas, Michigan, Minnesota, Missouri, Nebraska, North Dakota, Ohio, South Dakota, and Wisconsin.

Region—Northeast Connecticut, Maine, Massachusetts, New Hampshire, New Jersey, New York, Pennsylvania, Rhode Island, and Vermont.

Region—South Alabama, Arkansas, Delaware, District of Columbia, Florida, Georgia, Kentucky, Louisiana, Maryland, Mississippi, North Carolina, Oklahoma, South Carolina, Tennessee, Texas, Virginia, and West Virginia.

Region—West Alaska, Arizona, California, Colorado, Hawaii, Idaho, Montana, Nevada, New Mexico, Oregon, Utah, Washington, and Wyoming.

Regions Data are presented for four major regions: Northeast, Midwest, South, and West.

Relative importance (Consumer Price Index) BLS publishes what is called a "relative importance" for each commodity and commodity grouping. The relative importance of an item represents its basic value weight, including any imputations, multiplied by the relative of price change from the weight date to the date of the relative importance calculation, expressed as a percentage of the total value weight for the "all commodities" category.

Represented by unions (Current Population Survey) Data refer to union members, as well as workers who reported no union affiliation but whose jobs are covered by a union or an employee association contract.

Respiratory condition due to toxic agents (Safety and Health statistics) Examples: Pneumonitis, pharyngitis, rhinitis or acute congestion due to chemicals, dusts, gases, or fumes; farmer's lung.

Retirement plans (National Compensation Survey) Includes defined benefit pension plans and defined contribution retirement plans.

Sample A subset of a universe; usually selected randomly and considered representative of the universe.

Sample frame A listing of all units in the universe from which a sample can be drawn.

Seasonally adjusted Seasonal adjustment removes the effects of events that follow a more or less regular pattern each year. These adjustments make it easier to observe the cyclical and other nonseasonal movements in a data series.

Self-employed persons (Current Population Survey and American Time Use Survey) Those persons who work for profit or fees in their own business, profession, trade, or farm. Only the unincorporated self-employed are included in the self-employed category.

Secondary or simultaneous activity (American Time Use Survey) A secondary or simultaneous activity is an activity done at the same time as a primary activity. With the exception of the care of children under age 13, information on secondary activities is not systematically collected in the American Time Use Survey.

Separation (Job Openings and Labor Turnover Survey) See Turnover.

Separations rate (Job Openings and Labor Turnover Survey) See Turnover rate.

Series report A form-based application that uses BLS time series identifiers as input in extracting data from each survey-specific database according to a specified set of date ranges and output options.

Service-producing industries (Standard Industrial Classification) Includes transportation; communications; electric, gas, and sanitary services; wholesale trade; retail trade; finance, insurance, and real estate; and services.

Service-providing industries (North American Industry Classification System) Includes trade, transportation, and utilities; information; financial activities; professional and business services; education and health services; leisure and hospitality; other services.

Short-term disability insurance Provides short-term (typically 26 weeks) income protection to employees who are unable to work due to a non-work-related accident or illness.

Shortage (as in shortage of workers) Shortages occur in a market economy when the demand for workers for a particular occupation is greater than the supply of workers who are qualified, available, and willing to do that job.

Slowdown An effort, typically organized by a union, in which employees decrease productivity in order to bring pressure upon management. Generally a slowdown is used as an alternative to a strike and is seen as less disruptive.

Source of injury or illness (Safety and Health statistics) The object, substance, exposure, or bodily motion that directly produced or inflicted the disabling condition cited. Examples include lifting a heavy box; exposure to a toxic substance, fire or flame; and bodily motion of an injured or ill worker.

Stage-of-processing indexes (Producer Price Index) Stage-of-processing (SOP) price indexes regroup commodities at the subproduct class (6-digit) level according to the class of buyer and the amount of physical processing or assembling the products have undergone. The PPI publishes aggregate price indexes organized by commodity-based processing stage. The three stages of processing include Finished Goods; Intermediate Materials, Supplies, and Components; and Crude Materials for Further Processing.

Standard Industrial Classification (SIC) system The SIC system has been used throughout the Federal Government to group establishments into industries. The SIC system is being gradually replaced by the North American Industry Classification System (NAICS). More information on the SIC system can be found in the Standard Industrial Classification Manual, 1987 (Executive Office of the President, Office of Management and Budget), available in many libraries.

Standard Occupational Classification (SOC) system This system is being adopted by Federal statistical agencies to classify workers into occupational categories for the purpose of collecting, calculating, or disseminating data. All workers are classified into 1 of more than 800 occupations according to their occupational definition. To facilitate classification, occupations are combined to form 23 major groups, 96 minor groups, and 449 broad occupations. Each broad occupation includes detailed occupations) requiring similar job duties, skills, education, or experience.

Standard tables (Consumer Expenditure Survey) Standard tables contain annual expenditure data organized by various demographic characteristics. The following standard tables are available: age of reference person, composition of consumer unit, education of reference person, higher income before taxes, Hispanic or Latino origin of reference person, housing tenure and type of area, income before taxes, number of earners in consumer unit, occupation of reference person, population size of area of residence, quintiles of income before taxes, race of reference person, region of residence, size of consumer unit, and selected age of reference person.

Strike A temporary stoppage of work by a group of workers (not necessarily union members) to express a grievance or enforce a demand. A strike is initiated by the workers of an establishment.

Supplemental pay (National Compensation Survey) Supplemental pay includes overtime and premium pay for work in addition to the regular work schedule (such as weekends and holidays), shift differentials, and nonproduction bonuses (such as referral bonuses and lump-sum payments provided in lieu of wage increases).

Supply of workers Often refers to the labor force. The concept focuses on worker characteristics, especially their education and training, but also characteristics such as experience (often considered to be correlated with age), physical strength (often considered to be inversely correlated with age), ability to work in teams, etc. Some demographic characteristics that are not to be considered in hiring and promotion decisions, but that are studied, include gender, race, ethnicity, parental and marital statuses.

Survey reference week (Current Population Survey) The CPS, a survey of households, asks respondents about their labor market activities during a specific week each month. That week, called the survey reference week, is defined as the 7-day period, Sunday through Saturday, which includes the 12th of the month.

Survivor benefits A series of payments to the dependents of deceased employees. Survivor benefits come in two types: First, the "transition" type pays the named beneficiary a monthly amount for a short period (usually 24 months). Transition benefits may then be followed by "bridge benefits," which are a series of payments that last until a specific date, usually the surviving spouse's 62nd birthday.

Temporary help agency Establishment primarily engaged in supplying workers to client businesses for limited periods of time to supplement the work force of the client; the individuals provided are employees of the temporary help service establishment, but these establishments do not provide direct supervision of their employees.

Terms of trade Allocation of inputs into two or more economies that take advantage of differences in comparative advantages and, through specialization, improve the production of the economies. Note that a change in the terms of trade should cause all domestic production to change (that is, reallocates all inputs), rather than just imports.

Time off benefit Provides paid or unpaid leave for specific uses, such as lunch periods, holidays and vacations, and maternity and paternity leave.

Time/Index series A way of expressing, in percentage terms, the change in some variable from a given point in time to another point in time. For example, suppose output increased by 10 percent from an initial year (1987) to a subsequent year (1988). The index for the base year of 1987 in this example would be 100.0, while the index for 1988 would be 110.0. Conversely, if output had declined in 1988 by 10 percent, the 1988 index value would be 90.0.

Touchtone Data Entry (TDE) An automated method of collecting data in which respondents call a toll-free number and enter their data using a touchtone telephone.

Transaction price The market sale price of a good or input shows what has to be given in exchange to obtain a good or service. It is usually denoted in money terms, although payment need not be in a monetary form. The relative price is expressed in terms of the quantity of some other good which has to be given in exchange for the original good. Thus, if all prices increase at the same rate, absolute prices will rise but relative prices will remain unchanged.

Turnover (Job Openings and Labor Turnover Survey) Separation of an employee from an establishment (voluntary, involuntary, or other).

Turnover rate (Job Openings and Labor Turnover Survey) The number of total separations during the month divided by the number of employees who worked during or received pay for the pay period that includes the 12th of the month (monthly turnover); the number of total separations for the year divided by average monthly employment for the year (annual turnover).

Unemployed persons (Current Population Survey) Persons aged 16 years and older who had no employment during the reference week, were available for work, except for temporary illness, and had made specific efforts to find employment sometime during the 4-week period ending with the reference week. Persons who were waiting to be recalled to a job from which they had been laid off need not have been looking for work to be classified as unemployed.

Unemployment rate The unemployment rate represents the number unemployed as a percent of the labor force.

Union membership data Refers to wage and salary workers who report that they are members of a labor union or an employee association similar to a union.

Unit labor costs (Productivity and Costs) Unit labor costs show the growth in compensation relative to that of real output. These costs are calculated by dividing total labor compensation by real output. Changes in unit labor costs can be approximated by subtracting the change in productivity from the change in hourly compensation.

Unit value indexes Unit value indexes are calculated by dividing the total value of goods in a commodity area by the total quantity of goods in that commodity area.

Universe The total number of units (for example, individuals, households, or businesses) in the population of interest.

Unpaid family workers (Current Population Survey and American Time Use Survey) Persons who work without pay for 15 or more hours per week on a farm or in a business operated by a member of the household to whom they are related by birth or marriage.

Usual hours (Current Population Survey) Respondents are asked the number of hours per week they usually work. This provides a measure of the usual full-time or part-time status of employed persons. All employed persons, both those who were at work and those who were absent from work, are asked about the number of hours they usually work.

Usual weekly earnings (Current Population Survey) Wage and salary earnings before taxes and other deductions; includes any overtime pay, commissions, or tips usually received (at the main job, in the case of multiple jobholders). Earnings reported on a basis other than weekly (for example, annual, monthly, hourly) are converted to weekly. The term "usual" is as perceived by the respondent. If the respondent asks for a definition of usual, interviewers are instructed to define the term as more than half the weeks worked during the past 4 or 5 months. Data refer to wage and salary workers only, excluding all self-employed persons (regardless of whether their businesses were incorporated) and all unpaid family workers.

Vacancy (Job Openings and Labor Turnover Survey) See Job opening.

Vacancy rate (Job Openings and Labor Turnover Survey) See Job openings rate.

Wage and salary workers Workers who receive wages, salaries, commissions, tips, payment in kind, or piece rates. The group includes employees in both the private and public sectors.

Wages and salaries Hourly straight-time wage rate or, for workers not paid on an hourly basis, straight-time earnings divided by the corresponding hours. Straight-time wage and salary rates are total earnings before payroll deductions, excluding premium pay for overtime and for work on weekends and holidays, shift differentials, and nonproduction bonuses such as lump-sum payments provided in lieu of wage increases.

Weekly hours The expected or actual period of employment for the week, usually expressed in number of hours. Some uses of the term may relate to the outside dimensions of a week (for example, 7 consecutive days).

Wholesale Price Index (WPI) The Wholesale Price Index (WPI) was the original name of the Producer Price Index (PPI) program from its inception in 1902 until 1978, when it was renamed (PPI). At the same time, emphasis was shifted from one index encompassing the whole economy, to three main indexes covering the stages of production in the economy. By changing emphasis, BLS greatly reduced the double-counting phenomenon inherent in aggregate commodity-based indexes.

Work levels (National Compensation Survey) The National Compensation Survey produces earnings data by levels of work within an occupation. The duties and responsibilities of a job are evaluated using four factors (such as knowledge, and complexity of the work) to determine a work level. Levels vary by occupation, ranging from 1 to 15. For example, level 1 may represent an entry level, while level 15 may represent master-level skills.

Work relationship (Safety and Health Statistics) An employee must have had a verifiable work relationship with his or her employer to be included in the Census of Fatal Occupational Injuries. A work relationship exists if an event or exposure results in fatal injury or illness to a person under the following conditions: (1) ON the employer's premises and the person was there to work; or (2) OFF the employer's premises and the person was there to work, or the event or exposure was related to the person's work status as an employee. The employer's premises include buildings, grounds, parking lots, and other facilities and property used in the conduct of business. Work is defined as legal duties, activities, or tasks that produce a product as a result and that are done in exchange for money, goods, services, profit, or benefit.

Work stoppage A strike or a lockout.

Worklife estimates Estimates of the number of years individuals would spend in the labor force based on mortality conditions, labor force entry and exit rates, and demographic characteristics. BLS has not produced work life estimates since February 1986.

Labor Statistics

Absence rate (Current Population Survey) The ratio of workers with absences to total full-time wage and salary employment. Absences are defined as instances when persons who usually work 35 or more hours per week worked less than 35 hours during the reference week for one of the following reasons: own illness, injury, or medical problems; childcare problems; other family or personal obligations; civic or military duty; and maternity or paternity leave.

Accidental death and dismemberment (National Compensation Survey—Benefits) A term used to describe a policy that pays additional benefits to the beneficiary if the cause of death is due to a non-work-related accident. Fractional amounts of the policy will be paid out if the covered employee loses a bodily appendage or sight because of an accident.

All other occupational illnesses Illnesses other than skin diseases or disorders, respiratory conditions, or poisoning. Examples include anthrax, brucellosis, infectious hepatitis, malignant and benign tumors, food poisoning, histoplasmosis, coccidioidomycosis.

Alternative employment arrangements (Current Population Survey) BLS has collected data for workers in four types of alternative employment arrangements: 1) independent contractors, 2) on-call workers, 3) temporary help agency workers, and 4) workers provided by contract firms. More information

Average hours per day (American Time Use Survey) This term refers to the average number of hours spent in a 24-hour day (between 4 a.m. on the diary day and 4 a.m. on the interview day) doing a specified activity.

Average hours per day, population (American Time Use Survey) The average number of hours per day is computed using all responses from a given population, including respondents who did not do a particular activity on their diary day.

Average hours per day, persons reporting the activity on the diary day (American Time Use Survey) The average number of hours per day is computed using only responses from those who engaged in a particular activity on their diary day.

Base period A point in time used as a reference point for comparison with some later period.

Benefit incidence A measure of the availability of a benefit. The National Compensation Survey (NCS) presents data on the percent of workers with access to, and who participate in, employee benefits. Access is defined as the percent of workers in an occupation who are offered a benefit. For example, an employee may have access to an employer-sponsored fitness center, but may or may not use it. Employees in contributory plans are counted as participating in an insurance plan or a retirement plan if they have paid required contributions and met any applicable service requirements. Employees in noncontributory plans are counted as participating regardless of whether they have fulfilled their service requirements.

Benefits Nonwage compensation provided to employees. The National Compensation Survey groups benefits into five categories: paid leave (vacations, holidays, sick leave); supplementary pay (premium pay for overtime and work on holidays and weekends, shift differentials, nonproduction bonuses); retirement (defined benefit and defined contribution plans); insurance (life insurance, health benefits, short-term disability, and long-term disability insurance) and legally required benefits (Social Security and Medicare, Federal and State unemployment insurance taxes, and workers' compensation).

Blue-collar and service occupations (National Compensation Survey) Includes precision production, craft, and repair occupations; machine operators and inspectors; transportation and moving occupations; handlers, equipment cleaners, helpers, and laborers; and service occupations.

Business sector (Productivity and Costs) The business sector is a subset of the domestic economy and excludes the economic activities of the following: general government, private households, and nonprofit organizations serving individuals. The business sector accounted for about 78 percent of the value of gross domestic product (GDP) in 2000.

Capital services A chain-type index of service flows derived from the stock of physical assets and software. Assets include equipment and software, structures, land, and inventories. Capital services are estimated as a capital-income weighted average of the growth rates of each asset. Capital services differ from capital stocks because short-lived assets such as equipment and software provide more services per unit of stock than long-lived assets such as land.

Civilian noninstitutional population (Current Population Survey) Included are persons 16 years of age and older residing in the 50 states and the District of Columbia who do not live in institutions (for example, correctional facilities, long-term care hospitals, and nursing homes) and who are not on active duty in the Armed Forces.

Civilian workers (National Compensation Survey) The National Compensation Survey defines Civilian Workers as the sum of all private industry and State and local government workers. Federal Government, military and agricultural workers are excluded.

Cohort (National Longitudinal Surveys) A cohort in the BLS National Longitudinal Surveys (NLS) program is a group of people, defined by year of birth, that make up a particular study. For example, the National Longitudinal Survey of Youth 1979 (NLSY79) cohort consists of people born between January 1, 1957, and December 31, 1964.

Collective bargaining Method whereby representatives of employees (unions) and employers negotiate the conditions of employment, normally resulting in a written contract setting forth the wages, hours, and other conditions to be observed for a stipulated period (e.g., 3 years). The term also applies to union-management dealings during the term of the agreement.

Comparative advantage When one nation's opportunity cost of producing an item is less than another nation's opportunity cost of producing that item. A good or service with which a nation has the largest absolute advantage (or smallest absolute disadvantage) is the item for which they have a comparative advantage.

Compensation (National Compensation Survey) A term used to encompass the entire range of wages and benefits, both current and deferred, that employees receive in return for their work. In the Employment Cost Index (ECI), compensation includes the employer's cost of wages and salaries, plus the employer's cost of providing employee benefits.

Complete income reporters (Consumer Expenditure Survey) The distinction between complete and incomplete income reporters generally is based on whether the respondent provided values for major sources of income, such as wages and salaries, self-employment income, and Social Security income. Even complete income reporters may not have provided a full accounting of all income from all sources. In the current survey, across-the-board zero income reporting was designated as invalid, and the consumer unit was categorized as an incomplete reporter. In all tables, income data are for complete income reporters only.

Computer-assisted telephone interviewing (CATI) A structured system of microdata collection by telephone that speeds up the collection and editing of microdata; it also permits the interviewer to educate the respondents on the importance of timely and accurate data.

Consumer unit (Consumer Expenditure Survey) A consumer unit is defined as either (1) all members of a particular household who are related by blood, marriage, adoption, or other legal arrangements; (2) a person living alone or sharing a household with others or living as a roomer in a private home or lodging house or in permanent living quarters in a hotel or motel, but who is financially independent; or (3) two or more persons living together who pool their income to make joint expenditure decisions. Financial independence is determined by the three major expense categories: housing, food, and other living expenses. To be considered financially independent, a respondent must provide at least two of the three major expense categories.

Contingent workers (Current Population Survey) Workers who do not have an implicit or explicit contract for long-term employment. BLS uses three alternative measures of contingent workers that vary in scope. More information

Contract escalation Producer Price Index (PPI) data are commonly used in escalating purchase and sales contracts. These contracts typically specify dollar amounts to be paid at some point in the future. It is often desirable to include an escalation clause that accounts for changes in input prices. For example, a long-term contract for bread may be escalated for changes in wheat prices by applying the percent change in the PPI for wheat to the contracted price for bread. Consumer Price Index (CPI) data can also be used in escalation. For example, the CPI may be used to escalate lease payments or child support payments. More information

Cost-of-living index A cost-of-living index measures differences in the price of goods and services, and allows for substitutions to other items as prices change. A consumer price index measures a price change for a constant market basket of goods and services from one period to the next within the same city (or in the Nation). The CPIs are not true cost-of-living indexes and should not be used for place-to-place comparisons.

Defined benefit pension plan A retirement plan that uses a specific predetermined formula to calculate the amount of an employee's future benefit. The most common type of formula is based on the employee's terminal earnings. Under this formula, benefits are based on a percentage of average earnings during a specified number of years at the end of a worker's career—for example, the highest 5 out of the last 10 years—multiplied by the maximum number of years of credited service under the plan. In recent years, a new type of defined benefit plan, a cash balance plan, has become more prevalent. Under this type of plan, benefits are computed as a percentage of each employee's account balance. Employers specify a contribution—usually based on a percentage of the employee's earnings—and a rate of interest on that contribution that will provide a predetermined amount at retirement, usually in the form of a lump sum. In the private sector, defined benefit plans are typically funded exclusively by employer contributions. In the public sector, defined benefit plans often require employee contributions.

Defined contribution plan A retirement plan in which the amount of the employer's annual contribution is specified. Individual accounts are set up for participants and benefits are based on the amounts credited to these accounts (through employer contributions and, if applicable, employee contributions) plus any investment earnings on the money in the account. Only employer contributions to the account are guaranteed, not the future benefits. In defined contribution plans, future benefits fluctuate on the basis of investment earnings. The most common type of defined contribution plan is a savings and thrift plan. Under this type of plan, the employee contributes a predetermined portion of his or her earnings (usually pretax) to an individual account, all or part of which is matched by the employer.

Deflator A value that allows data to be measured over time in terms of some base period; or, in more obscure terms, an implicit or explicit price index used to distinguish between those changes in the money value of gross national product which result from a change in prices and those which result from a change in physical output. The import and export price indexes produced by the International Price Program are used as deflators in the U.S. national accounts. For example, the Gross Domestic Product (GDP) equals consumption expenditures plus net investment plus government expenditures plus exports minus imports. Various price indexes are used to "deflate" each component of the GDP in order to make the GDP figures comparable over time. Import price indexes are used to deflate the import component (i.e., import volume is divided by the Import Price index) and the export price indexes are used to deflate the export component (i.e., export volume is divided by the Export Price index).

Demand for additional workers (Employment Projections) Job openings resulting from employment growth and the need to replace workers who leave an occupation.

Designated person (American Time Use Survey) One individual age 15 or older who is randomly selected from each sampled household to participate in the American Time Use Survey. The designated person is interviewed by telephone once about only his or her activities on the day before the interview. No other household member may respond for the designated person.

Diary day (American Time Use Survey) The diary day is the day about which the designated person reports his or her activities for the American Time Use Survey. For example, the diary day of a designated person interviewed on Tuesday is Monday.

Disability insurance Includes paid sick leave, short-term disability benefits, and long-term disability benefits.

Discharge (Job Openings and Labor Turnover Survey) A separation of an employee from an establishment that is initiated by the employer; an involuntary separation

Discouraged workers (Current Population Survey) Persons not in the labor force who want and are available for a job and who have looked for work sometime in the past 12 months (or since the end of their last job if they held one within the past 12 months), but who are not currently looking because they believe there are no jobs available or there are none for which they would qualify.

Displaced workers (Current Population Survey) Persons 20 years and over who lost or left jobs because their plant or company closed or moved, there was insufficient work for them to do, or their position or shift was abolished.

Division, geographic or census One of nine geographic areas of the United States defined by the Census Bureau and widely used by BLS for presenting regional data.

Duration of unemployment (Current Population Survey) The length of time in weeks (through the current reference week) that persons classified as unemployed had been looking for work. For persons on layoff who are counted as unemployed, duration of unemployment represents the number of full weeks they had been on layoff. The data do not represent completed spells of unemployment. (See Unemployed persons.)

Earnings Remuneration (pay, wages) of a worker or group of workers for services performed during a specific period of time. The term usually carries a defining word or phrase, such as straight-time average hourly earnings. Because a statistical concept is usually involved in the term and its variations, the producers and users of earnings data should define them clearly. In the absence of such definitions, the following may serve as rough guidelines:
- Hourly, daily, weekly, annual: period of time to which earnings figures, as stated or computed,

relate. The context in which annual earnings (sometimes weekly earnings) are used may indicate whether the reference includes earnings from one employer only or from all employment plus other sources of income.
- Average: usually refers to the arithmetic mean; that is, total earnings (as defined) of a group of workers (as identified) divided by the number of workers in the group.
- Gross: usually refers to total earnings, before any deductions (such as tax withholding) including, where applicable, overtime payments, shift differentials, production bonuses, cost-of-living allowances, commissions, etc.
- Straight-time: usually refers to gross earnings excluding overtime payments and (with variations at this point) shift differentials and other monetary payments. (Also see Wages and Salaries.)

Educational attainment The highest diploma or degree, or level of work towards a diploma or degree, an individual has completed.

Educational attainment cluster (Employment Projections) Six clusters are defined based on the distribution of educational attainment across occupations. The clusters are as follows: high school occupations, high school/some college occupations, some college occupations, high school/some college/college occupations, some college/college occupations, and college occupations.

Employed persons (American Time Use Survey) Same as definition for Employed persons (Current Population Survey), EXCEPT that in the American Time Use Survey, the definition includes persons 15 years and over and the reference period is the last 7 days prior to the American Time Use Survey interview.

Employed persons (Current Population Survey) Persons 16 years and over in the civilian noninstitutional population who, during the reference week, (a) did any work at all (at least 1 hour) as paid employees; worked in their own business, profession, or on their own farm, or worked 15 hours or more as unpaid workers in an enterprise operated by a member of the family; and (b) all those who were not working but who had jobs or businesses from which they were temporarily absent because of vacation, illness, bad weather, childcare problems, maternity or paternity leave, labor-management dispute, job training, or other family or personal reasons, whether or not they were paid for the time off or were seeking other jobs. Each employed person is counted only once, even if he or she holds more than one job. Excluded are persons whose only activity consisted of work around their own house (painting, repairing, or own home housework) or volunteer work for religious, charitable, and other organizations.

Employer (Quarterly Census of Employment and Wages) A person or business employing one or more persons for wages or salary; the legal entity responsible for payment of quarterly unemployment insurance taxes or for reimbursing the State fund for unemployment insurance benefits costs in lieu of paying the quarterly taxes.

Employer costs for employee compensation (National Compensation Survey) The Employer Costs for Employee Compensation (ECEC) series shows employer costs per hour worked for wages and salaries and individual benefits. Cost data are presented in both dollar amounts and as percentages of compensation.

Employment Cost Index (National Compensation Survey) The Employment Cost Index (ECI) is a measure of the change in the cost of labor, free from the influence of employment shifts among occupations and industries. The series measures changes in compensation costs (wages and salaries and employer costs for employee benefits).

Employment-population ratio (Current Population Survey) The proportion of the civilian noninstitutional population aged 16 years and over that is employed.

Establishment The physical location of a certain economic activity—for example, a factory, mine, store, or office. A single establishment generally produces a single good or provides a single service. An enterprise (a private firm, government, or nonprofit organization) can consist of a single establishment or multiple establishments. All establishments in an enterprise may be classified in one industry (e.g., a chain), or they may be classified in different industries (e.g., a conglomerate).

Event or exposure (Safety and Health Statistics) Signifies the manner in which an occupational injury or illness was produced or inflicted—for example, overexertion while lifting, or a fall from a ladder.

Expenditure shares (Consumer Expenditure Survey) Expenditure shares are the portions of total expenditures (as percentages) allotted to each expenditure category. Tables organized by various demographic characteristics are available.

Expenditures (Consumer Expenditure Survey) Expenditures consist of the transaction costs, including excise and sales taxes, of goods and services acquired during the interview or recordkeeping period. Expenditure estimates include expenditures for gifts, but exclude purchases or portions of purchases directly assignable to business purposes. Also excluded are periodic credit or installment payments on goods or services already acquired. The full cost of each purchase is recorded even though full payment may not have been made at the date of purchase. Expenditure categories include food, alcoholic beverages, housing, apparel and services, transportation, health care, entertainment, personal care products and services, reading, education, tobacco products and smoking supplies, cash contributions, personal insurance and pensions, and miscellaneous).

Export A domestic good or service that is sold to a foreign resident from a U.S. resident. Exports include government and nongovernment goods and services; however they exclude goods and services sold to the U.S. military and diplomatic and consular institutions abroad. Exports do include goods and services that were previously imported.

Extended mass layoff Layoff of at least 31 days in duration and involving 50 or more individuals from a single establishment filing initial claims for unemployment insurance during a consecutive 5-week period.

Fatality rate (Safety and Health Statistics) Represents the number of fatal injuries per 100,000 workers, calculated as follows: (N/W) × 100,000, where N = number of fatal injuries, W = number of workers employed, and 100,000 = base to express the fatality rate per 100,000 workers.

Federal Information Processing Standards (FIPS) Standards for information processing issued by the National Institute of Standards and Technology of the U.S. Department of Commerce; includes a numeric designation for geographic areas such as States, counties, and metropolitan areas.

Flexible benefits A type of plan under Section 125 of the Internal Revenue Code that provides employees a choice between permissible taxable benefits, including cash, and nontaxable benefits such as life and health insurance, vacations, retirement plans, and child care. Although a common core of benefits may be required, the employee can determine how his or her remaining benefit dollars are to be allocated for each type of benefit from the total amount promised by the employer.

Full-time employees (National Compensation Survey) Employees are classified as full time or part time as defined by their employer.

Full-time workers (Current Population Survey and American Time Use Survey) Persons who work 35 hours or more per week.

Goods-producing industries (Standard Industrial Classification) Includes manufacturing, mining, and construction.

Goods-producing industries (North American Industry Classification System) Includes manufacturing, construction, and natural resources and mining.

Health insurance plan Insurance plans that include coverage for one or more of the following: medical care, dental care, and vision care.

Hire (Job Openings and Labor Turnover Survey) Any addition to an establishment's payroll, including newly hired and rehired employees.

Hires rate (Job Openings and Labor Turnover Survey) The number of hires during the month divided by the number of employees who worked during or received pay for the pay period that includes the 12th of the month.

Hispanic or Latino ethnicity Refers to persons who identified themselves in the enumeration process as being Spanish, Hispanic, or Latino. Persons of Hispanic or Latino ethnicity may be of any race.

Hourly compensation (Productivity and Costs) Compensation costs are defined as the sum of wage and salary accruals and supplements to wages and salaries. Wage and salary accruals consist of the monetary remuneration of employees, including the compensation of corporate officers; commissions, tips, and bonuses; voluntary employee contributions to certain deferred compensation plans, such as 401(k) plans; employee gains from exercising nonqualified stock options; and receipts in kind that represent income. Supplements to wages and salaries consist of employer contributions for social insurance and employer payments (including payments in kind) to private pension and profit-sharing plans, group health and life insurance plans, privately administered workers' compensation plans. For employees (wage and salary workers), hourly compensation is measured relative to hours at work and includes payments made by employers for time not at work, such as vacation, holiday, and sick pay. Because compensation costs for the business and nonfarm business sectors would otherwise be severely understated, an estimate of the hourly compensation of proprietors of unincorporated businesses is made by assuming that their hourly compensation is equal to that of employees in the same sector.

Hourly compensation costs (International Labor Comparisons) Hourly compensation costs, as measured in the BLS international comparison series, are defined as (1) all payments made directly to workers—pay for time worked (basic time and piece rates plus overtime premiums, shift differentials, other premiums and bonuses paid regularly each pay period, and cost-of-living adjustments), pay for time not worked (such as for vacations and holidays), seasonal or irregular bonuses and other special payments, selected social allowances, and the cost of payments in kind—before payroll deductions of any kind, and (2) employer expenditures for legally required insurance programs and contractual and private benefit plans (such as retirement plans, health insurance, unemployment insurance, and family allowances). In addition, for some countries, compensation is adjusted for other taxes on payrolls or employment (or reduced to reflect subsidies), even if they do not finance programs that directly benefit workers, because such taxes are regarded as labor costs. The BLS definition of hourly compensation costs used in its international comparisons series is based on the International Labour Office standard definition of total labor costs. However, it does not include all items of total labor costs; the items excluded are the costs of recruitment, employee training, and plant facilities and services, such as cafeterias and medical clinics. Hourly compensation costs include all the items of compensation covered in the BLS series Employer Costs for Employee Compensation, the Employment Cost Index, and the index of hourly compensation (published with the index of labor productivity); hourly compensation costs also include the costs of payments in kind and other taxes and subsidies, which may not be included in the other BLS compensation series. The classification of the compensation items and the terminology used in the definitions differ among the series.

Hours at work (Productivity and Costs) For productivity measurement, the proper measure of hours is "hours at work," which include paid time working, traveling between job sites, coffee breaks, and machine downtime. Hours at work, however, exclude hours for which employees are paid but not at work (examples: vacation time, holidays, and paid sick leave).

Hours worked (Current Population Survey) There are two different hours concepts measured in the CPS: usual hours and actual hours at work. Usual hours refer to a person's normal work schedule versus their actual hours at work during the survey reference week. For example, a person who normally works 40 hours per week, but was off for a 1-day holiday during the reference week, would report his or her usual hours as 40 but actual hours at work for the reference week as 32.

Import A good or service that is sold to a U.S. resident from a foreign resident. Imports include government and nongovernment goods and services; however they exclude goods and services to the U.S. military, diplomatic, and consular institutions abroad. Imports do include goods and services that were previously exported.

Incidence rate (Safety and Health Statistics) Represents the number of injuries and/or illnesses per 100 full-time workers, calculated as follows: (N/EH) × 200,000, where N = number of injuries and/or illnesses, EH = total hours worked by all employees during the calendar year, and 200,000 = base for 100 full-time equivalent workers (working 40 hours per week, 50 weeks per year).

Income before taxes (Consumer Expenditure Survey) Income before taxes is the total money earnings and selected money receipts of all consumer unit members aged 14 years or older during the 12 months prior to the interview date. It includes the following components: wages and salaries; self-employment income; Social Security, private and government retirement; interest, dividends, rental income, and other property income; unemployment, workers' compensation and veteran's benefits; public assistance, supplemental security income, and food stamps; regular contributions for support (including alimony and child support); other income (including cash scholarships, fellowships or stipends not based on working, and meals and rent as pay).

Industry A group of establishments that produce similar products or provide similar services. For example, all establishments that manufacture automobiles are in the same industry. A given industry, or even a particular establishment in that industry, might have employees in dozens of occupations. The North American Industry Classification System (NAICS) groups similar establishments into industries. NAICS is replacing the former Standard Industrial Classification (SIC) system.

Inflation Inflation has been defined as a process of continuously rising prices, or equivalently, of a continuously falling value of money.

Initial claimant A person who files any notice of unemployment to initiate a request either for a determination of entitlement to and eligibility for compensation, or for a subsequent period of unemployment within a benefit year or period of eligibility.

Item specification The description of a good or service that includes all price-determining characteristics and any other information necessary to distinguish the item from all others.

Job leavers (Current Population Survey) Unemployed persons who quit or otherwise terminated their employment voluntarily and immediately began looking for work.

Job losers (Current Population Survey) Unemployed persons who involuntarily lost their last job or who had completed a temporary job. This includes persons who were on temporary layoff expecting to return to work, as well as persons not on temporary layoff. (See Unemployed persons.) Those not on temporary layoff include permanent job losers and persons whose temporary jobs had ended. (See Permanent job losers.)

Job opening (Job Openings and Labor Turnover Survey) A specific position of employment to be filled at an establishment; conditions include the following: there is work available for that position, the job could start within 30 days, and the employer is actively recruiting for the position.

Job openings rate (Job Openings and Labor Turnover Survey) The number of job openings on the last business day of the month divided by the sum of the number of employees who worked during or received pay for the pay period that includes the 12th of the month and the number of job openings on the last business day of the month.

Job tenure (Current Population Survey) The length of time an employee has worked for his or her current employer. The data do not represent completed spells of tenure.

Labor dispute See Labor Management Dispute.

Labor force (Current Population Survey) The labor force includes all persons classified as employed or unemployed in accordance with the definitions contained in this glossary.

Labor force participation rate The labor force as a percent of the civilian noninstitutional population.

Labor management dispute A conflict between employees, typically represented by a union, and management or the employer. This general term covers all types of conflicts from a grievance to a strike or a lockout. Labor management disputes are more common during collective bargaining or union contract negotiations.

Labor productivity Labor productivity refers to the relationship between output and the labor time used in generating that output. It is the ratio of output per hour.

Laspeyres index Sum(p2q1)/Sum(p1q1): A weighted aggregative index showing the ratio of expenditures in the current period (p2q1, where p2 is the current period price and q1 is the base period quantity) to the expenditure in the base period (p1q1, where p1 is the base period price and q1 is the base period quantity) to purchase the identical market basket of items. It answers the question "How much more or less does it cost now to purchase the same items as in the base period?" The main shortcoming of the Laspeyres index is that it does not track actual expenditures because consumers adjust their buying in response to changes in relative price, which changes the composition of the market basket. This invalid assumption that consumer demand is totally price inelastic causes the index to overstate the actual effect on consumers when there is a change in prices.

Layoff (Job Openings and Labor Turnover Survey) A separation of an employee from an establishment that is initiated by the employer; an involuntary separation; a period of forced unemployment

Layoff and discharges rate (Job Openings and Labor Turnover Survey) The number of layoffs and discharges during the month divided by the number of employees who worked during or received pay for the pay period that includes the 12th of the month.

Legally required benefits (National Compensation Survey) Legally required benefits include the employer's costs for Social Security, Medicare, Federal and State unemployment insurance, and workers' compensation.

Life insurance A contract that pays the beneficiary a set sum of money upon the death of the policyholder. These plans pay benefits usually in the form of a lump sum, but they may be distributed as an annuity.

Locality of origin indexes U.S. import price indexes based on country or region, rather than product type.

Location quotient Ratio that compares the concentration of a resource or activity, such as employment, in a defined area to that of a larger area or base. For example, location quotients can be used to compare State employment by industry to that of the nation. More information

Lockout A temporary withholding or denial of employment during a labor dispute in order to enforce terms of employment upon a group of employees. A lockout is initiated by the management of an establishment.

Long-term disability insurance (National Compensation Survey—benefits) Provides a monthly benefit to employees who, due to a non-work-related injury or illness, are unable to perform the duties of their normal occupation or any other, for periods of time extending beyond their short-term disability or sickness and accident insurance.

Longitudinal data (National Longitudinal Surveys and Business Employment Dynamics) Data in which the same units are observed over multiple time periods. Another term for longitudinal data is panel data. For example, the BLS National Longitudinal Surveys (NLS) program collects data from several groups of individuals over many years on an annual or biennial basis.

Lost-worktime cases (Safety and Health Statistics) Cases involving days away from work, or days of restricted work activity, or both.

Lost-worktime cases involving days away from work (Safety and Health Statistics) Cases resulting in days away from work, or a combination of days away from work and days of restricted work activity.

Lost-worktime cases involving restricted work activity (Safety and Health Statistics) Cases resulting in restricted work activity only.

Lost-worktime rate (Current Population Survey) Hours absent as a percent of hours usually worked. Absences are defined as instances when persons who usually work 35 or more hours per week worked less than 35 hours during the reference week for one of the following reasons: own illness, injury, or medical problems; childcare problems; other family or personal obligations; civic or military duty; and maternity or paternity leave.

Lump-sum payments (National Compensation Survey) Payments made to employees in lieu of a general wage rate increase. The payment may be a fixed amount as set forth in a labor agreement or an amount determined by a formula—for example, 2.5 percent of an employee's earnings during the prior year. Lump-sum payments are not incorporated into an employee's base pay rate or salary, but are considered as nonproduction bonuses in the Employment Cost Index and Employer Costs for Employee Compensation series.

Marginally attached workers (Current Population Survey) Persons not in the labor force who want and are available for work, and who have looked for a job sometime in the prior 12 months (or since the end of their last job if they held one within the past 12 months), but were not counted as unemployed because they had not searched for work in the 4 weeks preceding the survey. Discouraged workers are a subset of the marginally attached. (See Discouraged workers.)

Market basket (Consumer Price Index) The market basket is a package of goods and services that consumers purchase for day-to-day living. The weight of each item is based on the amount of expenditure reported by a sample of households.

Mass layoff A situation in which 50 or more persons have filed initial claims for unemployment insurance benefits against an establishment during a consecutive 5-week period.

Mean wage (Occupational Employment Statistics) An average wage; an occupational mean wage estimate is calculated by summing the wages of all the employees in a given occupation and then dividing the total wages by the number of employees.

Median days away from work (Safety and Health Statistics) The measure used to summarize the varying lengths of absences from work among the cases with days away from work. The median is the point at which half of the cases involved more days away from work and half involved less days away from work.

Median wage An occupational median wage estimate is the boundary between the highest paid 50 percent and the lowest paid 50 percent of workers in that occupation. Half of the workers in a given occupation earn more than the median wage, and half the workers earn less than the median wage.

Medical care coverage A type of insurance coverage that provides for the payment of benefits as a result of sickness or injury. Medical care coverage can be provided in a hospital or a doctor's office. There are two main types of medical care plans. An indemnity plan—also called a fee-for-service plan—reimburses the patient or the provider as expenses are incurred. The most common type of indemnity plan is a preferred provider organization (PPO). A PPO provides coverage to the enrollee through a network of selected health care providers (such as hospitals and physicians). Enrollees may go outside the network, but would incur higher costs in the form of higher deductibles and higher coinsurance rates than if they stayed within the network. The second type of medical care plan is called a prepaid plan—also called a health maintenance organization. A prepaid plan assumes both the financial risks associated with providing comprehensive medical services and the responsibility for health care delivery in a particular geographic area, usually in return for a fixed prepaid fee from its members.

Metropolitan statistical areas (MSAs) The general concept of an MSA is one of a large population nucleus, together with adjacent communities which have a high degree of economic and social integration with that nucleus. These are defined by the Office of Management and Budget as a standard for Federal agencies in the preparation and publication of statistics relating to metropolitan areas. More information

Most significant source of postsecondary education or training (Employment Projections) An occupation is classified into 1 of 11 categories that best describes the postsecondary education or training needed by most workers to become fully qualified in the occupation. The categories are as follows: first professional degree; doctoral degree; master's degree; bachelor's or higher degree, plus work experience; bachelor's degree; associate degree; postsecondary vocational award; work experience in a related occupation; long-term on-the-job training; moderate-term on-the-job training; and short-term on-the-job training.

Multifactor productivity For the *private business and private nonfarm business* sectors, the growth rate of multifactor productivity is measured as the growth rate of output less the growth rate of combined inputs of labor and capital. Labor is measured by a weighted average of the number of hours worked classified by education, work experience, and gender. Capital services measure the flow of services from the stocks of equipment and software, structures, land, and inventories. For the *manufacturing* sector, multifactor productivity is the growth rate of output less the combined inputs of labor, capital, and intermediate purchases. Labor is measured by the number of hours worked. Capital services measure the flow of services from the stocks of equipment and software, structures, land, and inventories. Intermediate purchases are composed of materials, fuels, electricity, and purchased services.

Multiple jobholders (Current Population Survey and American Time Use Survey) Employed persons who, during the reference week, either had two or more jobs as a wage and salary worker, were self-employed and also held a wage and salary job, or worked as an unpaid family worker and also held a wage and salary job. Excluded are self-employed persons with multiple businesses and persons with multiple jobs as unpaid family workers.

Nature of injury or illness Names the principal physical characteristic of a disabling condition, such as sprain/strain, cut/laceration, or carpal tunnel syndrome.

New entrants (Current Population Survey) Unemployed persons who never worked before and who are entering the labor force for the first time.

Nonfarm business sector (Productivity and Costs) The nonfarm business sector is a subset of the domestic economy and excludes the economic activities of the following: general government, private households, nonprofit organizations serving individuals, and farms. The nonfarm business sector accounted for about 77 percent of the value of gross domestic product (GDP) in 2000.

Nonfinancial corporations (Productivity and Costs) The nonfinancial corporate business sector is a subset of the domestic economy and excludes the economic activities of the following: general government, private households, nonprofit organizations serving individuals, and those corporations classified as offices of bank holding companies, offices of other holding companies, or offices in the finance and insurance sector. Nonfinancial corporations accounted for about 54 percent of the value of gross domestic product (GDP) in 2000.

Nonlabor payments (Productivity and Costs) These payments include profits, consumption of fixed capital, taxes on production and imports less subsidies, net interest and miscellaneous payments, business current transfer payments, rental income of persons, and the current surplus of government enterprises.

North American Industry Classification System (NAICS) The successor to the Standard Industrial Classification (SIC) system; this system of classifying business establishments is being adopted by the United States, Canada, and Mexico. More information

Not employed (American Time Use Survey) The term refers to persons who are classified as unemployed as well as those classified as not in the labor force (using Current Population Survey definitions).

Not in the labor force (Current Population Survey) Includes persons aged 16 years and older in the civilian noninstitutional population who are neither employed nor unemployed in accordance with the definitions contained in this glossary. Information is collected on their desire for and availability for work, job search activity in the prior year, and reasons for not currently searching. (See Marginally attached workers.)

Not seasonally adjusted This term is used to describe data series that have not been subjected to the seasonal adjustment process. In other words, the effects of regular or seasonal patterns have not been removed from these series.

Occupation A set of activities or tasks that employees are paid to perform. Employees that perform essentially the same tasks are in the same occupation, whether or not they work in the same industry. Some occupations are concentrated in a few particular industries; other occupations are found in many industries. (See Industry.)

Occupational groups A group of related occupations; examples: sales occupations and service occupations.

Occupational illness Any abnormal condition or disorder, other than one resulting from an occupational injury, caused by exposure to factors associated with employment. It includes acute and chronic illnesses or diseases which may be caused by inhalation, absorption, ingestion, or direct contact.

Occupational injury Any injury such as a cut, fracture, sprain, amputation, etc., which results from a work-related event or from a single instantaneous exposure in the work environment.

Occupational Injury and Illness Classification System (Safety and Health Statistics) Defines many of the data elements—such as nature, part, event, and source—that are used in the production of safety and health statistics by BLS. More information

On-call employees Employees who are not permanent, but are called to work as needed, often on short notice, although they can be scheduled to work for several days or weeks in a row.

Other separation (Job Openings and Labor Turnover Survey) A separation of an employee from an establishment for miscellaneous reasons, including retirement, death, separation due to employee disability, or transfer to another location of the enterprise.

Other separations rate (Job Openings and Labor Turnover Survey) The number of other separations during the month divided by the number of employees who worked during or received pay for the pay period that includes the 12th of the month.

Paid leave (National Compensation Survey) Paid leave includes vacations, holidays, sick leave, and other leave with pay.

Panel data (National Longitudinal Surveys and Business Employment Dynamics) See Longitudinal data.

Part of body affected (Safety and Health Statistics) Directly linked to the nature of injury or illness cited, such as back, finger, or eye.

Part-time workers (Current Population Survey and American Time Use Survey) Persons who work less than 35 hours per week.

Pay period that includes the 12th of the month Standard measurement period for all Federal agencies collecting employment data from business establishments; time unit that employers use to pay employees that overlaps the 12th of the month; length of the pay period does not matter, as long as the 12th of the month is included in the pay period: For establishments with a Monday-through-Friday pay period, if the 12th of the month falls on a Saturday, it should be taken as the last day of the requested pay period, and if the 12th of the month falls on a Sunday, it should be taken as the first day of the requested pay period.

Payroll employment (Current Employment Statistics) Employment is the total number of persons on establishment payrolls employed full or part time who received pay for any part of the pay period which includes the 12th day of the month. Temporary and intermittent employees are included, as are any workers who are on paid sick leave, on paid holiday, or who work during only part of the specified pay period. A striking worker who only works a small portion of the survey period, and is paid, would be included as employed under the CES definitions. Persons on the payroll of more than one establishment are counted in each establishment. Data exclude proprietors, self-employed, unpaid family or volunteer workers, farm workers, and domestic workers. Persons on layoff the entire pay period, on leave without pay, on strike for the entire period or who have not yet reported for work are not counted as employed. Government employment covers only civilian workers. With the release of NAICS-based estimates in June 2003, the scope and definition of Federal Government employment estimates changed due to a change in source data and estimation methods. The previous series was an end-of-month federal employee count produced by the Office of Personnel Management, and it excluded some workers, mostly employees who work in Department of Defense-owned establishments such as military base commissaries. Beginning in June 2003, the CES national series began to include these workers. Also, Federal Government employment is now estimated from a sample of Federal establishments, is benchmarked annually to counts from unemployment insurance tax records, and reflects employee counts as of the pay period including the 12th of the month, consistent with other CES industry series. The historical time series for Federal Government employment was revised to reflect these changes.

Percentile wage estimate Shows what percentage of workers in an occupation earn less than a given wage and what percentage earn more. For example, a 25th percentile wage of $15.00 indicates that 25% of workers (in a given occupation in a given area) earn less than $15.00; therefore 75% of workers earn more than $15.00.

Permanent job losers (Current Population Survey) Unemployed persons whose employment ended involuntarily and who began looking for work.

Primary activity (American Time Use Survey) A primary activity is the main activity a respondent was doing at a specified time. Most published time use estimates reflect time spent in primary activities only.

Price index A price index is a tool that simplifies the measurement of price movements in a numerical series. Movements are measured with respect to the base period, when the index is set to 100.

Producer Price Index (PPI) A family of indexes that measure the average change over time in selling prices received by domestic producers of goods and services. PPIs measure price change from the perspective of the seller. This contrasts with other measures that measure price change from the purchaser's perspective, such as the Consumer Price Index (CPI). Sellers' and purchasers' prices may differ due to government subsidies, sales and excise taxes, and distribution costs.

Productivity A measure of economic efficiency that shows how effectively economic inputs are converted into output. Productivity is measured by comparing the amount of goods and services produced with the inputs that were used in production.

Professional employer organization (PEO) A business that supplies management and administrative services with regard to human resource responsibilities for employers; it serves as the co-employer of the client's employees for payroll, benefits, and related purposes. PEOs are referred to as "employee leasing companies" in the Standard Industrial Classification Manual.

Quit (Job Openings and Labor Turnover Survey) A separation of an employee from an establishment that is initiated by the employee; a voluntary separation; a resignation from a job or position.

Quits rate (Job Openings and Labor Turnover Survey) The number of quits during the month divided by the number of employees who worked during or received pay for the pay period that includes the 12th of the month.

Race (Current Population Survey) The CPS provides data by race, with the race given by the household respondent. Since 2003, respondents are allowed to choose more than one race; previously, multiracial persons were required to select a single primary race.

Persons who select more than one race are classified separately in the category "two or more races." Persons who select one race only are classified in one of the following five categories: 1) white, 2) black or African American, 3) Asian, 4) Native Hawaiian and other Pacific Islander, and 5) American Indian or Alaska Native. Only data for whites, blacks, and Asians are currently published because the number of survey respondents for the other racial categories is not large enough to produce statistically reliable estimates.

Recordable injuries and illnesses (Safety and Health statistics) Recordable cases include work-related injuries and illnesses that result in one or more of the following: death, loss of consciousness, days away from work, restricted work activity or job transfer, medical treatment (beyond first aid), significant work-related injuries or illnesses that are diagnosed by a physician or other licensed heath care professional (these include any work-related case involving cancer, chronic irreversible disease, a fracture or cracked bone, or a punctured eardrum); additional criteria include any needle-stick injury or cut from a sharp object that is contaminated with another person's blood or other potentially infectious material, any case requiring an employee to be medically removed under the requirements of an OSHA health standard, tuberculosis infection as evidenced by a positive skin test or diagnosis by a physician or other licensed health care professional after exposure to a known case of active tuberculosis.

Reentrants (Current Population Survey) Unemployed persons who previously worked but were out of the labor force prior to beginning their job search.

Reference person (Consumer Expenditure Survey) The first member mentioned by the respondent when asked to "Start with the name of the person or one of the persons who owns or rents the home." It is with respect to this person that the relationship of the other consumer unit members is determined.

Region—Midwest Illinois, Indiana, Iowa, Kansas, Michigan, Minnesota, Missouri, Nebraska, North Dakota, Ohio, South Dakota, and Wisconsin.

Region—Northeast Connecticut, Maine, Massachusetts, New Hampshire, New Jersey, New York, Pennsylvania, Rhode Island, and Vermont.

Region—South Alabama, Arkansas, Delaware, District of Columbia, Florida, Georgia, Kentucky, Louisiana, Maryland, Mississippi, North Carolina, Oklahoma, South Carolina, Tennessee, Texas, Virginia, and West Virginia.

Region—West Alaska, Arizona, California, Colorado, Hawaii, Idaho, Montana, Nevada, New Mexico, Oregon, Utah, Washington, and Wyoming.

Regions Data are presented for four major regions: Northeast, Midwest, South, and West.

Relative importance (Consumer Price Index) BLS publishes what is called a "relative importance" for each commodity and commodity grouping. The relative importance of an item represents its basic value weight, including any imputations, multiplied by the relative of price change from the weight date to the date of the relative importance calculation, expressed as a percentage of the total value weight for the "all commodities" category.

Represented by unions (Current Population Survey) Data refer to union members, as well as workers who reported no union affiliation but whose jobs are covered by a union or an employee association contract.

Respiratory condition due to toxic agents (Safety and Health statistics) Examples: Pneumonitis, pharyngitis, rhinitis or acute congestion due to chemicals, dusts, gases, or fumes; farmer's lung.

Retirement plans (National Compensation Survey) Includes defined benefit pension plans and defined contribution retirement plans.

Sample A subset of a universe; usually selected randomly and considered representative of the universe.

Sample frame A listing of all units in the universe from which a sample can be drawn.

Seasonally adjusted Seasonal adjustment removes the effects of events that follow a more or less regular pattern each year. These adjustments make it easier to observe the cyclical and other nonseasonal movements in a data series.

Self-employed persons (Current Population Survey and American Time Use Survey) Those persons who work for profit or fees in their own business, profession, trade, or farm. Only the unincorporated self-employed are included in the self-employed category.

Secondary or simultaneous activity (American Time Use Survey) A secondary or simultaneous activity is an activity done at the same time as a primary activity. With the exception of the care of children under age 13, information on secondary activities is not systematically collected in the American Time Use Survey.

Separation (Job Openings and Labor Turnover Survey) See Turnover.

Separations rate (Job Openings and Labor Turnover Survey) See Turnover rate.

Series report A form-based application that uses BLS time series identifiers as input in extracting data from each survey-specific database according to a specified set of date ranges and output options.

Service-producing industries (Standard Industrial Classification) Includes transportation; communications; electric, gas, and sanitary services; wholesale trade; retail trade; finance, insurance, and real estate; and services.

Service-providing industries (North American Industry Classification System) Includes trade, transportation, and utilities; information; financial activities; professional and business services; education and health services; leisure and hospitality; other services.

Short-term disability insurance Provides short-term (typically 26 weeks) income protection to employees who are unable to work due to a non-work-related accident or illness.

Shortage (as in shortage of workers) Shortages occur in a market economy when the demand for workers for a particular occupation is greater than the supply of workers who are qualified, available, and willing to do that job.

Slowdown An effort, typically organized by a union, in which employees decrease productivity in order to bring pressure upon management. Generally a slowdown is used as an alternative to a strike and is seen as less disruptive.

Source of injury or illness (Safety and Health statistics) The object, substance, exposure, or bodily motion that directly produced or inflicted the disabling condition cited. Examples include lifting a heavy box; exposure to a toxic substance, fire or flame; and bodily motion of an injured or ill worker.

Stage-of-processing indexes (Producer Price Index) Stage-of-processing (SOP) price indexes regroup commodities at the subproduct class (6-digit) level according to the class of buyer and the amount of physical processing or assembling the products have undergone. The PPI publishes aggregate price indexes organized by commodity-based processing stage. The three stages of processing include Finished Goods; Intermediate Materials, Supplies, and Components; and Crude Materials for Further Processing.

Standard Industrial Classification (SIC) system The SIC system has been used throughout the Federal Government to group establishments into industries. The SIC system is being gradually replaced by the North American Industry Classification System (NAICS). More information on the SIC system can be found in the Standard Industrial Classification Manual, 1987 (Executive Office of the President, Office of Management and Budget), available in many libraries.

Standard Occupational Classification (SOC) system This system is being adopted by Federal statistical agencies to classify workers into occupational categories for the purpose of collecting, calculating, or disseminating data. All workers are classified into 1 of more than 800 occupations according to their occupational definition. To facilitate classification, occupations are combined to form 23 major groups, 96 minor groups, and 449 broad occupations. Each broad occupation includes detailed occupations) requiring similar job duties, skills, education, or experience.

Standard tables (Consumer Expenditure Survey) Standard tables contain annual expenditure data organized by various demographic characteristics. The following standard tables are available: age of reference person, composition of consumer unit, education of reference person, higher income before taxes, Hispanic or Latino origin of reference person, housing tenure and type of area, income before taxes, number of earners in consumer unit, occupation of reference person, population size of area of residence, quintiles of income before taxes, race of reference person, region of residence, size of consumer unit, and selected age of reference person.

Strike A temporary stoppage of work by a group of workers (not necessarily union members) to express a grievance or enforce a demand. A strike is initiated by the workers of an establishment.

Supplemental pay (National Compensation Survey) Supplemental pay includes overtime and premium pay for work in addition to the regular work schedule (such as weekends and holidays), shift differentials, and nonproduction bonuses (such as referral bonuses and lump-sum payments provided in lieu of wage increases).

Supply of workers Often refers to the labor force. The concept focuses on worker characteristics, especially their education and training, but also characteristics such as experience (often considered to be correlated with age), physical strength (often considered to be inversely correlated with age), ability to work in teams, etc. Some demographic characteristics that are not to be considered in hiring and promotion decisions, but that are studied, include gender, race, ethnicity, parental and marital statuses. More information (PDF)

Survey reference week (Current Population Survey) The CPS, a survey of households, asks respondents about their labor market activities during a specific week each month. That week, called the survey reference week, is defined as the 7-day period, Sunday through Saturday, which includes the 12th of the month.

Survivor benefits A series of payments to the dependents of deceased employees. Survivor benefits come in two types: First, the "transition" type pays the named beneficiary a monthly amount for a short period (usually 24 months). Transition benefits may then be followed by "bridge benefits," which are a series of payments that last until a specific date, usually the surviving spouse's 62nd birthday.

Temporary help agency Establishment primarily engaged in supplying workers to client businesses for limited periods of time to supplement the work force of the client; the individuals provided are employees of the temporary help service establishment, but these establishments do not provide direct supervision of their employees.

Terms of trade Allocation of inputs into two or more economies that take advantage of differences in comparative advantages and, through specialization, improve the production of the economies. Note that a change in the terms of trade should cause all domestic production to change (that is, reallocates all inputs), rather than just imports.

Time off benefit Provides paid or unpaid leave for specific uses, such as lunch periods, holidays and vacations, and maternity and paternity leave.

Time/Index series A way of expressing, in percentage terms, the change in some variable from a given point in time to another point in time. For example, suppose output increased by 10 percent from an initial year (1987) to a subsequent year (1988). The index for the base year of 1987 in this example would be 100.0, while the index for 1988 would be 110.0. Conversely, if output had declined in 1988 by 10 percent, the 1988 index value would be 90.0.

Touchtone Data Entry (TDE) An automated method of collecting data in which respondents call a toll-free number and enter their data using a touchtone telephone.

Transaction price The market sale price of a good or input shows what has to be given in exchange to obtain a good or service. It is usually denoted in money terms, although payment need not be in a monetary form. The relative price is expressed in terms of the quantity of some other good which has to be given in exchange for the original good. Thus, if all prices increase at the same rate, absolute prices will rise but relative prices will remain unchanged.

Turnover (Job Openings and Labor Turnover Survey) Separation of an employee from an establishment (voluntary, involuntary, or other).

Turnover rate (Job Openings and Labor Turnover Survey) The number of total separations during the month divided by the number of employees who worked during or received pay for the pay period that includes the 12th of the month (monthly turnover); the number of total separations for the year divided by average monthly employment for the year (annual turnover).

Unemployed persons (Current Population Survey) Persons aged 16 years and older who had no employment during the reference week, were available for work, except for temporary illness, and had made specific efforts to find employment sometime during the 4-week period ending with the reference week. Persons who were waiting to be recalled to a job from which they had been laid off need not have been looking for work to be classified as unemployed.

Unemployment rate The unemployment rate represents the number unemployed as a percent of the labor force.

Union membership data Refers to wage and salary workers who report that they are members of a labor union or an employee association similar to a union.

Unit labor costs (Productivity and Costs) Unit labor costs show the growth in compensation relative to that of real output. These costs are calculated by dividing total labor compensation by real output. Changes in unit labor costs can be approximated by subtracting the change in productivity from the change in hourly compensation.

Unit value indexes Unit value indexes are calculated by dividing the total value of goods in a commodity area by the total quantity of goods in that commodity area.

Universe The total number of units (for example, individuals, households, or businesses) in the population of interest.

Unpaid family workers (Current Population Survey and American Time Use Survey) Persons who work without pay for 15 or more hours per week on a farm or in a business operated by a member of the household to whom they are related by birth or marriage.

Usual hours (Current Population Survey) Respondents are asked the number of hours per week they usually work. This provides a measure of the usual full-time or part-time status of employed persons. All employed persons, both those who were at work and those who were absent from work, are asked about the number of hours they usually work.

Usual weekly earnings (Current Population Survey) Wage and salary earnings before taxes and other deductions; includes any overtime pay, commissions, or tips usually received (at the main job, in the case of multiple jobholders). Earnings reported on a basis other than weekly (for example, annual, monthly, hourly) are converted to weekly. The term "usual" is as perceived by the respondent. If the respondent asks for a definition of usual, interviewers are instructed to define the term as more than half the weeks worked during the past 4 or 5 months. Data refer to wage and salary workers only, excluding all self-employed persons (regardless of whether their businesses were incorporated) and all unpaid family workers.

Vacancy (Job Openings and Labor Turnover Survey) See Job opening.

Vacancy rate (Job Openings and Labor Turnover Survey) See Job openings rate.

Wage and salary workers Workers who receive wages, salaries, commissions, tips, payment in kind, or piece rates. The group includes employees in both the private and public sectors.

Wages and salaries Hourly straight-time wage rate or, for workers not paid on an hourly basis, straight-time earnings divided by the corresponding hours. Straight-time wage and salary rates are total earnings before payroll deductions, excluding premium pay for overtime and for work on weekends and holidays, shift differentials, and nonproduction bonuses such as lump-sum payments provided in lieu of wage increases. (See Earnings.)

Weekly hours The expected or actual period of employment for the week, usually expressed in number of hours. Some uses of the term may relate to the outside dimensions of a week (for example, 7 consecutive days).

Wholesale Price Index (WPI) The Wholesale Price Index (WPI) was the original name of the Producer Price Index (PPI) program from its inception in 1902 until 1978, when it was renamed (PPI). At the same time, emphasis was shifted from one index encompassing the whole economy, to three main indexes covering the stages of production in the economy. By changing emphasis, BLS greatly reduced the double-counting phenomenon inherent in aggregate commodity-based indexes.

Work levels (National Compensation Survey) The National Compensation Survey produces earnings data by levels of work within an occupation. The duties and responsibilities of a job are evaluated using four factors (such as knowledge, and complexity of the work) to determine a work level. Levels vary by occupation, ranging from 1 to 15. For example, level 1 may represent an entry level, while level 15 may represent master-level skills.

Work relationship (Safety and Health Statistics) An employee must have had a verifiable work relationship with his or her employer to be included in the Census of Fatal Occupational Injuries. A work relationship exists if an event or exposure results in fatal injury or illness to a person under the following conditions: (1) ON the employer's premises and the person was there to work; or (2) OFF the employer's premises and the person was there to work, or the event or exposure was related to the person's work status as an employee. The employer's premises include buildings, grounds, parking lots, and other facilities and property used in the conduct of business. Work is defined as legal duties, activities, or tasks that produce a product as a result and that are done in exchange for money, goods, services, profit, or benefit.

Work stoppage A strike or a lockout.

Worklife estimates Estimates of the number of years individuals would spend in the labor force based on mortality conditions, labor force entry and exit rates, and demographic characteristics.

Small Business Administration

504 The 504 Certified Development Loan program provides small businesses with longterm, fixed-rate financing for the purchase of land, buildings and long-life capital equipment.

7(a) The 7(a) Loan Guaranty program is SBA's primary loan program. It provides general loan financing for a wide variety of purposes.

8(a) The 8(a) Business Development program assists firms owned and controlled by socially and economically disadvantaged individuals to enter and succeed in the economic mainstream.

7(m) The 7(m) Microloan program provides small, short-term loans to small business concerns and certain types of not-for-profit childcare centers.

A-123 Designation for OMB Circular on "Internal Control Systems." It prescribes policies and procedures to be followed by executive departments and agencies in establishing, maintaining, evaluating, improving, and reporting on internal controls in their program and administrative activities.

AA Associate Administrator.

AFMAC The Audit and Financial Management Advisory Committee assists the Administrator in overseeing SBA's financial operations.

AFR The Agency Financial Report is one of the annual PAR reports.

APR The Annual Performance Report, required by the Government Performance and Results Act presents a federal agency's progress in achieving the goals in its strategic plan and performance budget.

ARC The America's Recovery Capital Loan program is a temporary guaranty loan program authorized by the American Recovery and Reinvestment Act of 2009.

ARRA The American Recovery and Reinvestment Act of 2009 is most often referred to as the Recovery Act in SBA documents.

BATF The Business Assistance Trust Fund is a trust fund in the U.S. Treasury maintained to receive and account for donations made by private entities for activities to assist small business.

BD Business Development. The Office of Business Development uses SBA's statutory authority to provide business development and federal contract support to small disadvantaged firms.

BDMIS The Business Development Management Information System automates the certification and annual review process for the 8(a) program.

BLIF The Business Loan and Investment Fund is operated by the Treasury Department to maintain the accounting records of loans approved prior to 1992.

CA Capital Access (See OCA).

CDC Certified Development Company, refers to the Section 504 Certified Development Company debenture program.

CFO Chief Financial Officer. The CFO is responsible for the financial leadership of the Agency. This includes responsibility for all Agency disbursements, management and coordination of Agency planning, budgeting, analysis and accountability processes.

CFR the Code of Federal Regulations is the codification of the general and permanent rules published in the Federal Register by the executive departments and agencies of the federal government.

CIO Chief Information Officer. The CIO is responsible for the management of information technology for the Agency, including the design, implementation and continuing successful operation(s) of information programs and initiatives.

CLA The Office of Congressional and Legislative Affairs assists in the development and enactment of SBA legislative proposals and serves as the liaison for SBA's communications on all legislative and congressional activities.

COOP The Continuity of Operations Plan is a predetermined set of instructions or procedures that describes how an organization's essential functions will be sustained for up to 30 days following a disaster and then return to normal operations.

CRC The Civil Rights Center administers and enforces various federal statutes, regulations and Executive Orders that relate to nondiscrimination and equal opportunity.

CY Current Year.

DAP Disaster Assistance Plan. Executive Order 13411 mandates that federal agencies create a single application that fulfills the information requirements of all applicable federal disaster assistance programs.

DCIA The Debt Collection Improvement Act is a federal law to maximize collections of delinquent debts owed to the government.

DCMS The Disaster Credit Management System is the electronic system used by the SBA to process loan applications for all new disaster declarations.

DFP The Dealer Floor Plan is a small pilot program to make revolving loans to retail dealerships, including automobile dealers that began in July 2009.

DLF The Disaster Loan Fund assists eligible small businesses impacted by disasters.

ECCB The Enterprise Change Control Board is in charge of the administration of the centralized network accounts for the SBA.

EEO Equal Employment Opportunity.

ELA The Electronic Loan Application simplifies the application process by providing electronic loan applications.

EVB Entrepreneurship Boot Camp for Veterans with Disabilities.

FASAB The Federal Accounting Standards Advisory Board promulgates accounting principles for federal government reporting entities.

FCRA The Federal Credit Reform Act is a law enacted to provide a more realistic picture of the cost of U.S. government direct loans and loan guaranties.

FECA The Federal Employees Compensation Act provides compensation benefits to federal civilian employees for workrelated injuries or illnesses and to their surviving dependents.

FEMA The Federal Emergency Management Agency is the agency that is tasked with responding to, planning for, recovering from and mitigating against disasters.

FERS The Federal Employees' Retirement System is a three-tiered retirement plan for federal employees hired after 1984, composed of Social Security benefits, a basic benefit plan, and contributions to a TSP.

FEVS Federal Employee Viewpoint Survey.

FFMIA The Federal Financial Management Improvement Act requires each agency to implement and maintain financial management systems that comply substantially with federal financial management systems requirements, applicable federal accounting standards, and the USSGL.

FHCS The Federal Human Capital Survey is administered by OPM to measure federal employees' perceptions about how effectively agencies have managed their workforces.

FICA Federal Insurance Contributions Act.

FMFIA The Federal Managers Financial Integrity Act primarily requires ongoing evaluations and reports on the adequacy of the internal accounting and administrative control systems of executive agencies.

FPDS Federal Procurement Data System.

FRIS The Financial Reporting Information System is SBA's consolidated general ledger system.

FTA Fiscal and Transfer Agent.

FY Fiscal Year. The federal government fiscal year begins October 1 and ends the following September 30.

GAO The Government Accountability Office is the audit, evaluation and investigative arm of Congress.

GCBD Office of Government Contracting and Business Development. GCBD works to create an environment for maximum participation by small, disadvantaged and women-owned business in federal government contract awards and large prime subcontract awards.

GDP Gross Domestic Product.

GPRA-Mod GPRA (Government Performance and Results Act) Modernization Act of 2010.

GS General Schedule.

GSA General Services Administration.

GWAC Government-wide Acquisition Contract.

HUBZone The Historically Underutilized Business Zone program encourages economic development by the establishment of federal contract award preferences for small businesses located in historically underutilized business zones.

IP Improper Payments (See IPIA).

IPA Independent Public Accountant is a firm or person, other than the agency's IG, who meets the independence standards specified in GSA, and is engaged to perform the audit of a federal agency or for other purposes.

IPIA The Improper Payment Information Act is a federal law enacted in 2002 to identify and reduce erroneous payments in the government's programs and activities.

IT Information Technology, refers to matters concerned with the design, development, installation and implementation of information systems and applications.

IV&V Independent Validation and Verification is a review of SBA Office of Financial Analysis and Modeling (OFAM) Financial Models for accuracy and proper functioning by an outside expert.

Jobs Act The Small Business Jobs Act of 2010, most often referred to as the Jobs Act in SBA documents, may also be referred to as SBJA.

LAS The Loan Accounting System is SBA's loan origination servicing and disbursement system.

LLG Liability for Loan Guaranties, net present value of expected future cash flows for outstanding guaranties.

LMAS The Loan Management and Accounting System is the financial management system that supports loan accounting.

LMS The Loan Monitoring System aids the SBA in managing its core loan guaranty programs and serves as one of the building blocks in the overall systems modernization project.

MAS Multiple Awards Schedule.

MAX OMB uses the MAX Budget Information System to collect, validate, analyze, model and publish budget Information.

MD&A Management's Discussion and Analysis. The MD&A is considered required supplementary information for federal financial statements and is designed to provide a high level overview of the Agency.

MED Minority Enterprise Development.

MRA Master Reserve Account. SBA's fiscal agent maintains this escrow fund to facilitate the operation of the Certified Development Company program.

MRF Master Reserve Fund. SBA's fiscal and transfer agent maintains this reserve fund to facilitate the operation of the 7(a) secondary market program.

NAICS North American Industry Classification System. NAICS is the standard used by federal statistical agencies in classifying business establishments for the purpose of collecting, analyzing, and publishing statistical data related to the U.S. business economy.

NGPC National Guaranty Purchase Center is SBA's centralized loan guaranty purchase processing center.

NIST The National Institute of Standards and Technology is an agency of the U.S. Department of Commerce.

NPV Net Present Value.

NWBC The National Women's Business Council is a bi-partisan federal advisory council created to serve as an independent source of advice and policy recommendations to the President, Congress, and the SBA on economic issues of importance to women business owners.

OCA The Office of Capital Access is the SBA office responsible for small business program loans, lender oversight, and the surety bond program.

OCPL The Office of Communications and Public Liaison is the SBA office that provides communication for the Agency's programs and priorities to small businesses, their partners, and the public at large.

OCRM The Office of Credit Risk Management is the SBA office that manages program credit risk, monitors lender performance, and enforces lending program requirements.

ODA The Office of Disaster Assistance is the SBA office that promotes economic recovery in disaster ravaged areas. SBA disaster loans are the primary form of federal assistance for nonfarm, private sector disaster losses for individuals and businesses.

OED The Office of Entrepreneurial Development is the SBA office that provides business counseling and training through its resource partner network composed of small business development centers, women's business centers and SCORE, as well as through online training and related resources through SBA's website.

OFA The Office of Financial Assistance is the SBA office that administers various loan programs to assist small businesses.

OFO The Office of Field Operations is the SBA office that represents field offices, including regional and district offices, at headquarters.

OGC The Office of General Counsel provides legal advice for senior management and legal support for all Agency programs, initiatives and administrative responsibilities.

OGM The Office of Grants Management is the SBA office that awards and administers all grants under SBA's authorization and appropriations, with the exception of the small business development centers and women's business center grants which are awarded and administered by respective program offices.

OHA The Office of Hearings and Appeals is the SBA office that provides an independent, quasi-judicial appeal of certain SBA program decisions.

OHCM The Office of Human Capital Management is the SBA office that supports the strategic management of human capital in the accomplishment of the Agency's mission.

OIC The Office of Internal Control, part of the SBA Office of the Chief Financial Officer, has the lead in making sure managers can comply with internal control standards.

OIG The Office of Inspector General, conducts and supervises audits, inspections and investigations relating to SBA programs and operations.

OII The Office of Investment and Innovation is the SBA office that assists small businesses through the administration of the Small Business Investment Company program and the Small Business Innovation Research program. OIT — The Office of International Trade is the SBA office that promotes small business ability to compete in the global marketplace and delivers export technical assistance and trade finance.

OMB The U.S. Office of Management and Budget is the White House office that oversees preparation of the federal budget and supervises its administration in Executive Branch agencies.

ONAA The Office of Native American Affairs is the SBA office that coordinates Native American initiatives and develops policies and procedures to ensure that SBA assistance is made available to American Indians, Native Alaskans, and Native Hawaiians.

OPM The U.S. Office of Personnel Management is the federal government's human resources agency.

ORACLE ORACLE is the accounting program used by SBA's Administrative Accounting Division.

ORCA Online Representation and Certification Application is an e-government initiative that was designed to replace the paperbased representations and certifications process.

OVBD The Office of Veterans Business Development is the SBA office that works to enhance and increase successful small business ownership by veterans.

PAR The Performance and Accountability Report is the annual report that presents financial, budgetary and performance information to OMB, Congress and the public.

PCECGF The Pollution Control Equipment Contract Guaranty Fund supports costs associated with the credit portfolio of preOctober 1991 pollution control equipment loans and guaranties being liquidated by the SBA.

PIA Privacy Impact Assessment is part of the Privacy Impact Statement from the Privacy Act.

PII Personally Identifiable Information is any information that can identify a person.

PLP Preferred Lender program, covers certified or preferred lenders that receive full delegation of lending authority.

POA&M Plan of Action and Milestones.

PPS Probability Proportional to Size.

PY Prior Year.

QA Quality Assurance, functions to assure that project deliverables meet SBA's requirements and quality standards.

QAR Quality Assurance Review.

Recovery Act The American Recovery and Reinvestment Act of 2009, most often referred to as the Recovery Act in SBA documents, may also be referred to as ARRA.

SAS The Statement on Auditing Standards, establishes standards and provides guidance on the design and selection of an audit sample and the evaluation of the sample results.

SAT Senior Assessment Team.

SBA The U.S. Small Business Administration is a federal agency of the Executive Branch whose mission is to aid, counsel and protect the interests of small businesses and help families and businesses recover from disasters.

SBA Express The loan program provides selected lenders with a 50 percent guaranty on their loans in exchange for the ability to primarily use their own application and documentation forms, making it easier and faster for lenders to provide small business loans of $250,000 or less.

SBDC The Small Business Development Center program delivers management and technical assistance, economic development and management training to existing and prospective small businesses through cooperative agreements with universities and colleges and government organizations.

SBG The Surety Bond Guarantee program provides guaranties, bid, performance and payment bonds for contracts up to $2 million for eligible small businesses that cannot obtain surety bonds through regular commercial channels.

SBGRF Surety Bond Guaranty Revolving Fund. All the contractor and surety fees collected by the SBA are deposited in the SBGRF at the Treasury Department, which is used to pay claims.

SBIC The Small Business Investment Company program provides long-term loans, debt-equity investments and management assistance to small businesses, particularly during their growth stages.

SBIR The Small Business Innovation Research program supports scientific excellence and technological innovation through the investment of federal research funds.

SBLC A Small Business Lending Company is a non-depository small business lending company listed by the SBA Office of Capital Access.

SBPRA Small Business Paperwork Relief Act of 1992.

SBREFA Small Business Regulatory Enforcement Fairness Act.

SCORE A volunteer organization sponsored by the SBA that offers counseling and training for small business owners who are starting, building or growing their businesses.

SDB A Small Disadvantaged Business is a small business owned and controlled by individual(s) who are socially and economically disadvantaged.

SDM System Development Methodology. A software development methodology or system development methodology in software engineering is a framework that is used to structure, plan, and control the process of developing an information system.

SES Senior Executive Service.

SFFAS Statements of Federal Financial Accounting Standards, agreed upon specific standards and concepts published in the Federal Register.

SOP Standard Operating Procedure. SOPs are the primary source of the Agency's internal control.

SOX The Sarbanes-Oxley Act of 2002 introduced major changes to the regulations of financial practice and corporate governance.

Transportation

402 Program (Highway Safety Program) Program 402 funds may be used for nonconstruction ITS/CVO activities that support the selection and implementation of safety construction and traffic operational improvements.

AAMVAnet (American Association of Motor Vehicle Administrators network) A computer network which will route information between participating State Agencies and carriers.

ABS Antilock brake system.

ANSI (American National Standards Institute) The standards development organization involved with Commercial Vehicle Operations electronic data interchange transactions (EDI). This organization provides an infrastructure for defining and maintaining open EDI standards.

Architecture The overall structure and unifying design characteristics of a system.

ASAP (Automated Safety Assessment Program) Will collect data from motor carriers and determines the motor carrier's compliance with Federal Motor Carrier Safety Regulations.

ASAP MCDC (Automated Safety Assessment Program Motor Carrier Data Collection) Will collect data from motor carriers and determines the motor carrier's compliance with Federal Motor Carrier Safety Regulations. This program will consist of menu-driven software that will be provided to eligible motor carriers which could then be downloaded to the Office of Motor Carriers for validation and analysis.

Aspen A local roadside computer system used to collect inspection data which are then typically forwarded to SafetyNet.

ATA (American Trucking Associations) A national trade association of the trucking industry. Its mission is to educate public officials about the trucking industry and to supply current, accurate information to ensure compliance with federal, state, and local laws.

AVALANCHE A distributed system for managing safety data on both interstate and intrastate motor carriers and for the Federal and State offices to electronically exchange data on interstate carriers with MCMIS.

AVC Automated Vehicle Classification.

AVI Automatic Vehicle Identification.

AVL (Automatic Vehicle Location) A technology involving global positioning systems which will enable real-time identification of a vehicle's location relative to a map.

Awareness Seminars A facilitated workshop/discussion group whose purpose is to identify training requirements for implementing the ITS/CVO program.

Bus A motor vehicle consisting primarily of a transport device designed for carrying more than ten persons. Any motor vehicle designed, constructed, and or used for the transportation of passengers, including taxi cabs.

CAPRI State Compliance Review.

Carrier Operations An ITS/CVO Program Area which includes public sector programs and services designed to help manage the flow of commercial vehicles including travel information services and hazardous material incident response services. Private sector programs and services include global positioning systems, satellite technology integrated with computer-aided dispatch, and engine diagnostic systems.

CAT (Carrier Automated Transactions) This system will be one way for carriers to apply for and receive credentials electronically as well as file fuel tax returns. Currently, software is being developed and pilot tested.

CDL/DL Commercial Driver's License/Driver's License.

CDLIS (Commercial Driver License Information System) This system will provide a pointer to past performance records for commercial drivers.

Clearinghouse Processes information received electronically from states to compute fees due/owed each jurisdiction and facilitates periodic funds transfers. For example, carriers may register with a "base state" for their International Registration Plan (IRP) and/or their International Fuel Tax Agreement (IFTA) and that base state would then interface with a clearinghouse to apportion fees owed from and due to other states.

CMAQ (Congestion Mitigation and Air Quality Improvement) CVO traffic management activities and electronic screening, particularly in urban areas, would qualify for this funding.

COACH A JHU/APL document providing CVISN pilot state agencies, motor carriers, and developers of CVISN Core Infrastructure systems with a comprehensive checklist of what is required to be compatible with CVISN operational concepts and architecture.

Comprehensive Skills Matrix The skills matrix resulted from the awareness seminars as a document to be used for planning and executing a comprehensive ITS/CVO training program. The matrix identifies knowledge, skills, and competencies that enable an individual to perform a role in the implementation of ITS/CVO program activities.

Computer-Aided Dispatch A system using digital mapping and optimization algorithms to determine the most direct route between origin and destination, or for a series of stops.

Credentials Administration An ITS/CVO Program Area which includes programs and services designed to improve the deskside procedures and systems for managing motor carrier regulation. These include electronic application, purchasing, and issuance of credentials, automated tax reporting and filing, and interagency and interstate data exchange.

CVIEW (State Commercial Vehicle Information Exchange Window) A system that some states have chosen to implement to collect information from the commercial safety, credentialing, and tax systems to formulate segments of the interstate carrier, vehicle, and driver snapshots and reports for exchange within the state (e.g., with roadside sites) and with the SAFER system.

CVIS (Commercial Vehicle Information System) An information system being used to determine the feasibility of linking safety fitness to vehicle registration.

CVISN (Commercial Vehicle Information Systems and Networks) CVISN is the collection of state, federal and private sector information systems and communications networks that support commercial vehicle operations (CVO). Many improvement initiatives are currently underway to develop new systems and upgrade existing systems to add new capabilities and allow electronic exchange of information using open interface standards. This will enable delivery of new electronic services to states and carriers in the broad areas of safety, credentials, electronic clearance, and improved carrier operations.

CVO (Commercial Vehicle Operations) Includes all the operations associated with moving goods and passengers via commercial vehicles over the North American highway system and the activities necessary to regulate these operations.

CVSA (Commercial Vehicle Safety Alliance) A non-profit organization of federal, state, and provincial government agencies and representatives from industry in the United States, Canada, and Mexico dedicated to improving commercial vehicle safety. The Alliance seeks to bring together state/provincial officials with industry interest and federal governments in a unique discussion and problem solving interchange.

DACUM Derived from Developing A curriculum, DACUM is an analysis methodology originally developed by Ohio State University for analyzing educational curriculum requirements in a cost-effective and timely manner, and is an approach often used by universities to design educational curriculum and course content.

Data Type The size and type of a data element. An interpretation applied to a string of bits, such as integer, real, or character.

Database A collection of interrelated data stored with controlled redundancy to serve one or more applications; the data is stored so that it is independent of programs that use the data; a common and controlled approach is used in adding new data, and in modifying and retrieving existing data within a database.

DMV Department of Motor Vehicles.

DOT (Department of Transportation) Coordinates development of uniform standards for reliable electronic information to support CVISN and other CVO services.

DSRC (Dedicated Short Range Communications) Used to provide data communications between a moving vehicle and the roadside to support the screening process. This is accomplished by means of a transponder (e.g., tag) mounted in the cab of the vehicle and a reader and antenna installed at the roadside.

EDI (Electronic Data Interchange) The exchange of routine business transactions in a computer-processable format, covering such traditional applications as inquiries, planning, purchasing, acknowledgments, pricing, order status, scheduling, test results, shipping and receiving, invoices, payments and financial reporting.

EFT (Electronic Funds Transfer) An electronic mechanism which allows for transfer of funds from one bank to another. For example, for electronic credentialing one option is to pay for your credentials by transferring money from your bank to the credentialing agency's bank via EFT.

Electronic Clearance The process that allows commercial vehicles, whether operating intrastate or interstate, to pass a check point (e.g., weigh station) at mainline speeds without stopping to be checked for proper credentials, weight, and safety status.

Electronic Screening An ITS/CVO Program Area which includes programs and services designed to facilitate the verification of size, weight, and credential information including automated screening and clearance of commercial vehicles and international electronic border clearance.

Electronic Trip Recorders Also known as onboard computers, these recorders automatically monitor and record information on the performance of the vehicle and/or driver.

Enforcement Officers and Commanders Includes any State or local law enforcement officers and commanders with responsibility for commercial vehicle operations such as highway patrol, state police, etc.

Fedwire The Federal Reserve funds transfer system. Fedwire is used for transferring reserve account balances of depository institutions and government securities.

FHWA (Federal Highway Administration) The lead Federal agency for the ITS/CVO program.

FHWA GOE (Federal Highway Administration General Operating Expenditures) Funds are available for research and development, field operational tests, architecture and standards evaluation, and program system support. Approximately $34.7 million total spent on ITS/CVO in 1997.

GPS (Global Positioning System) A system which locates vehicles using trilateration from multiple satellite-based transmitters.

HazMat Hazardous Materials.

Help, Inc. (Heavy Vehicle Electronic License Plate Inc.) A non-profit partnership between motor carriers and government agencies in eleven western states.

IBC International Border Crossing.

ICC Interstate Commerce Commission.

IFTA International Fuel Tax Agreement.

IM (Interstate Maintenance) ITS/CVO projects in interstate construction zones, such as weigh station upgrades and traffic management systems, may be eligible for this funding.

Incident Management Projects Activities to enable more rapid detection, response, and clearance of incidents from highways, and efforts to spread information about the incident to encourage drivers to seek alternate routes and reduce traffic congestion.

Interstate Applications Via Internet browser, access governmental or private web sites to apply for credentials and perform other Commercial Vehicle-related functions.

Interstate Highway A traffic way on the Interstate System.

Interstate Motor Carrier A motor carrier engaged in interstate commerce whose vehicle(s) transports property or passengers between or through two or more states or other jurisdictions (see "Jurisdiction").

Interstate Operation Vehicle movement between or through two or more jurisdictions.

Intelligent Transportation System (ITS) Transportation systems which utilize information, communication, sensor, and control technologies to achieve improved levels of performance and safety on America's highways.

IRP International Registration Plan.

ISTEA (Intermodal Surface Transportation Efficiency Act) Passed by Congress in 1991 and calls for the creation of an economically efficient and environmentally sound transportation system that will move people and goods in an energy efficient manner and will provide the foundation for a competitive American transportation industry.

ITDS International Trade Data System.

ITS (Intelligent Transportation Systems) Intelligent Transportation Systems integrate advanced computer information processing, communications, sensors, and electronics technologies and management strategies to increase the safety and efficiency of the surface transportation system.

ITS America The only Congressionally-mandated, national public/private organization established to coordinate the development and deployment of Intelligent Transportation Systems (ITS) in the United States. ITS America's members include federal, state, local and foreign government agencies, national and international corporations involved in the development of ITS, universities, independent research organizations, and public interest groups.

ITS/CVO (Intelligent Transportation Systems/ Commercial Vehicle Operations) The ITS/CVO program is a voluntary effort involving public and private partnerships focused on improving highway safety and motor carrier productivity through the use of technology. The Federal Highway Administration is the lead Federal agency for the program and the Office of Motor Carrier's ITS/CVO Division is directly responsible for oversight of the program.

ITS/CVO Mainstreaming Initiative The Mainstreaming initiative is intended to organize and manage ITS/CVO deployment and communicate the ITS/CVO program to all stakeholders to gain support and participation. Mainstreaming efforts are underway in more than 35 states.

ITS/CVO Program Management The individuals with overall ITS/CVO program management responsibilities, including Federal, State or Private organizations.

ITS/CVO Technical Design and Implementation Individual with responsibility for the design and implementation of ITS/CVO technology.

ITS/CVO Technical Project Management Individuals with management responsibility for technical aspects of ITS/CVO implementation, including Federal, State, and Private organizations.

ITS/CVO Systems Design and Integration Individuals with responsibility for the design and integration of systems for ITS/CVO implementation.

ITS/CVO Technical Support Individuals with responsibility for technical support to the implementation of ITS/CVO technology.

ITS Deployment Incentive Funds Proposed Federal funding source for deployment grants.

JPO (Joint Program Office for Intelligent Transportation Systems) Coordinates ITS activities of all Department of Transportation modal administrations.

Jurisdiction Jurisdiction means a state territory, or possession of the United States, the District of Columbia, or a state, province, or territory of a country.

LPR SSWIM License Plate Reader Slow Speed Weigh In Motion.

MACS Advantage CVO Maintime Automated Clearance System.

MAPS (Multijurisdictional Automated Preclearance System) A public-private partnership between government and the trucking industry in Idaho, Oregon, Utah, and Washington. MAPS jurisdictions are building compatible systems for electronic screening and "one-stop shopping."

MCMIS (Motor Carrier Management Information System) A federal agency which collects and stores roadside inspection data.

MCSAP (Motor Carrier Safety Assistance Program) A grant program established to assist with state enforcement of safety, size, and weight regulations with goals of reducing commercial motor vehicle crashes. This program represents a key funding source for implementing ITS/CVO safety assurance projects.

Motor Carrier A person (an individual, partnership, association, corporation, business trust, or any other organized group of individuals) which is responsible for the safety fitness of a commercial motor vehicle engaged in commerce on roads and highways.

Motor Vehicle Any vehicle, machine, tractor, trailer or semitrailer propelled or drawn by mechanical power and used upon the highways in the transportation of passengers or property.

MPO Metropolitan Planning Organization.

MVA Motor Vehicle Administration.

NATAP North American Trade Automation Prototype.

NCIC National Crime Information Center.

NHS (National Highway System) ITS/CVO operational improvements eligible for NHS funding include traffic surveillance and control equipment, motorist information systems, and incident management programs. Electronic screening systems may also qualify for NHS funding.

NIER National Institute for Environmental Renewal.

NLETS National Law Enforcement Telecommunications System.

NMVTIS (National Motor Vehicle Titling Information System) The National Motor Vehicle Title Information System (NMVTIS) is an information-sharing system required by the Anti-Car Theft Act of 1992, enacted to deter trafficking of stolen vehicles by strengthening law enforcement against auto theft, combating automobile title fraud, preventing "chop shop" related thefts, and inspecting exports for stolen vehicles.

O & M Operations and Maintenance.

OMC (Office of Motor Carriers) This is a division of the U.S. Department of Transportation's (USDOT) Federal Highway Administration (FHWA). OMC is responsible for issues concerning the nation's motor carrier industry and is organized as follows:

- Headquarters—OMC's main office is at the USDOT building in Washington, D.C.
- Regional—There are nine OMC regions in the United States. Regional offices report to headquarters.
- Division—Each state has a division office which works closely with state motor carrier safety and registration officials. Division offices report to the Regional offices.

One-Stop Shopping Refers to the ability to obtain all required tax and regulatory credentials from a single source.

OOS Out of Service.

Open Standards Technology standards for each ITS/CVO technology that define requirements and design and are available to all ITS/CVO stakeholders for use in the design and implementation of ITS/CVO technology.

OS/OW Oversize/Overweight Permits.

PASS (Port of Entry Advanced Sorting System) An operational test of WIM, AVI, AVC, OBC, and two way communication systems to pre-clear trucks on mainline I-5 at Ashland (Oregon) port of entry.

PrePass™ A sophisticated intelligent transportation system that electronically identifies subscribing commercial vehicles, verifies state-required operating credentials and checks both axle and gross weight as commercial vehicles bypass designated weigh stations. The system is being implemented in California, New Mexico, Arizona, and Wyoming.

PRISM Performance and Registration Information Systems Management (Formerly CVIS).

Process A repetitive, well-defined set of logical tasks that support one function, can be defined in terms of inputs and outputs, and have a definable beginning and end. Processes can be decomposed into processes and are triggered by an event and carried out by a business segment to achieve a stated purpose. A low-level process may be replicated across the business segment.

PUC Public Utility Commission.

R & D Research and Development.

Regional Champion A full-time program coordinator hired by regional forums to facilitate the work of the forum and explain ITS/CVO services to administrators, legislators, motor carriers, and the general public.

Regional Forum There are seven regional forums which correspond to major "trucksheds" which are defined by freight generation and truck traffic volumes. They are responsible for providing policy and program direction for their state programs. Each forum hires a regional champion to facilitate the work of the forum.

Regulated Motor Carrier A carrier subject to economic regulation by the Interstate Commerce Commission.

Road That part of a traffic way which includes both the roadway and any shoulder alongside the roadway.

Roadside The part of the traffic way between the outer edge of the shoulder and the edge of the traffic way; off the road, but inside the traffic way and not part of the median.

Roadside Inspection An inspection of a commercial vehicle or driver that occurs at the roadside.

Roadway That part of a traffic way designed, improved, and ordinarily used for motor vehicle travel or, where various classes of motor vehicles are segregated, that part of a traffic way used by a particular class. Separate roadways may be provided for northbound and southbound traffic or for trucks and automobiles. Bridle paths and bicycle paths are not included in this definition.

SAFER (Safety and Fitness Electronic Records) An on-line system that will be available to users over a nationwide data network which will return a standard carrier safety fitness snapshot or record to the requester within a few seconds.

SAFESTAT a performance-based program to measure a motor carrier's safety performance and to determine when an on site review of a carrier's operation is necessary.

Safety Assurance An ITS/CVO Program Area which includes programs and services designed to assure the safety of commercial drivers, vehicles, and cargo. These include automated roadside safety inspections and carrier reviews, safety information systems, and on-board safety monitoring.

Safety Inspectors Includes any individual responsible for inspection of commercial vehicles whether contractor or state personnel.

SafetyNet A distributed system for managing safety data on both interstate and intrastate motor carriers and for the Federal and State offices to electronically exchange data on interstate carriers with MCMIS.

SafeVUE (SAFER and CVIEW Visual User Environment) Carriers will be able to retrieve own snapshots and records generated by SAFER and CVIEW systems.

SEA Safety Evaluation Area.

SENTRI Secure Electronic Network for Travelers' Rapid Inspection.

SIB (State Infrastructure Bank) A pilot program established in 1995 to assist participating states with ITS/CVO projects.

Smart Card Plastic cards with an embedded integrated circuit chip containing memory and microprocessor.

SME Subject Matter Experts- those individuals possessing unique expertise regarding technology or implementation of ITS/CVO.

Snapshot A packet of safety data which can be made available at roadside inspection stations via SAFER and/or CVIEW. Snapshots contain safety information on carriers, vehicles, and drivers.

SPR (State Planning and Research) Technical and organizational ITS/CVO activities may be eligible for this program.

Stakeholders/Users Including but not limited to Shippers, State Agency Managers and Administrators, and others not included in other specific user groups.

STP (Surface Transportation Program) ITS/CVO activities eligible for STP funding may include highway safety programs, planning activities, and capital and operating costs for traffic management facilities and programs.

System A group of interacting, interrelated, interdependent elements forming a complex whole to accomplish some function. Some examples include an automated roadside safety inspection process, on-board cargo monitoring system, an electronic credentialing system.

Technology The application of science and/or engineering which results in products such as computers, wireless communications, databases and networks, sensors, portable diagnostic devices, etc.

Transparent Borders The ability of commercial vehicles to travel unimpeded across state borders.

Transponder An electronic tag mounted in a motor vehicle that has electronically stored information that can be retrieved by a roadside reader.

Truck A motor vehicle designed to carry an entire load. It may consist of a chassis and body, a chassis, cab and body, or it may be of integral construction so that the body and chassis form a single unit.

Truck Combination A truck consisting primarily of a transport device which is a single-unit truck or truck tractor with one or more attached trailers.

Truck Tonnage The weight of freight, measured in tons, transported by a truck.

Truck Tractor A motor vehicle consisting of a single motorized transport device designed primarily for drawing trailers.

Trucking and Motor Coach Industry Includes all trucking operators and drivers and motor coach or busing operations for commercial vehicle operations on the highways.

UCR (Unified Carrier Register) The state component of the carrier registration system.

VAN (Value Added Network) A communications facility which transmits, receives, and stores EDI messages. This network can be considered as an "electronic mailbox," where business information is passed between users.

VIN Vehicle Identification Number.

VMS Variable Message Sign.

VMT Vehicle Miles Traveled.

VRC Vehicle to Roadside Communication

WIM (Weigh-in-Motion) Measures dynamic axle weight at highway or slower speeds. Weigh-in-Motion refers to various technologies that enable vehicle weights to be determined without the need for a vehicle to physically stop on a scale.

Veterans Affairs

1151 Benefits VA awarded monthly compensation benefits for disability or death incurred as the result of VA hospital care, medical or surgical treatment or examination, but only if the disability or death was proximately caused by negligence or an unforeseen event.

Access Access is the veteran's ability to obtain medical care at his/her desired location. The ease of access is determined by components, such as availability of health care services, location of health care facilities, transportation, hours of operation, and cost-effective delivery of health care. Efforts to improve access often focus on improving efficiency of health care delivery processes.

Adjunct Condition An adjunct condition, for medical treatment purposes, is a non-service-connected condition that may be associated with and held to be aggravating an adjudicated service-connected condition. VA bills health insurance plans for treatment of an adjunct condition and as applicable, may charge a copay for treatment of the adjunct condition.

Adult Day Health Care Adult Day Health Care is a therapeutic day care program, provides medical and rehabilitation services to disabled veterans in a congregate setting.

Aid and Attendance (A&A) A VA compensation or pension benefit awarded to a veteran determined to be in need of the regular aid and attendance of another person to perform basic functions of everyday life. A veteran may qualify for aid and attendance benefits if he or she:
- Is blind or so nearly blind as to have corrected visual acuity of 5/200 or less, in both eyes, or concentric contraction of the visual field to 5 degrees or less; or
- Is a patient in a nursing home because of mental or physical incapacity; or
- Proves a need for aid and attendance under established criteria

Allowable Deductions Allowable deductions are those payments made by veterans for certain nonreimbursed medical expenses, funeral and burial expenses and educational expenses. Veterans are able to exclude allowable deductions from their total gross household income in determining their eligibility for VA health care benefits.

Appeal A process used to request VA reconsider a previous authorization or claim decision.

Applicant A person who has submitted a formal request for VA health care benefits and/or for enrollment in the VA health care system.

Asset Property or resource of an individual which includes: cash, stocks and bonds, individual retirement accounts, income producing property, etc.

Bereavement Counseling Bereavement counseling is assistance and support to people with emotional and psychological stress after the death of a loved one. Bereavement counseling includes a broad range of transition services, including outreach, counseling, and referral services to family members.

Catastrophically Disabled A veteran who has a permanent, severely disabling injury, disorder, or disease that compromises the ability to carry out the activities of daily living to such a degree that he/she requires personal or mechanical assistance to leave home or bed, or requires constant supervision to avoid physical harm to self or others.

Chronic Care Long-term care of individuals with long-standing, persistent diseases or conditions. Chronic care includes care specific to the problem, as well as other measures to encourage self-care, promote health, and prevent loss of function.

Combat Service A status applied for a veteran who served on active duty in a theater of combat operations during a period of war recognized by the VA.

Commonwealth Army Veterans The term "Commonwealth Army veterans" refers to persons who served before July 1, 1946, in the organized military forces of the Government of the Philippines. These Filipino forces were made a part of the U.S. Armed Forces by a military order of the President dated July 26, 1941. Finally these veterans were discharged or released from this period of service under conditions other than dishonorable.

Community Residential Care Community Residential Care provides health care supervision to eligible veterans not in need of hospital or nursing home care but who, because of medical and/or psychosocial health conditions as determined through a statement of needed care, are not able to live independently and have no suitable family or significant others to provide the needed supervision and supportive care. The veteran must be capable of self-preservation with minimal assistance and exhibit socially acceptable behavior.

Compensable Disabilities A VA rated service-connected disability for which monetary compensation is authorized for payment. You might even be entitled to compensation when your disabilities are rated 0% disabling.

Here are the three situations that would be compensable.

- You have a condition rated 10% disabling or greater.
- Your have a condition rated at 0%, but it's a disability that entitles you to *special monthly compensation*.
- You have two or more 0% disabilities, and their *combined* effect interferes with your ability to work. (In this case, we'd pay you at the 10% rate.)

Congressional Appropriation The funding allocated by Congress to VA for providing benefits and medical services to eligible VA beneficiaries.

Consultation Service provided by a physician whose opinion or advice regarding evaluation and/or management of a specific problem is requested by another physician.

Contract Provider Any hospital, skilled nursing facility, extended care facility, individual, organization, or agency that has a contractual agreement with VA for providing medical services to veterans.

Copay A specific monetary charge for either medical services or outpatient medications provided by VA to veterans whose financial assessment determines they are able to pay.

Covered Benefit Medically necessary care and services included in the Medical Benefits Package as defined within 38 Code of Federal Regulation (CFR) 17.38.

Diagnosis The identity of a medical condition, cause or disease.

Deductible An amount that a veteran must pay for covered services in a specified time period before VA benefits begin.

Dependent Spouse or unmarried child (to include a biological, legally adopted, or stepchild under the age of 18, or between the ages of 18 and 23 and attending school, or a child who was permanently and totally disabled before the age of 18).

Disenrollment The discontinuation of a veteran's enrolled status. Disenrollment may result because the veteran requests not to participate in VA enrollment, or when VA determines that certain Priority Groups will no longer be provided services. Requests to disenroll must be in writing.

Domiciliary A VA facility that provides care on an ambulatory self-care basis for veterans disabled by age or disease who are not in need of acute hospitalization and who do not need the skilled nursing services provided in a nursing home.

Durable Medical Equipment Equipment intended for frequent use in the treatment of a medical condition or injury. Examples include wheelchairs, hospital beds, walkers, etc.

Earned Income Money you receive from working

Emergency An emergency medical condition is a medical condition manifesting itself by acute symptoms of sufficient severity such that a prudent layperson, who possesses an average knowledge of health and medicine, could reasonably expect the absence of immediate medical attention to result in 1) placing the health of the individual in serious jeopardy, 2) serious impairment to bodily functions, or 3) serious dysfunction of any bodily organ or part.

Enrollee A veteran who has applied for VA medical services under 38 United States Code (U.S.C.) 1710 and 38 CFR 17.36, has been accepted for such care, and who has received confirmation of enrollment in the VA health care system.

Enrollment The process for providing veterans access to VA health care benefits covered by the medical benefits package.

Enrollment Group Thresholds (EGT) The enrollment Priority Group level, as determined by the Secretary Veterans Affairs, at which veterans will be accepted for enrollment into the VA health care system.

Environmental Contaminants / Gulf War Illness Gulf War veterans were exposed to a wide variety of environmental hazards and potential harmful substances during their service in Southwest Asia. These include depleted uranium, pesticides, the anti-nerve gas pill pyridostigmine bromide, infectious diseases, chemical and biological warfare agents, and vaccinations (including anthrax and botulinum toxoid), and oil well free smoke and petroleum products. VA recognizes that there are other health risk factors encountered by Gulf War veterans. Veterans with service during the Gulf War are eligible to receive treatment for conditions related to this service. If the treatment provided is for an illness or symptom that may possibly be associated with environmental contamination, copay for medical care and medication copay will not be charged.

Conditions Associated with Environmental Contaminants:

- Persistent fatigue
- Skin rash
- Headache
- Arthralgias/myalgias

- Sleep disturbance
- Forgetfulness
- Joint pain
- Shortness of breath/chest pain
- Feverishness
- Amyotrophic Lateral Sclerosis

Financial Assessment A means of collecting income and asset information used to determine a veteran's eligibility for health care benefits.

Formulary A formulary is a list of medicines from which your VA provider can choose to treat your medical condition. This list of medicines has been looked at and approved by a group of highly trained VA physicians and clinical pharmacists. New medicines are usually added to the formulary based on a complete review of published medical studies as well as available patient safety data.

Medicines are grouped by VA as Formulary, Formulary-Restricted or Non-Formulary. Formulary-Restricted medicines usually can be used only by those providers with specific experience in how these medicines are prescribed and monitored. For example, oncologists usually are the only VA providers who can prescribe medicines used to treat cancer. Non-Formulary medicines are prescribed for those patients who either have failed or could not tolerate any of the VA Formulary medicines.

Geographic Means Test (GMT) Thresholds Copay Required A copay status assigned to a veteran whose household income is above the VA means test income thresholds but below the GMT income thresholds. GMT copay for inpatient care is reduced by 80%, all other copay amounts remain the same. GMT income thresholds are based upon established geographic income thresholds.

GMT—Below the Means Test Thresholds Veterans whose household income and net worth are below the VA National income thresholds such that they are unable to defray the expenses of care; therefore, they are not subject to copay charges for hospital and outpatient medical services.

GMT—Above the Means Test and GMT Thresholds Veterans whose household income and/or net worth are ABOVE the VA National income thresholds and income ABOVE the geographically-based income thresholds for their resident location who do not otherwise qualify for placement in a higher enrollment Priority Group. These veterans must agree to pay copays for hospital care and outpatient medical services.

GMT—Above the Means Test and Below the GMT Thresholds Veterans with household income and/or net worth are ABOVE the VA National income thresholds and income BELOW the geographically-based income thresholds for their resident location who do not otherwise qualify for placement in a higher enrollment Priority Group. These veterans must also agree to pay copays for hospital care and outpatient medical services, but their inpatient medical care copays are reduced 80 percent.

Geriatric Evaluation Geriatric evaluation, which is part of the basic benefits package, is the comprehensive assessment of a veteran's ability to care for him/herself, physical health, and social environment, which leads to a plan of care. The plan could include treatment, rehabilitation, health promotion, and social services.

Gross Household Income Generally, gross income of the veteran, spouse and dependent children is counted for determining a veteran's eligibility for VA health care benefits. This includes earned and unearned income but excludes most need-based payments such as welfare, Supplemental Security Income (SSI).

Gross Income Income before allowable expenses are subtracted.

Hardship A "hardship" exist when there is a significant change in your family income and net worth from the previous calendar year to the present year.

You could have been working in the previous year and due to a recent disability are no longer able to work. Chances are this type of situation would create a significant change in your family's income.

Head or Neck Cancer Veterans with cancer of the head and neck and a history of receipt of Nasopharyngeal (NP) radium therapy are eligible for treatment. There are very specific dates and locations where this activity occurred. Eligibility for this special class needs to be verified. (Not all veterans receiving head and neck cancer treatment fall into this treatment category.)

During the 1920s, nasopharyngeal (NP) radium therapy was developed to treat hearing loss caused by repeated ear infections. Radium-tipped rods were inserted into the nostrils and left in place for several minutes. Military physicians used NP radium to treat aerotitis media (barotrauma) in submariners, aviators, and divers. It is estimated that between 8,000 and 20,000 military personnel received NP radium treatments during World War II and until the 1960s. Veterans also included are those with documentation of NP radium treatment in active military, naval or air service; those who served as an aviator in the active military, naval or air service before the end of the Korean conflict; or underwent submarine training in active naval service before January 1, 1965. Veterans with exposure to NP radium treatments are eligible to receive treatment for conditions related to this exposure, including head and neck cancer. If the veteran is being treated for any condition during this episode of care that is related to Head and Neck Cancer; the veteran does not have to pay a copay for the visit or the medication.

Health Insurance Portability and Accountability Act (HIPAA) HIPAA is a federal law enacted in 1996. It was designated to improve availability and portability of health coverage and the efficiency of the health care system by standardizing the electronic exchange of health information and protecting the security and privacy of member-identifiable health information.

Home Health Care Skilled nursing and other therapeutic services provided by VA or a home health care agency in a home setting as an alternative to confinement in a hospital or skilled nursing facility.

Homemaker/Home Health Aide Services The Homemaker/Home Health Aide (H/HHA) Program provides services as an "alternative" to nursing home care. The H/HHA Coordinator along with the interdisciplinary team makes a clinical judgment that the veteran would, in the absence of H/HHA services, require nursing home equivalent care.

Hospice/Palliative Care Hospice/Palliative Care programs offer pain management, symptom control, and other medical services to terminally ill veterans or veterans in the late stages of the chronic disease process.

Hostilities "Hostilities" means any armed conflict in which the members pf the Armed Forces are subjected to combat conditions comparable to a period of war. The periods of armed conflict are determined by the Secretary of VA in consultation with the Secretary of Defense.

Housebound Benefit The VA's Housebound benefit is an additional amount available to eligible veterans and dependents who are entitled to VA pension or VA compensation. The housebound allowance may be paid to veterans, dependent spouses, or surviving spouses who because of their physical limitations, are unable to walk or travel beyond their home and are reasonably certain the disabilities or confinement will continue throughout his or her lifetime. Certain restrictions apply. For more information and eligibility criteria on this benefit call 800-827-1000, 800-827-1000 or go to http://www.vba.va.gov/bln/21/Benefits/.

Housing and Urban Development Geographic Index Congress wanted to grant relief from making VA copay for some veterans with marginal incomes, recognizing that income alone is not always a fair measure of one's standard of living because of sometimes large differences in the cost of living in different areas of the country. Congress modified VA's system of determining veterans' ability to pay for health care by creating a geographically-based income limit and reducing inpatient copay for those veterans whose income falls below these new geographic income thresholds. The new geographic income thresholds are adjusted for all standard metropolitan statistical areas (SMSAs) and are updated periodically to reflect economic changes within the SMSAs. The geographic means test thresholds are based upon the geographically based low- income thresholds set by the U.S. Department of Housing and Urban Development (HUD) for public housing benefits.

Inpatient Care Services received during a patient's hospital stay.

Ionizing Radiation Atomic veterans may have been exposed to ionizing radiation in a variety of ways at various locations. Veterans exposed at a nuclear device testing site (the Pacific Islands, e.g., Bikini, NM, NV, etc.) or in Hiroshima and/or Nagasaki, Japan, may be included. Atomic veterans with exposure to ionizing radiation are eligible to receive treatment for conditions related to this exposure. VA has recognized the following conditions by statute or regulation as being associated with radiation exposure:

Conditions Associated with Ionizing Radiation:
- Leukemia
- Thyroid Cancer
- Breast Cancer
- Lung Cancer
- Bone Cancer
- Primary Liver Cancer
- Skin Cancer
- Esophageal Cancer
- Stomach Cancer
- Colon Cancer
- Pancreatic Cancer
- Kidney Cancer Urinary Bladder Cancer
- Salivary Gland Cancer
- Multiple myeloma
- Posterior Subcapsular Cataracts
- Non-malignant Thyroid Nodular Disease
- Ovarian Cancer
- Parathyroid Adenoma
- Tumors of the brain and central nervous system
- Lymphomas other than Hodgkin's Disease
- Cancer of the Rectum
- Cancer of the Small Intestine
- Cancer of the Pharynx
- Cancer of the Bile Duct
- Cancer of the Gall Bladder
- Cancer of the Renal Pelvis, Ureters and Urethra
- Cancer of the Prostate
- All Other Cancers

Low-Income Thresholds Veterans with gross household income under the "low income thresholds" are eligible to receive certain health related benefits at no cost to the veteran. The low income thresholds is set by law and varies according to the veteran's family size and benefit applied for.

Means Test The formal financial assessment process used by VA to measure a veteran's gross household income and assets. The means test determines veterans copay responsibilities and helps to determine enrollment priority.

Means Test Copay Exempt Veterans not required to make copays for medical care provided by VA include:
- Veterans with a compensable service-connected rating or
- Veterans in receipt of VA pension benefits or whose income does not exceed the applicable VA means test income thresholds;
- Veterans requiring services/medications for treatment of a service-connected condition; or for conditions related to exposure to ionizing radiation, sexual trauma experienced while in the military; nose or throat radium treatments while in the military requiring services/medication for head or neck cancer; or for participation in Project 112/SHAD experiments;
- Former POWs;
- Veterans in receipt of a Purple Heart medal, WWI veterans and veterans who were discharged from the military for a disability that was incurred or aggravated in the line of duty; and
- Combat veterans who were discharged after November, 11, 1998, who require services/medications for conditions that are potentially related to combat service, as follows:

    If discharged on or after January 28, 2003 for five years post discharge.

    If discharged from active duty before January 28, 2003, and if application for enrollment is made on or after January 28, 2008, until January 27, 2011.

Means Test Copay Required A copay status assigned to a veteran who is required to make medical care copay based on financial status relative the applicable means test income thresholds.

Medicaid A jointly funded federal and state program that provides hospital expense and medical expense coverage to persons with low-income and certain aged and disabled individuals.

Medical Benefits Package The term "Medical Benefits Package" refers to a group of health care services that are provided to all enrolled veterans.

Medical Need The determination that care or service(s) are required to promote, preserve, or restore a veteran's health as specified within 38 CFR 17.38(b). A treatment, procedure, supply, or service is considered medically necessary as determined by the patient's care provider and in accordance with generally accepted standards of clinical practice.

Medicare A federal program that provides health care coverage for people aged 65 and older, as well as some younger individuals with specific health problems. Medicare Part A covers hospitalization, extended care and nursing home care; Medicare Part B covers outpatient services, and is subject to a monthly premium.

Military Sexual Trauma (MST) Sexual trauma experienced while on active duty in the military. Sexual trauma is defined as sexual harassment, sexual assault, rape and other acts of violence. Sexual harassment is further defined as repeated unsolicited, verbal or physical contact of a sexual nature, which is threatening in nature. If the veteran is being treated for any condition during this episode of care that the provider believes is related to MST; the veteran does not have to pay a copay for the visit or the medication. http://www.va.gov/womenvet/page.cfm?pg=23

Nasopharyngeal Radium Therapy Because it was effective in treating otitis media, military physicians used NP radium to treat aerotitis media (barotrauma) in submariners, aviators, and divers due to enlarged tissue in the throat combined with rapid pressure changes. It is estimated that between 8,000 and 20,000 military personnel received NP radium treatments during World War II and until the 1960s.

Net Worth Simply put, "net worth" means the market value of everything you own, minus what you owe.

There are exclusions, not everything you own or owe is considered. VA has some very specific guidelines on how it computes net worth. The VA Means Test uses the same rules as VA pension to determine your net worth.

Noncompensable Noncompensable refers awards of service-connection which VA determines do not warrant the award of monetary compensation.

Nonservice-Connected Pension A monetary support benefit awarded to permanently and totally disabled, low-income veterans with 90 days or more of active military service, of which at least one day was during wartime. Veterans of a period of war who are age 65 or older and meet service and income requirements are also eligible to receive a pension, regardless of current physical condition. Payments are made to qualified veterans to bring their total income, including other retirement or Social Security income, to a level set by Congress. For more information, go to http://www.va.gov and click on Compensation and Pension Benefits.

Nonservice-Connected Veteran An eligible veteran who has been discharged from active military duty, and does not have a VA adjudicated illness or injury incurred in or aggravated by military service.

Nursing Home The term "nursing home care" means the accommodation of convalescents or other persons who are not acutely ill and not in need of hospital care, but who require nursing care and related medical services, if such nursing care and medical services are prescribed by, or are performed under the general direction of, persons duly licensed to provide such care. Such term includes services furnished in skilled nursing care facilities, in intermediate care facilities, and in combined facilities. It does not include domiciliary care.

Open Enrollment The process of accepting applications for enrollment at any time during the year.

Other Than Dishonorable Conditions All veterans are potentially eligible for most veterans' health care benefits are based solely on active military service in the Army, Navy, Air Force, Marines, or Coast Guard (or Merchant Marines during WWII), and discharged under other than dishonorable conditions.

Outpatient Care Refers to health care a patient receives without being admitted to a hospital. Examples include office visits, x-rays, lab tests and some surgical procedures.

Palliative Care Care provided primarily to relieve symptoms of a disease or condition rather than for curative purposes.

Pension Benefit VA pension is a monetary award paid on a monthly basis to veterans with low income who are permanently and totally disabled, or are age 65 and older, may be eligible for monetary support if they have 90 days or more of active military service, at least one day of which was during a period or war. Payments are made to qualified veterans to bring their total income, including other retirement or Social Security income, to a level set by Congress annually. Veterans of a period of war who are age 65 or older and meet service and income requirements are also eligible to receive a pension, regardless of current physical condition.

Preferred Facility The veteran identified VA health care location where the veteran prefers to receive care. A preferred facility may be any VA health care location, for example, VA health care facility, independent clinic, or community based outpatient clinic. If VA is unable to provide your needed health care, that facility will make arrangements to refer you to another VA health care facility or to one of VA's private sector affiliates to provide the required care.

Preventive Care Health Care that emphasizes prevention, early detection, and treatment.

Primary Care Provider The clinician who is responsible for the supervision, coordination, and provision of the veteran's medical care. This clinician provides routine health services and is the veteran's first point of contact when the veteran becomes sick. The primary care provider can easily refer patients to a specialist (such as a surgeon) should they require care outside the scope of his or her expertise.

Project 112/SHAD Project SHAD, an acronym for Shipboard Hazard and Defense, was part of a larger effort called Project 112, which was conducted during the 1960s. Project SHAD encompassed tests designed to identify US warships' vulnerabilities to attacks with chemical or biological warfare agents and to develop procedures to respond to such attacks while maintaining a war-fighting capability.

Prosthetic Devices A device which replaces all or a portion of a part of the human body. A prosthetic device can be used when a part of the body is permanently damaged, is absent, or is malfunctioning.

Public Law (PL) 104-262 The public law passed by Congress in October 1996, also known as the *Veteran's Health Care Eligibility Reform Act of 1996*. This law established national standards of access and equitable health care services to veterans and required that most veterans be enrolled to receive care.

Public Law (PL) 107-135 "Department of Veterans Affairs Health Care Programs Enhancement Act of 2001" provides for chiropractic care and services for veterans through Department of Veterans Affairs medical centers and clinics.

Public Law (PL) 110-329 Also known as Consolidated Security, Disaster Assistance, and Continuing Appropriations Act, passed by Congress September 30, 2008. This act provided VA additional funding to allow expanded enrollment opportunity for certain Priority 8 veterans who may have been previously denied enrollment in VA's health care system because their income exceeded VA's means tests thresholds.

Purple Heart A "Purple Heart" is a medal given by the military to a service person injured as a direct result of combat.

Radiation Risk Activity On site participation in a test involving the atmospheric detonation of a nuclear device.

- Participation in the occupation of Hiroshima or Nagasaki from August 6, 1945 through July 1, 1946.
- Internment as a Prisoner of War in Japan (or service or active duty in Japan immediately following such internment.
- Service at Department of Energy plants at Paducah, KY, Portsmouth, OH, or the K25 area at Oak Ridge, TN for at least 250 days before February 1, 1992.
- Service at Longshot, Milrow, or Cannikin underground nuclear tests at Amchitka Island, AK prior to January 1, 1974.

Referral The process of referring a veteran from one practitioner to another for health care services.

Regular Filipino Scouts The Filipino Scouts were guerilla forces considered part of the Commonwealth Army of the Philippines. They were organized under commanders appointed, designated, or later recognized by the U.S. Army.

Respite care Respite care gives the caregiver of a veteran a planned period of relief from the physical and emotional demands associated with providing care.

Restore Health The process of improving a veteran's quality of life or daily function level that has been lost due to illness or injury.

Secondary Condition A secondary condition, for medical treatment purposes, may be the result of an adjudicated service-connected condition. Veterans are encouraged to file compensation claims for non-rated secondary conditions. Non-rated secondary conditions are billable as a non-service-connected condition.

NOTE: If awarded service-connection for the secondary condition, VA may reimburse all copays related to such service-connection retroactive to the date of the original claim filing.

Service-connected Generally a service-connected disability is a disability that VA determines was incurred or aggravated while on active duty in the military and in the line of duty. A service-connected rating is an official ruling by VA that your illness/condition is directly related to your active military service. Service-connected ratings are established by VA Regional Offices located throughout the country.

Service-Connected Veteran A veteran who has an illness or injury incurred in or aggravated by military service as determined by VA.

Sexual Trauma Sexual Harassment, Sexual Assault, Rape and other acts of violence. Repeated unsolicited, verbal or physical contact of a sexual nature, which is threatening in nature.

Southwest Asia An area of land located in the southwestern part of Asia to include the Persian Gulf, Red Sea, Gulf of Oman, Gulf of Aden, the portion of the Arabian Sea that lies north of 10 degrees North latitude and west of 68 degrees East longitude, as well as the total land areas of Iraq, Kuwait, Saudi Arabia, Oman, Bahrain, Qatar, and the United Arab Emirates.

Special (New) Philippine Scouts The term "New Philippine Scouts" refers to non-commissioned Philippine Scouts who—
- Enlisted on or after October 5, 1945,
- Served under Section 14 of the U.S. Armed Forces Voluntary Recruitment Act of 1945, *AND*
- Was discharged from this period of service under conditions other than dishonorable.

State Veterans Homes The eligibility for State Veterans Homes varies from state to state. But typically veterans and sometimes their spouse, can be admitted to a State Veterans Home. The costs of living in a State Veterans Home are usually paid by Medicaid, long term care insurance, and private funds. VA pays a modest share of the cost for each veteran living in a State Veterans Home. You can find information on the State Veterans Home(s) for your state by looking in the state government pages of the telephone book. VA social workers at the VA medical center where you're being treated can also provide information about State Veterans Homes.

Urgent Care Services received for an unexpected illness or injury that is not life threatening but requires immediate outpatient medical care that cannot be postponed. An urgent situation requires prompt medical attention to avoid complications and unnecessary suffering or severe pain, such as a high fever.

VA Form 10-10EZ, Application for Health Benefits The VA form completed by veterans to apply for VA health care benefits. The form includes demographic, military, insurance and financial information

VA Form 10-10EZR, Health Benefits Renewal The VA Form used by veterans to submit their updated personal, insurance and financial information to VA.

Veteran The term "Veteran" means a person who served in the active military, naval, or air service, and who was discharged or released under conditions other than dishonorable.

Water Quality

Acre-foot A volume of water equal to 1 foot in depth and covering 1 acre; equivalent to 43,560 cubic feet or 325,851 gallons.

Algae Chlorophyll-bearing nonvascular, primarily aquatic species that have no true roots, stems, or leaves; most algae are microscopic, but some species can be as large as vascular plants.

Alluvial aquifer A water-bearing deposit of unconsolidated material (sand and gravel) left behind by a river or other flowing water.

Alluvium Deposits of clay, silt, sand, gravel or other particulate rock material left by a river in a streambed, on a flood plain, delta, or at the base of a mountain.

Amalgamation The dissolving or blending of a metal (commonly gold and silver) in mercury to separate it from its parent material.

Ammonia A compound of nitrogen and hydrogen (NH3) that is a common by-product of animal waste. Ammonia readily converts to nitrate in soils and streams.

Anomalies As related to fish, externally visible skin or subcutaneous disorders, including deformities, eroded fins, lesions, and tumors.

Anthropogenic Occurring because of, or influenced by, human activity.

Aquatic guidelines Specific levels of water quality which, if reached, may adversely affect aquatic life. These are nonenforceable guidelines issued by a governmental agency or other institution.

Aquatic-life criteria Water-quality guidelines for protection of aquatic life. Often refers to U.S. Environmental Protection Agency water-quality criteria for protection of aquatic organisms. *See also* Water-quality guidelines, Water-quality criteria, and Freshwater chronic criteria.

Aquifer A water-bearing layer of soil, sand, gravel, or rock that will yield usable quantities of water to a well.

Artificial recharge Augmentation of natural replenishment of ground-water storage by some method of construction, spreading of water, or by pumping water directly into an aquifer.

Atmospheric deposition The transfer of substances from the air to the surface of the Earth, either in wet form (rain, fog, snow, dew, frost, hail) or in dry form (gases, aerosols, particles).

Background concentration A concentration of a substance in a particular environment that is indicative of minimal influence by human (anthropogenic) sources.

Bank The sloping ground that borders a stream and confines the water in the natural channel when the water level, or flow, is normal.

Base flow Sustained, low flow in a stream; ground-water discharge is the source of base flow in most places.

Basic fixed sites Sites on streams at which streamflow is measured and samples are collected for temperature, salinity, suspended sediment, major ions and metals, nutrients, and organic carbon to assess the broad-scale spatial and temporal character and transport of inorganic constituents of streamwater in relation to hydrologic conditions and environmental settings.

Basin *See* Drainage basin.

Basin and range physiography A region characterized by a series of generally north-trending mountain ranges separated by alluvial valleys.

Bed sediment The material that temporarily is stationary in the bottom of a stream or other watercourse.

Bed sediment and tissue studies Assessment of concentrations and distributions of trace elements and hydrophobic organic contaminants in streambed sediment and tissues of aquatic organisms to identify potential sources and to assess spatial distribution.

Bedload Sediment that moves on or near the streambed and is in almost continuous contact with the bed.

Bedrock General term for consolidated (solid) rock that underlies soils or other unconsolidated material.

Benthic Refers to plants or animals that live on the bottom of lakes, streams, or oceans.

Benthic invertebrates Insects, mollusks, crustaceans, worms, and other organisms without a backbone that live in, on, or near the bottom of lakes, streams, or oceans.

Best management practice (BMP) An agricultural practice that has been determined to be an effective, practical means of preventing or reducing nonpoint source pollution.

Bioaccumulation The biological sequestering of a substance at a higher concentration than that at which it occurs in the surrounding environment or medium. Also, the process whereby a substance enters organisms through the gills, epithelial tissues, dietary, or other sources.

Bioavailability The capacity of a chemical constituent to be taken up by living organisms either through physical contact or by ingestion.

Biochemical Refers to chemical processes that occur inside or are mediated by living organisms.

Biochemical oxygen demand (BOD) The amount of oxygen, measured in milligrams per liter, that is removed from aquatic environments by the life processes of microorganisms.

Biodegradation Transformation of a substance into new compounds through biochemical reactions or the actions of microorganisms such as bacteria.

Biomass The amount of living matter, in the form of organisms, present in a particular habitat, usually expressed as weight per unit area.

Biota Living organisms.

Blue-baby syndrome A condition that can be caused by ingestion of high amounts of nitrate resulting in the blood losing its ability to effectively carry oxygen. It is most common in young infants and certain elderly people.

Breakdown product A compound derived by chemical, biological, or physical action upon a pesticide. The breakdown is a natural process which may result in a more toxic or a less toxic compound and a more persistent or less persistent compound.

Canopy angle Generally, a measure of the openness of a stream to sunlight. Specifically, the angle formed by an imaginary line from the highest structure (for example, tree, shrub, or bluff) on one bank to eye level at midchannel to the highest structure on the other bank.

Carbonate rocks Rocks (such as limestone or dolostone) that are composed primarily of minerals (such as calcite and dolomite) containing the carbonate ion (CO_3^{2-}).

Center pivot irrigation An automated sprinkler system involving a rotating pipe or boom that supplies water to a circular area of an agricultural field through sprinkler heads or nozzles.

Channelization Modification of a stream, typically by straightening the channel, to provide more uniform flow; often done for flood control or for improved agricultural drainage or irrigation.

Chlordane Octachloro-4,7-methanotetrahydroindane. An organochlorine insecticide no longer registered for use in the U.S. Technical chlordane is a mixture in which the primary components are cis- and trans-chlordane, cis- and trans-nonachlor, and heptachlor.

Chlorinated solvent A volatile organic compound containing chlorine. Some common solvents are trichloroethylene, tetrachloroethylene, and carbon tetrachloride.

Chlorofluorocarbons A class of volatile compounds consisting of carbon, chlorine, and fluorine. Commonly called freons, which have been used in refrigeration mechanisms, as blowing agents in the fabrication of flexible and rigid foams, and, until several years ago, as propellants in spray cans.

Chrysene See Polycyclic aromatic hydrocarbon (PAH).

Clastic Rock or sediment composed principally of broken fragments that are derived from preexisting rocks which have been transported from their place of origin, as in sandstone.

Climate The sum total of the meteorological elements that characterize the average and extreme conditions of the atmosphere over a long period of time at any one place or region of the Earth's surface.

Combined sewer overflow A discharge of untreated sewage and stormwater to a stream when the capacity of a combined storm/sanitary sewer system is exceeded by storm runoff.

Community In ecology, the species that interact in a common area.

Concentration The amount or mass of a substance present in a given volume or mass of sample. Usually expressed as microgram per liter (water sample) or micrograms per kilogram (sediment or tissue sample).

Confined aquifer (artesian aquifer) An aquifer that is completely filled with water under pressure and that is overlain by material that restricts the movement of water.

Confining layer A layer of sediment or lithologic unit of low permeability that bounds an aquifer.

Confluence The flowing together of two or more streams; the place where a tributary joins the main stream.

Constituent A chemical or biological substance in water, sediment, or biota that can be measured by an analytical method.

Consumptive use The quantity of water that is not available for immediate reuse because it has been evaporated, transpired, or incorporated into products, plant tissue, or animal tissue. Also referred to as "water consumption."

Contamination Degradation of water quality compared to original or natural conditions due to human activity.

Contributing area The area in a drainage basin that contributes water to streamflow or recharge to an aquifer.

Criterion A standard rule or test on which a judgment or decision can be based.

Crystalline rocks Rocks (igneous or metamorphic) consisting wholly of crystals or fragments of crystals.

Cubic foot per second (ft 3/s, or cfs) Rate of water discharge representing a volume of 1 cubic foot passing a given point during 1 second, equivalent to approximately 7.48 gallons per second or 448.8 gallons per minute or 0.02832 cubic meter per second.

Degradation products Compounds resulting from transformation of an organic substance through chemical, photochemical, and/or biochemical reactions.

Denitrification A process by which oxidized forms of nitrogen such as nitrate (NO_3^-) are reduced to form nitrites, nitrogen oxides, ammonia, or free nitrogen: commonly brought about by the action of denitrifying bacteria and usually resulting in the escape of nitrogen to the air.

Detect To determine the presence of a compound.

Detection limit The concentration below which a particular analytical method cannot determine, with a high degree of certainty, a concentration.

Diatoms Single-celled, colonial, or filamentous algae with siliceous cell walls constructed of two overlapping parts.

DDT Dichloro-diphenyl-trichloroethane. An organochlorine insecticide no longer registered for use in the United States.

Dieldrin An organochlorine insecticide no longer registered for use in the United States. Also a degradation product of the insecticide aldrin.

Discharge Rate of fluid flow passing a given point at a given moment in time, expressed as volume per unit of time.

Dissolved constituent Operationally defined as a constituent that passes through a 0.45-micrometer filter.

Dissolved solids Amount of minerals, such as salt, that are dissolved in water; amount of dissolved solids is an indicator of salinity or hardness.

Diversion A turning aside or alteration of the natural course of a flow of water, normally considered physically to leave the natural channel. In some States, this can be a consumptive use direct from another stream, such as by livestock watering. In other States, a diversion must consist of such actions as taking water through a canal, pipe, or conduit.

Drainage area The drainage area of a stream at a specified location is that area, measured in a horizontal plane, which is enclosed by a drainage divide.

Drainage basin The portion of the surface of the Earth that contributes water to a stream through overland run-off, including tributaries and impoundments.

Drawdown The difference between the water level in a well before pumping and the water level in the well during pumping. Also, for flowing wells, the reduction of the pressure head as a result of the discharge of water.

Drinking-water standard or guideline A threshold concentration in a public drinking-water supply, designed to protect human health. As defined here, standards are U.S. Environmental Protection Agency regulations that specify the maximum contamination levels for public water systems required to protect the public welfare; guidelines have no regulatory status and are issued in an advisory capacity.

Drip irrigation An irrigation system in which water is applied directly to the root zone of plants by means of applicators (orifices, emitters, porous tubing, perforated pipe, and so forth) operated under low pressure. The applicators can be placed on or below the surface of the ground or can be suspended from supports.

Drought Commonly defined as being a time of less-than-normal or less-than-expected precipitation.

Ecological studies Studies of biological communities and habitat characteristics to evaluate the effects of physical and chemical characteristics of water and hydrologic conditions on aquatic biota and to determine how biological and habitat characteristics differ among environmental settings in NAWQA Study Units.

Ecoregion An area of similar climate, landform, soil, potential natural vegetation, hydrology, or other ecologically relevant variables.

Ecosystem The interacting populations of plants, animals, and microorganisms occupying an area, plus their physical environment.

Effluent Outflow from a particular source, such as a stream that flows from a lake or liquid waste that flows from a factory or sewage-treatment plant.

Endocrine system The collection of ductless glands in animals that secrete hormones, which influence growth, gender and sexual maturity.

Environmental framework Natural and human-related features of the land and hydrologic system, such as geology, land use, and habitat, that provide a unifying framework for making comparative assessments of the factors that govern water-quality conditions within and among Study Units.

Environmental sample A water sample collected from an aquifer or stream for the purpose of chemical, physical, or biological characterization of the sampled resource.

Environmental setting Land area characterized by a unique combination of natural and human-related factors, such as row-crop cultivation or glacial-till soils.

Ephemeral stream A stream or part of a stream that flows only in direct response to precipitation or snowmelt. Its channel is above the water table at all times.

EPT richness index An index based on the sum of the number of taxa in three insect orders, Ephemeroptera (mayflies), Plecoptera (stoneflies), and Trichoptera (caddisflies), that are composed primarily of species considered to be relatively intolerant to environmental alterations.

Equal-width increment (EWI) sample A composite sample across a section of stream with equal spacing between verticals and equal transit rates within each vertical that yields a representative sample of stream conditions.

Erosion The process whereby materials of the Earth's crust are loosened, dissolved, or worn away and simultaneously moved from one place to another.

Eutrophication The process by which water becomes enriched with plant nutrients, most commonly phosphorus and nitrogen.

Evaporite minerals (deposits) Minerals or deposits of minerals formed by evaporation of water containing salts. These deposits are common in arid climates.

Evapotranspiration A collective term that includes water lost through evaporation from the soil and surface-water bodies and by plant transpiration.

FDA action level A regulatory level recommended by the U.S. Environmental Protection Agency for enforcement by the FDA when pesticide residues occur in food commodities for reasons other than the direct application of the pesticide. Action levels are set for inadvertent pesticide residues resulting from previous legal use or accidental contamination. Applies to edible portions of fish and shellfish in interstate commerce.

Fecal bacteria Microscopic single-celled organisms (primarily fecal coliforms and fecal streptococci) found in the wastes of warm-blooded animals. Their presence in water is used to assess the sanitary quality of water for body-contact recreation or for consumption. Their presence indicates contamination by the wastes of warm-blooded animals and the possible presence of pathogenic (disease producing) organisms.

Fecal coliform See Fecal bacteria.

Fertilizer Any of a large number of natural or synthetic materials, including manure and nitrogen, phosphorus, and potassium compounds, spread on or worked into soil to increase its fertility.

Fish community See Community.

Fixed sites NAWQA's most comprehensive monitoring sites. *See also* Basic Fixed Sites and Intensive Fixed Sites.

Flood Any relatively high streamflow that overtops the natural or artificial banks of a stream.

Flood irrigation The application of irrigation water where the entire surface of the soil is covered by ponded water.

Flood plain The relatively level area of land bordering a stream channel and inundated during moderate to severe floods.

Flowpath An underground route for ground-water movement, extending from a recharge (intake) zone to a discharge (output) zone such as a shallow stream.

Flowpath study Network of clustered wells located along a flowpath extending from a recharge zone to a discharge zone, preferably a shallow stream. The studies examine the relations of land-use practices, ground-water flow, and contaminant occurrence and transport. These studies are located in the area of one of the land-use studies.

Fluvial deposit A sedimentary deposit consisting of material transported by suspension or laid down by a river or stream.

Freshwater chronic criteria The highest concentration of a contaminant that freshwater aquatic organisms can be exposed to for an extended period of time (4 days) without adverse effects. *See also* Water-quality criteria.

Fumigant A substance or mixture of substances that produces gas, vapor, fume, or smoke intended to destroy insects, bacteria, or rodents.

Furrow irrigation A type of surface irrigation where water is applied at the upper end of a field and flows in furrows to the lower end.

Gaging station A particular site on a stream, canal, lake, or reservoir where systematic observations of hydrologic data are obtained.

Geothermal Relating to the Earth's internal heat; commonly applied to springs or vents discharging hot water or steam.

Granitic rock A coarse-grained igneous rock.

Ground water In general, any water that exists beneath the land surface, but more commonly applied to water in fully saturated soils and geologic formations.

Habitat The part of the physical environment where plants and animals live.

Headwaters The source and upper part of a stream.

Health advisory Nonregulatory levels of contaminants in drinking water that may be used as guidance in the absence of regulatory limits. Advisories consist of estimates of concentrations that would result in no known or anticipated health effects (for carcinogens, a specified cancer risk) determined for a child or for an adult for various exposure periods.

Herbicide A chemical or other agent applied for the purpose of killing undesirable plants. *See also* Pesticide.

Human health advisory Guidance provided by U.S. Environmental Protection Agency, State agencies or scientific organizations, in the absence of regulatory limits, to describe acceptable contaminant levels in drinking water or edible fish.

Hydrograph Graph showing variation of water elevation, velocity, streamflow, or other property of water with respect to time.

Hydrologic cycle The circulation of water from the sea, through the atmosphere, to the land, and thence back to the sea by overland and subterranean routes.

Index of Biotic Integrity (IBI) An aggregated number, or index, based on several attributes or metrics of a fish community that provides an assessment of biological conditions.

Indicator sites Stream sampling sites located at outlets of drainage basins with relatively homogeneous land use and physiographic conditions; most indicator-site basins have drainage areas ranging from 20 to 200 square miles.

Infiltration Movement of water, typically downward, into soil or porous rock.

Insecticide A substance or mixture of substances intended to destroy or repel insects.

Instantaneous discharge The volume of water that passes a point at a particular instant of time.

Instream use Water use taking place within the stream channel for such purposes as hydroelectric power generation, navigation, water-quality improvement, fish propagation, and recreation. Sometimes called nonwithdrawal use or in-channel use.

Integrator or mixed-use site Stream sampling site located at an outlet of a drainage basin that contains multiple environmental settings. Most integrator sites are on major streams with relatively large drainage areas.

Intensive fixed sites Basic Fixed Sites with increased sampling frequency during selected seasonal periods and analysis of dissolved pesticides for 1 year. Most NAWQA Study Units have one to two integrator Intensive Fixed Sites and one to four indicator Intensive Fixed Sites.

Intermittent stream A stream that flows only when it receives water from rainfall runoff or springs, or from some surface source such as melting snow.

Intolerant organisms Organisms that are not adaptable to human alterations to the environment and thus decline in numbers where human alterations occur. *See also* Tolerant species.

Invertebrate An animal having no backbone or spinal column. *See also* Benthic invertebrate.

Irrigation return flow The part of irrigation applied to the surface that is not consumed by evapotranspiration or uptake by plants and that migrates to an aquifer or surface-water body.

Karst A type of topography that results from dissolution and collapse of carbonate rocks such as limestone and dolomite, and characterized by closed depressions or sinkholes, caves, and underground drainage.

Kill Dutch term for stream or creek.

Land-use study A network of existing shallow wells in an area having a relatively uniform land use. These studies are a subset of the Study-Unit Survey and have the goal of relating the quality of shallow ground water to land use. *See also* Study-Unit Survey.

Leaching The removal of materials in solution from soil or rock to ground water; refers to movement of pesticides or nutrients from land surface to ground water.

Load General term that refers to a material or constituent in solution, in suspension, or in transport; usually expressed in terms of mass or volume.

Loess Homogeneous, fine-grained sediment made up primarily of silt and clay, and deposited over a wide area (probably by wind).

Long-term monitoring Data collection over a period of years or decades to assess changes in selected hydrologic conditions.

Main stem The principal course of a river or a stream.

Major ions Constituents commonly present in concentrations exceeding 1.0 milligram per liter. Dissolved cations generally are calcium, magnesium, sodium, and potassium; the major anions are sulfate, chloride, fluoride, nitrate, and those contributing to alkalinity, most generally assumed to be bicarbonate and carbonate.

Maximum contaminant level (MCL) Maximum permissible level of a contaminant in water that is delivered to any user of a public water system. MCLs are enforceable standards established by the U.S. Environmental Protection Agency.

Mean The average of a set of observations, unless otherwise specified.

Mean discharge (MEAN) The arithmetic mean of individual daily mean discharges during a specific period, usually daily, monthly, or annually.

Median The middle or central value in a distribution of data ranked in order of magnitude. The median is also known as the 50th percentile.

Metabolite A substance produced in or by biological processes.

Metamorphic rock Rock that has formed in the solid state in response to pronounced changes of temperature, pressure, and chemical environment.

Method detection limit The minimum concentration of a substance that can be accurately identified and measured with present laboratory technologies.

Micrograms per liter (µg/L) A unit expressing the concentration of constituents in solution as weight (micrograms) of solute per unit volume (liter) of water; equivalent to one part per billion in most streamwater and ground water. One thousand micrograms per liter equals 1 mg/L.

Midge A small fly in the family Chironomidae. The larval (juvenile) life stages are aquatic.

Milligram (mg) A mass equal to 10-3 grams.

Milligrams per liter (mg/L) A unit expressing the concentration of chemical constituents in solution as weight (milligrams) of solute per unit volume (liter) of water; equivalent to one part per million in most streamwater and ground water. One thousand micrograms per liter equals 1 mg/L.

Minimum reporting level (MRL) The smallest measured concentration of a constituent that may be reliably reported using a given analytical method. In many cases, the MRL is used when documentation for the method detection limit is not available.

Monitoring Repeated observation or sampling at a site, on a scheduled or event basis, for a particular purpose.

Monitoring well A well designed for measuring water levels and testing ground-water quality.

Monocyclic aromatic hydrocarbons Single-ring aromatic compounds. Constituents of lead-free gasoline; also used in the manufacture of monomers and plasticizers in polymers.

Mouth The place where a stream discharges to a larger stream, a lake, or the sea.

National Academy of Sciences/National Academy of Engineering (NAS/NAE) recommended maximum concentration in water Numerical guidelines recmmended by two joint NAS/NAE committees for the protection of freshwater and marine aquatic life, respectively. These guidelines were based on available aquatic toxicity studies, and were considered preliminary even at the time (1972). The guidelines used in the summary reports are for freshwater.

Nitrate An ion consisting of nitrogen and oxygen (NO3-). Nitrate is a plant nutrient and is very mobile in soils.

Noncontact water recreation Recreational activities, such as fishing or boating, that do not include direct contact with the water.

Nonpoint source A pollution source that cannot be defined as originating from discrete points such as pipe discharge. Areas of fertilizer and pesticide applications, atmospheric deposition, manure, and natural inputs from plants and trees are types of nonpoint source pollution.

Nonpoint-source contaminant A substance that pollutes or degrades water that comes from lawn or cropland runoff, the atmosphere, roadways, and other diffuse sources.

Nonpoint-source water pollution Water contamination that originates from a broad area (such as leaching of agricultural chemicals from crop land) and enters the water resource diffusely over a large area.

Nonselective herbicide Kills or significantly retards growth of most higher plant species.

Nutrient Element or compound essential for animal and plant growth. Common nutrients in fertilizer include nitrogen, phosphorus, and potassium.

Occurrence and distribution assessment Characterization of the broad-scale spatial and temporal distributions of water-quality conditions in relation to major contaminant sources and background conditions for surface water and ground water.

Organic detritus Any loose organic material in streams—such as leaves, bark, or twigs—removed and transported by mechanical means, such as disintegration or abrasion.

Organochlorine compound Synthetic organic compounds containing chlorine. As generally used, term refers to compounds containing mostly or exclusively carbon, hydrogen, and chlorine. Examples include organochlorine insecticides, polychlorinated biphenyls, and some solvents containing chlorine.

Organochlorine insecticide A class of organic insecticides containing a high percentage of chlorine. Includes dichlorodiphenylethanes (such as DDT), chlorinated cyclodienes (such as chlordane), and chlorinated benzenes (such as lindane). Most organochlorine insecticides were banned because of their carcinogenicity, tendency to bioaccumulate, and toxicity to wildlife.

Organochlorine pesticide See Organochlorine insecticide.

Organophosphate insecticides A class of insecticides derived from phosphoric acid. They tend to have high acute toxicity to vertebrates. Although readily metabolized by vertebrates, some metabolic products are more toxic than the parent compound.

Organonitrogen herbicides A group of herbicides consisting of a nitrogen ring with associated functional groups and including such classes as triazines and acetanilides. Examples include atrazine, cyanazine, alachlor, and metolachlor.

Organophosphorus insecticides Insecticides derived from phosphoric acid and are generally the most toxic of all pesticides to vertebrate animals.

Outwash Soil material washed down a hillside by rainwater and deposited upon more gently sloping land.

Overland flow The part of surface runoff flowing over land surfaces toward stream channels.

Part per million (ppm) Unit of concentration equal to one milligram per kilogram or one milligram per liter.

Perennial stream A stream that normally has water in its channel at all times.

Periphyton Organisms that grow on underwater surfaces, including algae, bacteria, fungi, protozoa, and other organisms.

Pesticide A chemical applied to crops, rights of way, lawns, or residences to control weeds, insects, fungi, nematodes, rodents or other "pests."

pH The logarithm of the reciprocal of the hydrogen ion concentration (activity) of a solution; a measure of the acidity (pH less than 7) or alkalinity (pH greater than 7) of a solution; a pH of 7 is neutral.

Phenols A class of organic compounds containing phenol (C_6H_5OH) and its derivatives. Used to make resins, weed killers, and as a solvent, disinfectant, and chemical intermediate. Some phenols occur naturally in the environment.

Phosphorus A nutrient essential for growth that can play a key role in stimulating aquatic growth in lakes and streams.

Photosynthesis Synthesis of chemical compounds by organisms with the aid of light. Carbon dioxide is used as raw material for photosynthesis and oxygen is a product.

Phthalates A class of organic compounds containing phthalic acid esters [$C_6H_4(COOR)_2$] and derivatives. Used as plasticizers in plastics. Also used in many other products (such as detergents, cosmetics) and industrial processes (such as defoaming agents during paper and paperboard manufacture, and dielectrics in capacitors).

Physiography A description of the surface features of the Earth, with an emphasis on the origin of landforms.

Phytoplankton See Plankton.

Picocurie (pCi) One trillionth (10^{-12}) of the amount of radioactivity represented by a curie (Ci). A curie is the amount of radioactivity that yields 3.7×10^{10} radioactive disintegrations per second (dps). A picocurie yields 2.22 disintegrations per minute (dpm) or 0.037 dps.

Plankton Floating or weakly swimming organisms at the mercy of the waves and currents. Animals of the group are called zooplankton and the plants are called phytoplankton.

Point source A source at a discrete location such as a discharge pipe, drainage ditch, tunnel, well, concentrated livestock operation, or floating craft.

Point-source contaminant Any substance that degrades water quality and originates from discrete locations such as discharge pipes, drainage ditches, wells, concentrated livestock operations, or floating craft.

Pollutant Any substance that, when present in a hydrologic system at sufficient concentration, degrades water quality in ways that are or could become harmful to human and/or ecological health or that impair the use of water for recreation, agriculture, industry, commerce, or domestic purposes.

Polychlorinated biphenyls (PCBs) A mixture of chlorinated derivatives of biphenyl, marketed under the trade name Aroclor with a number designating the chlorine content (such as Aroclor 1260). PCBs were used in transformers and capacitors for insulating purposes and in gas pipeline systems as a lubricant. Further sale for new use was banned by law in 1979.

Polycyclic aromatic hydrocarbon (PAH) A class of organic compounds with a fused-ring aromatic structure. PAHs result from incomplete combustion of organic carbon (including wood), municipal solid waste, and fossil fuels, as well as from natural or anthropogenic introduction of uncombusted coal and oil. PAHs include benzo(a)pyrene, fluoranthene, and pyrene.

Pool A small part of the stream reach with little velocity, commonly with water deeper than surrounding areas.

Postemergence herbicide Herbicide applied to foliage after the crop has sprouted to kill or significantly retard the growth of weeds.

Precipitation Any or all forms of water particles that fall from the atmosphere, such as rain, snow, hail, and sleet.

Preemergence herbicide Herbicide applied to bare ground after planting the crop but prior to the crop sprouting above ground to kill or significantly retard the growth of weed seedlings.

Public-supply withdrawals Water withdrawn by public and private water suppliers for use within a general community. Water is used for a variety of purposes such as domestic, commercial, industrial, and public water use.

Quality assurance Evaluation of quality-control data to allow quantitative determination of the quality of chemical data collected during a study. Techniques used to collect, process, and analyze water samples are evaluated.

Radon A naturally occurring, colorless, odorless, radioactive gas formed by the disintegration of the element radium; damaging to human lungs when inhaled.

Recharge Water that infiltrates the ground and reaches the saturated zone.

Reference site A NAWQA sampling site selected for its relatively undisturbed conditions.

Relative abundance The number of organisms of a particular kind present in a sample relative to the total number of organisms in the sample.

Retrospective analysis Review and analysis of existing data in order to address NAWQA objectives, to the extent possible, and to aid in the design of NAWQA studies.

Riffle A shallow part of the stream where water flows swiftly over completely or partially submerged obstructions to produce surface agitation.

Riparian Areas adjacent to rivers and streams with a high density, diversity, and productivity of plant and animal species relative to nearby uplands.

Riparian zone Pertaining to or located on the bank of a body of water, especially a stream.

Runoff Excess rainwater or snowmelt that is transported to streams by overland flow, tile drains, or ground water.

Secondary maximum contaminant level (SMCL) The maximum contamination level in public water systems that, in the judgment of the U.S. Environmental Protection Agency (USEPA), are required to protect the public welfare. SMCLs are secondary (nonenforceable) drinking water regulations established by the USEPA for contaminants that may adversely affect the odor or appearance of such water.

Sediment Particles, derived from rocks or biological materials, that have been transported by a fluid or other natural process, suspended or settled in water.

Sediment guideline Threshold concentration above which there is a high probability of adverse effects on aquatic life from sediment contamination, determined using modified USEPA (1996) procedures.

Sediment quality guideline Threshold concentration above which there is a high probability of adverse effects on aquatic life from sediment contamination, determined using modified USEPA (1996) procedures.

Selective herbicide Kills or significantly retards growth of an unwanted plant species without significantly damaging desired plant species.

Semipermeable membrane device (SPMD) A long strip of low-density, polyethylene tubing filled with a thin film of purified lipid such as triolein that simulates the exposure to and passive uptake of highly lipid-soluble organic compounds by biological membranes.

Semivolatile organic compound (SVOC) Operationally defined as a group of synthetic organic compounds that are solvent-extractable and can be determined by gas chromatography/mass spectrometry. SVOCs include phenols, phthalates, and Polycyclic aromatic hydrocarbons (PAHs).

Sideslope gradient The representative change in elevation in a given horizontal distance (usually about 300 yards) perpendicular to a stream; the valley slope along a line perpendicular to the stream (near the water-quality or biological sampling point).

Siliciclastic rocks Rocks such as shale and sandstone which are formed by the compaction and cementation of quartz-rich mineral grains.

Sinuosity The ratio of the channel length between two points on a channel to the straight-line distance between the same two points; a measure of meandering.

Sole-source aquifer A ground-water system that supplies at least 50 percent of the drinking water to a particular human population; the term is used to denote special protection requirements under the Safe Drinking Water Act and may be used only by approval of the U.S. Environmental Protection Agency.

Solid-phase extraction A procedure to isolate specific organic compounds onto a bonded silica extraction column.

Solute See Solution.

Solution Formed when a solid, gas, or another liquid in contact with a liquid becomes dispersed homogeneously throughout the liquid. The substance, called a solute, is said to dissolve. The liquid is called the solvent.

Solvent See Solution.

Sorption General term for the interaction (binding or association) of a solute ion or molecule with a solid.

Source rocks The rocks from which fragments and other detached pieces have been derived to form a different rock.

Species Populations of organisms that may interbreed and produce fertile offspring having similar structure, habits, and functions.

Species diversity An ecological concept that incorporates both the number of species in a particular sampling area and the evenness with which individuals are distributed among the various species.

Species (taxa) richness The number of species (taxa) present in a defined area or sampling unit.

Specific conductance A measure of the ability of a liquid to conduct an electrical current.

Split sample A sample prepared by dividing it into two or more equal volumes, where each volume is considered a separate sample but representative of the entire sample.

Stage The height of the water surface above an established datum plane, such as in a river above a predetermined point that may (or may not) be near the channel floor.

Statistics A branch of mathematics dealing with the collection, analysis, interpretation, and presentation of masses of numerical data.

Stratification Subdivision of the environmental framework. The Study Unit is divided into subareas that exhibit reasonable homogeneous environmental conditions, as determined by both natural and human influences.

Stream-aquifer interactions Relations of water flow and chemistry between streams and aquifers that are hydraulically connected.

Streamflow A type of channel flow, applied to that part of surface runoff in a stream whether or not it is affected by diversion or regulation.

Stream mile A distance of 1 mile along a line connecting the midpoints of the channel of a stream.

Stream order A ranking of the relative sizes of streams within a watershed based on the nature of their tributaries. The smallest unbranched tributary is called first order, the stream receiving the tributary is called second order, and so on.

Stream reach A continuous part of a stream between two specified points.

Study Unit A major hydrologic system of the United States in which NAWQA studies are focused. Study Units are geographically defined by a combination of ground- and surface-water features and generally encompass more than 4,000 square miles of land area.

Study-Unit Survey Broad assessment of the water-quality conditions of the major aquifer systems of each Study Unit. The Study-Unit Survey relies primarily on sampling existing wells and, wherever possible, on existing data collected by other agencies and programs. Typically, 20 to 30 wells are sampled in each of three to five aquifer subunits.

Subsidence Compression of soft aquifer materials in a confined aquifer due to pumping of water from the aquifer.

Substrate size The diameter of streambed particles such as clay, silt, sand, gravel, cobble and boulders.

Subsurface drain A shallow drain installed in an irrigated field to intercept the rising ground-water level and maintain the water table at an acceptable depth below the land surface.

Surface water An open body of water, such as a lake, river, or stream.

Survey Sampling of any number of sites during a given hydrologic condition.

Suspended (as used in tables of chemical analyses) The amount (concentration) of undissolved material in a water-sediment mixture. It is associated with the material retained on a 0.45- micrometer filter.

Suspended sediment Particles of rock, sand, soil, and organic detritus carried in suspension in the water column, in contrast to sediment that moves on or near the streambed.

Suspended-sediment concentration The velocity-weighted concentration of suspended sediment in the sampled zone (from the water surface to a point approximately 0.3 foot above the bed) expressed as milligrams of dry sediment per liter of water-sediment mixture (mg/L).

Suspended solids Different from suspended sediment only in the way that the sample is collected and analyzed.

Synoptic sites Sites sampled during a short-term investigation of specific water-quality conditions during selected seasonal or hydrologic conditions to provide improved spatial resolution for critical water-quality conditions.

Tailings Rock that remains after processing ore to remove the valuable minerals.

Taxa richness See Species richness.

Taxon (plural taxa) Any identifiable group of taxonomically related organisms.

Tertiary-treated sewage The third phase of treating sewage that removes nitrogen and phosphorus before it is discharged.

Tier 1 sediment guideline Threshold concentration above which there is a high probability of adverse effects on aquatic life from sediment contamination, determined using modified USEPA (1996) procedures.

Tile drain A buried perforated pipe designed to remove excess water from soils.

Tissue study The assessment of concentrations and distributions of trace elements and certain organic contaminants in tissues of aquatic organisms.

Tolerant species Those species that are adaptable to (tolerant of) human alterations to the environment and often increase in number when human alterations occur.

Total concentration Refers to the concentration of a constituent regardless of its form (dissolved or bound) in a sample.

Total DDT The sum of DDT and its metabolites (breakdown products), including DDD and DDE.

Trace element An element found in only minor amounts (concentrations less than 1.0 milligram per liter) in water or sediment; includes arsenic, cadmium, chromium, copper, lead, mercury, nickel, and zinc.

Tracer A stable, easily detected substance or a radioisotope added to a material to follow the location of the substance in the environment or to detect any physical or chemical changes it undergoes.

Triazine herbicide A class of herbicides containing a symmetrical triazine ring (a nitrogen-heterocyclic ring composed of three nitrogens and three carbons in an alternating sequence). Examples include atrazine, propazine, and simazine.

Triazine pesticide See Triazine herbicide.

Tributary A river or stream flowing into a larger river, stream or lake.

Tritium A radioactive form of hydrogen with atoms of three times the mass of ordinary hydrogen; used to determine the age of water.

Turbidity Reduced clarity of surface water because of suspended particles, usually sediment.

Unconfined aquifer An aquifer whose upper surface is a water table; an aquifer containing unconfined ground water.

Unconsolidated deposit Deposit of loosely bound sediment that typically fills topographically low areas.

Un-ionized The neutral form of an ionizable compound (such as an acid or a base).

Un-ionized ammonia The neutral form of ammonia-nitrogen in water, usually occurring as NH_4OH. Un-ionized ammonia is the principal form of ammonia that is toxic to aquatic life. The relative proportion of un-ionized to ionized ammonia (NH_4^+) is controlled by water temperature and pH. At temperatures and pH values typical of most natural waters, the ionized form is dominant.

Upgradient Of or pertaining to the place(s) from which ground water originated or traveled through before reaching a given point in an aquifer.

Upland Elevated land above low areas along a stream or between hills; elevated region from which rivers gather drainage.

Uranium A heavy silvery-white metallic element, highly radioactive and easily oxidized. Of the 14 known isotopes of uranium, U238 is the most abundant in nature.

Urban site A site that has greater than 50 percent urbanized and less than 25 percent agricultural area.

Volatile organic compounds (VOCs) Organic chemicals that have a high vapor pressure relative to their water solubility. VOCs include components of gasoline, fuel oils, and lubricants, as well as organic solvents, fumigants, some inert ingredients in pesticides, and some by-products of chlorine disinfection.

Wasteway A waterway used to drain excess irrigation water dumped from the irrigation delivery system.

Water budget An accounting of the inflow, outflow, and storage changes of water in a hydrologic unit.

Water column studies Investigations of physical and chemical characteristics of surface water, which include suspended sediment, dissolved solids, major ions, and metals, nutrients, organic carbon, and dissolved pesticides, in relation to hydrologic conditions, sources, and transport.

Water-quality criteria Specific levels of water quality which, if reached, are expected to render a body of water unsuitable for its designated use. Commonly refers to water-quality criteria established by the U.S. Environmental Protection Agency. Water-quality criteria are based on specific levels of pollutants that would make the water harmful if used for drinking, swimming, farming, fish production, or industrial processes.

Water-quality guidelines Specific levels of water quality which, if reached, may adversely affect human health or aquatic life. These are nonenforceable guidelines issued by a governmental agency or other institution.

Water-quality standards State-adopted and U.S. Environmental Protection Agency-approved ambient standards for water bodies. Standards include the use of the water body and the water-quality criteria that must be met to protect the designated use or uses.

Watershed See Drainage basin.

Water table The point below the land surface where ground water is first encountered and below which the earth is saturated. Depth to the water table varies widely across the country.

Water year The continuous 12-month period, October 1 through September 30, in U.S. Geological Survey reports dealing with the surface-water supply. The water year is designated by the calendar year in which it ends and which includes 9 of the 12 months. Thus, the year ending September 30, 1980, is referred to as the "1980" water year.

Weather The state of the atmosphere at any particular time and place.

Wetlands Ecosystems whose soil is saturated for long periods seasonally or continuously, including marshes, swamps, and ephemeral ponds.

Withdrawal The act or process of removing; such as removing water from a stream for irrigation or public water supply.

Yield The mass of material or constituent transported by a river in a specified period of time divided by the drainage area of the river basin.

Zooplankton See Plankton.

CPSIA information can be obtained
at www.ICGtesting.com
Printed in the USA
BVOW09*1118031217
501741BV00005B/9/P